Webster's
ATLAS
and zip code directory

A Merriam-Webster®

G. & C. MERRIAM COMPANY
Springfield, Massachusetts, U.S.A.

Hammond Publications Advisory Board

Library of Congress Cataloging in Publication Data
Main entry under title:
Webster's atlas and zip code directory.
 "A Merriam-Webster."
 Maps by Hammond Incorporated.
 Includes indexes.
 Bibliography: p.
 1. Atlases.   2. Zip code — United States — Maps.
3. [United States — Zip code — Maps] .   I. Hammond
Incorporated.
G1021.W35   1978   912   78-17495
ISBN 0-87779-288-7

Contents

Gazetteer-Index of the World

This alphabetical list of grand divisions, countries, states, colonial possessions, etc., gives area, population, capital or chief town, and index references and page numbers on which they are shown on the largest scale. The index reference shows the square on the respective map in which the name of the entry may be located.

Country	Area (Sq. Miles)	Population	Capital or Chief Town	Index Ref.	Plate No.
Afars and Issas, Terr.	8,880	109,000	Djibouti	H 5	111
*Afghanistan	250,775	19,280,000	Kabul	A 2	68
Africa	11,707,000	431,900			102
Alabama, U.S.A.	51,609	3,444,165	Montgomery		194
Alaska, U.S.A.	586,412	302,173	Juneau		196
*Albania	11,100	2,482,000	Tiranë	E 5	45
Alberta, Canada	255,285	1,627,874	Edmonton		182
*Algeria	919,591	16,776,000	Algiers	D 3	106
American Samoa	76	30,000	Pago Pago	J 7	87
Andorra	188	26,558	Andorra la Vella	G 1	33
Angola	481,351	6,761,000	Luanda	C 6	115
Antarctica	5,500,000				5
Antigua & Dependencies	171	73,000	St. Johns	E11	161
*Argentina	1,072,070	23,983,000	Buenos Aires		143
Arizona, U.S.A.	113,909	1,772,482	Phoenix		198
Arkansas, U.S.A.	53,104	1,923,295	Little Rock		202
Ascension	34	1,146	Georgetown	A 5	102
Asia	17,128,500	2,535,333,000			54
*Australia	2,967,909	13,684,900	Canberra		88
*Austria	32,375	7,540,000	Vienna		41
*Bahamas	5,382	197,000	Nassau	C 1	156
*Bahrain	240	300,000	Manama	F 4	59
*Bangladesh	55,126	82,900,000	Dacca	G 4	68
*Barbados	166	253,620	Bridgetown	B 8	161
*Belgium	11,781	9,813,000	Brussels		27
Belize	8,867	122,000	Belmopan	C 2	154
*Benin	43,483	3,200,000	Porto-Novo	E 7	106
Bermuda	21	52,000	Hamilton	H 3	156
Bhutan	18,147	1,200,000	Thimphu	G 3	68
*Bolivia	424,163	4,804,000	La Paz, Sucre		136
*Botswana	224,764	700,000	Gaborone	C 4	118
*Brazil	3,284,426	90,840,000	Brasília		132
British Columbia, Canada	366,255	2,184,621	Victoria		184
British Indian Ocean Terr.	29	600	London (U.K.)	L10	54
Brunei	2,226	155,000	Bandar Seri Begawan	E 4	85
*Bulgaria	42,823	8,800,000	Sofia	F 4	45
*Burma	261,789	31,240,000	Rangoon	B 2	72
*Burundi	10,747	4,100,000	Bujumbura	E 4	115
California, U.S.A.	158,693	19,953,134	Sacramento		204
*Cambodia	69,898	8,110,000	Phnom Penh	E 4	72
*Cameroon	183,568	6,600,000	Yaoundé	B 2	115
*Canada	3,851,809	21,568,311	Ottawa		162
Canal Zone	647	44,650	Balboa Heights	G 6	154
*Cape Verde	1,557	302,000	Praia	B 8	106
Cayman Islands	100	10,652	Georgetown	B 3	156
*Central African Empire	236,293	1,800,000	Bangui	C 2	115
Central America	197,575	19,800,000			154
*Ceylon (Sri Lanka)	25,332	14,000,000	Colombo	E 7	68
*Chad	495,752	4,178,000	N'Djamena	C 4	111
Channel Islands	74	128,000	St. Helier	E 7	13
*Chile	292,257	8,834,820	Santiago		138
*China (mainland)	3,691,000	853,000,000	Peking		77
China (Taiwan)	13,971	16,426,386	Taipei	K 7	77
*Colombia	439,513	21,117,000	Bogotá		126
Colorado, U.S.A.	102,247	2,207,259	Denver		208
*Comoro Islands	719	266,000	Moroni	G 2	118
*Congo	132,046	1,400,000	Brazzaville	B 4	115
Connecticut, U.S.A.	5,009	3,032,217	Hartford		210
Cook Islands	91	17,046	Avarua	K 7	87
*Costa Rica	19,575	1,800,000	San José	E 5	154
*Cuba	44,206	8,553,395	Havana		158
*Cyprus	3,473	639,000	Nicosia	E 5	63
*Czechoslovakia	49,373	14,900,000	Prague		41
Delaware, U.S.A.	2,057	548,104	Dover		245
*Denmark	16,629	5,065,313	Copenhagen		21
District of Columbia, N.S.A.	67	756,510	Washington	F 5	245
Dominica	290	70,302	Roseau	E 7	161
*Dominican Republic	18,704	4,011,589	Santo Domingo		158
*Ecuador	109,483	6,144,000	Quito		128
*Egypt	386,659	37,900,000	Cairo	E 2	111
*El Salvador	8,260	3,418,455	San Salvador	C 4	154
England, U.K.	50,516	46,417,600	London		13
*Equatorial Guinea	10,831	320,000	Malabo	A 3	115
*Ethiopia	471,776	27,946,000	Addis Ababa	G 5	111
Europe	4,057,000	666,116,000			7
Faerøe Islands, Den.	540	38,000	Tórshavn	B 2	21
Falkland Islands	4,618	2,000	Stanley	E 8	120
*Fiji	7,055	569,468	Suva	H 8	87
*Finland	130,128	4,729,000	Helsinki		18
Florida, U.S.A.	58,560	6,789,443	Tallahassee		212
*France	210,038	53,300,000	Paris		28
French Guiana	35,135	48,000	Cayenne	E 3	131
French Polynesia	1,544	135,000	Papeete	L 8	87
*Gabon	103,346	526,000	Libreville	B 4	115
*Gambia	4,127	524,000	Banjul	A 6	106
Georgia, U.S.A.	58,876	4,589,575	Atlanta		216
*Germany, East (German Democratic Republic)	41,768	16,850,000	Berlin		22
*Germany, West (Federal Republic of)	95,985	61,644,600	Bonn		22
*Ghana	92,099	9,900,000	Accra	D 7	106
Gibraltar	2.28	30,000	Gibraltar	D 4	33
Gilbert Islands	354	47,711	Bairiki	J 6	87
*Great Britain and Northern Ireland (United Kingdom)	94,399	56,076,000	London		10
*Greece	50,944	9,046,000	Athens	F 6	45
Greenland	840,000	54,000	Godthåb	B12	4
*Grenada	133	96,000	St. George's	D 9	161
Guadeloupe & Dependencies	687	324,000	Basse-Terre	A 5	161
Guam	212	111,000	Agaña	F 4	87
*Guatemala	42,042	5,200,000	Guatemala	B 3	154
*Guinea	94,925	4,500,000	Conakry	B 6	106
*Guinea-Bissau	13,948	517,000	Bissau	A 6	106
*Guyana	83,000	763,000	Georgetown	B 3	131
*Haiti	10,694	4,867,190	Port-au-Prince		158
Hawaii, U.S.A.	6,450	769,913	Honolulu		218
*Holland (Netherlands)	15,892	13,800,000	Amsterdam, The Hague		27
*Honduras	43,277	2,495,000	Tegucigalpa	D 3	154
Hong Kong	403	4,400,000	Victoria	H 7	77
*Hungary	35,919	10,590,000	Budapest		41
*Iceland	39,768	220,000	Reykjavík	B 1	21
Idaho, U.S.A.	83,557	713,008	Boise		220
Illinois, U.S.A.	56,400	11,113,976	Springfield		222
*India	1,269,339	605,614,000	New Delhi		68
Indiana, U.S.A.	36,291	5,193,669	Indianapolis		227
*Indonesia	788,430	131,255,000	Djakarta		85
Iowa, U.S.A.	56,290	2,825,041	Des Moines		229
*Iran	636,293	32,900,000	Tehran		66
*Iraq	172,476	11,400,000	Baghdad		66
*Ireland	27,136	3,109,000	Dublin		17
Ireland, Northern, U.K.	5,452	1,537,200	Belfast		17
Isle of Man, U.K.	227	59,000	Douglas	C 3	13
*Israel	7,847	3,459,000	Jerusalem		65
*Italy	116,303	56,110,000	Rome		34
*Ivory Coast	127,520	6,673,013	Abidjan	C 7	106
*Jamaica	4,411	1,972,000	Kingston		158
*Japan	145,730	112,200,000	Tokyo		81
*Jordan	37,737	2,700,000	Amman		65
Kansas, U.S.A.	82,264	2,249,071	Topeka		232
Kentucky, U.S.A.	40,395	3,219,311	Frankfort		237
*Kenya	224,960	13,300,000	Nairobi	G 3	115
Korea, North	46,540	17,000,000	P'yŏngyang		81
Korea, South	38,175	34,688,079	Seoul		81
*Kuwait	6,532	1,100,000	Al Kuwait	E 4	59
*Laos	91,428	3,500,000	Vientiane	D 3	72
*Lebanon	4,015	3,207,000	Beirut	F 6	63
*Lesotho	11,720	1,100,000	Maseru	D 5	118
*Liberia	43,000	1,600,000	Monrovia	C 7	106
*Libya	679,358	2,500,000	Tripoli	C 2	111
Liechtenstein	61	25,000	Vaduz	J 2	39
Louisiana, U.S.A.	48,523	3,643,180	Baton Rouge		238
*Luxembourg	999	358,000	Luxembourg	J 9	27

*Members of the United Nations

GAZETTEER-INDEX OF THE WORLD

Country	Area (Sq. Miles)	Population	Capital or Chief Town	Index Ref.	Plate No.
Macao	6	300,000	Macao	H 7	77
*Madagascar	226,657	7,700,000	Tananarive	H 3	118
Maine, U.S.A.	33,215	993,663	Augusta		242
*Malawi	45,747	5,100,000	Lilongwe	F 6	115
Malaya, Malaysia	50,806	9,000,000	Kuala Lumpur	D 6	72
*Malaysia	128,308	12,368,000	Kuala Lumpur		72,85
*Maldives	115	136,000	Male	L 9	54
*Mali	464,873	5,800,000	Bamako	C 6	106
*Malta	122	319,000	Valletta	E 7	34
Manitoba, Canada	251,000	988,247	Winnipeg		179
Martinique	425	332,000	Fort-de-France	D 5	161
Maryland, U.S.A.	10,577	3,922,399	Annapolis		245
Massachusetts, U.S.A.	8,257	5,689,170	Boston		249
*Mauritania	452,702	1,318,000	Nouakchott	B 5	106
*Mauritius	790	899,000	Port Louis	G 5	118
Mayotte	144	40,000	Mamoutzou	G 2	119
*Mexico	761,601	48,313,438	Mexico City		150
Michigan, U.S.A.	58,216	8,875,083	Lansing		250
Midway Islands	2	2,220		J 3	87
Minnesota, U.S.A.	84,068	3,805,069	St. Paul		254
Mississippi, U.S.A.	47,716	2,216,912	Jackson		256
Missouri, U.S.A.	69,686	4,677,399	Jefferson City		261
Monaco	368 acres	23,035	Monaco	G 6	28
*Mongolia	606,163	1,500,000	Ulan Bator		77
Montana, U.S.A.	147,138	694,409	Helena		262
Montserrat	40	12,300	Plymouth	F 3	156
*Morocco	241,224	18,000,000	Rabat	C 2	106
*Mozambique	308,641	9,300,000	Maputo	E 5	118
Nauru	7.7	8,000	Yaren dist.	G 6	87
Nebraska, U.S.A.	77,227	1,483,791	Lincoln		264
*Nepal	54,663	12,900,000	Kathmandu	E 3	68
*Netherlands	15,892	13,800,000	Amsterdam, The Hague		27
Netherlands Antilles	390	220,000	Willemstad	E 4	156
Nevada, U.S.A.	110,540	488,738	Carson City		266
New Brunswick, Canada	28,354	534,557	Fredericton		170
New Caledonia & Dep.	7,335	136,000	Nouméa	G 8	87
Newfoundland, Canada	156,185	522,104	St. John's		166
New Hampshire, U.S.A.	9,304	737,681	Concord		268
New Hebrides	5,700	80,000	Vila	G 7	87
New Jersey, U.S.A.	7,836	7,168,164	Trenton		273
New Mexico, U.S.A.	121,666	1,016,000	Santa Fe		274
New York, U.S.A.	49,576	18,241,266	Albany		276
*New Zealand	103,736	3,121,904	Wellington		100
*Nicaragua	45,698	1,984,000	Managua	D 4	154
*Niger	489,189	4,700,000	Niamey	F 5	106
*Nigeria	379,628	83,800,000	Lagos	F 6	106
Niue	100	2,992	Alofi	K 7	87
North America	9,363,000	314,000,000			146
North Carolina, U.S.A.	52,586	5,082,059	Raleigh		281
North Dakota, U.S.A.	70,665	617,761	Bismarck		282
Northern Ireland, U.K.	5,452	1,537,200	Belfast		17
Northwest Territories, Canada	1,304,903	34,807	Yellowknife		187
*Norway	125,053	4,027,000	Oslo		18
Nova Scotia, Canada	21,425	788,960	Halifax		168
Ohio, U.S.A.	41,222	10,652,017	Columbus		284
Oklahoma, U.S.A.	69,919	2,559,253	Oklahoma City		288
*Oman	120,000	800,000	Muscat	G 5	59
Ontario, Canada	412,582	7,703,106	Toronto		175,177
Oregon, U.S.A.	96,981	2,091,385	Salem		291
Pacific Islands, U.S. Trust Terr. of the	707	120,000	Tanapag	F 5	87
*Pakistan	310,403	72,370,000	Islamabad		68
*Panama	29,209	1,425,343	Panamá	G 6	154
*Papua New Guinea	183,540	2,800,000	Port Moresby		85,87
*Paraguay	157,047	2,314,000	Asunción		144
Pennsylvania, U.S.A.	45,333	11,793,909	Harrisburg		294
*Persia (Iran)	636,293	32,900,000	Tehran		66
*Peru	496,222	13,586,300	Lima		128
*Philippines	115,707	43,751,000	Manila		82
Pitcairn Islands	18	67	Adamstown	O 8	87
*Poland	120,725	34,364,000	Warsaw		47
*Portugal	35,549	8,825,000	Lisbon		33
Prince Edward Island, Canada	2,184	111,641	Charlottetown	E 2	168
Puerto Rico	3,435	2,712,033	San Juan		161
*Qatar	4,247	150,000	Doha	F 4	59
Québec, Canada	594,860	6,027,764	Québec		172,174
Réunion	969	475,700	St-Denis	F 5	118
Rhode Island, U.S.A.	1,214	949,723	Providence		249
Rhodesia	150,803	6,600,000	Salisbury	D 3	118
*Rumania	91,699	21,500,000	Bucharest	F 3	45
*Rwanda	10,169	4,241,000	Kigali	E 4	115

Country	Area (Sq. Miles)	Population	Capital or Chief Town	Index Ref.	Plate No.
Sabah, Malaysia	28,460	633,000	Kota Kinabalu	F 4	85
St. Christopher-Nevis-Anguilla	138	56,000	Basseterre		155,161
St. Helena	47	4,707	Jamestown	B 6	102
St. Lucia	238	110,000	Castries	G 6	161
St-Pierre and Miquelon	93.5	6,000	St-Pierre	C 4	166
St. Vincent	150	89,129	Kingstown	A 8	161
San Marino	23.4	20,000	San Marino	D 3	34
*São Tomé e Príncipe	372	80,000	São Tomé	F 8	106
Sarawak, Malaysia	48,050	950,000	Kuching	E 5	85
Saskatchewan, Canada	251,700	926,242	Regina		181
*Saudi Arabia	829,995	7,200,000	Riyadh, Mecca	D 4	59
Scotland, U.K.	30,414	5,261,000	Edinburgh		15
*Senegal	75,954	5,085,388	Dakar	A 5	106
*Seychelles	145	60,000	Victoria	H 5	118
*Siam (Thailand)	198,455	42,700,000	Bangkok	D 3	72
*Sierra Leone	27,925	3,100,000	Freetown	B 7	106
*Singapore	226	2,300,000	Singapore	F 6	72
Solomon Islands	11,500	196,708	Honiara	F 6	87
*Somalia	246,200	3,170,000	Mogadishu	H 3	115
*South Africa	458,179	24,400,000	Cape Town, Pretoria	C 5	118
South America	6,875,000	186,000,000			120
South Carolina, U.S.A.	31,055	2,590,516	Columbia		296
South Dakota, U.S.A.	77,047	666,257	Pierre		298
South-West Africa	317,827	883,000	Windhoek	B 3	118
*Spain	194,881	36,000,000	Madrid		33
*Sri Lanka	25,332	14,000,000	Colombo	E 7	68
*Sudan	967,494	18,347,000	Khartoum	E 4	111
*Surinam	55,144	389,000	Paramaribo	C 3	131
*Swaziland	6,705	500,000	Mbabane	E 5	118
*Sweden	173,665	8,236,461	Stockholm		18
Switzerland	15,943	6,489,000	Bern		39
*Syria	71,498	7,585,000	Damascus	G 5	63
*Tanzania	363,708	15,506,000	Dar es Salaam	F 5	115
Tennessee, U.S.A.	42,244	3,924,164	Nashville		237
Texas, U.S.A.	267,339	11,196,730	Austin		302
*Thailand	198,455	42,700,000	Bangkok	D 3	72
*Togo	21,622	2,300,000	Lomé	E 7	106
Tokelau	3.9	1,603	Fakaofo	J 6	87
Tonga	270	102,000	Nuku'alofa	J 8	87
Transkei	14,180	1,500,000	Umtata	D 6	118
*Trinidad and Tobago	1,980	1,040,000	Port of Spain	A10	161
Tristan da Cunha	38	292	Edinburgh	G10	2
*Tunisia	63,170	5,776,000	Tunis	F 2	106
*Turkey	300,946	40,284,000	Ankara		63
Turks and Caicos Is.	166	6,000	Cockburn Town	D 2	156
Tuvalu	10	5,887	Fongafale	H 6	87
*Uganda	91,076	11,400,000	Kampala	F 3	115
*Ukrainian S.S.R., U.S.S.R.	233,089	49,438,000	Kiev	D 5	52
*Union of Soviet Socialist Republics	8,649,490	258,402,000	Moscow		48,52
*United Arab Emirates	32,278	240,000	Abu Dhabi	F 5	58
*United Kingdom	94,399	56,076,000	London		10
United States of America, land land and water	3,554,609 3,615,123	203,235,298	Washington, D.C.		188
*Upper Volta	105,869	6,144,013	Ouagadougou	D 6	106
*Uruguay	72,172	2,900,000	Montevideo		145
Utah, U.S.A.	84,916	1,059,273	Salt Lake City		304
Vatican City	116 acres	704		B 6	34
*Venezuela	352,143	10,398,907	Caracas		124
Vermont, U.S.A.	9,609	444,732	Montpelier		268
Vietnam	128,405	46,600,000	Hanoi	E 3	72
Virginia, U.S.A.	40,817	4,648,494	Richmond		307
Virgin Islands, British	59	10,484	Road Town	H 1	156
Virgin Islands, U.S.A.	133	62,468	Charlotte Amalie		161
Wake Island, U.S.A.	2.5	437		G 4	87
Wales, U.K.	8,017	2,778,000	Cardiff		13
Washington, U.S.A.	68,192	3,409,169	Olympia		310
*Western Samoa	1,133	159,000	Apia	J 7	87
West Virginia, U.S.A.	24,181	1,744,237	Charleston		312
*White Russian S.S.R. (Byelorussian S.S.R.), U.S.S.R.	80,154	9,522,000	Minsk	C 4	52
Wisconsin, U.S.A.	56,154	4,417,933	Madison		317
World	57,970,000	4,240,700,000			1,2
Wyoming, U.S.A.	97,914	332,416	Cheyenne		319
*Yemen Arab Republic	77,220	5,600,000	San'a	D 7	59
*Yemen, Peoples Dem. Rep. of	111,101	1,700,000	Aden	E 7	59
*Yugoslavia	98,766	21,520,000	Belgrade	C 3	45
Yukon Territory, Canada	207,076	18,388	Whitehorse	E 3	187
*Zaire	918,962	25,600,000	Kinshasa	D 4	115
*Zambia	290,586	4,936,000	Lusaka	E 7	115

Introduction to the Maps and Indexes

The following notes have been added to aid the reader in making the best use of this atlas. Though he may be familiar with maps and map indexes, the publisher believes that a quick review of the material below will add to his enjoyment of this reference work.

Arrangement — The Plan of the Atlas. The atlas has been designed with maximum convenience for the user as its objective. All geographically related information pertaining to a country or region appears on adjacent pages, eliminating the task of searching throughout the entire volume for data on a given area. Thus, the reader will find, conveniently assembled, political, topographic, economic and special maps of a political area or region, accompanied by detailed map indexes, statistical data, and illustrations of the national flags of the area.

The sequence of country units in this American-designed atlas is international in arrangement. Units on the world as a whole are followed by a section on the polar regions which, in turn, is followed by pages devoted to Europe and its countries. Every continent map is accompanied by special population distribution, climatic and vegetation maps of that continent. Following the maps of the European continent and its countries, the geographic sequence plan proceeds as follows: Asia, the Pacific and Australia, Africa, South America, North America, and ends with detailed coverage on the United States.

Political Maps — The Primary Reference Tool. The most detailed maps in each country unit are the *political maps*. It is our feeling that the reader is likely to refer to these maps more often than to any other in the book when confronted by such questions as — Where? How big? What is it near? Answering these common queries is the function of the political maps. Each political map stresses *political* phenomena — countries, internal political divisions, boundaries, cities and towns. The major political unit or units, shown on the map, are banded in distinctive colors for easy identification and delineation. First-order political subdivisions (states, provinces, counties on the state maps) are shown, scale permitting.

The reader is advised to make use of the *legend* appearing under the title on each political map. Map *symbols*, the special "language" of maps, are explained in the legend. Each variety of dot, circle, star or interrupted line has a special meaning which should be clearly understood by the user so that he may interpret the map data correctly.

Each country has been portrayed at a *scale* commensurate with its political, areal, economic or tourist importance. In certain cases, a whole map unit may be devoted to a single nation if that nation is considered to be of prime interest to most atlas users. In other cases, several nations will be shown on a single map if, as separate entities, they are of lesser relative importance. Areas of dense settlement and important significance within a country have been enlarged and portrayed in inset maps inserted on the margins of the main map. The reader is advised to refer to the linear or "bar" scale appearing on each map or map inset in order to ascertain the basic scale of the map or to determine the distance between points.

The *projection* system used for each map is noted near the title of the map. Map projections are the special graphic systems used by cartographers to render the curved three-dimensional surface of the globe on a flat surface. Optimum map projections determined by the attributes of the area have been used by the publishers for each map in the atlas.

A word here as to the choice of place names on the maps. Throughout the atlas names appear, with a few exceptions, in their local official spellings. However, conventional Anglicized spellings are used for major geographical divisions and for towns and topographic features for which English forms exist; i.e., "Spain" instead of "España" or "Munich" instead of "München." Names of this type are normally followed by the local official spelling in parentheses. As an aid to the user the indexes are cross-referenced for all current and most former spellings of such names.

Names of cities and towns in the United States follow the forms listed in the *Directory of Post Offices* of the United States Postal Service. Domestic physical names follow the decisions of the Board on Geographic Names, U.S. Department of the Interior, and of various state geographic name boards.

It is the belief of the publishers that the boundaries shown in a general reference atlas should reflect current geographic and political realities. This policy has been followed consistently in the atlas. The presentation of *de facto* boundaries in cases of territorial dispute between various nations does not imply the political endorsement of such boundaries by the publisher, but simply the honest representation of boundaries as they exist at the time of the printing of the atlas maps.

Indexes — Pinpointing a Location. Each political map is accompanied by a comprehensive index of the place names appearing on the map. If you are unfamiliar with the location of a particular geographical place and wish to find its position within the confines of the subject area of the map, consult the map index as your first step. The name of the feature sought will be found in its proper alphabetical sequence with a key reference letter-number combination corresponding to its location on the map. After noting the key reference letter-number combination for the place name, turn to the map. The place name will be found within the square formed by the two lines of latitude and the two lines of longitude which enclose the co-ordinates — i.e., the marginal letters and numbers. The diagram below illustrates the system of indexing.

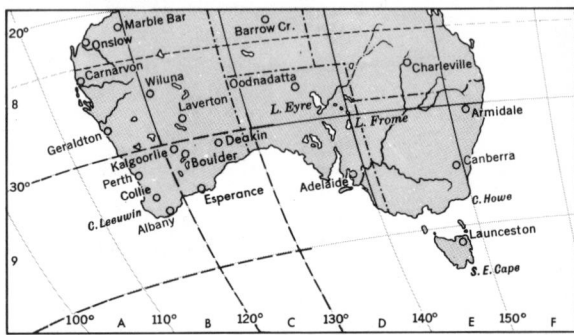

In the case of maps consisting entirely of insets, the place name is found near the intersection point of the imaginary lines connecting the co-ordinates at right angles. See below.

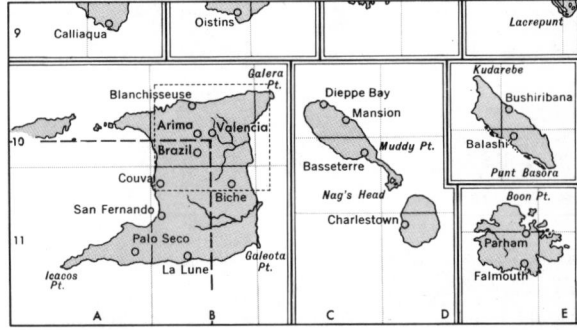

Where space on the map has not permitted giving the complete form of the place name, the complete form is shown in the index. Where a place is known by more than one name or by various spellings of the same name, the different forms have been included in the index. Physical features are listed under their proper names and not according to their generic terms; that is to say, Rio Negro will be found under Negro and not under Rio Negro. On the other hand, Rio Grande will be found under Rio Grande. Accompanying most index entries for cities and towns, and for other political units, are *population figures* for the particular entries. The large number of population figures in the atlas makes this work one of the most comprehensive statistical sources available to the public today. The population figures have been taken from the latest official censuses and estimates of the various nations.

Population and area figures for countries and major political units are listed in bold type *fact lists* on the margins of the indexes. In addition, the capital, largest city, highest point, monetary unit, principal languages and the prevailing religions of the country concerned are also listed. The Gazetteer-Index of the World on the preceding pages provides a quick reference index for countries and other important areas. Though population and area figures for each major unit area also found in the map section, the Gazetteer-Index provides a conveniently arranged statistical comparison contained in two pages.

All index entries for cities and towns in the United States are preceded by a five-digit postal ZIP code number applying to the community. This useful feature permits the reader to address his mail so that it will be routed and delivered more efficiently and quickly by the U.S. Postal Service. A dagger (†) designates those places that do not possess a post office. The ZIP code number listed in such cases refers to that of the nearest post office. An asterisk (*) marks those larger cities which are divided into multiple ZIP code areas. Using the single ZIP code number listed in such cases will direct your letter to the proper city with dispatch. However, if the precise ZIP code number of the address within the city is needed, it is suggested that the reader refer to the latest National ZIP Code Directory at his local post office. This detailed guide lists every street in a multiple ZIP code city with the proper ZIP code for the street.

Relief Maps. Accompanying each political map is a relief map of the area. The purpose of the relief map is to illustrate the surface configuration (TOPOGRAPHY) of the region. A shading technique in color simulates the relative ruggedness of the terrain — plains, plateaus, valleys, hills and mountains. Graded colors, ranging from greens for lowlands, yellows for intermediate elevations to browns in the highlands, indicate the height above sea level of each part of the land. A vertical scale at the margin of the map shows the approximate height in meters and feet represented by each color.

Economic Maps — Agriculture, Industry and Resources. One of the most interesting features that will be found in each country unit is the economic map. From this map one can determine the basic activities of a nation as expressed through its economy. A perusal of the map yields a full understanding of the area's economic geography and natural resources.

The agricultural economy is manifested in two ways: color bands and commodity names. The color bands express broad categories of *dominant land use*, such as, cereal belts, forest lands, livestock range lands, nonagricultural wastes. The red commodity names, on the other hand, pinpoint the areas of production of *specific* crops; i.e., wheat, cotton, sugar beets, etc.

Major mineral occurrences are denoted by standard letter symbols appearing in blue. The relative size of the letter symbols signifies the relative importance of the deposit.

The manufacturing sector of the economy is presented by means of diagonal line patterns expressing the various *industrial areas* of consequence within a country. The products of each major industrial area are listed in boxes at the margin of the map.

The fishing industry is represented by names of commercial fish species appearing offshore in blue letters. Major waterpower sites are designated by blue symbols.

The publishers have tried to make this work the most comprehensive and useful atlas available, and it is hoped that it will prove a valuable reference work. Any constructive suggestions from the reader will be welcomed.

Sources and Acknowledgments

A multitude of sources goes into the making of a large-scale reference work such as this. To list them all would take many pages and would consume space better devoted to the maps and reference materials themselves. However, certain general sources were very useful in preparing this work and are listed below.

STATISTICAL OFFICE OF THE UNITED NATIONS.
Demographic Yearbook. New York. Issued annually.

STATISTICAL OFFICE OF THE UNITED NATIONS.
Statistical Yearbook. New York. Issued annually.

THE GEOGRAPHER, U.S. DEPARTMENT OF STATE.
International Boundary Study papers. Washington. Various dates.

THE GEOGRAPHER, U.S. DEPARTMENT OF STATE.
Geographic Notes. Washington. Various dates.

UNITED STATES BOARD ON GEOGRAPHIC NAMES.
Decisions on Geographic Names in the United States. Washington. Various dates.

UNITED STATES BOARD ON GEOGRAPHIC NAMES.
Official Standard Names Gazetteers. Washington. Various dates.

CANADIAN PERMANENT COMMITTEE ON GEOGRAPHICAL NAMES.
Gazetteer of Canada series. Ottawa. Various dates.

UNITED STATES POSTAL SERVICE.
Directory of Post Offices. Washington. 1970.

UNITED STATES POSTAL SERVICE.
National Zip Code Directory. Washington. 1970-1971.

UNITED STATES POSTAL SERVICE.
Postal Bulletin. Washington. Issued weekly.

UNITED STATES DEPARTMENT OF THE INTERIOR. BUREAU OF MINES.
Minerals Yearbook. 4 vols. Washington. Various dates.

UNITED STATES GEOLOGICAL SURVEY.
Elevations and distances in the United States. Washington. 1969.

UNITED STATES DEPARTMENT OF COMMERCE. JOINT PUBLICATIONS RESEARCH SERVICE.
JPRS reports dealing with foreign geography. Washington. Various dates.

CARTACTUAL.
Cartactual — Topical Map Service. Budapest. Issued bi-monthly.

AMERICAN GEOGRAPHICAL SOCIETY.
Focus. New York. Issued ten times a year.

A sample list of sources used for specific countries follows:

Algeria
COMMISSARIAT NATIONAL AU RECENSEMENT DE LA POPULATION.
Résultats Préliminaires du Recensement Général de la Population Effectué en 1966. Oran.

Barbados
BARBADOS STATISTICAL SERVICE.
1970 Census. St. Michael.

Chile
INSTITUTO NACIONAL DE ESTADÍSTICAS.
XIV Censo Nacional de Población y III de Vivienda. 1970. Santiago.

Dominican Republic
OFICINA NACIONAL DE ESTADÍSTICA.
Censo Nacional de Población y Habitación. 9 y 10 Enero de 1970. Santo Domingo.

France
INSTITUT NATIONAL DE LA STATISTIQUE ET DES ÉTUDES ÉCONOMIQUES.
Recensement de 1968. Population de la France. Paris.

Ghana
CENSUS OFFICE.
1970 Population Census of Ghana. Accra.

Iran
IRANIAN STATISTICAL CENTER.
National Census of Population and Housing, 1966. Tehran.

Ireland
THE CENTRAL STATISTICS OFFICE.
Census of Population of Ireland 1966. Dublin.

Kenya
MINISTRY OF ECONOMIC PLANNING AND DEVELOPMENT. STATISTICS DIVISION.
Provisional Results of the 1969 Population Census. Nairobi.

Kuwait
MINISTRY OF GUIDANCE & INFORMATION.
Population Census 1970. Kuwait.

Mexico
DIRECCIÓN GENERAL DE ESTADÍSTICA.
IX Censo General de Población 1970. México, D.F.

New Caledonia
INSTITUT NATIONAL DE LA STATISTIQUE ET DES ÉTUDES ÉCONOMIQUES (France).
Recensement de 1969. Paris.

Panama
DIRECCIÓN DE ESTADÍSTICA Y CENSO.
Censos Nacionales de 1970. Panamá.

Rhodesia
CENTRAL STATISTICAL OFFICE.
1969 Population Censuses. Salisbury.

Tanzania
CENTRAL STATISTICAL BUREAU.
1967 Population Census. Dar es Salaam.

Togo
DIRECTION DE LA STATISTIQUE.
Résultats Provisoires du Recensement Général de la Population 1970. Lomé.

U.S.S.R.
CENTRAL STATISTICAL ADMINISTRATION.
Preliminary Results of the All-Union Census of Population 1970. Moscow.

United States
BUREAU OF THE CENSUS.
1970 Census of Population. Washington.

CORPS OF ENGINEERS.
Reservoir status lists and maps. Various districts.

Zaire
MINISTÈRE DE L'INTÉRIEUR ET DES AFFAIRES COUTUMIÈRES.
Recensement Général de la Population 1970. Kinshasa.

Zambia
CENTRAL STATISTICAL OFFICE.
Population and Housing Census — 1969. Lusaka.

VIII

Glossary of Abbreviations

A

A. A. F. — Army Air Field
Acad. — Academy
A. C. T. — Australian Capital Territory
adm. — administration; administrative
adm. city-co. — administrative city-county
A. F. B. — Air Force Base
Afgh., Afghan. — Afghanistan
Afr. — Africa
A. & I. — Terr. of the Afars and Issas
Ala. — Alabama
Alb. — Albania
Alg. — Algeria
Alta. — Alberta
Amer. — American
Amer. Samoa — American Samoa
And. — Andorra
Ant. — Antarctica
Ar. — Arabia
arch. — archipelago
Arg. — Argentina
Ariz. — Arizona
Ark. — Arkansas
A. S. S. R. — Autonomous Soviet
　　　　Socialist Republic
aut. — autonomous
Aut. Obl. — Autonomous Oblast
aut. prov. — autonomous province

B

B. — bay
Bah. Is. — Bahama Islands
Barb. — Barbados
Battlef. — Battlefield
Bch. — Beach
Belg. — Belgium
Berm. — Bermuda
Bol. — Bolivia
Bots. — Botswana
Br. — Branch
Br. — British
Braz. — Brazil
Br. Col. — British Columbia
Br. Ind. Oc. Terr. — British Indian
　　　　Ocean Territory
Bulg. — Bulgaria

C

C. — cape
Calif. — California
can. — canal
cap. — capital
Cent. Afr. Rep. — Central African
　　　　Republic
Cent. Amer. — Central America
C. G. Sta. — Coast Guard Station
C. H. — Court House
chan. — channel
Chan. Is. — Channel Islands
Chem. Ctr. — Chemical Center
co. — county
C. of G. H. — Cape of Good Hope
Col. — Colombia
Colo. — Colorado
comm. — commissary
Conn. — Connecticut
cont. — continent
cord. — cordillera (mountain range)
C. Rica — Costa Rica
C. S. — County Seat
C. Verde Is. — Cape Verde Islands
Cy. — City
C. Z. — Canal Zone
Czech. — Czechoslovakia

D

D. C. — District of Columbia
Del. — Delaware
Dem. — Democratic
Den. — Denmark
depr. — depression
dept. — department
des. — desert
dist., dist's — district, districts
div. — division
Dom. Rep. — Dominican Republic
dry riv. — dry river

E

E. — East
Ec., Ecua. — Ecuador
E. Ger. — East Germany
elec. div. — electoral division

El Salv. — El Salvador
Eng. — England
Eq. Guin. — Equatorial Guinea
escarp. — escarpment
est. — estuary
Eth. — Ethiopia

F

Falk. Is. — Falkland Islands
Fin. — Finland
Fk., Fks. — Fork, Forks
Fla. — Florida
for. — forest
Fr. — France, French
Fr. Gui. — French Guiana
Fr. Poly. — French Polynesia
Ft. — Fort

G

G. — gulf
Ga. — Georgia
Game Res. — Game Reserve
Ger. — Germany
geys. — geyser
Gibr. — Gibraltar
Gilb. & Ell. Is. — Gilbert and Ellice
　　　　Islands
glac. — glacier
gov. — governorate
Gr. — Group
Greenl. — Greenland
Gt. Brit. — Great Britain
Guad. — Guadeloupe
Guat. — Guatemala
Guy. — Guyana

H

har., harb., hbr. — harbor
hd. — head
highl. — highland, highlands
Hist. — Historic, Historical
Hond. — Honduras
Hts. — Heights
Hung. — Hungary

I

i., isl., isle — island, isle
Ice., Icel. — Iceland
Ida. — Idaho
Ill. — Illinois
Ind. — Indiana
ind. city — independent city
Indon. — Indonesia
Ind. Res. — Indian Reservation
int. div. — internal division
inten. — intendency
interm. str. — intermittent stream
Int'l — International
Ire. — Ireland
is., isls. — islands
Isr. — Israel
isth. — isthmus

J

Jam. — Jamaica
Jct. — Junction

K

Kans. — Kansas
Ky. — Kentucky

L

L. — Lake, Loch, Lough
La. — Louisiana
Lab. — Laboratory
lag. — lagoon
Ld. — Land
Leb. — Lebanon
Les. — Lesotho
Liecht. — Liechtenstein
Lux. — Luxembourg

M

Malag. Rep. — Malagasy Republic
Man. — Manitoba
Mart. — Martinique
Mass. — Massachusetts
Maur. — Mauritania
Md. — Maryland
met. area — metropolitan area
Mex. — Mexico
Mich. — Michigan
Minn. — Minnesota
Miss. — Mississippi

Mo. — Missouri
Mon. — Monument
Mong. — Mongolia
Mont. — Montana
Mor. — Morocco
Moz., Mozamb. — Mozambique
mt. — mount
mtn. — mountain

N

N., No. — North, Northern
N. Amer. — North America
N. A. S. — Naval Air Station
Nat'l — National
Nat'l Cem. — National Cemetery
Nat'l Mem. Park — National Memorial
　　　　Park
Nat'l Mil. Park — National Military
　　　　Park
Nat'l Pkwy. — National Parkway
Nav. Base — Naval Base
Nav. Sta. — Naval Station
N. B., N. Br. — New Brunswick
N. C. — North Carolina
N. Dak. — North Dakota
Nebr. — Nebraska
Neth. — Netherlands
Neth. Ant. — Netherlands Antilles
Nev. — Nevada
New Cal. — New Caledonia
Newf. — Newfoundland
New Hebr. — New Hebrides
N. H. — New Hampshire
Nic. — Nicaragua
N. Ire. — Northern Ireland
N. J. — New Jersey
N. Mex. — New Mexico
Nor. — Norway, Norwegian
No. Terr. — Northern Territory
　　　　(Australia)
N. S. — Nova Scotia
N. S. W. — New South Wales
N. W. T. — Northwest Territories
　　　　(Canada)
N. Y. — New York
N. Z. — New Zealand

O

Obl. — Oblast
O. F. S. — Orange Free State
Okla. — Oklahoma
Okr. — Okrug
Ont. — Ontario
Ord. Depot — Ordnance Depot
Oreg. — Oregon

P

Pa. — Pennsylvania
Pac. — Pacific
Pac. Is. — Pacific Islands,
　　　　Territory of the
Pak. — Pakistan
Pan. — Panama
Par. — Paraguay
par. — parish
passg. — passage
P.D.R. Yemen — Peoples Democratic
　　　　Republic of Yemen
P. E. I. — Prince Edward Island
pen. — peninsula
Phil., Phil. Is. — Philippines
Pk. — Park
pk. — peak
plat. — plateau
Port. — Portugal, Portuguese
P. Rico — Puerto Rico
pref. — prefecture
prom. — promontory
prov. — province, provincial
prov. dist. — provincial district
pt. — point

Q

Que. — Québec
Queens. — Queensland

R

R. — River
ra. — range
Rec., Recr. — Recreation, Recreational
reg. — region
Rep. — Republic
Rep. of Congo — Republic of Congo
res. — reservoir
Res. — Reservation, Reserve

Rhod. — Rhodesia
R. I. — Rhode Island
riv. — river
Rum. — Rumania

S

S. — South
Sa. — Sierra, Serra
S. Afr., S. Africa — South Africa
salt dep. — salt deposit
salt des. — salt desert
S. Amer. — South America
São T. & Pr. — São Tomé
　　　　and Príncipe
Sask. — Saskatchewan
Saudi Ar. — Saudi Arabia
S. Aust., S. Austral. — South Australia
S. C. — South Carolina
Scot. — Scotland
Sd. — Sound
S. Dak. — South Dakota
Sen. — Senegal
sen. dist. — senatorial district
Seych. — Seychelles
S. F. S. R. — Soviet Federated Socialist
　　　　Republic
Sing. — Singapore
S. Leone — Sierra Leone
S. Marino — San Marino
Sol. Is. Prot. — Solomon Islands
　　　　Protectorate, British
Sp. — Spanish
Spr., Sprs. — Spring, Springs
S. S. R. — Soviet Socialist Republic
St., Ste. — Saint, Sainte
Sta. — Station
St. Chr.-N.-A. — Saint Christopher-
　　　　Nevis-Anguilla
St. P. & M. — Saint Pierre and
　　　　Miquelon
str., strs. — strait, straits
Sur. — Surinam
S. W. Afr. — South-West Africa
Swaz. — Swaziland
Switz. — Switzerland

T

Tanz. — Tanzania
Tas. — Tasmania
Tenn. — Tennessee
terr., terrs. — territory, territories
Terr. N. G. — New Guinea, Territory of
Tex. — Texas
Thai. — Thailand
Trin. & Tob. — Trinidad and Tobago
Tun. — Tunisia
twp. — township

U

U. A. E. — Union of (United)
　　　　Arab Emirates
U. K. — United Kingdom
Upp. Volta — Upper Volta
urb. area — urban area
Urug. — Uruguay
U. S. — United States
U. S. S. R. — Union of Soviet Socialist
　　　　Republics

V

Va. — Virginia
Vall. — Valley
Ven., Venez. — Venezuela
V. I. (Br.) — Virgin Islands (British)
V. I. (U. S.) — Virgin Islands (U. S.)
Vic. — Victoria
Vill. — Village
vol. — volcano
Vt. — Vermont

W

W. — West, Western
Wash. — Washington
W. Aust., W. Austral. — Western
　　　　Australia
W. Ger. — West Germany
Wis. — Wisconsin
W. Samoa — Western Samoa
W. Va. — West Virginia
Wyo. — Wyoming

Y

Yugo. — Yugoslavia
Yukon — Yukon Territory

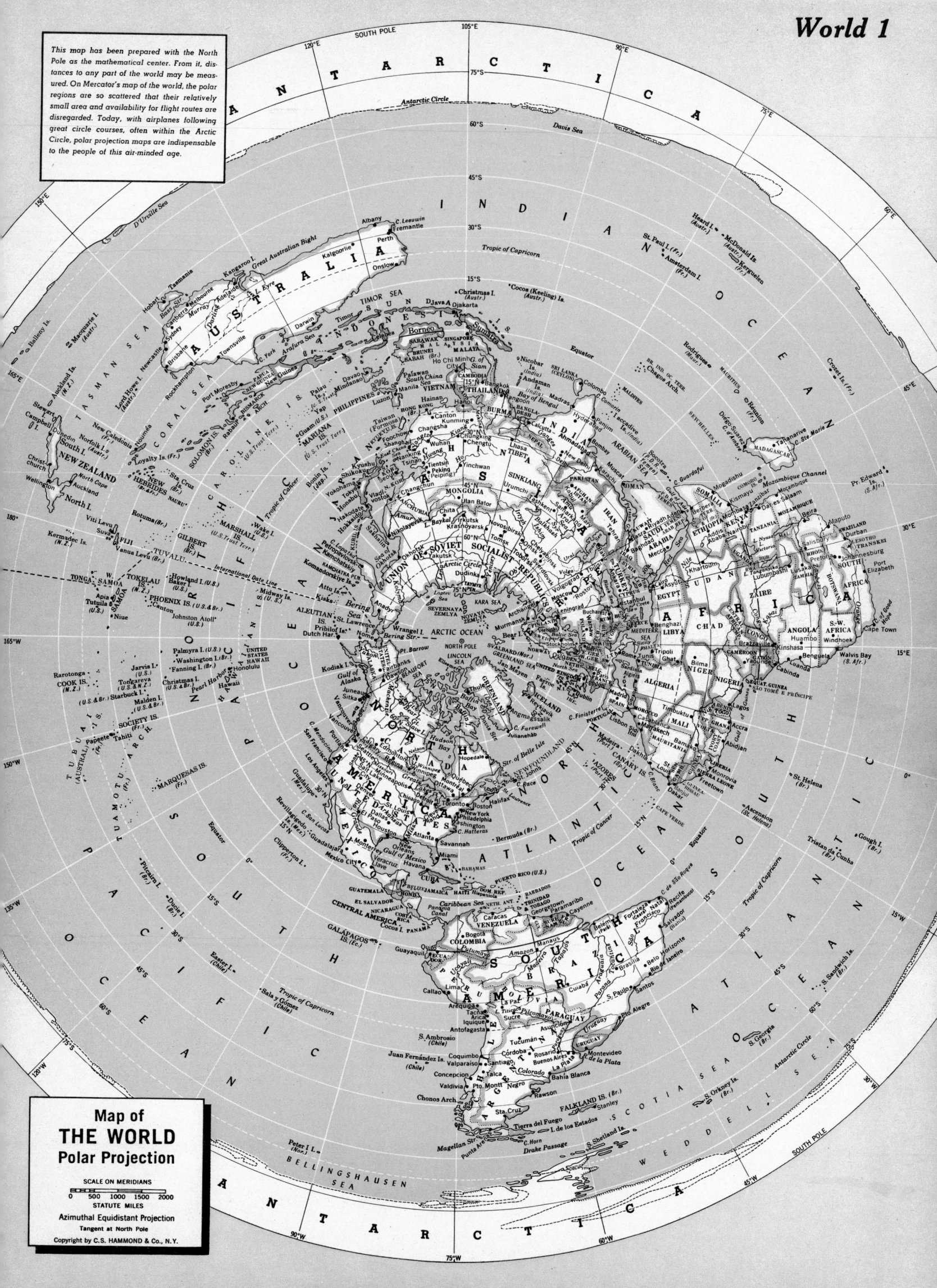

This map has been prepared with the North Pole as the mathematical center. From it, distances to any part of the world may be measured. On Mercator's map of the world, the polar regions are so scattered that their relatively small area and availability for flight routes are disregarded. Today, with airplanes following great circle courses, often within the Arctic Circle, polar projection maps are indispensable to the people of this air-minded age.

Map of THE WORLD Polar Projection

SCALE ON MERIDIANS

0   500   1000   1500   2000

STATUTE MILES

Azimuthal Equidistant Projection

Tangent at North Pole

Copyright by C.S. HAMMOND & Co., N.Y.

THE WORLD

BRIESEMEISTER ELLIPTICAL
EQUAL-AREA PROJECTION

Capitals of Countries .... ⊛
International Boundaries .... – – –

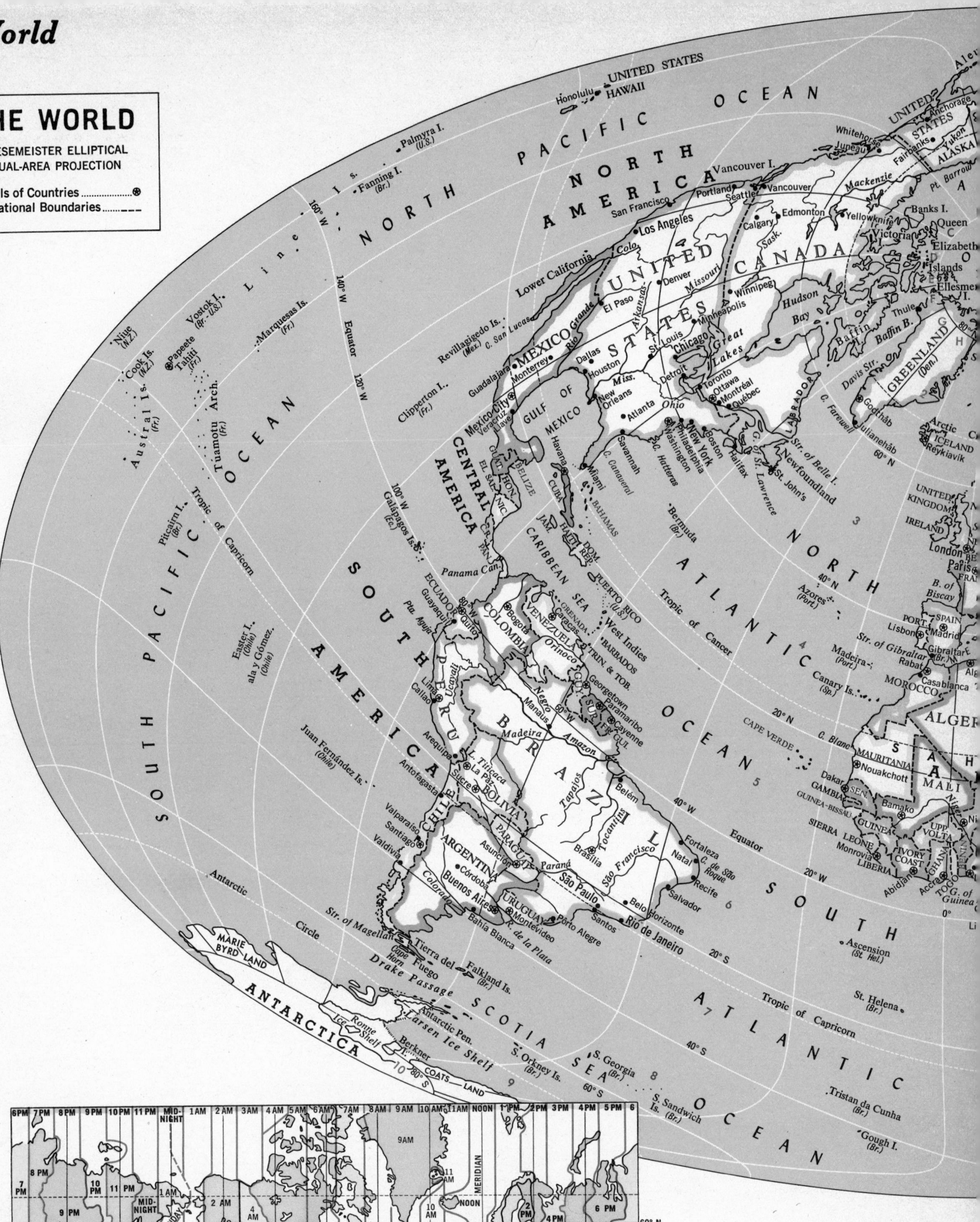

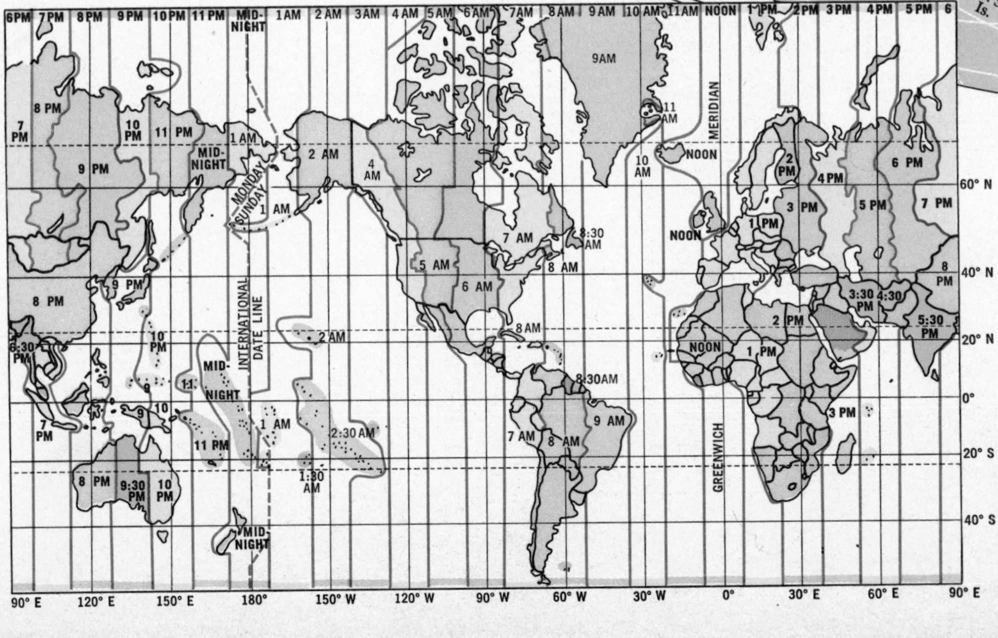

Oceans and Seas

NORTH PACIFIC OCEAN
NORTH PACIFIC OCEAN
SOUTH PACIFIC OCEAN
NORTH ATLANTIC OCEAN
SOUTH ATLANTIC OCEAN
CARIBBEAN SEA
GULF OF MEXICO
SCOTIA SEA
DRAKE PASSAGE

North America

UNITED STATES
HAWAII
Honolulu
CANADA
ALASKA
Anchorage
Fairbanks
Juneau
Whitehorse
Yukon
Mackenzie
Barrow
Pt. Barrow
Banks I.
Yellowknife
Edmonton
Calgary
Victoria
Vancouver
Vancouver I.
Seattle
Portland
San Francisco
Los Angeles
Denver
El Paso
Colo.
Arkansas
Missouri
Rio Grande
Dallas
Houston
New Orleans
St. Louis
Chicago
Great Lakes
Detroit
Minneapolis
Winnipeg
Hudson Bay
Baffin I.
Baffin B.
Thule
Davis Str.
GREENLAND (Den.)
Godthåb
Julianehåb
C. Farewell
Toronto
Ottawa
Montréal
Québec
Atlanta
Savannah
C. Hatteras
Washington
Philadelphia
New York
Boston
Halifax
St. John's
Newfoundland
Labrador
Str. of Belle I.
Miami
C. Canaveral
Bahamas
Cuba
Havana
BAHAMAS
Bermuda
Queen Elizabeth Islands
Ellesmere I.
Arctic C.
ICELAND
Reykjavik

Central America / Mexico

MEXICO
Mexico City
Veracruz
Guadalajara
Monterrey
Lower California
C. San Lucas
Revillagigedo Is. (Mex.)
Clipperton I. (Fr.)
CENTRAL AMERICA
GUATEMALA
BELIZE
HONDURAS
EL SALVADOR
NIC.
JAMAICA
HAITI
DOM. REP.
PUERTO RICO (U.S.)
WEST INDIES
Panama Can.
GUADELOUPE
BARBADOS
TRIN. & TOB.

South America

SOUTH AMERICA
COLOMBIA
Bogotá
ECUADOR
Quito
Guayaquil
Galápagos Is. (Ec.)
Pta. Aguja
PERU
Callao
Lima
Arequipa
Antofagasta
VENEZUELA
Orinoco
GUYANA
SUR.
FR. GU.
Georgetown
Paramaribo
Cayenne
Negro
Manaus
BRAZIL
Amazon
Madeira
Tapajos
Tocantins
Belém
Fortaleza
C. de São Roque
Natal
Recife
Salvador
São Francisco
Brasília
Belo Horizonte
Rio de Janeiro
Santos
São Paulo
Porto Alegre
BOLIVIA
La Paz
Sucre
L. Titicaca
Ucayali
PARAGUAY
Asunción
Paraná
ARGENTINA
Córdoba
Buenos Aires
URUGUAY
Montevideo
R. de la Plata
Bahía Blanca
Colorado
CHILE
Valparaíso
Santiago
Valdivia
Juan Fernández Is. (Chile)
Easter I. (Chile)
Sala y Gómez (Chile)
Tierra del Fuego
Cape Horn
Falkland Is. (Br.)
Str. of Magellan

Pacific Islands

Niue (N.Z.)
Cook Is. (N.Z.)
Austral Is. (Fr.)
Papeete
Tahiti (Fr.)
Tuamotu Arch. (Fr.)
Marquesas Is. (Fr.)
Vostok I. (Br. U.S.)
Pitcairn I. (Br.)
Line Is.
Fanning I. (Br.)
Palmyra I. (U.S.)

Atlantic Islands / Africa

Azores (Port.)
Madeira (Port.)
Canary Is. (Sp.)
CAPE VERDE
C. Blanc
UNITED KINGDOM
IRELAND
London
Paris
B. of Biscay
SPAIN
PORT.
Lisbon
Madrid
Gibraltar
Str. of Gibraltar
Rabat
Casablanca
MOROCCO
ALGERIA
SAHARA
MAURITANIA
Nouakchott
MALI
SENEGAL
Dakar
GAMBIA
GUINEA-BISSAU
GUINEA
Bamako
SIERRA LEONE
Monrovia
LIBERIA
IVORY COAST
Abidjan
Accra
GHANA
UPPER VOLTA
TOGO
G. of Guinea
Ascension (St. Hel.)
St. Helena (Br.)
Tristan da Cunha (Br.)
Gough I. (Br.)

Antarctica

ANTARCTICA
MARIE BYRD LAND
COATS LAND
Ronne Ice Shelf
Larsen Ice Shelf
Berkner I.
Antarctic Pen.
S. Orkney Is. (Br.)
S. Georgia (Br.)
S. Sandwich Is. (Br.)
Antarctic Circle

Lines

Equator
Tropic of Cancer
Tropic of Capricorn
160° W, 140° W, 120° W, 100° W, 80° W, 60° W, 40° W, 20° W, 0°, 20° E
20° N, 40° N, 60° N, 20° S, 40° S

Time Zones Chart

6PM 7PM 8PM 9PM 10PM 11PM MIDNIGHT 1AM 2AM 3AM 4AM 5AM 6AM 7AM 8AM 9AM 10AM 11AM NOON 1PM 2PM 3PM 4PM 5PM 6

MERIDIAN
GREENWICH
INTERNATIONAL DATE LINE
MONDAY / SUNDAY

90° E, 120° E, 150° E, 180°, 150° W, 120° W, 90° W, 60° W, 30° W, 0°, 30° E, 60° E, 90° E
60° N, 40° N, 20° N, 20° S, 40° S

TIME ZONES

STANDARD TIME ZONES

Areas using half hour deviations.

Areas not using zone system.

NOTE: Standard time zones in the U.S.S.R. are always advanced one hour.

WORLD
LAND AREA 57,970,000 sq. mi.
WATER AREA 139,781,000 sq. mi.
TOTAL SURFACE AREA 197,751,000 sq. mi.
POPULATION 4,240,700,000

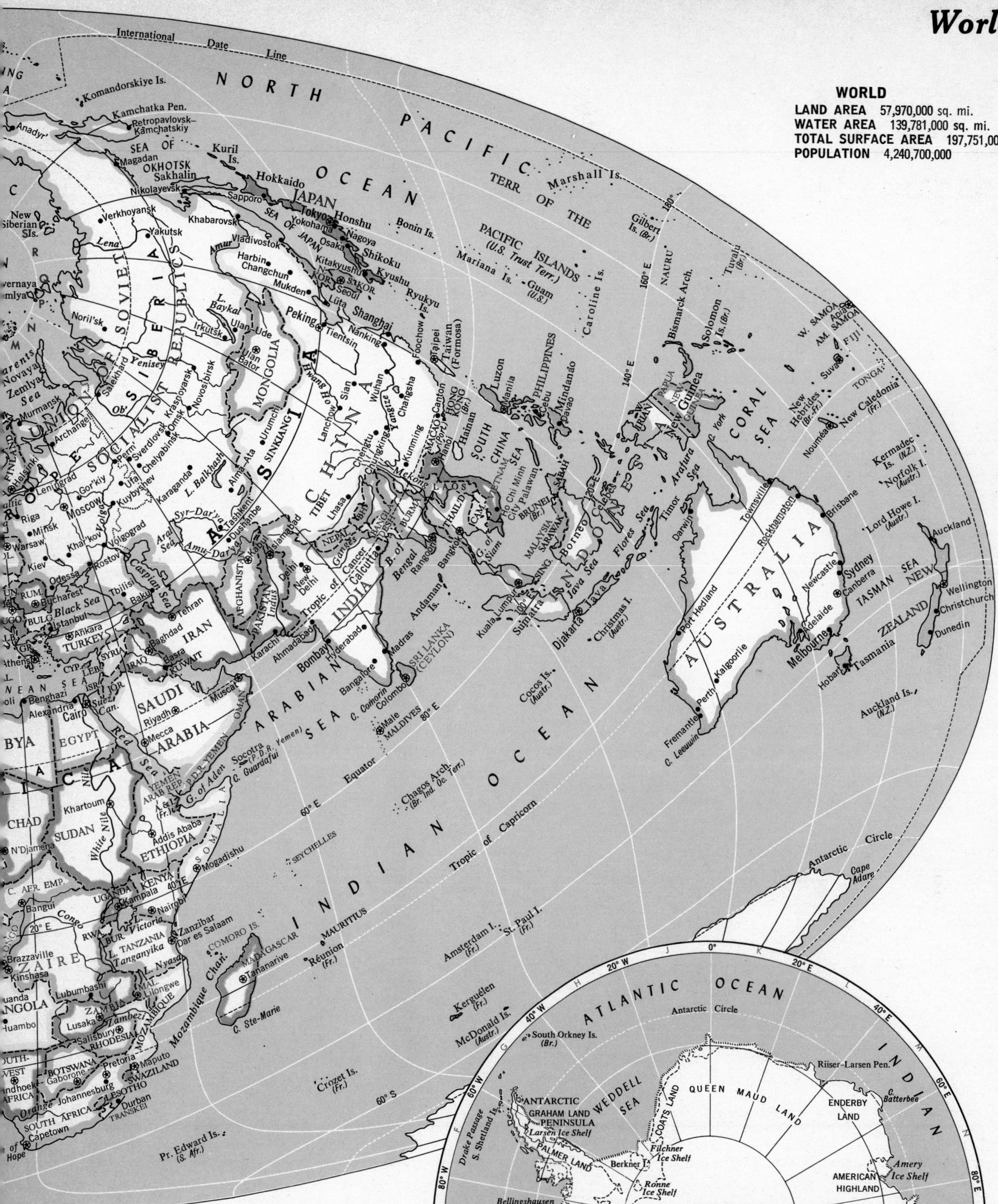

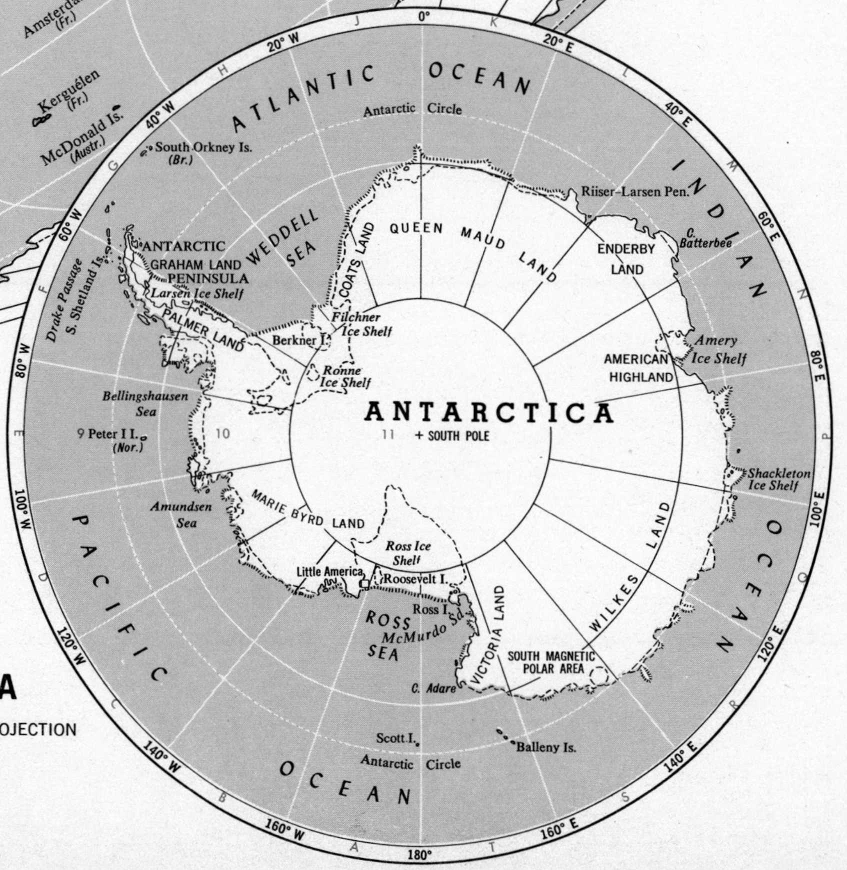

International Date Line

NORTH PACIFIC OCEAN

TERR. OF THE PACIFIC ISLANDS (U.S. Trust Terr.)

Komandorskiye Is.
Kamchatka Pen.
Retropavlovsk-Kamchatskiy
Anadyr'
New Siberian Is.
Vernaya
mlya
Kuril Is.
SEA OF OKHOTSK
Magadan
Sakhalin
Nikolayevsk
Hokkaido
Sapporo
Verkhoyansk
Yakutsk
Khabarovsk
Lena
Vladivostok
JAPAN
Tokyo
Yokohama
Honshu
Nagoya
Osaka
Kitakyushu
Kyushu
Shikoku
Ryukyu Is.
Amur
Harbin
Changchun
Mukden
KOR.
Seoul
S. KOR.
Peking
Tientsin
Nanking
Shanghai
Foochow
Taipei
Taiwan (Formosa)
Hong Kong (Br.)
Hainan
MONGOLIA
Ulan Bator
Ulan-Ude
Irkutsk
L. Baykal
Krasnoyarsk
Novosibirsk
Omsk
Sverdlovsk
Perm'
Chelyabinsk
Karaganda
Alma-Ata
Tashkent
SINKIANG
Urumchi
TIBET
Lhasa
CHINA
Lanchow
Sian
Wuhan
Yangtze
Changsha
Chungking
Kunming
Mekong
Hwang Ho
Canton
MACAO
Hanoi
VIETNAM
LAOS
BURMA
Rangoon
Mandalay
THAILAND
Bangkok
G. of Siam
CAMB.
Phnom Penh
Saigon
SOUTH CHINA SEA
Luzon
Manila
PHILIPPINES
Cebu
Mindanao
Davao
Palawan
BRUNEI (Br.)
MALAYSIA
SARAWAK
SABAH
SING.
Kuala Lumpur
Sumatra
Borneo
Celebes
Djakarta
Java
INDONESIA
Flores Sea
Timor
Timor Sea
Arafura Sea
NEW GUINEA
PAPUA
New Britain
Bismarck Arch.
Solomon Is. (Br.)
New Hebrides (Br.-Fr.)
New Caledonia (Fr.)
CORAL SEA
NAURU
Gilbert Is. (Br.)
Marshall Is.
Caroline Is.
Mariana Is.
Guam (U.S.)
Bonin Is.
W. SAMOA
AM. SAMOA
Apia
FIJI
Suva
TONGA
Kermadec Is. (N.Z.)
Norfolk I. (Austr.)
Lord Howe I. (Austr.)
Auckland
NEW ZEALAND
Wellington
Christchurch
Dunedin
TASMAN SEA
AUSTRALIA
Brisbane
Rockhampton
Townsville
C. York
Darwin
Port Hedland
Fremantle
Perth
C. Leeuwin
Kalgoorlie
Adelaide
Melbourne
Hobart
Tasmania
Sydney
Canberra
Newcastle

UNION OF SOVIET SOCIALIST REPUBLICS
SIBERIA
Novaya Zemlya
Barents Sea
Murmansk
Archangel
Leningrad
Moscow
Gor'kiy
Kuybyshev
Volgograd
Rostov
Khar'kov
Kiev
Minsk
Riga
Warsaw
Bucharest
Istanbul
Ankara
TURKEY
CYP.
LEB.
SYRIA
IRAQ
Baghdad
Basra
KUWAIT
IRAN
Tehran
Tabriz
AFGHANISTAN
Kabul
Kandahar
PAKISTAN
Karachi
Indus
Lahore
New Delhi
Delhi
NEPAL
BHUTAN
Ganges
INDIA
Calcutta
B. of Bengal
Bombay
Hyderabad
Bangalore
Madras
C. Comorin
SRI LANKA (CEYLON)
Colombo
Ahmadabad
Aral Sea
Syr-Dar'ya
Amu-Dar'ya
Dushanbe
Tashkent
Caspian Sea
Baku
Tbilisi
Black Sea
BULG.
RUM.
HUNG.
POL.
Athens
NEAN SEA
toli
Benghazi
Alexandria
Cairo
EGYPT
BYA
Suez Can.
Red Sea
Mecca
Riyadh
SAUDI ARABIA
Muscat
OMAN
YEMEN ARAB REP.
P.D.R. YEMEN
Aden
G. of Aden
Socotra (P.D.R. Yemen)
C. Guardafui
SOMALIA
Mogadishu
Addis Ababa
ETHIOPIA
SUDAN
Khartoum
White Nile
Nile
N'Djamena
CHAD
C. AFR. EMP.
Bangui
UGANDA
KENYA
Kampala
Nairobi
Victoria
Zanzibar
Dar es Salaam
TANZANIA
L. Tanganyika
L. Victoria
L. Nyasa
BUR.
RWA.
ZAIRE
Kinshasa
Brazzaville
Lubumbashi
ANGOLA
ZAMBIA
Lusaka
Zambezi
RHODESIA
Salisbury
MOZAMBIQUE
MAL.
Lilongwe
MADAGASCAR
Tananarive
COMORO Is.
Mozambique Chan.
C. Ste-Marie
C. Delgado
BOTSWANA
Gaborone
SOUTH-WEST AFRICA
Windhoek
Pretoria
Johannesburg
Orange
SOUTH AFRICA
LESOTHO
SWAZILAND
Durban
TRANSKEI
Capetown
C. of Good Hope
Pr. Edward Is. (S. Afr.)

Tropic of Cancer
Tropic of Capricorn
Equator
Antarctic Circle

INDIAN OCEAN
ARABIAN SEA
Andaman Is.
Nicobar Is.
MALDIVES
Male
SEYCHELLES
Chagos Arch. (Br. Ind. Oc. Terr.)
Cocos Is. (Austr.)
Christmas I. (Austr.)
MAURITIUS
Réunion (Fr.)
Amsterdam I. (Fr.)
St. Paul I. (Fr.)
Kerguélen (Fr.)
McDonald Is. (Austr.)
Crozet Is. (Fr.)
Pr. Edward Is.

40° E   60° E   80° E   100° E   120° E   140° E   160° E   180°   160° W

ANTARCTICA
AZIMUTHAL EQUIDISTANT PROJECTION

ATLANTIC OCEAN
Antarctic Circle
South Orkney Is. (Br.)
S. Shetland Is.
Drake Passage
ANTARCTIC PENINSULA
GRAHAM LAND
PALMER LAND
Larsen Ice Shelf
WEDDELL SEA
COATS LAND
QUEEN MAUD LAND
ENDERBY LAND
C. Batterbee
Riiser-Larsen Pen.
Filchner Ice Shelf
Berkner I.
Ronne Ice Shelf
AMERICAN HIGHLAND
Amery Ice Shelf
Bellingshausen Sea
Peter I I. (Nor.)
ANTARCTICA
+ SOUTH POLE
Shackleton Ice Shelf
WILKES LAND
Amundsen Sea
MARIE BYRD LAND
Ross Ice Shelf
Little America
Roosevelt I.
Ross I.
McMurdo
ROSS SEA
VICTORIA LAND
SOUTH MAGNETIC POLAR AREA
C. Adare
Cape Adare
Scott I.
Balleny Is.
Antarctic Circle
PACIFIC OCEAN
INDIAN OCEAN

20° W   0°   20° E   40° E   60° E   80° E   100° E   120° E   140° E   160° E   180°   160° W   140° W   120° W   100° W   80° W   60° W   40° W

4 Arctic Ocean

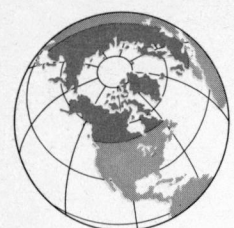

ARCTIC ICE

Approximate Limit of Pack Ice in September

Approximate Limit of Pack Ice in March

© C.S. Hammond & Co.

ARCTIC OCEAN

AZIMUTHAL EQUIDISTANT PROJECTION

SCALE OF MILES
0 100 200 400 600

SCALE OF KILOMETRES
0 200 400 600 800 1000

Copyright by C.S. Hammond & Co., N.Y.

EXPLORERS' ROUTES

Peary 1909
Byrd 1926
Amundsen, Ellsworth & Nobile 1926
Anderson in U.S.S. Nautilus 1958

By ship   By sledge
By airplane   By dirigible
By nuclear submarine

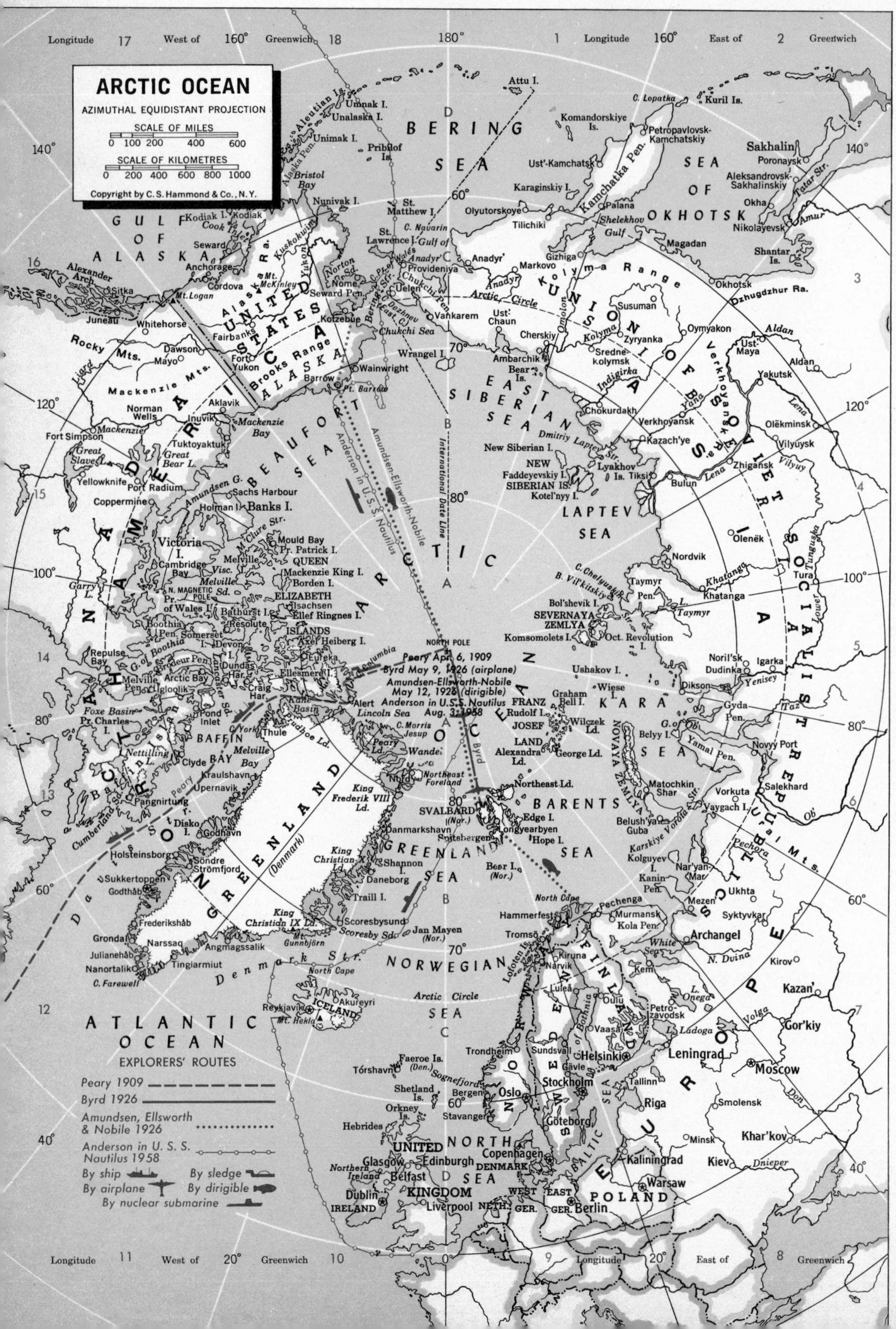

ANTARCTICA
AZIMUTHAL EQUIDISTANT PROJECTION

SCALE OF MILES
0 200 400 600 800

SCALE OF KILOMETRES
0 200 400 600 800 1000

© C. S. HAMMOND & Co., N.Y.

Map labels

ATLANTIC OCEAN · INDIAN OCEAN · PACIFIC OCEAN · SCOTIA SEA · WEDDELL SEA · BELLINGSHAUSEN SEA · Amundsen Sea · Ross Sea · Davis Sea · Tasman Sea

SOUTH AMERICA · NEW ZEALAND · AUSTRALIA · Tasmania · Melbourne · Hobart · Dunedin

Bouvet I. (Nor.) · Prince Edward Is. (S. Afr.) · Antarctic Circle · South Pole · SOUTH POLAR PLATEAU · AREA OF POLE OF INACCESSIBILITY · SOUTH-MAGNETIC POLAR AREA

Amundsen-Scott Sta.
Amundsen Dec. 14, 1911
Scott Jan. 17, 1912
Byrd Nov. 29, 1929 (airplane)
Fuchs Jan. 20, 1958

Queen Maud Land · New Schwabenland · Enderby Land · Mac-Robertson Land · American Highland · Wilkes Land · Victoria Land · Marie Byrd Land · Ellsworth Land · Palmer Land · English Coast · Coats Land

Vinson Massif 16,864 · Mt. Siple 10,171 · Mt. Sidley 13,717 · Mt. Lister 13,205 · Mt. Markham 14,272 · Mt. Kirkpatrick 14,856 · Mt. Sabine 12,202 · Mt. Levick 9,101 · Mt. Barr Smith 4,108 · Gaussberg

Byrd Sta. · Little America · Roosevelt I. · Scott · McMurdo · Mawson · Davis · Mirnyy · Dumont d'Urville · Lazarev · Sanae · Grytviken · Stanley

Ross Ice Shelf · Filchner Ice Shelf · Edith Ronne Ice Shelf · Amery Ice Shelf · Shackleton Ice Shelf · West Ice Shelf · Getz Ice Shelf · Larsen Ice Shelf

Falkland Is. (Br.) · South Georgia (Br.) · South Sandwich Is. (Br.) · South Orkney Is. (Br.) · South Shetland Is. · Elephant I. · King George I. · Joinville I. · James Ross I. · Adelaide I. · Alexander I. · Charcot I. · Peter I I. (Nor.) · Thurston I. · Roosevelt I. · Berkner I. · Balleny Is. · Scott I. · Macquarie I. (Australia) · Campbell I. (N.Z.) · Auckland Is. (N.Z.) · Antipodes Is. (N.Z.) · Bounty Is. (N.Z.) · Stewart I.

Drake Passage · Bransfield Str. · Ronne Entr. · Lützow-Holm Bay · Amundsen Bay · Edward VIII Bay · Prydz Bay · Vincennes Bay · Sulzberger Bay · Marguerite Bay · Hilton Inlet · Hope Bay · Kainan Bay · Farr Bay · Bass Str.

Limit of Drift Ice · C. Norvegia · C. Batterbee · C. Darnley · C. Daly · C. Goodenough · C. Keltie · C. Adare · C. Dart

PRINCESS MARTHA COAST · PRINCESS ASTRID COAST · PRINCESS RAGNHILD COAST · PRINCE OLAV COAST · KEMP COAST · CAIRD COAST · LUITPOLD COAST · QUEEN MARY COAST · WILHELM II COAST · BUDD COAST · SABRINA COAST · BANZARE COAST · CLARIE COAST · ADÉLIE COAST · GEORGE V COAST · OATES COAST · WALGREEN COAST · HOLLICK-KENYON PLATEAU · EIGHTS COAST · HOBBS COAST

Explorers' routes / Scott 1910-13 · Byrd 1928-30 · Amundsen 1911-12

Index

Adare (cape)	B 9	Luitpold Coast (region)	B17
Adelaide (isl.)	C15	Lützow-Holm (bay)	C 3
Adélie Coast (region)	C 7	Mackenzie (bay)	C 4
Alexander (isl.)	B15	Mac-Robertson Land (region)	C 4
American Highland	B 4	Marguerite (bay)	C15
Amery Ice Shelf	C 4	Marie Byrd Land (region)	B12
Amundsen (bay)	C 3	Markham (mt.)	A 8
Amundsen (sea)	B13	Mawson	C 4
Antarctic (pen.)	C15	McMurdo (sound)	B 9
Balleny (isls.)	C 9	Mertz (glacier)	C 8
Banzare Coast (region)	C 7	Mirnyy	C 5
Barr Smith (mt.)	C 5	New Schwabenland	B 1
Batterbee (cape)	C 4	Ninnis (glacier)	C 8
Beardmore (glacier)	A 8	Norvegia (cape)	B18
Bellingshausen (sea)	C14	Oates Coast (region)	B 8
Berkner (isl.)	B16	Palmer (arch.)	C15
Biscoe (isls.)	C15	Palmer Land (region)	B15
Bouvet (isl.)	D 1	Palmer Station	C15
Bransfield (strait)	C15	Peter I (isl.)	C14
Budd Coast (region)	C 6	Prince Edward (isls.)	E 2
Byrd Station	A12	Prince Olav Coast (region)	C 3
Caird Coast (region)	B17	Princess Astrid Coast (region)	B 1
Charcot (isl.)	C15	Princess Martha Coast (region)	B18
Clarie Coast (region)	C 7	Princess Ragnhild Coast (region)	B18
Coats Land (region)	B18	Prydz (bay)	C 4
Colbeck (cape)	B10	Queen Mary Coast (region)	C 5
Coronation (isl.)	C16	Queen Maud Land (region)	B 1
Daly (cape)	C 4	Riiser-Larsen (pen.)	C 2
Darnley (cape)	C 4	Ronne Entrance (bay)	B15
Dart (cape)	B12	Roosevelt (isl.)	A10
Davis (sea)	C 5	Ross (isl.)	B 9
Drake (passage)	C15	Ross (sea)	B10
Dumont d'Urville (sta.)	C 7	Ross Ice Shelf	A10
Edith Ronne Ice Shelf	B16	Sabine (mt.)	B 9
Edward VII (pen.)	B11	Sabrina Coast (region)	C 6
Eights Coast (region)	B14	Sanae (sta.)	B18
Elephant (isl.)	C16	Scotia (sea)	D16
Ellsworth Land (reg.)	A14	Scott (isl.)	C10
Enderby Land (region)	B14	Shackleton Ice Shelf	C 5
English Coast (reg.)	B15	Sidley (mt.)	B12
Executive Committee (range)	B12	Siple (mt.)	B12
Farr (bay)	C 5	South Georgia (isl.)	D17
Filchner Ice Shelf	B16	South Magnetic Polar Area	C 8
Ford (ranges)	B11	South Orkney (isls.)	C16
Gaussberg (mt.)	C 5	South Polar (plateau)	A 1
George V Coast (region)	C 8	South Pole	A 4
Getz Ice Shelf	B12	South Sandwich (isls.)	D17
Goodenough (cape)	C 7	South Shetland (isls.)	C15
Graham Land (region)	C15	Sulzberger (bay)	B11
Grytviken	D17	Thurston (isl.)	C14
Hilton Inlet (bay)	B16	Transantarctic (mts.)	A11
Hobbs Coast (region)	B12	Victoria Land (region)	B 8
Hollick-Kenyon (plateau)	B13	Vincennes (bay)	C 6
Hope (bay)	C15	Vinson Massif (mt.)	B14
Joinville (isl.)	C16	Walgreen Coast (region)	B13
Kainan (bay)	B10	Weddell (sea)	C17
Keltie (cape)	C 7	West Ice Shelf	C 5
Kemp Coast (region)	C 3	Wilhelm II Coast (region)	C 5
King George (isl.)	C16	Wilkes Land (region)	C 7
Kirkpatrick (mt.)	A 8		
Knox Coast (region)	C 6		
Larsen Ice Shelf	C16		
Lazarev (sta.)	C 1		
Levick (mt.)	B 8		
Lister (mt.)	B 8		
Little America	B10		

EXPLORERS' ROUTES

Palmer 1820 —+—+—+—
Amundsen 1910-12 ·········
Scott 1910-13 ··········
Byrd 1928-30 ———————
Fuchs 1957-58 ooooooooo
By ship · By sledge · By airplane · By snow tractor

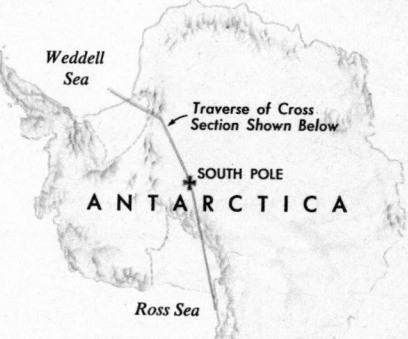

Weddell Sea
Traverse of Cross Section Shown Below
✛ SOUTH POLE
ANTARCTICA
Ross Sea

ANTARCTIC CROSS SECTION: WEDDELL SEA TO ROSS SEA

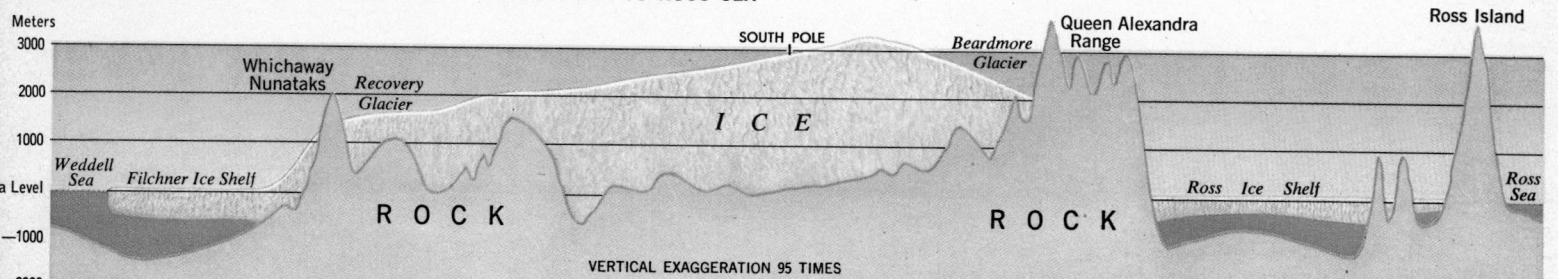

Meters 3000 / 2000 / 1000 / Sea Level / -1000 / -2000

Weddell Sea · Filchner Ice Shelf · Whichaway Nunataks · Recovery Glacier · ICE · SOUTH POLE · Beardmore Glacier · Queen Alexandra Range · Ross Ice Shelf · Ross Island · Ross Sea · ROCK · ROCK

VERTICAL EXAGGERATION 95 TIMES

Information Based on American Geographical Society's "Antarctic Map Folio Series"

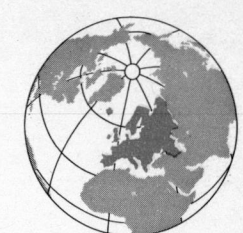

AREA 4,057,000 sq. mi.
POPULATION 666,116,000
LARGEST CITY London
HIGHEST POINT El'brus 18,481 ft.
LOWEST POINT Caspian Sea -92 ft.

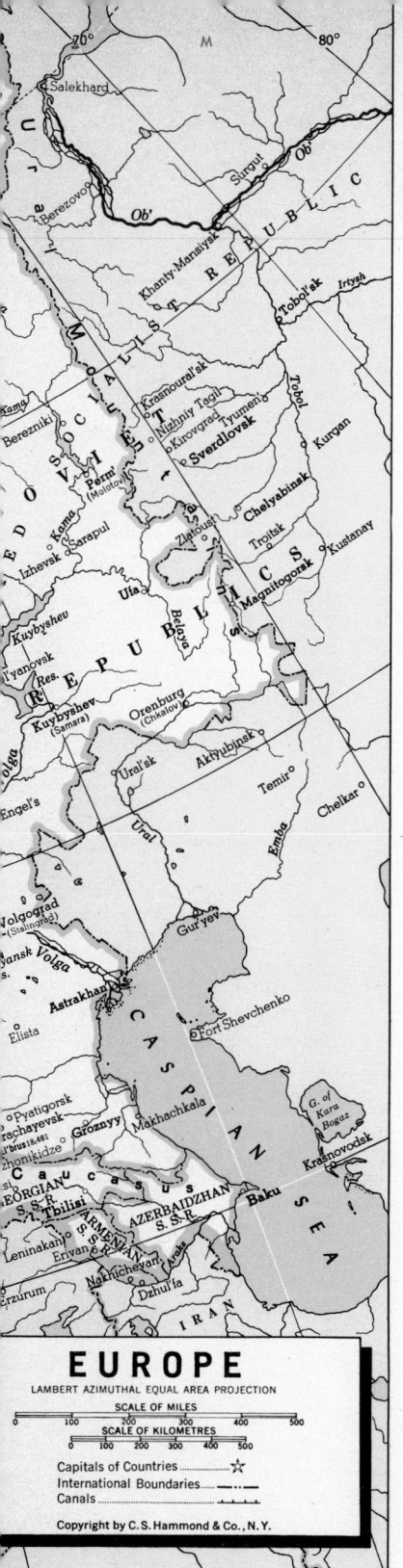

EUROPE

LAMBERT AZIMUTHAL EQUAL AREA PROJECTION

SCALE OF MILES
0   100   200   300   400   500

SCALE OF KILOMETRES
0   100   200   300   400   500

Capitals of Countries .... ☆
International Boundaries ...... ▬ ▬ ▬
Canals ....

Copyright by C.S. Hammond & Co., N.Y.

POPULATION DISTRIBUTION

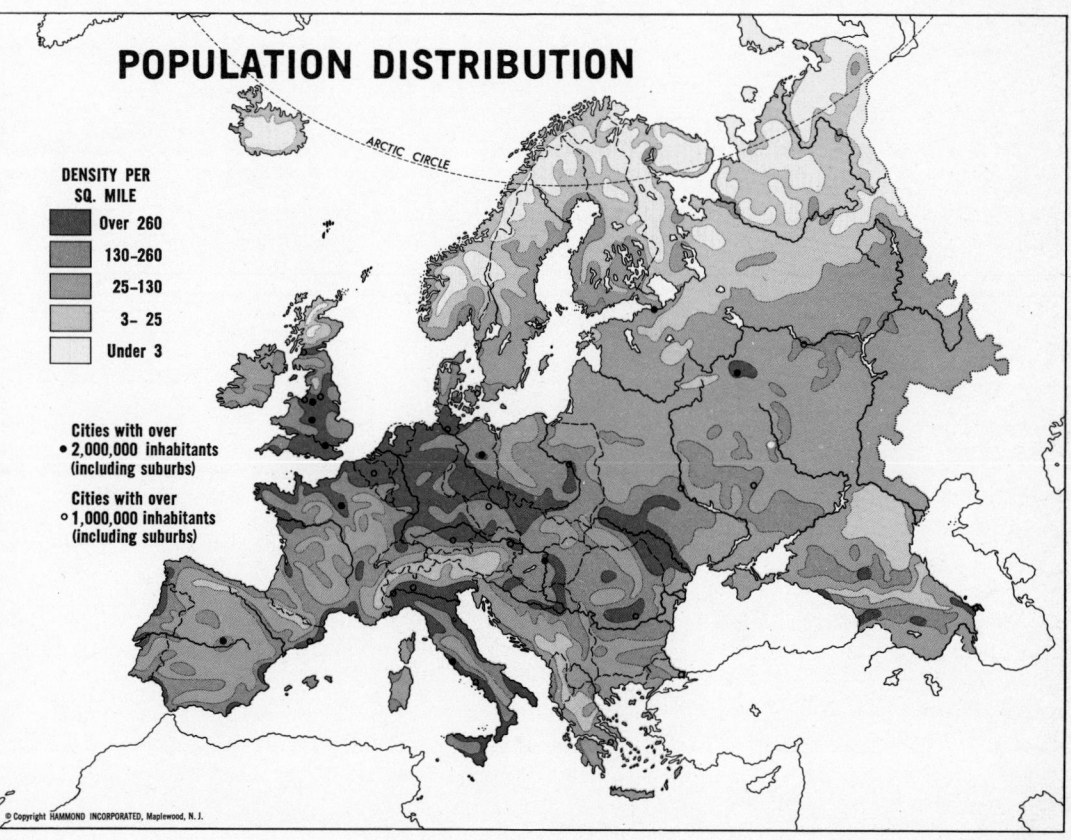

DENSITY PER
SQ. MILE

Over 260
130–260
25–130
3– 25
Under 3

● Cities with over
2,000,000 inhabitants
(including suburbs)

○ Cities with over
1,000,000 inhabitants
(including suburbs)

© Copyright HAMMOND INCORPORATED, Maplewood, N.J.

VEGETATION

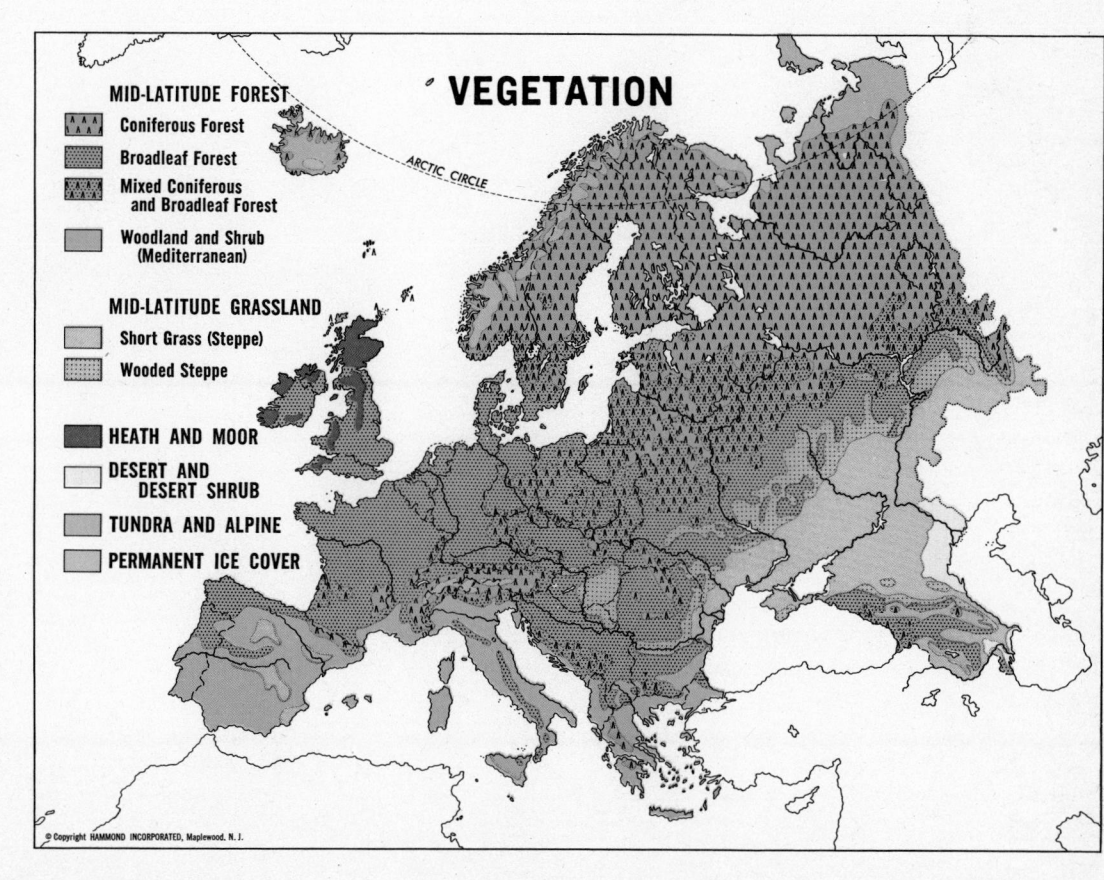

MID-LATITUDE FOREST

Coniferous Forest
Broadleaf Forest
Mixed Coniferous
and Broadleaf Forest
Woodland and Shrub
(Mediterranean)

MID-LATITUDE GRASSLAND

Short Grass (Steppe)
Wooded Steppe

HEATH AND MOOR
DESERT AND
DESERT SHRUB
TUNDRA AND ALPINE
PERMANENT ICE COVER

© Copyright HAMMOND INCORPORATED, Maplewood, N.J.

VEGETATION/RELIEF

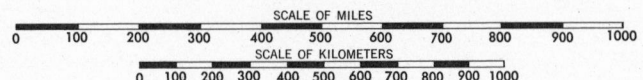

SCALE OF MILES

0 100 200 300 400 500 600 700 800 900 1000

SCALE OF KILOMETERS

0 100 200 300 400 500 600 700 800 900 1000

Capitals of Countries....................⊛
International Boundaries............------
Canals...-----
Elevations in Feet   Depths in Fathoms

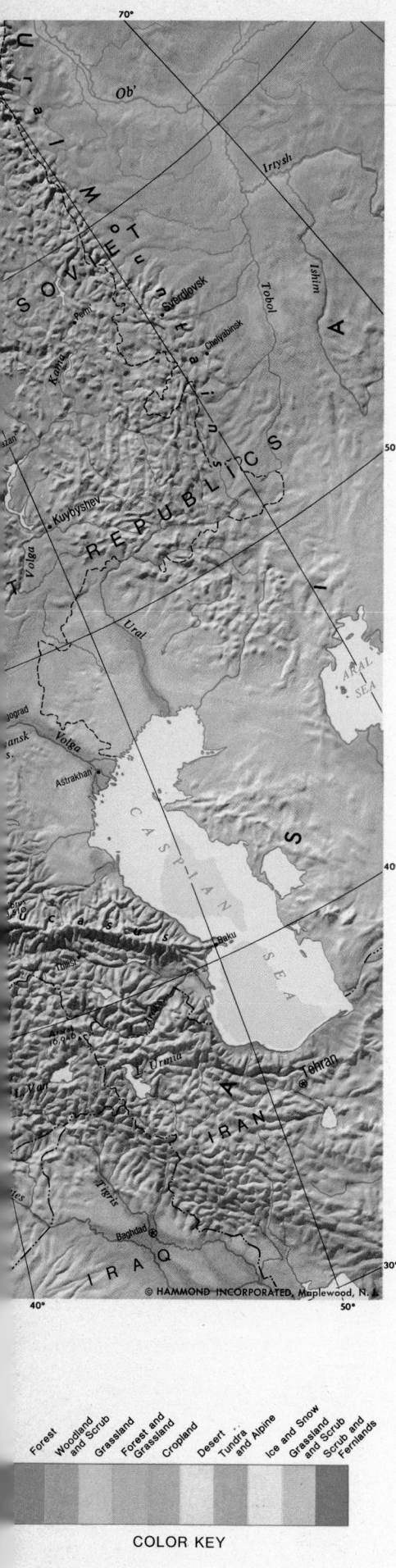

COLOR KEY

Forest / Woodland and Scrub / Grassland / Forest and Grassland / Cropland / Desert / Tundra and Alpine / Ice and Snow / Grassland and Scrub and Fernlands

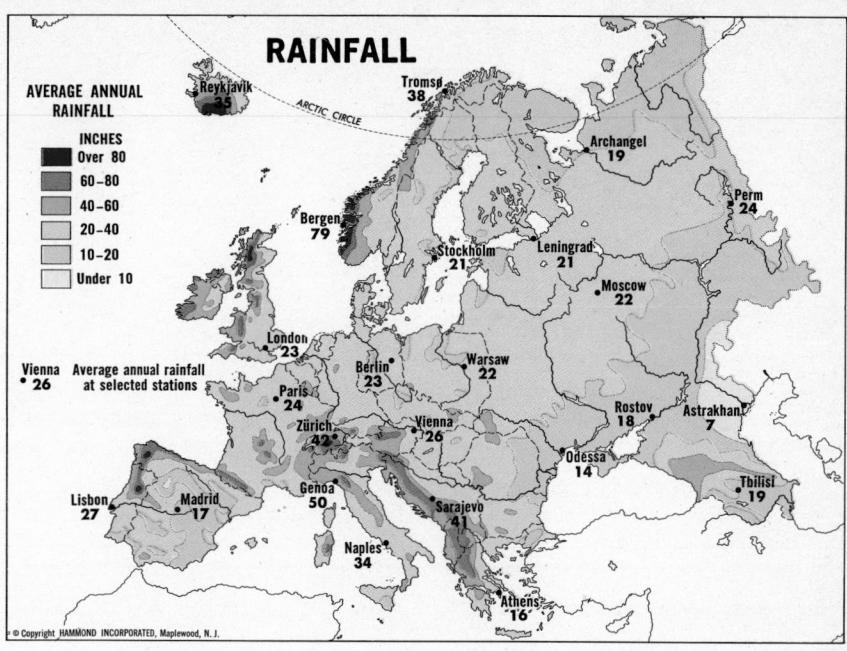

RAINFALL

AVERAGE ANNUAL RAINFALL

INCHES
- Over 80
- 60–80
- 40–60
- 20–40
- 10–20
- Under 10

Reykjavík 35
Tromsø 38
Archangel 19
Perm 24
Bergen 79
Stockholm 21
Leningrad 21
Moscow 22
London 23
Vienna •26 Average annual rainfall at selected stations
Berlin 23
Warsaw 22
Paris 24
Zürich 42
Vienna 26
Rostov 18
Astrakhan 7
Odessa 14
Tbilisi 19
Lisbon 27
Madrid 17
Genoa 50
Sarajevo 41
Naples 34
Athens 16

© Copyright HAMMOND INCORPORATED, Maplewood, N. J.

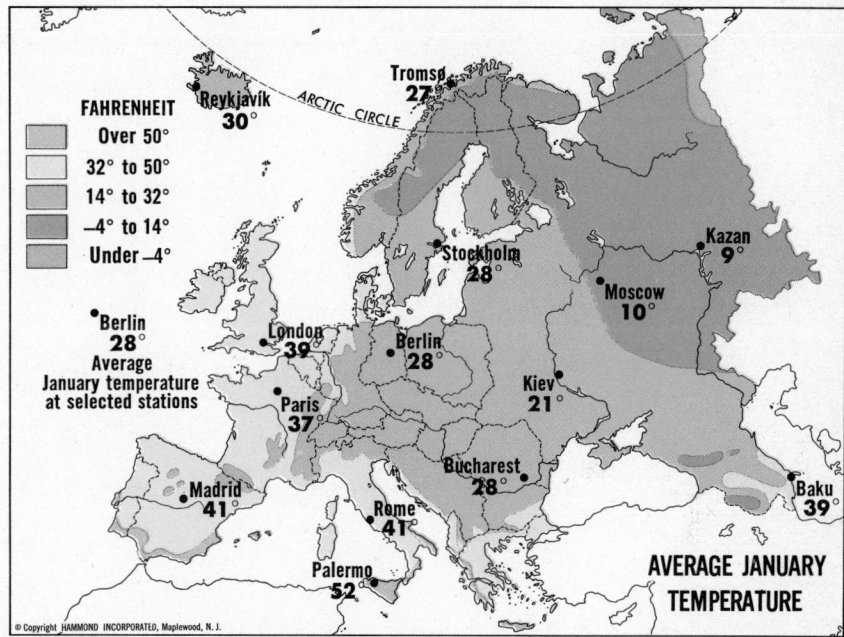

FAHRENHEIT
- Over 50°
- 32° to 50°
- 14° to 32°
- –4° to 14°
- Under –4°

Reykjavík 30
Tromsø 27
Stockholm 28
Kazan 9°
Moscow 10°
Berlin 28° Average January temperature at selected stations
London 39
Berlin 28°
Kiev 21°
Baku 39°
Paris 37
Madrid 41
Bucharest 28°
Rome 41
Palermo 52

AVERAGE JANUARY TEMPERATURE

© Copyright HAMMOND INCORPORATED, Maplewood, N. J.

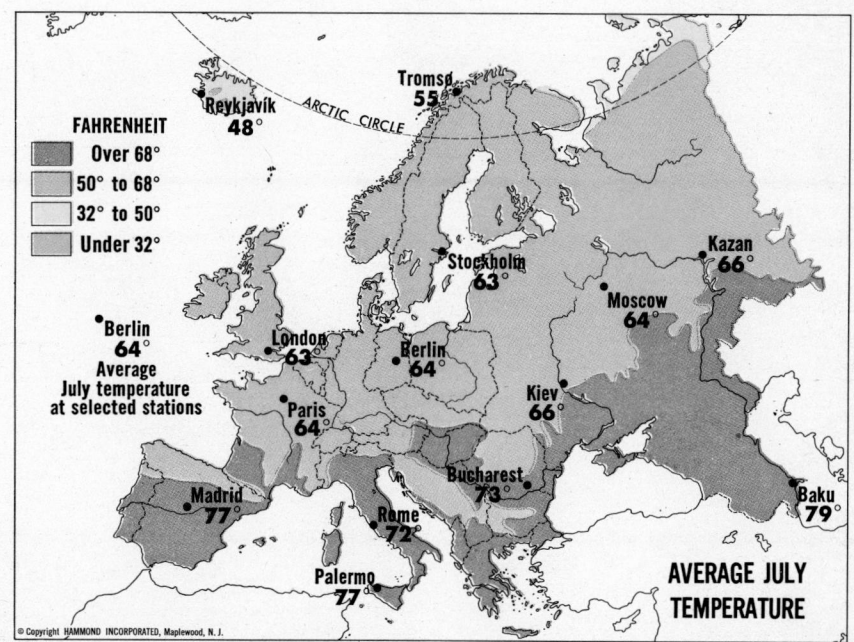

FAHRENHEIT
- Over 68°
- 50° to 68°
- 32° to 50°
- Under 32°

Reykjavík 48
Tromsø 55
Stockholm 63
Kazan 66°
Moscow 64°
Berlin 64° Average July temperature at selected stations
London 63
Berlin 64°
Kiev 66°
Baku 79°
Paris 64
Madrid 77
Bucharest 73
Rome 72
Palermo 77

AVERAGE JULY TEMPERATURE

© Copyright HAMMOND INCORPORATED, Maplewood, N. J.

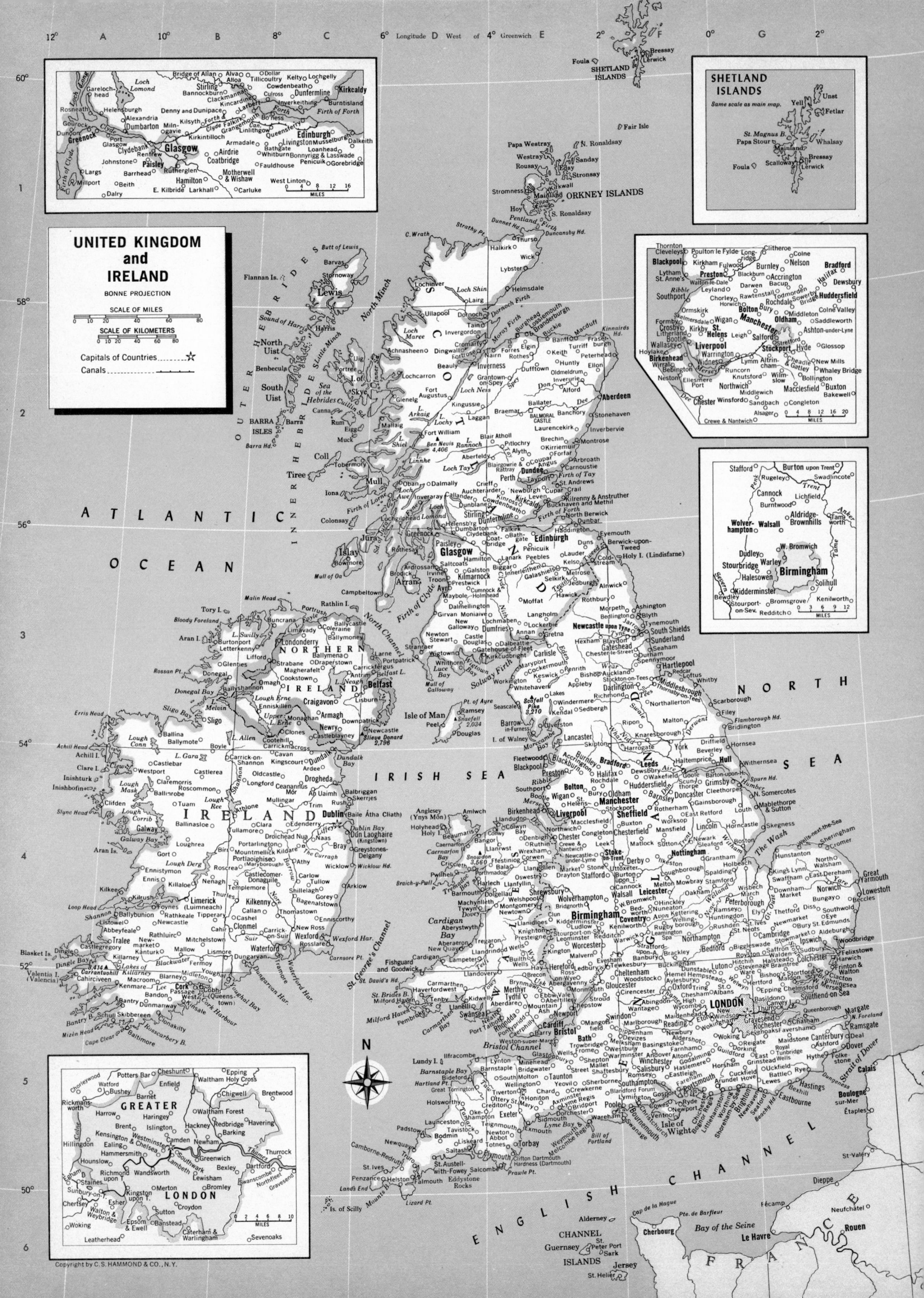

UNITED KINGDOM and IRELAND

BONNE PROJECTION

SCALE OF MILES

SCALE OF KILOMETERS

Capitals of Countries .... ★
Canals ....

SHETLAND ISLANDS

Same scale as main map.

UNITED KINGDOM

AREA 94,399 sq. mi.
POPULATION 56,076,000
CAPITAL London
LARGEST CITY London
HIGHEST POINT Ben Nevis 4,406 ft.
MONETARY UNIT pound sterling
MAJOR LANGUAGES English, Gaelic, Welsh
MAJOR RELIGIONS Protestantism, Roman Catholicism

IRELAND

AREA 27,136 sq. mi.
POPULATION 3,109,000
CAPITAL Dublin
LARGEST CITY Dublin
HIGHEST POINT Carrantuohill 3,415 ft.
MONETARY UNIT Irish pound
MAJOR LANGUAGES English, Gaelic (Irish)
MAJOR RELIGION Roman Catholicism

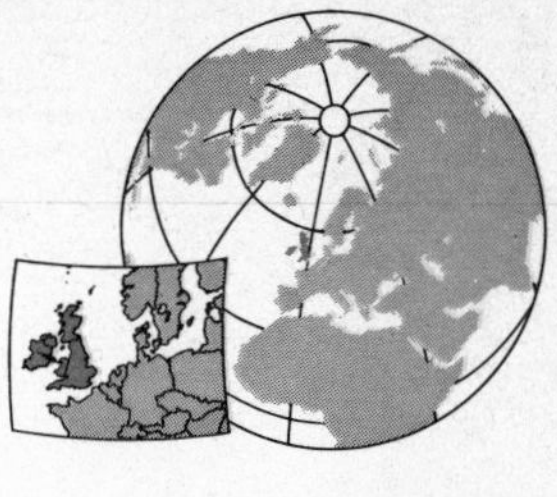

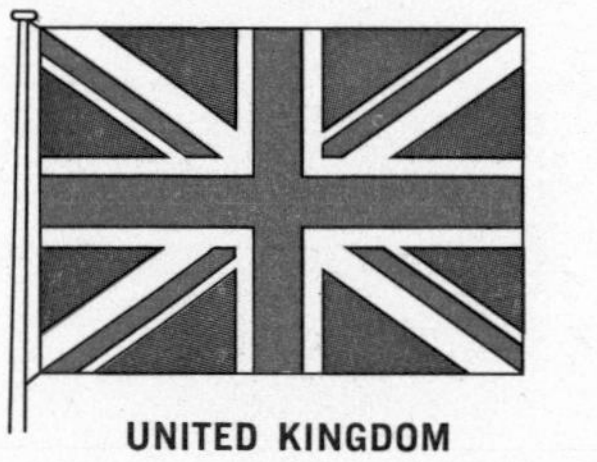

UNITED KINGDOM

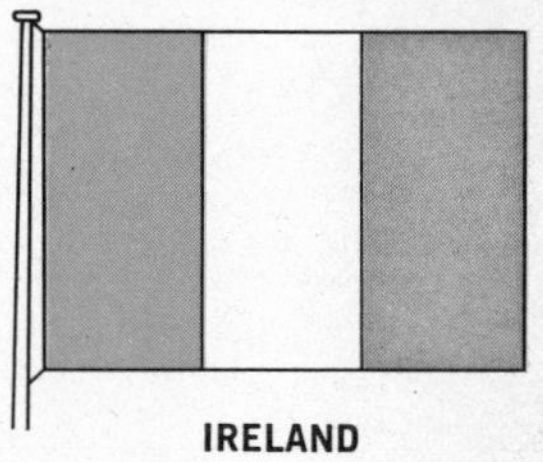

IRELAND

ENGLAND

COUNTIES

Avon, 920,200 . . . E 6
Bedfordshire, 491,700 . . . G 5
Berkshire, 659,000 . . . F 6
Buckinghamshire, 512,000 . . . G 6
Cambridgeshire, 563,000 . . . G 5
Cheshire, 916,400 . . . E 4
Cleveland, 567,900 . . . F 3
Cornwall, 405,200 . . . C 7
Cumbria, 473,600 . . . D 3
Derbyshire, 887,600 . . . F 5
Devon, 942,100 . . . D 7
Dorset, 575,800 . . . E 7
Durham, 610,400 . . . F 3
East Sussex, 655,600 . . . H 7
Essex, 1,426,200 . . . H 6
Gloucestershire, 491,500 . . . E 6
Greater London, 7,028,200 . . . H 8
Greater Manchester, 2,684,100 . . . H 2
Hampshire, 1,456,100 . . . F 6
Hereford and Worcester, 594,200 . . . E 5
Hertfordshire, 937,300 . . . G 6
Humberside, 848,600 . . . G 4
Isle of Wight, 111,300 . . . F 7
Isles of Scilly, 1,900 . . . A 7
Kent, 1,448,100 . . . H 6
Lancashire, 1,375,500 . . . E 4
Leicestershire, 837,900 . . . F 5
Lincolnshire, 524,500 . . . G 4
London, Greater, 7,028,200 . . . H 8
Manchester, Greater, 2,684,100 . . . H 2
Merseyside, 1,578,000 . . . G 2
Norfolk, 662,500 . . . H 5
Northamptonshire, 505,900 . . . G 5
Northumberland, 287,300 . . . E 2
North Yorkshire, 653,000 . . . F 3
Nottinghamshire, 977,500 . . . F 4
Oxfordshire, 541,800 . . . F 6
Salop, 359,000 . . . E 5
Somerset, 404,400 . . . E 6
South Yorkshire, 1,318,300 . . . F 4
Staffordshire, 997,600 . . . E 5
Suffolk, 577,600 . . . H 5
Surrey, 1,002,900 . . . G 6
Sussex, East, 655,600 . . . H 7
Sussex, West, 623,400 . . . G 7
Tyne and Wear, 1,182,900 . . . H 3
Warwickshire, 471,000 . . . F 5
West Midlands, 2,743,300 . . . F 5
West Sussex, 623,400 . . . G 7
West Yorkshire, 2,072,500 . . . J 1
Wiltshire, 512,800 . . . E 6
Yorkshire, North, 653,000 . . . F 3
Yorkshire, South, 1,318,300 . . . F 4
Yorkshire, West, 2,072,500 . . . J 1

CITIES and TOWNS

Abingdon, 20,130 . . . F 6
Accrington, 36,470 . . . H 1
Adwick le Street, 17,650 . . . K 2
Aldeburgh, 2,750 . . . J 5
Aldershot, 33,750 . . . G 8
Aldridge Brownhills, 89,370 . . . E 5
Alfreton, 21,560 . . . F 4
Alnwick, 7,300 . . . F 2
Altrincham, 40,800 . . . H 2
Amersham, ⊙17,254 . . . G 7
Andover, 27,620 . . . F 6
Appleby, 2,240 . . . E 3
Arnold, 35,090 . . . F 4
Arundel, 2,390 . . . G 7
Ashford, 36,380 . . . H 6
Ashington, 24,720 . . . F 2
Ashton-under-Lyne, 48,500 . . . H 2
Axminster, ⊙4,515 . . . D 7
Aycliffe, ⊙20,203 . . . F 3
Aylesbury, 41,420 . . . G 7
Bacup, 14,990 . . . H 1
Bakewell, 4,100 . . . J 2
Banbury, 31,060 . . . F 5
Banstead, 44,100 . . . H 8
Barking, 153,800 . . . H 8
Barnet, 305,200 . . . H 7
Barnsley, 74,730 . . . J 2
Barnstaple, 17,820 . . . D 6
Barrow-in-Furness, 73,400 . . . D 3
Barton-upon-Humber, 7,750 . . . G 4
Basildon, 135,720 . . . J 8
Basingstoke, 60,910 . . . F 6
Bath, 83,100 . . . E 6
Batley, 41,630 . . . J 1
Battle, ⊙4,987 . . . H 7
Bebington, 62,500 . . . G 2
Bedford, 74,390 . . . G 5
Bedlington, 27,200 . . . F 2
Bedworth, 41,600 . . . F 5
Beeston and Stapleford, 65,360 . . . F 5
Benfleet, 49,180 . . . J 8
Bentley with Arksey, 22,320 . . . F 4
Berkhamsted, 15,920 . . . G 7
Beverley, 16,920 . . . G 4
Bexhill, 34,680 . . . H 7
Bexley, 213,500 . . . H 8
Biddulph, 18,720 . . . H 2
Birkenhead, 135,750 . . . G 2
Birmingham, 1,058,800 . . . F 5
Bishop Auckland, 32,940 . . . E 3
Bishop's Stortford, 21,720 . . . H 6
Blackburn, 101,670 . . . H 1
Blackpool, 149,000 . . . G 1
Blaydon, 31,940 . . . H 3
Blyth, 35,390 . . . F 2
Bodmin, 10,430 . . . C 7
Bognor Regis, 34,620 . . . G 7
Boldon, 24,430 . . . J 3
Bolton, 154,480 . . . H 2
Bootle, 71,160 . . . G 2
Boston, 26,700 . . . G 5
Bournemouth, 144,100 . . . F 7
Bracknell, ⊙34,067 . . . G 8
Bradford, 458,900 . . . J 1
Braintree and Bocking, 26,300 . . . H 6
Brent, 256,500 . . . H 8
Brentwood, 58,690 . . . J 8
Bridgwater, 26,700 . . . E 6
Bridlington, 26,920 . . . G 3
Bridport, 6,660 . . . E 7
Brigg, 4,870 . . . G 4
Brighowe, 35,320 . . . J 1
Brightlingsea, 7,170 . . . J 6
Brighton, 156,500 . . . G 7
Bristol, 416,300 . . . E 6
Broadstairs and Saint Peter's, 21,670 . . . J 6
Bromley, 299,100 . . . H 8
Bromsgrove, 41,430 . . . E 5
Buckfastleigh, 2,870 . . . C 7
Buckingham, 5,290 . . . G 6
Bude-Stratton, 5,750 . . . C 7
Bungay, 4,120 . . . J 5
Burgess Hill, 20,030 . . . G 7
Burnham-on-Crouch, 4,920 . . . H 6
Burnley, 74,300 . . . H 1
Burntwood, ⊙23,088 . . . F 5
Burton upon Trent, 49,480 . . . F 5
Bury, 69,550 . . . H 2
Bury Saint Edmunds, 26,800 . . . H 5
Bushey, 24,500 . . . H 7
Buxton, 20,050 . . . J 2
Caister-on-Sea, ⊙6,287 . . . J 5
Camborne-Redruth, 43,970 . . . B 7
Cambridge, 106,400 . . . G 5
Camden, 185,800 . . . H 8
Cannock, 56,440 . . . E 5
Canterbury, 115,600 . . . H 6
Canvey Island, 29,550 . . . J 8
Carlisle, 99,600 . . . D 3
Carlton, 46,690 . . . F 5
Caterham and Warlingham, 35,840 . H 8
Chatham, 59,550 . . . J 8
Cheadle and Gatley, 62,460 . . . H 2
Chelmsford, 58,320 . . . J 7
Cheltenham, 75,910 . . . E 6
Chertsey, 45,070 . . . G 8
Chesham, 20,830 . . . G 7
Cheshunt, 45,750 . . . H 7
Chester, 117,200 . . . G 2
Chesterfield, 69,480 . . . J 2
Chester-le-Street, 20,720 . . . J 3
Chichester, 20,940 . . . G 7
Chigwell, 54,220 . . . H 8
Chippenham, 18,550 . . . E 6
Chorley, 31,800 . . . G 2
Christchurch, 31,610 . . . F 7
Cirencester, 14,500 . . . E 6
Clacton, 39,380 . . . J 6
Clay Cross, 9,630 . . . J 2
Cleator Moor, ⊙7,686 . . . D 3
Cleethorpes, 37,200 . . . H 4
Clevedon, 15,140 . . . D 6
Clun, ⊙1,261 . . . D 6
Coalville, 28,740 . . . F 5
Cockermouth, 6,480 . . . D 3
Colchester, 79,600 . . . H 6
Colne, 19,030 . . . H 1
Colne Valley, 21,190 . . . J 2
Congleton, 21,500 . . . H 2
Consett, 35,080 . . . H 3
Corby, 48,850 . . . G 5
Coventry, 336,800 . . . F 5
Cowes, 19,190 . . . F 7
Crawley, 72,600 . . . G 6
Crewe and Nantwich, 98,100 . . . E 4
Cromer, 5,720 . . . J 5
Crook and Willington, 21,120 . . . E 3
Crosby, 56,750 . . . G 2
Croydon, 330,600 . . . H 8
Cuckfield, 26,500 . . . G 6
Darlington, 85,120 . . . F 3
Dartford, 44,130 . . . J 8
Darton, 15,710 . . . J 2
Darwen, 29,290 . . . H 1
Deal, 26,840 . . . J 6
Dearne, 24,780 . . . K 2
Denton, 38,110 . . . H 2
Derby, 213,700 . . . F 5
Dewsbury, 50,560 . . . J 1
Didcot, ⊙14,277 . . . F 6
Doncaster, 81,530 . . . F 4
Dorking, 22,410 . . . G 8
Dover, 34,160 . . . J 6
Downham Market, 4,120 . . . H 5
Droitwich, 13,950 . . . E 5
Dronfield, 20,000 . . . J 2
Dudley, 187,110 . . . E 5
Dunstable, 32,090 . . . G 6
Durham, 88,800 . . . J 3
Ealing, 293,800 . . . H 8
Eastbourne, 73,200 . . . H 7
East Grinstead, 19,420 . . . G 6
Eastleigh, 46,340 . . . F 7
East Retford, 18,260 . . . G 4
Egham, 30,320 . . . G 8
Egremont, ⊙7,253 . . . D 3
Eling, ⊙20,006 . . . F 7
Ellesmere, ⊙2,630 . . . E 5
Ellesmere Port, 63,870 . . . G 2
Enfield, 260,900 . . . H 7
Epsom and Ewell, 70,700 . . . G 8
Esher, 63,970 . . . H 8
Eston, ⊙46,219 . . . F 3
Eton, 4,950 . . . G 8
Evesham, 14,090 . . . F 5
Exeter, 93,300 . . . D 7
Exminster, ⊙3,181 . . . D 7
Exmouth, 26,840 . . . D 7
Falmouth, 17,530 . . . B 7
Fareham, 86,300 . . . F 7
Farnborough, 43,520 . . . G 8
Farnham, 33,140 . . . G 8
Farnworth, 26,110 . . . H 2
Faversham, 15,010 . . . H 6
Felixstowe, 19,460 . . . J 6
Felling, 38,990 . . . J 3
Filey, 5,660 . . . G 3
Fleet, 22,930 . . . G 8
Fleetwood, 30,070 . . . D 4
Folkestone, 45,610 . . . J 6
Formby, 24,850 . . . G 2
Framlingham, ⊙2,258 . . . J 5
Frimley and Camberley, 47,390 . . . G 8
Fulwood, 22,910 . . . G 1
Gainsborough, 17,440 . . . G 4
Gateshead, 91,230 . . . J 3
Gillingham, Dorset, ⊙4,050 . . . E 6
Gillingham, Kent, 93,900 . . . J 8
Glastonbury, 6,580 . . . E 6
Glossop, 24,820 . . . J 2
Gloucester, 91,600 . . . E 6
Godalming, 18,840 . . . G 8
Golborne, 28,720 . . . G 2
Goole, 17,920 . . . G 4
Gosport, 82,300 . . . F 7
Grange, 3,520 . . . E 3
Grantham, 27,830 . . . G 5
Gravesend, 53,500 . . . J 8
Great Baddow, ⊙18,755 . . . J 7
Great Torrington, 3,430 . . . C 7
Great Yarmouth, 49,410 . . . J 5
Greenwich, 207,200 . . . H 8
Grimsby, 93,800 . . . G 4
Guildford, 58,470 . . . G 8
Guisborough, 14,860 . . . F 3
Hackney, 192,500 . . . H 8
Hale, 17,080 . . . H 2
Halesowen, 54,120 . . . E 5
Halifax, 88,580 . . . J 1
Haltemprice, 54,850 . . . G 4
Haltwhistle, ⊙3,511 . . . E 2
Hammersmith, 170,000 . . . H 8
Haringey, 228,200 . . . H 8
Harlow, 79,160 . . . H 7
Harrogate, 64,620 . . . J 1
Harrow, 200,200 . . . G 8
Hartlepool, 97,100 . . . F 3
Harwich, 15,280 . . . J 6
Haslingden, 15,140 . . . H 1
Hastings, 74,600 . . . H 7
Hatfield, ⊙25,359 . . . H 7
Havant and Waterloo, 112,430 . . . G 7
Haverhill, 14,550 . . . H 5
Havering, 239,200 . . . J 8
Hayle, ⊙5,378 . . . B 7
Hazel Grove and Bramhall, 40,400 . . . H 2
Heanor, 24,590 . . . F 4
Hebburn, 23,150 . . . J 3
Hedon, 3,010 . . . G 4
Hemel Hempstead, 71,150 . . . G 7
Hereford, 47,800 . . . E 5
Hertford, 20,760 . . . H 7
Hetton, 16,810 . . . J 3
Hexham, 9,820 . . . E 3
Heywood, 31,720 . . . H 2
High Wycombe, 61,190 . . . G 8
Hillingdon, 230,800 . . . G 8
Hinckley, 49,310 . . . F 5
Hinderwell, ⊙2,551 . . . G 3
Hitchin, 29,190 . . . G 6
Hoddesdon, 27,510 . . . H 7
Holmfirth, 19,790 . . . J 2
Horley, ⊙18,593 . . . H 8
Hornsea, 7,280 . . . G 4
Horsham, 26,770 . . . G 6
Horwich, 16,670 . . . G 2
Houghton-le-Spring, 33,150 . . . J 3
Hounslow, 199,100 . . . G 8
Hove, 72,000 . . . G 7
Hoylake, 32,000 . . . G 2
Hoyland Nether, 15,500 . . . J 2
Hucknall, 27,110 . . . F 4
Huddersfield, 130,060 . . . J 2
Hugh Town, ⊙1,958 . . . A 8
Hull, 276,600 . . . G 4
Hunstanton, 4,140 . . . H 5
Huntingdon and Godmanchester, 17,200 . . . G 5
Huyton-with-Roby, 65,950 . . . G 2
Hyde, 37,040 . . . H 2
Ilfracombe, 9,350 . . . C 6
Ilkeston, 33,690 . . . F 5
Immingham, ⊙10,259 . . . G 4
Ipswich, 121,500 . . . J 5
Islington, 171,600 . . . H 8
Jarrow, 28,510 . . . J 3
Kendal, 22,440 . . . E 3
Kenilworth, 19,730 . . . F 5
Kensington and Chelsea, 161,400 . . G 8
Keswick, 4,790 . . . D 3
Kettering, 44,480 . . . G 5
Keynsham, 18,970 . . . E 6
Kidderminster, 49,960 . . . E 5
Kidsgrove, 22,690 . . . E 4
King's Lynn, 29,990 . . . H 5
Kingston upon Thames, 135,600 . . H 8
Kingswood, 30,450 . . . E 6
Kirkburton, 20,320 . . . J 2
Kirkby, 59,100 . . . G 2
Kirkby Lonsdale, ⊙1,506 . . . E 3
Kirkby Stephen, ⊙1,539 . . . E 3
Knutsford, 14,840 . . . H 2
Lambeth, 290,300 . . . H 8
Lancaster, 126,300 . . . E 3
Leatherhead, 40,830 . . . G 8
Leeds, 744,500 . . . J 1
Leek, 19,460 . . . H 2
Leicester, 289,400 . . . F 5
Leigh, 46,390 . . . H 2
Leighton-Linslade, 22,590 . . . F 7
Letchworth, 31,520 . . . G 6
Lewes, 14,170 . . . H 7
Lewisham, 237,300 . . . H 8
Leyland, 23,690 . . . G 1
Lichfield, 23,690 . . . F 5
Lincoln, 73,700 . . . G 4
Liskeard, 5,360 . . . C 7
Litherland, 23,530 . . . G 2
Littlehampton, 20,320 . . . G 7

(continued on following page)

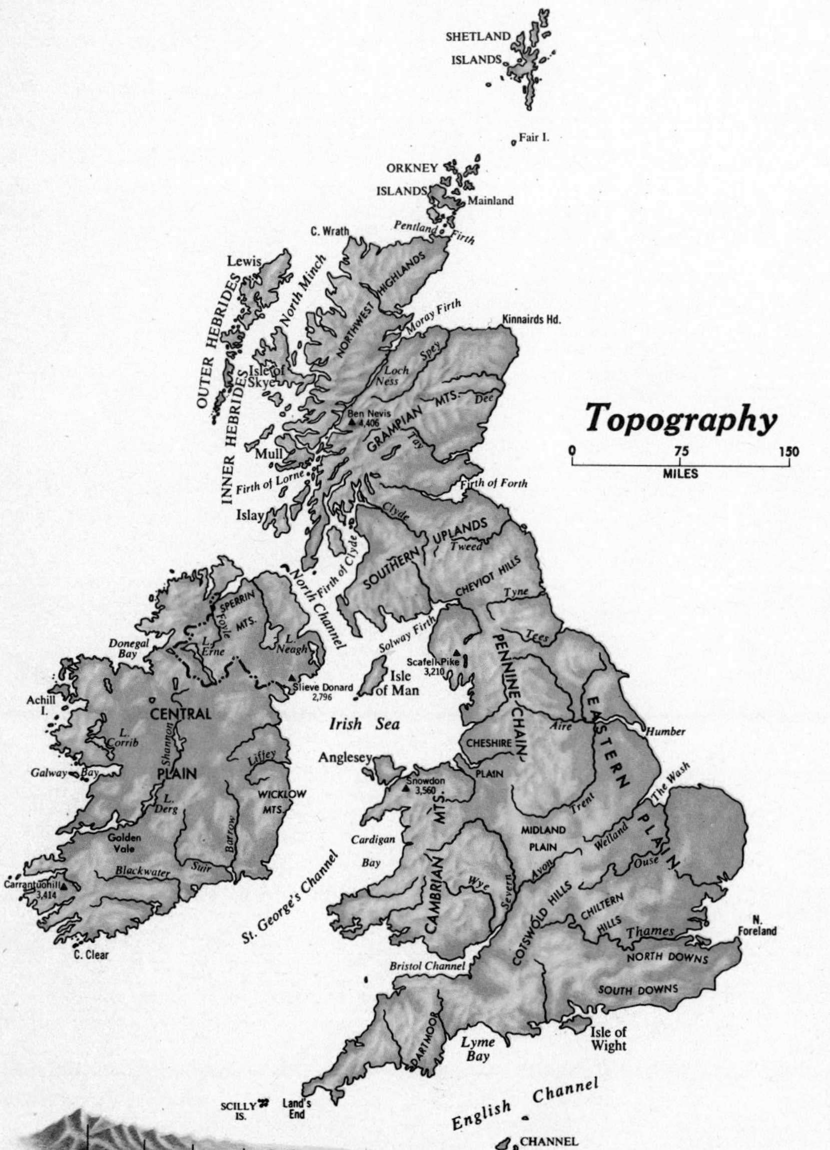
SHETLAND ISLANDS
Fair I.
ORKNEY ISLANDS
Mainland
C. Wrath
Pentland Firth
Lewis
OUTER HEBRIDES
North Minch
NORTHWEST HIGHLANDS
Moray Firth
Kinnairds Hd.
Spey
Loch Ness
Isle of Skye
INNER HEBRIDES
Ben Nevis 4,406
GRAMPIAN MTS.
Dee
Tay
Mull
Firth of Lorne
Firth of Forth
Islay
Clyde
Firth of Clyde
SOUTHERN UPLANDS
Tweed
CHEVIOT HILLS
Tyne
North Channel
SPERRIN MTS.
L. Erne
L. Neagh
Slieve Donard 2,796
Donegal Bay
Solway Firth
Scafell Pike 3,210
Isle of Man
PENNINE CHAIN
Tees
EASTERN PLAIN
Achill I.
CENTRAL PLAIN
L. Corrib
Shannon
Liffey
Irish Sea
Aire
Humber
Galway Bay
WICKLOW MTS.
Anglesey
CHESHIRE PLAIN
Snowdon 3,560
Trent
The Wash
L. Derg
Barrow
Golden Vale
Blackwater
Suir
Cardigan Bay
CAMBRIAN MTS.
MIDLAND PLAIN
Welland
Ouse
Carrantuohill 3,414
St. George's Channel
Wye
Severn
Avon
COTSWOLD HILLS
CHILTERN HILLS
Thames
N. Foreland
C. Clear
Bristol Channel
NORTH DOWNS
SOUTH DOWNS
DARTMOOR
Lyme Bay
Isle of Wight
SCILLY IS.
Land's End
English Channel
CHANNEL ISLANDS
Topography
0 75 150
MILES
5,000 m. 16,404 ft.
2,000 m. 6,562 ft.
1,000 m. 3,281 ft.
500 m. 1,640 ft.
200 m. 656 ft.
100 m. 328 ft.
Sea Level
Below

ENGLAND

AREA 50,516 sq.mi.
POPULATION 46,417,600
CAPITAL London
LARGEST CITY London
HIGHEST POINT Scafell Pike 3,210 ft.

WALES

AREA 8,017 sq. mi.
POPULATION 2,778,000
LARGEST CITY Cardiff
HIGHEST POINT Snowdon 3,560 ft.

SCOTLAND

AREA 30,414 sq. mi.
POPULATION 5,261,000
CAPITAL Edinburgh
LARGEST CITY Glasgow
HIGHEST POINT Ben Nevis 4,406 ft.

NORTHERN IRELAND

AREA 5,452 sq. mi.
POPULATION 1,537,200
CAPITAL Belfast
LARGEST CITY Belfast
HIGHEST POINT Slieve Donard 2,796 ft.

12 United Kingdom and Ireland

(continued)

Liverpool, 539,700 G 2
Loftus, 7,850 G 3
London (cap.), 7,028,200 H 8
London, ★12,332,900 H 8
Long Eaton, 33,560 F 5
Longbenton, 50,120 J 3
Looe, 4,060 C 7
Loughborough, 49,010 F 5
Lowestoft, 53,260 J 5
Ludlow, ⊙7,466 E 5
Luton, 164,500 G 6
Lydd, 4,670 H 7
Lyme Regis, 3,460 E 7
Lymington, 36,780 F 7
Lynton, 1,770 D 6
Lytham Saint Anne's, 42,120 G 1
Mablethorpe and Sutton, 6,750 H 4
Macclesfield, 45,420 H 2
Maidenhead, 48,210 G 8
Maidstone, 72,110 J 8
Maldon, 14,350 H 6
Malmesbury, 2,550 E 6
Malton, 4,010 G 3
Malvern, 30,420 E 5
Manchester, 490,000 H 2
Mangotsfield, 23,000 E 6
Mansfield, 58,450 K 2
Mansfield Woodhouse, 25,400 F 4
March, 14,560 H 5
Margate, 50,290 J 6
Market Harborough, 15,230 G 5
Marlborough, 6,370 F 6
Matlock, 20,300 J 2
Melton Mowbray, 20,680 G 5
Merton, 169,400 H 8
Middlesbrough, 153,900 F 3
Middleton, 53,340 H 2
Middlewich, 7,600 H 2
Mildenhall, ⊙9,269 H 5
Millom, ⊙7,101 D 3
Milton Keynes, 89,900 F 5
Minehead, 8,230 D 6
Moretonhampstead, ⊙1,440 C 7
Morpeth, 14,450 F 2
Mundesley, ⊙1,536 J 5
Nelson, 31,220 H 1
Neston, 18,210 G 2
Newark, 24,760 G 4
Newbury, 24,850 F 6
Newcastle upon Tyne, 295,800 H 3
Newcastle-under-Lyme, 75,940 E 4
Newham, 228,900 H 8
Newhaven, 9,970 H 7
Newport, 22,430 F 7
New Romney, 3,830 J 7
Newton Abbot, 19,940 D 7
Newton-le-Willows, 21,780 H 2
New Windsor, 29,660 G 8
Northallerton F 3
Northam, 8,310 C 6
Northampton, 128,290 F 5
Northfleet, 27,150 J 8
North Sunderland, ⊙1,725 F 2
Northwich, 17,710 H 2
Norton, 5,580 G 3
Norton-Radstock, 15,900 E 6
Norwich, 119,200 J 5
Nottingham, 280,300 F 5
Nuneaton, 69,210 F 5
Oadby, 20,700 F 5
Oakham, 7,280 G 5
Okehampton, 4,000 D 7
Oldham, 103,690 H 2
Ormskirk, 28,860 G 2
Oswaldtwistle, 14,270 H 1
Oxford, 117,400 F 6
Padstow, ⊙2,802 B 7
Penryn, 5,660 B 7
Penzance, 19,360 B 7
Peterborough, 118,900 G 5
Peterlee, ⊙21,846 J 3
Plymouth, 259,100 C 7
Polperro, ⊙1,491 C 7
Poole, 110,600 E 7
Porlock, ⊙1,290 D 6
Portishead, 9,680 E 6
Portland, 14,860 E 7
Portslade-by-Sea, 18,040 G 7
Portsmouth, 198,500 F 7
Potters Bar, 24,670 H 7
Poulton-le-Fylde, 16,340 G 1
Preston, 94,760 G 1
Prestwich, 32,850 H 2
Queenborough, 31,550 H 6
Radcliffe, 29,630 H 2
Ramsbottom, 16,710 H 2
Ramsgate, 40,090 J 6
Rawtenstall, 20,950 H 1
Rayleigh, 26,740 J 8
Reading, 131,200 G 8
Redbridge, 231,600 H 8
Redcar, ⊙46,325 F 3
Redditch, 44,750 E 5
Reigate, 55,600 H 8
Richmond upon Thames, 166,800 H 8
Rickmansworth, 29,030 G 8
Ripley, 18,060 F 4
Rochdale, 93,780 H 2
Rochester, 56,030 J 8
Rothbury, ⊙1,818 E 2
Rotherham, 84,770 K 2
Royal Leamington Spa, 44,950 F 5
Royal Tunbridge Wells, 44,800 H 6
Rugby, 60,380 F 5
Rugeley, 24,440 E 5
Runcorn, 42,730 G 2
Rushden, 21,840 G 5
Ryde, 23,170 F 7
Rye, 4,530 H 7
Ryton, 15,170 H 3
Saddleworth, 21,340 J 2
Saint Agnes, ⊙4,747 B 7
Saint Albans, 123,800 H 7
Saint Austell-with-Fowey, 32,710 C 7
Saint Columb Major, ⊙3,953 B 7
Saint Helens, 104,890 G 2
Saint Ives, Cornwall, 9,760 B 7
Saint Neots, 17,940 G 5
Salcombe, 2,370 D 7
Sale, 59,060 H 2
Salford, 261,100 H 2
Salisbury, 35,460 F 6
Saltburn and Marske-by-the-Sea, 21,170 G 3
Sandbach, 14,280 H 2
Sandown-Shanklin, 14,800 F 7
Sandwich, 4,420 J 6
Saxmundham, 1,820 J 5
Scarborough, 43,300 G 3
Scunthorpe, 68,100 G 4
Seaford, 18,020 H 7
Seaham, 22,470 J 3
Seascale, ⊙2,106 D 3
Seaton, 4,500 D 7
Seaton Valley, 35,880 J 3
Sedbergh, ⊙2,741 E 3
Selsey, ⊙6,491 G 7
Sevenoaks, 18,160 J 8
Shaftesbury, 4,180 E 7
Sheffield, 558,000 J 2
Sherborne, 9,230 E 7
Sheringham, 4,940 J 5
Shildon, 15,360 F 3
Shoreham-by-Sea, 19,620 G 7
Shrewsbury, 56,120 E 5
Silloth, ⊙2,662 D 3
Sittingbourne and Milton, 32,830 H 6
Skelmersdale, 35,850 G 2
Skelton and Brotton, 15,930 G 3
Sleaford, 8,050 G 5
Slough, 89,060 G 8
Solihull, 108,230 F 5
Southampton, 213,700 F 7
Southend-on-Sea, 159,300 H 6
Southport, 86,030 G 1
South Shields, 96,900 J 3
Southwark, 224,900 H 8
Southwold, 1,960 J 5
Sowerby Bridge, 15,700 H 1
Spalding, 17,040 G 5
Spenborough, 41,460 J 1
Spennymoor, 19,050 F 3
Stafford, 54,860 E 5
Staines, 56,380 G 8
Stamford, 14,980 G 5
Stanley, 42,280 H 3
Staveley, 17,620 K 2
Stevenage, 72,600 G 6
Stockport, 138,350 H 2
Stockton-on-Tees, 165,400 F 3
Stoke-on-Trent, 256,200 E 4
Stourbridge, 56,530 E 5
Stourport-on-Severn, 19,430 E 5
Stowmarket, 9,020 J 5
Stratford-upon-Avon, 20,080 F 5
Stretford, 52,450 H 2
Stroud, 19,600 E 6
Sudbury, 8,860 H 5
Sunbury-on-Thames, 40,070 G 8
Sunderland, 214,820 J 3
Sutton, 166,700 H 8
Sutton Bridge, ⊙3,113 H 5
Sutton in Ashfield, 40,330 K 2
Swadlincote, 21,060 F 5
Swanage, 8,000 E 7
Swindon, 90,680 F 6
Tamworth, 46,960 F 5
Taunton, 37,570 D 6
Tavistock, ⊙7,620 C 7
Telford, ⊙79,451 E 5
Tenbury, ⊙2,151 E 5
Tewkesbury, 9,210 E 6
Thetford, 15,690 H 5
Thirsk, ⊙2,884 F 3
Thornaby-on-Tees, ⊙42,385 F 3
Thorne, ⊙16,694 F 4
Thornton Cleveleys, 27,090 G 1
Thurrock, 127,700 J 8
Tiverton, 16,190 D 7
Todmorden, 14,540 H 1
Tonbridge, 31,410 H 8
Torbay, 109,900 D 7
Torpoint, 6,840 C 7
Tower Hamlets, 146,100 H 8
Tow Law, 2,460 H 4
Trowbridge, 20,120 E 6
Truro, 15,690 B 7
Turton, 22,800 H 2
Tynemouth, 67,090 J 3
Upton upon Severn, ⊙2,048 E 5
Urmston, 44,130 H 2
Uttoxeter, 9,100 E 5
Ventnor, 6,980 F 7
Wainfleet All Saints, ⊙1,116 H 4
Wakefield, 306,500 J 2
Wallasey, 94,520 G 2
Wallsend, 45,490 J 3
Walsall, 182,430 E 5
Waltham Forest, 223,700 H 8
Waltham Holy Cross, 14,810 H 7
Walton and Weybridge, 51,270 G 8
Walton-le-Dale, 27,660 G 1
Wandsworth, 284,600 H 8
Wantage, 8,490 F 6
Ware, 14,900 H 7
Wareham, 4,630 E 7
Warley, 161,260 E 5
Warminster, 14,440 E 6
Warrington, 65,320 G 2
Warwick, 17,870 F 5
Washington, 27,720 J 3
Watchet, 2,980 D 6
Watford, 77,000 H 7
Wellingborough, 39,570 G 5
Wells, 8,960 E 6
Wells-next-the-Sea, 2,450 H 5
Welwyn, 39,900 H 7
Wem, ⊙3,411 E 5
West Bridgford, 28,340 F 5
West Bromwich, 162,740 F 5
West Mersea, 4,730 H 6
Westminster, 216,100 H 8
Weston-super-Mare, 51,960 D 6
Weymouth and Melcombe Regis, 41,080 E 7
Whickham, 29,710 J 3
Whitchurch, ⊙7,142 E 5
Whitehaven, 26,260 D 3
Whitley Bay, 37,010 J 3
Widnes, 58,330 G 2
Wigan, 80,920 G 2
Wigston, 31,650 F 5
Wilmslow, 31,250 H 2
Wilton, 4,090 F 6
Winchester, 88,900 F 6
Windermere, 7,860 E 3
Winsford, 26,920 G 2
Wirral, 27,510 G 2
Wisbech, 16,990 H 5
Witham, 19,730 H 6
Withernsea, 6,300 H 4
Wivenhoe, 5,630 J 6
Woking, 79,300 G 8
Wokingham, 22,390 G 8
Wolverhampton, 266,400 E 5
Wombwell, 17,850 K 2
Woodhall Spa, 2,420 G 4
Woodley and Sandford, ⊙24,581 G 8
Woodstock, 2,070 F 6
Wooler, ⊙1,833 F 2
Worcester, 73,900 E 5
Workington, 28,260 D 3
Worksop, 36,590 F 4
Worsbrough, 15,180 J 2
Worsley, 49,530 H 2
Worthing, 89,100 G 7
Wymondham, 9,390 J 5
Yateley, ⊙16,505 G 8
Yeovil, 26,180 E 7
York, 101,900 F 4

OTHER FEATURES

Aire (riv.) F 4
Atlantic Ocean A 7
Avon (riv.) F 5
Avon (riv.) F 7
Axe Edge (mt.) H 2
Barnstaple (bay) C 6
Beachy (head) H 7
Bigbury (bay) C 7
Blackwater (riv.) H 6
Bristol (chan.) C 6
Brown Willy (mt.) C 7
Cheviot (hills) E 2
Cheviot, The (mt.) E 2
Chiltern (hills) G 6
Cleveland (hills) F 3
Colne (riv.) G 8
Cornwall (cape) B 7
Cotswold (hills) E 6
Cross Fell (mt.) E 3
Cumbrian (mts.) D 3
Dart (riv.) D 7
Dartmoor National Park C 7
Dee (riv.) D 4
Derwent (riv.) G 3
Derwent (riv.) H 3
Don (riv.) F 4
Dorset Heights (hills) E 7
Dove (riv.) J 2
Dover (str.) J 7
Dungeness (prom.) J 7
Dunkery (hill) D 6
Eddystone (rocks) C 7
Eden (riv.) E 3
English (chan.) D 8
Esk (riv.) D 2
Exe (riv.) D 7
Exmoor National Park D 6
Fens, The (reg.) G 5
Flamborough (head) G 3
Formby (head) G 2
Foulness Island (pen.) J 6
Gibraltar (pt.) H 4
Great Ouse (riv.) H 5
Hartland (pt.) C 6
High Willhays (mt.) C 7
Hodder (riv.) H 1
Holderness (pen.), 43,900 G 4
Holy (isl.), 189 F 2
Humber (riv.) G 4
Irish (sea) B 4
Kennet (riv.) F 6
Lake District National Park D 3
Land's End (prom.) B 7
Lea (riv.) G 6
Lincoln Wolds (hills) G 4
Lindisfarne (Holy) (isl.), 189 F 2
Liverpool (bay) D 4
Lizard, The (pen.), 7,371 B 8
Lundy (isl.), 49 C 6
Lune (riv.) E 3
Lyme (bay) D 7
Manacle (pt.) C 7
Medway (riv.) H 6
Mendip (hills) E 6
Mersea (isl.), 4,423 J 6
Mersey (riv.) G 2
Morecambe (bay) D 3
Mounts (bay) B 7
Naze, The (prom.) J 6
Nene (riv.) H 5
New (for.) F 6
North (sea) J 4
North Downs (hills) G 6
North Foreland (prom.) J 6
Northumberland National Park E 2
North York Moors National Park G 3
Orford Ness (prom.) J 5
Ouse (riv.) G 4
Ouse (riv.) G 6
Parrett (riv.) E 6
Peak District National Park F 4
Peak, The (mt.) J 2
Peel Fell (mt.) E 2
Pennine Chain (range) E 3
Plymouth (sound) C 7
Portland, Bill of (pt.) E 7
Prawle (pt.) D 7
Purbeck, Isle of (pen.), 39,500 F 7
Ribble (riv.) E 4
Saint Alban's (head) F 7
Saint Bees (head) D 3
Saint Martin's (isl.), 106 A 8
Saint Mary's (isl.), 1,958 A 8
Scafell Pike (mt.) D 3
Scilly (isls.), 1,900 A 7
Selsey Bill (prom.) G 7
Severn (riv.) E 6
Sheppey (isl.), 31,550 J 6
Sherwood (for.) F 4
Skiddaw (mt.) D 3
Solent (chan.) F 7
Solway (firth) D 3
South Downs (hills) G 7
Spithead (chan.) F 7
Spurn (head) H 4
Stonehenge (ruins) F 6
Stour (riv.) E 7
Stour (riv.) H 6
Stour (riv.) J 6
Swale (riv.) F 3
Tamar (riv.) C 7
Taw (riv.) D 7
Tees (riv.) F 3
Test (riv.) F 6
Thames (riv.) H 6
Tintagel (head) C 7
Torridge (riv.) C 7
Trent (riv.) G 4
Tresco (isl.), 246 A 8
Tweed (riv.) E 2
Tyne (riv.) F 3
Ure (riv.) F 3
Ver (riv.) H 7
Walney, Isle of (isl.), 11,241 D 3
Wash, The (bay) H 5
Weald, The (reg.) H 6
Wear (riv.) F 3
Weaver (riv.) G 2
Welland (riv.) G 5
Wey (riv.) G 6
Wharfe (riv.) E 3
Wirral (pen.), 432,900 G 2
Witham (riv.) G 4
Wolds, The (hills) G 4
Wye (riv.) D 5
Wyre (riv.) G 1
Yare (riv.) J 5
Yorkshire Dales National Park E 3

CHANNEL ISLANDS

CITIES and TOWNS

Saint Anne E 8
Saint Helier (cap.), Jersey, ⊙28,135 E 8
Saint Peter Port (cap.), Guernsey, ⊙16,303 E 8
Saint Sampson's, ⊙6,534 E 8

OTHER FEATURES

Alderney (isl.), 1,686 E 8
Guernsey (isl.), 51,351 E 8
Herm (isl.), 96 E 8
Jersey (isl.), 72,629 E 8
Sark (isl.), 590 E 8

ISLE of MAN

CITIES and TOWNS

Castletown, 2,820 C 3
Douglas (cap.), 20,389 C 3
Laxey, 1,170 C 3
Michael, 408 C 3
Onchan, 4,807 C 3
Peel, 3,081 C 3
Port Erin, 1,714 C 3
Port Saint Mary, 1,508 C 3
Ramsey, 5,048 C 3

OTHER FEATURES

Ayre (pt.) C 3
Calf of Man (isl.) C 3
Langness (prom.) C 3
Snaefell (mt.) C 3
Spanish (head) C 3

WALES

COUNTIES

Clwyd, 376,000 D 4
Dyfed, 323,100 C 6
Gwent, 439,600 D 6
Gwynedd, 225,100 C 4
Mid Glamorgan, 540,400 D 6
Powys, 101,500 D 5
South Glamorgan, 389,200 A 7
West Glamorgan, 371,900 D 6

CITIES and TOWNS

Aberaeron, 1,340 C 5
Abercarn, 18,370 B 6
Aberdare, 38,030 A 6
Abertillery, 20,550 B 6
Amlwch, 3,630 C 4
Bala, 1,650 D 5
Bangor, 16,030 C 4
Barmouth, 2,070 C 5
Barry, 42,780 B 7
Beaumaris, 2,090 C 4
Bedwellty, 25,460 B 6
Bethesda, 4,180 D 4
Betws-y-Coed, 720 D 4
Brecknock (Brecon), 6,460 D 6
Brecon, 6,460 D 6
Bridgend, 14,690 A 7
Brynmawr, 5,970 B 6
Builth Wells, 1,480 D 5
Burry Port, 5,990 C 6
Caernarfon, 8,840 C 4
Caerphilly, 42,190 B 6
Cardiff, 281,500 B 7
Cardigan, 3,830 C 5
Chepstow, 8,260 E 6
Chirk, ⊙3,564 D 5
Colwyn Bay, 25,370 D 4
Criccieth, 1,590 C 5
Cwmamman, 3,950 D 6
Cwmbran, 32,980 B 6
Denbigh, 8,420 D 4
Dolgellau, 2,430 D 5
Ebbw Vale, 25,670 B 6
Ffestiniog, 5,510 D 5
Fishguard and Goodwick, 5,020 B 5
Flint, 15,070 G 2
Gelligaer, 33,820 A 6
Harlech, ⊙332 C 5
Haverfordwest, 8,930 B 6
Hawarden, ⊙20,389 G 2
Hay, 1,200 D 5
Holywell, 8,570 G 2
Kidwelly, 3,090 C 6
Knighton, 2,190 D 5
Llandeilo, 1,780 C 6
Llandovery, 2,040 D 5
Llandrindod Wells, 3,460 D 5
Llandudno, 17,700 D 4
Llanelli, 25,870 C 6
Llanfairfechan, 3,800 D 4
Llangefni, 4,070 C 4
Llangollen, 3,050 D 5
Llanguicke, ⊙15,029 D 6
Llanidloes, 2,390 D 5
Llantrisant, ⊙27,490 A 7
Llanwrtyd Wells, 460 D 5
Llwchwr, 27,530 D 6
Machynlleth, 1,830 D 5
Maesteg, 21,100 D 6
Menai Bridge, 2,730 C 4
Merthyr Tydfil, 61,500 A 6
Milford Haven, 13,960 B 6
Mold, 8,700 G 2
Montgomery, 1,000 D 5
Mountain Ash, 27,710 A 6
Mynyddislwyn, 15,590 B 6
Narberth, 970 C 6
Neath, 27,280 D 6
Nefyn, ⊙2,086 C 5
Newcastle Emlyn, 690 C 5
Newport, Dyfed, ⊙1,062 C 5
Newport, Gwent, 110,090 B 6
New Quay, 760 C 5
Newtown, 6,400 D 5
Neyland, 2,690 B 6
Ogmore and Garw, 19,680 A 6
Pembroke, 14,570 C 6
Penarth, 24,180 B 7
Penmaenmawr, 4,050 C 4
Pontypool, 36,710 B 6
Pontypridd, 34,180 A 6
Porthcawl, 14,980 D 6
Porthmadog, 3,900 C 5
Port Talbot, 58,200 D 6
Prestatyn, 15,480 D 4
Presteigne, 1,330 D 5
Pwllheli, 4,020 C 5
Rhondda, 85,400 A 6
Rhyl, 22,150 D 4
Risca, 15,780 B 6
Ruthin, 4,780 D 4
Saint David's, ⊙1,638 B 6
Swansea, 190,800 C 6
Tenby, 4,930 C 6
Tredegar, 17,450 B 6
Tywyn, 3,850 C 5
Welshpool, 7,370 D 5
Wrexham, 39,530 E 4

OTHER FEATURES

Anglesey (isl.), 64,500 C 4
Aran Fawddwy (mt.) C 5
Bardsey (isl.), 9 C 5
Berwyn (mts.) D 5
Black (mts.) D 6
Braich-y-Pwll (prom.) C 5
Brecon Beacons (mt.) D 6
Brecon Beacons National Park D 6
Caldy (isl.), 70 C 6
Cambrian (mts.) D 5
Cardigan (bay) C 5
Carmarthen (bay) C 6
Cemmaes (head) C 5
Dee (riv.) D 4
Dovey (riv.) D 5
Ely (riv.) B 7
Gower (pen.), 17,220 C 6
Great Ormes (head) C 4
Holy (isl.), 13,715 C 4
Lleyn (pen.), 25,800 C 5
Menai (str.) C 4
Milford Haven (inlet) B 6
Pembrokeshire Coast National Park C 6
Plynlimon (mt.) D 5
Preseli (mts.) C 6
Radnor (for.) D 5
Rhymney (riv.) B 6
Saint Brides (bay) B 6
Saint David's (head) B 6
Saint George's (chan.) B 5
Saint Gowans (head) C 6
Severn (riv.) E 5
Snowdon (mt.) D 4
Snowdonia National Park D 4
Taff (riv.) B 7
Teifi (riv.) C 5
Towy (riv.) D 6
Tremadoc (bay) C 5
Usk (riv.) B 6
Wye (riv.) D 5
Ynys Môn (Anglesey) (isl.), 64,500 C 4

★Population of met. area.
⊙Population of parish.

SCOTLAND
(map on page 15)

REGIONS

Borders, 99,409 E 5
Central, 269,281 D 4
Dumfries and Galloway, 143,667 E 5
Fife, 336,339 E 4
Grampian, 448,772 F 3
Highland, 182,044 D 3
Lothian, 754,008 E 5
Orkney (islands area), 17,675 E 1
Shetland (islands area), 18,494 F 2
Strathclyde, 2,504,909 C 4
Tayside, 401,987 E 4
Western Isles (islands area), 29,615 A 3

CITIES and TOWNS

Aberchirder, 877 F 3
Aberdeen, 210,362 F 3
Aberdour, 1,576 D 1
Aberfeldy, 1,552 E 4
Aberfoyle, 793 D 4
Aberlady, 737 F 4
Aberlour, 842 E 3
Abernethy, 776 E 4
Aboyne, 1,040 F 3
Acharacle, ⊙764 C 4
Achiltibuie, ⊙1,564 C 3
Achnasheen, ⊙1,078 C 3
Ae, 239 E 5
Airdrie, 38,491 C 2
Alexandria, 9,758 A 1
Alford, 764 F 3
Alloa, 13,558 C 1
Alness, 2,560 D 3
Altnaharra, ⊙1,227 D 2
Alva, 4,593 C 1
Alyth, 1,738 E 4
Ancrum, 266 F 5
Annan, 6,250 E 6
Annat, ⊙550 C 3
Annbank Station, 2,530 D 5
Applecross, ⊙550 C 3
Arbroath, 22,706 F 4
Ardavasar, ⊙449 B 3
Ardersier, 942 E 3
Ardgay, 193 D 3
Ardrishaig, 946 C 4
Ardrossan, 11,072 D 5
Armadale, 7,200 C 2
Arrochar, 543 D 4
Ascog, 230 A 2
Auchenblae, 339 F 4
Auchencairn, 215 E 6
Auchinleck, 4,883 D 5
Auchterarder, 1,738 E 4
Auchtermuchty, 1,426 E 4
Auldearn, 405 E 3
Aviemore, 1,224 E 3
Avoch, 776 D 3
Ayr, 47,990 D 5
Ayton, 410 F 5
Bailivanish, 347 A 3
Baillieston, 7,671 B 2
Balallan, 283 B 2
Balerno, 3,576 D 2
Balfron, 1,149 B 1
Ballantrae, 262 C 5
Ballater, 981 F 3
Ballingry, 4,332 D 1
Ballinluig, 188 E 4
Balloch, Highland, 572 D 3
Balloch, Strathclyde, 1,484 B 1
Baltasound, 246 G 2
Banchory, 2,435 F 3
Banff, 3,832 F 3
Bankfoot, 868 E 4
Bankhead, 1,492 F 3
Bannockburn, 5,889 C 1
Barrhead, 18,736 B 2
Barrhill, 236 D 5
Barvas, 279 B 2
Bathgate, 14,038 C 2
Bayble, 543 B 2
Bearsden, 25,128 B 2
Beattock, 309 E 5
Beauly, 1,141 D 3
Beith, 5,859 D 5
Bellsbank, 3,066 D 5
Bellshill, 18,166 C 2
Berriedale, ⊙1,927 E 2
Bieldside, 1,137 F 3
Biggar, 1,718 E 5
Birnam, 659 E 4
Bishopbriggs, 21,570 B 2
Bishopton, 2,931 B 2
Blackburn, 7,636 C 2
Blackford, 529 E 4
Blair Atholl, 437 E 4
Blairgowrie and Rattray, 5,681 E 4
Blanefield, 835 B 1
Blantyre, 13,992 B 2
Blyth Bridge, ⊙441 E 5
Bo'ness, 12,959 C 1
Boat of Garten, 406 E 3
Boddam, 1,429 G 3
Bonar Bridge, 519 D 3
Bonhill, 4,385 B 1
Bonnybridge, 5,701 C 1
Bonnyrigg and Lasswade, 7,429 D 2
Bowmore, 947 B 5
Braemar, 394 E 3
Breasclete, 234 B 2
Brechin, 6,759 F 4
Bridge of Allan, 4,638 C 1
Bridge of Don, 4,086 F 3
Bridge of Weir, 4,724 A 2
Brightons, 3,106 C 1
Broadford, 310 B 3
Brodick, 630 C 5
Brora, 1,436 E 2
Broxburn, 7,776 D 1
Buchlyvie, 412 B 1
Buckhaven and Methil, 17,930 F 4
Buckie, 8,145 E 3
Bucksburn, 6,567 F 3
Bunessan, ⊙585 B 4
Burghead, 1,321 E 3
Burnmouth, 300 F 5
Burntisland, 5,626 D 1
Cairndow, ⊙874 D 4
Cairnryan, 199 D 6
Callander, 1,805 D 4
Cambuslang, 14,607 B 2
Campbeltown, 6,428 C 5
Cannich, 203 D 3
Canonbie, 234 F 5
Caol, 3,719 C 4
Carbost, ⊙772 B 3
Cardenden, 6,802 D 1
Carloway, 178 B 2
Carluke, 8,864 E 5
Carnoustie, 6,838 F 4
Carnwath, 1,246 E 5
Carradale, 262 C 5
Carrbridge, 416 E 3
Carron, 2,626 C 1
Carsphairn, 186 D 5
Castlebay, 284 A 4
Castle Douglas, 3,384 E 6
Castle Kennedy, 307 D 6
Castletown, 902 E 2
Catrine, 2,681 D 5
Cawdor, 111 E 3
Chirnside, 888 F 5
Chryston, 8,322 C 2
Clackmannan, 3,248 C 1
Clarkston, 8,404 B 2
Closeburn, 225 E 5
Clovulin, ⊙315 C 4
Clydebank, 47,538 B 2
Coalburn, 1,460 E 5
Coatbridge, 50,806 C 2
Cockburnspath, 233 F 5
Cockenzie and Port Seton, 3,539 D 1
Coldingham, 423 F 5
Coldstream, 1,393 F 5
Coll, 305 B 2
Colmonell, 218 D 5
Comrie, 1,119 E 4
Connel, 300 C 4
Cononbridge, 914 D 3
Corpach, 1,296 C 4
Coupar Angus, 2,010 E 4
Cove and Kilcreggan, 1,402 A 1
Cove Bay, 765 F 3
Cowdenbeath, 10,215 D 1
Cowie, 2,751 C 1
Craigellachie, 382 E 3
Craignure, ⊙544 C 4
Crail, 1,033 F 4
Crawford, 384 E 5
Creetown, 769 D 6
Crieff, 5,718 E 4
Crimond, 313 G 3
Crinan, ⊙462 C 4
Cromarty, 492 E 3
Crosshill, 535 D 5
Crossmichael, 317 D 6
Cruden Bay, 528 G 3
Cullen, 1,199 F 3
Culross, 504 C 1
Cults, 3,336 F 3
Cumbernauld, 41,200 C 1
Cumnock and Holmhead, 6,298 D 5
Cupar, 6,607 E 4
Currie, 6,764 D 2
Dailly, 1,258 D 5
Dalbeattie, 3,659 E 6
Daliburgh, 261 A 3
Dalkeith, 9,713 D 2
Dalmally, 283 D 4
Dalmellington, 1,949 D 5
Dalry, 5,833 D 5
Dalrymple, 1,336 D 5
Darvel, 3,177 D 5
Daviot, ⊙513 D 3
Denholm, 581 F 5
Denny and Dunipace, 10,424 C 1
Dervaig, ⊙1,081 B 4
Dingwall, 4,275 D 3
Dollar, 2,573 E 4
Dornoch, 880 D 3
Douglas, 1,843 E 5
Doune, 859 D 4
Drongan, 3,609 D 5
Drumbeg, ⊙833 C 2
Drummore, 336 D 6
Drumnadrochit, 359 D 3
Drymen, 659 B 1
Dufftown, 1,481 E 3
Dumbarton, 25,469 B 1
Dumfries, 29,259 E 5
Dunbar, 4,609 F 4
Dunbeath, 161 E 2
Dunbeg, 939 C 4
Dunblane, 5,222 E 4
Dundee, 194,732 F 4
Dundonald, 2,256 D 5
Dunfermline, 52,098 D 1
Dunkeld, 273 E 4
Dunning, 564 E 4
Dunoon, 8,759 A 2
Dunragit, 323 D 6
Duns, 1,812 F 5
Duntochter, 3,532 B 2
Dunure, 452 D 5
Dunvegan, 301 B 3
Dyce, 2,733 F 3
Eaglesfield, 581 E 5
Eaglesham, 2,788 D 5
Earlston, 1,415 F 5
East Calder, 2,690 D 2
East Kilbride, 71,200 B 2
East Linton, 882 F 5
Eastriggs, 1,455 E 5
Ecclefechan, 844 E 5
Edinburgh (cap.), 470,085 D 1
Edzell, 658 F 4
Elderslie, 5,204 B 2
Elgin, 17,042 E 3
Elie and Earlsferry, 807 F 4
Ellon, 2,855 F 3
Embo, 260 E 3
Errol, 762 E 4
Evanton, 562 D 3
Eyemouth, 2,704 F 5
Fairlie, 1,029 D 5
Falkirk, 36,901 C 1
Falkland, 998 E 4
Fallin, 3,159 C 1
Fauldhouse, 5,247 C 2
Ferness, ⊙287 E 3
Ferryden, 740 F 4
Findhorn, 664 E 3
Findochty, 1,229 E 3
Fintry, 296 B 1
Fochabers, 1,238 E 3
Forfar, 11,179 F 4
Forres, 5,317 E 3
Fort Augustus, 670 D 3
Forth, 2,929 C 2
Fortrose, 1,150 D 3
Fort William, 4,370 C 4
Foyers, 276 D 3
Fraserburgh, 10,930 G 3
Friockheim, 807 F 4
Furnace, 220 C 4
Fyvie, 405 F 3
Gairloch, 125 C 3
Galashiels, 12,808 F 5
Galston, 4,256 D 5
Gardenstown, 892 F 3
Garelochhead, 1,552 A 1
Gargunnock, 457 B 1
Garlieston, 385 D 6
Garmouth, 352 E 3
Garrabost, 307 B 2
Gartmore, 253 B 1
Gatehouse-of-Fleet, 835 D 6
Giffnock, 10,987 B 2
Gifford, 575 F 5
Girvan, 7,597 D 5
Glamis, 190 F 4
Glasgow, 880,617 B 2
Glasgow, ★1,674,789 B 2
Glenbarr, ⊙691 C 5
Glencaple, 275 E 5
Glencoe, 195 C 4
Glenelg, ⊙1,468 C 3
Glenluce, 725 D 6
Glenrothes, 31,400 E 4
Golspie, 1,374 E 3
Gordon, 320 F 5
Gorebridge, 3,426 D 2
Gourock, 11,192 A 1
Grangemouth, 24,430 C 1
Grantown-on-Spey, 1,578 E 3
Greenlaw, 574 F 5
Greenock, 67,275 A 2
Gretna, 1,907 E 5
Gullane, 1,701 F 4
Haddington, 6,767 F 5
Halkirk, 679 E 2
Hamilton, 45,495 C 2
Hamnavoe, 307 G 2
Harthill, 4,712 C 2
Hatton, 315 G 3
Hawick, 16,484 F 5
Heathhall, 1,365 E 5
Helensburgh, 13,327 A 1
Helmsdale, 727 E 2
Hill of Fearn, 233 D 3
Hillside, 692 F 4
Hillswick, ⊙696 G 2
Hopeman, 1,248 E 3
Huntly, 4,078 F 3
Hurlford, 4,294 D 5
Inchnadamph, ⊙833 D 2
Innellan, 922 A 2
Innerleithen, 2,293 E 5
Insch, 881 F 3
Inveraray, 473 C 4
Inverbervie, 853 F 4
Invercassley, ⊙1,067 D 3
Invergordon, 2,385 D 3
Invergowrie, 1,389 E 4
Inverie, ⊙1,468 C 3
Inverkeithing, 6,102 D 1
Inverness, 35,801 D 3
Inverurie, 5,534 F 3
Irvine, 48,500 D 5
Isle of Whithorn, 222 D 6
Jedburgh, 3,953 F 5
John O'Groats, 195 E 2
Johnshaven, 544 F 4
Johnstone, 23,251 B 2
Kames, 230 C 5
Keiss, 344 E 2
Keith, 4,192 F 3
Kelso, 4,934 F 5
Kelty, 6,573 D 1
Kemnay, 1,042 F 3
Kenmore, 211 E 4
Kilbarchan, 2,669 A 2
Kilbirnie, 8,259 A 2
Kilchoan, ⊙764 B 4
Kildonan, ⊙1,105 E 2
Killearn, 1,086 B 1
Killin, 600 D 4
Kilmacolm, 3,348 A 2
Kilmarnock, 50,175 D 5
Kilmaurs, 2,518 D 5
Kilninver, ⊙247 C 4
Kilrenny and Anstruther, 2,951 F 4
Kilsyth, 10,210 B 1
Kilwinning, 8,460 D 5
Kinbrace, ⊙1,105 E 2
Kincardine, 3,278 C 1
Kinghorn, 2,163 D 1
Kingussie, 1,036 D 3
Kinlochewe, ⊙1,794 C 3
Kinlochleven, 1,243 D 4
Kinloch Rannoch, 241 D 4
Kinloss, 2,378 E 3
Kinross, 2,829 E 4
Kintore, 970 F 3
Kippen, 529 B 1
Kirkcaldy, 50,207 D 1
Kirkcolm, 346 C 6
Kirkconnel, 3,318 E 5
Kirkcowan, 354 D 6
Kirkcudbright, 2,690 E 6
Kirkhill, 210 D 3
Kirkintilloch, 26,664 B 2
Kirkmuirhill, 2,575 E 5
Kirkton of Glenisla, ⊙331 E 4
Kirkwall, 4,777 E 2
Kirriemuir, 4,295 E 4
Kyleakin, 268 C 3
Kyle of Lochalsh, 687 C 3
Kylestrome, ⊙745 D 2
Ladybank, 1,216 E 4
Laggan, 393 D 3
Lairg, 572 D 2
Lamlash, 613 C 5
Lanark, 8,842 E 5
Langholm, 2,509 E 5
Larbert, 4,922 C 1
Largs, 9,461 A 2
Larkhall, 15,926 E 5
Lauder, 639 F 5
Laurencekirk, 1,416 F 4

(continued)

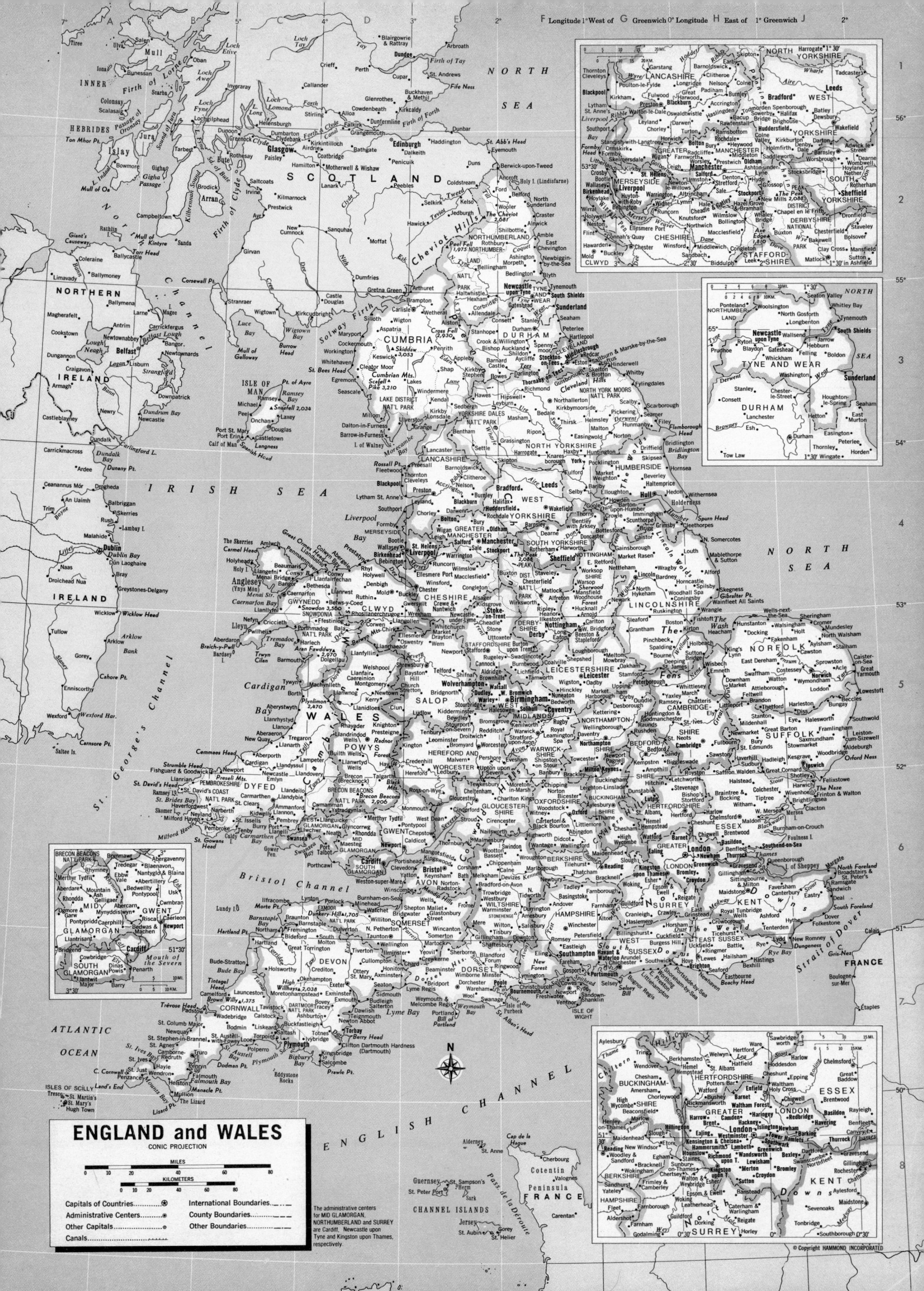

ENGLAND and WALES
CONIC PROJECTION

MILES
KILOMETERS

Capitals of Countries.............⊛
Administrative Centers............◉
Other Capitals.....................⊚
Canals.............................

International Boundaries.........
County Boundaries...............
Other Boundaries................

The administrative centers
for MID GLAMORGAN,
NORTHUMBERLAND and SURREY
are Cardiff, Newcastle upon
Tyne and Kingston upon Thames,
respectively.

© Copyright HAMMOND INCORPORATED

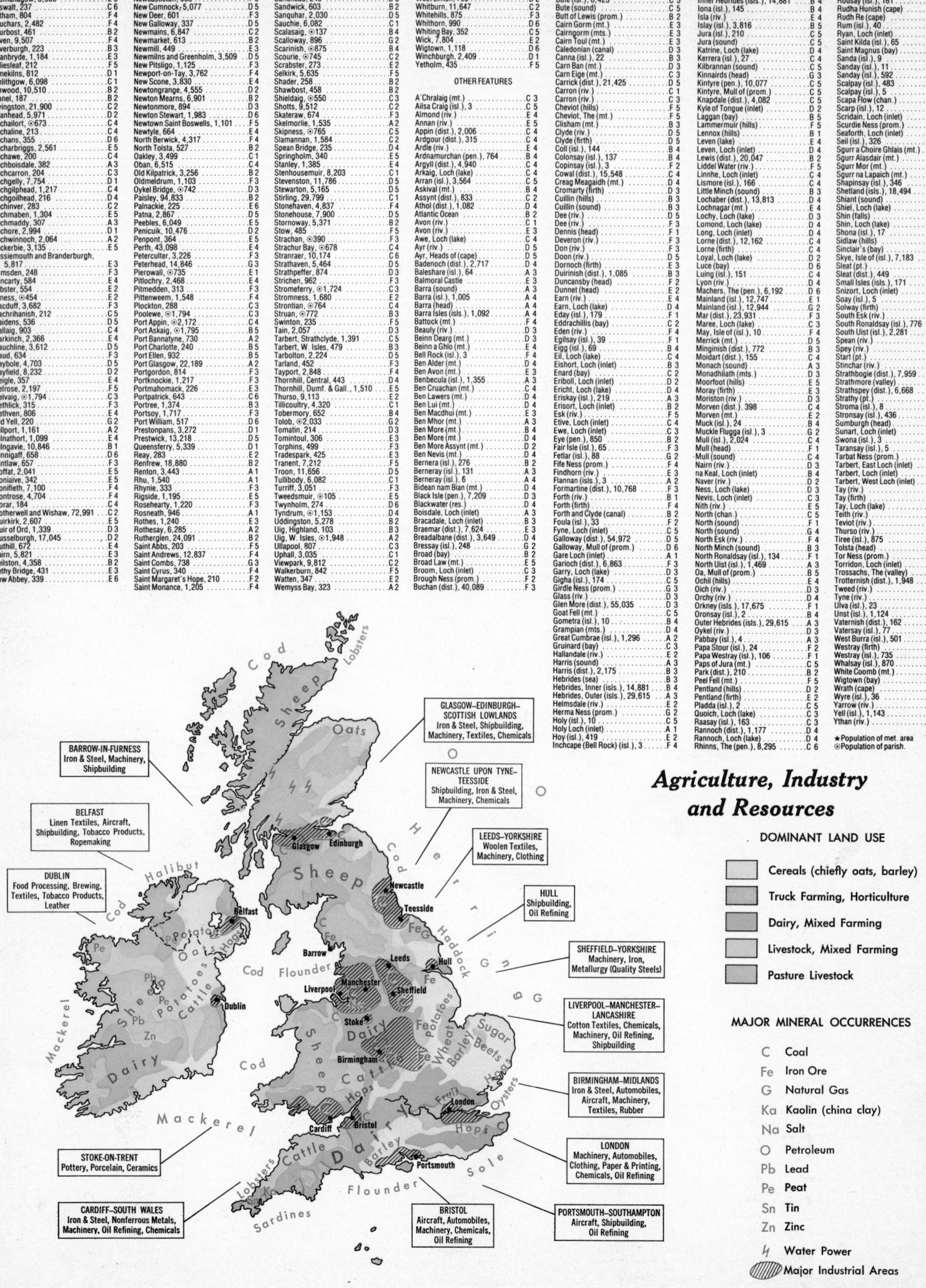

Agriculture, Industry and Resources

DOMINANT LAND USE

- Cereals (chiefly oats, barley)
- Truck Farming, Horticulture
- Dairy, Mixed Farming
- Livestock, Mixed Farming
- Pasture Livestock

MAJOR MINERAL OCCURRENCES

- C Coal
- Fe Iron Ore
- G Natural Gas
- Ka Kaolin (china clay)
- Na Salt
- O Petroleum
- Pb Lead
- Pe Peat
- Sn Tin
- Zn Zinc
- Water Power
- Major Industrial Areas

GLASGOW–EDINBURGH–SCOTTISH LOWLANDS
Iron & Steel, Shipbuilding, Machinery, Textiles, Chemicals

NEWCASTLE UPON TYNE–TEESSIDE
Shipbuilding, Iron & Steel, Machinery, Chemicals

LEEDS–YORKSHIRE
Woolen Textiles, Machinery, Clothing

HULL
Shipbuilding, Oil Refining

SHEFFIELD–YORKSHIRE
Machinery, Iron, Metallurgy (Quality Steels)

LIVERPOOL–MANCHESTER–LANCASHIRE
Cotton Textiles, Chemicals, Machinery, Oil Refining, Shipbuilding

BIRMINGHAM–MIDLANDS
Iron & Steel, Automobiles, Aircraft, Machinery, Textiles, Rubber

LONDON
Machinery, Automobiles, Clothing, Paper & Printing, Chemicals, Oil Refining

BARROW-IN-FURNESS
Iron & Steel, Machinery, Shipbuilding

BELFAST
Linen Textiles, Aircraft, Shipbuilding, Tobacco Products, Ropemaking

DUBLIN
Food Processing, Brewing, Textiles, Tobacco Products, Leather

STOKE-ON-TRENT
Pottery, Porcelain, Ceramics

CARDIFF–SOUTH WALES
Iron & Steel, Nonferrous Metals, Machinery, Oil Refining, Chemicals

BRISTOL
Aircraft, Automobiles, Machinery, Chemicals, Oil Refining

PORTSMOUTH–SOUTHAMPTON
Aircraft, Shipbuilding, Oil Refining

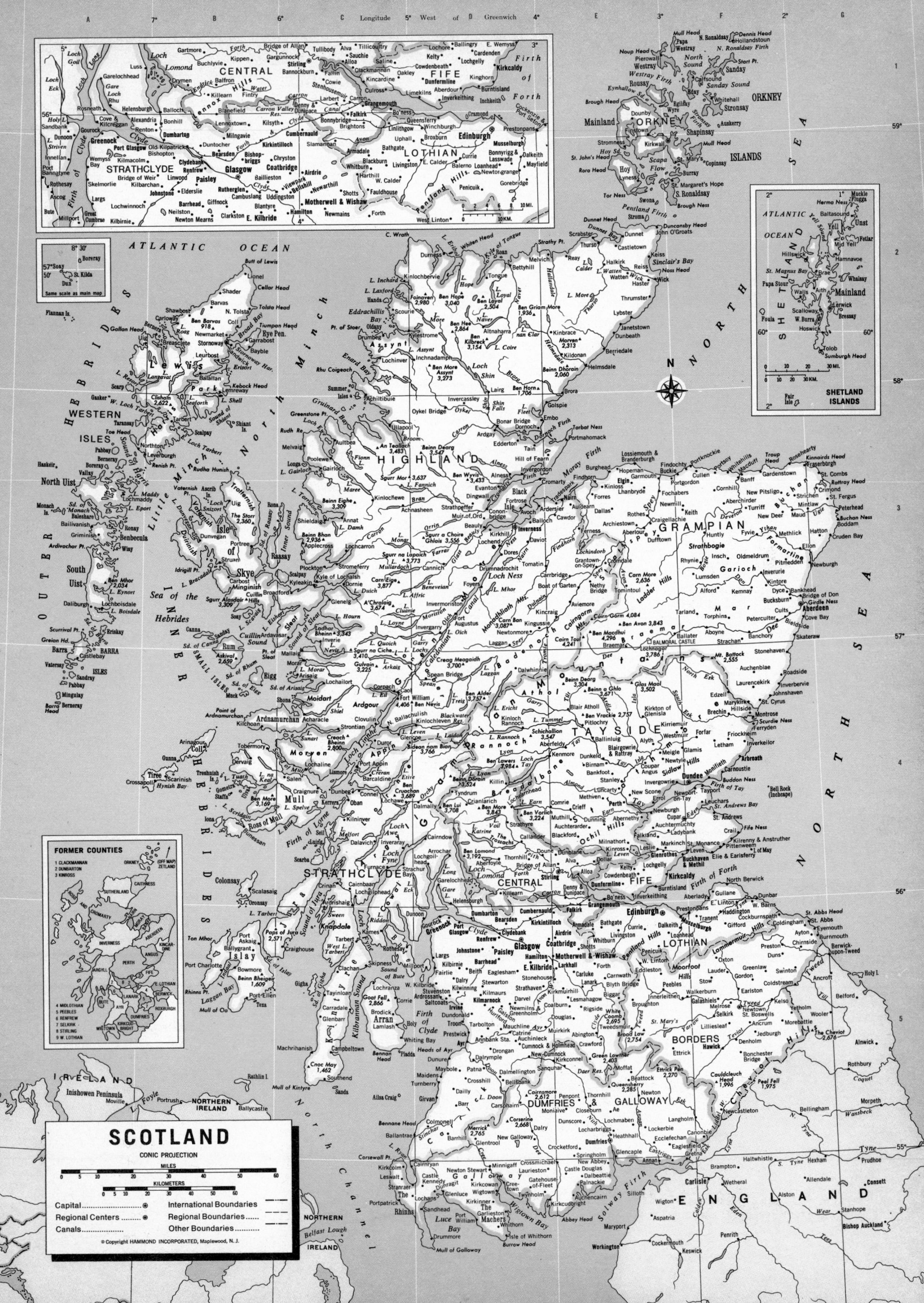

SCOTLAND

CONIC PROJECTION

Capital .... ★
Regional Centers .... ⊛
Canals ....

International Boundaries ...... — — —
Regional Boundaries .... — · —
Other Boundaries ....

© Copyright HAMMOND INCORPORATED, Maplewood, N.J.

FORMER COUNTIES

1 CLACKMANNAN
2 DUMBARTON
3 KINROSS
4 MIDLOTHIAN
5 PEEBLES
6 RENFREW
7 SELKIRK
8 STIRLING
9 W. LOTHIAN

SHETLAND ISLANDS

16 United Kingdom and Ireland

(continued)

IRELAND

COUNTIES

Carlow, 34,237 .... H 6
Cavan, 52,618 .... G 4
Clare, 75,008 .... D 6
Cork, 352,883 .... D 7
Donegal, 108,344 .... K 2
Dublin, 852,219 .... J 5
Galway, 149,223 .... D 5
Kerry, 112,772 .... B 7
Kildare, 71,977 .... H 5
Kilkenny, 61,473 .... G 6
Laoighis, 45,259 .... G 6
Leitrim, 28,360 .... E 3
Leix (Laoighis), 45,259 .... G 6
Limerick, 140,459 .... D 7
Longford, 28,250 .... F 4
Louth, 74,951 .... J 4
Mayo, 109,525 .... C 4
Meath, 71,729 .... H 4
Monaghan, 46,242 .... H 3
Offaly, 51,829 .... F 5
Roscommon, 53,519 .... E 4
Sligo, 50,275 .... D 3
Tipperary, 123,565 .... F 6
Waterford, 77,315 .... F 7
Westmeath, 53,570 .... G 5
Wexford, 86,351 .... H 7
Wicklow, 66,295 .... J 5

CITIES and TOWNS

Abbeydorney, 188 .... B 7
Abbeyfeale, 1,337 .... C 7
Abbeylara, ‡290 .... F 4
Abbeyleix, 1,033 .... G 6
Achill Sound, ‡1,163 .... B 4
Aclare, ‡336 .... D 3
Adare, 545 .... D 6
Aghada-Farsid-Rostellan, 461 .... E 8
Aghadoe, ‡497 .... B 7
Aghagower, ‡693 .... C 4
Ahascragh, 221 .... E 5
Annagry, 201 .... E 1
Annascaul, 236 .... B 7
An Uaimh, 4,605 .... H 4
An Uaimh, *6,665 .... H 4
Ardagh, Limerick, 213 .... C 7
Ardagh, Longford, ‡974 .... F 4
Ardara, 683 .... E 2
Ardee, *3,183 .... H 4
Ardee, 3,096 .... H 4
Ardfert, 286 .... B 7
Ardfinnan, 510 .... F 7
Ardmore, 233 .... F 8
Ardrahan, ‡239 .... D 5
Arklow, 6,948 .... J 6
Arthurstown, 1,188 .... H 7
Arva, 370 .... F 4
Ashford, 341 .... J 5
Askeaton, 844 .... D 6
Athboy, 705 .... H 4
Athea, 328 .... C 7
Athenry, 1,240 .... D 5
Athleague, ‡955 .... E 4
Athlone, 9,825 .... F 5
Athlone, *11,611 .... F 5
Athy, 4,270 .... H 6
Athy, *4,654 .... H 6
Aughrim, 451 .... J 6
Avoca, ‡620 .... J 6
Bagenalstown (Muinebeag), 2,321 .... H 6
Baile Átha Cliath (Dublin) (cap.), 567,866 .... K 5
Bailieborough, 1,293 .... G 4
Balbriggan, 3,741 .... J 4
Balla, 293 .... C 4
Ballaghaderreen, 1,121 .... E 4
Ballina, Mayo, 6,063 .... C 3
Ballina, *6,369 .... C 3
Ballina, Tipperary, 336 .... E 6
Ballinagh, 459 .... G 4
Ballinakill, 300 .... G 6
Ballineen .... D 8
Ballinamore, 808 .... F 3
Ballinasloe, 5,969 .... E 5
Ballincollig-Carrigrohane, 2,110 .... D 8
Ballindine, 232 .... C 4
Ballingarry, Limerick, 422 .... D 7
Ballingarry, Tipperary, ‡574 .... F 6
Ballinlough, 242 .... D 4
Ballinrobe, 1,272 .... C 4
Ballintober, ‡867 .... E 4
Ballintra, 197 .... E 2
Ballisodare, 486 .... E 3
Ballivor, 287 .... H 4
Ballybay, 754 .... G 3
Ballybay, *1,159 .... G 3
Ballybofey-Stranorlar, 2,214 .... F 2
Ballybunion, 1,287 .... B 7
Ballycanew, ‡460 .... J 6
Ballycarney, ‡294 .... J 6
Ballycastle, ‡724 .... C 3
Ballyconnell, 421 .... F 3
Ballycotton, 389 .... F 8
Ballydehob, 253 .... C 8
Ballyduff, 406 .... B 7
Ballygar, 359 .... E 4
Ballygeary, 725 .... J 7
Ballyhaise, 274 .... G 3
Ballyhaunis, 1,093 .... D 4
Ballyheigue, 450 .... B 7
Ballyjamesduff, 673 .... G 4
Ballylanders, 266 .... E 7
Ballylongford, 504 .... B 6
Ballymahon, 707 .... F 4
Ballymakeery, 272 .... C 8
Ballymore, ‡447 .... F 5
Ballymore Eustace, 433 .... J 5
Ballymote, 952 .... D 3
Ballyporeen, ‡810 .... E 7
Ballyragget, 519 .... G 6
Ballyroan, ‡478 .... G 6
Ballyshannon, 2,325 .... E 3
Ballytore, ‡580 .... H 5
Baltimore, 200 .... C 9
Baltinglass, 909 .... H 6
Baltray, 236 .... J 4
Banagher, 1,052 .... F 5
Bandon, 2,257 .... D 8
Bandon, *4,071 .... D 8
Bannow, ‡798 .... H 7
Bansha, 184 .... E 7
Bantry, 2,579 .... C 8
Barna, ‡1,734 .... C 5
Belmullet, 744 .... B 3
Belturbet, 1,092 .... G 3
Bennettsbridge, 367 .... G 6
Birr, 3,319 .... F 5
Birr, *3,881 .... F 5
Blanchardstown, 3,279 .... H 5
Blarney, 1,128 .... D 8
Blessington, 637 .... J 5
Boherbue, 372 .... C 7
Borris, 430 .... H 6
Borris-in-Ossory, 276 .... F 6
Borrisokane, 769 .... E 6
Borrisoleigh, 471 .... E 6
Boyle, 1,727 .... E 4
Boyle, *1,939 .... E 4
Bray, 14,467 .... K 5
Bray, *15,841 .... K 5
Bri Chualann (Bray), 14,467 .... K 5
Broadford, 226 .... C 7
Brosna, 250 .... C 7
Bruff, 547 .... D 7
Bruree, 243 .... D 7
Bunbeg-Derrybeg, 878 .... E 1
Bunclody-Carrickduff, 929 .... H 6
Buncrana, 2,955 .... G 1
Buncrana, *3,334 .... G 1
Bundoran, 1,337 .... E 3
Burtonport, ‡1,288 .... E 2
Buttevant, 1,045 .... D 7
Cahir, 1,747 .... F 7
Cahirciveen, 1,547 .... A 8
Callan, 1,283 .... G 7
Camolin, 306 .... J 6
Campile, 231 .... H 7
Cappamore, 567 .... E 6
Cappawhite, 305 .... E 6
Cappoquin, 872 .... F 7
Carbury, ‡894 .... H 5
Carlingford, 559 .... J 3
Carlow, 9,588 .... H 6
Carlow, *10,399 .... H 6
Carndonagh, 1,146 .... G 1
Carnew, 570 .... H 6
Carrickmacross, 2,100 .... H 4
Carrickmacross, *2,475 .... H 4
Carrick-on-Shannon, 1,854 .... F 4
Carrick-on-Suir, 5,006 .... F 7
Carrigaholt, ‡493 .... B 6
Carrigaline, 951 .... E 8
Carrigallen, 230 .... F 4
Carrigart, ‡753 .... F 1
Carrigtwohill, 622 .... E 8
Carrowkeel, ‡326 .... G 1
Cashel, 2,692 .... F 7
Castlebar, 5,979 .... C 4
Castlebar, *6,476 .... C 4
Castlebellingham, 407 .... J 4
Castleblayney, 2,118 .... H 3
Castleblayney, *2,395 .... H 3
Castlecomer-Donaguile, 1,244 .... G 6
Castledermot, 583 .... H 6
Castlefin, 610 .... F 2
Castlegregory, 216 .... A 7
Castleisland, 1,929 .... B 7
Castlemartyr, 491 .... E 8
Castlepollard, 693 .... G 4
Castlerea, 1,752 .... D 4
Castletown, ‡504 .... F 6
Castletownbere, 812 .... B 8
Castletownroche, 399 .... D 7
Castletownshend, 170 .... C 9
Causeway, 215 .... B 7
Cavan, 3,273 .... G 3
Cavan, *4,312 .... G 3
Ceanannus Mór, 2,391 .... G 4
Ceanannus Mór, *2,653 .... G 4
Celbridge, 1,568 .... H 5
Charlestown-Bellahy, 677 .... D 4
Charleville (Rathluirc), 2,232 .... D 7
Clara, 2,156 .... F 5
Claregalway, ‡594 .... D 5
Claremorris, 1,718 .... C 4
Clashmore, ‡379 .... F 8
Clifden, 790 .... B 5
Cloghan, 404 .... F 5
Clogh-Chatsworth, 324 .... G 6
Clogheen, 530 .... F 7
Clogherhead, 649 .... J 4
Clonakilty, 2,430 .... D 8
Clonaslee, 285 .... F 5
Clondalkin, 7,009 .... J 5
Clonegal, 202 .... H 6
Clones, 2,164 .... G 3
Clonfert, ‡430 .... E 5
Clonmany, ‡936 .... G 1
Clonmel, 11,622 .... F 7
Clonmel, *12,291 .... F 7
Clonmellon, 328 .... H 4
Clonroche, 222 .... H 7
Clontuskert, 351 .... E 4
Cloone, ‡460 .... F 4
Cloughjordan, 480 .... E 6
Cloyne, 654 .... E 8
Coachford, 290 .... D 8
Cóbh, 6,076 .... E 8
Cóbh, *7,141 .... E 8
Coill Dubh, 920 .... H 5
Collon, 262 .... J 4
Collooney, 546 .... E 3
Cong, 233 .... C 4
Convoy, 654 .... F 2
Coolaney, ‡352 .... D 3
Coolgreany, ‡603 .... J 6
Cootehill, 1,415 .... G 3
Cootehill, *1,542 .... G 3
Cork, 128,645 .... E 8
Cork, *134,430 .... E 8
Corofin, 342 .... C 6
Courtmacsherry, 210 .... D 8
Courtown Harbour, 291 .... J 6
Creeslough, 269 .... F 1
Crookhaven, ‡400 .... B 9
Croom, 756 .... D 6
Crosshaven, 1,222 .... E 8
Crossmolina, 1,077 .... C 3
Crusheen, ‡405 .... D 6
Culdaff, ‡621 .... G 1
Daingean, 492 .... G 5
Delvin, 223 .... G 4
Dingle, 1,401 .... A 7
Doaghbeg, ‡701 .... F 1
Donabate, 426 .... J 5
Donegal, 1,725 .... F 2
Doneraile, 799 .... D 7
Dooagh-Keel, 649 .... A 4
Doon, 387 .... E 6
Douglas, ‡4,448 .... D 8
Drimoleague, 415 .... C 8
Drishane, ‡1,548 .... C 7
Drogheda, 19,762 .... J 4
Drogheda, *20,095 .... J 4
Droichead Nua, 5,053 .... H 5
Droichead Nua, *6,444 .... H 5
Dromahair, 177 .... E 3
Drumcar, ‡1,215 .... J 4
Drumconrath, ‡1,044 .... H 4
Drumkeerin, ‡467 .... E 3
Drumlish, 205 .... F 4
Drumshanbo, 576 .... E 3
Dublin (cap.), 567,866 .... K 5
Dublin, *679,748 .... K 5
Duleek, 658 .... J 4
Duncannon, 228 .... H 7
Dundalk, 21,672 .... H 3
Dundalk, *23,816 .... H 3
Dunfanaghy, 303 .... F 1
Dungarvan, 5,583 .... F 7
Dungloe, 940 .... E 2
Dunkineely, 288 .... E 2
Dún Laoghaire, 53,171 .... K 5
Dún Laoghaire, *98,379 .... K 5
Dunlavin, 423 .... H 5
Dunleer, 855 .... J 4
Dunmanway, 1,392 .... C 8
Dunmore, 522 .... D 4
Dunmore East, 656 .... G 7
Dunshaughlin, ‡283 .... H 5
Durrow, Laoighis, 596 .... G 6
Durrow, Offaly, ‡441 .... F 5
Easky, 184 .... D 3
Edenderry, 2,953 .... G 5
Edenderry, *3,116 .... G 5
Elphin, 489 .... E 4
Emyvale, 281 .... G 3
Ennis, 5,972 .... D 6
Ennis, *10,840 .... D 6
Enniscorthy, 5,704 .... J 7
Enniscorthy, *6,642 .... J 7
Enniskerry, 772 .... J 5
Ennistymon, 1,013 .... C 6
Eyrecourt, 314 .... E 5
Fahan, ‡1,023 .... G 1
Falcarragh, 506 .... E 1
Feakle, ‡398 .... D 6
Fenit, 360 .... B 7
Ferbane, 1,064 .... F 5
Fermoy, 3,237 .... E 7
Fermoy, *4,033 .... E 7
Ferns, 712 .... J 6
Fethard, Tipperary, 1,064 .... F 7
Fethard, Wexford, ‡637 .... H 7
Foxford, 868 .... C 4
Foynes, 624 .... C 6
Frankford (Kilcormac), 1,089 .... F 5
Frenchpark, ‡693 .... E 4
Freshford, 585 .... G 6
Galbally, 258 .... E 7
Galway, 27,726 .... C 5
Galway, *29,375 .... C 5
Geashill, ‡751 .... G 5
Glandore, ‡695 .... C 8
Glanmire-Riverstown, 1,113 .... E 8
Glanworth, 335 .... E 7
Glenamaddy, 315 .... D 4
Glenbeigh, 266 .... B 7
Glencolumbkille, ‡787 .... D 2
Glengarriff, 244 .... C 8
Glenties, 734 .... E 2
Glenville, ‡264 .... D 7
Glin, 623 .... C 6
Golden, ‡640 .... F 7
Gorey, 2,946 .... J 6
Gorey, *3,024 .... J 6
Gormanston, ‡1,384 .... J 4
Gort, 975 .... D 5
Gowran, 402 .... G 6
Graiguenamanagh-Tinnahinch, 1,303 .... H 6
Granard, 1,054 .... F 4
Greencastle, 322 .... H 1
Greenore, 882 .... J 4
Greystones-Delgany, 4,517 .... K 5
Gurteen, 165 .... D 3
Hacketstown, 574 .... H 6
Headford, 673 .... C 5
Holycross, ‡902 .... F 6
Hospital, 525 .... E 7
Inchigeelagh, ‡516 .... C 8
Inishannon, 190 .... D 8
Inistioge, 179 .... G 7
Inniscrone, 582 .... C 3
Johnstown, 303 .... G 6
Kanturk, 2,063 .... D 7
Keel-Dooagh, 649 .... A 4
Kells, ‡423 .... G 6
Kells (Ceanannus Mór), 2,391 .... G 4
Kenmare, 903 .... B 8
Kilbaha, ‡471 .... B 6
Kilbeggan, 635 .... G 5
Kilcar, 273 .... D 2
Kilcock, 827 .... H 5
Kilconnell, ‡629 .... E 5
Kilcoole, 679 .... K 5
Kilcormac, 1,089 .... F 5
Kilcullen, 880 .... H 5
Kildare, 3,137 .... H 5
Kildysart, 239 .... C 6
Kilfenora, ‡441 .... C 6
Kilfinane, 561 .... D 7
Kilgarvan, 228 .... B 8
Kilkee, 1,287 .... B 6
Kilkelly, 225 .... D 4
Kilkenny, 9,838 .... G 6
Kilkenny, *13,306 .... G 6
Killala, 368 .... C 3
Killaloe, 871 .... D 6
Killarney, 7,184 .... C 7
Killarney, *7,541 .... C 7
Killavullen, 221 .... D 7
Killenaule, 592 .... F 6
Killeshandra, 432 .... F 3
Killimor, 221 .... E 5
Killinaboy, ‡297 .... C 6
Killorglin, 1,150 .... B 7
Killucan-Rathwire, 290 .... G 4
Killybegs, 1,094 .... E 2
Kilmacrennan, 274 .... F 1
Kilmacthomas, 396 .... G 7
Kilmallock, 1,170 .... D 7
Kilmeadan, ‡262 .... G 7
Kilmihill, 284 .... C 6
Kilmoganny, 181 .... G 7
Kilmore Quay, 273 .... H 7
Kilmurry, ‡387 .... C 6
Kilnaleck, 273 .... G 4
Kilronan, 243 .... B 5
Kilrush, 2,671 .... C 6
Kilsheelan, ‡665 .... F 7
Kiltimagh, 978 .... C 4
Kilworth, 360 .... E 7
Kingscourt, 1,016 .... H 4
Kingstown (Dún Laoghaire), 53,171 .... K 5
Kinlough, 160 .... E 3
Kinnegad, 362 .... G 5
Kinnitty, ‡420 .... F 5
Kinsale, 1,622 .... D 8
Kinsale, *1,989 .... D 8
Kinvara, 293 .... D 5
Knightstown, 236 .... A 8
Knock, ‡1,202 .... D 4
Knocklong, 248 .... D 7
Knocknagashel, 168 .... C 7
Labasheeda, ‡468 .... C 6
Laghey, ‡625 .... E 2
Lahinch, 455 .... C 6
Lanesborough-Ballyleague, 906 .... E 4
Laracor, ‡404 .... H 4
Laytown-Bettystown-Mornington, 1,882 .... J 4
Leenane, ‡271 .... B 4
Leighlindridge, 379 .... H 6
Leitrim, ‡544 .... F 3
Leixlip, 2,402 .... H 5
Letterkenny, 4,930 .... F 2
Letterkenny, *5,207 .... F 2
Lifford, 1,121 .... F 2
Limerick, 57,161 .... D 6
Limerick, *63,002 .... D 6
Liscarroll, 231 .... D 7
Lisdoonvarna, 459 .... C 5
Lismore, 884 .... F 7
Lismore, *1,041 .... F 7
Listowel, 3,021 .... C 7
Littleton, 322 .... F 6
Longford, 3,876 .... F 4
Longford, *4,791 .... F 4
Lorrha, ‡685 .... E 5
Loughrea, 3,075 .... E 5
Louisburgh, 310 .... B 4
Louth, 208 .... J 4
Lucan-Doddsborough, 4,245 .... J 5
Luimneach (Limerick), 57,161 .... D 6
Lusk, 553 .... J 4
Macroom, 2,256 .... C 8
Malahide, 3,834 .... J 5
Malin, ‡552 .... G 1
Mallow, 5,901 .... D 7
Mallow, *6,506 .... D 7
Manorhamilton, 858 .... E 3
Manulla, ‡660 .... C 4
Maryborough (Portlaoighise), 3,902 .... G 5
Maynooth, 1,296 .... H 5
Meathas Truim, 546 .... G 4
Midleton, 3,075 .... E 8
Midleton, *4,666 .... E 8
Milford, 763 .... F 1
Millstreet, 1,319 .... D 7
Milltown, 260 .... A 7
Miltown-Malbay, 677 .... C 6
Minard, ‡397 .... A 7
Mitchelstown, 2,783 .... E 7
Moate, 1,378 .... F 5
Mohill, 868 .... F 4
Monaghan, 5,256 .... G 3
Monasterevan, 1,619 .... H 5
Moneygall, 282 .... F 6
Monivea, ‡405 .... D 5
Mooncoin, 413 .... G 7
Mount Bellew, 275 .... D 5
Mountcharles, 445 .... E 2
Mountmellick, 2,595 .... G 5
Mountmellick, *2,864 .... G 5
Mountrath, 1,098 .... F 5
Moville, 1,089 .... G 1
Moycullen, ‡498 .... C 5
Moynalty, ‡583 .... H 4
Muff, 240 .... G 1
Muinebeag, 2,321 .... H 6
Mullagh, 293 .... H 4
Mullaghmore, ‡629 .... D 3
Mullinahone, 262 .... F 7
Mullinavat, 343 .... G 7
Mullingar, 6,790 .... G 4
Mullinger, *9,245 .... G 4
Naas, 5,078 .... H 5
Navan (An Uaimh), 4,605 .... H 4
Nenagh, 5,085 .... E 6
Nenagh, *5,174 .... E 6
Newbliss, ‡547 .... G 3
Newbridge (Droichead Nua), 5,053 .... H 5
Newcastle, 2,549 .... D 7
Newcastle, *2,680 .... D 7
Newmarket, 886 .... C 7
Newmarket-on-Fergus, 1,052 .... D 6
New Pallas, ‡1,271 .... E 6
Newport, Mayo, 420 .... C 4
Newport, Tipperary, 582 .... E 6
New Ross, 4,775 .... H 7
New Ross, *5,153 .... H 7
Newtownforbes, ‡495 .... F 4
Newtownmountkennedy, 882 .... J 5
Newtownsandes, 268 .... C 6
O'Briensbridge-Montpelier, 237 .... D 6
Oldcastle, 759 .... G 4
Old Leighlin, ‡309 .... G 6
Oola, 348 .... E 6
Oranmore, 440 .... D 5
Oughterard, 628 .... C 5
Passage East, 408 .... G 7
Passage West, 2,709 .... E 8
Patrickswell, 415 .... D 6
Pettigo, 332 .... F 2
Piltown, 456 .... G 7
Portarlington, 3,117 .... G 5
Portlaoighise, 3,902 .... G 5
Portlaoighise, *6,470 .... G 5
Portlaw, 1,166 .... G 7
Portmarnock, 1,726 .... J 5
Portumna, 913 .... E 5
Queenstown (Cóbh), 6,076 .... E 8
Rahan, ‡531 .... F 5
Ramelton, 807 .... F 1
Raphoe, 945 .... F 2
Rathangan, 868 .... G 5
Rathcoole, 1,740 .... J 5
Rathcormac, 191 .... E 7
Rathdowney, 892 .... F 6
Rathdrum, 1,141 .... J 6
Rathgormuck, ‡231 .... F 7
Rathkeale, 1,543 .... D 7
Rathluirc, 2,232 .... D 7
Rathmore, 437 .... J 5
Rathmullen, 486 .... F 1
Rathnew-Merrymeeting, 954 .... J 6
Rathowen, ‡294 .... F 4
Rathvilly, 230 .... H 6
Ratoath, 300 .... J 5
Riverstown, 236 .... E 3
Rockcorry, 233 .... H 3
Rosapenna, ‡822 .... F 1
Roscommon, 1,556 .... E 4
Roscommon, *2,821 .... E 4
Roscrea, 3,855 .... F 6
Rosscarbery, 309 .... C 8
Rosses Point, 464 .... D 3
Rosslare, 588 .... J 7
Rosslare Harbour (Ballygeary), 725 .... J 7
Roundstone, 204 .... A 5
Roundwood, 260 .... J 5
Rush, 2,633 .... J 4
Saint Johnston, 463 .... F 2
Scarriff, 619 .... E 6
Schull, 457 .... B 8
Scotstown, 264 .... H 3
Shanagolden, 231 .... C 6
Shannon Airport, 3,657 .... D 6
Shannon Bridge, 188 .... F 5
Shercock, 313 .... G 4
Shillelagh, 246 .... J 6
Shinrone, 365 .... F 5
Shrule, 288 .... C 4
Sixmilebridge, 567 .... D 6
Skerries, 3,044 .... J 4
Skibbereen, 2,104 .... C 8
Slane, 483 .... H 4
Sligo, 14,080 .... E 3
Sligo, *14,456 .... E 3
Sneem, 285 .... B 8
Spiddal, ‡819 .... C 5
Stepaside, 748 .... J 5
Stradbally, Laoighis, 891 .... G 5
Stradbally, Waterford, 158 .... F 7
Strokestown, 563 .... E 4
Swanlinbar, 257 .... F 3
Swinford, 1,105 .... C 4
Swords, 4,133 .... J 5
Taghmon, 369 .... H 7
Tallaght, 6,174 .... J 5
Tallow, 883 .... F 7
Tarbert, 485 .... C 6
Teltown, ‡739 .... H 4
Templemore, 2,174 .... F 6
Templetuohy, 197 .... F 6
Termonfeckin, 328 .... J 4
Thomastown, 1,270 .... G 7
Thurles, 6,840 .... F 6
Thurles, *7,087 .... F 6
Timoleague, 257 .... D 8
Tinahely, 450 .... H 6
Tipperary, 4,631 .... E 7
Tipperary, *4,717 .... E 7
Toomevara, 272 .... E 6
Tralee, 12,287 .... B 7
Tralee, *13,263 .... B 7
Tramore, 3,792 .... G 7
Trim, 1,700 .... H 4
Trim, *2,255 .... H 4
Tuam, 3,808 .... D 4
Tuam, *4,952 .... D 4
Tubbercurry, 959 .... D 3
Tulla, 415 .... D 6
Tullamore, 6,809 .... G 5
Tullamore, *7,474 .... G 5
Tullaroan, ‡301 .... G 6
Tullow, 1,838 .... H 6
Tullow, *1,945 .... H 6
Tynagh, ‡452 .... E 5
Tyrrellspass, 289 .... G 5
Urlingford, 652 .... F 6
Virginia, 583 .... G 4
Waterford, 31,968 .... G 7
Waterford, *33,676 .... G 7
Waterville, 547 .... A 8
Westport, 3,023 .... C 4
Wexford, 11,849 .... H 7
Wexford, *13,293 .... H 7
Whitegate, 370 .... E 8
Wicklow, 3,786 .... K 6
Wicklow, *3,915 .... K 6
Woodenbridge, ‡620 .... J 6
Woodford, 198 .... E 5
Youghal, 5,445 .... F 8
Youghal, *5,626 .... F 8

OTHER FEATURES

Achill (isl.), 3,129 .... A 4
Allen (lake) .... E 3
Allen, Bog of (marsh) .... H 5
Aran (isl.), 773 .... D 2
Aran (isls.), 1,499 .... B 5
Arklow (bank) .... K 6
Arrow (lake) .... E 3
Awbeg (riv.) .... D 7
Ballinskelligs (bay) .... A 8
Ballycotton (bay) .... F 8
Ballyheige (bay) .... B 7
Ballyhoura (hills) .... E 7
Ballyteige (bay) .... H 7
Bandon (riv.) .... D 8
Bann (riv.) .... J 6
Bantry (bay) .... B 8
Barrow (riv.) .... H 7
Baurtregaum (mt.) .... A 7
Bear (isl.), 288 .... B 8
Blacksod (bay) .... A 3
Blackstairs (mt.) .... H 6
Blackwater (riv.) .... D 7
Blackwater (riv.) .... H 4
Blasket (isls.) .... A 7
Bloody Foreland (prom.) .... E 1
Blue Stack (mts.) .... E 2
Boderg (lake) .... E 4
Boggeragh (mts.) .... D 7
Boyne (riv.) .... J 4
Brandon (head) .... A 7
Bride (riv.) .... E 7
Broad Haven (harb.) .... B 3
Brosna (riv.) .... F 5
Bull, The (isl.), 5 .... A 8
Caha (mts.) .... B 8
Carlingford (inlet) .... J 3
Carnsore (pt.) .... J 7
Carrantuohill (mt.) .... B 7
Clare (riv.) .... D 5
Clare (isls.), 168 .... A 4
Clear (cape) .... B 9
Clear (isl.), 192 .... C 9
Clew (bay) .... B 4
Comeragh (mts.) .... F 7
Conn (lake) .... C 3
Connacht (prov.), 390,902 .... C 4
Connemara (dist.), 7,599 .... B 5
Cork (harb.) .... E 8
Corrib (lake) .... C 5
Courtmacsherry (bay) .... D 8
Curragh, The .... H 5
Dee (riv.) .... H 4
Deel (riv.) .... D 7
Deele (riv.) .... F 2
Derg (lake) .... E 6
Derravaragh (lake) .... G 4
Derryveagh (mts.) .... E 2
Dingle (bay) .... A 7
Donegal (bay) .... D 3
Drum (hills) .... F 7
Dublin (bay) .... J 5
Dundalk (bay) .... J 4
Dunmanus (bay) .... B 8
Dursey (isl.), 38 .... A 8
Ennell (lake) .... G 5
Erne (riv.) .... E 3
Errigal (mt.) .... E 1
Erris (head) .... A 3
Fanad (head) .... F 1
Fastnet Rock (isl.), 3 .... B 9
Feale (riv.) .... C 7
Fergus (riv.) .... D 6
Finn (riv.) .... F 2
Finn (riv.) .... G 3
Flesk (riv.) .... C 7
Foyle (inlet) .... G 1
Foyle (riv.) .... G 2
Galley (head) .... D 9
Galtee (mts.) .... E 7
Galtymore (mt.) .... E 7
Galway (bay) .... C 5
Gara (lake) .... D 4
Garadice (lake) .... F 3
Gill (lake) .... E 3
Glyde (riv.) .... H 4
Golden Vale (plain) .... E 7
Gorumna (isl.), 1,108 .... B 5
Gowna (lake) .... G 4
Grand (canal) .... G 5
Greenore (pt.) .... J 7
Gweebarra (bay) .... D 2
Hags (head) .... B 6
Helvick (head) .... G 7
Hook (head) .... H 7
Horn (head) .... E 1
Iar Connacht (dist.), 10,774 .... C 5
Inishbofin (isl.), 236 .... A 4
Inishbofin (isl.), 103 .... E 1
Inisheer (isl.), 313 .... B 5
Inishmaan (isl.), 319 .... C 5
Inishmore (isl.), 864 .... B 5
Inishowen (head) .... H 1
Inishowen (pen.), 24,109 .... G 1
Inishtrahull (isl.), 3 .... G 1
Inishturk (isls.), 83 .... A 4
Inny (riv.) .... A 8
Inny (riv.) .... F 4
Inver (bay) .... E 2
Ireland's Eye (isl.) .... K 5
Irish (sea) .... K 4
Joyce's Country (dist.), 2,021 .... B 4
Kenmare (riv.) .... A 8
Kerry (head) .... A 7
Key (lake) .... E 3
Kilkieran (bay) .... B 5
Killala (bay) .... C 3
Killary (harb.) .... A 4
Kinsale (harb.) .... E 8
Kippure (mt.) .... J 5
Knockboy (mt.) .... B 8
Knockmealdown (mts.) .... F 7
Lady's Island Lake (inlet) .... J 7
Lambay (isl.), 24 .... K 4
Laune (riv.) .... B 7
Leane (lake) .... B 7
Leane (lake) .... G 4
Lee (riv.) .... D 8
Leinster (mt.) .... H 6
Leinster (prov.), 1,498,140 .... G 5
Lettermullan (isl.), 221 .... B 5
Liffey (riv.) .... H 5
Liscannor (bay) .... B 6
Long Island (bay) .... B 9
Loop (head) .... A 6
Lugnaquillia (mt.) .... J 5
Macgillicuddy's Reeks (mts.) .... B 7
Macnean (lake) .... F 3
Maigue (riv.) .... D 6
Maine (riv.) .... C 7
Malin (head) .... F 1
Mask (lake) .... C 4
Maumturk (mts.) .... B 5
Melvin (lake) .... E 3
Mizen (head) .... B 9
Moher (cliffs) .... B 6
Monavullagh (mts.) .... F 7
Moy (riv.) .... C 3
Mulkear (riv.) .... E 6
Mullaghareirk (mts.) .... C 7
Mulroy (bay) .... F 1
Munster (prov.), 882,002 .... D 7
Mweelrea (mt.) .... B 4
Mweenish (isl.), 198 .... B 5
Nagles (mts.) .... E 7
Nenagh (riv.) .... E 6
Nephin (mt.) .... C 3
Nore (riv.) .... G 7
North (sound) .... B 5
Omey (isl.), 34 .... A 5
Oughter (lake) .... G 3
Ovoca (riv.) .... J 6
Owenmore (riv.) .... D 3
Owey (isl.), 51 .... D 1
Paps, The (mt.) .... C 7
Partry (mts.) .... C 4
Pollaphuca (res.) .... J 5
Punchestown .... H 5
Rathlin O'Birne (isl.), 3 .... C 2
Ree (lake) .... F 5
Roaringwater (bay) .... B 9
Rosses (bay) .... D 1
Rosskeeragh (pt.) .... D 3
Royal (canal) .... G 4
Saint Finan's (bay) .... A 8
Saint George's (chan.) .... K 7
Saint John's (pt.) .... D 2
Saltee (isls.) .... H 7
Seven (heads) .... D 8
Seven Hogs, The (isls.) .... A 7
Shannon (riv.) .... E 6
Sheeffry (hills) .... B 4
Sheelin (lake) .... G 4
Sheep Haven (harb.) .... F 1
Sheeps (head) .... B 8
Sherkin (isl.), 82 .... C 9
Silvermine (mts.) .... E 6
Slaney (riv.) .... H 7
Slieve Aughty (mts.) .... D 5
Slieve Bloom (mts.) .... F 5
Slieve Gamph (mts.) .... D 3
Slievenaman (mt.) .... F 7
Sligo (bay) .... D 3
Slyne (head) .... A 5
South (sound) .... C 5
Stacks (mts.) .... B 7
Suck (riv.) .... E 5
Suir (riv.) .... G 7
Swilly (inlet) .... F 1
Tara (hill) .... H 4
Tory (isl.), 273 .... E 1
Tory (sound) .... E 1
Tralee (bay) .... B 7
Trawbreaga (bay) .... F 1
Ulster (part) (prov.), 207,204 .... G 2
Valencia (Valentia) (isl.), 770 .... A 8
Valentia (isl.), 770 .... A 8
Waterford (harb.) .... G 7
Wexford (bay) .... J 7
Wicklow (head) .... K 6
Wicklow (mts.) .... J 6
Youghal (bay) .... F 8

NORTHERN IRELAND

COUNTIES

Antrim, 37,600 .... J 2
Ards, 52,100 .... K 2
Armagh, 47,500 .... H 3
Ballymena, 52,200 .... J 2
Ballymoney, 22,700 .... J 1
Bainbridge, 28,800 .... J 3
Belfast, 368,200 .... J 2
Carrickfergus, 27,500 .... K 2
Castlereagh, 63,600 .... K 2
Coleraine, 44,900 .... H 1
Cookstown, 27,500 .... H 2
Craigavon, 71,200 .... J 3
Down, 48,800 .... K 3
Dungannon, 43,000 .... H 3
Fermanagh, 50,900 .... F 3
Larne, 29,000 .... K 2
Limavady, 25,000 .... H 1
Lisburn, 80,800 .... J 2
Londonderry, 86,600 .... G 2
Magherafelt, 32,200 .... H 2
Mourne (Newry and Mourne), 75,300 .... J 3
Moyle, 13,400 .... J 1
Newtownabbey, 71,500 .... J 2
North Down, 59,600 .... K 2
Omagh, 41,800 .... G 2
Strabane, 35,500 .... G 2

CITIES and TOWNS

Ahoghill, ‡1,929 .... J 2
Annalong, 1,001 .... K 3
Antrim, 8,351 .... J 2
Ardglass, 1,052 .... K 3
Armagh, 13,606 .... H 3
Armoy, ‡1,051 .... J 1
Augher, ‡1,986 .... G 3
Aughnacloy, ‡1,885 .... H 3
Ballycastle, 2,899 .... J 1
Ballyclare, 5,155 .... J 2
Ballygawley, ‡2,165 .... G 3
Ballykelly, 1,116 .... G 1
Ballymena, 23,386 .... J 2
Ballymoney, 5,697 .... J 1
Ballynahinch, 3,485 .... J 3
Banbridge, 7,968 .... J 3
Bangor, 35,260 .... K 2
Belfast (cap.), 353,700 .... J 2
Belfast, *551,940 .... J 2
Bellaghy, ‡2,265 .... H 2
Belleek, ‡2,487 .... E 3
Beragh, ‡2,137 .... G 2
Bessbrook, 2,619 .... J 3
Brookeborough, ‡2,534 .... G 3
Broughshane, 1,288 .... J 2
Bushmills, 1,288 .... J 1
Caledon, ‡1,828 .... H 3
Carnlough, 1,416 .... J 2
Carrickfergus, 16,603 .... K 2
Carrowdore, 2,548 .... K 2
Castledawson, 1,162 .... H 2
Castlederg, 1,766 .... F 2
Castlewellan, 1,488 .... K 3
Claudy, ‡2,507 .... G 2
Clogher, ‡1,888 .... G 3
Coalisland, 3,614 .... H 2
Coleraine, 16,354 .... H 1
Comber, 5,575 .... K 2
Cookstown, 6,965 .... H 2
Craigavon, 12,740 .... J 3
Crossgar, 1,098 .... K 3
Crossmaglen, 1,085 .... H 3
Crumlin, 1,450 .... J 2
Cullybackey, 1,649 .... J 2
Derrygonnelly, ‡2,539 .... F 3
Dervock, ‡1,191 .... J 1
Donaghadee, 4,008 .... K 2
Downpatrick, 7,918 .... K 3
Draperstown, ‡2,247 .... H 2
Dromore, Bainbridge, 2,848 .... J 3
Dromore, Omagh, ‡2,224 .... G 3
Drumquin, ‡1,982 .... F 2
Dundrum, ‡2,245 .... K 3
Dungannon, 8,190 .... H 3
Dungiven, 1,536 .... H 2
Dunnamanagh, ‡2,242 .... G 2
Ederny and Kesh, ‡2,497 .... F 2
Enniskillen, 9,679 .... F 3
Feeny, ‡1,459 .... H 2
Fintona, 1,190 .... G 3
Fivemiletown, ‡1,649 .... G 3
Garvagh, ‡2,363 .... H 2
Gilford, 1,592 .... J 3
Glenarm, ‡1,728 .... J 2
Glenavy, ‡2,360 .... J 2
Glynn, ‡1,872 .... K 2
Gortin, ‡2,033 .... G 2
Greyabbey, ‡2,646 .... K 2
Hillsborough, 1,021 .... J 3
Holywood, 9,892 .... K 2
Irvinestown, 1,457 .... F 3
Keady, 2,145 .... H 3
Kells, ‡2,560 .... J 2
Kesh, ‡2,497 .... F 3
Kilkeel, 4,090 .... K 3
Killough, ‡3,295 .... K 3
Killyleagh, 2,359 .... K 3
Kilrea, 1,196 .... H 2
Kircubbin, 1,075 .... K 3
Larne, 18,482 .... K 2
Limavady, 6,004 .... H 1
Lisburn, 31,836 .... J 2
Lisnaskea, 1,443 .... G 3
Londonderry, 51,200 .... G 2
Loughbrickland, ‡2,056 .... J 3
Maghera, 2,085 .... H 2
Magherafelt, 4,704 .... H 2
Markethill, ‡2,352 .... H 3
Millisle, 1,172 .... K 2
Moneymore, 1,178 .... H 2
Moy, ‡2,349 .... H 3
Moygashel, 1,086 .... H 3
Newcastle, 4,647 .... J 3
Newry, 20,279 .... J 3
Newtownabbey, 58,114 .... K 2
Newtownards, 15,484 .... K 2
Newtownbutler, ‡2,663 .... G 3
Newtownhamilton, ‡1,936 .... H 3
Newtownstewart, 1,433 .... G 2
Omagh, 14,594 .... G 2
Pomeroy, ‡1,786 .... H 2
Portaferry, 1,730 .... K 3
Portavogie, 1,310 .... K 3
Portglenone, ‡2,061 .... H 2
Portrush, 5,376 .... H 1
Portstewart, 5,085 .... H 1
Randalstown, 2,799 .... J 2
Rathfriland, 1,886 .... J 3
Rostrevor, 1,617 .... J 3
Saintfield, ‡2,198 .... K 3
Sion Mills, 1,588 .... G 2
Sixmilecross, ‡1,980 .... G 2
Stewartstown, ‡1,759 .... H 2
Strabane, 9,413 .... G 2
Strangford, ‡1,987 .... K 3
Tandragee, 1,725 .... J 3
Tempo, ‡2,282 .... G 3
Trillick, ‡2,167 .... G 3
Warrenpoint, 4,291 .... J 3
Whitehead, 2,642 .... K 2

OTHER FEATURES

Bann (riv.) .... H 2
Belfast (inlet) .... K 2
Blackwater (riv.) .... H 3
Bush (riv.) .... H 1
Derg (riv.) .... F 2
Divis (mt.) .... J 2
Dundrum (bay) .... K 3
Erne (lake) .... F 3
Foyle (inlet) .... G 1
Foyle (riv.) .... G 2
Giant's Causeway .... H 1
Lagan (riv.) .... K 2
Larne (inlet) .... K 2
Magee, Island (pen.), 1,581 .... K 2
Magilligan (pt.) .... H 1
Main (riv.) .... J 2
Mourne (mts.) .... J 3
Mourne (riv.) .... G 2
Neagh (lake) .... J 2
North (chan.) .... K 1
Rathlin (isl.), 109 .... J 1
Red (bay) .... K 1
Roe (riv.) .... H 1
Saint John's (pt.) .... K 3
Slieve Donard (mt.) .... K 3
Sperrin (mts.) .... G 2
Strangford (inlet) .... K 3
Torr (head) .... K 1
Ulster (part) (prov.), 1,537,200 .... G 2
Upper Lough Erne (lake) .... F 3

*City and suburbs.
‡Population of district.

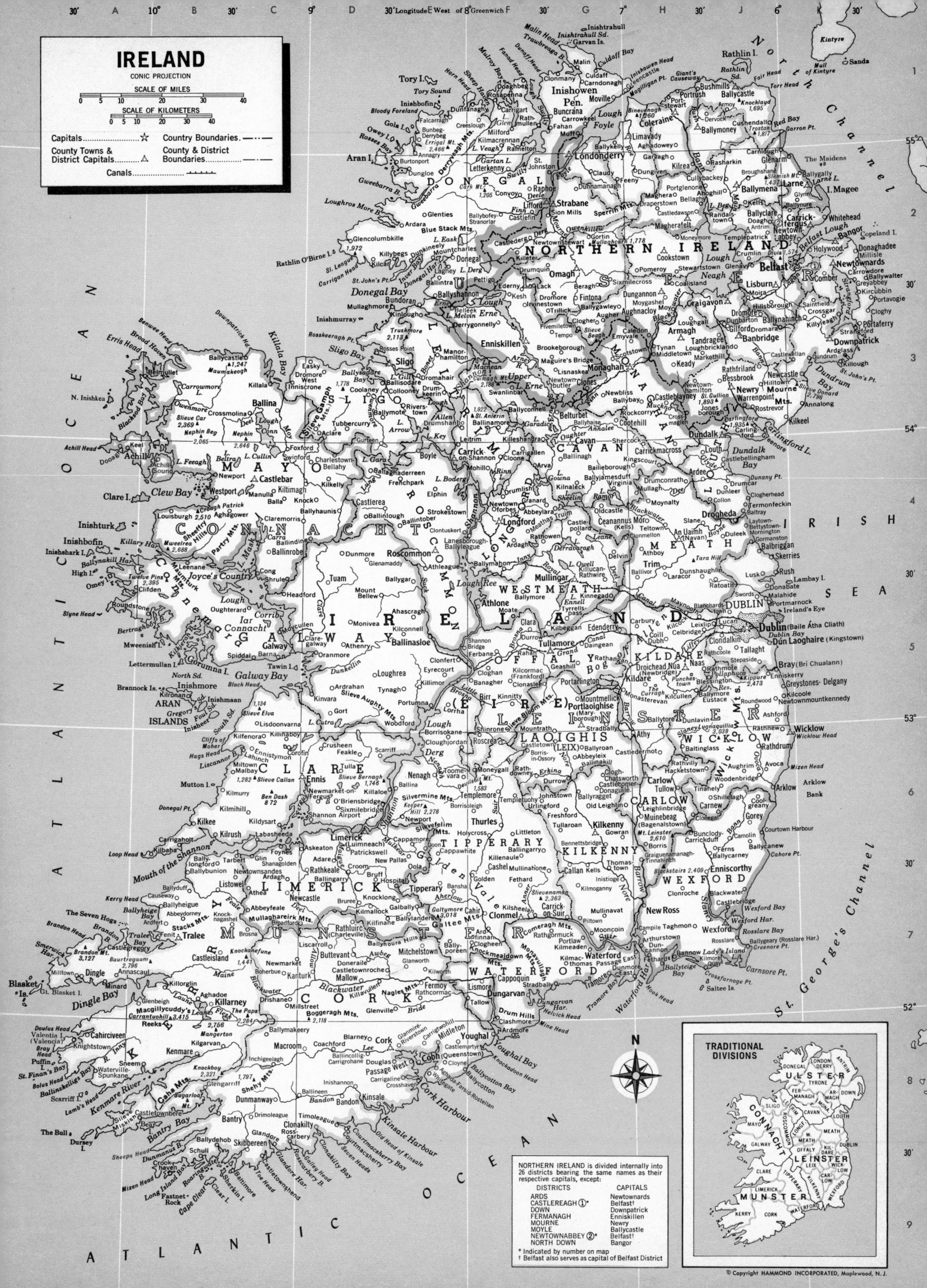

SVALBARD

NORWAY, SWEDEN, FINLAND and DENMARK

CONIC PROJECTION

SCALE OF MILES

SCALE OF KILOMETRES

NORWAY

EA 125,053 sq. mi.
PULATION 4,027,000
PITAL Oslo
RGEST CITY Oslo
GHEST POINT Glittertind 8,110 ft.
ONETARY UNIT krone
AJOR LANGUAGE Norwegian
AJOR RELIGION Protestantism

SWEDEN

AREA 173,665 sq. mi.
POPULATION 8,236,461
CAPITAL Stockholm
LARGEST CITY Stockholm
HIGHEST POINT Kebnekaise 6,946 ft.
MONETARY UNIT krona
MAJOR LANGUAGE Swedish
MAJOR RELIGION Protestantism

FINLAND

AREA 130,128 sq. mi.
POPULATION 4,729,000
CAPITAL Helsinki
LARGEST CITY Helsinki
HIGHEST POINT Mt. Haltia 4,343 ft.
MONETARY UNIT markka
MAJOR LANGUAGES Finnish, Swedish
MAJOR RELIGION Protestantism

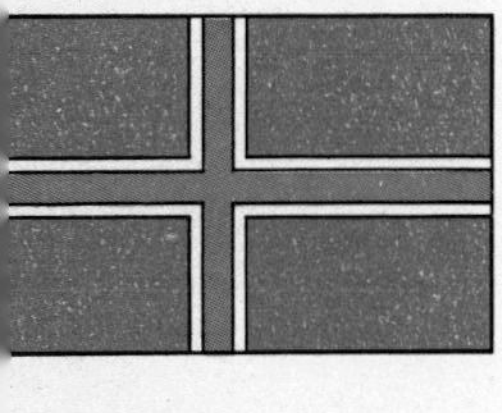

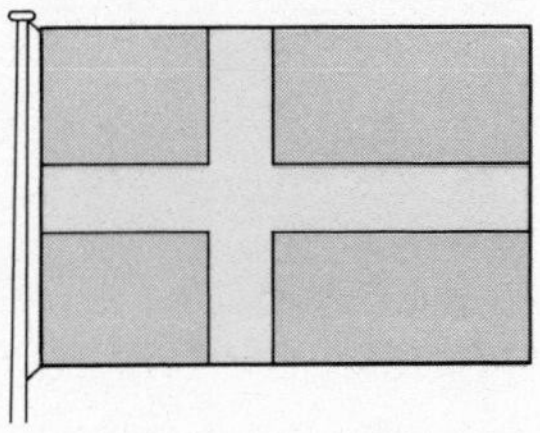

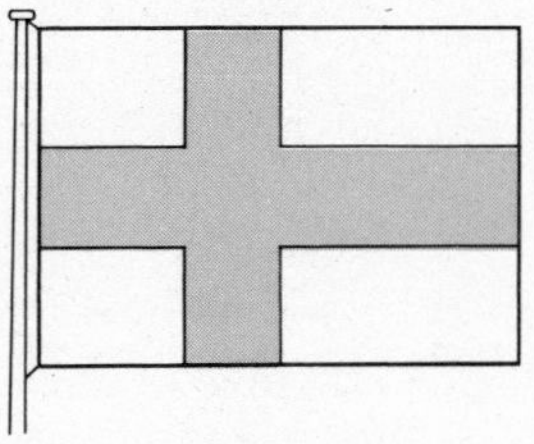

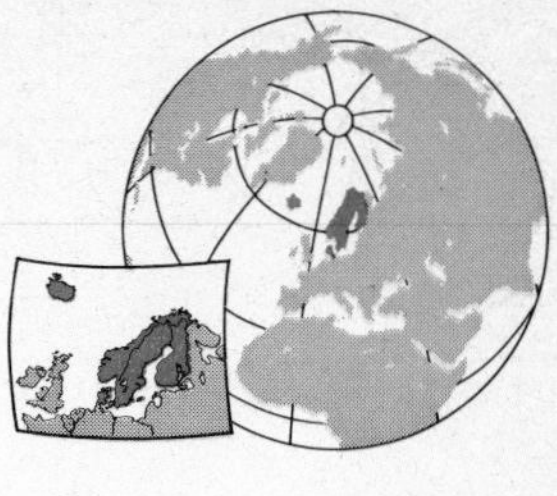

FINLAND

PROVINCES

venanmaa, 22,380	L 6
nd (Ahvenanmaa), 22,380	L 6
ne, 662,500	O 6
ki-Suomi, 241,770	O 5
pio, 252,023	P 5
ni, 346,478	Q 6
pi, 196,792	P 3
kkeli, 211,453	P 6
u, 406,309	P 4
njois-Karjala, 179,065	Q 5
ku-Pori, 697,988	N 6
simaa, 1,085,625	O 6
sa, 425,283	N 5

CITIES and TOWNS

nekoski, 10,725	O 5
(Turku), 164,857	N 6
vus, 10,285	N 5
gå, 18,740	O 6
näs, 7,391	N 6
Espoo, 117,090	O 6
Forssa, 18,442	N 6
Haapajärvi, 7,791	O 5
Hämeenlinna, 40,761	O 6
Hamina, 11,055	P 6
Hangö, 10,374	N 7
Hanko (Hangö), 10,374	N 7
Harjavalta, 8,445	M 6
Heinola, 15,350	P 6
Helsinki (cap.), 502,961	O 6
Helsinki, *794,746	O 6
Huutokoski, ☆6,458	P 5
Hyvinkää, 35,865	O 6
Iisalmi, 21,159	P 5
Ikaalinen, 8,364	N 6
Ilomantsi, 2,211	R 5
Imatra, 35,590	Q 6
Ivalo, 2,661	P 2
Jakobstad, 20,397	N 5
Joensuu, 41,429	R 5
Jyväskylä, 61,209	O 5
Jyväskylä, *84,185	O 5
Kajaani, 20,583	P 4
Kalajoki, 3,624	N 4
Karis, 8,152	N 6
Karjaa (Karis), 8,152	N 6
Karkkila, 8,678	N 6
Kauttua, 3,297	M 6
Kelloselkä, ☆8,200	Q 3
Kemi, 27,893	O 4
Kemijärvi, 12,951	P 3
Kerava, 19,966	O 6
Kokemäki, 10,188	N 6
Kokkola, 22,096	N 5
Kotka, 34,026	P 6
Kotka, *60,235	P 6
Kouvola, 29,383	P 6
Kouvola, *59,507	P 6
Kristiinankaupunki (Kristinestad), 9,331	N 5
Kristinestad, 9,331	N 5
Kuhmo, 4,150	Q 4
Kuopio, 71,684	Q 5
Kuopio, *74,600	Q 5
Kurikka, 11,177	M 5
Kuusamo, 4,449	Q 4
Lahti, 94,864	O 6
Lahti, *112,129	O 6
Lappeenranta, 52,682	P 6
Lieksa, 20,274	R 5
Loimaa, 6,575	N 6
Lovisa, 8,674	P 6
Maarianhamina (Mariehamn), 9,574	M 7
Mänttä, 7,910	O 6
Mariehamn, 9,574	M 7
Mikkeli, 27,112	P 6
Naantali, 7,814	M 6
Nokia, 22,308	N 6
Nurmes, 11,721	Q 5
Nykarleby, 7,408	N 5
Oulainen, 7,322	O 4
Oulu, 93,707	O 4
Oulu, *103,044	O 4
Outokumpu, 10,736	Q 5
Parkano, 8,518	N 6
Pello, 1,960	O 3
Pieksämäki, 12,923	P 5
Pietarsaari (Jakobstad), 20,397	N 5
Pori, 80,343	M 6
Pori, *86,635	M 6
Porkkala, ☆15,558	O 7
Porvoo (Borgå), 18,740	O 6
Posio, ☆6,205	Q 3
Pudasjärvi, ☆12,594	P 4
Raahe, 15,379	O 4
Rauma, 29,081	M 6
Riihimäki, 24,106	O 6
Rovaniemi, 28,411	O 3
Saarijärvi, 2,714	O 5
Salo, 19,176	N 6
Savonlinna, 28,336	Q 6
Seinäjoki, 22,123	N 5
Sodankylä, 3,304	P 3
Sotkamo, 2,316	Q 4
Suolahti, 5,936	O 5
Suonenjoki, 9,286	P 5
Tammisaari (Ekenäs), 7,391	N 6
Tampere, 168,118	N 6
Tampere, *220,920	N 6
Toijala, 8,080	N 6
Tornio, 19,971	O 4
Turku, 164,857	N 6
Turku, *217,423	N 6
Turtola, ☆5,852	O 3
Ulvila, ☆8,040	N 6
Uusikaarlepyy (Nykarleby), 7,408	N 5
Uusikaupunki, 11,915	M 6
Vaasa, 54,402	M 5
Vaasa, *58,224	M 5
Valkeakoski, 22,588	N 6
Vammala, 16,363	N 6
Varkaus, 24,450	Q 5
Vasa (Vaasa), 54,402	M 5
Vuotso, ☆10,186	P 2
Ylivieska, 10,827	O 4

OTHER FEATURES

Åland (isls.), 22,380	L 6
Baltic (sea)	K 9
Bothnia (gulf)	M 5
Finland (gulf)	P 7
Hailuoto (isl.), 926	O 4
Haltia (mt.)	M 2
Hangöudd (prom.)	N 7
Haukivesi (lake)	Q 5
Iijoki (riv.)	O 4
Inarijärvi (lake)	P 2
Ivalojoki (riv.)	P 2
Juojärvi (lake)	Q 5
Kalajoki (riv.)	O 4
Kallavesi (lake)	P 5
Karlö (Hailuoto) (isl.), 926	O 4
Keitele (lake)	O 5
Kemijärvi (lake)	Q 3
Kemijoki (riv.)	O 3
Kiantajärvi (lake)	Q 4
Kilpisjärvi (lake)	M 2
Kitinen (riv.)	P 3
Kivijärvi (lake)	O 5
Koitere (lake)	R 5
Kuusamojärvi (lake)	Q 4
Längelmävesi (lake)	O 6
Lapland (reg.), 196,792	O 2
Lappajärvi (lake)	O 5
Lapuanjoki (riv.)	N 5
Lestijärvi (lake)	O 5
Lokka (res.)	Q 3
Muojärvi (lake)	R 4
Muonio (riv.)	M 2
Näsijärvi (lake)	O 6
Onkivesi (lake)	P 5
Orihvesi (lake)	Q 5
Oulujärvi (lake)	P 4
Oulujoki (riv.)	O 4
Ounasjoki (riv.)	O 3
Päijänne (lake)	O 6
Pielinen (lake)	Q 5
Puruvesi (lake)	Q 6
Puulavesi (lake)	P 5
Pyhäjärvi (lake)	O 5
Pyhäjärvi (lake)	M 6
Saimaa (lake)	Q 6
Siikajoki (riv.)	O 4
Simojärvi (lake)	P 3
Simojoki (riv.)	O 4
Tana (riv.)	P 2
Tornio (riv.)	O 3
Vallgrund (isl.), 1,480	M 5
Ylikitka (lake)	Q 3

NORWAY

COUNTIES

Akershus, 355,196	G 6
Aust-Agder, 86,216	E 7
Buskerud, 209,684	F 6
Finnmark, 79,373	O 2
Hedmark, 183,465	G 6
Hordaland, 386,492	E 6
Møre og Romsdal, 231,944	E 5
Nordland, 243,233	J 3
Nord-Trøndelag, 122,886	H 4
Oppland, 178,259	F 6
Oslo (city), 462,732	D 3
Østfold, 228,546	G 7
Rogaland, 287,653	E 7
Sogn og Fjordane, 103,135	E 6
Sør-Trøndelag, 241,361	G 5
Telemark, 158,853	F 7
Troms, 144,111	L 2
Vest-Agder, 131,659	E 7
Vestfold, 182,433	G 7

CITIES and TOWNS

Ålesund, 40,868	D 5
Ålgård, 2,322	D 7
Alta, 5,582	N 2
Åndalsnes, 2,574	F 5
Årdalstangen, 2,360	F 6
Arendal, 11,701	F 7
Arendal, *21,228	F 7
Årnes, 2,267	G 6
Askim, 8,413	E 4
Bamble, ⊙7,031	F 7
Barentsburg	C 2
Bergen, 213,434	D 6
Bodø, 31,077	J 3
Borge, ⊙3,294	H 2
Brate, ⊙2,107	G 7
Brønnøysund, 3,130	G 4
Dombås, 1,114	F 5
Drammen, 50,777	C 4
Drammen, *56,521	C 4
Drøbak, 4,538	D 4
Eidsvoll, 2,906	G 6
Eigersund, 11,379	D 7
Elverum, 7,391	G 6
Farsund, 8,908	E 7
Flekkefjord, 8,750	E 7
Flora, 8,822	D 6
Fredrikstad, 29,024	D 4
Fredrikstad, *51,141	D 4
Gjøvik, 25,963	G 6
Grimstad, 13,091	F 7
Halden, 27,087	G 7
Hamar, 16,418	G 6
Hamar, *25,138	G 6
Hammerfest, 7,610	N 1
Hammerfest, *8,005	N 1
Harstad, 21,125	K 2
Hauge, 2,079	E 7
Haugesund, 27,386	D 7
Haugesund, *29,277	D 7
Hermansverk, 706	E 6
Holmestrand, 8,246	C 4
Holmsbu, 273	D 4
Honningsvag, 3,780	O 1
Horten, 13,746	D 4
Horten, *17,246	D 4
Kirkenes, 4,466	Q 2
Kongsberg, 19,854	F 7
Kongsvinger, 16,146	H 6
Kopervik, 4,221	D 7
Kornsjø, ⊙6,079	G 7
Kragerø, 5,249	F 7
Kristiansand, 59,488	F 8
Kristiansund, 18,847	E 5
Kvinnherad, ⊙2,898	E 6
Larvik, 9,097	C 4
Larvik, *19,202	C 4
Lenvik, ☆11,098	L 2
Levanger, 5,066	G 5
Lillehammer, 21,248	F 6
Lillesand, 3,028	F 7
Lillestrøm, ⊙11,550	E 3
Løkken, 1,942	F 5
Longyearbyen	D 2
Lysaker, ☆81,612	D 3
Mandal, 11,579	E 7
Meråker, ⊙2,907	G 5
Mo, 21,033	J 3
Molde, 20,334	E 5
Mosjøen, 9,341	H 4
Moss, 25,786	D 4
Moss, *27,430	D 4
Mysen, 3,760	G 7
Namsos, 11,452	G 4
Narvik, 19,582	K 2
Nesttun, ⊙11,519	D 6
Nittedal, ⊙8,889	D 3
Notodden, 12,970	F 7
Nøtterøy, 11,944	D 4
Ny-Ålesund	C 2
Odda, 7,401	E 6
Oppdal, 2,173	F 5
Orkanger, 3,685	F 5
Oslo (cap.), 462,732	D 3
Oslo, *645,413	D 3
Otta, 1,916	F 6
Porsgrunn, 31,709	G 7
Rakkestad, 2,392	G 7
Ringerike, 30,156	C 3
Risør, 6,560	F 7
Rjukan, 5,334	F 7
Røros, 3,041	G 5
Ryggebyen, 1,954	D 4
Sandefjord, 33,350	C 4
Sandnes, 33,934	D 7
Sandvika, ☆34,337	C 3
Sarpsborg, 12,889	D 4
Sarpsborg, *36,449	D 4
Selje, ⊙3,386	D 5
Setermoen, 2,114	L 2
Ski, 9,081	D 4
Skien, 47,105	F 7
Skudeneshavn, 2,206	D 7
Stavanger, 86,639	D 7
Stavern, 2,604	D 4
Steinkjer, 20,553	G 4
Stor-Elvdal, ⊙2,993	G 6
Sunndalsøra, 5,114	F 5
Sveagruva	D 2
Svelvik, 2,256	D 4
Svolvaer, 3,942	J 2
Tana, ⊙1,893	Q 1
Tønsberg, 9,964	D 4
Tønsberg, *36,374	D 4
Tromsø, 43,830	L 2
Trondheim, 134,910	F 5
Ullensvang, ⊙2,326	E 6
Vadsø, 6,019	Q 1
Vanylven, ⊙1,966	E 5
Vardø, 3,875	R 1
Vik, 1,019	E 6
Volda, 3,511	E 5
Voss, 5,944	E 6

OTHER FEATURES

Alsten (isl.), 5,154	H 4
Andøy (isl.), 7,537	J 2
Arnøy (isl.), 887	M 1
Barduelv (riv.)	L 2
Bellsund	C 2
Bjørnafjorden (fjord)	D 6
Bjornøya (isl.)	D 3
Boknafjord (fjord)	D 7
Bremanger (isl.), 1,862	D 6
Dønna (isl.), 1,671	H 3
Dovrefjeld (hills)	F 5
Edgeøya (isl.)	E 2
Femundsjø (lake)	G 5
Folda (fjord)	G 4
Folda (fjord)	J 3
Frohavet (bay)	F 5
Frøya (isl.), 3,417	F 5
Glittertind (mt.)	F 6
Glomma (riv.)	G 6
Haltia (mt.)	M 2
Hardanger (plat.)	E 6
Hardangerfjord (fjord)	D 7
Hinlopen (str.)	C 1
Hinnøy (isl.), 29,944	K 2
Hitra (isl.), 2,929	F 5
Hopen (isl.)	E 2
Isfjorden (fjord)	C 2
Jostedalsbreen (glac.)	E 6
Karmøy (isl.), 23,136	D 7
Kjölen (mts.)	K 3
Kongsfjorden (fjord)	B 2
Kvaløy (isl.), 8,457	O 1
Lågen (riv.)	G 6
Laksefjorden (fjord)	P 1
Langøy (isl.), 15,685	J 2
Lapland (reg.), 466,717	K 2
Leka (isl.), 724	G 4
Lindesnes (cape)	E 8
Lista (pen.), 8,304	E 7
Lofoten (isls.), 26,587	H 2
Lopphavet (bay)	M 1
Magerøy (isl.), 5,043	P 1
Moskenesøy (isl.), 2,003	H 3
Namsen (riv.)	H 4
Nordaustlandet (isl.)	D 1
Nordfjord (fjord)	E 6
Nordkapp (pt.)	C 1
Nordkyn (headland)	Q 1
Nordkyn (pen.), 1,669	P 1
North (pt.)	P 1
Norwegian (sea)	F 3
Ofotfjorden (fjord)	K 2
Oslofjord (fjord)	D 4
Otterelv (riv.)	E 7
Otterøy (isl.), 1,702	E 5
Pasvikelv (riv.)	Q 2
Platen, Kapp (pt.)	D 1
Porsangerfjord (fjord)	O 1
Ran (fjord)	H 3
Rauma (riv.)	F 5
Ringvassøy (isl.), 1,301	L 2
Romsdalsfjorden (fjord)	E 5
Saltfjorden (fjord)	J 3
Seiland (isl.), 559	N 1
Senja (isl.), 9,858	K 2
Skagerrak (str.)	F 8
Smøla (isl.), 2,486	F 5
Sognefjorden (fjord)	D 6
Sørkapp (pt.)	C 2
Sør Kvaløy (isl.), 3,542	K 2
Sorøy (isl.), 1,808	N 1
Spitsbergen (isl.)	C 2
Storfjorden (fjord)	D 2
Sulitjelma (mt.)	K 3
Svalbard (isls.), 3,431	C 3
Tana (riv.)	P 1
Tanafjord (fjord)	Q 1
Tokke (riv.)	F 7
Trondheimsfjorden (fjord)	G 5
Tyrifjord (lake)	C 3
Vaerøy (isl.), 1,088	H 3
Vagåvatn (lake)	F 6
Vannøy (isl.), 1,219	L 1
Varanger Halvøy (pen.), 19,320	Q 1
Varangerfjord (fjord)	Q 2
Vega (isl.), 1,426	G 4
Vesterålen (isls.), 61,564	J 2
Vestfjord (fjord)	H 3
Vestvågoy (isl.), 10,798	H 3
Vikna (isls.), 3,410	G 4

(continued on following page)

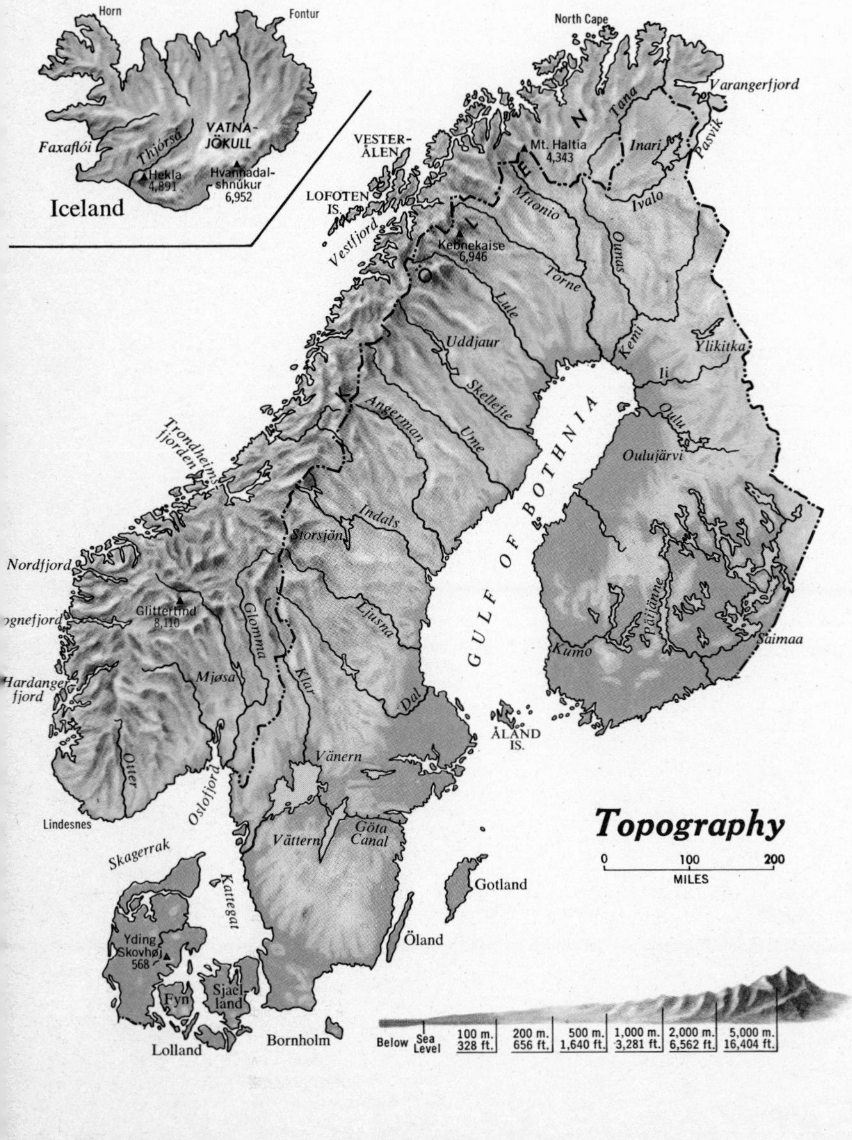
Horn
Fontur
Faxaflói
Thjórsá
VATNA-JÖKULL
Hekla 4,891
Hvannadal-shnúkur 6,952
Iceland
North Cape
Varangerfjord
Tana
Pasvik
Inari
Mt. Haltia 4,343
VESTER-ÅLEN
LOFOTEN IS.
Vestfjord
Kebnekaise 6,946
Muonio
Ounas
Ivalo
Torne
Lule
Kemi
Ylikitka
Ii
Uddjaur
Skellefte
Ångerman
Ume
Oulu
Oulujärvi
GULF OF BOTHNIA
Trondheimsfjorden
Indals
Storsjön
Nordfjord
Glittertind 8,110
Sognefjord
Glomma
Ljusna
Päijänne
Saimaa
Kumo
Hardangerfjord
Mjøsa
Klar
Dal
ÅLAND IS.
Vänern
Otter
Oslofjord
Lindesnes
Topography
0 100 200 MILES
Vättern
Göta Canal
Skagerrak
Kattegat
Gotland
Yding Skovhøj 568
Öland
Fyn
Sjælland
Lolland
Bornholm
Below Sea Level
100 m. 328 ft.
200 m. 656 ft.
500 m. 1,640 ft.
1,000 m. 3,281 ft.
2,000 m. 6,562 ft.
5,000 m. 16,404 ft.

20 Norway, Sweden, Finland, Denmark and Iceland
(continued)

SWEDEN

COUNTIES

Älvsborg, 420,199 . . . H 7
Blekinge, 154,968 . . . J 8
Gävleborg, 294,696 . . . K 6
Göteborg och Bohus, 714,478 . . . G 7
Gotland, 54,624 . . . L 8
Halland, 222,967 . . . H 8
Jämtland, 133,755 . . . J 5
Jönköping, 302,161 . . . H 8
Kalmar, 241,005 . . . K 8
Kopparberg, 283,353 . . . J 6
Kristianstad, 273,924 . . . J 8
Kronoberg, 170,307 . . . J 8
Malmöhus, 739,729 . . . H 9
Norrbotten, 266,033 . . . L 3
Örebro, 273,897 . . . J 7
Östergötland, 389,416 . . . J 7
Skaraborg, 264,316 . . . H 7
Södermanland, 252,017 . . . K 7
Stockholm, 1,500,736 . . . L 7
Uppsala, 233,131 . . . K 7
Värmland, 284,620 . . . H 7
Västerbotten, 237,679 . . . K 4
Västernorrland, 268,268 . . . K 5
Västmanland, 260,182 . . . K 7

CITIES and TOWNS

Åhus, 4,083 . . . J 9
Alingsås, 18,761 . . . H 7
Älmhult, 7,001 . . . H 8
Alvesta, 7,544 . . . J 8
Älvsbyn, 3,902 . . . M 4
Åmål, 9,331 . . . H 7
Ånge, 3,874 . . . J 5
Ängelholm, 14,853 . . . H 8
Arboga, 11,932 . . . J 7
Årjäng, ⊙2,171 . . . H 7
Arvidsjaur, 3,541 . . . L 4
Arvika, 12,975 . . . H 7
Åseda, 2,491 . . . J 8
Åsele, 2,249 . . . K 4
Askersund, 2,788 . . . J 7
Åtvidaberg, 8,385 . . . K 7
Avesta, 19,915 . . . J 6
Bålsta, 4,972 . . . G 1
Båstad, 2,395 . . . H 8
Bengtsfors, 3,389 . . . H 7
Boden, 18,642 . . . M 4
Bollnäs, 13,003 . . . K 6
Borås, 73,344 . . . H 8
Borås, *104,451 . . . H 8
Borgholm, 2,424 . . . K 8
Borlänge, 35,436 . . . J 6
Bräcke, 2,104 . . . J 5
Brunflo, 2,380 . . . J 5
Bureå, 2,031 . . . M 4
Charlottenberg, 1,942 . . . H 6
Danderyd, ☆27,103 . . . H 1
Dannemora, 464 . . . K 6
Edsbyn, 4,068 . . . J 6
Eksjö, 9,214 . . . J 8
Emmaboda, 3,860 . . . J 8
Enköping, 19,066 . . . G 1
Eskilstuna, 68,596 . . . K 7
Eslöv, 13,186 . . . H 9
Fagersta, ☆15,730 . . . J 6
Falkenberg, 13,476 . . . H 8
Falköping, 15,681 . . . H 7
Falun, 28,788 . . . J 6
Filipstad, 7,420 . . . H 7
Finspång, 16,181 . . . J 7
Flen, 6,768 . . . K 7
Forshaga, 4,297 . . . H 7
Frösö, 8,936 . . . J 5
Frövi, 2,586 . . . J 7
Gällivare, 7,773 . . . M 3
Gamleby, 3,521 . . . J 8
Gävle, 65,326 . . . K 6
Gimo, 2,905 . . . K 6
Gnesta, 2,908 . . . G 2
Göteborg, 442,507 . . . G 8
Göteborg, *692,210 . . . G 8
Gränna, 2,052 . . . J 8
Hagfors, 8,315 . . . H 6
Hällefors, 7,953 . . . J 7
Hallsberg, 7,559 . . . J 7
Hallstahammar, 13,818 . . . K 7
Hallstavik, 5,069 . . . L 6
Halmstad, 49,725 . . . H 8
Hälsingborg, 82,008 . . . H 8
Hälsingborg, *101,352 . . . H 8
Haparanda, 4,246 . . . N 4
Härnösand, 18,683 . . . L 5
Hässleholm, 16,984 . . . H 8
Hedemora, 6,628 . . . K 6
Hjo, 4,078 . . . J 7
Höganäs, 10,554 . . . H 8
Holmsund, 4,717 . . . M 5
Hudiksvall, 14,351 . . . K 6
Hultsfred, 5,417 . . . K 8
Järna, 5,715 . . . G 2
Jokkmokk, 2,966 . . . L 3
Jönköping, 80,693 . . . H 8
Jönköping, *108,182 . . . H 8
Kalmar, 34,918 . . . K 8
Karlshamn, 17,193 . . . J 8
Karlskoga, ☆37,733 . . . J 7
Karlskrona, 33,873 . . . J 8
Karlstad, 52,044 . . . H 7
Katrineholm, 22,616 . . . K 7
Kinna, 12,467 . . . H 8
Kiruna, 23,279 . . . L 3
Kisa, 3,951 . . . J 8
Köping, 21,740 . . . J 7
Kopparberg, 4,014 . . . J 7
Kramfors, 7,267 . . . L 5
Kristianstad, 29,013 . . . J 9
Kristinehamn, 21,043 . . . H 7
Kumla, 10,734 . . . J 7
Kungälv, ☆28,322 . . . G 8
Kungsbacka, ☆39,778 . . . G 8
Laholm, 3,695 . . . H 8
Landskrona, 30,110 . . . H 9
Långsele, 2,320 . . . K 5
Långshyttan, 2,793 . . . K 6
Laxå, 5,847 . . . J 7
Leksand, 4,200 . . . J 6
Lidingö, 29,799 . . . H 1
Lidköping, 21,300 . . . H 7
Lindesberg, 7,171 . . . J 7
Linköping, 77,063 . . . K 7
Linköping, *110,060 . . . K 7
Ljungby, 12,596 . . . J 8
Ljusdal, 6,489 . . . J 6
Ljusne, 3,748 . . . K 6
Ludvika, 18,266 . . . J 6
Luleå, 36,743 . . . N 4
Lund, 76,516 . . . H 9
Lycksele, 7,879 . . . L 4
Lysekil, 6,783 . . . G 7
Malmberget, 10,315 . . . M 3
Malmköping, 2,189 . . . F 1
Malmö, 240,283 . . . H 9
Malmö, *453,339 . . . H 9
Malung, 6,028 . . . H 6
Mariefred, 2,013 . . . F 1
Mariestad, 16,637 . . . H 7
Markaryd, 4,121 . . . H 8
Marstrand, 1,072 . . . G 8
Mellerud, 3,368 . . . H 7
Mjölby, 12,245 . . . J 7
Mölndal, ☆46,925 . . . H 8
Mönsterås, 5,430 . . . K 8
Mora, 7,891 . . . J 6
Motala, 28,942 . . . J 7
Nacka, 22,569 . . . H 1
Nässjö, 19,434 . . . J 8
Nora, 4,681 . . . J 7
Norberg, 5,392 . . . K 6
Norrköping, 91,034 . . . K 7
Norrköping, *119,984 . . . K 7
Norrtälje, 12,735 . . . L 7
Nybro, 12,875 . . . J 8
Nyköping, 30,943 . . . K 7
Nynäshamn, 10,955 . . . L 7
Ockelbo, 2,669 . . . K 6
Olofström, 10,482 . . . J 8
Örebro, 87,125 . . . J 7
Örebro, *117,399 . . . J 7
Örnsköldsvik, 28,428 . . . L 5
Orrefors, 921 . . . J 8
Orsa, 4,799 . . . J 6
Oskarshamn, 17,143 . . . K 8
Östersund, 27,320 . . . J 5
Östhammar, 2,668 . . . L 6
Överum, 2,483 . . . K 7
Oxelösund, 15,085 . . . K 7
Piteå, 15,067 . . . M 4
Ramnäs, 1,920 . . . J 7
Rättvik, 3,918 . . . J 6
Rimbo, 3,237 . . . L 7
Ronneby, 11,801 . . . J 8
Säffle, 11,609 . . . H 7
Sala, 10,476 . . . K 7
Saltsjöbaden, 7,055 . . . J 1
Sandviken, 28,410 . . . K 6
Säter, 3,973 . . . J 6
Sävsjö, 4,846 . . . J 8
Sigtuna, 4,214 . . . H 1
Simrishamn, 5,502 . . . J 9
Skanör med Falsterbo, 3,127 . . . H 9
Skara, 10,284 . . . H 7
Skellefteå, 27,456 . . . M 4
Skövde, 29,040 . . . H 7
Smedjebacken, 8,395 . . . J 6
Söderhamn, 13,721 . . . K 6
Söderköping, 4,688 . . . K 7
Södertälje, 57,494 . . . G 1
Sollefteå, 8,414 . . . K 5
Sollentuna, ☆44,582 . . . H 1
Solna, ☆52,854 . . . H 1
Sölvesborg, 6,797 . . . J 9
Stockholm (cap.), 661,536 . . . G 1
Stockholm, *1,364,056 . . . G 1
Storuman, 2,456 . . . K 4
Storvik, 2,615 . . . K 6
Strängnäs, 9,509 . . . F 1
Strömstad, 4,447 . . . G 7
Strömsund, 3,578 . . . K 5
Sundbyberg, ☆26,456 . . . G 1
Sundsvall, 53,599 . . . K 5
Sunne, 3,686 . . . H 7
Sveg, 2,298 . . . J 5
Svenljunga, 2,786 . . . H 8
Täby, ☆42,493 . . . H 1
Tidaholm, 7,663 . . . J 7
Tierp, 4,497 . . . K 6
Timrå, 11,055 . . . K 5
Tomelilla, 4,923 . . . J 9
Torsby, 3,094 . . . H 6
Torshälla, 8,363 . . . K 7
Tranås, 15,150 . . . J 7
Trelleborg, 34,504 . . . H 9
Trollhättan, 41,016 . . . H 7
Trosa, 2,173 . . . K 7
Uddevalla, 35,459 . . . G 7
Ulricehamn, 7,699 . . . H 8
Umeå, 47,692 . . . M 5
Uppsala, 92,624 . . . K 7
Uppsala, *139,883 . . . L 7
Vaggeryd, 3,820 . . . J 8
Valdemarsvik, 3,545 . . . K 7
Vänersborg, 19,465 . . . G 7
Vännäs, 4,066 . . . L 5
Vansbro, 2,701 . . . H 6
Vara, 2,827 . . . H 7
Varberg, 17,768 . . . G 8
Värnamo, 14,962 . . . J 8
Västerås, 99,343 . . . K 7
Västerås, *118,073 . . . K 7
Västerhaninge, 12,966 . . . H 1
Västervik, 20,168 . . . K 8
Vaxholm, ☆28,678 . . . J 1
Växjö, 39,019 . . . J 8
Vetlanda, 12,024 . . . J 8
Vilhelmina, 3,632 . . . K 4
Vimmerby, 7,201 . . . J 8
Virserum, 2,591 . . . J 8
Visby, 19,245 . . . L 8
Ystad, 14,164 . . . H 9

OTHER FEATURES

Ångermanälven (riv.) . . . K 5
Åsnen (lake) . . . J 8
Baltic (sea) . . . K 9
Bolmen (lake) . . . H 8
Bothnia (gulf) . . . N 4
Dalälven (riv.) . . . K 6
Fårö (isl.), 727 . . . L 8
Göta (canal) . . . J 7
Göta (riv.) . . . H 7
Gotland (isl.), 53,053 . . . L 8
Gräsö (isl.), 618 . . . L 6
Hanöbukten (bay) . . . J 9
Hjälmaren (lake) . . . J 7
Hoburg (cliff) . . . L 8
Hornslandet (pen.) . . . K 6
Indalsälven (riv.) . . . H 5
Kalixälv (riv.) . . . N 3
Kalmarsund (sound) . . . K 8
Kattegat (str.) . . . G 8
Kebnekaise (mt.) . . . L 3
Kjölen (mts.) . . . K 3
Klarälv (riv.) . . . H 6
Lapland (reg.), 503,712 . . . M 2
Ljusnan (riv.) . . . H 5
Luleälv (riv.) . . . M 3
Mälaren (lake) . . . G 1
Muonioälv (riv.) . . . M 2
Öland (isl.), 22,561 . . . K 8
Öresund (sound) . . . H 9
Ornö (isl.), 175 . . . J 2
Österdalälven (riv.) . . . H 6
Piteälv (riv.) . . . M 4
Siljan (lake) . . . J 6
Skagerrak (str.) . . . F 8
Sommen (lake) . . . J 7
Stora Lulevatten (lake) . . . L 3
Storsjön (lake) . . . J 5
Sulitjelma (mt.) . . . K 3
Torneälv (riv.) . . . M 3
Uddjaur (lake) . . . L 4
Umeälv (riv.) . . . L 4
Vänern (lake) . . . H 7
Västerdalälven (riv.) . . . H 6
Vättern (lake) . . . J 7

*City and suburbs.
☆Population of commune.
⊙Population of parish.

DENMARK

INTERNAL DIVISIONS

Århus (county), 525,167 . . . D 5
Bornholm (county), 47,405 . . . F 9
Copenhagen (commune), 634,500 . . . F 6
Færøe Islands, 38,000 . . . B 2
Frederiksberg (commune), 102,751 . . . F 6
Frederiksborg (county), 252,557 . . . F 5
Fyn (county), 430,958 . . . D 7
København (Copenhagen) (commune), 634,500 . . . F 6
København (county), 609,469 . . . F 6
Nordjylland (county), 455,062 . . . D 4
Ribe (county), 196,894 . . . B 6
Ringkøbing (county), 240,014 . . . B 5
Roskilde (county), 147,434 . . . E 6
Sønderjylland (county), 237,270 . . . C 7
Storstrøm (county), 251,815 . . . E 7
Vejle (county), 304,358 . . . C 6
Vestsjælland (county), 256,997 . . . E 6
Viborg (county), 220,214 . . . B 4

CITIES and TOWNS

Åbenrå, 15,156 . . . C 7
Åbybro, 6,309 . . . C 3
Ærøskøbing, 1,228 . . . D 8
Agerbæk, 804, . . . B 6
Åkirkeby, 1,549 . . . F 9
Ålborg, 82,346 . . . D 4
Ålborg, *153,307 . . . D 4
Ålestrup, 5,228 . . . C 4
Allingåbro, 1,352 . . . D 5
Allinge-Sandvig, 2,023 . . . F 8
Ansager, 1,123 . . . B 6
Arden, 1,353 . . . C 4
Århus, 109,498 . . . D 5
Århus, *232,173 . . . D 5
Års, 5,075 . . . C 4
Årup, †5,033 . . . D 7
Aså, 1,348 . . . D 3
Askov, 725 . . . C 7
Asnæs, 2,493 . . . E 6
Assens, Århus, 1,266 . . . D 4
Assens, Fyn, †10,777 . . . D 7
Augustenborg, 3,537 . . . D 8
Auning, 1,367 . . . D 5
Avlum, 3,694 . . . B 5
Bælum, 1,922 . . . D 4
Bagenkop, 774 . . . D 8
Ballerup, †50,128 . . . F 6
Bandholm, 1,248 . . . E 8
Bested, 1,886 . . . B 4
Birkerød, †20,835 . . . F 6
Bjerringbro, 6,469 . . . C 5
Bogense, †6,450 . . . D 6
Bolderslev, 729 . . . C 8
Børkop, †9,053 . . . C 6
Borup, 2,344 . . . E 7
Brabrand, 12,514 . . . C 5
Brædstrup, 3,925 . . . C 6
Bramminge, 5,937 . . . B 7
Brande, 6,814 . . . B 6
Bredebro, †3,747 . . . B 7
Broager, †5,387 . . . C 8
Brønderslev, 10,274 . . . C 3
Brøns, 867 . . . B 7
Brørup, 4,066 . . . C 7
Brovst, †8,086 . . . C 3
Christiansfeld, 958 . . . C 7
Copenhagen (cap.), 634,500 . . . F 6
Copenhagen, *1,346,720 . . . F 6
Dronninglund, 9,179 . . . D 3
Dybvad, 793 . . . D 3
Ebeltoft, 3,168 . . . D 5
Egernsund, 1,360 . . . C 8
Egtved, 2,857 . . . C 6
Ejby, 3,265 . . . D 7
Esbjerg, 62,483 . . . B 7
Fåborg, 5,630 . . . D 7
Fakse, 7,268 . . . F 7
Fakse Ladeplads, 1,639 . . . F 7
Farsø, 4,126 . . . C 4
Farum, †9,583 . . . F 6
Fjerritslev, 2,686 . . . C 3
Fredensborg, 3,977 . . . F 6
Fredericia, 34,464 . . . C 6
Frederiksberg, 102,751 . . . F 6
Frederikshavn, 24,640 . . . D 3
Frederikssund, 7,835 . . . E 6
Frederiksværk, 4,385 . . . E 6
Fuglebjerg, 5,082 . . . E 7
Gedser, 1,195 . . . F 8
Gedsted, 1,924 . . . C 4
Gelsted, 2,461 . . . C 7
Gentofte, †78,641 . . . F 6
Gilleleje, 4,300 . . . F 5
Give, 8,573 . . . C 6
Gjerlev, 1,209 . . . D 4
Glamsbjerg, †5,677 . . . D 7
Glostrup, †28,169 . . . F 6
Glumsø, 819 . . . E 7
Glyngøre, 1,047 . . . C 4
Gørding, 2,422 . . . B 7
Gørlev, 2,437 . . . E 6
Græsted, 2,899 . . . F 5
Gram, 3,935 . . . C 7
Gråsten, †6,336 . . . C 8
Grenå, 13,277 . . . D 5
Grindsted, 9,345 . . . B 6
Gylling, 990 . . . D 6
Haderslev, 20,291 . . . C 7
Hadsten, 6,919 . . . C 5
Hadsund, 6,862 . . . D 4
Hals, 3,016 . . . D 3
Hammel, 7,456 . . . C 5
Hammerum, 2,415 . . . C 5
Hanstholm, 3,358 . . . B 3
Harboør, 2,224 . . . A 4
Hårby, †4,671 . . . D 7
Hårlev, 980 . . . F 7
Hasle, 1,542 . . . F 8
Haslev, 10,173 . . . E 7
Havdrup, 5,163 . . . F 6
Hedensted, 4,791 . . . C 6
Hellebæk, 2,240 . . . F 5
Helsinge, 4,707 . . . F 6
Helsingør, 30,211 . . . F 6
Herning, 32,512 . . . B 5
Hillerød, 23,500 . . . F 6
Hinnerup, †5,614 . . . D 5
Hirtshals, 8,598 . . . C 2
Hjallerup, 1,385 . . . C 3
Hjerm, 1,421 . . . B 5
Hjørring, 15,699 . . . C 3
Hobro, 8,845 . . . C 4
Højer, 1,407 . . . B 8
Højslev, 2,863 . . . C 4
Holbæk, 17,892 . . . E 6
Holeby, 4,359 . . . E 8
Holstebro, 24,009 . . . B 5
Holsted, 2,773 . . . B 6
Høng, †7,355 . . . E 7
Hornslet, 3,371 . . . D 5
Horsens, 35,621 . . . C 6
Hørsholm, 18,060 . . . F 6
Hørve, 2,829 . . . E 6
Hov, 607 . . . D 6
Humlum, 2,357 . . . B 4
Hundested, †6,301 . . . E 6
Hurup, 2,560 . . . B 4
Hvidbjerg, 2,361 . . . B 4
Hvide Sande, 1,775 . . . A 6
Hviding, 750 . . . B 7
Ikast, 11,110 . . . C 5
Jelling, 4,780 . . . C 6
Jerslev, 2,672 . . . D 3
Juelsminde, 7,245 . . . D 6
Jyderup, 3,246 . . . E 6
Kalundborg, 11,762 . . . D 6
Karby, 2,302 . . . B 4
Karise, 1,733 . . . F 7
Karup, 1,891 . . . C 5
Kastrup . . . F 6
Kerteminde, †10,296 . . . D 7
Kibæk, 1,179 . . . B 5
Kjellerup, 3,506 . . . C 5
Klaksvík, Færøe Is., 3,894 . . . B 2
København (Copenhagen), (cap.), 634,500 . . . F 6
Køge, 17,360 . . . F 7
Kolding, 39,609 . . . C 7
Kolind, 2,590 . . . D 5
Kørsør, 15,550 . . . E 7
Kværndrup, 1,963 . . . D 7
Langå, 2,801 . . . C 5
Lem, 1,060 . . . B 5
Lemvig, 6,766 . . . B 4
Løgstør, 3,666 . . . C 4
Løgumkloster, 2,089 . . . B 7
Lohals, 634 . . . D 7
Løjt Kirkeby, 2,724 . . . C 7
Løkken, 1,388 . . . C 3
Løsning, 2,418 . . . C 6
Lundby, 2,392 . . . E 7
Lunderskov, †4,402 . . . C 7
Lyngby, †61,245 . . . F 6
Malling, 4,332 . . . D 5
Mariager, 3,733 . . . D 4
Maribo, 5,235 . . . E 8
Marstal, 4,095 . . . D 8
Middelfart, 9,015 . . . C 7
Møgeltønder, 1,181 . . . B 8
Næstved, 24,831 . . . E 7
Nakskov, 15,994 . . . E 8
Neksø, 3,499 . . . F 9
Nibe, 2,786 . . . C 4
Nordborg, 3,016 . . . C 7
Nordby, 2,353 . . . B 7
Nørre Åby, †5,195 . . . C 7
Nørre Alslev, 1,939 . . . E 8
Nørre Broby, 858 . . . D 7
Nørre Nebel, 867 . . . B 6
Nørre Snede, 3,019 . . . C 6
Nørresundby, 23,848 . . . D 3
Nørre Vorupør, 632 . . . B 4
Nyborg, 11,698 . . . D 7
Nykøbing, Storstrøm, 17,364 . . . E 8
Nykøbing, Vestsjælland, 4,905 . . . E 6
Nykøbing, Viborg, 8,710 . . . B 4
Nysted, 1,211 . . . E 8
Odder, 8,144 . . . D 6
Odense, 102,698 . . . D 7
Odense, *163,593 . . . D 7
Ølgod, 7,091 . . . B 6
Ørsted, 1,925 . . . D 5
Øster Vrå, 931 . . . D 3
Otterup, †10,462 . . . D 7
Ovtrup, 549 . . . B 6
Pandrup, 1,383 . . . C 3
Pedersborg, 1,560 . . . E 7

Agriculture, Industry and Resources

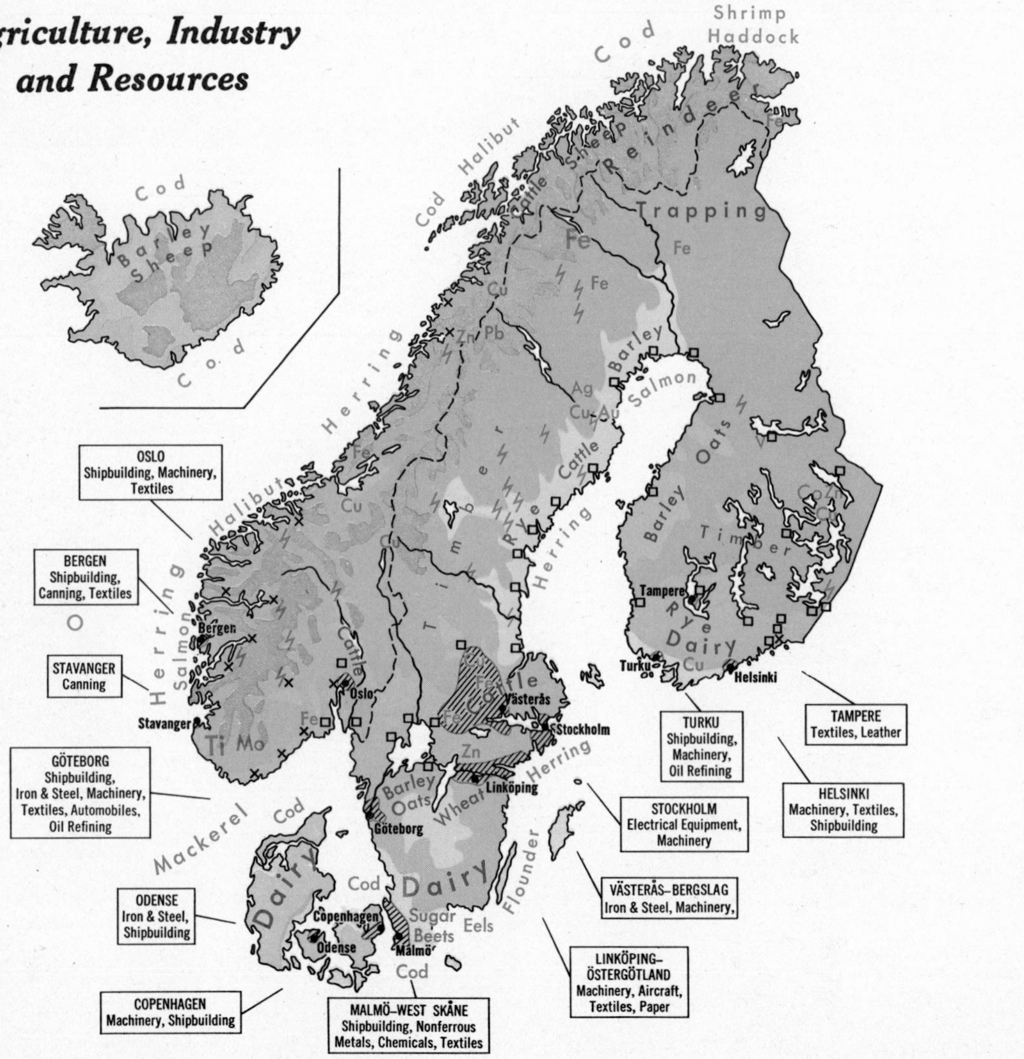
Cod
Shrimp
Haddock
Barley
Sheep
Halibut
Cattle
Sheep
Reindeer
Trapping
Fe
Cu
Herring
Barley
Salmon
Ag
Cu Au
Cattle
Oats
Timber
Rye
Zn
Pb
OSLO
Shipbuilding, Machinery, Textiles
BERGEN
Shipbuilding, Canning, Textiles
STAVANGER
Canning
GÖTEBORG
Shipbuilding, Iron & Steel, Machinery, Textiles, Automobiles, Oil Refining
ODENSE
Iron & Steel, Shipbuilding
COPENHAGEN
Machinery, Shipbuilding
MALMÖ–WEST SKÅNE
Shipbuilding, Nonferrous Metals, Chemicals, Textiles
LINKÖPING–ÖSTERGÖTLAND
Machinery, Aircraft, Textiles, Paper
VÄSTERÅS–BERGSLAG
Iron & Steel, Machinery,
STOCKHOLM
Electrical Equipment, Machinery
TURKU
Shipbuilding, Machinery, Oil Refining
HELSINKI
Machinery, Textiles, Shipbuilding
TAMPERE
Textiles, Leather
Tampere
Turku
Helsinki
Oslo
Bergen
Stavanger
Västerås
Stockholm
Linköping
Göteborg
Copenhagen
Odense
Malmö
Ti
Mo
Mackerel
Wheat
Oats
Dairy
Flounder
Sugar Beets
Eels

DOMINANT LAND USE

Cash Cereals, Dairy
Dairy, Cattle, Hogs
Dairy, General Farming
General Farming (chiefly cereals)
Nomadic Sheep Herding
Forests, Limited Mixed Farming
Nonagricultural Land

MAJOR MINERAL OCCURRENCES

Ag Silver
Au Gold
Co Cobalt
Cu Copper
Fe Iron Ore
Mo Molybdenum
O Petroleum
Pb Lead
Ti Titanium
V Vanadium
Zn Zinc

Water Power
Major Industrial Areas
× Electrochemical & Electrometallurgical Centers
□ Paper, Pulp & Sawmilling Centers

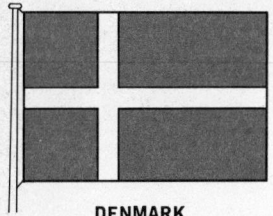

DENMARK

ICELAND

DENMARK	
AREA	16,629 sq. mi
POPULATION	5,065,313
CAPITAL	Copenhagen
LARGEST CITY	Copenhagen
HIGHEST POINT	Yding Skovhøj 568 ft.
MONETARY UNIT	krone
MAJOR LANGUAGE	Danish
MAJOR RELIGION	Protestantism

ICELAND	
AREA	39,768 sq. mi.
POPULATION	220,000
CAPITAL	Reykjavík
LARGEST CITY	Reykjavík
HIGHEST POINT	Hvannadalshnúkur 6,952 ft.
MONETARY UNIT	króna
MAJOR LANGUAGE	Icelandic
MAJOR RELIGION	Protestantism

Præstø, 4,926 ....E 7
Ramme, 1,560 ....B 4
Randers, 41,253 ....C 5
Ranum, 2,320 ....C 4
Ribe, 8,224 ....B 7
Ringe, 6,907 ....D 7
Ringkøbing, 6,536 ....B 5
Ringsted, 12,499 ....E 7
Rødby, 4,751 ....E 8
Rødding, 2,826 ....B 7
Rødekro, 17,874 ....C 7
Rødkærsbro, 992 ....C 5
Rødvig Ladeplads, 1,068 ....F 7
Rømø, 817 ....B 7
Rønde, 4,487 ....D 5
Rønne, 12,440 ....F 9
Rørby, 1,081 ....E 6
Roskilde, 39,984 ....E 6
Roslev, 1,260 ....B 4
Rudkøbing, 17,069 ....D 8
Ruds Vedby, 954 ....E 6
Ry, 5,945 ....C 5
Ryomgård, 947 ....D 5
Sæby, 4,378 ....D 3
Sakskøbing, 2,523 ....E 8
Silkeborg, 26,129 ....C 5
Sindal, 18,695 ....C 3
Skælskør, 8,776 ....E 7
Skærbæk, 3,016 ....B 7
Skagen, 11,699 ....D 2
Skals, 1,968 ....C 4
Skanderborg, 11,227 ....D 5
Skårup, 2,215 ....D 7
Skibby, 14,585 ....E 6
Skive, 17,980 ....B 4
Skjern, 6,058 ....B 6
Skodborg, 1,728 ....C 7
Skørping, 2,347 ....C 4
Slagelse, 23,169 ....E 7
Slangerup, 2,701 ....E 6
Snedsted, 2,571 ....B 4
Søllested, 857 ....D 8
Sønderborg, 23,069 ....C 7
Sønderho, 352 ....B 7
Sønder Nissum, 1,236 ....A 5
Sønder Omme, 2,449 ....B 6
Søndersø, 19,479 ....D 7
Sorø, 5,591 ....E 7
Stege, 3,872 ....F 8
Stenlille, 1,617 ....E 6
Stenstrup, 1,993 ....D 7
Støholm, 1,178 ....C 5
Store Heddinge, 2,245 ....F 7
Støvring, 1,980 ....C 4
Strandby, 1,752 ....D 3
Struer, 9,263 ....B 5
Stubbekøbing, 2,061 ....E 8
Sulsted, 5,006 ....C 4
Svaneke, 1,164 ....F 8
Svendborg, 23,149 ....D 7
Svenstrup, 3,530 ....C 4
Svinninge, 15,681 ....E 6
Tarm, 2,702 ....B 6
Tårnby, 145,868 ....F 6
Tåstrup, 129,154 ....E 6
Them, 2,419 ....C 5
Thisted, 8,032 ....B 4
Thyborøn, 2,404 ....B 4
Thyregod, 2,442 ....C 6
Tim, 1,175 ....B 5
Tinglev, 2,695 ....C 8
Tistrup, 653 ....B 6
Toftlund, 3,311 ....B 7
Tølløse, 18,036 ....E 6
Tommerup, 16,076 ....D 7
Tønder, 7,489 ....B 8
Tørring, 2,039 ....C 6
Tørshavn (cap.), Færøe Is., 9,738 ....A 3
Tranbjerg, 701 ....D 7
Troense, 631 ....D 7
Trustrup, 801 ....D 5
Tversted, 1,973 ....C 3
Uldum, 1,182 ....C 6
Ulfborg, 2,053 ....B 5
Vamdrup, 4,760 ....C 7
Varde, 11,456 ....B 6
Vejen, 12,440 ....C 7
Vejle, 31,763 ....C 6
Vemb, 1,937 ....B 5
Vester Skerninge, 503 ....D 7
Vestervig, 2,513 ....B 4
Viborg, 25,468 ....C 5
Viby, 1,038 ....F 7
Videbæk, 110,368 ....B 5
Vig, 2,678 ....E 6
Vildbjerg, 2,698 ....B 5
Vinderup, 17,857 ....B 5
Vodskov, 2,327 ....D 3
Vojens, 6,975 ....C 7
Vorbasse, 1,952 ....B 6
Vordingborg, 11,640 ....E 8
Vrå, 4,371 ....C 3

OTHER FEATURES

Ærø (isl.), 9,295 ....D 8
Ålborg (bay) ....D 4
Als (isl.), 50,518 ....C 8
Amager (isl.), 177,818 ....F 6
Anholt (isl.), 196 ....E 4
Årø (isl.), 259 ....C 7
Bågø (isl.), 113 ....C 7
Blåvands Huk (point) ....A 6
Bornholm (isl.), 47,405 ....F 9
Dovns Klint (prom.) ....D 8
Endelave (isl.), 257 ....D 6
Eysturoy (isl.), Færøe Is., 7,714 ....B 2
Færøe (isls.), 38,000 ....B 2
Fakse (bay) ....F 7
Falster (isl.), 49,405 ....E 8
Fanø (isl.), 2,705 ....B 7
Fehmarn (strait) ....E 8
Fejø (isl.), 933 ....E 8

Femø (isl.), 381 ....E 8
Frisian, North (isls.), 3,653 ....B 7
Fyn (isl.), 397,234 ....D 7
Fyns Hoved (prom.) ....D 6
Gedser Odde (point) ....E 8
Gelså (river) ....C 7
Gilbjerg Hoved (prom.) ....F 5
Gjerrild Klint (prom.) ....D 5
Gudenå (river) ....C 5
Horsens (fjord) ....D 6
Isefjord (fjord) ....E 6
Jammerbugt (bay) ....C 3
Jutland (Jylland) (pen.), 2,088,642 ....C 5
Jyske Ås (hills) ....D 3
Kattegat (strait) ....E 4
Knøsen (mt.) ....D 3
Knudshoved (prom.) ....D 7
Køge (bay) ....F 7
Læsø (isl.), 2,722 ....D 3
Langeland (isl.), 17,132 ....D 8
Langelands Bælt (channel) ....D 8
Lille Bælt (channel) ....C 7
Lilleå (river) ....C 5
Limfjorden (fjord) ....A, D 4
Løgstør Bredning ....C 4
Lolland (isl.), 74,819 ....E 8
Mariager (fjord) ....D 4
Mollebjerg (mt.) ....C 6
Møn (isl.), 12,436 ....F 8
Møns Klint (prom.) ....F 8
Mors (isl.), 25,026 ....B 4
Nissum (fjord) ....A 5
North Frisian (isls.), 3,653 ....B 7
Odense (fjord) ....D 7
Omme (river) ....E 7
Omø (isl.), 241 ....E 7
Øresund (sound) ....F 6
Ringkøbing (fjord) ....B 6
Rømø (isl.), 817 ....B 7
Rosnaes (prom.) ....E 7
Samsø (isl.), 5,192 ....D 6
Samsø Bælt (channel) ....D 6
Sandøy (isl.), Færøe Is., 1,684 ....B 3
Sejerø (isl.), 561 ....E 6
Sjælland (isl.), 2,116,294 ....E 6
Sjællands Odde (point) ....E 5
Skagens Odde (The Skaw) (point) ....D 2
Skagerrak (strait) ....C 2
Skive (river) ....C 5
Stevns Klint (prom.) ....F 7
Storå (river) ....B 5
Store Bælt (channel) ....D 7
Streymoy (isl.), Færøe Is., 14,078 ....A 2
Sudhuroy (isl.), Færøe Is., 5,734 ....B 3
Suså (river) ....E 7
Tannis (bay) ....C 2
Tranebjerg (mt.) ....B 6
Varde (river) ....B 6
Vejle (fjord) ....C 6
Vigsø (bay) ....B 3
Vorgod (river) ....B 6
Yding Skovhøj (mt.) ....C 6

ICELAND

CITIES and TOWNS

Akranes, 4,253 ....B 1
Akureyri, 10,755 ....C 1
Hafnarfjördhur, 9,696 ....B 1
Húsavík, 1,993 ....C 1
Ísafjördhur, 2,680 ....B 1
Keflavík, 5,663 ....B 1
Neskaupstadhur (Nes), 1,552 ....D 1
Olafsfjördhur, 1,086 ....C 1
Reykjavík (capital), 81,693 ....B 1
Reykjavík, *98,521 ....B 1
Saudhárkrókur, 1,600 ....C 1
Seydhisfjördhur, 884 ....D 1
Siglufjördhur, 2,161 ....C 1
Vestmannaeyjar, 5,186 ....B 2

OTHER FEATURES

Bjargtangur (point) ....A 1
Breidhafjördhur (fjord) ....B 1
Faxaflói (bay) ....B 1
Fontur (prom.) ....D 1
Gerpir (cape) ....D 1
Grímsey (isl.), 79 ....C 1
Hekla (volcano) ....C 1
Hofsjökull (glacier) ....C 1
Horn (cape) ....B 1
Hornafjördhur (fjord) ....D 1
Húnaflói (fjord) ....C 1
Hvannadalshnúkur ....D 1
Hvítá (river) ....B 1
Ísafjördhur (fjord) ....B 1
Jökulsá (river) ....C 1
Lagarfljót (stream) ....D 1
Langjökull (glacier) ....C 1
North (Horn) (cape) ....C 1
Öndverdharnes (cape) ....A 1
Reykjanesta (cape) ....A 1
Rifstangi (cape) ....C 1
Skagata (cape) ....B 1
Skjálfandafljót (river) ....C 1
Surtsey (isl.) ....B 2
Thjórsá (river) ....C 1
Vatnajökull (glacier) ....C 1
Vopnafjörd (fjord) ....D 1

*City and suburbs.
†Population of rural municipality.

Longitude 10° East of Greenwich 11°

DENMARK and ICELAND

CONIC PROJECTION

SCALE OF MILES
0 10 20 30 40 50

SCALE OF KILOMETERS
0 10 20 30 40 50

Capitals of Countries _____☆
Capitals of Counties (amter) ____△
International Boundaries _____
Internal Boundaries _____

Denmark is divided into fourteen counties plus Copennagen and Frederiksberg communes.

© Copyright HAMMOND INCORPORATED, Maplewood, N.J.

FAERØE ISLANDS
Streymoy
Klaksvík
Eysturoy
Tórshavn
Sandoy
Sudhuroy
0 15 30
MILES

Same scale as main map
BORNHOLM

WEST GERMANY

AREA 95,985 sq. mi
POPULATION 61,644,600
CAPITAL Bonn
LARGEST CITY Berlin (West)
HIGHEST POINT Zugspitze 9,718 ft.
MONETARY UNIT Deutsche mark
MAJOR LANGUAGE German
MAJOR RELIGIONS Protestantism, Roman Catholicism

EAST GERMANY

AREA 41,768 sq. mi.
POPULATION 16,850,000
CAPITAL Berlin (East)
LARGEST CITY Berlin (East)
HIGHEST POINT Fichtelberg 3,983 ft.
MONETARY UNIT East German mark
MAJOR LANGUAGE German
MAJOR RELIGIONS Protestantism, Roman Catholicism

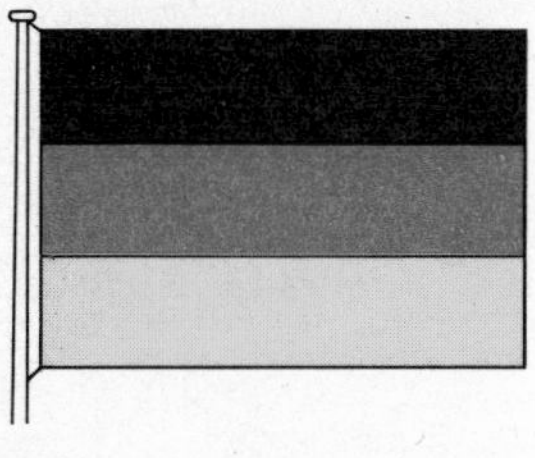

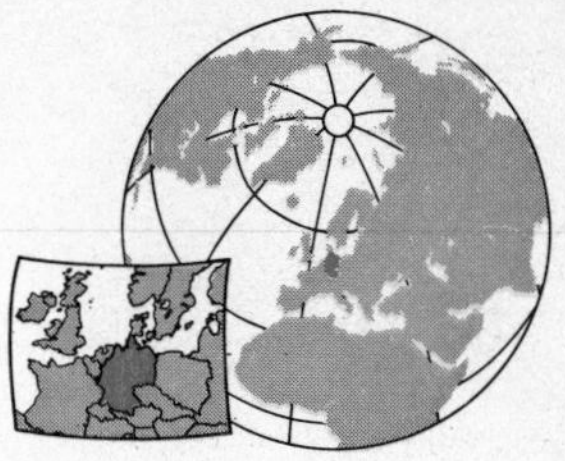

Topography

0 50 100
MILES

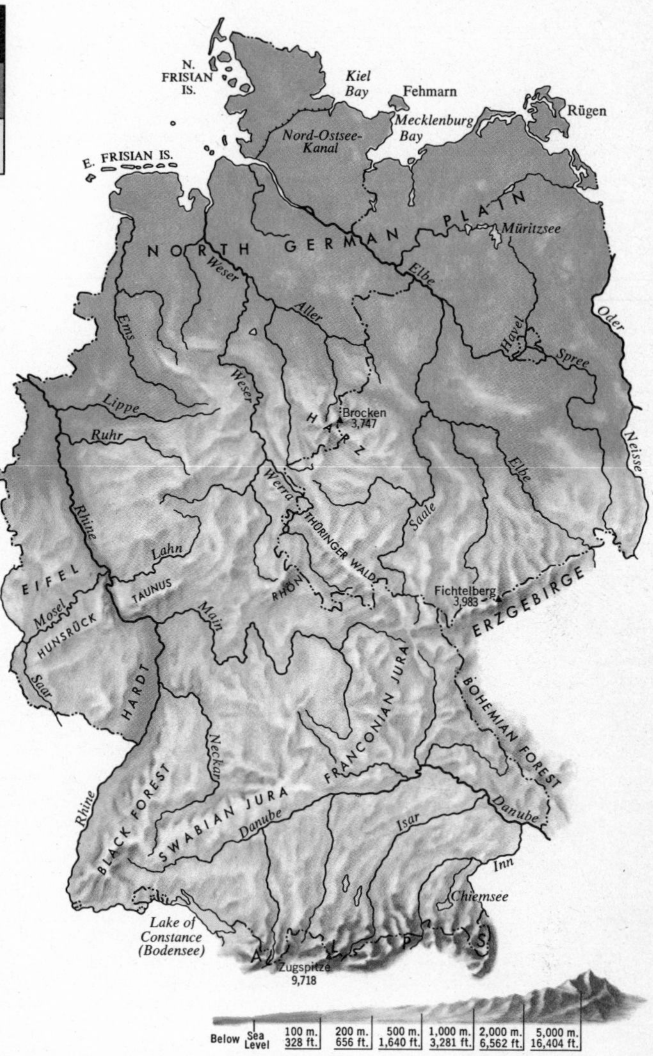
N. FRISIAN IS.
Kiel Bay
Fehmarn
Rügen
Mecklenburg Bay
Nord-Ostsee-Kanal
E. FRISIAN IS.
NORTH GERMAN PLAIN
Müritzsee
Weser
Aller
Elbe
Oder
Ems
Havel
Spree
Lippe
Brocken 3,747
HARZ
Ruhr
Neisse
Werra
Saale
Rhine
Lahn
THÜRINGER WALD
EIFEL
TAUNUS
RHÖN
Fichtelberg 3,983
ERZGEBIRGE
Mosel
HUNSRÜCK
Main
Saar
HARDT
FRANCONIAN JURA
BOHEMIAN FOREST
Neckar
BLACK FOREST
SWABIAN JURA
Danube
Isar
Inn
Chiemsee
Lake of Constance (Bodensee)
ALPS
Zugspitze 9,718
Below Sea Level
100 m. 328 ft.
200 m. 656 ft.
500 m. 1,640 ft.
1,000 m. 3,281 ft.
2,000 m. 6,562 ft.
5,000 m. 16,404 ft.

EAST GERMANY

DISTRICTS

Berlin, 1,094,147	F 4
Cottbus, 872,242	F 3
Dresden, 1,845,459	E 3
Erfurt, 1,247,213	D 3
Frankfurt, 688,637	F 2
Gera, 738,847	D 3
Halle, 1,890,187	D 3
Karl-Marx-Stadt, 1,994,115	E 3
Leipzig, 1,457,817	E 3
Magdeburg, 1,297,881	D 2
Neubrandenburg, 628,686	E 2
Potsdam, 1,124,892	E 2
Rostock, 867,806	E 1
Schwerin, 592,334	D 2
Suhl, 550,497	D 3

CITIES and TOWNS

Aken, 11,742	D 3
Altenburg, 51,193	E 3
Angermünde, 11,786	E 2
Anklam, 19,099	E 2
Annaberg-Buchholz, 26,561	E 3
Apolda, 28,649	D 3
Arnstadt, 29,462	D 3
Aschersleben, 36,674	D 3
Aue, 32,622	E 3
Auerbach, 18,168	E 3
Bad Doberan, 12,541	D 1
Bad Dürrenberg, 15,192	D 3
Bad Freienwalde, 11,497	F 2
Bad Langensalza, 166,282	D 3
Bad Salzungen, 17,277	C 3
Barth, 12,069	E 1
Bautzen, 45,851	F 3
Bergen, 13,244	E 1
Berlin (East) (cap.), 1,094,147	F 4
Bernau bei Berlin, 15,749	E 2
Bernburg, 44,428	D 3
Bischofswerda, 11,540	F 3
Bitterfeld, 27,062	E 3
Blankenburg am Harz, 18,784	D 3
Boizenburg an der Elbe, 12,428	D 2
Borna, 21,807	E 3
Brandenburg, 94,071	E 2
Burg bei Magdeburg, 29,027	D 2
Calbe, 15,976	D 3
Chemnitz (Karl-Marx-Stadt), 303,811	E 3
Coswig, Dresden, 22,149	E 3
Coswig, Halle, 12,473	E 3
Cottbus, 94,293	F 3
Crimmitschau, 28,845	E 3
Delitzsch, 24,076	E 3
Demmin, 17,270	E 2
Dessau, 100,820	E 3
Döbeln, 27,624	E 3
Dresden, 507,692	E 3
Ebersbach, 12,694	F 3
Eberswalde-Finow, 47,141	E 2
Eilenburg, 22,245	E 3
Eisenach, 49,954	D 3
Eisenberg, 13,450	D 3
Eisenhüttenstadt, 46,455	F 2
Eisleben, 29,297	D 3
Erfurt, 202,979	D 3
Falkensee, 25,295	E 3
Falkenstein, 14,367	E 3
Finsterwalde, 22,466	E 3
Forst, 28,084	F 3
Frankfurt an der Oder, 70,817	F 2
Freiberg, 50,815	E 3
Freital, 46,061	E 3
Friedland	E 2
Fürstenwalde, 31,065	F 2
Gardelegen, 12,987	D 2
Genthin, 15,916	E 2
Gera, 113,108	E 3
Glauchau, 30,927	E 3
Görlitz, 84,658	F 3
Gotha, 59,243	D 3
Greifswald, 53,940	E 1
Greiz, 37,612	E 3
Grevesmühlen, 12,005	D 2
Grimma, 17,100	E 3
Grimmen, 14,571	E 1
Grossenhain, 18,712	E 3
Grossräschen, 12,889	E 3
Guben (Wilhelm-Pieck-Stadt), 32,731	F 3
Güstrow, 36,824	E 2
Hagenow, 11,254	D 2
Halberstadt, 46,669	D 3
Haldensleben, 19,194	D 2
Halle, 241,425	D 3
Havelberg	D 2
Heidenau, 21,315	E 3
Heiligenstadt, 13,931	D 3
Hennigsdorf bei Berlin, 24,853	E 3
Hettstedt, 20,291	D 3
Hildburghausen, 11,372	D 3
Hoyerswerda, 64,904	F 3
Ilmenau, 22,021	D 3
Jena, 99,431	D 3
Johanngeorgenstadt, 10,328	E 3
Jüterbog, 13,477	E 3
Kamenz, 18,221	F 3
Karl-Marx-Stadt, 303,811	E 3
Kleinmachnow, 14,059	E 4
Klingenthal, 13,614	E 3
Königs Wusterhausen, 11,825	E 2
Köpenick, 130,987	F 4
Köthen, 35,451	E 3
Kühlungsborn	D 1
Lauchhammer, 26,939	E 3
Leipzig, 570,972	E 3
Lichtenberg, 192,063	F 4
Limbach-Oberfrohna, 25,706	E 3
Löbau, 18,077	F 3
Lübbcn, 14,224	E 3
Lübbenau, 22,350	F 3
Luckenwalde, 28,544	E 2
Ludwigslust, 13,280	D 2
Magdeburg, 276,089	D 2
Markkleeberg, 22,380	E 3
Meerane, 25,037	E 3
Meiningen, 26,134	D 3
Meissen, 43,561	E 3
Merseburg, 54,269	D 3
Meuselwitz, 13,585	E 3
Mittweida, 19,259	E 3
Mühlhausen (Thomas-Müntzer-Stadt), 44,106	D 3
Nauen, 11,940	E 2
Naumburg, 36,358	D 3
Neubrandenburg, 59,971	E 2
Neuenhagen bei Berlin, 12,603	F 4
Neuruppin, 24,888	E 2
Neustrelitz, 27,074	E 2
Nordhausen, 44,442	D 3
Oelsnitz, 15,084	E 3
Oelsnitz im Erzgebirge, 16,063	E 3
Olbernhau, 13,479	E 3
Oranienburg, 24,452	E 2
Oschatz, 18,974	E 3
Oschersleben, 17,377	D 2
Pankow, 136,527	F 3
Parchim, 22,927	D 2
Pasewalk, 15,099	F 2
Peenemünde	E 1
Perleberg, 15,029	D 2
Pirna, 49,771	E 3
Plauen, 80,353	E 3
Pössneck, 18,648	D 3
Potsdam, 117,236	E 2
Prenzlau, 22,738	E 2
Pritzwalk, 11,887	E 2
Quedlinburg, 29,796	D 3
Radeberg, 18,528	E 3
Radebeul, 38,383	E 3
Rathenow, 32,011	E 2
Reichenbach, 27,440	E 3
Ribnitz-Damgarten, 17,254	E 1
Riesa, 49,989	E 3
Rosslau, 16,520	E 3
Rostock, 210,167	E 1
Rüdersdorf bei Berlin, 11,068	E 2
Rudolstadt, 31,698	D 3
Saalfeld, 33,648	D 3
Salzwedel, 21,741	D 2
Sangerhausen, 32,721	D 3
Sassnitz, 13,857	E 1
Schkeuditz, 15,585	E 3
Schmalkalden, 15,017	D 3
Schmölln, 13,406	E 3
Schneeberg, 20,376	E 3
Schönebeck, 45,197	D 2
Schwedt, 45,729	F 2
Schwerin, 104,984	D 2
Sebnitz, 13,470	F 3
Senftenberg, 29,953	F 3
Sömmerda, 20,712	D 3
Sondershausen, 23,383	D 3
Sonneberg, 29,193	D 3
Spremberg, 22,862	F 3
Stassfurt, 26,225	D 3
Stendal, 39,647	D 2
Stralsund, 72,167	E 1
Strausberg, 21,334	F 2
Suhl, 36,642	D 3
Tangermünde, 12,898	D 2
Teltow, 16,171	E 4
Templin, 11,718	E 2
Teterow, 11,156	E 2
Thale, 17,248	D 3
Torgau, 21,613	E 3
Torgelow, 14,320	F 2
Treptow, 127,448	F 4
Ueckermünde, 11,423	F 2
Waldheim, 11,925	E 3
Waltershausen, 13,893	D 3
Waren, 22,921	E 2
Weida, 11,816	D 3
Weimar, 63,144	D 3
Weissenfels, 43,191	D 3
Weissensee, 78,451	F 3
Weisswasser, 25,910	F 3
Werdau, 22,249	E 3
Wernigerode, 34,658	D 3
Wilhelm-Pieck-Stadt, 32,731	F 3
Wismar, 56,765	D 2
Wittenberg, 51,364	E 3
Wittenberge, 32,907	D 2
Wittstock, 10,799	E 2
Wolgast, 16,384	E 1
Wurzen, 20,501	E 3
Zehdenick, 12,651	E 2
Zeitz, 44,582	E 3
Zella-Mehlis, 16,301	D 3
Zerbst, 19,356	E 3
Zeulenroda, 13,452	D 3
Zittau, 42,298	F 3
Zwickau, 123,069	E 3

OTHER FEATURES

Altmark (reg.), 267,229	D 2
Arkona (cape)	E 1
Baltic (sea)	E 1
Black Elster (riv.)	E 3
Brandenburg (reg.), 7,130,055	E 2
Elbe (riv.)	D 2
Elde (riv.)	D 2
Elster, Black (riv.)	E 3
Elster, White (riv.)	E 3
Erzgebirge (mts.)	E 3
Fichtelberg (mt.)	E 3
Harz (mts.)	D 3
Havel (riv.)	E 2
Lusatia (reg.), 594,784	F 3
Mecklenburg (bay)	D 1
Mecklenburg (reg.), 1,925,669	E 2
Mulde (riv.)	E 3
Neisse (riv.)	F 3
Oder (riv.)	F 2
Peene (riv.)	E 2
Pomerania (reg.), 630,524	E 2
Pomeranian (bay)	F 1
Rhön (mts.)	D 3
Rügen (isl.), 85,651	E 1
Saale (riv.)	D 3
Saxony (reg.), 5,148,714	E 3
Spree (riv.)	F 3
Spreewald (for.)	F 3
Thüringer Wald (for.)	D 3
Thuringia (reg.), 2,686,322	D 3
Ücker (riv.)	E 2
Unstrut (riv.)	D 3
Usedom (isl.)	F 1
Warnow (riv.)	D 2
Werra (riv.)	D 3
White Elster (riv.)	E 3

WEST GERMANY

STATES

Baden-Württemberg, 9,152,700	C 4
Bavaria, 10,810,400	D 4
Berlin (West) (free city), 1,984,800	E 4
Bremen, 716,800	C 2
Hamburg, 1,717,400	D 2
Hesse, 5,549,800	C 3
Lower Saxony, 7,238,500	C 2
North Rhine-Westphalia, 17,129,600	B 3
Rhineland-Palatinate, 3,665,800	B 4
Saarland, 1,096,300	B 4
Schleswig-Holstein, 2,582,400	C 1

CITIES and TOWNS

Aachen, 242,453	B 3
Aalen, 64,735	D 4
Ahaus, 27,126	B 2
Ahlen, 54,214	B 3
Ahrensburg, 24,964	D 2
Alfeld, 24,273	C 2
Alsdorf, 47,473	B 3
Alsfeld, 18,091	C 3
Altena, 26,753	B 3
Altona	C 2
Altötting, 11,010	E 4
Alzey, 15,190	C 4
Amberg, 46,934	D 4
Andernach, 27,132	B 3
Ansbach, 39,117	D 4
Arnsberg, 80,287	C 3
Arolsen, 15,619	C 3
Aschaffenburg, 55,398	C 4
Augsburg, 249,943	D 4
Aurich, 34,194	B 2
Backnang, 29,614	C 4
Bad Driburg, 17,478	C 3
Bad Dürkheim, 16,133	C 4
Bad Ems, 10,487	B 3
Baden-Baden, 49,718	C 4
Bad Gandersheim, 11,614	D 3
Bad Harzburg, 25,786	D 3
Bad Hersfeld, 29,248	C 3
Bad Homburg vor der Höhe, 51,196	C 3
Bad Honnef, 20,903	B 3
Bad Kissingen, 22,279	D 3
Bad Kreuznach, 42,588	B 4
Bad Lauterberg im Harz, 14,715	D 3
Bad Lippspringe, 10,961	C 3
Bad Mergentheim, 19,895	C 4
Bad Münstereifel, 14,340	B 3
Bad Nauheim, 25,916	C 3
Bad Neuenahr-Ahrweiler, 26,371	B 3
Bad Neustadt an der Saale, 11,107	D 3
Bad Oldesloe, 19,640	D 2
Bad Pyrmont, 21,896	C 3
Bad Reichenhall, 13,048	E 5
Bad Salzuflen, 50,924	C 2
Bad Schwartau, 18,696	D 2
Bad Segeberg, 13,320	D 2
Bad Tölz, 12,458	D 5
Bad Vilbel, 25,012	C 3
Bad Waldsee, 14,296	C 5
Bad Wildungen, 15,418	C 3
Bad Wimpfen, 5,536	C 4
Baiersbronn, 14,845	C 4
Balingen, 29,310	C 4
Bamberg, 74,236	D 4
Bassum, 14,113	C 2
Bayreuth, 67,035	D 4
Bayrischzell, 1,639	E 5
Bebra, 15,740	C 3
Bendorf, 15,943	B 3
Bensheim, 32,653	C 4
Bentheim, 13,681	B 2
Berchtesgaden, 8,558	E 5
Bergisch Gladbach, 99,517	B 3
Berleburg (Bad Berleburg), 20,415	C 3
Berlin (West), 1,984,837	E 4
Biberach an der Riss, 28,891	C 4
Bielefeld, 316,058	C 2
Bietigheim-Bissingen, 34,042	C 4
Bingen, 24,541	B 4
Birkenfeld, 5,883	B 4
Blaubeuren, 11,652	C 4
Böblingen, 40,547	C 4
Bocholt, 65,460	B 3
Bochum, 414,842	B 3
Bonn (cap.), 283,711	B 3
Boppard, 16,888	B 3
Borghorst, 17,238	B 2
Borken, 30,212	B 3
Bottrop, 101,495	B 3
Brake, 18,089	C 2
Bramsche, 24,119	B 2
Braunschweig (Brunswick), 268,519	D 2
Breisach am Rhein, 9,230	B 4
Bremen, 572,969	C 2
Bremerhaven, 143,836	C 2
Bremervörde, 17,565	C 2
Bretten, 22,140	C 4
Brilon, 24,595	C 3
Bruchsal, 38,929	C 4
Brühl, 44,305	B 3
Brunsbüttel, 11,451	C 2
Brunswick, 268,519	D 2
Buchholz in der Nordheide, 25,713	C 2
Bückeburg, 21,393	C 2
Büdingen, 16,845	C 3
Bühl, 21,596	C 4
Büren, 17,352	C 3
Burg auf Fehmarn, 5,874	D 1
Burghausen, 16,892	E 4
Burgsteinfurt, 31,367	B 2
Butzbach, 20,592	C 3
Buxtehude, 30,249	C 2
Celle, 74,347	D 2
Cham, 12,423	E 4
Charlottenburg, 201,732	E 4
Clausthal-Zellerfeld, 16,690	D 3
Cloppenburg, 19,757	B 2
Coburg, 46,244	D 3
Coesfeld, 30,617	B 3
Cologne, 1,013,771	B 3
Crailsheim, 24,506	D 4
Cuxhaven, 60,353	C 2
Dachau, 33,207	D 4
Dahlem	E 4
Darmstadt, 137,018	C 4
Deggendorf, 25,188	E 4
Delmenhorst, 71,488	C 2
Detmold, 65,629	C 3
Diepholz, 14,201	C 2
Dillenburg, 14,068	C 3
Dillingen an der Donau, 11,601	D 4
Dingolfing, 13,325	E 4
Dinkelsbühl, 10,034	D 4
Donaueschingen, 17,578	C 5
Donauwörth, 17,077	D 4
Dorsten, 65,718	B 3
Dortmund, 630,609	B 3
Duderstadt, 23,255	D 3
Dudweiler, 27,877	B 4
Duisburg, 591,635	B 3
Dülmen, 37,013	B 3
Düren, 87,774	B 3
Düsseldorf, 664,336	B 3
Eberbach, 15,834	C 4
Ebingen, 22,594	C 4
Eckernförde, 22,938	D 1
Ehingen, 21,600	C 4
Eichstätt, 13,080	D 4
Einbeck, 29,821	C 3
Eiserfeld, 22,346	C 3
Ellwangen, 21,994	D 4
Elmshorn, 41,355	C 2
Emden, 53,509	B 2
Emmendingen, 24,722	B 4
Emmerich, 29,113	B 3
Erlangen, 100,671	D 4
Eschwege, 24,882	C 3
Eschweiler, 53,603	B 3
Espelkamp, 22,670	C 2
Essen, 677,568	B 3
Esslingen am Neckar, 95,298	C 4
Ettlingen, 35,159	C 4
Euskirchen, 43,558	B 3
Eutin, 17,701	D 1
Fellbach, 42,501	C 4
Flensburg, 93,213	C 1
Forchheim, 23,430	D 4
Frankenberg-Eder, 15,337	C 3
Frankenthal, 43,684	C 4
Frankfurt am Main, 636,157	C 3
Frechen, 41,453	B 3
Freiburg im Breisgau, 175,371	B 5
Freising, 31,524	D 4
Freudenstadt, 19,454	C 4
Friedberg, 24,762	C 3
Friedrichshafen, 51,544	C 5
Fritzlar, 15,079	C 3
Fulda, 58,976	C 3
Fürstenfeldbruck, 27,194	D 4
Fürth, 101,639	D 4
Füssen, 10,506	D 5
Gaggenau, 28,846	C 4
Garmisch-Partenkirchen, 26,831	D 5
Gatow	E 4
Geesthacht, 24,745	D 2
Geislingen an der Steige, 28,693	C 4
Geldern, 24,082	B 3
Gelnhausen, 17,889	C 3
Gelsenkirchen, 322,584	B 3
Geretsried, 17,330	D 5
Germersheim, 12,041	C 4
Gerolstein, 6,857	B 3
Giessen, 75,481	C 3
Gifhorn, 31,635	D 2
Glückstadt, 12,159	C 2
Goch, 28,213	B 3
Göggingen, 15,980	D 4
Göppingen, 54,365	C 4
Goslar, 53,957	D 3
Göttingen, 123,797	D 3
Grevenbroich, 56,392	B 3
Griesheim, 18,548	C 4
Gronau, 40,527	B 2
Gummersbach, 49,316	B 3
Günzburg, 13,528	D 4
Gunzenhausen, 13,565	D 4
Gütersloh, 77,128	C 3
Haar, 18,824	D 4
Hagen, 229,224	B 3
Haltern, 29,750	B 3
Hamburg, 1,717,383	D 2
Hameln, 61,066	C 2
Hamm, 172,210	B 3
Hammelburg, 12,350	C 3
Hanau, 86,676	C 3
Hannover, 552,955	C 2
Harburg-Wilhelmsburg	C 2
Hassloch, 17,752	C 4
Haunstetten, 21,810	D 4
Hechingen, 15,926	C 4
Heide, 21,918	C 1
Heidelberg, 129,368	C 4
Heidenheim an der Brenz, 49,943	D 4
Heilbronn, 113,177	C 4
Helmstedt, 28,095	D 2
Hennef, 27,815	B 3
Herford, 64,385	C 2
Herne, 190,561	B 3
Hildesheim, 105,290	D 2
Hockenheim, 16,890	C 4
Hof, 54,357	D 3
Hofgeismar, 13,380	C 3
Holzminden, 23,650	C 3
Homburg, 41,861	B 4
Horn-Bad Meinberg, 16,927	C 3
Höxter, 32,759	C 3
Hünfeld, 13,873	C 3
Hürth, 51,692	B 3
Husum, 24,984	C 1
Hüttental, 39,561	C 3
Ibbenbüren, 42,202	B 2
Idar-Oberstein, 37,179	B 4
Immenstadt im Allgäu, 13,720	C 5
Ingolstadt, 88,500	D 4
Iserlohn, 96,174	B 3
Isny im Allgäu, 12,367	D 5
Itzehoe, 35,077	C 2
Jever, 12,096	B 2
Jülich, 31,564	B 3
Kaiserslautern, 100,886	B 4
Karlsruhe, 280,448	C 4
Kassel, 205,534	C 3
Kaufbeuren, 42,224	D 5
Kehl, 29,861	B 4
Kelheim, 11,996	D 4
Kempten, 56,944	D 5
Kevelaer, 20,971	B 3
Kiel, 262,164	D 1
Kirchheim unter Teck, 31,666	C 4
Kitzingen, 19,116	C 4
Kleve, 44,043	B 3
Koblenz, 118,394	B 3
Köln (Cologne), 1,013,771	B 3
Königswinter, 34,586	B 3
Konstanz, 70,152	C 5
Korbach, 22,998	C 3
Kornwestheim, 27,771	C 4
Krefeld, 228,463	B 3
Kronach, 11,538	D 3
Kulmbach, 25,711	D 3
Lage, 31,724	C 3
Lahnstein (Oberlahnstein), 19,725	B 3
Lahr, 35,570	B 4
Lampertheim, 31,993	C 4
Landau in der Pfalz, 37,661	C 4
Landsberg am Lech, 15,862	D 4
Landshut, 55,858	E 4
Langen, 30,227	C 4
Langenhagen, 47,092	C 2
Lauenburg an der Elbe, 11,077	D 2
Lauf an der Pegnitz, 19,443	D 4
Lauingen, 8,778	D 4
Lauterbach, 15,077	C 3
Leer, 32,785	B 2
Lehrte, 38,272	D 2
Lemgo, 39,664	C 2
Lengerich, 20,836	B 2
Leverkusen, 165,947	B 3
Lichtenfels, 13,719	D 3
Limburg an der Lahn, 28,606	C 3
Lindau, 23,930	C 5
Lingen, 43,785	B 2
Lippstadt, 63,040	C 3
Lohr am Main, 16,435	C 4
Lörrach, 44,179	B 5

(continued on following page)

GERMANY Before World War I 1871-1914

GERMANY Between Wars 1919-1937

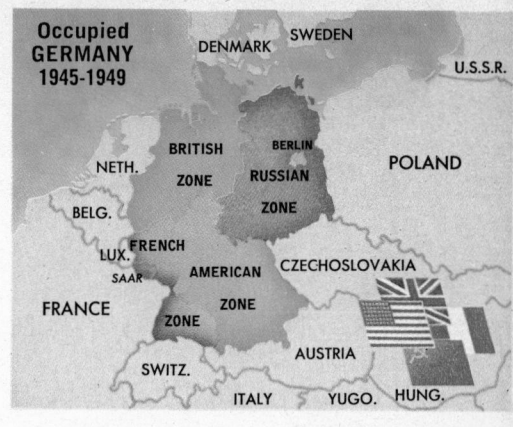

Occupied GERMANY 1945-1949

Lübeck, 232,270 ... D 2
Lüdenscheid, 76,213 ... B 3
Ludwigsburg, 83,622 ... C 4
Ludwigshafen am Rhein, 170,374 .. C 4
Lüneburg, 64,586 ... D 2
Lünen, 85,685 ... B 3
Mainz, 183,880 ... C 4
Mannheim, 314,086 ... C 4
Marbach am Neckar, 12,131 ... C 4
Marburg an der Lahn, 72,458 ... C 3
Marktredwitz, 16,404 ... D 3
Marl, 91,930 ... B 3
Mayen, 21,018 ... B 3
Mechernich, 21,498 ... B 3
Melle, 41,339 ... C 2
Melsungen, 13,444 ... C 3
Memmingen, 34,612 ... D 5
Meppen, 27,308 ... B 2
Merzig, 30,197 ... B 4
Meschede, 32,472 ... C 3
Metzingen, 19,224 ... C 4
Michelstadt, 13,591 ... C 4
Minden, 78,887 ... C 2
Mittenwald, 8,831 ... D 5
Mölln, 15,780 ... D 2
Mönchengladbach, 261,367 ... B 3
Monschau, 10,910 ... B 3
Moosburg an der Isar, 12,196 ... D 4
Mosbach, 23,663 ... C 4
Mühldorf am Inn, 12,638 ... E 4
Mülheim an der Ruhr, 189,259 .. B 3
Müllheim, 12,183 ... B 5
München (Munich), 1,314,865 ... D 4
Münden, 27,018 ... C 3
Munich, 1,314,865 ... D 4
Münster, 264,546 ... B 3
Nagold, 19,047 ... C 4
Neckarsulm, 20,112 ... C 4
Neheim-Hüsten, 36,373 ... C 3
Neuburg an der Donau, 19,400 ... C 4
Neu-Isenburg, 35,631 ... C 3
Neumarkt in der Oberpfalz, 29,713 ... D 4
Neumünster, 84,777 ... C 1
Neunkirchen, 54,992 ... B 4
Neuss, 148,198 ... B 3

Neustadt (Titisee-Neustadt), 11,129 ... C 5
Neustadt an der Weinstrasse, 51,011 ... B 4
Neustadt bei Coburg, 12,665 ... D 3
Neustadt in Holstein, 15,333 ... D 1
Neu-Ulm, 31,660 ... D 4
Neuwied, 62,029 ... B 3
Nienburg, 30,978 ... C 2
Norden, 24,207 ... B 2
Nordenham, 31,457 ... C 2
Nordhorn, 49,598 ... B 2
Nördlingen, 16,480 ... C 4
Northeim, 32,665 ... C 3
Nuremberg, 499,060 ... D 4
Nürnberg (Nuremberg), 499,060 ... D 4
Nürtingen, 34,333 ... C 4
Oberammergau, 4,704 ... D 5
Oberhausen, 237,147 ... B 3
Oberlahnstein, 19,725 ... B 3
Oberstdorf, 11,687 ... D 5
Oberursel, 39,802 ... C 4
Ochsenfurt, 11,223 ... D 4
Offenbach am Main, 115,251 ... C 3
Offenburg, 51,553 ... B 4
Oldenburg, 134,706 ... C 2
Oldenburg in Holstein, 9,201 ... D 1
Opladen, 42,789 ... B 3
Osnabrück, 161,671 ... C 2
Osterholz-Scharmbeck, 22,734 ... C 2
Osterode am Harz, 29,668 ... C 3
Paderborn, 103,705 ... C 3
Papenburg, 27,039 ... B 2
Passau, 50,920 ... E 4
Peine, 49,450 ... C 2
Penzberg, 11,100 ... D 5
Pfaffenhofen an der Ilm, 13,684 ... D 4
Pforzheim, 108,635 ... C 4
Pfullingen, 16,195 ... C 4
Pinneberg, 36,844 ... C 2
Pirmasens, 53,651 ... B 4
Plettenberg, 29,273 ... C 3
Porz am Rhein, 74,915 ... B 3
Preetz, 15,305 ... D 1
Puttgarden, ... D 1
Radolfzell, 23,274 ... C 5

Rastatt, 38,030 ... C 4
Rastede, 16,905 ... C 2
Ratingen, 86,028 ... B 3
Ratzeburg, 12,189 ... D 2
Ravensburg, 42,725 ... C 5
Recklinghausen, 122,437 ... B 3
Regensburg, 131,886 ... E 4
Remagen, 14,627 ... B 3
Remscheid, 133,145 ... B 3
Rendsburg, 34,407 ... C 1
Reutlingen, 95,289 ... C 4
Rheine, 71,539 ... B 2
Rheinfelden, 27,500 ... B 5
Rheydt, 100,077 ... B 3
Rinteln, 25,595 ... C 2
Rosenheim, 38,419 ... D 5
Rotenburg, 19,155 ... C 2
Rotenburg an der Fulda, 14,438 ... C 3
Roth bei Nürnberg, 17,782 ... D 4
Rothenburg ob der Tauber, 11,609 ... D 4
Rottenburg am Neckar, 30,583 ... C 4
Rottweil, 24,534 ... C 4
Rüsselsheim, 62,067 ... C 4
Saarbrücken, 205,336 ... B 4
Saarlouis, 39,974 ... B 4
Säckingen, 13,956 ... C 5
Sankt Goar, 3,511 ... B 3
Sankt Ingbert, 43,263 ... B 4
Sankt Wendel, 27,558 ... B 4
Saulgau, 15,403 ... C 5
Schleswig, 30,974 ... C 1
Schlüchtern, 13,801 ... C 3
Schöneberg, 169,835 ... E 4
Schöningen, 16,348 ... D 2
Schramberg, 19,677 ... C 4
Schwabach, 33,136 ... D 4
Schwäbisch Gmünd, 56,422 ... C 4
Schwäbisch Hall, 32,129 ... C 4
Schwandorf im Bayern, 22,547 ... E 4
Schweinfurt, 56,164 ... D 3
Schwelm, 31,850 ... B 3
Schwenningen-Villingen, 80,646 ... C 4
Schwetzingen, 18,286 ... C 4
Seesen, 23,577 ... C 3

Selb, 16,723 ... E 3
Sennestadt, 20,187 ... C 3
Siegburg, 34,943 ... B 3
Siegen, 116,552 ... C 3
Sigmaringen, 15,437 ... C 4
Sindelfingen, 54,134 ... C 4
Singen, 45,566 ... C 5
Soest, 40,308 ... C 3
Solingen, 171,810 ... B 3
Soltau, 19,949 ... C 2
Sonthofen, 17,821 ... D 5
Spandau, 197,687 ... E 4
Speyer, 44,471 ... C 4
Springe, 30,968 ... C 2
Stade, 42,097 ... C 2
Stadthagen, 23,003 ... C 2
Starnberg, 13,774 ... D 5
Stolberg, 57,379 ... B 3
Straubing, 43,774 ... E 4
Stuttgart, 600,421 ... C 4
Sulzbach-Rosenberg, 18,596 ... D 4
Tailfingen, 17,278 ... C 4
Tegel, ... E 3
Telgte, 15,165 ... C 3
Tempelhof, 159,730 ... F 4
Timmendorfer Strand, 10,690 ... D 1
Traunstein, 14,088 ... E 5
Travemünde, ... D 1
Treuchtlingen, 11,939 ... D 4
Trier, 100,338 ... B 4
Tübingen, 71,348 ... C 4
Tuttlingen, 32,342 ... C 5
Überlingen, 17,735 ... C 5
Uelzen, 37,550 ... D 2
Uetersen, 16,330 ... C 2
Ulm, 98,237 ... C 4
Uslar, 17,251 ... C 3
Varel, 24,435 ... C 2
Vechta, 21,786 ... C 2
Verden, 24,247 ... C 2
Viersen, 84,220 ... B 3
Villingen-Schwenningen, 80,646 ... B 4
Völklingen, 47,271 ... B 4
Waldkirch, 19,009 ... B 4
Waldkraiburg, 20,140 ... E 4
Waldshut-Tiengen, 22,046 ... C 5
Walldürn, 10,819 ... C 4

Walsrode, 23,423 ... C 2
Wangen im Allgäu, 23,127 ... C 5
Wanne-Eickel, 99,156 ... B 3
Warburg, 22,150 ... C 3
Warendorf, 32,273 ... B 3
Wedel, 30,045 ... C 2
Weiden in der Oberpfalz, 42,697 ... D 4
Weilburg, 12,652 ... C 3
Weilheim im Oberbayern, 15,347 .. D 5
Weingarten, 21,143 ... C 5
Weinheim, 41,005 ... C 4
Weissenburg im Bayern, 16,083 .. D 4
Wertheim, 20,942 ... C 4
Wesel, 56,584 ... B 3
Westerland, 9,652 ... C 1
Westerstede, 16,977 ... B 2
Wetzlar, 35,308 ... C 3
Wiedenbrück (Rheda-Wiedenbrück), 37,371 ... B 3
Wiehl, 19,004 ... B 3
Wiesbaden, 250,592 ... C 3
Wildbad im Schwarzwald, 11,611 .. C 4
Wildeshausen, 12,055 ... C 2
Wilhelmshaven, 103,417 ... B 2
Witten, 108,771 ... B 3
Witzenhausen, 16,877 ... C 3
Wolfenbüttel, 51,386 ... D 2
Wolfsburg, 126,298 ... D 2
Worms, 75,732 ... C 4
Wunstorf, 36,795 ... C 2
Wuppertal, 405,369 ... B 3
Würzburg, 112,584 ... C 4
Xanten, 15,688 ... B 3
Zirndorf, 13,661 ... D 4
Zülpich, 16,171 ... B 3
Zweibrücken, 35,978 ... B 4
Zwischenahn, 22,581 ... C 2

OTHER FEATURES

Aller (riv.) ... C 2
Allgäu (reg.), 326,220 ... D 5
Altmühl (riv.) ... D 4
Ammersee (lake) ... D 4

Amrum (isl.), 1,956 ... C 1
Baltrum (isl.), 661 ... B 2
Bavarian (for.) ... E 4
Bavarian Alps (range) ... D 5
Black (for.) ... B 4
Bodensee (Constance) (lake) ... C 5
Bohemian (for.) ... E 4
Borkum (isl.), 8,495 ... B 2
Breisgau (reg.), 667,285 ... B 5
Chiemsee (lake) ... E 5
Constance (lake) ... C 5
Danube (riv.) ... C 4
Donau (Danube) (riv.) ... C 4
East Friesland (reg.), 579,756 ... B 2
East Frisian (isls.), 20,451 ... B 2
Eder (res.) ... C 3
Elbe (riv.) ... D 2
Ems (riv.) ... B 2
Fehmarn (isl.), 12,455 ... D 1
Feldberg (mt.) ... B 5
Fichtelgebirge (range) ... D 3
Föhr (isl.), 10,251 ... C 1
Franconian Jura (range) ... D 4
Frisian, East (isls.), 20,451 ... B 2
Frisian, North (isls.), 37,946 ... B 1
Grosser Arber (mt.) ... E 4
Halligen (isls.), 4,864 ... C 1
Hardt (mts.) ... B 4
Harz (mts.) ... D 2
Hase (riv.) ... B 2
Hegau (reg.), 128,257 ... C 5
Helgoland (bay) ... C 1
Helgoland (isl.), 2,377 ... B 1
Hunsrück (mts.) ... B 4
Hunte (riv.) ... C 2
Iller (riv.) ... D 4
Inn (riv.) ... E 4
Isar (riv.) ... D 4
Kaiserstuhl (mt.) ... B 5
Kiel (bay) ... D 1
Kiel (Nord-Ostsee) (canal) ... C 1
Königssee (lake) ... E 5
Lahn (riv.) ... C 3
Langeoog (isl.), 2,535 ... B 2
Lech (riv.) ... D 4

Leine (riv.) ... C 2
Lippe (riv.) ... C 3
Lüneburger Heide (dist.) ... C 2
Main (riv.) ... C 4
Mecklenburg (bay) ... D 1
Mosel (riv.) ... B 3
Naab (riv.) ... D 4
Neckar (riv.) ... C 4
Norderney (isl.), 8,307 ... B 2
Nord-Ostsee (canal) ... C 1
Nordstrand (isl.), 2,729 ... C 1
North (sea) ... B 2
North Friesland (reg.), 156,415 ... C 1
North Frisian (isls.), 37,946 ... B 1
Odenwald (for.) ... C 4
Oker (riv.) ... D 2
Pellworm (isl.), 1,261 ... C 1
Regen (riv.) ... E 4
Regnitz (riv.) ... D 4
Rhine (riv.) ... B 3
Rhön (mts.) ... D 3
Ruhr (riv.) ... B 3
Saar (riv.) ... B 4
Sauer (riv.) ... B 4
Sauerland (reg.), 576,236 ... B 3
Schneeberg (mt.) ... D 3
Schwarzwald (Black) (for.) ... B 4
Spessart (range) ... C 4
Spiekeroog (isl.), 732 ... B 2
Starnberger (lake) ... D 5
Swabian Jura (range) ... C 4
Sylt (isl.), 20,875 ... C 1
Tauber (riv.) ... C 4
Taunus (range) ... C 3
Tegernsee (lake) ... D 5
Teutoburger Wald (for.) ... C 2
Vogelsberg (mts.) ... C 3
Walchensee (lake) ... D 5
Wangerooge (isl.), 1,700 ... B 2
Watzmann (mt.) ... E 5
Weser (riv.) ... C 2
Westerwald (for.) ... B 3
Würmsee (Starnbergersee) (lake) ... D 5
Zugspitze (mt.) ... D 5

Agriculture, Industry and Resources

DOMINANT LAND USE

- Wheat, Sugar Beets
- Cereals (chiefly rye, oats, barley)
- Potatoes, Rye
- Dairy, Livestock
- Mixed Cereals, Dairy
- Truck Farming
- Grapes, Fruit
- Forests

MAJOR MINERAL OCCURRENCES

Ag Silver
Ba Barite
C Coal
Cu Copper
Fe Iron Ore
G Natural Gas
Gr Graphite
K Potash

Lg Lignite
Mg Magnesium
Na Salt
O Petroleum
Pb Lead
U Uranium
Zn Zinc

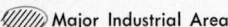 Water Power

Major Industrial Areas

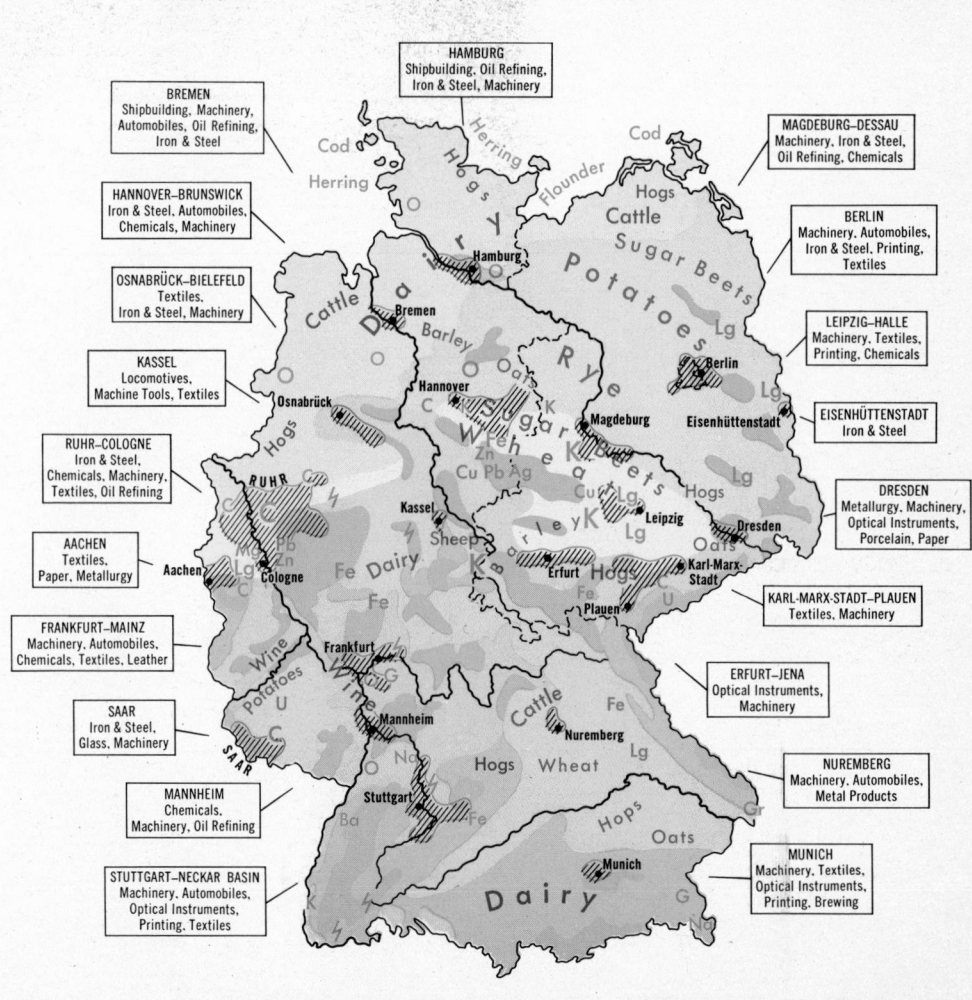

HAMBURG — Shipbuilding, Oil Refining, Iron & Steel, Machinery

BREMEN — Shipbuilding, Machinery, Automobiles, Oil Refining, Iron & Steel

MAGDEBURG–DESSAU — Machinery, Iron & Steel, Oil Refining, Chemicals

HANNOVER–BRUNSWICK — Iron & Steel, Automobiles, Chemicals, Machinery

BERLIN — Machinery, Automobiles, Iron & Steel, Printing, Textiles

OSNABRÜCK–BIELEFELD — Textiles, Iron & Steel, Machinery

LEIPZIG–HALLE — Machinery, Textiles, Printing, Chemicals

KASSEL — Locomotives, Machine Tools, Textiles

EISENHÜTTENSTADT — Iron & Steel

RUHR–COLOGNE — Iron & Steel, Chemicals, Machinery, Textiles, Oil Refining

DRESDEN — Metallurgy, Machinery, Optical Instruments, Porcelain, Paper

AACHEN — Textiles, Paper, Metallurgy

KARL-MARX-STADT–PLAUEN — Textiles, Machinery

FRANKFURT–MAINZ — Machinery, Automobiles, Chemicals, Textiles, Leather

ERFURT–JENA — Optical Instruments, Machinery

SAAR — Iron & Steel, Glass, Machinery

NUREMBERG — Machinery, Automobiles, Metal Products

MANNHEIM — Chemicals, Machinery, Oil Refining

MUNICH — Machinery, Textiles, Optical Instruments, Printing, Brewing

STUTTGART–NECKAR BASIN — Machinery, Automobiles, Optical Instruments, Printing, Textiles

NETHERLANDS
REA 15,892 sq. mi.
PULATION 13,800,000
PITALS The Hague, Amsterdam
RGEST CITY Amsterdam
GHEST POINT Vaalserberg 1,056 ft.
ONETARY UNIT guilder (florin)
AJOR LANGUAGE Dutch
AJOR RELIGIONS Protestantism, Roman Catholicism

BELGIUM
AREA 11,781 sq. mi.
POPULATION 9,813,000
CAPITAL Brussels
LARGEST CITY Brussels (greater)
HIGHEST POINT Botrange 2,277 ft.
MONETARY UNIT Belgian franc
MAJOR LANGUAGES French (Walloon), Flemish
MAJOR RELIGION Roman Catholicism

LUXEMBOURG
AREA 999 sq. mi.
POPULATION 358,000
CAPITAL Luxembourg
LARGEST CITY Luxembourg
HIGHEST POINT Ardennes Plateau 1,825 ft.
MONETARY UNIT Luxembourg franc
MAJOR LANGUAGES Luxembourgeois (Letzeburgisch), French, German
MAJOR RELIGION Roman Catholicism

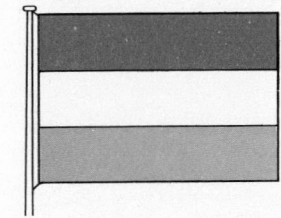

BELGIUM

PROVINCES

ntwerp, 1,533,249 . . . F 6
abant, 2,176,373 . . . F 7
ast Flanders, 1,310,117 . . . D 7
ainault, 1,317,453 . . . D 7
ège, 1,008,905 . . . H 7
mburg, 652,547 . . . G 7
uxembourg, 217,310 . . . G 9
amur, 380,561 . . . F 8
est Flanders, 1,054,429 . . . B 7

☆CITIES and TOWNS

alst, 46,659 . . . D 7
alter, 9,173 . . . C 6
arlen (Arlon), 13,745 . . . H 9
arschot, 12,474 . . . F 7
at (Ath), 11,842 . . . D 7
dinkerke, 2,577 . . . A 6
ken, 8,677 . . . G 7
lost (Aalst), 46,659 . . . D 7
may, 7,617 . . . G 7
ndenne, 8,091 . . . G 8
Anderlecht, 103,796 . . . B 9
Anderlues, 12,176 . . . E 8
Antoing, 3,426 . . . C 7
Antwerp, 224,543 . . . E 6
Antwerp, *928,000 . . . E 6
Ant2erpen (Antwerp), 224,543 . . . E 6
Ardooie, 7,081 . . . C 7
Arendonk, 9,919 . . . G 6
Arlon, 13,745 . . . H 9
As, 5,496 . . . H 6
Asse, 6,583 . . . E 7
Assesse, 1,147 . . . G 8
Ath, 11,842 . . . D 7
Athus, 7,445 . . . H 9
Audenarde (Oudenaarde), 26,615 . . D 7
Auderghem, 34,546 . . . C 9
Autelbas, 1,501 . . . H 9
Auvelais, 8,287 . . . F 8
Aywaille, 3,850 . . . H 8
Baerle-Duc, 2,121 . . . F 6
Balen, 15,110 . . . G 6
Barvaux, 1,934 . . . H 8
Basècles, 4,164 . . . D 7
Bastenaken (Bastogne), 6,816 . . . H 9
Bastogne, 6,816 . . . H 9
Beaumont, 1,790 . . . E 8
Beauraing, 2,755 . . . F 8
Berchem, 50,241 . . . F 6
Berchem-Sainte-Agathe, 19,087 . . B 9
Bergen (Mons), 59,362 . . . E 8
Bertrix, 4,562 . . . G 9
Beveren, 15,913 . . . E 6
Bilzen, 7,178 . . . G 7
Binche, 10,098 . . . E 8
Blankenberge, 13,969 . . . C 6
Bocholt, 6,497 . . . H 6
Boom, 16,584 . . . E 6
Borgerhout, 49,002 . . . E 6
Borgloon, 3,412 . . . G 7
Borgworm (Waremme), 10,956 . . G 7
Bouillon, 2,944 . . . G 9
Bourg-Léopold (Leopoldsburg), 9,593 . . . G 6
Boussu, 11,474 . . . D 8
Bovigny, 972 . . . H 8
Braine-l'Alleud, 18,531 . . . E 7
Braine-le-Comte, 11,957 . . . D 7
Bredene, 9,244 . . . B 6
Bree, 10,389 . . . H 6
Bruges, 117,220 . . . C 6
Brugge (Bruges), 117,220 . . . C 6
Brussels (cap.), *1,054,970 . . . C 9
Bruxelles (Brussels) (cap.), *1,054,970 . . . C 9
Charleroi, 23,689 . . . E 8
Charleroi, *458,000 . . . E 8
Châtelet, 14,752 . . . F 8
Châtelineau, 19,004 . . . F 8
Chièvres, 3,283 . . . D 7
Chimay, 3,288 . . . E 8
Ciney, 7,536 . . . G 8
Comblain-au-Pont, 3,582 . . . G 8
Comines, 8,192 . . . B 7
Couillet, 14,284 . . . E 8
Courcelles, 17,015 . . . E 8
Courtrai, 44,961 . . . C 7
Couvin, 4,234 . . . F 8
Cul-des-Sarts, 910 . . . E 9
Deinze, 16,711 . . . D 7
Denderleeuw, 9,925 . . . E 7
Dendermonde, 22,119 . . . E 6
De Panne, 6,985 . . . B 6
Dessel, 7,505 . . . G 6
Deurne, 80,766 . . . F 6
Diegem, 4,906 . . . C 9
Diest, 10,799 . . . F 7
Diksmuide, 6,669 . . . B 6
Dilbeek, 15,108 . . . B 9
Dinant, 9,747 . . . G 8
Dison, 8,466 . . . H 7
Dixmude (Diksmuide), 6,669 . . . B 6
Doel, 1,332 . . . E 6
Doornik (Tournai), 32,794 . . . C 7
Dour, 10,059 . . . D 8
Drogenbos, 4,840 . . . B 10
Drongen, 9,120 . . . D 6
Duffel, 13,802 . . . F 6
Ecaussinnes-d'Enghien, 6,630 . . . E 7
Edingen (Enghien), 4,115 . . . D 7
Eeklo, 19,144 . . . D 6
Eernegem, 5,778 . . . B 6
Eigenbrakel (Braine-l'Alleud), 18,531 . . . E 7
Ekeren, 27,648 . . . E 6
Ellezelles, 3,556 . . . D 7
Enghien, 4,115 . . . D 7
Ensival, 5,266 . . . H 7
Erquelinnes, 4,471 . . . E 8
Esneux, 6,183 . . . H 7
Essen, 10,795 . . . F 6
Etalle, 1,185 . . . H 9
Etterbeek, 51,030 . . . B 9
Eupen, 14,879 . . . J 7
Evere, 26,957 . . . C 9
Evergem, 12,886 . . . D 6
Flémalle-Haute, 8,135 . . . G 7
Fleurus, 8,523 . . . F 8
Florennes, 4,107 . . . F 8
Florenville, 2,529 . . . G 9
Forest, 55,135 . . . B 9
Fosses-la-Ville, 3,972 . . . F 8
Frameries, 11,224 . . . D 8
Frasnes-lez-Buissenal, 2,694 . . . D 7
Furnes (Veurne), 9,496 . . . B 6
Ganshoren, 21,147 . . . B 9
Gaurain-Ramecroix, 3,507 . . . D 7
Gedinne, 1,073 . . . F 9
Geel, 29,346 . . . F 6
Geldenaken (Jodoigne), 4,132 . . . F 7
Gembloux, 11,249 . . . F 7
Gemmenich, 2,501 . . . H 7
Genk, 57,913 . . . H 7
Gent (Ghent), 148,860 . . . D 6
Gentbrugge, 22,214 . . . D 6
Geraardsbergen, 17,533 . . . D 7
Ghent, 148,860 . . . D 6
Ghent, *477,000 . . . D 6
Gilly, 23,241 . . . E 8
Gosselies, 10,724 . . . E 8
Grammont (Geraardsbergen), 17,533 . . . D 7
Haacht, 4,436 . . . F 7
Hal (Halle), 20,017 . . . E 7
Halen, 5,322 . . . G 7
Halle, 20,017 . . . E 7
Hamme, 17,559 . . . E 6
Hamont, 6,893 . . . H 6
Hannuit (Hannut), 7,232 . . . G 7
Hannut, 7,232 . . . G 7
Harelbeke, 18,498 . . . C 7
Hasselt, 39,663 . . . G 7
Havelange, 1,632 . . . G 8
Heer, 569 . . . F 8
Heist-Knokke, 27,582 . . . C 6
Heist-op-den-Berg, 13,472 . . . F 6
Herbeumont, 573 . . . G 9
Herentals, 18,639 . . . F 6
Herselt, 7,412 . . . F 6
Herstal, 29,600 . . . H 7
Herve, 4,118 . . . H 7
Hoboken, 33,693 . . . E 6
Hoei (Huy), 12,736 . . . G 8
Hoeselt, 6,884 . . . G 7
Hoogstraten, 4,381 . . . F 6
Hornu, 10,712 . . . D 8
Houffalize, 1,315 . . . H 8
Huy, 12,736 . . . G 8
Ieper, 20,825 . . . B 7
Ingelmunster, 10,245 . . . C 7
Ixelles, 86,450 . . . C 9
Izegem, 22,928 . . . C 7
Jambes, 15,840 . . . F 8
Jemappes, 18,632 . . . D 8
Jemeppe, 12,243 . . . G 7
Jette, 40,013 . . . B 9
Jodoigne, 4,132 . . . F 7
Jumet, 28,029 . . . E 8
Kain, 5,032 . . . C 7
Kalmthout, 12,724 . . . F 6
Kapellen, 13,352 . . . E 6
Kessel-Lo, 23,104 . . . F 7
Knokke-Heist, 27,582 . . . C 6
Koekelare, 7,807 . . . B 6
Koekelberg, 17,570 . . . B 9
Koersel, 11,173 . . . G 6
Kontich, 14,432 . . . E 6
Kortemark, 5,904 . . . C 6
Kortrijk (Courtrai), 44,961 . . . C 7
Kraainem, 11,390 . . . C 9
La Louvière, 23,310 . . . E 8
La Louvière, *113,259 . . . E 8
Lanaken, 8,659 . . . H 7
Landen, 5,740 . . . G 7
Langemark, 5,457 . . . B 7
La Roche-en-Ardenne, 1,908 . . . G 8
Lede, 10,316 . . . D 7
Ledeberg, 10,338 . . . D 7
Lens, 1,758 . . . D 7
Leopoldsburg, 9,593 . . . G 6
Lessen (Lessines), 8,906 . . . D 7
Lessines, 8,906 . . . D 7
Leuven (Louvain), 30,623 . . . F 7
Leuze, 7,185 . . . D 7
Libramont, 2,975 . . . G 9
Lichtervelde, 7,459 . . . C 6
Liedekerke, 10,482 . . . D 7
Liège, 145,573 . . . H 7
Liège, *622,000 . . . H 7
Lier, 28,416 . . . F 6
Lierneux, 2,740 . . . H 8
Lierre (Lier), 28,416 . . . F 6
Limbourg, 3,762 . . . J 7
Limburg (Limbourg), 3,762 . . . J 7
Linkebeek, 4,265 . . . 1 0
Lokeren, 26,740 . . . D 6
Lommel, 21,984 . . . G 6
Looz (Borgloon), 3,412 . . . G 7
Louvain, 30,623 . . . F 7
Luik (Liège), 145,573 . . . H 7
Maaseik, 8,622 . . . H 6
Machelen, 7,057 . . . C 9
Maldegem, 14,474 . . . C 6
Malines (Mechelen), 65,466 . . . F 6
Malmédy, 6,464 . . . J 8
Marche-en-Famenne, 4,567 . . . G 8
Marchin, 4,206 . . . G 8
Marcinelle, 27,228 . . . E 8
Mariembourg, 1,783 . . . E 8
Martelange, 1,526 . . . H 9
Mechelen, 65,466 . . . F 6
Meerhout, 8,567 . . . G 6
Meerle, 2,911 . . . F 6
Melsbroek, 2,027 . . . D 9
Menen, 22,037 . . . C 7
Menin (Menen), 22,037 . . . C 7
Merchtem, 8,998 . . . E 7
Merelbeke, 13,837 . . . D 7
Merksem, 39,768 . . . E 6
Merksplas, 5,065 . . . F 6
Messancy, 3,150 . . . H 9
Mettet, 3,372 . . . F 8
Meulebeke, 10,458 . . . C 7
Moeskroen (Mouscron), 37,311 . . . C 7
Mol, 28,823 . . . G 6
Molenbeek-Saint-Jean, 68,411 . . . B 9
Mons, 59,362 . . . E 8
Montegnée, 11,823 . . . G 7
Montignies-sur-Sambre, 23,572 . . F 8
Mortsel, 28,012 . . . E 6
Mouscron, 37,311 . . . C 7
Namen (Namur), 32,269 . . . F 8
Namur, 32,269 . . . F 8
Neerlinter, 2,912 . . . G 7
Neerpelt, 8,771 . . . G 6
Neufchâteau, 2,670 . . . G 9
Nieuport (Nieuwpoort), 8,273 . . . B 6
Nieuwpoort, 8,273 . . . B 6
Nijvel (Nivelles), 16,126 . . . E 7
Ninove, 12,428 . . . D 7
Nivelles, 16,126 . . . E 7
Oostende (Ostend), 71,227 . . . B 6
Oostkamp, 8,999 . . . C 6
Ophoven, 2,577 . . . H 6
Opwijk, 9,699 . . . E 7
Ostend, 71,227 . . . B 6
Oudenaarde, 26,615 . . . D 7
Oud-Turnhout, 9,245 . . . F 6
Ougrée, 20,574 . . . G 7
Overijse, 16,181 . . . F 7
Overpelt, 10,470 . . . G 6
Peer, 7,201 . . . G 6
Péruwelz, 7,878 . . . D 8
Perwez, 2,905 . . . F 7
Philippeville, 2,076 . . . E 8
Poperinge, 12,671 . . . B 7
Poppel, 2,272 . . . G 6
Putte, 6,953 . . . F 6
Quaregnon, 17,688 . . . D 8
Quiévrain, 5,510 . . . D 8
Raeren, 3,655 . . . J 7
Rance, 1,464 . . . E 8
Rebecq-Rognon, 3,744 . . . E 7
Renaix (Ronse), 25,056 . . . D 7
Retie, 6,619 . . . G 6
Rièzes, 276 . . . E 9
Rochefort, 4,357 . . . G 8
Roeselare, 40,428 . . . C 7
Roeulx, 2,628 . . . E 8
Ronse, 25,056 . . . D 7
Roulers (Roeselare), 40,428 . . . C 7
Ruisbroek, 5,824 . . . B 9
Saint-Georges-sur-Meuse, 6,003 . . G 7
Saint-Gérard, 1,627 . . . F 8
Saint-Gilles, 55,055 . . . B 9
Saint-Hubert, 3,091 . . . G 8
Saint-Josse-ten-Noode, 23,633 . . . C 9
Saint-Léger, 1,586 . . . H 9
Saint-Trond (Sint-Truiden), 21,473 . . . G 7
Saint-Vith (Sankt Vith), 3,001 . . . J 8
Sankt Vith, 3,001 . . . J 8
Schaerbeek, 118,950 . . . C 9
Schoten, 29,914 . . . F 6
Seraing, 40,545 . . . G 7
's-Gravenbrakel (Braine-le-Comte), 11,957 . . . D 7
Sint-Amandsberg, 25,071 . . . D 6
Sint-Lenaarts, 4,606 . . . F 6
Sint-Niklaas, 49,214 . . . E 6
Sint-Pieters-Leeuw, 16,856 . . . B 9
Sint-Truiden, 21,473 . . . G 7
Sivry, 1,373 . . . E 8
Soignies, 12,006 . . . D 7
Spa, 9,504 . . . H 8
Staden, 5,499 . . . B 7
Stavelot, 4,723 . . . H 8
Steenokkerzeel, 4,037 . . . C 9
Strombeek-Bever, 11,233 . . . C 9
Tamines, 7,885 . . . F 8
Tamise (Temse), 14,950 . . . E 6
Templeuve, 3,902 . . . C 7
Temse, 14,950 . . . E 6
Termonde (Dendermonde), 22,119 . E 6
Tessenderlo, 11,778 . . . G 6
Theux, 5,316 . . . H 8
Thuin, 5,777 . . . E 8

(continued on following page)

Agriculture, Industry and Resources

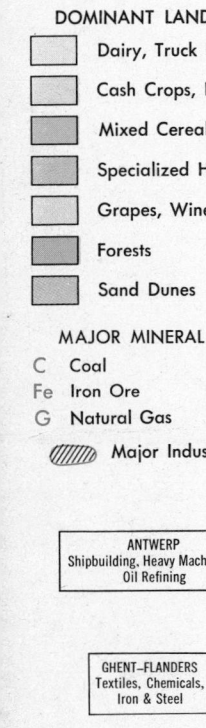

DOMINANT LAND USE
Dairy, Truck Farming
Cash Crops, Livestock
Mixed Cereals, Dairy
Specialized Horticulture
Grapes, Wine
Forests
Sand Dunes
MAJOR MINERAL OCCURRENCES
C Coal
Fe Iron Ore
G Natural Gas
Na Salt
O Petroleum
Major Industrial Areas
AMSTERDAM–HAARLEM
Shipbuilding, Machinery, Iron & Steel
ROTTERDAM
Shipbuilding, Machinery, Oil Refining
ENSCHEDE
Textiles, Cotton Industry
EINDHOVEN
Electrical Machinery, Automobiles
ANTWERP
Shipbuilding, Heavy Machinery, Oil Refining
LIÈGE
Iron & Steel, Machinery, Nonferrous Metals, Armaments
GHENT–FLANDERS
Textiles, Chemicals, Iron & Steel
VERVIERS
Textiles
BRUSSELS
Metallurgy, Textiles, Chemicals
LUXEMBOURG
Iron & Steel, Machinery, Chemicals
MONS–CHARLEROI
Iron & Steel, Metallurgy, Machinery, Chemicals
Mussels
Dairy
Cattle
Potatoes
Flowers
Flounder
Herring
Haarlem
Amsterdam
Enschede
Rotterdam
Hogs
Shrimp
Flax
Cattle
Oysters
Sugar Beets
Oats
Eindhoven
Sprats
Antwerp
Ghent
Rye
Brussels
Wheat
Liège
Verviers
Mons
Charleroi
Luxembourg

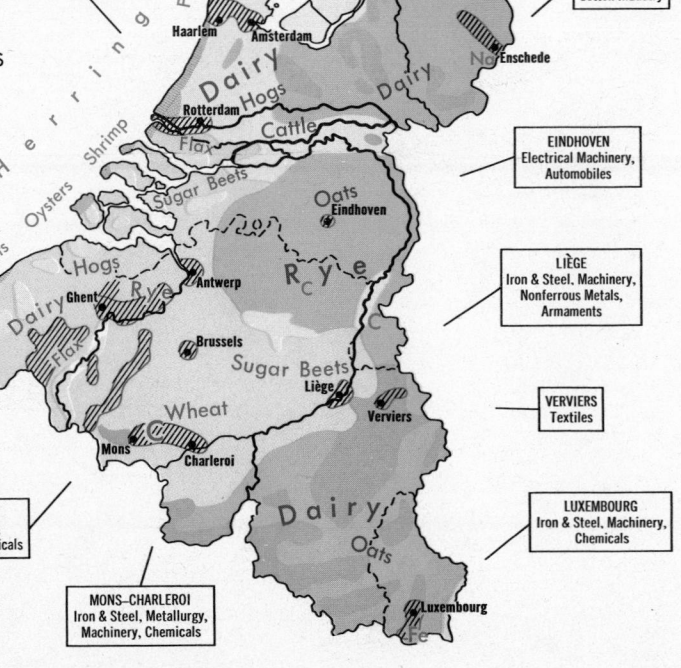

26 Netherlands, Belgium and Luxembourg

(continued)

Tielt, Brabant, 3,743 .... F 7
Tielt, West Flanders, 14,077 .... C 7
Tienen, 24,134 .... F 7
Tirlemont (Tienen), 24,134 .... F 7
Tongeren, 20,136 .... G 7
Tongres (Tongeren), 20,136 .... G 7
Torhout, 15,156 .... C 6
Tournai, 32,794 .... C 7
Tronchiennes (Drongen), 9,120 .... D 6
Tubeke (Tubize), 11,507 .... E 7
Tubize, 11,507 .... E 7
Turnhout, 38,007 .... F 6
Uccle, 78,909 .... B 9
Ukkel (Uccle), 78,909 .... B 9
Verviers, 33,587 .... H 7
Veurne, 9,496 .... B 6
Vielsalm, 3,587 .... H 8
Villers-devant-Orval, 733 .... G 9
Vilvoorde, 34,633 .... F 7
Vilvorde (Vilvoorde), 34,633 .... F 7
Virton, 3,558 .... H 9
Visé, 6,880 .... H 7
Vorst (Forest), 55,135 .... B 9
Waarschoot, 7,905 .... D 6
Waasten (Warneton), 3,167 .... B 7
Waha, 2,804 .... G 8
Waimes, 2,877 .... J 8
Walcourt, 2,005 .... F 8
Wandre, 6,853 .... H 7
Waregem, 17,725 .... C 7
Waremme, 10,956 .... G 7
Warneton, 3,167 .... B 7
Wasmes, 13,553 .... D 7
Waterloo, 17,764 .... E 7
Watermael-Boitsfort, 25,123 .... C 9
Watervliet, 1,714 .... D 6
Waver (Wavre), 11,767 .... F 7
Wavre, 11,767 .... F 7
Weismes (Waimes), 2,877 .... J 8
Wemmel, 12,631 .... B 9
Wenduine, 1,930 .... C 6
Wervik, 12,672 .... B 7
Westende, 4,854 .... B 6
Westerlo, 14,173 .... F 6
Wetteren, 20,816 .... D 7
Wezembeek-Oppem, 10,899 .... D 9
Wezet (Visé), 6,880 .... H 7
Willebroek, 15,726 .... E 6
Wilrijk, 43,485 .... E 6
Wingene, 7,140 .... C 6
Woluwe-Saint-Lambert, 47,360 .... C 9
Woluwe-Saint-Pierre, 40,884 .... C 9
Wolvertem, 5,482 .... E 7
Ypres (Ieper), 20,825 .... B 7
Yvoir, 2,628 .... F 8
Zaventem, 10,625 .... C 9
Zeebrugge .... C 6
Zele, 18,585 .... E 6
Zellik, 6,659 .... B 9
Zelzate, 12,785 .... D 6
Zinnik (Soignies), 12,006 .... D 7
Zonhoven, 13,484 .... G 6
Zottegem, 21,461 .... D 7

OTHER FEATURES

Albert (canal) .... F 6
Ardennes (for.) .... F 9
Botrange (mt.) .... J 8
Dender (riv.) .... D 7
Deûle (riv.) .... B 7
Dyle (riv.) .... F 7
Hohe Venn (plat.) .... H 8
Lesse (riv.) .... F 8
Lys (riv.) .... B 7
Mark (riv.) .... F 6
Meuse (riv.) .... F 8
Nethe (riv.) .... F 6
North (sea) .... D 4
Ourthe (riv.) .... H 8
Rupel (riv.) .... F 7
Sambre (riv.) .... D 8
Schelde (Scheldt) (riv.) .... C 7
Scheldt (riv.) .... C 7
Schnee Eifel (plat.) .... J 8
Semois (riv.) .... G 9
Senne (riv.) .... E 7
Vaalserberg (mt.) .... J 7
Vesdre (riv.) .... H 7
Weisserstein (mt.) .... J 8
Yser (riv.) .... B 7
Zitterwald (plat.) .... J 8

LUXEMBOURG

CITIES and TOWNS

Bascharage, 2,526 .... H 9
Clervaux, 916 .... J 8
Diekirch, ☆5,059 .... J 9
Differdange, 9,287 .... H 9
Dudelange, ☆14,615 .... 1 0
Echternach, ☆3,792 .... J 9
Esch-sur-Alzette, ☆27,574 .... J 9
Esch-sur-Sauer, ☆241 .... H 9
Ettelbruck, ☆5,990 .... J 9
Grevenmacher, ☆2,918 .... J 9
Hesperange, 619 .... J 9
Luxembourg (cap.), 78,272 .... J 9
Mersch, 1,869 .... J 9
Mertert, 914 .... J 9
Pétange, 6,234 .... H 9
Redange, 1,006 .... H 9
Remich, ☆12,138 .... J 9
Troisvierges, 910 .... J 9
Vianden, ☆1,520 .... J 9
Wasserbillig, 2,097 .... J 9
Wiltz, 1,601 .... H 9

OTHER FEATURES

Alzette (riv.) .... J 9
Clerf (riv.) .... J 8
Eisling (mts.) .... H 9
Mosel (riv.) .... J 9
Our (riv.) .... J 9
Sauer (riv.) .... J 9

NETHERLANDS

PROVINCES

Drenthe, 405,924 .... K 3
Friesland, 560,614 .... H 2
Gelderland, 1,639,997 .... H 4
Groningen, 540,062 .... K 2
Limburg, 1,051,620 .... H 6
North Brabant, 1,967,261 .... F 5
North Holland, 2,295,875 .... F 3
Overijssel, 985,569 .... J 4
South Holland, 3,048,648 .... E 5
Utrecht, 867,909 .... G 4
Zeeland, 332,286 .... D 6

☆CITIES and TOWNS

Aalsmeer, 20,779 .... F 4
Aalst, 13,219 .... G 6
Aalten, 17,486 .... K 5
Aardenburg, 3,869 .... C 6
Akkrum, 5,044 .... H 2
Alkmaar, 65,199 .... F 3
Almelo, 62,634 .... K 4
Amersfoort, 87,784 .... G 4
Amstelveen, 71,803 .... B 5
Amsterdam (cap.), 751,156 .... B 4
Amsterdam, *987,205 .... B 4
Andijk, 5,301 .... G 3
Apeldoorn, 134,055 .... H 4
Apeldoorn, *237,231 .... H 4
Appingedam, 13,295 .... K 2
Arnhem, 126,051 .... H 4
Arnhem, *281,126 .... H 4
Assen, 43,783 .... K 3
Asten, 12,295 .... H 6
Axel, 12,072 .... D 6
Baarle-Nassau, 5,583 .... F 6
Baarn, 25,045 .... G 4
Barneveld, 34,189 .... H 4
Bath .... E 6
Beilen, 12,948 .... K 3
Bergeijk (Hof), 9,009 .... G 6
Bergen, 14,306 .... F 3
Bergen op Zoom, 40,770 .... E 5
Bergum, 28,047 .... H 2
Berkel, 9,367 .... F 5
Berkhout, 5,167 .... F 3
Beverwijk, 37,551 .... F 4
Blerick .... J 6
Bloemendaal, 17,940 .... E 4
Blokzijl .... H 3
Bodegraven, 15,848 .... F 4
Bolsward, 9,934 .... H 2
Borculo, 9,859 .... J 4
Borger, 12,017 .... K 3
Borne, 18,216 .... K 4
Boskoop, 12,985 .... F 4
Boxmeer, 12,662 .... H 5
Boxtel, 22,465 .... G 5
Breda, 118,086 .... F 5
Breda, *151,182 .... F 5
Breezand .... F 3
Breskens .... C 6
Brielle, 10,620 .... E 5
Broek, 2,633 .... C 4
Brouwershaven, 3,263 .... D 5
Brummen, 20,460 .... J 4
Buiksloot .... B 4
Bussum, 37,848 .... G 4
Callantsoog, 2,541 .... F 3
Coevorden, 13,089 .... K 3
Colijnsplaat .... D 5
Culemborg, 17,682 .... G 5
Cuyk, 15,366 .... H 5
Dalen, 5,084 .... K 3
De Bilt, 32,588 .... G 4
Dedemsvaart, 12,975 .... J 3
De Koog .... F 2
Delft, 86,103 .... E 4
Delfzijl, 23,316 .... K 2
Den Burg, 12,132 .... F 2
Denekamp, 11,533 .... L 4
Den Helder, 60,421 .... F 3
Deurne, 26,539 .... H 6
Deventer, 65,557 .... J 4
De Wijk, 4,631 .... J 3
Diemen, 13,704 .... C 5
Dieren .... J 4
Diever, 3,162 .... J 3
Dinxperlo, 7,296 .... K 5
Dirksland, 6,495 .... E 5
Doesburg, 9,759 .... J 4
Doetinchem, 34,915 .... J 5
Dokkum, 11,203 .... H 2
Domburg, 3,874 .... C 5
Dongen, 19,219 .... F 5
Doorn, 11,966 .... G 4
Dordrecht, 101,840 .... F 5
Dordrecht, *186,793 .... F 5
Drachten, 45,390 .... J 2
Driebergen, 17,022 .... G 4
Dronten, 16,544 .... H 3
Druten, 11,113 .... H 5
Echt, 17,035 .... H 6
Edam-Volendam, 21,507 .... G 4
Ede, 79,897 .... H 4
Egmond aan Zee, 5,734 .... E 3
Eindhoven, 192,562 .... G 6
Eindhoven, *358,234 .... G 6
Elburg, 18,082 .... H 4
Elst, 16,686 .... H 5
Emmeloord, 34,467 .... H 3
Emmen, 86,700 .... K 3
Enkhuizen, 13,430 .... G 3
Enschede, 141,597 .... K 4
Enschede, *239,015 .... K 4
Epe, 32,267 .... H 4
Erica .... K 3
Ermelo, 23,835 .... H 4
Etten, 26,167 .... F 5
Europoort .... E 5
Flushing, 43,806 .... C 6
Franeker, 11,415 .... H 2
Geertruidenberg, 6,185 .... F 5
Geldermalsen, 8,952 .... G 5
Geldrop, 25,879 .... H 6
Geleen, 35,910 .... H 7
Gemert, 15,267 .... H 5
Gendringen, 19,086 .... J 5
Genemuiden, 6,058 .... H 3
Gennep, 14,773 .... H 5
Giessendam-Hardinxveld, 15,523 .... F 5
Giethoorn .... J 3
Goes, 28,505 .... D 6
Goirle, 13,447 .... G 5
Goor, 11,435 .... K 4
Gorinchem, 28,337 .... G 5
Gorredijk .... J 2
Gouda, 56,403 .... F 4
Graauw .... E 6
Gramsbergen, 5,866 .... K 3
Grave, 9,492 .... H 5
Groenlo, 8,693 .... K 4
Groesbeek, 18,094 .... H 5
Groningen, 163,357 .... K 2
Groningen, *201,662 .... K 2
Grouw, 8,567 .... H 2
Haamstede, 4,575 .... D 5
Haarlem, 164,672 .... F 4
Haarlem, *232,048 .... F 4
Haarlemmermeer (Hoofddorp), 72,046 .... F 4
Hague, The (cap.), 479,369 .... E 4
Hague, The, *682,452 .... E 4
Halfweg, 4,456 .... A 4
Hallum .... H 2
Hardenberg, 28,489 .... J 3
Harderwijk, 28,508 .... H 4
Hardinxveld-Giessendam, 15,523 .... G 5
Harlingen, 14,533 .... G 2
Hasselt, 5,817 .... J 3
Hattem, 11,074 .... H 4
Heemstede, 27,376 .... F 4
Heer .... H 7
Heerde, 16,833 .... H 4
Heerenveen, 34,948 .... H 3
Heerlen, 71,500 .... J 7
Heiloo, 20,524 .... F 3
Hellendoorn, 32,068 .... J 4
Hellevoetsluis, 14,186 .... E 5
Helmond, 59,249 .... H 6
Hengelo, Gelderland, 8,015 .... J 4
Hengelo, Overijssel, 72,281 .... K 4
Heusden, 5,542 .... G 5
Hillegom, 17,489 .... E 4
Hilvarenbeek, 8,408 .... G 6
Hilversum, 94,041 .... G 4
Hilversum, *110,498 .... G 4
Hindeloopen, 830 .... G 3
Hippolytushoef, 7,847 .... G 3
Hoek .... D 6
Hoek van Holland (Hook of Holland) .... D 4
Hoensbroek, 22,441 .... H 7
Hof (Bergeijk), 9,009 .... G 6
Holijsloot .... C 4
Hollum .... H 2
Holwerd .... H 2
Hoofddorp (Haarlemmermeer), 72,046 .... F 4
Hoogeveen, 42,673 .... J 3
Hoogezand-Sappemeer, 33,860 .... K 2
Hoogkarspel, 5,112 .... G 3
Hook of Holland .... D 4
Hoorn, 24,609 .... G 3
Horst, 16,242 .... H 6
Huissen, 11,049 .... H 5
Huizen, 25,603 .... G 4
Hulst, 17,283 .... E 6
IJlst, 2,366 .... H 2
IJmuiden, 6,633 .... E 4
IJsselstein, 15,450 .... F 4
Ilpendam, 3,310 .... C 4
Joure, 14,329 .... H 3
Kampen, 29,488 .... H 3
Katwijk aan Zee, 37,437 .... E 4
Kerkdriel, 7,584 .... G 5
Kerkrade, 46,609 .... J 7
Kesteren, 8,257 .... G 5
Kloosterveen, 8,247 .... K 3
Kollum, 11,887 .... J 2
Krimpen aan den IJssel, 26,396 .... F 5
Landsmeer, 8,082 .... C 4
Laren, 13,615 .... G 4
Leek, 15,713 .... J 2
Leerdam, 15,030 .... F 5
Leeuwarden, 85,074 .... H 2
Leiden, 99,891 .... E 4
Leiden, *167,554 .... E 4
Lelystad .... H 4
Lemmer, 10,013 .... H 3
Lisse, 19,182 .... F 4
Lith, 5,088 .... G 5
Lochem, 17,274 .... J 4
Lonneker .... K 4
Loon op Zand, 18,000 .... G 5
Losser, 20,688 .... L 4
Maarssen, 18,346 .... F 4
Maasbree, 9,462 .... H 6
Maassluis, 28,170 .... E 5
Maastricht, 111,044 .... H 7
Maastricht, *145,862 .... H 7
Makkum .... G 2
Margraten, 3,318 .... H 7
Medemblik, 6,432 .... G 3
Meerssen, 8,414 .... H 7
Meppel, 21,057 .... J 3
Middelburg, 36,372 .... C 6
Middelharnis, 14,245 .... E 5
Middenmeer .... F 3
Millingen aan den Rijn, 5,035 .... J 5
Moerdijk .... F 5
Monnikendam, 8,127 .... C 4
Montfoort, 3,442 .... G 4
Muiden, 6,567 .... G 4
Muntendam, 4,147 .... K 2
Naaldwijk, 24,117 .... E 4
Naarden, 17,319 .... G 4
Nagele .... H 3
Neede, 10,842 .... K 4
Nes, 3,012 .... H 2
Nieuw-Buinen .... K 3
Nieuwendam .... C 4
Nieuwe-Pekela, 5,086 .... L 2
Nieuweschans, 1,813 .... L 2
Nieuwkoop, 8,923 .... F 4
Nijkerk, 21,615 .... H 4
Nijmegen, 148,493 .... H 5
Nijmegen, *213,981 .... H 5
Nijverdal .... J 4
Noordwijk, 22,386 .... E 4
Norg, 6,041 .... J 2
Numansdorp, 7,072 .... E 5
Nunspeet, 21,340 .... H 4
Odoorn, 11,973 .... K 3
Oisterwijk, 16,263 .... G 5
Oldenzaal, 26,624 .... K 4
Olst, 8,480 .... J 4
Ommen, 16,136 .... J 3
Onstwedde .... K 2
Oostburg, 18,461 .... C 6
Oosterend .... G 2
Oosterhout, 40,077 .... F 5
Oostmahorn .... J 2
Oost-Vlieland, 1,070 .... F 2
Oostzaan, 6,336 .... C 4
Ootmarsum, 3,901 .... K 4
Oss, 45,643 .... H 5
Otterlo .... H 4
Oud-Beijerland, 14,251 .... E 5
Ouddorp, 9,091 .... D 5
Oudenbosch, 11,061 .... E 5
Oude-Pekela, 8,067 .... K 2
Oudewater, 6,870 .... F 4
Purmerend, 32,614 .... F 4
Putten, 18,243 .... H 4
Raalte, 23,598 .... J 4
Renkum, 34,547 .... H 5
Reusel, 6,901 .... G 6
Rheden, 49,755 .... J 4
Rhenen, 16,893 .... H 5
Ridderkerk, 45,069 .... F 5
Rijnsburg, 10,698 .... F 4
Rijssen, 20,008 .... J 4
Rijswijk, 54,123 .... E 4
Roden, 16,437 .... J 2
Roermond, 36,695 .... J 6
Roosendaal, 51,685 .... F 5
Rotterdam, 614,767 .... E 5
Rotterdam, *1,016,505 .... E 5
Rutten .... H 3
Ruurlo, 7,557 .... J 4
Sappemeer-Hoogezand, 33,860 .... K 2
Schagen, 13,929 .... F 3
Scheveningen .... E 4
Schiedam, 78,068 .... E 5
Schiermonnikoog, 845 .... J 1
Schijndel, 18,658 .... G 5
Schiphol .... B 5
Schoonebeek, 7,556 .... K 3
Schoonhoven, 10,753 .... F 5
's Gravendeel, 7,242 .... E 5
's Gravenhage (The Hague) (cap.), 479,369 .... E 4
's Gravenhage, *682,452 .... E 4
's Gravenzande, 15,833 .... E 4
's Heerenberg, 18,326 .... J 5
's Hertogenbosch, 86,184 .... G 5
Sint Annaland .... E 5
Sint Jacobiparochie .... H 2
Sittard, 34,278 .... H 6
Sliedrecht, 21,839 .... F 5
Slochteren, 13,447 .... K 2
Sloten, Friesland, 688 .... H 3
Sloten, North Holland .... B 5
Sloterdijk .... B 4
Sluis, 3,140 .... C 6
Smilde (Kloosterveen), 8,247 .... K 3
Sneek, 28,123 .... H 2
Soest, 40,165 .... G 4
Soesterberg .... G 4
Stadskanaal, 13,946 .... L 3
Staphorst, 11,608 .... J 3
Staveren, 907 .... G 3
Steenbergen, 12,930 .... E 5
Steenwijk, 20,721 .... J 3
Steenwijkerwold (Kerkbuurt en Thij) .... J 3
Stiens, 7,711 .... H 2
Swifterbant .... H 3
Tegelen, 18,386 .... J 6
Ter Apel .... L 3
Termunten, 4,803 .... K 2
Terneuzen, 33,731 .... D 6
Tholen, 17,213 .... E 5
Tiel, 24,974 .... G 5
Tilburg, 151,513 .... G 5
Tilburg, *212,510 .... G 5
Twello, 22,542 .... J 4
Uden, 28,946 .... H 5
Uitgeest, 8,897 .... F 3
Uithoorn, 22,812 .... F 4
Uithuizen, 5,194 .... K 2
Ulrum, 3,665 .... J 2
Urk, 9,397 .... H 3
Utrecht, 250,887 .... G 4
Utrecht, *464,357 .... G 4
Vaals, 11,057 .... H 7
Valkenswaard, 27,121 .... H 6
Van Ewijcksluis .... F 3
Veendam, 26,168 .... K 2
Veenendaal, 35,845 .... G 4
Veenhuizen .... J 2
Veere, 4,252 .... D 5
Veghel, 22,308 .... H 5
Velp .... J 5
Velsen, 64,035 .... F 4
Venlo, 61,659 .... J 6
Venraij, 31,526 .... H 6
Vianen, 12,821 .... G 5
Vlaardingen, 78,311 .... E 5
Vlagtwedde, 16,719 .... L 3
Vlijmen, 13,515 .... G 5
Vlissingen (Flushing), 43,806 .... C 6
Volendam-Edam, 21,507 .... G 4
Voorburg, 45,209 .... E 4
Voorst, 22,542 .... J 4
Vorden, 7,276 .... J 4
Vriezenveen, 16,025 .... K 4
Vught, 23,261 .... G 5
Waalwijk, 25,977 .... F 5
Wageningen, 28,659 .... H 5
Wamel, 8,979 .... H 5
Weert, 36,850 .... H 6
Weesp, 17,037 .... C 5
Westkapelle, 2,494 .... C 5
West-Terschelling, 4,542 .... G 2
Wierden, 20,618 .... K 4
Wijhe, 6,888 .... J 4
Wijk bij Duurstede, 7,927 .... G 5
Wijk en Aalburg, 9,266 .... F 5
Willemstad, 2,769 .... F 5
Winschoten, 19,760 .... L 2
Winsum, 5,007 .... K 2
Winterswijk, 27,413 .... K 5
Woensdrecht, 9,101 .... E 6
Woerden, 22,064 .... F 4
Wolvega, 22,812 .... J 3
Workum, 4,135 .... G 3
Zaandam (Zaanstad), 124,795 .... B 4
Zaandam (Zaanstad), *137,371 .... B 4
Zaltbommel, 8,010 .... G 5
Zandvoort, 16,289 .... E 4
Zeist, 58,630 .... G 4
Zevenaar, 26,560 .... J 5
Zevenbergen, 13,307 .... E 5
Zierikzee, 8,816 .... D 5
Zundert, 12,444 .... F 6
Zutphen, 29,188 .... J 4
Zwartsluis, 4,391 .... H 3
Zwijndrecht, 38,271 .... E 5
Zwolle, 77,826 .... J 3

OTHER FEATURES

Alkmaardermeer (lake) .... F 3
Ameland (isl.), 3,012 .... H 2
Bergumermeer (lake) .... J 2
Beulaker Wijde (lake) .... H 3
Borndiep (chan.) .... H 2
De Fluessen (lake) .... G 3
De Honte (bay) .... D 6
De Peel (reg.), 187,302 .... H 6
De Twente (reg.), 493,855 .... K 4
De Zaan (riv.) .... B 4
Dollart (bay) .... L 2
Dommel (riv.) .... H 6
Duiveland (isl.), 7,515 .... D 5
Eastern Scheldt (est.) .... D 5
Eems (riv.) .... K 2
Eijerlandsche Gat (str.) .... F 2
Flevoland Polders, 35,618 .... G 4
Friesche Gat (chan.) .... J 2
Frisian, West (isls.), 21,601 .... G 2
Galgenberg (hill) .... H 4
Goeree (isl.), 9,091 .... D 5
Grevelingen (str.) .... E 5
Griend (isl.) .... G 2
Groninger Wad (sound) .... J 2
Groote IJ Polder .... B 4
Haarlemmermeer Polder, 72,046 .... B 5
Haringvliet (str.) .... E 5
Het IJ (est.) .... C 4
Hoek van Holland (cape) .... D 5
Hondsrug (hills) .... K 3
Houtrak Polder .... A 4
Hunse (riv.) .... K 3
IJmeer (bay) .... C 4
IJssel (riv.) .... J 4
IJsselmeer (lake) .... G 3
Lauwers (chan.) .... J 1
Lauwers Zee (bay) .... J 2
Lek (riv.) .... F 5
Lemelerberg (hill) .... J 4
Linde (riv.) .... J 3
Lower Rhine (riv.) .... H 5
Maas (riv.) .... G 5
Mark (riv.) .... F 6
Marken (isl.), 2,018 .... G 4
Markerwaard Polder .... G 3
Marsdiep (chan.) .... F 3
Noordergat (chan.) .... F 2
North (sea) .... E 3
North Beveland (isl.), 6,292 .... D 5
North East Polder, 34,467 .... H 3
North Holland (canal) .... C 4
North Sea (canal) .... F 4
Old Rhine (riv.) .... E 4
Ooster Eems (chan.) .... K 1
Oostzaan Polder, 6,336 .... B 4
Orange (canal) .... K 3
Overflakkee (isl.), 29,654 .... E 5
Pinkegat (chan.) .... H 2
Regge (riv.) .... K 4
Rhine (riv.) .... J 5
Roer (riv.) .... J 6
Rottumeroog (isl.), 2,313 .... J
Schiermonnikoog (isl.), 845 .... J
Schouwen (isl.), 18,919 .... D 5
Simonszand (isl.) .... J 1
Slotermeer (lake) .... H 3
Sneekermeer (lake) .... H
South Beveland (isl.), 71,708 .... D
Terschelling (isl.), 4,542 .... G
Texel (isl.), 12,132 .... F
Tjeukemeer (lake) .... H
Vaalserberg (mt.) .... J
Vecht (riv.) .... F
Vechte (riv.) .... J
Veeregat (chan.) .... D
Veluwe (reg.), 756,956 .... H
Vlieland (isl.), 1,070 .... F
Vile Stroom (str.), ... G
Voorne (isl.), 50,601 .... D
Waal (riv.) .... G
Waddenzee (sound) .... G
Walcheren (isl.), 102,719 C
Wester Eems (chan.) .... K
Western Scheldt (De Honte) (bay) .... D
West Frisian (isls.), 21,601 .... F
Westgat (chan.) .... F
Wieringermeer Polder, 11,870 .... G
Wilhelmina (canal) .... G
Willems (canal) .... G

*City and suburbs.
☆Population of communes. All populations of cities in Belgium & Netherlands are communes.

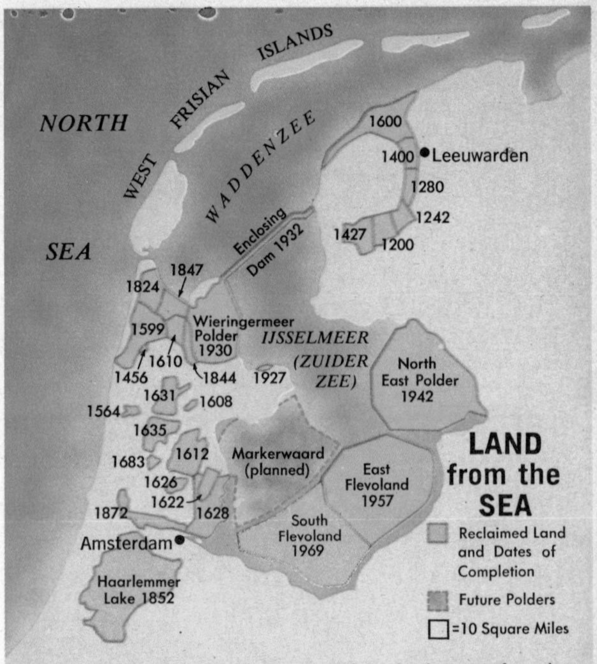

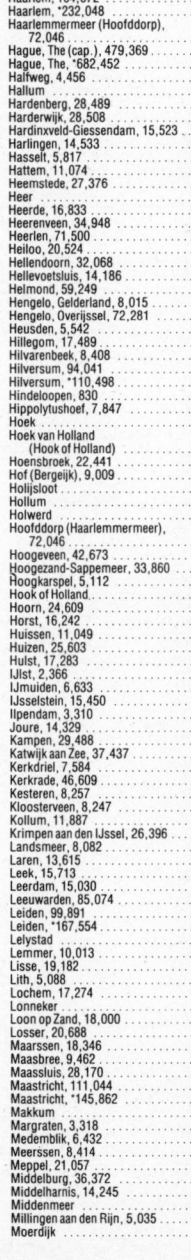

WEST FRISIAN ISLANDS
NORTH SEA
WADDENZEE
Enclosing Dam 1932
1600
1400
Leeuwarden
1280
1242
1427
1200
1847
1824
1599
Wieringermeer Polder 1930
IJSSELMEER (ZUIDER ZEE)
North East Polder 1942
1610
1456
1844
1927
1631
1608
1564
1635
1612
1683
Markerwaard (planned)
East Flevoland 1957
1626
1622
1628
1872
South Flevoland 1969
Amsterdam
Haarlemmer Lake 1852
LAND from the SEA
Reclaimed Land and Dates of Completion
Future Polders
=10 Square Miles

For centuries the Dutch have been renowned for the drainage of marshes and the construction of polders, i.e., arable land reclaimed from the sea. Future projects will convert much of the present IJsselmeer to agricultural land.

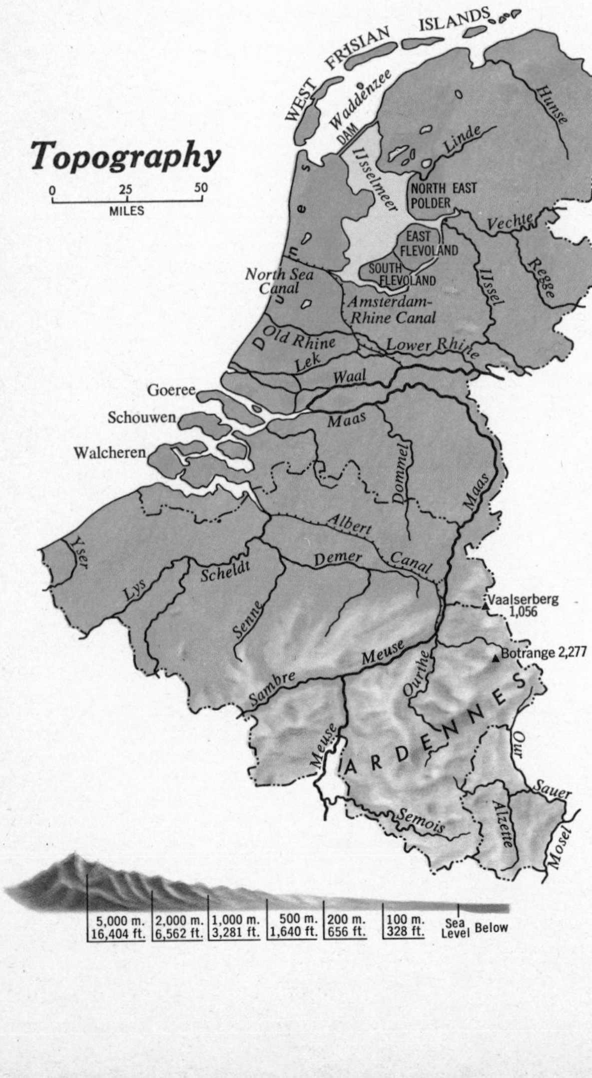

Topography
0 25 50
MILES
WEST FRISIAN ISLANDS
Waddenzee
DAM
IJsselmeer
Hunse
Linde
NORTH EAST POLDER
EAST FLEVOLAND
SOUTH FLEVOLAND
Vechte
Regge
IJssel
Dunes
North Sea Canal
Amsterdam-Rhine Canal
Old Rhine
Lower Rhine
Lek
Waal
Goeree
Schouwen
Walcheren
Maas
Dommel
Albert
Canal
Demer
Scheldt
Lys
Yser
Senne
Vaalserberg 1,056
Botrange 2,277
Meuse
Ourthe
Sambre
ARDENNES
Our
Sauer
Semois
Alzette
Mosel
5,000 m. 16,404 ft.
2,000 m. 6,562 ft.
1,000 m. 3,281 ft.
500 m. 1,640 ft.
200 m. 656 ft.
100 m. 328 ft.
Sea Level
Below

NETHERLANDS, BELGIUM and LUXEMBOURG

CONIC PROJECTION

SCALE OF MILES

0 5 10 20 30 40

SCALE OF KILOMETRES

0 5 10 20 30 40 50

Capitals of Countries _____ ☆
Provincial Capitals _____ △
International Boundaries _____
Provincial Boundaries _____
Canals _____

Copyright by C. S. Hammond & Co., N.Y.

AMSTERDAM

BRUSSELS

FRANCE

CONIC PROJECTION

SCALE OF MILES

SCALE OF KILOMETRES

Capitals of Countries
Capitals of Departments
International Boundaries
Department Boundaries
Canals

© C.S. HAMMOND & Co., N.Y.

PARIS and ENVIRONS

CORSICA

Same Scale as Main Map

DEPARTMENTS

Ain, 339,262 ....F 4
Aisne, 526,346 ....E 3
Allier, 386,533 ....E 4
Alpes-de-Haute-Provence, 104,813 ....G 5
Alpes-Maritimes, 722,070 ....G 6
Ardèche, 256,927 ....F 5
Ardennes, 309,380 ....F 3
Ariège, 138,478 ....D 6
Aube, 270,325 ....E 3
Aude, 278,323 ....E 6
Aveyron, 281,568 ....E 5
Bas-Rhin, 827,367 ....G 3
Belfort (terr.), 118,450 ....G 4
Bouches-du-Rhône, 1,470,271 ....F 6
Calvados, 519,695 ....C 3
Cantal, 169,330 ....E 5
Charente, 331,016 ....D 5
Charente-Maritime, 483,622 ....C 5
Cher, 304,601 ....E 4
Corrèze, 237,858 ....D 5
Corse-du-Sud, 121,771 ....B 7
Côte-d'Or, 421,192 ....F 4
Côtes-du-Nord, 506,102 ....B 3
Creuse, 156,876 ....D 4
Deux-Sèvres, 326,462 ....C 4
Dordogne, 374,073 ....D 5
Doubs, 426,363 ....G 4
Drôme, 342,891 ....F 5
Essonne, 674,157 ....E 3
Eure, 383,385 ....D 3
Eure-et-Loir, 302,207 ....D 3
Finistère, 768,929 ....A 3
Gard, 478,544 ....F 6
Gers, 181,577 ....D 6
Gironde, 1,009,390 ....C 5
Haut-Rhin, 585,018 ....G 4
Haute-Corse, 148,060 ....B 6
Haute-Garonne, 690,712 ....D 6
Haute-Loire, 208,337 ....E 5
Haute-Marne, 214,336 ....F 3
Haute-Saône, 214,176 ....G 4
Haute-Savoie, 378,550 ....G 5
Haute-Vienne, 341,589 ....D 5
Hautes-Alpes, 91,790 ....G 5
Hautes-Pyrénées, 225,730 ....D 6
Hauts-de-Seine, 1,461,619 ....A 2
Hérault, 591,397 ....E 6
Ille-et-Vilaine, 652,722 ....C 3
Indre, 247,178 ....D 4
Indre-et-Loire, 437,870 ....D 4
Isère, 768,450 ....F 5
Jura, 233,547 ....F 4
Landes, 277,381 ....C 5
Loir-et-Cher, 267,896 ....D 4
Loire, 722,383 ....F 5
Loire-Atlantique, 861,452 ....C 4
Loiret, 430,629 ....E 4
Lot, 151,198 ....D 5
Lot-et-Garonne, 290,592 ....D 5
Lozère, 77,258 ....E 5
Maine-et-Loire, 584,709 ....C 4
Manche, 451,939 ....C 3
Marne, 485,388 ....F 3
Mayenne, 252,762 ....C 3
Meurthe-et-Moselle, 705,413 ....G 3
Meuse, 209,513 ....F 3
Morbihan, 540,474 ....B 4
Moselle, 971,314 ....G 3
Nièvre, 247,702 ....E 4
Nord, 2,417,899 ....E 2
Oise, 540,988 ....E 3
Orne, 288,524 ....C 3
Paris, 2,590,771 ....B 2
Pas-de-Calais, 1,397,159 ....E 2
Puy-de-Dôme, 547,743 ....E 5
Pyrénées-Atlantiques, 508,734 ....C 6
Pyrénées-Orientales, 281,976 ....E 6
Rhône, 1,325,611 ....F 5
Saône-et-Loire, 550,362 ....F 4
Sarthe, 461,839 ....D 3
Savoie, 288,921 ....G 5
Seine-et-Marne, 604,340 ....E 3
Seine-Maritime, 1,113,977 ....D 3
Seine-Saint-Denis, 1,251,792 ....B 1
Somme, 512,113 ....E 3
Tarn, 332,011 ....E 6
Tarn-et-Garonne, 183,572 ....D 5
Val-de-Marne, 1,121,340 ....B 2
Val-d'Oise, 693,269 ....E 3
Var, 555,926 ....G 6
Vaucluse, 353,966 ....F 6
Vendée, 421,250 ....C 4
Vienne, 340,256 ....D 4
Vosges, 388,201 ....G 3
Yonne, 283,376 ....E 4
Yvelines, 853,386 ....D 3

CITIES and TOWNS

Abbeville, 23,770 ....D 2
Agde, 8,812 ....E 6
Agen, 34,592 ....D 5
Aix-en-Provence, 74,948 ....F 6
Aix-les-Bains, 20,594 ....G 5
Ajaccio, 38,776 ....B 7
Albert, 10,937 ....E 2
Albertville, 15,422 ....G 5
Albi, 38,867 ....E 6
Alençon, 30,368 ....D 3
Aléria, 1,000 ....B 6
Alès, 31,948 ....E 5
Ambérieu-en-Bugey, 8,570 ....F 5
Amboise, 8,408 ....D 4
Amiens, 116,107 ....D 3
Angers, 127,415 ....C 4
Angoulême, 46,584 ....D 5
Annecy, 53,361 ....G 5
Annonay, 19,591 ....F 5
Antibes, 47,393 ....G 6
Antony, 56,556 ....B 2
Apt, 8,502 ....F 6
Arcachon, 14,852 ....C 5
Argentan, 14,418 ....D 3
Argenteuil, 87,106 ....A 1
Arles, 33,575 ....F 6
Armentières, 24,460 ....E 2
Arras, 48,494 ....E 2
Asnières, 79,942 ....A 1
Aubagne, 17,055 ....F 6
Aubenas, 10,480 ....F 5
Aubervilliers, 73,559 ....B 1
Aubusson, 5,641 ....E 4
Auch, 18,072 ....D 6
Audincourt, 13,487 ....G 4
Aulnay-sous-Bois, 61,384 ....B 1
Auray, 8,180 ....B 4
Aurignac, 783 ....D 6
Aurillac, 26,776 ....E 5
Autun, 17,194 ....F 4
Auxerre, 33,700 ....E 4
Avallon, 6,615 ....E 4
Avesnes-sur-Helpe, 6,253 ....F 2
Avignon, 78,871 ....F 6
Avion, 22,390 ....E 2
Avranches, 9,751 ....C 3
Bagnères-de-Bigorre, 9,139 ....D 6
Bagnères-de-Luchon, 4,079 ....D 6
Bagnolet, 33,607 ....B 2
Bagnols-sur-Cèze, 15,336 ....F 5
Bar-le-Duc, 18,874 ....F 3
Bar-sur-Seine, 2,642 ....F 3
Barfleur, 825 ....C 3
Bastia, 48,800 ....B 6
Bayeux, 11,190 ....C 3
Bayonne, 39,761 ....C 6
Beaucaire, 8,820 ....F 6
Beaune, 16,441 ....F 4
Beauvais, 46,284 ....E 3
Bédarieux, 6,929 ....E 6
Belfort, 53,001 ....G 4
Belley, 5,958 ....F 5
Berck, 13,658 ....D 2
Bergerac, 24,184 ....D 5
Berney, 9,298 ....D 3
Besançon, 107,939 ....G 4
Bessèges, 5,421 ....F 5
Béthune, 26,144 ....E 2
Béziers, 74,517 ....E 6
Biarritz, 26,628 ....C 6
Blois, 39,279 ....D 4
Bobigny, 39,321 ....B 1
Bolbec, 12,517 ....D 3
Bondy, 51,555 ....B 1
Bordeaux, 263,808 ....C 5
Bordeaux, †648,000 ....C 5
Boulogne-Billancourt, 108,846 ....A 2
Boulogne-sur-Mer, 49,064 ....D 2
Bourg-en-Bresse, 35,064 ....F 4
Bourges, 67,137 ....E 4
Bressuire, 8,010 ....C 4
Brest, 150,696 ....A 3
Briançon, 7,551 ....G 5
Briare, 4,725 ....E 4
Brignoles, 8,010 ....G 6
Brive-la-Gaillarde, 45,314 ....D 5
Bruay-en-Artois, 38,608 ....E 2
Caen, 106,790 ....C 3
Cahors, 17,775 ....D 5
Calais, 70,153 ....D 2
Caluire-et-Cuire, 37,541 ....F 5
Calvi, 2,523 ....B 6
Cambrai, 37,290 ....E 2
Cannes, 66,590 ....G 6
Carcassonne, 40,580 ....D 6
Carentan, 5,207 ....C 3
Carmaux, 13,423 ....E 5
Carpentras, 18,092 ....F 5
Castelnaudary, 8,550 ....E 6
Castelsarrasin, 7,912 ....D 6
Castres, 35,975 ....E 6
Cavaillon, 14,815 ....F 6
Cayeux-sur-Mer, 2,489 ....D 2
Chalon-sur-Saône, 47,004 ....F 4
Châlons-sur-Marne, 48,558 ....F 3
Chambéry, 49,858 ....F 5
Chambord, 200 ....D 4
Chamonix-Mont Blanc, 5,907 ....G 5
Champigny-sur-Marne, 70,353 ....C 2
Chantilly, 10,156 ....E 3
Charenton-le-Pont, 22,220 ....B 2
Charleville-Mézières, 55,230 ....F 3
Chartres, 34,128 ....D 3
Château-du-Loir, 5,239 ....D 4
Château-Gontier, 7,881 ....C 4
Château-Renault, 5,082 ....D 4
Château-Thierry, 10,858 ....E 3
Châteaubriant, 11,196 ....C 4
Châteaudun, 13,715 ....D 3
Châteauneuf-sur-Loire, 4,603 ....E 4
Châteauroux, 48,867 ....D 4
Châtellerault, 33,491 ....D 4
Châtillon, 24,468 ....B 2
Châtillon-sur-Seine, 6,128 ....F 4
Chatou, 22,495 ....A 1
Chaumont, 25,602 ....F 3
Chauny, 13,714 ....E 3
Chelles, 22,111 ....C 1
Cherbourg, 37,933 ....C 3
Chinon, 5,435 ....D 4
Choisy-le-Roi, 41,080 ....B 2
Cholet, 40,224 ....C 4
Clamart, 54,866 ....A 2
Clermont, 7,119 ....E 3
Clermont-Ferrand, 145,856 ....E 5
Clichy, 52,398 ....B 1
Cluny, 3,552 ....F 4
Cluses, 12,391 ....G 4
Cognac, 21,137 ....C 5
Colmar, 58,623 ....G 3
Colombes, 80,224 ....A 1
Commentry, 8,129 ....E 4
Commercy, 7,043 ....F 3
Compiègne, 28,881 ....E 3
Concarneau, 16,458 ....A 4
Cosne-sur-Loire, 8,931 ....E 4
Coudekerque-Branche, 22,972 ....E 2
Coulommiers, 11,182 ....E 3

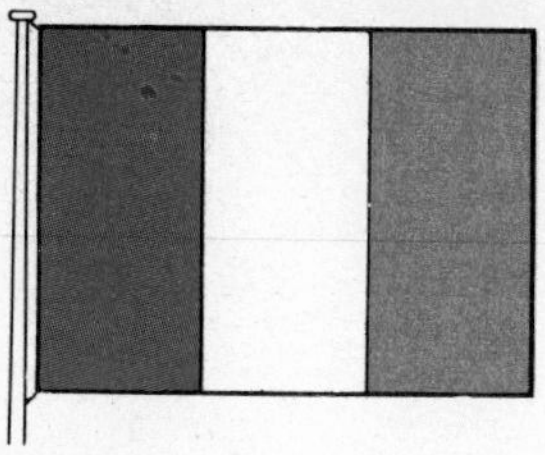

AREA 210,038 sq. mi.
POPULATION 53,300,000
CAPITAL Paris
LARGEST CITY Paris
HIGHEST POINT Mont Blanc 15,771 ft.
MONETARY UNIT franc
MAJOR LANGUAGE French
MAJOR RELIGION Roman Catholicism

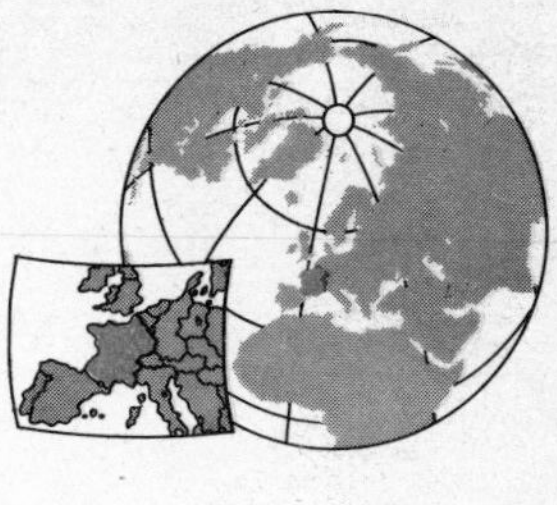

Topography

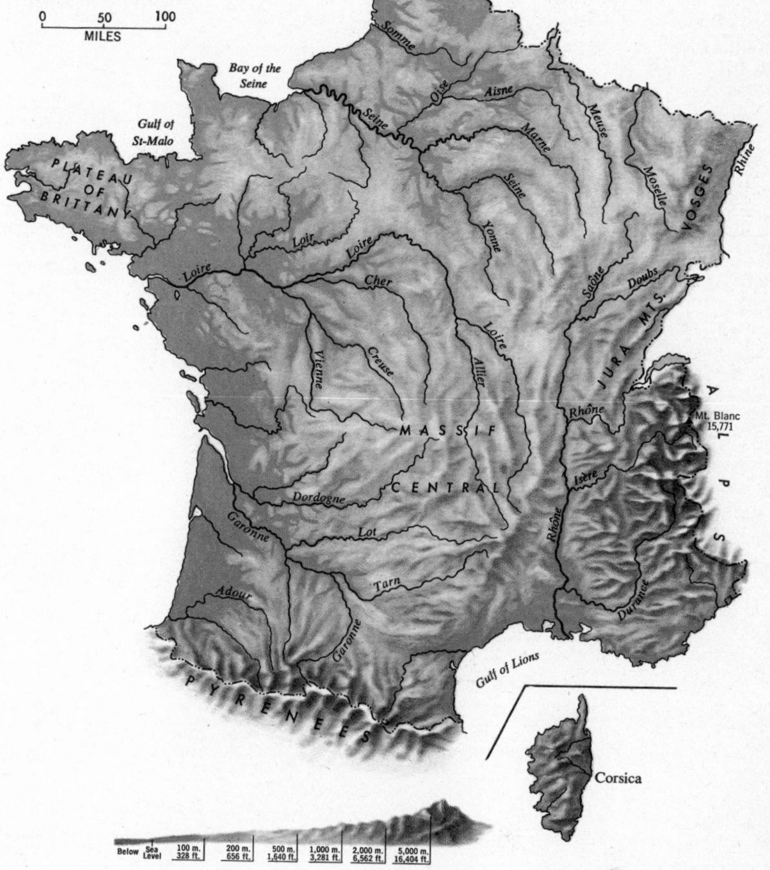
0 50 100
MILES
Bay of the Seine
Gulf of St-Malo
PLATEAU OF BRITTANY
Somme
Oise
Aisne
Seine
Marne
Meuse
Moselle
Rhine
VOSGES
Yonne
Loir
Loire
Cher
Saône
Doubs
JURA MTS.
Vienne
Creuse
Allier
MASSIF CENTRAL
Rhône
Mt. Blanc 15,771
A L P S
Isère
Dordogne
Garonne
Lot
Tarn
Adour
Durance
Gulf of Lions
PYRENEES
Corsica
Below Sea Level
100 m. 328 ft.
200 m. 656 ft.
500 m. 1,640 ft.
1,000 m. 3,281 ft.
2,000 m. 6,562 ft.
5,000 m. 16,404 ft.

HISTORIC PROVINCES

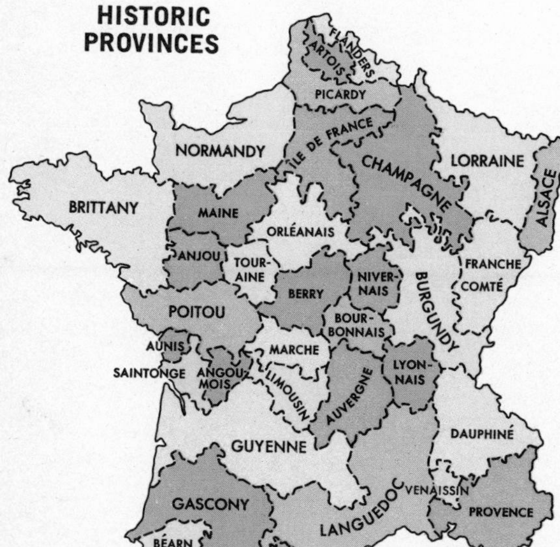
FLANDERS
ARTOIS
PICARDY
NORMANDY
ILE DE FRANCE
CHAMPAGNE
LORRAINE
ALSACE
BRITTANY
MAINE
ORLÉANAIS
ANJOU
TOUR-AINE
BERRY
NIVER-NAIS
BURGUNDY
FRANCHE COMTÉ
POITOU
BOUR-BONNAIS
AUNIS
MARCHE
SAINTONGE
ANGOU-MOIS
LIMOUSIN
AUVERGNE
LYON-NAIS
GUYENNE
DAUPHINÉ
GASCONY
VENAISSIN
LANGUEDOC
PROVENCE
BÉARN
FOIX
ROUSSILLON

A resident of the city of Caen thinks of himself as a Norman rather than as a citizen of the modern department of Calvados. In spite of the passing of nearly two centuries, the historic provinces which existed before 1790 command the local patriotism of most Frenchmen.

Courbevoie, 57,998 ....A 1
Coutances, 8,599 ....C 3
Coutras, 4,251 ....C 5
Creil, 31,792 ....E 3
Crépy-en-Valois, 8,506 ....E 3
Créteil, 48,757 ....B 2
Cusset, 12,286 ....E 4
Dax, 18,185 ....C 6
Deauville, 5,103 ....C 3
Decazeville, 9,581 ....E 5
Denain, 27,840 ....E 2
Dieppe, 29,829 ....D 3
Digne, 11,973 ....G 5
Digoin, 9,585 ....F 4
Dijon, 143,120 ....F 4
Dinan, 12,939 ....B 3
Dinard, 9,042 ....B 3
Dôle, 25,620 ....F 4
Domrémy-la-Pucelle, 184 ....F 3
Douai, 47,347 ....E 2
Douarnenez, 18,442 ....A 3
Draguignan, 16,139 ....G 6
Drancy, 69,226 ....B 1
Dreux, 28,156 ....D 3
Dunkirk (Dunkerque), 26,038 ....E 2
Elbeuf, 19,110 ....D 3
Embrun, 3,986 ....G 5
Épernay, 26,094 ....E 3
Épinal, 36,219 ....G 3
Épinay-sur-Seine, 41,538 ....B 1
Étampes, 15,542 ....E 3
Étaples, 9,092 ....D 2
Eu, 7,866 ....D 3
Évreux, 41,004 ....D 3
Évry, 7,047 ....E 3
Falaise, 6,977 ....C 3
Fécamp, 21,098 ....D 3
Figeac, 8,462 ....D 5
Firminy, 24,545 ....F 5
Flers, 16,677 ....C 3
Foix, 9,061 ....D 6
Fontainebleau, 17,565 ....E 3
Fontenay-le-Comte, 10,884 ....C 4
Fontenay-sous-Bois, 38,737 ....C 2
Forbach, 23,062 ....G 3
Fougères, 25,745 ....C 3
Fourmies, 14,895 ....F 2
Fréjus, 22,567 ....G 6
Gagny, 35,745 ....C 1
Gap, 22,027 ....G 5
Gardanne, 12,601 ....F 6
Gennevilliers, 45,925 ....B 1
Gentilly, 18,638 ....B 2
Gex, 3,078 ....G 4
Gien, 11,655 ....E 4
Gisors, 7,024 ....D 3
Givet, 7,697 ....F 2
Givors, 17,545 ....F 5
Granville, 12,315 ....C 3
Grasse, 24,398 ....G 6
Graulhet, 10,318 ....E 6
Gray, 7,782 ....F 4
Grenoble, 161,230 ....F 5
Guebwiller, 10,684 ....G 4
Guéret, 12,441 ....D 4
Guingamp, 9,091 ....B 3
Guise, 6,732 ....E 3
Haguenau, 22,335 ....G 3
Ham, 5,565 ....E 3
Harfleur, 15,503 ....D 3
Hautmont, 17,818 ....F 2
Hayange, 10,218 ....F 3
Hazebrouck, 16,768 ....E 2
Hendaye, 7,536 ....C 6
Hénin-Liétard, 25,067 ....E 2
Hennebont, 7,605 ....B 4
Héricourt, 7,376 ....G 4
Hirson, 11,764 ....F 3
Honfleur, 9,017 ....D 3
Hyères, 27,600 ....G 6
Issoire, 11,745 ....E 5
Issoudun, 14,559 ....D 4
Issy-les-Moulineaux, 50,260 ....A 2
Istres, 8,713 ....F 6
Ivry-sur-Seine, 60,342 ....B 2
Joigny, 9,609 ....E 3
La Baule-Escoublac, 11,962 ....B 4
La Ciotat, 19,485 ....F 6
La Courneuve, 42,812 ....B 1
La Flèche, 9,536 ....C 4
La Grand-Combe, 8,608 ....E 5
La Roche-sur-Yon, 32,279 ....C 4
La Rochelle, 72,075 ....C 4
La Seyne-sur-Mer, 42,958 ....F 6
La Tour-du-Pin, 5,649 ....F 5
L'Aigle, 7,478 ....D 3
Landerneau, 12,356 ....B 3
Langeac, 4,584 ....E 5
Langres, 8,945 ....F 4
Lannion, 10,066 ....B 3
Laon, 25,623 ....E 3
Laval, 45,051 ....C 3
Lavelanet, 8,512 ....E 6
Le Blanc-Mesnil, 48,212 ....B 1
Le Bourget, 9,625 ....B 1
Le Cateau, 8,922 ....E 2
Le Chesnay, 13,586 ....A 2
Le Creusot, 33,581 ....F 4
Le Croisic, 4,092 ....B 4
Le Havre, 198,021 ....C 3
Le Mans, 140,520 ....C 3
Le Puy, 24,816 ....F 5
Le Teil, 7,872 ....F 5
Le Touquet-Paris-Plage, 4,403 ....D 2
Le Tréport, 6,194 ....D 2
Lens, 41,800 ....E 2
Les Andelys, 6,292 ....D 3
Les Sables-d'Olonne, 17,856 ....B 4
Levallois-Perret, 58,890 ....B 1
Lézignan-Corbières, 7,101 ....E 6
Libourne, 19,981 ....C 5
Liévin, 35,733 ....E 2
Lille, 189,697 ....E 2
Lille, †1,042,000 ....E 2
Limoges, 127,605 ....D 5
Limoux, 9,150 ....E 6
Lisieux, 23,337 ....D 3
Livry-Gargan, 32,015 ....C 1
Lodève, 6,899 ....E 6
Longwy, 21,052 ....F 3
Lons-le-Saunier, 18,649 ....F 4
Lorient, 66,023 ....B 4
Loudun, 6,118 ....D 4
Lourdes, 17,627 ....C 6
Louviers, 15,159 ....D 3
Lunel, 10,178 ....E 6
Lunéville, 22,961 ....G 3
Luxeuil-les-Bains, 9,203 ....G 4
Lyon, 524,500 ....F 5
Lyon, †1,305,000 ....F 5
Mâcon, 33,266 ....F 4
Maisons-Alfort, 53,118 ....B 2
Maisons-Laffitte, 24,041 ....A 1
Malakoff, 36,198 ....B 2
Manosque, 13,352 ....G 6
Mantes-la-Jolie, 25,842 ....D 3
Marmande, 12,145 ....C 5
Marseille, 880,527 ....F 6
Marseille, †1,015,000 ....F 6
Martigues, 17,771 ....F 6
Maubeuge, 31,992 ....F 2
Mayenne, 10,010 ....C 3
Mazamet, 14,650 ....E 6
Meaux, 29,966 ....E 3
Melun, 33,345 ....E 3
Mende, 9,424 ....E 5
Menton, 23,401 ....G 6
Metz, 105,533 ....G 3
Meudon, 30,735 ....A 2
Millau, 21,420 ....E 5
Moissac, 7,694 ....D 5
Mont-de-Marsan, 22,771 ....C 6
Mont-Dore, 2,045 ....E 5
Mont-Saint-Michel, 72 ....C 3
Montargis, 18,087 ....E 3
Montauban, 33,945 ....D 5
Montbéliard, 23,402 ....G 4
Montbrison, 8,733 ....E 5
Montceau-les-Mines, 18,621 ....F 4
Montdidier, 5,785 ....E 3
Montélimar, 23,831 ....F 5
Montfort, 2,563 ....C 3
Montigny-lès-Metz, 24,417 ....G 3
Montluçon, 57,638 ....E 4
Montpellier, 152,105 ....E 6
Montreuil, 95,420 ....B 2
Montrouge, 44,788 ....B 2
Morlaix, 16,750 ....B 3
Moulins, 25,778 ....E 4
Moûtiers, 4,066 ....G 5
Moyeuvre-Grande, 14,559 ....G 3
Mulhouse, 115,632 ....G 4
Muret, 10,515 ....D 6
Nancy, 121,910 ....G 3
Nanterre, 90,124 ....A 1
Nantes, 253,105 ....C 4
Narbonne, 35,236 ....E 6
Nemours, 8,081 ....E 3
Neufchâteau, 7,656 ....F 3
Neufchâtel-en-Bray, 5,734 ....D 3
Neuilly-sur-Seine, 70,787 ....B 1
Nevers, 42,092 ....E 4
Nice, 301,400 ....G 6
Nîmes, 115,561 ....F 6
Niort, 46,749 ....C 4
Nogent-le-Rotrou, 11,040 ....D 3
Nogent-sur-Seine, 4,271 ....E 3
Noisy-le-Sec, 34,058 ....B 1
Noyon, 11,567 ....E 3
Nyons, 4,311 ....F 5
Oloron-Sainte-Marie, 12,597 ....C 6
Orange, 17,582 ....F 5
Orléans, 94,382 ....D 3
Orly, 30,151 ....B 2
Orthez, 8,778 ....C 6
Oullins, 26,520 ....F 5
Oyonnax, 19,571 ....F 4
Pamiers, 13,183 ....D 6
Pantin, 47,580 ....B 1
Paray-le-Monial, 10,324 ....F 4
Paris (cap.), 2,580,010 ....B 2
Paris, *7,953,065 ....B 2
Paris, †9,283,000 ....B 2
Parthenay, 11,177 ....C 4
Pau, 71,865 ....C 6
Périgueux, 36,991 ....D 5
Perpignan, 100,086 ....E 6
Pessac, 35,343 ....C 5
Ploërmel, 3,720 ....B 4
Poitiers, 68,082 ....D 4
Pont-à-Mousson, 13,283 ....G 3
Pont-l'Abbé, 6,227 ....A 4
Pont-l'Évêque, 2,823 ....D 3
Pontarlier, 16,250 ....G 4
Pontivy, 9,674 ....B 3
Pontoise, 16,633 ....E 3
Port-de-Bouc, 13,447 ....F 6
Port-Louis, 3,921 ....B 4

(continued on following page)

(continued)

OTHER FEATURES

*City and suburbs.
†Population of metropolitan area.

MONACO

CITIES and TOWNS

MONACO
AREA 368 acres
POPULATION 23,035

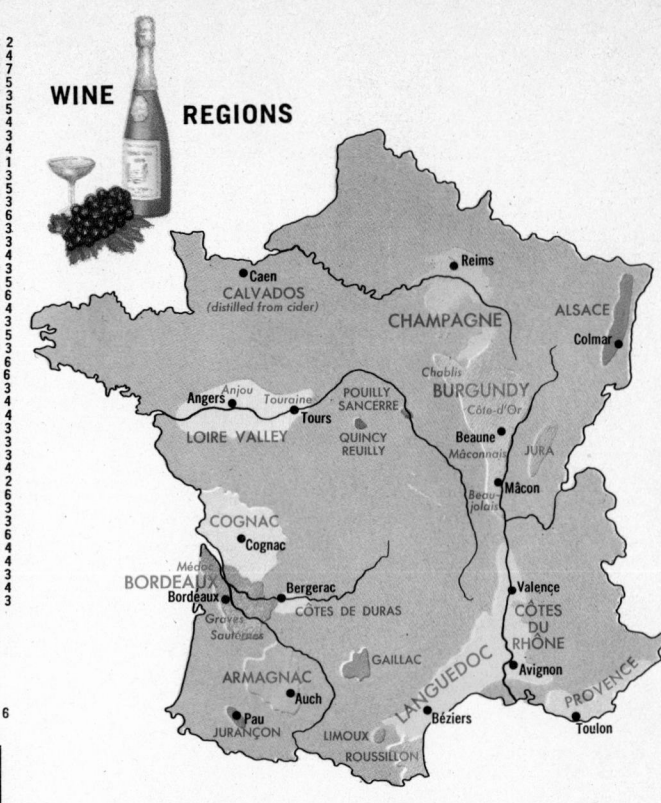

WINE
REGIONS
Caen
CALVADOS
(distilled from cider)
Reims
CHAMPAGNE
ALSACE
Colmar
Chablis
BURGUNDY
Côte-d'Or
Anjou
Angers
Touraine
Tours
POUILLY
SANCERRE
LOIRE VALLEY
QUINCY
REUILLY
Beaune
Mâconnais
JURA
Beaujolais
Mâcon
COGNAC
Cognac
Médoc
BORDEAUX
Bordeaux
Bergerac
Graves
Sauternes
CÔTES DE DURAS
Valence
CÔTES
DU
RHÔNE
GAILLAC
ARMAGNAC
Auch
LANGUEDOC
Avignon
PROVENCE
Pau
JURANÇON
LIMOUX
Béziers
Toulon
ROUSSILLON

Climate, soil and variety of grape planted determine the quality of wine. Long, hot and fairly dry summers with cool, humid nights constitute an ideal climate. The nature of the soil is such a determining influence that identical grapes planted in Bordeaux, Burgundy and Champagne, will yield wines of widely different types.

Agriculture, Industry and Resources

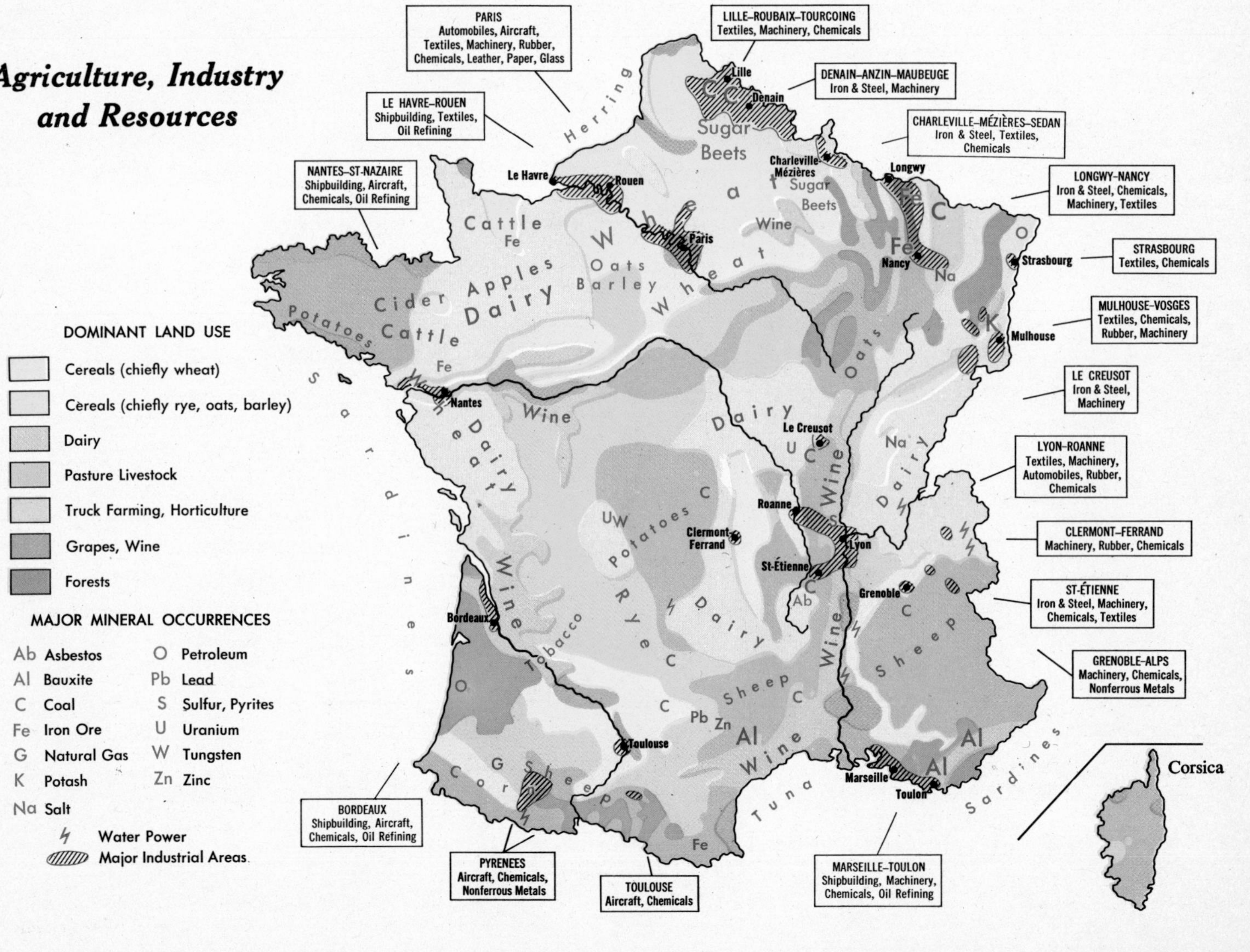
DOMINANT LAND USE
Cereals (chiefly wheat)
Cereals (chiefly rye, oats, barley)
Dairy
Pasture Livestock
Truck Farming, Horticulture
Grapes, Wine
Forests
MAJOR MINERAL OCCURRENCES
Ab Asbestos
Al Bauxite
C Coal
Fe Iron Ore
G Natural Gas
K Potash
Na Salt
O Petroleum
Pb Lead
S Sulfur, Pyrites
U Uranium
W Tungsten
Zn Zinc
Water Power
Major Industrial Areas
PARIS
Automobiles, Aircraft, Textiles, Machinery, Rubber, Chemicals, Leather, Paper, Glass
LILLE–ROUBAIX–TOURCOING
Textiles, Machinery, Chemicals
DENAIN–ANZIN–MAUBEUGE
Iron & Steel, Machinery
LE HAVRE–ROUEN
Shipbuilding, Textiles, Oil Refining
CHARLEVILLE–MÉZIÈRES–SEDAN
Iron & Steel, Textiles, Chemicals
NANTES–ST-NAZAIRE
Shipbuilding, Aircraft, Chemicals, Oil Refining
LONGWY–NANCY
Iron & Steel, Chemicals, Machinery, Textiles
STRASBOURG
Textiles, Chemicals
MULHOUSE–VOSGES
Textiles, Chemicals, Rubber, Machinery
LE CREUSOT
Iron & Steel, Machinery
LYON–ROANNE
Textiles, Machinery, Automobiles, Rubber, Chemicals
CLERMONT–FERRAND
Machinery, Rubber, Chemicals
ST-ÉTIENNE
Iron & Steel, Machinery, Chemicals, Textiles
GRENOBLE–ALPS
Machinery, Chemicals, Nonferrous Metals
BORDEAUX
Shipbuilding, Aircraft, Chemicals, Oil Refining
PYRENEES
Aircraft, Chemicals, Nonferrous Metals
TOULOUSE
Aircraft, Chemicals
MARSEILLE–TOULON
Shipbuilding, Machinery, Chemicals, Oil Refining
Lille
Denain
Herring
Sugar Beets
Charleville-Mézières
Longwy
Le Havre
Rouen
Paris
Nancy
Strasbourg
Mulhouse
Cattle
Cider Apples
Dairy
Potatoes
Oats
Barley
Wheat
Wine
Nantes
Le Creusot
Roanne
Clermont-Ferrand
Lyon
St-Étienne
Grenoble
Bordeaux
Tobacco
Rye
Sheep
Toulouse
Marseille
Toulon
Tuna
Sardines
Corsica

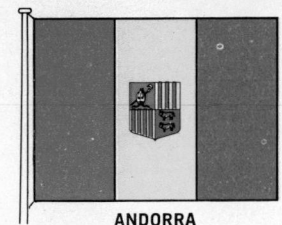
ANDORRA

SPAIN

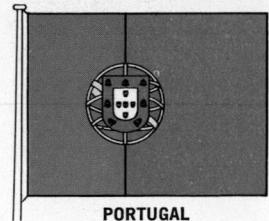
PORTUGAL

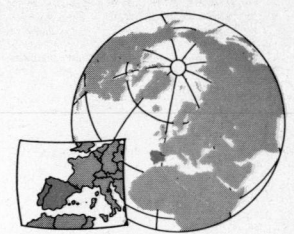

SPAIN

AREA 194,881 sq. mi.
POPULATION 36,000,000
CAPITAL Madrid
LARGEST CITY Madrid
HIGHEST POINT Pico de Teide 12,172 ft. (Canary Is.);
Mulhacén 11,411 ft. (mainland)
MONETARY UNIT peseta
MAJOR LANGUAGES Spanish, Catalan,
Basque, Galician, Valencian
MAJOR RELIGION Roman Catholicism

ANDORRA

AREA 188 sq. mi.
POPULATION 26,558
CAPITAL Andorra la Vella
MONETARY UNIT French franc, Spanish peseta
MAJOR LANGUAGE Catalan
MAJOR RELIGION Roman Catholicism

PORTUGAL

AREA 35,549 sq. mi.
POPULATION 8,825,000
CAPITAL Lisbon
LARGEST CITY Lisbon
HIGHEST POINT Malhão da Estrêla 6,532 ft.
MONETARY UNIT escudo
MAJOR LANGUAGE Portuguese
MAJOR RELIGION Roman Catholicism

GIBRALTAR

AREA 2.28 sq. mi.
POPULATION 30,000
CAPITAL Gibraltar
MONETARY UNIT pound sterling
MAJOR LANGUAGES English, Spanish
MAJOR RELIGION Roman Catholicism

Agriculture, Industry and Resources

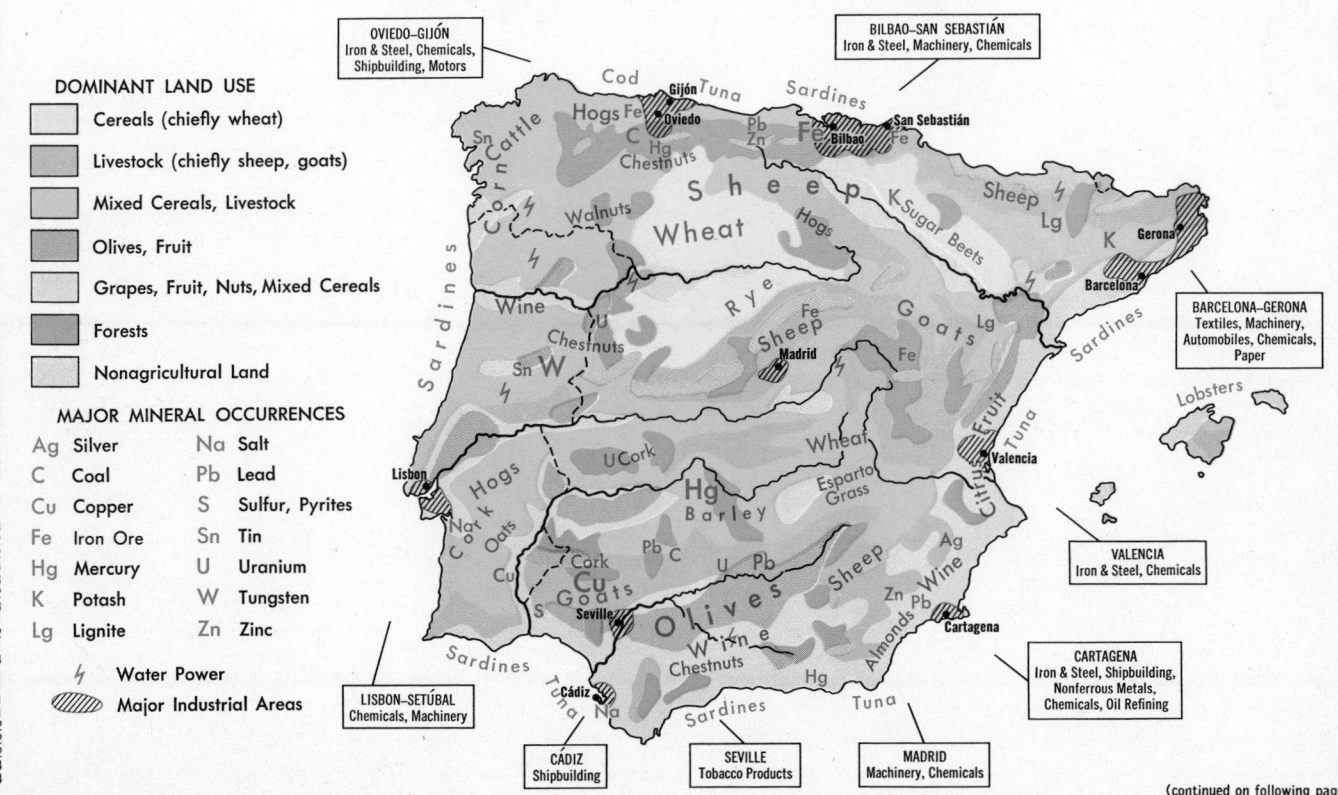

OVIEDO–GIJÓN
Iron & Steel, Chemicals,
Shipbuilding, Motors

BILBAO–SAN SEBASTIÁN
Iron & Steel, Machinery, Chemicals

BARCELONA–GERONA
Textiles, Machinery,
Automobiles, Chemicals,
Paper

VALENCIA
Iron & Steel, Chemicals

CARTAGENA
Iron & Steel, Shipbuilding,
Nonferrous Metals,
Chemicals, Oil Refining

LISBON–SETÚBAL
Chemicals, Machinery

CADIZ
Shipbuilding

SEVILLE
Tobacco Products

MADRID
Machinery, Chemicals

DOMINANT LAND USE

Cereals (chiefly wheat)
Livestock (chiefly sheep, goats)
Mixed Cereals, Livestock
Olives, Fruit
Grapes, Fruit, Nuts, Mixed Cereals
Forests
Nonagricultural Land

MAJOR MINERAL OCCURRENCES

Ag Silver
C Coal
Cu Copper
Fe Iron Ore
Hg Mercury
K Potash
Lg Lignite
Na Salt
Pb Lead
S Sulfur, Pyrites
Sn Tin
U Uranium
W Tungsten
Zn Zinc

⚡ Water Power
▨ Major Industrial Areas

(continued on following page)

SPAIN (continued)

Salt, 5,572 ...H 1
Sama, 9,863 ...D 1
San Carlos de la Rápita, 8,946 ...G 2
San Clemente, 6,016 ...E 3
San Felíu de Guixols, 12,006 ...H 2
San Fernando, 59,309 ...C 4
San Ildefonso, 3,198 ...E 2
San Lorenzo de El Escorial, 8,098 ...E 2
Sanlúcar de Barrameda, 29,483 ...C 4
Sanlúcar la Mayor, 6,121 ...C 4
San Roque, 8,224 ...D 4
San Sebastián, 159,557 ...E 1
Santa Cruz de la Palma, 10,393 ...B 4
Santa Cruz de Mudela, 6,354 ...E 3
Santa Cruz de Tenerife, 74,910 ...B 4
Santa Eugenia, 5,946 ...B 1
Santafé, 8,990 ...E 4
Santander, 130,019 ...D 1
Santiago, 51,620 ...B 1
Santo Domingo de la Calzada, 5,638 ...E 1
Santoña, 9,546 ...E 1
San Vicente de Alcántara, 7,006 ...C 3
Saragossa, 449,319 ...F 2
Saragossa, ★500,000 ...F 2
Segorbe, 6,962 ...G 2
Segovia, 41,880 ...D 2
Seo de Urgel, 6,604 ...G 1
Sestao, 37,312 ...E 1
Seville, 511,447 ...D 4
Seville, ★560,000 ...D 4
Sitges, 8,906 ...G 2
Socuéllamos, 12,610 ...E 3
Sóller, 6,470 ...H 3
Solsona, 5,346 ...G 2
Sonseca, 6,594 ...D 3
Soria, 24,744 ...E 2
Sotrondio, 5,914 ...D 1
Sueca, 20,019 ...F 3
Tabernes de Valldigna, 13,962 ...G 3

Tafalla, 8,858 ...F 1
Talavera de la Reina, 39,889 ...D 2
Tarancón, 8,238 ...E 2
Tarazona, 11,067 ...E 2
Tarazona de la Mancha, 5,952 ...F 3
Tarifa, 9,201 ...D 4
Tarragona, 53,548 ...G 2
Tarrasa, 134,481 ...G 2
Tárrega, 9,036 ...G 2
Tauste, 6,832 ...F 2
Telde, 13,257 ...B 5
Teruel, 20,614 ...F 2
Tobarra, 5,887 ...F 3
Toledo, 43,905 ...D 3
Tolosa, 15,164 ...E 1
Tomelloso, 26,041 ...E 3
Tordesillas, 5,815 ...D 2
Toro, 8,455 ...D 2
Torredonjimeno, 12,507 ...D 4
Torrejón de Ardoz, 21,081 ...F 4
Torrelavega, 19,933 ...D 1
Torremolinos, 20,484 ...D 4
Torrente, 38,397 ...F 3
Torrevieja, 9,431 ...F 4
Torrijos, 6,362 ...D 2
Torrox, 5,583 ...E 4
Tortosa, 20,030 ...G 2
Totana, 12,714 ...F 4
Trigueros, 6,280 ...C 4
Trujillo, 9,024 ...D 3
Tudela, 20,942 ...F 1
Ubeda, 28,306 ...E 3
Ubrique, 13,166 ...D 4
Utiel, 9,168 ...F 3
Utrera, 28,287 ...D 4
Valdemoro, 6,263 ...F 4
Valdepeñas, 24,018 ...E 3
Valencia, 626,675 ...F 3
Valencia, ★700,000 ...F 3
Valencia de Alcántara, 5,963 ...C 3
Valladolid, 227,511 ...D 2
Vall de Uxó, 23,976 ...F 3
Vallecas ...G 4
Valls, 14,189 ...G 2
Valverde del Camino, 10,566 ...C 4
Vejer de la Frontera, 6,184 ...C 4

OTHER FEATURES

Alborán (isl.) ...E 5
Alcaraz, Sierra de (range) ...E 3
Alcudia (bay) ...H 3
Almanzor (mt.) ...D 2
Almanzora (riv.) ...E 3
Andalusia (reg.), 5,971,277 ...C 4
Aneto (peak) ...G 1
Aragón (reg.), 1,152,710 ...F 2
Arosa, Ría de (est.) ...B 1

Vélez-Málaga, 20,794 ...E 4
Vendrell, 7,951 ...G 2
Vera, 4,903 ...F 4
Vergara, 11,541 ...E 1
Vicálvaro ...G 4
Vich, 23,449 ...H 2
Vigo, 114,526 ...B 1
Villacañas, 9,883 ...E 3
Villacarrillo, 9,452 ...E 3
Villafranca de Los Barros, 12,610 ...C 3
Villafranca del Penedés, 16,875 ...G 2
Villagarcía, 6,601 ...B 1
Villajoyosa, 12,573 ...F 4
Villanueva de Córdoba, 11,270 ...D 3
Villanueva del Arzobispo, 8,076 ...E 3
Villanueva de la Serena, 16,687 ...D 3
Villanueva de los Infantes, 8,154 ...E 3
Villanueva y Geltrú, 35,714 ...G 2
Villarreal de los Infantes, 29,482 ...G 3
Villarrobledo, 19,698 ...E 3
Villarrubia de los Ojos, 9,144 ...E 3
Villaverde ...F 4
Villena, 23,483 ...F 3
Vinaroz, 13,727 ...G 2
Vitoria, 124,791 ...E 1
Yecla, 19,352 ...F 3
Zafra, 11,583 ...C 3
Zalamea la Serena, 6,017 ...D 3
Zamora, 48,791 ...D 2
Zaragoza (Saragossa), 449,319 ...F 2

OTHER FEATURES

Asturias (reg.), 1,045,635 ...C 1
Autza (mt.) ...F 1
Balaitous (mt.) ...F 1
Balearic (Baleares) (isls.), 558,287 ...H 3
Barbate (riv.) ...D 4
Biscay (gulf) ...E 1
Cabrera (isl.) ...H 3
Cádiz (gulf) ...C 4
Cala Burras (pt.) ...H 3
Canary (isls.), 1,170,224 ...B 4
Cantabrian (range) ...C 1
Catalonia (reg.), 5,122,567 ...G 2
Cinca (riv.) ...G 2
Columbretes (isls.), 2 ...G 3
Costa Brava (reg.) ...H 2
Costa de Sola (Costa del Sol) (reg.) ...D 4
Creus (cape) ...H 1
Cuenca, Sierra de (range) ...E 2
Demanda, Sierra de la (range) ...E 1
Douro (riv.) ...C 2
Duero (Douro) (riv.) ...C 2
Ebro (riv.) ...F 2
Eresma (riv.) ...D 2
Esla (riv.) ...D 2
Estats (peak) ...G 1
Estremadura (reg.), 1,145,376 ...C 3
Finisterre (cape) ...B 1
Formentera (isl.), 2,965 ...G 3
Formentor (cape) ...H 3
Fuerteventura (isl.), 18,192 ...C 4
Galicia (reg.), 2,583,674 ...B 1
Gata (cape) ...F 4
Gata (mts.) ...C 2
Genil (riv.) ...D 4
Gibraltar (str.) ...D 5
Gomera (isl.), 19,339 ...B 5
Gran Canaria (isl.), 519,606 ...B 5
Gredos, Sierra de (range) ...D 2
Guadalimar (riv.) ...E 3
Guadalquivir (riv.) ...C 4
Guadarrama, Sierra de (range) ...E 2
Guadiana (riv.) ...D 3
Gúdar, Sierra de (range) ...F 2

Henares (riv.) ...G 4
Hierro (isl.), 5,503 ...A 5
Ibiza (isl.), 45,075 ...G 3
Jalón (riv.) ...E 2
Jarama (riv.) ...F 4
Júcar (riv.) ...F 3
Lanzarote (isl.), 41,912 ...C 4
La Palma (isl.), 65,291 ...A 4
León (reg.), 1,172,262 ...C 2
Llobregat (riv.) ...G 2
Majorca (isl.), 462,995 ...H 3
Mallorca (Majorca) (isl.), 462,995 ...H 3
Mancha, La (reg.) ...E 3
Manzanares (riv.) ...F 4
Marismas, Las (marsh) ...C 4
Mar Menor (lag.) ...F 4
Mayor (cape) ...D 1
Menorca (Minorca) (isl.), 50,217 ...J 2
Minho (riv.) ...B 1
Minorca (isl.), 50,217 ...J 2
Moncayo, Sierra de (range) ...F 2
Mont Rouge (peak) ...G 1
Montserrat (mt.) ...G 2
Morena, Sierra (range) ...D 3
Mulhacén (mt.) ...E 4
Murcia (reg.), 1,167,339 ...F 3
Nao (cape) ...G 3
Navia (riv.) ...C 1
Nevada, Sierra (mts.) ...E 4
New Castile (reg.), 5,164,026 ...E 3
Odiel (riv.) ...C 4
Old Castile (reg.), 2,153,785 ...D 2
Orbigo (riv.) ...D 1
Palos (cape) ...F 4
Peñalara (mt.) ...E 2
Peñas (cape) ...D 1
Peña Vieja (mt.) ...D 1
Penibética, Sistema (range) ...E 4
Perdido (mt.) ...G 1
Pyrenees (range) ...G 1
Rosas (gulf) ...H 1
San Jorge (gulf) ...G 2
Segre (riv.) ...G 2
Segura (riv.) ...F 3
Sil (riv.) ...C 1
Tagus (riv.) ...F 3
Tajo (Tagus) (riv.) ...F 3
Teide, Pico de (peak) ...B 5
Tenerife (isl.), 500,381 ...B 5
Ter (riv.) ...H 1
Tinto (riv.) ...C 4
Toledo (mts.) ...C 3
Tortosa (cape) ...G 2

Trafalgar (cape) ...C 4
Turia (riv.) ...F 3
Ulla (riv.) ...B 1
Urgel, Llanos de (plain) ...G 2
Valencia (gulf) ...G 3
Valencia (reg.), 3,073,255 ...F 3
Valencia, Albufera de (lag.) ...F 3
Vascongadas (reg.), 1,878,636 ...E 1

PORTUGAL

PROVINCES

Algarve, 266,621 ...B 4
Alto Alentejo, 304,542 ...C 3
Baixo Alentejo, 267,733 ...C 4
Beira Alta, 545,904 ...C 2
Beira Baixa, 275,379 ...C 2
Beira Litoral, 976,826 ...B 2
Douro Litoral, 1,518,804 ...B 2
Estremadura, 2,121,562 ...A 3
Madeira, 253,220 ...
Minho, 867,296 ...B 1
Ribatejo, 467,730 ...B 3
Trás-os-Montes e Alto Douro, 511,722 ...C 2

Topography

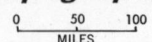

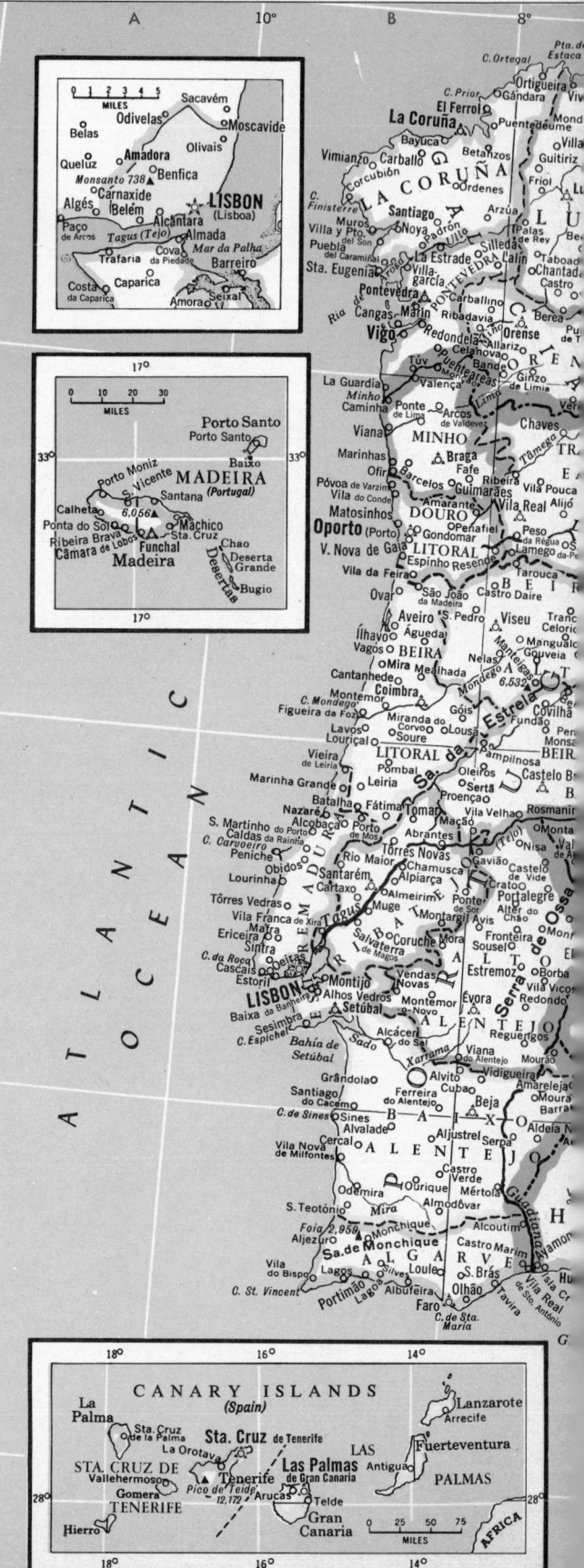

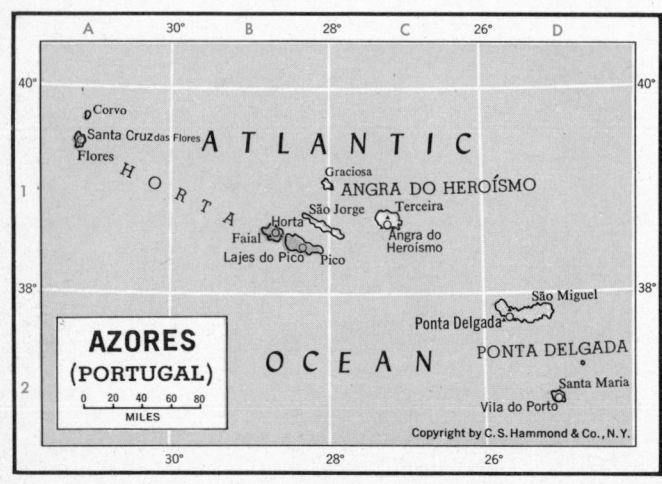

AZORES

INTERNAL DIVISIONS

Angra do Heroismo (dist.), 83,500 ...C 1
Horta (dist.), 38,700 ...A 1
Ponta Delgada (dist.), 153,700 ...D 2

CITIES and TOWNS

Angra do Heroismo, 13,795 ...C 1
Horta, 6,145 ...B 1
Lajes do Pico, 2,147 ...B 1
Ponta Delgada, 20,195 ...C 2
Santa Cruz das Flores, 1,880 ...A 1
Vila do Porto, 4,149 ...D 2

OTHER FEATURES

Azores (isls.), 275,900 ...A 2
Corvo (isl.), 469 ...A 1
Faial (isl.), 17,474 ...B 1
Flores (isl.), 5,302 ...A 1
Graciosa (isl.), 7,188 ...C 1
Pico (isl.), 18,014 ...C 1
Santa Maria (isl.), 9,487 ...D 2
São Jorge (isl.), 12,853 ...B 1
São Miguel (isl.), 149,873 ...C 1
Terceira (isl.), 70,368 ...C 1

Copyright by C. S. Hammond & Co., N.Y.

CITIES and TOWNS

...tes, 11,775 ....B 3	Borba, 4,879 ....C 3
...da, 9,343 ....B 3	Braga, 48,735 ....B 2
...eira, 7,479 ....B 4	Bragança, 9,310 ....B 2
...er do Sal, 13,187 ....B 3	Caldas da Rainha, 13,070 ....B 3
...tara, 23,699 ....A 1	Câmara de Lobos, 14,068 ....A 2
...228 ....C 4	Campo Maior, 7,405 ....C 3
... Nova de São Bento,	Cantanhede, 6,734 ....B 2
...18,010 ....B 3	Caparica, 13,315 ....A 1
... Vedros, 7,915 ....A 1	Carnaxide, 38,309 ....A 1
...rel, 7,473 ....B 3	Cartaxo, 6,628 ....B 3
...da, 38,990 ....A 1	Cascais, 14,925 ....A 1
...rim, 8,780 ....A 1	Castelo Branco, 18,740 ....C 2
...ça, 7,623 ....B 2	Cercal, 5,021 ....B 4
...ora, 65,870 ....B 2	Chaves, 11,465 ....C 2
... 6,067 ....B 2	Coimbra, 55,985 ....B 2
...a, 10,330 ....A 1	Coruche, 17,461 ....B 3
... 19,905 ....A 1	Cova da Piedade, 21,000 ....A 1
...1,686 ....C 3	Covilhã, 26,530 ....C 2
...ro, 53,690 ....B 1	Elvas, 10,305 ....C 3
...6,673 ....C 3	Espinho, 11,745 ....B 2
...14,760 ....C 3	Estoril, 15,740 ....A 1
...12,001 ....A 1	Estremoz, 9,565 ....C 3
... 19,043 ....A 1	Évora, 23,665 ....C 3
...a, 39,459 ....A 1	Faro, 20,470 ....B 4
	Fátima, 6,433 ....B 3
	Ferreira do Alentejo, 6,153 ....B 3

Figueira da Foz, 10,485 ....B 2	Montemor-o-Novo, 9,284 ....B 3
Funchal, 38,340 ....A 2	Montijo, 26,730 ....A 1
Fundão, 5,081 ....C 2	Moscavide, 21,765 ....A 1
Gondomar, 14,105 ....B 2	Moura, 9,351 ....C 3
Grândola, 9,698 ....B 3	Nazaré, 8,553 ....B 3
Guarda, 9,735 ....C 2	Odemira, 6,793 ....B 4
Guimarães, 24,280 ....B 2	Odivelas, 26,020 ....A 1
Ilhavo, 11,083 ....B 2	Oeiras, 14,880 ....A 1
Lagoa, 5,694 ....B 4	Olhão, 11,155 ....C 4
Lagos, 10,359 ....B 4	Olivais, 55,138 ....A 1
Lamego, 10,350 ....C 2	Ovar, 16,004 ....B 2
Lavos, 5,051 ....B 2	Paço de Arcos, 11,791 ....A 1
Leiria, 7,540 ....B 3	Penafiel, 6,463 ....B 2
Loulé, 12,777 ....B 4	Peniche, 12,555 ....B 3
Louriçal, 6,087 ....B 2	Peso da Régua, 5,376 ....C 2
Lourinhã, 7,340 ....B 3	Pombal, 12,508 ....B 2
Lousã, 7,341 ....B 2	Ponta do Sol, 5,599 ....A 2
Machico, 10,905 ....A 2	Ponte de Sor, 9,951 ....B 3
Mafra, 7,149 ....A 1	Portalegre, 10,970 ....C 3
Marinha Grande, 18,548 ....B 3	Portimão, 10,308 ....B 4
Matosinhos, 22,505 ....B 2	Porto (Oporto), 350,000 ....B 2
Mira, 12,740 ....B 2	Póvoa de Varzim, 17,415 ....B 2
Mirandela, 5,203 ....C 2	Queluz, 25,845 ....A 1
Monchique, 8,155 ....B 4	Redondo, 6,858 ....C 3
Montargil, 5,070 ....B 3	Reguengos de Monsaraz, 5,806 ....C 3
	Ribeira Brava, 7,416 ....A 2

Rio Maior, 10,206 ....B 3	Vila do Conde, 16,485 ....B 2
Sacavém, 12,625 ....A 1	Vila Franca de Xira, 13,070 ....B 3
Salvaterra de Magos, 6,265 ....B 3	Vila Nova de Gaia, 50,805 ....B 2
Santa Cruz, 6,348 ....A 2	Vila Real, 10,050 ....C 2
Santarém, 16,850 ....B 3	Vila Real de Santo António,
Santiago do Cacem, 5,887 ....B 3	10,320 ....C 4
São Brás de Alportel, 7,632 ....C 4	Viseu, 16,140 ....C 2
São João da Madeira, 14,225 ....B 2	
São Teotónio, 6,146 ....B 4	**OTHER FEATURES**
São Vicente, 5,147 ....A 2	
Serpa, 7,991 ....C 3	Atlantic Ocean ....A 3
Sertã, 6,043 ....B 3	Carvoeiro (cape) ....A 2
Sesimbra, 8,041 ....A 1	Desertas (isls.) ....A 2
Setúbal, 49,670 ....B 3	Douro (riv.) ....C 2
Silves, 9,493 ....B 4	Espichel (cape) ....B 3
Sines, 6,996 ....B 4	Estrela, Serra da (mts.) ....C 2
Sintra, 15,994 ....A 1	Guadiana (riv.) ....C 4
Soure, 7,620 ....B 2	Lima (riv.) ....B 2
Tavira, 10,263 ....C 4	Madeira (isl.) 253,220 ....A 2
Tomar, 10,905 ....B 3	Madeira (isls.) 249,300 ....A 2
Tôrres Novas, 13,806 ....B 3	Minho (riv.) ....B 2
Tôrres Vedras, 14,833 ....B 3	Mondego (riv.) ....B 2
Vagos, 5,088 ....B 2	Monchique, Serra de (mts.) ....B 4
Vendas Novas, 8,979 ....B 3	Monsanto (mt.) ....C 2
Viana do Castelo, 12,510 ....B 2	Monsanto (mt.) ....A 1
Vila da Feira, 5,222 ....B 2	Ossa, Serra da (mts.) ....C 3

Palma, Mar da (bay) ....A 1	
Porto Santo (isl.), 3,927 ....B 2	
Roca (cape) ....A 1	
Sado (riv.) ....B 3	
Saint Vincent (cape) ....B 4	
Santa Maria (cape) ....C 4	
Setubal (bay) ....B 3	
Tagus (riv.) ....C 3	
Tâmega (riv.) ....C 2	
Tejo (Tagus) (riv.) ....C 3	
Xarrama (riv.) ....B 3	

ANDORRA

CITIES and TOWNS

Andorra la Vella (cap.), 12,000 ....G 1

GIBRALTAR

Gibraltar, 29,927 ....D 4

PHYSICAL FEATURES

Europa (pt.) ....D 4

★ Population of metropolitan area

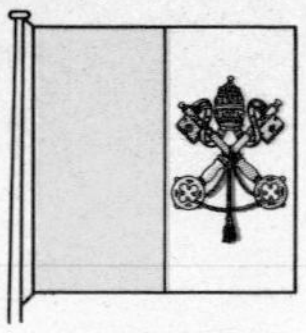

ATICAN CITY

REA 116 acres
OPULATION 704

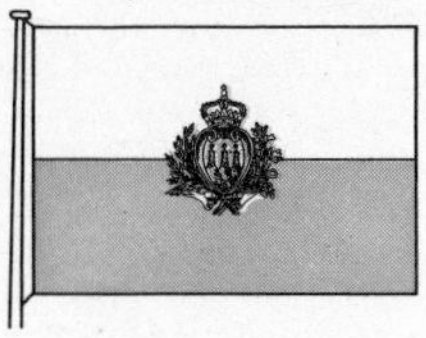

SAN MARINO

REA 23.4 sq. mi.
OPULATION 20,000

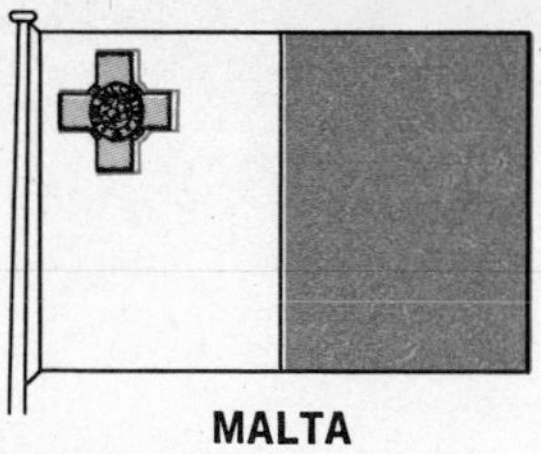

MALTA

AREA 122 sq. mi.
POPULATION 319,000
CAPITAL Valletta
LARGEST CITY Sliema
HIGHEST POINT 787 ft.
MONETARY UNIT Maltese pound
MAJOR LANGUAGES Maltese, English
MAJOR RELIGION Roman Catholicism

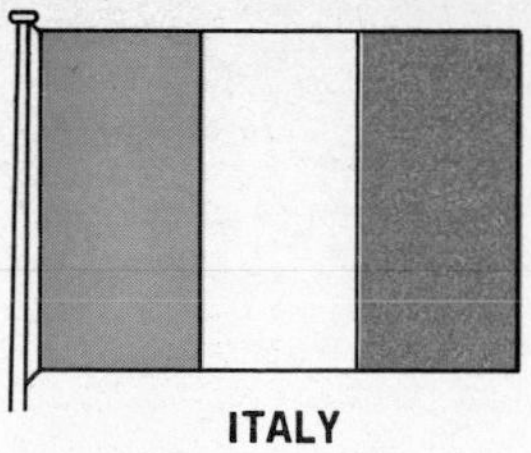

ITALY

AREA 116,303 sq. mi.
POPULATION 56,110,000
CAPITAL Rome
LARGEST CITY Rome
HIGHEST POINT Dufourspitze (Mte. Rosa) 15,203 ft.
MONETARY UNIT lira
MAJOR LANGUAGE Italian
MAJOR RELIGION Roman Catholicism

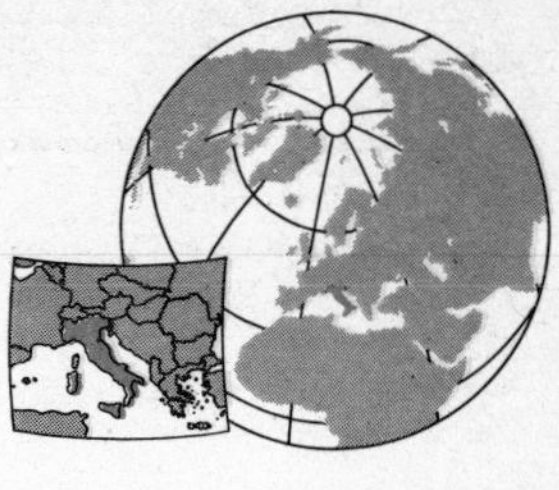

ITALY

REGIONS

ruzzi, 1,166,664	D 3
sta, 109,150	A 2
ulia (Puglia), 3,582,787	F 4
silicata, 603,064	F 4
labria, 1,988,051	F 5
mpania, 5,059,348	E 4
nilia-Romagna, 3,846,755	C 2
iuli-Venezia Giulia, 1,213,532	D 1
tium (Lazio), 4,689,482	D 3
guria, 1,853,578	B 2
mbardy, 8,543,657	B 2
arche, 1,359,907	D 3
olise, 319,807	E 4
edmont, 4,432,313	A 2
rdinia, 1,473,800	B 4
cily, 4,680,715	D 6
entino-Alto Adige, 841,886	C 1
scany, 3,473,097	C 3
nbria, 775,783	D 3
enetia (Veneto), 2,109,502	C 2

PROVINCES

grigento, 454,045	D 6
essandria, 483,183	B 2
ncona, 416,611	D 3
sta, 109,150	A 2
ezzo, 306,340	C 3
scoli Piceno, 340,758	D 3
sti, 218,547	B 2
vellino, 427,509	E 4
ri, 1,351,288	F 4
lluno, 221,155	D 1
enevento, 286,499	E 4
rgamo, 829,019	B 2
Bologna, 918,844	C 2
Bolzano-Bozen, 414,041	C 1
Brescia, 957,686	C 2
Brindisi, 366,027	G 4
Cagliari, 802,888	B 5
Caltanissetta, 282,069	D 6
Campobasso, 227,641	E 4
Caserta, 677,959	E 4
Catania, 938,273	E 6
Catanzaro, 718,069	F 5
Chieti, 351,567	E 3
Como, 720,463	B 2
Cosenza, 691,659	F 5
Cremona, 334,281	B 2
Cuneo, 540,504	A 2
Enna, 202,131	E 6
Ferrara, 383,639	C 2
Florence, 1,146,367	C 3
Foggia, 657,292	E 4
Forlì, 565,470	D 2
Frosinone, 422,630	D 4
Genoa, 1,087,973	B 2
Gorizia,	D 2
Grosseto, 216,315	C 3
Imperia, 225,127	B 3
Isernia, 92,166	E 4
L'Aquila, 293,066	D 3
La Spezia, 244,435	B 2
Latina, 376,238	D 4
Lecce, 696,503	G 4
Leghorn, 335,265	C 3
Lucca, 380,356	C 3
Macerata, 286,155	D 3
Mantua, 376,892	C 2
Massa-Carrara, 200,955	C 2
Matera, 194,629	F 4
Messina, 654,703	E 5
Milan, 3,903,685	B 2
Modena, 553,852	C 2
Naples, 2,709,929	E 4
Novara, 496,811	B 2
Nuoro, 273,021	B 4
Padua, 762,998	C 2
Palermo, 1,124,015	D 5
Parma, 395,497	C 2
Pavia, 526,389	B 2
Perugia, 552,936	D 3
Pesaro e Urbino, 316,383	D 3
Pescara, 264,981	E 3
Piacenza, 284,881	B 2
Pisa, 375,933	C 3
Pistoia, 254,335	C 2
Pordenone, 253,906	D 2
Potenza, 408,435	E 4
Ragusa, 255,047	E 6
Ravenna, 351,876	D 2
Reggio di Calabria, 578,323	E 5
Reggio nell'Emilia, 392,696	C 2
Rieti, 143,162	D 3
Rome, 3,490,377	F 6
Rovigo, 251,908	C 2
Salerno, 957,452	E 4
Sassari, 397,891	B 4
Savona, 296,043	B 2
Siena, 257,221	C 3
Sondrio, 169,149	B 1
Syracuse, 365,039	E 6
Taranto, 511,677	F 4
Teramo, 257,080	D 3
Terni, 222,847	D 3
Trapani, 405,393	D 5
Trento, 427,845	C 1
Treviso, 668,620	D 2
Trieste, 300,304	E 2
Turin, 2,287,016	A 2
Udine, 516,910	D 1
Varese, 725,823	B 2
Venice, 807,251	D 2
Vercelli, 406,252	B 2
Verona, 733,595	C 2
Vicenza, 677,884	C 2
Viterbo, 257,075	C 3

CITIES and TOWNS

Acireale, 34,081	E 6
Acqui Terme, 20,099	B 2
Acri, 8,150	F 5
Adrano, 31,988	E 6
Adria, 11,951	D 2
Agira, 11,262	E 6
Agrigento, 40,513	D 6
Agropoli, 9,413	E 4
Alassio, 13,512	A 2
Alba, 23,522	B 2
Albano Laziale, 15,561	F 7
Albenga, 13,397	B 3
Albino, 8,837	B 2
Alcamo, 41,448	D 6
Alessandria, 78,644	B 2
Alghero, 28,454	B 4
Altamura, 44,879	F 4
Amalfi, 4,205	E 4
Amantea, 6,132	E 5
Ancona, 88,427	D 3
Andria, 76,405	F 4
Anzio, 14,966	D 4
Aosta, 35,053	A 2
Aprilia, 18,412	D 4
Aragona, 11,213	D 6
Arezzo, 56,693	C 3
Argenta, 6,682	D 2
Ariano Irpino, 9,796	E 4
Ariccia, 7,287	F 7
Ascoli Piceno, 43,041	D 3
Assisi, 4,630	D 3
Asti, 62,277	B 2
Augusta, 32,501	E 6
Avellino, 44,750	E 4
Aversa, 46,536	E 4
Avezzano, 26,456	D 3
Avola, 29,089	E 6
Bagheria, 32,465	D 5
Barcellona Pozzo di Gotto, 25,280	E 5
Bari, 339,110	F 4
Barletta, 75,116	F 4
Bassano del Grappa, 33,002	C 2
Bellagio, 3,258	B 2
Belluno, 22,180	D 1
Benevento, 48,523	E 4
Bergamo, 127,553	B 2
Biancavilla, 18,743	E 6
Biella, 46,453	B 2
Bisceglie, 45,014	F 4
Bitonto, 39,714	F 4
Bologna, 493,282	C 2
Bolzano, 102,806	C 1
Bondeno, 7,451	C 2
Bordighera, 8,994	A 3
Borgomanero, 16,655	B 2
Borgo San Lorenzo, 7,699	C 2
Bosa, 8,045	B 4
Bra, 18,399	A 2
Bracciano, 7,681	C 3
Brescia, 189,092	C 2
Bressanone, 12,261	C 1
Brindisi, 76,612	G 4
Bronte, 17,823	E 6
Busto Arsizio, 72,400	B 2
Cagliari, 211,015	B 5
Caltagirone, 34,444	E 6
Caltanissetta, 52,838	D 6
Camaiore, 8,578	C 3
Campobasso, 35,551	E 4
Campo Tures, 1,325	C 1
Canicattì, 28,761	E 6
Canosa di Puglia, 30,263	E 4
Cantù, 28,617	B 2
Capua, 13,938	E 4
Caravaggio, 11,298	B 2
Carbonia, 23,031	B 5
Carini, 14,255	D 5
Carloforte, 6,671	B 5
Carmagnola, 16,469	A 2
Carpi, 41,789	C 2
Carrara, 56,236	C 2
Casale Monferrato, 35,156	B 2
Casalmaggiore, 6,374	C 2
Cascina-Navacchio, 28,263	C 3
Caserta, 51,621	E 4
Cassano allo Ionio, 9,661	F 5
Cassino, 14,747	D 4
Castelfranco Veneto, 16,042	D 2
Castel Gandolfo, 2,965	F 7
Castellammare del Golfo, 13,144	D 5
Castellammare di Stabia, 64,341	E 4
Castel San Pietro Terme, 6,985	C 2
Castelvetrano, 29,167	D 6
Castrovillari, 15,207	F 5
Catania, 403,390	E 6
Catanzaro, 52,054	F 5
Cava de'Tirreni, 33,868	E 4
Cavarzere, 7,917	D 2
Cecina, 19,415	C 3
Cefalù, 11,043	E 5
Ceglie Messapico, 17,512	F 4
Celano, 9,531	D 3
Cerignola, 44,648	E 4
Cernobbio, 8,026	B 2
Cesena, 49,915	D 2
Cesenatico, 12,805	D 2
Chiari, 12,017	C 2
Chiavari, 29,950	B 2
Chieri, 27,548	A 2
Chieti, 31,895	E 3
Chioggia, 24,044	D 2
Chivasso, 21,369	A 2
Ciampino, 36,728	F 7
Cittadella, 9,321	C 2
Città di Castello, 18,880	C 3
Cittanova, 11,045	F 5
Cividale del Friuli, 8,345	D 1
Civitavecchia, 41,305	C 3
Clusone-Fiorine, 6,428	C 2
Codroipo, 6,117	D 2
Colle di Val d'Elsa, 8,657	C 3
Comacchio, 10,437	D 2
Comiso, 24,508	E 6
Como, 73,257	B 2
Conegliano, 28,635	D 2
Conversano, 16,805	F 4
Corato, 38,163	F 4
Cori, 6,829	F 7
Corigliano Calabro, 14,518	F 5
Corleone, 11,057	D 6
Correggio, 11,415	C 2
Cortina d'Ampezzo, 7,285	D 1
Cosenza, 94,565	F 5
Courmayeur, 1,401	A 2
Crema, 26,061	B 2
Cremona, 75,988	B 2
Crotone, 44,081	F 5
Cuneo, 41,633	A 2
Cuorgnè, 6,752	A 2
Desenzano del Garda, 14,624	C 2
Diano Marina, 6,001	B 3
Domodossola, 18,562	A 1
Dorgali, 6,714	B 4
Eboli, 19,787	E 4
Empoli, 30,526	C 3
Enna, 27,351	E 6
Este, 12,992	C 2
Fabriano, 18,355	D 3
Faenza, 36,241	D 2
Fano, 31,238	D 3
Fasano, 21,247	F 4
Favara, 27,940	D 6
Feltre, 11,806	C 1
Fermo, 17,521	D 3
Ferrandina, 8,372	F 4
Ferrara, 97,507	C 2
Fidenza, 18,064	B 2
Fiesole, 3,772	C 3
Finale Emilia, 7,474	C 2
Finale Ligure, 11,461	B 2
Firenze (Florence), 441,654	C 3
Fiumicino, 13,180	F 7
Florence, 441,654	C 3
Floridia, 16,562	E 6
Foggia, 136,436	E 4
Foligno, 26,887	D 3
Fondi, 16,472	D 4
Forlì, 83,303	D 2
Formia, 18,978	D 4
Fossano, 15,857	A 2
Fossombrone, 5,882	D 3
Francavilla Fontana, 30,347	F 4
Frascati, 14,217	F 7
Frosinone, 34,066	D 4
Gaeta, 21,973	D 4
Galatina, 22,137	G 4
Galatone, 13,880	F 4
Gallarate, 43,773	B 2
Gallipoli, 16,878	F 4
Gela, 66,845	E 6
Gemona, 6,863	D 1
Genoa, 787,011	B 2
Genova (Genoa), 787,011	B 2
Genzano di Roma, 14,147	F 7
Giarre, 18,233	E 6
Gioia del Colle, 23,299	F 4
Giovinazzo, 17,768	F 4
Giulianova, 17,926	E 3
Gorizia, 35,912	D 2
Gravina in Puglia, 32,006	F 4
Grosseto, 48,309	C 3
Grottaferrata, 10,639	F 7
Grottaglie, 23,556	F 4
Guastalla, 7,639	C 2
Gubbio, 12,371	D 3
Guidonia, 8,413	F 6
Iesi, 33,011	D 3
Iglesias, 24,472	B 5
Imola, 42,111	C 2
Imperia, 37,585	B 3
Isernia, 12,290	E 4
Ivrea, 26,530	B 2
Ladispoli, 6,625	E 6
La Maddalena, 10,405	B 4
Lanciano, 19,652	E 3
L'Aquila, 36,233	D 3
La Spezia, 121,254	B 2
Latina, 53,003	D 4
Lavello, 11,486	E 4
Lecce, 80,114	G 4
Lecco, 53,165	B 2
Leghorn, 170,369	C 3
Legnago, 15,534	C 2
Lendinara, 7,079	C 2
Lentini, 31,429	E 6
Leonforte, 16,317	E 6
Licata, 40,997	D 6
Lido di Ostia, 61,492	F 7
Lido di Venezia, 18,794	D 2
Livigno, 2,135	C 1
Livorno (Leghorn), 170,369	C 3
Lodi, 42,489	B 2
Lonigo, 6,368	C 2
Lucca, 54,280	C 3
Lucera, 29,355	E 4
Lugo, 19,497	D 2
Macerata, 33,470	D 3
Macomer, 9,433	B 4
Maglie, 13,326	G 4
Manduria, 25,194	F 4
Manfredonia, 44,463	F 4
Mantua, 59,529	C 2
Marino, 12,135	F 7
Marsala, 34,150	D 6
Martina Franca, 31,811	F 4
Massa, 56,591	C 2
Massafra, 22,610	F 4
Massa Marittima, 6,438	C 3
Matera, 43,026	F 4
Mazara del Vallo, 37,441	D 6
Mazzarino, 14,981	E 6
Melfi, 13,355	E 4
Menfi, 12,386	D 6
Merano, 30,951	C 1
Mesagne, 26,955	G 4
Messina, 203,937	E 5
Mestre, 184,818	D 2
Milan, 1,724,557	B 2
Milazzo, 18,576	E 5
Minturno, 2,428	D 4
Mirandola, 11,551	C 2
Mira Taglio, 10,194	D 2
Mistretta, 6,631	E 6
Modena, 149,029	C 2
Modica, 31,074	E 6
Mola di Bari, 23,778	F 4
Molfetta, 63,250	F 4
Moncalieri, 49,953	A 2
Mondovì Breo, 12,524	A 2
Monfalcone, 29,589	D 2
Monopoli, 29,776	F 4
Monreale, 19,348	D 5
Monselice, 9,047	C 2
Montebelluna, 9,573	D 2
Montefiascone, 6,885	D 3
Monterotondo, 15,869	F 6
Monte Sant'Angelo, 17,756	F 4
Montevarchi, 16,849	C 3
Monza, 110,735	B 2
Mortara, 13,929	B 2
Naples, 1,214,775	E 4
Nardò, 24,142	F 4
Narni, 6,213	D 3
Naro, 13,171	D 6
Nettuno, 20,927	D 4
Nicastro, 27,206	F 5
Nicosia, 13,982	E 6
Niscemi, 23,925	E 6
Nizza Monferrato, 7,532	B 2
Nocera Inferiore, 44,415	E 4
Noto, 21,606	E 6
Novara, 92,634	B 2
Novi Ligure, 29,944	B 2
Nuoro, 30,551	B 4
Olbia, 20,998	B 4
Oliena, 7,030	B 4
Orbetello, 6,884	C 3
Oristano, 20,966	B 5
Ortona, 11,966	E 3
Orvieto, 8,813	D 3
Osimo, 12,034	D 3
Ostia Antica, 2,583	F 7
Ostuni, 27,241	F 4
Otranto, 3,707	G 4
Ozieri, 9,149	B 4
Pachino, 20,427	E 6
Padua, 210,950	C 2
Palazzolo Acreide, 8,981	E 6
Palermo, 556,374	D 5
Palestrina, 9,239	F 7
Palma di Montechiaro, 22,381	D 6
Palmi, 14,405	E 5
Paola, 11,330	E 5
Parma, 151,967	C 2
Partanna, 10,303	D 6
Partinico, 25,447	D 6
Paterno, 41,504	E 6
Patti, 7,500	E 5
Pavia, 80,639	B 2
Penne, 5,889	D 3
Pergine Valsugana, 6,248	C 1
Perugia, 65,975	D 3
Pesaro, 72,104	D 3
Pescara, 125,391	E 3
Pescia, 9,918	C 3
Piacenza, 100,001	B 2
Piazza Armerina, 21,754	E 6
Pietrasanta, 6,620	B 3
Pinerolo, 33,935	A 2
Piombino, 35,641	C 3
Piove di Sacco, 7,035	C 2
Pisa, 91,156	C 3
Pisticci, 11,239	F 4
Pistoia, 55,403	C 2
Poggibonsi, 21,271	C 3
Pomezia, 11,915	F 7
Pontecorvo, 5,986	D 4
Pordenone, 43,230	D 2
Porto Civitanova, 25,773	D 3
Porto Empedocle, 15,986	D 6
Portoferraio, 7,579	C 3
Portofino, 720	B 2
Portogruaro, 12,258	D 2
Portomaggiore, 6,343	C 2
Porto Torres, 15,422	B 4
Potenza, 46,869	E 4
Pozzallo, 12,199	E 6
Pozzuoli, 53,546	D 4
Prato, 108,385	C 3
Prima Porta, 11,393	F 6
Priverno, 9,950	D 4
Putignano, 19,290	F 4
Quartu Sant'Elena, 29,715	B 5
Ragusa, 55,751	E 6
Rapallo, 22,272	B 2
Ravenna, 75,153	D 2
Recanati, 10,176	D 3
Reggio di Calabria, 110,291	E 5
Reggio nell'Emilia, 102,337	C 2
Rho, 39,206	B 2
Riesi, 15,855	E 6
Rieti, 26,775	D 3
Rimini, 101,579	D 2
Rionero in Vulture, 11,230	E 4
Riva del Garda, 8,513	C 2
Rome (cap.), 2,535,018	F 6
Ronciglione, 5,900	C 3
Rossano, 12,119	F 5
Rovereto, 26,827	C 2
Rovigo, 31,124	C 2
Ruvo di Puglia, 23,133	F 4
Sala Consilina, 8,177	E 4
Salemi, 10,180	D 6
Salerno, 146,534	E 4
Salsomaggiore Terme, 13,677	B 2
Saluzzo, 13,929	A 2
Sambiase, 10,567	F 5
San Bartolomeo in Galdo, 6,943	E 4
San Benedetto del Tronto, 40,108	E 3
San Cataldo, 19,609	D 6
San Giovanni in Fiore, 16,116	F 5

(continued on following page)

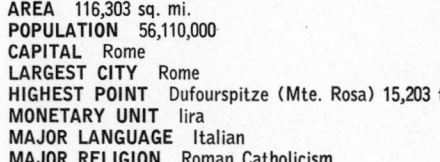

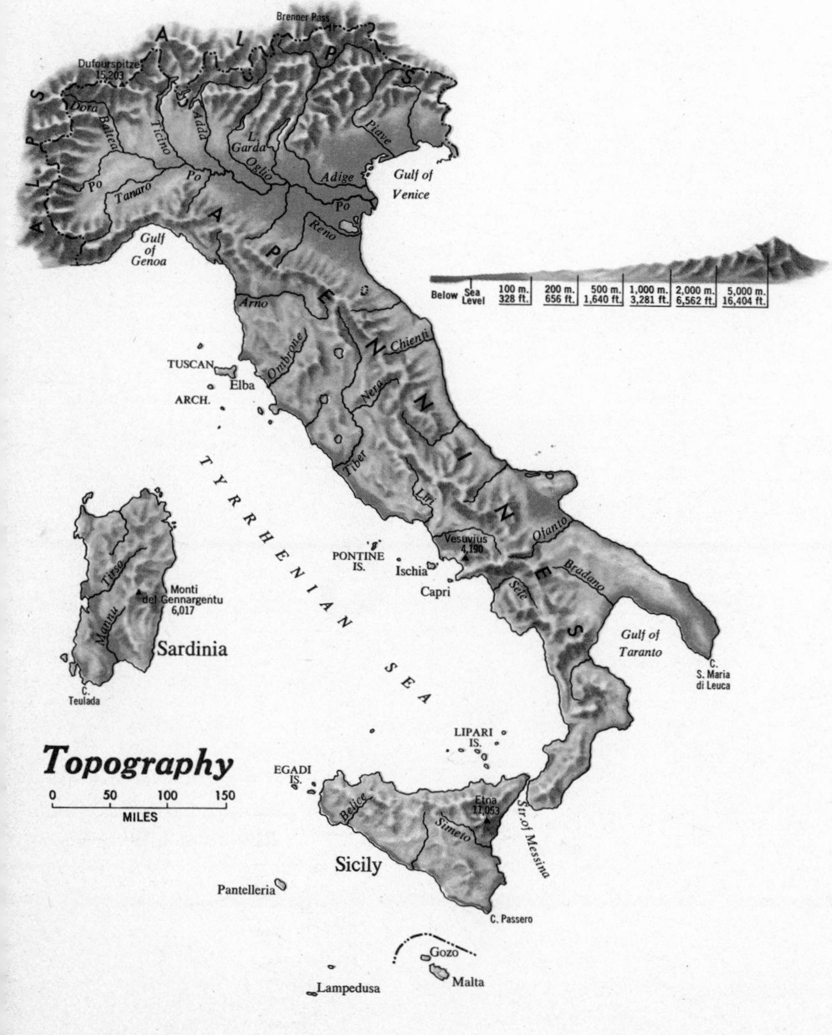
Brenner Pass
Dufourspitze 15,203
A L P S
Dora Baltea
Ticino
Adda
L. Garda
Oglio
Piave
Adige
Po
Tanaro
Gulf of Venice
Reno
Gulf of Genoa
A P E N N I N E S
Arno
Ombrone
Chienti
Tiber
Liri
TUSCAN ARCH.
Elba
T Y R R H E N I A N   S E A
PONTINE IS.
Ischia
Vesuvius 4,190
Capri
Ofanto
Bradano
Sele
Gulf of Taranto
C. S. Maria di Leuca
Tirso
Monti del Gennargentu 6,017
Sardinia
C. Teulada
LIPARI IS.
EGADI IS.
Sicily
Etna 11,053
Str. of Messina
Belice
Simeto
C. Passero
Pantelleria
Gozo
Malta
Lampedusa
Below Sea Level
100 m. 328 ft.
200 m. 656 ft.
500 m. 1,640 ft.
1,000 m. 3,281 ft.
2,000 m. 6,562 ft.
5,000 m. 16,404 ft.
Topography
0 50 100 150
MILES

Agriculture, Industry and Resources

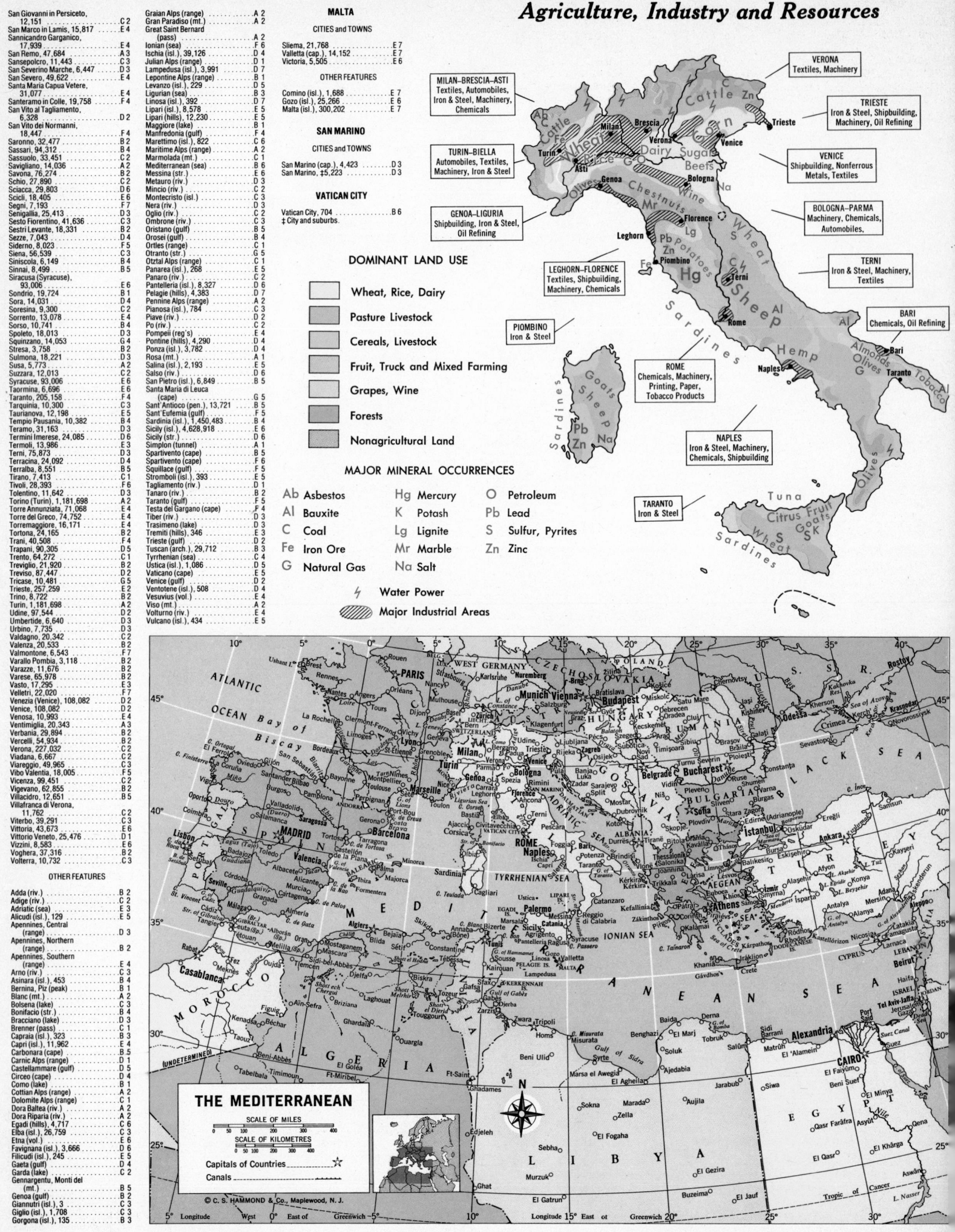

VERONA
Textiles, Machinery

TRIESTE
Iron & Steel, Shipbuilding, Machinery, Oil Refining

VENICE
Shipbuilding, Nonferrous Metals, Textiles

BOLOGNA–PARMA
Machinery, Chemicals, Automobiles,

TERNI
Iron & Steel, Machinery, Textiles

BARI
Chemicals, Oil Refining

MILAN–BRESCIA–ASTI
Textiles, Automobiles, Iron & Steel, Machinery, Chemicals

TURIN–BIELLA
Automobiles, Textiles, Machinery, Iron & Steel

GENOA–LIGURIA
Shipbuilding, Iron & Steel, Oil Refining

LEGHORN–FLORENCE
Textiles, Shipbuilding, Machinery, Chemicals

PIOMBINO
Iron & Steel

ROME
Chemicals, Machinery, Printing, Paper, Tobacco Products

NAPLES
Iron & Steel, Machinery, Chemicals, Shipbuilding

TARANTO
Iron & Steel

DOMINANT LAND USE

Wheat, Rice, Dairy
Pasture Livestock
Cereals, Livestock
Fruit, Truck and Mixed Farming
Grapes, Wine
Forests
Nonagricultural Land

MAJOR MINERAL OCCURRENCES

Ab Asbestos
Al Bauxite
C Coal
Fe Iron Ore
G Natural Gas
Hg Mercury
K Potash
Lg Lignite
Mr Marble
Na Salt
O Petroleum
Pb Lead
S Sulfur, Pyrites
Zn Zinc

Water Power
Major Industrial Areas

THE MEDITERRANEAN

SCALE OF MILES
0   100   200   400

SCALE OF KILOMETRES
0   50 100   200   300   400

Capitals of Countries ....★
Canals

© C. S. HAMMOND & Co., Maplewood, N.J.

SWITZERLAND
AREA 15,943 sq. mi.
POPULATION 6,489,000
CAPITAL Bern
LARGEST CITY Zürich
HIGHEST POINT Dufourspitze (Mte. Rosa) 15,203 ft.
MONETARY UNIT Swiss franc
MAJOR LANGUAGES German, French, Italian, Romansch
MAJOR RELIGIONS Protestantism, Roman Catholicism

LIECHTENSTEIN
AREA 61 sq. mi.
POPULATION 25,000
CAPITAL Vaduz
LARGEST CITY Vaduz
HIGHEST POINT Naafkopf 8,445 ft.
MONETARY UNIT Swiss franc
MAJOR LANGUAGE German
MAJOR RELIGION Roman Catholicism

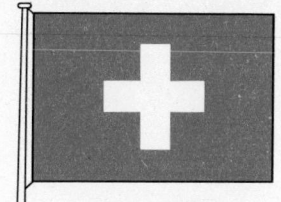
SWITZERLAND

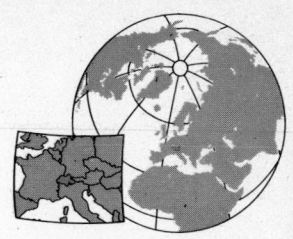

LIECHTENSTEIN

LANGUAGES

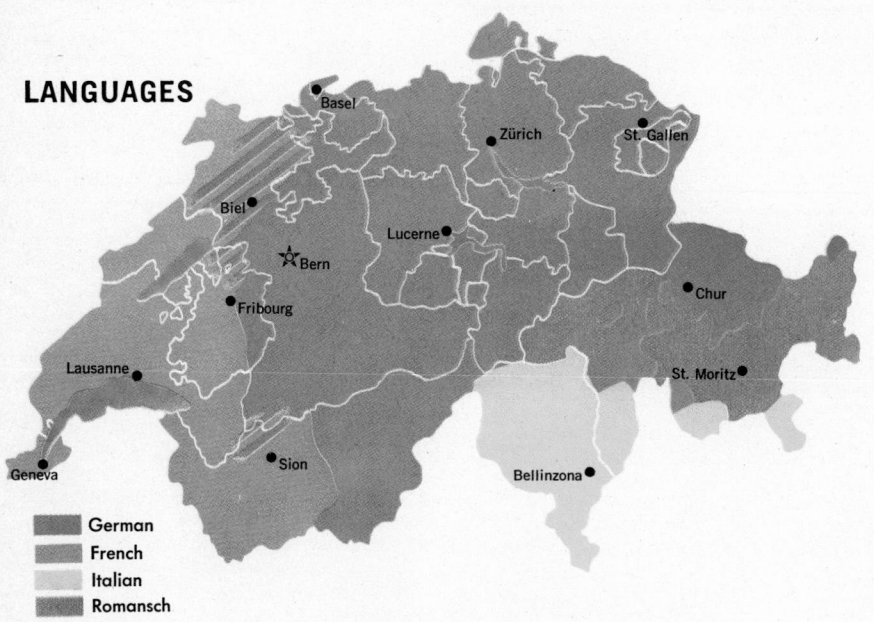

- German
- French
- Italian
- Romansch

Switzerland is a multilingual nation with four official languages. 70% of the people speak German, 19% French, 10% Italian and 1% Romansch.

SWITZERLAND

CANTONS

Aargau, 433,284	F 2
Appenzell, Ausser Rhoden, 49,023	H 2
Appenzell, Inner Rhoden, 13,124	H 2
Baselland, 204,889	E 2
Baselstadt, 234,945	E 1
Bern, 983,296	D 2
Fribourg, 180,309	D 3
Geneva (Genève), 331,599	B 4
Glarus, 38,155	H 3
Graubünden, 162,086	H 3
Grisons (Graubünden), 162,086	H 3
Lucerne (Luzern), 289,641	F 2
Luzern, 289,641	F 2
Neuchâtel, 169,173	C 3
Nidwalden, 25,634	F 3
Obwalden, 24,509	F 3
Sankt Gallen, 384,475	H 2
Schaffhausen, 72,854	G 1
Schwyz, 92,072	G 2
Soleure (Solothurn), 224,133	E 2
Solothurn, 224,133	E 2
Thurgau, 182,835	H 1
Ticino, 245,458	G 4
Uri, 34,091	G 3
Valais, 206,563	D 4
Vaud, 511,851	B 3
Zug, 67,996	G 2
Zürich, 1,107,788	G 2

CITIES and TOWNS

Aadorf, 3,022	G 2
Aarau, 16,881	F 2
Aarau, ‡51,800	F 2
Aarberg, 3,122	D 2
Aarburg, 5,943	E 2
Adelboden, 3,326	E 3
Aeschi bei Spiez, 1,402	E 3
Affoltern am Albis, 7,363	F 2
Affoltern im Emmental, 1,223	E 2
Aigle, 6,532	C 4
Airolo, 2,140	G 3
Alle, 1,615	D 2
Allschwil, 17,638	D 1
Alpnach, 3,277	F 3
Altdorf, 8,647	G 3
Altstätten, 9,084	J 2
Amriswil, 7,601	H 1
Andeer, 714	H 3
Andermatt, 1,589	G 3
Appenzell, 5,217	H 2
Apples, 652	B 3
Arbedo-Castione, 2,456	G 4
Arbon, 12,227	H 1
Arbon, ‡15,400	H 1
Ardon, 1,498	D 4
Arosa, 2,717	J 3
Arth, 7,580	F 2
Ascona, 4,086	G 4
Attalens, 1,116	C 3
Aubonne, 1,983	B 4
Avenches, 2,235	D 3
Baar, 14,074	F 2
Baden, 14,115	F 2
Baden, ‡66,800	F 2
Bad Ragaz, 3,713	H 2
Baierna, 3,885	G 5
Ballaigues, 868	B 3
Balsthal, 5,607	E 2
Bäretswil, 2,733	G 2
Basel, 199,600	E 1
Basel, ‡379,700	E 1
Bassecourt, 2,985	D 2
Bätterkinden, 1,757	E 2
Baulmes, 811	C 3
Bauma, 3,159	G 2
Beatenberg, 1,263	E 3
Begnins, 981	B 4
Beinwil am See, 2,520	F 2
Belfaux, 1,075	D 3
Bellinzona, 16,979	H 4
Bellinzona, ‡31,000	H 4
Belp, 6,981	D 3
Bern (cap.), 154,700	D 3
Bern, ‡285,300	D 3
Beromünster, 1,552	F 2
Bex, 5,069	D 4
Biasca, 4,696	H 4
Biberist, 7,769	D 2
Biel, 63,400	D 2
Biel, ‡89,900	D 2
Bière, 1,252	B 3
Binningen, 15,344	D 1
Bischofszell, 4,233	H 1
Blumenstein, 1,049	E 3
Bodio, 1,425	G 4
Bolligen, 26,121	E 3
Boltigen, 1,519	D 3
Boncourt, 1,528	C 2
Bonfol, 888	D 2
Bönigen, 1,738	E 3
Boswil, 1,904	F 2
Boudry, 4,372	C 3
Bourg Saint-Pierre, 236	C 5
Breil-Brigels, 1,215	H 3
Breitenbach, 2,455	E 2
Bremgarten, 4,873	F 2
Brienz, 2,796	F 3
Brig, 5,191	F 4
Brissago, 2,120	G 4
Brittnau, 2,888	E 2
Brugg, 8,635	F 2
Brusio, 1,344	K 4
Bubendorf, 2,070	E 2
Bubikon, 3,244	G 2
Buchs, 8,454	H 2
Bülach, 11,043	G 1
Bulle, 7,556	D 3
Buochs, 3,232	F 3
Büren an der Aare, 3,085	D 2
Burgdorf, 15,888	E 2
Burgdorf, ‡18,400	E 2
Bürglen, Thurgau, 1,920	H 1
Bürglen, Uri, 3,401	G 3
Bussigny-près-Lausanne, 4,509	B 3
Bütschwil, 3,270	H 2
Buttes, 801	C 3
Carouge, 14,055	B 4
Castagnola, 4,430	G 4
Cazis, 1,687	H 3
Cernier, 1,717	C 2
Chalais, 1,651	E 4
Cham, 8,209	F 2
Chamoson, 2,049	D 4
Champéry, 926	C 4
Charmey, 1,155	D 3
Château-d'Oex, 3,203	D 4
Châtel-Saint-Denis, 2,842	C 3
Chavornay, 1,521	C 3
Chexbres, 16,072	C 3
Chiasso, 8,868	G 5
Chur, 32,400	J 3
Churwalden, 1,052	J 3
Claro, 1,143	G 4
Concise, 650	C 3
Conthey, 4,259	D 4
Coppet, 1,097	B 4
Corcelles-près-Payerne, 1,256	C 3
Corgémont, 1,645	D 2
Cossonay, 1,529	B 3
Courgenay, 1,954	D 2
Courroux, 1,788	D 2
Courtelary, 1,462	C 2
Courtételle, 1,864	D 2
Couvet, 3,481	C 3
Cully, 1,535	C 4
Davos, 10,238	J 3
Degersheim, 3,400	H 2
Delémont, 11,797	D 2
Derendingen, 4,917	E 2
Diemtigen, 1,913	D 3
Diessenhofen, 2,532	G 1
Dietikon, 22,705	F 2
Disentis-Mustér, 2,319	G 3
Dombresson, 1,109	C 2
Dornach, 5,258	E 2
Dübendorf, 19,639	G 2
Düdingen, 4,932	D 3
Dürnten, 4,820	G 2
Dürrenroth, 1,084	E 2
Ebnat-Kappel, 5,131	H 2
Echallens, 1,643	C 3
Egg, 5,250	G 2
Eggiwil, 2,391	E 3
Eglisau, 2,160	G 1
Egnach, 3,466	H 1
Einsiedeln, 10,020	G 2
Elgg, 2,970	G 2

(continued on following page)

Agriculture, Industry and Resources

DOMINANT LAND USE

- Cereals, Dairy
- Pasture Livestock
- General Farming, Livestock
- Fruit, Truck, Mixed Farming
- Forests
- Nonagricultural Land

⚡ Water Power
▨ Major Industrial Areas

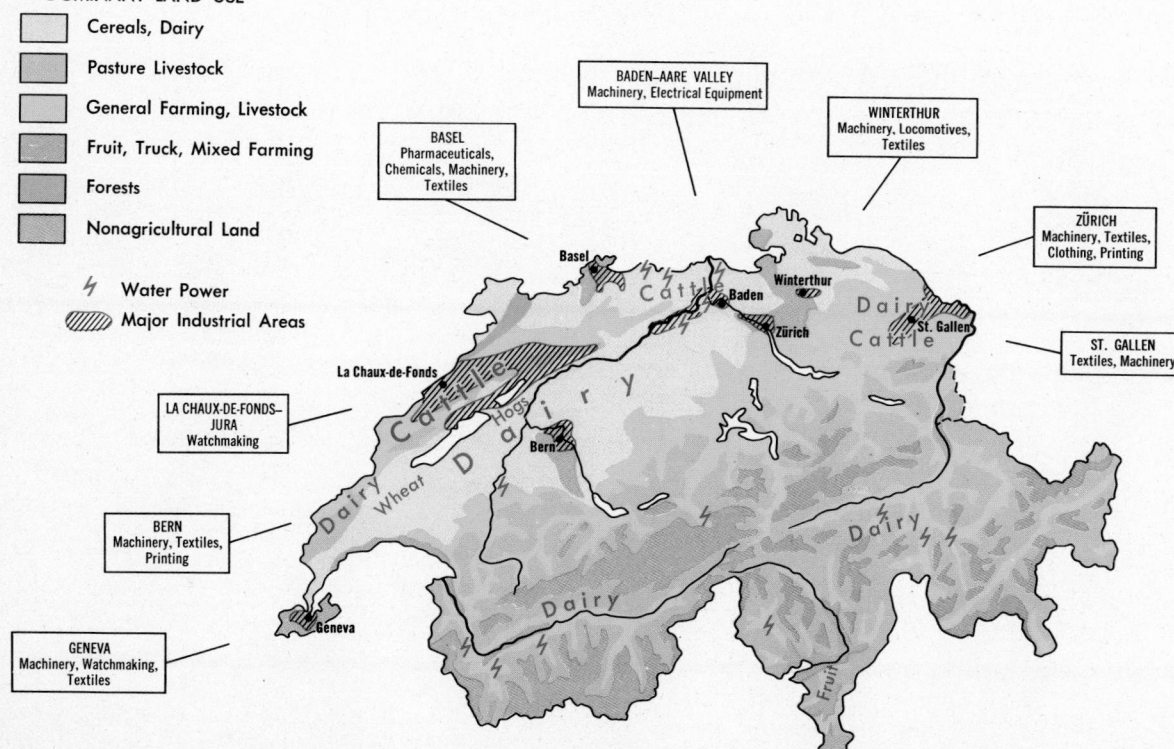

BADEN–AARE VALLEY Machinery, Electrical Equipment

WINTERTHUR Machinery, Locomotives, Textiles

BASEL Pharmaceuticals, Chemicals, Machinery, Textiles

ZÜRICH Machinery, Textiles, Clothing, Printing

ST. GALLEN Textiles, Machinery

LA CHAUX-DE-FONDS–JURA Watchmaking

BERN Machinery, Textiles, Printing

GENEVA Machinery, Watchmaking, Textiles

Topography

0 20 40
MILES

```
Below    100 m.   200 m.   500 m.   1,000 m.  2,000 m.  5,000 m.
Sea      328 ft.  656 ft.  1,640 ft. 3,281 ft. 6,562 ft. 16,404 ft.
Level
```

SWITZERLAND (continued)

Elm, 795 ....H3	Küttigen, 4,181 ....F2	Neuchâtel, 38,400 ....C3	Schiers, 2,342 ....J3
Emmen, 22,040 ....F2	L'Abbaye, 1,319 ....B3	Neuchâtel, ±61,700 ....C3	Schinznach-Dorf, 1,154 ....F2
Engelberg, 2,841 ....F3	La Chaux-de-Fonds, 42,500 ....C2	Neuenegg, 3,452 ....D3	Schlarigna-Celerina, 983 ....J3
Engi, 837 ....H3	Lachen, 4,914 ....G2	Neuhausen am Rheinfall,	Schleitheim, 1,544 ....G1
Ennenda, 2,762 ....H3	La Neuveville, 1,811 ....D2	12,103 ....G1	Schlieren, 11,869 ....F2
Entlebuch, 3,310 ....F3	Langenthal, 13,077 ....E2	Neunkirch, 1,239 ....G1	Schönenwerd, 4,793 ....E2
Erlach, 1,052 ....D2	Langenthal, ±22,100 ....E2	Niederbipp, 3,293 ....E2	Schüpfheim, 3,773 ....F3
Erlenbach im Simmental,	Langnau am Albis, 4,879 ....F2	Niederurnen, 3,354 ....G2	Schwanden, 2,823 ....H2
1,436 ....E3	Langnau in Emmental, 8,950 ....E3	Nunningen, 1,450 ....E2	Schwyz, 12,194 ....G3
Ermatingen, 1,787 ....H1	La Roche, 1,069 ....D3	Nyon, 11,424 ....B4	Scuol, 1,686 ....K3
Erstfeld, 4,516 ....G3	La Sarraz, 1,190 ....C3	Oberägeri, 2,992 ....G2	Sedrun, 1,273 ....G3
Eschenbach, 3,387 ....G2	La Tour-de-Peilz, 8,864 ....C4	Oberburg, 3,015 ....E2	Seewis im Prättigau,
Escholzmatt, 3,161 ....E3	Läufelfingen, 1,243 ....E2	Oberdiessbach, 2,145 ....E3	923 ....J3
Estavayer-le-Lac, 3,439 ....C3	Laufen, 4,723 ....D2	Oberdorf, 1,210 ....E2	Sembrancher, 712 ....D4
Evolène, 1,403 ....D4	Laupen, 2,139 ....D3	Oberriet, 6,123 ....J2	Sempach, 1,619 ....F2
Faido, 1,866 ....G3	Lauperswil, 2,542 ....E3	Oberuzwil, 4,659 ....H2	Semsales, 829 ....D3
Finhaut, 681 ....C4	Lausanne, 136,100 ....C3	Oensingen, 3,387 ....E2	Sent, 704 ....K3
Flawil, 8,474 ....H2	Lausanne, ±228,700 ....C3	Olion, 4,470 ....D4	Seon, 3,628 ....F2
Fleurier, 4,124 ....C3	Lauterbrunnen, 3,431 ....E3	Olten, 21,200 ....E2	Sevelen, 2,742 ....H2
Flims, 1,936 ....H3	Lavey-Morcles, 734 ....C4	Olten, ±49,000 ....E2	Sierre, 11,017 ....D4
Flüelen, 1,731 ....G3	Le Brassus, 5,465 ....B3	Orbe, 4,522 ....C3	Signau, 2,642 ....E3
Flums, 4,474 ....H2	Le Châble, 4,541 ....D4	Ormont-Dessous, 884 ....D4	Sigriswil, 3,540 ....E3
Frauenfeld, 17,576 ....G1	Le Lieu, 924 ....B3	Oron-la-Ville, 764 ....C3	Silenen, 2,338 ....G3
Fribourg, 41,600 ....D3	Le Locle, 14,452 ....C2	Orsières, 2,470 ....D4	Sils im Domleschg, 762 ....H3
Fribourg, ±53,500 ....D3	Le Mont-sur-Lausanne,	Osogna, 750 ....H4	Silvaplana, 714 ....J4
Frick, 3,112 ....E1	2,692 ....C3	Ouchy, 2,500 ....C4	Sins, 2,435 ....F2
Frutigen, 5,796 ....E3	Lengnau, 4,736 ....D2	Payerne, 6,899 ....C3	Sion, 21,925 ....D4
Fully, 3,643 ....D4	Lenk, 1,876 ....D4	Peseux, 5,578 ....C3	Sirnach, 3,706 ....G2
Gais, 2,344 ....H2	Le Noirmont, 1,516 ....C2	Pfäffikon, 7,586 ....G2	Sissach, 4,938 ....E2
Gampel, 1,021 ....E4	Lens, 2,052 ....D4	Pfaffnau, 2,584 ....E2	Solothurn (Soleure),
Geiterkinden, 5,157 ....E2	Lenzburg, 7,594 ....F2	Pieterlen, 3,485 ....D2	17,708 ....E2
Geneva (Genève), 163,100 ....B4	Les Bois, 1,110 ....C2	Pontresina, 1,646 ....J3	Solothurn, ±35,600 ....E2
Geneva (Genève), ±320,200 ....B4	Les Ponts-de-Martel, 1,327 ....C2	Porrentruy, 7,827 ....D1	Somvix, 1,555 ....G3
Gersau, 1,753 ....G2	Les Verrières, 898 ....B3	Poschiavo, 3,563 ....J4	Sonvico, 1,129 ....G4
Gimel, 1,205 ....B3	Leuk, 2,796 ....D4	Pratteln, 15,127 ....E1	Spiez, 9,911 ....E3
Giornico, 1,389 ....G4	Leukerbad, 1,056 ....D4	Pully, 15,917 ....C4	Stäfa, 9,937 ....G2
Giswil, 2,760 ....F3	Leysin, 2,752 ....C4	Quinto, 1,490 ....G3	Stalden, 1,121 ....E4
Giubiasco, 5,796 ....H4	Liestal, 12,500 ....E2	Rafz, 2,215 ....G1	Stans, 5,180 ....F3
Gland, 2,404 ....B4	Liestal-Sissach, ±40,800 ....E2	Ramsen, 1,217 ....G1	Steckborn, 3,752 ....G1
Glarus, 6,199 ....H2	Linthal, 1,458 ....H3	Rapperswil, 8,713 ....G2	Steffisburg, 12,621 ....E3
Glattfelden, 2,857 ....F1	Littau, 13,495 ....F2	Raron, 1,257 ....E4	Stein, 1,763 ....E1
Gordola, 2,586 ....G4	Locarno, 14,143 ....G4	Rechthalten, 878 ....D3	Stein am Rhein, 2,751 ....G1
Göschenen, 888 ....G3	Locarno, ±39,200 ....G4	Regensdorf, 8,566 ....F2	Sulgen, 1,834 ....H1
Gossau, 12,793 ....H2	Lodrino, 1,075 ....G4	Reichenbach im Kandertal,	Sulz, 1,021 ....F1
Grabs, 4,245 ....H2	Lucens, 2,144 ....C3	2,900 ....E3	Sumiswald, 5,334 ....E2
Grandson, 2,135 ....C3	Lucerne, 70,200 ....F2	Reiden, 3,275 ....E2	Sursee, 7,052 ....F2
Grenchen, 20,051 ....D2	Lucerne, ±158,600 ....F2	Reinach, 5,862 ....F2	Tafers, 2,021 ....D3
Grenchen, ±28,300 ....D2	Lugano, 22,280 ....G4	Renens, 17,391 ....C3	Tamins, 828 ....H3
Grindelwald, 3,511 ....E3	Lugano, ±64,200 ....G4	Rheinau, 2,075 ....G1	Täuffelen, 1,761 ....D2
Grono, 845 ....H4	Lungern, 1,813 ....F3	Rheineck, 3,275 ....J2	Tavannes, 3,869 ....D2
Grosswangen, 2,213 ....F2	Luthern, 1,706 ....E2	Rheinfelden, 6,866 ....E1	Tavetsch (Sedrun), 1,273 ....G3
Gruyères, 1,234 ....D3	Lutry, 4,904 ....C4	Richterswil, 7,380 ....G2	Thalwil, 13,591 ....F2
Gryon, 752 ....D4	Lützelflüh, 3,842 ....E3	Riehen, 21,026 ....E1	Thayngen, 3,640 ....G1
Gstaad, ...D4	Luzern (Lucerne), 70,200 ....F2	Riggisberg, 2,193 ....E3	Therwil, 5,412 ....E1
Gsteig, 865 ....D4	Lyss, 8,131 ....D2	Riva San Vitale, 1,607 ....G5	Thun, 37,000 ....E3
Guggisberg, 1,739 ....D3	Maienfeld, 1,542 ....J3	Rivera, 1,146 ....G4	Thun, ±63,600 ....E3
Gurtnellen, 1,048 ....G3	Malans, 1,294 ....J3	Roche, 848 ....C4	Thusis, 2,381 ....H3
Hallau, 1,836 ....F1	Malters, 5,100 ....F2	Roggwil, 3,403 ....E2	Trachselwald, 1,199 ....E2
Heiden, 3,716 ....H2	Malvaglia, 1,099 ....H4	Rolle, 3,658 ....B4	Tramelan, 5,549 ....D2
Heimberg, 3,046 ....E3	Männedorf, 7,419 ....G2	Romanshorn, 8,329 ....H1	Treyvaux, 946 ....D3
Hérémence, 1,484 ....D4	Marbach, 1,265 ....E3	Romont, 3,276 ....C3	Trimmis, 1,109 ....J3
Herisau, 14,597 ....H2	Martigny, 10,478 ....C4	Rorschach, 11,963 ....H1	Trin, 714 ....H3
Herzogenbuchsee, 5,140 ....E2	Meilen, 9,881 ....G2	Rorschach, ±24,200 ....H1	Trub, 1,833 ....E3
Hinwil, 6,547 ....G2	Meiringen, 3,759 ....F3	Rosenlaui, ...F3	Trun, 1,607 ....G3
Hochdorf, 5,222 ....F2	Melide, 1,315 ....G4	Rothrist, 5,883 ....E2	Turbenthal, 2,939 ....G2
Horgen, 15,691 ....F2	Mellingen, 3,211 ....F2	Rougemont, 824 ....D4	Uetendorf, 3,132 ....E3
Huttwil, 4,800 ....E2	Mels, 5,969 ....H2	Roveredo, 2,037 ....H4	Unterägeri, 4,671 ....G2
Igis, 5,283 ....J3	Mendrisio, 6,223 ....G5	Rüeggisberg, 1,857 ....D3	Unterkulm, 2,596 ....F2
Ilanz, 1,783 ....H3	Menzingen, 3,483 ....G2	Rüschegg, 1,346 ....D3	Unterseen, 4,192 ....E3
Illnau, 13,693 ....G2	Menznau, 2,185 ....F2	Ruswil, 4,756 ....F2	Untervaz, 1,230 ....J3
Ingenbohl, 5,111 ....G2	Mesocco, 1,376 ....H4	Rüthi, 1,493 ....J2	Urnäsch, 2,313 ....H2
Innertkirchen, 1,064 ....F3	Minusio, 5,027 ....G4	Rüti, Zürich, 9,546 ....G2	Uster, 21,819 ....G2
Ins, 2,435 ....D2	Möhlin, 6,003 ....E1	Saanen, 5,840 ....D4	Utzenstorf, 3,193 ....E2
Interlaken, 4,735 ....E3	Mollis, 2,628 ....H2	Saas Fee, 895 ....E4	Uznach, 3,984 ....G2
Intragna, 830 ....G4	Montana, 1,725 ....D4	Sachseln, 3,059 ....F3	Uzwil, 9,133 ....H2
Jaun, 689 ....D3	Monthey, 10,114 ....C4	Saignelégier, 1,745 ....D2	Vallorbe, 4,028 ....B3
Jegenstorf, 2,858 ....D2	Montreux, 20,421 ....C4	Saint-Blaise, 2,586 ....D2	Vals, 1,037 ....H3
Jenaz, 1,124 ....J3	Morges, 11,931 ....B3	Sainte-Croix, 6,240 ....B3	Vaz-Obervaz, 2,003 ....J3
Jona, 9,286 ....G2	Morges, ±17,200 ....B3	Saint-Imier, 6,740 ....C2	Vechigen, 3,595 ....D4
Jungfraujoch, ...E3	Moudon, 3,773 ....C3	Saint-Martin, 1,120 ....E4	Vernayaz, 1,356 ....C4
Jussy, 692 ....B4	Moutier, 8,794 ....D2	Saint-Maurice, 3,808 ....C4	Versoix, 5,627 ....C4
Kaltbrunn, 2,751 ....G2	Müllheim, 1,620 ....G1	Saint Moritz, 5,699 ....J3	Vevey, 17,957 ....C4
Kandersteg, 957 ....E4	Mümliswil-Ramiswil,	Saint Niklaus, 2,043 ....E4	Vevey-Montreux, ±62,300 ....C4
Kerns, 3,807 ....F3	2,702 ....E2	Saint-Prex, 2,306 ....B4	Villeneuve, 3,705 ....C4
Kerzers, 2,688 ....D3	Münchenbuchsee, 6,459 ....E2	Saint Stephan, 1,213 ....D3	Visp, 5,252 ....E4
Kirchberg, Bern, 3,595 ....E2	Münsingen, 8,350 ....E3	Saint-Ursanne, 1,073 ....D2	Vouvry, 1,851 ....C4
Kirchberg, St. Gallen,	Muotathal, 2,763 ....G3	Samedan, 2,574 ....J3	Wädenswil, 15,695 ....G2
6,309 ....G2	Muri, 4,853 ....F2	Sankt Gallen, 81,900 ....H2	Wahlern, 4,832 ....D3
Kleinlützel, 1,271 ....D2	Muri bei Bern, 3,057 ....E3	Sankt Gallen, ±90,400 ....H2	Wald, 8,185 ....G2
Klingnau, 2,545 ....F1	Mürren, ...E3	Sargans, 4,058 ....H2	Waldenburg, 1,449 ....E2
Klosters, 3,534 ....J3	Murten, 4,256 ....D3	Sarnen, 6,952 ....F3	Waldkirch, 2,669 ....H2
Kloten, 16,388 ....F2	Müstair, 645 ....K3	Satigny, 1,877 ....A4	Wallenstadt, 3,446 ....H2
Koblenz, 1,439 ....F1	Muttenz, 15,518 ....E1	Savièse, 3,585 ....D4	Walzenhausen, 2,082 ....J2
Kölliken, 3,219 ....F2	Näfels, 3,739 ....H2	Savognin, 820 ....J3	Wangen an der Aare, 2,013 ....E2
Köniz, 33,800 ....D3	Naters, 5,517 ....E4	Saxon, 2,409 ....D4	Wängi, 2,730 ....H1
Kreuzlingen, 15,760 ....H1	Nebikon, 1,378 ....F2	Schaffhausen, 36,800 ....G1	Wartau, 3,604 ....H2
Kriens, 20,409 ....F2	Nesslau, 1,934 ....H2	Schaffhausen, ±55,800 ....G1	Wassen, 764 ....G3
Küblis, 796 ....J3	Netstal, 2,771 ....H2	Schangnau, ...E3	Wattwil, 8,566 ....H2
Küsnacht, 12,193 ....F2		Schänis, 2,355 ....H2	Weesen, 1,308 ....H2
Küssnacht am Rigi, 7,956 ....F2			Weggis, 2,517 ....F2

Weinfelden, 8,621 ....H1	Zizers, 1,913 ....J3	Bielersee (lake) D2
Wettingen, 19,900 ....F2	Zofingen, 9,292 ....F2	Bietschhorn (mt.) E4
Wetzikon, 13,469 ....G2	Zollikofen, 9,069 ....E3	Birs (riv.) D2
Wil, 14,646 ....H2	Zollikon, 12,117 ....G2	Blinnenhorn (mt.) F4
Wil, ±20,500 ....H2	Zug, 22,972 ....G2	Blümlisalp (mt.) E3
Wilchingen, 1,066 ....F1	Zug, ±51,300 ....G2	Bodensee (Constance)
Wilderswil, 1,666 ....E3	Zuoz, 1,165 ....J3	(lake) H1
Wildhaus, 1,104 ....H2	Zürich, 401,600 ....F2	Borgne (riv.) D4
Willisau, 2,728 ....F2	Zürich, ±718,100 ....F2	Breithorn (mt.) E4
Wimmis, 1,833 ....E3	Zurzach, 3,098 ....F1	Breithorn (mt.) E5
Windisch, 7,444 ....F2	Zweisimmen, 2,738 ....D3	Brienzer Rothorn (mt.) F3
Winterthur, 93,500 ....G1		Brienzer (lake) E3
Winterthur, ±110,100 ....G1	OTHER FEATURES	Broye (riv.) D2
Wohlen, 12,024 ....F2		Buchegg (mts.) D2
Wohlen, ±16,000 ....F2	Aa (riv.) F3	Buin (peak) K3
Wohlen bei Bern, 4,190 ....D3	Aare (riv.) E3	Campo Tencia (peak) G3
Wolfenschiessen, 1,470 ....F3	Agerisee (lake) G2	Chasseron (mt.) C3
Wolhusen, 3,556 ....F2	Aiguille d' Argentière	Churfirsten (mt.) H2
Worb, 9,526 ....E3	(mt.) C5	Clariden (mt.) H3
Wynigen, 1,986 ....E2	Aletschhorn (mt.) E4	Constance (lake) H1
Yverdon, 20,538 ....C3	Aroser Rothorn (mt.) J3	Cornettes de Bise (mts.) C4
Yvonand, 1,321 ....C3	Ault (peak) H3	Dammastock (mt.) F3
Zell, Luzern, 1,590 ....E2	Balmhorn (mt.) E4	Davos (valley) J3
Zell, Zürich, 4,008 ....G2	Bernese Oberland (reg.) E3	Dent Blanche (mt.) D4
Zermatt, 3,101 ....E4	Bernina (peak) J4	Dent de Lys (mt.) D3
Zernez, 906 ....K3	Bernina (pass) K4	Dent de Ruth (mt.) D3

SWITZERLAND and LIECHTENSTEIN

CONIC PROJECTION

SCALE OF MILES

0 5 10 20 30

SCALE OF KILOMETRES

0 5 10 20 30 40 50

Capitals of Countries .... ☆
Capitals of Cantons .... ◉
International Boundaries .... ▬ ▪ ▬ ▪
Canals .... ▭▭▭

Copyright by C.S. Hammond & Co., N.Y.

Dent d'Hérens (mt.)	E 5	Great Saint Bernard (mt.)	D 5	Oberalp (pass)	G 3	Saint Gotthard (pass)	G 3	Sustenhorn (mt.)	G 3	Wandfluhhorn (mt.)	G 4

Dent d'Hérens (mt.) ....E 5
Dents du Midi (mt.) ....C 4
Diablerets (mt.) ....D 4
Doldenhorn (mt.) ....D 4
Dolent (mt.) ....C 5
Dom (mt.) ....E 4
Doubs (riv.) ....C 2
Drance (riv.) ....D 5
Dufourspitze (mt.) ....K 3
Emmental (riv.) ....E 3
Engadine (riv.) ....K 3
Err (peak) ....J 3
Finsteraarhorn (mt.) ....F 3
Finsteraarhorn (pass) ....K 3
Fletschhorn (mt.) ....F 4
Fluchthorn (mt.) ....K 3
Flüela (pass) ....J 3
Furka (pass) ....F 3
Generoso (mt.) ....H 5
Geneva (riv.) ....C 4
Glärnisch (mt.) ....H 3
Glarus Alps (mts.) ....H 3
Grand Combin (mt.) ....D 5
Grande Dixence (dam) ....D 4
Grand Muveran (mt.) ....D 4
Grauehörner (mts.) ....H 3

Great Saint Bernard (mt.) ....D 5
Great Saint Bernard (pass) ....D 5
Greifensee (lake) ....G 2
Greina (pass) ....G 3
Grimsel (pass) ....F 3
Gross Emme (riv.) ....E 2
Gross Litzner (mt.) ....K 3
Hinterrhein (riv.) ....H 3
Hochwang (mt.) ....J 3
Hohenstollen (mt.) ....F 3
Hörnli (mt.) ....G 2
Inn (riv.) ....K 3
Jorat (mt.) ....C 3
Jungfrau (mt.) ....E 3
Jura (mts.) ....B 3
Kaiseregg (mt.) ....D 3
Kesch (peak) ....J 3
La Dôle (mt.) ....B 4
Landquart (riv.) ....J 3
Le Chasseral (mt.) ....C 3
Le Gros Crêt (mt.) ....B 3
Léman (Geneva) (lake) ....C 4
Leone (mt.) ....F 4
Lepontine Alps (range) ....G 4

Limmat (riv.) ....F 2
Linard (peak) ....K 3
Linden (mt.) ....F 2
Linth (riv.) ....G 2
Lötschberg (tunnel) ....E 4
Lower Engadine (valley) ....K 3
Lucerne (lake) ....F 3
Lugano (lake) ....H 5
Madrisahorn (mt.) ....J 3
Maggia (riv.) ....G 4
Maggiore (lake) ....G 4
Männlifluh (mt.) ....E 4
Marmontana (mt.) ....H 4
Matterhorn (mt.) ....E 5
Mauvoisin (dam) ....D 4
Moësa (riv.) ....H 4
Morat (lake) ....D 3
Muota (riv.) ....G 3
Murg (riv.) ....G 1
Murtaröl (peak) ....K 3
Muttler (mt.) ....K 3
Naafkopf (mt.) ....J 2
Napf (mt.) ....E 3
National Park ....K 3
Neuchâtel (lake) ....C 3
Noirmont (mt.) ....B 4

Oberalp (pass) ....G 3
Oberalpstock (mt.) ....G 3
Ochsen (mt.) ....K 3
Ofen (pass) ....K 3
Ofenhorn (mt.) ....F 4
Orbe (riv.) ....C 4
Pennine Alps (range) ....E 5
Pilatus (mt.) ....F 3
Poschiavo (valley) ....K 4
Pragel (pass) ....G 3
Quartaval (peak) ....K 3
Reuss (riv.) ....F 2
Rhaetian Alps (range) ....J 3
Rheinwaldhorn (mt.) ....H 4
Rhine (riv.) ....H 2
Rhône (riv.) ....J 2
Rigi (mt.) ....F 2
Rimpfischhorn (mt.) ....E 5
Ringelspitz (mt.) ....H 3
Risoux (mt.) ....B 3
Rosa (mt.) ....E 5
Rosstock (mt.) ....F 3
Rothorn (mt.) ....E 3

Saint Gotthard (pass) ....G 3
Saint Gotthard (tunnel) ....G 3
San Bernardino (pass) ....H 3
Säntis (mt.) ....H 2
Sarine (Saane) (riv.) ....D 3
Sarnen (lake) ....F 3
Schesaplana (mt.) ....J 3
Scherhorn (mt.) ....G 3
Schreckhorn (mt.) ....F 3
Schwarzhorn (mt.) ....F 3
Schwarzhorn (mt.) ....F 3
Seez (riv.) ....H 2
Sempach (lake) ....F 2
Septimer (pass) ....J 4
Sesvenna (peak) ....K 3
Sihlsee (lake) ....G 2
Silvretta (mts.) ....K 3
Simplon (pass) ....F 4
Simplon (tunnel) ....F 4
Sol (peak) ....H 3
Sonnenhorn (mt.) ....G 4
Splügen (pass) ....H 4
Stockhorn (mt.) ....E 3
Sulzfluh (mt.) ....J 3
Susten (pass) ....G 3

Sustenhorn (mt.) ....G 3
Tamaro (mt.) ....G 4
Tamina (riv.) ....H 3
Tendre (peak) ....B 3
Terri (mt.) ....G 3
Thunersee (lake) ....E 3
Thur (riv.) ....G 1
Ticino (riv.) ....G 4
Titlis (mt.) ....F 3
Tödi (mt.) ....G 3
Toggenburg (dist.) ....H 2
Töss (riv.) ....G 2
Tour d'Ai (mt.) ....C 4
Umbrail (pass) ....K 3
Untersee (lake) ....H 1
Unterwalden (reg.) ....F 3
Upper Engadine (valley) ....J 4
Urirotstock (mt.) ....G 3
Vadret (peak) ....K 3
Valserrhein (riv.) ....H 3
Vanil Noir (mt.) ....D 4
Velan (mt.) ....D 5
Visp (riv.) ....E 4
Vorab (mt.) ....H 3
Vorderrhein (riv.) ....H 3
Wallenstadt (lake) ....H 2

Wandfluhhorn (mt.) ....G 4
Weissenstein (mts.) ....D 2
Weisshorn (mt.) ....E 4
Weisshorn (mt.) ....J 3
Weissmies (mt.) ....F 4
Wetterhorn (mt.) ....F 3
Wildhorn (mt.) ....D 4
Wildstrubel (mt.) ....E 4
Zellersee (lake) ....G 1
Zugersee (lake) ....F 2
Zürichsee (lake) ....G 2

LIECHTENSTEIN

CITIES and TOWNS

Schaan, 3,890 ....H 2
Triesen, 2,637 ....H 2
Vaduz (cap.), 7,500 ....H 2

OTHER FEATURES

Naafkopf (mt.) ....J 2
Ochsenkopf (mt.) ....J 2
Rhätikon (mts.) ....J 2
Rhine (riv.) ....J 2
Vorderrhein (riv.) ....H 2
Wildhorn (mt.) ....J 2

‡ City and suburbs.

AUSTRIA

PROVINCES

Burgenland, 272,119 ... D3
Carinthia, 525,728 ... B3
Lower Austria, 1,414,161 ... C2
Salzburg, 401,766 ... B3
Styria, 1,192,442 ... C3
Tirol, 540,771 ... A3
Upper Austria, 1,223,444 ... C2
Vienna (city), 1,614,841 ... D2
Vorarlberg, 271,473 ... A3

CITIES and TOWNS

Achenkirch, 1,763 ... A3
Admont, 3,126 ... C3
Aigen im Mühlkreis, 1,822 ... B2
Allentsteig, 2,783 ... C2
Alt Aussee, 1,951 ... B3
Altheim, 4,766 ... B2
Althofen, 3,886 ... C3
Amstetten, 13,330 ... C2
Andau, 3,058 ... D3
Arnoldstein, 6,740 ... B3
Aspang Markt, 2,316 ... C3
Attnang-Puchheim, 7,837 ... B2
Bad Aussee, 5,039 ... B3
Baden, 22,631 ... D2
Badgastein, 5,228 ... B3
Bad Goisern, 6,360 ... B3
Bad Hofgastein, 5,525 ... B3
Bad Ischl, 12,740 ... B3
Bad Sankt Leonhard im Lavanttal, 4,882 ... C3
Berndorf, 8,371 ... C3
Bischofshofen, 9,417 ... B3
Bludenz, 12,050 ... A3
Bramberg am Wildkogel, 3,129 ... B3
Braunau am Inn, 16,432 ... B2
Bregenz, 22,839 ... A3
Bruck an der Leitha, 7,506 ... D2
Bruck an der Mur, 16,359 ... C3
Deutsch Feistritz, 3,820 ... C3
Deutschkreutz, 3,673 ... D3
Deutsch Landsberg, 6,614 ... C3
Deutsch Wagram, 4,481 ... D2
Dölsach, 1,752 ... B3
Dornbirn, 33,810 ... A3
Ebenfurth, 2,272 ... D2
Ebensee, 9,413 ... B3

Heiligenblut, 1,324 ... B3
Hermagor-Preseggersee, 7,531 ... B3
Herzogenburg, 7,299 ... C2
Hieflau, 1,699 ... C3
Hohenau an der March, 3,591 ... D2
Hohenberg, 2,016 ... C3
Hohenems, 11,487 ... A3
Hollabrunn, 6,563 ... C2
Hopfgarten in Nordtirol, 4,784 ... B3
Horn, 6,264 ... C2
Hüttenberg, 3,251 ... C3
Imst, 5,855 ... A3
Innsbruck, 115,800 ... A3
Innsbruck, *167,200 ... A3
Jenbach, 5,868 ... A3
Jennersdorf, 4,210 ... D3
Judenburg, 11,346 ... C3
Kapfenberg, 26,001 ... C3
Kappl, 2,156 ... A3
Kaprun, 2,604 ... B3
Kindberg, 6,128 ... C3
Kirchdorf an der Krems, 3,471 ... C3
Kitzbühel, 7,995 ... B3
Klagenfurt, 74,326 ... C3
Klagenfurt, *112,600 ... C3
Klosterneuburg, 21,912 ... D2
Knittelfeld, 14,517 ... C3
Köflach, 12,612 ... C3
Königswiesen, 2,921 ... C2
Korneuburg, 8,892 ... D2
Kössen, 2,764 ... B3
Kötschach-Mauthen, 3,740 ... B3
Krems an der Donau, 21,733 ... C2
Krimml, 794 ... B3
Kufstein, 12,766 ... A3
Kundl, 3,020 ... A3
Laa an der Thaya, 5,455 ... C2
Laakirchen, 15,239 ... B3
Lambach, 3,301 ... C2
Landeck, 7,388 ... A3
Längenfeld, 2,838 ... A3
Langenlois, 4,957 ... C2
Langenwang, 4,170 ... C3
Lavamünd, 4,120 ... C3
Leibnitz, 6,646 ... C3
Lenzing, 5,385 ... B3
Leoben, 35,153 ... C3
Leonfelden, 2,712 ... C2
Lienz, 11,696 ... B3
Liezen, 6,244 ... C3
Lilienfeld, 3,126 ... C3
Linz, 205,700 ... C2

Ratten, 1,368 ... C3
Rechnitz, 3,412 ... D3
Reichenau an der Rax, 4,053 ... C3
Retz, 4,780 ... C2
Reutte, 5,006 ... A3
Ried im Innkreis, 10,534 ... B2
Rohrbach in Oberösterreich, 1,755 ... B2
Rottenmann, 4,781 ... C3
Rust, 1,704 ... D3
Saalfelden am Steinernen Meer, 10,172 ... B3
Salzburg, 122,100 ... B3
Salzburg, *213,430 ... B3
Sankt Aegyd am Neuwalde, 3,165 ... C3
Sankt Anton am Arlberg, 2,086 ... A3
Sankt Johann in Tirol, 5,942 ... B3
Sankt Michael im Lungau, 2,839 ... B3
Sankt Michael in Obersteiermark, 3,717 ... C3
Sankt Paul im Lavanttal, 6,721 ... C3
Sankt Pölten, 43,300 ... C2
Sankt Valentin, 8,715 ... C2
Sankt Veit an der Glan, 11,047 ... C3
Sankt Wolfgang im Salzkammergut, 2,476 ... B3
Schärding, 5,874 ... B2
Scheibbs, 4,419 ... C2
Schladming, 3,460 ... B3
Schrems, 5,393 ... C2
Schruns, 3,607 ... A3
Schwarzach im Pongau, 3,616 ... B3
Schwaz, 10,253 ... A3
Schwertberg, 3,881 ... C2
Sierning, 8,162 ... C2
Sigmundsherberg, 945 ... C2
Sillian, 1,988 ... B3
Solbad Hall in Tirol, 12,335 ... A3
Spital am Pyhrn, 2,315 ... C3
Spittal an der Drau, 13,690 ... B3
Spitz, 1,504 ... C2
Steinach, 2,698 ... A3
Steyr, 40,578 ... C2
Stockerau, 12,634 ... D2
Strassburg, 2,850 ... C3
Tamsweg, 5,060 ... B3
Telfs, 9,707 ... A3
Ternitz, 10,287 ... C3
Traiskirchen, 8,878 ... C2
Traun, 20,843 ... C2
Trieben, 4,639 ... C3
Trofaiach, 8,731 ... C3

Tulln, 7,705 ... D2
Velden am Wörthersee, 7,306 ... C3
Vienna (cap.), 1,700,000 ... D2
Vienna, *1,858,700 ... D2
Villach, 50,979 ... B3
Vils, 1,325 ... A3
Vöcklabruck, 10,627 ... B2
Voitsberg, 11,094 ... C3
Völkermarkt, 10,772 ... C3
Vordernberg, 2,508 ... C3
Waidhofen an der Thaya, 4,200 ... C2
Waidhofen an der Ybbs, 5,218 ... C3
Weitensfeld-Flattnitz, 5,206 ... B3
Weitra, 3,250 ... C2
Weiz, 8,421 ... C3
Wels, 47,279 ... C2
Weyer Markt, 2,518 ... C3
Wiener Neustadt, 34,774 ... D3
Wildon, 2,002 ... C3
Wilhelmsburg, 6,307 ... C2
Windischgarsten, 1,805 ... C3
Wolfsberg, 31,176 ... C3
Wörgl, 7,811 ... A3
Ybbs an der Donau, 6,422 ... C2
Zams, 3,120 ... A3
Zell am See, 7,456 ... B3
Zell am Ziller, 1,882 ... A3
Zeltweg, 8,431 ... C3
Zirl, 4,157 ... A3
Zistersdorf, 3,412 ... D2
Zwettl-Niederösterreich, 11,624 ... C2

OTHER FEATURES

Allgäu Alps (mts.) ... A3
Bavarian Alps (mts.) ... A3
Bodensee (Constance) (lake) ... A3
Brenner (pass) ... A3
Carnic Alps (mts.) ... B3
Constance (lake) ... A3
Danube (riv.) ... C2
Donau (Danube) (riv.) ... C2
Drau (riv.) ... C3
Enns (riv.) ... C3
Grossglockner (mt.) ... B3
Hohe Tauern (range) ... B3
Inn (riv.) ... B2
Karawanken (range) ... C3
March (riv.) ... D2
Mühlviertel (reg.), 214,012 ... C2
Mur (riv.) ... B3

Neusiedler See (lake) ... D3
Niedere Tauern (range) ... B3
Ötztal Alps (mts.) ... A3
Raab (riv.) ... C3
Rhine (riv.) ... A3
Salzach (riv.) ... B3
Salzkammergut (reg.), 112,566 ... B3
Semmering (pass) ... C3
Thaya (riv.) ... C2
Traun (riv.) ... C2
Wildspitze (mt.) ... A3
Zugspitze (mt.) ... A3

CZECHOSLOVAKIA

REPUBLICS

Czech Socialist Rep., 9,964,338 ... B1
Slovak Socialist Rep., 4,670,409 ... E2

REGIONS

Bratislava (city), 333,000 ... D2
Jihocesky, 662,002 ... C2
Jihomoravsky, 1,966,850 ... D2
Praha (city), 1,161,200 ... C1
Severocesky, 1,122,035 ... C1
Severomoravsky, 1,849,286 ... E1
Stredocesky, 1,193,041 ... C2
Stredoslovensky, 1,436,351 ... E2
Vychodocesky, 1,214,581 ... C1
Vychodoslovensky, 1,298,481 ... F2
Zapadocesky, 865,094 ... B2
Zapadoslovensky, 1,610,542 ... D2

CITIES and TOWNS

Aš, 12,000 ... B1
Bánovce nad Bebravou, 11,400 ... E2
Banska Bystrica, 53,000 ... E2
Banska Stiavnica, 7,486 ... E2
Bardejov, 11,100 ... F2
Benesov, 11,100 ... C2
Beroun, 17,600 ... B2
Bilina, 17,800 ... B1
Blansko, 13,800 ... D2
Boskovice, 8,531 ... D2
Brandys nad Labem-Stará Boleslav, 15,500 ... C1
Bratislava, 333,000 ... D2
Breclav, 21,100 ... D2
Brezno, 14,800 ... E2
Brno, 335,700 ... D2
Broumov, 7,782 ... D1
Bruntal, 12,300 ... D2
Bystrice nad Pernstejnem, 6,471 ... D2
Bystrice pod Hostynem, 6,681 ... D2
Bytca, 6,922 ... E2
Cadca, 16,800 ... E2
Calovo, 6,591 ... D3
Caslav, 10,200 ... C2
Ceska Lipa, 18,600 ... C1
Ceska Trebova, 14,700 ... D2
Ceske Budejovice, 80,800 ... C2
Cesky Brod, 6,640 ... C1
Cesky Krumlov, 12,000 ... C2
Cesky Tesin, 17,200 ... E2

Cheb, 27,000 ... B1
Chocen, 8,198 ... D1
Chodov, 14,400 ... B1
Chomutov, 44,200 ... B1
Chotebor, 6,692 ... C2
Chrudim, 18,800 ... C2
Cierny Balog, 6,435 ... E2
Decin, 46,500 ... C1
Detva, 13,100 ... E2
Dobris, 6,378 ... C2
Dobruska, 5,779 ... D1
Dolny Kubin, 9,900 ... E2
Domazlice, 9,100 ... B2
Dubnica nad Vahom, 11,300 ... E2
Duchcov, 9,712 ... B1
Dunajská Streda, 13,000 ... D3
Dvory nad Zitavou, 5,847 ... E3
Dvur Králové nad Labem, 16,800 ... C1
Falknov (Sokolov), 23,900 ... B1
Fil'akovo, 7,822 ... E2
Frenstat pod Radhostem, 8,516 ... E2
Frydek-Mistek, 43,800 ... E2
Frydlant v Cechach, 5,948 ... C1
Frydant nad Ostravici, 6,250 ... E2
Galanta, 12,300 ... D2
Gottwaldov, 84,300 ... D2
Handlova, 16,200 ... E2
Havirov, 85,000 ... E2
Havlickuv Brod, 19,200 ... C2
Hlinsko, 8,890 ... D2
Hlohovec, 15,200 ... D2
Hlucin, 15,300 ... E2

Topography

0   50   100
MILES

5,000 m. / 16,404 ft. — 2,000 m. / 6,562 ft. — 1,000 m. / 3,281 ft. — 500 m. / 1,640 ft. — 200 m. / 656 ft. — 100 m. / 328 ft. — Sea Level — Below

---

Eferding, 3,014 ... B2
Eggenburg, 3,730 ... C2
Ehrwald, 2,198 ... A3
Eisenerz, 11,563 ... C3
Eisenkappel-Vellach, 3,761 ... C3
Eisenstadt, 10,059 ... D3
Eisenstadt, *43,582 ... D3
Engelhartszell, 1,238 ... C2
Enns, 9,622 ... C2
Feldbach, 3,887 ... C3
Feldkirch, 21,214 ... A3
Feldkirchen in Kärnten, 11,188 ... C3
Fels am Wagram, 1,896 ... C2
Ferlach, 7,621 ... C3
Fieberbrunn, 3,651 ... B3
Fohnsdorf, 11,169 ... C3
Frankenmarkt, 2,960 ... B3
Frauenkirchen, 2,749 ... D3
Freistadt, 5,956 ... C2
Friedberg, 2,504 ... C3
Friesach, 7,257 ... C3
Frohnleiten, 5,081 ... C3
Fulpmes, 2,553 ... A3
Fürstenfeld, 6,054 ... C3
Gaming, 4,181 ... C3
Gänserndorf, 4,211 ... D2
Gleisdorf, 4,921 ... C3
Gloggnitz, 7,078 ... C3
Gmünd, Carinthia, 2,267 ... B3
Gmünd, Lower Austria, 6,323 ... C2
Gmunden, 12,270 ... B3
Golling an der Salzach, 3,293 ... B3
Götzis, 7,931 ... A3
Gratwein, 2,747 ... C3
Graz, 251,900 ... C3
Graz, *314,200 ... C3
Grein, 2,767 ... C2
Gries am Brenner, 1,396 ... A3
Grieskirchen, 4,519 ... B2
Gross Siegharts, 3,288 ... C2
Grünburg, 3,775 ... C3
Gurk, 1,689 ... C3
Güssing, 3,675 ... D3
Haag, 5,060 ... C2
Hainburg an der Donau, 6,009 ... D2
Hainfeld, 3,897 ... C2
Hallein, 14,371 ... B3
Hallstatt, 1,303 ... B3
Hartberg, 5,702 ... C3
Haslach an der Mühl, 2,636 ... C2
Heidenreichstein, 4,340 ... C2

Linz, *356,600 ... C2
Lofer, 1,687 ... B3
Lustenau, 15,239 ... A3
Mallnitz, 1,008 ... B3
Mannersdorf am Leithagebirge, 4,012 ... D3
Marchegg, 2,678 ... D2
Mariazell, 2,298 ... C3
Matrei in Osttirol, 4,003 ... B3
Mattersburg, 5,417 ... D3
Mattighofen, 4,344 ... B2
Mauerkirchen, 2,960 ... B2
Mautern in Steiermark, 2,536 ... C3
Mauthausen, 4,419 ... C2
Mauthen-Kötschach, 3,740 ... B3
Mayrhofen, 3,174 ... A3
Melk, 5,108 ... C2
Mistelbach an der Zaya, 6,306 ... D2
Mittersill, 4,361 ... B3
Mödling, 18,712 ... D2
Mondsee, 2,141 ... B3
Murau, 2,710 ... C3
Mürzzuschlag, 11,564 ... C3
Nassereith, 1,888 ... A3
Nauders, 1,302 ... A3
Neuberg an der Mürz, 2,183 ... C3
Neumarkt am Wallersee, 3,267 ... B3
Neumarkt in Steiermark, 1,835 ... C3
Neunkirchen, 10,922 ... C3
Neusiedl am See, 3,999 ... D3
Neustift im Stubaital, 2,789 ... A3
Ober Grafendorf, 4,109 ... C2
Obervellach, 2,420 ... B3
Oberwart, 5,661 ... C3
Oberwölz, 870 ... C3
Paternion, 5,805 ... B3
Perg, 4,872 ... C2
Peuerbach, 2,161 ... B2
Pfunds, 2,043 ... A3
Pinkafeld, 4,610 ... C3
Pöchlarn, 3,199 ... C2
Pöllau, 1,811 ... C3
Pörtschach am Wörthersee, 2,511 ... C3
Poysdorf, 5,774 ... D2
Pregarten, 3,249 ... C2
Raabs an der Thaya, 4,194 ... C2
Radenthein, 6,847 ... B3
Radkersburg, 2,000 ... C3
Radstadt, 3,585 ... B3
Rankweil, 8,440 ... A3

AUSTRIA
AREA 32,375 sq. mi.
POPULATION 7,540,000
CAPITAL Vienna
LARGEST CITY Vienna
HIGHEST POINT Grossglockner 12,457 ft.
MONETARY UNIT schilling
MAJOR LANGUAGE German
MAJOR RELIGION Roman Catholicism

CZECHOSLOVAKIA
AREA 49,373 sq. mi.
POPULATION 14,900,000
CAPITAL Prague
LARGEST CITY Prague
HIGHEST POINT Gerlachovka 8,707 ft.
MONETARY UNIT koruna
MAJOR LANGUAGES Czech, Slovak
MAJOR RELIGIONS Roman Catholicism,
Protestantism

HUNGARY
AREA 35,919 sq. mi.
POPULATION 10,590,000
CAPITAL Budapest
LARGEST CITY Budapest
HIGHEST POINT Kékes 3,330 ft.
MONETARY UNIT forint
MAJOR LANGUAGE Hungarian
MAJOR RELIGIONS Roman Catholicism,
Protestantism

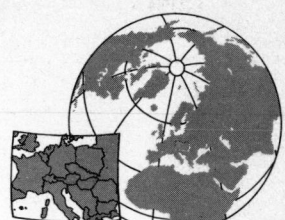

AUSTRIA

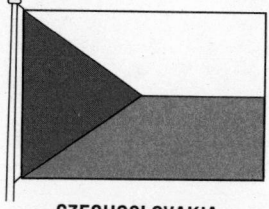

CZECHOSLOVAKIA

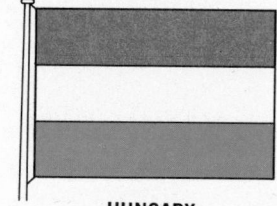

HUNGARY

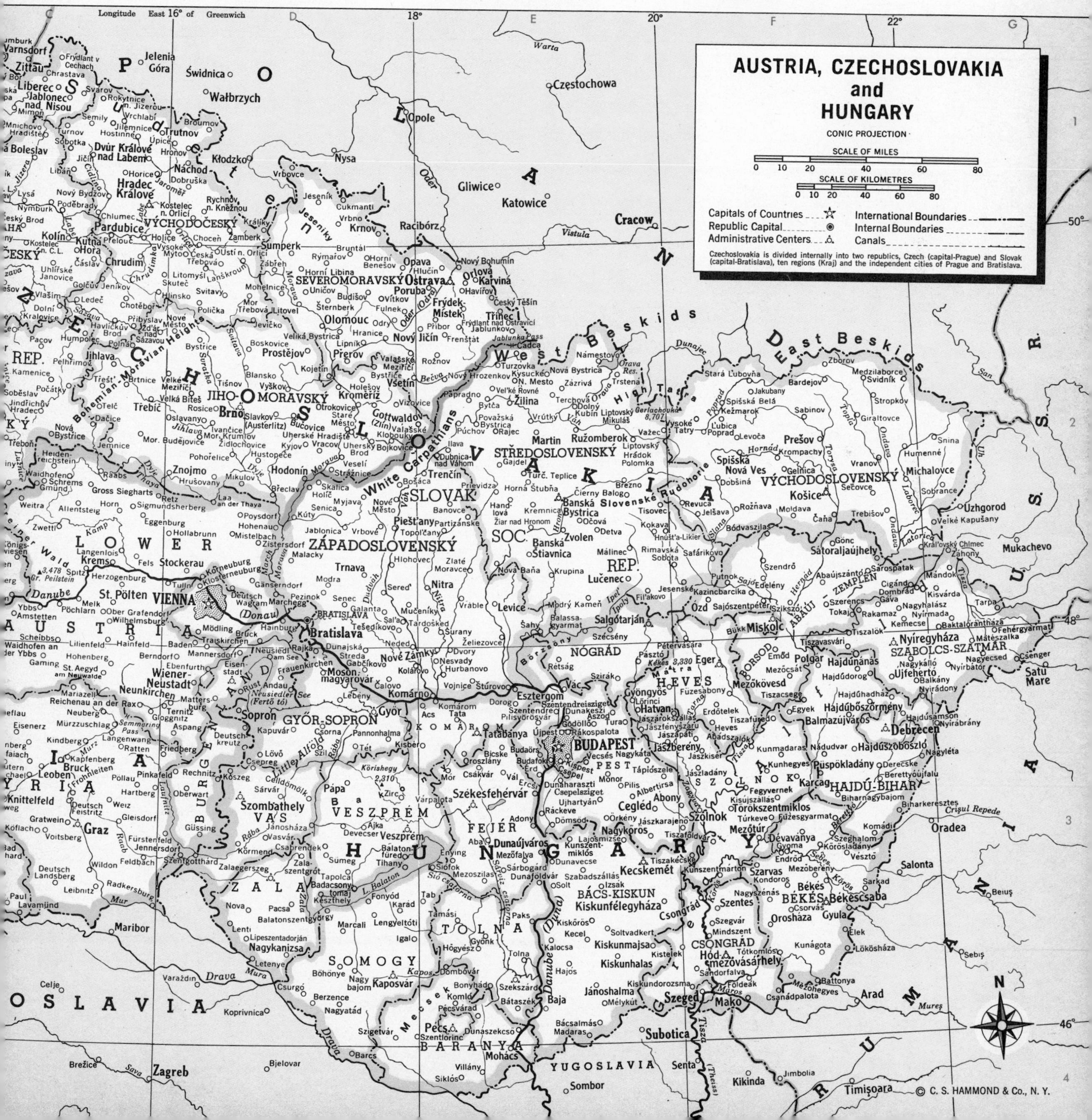

AUSTRIA, CZECHOSLOVAKIA and HUNGARY

CONIC PROJECTION

SCALE OF MILES
0 10 20 40 60 80

SCALE OF KILOMETRES
0 10 20 40 60 80

Capitals of Countries ⋯⋯☆
Republic Capital ⋯⋯◉
Administrative Centers ⋯⋯△
International Boundaries ⎯⎯⎯
Internal Boundaries ⎯ ⎯ ⎯
Canals ⎯⎯⎯

Czechoslovakia is divided internally into two republics, Czech (capital-Prague) and Slovak (capital-Bratislava), ten regions (Kraj) and the independent cities of Prague and Bratislava.

© C. S. HAMMOND & Co., N.Y.

(continued)

Hnušťa-Likier E 2
Hodonín, 22,600 D 2
Holešov, 9,091 D 2
Holíč, 7,602 D 2
Holice, 6,151 C 1
Horažďovice B 2
Hořice v Podkrkonoší, 7,715 C 1
Horná Štubňa E 2
Horní Benešov D 2
Horní Libina D 2
Hořovice, 5,665 C 2
Horšovský Týn B 2
Hostinné C 1
Hradec Králové, 85,600 C 1
Hranice, 13,300 D 2
Hronov, 9,767 D 1
Hrušovany D 2
Humenné, 22,200 G 2
Humpolec, 7,810 C 2
Hurbanovo E 3
Hustopeče D 2
Ilava E 2
Ivančice, 7,314 D 2
Jablonec nad Nisou, 36,300 C 1
Jablonica D 2
Jablunkov, 9,405 E 2
Jáchymov B 1
Jakubany F 2
Jaroměř, 11,600 C 1
Jelšava F 2
Jemnice C 2
Jeseník, 10,900 D 1
Jesenské F 2
Jevíčko D 2
Jičín, 13,200 C 1
Jihlava, 44,500 C 2
Jilemnice C 1
Jindřichův Hradec, 15,700 C 2
Jirkov, 11,400 B 1
Kadaň, 18,100 B 1
Kamenice C 2
Kaplice C 2
Karlovy Vary, 43,300 B 1
Karviná, 79,100 E 2
Kdyně B 2
Kežmarok, 11,000 F 2
Kladno, 61,200 B 1
Klatovy, 18,500 B 2
Kojetín, 5,852 D 2
Kokava nad Rimavicou, 5,391 E 2
Kolárovo, 10,500 D 3
Kolín, 29,100 C 1
Komárno, 28,200 D 3
Košice, 169,100 F 2
Kostelec nad Orlicí, 5,575 D 1
Kráľovský Chlmec, 5,329 G 2
Kralupy nad Vltavou, 16,900 C 1
Kraslice, 6,733 B 1
Kremnica, 5,941 E 2
Krnov, 25,000 D 1
Kroměříž, 23,200 D 2
Krompachy, 6,332 F 2
Krupina, 6,627 E 2
Krupka, 8,301 B 1
Kutná Hora, 19,200 C 2
Kyjov, 10,700 D 2
Kynšperk, 5,524 B 1
Kysucké Nové Mesto, 11,700 E 2
Lanškroun, 8,683 D 2
Levice, 19,000 E 2
Levoča, 10,100 F 2
Libáň C 1
Liberec, 75,600 C 1
Libochovice B 1
Lidice C 1
Lipník nad Bečvou, 7,358 D 2
Liptovský Hrádok E 2
Liptovský Mikuláš, 19,400 E 2
Lišov C 2
Litoměřice, 19,700 C 1
Litomyšl, 8,112 D 2
Litovel, 5,805 D 2
Litvínov, 23,300 B 1
Lomnice C 2
Louny, 15,200 B 1
Lovosice, 9,323 C 1
Ľubica F 2
Lučenec, 23,300 E 2
Lysá nad Labem, 9,920 C 1
Malacky, 13,200 D 2
Mariánské Lázně, 14,600 B 2
Martin, 47,800 E 2
Medzilaborce F 2
Mělník, 17,800 C 1
Michalovce, 23,600 G 2
Mikulov, 6,267 D 2
Milevsko, 7,091 C 2
Mimoň, 6,773 C 1
Mladá Boleslav, 36,900 C 1
Mladá Vožice C 2
Mnichovo Hradiště, 5,239 C 1
Modra, 7,219 D 2
Modrý Kameň, 6,200 E 2
Mohelnice, 6,050 D 2
Moldava nad Bodvou, 5,397 F 2
Moravská Třebová, 9,052 D 2
Moravské Budějovice, 5,576 D 2
Most, 59,400 B 1
Mučeníky D 2
Myjava, 6,657 D 2
Náchod, 19,300 D 1
Námestovo E 2
Neded D 2
Nejdek, 8,187 B 1
Nepomuk B 2
Nesvady, 5,453 E 3
Netolice C 2
Nitra, 50,000 E 2
Nová Baňa, 6,218 E 2
Nová Bystrica E 2
Nová Bystřice C 2
Nové Hrady C 2
Nové Město na Moravě, 6,581 D 2
Nové Mesto nad Váhom, 15,900 D 2
Nové Strašecí B 1
Nové Zámky, 27,300 D 3
Nový Bohumín, 16,700 E 2
Nový Bor, 7,621 C 1
Nový Bydžov, 6,824 C 1
Nový Hrozenkov E 2
Nový Jičín, 21,400 E 2
Nymburk, 13,600 C 1
Nýřany, 6,204 B 2
Nýrsko B 2
Odry D 2
Olomouc, 82,800 D 2
Opava, 53,800 E 2
Orlová, 25,500 E 2
Ostrava, 293,500 E 2
Ostrov, 18,200 B 1
Pardubice, 78,500 C 1
Partizánske, 15,100 E 2
Pelhřimov, 11,900 C 2
Pezinok, 13,100 D 2
Piešťany, 25,400 D 2
Písek, 25,100 C 2
Plzeň, 155,000 B 2
Počátky C 2
Podbořany B 1
Poděbrady, 13,400 C 1
Pohořelice D 2
Polička, 6,529 D 2
Polná C 2
Polomka E 2
Poprad, 25,800 F 2
Považská Bystrica, 19,300 E 2
Prachatice, 7,900 B 2
Prague (Praha) (cap.), 1,161,200 C 1
Přelouč, 6,251 C 1
Přerov, 43,500 D 2
Prešov, 61,000 F 2
Přeštice B 2
Příbor, 7,726 E 2
Příbram, 31,300 B 2
Prievidza, 30,900 E 2
Prostějov, 44,200 D 2
Protivín C 2
Púchov, 9,306 E 2
Radnice B 2
Rajec E 2
Rakovník, 14,200 B 1
Revúca, 5,901 F 2
Říčany u Prahy, 8,407 C 2
Rimavská Sobota, 5,800 E 2
Rokycany, 12,800 B 2
Rokytnice nad Jizerou C 1
Rosice D 2
Roudnice nad Labem, 11,800 C 1
Rožňava, 12,400 F 2
Rožnov pod Radhoštěm, 11,600 E 2
Rumburk C 1
Ružomberok, 22,600 E 2
Rychnov nad Kněžnou, 7,500 D 1
Rýmařov, 7,522 D 2
Sabinov, 5,473 F 2
Šafárikovo F 2
Šahy, 5,049 E 2
Šaľa, 15,200 D 2
Sečovce, 5,744 F 2
Sedlčany C 2
Semily, 8,200 C 1
Senec, 8,544 D 2
Senica, 12,300 D 2
Sereď, 12,500 D 2
Skalica, 11,100 D 2
Skuteč D 2
Slaný, 13,200 C 1
Slavkov D 2
Snina, 10,900 G 2
Soběslav, 6,140 C 2
Sobotka C 1
Sobrance G 2
Sokolov, 23,900 B 1
Spišská Belá F 2
Spišská Nová Ves, 26,100 F 2
Stará Ľubovňa, 5,800 F 2
Staré Město, 6,293 D 2
Šternberk, 13,700 D 2
Stod B 2
Strakonice, 19,000 B 2
Strážnice, 5,482 D 2
Stříbro B 2
Stropkov, 5,645 F 2
Štúrovo, 8,287 E 3
Šumperk, 25,900 D 1
Šurany, 6,693 E 2
Sušice, 10,300 B 2
Svárov C 1
Svidník, 4,600 F 2
Svitavy, 15,000 D 2
Tábor, 28,100 C 2
Tachov, 11,400 B 2
Telč, 5,285 C 2
Teplice, 52,300 B 1
Tišnov, 8,263 D 2
Topoľčany, 17,500 D 2
Třebíč, 23,900 C 2
Trebišov, 13,700 F 2
Třeboň, 6,068 C 2
Trenčín, 38,800 E 2
Třešť, 5,053 C 2
Třinec, 32,000 E 2
Trnava, 48,600 D 2
Trutnov, 24,500 D 1
Turnov, 13,600 C 1
Turzovka, 6,107 E 2
Uherské Hradiště, 32,100 D 2
Uherský Brod, 12,800 D 2
Uničov, 10,800 D 2
Úpice, 6,323 C 1
Ústí nad Labem, 74,900 C 1
Ústí nad Orlicí, 13,700 D 2
Valašské Meziříčí, 19,400 D 2
Varnsdorf, 14,700 C 1
Važec E 2
Vejprty B 1
Velká Bíteš D 2
Velká Bystřice D 2
Veľké Kapušany G 2
Velké Meziříčí, 7,590 D 2
Veľké Rovné E 2
Veselí nad Lužnicí C 2
Veselí nad Moravou, 11,500 D 2
Vimperk, 5,749 B 2
Vítkov, 5,138 D 2
Vizovice D 2
Vlašim, 8,873 C 2
Vodňany, 5,620 C 2
Vojnice E 3
Volary B 2
Volyně B 2
Votice C 2
Vráble E 2
Vracov D 2
Vranov nad Teplou, 14,700 F 2
Vrbno pod Pradědem, 5,594 D 1
Vrbovce D 1
Vrbové D 2
Vrchlabí, 11,700 C 1
Vrútky, 5,756 E 2
Vsetín, 24,100 D 2
Vyškov, 15,100 D 2
Vysoké Mýto, 8,830 D 2
Vysoké Tatry F 2
Vyšší Brod C 2
Zábřeh, 11,300 D 2
Žamberk, 5,040 D 1
Žatec, 17,400 B 1
Zázrivá E 2
Zbiroh B 2
Zborov F 2
Žďár nad Sázavou, 17,800 C 2
Želiezovce, 5,478 E 2
Žiar nad Hronom, 14,800 E 2
Židlochovice D 2
Žilina, 56,000 E 2
Zlaté Moravce, 10,300 E 2
Zlín (Gottwaldov), 84,300 D 2
Žlutice B 1
Znojmo, 28,500 D 2
Zvolen, 29,000 E 2

OTHER FEATURES

Berounka (riv.) C 2
Beskids, East (mts.) F 1
Beskids, West (mts.) E 2
Bohemian (for.) B 2
Bohemian-Moravian Heights (hills) C 2
Danube (riv.) C 2
Dunajec (riv.) F 2
Dyje (riv.) D 2
Erzgebirge (mts.) B 1
Gerlachovka (mt.) E 2
Hornád (riv.) F 2
Hron (riv.) E 2
Ipeľ (riv.) E 2
Jablunka (pass) E 2
Jeseníky (mts.) D 1
Jihlava (riv.) D 2
Krušné Hory (Erzgebirge) (mts.) B 1
Labe (riv.) C 1
Lipno (res.) C 2
Lužnice (riv.) C 2
Moldau (Vltava) (riv.) C 2
Morava (riv.) D 2
Nitra (riv.) E 2
Oder (Odra) (riv.) D 2
Ohře (riv.) B 1
Ondava (riv.) F 2
Orava (riv.) E 2
Orlická (res.) C 2
Sázava (riv.) C 2
Slovenské Rudohorie (mts.) E 2
Sudeten (mts.) C 1
Svitava (riv.) D 2
Svratka (riv.) D 2
Tatra, High (mts.) E 2
Torysa (riv.) F 2
Úhlava (riv.) B 2
Váh (riv.) D 2
Vltava (riv.) C 2
White Carpathians (mts.) E 2

HUNGARY

COUNTIES

Bács-Kiskun, 574,009 E 3
Baranya, 424,857 E 4
Békés, 446,405 F 3
Borsod-Abaúj-Zemplén, 779,424 F 2
Budapest (city), 2,051,354 E 3
Csongrád, 441,399 F 3
Fejér, 390,655 E 3
Gy"or-Sopron, 403,860 D 3
Hajdú-Bihar, 531,508 F 3
Heves, 347,270 F 3
Komárom, 301,760 E 3
Nógrád, 240,129 E 3
Pest, 875,462 E 3
Somogy, 363,075 D 3
Szabolcs-Szatmár, 590,211 G 3
Szolnok, 449,001 F 3
Tolna, 258,789 E 3
Vas, 280,125 D 3
Veszprém, 412,298 D 3
Zala, 266,779 D 3

CITIES and TOWNS

Aba, 4,271 E 3
Abádszalók, 6,386 F 3
Abaújszántó, 4,209 F 2
Abony, 15,624 E 3
Ács, 8,423 E 3
Ajka, 20,263 D 3
Albertirsa, 11,252 E 3
Aszód, 6,218 E 3
Bácsalmás, 9,025 E 3
Badacsonytomaj, 2,933 D 3
Baja, 34,650 E 3
Baktalórántháza, 3,736 G 2
Balassagyarmat, 15,147 E 2
Balatonfüred, 9,736 D 3
Balatonszentgyörgy, 1,416 D 3
Balkány, 7,667 G 3
Balmazújváros, 17,371 F 3
Barcs, 7,703 D 4
Bátaszék, 7,274 E 3
Battonya, 9,324 F 3
Békés, 21,032 F 3
Békéscsaba, 57,060 F 3
Berettyóújfalu, 13,999 F 3
Berzence, 3,406 D 3
Bicske, 10,720 E 3
Biharkeresztes, 4,788 F 3
Biharnagybajom, 4,093 F 3
Bódvaszilas, 1,280 F 2
Böhönye, 3,215 D 3
Bonyhád, 12,377 E 3
Budafok, 40,623 E 3
Budaörs, 13,958 E 3
Budapest (cap.), 2,051,354 E 3
Cegléd, 38,040 E 3
Celldömölk, 10,493 D 3
Cigánd, 4,767 F 2
Csabrendek, 3,045 D 3
Csákvár, 5,238 E 3
Csanádpalota, 4,642 F 3
Csenger, 4,792 G 3
Csepel, 71,693 E 3
Csepreg, 4,079 D 3
Csongrád, 20,264 E 3
Csorna, 9,508 D 3
Csorvás, 6,826 F 3
Csurgó, 5,463 D 3
Debrecen, 179,755 F 3
Derecske, 9,579 F 3
Dévaványa, 11,208 F 3
Devecser, 5,482 D 3
Dombóvár, 16,670 E 3
Dombrád, 6,328 F 2
Dömsöd, 6,545 E 3
Dorog, 10,754 E 3
Dunaföldvár, 10,318 E 3
Dunaharaszti, 15,788 E 3
Dunakeszi, 19,280 E 3
Dunaszekcs"o, 2,999 E 3
Dunaújváros, 44,721 E 3
Dunavecse, 4,521 E 3
Edelény, 9,559 F 2
Eger, 45,236 F 3
Egyek, 7,956 F 3
Elek, 6,032 F 3
Endr"od, 8,136 F 3
Enying, 7,518 E 3
Érd, 31,188 E 3
Erd"otelek, 4,250 F 3
Esztergom, 26,965 E 3
Fegyvernek, 7,331 F 3
Fehérgyarmat, 6,688 G 3
Földeák, 3,855 F 3
Fonyód, 3,957 D 3
Füzesabony, 6,965 F 3
Füzesgyarmat, 7,097 F 3
Gödöll"o, 21,418 E 3
Gönc, 2,875 F 2
Gyoma, 10,392 F 3
Gyöngyös, 33,117 E 3
Gy"onk, 2,507 E 3
Gy"or, 114,709 D 3
Gyula, 26,438 F 3
Hajdúböszörmény, 30,464 F 3
Hajdúdorog, 10,118 F 3
Hajdúhadház, 13,626 F 3
Hajdúnánás, 17,906 F 3
Hajdúsámson, 7,492 F 3
Hajdúszoboszló, 22,003 F 3
Hajós, 5,113 E 3
Hatvan, 21,984 E 3
Heves, 10,943 F 3
Hódmez"ovásárhely, 52,777 F 3
H"ogyész, 3,534 E 3
Igal, 1,813 D 3
Izsák, 7,686 E 3
Jánoshalma, 12,534 E 3
Jánosháza, 3,274 D 3
Jászapáti, 10,424 E 3
Jászárokszállás, 10,139 E 3
Jászberény, 29,793 E 3
Jászfényszaru, 6,869 E 3
Jászkarajen"o, 4,101 E 3
Jászkisér, 6,816 F 3
Jászladány, 7,823 F 3
Kalocsa, 16,084 E 3
Kaposvár, 58,524 D 3
Kapuvár, 10,570 D 3
Karád, 2,754 D 3
Karcag, 24,638 F 3
Kazincbarcika, 25,948 F 2
Kecel, 10,493 E 3
Kecskemét, 77,963 E 3
Kemecse, 4,583 F 2
Keszthely, 17,082 D 3
Kisbér, 4,562 D 3
Kisk"orös, 14,150 E 3
Kiskunfélegyháza, 34,073 E 3
Kiskunhalas, 26,668 E 3
Kiskunmajsa, 14,439 E 3
Kispest, 65,106 E 3
Kistelek, 8,544 E 3
Kisújszállás, 13,470 F 3
Kisvárda, 13,725 G 2
Komádi, 8,765 F 3
Komárom, 11,300 E 3
Komló, 28,191 E 3
Kondoros, 7,319 F 3
Körmend, 9,942 D 3
Körösladány, 6,565 F 3
K"oszeg, 10,238 D 3
Kunágota, 4,622 F 3
Kunhegyes, 10,116 F 3
Kunmadaras, 7,343 F 3
Kunszentmárton, 11,103 F 3
Kunszentmiklós, 7,952 E 3
Lajosmizse, 12,872 E 3
Lébény, 6,190 D 3
Lengyeltóti, 3,389 D 3
Lenti, 4,476 D 3
Letenye, 4,395 D 3
Lispeszentadorján, 722 D 3
Lökösháza, 2,514 F 3
L"orinci, 10,679 E 3
Löv"o, 1,671 D 3
Madaras, 4,519 E 3
Makó, 30,073 F 3
Mándok, 5,093 G 2
Marcali, 8,282 D 3
Mátészalka, 12,413 G 3
Mélykút, 7,640 E 3
Mez"oberény, 12,702 F 3
Mez"ocsát, 6,729 F 3
Mez"ofalva, 5,008 E 3
Mez"ohegyes, 8,631 F 3
Mez"okövesd, 17,899 F 3
Mez"oszilas, 2,792 E 3
Mez"otúr, 21,851 F 3
Mindszent, 8,730 F 3
Miskolc, 194,648 F 2
Mohacs, 19,717 E 4
Monor, 16,838 E 3
Mór, 12,066 E 3
Mosonmagyaróvár, 24,440 D 3
Nádudvar, 9,447 F 3
Nagyatád, 10,358 D 3
Nagybajom, 4,402 D 3
Nagyecsed, 8,225 G 3
Nagyhalász, 6,437 F 2
Nagykálló, 11,282 F 3
Nagykanizsa, 39,559 D 3
Nagykáta, 11,922 E 3
Nagyk"orös, 25,927 E 3
Nagyszénás, 7,124 F 3
Nova, 1,329 D 3
Nyírábrány, 4,509 G 3
Nyíradony, 7,146 G 3
Nyírbátor, 11,022 G 3
Nyíregyháza, 73,013 F 3
Nyírmada, 4,744 F 2
Örkény, 5,013 E 3
Orosháza, 33,471 F 3
Oroszlány, 18,249 E 3
Ózd, 38,620 F 2
Pacsa, 1,984 D 3
Paks, 12,385 E 3
Pannonhalma, 3,731 D 3
Pápa, 28,640 D 3
Pásztó, 7,962 E 3
Pécs, 160,488 E 3
Pécsvárad, 3,672 E 3
Pétervására, 2,753 F 3
Pilis, 9,055 E 3
Pilisvörösvár, 10,217 E 3
Polgár, 9,429 F 3
Püspökladány, 15,730 F 3
Putnok, 7,103 F 2
Ráckeve, 7,534 E 3
Rajka, 2,448 D 3
Rakamaz, 5,407 F 2
Rákospalota, 60,983 E 3
Rétság, 1,591 E 3
Sajószentpéter, 13,992 F 2
Salgótarján, 40,095 E 2
Sándorfalva, 5,949 F 3
Sárbogárd, 11,178 E 3
Sarkad, 11,937 F 3
Sárospatak, 14,061 F 2
Sárvár, 12,754 D 3
Sátoraljaújhely, 16,982 F 2
Siklós, 7,083 E 4
Siófok, 17,315 E 3
Solt, 6,911 E 3
Soltvadkert, 7,934 E 3
Sopron, 44,956 D 3
Sümeg, 6,229 D 3
Szabadszállás, 8,223 E 3
Szarvas, 19,521 F 3
Szécsény, 5,690 E 2
Szeged, 166,040 E 3
Szeghalom, 9,736 F 3
Szegvár, 6,395 F 3
Székesfehérvár, 73,949 E 3
Szekszárd, 24,364 E 3
Szendr"o, 4,098 F 2
Szentendre, 12,859 E 3
Szentes, 33,436 F 3
Szentgotthárd, 5,837 D 3
Szentl"orinc, 3,926 E 3
Szerencs, 8,612 F 2
Szigetvár, 10,412 D 3
Szikszó, 6,419 F 2
Szil, 2,073 D 3
Szirák, 1,435 E 3
Szolnok, 61,559 F 3
Szombathely, 64,485 D 3
Tab, 3,922 E 3
Tamási, 7,602 E 3
Tápiószele, 5,575 E 3
Tapolca, 11,223 D 3
Tarpa, 3,436 G 2
Tata, 20,565 E 3
Tatabánya, 65,274 E 3
Tét, 4,441 D 3
Tihany, 1,390 D 3
Tiszacsege, 6,263 F 3
Tiszaföldvár, 12,560 F 3
Tiszafüred, 12,259 F 3
Tiszakécske, 12,378 E 3
Tiszalök, 6,230 F 2
Tiszavasvári, 13,292 F 3
Tokaj, 4,845 F 2
Tolna, 8,997 E 3
Törökszentmiklós, 24,301 F 3
Tótkomlós, 8,803 F 3
Tura, 8,235 E 3
Túrkeve, 11,640 F 3
Újfehértó, 14,412 F 3
Újpest, 80,384 E 3
Vác, 28,847 E 3
Vál, 2,488 E 3
Várpalota, 25,312 E 3
Vasvár, 4,275 D 3
Vecsés, 19,193 E 3
Veszprém, 36,938 D 3
Vészt"o, 9,815 F 3
Villány, 2,764 E 4
Záhony, 3,049 G 2
Zalaegerszeg, 39,252 D 3
Zalaszentgrót, 5,346 D 3
Zirc, 5,980 D 3

OTHER FEATURES

Bakony (mts.) D 3
Balaton (lake) D 3
Berettyó (riv.) F 3
Bükk (mts.) F 2
Csepelsziget (isl.) E 3
Danube (riv.) E 3
Dráva (riv.) D 3
Duna (Danube) (riv.) E 3
Fert"o tó (Neusiedler See) (lake) D 3
Great Alfold (plain) F 3
Hernád (riv.) F 2
Kapos (riv.) D 3
Kékes (mt.) E 3
Körös (riv.) F 3
Maros (riv.) F 3
Mátra (mts.) E 3
Mecsek (mts.) D 3
Mura (riv.) D 3
Rába (riv.) D 3
Sajó (riv.) F 2
Sárviz csatorna (canal) E 3
Sió csatorna (canal) E 3
Szentendreisziget (isl.) E 3
Tisza (riv.) F 3
Zala (riv.) D 3

*City and suburbs.
☆Population of Austrian cities are communes.

Agriculture, Industry and Resources

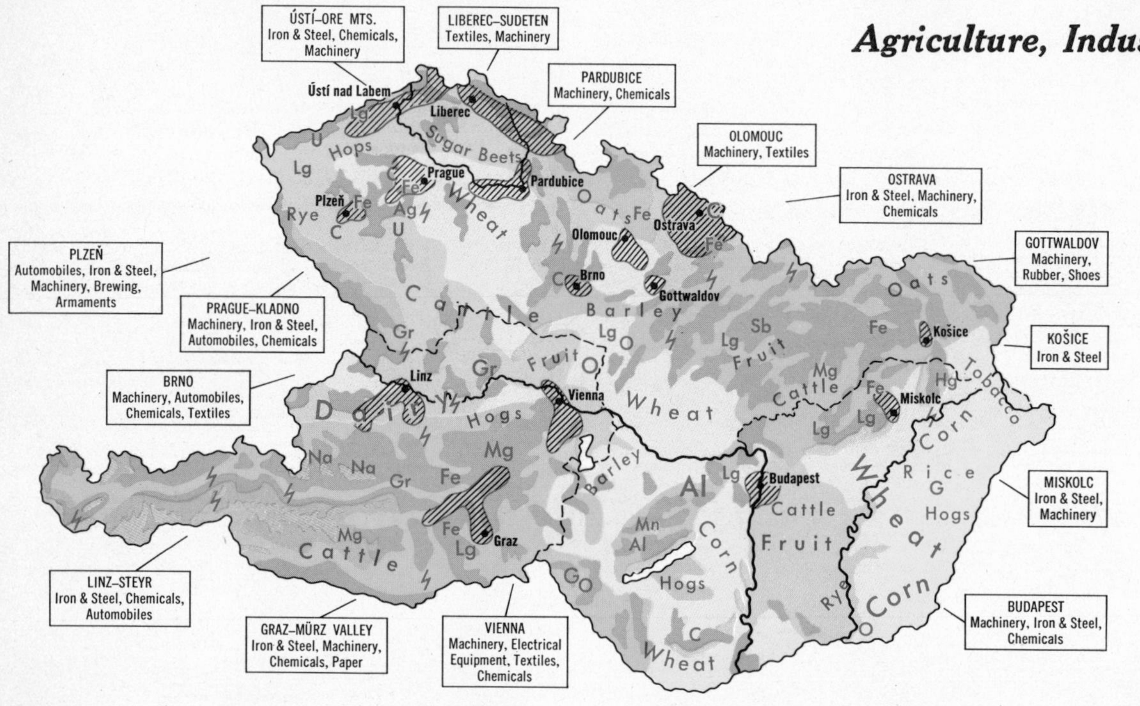

ÚSTÍ–ORE MTS. Iron & Steel, Chemicals, Machinery
LIBEREC–SUDETEN Textiles, Machinery
PARDUBICE Machinery, Chemicals
OLOMOUC Machinery, Textiles
OSTRAVA Iron & Steel, Machinery, Chemicals
PLZEŇ Automobiles, Iron & Steel, Machinery, Brewing, Armaments
PRAGUE–KLADNO Machinery, Iron & Steel, Automobiles, Chemicals
GOTTWALDOV Machinery, Rubber, Shoes
KOŠICE Iron & Steel
BRNO Machinery, Automobiles, Chemicals, Textiles
MISKOLC Iron & Steel, Machinery
LINZ–STEYR Iron & Steel, Chemicals, Automobiles
GRAZ–MÜRZ VALLEY Iron & Steel, Machinery, Chemicals, Paper
VIENNA Machinery, Electrical Equipment, Textiles, Chemicals
BUDAPEST Machinery, Iron & Steel, Chemicals
Ústí nad Labem
Liberec
Prague
Pardubice
Plzeň
Olomouc
Ostrava
Brno
Gottwaldov
Košice
Linz
Vienna
Miskolc
Budapest
Graz
Hops
Sugar Beets
Oats
Wheat
Rye
Cattle
Barley
Fruit
Dairy
Hogs
Tobacco
Corn
Rice

DOMINANT LAND USE

- Cereals (chiefly wheat, corn)
- Other Cereals, Livestock, Dairy
- General Farming, Livestock
- General Farming, Truck Farming
- Pasture Livestock
- Grapes, Wine
- Forests
- Nonagricultural Land

MAJOR MINERAL OCCURRENCES

Ag	Silver	Lg	Lignite
Al	Bauxite	Mg	Magnesium
C	Coal	Mn	Manganese
Fe	Iron Ore	Na	Salt
G	Natural Gas	O	Petroleum
Gr	Graphite	Sb	Antimony
Hg	Mercury	U	Uranium

Water Power

Major Industrial Areas

YUGOSLAVIA

AREA 98,766 sq. mi.
POPULATION 21,520,000
CAPITAL Belgrade
LARGEST CITY Belgrade
HIGHEST POINT Triglav 9,393 ft.
MONETARY UNIT Yugoslav dinar
MAJOR LANGUAGES Serbo-Croatian, Slovenian, Macedonian, Montenegrin, Albanian
MAJOR RELIGIONS Eastern Orthodoxy, Roman Catholicism, Islam

ALBANIA

AREA 11,100 sq. mi.
POPULATION 2,482,000
CAPITAL Tiranë
LARGEST CITY Tiranë
HIGHEST POINT Korab 9,026 ft.
MONETARY UNIT lek
MAJOR LANGUAGE Albanian
MAJOR RELIGIONS Islam, Eastern Orthodoxy, Roman Catholicism

RUMANIA

AREA 91,699 sq. mi.
POPULATION 21,500,000
CAPITAL Bucharest
LARGEST CITY Bucharest
HIGHEST POINT Moldoveanul 8,343 ft.
MONETARY UNIT leu
MAJOR LANGUAGES Rumanian, Hungarian
MAJOR RELIGION Eastern Orthodoxy

BULGARIA

AREA 42,823 sq. mi.
POPULATION 8,800,000
CAPITAL Sofia
LARGEST CITY Sofia
HIGHEST POINT Musala 9,597 ft.
MONETARY UNIT lev
MAJOR LANGUAGE Bulgarian
MAJOR RELIGION Eastern Orthodoxy

GREECE

AREA 50,944 sq. mi.
POPULATION 9,046,000
CAPITAL Athens
LARGEST CITY Athens
HIGHEST POINT Olympus 9,570 ft.
MONETARY UNIT drachma
MAJOR LANGUAGE Greek
MAJOR RELIGION Eastern (Greek) Orthodoxy

BULGARIA

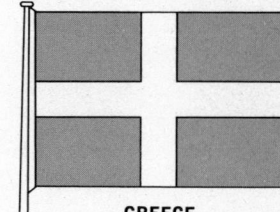

GREECE

YUGOSLAVIA

ALBANIA

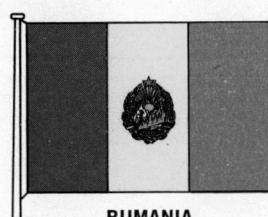

RUMANIA

DOMINANT LAND USE

- Cereals (chiefly wheat, corn)
- Mixed Farming, Horticulture
- Pasture Livestock
- Tobacco, Cotton
- Grapes, Wine
- Forests
- Nonagricultural Land

Agriculture, Industry and Resources

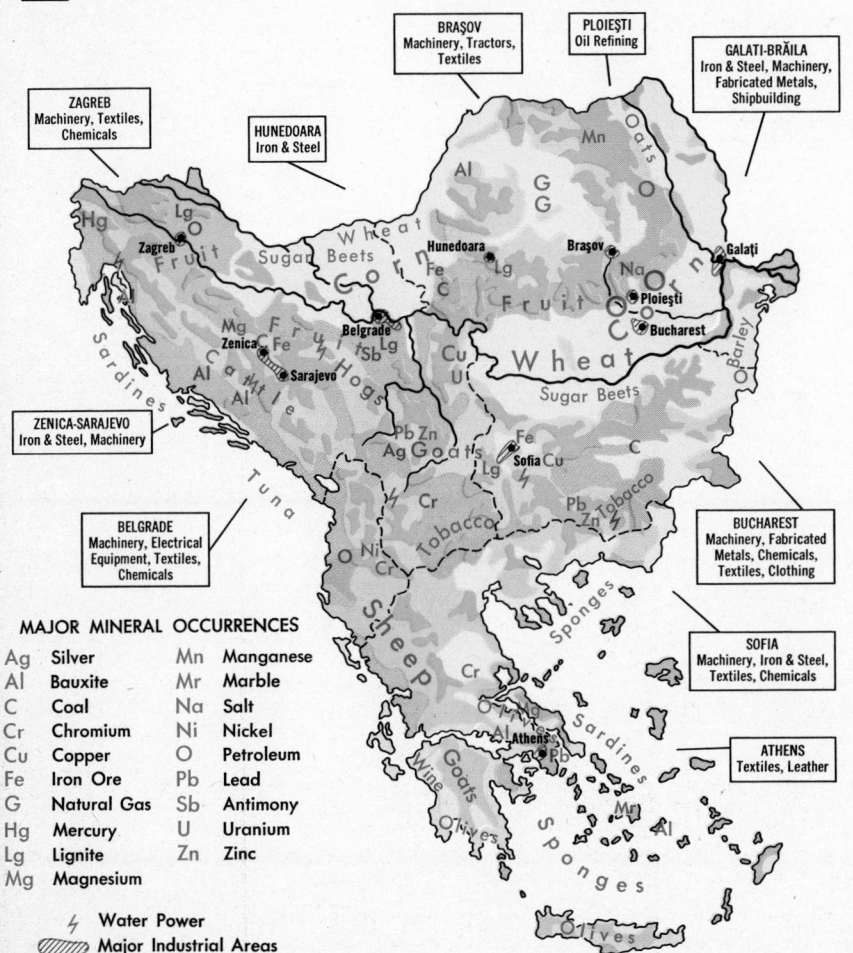

BRAŞOV
Machinery, Tractors, Textiles

PLOIEŞTI
Oil Refining

GALATI-BRĂILA
Iron & Steel, Machinery, Fabricated Metals, Shipbuilding

ZAGREB
Machinery, Textiles, Chemicals

HUNEDOARA
Iron & Steel

ZENICA-SARAJEVO
Iron & Steel, Machinery

BELGRADE
Machinery, Electrical Equipment, Textiles, Chemicals

BUCHAREST
Machinery, Fabricated Metals, Chemicals, Textiles, Clothing

SOFIA
Machinery, Iron & Steel, Textiles, Chemicals

ATHENS
Textiles, Leather

MAJOR MINERAL OCCURRENCES

Ag	Silver	Mn	Manganese
Al	Bauxite	Mr	Marble
C	Coal	Na	Salt
Cr	Chromium	Ni	Nickel
Cu	Copper	O	Petroleum
Fe	Iron Ore	Pb	Lead
G	Natural Gas	Sb	Antimony
Hg	Mercury	U	Uranium
Lg	Lignite	Zn	Zinc
Mg	Magnesium		

⚡ Water Power
▨ Major Industrial Areas

ALBANIA

CITIES and TOWNS

Berat, 22,000	D 5
Bajram Curi, 1,795	D 4
Burrel, 3,150	D 5
Çorovodë, 1,790	E 5
Delvinë, 5,700	D 6
Durrës, 47,900	D 5
Elbasan, 35,300	E 5
Ersekë, 2,150	E 5
Fier, 17,900	D 5
Gjirokastër, 15,000	D 5
Kavajë, 17,700	D 5
Korcë, 43,700	E 5
Kruë, 6,700	D 5
Kucovë (Stalin), 12,300	D 5
Kukës, 3,900	E 4
Leskovik, 1,625	E 5
Lezh, 3,000	D 5
Lushnje, 16,000	D 5
Peqin, 3,800	D 5
Përmet, 4,000	E 5
Peshkopi, 5,500	E 5
Pogradec, 8,900	E 5
Pukë, 1,700	E 4
Sárandë, 7,700	E 6
Shijak, 5,100	D 5
Shkodër, 47,000	D 5
Stalin, 12,300	D 5
Tepelenë, 2,500	D 5
Tiranë (Tiranä) (cap.), 170,000	E 5
Vlorë, 46,900	D 5

OTHER FEATURES

Adriatic (sea)	B 4
Drin (riv.)	E 4
Korab (mt.)	E 5
Ohrid (lake)	E 5
Otranto (str.)	D 5
Prespa (lake)	E 5
Sazan (isl.)	D 5
Scutari (lake)	D 4
Tomor (mt.)	E 5
Vijosë (riv.)	D 5

BULGARIA

CITIES and TOWNS

Alfatar, 3,650	H 4
Akhtopol, 1,058	H 4
Alfatar, 4,042	H 4
Ardino, 2,558	G 5
Asenovgrad, 37,411	G 5
Aytos, 17,769	H 4
Balchik, 8,714	H 4
Bansko, 7,851	F 5
Belogradchik, 5,174	F 4
Berkovitsa, 11,553	F 4
Blagoyevgrad, 32,744	F 5
Botevgrad, 12,051	G 4
Bregovo, 4,725	F 3
Breznik, 4,093	F 4
Burgas, 122,212	H 4
Byala, 9,347	G 4
Byala Slatina, 14,942	F 4
Chirpan, 17,857	G 4
Devin, 4,475	F 5
Dimitrovgrad, 41,787	G 4
Dobrich (Tolbukhin), 55,111	H 4
Dryanovo, 8,187	G 4
Elena, 4,071	G 4
Elin Pelin, 8,074	F 4
Elkhovo, 11,315	H 4
Gabrovo, 57,758	G 4
General Toshevo, 8,251	H 4
Godech, 4,074	F 4
Gorna Dzhumaya (Blagoyevgrad), 32,744	F 5
Gorna Oryakhovitsa, 26,290	G 4
Gotse Delchev, 14,457	F 5
Grudovo, 9,177	H 4
Ikhtiman, 10,325	F 4
Isperikh, 8,445	H 4
Ivaylovgrad, 2,907	H 5
Karapelit, 2,033	H 4
Karlovo (Levskigrad), 20,287	G 4
Karnobat (Polyanovgrad), 18,727	H 4
Kavarna, 8,291	H 4
Kazanlŭk, 44,418	G 4
Kharmanlii, 15,478	H 5
Khaskovo, 57,682	G 5
Kolarovgrad (Shumen), 59,362	H 4
Kotel, 7,209	H 4
Krumovgrad, 2,230	G 5
Kubrat, 7,531	H 4
Kula, 6,474	F 4
Kürdzhali, 33,319	G 5
Kyustendil, 38,199	F 4
Levskigrad, 20,287	G 4
Lom, 28,189	F 4
Lovech, 30,843	G 4
Lukovit, 9,716	G 4
Malico Tŭrnovo, 3,744	H 4
Maritsa, 8,532	H 4
Michurin, 2,783	H 4
Mikhaylovgrad, 27,240	F 4
Momchilgrad, 6,084	G 5
Nesebŭr, 2,333	H 4
Nikopol, 5,763	G 4
Nova Zagora, 19,257	H 4
Novi Pazar, 12,476	H 4
Omurtag, 8,148	H 4
Oryakhovo, 7,498	F 4
Panagyurishte, 18,298	F 4
Pazardzhik, 55,410	G 4
Pernik, 75,844	F 4
Peshtera, 14,606	G 4
Petrich, 20,653	F 5
Pirdop, 8,252	G 4
Pleven, 79,234	G 4
Plovdiv, 234,547	G 4
Polyanovgrad, 18,727	H 4
Pomorie, 9,567	H 4
Popina, 2,699	H 3
Popovo, 15,609	H 4
Provadiya, 13,837	H 4
Radomir, 8,458	F 4
Razgrad, 26,297	H 4
Razlog, 10,425	F 5
Rositsa, 1,505	H 4
Ruse, 142,894	H 4
Samokov, 21,585	F 4
Sandanski, 14,590	F 5
Sevlievo, 20,396	G 4
Shabla, 3,788	J 4
Shumen, 59,362	H 4
Silistra, 32,996	H 3
Simeonovgrad (Maritsa), 8,532	H 4
Sliven, 68,331	H 4
Smolyan, 17,479	G 5
Smyadovo, 5,349	H 4
Sofia (cap.), 840,113	F 4
Sofia, *923,400	F 4
Sozopol, 3,257	H 4
Stanke Dimitrov, 35,813	F 4
Stara Zagora, 100,565	G 4
Sveti Vrach (Sandanski), 14,590	F 5
Svilengrad, 12,438	G 5
Svishtov, 21,522	G 4
Teteven, 9,807	G 4
Tolbukhin, 55,111	H 4
Topolovgrad, 6,633	H 4
Troyan, 18,982	G 4
Trŭn, 2,922	F 4
Tŭrgovishte, 25,528	H 4
Tutrakan, 9,909	H 4
Varna, 200,821	H 4
Veliko Tŭrnovo, 37,269	G 4
Vidin, 36,820	F 4
Vratsa, 39,052	F 4
Yambol, 58,405	H 4
Zlatograd, 6,508	G 5

OTHER FEATURES

Balkan (mts.)	G 4
Black (sea)	J 4
Danube (Dunav) (riv.)	H 4
Emine (cape)	H 4
Iskŭr (riv.)	F 4
Kaliakra (cape)	J 4
Lom (riv.)	F 4
Maritsa (riv.)	G 4
Mesta (riv.)	F 5
Musala (mt.)	F 4
Osŭm (riv.)	G 4
Rhodope (mts.)	F 5
Ruen (mt.)	F 4
Struma (riv.)	F 5
Timok (riv.)	F 3
Tundzha (riv.)	H 4
Vit (riv.)	G 4

GREECE

REGIONS

Aegean Islands, 477,476	G 6
Áyion Óros (aut. dist.), 2,687	G 5
Central Greece and Euboea, 2,823,658	G 8
Crete, 483,258	G 8
Epirus, 352,604	E 6
Greater Athens, 1,852,709	F 7
Ionian Islands, 212,573	D 6
Macedonia, 1,890,654	F 5
Pelopónnisos, 1,096,390	F 7
Thessalía, 695,385	F 6
Thrace, 356,555	G 5

CITIES and TOWNS

Agrínion, 24,763	E 6
Aíyina, 4,989	F 7
Aíyion, 17,762	F 6
Alexandroúpolis, 18,712	H 5
Alivérion, 3,523	G 6
Almirós, 6,010	F 6
Amaliás, 15,468	E 7
Amfilokhía, 5,408	E 6
Amfissa, 6,076	F 6
Ándissa, 2,530	H 6
Andravídha, 3,155	E 6
Ándros, 2,032	G 7
Áno Viánnos, 1,820	G 8
Anóyia, 2,461	G 8
Ardhéa, 3,222	F 5
Argalastí, 1,864	F 6
Árgos, 16,712	F 7
Argostólion, 7,322	E 6
Arkhángelos, 2,918	J 7
Arnaía, 2,612	F 5
Árta, 16,899	E 6
Astipálaia, 1,205	H 7
Atalándi, 4,552	F 6
Athens (cap.), 627,564	F 7
Athens, *2,347,000	F 7
Áyios Matthaíos, 1,892	D 6
Áyios Nikólaos, 3,709	G 8
Candia (Iráklion), 63,458	G 8
Canea (Khaniá), 38,467	G 8
Chalcis (Khalkís), 24,745	F 6
Corinth, 15,892	F 7
Dhelvinákion, 1,076	E 6
Dhidhimótikhon, 7,287	H 5
Dhíkaia, 1,181	H 5
Dhimitsána, 1,300	F 7
Dhomokós, 2,017	F 6
Dráma, 32,195	F 5
Édhessa, 15,534	F 5
Elassón, 6,501	F 6
Elevtheroúpolis, 5,448	G 5
Ermoúpolis, 14,402	G 7
Fársala, 6,396	F 6
Filiátes, 3,065	E 6
Filiatrá, 6,753	E 7
Flórina, 11,933	E 5
Gargaliánoi, 6,637	E 7
Grevená, 6,892	E 6
Idhra, 2,546	F 7
Ierápetra, 6,488	G 8
Igoumenítsa, 3,235	E 6
Ioánnina, 34,997	E 6
Iráklion, 63,458	G 8
Istiaía, 3,882	F 6
Itháki, 2,632	E 6
Kalámai, 38,211	E 7
Kalampáka, 4,640	E 6
Kalávrita, 2,039	F 6
Kálimnos, 10,211	H 7
Kardhítsa, 23,708	E 6
Kariá, 1,739	E 6
Kariaí, 429	G 5
Káristos, 3,523	G 6
Karpenísion, 3,523	E 6
Kastéllion, 2,071	H 8
Kastéllion, 1,351	G 8
Kastoría, 10,162	E 5
Kateríni, 28,046	F 5
Kaválla, 44,517	G 5
Kéa, 1,788	G 7
Khalkís, 24,745	F 6
Khaniá, 38,467	G 8
Khíos, 24,053	G 6
Kiáton, 6,069	F 6
Kilkís, 10,963	F 5
Kími, 3,252	G 6
Kiparissía, 4,602	E 7
Kíthira, 469	F 7
Komotiní, 28,355	G 5
Kónitsa, 3,485	E 5
Koropí, 7,862	F 7
Kos, 8,138	H 7

(continued on following page)

(continued)

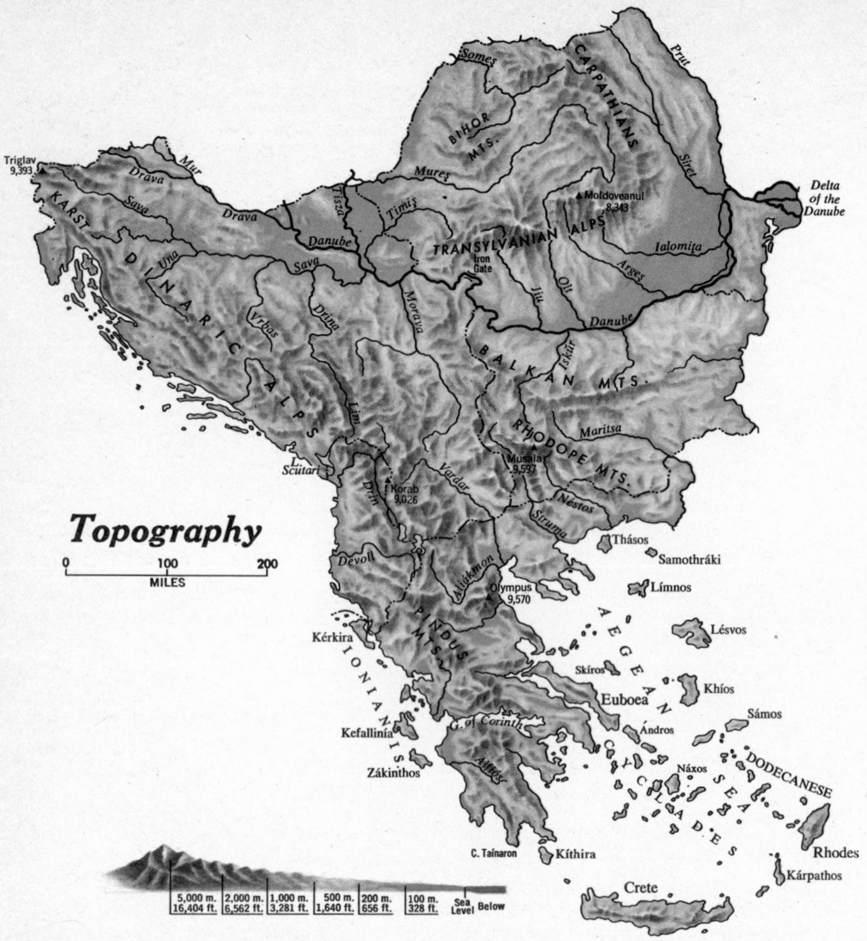
Topography
0 100 200
MILES
Triglav 9,393
Drava
Mur
Sava
KARST
DINARIC ALPS
Una
Vrbas
Drina
Danube
Tisza
Timiş
Someş
Mureş
BIHOR MTS.
CARPATHIANS
Prut
Siret
Moldoveanul 8,343
TRANSYLVANIAN ALPS
Iron Gate
Jiu
Olt
Argeş
Ialomiţa
Delta of the Danube
Morava
Iskăr
BALKAN MTS.
Maritsa
RHODOPE MTS.
Musala 9,597
Nestos
Struma
Lim
L. Scutari
Drin
Korab 9,026
Vardar
Devoll
Aliákmon
Olympus 9,570
PINDUS MTS.
Thásos
Samothráki
Límnos
Lésvos
AEGEAN SEA
Kérkira
IONIAN SEA
Skíros
Euboea
Khíos
Sámos
G. of Corinth
Kefallinía
Zákinthos
Ándros
Náxos
DODECANESE
CYCLADES
Alfiós
C. Taínaron
Kíthira
Rhodes
Kárpathos
Crete
5,000 m. 16,404 ft.
2,000 m. 6,562 ft.
1,000 m. 3,281 ft.
500 m. 1,640 ft.
200 m. 656 ft.
100 m. 328 ft.
Sea Level
Below

GREECE (continued)

Kozáni, 21,537 F 5
Kranídhion, 3,942 F 7
Lamía, 21,509 F 6
Langadhás, 6,739 F 5
Lárisa, 55,391 F 6
Lávrion, 6,553 G 7
Leonídhion, 3,297 F 7
Levádhia, 12,609 F 6
Levkás, 6,552 E 6
Limenária, 1,999 G 5
Limín Vathéos, 5,469 H 7
Límni, 2,394 F 6
Litókhoron, 5,032 F 5
Lixoúrion, 3,977 E 6
Loutrá Aidhipsoú, 1,859 F 6
Marathón, 2,167 G 6
Megalópolis, 2,235 E 7
Mégara, 15,450 F 6
Meligalá, 1,960 F 7
Mesolóngion, 11,266 E 6
Messíni, 8,249 E 7
Métsovon, 2,976 E 6
Mikínai, 361 F 7
Mílos, 944 G 7
Mírina, 3,460 G 6
Missolonghi (Mesolóngion), 11,266 E 6
Míthimna, 1,828 G 6
Mitilíni, 25,758 H 6
Moláoi, 2,526 F 7
Monólithos, 496 H 7
Moúdhros, 1,236 G 6
Náousa, 15,492 F 5
Návpaktos, 7,080 E 6
Návplion, 8,918 F 7
Náxos, 2,458 G 7
Néa Filippiás, 3,001 E 6
Neápolis, 2,464 F 7
Neméa, 4,720 F 7
Néon Karlóvasi, 5,308 H 7
Nigríta, 9,979 F 5
Olimbía, 771 E 7
Orestiás, 10,281 H 5
Paramithiá, 2,827 E 6
Pátrai, 95,364 E 6
Péta, 2,522 E 6
Pigádhia, 1,281 H 8
Pílos, 2,434 E 7
Piraiévs (Piraeus), 183,877 F 7
Pírgos, 20,558 E 7
Piryí, 1,914 G 6
Píthion, 1,535 H 5
Plomárion, 5,172 H 6
Políkastron, 3,821 F 5
Polikhnitos, 5,131 G 6
Políyiros, 3,541 F 5
Póros, 4,392 F 7
Préveza, 11,172 E 6
Psakhná, 4,433 F 6
Ptolemaís, 12,747 E 5
Réthimnon, 14,999 G 8
Ródhos (Rhodes), 27,393 J 7
Salamís, 11,161 F 6
Salonika (Thessaloníki), 448,000 F 5
Sámi, 1,065 E 6
Samothráki, 1,555 G 5
Sápai, 2,589 G 5
Sérrai, 40,063 F 5
Sérvia, 4,132 F 5
Siátista, 4,737 E 5
Sidhirókastron, 8,177 F 5
Símí, 2,982 H 7
Sitía, 5,327 H 8
Skíros, 2,411 G 6
Skópelos, 2,955 F 6
Souflíon, 6,693 H 5
Sparta, 10,412 F 7
Spétsai, 3,314 F 7
Stilís, 4,673 F 6
Thebes (Thívai), 15,779 F 6
Thessaloníki, 448,000 F 5
Thásos, 1,875 G 5
Thíra, 1,481 G 7
Thívai, 15,779 F 6
Timbákion, 2,816 G 8
Tínos, 2,888 G 7
Tírnavos, 10,805 F 6
Tríkkala, 27,876 E 6
Trípolis, 18,500 F 7
Vartholomión, 3,244 E 7
Vathí, 3,161 H 7
Velvendós, 4,158 F 5
Véroia, 25,765 F 5
Vólos, 49,221 F 6
Vólos, *67,424 F 6
Vónitsa, 2,996 E 6
Vrondádhes, 4,685 G 6
Xánthi, 26,377 G 5
Yiannitsá, 19,693 F 5
Yíthion, 4,992 F 7
Zákinthos, 9,506 E 7
Zante (Zúkinthos), 9,506 E 7

OTHER FEATURES

Aegean (sea) G 6
Akrítas (cape) E 7
Aktí (pen.) G 5
Amorgós (isl.), 2,396 G 7
Anáfi (isl.), 471 G 7
Andikíthira (isl.), 178 F 8
Ándros (isl.), 12,928 G 7
Arda (riv.) G 5
Argolís (gulf) F 7
Astipálaia (isl.), 1,539 H 7
Áthos (mt.) G 5
Áyios Evstrátios (isl.), 1,061 G 6
Áyios Yeóryios (cape) G 7
Cephalonia (Kefallinía) (isl.), 39,793 E 6
Chios (Khíos) (isl.), 60,061 G 6
Corfu (Kérkira) (isl.), 99,092 D 6
Corinth (gulf) F 6
Crete (isl.), 483,075 G 8
Crete (sea) G 7
Cyclades (isls.), 99,959 G 7
Dhrépanon (cape) G 6
Dodecanese (isls.), 123,021 H 8
Euboea (isl.), 163,215 G 6
Évros (riv.) H 5
Gávdhos (isl.), 172 F 8
Ikaría (isl.), 9,577 G 7
Ionian (sea) D 7
Íos (isl.), 1,343 G 7
Itháki (Ithaca) (isl.), 5,210 E 6
Kálimnos (isl.), 10,211 H 7
Kafirévs (cape) G 6
Kárpathos (isl.), 6,689 H 8
Kásos (isl.), 1,422 H 8
Kassándra (pen.) F 6
Kéa (isl.), 2,361 G 7
Kefallinía (isl.), 39,793 E 6
Kérkira (isl.), 99,092 D 6
Khálki (isl.), 501 H 7
Khani, (gulf) G 8
Khíos (isl.), 60,061 G 6
Kiparissía (gulf) E 7
Kíthira (isl.), 5,340 F 7
Kíthnos (isl.), 2,064 G 7
Kos (isl.), 18,187 H 7
Kriós (cape) F 8
Lakonía (gulf) F 7
Léros (isl.), 6,611 H 7
Lésvos (isl.), 117,371 G 6
Levítha (isl.), 7 H 7
Levkás (isl.), 2,697 E 6
Límnos (isl.), 21,808 G 6
Maléa (cape) F 7
Matapan (Taínaron) (cape) F 7
Merabéllou (gulf) H 8
Mesará (gulf) G 8
Messíni (gulf) E 7
Míkonos (isl.), 3,633 G 7
Mílos (isl.), 4,910 G 7
Mirtóön (sea) F 7
Náxos (isl.), 16,703 G 7
Néstos (riv.) G 5
Nísiros (isl.), 1,788 H 7
Northern Sporades (isls.), 9,810 F 6
Ólimbos (mt.) F 5
Óssa (mt.) F 6
Parnassus (mt.) F 6
Páros (isl.), 7,830 G 7
Pátmos (isl.), 2,564 H 7
Paxoí (isl.), 2,678 D 6
Píndus (mts.) E 6
Piniós (riv.) E 6
Prespa (lake) E 5
Psará (isl.), 576 G 6
Rhodes (isl.), 63,951 H 7
Rhodope (mts.) G 5
Salonika (Thermaic) (gulf) F 6
Sámos (isl.), 41,124 H 7
Samothráki (isl.), 3,830 G 5
Saría (isl.), 18 H 8
Saronic (gulf) F 7
Sérifos (isl.), 1,878 G 7
Sídheros (cape) H 8
Sífnos (isl.), 2,258 G 7
Sími (isl.), 3,123 H 7
Síros (isl.), 19,570 G 7
Sithoniá (pen.) F 6
Skíros (isl.), 2,882 G 6
Spátha (cape) F 8
Strimón (gulf) G 5
Strofádhes (isls.), 10 E 7
Taínaron (cape) F 7
Thásos (isl.), 15,916 G 5
Thermaic (gulf) F 6
Thíra (isl.), 7,751 G 7
Tílos (isl.), 789 H 7
Tínos (isl.), 9,273 G 7
Toronaic (gulf) F 6
Vardar (riv.) E 5
Voïvïïs (lake) F 6
Vólvi (lake) F 5
Voúxa (cape) F 8
Zákinthos (Zante) (isl.), 35,499 E 7

RUMANIA

CITIES and TOWNS

Aiud, 11,886 F 2
Alba Iulia, 22,225 F 2
Alexandria, 21,907 G 3
Anina, 11,837 E 3
Arad, 132,757 E 2
Arad, *137,444 E 2
Babadag, 5,549 J 3
Bacău, 73,481 H 2
Bacău, *87,465 H 2
Baia Mare, 62,769 F 2
Baia Mare, *108,709 F 2
Băileşti, 15,932 F 3
Balş, 6,956 G 3
Beiuş, 6,467 F 2
Bîrlad, 41,061 H 2
Bîrlad, *52,497 H 2
Bistriţa, 25,534 G 2
Blaj, 8,731 F 2
Botoşani, 35,185 H 2
Botoşani, *50,204 H 2
Brad, 9,963 F 2
Brăila, 147,495 H 3
Braşov, 175,264 G 3
Braşov, *264,537 G 3
Bucharest (Bucureşti) (cap.), 1,431,993 G 3
Bucharest, *1,518,725 G 3
Buhuşi, 12,382 H 2
Buzău, 56,380 H 3
Buzău, *82,454 H 3
Buziaş, 5,140 E 3
Călafat, 8,069 F 3
Călăraşi, 35,698 H 3
Caracal, 22,715 G 3
Caransebeş, 15,195 F 3
Carei, 16,780 F 2
Cernavodă, 8,802 J 3
Cîmpia Turzii, 11,514 F 2
Cîmpina, 22,862 H 3
Cîmpulung, 24,891 G 3
Cîmpulung Moldovenesc, 13,627 G 2
Cisnădie, 12,246 F 3
Cluj, 193,375 F 2
Cluj, *223,519 F 2
Comăneşti, 12,392 H 2
Constanţa, 165,245 J 3
Constanţa, *202,024 J 3
Corabia, 11,502 G 4
Craiova, 166,249 F 3
Craiova, *174,669 F 3
Curtea de Argeş, 10,764 G 3
Dej, 26,968 F 2
Deva, 26,952 F 3
Deva, *45,836 F 3
Dorohoi, 14,771 H 2
Drăgăşani, 9,963 G 3
Făgăraş, 22,941 G 3
Fălticeni, 13,305 H 2
Feteşti, 21,425 H 3
Focşani, 35,075 H 3
Focşani, *40,701 H 3
Găeşti, 7,179 G 3
Galaţi, 160,097 H 3
Gheorgheni, 11,969 G 2
Gherla, 7,617 G 2
Giurgiu, 39,225 G 3
Giurgiu, *55,471 G 3
Haţeg, 3,853 F 3
Hîrşova, 4,761 J 3
Hunedoara, 68,303 F 3
Hunedoara, *100,953 F 3
Huşi, 20,703 J 2
Iaşi, 173,569 H 2
Iaşi, *196,167 H 2
Isaccea, 5,203 J 3
Jimbolia, 11,281 E 3
Lipova, 10,064 E 2
Lugoj, 35,388 F 3
Lupeni, 29,377 F 3
Mangalia, 4,792 J 4
Medgidia, 27,989 J 3
Mediaş, 46,396 G 2
Miercurea Ciuc, 11,996 G 2
Mizil, 7,460 H 3
Moineşti, 12,934 H 2
Moldova Nouă, 3,582 E 3
Moreni, 11,687 G 3
Năsăud, 5,725 G 2
Ocna Mureş, 10,701 G 2
Odobeşti, 4,977 H 3
Odorhei, 14,162 G 2
Olteniţa, 14,111 H 3
Oradea, 132,266 E 2
Oradea, *136,375 E 2
Orăştie, 10,488 F 3
Oraşul Gheorghe Gheorghiu-Dej, 35,689 H 2
Oraviţa, 8,175 E 3
Orşova, 6,527 F 3
Panciu, 7,679 H 3
Paşcani, 15,008 H 2
Petrila, 24,804 F 3
Petroşeni, 35,237 F 3
Petroşeni, *130,111 F 3
Piatra Neamţ, 45,925 G 2
Piatra Neamţ, *58,397 G 2
Piteşti, 60,094 G 3
Piteşti, *78,784 G 3
Ploieşti, 156,382 H 3
Ploieşti, *191,663 H 3
Pucioasa, 9,259 G 3
Rădăuţi, 15,949 G 2
Reghin, 23,317 G 2
Reşiţa, 58,683 E 3
Reşiţa, *121,458 E 3
Rîmnicu Sărat, 22,325 H 3
Rîmnicu Vîlcea, 23,880 F 3
Roman, 38,990 H 2
Roman, *49,496 H 2
Roşiori de Vede, 21,707 G 3
Săcele, 22,822 G 3
Salonta, 16,276 E 2
Satu Mare, 68,257 F 2
Sebeş, 11,628 F 3
Sfîntu Gheorge, 20,759 G 3
Sibiu, 117,020 G 3
Sighetul-Marmaţiei, 29,768 F 2
Sighişoara, 25,100 G 2
Şimleu Silvaniei, 8,560 F 2
Sinaia, 9,006 G 3
Sînnicolau Mare, 9,956 E 2
Siret, 5,664 H 2
Slănic, 6,842 G 3
Slatina, 13,381 G 3
Slobozia, 9,632 H 3
Solca, 2,348 G 2
Strehaia, 8,545 F 3
Suceava, 37,715 G 2
Suceava, *76,327 G 2
Sulina, 3,622 J 3
Techirghiol, 2,705 J 3
Tecuci, 28,458 H 3
Timişoara, 184,797 E 3
Timişoara, *194,159 E 3
Tîrgovişte, 29,754 G 3
Tîrgovişte, *48,005 G 3
Tîrgu Jiu, 30,837 F 3
Tîrgu Jiu, *33,019 F 3
Tîrgu Mureş, 86,458 G 2
Tîrgu Mureş, *104,922 G 2
Tîrgu Neamţ, 10,373 G 2
Tîrgu Ocna, 11,227 H 2
Tîrgu Secuiesc, 7,500 H 2
Tîrnăveni, 20,354 F 2
Topliţa, 8,944 G 2
Tulcea, 35,552 J 3
Turda, 42,318 F 2
Turda, *69,768 F 2
Turnu Măgurele, 26,409 G 4
Turnu Severin, 45,394 F 3
Turnu Severin, *52,497 F 3
Urlaţi, 8,658 H 3
Urziceni, 6,061 H 3
Vasile Roaită, 3,286 J 3
Vaslui, 14,850 H 2
Vatra Dornei, 10,822 G 2
Vişeu de Sus, 13,956 F 2
Zalău, 13,378 F 2
Zărneşti, 6,673 G 3
Zimnicea, 12,445 G 4

OTHER FEATURES

Argeş (riv.) G 3
Buzău (riv.) H 3
Carpathian (mts.) G 2
Crişul Alb (riv.) F 2
Crişul Repede (riv.) F 2
Danube (river) H 4
Ialomiţa (marshes) H 3
Jiu (riv.) F 3
Moldoveanul (mt.) G 3
Mureş (riv.) E 2
Negoiul (mt.) G 3
Olt (riv.) G 3
Pietrosul (mt.) G 2
Prut (riv.) J 2
Siret (riv.) H 2
Someş (riv.) F 2
Timiş (riv.) E 3
Transylvanian Alps (mts.) G 3

YUGOSLAVIA

INTERNAL DIVISIONS

Bosnia and Hercegovina (rep.), 3,594,000 C 3
Croatia (rep.), 4,281,000 C 3
Kosovo-Mitohiyan (aut. prov.), 1,089,000 E 4
Macedonia (rep.), 1,506,000 E 5
Montenegro (rep.), 471,894 D 4
Serbia (rep.), 7,637,800 E 3
Slovenia (rep.), 1,624,900 B 2
Voyvodina (aut. prov.), 1,880,000 D 3

CITIES and TOWNS

Aleksinac, 8,828 E 4
Apatin, 17,000 D 3
Bačka Topola, 14,000 D 3
Bakar B 3
Banja Luka, 55,000 C 3
Bar, 2,184 D 4
Bečej, 22,000 E 3
Bela Crkva, 11,000 E 3
Belgrade (Beograd) (cap.), 745,000 E 3
Belgrade, *1,050,000 E 3
Bihać, 17,000 B 3
Bijeljina, 19,000 D 3
Bijelo Polje, 5,856 D 4
Bileća, 2,491 D 4
Biograd, 2,418 B 4
Bitola (Bitolj), 52,000 E 5
Bjelovar, 16,000 C 3
Bled, 4,156 A 2
Bor, 19,000 E 3
Bosanska Dubica, 6,259 C 3
Bosanska Gradiška, 6,363 C 3
Bosanska Kostajnica, 2,034 B 3
Bosanska Krupa, 6,191 C 3
Bosanski Brod, 7,350 D 3
Bosanski Novi, 7,023 C 3
Bosanski Petrovac, 3,473 C 3
Bosanski Šamac, 3,654 D 3
Brčko, 20,000 D 3
Brežice, 2,641 B 3
Brod, 30,000 D 3
Bugojno, 5,453 C 3
Buje, 1,955 A 3
Čačak, 30,000 E 4
Čapljina, 3,275 C 4
Caribrod (Dimitrovgrad), 3,665 F 4
Celje, 28,000 B 2
Cetinje, 9,359 D 4
Ćuprija, 12,000 E 4
Debar, 6,323 E 5
Derventa, 9,843 C 3
Dimitrovgrad, 3,665 F 4
Djakovica, 22,000 E 4
Djakovo, 13,000 D 3
Donji Vakuf, 3,764 C 3
Drvar, 3,646 C 3
Dubrovnik, 24,000 C 4
Fiume (Rijeka), 108,000 B 3
Foča, 6,763 D 4
Fojnica, 1,549 C 4
Gacko, 1,368 D 4
Gevgelija, 7,332 F 5
Glamoč, 1,626 C 3
Gnjilane, 14,000 E 4
Gornji Vafuf, 1,860 C 4
Gospić, 6,767 B 3
Gostivar, 14,000 E 5
Gračac, 2,183 B 3
Gračanica, 7,656 D 3
Gradačac, 5,878 D 3
Grubišno Polje, 2,655 C 3
Gusinje, 2,756 D 4
Hercegnovi, 3,797 D 4
Ivangrad, 6,969 E 4
Jajce, 6,853 C 3
Jesenice, 16,000 A 2
Kamnik, 5,062 B 2
Kanjiža, 10,000 D 2
Kardeljevo, 3,267 C 4
Karlovac, 35,000 B 3
Kavadarci, 13,000 E 5
Kičevo, 11,000 E 5
Kikinda, 32,000 E 3
Kladanj, 2,825 D 3
Ključ, 2,320 C 3
Knin, 5,116 C 3
Knjaževac, 7,448 F 4
Kočevje, 5,819 B 3
Konjic, 5,927 D 4
Koper, 12,000 A 3
Koprivnica, 12,000 C 2
Korčula, 2,458 C 4
Kosovska Mitrovica, 29,000 E 4
Kostajnica, 2,080 C 3
Kotor, 4,764 D 4
Kragujevac, 56,000 E 3
Kraljevo (Rankovićevo), 26,000 E 4
Kranj, 23,000 B 2
Križevci, 6,642 C 2
Krk, 1,280 B 3
Krško, 3,518 B 3
Kruševac, 31,000 E 4
Kumanovo, 33,000 E 4
Leskovac, 37,000 E 4
Livno, 5,181 C 4
Ljubljana, 183,000 B 3
Ljubuški, 2,168 C 4
Loznica, 12,000 D 3
Maglaj, 4,556 D 3
Makarska, 3,634 C 4
Maribor, 89,000 B 2
Mladenovac, 12,000 E 3
Modriča, 5,053 D 3
Mostar, 53,000 D 4
Našice, 4,187 C 3
Negotin, 8,635 F 3
Nevesinje, 2,349 D 4
Nikšić, 25,000 D 4
Niš, 92,000 E 4
Nova Gradiška, 9,229 C 3
Novi, 2,075 B 3
Novi Pazar, 23,000 E 4
Novi Sad, 119,000 D 3
Novo Mesto, 6,885 B 3
Novska, 3,483 C 3
Ogulin, 3,522 B 3
Ohrid, 18,000 E 5
Omiš, 2,171 C 4
Opatija, 7,974 A 3
Osijek, 78,000 D 3
Pag, 2,431 B 3
Pančevo, 49,000 E 3
Paraćin, 17,000 E 4
Peć, 30,000 E 4
Petrinja, 7,366 B 3
Piran, 5,474 A 3
Pirot, 20,000 F 4
Plav, 2,535 D 4
Pljevlja, 12,000 D 4
Podgorica (Titograd), 37,000 D 4
Pola (Pula), 40,000 A 3
Poreč, 3,006 A 3
Postojna, 4,857 B 3
Požarevac, 23,000 E 3
Požega, 14,000 C 3
Preševo, 5,680 E 4
Priboj, 5,490 D 4
Prijedor, 13,000 C 3
Prijepolje, 4,566 D 4
Prilep, 40,000 E 5
Priština, 43,000 E 4
Prizren, 29,000 E 4
Prokuplje, 15,000 E 4
Prozor, 1,052 C 4
Ptuj, 7,392 C 2
Pula, 40,000 A 3
Rab, 1,548 B 3
Rača, 1,351 E 3
Radeče, 1,500 B 2
Radoviš, 6,246 F 5
Ragusa (Dubrovnik), 24,000 C 4
Rankovićevo, 26,000 E 4
Raška, 2,278 E 4
Rijeka, 108,000 B 3
Rogatica, 3,040 D 4
Rovinj, 7,155 A 3
Ruma, 21,000 D 3
Šabac, 30,000 D 3
Sanski Most, 5,096 C 3
Sarajevo, 223,000 D 4
Senj, 3,903 B 3
Senta, 22,000 D 3
Šibenik, 27,000 C 4
Sinj, 4,134 C 4
Sisak, 29,000 C 3
Škofja Loka, 3,429 A 2
Skopje, 230,000 E 5
Skradin, 1,118 C 4
Smederevo, 29,000 E 3
Sombor, 31,000 D 3
Split, 106,000 C 4
Srebrenica, 1,859 D 3
Sremska Mitrovica, 22,000 D 3
Sremski Karlovci, 6,390 D 3
Stari Majdan, 1,445 C 3
Štip, 22,000 F 5
Stolac, 2,970 D 4
Struga, 6,857 E 5
Strumica, 17,000 F 5
Subotica, 76,000 D 2
Surdulica, 5,007 F 4
Svetozarevo, 22,000 E 4
Svilajnac, 5,895 E 3
Tešanj, 3,148 C 3
Tetovo, 27,000 E 5
Titograd, 37,000 D 4
Titovo Užice, 26,000 D 4
Titov Veles, 29,000 E 5
Travnik, 12,000 C 3
Trbovlje, 16,000 B 2
Trebinje, 4,073 D 4
Trogir, 5,003 C 4
Tržič, 4,881 B 2
Tuzla, 55,000 D 3
Ulcinj, 5,705 D 5
Valjevo, 27,000 D 3
Varaždin, 28,000 B 2
Vareš, 7,647 D 3
Veliki Bečkerek (Zrenjanin), 56,000 E 3
Vinkovci, 24,000 D 3
Virovitica, 10,000 C 3
Višegrad, 3,309 D 4
Vranje, 18,000 F 4
Vrbas, 19,000 D 3
Vršac, 32,000 E 3
Vukovar, 25,000 D 3
Žabari, 1,984 E 3
Zadar, 28,000 B 3
Zagreb, 503,000 B 3
Zaječar, 18,000 F 4
Zara (Zadar), 28,000 B 3
Zenica, 50,000 C 3
Žepče, 2,709 D 3
Zrenjanin, 56,000 E 3
Zvornik, 5,444 D 3

OTHER FEATURES

Adriatic (sea) B
Bobotov Kuk (mt.) D
Bosna (riv.) D
Brač (isl.), 14,227 C
Čazma (riv.) C
Cres (isl.), 4,949 B
Danube (riv.) E
Dinaric Alps (mts.) B
Drava (riv.) C
Drina (riv.) D
Dugi Otok (isl.), 4,873 B
Hvar (isl.), 12,147 C
Ibar (riv.) E
Kamenjak (cape) A
Korab (mt.) E
Korčula (isl.), 10,245 C
Kornat (isl.), 6 B
Krk (isl.), 14,548 B
Kvarner (gulf) B
Lastovo (Lagosta) (isl.), 1,449 C
Lim (riv.) D
Lošinj (isl.), 5,068 B
Mljet (isl.), 1,963 C
Morava (riv.) E
Mur (riv.) B
Neretva (riv.) D
Ohrid (lake) E
Pag (isl.), 8,017 B
Pelagruž (Pelagosa) (isl.) C
Prespa (lake) E
Rab (isl.), 8,400 B
Ruen (mt.) F
Sava (riv.) D
Scutari (lake) D
Solta (isl.), 2,735 C
Tara (riv.) D
Timok (riv.) F
Tisza (riv.) E
Triglav (mt.) A
Una (riv.) C
Vardar (riv.) E
Vis (isl.), 7,004 C
Vrbas (riv.) C
Žirje (isl.), 506 B

*City and suburbs.

THE
BALKAN STATES

CONIC PROJECTION

SCALE OF MILES

0 25 50 75 100 125 150 175

SCALE OF KILOMETRES

0 25 50 75 100 125 150 175

Capitals of Countries _____ ☆
Administrative Centers _____ ▲
International Boundaries _____
Major Internal Boundaries _____
Minor Internal Boundaries _____
Canals _____

BULGARIA and GREECE are divided into counties and
departments, respectively. Because of the scale no
attempt has been made to delimit and name these subdivisions; their administrative centers have, however,
been designated.
    The larger divisions named in Greece are well-known
geographical regions, without administrative function.
    RUMANIA consists of thirty-nine counties and
three cities of regional status, Bucharest, Constanța
and Petroșeni. Scale does not permit delimiting
these counties.
    ALBANIA is divided into twenty-seven districts. Scale
does not permit the delimitation of these divisions.
    YUGOSLAVIA is a federation of six republics. The
Serbian republic includes an autonomous province
(Voyvodina), and an autonomous region (Kosovo-
Mitohiyan).

© C. S. HAMMOND & Co., N.Y.

Topography

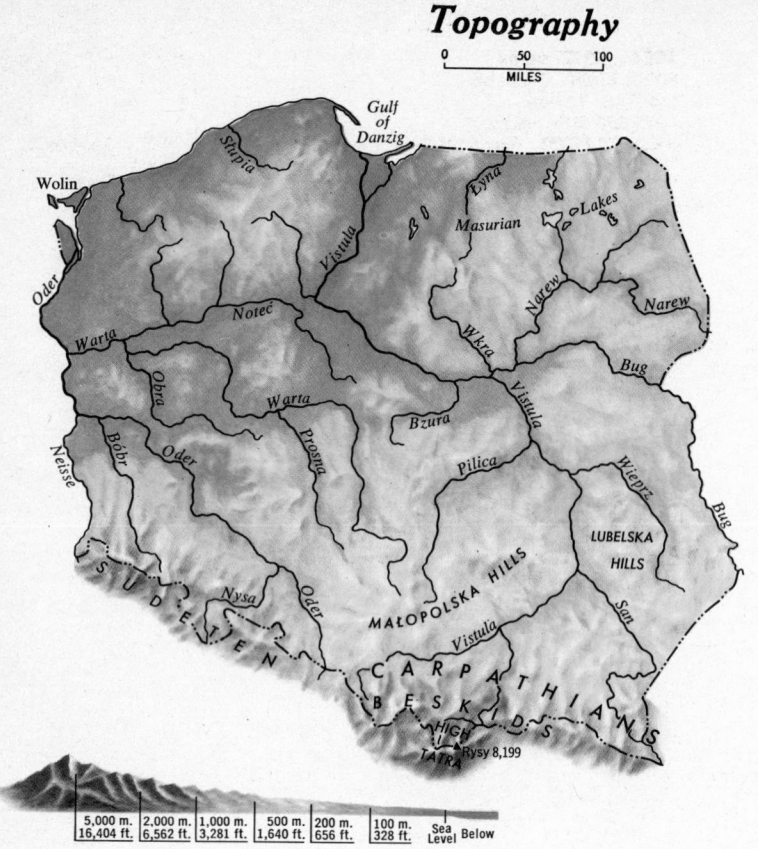

0 50 100
MILES

5,000 m. / 16,404 ft. | 2,000 m. / 6,562 ft. | 1,000 m. / 3,281 ft. | 500 m. / 1,640 ft. | 200 m. / 656 ft. | 100 m. / 328 ft. | Sea Level | Below

POLAND 1938

0 50 100
MILES

POLAND 1945

0 50 100
MILES

PROVINCES		
Biała Podlaska, 283,200	F 2	
Białystok, 613,800	F 2	
Bielsko, 765,500	D 4	
Bydgoszcz, 982,100	C 2	
Chełm, 221,000	F 3	
Ciechanów, 398,500	E 2	
Cracow, 1,097,600	E 4	
Cracow (city), 651,300	E 4	
Częstochowa, 723,200	D 3	
Elbląg, 419,800	D 1	
Gdańsk, 1,220,500	D 1	
Gorzów, 428,700	B 2	
Jelenia Góra, 483,400	B 3	
Kalisz, 640,300	C 3	
Katowice, 3,439,700	D 3	
Kielce, 1,030,400	E 3	
Konin, 423,700	D 2	
Koszalin, 428,500	C 1	
Krosno, 418,000	E 4	
Legnica, 405,600	C 3	
Leszno, 340,600	C 3	
Łódź, 1,063,700	D 3	
Łódź (city), 777,800	D 3	
Łomża, 320,600	F 2	
Lublin, 875,300	F 3	
Nowy Sącz, 600,300	E 4	
Olsztyn, 654,400	E 2	
Opole, 961,600	C 3	
Ostrołęka, 360,700	E 2	
Piła, 414,000	C 2	
Piotrków, 581,900	D 3	
Płock, 479,700	D 2	
Poznań, 1,156,500	C 2	
Przemyśl, 373,100	F 4	
Radom, 674,400	E 3	
Rzeszów, 602,200	F 4	
Siedlce, 602,100	F 2	
Sieradz, 388,500	D 3	
Skierniewice, 388,300	E 3	
Słupsk, 352,900	C 1	
Suwałki, 412,700	F 1	
Szczecin, 841,400	B 2	
Tarnobrzeg, 532,200	E 3	
Tarnów, 573,900	E 4	
Toruń, 580,500	D 2	
Wałbrzych, 709,600	C 3	
Warsaw, 2,117,700	E 2	
Warsaw (city), 1,377,100	E 2	
Włocławek, 402,000	D 2	
Wrocław, 1,014,600	C 3	
Zamość, 472,300	F 3	
Zielona Góra, 575,000	B 3	

CITIES and TOWNS	
Aleksandrów Łódzki, 14,800	D 3
Andrespol, 12,500	D 3
Andrychów, 14,300	D 4
Augustów, 20,200	F 2
Bartoszyce, 15,700	E 1
Będzin, 42,500	B 3
Bełchatów, 9,230	D 3
Bełżyce, 5,333	F 3
Biała Podlaska, 26,700	F 3
Białogard, 20,800	C 1
Białystok, 182,300	F 2
Bielawa, 31,300	C 3
Bielsk Podlaski, 14,600	F 2
Bielsko-Biała, 114,200	D 4
Biłgoraj, 13,600	F 3
Błonie, 12,500	E 2
Bochnia, 15,000	E 4
Bogatynia, 12,300	B 3
Boguszów-Gorce, 11,900	C 3
Bolesławiec, 31,400	B 3
Braniewo, 12,400	D 1
Brodnica, 17,700	D 2
Brzeg, 31,500	C 3
Brzeg Dolny, 10,900	C 3
Brzesko, 10,800	E 3

Agriculture, Industry and Resources

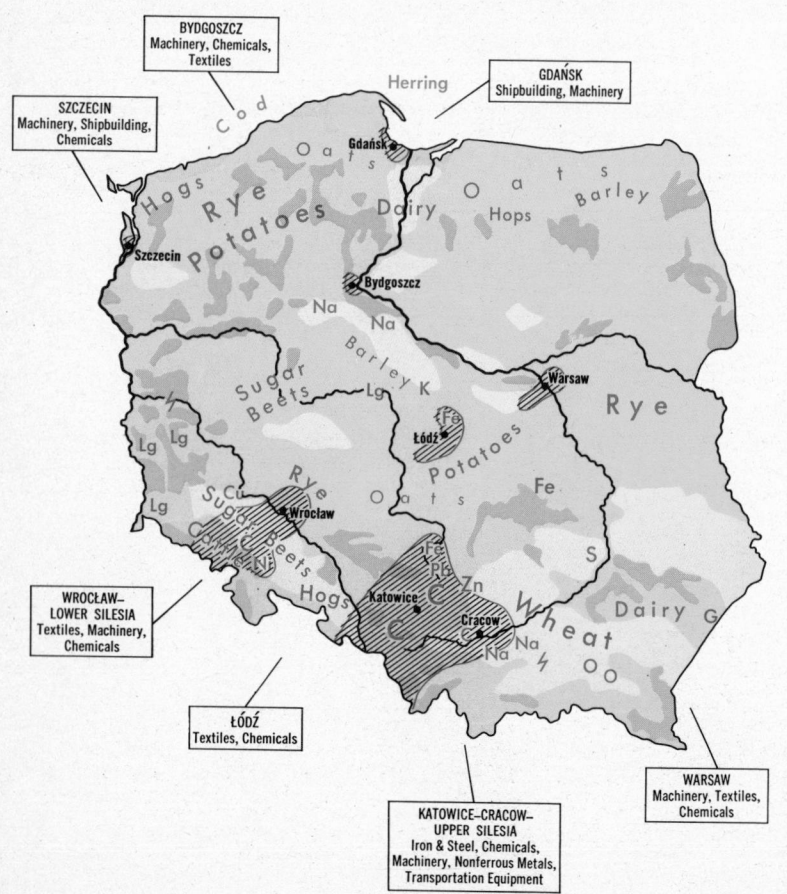

BYDGOSZCZ
Machinery, Chemicals, Textiles

GDAŃSK
Shipbuilding, Machinery

SZCZECIN
Machinery, Shipbuilding, Chemicals

WROCŁAW–LOWER SILESIA
Textiles, Machinery, Chemicals

ŁÓDŹ
Textiles, Chemicals

KATOWICE–CRACOW–UPPER SILESIA
Iron & Steel, Chemicals, Machinery, Nonferrous Metals, Transportation Equipment

WARSAW
Machinery, Textiles, Chemicals

DOMINANT LAND USE

- Cereals (chiefly wheat)
- Rye, Oats, Barley, Potatoes
- General Farming, Livestock
- Forests

MAJOR MINERAL OCCURRENCES

C	Coal	Na	Salt
Cu	Copper	Ni	Nickel
Fe	Iron Ore	O	Petroleum
G	Natural Gas	Pb	Lead
K	Potash	S	Sulfur
Lg	Lignite	Zn	Zinc

⚡ Water Power

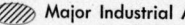 Major Industrial Areas

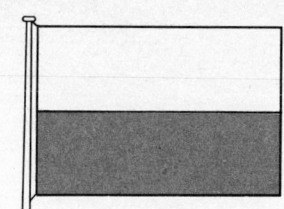

AREA 120,725 sq. mi.
POPULATION 34,364,000
CAPITAL Warsaw
LARGEST CITY Warsaw
HIGHEST POINT Rysy 8,199 ft.
MONETARY UNIT zloty
MAJOR LANGUAGE Polish
MAJOR RELIGION Roman Catholicism

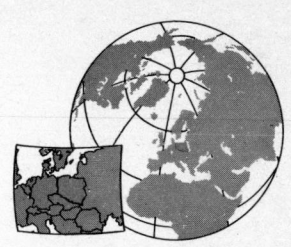

Brzozów, 8,591 F 4
Busko-Zdrój, 11,400 E 3
Bydgoszcz, 305,500 C 2
Bytom, 192,000 A 3
Bytów, 10,900 C 1
Chełm, 40,000 F 3
Chełmno, 18,100 D 2
Chełmża, 14,500 D 2
Chodzież, 14,300 C 2
Chojnice, 24,000 C 2
Chojnów, 11,100 B 3
Chorzów, 154,300 B 4
Choszczno, 10,200 B 2
Chrzanów, 29,300 B 4
Ciechanów, 23,500 E 2
Cieplice Śląskie-Zdrój, 15,600 B 3
Cieszyn, 25,600 D 4
Cracow (Kraków), 651,300 E 4
Czechowice-Dziedzice, 25,700 D 4
Czeladź, 32,700 B 4
Czerwionka, 10,600 A 4
Częstochowa, 193,400 D 3
Dąbrowa Górnicza, 62,400 B 3
Dąbrowa Tarnowska, 9,703 E 3
Darłowo, 11,500 C 1
Dębica, 23,600 E 3
Dęblin, 14,900 E 3
Dębno, 11,000 B 2
Działdowo, 10,500 E 2
Dzierżoniów, 33,400 C 3
Elbląg, 91,400 D 1
Ełk, 27,900 F 2
Gdańsk, 394,000 D 1
Gdynia, 207,600 D 1
Giżycko, 18,500 E 1
Gliwice, 178,300 A 4
Głogów, 22,700 C 3
Głowno, 13,200 D 2
Głubczyce, 11,500 C 3
Głuchołazy, 13,400 C 3
Gniezno, 51,300 C 2
Goldap, 8,886 F 1
Goleniów, 15,000 B 2
Góra, 9,905 C 3
Gorlice, 16,000 E 4
Gorzów Wielkopolski, 76,200 B 2
Gostyń, 13,300 C 3
Gostynin, 12,200 D 2
Grajewo, 11,400 F 2
Grodziec, 10,200 B 3
Grodzisk Mazowiecki, 21,000 E 2
Grójec, 10,400 E 3
Grudziądz, 76,600 D 2
Gryfice, 13,600 B 2
Gryfino, 7,446 B 2
Gubin, 15,000 B 3
Hajnówka, 14,600 F 2
Hrubieszów, 15,500 F 3
Iława, 17,100 D 2
Iłża, 4,419 E 3
Inowrocław, 55,900 D 2
Janów Lubelski, 5,944 F 3
Jarocin, 18,300 C 3
Jarosław, 29,500 F 4
Jasło, 17,800 E 4
Jastrzębie-Zdrój, 34,400 D 3
Jawon, 15,700 C 3
Jaworzno, 64,500 B 4
Jędrzejów, 13,700 E 3
Jelenia Góra, 56,200 B 3
Kalisz, 82,400 D 3
Kamienna Góra, 21,200 B 3
Kamień Pomorski, 8,725 B 2
Kartuzy, 10,800 C 1
Katowice, 317,700 B 4
Kazimierza Wielka, 8,571 E 3
Kędzierzyn, 34,200 D 3
Kępno, 10,300 C 3
Kętrzyn, 19,600 E 1
Kęty, 12,000 D 4
Kielce, 138,700 E 3
Kłobuck, 12,500 D 3
Kłodzko, 26,300 C 3
Kluczbork, 18,200 D 3
Knurów, 30,600 A 4
Kolno, 7,980 F 2
Koło, 13,400 D 2
Kołobrzeg, 26,600 B 1
Konin, 42,800 D 2
Końskie, 13,700 E 3
Konstantynów Łódzki, 13,000 D 3
Kościan, 19,000 C 2
Kościerzyna, 15,500 C 1
Kostrzyń, 11,700 B 2
Koszalin, 66,800 C 1
Kowary, 11,400 B 3
Koźle, 13,300 D 3
Krapkowice, 14,200 D 3
Kraśnik, 14,700 F 3
Kraśnik Fabryczny, 13,800 F 3
Krasnystaw, 12,700 F 3
Krosno, 27,200 E 4
Krotoszyn, 22,200 C 3
Krynica, 10,400 E 4
Kutno, 30,600 D 2
Kwidzyn, 23,400 D 2
Łańcut, 12,300 F 3
Łaziska Górne, 10,900 A 4
Lębork, 25,300 C 1
Łęczyca, 13,900 D 2
Lędziny, 12,800 B 4
Legionowo, 21,000 E 2
Legnica, 76,800 C 3
Leszczyny, 12,100 A 4
Leszno, 34,600 C 3
Leżajsk, 9,647 F 3
Libiąż, 10,700 D 3
Lidzbark Warmiński, 13,200 E 1
Lipno, 11,100 D 2
Łódź, 777,800 D 3
Łomża, 26,400 F 2
Łosice, 4,197 F 2
Łowicz, 21,100 D 2
Lubaczów, 8,298 F 3
Lubań, 17,500 B 3
Lubartów, 10,300 F 3
Lubin, 31,900 C 3
Lublin, 254,700 F 3
Lubliniec, 20,100 D 3
Luboń, 17,000 C 2
Lubsko, 13,000 B 3
Łuków, 16,300 F 3
Malbork, 31,500 D 1
Maków Mazowiecki, 7,694 E 2
Międzyrzec Podlaski, 13,800 F 3
Międzyrzecz, 15,200 B 2
Mielec, 27,700 E 3
Mikołów, 21,800 B 4
Mińsk Mazowiecki, 24,900 E 2
Mława, 20,600 E 2
Mońki, 9,560 F 2
Morąg, 9,681 E 2
Mrągowo, 13,700 E 2
Myślenice, 12,400 E 4
Mysłowice, 45,100 B 4
Myszków, 18,300 D 3
Nakło nad Notecią, 17,000 C 2
Namysłów, 11,200 C 3
Nidzica, 10,000 E 2
Nisko, 10,300 E 3
Nowa Ruda, 18,300 C 3
Nowa Sól, 34,000 B 3
Nowy Dwór Gdański, 7,146 D 1
Nowy Dwór Mazowiecki, 17,200 E 2
Nowy Sącz, 42,100 E 4
Nowy Targ, 22,600 E 4
Nysa, 33,100 C 3
Oborniki, 10,300 C 2
Oława, 18,500 C 3
Olecko, 9,120 F 1
Oleśnica, 28,100 C 3
Olkusz, 16,500 D 3
Olsztyn, 104,300 E 2
Opatów, 9,784 E 3
Opoczno, 12,400 E 3
Opole, 87,800 C 3
Ostróda, 21,600 E 2
Ostrołęka, 23,000 E 2
Ostrów Mazowiecka, 15,200 F 2
Ostrów Wielkopolski, 50,300 C 3
Ostrowiec Świętokrzyski, 51,400 E 3
Oświęcim, 40,200 D 3
Otwock, 40,200 E 2
Ozorków, 18,400 D 3
Pabianice, 63,500 D 3
Parczew, 6,952 F 3
Pasłęk, 8,030 D 1
Piaseczno, 20,500 E 2
Piekary Śląskie, 36,600 B 3
Piła, 44,500 C 2
Pińczów, 7,080 E 3
Pionki, 14,000 E 3
Piotrków Trybunalski, 60,800 D 3
Pisz, 11,400 E 2
Pleszew, 13,700 C 3
Płock, 74,100 D 2
Płońsk, 11,900 E 2
Police, 13,200 B 2
Polkowice, 10,600 C 3
Poznań, 495,200 C 2
Prudnik, 20,400 C 3
Pruszcz Gdański, 13,100 D 1
Pruszków, 43,500 E 2
Przasnysz, 11,400 E 2
Przemyśl, 53,800 F 4
Puławy, 36,400 F 3
Pułtusk, 12,600 E 2
Pyskowice, 23,300 A 3
Rabka, 10,800 D 4
Racibórz, 40,600 C 3
Radom, 166,000 E 3
Radomsko, 31,600 D 3
Radziejów, 4,165 D 2
Radzionków, 28,200 A 3
Rawicz, 14,300 C 3
Ruda Śląska, 146,200 A 4
Rumia, 23,800 D 1
Rybnik, 44,000 D 3
Rydułtowy, 19,500 D 3
Rypin, 10,200 D 2
Rzeszów, 83,900 F 4
Sandomierz, 17,300 E 3
Sanok, 22,100 F 4
Siedlce, 39,600 F 2
Siemianowice Śląskie, 67,800 A 4
Sieradz, 19,000 D 3
Sierpc, 12,900 D 2
Skarżysko-Kamienna, 39,700 E 3
Skawina, 16,400 D 4
Skierniewice, 25,800 E 2
Sławno, 10,900 C 1
Słubice, 12,200 B 2
Słupca, 8,634 D 2
Słupsk, 69,900 C 1
Sochaczew, 21,000 D 2
Sokółka, 10,300 F 2
Sokołów Podlaski, 9,569 F 2
Solec Kujawski, 10,800 D 2
Sopot, 48,500 D 1
Sosnowiec, 148,300 B 4
Śrem, 16,400 C 2
Środa Wielkopolska, 15,000 C 2
Stalowa Wola, 31,100 F 3
Starachowice, 43,700 E 3
Stargard Szczeciński, 45,600 B 2
Starogard Gdański, 34,200 D 2
Staszów, 8,449 E 3
Strzegom, 14,400 C 3
Strzelce Opolskie, 15,000 D 3
Strzemieszyce Wielkie, 11,500 B 3
Sulechów, 10,500 B 2
Suwałki, 26,500 F 1
Swarędz, 12,200 C 2
Świdnica, 48,200 C 3
Świdnik, 23,100 F 3
Świdwin, 12,600 B 2
Świebodzice, 18,900 C 3
Świebodzin, 15,200 B 2
Świecie, 18,300 D 2
Świętochłowice, 57,200 A 4
Świnoujście, 28,800 A 2
Szamotuły, 14,800 C 2
Szczecin, 355,600 B 2
Szczecinek, 29,500 C 2
Szczytno, 17,900 E 2
Szprotawa, 11,500 B 3
Szydłowiec, 6,240 E 3
Tarnobrzeg, 21,300 E 3
Tarnów, 87,200 E 4
Tarnowskie Góry, 35,000 A 3
Tczew, 42,100 D 1
Tomaszów Lubelski, 12,800 F 3
Tomaszów Mazowiecki, 55,600 E 3
Toruń, 139,000 D 2
Trzcianka, 11,200 C 2
Trzebinia-Siersza, 19,600 C 4
Tuchola, 9,439 D 2
Turek, 18,700 D 2
Tychy, 72,800 B 4
Ursus, 30,900 E 2
Wąbrzeźno, 11,900 D 2
Wadowice, 12,000 D 4
Wągrowiec, 16,000 C 2
Wałbrzych, 127,400 C 3
Wałcz, 19,200 C 2
Warsaw (Warszawa) (cap.), 1,377,100 E 2
Węgorzewo, 8,522 E 1
Wejherowo, 34,600 C 1
Wieliczka, 14,000 E 3
Wieluń, 14,900 D 3
Wieruszów, 3,650 D 3
Włocławek, 79,900 D 2
Włodawa, 7,354 F 3
Wodzisław Śląski, 27,500 D 4
Wołomin, 24,100 E 2
Wołów, 10,600 C 3
Wrocław, 557,200 C 3
Września, 18,400 C 2
Wschowa, 10,100 C 3
Wysokie Mazowieckie, 5,296 F 2
Wyszków, 12,200 E 2
Ząbki, 16,200 E 2
Ząbkowice Śląskie, 14,400 C 3
Zabrze, 200,700 A 4
Żagań, 21,700 B 3
Zagórze, 13,000 B 4
Zakopane, 27,200 D 4
Zambrów, 14,500 E 2
Zamość, 35,600 F 3
Żary, 28,500 B 3
Zawiercie, 39,800 D 3
Zduńska Wola, 29,500 D 3
Zgierz, 44,100 D 3
Zgorzelec, 28,800 B 3
Zielona Góra, 75,000 B 3
Złocieniec, 10,400 C 2
Złotoryja, 12,400 C 3
Złotów, 12,100 C 2
Zwoleń, 5,216 E 3
Żyrardów, 33,300 E 2
Żywiec, 22,900 D 4

OTHER FEATURES

Baltic (sea) B 1
Beskids (mts.) D 4
Brda (river) C 2
Brynica (river) B 3
Bug (river) F 2
Danzig (gulf) D 1
Dukla (pass) E 4
Dunajec (river) E 4
Gwda (river) C 2
Hel (pen.) D 1
High Tatra (mts.) D 4
Kłodnica (river) A 4
Łyna (river) E 1
Mamry (lake) F 1
Masurian (lakes) E 2
Narew (river) E 2
Neisse (river) B 3
Noteć (river) B 2
Nysa Kłodzka (river) C 3
Nysa Łużycka (Neisse) (riv.) B 3
Oder (Odra) (river) B 2
Orava (res.) D 4
Pilica (river) D 3
Pomeranian (bay) B 1
Prosna (river) C 3
Przemsza (river) B 4
Rysy (mt.) D 4
San (river) F 3
Słupia (river) C 1
Śniardwy (lake) E 2
Sudeten (mts.) B 3
Uznam (Usedom) (isl.) B 2
Vistula (river) D 2
Warmia (reg.) D 1
Warta (river) B 2
Wieprz (river) F 3
Wisła (Vistula) (river) D 2
Wkra (river) E 2
Wolin (isl.) B 2

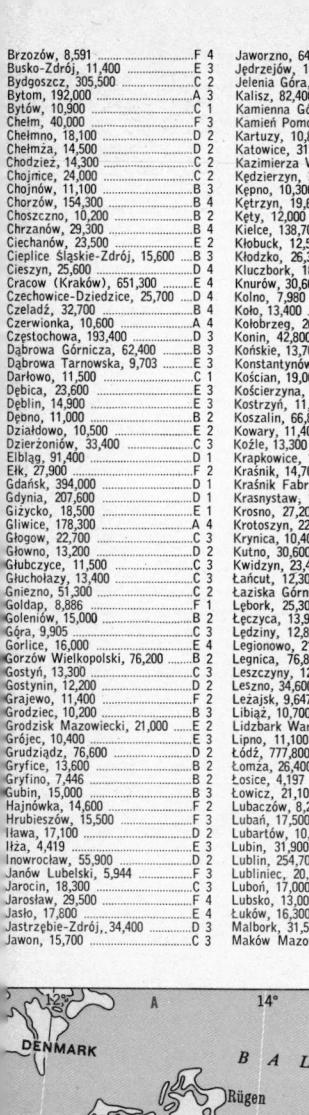

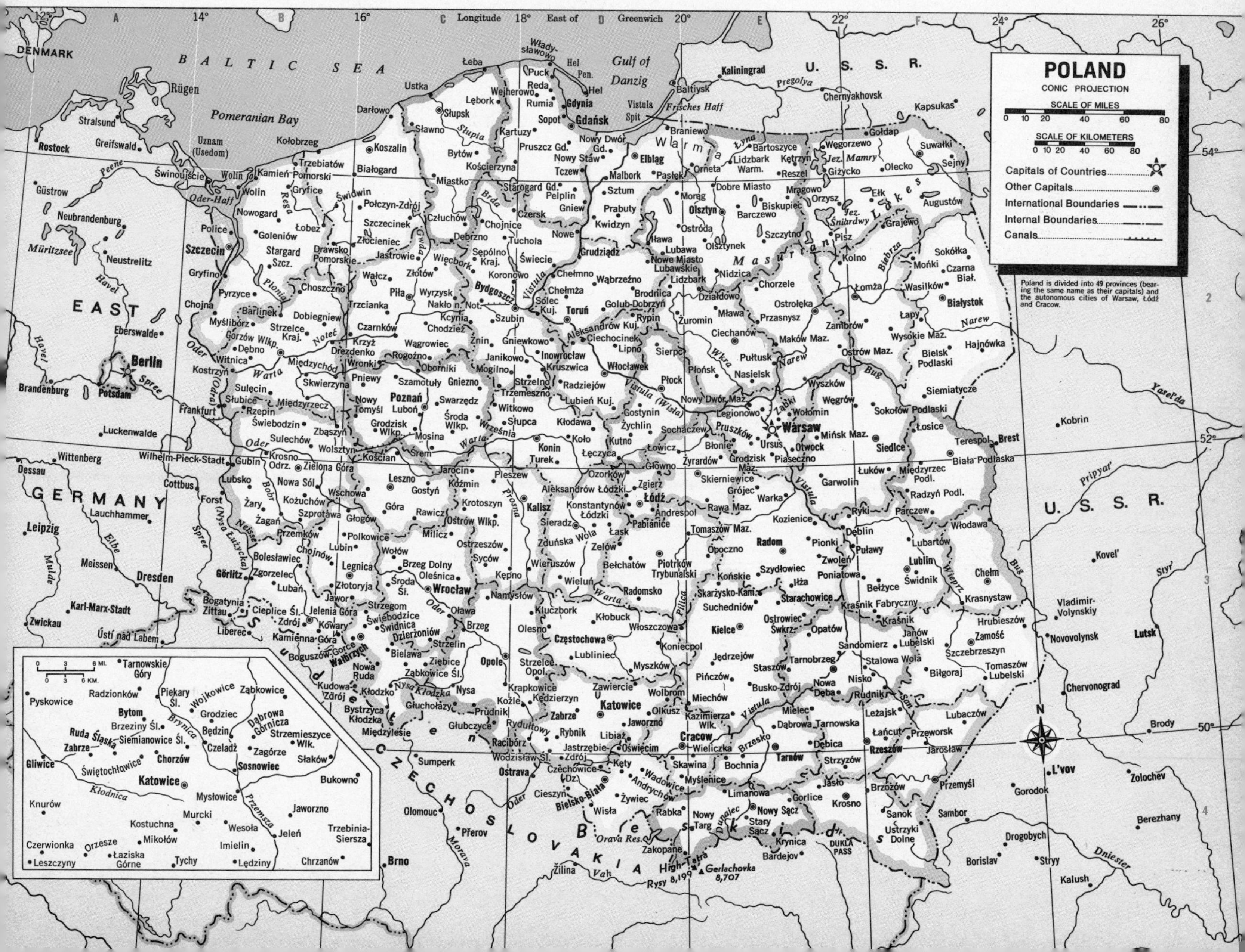

POLAND
CONIC PROJECTION
SCALE OF MILES
0 10 20 40 60 80
SCALE OF KILOMETERS
0 10 20 40 60 80
Capitals of Countries
Other Capitals
International Boundaries
Internal Boundaries
Canals
Poland is divided into 49 provinces (bearing the same name as their capitals) and the autonomous cities of Warsaw, Łódź and Cracow.
Longitude East of Greenwich
BALTIC SEA
Gulf of Danzig
Pomeranian Bay
U. S. S. R.
EAST GERMANY
CZECHOSLOVAKIA

UNION REPUBLICS

Armenian S.S.R., 2,491,900 .... E 6
Azerbaidzhan S.S.R.,
5,117,100 .... E 5
Estonian S.S.R., 1,356,100 .... C 4
Georgian S.S.R., 4,686,000 .... D 5
Kazakh S.S.R., 14,185,000 .... F 5
Kirgiz S.S.R., 2,932,800 .... H 5
Latvian S.S.R., 2,364,100 .... C 4
Lithuanian S.S.R.,
3,128,000 .... C 4
Moldavian S.S.R., 3,823,000 .... D 5
Russian S.F.S.R.,
133,913,000 .... D 4
Tadzhik S.S.R., 2,900,000 .... H 6
Turkmen S.S.R., 2,158,880 .... F 6
Ukrainian S.S.R.,
49,438,000 .... C 5
Uzbek S.S.R., 11,960,000 .... G 5
White Russian S.S.R.,
9,522,000 .... C 5

INTERNAL DIVISIONS

Abkhaz A.S.S.R., 487,000 .... E 5
Adygey Aut. Oblast,
385,000 .... D 5
Adzhar A.S.S.R., 310,000 .... E 5
Aginsk-Buryat Nat'l Okrug,
66,000 .... M 4
Bashkir A.S.S.R., 3,818,000 .... F 4
Buryat A.S.S.R., 812,000 .... M 4
Chechen-Ingush A.S.S.R.,
1,065,000 .... E 5

Chukchi Nat'l Okrug,
101,000 .... R 3
Chuvash A.S.S.R.,
1,224,000 .... E 4
Dagestan A.S.S.R.,
1,429,000 .... E 5
Evenki Nat'l Okrug,
13,000 .... K 3
Gorno-Altay Aut. Oblast,
168,000 .... J 4
Gorno-Badakhshan Aut. Oblast,
98,000 .... H 6
Jewish Aut. Oblast,
172,000 .... O 5
Kabardin-Balkar A.S.S.R.,
588,000 .... E 5
Kalmuck A.S.S.R.,
268,000 .... E 5
Karachay-Cherkess Aut. Oblast,
345,000 .... E 5
Karakalpak A.S.S.R.,
702,000 .... G 5
Karelian A.S.S.R.,
713,000 .... D 3
Khakass Aut. Oblast,
446,000 .... J 4
Khanty-Mansi Nat'l Okrug,
271,000 .... H 3
Komi A.S.S.R., 965,000 .... F 3
Komi-Permyak Nat'l Okrug,
212,000 .... F 4
Koryak Nat'l Okrug,
31,000 .... R 3
Mari A.S.S.R., 685,000 .... F 4
Mordvinian A.S.S.R.,
1,029,000 .... E 4

Nagorno-Karabakh Aut. Oblast,
150,000 .... E 5
Nakhichevan' A.S.S.R.,
202,000 .... E 6
Nenets Nat'l Okrug, 39,000 .... F 3
North Ossetian A.S.S.R.,
552,000 .... E 5
South Ossetian Aut. Oblast,
99,000 .... E 5
Tatar A.S.S.R., 3,131,000 .... F 4
Taymyr Nat'l Okrug, 38,000 .... K 2
Tuvinian A.S.S.R., 231,000 .... K 4
Udmurt A.S.S.R., 1,418,000 .... F 4
Ust'-Ordynsk-Buryat Nat'l Okrug,
146,000 .... L 4
Yakut A.S.S.R., 664,000 .... N 3
Yamal-Nenets Nat'l Okrug,
80,000 .... H 3

CITIES and TOWNS

Abakan, 90,000 .... J 4
Achinsk, 97,000 .... K 4
Adimi .... O 5
Bagdarin .... M 4
Akmolinsk (Tselinograd),
180,000 .... H 4
Aktyubinsk, 150,000 .... F 4
Aldan, 19,000 .... N 4
Aleksandrovsk-Sakhalinskiy,
22,000 .... P 5
Aleysk, 32,000 .... J 4
Alga, 17,000 .... F 5
Allakh-Yun' .... H 5
Alma-Ata, 730,000 .... H 5

Ambarchik .... R 3
Amderma .... F 3
Amursk, 15,000 .... O 4
Anadyr', 8,000 .... S 3
Andizhan, 188,000 .... H 5
Angarsk, 203,000 .... L 4
Anzhero-Sudzhensk,
106,000 .... J 4
Aral'sk, 26,000 .... G 5
Archangel, 343,000 .... E 3
Arkalyk, 55,000 .... G 4
Armavir, 145,000 .... E 5
Artem, 61,000 .... O 5
Artemovskiy .... M 4
Arzamas, 67,000 .... E 4
Ashkhabad, 253,000 .... F 6
Ashkhabad, *256,000 .... F 6
Asino, 30,000 .... J 4
Astrakhan, 410,000 .... E 5
Atbasar, 41,000 .... G 4
Atka .... Q 3
Ayaguz, 40,000 .... J 5
Ayan .... O 4
Aykhal .... M 3
Baku, 852,000 .... F 5
Baku, *1,266,000 .... F 5
Balashov, 83,000 .... E 4
Balkhash, 76,000 .... H 5
Balturino, 10,000 .... K 4
Barabinsk, 40,000 .... H 4
Baranovichi, 101,000 .... C 4
Barnaul, 439,000 .... J 4
Batumi, 101,000 .... E 5
Baykit .... K 3
Baykonur .... G 5

Bayram-Ali, 33,000 .... G 6
Belgorod, 151,000 .... D 4
Belogorsk, 57,000 .... N 4
Belomorsk, 18,000 .... D 3
Beloretsk, 67,000 .... F 4
Belovo, 108,000 .... J 4
Berdichev, 71,000 .... C 5
Berdsk, 53,000 .... J 4
Berezniki, 146,000 .... F 4
Berezovo, 6,000 .... G 3
Beringovskiy .... T 3
Bilibino, 13,000 .... R 3
Birobidzhan, 56,000 .... O 5
Biysk, 186,000 .... J 4
Blagoveshchensk,
128,000 .... N 4
Bobruysk, 138,000 .... D 4
Bodaybo, 19,000 .... M 4
Borisoglebsk, 64,000 .... E 4
Borzya, 28,000 .... M 4
Boshchakul' .... H 4
Bratsk, 155,000 .... L 4
Brest, 122,000 .... C 4
Bryansk, 318,000 .... D 4
Bugul'ma, 72,000 .... F 4
Bukhara, 112,000 .... G 5
Bulun .... N 2
Buzuluk, 67,000 .... F 4
Chagda .... N 4
Chapayevo .... F 4
Chapayevsk, 86,000 .... F 4
Chardzhou, 96,000 .... G 6
Chardara .... H 4
Cheboksary, 216,000 .... E 4
Chelkar, 25,000 .... F 5
Chelyabinsk,
875,000 .... G 4

Cheremkhovo, 99,000 .... L 4
Cherepovets, 188,000 .... D 4
Cherkessk, 67,000 .... E 5
Chernigov, 159,000 .... D 4
Chernovtsy, 187,000 .... C 5
Chernyshevsk, 10,000 .... M 4
Chernyshevskiy,
10,000 .... M 3
Cherskiy .... Q 3
Chimbay, 20,000 .... F 5
Chimkent, 247,000 .... G 5
Chirchik, 107,000 .... H 5
Chita, 241,000 .... M 4
Chokurdakh .... P 2
Chul'man .... N 4
Chumikan .... O 4
Dalnegorsk, 33,500 .... O 5
Dalnerechensk, 30,000 .... O 5
Daugavpils, 100,400 .... C 4
Dikson .... J 2
Dimitrovgrad, 81,000 .... F 4
Dnepropetrovsk,
862,000 .... D 5
Dolinsk, 18,000 .... P 5
Donetsk, 879,000 .... D 5
Drogobych, 56,000 .... C 5
Druzhina .... P 3
Dudinka, 22,000 .... J 3
Dushanbe, 376,000 .... G 6
Dzerzhinsk, 221,000 .... E 4
Dzhalal-Abad, 44,000 .... H 5
Dzhalinda .... N 4
Dzhambul, 187,000 .... H 5
Dzhetygara, 39,000 .... G 4
Dzhezkazgan, 62,000 .... G 5
Ekibastuz, 46,000 .... H 4

Ekimchan .... O 4
El'dikan .... O 3
Elista, 50,000 .... E 5
Engel's, 130,000 .... E 4
Erivan, 767,000 .... E 5
Evensk .... Q 3
Fergana, 111,000 .... H 5
Fort-Shevchenko,
12,000 .... F 5
Frolovo, 30,000 .... E 5
Frunze, 430,600 .... H 5
Gasan-Kuli .... F 6
Gizhiga .... Q 3
Gol'chikha .... J 2
Gomel, 272,000 .... D 4
Gor'kiy, 1,170,000 .... E 4
Gorno-Altaysk,
34,000 .... J 4
Grodno, 132,000 .... C 4
Groznyy, 341,000 .... E 5
Gubakha, 40,000 .... F 4
Gulistan, 37,000 .... G 5
Gur'yev, 114,000 .... F 5
Gusinoozersk, 10,000 .... L 4
Gydy .... H 2
Igarka, 22,000 .... J 3
Ilanskiy, 24,000 .... K 4
Iliysk, 17,000 .... H 5
Indiga .... E 3
Inta, 50,000 .... F 3
Iolotan', 10,000 .... G 6
Irkutsk, 451,000 .... L 4
Ishim, 56,000 .... G 4
Ishimbay, 54,000 .... F 4
Isil'-Kul', 26,000 .... H 4
Ivano-Frankovsk, 105,000 .... C 5

UNION OF SOVIET SOCIALIST REPUBLICS

CONIC PROJECTION

SCALE OF MILES

0   100 200 300 400 500 600

SCALE OF KILOMETERS

0 100 200 300 400 500 600

Capitals
● National
★ Union Republic
⊙ A.S.S.R.
⊙ Autonomous Oblast
⊙ National Okrug

Boundaries

ADMINISTRATIVE DIVISIONS NOT NAMED ON MAP

Division	Ref.	Division	Ref.
1. Abkhaz A.S.S.R.	E5	13. Khakass Aut. Oblast	J4
2. Adygey Aut. Oblast	D5	14. Komi-Permyak Nat'l Okrug	F4
3. Adzhar A.S.S.R.	E5	15. Mari A.S.S.R.	E4
4. Aginsk-Buryat Nat'l Okrug	M4	16. Mordvinian A.S.S.R.	E4
5. Chechen-Ingush A.S.S.R.	E5	17. Nagorno-Karabakh Aut. Oblast	E6
6. Chuvash A.S.S.R.	E4	18. Nakhichevan' A.S.S.R.	E6
7. Gorno-Altay Aut. Oblast	J4	19. North Ossetian A.S.S.R.	E5
8. Gorno-Badakhshan Aut. Oblast	H6	20. South Ossetian Aut. Oblast	E5
9. Jewish Aut. Oblast	O5	21. Tatar A.S.S.R.	F4
10. Kabardin-Balkar A.S.S.R.	E5	22. Tuvinian A.S.S.R.	K4
11. Karachay-Cherkess Aut. Oblast	E5	23. Udmurt A.S.S.R.	F4
12. Karakalpak A.S.S.R.	G5	24. Ust'-Ordynsk-Buryat Nat'l Okrug	J4

AREA 8,649,490 sq. mi.
POPULATION 258,402,000
CAPITAL Moscow
LARGEST CITY Moscow
HIGHEST POINT Communism Peak 24,590 ft.
MONETARY UNIT ruble
MAJOR LANGUAGES Russian, Ukrainian, White Russian, Uzbek, Azerbaidzhani, Tatar, Georgian, Lithuanian, Armenian, Yiddish, Latvian, Mordvinian, Kirgiz, Tadzhik, Estonian, Kazakh, Moldavian, German, Chuvash, Turkmenian, Bashkir
MAJOR RELIGIONS Eastern (Russian) Orthodoxy, Islam, Judaism, Protestantism (Baltic States)

UNION REPUBLICS

	AREA (sq. mi.)	POPULATION	CAPITAL and LARGEST CITY
RUSSIAN S.F.S.R.	6,592,812	133,913,000	Moscow 7,632,000
KAZAKH S.S.R.	1,048,300	14,185,000	Alma-Ata 836,000
UKRAINIAN S.S.R.	233,089	49,438,000	Kiev 1,947,000
TURKMEN S.S.R.	188,455	2,158,880	Ashkhabad 280,000
UZBEK S.S.R.	173,591	11,960,000	Tashkent 1,595,000
WHITE RUSSIAN S.S.R.	80,154	9,522,000	Minsk 1,147,000
KIRGIZ S.S.R.	76,641	2,932,800	Frunze 474,000
TADZHIK S.S.R.	55,251	2,900,000	Dushanbe 422,000
AZERBAIDZHAN S.S.R.	33,436	5,117,100	Baku 1,383,000
GEORGIAN S.S.R.	26,911	4,686,000	Tbilisi 1,006,000
LITHUANIAN S.S.R.	25,174	3,128,000	Vilna 420,000
LATVIAN S.S.R.	24,595	2,364,100	Riga 796,000
ESTONIAN S.S.R.	17,413	1,356,100	Tallinn 392,000
MOLDAVIAN S.S.R.	13,012	3,823,000	Kishinev 432,000
ARMENIAN S.S.R	11,506	2,491,900	Erivan 899,000

Topography

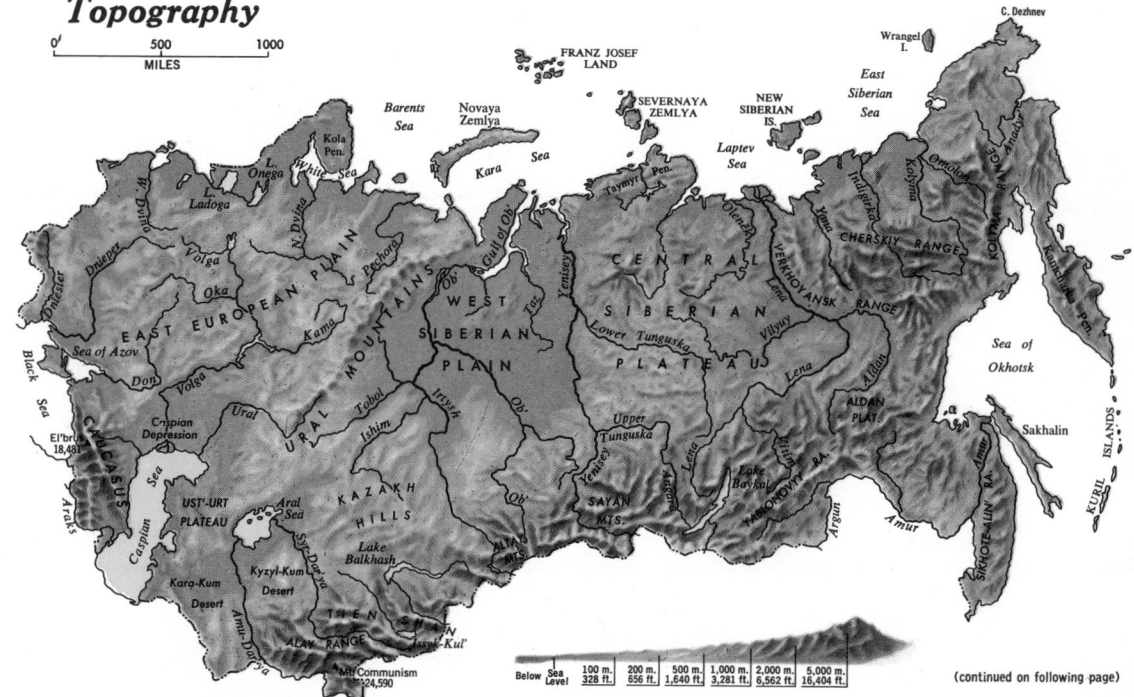

(continued on following page)

Agriculture, Industry and Resources

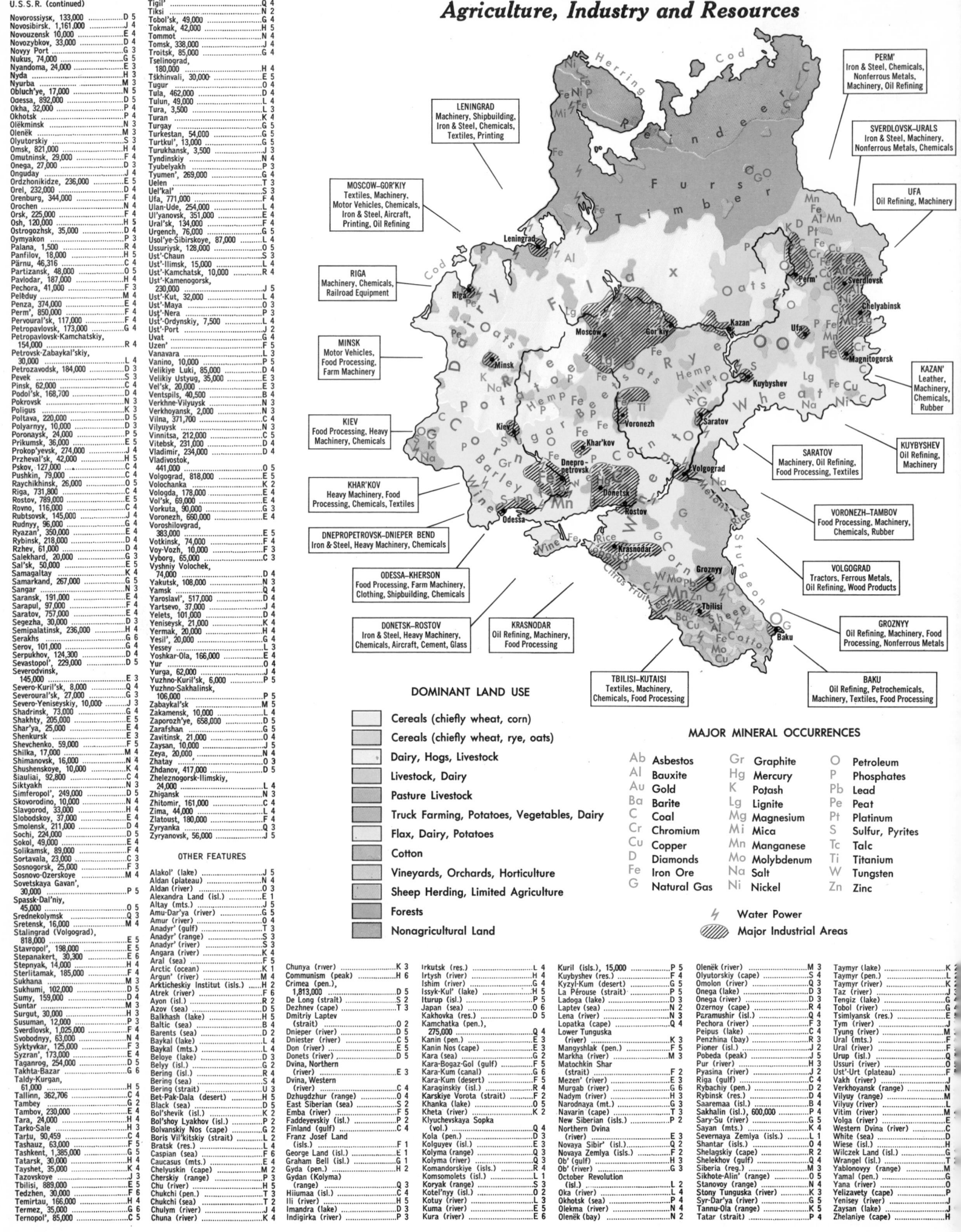

DOMINANT LAND USE

- Cereals (chiefly wheat, corn)
- Cereals (chiefly wheat, rye, oats)
- Dairy, Hogs, Livestock
- Livestock, Dairy
- Pasture Livestock
- Truck Farming, Potatoes, Vegetables, Dairy
- Flax, Dairy, Potatoes
- Cotton
- Vineyards, Orchards, Horticulture
- Sheep Herding, Limited Agriculture
- Forests
- Nonagricultural Land

MAJOR MINERAL OCCURRENCES

Ab Asbestos · Al Bauxite · Au Gold · Ba Barite · C Coal · Cr Chromium · Cu Copper · D Diamonds · Fe Iron Ore · G Natural Gas · Gr Graphite · Hg Mercury · K Potash · Lg Lignite · Mg Magnesium · Mi Mica · Mn Manganese · Mo Molybdenum · Na Salt · Ni Nickel · O Petroleum · P Phosphates · Pb Lead · Pe Peat · Pt Platinum · S Sulfur, Pyrites · Tc Talc · Ti Titanium · W Tungsten · Zn Zinc

Water Power · Major Industrial Areas

Agriculture, Industry and Resources

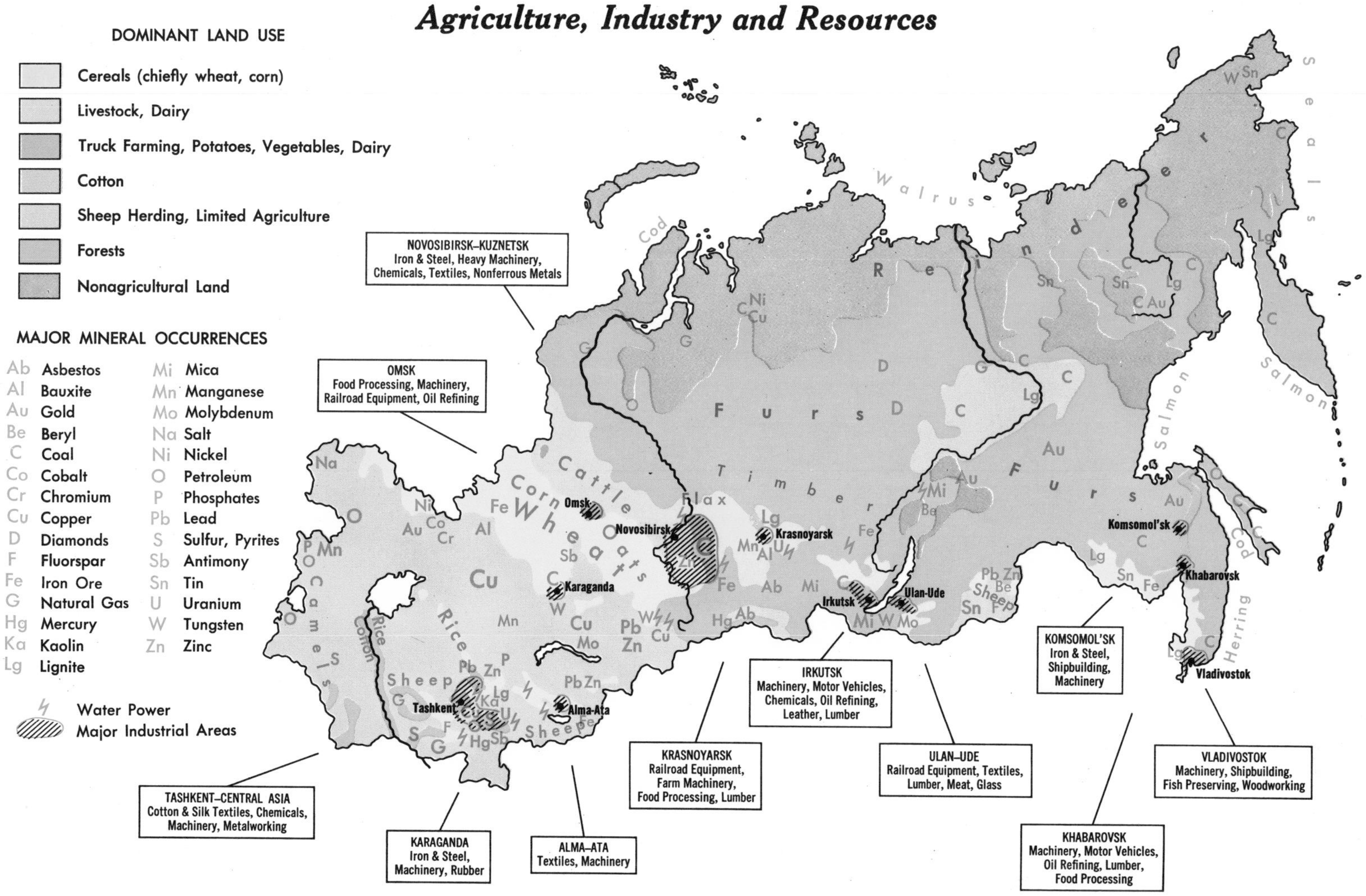

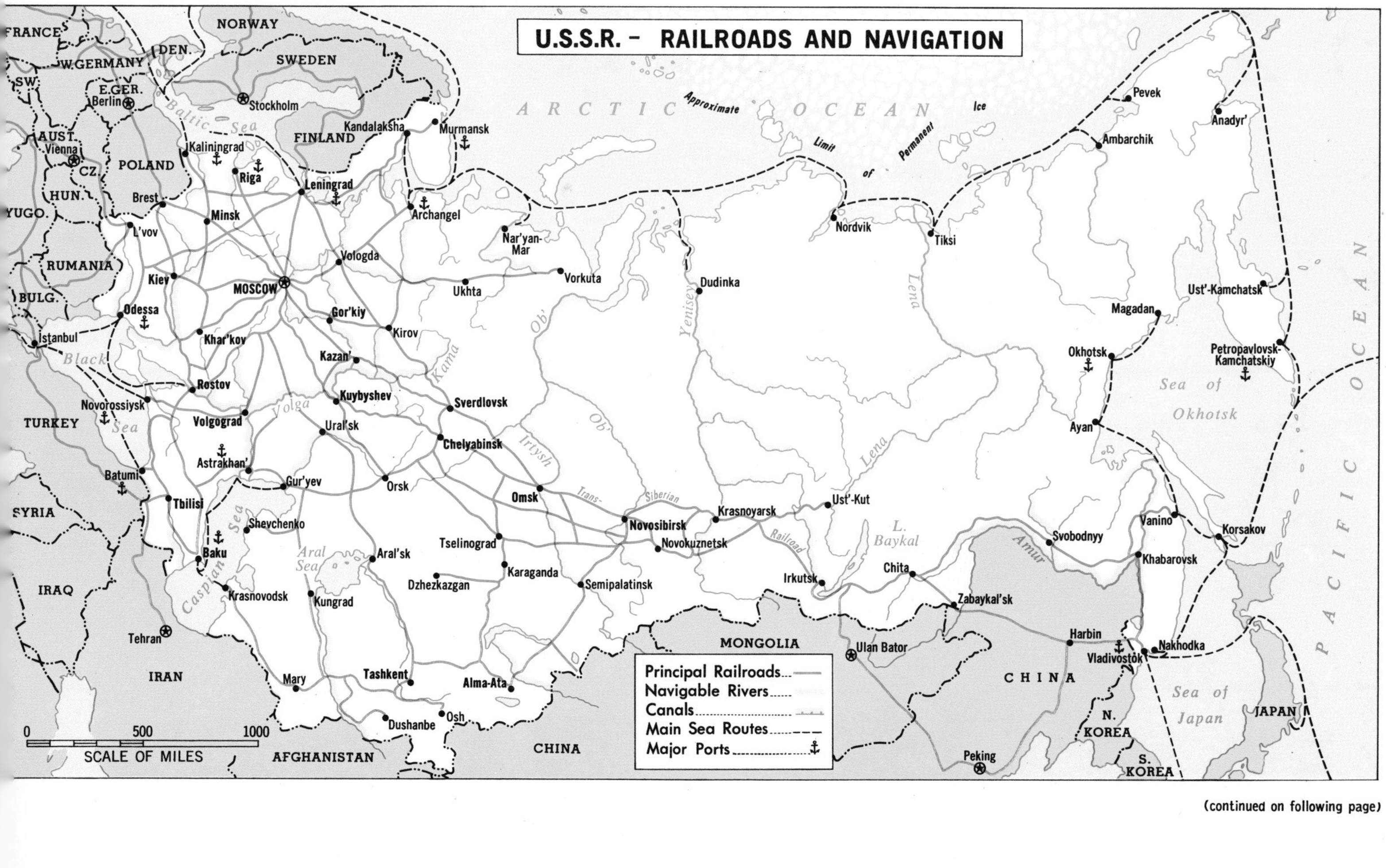

DOMINANT LAND USE

- Cereals (chiefly wheat, corn)
- Livestock, Dairy
- Truck Farming, Potatoes, Vegetables, Dairy
- Cotton
- Sheep Herding, Limited Agriculture
- Forests
- Nonagricultural Land

MAJOR MINERAL OCCURRENCES

Ab	Asbestos	Mi	Mica
Al	Bauxite	Mn	Manganese
Au	Gold	Mo	Molybdenum
Be	Beryl	Na	Salt
C	Coal	Ni	Nickel
Co	Cobalt	O	Petroleum
Cr	Chromium	P	Phosphates
Cu	Copper	Pb	Lead
D	Diamonds	S	Sulfur, Pyrites
F	Fluorspar	Sb	Antimony
Fe	Iron Ore	Sn	Tin
G	Natural Gas	U	Uranium
Hg	Mercury	W	Tungsten
Ka	Kaolin	Zn	Zinc
Lg	Lignite		

- Water Power
- Major Industrial Areas

NOVOSIBIRSK–KUZNETSK
Iron & Steel, Heavy Machinery,
Chemicals, Textiles, Nonferrous Metals

OMSK
Food Processing, Machinery,
Railroad Equipment, Oil Refining

TASHKENT–CENTRAL ASIA
Cotton & Silk Textiles, Chemicals,
Machinery, Metalworking

KARAGANDA
Iron & Steel,
Machinery, Rubber

ALMA–ATA
Textiles, Machinery

KRASNOYARSK
Railroad Equipment,
Farm Machinery,
Food Processing, Lumber

IRKUTSK
Machinery, Motor Vehicles,
Chemicals, Oil Refining,
Leather, Lumber

ULAN–UDE
Railroad Equipment, Textiles,
Lumber, Meat, Glass

KHABAROVSK
Machinery, Motor Vehicles,
Oil Refining, Lumber,
Food Processing

KOMSOMOL'SK
Iron & Steel,
Shipbuilding,
Machinery

VLADIVOSTOK
Machinery, Shipbuilding,
Fish Preserving, Woodworking

U.S.S.R. - RAILROADS AND NAVIGATION

Legend:
- Principal Railroads
- Navigable Rivers
- Canals
- Main Sea Routes
- Major Ports

Map labels (countries/cities): FRANCE, NORWAY, DEN., W. GERMANY, SW., E. GER., Berlin, SWEDEN, Stockholm, AUST., Vienna, POLAND, Kaliningrad, Riga, FINLAND, Kandalaksha, Murmansk, ARCTIC OCEAN, Approximate, Ice, Pevek, Anadyr', Ambarchik, CZ., HUN., Brest, Minsk, Leningrad, Archangel, Nar'yan-Mar, Limit, of, Permanent, Nordvik, Tiksi, YUGO., RUMANIA, L'vov, Vologda, Ukhta, Vorkuta, Ust'-Kamchatsk, BULG., Kiev, MOSCOW, Kirov, Dudinka, Magadan, Istanbul, Odessa, Gor'kiy, Kazan', Okhotsk, Petropavlovsk-Kamchatskiy, Black, Khar'kov, Kama, Ob', Yenisey, Sea, Rostov, Kuybyshev, Sverdlovsk, Lena, Sea of Okhotsk, TURKEY, Novorossiysk, Volgograd, Ural'sk, Chelyabinsk, Ayan, Batumi, Tbilisi, Astrakhan', Gur'yev, Orsk, Omsk, Irtysh, Trans-Siberian Railroad, Krasnoyarsk, Ust'-Kut, Svobodnyy, Amur, Vanino, Korsakov, SYRIA, Shevchenko, Volga, Aral Sea, Tselinograd, Novosibirsk, Novokuznetsk, L. Baykal, Chita, Khabarovsk, PACIFIC OCEAN, IRAQ, Baku, Caspian Sea, Krasnovodsk, Kungrad, Aral'sk, Karaganda, Dzhezkazgan, Semipalatinsk, Irkutsk, Zabaykal'sk, Harbin, Nakhodka, IRAN, Tehran, Mary, Tashkent, Alma-Ata, Osh, Dushanbe, AFGHANISTAN, CHINA, MONGOLIA, Ulan Bator, Vladivostok, N. KOREA, S. KOREA, Peking, Sea of Japan, JAPAN

SCALE OF MILES — 0 · 500 · 1000

(continued on following page)

U.S.S.R. - EUROPEAN

UNION REPUBLICS

Armenian S.S.R., 2,491,900 ... F 6
Azerbaidzhan S.S.R., 5,117,100 ... G 6
Estonian S.S.R., 1,356,100 ... C 3
Georgian S.S.R., 4,686,000 ... F 6
Latvian S.S.R., 2,364,100 ... B 3
Lithuanian S.S.R., 3,128,000 ... B 3
Moldavian S.S.R., 3,823,000 ... C 5
Russian S.F.S.R., 133,913,000 ... F 3
Ukrainian S.S.R., 49,438,000 ... D 5
White Russian S.S.R., 9,522,000 ... C 4

INTERNAL DIVISIONS

Abkhaz A.S.S.R., 487,000 ... F 6
Adygey Aut. Oblast, 385,000 ... F 6
Adzhar A.S.S.R., 310,000 ... F 6
Bashkir A.S.S.R., 3,818,000 ... J 4
Chechen-Ingush A.S.S.R., 1,065,000 ... G 6
Chuvash A.S.S.R., 1,224,000 ... G 3
Crimean Oblast, 1,813,000 ... D 6
Dagestan A.S.S.R., 1,429,000 ... G 6
Kabardin-Balkar A.S.S.R., 588,000 ... F 6
Kalmuck A.S.S.R., 268,000 ... F 5
Karachay-Cherkess Aut. Oblast, 345,000 ... F 6
Karelian A.S.S.R., 713,000 ... D 2
Komi A.S.S.R., 965,000 ... H 2
Komi-Permyak Nat'l Okrug, 212,000 ... H 3
Mari A.S.S.R., 685,000 ... G 3
Mordvinian A.S.S.R., 1,029,000 ... G 4
Nagorno-Karabakh Aut. Oblast, 150,000 ... G 7
Nakhichevan' A.S.S.R., 202,000 ... F 7
Nenets Nat'l Okrug, 39,000 ... H 1
North Ossetian A.S.S.R., 552,000 ... F 6
South Ossetian Aut. Oblast, 99,000 ... F 6
Tatar A.S.S.R., 3,131,000 ... G 3
Trans-Carpathian Oblast, 1,057,000 ... B 5
Udmurt A.S.S.R., 1,418,000 ... H 3
Volyn Oblast, 974,000 ... C 4

CITIES and TOWNS

Abdulino, 27,000 ... H 4
Agdam, 21,300 ... G 6
Agryz, 21,000 ... H 3
Akhaltsikhe, 20,000 ... F 6
Akhtubinsk, 33,000 ... G 5
Akhtyrka, 42,000 ... E 4
Alagir, 18,000 ... F 6
Alatyr', 47,000 ... G 4
Aleksandriya, 69,000 ... D 5
Alekseyevka, 24,000 ... E 4
Aleksin, 61,000 ... E 4
Ali-Bayramly, 33,900 ... G 7
Al'met'yevsk, 87,000 ... H 3
Alushta, 21,000 ... D 6
Anapa, 25,000 ... E 6
Apatity, 40,000 ... D 1
Apsheronsk, 36,000 ... F 6
Archangel (Arkhangel'sk), 343,000 ... F 2
Armavir, 145,000 ... F 5
Arzamas, 67,000 ... F 3
Astrakhan', 410,000 ... G 5
Atkarsk, 30,000 ... G 4
Azov, 59,000 ... E 5
Bakhchisaray, 12,000 ... D 6
Bakhmach, 14,000 ... D 4
Baku, 852,000 ... H 6
Baku, *1,266,000 ... H 6
Balakhna, 36,000 ... F 3
Balaklava, 5,000 ... D 6
Balakovo, 103,000 ... G 4
Balashov, 83,000 ... F 4
Baltiysk, 18,000 ... A 4
Baranovichi, 101,000 ... C 4
Barysh, 21,000 ... G 4
Bataysk, 85,000 ... E 5
Batumi, 101,000 ... F 6
Belaya Tserkov', 109,000 ... C 5
Belebey, 35,000 ... H 4
Belev, 18,000 ... E 4
Belgorod, 151,000 ... E 4
Belgorod-Dnestrovskiy, 30,000 ... D 5
Belomorsk, 18,000 ... D 2
Beloretsk, 67,000 ... J 4
Bel'tsy, 101,800 ... C 5
Bendery, 72,300 ... C 5
Berdichev, 71,000 ... C 5
Berdyansk, 100,000 ... E 5
Beregovo, 30,000 ... B 5
Berezniki, 146,000 ... J 3
Beslan, 28,000 ... F 6
Bezhetsk, 31,000 ... E 3
Birsk, 36,000 ... J 3
Blagoveshchensk, 15,000 ... J 4
Bobruysk, 138,000 ... C 4
Bologoye, 32,000 ... D 3
Bor, 55,000 ... F 3
Borislav, 36,000 ... B 5
Borisoglebsk, 64,000 ... F 4
Borisov, 84,000 ... C 4
Borovichi, 55,000 ... D 3
Borzhomi, 17,000 ... F 6
Brest, 122,000 ... B 4
Bryansk, 318,000 ... D 4
Bugul'ma, 72,000 ... H 4
Buguruslan, 49,000 ... H 4
Buy, 25,000 ... F 3
Buynaksk, 41,000 ... G 6
Buzuluk, 67,000 ... H 4
Bykhov, 16,000 ... C 4
Cēsis, 17,700 ... C 3
Chadyr-Lunga, 20,200 ... C 5
Chapayevsk, 86,000 ... G 4
Chaykovskiy, 48,000 ... H 3
Cheboksary, 216,000 ... G 3
Cherepovets, 188,000 ... E 3
Cherkassy, 158,000 ... D 5
Cherkessk, 67,000 ... F 6
Chernigov, 159,000 ... D 4
Chernovtsy, 187,000 ... C 5
Chervonograd, 41,000 ... B 4
Chiatura, 30,000 ... F 6
Chistopol', 60,000 ... H 3
Chkalov (Orenburg), 344,000 ... J 4
Chortkov, 21,000 ... B 5
Chusovoy, 58,000 ... J 3
Danilov, 17,000 ... F 3
Daugavpils, 100,400 ... C 3
Davlekanovo, 22,000 ... H 4
Derbent, 57,000 ... G 6
Dimitrovgrad, 81,000 ... G 4
Dneprodzerzhinsk, 227,000 ... D 5
Dnepropetrovsk, 862,000 ... D 5
Dobrush, 17,000 ... D 4
Donetsk, 879,000 ... E 5
Drogobych, 56,000 ... B 5
Dubna, 43,700 ... E 3
Dubna, 8,000 ... E 4
Dvinsk (Daugavpils), 100,400 ... C 3
Dzerzhinsk, 221,000 ... F 3
Dzhankoy, 42,000 ... D 5
Elektrostal', 123,100 ... E 3
Elista, 50,000 ... F 5
Engel's, 130,000 ... G 4
Erivan, 767,000 ... F 6
Ertil', 20,000 ... F 4
Fastov, 42,000 ... C 4
Feodosiya, 65,000 ... D 5
Frolovo, 30,000 ... F 5
Furmanov, 44,000 ... F 3
Gagarin, 15,000 ... D 3
Gagra, 23,000 ... E 6
Galich, 20,000 ... F 3
Gandzha (Kirovabad), 189,800 ... G 6
Gatchina, 63,000 ... D 3
Gay, 35,000 ... J 4
Gaysin, 23,000 ... C 5
Gelendzhik, 24,000 ... E 6
Genichesk, 19,000 ... E 5
Georgiu-Dezh, 48,000 ... E 4
Glazov, 68,000 ... H 3
Glukhov, 30,000 ... D 4
Gomel', 272,000 ... D 4
Gori, 45,000 ... F 6
Gorki, 24,000 ... D 4
Gor'kiy, 1,170,000 ... F 3
Gorlovka, 335,000 ... E 5
Gornyatskiy, 30,000 ... K 1
Gorodets, 34,000 ... F 3
Gremyachinsk, 34,000 ... J 3
Grodno, 132,000 ... B 4
Groznyy, 341,000 ... G 6
Gryazi, 40,000 ... F 4
Gubakha, 40,000 ... J 3
Gubkin, 54,000 ... E 4
Gudauta, 14,000 ... F 6
Gukovo, 65,000 ... F 5
Gus'-Khrustal'nyy, 65,000 ... F 3
Ichnya, 14,000 ... D 4
Inta, 50,000 ... K 1
Inza, 20,000 ... G 4
Ishimbay, 54,000 ... J 4
Ivano-Frankovsk, 105,000 ... B 5
Ivanovo, 420,000 ... E 3
Izhevsk, 422,000 ... H 3
Izmail, 70,000 ... C 5
Izyum, 52,000 ... E 5
Jelgava, 55,300 ... B 3
Kadiyevka, 137,000 ... E 5
Kagul, 26,000 ... C 5
Kakhovka, 25,000 ... D 5
Kalach, 23,000 ... F 5
Kalinin, 345,000 ... E 3
Kaliningrad, 297,000 ... B 4
Kaliningrad, 105,900 ... E 3
Kalinkovichi, 22,000 ... C 4
Kaluga, 211,000 ... E 4
Kamenets-Podol'skiy, 57,000 ... C 5
Kamenka, 30,000 ... F 4
Kamensk-Shakhtinskiy, 68,000 ... F 5
Kamyshin, 97,000 ... F 4
Kanash, 45,000 ... G 3
Kandalaksha, 42,000 ... D 1
Kapsukas, 28,700 ... B 4
Kashin, 19,000 ... E 3
Kasimov, 37,000 ... F 4
Kaspiysk, 39,000 ... G 6
Kaunas, 306,200 ... B 4
Kazan', 869,000 ... G 3
Kazatin, 28,000 ... C 5
Kem', 21,000 ... D 2
Kerch', 128,000 ... E 5
Khachmas, 22,300 ... G 6
Khar'kov, 1,223,000 ... E 5
Khasavyurt, 54,000 ... G 6
Kherson, 261,000 ... D 5
Khmel'nitskiy, 113,000 ... C 5
Khorol, 13,000 ... D 5
Khvalynsk, 19,000 ... G 4
Kiev, 1,632,000 ... D 4
Kiliya, 26,000 ... C 5
Kimovsk, 44,000 ... E 4
Kimry, 53,000 ... E 3
Kinel', 38,000 ... H 4
Kineshma, 96,000 ... F 3
Kirov, 30,000 ... D 4
Kirov, 333,000 ... G 3
Kirovabad, 189,800 ... G 6
Kirovakan, 107,000 ... G 6
Kirovo-Chepetsk, 51,000 ... H 3
Kirovograd, 189,000 ... D 5
Kirovsk, 48,000 ... D 1
Kirsanov, 24,000 ... F 4
Kishinev, 356,900 ... C 5
Kislovodsk, 90,000 ... F 6
Kizel, 49,000 ... J 3
Kizlyar, 30,000 ... G 6
Klaipėda, 139,900 ... B 3
Klimovichi, 13,000 ... D 4
Klintsy, 58,000 ... D 4
Kobrin, 25,000 ... B 4
Kobuleti, 18,000 ... F 6
Kohtla-Järve, 68,318 ... C 3
Kolomna, 135,900 ... E 4
Kolpino, 70,000 ... D 3
Kommunarsk, 123,000 ... E 5
Komrat, 21,000 ... C 5
Kondopoga, 25,000 ... D 2
Königsberg (Kaliningrad), 297,000 ... B 4
Konotop, 68,000 ... D 4
Konstantinovka, 105,000 ... E 5
Korosten', 56,000 ... C 4
Kostroma, 223,000 ... F 3
Kotel'nich, 30,000 ... G 3
Kotel'nikovo, 21,000 ... F 5
Kotlas, 56,000 ... G 2
Kotovo, 20,000 ... G 4
Kotovsk, 38,000 ... C 5
Kotovsk, 32,000 ... F 4
Kovel', 35,000 ... C 4
Kovrov, 123,000 ... F 3
Kramatorsk, 150,000 ... E 5
Krasnoarmeysk, 21,000 ... G 4
Krasnodar, 464,000 ... E 6
Krasnograd, 18,000 ... E 5
Krasnokamsk, 55,000 ... H 3
Krasnovishersk, 16,000 ... J 2
Krasnyy Kut, 17,000 ... G 4
Krasnyy Luch, 103,000 ... E 5
Kremenchug, 148,000 ... D 5
Krichev, 26,000 ... D 4
Krivoy Rog, 573,000 ... D 5
Krolevets, 18,000 ... D 4
Kropotkin, 68,000 ... F 5
Krymsk, 44,000 ... E 6
Kuba, 18,900 ... G 6
Kudymkar, 20,000 ... H 3
Kulebaki, 48,000 ... F 4
Kumertau, 42,000 ... J 4
Kungur, 74,000 ... J 3
Kupyansk, 28,000 ... E 5
Kursk, 284,000 ... E 4
Kutaisi, 161,000 ... F 6
Kuvandyk, 24,000 ... J 4
Kuybyshev, 1,045,000 ... H 4
Kuznetsk, 84,000 ... G 4
Labinsk, 50,000 ... F 6
Lebedin, 29,000 ... D 4
Leninakan, 165,000 ... F 6
Leningrad, 3,513,000 ... C 3
Leningrad, *3,950,000 ... C 3
Leninogorsk, 45,000 ... H 4
Lenkoran', 35,500 ... G 7
L'gov, 28,000 ... E 4
Lida, 48,000 ... C 4
Liepāja, 92,800 ... B 3
Lipetsk, 289,000 ... E 4
Lisichansk, 118,000 ... E 5
Livny, 37,000 ... E 4
Lodeynoye Pole, 20,000 ... D 2
Lozovaya, 34,000 ... E 5
Lubny, 39,000 ... D 4
Luga, 30,000 ... C 3
Lutsk, 94,000 ... B 4
L'vov (Lwów), 553,000 ... B 5
Lys'va, 73,000 ... J 3
Lyubertsy, 139,400 ... E 3
Lyubotin, 38,000 ... E 4
Lyudinovo, 33,000 ... D 4
Makeyevka, 392,000 ... E 5
Makhachkala, 186,000 ... G 6
Makharadze, 24,000 ... F 6
Manturovo, 21,000 ... F 3
Marganets, 47,000 ... E 5
Mariupol' (Zhdanov), 417,000 ... E 5
Marks, 18,000 ... G 4
Maykop, 110,000 ... F 6
Mednogorsk, 41,000 ... J 4
Medvezh'yegorsk, 18,000 ... D 2
Melenki, 19,000 ... F 3
Meleuz, 28,000 ... J 4
Melitopol', 137,000 ... D 5
Memel (Klaipėda), 139,900 ... B 3
Merefa, 32,000 ... E 5
Michurinsk, 94,000 ... F 4
Mikhaylovka, 50,000 ... F 4
Millerovo, 38,000 ... F 5
Mineralnye Vody, 55,000 ... F 6
Mingechaur, 43,100 ... G 6
Minsk, 907,000 ... C 4
Minsk, *917,000 ... C 4
Mirgorod, 28,000 ... D 5
Mogilev, 202,000 ... C 4
Mogilev-Podol'skiy, 27,000 ... C 5
Molodechno, 50,000 ... C 4
Molotov (Perm'), 850,000 ... J 3
Monchegorsk, 49,000 ... D 1
Morshansk, 45,000 ... F 4
Moscow (Moskva) (cap.), 6,942,000 ... E 3
Moscow, *7,061,000 ... E 3
Mozhaysk, 20,300 ... E 3
Mozhga, 34,000 ... H 3
Mozyr', 49,000 ... C 4
Mtsensk, 24,000 ... E 4
Mukachevo, 57,000 ... B 5
Murmansk, 309,000 ... D 1
Murom, 99,000 ... F 3
Mytishchi, 118,700 ... E 3
Naberezhnye Chelny, 38,000 ... H 3
Nakhichevan', 33,200 ... F 7
Nal'chik, 146,000 ... F 6
Narva, 57,863 ... C 3
Nar'yan-Mar, 15,000 ... H 1
Neftekamsk, 35,000 ... J 3
Nelidovo, 30,000 ... D 3
Nerekhta, 28,000 ... F 3
Nevinnomyssk, 85,000 ... F 6
Nezhin, 56,000 ... D 4
Nikel', 17,000 ... C 1
Nikolayev, 331,000 ... D 5
Nikopol', 125,000 ... D 5
Nizhnekamsk, 49,000 ... H 3
Nizhniy Lomov, 19,000 ... F 4
Nosovka, 23,000 ... D 4
Novaya Kakhovka, 40,000 ... D 5
Novgorod, 128,000 ... D 3
Novoanninskiy, 21,000 ... F 4
Novocherkassk, 162,000 ... F 5
Novograd-Volynskiy, 36,000 ... C 4
Novogrudok, 20,000 ... C 4
Novokuybyshevsk, 104,000 ... G 4
Novomoskovsk, 134,000 ... E 4
Novopolotsk, 40,000 ... C 3
Novorossiysk, 133,000 ... E 6
Novoshakhtinsk, 102,000 ... E 5
Novotroitsk, 83,000 ... J 4
Novoukrainka, 22,000 ... D 5
Novovolynsk, 40,000 ... B 4
Novozybkov, 33,000 ... D 4
Nyandoma, 24,000 ... F 2
Obninsk, 49,000 ... E 3
Ochamchire, 20,000 ... F 6
Odessa, 892,000 ... D 5
Oktyabr'sk, 36,000 ... G 4
Oktyabr'skiy, 77,000 ... H 4
Olenegorsk, 21,000 ... D 1
Omutninsk, 29,000 ... H 3
Onega, 27,000 ... E 2
Ordzhonikidze, 236,000 ... F 6
Orel, 232,000 ... E 4
Orenburg, 344,000 ... J 4
Orgeyev, 25,900 ... C 5
Orsha, 101,000 ... C 4
Orsk, 225,000 ... J 4
Osipenko (Berdyansk), 100,000 ... E 5
Osipovichi, 19,000 ... C 4
Ostashkov, 22,000 ... D 3
Ostrogozhsk, 35,000 ... E 4
Ostrov, 19,000 ... C 3
Otradnyy, 46,000 ... H 4
Panevėžys, 73,500 ... B 3
Pärnu, 46,316 ... C 3
Pavlovo, 63,000 ... F 3
Pechora, 41,000 ... J 1
Penza, 374,000 ... F 4
Perm', 850,000 ... J 3
Pervomaysk, 59,000 ... D 5
Pervomayskiy, 18,000 ... F 4
Petrovsk, 32,000 ... G 4
Petrozavodsk, 184,000 ... E 2
Pinsk, 62,000 ... C 4
Piryatin, 18,000 ... D 4
Pochep, 16,000 ... D 4
Podol'sk, 168,700 ... E 3
Polonnoye, 23,000 ... C 4
Polotsk, 64,000 ... C 3
Poltava, 220,000 ... D 5
Postavy, 13,000 ... C 3
Poti, 48,000 ... F 6
Povorino, 22,000 ... F 4
Prikumsk, 36,000 ... F 6
Priluki, 57,000 ... D 4
Primorsko-Akhtarsk, 30,000 ... E 5
Priyutovo, 20,000 ... H 4
Promyshlennyy, 22,000 ... K 1
Pskov, 127,000 ... C 3
Pugachev, 38,000 ... G 4
Pushkin, 79,000 ... C 3
Pyatigorsk, 93,000 ... F 6
Pyatikhatki, 20,000 ... D 5
Radomyshl', 12,000 ... C 4
Rakhov, 11,000 ... B 5
Rakvere, 17,891 ... C 3
Rasskazovo, 40,000 ... F 4
Rechitsa, 48,000 ... C 4
Revel (Tallinn), 362,706 ... B 3
Rēzekne, 30,800 ... C 3
Riga, 731,800 ... B 3
Rogachev, 12,000 ... D 4
Romny, 48,000 ... D 4
Roslavl', 48,000 ... D 4
Rossosh', 36,000 ... E 4
Rostov, 32,000 ... E 3
Rostov, 789,000 ... E 5
Rovno, 116,000 ... C 4
Rtishchevo, 40,000 ... F 4
Rubezhnoye, 58,000 ... E 5
Rustavi, 98,000 ... G 6
Ruzayevka, 38,000 ... G 4
Ryazan', 350,000 ... E 4
Rybinsk, 218,000 ... E 3
Rybnitsa, 32,400 ... C 5
Rzhev, 61,000 ... D 3
Safonovo, 44,000 ... D 3
Saki, 23,000 ... D 5
Salavat, 114,000 ... H 4
Sal'sk, 50,000 ... F 5
Sal'yany, 20,200 ... G 7
Samara (Kuybyshev), 1,045,000 ... H 4
Saransk, 191,000 ... G 4
Sarapul, 97,000 ... H 3
Saratov, 757,000 ... G 4
Sarny, 10,000 ... C 4
Sasovo, 28,000 ... F 4
Segezha, 30,000 ... D 2
Semenov, 25,000 ... F 3
Serdobel (Sortavala), 23,000 ... D 2
Serdobsk, 33,000 ... F 4
Serpukhov, 124,300 ... E 4
Sevastopol', 229,000 ... D 6
Severodonetsk, 90,000 ... E 5
Severodvinsk, 145,000 ... E 2
Severomorsk, 45,000 ... D 1
Shakhty, 205,000 ... F 5
Shakhun'ya, 22,000 ... G 3
Shar'ya, 25,000 ... G 3
Shchekino, 61,000 ... E 4
Shcherbakov (Rybinsk), 218,000 ... E 3
Sheki, 43,200 ... G 6
Shemakha, 17,900 ... G 6
Shepetovka, 39,000 ... C 4
Shostka, 64,000 ... D 4
Shumerlya, 33,000 ... G 3
Shuya, 69,000 ... F 3
Šiauliai, 92,800 ... B 3
Sibay, 42,000 ... J 4
Simferopol', 249,000 ... D 6
Skopin, 23,000 ... F 4
Slantsy, 40,000 ... C 3
Slavuta, 24,000 ... C 4
Slavyansk, 124,000 ... E 5
Slavyansk-na-Kubani, 52,000 ... E 5
Slobodskoy, 37,000 ... H 3
Slonim, 30,000 ... B 4
Slutsk, 36,000 ... C 4
Smela, 55,000 ... D 5
Smolensk, 211,000 ... D 4
Sochi, 224,000 ... E 6
Sokol, 49,000 ... F 3
Solikamsk, 89,000 ... J 3
Sol'-Iletsk, 25,000 ... J 4
Sorochinsk, 25,000 ... H 4
Soroki, 21,700 ... C 5
Sortavala, 23,000 ... D 2
Sosnogorsk, 25,000 ... H 2
Sovetsk, 38,000 ... B 4
Sovetsk, 19,000 ... G 3
Stalingrad (Volgograd), 818,000 ... F 5
Staraya Russa, 34,000 ... D 3
Staryy Oskol, 52,000 ... E 4
Stavropol', 198,000 ... F 5
Stepanakert, 30,300 ... G 7
Stepnoy (Elista), 50,000 ... G 5
Sterlitamak, 185,000 ... J 4
Stupino, 59,300 ... E 4
Sukhumi, 102,000 ... F 6
Sumgait, 124,400 ... G 6
Sumy, 159,000 ... E 4
Svetlogorsk, 40,000 ... C 4
Svetlograd, 30,000 ... F 5
Syktyvkar, 125,000 ... H 2
Syzran', 173,000 ... G 4
Taganrog, 254,000 ... E 5
Tallinn, 362,706 ... B 3
Tambov, 230,000 ... F 4
Tartu, 90,459 ... C 3
Tauragė, 19,500 ... B 3
Tbilisi, 889,000 ... F 6
Telavi, 23,000 ... G 6
Telšiai, 20,200 ... B 3
Temryuk, 28,000 ... E 5
Ternopol', 85,000 ... C 5
Teykovo, 34,000 ... F 3
Tiflis (Tbilisi), 889,000 ... F 6
Tighina (Bendery), 72,300 ... C 5
Tikhoretsk, 60,000 ... F 5
Tikhvin, 29,000 ... D 3
Timashevsk, 35,000 ... E 5
Tiraspol', 105,700 ... C 5
Togliatti, 251,000 ... G 4
Tokmak, 39,000 ... E 5
Torzhok, 47,000 ... D 3
Tskhinvali, 30,000 ... F 6
Tuapse, 51,000 ... E 6
Tula, 462,000 ... E 4
Tul'chin, 14,000 ... C 5
Tuymazy, 35,000 ... H 4
Tyrnyauz, 19,000 ... F 6
Uchaly, 18,000 ... J 4
Ufa, 771,000 ... J 4
Uglich, 36,000 ... E 3
Ukhta, 63,000 ... H 2
Ukmergė, 21,600 ... C 3
Ul'yanovsk, 351,000 ... G 4
Uman', 63,000 ... D 5
Uryupinsk, 37,000 ... F 4
Usman', 19,000 ... E 4
Uzhgorod, 65,000 ... B 5
Uzlovaya, 62,000 ... E 4
Valga, 16,795 ... C 3
Valmiera, 20,300 ... C 3
Valuyki, 29,000 ... E 4
Vasil'kov, 27,000 ... D 4
Velikiye Luki, 85,000 ... D 3
Velikiy Ustyug, 35,000 ... F 2
Vel'sk, 20,000 ... F 2
Ventspils, 40,500 ... B 3
Vichuga, 53,000 ... F 3
Viipuri (Vyborg), 65,000 ... C 2
Vilna (Vilnius), 371,700 ... C 4
Vinnitsa, 212,000 ... C 5
Vitebsk, 231,000 ... C 3
Vladimir, 234,000 ... F 3
Volgodonsk, 25,000 ... F 5
Volgograd, 818,000 ... F 5
Volkhov, 46,000 ... D 3
Volkovysk, 22,000 ... B 4
Vologda, 178,000 ... F 3
Vol'sk, 69,000 ... G 4
Volzhsk, 44,000 ... G 3
Volzhskiy, 142,000 ... G 5
Vorkuta, 90,000 ... K 1
Voronezh, 660,000 ... E 4
Voroshilovgrad, 383,000 ... F 5
Voskresensk, 66,900 ... E 3
Votkinsk, 74,000 ... H 3
Voznesensk, 36,000 ... D 5
Vyatskiye Polyany, 33,000 ... H 3
Vyaz'ma, 42,000 ... D 3
Vyborg, 65,000 ... C 2
Vyksa, 46,000 ... F 3
Vyshniy Volochek, 74,000 ... D 3
Yalta, 62,000 ... D 6
Yanaul, 18,000 ... J 3
Yaroslavl', 517,000 ... E 3
Yartsevo, 37,000 ... D 3
Yefremov, 47,000 ... E 4
Yelabuga, 36,000 ... H 3
Yelets, 101,000 ... E 4
Yenakiyevo, 92,000 ... E 5
Yershov, 20,000 ... G 4
Yessentuki, 65,000 ... F 6
Yevpatoria, 79,000 ... D 5
Yeysk, 64,000 ... E 5
Yoshkar-Ola, 166,000 ... G 3
Yur'yevets, 23,000 ... F 3
Zagorsk, 92,400 ... E 3
Zaporozh'ye, 658,000 ... E 5
Zelenodol'sk, 77,000 ... G 3
Zhdanov, 417,000 ... E 5
Zherdevka, 20,000 ... F 4
Zhigulevsk, 52,000 ... G 4
Zhitomir, 161,000 ... C 4
Zhlobin, 25,000 ... D 4
Zhmerinka, 34,000 ... C 5
Zhodino, 17,000 ... C 4
Znamenka, 30,000 ... D 5
Zolotonosha, 27,000 ... D 5
Zugdidi, 39,000 ... F 6
Zvenigorodka, 21,000 ... D 5

OTHER FEATURES

Apsheron (pen.) ... H 6
Araks (river) ... G 7
Azov (sea) ... E 5
Baltic (sea) ... B 3
Barents (sea) ... H 1
Belaya (river) ... H 3
Beloye (lake) ... E 2
Berezina (river) ... C 4
Black (sea) ... D 6
Bug (river) ... B 4
Bug (river) ... D 5
Caspian (sea) ... G 6
Caucasus (mts.) ... F 6
Central Ural (mts.) ... J 3
Chir (river) ... F 5
Crimea (pen.), 1,813,000 ... D 5
Dagö (Hiiumaa) (isl.) ... B 3
Denezhkin Kamen' (mt.) ... K 2
Desna (river) ... D 4
Dnieper (river) ... D 5
Dniester (river) ... C 5
Don (river) ... F 5
Donets (river) ... E 5
Dvina (bay) ... E 2
Dvina, Northern (river) ... F 2
Dvina, Western (river) ... C 3
Dykh-Tau (mt.) ... F 6
El'brus (mt.) ... F 6
Finland (gulf) ... C 3
Goryn' (river) ... C 4
Hiiumaa (isl.) ... B 3
Ilek (river) ... J 4
Il'men (lake) ... D 3
Izhma (river) ... H 2
Kakhovka (res.) ... D 5
Kama (river) ... H 3
Kandalaksha (gulf) ... D 1
Kanin (pen.) ... G 1
Kapydzhik (mt.) ... G 7
Kara (sea) ... K 1
Kazbek (mt.) ... F 6
Khoper (river) ... F 4
Kil'din (isl.) ... D 1
Kinel' (river) ... H 4
Kola (pen.) ... E 1
Kolguyev (isl.) ... G 1
Kolva (river) ... J 1
Kuban' (river) ... E 5
Kubeno (lake) ... E 3
Kura (river) ... G 6
Kuyto (lake) ... D 2
Ladoga (lake) ... D 2
Lapland (reg.) ... C 1
Lovat' (river) ... D 3
Mansel'ka (mts.) ... D 2
Manych-Gudilo (lake) ... F 5
Matveyev (isl.) ... J 1
Medveditsa (river) ... F 4
Mezen' (river) ... G 1
Mezhdusharskiy (isl.) ... G 1
Moksha (river) ... F 4
Moskva (river) ... E 3
Msta (river) ... D 3
Niemen (river) ... B 4
North Ural (mts.) ... K 1
Northern Dvina (river) ... F 2
Novaya Zemlya (isls.) ... H 1
Oka (river) ... F 4
Onega (bay) ... E 2
Onega (lake) ... E 2
Ösel (Saaremaa) (isl.) ... B 3
Pay-Yer (mt.) ... K 1
Pechora (river) ... H 1
Pechora (sea) ... H 1
Peipus (lake) ... C 3
Pinega (river) ... G 2
Ponoy (river) ... E 1
Pripet (marsh) ... C 4
Pripyat' (river) ... C 4
Prut (river) ... C 5
Psel (river) ... D 4
Riga (gulf) ... B 3
Russkiy Zavorot (cape) ... H 1
Rybachiy (pen.) ... D 1
Saaremaa (isl.) ... B 3
Samara (river) ... H 4
Seg (lake) ... D 2
Sevan (lake) ... G 6
Seym (river) ... D 4
Solovetskiye (isls.) ... E 1
South Ural (mts.) ... J 4
Suda (river) ... E 3
Sukhona (river) ... F 2
Sura (river) ... G 4
Svir' (river) ... D 2
Sysola (river) ... H 2
Tel'pos-Iz (mt.) ... K 2
Timan Ridge (mts.) ... H 1
Top (lake) ... D 1
Tuloma (river) ... D 1
Ufa (river) ... J 3
Undzha (river) ... F 3
Ural (mts.) ... J 2
Ural (river) ... J 4
Usa (river) ... K 1
Vaga (river) ... F 2
Valday (hills) ... D 3
Vaygach (isl.) ... K 1
Velikaya (river) ... C 3
Vetluga (river) ... G 3
Vodl (lake) ... E 2
Volga (river) ... E 3
Volga-Don (canal) ... F 5
Volkhov (river) ... D 3
Vorona (river) ... F 4
Vorskla (river) ... E 4
Vozhe (lake) ... F 2
Vyatka (river) ... H 3
Vychegda (river) ... G 2
Vyg (lake) ... E 2
Vym' (river) ... H 2
Western Dvina (river) ... C 3
White (sea) ... E 1
Yamantau (mt.) ... J 4
Yug (river) ... G 2
Yugorskiy (pen.) ... K 1

*City and suburbs.

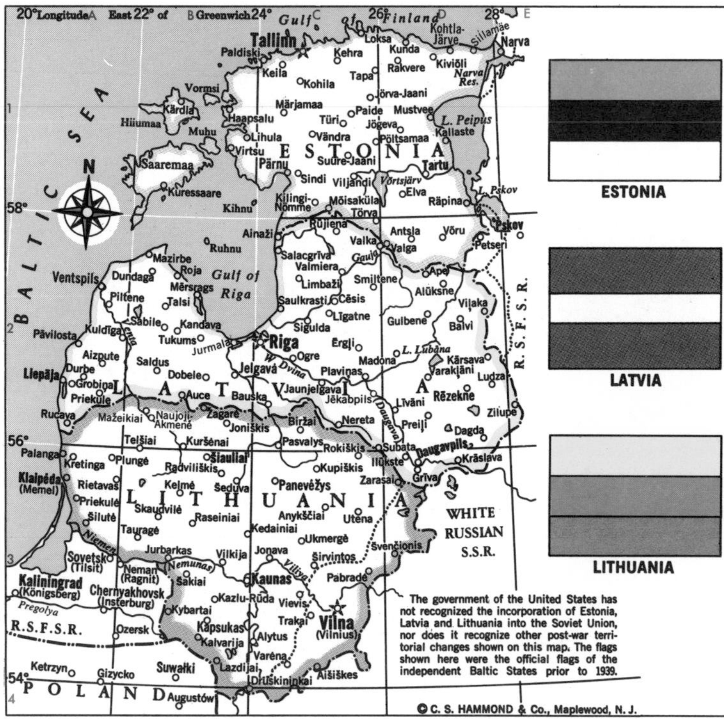
ESTONIA
LATVIA
LITHUANIA
BALTIC SEA
Gulf of Riga
WHITE RUSSIAN S.S.R.
R.S.F.S.R.
POLAND
The government of the United States has not recognized the incorporation of Estonia, Latvia and Lithuania into the Soviet Union, nor does it recognize other post-war territorial changes shown on this map. The flags shown here were the official flags of the independent Baltic States prior to 1939.
© C. S. HAMMOND & Co., Maplewood, N. J.

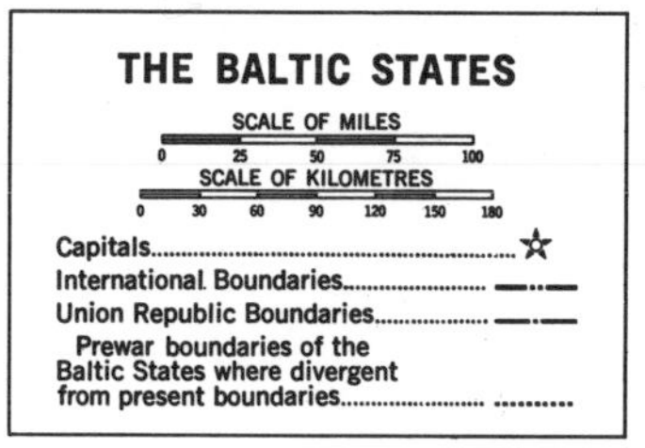
THE BALTIC STATES
SCALE OF MILES
SCALE OF KILOMETRES
Capitals
International Boundaries
Union Republic Boundaries
Prewar boundaries of the Baltic States where divergent from present boundaries

THE BALTIC STATES

Alytus, 27,900 ... C 3
Biržai, 11,400 ... C 2
Cēsis, 17,700 ... C 2
Daugava (Western Dvina) (riv.) ... C 2
Daugavpils, 100,400 ... D 3
Dobele, 10,100 ... B 2
Druskininkai, 11,200 ... C 3
Dvina, Western (river) ... C 2
Finland (gulf) ... D 1
Gauja (riv.) ... C 2
Haapsalu, 11,483 ... B 1
Hiiumaa (isl.) ... B 1
Jēkabpils, 22,400 ... C 2
Jelgava, 55,300 ... B 2
Jonava, 14,400 ... C 3
Jurmala, 53,800 ... B 2
Kapsukas, 28,700 ... B 3
Kaunas (cap.), Lithuania, 306,200 ... C 3
Kedainiai, 19,700 ... C 3
Kihnu (isl.) ... B 1
Kingisepp (Kuressaare), 12,140 ... B 1
Kiviõli, 11,153 ... D 1
Klaipėda, 139,900 ... A 3
Kohtla-Järve, 68,318 ... D 1
Kretinga, 13,000 ... A 3
Kuldīga, 12,300 ... A 2
Kuressaare, 12,140 ... B 1
Kuršėnai, 11,500 ... B 2
Liepāja, 92,800 ... A 2
Lubāna (lake) ... D 2
Mažeikiai, 13,400 ... A 2
Memel (Klaipėda), 139,900 ... A 3
Muhu (isl.) ... B 1
Narva, 57,863 ... E 1
Naujoji-Akmene, 10,200 ... B 2
Niemen (Nemunas) (riv.) ... A 3
Ogre, 15,700 ... C 2
Panevėžys, 73,500 ... C 3
Pärnu, 46,316 ... C 1
Peipus (lake) ... D 1
Plungė, 13,600 ... B 3
Radviliškis, 16,900 ... B 3
Rakvere, 17,891 ... D 1
Rēzekne, 30,800 ... D 2
Riga (cap.), Latvia, 731,800 ... C 2
Riga (gulf) ... B 2
Saaremaa (isl.) ... B 1
Saldus, 10,000 ... B 2
Šiauliai, 92,800 ... B 3
Sillamäe, 13,505 ... D 1
Silutė, 12,400 ... A 3
Tallinn (cap.), Estonia, 362,706 ... C 1
Tapa, 10,037 ... C 1
Tartu, 90,459 ... D 1
Tauragė, 19,500 ... B 3
Telšiai, 20,200 ... B 2
Tukums, 14,800 ... B 2
Ukmergė, 21,600 ... C 3
Utena, 13,300 ... C 3
Valga, 16,795 ... C 2
Valmiera, 20,300 ... C 2
Venta (riv.) ... B 2
Ventspils, 40,500 ... A 2
Viliya (riv.) ... C 3
Viljandi, 20,814 ... C 1
Vilna (Vilnius), 371,700 ... C 3
Vormsi (isl.) ... B 1
Võrtsjärv (lake) ... D 1
Voru, 15,398 ... D 1
Western Dvina (riv.) ... C 2

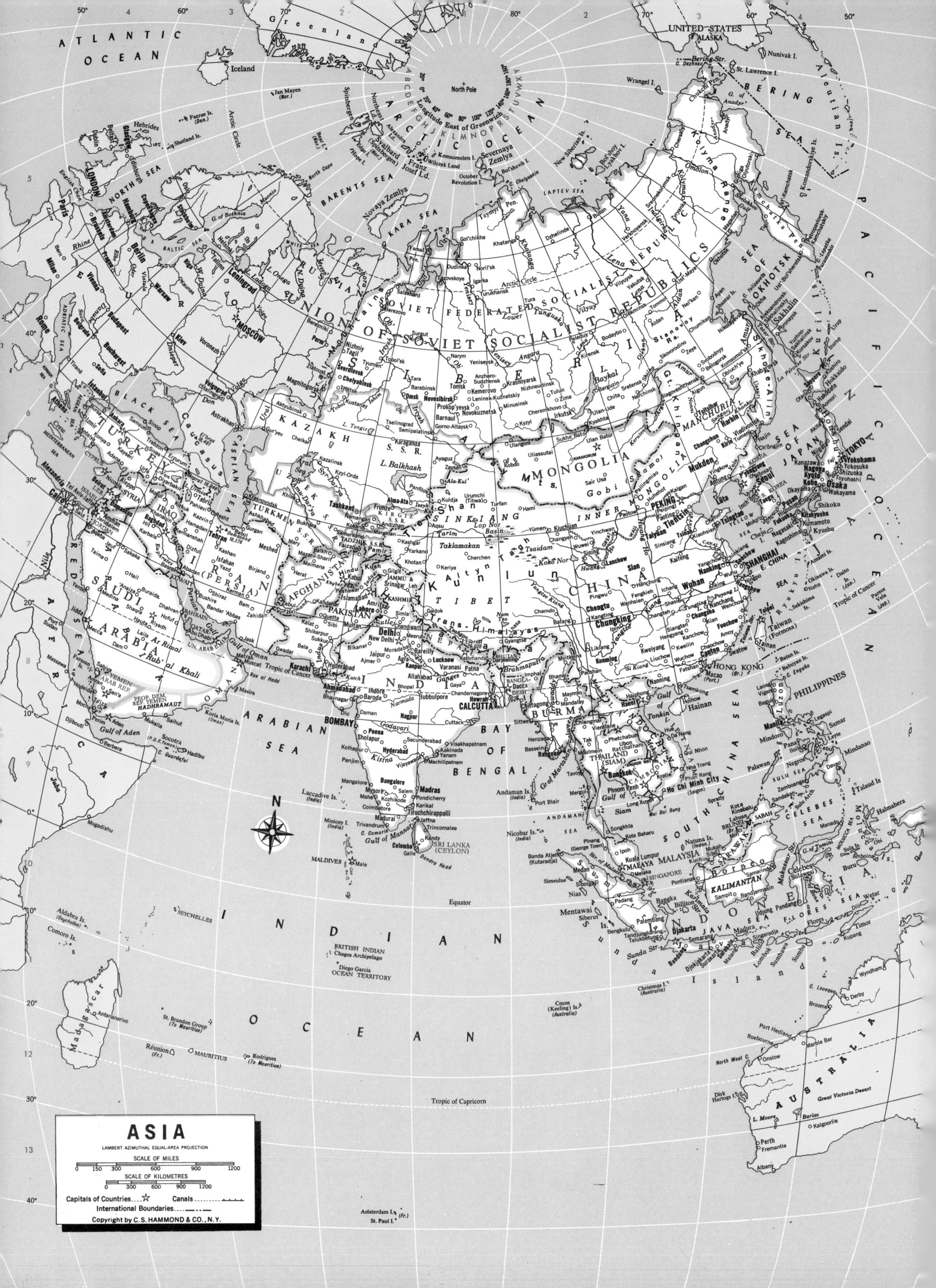

ASIA

LAMBERT AZIMUTHAL EQUAL-AREA PROJECTION

SCALE OF MILES

0   150   300   600   900   1200

SCALE OF KILOMETRES

0   300   600   900   1200

Capitals of Countries.... ☆   Canals........

International Boundaries........

Copyright by C.S. HAMMOND & CO., N.Y.

POPULATION DISTRIBUTION

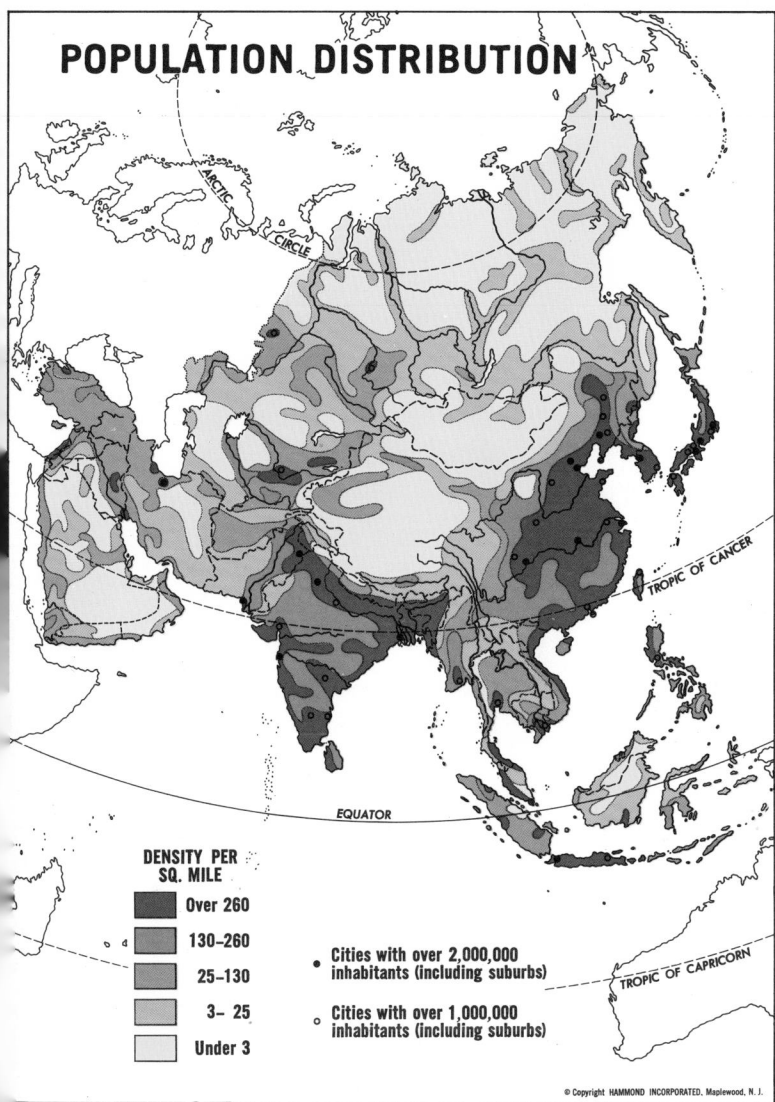

AREA 17,128,500 sq. mi.
POPULATION 2,535,333,000
LARGEST CITY Tokyo
HIGHEST POINT Mt. Everest 29,028 ft.
LOWEST POINT Dead Sea -1,296 ft.

DENSITY PER SQ. MILE
- Over 260
- 130–260
- 25–130
- 3–25
- Under 3

• Cities with over 2,000,000 inhabitants (including suburbs)
○ Cities with over 1,000,000 inhabitants (including suburbs)

© Copyright HAMMOND INCORPORATED, Maplewood, N.J.

VEGETATION

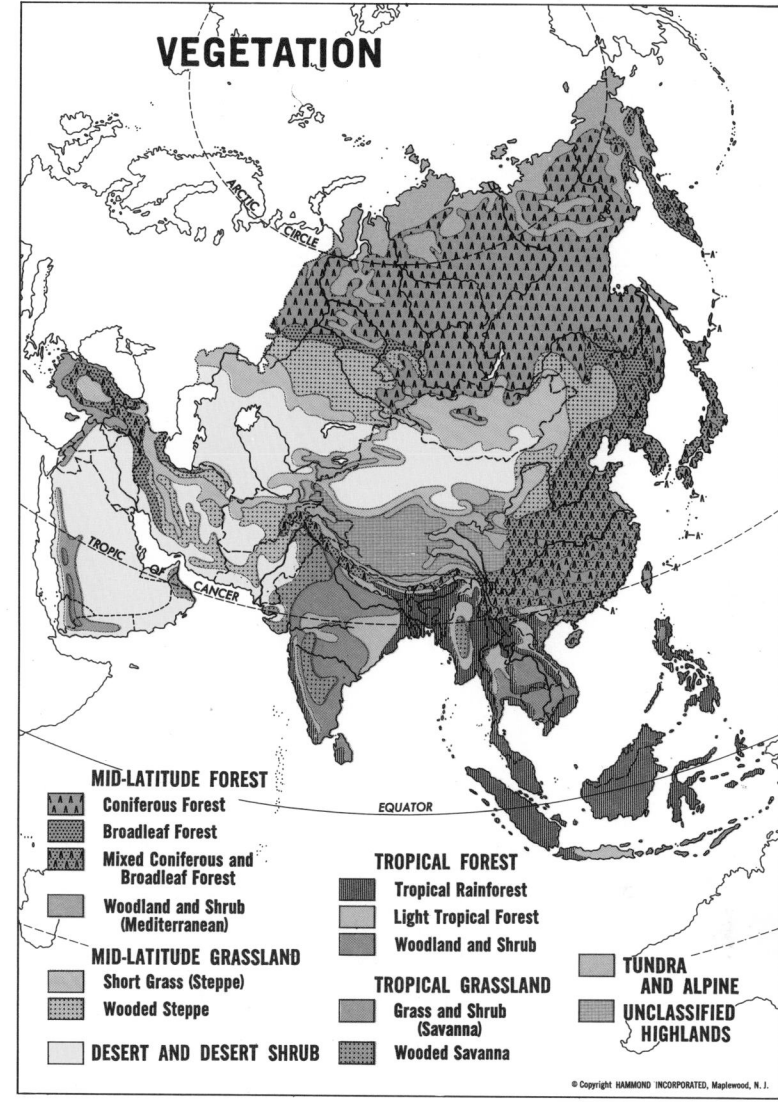

MID-LATITUDE FOREST
- Coniferous Forest
- Broadleaf Forest
- Mixed Coniferous and Broadleaf Forest
- Woodland and Shrub (Mediterranean)

MID-LATITUDE GRASSLAND
- Short Grass (Steppe)
- Wooded Steppe

DESERT AND DESERT SHRUB

TROPICAL FOREST
- Tropical Rainforest
- Light Tropical Forest
- Woodland and Shrub

TROPICAL GRASSLAND
- Grass and Shrub (Savanna)
- Wooded Savanna

TUNDRA AND ALPINE

UNCLASSIFIED HIGHLANDS

© Copyright HAMMOND INCORPORATED, Maplewood, N.J.

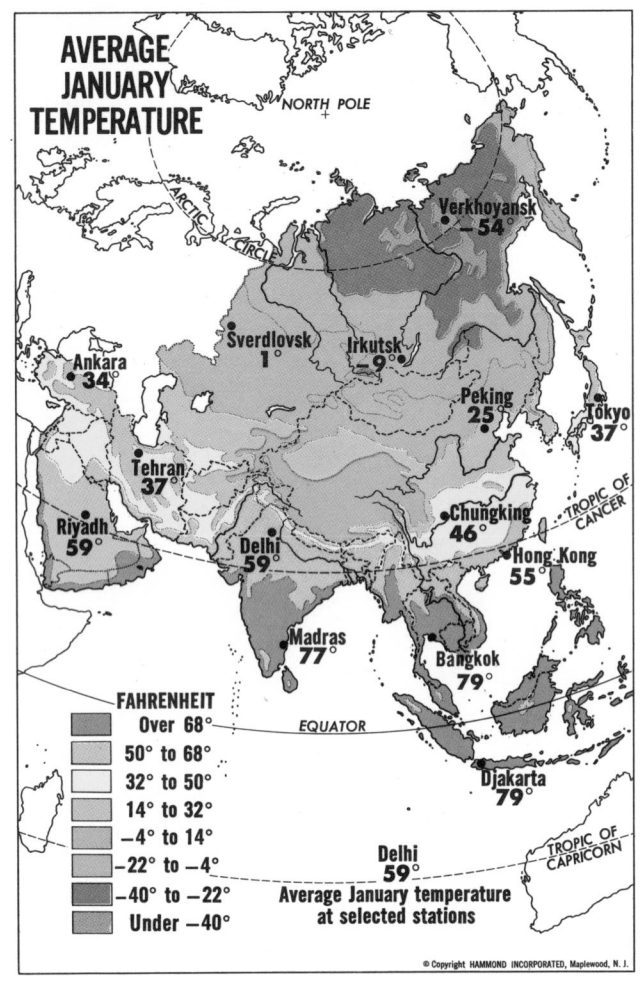

AVERAGE JANUARY TEMPERATURE

NORTH POLE

Verkhoyansk −54°

Sverdlovsk 1°   Irkutsk −9°

Ankara 34°

Peking 25°   Tokyo 37°

Tehran 37°

Riyadh 59°   Delhi 59°   Chungking 46°   Hong Kong 55°

Madras 77°   Bangkok 79°

EQUATOR

Djakarta 79°

TROPIC OF CANCER

TROPIC OF CAPRICORN

FAHRENHEIT
- Over 68°
- 50° to 68°
- 32° to 50°
- 14° to 32°
- −4° to 14°
- −22° to −4°
- −40° to −22°
- Under −40°

Delhi 59°
Average January temperature at selected stations

© Copyright HAMMOND INCORPORATED, Maplewood, N. J.

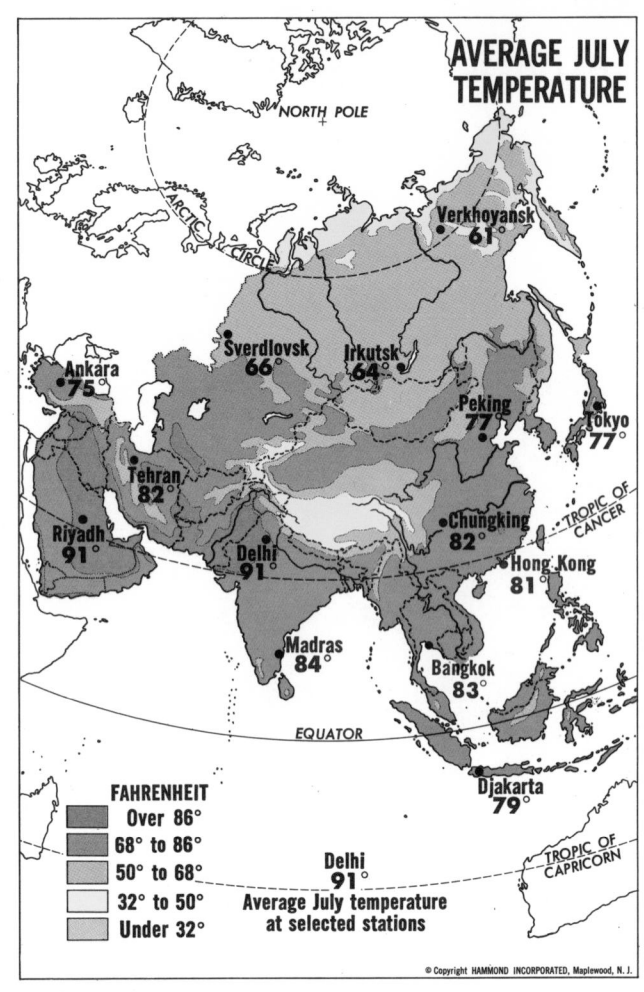

AVERAGE JULY TEMPERATURE

NORTH POLE

Verkhoyansk 61°

Sverdlovsk 66°   Irkutsk 64°

Ankara 75°

Peking 77°   Tokyo 77°

Tehran 82°

Riyadh 91°   Delhi 91°   Chungking 82°   Hong Kong 81°

Madras 84°   Bangkok 83°

EQUATOR

Djakarta 79°

TROPIC OF CANCER

TROPIC OF CAPRICORN

FAHRENHEIT
- Over 86°
- 68° to 86°
- 50° to 68°
- 32° to 50°
- Under 32°

Delhi 91°
Average July temperature at selected stations

© Copyright HAMMOND INCORPORATED, Maplewood, N. J.

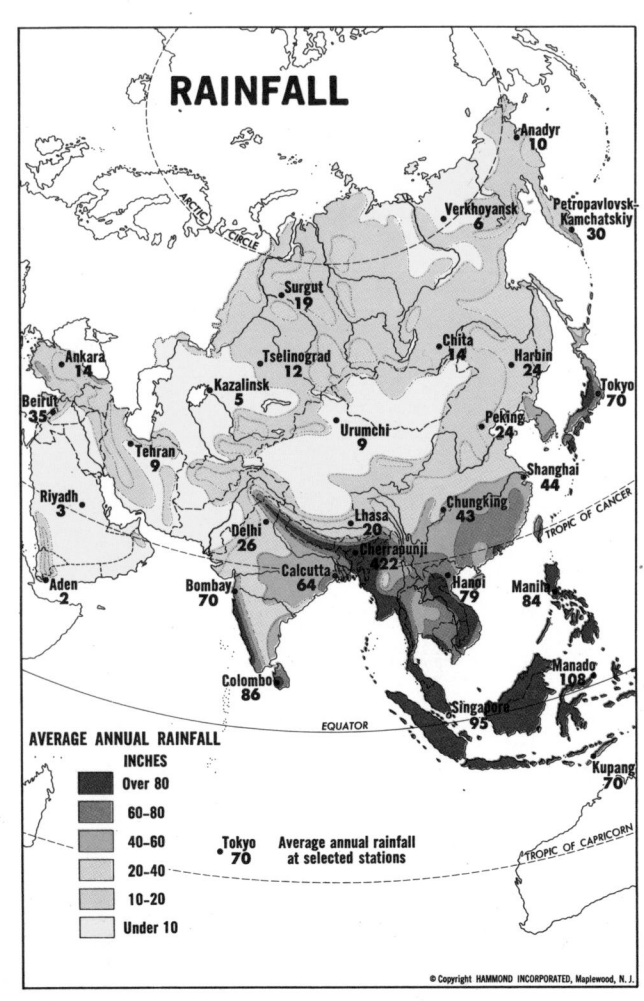

RAINFALL

Anadyr 10

Verkhoyansk 6   Petropavlovsk-Kamchatskiy 30

Surgut 19

Ankara 14   Chita 14   Harbin 24

Beirut 35   Tselinograd 12   Kazalinsk 5   Tokyo 70

Peking 24

Tehran 9   Urumchi 9   Shanghai 44

Riyadh 3   Lhasa 20   Chungking 43

Delhi 26   Cherrapunji 422   Hanoi 79   Manila 84

Bombay 70   Calcutta 64

Aden 2

Colombo 86   Manado 108

EQUATOR   Singapore 95

Kupang 70

TROPIC OF CANCER

TROPIC OF CAPRICORN

AVERAGE ANNUAL RAINFALL
INCHES
- Over 80
- 60–80
- 40–60
- 20–40
- 10–20
- Under 10

Tokyo 70   Average annual rainfall at selected stations

© Copyright HAMMOND INCORPORATED, Maplewood, N. J.

VEGETATION/RELIEF

SCALE OF MILES
0 150 300   600   900   1200   1500

SCALE OF KILOMETERS
0 150 300   600   900   1200   1500

Capitals of Countries.........................⊛
International Boundaries.....................
Canals...

Elevations in Feet   Depths in Fathoms

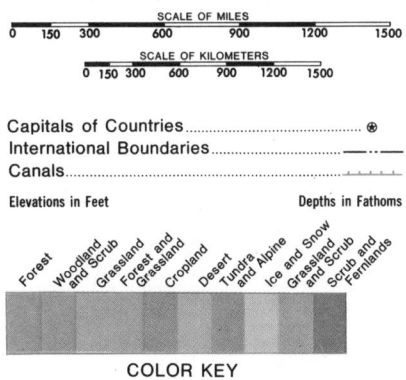

Forest · Woodland and Scrub · Grassland · Forest and Grassland · Cropland · Desert · Tundra and Alpine · Ice and Snow · Grassland and Scrub · Scrub and Fernlands

COLOR KEY

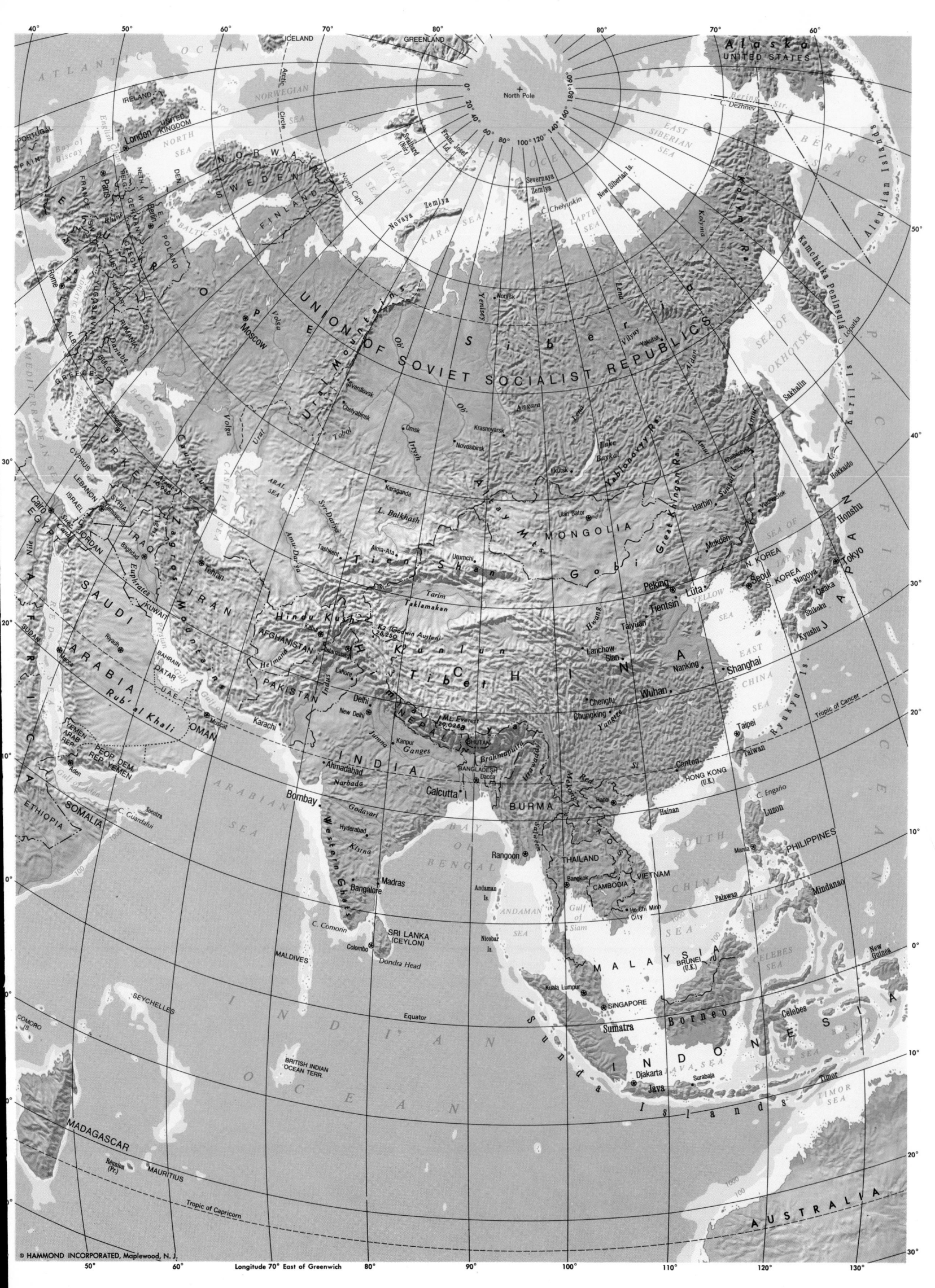

58 Near and Middle East

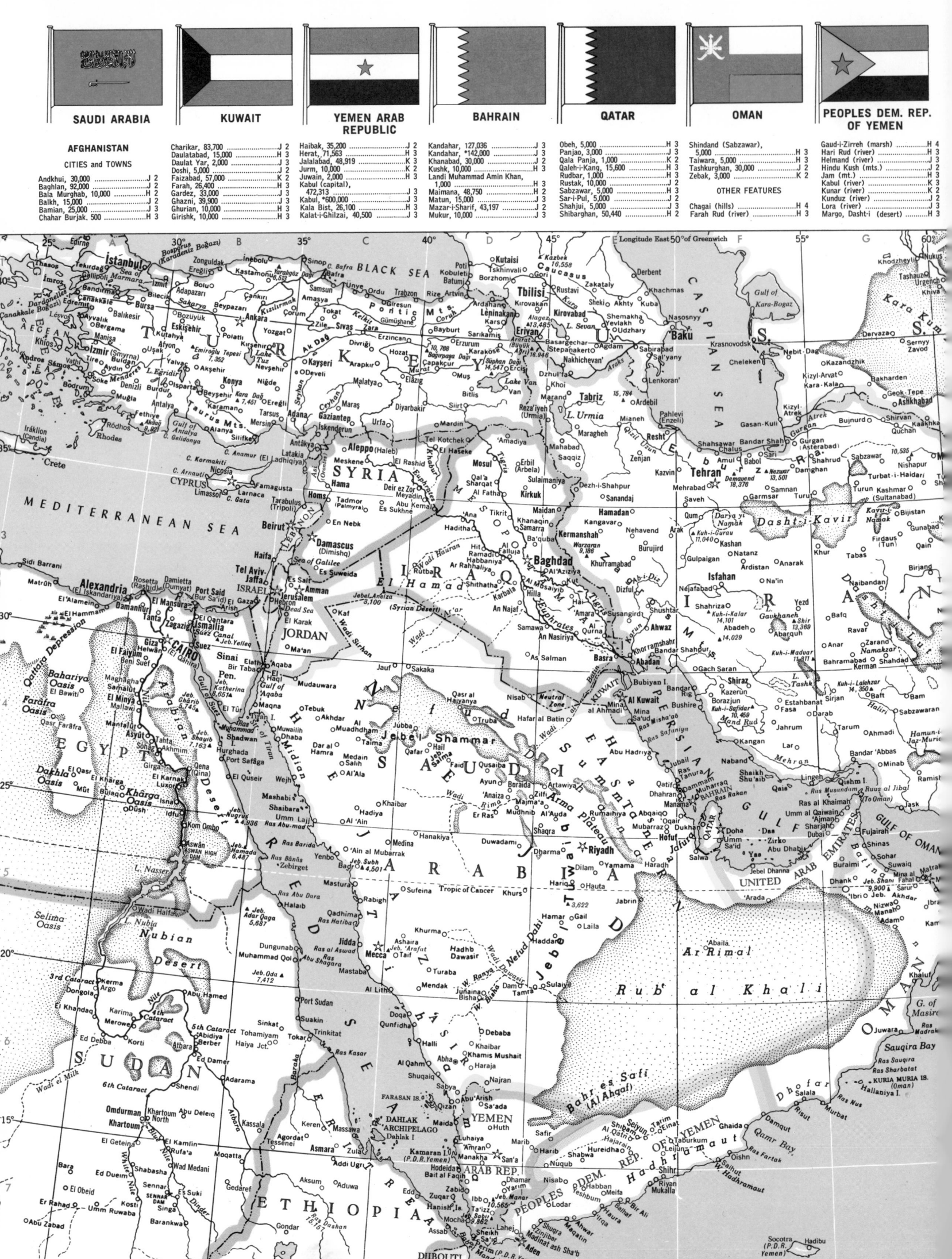

SAUDI ARABIA   **KUWAIT**   **YEMEN ARAB REPUBLIC**   **BAHRAIN**   **QATAR**   **OMAN**   **PEOPLES DEM. REP. OF YEMEN**

AFGHANISTAN

CITIES and TOWNS

Andkhui, 30,000	J 2	Charikar, 83,700	J 2
Baghlan, 92,000	J 2	Daulatabad, 15,000	H 3
Bala Murghab, 10,000	H 2	Daulat Yar, 2,000	H 3
Balkh, 15,000	J 2	Doshi, 5,000	J 2
Bamian, 25,000	J 3	Faizabad, 57,000	K 2
Chahar Burjak, 500	H 3	Farah, 26,400	H 3

Gardez, 33,000	J 3
Ghazni, 39,900	J 3
Ghurian, 10,000	H 3
Girishk, 10,000	H 3

Haibak, 35,200	J 2
Herat, 71,563	H 3
Jalalabad, 48,919	K 3
Jurm, 10,000	K 2
Juwain, 2,000	H 3
Kabul (capital), 472,313	J 3
Kabul, *600,000	J 3
Kala Bist, 26,100	H 3
Kalat-i-Ghilzai, 40,500	J 3

Kandahar, 127,036	J 3
Kandahar, *142,000	J 3
Khanabad, 30,000	J 2
Kushk, 10,000	H 2
Landi Muhammad Amin Khan, 1,000	K 3
Maimana, 48,750	H 2
Matun, *600,000	J 3
Mazar-i-Sharif, 43,197	J 2
Mukur, 10,000	J 3

Obeh, 5,000	H 3
Panjao, 3,000	J 3
Qala Panja, 1,000	K 2
Qaleh-i-Kang, 15,600	H 3
Rudbar, 1,000	H 3
Rustak, 10,000	J 2
Sabzawar, 5,000	H 3
Sar-i-Pul, 5,000	J 2
Shahjui, 5,000	J 3
Shibarghan, 50,440	H 2

Shindand (Sabzawar), 5,000	H 3
Taiwara, 5,000	H 3
Tashkurghan, 30,000	J 2
Zebak, 3,000	K 2

OTHER FEATURES

Chagai (hills)	H 4
Farah Rud (river)	H 3

Gaud-i-Zirreh (marsh)	H 4
Hari Rud (river)	H 3
Helmand (river)	H 3
Hindu Kush (mts.)	J 2
Jam (mt.)	H 3
Kabul (river)	K 3
Kunar (river)	K 2
Kunduz (river)	J 2
Lora (river)	J 3
Margo, Dasht-i (desert)	H 3

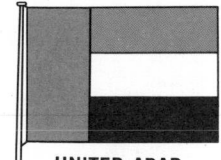

UNITED ARAB EMIRATES

Murghab (river) ....H 2
Namaksar (salt lake) ....H 3
Paropamisus (range) ....H 3
Pyandzh (river) ....K 2
Registan (desert) ....H 3

BAHRAIN

CITIES and TOWNS

Manama (capital),
  79,098 ....F 4
Muharraq, 34,430 ....F 4

IRAN

CITIES and TOWNS

Abadan, 272,962 ....E 3
Abadeh, 16,000 ....F 3

Abarquh, 8,000 ....F 3
Ahwaz, 206,375 ....E 3
Amul, 40,076 ....F 2
Anarak, 2,038 ....F 3
Arak, 71,925 ....E 3
Ardebil, 83,596 ....E 2
Ardistan, 6,645 ....F 3
Asterabad (Gurgan),
  51,181 ....F 2
Babol, 49,973 ....F 2

Bafq, 5,000 ....G 3
Baft, 6,000 ....G 4
Bahramabad, 21,000 ....G 3
Bam, 22,000 ....G 4
Bandar 'Abbas, 34,627 ......G 4
Bandar Shah, 13,000 ....F 2
Bandar Shahpur, 6,000 ......E 3
Barfrush (Babol),
  49,973 ....F 2
Birjand, 25,854 ....G 3

Borazjun, 20,000 ....F 4
Bujnurd, 31,248 ....G 2
Burujird, 71,476 ....E 3
Bushire, 26,032 ....F 4
Chalus, 15,000 ....F 2
Damghan, 13,000 ....F 2
Darab, 13,000 ....G 4
Dizful, 84,499 ....E 3
Duzdab (Zahidan),
  40,000 ....H 4

(continued on following page)

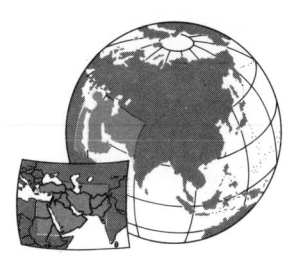

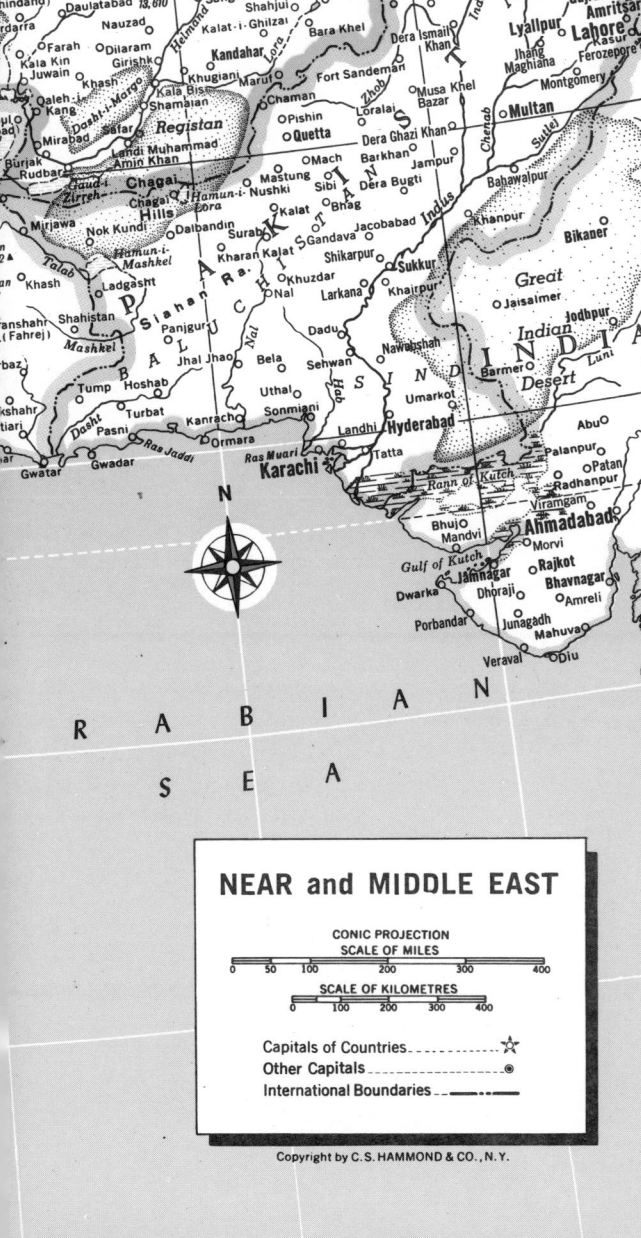

SAUDI ARABIA

AREA 829,995 sq. mi.
POPULATION 7,200,000
CAPITALS Riyadh, Mecca
MONETARY UNIT Saudi riyal
MAJOR LANGUAGE Arabic
MAJOR RELIGION Islam

YEMEN ARAB REPUBLIC

AREA 77,220 sq. mi.
POPULATION 5,600,000
CAPITAL San'a
MONETARY UNIT Yemeni rial
MAJOR LANGUAGE Arabic
MAJOR RELIGION Islam

BAHRAIN

AREA 240 sq. mi.
POPULATION 300,000
CAPITAL Manama
MONETARY UNIT Bahraini dinar
MAJOR LANGUAGE Arabic
MAJOR RELIGION Islam

UNITED ARAB EMIRATES

AREA 32,278 sq. mi.
POPULATION 240,000
CAPITAL Abu Dhabi
MONETARY UNIT dirham
MAJOR LANGUAGE Arabic
MAJOR RELIGION Islam

KUWAIT

AREA 6,532 sq. mi.
POPULATION 1,100,000
CAPITAL Al Kuwait
MONETARY UNIT Kuwaiti dinar
MAJOR LANGUAGE Arabic
MAJOR RELIGION Islam

PEOPLES DEMOCRATIC REPUBLIC OF YEMEN

AREA 111,101 sq. mi.
POPULATION 1,700,000
CAPITAL Aden
MONETARY UNIT Yemeni dinar
MAJOR LANGUAGE Arabic
MAJOR RELIGION Islam

QATAR

AREA 4,247 sq. mi.
POPULATION 150,000
CAPITAL Doha
MONETARY UNIT Qatari riyal
MAJOR LANGUAGE Arabic
MAJOR RELIGION Islam

OMAN

AREA 120,000 sq. mi.
POPULATION 800,000
CAPITAL Muscat
MONETARY UNIT Omani rial
MAJOR LANGUAGE Arabic
MAJOR RELIGION Islam

NEAR and MIDDLE EAST

CONIC PROJECTION
SCALE OF MILES

0 50 100 200 300 400

SCALE OF KILOMETRES

0 100 200 300 400

Capitals of Countries ....☆
Other Capitals ....◉
International Boundaries _____

Copyright by C.S. HAMMOND & CO., N.Y.

Topography

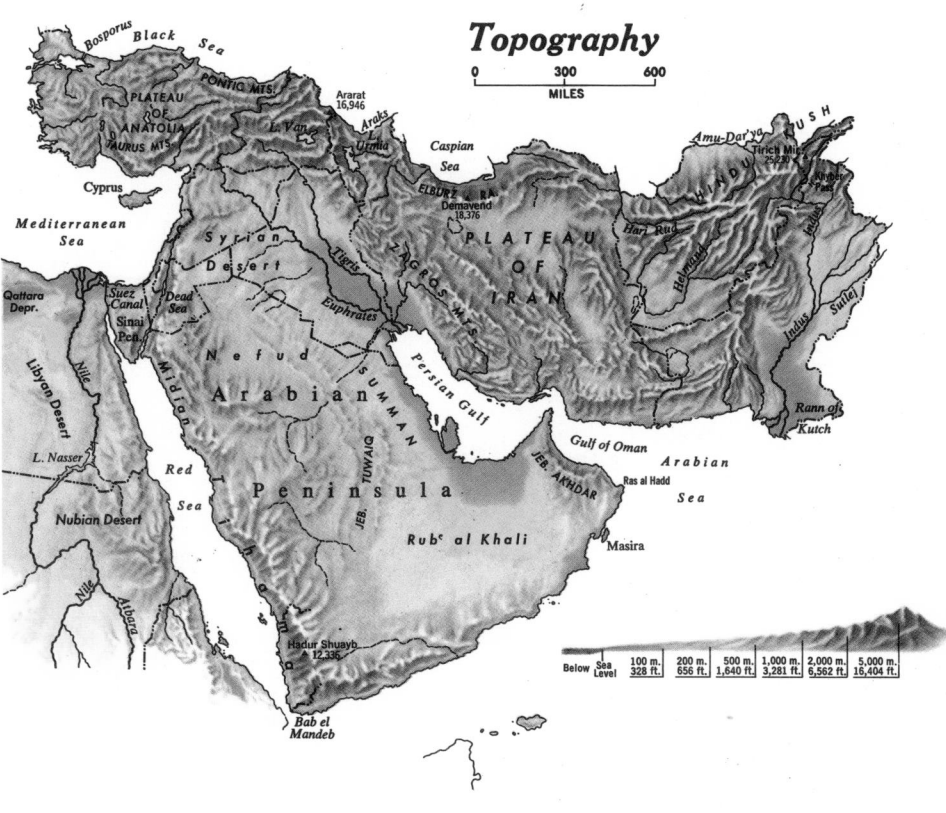

0   300   600
MILES

Below Sea Level | 100 m. 328 ft. | 200 m. 656 ft. | 500 m. 1,640 ft. | 1,000 m. 3,281 ft. | 2,000 m. 6,562 ft. | 5,000 m. 16,404 ft.

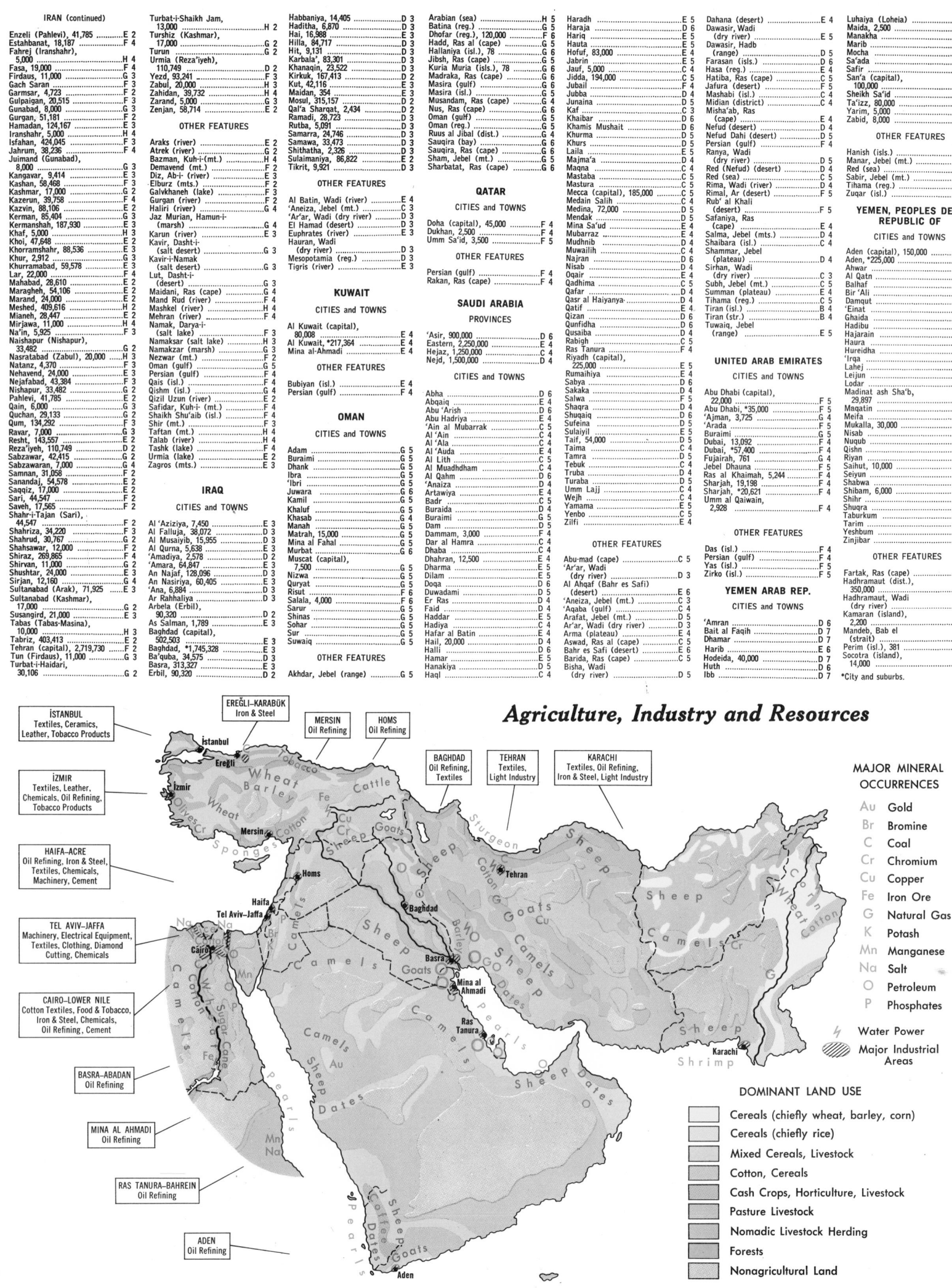

IRAN (continued)

Enzeli (Pahlevi), 41,785 ... E 2
Estahbanat, 18,187 ... F 4
Fahrej (Iranshahr), 5,000 ... H 4
Fasa, 19,000 ... F 4
Firdaus, 11,000 ... G 3
Gach Saran ... F 4
Garmsar, 4,723 ... F 2
Gulpaigan, 20,515 ... F 3
Gunabad, 8,000 ... G 3
Gurgan, 51,181 ... F 2
Hamadan, 124,167 ... E 3
Iranshahr, 5,000 ... H 4
Isfahan, 424,045 ... F 3
Jahrum, 38,236 ... F 4
Juimand (Gunabad), 8,000 ... G 3
Kangavar, 9,414 ... E 3
Kashan, 58,468 ... F 3
Kashmar, 17,000 ... G 2
Kazerun, 39,758 ... F 4
Kazvin, 88,106 ... E 2
Kerman, 85,404 ... G 3
Kermanshah, 187,930 ... E 3
Khaf, 5,000 ... H 3
Khoi, 47,648 ... E 2
Khorramshahr, 88,536 ... E 3
Khur, 2,912 ... G 3
Khurramabad, 59,578 ... E 3
Lar, 22,000 ... F 4
Mahabad, 28,610 ... E 2
Maragheh, 54,106 ... E 2
Marand, 24,000 ... E 2
Meshed, 409,616 ... H 2
Mianeh, 28,447 ... E 2
Mirjawa, 11,000 ... H 4
Na'in, 5,925 ... F 3
Naishapur (Nishapur), 33,482 ... G 2
Nasratabad (Zabul), 20,000 ... H 3
Natanz, 4,370 ... F 3
Nehavend, 24,000 ... E 3
Nejafabad, 43,384 ... F 3
Nishapur, 33,482 ... G 2
Pahlevi, 41,785 ... E 2
Qain, 6,000 ... G 3
Quchan, 29,133 ... G 2
Qum, 134,292 ... F 3
Ravar, 7,000 ... G 3
Resht, 143,557 ... E 2
Reza'iyeh, 110,749 ... D 2
Sabzawar, 42,415 ... G 2
Sabzawaran, 7,000 ... G 4
Samnan, 31,058 ... F 2
Sanandaj, 54,578 ... E 2
Saqqiz, 17,000 ... E 2
Sari, 44,547 ... F 2
Saveh, 17,565 ... F 2
Shahr-i-Tajan (Sari), 44,547 ... F 2
Shahriza, 34,220 ... F 3
Shahrud, 30,767 ... G 2
Shahsawar, 12,000 ... F 2
Shiraz, 269,865 ... F 4
Shirvan, 11,000 ... G 2
Shushtar, 24,000 ... E 3
Sirjan, 12,160 ... G 4
Sultanabad (Arak), 71,925 ... E 3
Sultanabad (Kashmar), 17,000 ... G 2
Susangird, 21,000 ... E 3
Tabas (Tabas-Masina), 10,000 ... H 3
Tabriz, 403,413 ... E 2
Tehran (capital), 2,719,730 ... F 2
Tun (Firdaus), 11,000 ... G 3
Turbat-i-Haidari, 30,106 ... G 2
Turbat-i-Shaikh Jam, 13,000 ... H 2
Turshiz (Kashmar), 17,000 ... G 2
Turun ... G 2
Urmia (Reza'iyeh), 110,749 ... D 2
Yezd, 93,241 ... F 3
Zabul, 20,000 ... H 3
Zahidan, 39,732 ... H 4
Zarand, 5,000 ... G 3
Zenjan, 58,714 ... E 2

OTHER FEATURES

Araks (river) ... E 2
Atrek (river) ... G 2
Bazman, Kuh-i-(mt.) ... H 4
Demavend (mt.) ... F 2
Diz, Ab-i- (river) ... E 3
Elburz (mts.) ... F 2
Galvkhaneh (lake) ... F 3
Gurgan (river) ... F 2
Haliri (river) ... G 4
Jaz Murian, Hamun-i- (marsh) ... G 4
Karun (river) ... E 3
Kavir, Dasht-i- (salt desert) ... G 3
Kavir-i-Namak (salt desert) ... G 3
Lut, Dasht-i- (desert) ... G 3
Maidani, Ras (cape) ... G 4
Mand Rud (river) ... F 4
Mashkel (river) ... H 4
Mehran (river) ... F 4
Namak, Darya-i- (salt lake) ... F 3
Namaksar (salt lake) ... H 3
Namakzar (marsh) ... G 3
Nezwar (mt.) ... F 2
Oman (gulf) ... G 5
Persian (gulf) ... F 4
Qais (isl.) ... F 4
Qishm (isl.) ... G 4
Qizil Uzun (river) ... E 2
Safidar, Kuh-i- (mt.) ... F 4
Shaikh Shu'aib (isl.) ... F 4
Shir (mt.) ... F 3
Taftan (mt.) ... H 4
Talab (river) ... H 4
Tashk (lake) ... F 4
Urmia (lake) ... E 2
Zagros (mts.) ... E 3

IRAQ

CITIES and TOWNS

Al 'Aziziya, 7,450 ... E 3
Al Falluja, 38,072 ... D 3
Al Musaiyib, 15,955 ... D 3
Al Qurna, 5,638 ... E 3
'Amadiya, 2,578 ... D 2
'Amara, 64,847 ... E 3
An Najaf, 128,096 ... D 3
An Nasiriya, 60,405 ... E 3
'Ana, 6,884 ... D 3
Ar Rahhaliya ... D 3
Arbela (Erbil), 90,320 ... D 2
As Salman, 1,789 ... D 3
Baghdad (capital), 502,503 ... E 3
Baghdad, *1,745,328 ... E 3
Ba'quba, 34,575 ... D 3
Basra, 313,327 ... E 3
Erbil, 90,320 ... D 2
Habbaniya, 14,405 ... D 3
Haditha, 6,870 ... D 3
Hai, 16,988 ... E 3
Hilla, 84,717 ... D 3
Hit, 9,131 ... D 3
Karbala', 83,301 ... D 3
Khanaqin, 23,522 ... D 3
Kirkuk, 167,413 ... D 2
Kut, 42,116 ... E 3
Maidan, 354 ... E 3
Mosul, 315,157 ... D 2
Qal'a Sharqat, 2,434 ... D 2
Ramadi, 28,723 ... D 3
Rutba, 5,091 ... D 3
Samarra, 24,746 ... D 3
Samawa, 33,473 ... D 3
Shithatha, 2,326 ... D 3
Sulaimaniya, 86,822 ... E 2
Tikrit, 9,921 ... D 3

OTHER FEATURES

Al Batin, Wadi (river) ... E 4
'Aneiza, Jebel (mt.) ... C 3
'Ar'ar, Wadi (dry river) ... D 3
El Hamad (desert) ... D 3
Euphrates (river) ... E 3
Hauran, Wadi (dry river) ... D 3
Mesopotamia (reg.) ... D 3
Tigris (river) ... E 3

KUWAIT

CITIES and TOWNS

Al Kuwait (capital), 80,008 ... E 4
Al Kuwait, *217,364 ... E 4
Mina al-Ahmadi ... E 4

OTHER FEATURES

Bubiyan (isl.) ... E 4
Persian (gulf) ... F 4

OMAN

CITIES and TOWNS

Adam ... G 5
Buraimi ... G 5
Dhank ... G 5
Ibra ... G 5
'Ibri ... G 5
Juwara ... G 6
Kamil ... G 5
Khaluf ... G 5
Khasab ... G 4
Manah ... G 5
Matrah, 15,000 ... G 5
Mina al Fahal ... G 5
Murbat ... G 6
Muscat (capital), 7,500 ... G 5
Nizwa ... G 5
Quryat ... G 5
Risut ... F 6
Salala, 4,000 ... F 6
Sarur ... G 5
Shinas ... G 5
Sohar ... G 5
Sur ... G 5
Suwaiq ... G 5

OTHER FEATURES

Akhdar, Jebel (range) ... G 5
Arabian (sea) ... H 5
Batina (reg.) ... G 5
Dhofar (reg.), 120,000 ... F 6
Hadd, Ras al (cape) ... G 5
Hallaniya (isl.), 78 ... G 6
Jibsh, Ras (cape) ... G 5
Kuria Muria (isls.), 78 ... G 6
Madraka, Ras (cape) ... G 6
Masira (gulf) ... G 6
Masira (isl.) ... G 5
Musandam, Ras (cape) ... G 4
Nus, Ras (cape) ... G 6
Oman (gulf) ... G 5
Oman (reg.) ... G 5
Ruus al Jibal (dist.) ... G 4
Sauqira (bay) ... G 6
Sauqira, Ras (cape) ... G 6
Sham, Jebel (mt.) ... G 5
Sharbatat, Ras (cape) ... G 6

QATAR

CITIES and TOWNS

Doha (capital), 45,000 ... F 4
Dukhan, 2,500 ... F 4
Umm Sa'id, 3,500 ... F 5

OTHER FEATURES

Persian (gulf) ... F 4
Rakan, Ras (cape) ... F 4

SAUDI ARABIA

PROVINCES

'Asir, 900,000 ... D 6
Eastern, 2,250,000 ... E 4
Hejaz, 1,250,000 ... C 4
Nejd, 1,500,000 ... D 4

CITIES and TOWNS

Abha ... D 6
Abqaiq ... E 4
Abu 'Arish ... D 6
Abu Hadriya ... E 4
'Ain al Mubarrak ... C 5
Al 'Ain ... C 4
Al 'Ala ... C 4
Al 'Auda ... E 4
Al Lith ... C 5
Al Muadhdham ... C 4
Al Qahm ... D 6
'Anaiza ... D 4
Artawiya ... E 4
Badr ... C 5
Buraida ... D 4
Buraimi ... G 5
Dam ... D 5
Dammam, 3,000 ... F 4
Dar al Hamra ... C 4
Dhaba ... C 4
Dhahran, 12,500 ... E 4
Dharma ... E 5
Dilam ... E 5
Doqa ... D 6
Duwadami ... D 5
Er Ras ... D 4
Faid ... D 4
Haddar ... E 5
Hadiya ... C 4
Hafar al Batin ... E 4
Hail, 20,000 ... D 4
Halli ... D 6
Hamar ... E 5
Hanakiya ... D 5
Haql ... C 4
Haradh ... E 5
Haraja ... D 6
Hariq ... E 5
Hauta ... E 5
Hofuf, 83,000 ... E 4
Jabrin ... E 5
Jauf, 5,000 ... C 4
Jidda, 194,000 ... C 5
Jubail ... F 4
Jubba ... D 4
Junaina ... D 5
Kaf ... C 3
Khaibar ... D 6
Khamis Mushait ... D 6
Khurma ... D 5
Khurs ... D 5
Laila ... E 5
Majma'a ... D 4
Maqna ... C 4
Mastaba ... C 5
Mastura ... C 5
Mecca (capital), 185,000 ... C 5
Medain Salih ... C 4
Medina, 72,000 ... D 5
Mendak ... D 5
Mina Sa'ud ... E 4
Mubarraz ... E 4
Mudhnib ... D 4
Muwailih ... C 4
Najran ... D 6
Nisab ... D 4
Oqair ... E 4
Qadhima ... C 5
Qafar ... D 4
Qasr al Haiyanya ... D 4
Qatif ... E 4
Qizan ... D 6
Qunfidha ... D 6
Qusaiba ... D 4
Rabigh ... C 5
Ras Tanura ... F 4
Riyadh (capital), 225,000 ... E 5
Rumaihiya ... E 4
Sabya ... D 6
Sakaka ... D 4
Salwa ... F 5
Shaqra ... D 4
Shuqaiq ... D 6
Sufeina ... D 5
Sulaiyil ... E 5
Taif, 54,000 ... D 5
Taima ... C 4
Tamra ... D 5
Tebuk ... C 4
Truba ... D 4
Turaba ... D 5
Umm Lajj ... C 4
Wejh ... C 4
Yamama ... E 5
Yenbo ... C 5
Zilfi ... E 4

OTHER FEATURES

Abu-mad (cape) ... C 5
'Ar'ar, Wadi (dry river) ... D 3
Al Ahqaf (Bahr es Safi) (desert) ... E 6
'Aneiza, Jebel (mt.) ... C 3
'Aqaba (gulf) ... C 4
Arafat, Jebel (mt.) ... D 5
Ar'ar, Wadi (dry river) ... D 3
Arma (plateau) ... E 4
Aswad, Ras al (cape) ... C 5
Bahr es Safi (desert) ... E 6
Barida, Ras (cape) ... C 5
Bisha, Wadi (dry river) ... D 5
Dahana (desert) ... E 4
Dawasir, Wadi (dry river) ... E 5
Dawasir, Hadb (range) ... D 5
Farasan (isls.) ... D 6
Hasa (reg.) ... E 4
Hatiba, Ras (cape) ... C 5
Jafura (desert) ... F 5
Mashabi (isl.) ... C 4
Midian (district) ... C 4
Misha'ab, Ras (cape) ... E 4
Nefud (desert) ... D 4
Nefud Dahi (desert) ... D 5
Persian (gulf) ... F 4
Ranya, Wadi (dry river) ... D 5
Red (Nefud) (desert) ... D 4
Red (sea) ... C 5
Rima, Wadi (river) ... D 4
Rimal, Ar (desert) ... F 5
Rub' al Khali (desert) ... F 5
Safaniya, Ras (cape) ... E 4
Salma, Jebel (mts.) ... D 4
Shaibara (isl.) ... C 4
Shammar, Jebel (plateau) ... D 4
Sirhan, Wadi (dry river) ... C 3
Subh, Jebel (mt.) ... C 5
Summan (plateau) ... E 4
Tihama (reg.) ... C 5
Tiran (isl.) ... B 4
Tiran (str.) ... B 4
Tuwaiq, Jebel (range) ... E 5

UNITED ARAB EMIRATES

CITIES and TOWNS

Abu Dhabi (capital), 22,000 ... F 5
Abu Dhabi, *35,000 ... F 5
'Ajman, 3,725 ... G 4
'Arada ... F 5
Buraimi ... G 5
Dubai, 13,092 ... F 4
Dubai, *57,400 ... F 4
Fujairah, 761 ... G 4
Jebel Dhauna ... F 5
Ras al Khaimah, 5,244 ... F 4
Sharjah, 19,198 ... F 4
Sharjah, *20,621 ... F 4
Umm al Qaiwain, 2,928 ... F 4

OTHER FEATURES

Das (isl.) ... F 4
Persian (gulf) ... F 4
Yas (isl.) ... F 5
Zirko (isl.) ... F 5

YEMEN ARAB REP.

CITIES and TOWNS

'Amran ... D 6
Bait al Faqih ... D 7
Dhamar ... D 7
Harib ... E 6
Hodeida, 40,000 ... D 7
Huth ... D 6
Ibb ... D 7
Luhaiya (Loheia) ... D 6
Maida, 2,500 ... D 6
Manakha ... D 6
Marib ... D 6
Mocha ... D 7
Sa'ada ... D 6
Safir ... E 6
San'a (capital), 100,000 ... D 6
Sheikh Sa'id ... D 7
Ta'izz, 80,000 ... D 7
Yarim, 5,000 ... D 7
Zabid, 8,000 ... D 7

OTHER FEATURES

Hanish (isls.) ... D 7
Manar, Jebel (mt.) ... D 7
Red (sea) ... C 5
Sabir, Jebel (mt.) ... D 7
Tihama (reg.) ... C 5
Zuqar (isl.) ... D 7

YEMEN, PEOPLES DEM. REPUBLIC OF

CITIES and TOWNS

Aden (capital), 150,000 ... E 7
Aden, *225,000 ... E 7
Ahwar ... E 7
Al Qatn ... E 6
Balhaf ... E 7
Bir 'Ali ... E 7
Damqut ... F 6
'Einat ... E 6
Ghaida ... F 6
Hadibu ... F 7
Hajarain ... E 6
Haura ... E 7
Hureidha ... E 6
'Irqa ... E 7
Lahej ... E 7
Leijun ... E 6
Lodar ... E 7
Madinat ash Sha'b, 29,897 ... E 7
Maqatin ... E 7
Meifa ... E 7
Mukalla, 30,000 ... E 7
Nisab ... E 7
Nuqub ... E 6
Qishn ... F 6
Riyan ... E 7
Saihut, 10,000 ... F 6
Seiyun ... E 6
Shabwa ... E 6
Shibam, 6,000 ... E 6
Shihr ... E 7
Shuqra ... E 7
Taburkum ... E 6
Tarim ... E 6
Yeshbum ... E 7
Zinjibar ... E 7

OTHER FEATURES

Fartak, Ras (cape) ... F 6
Hadhramaut (dist.), 350,000 ... E 7
Hadhramaut, Wadi (dry river) ... F 7
Kamaran (island), 2,200 ... D 6
Mandeb, Bab el (strait) ... D 7
Perim (isl.), 381 ... D 7
Socotra (island), 14,000 ... F 7

*City and suburbs.

Agriculture, Industry and Resources

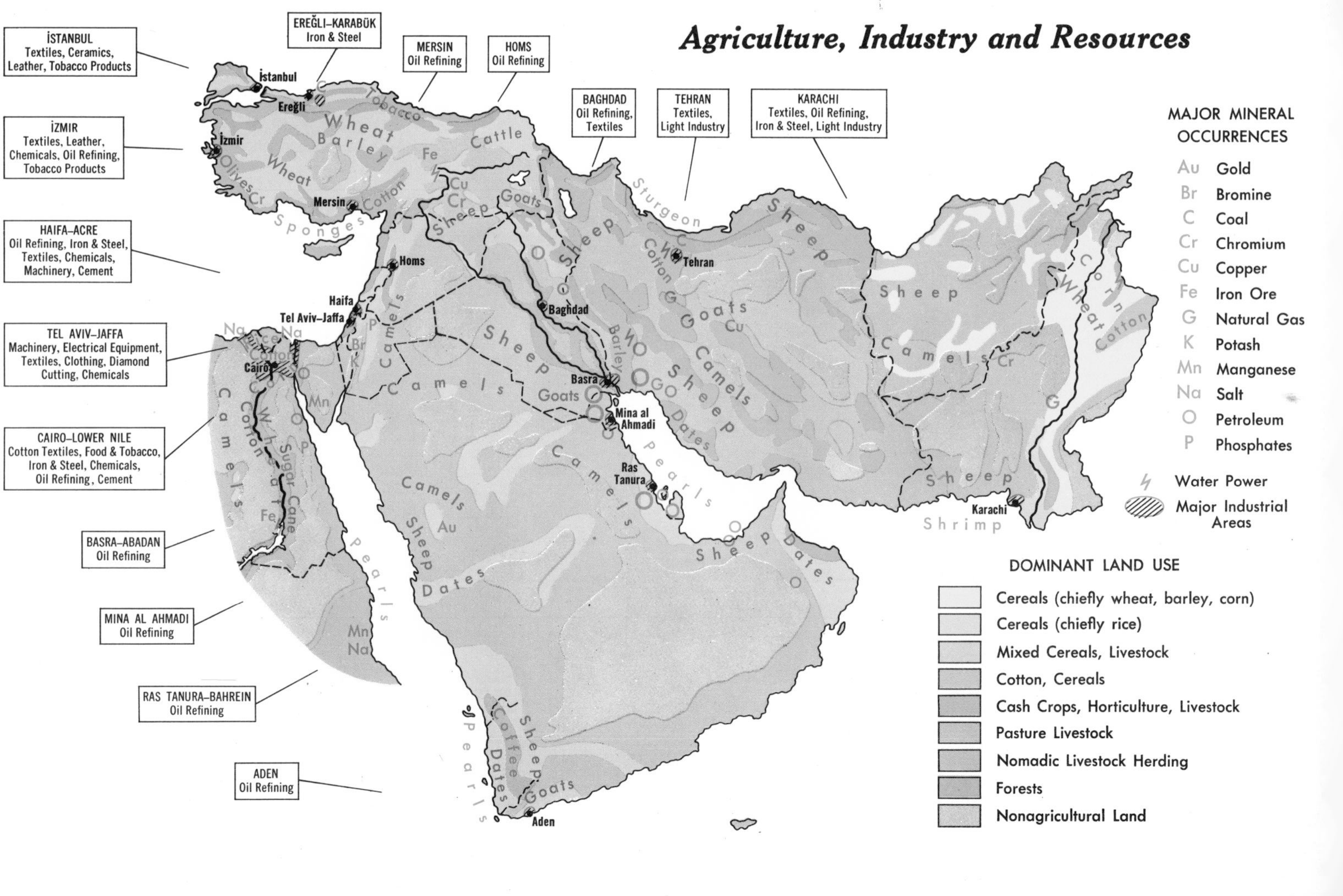

İSTANBUL
Textiles, Ceramics, Leather, Tobacco Products
EREĞLI–KARABÜK
Iron & Steel
MERSIN
Oil Refining
HOMS
Oil Refining
BAGHDAD
Oil Refining, Textiles
TEHRAN
Textiles, Light Industry
KARACHI
Textiles, Oil Refining, Iron & Steel, Light Industry
İZMIR
Textiles, Leather, Chemicals, Oil Refining, Tobacco Products
HAIFA–ACRE
Oil Refining, Iron & Steel, Textiles, Chemicals, Machinery, Cement
TEL AVIV–JAFFA
Machinery, Electrical Equipment, Textiles, Clothing, Diamond Cutting, Chemicals
CAIRO–LOWER NILE
Cotton Textiles, Food & Tobacco, Iron & Steel, Chemicals, Oil Refining, Cement
BASRA–ABADAN
Oil Refining
MINA AL AHMADI
Oil Refining
RAS TANURA–BAHREIN
Oil Refining
ADEN
Oil Refining
İstanbul
Ereğli
İzmir
Mersin
Homs
Haifa
Tel Aviv–Jaffa
Cairo
Baghdad
Tehran
Basra
Mina al Ahmadi
Ras Tanura
Karachi
Aden
Wheat
Barley
Cattle
Olives
Cotton
Sponges
Sheep
Goats
Camels
Sturgeon
Corn
Sugar Cane
Dates
Pearls
Coffee
Shrimp
MAJOR MINERAL OCCURRENCES
Au Gold
Br Bromine
C Coal
Cr Chromium
Cu Copper
Fe Iron Ore
G Natural Gas
K Potash
Mn Manganese
Na Salt
O Petroleum
P Phosphates
Water Power
Major Industrial Areas
DOMINANT LAND USE
Cereals (chiefly wheat, barley, corn)
Cereals (chiefly rice)
Mixed Cereals, Livestock
Cotton, Cereals
Cash Crops, Horticulture, Livestock
Pasture Livestock
Nomadic Livestock Herding
Forests
Nonagricultural Land

TURKEY

AREA 300,946 sq. mi.
POPULATION 40,284,000
CAPITAL Ankara
LARGEST CITY Istanbul
HIGHEST POINT Ararat 16,946 ft.
MONETARY UNIT Turkish lira
MAJOR LANGUAGE Turkish
MAJOR RELIGION Islam

SYRIA

AREA 71,498 sq. mi.
POPULATION 7,585,000
CAPITAL Damascus
LARGEST CITY Damascus
HIGHEST POINT Hermon 9,232 ft.
MONETARY UNIT Syrian pound
MAJOR LANGUAGES Arabic, French, Kurdish, Armenian
MAJOR RELIGIONS Islam, Christianity

LEBANON

AREA 4,015 sq. mi.
POPULATION 3,207,000
CAPITAL Beirut
LARGEST CITY Beirut
HIGHEST POINT Qurnet es Sauda 10,131 ft.
MONETARY UNIT Lebanese pound
MAJOR LANGUAGE Arabic, French
MAJOR RELIGIONS Christianity, Islam

CYPRUS

AREA 3,473 sq. mi.
POPULATION 639,000
CAPITAL Nicosia
LARGEST CITY Nicosia
HIGHEST POINT Troodos 6,406 ft.
MONETARY UNIT Cypriot pound
MAJOR LANGUAGES Greek, Turkish, English
MAJOR RELIGIONS Eastern (Greek) Orthodoxy, Islam

CYPRUS

CITIES and TOWNS

amagusta, 38,000 ....F 5
amagusta, *41,000 ....F 5
yrenia, 3,500 ....E 5
yrenia, *4,500 ....E 5
arnaca, 20,000 ....E 5
arnaca, *21,000 ....E 5
efka, 3,673 ....E 5
efkara, 2,075 ....E 5
imassol, 46,500 ....E 5
imassol, *50,000 ....E 5
orphou, 6,642 ....E 5
icosia (capital), 47,000 .....E 5
icosia, *112,000 ....E 5
aphos, 10,000 ....E 5
aphos, *11,500 ....E 5
ialousa, 2,541 ....F 5

OTHER FEATURES

ndreas (cape) ....F 5
rnauti (cape) ....E 5
amagusta (bay) ....F 5
ata (cape) ....F 5
reco (cape) ....F 5
lides (isls.) ....F 5
ormakiti (cape) ....E 5
arnaca (bay) ....E 5
Morphou (bay) ....E 5
overeign Base Area, 3,602...E 5
roodos (mt.) ....E 5

LEBANON

CITIES and TOWNS

Aleih, 18,630 ....F 6
myun, 7,926 ....F 5
a'albek, 15,560 ....G 5
atrun, 5,976 ....F 5
eirut (capital), 700,000 ....F 6
eirut, *840,000 ....F 6
n Naqura, 967 ....F 6
ermil, 2,652 ....G 5

Merj 'Uyun, 9,318 ....F 6
Rasheiya, 6,731 ....F 6
Rayak, 1,480 ....F 6
Saida, 32,200 ....F 6
Sidon (Saida), 32,200 ......F 6
Sur, 16,483 ....F 6
Tarabulus (Tripoli), 127,611 .F 5
Tyre (Sur), 16,483 ....F 6
Zahle, 53,121 ....G 5
Zegharta, 18,210 ....G 5

OTHER FEATURES

Hermon (mt.) ....F 6
Lebanon (range) ....F 6
Litani (Leontes) (river) .....F 6
Sauda, Qurnet es (mt.) ....G 5

SYRIA

GOVERNORATES

Aleppo, 1,131,854 ....G 4
Damascus, 1,060,484 ....G 6
Damascus (municipality), 630,063 ....G 6
Deir es Zor, 286,010 ....H 5
Der'a, 221,275 ....G 6
El Quneitra, 6,396 ....F 6
Es Suweida, 151,500 ....G 6
Hama, 390,084 ....G 5
Haseke, 309,279 ....J 4
Homs, 504,098 ....G 5
Idlib, 374,751 ....G 5
Latakia, 625,473 ....G 5
Rashid, 124,876 ....H 5

CITIES and TOWNS

Abu Kemal, 6,907 ....J 5
Aleppo, 566,770 ....G 4
A'zaz, 13,923 ....F 5
Baniyas, 8,537 ....F 5
Damascus (cap.), 789,840 ..G 6
Deir ez Zor, 60,335 ....H 5
Der'a, 20,465 ....G 6

Dimishq (Damascus) (capital), 789,840 ....G 6
Duma, 30,050 ....G 6
El Bab, 27,366 ....G 4
El Haseke, 23,074 ....J 4
El Ladhiqiya (Latakia), 72,378..F 5
El Quneitra, 206 ....F 6
El Rashid, 11,998 ....H 5
En Nebk, 16,334 ....G 5
Es Suweida, 17,592 ....G 6
Haleb (Aleppo), 566,770 ..G 4
Hama, 196,224 ....G 5
Harim, 6,837 ....G 4
Homs, 231,877 ....G 5
Idlib, 37,501 ....G 5
Jeble, 15,715 ....F 5
Jerablus, 8,610 ....G 4
Jisr esh Shughur, 13,131 ..G 5
Latakia, 72,378 ....F 5
Masyaf, 7,058 ....G 5
Membij, 13,796 ....G 4
Meyadin, 12,515 ....J 5
Palmyra (Tadmor), 10,670 ..H 5
Qamishliye, 31,448 ......J 4
Quteife, 4,993 ....G 6
Raqqa (El Rashid), 11,998 ..H 4
Safita, 9,650 ....G 5
Selemiya, 25,728 ....G 5
Tadmor, 10,670 ....H 5
Tartus, 19,137 ....F 5
Zebdani, 10,010 ....G 6

OTHER FEATURES

'Abdul 'Aziz, Jebel (mts.)..J 4
Abu Rujmein, Jebel (mts.)..H 5
'Asi (river) ....G 5
Druz, Jebel ed (mts.) .....G 6
Euphrates (El Furat) (river) ..J 5
Furat, El (river) ....J 5
Hermon (mt.) ....F 6
Khabur (river) ....J 5
Orontes ('Asi) (river) .....G 5
Ruad (island) ....F 5
Sharqi, Jebel esh (range) ..G 5
Tigris (river) ....K 4

TURKEY

PROVINCES

Adana, 902,712 ....F 4
Adıyaman, 267,288 ....H 4
Afyon-Karahisar, 502,248 ....D 3
Ağrı, 246,961 ....K 3
Amasya, 285,729 ....G 3
Ankara, 1,644,302 ....E 3
Antalya, 486,910 ....D 4
Artvin, 210,065 ....J 2
Aydın, 524,918 ....D 4
Balıkesir, 708,342 ....B 3
Bilecik, 139,041 ....D 2
Bingöl, 150,521 ....J 3
Bitlis, 154,069 ....J 3
Bolu, 383,939 ....D 2
Burdur, 194,950 ....D 4
Bursa, 755,504 ....C 2
Çanakkale, 350,317 ....B 2
Çankırı, 250,706 ....E 2
Çorum, 485,567 ....F 2
Denizli, 463,369 ....C 4
Diyarbakır, 475,916 ....H 4
Edirne, 303,234 ....B 2
Elâzığ, 322,727 ....H 3
Erzincan, 258,586 ......H 3
Erzurum, 628,001 ......J 3
Eskişehir, 415,101 ......D 3
Gaziantep, 521,026 ....G 4
Giresun, 428,015 ....H 2
Gümüşhane, 262,731 ..H 2
Hakkâri, 83,937 ....K 4
Hatay, 506,154 ....G 4
İçel, 511,273 ....F 4
Isparta, 266,240 ....D 4
İstanbul, 2,293,823 ....C 2
İzmir, 1,234,667 ....B 3
Kars, 606,313 ....K 2
Kastamonu, 441,638 ..E 2
Kayseri, 536,206 ....F 3
Kırklareli, 258,386 .....B 2
Kırşehir, 196,836 ....E 3
Kocaeli, 335,518 ....D 2
Konya, 1,122,622 ......E 4
Kütahya, 398,081 ......C 3

Malatya, 452,624 ....H 3
Manisa, 748,545 ....B 3
Maraş, 438,423 ....G 4
Mardin, 397,880 ....J 4
Muğla, 334,973 ....C 4
Muş, 198,716 ....J 3
Nevşehir, 203,316 ......F 3
Niğde, 362,044 ....F 4
Ordu, 543,863 ....G 2
Rize, 281,099 ....J 2
Sakarya, 404,078 ......D 2
Samsun, 755,946 ....F 2
Siirt, 281,832 ....J 4
Sinop, 266,069 ....F 2
Sivas, 705,186 ....G 3
Tekirdağ, 287,381 .....B 2
Tokat, 495,352 ....G 2
Trabzon, 595,782 ......H 2
Tunceli, 154,175 ....H 3
Urfa, 450,798 ....H 4
Uşak, 190,536 ....C 3
Van, 266,840 ....K 3
Yozgat, 437,883 ....F 3
Zonguldak, 650,191 ..D 2

CITIES and TOWNS

Abana, 2,455 ....F 1
Acıgol, 3,265 ....F 3
Acıpayam, 4,118 ....C 4
Adapazarı, 71,833 ....D 4
Adana, 289,919 ....F 4
Adapazarı, 86,124 .....D 2
Adilcevaz, 6,148 ....K 3
Adıyaman, 22,153 ....H 4
Afşin, 8,069 ....G 3
Afyon, 44,026 ....D 3
Ağlasun, 3,730 ....D 4
Ağlı, 3,425 ....E 2
Ağrı (Karaköse), 24,168 ..K 3
Ahlat, 5,879 ....K 3
Akçaabat, 7,600 ....H 2
Akçadağ, 5,995 ....G 3
Akçakale, 4,526 ....H 4
Akçakoca, 7,179 ....D 2
Akdağmadeni, 4,321 ..F 3
Akhisar, 46,167 ....B 3
Aksaray, 24,414 ......F 3

Akşehir, 25,269 ....D 3
Akseki, 2,505 ....D 4
Akviran, 3,786 ....E 4
Akyazı, 9,090 ....D 2
Alaca, 8,288 ....F 2
Alaçam, 7,833 ....F 2
Alanya, 12,436 ....D 4
Alaşehir, 16,012 ......C 3
Alexandretta (İskenderun), 69,382 ....G 4
Aliağa, 3,087 ....B 3
Alibeyköyü, 15,199 ..D 6
Almus, 4,110 ....G 2
Alpu, 2,709 ....D 3
Altındağ, 89,838 .....E 2
Altınova, 6,368 ....B 3
Altıntaş, 2,361 ....C 3
Amasya, 34,168 ......G 2
Anadoluhisari, 13,959 ..D 6
Anamur, 11,246 ......E 4
Andırın, 3,695 ....G 4
Ankara (capital), 905,660 ..E 3
Antakya, 57,855 .....G 4
Antalya, 71,833 ......D 4
Araç, 2,820 ....E 2
Aralık, 2,879 ....L 3
Arapkir, 7,056 ....H 3
Ardahan, 9,117 ......K 2
Ardeşen, 5,488 ......J 2
Arhavi, 4,500 ....J 2
Arnavutköy, 22,468 ..D 6
Arsin, 4,028 ....H 2
Artova, 2,863 ....G 2
Artvin, 9,847 ....J 2
Aşkale, 6,943 ....J 3
Aslanköy, 3,656 .....F 4
Avanos, 5,675 ....F 3
Ayancık, 5,320 ......F 2
Ayas, 3,873 ....E 2
Aybastı, 7,450 ......G 2
Aydın, 43,483 ....B 4
Ayvacık, 2,277 ......B 3
Ayvalık, 16,283 .....B 3
Babadağ, 5,511 .....C 4
Babaeski, 13,879 ...B 2
Bafra, 26,239 ....F 2
Bahçe, 2,264 ....G 4
Bakırköy, 65,285 ...D 6

Baklan, 2,680 ....C 4
Balâ, 3,646 ....E 3
Balıkesir, 69,341 ....B 3
Banaz, 3,495 ....C 3
Bandırma, 33,116 ..C 2
Barak, 3,117 ....G 4
Bartın, 14,259 ....E 2
Başkale, 4,007 ......K 3
Başmakçı, 5,093 ....D 4
Batman, 24,990 .....J 4
Bayburt, 15,184 ....H 2
Bayındır, 11,273 ....B 3
Bayramiç, 4,607 ....B 3
Bergama, 24,121 ...B 3
Besni, 11,625 ....G 4
Beşiktaş, 58,814 ....D 6
Beykoz, 37,730 .....D 5
Beylerbeyi, 21,741 ..D 6
Beyoğlu, 39,984 ....D 6
Beypazarı, 9,860 ...D 2
Beyşehir, 7,456 .....D 3
Biga, 12,063 ....B 2
Bigadiç, 4,820 ....C 3
Bilecik, 9,722 ....C 3
Bingöl (Çapakçur), 11,727 ..J 3
Birecik, 15,317 ......H 4
Bismil, 4,444 ....J 4
Bitlis, 18,725 ....J 3
Bodrum, 5,136 ......B 4
Boğazlıyan, 7,925 ..F 3
Bolu, 21,700 ....D 2
Bolvadin, 20,139 ...D 3
Bor, 14,309 ....F 4
Borçka, 3,763 ....J 2
Bornova, 30,445 ...B 3
Boyabat, 9,418 .....F 2
Bozdoğan, 6,739 ...C 4
Bozkır, 3,112 ....E 4
Bozkurt, 2,954 ......F 2
Bozova, 3,425 ......H 4
Bozüyük, 10,842 ...D 3
Bucak, 10,094 ......D 4
Bulancak, 9,343 ....G 2
Bulanık, 6,186 ......K 3
Buldan, 9,813 ......C 3
Bünyan, 8,467 .....F 3
Burdur, 29,268 ....D 4
Burhaniye, 12,597 ..B 3

(continued on following page)

Agriculture, Industry and Resources

DOMINANT LAND USE

- Cereals (chiefly wheat, barley), Livestock
- Cash Crops, Horticulture, Livestock
- Pasture Livestock
- Nomadic Livestock Herding
- Forests
- Nonagricultural Land

MAJOR MINERAL OCCURRENCES

- Ab Asbestos
- C   Coal
- Cr Chromium
- Cu Copper
- Fe Iron Ore
- Hg Mercury
- Na Salt
- O   Petroleum
- Pb Lead
- Sb Antimony
- Zn Zinc

⚡ Water Power
▨ Major Industrial Areas

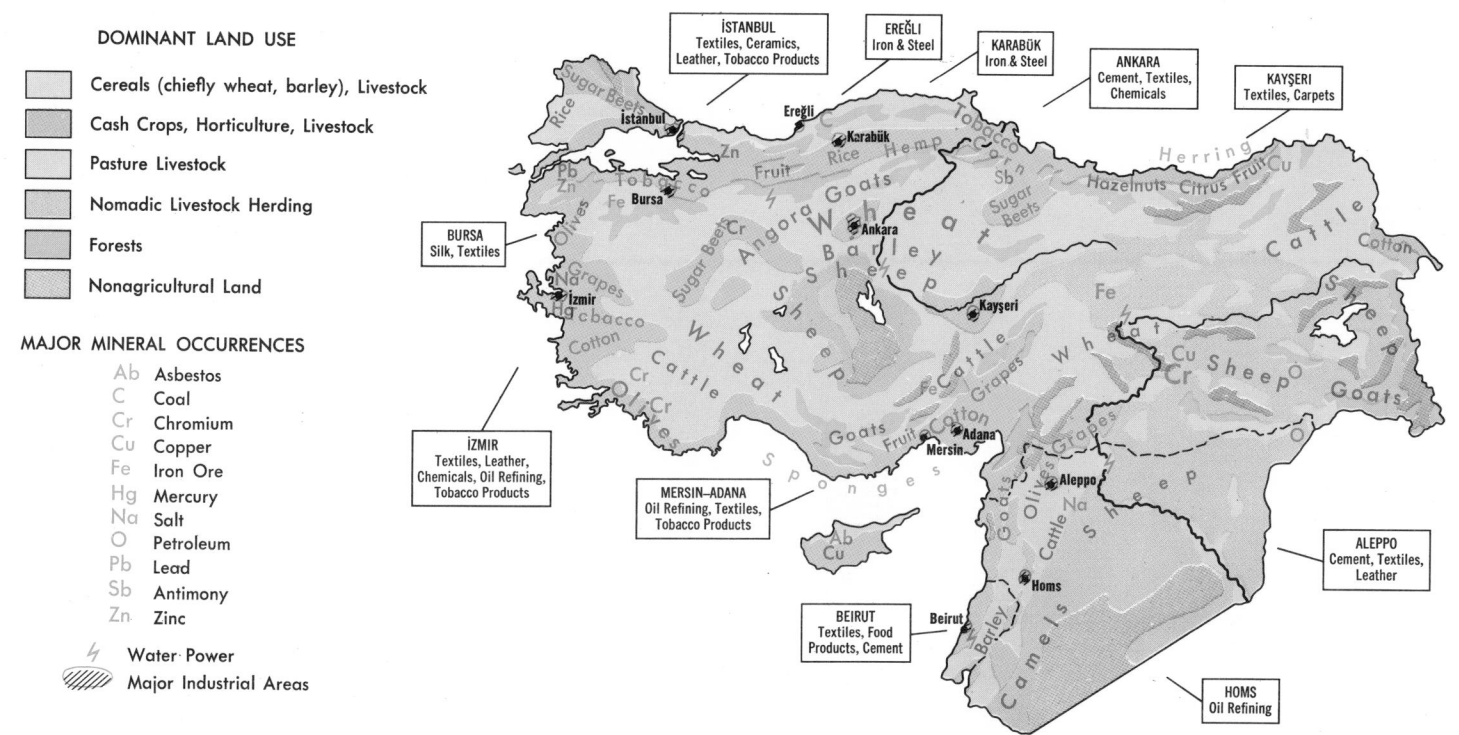

TURKEY (continued)

Bursa, 211,644	C 2
Büyükada, 5,261	D 6
Büyükdere	D 5
Çal, 2,925	C 3
Çalköy, 2,232	C 3
Çamlıdere, 3,132	E 2
Çan, 5,826	B 2
Çanakkale, 22,789	A 2
Çandır, 4,619	F 3
Çankaya, 161,804	E 3
Çankırı, 21,450	E 2
Çapakçur, 11,727	J 3
Çardak, 2,410	C 6
Çarşamba, 18,003	G 2
Çatalca, 5,811	C 2
Çay, 9,761	D 3
Çayeli, 11,496	J 2
Çayıralan, 4,357	F 3
Çebeci, 204,592	E 3
Çekerek, 3,286	F 2
Çelikhan, 3,305	H 3
Çemişkezek, 2,235	H 3
Çerkeş, 2,865	E 2
Çerkezköy, 5,355	C 2
Çermik, 5,420	H 3
Çeşme, 4,068	A 3
Çetinkaya, 2,525	G 3
Cevizli, 2,580	D 4
Ceyhan, 41,124	F 4
Ceylanpınar, 12,508	H 4
Cide, 2,130	E 2
Cifteler, 5,901	D 3
Cihanbeyli, 6,739	E 3
Çıldır, 2,040	K 2
Çimin, 4,405	H 3
Çine, 8,271	B 4
Çivril, 5,780	C 3
Cizre, 8,662	K 4
Çölemerik, 6,129	K 4
Çorlu, 27,187	B 2
Çorum, 41,574	F 2
Çubuk, 8,857	E 2
Çukur, 4,045	F 2
Çumra, 10,299	E 4
Darende, 8,912	G 3
Demirci, 10,050	C 3
Demirkent, 3,855	E 4
Demirköy, 3,309	B 2
Denizli, 64,331	C 4
Derik, 6,684	J 4
Derinkuyu, 4,056	F 3
Develi, 13,411	F 3
Devrek, 5,058	D 2
Dicle, 3,577	J 3
Dikili, 5,805	B 3
Dinar, 11,298	C 3
Dirmil, 2,736	C 4
Divriği, 9,160	G 3
Diyadin, 2,934	K 3
Diyarbakır, 102,653	H 3
Doğanbey, 3,058	D 4
Doğanhisar, 5,966	D 3
Doğanşehir, 4,944	G 3
Döger, 2,913	D 3
Doğubeyazıt, 8,523	K 3
Dörtyol, 11,595	F 4
Dumlu, 3,416	J 2
Dursunbey, 6,533	C 3
Düzce, 22,274	D 2
Eceabat, 2,842	B 2
Edremit, 26,003	B 3
Eğridir, 8,912	D 4
Eldivan, 3,344	E 2
Eleşkirt, 6,019	K 3
Emet, 4,815	C 4
Emirdağ, 10,914	D 3
Emirgazi, 3,509	E 3
Enez, 1,808	A 2
Erbaa, 13,168	G 2
Erciş, 14,072	K 3
Erdek, 7,813	B 2
Erdemli, 10,304	E 4
Ereğli, 38,362	D 2
Ereğli, 18,978	E 3
Erenköy, 35,980	D 6
Ergani, 10,528	H 3
Erkilet, 3,223	F 3
Ermenak, 8,017	D 4
Eruh, 3,298	K 4
Erzin, 10,257	F 4
Erzincan, 45,197	H 3
Erzurum, 105,317	J 3
Eskimalatya, 4,244	H 3
Eskişehir, 173,882	D 3
Eşme, 5,035	C 3
Espiye, 5,318	H 2
Eynesil, 5,210	H 2
Eyüp, 58,244	D 6
Ezbider, 3,185	H 2
Ezine, 7,819	B 3
Fakılı, 3,377	F 3
Fatih, 71,965	D 6
Fatsa, 9,738	G 2
Feke, 3,030	F 4
Fethiye, 8,386	C 4
Fevzipaşa, 3,917	G 4
Fındıklı, 3,928	J 2
Finike, 4,352	C 4
Foça, 2,953	B 3
Gallipoli, 12,945	B 2
Gaziantep, 160,152	G 4
Gazipaşa, 3,524	D 4
Gebze, 9,269	C 2
Gediz, 7,486	C 3
Gelibolu (Gallipoli), 12,945	B 2
Gemerek, 4,660	G 3
Gemlik, 15,716	C 2
Genç, 3,114	J 3
Genezin, 4,691	F 3
Gerciüş, 2,593	J 4
Gerede, 6,677	E 2
Germencik, 7,344	B 3
Gerze, 5,387	F 2
Gevaş, 4,019	K 3
Geyve, 5,001	D 2
Giresun, 25,331	H 2
Göksun, 4,511	G 3
Gölbaşı, 5,044	G 4
Gölcük, 21,544	C 2
Göle, 3,826	K 2
Gölhisar, 5,562	C 4
Gölköy, 5,852	H 2
Gölmarmara, 8,301	B 3
Gölpazarı, 3,960	D 2
Gönen, 11,666	B 2
Gördes, 5,665	C 3
Görele, 5,687	H 2
Göynük, 2,084	D 2
Güdül, 4,385	E 2
Gülnar, 4,983	E 4
Gülşehir, 3,549	F 3
Gümüş, 2,949	F 2
Gümüşhacıköy, 10,199	F 2
Gümüşhane, 8,092	H 2
Güney, 7,416	C 3
Gürün, 6,374	G 3
Hacılar, 10,149	F 3
Hadım, 7,176	E 4
Hafik, 2,634	G 3
Hakkâri (Çölemerik), 6,129	K 4
Halfeti, 2,622	G 4
Hani, 4,802	H 3
Harput, 2,205	H 3
Haruniye, 5,198	G 4
Hatay (Antakya), 57,855	G 4
Havran, 7,205	B 3
Havza, 10,338	F 2
Haymana, 5,396	E 3
Hayrabolu, 9,444	B 2
Hazro, 3,483	H 3
Hekimhan, 4,288	G 3
Helete, 3,636	G 4
Hendek, 10,788	D 2
Hilvan, 3,390	H 3
Hınıs, 5,263	J 3
Hisarönü, 3,730	E 2
Hopa, 5,703	J 2
Horasan, 5,236	J 3
Hozat, 4,540	H 3
İçel (Mersin), 86,692	F 4
İçme, 2,680	H 3
Iğdır, 15,701	K 2
Ilgaz, 2,924	E 2
Ilgın, 10,196	D 3

Turkey is divided into provinces bearing the same names as their capital towns, except:

Province	Capital	
AFYON-KARAHISAR	Afyon	D 3
AĞRI	Karaköse	K 3
BINGÖL	Çapakçur	J 3
HAKKÂRI	Çölemerik	K 4
HATAY	Antakya	G 4
İÇEL	Mersin	F 4
KOCAELI	İzmit	C 2
SAKARYA	Adapazarı	D 2
TUNCELI	Kalan	H 3

Ilıca, 7,612 ....J 3
İmranlı, 3,176 ....H 3
İmroz, 2,721 ....B 2
İncesu, 5,775 ....F 3
İnebolu, 5,935 ....E 2
İnegöl, 27,777 ....C 2
İnönü, 4,246 ....D 3
İpsala, 6,544 ....B 2
İpsile, 2,246 ....G 2
İskenderun, 69,382 ....G 4
İskilip, 12,400 ....F 2
İslâhiye, 13,775 ....G 4
Isparta, 42,901 ....D 4
İspir, 2,294 ....J 2
İstanbul, 1,742,978 ....D 6
İstanbul, *2,043,447 ....D 6
İzmir, 263,521 ....B 3
İzmir, *411,626 ....B 3
İzmit, 89,547 ....C 2
İznik, 8,213 ....C 2
Kadıköy, 81,945 ....D 6
Kadınhanı, 8,398 ....E 3
Kadirli, 15,926 ....F 4
Kağıthane, 56,157 ....D 6
Kağızman, 9,417 ....K 2
Kâhta, 6,885 ....H 4
Kalan, 5,825 ....H 3
Kale, 3,166 ....C 4
Kalecik, 4,022 ....E 2
Kaman, 10,067 ....E 3
Kandıra, 5,992 ....D 2
Kangal, 4,412 ....G 3
Karabük, 46,169 ....E 2
Karacabey, 18,368 ....C 2
Karahallı, 4,987 ....C 3
Karakoçan, 2,965 ....J 3
Karaköse, 24,168 ....K 3
Karaman, 26,051 ....E 4
Karamanlı, 4,694 ....C 4
Karapınar, 12,989 ....E 4
Karasu, 7,060 ....D 2
Karataş, 3,686 ....F 4
Karayaka, 3,631 ....G 2
Kargı, 3,954 ....F 2
Kars, 41,376 ....K 2
Karşıyaka, 82,574 ....B 3
Kartal, 20,139 ....D 6
Kastamonu, 23,485 ....F 2
Kavak, 2,135 ....C 5
Kavak, 2,473 ....F 2
Kayseri, 126,653 ....F 3
Kazanlı, 3,360 ....F 4

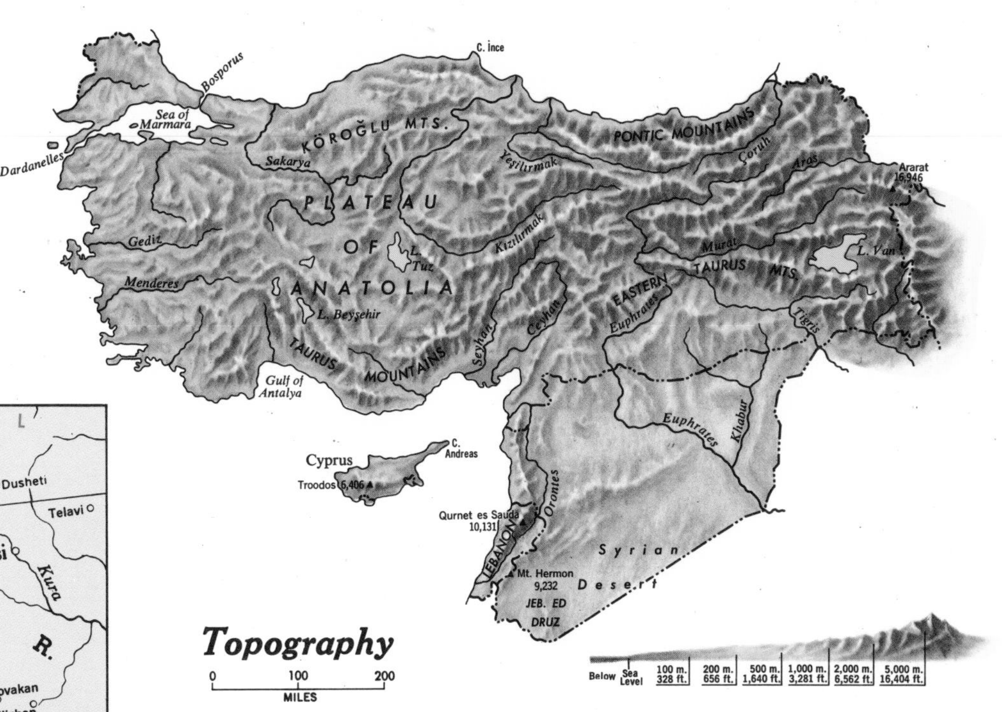

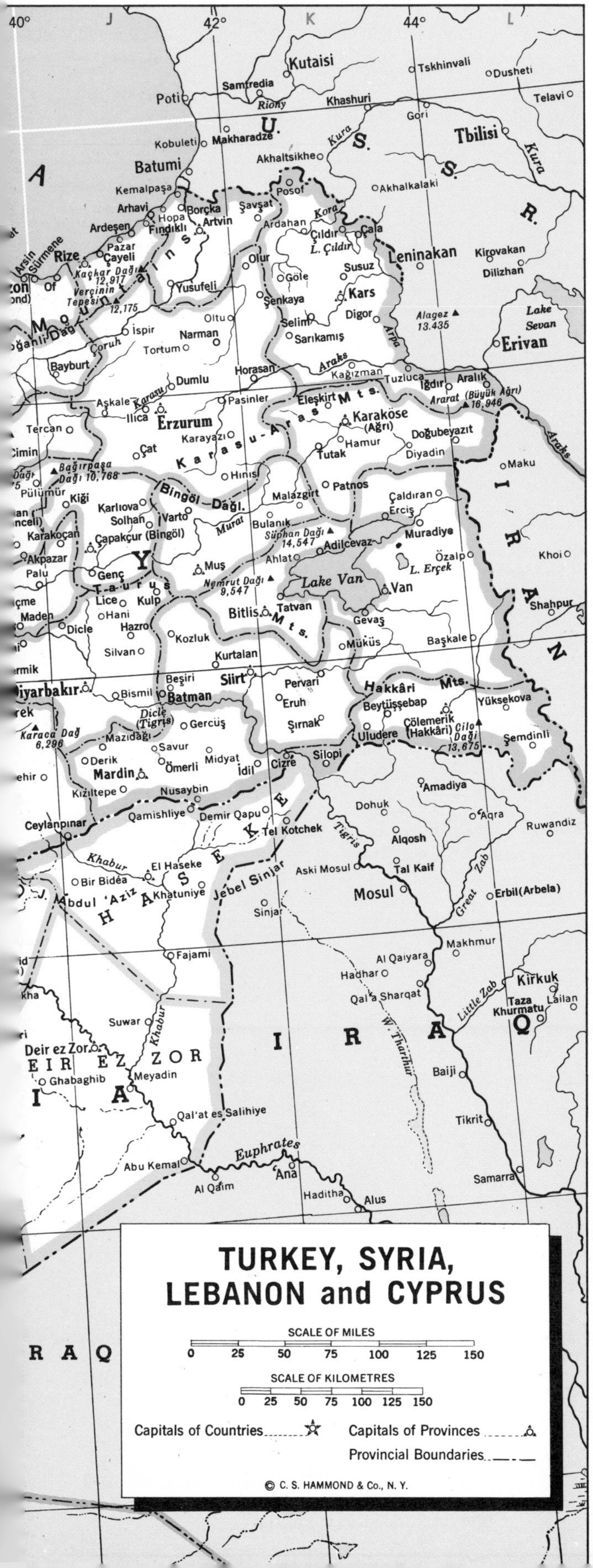

Kazımkarabekir, 3,561 ....E 4
Keban, 2,746 ....H 3
Keçiborlu, 5,430 ....D 4
Kelkit, 4,340 ....H 2
Kemaliye, 2,384 ....H 3
Kemerburgaz, 3,453 ....D 5
Kemerhisar, 5,127 ....F 3
Kepsut, 4,111 ....C 3
Keşan, 20,293 ....B 2
Keşap, 4,402 ....H 2
Keskin, 7,453 ....E 3
Kiğı, 2,241 ....J 3
Kilimli, 21,020 ....E 2
Kilis, 38,095 ....G 4
Kınık, 7,718 ....B 3
Kırıkhan, 23,405 ....G 4
Kırıkkale, 57,669 ....E 3
Kırkağaç, 12,162 ....B 3
Kırklareli, 24,790 ....B 2
Kırşehir, 24,861 ....F 3
Kızılcahamam, 5,202 ....E 2
Kızılhisar, 9,359 ....C 4
Kızıltepe, 9,589 ....J 4
Kızıltoprak, 46,364 ....D 6
Kocaeli (İzmit), 89,547 ....C 2
Konya, 157,934 ....E 4
Korkuteli, 5,602 ....D 4
Köyceğiz, 3,409 ....C 4
Koyulhisar, 2,538 ....G 2
Kozan, 20,236 ....F 4
Kozlu, 25,742 ....D 2
Kozluk, 3,742 ....J 3
Küçükköy, 14,564 ....C 6
Kula, 8,599 ....C 3
Kulp, 3,375 ....J 3
Kulu, 8,905 ....E 3
Kumluca, 4,348 ....D 4
Kurşunlu, 3,068 ....E 2
Kurtalan, 3,422 ....J 3
Kuşadası, 7,388 ....B 4
Kütahya, 49,301 ....C 3
Kuyucak, 4,993 ....C 4
Lâdik, 6,658 ....F 2
Lapseki, 3,264 ....C 6
Lice, 7,643 ....J 3
Lüleburgaz, 25,667 ....B 2
Maden, 10,166 ....H 3
Mağara, 2,906 ....G 4
Mahmudiye, 4,900 ....D 3
Malatya, 104,428 ....H 3
Malazgirt, 7,826 ....K 3
Malkara, 10,763 ....B 2
Maltepe, 16,626 ....D 6
Manavgat, 6,308 ....D 4
Manisa, 69,711 ....B 3
Maraş, 63,284 ....G 4
Mardin, 30,974 ....J 4
Marmaris, 3,641 ....C 4
Mazıdağı, 2,435 ....J 4
Mecitözü, 5,611 ....F 2
Menemen, 16,588 ....B 3
Menye, 2,861 ....C 3
Mersin, 86,692 ....F 4
Merzifon, 23,410 ....F 2
Mesudiye, 2,547 ....G 2
Midyat, 10,391 ....J 4
Mihaliççık, 3,704 ....D 3
Milâs, 12,987 ....B 4
Mucur, 5,683 ....F 3
Mudanya, 6,849 ....C 2
Mudurnu, 3,727 ....D 2
Muğla, 16,408 ....C 4
Muradiye, 2,318 ....K 3
Muş, 15,687 ....J 3
Mustafa Kemalpaşa, 23,179 ....C 3
Mut, 6,556 ....E 4
Muttalip, 3,926 ....D 3
Nallıhan, 3,511 ....D 2
Narman, 3,160 ....J 2
Nazilli, 41,330 ....C 4
Nevşehir, 21,121 ....F 3
Nigde, 21,663 ....F 4
Niksar, 12,577 ....G 2
Nizip, 22,675 ....G 4
Nurhak, 3,240 ....G 4
Nusaybin, 7,584 ....J 4
ödemiş, 30,580 ....C 3
Of, 3,508 ....J 2
Oğuzeli, 5,577 ....G 4
ömerli, 2,381 ....J 4
Oltu, 5,995 ....J 2
Ordu, 27,303 ....G 2
Orhaneli, 2,377 ....C 3
Orta, 2,833 ....E 2
Ortaca, 5,084 ....C 4
Ortakaraviran, 3,688 ....E 4
Ortaköy, 2,651 ....F 3
Osmancık, 8,236 ....F 2
Osmaniye, 34,027 ....G 4
özalp, 2,232 ....K 3
Palu, 4,035 ....H 3
Pasinler, 9,277 ....J 3
Patnos, 5,653 ....K 3
Pazar, 3,962 ....G 2
Pazar, 5,859 ....J 2
Pazarcık, 6,098 ....G 4
Pazaryer, 5,318 ....C 3
Pera (Beyoğlu), 39,984 ....D 6
Perşembe, 4,390 ....G 2
Pertek, 3,578 ....H 3
Pervari, 2,778 ....K 4
Pınarbaşı, 6,328 ....G 3
Pınarhisar, 2,672 ....B 2
Polatlı, 22,558 ....E 3
Pozantı, 2,976 ....F 4
Pülümür, 2,320 ....H 3
Pütürge, 2,843 ....H 3
Reşadiye, 4,546 ....G 2
Reyhanlı, 16,469 ....G 4
Rize, 26,989 ....J 2
Şabanözü, 2,247 ....E 2
Safranbolu, 9,712 ....E 2
Saimbeyli, 2,616 ....G 4
Sakarya (Adapazarı), 86,124 ....D 2
Salihli, 28,909 ....C 3
Samandağı, 15,990 ....F 4
Samsun, 107,510 ....F 2
Sandıklı, 10,192 ....D 3
Sapanca, 6,873 ....D 2
Şaphane, 3,449 ....C 3
Sarayköy, 7,759 ....C 4
Sarayönü, 6,574 ....E 3
Sarıkamış, 16,618 ....K 2
Sarıkaya, 2,309 ....F 3
Sarıoğlan, 2,818 ....F 3
Sarıyer, 24,500 ....D 5
Şarkikaraağaç, 4,585 ....D 3
Şarkışla, 6,766 ....G 3
Şarköy, 4,299 ....B 2
Savastepe, 5,581 ....B 3
Şavşat, 2,301 ....K 2
Savur, 4,046 ....J 4
Şebinkarahisar, 9,764 ....H 2
Şefaatlı, 4,081 ....F 3
Seferihisar, 5,269 ....B 3
Selçuk, 10,227 ....B 3
Selim, 2,939 ....K 2
Selimiye, 2,144 ....B 4
Senirkent, 7,706 ....D 3
Şenkaya, 2,416 ....K 2
Şereflikoçhisar, 11,683 ....E 3
Serik, 7,336 ....D 4
Seydişehir, 6,683 ....D 4
Seyitgazi, 2,612 ....D 3
Siirt, 25,480 ....J 4
Şile, 2,788 ....C 2
Silifke, 11,864 ....E 4
Silivri, 6,114 ....C 2
Silopi, 2,645 ....K 4
Silvan, 12,158 ....J 3
Simav, 8,003 ....C 3
Sincanlı, 3,473 ....D 3
Sındırgı, 6,304 ....C 3
Sinop, 13,354 ....F 2
Şiran, 2,080 ....H 2
Şırnak, 4,936 ....K 4
Sivas, 108,320 ....G 3
Sivaslı, 3,895 ....C 3
Siverek, 27,527 ....H 4
Sivrihisar, 7,442 ....D 3
Smyrna (İzmir), 263,521 ....B 3
Söğüt, 3,008 ....D 3
Söke, 27,558 ....B 4
Soma, 18,633 ....B 3
Sorgun, 6,144 ....F 3
Şuhut, 6,099 ....D 3
Sulakyurt, 2,038 ....E 2
Sultandağı, 5,643 ....D 3
Sultanhanı, 4,116 ....E 3
Suluova, 9,687 ....F 2
Sungurlu, 12,886 ....F 2
Sürmene, 5,286 ....J 2
Sürüç, 9,015 ....H 4
Suşehri, 7,063 ....H 2
Susurluk, 11,268 ....C 3
Susuz, 3,004 ....K 2
Sütçüler, 2,401 ....D 4
Suvarlı, 2,739 ....G 4
Tarsus, 57,737 ....F 4
Taşkent, 5,102 ....E 4
Taşköprü, 7,113 ....F 4
Taşova, 4,021 ....B 2
Tatvan, 10,786 ....K 3
Tavas, 8,408 ....C 4
Tavşanlı, 13,652 ....C 3
Tefenni, 2,893 ....C 4
Tekirdağ, 27,069 ....B 2
Tercan, 2,448 ....J 3
Terme, 8,618 ....G 2
Tire, 27,243 ....B 3
Tirebolu, 5,722 ....H 2
Tokat, 37,368 ....G 2
Tomarza, 4,108 ....F 3
Tömük, 4,610 ....F 4
Tonya, 6,126 ....H 2
Torbalı, 11,712 ....B 3
Tortum, 2,304 ....J 2
Torul, 2,261 ....H 2
Tosya, 14,119 ....F 2
Trabzon, 65,516 ....H 2
Trebizond (Trabzon), 65,516 ....H 2
Tunceli (Kalan) 5,825 ....H 3
Turgutlu, 35,674 ....B 3
Turhal, 22,658 ....F 2
Türkoğlu, 5,941 ....G 4
Tutak, 2,314 ....K 3
Tuzluca, 3,234 ....K 3
Tuzlukçu, 4,423 ....D 3
Ula, 4,616 ....C 4
Ulubey, 4,204 ....C 3
Uluborlu, 6,447 ....D 3
Ulukışla, 4,708 ....F 4
Umurbey, 2,536 ....C 6
Unye, 15,039 ....G 2
Urfa, 73,498 ....H 4
Ürgüp, 5,607 ....F 3
Urla, 12,454 ....B 3
Uşak, 35,517 ....C 3
Üsküdar, 84,358 ....D 6
Üzümlü, 4,407 ....D 4
Uzunköprü, 20,237 ....B 2
Vakfikebir, 5,032 ....H 2
Van, 31,431 ....K 3
Varto, 2,804 ....J 3
Vezirköprü, 9,431 ....F 2
Viranşehir, 11,063 ....H 4
Vize, 6,998 ....B 2
Yahyalı, 10,283 ....F 3
Yalova, 14,241 ....C 2
Yalvaç, 10,912 ....D 3
Yatağan, 3,406 ....C 4
Yayladağ, 2,841 ....F 5
Yenice, 4,866 ....E 2
Yenice, 3,281 ....F 4
Yeniceoba, 4,051 ....E 3
Yeniköy, 22,229 ....D 6
Yenimahalle, 66,079 ....E 3
Yenişehir, 11,352 ....C 2
Yerkesik, 2,729 ....C 4
Yerköy, 11,962 ....F 3
Yeşilhisar, 8,647 ....F 3
Yeşilköy, 16,857 ....D 6
Yeşilova, 2,588 ....C 4
Yeşilova, 4,880 ....E 3
Yeşilyurt, 7,436 ....H 2
Yıldızeli, 5,921 ....G 3
Yozgat, 23,081 ....F 3
Yüksekova, 2,768 ....L 4
Yunak, 4,452 ....D 3
Yusufeli, 2,183 ....J 2
Zara, 7,661 ....G 3
Zeytinburnu, 102,874 ....D 6
Zeytindağ, 3,460 ....B 3
Zile, 26,113 ....G 2
Zonguldak, 55,404 ....D 2

OTHER FEATURES

Abydos (ruins) ....B 6
Acı (lake) ....C 4
Adalar (island), 5,261 ....D 6
Aegean (sea) ....A 3
Ak Dağ (mts.) ....G 3
Akşehir (lake) ....D 3
Aksu (river) ....D 4
Aladağ (mt.) ....F 4
Alexandretta (gulf) ....F 4
Amanos (mts.) ....G 4
Anamur (cape) ....E 5
Ankara (river) ....D 3
Antalya (gulf) ....D 4
Anti-Taurus (mountains) ....F 4
Apolyont (lake) ....C 2
Araks (river) ....K 2
Ararat (mt.) ....L 3
Arpa (river) ....K 2
Baba (cape) ....A 3
Bafa (lake) ....B 4
Bafra (cape) ....G 2
Balik (lake) ....G 2
Balkar (mts.) ....F 4
Batı Fırat (river) ....H 3
Beyşehir (lake) ....D 4
Bingöl Dağları (mountains) ....J 3
Bosporus (strait) ....D 5
Bozcaada (island), 2,141 ....A 3
Burdur (lake) ....D 4
Burgaz, (island), 2,919 ....D 6
Büyük Ağrı (Ararat) (mountain) ....L 3
Çanakkale Boğazı (Dardanelles) (strait) ....B 6
Canik (mts.) ....G 2
Ceyhan (river) ....F 4
Cıldır (lake) ....K 2
Cilo Dağı (mt.) ....K 4
Çoruh (river) ....J 2
Çorum (river) ....F 2
Dardanelles (strait) ....B 6
Dedegöl Tepesi (mt.) ....D 4
Deliceırmak (river) ....F 3
Devrez (river) ....E 2
Dicle (river) ....J 4
Eastern Taurus (mountains) ....J 3
Edremit (gulf) ....B 3
Eğridir (lake) ....D 4
Emiroğlu Tepesi (mt.) ....D 3
Ephesus (ruins) ....B 4
Erçek (lake) ....K 3
Erciyas Dağı (mt.) ....F 3
Ergene (river) ....B 2
Euphrates (Fırat) (river) ....H 4
Filyos (river) ....D 2
Fırat (river) ....G 4
Gediz (river) ....B 3
Gelidonya (cape) ....D 4
Gökırmak (river) ....E 2
Göksu (river) ....E 4
Hasan Dağı (mt.) ....E 3
Heybeli (island), 7,039 ....D 6
Honaz Dağı (mt.) ....C 4
Hoyran (lake) ....D 3
Iğneada (cape) ....C 2
Ilium (ruins) ....B 6
İmrali (island) ....C 2
İmroz (island), 5,941 ....A 2
İnce (cape) ....F 1
İstranca (mts.) ....B 2
İzmar (gulf) ....B 3
İznik (lake) ....C 2
Kaçkar Dağı (mt.) ....J 2
Karaca Dağ (mt.) ....H 4
Karadeniz Boğazı (Bosporus) (strait) ....C 2
Karasu (river) ....J 3
Kelkit (river) ....G 2
Kerme (gulf) ....B 4
Keşiş Tepesi (mt.) ....H 3
Kınalı (island) ....D 6
Kirmastı (river) ....C 3
Kızılırmak (river) ....E 2
Koca (river) ....C 3
Koca (river) ....C 6
Kora (river) ....K 2
Köroğlu (mts.) ....E 2
Köroğlu Tepe (mt.) ....E 2
Küre (mts.) ....E 2
Kuşada (gulf) ....B 4
Mandalya (gulf) ....B 4
Manyas (lake) ....B 2
Marmara (island), 4,917 ....B 2
Marmara (sea) ....C 2
Medetsız Tepe (mt.) ....F 4
Menderes (river) ....C 4
Meriç (river) ....B 2
Murat (river) ....H 3
Murat Dağı (mt.) ....C 3
Nuruhak Dağı (mt.) ....G 3
Pontic (mts.) ....H 2
Porsuk (river) ....D 3
Sakarya (river) ....D 2
Saros (gulf) ....B 5
Seyhan (river) ....F 4
Simav (river) ....C 3
Sinop (cape) ....F 1
Sultan (mts.) ....D 3
Süphan Dağı (mt.) ....K 3
Taurus (mts.) ....D 4
Tigris (Dicle) (river) ....J 4
Troy (Ilium) (ruins) ....B 6
Tuz (lake) ....E 3
Uludağ (mt.) ....C 3
Van (lake) ....K 3
Yaralıgöz Dağı (mt.) ....F 2
Yesilırmak (river) ....G 2

*City and suburbs.

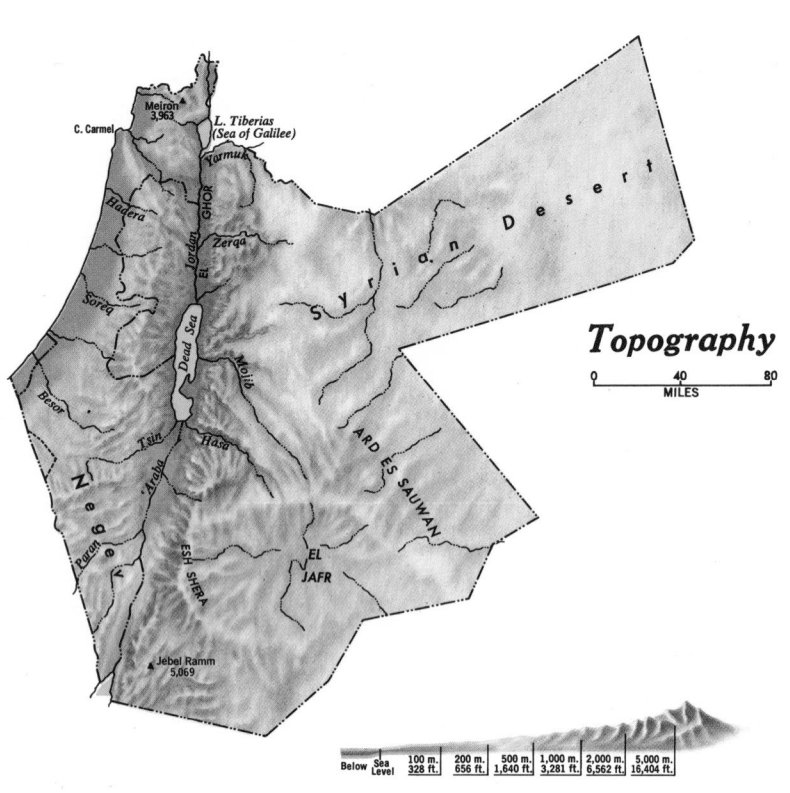

Topography

```
0        40      80
       MILES
```

```
Below  Sea    100 m.   200 m.   500 m.   1,000 m.  2,000 m.  5,000 m.
       Level  328 ft.  656 ft.  1,640 ft. 3,281 ft. 6,562 ft. 16,404 ft.
```

ISRAEL

DISTRICTS

Central, 572,300 .... B 3
Haifa, 480,800 .... C 2
Jerusalem, 338,600 .... B 4
Northern, 473,700 .... C 2
Southern, 351,300 .... B 5
Tel Aviv, 905,100 .... B 3

CITIES and TOWNS

Acre, 34,400 .... C 2
Afiqim, 1,243 .... D 2
'Afula, 17,400 .... C 2
Ahuzzam, 407 .... B 4
Akko (Acre), 34,400 .... C 2
Arad, 5,400 .... C 5
'Arrabe, 6,000 .... C 2
Ashdod, 40,500 .... B 4
Ashdot Ya'aqov, 1,197 ...... D 2
Ashqelon, 43,100 .... A 4
Atlit, 1,516 .... B 2
Avihayil, 579 .... B 3
Bat Shelomo, 218 .... B 2
Bat Yam, 114,000 .... B 3
Be'eri, 390 .... A 5
Beersheba, 104,000 .... D 4
Be'er Tuveya, 602 .... B 4
Beit Guvrin, ... B 4
Bene Beraq, 74,100 .... B 3
Bet Dagan, 2,932 .... B 4
Bet Hagaddi, 566 .... B 5
Bet Qama, 228 .... B 5
Bet She'an, 11,300 .... D 3
Bet Shemesh, 10,100 .... C 4
Binyamina, 2,701 .... B 2
Carmiel, ... C 2
Dafna, 577 .... D 1
Dalyat al-Karmel, 6,200 ... C 2
Dan, 498 .... D 1
Dimona, 23,700 .... D 4
Dor, 195 .... B 2
'Ein Harod, 1,372 .... C 2
Elath (Elat), 12,800 ...... D 5
El 'Auja .... D 5
Elyakim, 568 .... C 2
Elyashiv, 435 .... B 3
Even Yehuda, 3,464 .... B 3
Gal'on, 356 .... B 4
Gan Yavne, 2,668 .... B 4
Gat, 430 .... B 4
Gedera, 5,400 .... B 4
Gesher, 360 .... C 2
Gesher Haziv, 238 .... C 1
Gevar'am, 283 .... A 4
Gilat, 561 .... B 5
Ginnosar, 473 .... D 2
Giv'atayim, 48,500 .... B 3
Giv'at Brenner, 1,505 ..... B 4
Giv'at Hayyim, 1,360 ...... B 3
Gosh Halav (Jish), 1,498 .. C 1
Habonim, 189 .... B 2
Hadera, 31,900 .... B 3
Haifa, 225,000 .... B 2
Haifa, *353,700 .... B 2
Hatseva .... D 5
Hazerim, 127 .... B 5
Helez, 466 .... B 4

Herzeliyya, 41,200 .... B 3
Hod Hasharon, 13,500 ...... B 3
Hodiyya, 400 .... B 4
Holon, 110,300 .... B 3
Iksal, 2,156 .... C 2
Jerusalem (cap.), 344,200 . C 4
Jish, 1,498 .... C 1
Kafar Kanna, 5,200 .... C 2
Kafar Yasif, 2,975 .... C 2
Karkur-Pardes Hanna, 13,600 C 3
Kefar Atta, 27,000 .... C 2
Kefar Blum, 565 .... D 1
Kefar Gil'adi, 701 .... C 1
Kefar Ruppin, 306 .... D 2
Kefar Sava, 26,500 .... B 3
Kefar Vitkin, 808 .... B 3
Kefar Yona, 2,372 .... B 3
Kefar Zekhariya, 420 ...... B 4
Kinneret, 909 .... D 2
Kurnub .... C 5
Lod (Lydda), 30,500 .... B 4
Lydda, 30,500 .... B 4
Magen, 149 .... A 5
Malkiya .... D 1
Mash 'Abbe Sade, 238 ...... B 6
Mavqi'im, 177 .... B 4
Megiddo .... C 2
Me'ona, 317 .... C 1
Metula, 261 .... D 1
Migdal, 688 .... C 2
Mikhmoret, 608 .... B 3
Mishmar Hanegev, 336 ...... B 5
Mishmar Hayarden .... D 1
Mivtahim, 398 .... A 5
Mizpe Ramon, 331 .... D 5
Moza Illit, 219 .... C 4
Mughar, 4,010 .... C 2
Muqeible, 459 .... C 2
Nahariyya, 24,000 .... C 1
Nazareth, 33,300 .... C 2
Negba, 453 .... B 4
Nesher, 9,400 .... C 2
Nes Ziyyona, 11,700 .... B 4
Netanya, 70,700 .... B 3
Nevatim, 436 .... B 5
Newe Yam, 211 .... B 2
Nir Am, 331 .... B 4
Nir Yitzhaq, 209 .... A 5
Nizzanim, 479 .... B 4
Oron .... C 6
Pardes Hanna-Karkur, 13,600 C 3
Peduyim, 361 .... B 5
Petah Tiqwa, 103,000 ...... B 3
Qadima, 2,937 .... B 3
Qedma, 157 .... B 4
Qiryat Bialik, 18,000 ..... C 2
Qiryat Gat, 19,200 .... B 4
Qiryat Haayin, 25,600 ..... C 2
Qiryat Motzkin, 17,600 .... C 2
Qiryat Shemona, 15,200 .... C 1
Qiryat Tiv'on, 9,800 ...... C 2
Qiryat Yam, 19,800 .... C 2
Ra'anana, 14,900 .... B 3
Ramat Gan, 120,200 .... B 3
Ramat Hasharon, 20,100 .... B 3
Rame, 2,986 .... C 2
Ramla, 34,100 .... B 4
Rehovot, 39,200 .... B 4
Re'im, 155 .... A 5
Revadim, 175 .... B 4

Revivim, 258 .... D 5
Rishon Le Ziyyon, 51,900 .. B 4
Rosh Pinna, 700 .... D 2
Ruhama, 497 .... B 4
Sa'ad, 418 .... B 5
Safad (Zefat), 13,600 ..... C 2
Sakhnin, 8,400 .... C 2
Sede Boqer .... D 5
Sedom .... C 5
Sedot Yam, 511 .... B 2
Shave Ziyyon, 269 .... C 1
Shefar'am, 11,800 .... C 2
Shefayim, 614 .... B 3
Shoval, 393 .... B 4
Tayibe, 11,700 .... C 3
Tel Aviv-Jaffa, 357,600 ... B 3
Tel Aviv-Jaffa, *1,156,800 B 3
Tiberias, 23,800 .... D 2
Tirat Hakarmel, 14,400 .... B 2
Tirat Zevi, 353 .... D 3
Tur'an, 2,304 .... C 2
Umm el Fahm, 13,300 .... C 2
Urim, 203 .... B 5
Uzza, 487 .... B 4
Yad Mordekhai, 416 .... A 4
Yagur, 1,266 .... C 2
Yahav .... D 5
Yavne, 10,100 .... B 4
Yavne'el, 1,580 .... D 2
Yehud, 8,900 .... B 3
Yeroham, 5,800 .... D 5
Yesodot, 293 .... B 4
Yesud Hama'ala, 428 .... D 1
Yiftah .... D 1
Yirka, 2,715 .... C 2
Yoqne'am, 2,884 .... C 2
Yotvata .... D 5
Zavdi'el, 396 .... B 4
Ze'elim, 148 .... A 5
Zefat, 13,600 .... C 2
Zikhron Ya'aqov, 6,500 .... B 2
Zippori, 241 .... C 2

OTHER FEATURES

'Araba, Wadi (dry riv.) ... D 5
Beer Sheva (dry riv.) ..... B 5
Besor (riv.) .... B 5
Carmel (cape) .... C 2
Carmel (mt.) .... C 2
Dead (sea) .... C 4
'Ein Gedi (well) .... C 5
Galilee, Sea of (Tiberias)
   (lake) .... D 2
Galilee (reg.) .... C 2
Gerar (dry riv.) .... B 5
Hadera (dry riv.) .... B 3
Haniqra, Rosh (cape) ...... C 1
Jordan (riv.) .... D 3
Judaea (reg.) .... B 5
Lakhish (dry riv.) .... B 4
Meiron (mt.) .... C 1
Negev (reg.) .... D 5
Qishon (riv.) .... C 2
Ramon (mt.) .... D 5
Rubin (dry riv.) .... B 4
Tabor (mt.) .... C 2
Tiberias (lake) .... D 2
Yarmuk (riv.) .... D 2
Yarqon (riv.) .... B 3
```

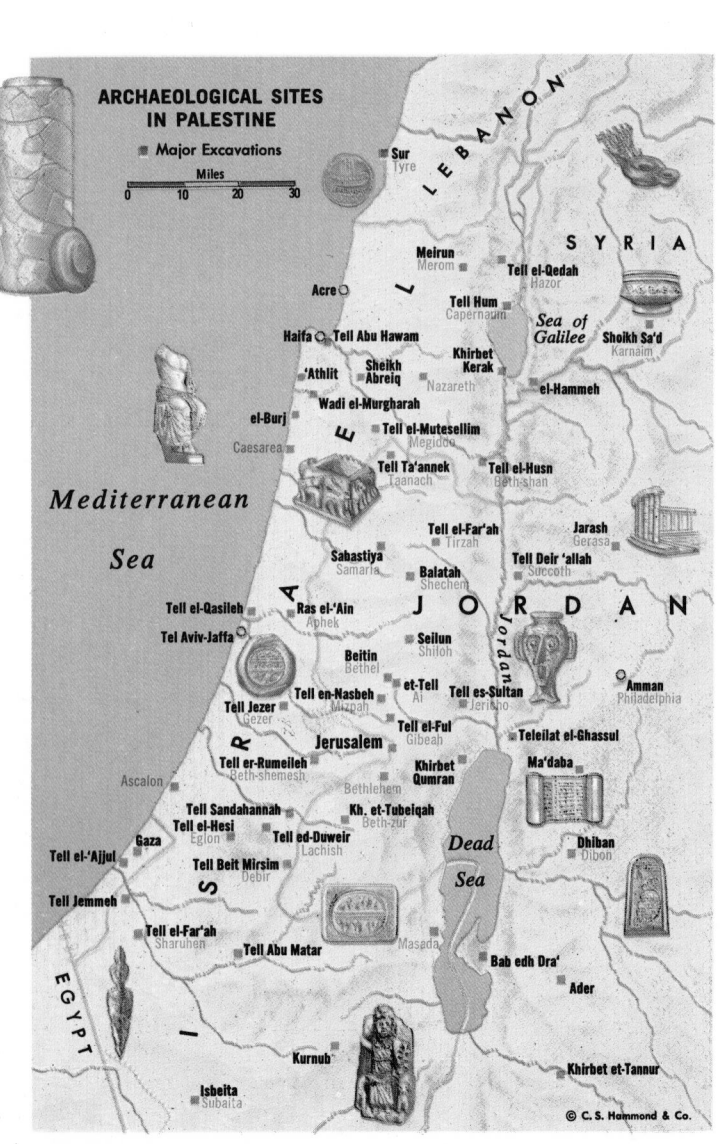

## ARCHAEOLOGICAL SITES IN PALESTINE

■ Major Excavations

```
        Miles
0   10   20    30
```

© C. S. Hammond & Co.

Agriculture, Industry and Resources

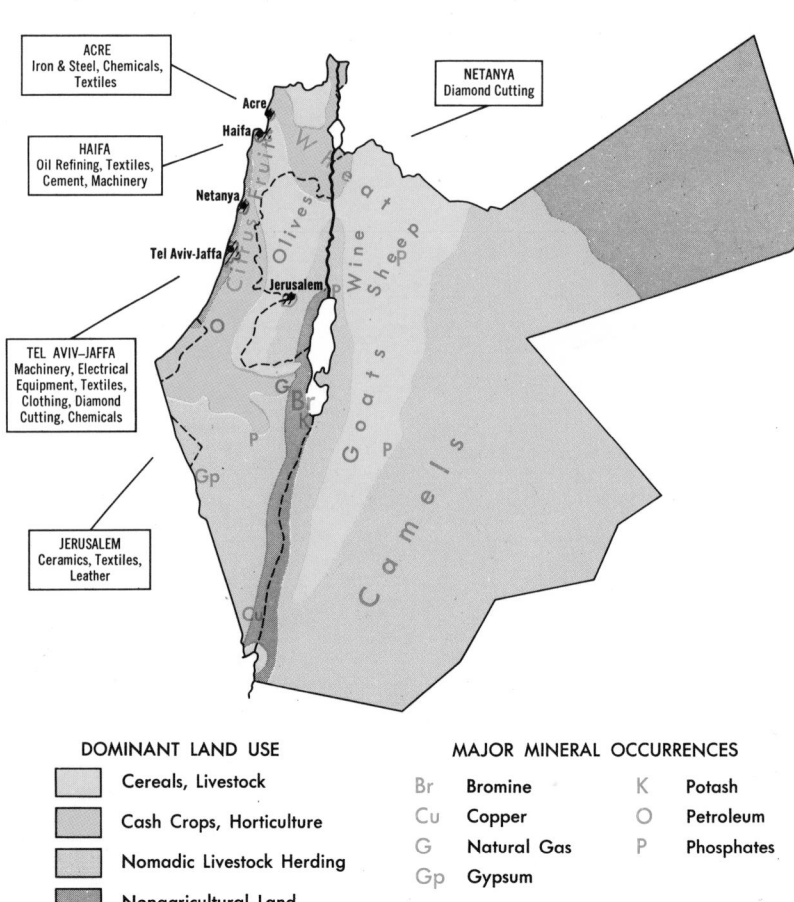

ACRE
Iron & Steel, Chemicals, Textiles

NETANYA
Diamond Cutting

HAIFA
Oil Refining, Textiles, Cement, Machinery

TEL AVIV–JAFFA
Machinery, Electrical Equipment, Textiles, Clothing, Diamond Cutting, Chemicals

JERUSALEM
Ceramics, Textiles, Leather

DOMINANT LAND USE

- Cereals, Livestock
- Cash Crops, Horticulture
- Nomadic Livestock Herding
- Nonagricultural Land

MAJOR MINERAL OCCURRENCES

Br Bromine
Cu Copper
G   Natural Gas
Gp Gypsum
K   Potash
O   Petroleum
P   Phosphates

▨ Major Industrial Areas
```

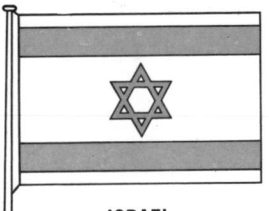

ISRAEL

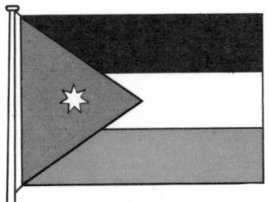

JORDAN

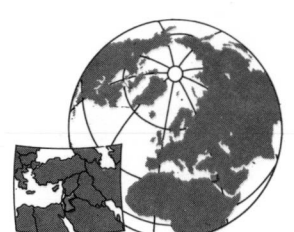

ISRAEL
AREA 7,847 sq. mi.
POPULATION 3,459,000
CAPITAL Jerusalem
LARGEST CITY Tel Aviv-Jaffa
HIGHEST POINT Meiron 3,963 ft.
MONETARY UNIT Israeli pound
MAJOR LANGUAGES Hebrew, Arabic
MAJOR RELIGIONS Judaism, Islam, Christianity

JORDAN
AREA 37,737 sq. mi.
POPULATION 2,700,000
CAPITAL Amman
LARGEST CITY Amman
HIGHEST POINT Jeb. Ramm 5,755 ft.
MONETARY UNIT Jordanian dinar
MAJOR LANGUAGE Arabic
MAJOR RELIGION Islam

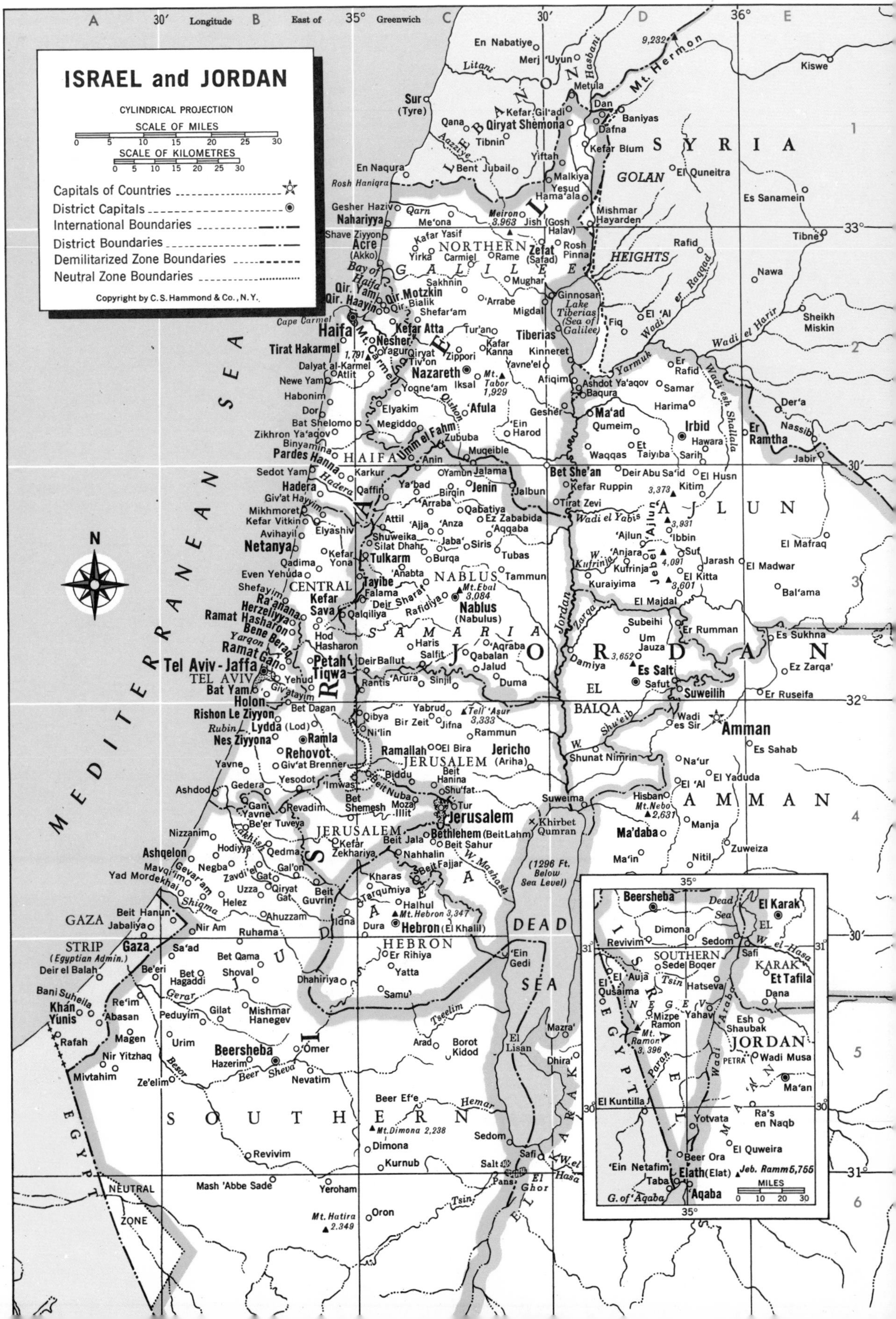

ISRAEL and JORDAN
CYLINDRICAL PROJECTION
SCALE OF MILES
0 5 10 15 20 25 30
SCALE OF KILOMETRES
0 5 10 15 20 25 30

Capitals of Countries .... ☆
District Capitals .... ◉
International Boundaries ....
District Boundaries ....
Demilitarized Zone Boundaries .....
Neutral Zone Boundaries ....

Copyright by C. S. Hammond & Co., N.Y.

JORDAN

GOVERNORATES

...un, 506,000	D 3
...man, 1,000,000	D 4
...alqa, 113,000	D 4
...arak, 93,000	E 5
...bron, 145,000	C 5
...usalem, 288,000	C 4
...an, 62,000	D 5
...blus, 414,000	C 3

CITIES and TOWNS

...a, 1,322	C 3
...un, ‡42,000	D 3
...man (cap.), 615,000	D 4
...abta, 3,426	C 2
...in, 914	D 2
...jara, 3,163	C 3
...za, 807	A 5
...qaba, 1,127	C 3
...ba (Jericho), 5,312	C 4
...aba, 4,231	C 3
...ara, 849	C 3
...il, 3,808	D 4
...ama, 769	E 3
...qura, 3,042	D 2
...t Fajjar, 2,474	C 4
...t Hanina, 1,177	C 4
...t Jala, 6,041	C 4
...t Lahm (Bethlehem), 14,439	C 4
...t Nuba, 1,350	C 4
...t Sahur, 5,380	C 4
...hlehem, 14,439	C 4
...ddu, 1,259	C 4
...qin, 2,036	C 3
...Zeit, 2,311	C 4
...rqa, 2,477	D 3
...miya, 483	D 3
...na, 844	E 5
...r Abu Sa'id, 1,927	D 3
...r Ballut, 1,058	C 4
...r Sharaf, 973	C 3
...ahiriya, 4,875	B 5
...ira*	D 5
...ma, 524	C 3
...ra, 4,954	C 4
...Al, 492	D 4
...Bira, 9,674	C 4
...Bira, *13,037	C 4
...Husn, 3,728	D 3
...Karak, 10,000	E 4
...Khalil (Hebron), 38,309	C 4
...kitta, 987	D 3
...Madwar, 164	E 3
...Mafraq, 15,500	E 3
...Majdal, 259	D 3
...Quweira, 268	D 6
...Yaduda, 251	D 4
...Rafid, 787	D 2
...Rihiya, 679	C 5
...Rumman, 293	D 3
...Ruseifa, 6,200	E 3
...h Shaubak, *4,634	D 5
...Sahab, 2,580	E 4
...Salt, 24,000	D 3
...Sukhna, 649	E 3
...Taiyiba, 2,606	D 2
...Zababida, 1,474	C 3
...Zarqa, 226,000	E 3
...ica, 162	C 4
...ahul, 6,041	C 4
...aris, 641	D 2
...awara, 2,342	D 2
...ebron, 38,309	C 4
...sban, 718	D 4
...bin, 1,364	D 3
...nwas, 1,955	B 4
...old, 125,000	D 2
...aba*, 2,817	C 3
...abir, 132	E 2
...alama, 784	C 3
...lbun, 914	C 3
...alud, 221	C 3
...arash, ‡29,000	D 3
...enin, 8,346	C 3
...enin, *13,365	C 3
...ericho, 5,312	C 4
...ericho, *6,931	C 4
...fna, 655	C 4

Kharas, 1,364	C 4
Kitim, 1,026	D 3
Kufrinja, 3,922	D 3
Kuraiyima	D 3
Ma'ad, 125	D 2
Ma'an, 9,500	D 5
Ma'daba, 22,600	D 4
Ma'in, 1,271	D 4
Manja, 353	D 4
Mazra	C 5
Nablus (Nabulus), 41,799	C 3
Nablus, *44,223	C 3
Nahhalin, 1,109	C 4
Na'ur, 2,382	D 4
Ni'lin, 1,227	C 4
Nitil, 348	D 4
Qabalan, 1,970	C 3
Qabatiya, 6,005	C 3
Qaffin, 2,480	C 3
Qalqiliya, 8,926	C 3
Qumeim, 955	D 2
Rafidiya, 1,123	C 3
Ramallah, 12,134	C 4
Rammun, 1,198	C 4
Rantis, 897	C 4
Ra's en Naqb, 225	E 5
Safi	E 5
Safut, 4,210	D 3
Salfit, 3,201	C 3
Samu', 3,784	C 5
Sarih, 3,390	D 3
Shu'fat, 14,000	C 4
Silat Dhahr, 2,104	C 3
Sinjil, 1,823	C 3
Siris, 1,285	C 3
Subeihi, 514	D 3
Suf	D 3
Suweilih, 3,457	D 3
Suweima, 315	D 4
Tammun, 2,952	C 3
Tarqumiya, 2,412	C 4
Tubas, 5,262	C 3
Tulkarm, 10,255	C 3
Tulkarm, *15,275	C 3
Tur, 12,200	C 4
Um Jauza, 582	D 3
Wadi es Sir, 4,455	D 4
Wadi Musa, 654	E 5
Waqqas, 2,321	D 3
Ya'bad, 4,857	C 3
Yabrud, 277	C 4
Yamun, 4,384	C 3
Yatta, 7,281	C 5
Zububa, 633	C 2
Zuweiza, 126	D 4

OTHER FEATURES

'Ajlun (range)	D 3
'Aqaba (gulf)	D 6
'Araba, Wadi (dry riv.)	D 5
Dead (sea)	C 4
Ebal (mt.)	C 3
El Ghor (reg.)	C 5
El Lisan (pen.)	C 5
Hebron (dist.)	C 4
Jordan (riv.)	D 3
Judaea (reg.)	C 4
Khirbet Qumran (site)	D 4
Nebo (mt.)	D 4
Petra (ruins)	D 5
Ramm, Jebel (mt.)	D 5
Samaria (reg.)	C 3
Tell 'Asur (mt.)	C 4
Zarqa' (riv.)	D 3

GAZA STRIP

CITIES and TOWNS

'Abasan, 1,481	A 5
Bani Suheila, 7,561	A 5
Beit Hanun, 4,756	A 4
Deir el Balah, 10,854	A 5
Deir el Balah, *18,118	A 5
Gaza, 87,793	A 5
Gaza, *118,272	A 5
Jabaliya, 10,508	A 4
Jabaliya, *43,604	A 4
Khan Yunis, 29,522	A 5
Khan Yunis, *52,997	A 5
Rafah, 10,812	A 5
Rafah, *49,812	A 5

*City and suburbs.
‡Population of subdivision.

IRAN

INTERNAL DIVISIONS

Bakhtiari (governorate),
298,448 .... F 4
Boyer Ahmedi and Kahkiluye
(governorate) .... G 5
Central (province), 4,979,081 ... G 3
East Azerbaijan (province),
2,596,439 .... E 1
Fars (province), 1,429,804 ...... H 6
Gilan (province), 1,752,504 ..... F 2
Hamadan (governorate),
889,888 .... F 3
Ilam (governorate) .... E 4
Isfahan (province),
1,703,701 .... H 4
Kerman (province), 761,851 ...... K 6
Kermanshah (prov.), 924,717 ..... E 3
Khurasan (prov.), 2,497,381 ..... K 3
Khuzistan (prov.), 1,578,079 .... F 5
Kurdistan (province), 619,573 ... E 3
Luristan (governorate)
686,307 .... F 4
Mazanderan (province),
1,841,637 .... H 2
Ports and Islands
(province), 346,410 .... H 7
Samnan (governorate),
207,786 .... J 3
Seistan and Baluchistan (prov.),
454,996 .... M 6
Southern Coast (province),
251,921 .... G 6
West Azerbaijan (province),
1,087,182 .... D 1
Yezd (governorate) .... J 5
Zenjan (governorate) .... F 2

CITIES and TOWNS

Abadan, 272,962 .... F 5
Abadeh, 16,000 .... H 5
Abarquh, 8,000 .... H 5
Abhar, 11,000 .... F 2
Ahar, 24,000 .... E 1
Ahwaz, 206,375 .... F 5
Amul, 40,076 .... H 2
Anarak, 2,038 .... H 4
Andimeshk, 16,000 .... F 4
Aradan, 18,925 .... H 3
Arak, 71,925 .... F 3
Ardabil, 83,596 .... E 1
Ardistan, 6,645 .... H 4
Asadabad, 7,000 .... F 3
Asterabad (Gurgan)
51,181 .... J 2
Azarshahr, 6,000 .... D 2
Azna, 5,000 .... F 4
Babol, 49,973 .... H 2
Babulsar, 12,000 .... H 2
Bafq, 5,000 .... J 5
Baft, 6,000 .... K 6
Bahramabad, 21,000 .... K 5
Bam, 22,000 .... L 6
Bandar 'Abbas, 34,627 .... J 7
Bandar Ma'shur,
17,000 .... F 5
Bandar Shah, 13,000 .... H 2
Bandar Shahpur, 6,000 .... F 5
Behbehan, 39,874 .... G 5
Behshahr, 26,032 .... H 2
Bijar, 12,000 .... E 3
Birjand, 25,854 .... L 4
Borazjun, 20,000 .... G 6
Bujnurd, 31,248 .... K 2
Bukan, 9,000 .... D 2
Burujird, 71,476 .... F 3

Bushire, 26,032 .... G 6
Chalus, 15,000 .... G 2
Dalijan, 6,000 .... G 4
Damghan, 13,000 .... J 2
Darab, 13,000 .... J 6
Daran, 4,609 .... G 4
Darreh Gaz, 11,000 .... L 2
Daulatabad (Malayer), 28,434 .... F 3
Deh Haqq, 4,115 .... H 4
Demavend, 5,391 .... H 3
Dizful, 84,499 .... F 4
Duzdab (Zahidan), 40,000 .... M 6
Enzeli (Pahlevi), 41,785 .... F 2
Estahbanat, 18,187 .... H 6
Fahrej (Iranshahr), 5,000 .... M 7
Fariman, 8,000 .... L 3
Farrashband, 3,532 .... G 6
Fasa, 19,000 .... H 6
Firdaus, 11,000 .... K 3
Firuzabad, 8,718 .... G 6
Firuzkuh, 4,684 .... H 3
Fumen, 9,000 .... F 2
Gach Saran ....G 5
Ganaveh, 9,000 .... G 6
Garmsar, 6,000 .... H 3
Golshan (Tabas), 10,000 .... K 4
Gulpaigan, 20,515 .... G 4
Gumishan, 6,000 .... J 2
Gunbad-i-Qabus, 40,667 .... K 3
Gurgan, 51,181 .... J 2
Haft Kel, 10,000 .... F 5
Hamadan, 124,167 .... F 3
Hashtgar, 5,000 .... F 2
Homayunshahr, 46,836 .... G 4
Ilam, 15,000 .... E 4
Iranshahr, 5,000 .... M 7
Isfahan, 424,045 .... H 4
Jahrum, 38,236 .... H 6

Kangavar, 9,414 .... F 3
Karaj, 44,243 .... G 3
Kashan, 58,468 .... G 3
Kashmar, 17,000 .... L 3
Kazerun, 39,758 .... G 6
Kazvin, 88,106 .... F 3
Kerman, 85,404 .... K 5
Kermanshah, 187,930 .... E 3
Khaf, 5,000 .... L 3
Khoi, 47,648 .... D 1
Khorramshahr, 88,536 .... F 5
Khunsar, 10,947 .... G 4
Khur, 2,912 .... J 4
Lahijan, 25,725 .... F 2
Lar, 22,000 .... J 7
Mahabad, 28,610 .... D 2
Mahallat, 12,000 .... G 4
Mahan, 15,000 .... K 5
Maibud, 15,000 .... J 4
Maku, 15,000 .... D 1
Malayer, 28,434 .... F 3
Maragheh, 54,106 .... D 1
Marand, 24,000 .... D 1
Marvdasht, 25,498 .... H 6
Masjid-i-Sulaiman, 64,488 .... F 5
Meshed, 409,616 .... L 2
Meshed-i-Sar (Babulsar)
12,000 .... H 2
Meshkinshahr, 9,000 .... E 1
Mianeh, 28,447 .... E 2
Mirjawa, 11,000 .... M 6
Miyanduab, 19,000 .... D 1
Naft-i-Shah, 3,043 .... E 4
Na'in, 5,925 .... H 4
Nasratabad (Zabul), 20,000 ...... M 5
Natanz, 4,370 .... H 4
Naushahr, 8,000 .... G 2
Nehavend, 24,000 .... F 3

Nejafabad, 43,384 .... G 4
Niriz, 16,114 .... J 6
Pahlevi (Enzeli), 41,785 .... F 2
Qain, 6,000 .... L 4
Qasr-i-Shirin, 15,904 .... E 3
Quchan, 29,133 .... L 2
Qum, 134,292 .... G 3
Rafsenjan (Bahramabad),
21,000 .... K 5
Rai, 102,825 .... G 3
Ram Hormuz, 9,000 .... F 5
Ramsar, 12,000 .... G 2
Resht, 143,557 .... F 2
Reza'iyeh, 110,749 .... D 2
Sabzawar, 42,415 .... K 2
Sabzawaran, 7,000 .... K 6
Saidabad (Sirjan), 20,000 .... J 6
Samnan, 31,058 .... J 3
Sanandaj, 54,578 .... E 3
Sang-i-Sar, 9,000 .... J 3
Saqqiz, 17,000 .... E 2
Sarab, 16,000 .... E 2
Sardasht, 6,000 .... D 2
Sari, 44,547 .... H 2
Savanat (Estahbanat),
18,187 .... H 6
Saveh, 17,565 .... G 3
Shahabad, 12,000 .... E 3
Shahdegan, 6,000 .... F 5
Shahi, 38,898 .... H 2
Shahpur, 22,000 .... D 1
Shahr-i-Kurd, 24,000 .... G 4
Shahraza, 34,220 .... H 4
Shahrud, 30,767 .... J 2
Shahsawar, 12,000 .... G 2
Shiraz, 269,865 .... H 6
Shirvan, 11,000 .... F 1

Shushtar, 24,000 .... F 4
Sinneh (Sanandaj), 54,578 .... E 3
Sirjan, 20,000 .... J 6
Sultanabad (Kashmar),
17,000 .... L 3
Sunqur, 10,433 .... E 3
Susangird, 21,000 .... F 5
Tabas, 10,000 .... K 4
Tabriz, 403,413 .... D 1
Taft, 7,000 .... J 5
Tajrish, 157,486 .... G 3
Takistan, 13,485 .... F 2
Tehran (capital), 2,719,730 ..... G 3
Tuiserkan, 12,000 .... F 3
Tun (Firdaus), 11,000 .... K 3
Turbat-i-Haidari, 30,106 .... L 3
Turbat-i-Shaikh Jam, 13,000 ..... M 3
Urmia (Reza'iyeh), 110,749 ...... D 2
Ushnuiyeh, 5,000 .... D 2
Veramin, 11,083 .... G 3
Yezd, 93,241 .... J 4
Zahidan, 39,732 .... M 6
Zarand, 5,000 .... K 5
Zarghan, 7,000 .... H 6
Zenjan, 58,714 .... F 2

OTHER FEATURES

Ab-i-Diz (river) .... F 4
Aji Chai (river) .... D 1
Arabi (isl.) .... D 7
Aras (Araks) (river) .... D 1
Atrek (river) .... K 2
Bakhtegan (lake) .... J 6
Baluchistan (region) .... M 7
Bampur (river) .... M 7
Behistun (ruins) .... E 3
Caspian (sea) .... F 1

Darya-yi-Namak (salt lake) ...... G 3
Dasht-i-Kavir (salt desert) ..... H 3
Dasht-i-Lut (desert) .... K 5
Demavend (mt.) .... H 3
Dez (Ab-i-Diz) (river) .... F 4
Elburz (range) .... H 2
Farsi (isl.) .... F 6
Gurgan (river) .... J 2
Hamun-i-Helmand (marsh) .... N 6
Hamun-i-Jaz-Murian
(marsh) .... L 7
Hamun-i-Sabari (lake) .... N 5
Hanjam (isl.) .... J 7
Hari Rud (river) .... M 3
Hashtadan (reg.) .... M 4
Hormuz (strait) .... J 7
Kalar, Kuh-i (mt.) .... G 2
Karkheh (river) .... F 4
Karun (river) .... F 5
Kashaf Rud (river) .... L 2
Kharg (isl.), 647 .... F 6
Kuh, Ras el (cape) .... J 7
Kuh-i-Aladagh (mts.) .... K 2
Kuh-i-Bagraband (mts.) .... M 8
Kuh-i-Bazqush (mts.) .... E 2
Kuh-i-Dinar (mts.) .... G 5
Kuh-i-Gugird (mts.) .... G 3
Kuh-i-Jagatai (mts.) .... K 2
Kuh-i-Shah Jehan (mts.) .... K 2
Kur Rud (river) .... H 6
Kurang (river) .... G 4
Laristan (region) .... J 7
Maidani (cape) .... G 7
Makran (region) .... M 8
Mand Rud (river) .... G 6
Mashkel (river) .... N 7
Mehran (river) .... J 7
Mura, Qal'eh-i- (river) .... M 4
Namaksar (lake) .... M 4

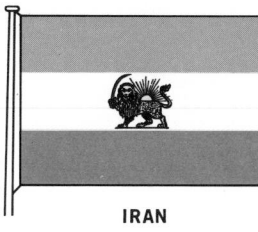

IRAN

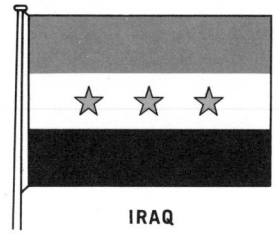

IRAQ

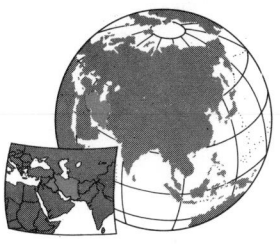

IRAN

AREA 636,293 sq. mi.
POPULATION 32,900,000
CAPITAL Tehran
LARGEST CITY Tehran
HIGHEST POINT Demavend 18,376 ft.
MONETARY UNIT Iranian rial
MAJOR LANGUAGES Persian, Azerbaijani, Kurdish
MAJOR RELIGIONS Islam, Zoroastrianism

IRAQ

AREA 172,476 sq. mi.
POPULATION 11,400,000
CAPITAL Baghdad
LARGEST CITY Baghdad
HIGHEST POINT Haji Ibrahim 11,811 ft.
MONETARY UNIT Iraqi dinar
MAJOR LANGUAGES Arabic, Kurdish
MAJOR RELIGION Islam

Topography

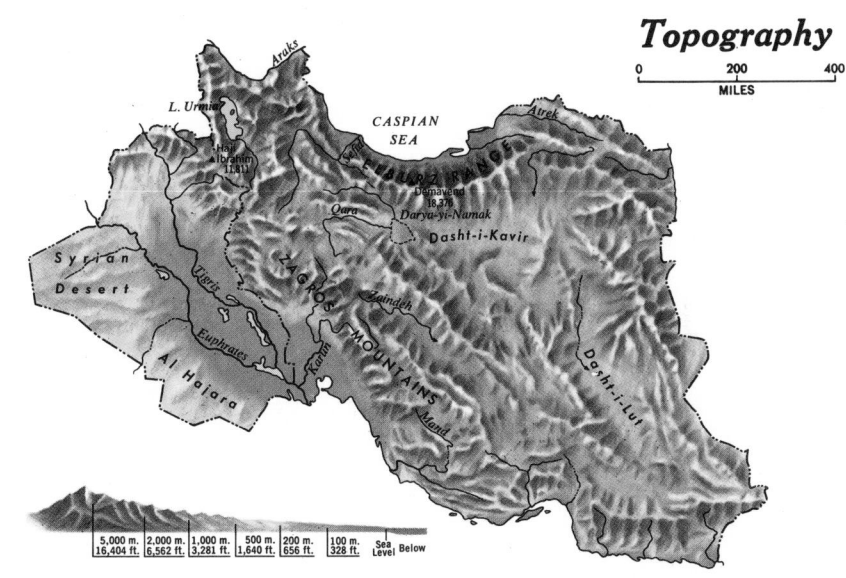

5,000 m. / 16,404 ft. — 2,000 m. / 6,562 ft. — 1,000 m. / 3,281 ft. — 500 m. / 1,640 ft. — 200 m. / 656 ft. — 100 m. / 328 ft. — Sea Level — Below

Agriculture, Industry and Resources

DOMINANT LAND USE

- Cereals, Livestock
- Cash Crops, Horticulture, Livestock
- Pasture Livestock
- Nomadic Livestock Herding
- Forests
- Nonagricultural Land

MAJOR MINERAL OCCURRENCES

C	Coal
Cr	Chromium
Cu	Copper
Fe	Iron Ore
G	Natural Gas
Mn	Manganese
Na	Salt
O	Petroleum
Pb	Lead
S	Sulfur, Pyrites

⚡ Water Power
〰 Major Industrial Areas

TABRIZ — Textiles, Carpets
TEHRAN — Textiles, Light Industry
MOSUL — Textiles, Cement
BAGHDAD — Oil Refining, Textiles
BASRA — Oil Refining
ABADAN — Oil Refining
ISFAHAN — Textiles, Carpets

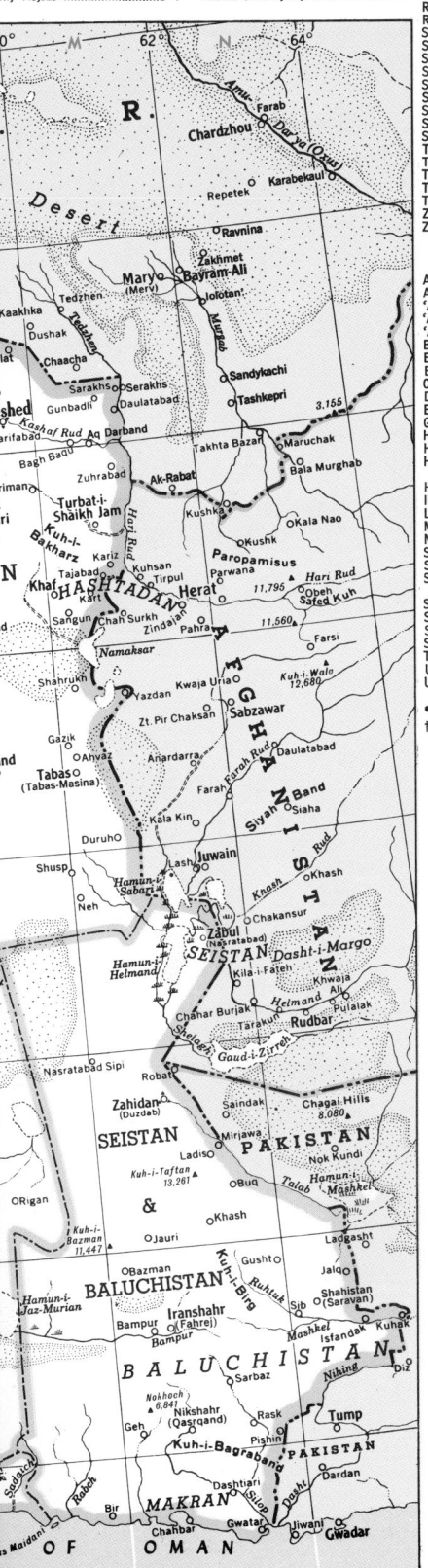

INDIAN SUBCONTINENT and AFGHANISTAN

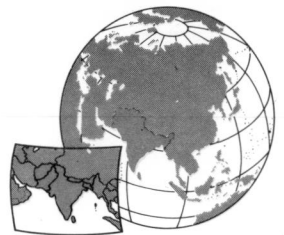

INDIA

AREA 1,269,339 sq. mi.
POPULATION 605,614,000
CAPITAL New Delhi
LARGEST CITY Calcutta (greater)
HIGHEST POINT K2 (Godwin Austen) 28,250 ft.
MONETARY UNIT Indian rupee
MAJOR LANGUAGES Hindi, English, Bihari, Telugu, Marathi, Bengali, Tamil, Gujarati, Rajasthani, Kanarese, Malayalam, Oriya, Punjabi, Assamese, Kashmiri, Urdu
MAJOR RELIGIONS Hinduism, Islam, Christianity, Sikhism, Buddhism, Jainism, Zoroastrianism, Animism

PAKISTAN

AREA 310,403 sq. mi.
POPULATION 72,370,000
CAPITAL Islamabad
LARGEST CITY Karachi
HIGHEST POINT Tirich Mir 25,230 ft.
MONETARY UNIT Pakistani rupee
MAJOR LANGUAGES Urdu, English, Punjabi, Pushtu, Sindhi, Baluchi, Brahui
MAJOR RELIGIONS Islam, Hinduism, Sikhism, Christianity, Buddhism

SRI LANKA (CEYLON)

AREA 25,332 sq. mi.
POPULATION 14,000,000
CAPITAL Colombo
LARGEST CITY Colombo
HIGHEST POINT Pidurutalagala 8,281 ft.
MONETARY UNIT Sri Lanka rupee
MAJOR UNIT Sinhala, Tamil, English
MAJOR RELIGIONS Buddhism, Hinduism, Christianity, Islam

AFGHANISTAN

AREA 250,775 sq. mi.
POPULATION 19,280,000
CAPITAL Kabul
LARGEST CITY Kabul
HIGHEST POINT Noshaq 24,581 ft.
MONETARY UNIT afghani
MAJOR LANGUAGES Pushtu, Dari, Uzbek
MAJOR RELIGION Islam

NEPAL

AREA 54,663 sq. mi.
POPULATION 12,900,000
CAPITAL Kathmandu
LARGEST CITY Kathmandu
HIGHEST POINT Mt. Everest 29,028 ft.
MONETARY UNIT Nepalese rupee
MAJOR LANGUAGES Nepali, Maithili, Tamang, Newari, Tharu
MAJOR RELIGIONS Hinduism, Buddhism

MALDIVES

AREA 115 sq. mi.
POPULATION 136,000
CAPITAL Male
LARGEST CITY Male
HIGHEST POINT 20 ft.
MONETARY UNIT Maldivian rupee
MAJOR LANGUAGE Divehi
MAJOR RELIGION Islam

BHUTAN

AREA 18,147 sq. mi.
POPULATION 1,200,000
CAPITAL Thimphu
LARGEST CITY Thimphu
HIGHEST POINT Kula Kangri 24,784 ft.
MONETARY UNIT tikchung
MAJOR LANGUAGES Dzongka, Nepali
MAJOR RELIGIONS Buddhism, Hinduism

BANGLADESH

AREA 55,126 sq. mi.
POPULATION 82,900,000
CAPITAL Dacca
LARGEST CITY Dacca
HIGHEST POINT Mowdok Mual 3,292 ft.
MONETARY UNIT taka
MAJOR LANGUAGES Bengali, English
MAJOR RELIGIONS Islam, Hinduism, Christianity

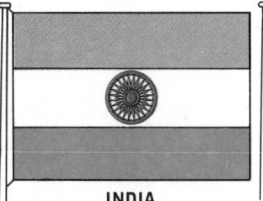
INDIA

PAKISTAN

SRI LANKA (CEYLON)

BHUTAN

AFGHANISTAN

MALDIVES

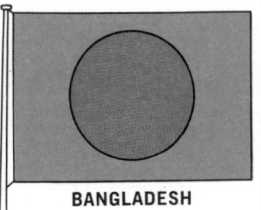
BANGLADESH

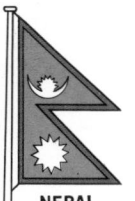
NEPAL

(continued on following page)

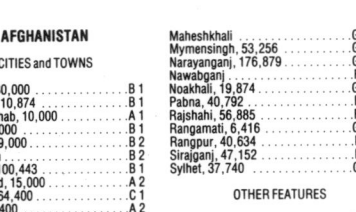

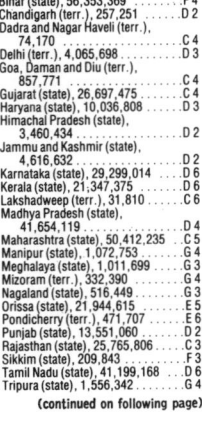

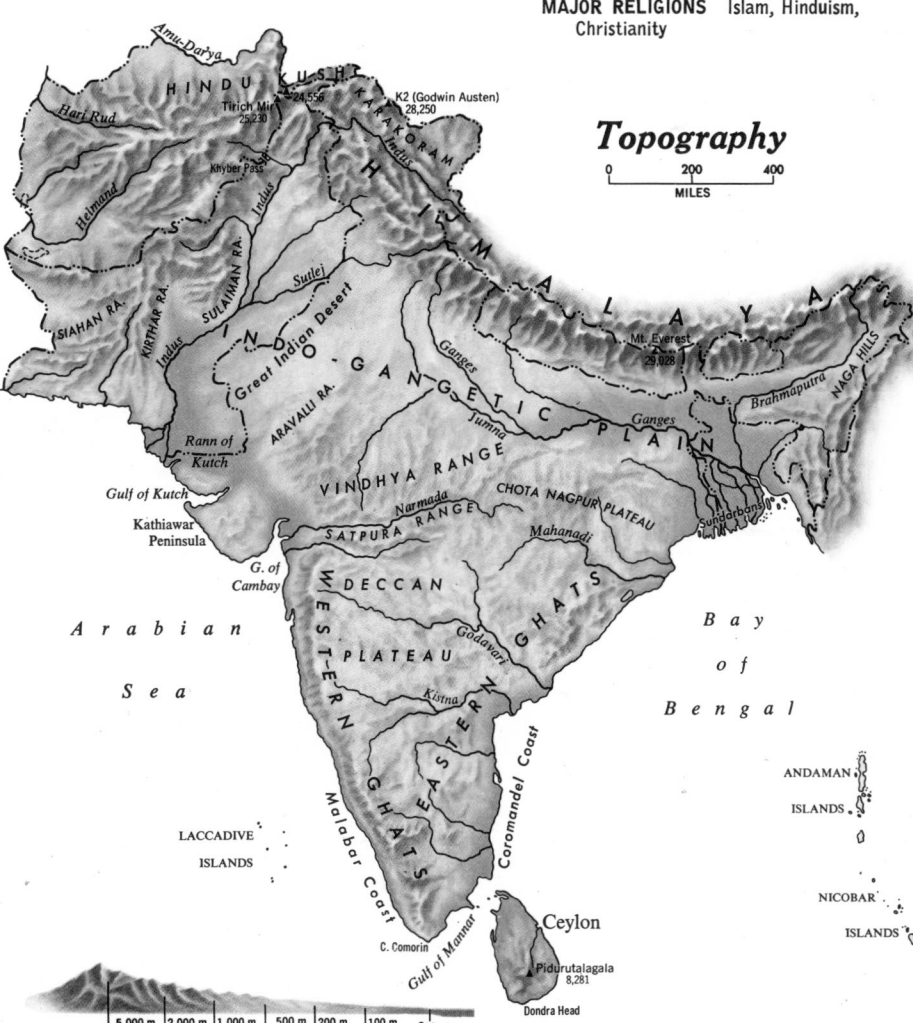

Topography

0   200   400
MILES

| 5,000 m. | 2,000 m. | 1,000 m. | 500 m. | 200 m. | 100 m. | Sea Level | Below |
| 16,404 ft. | 6,562 ft. | 3,281 ft. | 1,640 ft. | 656 ft. | 328 ft. | | |

(continued)

Uttar Pradesh (state), 88,341,144 . . . D 3
West Bengal (state), 44,312,011 . . . F 4

CITIES and TOWNS

Abu, 9,840 . . . C 4
Abu Road, 25,331 . . . C 4
Achalpur, 42,326 . . . D 4
Achalpur, □66,451 . . . D 4
Adilabad, 30,368 . . . D 5
Adoni, 85,311 . . . D 5
Agartala, 59,625 . . . G 4
Agartala, □100,264 . . . G 4
Agra, 591,917 . . . D 3
Agra, □634,622 . . . D 3
Ahmadabad, 1,591,832 . . . C 4
Ahmadabad, □1,741,522 . . . C 4
Ahmadnagar, 118,236 . . . C 5
Ahmadnagar, □148,405 . . . C 5
Ahwa, ‡94,185 . . . C 4
Aizwal, 31,740 . . . G 4
Ajanta . . . D 4
Ajmer, 262,851 . . . C 3
Ajmer, □264,291 . . . C 3
Akola, 168,438 . . . D 4
Alibag, 11,913 . . . C 5
Aligarh, 252,314 . . . D 3
Allahabad, 490,622 . . . E 3
Allahabad, □513,036 . . . E 3
Alleppey, 160,166 . . . D 7
Almora, 19,671 . . . D 3
Almora, □20,881 . . . D 3
Alwar, 100,378 . . . D 3
Amalner, 55,544 . . . C 4
Ambala, 83,633 . . . D 2
Ambala, □186,168 . . . D 2
Ambikapur, 23,087 . . . E 4
Ambikapur, □23,740 . . . E 4
Amravati, 193,800 . . . D 4
Amreli, 39,520 . . . C 4
Amreli, □43,794 . . . C 4
Amritsar, 407,628 . . . C 2
Amritsar, □458,029 . . . C 2
Anakapalle, 57,273 . . . E 5
Anantapur, 80,069 . . . D 6
Anantnag, 27,643 . . . D 2
Arcot, 30,230 . . . D 6
Arcot, □75,911 . . . D 6
Arrah, 92,919 . . . E 3
Aruppukkottai, 62,223 . . . D 7
Arvi, 26,494 . . . D 4
Asansol, 155,968 . . . F 4
Asansol, □241,792 . . . F 4
Aurangabad, Bihar, 18,714 . . . E 4
Aurangabad, Maharashtra, 150,483 . . . D 5
Aurangabad, □165,253 . . . D 5
Azamgarh, 40,963 . . . E 3
Badagara, 53,938 . . . D 6
Bagalkot, 51,746 . . . D 5
Bahraich, 73,931 . . . E 3
Baidyabati, 54,130 . . . F 1
Balaghat, 27,872 . . . E 4
Balaghat, □33,346 . . . E 4
Balasore, 46,239 . . . F 4
Ballia, 47,101 . . . E 3
Bally, 38,892 . . . F 1
Balotra, 17,595 . . . C 3
Balrampur, 36,191 . . . E 3
Baltit . . . C 1
Banda, 50,575 . . . D 3
Bandra . . . B 7
Bangalore, 1,540,741 . . . D 6
Bangalore, □1,653,779 . . . D 6
Bankura, 79,129 . . . F 4
Bansberia, 61,748 . . . F 1
Banswara, 27,363 . . . C 4
Baramati, 27,912 . . . C 5
Baramula, 26,334 . . . C 2
Barasat, 42,642 . . . F 1
Barasat, □95,726 . . . F 1
Bareilly, 296,248 . . . D 3
Bareilly, □326,106 . . . D 3
Baripada, 28,725 . . . F 4
Barmer, 38,630 . . . C 3
Barnagore, 136,842 . . . F 1
Baroda, 466,696 . . . C 4
Baroda, □467,487 . . . C 4
Barpeta, 26,479 . . . G 3
Barpeta, □43,466 . . . G 3
Barrackpore, 96,889 . . . F 1
Barrackpore, □198,255 . . . F 1
Barsi, 62,374 . . . D 5
Barwani, 22,099 . . . D 4
Basim, 32,496 . . . D 4
Basirhat, 63,816 . . . F 4
Bassein, 30,594 . . . C 5
Bassein, □44,909 . . . C 5
Batala, 58,200 . . . D 2
Batala, □76,488 . . . D 2
Beawar, 66,114 . . . C 3
Belgaum, 192,427 . . . C 5
Belgaum, □213,872 . . . C 5
Bellary, 125,183 . . . D 5
Benares (Varanasi), 583,856 . . . E 3
Berhampore, 72,605 . . . F 4
Berhampore, □78,909 . . . F 4
Berhampur, 117,662 . . . F 5
Bettiah, 51,018 . . . E 3
Betul, 30,862 . . . D 4
Bhadrak, 40,487 . . . F 4
Bhadravati, 40,203 . . . D 6
Bhadravati, □101,358 . . . D 6
Bhadreswar, 45,586 . . . F 1
Bhagalpur, 172,202 . . . F 4
Bhandara, 39,423 . . . E 4
Bharatpur, 68,036 . . . D 3
Bharatpur, □69,902 . . . D 3
Bhatinda, 53,684 . . . C 2
Bhatinda, □65,318 . . . C 2
Bhatkal, 18,732 . . . C 6
Bhatpara, 204,750 . . . F 1
Bhavnagar, 225,358 . . . C 4
Bhavnagar, □225,974 . . . C 4
Bhawanipatna, 22,808 . . . E 5
Bhawanipatna, □23,264 . . . E 5
Bhilai, 157,173 . . . E 4
Bhilwara, 82,155 . . . C 3
Bhimavaram, 63,762 . . . E 5
Bhimunipatnam, 14,291 . . . E 5
Bhir (Bir), 49,965 . . . D 5
Bhiwandi, 79,576 . . . C 5
Bhiwani, 73,086 . . . D 3
Bhopal, 298,022 . . . D 4
Bhopal, □384,859 . . . D 4
Bhubaneswar, 105,491 . . . F 4
Bhuj, 52,177 . . . B 4
Bhuj, □52,861 . . . B 4
Bhusawal, 96,800 . . . D 4
Bhusawal, □104,708 . . . D 4
Bidar, 50,670 . . . D 5
Bihar, 100,046 . . . F 3
Bijapur, Karnataka, 103,931 . . . D 5
Bijapur, □7,138 . . . E 5
Bijnor, 43,290 . . . D 3
Bikaner, 188,518 . . . C 3
Bikaner, □208,894 . . . C 3
Bilaspur, 98,410 . . . E 4
Bilaspur, □130,740 . . . E 4
Bina-Itawa, 33,106 . . . D 4
Bina-Itawa, □33,476 . . . D 4
Bir, 49,965 . . . D 5
Birmitrapur, 28,063 . . . E 4
Bobbili, 30,649 . . . E 5
Bodhan, 37,589 . . . D 5
Bodinayakkanur, 54,176 . . . D 6
Bolangir, 35,748 . . . E 4
Bombay (Greater), °5,970,575 . . . B 7
Broach, 91,589 . . . C 4
Broach, □92,251 . . . C 4
Budaun, 72,204 . . . D 3
Budge-Budge, 51,039 . . . F 2
Budge-Budge, □62,752 . . . F 2
Bulsar, 43,254 . . . C 4
Bulsar, □63,069 . . . C 4
Bundi, 34,279 . . . D 3
Bundi, □34,492 . . . D 3
Bunji . . . C 1
Burdwan, 143,318 . . . F 4
Burhanpur, 105,246 . . . D 4
Burhanpur, □105,335 . . . D 4
Calcutta, 3,148,746 . . . F 2
Calcutta, □7,031,382 . . . F 2
Calicut (Kozhikode), 333,979 . . . D 6
Cambay, 62,097 . . . C 4
Cannanore, 55,162 . . . C 6
Cawnpore (Kanpur), 1,154,388 . . . E 3
Chaibasa, 35,386 . . . F 4
Chamba, 11,814 . . . D 2
Champdani, 58,596 . . . F 1
Chanda, 75,134 . . . D 5
Chanderi, 10,294 . . . D 4
Chanderi, □10,354 . . . D 4
Chandernagore, 75,238 . . . F 1
Chandigarh, 218,743 . . . D 2
Chandigarh, □232,940 . . . D 2
Chapra, 83,101 . . . F 3
Chembur . . . B 7
Cherrapunji, ‡83,987 . . . G 3
Chhatarpur, 32,271 . . . D 4
Chhindwara, 53,492 . . . D 4
Chhindwara, □53,508 . . . D 4
Chidambaram, 48,811 . . . E 6
Chidambaram, □57,658 . . . E 6
Chik Ballapur, 29,227 . . . D 6
Chikmagalur, 41,639 . . . D 6
Chilas . . . C 1
Chingleput, 38,419 . . . E 6
Chiplun, 20,942 . . . C 5
Chirala, 54,487 . . . E 5
Chitorgarh, 25,917 . . . C 4
Chitradurga, 50,254 . . . D 6
Chittoor, 63,035 . . . D 6
Churu, 52,502 . . . D 3
Churu, □53,185 . . . D 3
Chushul . . . D 2
Cocanada (Kakinada), 164,200 . . . E 5
Cochin, 439,066 . . . D 6
Coimbatore, 356,368 . . . D 6
Coimbatore, □736,203 . . . D 6
Colachel, 18,819 . . . D 7
Cooch Behar, 53,684 . . . F 3
Cooch Behar, □62,664 . . . F 3
Coondapoor, 23,831 . . . C 6
Cuddalore, 101,335 . . . E 6
Cuddapah, 66,195 . . . D 6
Cuttack, 194,068 . . . F 4
Cuttack, □205,759 . . . F 4
Dabhoi, 37,892 . . . C 4
Daltonganj, 32,367 . . . E 4
Damoh, 59,489 . . . D 4
Damoh, □59,983 . . . D 4
Dankhar Gömpa, ‡7,196 . . . D 2
Darbhanga, 132,059 . . . F 3
Darjeeling, 42,873 . . . F 3
Datia, 36,439 . . . D 3
Datia, □37,436 . . . D 3
Davangere, 121,110 . . . D 6
Deesa, 28,324 . . . C 4
Dehra Dun, 166,073 . . . D 2
Dehra Dun, □203,464 . . . D 2
Delhi, 3,287,883 . . . D 3
Delhi, □3,647,023 . . . D 3
Deoghar, Bihar, 40,356 . . . F 4
Deoghar, □45,060 . . . F 4
Deolali, 55,436 . . . C 5
Deolali, □86,054 . . . C 5
Deoria, 38,161 . . . E 3
Dewas, 51,545 . . . D 4
Dewas, □51,866 . . . D 4
Dhamtari, 34,546 . . . E 4
Dhamtari, □43,362 . . . E 4
Dhanbad, 79,838 . . . F 4
Dhanbad, □434,031 . . . F 4
Dhar, 36,172 . . . C 4
Dharmsala, 10,939 . . . D 2
Dharwar-Hubli, 379,166 . . . C 5
Dholpur, 31,865 . . . D 3
Dhond, 16,583 . . . C 5
Dhond, □35,970 . . . C 5
Dhoraji, 59,773 . . . C 4
Dhoraji, □60,080 . . . C 4
Dhubri, 36,503 . . . G 3
Dhubri, □45,589 . . . G 3
Dhulia, 137,129 . . . C 4
Dibrugarh, 80,348 . . . G 3
Dindigul, 128,429 . . . D 6
Diphu, 10,200 . . . G 3
Dispur, 1,725 . . . G 3
Dohad, 44,506 . . . C 4
Dohad, □69,224 . . . C 4
Dum Dum, 31,363 . . . F 1
Dum Dum, □273,812 . . . F 1
Dungarpur, 19,773 . . . C 4
Durg, 67,892 . . . E 4
Durg-Bhilai, □245,124 . . . E 4
Durgapur, 206,638 . . . F 4
Dwarka, 17,801 . . . B 4
Eluru, 127,023 . . . E 5
English Bazar, 61,335 . . . F 3
English Bazar, □68,026 . . . F 3
Erode, 105,111 . . . D 6
Erode, □169,613 . . . D 6
Etawah, 85,894 . . . D 3
Faizabad-cum-Ayodhya, 102,835 . . . E 3
Faizabad-cum-Ayodhya, □109,806 . . . E 3
Fatehgarh, 102,768 . . . D 3
Fatehgarh, □110,835 . . . D 3
Fatehpur, Rajasthan, 34,929 . . . C 3
Fatehpur, Uttar Pradesh, 54,665 . . . E 3
Ferozepore, 49,545 . . . C 2
Ferozepore, □92,661 . . . C 2
Firozabad, 133,863 . . . D 3
Gadag-Betgeri, 95,426 . . . D 5
Gadwal, 21,828 . . . D 5
Gandhinagar, 24,055 . . . C 4
Ganganagar, 90,042 . . . C 3
Gangtok, 12,000 . . . F 3
Garden Reach, 154,913 . . . F 2
Garulia, 44,271 . . . F 1
Gauhati, 123,783 . . . G 3
Gauhati, □200,377 . . . G 3
Gaya, 179,884 . . . F 4
Ghat Kopar, 34,256 . . . B 7
Ghaziabad, 118,836 . . . D 3
Ghaziabad, □127,700 . . . D 3
Ghazipur, 45,635 . . . E 3
Gilgit . . . C 1
Goalpara, 16,703 . . . G 3
Godhra, 66,403 . . . C 4
Godhra, □66,853 . . . C 4
Gonda, 52,662 . . . E 3
Gondal, 54,928 . . . C 4
Gondal, □55,329 . . . C 4
Gorakhpur, 230,911 . . . E 3
Goregaon . . . B 7
Gudur, 33,778 . . . D 6
Gulbarga, 145,588 . . . D 5
Guna, 40,006 . . . D 4
Guna, □42,330 . . . D 4
Guntakal, 66,320 . . . D 5
Guntur, 269,991 . . . E 5
Gwalior, 384,772 . . . D 3
Gwalior, □406,140 . . . D 3
Haflong, 5,197 . . . G 3
Harda, 28,504 . . . D 4
Hardoi, 46,639 . . . E 3
Hardwar, 77,864 . . . D 2
Hardwar, □79,277 . . . D 2
Hassan, 51,325 . . . D 6
Hathras, 74,349 . . . D 3
Hazaribagh, 54,818 . . . F 4
Hindupur, 42,959 . . . D 6
Hinganghat, 44,349 . . . D 4
Hingoli, 31,948 . . . D 5
Hissar, 89,437 . . . D 3
Honavar, 12,444 . . . C 6
Hooghly-Chinsura, 105,241 . . . F 1
Hoshangabad, 27,011 . . . D 4
Hoshangabad, □29,434 . . . D 4
Hospet, 65,196 . . . D 5
Howrah, 737,877 . . . F 2
Hubli-Dharwar, 379,166 . . . C 5
Hunza (Baltit) . . . C 1
Hyderabad, 1,607,396 . . . D 5
Hyderabad, □1,796,339 . . . D 5
Ichchapuram, 15,850 . . . F 5
Imphal, 100,366 . . . G 4
Indore, 543,381 . . . D 4
Indore, □560,936 . . . D 4
Itanagar, ‡18,787 . . . G 3
Itarsi, 44,191 . . . D 4
Itarsi, □46,866 . . . D 4
Jabalpur, 426,224 . . . D 4
Jabalpur, □534,845 . . . D 4
Jagdalpur, 31,344 . . . E 5
Jagdalpur, □36,932 . . . E 5
Jagtial, 30,900 . . . D 5
Jaipur, 615,258 . . . D 3
Jaipur, □636,768 . . . D 3
Jaisalmer, 16,578 . . . C 3
Jajpur, 16,707 . . . F 4
Jalgaon, 106,711 . . . D 4
Jalna, 91,099 . . . D 4
Jalor, 15,478 . . . C 3
Jalpaiguri, 55,159 . . . F 3
Jamalpur, 61,731 . . . F 3
Jammu, 155,338 . . . D 2
Jammu, □164,207 . . . D 2
Jamnagar, 214,816 . . . B 4
Jamnagar, □227,640 . . . B 4
Jamshedpur, 341,576 . . . F 4
Jamshedpur, □456,146 . . . F 4
Jaora, 37,235 . . . D 4
Jaora, □37,499 . . . D 4
Jaunpur, 80,737 . . . E 3
Jeypore, 34,319 . . . E 5
Jhalawar, 20,035 . . . D 4
Jhansi, 173,292 . . . D 3
Jhansi, □198,135 . . . D 3
Jhunjhunu, 32,024 . . . D 3
Jind, 38,161 . . . D 3
Jodhpur, 317,612 . . . C 3
Jorhat, 30,247 . . . G 3
Jorhat, □70,674 . . . G 3
Jubbulpore (Jabalpur), 426,224 . . . D 4
Juhu . . . B 7
Jullundur, 296,106 . . . D 2
Jullundur, □329,830 . . . D 2
Junagadh, 95,485 . . . B 4
Junagadh, □95,900 . . . B 4
Kadayanallur, 50,295 . . . D 7
Kadiri, 33,810 . . . D 6
Kakinada, 164,200 . . . E 5
Kalyan, 99,547 . . . C 5
Kamarhati, 169,404 . . . F 1
Kamptee, 53,412 . . . D 4
Kamptee, □64,383 . . . D 4
Kanchipuram, 110,657 . . . E 6
Kanchipuram, □119,693 . . . E 6
Kandla, 17,995 . . . C 4
Kandukur, 16,654 . . . E 5
Kanker, □10,646 . . . E 4
Kannauj, 28,187 . . . D 3
Kanpur, 1,154,388 . . . E 3
Kanpur, □1,275,242 . . . E 3
Karad, 42,329 . . . C 5
Karaikudi, 55,449 . . . D 7
Karaikudi, □88,371 . . . D 7
Karanja, 31,150 . . . D 4
Kargil, 2,390 . . . D 2
Karikal, 26,080 . . . E 6
Karkal, 18,593 . . . C 6
Karnal, 92,784 . . . D 3
Karur, 65,706 . . . D 6
Karwar, 27,770 . . . C 6
Kasaragod, 34,984 . . . C 6
Kasganj, 46,467 . . . D 3
Katarnian Ghat . . . E 3
Katihar, 67,014 . . . F 3
Katihar, □80,121 . . . F 3
Katni (Murwara), 54,864 . . . E 4
Kavali, 29,616 . . . E 6
Kavaratti, 4,420 . . . C 6
Kendrapara, 20,079 . . . F 4
Keonjhar, 19,340 . . . F 4
Khamgaon, 53,692 . . . D 4
Khamman, 56,919 . . . D 5
Khandwa, 84,517 . . . D 4
Khandwa, □85,403 . . . D 4
Kharagpur, 61,783 . . . F 4
Kharagpur, □135,218 . . . F 4
Khardah, 32,302 . . . F 1
Khurda, 15,879 . . . F 4
Kirkee, 65,497 . . . C 5
Kishangarh, 37,405 . . . D 3
Kohima, 21,545 . . . G 3
Kolar, 43,418 . . . D 6
Kolar Gold Fields, 76,112 . . . D 6
Kolar Gold Fields, □118,861 . . . D 6
Kolhapur, 259,050 . . . C 5
Kolhapur, □267,513 . . . C 5
Konnagar, 34,424 . . . F 1
Koppal, 27,277 . . . D 5
Koraput, 21,505 . . . E 5
Kota, 212,991 . . . D 3
Kottayam, 59,714 . . . D 7
Kotturu, 12,873 . . . D 6
Kovur, 16,846 . . . E 6
Kozhikode, 333,979 . . . D 6
Krishnanagar, 85,923 . . . F 4
Kumbakonam, 113,130 . . . D 6
Kumbakonam, □119,655 . . . D 6
Kumta, 19,112 . . . C 6
Kurla . . . B 7
Kurnool, 136,710 . . . D 5
Latur, 70,156 . . . D 5
Leh, 5,519 . . . D 2
Lohardaga, 17,087 . . . E 4
Lucknow, 749,239 . . . E 3
Lucknow, □813,982 . . . E 3
Ludhiana, 397,850 . . . D 2
Ludhiana, □401,176 . . . D 2
Lumding, 29,253 . . . G 3
Machilipatnam, 112,612 . . . E 5
Madhubani, 32,919 . . . F 3
Madras, 2,469,449 . . . E 6
Madras, □3,169,930 . . . E 6
Madurai, 549,114 . . . D 7
Madurai, □711,501 . . . D 7
Mahabaleshwar, 7,318 . . . C 5
Mahbubnagar, 51,756 . . . D 5
Mahe, 8,972 . . . D 6
Mahoba, 29,707 . . . D 3
Mahuva, 39,497 . . . C 4
Mahuva, □41,588 . . . C 4
Malad . . . B 6
Malegaon, 191,847 . . . C 4
Maler Kotla, 48,536 . . . D 2
Maler Kotla, □48,859 . . . D 2
Malkapur, 35,476 . . . D 4
Malvan, 17,579 . . . C 5
Mandi, 16,849 . . . D 2
Mandla, 24,406 . . . E 4
Mandla, □27,465 . . . E 4
Mandsaur, 52,347 . . . C 4
Mandsaur, □56,988 . . . C 4
Mandvi, 27,849 . . . B 4
Mangalore, 165,174 . . . C 6
Mangalore, □215,122 . . . C 6
Mangrol, 27,183 . . . B 4
Mangrol, □28,483 . . . B 4
Manmad, 29,571 . . . C 4
Manmad, □40,061 . . . C 4
Mannargudi, 42,783 . . . E 6
Margao, 41,655 . . . C 5
Margao, □48,593 . . . C 5
Marmagao, 44,065 . . . C 5
Mathura, 132,028 . . . D 3
Mathura, □140,150 . . . D 3
Mau, 64,058 . . . E 3
Mayuram, 60,195 . . . D 6
Meerut, 270,993 . . . D 3
Meerut, □367,754 . . . D 3
Mehsana, 51,598 . . . C 4
Mehsana, □51,713 . . . C 4
Mercara, 19,357 . . . D 6
Mhow, 59,037 . . . D 4
Mhow, □63,739 . . . D 4
Midnapore, 71,326 . . . F 4
Miraj, 77,606 . . . D 5
Mirpur . . . C 2
Mirzapur-cum-Vindhyachal, 105,939 . . . E 4
Modasa, 22,483 . . . C 4
Monghyr, 102,474 . . . F 3
Moradabad, 258,590 . . . D 3
Moradabad, □272,652 . . . D 3
Morvi, 60,976 . . . C 4
Mulund . . . B 6
Murwara, 54,864 . . . E 4
Murwara, □86,535 . . . E 4
Muzaffarabad . . . C 2
Muzaffarnagar, 114,783 . . . D 3
Muzaffarpur, 126,379 . . . E 3
Mysore, 355,685 . . . D 6
Nadiad, 108,269 . . . C 4
Nagapattinam, 68,026 . . . E 6
Nagapattinam, □74,019 . . . E 6
Nagar . . . D 1
Nagaur, 36,448 . . . C 3
Nagercoil, 141,288 . . . D 7
Nagina, 37,066 . . . D 3
Nagpur, 866,076 . . . D 4
Nagpur, □930,459 . . . D 4
Nahan, 16,017 . . . D 2
Naihati, 82,080 . . . F 1
Naini Tal, 23,986 . . . D 3
Naini Tal, □25,167 . . . D 3
Nainpur, 14,683 . . . E 4
Nalgonda, 33,126 . . . D 5
Nander, 126,538 . . . D 5
Nandurbar, 54,070 . . . C 4
Nandyal, 63,149 . . . D 5
Narayanpet, 21,744 . . . D 5
Narnaul, 31,875 . . . D 3
Narsinghgarh, 13,814 . . . D 4
Narsinghpur, 25,552 . . . D 4
Nasik, 176,091 . . . C 5
Nasik, □271,681 . . . C 5
Nasirabad, 25,732 . . . C 3
Navsari, 72,979 . . . C 4
Navsari, □80,101 . . . C 4
Nellore, 133,590 . . . E 6
New Delhi (cap.), 301,801 . . . D 3
Nimach, 47,113 . . . D 4
Nimach, □49,748 . . . D 4
Nirmal, 28,529 . . . D 5
Nizamabad, 115,640 . . . D 5
North Lakhimpur, 20,094 . . . G 3
Nova Goa (Panjim), 34,953 . . . C 5
Nowgong, Assam, 56,537 . . . G 3
Nowgong, □11,459 . . . D 3
Okha Port, 10,687 . . . B 4
Ongole, 53,330 . . . E 5
Ootacamund, 63,310 . . . D 6
Orai, 42,513 . . . D 3
Osmanabad, 27,279 . . . D 5
Pachmarhi, 1,212 . . . D 4
Pachmarhi, □9,224 . . . D 4
Palanpur, 42,114 . . . C 4
Palayankottai, 70,070 . . . D 7
Palghat, 95,788 . . . D 6
Pali, 49,834 . . . C 3
Palni, 49,575 . . . D 6
Palni, □51,664 . . . D 6
Panchur, 59,021 . . . F 2
Pandharpur, 53,638 . . . D 5
Panihati, 148,046 . . . F 1
Panipat, 87,981 . . . D 3
Panjim, 34,953 . . . C 5
Panjim, □59,258 . . . C 5
Panna, 22,316 . . . E
Panna, □24,367 . . . E
Panruti, 34,065 . . . D 6
Parbhani, 61,570 . . . D 5
Parlakhemundi, 26,917 . . . E 5
Partabgarh, 17,402 . . . C
Parvatipuram, 30,025 . . . E 5
Pasighat, 5,116 . . . G 3
Patan, 64,519 . . . C 4
Patan, □75,520 . . . C 4
Patiala, 148,686 . . . D
Patiala, □151,041 . . . D 2
Patna, 473,001 . . . F
Patna, □491,217 . . . F
Phalodi, 17,379 . . . C
Pilibhit, 68,273 . . . D
Pondicherry, 90,637 . . . E
Pondicherry, □153,325 . . . E
Ponnani, 35,723 . . . D
Poona, 856,105 . . . C
Poona, □1,135,034 . . . C
Porbandar, 96,881 . . . B
Porbandar, □106,727 . . . B
Port Blair, 26,218 . . . G
Porto Novo, 17,412 . . . E
Proddatur, 70,822 . . . D
Pudukkottai, 66,384 . . . D
Puri, 72,676 . . . F
Purnea, 56,484 . . . F
Purnea, □71,311 . . . F
Purulia, 57,708 . . . F
Puttur, 17,483 . . . D
Quilon, 124,208 . . . D
Radhanpur, 18,360 . . . C
Raichur, 79,831 . . . D
Raigarh, 46,745 . . . E
Raigarh, □48,049 . . . E
Raipur, 174,518 . . . E
Raipur, □205,986 . . . E
Rajahmundry, 165,912 . . . E
Rajahmundry, □188,805 . . . E
Rajapalaiyam, 86,952 . . . D
Rajapur, 9,017 . . . C
Rajkot, 300,612 . . . C
Rajnandgaon, 41,183 . . . E
Rajnandgaon, □55,827 . . . E
Rajpipla, 25,769 . . . C
Rajpur, 34,393 . . . F
Rajpura, 14,840 . . . D
Rameswaram, 16,755 . . . D
Rampur, Uttar Pradesh, 161,417 . . . D
Ranchi, 175,934 . . . F

BRITISH INDIA
U.S.S.R.
GILGIT AGENCY
AFGHANISTAN
KASHMIR & JAMMU
N.W. FRONTIER PROV.
PUNJAB
BALUCHISTAN
Indus
PUNJAB STATES
TIBET
CHINA
IRAN
BAHAWALPUR (PUNJ. ST.)
DELHI
RAMPUR
UNITED PROVINCES
NEPAL
SIKKIM
BHUTAN
ASSAM
Brahmaputra
PUNJ. ST.
RAJPUTANA
AJMER-MERWARA
E. ST.
KHASI HILLS
Gwadar (Oman)
SIND
Ganges
GWALIOR
BENARES
CENTRAL INDIA
BIHAR
MANIPUR
BENGAL
TRIPURA (E. ST.)
WESTERN INDIA
EASTERN STATES
Arabian Sea
Chandernagore (Fr.)
BURMA
GUJARAT ST.
CENTRAL PROVINCES
E. ST.
Diu (Port.)
Damão (Port.)
BERAR
ORISSA
BOMBAY
EASTERN STATES
Bay of Bengal
HYDERABAD
DECCAN STATES
Yanaon (Fr.)
Gôa (Port.)
MADRAS
MYSORE
Bangalore (Br.)
COORG
Andaman Islands (Br.)
Mahé (Fr.)
Pondichéry (Fr.)
Karikal (Fr.)
M. ST.
Laccadive Islands (Madras)
Cochin (Br.)
MADRAS STATES
Nicobar Islands (Br.)
CEYLON
British India. The provinces of British India were directly administered by Britain. A few areas were leased from the Indian princes.
Indian States. The Indian States, sometimes referred to as the "Native" or "Princely States," were under the nominal control of maharajas or other hereditary princes.
Possessions of Other Countries in India
State or Provincial Boundaries
Other Internal Boundaries

Indian Subcontinent and Afghanistan 71

Ranchi, □255,551 .... F 4
Ratangarh, 31,506 .... C 3
Ratlam, 106,666 .... C 4
Ratlam, □119,247 .... C 4
Ratnagiri, 37,551 .... C 5
Raurkela, 47,076 .... F 4
Raurkela, □172,502 .... F 4
Raxaul, 12,064 .... E 3
Rayagada, 25,064 .... E 5
Rewa, 69,182 .... E 4
Rewari, 43,885 .... D 3
Rishra, 63,486 .... F 1
Sadiya, ‡64,252 .... H 3
Sagar, 118,574 .... D 4
Sagar, □154,785 .... D 4
Saharanpur, 225,396 .... D 3
Salem, 308,716 .... D 6
Salem, □416,440 .... D 6
Samalkot, 34,607 .... E 5
Sambalpur, 64,675 .... E 4
Sambalpur, □105,085 .... E 4
Sambhal, 86,323 .... D 3
Sangamner, 28,594 .... C 5
Sangli, 115,138 .... C 5
Sangli, □201,597 .... C 5
Santa Cruz .... B 7
Santipur, 61,166 .... F 4
Sardarshahr, 37,703 .... C 3
Sardarshahr, □38,346 .... C 3
Sarnath .... E 3
Sasaram, 48,282 .... E 4
Satara, 66,433 .... C 5
Satna, 57,531 .... E 4
Satna, □62,162 .... E 4
Savantvadi, 16,873 .... C 5
Savanur, 18,302 .... D 6
Sawi, ‡13,504 .... G 7
Secunderabad, 250,636 .... D 5
Secunderabad, □345,052 .... D 5
Sehore, 35,657 .... D 4
Sehore, □36,136 .... D 4
Seoni, 38,396 .... D 4
Serampore, 102,023 .... F 1
Seringapatam, 14,100 .... D 6
Shahdol, 28,490 .... E 4
Shahdol, □32,236 .... E 4
Shahjahanpur, 135,604 .... E 3
Shahjahanpur, □144,065 .... E 3
Shajapur, 25,189 .... D 4
Sheopur, 16,418 .... D 3
Sheopur, □19,077 .... D 3
Shillong, 87,659 .... G 3
Shillong, □122,752 .... G 3
Shimoga, 102,709 .... D 6
Shivpuri, 42,120 .... D 3
Shivpuri, □50,858 .... D 3
Sholapur, 398,361 .... D 5
Shorapur, 21,056 .... D 5
Sibsagar, 27,426 .... H 3
Sidhi, 8,341 .... E 4
Sidhi, □9,364 .... E 4
Sidhpur, 40,521 .... C 4
Sidhpur, □41,334 .... C 4
Sikar, 70,987 .... D 3
Silchar, 52,596 .... G 4
Siliguri, 97,484 .... F 3
Silvassa .... C 4
Simla, 55,368 .... D 2
Sirohi, 18,774 .... C 4
Sironj, 22,413 .... D 4
Sirsa, 48,808 .... D 3
Sirsi, 28,576 .... D 6
Sitapur, 66,715 .... E 3
Skardu .... D 1
South Suburban, 272,600 .... F 2
Srikakulam, 45,179 .... E 5
Srinagar, 403,413 .... D 2
Srinagar, □423,253 .... D 2
Sundargarh, 17,244 .... E 4
Surat, 471,656 .... C 4
Surat, □493,001 .... C 4
Suratgarh, 14,491 .... C 3
Suratgarh, □17,843 .... C 3
Surendranagar, 66,667 .... C 4
Tanda, 41,611 .... E 3
Tehri, 5,480 .... D 2
Tellicherry, 68,759 .... C 6
Tenali, 102,937 .... E 5
Tezpur, 39,870 .... G 3
Thana, 170,675 .... B 6
Thana, □207,352 .... B 6
Thanjavur, 140,547 .... D 6
Tinsukia, 54,911 .... H 3
Tiruchchirappalli, 307,400 .... D 6
Tiruchchirappalli, □464,624 .... D 6
Tiruchendur, 18,126 .... D 7
Tiruchendur, □55,636 .... D 7
Tirunelveli, 108,498 .... D 7
Tirunelveli, □266,688 .... D 7
Tirupati, 65,843 .... D 6
Tiruppattur, 40,357 .... D 6
Tiruvannamalai, 61,370 .... D 6
Titagarh, 88,218 .... F 1
Titlagarh, 14,504 .... E 4
Titlagarh, □15,840 .... E 4
Tollygunge .... F 2
Tonk, 55,866 .... D 3
Tranquebar, 17,318 .... E 6
Trichur, 76,241 .... D 6
Trivandrum, 409,627 .... D 7
Trombay .... B 7
Tumkur, 70,476 .... D 6
Tuni, 28,344 .... E 5
Tura, 15,489 .... G 3
Tuticorin, 155,310 .... D 7
Tuticorin, □181,913 .... D 7
Udaypur, 161,278 .... C 4
Udhampur, 16,392 .... D 2
Udipi, 29,753 .... C 6
Ujjain, 203,278 .... D 4
Ujjain, □208,561 .... D 4
Ulhasnagar, 168,462 .... C 5
Ulhasnagar, □396,384 .... C 5
Umrer, 27,092 .... D 4
Unnao, 38,195 .... E 3
Uttarpara-Kotrung, 67,568 .... F 1
Vaniyambadi, 51,810 .... D 6
Vaniyambadi, □57,686 .... D 6
Varanasi, 583,856 .... E 3
Varanasi, □606,721 .... E 3
Vellore, 139,082 .... D 6
Vellore, □178,554 .... D 6
Vengurla, 11,805 .... C 5
Venkatagiri, 17,546 .... D 6
Veraval, 58,771 .... C 4
Vidisha, 43,212 .... D 4
Vijayawada, 317,258 .... D 5
Vijayawada, □344,607 .... D 5
Villupuram, 60,242 .... D 6
Vinukonda, 16,259 .... D 5
Viramgam, 43,790 .... C 4
Visakhapatnam, 352,504 .... E 5
Visakhapatnam, □363,467 .... E 5
Visnagar, 34,863 .... C 4
Vizagapatam (Visakhapatnam), 352,504 .... E 5
Vizianagaram, 86,608 .... E 5
Warangal, 207,520 .... D 5
Wardha, 69,037 .... D 4
Wun, 24,455 .... D 5
Yanam, 8,291 .... E 5
Yasin .... C 1
Yellamanchili, 15,318 .... E 5
Yeola, 24,533 .... C 4
Yeotmal, 64,836 .... D 4
Ziro, ‡62,127 .... G 3

OTHER FEATURES

Abor (hills) .... G 3
Adam's Bridge (sound) .... D 7
Agatti (isl.), 3,155 .... C 6
Amindiri (isl.), 4,542 .... C 6
Amindivi (isls.), 13,359 .... C 6
Amini (Amindiri) (isl.), 4,542 .... C 6
Andaman (isls.), 93,468 .... G 6
Andaman (sea) .... G 6
Androth (isl.), 5,425 .... C 6
Angedeva (isl.) .... C 6
Anjidiv (Angedeva) (isl.) .... C 6
Arabian (sea) .... B 5
Back (bay) .... B 7
Baltistan (reg.) .... D 1
Bengal, Bay of (sea) .... F 5
Berar (reg.), 5,729,342 .... D 4
Brahmaputra (riv.) .... G 3
Butcher (isl.) .... B 7
Cambay (gulf) .... C 4
Car Nicobar (isl.), 13,504 .... G 7
Chambal (riv.) .... D 3
Chenab (riv.) .... C 2
Chetlat (isl.), 1,200 .... C 6
Chilka (lake) .... F 5
Coco (chan.) .... G 6
Colaba (pt.) .... B 7
Colair (lake) .... E 5
Comorin (cape) .... D 7
Coromandel Coast (reg.) .... E 6
Daman (dist.), 38,739 .... C 4
Damodar (riv.) .... F 4
Deccan (plat.) .... D 6
Diu (dist.), 23,912 .... C 4
Eastern Ghats (mts.) .... D 6
Elephanta (isl.) .... B 7
Ganga (Ganges) (riv.) .... F 3
Ganges, Mouths of the (delta) .... F 4
Ganges (riv.) .... F 3
Ghaghara (riv.) .... E 3
Goa (dist.), 795,120 .... C 5
Godavari (riv.) .... D 5
Godwin Austen (K2) (mt.) .... D 1
Golconda (ruins) .... D 5
Great (chan.) .... G 7
Great Indian (des.) .... C 3
Great Nicobar (isl.) .... G 7
Himalaya (mts.) .... D 2
Hindu Kush (mts.) .... C 1
Hooghly (riv.) .... F 2
Indus (riv.) .... B 3
Jhelum (riv.) .... C 2
Jumna (riv.) .... E 3
K2 (mt.) .... D 1
Kadmat (isl.), 2,416 .... C 6
Kalpeni (isl.), 3,152 .... C 7
Kamet (mt.) .... D 2
Kanchenjunga (mt.) .... F 3
Karakoram (mts.) .... D 1
Kaveri (riv.) .... D 6
Khasi (hills) .... G 3
Kiltan (isl.), 2,046 .... C 6
Kistna (riv.) .... D 5
Krishna (Kistna) (riv.) .... D 5
Kunlun (range) .... D 1
Kutch (gulf) .... B 4
Kutch, Rann of (salt marsh) .... B 4
Laccadive (isls.), 13,109 .... C 6
Ladakh (reg.), 105,291 .... D 2
Little Andaman (isl.) .... G 6
Little Nicobar (isl.) .... G 7
Mahanadi (riv.) .... E 4
Malabar (hill) .... B 7
Malabar Coast (reg.) .... C 6
Mannar (gulf) .... D 7
Middle Andaman (isl.) .... G 6
Minicoy (isl.), 5,342 .... C 7
Miri (hills) .... G 3
Mishmi (hills) .... H 3
Nancowry (isl.), 8,161 .... G 7
Nanda Devi (mt.) .... D 2
Nanga Parbat (mt.) .... D 1
Narmada (riv.) .... D 4
Nicobar (isls.), 21,665 .... G 7
North Andaman (isl.), 60,312 .... G 6
Palk (str.) .... D 7
Penganga (riv.) .... D 5
Periyar (lake) .... D 7
Pitti (isl.), 112 .... C 6
Pulicat (lake) .... E 6
Rakaposhi (mt.) .... C 1
Salsette (isl.) .... B 7
Sambhar (lake) .... C 3
Satpura (range) .... D 4
Shipki (pass) .... D 2
South Andaman (isl.) .... G 6
Sundarbans (reg.) .... F 4
Sutlej (riv.) .... C 3
Ten Degree (chan.) .... G 7
Towers of Silence .... B 7
Travancore (reg.), 11,447,938 .... D 7
Tungabhadra (riv.) .... D 5
Vindhya (range) .... D 4
Western Ghats (mts.) .... C 5
Zaskar (mts.) .... D 2

MALDIVES

Maldives, 136,000 .... C 7

NEPAL

CITIES and TOWNS

Baitadi, ‡128,696 .... E 3
Bhaktapur, 40,112 .... F 3
Bhaktapur, ‡110,157 .... F 3
Bhojpur, ‡194,506 .... F 3
Biratnagar, 45,100 .... F 3
Birganj, 12,999 .... F 3
Dailekh, ‡156,072 .... E 3
Dhangarhi .... E 3
Dhankuta, ‡107,649 .... F 3
Doti, ‡166,070 .... E 3
Janakpur, 14,294 .... F 3
Jumla, ‡122,753 .... E 3
Kathmandu (cap.), 150,402 .... E 3
Kathmandu, ‡353,752 .... E 3
Lalitpur, 59,049 .... E 3
Lalitpur, ‡154,998 .... E 3
Mukhtinath .... E 3
Mustang, ‡26,944 .... E 3
Nepalganj, 23,523 .... E 3
Palpa, ‡212,633 .... E 3
Pokhara, 20,611 .... E 3
Pyuthan, ‡137,338 .... E 3
Ramechhap, ‡157,349 .... F 3
Ridi .... E 3
Sallyana, ‡141,457 .... E 3

OTHER FEATURES

Annapurna (mt.) .... E 3
Bheri (riv.) .... E 3
Dhaulagiri (mt.) .... E 3
Everest (mt.) .... F 3
Himalaya (mts.) .... D 2
Kanchenjunga (mt.) .... F 3

PAKISTAN

PROVINCES

Baluchistan, 2,409,000 .... B 3
Federal Capital Territory, 235,000 .... C 2
North-West Frontier, 10,909,000 .... C 2
Punjab, 37,374,000 .... C 2
Sind, 13,965,000 .... B 3

CITIES and TOWNS

Abbottabad, 31,036 .... C 2
Ahmadpur East, 32,423 .... C 3
Attock .... C 2
Bahawalnagar, 36,290 .... C 2
Bahawalpur, 133,956 .... C 3
Bahawalpur, *181,000 .... C 3
Bannu, 31,623 .... C 2
Bela, 3,139 .... B 3
Bhera, 17,992 .... C 2
Campbellpore, 19,041 .... C 2
Chagai, ‡41,263 .... A 3
Chaman, 12,208 .... B 2
Chiniot, 47,099 .... C 2
Chitral .... C 1
Dadu, 19,142 .... B 3
Dera Ghazi Khan, 47,105 .... C 3
Dera Ismail Khan, 46,140 .... C 2
Diplo .... B 4
Dir .... C 1
Fort Sandeman, 8,058 .... B 2
Gujranwala, 360,419 .... C 2
Gujrat, 100,581 .... C 2
Gwadar, 8,146 .... A 4
Hyderabad, 628,310 .... B 3
Hyderabad, *834,000 .... B 3
Islamabad (cap.), 77,318 .... C 2
Jacobabad, 35,278 .... B 3
Jhang-Maghiana, 135,722 .... C 2
Jhelum, 52,585 .... C 2
Kalat, 5,321 .... B 3
Karachi, 3,498,634 .... B 4
Karachi, *3,650,000 .... B 4
Kasur, 102,531 .... C 2
Khairpur, 34,144 .... B 3
Khanewal, 49,093 .... C 2
Khanpur, 31,465 .... C 3
Kharan Kalat, 2,692 .... A 3
Khushab, 24,851 .... C 2
Kohat, 49,854 .... C 2
Kotri, 20,262 .... B 3
Lahore, 2,165,372 .... C 2
Larkana, 48,008 .... B 3
Leiah, 19,608 .... C 2
Loralai, 5,519 .... B 2
Lyallpur, 822,263 .... C 2
Lyallpur, *1,104,000 .... C 2
Mach, 4,921 .... B 3
Malakand .... C 2
Mardan, 115,218 .... C 2
Mardan, *131,000 .... C 2
Mastung, 5,962 .... B 3
Mianwali, 31,398 .... C 2
Miram Shah .... C 2
Mirpur Khas, 60,861 .... B 3
Montgomery, 106,213 .... C 2
Montgomery, *118,000 .... C 2
Multan, 542,195 .... C 2
Multan, *723,000 .... C 2
Murree, 13,486 .... C 2
Nal .... B 3
Nawabshah, 45,651 .... B 3
Nok Kundi, 861 .... A 3
Nowshera, 43,757 .... C 2
Nushki, 3,153 .... B 3
Ormara .... A 3
Pasni, 7,483 .... A 3
Peshawar, 268,366 .... C 2
Peshawar, *331,000 .... C 2
Quetta, 156,000 .... B 2
Rahimyar Khan, 43,548 .... C 3
Rahimyar Khan, *130,000 .... C 3
Rawalpindi, 615,392 .... C 2
Risalpur, 11,291 .... C 2
Rohri, 19,072 .... B 3
Saidu, 15,920 .... C 2
Sargodha, 201,407 .... C 2
Sargodha, *225,000 .... C 2
Shikarpur, 53,910 .... B 3
Sialkot, 203,779 .... C 2
Sibi, 13,327 .... B 3
Sonmiani .... B 3
Sukkur, 158,876 .... B 3
Tando Adam, 31,246 .... B 3
Tatta, 12,786 .... B 4
Turbat, 4,578 .... A 3
Uch, 5,483 .... B 3
Umarkot, 5,878 .... B 3
Wana .... C 2

OTHER FEATURES

Arabian (sea) .... B 5
Bolan (pass) .... B 3
Chagai (hills) .... A 3
Chenab (riv.) .... C 2
Hindu Kush (mts.) .... B 1
Indus (riv.) .... B 3
Jhelum (riv.) .... C 2
Khyber (pass) .... C 2
Kunar (riv.) .... C 1
Kutch, Rann of (salt marsh) .... B 4
Mashkel (riv.) .... A 3
Mohenjo Daro (ruins) .... B 3
Muari, Ras (cape) .... B 4
Ravi (riv.) .... C 2
Siahan (range) .... A 3
Sulaiman (range) .... C 3
Sutlej (riv.) .... C 3
Talab (riv.) .... A 3
Taxila (ruins) .... C 2
Tirich Mir (mt.) .... C 1
Zhob (riv.) .... B 2

SRI LANKA (CEYLON)

CITIES and TOWNS

Anuradhapura, 34,836 .... E 7
Badulla, 34,658 .... E 7
Batticaloa, 36,761 .... E 7
Colombo (cap.), 618,000 .... D 7
Colombo, *852,098 .... D 7
Galle, 72,720 .... D 7
Hambantota, 6,908 .... E 7
Jaffna, 112,000 .... E 7
Kalmunai, 19,176 .... E 7
Kalutara, 28,748 .... D 7
Kandy, 93,602 .... E 7
Kurunegala, 25,189 .... E 7
Mannar, 11,157 .... E 7
Matara, 36,641 .... E 7
Moratuwa, 96,489 .... D 7
Mullaittivu, 4,930 .... E 7
Negombo, 57,115 .... D 7
Nuwara Eliya, 16,347 .... E 7
Polonnaruwa, 9,551 .... E 7
Puttalam, 17,982 .... D 7
Ratnapura, 29,116 .... D 7
Sigiriya, 1,446 .... E 7
Trincomalee, 41,780 .... E 7
Vavuniya, 15,639 .... E 7

OTHER FEATURES

Adam's (peak) .... E 7
Adam's Bridge (shoals) .... D 7
Dondra (head) .... E 7
Kirigalpota (mt.) .... E 7
Mannar (gulf) .... D 7
Palk (str.) .... D 7
Pedro (pt.) .... E 6
Pidurutalagala (mt.) .... E 7

*City and suburbs.
‡Population of district.
□Population of urban areas.

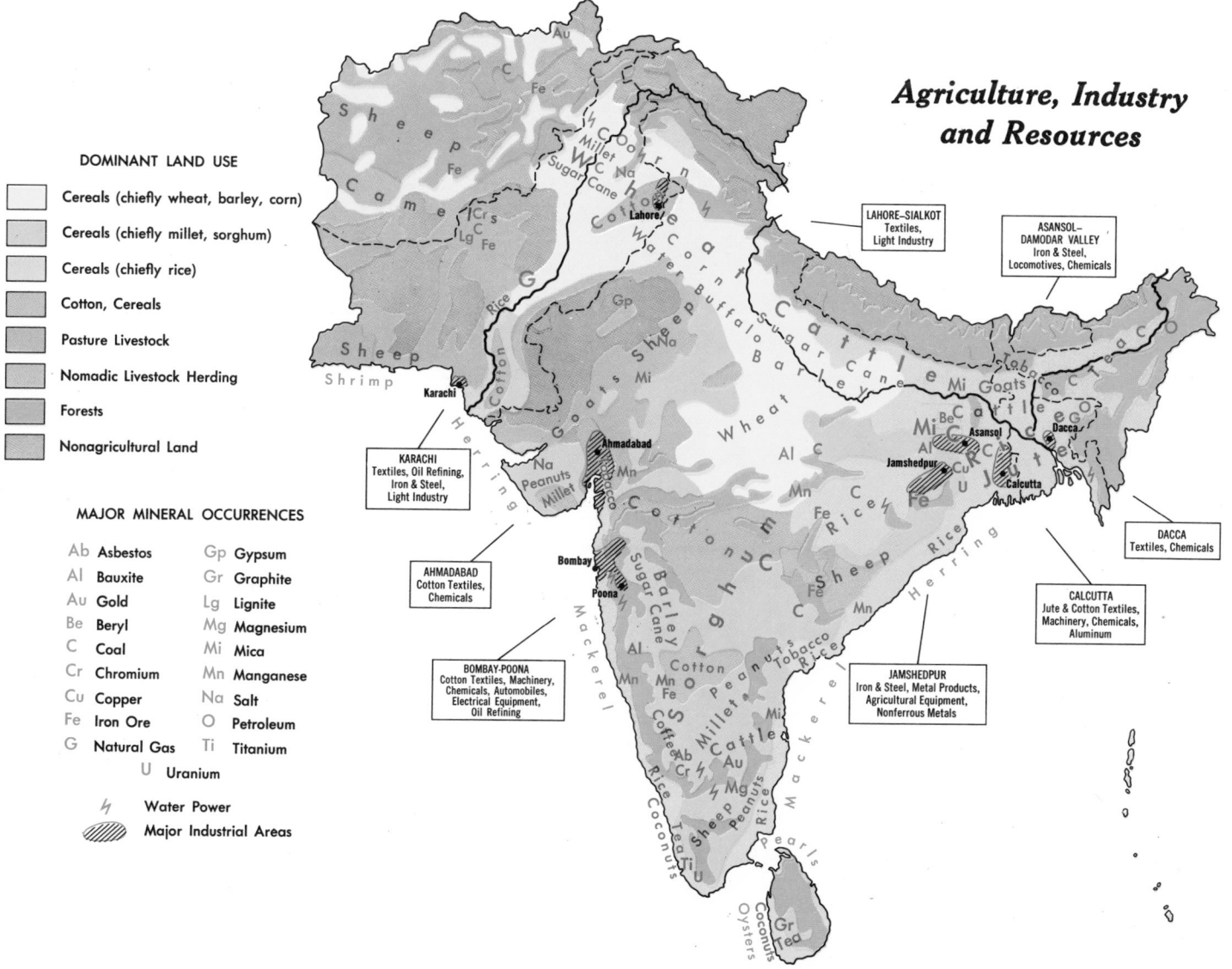

Agriculture, Industry and Resources

DOMINANT LAND USE

- Cereals (chiefly wheat, barley, corn)
- Cereals (chiefly millet, sorghum)
- Cereals (chiefly rice)
- Cotton, Cereals
- Pasture Livestock
- Nomadic Livestock Herding
- Forests
- Nonagricultural Land

MAJOR MINERAL OCCURRENCES

- Ab Asbestos
- Al Bauxite
- Au Gold
- Be Beryl
- C Coal
- Cr Chromium
- Cu Copper
- Fe Iron Ore
- G Natural Gas
- Gp Gypsum
- Gr Graphite
- Lg Lignite
- Mg Magnesium
- Mi Mica
- Mn Manganese
- Na Salt
- O Petroleum
- Ti Titanium
- U Uranium

Water Power

Major Industrial Areas

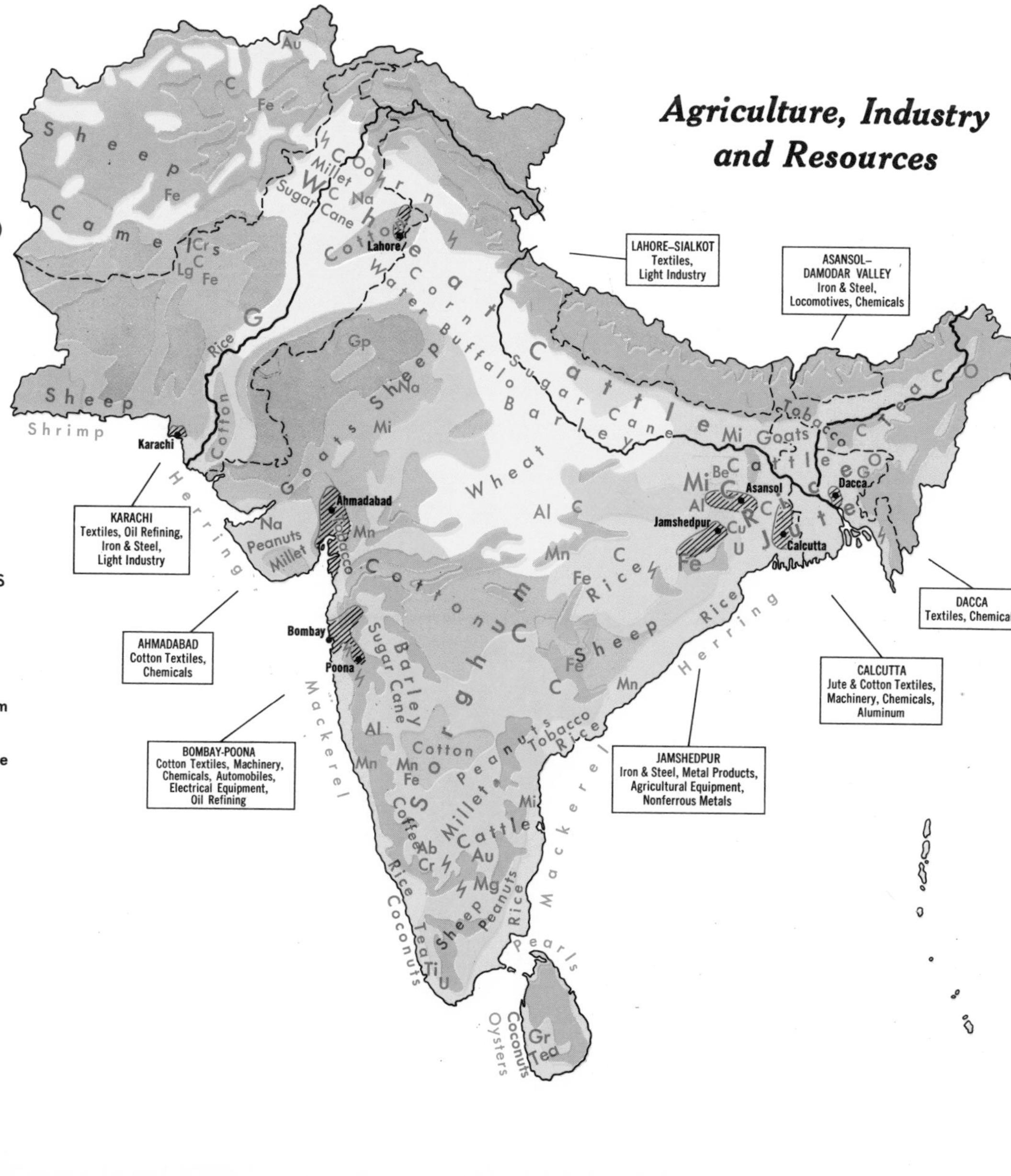

LAHORE–SIALKOT
Textiles, Light Industry
ASANSOL–DAMODAR VALLEY
Iron & Steel, Locomotives, Chemicals
KARACHI
Textiles, Oil Refining, Iron & Steel, Light Industry
AHMADABAD
Cotton Textiles, Chemicals
BOMBAY-POONA
Cotton Textiles, Machinery, Chemicals, Automobiles, Electrical Equipment, Oil Refining
JAMSHEDPUR
Iron & Steel, Metal Products, Agricultural Equipment, Nonferrous Metals
CALCUTTA
Jute & Cotton Textiles, Machinery, Chemicals, Aluminum
DACCA
Textiles, Chemicals
Lahore
Karachi
Ahmadabad
Bombay
Poona
Jamshedpur
Asansol
Calcutta
Dacca
Sheep
Camels
Shrimp
Herring
Mackerel
Pearls
Coconuts
Oysters
Wheat
Cotton
Rice
Cattle
Goats
Tea
Sugar Cane
Peanuts
Millet
Barley
Coffee

BURMA, THAILAND,
INDOCHINA
and MALAYA

CONIC PROJECTION

SCALE OF MILES

SCALE OF KILOMETRES

International Boundaries _____
Division and State Boundaries_____
Capitals of Countries _____ ☆
Division and State Capitals _____ ●

Copyright by C.S. HAMMOND & Co., N.Y.

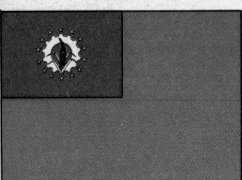

BURMA

THAILAND

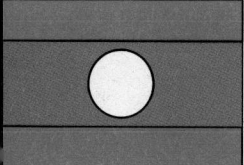

LAOS

CAMBODIA

VIETNAM

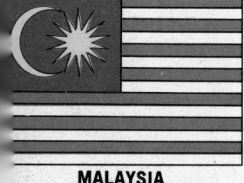

MALAYSIA

SINGAPORE

BURMA

AREA 261,789 sq. mi.
POPULATION 31,240,000
CAPITAL Rangoon
LARGEST CITY Rangoon
HIGHEST POINT Hkakabo Razi 19,296 ft.
MONETARY UNIT kyat
MAJOR LANGUAGES Burmese, Karen, Shan, Kachin, Chin, Kayah, English
MAJOR RELIGIONS Buddhism, Tribal religions

THAILAND

AREA 198,455 sq. mi.
POPULATION 42,700,000
CAPITAL Bangkok
LARGEST CITY Bangkok
HIGHEST POINT Doi Inthanon 8,452 ft.
MONETARY UNIT baht
MAJOR LANGUAGES Thai, Lao, Chinese, Khmer, Malay
MAJOR RELIGIONS Buddhism, Tribal religions

LAOS

AREA 91,428 sq. mi.
POPULATION 3,500,000
CAPITAL Vientiane
LARGEST CITY Vientiane
HIGHEST POINT Phu Bia 9,252 ft.
MONETARY UNIT kip
MAJOR LANGUAGES Lao, French
MAJOR RELIGIONS Buddhism, Tribal religions

CAMBODIA

AREA 69,898 sq. mi.
POPULATOIN 8,110,000
CAPITAL Phnom Penh
LARGEST CITY Phnom Penh
HIGHEST POINT 5,948 ft.
MONETARY UNIT riel
MAJOR LANGUAGES Khmer (Cambodian), French
MAJOR RELIGION Buddhism

VIETNAM

AREA 128,405 sq. mi.
POPULATION 46,600,000
CAPITAL Hanoi
LARGEST CITY Ho Chi Minh City (Saigon)
HIGHEST POINT Fan Si Pan 10,308 ft.
MONETARY UNIT dong
MAJOR LANGUAGES Vietnamese, Thai, Muong, Meo, Yao, Khmer, French, Chinese, Cham
MAJOR RELIGIONS Buddhism, Taoism, Confucianism, Roman Catholicsm, Cao-Dai

MALAYSIA

AREA 128,308 sq. mi.
POPULATION 12,368,000
CAPITAL Kuala Lumpur
LARGEST CITY Kuala Lumpur
HIGHEST POINT Mt. Kinabalu 13,455 ft.
MONETARY UNIT Malaysian dollar
MAJOR LANGUAGES Malay, Chinese, English, Tamil, Dayak, Kadazan
MAJOR RELIGIONS Islam, Confucianism, Buddhism, Tribal religions, Hinduism, Taoism, Christianity, Sikhism

SINGAPORE

AREA 226 sq. mi.
POPULATION 2,300,000
CAPITAL Singapore
LARGEST CITY Singapore
HIGHEST POINT Bukit Timah 581 ft.
MONETARY UNIT Singapore dollar
MAJOR LANGUAGES Chinese, Malay, Tamil, English, Hindi
MAJOR RELIGIONS Confucianism, Buddhism, Taoism, Hinduism, Islam, Christianity

Topography

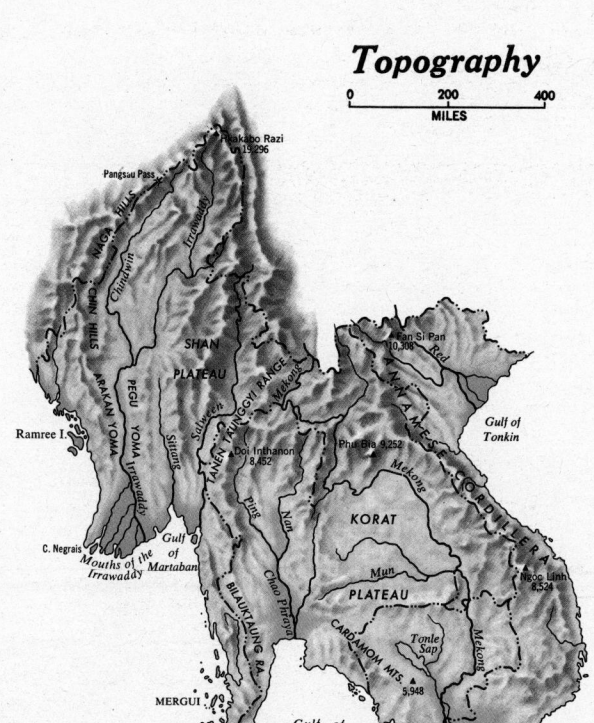

0   200   400
MILES

5,000 m. / 16,404 ft. | 2,000 m. / 6,562 ft. | 1,000 m. / 3,281 ft. | 500 m. / 1,640 ft. | 200 m. / 656 ft. | 100 m. / 328 ft. | Sea Level | Below

BURMA

INTERNAL DIVISIONS

Arakan (state) ....B 3
Chin (state) ....B 2
Irrawaddy (div.) ....B 3
Kachin (state) ....C 1
Karen (state) ....C 3
Kayah (state) ....C 3
Magwe (div.) ....B 2
Mandalay (div.) ....B 2
Mon (state) ....C 3
Pegu (div.) ....C 3
Rangoon (div.) ....C 3
Sagaing (div.) ....B 1
Shan (state) ....C 2
Tenasserim (div.) ....C 4

CITIES and TOWNS

Akyab (Sittwe), 42,329 ....A 3
Allanmyo, 15,580 ....B 3
Amarapura, 11,268 ....B 2
Amherst, 6,000 ....C 3
Bassein, 105,000 ....B 3
Bhamo, 9,821 ....C 1
Chauk, 24,464 ....B 2
Danubyu, 9,833 ....B 3
Fort Hertz (Putao) ....C 1
Gyobingauk, 9,922 ....C 3
Haka ....B 2
Henzada, 100,000 ....B 3
Insein, 27,030 ....C 3
Kalemyo, 3,158 ....B 2
Kalewa, 2,230 ....B 2
Kama, 3,523 ....B 3
Kamayut, 23,032 ....C 3
Kambalu, 3,281 ....B 2
Kani, 2,600 ....B 2
Katha, 7,648 ....C 1
Kawlin, 3,735 ....B 2
Kyaikto, 13,154 ....C 3
Kyangin, 6,073 ....B 3
Kyaukpadaung, 5,480 ....B 2
Kyaukpyu, 7,335 ....B 3
Kyaukse, 8,659 ....C 2
Kyewbwe, 3,150 ....C 3
Labutta, 12,982 ....B 3
Lashio ....C 2
Letpadan, 15,896 ....C 3
Loi-kaw ....C 3
Madauk, 4,618 ....C 3
Magwe, 13,270 ....B 2
Mahlaing, 6,543 ....B 2
Mandalay, #300,000 ....C 2
Martaban, 5,661 ....C 3
Ma-ubin, 23,362 ....B 3
Maungdaw, 3,772 ....B 2
Mawlaik, 2,993 ....B 2
Maymyo, 22,287 ....C 2
Meiktila, 19,474 ....B 2
Mergui, 33,697 ....C 4
Minbu, 9,096 ....B 2
Minbya, 5,783 ....B 2
Minhla, 6,470 ....B 3
Mogaung, 2,920 ....C 1
Mogok, 8,334 ....C 2
Monywa, 26,297 ....B 2
Moulmein, #175,000 ....C 3
Mudon, 20,136 ....C 3
Myanaung, 11,155 ....B 3
Myaungmya, 24,532 ....B 3
Myebon, 3,499 ....B 2
Myingyan, 36,439 ....B 2
Myitkyina, 12,382 ....C 1
Myitnge, 3,888 ....C 2
Myohaung, 6,534 ....B 2
Nyaunglebin, 12,155 ....C 3
Pa-an, 4,139 ....C 3
Pagan, 2,824 ....B 2
Pakokku, 30,943 ....B 2
Palaw, 5,596 ....C 4
Papun ....C 3
Paungde, 17,286 ....B 3
Pegu, 47,378 ....C 3

Putao ....C 1
Pyapon, 19,174 ....B 3
Pye, 36,997 ....A 3
Pyinmana, 22,025 ....C 3
Pyu, 10,443 ....C 3
Rangoon (capital), *1,700,000....C 3
Rathedaung, 2,969 ....B 2
Sagaing, 15,382 ....B 2
Sandoway, 5,172 ....B 3
Shwebo, 17,827 ....B 2
Shwegyin, 5,439 ....C 3
Shwenyaung ....C 2
Singkaling Hkamti ....B 1
Singu, 4,027 ....C 2
Sittwe, 42,329 ....A 3
Syriam, 15,296 ....C 3
Taungdwingyi, 16,233 ....B 2
Taunggyi ....C 2
Taungup, 4,065 ....B 3
Tavoy, 40,312 ....C 4
Tenasserim, 1,086 ....C 5
Tharrawaddy, 8,977 ....C 3
Thaton, 38,047 ....C 3
Thayetmyo, 11,649 ....B 3
Thazi, 7,531 ....C 2
Thongwa, 10,829 ....C 3
Thonze, 14,443 ....B 3
Toungoo, 31,589 ....C 3
Victoria Point, 1,520 ....C 5
Wakema, 20,716 ....B 3
Yamethin, 11,167 ....C 2
Yandoon, 15,245 ....B 3
Ye, 12,852 ....C 4
Yenangyaung, 24,416 ....B 2
Yesagyo, 7,880 ....B 2
Ye-u, 5,307 ....B 2

OTHER FEATURES

Amya (pass) ....C 4
Andaman (sea) ....B 5
Arakan Yoma (mts.) ....B 3
Bengal (bay) ....B 3
Bilauktaung (range) ....C 4
Chaukan (pass) ....C 1
Cheduba (isl.), 2,621 ....B 3
Chin (hills) ....B 2
Chindwin (river) ....B 2
Coco (chan.) ....B 4
Combermere (bay) ....B 3
Dawna (range) ....C 3
Great Coco (isl.) ....B 4
Great Tenasserim (river) ....C 4
Hkakabo Razi (mt.) ....C 1
Indawgyi (lake) ....C 1
Inle (lake) ....C 2
Irrawaddy (river) ....B 3
Irrawaddy, Mouths of the (delta) ....B 4
Kaladan (river) ....B 2
Khao Luang (mt.) ....C 5
Loi Leng (mt.) ....C 2
Manipur (river) ....B 2
Martaban (gulf) ....C 4
Mekong (river) ....D 2
Mergui (arch.) ....C 5
Mon (river) ....C 3
Mu (river) ....B 2
Nam Hka (river) ....B 2
Nam Pawn (river) ....C 2
Nam Teng (river) ....C 2
Negrais (cape) ....B 3
Pakchan (river) ....C 5
Pangsau (pass) ....B 1
Pegu Yoma (mts.) ....B 3
Preparis (isl.) ....B 4
Ramree (isl.), 11,133 ....B 3
Salween (river) ....C 3
Shan (plateau) ....C 2
Sittang (river) ....C 3
Taungthonton (mt.) ....B 1
Tavoy (point) ....C 4
Tenasserim (isl.) ....C 4
Three Pagodas (pass) ....C 4
Victoria (mt.) ....B 2

(continued on following page)

CAMBODIA

CITIES and TOWNS

Banam, †87,048 E 5
Battambang, 38,846 D 4
Cheom Ksan E 4
Chhlong, †46,108 E 4
Chong Kal, †16,918 D 4
Kampot, 12,558 E 5
Kep, 7,565 E 5
Khemarak Phouinville D 5
Kohnieh E 4
Kompong Cham, 28,534 E 4
Kompong Chhnang, 12,847 D 4
Kompong Kleang E 4
Kompong Som, 6,578 D 5
Kompong Speu, 7,453 E 5
Kompong Thom, 9,682 E 4
Kompong Trabek, †108,227 E 5
Koulen E 4
Kratie, 11,908 E 4
Krauchmar, †63,262 E 4
Moung, †88,321 D 4
Pailin, †15,536 D 4
Phnom Penh (capital), *500,000 E 5
Phsar Babau D 4
Phsar Oudong, †50,456 E 5
Phum Rovieng, †21,151 E 4
Phum Troun E 4
Poipet D 4
Prek Po E 5
Prey Veng, 8,792 E 5
Pursat, 14,329 D 4
Ream D 5
Sambor, †11,213 E 4
Siem Pang, †8,959 E 4
Siem Reap, 10,230 D 4
Sisophon, †29,581 D 4
Sre Khtum E 4
Stung Treng, 3,369 E 4
Suong E 5
Svay Rieng, 11,184 E 5
Takeo, 11,312 E 5
Virachei, †16,912 E 4

OTHER FEATURES

Angkor Wat (ruins) E 4
Dang Raek, Phanom (mts.) D 4
Joncs (plain) E 5
Kas Kong (isl.) D 5
Kas Tang (isl.) D 5
Kong, Kas (isl.) D 5
Mekong (river) E 4
Phanom Dang Raek (mts.) D 4
Preapatang (rapids) E 4
Rong, Koh (isl.) D 5
Samit (point) D 5
Se Khong (river) E 4
Se San (river) E 4
Siam (gulf) D 5
Srepok (river) E 4
Stung Sen (river) E 4
Tang, Kas (isl.) D 5
Tonle Sap (lake) D 4

LAOS

CITIES and TOWNS

Attopeu, 2,750 E 4
Ban Bung Sai E 4
Borikhane D 3
Botene D 3
Boun Neua, 2,500 D 2
Boun Tai, †1,681 D 2
Champassak, 3,500 E 4
Houei Sai, 1,500 D 2
Hua Muong D 2
Keng Kok, 2,000 E 3
Kham Keut, †31,206 E 3
Khone E 4
Khong, 1,750 E 4
Khong Sédone, 2,000 E 4
Luang Prabang, 7,596 D 3
Mahaxay, 2,000 E 3
Muong Beng, †2,305 D 2
Muong Bo D 3
Muong Hai, †476 D 2
Muong Hôm D 3
Muong Lan, †836 D 3
Muong May E 4
Muong Phalane E 3
Muong Phine E 3
Muong Phong D 3
Muong Sai, 2,000 D 2
Muong Sing, 1,091 D 2
Muong Son D 2
Muong Song Khone, 2,000 E 3
Muong Wapi E 4
Muong Yo D 2
Nam Tha, 1,459 D 2
Napé E 3
Nong Het E 3
Ou Neua, †4,300 D 2
Pak Beng, †2,964 D 2
Pak Hin Boun, 1,750 E 3
Pak Sane, 2,500 D 3
Paklay, 2,000 D 3
Pakse, 8,000 E 4
Phiafay, †17,216 E 4
Phon Tiou E 3
Phong Saly, 2,500 D 2
Sam Neua, 3,000 E 2
Saravane, 2,350 E 4
Savannakhet, 8,500 E 3
Sayaboury, 2,500 D 3
Tchepone, 1,250 E 3
Tha-deua D 3
Thakhek, 5,500 E 3
Tourakom D 3
Vang Vieng, 1,250 D 3
Vien Phou Kha D 2
Vientiane (capital), 132,253 D 3
Vientiane, *162,297 D 3
Xieng Khouang, 3,500 D 3

OTHER FEATURES

Bolovens (plateau) E 4
Hou, Nam (river) D 2
Jars (plain) D 3
Mekong (river) D 3
Nam Hou (river) D 2
Nam Tha (river) D 2
Phu Bia (mt.) D 3
Phu Co Pi (mt.) E 3
Phu Loi (mt.) D 2
Rao Co (mt.) E 3
Se Khong (river) E 4
Tha, Nam (river) D 2
Tran Ninh (plateau) D 3

MALAYSIA

STATES

Federal Territory D 7
Johor, 1,236,412 D 7
Kedah, 885,775 D 6
Kelantan, 645,200 D 6
Melaka, 391,003 D 7
Negeri Sembilan, 488,318 D 7
Pahang, 405,156 D 7
Perak, 1,568,024 D 6
Perlis, 113,350 D 6
Pinang, 724,169 D 6
Selangor, 1,339,142 D 7
Terengganu, 360,388 D 6

CITIES and TOWNS

Alor Gajah, 2,135 D 7
Alor Setar, 52,915 D 6
Baling, 4,121 D 6
Bandar Maharani, 39,046 D 7
Bandar Penggaram, 39,294 D 7
Batu Gajah, 10,143 D 6
Bentong, 18,845 D 7
Butterworth, 42,504 D 6
Cameron Highlands D 6
Chukai, 10,803 D 6
Gemas, 4,873 D 7
George Town (Pinang), 234,903 C 6
Ipoh, 125,770 D 6
Johor Baharu, 74,909 F 5
Kampar, 24,602 D 6
Kangar, 6,064 D 6
Kelang, 75,649 D 7
Keluang, 31,181 D 7
Kota Baharu, 38,103 D 6
Kota Tinggi, 7,475 F 5
Kuala Dungun, 12,515 D 6
Kuala Lipis, 8,753 D 6
Kuala Lumpur (cap.), 325,000 D 7
Kuala Pilah, 12,024 D 7
Kuala Selangor, 2,285 D 7
Kuala Terengganu, 29,446 D 6
Kuantan, 23,034 D 7
Kulai, 7,759 F 5
Lumut, 2,947 D 6
Melaka (Malacca), 69,848 D 7
Mersing, 7,228 E 7
Pekan, 2,070 D 7
Pekan Nanas, 7,129 E 5
Pinang, 234,903 C 6
Pontian Kechil, 8,459 E 5
Port Dickson, 4,416 D 7
Port Swettenham, 16,925 D 7
Port Weld, 2,260 D 6
Raub, 15,363 D 7
Segamat, 18,445 D 7
Seremban, 52,091 D 7
Shah Alam D 7
Sungei Petani, 22,916 C 6
Taiping, 48,206 D 6
Tanah Merah, 775 D 6
Telok Anson, 37,042 D 6
Tumpat, 8,946 D 6

OTHER FEATURES

Aur, Pulau (isl.), 415 E 7
Belumut, Gunong (mt.) D 7
Gelang, Tanjong (point) D 7
Johor (river) F 5
Johore (str.) E 6
Kelantan (river) D 6
Langkawi, Pulau (isl.), 16,535 C 6
Ledang, Gunong (mt.) D 7
Lima, Pulau (isl.) F 6
Malacca (str.) D 7
Malaya (region), 9,000,000 E 6
Pahang (river) D 7
Pangkor, Pulau (isl.), 2,580 D 6
Perak, Gunong (mt.) D 6
Perhentian (isls.), 447 D 6
Pulai (river) E 5
Pinang, Pulau (isl.), 338,898 C 6
Ramunia, Tanjong (point) F 6
Redang, Pulau (isl.), 470 D 6
Sedili Kechil, Tanjong (point) F 5
Tahan, Gunong (mt.) D 6
Temiang, Bukit (mt.) D 6
Tenggol, Pulau (isl.), 2,386 D 6
Tinggi, Pulau (isl.), 440 E 7

SINGAPORE

CITIES and TOWNS

Jurong E 6
Nee Soon, 6,043 F 6
Paya Lebar, 45,440 F 6
Serangoon, 3,798 F 6
Singapore (cap.), *1,987,900 F 6
Woodlands, 737 E 6

OTHER FEATURES

Johore (str.) E 6
Keppel (harb.) F 6
Main (str.) F 6
Singapore (str.) F 6
Tekong Besar, Pulau (isl.), 4,074 F 6

THAILAND (SIAM)

CITIES and TOWNS

Amnat, 11,335 E 4
Ang Thong, 6,458 C 4
Ayutthaya, 24,597 D 4
Ban Aranyaprathet, 11,112 D 4
Ban Kantang, 5,076 C 5
Ban Khlong Yai, 3,815 D 5
Ban Pak Phanang, 11,963 D 5
Ban Pua, 12,317 D 3
Ban Sattahip, 22,942 D 4
Ban Tha Uthen, 7,297 E 3
Bang Lamung, 9,087 D 4
Bang Saphan, 6,959 C 4
Bangkok (capital), 1,299,528 D 4
Bangkok, *2,000,000 D 4
Banphot Phisai, 6,036 C 3
Buriram, 12,579 D 4
Chachoengsao, 19,809 G 4
Chai Badan, 6,158 D 4
Chai Buri, †31,135 D 3
Chainat, 4,652 D 4
Chaiya, 3,607 C 5
Chaiyaphum, 9,633 D 4
Chang Khoeng, 6,037 C 3
Chanthaburi, 10,780 D 4
Chiang Dao, 8,017 C 3
Chiang Khan, 5,810 D 3
Chiang Rai, 11,663 C 3
Chiang Saen, 5,443 C 2
Chiengmai, 65,600 C 3
Chon Buri, 32,496 D 4
Chumphon, 9,342 C 5
Dan Sai, 6,710 D 3
Den Chai, 12,732 C 3
Hat Yai, 35,504 C 6
Hua Hin, 17,078 D 4
Kabin Buri, 3,703 D 4
Kalasin, 11,043 D 3
Kamphaeng Phet, 7,171 C 3
Kanchanaburi, 12,957 C 4
Khemmarat, 5,426 E 3
Khon Kaen, 19,591 D 3
Khorat (Nakhon Ratchasima), 41,037 D 4
Khu Khan, †122,206 E 4
Kra Buri, 3,717 C 5
Krung Thep (Bangkok) (cap.), 1,299,528 D 4
Kumphawapi, 20,759 D 3
Lae, 5,743 D 3
Lampang, 36,488 C 3
Lamphun, 10,602 C 3
Lang Suan, 4,108 C 5
Loei, 7,301 D 3
Lom Sak, 8,386 D 3
Lop Buri, 21,244 D 4
Maha Sarakham, 15,680 D 3
Mukdahan, 17,738 E 3
Nakhon Nayok, 8,048 D 4
Nakhon Pathom, 28,426 C 4
Nakhon Phanom, 14,799 E 3
Nakhon Ratchasima, 41,037 D 4
Nakhon Sawan, 34,947 D 4
Nakhon Si Thammarat, 25,919 D 5
Nan, 13,843 D 3
Nang Rong, 15,623 D 4
Narathiwat, 17,508 D 6
Ngao, †32,643 D 3
Nong Khai, 21,120 D 3
Pattani, 16,804 D 6
Phanat Nikhom, 9,307 D 4
Phangnga, 4,782 C 5
Phatthalung, 10,420 D 6
Phayao, 17,959 C 3
Phet Buri, 24,654 C 4
Phetchabun, 5,947 D 3
Phichai, 5,258 D 3
Phichit, 9,258 D 3
Phitsanulok, 30,364 D 3
Phon Phisai, 6,745 D 3
Phrae, 16,005 D 3
Phuket, 28,163 C 6
Phutthaisong, 9,315 D 4
Prachin Buri, 13,420 D 4
Prachuap Khiri Khan, 6,303 C 5
Pran Buri, 7,795 D 4
Rahaeng (Tak), 13,274 C 3
Ranong, 5,993 C 5
Rat Buri, 20,383 C 4
Rayong, 9,680 D 4
Roi Et, 12,930 D 3
Rong Kwang, †39,375 D 3
Sakon Nakhon, 16,457 E 3
Samut Prakan, 21,769 D 4
Samut Sakhon, 27,802 D 4
Samut Songkhram, 12,801 C 4
Sara Buri, 17,572 D 4
Satun, 4,369 C 6
Sawankhalok, 7,880 C 3
Selaphum, 10,395 E 3
Sing Buri, 8,384 D 4
Singora (Songkhla), 31,014 D 6
Sisaket, 9,519 E 4
Songkhla, 31,014 D 6
Sukhothai, 8,627 D 3
Suphan Buri, 13,859 C 4
Surat Thani, 19,738 C 5
Surin, 13,860 D 4
Suwannaphum, 15,731 D 4
Tak, 13,274 C 3
Takua Pa, 6,308 C 5
Thoen, 17,283 C 3
Thonburi, 403,818 D 4
Thonburi, *460,000 D 4
Trang, 17,158 C 6
Trat, 3,813 D 4
Ubon, 27,092 E 4
Udon Thani, 29,965 D 3
Uthai Thani, 10,729 C 4
Uttaradit, 9,120 D 3
Warin Chamrap, 7,067 E 4
Yala, 18,083 D 6
Yasothon, 9,717 D 4

OTHER FEATURES

Amya (pass) C 4
Bilauktaung (range) C 4
Chao Phraya, Mae Nam (river) D 4
Chi, Mae Nam (river) D 3
Chong Pak Phra (cape) C 5
Dang Raek, Phanom (mts.) D 4
Doi Inthanon (mt.) C 3
Doi Pha Hom Pok (mt.) C 2
Doi Pia Fai (mt.) C 4
Kao Prawa (mt.) C 3
Khao Luang (mt.) C 5
Khwae Noi, Mae Nam (river) C 4
Ko Chang (isl.) D 4
Ko Kut (isl.) D 5
Ko Lanta (isl.), 9,486 C 5
Ko Phangan (isl.) C 5
Ko Phuket (isl.), 75,652 C 5
Ko Samui (isl.), 30,818 C 5
Ko Tao (isl.) C 5
Ko Terutao (isl.) C 6
Ko Thalu (isls.) C 5
Kra (isthmus) C 5
Laem Pho (cape) D 6
Laem Talumphuk (cape) D 5
Luang (mt.) C 5
Mae Klong, Mae Nam (river) C 4
Mekong (river) E 3
Mulayit Taung (mt.) C 3
Mun, Mae Nam (river) D 4
Nan, Mae Nam (river) D 3
Nong Lahan (lake) D 3
Pa Sak, Mae Nam (river) D 4
Pakchan (river) C 5
Phanom Dang Raek (mts.) D 4
Ping, Mae Nam (river) C 3
Samui (str.) D 5
Siam (gulf) D 5
Tapi, Mae Nam (river) C 5
Tha Chin, Mae Nam (river) C 4
Thale Luang (lagoon) D 6
Three Pagodas (pass) C 4
Wang, Mae Nam (river) C 3

VIETNAM

CITIES and TOWNS

An Khe F 4
An Loc, 15,276 E 5
Bac Can E 2
Bac Lieu (Vinh Loi), 53,841 E 5
Bac Ninh, 22,560 E 2
Ba Don E 3
Bai Thuong E 3
Ban Me Thuot, 68,771 F 4
Bao Ha D 2
Bao Lac E 2
Bien Hoa, 87,135 E 5
Binh Dinh F 4
Binh Son F 4
Bong Son F 4
Bu Dop E 4
Cam Ranh, 84,281 F 5
Can Tho, 92,132 E 5
Cao Bang E 2
Cao Lanh, 16,482 E 5
Cap Saint-Jacques (Vung Tau), 79,270 E 5
Chau Phu, 37,175 E 5
Cheo Reo E 4
Chu Lai F 4
Co Lieu E 3
Con Cuong E 3
Cua Rao E 3
Dak Bla E 4
Da Lat, 83,992 F 5
Dam Doi E 5
Da Nang, 363,343 E 3
Dien Bien Phu D 2
Di Linh F 5
Dong Hoi E 3
Duong Dong D 5
Go Cong, 33,191 E 5
Go Quao E 5
Ha Giang E 2
Haiphong, 182,496 E 2
Haiphong, ‡*600,000 E 2
Ham Tan, 19,323 E 5
Hanoi (capital), 414,620 E 2
Hanoi, ‡*1,400,000 E 2
Ha Tien E 5
Ha Tinh E 3
Hoa Binh E 2
Hoa Da F 5
Ho Chi Minh City, 1,706,869 E 5
Hoi An, 45,059 F 4
Hoi Xuan E 2
Hon Chong E 5
Hon Gay, †100,000 E 2
Hue, 170,884 E 3
Huong Khe E 3
Ke Bao E 2
Khanh Hoa F 4
Khanh Hung, 59,015 E 5
Kontum, 33,554 E 4
Lai Chau D 2
Lang Mo E 3
Lang Son, 15,071 E 2
Lao Cai E 2
Loc Chou E 3
Loc Ninh E 5
Long Xuyen, 72,658 E 5
Luc An Chau E 2
Moc Hoa, 3,191 E 5
Mo Duc F 4
Mon Cay E 2
Muong Khuong E 2
My Tho, 109,967 E 5
Nam Dinh, ‡125,000 E 2
Nghia Lo D 2
Nha Trang, 103,184 F 4
Ninh Binh E 2
Phan Rang, 33,377 F 5
Phan Ri F 5
Phan Thiet, 80,122 F 5
Phoc Tuy, 16,419 E 5
Phuc Loi E 3
Phu Cuong, 28,267 E 5
Phu Dien E 3
Phu Lang Thuong E 2
Phu Loc E 5
Phuly E 2
Phu My F 4
Phu Qui E 3
Phu Rieng E 5
Phu Tho, 10,888 E 2
Phu Vinh (Tra Vinh), 48,485 E 5
Pleiku, 23,720 E 4
Pleime E 4
Quang Nam E 4
Quang Khe E 3
Quang Ngai, 14,119 F 4
Quang Tri, 15,874 E 3
Quang Yen E 2
Quan Long, 59,331 E 5
Qui Nhon, 116,821 F 4
Rach Gia, 66,745 E 5
Ron E 3
Sa Dec, 51,867 E 5
Saigon (Ho Chi Minh City), 1,706,869 E 5
Song Cau F 4
Son Ha F 4
Son La D 2
Son Tay, 19,213 E 2
Tam Ky, 38,532 F 4
Tam Quan F 4
Tan An, 38,082 E 5
Tay Ninh, 22,957 E 5
Thai Binh, 14,739 E 2
Thai Nguyen, ‡110,000 E 2
Thanh Hoa, 31,211 E 3
That Khe E 2
Tien Yen E 2
Tra Vinh, 48,485 E 5
Truc Giang, 68,629 E 5
Trung Khanh Phu E 2
Tuyen Quang E 2
Tuy Hoa, 63,552 F 4
Van Gia F 4
Van Hoa E 2
Van Yen E 2
Vinh, 43,954 E 3
Vinh Loi, 53,841 E 5
Vinh Long, 30,667 E 5
Vinh Yen E 2
Vo Dat E 5
Vu Liet E 3
Vung Tau, 79,270 E 5
Yen Bai E 2
Yen Minh E 2

OTHER FEATURES

Bach Long Vi, Dao (isl.) F 2
Batangan (cape) F 4
Bên Gôi (bay) F 4
Black (river) D 2
Ca Mau (Mui Bai Bung) (pt.) E 5
Cam Ranh (bay) F 5
Cat Ba, Dao (isl.) E 2
Chon May (bay) F 3
Chu Yang Sin (mt.) F 4
Con Son (isls.), 3,147
Cu Lao Hon (isls.)
Dama, Poulo (isls.)
Dao Bach Long Vi (isl.)
Dao Phu Quoc (isl.)
Darlac (plateau)
Dent du Tigre (mt.)
Deux Frères, Les (isls.)
Fan Si Pan (mt.)
Hon Khoai (isl.)
Hon Panjang (isl.)
Ia Drang (riv.)
Joncs (plain)
Ke Ga (point)
Kontum (plateau)
Lang Bian (mts.)
Lay (cape)
Mekong, Mouths of the (delta)
Mui Bai Bung (pt.)
Mui Dinh (cape)
Mui Duong (cape)
Nam Tram (cape)
Nightingale (Bach Long Vi) (isl.)
Nui Ba Den (mt.)
Phu Quoc, Dao (isl.)
Poulo Dama (isls.)
Poulo Way (isls.)
Rao Co (mt.)
Red (river)
Se San (river)
Siam (gulf)
Sip Song Chau Thai (mts.)
Song Ba (river)
Song Bo (Black) (river)
Song Ca (river)
Song Cai (river)
Song Coi (Red) (river)
South China (sea)
Tigre (isl.)
Tonkin (gulf)
Varella (cape)
Way, Poulo (isls.)

★See page 84 for other Malaysian entries.
*City and suburbs.
†Population of district.

‡City populations courtesy of Kingsley Davis, Office of Int'l Pop. & Urban Research, Inst. of Int'l Studies, Univ. of California.

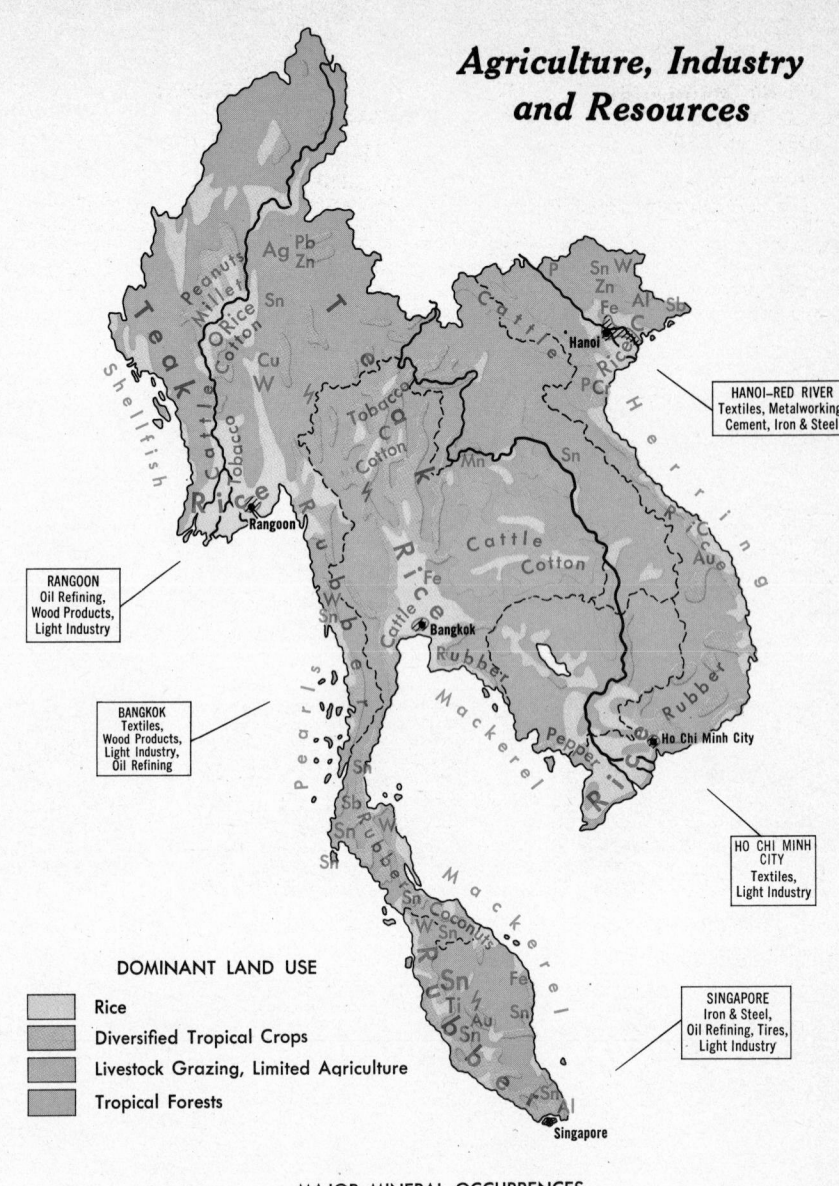

Agriculture, Industry and Resources

Hanoi
HANOI–RED RIVER Textiles, Metalworking, Cement, Iron & Steel
Rangoon
RANGOON Oil Refining, Wood Products, Light Industry
Bangkok
BANGKOK Textiles, Wood Products, Light Industry, Oil Refining
Ho Chi Minh City
HO CHI MINH CITY Textiles, Light Industry
Singapore
SINGAPORE Iron & Steel, Oil Refining, Tires, Light Industry
Teak
Rice
Cattle
Cotton
Tobacco
Rubber
Peanuts
Millet
Shellfish
Pearls
Mackerel
Herring
Coconuts
Pepper
DOMINANT LAND USE
Rice
Diversified Tropical Crops
Livestock Grazing, Limited Agriculture
Tropical Forests
MAJOR MINERAL OCCURRENCES
Ag Silver
Al Bauxite
Au Gold
C Coal
Cr Chromium
Cu Copper
Fe Iron Ore
Mn Manganese
O Petroleum
P Phosphates
Pb Lead
Sb Antimony
Sn Tin
Ti Titanium
W Tungsten
Zn Zinc
Water Power
Major Industrial Areas

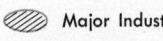

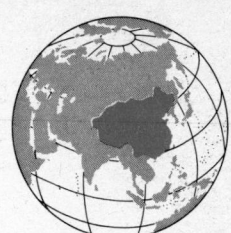

CHINA (MAINLAND)
AREA 3,691,000 sq. mi.
POPULATION 853,000,000
CAPITAL Peking
LARGEST CITY Shanghai
HIGHEST POINT Mt. Everest 29,028 ft.
MONETARY UNIT yüan
MAJOR LANGUAGES Chinese, Chuang, Uigur, Yi, Tibetan, Miao, Mongol, Kazakh
MAJOR RELIGIONS Confucianism, Buddhism, Taoism, Islam

CHINA (TAIWAN)
AREA 13,971 sq. mi.
POPULATION 16,426,386
CAPITAL Taipei
LARGEST CITY Taipei
HIGHEST POINT Hsinkao Shan 12,959 ft.
MONETARY UNIT new Taiwan yüan (dollar)
MAJOR LANGUAGES Chinese, Formosan
MAJOR RELIGIONS Confucianism, Buddhism, Taoism, Christianity, Tribal religions

MONGOLIA
AREA 606,163 sq. mi.
POPULAIOTN 1,500,000
CAPITAL Ulan Bator
LARGEST CITY Ulan Bator
HIGHEST POINT Tabun Bogdo 14,288 ft.
MONETARY UNIT tugrik
MAJOR LANGUAGES Khalkha Mongolian, Kazakh (Turkic)
MAJOR RELIGION Buddhism

HONG KONG
AREA 403 sq. mi.
POPULATION 4,400,000
CAPITAL Victoria
MONETARY UNIT Hong Kong dollar
MAJOR LANGUAGES Chinese, English
MAJOR RELIGIONS Confucianism, Buddhism, Christianity

MACAO
AREA 6 sq. mi.
POPULATION 300,000
CAPITAL Macao
MONETARY UNIT pataca
MAJOR LANGUAGES Chinese, Portuguese
MAJOR RELIGIONS Confucianism, Buddhism, Taoism, Christianity

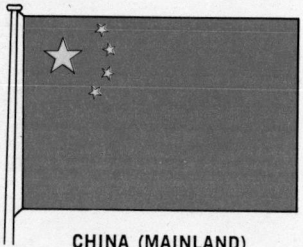
CHINA (MAINLAND)

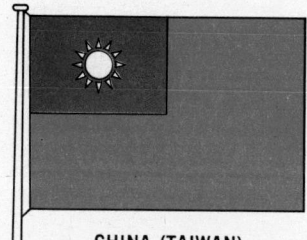
CHINA (TAIWAN)

MONGOLIA

CHINA AND MONGOLIA TRANSPORTATION

CHINA (continued)

Hsünkow .... L 2
Huhehot, 700,000 .... H 3
Huma .... L 1
Hunchun, 13,246 .... M 3
Hunkiang .... L 3
Huocheng .... B 3
Hwainan, 350,000 .... J 5
Hwaiteh, 60,000 .... K 3
Hwangchung .... F 4
Hwangling .... G 4
Hwangshih, 200,000 .... J 5
Hwangyüan .... F 4
Hweili .... F 6
Hwohsien .... H 4
Ichang, 150,000 .... H 5
Ichun, 200,000 .... L 2
Ierhsieh .... I 2
Iliang .... F 7
Ining (Kuldja), 160,000 .... B 3
Ipin, 275,000 .... F 6
Ishan .... G 7
Jechiang (Charkhliq) .... C 4
Jyekundo .... E 5
Kaifeng, 330,000 .... J 5
Kailu .... K 3
Kalgan, 1,000,000 .... J 3
Kanchow, 135,000 .... J 6
Kangting .... F 6
Kantse .... F 5
Kaohsiung, 719,899 .... J 7
Karamai, 43,000 .... B 2
Kashgar, 175,000 .... A 4
Kashing, 132,000 .... K 5
Keelung, 304,740 .... J 7
Kelpin (Koping) .... A 3
Kenho .... K 1
Keriya .... B 4
Khabakhe .... C 2
Khana Abasa ....
Khetinsiring .... D 5
Khobuk-Saur (Hofeng) .... C 2
Khotan .... A 4
Kiamusze, 275,000 .... L 2
Kian, 100,000 .... J 6
Kiangling .... H 5
Kiaoho .... L 3
Kiaohsien .... K 4
Kiayükwan .... E 4
Kienko .... G 5
Kienow .... J 6
Kienshui .... F 7
Kienyang, 50,000 .... H 6
Kinghung .... E 7
Kingku .... E 7
Kingpeng .... J 3
Kingtehci en, 300,000 .... J 6
Kingyang .... G 4
Kinhwa, 46,200 .... J 6
Kinta .... E 3
Kirin, 1,200,000 .... L 3
Kishow .... G 6
Kisi, 350,000 .... M 2

Kitai .... C 3
Kiuchüan, 50,000 .... E 4
Kiukiang, 120,000 .... J 6
Kiungshan .... H 8
Kokiu, 250,000 .... F 7
Kongmoon, 150,000 .... H 7
Koping .... A 3
Kucha .... B 3
Kueitun .... C 3
Kulang .... F 4
Kuldja, 160,000 .... B 3
Kungliu .... B 3
Kunming, 1,700,000 .... F 7
Kurla .... C 3
Kütsing .... F 7
Kuyang .... G 3
Kuyüan .... F 4
Kwanghwa .... G 3
Kwangnan .... F 7
Kwangwha ....
Kweilin, 225,000 .... G 6
Kweiping .... G 7
Kweisui (Huhehot), 700,000 .... H 3
Kweiyang, 1,500,000 .... G 6
Kweiyang .... H 6
Laiyang .... K 4
Lanchow, 1,500,000 .... F 4
Lantsang .... E 7
Leiyang .... H 6
Lhakang Dzong .... D 6
Lhasa, 175,000 .... D 6
Lhatse Dzong .... C 6
Lhuntse Dzong .... D 6
Lhsien .... H 6
Likiang .... F 6
Linchwan, 45,000 .... J 6
Linfen .... H 4
Lingling .... H 6
Linhai .... K 6
Linho .... G 3
Linhsien .... H 4
Linkow .... M 2
Linping .... B 5
Linsi .... K 3
Linsia, 75,000 .... F 4
Lintsang .... E 7
Lintsing, 45,000 .... J 4
Liping .... G 6
Lishui .... K 6
Ltang .... F 6
Liuchow, 250,000 .... G 6
Loho, 55,000 .... H 5
Loshan, 250,000 .... F 6
Loyang, 750,000 .... H 5
Luchow, 225,000 .... F 6
Luhsi .... E 7
Lukchun .... D 3
Lungchen, 14,000 .... L 2
Lungyen .... J 6
Lupeh .... L 3
Lüshun (Port Arthur) (in Lüta) .... K 4

Lüta, ‡4,000,000 .... K 4
Maerhkang .... F 5
Mahai .... D 4
Manass .... C 3
Manchouli, 30,000 .... J 2
Mangyal .... D 4
Mani .... D 5
Manning (Wanning) .... A 8
Maralbashi .... A 4
Markham Dzong .... E 6
Mato .... E 5
Meihsien .... J 7
Mendong Gomba .... C 6
Menyüan .... F 4
Merket .... A 4
Mienning .... F 6
Mienyang .... F 6
Minhsien .... F 5
Mintsin .... F 4
Mishan .... M 2
Moho .... K 1
Mowming, 15,000 .... G 7
Moyü (Qara Qash) .... B 4
Mukden, 3,750,000 .... K 3
Muli .... F 6
Mutankiang, 400,000 .... M 3
Nachü .... D 5
Nanchang, 900,000 .... J 6
Nanchi, 50,000 .... J 6
Nanchung, 275,000 .... G 5
Nangtsien .... E 5
Nanhsiung .... H 6
Nanking, 2,000,000 .... J 5
Nanning, 375,000 .... G 7
Narping, 53,445 .... F 6
Nanyang, 75,000 .... H 5
Neikiang, 240,000 .... F 6
Nenkiang .... L 2
Ningan ....
Ningpo, 350,000 .... K 6
Ningsia (Yinchwan), 175,000 .... F 4
Ningsiang .... H 6
Ningteh .... J 6
Ningtu .... J 6
Ningwu .... H 4
Noho .... K 2
Noma .... B 5
Omin (Durbuljin) .... C 2
Owpu .... D 5
Pachen ....
Pachu (Maralbashi) .... A 4
Pachung .... G 5
Paicheng (Bai) .... B 3
Paicheng, 75,000 .... K 3
Pailingmiao .... H 3
Paiyin, 50,000 .... F 4
Paiyü .... E 5
Pakhoi, 175,000 .... G 7
Pangkiang .... H 3
Paochang .... H 3
Paoki, 275,000 .... G 5
Paoshan .... E 7
Paoting, 350,000 .... J 4
Paotow, 800,000 .... G 3

Pehan, 130,000 .... L 2
Peihai (Pakhoi), 175,000 .... G 7
Peiping (Peking) (cap.), ‡8,000,000 .... J 3
Peking (cap.) ‡8,000,000 .... J 3
Penglai .... K 4
Pengpu, 400,000 .... J 5
Penki, 750,000 .... K 3
Phongdo Dzong .... D 5
Pichieh .... G 6
Pikiang .... E 6
Pingchüan .... K 3
Pingliang, 60,000 .... G 4
Pinglo .... H 7
Pingsiang, 7,000 .... G 7
Pingsiang, 210,000 .... H 6
Pingtung, 153,953 .... J 7
Pingwu .... G 5
Pingyao .... H 4
Pinyang .... K 6
Pishan (Guma) .... A 4
Pohsien, 75,000 .... J 5
Pokotu .... K 2
Poli .... M 2
Port Arthur (in Lüta) .... K 4
Poseh .... G 7
Pucheng ....
Puerh .... F 7
Putien .... J 6
Qara Qash .... B 4
Qara Shahr .... C 3
Qaraqum .... C 3
Qarghaliq .... A 4
Rima .... E 6
Rudok .... B 5
Rungmar Thok .... C 5
Saka .... C 6
Sanga Cho Dzong .... K 1
Sanho ....
Sanming .... J 6
Santai .... F 5
Shahyar .... B 3
Shangchih .... L 3
Shanghai, ‡8,500,000 .... K 5
Shanghang .... J 7
Shanghsien .... H 5
Shangjao, 100,000 .... J 6
Shangkiu, 250,000 .... J 5
Shangnan ....
Shangshui, 100,000 .... J 5
Shanhaikwan .... K 3
Shanshan .... D 3
Shantan .... E 4
Shaohing, 225,000 .... K 6
Shaoyang, 275,000 .... H 6
Shasi, 125,000 .... H 5
Shentsa Dzong .... C 5
Shenyang (Mukden), 3,750,000 .... K 3
Shigatse, 26,000 .... C 6
Shihchü ....
Shihchüan .... G 5
Shihhotzu, 70,000 .... C 3
Shihkiachwang, 1,500,000 .... J 4

Shihtsuishan, 60,000 .... G 4
Shiukwan, 125,000 .... H 7
Shobando ....
Shwangcheng .... K 3
Shwangliao .... K 3
Shwangyashan, 150,000 .... M 2
Siaho .... F 4
Siakwan, 26,200 .... E 6
Sian, 1,900,000 .... G 5
Siangfan, 150,000 .... H 5
Siangtan, 300,000 .... H 6
Siangyin .... H 6
Sichang .... F 6
Sienyang, 120,000 .... G 5
Silin .... G 7
Silinhot, 20,000 .... J 3
Sinchu, 188,062 .... K 7
Singi Obo .... D 5
Singsingsia .... D 3
Singtai, 75,000 .... J 4
Sinhailien (Lienyünkang), 300,000 .... J 5
Sinhsien .... H 4
Sinhwa .... H 6
Sining, 250,000 .... F 4
Sinsiang, 300,000 .... H 4
Sinyang, 125,000 .... H 5

Siushui .... J 6
Soche (Yarkand), 80,000 .... A 4
Solun .... K 2
Soochow, 1,300,000 .... K 5
Süchow, 1,500,000 .... J 5
Suhsien .... J 5
Suihsien .... H 5
Suihwa, 36,000 .... L 2
Suining, 75,000 .... F 5
Suiteh .... G 4
Sungpan .... F 5
Sutsien .... J 5
Süyung .... F 6
Swatow, 400,000 .... J 7
Szeping, 180,000 .... K 3
Tacheng (Chuguchak) .... B 2
Tahsien .... G 5
Taian, 20,000 .... J 4
Taichao ....
Taichung, 407,054 .... J 7
Tainan, 441,556 .... J 7
Taipei (cap.), 1,604,543 .... K 7
Taitung, 69,984 .... K 7
Taiyüan, 2,725,000 .... H 4
Taklakhar .... B 5
Talai, 20,000 .... K 2
Tali .... E 6

Tangshan, 1,200,000 .... J 4
Tanhsien ....
Tantung, 450,000 ....
Taoan, 75,000 ....
Taocheng ....
Taofu ....
Tapanshang ....
Tardin ....
Tash Qurghan ....
Tashigong ....
Tatsaitan ....
Tatung, 300,000 ....
Tayü ....
Tehchow, 45,000 ....
Tehko ....
Telingha ....
Tengchang ....
Tengkow ....
Tepao ....
Thok Daurakpa ....
Thok Jalung ....
Tiehling, 52,945 ....
Tienshui, 100,000 ....
Tientsin, ‡4,500,000 ....
Tinghai ....
Tingri Dzong C

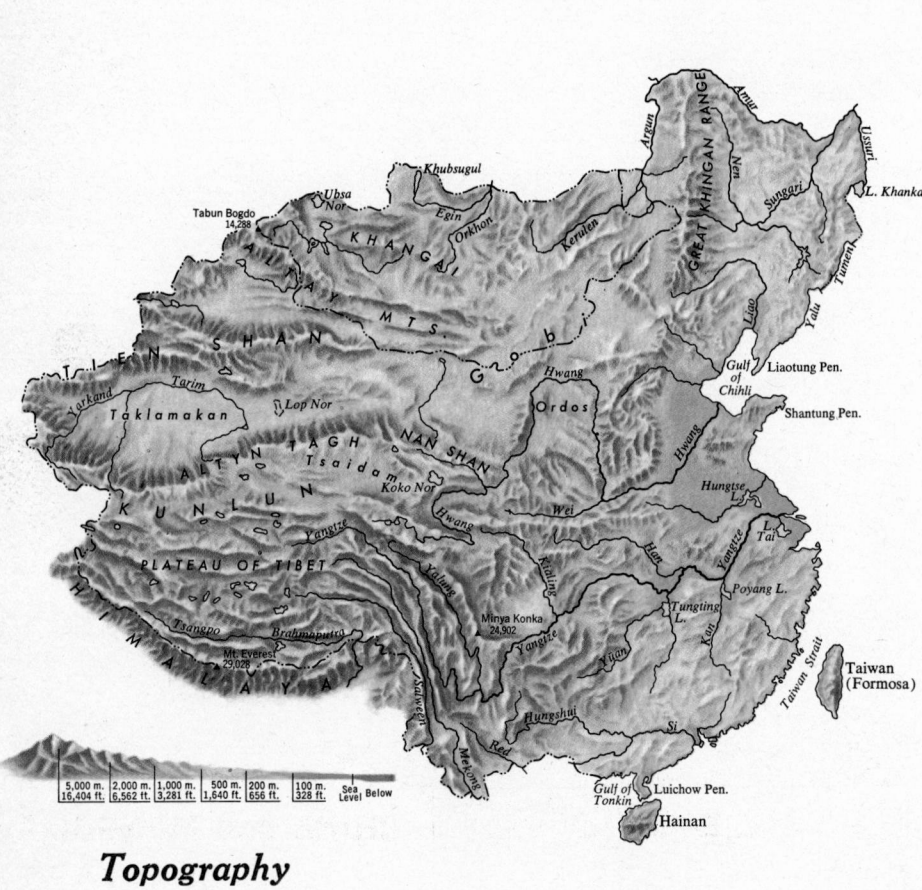

Topography

5,000 m. / 16,404 ft. — 2,000 m. / 6,562 ft. — 1,000 m. / 3,281 ft. — 500 m. / 1,640 ft. — 200 m. / 656 ft. — 100 m. / 328 ft. — Sea Level — Below

0 — 300 — 600 MILES

(continued on following page)

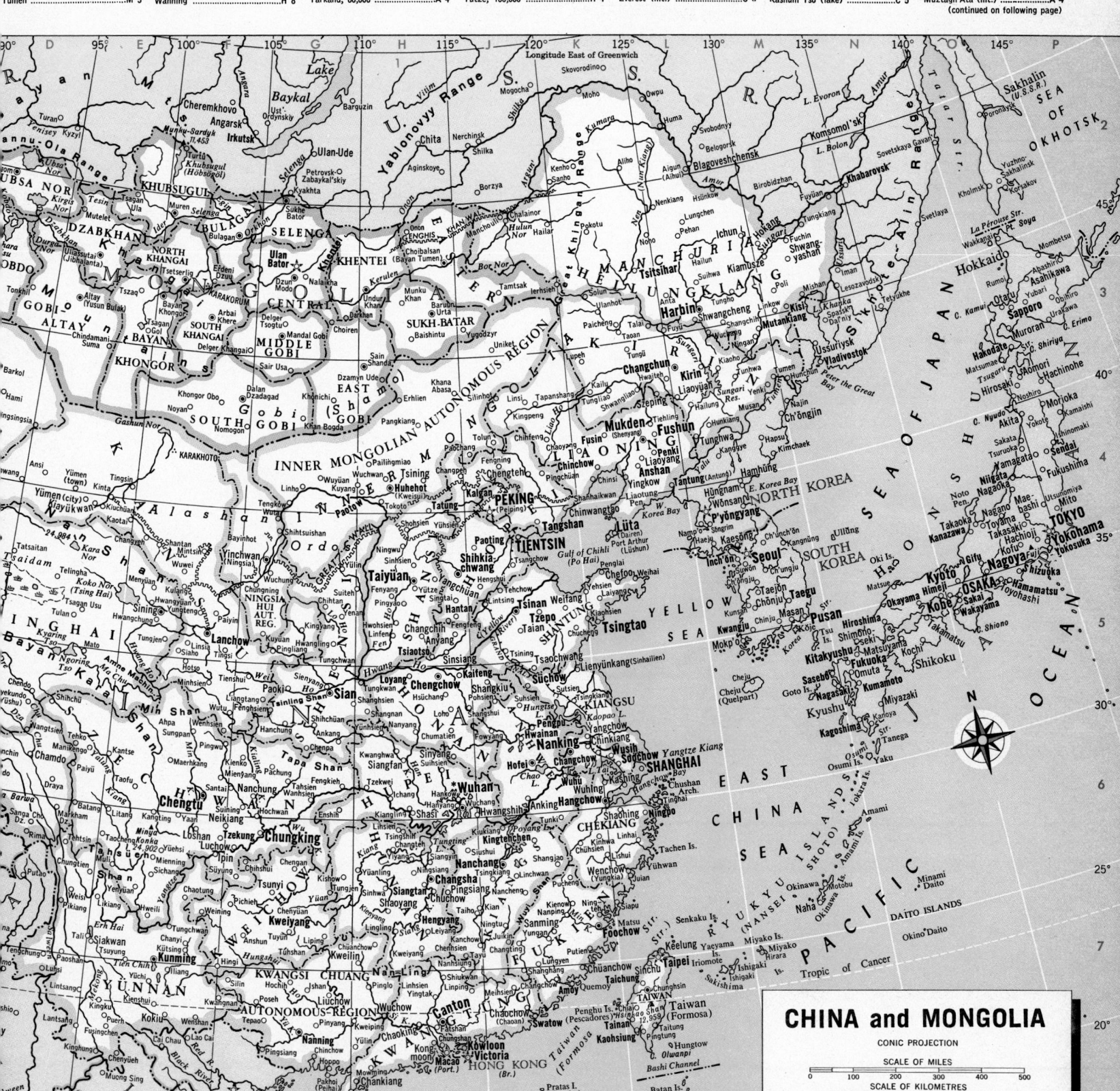

CHINA and MONGOLIA

CONIC PROJECTION

SCALE OF MILES
0 100 200 300 400 500

SCALE OF KILOMETRES
0 100 200 300 400 500

Capitals of Countries ... ☆ International Boundaries ... _____
Provincial Capitals ... ◉ Provincial Boundaries ... _ _ _ _ _
Canals ... - - - - - Walls ... ▨▨▨▨

*Wuhan municipality consists of Hankow, Hanyang and Wuchang

© Copyright by C.S. HAMMOND & CO., N.Y.

CHINA (continued)

Nam Tso (lake) .... D 5
Namcha Barwa (mt.) .... E 6
Nan Shan (range) .... E 4
Nen (river) .... K 2
Nganglaring Tso (lake) .... B 5
Ngangtse Tso (lake) .... C 5
Ngoring Tso (lake) .... E 5
Nyenchen Tanglha (range) .... C 6
Olwanpi (cape) .... K 7
Ordos (desert) .... G 4
Pangong Tso (lake) .... A 5
Penghu (isls.), 113,503 .... J 7
Pescadores (Penghu)
   (isls.), 113,503 .... J 7
Pobeda (peak) .... B 3
Po Hai (Chihli) (gulf) .... K 4
Poyang (lake) .... J 6
Pratas (isl.) .... J 7
Quemoy (isl.), 60,000 .... J 7
Red (river) .... F 7
Salween (river) .... E 6
Shamo (Gobi) (des.) .... G 3
Si Kiang (river) .... H 7
Siang Kiang (river) .... H 6
Sinkao Shan (mt.) .... K 7
South China (sea) .... H 7
Sungari (river) .... M 2
Sutlej (river) .... A 5
Tachen (isls.) .... K 6
Tahsüeh Shan (range) .... F 6
Tai (lake) .... J 5
Taiwan (isl.), 12,888,478 .... K 7
Taiwan (str.) .... J 7
Taklamakan (desert) .... B 4
Tanglha (range) .... C 5
Tangra Tso (lake) .... C 5
Tapa Shan (range) .... G 5
Tarbagatay (range) .... B 2
Tarim (river) .... C 3
Tarok Tso (lake) .... B 5
Tien Chih (lake) .... F 7
Tien Shan (range) .... B 3
Tonkin (gulf) .... G 8
Trans-Himalayas (range) .... C 5
Tsaidam (swamp) .... E 4
Tsangpo (river) .... C 6
Tsing Hai (Koko Nor) (lake)... E 4
Tsinling Shan (range) .... G 5

Tungsha (Pratas) (isl.) .... J 7
Tungting (lake) .... H 6
Turfan (depr.) .... C 3
Ulan Muren (river) .... D 5
Ulugh Muztagh (mt.) .... C 4
Ulyungur Nor (lake) .... C 2
Urungu (river) .... C 2
Ussuri (river) .... M 2
Wei Ho (river) .... G 5
West Korea (bay) .... K 4
Wu Kiang (river) .... G 6
Yalu (river) .... L 3
Yalung Kiang (river) .... E 5
Yamdrok Tso (lake) .... D 6
Yangtze Kiang (river) .... K 5
Yarkand (river) .... A 4
Yellow (Hwang Ho) (river) .... J 4
Yellow (sea) .... K 4
Yü Kiang (river) .... G 6
Yüan Kiang (river) .... G 6
Zilling Tso (lake) .... C 5

HONG KONG

CITIES and TOWNS

Kowloon, 692,800 .... H 7
Victoria (cap.), 694,500 .... H 7
Victoria, *1,034,000 .... H 7

MACAO

CITIES and TOWNS

Macao (cap.), 262,000 .... H 7

MONGOLIA

PROVINCES

Bayan Khongor, 43,600 .... E 2

Bayan Ulegei, 45,100 .... C 2
Bulagan, 31,200 .... G 2
Central, 50,400 .... G 2
Dzabkhan, 56,800 .... G 2
Eastern, 34,300 .... H 2
East Gobi, 26,300 .... G 3
Gobi-Altay, 40,500 .... D 2
Khentei, 35,400 .... G 2
Khubsugul, 61,100 .... E 1
Kobdo, 44,800 .... D 2
Middle Gobi, 27,500 .... G 2
North Khangai, 60,300 .... F 2
Selenga, 43,300 .... G 2
South Gobi, 21,900 .... G 3
South Khangai, 53,800 .... F 2
Sukh-Batar, 30,400 .... H 2
Ubsa Nor, 49,000 .... D 2

CITIES and TOWNS

Arbai Khere, 6,000 .... F 2
Altay, 7,000 .... H 2
Baishintu .... H 2
Baruun Urta, 6,000 .... H 2
Bayan Khongor, 4,400 .... F 2
Bayan Tumen (Choibalsan),
   14,000 .... H 2
Bayan Ulegei, 8,000 .... D 2
Bulagan, 8,000 .... G 2
Chindamani Suma .... E 2
Choibalsan, 14,000 .... H 2
Dalan Dzadagad, 4,000 .... G 3
Darkhan, 30,000 .... G 2
Delger Khangai .... F 2
Delger Tsogtu .... G 2
Dzamyn Ude .... G 3
Dzun Modo, 6,000 .... G 2
Erdeni Dzuu .... F 2
Jibhalanta (Uliassutai), 7,000... E 2
Jirgalanta (Kobdo), 11,000 .... D 2
Khan Bogda .... G 3
Khongor Obo .... G 2
Khonichi .... G 3
Kobdo, 11,000 .... D 2
Mandal Gobi, 5,000 .... G 2
Munku Khan .... H 2
Muren, 9,000 .... F 2
Nalaikha, 14,000 .... G 2
Nomogon .... F 3

Noyan .... F 3
Onon .... H 2
Sain Shanda, 7,000 .... H 3
Sair Usa .... G 3
Sukhe Bator, 9,000 .... G 2
Suok .... C 2
Tamtsak .... J 2
Tsagan Ula .... F 2
Tsetserlig, 14,000 .... F 2
Tszaq .... G 2
Ulan Bator (cap.), 268,800 .... G 2
Ulangom, 10,000 .... D 2
Uliassutai, 7,000 .... E 2
Undur Khan, 7,000 .... H 2
Yugodzyr .... H 2
Yusun Bulak (Altay), 7,000 .... E 2

OTHER FEATURES

Altay (mts.) .... J 2
Bor Nor (lake) .... J 2
Durga Nor (lake) .... D 2
Dzabkhan (river) .... D 2
Egin (river) .... F 1
Genghis Khan Wall (ruins) .... H 2
Gobi (desert) .... F 3
Höbsögöl (Khubsugul) (lake)... F 1
Ider (river) .... F 2
Karakorum (ruins) .... F 2
Kerulen (river) .... H 2
Khangai (mts.) .... F 2
Khara Usu (lake) .... D 2
Khentei (mts.) .... G 2
Khubsugul (lake) .... F 1
Kirgis Nor (lake) .... D 2
Kobdo (river) .... D 2
Munku-Sardyk (mt.) .... F 1
Onon (river) .... H 2
Orkhon (river) .... F 2
Selenga (river) .... F 2
Shamo (Gobi) (des.) .... G 3
Tabun Bogdo (mt.) .... D 2
Tannu-Ola (range) .... D 1
Tesin (river) .... D 1
Ubsa Nor (lake) .... D 1

*City and suburbs.
‡Popuation of municipality.

†Populations of mainland cities over 100,000 courtesy of Kingsley Davis, Office of Int'l Pop. & Urban Research, Inst. of Int'l Studies, Univ. of California.

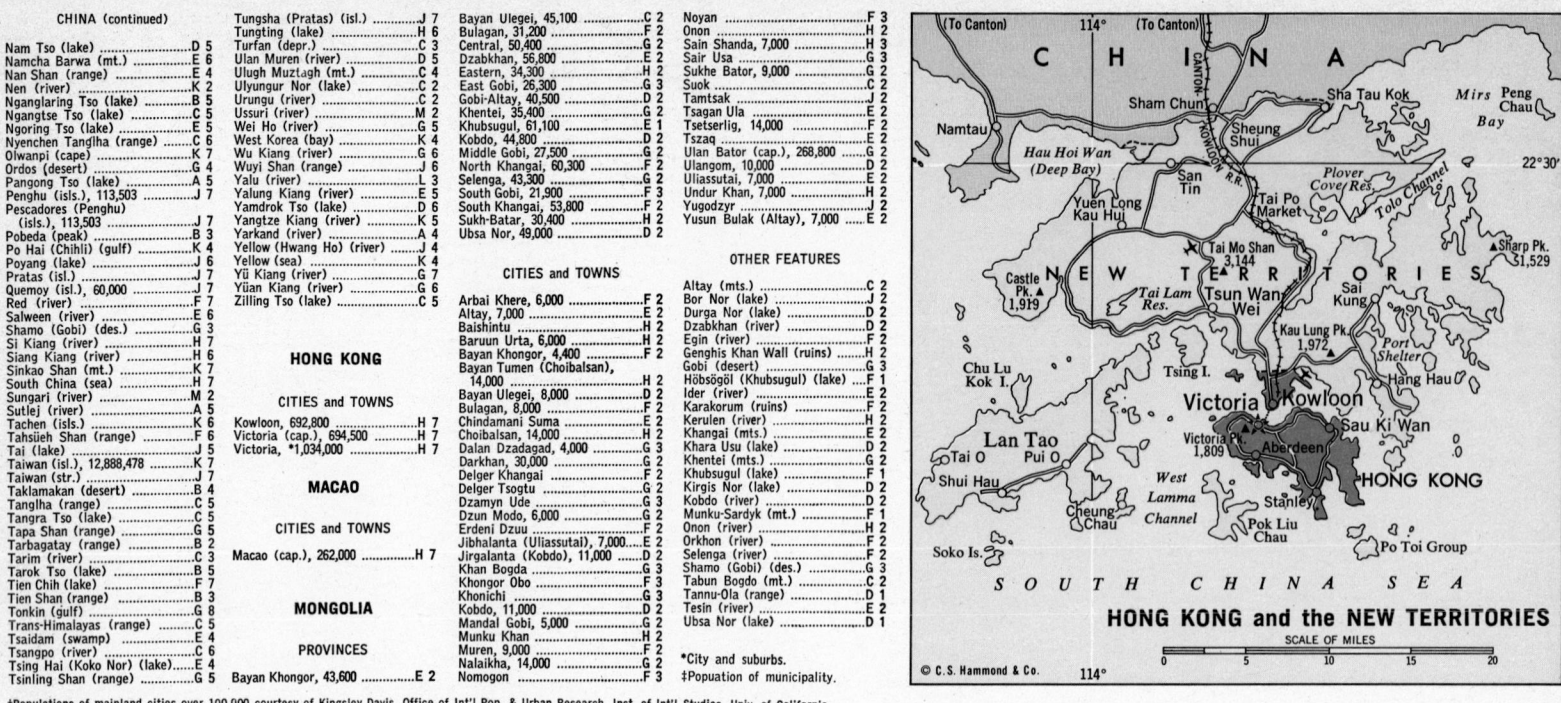

HONG KONG and the NEW TERRITORIES

SCALE OF MILES

0   5   10   15   20

© C.S. Hammond & Co.

114°

Agriculture, Industry and Resources

DOMINANT LAND USE

- Cereals (chiefly wheat, millet)
- Cereals (chiefly wheat, rice, barley)
- Cereals (chiefly rice, barley)
- Livestock Herding, Limited Agriculture
- Forests
- Nonagricultural Land

MAJOR MINERAL OCCURRENCES

- Ab Asbestos
- Ag Silver
- Al Bauxite
- Au Gold
- C   Coal
- Cu Copper
- F   Fluorspar
- Fe Iron Ore
- G   Natural Gas
- Gp Gypsum
- Hg Mercury
- J   Jade
- Mg Magnesium
- Mn Manganese
- Mo Molybdenum
- Na Salt
- O   Petroleum
- Pb Lead
- Sb Antimony
- Sn Tin
- Tc Talc
- U   Uranium
- W   Tungsten
- Zn Zinc

- ⚡ Water Power
- ▨ Major Industrial Areas

URUMCHI
Cement,
Agricultural Machinery

LANCHOW
Oil Refining,
Cement, Chemicals

PAOTOW
Iron & Steel

TAIYÜAN
Iron & Steel, Machinery,
Chemicals, Cement

HARBIN
Food Processing,
Electric Motors,
Bearings, Machinery

CHANGCHUN
Automobiles, Trucks,
Locomotives, Chemicals,
Tools, Cement

MUKDEN–ANSHAN
Iron & Steel, Machinery,
Tools, Ballbearings,
Electrical Equipment,
Chemicals

LÜTA
Steel, Railroad Equipment,
Shipbuilding, Cement,
Chemicals

PEKING–TIENTSIN
Iron & Steel, Machinery, Cement,
Textiles, Chemicals

TSINGTAO
Textiles, Tires,
Locomotives

SHANGHAI-NANKING
Iron & Steel, Machinery, Tools,
Shipbuilding, Textiles, Food
Processing, Chemicals, Paper,
Cement

WUHAN
Iron & Steel, Machinery,
Chemicals, Cement

FOOCHOW
Chemicals

SIAN
Textiles, Cement,
Electrical Equipment

CHUNGKING-RED BASIN
Iron & Steel, Machinery, Chemicals,
Sugar Refining, Fertilizer

CHANGSHA
Nonferrous Metals,
Electrical Equipment,
Iron & Steel, Tools, Cement

CANTON
Textiles, Sugar Refining,
Cement, Shipbuilding, Paper

HONG KONG
Textiles, Clothing,
Light Industry,
Shipbuilding

NANCHANG
Aircraft

TAIPEI
Machinery, Chemicals,
Textiles, Shipbuilding

TAINAN–KAOHSIUNG
Machinery, Oil Refining,
Nonferrous Metals,
Sugar Refining

JAPAN	NORTH KOREA	SOUTH KOREA
[ARE]A 145,730 sq. mi.	**AREA** 46,540 sq. mi.	**AREA** 38,175 sq.mi.
[POP]ULATION 112,200,000	**POPULATION** 17,000,000	**POPULATION** 34,688,079
[CAP]ITAL Tokyo	**CAPITAL** P'yŏngyang	**CAPITAL** Seoul
[LAR]GEST CITY Tokyo	**LARGEST CITY** P'yŏngyang	**LARGEST CITY** Seoul
[HIG]HEST POINT Fuji 12,389 ft.	**HIGHEST POINT** Paektu 9,003 ft.	**HIGHEST POINT** Halla 6,398 ft.
[MO]NETARY UNIT yen	**MONETARY UNIT** wŏn	**MONETARY UNIT** wŏn
[MA]JOR LANGUAGE Japanese	**MAJOR LANGUAGE** Korean	**MAJOR LANGUAGE** Korean
[MA]JOR RELIGIONS Buddhism, Shintoism	**MAJOR RELIGIONS** Confucianism, Buddhism, Christianity, Ch'ŏndogyo	**MAJOR RELIGIONS** Confucianism, Buddhism, Ch'ŏndogyo, Christianity

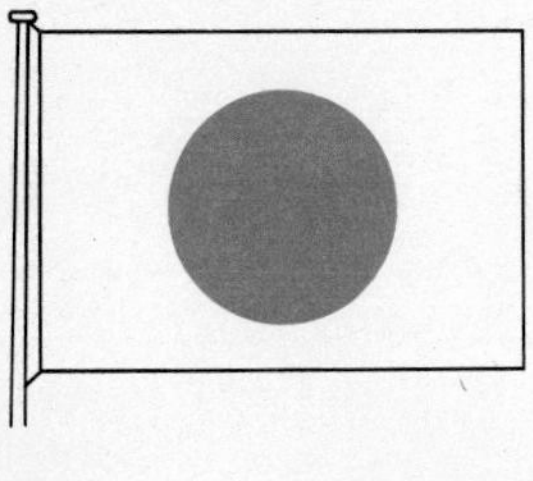

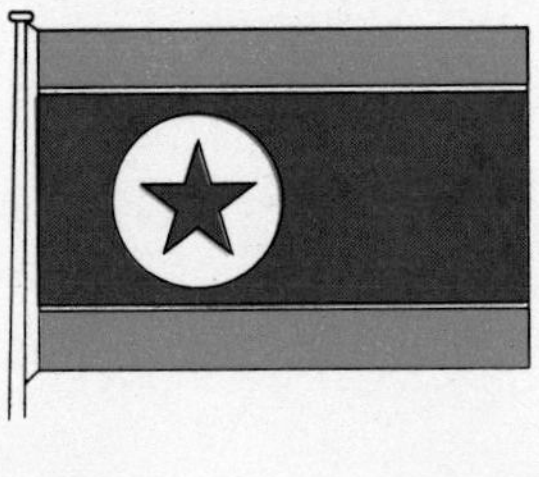

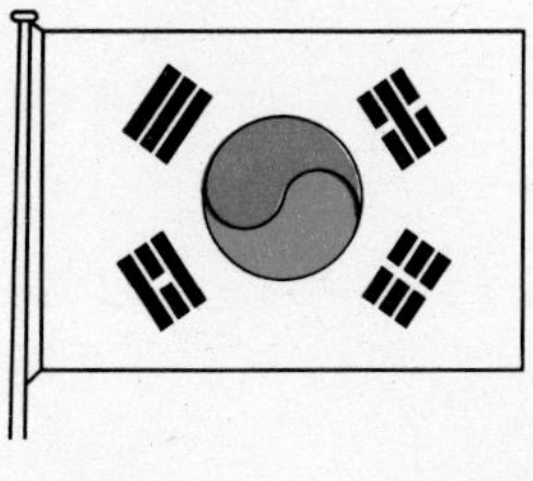

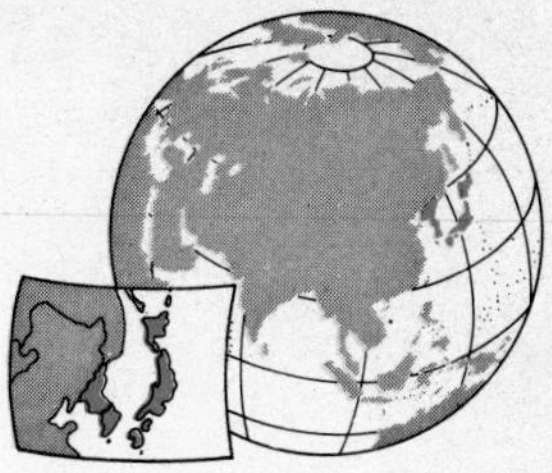

JAPAN

PREFECTURES

5,923,499	H 6
1,232,493	J 4
ri, 1,468,571	K 3
, 4,149,132	P 2
e, 1,465,205	F 7
773,597	G 5
ka, 4,292,997	D 7
shima, 1,970,675	K 5
1,867,970	H 6
ma, 1,756,489	J 5
hima, 2,646,353	E 6
aido, 5,338,043	K 2
o, 4,991,910	H 7
ki, 2,342,173	K 5
awa, 1,069,871	H 5
, 1,385,566	K 4
wa, 961,285	G 6
shima, 1,723,900	E 8
gawa, 3,697,619	O 2
, 808,367	F 7
moto, 1,715,011	E 7
, 2,424,830	J 7
1,625,992	H 6
gi, 1,955,274	K 4
zaki, 1,085,057	E 8
no, 2,017,544	J 5
saki, 1,571,919	D 7
, 1,077,301	J 8
ta, 2,391,963	J 5
1,190,307	E 7
ama, 1,814,300	F 6
awa, 1,042,502	N 6
a, 8,278,844	J 8
, 837,680	E 7
Saitama, 4,821,349	O 2
Shiga, 985,515	J 7
Shimane, 768,876	F 6
Shizuoka, 3,308,796	H 6
Tochigi, 1,698,002	K 5
Tokushima, 805,090	G 7
Tokyo, 11,669,167	O 2
Tottori, 581,318	G 6
Toyama, 1,070,793	H 5
Wakayama, 1,072,078	G 6
Yamagata, 1,220,308	K 4
Yamaguchi, 1,555,233	E 6
Yamanashi, 783,054	J 6

CITIES and TOWNS

Abashiri, 43,821	M 1
Ageo, 146,359	O 2
Aikawa, 13,546	H 4
Aizuwakamatsu, 108,676	J 5
Ajigasawa, 18,094	J 3
Akabira, 26,363	K 2
Akashi, 234,905	H 8
Aki, 24,483	F 7
Akita, 261,242	J 4
Akkeshi, 16,778	M 2
Akune, 30,296	E 7
Amagasaki, 545,762	H 8
Amagi, 42,725	E 7
Anan, 60,369	G 7
Aomori, 264,187	K 3
Asahi, 34,028	K 6
Asahikawa, 320,526	L 2
Ashibetsu, 36,517	L 2
Ashikaga, 162,361	J 5
Ashiya, 76,211	H 8
Atami, 51,437	J 6
Atsugi, 108,952	O 2
Awaji, 9,622	H 8
Ayabe, 43,490	G 6
Beppu, 133,893	E 7
Bibai, 38,418	L 2
Chiba, 659,344	P 2
Chichibu, 61,797	J 5
Chigasaki, 152,024	O 3
Chitose, 61,031	K 2
Chofu, 175,858	O 2
Choshi, 90,375	K 6
Daito, 110,829	J 8
Ebetsu, 77,623	K 2
Esashi, Hokkaido, 10,172	L 1
Esashi, Hokkaido, 14,410	J 3
Esashi, Iwate, 36,338	K 4
Fuchu, Hiroshima, 50,217	F 6
Fuchu, Tokyo, 182,379	O 2
Fuji, 199,195	J 6
Fujieda, 90,356	J 6
Fujisawa, 265,938	O 3
Fukuchiyama, 60,004	G 6
Fukue, 32,016	D 7
Fukui, 231,365	G 5
Fukuoka, 1,002,214	D 7
Fukushima, 246,531	K 5
Fukuyama, 329,779	F 6
Funabashi, 423,106	P 2
Furukawa, 54,358	K 4
Gifu, 408,699	H 6
Gobo, 30,273	G 7
Gose, 37,555	J 8
Gosen, 39,378	J 5
Goshogawara, 49,048	K 3
Gotsu, 27,990	F 6
Habikino, 94,160	J 8
Haboro, 13,624	K 1
Hachinohe, 224,213	K 3
Hachioji, 322,558	O 2
Hagi, 52,724	E 6
Hakodate, 307,447	K 3
Hakui, 28,726	H 5
Hamada, 50,315	E 6
Hamamatsu, 468,886	H 6
Hanamaki, 65,829	K 4
Hanno, 55,925	O 2
Haramachi, 43,482	K 5
Hayama, 24,025	O 3
Higashiosaka, 524,731	J 8
Hikone, 85,068	H 6
Himeji, 436,099	G 6
Himi, 61,789	H 5
Hirakata, 297,618	J 7
Hirara, 29,292	L 7
Hirata, 30,943	F 6
Hiratsuka, 195,635	O 3
Hiroo, 11,399	L 2
Hirosaki, 164,924	K 3
Hiroshima, 852,607	E 6
Hitachi, 202,387	K 5
Hitachiota, 35,322	K 5
Hitoyoshi, 41,119	E 7
Hofu, 105,538	E 6
Hondo, 40,432	E 7
Honjo, 40,488	J 4
Hyuga, 53,449	E 7
Ibaraki, 210,286	J 7
Ibusuki, 32,338	E 8
Ichihara, 194,069	P 3
Ichikawa, 319,272	P 2
Ichinohe, 21,437	K 3
Ichinomiya, 238,457	H 6
Ichinoseki, 59,143	K 4
Ide, 9,112	J 7
Iida, 77,114	H 6
Iizuka, 75,417	E 7
Ikeda, Hokkaido, 12,306	L 2
Ikeda, Osaka, 100,263	H 7
Ikuno, 6,659	G 6
Imabari, 119,725	F 6
Imari, 60,914	D 7
Imazu, 11,520	G 6
Ina, 54,467	H 6
Isahaya, 73,339	D 7
Ise, 104,955	H 6
Ishigaki, 34,625	L 7
Ishige, 19,220	P 2
Ishinomaki, 115,084	K 4
Ishioka, 43,678	K 5
Itami, 171,979	H 7
Ito, 68,073	J 6
Itoigawa, 36,646	H 5
Itoman, 39,359	N 6
Iwaizumi, 20,218	K 4
Iwaki, 330,210	K 5
Iwakuni, 111,071	E 6
Iwami, 16,062	G 6
Iwamizawa, 72,303	L 2
Iwanai, 25,823	K 2
Iwasaki, 4,439	J 3
Iwata, 67,665	H 6
Iwatsuki, 83,825	O 2
Iyo, 27,808	F 7
Izuhara, 18,460	D 6
Izumi, 118,234	J 8
Izumiotsu, 66,243	J 8
Izumisano, 86,139	G 6
Izumo, 71,568	F 6
Joyo, 58,916	J 7
Kadoma, 143,235	J 7
Kaga, 61,598	H 5
Kagoshima, 456,818	E 8
Kaizuka, 79,506	H 8
Kakogawa, 169,297	G 6
Kamaishi, 68,982	L 4
Kamakura, 165,548	O 3
Kameoka, 58,184	J 7
Kaminoyama, 37,860	J 4
Kamiyaku, 8,666	E 8
Kamo, 8,954	J 7
Kanazawa, 395,262	H 5
Kanonji, 44,134	F 6
Kanoya, 67,949	E 8
Kanuma, 81,800	J 5
Karatsu, 75,224	D 7
Kaseda, 24,969	D 8
Kashihara, Nara, 95,697	J 8
Kashihara, Osaka, 63,585	J 8
Kashiwa, 203,063	P 2
Kashiwazaki, 80,353	J 5
Kasugai, 213,856	H 6
Kasukabe, 121,639	O 2
Katsuta, 79,997	K 5
Katsuura, 26,755	K 6
Kawachinagano, 66,945	J 8
Kawagoe, 225,467	O 2
Kawaguchi, 345,547	J 6
Kawanishi, 115,771	H 7
Kawasaki, 1,015,022	O 2
Kesennuma, 66,618	K 4
Kikonai, 10,034	K 3
Kiryu, 134,240	J 5
Kisarazu, 96,839	P 3
Kishiwada, 174,947	J 8
Kitaibaraki, 44,332	K 5
Kitakata, 37,472	J 5
Kitakyushu, 1,058,067	E 6
Kitami, 91,514	L 2
Kizu, 11,891	J 7
Kobayashi, 38,325	E 8
Kobe, 1,360,530	H 7
Kochi, 280,960	F 7
Kodaira, 156,182	O 2
Kofu, 193,887	J 6
Kokubu, 31,658	E 8
Komagane, 30,318	H 6
Komatsu, 100,276	H 5
Koriyama, 264,610	K 5
Koshigaya, 195,915	P 2
Kuji, 38,126	K 3
Kuki, 45,799	O 2
Kumagaya, 131,486	J 5
Kumamoto, 488,053	E 7
Kumano, 27,025	G 7
Kumiyama, 11,539	J 7
Kurashiki, 392,770	F 6
Kurayoshi, 50,786	F 6
Kure, 242,652	F 6
Kurume, 204,474	E 7
Kushikino, 30,457	E 8
Kushima, 30,036	E 8
Kushimoto, 18,998	G 7
Kushiro, 206,689	M 2
Kutchan, 18,668	K 2
Kyonan, 13,066	O 3
Kyoto, 1,461,050	J 7
Machida, 255,303	O 2
Maebashi, 250,241	J 5
Maibara, 12,834	G 6
Maizuru, 97,775	G 6
Makurazaki, 29,689	O 3
Mashike, 9,312	K 2
Masuda, 50,732	E 6
Matsubara, 132,662	H 8
Matsudo, 344,552	P 2
Matsue, 127,446	F 6
Matsumae, 18,307	J 3
Matsumoto, 185,577	H 5
Matsusaka, 108,891	H 6
Matsuto, 36,170	H 5
Matsuyama, 367,313	F 7
Mihara, 83,680	F 6
Miki, 55,730	H 7
Mikuni, 21,603	G 5
Minamata, 36,782	E 7
Minobu, 10,346	J 6
Minoo, 79,620	J 7
Misawa, 37,434	K 3
Mishima, 22,404	J 7
Mitaka, 164,852	O 2
Mito, 197,950	K 5
Mitsukaido, 38,820	P 2
Miura, 47,890	O 3
Miyako, 61,912	L 4
Miyakonojo, 118,284	E 8
Miyazaki, 234,348	E 8
Miyazu, 30,194	G 6
Miyoshi, 37,195	F 6
Mizusawa, 52,271	K 4
Mobara, 64,942	K 6
Mombetsu, 32,821	L 1
Mooka, 47,347	K 5
Mori, 17,030	K 2
Moriguchi, 178,379	J 7
Morioka, 216,211	K 4
Motobu, 17,809	N 6
Muko, 45,886	J 7
Murakami, 32,939	J 4
Muroran, 158,714	K 2
Muroto, 26,660	G 7
Musashino, 139,493	O 2
Mutsu, 44,651	K 3
Nachikatsuura, 23,597	H 7
Nagahama, Ehime, 13,144	F 7
Nagahama, Shiga, 53,966	H 6
Nagano, 306,643	J 5
Nagaoka, Kyoto, 65,557	J 7
Nagaoka, Niigata, 171,742	J 5
Nagasaki, 450,195	D 7
Nagato, 27,327	E 6
Nago, 45,207	N 6
Nagoya, 2,079,694	H 6
Naha, 295,091	N 6
Nakaminato, 33,144	K 5
Nakamura, 34,426	F 7
Nakasato, 14,247	K 3
Nakatsu, 59,111	E 7
Nanao, 49,491	H 5
Nankoku, 42,828	F 7
Naoetsu, 123,416	H 5
Nara, 257,482	J 8
Narashino, 117,851	P 2
Nayoro, 35,145	L 1
Naze, 46,337	O 5
Nemuro, 45,817	M 2
Neyagawa, 254,316	J 7
Nichinan, 52,171	E 8
Niigata, 423,204	J 5
Niihama, 131,707	F 6
Niimi, 30,014	F 6
Niitsu, 58,970	J 5
Nikko, 26,279	J 5
Nishinomiya, 400,590	H 8
Nishinoomote, 24,266	E 8
Nobeoka, 134,530	E 7
Noboribetsu, 50,890	K 2
Noda, 78,194	P 2
Nogata, 58,551	E 7
Nose, 9,751	J 7
Noshiro, 59,218	J 3
Noto, 15,815	H 5
Numata, 45,254	J 5
Numazu, 199,325	J 6
Obama, 33,891	G 6
Obihiro, 141,776	L 2
Oda, 37,450	F 6

(continued on following page)

Agriculture, Industry and Resources

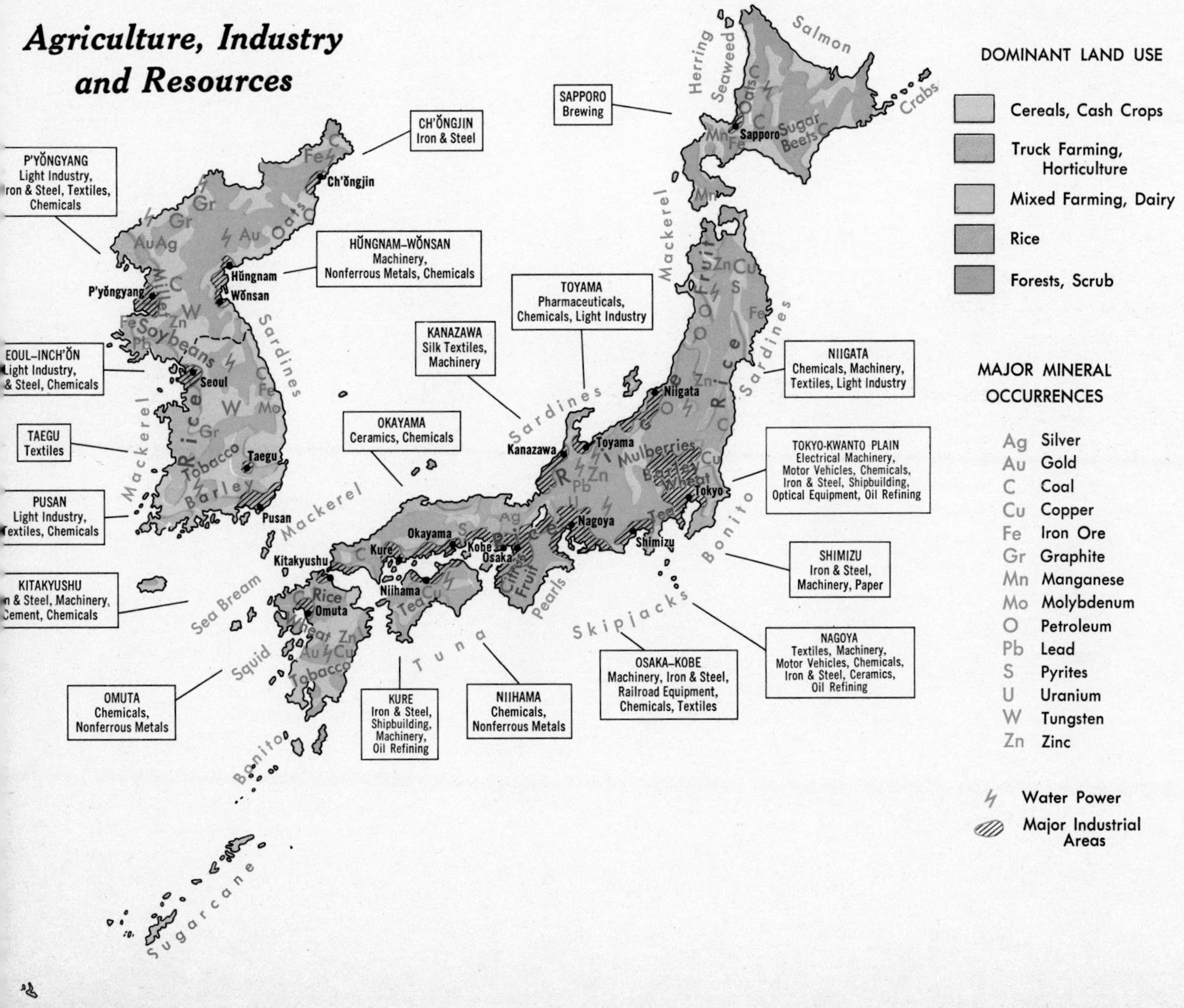

P'YŎNGYANG
Light Industry,
Iron & Steel, Textiles,
Chemicals
CH'ŎNGJIN
Iron & Steel
HŬNGNAM–WŎNSAN
Machinery,
Nonferrous Metals, Chemicals
SEOUL–INCH'ŎN
Light Industry,
Iron & Steel, Chemicals
TAEGU
Textiles
PUSAN
Light Industry,
Textiles, Chemicals
KITAKYUSHU
Iron & Steel, Machinery,
Cement, Chemicals
OMUTA
Chemicals,
Nonferrous Metals
KURE
Iron & Steel,
Shipbuilding,
Machinery,
Oil Refining
NIIHAMA
Chemicals,
Nonferrous Metals
OSAKA–KOBE
Machinery, Iron & Steel,
Railroad Equipment,
Chemicals, Textiles
NAGOYA
Textiles, Machinery,
Motor Vehicles, Chemicals,
Iron & Steel, Ceramics,
Oil Refining
SHIMIZU
Iron & Steel,
Machinery, Paper
TOKYO-KWANTO PLAIN
Electrical Machinery,
Motor Vehicles, Chemicals,
Iron & Steel, Shipbuilding,
Optical Equipment, Oil Refining
NIIGATA
Chemicals, Machinery,
Textiles, Light Industry
OKAYAMA
Ceramics, Chemicals
KANAZAWA
Silk Textiles,
Machinery
TOYAMA
Pharmaceuticals,
Chemicals, Light Industry
SAPPORO
Brewing
Ch'ŏngjin
Hŭngnam
Wŏnsan
P'yŏngyang
Seoul
Taegu
Pusan
Kitakyushu
Omuta
Kure
Niihama
Okayama
Kobe
Osaka
Nagoya
Kanazawa
Toyama
Niigata
Tokyo
Shimizu
Sapporo
Salmon
Herring
Seaweed
Crabs
Sugar Beets
Oats
Mackerel
Sardines
Fruit
Rice
Soybeans
Millet
Tobacco
Barley
Mulberries
Wheat
Tea
Pearls
Bonito
Skipjacks
Tuna
Squid
Sea Bream
Sugarcane
DOMINANT LAND USE
Cereals, Cash Crops
Truck Farming, Horticulture
Mixed Farming, Dairy
Rice
Forests, Scrub
MAJOR MINERAL OCCURRENCES
Ag Silver
Au Gold
C Coal
Cu Copper
Fe Iron Ore
Gr Graphite
Mn Manganese
Mo Molybdenum
O Petroleum
Pb Lead
S Pyrites
U Uranium
W Tungsten
Zn Zinc
Water Power
Major Industrial Areas

(continued)

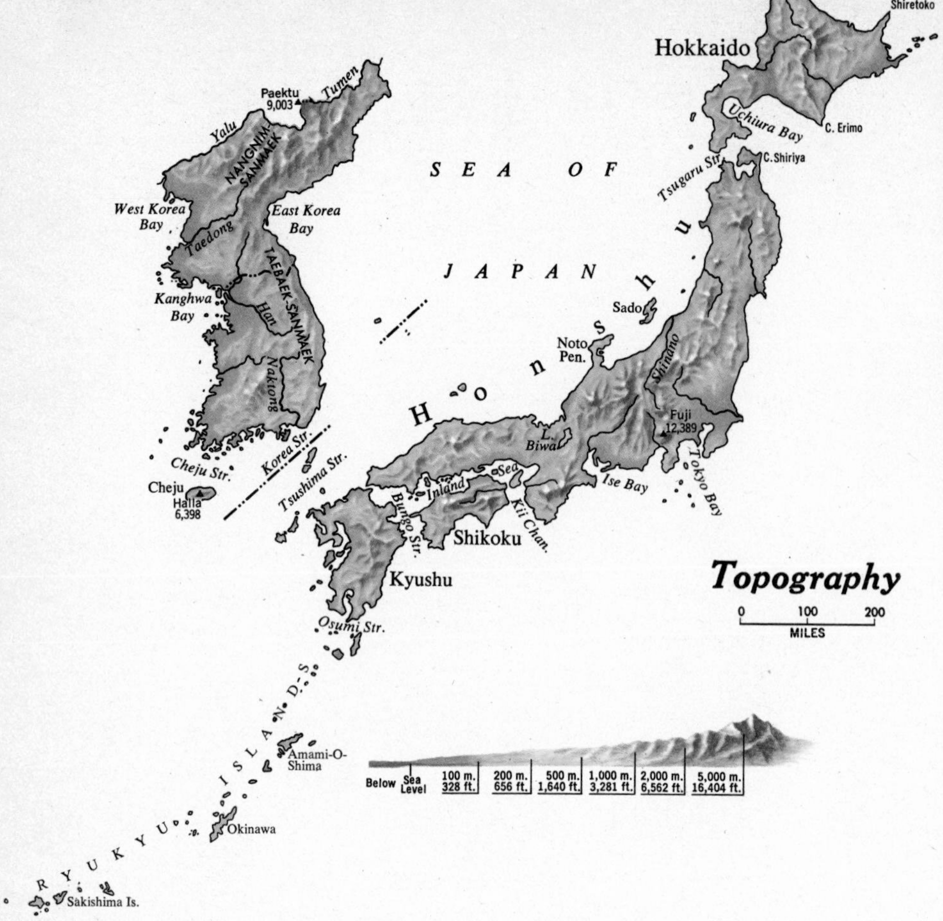
Pt. Soya
C. Shiretoko
Hokkaido
Uchiura Bay
C. Erimo
C. Shiriya
Tsugaru Str.
SEA OF JAPAN
Honshu
Sado
Noto Pen.
Shinano
Fuji 12,389
Tokyo Bay
Biwa
Ise Bay
Inland Sea
Kii Chan.
Shikoku
Bungo Str.
Kyushu
Osumi Str.
Tsushima Str.
Korea Str.
Cheju Str.
Cheju
Halla 6,398
Paektu 9,003
Tumen
Yalu
NANGNIM SANMAEK
West Korea Bay
East Korea Bay
Taedong
TAEBAEK-SANMAEK
Kanghwa Bay
Han
Naktong
RYUKYU ISLANDS
Amami-O-Shima
Okinawa
Sakishima Is.
Topography
0 100 200
MILES
Below Sea Level
100 m. 328 ft.
200 m. 656 ft.
500 m. 1,640 ft.
1,000 m. 3,281 ft.
2,000 m. 6,562 ft.
5,000 m. 16,404 ft.

Odate, 71,828	K 3
Odawara, 173,521	J 6
Ofunato, 39,629	K 4
Oga, 39,621	J 4
Ogaki, 140,424	H 6
Ogi, 4,717	J 5
Ohata, 12,632	K 3
Oita, 320,236	E 7
Ojiya, 44,375	J 5
Okawa, 50,397	E 7
Okaya, 61,776	H 5
Okayama, 513,452	F 6
Okazaki, 234,506	H 6
Omagari, 40,581	K 4
Omiya, 327,696	O 2
Omu, 7,407	L 1
Omura, Bonin Is., 1,507	M 3
Omura, Nagasaki, 60,919	E 7
Omuta, 165,971	E 7
Onagawa, 16,945	K 4
Ono, 41,918	H 6
Onoda, 43,804	E 6
Onomichi, 102,954	F 6
Osaka, 2,778,975	J 8
Ota, 110,724	J 5
Otaru, 184,403	K 2
Otawara, 42,331	K 5
Otsu, 191,474	J 7
Owase, 31,798	H 6
Oyabe, 35,791	H 5
Oyama, 120,259	J 5
Ozu, 37,296	F 7
Rausu, 8,249	M 1
Rikuzentakata, 29,440	K 4
Rumoi, 36,878	K 2
Ryotsu, 22,109	J 4
Ryugasaki, 40,569	P 2
Sabae, 57,252	H 5
Saga, 150,260	E 7
Sagamihara, 377,341	O 2
Saigo, 14,408	F 5
Saiki, 52,863	E 7
Saito, 37,054	E 7
Sakado, 51,230	O 2
Sakai, Ibaraki, 24,347	P 1
Sakai, Osaka, 750,671	J 8
Sakaide, 67,624	G 6
Sakaiminato, 35,819	F 6
Sakata, 97,723	J 4
Saku, 56,145	J 5
Sakurai, 54,315	J 8
Sanda, 35,261	H 7
Sanjo, 81,806	J 5
Sapporo, 1,240,617	K 2
Sarufutsu, 3,552	L 1
Sasebo, 250,723	D 7
Satte, 43,083	O 1
Sawara, 48,669	K 6
Sayama, 98,548	O 2
Sendai, Kagoshima, 61,790	E 8
Sendai, Miyagi, 615,473	K 4
Shari, 15,996	M 2
Shibata, 74,025	J 5
Shibetsu, 30,028	M 2
Shimabara, 45,178	E 7
Shimizu, 243,045	J 6
Shimoda, 31,700	J 6
Shimonoseki, 266,596	E 6
Shingu, 39,023	H 7
Shinjo, 42,229	K 4
Shiogama, 59,236	K 4
Shiroishi, 40,862	K 4
Shizunai, 24,832	L 2
Shizuoka, 446,952	H 6
Shobara, 23,867	F 6
Soka, 167,176	O 2
Soma, 37,550	K 5
Sonobe, 14,827	J 7
Suita, 300,949	J 7
Sukagawa, 54,925	K 5
Sukumo, 25,338	F 7
Sumoto, 44,135	G 6
Sunagawa, 26,023	K 2
Susaki, 31,016	F 7
Suttsu, 6,511	J 2
Suwa, 49,595	H 6
Suzu, 28,238	H 5
Suzuka, 141,829	H 6
Tachikawa, 138,097	O 2
Tajimi, 68,901	H 6
Takaishi, 66,824	H 8
Takamatsu, 298,997	G 6
Takaoka, 169,618	H 5
Takarazuka, 162,622	H 7
Takasaki, 211,348	J 5
Takatsuki, 330,571	J 7
Takawa, 61,465	E 7
Takayama, 60,506	H 5
Takefu, 65,013	G 6
Tanabe, Kyoto, 30,025	J 7
Tanabe, Wakayama, 67,001	G 7
Tateyama, 56,139	K 6
Tendo, 48,077	K 4
Tenri, 62,908	J 8
Teshio, 6,509	K 1
Toba, 29,346	H 6
Tobetsu, 17,351	K 2
Togane, 33,404	K 6
Toi, 6,982	J 6
Tojo, 13,795	F 6
Tokushima, 239,285	G 7
Tokuyama, 106,963	F 6
Tokyo (cap.), 8,642,800	O 2
Tokyo, *11,635,201	O 2
Tomakomai, 132,480	K 2
Tomiyama, 7,390	O 3
Tondabayashi, 91,393	J 8
Tosa, 30,679	F 7
Tosashimizu, 24,858	F 7
Tosu, 50,732	E 7
Tottori, 122,312	G 6
Towada, 54,369	K 3
Toyama, 290,145	H 5
Toyohashi, 284,597	H 6
Toyonaka, 398,363	J 7
Toyooka, 46,211	G 6
Toyota, 248,774	H 6
Tsu, 139,537	H 6
Tsubame, 43,265	J 5
Tsuchiura, 104,031	J 5
Tsuruga, 60,210	G 6
Tsurugi, 15,253	H 5
Tsuruoka, 95,933	J 4
Tsuyama, 79,907	F 6
Ube, 161,971	E 6
Ueda, 105,147	J 5
Ugo, 21,956	K 4
Uji, 133,396	J 7
Uozu, 48,419	H 5
Urakawa, 20,213	L 2
Urawa, 331,145	O 2
Ushibuka, 24,252	D 7
Usuki, 39,161	F 7
Utsunomiya, 344,417	K 5
Uwajima, 70,433	F 7
Wajima, 33,232	H 5
Wakasa, 6,989	G 6
Wakayama, 389,677	G 6
Wakkanai, 55,464	K 1
Warabi, 76,312	O 2
Yaizu, 94,102	J 6
Yakumo, 19,260	J 2
Yamagata, 219,773	K 4
Yamaguchi, 106,099	E 6
Yamato, 145,877	O 2
Yamatokoriyama, 71,000	J 8
Yamatotakada, 58,638	J 8
Yao, 261,642	J 8
Yatabe, 22,225	P 2
Yatsushiro, 103,693	E 7
Yawata, 50,131	J 7
Yawatahama, 45,260	F 7
Yoichi, 25,816	K 2
Yokawa, 8,012	H 7
Yokkaichi, 247,000	H 6
Yokohama, 2,621,648	O 3
Yokosuka, 389,559	O 3
Yokote, 43,030	K 4
Yonago, 118,332	F 6
Yonezawa, 91,975	K 5
Yono, 71,045	O 2
Yubari, 50,131	L 2
Yubetsu, 6,693	L 1
Yukuhashi, 53,751	E 7
Yuzawa, 38,005	K 4
Zushi, 56,298	O 3

OTHER FEATURES

Abashiri (riv.)	M 1
Abukuma (riv.)	K 4
Agano (riv.)	J 4
Akan National Park	M 2
Amakusa (isls.), 175,495	D 7
Amami (isls.), 155,884	N 5
Amami-O-Shima (isl.), 85,168	N 5
Ara (riv.)	O 2
Asahi (mt.)	J 4
Asama (mt.)	J 5
Ashizuri (cape)	F 7
Aso (mt.)	E 7
Aso National Park	E 7
Atsumi (bay)	H 6
Awa (isl.), 674	J 4
Awaji (isl.), 172,118	H 8
Bandai (mt.)	K 5
Bandai-Asahi National Park	J 4
Biwa (lake)	H 6
Bonin (isls.), 1,507	M 3
Boso (pen.), 976,493	K 6
Bungo (str.)	F 7
Chichi (isl.), 1,507	M 3
Chichibu-Tama National Park	J 6
Chokai (mt.)	J 4
Chubu-Sangaku National Park	H 5
Dai (mt.)	F 6
Daimanji (mt.)	F 5
Daio (cape)	H 6
Daisen-Oki National Park	F 6
Daisetsu (mt.)	L 2
Daisetsu-Zan National Park	L 2
Dogo (isl.), 23,605	F 5
Dozen (isls.), 6,160	F 5
East China (sea)	C 8
Edo (riv.)	P 2
Erimo (cape)	L 3
Esan (pt.)	K 3
Fuji (mt.)	J 6
Fuji (riv.)	J 6
Fuji-Hakone-Izu National Park	H 6
Gassan (mt.)	J 4
Goto (isls.), 126,261	D 7
Habomai (isls.)	N 2
Hachiro (lag.)	J 3
Haha (isl.)	M 3
Hakken (mt.)	H 6
Haku (mt.)	H 5
Hakusan National Park	H 5
Harima (sea)	G 6
Hida (riv.)	H 6
Hodaka (mt.)	H 5
Hokkaido (isl.), 5,312,404	L 2
Honshu (isl.), 88,578,094	J 5
Ie (isl.), 5,262	N 6
Iheya (isl.), 1,640	N 6
Iki (isl.), 41,873	D 7
Ina (riv.)	H 7
Inawashiro (lake)	K 5
Inubo (cape)	K 6
Iriomote (isl.), 3,469	K 7
Iro (cape)	J 6
Ise (bay)	H 6
Ise-Shima National Park	H 6
Ishigaki (isl.), 34,625	L 7
Ishikari (bay)	K 2
Ishikari (riv.)	L 2
Ishizuchi (mt.)	F 7
Iwaki (mt.)	K 3
Iwate (mt.)	K 4
Iwo (isl.)	M 4
Iyo (sea)	E 7
Izu (isls.), 32,459	J 6
Izu (pen.), 274,136	J 6
Japan (sea)	G 4
Joshinetsu-Kogen National Park	J 5
Kagoshima (bay)	E 8
Kamui (cape)	K 2
Kariba (mt.)	K 2
Kasumiga (lag.)	K 5
Kazan-retto (Volcano) (isls.)	M 4
Kerama (isls.), 1,687	M 6
Kii (chan.)	G 7
Kikai (isl.), 11,464	O 5
Kino (riv.)	G 6
Kirishima-Yaku National Park	E 7
Kita Iwo (isl.)	M 4
Kitakami (riv.)	K 4
Komaga (mt.)	K 2
Korea (str.)	D 6
Koshiki (isls.), 8,979	D 8
Kuchino (isl.)	O 4
Kuju (mt.)	E 7
Kume (isl.), 4,740	M 6
Kutcharo (lake)	M 2
Kyushu (isl.), 11,775,985	E 7
Meakan (mt.)	L 2
Minami Iwo (isl.)	M 5
Miura (pen.), 517,772	O 3
Miyako (isl.), 40,160	L 7
Miyako (isls.), 57,739	L 7
Mogami (riv.)	K 4
Motsuta (cape)	J 2
Muko (isl.)	M 3
Muko (riv.)	H 7
Muroto (pt.)	G 7
Mutsu (bay)	K 3
Naka (riv.)	K 5
Nampo-Shoto (isls.), 1,507	M 3
Nansei Shoto (Ryukyu) (isls.), 1,198,386	M 6
Nantai (mt.)	J 5
Nasu (mt.)	J 5
Nemuro (str.)	M 1
Nii (isl.), 3,666	J 6
Nikko National Park	J 5
Nishino (isl.)	M 3
Nojima (cape)	K 6
Nosappu (pt.)	N 2
Noto (pen.), 290,628	H 5
Nyudo (cape)	J 4
Oani (riv.)	K 3
Obitsu (riv.)	P 3
Oga (pen.), 39,621	J 4
Ogasawara-gunto (Bonin) (isls.), 1,507	M 3
Okhotsk (sea)	M 1
Oki (isls.), 29,765	F 5
Okinawa (isl.), 924,540	N 6
Okinawa (isls.), 936,895	N 6
Okinoerabu (isl.), 16,883	N 5
Okushiri (isl.), 5,746	J 2
Oma (cape)	K 3
Omono (riv.)	J 4
Ono (riv.)	E 7
Ontake (mt.)	H 6
Osaka (bay)	H 8
O-Shima (isl.), 11,096	J 6
Osumi (isls.), 62,453	E 8
Osumi (pen.), 33,575	E 8
Osumi (str.)	E 8
Otakine (mt.)	K 5
Rebun (isl.), 6,525	K 1
Rikuchu-Kaigan National Park	L 4
Rishiri (isl.), 13,368	K 1
Ryukyu (isls.), 1,198,386	L 7
Sado (isl.), 87,504	J 4
Sagami (bay)	O 3
Sagami (riv.)	O 2
Sagami (sea)	J 6
Saikai National Park	D 7
Sakishima (isls.), 63,361	K 7
San'in Kaigan National Park	G 6
Sata (cape)	E 8
Setonaikai National Park	H 7
Shikoku (isl.), 3,928,607	F 7
Shikotan (isl.)	N 2
Shikotsu (lake)	K 2
Shikotsu-Toya National Park	K 2
Shimane (pen.), 199,148	F 6
Shimokita (pen.), 95,574	K 3
Shinano (riv.)	J 5
Shiono (cape)	H 7
Shiragami (cape)	J 3
Shirane (mt.)	J 5
Shirane (mt.)	H 6
Shiretoko (cape)	M 1
Shiriya (cape)	K 3
Soya (pt.)	L 1
Suo (sea)	E 7
Suruga (bay)	J 6
Suwanose (isl.)	O 4
Suzu (pt.)	H 5
Takeshima (isls.)	F 5
Tama (riv.)	O 2
Tanega (isl.), 46,345	E 8
Tappi (cape)	K 3
Tarama (isl.), 1,805	L 7
Tazawa (lake)	K 4
Teshio (mt.)	L 1
Teshio (riv.)	L 1
Tobi (isl.)	J 4
Tokachi (mt.)	L 2
Tokachi (riv.)	L 2
Tokara (isls.)	O 5
Tokuno (isl.), 35,396	O 5
Tokyo (bay)	O 2
Tone (riv.)	K 6
Tosa (bay)	F 7
Towada (lake)	K 3
Towada-Hachimantai National Park	K 3
Toya (lake)	K 2
Toyama (bay)	H 5
Tsu (isls.), 52,478	D 6
Tsugaru (str.)	K 3
Tsurugi (mt.)	G 7
Tsushima (str.)	
Uchiura (bay)	
Unzen (mt.)	
Unzen-Amakusa National Park	
Volcano (isls.)	
Wakasa (bay)	
Yaeyama (isls.), 5,622	
Yaku (isl.), 16,108	
Yodo (riv.)	
Yonaguni (isl.), 2,153	
Yoron (isl.), 6,973	
Yoshino (riv.)	
Yoshino-Kumano National Park	
Zao (mt.)	

KOREA (NORTH)

CITIES and TOWNS

Ch'ŏngjin, 306,000	
Chŏngju	
Haeju, 140,000	
Hamhŭng, 484,000	
Heijo (P'yŏngyang) (cap.), 1,250,000	

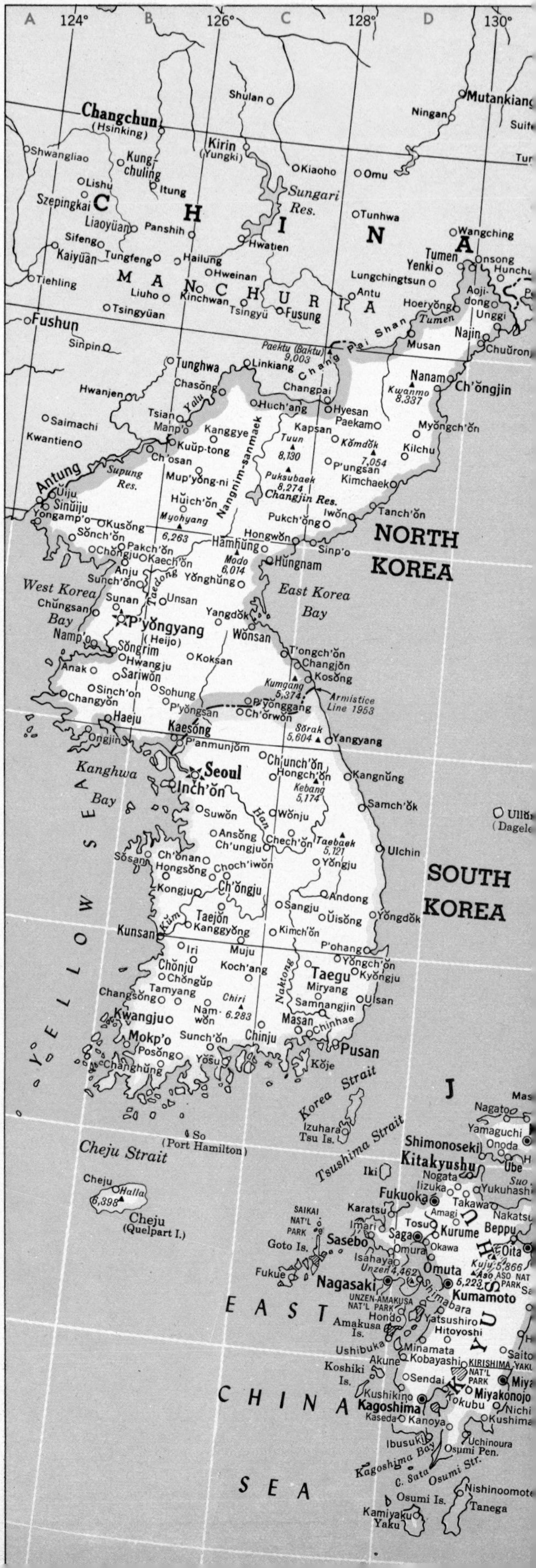
124°
126°
128°
130°
Changchun (Hsinking)
Kirin (Yungki)
C H I N A
M A N C H U R I A
Mutankiang
Sungari Res.
Tunhwa
Fushun
Paektu (Baktu) 9,003
NORTH KOREA
SOUTH KOREA
Ch'ŏngjin
Hamhŭng
P'yŏngyang (Heijo)
Wŏnsan
Kaesŏng
Armistice Line 1953
Seoul
Inch'ŏn
Kanghwa Bay
West Korea Bay
East Korea Bay
YELLOW SEA
Taegu
Pusan
Kwangju
Mokp'o
Korea Strait
Cheju Strait
Cheju (Quelpart I.)
Tsushima Strait
Kitakyushu
Fukuoka
Nagasaki
Kumamoto
Kagoshima
EAST CHINA SEA

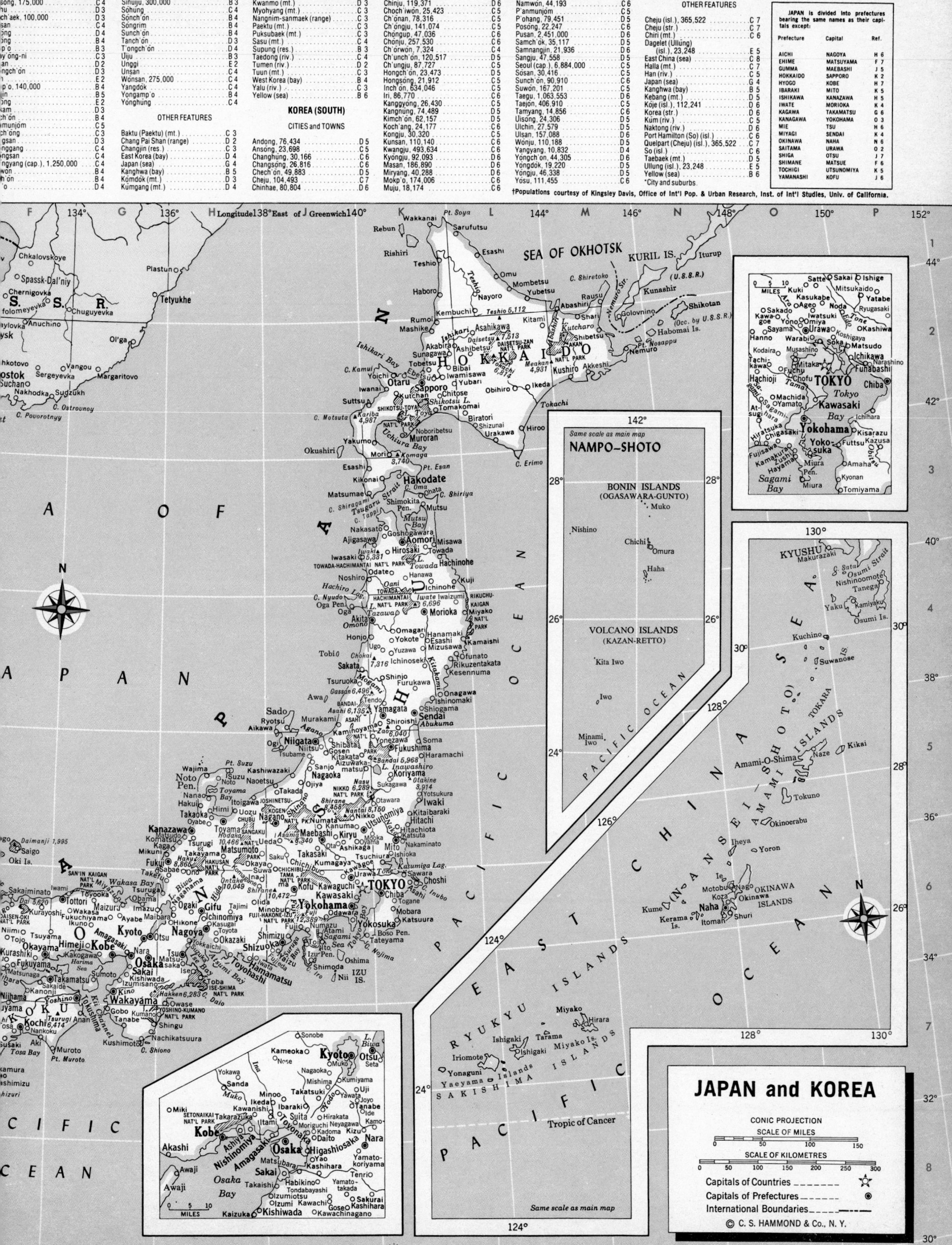

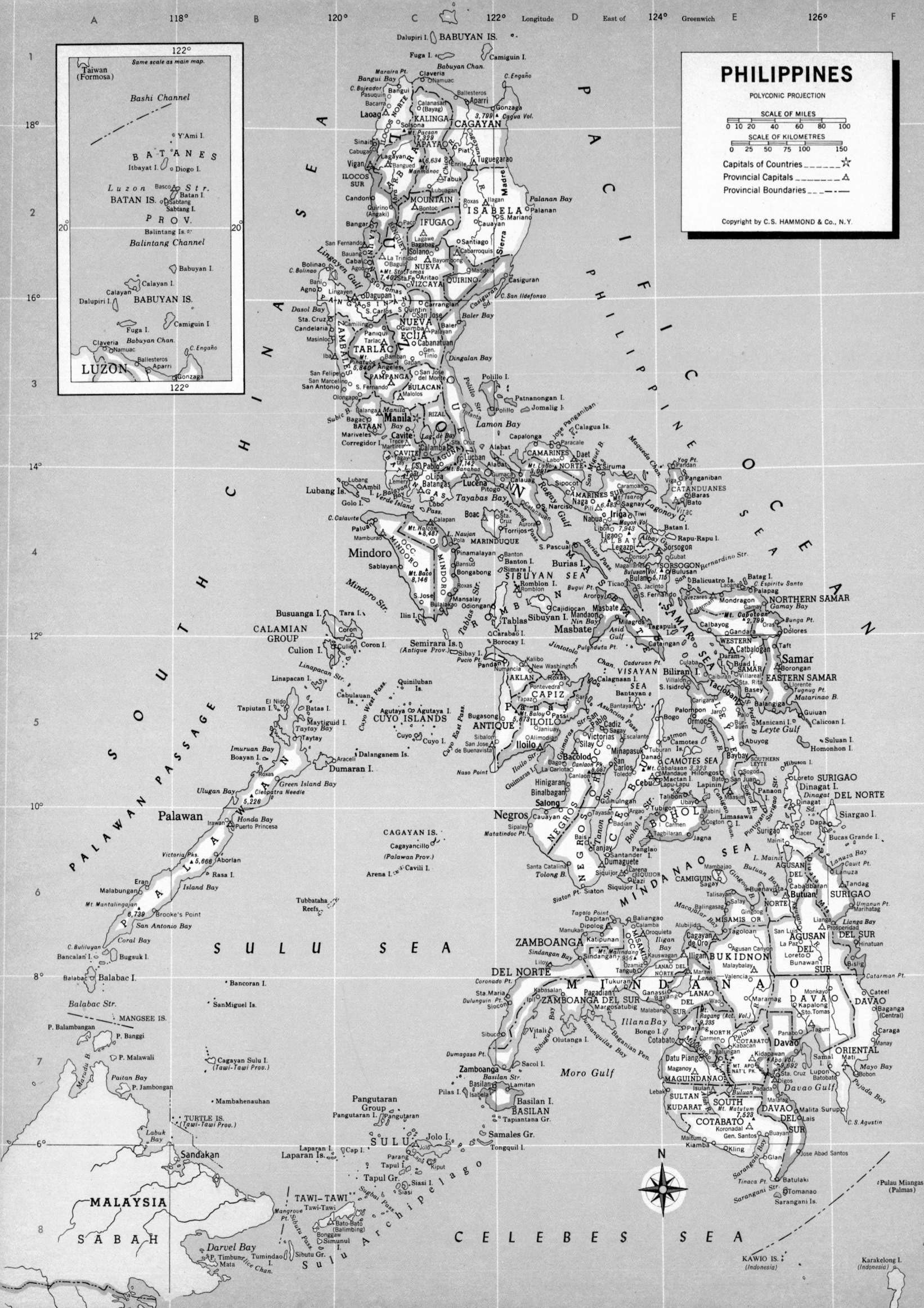

Philippines 83

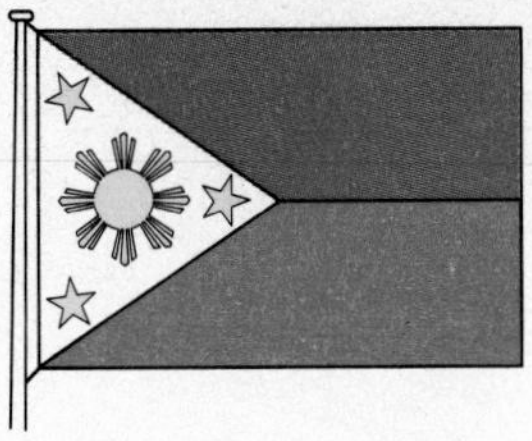

AREA 115,707 sq. mi.
POPULATION 43,751,000
CAPITAL Manila
LARGEST CITY Manila
HIGHEST POINT Apo 9,692 ft.
MONETARY UNIT piso
MAJOR LANGUAGES Pilipino (Tagalog), English, Spanish, Bisayan, Ilocano, Bikol
MAJOR RELIGIONS Roman Catholicism, Islam, Protestantism, Tribal religions

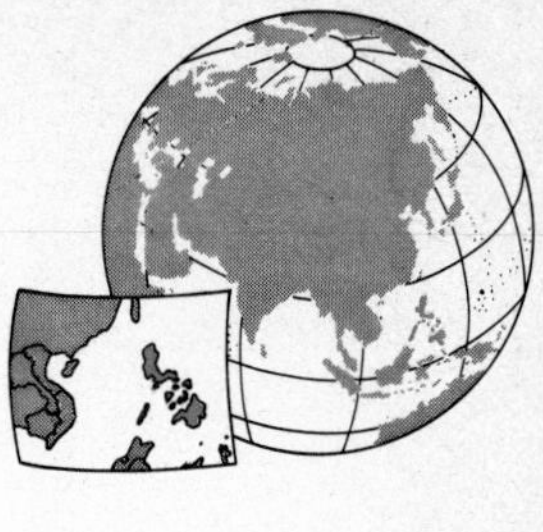

PROVINCES

Abra, 145,508 . . . . . C 2
Agusan del Norte, 278,053 . . . . . E 6
Agusan del Sur, 174,682 . . . . . E 6
Aklan, 263,358 . . . . . D 5
Albay, 673,981 . . . . . D 4
Antique, 289,172 . . . . . D 5
Basilan, 143,829 . . . . . D 7
Bataan, 216,210 . . . . . C 3
Batanes, 11,398 . . . . . A 2
Batangas, 926,308 . . . . . C 4
Benguet, 263,550 . . . . . C 2
Bohol, 683,297 . . . . . E 6
Bukidnon, 414,762 . . . . . E 6
Bulacan, 836,431 . . . . . C 3
Cagayan, 581,237 . . . . . C 1
Camarines Norte, 262,207 . . . . . D 3
Camarines Sur, 948,436 . . . . . D 4
Camiguin, 53,913 . . . . . E 6
Capiz, 394,041 . . . . . D 5
Catanduanes, 162,302 . . . . . E 4
Cavite, 520,180 . . . . . C 3
Cebu, 1,634,182 . . . . . D 5
Davao, 442,543 . . . . . E 7
Davao del Sur, 785,398 . . . . . E 7
Davao Oriental, 247,995 . . . . . F 7
Eastern Samar, 271,000 . . . . . E 5
Ifugao, 92,487 . . . . . C 2
Ilocos Norte, 343,427 . . . . . C 1
Ilocos Sur, 385,139 . . . . . C 2
Iloilo, 1,167,973 . . . . . D 5
Isabela, 648,123 . . . . . C 2
Kalinga-Apayao, 136,249 . . . . . C 1
Laguna, 699,736 . . . . . C 3
Lanao del Norte, 349,942 . . . . . E 6
Lanao del Sur, 455,508 . . . . . E 7
La Union, 373,682 . . . . . C 2
Leyte, 1,110,626 . . . . . E 5
Maguindanao, 476,338 . . . . . E 7
Manila, 3,868,239 . . . . . C 3
Marinduque, 144,109 . . . . . C 4
Masbate, 492,908 . . . . . D 4
Misamis Occidental, 319,855 . . . . . D 6
Misamis Oriental, 472,756 . . . . . E 6
Mountain, 93,112 . . . . . C 2
Negros Occidental, 1,503,782 . . . . . D 6
Negros Oriental, 652,264 . . . . . D 6
North Cotabato . . . . . E 7
Northern Samar, 306,114 . . . . . E 4
Nueva Ecija, 851,294 . . . . . C 3
Nueva Vizcaya, 169,198 . . . . . C 2
Occidental Mindoro, 144,032 . . . . . C 4
Oriental Mindoro, 328,364 . . . . . C 4
Palawan, 236,635 . . . . . B 6
Pampanga, 907,275 . . . . . C 3
Pangasinan, 1,386,143 . . . . . C 3
Quezon, 983,324 . . . . . C 3
Quirino, 52,767 . . . . . C 2
Rizal, 307,238 . . . . . C 3
Romblon, 167,082 . . . . . D 4
Siquijor, 62,976 . . . . . D 6
Sorsogon, 427,047 . . . . . E 4
South Cotabato, 466,110 . . . . . E 7
Southern Leyte, 251,425 . . . . . E 5
Sultan Kudarat, 191,315 . . . . . E 7
Sulu, 315,421 . . . . . C 7
Surigao del Norte, 238,714 . . . . . F 5
Surigao del Sur, 258,680 . . . . . F 6
Tarlac, 559,708 . . . . . C 3
Tawi-Tawi, 110,196 . . . . . B 8
Western Samar, 442,244 . . . . . E 5
Zambales, 343,034 . . . . . C 3
Zamboanga del Norte, 409,379 . . . . . D 6
Zamboanga del Sur, 890,189 . . . . . D 7

CITIES and TOWNS

Angeles, 175,694 . . . . . C 3
Aparri, 14,597 . . . . . C 1
Bacolod, 196,492 . . . . . D 5
Bago, 71,653 . . . . . D 5
Baguio, 100,209 . . . . . C 2
Bais, 40,095 . . . . . D 6
Balanga, 1,298 . . . . . C 3
Baler, ◆14,632 . . . . . C 3
Balimbing (Bato-Bato), 3,880 . . . . . C 8
Bangued, 10,482 . . . . . C 2
Bantayan, 11,771 . . . . . D 5
Basco, ◆3,757 . . . . . A 2
Basilan, 171,266 . . . . . C 7
Batangas, 125,304 . . . . . C 4
Bato-Bato, 3,880 . . . . . C 8
Baybay, 11,989 . . . . . E 5
Bayombong, 11,697 . . . . . C 2
Binalbagan, 17,456 . . . . . D 5
Bislig, 26,625 . . . . . F 6
Boac, 3,497 . . . . . C 4
Bogo, 11,069 . . . . . E 5
Bontoc, 3,336 . . . . . C 2
Buenavista, 9,211 . . . . . E 6
Bulan, 19,716 . . . . . D 4
Burauen, 12,172 . . . . . E 5
Butuan, 173,429 . . . . . E 6
Cabanatuan, 117,995 . . . . . C 3
Cabarroquis . . . . . C 2
Cadiz, 130,199 . . . . . D 5
Cagayan de Oro, 163,163 . . . . . E 6
Calamba, Laguna, 22,750 . . . . . C 3
Calapan, 11,376 . . . . . C 4
Calbayog, 101,748 . . . . . E 4
Camiling, 12,996 . . . . . C 3
Canlaon, 23,598 . . . . . D 5
Carigara, 11,824 . . . . . E 5
Catarman, 13,018 . . . . . E 4
Catbalogan, 18,413 . . . . . E 5
Catmon, ◆14,837 . . . . . E 5
Cavite, 75,739 . . . . . C 3
Cebu, 418,517 . . . . . D 5
Cotabato, 61,184 . . . . . D 7
Daet, 23,739 . . . . . D 3
Dagupan, 83,582 . . . . . C 2
Danao, 47,662 . . . . . D 5
Dapitan, 37,781 . . . . . D 6
Davao, 515,520 . . . . . E 7
Digos, 17,334 . . . . . E 7
Dipolog, 46,368 . . . . . D 6
Dumaguete, 52,000 . . . . . D 6
Escalante, 16,324 . . . . . D 5
Ganassi, ◆13,227 . . . . . D 7
Gapan, 11,958 . . . . . C 3
General Santos, 108,285 . . . . . E 7
Gingoog, 65,522 . . . . . E 6
Gubat, 11,369 . . . . . E 4
Guimba, 10,077 . . . . . C 3
Gumaca, 9,459 . . . . . D 4
Hinigaran, 10,864 . . . . . D 5
Iba, 4,486 . . . . . B 3
Ilagan, 11,494 . . . . . C 2
Iligan, 129,454 . . . . . E 6
Iloilo, 247,956 . . . . . D 5
Iriga, 77,382 . . . . . D 4
Isabela, 12,879 . . . . . C 7
Isulan, 10,075 . . . . . E 7
Jolo, 46,586 . . . . . C 8
Jose Panganiban, 9,970 . . . . . D 3
Kalibo, 10,564 . . . . . D 5
Kauswagan, ◆12,316 . . . . . E 6
Kidapawan, 11,344 . . . . . E 7
Koronadal, 14,003 . . . . . E 7
La Carlota, 38,321 . . . . . D 5
Lagawe, 3,038 . . . . . C 2
Lais, 15,209 . . . . . E 7
Laoag, 61,727 . . . . . C 1
Lapu-Lapu, 69,268 . . . . . E 5
La Trinidad, ◆18,551 . . . . . C 2
Lazi, ◆14,875 . . . . . D 6
Legazpi, 84,090 . . . . . D 4
Lianga, 12,689 . . . . . E 6
Lingayen, 15,333 . . . . . C 2
Lipa, 112,006 . . . . . C 4
Loreto, Agusan del Sur, ◆13,057 . . . . . E 6
Lucban, 18,466 . . . . . C 3
Lucena, 77,006 . . . . . C 4
Maasin, 12,661 . . . . . E 5
Maganoy, 1,648 . . . . . E 7
Mainit, 3,559 . . . . . E 6
Malabang, 9,244 . . . . . D 7
Malaybalay, 10,193 . . . . . E 6
Malita, 9,705 . . . . . E 7
Malolos, 73,996 . . . . . C 3
Mandaue, 58,579 . . . . . E 5
Manila (cap.), 1,438,252 . . . . . C 3
Manila (Metro.), *4,337,140 . . . . . C 3
Marawi, 55,708 . . . . . E 6
Mariveles, 4,502 . . . . . C 3
Masbate, 17,749 . . . . . D 4
Mati, 16,186 . . . . . F 7
Mondragon, ◆14,974 . . . . . E 4
Naga, 79,846 . . . . . D 4
Olongapo, 134,453 . . . . . C 3
Ormoc, 84,563 . . . . . E 5
Oroquieta, 38,575 . . . . . D 6
Ozamiz, 64,643 . . . . . D 6
Padada, ◆14,402 . . . . . E 7
Pagadian, 57,615 . . . . . D 7
Paniqui, 11,789 . . . . . C 3
Parang, Sulu, ◆21,115 . . . . . C 8
Prosperidad, 3,043 . . . . . F 6
Puerto Princesa, 12,278 . . . . . B 6
Romblon, 4,241 . . . . . D 4
Roxas, Capiz, 67,648 . . . . . D 5
Roxas, Isabela, 9,849 . . . . . C 2
Sablayan, ◆18,256 . . . . . C 4
Sagay, Negros Occ., 36,855 . . . . . D 5
Sagnay, ◆16,968 . . . . . D 4
Salong, 35,137 . . . . . D 5
San Antonio, 13,270 . . . . . B 3
San Carlos, Negros Occ., 90,058 . . . . . D 5
San Carlos, Pangasinan, 84,333 . . . . . C 3
San Fernando, La Union, 11,084 . . . . . C 2
San Fernando, Pampanga, 84,362 . . . . . C 3
San Isidro, ◆23,569 . . . . . E 5
San Jose, Nueva Ecija, 70,314 . . . . . C 3
San Jose, Occ. Mindoro, 10,388 . . . . . C 4
San Mariano, ◆20,227 . . . . . D 2
San Pablo, Laguna, 125,720 . . . . . C 3
Santa Cruz, Davao del Sur, 9,787 . . . . . E 7
Santa Cruz, Laguna, 47,114 . . . . . C 3
Santa Rita, ◆20,713 . . . . . E 5
Santiago, ◆49,688 . . . . . C 2
Siasi, 9,930 . . . . . C 8
Silay, 69,200 . . . . . D 5
Sindangan, 10,965 . . . . . D 6
Sipalay, ◆34,771 . . . . . D 6
Sipocot, ◆38,153 . . . . . D 4
Siquijor, 766 . . . . . D 6
Solano, 14,274 . . . . . C 2
Solsona, ◆12,803 . . . . . C 1
Sorsogon, 19,008 . . . . . E 4
Surigao, 26,099 . . . . . E 6
Tacloban, 76,531 . . . . . E 5
Tagaytay, 10,907 . . . . . C 3
Tagbilaran, 33,005 . . . . . E 6
Tagum, 17,161 . . . . . E 7
Tangub, 30,918 . . . . . D 6
Tanjay, 12,676 . . . . . D 6
Tarlac, 23,547 . . . . . C 3
Toledo, 67,727 . . . . . D 5
Tuguegarao, 14,116 . . . . . C 2
Tukuran, ◆19,274 . . . . . D 7
Victorias, 13,416 . . . . . D 5
Vigan, 30,252 . . . . . C 2
Virac, 10,314 . . . . . E 4
Zamboanga, 240,066 . . . . . C 7

OTHER FEATURES

Abra (riv.) . . . . . C 2
Agusan (riv.) . . . . . E 6
Agutaya (isl.), 2,464 . . . . . C 5
Alabat (isl.), 22,666 . . . . . D 3
Ambil (isl.), 323 . . . . . C 4
Apo (vol.) . . . . . E 7
Asid (gulf) . . . . . D 4
Babuyan (isls.), 7,749 . . . . . A 2
Baganian (pen.), 22,755 . . . . . D 7
Balabac (isl.), 4,946 . . . . . A 7
Balayan (bay) . . . . . C 4
Balicuatro (isls.), 6,349 . . . . . E 4
Balintang (chan.) . . . . . A 2
Baloy (mt.) . . . . . D 5
Bancalan (isl.), 398 . . . . . A 6
Bantayan (isl.), 57,311 . . . . . D 5
Banton (isl.), 6,447 . . . . . D 4
Bashi (chan.) . . . . . A 1
Basilan (isl.), 147,871 . . . . . D 7
Batag (isl.), 4,142 . . . . . E 4
Batan, Albay (isl.), 11,779 . . . . . E 4
Batan, Batanes (isl.), 6,831 . . . . . B 2
Batan (isls.), 11,398 . . . . . A 2
Batas (isl.), 204 . . . . . B 5
Bay, Laguna de (lake) . . . . . C 3
Biliran (isl.), 82,033 . . . . . E 5
Bohol (isl.), 613,532 . . . . . E 6
Bojeador (cape) . . . . . C 1
Bongo (isl.), 2,077 . . . . . D 7
Borocay (isl.), 2,660 . . . . . D 5
Buad (isl.), 12,064 . . . . . E 5
Bucas Grande (isl.), 6,213 . . . . . F 6
Bugsuk (isl.), 831 . . . . . A 6
Buliluyan (cape) . . . . . A 6
Bunga (pt.) . . . . . E 4
Burias (isl.), 53,299 . . . . . D 4
Busuanga (isl.), 16,136 . . . . . B 4
Cabalasan (mt.) . . . . . E 5
Cabulauan (isls.), 570 . . . . . C 5
Cagayan (isls.), 3,598 . . . . . C 6
Cagayan (riv.) . . . . . C 2
Cagayan Sulu (isl.), 12,577 . . . . . B 7
Cagua (vol.) . . . . . D 1
Calagnaan (isl.), 2,690 . . . . . D 5
Calagua (isls.), 1,890 . . . . . D 3
Calamian Group (isls.), 26,864 . . . . . B 4
Calayan (isl.), 5,075 . . . . . A 2
Calicoan (isl.), 2,966 . . . . . E 5

Topography

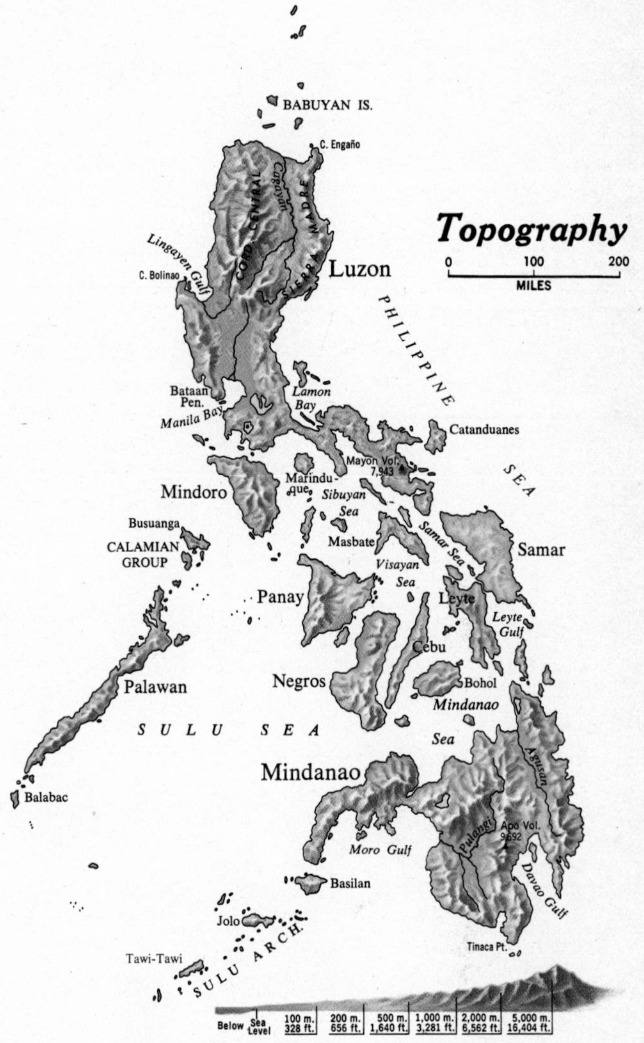

0 100 200
MILES
BABUYAN IS.
C. Engaño
Luzon
C. Bolinao
Lingayen Gulf
CORD. CENTRAL
SIERRA MADRE
PHILIPPINE SEA
Bataan Pen.
Manila Bay
Lamon Bay
Catanduanes
Mayon Vol. 7,943
Mindoro
Marinduque
Sibuyan Sea
Busuanga
CALAMIAN GROUP
Masbate
Samar Sea
Samar
Visayan Sea
Panay
Leyte
Leyte Gulf
Cebu
Negros
Bohol
Palawan
Mindanao Sea
SULU SEA
Mindanao
Apo Vol. 9,692
Moro Gulf
Davao Gulf
Balabac
Basilan
Jolo
Tawi-Tawi
SULU ARCH.
Tinaca Pt.
Below Sea Level
100 m. 328 ft.
200 m. 656 ft.
500 m. 1,640 ft.
1,000 m. 3,281 ft.
2,000 m. 6,562 ft.
5,000 m. 16,404 ft.

Agriculture, Industry and Resources

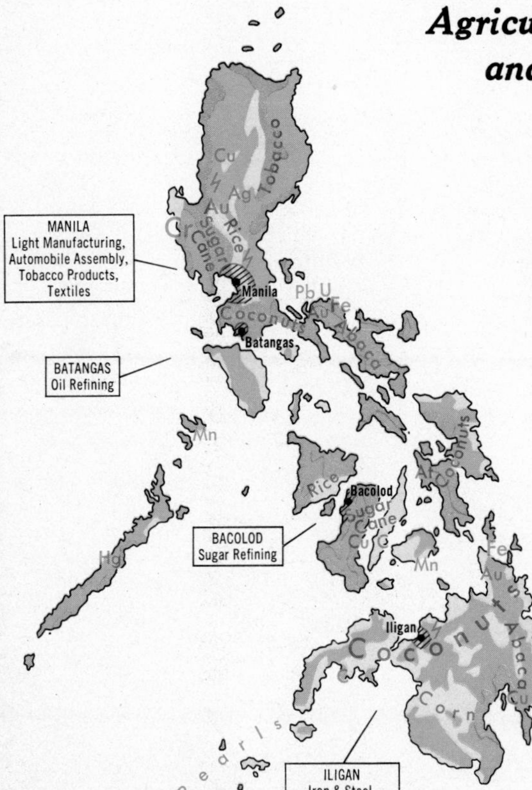

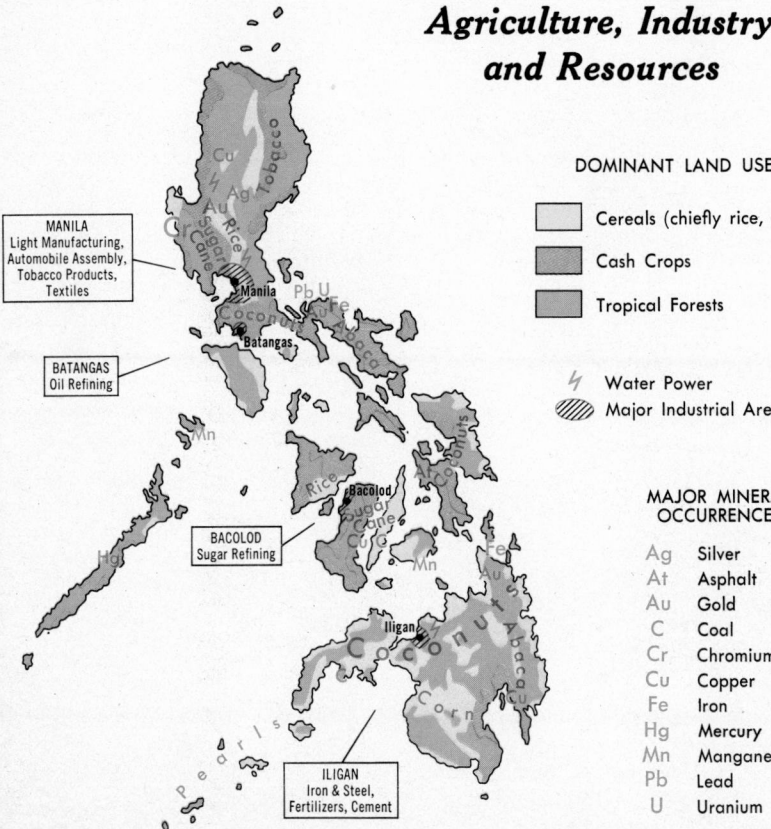

MANILA
Light Manufacturing, Automobile Assembly, Tobacco Products, Textiles
BATANGAS
Oil Refining
BACOLOD
Sugar Refining
ILIGAN
Iron & Steel, Fertilizers, Cement
Manila
Batangas
Bacolod
Iligan
Tobacco
Rice
Sugar Cane
Coconuts
Abaca
Corn
Pearls

DOMINANT LAND USE

- Cereals (chiefly rice, corn)
- Cash Crops
- Tropical Forests

- Water Power
- Major Industrial Areas

MAJOR MINERAL OCCURRENCES

- Ag Silver
- At Asphalt
- Au Gold
- C Coal
- Cr Chromium
- Cu Copper
- Fe Iron
- Hg Mercury
- Mn Manganese
- Pb Lead
- U Uranium

Camiguin, Cagayan (isl.), 1,741 . . . . . B 3
Camiguin, Camiguin (isl.), 53,913 . . . . . E 6
Camotes (isls.), 55,479 . . . . . E 5
Camotes (sea) . . . . . E 5
Canigao (chan.) . . . . . E 5
Canlaon (peak) . . . . . D 5
Capotoan (mt.) . . . . . E 4
Carabao (isl.), 4,562 . . . . . D 4
Catanduanes (isl.), 160,614 . . . . . E 4
Cebu (isl.), 1,426,804 . . . . . D 5
Celebes (sea) . . . . . D 8
Cleopatra Needle (mt.) . . . . . B 5
Coron (isl.), 477 . . . . . C 5
Corregidor (isl.), 91 . . . . . C 3
Culion (isl.), 5,580 . . . . . B 5
Cuyo (isl.), 9,489 . . . . . C 5
Cuyo (isls.), 16,737 . . . . . C 5
Dalanganem (isls.), 512 . . . . . C 5
Daram (isl.), 26,087 . . . . . E 5
Davao (gulf) . . . . . E 7
Dinagat (isl.), 23,337 . . . . . E 5
Diuata (mts.) . . . . . E 6
Dumanquilas (bay) . . . . . D 7
Dumaran (isl.), 3,996 . . . . . C 5
Engaño (cape) . . . . . D 1
Espiritu Santo (cape) . . . . . E 4
Fuga (isl.), 967 . . . . . A 3
Golo (isl.), 1,300 . . . . . C 4
Guimaras (isl.), 71,067 . . . . . D 5
Halcon (mt.) . . . . . C 4
Hibuson (isl.), 531 . . . . . E 5
Homonhon (isl.), 2,316 . . . . . E 5
Honda (bay) . . . . . B 6
Iligan (bay) . . . . . E 6
Ilin (isl.), 6,647 . . . . . C 4
Illana (bay) . . . . . D 7
Imuruan (bay) . . . . . B 5
Island (bay) . . . . . B 6
Itbayat (isl.), 2,760 . . . . . A 2
Jintotolo (chan.) . . . . . D 5
Jolo (isl.), 208,110 . . . . . C 7
Jomalig (isl.), 1,792 . . . . . D 3
Lagonoy (gulf) . . . . . E 4
Lamon (bay) . . . . . C 3
Lanao (lake) . . . . . E 7
Laparan (isls.) . . . . . B 8
Lapinin (isl.), 9,229 . . . . . E 5
Leyte (gulf) . . . . . E 5
Leyte (isl.), 1,223,667 . . . . . E 5
Limasawa (isl.), 2,116 . . . . . E 6
Linapacan (isl.), 1,121 . . . . . B 5
Lingayen (gulf) . . . . . C 2
Lubang (isls.), 19,904 . . . . . B 4
Luzon (isl.), 17,862,660 . . . . . C 3
Luzon (str.) . . . . . A 2
Macajalar (bay) . . . . . E 6
Mactan (isl.), 70,729 . . . . . E 5
Malindang (mt.) . . . . . D 6
Mangsee (isls.), 246 . . . . . A 7
Manicani (isl.), 1,555 . . . . . E 5
Manila (bay) . . . . . C 3
Mantalingajan (mt.) . . . . . A 6
Maqueda (chan.) . . . . . D 3
Maraira (pt.) . . . . . C 1
Marinduque (isl.), 140,924 . . . . . C 4
Masbate (isl.), 387,721 . . . . . D 4
Mayon (vol.) . . . . . D 4
Maytiguid (isl.), 632 . . . . . B 5
Mindanao (isl.), 6,871,696 . . . . . D 7
Mindanao (riv.) . . . . . E 7
Mindanao (sea) . . . . . D 6
Mindoro (isl.), 437,817 . . . . . C 4
Mindoro (str.) . . . . . C 4
Mompog (passage) . . . . . D 4
Moro (gulf) . . . . . D 7
Mount Apo National Park . . . . . E 7
Naso (pt.) . . . . . C 5
Negros (isl.), 2,080,153 . . . . . D 6
Olutanga (isl.), 16,680 . . . . . D 7
Pacsan (mt.) . . . . . C 2
Palawan (isl.), 146,430 . . . . . B 6
Palawan (passage) . . . . . A 6
Panaon (isl.), 31,149 . . . . . E 5
Panay (isl.), 2,010,297 . . . . . D 5
Panglao (isl.), 29,121 . . . . . D 6
Pangutaran (isl.), 12,883 . . . . . C 7
Pangutaran Group (isls.), 16,172 . . . . . C 7
Patnanongan (isl.), 3,680 . . . . . D 3
Philippine (sea) . . . . . D 3
Pilas (isl.), 8,666 . . . . . C 7
Pinatubo (mt.) . . . . . C 3
Polillo (isl.), 27,716 . . . . . C 3
Pujada (bay) . . . . . F 7
Pulangi (riv.) . . . . . E 7
Quiniluban (isls.), 653 . . . . . C 5
Ragang (vol.) . . . . . E 7
Ragay (gulf) . . . . . D 4
Rapu-Rapu (isl.), 8,007 . . . . . E 4
Romblon (isl.), 19,728 . . . . . D 4
Sabtang (isl.), 1,359 . . . . . B 2
Sacol (isl.), 7,994 . . . . . D 7
Samal (isl.), 30,897 . . . . . E 7
Samales Group (isls.), 9,095 . . . . . D 7
Samar (isl.), 861,765 . . . . . E 5
Samar (sea) . . . . . E 4
San Agustin (cape) . . . . . F 7
San Bernardino (str.) . . . . . E 4
San Miguel (bay) . . . . . D 3
San Pedro (bay) . . . . . E 5
Santo Tomas (mt.) . . . . . C 2
Sarangani (isls.), 6,791 . . . . . E 8
Semirara (isls.), 7,932 . . . . . C 5
Siargao (isl.), 40,632 . . . . . F 6
Siasi (isl.), 24,026 . . . . . C 8
Sibay (isl.), 1,544 . . . . . C 5
Sibuguey (bay) . . . . . D 7
Sibutu Group (isls.), 13,738 . . . . . B 8
Sibuyan (isl.), 32,079 . . . . . D 4
Sibuyan (sea) . . . . . D 4
Sierra Madre (mts.) . . . . . D 2
Simara (isl.), 7,805 . . . . . D 4
Simunul (isl.), 8,401 . . . . . B 8
Siquijor (isl.), 62,976 . . . . . D 6
South China (sea) . . . . . B 3
Subic (bay) . . . . . C 3
Sulu (arch.), 413,040 . . . . . B 8
Sulu (sea) . . . . . B 6
Suluan (isl.), 966 . . . . . F 5
Taal (lake) . . . . . C 4
Tablas (isl.), 89,642 . . . . . D 4
Tablas (str.) . . . . . C 4
Tagapula (isl.), 5,691 . . . . . E 4
Tagolo (pt.) . . . . . D 6
Tanon (str.) . . . . . D 6
Tapiantana Group (isls.), 6,697 . . . . . D 7
Tapul (isl.), 8,830 . . . . . C 8
Tapul Group (isls.), 72,119 . . . . . C 8
Tara (isl.), 449 . . . . . C 4
Tawi-Tawi (isl.), 13,216 . . . . . B 8
Tayabas (bay) . . . . . C 4
Ticao (isl.), 62,270 . . . . . D 4
Tinaca (pt.) . . . . . E 8
Tongquil (isl.), 2,599 . . . . . D 8
Tumindao (isl.), 2,389 . . . . . B 8
Turtle (isls.), 389 . . . . . B 7
Verde Island (passage) . . . . . C 4
Victoria (peaks) . . . . . B 6
Visayan (sea) . . . . . D 5
Vitali (isl.), 6,026 . . . . . D 7

*City and suburbs.
◆Population of municipality.

BRUNEI
CITIES and TOWNS

Bandar Seri Begawan (cap.), 37,000 .....E 4

INDONESIA
CITIES and TOWNS

Agats, 300 .....K 7
Amahai, 18,017 .....H 6
Amboina, 70,000 .....H 6
Ambon (Amboina), 70,000 .....H 6
Balikpapan, 113,000 .....F 6
Banda Atjeh, 49,000 .....A 4
Bandanaira, 13,686 .....H 6
Bandjarmasin, 264,000 .....E 6
Bandung, 1,006,000 .....H 2
Bangil, 34,112 .....K 2
Bangkalan, 129,536 .....K 2
Banjuwangi, 53,576 .....L 2
Bantul, 30,572 .....J 2
Barabai, 9,366 .....F 6
Barus, †35,716 .....B 5
Batang, 57,561 .....J 2
Batavia (Djakarta) (cap.), 3,429,000 .....H 1
Baturadja, 126,706 .....C 6
Batusangkar, 10,437 .....C 6
Bekasi, 32,012 .....H 2
Bengkajang, †17,029 .....D 5
Bengkalis, †36,433 .....C 5
Bengkulu, 31,000 .....C 6
Benteng, 7,035 .....F 7
Bindjai, 56,000 .....B 5
Bitung, 15,249 .....H 5
Blitar, 78,000 .....K 2
Blora, 49,296 .....K 2
Bodjonegoro, 161,749 .....J 2
Bogor, 170,000 .....H 2
Bondowoso, 144,215 .....L 2
Bonthain, 140,289 .....F 7
Brebes, 172,971 .....H 2
Bukittinggi, 62,000 .....C 6
Bula, 3,116 .....J 6
Bulukumba, 14,137 .....F 7
Bumiaju, 152,780 .....H 2
Demak, 142,915 .....J 2
Denpasar, 152,000 .....F 7
Dili, 9,753 .....H 7
Djailolo, 110,170 .....H 5
Djajapura, 14,462 .....K 6
Djakarta (cap.), 3,429,000 .....H 1
Djakarta, *5,692,000 .....H 1
Djambi (Telanaipura) 139,000 .....C 6
Djeneponto, 10,350 .....F 7
Djepara, 154,025 .....J 2
Djombang, 157,370 .....K 2
Dompu, 8,886 .....F 7
Fakfak, 2,430 .....J 6
Galela, 17,384 .....H 5
Garut, 167,542 .....H 2
Gorontalo, 88,000 .....G 5
Gresik, 36,790 .....K 2
Hollandia (Djajapura), 14,462 .....K 6
Indramaju, 156,117 .....H 2

Isimu, 4,304 .....G 5
Kaimana, 1,128 .....J 6
Kajuagung, 15,000 .....D 6
Kalianda, 131,073 .....D 6
Kampung Baru (Tolitoli), 8,333 .....G 5
Karangasem, 16,022 .....F 7
Kau, †7,497 .....H 5
Kebumen, †64,874 .....J 2
Kediri, 196,000 .....K 2
Kendal, 23,129 .....J 2
Kendari, 191,065 .....G 6
Kendawangan, 6,845 .....D 6
Klaten, 33,400 .....J 2
Kolaka, 118,671 .....G 6
Kotaagung, 125,314 .....C 7
Kragan, 23,786 .....K 2
Krawang, 49,867 .....H 2
Kualakurun, 11,489 .....E 6
Kudus, 62,130 .....J 2
Kumai, 8,835 .....E 6
Kuningan, 177,181 .....H 2
Kupang, 17,171 .....G 8
Kutaradja (Banda Atjeh), 49,000 .....A 4
Kutoardjo, 44,962 .....J 2
Labuan, †22,259 .....J 2
Lahat, 125,781 .....C 6
Lamongan, 134,825 .....K 2
Langsa, 147,044 .....B 5
Lawang, 140,239 .....K 2
Longiram, 7,576 .....F 5
Longnawan, 116,234 .....F 5
Lubuklinggau, 14,890 .....C 6
Lubuksikaping, 11,778 .....B 5
Lumadjang, 55,700 .....K 2
Madiun, 152,000 .....J 2
Madjalengka, †47,055 .....H 2
Madjene, †37,722 .....F 6
Magelang, 119,000 .....J 2
Magetan, 154,159 .....J 2
Makassar (Udjung Pandang), 473,000 .....F 7
Malang, 419,000 .....K 2
Malili, 5,735 .....G 6
Malinau, 9,677 .....F 5
Mamudju, 147,309 .....F 6
Manado, 129,000 .....G 5
Manokwari, 10,461 .....J 6
Marabahan, 8,893 .....E 6
Martapura, 153,216 .....F 6
Masamba, †15,152 .....G 6
Medan, 590,000 .....B 5
Menggala, 20,343 .....D 6
Merak, †36,293 .....J 1
Merauke, 5,989 .....K 7
Mindiptana, 1,577 .....K 7
Modjokerto, 64,000 .....K 2
Muarabungo, 10,706 .....C 6
Muaratewah, 6,135 .....F 6
Muntok, †25,883 .....D 6
Namlea, 16,018 .....H 6
Nangapinoh, 13,298 .....E 6
Nangatajap, 18,285 .....E 6
Negara, 10,161 .....F 6
Ngabang, †24,516 .....D 5
Ngawi, 29,220 .....J 2
Padang, 178,000 .....B 6
Padangpandjang, 32,000 .....B 6
Padangsidimpuan, †71,704 .....B 5
Painan, 12,060 .....C 6

Pajakumbuh, †74,393 .....C 6
Pakanbaru, 87,000 .....C 5
Palangkaraja, 9,000 .....E 6
Palelèh, 5,466 .....G 5
Palembang, 585,000 .....D 6
Pamangkat, 151,871 .....D 5
Pamekasan, 142,650 .....L 2
Pameungpeuk, 124,662 .....H 2
Panarukan, 6,846 .....L 2
Pandeglang, 124,823 .....J 2
Pangkalanberandan, 123,806 .....B 5
Pangkalpinang, 74,000 .....D 6
Pare, 185,528 .....K 2
Parepare, 84,000 .....F 6
Pariaman, 145,812 .....B 6
Pasuruan, 78,000 .....K 2
Pati, †56,749 .....J 2
Patjitan, 44,383 .....J 2
Pekalongan, 125,000 .....J 2
Pemalang, 193,609 .....J 2
Pematangsiantar, 142,000 .....B 5
Perabhumulih, 41,951 .....C 6
Pinrang, 23,818 .....F 6
Piru, 123,633 .....H 6
Ponorogo, 49,993 .....J 2
Pontianak, 185,000 .....D 6
Poso, 141,292 .....G 6
Praja, 26,729 .....F 7
Prapat, 5,552 .....B 5
Probolinggo, 85,000 .....K 2
Purbolinggo, 31,719 .....J 2
Purwakarta, 188,680 .....H 2
Purwodadi, 154,648 .....J 2
Purwokerto, 22,623 .....H 2
Purworedjo, 23,209 .....J 2
Putussibau, 18,357 .....E 5
Rangkasbitung, †51,176 .....G 2
Rantauprapat, 25,707 .....B 5
Rembang, 39,939 .....K 2
Rengat, 122,982 .....C 6
Ruteng, 15,814 .....G 7
Sabang, 6,747 .....B 4
Salatiga, 72,000 .....J 2
Samarinda, 87,000 .....F 6
Sambas, 153,290 .....D 5
Sampang, 47,596 .....L 2
Sanana, 23,388 .....H 6
Sanggau, 128,039 .....E 5
Sangkulirang, 6,108 .....F 5
Saparua, 53,390 .....H 6
Saumlaki, †22,732 .....J 7
Sawahlunto, 15,000 .....C 6
Semarang, 619,000 .....J 2
Semitau, 19,255 .....E 5
Sengkang, †17,948 .....F 6
Serang, †43,661 .....G 1
Serui, 2,743 .....K 6
Sibolga, 48,000 .....B 5
Sidoardjo, 140,591 .....K 2
Sigli, 4,050 .....B 4
Sindjai, 18,390 .....F 7
Singaradja, 57,000 .....F 7
Singkawang, 161,107 .....D 5
Sintang, 125,067 .....E 5
Situbondo, 30,000 .....L 2
Sorong, 9,151 .....J 6
Sragen, 32,310 .....J 2
Subang, 122,825 .....H 2
Sukabumi, 90,000 .....H 2
Sukadana, 6,899 .....E 6
Sumbawa Besar, †22,308 .....F 7

Sumedang, †74,062 .....H 2
Sumenep, 33,628 .....L 2
Surabaja, 1,241,000 .....K 2
Surakarta, 453,000 .....J 2
Tandjungbalai, 36,000 .....C 5
Tandjungkarang-Telukbetung, 164,000 .....D 7
Tandjungpandan, 139,253 .....D 6
Tandjungpriok, †140,573 .....H 1
Tandjungpura, 120,726 .....B 5
Tangerang, †81,042 .....G 1
Tapaktuan, 9,650 .....F 5
Tarakan, 24,807 .....F 5
Tarutung, †41,041 .....B 5
Tasikmalaja, †101,466 .....H 2
Tebingtinggi, 32,000 .....B 5
Tegal, 110,000 .....J 2
Telanaipura, 139,000 .....C 6
Temanggung, 8,107 .....J 2
Tenggarong, †15,516 .....F 6
Ternate, 23,500 .....H 5
Tjiamis, †80,018 .....H 2
Tjiandjur, †77,927 .....H 2
Tjidulang, †32,475 .....H 2
Tjilatjap, 78,619 .....H 2
Tjimahi, †90,718 .....H 2
Tjirebon, 176,000 .....H 2
Tjurup, 14,480 .....C 6
Tobelo, 114,430 .....H 5
Tolitoli, 8,333 .....G 5
Tondano, 129,584 .....H 5
Trenggalek, †37,762 .....K 2
Tual, 48,123 .....J 6
Tulungagung, 43,115 .....K 2
Turen, †57,711 .....K 2
Udjung Pandang, 473,000 .....F 7
Wahai, 18,781 .....H 6
Wonogiri, †45,704 .....J 2
Wonosobo, 33,917 .....J 2

OTHER FEATURES

Alas (str.) .....F 7
Anambas (isls.), 15,700 .....D 5
Arafura (sea) .....J 8
Aru (isls.), 27,006 .....J 7
Asahan (river) .....B 5
Babar (isls.), 14,133 .....H 7
Bali (isl.), 2,196,000 .....F 7
Bali (sea) .....F 7
Banda (sea) .....H 7
Banggai (arch.), 144,747 .....G 6
Bangka (isl.), 384,000 .....D 6
Banjak (isls.), 1,696 .....A 5
Barisan (mts.) .....C 6
Barito (river) .....E 6
Batjan (isl.), 21,861 .....H 6
Batu (isls.), 60,806 .....B 6
Bawean (isl.), 47,589 .....K 1
Belitung (Billiton) (isl.), 126,000 .....D 6
Bengalen (passage) .....A 4
Berau (bay) .....J 6
Biak (isl.), 31,139 .....K 6
Billiton (isl.), 126,000 .....D 6
Binongko (isl.), 10,580 .....G 7
Bintan (isl.), 65,301 .....C 5
Bone (gulf) .....F 6
Borneo (isl.) .....E 5
Borneo (Kalimantan) (reg.), 4,243,000 .....E 6

Bosch, van den (cape) .....J 6
Bunguran (Natuna) (isls.), 15,261 .....D 5
Buru (isl.), 16,018 .....H 6
Butung (isl.), 311,000 .....G 6
Celebes (isl.), 7,665,000 .....G 6
Celebes (sea) .....G 5
Ceram (isl.), 73,453 .....H 7
Damar (isl.) .....H 7
Dampier (str.) .....J 6
Diamond (point) .....B 4
Digul (river) .....K 7
Djaja (mt.) .....K 6
Djajawidjaja (range) .....K 6
Djemadja (isl.), 3,874 .....D 5
Doberai (pen.) .....J 6
Dolak (isl.) .....K 7
Enggano (isl.), 686 .....C 7
Ewab (isls.), 76,606 .....J 7
Flores (isl.), 1,108,000 .....G 7
Flores (sea) .....F 7
Frederik Hendrik (Dolak) (isl.) .....K 7
Gebe (isl.), 5,410 .....H 6
Geelvink (Sarera) (bay) .....K 6
Good Hope (cape) .....J 5
Gorong (isls.), 33,241 .....J 6
Halmahera (isl.), †97,133 .....H 5
Idenburg (river) .....K 6
Japen (isl.), 23,701 .....K 6
Java (head) .....C 7
Java (isl.), 69,323,000 .....J 2
Java (sea) .....D 6
Kabaena (isl.), 14,380 .....G 7
Kabia (Salajar) (isl.), 107,000 .....G 7
Kai (Ewab) (isls.), 76,606 .....J 7
Kalao (isl.), 670 .....G 7
Kalaotoa (isl.), 2,031 .....G 7
Kalimantan (reg.), 4,243,000 .....E 5
Kangean (isls.), 52,893 .....F 7
Kapuas (river) .....D 6
Karakelong (isl.), 15,276 .....H 5
Karimata (arch.), 1,623 .....D 6
Karimundjawa (isls.), 1,611 .....J 1
Kerintji (mt.) .....C 6
Kisar (isl.), 16,569 .....H 7
Komodo (isl.) .....F 7
Krakatau (Rakata) (isl.) .....C 7
Laut (isl.), 42,099 .....F 6
Leuser (mt.) .....B 5
Lingga (arch.), 39,307 .....D 5
Lingga (isl.), 14,309 .....D 5
Lombok (isl.), 1,602,000 .....F 7
Madura (isl.), 2,650,000 .....K 2
Mahakam (river) .....F 6
Makassar (str.) .....F 6
Malacca (str.) .....C 5
Mamberamo (river) .....K 6
Maoke (mts.) .....K 6
Mapia (isl.) .....J 5
Mentawai (isls.), 23,649 .....B 6
Misool (isl.), 3,022 .....J 6
Molucca (sea) .....H 6
Moluccas (isls.), 973,000 .....H 6
Morotai (isl.), 19,523 .....H 5
Muli (str.) .....K 7
Müller (mts.) .....E 5
Muna (isl.), 139,000 .....G 6
Musi (river) .....C 6
Natuna (isls.), 15,261 .....D 5
Ngundju (cape) .....F 8
Nias (isl.), 388,000 .....B 5

Obi (isls.), 6,358 .....H 6
Ombai (str.) .....H 7
Perkam (cape) .....K 6
Puting (cape), Borneo .....E 6
Puting (cape), Sumatra .....C 7
Radja Ampat Group (isls.), 17,158 .....H 6
Raja (isl.) .....C 7
Rakata (isl.) .....C 7
Rantekombola (mt.) .....F 6
Riau (arch.), 342,000 .....C 5
Rokan (river) .....C 5
Roti (isl.), 68,330 .....G 8
Rouffaer (river) .....K 6
Salajar (isl.), 107,000 .....G 7
Salawati (isl.), 5,125 .....J 6
Sandalwood (Sumba) (isl.), 311,000 .....F 7
Sangihe (isl.), 83,585 .....H 5
Sangihe (isls.), 126,931 .....H 5
Sarera (bay) .....K 6
Sawu (isl.), 78,785 .....G 8
Sawu (sea) .....G 7
Schouten (isls.), 41,647 .....K 6
Schwaner (mts.) .....E 6
Seaflower (channel) .....B 6
Sebuko (isl.) .....F 5
Selatan (cape) .....E 6
Semeru (mt.) .....K 2
Siau (isl.), 29,762 .....H 5
Siberut (str.) .....A 5
Simeulue (isl.), 25,951 .....A 5
Singkep (isl.), 17,712 .....D 5
Sipora (isl.), 5,671 .....B 6
Slamet (mt.) .....J 2
Sorik Merapi (mt.) .....B 5
South Natuna (isls.), 3,318 .....D 5
Sudirman (range) .....K 6

Sula (isls.), 30,779 .....H 6
Sulawesi (Celebes) (isl.), 7,665,000 .....G 6
Sumatra (isl.), 17,345,000 .....C 6
Sumba (isl.), 311,000 .....F 7
Sumba (str.) .....F 7
Sumbawa (isl.), 625,000 .....F 7
Sunda (str.) .....C 7
Tahulandang (isl.), 13,584 .....H 5
Talaud (isls.), 28,738 .....H 5
Taliabu (isl.), 7,391 .....G 6
Tambelan (isls.), 3,551 .....D 5
Tanimbar (isls.), 41,233 .....J 7
Tidore (isl.), 24,064 .....H 5
Timor (sea) .....H 7
Timor (reg.), 1,466,000 .....G 7
Toba (lake) .....B 5
Tolo (gulf) .....G 6
Tomini (gulf) .....G 6
Tukangbesi (isls.), 59,775 .....G 7
Vals (cape) .....K 7
Vogelkop (Doberai) (pen.) .....J 6
Waigeo (isl.), 9,011 .....J 6
Wangiwangi (isl.), 19,719 .....G 7
Weh (isl.) .....A 4
West Irian (reg.), 933,000 .....K 6
Wetar (isl.), 11,383 .....H 7

MALAYSIA★
STATES

Sabah, 633,000 .....
Sarawak, 950,000 .....

CITIES and TOWNS

Beaufort, †25,408 .....

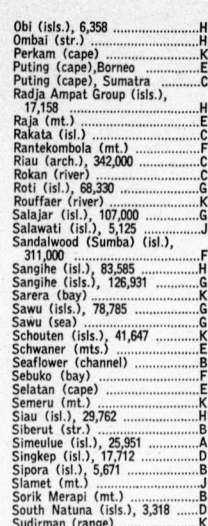
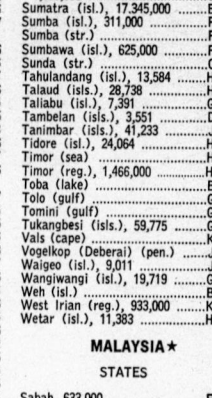

Topography

0 300 600
MILES

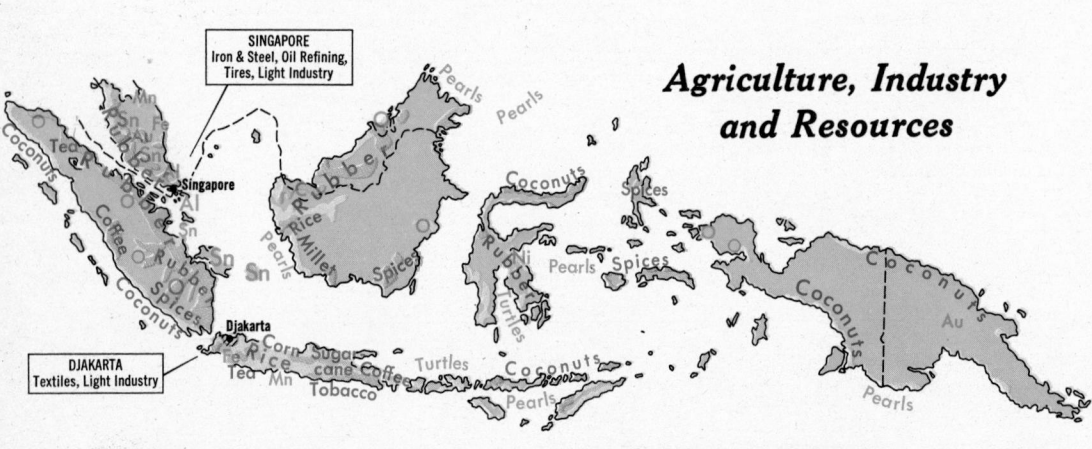

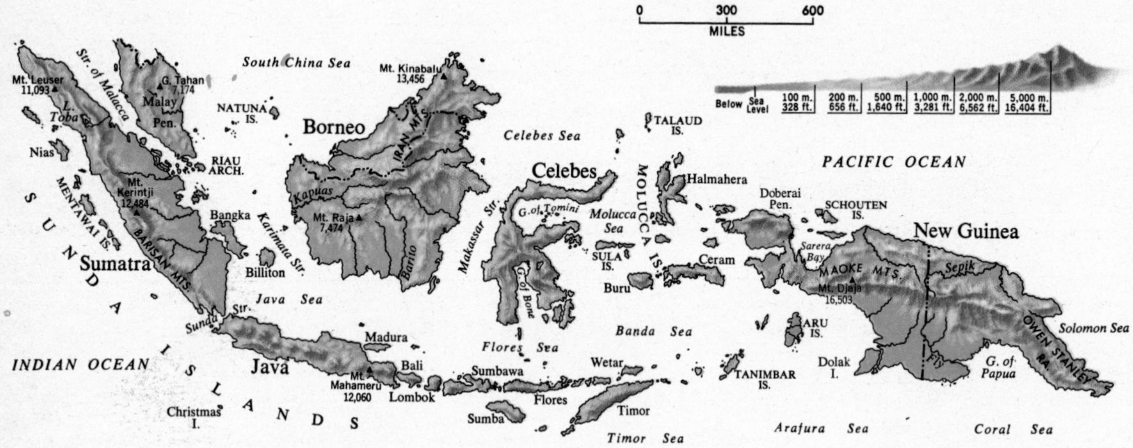

Agriculture, Industry and Resources

SINGAPORE
Iron & Steel, Oil Refining, Tires, Light Industry

DJAKARTA
Textiles, Light Industry

DOMINANT LAND USE
- Cereals (chiefly rice, corn)
- Diversified Tropical Crops
- Forests

MAJOR MINERAL OCCURRENCES
Al Bauxite
Au Gold
C Coal
Fe Iron Ore
Mn Manganese
Ni Nickel
O Petroleum
Sn Tin
Major Industrial Areas

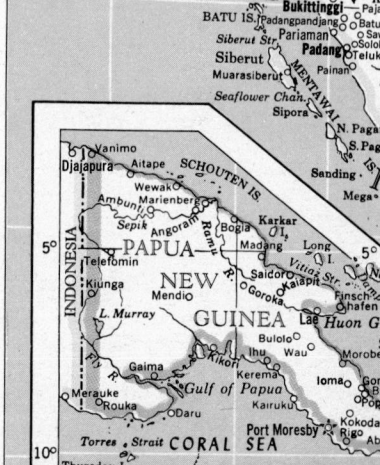

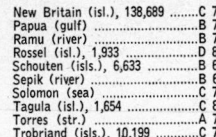

INDONESIA

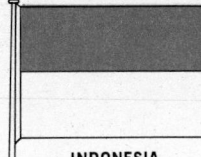

PAPUA NEW GUINEA

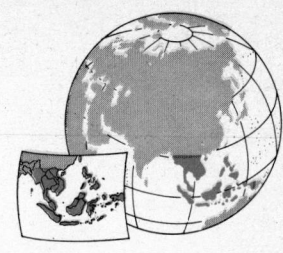

INDONESIA
AREA 788,430 sq. mi.
POPULATION 131,255,000
CAPITAL Djakarta
LARGEST CITY Djakarta
HIGHEST POINT Mt. Djaja 16,503 ft.
MONETARY UNIT rupiah
MAJOR LANGUAGES Bahasa Indonesia, Indonesian and Papuan languages, English
MAJOR RELIGIONS Islam, Tribal religions, Christianity, Hinduism

PAPUA NEW GUINEA
AREA 183,540 sq. mi.
POPULATION 2,800,000
CAPITAL Port Moresby
LARGEST CITY Port Moresby
HIGHEST POINT Mt. Wilhelm 15,400 ft.
MONETARY UNIT kina
MAJOR LANGUAGES Pidgin English, Hiri Motu, English
MAJOR RELIGIONS Tribal religions, Christianity

BRUNEI
AREA 2,226 sq. mi.
POPULATION 155,000
CAPITAL Bandar Seri Begawan

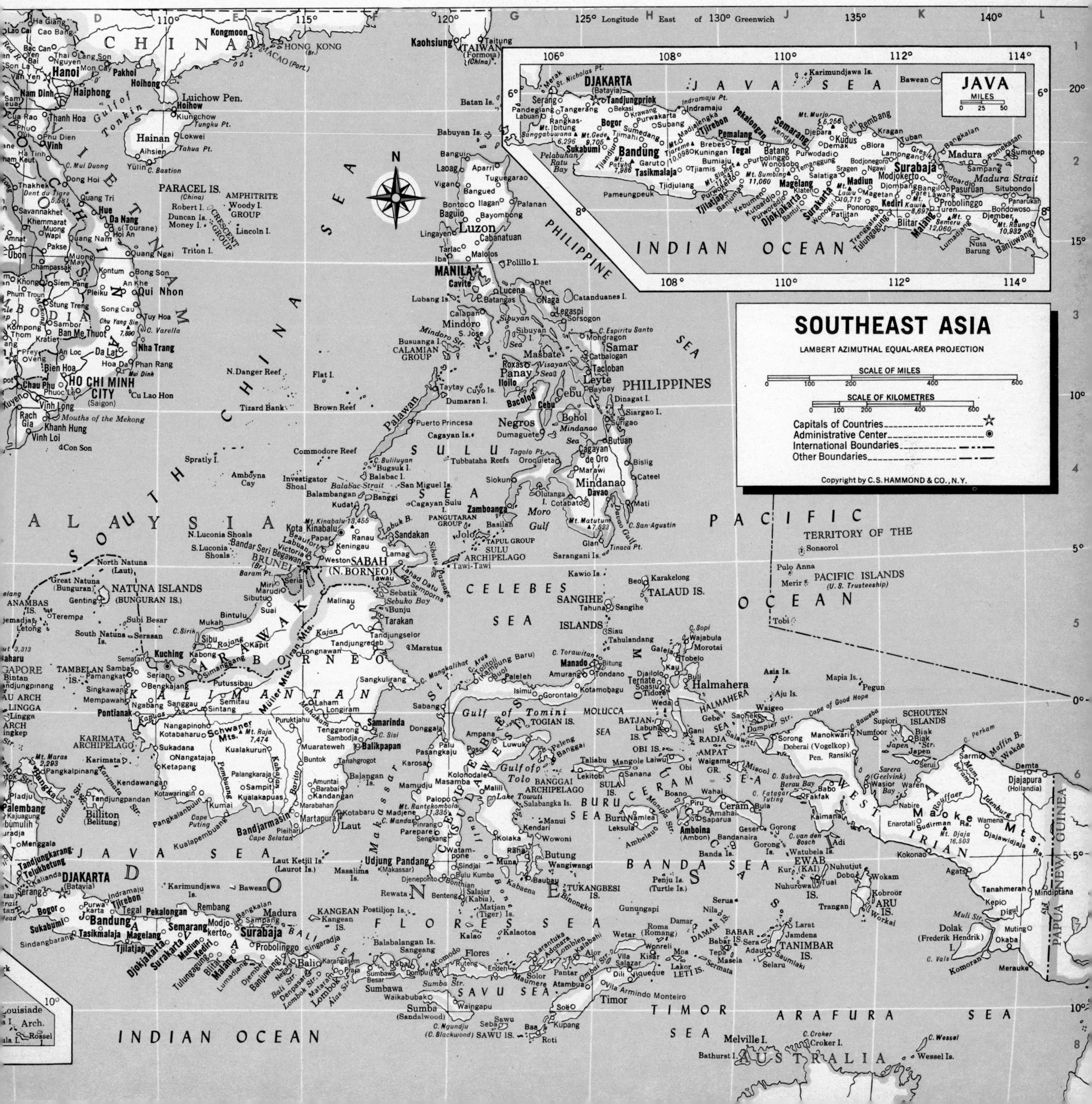

JAVA
MILES
0   25   50

SOUTHEAST ASIA
LAMBERT AZIMUTHAL EQUAL-AREA PROJECTION

SCALE OF MILES
0   100   200   400   600

SCALE OF KILOMETRES
0 100 200 400 600

Capitals of Countries _____ ★
Administrative Center _____ ◉
International Boundaries _____
Other Boundaries _____

Copyright by C.S. HAMMOND & CO., N.Y.

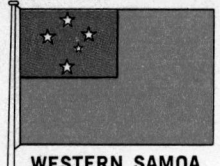 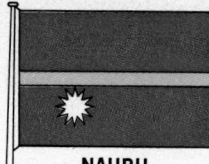 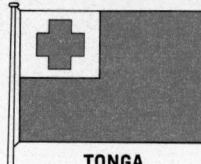 

| WESTERN SAMOA | NAURU | TONGA | FIJI |

WESTERN SAMOA

AREA 1,133 sq. mi.
POPULATION 159,000
CAPITAL Apia
LARGEST CITY Apia
HIGHEST POINT Mt. Silisili 6,094 ft.
MONETARY UNIT tala
MAJOR LANGUAGES Samoan, English
MAJOR RELIGIONS Protestantism,
   Roman Catholicism

NAURU

AREA 7.7 sq. mi.
POPULATION 8,000
CAPITAL Yaren (district)
MONETARY UNIT Australian dollar
MAJOR LANGUAGES Nauruan, English
MAJOR RELIGION Protestantism

TONGA

AREA 270 sq. mi.
POPULATION 102,000
CAPITAL Nuku'alofa
LARGEST CITY Nuku'alofa
HIGHEST POINT 3,389 ft.
MONETARY UNIT pa'anga
MAJOR LANGUAGES Tongan, English
MAJOR RELIGION Protestantism

FIJI

AREA 7,055 sq. mi.
POPULATION 569,468
CAPITAL Suva
LARGEST CITY Suva
HIGHEST POINT Tomaniivi 4,341 ft.
MONETARL UNIT Fijian dollar
MAJOR LANGUAGES Fijian, Hindi, English
MAJOR RELIGIONS Protestantism, Hinduism

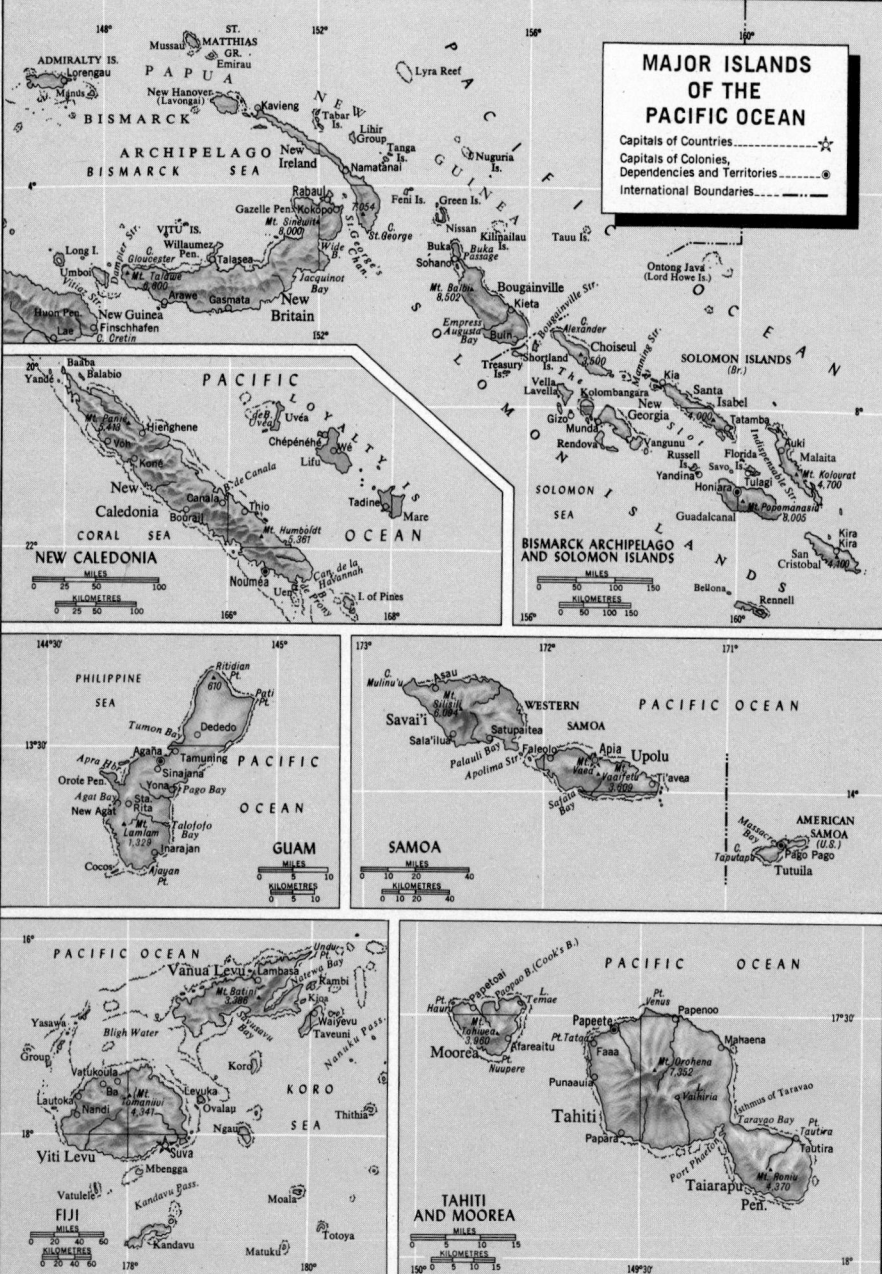

MAJOR ISLANDS
OF THE
PACIFIC OCEAN
Capitals of Countries ....☆
Capitals of Colonies,
Dependencies and Territories ....◉
International Boundaries ....———

Copyright by C. S. Hammond & Co., N.Y.

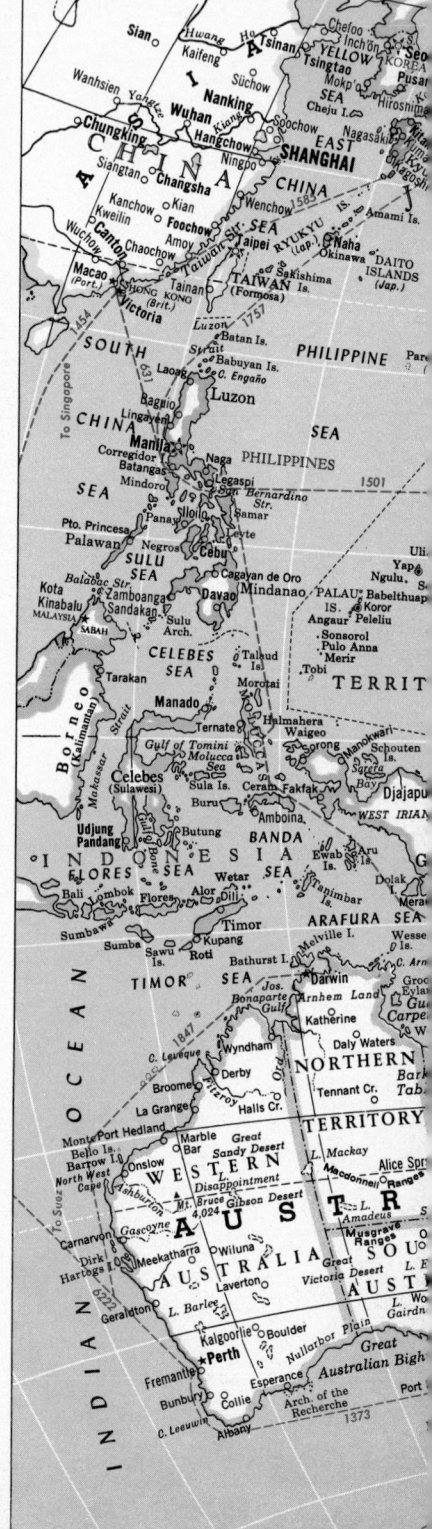

Abaing (atoll), 3,271 ....H 5
Abemama (atoll), 2,126 ....H 5
Adamstown, 74 ....N 8
Adelaide, ‡727,916 ....D 9
Admiralty (isls.), 21,588 ....E 6
Agaña, 2,131 ....E 4
Agrihan (isl.), 64 ....E 4
Ahau, 414 ....H 7
Ailinglapalap (atoll), 1,281 ....G 5
Ailuk (atoll), 371 ....H 4
Aitutaki (atoll), 2,579 ....K 7
Alamagan (isl.), 48 ....E 4
Albany, 25,112 ....B 9
Albury, 25,419 ....E 9
Alice Springs, 6,037 ....D 7
Alofi, 1,117 ....K 7
Amanu (atoll), 117 ....N 7
Ambrym (isl.), 4,200 ....G 7
American Samoa, 30,000 ....J 7
Anaa (atoll), 360 ....M 7
Anatahan (isl.), 23 ....E 4
Aneityum (isl.), 300 ....G 8
Angaur (isl.), 533 ....D 5
Apataki (atoll), 108 ....M 7
Apia, 27,000 ....J 7
Armidale, 14,984 ....F 9
Arnhem Land (reg.) ....D 7
Arno (atoll), 1,198 ....H 5
Arorae (isl.), 1,830 ....H 6
Atafu (atoll), 615 ....J 6
Atiu (isl.), 1,327 ....L 8
Atuona, 663 ....M 7
Auckland, 152,200 ....H 9
Auki, 5,234 ....G 6
Austral (isls.), 5,053 ....L 8
Australia, 13,684,900 ....C 8
Australian Cap. Terr., 204,200 ....F 9
Avarua, 4,100 ....L 8
Babelthuap (isl.), 5,222 ....D 5
Bairiki, 1,300 ....H 6
Baker (isl.) ....J 5
Ballarat, *56,290 ....E 9
Banks (isls.), 3,250 ....G 7
Belep (isls.), 551 ....F 7
Bendigo, *42,208 ....E 9
Beru (atoll), 2,412 ....H 6
Bikini (atoll) ....G 4
Bismarck (arch.), 209,051 ....E 6
Blackall, 2,004 ....E 7
Blue Mountains, 30,731 ....E 9
Bora-Bora, 2,572 ....L 7
Bougainville (isl.), 72,661 ....F 6
Boulder, 5,234 ....C 9
Bourail, 672 ....F 7
Bowen, 5,144 ....E 7
Brisbane, ‡718,822 ....F 8
Broken Hill, 30,014 ....E 8
Broome, 1,570 ....C 7
Bunbury, 15,459 ....B 9
Bundaberg, 25,402 ....E 8
Butaritari (atoll), 2,714 ....H 5
Cairns, 29,326 ....E 7
Canberra, *204,200 ....F 9
Canton (isl.), 421 ....J 6
Carnarvon, 2,956 ....B 8
Caroline (isls.), 54,563 ....E 5
Charleville, 4,871 ....E 8
Charters Towers, 7,602 ....E 7
Chatham (isls.), 520 ....J 10
Chichi (isl.), 203 ....E 3
Choiseul (isl.), 6,600 ....F 6
Christchurch, 165,000 ....H10
Christmas (isl.), 367 ....L 5
Cloncurry, 2,149 ....E 7
Collie, 7,628 ....B 9
Cook (isls.), 17,046 ....K 7
Coral (sea) ....F 7
Cunnamulla, 1,980 ....E 8
Daito (isls.), 3,896 ....D 3
Daly Waters, ‡265 ....D 7
Danger (Pukapuka) (atoll),
   684 ....K 7
Daru, 3,663 ....E 6
Darwin, 18,042 ....D 7
D'Entrecasteaux (isls.), 32,288 ....F 6
Derby, 1,424 ....C 7
Devonport, 14,874 ....E10
Dunedin, 77,800 ....H10
Easter (isl.), 1,598 ....Q 8
Eauripik (atoll), 158 ....E 5
Ebon (atoll), 731 ....G 5
Efate (isl.), 10,000 ....G 7
Elato (atoll), 35 ....E 5
Ellice Islands (Tuvalu), 5,887 ....H 6
Enderbury (isl.) ....J 6
Eniwetok (atoll) ....G 4
Erromanga (isl.), 600 ....G 7
Esperance, 2,677 ....C 9
Espiritu Santo (isl.), 10,000 ....G 7
Fais (isl.), 230 ....E 5
Fakaofo (isl.), 740 ....J 6
Fakarava (atoll), 230 ....M 7
Fanning (isl.), 376 ....L 5
Faraulep (atoll), 178 ....E 5
Fatuhiva (isl.), 459 ....N 7
Fiji, 569,468 ....H 8
Fly (riv.) ....E 6
Fongafale, 826 ....H 6
Fremantle, 25,284 ....B 9
French Polynesia, 135,000 ....L 8
Funafuti (atoll), 826 ....H 6
Furneaux Group (isls.), 1,234 ....E 9
Gambier (isls.), 516 ....N 8
Garapan, 4,100 ....E 4
Gardner (isl.), 23 ....J 6
Geelong, *105,059 ....E 9
Geraldton, 12,125 ....B 9
Gilbert (isls.), 44,205 ....H 5
Gilbert Islands, 47,711 ....J 6
Gisborne, 25,600 ....H 9
Grafton, 15,951 ....F 8
Great Barrier (reef) ....E 7
Greenwich (Kapingamarangi)
   (atoll), 411 ....F 5
Greymouth, 8,590 ....H10
Guadalcanal (isl.), 23,922 ....F 7
Guam (isl.), 111,000 ....E 4
Gympie, 11,279 ....F 8
Ha'apai Group (isls.), 10,591 ....J 8
Halls Creek, ‡577 ....C 7
Hamilton, 67,700 ....H 9
Hao (atoll), 812 ....N 7
Hastings, 28,100 ....H 9
Hawaii (isl.), 63,468 ....L 3
Hawaii (state), 769,913 ....K 4
Hawaiian (isls.), 772,133 ....J 3
Hikueru (atoll), 115 ....M 7
Hilo, 26,353 ....L 4
Hivaoa (isl.), 1,027 ....N 6
Hobart, 53,257 ....E 10
Honiara, 11,389 ....F 6
Honolulu, 324,871 ....L 3
Honolulu, *630,528 ....L 3
Hoorn (isls.), 3,500 ....J 7
Howland (isl.) ....J 5
Huahine (isl.), 2,814 ....L 7
Hughenden, 2,033 ....E 8
Hull (isl.), 583 ....J 6
Ifalik (atoll), 321 ....E 5
Invercargill, 45,300 ....H10

Ipswich, 54,531 ....F 8
Iwo (isl.) ....E 3
Jaluit (atoll), 932 ....G 5
Jarvis (isl.) ....K 6
Johnston (atoll), 1,007 ....L 4
Kalgoorlie, *19,908 ....B 9
Kandavu (isl.), 6,600 ....H 7
Kangaroo (isl.), 3,375 ....D 9
Kapingamarangi (atoll), 411 ....F 5
Katherine, 1,302 ....D 7
Kauai (isl.), 29,524 ....L 3
Kavieng, 3,342 ....F 6
Kermadec (isls.), 9 ....J 9
Kieta, 755 ....F 6
Kili (atoll), 320 ....G 5
King (isl.), 2,462 ....E10
Kingman Reef (isl.) ....K 5
Koror, 5,541 ....D 5
Kosrae (isl.), 3,648 ....G 5
Kwajalein (atoll), 3,841 ....G 5
Lae, 12,392 ....E 6
Lamotrek (atoll), 203 ....E 5
Lanai (isl.), 2,204 ....L 3
Lau Group (isls.), 15,988 ....J 7
Launceston, 37,217 ....E10
Laverton, ‡206 ....C 8
Lavongai (isl.), 7,829 ....E 6
Levuka, 1,685 ....H 7
Lifu (isl.), 6,837 ....G 8
Line (isls.), 1,180 ....K 5
Lismore, 19,734 ....F 8
Lithgow, 13,165 ....F 9
Little Makin (isl.), 1,387 ....H 5
Longreach, 3,871 ....E 8
Lord Howe (isl.), 267 ....G 8
Lord Howe (Ontong Java)
   (isl.), 900 ....G 6
Louisiade (archipelago), 11,451 ....F 7

Loyalty (isls.), 12,248 ....G 8
Luganville, 3,500 ....G 7
Mackay, 24,578 ....E 7
Madang, 6,601 ....E 6
Maitland, 28,428 ....F 9
Majuro (atoll), 5,957 ....H 5
Makatea (isl.), 55 ....M 7
Makin (Butaritari) (atoll),
   2,714 ....H 5
Malaita (isl.), 54,000 ....G 6
Malekula (isl.), 11,200 ....G 7
Maloelap (atoll), 494 ....H 5
Mangaia (isl.), 2,002 ....L 8
Mangareva (isl.), 516 ....N 8
Manihiki (atoll), 584 ....K 7
Manra (Sydney) (isl.) ....J 6
Manua (isls.), 2,112 ....K 7
Manuae (isl.), 15 ....L 8
Manus (isl.), 11,088 ....E 6
Marble Bar, ‡567 ....C 8
Marcus (isl.) ....E 3
Maré (isl.), 3,410 ....G 8
Mariana (isls.), 11,827 ....E 4
Mariana Trench ....E 4
Marquesas (isls.), 5,174 ....N 6
Marshall (isls.), 19,328 ....G 5
Marutea (atoll) ....N 8
Maryborough, 20,393 ....F 8
Matautu 566 ....J 7
Maui (isl.), 38,691 ....L 3
Mauke (isl.), 671 ....L 8
Meekatharra, ‡1,011 ....B 8
Mehetia (isl.) ....M 7
Melanesia (reg.) ....F 6
Melbourne, 12,110,168 ....E 9
Micronesia (reg.) ....E 5
Midway (isls.), 2,220 ....J 3
Mili (atoll), 360 ....H 5

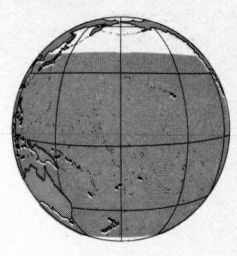

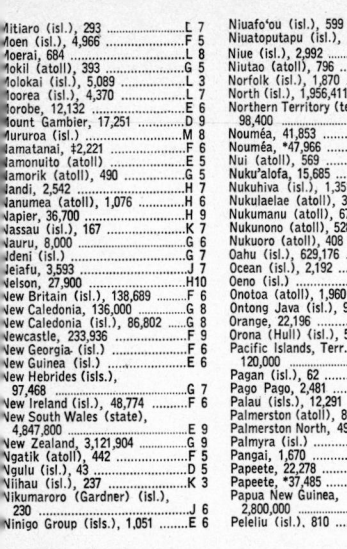

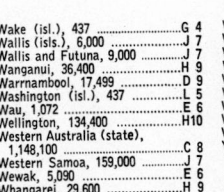

PACIFIC OCEAN

LAMBERT AZIMUTHAL EQUAL-AREA PROJECTION

Copyright by C. S. HAMMOND & Co., N.Y.

NAUTICAL MILES
0 200 400 600 800 1000 1200

STATUTE MILES
0 200 400 600 800 1000 1200

KILOMETRES
0 200 400 600 800 1000 1200

Capitals of Countries .... ★
Capitals of Colonies, Dependencies, States and Territories ... ★
Administrative Centers .... ⊛

International Boundaries
Internal Boundaries
Distances Between Points 5444
(nautical miles)

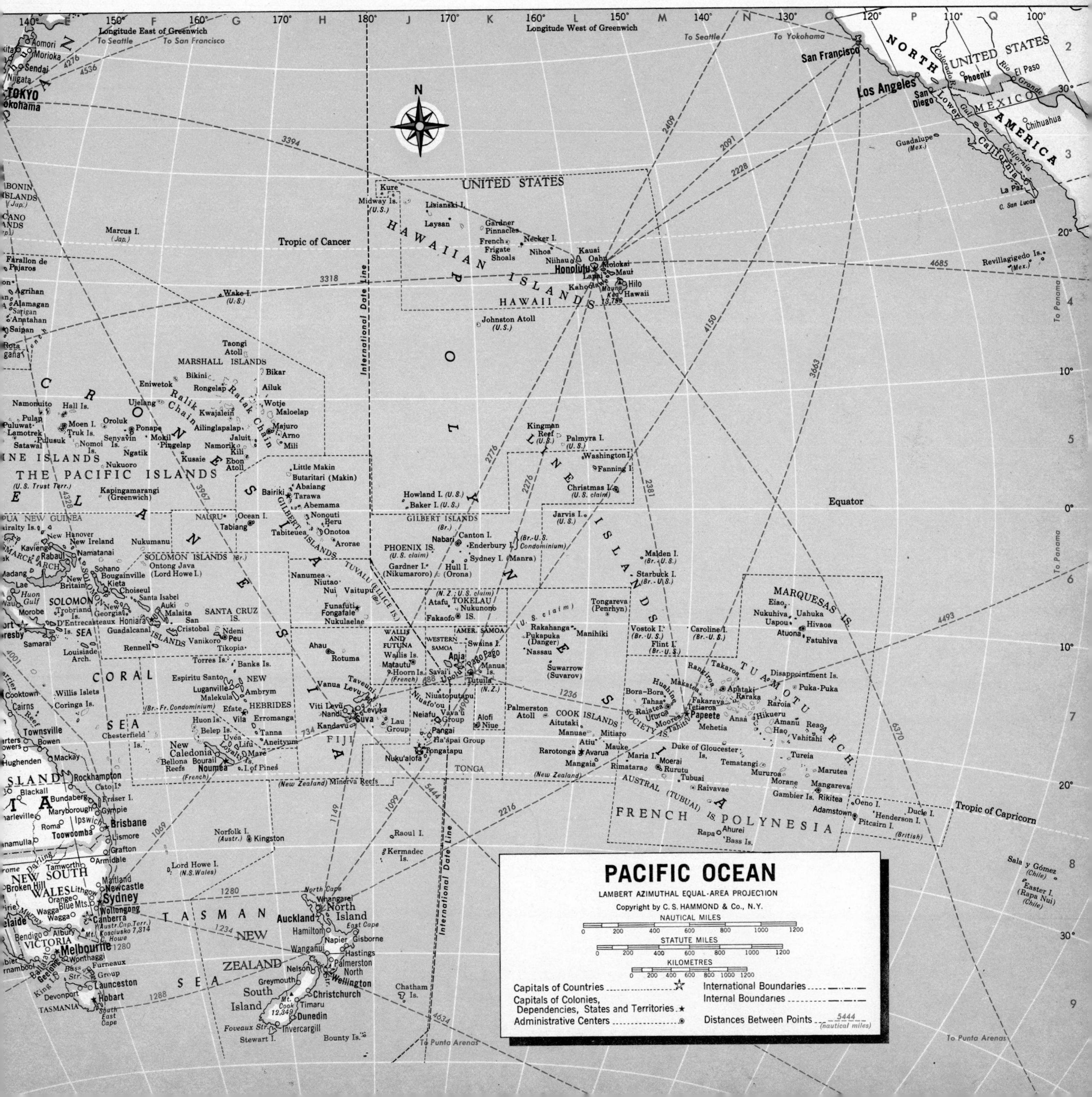

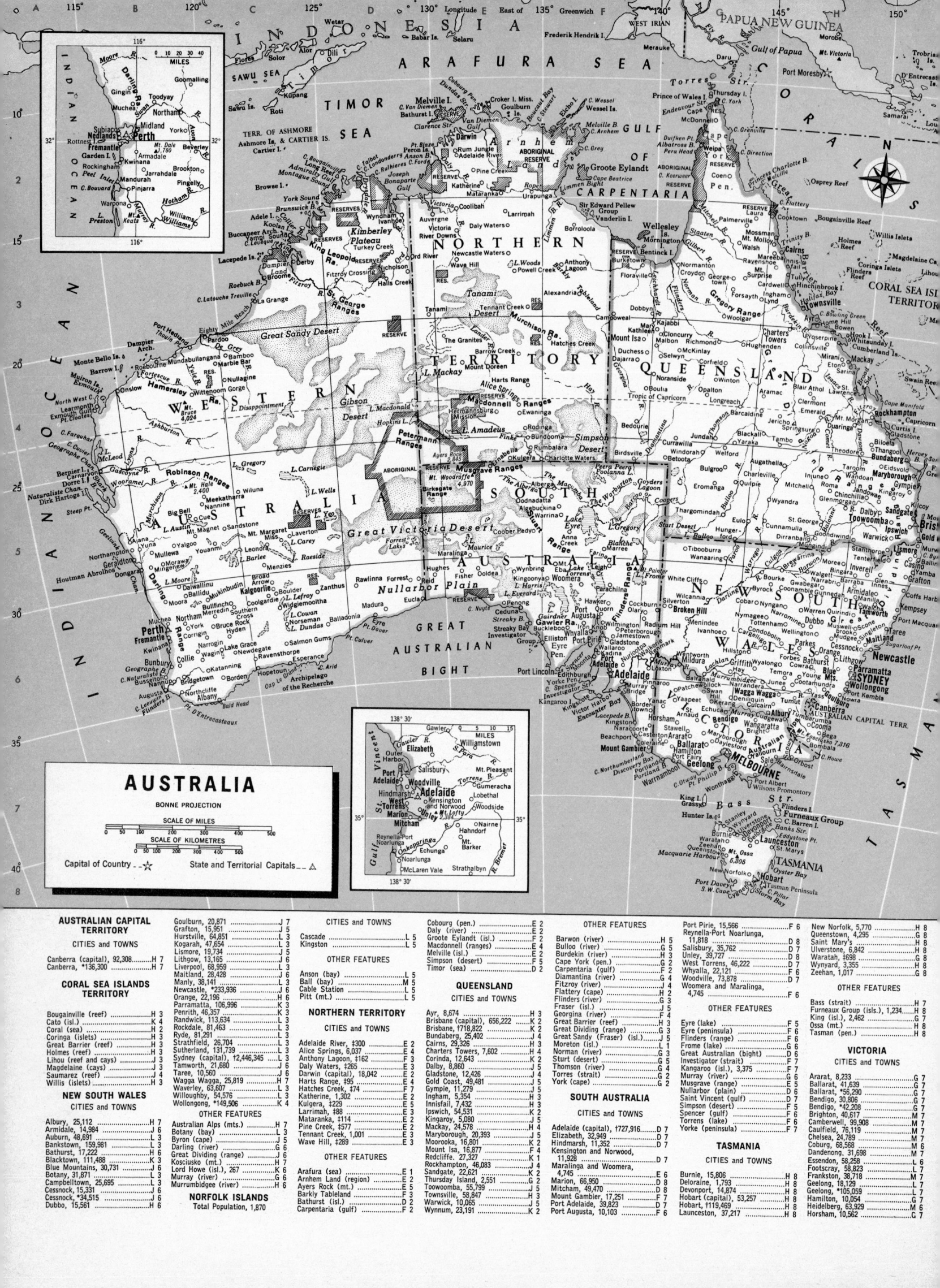

AUSTRALIA

BONNE PROJECTION

SCALE OF MILES

SCALE OF KILOMETRES

Capital of Country ⭐ State and Territorial Capitals ▲

AUSTRALIAN CAPITAL TERRITORY

CITIES and TOWNS

Canberra (capital), 92,308 ... H 7
Canberra, *136,300 ... H 7

CORAL SEA ISLANDS TERRITORY

Bougainville (reef) ... H 3
Cato (isl.) ... K 4
Coral (sea) ... H 2
Coringa (islets) ... H 3
Great Barrier (reef) ... H 3
Holmes (reef) ... J 3
Lihou (reef and cays) ... J 3
Magdelaine (cays) ... J 3
Saumarez (reef) ... J 4
Willis (islets) ... J 3

NEW SOUTH WALES

CITIES and TOWNS

Albury, 25,112 ... H 7
Armidale, 14,984 ... J 6
Auburn, 48,691 ... L 3
Bankstown, 159,981 ... L 3
Bathurst, 17,222 ... J 6
Blacktown, 111,488 ... K 3
Blue Mountains, 30,731 ... J 6
Botany, 31,871 ... L 4
Campbelltown, 25,695 ... J 6
Cessnock, 15,331 ... J 6
Cessnock, *34,515 ... H 6
Dubbo, 15,561 ... H 6

Goulburn, 20,871 ... J 7
Grafton, 15,951 ... J 5
Hurstville, 64,851 ... L 3
Kogarah, 47,654 ... L 3
Lismore, 19,734 ... J 5
Lithgow, 13,165 ... J 6
Liverpool, 89,959 ... L 3
Maitland, 28,428 ... J 6
Manly, 38,141 ... L 3
Newcastle, *233,936 ... J 6
Orange, 22,196 ... H 6
Parramatta, 106,996 ... K 3
Penrith, 46,357 ... K 3
Randwick, 113,634 ... L 3
Rockdale, 81,463 ... L 3
Ryde, 81,291 ... L 3
Strathfield, 26,704 ... L 3
Sutherland, 131,739 ... L 3
Sydney (capital), †2,446,345 ... L 3
Tamworth, 21,680 ... J 6
Taree, 10,560 ... J 6
Wagga Wagga, 25,819 ... H 7
Waverley, 63,607 ... L 3
Willoughby, 54,576 ... L 3
Wollongong, *149,506 ... K 4

OTHER FEATURES

Australian Alps (mts.) ... H 7
Botany (bay) ... L 3
Byron (cape) ... J 5
Darling (river) ... J 6
Great Dividing (range) ... J 6
Kosciusko (mt.) ... H 7
Lord Howe (isl.), 267 ... K 7
Murray (river) ... G 6
Murrumbidgee (river) ... H 6

NORFOLK ISLANDS

Total Population, 1,870

CITIES and TOWNS

Cascade ... L 5
Kingston ... L 5

OTHER FEATURES

Anson (bay) ... L 5
Ball (bay) ... M 5
Cable Station ... L 5
Pitt (mt.) ... L 5

NORTHERN TERRITORY

CITIES and TOWNS

Adelaide River, ‡300 ... E 2
Alice Springs, 6,037 ... E 4
Anthony Lagoon, ‡162 ... F 3
Daly Waters, ‡265 ... E 3
Darwin (capital), 18,042 ... E 2
Harts Range, ‡95 ... E 4
Hatches Creek, ‡74 ... E 4
Katherine, 1,302 ... E 2
Kulgera, ‡229 ... E 5
Larrimah, ‡88 ... E 3
Mataranka, ‡114 ... E 2
Pine Creek, ‡577 ... E 2
Tennant Creek, 1,001 ... E 3
Wave Hill, ‡289 ... E 3

OTHER FEATURES

Arafura (sea) ... E 1
Arnhem Land (region) ... E 2
Ayers Rock (mt.) ... E 5
Barkly Tableland ... F 3
Bathurst (isl.) ... E 2
Carpentaria (gulf) ... F 2
Cobourg (pen.) ... E 2
Daly (river) ... E 2
Groote Eylandt (isl.) ... F 2
Macdonnell (ranges) ... E 4
Melville (isl.) ... E 2
Simpson (desert) ... F 5
Timor (sea) ... D 2

QUEENSLAND

CITIES and TOWNS

Ayr, 8,674 ... H 3
Brisbane (capital), 656,222 ... K 2
Brisbane, †718,822 ... K 2
Bundaberg, 25,402 ... J 4
Cairns, 29,326 ... H 3
Charters Towers, 7,602 ... H 4
Corinda, 12,643 ... J 4
Dalby, 8,860 ... J 5
Gladstone, 12,426 ... J 4
Gold Coast, 49,481 ... J 5
Gympie, 11,279 ... J 5
Ingham, 5,354 ... H 3
Innisfail, 7,432 ... H 3
Ipswich, 54,531 ... K 2
Kingaroy, 5,080 ... J 5
Mackay, 24,578 ... H 4
Maryborough, 20,393 ... J 4
Moorooka, 16,801 ... K 2
Mount Isa, 16,877 ... F 4
Redcliffe, 27,327 ... K 1
Rockhampton, 46,083 ... J 4
Sandgate, 22,621 ... K 2
Thursday Island, 2,551 ... G 2
Toowoomba, 55,799 ... J 5
Townsville, 58,847 ... H 3
Warwick, 10,065 ... J 5
Wynnum, 23,191 ... K 2

OTHER FEATURES

Barwon (river) ... H 5
Bulloo (river) ... G 5
Burdekin (river) ... H 3
Cape York (pen.) ... G 2
Carpentaria (gulf) ... F 2
Diamantina (river) ... G 4
Fitzroy (river) ... J 4
Flinders (cape) ... H 2
Flinders (river) ... G 3
Fraser (isl.) ... J 4
Georgina (river) ... F 4
Great Barrier (reef) ... H 2
Great Dividing (range) ... G 3
Great Sandy (Fraser) (isl.) ... L 1
Moreton (isl.) ... L 1
Norman (river) ... G 3
Sturt (desert) ... G 5
Thomson (river) ... G 4
Torres (strait) ... G 2
York (cape) ... G 2

SOUTH AUSTRALIA

CITIES and TOWNS

Adelaide (capital), †727,916 ... D 7
Elizabeth, 32,949 ... D 7
Hindmarsh, 11,352 ... D 7
Kensington and Norwood, 11,928 ... D 7
Maralinga and Woomera, 4,745 ... E 6
Marion, 66,950 ... D 8
Mitcham, 49,470 ... D 8
Mount Gambier, 17,251 ... F 7
Port Adelaide, 39,823 ... D 7
Port Augusta, 10,103 ... F 6

Port Pirie, 15,566 ... F 6
Reynella-Port Noarlunga, 11,818 ... D 8
Salisbury, 35,762 ... D 7
Unley, 39,727 ... D 8
West Torrens, 46,222 ... D 7
Whyalla, 22,121 ... F 6
Woodville, 73,878 ... D 7
Woomera and Maralinga, 4,745 ... F 6

OTHER FEATURES

Eyre (lake) ... F 5
Eyre (peninsula) ... F 6
Flinders (range) ... F 6
Frome (lake) ... F 6
Great Australian (bight) ... D 6
Investigator (strait) ... F 7
Kangaroo (isl.), 3,375 ... F 7
Murray (river) ... G 6
Musgrave (range) ... E 5
Nullarbor (plain) ... D 6
Saint Vincent (gulf) ... D 7
Simpson (desert) ... F 5
Spencer (gulf) ... F 6
Torrens (lake) ... F 6
Yorke (peninsula) ... F 7

TASMANIA

CITIES and TOWNS

Burnie, 15,806 ... H 8
Deloraine, 1,793 ... H 8
Devonport, 14,874 ... H 8
Hobart (capital), 53,257 ... H 8
Hobart, †119,469 ... H 8
Launceston, 37,217 ... H 8

New Norfolk, 5,770 ... H 8
Queenstown, 4,295 ... G 8
Saint Mary's ... H 8
Ulverstone, 6,842 ... H 8
Waratah, 698 ... G 8
Wynyard, 3,355 ... G 8
Zeehan, 1,017 ... G 8

OTHER FEATURES

Bass (strait) ... H 7
Furneaux Group (isls.), 1,234 ... H 8
King (isl.), 2,462 ... G 7
Ossa (mt.) ... G 8
Tasman (pen.) ... H 8

VICTORIA

CITIES and TOWNS

Ararat, 8,233 ... G 7
Ballarat, 41,639 ... G 7
Ballarat, *56,290 ... G 7
Bendigo, 30,806 ... G 7
Bendigo, *42,208 ... G 7
Brighton, 40,617 ... M 7
Camberwell, 99,908 ... M 7
Caulfield, 76,119 ... M 7
Chelsea, 24,789 ... M 7
Coburg, 69,568 ... M 7
Dandenong, 31,698 ... M 7
Essendon, 58,258 ... M 7
Footscray, 58,823 ... L 7
Frankston, 38,718 ... M 7
Geelong, 18,129 ... G 7
Geelong, *105,059 ... L 7
Hamilton, 10,054 ... G 7
Heidelberg, 63,929 ... M 6
Horsham, 10,562 ... G 7

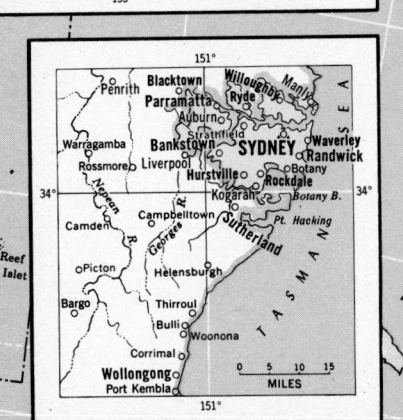

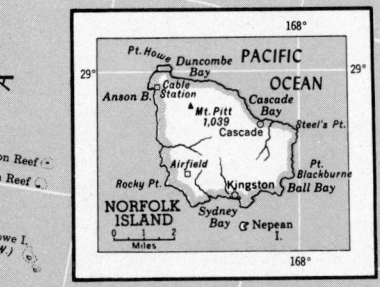

AREA   2,967,909 sq. mi.
POPULATION   13,684,900
CAPITAL   Canberra
LARGEST CITY   Sydney
HIGHEST POINT   Mt. Kosciusko 7,316 ft.
LOWEST POINT   Lake Eyre -39 ft.
MONETARY UNIT   Australian dollar
MAJOR LANGUAGE   English
MAJOR RELIGIONS   Protestantism, Roman Catholicism

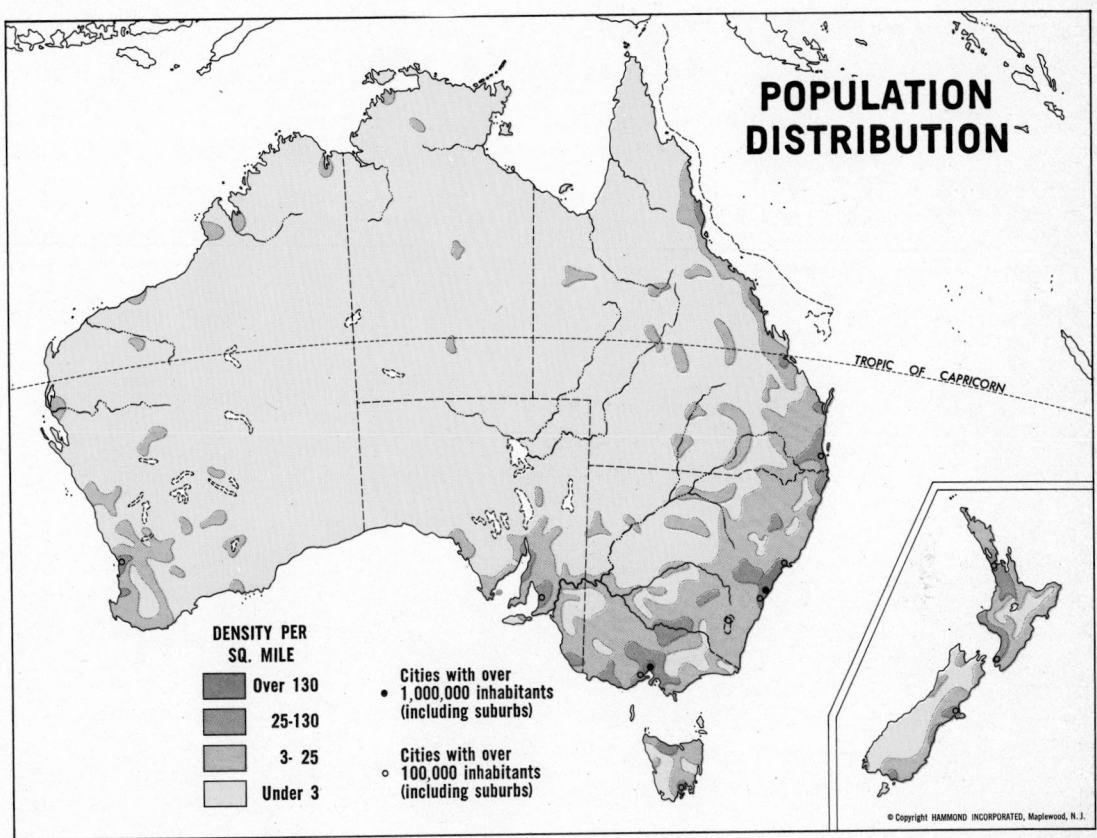

POPULATION DISTRIBUTION

TROPIC OF CAPRICORN

DENSITY PER SQ. MILE

- Over 130
- 25-130
- 3- 25
- Under 3

• Cities with over 1,000,000 inhabitants (including suburbs)

○ Cities with over 100,000 inhabitants (including suburbs)

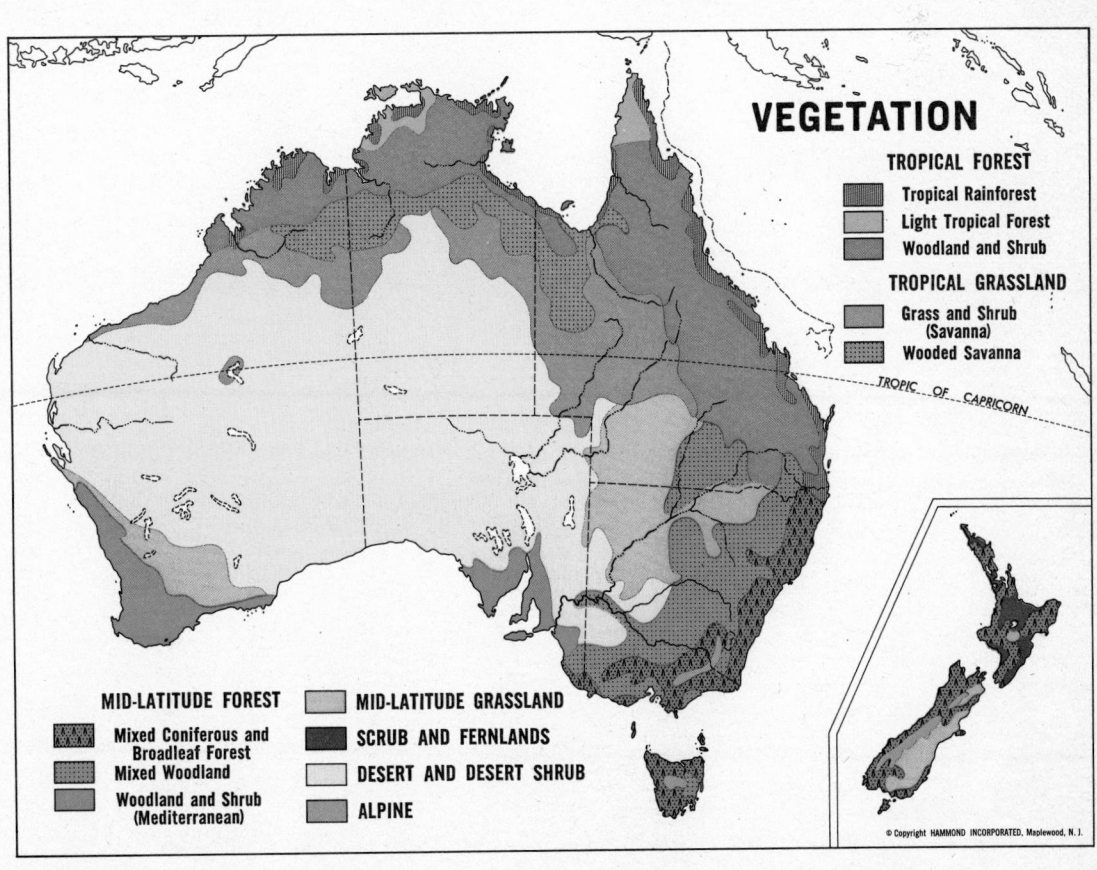

VEGETATION

TROPICAL FOREST
- Tropical Rainforest
- Light Tropical Forest
- Woodland and Shrub

TROPICAL GRASSLAND
- Grass and Shrub (Savanna)
- Wooded Savanna

TROPIC OF CAPRICORN

MID-LATITUDE FOREST
- Mixed Coniferous and Broadleaf Forest
- Mixed Woodland
- Woodland and Shrub (Mediterranean)

MID-LATITUDE GRASSLAND

SCRUB AND FERNLANDS

DESERT AND DESERT SHRUB

ALPINE

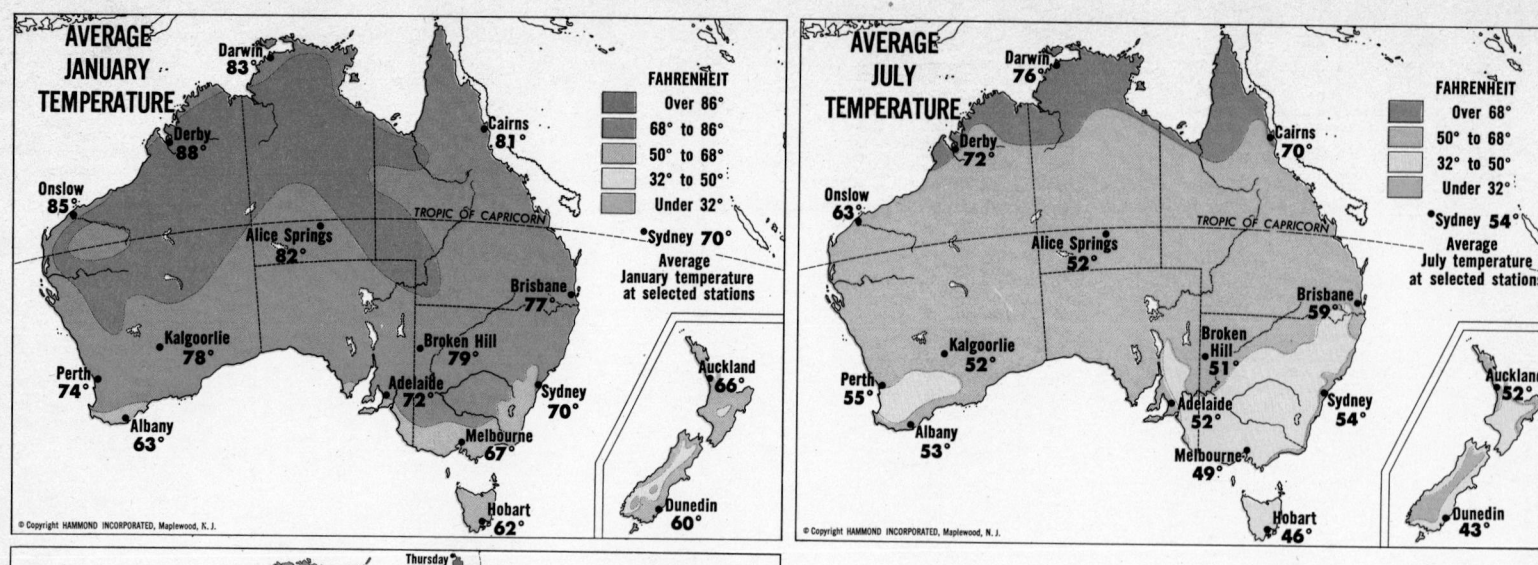

AVERAGE
JANUARY
TEMPERATURE
FAHRENHEIT
Over 86°
68° to 86°
50° to 68°
32° to 50°
Under 32°
Sydney 70°
Average
January temperature
at selected stations
TROPIC OF CAPRICORN
Darwin 83°
Derby 88°
Cairns 81°
Onslow 85°
Alice Springs 82°
Brisbane 77°
Kalgoorlie 78°
Broken Hill 79°
Perth 74°
Adelaide 72°
Sydney 70°
Albany 63°
Melbourne 67°
Hobart 62°
Auckland 66°
Dunedin 60°
© Copyright HAMMOND INCORPORATED, Maplewood, N. J.

AVERAGE
JULY
TEMPERATURE
FAHRENHEIT
Over 68°
50° to 68°
32° to 50°
Under 32°
Sydney 54°
Average
July temperature
at selected stations
TROPIC OF CAPRICORN
Darwin 76°
Derby 72°
Cairns 70°
Onslow 63°
Alice Springs 52°
Brisbane 59°
Kalgoorlie 52°
Broken Hill 51°
Perth 55°
Adelaide 52°
Sydney 54°
Albany 53°
Melbourne 49°
Hobart 46°
Auckland 52°
Dunedin 43°
© Copyright HAMMOND INCORPORATED, Maplewood, N. J.

RAINFALL
Thursday Island 66
Darwin 60
Cairns 86
Derby 23
Tennant Creek 15
Cloncurry 19
Mackay 63
Onslow 12
Alice Springs 12
TROPIC OF CAPRICORN
William Creek 5
Brisbane 45
Geraldton 19
Kalgoorlie 9
Broken Hill 9
Perth 36
Albany 37
Adelaide 20
Albury 28
Sydney 47
Melbourne 26
Auckland 48
Hokitika 116
Wellington 48
Hobart 25
Dunedin 36
AVERAGE ANNUAL RAINFALL
INCHES
Over 80
60-80
40-60
20-40
10-20
Under 10
Average annual rainfall
at selected stations
Sydney 47
© Copyright HAMMOND INCORPORATED, Maplewood, N. J.

Agriculture, Industry and Resources

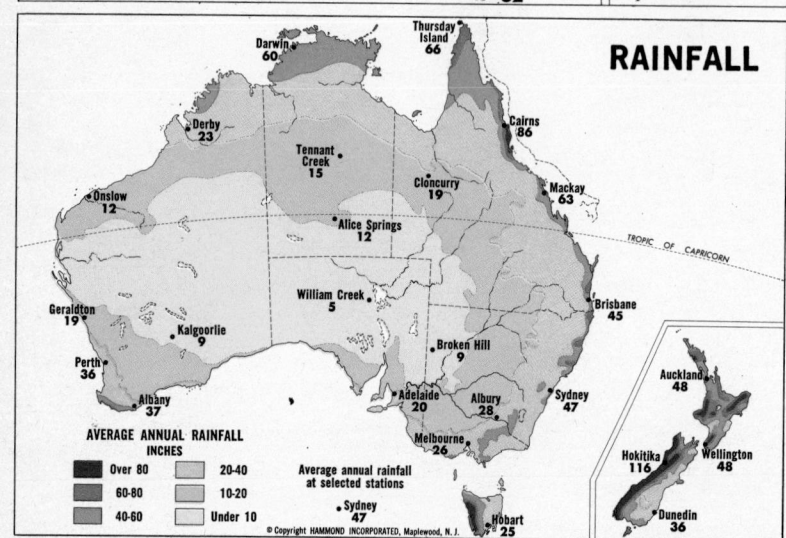

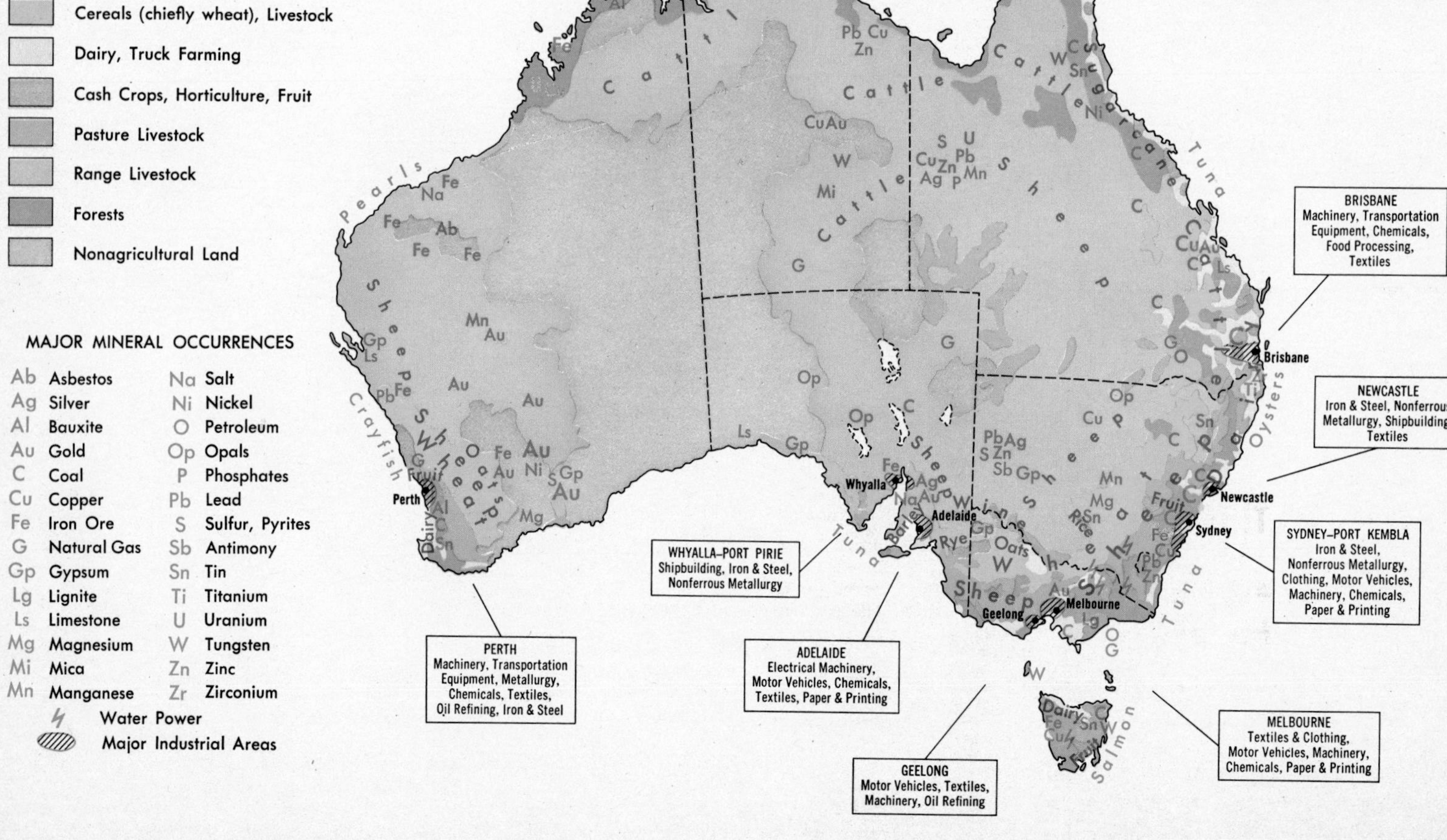

DOMINANT LAND USE
Cereals (chiefly wheat), Livestock
Dairy, Truck Farming
Cash Crops, Horticulture, Fruit
Pasture Livestock
Range Livestock
Forests
Nonagricultural Land
MAJOR MINERAL OCCURRENCES
Ab Asbestos
Ag Silver
Al Bauxite
Au Gold
C Coal
Cu Copper
Fe Iron Ore
G Natural Gas
Gp Gypsum
Lg Lignite
Ls Limestone
Mg Magnesium
Mi Mica
Mn Manganese
Na Salt
Ni Nickel
O Petroleum
Op Opals
P Phosphates
Pb Lead
S Sulfur, Pyrites
Sb Antimony
Sn Tin
Ti Titanium
U Uranium
W Tungsten
Zn Zinc
Zr Zirconium
Water Power
Major Industrial Areas
Pearls
Cattle
Sheep
Wheat
Sugarcane
Tuna
Oysters
Crayfish
Salmon
Rice
Oats
Fruit
Dairy
Rye
Perth
Whyalla
Adelaide
Geelong
Melbourne
Sydney
Newcastle
Brisbane
BRISBANE
Machinery, Transportation Equipment, Chemicals, Food Processing, Textiles
NEWCASTLE
Iron & Steel, Nonferrous Metallurgy, Shipbuilding, Textiles
SYDNEY–PORT KEMBLA
Iron & Steel, Nonferrous Metallurgy, Clothing, Motor Vehicles, Machinery, Chemicals, Paper & Printing
MELBOURNE
Textiles & Clothing, Motor Vehicles, Machinery, Chemicals, Paper & Printing
GEELONG
Motor Vehicles, Textiles, Machinery, Oil Refining
ADELAIDE
Electrical Machinery, Motor Vehicles, Chemicals, Textiles, Paper & Printing
WHYALLA–PORT PIRIE
Shipbuilding, Iron & Steel, Nonferrous Metallurgy
PERTH
Machinery, Transportation Equipment, Metallurgy, Chemicals, Textiles, Oil Refining, Iron & Steel

120° 125° 130° 135° 140° 145° 150°

ARAFURA   SEA

INDONESIA
Sumba
Timor
TIMOR
SEA
Ashmore Is. TERR. OF ASHMORE
Cartier I. & CARTIER IS.

Melville I.
Cobourg
Pen.
Darwin
C. Wessel

New Guinea
PAPUA
NEW
GUINEA
Port Moresby
Torres Strait
C. York

INDIAN
OCEAN

Arnhem
Land
Groote
Eylandt

Gulf of
Carpentaria

Cape
York
Peninsula
Mitchell

CORAL
SEA
Great
Barrier
Reef

Kimberley
Plateau
Ord
Derby
Fitzroy

NORTHERN
Victoria
Barkly Tableland

Mt. Bartle Frere
5,287
Cairns
Townsville

Great
Port Hedland
Fortescue
Hamersley Ra.
Mt. Bruce
4,024
th West
C.
Geraldton

Great Sandy Desert
WESTERN

TERRITORY
Tanami
Desert

Lake
Mackay
Macdonnell Ranges
Alice Springs
Finke
Ayers Rock
2,845

Mt. Isa

QUEENSLAND
Georgina
Flinders

Dividing

Mackay

Rockhampton
Lake
Disappointment
Tropic of Capricorn
Gibson Desert

AUSTRALIA
Lake
Carnegie

Simpson
Desert
Diamantina

Barcoo
Grey Range
Warrego

Range
Bundaberg
Toowoomba
Brisbane
Gold Coast

Great Victoria Desert
Lake
Barlee

SOUTH
AUSTRALIA
Musgrave Ranges

Lake
Eyre
Barcoo
Sturt
Desert

NEW SOUTH

Tamworth

Kalgoorlie-
Boulder
Nullarbor Plain

Lake
Torrens
Lake
Gairdner
Whyalla
Eyre
Pen.

Lake
Frome
Flinders Range
Broken Hill
Darling

WALES
Ranges

Perth
Fremantle
Bunbury
Darling Ra.
C. Leeuwin
Albany

Great
Australian Bight
100
1000

Spencer Gulf
Adelaide
Kangaroo I.
Mt. Lofty Ra.

Murray
Lachlan
Wagga Wagga
Albury
Bendigo
VICTORIA
Ballarat
Geelong
Mt. Gambier

Newcastle
Sydney
Wollongong
Canberra
AUSTRALIAN CAPITAL
TERRITORY
Gre
Mt. Kosciusko
7,316
C. Howe
Melbourne

INDIAN
OCEAN

King I.
Bass Strait
Furneaux
Group

TASMAN
SEA

Launceston
TASMANIA
Hobart
South Cape

© HAMMOND INCORPORATED, Maplewood, N.J.

110° 115° 120° 125° 130° 135° Longitude 140° East of Greenwich 145° 150° 155°

VEGETATION/RELIEF

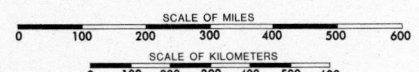

SCALE OF MILES
0 100 200 300 400 500 600
SCALE OF KILOMETERS
0 100 200 300 400 500 600

Capital of Country.......................... ⊛
State and Territorial Capitals.......... ⊚
International Boundaries...................
State and Territorial Boundaries........
Elevations in Feet   Depths in Fathoms

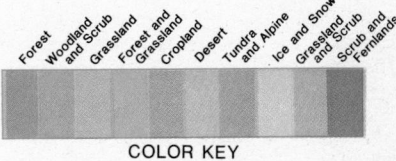

Forest
Woodland
and Scrub
Grassland
Forest and
Grassland
Cropland
Desert
Tundra
and Alpine
Ice and Snow
Grassland
and Scrub
Scrub and
Fernlands

COLOR KEY

AREA 975,920 sq. mi.
POPULATION 1,148,100
CAPITAL Perth
LARGEST CITY Perth
HIGHEST POINT Mt. Bruce 4,024 ft.

CITIES and TOWNS

Albany, 11,419	B 6
Armadale, 3,463	A 1
Augusta, ⊙3,238	A 6
Beverley, ⊙1,773	B 1
Boddington, ⊙761	B 2
Boulder, 5,234	C 5
Bridgetown, 1,569	B 6
Brookton, ⊙1,341	B 2
Broome, 1,570	C 2
Bruce Rock, ⊙2,142	B 1
Bunbury, 15,459	A 2
Busselton, 4,278	A 6
Capel, ⊙2,132	A 2
Carnamah, ⊙996	A 5
Carnarvon, 2,956	A 4
Collie, 7,628	B 2
Coolgardie, ⊙762	C 5
Coorow, ⊙808	B 5
Corrigin, ⊙2,099	B 6
Cranbrook, ⊙1,419	B 6
Cuballing, ⊙732	B 2
Cue, ⊙430	B 4
Cunderdin, ⊙2,114	B 5
Dalwallinu, ⊙2,425	B 5
Dampier, 1,080	B 3
Dandaragan, ⊙619	A 5
Denmark, ⊙1,775	B 6
Derby, 1,424	C 2
Donnybrook, 981	A 2
Esperance, 2,677	C 6
Exmouth Gulf, ⊙2,248	A 3
Fremantle, 25,284	A 1
Geraldton, 12,125	A 5
Gingin, ⊙1,021	A 1
Gnowangerup, 981	B 6
Goomalling, ⊙1,567	B 1
Gosnells, 7,135	A 1
Halls Creek, ⊙577	D 2
Harvey, 2,066	A 2
Jarrahdale, ⊙1,728	B 5
Kalamunda-Gooseberry Hill, 3,068	B 1
Kalgoorlie, 9,174	C 5
Kalgoorlie, ⊙19,908	C 5
Katanning, 3,506	B 6
Kellerberrin, 1,343	B 5
Kojonup, ⊙2,711	B 6
Kwinana, 1,272	A 1
Lake Grace, ⊙1,986	B 6
Learmonth,	A 3
Leonora, ⊙623	C 5
Mandurah, 2,730	A 2
Manjimup, 3,186	B 6
Marble Bar, ⊙567	C 3
Meekatharra, ⊙1,011	B 4
Menzies, ⊙404	C 5
Merredin, 3,599	B 5
Midland, 9,335	A 1
Mingenew, ⊙978	A 5
Moora, 1,185	B 5
Morawa, ⊙1,718	B 5
Mount Barker, 1,594	B 6
Mount Magnet, ⊙1,016	B 5
Mukinbudin, ⊙869	B 5
Mullewa, ⊙1,825	A 5
Nannup, ⊙1,272	B 6
Narrogin, 4,861	B 2
Nedlands, 23,320	A 1
Norseman, 1,863	C 6
Northam, 7,400	A 1
Northampton, ⊙2,021	A 5
Nullagine, ⊙211	C 3
Nungarin, ⊙539	B 5
Onslow,	A 3
Pardoo,	A 3
Pemberton, 930	B 6
Perenjori, ⊙1,311	B 5
Perth (cap.), ‡499,969	A 1
Pingelly, ⊙1,453	B 2
Port Hedland, 1,778	B 3
Quairading, ⊙1,687	B 1
Ravensthorpe, ⊙782	B 6
Rockingham, 3,767	A 1
Roebourne, 702	B 3
South Perth, 32,042	A 1
Subiaco, 16,621	A 1
Tableland, ⊙1,815	D 2
Three Springs, ⊙1,038	A 5
Toodyay, ⊙1,388	B 1
Wagin, 1,750	B 2
Wandering, ⊙611	B 2
Wanneroo, 612	A 1
Waroona, 1,013	A 2
Wickepin, ⊙1,380	B 2
Williams, ⊙1,193	B 2
Wiluna, ⊙219	C 4
Wundowie, 1,040	B 1
Wyalkatchem, ⊙1,252	B 1
Wyndham, 1,156	E 1
Yalgoo, ⊙392	A 5
Yampi Sound,	C 2
York, 1,421	B 1

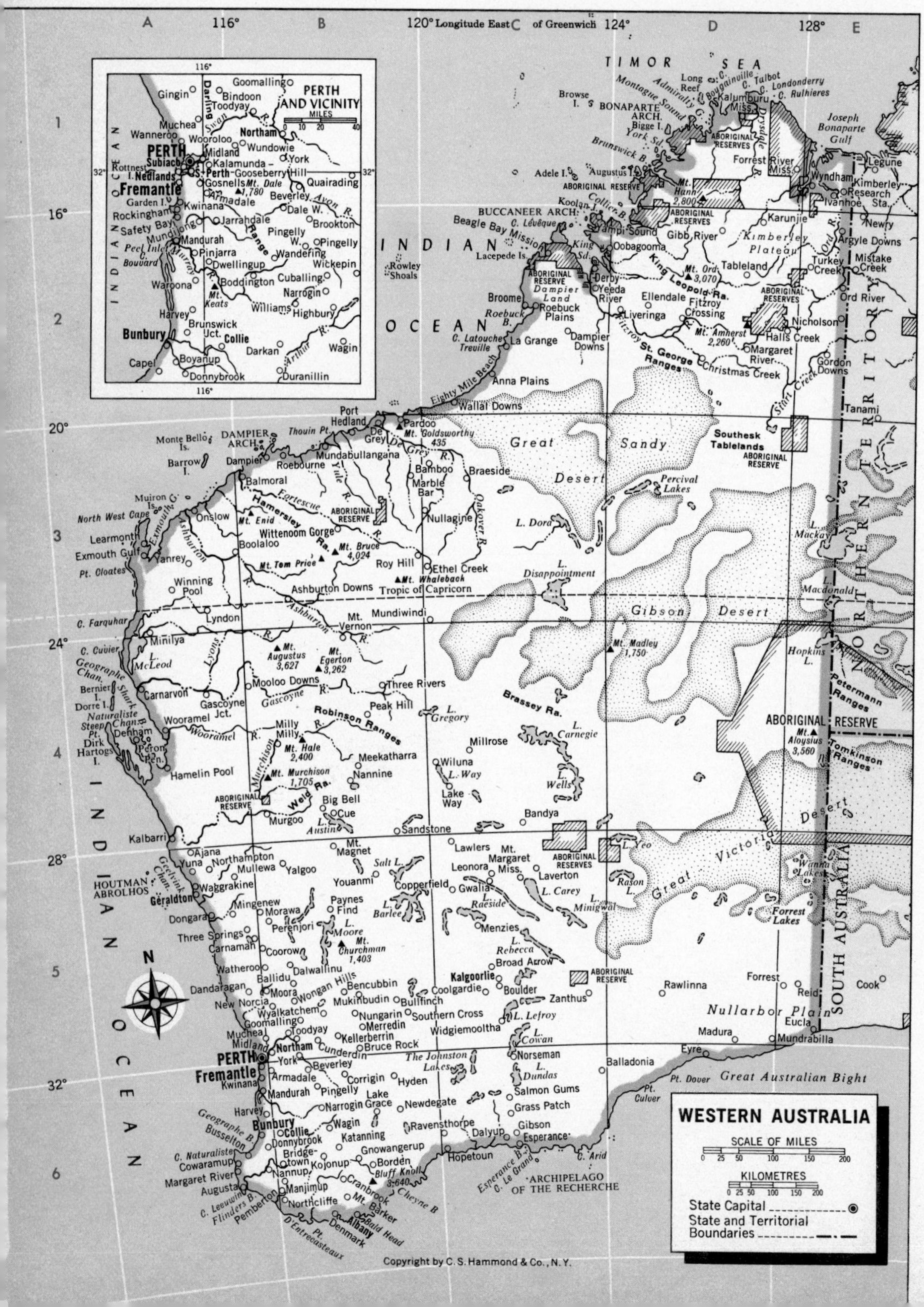

Topography

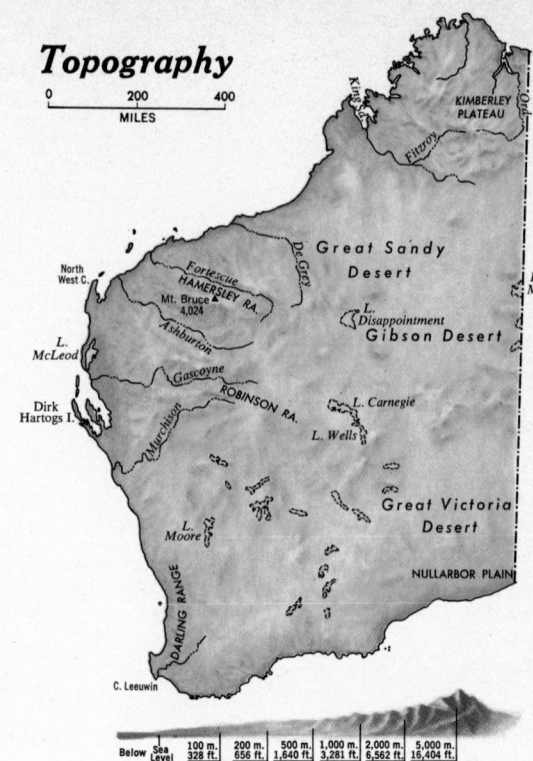

SCALE: 0 — 200 — 400 MILES

Below Sea Level | 100 m. 328 ft. | 200 m. 656 ft. | 500 m. 1,640 ft. | 1,000 m. 3,281 ft. | 2,000 m. 6,562 ft. | 5,000 m. 16,404 ft.

OTHER FEATURES

Adele (isl.)	C 1
Admiralty (gulf)	D 1
Aloysius (mt.)	E 4
Amherst (mt.)	D 2
Arid (cape)	C 6
Arthur (riv.)	B 2
Ashburton (riv.)	A 3
Augustus (isl.)	D 1
Augustus (mt.)	B 4
Austin (lake)	B 4
Avon (riv.)	A 1
Bald (head)	B 6
Barlee (lake)	B 5
Barrow (isl.)	A 3
Bernier (isl.)	A 4
Bigge (isl.)	D 1
Bluff Knoll (mt.)	B 6
Bonaparte (arch.)	D 1
Bougainville (cape)	D 1
Bouvard (cape)	A 2
Brassey (range)	C 4
Browse (isl.)	C 1
Bruce (mt.)	B 3
Brunswick (bay)	D 1
Buccaneer (arch.)	C 2
Carey (lake)	C 5
Carnegie (lake)	C 4
Cheyne (bay)	B 6
Churchman (mt.)	B 5
Cloates (pt.)	A 3
Collier (bay)	C 1
Cowan (lake)	C 5
Culver (pt.)	D 6
Cuvier (cape)	A 4
Dale (riv.)	B 1
Dampier (arch.)	B 3
Dampier Land (reg.)	C 2
Darling (range)	A 1
De Grey (riv.)	B 3
D'Entrecasteaux (pt.)	B 6
Dirk Hartogs (isl.)	A 4
Disappointment (lake)	C 3
Dora (lake)	C 3
Dorre (isl.)	A 4
Dover (pt.)	D 6
Drysdale (riv.)	D 1
Dundas (lake)	C 6
Egerton (mt.)	B 4
Eighty Mile (beach)	C 2
Enid (mt.)	B 3
Esperance (bay)	C 6
Exmouth (gulf)	A 3
Farquhar (cape)	A 4
Fitzroy (riv.)	D 2
Flinders (bay)	A 6
Fortescue (riv.)	B 3
Garden (isl.)	A 1
Gascoyne (riv.)	A 4
Geelvink (chan.)	A 5
Geographe (bay)	A 2
Geographe (chan.)	A 4
Gibson (des.)	D 3
Goldsworthy (mt.)	B 3
Great Australian (bight)	E 6
Great Sandy (des.)	C 3
Great Victoria (des.)	D 5
Gregory (lake)	B 4
Hale (mt.)	B 4
Hamersley (range)	B 3
Hann (range)	D 1
Hopkins (lake)	E 4
Houtman Abrolhos (isls.)	A 5
Indian Ocean	
Johnston, The (lakes)	
Joseph Bonaparte (gulf)	
Keats (mt.)	
Kimberley (plat.)	
King (sound)	
King Leopold (range)	
Koolan (isl.)	
Lacepede (isls.)	
Latouche Treville (cape)	
Leeuwin (cape)	
Lefroy (lake)	
Le Grand (cape)	
Lévêque (cape)	
Londonderry (cape)	
Long (reef)	
Lyons (riv.)	
Macdonald (lake)	
Mackay (lake)	
Madley (mt.)	
McLeod (lake)	
Minigwal (lake)	
Montague (sound)	
Monte Bello (isls.)	
Moore (lake)	
Muiron (isls.)	
Murchison (lake)	
Murchison (riv.)	
Murray (riv.)	
Naturaliste (cape)	
Naturaliste (chan.)	
North West (cape)	
Nullarbor (plain)	
Oakover (riv.)	
Ord (mt.)	
Ord (riv.)	
Peel (inlet)	
Percival (lakes)	
Peron (pen.)	
Petermann (ranges)	
Raeside (lake)	
Rason (lake)	
Rebecca (lake)	
Recherche (arch.)	
Robinson (ranges)	
Roebuck (bay)	
Rottnest (isl.)	
Rowley (shoals)	
Rulhieres (cape)	
Saint George (ranges)	
Salt (lake)	
Shark (bay)	
Southesk Tablelands	
Steep (pt.)	
Sturt (creek)	
Swan (riv.)	
Talbot (cape)	
Thouin (pt.)	
Timor (sea)	
Tomkinson (ranges)	
Tom Price (mt.)	
Wanna (lakes)	
Way (lake)	
Weld (range)	
Wells (lake)	
Whaleback (mt.)	
Wooramel (riv.)	
Yeo (lake)	
York (sound)	
Yule (riv.)	

⊙ Population of district.
‡ Population of met. area.
▢ Population of urban area.

WESTERN AUSTRALIA

SCALE OF MILES
0 25 50 100 150 200

KILOMETRES
0 25 50 100 150 200

State Capital ⊛
State and Territorial Boundaries ----

CITIES and TOWNS

Adelaide River, ☉300	B 2
...eron,	C 7
...exandria,	E 5
...ce Springs, 6,037	D 7
...roy Downs,	E 5
...dado,	D 8
...gas Downs,	D 8
Anthony Lagoon, ☉162	D 4
...eyonga,	C 8
...gadargada,	E 6
...ltunga,	D 7
...vergne,	B 3
...ron Downs, ☉231	E 5
...nka Banka,	C 5
...rrow Creek,	D 6
...tchelor, ☉551	B 2
...hurst Island Mission,	B 1
...rum,	C 3
...rrimbah,	C 3
...rrindudu,	A 5
...indooma,	E 4
...ramurra,	E 6
...alvert Hills,	E 4
...harlotte Waters,	C 8
...laravale,	B 3
...oniston,	C 7
...oolibah,	B 3
...eswell Downs,	E 4
...aly River, ☉237	B 2
...aly Waters, ☉265	C 4
...arwin (cap.), 18,042	B 2
...ouglas,	B 2
...lliott, ☉234	C 4
...enarra,	D 6
...dunda,	C 8
...a Downs,	D 5
Ewaninga,	D 8
Fitzroy,	B 4
Frewena,	D 5
Harts Range, ☉95	D 7
Hatches Creek, ☉74	D 6
Helen Springs,	C 4
Henbury,	C 8
Humpty Doo,	B 2
Inverway,	A 4
Katherine, 1,302	B 3
Kildurk,	A 4
Killarney,	A 4
Koolpinyah,	B 2
Kulgera, ☉229	C 8
Kurundi,	D 6
Lake Nash, ☉113	E 6
Larrimah, ☉88	C 3
Legune,	A 3
Limbunya,	B 4
Litchfield,	B 2
Lucy Creek,	E 7
Mainoru,	C 3
Mataranka, ☉114	C 3
Mistake Creek,	A 4
Montejinni,	C 4
Mount Cavanagh,	C 8
Mount Doreen,	B 7
Murray Downs,	D 6
Napperby,	C 7
Newcastle Waters,	C 4
Newry,	A 3
Nutwood Downs,	D 4
O.T. Downs,	D 4
Pine Creek, ☉577	C 2
Plenty River Mine,	D 7
Powell Creek,	C 5
Rankine Store,	E 5
Ringwood,	D 7
Robinson River,	E 4
Rockhampton Downs,	D 5
Rodinga,	D 8
Roper River Mission, ☉357	D 3
Roper Valley,	D 3
Rosewood,	A 4
Rum Jungle,	B 2
Soudan,	E 6
Stirling,	C 6
Tanami,	A 5
Tarlton Downs,	E 7
Tea Tree Well Store,	C 7
Tempe Downs,	C 8
Tennant Creek, 1,001	C 5
The Granites,	B 6
Top Springs,	C 4
Ucharonidge,	D 4
Umbeara,	C 8
Urapunga,	D 3
Utopia,	D 7
Victoria River Downs,	B 4
Waterloo,	A 4
Wave Hill, ☉289	B 4
White Quartz Hill,	D 7
Willeroo,	B 3
Willowra,	C 6
Wolloogorang, ☉87	F 4
Yambah,	C 7

OTHER FEATURES

Amadeus (lake)	B 8
Arafura (sea)	D 1
Arnhem (cape)	E 2
Arnhem Land (reg.)	D 2
Arnold (riv.)	D 3
Barkly Tableland	D 4
Bathurst (isl.)	A 1
Beagle (gulf)	A 2
Beatrice (cape)	E 3
Bennett (lake)	B 7
Bickerton (isl.)	E 2
Blaze (pt.)	A 2
Boucaut (bay)	D 1
Carpentaria (gulf)	E 3
Central Wedge (mt.)	C 7
Clarence (str.)	B 2
Cobourg (pen.)	C 1
Conner (mt.)	C 8
Croker (cape)	C 1
Daly (riv.)	B 2
Davenport (mt.)	B 7
Dobbie (mt.)	E 7
Drummond (mt.)	D 5
Dry (riv.)	C 3
Dundas (str.)	B 1
East Alligator (riv.)	C 2
Ehrenberg (range)	B 7
Elcho (isl.)	D 1
Ewing (mt.)	E 7
Finke (riv.)	C 8
Fitzmaurice (riv.)	B 3
Flora (riv.)	B 3
Ford (cape)	A 2
Georgina (riv.)	E 6
Goulburn (isls.)	C 1
Goyder (riv.)	D 2
Grey (cape)	E 2
Groote Eylandt (isl.)	D 2
Hale (riv.)	D 8
Hanson (riv.)	C 6
Hay (cape)	A 2
Hay (dry riv.)	E 7
Hogarth (mt.)	E 6
Hopkins (lake)	A 8
Joseph Bonaparte (gulf)	A 3
Katherine (riv.)	C 3
Lander (riv.)	C 6
Leisler (mt.)	A 7
Limmen (bight)	D 3
Limmen Bight (riv.)	D 4
Macdonald (lake)	B 7
Macdonnell (ranges)	C 7
MacKay (lake)	A 7
Mann (riv.)	D 2
Marshall (riv.)	D 7
Melville (bay)	E 2
Melville (isl.)	B 1
Murchison (range)	D 6
Napier (mt.)	A 4
Neale (lake)	A 8
Newcastle (creek)	C 4
Nicholson (riv.)	E 5
Old Marsh Bed	B 6
Olga (mt.)	B 8
Peron (isls.)	A 2
Petermann (ranges)	A 8
Port Darwin (inlet)	B 2
Ranken (riv.)	E 6
Robinson (riv.)	E 4
Roper (riv.)	C 3
Rose (riv.)	D 2
Sandover (riv.)	D 6
Simpson (des.)	E 8
Singleton (mt.)	C 7
Sir Edward Pellew Group (isls.)	D 3
South Alligator (riv.)	C 2
Stanley (mt.)	B 7
Stewart (cape)	D 1
Stirling (creek)	A 4
Sturt (plain)	C 4
Sylvester (lake)	D 5
Tanami (des.)	C 5
Timor (sea)	A 2
Todd (riv.)	D 8
Vanderlin (isl.)	E 3
Van Diemen (cape)	A 1
Van Diemen (gulf)	B 1
Victoria (riv.)	B 3
Warwick (chan.)	E 3
Wessel (cape)	E 1
Wessel (isls.)	E 1
West Baines (riv.)	A 4
White (lake)	A 6
Winnecke (creek)	B 5
Woods (lake)	C 4
Young (mt.)	D 3
Ziel (mt.)	C 7

☉ Population of district.

AREA 520,280 sq. mi.
POPULATION 98,400
CAPITAL Darwin
LARGEST CITY Darwin
HIGHEST POINT Mt. Ziel 4,955 ft.

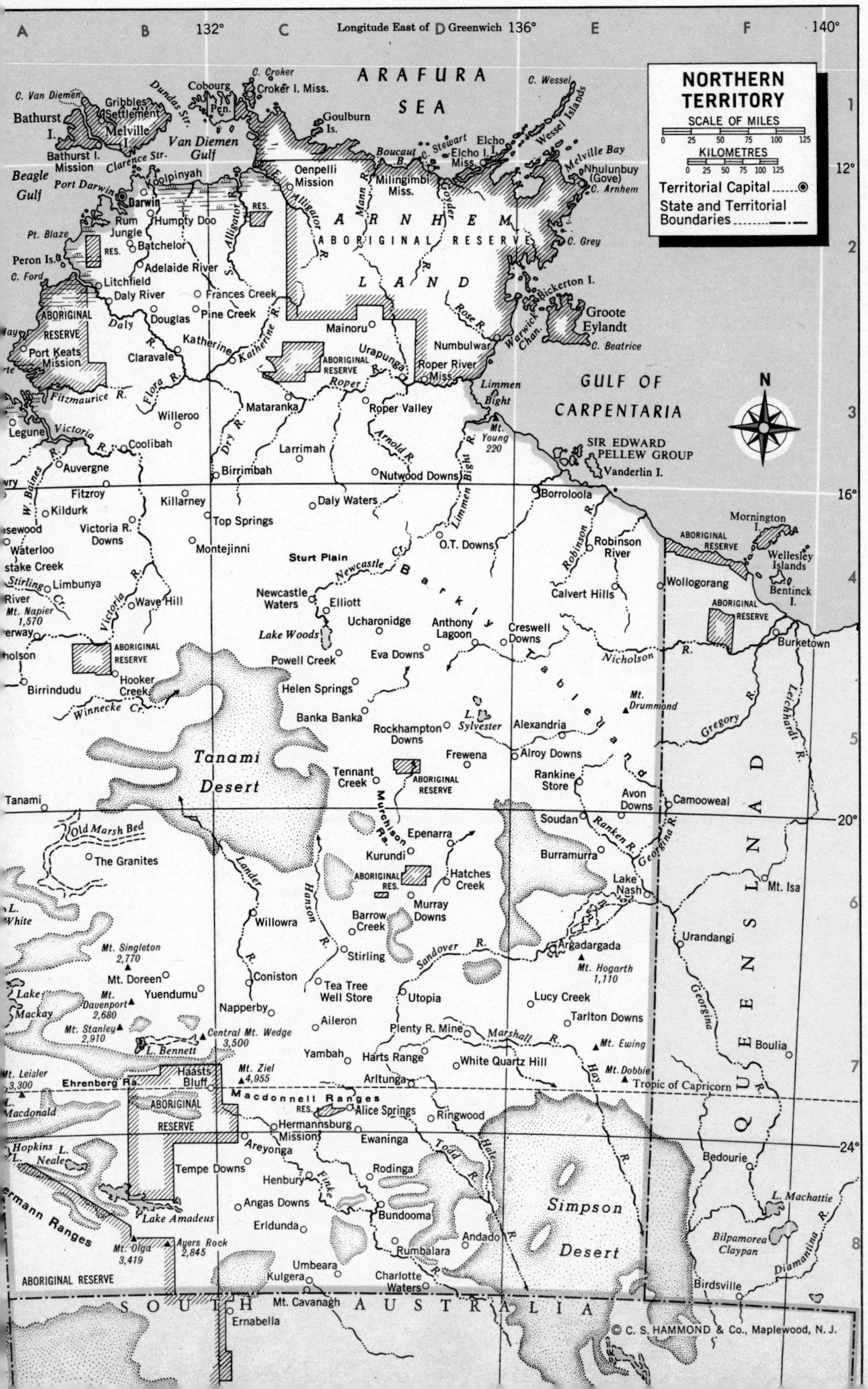

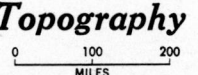

Topography

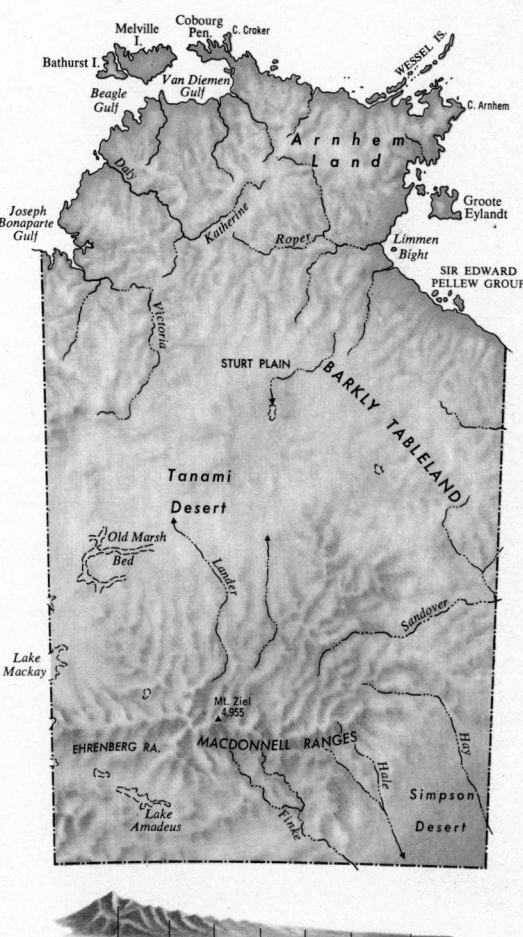

© C. S. HAMMOND & Co., Maplewood, N.J.

AREA 380,070 sq. mi.
POPULATION 1,247,100
CAPITAL Adelaide
LARGEST CITY Adelaide
HIGHEST POINT Mt. Woodroffe 4,970 ft.

CITIES and TOWNS

Adelaide (cap.), ‡727,916 ..B 6
Angaston, 1,887 ....F 6
Balaklava, 1,199 ....F 6
Barmera, 1,484 ....G 6
Beachport, ⊙1,903 ....F 7
Berri, 2,232 ....G 6
Bordertown, 1,758 ....G 7
Brighton, 22,620 ....A 8
Burnside, 38,758 ....B 8
Burra, 1,342 ....F 5
Campbelltown, 32,083 ......B 7
Ceduna, 1,406 ....D 5
Clare, 1,579 ....F 5
Cleve, ⊙2,817 ....E 5
Colonel Light Gardens,
   3,404 ....A 8
Coober Pedy ....D 3
Crystal Brook, 1,235 ....F 5
Elizabeth, 32,949 ....B 7
Elliston, ⊙1,424 ....D 5
Enfield, 80,261 ....B 7
Gawler, 6,645 ....B 6
Gladstone, 1,035 ....F 5
Glenelg, 14,762 ....A 8
Gumeracha, ⊙2,654 ....C 7
Hindmarsh, 11,352 ....A 7
Hope Valley-Tea Tree
   Gully, ⊙21,314 ....B 7
Jamestown, 1,282 ....F 5
Kadina, 3,022 ....E 5
Kapunda, 1,119 ....F 6
Keith, 1,097 ....G 7
Kensington and Norwood,
   11,928 ....B 8
Kimba, ⊙1,703 ....E 5
Kingscote, 1,071 ....E 6
Kingston, 1,065 ....G 7
Lameroo, ⊙1,947 ....G 6
Leigh Creek, 1,014 ....F 4
Lobethal, 1,098 ....C 7
Loxton, 2,418 ....G 6
Maitland, 1,017 ....E 6
Mannum, 2,034 ....F 6
Maralinga and Woomera,
   4,745 ....B 3
Marion, 66,950 ....A 8
Meadows, ⊙2,824 ....B 8
Meningie, ⊙4,104 ....F 6
Millicent, 4,533 ....F 7
Minlaton, ⊙2,504 ....E 6
Mitcham, 49,470 ....B 3
Moonta, 1,122 ....E 5
Mount Barker, 1,934 ....C 8
Mount Gambier, 17,251 ....F 6
Murray Bridge, 5,957 ....F 6
Nangwarry, 977 ....G 7
Naracoorte, 4,378 ....G 7
Nuriootpa, 2,041 ....F 6
Orroroo, ⊙1,228 ....F 5
Payneham, 16,844 ....B 7
Penola, 1,383 ....G 7
Peterborough, 3,117 ....F 5
Pinnaroo, ⊙1,717 ....G 6
Port Adelaide, 39,823 ......A 7

Port Augusta, 10,103 ....E 5
Port Lincoln, 8,888 ....E 6
Port Pirie, 15,566 ....E 5
Prospect, 21,411 ....B 7
Radium Hill ....G 5
Renmark, 6,275 ....G 5
Reynella-Port Noarlunga,
   11,818 ....A 8
Robe, ⊙941 ....F 7
Salisbury, 35,762 ....B 7
Snowtown, ⊙1,694 ....E 5
Stirling-Bridgewater,
   4,487 ....B 8
Strathalbyn, 1,449 ....F 6
Streaky Bay, ⊙2,134 ....D 5
Tailem Bend, 1,947 ....F 6
Tanunda, 1,986 ....C 6
Thebarton, 12,296 ....A 7
Tumby Bay, ⊙2,793 ....E 6
Unley, 39,727 ....B 8
Victor Harbor, 3,128 ....F 6
Waikerie, ⊙3,818 ....F 6
Wallaroo, 2,094 ....E 5
West Torrens, 46,222 ......A 8
Whyalla, 22,121 ....E 5
Willunga, ⊙2,190 ....F 6
Wilmington, ⊙828 ....F 6
Woodville, 73,878 ....A 7
Woomera and Maralinga,
   4,745 ....E 4
Yorketown, ⊙2,734 ....E 6

OTHER FEATURES

Acraman (lake) ....D 5
Alberga, The (riv.) ....D 2
Alexandrina (lake) ....F 6
Anxious (bay) ....D 5
Arckaringa (creek) ....D 2
Barcoo (creek) ....F 3
Barossa (res.) ....C 6
Birksgate (range) ....A 2
Blanche (lake) ....F 3
Brady (mt.) ....D 3
Cadibarrawirracanna
   (lake) ....D 3
Callabonna (lake) ....F 3
Catastrophe (cape) ....D 6
Coffin (bay) ....D 6
Coffin Bay (pen.) ....D 6
Coopers (Barcoo) (creek) ..F 3
Coorong, The (lag.) ....F 6
Dey Dey (lake) ....B 3
Encounter (bay) ....F 6
Everard (lake) ....D 4
Everard (ranges) ....D 2
Eyre (pen.) ....D 5
Eyre North (lake) ....E 3
Eyre South (lake) ....E 3
Finke (riv.) ....C 1
Flinders (range) ....F 4
Frome (lake) ....G 4
Gairdner (lake) ....D 4
Gawler (ranges) ....E 5
Gawler (riv.) ....E 5
Gilles (lake) ....E 5
Goyders (lag.) ....F 2
Great Australian (bight) ...A 5
Great Victoria (des.) ....B 3
Gregory (lake) ....F 3

Hack (mt.)
Hamilton, The (riv.)
Harris (lake)
Head of Bight (bay)
Indian Ocean
Investigator (str.)
Investigator Group (isls.)
Island (lag.)
Jaffa (cape)
Kangaroo (isl.), 3,375
Lacepede (bay)
Little Para (riv.)
Lofty (mt.)
Macfarlane (lake)
Macumba, The (riv.)
Maurice (lake)
Meramangye (lake)
Morris (mt.)
Mount Bold (res.)
Murray (riv.)
Musgrave (ranges)
Neales, The (riv.)
Neptune (isls.)
Northumberland (cape)
Nukey Bluff (mt.)
Nullarbor (plain)
Nurrari (lakes)
Nuyts (arch.)
Nuyts (cape)
Onkaparinga (riv.)
Peera Peera Poolanna
   (lake)
Saint Mary (peak)
Saint Vincent (gulf)
Serpentine (lakes)
Simpson (des.)
Sir Joseph Banks Group
   (isls.)
South Para (riv.)
Spencer (cape)
Spencer (gulf)
Stevenson, The (riv.)
Streaky (bay)
Strzelecki (creek)
Stuart (range)
Sturt (des.)
Sturt (riv.)
The Alberga (riv.)
The Coorong (lag.)
The Hamilton (riv.)
The Macumba (riv.)
The Neales (riv.)
The Stevenson (riv.)
The Warburton (riv.)
Thistle (isl.)
Torrens (lake)
Torrens (riv.)
Warburton, The (riv.)
Warren (res.)
Whidbey (isls.)
Wilkinson (lakes)
Wilson Bluff (prom.)
Woodroffe (mt.)
Wright (lake)
Yarle (lake)
Yorke (pen.)

⊙ Population of district.
‡ Population of met. area.

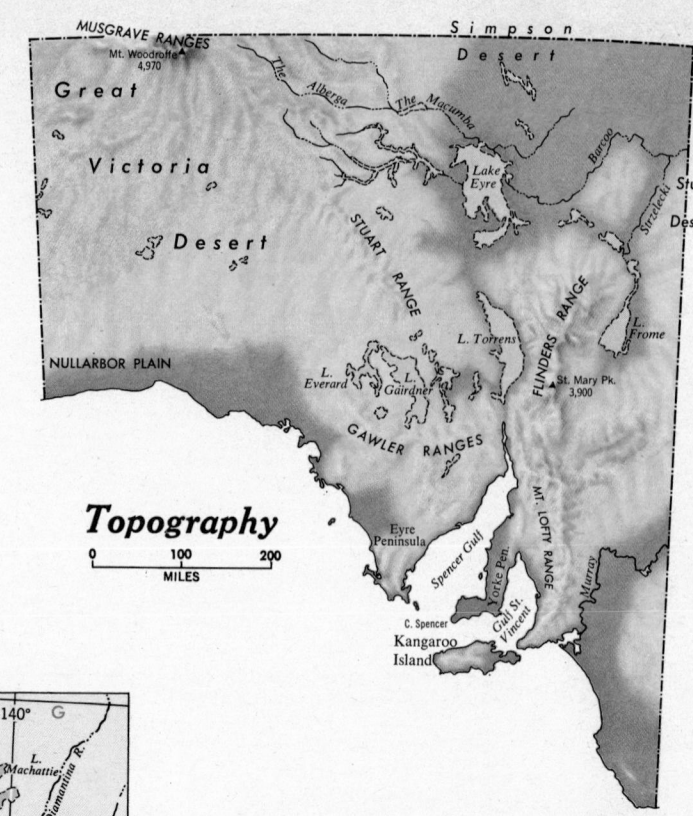

Topography

0   100   200
MILES

Below Sea Level | 100 m. 328 ft. | 200 m. 656 ft. | 500 m. 1,640 ft. | 1,000 m. 3,281 ft. | 2,000 m. 6,562 ft. | 5,000 m. 16,404 ft.

SOUTH AUSTRALIA

SCALE OF MILES
0   25   50   100   150

KILOMETRES
0   25 50   75 100   150

State Capital ....⊙
State and Territorial
Boundaries ....

ADELAIDE AND VICINITY

MILES
0   1   2   3   4

CORAL SEA ISLANDS TERR
Total Population
3

PHYSICAL FEATURES

...gainville (reef) ....C 2
...ders (reefs) ....D 3
...at Barrier (reef) ....C 3
...alds (cays) ....D 3
...mes (reef) ....C 3
...ion (reef) ....E 3
...prey (reef) ....C 2
...marez (reef) ....E 4

QUEENSLAND

CITIES and TOWNS

...ot, 16,450 ....E 2
...8,674 ....C 3
...moral, 15,758 ....D 5
...ela, 3,537 ....D 5
...ven, 5,144 ....D 3
...sbane (cap.) 656,222 ....D 2
...sbane, ‡718,822 ....D 2
...rns, 29,326 ....C 3
...daberg, 25,402 ....D 5
...oundra, 3,657 ....E 5
...mp Hill, 12,392 ....E 3
...dwell, ⊙5,640 ....C 3
...arleville, 4,871 ....C 5
...arters Towers, 7,602 ....C 4
...ermside, 26,189 ....D 2
...mp Hill, 12,392 ....E 3
...oppers Plains, 16,817 ....D 3
...inda, 12,643 ....D 5
...by, 8,860 ....D 5
...st Brisbane, 10,780 ....E 3
...bin, 13,224 ....D 3
...a, ⊙6,120 ....E 3
...ebung, 17,850 ....D 2
...dstone, 12,426 ....D 4
...d Coast, 49,481 ....E 6
...ondiwindi, 3,529 ....D 6
...enslopes, 13,351 ....E 3
...mpie, 11,279 ....E 5
...land Park, 22,645 ....D 3
...ne Hill, 3,507 ....C 3
...a, 18,705 ....C 3
...oroopilly, 15,321 ....D 3
...ham, 5,354 ....C 3
...sfail, 7,432 ....C 3
...garoy, 5,080 ....D 5
...greach, 3,871 ....B 4

Mackay, 24,578 ....D 4
Mareeba, 4,799 ....C 3
Maryborough, 20,393 ....E 5
Mary Kathleen ....A 4
Mirani, ⊙5,379 ....D 4
Mitchelton, 13,998 ....D 2
Moorooka, 16,801 ....D 3
Mount Isa, 16,877 ....A 4
Mount Morgan, 4,055 ....D 4
Nambour, 6,219 ....E 5
Newmarket, 12,212 ....D 2
Nundah, 15,609 ....E 2
Redcliffe, 27,327 ....E 5
Rockhampton, 46,083 ....D 4
Roma, 5,996 ....D 5
Sandgate, 22,621 ....D 2
Stafford, 17,692 ....D 2
Stanthorpe, 3,641 ....D 6
Taroom, ⊙3,367 ....D 5
Toowoomba, 52,139 ....D 5
Townsville, 58,847 ....C 3
Warwick, 10,065 ....D 6
Weipa, ... B 2
Windsor, 14,023 ....D 2
Wynnum, 23,191 ....E 5
Yeppoon, 3,418 ....D 4
Yeronga, 11,769 ....D 3

OTHER FEATURES

Albatross (bay) ....B 2
Alice (riv.) ....C 4
Archer (riv.) ....B 2
Balonne (riv.) ....D 6
Banks (isl.) ....B 1
Barcoo (creek) ....B 5
Barkly Tableland ....A 4
Bartle Frere (mt.) ....C 3
Beal (range) ....B 5
Belyando (riv.) ....C 4
Bentinck (isl.) ....A 3
Bigge (range) ....D 5
Bowling Green (cape) ....C 3
Bramble (bay) ....E 2
Brisbane (riv.) ....D 2
Brisbane Airport ....E 2
Broad (sound) ....D 4
Bulimba (creek) ....E 3
Bulloo (lake) ....B 6
Bulloo (riv.) ....B 6
Bunker Group (isls.) ....E 4
Burdekin (riv.) ....C 3
Cabbage Tree (creek) ....D 2
Cape York (pen.) ....B 2
Capricorn (chan.) ....D 4
Capricorn Group (isls.) ......E 4
Carnarvon (range) ....D 5
Carpentaria (gulf) ....A 2

Carapundy (swamp) ....B 6
Clarke (range) ....C 4
Cloncurry (riv.) ....B 4
Coleman (riv.) ....B 2
Comet (riv.) ....D 5
Condamine (riv.) ....D 5
Coopers (Barcoo) (creek) .....B 5
Coral (sea) ....C 1
Culgoa (riv.) ....C 6
Cumberland (isls.) ....D 4
Curtis (isl.) ....D 4
Darling Downs ....D 5
Dawson (riv.) ....D 5

Diamantina (riv.) ....B 4
Direction (cape) ....B 2
Downfall (creek) ....D 2
Drummond (range) ....C 5
Duifken (pt.) ....B 2
Endeavour (str.) ....B 1
Enoggera (creek) ....D 2
Fitzroy (riv.) ....D 4
Flattery (cape) ....C 2
Flinders (riv.) ....B 3
Fraser (isl.) ....E 5
Galilee (lake) ....C 4
Georgina (riv.) ....A 4

AREA 666,991 sq. mi.
POPULATION 2,015,300
CAPITAL Brisbane
LARGEST CITY Brisbane
HIGHEST POINT Mt. Bartle Frere 5,287 ft.

QUEENSLAND
SCALE OF MILES
0   50   100   150   200
KILOMETRES
0   50 100 150 200
Territorial Capital ....⊙
State and Territorial
Boundaries ....

BRISBANE
AND
VICINITY
MILES
0   1   2

BRISBANE

Copyright by C. S. Hammond & Co., N.Y.

Topography

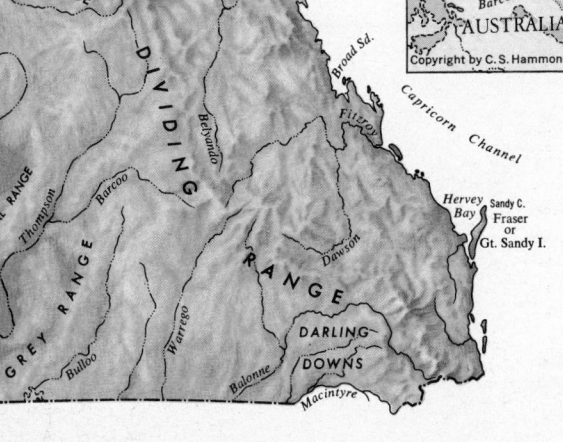

0   100   200
MILES

5,000 m. | 2,000 m. | 1,000 m. | 500 m. | 200 m. | 100 m. | Sea | Below
16,404 ft. | 6,562 ft. | 3,281 ft. | 1,640 ft. | 656 ft. | 328 ft. | Level |

Gilbert (riv.) ....B 3
Great Dividing (range) ....C 4
Great Sandy (Fraser) (isl.) ..E 5
Gregory (range) ....B 3
Gregory (riv.) ....A 3
Grenville (cape) ....B 1
Grey (range) ....B 5
Halifax (bay) ....C 3
Hamilton (riv.) ....B 4
Hervey (bay) ....E 5
Hinchinbrook (isl.) ....C 3
Holroyd (riv.) ....B 2
Hook (isl.) ....D 4
Isaacs (riv.) ....D 4
Kedron (brook) ....D 2
Keerweer (cape) ....B 2
Leichhardt (range) ....C 4
Leichhardt (riv.) ....A 3
Machattie (lake) ....B 5
Macintyre (riv.) ....D 6
Manifold (cape) ....D 4
Maranoa (riv.) ....C 5

Mary (riv.) ....E 5
McIlwraith (range) ....B 2
Melville (cape) ....C 2
Mitchell (riv.) ....B 2
Moonah (creek) ....A 4
Moreton (bay) ....E 5
Moreton (isl.) ....E 5
Mornington (isl.) ....A 3
Nicholson (riv.) ....A 3
Nogoa (riv.) ....C 5
Norman (riv.) ....B 3
Norman (cape) ....D 4
Normandy (riv.) ....B 2
Northumberland (isls.) ....D 4
Oxley (creek) ....D 3
Palmer (riv.) ....C 2
Paroo (riv.) ....C 6
Peak (range) ....C 4
Pera (head) ....B 2
Prince of Wales (isl.) ....B 1
Princess Charlotte (bay) .....C 2
Sandy (cape) ....E 5

Selwyn (range) ....B 4
Sidmouth (cape) ....C 2
Simpson (des.) ....A 5
Staaten (riv.) ....B 3
Sturt (des.) ....B 3
Suttor (riv.) ....C 4
Swain (reefs) ....E 4
Thompson (riv.) ....B 5
Torres (str.) ....B 1
Trinity (bay) ....C 3
Tully (falls) ....C 3
Warrego (range) ....C 5
Warrego (riv.) ....C 5
Wellesley (isls.) ....A 3
Whitsunday (isl.) ....D 4
Wide (bay) ....E 5
Willies (range) ....C 6
Wilson (riv.) ....B 5
Yamma Yamma (lake) ....B 5
York (cape) ....B 1

⊙ Population of district.
‡ Population of met. area.

AUSTRALIAN CAPITAL TERRITORY
Total Population
136,300

CITIES AND TOWNS

Canberra (cap.),		
Australia, 92,308		E 4
Canberra, ‡136,300		E 4
Jervis Bay		F 4

OTHER FEATURES

Saint George (head) .... F 4

NEW SOUTH WALES
CITIES and TOWNS

Aberdeen, 1,127	F 3	Ashford, ⊙2,930	F 1	Barooga,	C 4	Belmore,	J 3	Blayney, 1,909	E 3	Boorowa, 1,181	E 4
Abermain,	F 3	Ashley,	E 1	Barraba, 1,425	F 2	Bemboka,	E 5	Blue Mountains, 30,731	F 3	Boree Creek,	D 4
Adaminaby,	E 5	Attunga,	F 2	Barringun,	C 1	Benanee,	B 4	Bobadah,	D 3	Botany, 31,871	K 3
Adelong,	D 4	Auburn, 48,691	J 3	Baryulgil,	G 1	Bendemeer,	E 2	Bodalla,	F 5	Bourke, 3,262	C 2
Albert,	D 3	Baan Baa,	E 2	Batemans Bay–		Bermagui,	F 5	Bogan Gate,	D 3	Bowral, 5,210	E 4
Albury, 25,112	D 5	Ballina, 4,931	G 1	Batehaven, 1,445	F 4	Berrigan, ⊙6,641	C 4	Boggabilla,	F 1	Bowraville, 883	G 2
Alstonville,	G 1	Balpunga,	A 3	Bathurst, 17,222	E 3	Berry,	F 4	Boggabri, 1,199	F 2	Braidwood,	E 4
Ardlethan,	D 4	Balranald, 1,490	B 4	Batlow, 1,448	D 4	Bibbenluke, ⊙2,220	E 5	Bomaderry-Nowra, 9,633	F 4	Branxton-Greta, 2,539	F 3
Ariah Park,	D 4	Bangalow,	G 1	Baulkham Hills, 24,873	H 3	Bigga,	E 4	Bombala, 1,495	E 5	Bredbo,	E 5
Armidale, 14,984	F 2	Bankstown, 159,981	J 3	Bega, 3,925	E 5	Binda,	E 4	Bonalbo,	G 1	Brewarrina, 1,255	D 2
Ashfield, 41,933	J 3	Baradine,	E 2	Bellata,	E 1	Bingara, 1,504	F 1	Bondi,	K 3	Bribbaree,	D 4
		Barellan,	D 4	Bellbird-Cessnock,		Binnalong,	E 4	Bonnyrigg,	H 3	Broken Hill, 30,036,	A 3
		Bargo,	F 4	15,331	F 3	Binnaway,	E 2	Booligal,	C 3	Browning,	
		Barham, 1,139	C 4	Bellingen, 1,390	G 2	Birriwa,	E 3	Boomi, ⊙2,654	E 1	Brunswick Heads, 1,068	G 1
		Barmedman,	D 4	Belmont,	F 3	Blacktown, 111,488	H 3	Booroorban,	C 4	Bugaldie,	E 2

NEW SOUTH WALES

AREA 309,433 sq. mi.
POPULATION 4,847,800
CAPITAL Sydney
LARGEST CITY Sydney
HIGHEST POINT Mt. Kosciusko
7,316 ft.

VICTORIA

AREA 87,884 sq. mi.
POPULATION 3,713,200
CAPITAL Melbourne
LARGEST CITY Melbourne
HIGHEST POINT Mt. Bogong
6,508 ft.

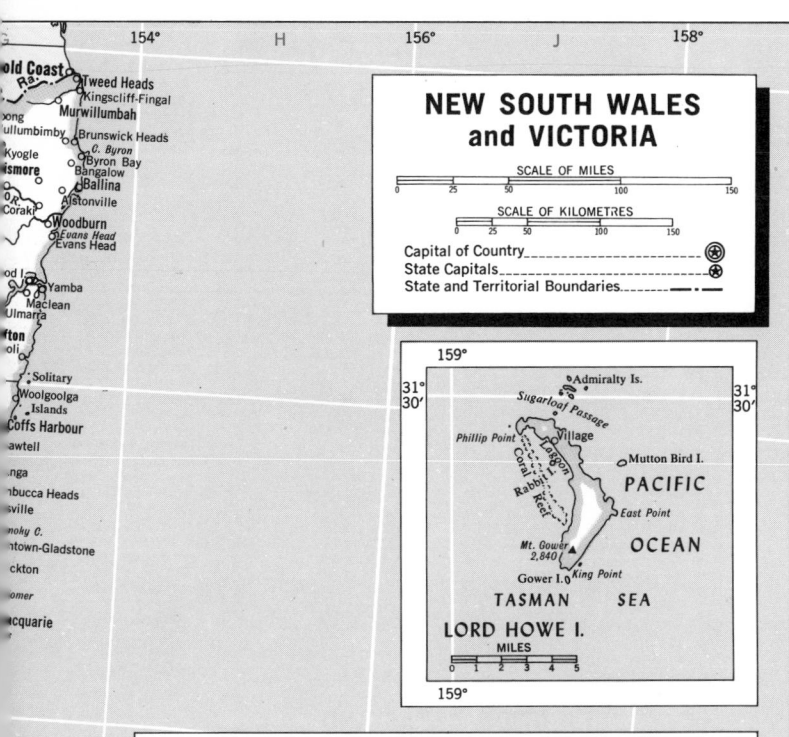

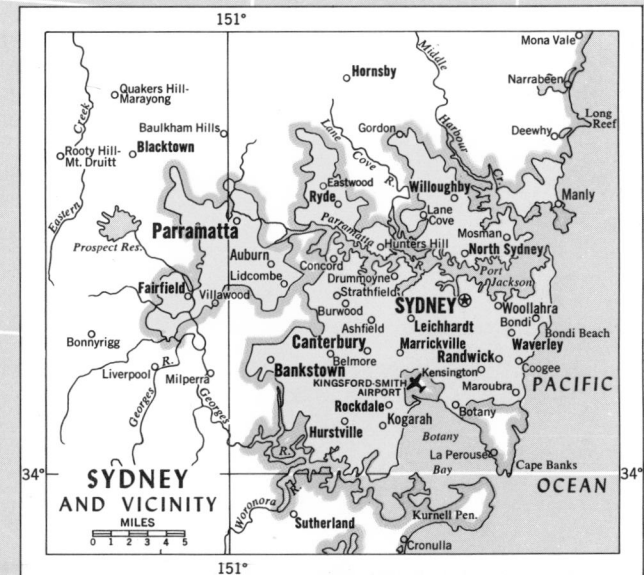

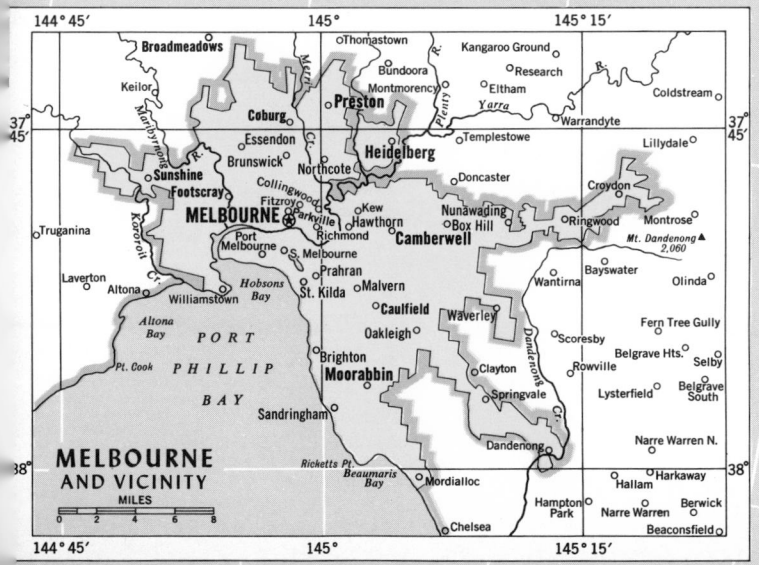

Topography

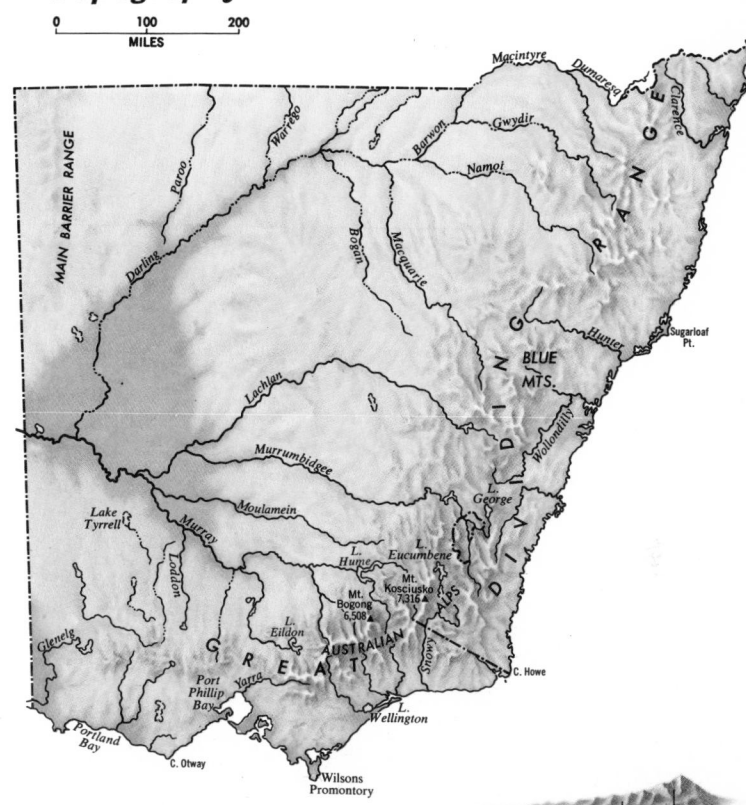

IRRIGATION AREAS AND ARTESIAN BASINS IN AUSTRALIA

Permanent Rivers

Non-Permanent Rivers

Major Irrigation and Other Water Supply Areas

Basins Where Artesian Water Is Generally Available

Flowing Water Bores

Major Dams

Prepared from Atlas of Australian Resources.

AREA 26,383 sq. mi.
POPULATION 410,800
CAPITAL Hobart
LARGEST CITY Hobart
HIGHEST POINT Mt. Ossa 5,305 ft.

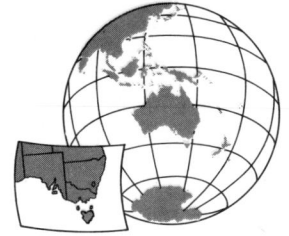

Gordon (riv.) .... B 4	Long (pt.) .... E 3	Pieman (riv.) .... B 3	Stanley (mt.) .... A 1
Great (lake) .... C 3	Low Rocky (pt.) .... B 4	Pillar (cape) .... E 5	Stokes (pt.) .... A 1
Great Western Tiers (mts.)..C 3	Lyell (mt.) .... B 4	Port Davey (inlet) ...... B 5	Stony (head) .... C 2
Grim (cape) .... A 2	Maatsuyker (isls.) ...... C 5	Portland (cape) .... D 2	Storm (bay) .... D 5
Hartz (mt.) .... C 5	Macquarie (harb.) .... B 4	Ramsay (mt.) .... B 3	Strzelecki (mt.) .... D 2
Hibbs (pt.) .... B 4	Macquarie (riv.) .... D 3	Raoul (cape) .... D 5	Swan (isl.) .... E 2
High Rocky (pt.) .... B 4	Maria (isl.) .... E 4	Reid (rocks) .... B 1	Tamar (riv.) .... D 3
Hogan Group (isls.) ..... D 1	Marion (bay) .... E 4	Ringarooma (bay) .... D 2	Tasman (head) .... D 5
Hummock (isl.) .... D 2	Mersey (riv.) .... C 3	Robbins (isl.) .... B 2	Tasman (pen.) .... E 5
Hunter (isl.) .... A 2	Munro (mt.) .... E 2	Rocky (cape) .... B 2	Tasman (sea) .... E 4
Hunter (isls.) .... B 2	Naturaliste (cape) ...... E 2	Saint Clair (lake) ...... C 4	Three Hummock (isl.) .... B 2
Huon (riv.) .... C 5	Nive (riv.) .... C 4	Saint Helens (pt.) ...... E 3	Tooms (lake) .... D 4
Indian Ocean .... A 4	Norfolk (bay) .... D 4	Saint Vincent (cape) .... B 5	Vansittart (isl.) .... E 2
Kent Group (isls.) ...... D 1	North (pt.) .... E 1	Sandy (cape) .... A 3	Walker (isl.) .... B 2
King (isl.), 2,462 .... A 1	North Bruny (isl.) ...... D 5	Schouten (isl.) .... E 4	Waterhouse (isl.) .... D 2
King (riv.) .... B 4	North Esk (riv.) .... D 3	Sorell (lake) .... D 4	West (pt.) .... A 2
King William (lake) ..... C 4	Ossa (mt.) .... C 3	Sorell (cape) .... B 2	West Sister (isl.) ...... D 1
Lake (riv.) .... D 3	Ouse (riv.) .... C 4	Sorell (lake) .... D 4	Wickham (cape) .... A 1
Legges Tor (mt.) .... D 3	Oyster (bay) .... E 4	South (cape) .... C 5	
Leven (riv.) .... B 3	Peron (cape) .... D 4	South Bruny (isl.) ...... D 5	
Lodi (cape) .... E 3	Phoques (bay) .... A 1	South East (cape) ...... C 5	
Lofty (range) .... B 3	Picton (mt.) .... C 5	South West (cape) ...... B 5	

⊙ Population of district.
‡ Population of met. area.

Topography

0   30   60
MILES

Below Sea Level | 100 m. 328 ft. | 200 m. 656 ft. | 500 m. 1,640 ft. | 1,000 m. 3,281 ft. | 2,000 m. 6,562 ft. | 5,000 m. 16,404 ft.

CITIES and TOWNS

Adventure Bay, ...D 5	Rosebery, 1,774 ....B 3
Avoca, ...D 3	Ross, ⊙617 ....D 4
Bagdad, ...D 4	Saint Leonards, ⊙13,660..D 3
Barrington, ...C 3	Scottsdale, 1,698 ....D 3
Beaconsfield, 1,028 ....C 3	Smithton, 2,698 ....A 2
Bell Bay, ...C 3	Somerset, 2,236 ....B 3
Bicheno, ...E 3	Sorell, 1,652 ....D 4
Boat Harbour, ...B 2	Strahan, ⊙470 ....B 4
Bothwell, ⊙1,008 ....C 4	Temma, ...A 3
Bracknell, ...C 3	Ulverstone, 6,842 ....C 3
Branxholm, ...D 3	Waratah, ⊙698 ....B 3
Bridgewater, ...D 4	Westbury, ⊙4,964 ....C 3
Bridport, ...D 3	Wynyard, 3,355 ....B 3
Brighton, 1,150 ....D 4	Zeehan, 1,017 ....B 3
Burnie, 15,806 ....B 3	
Bushy Park, ...C 4	
Cambridge, ...D 4	OTHER FEATURES
Campbell Town, ⊙1,753 ...D 3	
Chudleigh, ...C 3	Anderson (bay) ....D 2
Colebrook, ...D 4	Anne (mt.) ....C 4
Conara Junction, ...D 3	Anser Group (isls.) ....C 1
Cornwall, ...E 3	Arthur (lake) ....D 4
Cranbrook, ...D 4	Arthur (range) ....C 5
Cressy, ...C 3	Arthur (riv.) ....B 3
Currie, ...A 1	Babel (isls.) ....E 1
Cygnet, ...C 5	Banks (str.) ....D 2
Deloraine, 1,793 ....C 3	Barn Bluff (mt.) ....B 3
Derby, ...D 3	Barren (cape) ....E 2
Derwent Bridge, ...C 4	Bass (str.) ....C 1
Devonport, 14,874 ....C 3	Bathurst (harb.) ....C 5
Dover, ...C 5	Cape Barren (isl.) ....E 2
Dunalley, ...D 4	Chappell (isls.) ....D 2
Egg Lagoon, ...A 1	Circular (head) ....B 2
Ellendale, ...C 4	Clarke (isl.) ....E 2
Elliott, ...B 3	Clyde (riv.) ....D 4
Emita, ...D 2	Cox (bight) ....C 5
Evandale, ⊙1,554 ....D 3	Cradle (mt.) ....B 3
Fingal, ⊙3,791 ....E 3	Crescent (lake) ....D 4
Flowerdale, ...B 2	Curtis Group (isls.) ....C 1
Forest, ...B 2	D'Aguilar (range) ....B 4
Forth, ...C 3	Davey (riv.) ....B 4
Franklin, ...C 5	Deal (isl.) ....D 1
George Town, 4,086 ....C 3	Dee (riv.) ....C 4
Glenorchy, 37,770 ....D 4	Denison (range) ....C 4
Gormanston, ⊙540 ....B 4	D'Entrecasteaux (chan.) ...D 5
Hamilton, ⊙4,202 ....C 4	Derwent (riv.) ....C 4
Hobart (cap.), 53,257 ....D 4	Donaldson (riv.) ....B 3
Hobart, ‡119,469.............D 4	East Sister (isl.) ....E 1
Latrobe, 2,241 ....C 3	Echo (lake) ....C 4
Lauderdale, 916 ....D 4	Eddystone (pt.) ....E 2
Launceston, 37,217 ....C 3	Elliott (bay) ....B 5
Launceston, ‡60,456 ....C 3	Fires (bay) ....E 3
Lilydale, ⊙7,841 ....C 3	Florence (riv.) ....C 4
Longford, 1,688 ....C 3	Forestier (cape) ....E 4
New Norfolk, 5,707 ....C 4	Forestier (pen.) ....E 4
Nugent, ⊙540 ....D 4	Forth (riv.) ....C 3
Penguin, 2,149 ....C 3	Frankland (cape) ....D 1
Perth, 1,002 ....D 3	Frankland (range) ....B 4
Queenstown, 4,295 ....B 4	Franklin (riv.) ....B 4
Richmond, ⊙1,658 ....D 4	Frenchmans Cap (mt.) ....B 4
Ringarooma, ⊙2,866 ....D 3	Freycinet (pen.) ....E 4
	Furneaux Group (isls.),
	1,234 ....E 1

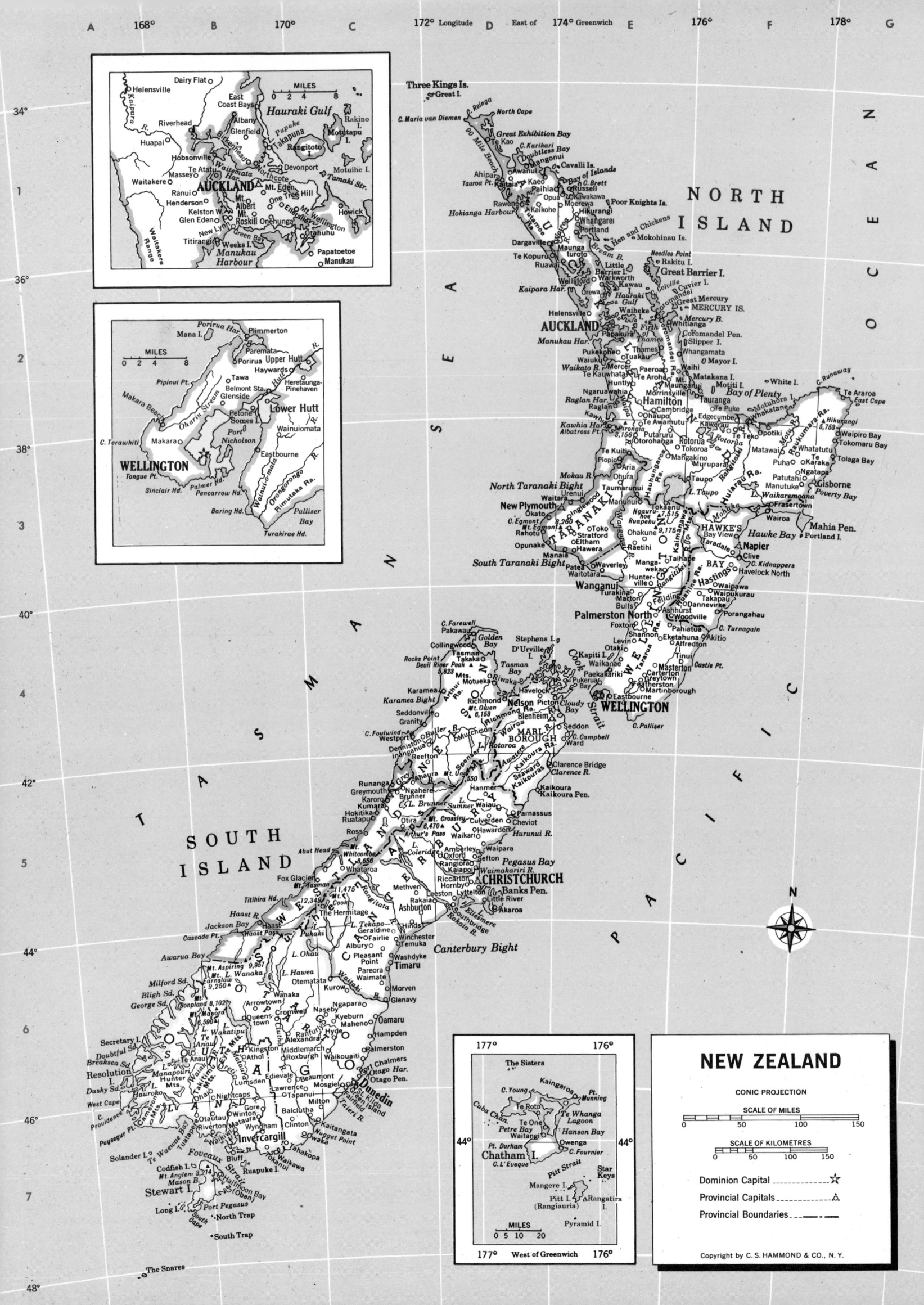

Topography

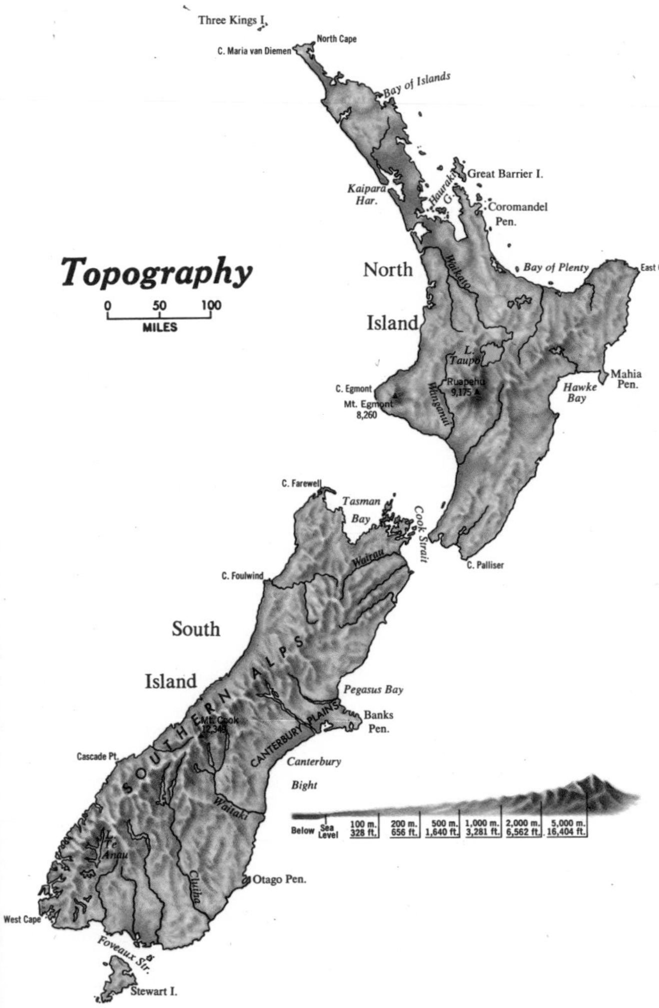

Three Kings I.
North Cape
C. Maria van Diemen
Bay of Islands
Great Barrier I.
Kaipara Har.
Hauraki G.
Coromandel Pen.
North Island
Bay of Plenty
East Cape
Waikato
L. Taupo
Ruapehu 9,175
C. Egmont
Mt. Egmont 8,260
Mahia Pen.
Hawke Bay
C. Farewell
Tasman Bay
Cook Strait
C. Palliser
C. Foulwind
Wairau
South Island
Pegasus Bay
Banks Pen.
Mt. Cook 12,349
Canterbury Bight
Cascade Pt.
SOUTHERN ALPS
CANTERBURY PLAINS
Waitaki
Clutha
Otago Pen.
West Cape
Foveaux Str.
Stewart I.
0 50 100
MILES
Below Sea Level
100 m. 328 ft.
200 m. 656 ft.
500 m. 1,640 ft.
1,000 m. 3,281 ft.
2,000 m. 6,562 ft.
5,000 m. 16,404 ft.

AREA 103,736 sq. mi.
POPULATION 3,121,904
CAPITAL Wellington
LARGEST CITY Auckland
HIGHEST POINT Mt. Cook 12,349 ft.
MONETARY UNIT New Zealand dollar
MAJOR LANGUAGES English, Maori
MAJOR RELIGION Protestantism

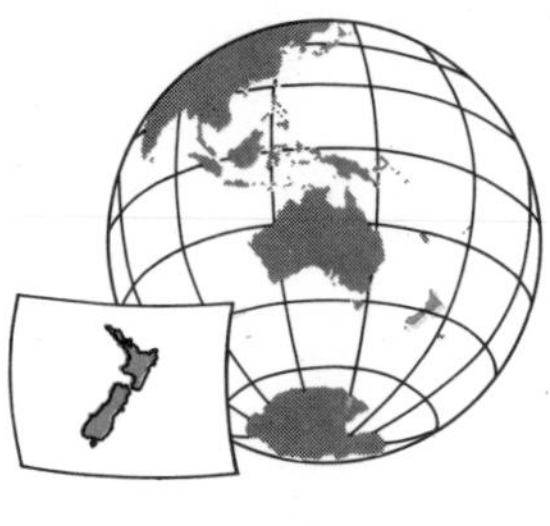

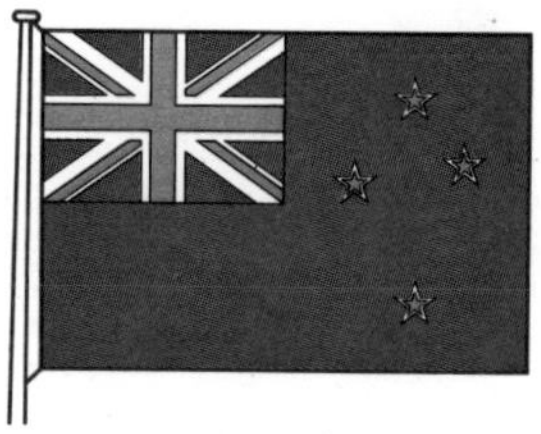

DISTRICTS

Auckland (prov. dist.), 1,189,811 ... E 2
Canterbury (prov. dist.), 385,981 ... C 5
Hawke's Bay (prov. dist.), 128,300 ... F 3
Marlborough (prov. dist.), 30,200 ... D 4
Nelson (prov. dist.), 68,300 ... D 4
Otago (prov. dist.), 290,100 ... A 6
Otago (land dist.), 183,200 ... B 6
Southland (land dist.), 106,900 ... A 6
Taranaki (prov. dist.), 101,200 ... E 3
Wellington (prov. dist.), 537,100 ... E 4
Westland (prov. dist.), 24,100 ... C 5

CITIES and TOWNS

Alexandra, 3,160 ... B 6
Ashburton, 12,950 ... C 5
Ashhurst, 922 ... E 4
Auckland, 152,200 ... B 1
Auckland, †588,400 ... B 1
Balclutha, 4,570 ... B 7
Bay View, 945 ... F 3
Belmont Hill, 1,119 ... B 2
Birkenhead, 12,800 ... B 1
Blenheim, 13,950 ... D 4
Bluff, 3,300 ... B 7
Bulls, 1,803 ... E 4
Cambridge, 6,060 ... E 2
Carterton, 3,640 ... E 4
Christchurch, 165,000 ... D 5
Christchurch, †256,300 ... D 5
Clive, 1,017 ... F 3
Cromwell, 1,062 ... B 6
Dannevirke, 5,780 ... F 4
Dargaville, 3,910 ... D 1
Devonport, 11,100 ... C 1
Dunedin, 77,800 ... C 6
Dunedin, †109,800 ... C 6
Eastbourne, 4,610 ... B 3
East Coast Bays, 13,150 ... B 1
Edgecumbe, 1,277 ... F 2
Ellerslie, 4,260 ... B 1
Eltham, 2,319 ... E 3
Fairfield, 1,106 ... C 6
Featherston, 1,857 ... E 4
Feilding, 9,360 ... E 4
Foxton, 2,830 ... E 4
Geraldine, 1,876 ... C 6
Gisborne, 25,600 ... G 3
Gisborne, †28,500 ... G 3
Glen Eden, 6,230 ... B 1
Glenfield, 16,450 ... B 1
Gore, 8,380 ... B 7
Green Bay, 2,022 ... B 1
Green Island, 5,990 ... C 7
Greymouth, 8,590 ... C 5
Greytown, 1,715 ... E 4
Hamilton, 67,700 ... E 2
Hamilton, †68,000 ... E 2
Hastings, 28,100 ... F 3
Hastings, †39,200 ... F 3
Havelock North, 5,950 ... F 3
Hawera, 8,210 ... E 3
Helensville, 1,305 ... B 1
Henderson, 5,780 ... B 1
Heretaunga-Pinehaven, 4,990 ... C 2
Hikurangi, 1,091 ... E 1
Hobsonville, 1,612 ... B 1
Hokitika, 3,310 ... C 5
Hornby, 6,780 ... D 5
Howick, 9,890 ... C 1
Huntly, 5,420 ... E 2
Hutt, †118,400 ... B, C 2
Inglewood, 2,003 ... E 3
Invercargill, 45,300 ... B 7
Invercargill, †47,800 ... B 7
Kaiapoi, 3,610 ... D 5
Kaikohe, 3,120 ... D 1
Kaikoura, 1,571 ... D 5
Kaitaia, 3,110 ... D 1
Kaitangata, 1,208 ... C 7
Kawakawa, 1,032 ... E 1
Kawerau, 6,010 ... F 3
Kelston West, 5,490 ... B 1
Levin, 11,950 ... E 4
Lower Hutt, 58,700 ... C 2
Lyttelton, 3,510 ... D 5
Mangakino, 1,466 ... E 3
Manukau, 84,700 ... C 1
Martinborough, 1,462 ... E 4
Marton, 4,780 ... E 4
Massey ... B 1
Masterton, 17,950 ... E 4
Mataura, 2,720 ... B 7
Milton, 1,861 ... C 7
Moerewa, 1,090 ... E 1
Morrinsville, 4,530 ... E 2
Mosgiel, 8,100 ... C 6
Motueka, 3,840 ... D 4
Mount Albert, 25,700 ... B 1
Mount Eden, 18,400 ... B 1
Mount Maunganui, 7,210 ... F 2
Mount Roskill, 34,400 ... B 1
Mount Wellington, 19,650 ... C 1
Murupara, 2,670 ... F 3
Napier, 36,700 ... F 3
Napier, †39,900 ... F 3
Nelson, 27,900 ... D 4
Nelson, †28,400 ... D 4
New Lynn, 10,150 ... B 1
New Plymouth, 32,300 ... D 3
New Plymouth, †35,800 ... D 3
Ngaruawahia, 3,790 ... E 2
Northcote, 8,640 ... B 1
Oamaru, 13,350 ... C 6
Ohai, 939 ... A 6
Ohakune, 1,458 ... E 3
One Tree Hill, 12,900 ... B 1
Onehunga, 16,050 ... B 1
Opotiki, 2,560 ... F 3
Opua, 151 ... D 1
Orewa, 1,357 ... E 2
Otahuhu, 10,000 ... C 1
Otaki, 3,660 ... E 4
Otematata, 3,890 ... B 6
Otorohanga, 1,951 ... E 3
Paekakariki, 1,934 ... E 4
Pahiatua, 2,590 ... E 4
Palmerston North, 49,200 ... E 4
Palmerston North, †50,900 ... E 4
Papakura, 12,950 ... E 2
Papatoetoe, 21,400 ... C 1
Patea, 2,013 ... E 3
Petone, 10,200 ... B 2
Picton, 2,610 ... D 4
Pinehaven (Heretaunga-Pinehaven), 4,990 ... C 2
Plimmerton-Paremata, 3,910 ... B 2
Porirua, 24,900 ... B 2
Port Chalmers, 3,040 ... C 6
Pukekohe, 6,800 ... E 2
Pukerua Bay, 1,220 ... E 4
Putaruru, 4,500 ... E 3
Queenstown, 1,634 ... B 6
Raetihi, 1,376 ... E 3
Raglan, 1,019 ... E 2
Ranfurly, 946 ... B 6
Rangiora, 4,270 ... D 5
Ranui, 1,897 ... B 1
Reefton, 1,730 ... C 5
Riccarton, 7,220 ... D 5
Richmond, 4,870 ... D 4
Riverton, 1,258 ... A 7
Riwaka, 993 ... D 4
Rotorua, 27,600 ... F 3
Rotorua, †35,300 ... F 3
Runanga, 1,683 ... C 5
Saint Kilda, 6,720 ... C 7
Shannon, 1,544 ... E 4
Stratford, 5,470 ... E 3
Taihape, 2,880 ... E 3
Takapuna, 23,800 ... B 1
Taradale ... F 3
Taumarunui, 6,080 ... E 3
Taupo, 8,530 ... F 3
Tauranga, 25,500 ... F 2
Tauranga, †33,500 ... F 2
Tawa, 10,200 ... B 2
Te Anau, 951 ... A 6
Te Aroha, 3,220 ... E 2
Te Atatu ... B 1
Te Awamutu, 6,780 ... E 3
Te Karaka, 637 ... F 3
Te Kuiti, 4,830 ... E 3
Temuka, 3,190 ... C 6
Te Puke, 3,090 ... F 2
Thames, 5,680 ... E 2
The Hermitage, 306 ... C 5
Timaru, 27,800 ... C 6
Timaru, †28,400 ... C 6
Titirangi, 5,740 ... B 1
Tokoroa, 12,450 ... F 3
Tuakau, 1,677 ... E 2
Tuatapere, 954 ... A 7
Upper Hutt, 19,750 ... B 2
Waihi, 3,170 ... F 2
Waikanae, 1,570 ... E 4
Waimate, 3,300 ... C 6
Wainuiomata, 15,000 ... B 3
Waipawa, 1,848 ... F 3
Waipukurau, 3,670 ... F 4
Wairoa, 5,190 ... F 3
Waitangi, 179 ... D 7
Waitara, 4,870 ... E 3
Waiuku, 1,759 ... E 2
Wanganui, 36,400 ... E 3
Wanganui, †38,500 ... E 3
Warkworth, 1,200 ... E 2
Waverley, 1,062 ... E 3
Wellington (capital), 134,400 ... A 3
Wellington, †175,500 ... A 3
Wellsford, 1,431 ... E 2
Westport, 5,230 ... C 4
Whakatane, 9,080 ... F 2
Whangarei, 29,600 ... E 1
Whangarei, †31,600 ... E 1
Winton, 1,740 ... B 7
Woodville, 1,529 ... F 4

OTHER FEATURES

Abut (head) ... B 5
Arthur (range) ... D 4
Arthur's (pass) ... C 5
Aspiring (mt.) ... B 6
Awarua (bay) ... A 6
Banks (pen.) ... D 5
Bligh (sound) ... A 6
Breaksea (sound) ... A 6
Bream (bay) ... E 1
Brett (cape) ... E 1
Brunner (lake) ... C 5
Buller (river) ... D 4
Cameron (mts.) ... A 7
Campbell (cape) ... E 4
Canterbury (bight) ... D 6
Cascade (point) ... A 6
Castle (point) ... F 4
Chatham (isl.), 467 ... D 7
Chatham (isls.), 520 ... D 7
Christina (mt.) ... B 6
Clarence (river) ... E 5
Cloudy (bay) ... E 4
Clutha (river) ... B 6
Codfish (isl.) ... A 7
Coleridge (lake) ... C 5
Colville (cape) ... E 2
Cook (mt.) ... C 5
Cook (strait) ... E 4
Coromandel (pen.) ... E 2
Coromandel (range) ... E 2
Crossley (mt.) ... C 5
Cuvier (isl.), 12 ... E 2
D'Urville (isl.), 91 ... D 4
Devil River (peak) ... D 4
Durham (pt.) ... D 7
Dusky (sound) ... A 6
Earnslaw (mt.) ... B 6
East (cape) ... G 2
Egmont (mt.) ... D 3
Ellesmere (lake) ... D 6
Eyre (mts.) ... B 6
Farewell (cape) ... D 4
Foulwind (cape) ... C 4
Foveaux (strait) ... A 7
George (sound) ... A 6
Golden (bay) ... D 4
Great Barrier (isl.), 272 ... F 2
Great Mercury (isl.), 7 ... E 2
Grey (river) ... C 5
Hauhangaroa (range) ... E 3
Hauraki (gulf) ... E 2
Hawea (lake) ... B 6
Hawke's (bay) ... F 3
Hen and Chickens (isls.) ... E 1
Hikurangi (mt.) ... G 2
Hokianga (harb.) ... D 1
Hunter (mts.) ... A 6
Hurunui (river) ... D 5
Hutt (river) ... C 2
Islands, Bay of (bay) ... E 1
Jackson (bay) ... B 5
Kaikoura (pen.) ... D 5
Kaikoura (range) ... D 4
Kaimanawa (mts.) ... E 3
Kaipara (harb.) ... D 2
Kapiti (isl.), 2 ... E 4
Karamea (bight) ... C 4
Karikari (cape) ... D 1
Kawau (isl.), 103 ... E 2
Kawhia (harb.) ... E 3
Kidnappers (cape) ... F 3
Little Barrier (isl.), 4 ... E 2
Mahia (pen.) ... G 3
Mana (isl.), 5 ... B 2
Manapouri (lake) ... A 6
Manukau (harb.) ... D 2
Maria van Diemen (cape) ... D 1
Mason (bay) ... A 7
Matakana (isl.), 396 ... F 2
Mataura (river) ... B 6
Mayor (isl.), 47 ... F 2
Mercury (bay) ... F 2
Mercury (isls.), 7 ... F 2
Milford (sound) ... A 6
Mokau (river) ... E 3
Mokohinau (isls.), 7 ... E 1
Motiti (isl.), 7 ... F 2
Motuhora (isl.) ... F 2
Motuihe (isl.), 6 ... C 1
Motutapu (isl.), 27 ... C 1
Munning (point) ... E 7
Needles (point) ... E 2
Ninety-Mile (beach) ... D 1
North (isl.), 1,956,411 ... F 1
North Taranaki (bight) ... D 3
Nugget (point) ... C 7
Ohariu (stream) ... B 2
Otago (pen.), ... C 6
Owen (mt.) ... D 4
Palliser (bay) ... C 3
Palliser (cape) ... E 4
Pegasus (bay) ... D 5
Pitt (isl.), 53 ... E 7
Plenty (bay) ... F 2
Poor Knights (isls.) ... E 1
Port Nicholson (inlet) ... B 3
Port Pegasus (inlet) ... B 7
Portland (isl.), 14 ... G 3
Poverty (bay) ... G 3
Pukaki (lake) ... B 6
Pupuke (lake) ... B 1
Puysegur (point) ... A 7
Pyramid (isl.) ... E 7
Rakino (isl.), 5 ... C 1
Rakitu (isl.), 2 ... E 2
Rangatira (isl.) ... E 7
Rangiauria (Pitt) (isl.), 53 ... E 7
Rangitoto (isl.), 48 ... C 1
Raukumara (range) ... F 3
Reinga (cape) ... D 1
Resolution (isl.) ... A 6
Richmond (range) ... D 4
Rimutaka (range) ... B 3
Rocks (point) ... C 4
Rotorua (lake) ... E 3
Ruahine (range) ... E 4
Ruapehu (mt.) ... E 3
Ruapuke (isl.) ... B 7
Runaway (cape) ... G 2
Secretary (isl.) ... A 6
Slipper (isl.), 4 ... E 2
Somes (isl.), 2 ... B 2
South (isl.), 798,681 ... B 5
South Taranaki (bight) ... D 3
Southern Alps (range) ... C 5
Spenser (mts.) ... D 5
Stephens (isl.), 9 ... D 4
Stewart (isl.), 332 ... A 7
Sumner (lake) ... D 5
Taieri (river) ... C 7
Tasman (bay) ... D 4
Tasman (mt.) ... C 5
Tasman (sea) ... B 3
Taupo (lake) ... E 3
Tauroa (point) ... D 1
Te Anau (lake) ... A 6
Tekapo (lake) ... C 5
Three Kings (isls.) ... C 1
Titihiri (head) ... B 5
Tongue (point) ... A 3
Turnagain (cape) ... F 4
Tutumoe (range) ... D 1
Una (mt.) ... D 5
Waiau (river) ... A 6
Waiheke (isl.), 2,013 ... E 2
Waikato (river) ... E 2
Waimakariri (river) ... D 5
Wairau (river) ... D 4
Wairoa (river) ... E 1
Waitaki (river) ... C 6
Wakatipu (lake) ... B 6
Wanaka (lake) ... B 6
Wanganui (river) ... E 3
West (cape) ... A 6
Whitcombe (mt.) ... C 5
White (isl.) ... F 2

†Population of urban area.

Agriculture, Industry and Resources

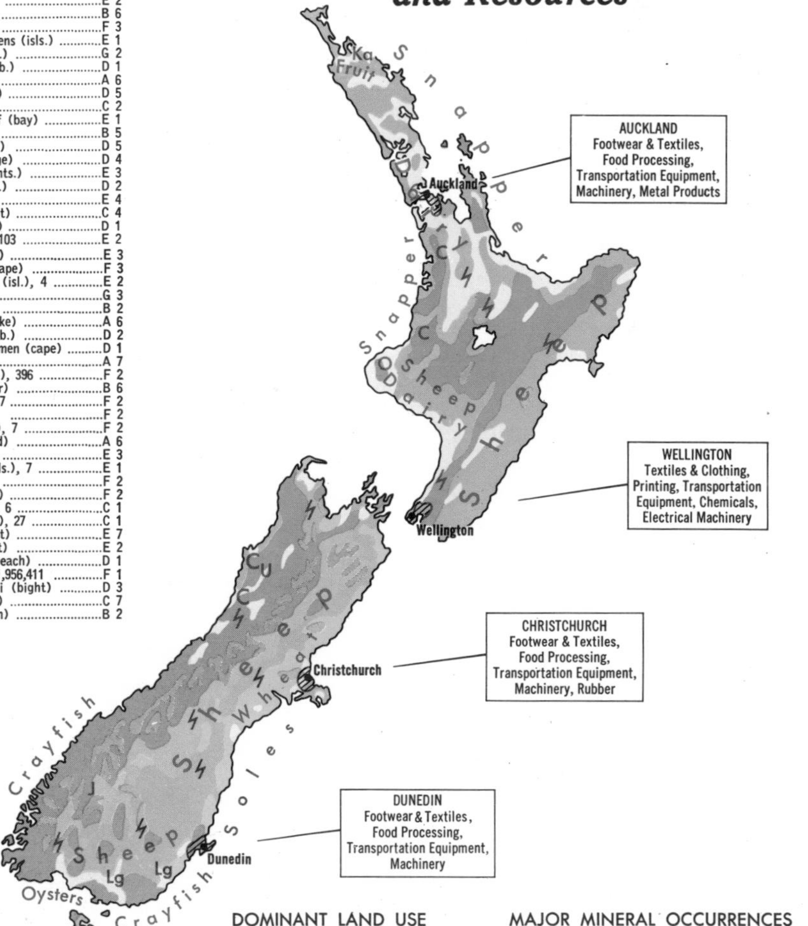

Ka
Fruit
Snapper
Auckland
AUCKLAND
Footwear & Textiles, Food Processing, Transportation Equipment, Machinery, Metal Products
Sheep
Dairy
WELLINGTON
Textiles & Clothing, Printing, Transportation Equipment, Chemicals, Electrical Machinery
Wellington
CHRISTCHURCH
Footwear & Textiles, Food Processing, Transportation Equipment, Machinery, Rubber
Christchurch
Wheat
Crayfish
Soles
DUNEDIN
Footwear & Textiles, Food Processing, Transportation Equipment, Machinery
Dunedin
Lg
Oysters

DOMINANT LAND USE

- Mixed Farming, Livestock
- Dairy
- Truck Farming, Horticulture
- Pasture Livestock (chiefly sheep)
- Livestock Herding
- Forests
- Nonagricultural Land

MAJOR MINERAL OCCURRENCES

- C Coal
- Lg Lignite
- J Jade
- O Petroleum
- Ka Kaolin
- U Uranium
- Water Power
- Major Industrial Areas

AFRICA
1939

British
French
Italian
Portuguese
Spanish
Belgian
Mandates

AFRICA
LAMBERT AZIMUTHAL EQUAL-AREA PROJECTION
SCALE OF MILES
0   100   200   400   600   800
SCALE OF KILOMETRES
0   200   400   600   800

Capitals .... ★ ◉   International Boundaries ....
Canals .... ═══   Mountain Peaks .... ▲

Copyright by C. S. Hammond & Co., N.Y.

CAPE VERDE
MILES
0   20   40   60

POPULATION DISTRIBUTION

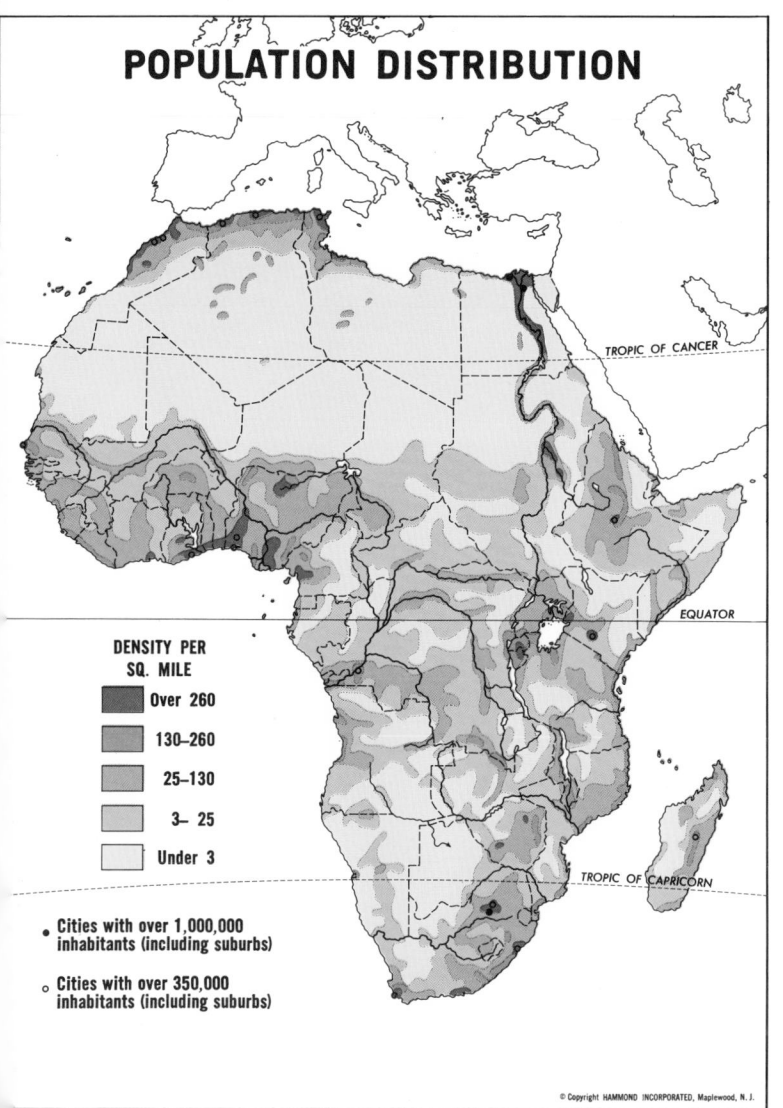

AREA 11,707,000 sq. mi.
POPULATION 431,900,000
LARGEST CITY Cairo
HIGHEST POINT Kilimanjaro 19,340 ft.
LOWEST POINT Qattara Depression -436 ft.

DENSITY PER SQ. MILE

- Over 260
- 130–260
- 25–130
- 3– 25
- Under 3

● Cities with over 1,000,000
  inhabitants (including suburbs)

○ Cities with over 350,000
  inhabitants (including suburbs)

© Copyright HAMMOND INCORPORATED, Maplewood, N. J.

VEGETATION

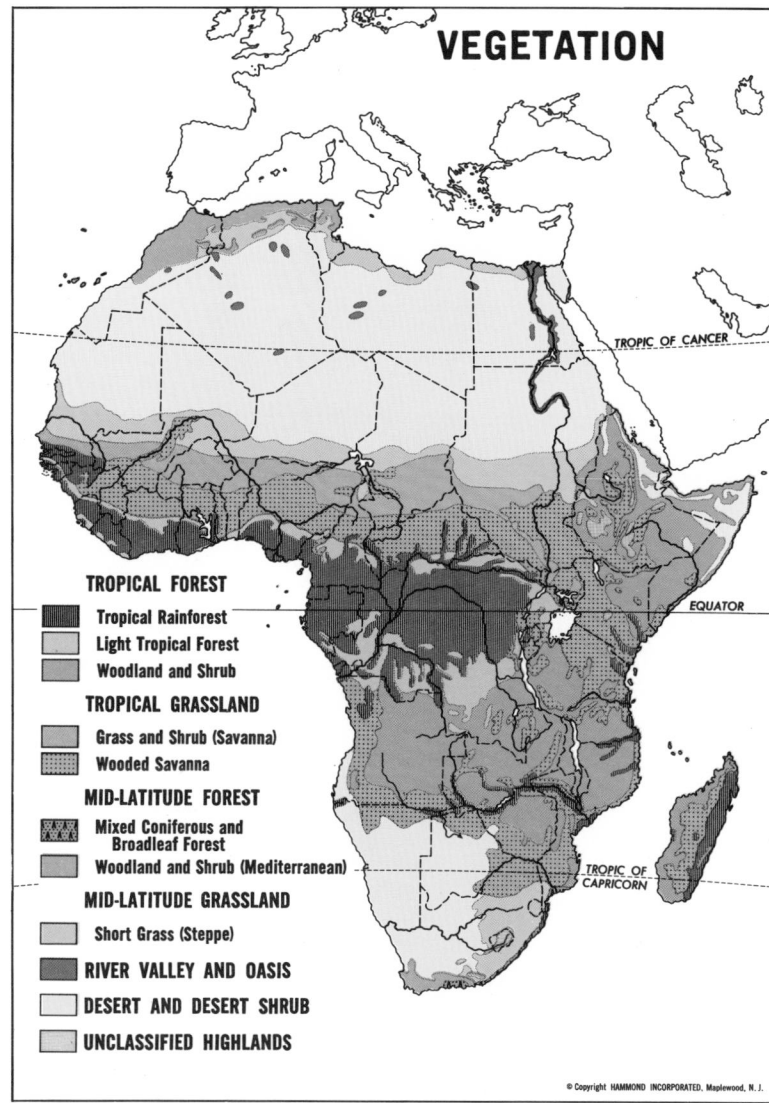

TROPICAL FOREST

- Tropical Rainforest
- Light Tropical Forest
- Woodland and Shrub

TROPICAL GRASSLAND

- Grass and Shrub (Savanna)
- Wooded Savanna

MID-LATITUDE FOREST

- Mixed Coniferous and Broadleaf Forest
- Woodland and Shrub (Mediterranean)

MID-LATITUDE GRASSLAND

- Short Grass (Steppe)

RIVER VALLEY AND OASIS

DESERT AND DESERT SHRUB

UNCLASSIFIED HIGHLANDS

© Copyright HAMMOND INCORPORATED, Maplewood, N. J.

cher, Chad .....E 3
okuta, Nigeria .....C 4
djan (cap.), Ivory Coast .....B 4
ra (cap.), Ghana .....B 4
is Ababa (cap.), Ethiopia .....F 4
n .....G 3
ra, Ethiopia .....G 3
dès, Niger .....C 3
Ihas (cape), S. Africa .....D 8
ggar (mts.), Algeria .....F 2
ert (lake) .....F 4
bra (isls.), Seychelles .....G 5
andria, Egypt .....C 1
eria .....C 1
ers (cap.), Algeria .....D 6
aulo, Angola .....D 6
ola .....C 1
aba, Algeria .....C 1
obón (Pagalu) (isl.), Equat.
  Guinea, 1,408 .....C 5
ananarivo (cap.),
  Madagascar .....G 6
sirabe, Madagascar .....G 6
sha, Tanzania .....F 5
nsion (isl.), St. Helena,
  146 .....A 5
ara, Ethiopia .....F 4
ân, Egypt .....F 2
ra, Sudan .....F 3
s (mts.) .....B 1
a, Libya .....E 2
l, Senegal .....A 3
ako (capital), Mali .....B 3
gui (cap.), Central African
  Empire .....D 4
ul (cap.), Gambia .....A 3
, Equat. Guinea .....D 4
ar, Algeria .....B 1
, Mozambique .....F 6
hazi, Libya .....D 1
uela, Angola .....D 6
n .....E 4
n City, Nigeria .....C 4
Suef, Egypt .....F 2
er, Sudan .....F 3
a, Niger .....D 3
ra, Algeria .....C 1
au (capital), Guinea-
  ssau .....A 3
rte, Tunisia .....C 1
c (cape), Mauritania .....A 2
kyre, Malawi .....F 6
mfontein (cap.), O.F.S.,
  Africa .....E 7
Nile (riv.) .....F 3
-Dioulasso, Upper Volta .....B 4
a, Zaire .....D 5
(cape), Tunisia .....D 1
(Annaba), Algeria .....C 1
uthatswana (aut. rep.),
  uth Africa .....E 7
wana .....E 7
ké, Ivory Coast .....B 4
zaville (cap.), Congo .....D 5
n Hill, Zambia .....E 6
anan, Liberia .....A 4

Bujumbura (capital),
  Burundi .....F 5
Bukavu, Zaire .....E 5
Bulawayo, Rhodesia .....E 7
Burundi .....F 5
Cabinda, Angola .....D 5
Cairo (capital), Egypt .....E 2
Calvinia, S. Africa .....D 8
Cameroon .....D 4
Canary (isls.), Spain .....A 2
Cape Coast, Ghana .....B 4
Cape of Good Hope (prov.),
  South Africa .....E 8
Cape Town (capital),
  South Africa .....D 8
Cape Verde .....G 8
Casablanca, Morocco .....B 1
Central African Empire .....D 4
Ceuta, Spain .....B 1
Chad .....D 3
Chad (lake) .....D 3
Chinguetti, Mauritania .....A 2
Comoro Islands .....G 6
Conakry (cap.), Guinea .....A 4
Congo .....D 5
Congo (riv.) .....B 4
Constantine, Algeria .....C 1
Cotonou, Benin .....C 4
Cradock, S. Africa .....E 8
Cyrenaica (reg.), Libya .....E 2
Dakar (cap.), Senegal .....A 3
Dakhla, Mauritania .....A 2
Damietta, Egypt .....F 1
Dar es Salaam (capital),
  Tanzania .....F 5
Diégo-Suarez, Madagascar .....G 6
Dire Dawa, Ethiopia .....G 4
Djibouti .....G 3
Djibouti (cap.), Djibouti .....G 3
Douala, Cameroon .....C 4
Durban, S. Africa .....E 8
East London, S. Africa .....E 8
Ebolowa, Cameroon .....D 4
Edward (lake) .....E 5
Egypt .....E 2
El Faiyûm, Egypt .....E 2
El Fasher, Sudan .....E 3
El Jadida, Morocco .....B 1
El Minya, Egypt .....E 2
El Obeid, Sudan .....E 3
Elgon (mt.) .....F 4
Entebbe, Uganda .....F 4
Enugu, Nigeria .....C 4
Equatorial Guinea .....D 4
Eritrea (reg.), Ethiopia .....F 3
Essaouira, Morocco .....B 1
Ethiopia .....F 4
Etosha Pan (salt dep.),
  S.W. Africa .....D 6
Fez, Morocco .....B 1
Fezzan (reg.), Libya .....D 2
Fianarantsoa, Madagascar .....G 7
Fifth Cataract, Sudan .....F 3
Fort Hall, Kenya .....F 5
Fourth Cataract, Sudan .....F 3
Freetown (capital),
  Sierra Leone .....A 4

Fria (cape), S.W. Africa .....D 6
Funchal (cap.), Madeira,
  Port. .....A 1
Gaborone (capital),
  Botswana .....E 7
Gabès, Tunisia .....D 1
Gabon .....D 5
Gambia .....A 3
Garoua, Cameroon .....D 4
Germiston, S. Africa .....E 7
Ghana .....B 4
Gondar, Ethiopia .....F 3
Good Hope (cape), S. Africa .....D 8
Grahamstown, S. Africa .....E 8
Guardafui (cape), Somalia .....H 3
Guinea .....A 3
Guinea (gulf) .....C 4
Guinea-Bissau .....A 3
Gwelo, Rhodesia .....E 6
Harar, Ethiopia .....G 4
Harghessa, Somalia .....G 4
Huambo, Angola .....D 6
Ibadan, Nigeria .....C 4
Ilorin, Nigeria .....C 4
Impfondo, Congo .....D 4
Ivory Coast .....B 4
Jinja, Uganda .....F 4
Johannesburg, South Africa .....E 7
Kaduna, Nigeria .....C 3
Kalahari (des.) .....D 7
Kambove, Zaire .....E 6
Kampala (capital),
  Uganda .....F 4
Kananga, Zaire .....E 5
Kankan, Guinea .....B 3
Kano, Nigeria .....C 3
Kaolack, Senegal .....A 3
Kariba (lake) .....E 6
Kasaï (riv.) .....D 5
Kasama, Zambia .....F 6
Kassala, Sudan .....F 3
Katanga (reg.), Zaire .....E 5
Kayes, Mali .....A 3
Kénitra, Morocco .....B 1
Kenya .....F 4
Kenya (mt.), Kenya .....F 5
Khartoum (capital),
  Sudan .....F 3
Kigali (cap.), Rwanda .....E 5
Kilimanjaro (mt.), Tanzania .....F 5
Kilwa Kivinje, Tanzania .....G 5
Kimberley, S. Africa .....E 7
Kinshasa (cap.), Zaire .....D 5
Kioga (lake), Uganda .....F 4
Kisangani, Zaire .....E 4
Kismayu, Somalia .....G 5
Kivu (lake) .....E 5
Kumasi, Ghana .....B 4
Laayoune, Morocco .....A 2
Lagos (cap.), Nigeria .....C 4
Las Palmas (cap.), Canary Is.,
  Spain .....A 2
Lesotho .....E 7
Liberia .....A 4
Libreville (cap.), Gabon .....C 4
Libya .....D 2
Libyan (des.) .....E 2

Likasi, Zaire .....E 6
Lilongwe (cap.), Malawi .....F 6
Limpopo (riv.) .....E 7
Livingstone, Zambia .....E 6
Lobito, Angola .....D 6
Lokoja, Nigeria .....C 4
Lomé (cap.), Togo .....C 4
Lourenço Marques (Maputo)
  (cap.), Mozambique .....F 7
Luanda (cap.), Angola .....D 5
Lubumbashi, Zaire .....E 6
Lusaka (cap.), Zambia .....E 6
Macías Nguema Biyogo (isl.),
  Equat. Guin. .....C 4
Madagascar .....G 6
Madeira (isls.), Port. .....A 1
Maiduguri, Nigeria .....D 3
Majunga, Madagascar .....G 6
Malabo (cap.), Equat.
  Guinea .....C 4
Malawi .....F 6
Mali .....B 3
Maputo (cap.), Mozambique .....F 7
Marrakech, Morocco .....A 1
Maseru (cap.), Lesotho .....E 8
Massawa, Ethiopia .....G 3
Matadi, Zaire .....D 5
Maun, Botswana .....E 6
Mauritania .....A 3
Mayotte (isl.) .....G 6
Mazabuka, Zambia .....E 6
Mbabane (cap.), Swaziland .....F 7
Mbandaka, Zaire .....D 4
Meknès, Morocco .....B 1
Melilla, Spain .....B 1
Merowe, Sudan .....F 3
Misurata, Libya .....D 1
Mmabatho (cap.), Bophutha-
  tswana, South Africa .....E 7
Mogadishu (Mogadiscio) (cap.),
  Somalia .....G 4
Mombasa, Kenya .....G 5
Monrovia (cap.), Liberia .....A 4
Morocco .....B 1
Moroni (capital), Comoro
  Islands .....G 6
Mossel Bay, S. Africa .....E 8
Mostaganem, Algeria .....C 1

Mozambique .....F 6
Mozambique (channel) .....G 6
Murzuk, Libya .....D 2
Naivasha, Kenya .....F 5
Nairobi (cap.), Kenya .....F 5
Namibia (South-West Africa) .....D 7
Nasser (lake), Egypt .....F 2
Natal (prov.), S. Africa .....F 7
N'Djamena (cap.), Chad .....D 3
Ndola, Zambia .....E 6
N'Gaoundéré, Cameroon .....D 4
Niamey (cap.), Niger .....C 3
Niger .....C, D 3
Niger (river) .....C 4
Nile (river) .....F 2
Nouakchott (capital),
  Mauritania .....A 3
Nubia (lake), Sudan .....F 2
Nubian (des.), Sudan .....F 2
Nyasa (lake) .....F 6
Obbia, Somalia .....G 4
Omdurman, Sudan .....F 3
Oran, Algeria .....C 1
Orange (river) .....D 7
Orange Free State (prov.),
  South Africa .....E 7
Ouagadougou (cap.),
  Upper Volta .....B 3
Oudtshoorn, S. Africa .....D 8
Oujda, Morocco .....B 1
Oyo, Nigeria .....C 4
Pagalu (isl.), Equat.
  Guinea, 1,408 .....C 5
Palmas (cape) .....B 4
Pemba (isl.), Tanzania .....G 5
Pietermaritzburg (cap.), Natal,
  S. Africa .....E 7
Pietersburg, S. Africa .....E 7
Pointe-Noire, Congo .....D 5
Port Elizabeth, S. Africa .....E 8
Port Francqui, Zaire .....E 5
Port Harcourt, Nigeria .....C 4
Port Said, Egypt .....F 1
Port Sudan, Sudan .....F 3
Porto-Novo (cap.), Benin .....C 4
Praia (cap.), Cape Verde .....G 8

Pretoria (capital),
  South Africa .....E 7
Qena, Egypt .....F 2
Quelimane, Mozambique .....F 6
Rabat (cap.), Morocco .....B 1
Red (sea) .....F 2
Rhodesia .....E 6
Río de Oro (reg.) .....A 2
Río Muni (terr.) .....D 4
  Equat. Guinea .....C 4
Rudolf (lake), Kenya .....F 4
Rufisque, Senegal .....A 3
Rwanda .....E 5
Ruwenzori (range) .....E 4
Sahara (desert) .....C 2
Saint Helena (isl.), 5,000 .....B 6
Saint-Louis, Senegal .....A 3
Salisbury (capital),
  Rhodesia .....F 6
Santa Cruz (cap.), Canary Is.,
  Spain .....A 2
São Tomé e Príncipe .....C 4
Sassandra, Ivory Coast .....B 4
Ségou, Mali .....B 3
Sekondi, Ghana .....B 4
Senegal .....A 3
Serowe, Botswana .....E 7
Sétif, Algeria .....C 1
Sfax, Tunisia .....D 1
Sidi-bel-Abbès, Algeria .....C 1
Sierra Leone .....A 4
Sinai (pen.), Egypt .....F 1
Sinoia, Rhodesia .....E 6
Sixth Cataract, Sudan .....F 3
Skikda, Algeria .....C 1
Sohâg, Egypt .....F 2
Somalia .....G 4
Songea, Tanzania .....F 6
Sousse, Tunisia .....D 1
South Africa .....E 7
South-West Africa .....D 7
Stanley (falls), Zaire .....E 4
Suez, Egypt .....F 1
Suez (canal), Egypt .....F 1
Swakopmund, S.W. Africa .....D 7
Swaziland .....F 7
Takoradi, Ghana .....B 4

Tamale, Ghana .....B 4
Tamatave, Madagascar .....G 6
Tana (lake), Ethiopia .....F 3
Tanga, Tanzania .....F 5
Tanganyika (lake) .....F 5
Tangier, Morocco .....B 1
Tanzania .....F 5
Taouz, Morocco .....B 1
Thiès, Senegal .....A 3
Third Cataract, Sudan .....E 3
Tibesti (mts.) .....D 2
Timbuktu, Mali .....B 3
Tlemcen, Algeria .....B 1
Togo .....C 4
Transkei (aut. rep.),
  South Africa .....E 8
Transvaal (prov.), South Africa .....E 7
Tripoli (cap.), Libya .....D 1
Tripolitania (region), Libya .....D 1
Tuléar, Madagascar .....G 7
Tunis (cap.), Tunisia .....D 1
Tunisia .....C 1
Ubangi (river) .....E 4
Uganda .....F 4
Uitenhage, S. Africa .....E 8
Umtali, Rhodesia .....F 6
Umtata (capital), Transkei,
  South Africa .....E 8
Upper Volta .....B 3
Vaal (riv.), S. Africa .....E 7
Verde (cape), Senegal .....A 3
Victoria (falls) .....E 6
Victoria (lake) .....F 5
Volta (lake), Ghana .....B 4
Volta (river) .....B 4
Wad Medani, Sudan .....F 3
Walvis Bay, S. Africa .....D 7
White Nile (river) .....F 3
Windhoek (cap.), S.-W. Africa .....D 7
Yaoundé (cap.), Cameroon .....D 4
Zaire .....E 4
Zaire (Congo) (riv.) .....E 4
Zambezi (river) .....E 6
Zambia .....E 6
Zanzibar, Tanzania .....G 5
Zanzibar (isl.), Tanzania .....G 5
Zimbabwe (Rhodesia) .....E 6
Zomba, Malawi .....F 6

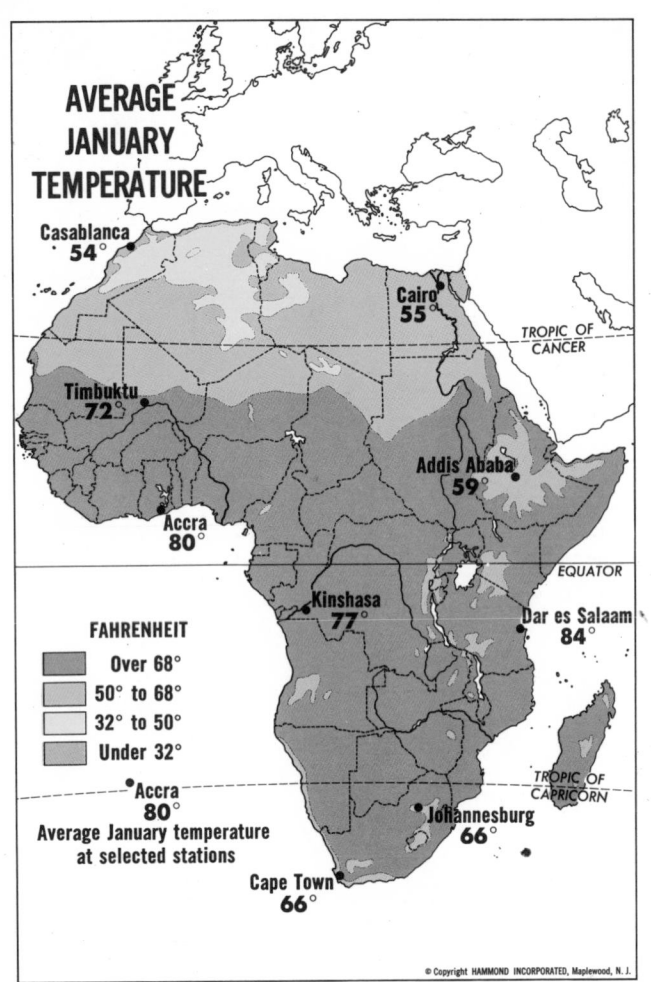

AVERAGE JANUARY TEMPERATURE

Casablanca 54°
Cairo 55°
Timbuktu 72°
Addis Ababa 59°
Accra 80°
Kinshasa 77°
Dar es Salaam 84°

TROPIC OF CANCER
EQUATOR
TROPIC OF CAPRICORN

FAHRENHEIT
- Over 68°
- 50° to 68°
- 32° to 50°
- Under 32°

• Accra 80°
Average January temperature at selected stations

Johannesburg 66°
Cape Town 66°

© Copyright HAMMOND INCORPORATED, Maplewood, N. J.

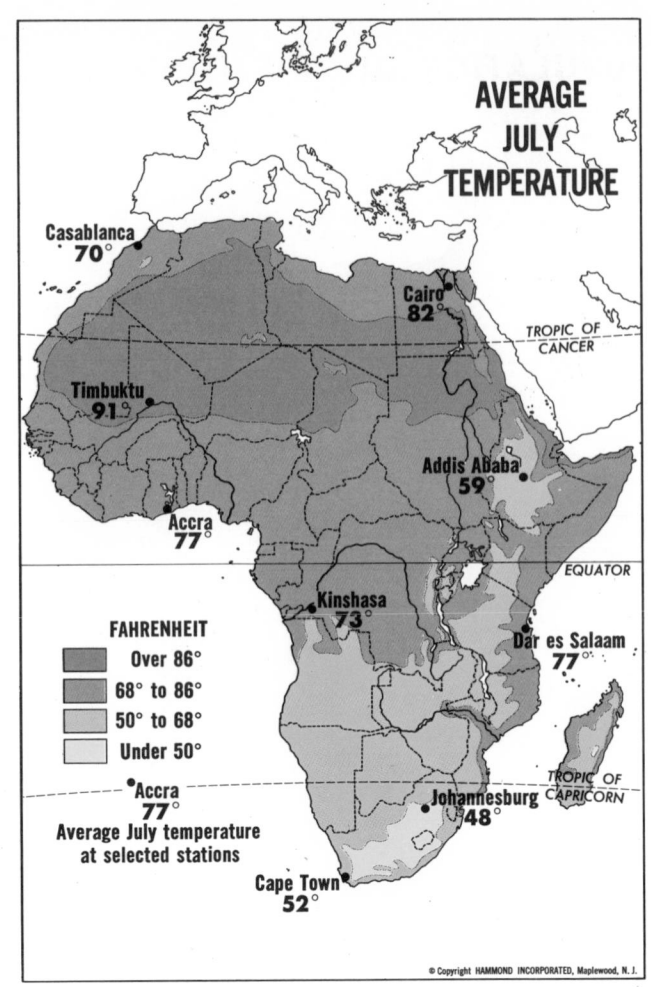

AVERAGE JULY TEMPERATURE

Casablanca 70°
Cairo 82°
Timbuktu 91°
Addis Ababa 59°
Accra 77°
Kinshasa 73°
Dar es Salaam 77°

TROPIC OF CANCER
EQUATOR
TROPIC OF CAPRICORN

FAHRENHEIT
- Over 86°
- 68° to 86°
- 50° to 68°
- Under 50°

• Accra 77°
Average July temperature at selected stations

Johannesburg 48°
Cape Town 52°

© Copyright HAMMOND INCORPORATED, Maplewood, N. J.

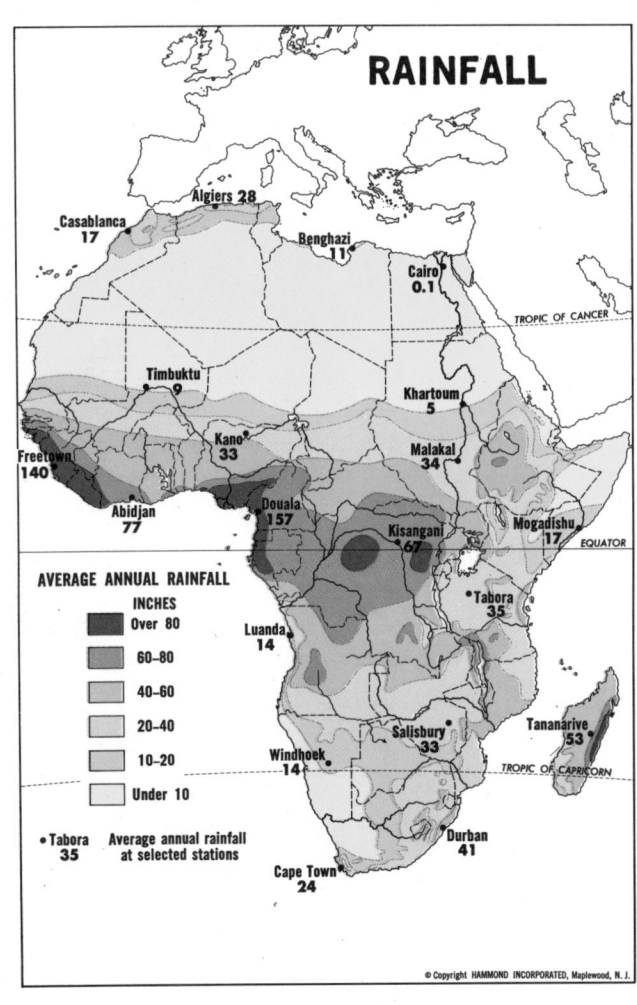

RAINFALL

Algiers 28
Casablanca 17
Benghazi 11
Cairo 0.1
Timbuktu
Khartoum 5
Kano 33
Malakal 34
Freetown 140
Abidjan 77
Douala 157
Kisangani 67
Mogadishu 17
Tabora 35
Luanda 14
Salisbury 33
Tananarive 53
Windhoek 14
Durban 41
Cape Town 24

TROPIC OF CANCER
EQUATOR
TROPIC OF CAPRICORN

AVERAGE ANNUAL RAINFALL
INCHES
- Over 80
- 60–80
- 40–60
- 20–40
- 10–20
- Under 10

• Tabora 35
Average annual rainfall at selected stations

© Copyright HAMMOND INCORPORATED, Maplewood, N. J.

VEGETATION/RELIEF

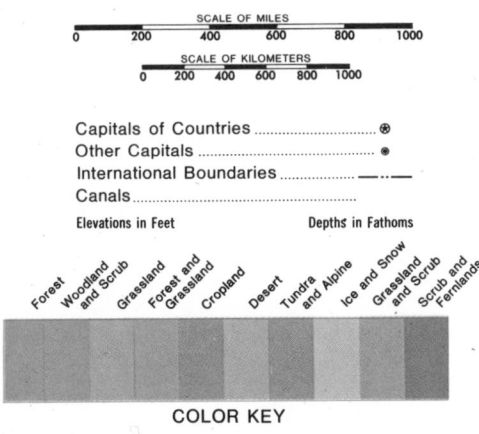

SCALE OF MILES
0   200   400   600   800   1000

SCALE OF KILOMETERS
0   200   400   600   800   1000

Capitals of Countries .... ⊛
Other Capitals .... ⊙
International Boundaries .... —·—·—
Canals ....

Elevations in Feet   Depths in Fathoms

Forest | Woodland and Scrub | Grassland | Forest and Grassland | Cropland | Desert | Tundra and Alpine | Ice and Snow | Grassland and Scrub | Scrub and Fernlands

COLOR KEY

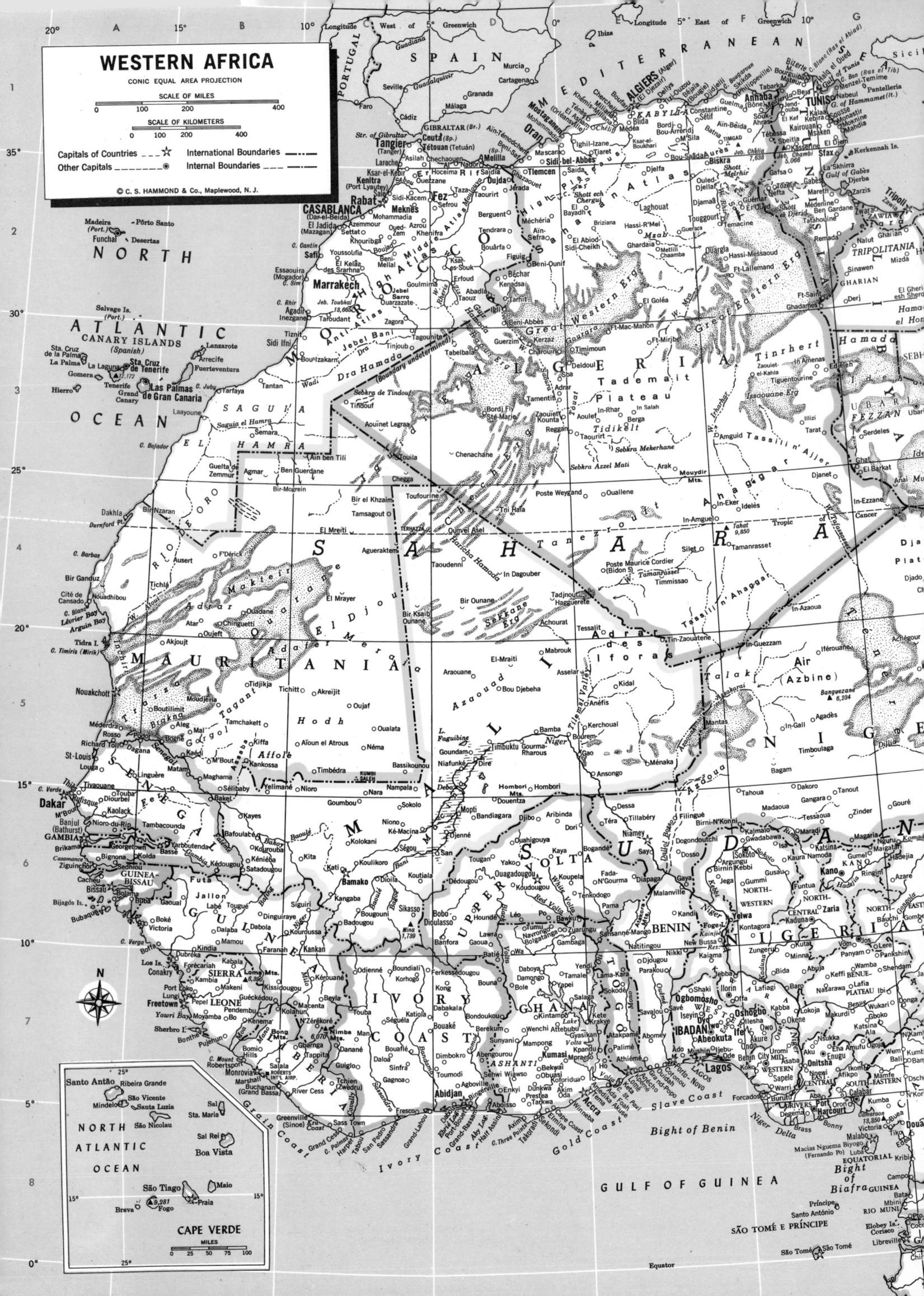

ALGERIA
A 919,591 sq. mi.
ULATION 16,776,000
ITAL Algiers
GEST CITY Algiers
HEST POINT Tahat 9,850 ft.
ETARY UNIT Algerian dinar
OR LANGUAGES Arabic, Berber, French
OR RELIGION Islam

BENIN
AREA 43,483 sq. mi.
POPULATION 3,200,000
CAPITAL Porto-Novo
LARGEST CITY Cotonou
HIGHEST POINT Atakora Mts. 2,083 ft.
MONETARY UNIT CFA franc
MAJOR LANGUAGES Fon, Somba, Yoruba, Bariba, French, Mina, Dendi
MAJOR RELIGIONS Tribal religions, Islam, Roman Catholicism

CAPE VERDE
AREA 1,557 sq. mi.
POPULATION 302,000
CAPITAL Praia
LARGEST CITY Praia
HIGHEST POINT 9,281 ft.
MONETARY UNIT Cape Verde escudo
MAJOR LANGUAGE Portuguese
MAJOR RELIGION Roman Catholicism

GAMBIA
A 4,127 sq. mi.
ULATION 524,000
TAL Bathurst
GEST CITY Bathurst
HEST POINT 100 ft.
ETARY UNIT dalasi
OR LANGUAGES Mandingo, Fulani, Wolof, English, Malinke
OR RELIGIONS Islam, Tribal religions, Christianity

GHANA
AREA 92,099 sq. mi.
POPULATION 9,900,000
CAPITAL Accra
LARGEST CITY Accra
HIGHEST POINT Togo Hills 2,900 ft.
MONETARY UNIT new cedi
MAJOR LANGUAGES Twi, Fante, Dagbani, Ewe, Ga, English, Hausa, Akan
MAJOR RELIGIONS Tribal religions, Christianity, Islam

GUINEA
AREA 94,925 sq. mi.
POPULATION 4,500,000
CAPITAL Conakry
LARGEST CITY Conakry
HIGHEST POINT Nimba Mts. 6,070 ft.
MONETARY UNIT syli
MAJOR LANGUAGES Fulani, Mandingo, Susu, French
MAJOR RELIGIONS Islam, Tribal religions

GUINEA-BISSAU
AREA 13,948 sq. mi.
POPULATION 517,000
CAPITAL Bissau
LARGEST CITY Bissau
HIGHEST POINT 689 ft.
MONETARY UNIT Guinea-Bissau peso
MAJOR LANGUAGES Balante, Fulani, Crioulo, Mandingo, Portuguese
MAJOR RELIGIONS Islam, Tribal religions, Roman Catholicism

IVORY COAST
A 127,520 sq. mi.
ILATION 6,673,013
TAL Abidjan
GEST CITY Abidjan
HEST POINT Nimba Mts. 5,745 ft.
ETARY UNIT CFA franc
OR LANGUAGES Bale, Bete, Senufu, French, Dioula
OR RELIGIONS Tribal religions, Islam

LIBERIA
AREA 43,000 sq. mi.
POPULATION 1,600,000
CAPITAL Monrovia
LARGEST CITY Monrovia
HIGHEST POINT Wutivi 5,584 ft.
MONETARY UNIT Liberian dollar
MAJOR LANGUAGES Kru, Kpelle, Bassa, Vai, English
MAJOR RELIGIONS Christianity, Tribal religions, Islam

MALI
AREA 464,873 sq. mi.
POPULATION 5,800,000
CAPITAL Bamako
LARGEST CITY Bamako
HIGHEST POINT Hombori Mts. 3,789 ft.
MONETARY UNIT Mali franc
MAJOR LANGUAGES Bambara, Senufu, Fulani, Soninke, French
MAJOR RELIGIONS Islam, Tribal religions

MAURITANIA
AREA 452,702 sq. mi.
POPULATION 1,318,000
CAPITAL Nouakchott
LARGEST CITY Nouakchott
HIGHEST POINT 2,972 ft.
MONETARY UNIT ouguiya
MAJOR LANGUAGES Arabic, French, Wolof, Tukolor
MAJOR RELIGION Islam

MOROCCO
AREA 241,224 sq. mi.
POPULATION 18,000,000
CAPITAL Rabat
LARGEST CITY Casablanca
HIGHEST POINT Jeb. Toubkal 13,665 ft.
MONETARY UNIT dirham
MAJOR LANGUAGES Arabic, Berber, French
MAJOR RELIGIONS Islam, Judaism, Christianity

NIGER
AREA 489,189 sq. mi.
POPULATION 4,700,000
CAPITAL Niamey
LARGEST CITY Niamey
HIGHEST POINT Banguezane 6,234 ft.
MONETARY UNIT CFA franc
MAJOR LANGUAGES Hausa, Songhai, Fulani, French, Tamashek, Djerma
MAJOR RELIGIONS Islam, Tribal religions

NIGERIA
AREA 379,628 sq. mi.
POPULATION 83,800,000
CAPITAL Lagos
LARGEST CITY Lagos
HIGHEST POINT Vogel 6,700 ft.
MONETARY UNIT naira
MAJOR LANGUAGES Hausa, Yoruba, Ibo, Ijaw, Fulani, Tiv, Kanuri, Ibibio, English, Edo
MAJOR RELIGIONS Islam, Christianity, Tribal religions

SÃO TOMÉ E PRÍNCIPE
AREA 372 sq. mi.
POPULATION 80,000
CAPITAL São Tomé
LARGEST CITY São Tomé
HIGHEST POINT Pico 6,640 ft.
MONETARY UNIT São Tomean escudo
MAJOR LANGUAGES Bantu languages, Portuguese
MAJOR RELIGIONS Tribal religions, Roman Catholicism

SENEGAL
AREA 75,954 sq. mi.
POPULATION 5,085,388
CAPITAL Dakar
LARGEST CITY Dakar
HIGHEST POINT Futa Jallon 1,640 ft.
MONETARY UNIT CFA franc
MAJOR LANGUAGES Wolof, Peul (Fulani), French, Mende, Mandingo, Dida
MAJOR RELIGIONS Islam, Tribal religions, Roman Catholicism

SIERRA LEONE
AREA 27,925 sq. mi.
POPULATION 3,100,000
CAPITAL Freetown
LARGEST CITY Freetown
HIGHEST POINT Loma Mts. 6,390 ft.
MONETARY UNIT leone
MAJOR LANGUAGES Mende, Temne, Vai, English, Krio (pidgin)
MAJOR RELIGIONS Tribal religions, Islam, Christianity

TOGO
AREA 21,622 sq. mi.
POPULATION 2,300,000
CAPITAL Lomé
LARGEST CITY Lomé
HIGHEST POINT Agou 3,445 ft.
MONETARY UNIT CFA franc
MAJOR LANGUAGES Ewe, French, Twi, Hausa
MAJOR RELIGIONS Tribal religions, Roman Catholicism, Islam

TUNISIA
AREA 63,170 sq. mi.
POPULATION 5,776,000
CAPITAL Tunis
LARGEST CITY Tunis
HIGHEST POINT Jeb. Chambi 5,066 ft.
MONETARY UNIT Tunisian dinar
MAJOR LANGUAGES Arabic, French
MAJOR RELIGION Islam

UPPER VOLTA
AREA 105,869 sq. mi.
POPULATION 6,144,013
CAPITAL Ouagadougou
LARGEST CITY Ouagadougou
HIGHEST POINT 2,352 ft.
MONETARY UNIT CFA franc
MAJOR LANGUAGES Mossi, Lobi, French, Samo, Gourounsi
MAJOR RELIGIONS Islam, Tribal religions, Roman Catholicism

Topography

0   200   400   600
MILES

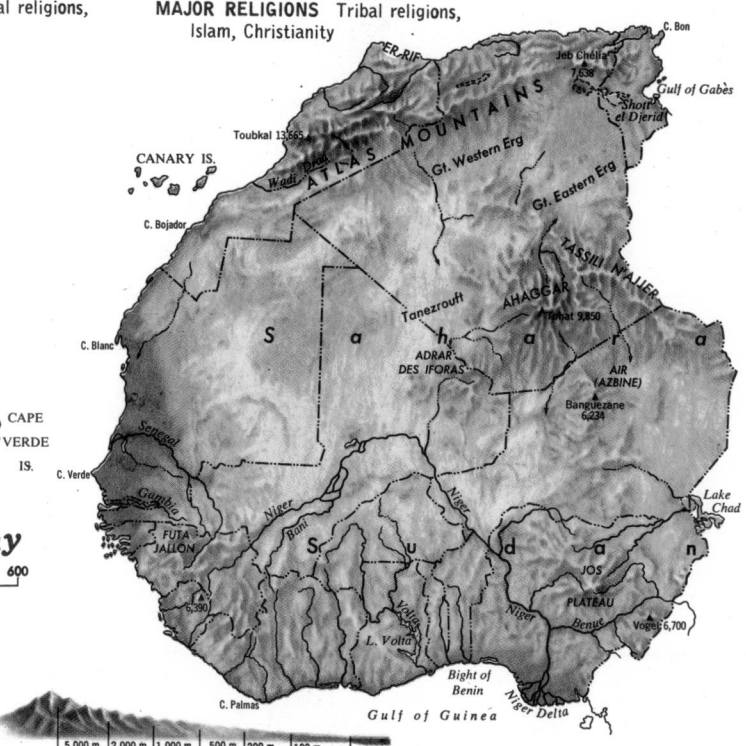

5,000 m. 2,000 m. 1,000 m. 500 m. 200 m. 100 m. Sea
16,404 ft. 6,562 ft. 3,281 ft. 1,640 ft. 656 ft. 328 ft. Level Below

(continued on following page)

(continued)

ALGERIA

CITIES and TOWNS

Abadla, 7,288 D 2
Adrar, 13,332 D 3
Aïn-Béïda, 30,757 F 1
Aïn-Sefra, 16,818 D 2
Aïn-Témouchent, 33,481 D 1
Algiers (cap.), 943,142 E 1
Algiers, *1,800,000 E 1
Amguid F 3
Annaba, 152,006 F 1
Annaba, *223,000 F 1
Aoulef, 11,285 E 3
Arak E 3
Batna, 69,090 F 1
Béchar, 46,505 D 2
Béjaïa, 64,876 F 1
Beni-Abbès, 3,943 D 2
Beni-Ounif, 5,271 D 2
Beni-Saf, 23,368 D 1
Berga E 3
Bidon 5 (Poste Maurice Cordier) E 4
Biskra, 59,275 F 2
Blida, 99,238 E 1
Bordj-Bou-Arréridj, 43,494 E 1
Bordj Fly Sainte-Marie D 3
Boufarik, 33,881 E 1
Bougie (Béjaïa), 64,876 F 1
Bou-Saâda, 26,262 E 1
Briziana, 7,498 E 2
Charouïn D 3
Cherchell, 27,464 E 1
Constantine, 243,558 F 1
Deldoul F 3
Dellys, 23,718 E 1
Djamaâ, 25,925 F 2
Djanet F 4
Djelfa, 30,304 E 2
Djidjelli, 35,371 F 1
Edjeleh F 3
El Abiod-Sidi-Cheikh, 10,512 E 2
El Asnam, 69,745 E 1
El Bayadh, 24,770 E 2
El Djezair (Algiers) (cap.), 943,142 E 1
El Goléa, 16,679 E 2
El Oued, 43,547 F 2
Fort-Lallemand F 2
Fort-Mac-Mahon E 3
Fort-Miribel E 3
Ghardaïa, 46,609 E 2
Ghazaouet, 20,785 D 2
Guelma, 39,817 F 1
Guémar, 20,394 F 2
Guerara, 14,173 E 2
Guerzim D 3
Hassi-Messaoud F 2
Hassi-R'Mel E 2
Idelès F 4
Ighil-Izane, 43,547 E 1
Igli, 2,912 D 2
Illizi, 4,000 F 3
In-Amenas F 3
In-Amguel E 4
In-Eker F 4
In-Rhar E 3
In Salah, 12,645 E 3
Kenadsa, 7,258 D 2
Kerzaz, 2,492 D 3
Khémis-Miliana, 36,530 E 1
Ksar-el-Boukhari, 30,338 E 1
Laghouat, 38,166 E 2
Mascara, 43,108 D 1
Méchéria, 12,151 D 2
Médéa, 53,567 E 1
Metlili Chaamba, 17,999 E 2
Miliana, 28,410 E 1
Mohammadia, 38,441 D 1
Mostaganem, 75,332 D 1
M'Sila, 36,930 E 1
Oran, 327,493 D 1
Oran, *393,000 D 1
Ouallene E 4
Ouargla, 48,323 F 2
Ouled-Djellal, 14,597 F 2
Philippeville (Skikda), 72,742 F 1
Poste Maurice Cordier E 4
Poste Weygand D 4
Reggan, 11,075 D 3
Saïda, 38,348 E 2
Sba D 3
Sétif, 98,337 F 1
Sidi-bel-Abbès, 91,527 D 1
Silet E 4
Skikda, 72,742 F 1
Souk-Ahras, 42,680 F 1
Tabelbala, 1,972 D 3
Tamanrasset, 16,298 F 4
Tamentit D 3
Taourirt E 3
Tarat F 3
Tarhit D 2
Tébessa, 46,148 F 1
Temacine F 2
Ténès, 22,881 E 1
Tiaret, 40,934 E 1
Tiguentourine F 3
Timimoun, 15,349 E 3
Tindouf, 3,414 C 3
Tizi-Ouzou, 53,546 E 1
Tlemcen, 87,210 D 2
Touggourt, 50,159 F 2
Zaouiet-el-Kahla, 1,080 F 3
Zaouïet-Kounta, 11,455 D 3

OTHER FEATURES

Adrar des Iforas (plat.) E 4
Ahaggar (range) F 4
Aouïnet Legraa (well) C 3
Atlas (mts.) E 2
Aurés (mts.) F 1
Azzel Mati, Sebkra (lake) E 3
Bougaroun (cape) F 1
Chech Erg (des.) D 3
Chélia (mt.) F 1
Chéliff (riv.) E 1
Chenachane (well) D 3
Chergui, Shott Ech (salt lake) E 2
Gourara (oasis), 28,893 E 3
Great Eastern Erg (des.) F 2
Great Western Erg (des.) E 2
High Plateaus (ranges) D 2
Iguidi Erg (des.) C 3
In-Ezzane (well) G 4
In-Guezzam (well) F 5
Irharhar, Wadi (dry riv.) F 3
Issaouane Erg (des.) F 3
Kabylia (reg.) E 1
Medjerda (riv.) F 1
Mekerhane, Sebkra (salt lake) E 3
Melrhir, Shott (salt lake) F 2
Mouydir (mts.) E 3
Mya, Wadi (dry riv.) E 2
Mzab (oasis), 52,500 E 2
Raoui Erg (des.) D 3
Rhir, Wadi (dry riv.) F 2
Sahara (des.) E 4
Saharan Atlas (mts.) E 2
Saoura, Wadi (dry riv.) D 3
Souf (oasis), 92,014 F 2
Tademait (plat.) E 3
Tahat (mt.) F 4
Tamanrasset, Wadi (dry river) E 4
Tanezrouft (des.) E 4
Tassili n'Ahaggar (plat.) E 4
Tassili n'Ajjer (plat.) F 3
Tidikelt (oasis), 17,280 E 3
Timgad (ruins) F 1
Timmissao (well) E 4
Tindouf, Sebkra de (salt lake) C 3
Tinrhert Hamada (des.) F 3
Tni Haïa (well) D 4
Touat (oasis), 35,537 E 3
Touila (well) C 3

BENIN

CITIES and TOWNS

Abomey, 19,000 E 7
Athiémé, 1,782 E 7
Cotonou, 120,000 E 7
Djougou, 7,000 E 7
Grand-Popo, 2,545 E 7
Kandi, 5,100 E 6
Malanville, 1,900 E 6
Natitingou, 2,260 E 6
Nikki E 7
Ouidah, 18,915 E 7
Parakou, 10,600 E 7
Porto-Novo (cap.), 80,000 E 7
Savalou, 5,000 E 7
Savé, 6,262 E 7

OTHER FEATURES

Atakora (mts.) E 6
Benin (bight) E 8
Guinea (gulf) E 8
Ouémé (riv.) E 7
Slave Coast (reg.) E 7

CAPE VERDE

CITIES and TOWNS

Mindelo, 7,312 A 7
Praia (cap.), 3,628 B 8
Ribeira Grande, †17,573 B 7
Sal Rei, †3,309 B 8
Santa Maria, †2,626 B 8

OTHER FEATURES

Boa Vista (isl.), 3,309 B 8
Brava (isl.), 8,646 B 8
Fogo (isl.), 25,457 B 8
Maio (isl.), 2,718 B 8
Sal (isl.), 2,626 B 7
Santa Luzia (isl.) B 8
Santo Antão (island), 36,703 A 7
São Nicolau (island), 13,894 B 8
São Tiago (island), 86,835 B 8
São Vicente (island), 21,361 B 7

GAMBIA

CITIES and TOWNS

Banjul (cap.), 31,800 A 6
Banjul, *48,333 A 6
Basse, 1,639 B 6
Brikama, 4,195 A 6
Georgetown, 1,592 A 6

GHANA

CITIES and TOWNS

Accra (cap.), 337,828 D 7
Accra, *848,825 D 7
Ada Foah, 3,332 E 7
Akim Oda, 19,666 D 7
Amedika Akuse, 3,638 E 7
Attebubu, 4,216 D 7
Axim, 5,619 D 8
Bawku, 12,719 D 6
Bekwai, 9,093 D 7
Berekum, 11,148 D 7
Bole, 3,118 D 7
Bolgatanga, 5,515 D 6
Cape Coast, 41,230 D 7
Daboya, 1,579 D 7
Damongo, 6,575 D 7
Dunkwa, 12,689 D 7
Elmina, 8,534 D 8
Enkyi, 4,007 D 7
Gambaga, 2,936 D 6
Gyasikan, 4,989 D 7
Half Assini, 4,575 D 8
Ho, 14,519 E 7
Keta, 16,719 E 7
Kete Krakye, 3,928 E 7
Kintampo, 4,678 D 7
Koforidua, 34,856 D 7
Kpandu, 8,070 D 7
Kumasi, 281,600 D 7
Kumasi, *340,200 D 7
Lawra, 3,237 D 6
Mampong, 7,943 D 7
Mpraeso, 5,193 D 7
Navrongo, 5,274 D 6
Obuasi, 22,818 D 7
Prestea, 13,246 D 7
Salaga, 4,199 D 7
Sehwi Wiawso, 4,430 D 7
Sekondi, 34,513 D 8
Sekondi-Takoradi, 128,200 D 8
Sekondi-Takoradi, *209,400 D 8
Sunyani, 12,160 D 7
Takoradi, 40,937 D 8
Tamale, 40,443 D 7
Tarkwa, 13,545 D 7
Tema, 14,937 E 7
Tumu, 2,773 D 6
Wa, 14,342 D 6
Wenchi, 10,672 D 7
Winneba, 25,376 D 7
Yapei, 515 D 7

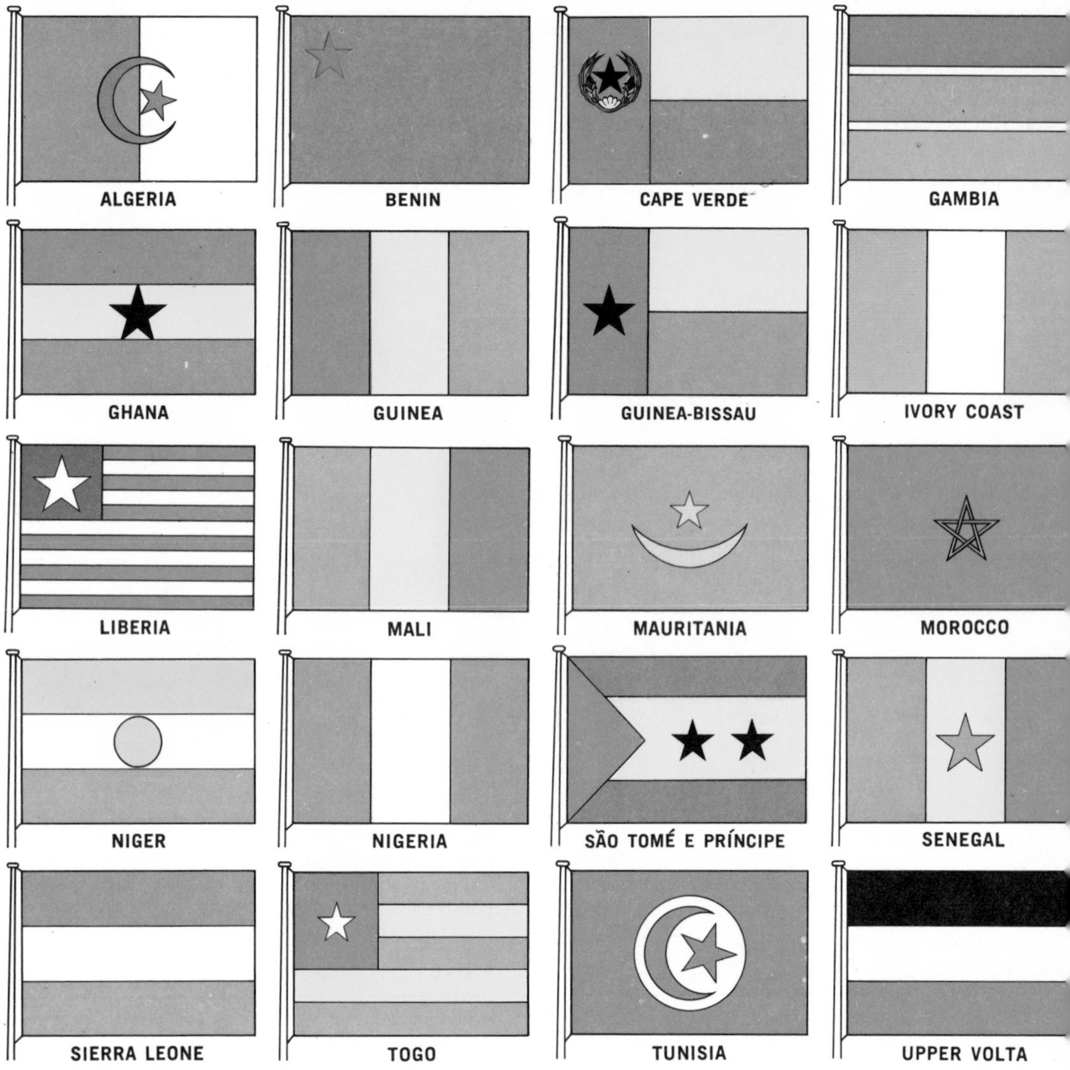

ALGERIA
BENIN
CAPE VERDE
GAMBIA
GHANA
GUINEA
GUINEA-BISSAU
IVORY COAST
LIBERIA
MALI
MAURITANIA
MOROCCO
NIGER
NIGERIA
SÃO TOMÉ E PRÍNCIPE
SENEGAL
SIERRA LEONE
TOGO
TUNISIA
UPPER VOLTA

Yendi, 16,096 D 7
Zuarungu, 1,278 D 6

OTHER FEATURES

Ashanti (region), 1,109,133 D 7
Black Volta (riv.) D 6
Gold Coast (reg.) D 8
Guinea (gulf) E 8
Oti (riv.) E 7
Saint Paul (cape) E 7
Three Points (cape) D 8
Volta (lake) D 7
Volta (riv.) E 7
White Volta (riv.) D 6

GUINEA

CITIES and TOWNS

Beyla, 6,035 C 7
Boffa, 1,014 B 6
Boké, 6,000 B 6
Conakry (capital), 43,000 B 7
Conakry, *197,267 B 7
Dabola, 5,600 B 6
Dalaba, 5,450 B 6
Dinguiraye, 2,600 B 6
Dubréka, 740 B 7
Faranah, 4,000 B 6
Forécariah, 5,250 B 7
Gaoual, 3,208 B 6
Guéckédou, 1,421 B 7
Kankan, 50,000 C 6
Kérouané C 7
Kindia, 25,000 B 6
Kissidougou, 12,000 B 7
Kouroussa, 6,100 C 6
Labé, 11,609 B 6
Macenta, 22,500 C 7
Mamou, 9,000 B 6
N'Zérékoré, 11,000 C 7
Siguiri, 12,000 C 6
Tougué, 9,810 B 6
Victoria, 1,913 B 6

OTHER FEATURES

Bafing (riv.) B 6
Futa Jallon (mts.) B 6
Los (isls.) B 7
Milo (riv.) C 7
Niger (riv.) C 6
Nimba (mts.) C 7
Verga (cape) B 6

GUINEA-BISSÀU

CITIES and TOWNS

Bissau (capital), 20,000 A 6
Bolama, †4,642 A 6
Buba B 6
Bubaque A 6
Cacheu, †70,233 A 6

OTHER FEATURES

Bijagós (isls.), 9,332 A 6

IVORY COAST

CITIES and TOWNS

Abengourou, 18,000 D 7
Abidjan (capital), 180,000 D 7
Abidjan, *425,000 D 7
Aboisso, 3,310 D 7
Agboville, 15,475 D 7
Bingerville, 2,500 D 7
Bondoukou, 5,216 D 7
Bouaflé, 5,000 C 7
Bouaké, 100,000 D 7
Bouna, 3,410 D 7
Boundiali, 3,608 C 7
Dabakala, 1,500 D 7
Dabou, 4,500 D 7
Daloa, 20,000 C 7
Danané, 5,200 C 7
Dimbokro, 10,260 D 7
Ferkessédougou, 9,110 D 7
Fresco, 719 C 7
Gagnoa, 18,000 C 7
Grand-Bassam, 12,330 D 7
Grand-Lahou, 4,040 C 8
Guiglo, 3,867 C 7
Katiola, 7,778 C 7
Kong, 4,073 D 7
Korhogo, 25,000 C 7
Man, 24,000 C 7
Odienné, 6,000 C 7
Port-Bouet D 7
San Pedro, 21 C 8
Sassandra, 5,300 D 7
Séguéla, 7,598 C 7
Sinfra, 5,965 C 7
Tabou, 3,030 C 8
Touba, 1,217 C 7
Toumodi, 3,000 D 7

OTHER FEATURES

Aby (lag.) D 8
Bandama (riv.) C 7
Cavally (riv.) C 7
Comoé (riv.) D 7
Ebrié (lag.) D 8
Ivory Coast (reg.) C 8
Sassandra (riv.) C 7

LIBERIA

CITIES and TOWNS

Bomi Hills, 2,441 B 7
Buchanan, 11,909 B 7
Gbarnga, 2,810 C 7
Grand Bassa (Buchanan), 11,909 B 7
Grand Cess C 8
Greenville, 3,962 C 8
Harper, 6,095 C 8
Kolahun C 7
Marshall B 7
Monrovia (capital), 85,000 B 7
Monrovia, *100,000 B 7
River Cess C 7
Robertsport, 2,417 B 7
Salala B 7
Sass Town C 8
Sinoe (Greenville), 3,962 C 8
Tappita C 7
Tchien, 945 C 7
Zwedru (Tchien), 945 C 7

OTHER FEATURES

Bong (mts.) B 7
Cavally (riv.) C 7
Grain Coast (reg.) B 8
Kru Coast (reg.), 21,280 C 8
Mano (riv.) B 7
Mount (cape) B 7
Nimba (mts.) C 7
Palmas (cape) C 8
Roberts International Airport B 7

MALI

CITIES and TOWNS

Anéfis E 5
Ansongo, 1,200 E 5
Araouane D 5
Badougou C 6
Bafoulabé, 1,300 B 6
Bamako (cap.), 88,500 C 6
Bamako, *182,000 C 6
Bamba D 5
Bandiagara, 6,700 D 6
Bou Djebeha D 5
Bougouni, 5,500 C 6
Bourem, 2,700 E 5
Dioila, 1,900 C 6
Dire, 3,300 D 5
Djenné, 8,200 D 6
Douentza, 7,100 D 6
Gao, 15,400 E 5
Goumbou, 5,000 C 6
Goundam, 10,000 D 5
Gourma-Rharous, 2,700 D 5
Hombori, 3,600 D 5
Kangaba, 6,200 C 6
Kati, 5,900 C 6
Kayes, 23,600 B 6
Ké-Macina, 3,100 C 6
Kéniéba, 800 B 6
Kerchoual E 5
Kidal, 1,200 E 5
Kita, 8,600 C 6
Kolokani, 7,300 C 6
Koulikoro, 10,000 C 6
Kourouba, 807 B 6
Koutiala, 11,300 C 6
Mabrouk D 5
Ménaka, 1,400 E 5
Mopti, 32,000 D 6
Nampala C 5
Nara, 2,500 C 5
Niafunké, 5,100 D 5
Niono, 4,000 C 6
Nioro, 11,000 C 5
San, 14,900 D 6
Satadougou, 180 B 6
Ségou, 27,200 C 6
Sikasso, 21,800 C 6
Sokolo, 3,457 C 6
Taoudenni D 4
Tessalit E 4
Timbuktu, 14,900 D 5
Tin-Zaouatene E 5
Yelimané, 1,700 B 5

OTHER FEATURES

Achourat (well) D 4
Adrar des Iforas (plat.) E 4
Asselar (well) D 5
Azaouad (reg.) D 5
Azaouak (dry riv.) E 5
Bafing (riv.) B 6
Bagoé (riv.) C 6
Bakoy (riv.) B 6
Bani (riv.) C 6
Baoulé (riv.) C 6
Bir Ounane (well) D 4
Chech Erg (des.) D 3
Debo (lake) D 5
El-Mraiti (well) D 5
Faguibine (lake) D 5
Falémé (riv.) B 6
Haricha Hamada (des.) D 4
Hombori (mts.) D 5
In Dagouber (well) D 4
Macina (depr.) D 6
Mina (mt.) C 6
Niger (riv.) D 5
Oum el Asel (well) D 4
Sahara (des.) D 4
Sekkane (des.) D 4
Tadjnout Hagguerete (well) D 4
Terhazza (ruins) C 4
Tilemsi (valley) E 5
Toufourine (well) C 4

MAURITANIA

CITIES and TOWNS

Aïoun el Atrous, 3,054 C 5
Akjoujt, 2,500 B 5
Akreïjit C 5
Aleg, 1,000 B 5
Atar, 7,120 B 4
Bassikounou C 5
Bir Mogrein, 1,052 B 4
Boghé, 2,316 B 5
Boutilimit, 3,000 B 5
Chinguetti, 600 B 4
Cité de Cansado A 4
Dakhla, 4,000 A 4
F'Dérick, †900 B 4
Kaédi, 11,000 B 5
Kankossa, †13,000 B 5
Kiffa, 2,600 B 5
Maghama, 3,157 B 5
Mal B 5
M'Bout, 1,400 B 5
Méderdra, 1,473 A 5
Moudjéria, 753 B 5
Néma, 2,946 C 5
Nouadhibou, 11,250 A 4
Nouakchott (capital), 14,500 A 5
Ouadane
Oualata, 1,285
Oujaf
Oujeft
Rosso, 3,923
Sélibaby, 2,600
Tamchakett, 641
Tamsagout
Tazadit
Tichitt, 1,000
Tidjikja, 5,900
Timbédra, 1,200

OTHER FEATURES

Adafer (reg.)
Adrar (reg.), 50,920
Affolé (reg.)
Agmar (well)
Agueraktem (well)
Aïn ben Tili (well)
Arguin (bay)
Assaba (reg.), 100,000
Atoui, Wadi (dry riv.)
Ausert (well)
Barbas (cape)
Ben Guerdane (well)
Bir el Khzaim (well)
Bir Ganduz (well)
Bir Nzaran (well)
Blanc (cape)
Brakna (reg.), 82,020
Chegga (well)
Djouf, El (des.)
Durnford (pt.)
El Mrayer (well)
El Mreïti (well)
Gorgol (reg.), 54,037
Hodh (reg.), 183,945
Iguidi Erg (des.)
Inchiri (reg.), 15,443
Kumbi Saleh (ruins)
Lévrier (bay)
Makteïr (des.)
Meraia (reg.)
Mirik (Timiris) (cape)
Ouarane (reg.)
Sahara (des.)
Senegal (riv.)
Tagant (reg.), 52,703
Tichlá (well)
Tidra (isl.)
Timiris (cape)
Touila (well)
Trarza (reg.), 105,737

MOROCCO

CITIES and TOWNS

Agadir, 16,695 C
Al Hoceima, 11,262 D
Asilah, 10,839 C
Azemmour, 12,449 C
Azrou, 14,143 C
Beni-Mellal, 28,933 C
Berguent, 2,607 D
Bouârfa, 8,775 D
Bou-Izakarn, 661 C

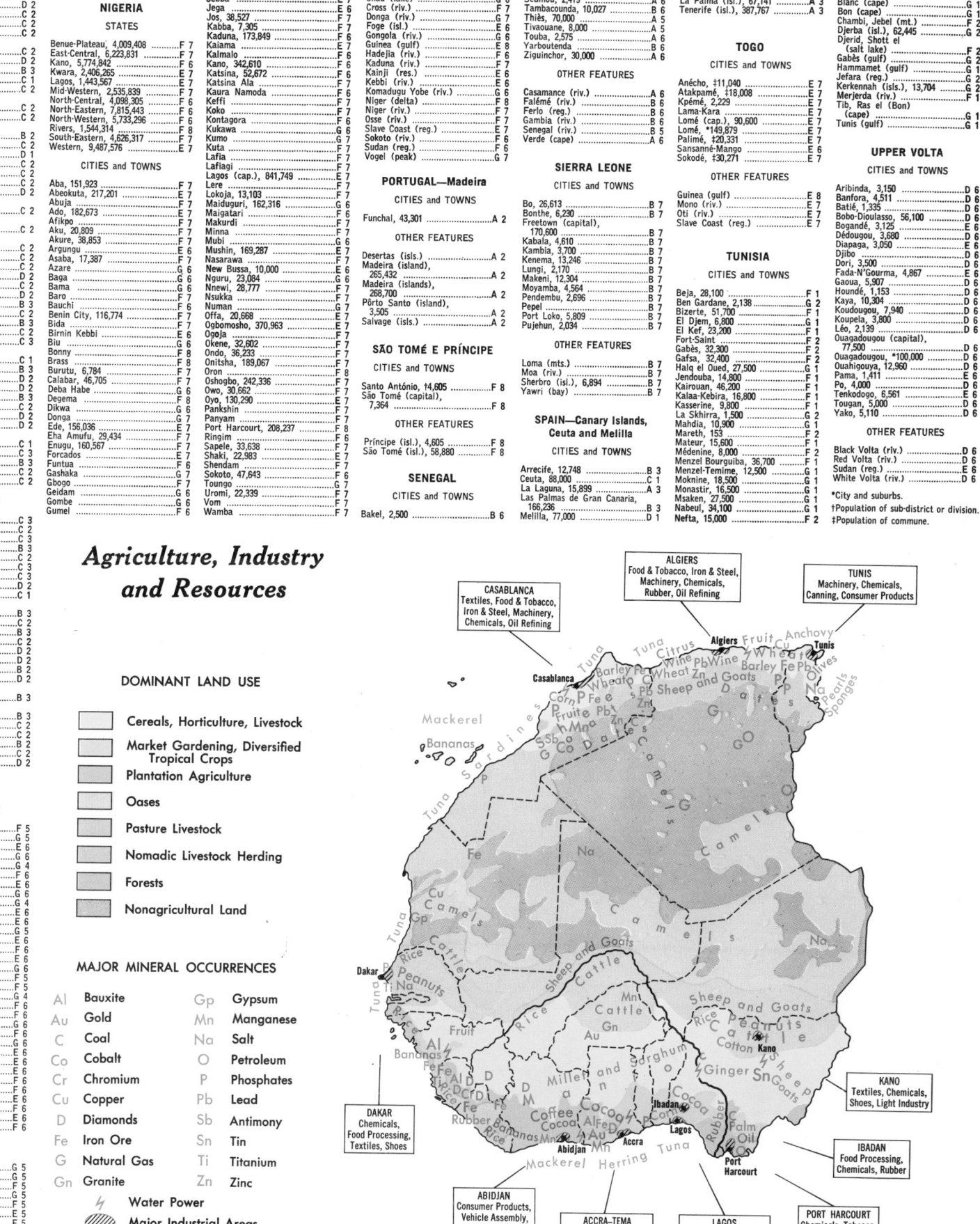

12,108 ....D 2	
...ma, 1,804 ....C 2	
...ne, 6,917 ....C 2	
..., 18,872 ....C 2	
...ne, 125,000 ....C 2	
...ibga, 40,838 ....C 2	
...l-Kebir,	
...35 ....C 2	
...une, 10,000 ....B 3	
...ne, 30,763 ....C 1	
...an (El Jadida),	
...02 ....C 2	
..., 235,000 ....C 2	
...or (Essaouira),	
...........................B 2	
...rmedia, 35,010 ....D 1	
...17,583 ....C 2	
...azate, 4,200 ....C 2	
...ane, 26,203 ....D 2	
...150,000 ....D 2	
...ean (Sidi-Kacem),	
...........................C 2	
...78	
...rayoune (Kénitra),	
(capital),	
...........................C 2	
...45	
...*435,000 ....C 2	
...25,000 ....C 2	
..., 1,102 ....D 2	
...75,799 ....D 2	
..., 1,000 ....B 3	
..., 21,478 ....D 2	
...ni, 12,751 ....B 3	
...acem, 19,478 ....C 2	
...aïte, 354 ....C 3	
...00	
...e (Tanger) ....C 1	
...900	
..., 2,153 ....B 3	
...t, 7,343 ....D 2	
...641 ....D 2	
..., 1,521 ....D 2	
...ant, 17,141 ....D 2	
...31,667 ....D 2	
...n, 1,563 ....D 2	
...n (Tetuán) ....C 1	
...00	
..., 7,694 ....B 3	
...ufia, 8,302 ....C 2	
..., 2,200 ....C 2	
OTHER FEATURES	

Agriculture, Industry and Resources

DOMINANT LAND USE

- Cereals, Horticulture, Livestock
- Market Gardening, Diversified Tropical Crops
- Plantation Agriculture
- Oases
- Pasture Livestock
- Nomadic Livestock Herding
- Forests
- Nonagricultural Land

MAJOR MINERAL OCCURRENCES

Al	Bauxite	Gp	Gypsum
Au	Gold	Mn	Manganese
C	Coal	Na	Salt
Co	Cobalt	O	Petroleum
Cr	Chromium	P	Phosphates
Cu	Copper	Pb	Lead
D	Diamonds	Sb	Antimony
Fe	Iron Ore	Sn	Tin
G	Natural Gas	Ti	Titanium
Gn	Granite	Zn	Zinc

⚡ Water Power

▨ Major Industrial Areas

CASABLANCA
Textiles, Food & Tobacco, Iron & Steel, Machinery, Chemicals, Oil Refining

ALGIERS
Food & Tobacco, Iron & Steel, Machinery, Chemicals, Rubber, Oil Refining

TUNIS
Machinery, Chemicals, Canning, Consumer Products

DAKAR
Chemicals, Food Processing, Textiles, Shoes

ABIDJAN
Consumer Products, Vehicle Assembly, Oil Refining

ACCRA–TEMA
Vehicle Assembly, Food Processing, Oil Refining, Chemicals

LAGOS
Machinery, Chemicals, Brewing

PORT HARCOURT
Chemicals, Tobacco, Light Industry, Oil Refining, Tires

IBADAN
Food Processing, Chemicals, Rubber

KANO
Textiles, Chemicals, Shoes, Light Industry

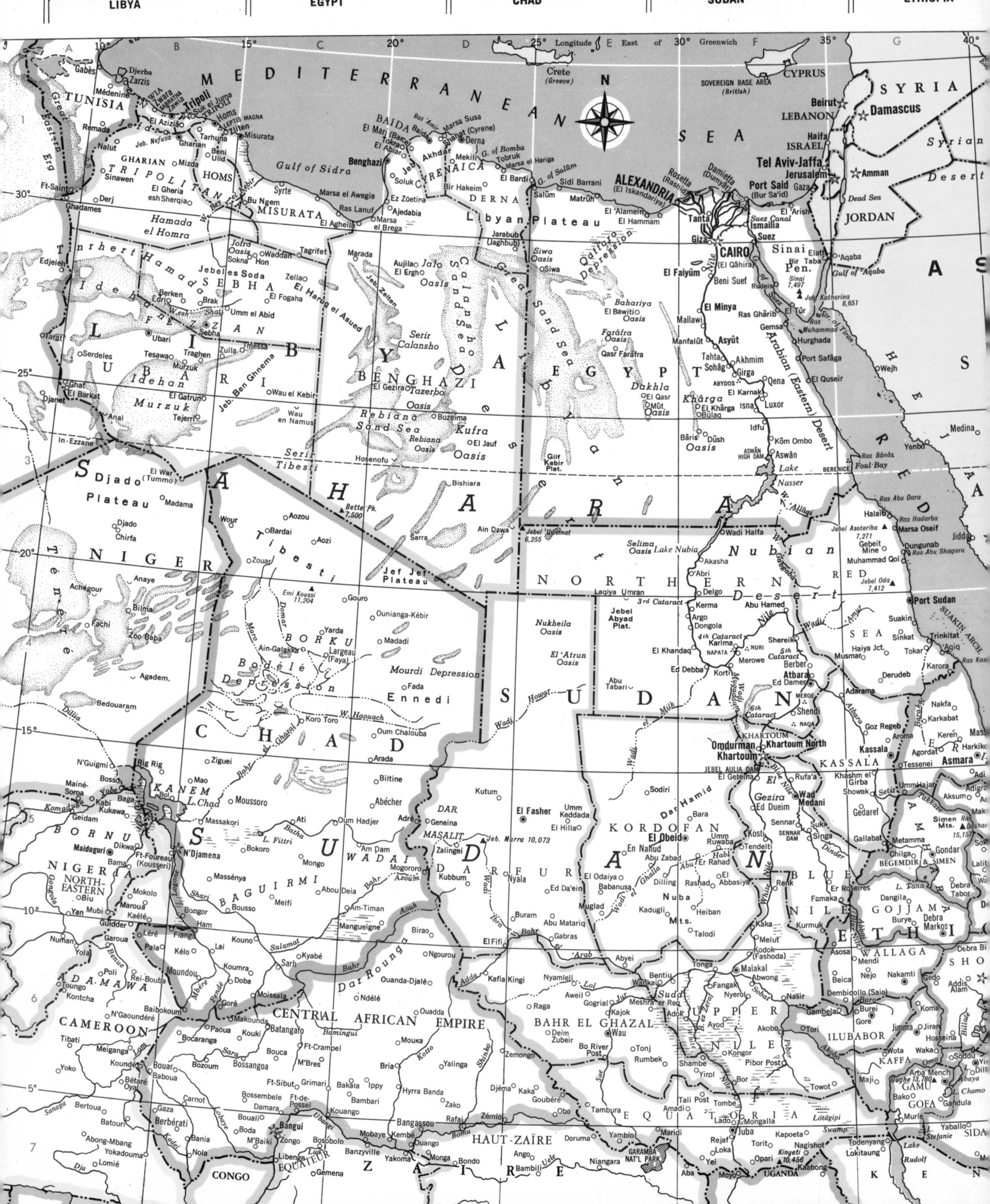

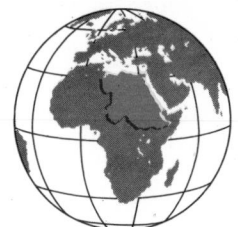

DJIBOUTI (flag label)

LIBYA
AREA 679,358 sq. mi.
POPULATION 2,500,000
CAPITAL Tripoli
LARGEST CITY Tripoli
HIGHEST POINT Bette Pk. 7,500 ft.
MONETARY UNIT Libyan dinar
MAJOR LANGUAGES Arabic, Berber, Italian
MAJOR RELIGION Islam

DJIBOUTI
AREA 8,880 sq. mi.
POPULATION 250,000
CAPITAL Djibouti
LARGEST CITY Djibouti
HIGHEST POINT Moussa Ali 6,768 ft.
MONETARY UNIT Djibouti franc
MAJOR LANGUAGES Arabic, Somali, Afar, French
MAJOR RELIGIONS Islam, Roman Catholicism

EGYPT
AREA 386,659 sq. mi.
POPULATION 37,900,000
CAPITAL Cairo
LARGEST CITY Cairo
HIGHEST POINT Jeb. Katherina 8,651 ft.
MONETARY UNIT Egyptian pound
MAJOR LANGUAGE Arabic
MAJOR RELIGIONS Islam, Coptic Christianity

CHAD
AREA 495,752 sq. mi.
POPULATION 4,178,000
CAPITAL N'Djamena
LARGEST CITY N'Djamena
HIGHEST POINT Emi Koussi 11,204 ft.
MONETARY UNIT CFA franc
MAJOR LANGUAGES Arabic, Bagirmi, French, Sara, Massa, Moudang
MAJOR RELIGIONS Islam, Tribal religions

SUDAN
AREA 967,494 sq. mi.
POPULATION 18,347,000
CAPITAL Khartoum
LARGEST CITY Khartoum
HIGHEST POINT Jeb. Marra 10,073 ft.
MONETARY UNIT Sudanese pound
MAJOR LANGUAGES Arabic, Dinka, Nubian, Beja, Nuer, English
MAJOR RELIGIONS Islam, Tribal religions

ETHIOPIA
AREA 471,776 sq. mi.
POPULATION 27,946,000
CAPITAL Addis Ababa
LARGEST CITY Addis Ababa
HIGHEST POINT Ras Dashan 15,157 ft.
MONETARY UNIT Ethiopian dollar
MAJOR LANGUAGES Amharic, Gallinya, Tigrinya, Somali, Sidamo, Arabic, Ge'ez, Italian
MAJOR RELIGIONS Coptic Christianity, Islam

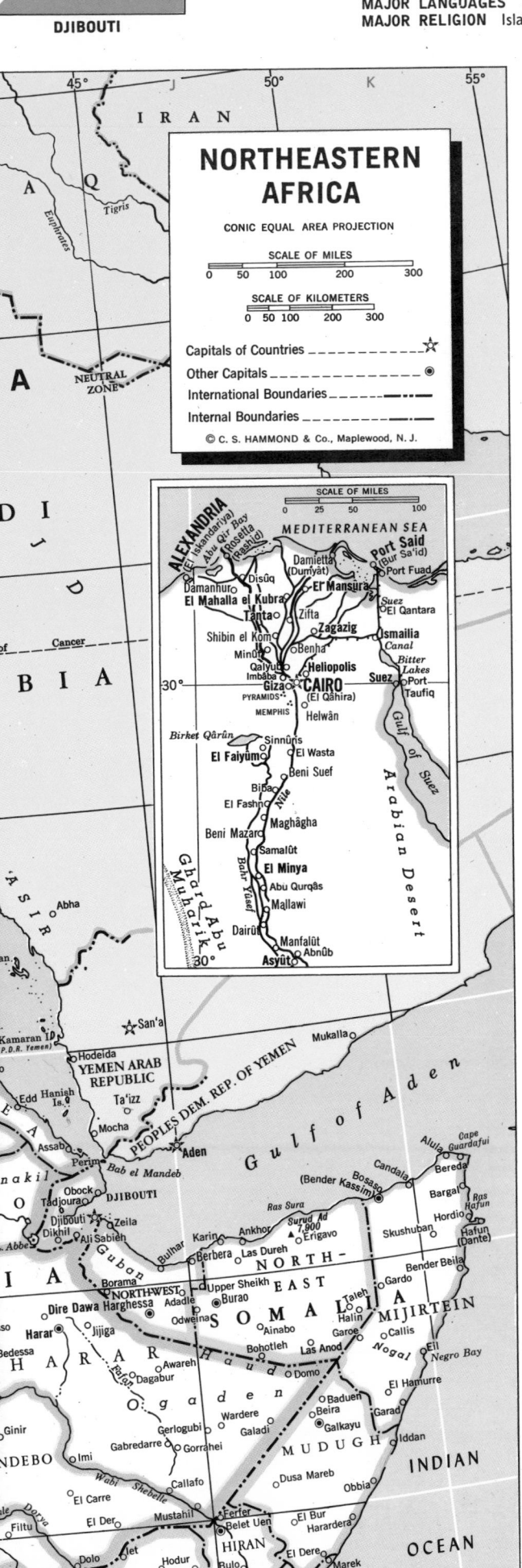

NORTHEASTERN AFRICA
CONIC EQUAL AREA PROJECTION

SCALE OF MILES
0 50 100 200 300

SCALE OF KILOMETERS
0 50 100 200 300

Capitals of Countries ....☆
Other Capitals ....◉
International Boundaries ....
Internal Boundaries ....

© C. S. HAMMOND & Co., Maplewood, N.J.

CHAD
CITIES and TOWNS
Abécher, 19,650	D 5
Abou Deïa, 1,100	C 5
Adré	D 5
Ain-Galakka	C 4
Am-Dam, 1,002	D 5
Am-Timan, 1,500	D 5
Aozi	C 3
Aozou	C 3
Arada	D 4
Ati, 6,000	C 5
Baïbokoum, 3,138	C 6
Bardai, 800	C 3
Biltine, 4,000	D 5
Bokoro, 4,700	C 5
Bol, 1,500	B 5
Bongor, 11,000	C 6
Bousso, 1,800	C 5
Doba, 7,375	C 6
Fada, 1,500	D 4
Faya (Largeau), 5,200	C 4
Fianga, 923	C 6
Goré	C 6
Gouro	C 4
Ham	C 5
Kélo, 6,067	C 6
Koro Toro	C 4
Koumra, 6,351	C 6
Kouno	C 6
Kyabé, 5,000	C 6
Lai, 8,000	C 6
Largeau, 5,200	C 4

Léré, 3,500	B 6
Madadi	D 4
Manqueigne, 1,700	D 5
Mao	C 5
Massakori, 2,000	C 5
Masséyna, 1,700	C 5
Melfi, 3,000	C 5
Mogororo	D 5
Moïssala, 3,000	C 6
Mongo, 7,000	C 5
Moundou, 34,100	C 6
Moussoro	C 5
N'Djamena (capital), 132,500	C 5
Oum Chalouba	D 4
Oum Hadjer, 4,500	C 5
Ounianga-Kébir	D 3
Pala, 4,200	B 6
Rig Rig, 286	B 5
Sarh, 35,000	C 6
Yaré	C 4
Ziguei	C 5
Zouar	C 3

OTHER FEATURES
Baguirmi (region), 81,666	C 5
Bahr el Ghazal (dry riv.)	C 4
Batha (riv.)	C 5
Bodélé (depr.)	C 4
Borku (region), 21,962	C 4
Chad (lake)	C 5

Domar (dry riv.)	C 4
Emi Koussi (mt.)	D 4
Ennedi (plat.)	D 4
Fittri (lake)	C 5
Haouach, Wadi (dry riv.)	C 4
Jef Jef (plat.)	D 3
Kanem (region), 261,108	C 5
Logone (riv.)	C 5
Maro (dry riv.)	C 5
Mbéré (riv.)	C 6
Mourdi (depr.)	D 4
Pendé (riv.)	C 6
Sahara (des.)	C 3
Salamat (riv.)	C 6
Sara (riv.)	C 6
Shari (riv.)	C 5
Sudan (reg.)	C 5
Tibesti (mts.)	C 3
Wadai (region) 314,775	D 5

DJIBOUTI
CITIES and TOWNS
Ali Sabieh, 2,000	H 5
Dikhil, 1,000	H 5
Djibouti (capital), 130,000	H 5
Obock, 582	H 5
Tadjoura, 2,000	H 5

OTHER FEATURES
Abbe (lake)	H 5
Aden (gulf)	J 5
Bab el Mandeb (str.)	H 5

EGYPT
CITIES and TOWNS
Abnûb, 27,751	J 4
Abu Qurqâs, 19,318	J 4
Akhmin, 41,580	F 2
Alexandria, 1,803,900	J 2
Aswân, 127,700	F 3
Asyût, 154,100	J 4
Bâris, 1,347	F 3
Benha, 52,686	J 3
Beni Mazar, 30,583	J 4
Beni Suef, 78,829	J 3
Biba, 20,773	J 4
Bôlaq, 928	F 2
Bur Sa'id (Port Said), 283,400	K 3
Cairo (cap.), 4,219,853	J 3
Dairût, 24,364	J 4
Damanhur, 146,300	J 3
Damietta, 71,780	J 3
Disûq, 39,473	J 3
Dumyât (Damietta), 71,780	J 3
Dôsh, 794	F 3
El 'Alamein, 593	E 1
El 'Arish, 29,973	F 1
El Bawiti, 2,478	E 2
El Fashn, 25,961	J 4
El Faiyûm, 133,800	J 3

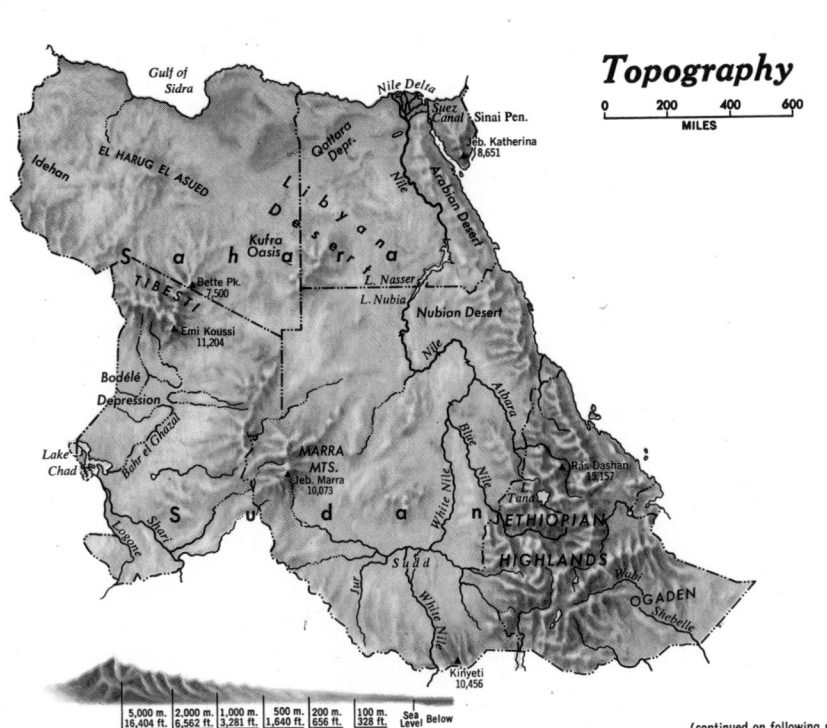

Topography
0 200 400 600
MILES

(continued on following page)

EGYPT (continued)

El Hammam, 3,664 E 1
El Iskandariya (Alexandria), 1,803,900 J 2
El Karnak, 14,121 F 2
El Khârga, 9,277 F 2
El Mahalla el Kubra, 225,700 J 3
El Mansûra, 191,700 K 3
El Minya, 112,800 J 4
El Qâhira (Cairo) (cap.), 4,219,853 J 3
El Qantara, 11,201 K 3
El Qasr, 1,789 E 2
El Quseir, 4,336 F 2
El Tûr, 418 F 2
El Wasta, 11,283 J 3
Gaza, 87,793 F 1
Gaza, *118,272 F 1
Gemsa, 225 F 2
Girga, 42,017 F 2
Giza, 571,249 J 3
Heliopolis, 124,774 J 3
Helwân, 94,385 J 3
Hurghada, 2,012 F 2
Idfu, 25,105 F 3
Imbâba, 226,300 J 3
Ismailia, 156,500 K 3
Isna, 25,342 F 2
Kôm Ombo, 21,783 F 3
Luxor, 35,074 F 2
Maghâgha, 28,650 J 4
Mallawi, 52,614 J 4
Manfalût, 28,540 J 4
Matrûh, 9,254 E 1
Minûf, 41,914 J 3
Mût, 3,496 E 2
Port Fuad, 12,881 K 3
Port Safâga, 1,448 F 2
Port Said, 283,400 K 3
Port Taufiq, 26,075 K 3
Qalyub, 43,202 J 3
Qasr Farâfra, 747 E 2
Qena, 57,417 F 2
Ras Ghârib, 5,857 F 2
Rashid (Rosetta), 32,368 J 2
Rosetta, 32,368 J 2
Rudeis F 2
Salûm, 1,348 E 1
Samalût, 17,368 J 4
Shibin el Kom, 54,910 J 3
Sidi Barrani, 1,583 E 1
Sinnûris, 31,831 J 3
Siwa, 3,839 E 2
Sohâg, 61,944 F 2
Suez, 264,500 K 3
Tahta, 36,165 F 2
Tanta, 230,400 J 3
Zagazig, 151,300 J 3
Zifta, 31,421 J 3

OTHER FEATURES

Abu Qir (bay) J 2
Abydos (ruins) F 2
'Allaqi, Wadi (dry riv.) F 3
'Aqaba (gulf) G 2
Arabian (des.) F 2
Aswân (dam) F 3
Aswân High (dam) F 3
Bahariya (oasis), 6,779 E 2
Bahr Yusef (stream) J 4
Bânâs, Ras (cape) G 3
Berenice (ruins) F 3
Birket Qârûn (lake) J 3
Bir Taba (well) F 2
Bitter (lakes) K 3
Dakhla (oasis), 21,586 E 2
Eastern (Arabian) (des.) F 2
Farâfra (oasis), 747 E 2
Foul (bay) G 3
Ghard Abu Muharik (des.) J 4
Gilf Kebir (plat.) E 3
Great Sand Sea (des.) E 2
Katherina, Jebel (mt.) F 2
Khârga (oasis), 12,346 F 2
Libyan (des.) E 2
Libyan (plat.) E 1
Mediterranean (sea) E 1
Memphis (ruins) J 3
Muhammad, Ras (cape) F 2
Nasser (lake) F 3
Nile (riv.) F 2
Pyramids (ruins) J 3
Qattâra (depr.) E 2
Red (sea) G 3
Sahara (des.) E 3
Salûm (gulf) E 1
Sinai (mt.) F 2
Sinai (pen.), 49,769 F 2
Siwa (oasis), 3,839 E 2
Suez (canal) K 3
Suez (gulf) F 2
Tiran (str.) F 2
'Uweinat, Jebel (mt.) E 3

ETHIOPIA

GOVERNORATES

Arusi, 1,092,565 G 6
Begemdir and Simen, 2,125,069 G 5
Eritrea, 1,757,912 G 4
Gamu-Gofa, 563,749 G 6
Gojjam, 1,414,944 G 5
Harar, 1,540,211 H 6
Ilubabor, 1,061,208 F 6
Kaffa, 876,836 G 6
Mendebo, 353,736 H 6
Shoa, 2,614,689 G 6
Sidamo, 2,242,515 G 7
Tigre, 3,104,451 H 5
Wallaga, 2,386,218 G 6
Wallo, 2,946,924 H 5

CITIES and TOWNS

Addis Ababa (capital), 644,120 G 6
Addis Alam, 7,789 G 6
Adigrat G 5
Adi Ugri G 5
Adola G 6
Adwa G 5
Agordat G 4
Aksum, 11,596 G 5
Ankober, 12,871 H 6
Arba Mench G 6
Asmara, 190,500 G 4
Asosa F 5
Assab H 5
Asselle, 9,523 G 6
Awareh H 6
Awash H 6
Bako G 6
Bedessa H 6
Beica F 6
Burei G 6
Burye, 18,139 G 5
Callafo H 6
Chilga G 5
Dagabur H 6
Dallol G 5
Dangila, 2,351 G 5
Debra Birhan G 6
Debra Markos, 20,096 G 5
Debra Tabor G 5
Dembidollo F 6
Dessye, 40,000 G 5
Dilla G 6
Dire Dawa, 40,000 H 6
Dolo H 7
Domo J 6
Edd H 5
El Carre H 6
El Der H 6
Filtu H 6
Gabredarre H 6
Galadi J 6
Gambela, 9,955 F 6
Gardula G 6
Gedo G 6
Gerlogubi H 6
Ginir H 6
Goba, 6,389 H 6
Gondar, 24,673 G 5
Gore G 6
Gorrahei H 6
Hadama, 7,293 G 6
Harar, 40,499 H 6
Harkiko G 4
Hosseina, 5,803 G 6
Imi H 6
Jijiga H 6
Jimma, 39,559 G 6
Jiran G 6
Karkabat G 4
Keren G 4
Koma G 6
Lalibela G 5
Magdala G 5
Maji G 6
Makale, 16,873 G 5
Massawa, 25,000 G 4
Masslo G 6
Mega G 7
Mendi G 6
Mersa Fatma H 5
Metamma G 5
Miesso, 32,960 H 6
Murle G 6
Mustahil H 6
Nakamti, 5,889 G 6
Nakfa G 4
Negelli G 6
Nejo G 6
Saio (Dembidollo) F 6
Soddu, 5,595 G 6
Sokota G 5
Tessenei G 4
Thio H 5
Tori F 6
Umm Hajar G 5
Waka G 6
Waldia G 5
Wardere J 6
Wota G 6
Yaballo G 6
Yirga Alam G 6
Zula G 4

OTHER FEATURES

Abaya (lake) G 6
Abbai (riv.) G 5
Abbe (lake) H 5
Akobo (riv.) F 6
Amhara (reg.) G 5
Assale (lake) H 5
Awash (riv.) H 5
Bale (mt.) G 6
Baraka (dry riv.) G 4
Baro (riv.) G 6
Billate (riv.) G 6
Blue Nile (Abbai) (riv.) G 5
Buri (pen.) H 4
Chamo (lake) G 6
Dahlak (arch.) H 4
Dahlak (isl.) H 4
Danakil (reg.) H 5
Dawa (riv.) H 7
Fafan (riv.) H 6
Ganale Dorya (riv.) H 6
Gughe (mt.) G 6
Haud (reg.) J 6
Kasar, Ras (cape) G 4
Ogaden (reg.) H 6
Omo (riv.) G 6
Ras Dashan (mt.) G 5
Red (sea) G 3
Rudolf (lake) G 7
Simen (mts.) G 5
Stefanie (lake) G 7
Takkaze (riv.) G 5
Tana (lake) G 5
Wabi (riv.) H 6
Wabi Shebelle (riv.) H 6
Zwai (lake) G 6

LIBYA

PROVINCES

Baida, 88,016 D 1
Benghazi, 278,826 D 2
Derna, 84,112 D 1
Gharian, 180,883 B 1
Homs, 136,679 B 1
Misurata, 145,894 C 1
Sebha, 47,436 B 2
Tripoli, 379,925 B 1
Ubari, 31,890 B 2
Zawia, 190,708 B 1

CITIES and TOWNS

Ajedabia, †15,430 D 1
Aujila, †2,993 D 2
Baida, 12,799 D 1
Barce (El Marj), 10,645 D 1
Benghazi, 137,295 C 1
Beni Ulid, †4,293 B 1
Berken, †3,114 B 2
Bir Hakeim D 1
Brak, †7,042 B 2
Bu Ngem C 1
Buzeima D 3
Cyrene (Shahat), †6,266 D 1
Derj, †2,272 B 1
Derna, 21,432 D 1
Edri, †4,271 B 2
El Abiar, †14,260 D 1
El Agheila, †852 C 1
El Azizia, †18,753 B 1
El Bardi, †3,755 D 1
El Barkat, †1,476 B 3
El Ergh D 2
El Fogaha, †607 C 2
El Gatrun, †1,660 B 3
El Gezira D 2
El Gheria esh Sherqia B 1
El Jauf, †4,330 D 3
El Marj, 10,645 D 1
Ez Zuetina, †2,430 D 1
Ghadames, †2,636 A 2
Gharian, †10,807 B 1
Ghat, †1,639 B 3
Homs, †13,864 B 1
Hon, †3,435 C 2
Jaghbub (Jarabub), †1,101 D 2
Jarabub, †1,101 D 2
Marada, †2,172 C 2
Marsa el Awegia C 1
Marsa el Brega, †2,797 D 1
Marsa el Hariga D 1
Marsa Susa, †2,062 D 1
Mekili, †703 D 1
Misurata, †36,850 C 1
Mizda, †2,508 B 1
Murzuk, †3,863 B 2
Nalut, †9,010 B 1
Ras Lanuf C 1
Sebha, †9,804 B 2
Serdeles B 2
Shahat, †6,266 D 1
Sinawen, †715 B 1
Sokna, †1,873 C 2
Soluk, †12,395 D 1
Suk el Juma, †81,123 B 1
Syrte, †7,093 C 1
Tagrifet C 2
Tarhuna, †25,502 B 1
Tejerri B 3
Tesawa B 2
Tmessa, 4,806 C 2
Tobruk, 15,867 D 1
Tokra, †5,900 D 1
Traghen, †2,952 B 2
Tripoli (capital), 247,365 B 1
Ubari, †1,711 B 2
Umm el Abid C 2
Waddan, †3,519 C 2
Wau el Kebir C 2
Zawia, †28,349 B 1
Zella, †2,560 C 2
Zliten, †17,950 C 1
Zuila, †1,839 C 2
Zwara, †14,578 B 1

OTHER FEATURES

Ain Dawa (well) D 3
Akhdar, Jebel (mts.) D 1
'Amir, Ras (cape) D 1
Anai (well), †1,795 B 3
Ben Ghnema, Jebel (mts.) C 2
Bette (peak) C 3
Bey el Kebir, Wadi (dry riv.) B 1
Bishiara (well) D 3
Bomba (gulf) D 1
Calansho, Serir (des.) D 2
Calansho Sand Sea (desert) D 2
Cyrenaica (region), 450,954 D 1
Fezzan (region), 79,326 B 2
Great Sand Sea (des.) D 2
Harug el Asued, El (mts.) C 2
Homra, Hamada el (desert) B 2
Hosenofu (well) D 3
Idehan (des.) B 2
Idehan Murzuk (des.) B 2
Jalo (oasis), 3,910 D 2
Jefara (reg.) B 1
Jofra (oasis), 8,827 C 2
Kufra (oasis), 5,509 D 3
Leptis Magna (ruins) B 1
Libyan (des.) D 2
Libyan (plat.) D 1
Mediterranean (sea) C 1
Nefusa, Jebel (mts.) B 1
Rebiana (oasis), †666 D 3
Rebiana Sand Sea (des.) D 3
Sabratha (ruins) B 1
Sahara (des.) D 3
Sarra (well) D 3
Shati, Wadi esh (dry riv.) B 2
Sidra (gulf) C 1
Soda, Jebel es (mts.) C 2
Tazerbo (oasis), †1,307 D 2
Tibesti, Serir (des.) C 3
Tinrhert Hamada (des.) B 2
Tripolitania (region), 1,034,089 B 1
'Uweinat, Jebel (mt.) E 3
Wau en Namus (well) C 3
Zelten, Jebel (mts.) D 2

SUDAN

PROVINCES

Bahr el Ghazal, 1,238,779 E 6
Blue Nile, 2,724,968 F 5
Darfur, 1,467,688 D 5
Equatoria, 1,129,388 E 6
Kassala F 4
Khartoum, 749,932 F 4
Kordofan, 2,022,201 E 5
Northern, 982,046 E 3
Red Sea G 4
Upper Nile, 1,110,769 F 6

CITIES and TOWNS

Abu Hamed F 4
Abu Matariq E 5
Abu Zabad E 5
Abwong F 6
Abyei E 6
Adarama G 4
Adok F 6
Akobo F 6
Amadi F 6
'Aqiq G 4
Argo, 2,329 F 4
Aroma, 3,451 G 4
Atbara, 36,000 F 4
Aweil, 2,438 E 6
Ayod F 6
Babanusa E 5
Bara, 4,885 E 5
Bentiu E 6
Berber, 10,977 F 4
Bor F 6
Bo River Post E 6
Buram E 5
Deim Zubeir E 6
Delgo F 3
Derudeb G 4
Dilling, 5,596 E 5
Dongola, 3,350 F 4
Dungunab G 3
Ed Da'ein E 5
Ed Damer, 5,458 F 4
Ed Debba F 4
Ed Dueim, 12,319 F 5
El Abbasiya, 2,846 F 5
El Fasher, 26,161 E 5
El Fifi D 5
El Geteina F 5
El Hilla E 5
El Khandaq F 4
El Obeid, 53,000 E 5
El Odaiya E 5
En Nahud, 16,499 E 5
Er Rahad, 6,706 F 5
Er Roseires, 3,927 F 5
Famaka F 5
Fangak F 6
Fashoda (Kodok), 9,100 F 6
Gabras E 5
Gallabat G 5
Gebeit Mine G 3
Gedaref, 17,537 G 5
Geneina, 11,817 D 5
Gogrial E 6
Goz Regeb G 4
Haiya Junction G 4
Halaib G 3
Heiban F 5
Juba, 10,660 F 7
Kadugli, 4,716 E 5
Kafia Kingi D 6
Kajok E 6
Kaka F 5
Kapoeta F 7
Karima, 5,989 F 4
Karora G 4
Kassala, 40,000 G 4
Kerma F 4
Khartoum (capital), 194,000 F 4
Khartoum North, 40,000 F 4
Khashm el Girba G 5
Kodok, 9,100 F 6
Kongor F 6
Korti F 4
Kosti, 22,688 F 5
Kubbum D 5
Kurmuk, 1,647 F 5
Kutum D 5
Lado F 6
Loka F 7
Malakal, 9,680 F 6
Maridi, 839 E 7
Marsa Oseif G 3
Melut, 334 F 5
Merowe, 1,620 F 4
Meshra' er Req E 6
Mongalla F 6
Muglad, 3,735 E 5
Muhammad Qol G 3
Musmar G 4
Nagishot F 7
Nasir F 6
Nimule F 7
Nyala, 12,278 E 5
Nyamlell E 6
Nyerol F 6
Omdurman, 206,000 F 4
Opari F 7
Pibor Post F 6
Port Sudan, 110,000 G 4
Raga E 6
Rashad, 1,683 F 5
Rejaf F 7
Renk F 5
Rufa'a, 9,137 F 5
Rumbek, 2,944 E 6
Sennar, 8,093 F 5
Shambe F 6
Shendi, 11,031 F 4
Shereik F 4
Showak, 2,171 G 5
Singa, 9,436 F 5
Sinkat, 5,175 G 4
Sodiri, 1,804 E 5
Suakin, 4,228 G 4
Suki, 7,388 F 5
Tali Post F 6
Talodi, 2,736 F 5
Tambura E 6
Tendelti, 7,555 F 5
Tokar, 16,802 G 4
Tombe F 6
Tonga F 6
Tonj, 2,071 E 6
Torit, 2,353 F 7
Towot F 6
Trinkitat G 4
Umm Keddada, 2,410 E 5
Umm Ruwaba, 7,805 F 5
Wadi Halfa, 11,006 F 3
Wad Medani, 48,000 F 5
Wau, 8,009 E 6
Yambio, 3,890 E 7
Yei, 739 F 7
Yirol, 1,895 F 6
Zalingei, 3,314 D 5

OTHER FEATURES

Abu Dara, Ras (cape) G 3
Abu Habl, Wadi (dry riv.) F 5
Abu Shagara, Ras (cape) G 3
Abu Tabari (well) E 4
Adda (riv.) D 6
Akobo (riv.) F 6
'Amur, Wadi (dry riv.) G 4
Asoteriba, Jebel (mt.) G 3
Atbara (riv.) G 4
Bahr Azoum (riv.) D 5
Bahr el 'Arab (riv.) E 6
Bahr ez Zeraf (riv.) F 6
Baraka (dry riv.) G 4
Blue Nile (riv.) F 5
Dar Hamid (region) F 5
Dar Masalit (reg.), 323,616 D 5
Dinder (riv.) G 5
El 'Atrun (oasis) E 4
Fifth Cataract F 4
Fourth Cataract F 4
Gabgaba, Wadi (dry riv.) F 3
Gezira, El (reg.) F 5
Ghalla, Wadi el (dry riv.) E 5
Hadarba, Ras (cape) G 3
Howar, Wadi (dry riv.) E 4
Ibra, Wadi (dry riv.) D 5
Jebel Abyad (plat.) E 4
Jebel Aulia (dam) F 4
Jur (riv.) E 6
Kasar, Ras (cape) G 4
Kinyeti (mt.) F 7
Laqiya 'Umran (well) E 3
Libyan (desert) E 3
Lol (dry riv.) E 6
Lotagipi (swamp) F 6
Marra, Jebel (mt.) D 5
Meroe (ruins) F 4
Milk, Wadi el (dry riv.) E 4
Muqaddam, Wadi (dry riv.) F 4
Napata (ruins) F 4
Naqa (ruins) F 4
Nile (riv.) F 4
Nuba (mts.) E 5
Nubia (lake) F 3
Nubian (des.) E 5
Nuri (ruins) F 4
Oda, Jebel (mt.) G 3
Pibor (riv.) F 6
Red (sea) G 3
Sahara (des.) E 3
Second Cataract F 3
Selima (oasis) E 3
Sennar (dam) F 5
Setit (riv.) G 5
Sixth Cataract F 4
Sobat (riv.) F 6
Suakin (arch.) G 4
Sudan (reg.) E 5
Sudd (swamp) F 6
Sue (riv.) E 6
Third Cataract E 4
'Uweinat, Jebel (mt.) E 3
White Nile (riv.) F 5

*City and suburbs.
†Population of sub-district or divisi[on]

Agriculture, Industry and Resources

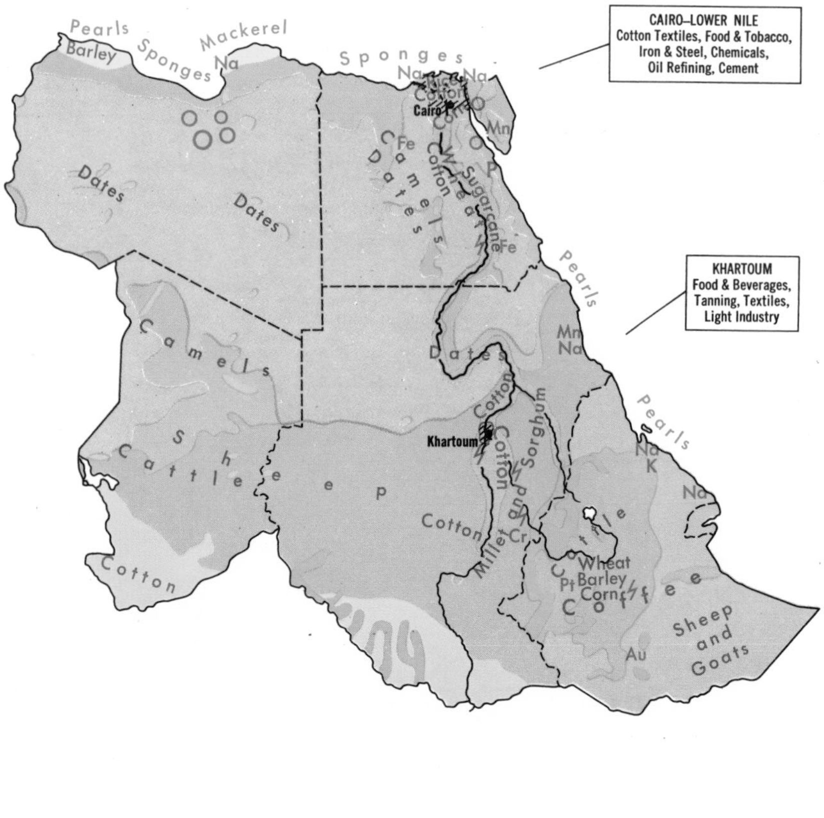

CAIRO–LOWER NILE
Cotton Textiles, Food & Tobacco, Iron & Steel, Chemicals, Oil Refining, Cement
KHARTOUM
Food & Beverages, Tanning, Textiles, Light Industry
Pearls
Mackerel
Barley
Sponges
Na
Cairo
Cotton
Dates
Camels
Sugarcane
Fe
Mn
Khartoum
Sorghum
Millet
Cattle
Sheep
Cr
Wheat
Barley
Corn
Coffee
Pt
Sheep and Goats
Au
K

DOMINANT LAND USE

Cereals, Horticulture, Livestock
Cash Crops, Mixed Cereals
Cotton, Cereals
Market Gardening, Diversified Tropical Crops
Plantation Agriculture
Oases
Pasture Livestock
Nomadic Livestock Herding
Forests
Nonagricultural Land

MAJOR MINERAL OCCURRENCES

Au Gold
Cr Chromium
Fe Iron Ore
K Potash
Mn Manganese
Na Salt
O Petroleum
P Phosphates
Pt Platinum

Water Power
Major Industrial Areas

ANGOLA
AREA 481,351 sq. mi.
POPULATION 6,761,000
CAPITAL Luanda
LARGEST CITY Luanda
HIGHEST POINT Mt. Moco 8,593 ft.
MONETARY UNIT Angolan escudo
MAJOR LANGUAGES Mbundu, Kongo, Lunda, Portuguese
MAJOR RELIGIONS Tribal religions, Roman Catholicism

BURUNDI
AREA 10,747 sq. mi.
POPULATION 4,100,000
CAPITAL Bujumbura
LARGEST CITY Bujumbura
HIGHEST POINT 8,858 ft.
MONETARY UNIT Burundi franc
MAJOR LANGUAGES Kirundi, French, Swahili
MAJOR RELIGIONS Tribal religions, Roman Catholicism, Islam

CAMEROON
AREA 183,568 sq.mi.
POPULATION 6,600,000
CAPITAL Yaoundé
LARGEST CITY Douala
HIGHEST POINT Cameroon 13,350 ft.
MONETARY UNIT CFA franc
MAJOR LANGUAGES Fang, Bamileke, Fulani, Duala, French, English
MAJOR RELIGIONS Tribal religions, Christianity, Islam

CENTRAL AFRICAN EMPIRE
AREA 236,293 sq. mi.
POPULATION 1,800,000
CAPITAL Bangui
LARGEST CITY Bangui
HIGHEST POINT Gao 4,659 ft.
MONETARY UNIT CFA franc
MAJOR LANGUAGES Banda, Gbaya, Sangho, French
MAJOR RELIGIONS Tribal religions, Christianity, Islam

CONGO
AREA 132,046 sq. mi.
POPULATION 1,400,000
CAPITAL Brazzaville
LARGEST CITY Brazzaville
HIGHEST POINT Leketi Mts. 3,412 ft.
MONETARY UNIT CFA franc
MAJOR LANGUAGES Kikongo, Bateke, Lingala, French
MAJOR RELIGIONS Christianity, Tribal religions, Islam

EQUATORIAL GUINEA
AREA 10,831 sq. mi.
POPULATION 320,000
CAPITAL Malabo
LARGEST CITY Malabo
HIGHEST POINT 9,868 ft.
MONETARY UNIT ekuele
MAJOR LANGUAGES Fang, Bubi, Spanish, English, Ibo
MAJOR RELIGIONS Tribal religions, Christianity

GABON
AREA 103,346 sq. mi.
POPULATION 526,000
CAPITAL Libreville
LARGEST CITY Libreville
HIGHEST POINT Ibounzi 5,165 ft.
MONETARY UNIT CFA franc
MAJOR LANGUAGES Fang and other Bantu languages, French
MAJOR RELIGIONS Tribal religions, Christianity, Islam

KENYA
AREA 224,960 sq. mi.
POPULATION 13,300,000
CAPITAL Nairobi
LARGEST CITY Nairobi
HIGHEST POINT Kenya 17,058 ft.
MONETARY UNIT Kenya shilling
MAJOR LANGUAGES Kikuyu, Luo, Kavirondo, Kamba, Swahili, English
MAJOR RELIGIONS Tribal religions, Christianity, Hinduism, Islam

MALAWI
AREA 45,747 sq. mi.
POPULATION 5,100,000
CAPITAL Lilongwe
LARGEST CITY Blantyre
HIGHEST POINT Mlanje 9,843 ft.
MONETARY UNIT Malawi kwacha
MAJOR LANGUAGES Chichewa, Yao, English, Nyanja, Tumbuka, Tonga, Ngoni
MAJOR RELIGIONS Tribal religions, Islam, Christianity

RWANDA
AREA 10,169 sq. mi.
POPULATION 4,241,000
CAPITAL Kigali
LARGEST CITY Kigali
HIGHEST POINT Karisimbi 14,780 ft.
MONETARY UNIT Rwanda franc
MAJOR LANGUAGES Kinyarwanda, French, Swahili
MAJOR RELIGIONS Tribal religions, Roman Catholicism, Islam

SOMALIA
AREA 246,200 sq. mi.
POPULATION 3,170,000
CAPITAL Mogadishu
LARGEST CITY Mogadishu
HIGHEST POINT Surud Ad 7,900 ft.
MONETARY UNIT Somali shilling
MAJOR LANGUAGES Somali, Arabic, Italian, English
MAJOR RELIGIONS Islam

TANZANIA
AREA 363,708 sq. mi.
POPULATION 15,506,000
CAPITAL Dar es Saláam
LARGEST CITY Dar es Salaam
HIGHEST POINT Kilimanjaro 19,340 ft.
MONETARY UNIT Tanzanian shilling
MAJOR LANGUAGES Nyamwezi-Sukuma, Swahili, English
MAJOR RELIGIONS Tribal religions, Christianity, Islam

UGANDA
AREA 91,076 sq. mi.
POPULATION 11,400,000
CAPITAL Kampala
LARGEST CITY Kampala
HIGHEST POINT Margherita 16,795 ft.
MONETARY UNIT Ugandan shilling
MAJOR LANGUAGES Luganda, Acholi, Teso, Nyoro, Soga, Nkole, English, Swahili
MAJOR RELIGIONS Tribal religions, Christianity, Islam

ZAIRE
AREA 918,962 sq. mi.
POPULATION 25,600,000
CAPITAL Kinshasa
LARGEST CITY Kinshasa
HIGHEST POINT Margherita 16,795 ft.
MONETARY UNIT zaire
MAJOR LANGUAGES Tshiluba, Mongo, Kikongo, Kingwana, Zande, Lingala, Swahili, French
MAJOR RELIGIONS Tribal religions, Christianity

ZAMBIA
AREA 290,586 sq. mi.
POPULATION 4,936,000
CAPITAL Lusaka
LARGEST CITY Lusaka
HIGHEST POINT Sunzu 6,782 ft.
MONETARY UNIT Zambian kwacha
MAJOR LANGUAGES Bemba, Tonga, Lozi, Luvale, Nyanja, English, Afrikaans
MAJOR RELIGIONS Tribal religions

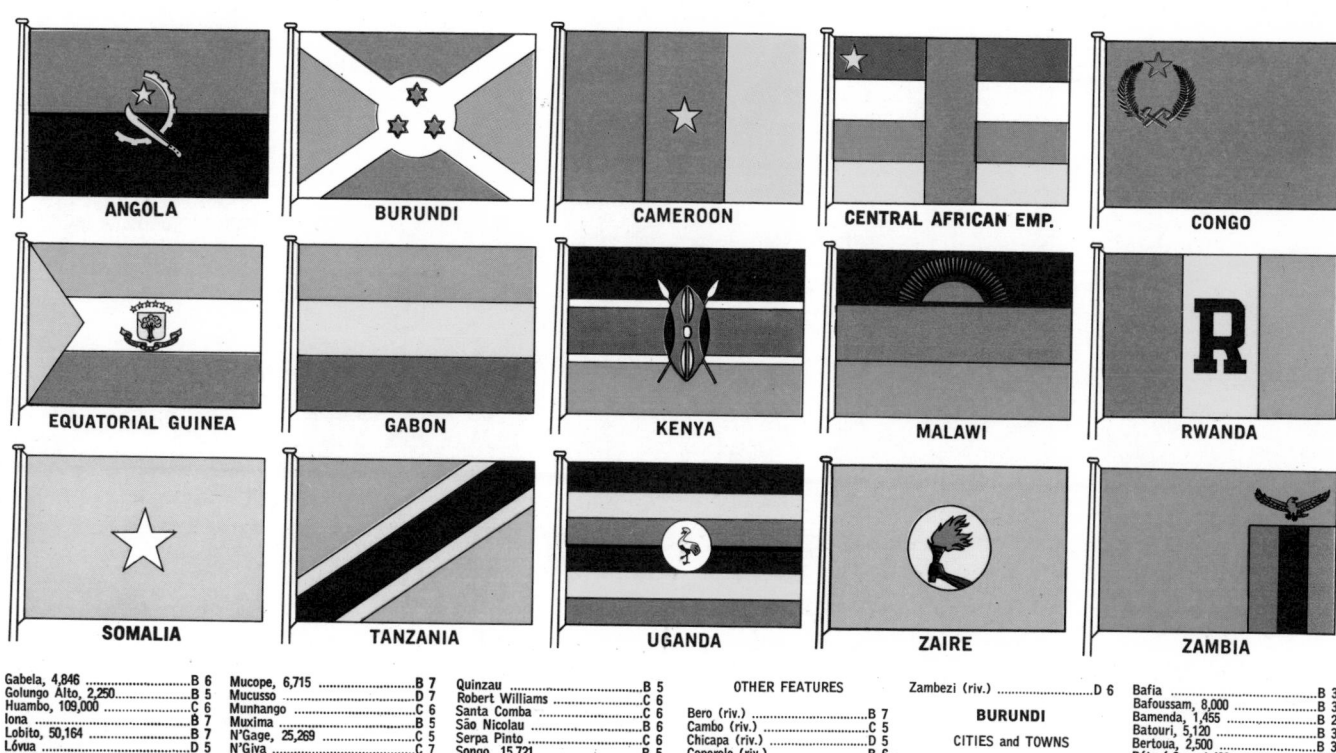

ANGOLA — BURUNDI — CAMEROON — CENTRAL AFRICAN EMP. — CONGO — EQUATORIAL GUINEA — GABON — KENYA — MALAWI — RWANDA — SOMALIA — TANZANIA — UGANDA — ZAIRE — ZAMBIA

(continued on following page)

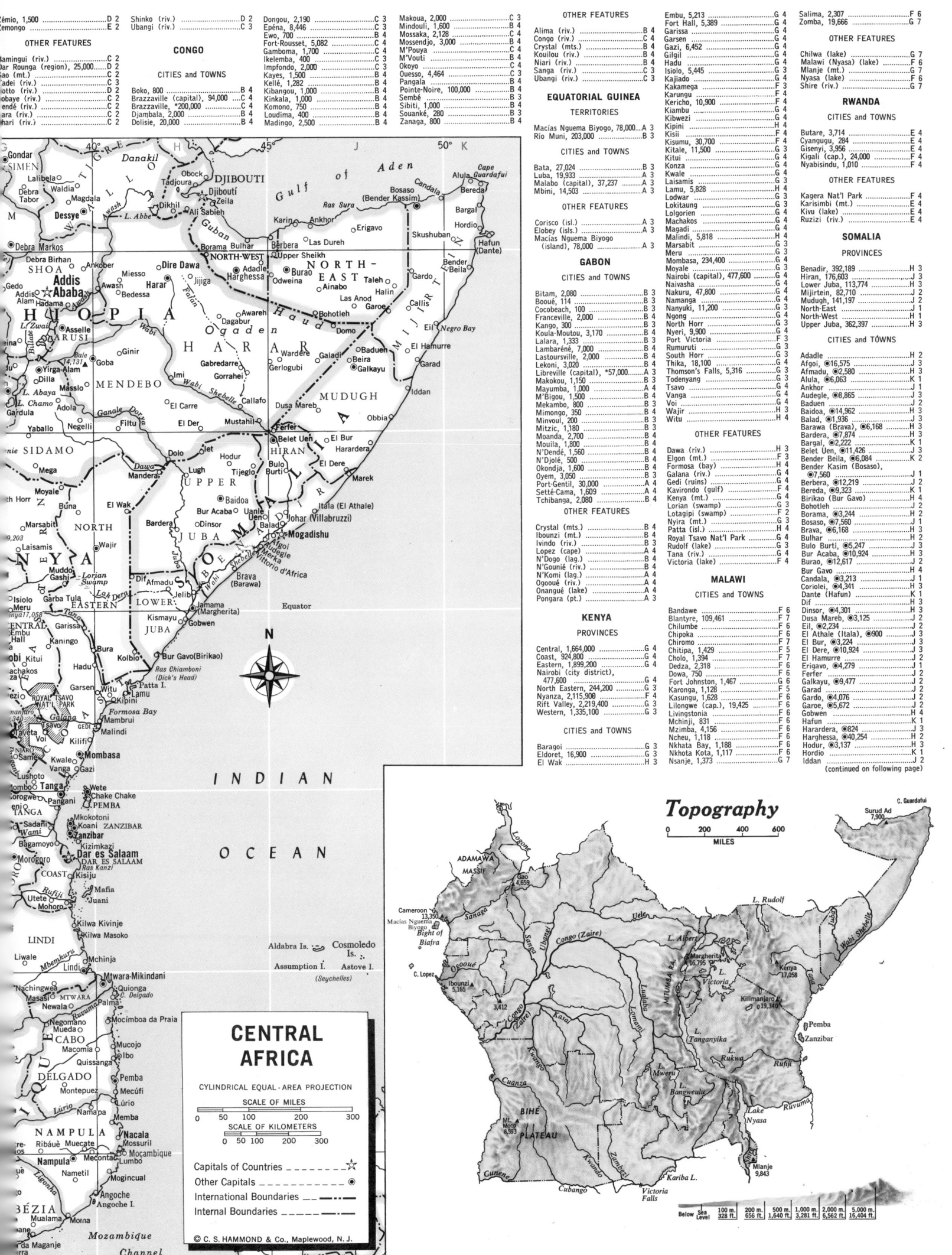

émio, 1,500 ....D 2
emongo ....E 2

OTHER FEATURES

amingui (riv.) ....C 2
lar Rounga (region), 25,000 ....C 2
adé (riv.) ....D 2
otto (riv.) ....D 2
obaye (riv.) ....C 2
ara (riv.) ....C 2
hari (riv.) ....C 2

Shinko (riv.) ....D 2
Ubangi (riv.) ....C 3

Dongou, 2,190 ....C 3
Epéna, 8,446 ....C 3
Ewo, 700 ....B 4
Fort-Rousset, 5,082 ....C 4
Gamboma, 1,700 ....C 4
Ikelemba, 400 ....C 4
Impfondo, 2,000 ....C 3
Kayes, 1,500 ....B 4
Kellé, 1,282 ....B 4
Kibangou, 1,150 ....B 4
Kinkala, 1,000 ....B 4
Komono, 750 ....B 4
Loudima, 400 ....B 4
Madingo, 2,500 ....B 4

Makoua, 2,000 ....C 3
Mindouli, 1,600 ....B 4
Mossaka, 2,128 ....C 4
Mossendjo, 3,000 ....B 4
M'Pouya ....C 4
M'Vouti ....B 4
Okoyo ....C 4
Ouesso, 4,464 ....B 3
Pangala ....B 4
Pointe-Noire, 100,000 ....B 3
Sembé ....B 3
Sibiti, 1,000 ....B 4
Souanké, 280 ....B 3
Zanaga, 800 ....B 4

CONGO
CITIES and TOWNS

Boko, 800 ....B 4
Brazzaville (capital), 94,000 ....B 4
Brazzaville, *200,000 ....B 4
Djambala, 2,000 ....C 4
Dolisie, 20,000 ....B 4

OTHER FEATURES

Alima (riv.) ....B 4
Congo (riv.) ....C 4
Crystal (mts.) ....A 3
Kouilou (riv.) ....B 4
Niari (riv.) ....B 4
Sanga (riv.) ....C 3
Ubangi (riv.) ....C 3

EQUATORIAL GUINEA
TERRITORIES

Macías Nguema Biyogo, 78,000 ....A 3
Río Muni, 203,000 ....B 3

CITIES and TOWNS

Bata, 27,024 ....B 3
Luba, 19,933 ....A 3
Malabo (capital), 37,237 ....A 3
Mbini, 14,503 ....A 3

OTHER FEATURES

Corisco (isl.) ....A 3
Elobey (isls.) ....A 3
Macías Nguema Biyogo
(island), 78,000 ....A 3

GABON
CITIES and TOWNS

Bitam, 2,080 ....B 3
Booué, 114 ....B 4
Cocobeach, 100 ....A 3
Franceville, 2,000 ....B 4
Kango, 300 ....B 3
Koula-Moutou, 3,170 ....B 4
Lalara, 1,333 ....B 4
Lambaréné, 7,000 ....B 4
Lastoursville, 2,000 ....B 4
Lekoni, 3,020 ....B 4
Libreville (capital), *57,000 ....A 3
Makokou, 1,150 ....B 4
Mayumba, 1,000 ....A 4
M'Bigou, 1,500 ....B 4
Mekambo, 800 ....B 4
Mimongo, 350 ....B 4
Minvoul, 200 ....B 3
Mitzic, 1,180 ....B 3
Moanda, 2,700 ....B 4
Mouila, 1,800 ....B 4
N'Dendé, 1,560 ....B 4
N'Djolé, 500 ....B 4
Okondja, 1,600 ....B 4
Oyem, 3,050 ....B 3
Port-Gentil, 30,000 ....A 4
Setté-Cama, 1,609 ....A 4
Tchibanga, 2,080 ....B 4

OTHER FEATURES

Crystal (mts.) ....B 3
Ibounzi (mt.) ....B 3
Ivindo (riv.) ....B 3
Lopez (cape) ....A 4
N'Dogo (lag.) ....A 4
N'Gounié (riv.) ....B 4
N'Komi (lag.) ....A 4
Ogooué (riv.) ....A 4
Onangué (lake) ....A 4
Pongara (pt.) ....A 3

KENYA
PROVINCES

Central, 1,664,000 ....G 4
Coast, 924,800 ....G 4
Eastern, 1,899,200 ....G 4
Nairobi (city district),
477,600 ....G 4
North Eastern, 244,200 ....G 3
Nyanza, 2,115,908 ....F 4
Rift Valley, 2,219,400 ....G 3
Western, 1,335,100 ....G 3

CITIES and TOWNS

Baragoi ....G 3
Eldoret, 16,900 ....G 3
El Wak ....H 3

Embu, 5,213 ....G 4
Fort Hall, 5,389 ....G 4
Garissa ....G 4
Garsen ....G 4
Gazi, 6,452 ....G 4
Gilgil ....G 4
Hadu ....G 4
Isiolo, 5,445 ....G 3
Kajiado ....G 4
Kakamega ....F 4
Karungu ....F 4
Kericho, 10,900 ....F 4
Kiambu ....G 4
Kibwezi ....G 4
Kipini ....H 4
Kisii ....F 4
Kisumu, 30,700 ....G 3
Kitale, 11,500 ....G 3
Kitui ....G 4
Konza ....G 4
Kwale ....G 4
Laisamis ....G 3
Lamu, 5,828 ....H 4
Lodwar ....F 3
Lokitaung ....G 3
Lolgorien ....F 4
Machakos ....G 4
Magadi ....G 4
Malindi, 5,818 ....H 4
Marsabit ....G 3
Meru ....G 3
Mombasa, 234,400 ....G 4
Moyale ....G 3
Nairobi (capital), 477,600 ....G 4
Naivasha ....G 4
Nakuru, 47,800 ....G 3
Namanga ....G 4
Nanyuki, 11,200 ....G 3
Ngong ....G 4
North Horr ....G 3
Nyeri, 9,900 ....G 4
Port Victoria ....F 3
Rumuruti ....G 3
South Horr ....G 3
Thika, 18,100 ....G 4
Thomson's Falls, 5,316 ....G 3
Todenyang ....G 3
Tsavo ....G 4
Vanga ....G 4
Voi ....G 4
Wajir ....G 3
Witu ....H 4

OTHER FEATURES

Dawa (riv.) ....H 3
Elgon (mt.) ....F 3
Formosa (bay) ....H 4
Galana (riv.) ....G 4
Gedi (ruins) ....H 4
Kavirondo (gulf) ....F 4
Kenya (mt.) ....G 4
Lorian (swamp) ....G 3
Lotagipi (swamp) ....F 2
Nyira (mt.) ....G 3
Patta (isl.) ....H 4
Royal Tsavo Nat'l Park ....G 4
Rudolf (lake) ....G 3
Tana (riv.) ....G 4
Victoria (lake) ....F 4

MALAWI
CITIES and TOWNS

Bandawe ....F 6
Blantyre, 109,461 ....F 7
Chilumbe ....F 6
Chipoka ....F 6
Chiromo ....F 7
Chitipa, 1,429 ....F 5
Cholo, 1,394 ....F 7
Dedza, 2,318 ....F 6
Dowa, 750 ....F 6
Fort Johnston, 1,467 ....G 6
Karonga, 1,128 ....F 5
Kasungu, 1,628 ....F 6
Lilongwe (cap.), 19,425 ....F 6
Livingstonia ....F 6
Mchinji, 831 ....F 6
Mzimba, 4,156 ....F 6
Ncheu, 1,118 ....F 6
Nkhata Bay, 1,188 ....F 6
Nkhota Kota, 1,117 ....F 6
Nsanje, 1,373 ....G 7

Salima, 2,307 ....F 6
Zomba, 19,666 ....G 7

OTHER FEATURES

Chilwa (lake) ....G 7
Malawi (Nyasa) (lake) ....F 6
Mlanje (mt.) ....G 7
Nyasa (lake) ....F 6
Shire (riv.) ....G 7

RWANDA
CITIES and TOWNS

Butare, 3,714 ....E 4
Cyangugu, 284 ....E 4
Gisenyi, 3,956 ....E 4
Kigali (cap.), 24,000 ....E 4
Nyabisindu, 1,010 ....F 4

OTHER FEATURES

Kagera Nat'l Park ....F 4
Karisimbi (mt.) ....E 4
Kivu (lake) ....E 4
Ruzizi (riv.) ....E 4

SOMALIA
PROVINCES

Benadir, 392,189 ....H 3
Hiran, 176,603 ....J 3
Lower Juba, 113,774 ....H 3
Mijirtein, 82,710 ....J 2
Mudugh, 141,197 ....J 2
North-East ....H 1
North-West ....H 1
Upper Juba, 362,397 ....H 3

CITIES and TOWNS

Adadle, ⊙16,575 ....H 2
Afgoi, ⊙16,575 ....J 3
Afmadu, ⊙2,580 ....H 3
Alula, ⊙6,063 ....K 1
Ankhor ....J 3
Audegle, ⊙8,865 ....J 3
Baduen ....J 2
Baidoa, ⊙14,962 ....H 3
Balad, ⊙1,936 ....J 3
Barawa (Brava), ⊙6,168 ....H 3
Bardera, ⊙7,874 ....H 3
Bargal, ⊙2,222 ....K 1
Belet Uen, ⊙11,426 ....J 3
Bender Beila, ⊙6,084 ....K 2
Bender Kasim (Bosaso),
⊙7,560 ....J 1
Berbera, ⊙12,219 ....H 1
Bereda, ⊙9,323 ....K 1
Birikao (Bur Gavo) ....H 4
Bohotleh ....J 2
Borama, ⊙3,244 ....H 1
Bosaso, ⊙7,560 ....J 1
Brava, ⊙6,168 ....H 3
Bulhar ....H 1
Bulo Burti, ⊙5,247 ....J 3
Bur Acaba, ⊙10,924 ....H 3
Burao, ⊙12,617 ....J 2
Bur Gavo ....H 4
Candala, ⊙3,213 ....K 1
Coriolei, ⊙4,341 ....J 3
Dante (Hafun) ....K 1
Dif ....H 3
Dinsor, ⊙4,301 ....H 3
Dusa Mareb, ⊙3,125 ....J 2
Eil, ⊙2,234 ....J 2
El Athale (Itala), ⊙900 ....J 3
El Bur, ⊙3,224 ....J 2
El Dere, ⊙10,924 ....J 2
El Hamurre ....J 1
Erigavo, ⊙4,279 ....J 1
Ferfer ....J 2
Galkayu, ⊙9,477 ....J 2
Garad ....J 2
Gardo, ⊙4,076 ....J 2
Garoe, ⊙5,672 ....J 2
Gobwen ....H 4
Hafun ....K 1
Harardera, ⊙824 ....J 3
Harghessa, ⊙40,254 ....H 1
Hodur, ⊙3,137 ....H 3
Hordio ....K 1
Iddan ....J 2

(continued on following page)

CENTRAL AFRICA

CYLINDRICAL EQUAL-AREA PROJECTION
SCALE OF MILES
0 50 100   200   300
SCALE OF KILOMETERS
0 50 100   200   300

Capitals of Countries .... ☆
Other Capitals .... ⊙
International Boundaries .... ——
Internal Boundaries .... ———

© C. S. HAMMOND & Co., Maplewood, N.J.

Topography

0   200   400   600
MILES

Below Sea Level | 100 m. 328 ft. | 200 m. 656 ft. | 500 m. 1,640 ft. | 1,000 m. 3,281 ft. | 2,000 m. 6,562 ft. | 5,000 m. 16,404 ft.

(continued)

SOMALIA (cantinued)

Iet, ◉1,370	H 3
Itala, ◉900	J 3
Jamama, ◉22,030	H 3
Jelib, ◉3,232	H 3
Johar, ◉13,156	H 3
Kismayu, ◉17,872	H 4
Las Anod, ◉2,441	J 2
Las Dureh	J 1
Las Khoreh, ◉2.245	J 1
Lugh, ◉3,768	H 3
Marek	J 3
Margherita (Jamama), ◉22,030	H 3
Merka, ◉56,385	H 3
Mogadishu, 172,677	J 3
Obbia, ◉2,106	J 2
Odweina, ◉1,422	J 2
Skushuban, ◉1,384	J 1
Taleh	J 2
Tijeglo, ◉5,459	H 3
Uanle Uen, ◉9,650	H 3
Upper Sheikh	J 2
Villabruzzi (Johar), ◉13,156	J 3
Vittorio d'Africa	H 3
Zeila, ◉1,226	H 1

OTHER FEATURES

Aden (gulf)	J 1
Chiamboni, Ras (cape)	H 4
Guardafui (cape)	K 1
Guban (reg.)	H 1
Hafun, Ras (cape)	K 1
Haud (plat.)	J 2
Juba (riv.)	H 3
Negro (bay)	J 2
Nogal (reg.)	J 2
Surud Ad (mt.)	J 1
Wabi Shebelle (riv.)	H 3

TANZANIA

REGIONS

Arusha	G 4
Coast	G 5
Dar es Salaam	G 5
Dodoma	G 5
Iringa	G 5
Kigoma	F 4
Kilimanjaro	G 4
Lindi	G 5
Mara	F 4
Mbeya	F 5
Morogoro	G 5
Mtwara	G 6
Mwanza	F 4
Pemba	H 5
Rukwa	F 5
Ruvuma	G 6
Shinyanga	F 4
Singida	F 5
Tabora	F 5
Tanga	G 5
West Lake	F 4
Zanzibar Mjini	H 5
Zanzibar Shambani North	G 5
Zanzibar Shambani South	G 5

CITIES and TOWNS

Arusha, 32,452	G 4
Bagamoyo, 5,112	G 5
Biharamulo, 1,011	F 4
Bukene, 2,288	F 4
Bukoba, 8,141	F 4
Chake Chake, 4,862	G 5
Chunya, 2,398	F 5
Dar es Salaam (capital), 272,821	G 5
Dodoma, 23,559	G 5
Geita, 3,066	F 4
Ifakara, †21,101	G 5
Iringa, 21,746	G 5
Itigi, †6,633	F 5
Kahama, 3,211	F 4
Kaliua, †13,071	F 5
Karema, †3,171	F 5
Kasanga, †10,462	F 5
Kibara, †18,827	F 4
Kibaya, †4,422	G 5
Kibondo	F 4
Kigoma-Ujiji, 21,369	E 4
Kilosa, 4,458	G 5
Kilwa Kivinje, 2,790	G 5
Kilwa Masoko	G 5
Kinyangiri, †14,111	G 4
Kipili, †2,964	F 5
Kisiju, †26,298	G 5
Kitunda, †2,491	F 5
Kizimkazi, 992	G 5
Koani, 1,102	G 5
Kondoa, 4,514	G 4
Kongwa, †27,411	G 5
Korogwe, 6,675	G 5
Lindi, 13,352	G 5
Liwale, †22,205	G 5
Longido, †1,998	G 4
Lushoto, 1,803	G 4
Mahenge, †32,047	G 5
Makumbako	G 5
Manyoni, †4,362	G 5
Mbamba Bay, †10,936	G 6
Mbeya, 12,479	F 5
Mbulu, †7,004	G 4
Mchinga, †5,778	H 5
Mkokotoni, 2,200	G 5
Mohoro-Kikobo, †6,112	G 5
Mombo, †29,782	G 4
Morogoro, 25,262	G 5
Moshi, 26,864	G 4
Mpanda, †4,220	F 5
Mpwapwa, 2,429	G 5
Mtwara-Mikindani, 20,413	H 6
Murongo, †20,118	F 4
Musoma, 15,412	F 4
Muwale	F 5
Mwadui, 7,383	F 4
Mwanza, 34,861	F 4
Mwaya, †15,940	F 5
Mwesi, †803	F 5
Nachingwea, 3,751	G 6
Newala, †7,458	G 6
Ngara	F 4
Njombe	F 5
Nzega, 2,386	F 4
Pangani, 2,955	G 5
Rungwa, †903	F 5
Sadani, †760	G 5
Same, †8,105	G 4
Sekenke	F 4
Shinyanga, 5,135	F 4
Singida, 9,478	F 4
Songea, 5,430	G 6
Sumbawanga, †34,106	F 5
Tabora, 21,012	F 5
Tanga, 61,058	G 4
Tukuyu, 4,089	F 5
Tunduru	G 6
Urambo, †16,625	F 4
Utete, †5,642	G 5
Uvinza, †12,812	F 5
Wete, 8,469	G 4
Zanzibar, 68,490	G 5
Zanzibar, *95,047	G 5

OTHER FEATURES

Eyasi (lake)	F 4
Gombe (riv.)	F 4
Great Ruaha (riv.)	G 5
Juani (isl.), 696	G 5
Kalambo (falls)	F 5
Kanzi (cape)	G 5
Kilimanjaro (mt.)	G 4
Kilombero (riv.)	G 5
Kungwe (mt.)	F 5
Mafia (isl.), 15,459	H 5
Manyara (lake)	G 4
Masai (steppe)	G 4
Mbarangandu (riv.)	G 5
Mbemkuru (riv.)	G 5
Meru (mt.)	G 4
Natron (lake)	G 4
Ngorongoro (crater)	F 4
Njombe (riv.)	F 5
Nyasa (lake)	F 6
Olduvai Gorge (canyon)	G 4
Pangani (riv.)	G 4
Pemba (isl.), 164,321	H 5
Rufiji (riv.)	G 5
Rukwa (lake)	F 5
Rungwa (riv.)	F 5
Rungwe (mt.)	F 5
Ruvuma (riv.)	G 4
Serengeti Nat'l Park	F 4
Tanganyika (lake)	E 5
Victoria (lake)	F 4
Wami (riv.)	G 5
Wembere (riv.)	F 4
Zanzibar (isl.), 190,494	G 5

UGANDA

CITIES and TOWNS

Arua, 4,645	F 3
Atura, 119	F 3
Butiaba, 1,216	F 3
Entebbe, 10,941	F 4
Fort Portal, 8,317	F 3
Gulu, 4,770	F 3
Hoima, 1,056	F 3
Jinja, 29,741	F 3
Kaabong	F 3
Kabale, 10,919	E 4
Kampala (capital), 330,000	F 3
Kasese, 1,564	F 3
Katwe, 2,057	F 4
Kilembe	F 3
Kitgum, 3,454	F 3
Lira, 2,929	F 3
Masaka, 4,785	F 4
Masindi, 1,571	F 3
Mbale, 23,539	F 3
Mbarara, 3.844	F 4
Moroto, 2.082	F 3
Moyo, 2,009	F 3
Mubende, 1,878	F 3
Namasagali	F 3
Pakwach, 1,467	F 3
Rhino Camp, 3,478	F 3
Soroti, 6,645	F 3
Tororo, 6,365	F 3
Yumbe, 949	F 3

OTHER FEATURES

Albert (lake)	F 3
Edward (lake)	E 4
Elgon (mt.)	F 3
George (lake)	F 4
Kioga (lake)	F 3
Margherita (mt.)	E 3
Murchison (falls)	F 3
Owen Falls (dam)	F 3
Queen Elizabeth Nat'l Park	F 4
Ruwenzori (range)	E 3
Sese (isls.)	F 4
Victoria (lake)	F 4

ZAIRE

PROVINCES

Bandundu, 2,600,556	C 4
Bas-Zaïre, 1,504,361	B 4
Equateur, 2,431,812	D 3
Haut-Zaïre, 3,356,419	E 3
Kasai-Occidental, 2,433,861	D 4
Kasai-Oriental, 1,872,231	D 5
Katanga, 2,753,714	E 5
Kinshasa (city), 1,323,039	C 4
Kivu, 3,361,883	E 4

CITIES and TOWNS

Aba	F 3
Abumombazi, †5,773	D 3
Aketi, 15,339	D 3
Ango	E 3
Avakubi	E 3
Bagata	C 4
Balangala	D 3
Bambesa	E 3
Bambili	E 3
Banana	B 5
Bandundu, 74,467	C 4
Banzyville, 6,608	D 3
Baraka	E 4
Basankusu, 5,613	C 3
Basoko	D 3
Basongo	D 4
Batama	E 3
Baudouinville	E 5
Befale, 3,407	D 3
Bena-Dibele	D 4
Beni	E 3
Bikoro, 6,491	C 4
Boende, 391	D 4
Bokungu, 4,952	D 4
Bolobo	C 4
Bolomba, 5,636	C 3
Boma, 33,143	B 5
Bomboma, 1,319	C 3
Bomongo, 4,827	C 3
Bondo, 453	D 3
Bongandanga, 4,476	D 3
Bosobolo, 2,809	D 3
Budjala, 415	C 3
Bukama	E 5
Bukavu, 134,861	E 4
Bumba, 5,182	D 3
Bunia, 12,410	E 3
Bunkeya	E 6
Busanga, †2,792	D 6
Businga, 2,827	D 3
Busu-Djanoa, †5,520	D 3
Buta, 10,845	D 3
Butembo, 9,980	E 3
Dekese	D 4
Demba	D 5
Dibaya	D 5
Dibaya-Lubue	C 4
Dilolo	D 6
Dimbelenge	D 5
Djolu, 2,516	D 3
Djugu	F 3
Djuma	C 4
Dongo, 559	C 3
Doruma	E 3
Dungu	E 3
Elila	E 4
Equateur	C 3
Etoile	E 6
Faradje	E 3
Feshi	C 5
Fizi	E 4
Gandajika	D 5
Gemena, 8,135	D 3
Goma, 14,115	E 4
Gombari	E 3
Gumba-Mobeka, †7,023	C 3
Idiofa	C 4
Ikela, 3,166	D 4
Imese, 115	C 3
Ingende, 6,730	C 4
Inongo	C 4
Irumu	E 3
Isangi	D 3
Isangila	B 5
Isiro, 17,430	E 3
Kabalo	E 5
Kabare	E 4
Kabinda	D 5
Kabongo	E 5
Kabunda	E 6
Kahemba	C 5
Kalehe	E 4
Kalemie, 29,934	E 5
Kalima	E 4
Kaloko	E 5
Kama	E 4
Kambove (with Shinkolobwe), 14,517	E 6
Kamina, 20,915	D 5
Kananga, 428,960	D 5
Kanda Kanda	D 5
Kaniama	D 5
Kapanga	D 5
Kasaji	D 6
Kasangulu	C 4
Kasenyi	E 3
Kasese	E 4
Kasongo	E 4
Kasongo-Lunda	C 5
Katako-Kombe	D 4
Katana	E 4
Katenga	E 5
Kazumba	D 5
Kenge	C 4
Kibombo	E 4
Kikwit, 111,960	C 5
Kilo	E 3
Kilwa	E 5
Kindu-Port Empain, 19,385	E 4
Kiniama	E 6
Kinshasa (capital), 1,323,039	C 4
Kipushi, 22,602	E 6
Kirundu	E 4
Kisangani, 229,596	E 3
Kolwezi, 45,192	E 6
Komba	D 3
Kongolo, 10,434	E 5
Kungu, 7,912	C 3
Kutu, †2,072	C 4
Kwamouth	C 4
Libenge, 2,632	C 3
Lienartville	E 3
Likasi, 146,394	E 6
Likati	D 3
Lisala, 574	D 3
Lodja, 7,227	D 4
Lokolama	D 4
Lomela, †7,757	D 4
Loto	D 4
Lotumbe	C 4
Luashi	D 6
Lubefu	D 4
Lubudi, 5,915	E 5
Lubumbashi, 318,000	E 6
Lubutu	E 4
Luebo	D 5
Luena	E 5
Luishia	E 6
Lukula	B 4
Lunyama	E 5
Luofu	E 4
Luozi	B 5
Luputa	D 5
Lusambo, 9,395	D 4
Lusangi	E 4
Madimba	C 5
Malonga	D 6
Mambasa	E 3
Manono, 12,234	E 5
Masi-Manimba	C 4
Masisi	E 4
Matadi, 110,436	B 5
Mbandaka, 107,910	C 3
Mbuji-Mayi, 256,154	D 5
Moanda	B 5
Moba	E 5
Moliro	E 5
Monga	D 3
Monkoto, 5,209	D 4
Monveda	D 3
Mungbere	E 3
Mushie, 12,118	C 4
Mutshatsha	D 6
Muyumba	E 5
Mwadingusha	E 6
Mwanza	E 5
Mwene Ditu	D 5
Mwenga	E 4
Niangara	E 3
Niemba	E 5
Nouvelle-Anvers, †4,330	C 3
Nyunzu	E 5
Oshwe	C 4
Panda	E 6
Pangi	E 4
Penge	D 5
Piana-Mwanga	E 5
Poie	D 4
Poko	E 3
Ponthierville	D 4
Port-Francqui	D 4
Punia	E 4
Pweto	E 5
Rutshuru	E 4
Sakania	E 6
Sampwe	E 5
Sandoa	D 5
Shabunda	E 4
Shinkolobwe (with Kambove), 14,517	E 6
Songololo	B 5
Thysville, 16,369	C 5
Titule	E 3
Tolo	C 4
Tondo	C 4
Tshela	B 4
Tshikapa	D 5
Tshofa	D 5
Uvira	E 4
Vanga	C 4
Wafania, 584	D
Waka, 264	D
Wamba	E
Watsa, 6,077	E
Yakoma, †5,685	D
Yangambi, 18,849	D
Zongo, †4,128	C

OTHER FEATURES

Albert (lake)	F
Albert Nat'l Park	E
Aruwimi (riv.)	E
Bomu (riv.)	D
Congo (riv.)	C
Edward (lake)	E
Elila (riv.)	E
Fimi (riv.)	C
Garamba Nat'l Park	E
Giri (riv.)	C
Itimbiri (riv.)	D
Ituri (for.)	E
Karisimbi (mt.)	E
Kasai (riv.)	C
Kivu (lake)	E
Kwa (riv.)	C
Kwango (riv.)	C
Kwilu (riv.)	C
Léopold II (lake)	C
Lindi (riv.)	E
Livingstone (falls)	B
Loange (riv.)	C
Lokoro (riv.)	C
Lomami (riv.)	D
Lomela (riv.)	D
Lowa (riv.)	E
Lua (riv.)	C
Lualaba (riv.)	E
Luapula (riv.)	E
Lubilash (riv.)	D
Lufira (riv.)	E
Luilaka (riv.)	D
Lukenie (riv.)	D
Lukuga (riv.)	E
Lulua (riv.)	D
Luvua (riv.)	E
Margherita (mt.)	E
Mweru (lake)	E
Marungu (mts.)	E
Ruwenzori (range)	E
Ruzizi (riv.)	E
Sankuru (riv.)	D
Stanley (falls)	E
Stanley Pool (lake)	C
Tanganyika (lake)	
Tshuapa (riv.)	
Tumba (lake)	
Ubangi (riv.)	
Uele (riv.)	
Ulindi (riv.)	
Upemba (lake)	
Upemba Nat'l Park	
Virunga (range)	
Zaire (Congo) (riv.)	

ZAMBIA

CITIES and TOWNS

Abercorn (Mbala), ‡5,200	
Balovale, 2,260	
Bancroft (Chililabombwe), ‡39,900	
Broken Hill (Kabwe), ‡67,200	
Chilanga, 2,510	
Chililabombwe, ‡39,900	
Chingola, ‡92,800	
Chinsali, 1,110	
Chipata, ‡13,300	
Chisamba, 790	
Choma, ‡11,300	
Feira, 310	
Fort Rosebery (Mansa), ‡5,700	
Isoka, 1,370	
Kabompo, 990	
Kabwe, ‡67,200	
Kafue, 2,490	
Kalabo, 2,420	
Kalomo, 2,560	
Kapiri Mposhi, 440	
Kasama, ‡8,900	
Kasempa, 670	
Kawambwa, 1,430	
Kitwe, ‡179,300	
Lealui	
Livingstone, ‡43,000	
Luanshya, ‡90,400	
Lukulu	
Lundazi, 1,750	
Lusaka (capital), ‡238,200	
Luwingu, 850	
Mankoya, 1,600	
Mansa, ‡5,700	
Mazabuka, ‡9,400	
Mbala, ‡5,200	
Mongu, ‡10,700	
Monze, ‡4,300	
Mpika, 660	
Mporokoso, 790	
Mpulungu, 1,830	
Mufulira, ‡101,200	
Mumbwa, 1,400	
Mwinilunga, 700	
Nakonde	
Namwala, 880	
Nchanga, 35,030	
Ndola, ‡150,800	
Nkana, 54,500	
Petauke, 1,640	
Roan Antelope, 36,300	
Senanga, 1,500	
Serenje, 1,650	
Sesheke, 910	
Solwezi, 1,930	

OTHER FEATURES

Bangweulu (lake)	
Barotseland (reg.), 417,000	
Chambeshi (riv.)	
Dongwe (riv.)	
Kabampo (riv.)	
Kafue (riv.)	
Kariba (dam)	
Kariba (lake)	
Kwando (riv.)	
Luangwa (riv.)	
Mosi-Ao-Tunya (Victoria) (falls)	
Mulungushi (dam)	
Mweru (lake)	
Sunzu (mt.)	
Tanganyika (lake)	
Victoria (falls)	
Zambezi (riv.)	

*City and suburbs.
†Population of sub-district or di
‡Population of urban area.
◉Population of municipality.

Agriculture, Industry and Resources

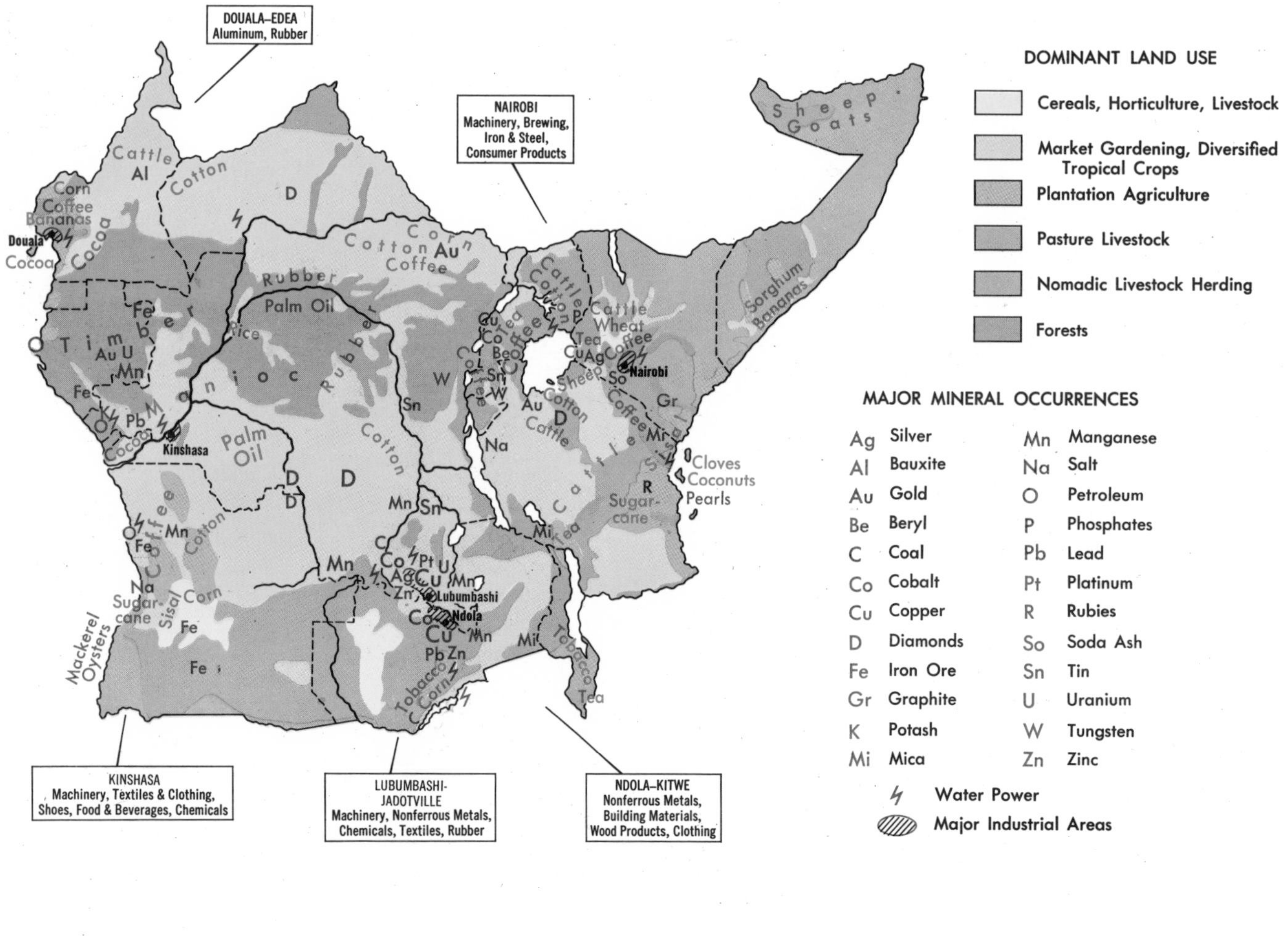
DOUALA–EDEA
Aluminum, Rubber
NAIROBI
Machinery, Brewing, Iron & Steel, Consumer Products
KINSHASA
Machinery, Textiles & Clothing, Shoes, Food & Beverages, Chemicals
LUBUMBASHI-JADOTVILLE
Machinery, Nonferrous Metals, Chemicals, Textiles, Rubber
NDOLA–KITWE
Nonferrous Metals, Building Materials, Wood Products, Clothing
Douala
Kinshasa
Lubumbashi
Ndola
Nairobi
Cloves
Coconuts
Pearls
Mackerel
Oysters
DOMINANT LAND USE
Cereals, Horticulture, Livestock
Market Gardening, Diversified Tropical Crops
Plantation Agriculture
Pasture Livestock
Nomadic Livestock Herding
Forests
MAJOR MINERAL OCCURRENCES
Ag Silver
Al Bauxite
Au Gold
Be Beryl
C Coal
Co Cobalt
Cu Copper
D Diamonds
Fe Iron Ore
Gr Graphite
K Potash
Mi Mica
Mn Manganese
Na Salt
O Petroleum
P Phosphates
Pb Lead
Pt Platinum
R Rubies
So Soda Ash
Sn Tin
U Uranium
W Tungsten
Zn Zinc
Water Power
Major Industrial Areas

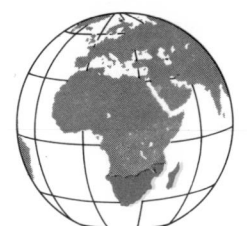

SOUTH-WEST AFRICA (NAMIBIA)
AREA 317,827 sq. mi.
POPULATION 883,000
CAPITAL Windhoek
LARGEST CITY Windhoek
HIGHEST POINT Brandberg 8,550 ft.
MONETARY UNIT rand
MAJOR LANGUAGES Ovambo, Hottentot, Herero, Afrikaans, English
MAJOR RELIGIONS Tribal religions, Protestantism

SOUTH AFRICA
AREA 458,179 sq. mi.
POPULATION 24,400,000
CAPITALS Cape Town, Pretoria
LARGEST CITY Johannesburg
HIGHEST POINT Injasuti 11,182 ft.
MONETARY UNIT rand
MAJOR LANGUAGES Afrikaans, English, Xhosa, Zulu, Sesotho
MAJOR RELIGIONS Protestantism, Roman Catholicism, Islam, Hinduism

LESOTHO
AREA 11,720 sq. mi.
POPULATION 1,100,000
CAPITAL Maseru
LARGEST CITY Maseru
HIGHEST POINT 11,425 ft.
MONETARY UNIT South African rand
MAJOR LANGUAGES Sesotho, English
MAJOR RELIGIONS Tribal religions, Christianity

BOTSWANA
AREA 224,764 sq. mi.
POPULATION 700,000
CAPITAL Gaborone
LARGEST CITIES Selebi-Pikwe
HIGHEST POINT Tsodilo Hill 5,922 ft.
MONETARY UNIT pula
MAJOR LANGUAGES Setswana, Shona, Bushman, English, Afrikaans
MAJOR RELIGIONS Tribal religions, Protestantism

MOZAMBIQUE
AREA 308,641 sq. mi.
POPULATION 9,300,000
CAPITAL Maputo
LARGEST CITY Maputo
HIGHEST POINT Mt. Binga 7,992 ft.
MONETARY UNIT Mozambique escudo
MAJOR LANGUAGES Makua, Thonga, Shona, Portuguese
MAJOR RELIGIONS Tribal religions, Roman Catholicism, Islam

SWAZILAND
AREA 6,705 sq. mi.
POPULATION 500,000
CAPITAL Mbabane
LARGEST CITY Mbabane
HIGHEST POINT Emlembe 6,109 ft.
MONETARY UNIT lilangeni
MAJOR LANGUAGES siSwati, English
MAJOR RELIGIONS Tribal religions, Christianity

RHODESIA (ZIMBABWE)
AREA 150,803 sq. mi.
POPULATION 6,600,000
CAPITAL Salisbury
LARGEST CITY Salisbury
HIGHEST POINT Mt. Inyangani 8,517 ft.
MONETARY UNIT Rhodesian dollar
MAJOR LANGUAGES English, Shona, Ndebele
MAJOR RELIGIONS Tribal religions, Protestantism

MADAGASCAR
AREA 226,657 sq. mi.
POPULATION 7,700,000
CAPITAL Antananarivo
LARGEST CITY Antananarivo
HIGHEST POINT Maromokotro 9,436 ft.
MONETARY UNIT Madagascar franc
MAJOR LANGUAGES Malagasy, French
MAJOR RELIGIONS Tribal religions, Roman Catholicism, Prostestantism

COMORO ISLANDS
AREA 719 sq. mi.
POPULATION 266,000
CAPITAL Moroni
LARGEST CITY Moroni
HIGHEST POINT Karthala 8,399 ft.
MONETARY UNIT CFA franc
MAJOR LANGUAGES Arabic, French, Swahili
MAJOR RELIGION Islam

MAURITIUS
AREA 790 sq. mi.
POPULATION 899,000
CAPITAL Port Louis
LARGEST CITY Port Louis
HIGHEST POINT 2,711 ft.
MONETARY UNIT Mauritian rupee
MAJOR LANGUAGES English, French, French Creole, Hindi, Urdu
MAJOR RELIGIONS Hinduism, Christianity, Islam

SEYCHELLES
AREA 145 sq. mi.
POPULATION 60,000
CAPITAL Victoria
LARGEST CITY Victoria
HIGHEST POINT Morne Seychellois 2,970 ft.
MONETARY UNIT Seychellois rupee
MAJOR LANGUAGES English, French, Creole
MAJOR RELIGION Roman Catholicism

RÉUNION
AREA 969 sq. mi.
POPULATION 475,700
CAPITAL St-Denis

MAYOTTE
AREA 144 sq. mi.
POPULATION 40,000
CAPITAL Mamoutzou

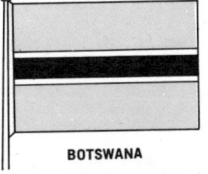
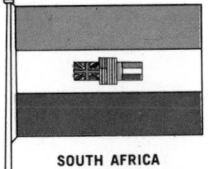
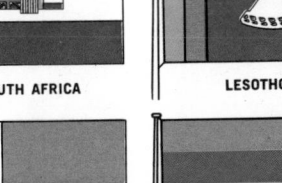
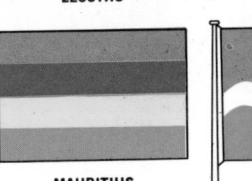
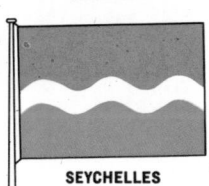

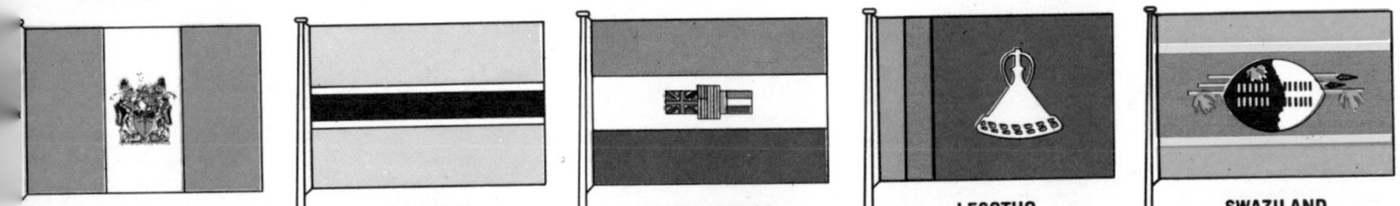

RHODESIA | BOTSWANA | SOUTH AFRICA | LESOTHO | SWAZILAND

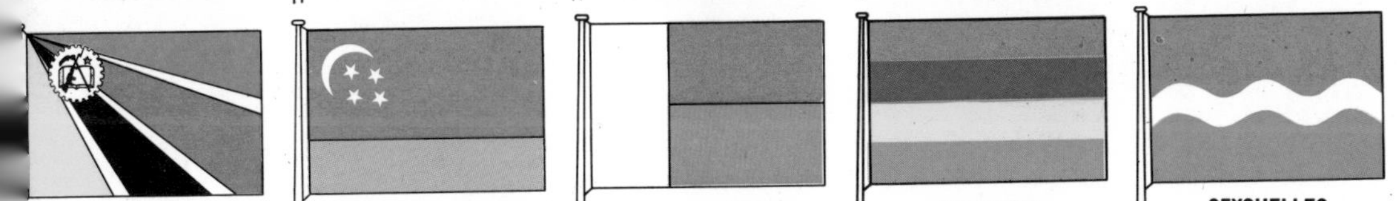

MOZAMBIQUE | COMORO ISLANDS | MADAGASCAR | MAURITIUS | SEYCHELLES

Agriculture, Industry and Resources

MAJOR MINERAL OCCURRENCES

Ab	Asbestos	D	Diamonds	Mn	Manganese	Sb	Antimony
Ag	Silver	Fe	Iron Ore	Na	Salt	Sn	Tin
Au	Gold	Gr	Graphite	Ni	Nickel	U	Uranium
Be	Beryl	Lt	Lithium	P	Phosphates	V	Vanadium
C	Coal	Mg	Magnesium	Pb	Lead	W	Tungsten
Cr	Chromium	Mi	Mica	Pt	Platinum	Zn	Zinc
Cu	Copper						

⚡ Water Power
▨ Major Industrial Areas

DOMINANT LAND USE
Cereals, Horticulture, Livestock
Market Gardening, Diversified Tropical Crops
Plantation Agriculture
Pasture Livestock
Nomadic Livestock Herding
Forests
Nonagricultural Land

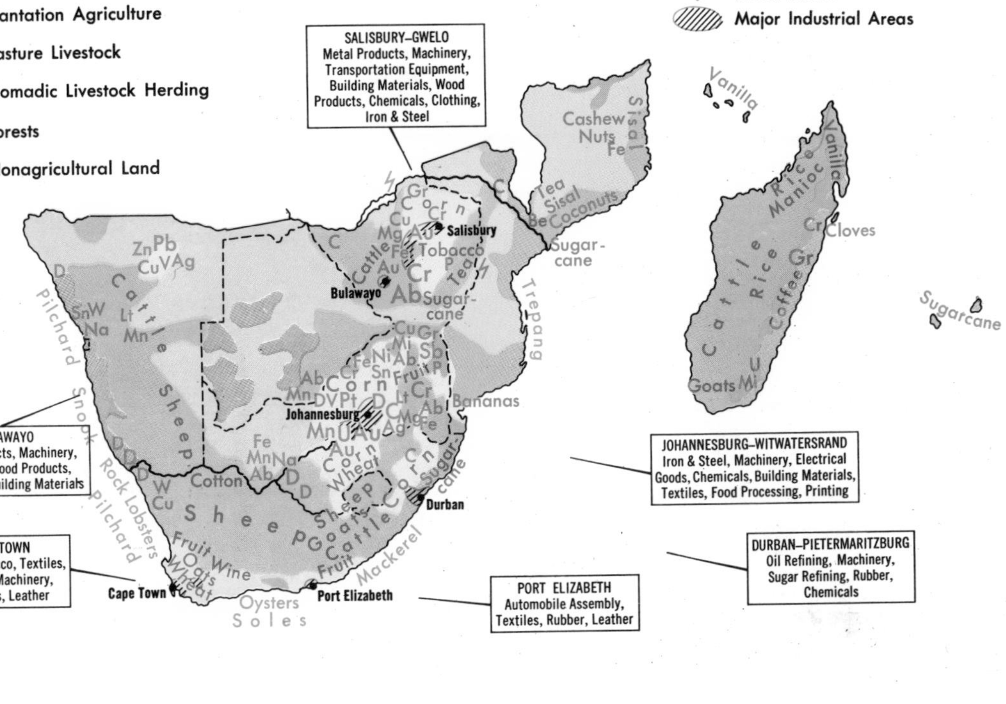

SALISBURY–GWELO
Metal Products, Machinery, Transportation Equipment, Building Materials, Wood Products, Chemicals, Clothing, Iron & Steel

BULAWAYO
Metal Products, Machinery, Clothing, Wood Products, Chemicals, Building Materials

CAPE TOWN
Food & Tobacco, Textiles, Clothing, Machinery, Chemicals, Leather

JOHANNESBURG–WITWATERSRAND
Iron & Steel, Machinery, Electrical Goods, Chemicals, Building Materials, Textiles, Food Processing, Printing

DURBAN–PIETERMARITZBURG
Oil Refining, Machinery, Sugar Refining, Rubber, Chemicals

PORT ELIZABETH
Automobile Assembly, Textiles, Rubber, Leather

Vanilla
Cashew Nuts
Sisal
Tea
Sisal
Coconuts
Sugar-cane
Rice
Manioc
Vanilla
Cloves
Sugarcane
Rice
Gr
Coffee
U
Goats
Salisbury
Bulawayo
Johannesburg
Durban
Cape Town
Port Elizabeth
Trepang

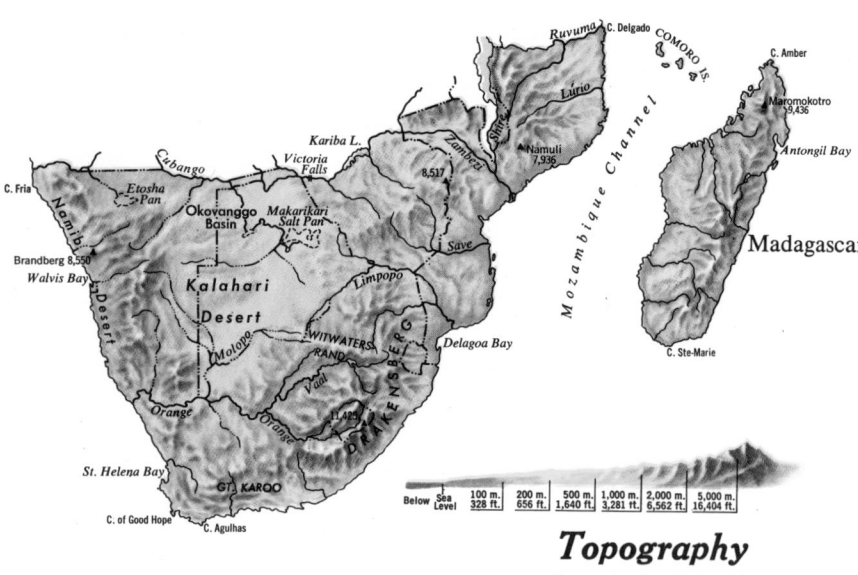

Topography

Below Sea Level | 100 m. 328 ft. | 200 m. 656 ft. | 500 m. 1,640 ft. | 1,000 m. 3,281 ft. | 2,000 m. 6,562 ft. | 5,000 m. 16,404 ft.

MILES
0 200 400 600

Kenhardt, 3,230 ... C 5
Kimberley, 105,258 ... C 5
Kimberley, □108,609 ... C 5
King William's Town, 15,798 ... D 6
Kirkwood, 5,151 ... F 7
Kleinmond, 1,115 ... F 7
Klerksdorp, 63,558 ... D 5
Kliprivier ...
Knysna, 13,479 ... C 6
Koffiefontein, 3,672 ... D 5
Kokstad, 10,227 ... D 6
Kommetjie ... E 7
Kraaifontein, 10,286 ... F 6
Kraal ... J 7
Kroonstad, 51,988 ... D 5
Krugersdorp, 92,725 ... H 6
Kuilsrivier, 8,132 ...
Kuruman, 5,758 ... C 5
Ladismith, 2,756 ...
Ladybrand, 8,757 ... D 5
Ladysmith, 28,920 ... D 5
Lambert's Bay, 3,247 ... B 6
Louis Trichardt, 8,906 ... E 4
Lydenburg, 7,427 ... E 4
Maclear, 3,279 ... D 6
Mafeking, 6,515 ... C 5
Malmesbury, 9,314 ... B 6
Margate, 4,410 ... E 6

Matatiele, 3,853 ... D 6
Messina, 12,121 ... D 4
Meyerton, 6,654 ... H 7
Middelburg, C. of Good Hope, 11,121 ... D 6
Middelburg, Transvaal, 26,942 ... D 5
Middelvlei ... G 7
Mmabatho ... D 5
Modderfontein, 8,538 ... H 6
Molteno, 5,825 ... D 5
Montagu, 5,504 ... C 6
Moorreesburg, 4,945 ... B 6
Mossel Bay, 17,574 ... C 6
Nababiep, 8,293 ...
Nelspruit, 25,092 ... E 5
Newcastle, 14,407 ... D 5
Nigel, 41,179 ... J 7
Noupoort, 7,403 ... D 6
Nylstroom, 6,906 ... D 4
Odendaalsrus, 15,603 ... D 5
Okiep, 4,983 ... B 5
Onrusrivier, 337 ...
Oudtshoorn, 26,907 ... C 6
Paarl, 49,244 ... B 6
Parow, 60,768 ... F 6
Parys, 17,447 ... D 5
Pietermaritzburg, 114,822 ... E 5

Pietermaritzburg, □174,179 ... E 5
Pietersburg, 27,174 ... D 4
Piet Retief, 10,056 ... E 5
Piketberg, 3,638 ... B 6
Pinelands, 11,769 ... E 6
Pinetown, 22,721 ... E 6
Pniel, 1,596 ...
Port Alfred, 8,640 ... D 5
Port Elizabeth, 392,231 ... D 6
Port Elizabeth, □413,961 ... D 6
Port Nolloth, 2,893 ...
Port Saint Johns, 1,817 ...
Port Shepstone, 5,581 ... E 6
Postmasburg, 9,020 ...
Potchefstroom, 57,443 ... D 5
Potgietersrus, 6,667 ...
Pretoria (cap.), 545,450 ... D 5
Pretoria, □573,283 ...
Prieska, 8,521 ...
Prince Albert, 3,346 ... C 6
Queenstown, 39,304 ... D 6
Randfontein, 50,481 ... H 6
Reitz, 5,650 ...
Richmond, 3,185 ...
Riversdale, 6,165 ...
Robertson, 10,237 ...
Roodeport, 115,366 ... H 6

Tsiroanomandidy, 11,444 ... H 3
Tsivory, 1,036 ... H 4
Tuléar, 37,072 ... G 4
Vangaindrano, 3,249 ... H 4
Vatomandry, 4,202 ... H 3
Vohémar, 4,289 ... J 2
Vohipeno, 2,736 ... H 4

OTHER FEATURES

Alaotra (lake) ... H 3
Amber (cape) ... H 2
Antongil (bay) ... J 3
Betsiboka (riv.) ... H 3
Mangoky (riv.) ... G 4
Mangoro (riv.) ... H 3
Maromokotro (mt.) ... H 2
Masoala (pen.) ... J 3
Mozambique (chan.) ... G 3
Nossi-Bé (isl.), 27,181 ... H 2
Onilahy (riv.) ... G 4
Saint-André (cape) ... G 3
Sainte-Marie (cape) ... G 5
Sainte-Marie (isl.), 9,604 ... J 3
Tsiafajavona (mt.) ... H 3
Tsiribihina (riv.) ... G 3

MAURITIUS

CITIES and TOWNS

Curepipe, 52,709 ... G 5
Mahébourg, 15,463 ... G 5
Port Louis (cap.), 136,802 ... G 5
Poudre d'Or, 1,208 ... G 5
Quatre Bornes, 51,638 ... G 5
Souillac, 2,606 ... G 5

OTHER FEATURES

Mascarene (isls.) ... F 5

MAYOTTE

CITIES and TOWNS

Mamoutzou (cap.), 1,090 ... H 2

MOZAMBIQUE

DISTRICTS

Cabo Delgado, 546,113 ... F 2
Gaza, 756,654 ... E 4
Inhambane, 748,575 ... E 4
Manica, 367,337 ... E 3
Maputo, 799,502 ... E 5
Nampula, 1,716,486 ... F 2
Niassa, 285,329 ... F 2
Sofala, 712,381 ... E 3
Tete, 488,668 ... E 3
Zambézia, 1,747,888 ... E 3

CITIES and TOWNS

Alto Molócuè, 415 ... F 3
Angoche, 1,714 ... G 3
Bartolomeu Dias, †6,102 ... F 4
Beira, 46,293 ... F 3
Beira, *130,398 ... F 3
Bela-Vista, 851 ... E 5
Caniçado, 530 ... E 4
Chemba, 588 ... E 3
Chibuto, 23,763 ... E 4
Chicoa, 6,564 ... E 3
Chigubo ...
Chimoio, 4,507 ... E 3
Chinde, 742 ... F 3
Cóbuè, †770 ... F 2
Dona Ana (Mutarara), 686 ... F 3
Entre-Rios, 430 ... F 2
Errego, 418 ... F 3
Espungabera, 405 ... E 4
Fingoè, 1,137 ... E 2
Funhalouro, †42,366 ... E 4
Furancungo, 188 ... E 2
Goba ...
Homoine, 1,122 ... E 4
Ibo, 1,015 ... G 2
Inhambane, 4,975 ... E 4
Inhaminga, 1,607 ... F 3
Inharrime, 856 ... F 4
Lichinga, 3,011 ... F 2
Lourenço Marques (Maputo) (cap.), 101,754 ... E 5
Lumbo, †11,080 ... G 3
Lúrio, †13,417 ... G 2
Mabalane, †13,158 ... E 4
Mabote, †28,970 ... E 4
Machanga, †15,754 ... F 4
Machaze, †42,255 ... E 4
Macia, 1,203 ... E 5
Macomia, 730 ... F 2
Magude, 1,502 ... E 5
Mague, 359 ... E 3

Malvérnia (Chicualacuala), 2,050 ... E 4
Mandie, †24,382 ... E 3
Mandimba, †7,634 ... F 2
Manhiça, 1,680 ... E 5
Maniamba, †2,045 ... F 2
Manjacaze, 641 ... E 5
Mapai ... E 4
Maputo (cap.), 101,754 ... E 5
Maputo, *378,348 ... E 5
Marromeu, 1,330 ... F 3
Marrupa, 824 ... F 2
Massangena, †3,301 ... E 4
Massinga, 517 ... F 4
Maxia, 331 ... F 2
Meconta, 1,051 ... F 3
Mecufi, 70 ... G 2
Mecula, 148 ... F 2
Memba, 379 ... G 2
Metangula, 1,502 ... F 2
Milange, 1,048 ... F 3
Moamba, 643 ... E 5
Moatize (Benga), 1,398 ... E 3
Moçambique, 1,730 ... G 3
Mocímboa da Praia, 935 ... G 2
Mocuba, 2,293 ... F 3
Mogincual, 133 ... G 3
Moma, 433 ... F 3
Montepuez, 2,837 ... F 2
Mopeia, 233 ... F 3
Morrumbala, 415 ... F 3
Morrumbene, 1,121 ... F 4
Mossuril, 231 ... G 2
Mualama, †34,992 ... F 3
Mucojo, †15,867 ... G 2
Muecate, 263 ... F 2
Mueda, 1,583 ... F 2
Mungári, 174 ... E 3
Nacala, 4,601 ... G 2
Namacurra, 399 ... F 3
Nampa, 440 ... F 2
Namarrói, 271 ... F 3
Nametil, 453 ... F 3
Nampula, 23,072 ... F 2
Negomano, †656 ... F 2
Nova Freixo (Cuamba), 1,416 ... F 2
Nova Luzitánia, 1,363 ... E 3
Nova Mambone, 883 ... F 4
Nova Sofala, 274 ... F 3
Pafúri, †2,599 ... E 4
Palma, 318 ... G 2
Panda, 309 ... F 4
Pebane, 325 ... F 3
Pemba, 3,629 ... G 2
Quelimane, 10,522 ... F 3
Quionga, †3,181 ... G 2
Quissanga, 135 ... G 2
Quissico, 2,615 ... F 4
Ribáuè, 437 ... F 2
Tete, 4,549 ... E 3
Unango, †9,377 ... F 2
Vila Coutinho, 451 ... E 2
Vila de Maganja, 267 ... F 3
Vila de Manica, 1,529 ... E 3
Vila de Sena, †21,074 ... E 3
Vila do Dondo, 2,112 ... F 3
Vila Fontes, 1,363 ... F 3
Vila Gouveia, 663 ... E 3
Vila Luísa, 1,342 ... E 5
Vilanculos, 887 ... F 4
Vila Paiva de Andrada, 435 ... E 3

OTHER FEATURES

Angoche (isl.) ... G 3
Bazaruto (isl.) ... F 4
Binga (mt.) ... E 3
Caça National Park ... E 3
Changane (riv.) ... E 4
Chilwa (lake) ... F 3
Delagoa (bay) ... E 5
Delgado (cape) ... G 2
Limpopo (riv.) ... F 4
Lugenda (riv.) ... F 2
Lúrio (riv.) ... F 2
Mazoe (riv.) ... E 3
Mozambique (chan.) ... G 3
Namuli (mt.) ... F 3
Nyasa (lake) ... F 2
Olifants (riv.) ... D 4
Ruvuma (riv.) ... F 2
São Sebastião (cape) ... F 4
Save (riv.) ... E 4
Shire (riv.) ... F 3
Zambezi (riv.) ... E 3

REUNION

CITIES and TOWNS

Le Port, 17,280 ... F 5

Saint-André, 8,712 ... G 5
Saint-Benoît, 7,731 ... G 5
Saint-Denis (cap.), 66,162 ... F 5
Saint-Denis, *85,992 ... F 5
Saint-Joseph, 9,424 ... G 6
Saint-Louis, 7,267 ... F 5
Saint-Pierre, 18,534 ... F 6

OTHER FEATURES

Bassas da India (isl.) ... F 4
Europa (isl.) ... G 4
Glorioso (isls.) ... H 2
Juan de Nova (isl.) ... G 3
Piton des Neiges (mt.) ... F 5

RHODESIA (ZIMBABWE)

CITIES and TOWNS

Beitbridge, 1,986 ... E 4
Bindura, 10,321 ... E 3
Bulawayo, 207,949 ... D 3
Bulawayo, □308,000 ... D 3
Chipinga, 2,350 ... E 4
Dett, 2,473 ... D 3
Eiffel Flats, 4,043 ... E 3
Enkeldoorn, 1,669 ... E 3
Fort Victoria, 11,218 ... E 4
Fort Victoria, □15,000 ... E 4
Gatooma, 19,695 ... D 3
Gatooma, □32,000 ... D 3
Gwaai, †2,710 ... D 3
Gwanda, 2,049 ... D 4
Gwelo, 44,583 ... D 3
Gwelo, □58,000 ... D 3
Hartley, 8,633 ... E 3
Inyanga, 733 ... E 3
Kariba, 3,943 ... E 3
Marandellas, 10,936 ... E 3
Marandellas, □13,000 ... E 3
Matopos, †11,330 ... D 4
Melsetter, 667 ... E 3
Mount Darwin, 904 ... E 3
Nuanetsi, †7,830 ... E 4
Plumtree, 2,041 ... D 4
Que Que, 31,765 ... D 3
Que Que, □41,000 ... D 3
Rusape, 5,286 ... E 3
Salisbury (cap.), 267,417 ... E 3
Salisbury, □503,000 ... E 3
Selukwe, 8,387 ... E 3
Shabani, 4,440 ... E 4
Shabani, □17,000 ... E 4
Shamva, 785 ... E 3
Sinoia, 12,803 ... D 3
Sinoia, □17,000 ... D 3
Somabula, 292 ... D 3
Tuli, †340 ... D 4
Umtali, 42,358 ... E 3
Umtali, □54,000 ... E 3
Umvuma, 1,525 ... D 3
Wankie, 10,276 ... D 3
Wankie, □26,000 ... D 3
West Nicholson, 1,929 ... D 4

OTHER FEATURES

Inyanga National Park ... E 3
Kariba (lake) ... D 3
Lundi (riv.) ... E 4
Mashonaland (reg.), 1,875,700 ... E 3
Matabeleland (reg.), 969,220 ... D 3
Mazoe (riv.) ... E 3
Mushandike National Park ... D 4
Sabi (riv.) ... E 4
Shangani (riv.) ... D 3
Shashi (riv.) ... D 4
Umvukwe (range) ... E 3
Victoria (falls) ... C 3
Zambezi (riv.) ... C 3
Zimbabwe National Park ... E 4

SEYCHELLES

CITIES and TOWNS

Anse Boileau, ⊙3,027 ... H 5
Anse Royale, ⊙2,827 ... H 5
Cascade, ⊙2,037 ... H 5
Victoria (cap.), 13,736 ... H 5
Victoria, *16,629 ... H 5

OTHER FEATURES

Aldabra (isls.), 100 ... H 1
Assumption (isl.), 61 ... H 1
Astove (isl.), 9 ... H 1
Cosmoledo (isls.), 15 ... H 1
Frigate (isl.), 30 ... J 5
La Digue (isl.), 1,985 ... J 5
Mahé (isl.), 45,420 ... H 5
North (isl.), 27 ... H 5
Praslin (isl.), 4,244 ... H 5

Silhouette (isl.), 417 ... H 5

SOUTH AFRICA

PROVINCES

Cape of Good Hope, 4,604,354 ... C 6
Natal, 4,245,675 ... E 5
Orange Free State, 1,674,139 ... D 4
Transvaal, 8,167,154 ... D 4

AUTONOMOUS REPUBLICS

Bophuthatswana, 847,198 ... D 5
Transkei, 1,967,289 ... D 6

CITIES and TOWNS

Aberdeen, 4,968 ... C 6
Adelaide, 7,227 ... D 6
Alberton, 23,988 ... H 6
Alexandra, 57,040 ... H 6
Alexander Bay, 2,675 ... B 5
Aliwal North, 12,311 ... D 6
Bank, 452 ... G 7
Barberton, 12,382 ... E 5
Barkly East, 4,023 ... D 6
Beaufort West, 17,862 ... C 6
Bellville, 49,026 ... F 6
Benoni, 151,294 ... J 6
Benoni, □164,543 ... J 6
Bethal, 17,337 ... E 5
Bethlehem, 29,918 ... D 5
Bloemfontein, 149,836 ... C 5
Bloemfontein, □182,329 ... C 5
Bloubergstrand, 378 ... E 6
Boksburg, 106,126 ... J 6
Botrivier, 743 ...
Brakpan, 73,210 ... J 6
Brandvlei, 1,337 ... C 5
Brits, 12,182 ... D 5
Britstown, 3,039 ... C 5
Burgersdorp, 8,340 ... D 6
Butterworth, 2,769 ... D 6
Caledon, 5,406 ... G 7
Calvinia, 6,386 ... B 6
Cape Town (cap.), 697,514 ... E 6
Cape Town, □833,731 ... E 6
Carnarvon, 5,199 ... C 6
Ceres, 9,230 ... B 6
Christiana, 6,882 ... D 5
Clanwilliam, 2,724 ... B 6
Colesberg, 7,088 ... D 6
Constantia, 7,220 ... E 6
Cradock, 20,822 ... D 6
De Aar, 18,057 ... C 5
Dibeng, 945 ... C 5
Douglas, 4,335 ... C 5
Dundee, 17,162 ... E 5
Durban, 736,852 ... E 5
Durban, □975,494 ... E 5
Durbanville, 7,438 ... E 6
East London, 119,727 ... D 6
East London, □126,671 ... D 6
Edenburg, 3,710 ... D 5
Edendale, 41,194 ... D 5
Edenvale, 25,126 ... H 6
Eersterivier, 1,459 ... F 6
Elliot, 3,739 ... D 6
Eloff, 1,134 ... J 6
Empangeni, 7,532 ... E 5
Ermelo, 19,036 ... E 5
Eshowe, 4,240 ... E 5
Estcourt, 10,922 ... D 5
Ficksburg, 9,504 ... D 5
Fort Beaufort, 11,640 ... D 6
Franschhoek, 1,216 ... F 6
Garies, 1,339 ... B 6
George, 24,625 ... C 6
Germiston, 221,972 ... H 6
Germiston, □293,257 ... H 6
Glencoe, 10,513 ... E 5
Goodwood, 31,592 ... F 6
Gordon's Bay, 1,112 ... F 7
Graaff-Reinet, 22,392 ... C 6
Grabouw, 4,286 ... F 7
Grahamstown, 41,302 ... D 6
Grassy Park, 32,709 ... E 6
Greytown, 9,028 ... E 5
Griquatown, 2,996 ... C 5
Harrismith, 16,082 ... D 5
Hawston, 2,501 ... G 7
Heidelberg, 12,521 ... F 7
Heilbron, 8,258 ... D 5
Hermanus, 4,956 ... G 7
Hopetown, 3,273 ... C 5
Howick, 12,429 ... E 5
Humansdorp, 4,215 ... C 6
Ingwavuma, 718 ... E 5
Jagersfontein, 4,142 ... D 5
Jameson Park, 2,280 ... J 7
Johannesburg, 654,232 ... H 6
Johannesburg, □1,417,818 ... H 6
Keimoes, 4,534 ... C 5
Kempton Park, 37,205 ... J 6

SOUTHERN AFRICA

CONIC PROJECTION

SCALE OF MILES
0 50 100 200 300

SCALE OF KILOMETERS
0 50 100 200 300

Capitals of Countries .... ☆
Other Capitals .... ⊙
International Boundaries ___ _ _ ___
Internal Boundaries ___ ..... ___

Copyright by C.S. HAMMOND & CO., N.Y.

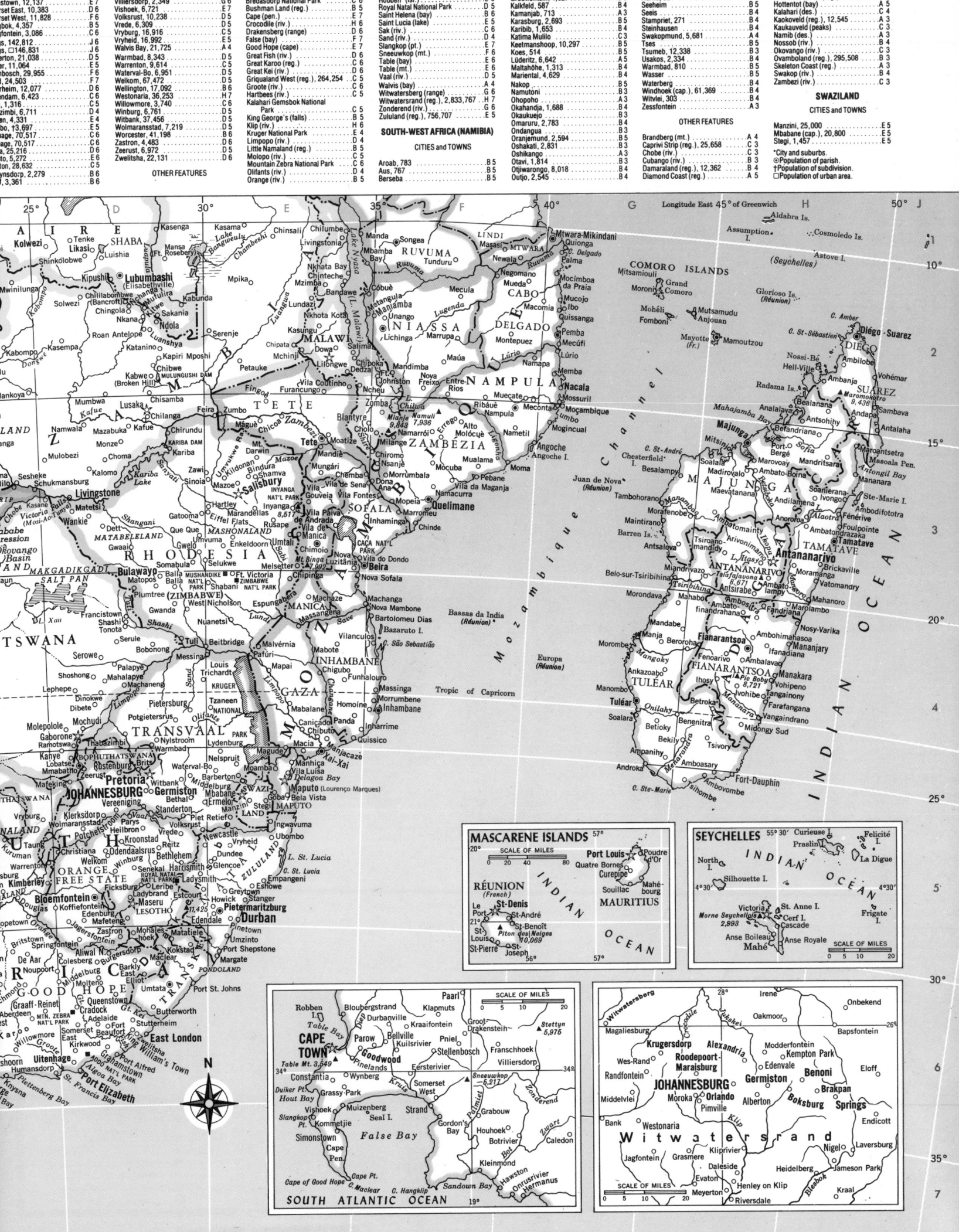

SOUTH AMERICA

LAMBERT AZIMUTHAL EQUAL-AREA PROJECTION

SCALE OF MILES

0   100   200   400   600

SCALE OF KILOMETRES

0 100 200   400   600

Capitals of Countries .... ☆
International Boundaries ._._._._
Canals ....

© C.S. HAMMOND & Co., N.Y.

GALAPAGOS ISLANDS
(ARCHIPIELAGO DE COLON)
(ECUADOR)

SCALE OF MILES

0   50   100   150

PACIFIC   OCEAN

POPULATION DISTRIBUTION

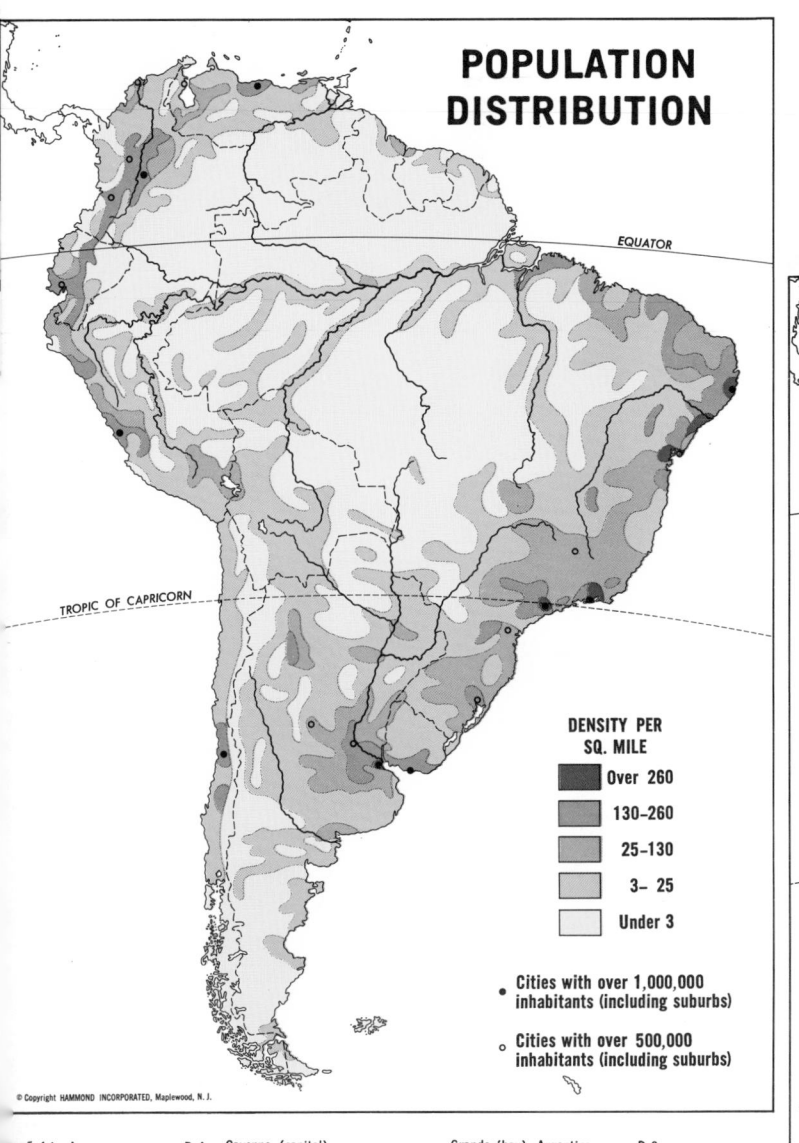

EQUATOR

TROPIC OF CAPRICORN

DENSITY PER SQ. MILE
- Over 260
- 130–260
- 25–130
- 3–25
- Under 3

● Cities with over 1,000,000 inhabitants (including suburbs)

○ Cities with over 500,000 inhabitants (including suburbs)

AREA 6,875,000 sq. mi.
POPULATION 186,000,000
LARGEST CITY Buenos Aires (greater)
HIGHEST POINT Cerro Aconcagua 22,831 ft.
LOWEST POINT Salina Grande -131 ft.

VEGETATION

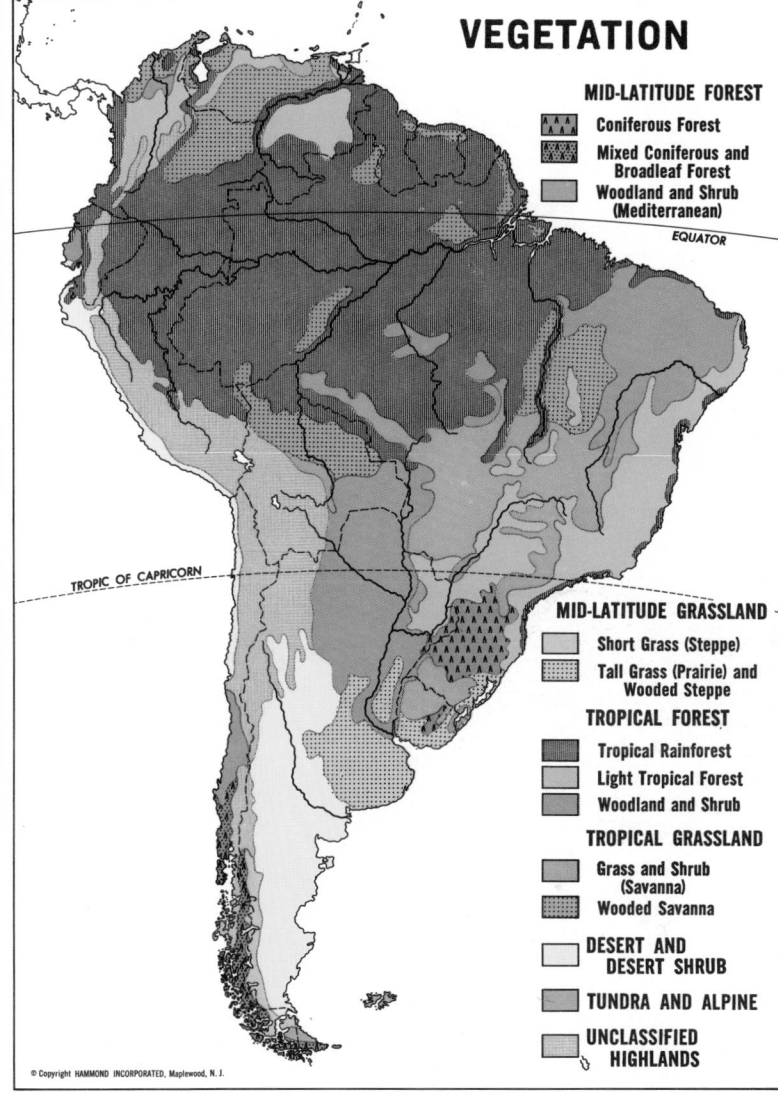

EQUATOR

TROPIC OF CAPRICORN

MID-LATITUDE FOREST
- Coniferous Forest
- Mixed Coniferous and Broadleaf Forest
- Woodland and Shrub (Mediterranean)

MID-LATITUDE GRASSLAND
- Short Grass (Steppe)
- Tall Grass (Prairie) and Wooded Steppe

TROPICAL FOREST
- Tropical Rainforest
- Light Tropical Forest
- Woodland and Shrub

TROPICAL GRASSLAND
- Grass and Shrub (Savanna)
- Wooded Savanna

DESERT AND DESERT SHRUB

TUNDRA AND ALPINE

UNCLASSIFIED HIGHLANDS

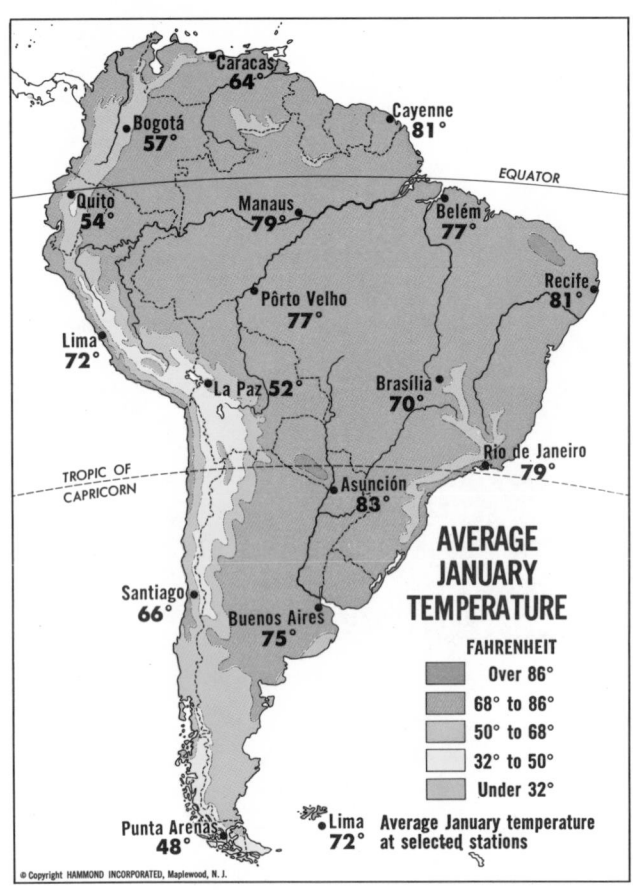

Caracas 64°
Bogotá 57°
Cayenne 81°
EQUATOR
Quito 54°
Manaus 79°
Belém 77°
Recife 81°
Pôrto Velho 77°
Lima 72°
La Paz 52°
Brasília 70°
TROPIC OF CAPRICORN
Rio de Janeiro 79°
Asunción 83°

AVERAGE JANUARY TEMPERATURE

FAHRENHEIT
Over 86°
68° to 86°
50° to 68°
32° to 50°
Under 32°

Santiago 66°
Buenos Aires 75°

• Lima 72° Average January temperature at selected stations

Punta Arenas 48°

© Copyright HAMMOND INCORPORATED, Maplewood, N. J.

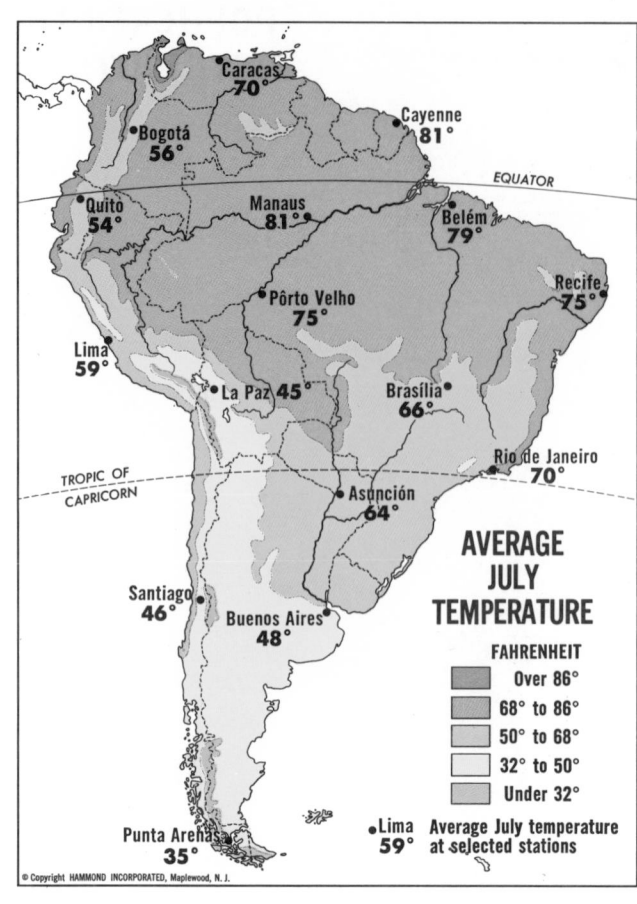

Caracas 70°
Bogotá 56°
Cayenne 81°
EQUATOR
Quito 54°
Manaus 81°
Belém 79°
Recife 75°
Pôrto Velho 75°
Lima 59°
La Paz 45°
Brasília 66°
TROPIC OF CAPRICORN
Rio de Janeiro 70°
Asunción 64°

AVERAGE JULY TEMPERATURE

FAHRENHEIT
Over 86°
68° to 86°
50° to 68°
32° to 50°
Under 32°

Santiago 46°
Buenos Aires 48°

• Lima 59° Average July temperature at selected stations

Punta Arenas 35°

© Copyright HAMMOND INCORPORATED, Maplewood, N. J.

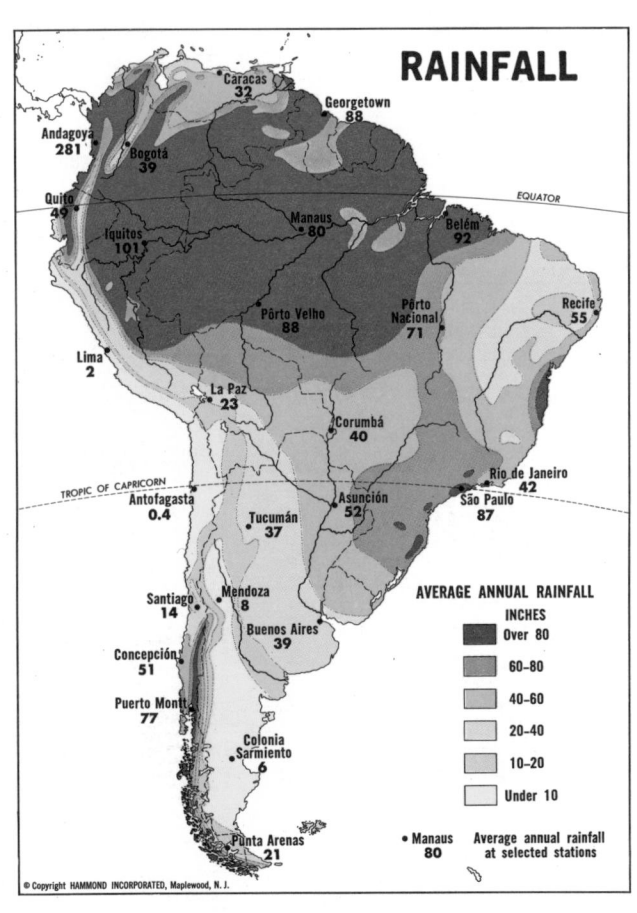

RAINFALL

Caracas 32
Georgetown 88
Andagoyá 281
Bogotá 39
Quito 49
EQUATOR
Iquitos 101
Manaus 80
Belém 92
Pôrto Velho 88
Pôrto Nacional 71
Recife 55
Lima 2
La Paz 23
Corumbá 40
TROPIC OF CAPRICORN
Rio de Janeiro 42
Antofagasta 0.4
Tucumán 37
Asunción 52
São Paulo 87

AVERAGE ANNUAL RAINFALL
INCHES
Over 80
60–80
40–60
20–40
10–20
Under 10

Santiago 14
Mendoza 8
Buenos Aires 39
Concepción 51
Puerto Montt 77
Colonia Sarmiento 6

• Manaus 80 Average annual rainfall at selected stations

Punta Arenas 21

© Copyright HAMMOND INCORPORATED, Maplewood, N. J.

VEGETATION/RELIEF

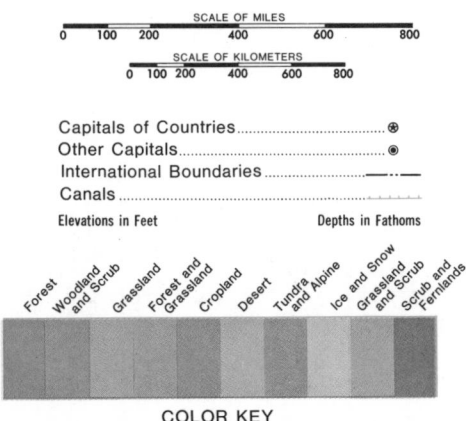

SCALE OF MILES
0   100 200   400   600   800

SCALE OF KILOMETERS
0 100 200   400   600   800

Capitals of Countries.....................⊕
Other Capitals.............................◉
International Boundaries................._____
Canals..

Elevations in Feet   Depths in Fathoms

Forest
Woodland and Scrub
Grassland
Forest and Grassland
Cropland
Desert
Tundra and Alpine
Ice and Snow
Grassland and Scrub
Scrub and Fernlands

COLOR KEY

INTERNAL DIVISIONS

Amazonas (terr.), 12,831..........E 5
Anzoátegui (state), 501,384 ....F 3
Apure (state), 158,487 ....D 4
Aragua (state), 429,344 ....E 3
Barinas (state), 193,914 ......D 3
Bolívar (state), 383,315 ......F 4
Carabobo (state), 512,173 ....D 2
Cojedes (state), 95,177 ....D 3
Delta Amacuro (terr.), 34,278 ..H 3
Dependencias Federales (terr.), 1,000 ....E 2
Distrito Federal, 2,009,561 ...E 2
Falcón (state), 408,051 ....D 2
Guárico (state), 330,147 .....E 3
Lara (state), 611,192 ....C 2
Mérida (state), 335,428 ....C 3
Miranda (state), 702,603......E 2
Monagas (state), 316,732 .....G 3
Nueva Esparta (state), 112,611 ....G 2
Portuguesa (state), 284,523 ....D 3
Sucre (state), 493,840 ....G 2
Táchira (state), 525,840 .....B 3
Trujillo (state), 382,441 ....C 3
Yaracuy (state), 222,041 .....D 2
Zulia (state), 1,342,994 .....B 2

CITIES and TOWNS

Acarigua, 30,683 ....D 3
Achaguas, 1,934 ....D 4
Adícora, 563 ....D 2
Aguada Grande, 1,601 ....D 2
Agua Fría, 539 ....D 2
Agua Linda, 25 ....E 5
Aguasay, 1,458 ....G 3
Altagracia, 7,362 ....C 2
Altagracia de Orituco, 13,013 ..E 3
Amuay, 998 ....D 2
Anaco, 23,105 ....F 3
Aparurén ....G 5
Apurito, 739 ....D 4
Arabopó ....H 5
Aragua de Barcelona, 8,241 ....F 3
Aragua de Maturín, 2,643 ....G 3
Araure, 12,316 ....D 3
Aricagua, 230 ....C 3
Arichuna, 983 ....E 4
Aripao, 400 ....F 4
Arismendi, 1,243 ....D 3
Aroa, 6,356 ....D 2
Atapirire, 203 ....F 3
Bachaquero, 14,490 ....C 2
Baragua, 831 ....D 2
Barbacoas, 1,579 ....E 3
Barcelona, 42,379 ....F 2
Barinas, 25,748 ....C 3
Barinitas, 7,208 ....C 3
Barquisimeto, 280,086 ....D 2
Barrancas, Barinas, 3,154 ....C 3
Barrancas, Monagas, 4,189 ....G 3
Betijoque, 3,915 ....C 3
Biruaca, 631 ....E 4
Biscucuy, 3,900 ....D 3
Bobare, 970 ....D 2
Bobures, 2,159 ....C 3
Boca de Aroa, 1,674 ....D 2
Boca del Mangle, 1,075 ....C 2
Boca del Pao, 283 ....F 3
Boconó, 10,430 ....C 3
Borbón, 373 ....F 2
Borojó, 367 ....C 2
Bruzual, 516 ....D 4
Buena Vista, Anzoátegui, 2,335 ..F 3
Buena Vista, Apure, 64 ....D 4
Buena Vista, Falcón, 786 .....D 2
Cabimas, 141,314 ....C 2
Cabruta, 813 ....E 4
Cabudare, 4,480 ....D 2
Cabure, 1,440 ....D 2
Cachipo, 1,091 ....G 3
Cacuri, 45 ....F 5
Cagua, 16,233 ....E 2
Caicara, 4,776 ....D 2
Caicara de Orinoco, 3,281 ....E 4
Calabozo, 15,739 ....E 3
Calderas, 857 ....C 3
Camaguán, 1,917 ....E 3
Camatagua, 1,419 ....E 3
Campo Claro, 1,620 ....G 2
Candelaria, 158 ....F 4
Cantaura, 14,068 ....F 3
Capatárida, 1,278 ....C 2
Capure, 459 ....G 3
Carabobo, Bolívar ....H 4
Carabobo, Carabobo, 2,319 ....D 3
Caracas (cap.), 786,710 ......E 2
Caracas, *2,064,033 ....E 2
Carache, 2,635 ....C 3
Carapa, 115 ....G 2
Caraco, 4,281 ....C 2
Caribén, 25 ....F 4
Caripe, 3,583 ....G 2
Caripito, 21,598 ....G 2
Carirubana, 3,421 ....C 2
Carmelo, 1,954 ....C 2
Carora, 23,227 ....C 2
Carrasquero, 1,353 ....B 2
Carúpano, 38,197 ....G 2
Casanay, 3,561 ....G 2
Casigua, Falcón, 406 ....C 2
Casigua, Zulia, 5,320 ....B 3
Caucagua, 4,705 ....E 2
Cazorla, 657 ....E 3
Chaguaramas, 1,363 ....E 3
Chichiriviche, 2,512 ....D 2
Chivacoa, 12,871 ....D 2
Choroní, 352 ....E 2
Churuguara, 4,458 ....C 2
Ciudad Bolívar, 63,266 ....G 3
Ciudad Bolivia, 2,080 ....C 3
Ciudad de Nutrias, 541 ....D 3
Ciudad Guayana, 127,681 ......G 3
Ciudad Ojeda, 53,745 ....C 2
Ciudad Piar, 4,598 ....G 4
Clarines, 2,018 ....F 3
Cojoro, 156 ....C 2
Colón, 169 ....E 6
Comunidad, 44 ....E 6
Coporito, 659 ....H 3
Coro, 45,506 ....D 2
Corozo Pando, 286 ....E 3
Cúa, 5,567 ....E 2
Cubiro, 1,742 ....D 3
Cuchivero, 122 ....F 4
Cumaná, 69,937 ....F 2
Cumanacoa, 7,354 ....F 2
Cunaviche, 596 ....E 4
Curiapo, 375 ....H 3
Dabajuro, 3,927 ....C 2
Delicias, 1,398 ....B 4
Democracia, 12 ....E 6
Dolores, 1,122 ....D 3
Duaca, 5,771 ....D 2
Ejido, 5,457 ....C 3
El Almacén, 31 ....F 4
El Amparo de Apure, 1,087 ....C 4
El Baúl, 1,550 ....D 3
El Callao, 5,039 ....H 4
El Calvario, 567 ....E 3
El Carmen ....E 7
El Chaparro, 1,703 ....F 3
El Cristo, 328 ....G 4
El Dorado, 2,094 ....H 4
El Empedrado, 1,739 ....C 3
El Guapo, 842 ....F 2
El Manteco, 999 ....H 4
El Miamo, 269 ....H 4
Elorza, 2,121 ....D 4
El Palmar, 1,986 ....G 4
El Pao, Anzoátegui, 586 ......F 3
El Pao, Bolívar, 2,115 ....G 3
El Pao, Cojedes, 1,081 ....D 3
El Perú, 1,487 ....H 4
El Pilar, 3,326 ....G 2
El Rastro, 748 ....E 3
El Roque, 348 ....D 2
El Samán de Apure, 1,099 .....D 4
El Socorro, 3,153 ....F 3
El Sombrero, 5,712 ....E 3
El Tigre, 41,961 ....F 3
El Tocuyo, 14,560 ....C 2
El Toro, 199 ....H 3
El Vigía, 8,874 ....C 3
El Vínculo, 1,224 ....D 1
Encontrados, 2,991 ....B 3
Espino, 470 ....F 3
Esperanza, 15 ....E 6
Garcitas, 3 ....D 3
Guaca, 11,353 ....G 2
Guachara, 462 ....D 4
Guadarrama, 461 ....D 3
Guana, 8 ....G 5
Guanare, 18,452 ....D 3
Guanarito, 1,048 ....D 3
Guanoco, 437 ....G 2
Guanta, 8,048 ....F 2
Guardatinajas, 704 ....E 3
Guarero, 646 ....B 2
Guarico, 3,653 ....D 2
Guariquén, 633 ....G 2
Guasdualito, 4,586 ....C 4
Guasimal, 303 ....D 4
Guasipati, 3,446 ....H 3
Guayabal, 40 ....E 3
Guayabal, 841 ....D 4
Güiria, 11,061 ....H 2
Guri, 158 ....G 3
Guzmán Blanco, 151 ....F 2
Higuerote, 3,852 ....E 2
Icabarú, 475 ....G 5
Independencia, 3,658 ....C 3
Irapa, 4,532 ....H 2
Juangriego, 4,505 ....G 2
Judibana, 4,375 ....D 2
Jusepín, 2,471 ....G 2
Kavanayen, 401 ....H 4
La Asunción, 5,517 ....G 2
La Canoa, 256 ....F 3
La Ceiba, Apure, 13 ....D 4
La Ceiba, Trujillo, 199 ......C 2
La Concepción, 18,015 ....B 2
La Concepción, 9,488 ....B 2
La Esmeralda, 30 ....F 5
La Esperanza, 4,771 ....D 3
La Grita, 7,866 ....B 3
La Guaira, 20,497 ....E 2
Lagunetas, 522 ....C 3
La Horqueta, 330 ....G 3
La Inglesa, 100 ....G 3
La Leona, 327 ....F 3
La Luz, 414 ....C 3
La Margarita ....G 2
La Paragua, 833 ....G 4
Las Bonitas, 306 ....E 4
Las Lajitas ....F 4

Las Mercedes, 5,410 ....E 3
Las Piedras, Falcón, 2,068 ....C 2
Las Piedras, Zulia, 2,069 ....B 2
Las Trincheras, 157 ....F 4
Las Vegas, 1,190 ....D 3
La Tigra, 234 ....H 4
La Trinidad, 141 ....D 4
La Trinidad de Arauca, 68 ....D 3
La Trinidad de Orichuna, 820 ....D 4
La Unión, 1,068 ....E 3
La Urbana, 444 ....E 4
La Vela de Coro, 4,963 ....D 2
La Victoria, Apure, 109 ....D 4
La Victoria, Aragua, 22,293 ....E 2
Libertad, Barinas, 1,218 ....D 3
Libertad, Cojedes, 1,000 ....D 3
Los Castillos, 92 ....G 3
Los Taques, 2,097 ....C 2
Los Teques, 36,073 ....E 2
Macareo Santo Niño, 376 ....H 3
Machiques, 11,115 ....B 3
Macuro, 899 ....H 2
Macuto, 7,041 ....E 2
Maiquetía, 75,687 ....E 2
Mantecal, Apure, 987 ....D 4
Mantecal, Bolívar, 21 ....F 4
Maparari, 1,330 ....D 2
Mapire, 658 ....F 4
Maporal, 224 ....C 4
Maracaibo, 625,101 ....C 2
Maracaibo, *655,000 ....C 2
Maracay, 185,655 ....E 2

Marigüitar, 3,075 ....G 2
Maripa, 802 ....F 4
Maroa, 417 ....E 6
Matu, 87 ....F 4
Maturín, 54,362 ....G 3
Mene de Mauroa, 3,597 ....C 2
Mene Grande, 11,673 ....C 3
Mérida, 46,339 ....C 3
Mesa Bolívar, 1,227 ....C 3
Mirimire, 1,473 ....D 2
Moitaco, 364 ....F 4
Morganito, 103 ....E 5
Morón, 7,079 ....D 2
Mucuchachí, 391 ....C 3
Mucuchíes, 1,034 ....C 3
Naricual, 656 ....F 2
Nirgua, 7,371 ....D 2
Nuevo Mamo, 284 ....G 3
Obispos, 651 ....D 3
Ocumare de la Costa, 1,332 ....E 2
Ocumare del Tuy, 15,006 ....E 2
Onoto, 1,090 ....F 3
Ortiz, 1,309 ....E 3
Ospino, 1,590 ....D 3
Palmarejo, 943 ....C 2
Palmarito, Apure, 1,176 ....D 4
Palmarito, Guárico, 74 ....F 3
Palmarito, Mérida, 903 ....C 3
Papelón, 414 ....D 3
Paraguaipoa, 1,443 ....C 2
Paraíso de Chabasquén, 2,324 ....D 3
Pariaguán, 6,236 ....F 3
Parmana, 322 ....F 4
Pedernales, 788 ....G 3
Pedregal, 1,483 ....C 2
Peraitepuí, 81 ....H 5
Piacoa, 377 ....H 3
Pimichín, 19 ....E 6
Píritu, Anzoátegui, 1,438 ....F 2
Píritu, Falcón, 1,859 ....D 2
Píritu, Portuguesa, 4,879 ....D 3
Platanal, 8 ....F 6
Porlamar, 21,787 ....G 2
Pozuelos, 6,488 ....F 2
Pregonero, 2,894 ....C 3
Pueblo Nuevo, 2,680 ....D 1
Puerto Ayacucho, 5,465 ....E 5
Puerto Cabello, 52,493 ....E 2
Puerto Cumarebo, 8,029 ....D 2
Puerto de Nutrias, 565 ....D 3
Puerto Hierro, 1,096 ....H 2
Puerto La Cruz, 59,033 ....F 2
Puerto Miranda, 374 ....E 4
Puerto Páez, 767 ....E 4
Puerto Píritu, 2,407 ....F 2
Punta Cardón, 7,461 ....C 2
Punta de Mata, 6,525 ....G 3
Punta de Piedras, 2,342 ....F 2
Punto Fijo, 34,457 ....D 2
Puruey, 343 ....F 4
Puruname, 8 ....E 6
Quibor, 7,046 ....D 3
Quiriquire, 7,393 ....G 3
Quisiro, 816 ....C 2
Río Caribe, 7,774 ....G 2
Río Chico, 2,612 ....F 2
Río Claro, 1,374 ....D 3
Río Tocuyo, 1,650 ....C 2
Rosario, 10,442 ....B 2
Rubio, 11,774 ....B 4
Sabaneta, Barinas, 1,997 ....D 3
Sabaneta, Falcón, 414 ....D 2
Samariapo, 19 ....E 5
San Antonio, Monagas, 3,337 ......G 2
San Antonio, Zulia, 510 ....C 3
San Antonio de Caparo, 1,412 ....C 4
San Antonio del Táchira, 14,247 ....B 4
San Antonio de Orinoco, 48 .....E 6
San Antonio de Tabasca, 434 ....G 3
Sanare, 3,599 ....D 3
San Carlos, Cojedes, 11,934 ....D 3
San Carlos, Zulia, 686 ....C 2
San Carlos del Zulia, 14,480 ....C 3
San Carlos de Río Negro, 474 ....E 7
San Casimiro, 3,485 ....E 3

San Cristóbal, 149,063 ....B 4
San Diego de Cabrutica, 455 ....F 3
San Felipe, Yaracuy, 28,744 ....D 2
San Felipe, Zulia, 570 ....B 3
San Félix, 424 ....C 2
San Fernando, 24,470 ....E 4
San Fernando de Atabapo, 898 ..E 5
San Francisco, 967 ....C 2
San Ignacio, 697 ....B 2
San José, Amazonas ....E 5
San José, Zulia, 2,991 ....B 3
San José de Amacuro, 22 ....H 3
San José de Areocuar, 1,000 ......G 2
San José de Guanipa, 20,746 ....G 3
San José de la Costa, 505 ....D 2
San José de Río Chico, 3,368 ......F 2
San José de Tiznados, 504 ....E 3
San Juan de Colón, 8,944 ....B 3
San Juan de las Galdonas, 1,104 ....G 2
San Juan de los Cayos, 1,191 .....D 2
San Juan de los Morros, 28,556 ....E 3
San Juan de Manapiare, 46 ......E 5
San Juan de Payara, 945 ....E 4
San Lorenzo, Falcón, 527 ....D 2
San Lorenzo, Zulia, 1,552 ....C 3
San Luis, 1,266 ....D 2
San Mateo, 1,849 ....F 3
San Mauricio, 43 ....E 3
San Pedro de las Bocas, 288 ...G 4
San Rafael, 6,390 ....C 2
San Rafael de Atamaica, 597 ....E 4
San Rafael de Orituco, 991 ....E 3
San Sebastián, 4,090 ....E 2
Santa Ana, Anzoátegui, 3,609 ....F 3
Santa Ana, Táchira, 3,677 ....B 4
Santa Bárbara, Amazonas ....E 6
Santa Bárbara, Barinas, 2,029 ....C 4
Santa Bárbara, Monagas, 1,720 ....G 3
Santa Bárbara, Zulia, 105 ....C 3
Santa Catalina, Barinas, 425 ....D 4
Santa Catalina, Delta Amacuro, 440 ....H 3
Santa Cruz, 3,224 ....C 3
Santa Cruz de Bucaral, 1,829 ....D 2
Santa Cruz del Zulia, 2,041 ....B 3
Santa Cruz de Mara, 1,919 ....C 2
Santa Cruz de Orinoco, 419 ....F 3
Santa Elena, 752 ....H 5
Santa Inés, Anzoátegui, 917 ....F 3
Santa Inés, Barinas, 257 ....C 3
Santa Isabel ....F 7
Santa Lucía, 563 ....D 3
Santa María, Bolívar, 468 ....G 3
Santa Mariá de Erebató, 468 ....F 5
Santa María de Ipire, 3,167 ....F 3
Santa María del Orinoco, 57 ....E 4
Santa Rita, Guárico, 306 ....E 3
Santa Rita, Zulia, 5,342 ....C 2

Santa Rosa, Anzoátegui, 1,036 ....F 3
Santa Rosa, Apure, 27 ....D 4
Santa Rosa, Barinas, 957 ....D 3
Santa Rosa de Amanadona, 163 ....E 7
Santa Rosalía, 239 ....F 4
Santa Teresa del Tuy, 6,958 ....E 2
San Timoteo, 2,823 ....C 3
San Tomé, 5,625 ....F 3
San Vicente, Amazonas, 14 .....E 5
San Vicente, Apure, 252 ....D 4
Sarare, 2,664 ....D 3
Seboruco, 2,440 ....B 3
Simaraña ....G 5
Sinamaica, 1,345 ....B 2
Siquisique, 2,579 ....D 2
Solano ....E 6
Soledad, 5,653 ....G 3
Sucre, 65 ....D 3

Suripa, 128 ....D 4
Tamatama, 35 ....F 6
Táriba, 9,835 ....B 4
Temblador, 2,041 ....G 3
Tia Juana, 5,846 ....C 2
Timotes, 2,548 ....C 3
Tinaco, 4,485 ....D 3
Tinaquillo, 8,142 ....D 3
Tocópero, 721 ....D 2
Tocuyo de la Costa, 3,351 ....D 2
Torunos, 676 ....C 3
Tovar, 9,614 ....C 3
Trujillo, 18,957 ....C 3
Tucacas, 3,853 ....D 2
Tucupido, 7,016 ....F 3
Tucupita, 9,922 ....H 3
Tumeremo, 3,926 ....H 4
Tupí, 91 ....D 2
Turén, 341 ....D 3
Turiamo, 31 ....E 2

Turmero, 7,639 ....E 2
Upata, 12,717 ....G 3
Urachiche, 3,630 ....D 2
Uracoa, 858 ....G 3
Urica, 1,577 ....F 3
Urimán, 237 ....G 5
Urumaco, 941 ....C 2
Uruyén ....G 5
Uverito, 336 ....F 3
Valencia, 177,199 ....E 2
Valencia, *224,552 ....E 2
Valera, 46,643 ....C 3
Valle de Guanape, 3,254 ....F 3
Valle de la Pascua, 24,308 ....F 3
Villa Bruzual, 10,278 ....D 3
Villa de Cura, 19,945 ....E 2
Villa Frontado, 1,597 ....G 2
Yaguaraparo, 2,673 ....G 2
Yaritagua, 14,740 ....D 2
Yavita, 49 ....E 6
Yerichaña ....F 5
Yoco, 2,181 ....G 2
Zanja de Lira, 58 ....E 3
Zaraza, 10,084 ....F 3
Zuata, 783 ....F 3

OTHER FEATURES

Amacuro (river) ....H 4
Angel (Salto Angel) (fall) ....G 5
Apongua (river) ....H 5
Apure (river) ....E 4
Arauca (river) ....E 4
Arichuna (river) ....D 4
Aro (river) ....F 4
Atabapo (river) ....E 6
Auyantepui (mt.) ....G 5
Baria (river) ....E 7
Blanquilla, La (isl.), 46 ....F 2
Bolívar (mt.) ....C 3
Bolívar (mt.) ....G 4
Canagua (river) ....C 3
Caño Capure (river) ....H 3
Caño Macareo (river) ....H 3
Caño Mánamo (river) ....G 3
Capanaparo (river) ....E 4
Caparo (river) ....C 4
Caroní (river) ....G 4
Carrao (river) ....G 5
Caruai (river) ....H 5
Casiquiare, Brazo (river) ....E 6
Catatumbo (river) ....B 3
Caura (river) ....F 5
Cerbatana, La (mts.) ....E 4
Chicanán (river) ....H 4
Chimantá–tepuí (mt.) ....G 5
Chivapure (river) ....E 4
Cinaruco (river) ....D 4
Coche (isl.) ....F 2
Codera (cape) ....F 2
Cojedes (river) ....D 3
Cuao (river) ....E 5
Cubagua (isl.) ....F 2
Cuchivero (river) ....F 4
Cuquenán (river) ....H 5
Curutú (river) ....G 5
Cuyuni (river) ....H 4
Delgado Chalbaud (mt.) ....G 6
Dragons Mouth (strait) ....H 2
Duida (mt.) ....F 6
Erebato (river) ....F 5
Gran Sabana, La (plain) ....G 5
Guainía (river) ....E 6
Guampí (mts.) ....F 4
Guanare (river) ....D 3
Guanare Viejo (river) ....D 3
Guanipa (river) ....G 3
Guárico (res.) ....E 3
Guárico (river) ....E 3
Guayapo (mts.) ....E 5
Güere (river) ....F 3

Guri (dam) ....G 4
Guri (res.) ....G 4
Hermanos, Los (isls.) ....F 2
Icabaru (river) ....G 5
Imataca (mts.) ....H 4
Imeri (mts.) ....F 7
La Blanquilla (isl.), 46 ....F 2
La Grand Sabana (plain) ....G 5
La Orchila (isl.), 35 ....F 2
Las Aves (isl.), 6 ....E 2
La Tortuga (isl.), 25 ....F 2
Los Hermanos (isls.) ....F 2
Los Monjes (isls.) ....C 1
Los Roques (isls.), 537 ....E 2
Los Testigos (isls.), 59 ....G 2
Macanao (pen.) ....F 2
Maigualida (mts.) ....F 4
Manapire (river) ....E 3
Maracaibo (lake) ....C 3
Margarita (isl.), 85,296 ....F 2
Mavaca (river) ....F 6
Médanos (isthmus) ....D 2
Merevari (river) ....E 4
Mérida (mts.) ....C 3
Meta (river) ....E 4
Monjes, Los (isls.) ....C 1
Morichal Largo (river) ....G 3
Neblina (Phelps) (pk.) ....E 7
Negro (river) ....E 7
Nuria (mts.) ....H 4
Ocamo (river) ....F 6
Orchila, La (isl.), 35 ....F 2
Orinoco (delta) ....H 3
Orinoco (river) ....G 3
Orituco (river) ....E 3
Pacaraima (mts.) ....G 5
Pao (river) ....D 3
Pao (river) ....F 3
Paragua (river) ....G 4
Paraguaná (peninsula), 104,535 ....C 1
Paria (gulf) ....H 2
Paria (pen.) ....G 2
Parida, La (Bolívar) (mt.) ....G 4
Parima (mts.) ....F 6
Perijá (mts.) ....B 2
Phelps (pk.) ....E 7
Portuguesa (river) ....D 3
Roques, Los (isls.), 537 ....E 2
Roraima (mt.) ....H 5
Salto Angel (fall) ....G 5
Sarare (river) ....C 4
Serpents Mouth (strait) ....H 3
Siapa (river) ....E 7
Sipapo (river) ....E 5
Suapure (river) ....E 4
Suripá (river) ....C 4
Tapirapecó (mts.) ....F 7
Testigos, Los (isls.), 59 ....G 2
Tigre (river) ....G 3
Tocuco (river) ....B 3
Tocuyo (river) ....D 2
Tortuga, La (isl.), 25 ....F 2
Tramán–tepuí (mt.) ....G 5
Triste (gulf) ....D 2
Turagua (mts.) ....F 4
Tuy (river) ....E 2
Unare (river) ....F 3
Valencia (lake) ....E 2
Venamo (mt.) ....H 4
Venamo (river) ....H 4
Venezuela (gulf) ....C 2
Ventuari (river) ....E 5
Votamo (river) ....F 6
Yatua (river) ....E 7
Yuruari (river) ....H 4
Zuata (river) ....F 3
Zulia (river) ....B 3

*City and suburbs.

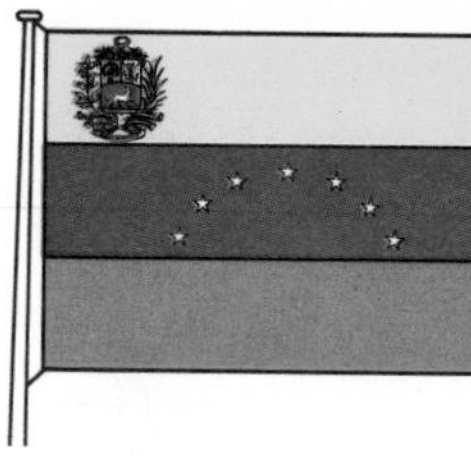

AREA 352,143 sq. mi.
POPULATION 10,398,907
CAPITAL Caracas
LARGEST CITY Caracas
HIGHEST POINT Pico Bolívar 16,427 ft.
MONETARY UNIT bolívar
MAJOR LANGUAGE Spanish
MAJOR RELIGION Roman Catholicism

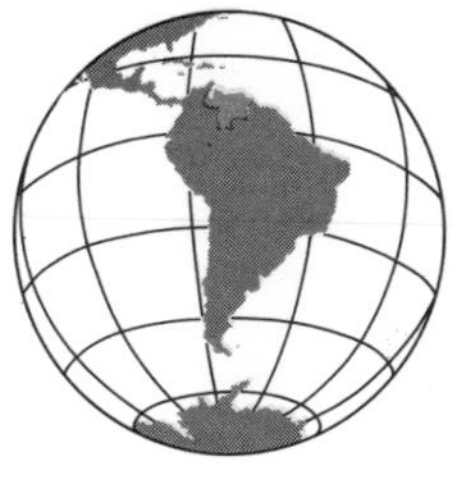

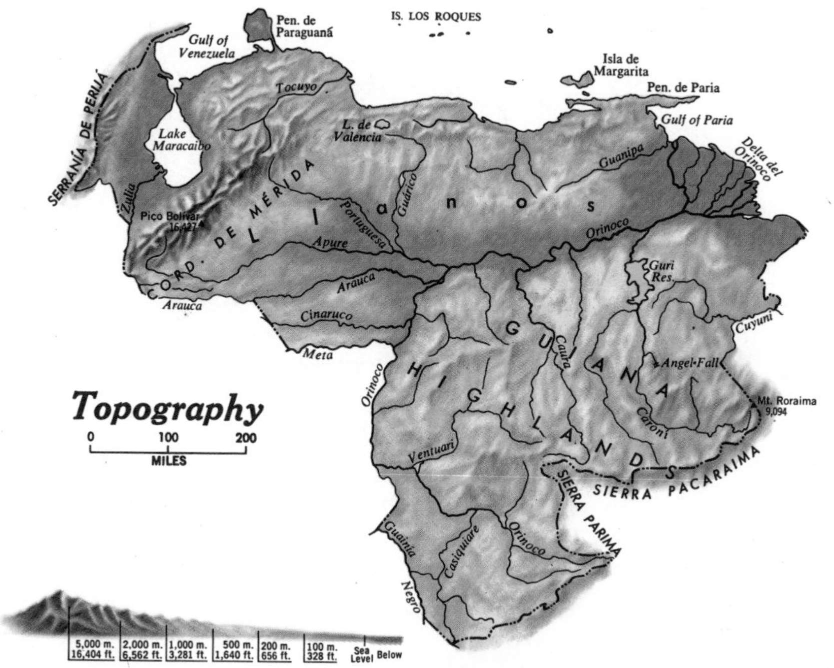

Topography
0 100 200
MILES
Pen. de Paraguaná
IS. LOS ROQUES
Isla de Margarita
Pen. de Paria
Gulf of Paria
Gulf of Venezuela
Delta del Orinoco
SERRANÍA DE PERIJÁ
Lake Maracaibo
Tocuyo
L. de Valencia
Guanipa
Zulia
Pico Bolívar 16,427
CORD. DE MÉRIDA
Llanos
Portuguesa
Guárico
Orinoco
Apure
Arauca
Guri Res.
Cuyuni
Cinaruco
Meta
Caura
GUIANA HIGHLANDS
Angel Fall
Caroní
Mt. Roraima 9,094
Ventuari
SIERRA PACARAIMA
SIERRA PARIMA
Casiquiare
Guainía
Negro
5,000 m. 16,404 ft.
2,000 m. 6,562 ft.
1,000 m. 3,281 ft.
500 m. 1,640 ft.
200 m. 656 ft.
100 m. 328 ft.
Sea Level
Below

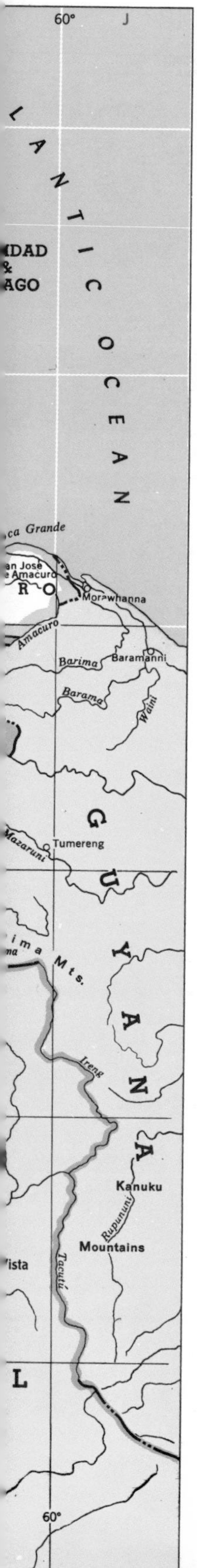

60°
J
ATLANTIC OCEAN
TRINIDAD & TOBAGO
GUYANA
Tumereng
Barima
Baramanni
Waini
Amacuro
Mazaruni
Ireng
Kanuku
Mountains
Rupununi
Tacutu

Agriculture, Industry and Resources

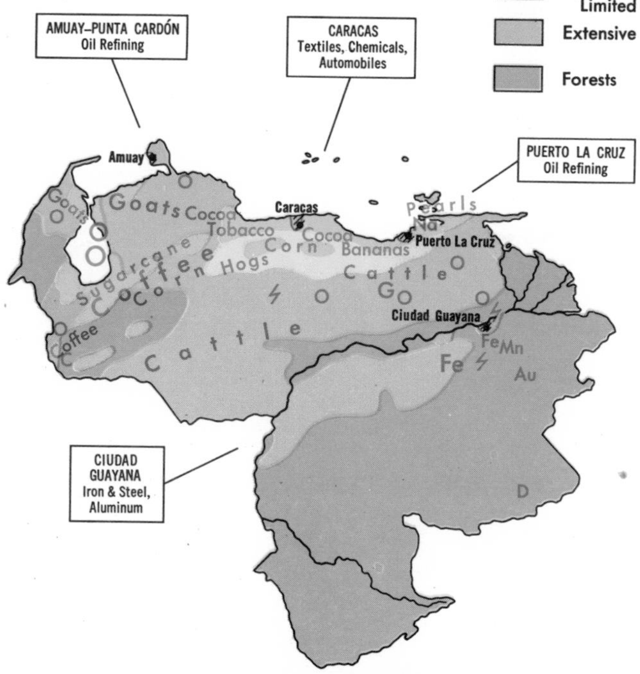

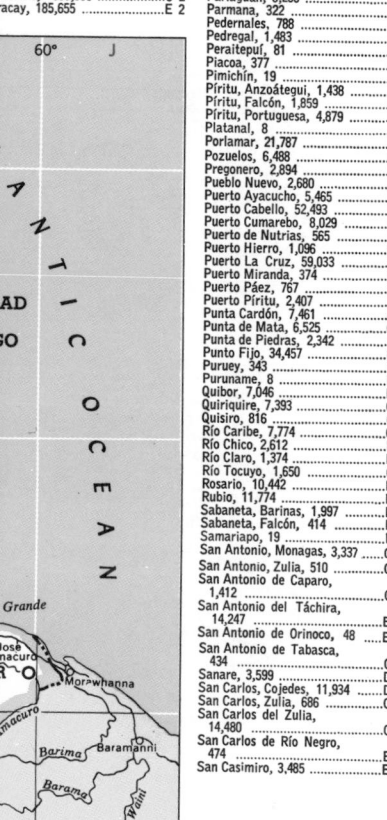

AMUAY–PUNTA CARDÓN
Oil Refining
CARACAS
Textiles, Chemicals, Automobiles
PUERTO LA CRUZ
Oil Refining
CIUDAD GUAYANA
Iron & Steel, Aluminum
Amuay
Caracas
Puerto La Cruz
Ciudad Guayana
Goats
Cocoa
Tobacco
Corn
Bananas
Pearls
Sugarcane
Coffee
Hogs
Cattle

DOMINANT LAND USE

- Diversified Tropical Crops (chiefly plantation agriculture)
- Upland Cultivated Areas
- Upland Livestock Grazing, Limited Agriculture
- Extensive Livestock Ranching
- Forests

MAJOR MINERAL OCCURRENCES

- Au Gold
- C Coal
- D Diamonds
- Fe Iron Ore
- G Natural Gas
- Mn Manganese
- Na Salt
- O Petroleum
- Water Power
- Major Industrial Areas

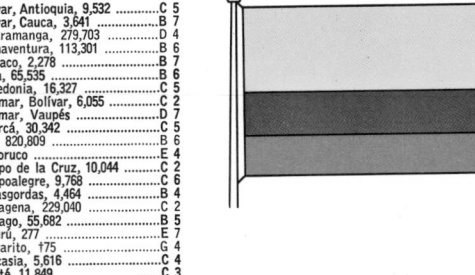

AREA 439,513 sq. mi.
POPULATION 21,117,000
CAPITAL Bogotá
LARGEST CITY Bogotá
HIGHEST POINT Pico Cristóbal Colón 19,029 ft.
MONETARY UNIT Colombian peso
MAJOR LANGUAGE Spanish
MAJOR RELIGION Roman Catholicism

INTERNAL DIVISIONS

Amazonas (intendency), 16,000...D 8
Antioquia (dept.), 3,031,000......C 4
Arauca (commissary), 32,000....E 4
Atlántico (dept.), 903,000 ....C 2
Bolívar (dept.), 849,000 ....C 3
Boyacá (dept.), 1,104,000 ....D 5
Caldas (dept.), 810,000 ....C 4
Caquetá (intendency), 157,000....C 7
Casanare (intendency), 90,000....E 5
Cauca (dept.), 696,000 ....B 6
Cesar (dept.), 357,000 ....D 3
Chocó (dept.), 210,000 ....B 4
Córdoba (dept.), 760,000 ....C 3
Cundinamarca (dept.),
   1,187,000 ....C 5
Distrito Especial, 2,416,000 ....C 5
Guainía (comm.), 5,000 ....F 6
Guajira, La (dept.), 173,000 ......D 2
Huila (dept.), 485,000 ....C 6
La Guajira (dept.), 173,000 ....D 2
Magdalena (dept.), 683,000 ....D 3
Meta (dept.), 248,000 ....D 6
Nariño (dept.), 787,000 ....B 7
Norte de Santander (dept.),
   615,000 ....D 4
Putumayo (comm.), 77,000 ....C 7
Quindío (dept.), 346,000 ....C 5
Risaralda (dept.), 512,000 ....C 5
San Andrés y Providencia
   (intendency), 27,000 ....B10
Santander (dept.), 1,137,000 .....D 4
Sucre (dept.), 361,000 ....C 3
Tolima (dept.), 902,000 ....C 5
Valle del Cauca (dept.),
   2,114,000 ....B 6
Vaupés (commissary), 18,000 ....C 7
Vichada (commissary), 9,000 ....F 5

CITIES and TOWNS

Acacías, 6,508 ....D 6
Acandí, 1,686 ....B 3
Agrado, 2,751 ....C 6
Agua de Dios, 7,401 ....C 5
Aguachica, 8,556 ....D 3
Aguadas, 10,822 ....C 5
Agustín Codazzi, 11,673 ....D 3
Aipe, 3,404 ....C 6
Algeciras, 3,778 ....C 6
Almaguer, 1,251 ....B 7
Amalfi, 4,667 ....C 4
Amanavén, 11,164 ....G 6
Andes, 11,135 ....B 5
Anserma, 14,129 ....B 5
Antioquia, 6,002 ....B 4
Anza, 680 ....C 4
Aracataca, 5,304 ....C 2
Araracuara ....E 8
Arauca, 4,280 ....E 4
Arauquita, 413 ....E 4
Arjona, 16,510 ....C 2
Armenia, 162,837 ....B 5
Armero, 17,495 ....C 5
Ayapel, 5,610 ....C 3
Bagadó, 865 ....B 5
Baranoa, 14,064 ....C 2
Baraya, 2,696 ....C 6
Barbacoas, 4,011 ....A 7
Barbosa, 6,018 ....D 5
Barichara, 2,798 ....D 4
Barrancabermeja, 59,625 ....C 4
Barrancas, 2,010 ....D 2
Barranco de Loba, 1,648 ....C 3
Barranquilla, 816,706 ....C 2
Belén de los Andaquíes, 1,420...C 7
Bello, 127,377 ....C 4
Boca del Pepé, 566 ....B 5
Bogotá (cap.), 2,037,904 ....D 5
Bogotá, *2,416,000 ....D 5

Bolívar, Antioquia, 9,532 ....C 5
Bolívar, Cauca, 3,641 ....B 7
Bucaramanga, 279,703 ....D 4
Buenaventura, 113,301 ....B 6
Buesaco, 2,278 ....B 7
Buga, 65,535 ....B 6
Caicedonia, 16,327 ....C 5
Calamar, Bolívar, 6,055 ....C 2
Calamar, Vaupés ....D 7
Calarcá, 30,342 ....C 5
Cali, 820,809 ....B 6
Camoruco ....E 4
Campo de la Cruz, 10,044 ....C 2
Campoalegre, 9,768 ....C 6
Cañasgordas, 4,464 ....B 4
Cartagena, 229,040 ....B 3
Cartago, 55,682 ....B 5
Carurú, 277 ....E 7
Casuarito, 175 ....G 4
Caucasia, 5,616 ....C 3
Cereté, 11,849 ....C 3
Cerro de San Antonio, 3,397 .....C 2
Chaparral, 13,261 ....C 6
Chimichagua, 5,093 ....D 3
Chinácota, 4,081 ....D 4
Chinchiná, 15,944 ....C 5
Chinú, 7,552 ....C 3
Chiquinquirá, 16,926 ....C 5
Chiriguaná, 6,516 ....D 3
Ciénaga, 142,893 ....C 2
Ciénaga de Oro, 8,047 ....C 3
Cisneros, 7,554 ....C 4
Colombia, 1,599 ....C 6
Colón, 1,133 ....B 7
Condoto, 4,094 ....B 5
Contratación, 3,117 ....D 4
Convención, 7,371 ....D 3
Corozal, 14,000 ....C 3
Cravo Norte, 566 ....F 4
Cúcuta, 207,091 ....D 4
Cumbal, 2,549 ....B 7
Cuñare ....D 7
Dabeiba, 4,218 ....B 4
Dagua, 4,635 ....B 6
Dibulla ....D 2
Duitama, 31,865 ....D 5
El Banco, 14,889 ....D 3
El Carmen, Chocó, 1,689 ....B 5
El Carmen, Norte de Santander,
   2,737 ....D 3
El Carmen de Bolívar, 19,196....C 3
El Cerrito, 12.200 ....C 5
El Cocuy, 2,869 ....D 4
El Tambo, 4,003 ....B 6
Envigado, 40,686 ....C 4
Espinal, 22,791 ....C 5
Facatativá, 20,742 ....C 5
Florencia, 17,709 ....C 7
Fonseca, 5,190 ....D 2
Fontibón ....C 5
Fresno, 7,058 ....C 5
Fundación, 14,128 ....D 2
Fusagasugá, 18,755 ....C 5
Gachalá, 1,253 ....D 3
Gamarra, 4,664 ....D 3
Garzón, 21,999 ....C 6
Gigante, 4,594 ....C 6
Girardot, 66,584 ....C 5
Gramalote, 3,098 ....D 4
Guacamaya ....C 6
Guamal, Magdalena, 4,695 ....C 3
Guamal, Meta, 2,113 ....D 6
Guape ....D 6
Guapí, 3,066 ....B 6
Guateque, 4,646 ....D 5
Honda, 19,945 ....C 5
Ibagué, 178,821 ....C 5
Inírida ....G 6
Ipiales, 23,320 ....B 7
Iscuandé, 1,777 ....A 6
Istmina, 3,996 ....B 5
Itagüí, 101,066 ....C 4

Ituango, 3,466 ....C 4
Juradó, 708 ....B 4
La Cruz, 4,014 ....B 7
La Dorada, 26,168 ....D 5
La Gloria, 2,915 ....D 3
La Palma, 4,594 ....C 5
La Plata, 5,863 ....C 6
La Unión, 3,875 ....B 7
Leticia, 4,013 ....F10
Líbano, 18,640 ....C 5
Lorica, 12,880 ....C 3
Los Andes, 1,392 ....M 7
Macaranaima ....E 7
Maganguá, 27,354 ....C 3
Maicao, 9,347 ....D 2
Maipures ....F 5
Majagual, 2,197 ....C 3
Málaga, 9,674 ....D 4
Manare ....E 4
Maní, 586 ....D 5
Manizales, 267,543 ....C 5
Matanza, 1,264 ....D 4
Medellín, 967,826 ....C 4
Medina, 893 ....D 5
Mercaderes, 2,376 ....B 7
Micay ....B 6
Miraflores, Boyacá, 3,257 ....D 5
Miraflores, Vaupés, 245 ....E 7
Miranda, 5,527 ....B 6
Mitú, 1,623 ....E 7
Mituas ....F 6
Mocoa, 2,510 ....C 7
Mompós, 10,965 ....C 3
Moniquirá, 4,882 ....D 5
Montería, 167,446 ....C 3
Morichal, †2,512 ....E 6
Mosquera, 766 ....A 6
Murindó, 319 ....B 4
Muzo, 792 ....D 5
Natagaima, 8,372 ....C 6
Naya ....B 6
Neiva, 111,727 ....C 6
Nóvita, 883 ....B 5
Nueva Antioquia, †236 ....F 5
Nunchía, 461 ....D 5
Nuquí, 1,500 ....B 5
Ocaña, 28,028 ....D 3
Orocué, 1,600 ....E 5
Ortega, 4,450 ....C 5
Pacho, 7,192 ....C 5
Pacoa, 1960 ....G 6
Páez, 1,570 ....C 6
Palmira, 164,394 ....B 6
Pamplona, 25,502 ....D 4
Pasto, 123,153 ....B 7
Patía, 3,045 ....B 6
Paz de Ariporo, 1,216 ....E 5
Paz de Río, 2,748 ....D 4
Pedraza, 1,757 ....C 2
Pereira, 224,421 ....C 5
Piedecuesta, 12,278 ....D 4

Pitalito, 10,818 ....B 7
Pivijay, 8,200 ....C 2
Planeta Rica, 5,959 ....C 3
Plato, 13,364 ....C 3
Popayán, 58,500 ....B 6
Pore, 193 ....D 5
Potosí, 1,149 ....C 7
Pradera, 11,223 ....B 6
Puente Nacional, 2,913 ....D 5
Puerto Asís, 2,902 ....C 7
Puerto Berrío, 15,812 ....C 4
Puerto Carreño, 1,115 ....G 4
Puerto Colombia, 7,143 ....C 2
Puerto Escondido, 1,543 ....B 3
Puerto Leguízamo, 3,014 ....C 8
Puerto López, La Guajira ....E 2
Puerto López, Meta, 3,586 ....D 5
Puerto Murillo, †1,014 ....G 4
Puerto Nariño, 1926 ....F 5
Puerto Rico, Caquetá, †10,328...C 7
Puerto Rico, Meta ....E 4
Puerto Rondón, 951 ....E 4
Puerto Salgar, 6,398 ....C 5
Puerto Tejada, 14,663 ....B 6
Puerto Wilches, 4,635 ....D 4
Pupiales, 2,432 ....B 7
Purificación, 7,044 ....C 6
Quibdó, 19,989 ....B 5
Remedios, 2,090 ....C 4
Remolino, 3,373 ....C 2
Restrepo, 2,603 ....D 5
Ricaurte, 866 ....A 7
Río de Oro, 2,482 ....D 3
Riohacha, 11,708 ....D 2
Rionegro, Antioquia, 2,708 ....C 4
Rionegro, Santander, 12,541 .....C 4
Riosucio, Caldas, 11,274 ....C 5
Riosucio, Chocó, 1,817 ....B 4
Roberto Payán, 402 ....A 7
Robles, 4,278 ....D 2
Rovira, 4,582 ....C 5
Sabanalarga, 20,254 ....C 2
Sácama, 54 ....D 4
Sahagún, 11,560 ....C 3
Salamina, 14,263 ....C 5
Salazar, 3,020 ....D 4
Samaniego, 3,181 ....B 7
San Agustín, 3,250 ....B 7
San Andrés, Antioquia, 1,773 ....C 4
San Andrés, San Andrés y
   Providencia, 9,040 ....A10
San Antero, 6,596 ....C 3
San Felipe, 187 ....G 7
San Francisco, 1,248 ....D 4
San Gil, 18,518 ....D 4
San Jacinto, 10,210 ....C 3
San José del Guaviare, 215 ....D 6
San José del Ocune, 105 ....D 5
San Juan del César, 9,347 ....D 2
San Marcos, 7,083 ....C 3
San Martín, 6,739 ....D 6
San Onofre, 10,737 ....C 3
San Pablo, 4,103 ....B 7
San Roque, 3,272 ....C 4

San Vicente del Caguán, 1,764...C 6
Sandoná, 6,776 ....B 7
Santa Bárbara, 7,779 ....C 5
Santa Isabel, 468 ....B 9
Santa Marta, 137,474 ....C 2
Santa Rosa de Cabal, 31,646 ....C 5
Santa Rosa de Osos, 6,860 ....C 4
Santander, 11,426 ....B 6
Santiago, 929 ....B 7
Sardinata, 2,964 ....D 3
Segovia, 9,274 ....C 4
Sevilla, 26,757 ....C 5
Sibundoy-Las Casas, 1,999 ....B 7
Silvia, 3,180 ....B 6
Simití, 2,825 ....C 3
Sincé, 10,631 ....C 3
Sincelejo, 44,001 ....C 3
Sipí, 155 ....B 5
Sitionuevo, 5,969 ....C 2
Soatá, 4,361 ....D 4
Socorro, 13,716 ....D 4
Sogamoso, 32,274 ....D 5
Soledad, 37,617 ....C 2
Sonsón, 35,955 ....C 5
Sopetrán, 3,646 ....C 4
Sucre, Bolívar, 3,035 ....C 3
Sucre, Caquetá ....C 7
Tadó, 1,947 ....B 5
Támara, 1,034 ....D 5
Tame, 3,063 ....E 4
Tibaná, 924 ....D 5
Tierralta, 4,415 ....C 3
Timaná, 2,999 ....C 6
Timbío, 4,145 ....B 6
Timbiquí, 1,406 ....B 6
Toledo, 2,314 ....D 4
Tolú, 7,954 ....C 3
Tuluá, 56,539 ....B 5
Tumaco, 25,145 ....A 7
Tunja, 40,451 ....D 5
Túquerres, 10,698 ....B 7
Turbaco, 14,293 ....B 3
Turbo, 7,375 ....B 3
Ubaté, 6,261 ....D 5
Uribia, 1,763 ....D 2
Urrao, 7,712 ....B 4
Valdivia, 2,264 ....C 4
Valledupar, 120,009 ....D 2
Vélez, 7,033 ....D 4
Venadillo, 6,931 ....C 5
Villanueva, 8,288 ....D 5
Villa Amazónica, 1,344 ....B 7
Villa Rosario, 5,184 ....D 4
Villavicencio, 45,277 ....D 5
Villeta, 5,280 ....C 5
Yarumal, 16,823 ....C 4
Yavaraté, †1,963 ....F 7
Yopal, 2,878 ....D 5
Yumbo, 15,270 ....B 6
Zapatoca, 7,305 ....D 4
Zaragoza, 2,134 ....C 4
Zarzal, 17,768 ....B 5
Zipaquirá, 22,648 ....D 5

OTHER FEATURES

Abibe (mts.) ....B 4
Aguja (cape) ....C 2
Albuquerque (cays) A10
Alicia (bank) ....B 8
Alto Ritacuva (mt.) ....D 4
Amazon (Amazonas) (river) ....E 9
Ancón de Sardinas (bay) ....A 7
Angostura (falls) ....F 6
Apaporis (river) ....E 8
Araracuara (mts.) ....E 7
Arauca (river) ....E 4
Ariari (river) ....D 6
Ariguaní (river) ....D 3
Ariporo (river) ....E 4
Atabapo (river) ....G 6
Atrato (river) ....B 4
Augusta (cape) ....C 2
Ayapel (mts.) ....C 3
Bajo Nuevo (shoal) ....C 8
Baudó (mts.) ....B 5
Baudó (river) ....B 5
Bita (river) ....F 5
Caguán (river) ....C 7
Cahuinari (river) ....E 8
Caquetá (river) ....E 8
Caraparaná (river) ....D 8
Casanare (river) ....E 4
Cauca (river) ....C 4
Cazueleja (mt.) ....C 6
Central (mts.) ....C 5
César (river) ....D 2
Chaira (lagoon) ....C 8
Chamusa (river) ....C 3
Charambirá (point) ....B 5
Chiribiquete (mts.) ....D 7
Chocó (bay) ....B 6
Cocha (lake) ....B 7
Cocuy (mts.) ....D 4
Coredó (Humboldt) (bay) ....B 4
Corrientes (cape) ....B 5
Courtown (Este Sudeste)
   (cays) A10
Cravo Norte (river) ....E 4
Cravo Sur (river) ....E 5
Cristóbal Colón (mt.) ....D 2
Cuemaní (river) ....D 7
Cupica (gulf) ....B 4
Cuquiari (river) ....G 7
Cusiana (river) ....D 5
Este Sudeste (cays) A10
Gallinas (point) ....E 1
Grande (isl.) ....B 4
Guainía (river) ....F 6
Guajira (pen.) ....E 1
Guapí (bay) ....A 6
Guaviare (river) ....E 5
Guayabero (river) ....D 6
Huila (mt.) ....C 6
Humboldt (Coredó) (bay) ....B 4
Igara-Paraná (river) ....D 8
Inírida (river) ....F 6
Isana (river) ....F 7

Lebrija (river) ....D 4
Llanos (plains) ....D 5
Losada (river) ....C 6
Macarena (mts.) ....D 6
Magdalena (river) ....C 3
Manacacías (river) ....D 5
Mapiripán (lake) ....E 6
Marzo (cape) ....B 4
Mesai (river) ....D 7
Meta (river) ....E 5
Metica (river) ....E 5
Miritiparaná (river) ....E 8
Morrosquillo (gulf) ....C 3
Muco (river) ....E 5
Naipo (isl.) ....C 4
Nechí (river) ....C 4
Occidental, Cordillera (mts.) .....B 5
Oriental, Cordillera (mts.) ....D 5
Orinoco (river) ....G 5
Orteguaza (river) ....C 7
Papunáua (river) ....E 6
Patía (river) ....B 7
Pauto (river) ....E 5
Perijá (mts.) ....D 2
Providencia (isl.), 2,318 ....B 9
Pupurí (river) ....F 7
Puracé (volcano) ....B 6
Putumayo (river) ....E 8
Quitasueño (bank) ....A 8
Riosucio (river) ....C 8
Roncador (cays) ....B 9
Saldaña (river) ....D 8
Salto Grande (falls) ....D 8
San Andrés (isl.), 14,413 ....A10
San Jorge (river) ....C 3
San Juan (river) ....B 5
Santa Marta, Nev. de (range)....D 2
Serrana (bank) ....B 9
Serranilla (bank) ....B 8
Sinú (river) ....B 3
Sogamoso (river) ....D 4
Solano (point) ....B 4
Suárez (river) ....D 4
Taraíra (river) ....F 8
Tequendama (falls) ....C 5
Tibugá (gulf) ....B 5
Tolima (mt.) ....C 5
Tomo (river) ....F 5
Tortugas (gulf) ....B 6
Truandó (river) ....B 4
Tumaco (inlet) ....A 6
Tunahí (mts.) ....E 7
Upía (river) ....E 5
Urabá (gulf) ....B 3
Uva (lake) ....E 6
Uva (river) ....E 7
Vaupés (river) ....E 7
Vela (river) ....D 1
Vela, Roca que (cay) ....B 8
Vichada (river) ....F 5
Yarí (river) ....D 7
Zapatosa (swamp) ....D 3

*City and suburbs.

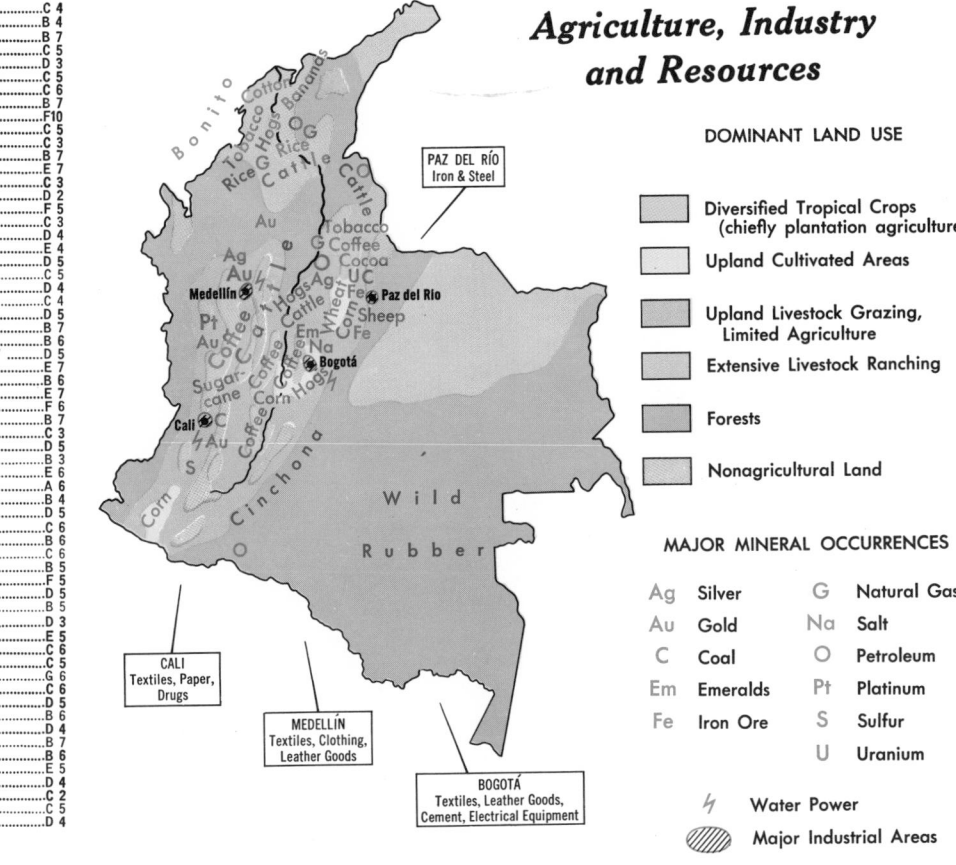

Agriculture, Industry and Resources

PAZ DEL RÍO
Iron & Steel

CALI
Textiles, Paper, Drugs

MEDELLÍN
Textiles, Clothing, Leather Goods

BOGOTÁ
Textiles, Leather Goods, Cement, Electrical Equipment

DOMINANT LAND USE

Diversified Tropical Crops (chiefly plantation agriculture)
Upland Cultivated Areas
Upland Livestock Grazing, Limited Agriculture
Extensive Livestock Ranching
Forests
Nonagricultural Land

MAJOR MINERAL OCCURRENCES

Ag Silver
Au Gold
C Coal
Em Emeralds
Fe Iron Ore
G Natural Gas
Na Salt
O Petroleum
Pt Platinum
S Sulfur
U Uranium

⚡ Water Power
Major Industrial Areas

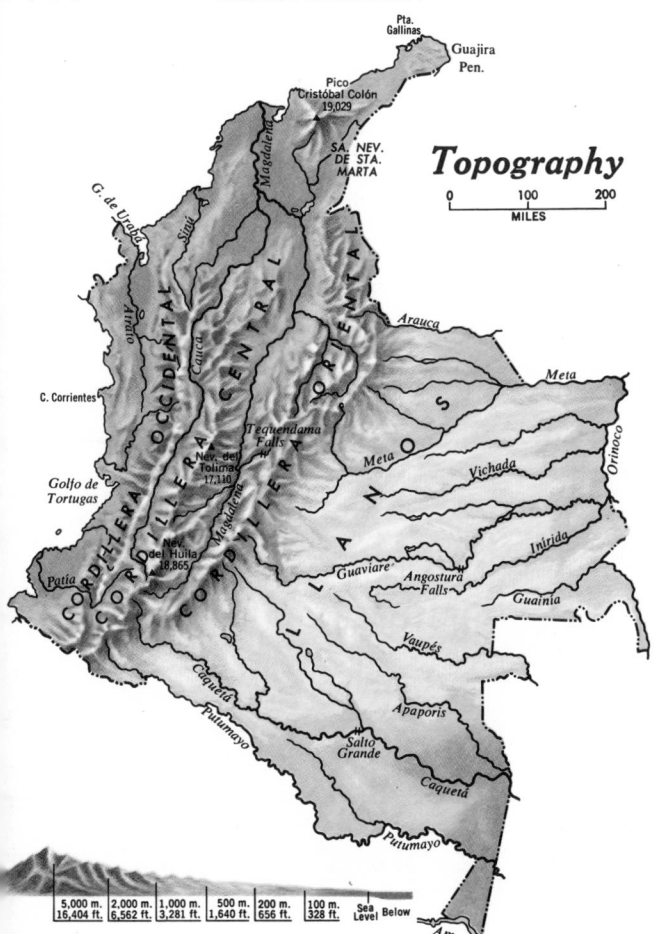

Topography

0   100   200
MILES

5,000 m. | 2,000 m. | 1,000 m. | 500 m. | 200 m. | 100 m. | Sea | Below
16,404 ft. | 6,562 ft. | 3,281 ft. | 1,640 ft. | 656 ft. | 328 ft. | Level |

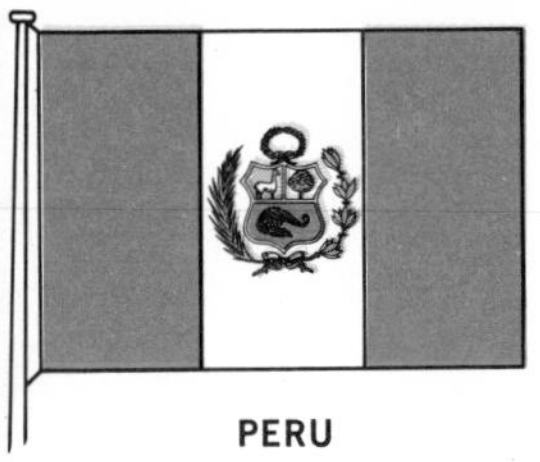

PERU

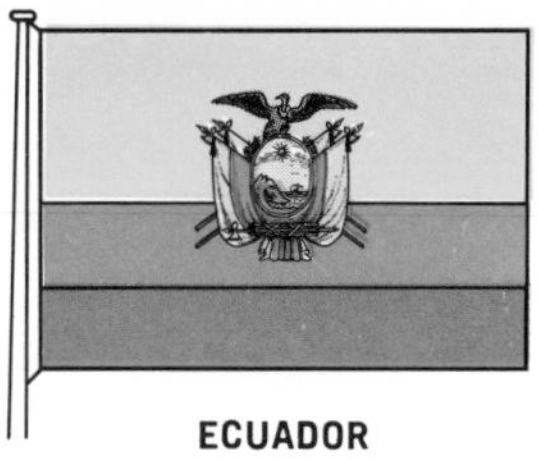

ECUADOR

PERU

AREA 496,222 sq. mi.
POPULATION 13,586,300
CAPITAL Lima
LARGEST CITY Lima
HIGHEST POINT Huascarán 22,205 ft.
MONETARY UNIT sol
MAJOR LANGUAGES Spanish, Quechua, Aymara
MAJOR RELIGION Roman Catholicism

ECUADOR

AREA 109,483 sq. mi.
POPULATION 6,144,000
CAPITAL Quito
LARGEST CITY Guayaquil
HIGHEST POINT Chimborazo 20,561 ft.
MONETARY UNIT sucre
MAJOR LANGUAGES Spanish, Quechua
MAJOR RELIGION Roman Catholicism

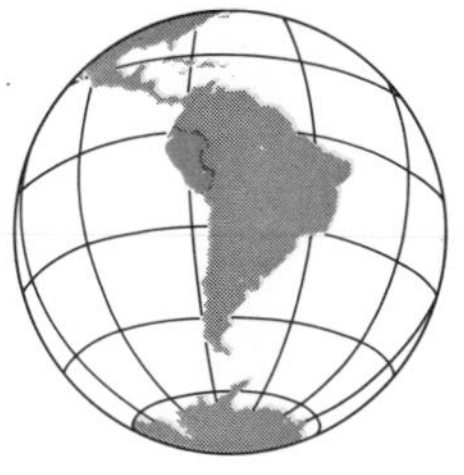

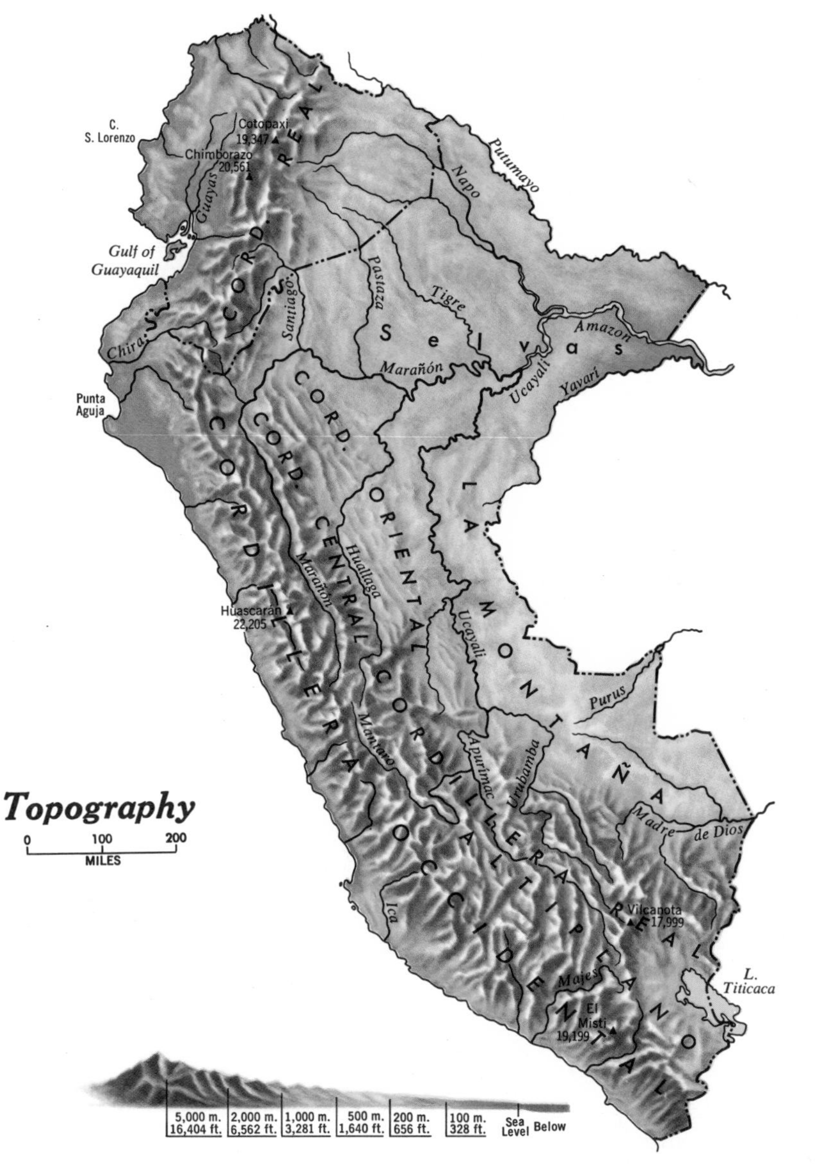
C. S. Lorenzo
Cotopaxi 19,347
Chimborazo 20,561
Guayas
CORD. REAL
Putumayo
Napo
Gulf of Guayaquil
Santiago
Pastaza
Tigre
Amazon
Chira
S e l v a s
Marañón
Ucayali
Yavari
Punta Aguja
CORD. OCCIDENTAL
CORD. CENTRAL
CORD. ORIENTAL
LA MONTAÑA
Huallaga
Marañón
Huascarán 22,205
Ucayali
Purus
Mantaro
CORDILLERA OCCIDENTAL
Apurímac
Urubamba
Madre de Dios
CORDILLERA REAL
ALTIPLANO
Ica
Vilcanota 17,999
L. Titicaca
Majes
El Misti 19,199
Topography
0 100 200
MILES
5,000 m. 16,404 ft.
2,000 m. 6,562 ft.
1,000 m. 3,281 ft.
500 m. 1,640 ft.
200 m. 656 ft.
100 m. 328 ft.
Sea Level
Below

PERU

DEPARTMENTS

Amazonas, 171,100 ....C 5
Ancash, 744,700 ....D 7
Apurímac, 330,400 ....F10
Arequipa, 518,300 ....F10
Ayacucho, 474,100 ....E 9
Cajamarca, 1,007,600 ....C 6
Callao (province), 335,400 ....D 9
Cuzco, 756,100 ....F 9
Huancavelica, 367,100 ....E 9
Huánuco, 430,100 ....D 7
Ica, 362.700 ....E10
Junín, 699,100 ....E 8
La Libertad, 784,900 ....C 6
Lambayeque, 485,500 ....B 6
Lima, 3,155,800 ....D 8
Loreto, 504,600 ....E 5
Madre de Dios, 24,200 ....G 8
Moquegua, 68,800 ....G11
Pasco, 188,000 ....E 8
Piura, 922,300 ....B 5
Puno, 848,200 ....G10
San Martín, 229,400 ....D 6
Tacna, 93,900 ....G11
Tumbes, 84,000 ....B 4

CITIES and TOWNS

Abancay, 9,053 ....F 9
Acarí, 1,428 ....E10
Acobamba, 2,167 ....E 9
Acolla, 4,415 ....E 8
Acomayo, Cuzco, 1,874 ....G 9
Acomayo, Huánuco, 1,198 ....E 7
Acora, 941 ....H11
Acuracay, 96 ....F 5
Aija, 1,710 ....D 7
Alca, 539 ....F10
Ambo, 1,606 ....D 8
Ancón, 3,760 ....D 8
Andahuaylas, 4,674 ....F 9
Andamarca, 339 ....E 8
Anta, 2,574 ....F 9
Antabamba, 2,294 ....F10
Aplao, 1,316 ....F11
Aquia, 897 ....D 8
Arequipa, 194,700 ....G11
Ascope, 3,845 ....C 6
Astillero ....H 9
Atalaya, 816 ....E 8
Atico, 297 ....F11
Ayabaca, 3,415 ....C 5
Ayacucho, 28,500 ....F 9
Ayavirí, 7,553 ....G10
Azángaro, 4,771 ....H10
agua, 2,343 ....C 5
alsapuerto, 203 ....D 5
ambamarca, 4,281 ....C 6
arranca, Lima, 11,320 ....C 8
arranca, Loreto, 184 ....D 5
artra Antiguo ....E 4
artra Nuevo ....E 4
ayóvar ....B 5
ellavista, 2,129 ....C 5
olívar, 1,057 ....D 6
olognesi ....F 6
olognesi, 516 ....F 8
orja, 300 ....D 5
retaña, 766 ....E 5
uldibuyo, 616 ....D 7
aballococha, 1,197 ....G 4
abana, 1,910 ....C 7
abo Blanco ....B 5
ahuapanas, 125 ....D 5
ailloma, 607 ....G10
ajabamba, 5,253 ....C 6
ajacay, 809 ....D 8
ajamarca, 28,200 ....C 6
ajatambo, 2,257 ....D 8
alca, 3,489 ....G 9
allalli, 133 ....G10
allao, 335,400 ....D 9
amaná, 5,120 ....F11
andarave, 859 ....G11
angallo, 1,578 ....E 9
anta, 2,491 ....D 8
apachica, 193 ....H10
arás, 4,033 ....D 7
aravelí, 1,954 ....F10
arhuás, 2,175 ....D 7
arumás, 727 ....G11
ascas, 2,403 ....C 6
asma, 4,975 ....C 7
astilla, 29,541 ....B 5
astrovirreyna, 784 ....E 9
atacaos, 12,135 ....B 5
elendín, 5,646 ....D 6
erro Azul, 1,571 ....D 9
erro de Pasco, 23,400 ....D 8
achapoyas, 6,860 ....D 6
ala, 1,054 ....E10
alhuanca, 2,840 ....F10
ancay, 6,145 ....D 8
ao ....C 7
epén, 16,119 ....C 6
icama, 1,362 ....C 6
iclayo, 140,800 ....C 6
ilca (Pucusana), 1,331 ....D 9
ilete, 1,105 ....C 6
imbote, 102,800 ....C 7
incha Alta, 26,500 ....D 9
iquián, 3,354 ....D 8
irinos, 490 ....C 5
ivay, 2,320 ....G10
orrillós, 31,703 ....D 9
osica ....D 8
ota, 4,961 ....C 6
ulucanas, 19,714 ....B 5
upaca, 2,180 ....E 9
uquibamba, 2,983 ....F10
uquibambilla, 1,423 ....F 9
Churín, 610 ....D 8
Cocachacra, 2,869 ....G11
Cocama ....G 8
Cojata, 763 ....H10
Colasay, 466 ....C 5
Colcamar, 1,370 ....D 6
Conaica, 1,408 ....E 9
Concepción, 4,184 ....E 8
Concordia, 66 ....E 5
Contamana, 4,708 ....E 6
Contumazá, 2,532 ....C 6
Coracora, 4,116 ....F10
Córdova, 620 ....E10
Corongo, 2,241 ....D 7
Cotahuasi, 1,618 ....F10
Culebras ....C 7
Cumaría ....F 7
Cutervo, 4,702 ....C 6
Cuyocuyo, 708 ....H10
Cuzco, 108,900 ....F 9
Desaguadero, 948 ....H11
Deustua, 416 ....G10
Dos de Mayo, 970 ....E 6
Echarate, 374 ....F 9
El Portugués ....C 7
Esperanza, 261 ....G 7
Ferreñafe, 12,112 ....C 6
Fitzcarrald ....G 8
Francisco de Orellana, 306 ....F 4
Guadalupe, 2,896 ....E 9
Güeppi ....E 3
Huacho, 29,400 ....D 8
Huacrachuco, 757 ....D 7
Hualgayoc, 1,223 ....C 6
Hualla, 2,586 ....F 9
Huallanca, Ancash, 491 ....D 7
Huallanca, Huánuco, 1,202 ....D 7
Huamachuco, 5,730 ....D 6
Huancabamba, 3,215 ....C 5
Huancané, 4,053 ....H10
Huancapi, 2,415 ....E 9
Huancavelica, 11,039 ....E 9
Huancayo, 95,000 ....E 9
Huanchaco, 1,006 ....C 7
Huanta, 5,728 ....E 9
Huánuco, 34,500 ....E 7
Huaral, 11,481 ....D 8
Huaráz, 20,345 ....D 7
Huari, 2,467 ....D 7
Huariaca, 1,534 ....E 8
Huarmey, 5,232 ....C 8
Huarochirí, 2,125 ....D 9
Huarocondo, 2,921 ....F 9
Huaura, 1,442 ....D 8
Huaylas, 1,258 ....C 7
Iberia, 526 ....F 5
Ica, 72,300 ....E10
Ichuña, 183 ....G11
Ilave, 4,278 ....H11
Ilo, 9,986 ....G11
Imperial, 6,345 ....D 9
Inambari, 9 ....H 9
Iñapari, 159 ....H 8
Intutu, 344 ....E 4
Iparia, 171 ....E 7
Iquitos, 76,100 ....F 4
Jaén, 4,420 ....C 5
Jauja, 12,751 ....E 8
Jayanca, 4,240 ....B 6
Jeberos, 1,842 ....D 5
Juanjuí, 5,105 ....D 6
Juli, 3,874 ....H11
Juliaca, 35,000 ....G10
Jumbilla, 876 ....C 5
Junín, 5,004 ....E 8
Lagunas, 3,637 ....E 5
La Huaca, 1,863 ....B 5
La Jalca, 1,401 ....D 6
La Joya, 1,305 ....G11
Lamas, 7,139 ....D 6
Lambayeque, 10,629 ....B 6
Lampa, 3,123 ....G10
Lamud, 2,609 ....C 6
Lanlacuni Bajo, 229 ....G 9
La Oroya, 32,600 ....D 8
Las Piedras, 13 ....H 9
Las Yaras, 367 ....G11
La Tina ....B 5
La Unión, 2,013 ....D 7
Leimebamba, 1,026 ....D 6
Lima (capital), *2,541,300 ....D 8
Limbani, 903 ....H10
Lircay, 2,077 ....E 9
Llata, 2,255 ....D 7
Lobitos, 3,071 ....B 5
Locumba, 349 ....G11
Lomas, 111 ....E10
Lucerna ....H 9
Lurín, 2,741 ....D 9
Machupicchu, 1,026 ....F 9
Macusani, 1,601 ....G10
Madre de Dios, †802 ....G 9
Máncora, 7,943 ....B 5
Manú, †686 ....G 9
Marcapata, 334 ....G 9
Marcona, 6,744 ....E10
Margos, 1,195 ....D 8
Masisea, 1,520 ....E 7
Matarani F11
Matucana, 2,883 ....D 8
Mavila ....H 8
Mazán, 411 ....F 4
Mazocruz, 156 ....H11
Mendoza, 1,002 ....D 6
Miraflores, 52,142 ....G11
Mishagua ....F 8
Moho, 1,377 ....H10
Mollendo, 12,483 ....F11
Monsefú, 11,141 ....C 6
Moquegua, 7,795 ....G11
Morales, 2,430 ....D 6
Morococha, 6,519 ....D 8
Morropón, 4,730 ....C 5
Motupe, 1,286 ....C 6
Moyobamba, 8,373 ....D 6
Nauta, 1,905 ....F 5
Nazca, 13,587 ....E10
Negritos, 14,810 ....B 5
Nueva Alejandría, †264 ....F 5
Nuñoa, 2,137 ....G10
Ocoña, 1,207 ....F11
Ocros, 1,204 ....D 8
Ollachea, 903 ....G 9
Ollantaytambo, 1,632 ....F 9
Olmos, 3,628 ....C 5
Omaguas ....F 4
Omas, 217 ....D 9
Omate, 856 ....G11
Orcotuna, 2,716 ....E 8
Orellana, 1,596 ....E 6
Otuzco, 4,311 ....C 6
Oxapampa, 2,535 ....E 8
Oyón, 2,171 ....D 8
Pacasmayo, 11,956 ....C 6
Pachiza, 1,307 ....D 6
Paijan, 5,815 ....C 6
Paita, 9,615 ....B 5
Palpa, 2,615 ....E10
Pampachiri, 448 ....F10
Pampacolca, 1,876 ....F10
Pampas, 2,495 ....E 9
Panao, 1,262 ....E 7
Pantoja, 528 ....E 3
Parinari, 126 ....E 5
Paruro, 1,905 ....F 9
Pataz, 324 ....D 6
Pativilca, 15,325 ....D 8
Paucarbamba, 715 ....E 9
Paucartambo, Cuzco, 1,928 ....E 8
Paucartambo, Pasco, 1,717 ....G 9
Pevas, 696 ....G 4
Picota, 2,014 ....D 6
Pimentel, 6,252 ....B 6
Pinquén ....G 9
Pisac, 1,230 ....G 9
Pisco, 27,300 ....D 9
Piura, 111,400 ....B 5
Pizacoma, 86 ....H11
Pomabamba, 2,522 ....D 7
Porvenir ....E 5
Poto, 161 ....H10
Pozuzo, 121 ....E 8
Puca Barranca ....F 4
Pucallpa, 45,600 ....E 7
Pucará, 1,119 ....G10
Pucaurco, 12 ....G 4
Pucusana, 1,331 ....D 9
Puerto Alianza ....D 5
Puerto América, 150 ....D 5
Puerto Arturo ....F 3
Puerto Bermúdez, 230 ....E 8
Puerto Caballas E10
Puerto Chicama, 3,002 ....C 6
Puerto Eten, 2,192 ....B 6
Puerto José Pardo ....D 4
Puerto Leguía, Loreto ....D 4
Puerto Leguía, Puno ....G 9
Puerto Maldonado, 3,518 ....H 9
Puerto Morín ....C 7
Puerto Ocopa, 1,304 ....E 8
Puerto Pardo ....F 7
Puerto Pizarro ....B 4
Puerto Portillo, 49 ....F 7
Puerto Prado, 419 ....E 8
Puerto Samanco, 1,733 ....C 7
Puerto Tahuantinsuyo ....G 9
Puerto Victoria ....E 7
Puno, 32,100 ....G10
Punta de Bombón, 3,943 ....F11
Punta Moreno ....C 6
Puquina, 1,030 ....G11
Puquio, 8,144 ....F10
Putina, 3,512 ....H10
Querecotillo, 6,205 ....B 5
Quicacha, 299 ....F10
Quilca, 171 ....F11
Quillabamba, 8,644 ....F 9
Quince Mil ....G 9
Ramón Castilla, †8,106 ....G 5
Recuay, 1,755 ....D 7
Requena, 3,931 ....F 5
Reventazón ....B 6
Rioja, 4,361 ....D 6
Salaverry, 4,605 ....C 7
San José, 2,612 ....B 6
San José de Sisa, 4,190 ....D 6
San Juan, 717 ....E10
San Lorenzo, 84 ....H 8
San Martín ....E 3
San Miguel, Ayacucho, 1,271 ....F 9
San Miguel, Cajamarca, 1,871 ....C 6
San Pedro de Lloc, 7,497 ....C 6
San Ramón, 3,016 ....E 8
San Vicente de Cañete, 7,184 ....D 9
Saña, 18,421 ....C 6
Sandia, 3,026 ....H10
Santa, 2,966 ....C 7
Santa Clotilde, 824 ....E 4
Santa Cruz, Cajamarca, 1,729 ....C 6
Santa Cruz, Loreto, 739 ....E 5
Santa Elena, 271 ....F 5
Santa Isabel de Sihuas, 118 ....F11
Santa María de Nanay, 123 ....F 4
Santiago, 1,613 ....E10
Santiago de Cao, 1,033 ....C 6
Santiago de-Chocorvos, 344 ....E 9
Santiago de Chuco, 4,649 ....C 7
Santo Tomás, Amazonas, 1,097 ....C 6
Santo Tomás, Cuzco, 1,659 ....G10
Santo Tomás de Andoas, 65 ....D 4
Saposoa, 4,456 ....D 6
Saquena, 688 ....F 5
Satipo, 2,499 ....E 8
Sauce, 1,761 ....D 6
Sayán, 1,764 ....D 8
Sechura, 5,157 ....B 5
Sicuani, 10,664 ....G10
Sihuas, 1,404 ....D 7
Sullana, 43,500 ....B 5
Sumbay G10
Sumbilca, 1,365 ....D 8
Supe, 2,499 ....D 8
Tacna, 41,200 ....G11
Tahuamanu, †4,011 ....H 8
Talara, 39,600 ....B 5
Tambo de Mora, 1,128 ....D 9
Tambo Grande, 4,404 ....B 5
Tamshiyacu, 1,623 ....F 5
Tarapoto, 13,907 ....D 6
Tarata, 2,673 ....H11
Tarma, 15,452 ....E 8
Tarqui ....E 3
Tayabamba, 1,519 ....D 7
Ticaco, 1,206 ....H11
Tingo María, 5,208 ....D 7
Tiruntán, 847 ....E 6
Tocache, 1,607 ....D 7
Tonegrama ....D 4
Topara, 1,437 ....D 9
Toquepala G11
Torata, 669 ....G11
Tournavista ....E 7
Trujillo, 156,200 ....C 7
Tumbes, 30,000 ....B 4
Ubinas, 348 ....G11
Uchiza, 1,006 ....D 7
Unini ....F 8
Urcos, 2,733 ....G 9
Urubamba, 3,325 ....F 9
Vinchos, 473 ....E 9
Virú, 2,647 ....C 7
Vitor, 117 ....G11
Yambrasbamba, 306 ....D 5
Yanahuanca, 962 ....D 8
Yanaoca, 1,146 ....G10
Yauca, 2,364 ....E10
Yauli, 1,696 ....D 8
Yauri, 2,834 ....G10
Yauyos, 1,456 ....E 9
Yunguyo, 2,506 ....H11
Yurimaguas, 11,655 ....E 5
Zarumilla, 3,499 ....B 4
Zorritos, 2,862 ....B 4

OTHER FEATURES

Acarí (river) E10
Aguaytía (river) ....E 7
Aguja (point) ....B 5
Amazon (river) ....F 4
Andes, Cordillera de los (mts.) F10
Apurímac (river) ....F 9
Azángaro (river) G10
Azul, Cordillera (mts.) ....E 7
Blanca, Cordillera (mts.) ....D 7
Blanco (cape) ....B 5
Blanco (river) ....F 6
Boquerón, El (pass) ....E 7
Cañete (river) ....D 9
Casma (river) ....C 7
Chimbote (bay) ....C 7
Chincha (isls.) ....D 9
Chira (river) ....B 5
Coles (point) G11
Cóndor, Cordillera del (mts.) ....C 5
Coropuna, Nudo (mt.) F10
Corrientes (river) ....E 4
El Boquerón (pass) ....E 7
El Misti (mt.) G11
Ene (river) ....E 8
Ferrol (pen.) ....C 7
Grande (river) E10
Guañape (isls.) ....C 7
Heath (river) ....H 9
Huallaga (river) ....D 5
Huasaga (river) ....D 4
Huascarán (mt.) ....D 7
Huayabamba (river) ....D 6
Ica (river) E10
Inambari (river) ....H 9
Independencia (bay) D10
Junín (lake) ....E 8
La Montaña (reg.) ....F 8
Lachay (Salinas) (point) ....D 8
Las Piedras (river) ....G 8
Las Viejas (isl.) D10
Lobos de Afuera (isls.) ....B 6
Lobos de Tierra (isl.) ....B 6
Locumba (river) G11
Madre de Dios (river) ....G 9
Majes (river) F11
Mantaro (river) ....E 8
Manú (river) ....G 8
Marañón (river) ....E 5
Mayo (river) ....D 6
Misti, El (mt.) G11
Montaña, La (reg.) ....F 8
Morona (river) ....D 5
Nanay (river) ....E 4
Napo (river) ....F 4
Negra, Cordillera (mts.) ....D 7
Negra (point) ....B 6
Ñermete (point) ....B 5
Nudo Coropuna (mt.) F10
Occidental, Cordillera (mts.) F10
Ocoña (river) F11
Oriental, Cordillera (mts.) H10
Pachitea (river) ....E 7
Paita (bay) ....B 5
Pampas (river) ....E 9
Paracas (pen.), †727 ....D 9
Parinacochas (lake) F10
Pariñas (point) ....B 5
Pastaza (river) ....D 5
Pativilca (river) ....D 8
Perené (river) ....E 8
Pichis (river) ....E 8
Piedras, Las (river) ....G 8
Pisco (bay) ....D 9
Pisco (river) ....D 9
Pirua (river) ....B 5
Puinagua, Canal de (river) ....E 5
Purus (river) ....G 8
Putumayo (river) ....G 4
Rímac (river) ....D 9
Salinas (Lachay) (point) ....D 8
Sama (river) G11

(continued on following page)

(continued)

PERU (continued)

San Gallán (isl.) ....D 9
San Lorenzo (isl.) ....D 9
San Nicolás (bay) E10
Santa (river) ....C 7
Santiago (river) ....D 4
Sechura (bay) ....B 5
Tahuamanu (river) ....H 8
Tambo (river) G11
Tambopata (river) ....H 9
Tapiche (river) ....E 6
Tigre (river) ....E 4
Titicaca (lake) H10
Tumbes (river) ....B 4
Ucayali (river) ....F 5
Urituyacu (river) ....D 5
Urubamba (river) ....F 8
Viejas, Las (isl.) D10
Vilcabamba, Cordillera (mts.) ..F 9
Vilcanota (mt.) G10
Vitor (river) F11
Yaguas (river) ....G 4
Yavarí (river) ....G 5
Yavero (river) ....F 9

ECUADOR

PROVINCES

Azuay, 274,642 ....C 4
Bolívar, 131,651 ....C 3
Cañar, 112,733 ....C 4
Carchi, 94,649 ....C 2
Chimborazo, 276,668 ....C 3
Cotopaxi, 154,971 ....C 3
El Oro, 160,650 ....C 4
Esmeraldas, 124,881 ....C 2
Galápagos, 2,391 ....C 8
Guayas, 979,223 ....B 4
Imbabura, 174,039 ....C 2
Loja, 285,448 ....C 4
Los Ríos, 250,062 ....C 3
Manabí, 612,542 ....B 3
Morona-Santiago, 25,503 ....C 4
Napo, 24,253 ....D 3
Pastaza, 13,693 ....D 3
Pichincha, 587,835 ....C 3
Tungurahua, 178,709 ....C 3
Zamora-Chinchipe, 11,464 ....C 5

CITIES and TOWNS

Alausí, 6,676 ....C 4
Ambato, 53,372 ....C 3
Andoas Nuevo ....D 4
Arapicos ....D 3
Archidona ....D 3
Arenillas, 3,925 ....B 4
Atuntaqui, 8,759 ....C 2
Azogues, 8,075 ....C 4
Baba, 693 ....C 3
Babahoyo, 16,444 ....C 3
Baeza, 213 ....D 3
Bahía de Caráquez, 8,845 ....B 3
Balao, 1,415 ....C 4
Balzar, 6,588 ....C 3
Bolívar, 410 ....C 2
Cajabamba, 2,094 ....C 3
Calceta 4,946 ....C 3
Cañar, 4,935 ....C 4
Canelos ....D 3
Cariamanga, 5,381 ....C 5
Carondelet, 318 ....C 2
Catacocha, 3,796 ....C 5
Catamayo, 4,097 ....C 4
Catarama, 2,424 ....C 3
Cayambe, 8,101 ....D 3
Celica, 3,467 ....B 4
Chone, 12,832 ....B 3
Chunchi, 2,388 ....C 4
Coca ....D 3
Cojimíes, 1,538 ....B 2
Cononaco ....E 3
Cuenca, 60,402 ....C 4
Cuyabeno ....E 3
Daule, 7,428 ....B 3
Edén ....E 3
El Ángel, 4,009 ....C 2
El Corazón, 1,118 ....C 3
El Progreso ....C 9
El Pun, 612 ....D 2
Esmeraldas, 33,403 ....B 2
Farfán ....D 2
Floreana B10
Girón, 1,914 ....C 4
Gualaceo, 3,065 ....C 4
Gualaquiza, 635 ....C 4
Guale ....B 3
Guamote, 2,640 ....C 4
Guano, 4,455 ....C 3
Guaranda, 9,900 ....C 3
Guayaquil, 738,591 ....B 4
Ibarra, 25,835 ....D 2
Jama, 1,743 ....B 3
Jipijapa, 13,367 ....B 3
La Libertad, 13,565 ....B 4
La Tola, 650 ....C 2
Latacunga, 14,856 ....C 3
Loja, 26,785 ....C 4
Loreto ....D 3
Macará, 5,027 ....C 5
Macas, 1,355 ....D 4
Machachi, 3,951 ....C 3
Machala, 29,036 ....B 4
Machalilla, 615 ....B 3
Manglaralto, 799 ....B 3
Manta, 33,622 ....B 3
Méndez, 527 ....C 4
Mera ....C 3
Miazal ....D 4
Milagro, 28,148 ....C 4
Montecristi, 4,540 ....B 3
Morona ....D 4
Mulaló, 427 ....C 3
Napo ....D 3
Nuevo Rocafuerte, 435 ....E 3
Otavalo, 8,630 ....C 2
Paján, 1,818 ....B 3
Palanda ....C 5
Papallacta ....D 3
Pasaje, 13,215 ....C 4
Paute, 1,511 ....C 4
Pedernales, 610 ....B 2
Pelileo, 2,545 ....C 3
Píllaro, 2,714 ....C 3
Piñas, 3,344 ....C 4
Playas, 5,067 ....B 4
Portoviejo, 32,228 ....B 3
Posorja, 2,086 ....B 4
Puerto Baquerizo Moreno ....C 9
Puerto de Cayo, 713 ....B 3
Pujilí, 2,534 ....C 3
Putumayo ....E 3
Puyo, 2,290 ....D 3
Quevedo, 20,602 ....C 3
Quito (capital), 496,410 ....C 3
Río Tigre ....D 4
Riobamba, 41,625 ....C 3
Rocafuerte, 4,349 ....B 3
Rosa Zárate, 1,662 ....C 2
Salinas, 5,460 ....B 4
San Gabriel, 6,803 ....D 2
San Lorenzo, 575 ....C 2
San Miguel, 2,410 ....C 3
San Miguel de Salcedo, 3,442 ....C 3
Sangolquí, 5,501 ....C 3
Santa Ana, 3,940 ....B 3
Santa Cruz ....B 9
Santa Elena, 4,241 ....B 4
Santa Isabel, 1,602 ....C 4
Santa Rosa, 8,935 ....C 4
Santa Rosa de Sucumbíos, 132 ....D 2
Santo Domingo de los Colorados, 6,951 ....C 3
Saraguro, 1,562 ....C 4
Sarayacu ....D 3
Sigsig, 1,228 ....C 4
Sigüe ....D 2
Sucre, 2,578 ....B 3
Sucúa, 1,153 ....C 4
Tabacundo, 2,009 ....C 2
Tachina ....C 2
Tena, 1,029 ....D 3
Tulcán, 16,448 ....D 2
Valdez, 3,358 ....C 2
Viche, 230 ....C 2
Villamil ....B 9
Vinces, 5,901 ....C 3
Yacuambí, 405 ....C 4
Yaguachi, 2,996 ....C 4
Yaupi ....D 4
Zamora, 1,030 ....C 5
Zapotillo, 460 ....B 5
Zaruma, 9,000 ....C 4
Zumba, 450 ....C 5

OTHER FEATURES

Aguarico (river) ....D 3
Albemarle (point) ....B 9
Ancón de Sardinas (bay) ....C 2
Antisana (mt.) ....D 3
Baltra (isl.) ....B 9
Banks (bay) ....B 9
Bobonaza (river) ....D 3
Cayambe (mt.) ....D 2
Chaves (Santa Cruz) (isl.), 626 ....C 9
Chimborazo (mt.) ....C 3
Cotopaxi (mt.) ....C 3
Cristóbal (point) ....B 9
Culpepper (isl.) ....B 8
Curaray (river) ....D 3
Darwin (Culpepper) (isl.) ....B 8
Esmeraldas (river) ....C 2
Española (isl.) C10
Fernandina (isl.) ....B 9
Floreana (Santa María) (isl.), 46 ....B10
Galápagos (isls.), 2,391 ....C 8
Galera (point) ....B 2
Genovesa (isl.) ....C 9
Guayaquil (gulf) ....B 4
Guayas (river) ....C 4
Isabel (bay) ....B 9
Isabela (isl.), 336 ....B 9
La Puntilla (cape) ....B 4
Manta (bay) ....B 3
Marchena (isl.) ....B 9
Mira (river) ....C 2
Napo (river) ....D 3
Naranjal (river) ....C 4
Pasado (cape) ....B 3
Pastaza (river) ....D 4
Pindo (river) ....D 3
Pinta (isl.) ....B 9
Pinzón (isl.) ....B 9
Puná (isl.), 5,459 ....B 4
Puntilla, La (cape) ....B 4
Putumayo (river) ....E 2
Rosa (cape) B10
San Cristóbal (isl.), 1,404 ....C 9
San Francisco (cape) ....B 2
Sangay (mt.) ....C 4
San Lorenzo (cape) ....B 3
San Miguel (river) ....D 2
San Salvador (isl.) ....B 9
Santa Cruz (isl.), 626 ....C 9
Santa Elena (bay) ....B 3
Santa Fé (isl.) ....C 9
Santa María (isl.), 46 ....B10
Santiago (San Salvador) (isl.) ....C 9
Tumbes (river) ....B 4
Wenman (isl.) ....B 8
Wolf (Wenman) (isl.) ....B 8
Zamora (river) ....B 4

*City and suburbs.
†Population of district.

FRENCH GUIANA

DISTRICTS

Cayenne, 36,187 ....E 3
St-Laurent-du-Maroni, 8,205 ....E 4

CITIES and TOWNS

Camopi, †276 ....E 4
Cayenne (cap.), 19,668 ....E 3
Cayenne, *24,581 ....E 3
Counamama ....E 3
Edmond ....E 3
Grand-Santi, 60 ....D 3
Guisambourg ....F 3
Inini ....E 4
Iracoubo, 504 ....E 3
Kaw, 258 ....E 3
Kourou, 868 ....E 3
Macouria (Tonate), 301 ....E 3
Mana, 568 ....E 3
Maripa ....E 4
Maripasoula, 166 ....D 4
Montsinéry, 107 ....E 3
Organobo ....E 3
Oscar ....E 4
Ouanary, 79 ....F 3
Ouaqui ....D 4
P. I. (Paul Isnard), †47 ....E 3
Paul Isnard, †47 ....E 3
Régina ....E 3
Rémire, 650 ....E 3
Roura, 84 ....E 3
Saint-Élie, 78 ....E 3
Saint-Georges-de-l'Oyapoc, 502....F 4
Saint-Jean ....D 3
Saint-Laurent-du-Maroni, 3,486...E 3
Saül, 81 ....E 4
Saut-Tigre ....E 3
Sinnamary, 1,355 ....E 3
Tonate, 301 ....E 3

OTHER FEATURES

Approuague (river) ....E 4
Béhague (point) ....F 3
Camopi (river) ....E 4
Chaîne Granitique (range) ....E 4
Comté (river) ....E 3
Connétable (isls.) ....F 3
Devil's (isl.) ....E 3
Granitique, Chaîne (range) ....E 4
Inini (river) ....E 4
Itany (river) ....D 4
Mana (river) ....E 3
Maroni (river) ....D 3
Marouini (river) ....D 4
Oyapock (river) ....E 4
Rémire (isls.) ....F 3
Salut (isls.) ....F 3
Sinnamary (river) ....E 3
Tampoc (river) ....E 4

GUYANA

DISTRICTS

East Berbice, 115,511 ....C 3
East Demerara, 256,908 ....B 2
Essequibo, 29,729 ....B 2
Essequibo Islands, 15,728 ....B 2
Mazaruni-Potaro, 12,029 ....A 2
North West, 12,809 ....A 2
Rupununi, 10,031 ....B 4
West Berbice, 26,524 ....C 2
West Demerara, 81,061 ....B 3

CITIES and TOWNS

Adventure, 507 ....B 2
Anna Regina, 848 ....B 2
Apoteri ....B 3
Arakaka ....B 2
Atkinson Field ....B 2
Aurora ....B 2
Baramanni ....B 2
Baramita ....A 2
Bartica, 2,352 ....B 2
Charity, 838 ....B 2
Christianburg-Wismar-Mackenzie, 5,843 ....B 2
Dadanawa ....B 4
Danielstown, 478 ....B 2
Enmore ....C 2
Enterprise ....B 2
Epira ....C 3
Five Stars ....A 2
Fort Wellington ....C 2
Georgetown (cap.), 97,190 ....C 2
Georgetown, *102,688 ....C 2
Imbaimadai ....A 3
Ituni ....B 3
Kamakusa ....A 3
Kamarang, 510 ....A 3
Kurupukari ....B 3
Lethem ....B 4
Lumid Pau ....B 4
Mabaruma, 343 ....B 1
Mahaica, 8,646 ....C 2
Mahaicony, 8,272 ....C 2
Morawhanna, 305 ....B 1
Mount Everard ....B 2
New Amsterdam, 14,300 ....C 2
Orealla ....C 3
Paradise ....C 3
Parika, 577 ....B 2
Pickersgill, 334 ....B 2
Port Kaituma ....B 2
Queenstown, 1,067 ....B 2
Rockstone ....B 2
Rosignol, 1,204 ....C 2
Skeldon, 4,367 ....C 3
Springlands, 181 ....C 2
Suddie, 512 ....B 2
Takama ....C 3
Tumatumari ....B 3
Tumereng ....B 2
Vreed-en-Hoop, 3,156 ....B 2
Yupukari ....B 4

OTHER FEATURES

Akarai (mts.) ....B 5
Amakara (river) ....A 2
Amuku (mts.) ....B 4
Barama (river) ....A 2
Barima (river) ....B 2
Berbice (river) ....B 3
Canje (river) ....C 2
Courantyne (river) ....C 3
Cuyuni (river) ....B 2
Demerara (river) ....B 3
Enwarak (mt.) ....B 3
Essequibo (river) ....B 3
Great (fall) ....B 3
Ireng (river) ....B 3
Kaieteur (fall) ....B 3
Kamaria (falls) ....B 2
Kanuku (mts.) ....B 4
Kurungiku (mts.) ....B 3

Agriculture, Industry and Resources

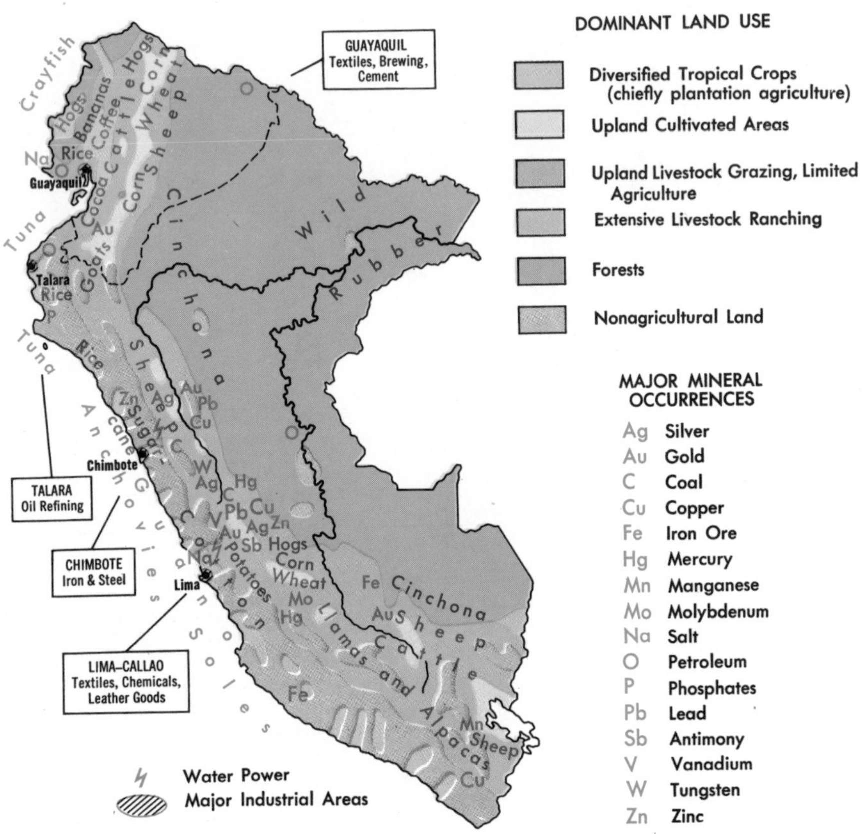
GUAYAQUIL
Textiles, Brewing, Cement
TALARA
Oil Refining
CHIMBOTE
Iron & Steel
LIMA-CALLAO
Textiles, Chemicals, Leather Goods
Guayaquil
Talara
Chimbote
Lima
Crayfish
Tuna
Anchovies
Sardines
Rice
Bananas
Coffee
Cocoa
Corn
Wheat
Sheep
Hogs
Goats
Cattle
Cotton
Sugarcane
Potatoes
Wild Rubber
Cinchona
Llamas and Alpacas
DOMINANT LAND USE
Diversified Tropical Crops (chiefly plantation agriculture)
Upland Cultivated Areas
Upland Livestock Grazing, Limited Agriculture
Extensive Livestock Ranching
Forests
Nonagricultural Land
MAJOR MINERAL OCCURRENCES
Ag Silver
Au Gold
C Coal
Cu Copper
Fe Iron Ore
Hg Mercury
Mn Manganese
Mo Molybdenum
Na Salt
O Petroleum
P Phosphates
Pb Lead
Sb Antimony
V Vanadium
W Tungsten
Zn Zinc
Water Power
Major Industrial Areas

Agriculture, Industry and Resources

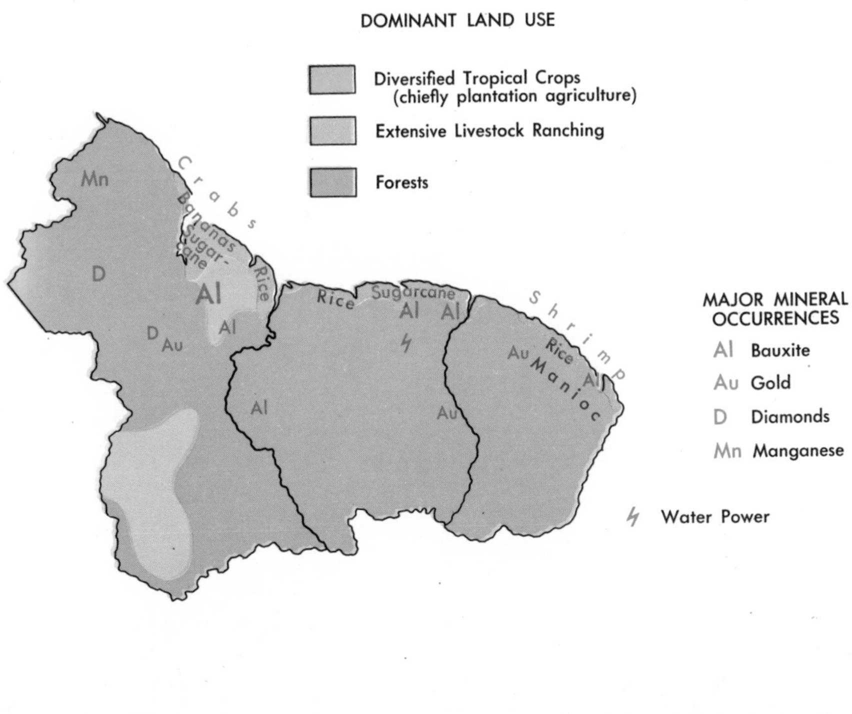
DOMINANT LAND USE
Diversified Tropical Crops (chiefly plantation agriculture)
Extensive Livestock Ranching
Forests
Crabs
Bananas
Sugarcane
Rice
Shrimp
Manioc
MAJOR MINERAL OCCURRENCES
Al Bauxite
Au Gold
D Diamonds
Mn Manganese
Water Power

GUYANA
AREA 83,000 sq. mi.
POPULATION 763,000
CAPITAL Georgetown
LARGEST CITY Georgetown
HIGHEST POINT Mt. Roraima 9,094 ft.
MONETARY UNIT Guyana dollar
MAJOR LANGUAGES English, Hindi
MAJOR RELIGIONS Christianity, Hinduism, Islam

SURINAM
AREA 55,144 sq. mi.
POPULATION 389,000
CAPITAL Paramaribo
LARGEST CITY Paramaribo
HIGHEST POINT Julianatop 4,200 ft.
MONETARY UNIT Surinam guilder
MAJOR LANGUAGES Dutch, Hindi, Indonesian
MAJOR RELIGIONS Christianity, Islam, Hinduism

FRENCH GUIANA
AREA 35,135 sq. mi.
POPULATION 48,000
CAPITAL Cayenne
LARGEST CITY Cayenne
HIGHEST POINT 2,723 ft.
MONETARY UNIT French franc
MAJOR LANGUAGE French
MAJOR RELIGIONS Roman Catholicism, Protestantism

GUYANA

Kuyuwini (river) .... B 4
Kwitaro (river) .... B 4
Leguan (isl.), 6,567 .... B 2
Marudi (mts.) .... B 5
Mazaruni (river) .... A 2
Moruka (river) .... B 2
New (river) .... C 4
Pakaraima (mts.) .... A 3
Playa (point) .... B 1
Pomeroon (river) .... B 2
Potaro (river) .... B 3
Puruni (river) .... B 2
Roraima (mt.) .... A 3
Rupununi (river) .... B 4
Sororieng (mt.) .... A 3
Surwakwima (fall) .... A 2
Takutu (river) .... B 4
Venamo (mt.) .... A 3
Waini (river) .... B 2
Wenamu (river) .... A 2

SURINAM

DISTRICTS

Brokopondo, 1,376 .... D 4
Commewijne, 18,796 .... D 3
Coronie, 4,069 .... C 3
Marowijne, 10,074 .... D 4
Nickerie, 24,730 .... C 3
Para .... D 3
Paramaribo, 122,634 .... D 2
Saramacca, 10,979 .... C 3
Suriname, 80,870 .... D 3

CITIES and TOWNS

Ajoewa .... C 4
Alalapadu .... C 4
Albina, 1,000 .... D 3
Asidonhoppo .... D 3
Berg-en-Dal .... D 3
Bitagron .... C 3
Brokopondo .... D 3
Burnside .... C 2
Calcutta, 1,100 .... D 3

Cottica .... D 3
Domburg, 1,200 .... D 3
Groningen, 600 .... D 3
Huwelijkszorg .... D 3
Kwakoegron .... D 3
Kwatta .... D 2
Lelydorp, 300 .... D 3
Magalie .... D 4
Marienburg, 3,500 .... D 3
Moengo, 2,100 .... D 3
Nieuw-Amsterdam, 1,400 .... D 3
Nieuw-Nickerie, 7,400 .... C 2
Paramaribo (cap.), 110,867 .... D 2
Paramaribo, *182,100 .... D 2
Paranam .... D 3
Saramaccapolder .... D 2
Totness, 1,300 .... C 3
Wageningen, 800 .... C 3
Zanderij .... D 3

OTHER FEATURES

Bakhuys (mts.) .... C 3
Coeroeni (river) .... C 4
Commewijne (river) .... D 3
Coppename (river) .... C 3
Corantijn (river) .... C 3
Cottica (river) .... D 3
Eilerts-de-Haan (mts.) .... C 4
Frederik Willem IV (falls) .... C 4
Julianatop (mt.) .... C 4
Kayser (mts.) .... D 4
Lely (mts.) .... D 3
Litani (river) .... D 4
Marowijne (river) .... D 3
Nickerie (river) .... C 3
Orange (mts.) .... D 4
Saramacca (river) .... D 3
Sipaliwini (river) .... C 4
Suriname (river) .... D 3
Tapanahoni (river) .... D 4
Toekomstig (res.) .... C 4
Van Blommestein (lake) .... D 3
Wilhelmina (mts.) .... C 4

*City and suburbs.
†Population of municipality.

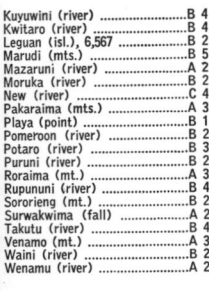

Topography

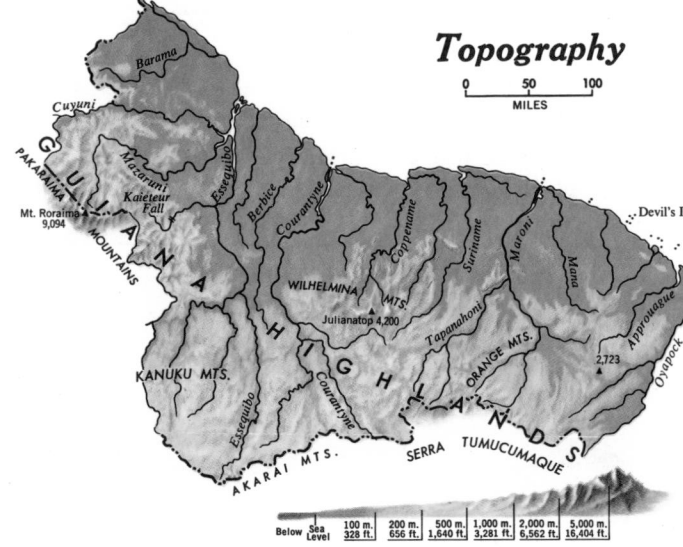

MILES 0 50 100

Mt. Roraima 9,094
GUIANA HIGHLANDS
PAKARAIMA MOUNTAINS
Cuyuni
Barama
Mazaruni
Kaieteur Fall
Essequibo
Berbice
Courantyne
Coppename
Suriname
Maroni
Mana
Approuague
Oyapock
Devil's I.
WILHELMINA MTS.
Julianatop 4,200
Tapanahoni
ORANGE MTS.
2,723
KANUKU MTS.
Essequibo
Courantyne
AKARAI MTS.
SERRA TUMUCUMAQUE

Below Sea Level | 100 m. 328 ft. | 200 m. 656 ft. | 500 m. 1,640 ft. | 1,000 m. 3,281 ft. | 2,000 m. 6,562 ft. | 5,000 m. 16,404 ft.

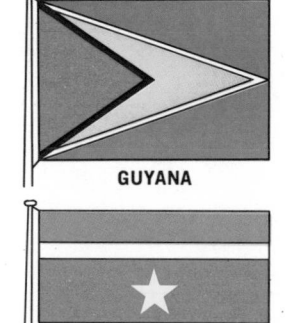

GUYANA

SURINAM

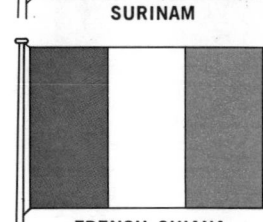

FRENCH GUIANA

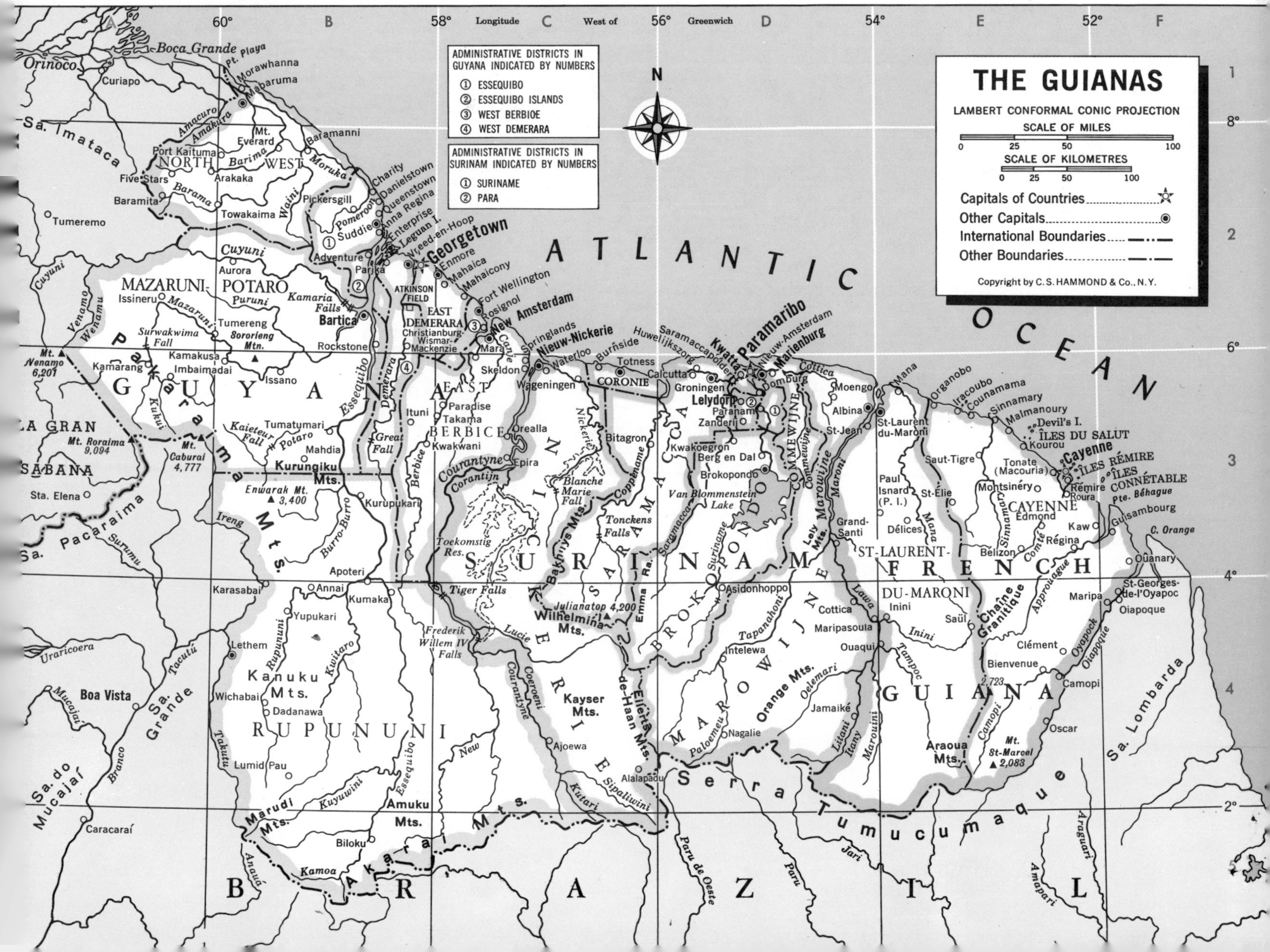

ADMINISTRATIVE DISTRICTS IN GUYANA INDICATED BY NUMBERS
① ESSEQUIBO
② ESSEQUIBO ISLANDS
③ WEST BERBICE
④ WEST DEMERARA

ADMINISTRATIVE DISTRICTS IN SURINAM INDICATED BY NUMBERS
① SURINAME
② PARA

THE GUIANAS
LAMBERT CONFORMAL CONIC PROJECTION
SCALE OF MILES
0 25 50 100
SCALE OF KILOMETRES
0 25 50 100

Capitals of Countries .... ☆
Other Capitals .... ◉
International Boundaries .... —·—
Other Boundaries .... ----

Copyright by C.S. HAMMOND & Co., N.Y.

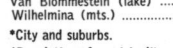

Longitude 60° B 58° C West of 56° D Greenwich 54° E 52° F

ATLANTIC OCEAN

Orinoco
Boca Grande playa
Curiapo
Morawhanna
pt.
Sa. Imataca
Amacuro
Amakura
Mabaruma
Mt. Everard
Batamanni
Port Kaituma
NORTH Barima WEST
Five Stars
Arakaka
Moruka
Baramita
Barama
Towakaima
Pickersgill
Charity
Waini
Pomeroon
Danielstown
Queenstown
Anna Regina
Enterprise
Suddie
Leguan I.
Tumeremo
Cuyuni
Aurora
MAZARUNI-POTARO
Puruni
Adventure
Parika
① Wsed-en-Hoop
Georgetown
Enmore
Mahaica
Mahaicony
② Kamaria Falls
Bartica
Tumereng
Sororieng Mtn.
ATKINSON FIELD
EAST DEMERARA
③ Christianburg-Wismar-Mackenzie
Fort Wellington
Rosignol
New Amsterdam
Issineru
Surwakwima Fall
Kamakusa
Imbaimadai
Rockstone
④ EAST
Springlands
Nieuw-Nickerie
Waterloo
Skeldon
Canje
Burnside
Huwelijkszorg
Saramaccapolder
Kwatta Paramaribo
Nieuw-Amsterdam
Marienburg
Cottica
Mt. Nenamo 6,201
Kamarang
Issano
BERBICE
Ituni
Paradise
Takama
Corentyn
Wageningen
CORONIE
Totness
Groningen
Lelydorp ②
Paranam ①
Zanderij
Moengo
Albina
Organobo
St-Jean
Mana
GUYANA
LA GRAN SABANA
Mt. Roraima 9,094
Mt. Caburaí 4,777
Kaieteur Fall
Potaro
Mahdia
Kurungiku
Great Fall
Kwakwani
Epira
Orealla
Bitagron
Kwakoegron
Berg en Dal
Brokopondo
Van Blommestein Lake
Grand-Santi
St-Laurent du-Maroni
Saut-Tigre
Tonate (Macouria)
Montsinéry
Paul Isnard (P.I.)
St-Élie
Délices
ÎLES DU SALUT
Kourou
Devil's I.
Sinnamary
Counamama
Vracoubo
Iracoubo
Malmanoury
CAYENNE
Roura
ÎLES RÉMIRE
ÎLES CONNÉTABLE
Pte. Béhague
Sta. Elena
Pacaraima
Enwarak Mt. 3,400
Surumu
Ireng
Burro-Burro
Kurupukari
Toekomstig Res.
Blanche Marie Fall
Tonckens Falls
SURINAM
Saramacca
BROKOPONDO
Asidonhoppo
Cottica
Lawa
Inini
Maripasoula
Saül
Chaîne Granitique
Edmond
Régina
Belizon
Guisambourg
C. Orange
Boa Vista
Karasabai
Annai
Kumaka
Tiger Falls
Apoteri
Frederik Willem IV Falls
Lucie
Wilhelmina Mts.
Julianatop 4,200
Emma
Tapanahoni
Nagalie
Intelewa
Ouaqui
Inini
Bienvenue
Clément
ST-LAURENT-DU-MARONI
FRENCH GUIANA
2,723
Approuague
Maripa
St-Georges-de-l'Oyapoc
Oiapoque
Oyapock
Uraricoera
Yupukari
Lethem
Wichabai
Dadanawa
KANUKU Mts.
RUPUNUNI
Kwitaro
Kwatari
New
Coeroeni
Kayser Mts.
Ajoewa
Eilerts-de-Haan Mts.
Sipaliwini
MAROWIJNE
Paloemeu
Litani
Itany
Oelemari
Tampoc
Jamaiké
Marouini
Camopi
Oscar
Ouanary
Sa. Lombarda
Boca Grande
Rio Branco
Caracaraí
Sa. do Mucajaí
Sa. Grande
Tacutu
Lumid Pau
Maruaí
Anauá
Kamoa
Biloku
AKARAI Mts.
Amuku Mts.
Essequibo
Kuyuwini
Amaku Mts.
Serra Tumucumaque
Mt. St-Marcel 2,083
Araoua Mts.
GUIANA
Paru de Osses
Jari
Camopi
Araguari
Amapari
Oyapock
B R A Z I L
N

BRAZIL

BIPOLAR OBLIQUE CONIC CONFORMAL PROJECTION

SCALE OF MILES
0 50 100 200 300

SCALE OF KILOMETRES
0 50 100 200 300

Capitals of Countries .... ⊛
State Capitals .... ◉
International Boundaries ....
State Boundaries ....

Copyright by C.S. HAMMOND & CO., N.Y.

BRAZIL
WESTERN PART
0 50 100 200
MILES

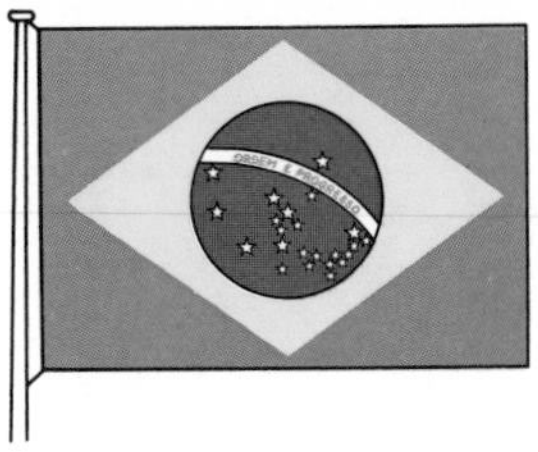

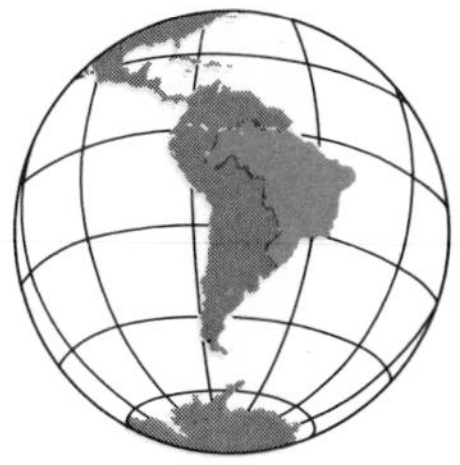

AREA 3,284,426 sq. mi.
POPULATION 90,840,000
CAPITAL Brasília
LARGEST CITY São Paulo (greater)
HIGHEST POINT Pico da Neblina 9,889 ft.
MONETARY UNIT cruzeiro
MAJOR LANGUAGE Portuguese
MAJOR RELIGION Roman Catholicism

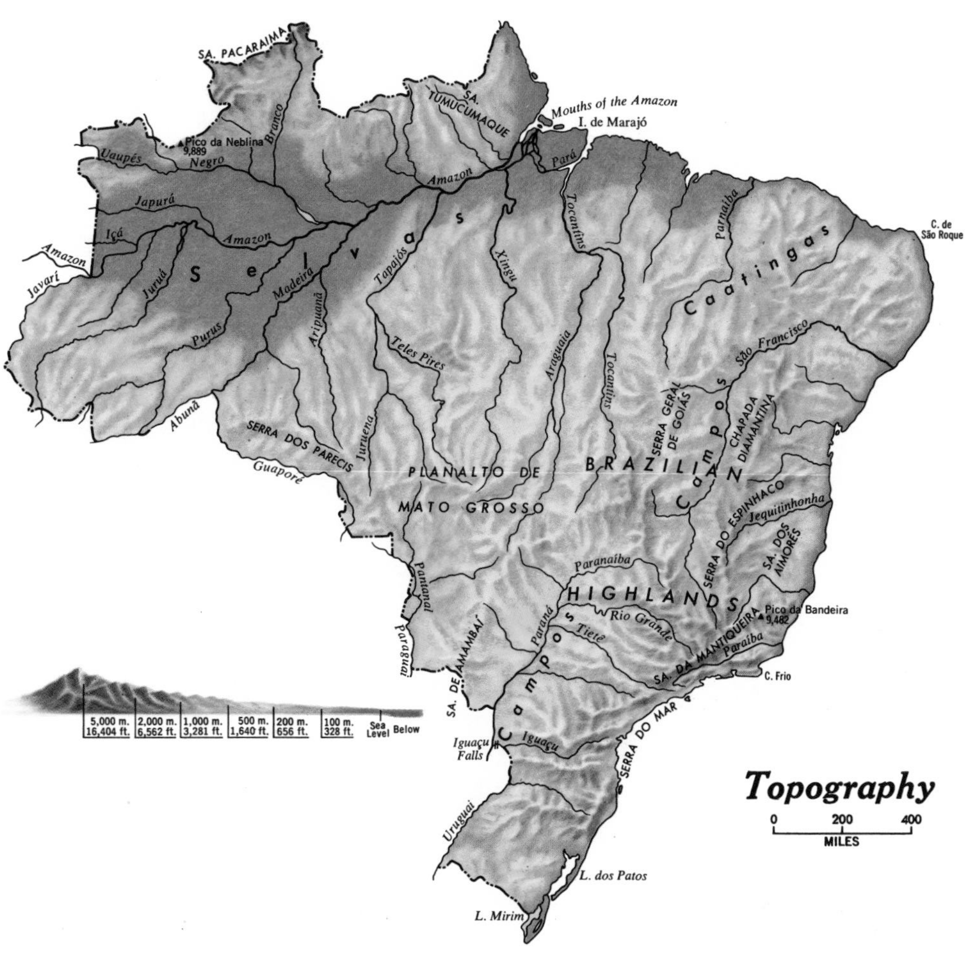

Topography

STATES and TERRITORIES

e, 196,000 ..... G10
goas, 1,381,000 ..... G 5
apá (terr.), 0,000 ..... D 2
azonas, 875,000 ..... G 9
ia, 6,778,000 ..... F 6
á, 3,764,000 ..... G 4
rito Santo, 446,000 ..... F 7
eral District, 48,000 ..... E 6
ás, 2,950,000 ..... D 6
poré (Rondônia) (terr.), ,000 ..... H10
anhão, 3,314,000 ..... E 4
o Grosso, 293,000 ..... B 6
as Gerais, ,230,000 ..... E 7, †D 2
á, 1,872,000 ..... C 4
aíba, 2,219,000 ..... G 4
aná, 6,743,000 ..... D 9, †B 4
nambuco, 645,000 ..... G 5
uí, 1,391,000 ..... F 4
de Janeiro, 347,000 ..... F 8, †E 3
Grande do Norte, 271,000 ..... G 4
Grande do Sul, 397,000 ..... C10
dônia (terr.), 07,000 ..... H10
aima (terr.), 40,000 ..... H 8
ta Catarina, 624,000 ..... D 9
Paulo, 5,081,000 ..... D 8, †B 2
gipe, 838,000 ..... G 5

CITIES and TOWNS

aeté, 7,988 ..... E 7
aetetuba, 11,196 ..... D 3
araú, 3,042 ..... F 3
opiara, 3,953 ..... G 4
orizal, 892 ..... C 6
u, 8,158 ..... G 4
uá, 600 ..... D 3
udos, 6,564 ..... †B 3
agoa Grande, 2,115 ..... H 4
agoinhas, 38,246 ..... G 6
cobaça, 1,812 ..... G 7
egre, 7,487 ..... †F 2
egrete, 33,735 ..... B10
ém Paraíba, 8,399 ..... †E 2
enquer, 7,027 ..... C 3
fenas, 16,051 ..... †C 2
fredo Chaves, 1,209 ..... F 8
tamira, 2,939 ..... C 3
to Araguaia, 2,077 ..... C 7
to Longa, 784 ..... F 4
to Parnaiba, 1,300 ..... E 5
tos, 5,056 ..... F 4
nambaí, 2,601 ..... C 8
narante, 3,199 ..... F 4
nargosa, 6,059 ..... F 6
nericana, 32,000 ..... †C 3
nparo, 14,348 ..... †C 3
ápolis, 48,847 ..... D 7
daraí, 2,510 ..... F 6
gra dos Reis, 10,634 ..... †D 3
icuns, 3,642 ..... D 7
drelândia, 4,617 ..... †D 2
tonina, 8,520 ..... †B 4
arecida, 15,290 ..... †D 3
iaí, 2,728 ..... †B 4
uidauana, 11,997 ..... C 8
acaju, *156,243 ..... G 5
acati, 11,016 ..... G 4
açatuba, 53,563 ..... †A 2
açuaí, 6,763 ..... F 7
aguacema, 1,745 ..... D 5
aguaiana, 568 ..... C 6
aguari, 35,520 ..... D 7
aioses, 1,487 ..... F 3
aranguá, 7,775 ..... D10
araquara, 58,076 ..... †B 2
aras, 23,898 ..... †C 3
ari, 4,004 ..... E 3
axá, 24,041 ..... E 7
coverde, 18,008 ..... G 5
eia Branca, 8.904 ..... G 4
ipuanã, 178 ..... B 5
raias, 1,446 ..... E 6
sis, 30,207 ..... †A 3
urora, 3,622 ..... G 4
aré, 20,334 ..... †B 3
acabal, *19,753 ..... E 4
agé, 47,930 ..... C10
ahia (Salvador), *892,392 ..... G 6
aião, 2,265 ..... D 3
aixo Guandu, 6,975 ..... F 7
alsas, 1,946 ..... E 4
ambuí, 8,148 ..... †C 2
arão de Cocais, 7,223 ..... †E 1
arbacena, 41,931 ..... †E 2
arcelos, 1,904 ..... H 9
ariri, 8,403 ..... †B 3
arra, 7,237 ..... F 5
arra-do-Bugres, 658 ..... B 6
arra-do-Corda, 3,723 ..... E 4
arra do Piraí, 29,398 ..... †E 3
arra Mansa, 47,398 ..... †D 3
arras, 3,388 ..... F 4
arreiras, 7,175 ..... E 6
arreirinha, 701 ..... B 3
arreirinhas, 2,184 ..... F 3
arreiros, 10,402 ..... H 5
arretos, 39,950 ..... †B 2
atalha, 15,559 ..... F 3
atatais, 15,266 ..... †C 2
aturité, 7,198 ..... G 4
auru, *110,961 ..... †B 3
ebedouro, 18,249 ..... †B 2
ela Vista, 8,878 ..... C 8
ela Vista de Goiás, 2,687 ..... D 7
elém, *563,996 ..... E 3
elmonte, 7,897 ..... G 6
elo Horizonte, *1,167,026 ..... †D 1
elo Horizonte, ‡1,300,000 ..... †D 1
eneditinos, 828 ..... F 4
enjamin Constant, 3,224 ..... G 9
ento Gonçalves, 13,662 ..... C10
ertolínia, 714 ..... F 4
Betim, 8,963 ..... †D 2
Bicas, 7,469 ..... †E 2
Birigui, 18,721 ..... †A 2
Blumenau, 46,591 ..... D 9
Boa Esperança, 9,263 ..... †D 2
Boa Vista, 10,180 ..... H 8
Bôca do Acre, 2,994 ..... G10
Bocaiúva, 5,952 ..... E 7
Boiaçu, 180 ..... H 8
Bom Conselho, 6,840 ..... G 5
Bom Despacho, 13,568 ..... †D 1
Bom Jesus, 1,431 ..... E 5
Bom Jesus da Lapa, 6,107 ..... F 6
Bom Retiro, 1,601 ..... D10
Bom Sucesso, 6,173 ..... †D 2
Borba, 1,304 ..... H 9
Botucatu, 33,878 ..... †B 3
Bragança, 12,848 ..... E 3
Bragança Paulista, 27,328 ..... †C 3
Brasiléia, 1,902 ..... G10
Brasília (capital), 130,968 ..... D 6
Brasília, ‡379,699 ..... D 6
Brasília, 3,182 ..... F 7
Brumado, 7,054 ..... F 6
Brusque, 16,127 ..... D 9
Buri, 2,666 ..... †B 3
Buriti, 1,951 ..... F 3
Buriti Alegre, 5,042 ..... D 7
Buriti dos Lopes, 1,812 ..... F 3
Cabedelo, 10,738 ..... H 4
Cabo Frio, 13,117 ..... †F 3
Caçador, 10,480 ..... D 9
Caçapava, 7,987 ..... †D 3
Caçapava do Sul, 6,712 ..... C10
Cáceres, 8,246 ..... B 7
Cachoeira, 11,415 ..... G 6
Cachoeira do Arari, 2,532 ..... D 3
Cachoeira do Sul, 38,661 ..... C10
Cachoeiro de Itapemirim, *110,301 ..... G 8
Caeté, 10,840 ..... †E 1
Caetıte, 4,823 ..... F 6
Cafelândia, 6,573 ..... †B 2
Caiapônia, 2,476 ..... C 7
Caicó, 15,826 ..... G 4
Cajàzeiras, 15,884 ..... G 4
Cajuru, 4,971 ..... †C 2
Camaquã, 9,732 ..... C10
Cambará, 6,028 ..... †A 3
Cametá, 5,695 ..... D 3
Camocim, 10,788 ..... F 3
Campanha, 6,178 ..... †D 2
Campina Grande, *157,149 ..... G 4
Campinas, *252,145 ..... †C 3
Campina Verde, 4,464 ..... D 7
Campo Belo, 15,742 ..... †D 2
Campo Florido, 1,307 ..... †B 1
Campo Formoso, 3,925 ..... F 5
Campo Grande, *111,205 ..... C 8
Campo Largo, 7,915 ..... †B 4
Campo Maior, 13,939 ..... F 4
Campos, *389,045 ..... †F 2
Campos Altos, 5,243 ..... †C 1
Cananéia, 1,948 ..... †C 4
Canavieiras, 10,264 ..... G 6
Cândido Mendes, 819 ..... E 3
Canguaretama, 4,261 ..... H 4
Canindé, 5,854 ..... G 4
Canoas, *122,040 ..... D10
Canoinhas, 9,252 ..... D 9
Cantagalo, 3,479 ..... †E 3
Canto do Buriti, 1,636 ..... F 5
Canutama, 977 ..... G 9
Capanema, 9,678 ..... E 3
Capão Bonito, 6,829 ..... †B 4
Capela, 5,172 ..... G 5
Caraguatatuba, 4,655 ..... †D 3
Carandaí, 2,792 ..... †E 2
Carangola, 11,896 ..... †E 2
Caratinga, *123,344 ..... †E 1
Caraúbas, 3,066 ..... G 4
Caravelas, 3,096 ..... G 7
Carinhanha, 2,163 ..... E 6
Carolina, 8,137 ..... E 4
Caruaru, *115,414 ..... G 5
Carutapera, 2,477 ..... E 3
Casa Branca, 8,980 ..... †C 2
Casa Nova, 1,525 ..... F 5
Cascatinha, 19,497 ..... †E 3
Cascavel, 3,336 ..... G 4
Cássia, 7,034 ..... †C 2
Castanhal, 9,528 ..... E 3
Castelo, 5,729 ..... F 8
Castelo do Piauí, 1,185 ..... F 4
Castro, 9,249 ..... †B 4
Castro Alves, 7,388 ..... G 6
Cataguases, 21,476 ..... †E 2
Catalão, 11,471 ..... D 7
Catanduva, 37,307 ..... †B 2
Catolé do Rocha, 5,217 ..... G 4
Cavalcante, 660 ..... D 6
Caxambu, 10,491 ..... †D 2
Caxias, *124,403 ..... F 4
Caxias do Sul, *110,241 ..... D10
Ceará (Fortaleza), *846,069 ..... G 3
Ceará-Mirim, 8,290 ..... H 4
Ceres, 6,895 ..... D 7
Cêrro Azul, 1,460 ..... †B 4
Chaves, 428 ..... D 3
Cicero Dantas, 2,972 ..... G 5
Coari, 5,908 ..... H 9
Codajás, 1,505 ..... H 9
Codó, *100,933 ..... E 4
Colatina, *140,729 ..... F 7
Colinas, 2,972 ..... F 4
Conceição da Barra, 2,229 ..... G 7
Conceição do Araguaia, 2,332 ..... D 5
Concórdia, 5,864 ..... D 9
Conde, 4,190 ..... G 5
Conselheiro Lafaiete, 29,208 ..... †E 2
Corinto, 12,247 ..... E 7
Cornélio Procópio, 17,524 ..... D 8
Coroatá, 7,720 ..... F 3
Coromandel, 5,148 ..... E 7
Corrente, 2,214 ..... E 5
Correntina, 2,636 ..... E 6
Corumbá, 36,744 ..... B 7
Coxim, 1,371 ..... C 7
Crateús, 14,572 ..... F 4
Crato, 27,649 ..... G 4
Criciúma, 25,331 ..... D10
Cristalina, 3,810 ..... E 7
Cruz Alta, 33,190 ..... C10
Cruzeiro, 27,005 ..... †D 3
Cruzeiro do Sul, 2,826 ..... G10
Cubatão, 18,885 ..... †C 3
Cuiabá, 43,112 ..... C 6
Curaça, 1,264 ..... G 5
Curitiba, *616,548 ..... †B 4
Currais Novos, 7,782 ..... G 4
Curuçá, 3,871 ..... E 3
Cururupu, 4,822 ..... E 3
Curvelo, 21,772 ..... E 7
Diamantina, 14,252 ..... F 7
Diamantino, 645 ..... B 6
Dianópolis, 2,145 ..... E 5
Divinópolis, 41,544 ..... †D 2
Dois Córregos, 7,272 ..... †B 3
Dom Pedrito, 15,429 ..... C10
Dores do Indaiá, 10,354 ..... E 7
Dourados, 10,757 ..... C 8
Duque de Caxias, *324,261 ..... †E 3
Eirunepé, 3,023 ..... G10
Eldorado, 1,524 ..... †B 4
Erechim, 24,941 ..... C 9
Erval, 1,404 ..... C11
Escada, 13,761 ..... H 5
Esperança, 9,105 ..... G 4
Esplanada, 3,792 ..... G 5
Estância, 16,106 ..... G 5
Exu, 2,549 ..... G 4
Faro, 1,434 ..... B 3
Feira de Santana, *136,000 ..... G 5
Fernandópolis, 14,375 ..... †A 2
Ferreira Gomes, 439 ..... D 2
Ferros, 2,456 ..... F 7
Flores, 2,102 ..... G 4
Floriano, 16,063 ..... F 4
Florianópolis, *130,012 ..... E 9
Formiga, 18,763 ..... †D 2
Formosa, 9,449 ..... E 6
Fortaleza, *846,069 ..... G 3
Foz do Iguaçu, 7,407 ..... C 9
Franca, 47,244 ..... †C 2
Fronteiras, 1,320 ..... F 4
Frutal, 8,252 ..... †B 2
Garanhuns, 34,050 ..... G 5
Garça, 18,155 ..... †B 3
Gilbués, 588 ..... E 5
Goiana, 19,026 ..... H 4
Goiandira, 3,169 ..... E 7
Goiânia, *345,085 ..... D 7
Goiás, 7,121 ..... D 6
Governador Valadares, *124,606 ..... F 7
Grajaú, 2,539 ..... E 4
Granja, 5,074 ..... F 3
Guacuí, 7,724 ..... †F 2
Guajará-Mirim, 7,115 ..... H10
Guamá, 2,470 ..... E 3
Guarabira, 15,848 ..... H 4
Guarapuava, *126,080 ..... C 9
Guaratinguetá, 38,293 ..... †D 3
Guarujá, 6,506 ..... †C 4
Guarulhos, *119,572 ..... †C 3
Guarus, 21,492 ..... †F 2
Guaxupé, 14,168 ..... †C 2
Guimarães, 1,512 ..... E 3
Guiratinga, 4,203 ..... C 7
Gurupá, 912 ..... D 3
Gurupi, 4,148 ..... D 5
Humaitá, 1,192 ..... H10
Ibaiti, 3,628 ..... †A 3
Ibiá, 6,999 ..... E 7
Ibipetuba, 2,298 ..... F 5
Ibitinga, 8,881 ..... †B 2
Icó, 5,586 ..... G 4
Icoraci, 11,512 ..... D 3
Igarapava, 9,083 ..... †C 2
Igarapé-Miri, 2,591 ..... D 3
Iguape, 5,465 ..... †C 4
Iguatu, 16,540 ..... G 4
Ijuí, 19,671 ..... C10
Ilhéus, *100,687 ..... G 6
Imbituba, 6,638 ..... D10
Imbituva, 3,290 ..... †A 4
Imperatriz, 9,004 ..... E 4
Inhumas, 8,298 ..... D 7
Ipameri, 8,987 ..... E 7
Ipiaú, 13,164 ..... G 6
Ipu, 7,724 ..... F 4
Irati, 12,764 ..... †A 4
Itabaiana, Paraíba, 11,847 ..... H 4
Itabaiana, Sergipe, 11,050 ..... G 5
Itaberaba, 8,555 ..... F 6
Itabira, 15,539 ..... F 7
Itabirito, 10,511 ..... †E 2
Itabuna, 54,268 ..... G 6
Itacoatiara, 8,818 ..... B 3
Itaguatins, 1,596 ..... D 4
Itaí, 1,601 ..... †B 3
Itajaí, 38,889 ..... D 9
Itajubá, 31,262 ..... †D 3
Itamarandiba, 2,404 ..... F 7
Itanhaém, 5,376 ..... †C 4
Itapecerica, 7,696 ..... †D 2
Itapecuru-Mirim, 3,385 ..... F 3
Itapemirim, 4,095 ..... F 8
Itaperuna, 18,095 ..... †F 2
Itapetininga, 29,468 ..... †B 3
Itapeva, 13,510 ..... †B 3
Itapicuru, 900 ..... G 5
Itapipoca, 7,186 ..... G 3
Itapira, 16,859 ..... †C 3
Itapiranga, 477 ..... B 3
Itápolis, 7,430 ..... †B 2
Itaporanga, 5,328 ..... G 4
Itaqui, 13,223 ..... B10
Itararé, 12,812 ..... †B 4
Itariri, 1,318 ..... †C 4
Itatiba, 12,336 ..... †C 3
Itaúna, 22,319 ..... †D 2
Itu, 23,435 ..... †C 3
Ituaçu, 1,431 ..... F 6
Ituberá, 4,097 ..... G 6
Ituiutaba, 29,724 ..... D 7
Itumbiara, 12,575 ..... D 7
Iturama, 1,518 ..... †A 1
Ituverava, 11,890 ..... †C 2
Jaboticabal, 20,231 ..... †B 2
Jacareí, 28,131 ..... †D 3
Jacarèzinho, 14,813 ..... †A 3
Jacobina, 12,373 ..... F 5
Jacupiranga, 2,144 ..... †B 4
Jaguaquara, 5,363 ..... F 6
Jaguarão, 12,336 ..... C11
Jaguariaíva, 6,465 ..... †B 4
Jaicós, 1,308 ..... F 4
Januária, 9,741 ..... E 6
Jaraguá, 3,813 ..... D 6
Jardim, 3,104 ..... G 4
Jataí, 14,022 ..... D 7
Jaú, 31,229 ..... †B 3
Jequié, 40,158 ..... F 6
Jequitinhonha, 5,410 ..... F 7
Jeremoabo, 3,177 ..... G 5
Joaçaba, 7,921 ..... D 9
João Pessoa, *189,096 ..... H 4
João Pinheiro, 3,433 ..... E 7
Joaquim Tavora, 3,574 ..... †B 3
Joinville, 44,255 ..... D 9
Juàzeiro, 21,196 ..... G 5
Juàzeiro do Norte, 53,421 ..... F 4
Juiz de Fora, *194,135 ..... †E 2
Jundiaí, *124,368 ..... †C 3
Lábrea, 2,080 ..... G10
Laguna, 17,451 ..... D10
Lajes, 35,112 ..... D 9
Lambari, 6,825 ..... †D 2
Lapa, 7,167 ..... D 9
Laranjeiras, 4,296 ..... G 5
Laranjeiras do Sul, 3,802 ..... C 9
Lavras, 23,793 ..... †D 2
Leme, 11,785 ..... †C 3
Lençóis, 2,483 ..... F 6
Leopoldina, 17,726 ..... †E 2
Lima Duarte, 3,554 ..... †E 2
Limeira, 45,256 ..... †C 3
Limoeiro, 21,252 ..... H 4
Limoeiro do Norte, 5,705 ..... G 4
Linhares, 5,751 ..... F 7
Lins, 32,204 ..... †B 2
Londrina, *226,332 ..... D 8
Lorena, 26,068 ..... †D 3
Luís Correia, 1,523 ..... F 3
Luz, 5,633 ..... †D 1
Luziânia, 4,849 ..... E 7
Luzilândia, 3,434 ..... F 3
Macaé, 19.830 ..... †F 3
Macapá, 27,585 ..... D 2
Macau, 11,876 ..... G 4
Macaúbas, 2,504 ..... F 6
Maceió, *221,250 ..... H 5
Machado, 8,373 ..... †C 2
Mafra, 12,981 ..... D 9
Magé, 10,712 ..... †E 3
Mallet, 1,816 ..... D 9
Manacapuru, 2,584 ..... H 9
Manaus, *249,797 ..... H 9
Manga, 2,000 ..... E 6
Manhuaçu, 10,546 ..... †E 2
Manhumirim, 9,477 ..... †E 2
Manicoré, 2,268 ..... H 9
Marabá, 8,533 ..... D 4
Maragogipe, 12,575 ..... G 6
Maranguape, 8,715 ..... G 3
Marapanim, 3,542 ..... E 3
Marechal-Deodoro, 5,269 ..... H 5
Mariana, 6,378 ..... †E 2
Marília, *107,305 ..... †A 3
Marques de Valença, 18,935 ..... †D 3
Massapê, 4,760 ..... G 3
Mata de São João, 8,117 ..... G 6
Mato Grosso, 520 ..... B 6
Maués, 4,161 ..... B 3
Mazagão, 919 ..... B 3
Miguel Alves, 4,537 ..... F 4
Mimoso do Sul, 5,278 ..... †F 2
Minas Novas, 1,708 ..... F 7
Mineiros, 5,105 ..... C 7
Miracema, 9,810 ..... †E 2
Mirador, 818 ..... B 4
Miranda, 2,075 ..... C 8
Mirassol, 13,674 ..... †B 2
Mocajuba, 1,352 ..... D 3
Mococa, 14,306 ..... †C 2
Mogi das Cruzes, *111,554 ..... †C 3
Mogi-Mirim, 18,345 ..... †C 3
Monte Alegre, 3,911 ..... C 3
Monte Alegre de Minas, 4,464 ..... D 7
Monte Aprazível, 7,235 ..... †A 2
Monte Azul, 4,860 ..... F 6
Monteiro, 6,028 ..... G 4
Montenegro, 14,491 ..... D10
Monte Santo, 1,607 ..... G 5
Montes Claros, *121,428 ..... E 7
Morrinhos, 9,879 ..... D 7
Morro do Chapéu, 2,039 ..... F 5
Mossoró, 38,833 ..... G 4
Mucugê, 723 ..... F 6
Mucuri, 603 ..... G 7
Mundo Novo, 3,237 ..... F 5
Muqui, 4,262 ..... F 8
Muriaé, 22,571 ..... †E 2
Muzambinho, 18,073 ..... †C 2
Natal, *239,590 ..... H 4

(continued on following page)

(continued)

Nazaré, 14,644 G 6
Neópolis, 7,356 G 5
Neves, 85,741 †E 3
Nioaque, 2,578 C 8
Niquelândia, 1,262 D 6
Niterói, *303,575 †E 3
Nossa Senhora do Livramento, 980 B 6
Nova Cruz, 6,780 H 4
Nova Era, 7,326 †E 1
Nova Friburgo, 49,901 †E 3
Nova Granada, 5,134 †B 2
Nova Iguaçu, *478,319 †E 3
Nova Iorque, 797 E 4
Nova Lima, 21,135 †E 2
Nova Russas, 4,666 F 4
Novo Hamburgo, 25,610 D10
Novo Horizonte, 8,581 †B 2
Óbidos, 5,901 C 3
Oeiras, 6,098 F 4
Olímpia, 14,629 †B 2
Olinda, *119,458 H 4
Oliveira, 12,919 †D 2
Oriximiná, 3,974 C 3
Orlândia, 6,898 †C 2
Orleães, 3,070 D10
Ourinhos, 25,717 †B 3
Ouro Fino, 8,044 †C 3
Ouro Prêto, 14,722 †E 2
Palmares, 17,327 H 5
Palmas, 5,540 C 9
Palmeira, 5,916 †B 4
Palmeira das Missoes, 8,017 C 9
Palmeiras, 2,040 F 6
Palmeiras de Goiás, 2,378 D 7
Pará (Belém), *563,996 E 3
Pará de Minas, 15,858 †D 1
Paracatu, 10,677 E 7
Paraguaçu Paulista, 11,391 D 8
Paraíba do Sul, 7,675 †E 3
Paranã, 970 E 6
Paranaguá, 27,728 †B 4
Paranaíba, 3,853 D 7
Parati, 3,046 †D 3
Paratinga, 2,403 F 6
Parintins, 9,068 B 3
Parnaguá, 508 E 5
Parnaíba, 39,951 F 3
Parnamirim, 1,589 F 4
Passagem Franca, 1,703 E 4
Passo Fundo, 47,299 D10
Passos, 28,555 †C 2
Patos, 27,275 G 4
Patos de Minas, 31,471 E 7
Patrocínio, 13,933 E 7
Pau dos Ferros, 4,298 G 4
Paulo de Faria, 2,722 †B 2
Peçanha, 3,602 F 7
Pederneiras, 8,053 †B 3
Pedra Azul, 8,238 F 6
Pedreiras, 10,189 E 4
Pedro Afonso, 3,175 E 5
Pedro Segundo, 3,160 F 4
Peixe, 822 D 6
Pelotas, *208,672 C10
Penalva, 5,339 E 3
Penápolis, 14,400 †A 2
Penedo, 17,084 G 5
Pernambuco (Recife), *1,100,464 H 5
Petrolina, 14,652 G 5
Petrópolis, *200,052 †E 3
Piaçabuçu, 4,864 H 5
Picos, 8,176 F 4
Piedade, 4,812 †C 3
Pilão Arcado, 1,457 F 5
Pilar, 7,201 H 5
Pindamonhangaba, 19,144 †D 3
Pinhal, 14,260 †C 3
Pinheiro, 6,537 E 3
Piquete, 10,543 †D 3
Piracanjuba, 3,869 D 7
Piracicaba, *137,184 †C 3
Piracuruca, 4,320 F 3
Piraí do Sul, 4,842 †B 4
Piraju, 10,658 †B 3
Pirajuí, 6,465 †B 2
Pirapora, 13,772 E 7
Pirassununga, 16,784 †C 3
Pirenópolis, 3,088 D 6
Pires do Rio, 8,390 D 7
Piripiri, 9,635 F 4
Pitangui, 7,421 †D 1
Piuí, 9,164 †D 2
Poções, 6,115 F 6
Poconé, 4,702 B 7
Poços de Caldas, 32,291 †C 2
Pompéia, 7,462 †A 3
Ponta de Pedras, 1,907 D 3
Ponta Grossa, *152,581 †B 4
Ponta Porã, 9,610 C 8
Ponte Nova, 22,536 †E 2
Porangatu, 2,886 D 5
Porciúncula, 4,868 †E 2
Portel, 1,821 D 3
Pôrto Alegre, *932,801 D10
Pôrto de Moz, 879 D 3
Pôrto Esperança, 486 B 7
Pôrto Feliz, 11,786 †C 3
Pôrto Franco, 1,750 E 4
Pôrto Murtinho, 4,476 B 8
Pôrto Nacional, 4,926 E 5
Pôrto Seguro, 2,697 G 7
Pôrto União, 9,954 D 9
Pôrto Velho, 19,387 H10
Posse, 1,953 E 6
Pouso Alegre, 18,852 †D 3
Poxoréu, 3,315 C 6
Prainha, 778 C 3
Prata, 4,725 D 7
Presidente Dutra, 3,349 E 4
Presidente Prudente, 54,055 D 8
Presidente Venceslau, 13,140 D 8
Promissão, 9,683 †B 2
Propriá, 15,947 G 5
Prudentópolis, 4,524 D 9
Quaraí, 10,575 C10
Queimadas, 3,553 F 5
Quipapá, 3,421 G 5
Quixadá, 8,747 G 4
Quixeramobim, 6,384 F 4
Raposos, 7,631 †E 2
Raul Soares, 6,194 †E 2

Recife, *1,100,464 H 5
Recife, ‡1,200,000 H 5
Registro, 4,913 †C 4
Remanso, 5,125 F 5
Resende, 13,544 †D 3
Riachão, 1,907 E 4
Ribeira, 603 †B 4
Ribeirão Prêto, *169,845 †C 2
Rio Bonito, 11,916 †E 3
Rio Branco, 17,245 G10
Rio Brilhante, 876 C 8
Rio Claro, 48,548 †C 3
Rio de Janeiro, *4,207,322 †E 3
Rio de Janeiro, ‡4,400,000 †E 3
Rio do Sul, 13,433 D 9
Rio Grande, *117,500 D11
Rio Negro, 10,225 D 9
Rio Pardo, 14,412 C10
Rio Pomba, 6,083 †E 2
Rio Real, 3,171 G 5
Rio Tinto, 16,811 H 4
Rio Verde, 11,268 D 7
Rolândia, 10,023 D 8
Rondônia, 1,293 H10
Rosário, 6,999 F 3
Rosário-do-Sul, 15,786 C10
Rosário-Oeste, 2,607 C 6
Russas, 7,102 G 4
Sabará, 10,004 †E 2
Sabinópolis, 4,101 F 7
Sacramento, 5,872 †C 1
Salgueiro, 8,936 G 5
Salinas, 5,186 F 7
Salinópolis, 4,101 E 3
Salto, 12,643 †C 3
Salvador, *892,392 G 6
Salvador, ‡892,392 G 6
Santa Cruz, 5,286 G 4
Santa Cruz do Rio Pardo, 13,889 †B 3
Santa Cruz do Sul, 18,898 C10
Santa Filomena, 652 E 5
Santa Maria, *141,610 C10
Santa Maria da Vitória, 3,208 F 6
Santana, 4,357 E 6
Santana do Ipanema, 8,139 G 5
Santana do Livramento, 37,666 C10
Santarém, *111,706 C 3
Santa Rita do Sapucaí, 8,464 †D 3
Santa Vitória do Palmar, 8,224 C11
Santiago, 15,140 C10
Santo Amaro, 17,226 G 6
Santo André, *289,442 †C 3

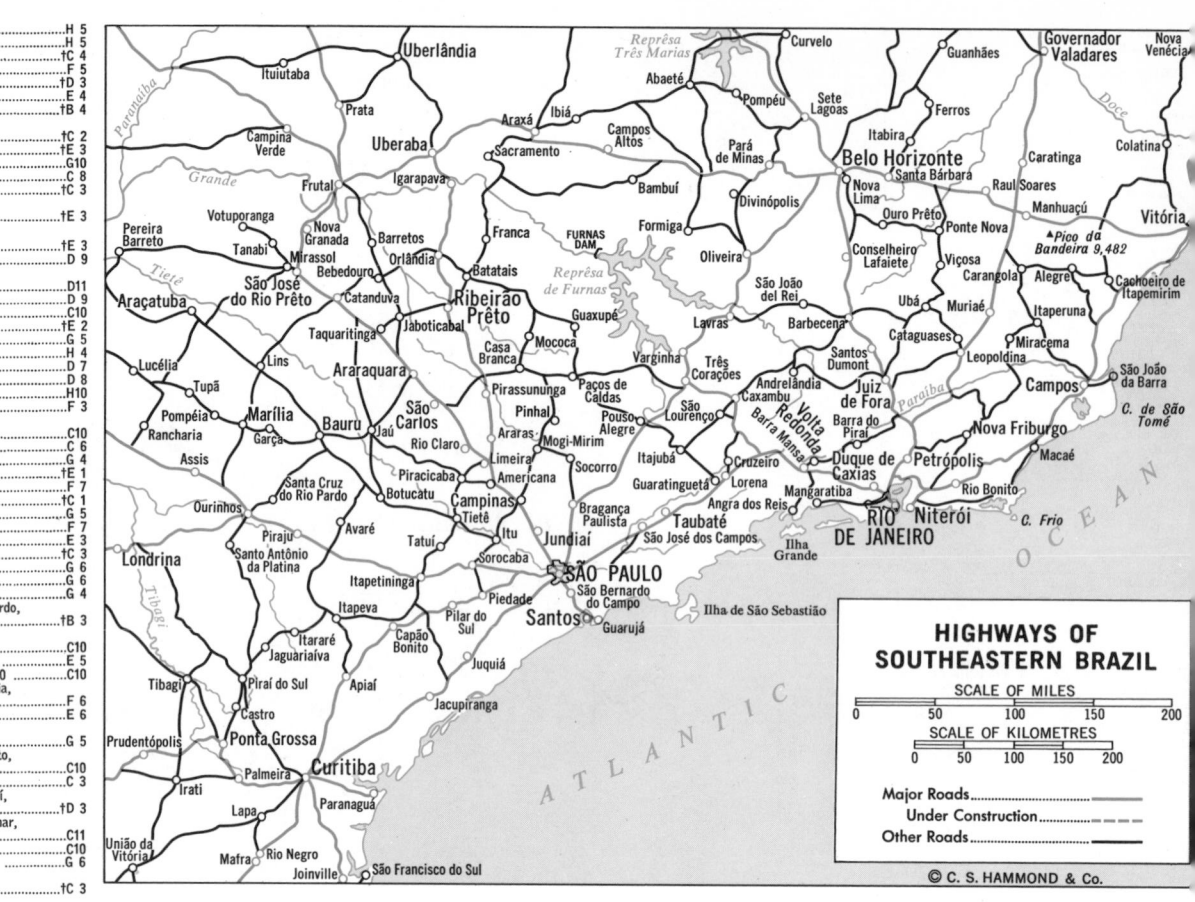

HIGHWAYS OF SOUTHEASTERN BRAZIL
SCALE OF MILES
0 50 100 150 200
SCALE OF KILOMETRES
0 50 100 150 200
Major Roads
Under Construction
Other Roads
© C. S. HAMMOND & Co.
Belo Horizonte
Uberlândia
Uberaba
Ribeirão Prêto
Campinas
SÃO PAULO
Santos
RIO DE JANEIRO
Niterói
Petrópolis
Juiz de Fora
Curitiba
Ponta Grossa
Londrina
Vitória
Governador Valadares
ATLANTIC OCEAN

Agriculture, Industry and Resources

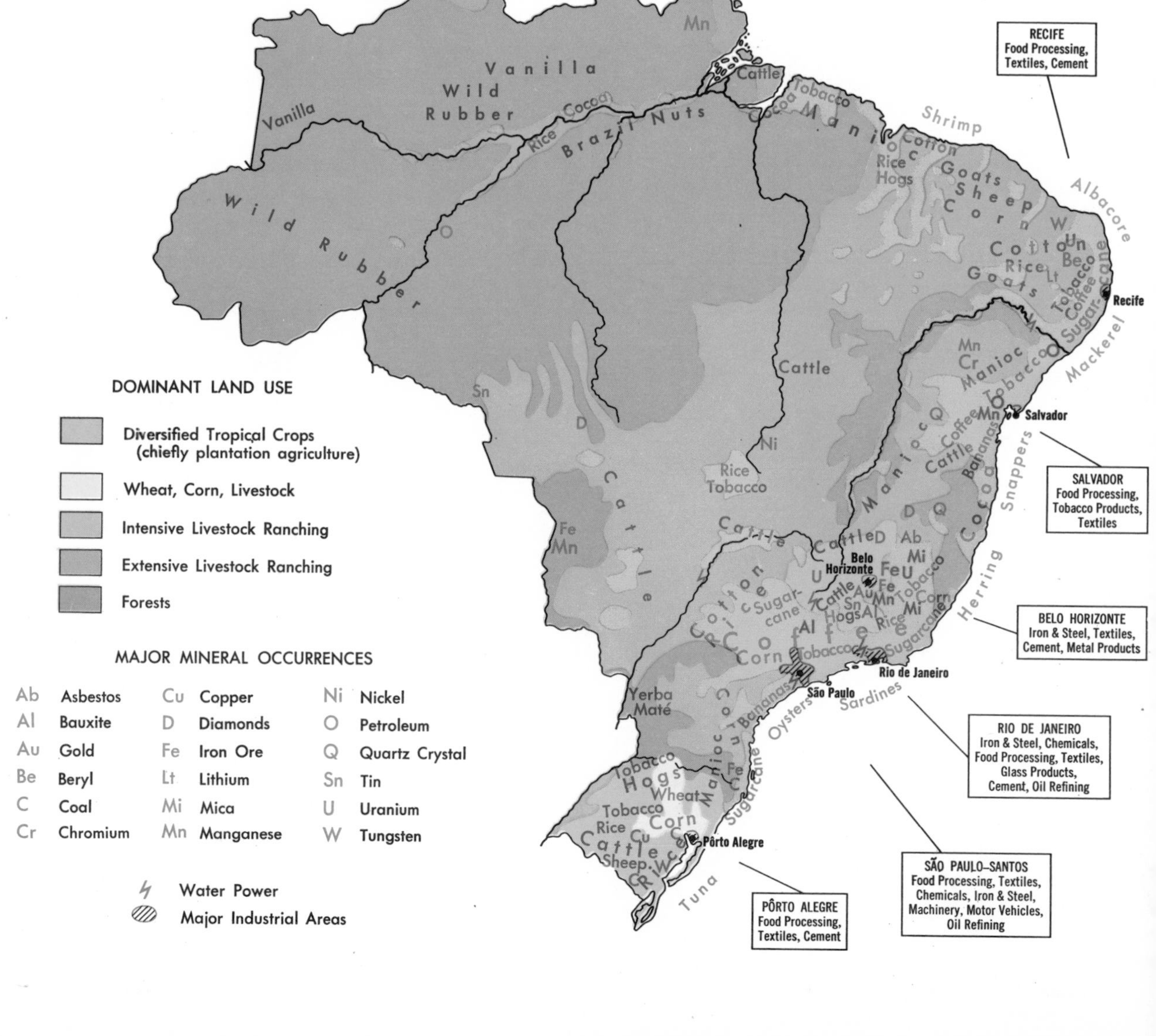

DOMINANT LAND USE
Diversified Tropical Crops (chiefly plantation agriculture)
Wheat, Corn, Livestock
Intensive Livestock Ranching
Extensive Livestock Ranching
Forests
MAJOR MINERAL OCCURRENCES
Ab Asbestos
Al Bauxite
Au Gold
Be Beryl
C Coal
Cr Chromium
Cu Copper
D Diamonds
Fe Iron Ore
Lt Lithium
Mi Mica
Mn Manganese
Ni Nickel
O Petroleum
Q Quartz Crystal
Sn Tin
U Uranium
W Tungsten
Water Power
Major Industrial Areas
RECIFE
Food Processing, Textiles, Cement
SALVADOR
Food Processing, Tobacco Products, Textiles
BELO HORIZONTE
Iron & Steel, Textiles, Cement, Metal Products
RIO DE JANEIRO
Iron & Steel, Chemicals, Food Processing, Textiles, Glass Products, Cement, Oil Refining
SÃO PAULO–SANTOS
Food Processing, Textiles, Chemicals, Iron & Steel, Machinery, Motor Vehicles, Oil Refining
PÔRTO ALEGRE
Food Processing, Textiles, Cement
Wild Rubber
Vanilla
Brazil Nuts
Cattle
Manioc
Cotton
Goats
Sheep
Corn
Rice
Hogs
Tobacco
Coffee
Sugarcane
Cacao
Bananas
Yerba Maté
Wheat
Shrimp
Albacore
Mackerel
Snappers
Herring
Sardines
Oysters
Tuna
Recife
Salvador
Belo Horizonte
Rio de Janeiro
São Paulo
Pôrto Alegre

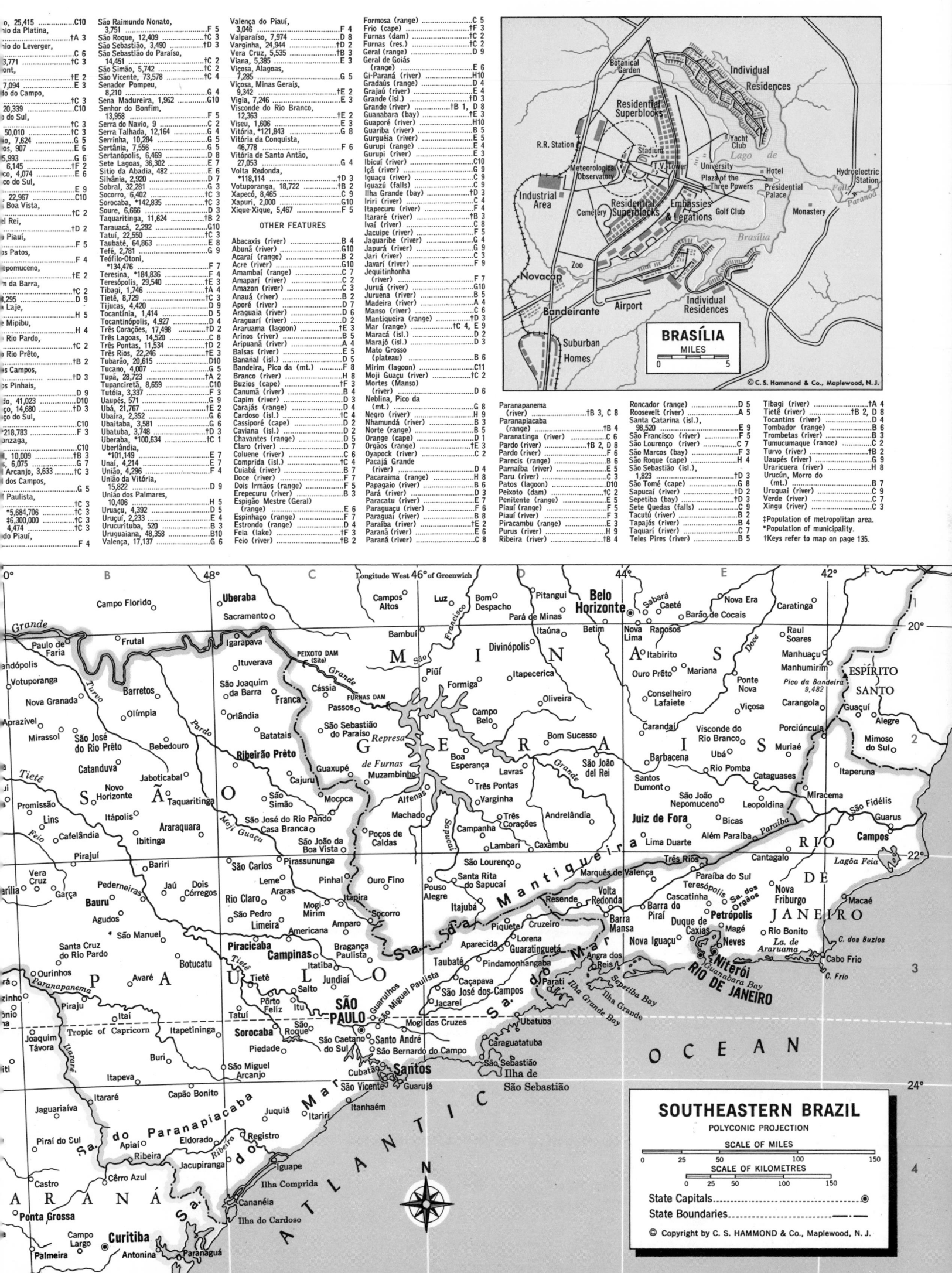

BRASÍLIA

MILES
0   5

© C. S. Hammond & Co., Maplewood, N. J.

SOUTHEASTERN BRAZIL

POLYCONIC PROJECTION

SCALE OF MILES
0   25   50   100   150

SCALE OF KILOMETRES
0   25   50   100   150

State Capitals .... ◉
State Boundaries ....

© Copyright by C. S. HAMMOND & Co., Maplewood, N. J.

DEPARTMENTS

Beni, 181,000 ....C 3
Chuquisaca, 427,400 ....C 6
Cochabamba, 741,100 ....B 5
La Paz, 1,433,000 ....A 4
Oruro, 317,700 ....A 5
Pando, 29,900 ....B 2
Potosí, 807,400 ....B 7
Santa Cruz, 432,300 ....E 5
Tarija, 191,600 ....D 7

CITIES and TOWNS

Abapó, 466 ....D 6
Acchilla, 208 ....A 5
Achacachi, 3,621 ....A 5

Aiquile, 3,465 ....C 6
Alcalá, 236 ....C 6
Alejandría ....C 3
Alto Seco ....D 6
Amarete, 992 ....C 5
Amboró ....C 4
Ananea, 302 ....A 4
Ancoraimes, 769 ....A 4
Andamarca ....A 5
Añimbo, 443 ....C 7
Anzaldo, 1,056 ....C 5
Apolo, 1,043 ....B 4
Aquío ....D 6
Araca ....B 5
Arampampa, 829 ....B 5
Arani, 2,200 ....C 5
Arcopongo ....B 5

Aroma, 1,254 ....B 6
Arque, 1,254 ....B 5
Arroyo Grande ....A 2
Ascención, 2,097 ....D 4
Asunción ....A 2
Asunta, 45 ....B 4
Atén, 199 ....A 4
Ayacucho, 729 ....D 5
Ayata, 479 ....A 4
Azurduy, 1,234 ....C 6

Barrera ....B 3
Baures, 592 ....B 3
Bella Flor ....B 2
Bella Vista ....E 3
Berenguela ....A 5
Bermejo ....C 8

Betanzos, 1,097 ....C 6
Bolívar ....B 3
Bolpebra ....A 2
Boyuibe, 537 ....D 7
Buena Hora ....E 4
Buena Vista ....B 2
Buena Vista, 435 ....D 5
Cabezas, 298 ....D 6
Cachuela Esperanza, 1,073 .C 2
Caiza, 838 ....C 7
Cajuata, 447 ....B 5
Calacoto, 415 ....A 5
Calamarca, 802 ....A 5
Callapa, 636 ....A 5
Calcha ....C 7
Camacho ....C 7

Camargo, 1,609 ....C 7
Camatindi ....D 7
Camiri, 4,969 ....D 7
Cañas ....C 8
Candelaria ....F 5
Canquella, 148 ....A 7
Capinota, 1,734 ....B 5
Capirenda ....D 7
Caquiaviri, 760 ....A 5
Carabuco, 626 ....A 4
Caracollo, 909 ....B 5
Caranavi ....B 4
Carandaití, 1,403 ....D 7
Carangas ....A 5
Caraparí, 351 ....D 7
Carmen ....B 2
Carrizal ....C 7

Cataricahua, 3,240 ....B 6
Cavari, 249 ....B 5
Cavinas ....A 6
Chachacomani, 159 ....A 6
Chaguaya, 643 ....C 7
Challacollo, 284 ....B 6
Challacota ....B 6
Challana ....B 6
Challapata, 2,529 ....B 6
Chapacura ....A 2
Chaquí, 291 ....C 6
Charagua, 1,185 ....D 7
Charaña, 794 ....A 5
Chayanta, 1,272 ....B 6
Chiguana, 154 ....A 7
Chiñijo, 27 ....C 7
Chivé ....C 7

Chocaya, 444 ....C 7
Choquecota ....A 5
Chorrillos ....B 3
Chulumani, 2,362 ....B 6
Chuma, 931 ....C 7
Chuquichambi ....B 6
Chuquichuqui ....C 6
Cliza, 3,121 ....C 5
Cobija, 2,537 ....A 2
Cocani ....C 6
Cocapata ....A 5
Cochabamba, 157,000 ....A 5
Cohoni, 890 ....B 5
Coipasa ....A 6
Collpa, 481 ....A 5
Colquechaca, 1,070 ....A 3
Colquiri, 806 ....B 5

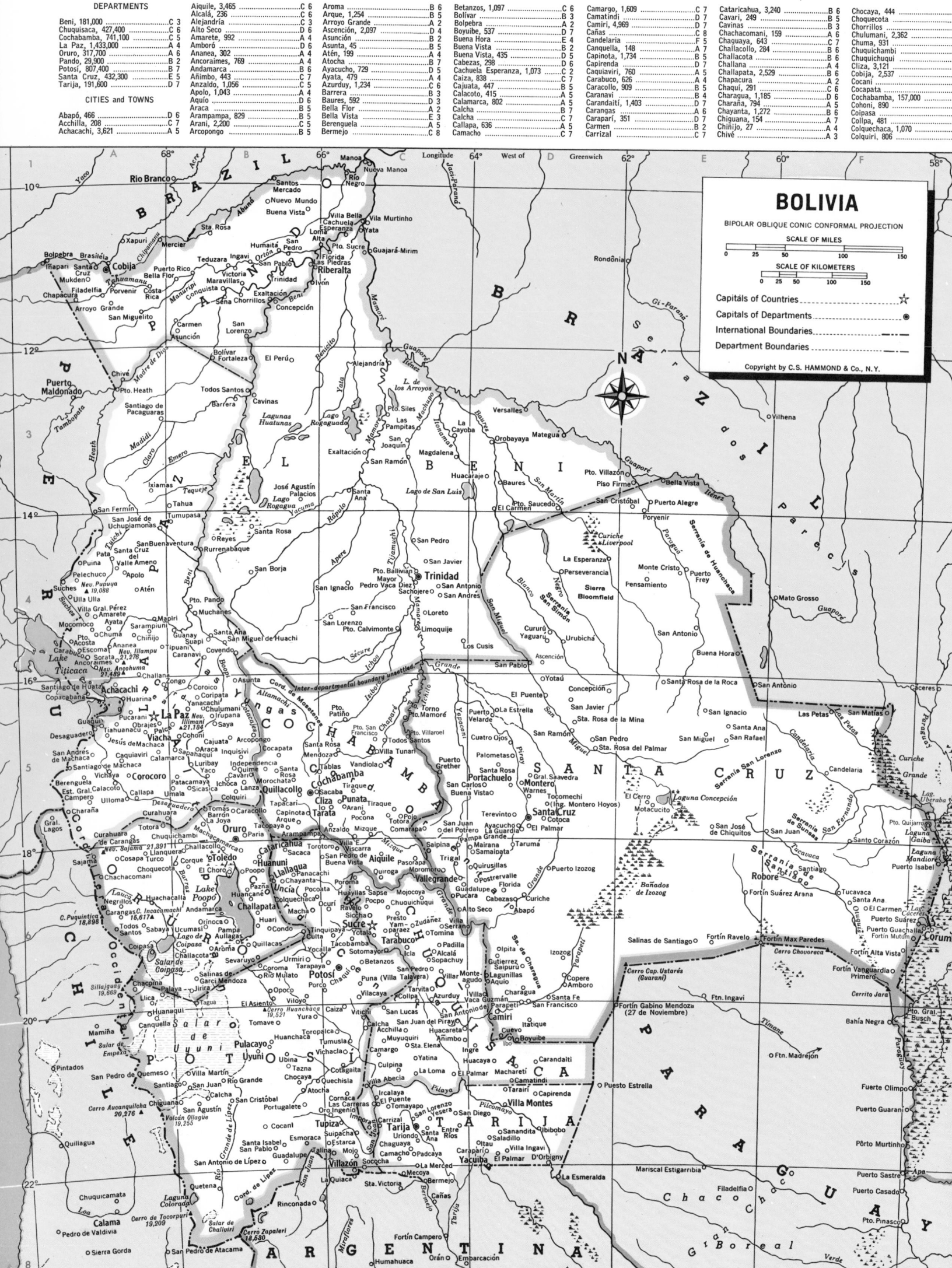

1,096 ....C 5
.... B 2
, 1,056 ....D 5
....B 6
....B 2
a, 1,981 ....A 5
....D 6
1,647 ....B 5
264 ....C 7
4,431 ....A 5
,235 ....B 5
....B 6
3 ....B 6
37 ....A 6
....A 2
1,353 ....C 7
5 ....D 5
71 ....B 4
os ....D 5
....D 7
81 ....C 7
....B 6
, 510 ....A 5
, de Carangas, 235 ....A 5
257 ....D 6
....D 4
ero, 201 ....A 5
....D 7
....B 6
, 232 ....D 3
....F 6
117 ....E 5
224 ....B 6
....D 7
, 437 ....D 5
, 832 ....D 7
....B 3
....C 7
....D 5
s, 1,011 ....C 7
20 ....A 4
....B 7
General Campero ....A 5
....C 7
1 ....B 2
n, 405 ....C 3
....A 2
....C 2
28 ....D 6
....B 3
a Vista ....F 6
mpero ....C 8
ax Paredes ....F 6
itum ....F 6
velo ....E 6
árez Arana ....F 6
nguardia Primero ....F 6
Saavedra, 1,006 ....D 5
e, 71 ....B 7
e, 2,355 ....C 6
574 ....B 4
,266 ....A 5
, 770 ....D 6
e, 673 ....D 3
a, 239 ....C 7
229 ....D 7
alla, 801 ....A 6
, 359 ....A 7
, 148 ....B 6
a ....B 7
5,696 ....B 6
070 ....B 6
1,151 ....A 5
206 ....C 6
....B 2
....D 7
....D 7
91 ....B 5
....C 6
274 ....C 7
encia, 1,742 ....B 5
....B 2
Montero Hoyos
nechi), 575 ....D 5
2 ....D 7
530 ....B 5
....D 6
....C 7
1,937 ....B 5
....D 7
....D 7
....C 2
292 ....A 3
....D 6
Machaca, 529 ....A 5
....B 6
ustín Palacios ....B 3
a ....C 3
alda ....D 8
anza ....D 4
lla ....D 5
lia, 470 ....D 5

La Joya, 401 ....B 5
La Loma ....C 7
La Merced ....C 8
La Paz (cap.), 525,000 ....B 5
Lagunillas, 840 ....D 6
Lanza, 526 ....B 5
Las Carreras, 155 ....C 7
Las Pampitas ....C 3
Las Petas ....F 5
Las Piedras ....C 2
Limoquije ....C 4
Llallagua, 6,719 ....B 6
Llanquera, 613 ....A 6
Llica, 560 ....A 6
Loma Alta ....B 2
Loreto, 589 ....C 4
Los Cusis ....D 4
Luribay, 392 ....B 5
Macha, 1,050 ....B 6
Machacamarca, 1,746 ....B 5
Machareti ....D 7
Magdalena, 1,724 ....C 3
Mairana, 508 ....D 6
Manoa ....C 1
Mapiri, 289 ....B 4
Maravillas ....B 2
Mategua, 38 ....D 3
Mayor Pedro Vaca Diez, 358 ....C 4
Mecoya ....C 8
Mendoza ....C 5
Mercier ....B 2
Mizque, 870 ....C 5
Mocomoco, 977 ....A 4
Mojo, 469 ....C 7
Mojocoya, 498 ....C 6
Monte Cristo ....E 4
Monteagudo, 971 ....D 6
Montero, 2,713 ....D 5
Morochata, 461 ....B 5
Moromoro, 556 ....C 6
Motacucito ....E 5
Muchanes ....B 4
Mukden ....A 2
Muyuquiri ....C 7
Negrillos, 85 ....A 6
Nueva Manoa ....C 1
Nuevo Mundo ....B 2
Obrajes ....A 5
Ocurí, 1,531 ....C 6
Opoco ....B 6
Orinoca ....B 6
Oro Ingenio ....C 7
Orobayaya ....D 3
Oruro, 86,985 ....B 5
Padcaya, 324 ....C 7
Padilla, 2,462 ....C 6
Palaya, 300 ....A 6
Palca, 887 ....A 5
Palometas ....D 5
Pampa Aullagas ....B 6
Pampa Grande, 727 ....D 5
Panacachi, 952 ....B 6
Paria, 335 ....B 5
Pasorapa, 1,016 ....C 6
Pata, 122 ....A 4
Patacamaya, 1,278 ....B 5
Pazña, 671 ....B 6
Pelechuco, 873 ....A 4
Pensamiento ....E 4
Perseverancia ....D 4
Piso Firme ....D 3
Pocoata, 859 ....B 6
Pocona, 518 ....C 5
Pocpo ....C 6
Pojo, 1,047 ....C 5
Poopó, 736 ....B 6
Porco, 817 ....B 6
Poroma, 171 ....C 6
Portachuelo, 2,456 ....D 5
Portugalete ....B 7
Porvenir ....A 2
Porvenir ....E 4
Postrervalle, 750 ....D 6
Potosí, 55,233 ....C 6
Presto, 725 ....C 6
Pucara, 762 ....C 6
Pucarani, 1,041 ....A 5
Puerto Acosta, 1,302 ....A 4
Puerto Alegre ....E 3
Puerto Ballivián ....C 4
Puerto Calvimonte ....C 4
Puerto Frey ....E 4
Puerto General Busch ....G 7
Puerto Grether ....C 5
Puerto Guachalla ....F 6
Puerto Heath ....A 3
Puerto Isabel ....G 6
Puerto Izozog ....D 6
Puerto Mamoré ....C 5
Puerto Pando ....B 4
Puerto Patiño ....C 5
Puerto Quijarro, 1,006 ....G 5

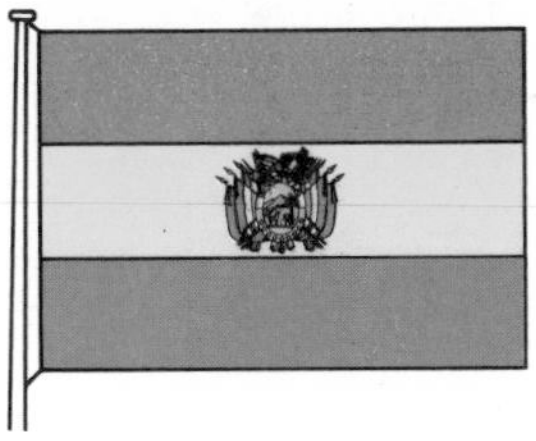

AREA 424, 163 sq. mi.
POPULATION 4,804,000
CAPITALS La Paz, Sucre
LARGEST CITY La Paz
HIGHEST POINT Nevada Ancohuma 21,489 ft.
MONETARY UNIT Bolivian peso
MAJOR LANGUAGES Spanish, Quechua, Aymara
MAJOR RELIGION Roman Catholicism

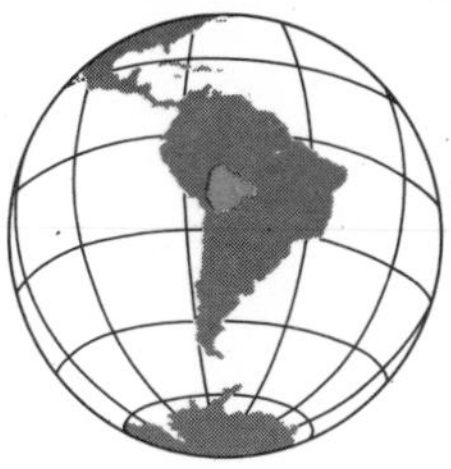

Puerto Rico ....B 2
Puerto San Francisco ....C 5
Puerto Saucedo ....D 3
Puerto Siles, 357 ....C 3
Puerto Suárez, 1,159 ....F 6
Puerto Sucre, 1,470 ....C 2
Puerto Torno ....C 5
Puerto Velarde ....D 5
Puerto Villaroel ....C 5
Puerto Villazón ....D 3
Puina ....A 4
Pulacayo, 7,984 ....B 7
Puna, 852 ....C 6
Punata, 5,014 ....C 5
Quechisla, 171 ....C 7
Quetena, 183 ....B 8
Quillacas, 1,170 ....B 6
Quillacollo, 9,123 ....B 5
Quime, 1,256 ....B 5
Quiroga ....C 6
Quirusillas, 433 ....D 6
Ravelo, 907 ....C 6
Reyes, 1,404 ....B 4
Riberalta, 6,549 ....C 2
Río Grande, 281 ....B 7
Río Mulato, 381 ....B 6
Río Negro ....C 1
Roboré, 3,715 ....F 6
Rurrenabaque, 1,225 ....B 4
Sabaya, 649 ....A 6
Sacaba, 2,752 ....C 5
Sacaca, 1,778 ....B 6
Sachojere, 401 ....C 4
Saipina, 573 ....C 6
Saipurú ....D 6
Sajama, 231 ....A 6
Saladillo ....D 7
Salinas de Garci Mendoza, 335 ....B 6
Salinas de Santiago ....E 6
Samaipata, 1,656 ....D 6
San Agustín ....B 7
San Andrés, 399 ....C 4
San Andrés de Machaca, 101 ....A 5
San Antonio, 436 ....C 4
San Antonio ....E 4
San Antonio de Lípez ....B 7
San Antonio del Parapetí, 497 ....D 7
San Borja, 708 ....B 4
San Buenaventura, 307 ....A 4
San Carlos, 570 ....D 5
San Cristóbal ....B 7
San Cristóbal ....E 3
San Diego ....D 7
San Fermín ....A 3
San Francisco, 185 ....C 4
San Francisco ....D 7
San Ignacio, 1,757 ....C 4
San Ignacio, 1,819 ....E 5
San Javier, 233 ....C 4
San Javier, 564 ....D 5
San Joaquín, 1,959 ....C 3
San José de Chiquitos, 1,933 ....E 6
San José de Uchupiamonas, 277 ....A 4
San Juan, 131 ....B 7
San Juan ....F 5
San Juan del Piray, 541 ....C 7
San Juan del Potrero, 263 ....C 5
San Lorenzo ....B 2
San Lorenzo, 496 ....C 4
San Lorenzo, 785 ....C 7
San Lucas, 925 ....C 7
San Matías, 887 ....F 5
San Miguel, 502 ....E 5
San Miguel de Huachi, 25 ....B 4
San Miguelito ....A 2
San Pablo ....B 2
San Pablo, 11 ....B 7
San Pablo ....D 4
San Pedro ....B 2
San Pedro, 262 ....C 4
San Pedro, 182 ....C 6

San Pedro, 80 ....D 5
San Pedro de Buena Vista, 1,094 ....C 6
San Pedro de Quemes ....A 7
San Rafael ....E 5
San Ramón, 1,161 ....C 3
San Ramón, 379 ....D 5
Sanandita, 379 ....D 7
Santa Ana, 171 ....B 4
Santa Ana, 2,225 ....C 3
Santa Ana ....C 7
Santa Ana, 275 ....E 5
Santa Ana, 663 ....F 6
Santa Cruz ....A 2
Santa Cruz, 108,720 ....D 5
Santa Cruz del Valle Ameno, 442 ....A 4
Santa Elena ....C 7
Santa Fe ....D 6
Santa Isabel ....B 7
Santa Rosa ....B 2
Santa Rosa, 765 ....B 4
Santa Rosa, 491 ....B 5
Santa Rosa ....C 5
Santa Rosa, 995 ....D 5
Santa Rosa de la Mina, 99 ....D 5
Santa Rosa de la Roca, 101 ....E 5
Santa Roso del Palmar, 441 ....E 5
Santiago, 172 ....A 7
Santiago, 765 ....F 6
Santiago de Huata, 948 ....A 5
Santiago de Machaca, 218 ....A 5
Santiago de Pacaguaras ....A 3
Santo Corazón ....F 5
Santos Mercado ....B 2
Sapahaqui, 55 ....B 5
Sapse ....C 6
Sarampiuni, 138 ....A 4
Saya, 339 ....B 5
Sena ....B 2
Sevaruyo, 475 ....B 6
Sicasica, 1,486 ....B 5
Siccha ....C 6
Socochа ....C 7
Sopachuy, 713 ....C 6
Sorata, 2,087 ....A 4
Sotomayor, 510 ....C 6
Suapi ....B 4
Suches ....A 4
Sucre (capital), 58,359 ....C 6
Suipacha ....C 7
Tablas ....C 5
Tacobamba ....C 6
Tacopaya, 795 ....B 5
Tagua ....B 6
Tahua, 114 ....B 3
Talina, 122 ....B 7
Tapacarí, 980 ....B 5
Tarabuco, 2,833 ....C 6
Tarairí ....D 7
Tarapaya, 357 ....B 6
Tarata, 3,016 ....C 5
Tarija, 20,851 ....C 7
Tarumá ....D 6
Tarvita, 404 ....C 6
Tazna ....B 7
Teduzara ....B 2
Terevinto ....D 5
Tiahuanacu, 1,227 ....A 5
Tinquipaya, 766 ....C 6
Tipuani ....B 4
Tiraque, 1,390 ....C 5
Tiraque, 234 ....C 5
Tocomechi (Ingeniero Montero Hoyos), 575 ....D 5
Todos Santos, 68 ....A 6
Todos Santos ....B 3
Todos Santos, 408 ....C 5
Toledo, 3,273 ....B 6
Tomás Barrón, 1,852 ....B 5
Tomave, 201 ....B 7
Tomayapo ....C 7

Topography

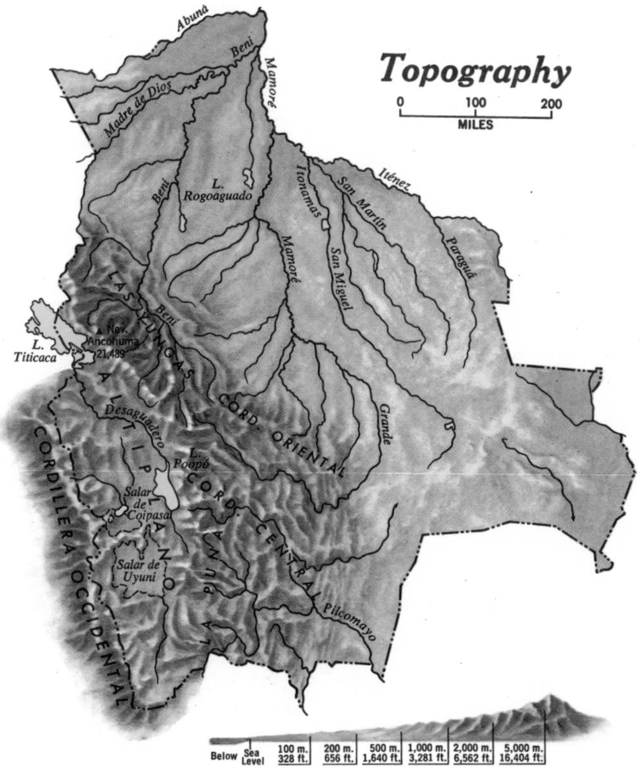
0 100 200
MILES
Abuná
Beni
Madre de Dios
Mamoré
L. Rogoaguado
Itonamas
San Martín
Iténez
Paraguá
San Miguel
Nev. Ancohuma 21,489
L. Titicaca
LAS YUNGAS
ALTIPLANO
Desaguadero
L. Poopó
Salar de Coipasa
Salar de Uyuni
CORD. ORIENTAL
CORD. CENTRAL
CORDILLERA OCCIDENTAL
PUNA
Grande
Pilcomayo
Below Sea Level
100 m. 328 ft.
200 m. 656 ft.
500 m. 1,640 ft.
1,000 m. 3,281 ft.
2,000 m. 6,562 ft.
5,000 m. 16,404 ft.

Tomina, 708 ....C 6
Toropalca ....B 7
Torotoro, 1,233 ....C 6
Totora, 210 ....A 5
Totora, 2,290 ....C 5
Trigal, 749 ....C 6
Trinidad ....B 2
Trinidad, 14,505 ....C 4
Tucavaca ....F 6
Tumupasa, 349 ....B 4
Tumusla ....C 7
Tupiza, 8,248 ....C 7
Turco, 131 ....A 6
Ubina ....B 7
Ucumasi ....B 6
Ulla Ulla, 52 ....A 4
Ulloma, 116 ....A 5
Umala, 481 ....B 5
Uncía, 4,507 ....B 6
Uriondo, 860 ....C 7
Urmiri ....B 6
Urubichá, 1,369 ....D 4
Uyuni, 6,968 ....B 7

Vallegrande, 5,094 ....C 6
Vandiola ....C 5
Versalles, 83 ....D 3
Viacha, 6,607 ....A 5
Vichacla, 317 ....C 7
Vichaya, 422 ....A 5
Victoria ....B 2
Vilacaya, 200 ....C 6
Villa Abecia, 539 ....C 7
Villa Bella, 88 ....C 2
Villa E. Viscarra, 658 ....C 6
Villa General Pérez, 802 ....A 4
Villa Ingavi, 122 ....D 7
Villa Martín, 543 ....B 7
Villa Montes, 3,105 ....D 7
Villa Serrano, 1,570 ....C 6
Villa Talavera (Puna), 852 ....C 6
Villa Tunari, 510 ....C 5
Villa Vaca Guzmán, 699 ....D 6
Villar, 322 ....C 6
Villazón, 6,261 ....C 7
Viloyo ....B 6
Vitichi, 1,515 ....C 7
Warnes, 1,571 ....D 5
Yaco, 835 ....B 5
Yacuiba, 5,027 ....D 7
Yaguarú ....D 4
Yamparáez, 725 ....C 6
Yanacachi ....B 5
Yata ....C 2
Yatina ....C 7
Yesera ....C 7
Yocalla ....B 6
Yotala, 1,554 ....C 6
Yotaú ....D 5
Yura, 136 ....B 7
Zongo, 141 ....B 5
Zudáñez, 1,868 ....C 6

OTHER FEATURES

Altamachi (river) ....B 5
Ancohuma, Nevada (mt.) ....A 4
Andes (mts.) ....A 3
Apere (river) ....C 4
Arroyas, Los (lake) ....C 3
Barras (river) ....B 6
Baures (river) ....D 3
Beni (river) ....B 2
Bermejo (river) ....C 8
Blanco (river) ....D 4
Bloomfield, Sierra (mts.) ....D 4
Boopi (river) ....B 4
Cáceres (lagoon) ....F 6
Candelaria (river) ....F 5
Capitán Ustarés, Cerro (mt.) ....E 6
Central, Cordillera (mts.) ....C 6
Challviri (salt depr.) ....B 8
Chaparé (river) ....C 5
Charagua (mts.) ....D 6
Chipamanu (river) ....A 2
Coipasa (lake) ....B 6
Coipasa (salt depr.) ....A 6
Colorada (lagoon) ....A 8
Concepción (lagoon) ....E 5
Cotacajes (river) ....B 5
Desaguadero (river) ....B 5
Empexa (salt depr.) ....A 7
Gaiba (lagoon) ....G 5
Grande (marsh) ....F 5
Grande (river) ....C 4

Grande (river) ....C 6
Grande de Lípez (river) ....B 7
Guaporé (river) ....C 3
Guaraní (Capitán Ustarés) (mt.) ....E 6
Heath (river) ....A 3
Huanchaca, Cerro (mt.) ....B 7
Huanchaca, Serranía de (mts.) ....E 4
Ichilo (river) ....C 5
Illampu, Nevada (mt.) ....A 4
Illimani, Nevada (mt.) ....B 5
Incacamachi, Cerro (mt.) ....A 6
Isiboro (river) ....C 5
Iténez (Guaporé) (river) ....C 3
Itonamas (river) ....C 3
Izozog (swamp) ....E 6
Las Petas (river) ....F 5
Las Yungas (region) ....B 5
Lauca (river) ....A 6
Lípez, Cordillera de (mts.) ....B 8
Liverpool (swamp) ....D 4
Machupo (river) ....C 3
Madidi (river) ....A 3
Madre de Dios (river) ....A 3
Mamoré (river) ....C 2
Mandioré (lagoon) ....G 6
Manuripi (river) ....B 2
Mizque (river) ....C 6
Mosetenes, Cordillera de (mts.) ....B 5
Negro (river) ....D 4
Occidental, Cordillera (mts.) ....A 6
Ollagüe (volcano) ....A 7
Oriental, Cordillera (mts.) ....C 5
Ortón (river) ....B 2
Otuquis (river) ....F 6
Paraguá (river) ....E 4
Paraguay (river) ....F 7
Parapetí (river) ....D 6
Petas, Las (river) ....F 5
Pilaya (river) ....C 7
Pilcomayo (river) ....D 7
Piray (river) ....D 5
Poopó (lake) ....B 6
Pupuya, Nevada (mt.) ....A 4
Puquintica, Cerro (mt.) ....A 6
Rápulo (river) ....C 4
Real, Cordillera (mts.) ....A 5
Rogagua (lake) ....B 3
Rogaguado (lake) ....C 3
Sajama, Nevada (mt.) ....A 6
San Fernando (river) ....F 5
San Juan (river) ....C 7
San Luis (lake) ....C 3
San Martín (river) ....D 3
San Miguel (river) ....D 4
San Simón, Serranía (mts.) ....D 4
Santiago, Serranía de (mts.) ....F 6
Sillajguay (mt.) ....A 6
Suches (river) ....A 4
Tahuamanu (river) ....A 2
Tarija (river) ....C 8
Titicaca (lake) ....A 4
Tocorpuri, Cerros de (mt.) ....A 8
Tucavaca (river) ....F 6
Tuichi (river) ....A 4
Uberaba (lagoon) ....F 5
Uyuni (salt depr.) ....B 7
Yacuma (river) ....B 3
Yapacani (river) ....C 5
Yata (river) ....C 3
Yungas, Las (region) ....B 5
Zapaleri, Cerro (mt.) ....B 8

Agriculture, Industry and Resources

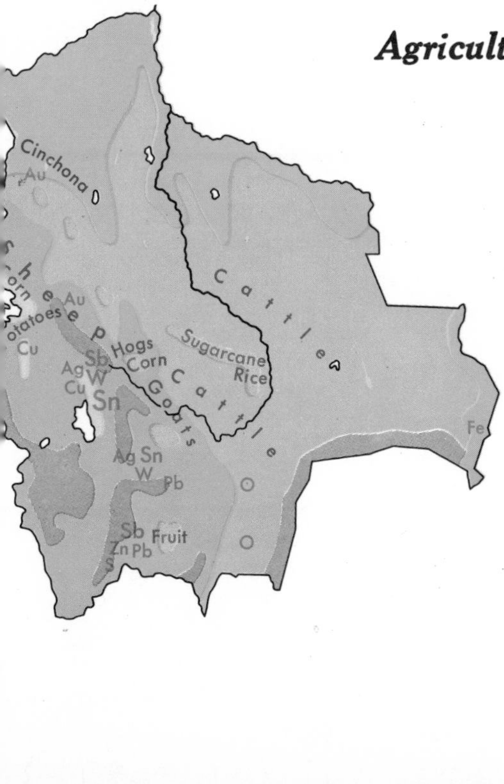
Cinchona
Au
Sheep
Potatoes
Cattle
Sugarcane
Rice
Hogs
Corn
Goats
Ag
W
Cu
Sn
Sb
Pb
Zn
Fruit
Fe

DOMINANT LAND USE

- Diversified Tropical Crops (chiefly plantation agriculture)
- Upland Cultivated Areas
- Upland Livestock Grazing, Limited Agriculture
- Extensive Livestock Ranching
- Forests
- Nonagricultural Land

MAJOR MINERAL OCCURRENCES

Ag	Silver	O	Petroleum	Sn	Tin
Au	Gold	Pb	Lead	W	Tungsten
Cu	Copper	S	Sulfur	Zn	Zinc
Fe	Iron Ore	Sb	Antimony		

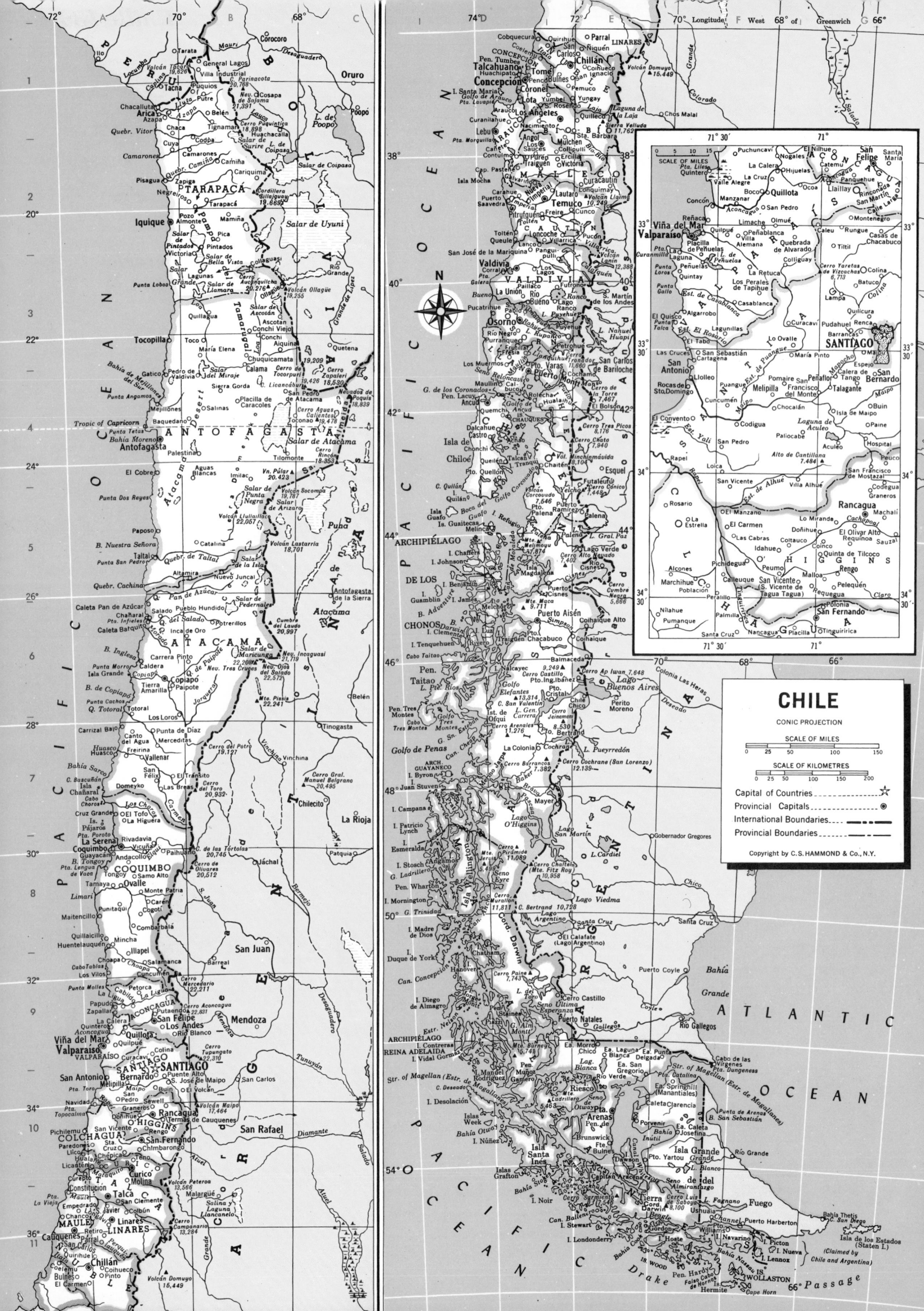

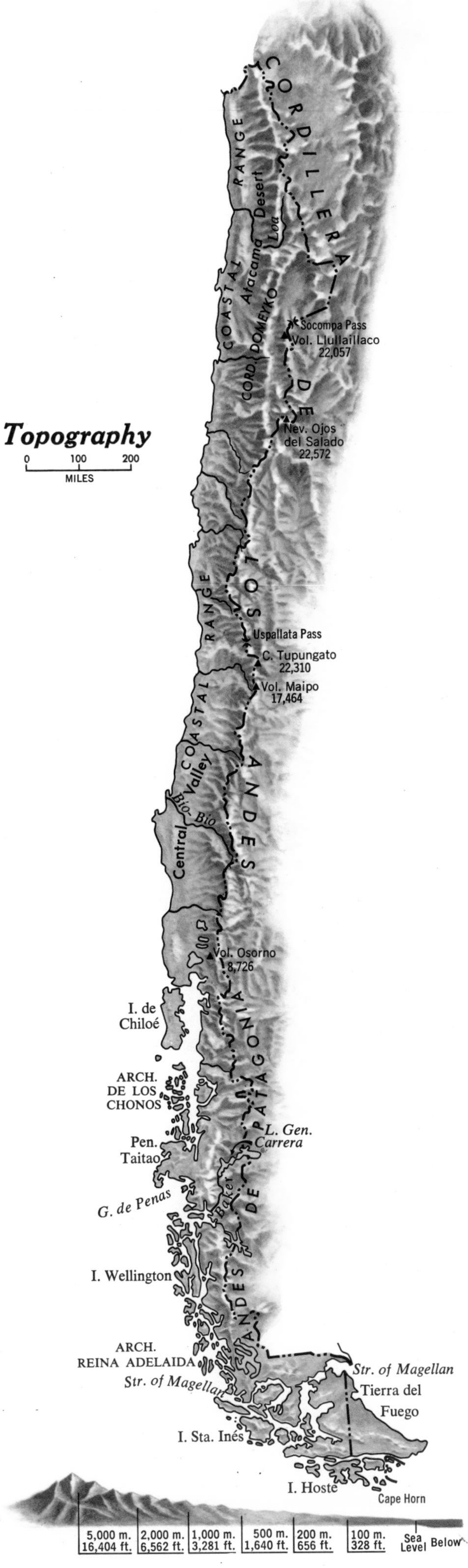

Topography
0 100 200
MILES
CORDILLERA DE LOS ANDES
COASTAL RANGE
Atacama Desert
Loa
CORD. DOMEYKO
Socompa Pass
Vol. Llullaillaco 22,057
Nev. Ojos del Salado 22,572
Uspallata Pass
C. Tupungato 22,310
Vol. Maipo 17,464
Central Valley
Bío Bío
Vol. Osorno 8,726
I. de Chiloé
ARCH. DE LOS CHONOS
Pen. Taitao
L. Gen. Carrera
G. de Penas
Baker
PATAGONIA
I. Wellington
ARCH. REINA ADELAIDA
Str. of Magellan
Str. of Magellan
Tierra del Fuego
I. Sta. Inés
I. Hoste
Cape Horn
5,000 m. 16,404 ft.
2,000 m. 6,562 ft.
1,000 m. 3,281 ft.
500 m. 1,640 ft.
200 m. 656 ft.
100 m. 328 ft.
Sea Level
Below

AREA 292,257 sq. mi.
POPULATION 8,834,820
CAPITAL Santiago
LARGEST CITY Santiago
HIGHEST POINT Ojos del Salado 22,572 ft.
MONETARY UNIT Chilean escudo
MAJOR LANGUAGE Spanish
MAJOR RELIGION Roman Catholicism

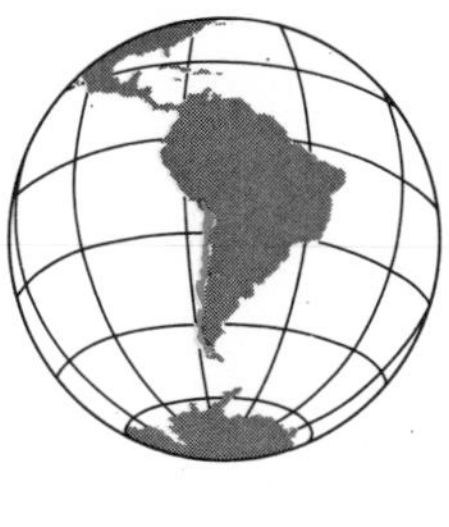

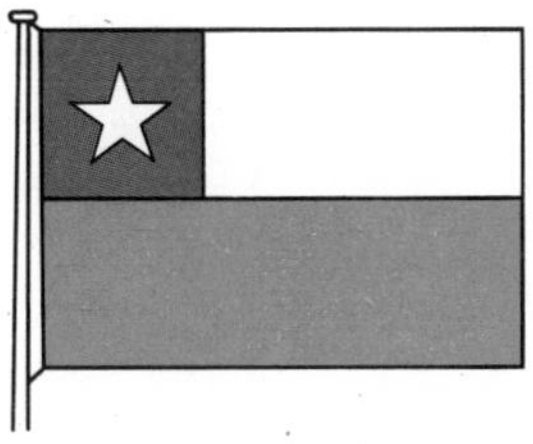

PROVINCES

Aconcagua, 160,821 ....A 9
Aisén, 51,022 ....D 6
Antofagasta, 250,665 ....B 4
Arauco, 98,810 ....D 1
Atacama, 152,326 ....B 6
Bío-Bío, 193,002 ....D 1
Cautín, 420,682 ....E 2
Chiloé, 110,728 ....D 4
Colchagua, 167,899 ....A10
Concepción, 638,118 ....D 1
Coquimbo, 336,821 ....A 8
Curicó, 113,710 ....A10
Linares, 189,010 ....A11
Llanquihue, 197,986 ....D 3
Magallanes, 88,706 ....E10
Malleco, 176,060 ....E 2
Maule, 82,339 ....A11
Ñuble, 314,738 ....E 1
O'Higgins, 306,739 ....A10
Osorno, 158,673 ....D 3
Santiago, 3,217,870 ....A 9
Talca, 231,088 ....A11
Tarapacá, 174,730 ....B 2
Valdivia, 275,404 ....D 3
Valparaíso, 726,953 ....A 9

CITIES and TOWNS

Achao, †11,501 ....D 4
Aculeo, 20 ....G 4
Aguas Blancas, †203 ....B 4
Aiquina, 105 ....B 3
Alcones, 682 ....F 5
Algarrobo, †3,941 ....F 3
Altamira, 93 ....B 5
Ancud, †22,127 ....D 4
Andacollo, †9,987 ....A 8
Angol, †35,995 ....D 1
Antofagasta, †126,252 ....A 4
Arauco, †20,018 ....D 1
Arica, †92,394 ....A 1
Ascotán, 23 ....B 3
Azapa, 225 ....A 1
Balmaceda, 735 ....E 6
Baquedano, 1,412 ....A 4
Barrancas, †184,241 ....G 3
Batuco, 1,125 ....G 3
Belén, †925 ....B 1
Boco, 1,655 ....F 2
Buin, †31,233 ....G 4
Bulnes, †16,107 ....E 1
Cabildo, †13,018 ....A 9
Calama, †71,983 ....B 3
Calbuco, †21,673 ....D 4
Caldera, †3,268 ....A 6
Calera de Tango, †6,198 ....G 4
Caleta Barquito, 932 ....A 6
Caleta Clarencia, 60 ....E10
Caleta Pan de Azúcar, 8 ....A 6
Caleu, 187 ....G 2
Calle Larga, †7,172 ....G 2
Calleuque ....F 5
Camarones, 259 ....B 2
Camiña, 234 ....B 2
Cañete, †15,179 ....D 2
Canto del Agua, 269 ....A 7
Capitán Pastene, 1,669 ....D 2
Carahue, †12,733 ....D 2
Carén, 225 ....A 8
Cariquima, 20 ....B 2
Carrera Pinto, 68 ....B 6
Carrizal Bajo, 207 ....A 7
Cartagena, †7,124 ....F 3
Casablanca, †12,292 ....F 3
Castro, †22,682 ....D 4
Catalina, †1,637 ....B 5
Catemu, †8,728 ....G 2
Cauquenes, †38,476 ....A11
Cerro Castillo, †537 ....E 9
Chaca, 37 ....B 1
Chacalluta, 75 ....A 1
Chaitén, †4,067 ....E 4
Chañaral, †36,949 ....A 6
Chanco, †12,433 ....A11
Chépica, †11,199 ....A10
Chile Chico, 1,926 ....E 6
Chillán, †102,361 ....A11
Chimbarongo, †17,592 ....A10
Choapa, 258 ....A 9
Chocalán, 187 ....F 4
Chonchi, †8,911 ....D 4
Chuquicamata, 24,798 ....B 3
Cobquecura, †6,298 ....D 1
Cochamó, †5,042 ....E 3
Codegua, †6,757 ....G 4
Codigua, 530 ....F 4
Codpa, †950 ....B 1
Coelemu, †11,967 ....D 1
Cogotí, 212 ....A 8
Coihaique, †24,032 ....E 6
Coihaique Alto, 24 ....E 6
Coihueco, †17,276 ....A11
Coinco, †4,942 ....G 5
Colbún, †12,924 ....A11
Colina, †18,058 ....G 3
Collaguasi, 8 ....B 3
Colliguay, 102 ....F 3
Collipulli, †15,058 ....E 2
Coltauco, †11,857 ....F 5
Combarbalá, †17,332 ....A 8
Concepción, †189,929 ....D 1
Conchi, 9 ....B 3
Conchi Viejo, 17 ....B 3
Concón, 5,381 ....F 2
Constitución, †23,543 ....A11
Contulmo, †13,987 ....D 2
Copiapó, †51,809 ....B 6
Coquimbo, †55,360 ....A 8
Coronel, †73,568 ....D 1
Corral, †5,533 ....D 3
Cruz Grande, 478 ....A 7
Cunco, †18,836 ....E 2
Cuncumén, Coquimbo, 1,052 ....A 9
Cuncumén, Santiago ....F 4
Curacautín, †15,862 ....E 2
Curacaví, †11,481 ....G 3
Curanilahue, †21,207 ....D 1
Curepto, †13,020 ....A10
Curicó, †59,621 ....A10
Cuya, 86 ....B 2
Dalcahue, †7,084 ....D 4
Domeyko, 1,814 ....A 7
Doñihue, †8,837 ....G 5
El Carmen, Ñuble, †13,226 ....A11
El Carmen, O'Higgins, 625 ....F 5
El Cobre, 7 ....A 4
El Convento, 733 ....F 4
El Manzano, 1,073 ....F 5
El Ñilhue, 341 ....G 1
El Olivar Alto, †5,414 ....G 5
El Quisco, †2,152 ....E 3
El Tabo, †2,180 ....F 3
El Tofo, 1,175 ....A 7
El Tránsito, 235 ....B 7
El Volcán, 250 ....B10
Empedrado, †7,887 ....A11
Ercilla, †8,061 ....E 2
Espejo, 3,481 ....G 3
Estancia Caleta Josefina, †1,042 ....F10
Estancia Laguna Blanca, 119 ....E 9
Estancia Morro Chico, †785 ....E 9
Estancia Punta Delgada, 233 ....E 9
Estancia San Gregorio, †1,156 ....E 9
Estancia Springhill (Manantiales), 291 ....F10
Freire, †23,313 ....E 2
Freirina, †5,523 ....A 7
Fresia, †15,359 ....D 3
Frutillar, †12,721 ....D 3
Fuerte Bulnes, 18 ....E10
Futaleufú, †2,366 ....E 4
Futrono, †7,109 ....E 3
Galvarino, †9,495 ....D 2
Gatico, 16 ....A 4
General Lagos, †810 ....B 1
Graneros, †13,523 ....G 5
Guayacán, 1,514 ....A 8
Hijuelas, †7,128 ....F 2
Hospital, 460 ....G 4
Huachipato, †16,336 ....D 1
Hualaihué, 391 ....E 4
Hualañé, †6,912 ....A10
Huara, †1,934 ....B 2
Huasco, †4,971 ....A 7
Huentelauquén, 355 ....A 8
Idahue, 1,832 ....F 5
Illapel, †20,660 ....A 8
Imalac, 27 ....B 4
Inca de Oro, 1,406 ....B 6
Iquique, †64,900 ....A 2
Isla de Maipo, †12,903 ....G 4
La Calera, †28,728 ....F 2
La Colonia, 41 ....D 7
La Cruz, †8,907 ....F 2
La Estrella, †3,707 ....F 5
La Higuera, †6,991 ....A 7
La Laguna, 316 ....F 2
La Ligua, †15,719 ....A 9
La Retuca, 173 ....F 3
La Serena, †71,898 ....A 8
La Unión, †32,010 ....D 3
Lago Ranco, †12,767 ....D 3
Lago Verde, 193 ....E 5
Lagunas, †5,653 ....B 3
Lagunillas, 468 ....F 3
Lampa, †10,220 ....G 3
Lanco, †14,479 ....D 2
Las Breas, 14 ....B 7
Las Cabras †12,119 ....F 5
Las Cruces, 612 ....F 3
Lautaro, †26,011 ....E 2
Lebu, †16,946 ....D 1
Licantén, †6,354 ....A10
Limache, †22,472 ....F 2
Linares, †61,011 ....A11
Llaillay, †14,074 ....G 2
Llico, 330 ....A10
Llolleo, 9,846 ....F 4
Lo Miranda, 2,270 ....G 5
Lo Ovalle, 129 ....F 3
Loica, 446 ....F 4
Loncoche, †17,539 ....D 2
Longaví, †15,909 ....A11
Lonquimay, †9,524 ....E 2
Los Andes, †30,408 ....B 9
Los Ángeles, †89,810 ....D 1
Los Lagos, †14,934 ....D 3
Los Loros, 269 ....A 6
Los Muermos, †9,296 ....D 3
Los Perales de Tapihue, 176 ....F 3
Los Sauces, †7,613 ....D 2
Los Vilos, †10,453 ....A 9
Lota, †51,548 ....D 1
Machalí, †28,415 ....G 5
Maipú, †117,872 ....G 3
Maitencillo, 31 ....A 8
Malloa, †9,742 ....G 5
Mamiña, 341 ....B 2
Manantiales, 291 ....F10
Manzanar, 248 ....F 2
Marchihue, †4,451 ....F 5
María Elena, 9,572 ....B 3
María Pinto, †5,980 ....G 3
Maullín, †14,544 ....D 4
Mayer, 29 ....E 7
Mejillones, †3,333 ....A 4
Melinca, 166 ....D 5
Melipilla, †49,306 ....F 4
Merceditas, 33 ....B 7
Mincha, †11,329 ....A 8
Molina, †30,398 ....A10
Montenegro, 327 ....G 2
Monte Patria, †18,927 ....A 8
Mulchén, †23,379 ....E 1
Nacimiento, †17,651 ....D 1
Nancagua, †11,076 ....F 6
Navidad, †6,618 ....A10
Negreiros, †1,144 ....B 2
Nilahue, 428 ....E 6
Ñiquén, †13,640 ....E 1
Nogales, †18,529 ....F 2
Nueva Imperial, †30,286 ....D 2
Nuevo Juncal, 2 ....B 5
Ocoa, 871 ....G 2
Ollagüe, 333 ....B 3
Olmué, †8,804 ....F 2
Osorno, †105,793 ....D 3
Ovalle, †53,433 ....A 8
Paihuano, †6,048 ....B 8
Paillaco, †13,612 ....D 3
Paine, †21,876 ....G 4
Paipote, 2,278 ....B 6
Palena, †2,508 ....E 5
Palestina, 7 ....B 4
Paliocabe, 77 ....F 4
Palmilla, †12,429 ....F 6
Panguipulli, †32,834 ....E 2
Panquehue, †4,230 ....G 2
Paposo, 87 ....A 5
Papudo, †2,594 ....A 9
Paredones, †7,404 ....A10
Parral, †30,427 ....A11
Pedro de Valdivia, 11,028 ....B 4
Pelequen, 1,068 ....G 5
Pemuco, †7,577 ....E 1
Peñablanca, 5,586 ....F 2
Peñaflor, †37,788 ....G 4
Penco, †33,962 ....D 1
Peñuelas, 359 ....F 3
Peralillo, †7,965 ....F 5
Petorca, †8,343 ....A 9
Petrohué, 40 ....E 3
Peuco, 211 ....G 4
Peumo, †11,308 ....F 5
Pica, †1,487 ....B 2
Pichidegua, †13,550 ....F 5
Pichilemu, †8,042 ....A10
Pintados, 144 ....B 2
Pinto, †8,687 ....A11
Pisagua, †1,880 ....A 2
Pitrufquén, †16,797 ....D 2
Placilla, †6,411 ....F 6
Placilla de Caracoles, 2 ....B 4
Placilla de Peñuelas, 1,495 ....F 2
Población, 1,026 ....F 5
Polonia ....G 6
Pomaire, 1,366 ....F 4
Porvenir, †3,600 ....E10
Potrerillos, 6,168 ....B 6
Pozo Almonte, †1,798 ....B 2
Puangue ....F 4
Pucatrihue, 60 ....D 3
Puchuncaví, †7,542 ....F 2
Pucón, †16,872 ....E 2
Pudahuel, 172 ....G 3
Pueblo Hundido, 2,123 ....B 6
Puente Alto, †81,031 ....B10
Puerto Aisén, †15,000 ....E 6
Puerto Bertrand, 52 ....E 7
Puerto Chacabuco, 130 ....D 6
Puerto Cisnes, †2,800 ....E 5
Puerto Cristal, 698 ....E 6
Puerto Ingeniero Ibáñez, †1,900 ....E 6
Puerto Montt, †86,750 ....E 4
Puerto Natales, †13,577 ....E 9
Puerto Palena, 105 ....D 5
Puerto Quellón, †7,734 ....D 4
Puerto Ramírez, 82 ....E 5
Puerto Saavedra, 805 ....D 2
Puerto Varas, †21,003 ....E 3
Puerto Williams, †949 ....F11
Puerto Yartou, 14 ....E10
Pumanque, †3,137 ....F 6
Punitaqui, †16,167 ....A 8
Punta Arenas, †64,958 ....E10
Punta de Díaz, 11 ....B 7
Puquios, 105 ....B 1
Purén, †11,604 ....D 2
Purranque, †18,201 ....D 3
Putaendo, †12,806 ....A 9
Putre, †855 ....B 1
Puyehue, 39 ....E 3
Quebrada de Alvarado, 429 ....F 2
Queilén, †6,055 ....D 4
Quemchi, †6,707 ....D 4
Queule, 235 ....D 2
Quilicura, †22,644 ....G 3
Quillagua, 288 ....B 3
Quillaicillo, 195 ....A 8
Quilleco, †16,043 ....E 1
Quillota, †49,202 ....F 2
Quilpué, †56,399 ....F 2
Quinta de Tilcoco, †6,513 ....G 5
Quintay, 166 ....F 3
Quintero, †11,847 ....F 2
Quirihue, †11,178 ....E 1
Rancagua, †95,030 ....G 5
Rapel, 699 ....F 4
Reñaca, 1,267 ....F 2
Renca, †67,168 ....G 3
Rengo, †28,230 ....G 5
Requegua, 1,699 ....G 5
Requíhoa, †10,730 ....G 5
Retiro, †15,146 ....A11
Rinconada San Martín, †4,118 ....G 2
Río Blanco, 456 ....B 9
Río Bueno, †28,469 ....D 3
Río Cisnes, 244 ....E 5
Río Negro, †15,582 ....D 3
Río Verde, †554 ....E10
Rivadavia, 443 ....A 7
Rocas de Santo Domingo, †4,114 ....F 4
Rolecha, 573 ....D 4
Rosario, †3,383 ....F 5
Rungue, 312 ....G 2
Salado, 1,375 ....A 6
Salamanca, †18,741 ....A 9
Salinas, 7 ....B 4
Samo Alto, †5,689 ....A 8
San Antonio, †53,100 ....F 3
San Bernardo, †117,766 ....G 4
San Carlos, †30,651 ....E 1
San Clemente, †23,273 ....A11
San Felipe, †34,292 ....G 2
San Félix, 495 ....A 7
Sán Fernando, †44,160 ....G 6
San Francisco de Mostazal, †11,439 ....G 4
San Francisco del Monte, †14,897 ....G 4
San Ignacio, †13,523 ....E 1
San Javier, †27,592 ....A11
San José de la Mariquina, 2,878 ....D 2
San José de Maipo, †9,601 ....B10
San Pablo, †7,978 ....D 3
San Pedro, Santiago, †8,255 ....F 4
San Pedro, Valparaíso, 1,420 ....F 2
San Pedro de Atacama, 515 ....C 4
San Rosendo, †14,337 ....E 1
San Sebastián, 494 ....F 3
San Vicente, 230 ....F 4
San Vicente (San Vicente de Tagua Tagua), †28,333 ....F 5
Santa Bárbara, †14,345 ....E 1
Santa Cruz, †19,338 ....F 6
Santa María, †8,162 ....G 2
Santiago (capital), 2,596,929 ....G 3
Sewell, 10,866 ....A10
Sierra Gorda, †8,805 ....B 4
Talagante, †23,619 ....G 4
Talca, †102,522 ....A11
Talcahuano, †150,011 ....D 1
Taltal, †7,417 ....A 5
Tamaya, 248 ....A 8
Tarapacá, 130 ....B 2
Temuco, †146,039 ....E 2
Teno, †17,675 ....A10
Termas de Cauquenes, 210 ....B10
Tierra Amarilla, †6,842 ....A 6
Tignamar, 226 ....B 1
Tilomonte, 3 ....B 4
Tiltil, †9,198 ....G 2
Tinguiririca, 1,012 ....G 6
Toco, †8,734 ....B 3
Toconao, 452 ....C 4
Tocopilla, †22,301 ....A 3
Toltén, †16,265 ....D 2
Tomé, †44,480 ....D 1
Tongoy, 935 ....A 8
Totoral, 109 ....A 6
Traiguén, †21,084 ....D 2
Valdivia, †90,942 ....D 3
Valle Alegre, 241 ....F 2
Vallenar, †41,907 ....A 7
Valparaíso, †251,459 ....E 2
Victoria, Malleco, †28,382 ....E 2
Victoria, Tarapacá, 4,943 ....B 3
Vicuña, †13,806 ....A 8
Villa Alemana, †37,547 ....F 2
Villa Alhué, †5,078 ....G 4
Villa Industrial, 28 ....B 1
Villarrica, †23,924 ....E 2
Viña del Mar, †184,332 ....F 2
Yumbel, †21,858 ....E 1
Yungay, †10,725 ....E 1
Zapallar, †2,894 ....A 9

OTHER FEATURES

Aconcagua (river) ....F 2
Aculeo (lagoon) ....G 4
Adventure (bay) ....D 5
Aguas Calientes (mt.) ....C 4
Alhué (river) ....F 4
Almirantazgo (bay) F11
Almeida (mts.) ....C 4
Almirante Montt (gulf) ....D 9
Alto Nevado (mt.) ....E 5
Ancho (channel) ....D 8
Ancud (gulf) ....D 4
Angamos (isl.) ....D 8
Angamos (point) ....A 4
Ap Iwan (mt.) ....E 6
Arauco (gulf) ....D 1
Arenales (mt.) ....D 7
Ascotán (salt deposit) ....B 3
Atacama (desert) ....B 4
Atacama (salt deposit) ....C 4
Aucanquilcha (mt.) ....B 3
Azapa (river) ....B 1
Baker (river) ....D 7
Ballenero (channel) E11
Barrancos (mt.) ....D 7
Bascuñán (cape) ....A 7
Beagle (channel) E11
Bella Vista (salt deposit) ....B 3
Benjamín (isl.), 16 ....D 5
Bertrand (mt.) ....D 8
Bío-Bío (river) ....E 2
Blanca (lagoon) E10
Blanco (lake) F10
Bravo (river) ....D 7
Brunswick (pen.) E10

(continued on following page)

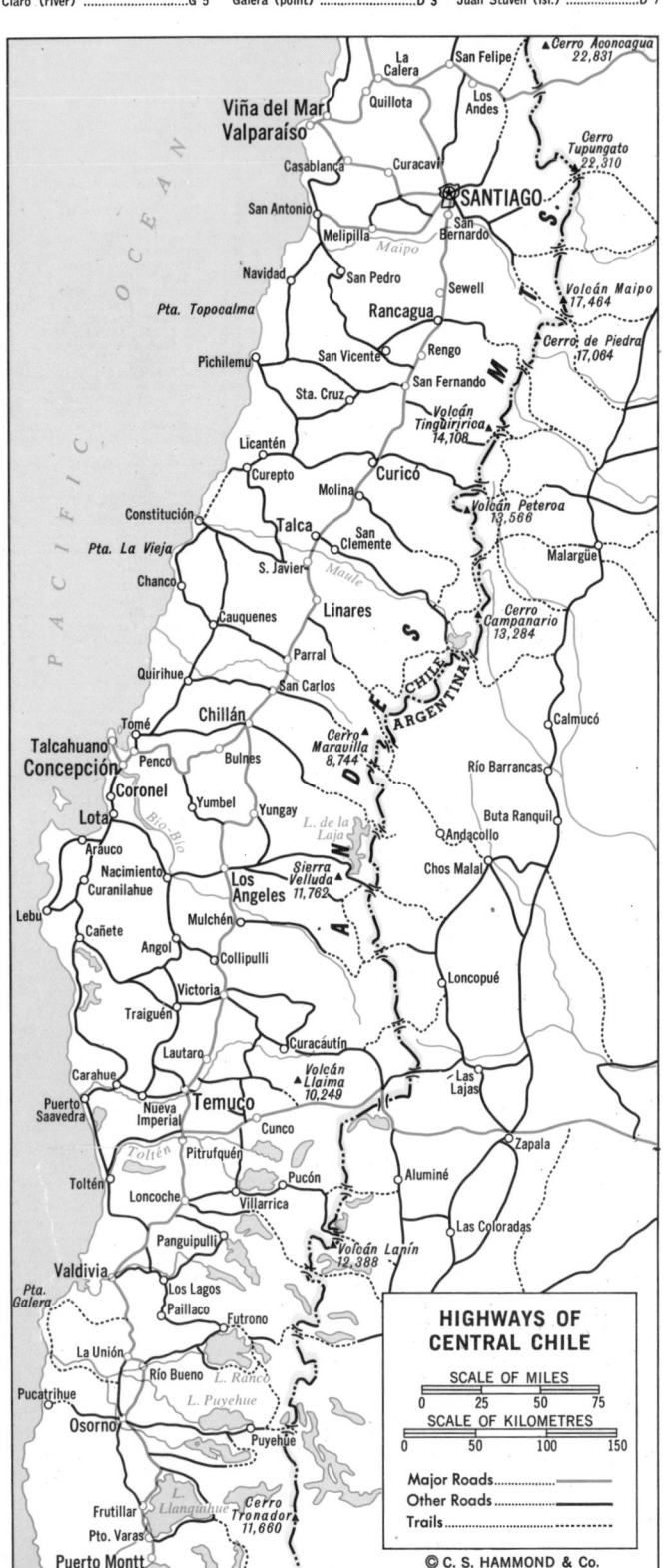

Bueno (river) ....D 3
Buenos Aires (lake) ....E 6
Burney (mt.) ....D 9
Byron (isl.) ....D 7
Cachapoal (river) ....G 5
Cachina (river) ....A 5
Cachos (point) ....A 6
Calafquén (lake) ....E 3
Camarones (river) ....A 2
Camiña (river) ....B 2
Campana (isl.) ....D 7
Campanario (mt.) B11
Cantillana (mt.) ....G 4
Capitán Aracena (isl.) E10
Carmen (river) ....A 7
Casablanca (river) ....F 3
Castillo (mt.) ....E 6
Catalina (point) F10
Chaffers (isl.) ....D 5
Chaltel (mt.) ....E 8
Chañaral (isl.) ....A 7
Chatham (isl.) ....D 9
Chato (mt.) ....E 4
Chauques (isls.),
  2,284 ....D 4
Cheap (channel) ....D 7
Chiloé (isl.), 68,710 ....D 4
Choapa (river) ....A 9
Chonos (arch.) ....D 6
Choros (cape) ....A 7
Choros, Los (river) ....A 7
Cisnes (river) ....D 5
Clarence (isl.), 8, ...E10
Claro (river) ....G 5

Clemente (isl.) ....D 6
Cochrane (lake) ....E 7
Cochrane (mt.) ....E 7
Cockburn (channel) E10
Colina (river) ....G 3
Concepción (channel) ....D 9
Cónico (mt.) ....E 4
Contreras (isl.) ....D 10
Cook (bay) E11
Copiapó (river) ....A 6
Corcovado (gulf) ....D 4
Corcovado (vol.) ....D 5
Coronados (gulf) ....D 5
Cumbre Negra (mt.) ....E 5
Curanmilla (point) ....E 2
Darwin (bay) ....D 6
Darwin (mts.) E11
Darwin (mts.) ....D 8
Dawson (isl.), 147 ....E10
Deseado (cape) D10
Desolación (isl.) ....D 9
Diego de Almagro (isl) ....D 9
Domeyko (mts.) ....B 4
Dos Reyes (point) ....A 5
Drake (passage) E11
Duque de York (isl.) ....C 9
Dungeness (point) F10
Elefantes (gulf) ....D 6
Elqui (river) ....A 8
Esmeralda (isl.) ....C 8
Eyre (bay) ....D 8
Fagnano (lake) F11
Fitz Roy (Chaltel) (mt.) ....E 8
Galera (point) ....D 3

Gallo (point) ....E 3
General Paz (lake) ....E 5
Gordon (isl.) E11
Grafton (isls.) D10
Grande (isl.), 2 ....A 6
Grande (river) F10
Grande (salt deposit) ....B 3
Grande de Tierra del Fuego
  (isl.), 5,467 ....E11
Guafo (gulf) ....D 5
Guafo (isl.) ....D 5
Guaitecas (isls.), 8 ....D 5
Guamblin (isl.), 851 ....D 5
Guayaneco (arch.) ....D 7
Hanover (isl.) ....D 9
Hardy (pen.) F11
Hermite (isl.) F11
Horn (cape) F11
Hornos, Falso (cape) F11
Hoste (isl.), 20, ...F11
Huasco (river) ....A 7
Imperial (river) ....D 2
Incaguasi (mt.) ....C 6
Inglesa (bay) ....A 6
Inútil (bay) E10
Isla (salt deposit) ....B 5
Itata (river) A11
James (isl.) ....D 8
Jeinemeni (mt.) ....E 6
Jervis (mt.) ....D 5
Johnson (isl.) ....D 5
Jorge Montt (isl.) ....D 9
Jorquera (river) ....B 6
Juan Stuven (isl.) ....D 7

DOMINANT LAND USE

Cereals, Livestock

Mediterranean Agriculture (cereals, fruit, livestock)

Pasture Livestock

Extensive Livestock Ranching

Limited Seasonal Grazing

Forests

Nonagricultural Land

MAJOR MINERAL OCCURRENCES

Ag Silver
Au Gold
C Coal
Cu Copper
Fe Iron Ore
G Natural Gas
Gp Gypsum

Hg Mercury
Id Iodine
Mn Manganese
Mo Molybdenum
N Nitrates
Na Salt
O Petroleum
S Sulfur

⚡ Water Power   ▨ Major Industrial Areas

La Ligua (river) ....A 9
Lacuy (pen.) ....D 4
Ladrillero (gulf) ....C 8
Ladrillero (mt.) E10
Laja (lagoon) ....E 1
Laja (river) ....E 1
Lanín (vol.) ....E 2
Lastarria (vol.) ....B 5
Lauca (river) ....B 1
Lavapié (point) ....D 1
Lengua de Vaca
  (point) ....A 8
Lennox (isl.) F11
Licancábur (mt.) ....B 4
Liles (point) ....F 2
Limarí (river) ....A 8
Llaima (mt.) ....E 2
Llamara
  (salt deposit) ....B 3
Llanquihue (lake) ....B 3
Llullaillaco (vol.) ....B 5
Lluta (river) ....B 1
Loa (river) ....B 3
Lobos (point) ....A 3
Londonderry (isl.) E11
Loros (point) ....E 3
Luis de Saboya (mt.) F11
Luz (isl.), 23 ....D 6
Macá (mt.) ....D 5
Madre de Dios (isl.) ....D 8
Magdalena (isl.) ....D 5
Magellan (Magallanes)
  (strait) D10
Maipo (river) ....F 4
Maipo (vol.) B10
Manso (river) ....E 4
Manuel Rodríguez (isl.) D10
Mapocho (river) ....G 3
Maricunga (salt deposit) ....B 6
Mataquito (river) A10
Maule (river) A11
Maullín (river) ....D 3
Mejillones del Sur (bay) ....A 4
Melchor (isl.), 12 ....D 6
Melimoyu (mt.) ....D 5
Merino Jarpa (isl.) ....D 7
Minchinmávida (vol.) ....E 4
Miraje (salt deposit) ....B 3
Mocha (isl.), 689 ....D 2
Molles (point) ....A 9
Morado (river) ....A 6
Moraleda (channel) ....D 5
Moreno (bay) ....A 4
Morguilla (point) ....D 1
Mornington (isl.) ....D 8
Morro (point) ....A 6
Muñoz Gamero (pen.) D10
Murallón (mt.) ....D 8
Nalcayec (isl.) ....D 6
Nassau (bay) F11
Navarino (isl.), 436 ....F11
Nelson (strait) ....D 9
Nevados de Poquis ....C 4
Noir (isl.) E11
Nuestra Señora (bay) ....A 5
Nueva (isl.) F11
Núñez (isl.) D10
O'Higgins (lake) ....D 7
Ofqui (isthmus) ....D 6
Ojos del Salado (mt.) ....B 6
Olivares (mt.) ....B 8
Ollagüe (vol.) ....C 3
Otway (bay) D10
Otway (sound) E10
Paine (mt.) ....D 9
Paipote (river) ....B 6
Pájaros (isls.) ....A 7
Palena (lake) ....E 5
Palena (river) ....D 5
Pan de Azúcar (river) ....B 5
Parinacota (mt.) ....B 1
Pascua (river) ....D 7
Patricio Lynch (isl.) ....D 7
Pedernales
  (salt deposit) ....B 5
Penas (gulf) ....D 7
Peñuelas (lake) ....F 2
Perquilauquén (river) A11
Peteroa (vol.) B10
Piazzi (isl.) ....D 9
Picton (isl.) F11
Pilmaiquén (river) ....D 3
Pintados (salt deposit) ....B 3
Pirámide (mt.) ....D 8

Poquis, Nevados de (mt.) ....C 4
Potro (mt.) ....B 7
Prat (isl.) ....D 7
Presidente Ríos (lake) ....D 6
Puangue (river) ....F 3
Puelo (river) ....E 4
Púlar (mt.) ....B 4
Punta Negra (salt deposit) .....B 5
Puquintica (mt.) ....B 1
Puyehue (lake) ....E 3
Quilán (cape) ....D 4
Quilán (isl.) ....D 5
Rahue (river) ....D 3
Ranco (lake) ....E 3
Rapel (river) ....F 4
Refugio (isl.) ....D 5
Reina Adelaida (arch.) ....D 9
Reloncaví (bay) ....D 4
Riesco (isl.), 264 ....E10
Rincón (mt.) ....C 4
Rivero (isl.) ....D 6
Rosario (river) ....F 3
Rupanco (lake) ....D 3
Salado (river) ....B 6
San Esteban (gulf) ....D 7
San Lorenzo (Cochrane)
  (mt.) ....E 7
San Martín (lake) ....E 7
San Pedro (point) ....A 5
San Valentín (mt.) ....D 6
Santa Inés (isl.) D10
Santa María (isl.), 74 ....D 1
Sarco (bay) ....A 7
Sarmiento (mt.) E11
Sillajaguay (mt.) ....B 2
Simpson (river) ....E 6
Skyring (bay) E10
Socompa (vol.) ....B 4
Staines (pen.) ....D 9
Stewart (isl.) E11
Stokes (bay) D10
Stosch (isl.) ....C 8
Surire (salt deposit) ....B 2
Tablas (cape) ....A 9
Tacora (vol.) ....B 1
Taitao (pen.) ....D 6
Talca (point) ....E 3
Talcán (isl.) ....D 4
Taltal (river) ....B 5
Tamarugal (plain) ....B 3
Tenquehuen (isl.) ....D 6
Tetas (point) ....A 4
Tierra del Fuego, Grande de
  (isl.), 5,467 ....E11
Tinquiririca (river) ....F 5
Tocorpuri (mt.) ....B 3
Toltén (river) ....D 2
Tongoy (bay) A10
Topocalma (point) A10
Toro (lake) ....D 9
Toro (mt.) ....B 9
Toro (point) A10
Torre, La (isl.) ....E 4
Tortolas (mt.) ....B 8
Totoral (river) ....A 6
Traiguén (isl.), 23 ....D 6
Tranqui (isl.) ....D 4
Tres Cruces (mt.) ....B 6
Tres Montes (cape) ....C 7
Tres Montes (gulf) ....D 6
Tres Montes (pen.) ....D 6
Trinidad (gulf) ....D 8
Tronador (mt.) ....E 3
Tumbes (point) ....A 4
Tupungato (mt.) ....B 9
Última Esperanza (sound) ......E 9
Velluda (mt.) ....E 1
Vidal Gormaz (isl.) ....D 9
Vieja, La (point) A11
Villarrica (lake) ....E 2
Vítor (river) ....A 1
Wager (isl.) D10
Wellington (isl.), 47 ....D 8
Wharton (pen.) ....D 8
Whiteside (channel) E10
Wollaston (isls.) F11
Wood (isl.) E11
Yali (river) ....F 4
Yaretas de Vizcachas ....G 3
Yelcho (lake) ....E 4
Zapaleri (mt.) ....C 4

†Population of commune.

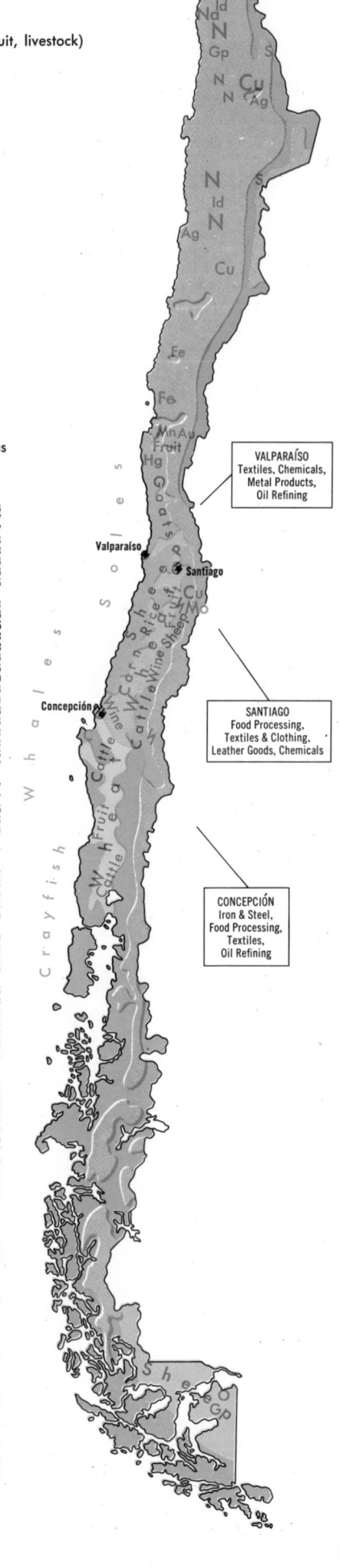

VALPARAÍSO
Textiles, Chemicals,
Metal Products,
Oil Refining

SANTIAGO
Food Processing,
Textiles & Clothing,
Leather Goods, Chemicals

CONCEPCIÓN
Iron & Steel,
Food Processing,
Textiles,
Oil Refining

HIGHWAYS OF CENTRAL CHILE

SCALE OF MILES
0   25   50   75

SCALE OF KILOMETRES
0   50   100   150

Major Roads ....
Other Roads ....
Trails ....

© C. S. HAMMOND & Co.

PROVINCES

es, 6,734,548 ....D 4
172,407 ....C 2
443 ....D 2
2,195 ....C 5
,759,997 ....D 3
543,226 ....E 2
deral (fed. dist.),
..................................H 7
803,505 ....E 3
78,458 ....D 1
783 ....C 1
158,489 ....C 4
28,270 ....C 2
325,535 ....C 4
91,094 ....F 2
1,008 ....C 4
192,595 ....C 5
552 ....D 1
352,461 ....C 3
74,251 ....C 3
52,853 ....C 6
,865,537 ....D 3
el Estero,
..................................D 2
Fuego, Antártida
el Atlántico Sur
13,452 ....C 7
780,348 ....C 2

TIES and TOWNS

ba, 1,391 ....C 1
26 ....F 6
,057 ....F 6
Acuña, 805 ....G 5
Adolfo Alsina, 5,836 ....D 4
Aguilares, 9,816 ....C 2
Aimogasta, 2,721 ....C 2
Alberti, 4,447 ....G 7
Alcaraz, 376 ....G 5
Alcorta, 3,781 ....F 6
Alejandra, 881 ....F 5
Allen, 11,389 ....C 4
Alpachiri, 733 ....D 4
Alta Gracia, 11,570 ....D 3
Aluminé, 744 ....B 4
Alvear, 4,252 ....E 2
Ameghino, 2,770 ....D 3
Aminga, 480 ....C 2
Añatuya, 11,753 ....D 2
Anchorena, 862 ....C 4
Andacollo, 587 ....B 4
Andalgalá, 3,260 ....C 2
Angélica, 434 ....E 5
Anguil, 734 ....D 4
Antofagasta de la Sierra,
462 ....C 2
Apóstoles, 6,507 ....E 2
Arrecifes, 7,635 ....F 6
Arribeños, 1,739 ....F 7
Arroyo Seco, 5,193 ....F 6
Ascensión, 1,775 ....F 7
Astra, 1,019 ....C 6
Avellaneda, †329,626 ....G 7
Ayacucho, 9,220 ....E 4
Azul, 28,609 ....E 4
Bahía Blanca, †150,354 ....D 4
Bahía Thetis, †438 ....C 7
Baibiene, 380 ....G 4
Baigorrita, 1,206 ....F 7
Balcarce, 15,210 ....E 4
Balnearia, 4,306 ....D 3
Bañado de Ovanta, 198 ....C 2
Bandera, 2,035 ....D 2
Baradero, 10,194 ....G 6
Barrancas, 1,953 ....F 6
Barranqueras, 19,779 ....E 2
Barreal, 1,790 ....C 3
Basavilbaso, 6,614 ....G 6
Batavia, 457 ....C 3
Beazley, 1,070 ....C 3
Belén, 5,469 ....C 2
Bella Vista, Corrientes, 8,334 ....E 2
Bella Vista, Tucumán, 6,816 ......D 2
Bell Ville, 15,796 ....D 3
Bernardo de Irigoyen, 1,400....F 2
Bolívar, 14,010 ....D 4
Bovril, 1,955 ....G 5
Bragado, 16,104 ....F 7
Buenos Aires (capital),
3,549,000 ....H 7
Buenos Aires, *9,070,000 ......H 7
Bustinza, 918 ....F 6
Cachi, 491 ....C 2
Cafayate, 2,407 ....C 2
Calchaqui, 2,782 ....F 5
Caleta Olivia, 3,639 ....C 6
Caleufú, 1,197 ....D 4
Camarones, 501 ....D 5
Campana, 14,452 ....G 6
Campo Gallo, 2,336 ....D 2
Cañada de Gómez, 12,354 ....F 6
Cañada Honda, 345 ....C 3
Canals, 5,359 ....D 3
Cañuelas, 5,614 ....G 7
Carabelas, 3,476 ....F 6
Carcaraña, 4,516 ....F 6
Carlos Casares, 7,558 ....F 7
Carlos Tejedor, 2,897 ....D 4
Carmen de Areco, 4,411 ....F 7
Carmen de Patagones,
5,423 ....D 5
Caseros, 4,975 ....D 4
Casilda, 11,023 ....F 6
Castelli, Buenos Aires, 3,263 .....H 7
Castelli, Chaco, 4,131 ....D 2
Catamarca, 45,929 ....C 2
Catriló, 1,794 ....D 4
Cayasta, 592 ....F 5
Cayastacito, 483 ....F 5
Cereales, 367 ....D 4
Ceres, 6,525 ....D 2
Chabas, 2,937 ....F 6
Chacabuco, 12,530 ....F 7
Chajarí, 9,075 ....G 5
Chamical, 3,756 ....C 3
Charadai, 1,872 ....D 2
Charata, 8,953 ....D 2
Chascomús, 9,105 ....H 7
Chepes, 2,941 ....C 3
Chicoana, 1,093 ....C 2
Chilecito, 9,809 ....C 2
Chivilcoy, 23,386 ....F 7
Choele-Choel, 3,079 ....C 4
Chos Malal, 2,874 ....C 4
Chumbicha, 2,188 ....C 2
Cinco Saltos, 10,196 ....C 4
Cipolletti, 19,862 ....C 4
Clarke, 506 ....F 6
Clodomira, 4,685 ....D 2
Clorinda, 10,043 ....E 2
Colón, Buenos Aires, 5,628 ....F 6

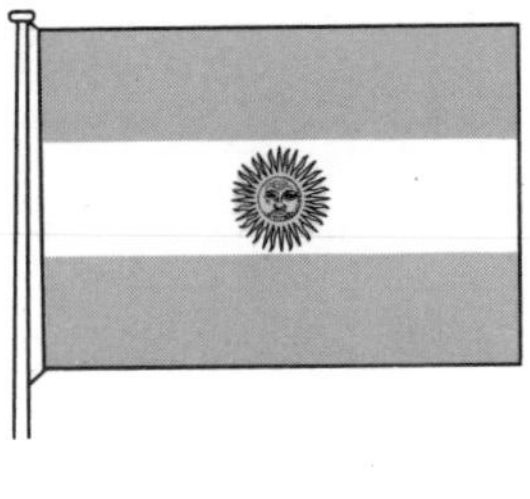

AREA 1,072,070
POPULATION 23,983,000
CAPITAL Buenos Aires
LARGEST CITY Buenos Aires
HIGHEST POINT Cerro Aconcagua 22,831 ft.
MONETARY UNIT Argentine peso
MAJOR LANGUAGE Spanish
MAJOR RELIGION Roman Catholicism

Agriculture, Industry and Resources

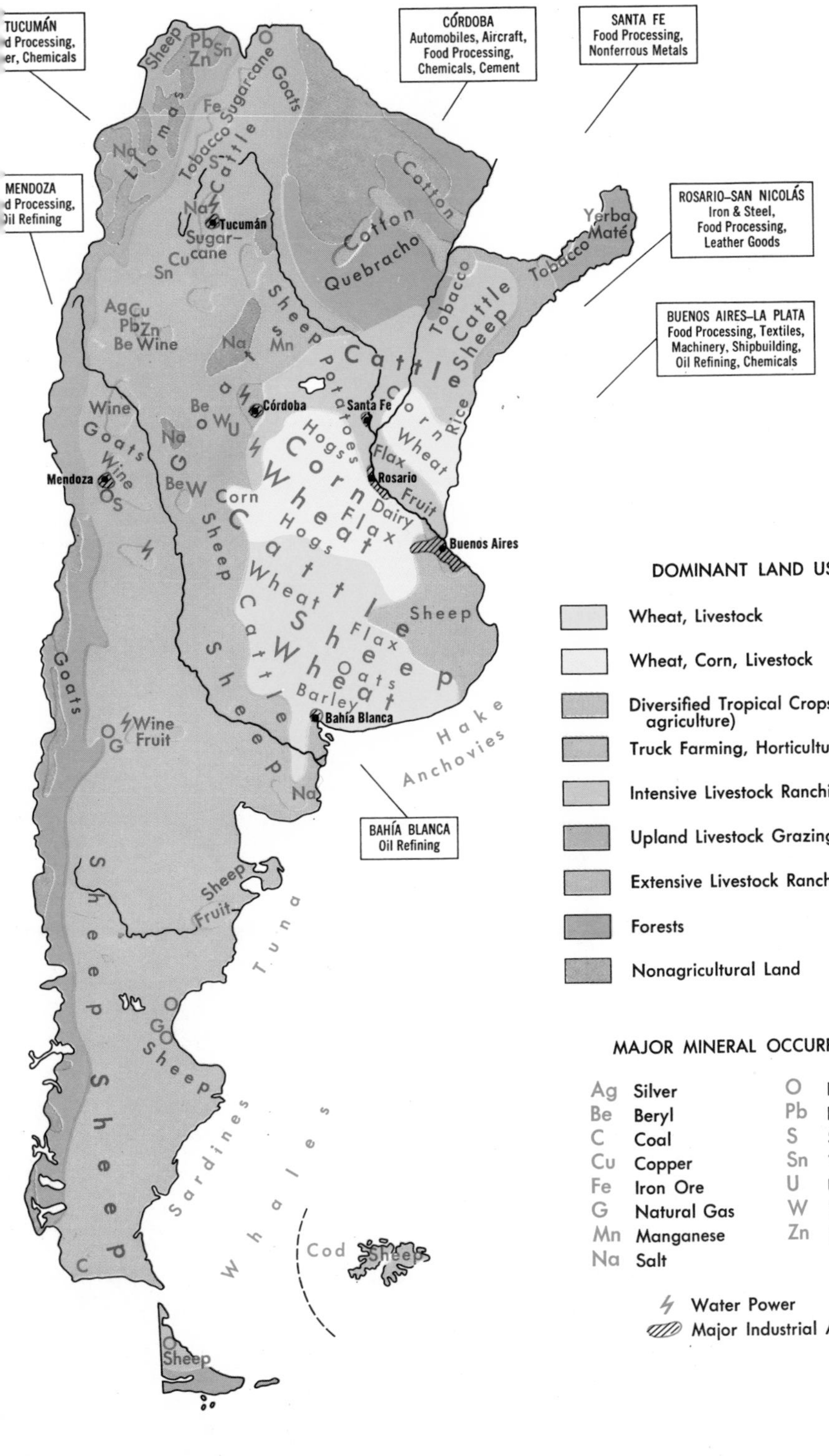
TUCUMÁN
d Processing,
er, Chemicals
MENDOZA
d Processing,
Oil Refining
CÓRDOBA
Automobiles, Aircraft, Food Processing, Chemicals, Cement
SANTA FE
Food Processing, Nonferrous Metals
ROSARIO–SAN NICOLÁS
Iron & Steel, Food Processing, Leather Goods
BUENOS AIRES–LA PLATA
Food Processing, Textiles, Machinery, Shipbuilding, Oil Refining, Chemicals
BAHÍA BLANCA
Oil Refining
Tucumán
Córdoba
Santa Fe
Rosario
Buenos Aires
Mendoza
Bahía Blanca
Cotton
Quebracho
Yerba Maté
Tobacco
Sugarcane
Sugar-cane
Cattle
Sheep
Goats
Llamas
Wine
Corn
Wheat
Flax
Hogs
Dairy
Fruit
Rice
Oats
Barley
Potatoes
Hake
Anchovies
Tuna
Sardines
Whales
Cod

DOMINANT LAND USE

- Wheat, Livestock
- Wheat, Corn, Livestock
- Diversified Tropical Crops (chiefly plantation agriculture)
- Truck Farming, Horticulture, Special Crops
- Intensive Livestock Ranching
- Upland Livestock Grazing, Limited Agriculture
- Extensive Livestock Ranching
- Forests
- Nonagricultural Land

MAJOR MINERAL OCCURRENCES

Ag	Silver	O	Petroleum
Be	Beryl	Pb	Lead
C	Coal	S	Sulfur
Cu	Copper	Sn	Tin
Fe	Iron Ore	U	Uranium
G	Natural Gas	W	Tungsten
Mn	Manganese	Zn	Zinc
Na	Salt		

Water Power
Major Industrial Areas

Colón, Entre Ríos, 6,813 ......G 6
Colonia Elisa, 1,338 ....E 2
Colonia Las Heras, 1,880 ......C 6
Comandante Fontana,
1,686 ....D 2
Comandante Luis Piedrabuena,
1,441 ....C 6
Comodoro Rivadavia, 35,966 ......C 6
Concepción, Corrientes, 2,593 ....E 2
Concepción, Tucumán, 15,832 .....C 2
Concepción del Uruguay,
36,486 ....G 6
Concordia, 56,654 ....G 5
Copacabana, 957 ....C 2
Córdoba, †589,153 ....D 3
Coronda, 4,656 ....F 6
Coronel Bogado, 1,264 ....F 6
Coronel Brandsen, 3,803 ....H 7
Coronel Dorrego, 7,245 ....D 4
Coronel Moldes, 1,695 ....C 2
Coronel Pringles, 12,844 ......D 4
Coronel Suárez, 11,133 ....D 4
Corral de Bustos, 3,900 ....D 3
Corrientes, 97,507 ....E 2
Cosquín, 7,746 ....D 3
Crespo, 5,706 ....F 6
Cruz del Eje, 15,563 ....C 3
Cuadro Nacional, 1,879 ....C 3
Curuzú Cuatiá, 16,567 ....G 5
Cutral-Có, 11,292 ....C 4
Deán Funes, 13,840 ....D 3
Del Carril, 475 ....G 7
Diamante, 10,948 ....F 6
Díaz, 1,288 ....F 6
Doblas, 902 ....D 4
Dolavón, 1,277 ....C 5
Dolores, 14,438 ....E 4
Dudignac, 1,503 ....F 7
Eduardo Castex, 4,020 ....D 4
El Bolsón, 2,607 ....B 5
El Calafate, 567 ....B 7
El Chorro, 377 ....D 1
Eldorado, 2,778 ....F 2
El Huecu, 298 ....B 4
Elisa, 579 ....F 5
El Maitén, 2,382 ....B 5
Elortondo, 3,514 ....F 6
El Pintado, 388 ....D 1
El Quebrachal, 1,212 ....D 2
Embarcación, 6,371 ....D 1
Emilio Ayarza, 1,357 ....F 7
Empedrado, 3,735 ....E 2
Enrique Carbó, 956 ....G 6
Ensenada, †35,030 ....H 7
Escobar, 3,693 ....G 7
Esperanza, 10,035 ....F 5
Esquel, 9,900 ....B 5
Esquina, 7,619 ....G 5
Famatina, 1,330 ....C 2
Federación, 4,247 ....G 5
Fernández, 3,115 ....D 2
Fiambalá, 1,450 ....C 2
Firmat, 4,051 ....F 6
Fives Lille, 667 ....F 5
Formosa, 36,499 ....E 2
French, 4,007 ....F 7
Frías, 11,862 ....D 2
Gaiman, 1,286 ....C 5
Gálvez, 2,475 ....F 6
Gálvez, 7,891 ....F 6
Gan Gan, 281 ....C 5
General Acha, 4,709 ....C 4
General Alvarado, 3,537 ....E 4
General Alvear, Buenos Aires,
2,548 ....F 7
General Alvear, Mendoza,
12,325 ....C 3
General Arenales, 2,182 ....F 7
General Belgrano, 3,789 ....G 7
General Campos, 1,400 ....G 5
General Conesa, 716 ....C 5
General Galarza, 2,435 ....G 6
General Juan Madariaga,
7,073 ....E 4
General José de San Martín,
5,390 ....E 2
General La Madrid, 3,572 ......D 4
General Las Heras, 3,820 ......G 7
General Lavalle, 1,663 ....E 4
Gral. M. M. de Güemes, 8,748....D 1
General O'Brien, 2,988 ....F 7
General Paz, 1,689 ....E 2
General Pico, 11,121 ....D 4
General Roca, 21,969 ....C 4
General San Martín, 2,501 .....D 4
General Villegas, 4,738 ....D 4
Gobernador Crespo, 6,000 ......F 5
Gobernador Gregores,
772 ....C 6
Gobernador Mansilla, 947 ......G 6
Godoy Cruz, 80,024 ....C 3
Goya, 30,011 ....G 4
Gualeguay, 16,542 ....G 6
Gualeguaychú, 29,863 ....G 6
Guandacol, 1,255 ....C 2
Guardia Mitre, 746 ....D 5
Guatrache, 1,259 ....D 4
Guaymallén, 85,718 ....C 3
Hasenkamp, 1,789 ....F 5
Helvecia, 3,390 ....F 5
Hernández, 283 ....F 6
Hernando, 4,869 ....D 3
Herradura, 1,679 ....E 2
Herrera, 1,685 ....D 2
Huinca Renancó, 4,391 ....D 3
Humahuaca, 2,530 ....C 1
Humberto, 3,434 ....F 5
Ibarreta, 4,366 ....D 2
Ibicuy, 3,356 ....G 6
Icaño, Catamarca, 1,114 ....C 2
Icaño, Santiago del Estero,
1,926 ....D 2
Iglesia, 575 ....C 3
Ingeniero Huergo, 3,083 ....C 4
Ingeniero Jacobacci, 2,656 ....C 5
Ingeniero Luiggi, 1,665 ....D 4
Intendente Alvear, 2,760 ......D 4
Irigoyen, 3,500 ....F 6
Itacaruaré, 422 ....F 2
Jáchal, 6,886 ....C 3
Jaramillo, 437 ....C 6
Jesús María, 6,284 ....D 3
Joaquín V. González, 3,274 ......D 2
Jobson, 7,667 ....F 5
José de San Martín, 1,143 .....B 5
José M. Micheo, 1,165 ....G 7
Juan B. Arruabarrena,
1,997 ....G 5
Juan B. Molino, 1,483 ....F 6
Juan Ortíz, 6,240 ....F 6
Juan Pujol, 625 ....G 5
Juárez, 7,602 ....D 4
Jujuy, 44,188 ....C 1
Juncal, 943 ....F 6
Junín, 36,149 ....F 7
Junín de los Andes, 1,183 .....B 4
La Banda, 23,772 ....D 2
Labougle, 503 ....G 5
Laboulaye, 9,032 ....D 3
La Clarita, 389 ....G 5
La Cumbre, 3,961 ....C 3
La Esmeralda, 348 ....G 5
La Falda, 2,847 ....D 3
La Gallareta, 3,736 ....F 5
Lago Argentino (El Calafate),
567 ....B 7
Laguna Paiva, 7,196 ....F 5
Lanús, 381,561 ....H 7
La Paz, Entre Ríos, 11,028 ....G 5
La Paz, Mendoza, 2,502 ....C 3
La Plata, †330,310 ....H 7
La Quiaca, 6,290 ....C 1
La Rioja, 35,431 ....C 2
Las Flores, 9,287 ....E 4
Las Lajas, 1,805 ....B 4
Las Lomitas, 1,650 ....D 1
Las Palmas, 3,590 ....E 2
Las Parejas, 1,973 ....F 6
Las Plumas, 182 ....C 5
Las Rosas, 6,153 ....F 6
Las Varillas, 5,950 ....D 3
La Toma, 2,352 ....C 3
Lavalle, 1,571 ....G 4
Leleque, 401 ....B 5
Lezama, 1,962 ....H 7
Libertador General San Martín,
Jujuy, 5,051 ....D 1
Libertador General San Martín,
Misiones, 2,267 ....E 2
Lincoln, 12,695 ....F 7
Lobería, 7,916 ....E 4
Lobos, 8,372 ....G 7
Lomas de Zamora, †275,219 .....G 7
Loncopué, 856 ....B 4
Los Antiguos, 709 ....B 6
Los Menucos, 1,749 ....C 5
Los Toldos, 5,342 ....F 7
Lucas González, 1,145 ....G 6
Luján, 19,176 ....G 7
Lules, 4,828 ....C 2
Macachín, 1,793 ....D 4
Maciel, 1,832 ....F 6
Magdalena, 4,114 ....H 7
Maipú, 5,469 ....E 4
Makallé, 1,462 ....E 2
Malabrigo, 1,532 ....F 4
Malargüe, 4,523 ....C 4
Manucho, 2,800 ....F 5
Maquinchao, 1,851 ....C 5
Mar del Plata, 141,886 ....E 4
Marcos Juárez, 9,556 ....D 3
Marcos Paz, 4,115 ....G 7
Margarita, 1,461 ....F 5
María Grande, 2,819 ....F 5
Mburucuyá, 2,555 ....E 2
Médanos, Buenos Aires,
2,229 ....D 4
Médanos, Entre Ríos, 647 ......G 6
Mencué, 208 ....C 5
Mendoza, 109,122 ....C 3
Mercedes, Buenos Aires,
16,932 ....G 7

(continued on following page)

Mercedes, Corrientes, 13,368 ....G 4
Mercedes, San Luis, 35,449 ....C 3
Merlo, 8,385 ....G 7
Metán, 12,849 ....D 2
Milagro, 1,967 ....C 3
Miñones, 204 ....G 5
Miramar (General Alvarado), 3,537 ....E 4
Moisés Ville, 3,166 ....E 5
Molinos, 174 ....C 2
Monte, 2,491 ....G 7
Monte Caseros, 12,930 ....G 5
Monte Comán, 4,278 ....C 3
Monte Quemado, 4,083 ....D 2
Monteros, 11,938 ....C 2
Monteros, 5,993 ....D 3
Mosconi, 333 ....F 7
Naré, 346 ....F 5
Navarro, 2,547 ....G 7
Necochea, 17,808 ....E 4
Nelson, 866 ....F 5
Neuquén, 16,738 ....C 4
Niquivil, 1,301 ....C 3
Nogoyá, 10,911 ....F 6
Norberto de la Riestra, 2,809 ....G 7
Norquincó, 602 ....B 5
Nueve (9) de Julio, 13,678 ....F 7
Obera, 12,322 ....F 2
Olavarría, 24,204 ....D 4
Oliva, 8,701 ....D 3
Olta, 1,226 ....C 3
Orán, 14,286 ....D 1
Ordoqui, 402 ....F 7
Palo Santo, 1,123 ....E 2
Pampa del Chañar, 1,521 ....C 2
Pampa del Infierno, 1,261 ....D 2
Paraná, 107,551 ....F 5
Paso de Indios, 1,067 ....C 5
Paso de los Libres, 15,054 ....E 2
Patquía, 839 ....C 3
Paz, 2,495 ....F 6
Pedernal, 250 ....G 5
Pehuajó, 13,537 ....D 4
Pellegrini, 2,310 ....D 4
Pérez, 3,433 ....F 6
Pergamino, 32,382 ....F 6
Perito Moreno, 1,587 ....B 6
Perugorria, 1,110 ....G 4
Pico Truncado, 1,527 ....C 6
Pigüé, 5,869 ....D 4
Pila, 1,009 ....H 7
Pilar, 2,508 ....F 5
Pipinas, 658 ....H 7
Pirané, 5,285 ....E 2
Plaza Huincul, 4,906 ....B 4
Pomán, 1,100 ....C 2
Posadas, 70,691 ....E 2
Pozo Hondo, 872 ....C 2
Presidencia de la Plaza, 4,568 ....D 2
Presidencia Roque Sáenz Peña, 14,381 ....D 2
Puán, 3,191 ....D 4
Puerto Coyle, 251 ....C 7
Puerto Deseado, 3,120 ....D 6
Puerto Madryn, 5,586 ....C 5
Puerto Pirámides, 425 ....D 5
Punta Alta, 19,852 ....D 4
Quebracho Coto, 271 ....D 2

Quemú-Quemú, 2,735 ....D 4
Quequén, 4,760 ....E 4
Quimilí, 2,902 ....D 2
Quines, 3,319 ....C 3
Quiroga, 1,827 ....F 7
Quitilipi, 5,217 ....D 2
Rafaela, 23,665 ....F 5
Raíces, 452 ....G 6
Ramallo, 4,824 ....F 6
Ranchos, 2,475 ....H 7
Rauch, 5,274 ....E 4
Rawson, Buenos Aires, 2,425 ....F 7
Rawson, Chubut, 4,109 ....D 5
Reconquista, 12,729 ....D 2
Recreo, 2,834 ....C 2
Resistencia, 84,036 ....E 2
Rigby, 737 ....F 6
Rinconada, 782 ....C 1
Río Colorado, Río Negro, 5,892 ....D 4
Río Cuarto, 48,706 ....D 3
Río Gallegos, 14,439 ....C 7
Río Grande, 5,103 ....C 7
Río Segundo, 5,873 ....C 3
Río Tercero, 10,683 ....D 3
Rivadavia, Mendoza, 14,358 ....C 3
Rivadavia, Salta, 215 ....D 1
Rivas, 429 ....F 7
Rojas, 6,608 ....F 6
Roldán, 3,402 ....F 6
Romang, 1,906 ....F 4
Roque Pérez, 2,841 ....G 7
Rosario, 1671,852 ....F 6
Rosario de la Frontera, 7,134 ....D 2
Rosario de Lerma, 4,241 ....C 2
Rosario del Tala, 7,350 ....G 6
Rufino, 10,987 ....D 3
Saforcada, 146 ....F 7
Saladas, 3,883 ....E 2
Saladillo, 7,586 ....G 7
Salta, 117,400 ....C 2
San Andrés de Giles, 5,392 ....G 7
San Antonio de Areco, 7,436 ....G 7
San Antonio de los Cobres, 1,439 ....C 1
San Antonio Oeste, 5,278 ....C 5
San Carlos, Corrientes, 1,858 ....E 2
San Carlos, Mendoza, 809 ....C 3
San Carlos, Santa Fe, 3,126 ....F 5
San Carlos de Bariloche, 15,995 ....B 5
San Cristóbal, 9,071 ....F 5
San Fernando, 191,644 ....G 7
San Francisco, Córdoba, 24,354 ....D 3
San Francisco del Chañar, 817 ....C 2
San Genaro, 2,821 ....F 5
San Ignacio, 2,106 ....E 2
San Isidro, 2,271 ....G 7
San Javier, Río Negro, 370 ....D 5
San Javier, Santa Fe, 2,961 ....F 5
San José, 2,188 ....C 2
San José de Feliciano, 3,721 ....G 5
San Juan, 106,564 ....C 3
San Julián, 3,649 ....C 7
San Justo, 6,571 ....F 5
San Lorenzo, 11,109 ....F 6
San Luis, 40,420 ....C 3

San Martín, 20,466 ....C 3
San Martín de los Andes, 4,567 ....B 5
San Martín Norte, 485 ....F 5
San Miguel, 1,300 ....G 2
San Nicolás, 25,029 ....F 6
San Pedro, Buenos Aires, 12,778 ....F 6
San Pedro, Jujuy, 15,354 ....D 1
San Rafael, 46,599 ....C 3
San Salvador, 2,108 ....G 6
San Sebastián, 13,154 ....C 7
Santa Catalina, 331 ....C 1
Santa Clara, 3,700 ....F 6
Santa Cruz, 1,178 ....C 7
Santa Elena, 8,174 ....F 5
Santa Fe, 1259,560 ....F 5
Santa Lucia, Buenos Aires, 1,831 ....
Santa Lucía, Corrientes, 2,930 ....E 2
Santa María, 2,826 ....C 2
Santa Rosa, Córdoba, 2,999 ....D 3
Santa Rosa, La Pampa, 14,623 ....C 4
Santa Rosa, San Luis, 2,880 ....C 3
Santa Victoria, 165 ....D 1
Santiago del Estero, 80,395 ....D 2
Santo Tomé, Corrientes, 10,121 ....E 2
Santo Tomé Santa Fe, 4,446 ....F 5
San Urbano, 1,721 ....F 6
Sarmiento, 4,922 ....C 6
Sauce, 3,448 ....G 5
Sauce Luna, 501 ....G 6
Seguí, 2,161 ....G 6
Selva, 1,070 ....D 2
Sierra Colorada, 541 ....C 5
Sierra Grande, 512 ....C 5
Solari, 1,636 ....G 4
Soledad, 794 ....F 5
Suipacha, 3,006 ....G 7
Sunchales, 5,048 ....E 2
Suncho Corral, 2,693 ....D 2
Susana, 484 ....F 5
Susques, 537 ....C 1
Tafí Viejo, 21,197 ....C 2
Tamberías, 1,129 ....C 3
Tandil, 32,309 ....E 4
Tapalqué, 3,018 ....D 4
Tartagal, 16,740 ....D 1
Telsen, 490 ....C 5
Tigre, 191,824 ....G 7
Tilcara, 1,675 ....D 1
Tinogasta, 3,557 ....C 2
Tintina, 1,500 ....D 2
Toay, 2,457 ....D 4
Tornquist, 2,782 ....D 4
Tostado, 5,234 ....D 2
Trelew, 11,852 ....C 5
Trenel, 1,242 ....D 4
Trenque Lauquen, 10,887 ....D 4
Tres Arroyos, 29,996 ....D 4
Tres Lomas, 3,425 ....D 4
Trevelin, 1,542 ....B 5
Tricao Malal, 370 ....B 4
Tucumán, 271,546 ....C 2
Tunuyán, 9,781 ....C 3
Ulapes, 438 ....C 3
Unión, 6,571 ....F 5
Urdinarrain, 3,484 ....G 6
Ushuaia, 4,950 ....C 7

Valcheta, 1,697 ....C 5
Valle Fértil, 1,293 ....C 3
Vedia, 3,676 ....F 7
Veinticinco (25) de Mayo, 9,063 ....F 7
Venado Tuerto, 15,947 ....D 3
Vergara, 1,077 ....H 7
Verónica, 2,405 ....H 7
Victoria, 15,108 ....F 6
Victorica, 2,475 ....C 4
Vicuña Mackenna, 3,032 ....D 3
Viedma, 7,253 ....D 5
Villa Ana, 5,413 ....E 2
Villa Ángela, 18,518 ....D 2
Villa Atamisqui, 1,122 ....C 2
Villa Atuel, 6,072 ....C 3
Villa Bustos, 1,314 ....C 2
Villa Cañas, 7,099 ....F 6
Villa Clara, 1,557 ....G 5
Villa Constitución, 9,183 ....F 6
Villa del Rosario, 4,461 ....D 2
Villa Dolores, 13,835 ....C 2
Villa Domínguez, 984 ....G 6
Villa Elisa, 2,715 ....G 6
Villa Federal, 5,256 ....F 5
Villa General Ramírez, 3,203 ....F 6
Villa General Roca, 325 ....G 5
Villaguay, 12,463 ....G 5
Villa Guillermina, 7,471 ....F 5
Villa Hernandarias, 2,788 ....F 5
Villalonga, 3,004 ....D 5
Villa Larroque, 1,993 ....G 6
Villa Mantero, 989 ....G 6
Villa María, 30,362 ....D 3
Villa Ocampo, 4,897 ....C 2
Villa Ojo de Agua, 1,505 ....D 2
Villa Regina, 11,360 ....C 4
Villa San Martín, 3,354 ....C 2
Villa Unión, 1,696 ....C 2
Vinchina, 395 ....C 2
Winifreda, 1,063 ....D 4
Yacimiento Río Turbio, 3,506 ....B 7
Yofré, 826 ....D 2
Zapala, 7,497 ....B 4
Zárate, 35,197 ....G 6
Zavalla, 1,799 ....F 6

OTHER FEATURES

Aconcagua (mt.) ....C 3
Alerces, Los (park) ....B 5
Andes (mts.) ....C 2
Argentino (lake) ....B 7
Arizaro (salt dep.) ....C 2
Arrecifes (river) ....C 7
Atacama, Puna de (reg.) ....C 2
Atuel (river) ....C 4
Barrancas (river) ....B 4
Bermejo (river) ....G 2
Blanca (bay) ....D 4
Brazo Sur (river) ....E 1
Buenos Aires (lake) ....B 6
Campanario (river) ....C 4
Chaco Austral (reg.) ....D 2
Chaco Central (reg.) ....D 1
Chato (mt.) ....B 5
Chico (river) ....C 6
Chico (river) ....C 6

Chubut (river) ....C 5
Colhué Huapí (lake) ....C 6
Colorado (river) ....D 4
Cónico (mt.) ....B 5
Corrientes (river) ....E 2
Coyle (river) ....B 7
Cuarto (river) ....D 3
Delgada (point) ....D 5
Desaguadero (river) ....C 3
Deseado (river) ....C 6
Diamante (river) ....C 3
Domuyo (vol.) ....B 4
Dos Bahías (cape) ....D 5
Dulce (river) ....D 2
El Chocón (river) ....C 4
Estados (isl.) ....D 7
Fagnano (lake) ....C 7
Famatina (mts.) ....C 2
Feliciano (river) ....G 5
Flores, Las (river) ....G 7
Gallegos (river) ....B 7
General Manuel Belgrano (mt.) ....C 2
Glaciares, Los (park) ....B 6
Gran Chaco (reg.) ....D 1
Grande (bay) ....C 7
Grande (falls) ....G 5
Grande (river) ....C 3
Gualeguay (river) ....G 6
Guayquiraró (river) ....G 5
Iguazú (falls) ....F 2
Iguazú (park) ....E 2
Incahuasi (mt.) ....B 4
Lanín (mt.) ....B 4
Lanín (park) ....B 4
Lanín (vol.) ....B 4
Laudo (mt.) ....C 2
Lechiguanas (isls.) ....G 6
Lennox (isl.) ....C 8
Limay (river) ....C 4
Llancanelo (lag.) ....C 4
Llullaillaco (mt.) ....C 2
Magallanes (Magellan) (str.) ....C 7
Maipo (vol.) ....C 4
Mar Chiquita (lake) ....D 3
Martín García (isl.), 1,575 ....H 7
Mendoza (river) ....C 3
Mercedario (mt.) ....B 3
Mogotes (point) ....E 4
Montemayor (plateau) ....C 5
Murallón (mt.) ....B 6
Nahuel Huapi (lake) ....B 5
Nahuel Huapi (park) ....B 5
Negro (river) ....D 4
Neuquén (river) ....C 4
Ninfas (point) ....D 5
Norte (point) ....D 5

Norte del Cabo San Antonio (point) ....
Nuevo (gulf) ....D 5
Ojos del Salado (mt.) ....
Olivares (mt.) ....
Pampa de las Tres Hermanas (plain) ....
Pampas (plain) ....
Paraná (river) ....
Patagonia (reg.) ....
Peteroa (vol.) ....
Pilcomayo (river) ....
Pissis (mt.) ....
Plata, Río de la (est.) ....
Pueyrredón (lake) ....
Puna de Atacama (reg.) ....
Quinto (river) ....
Rincón (mt.) ....
Saladillo (river) ....
Salado (river) ....
Salado (river) ....
Salado del Norte (river) ....
Sali (river) ....
Salto (river) ....
Samborombón (bay) ....
San Antonio (cape) ....
San Diego (cape) ....
San Jorge (gulf) ....
San Juan (river) ....
San Lorenzo (mt.) ....
San Martín (lake) ....
San Matías (gulf) ....
Santa Cruz (river) ....
Senguerr (river) ....
Staten (Estados) (isl.) ....
Sur del Cabo San Antonio (point) ....
Tarija (river) ....
Tercero (river) ....
Teuco (river) ....
Tierra del Fuego, Isla Grande de (isl.), 10,620 ....
Toro (mt.) ....
Tres Picos (mt.) ....
Tres Puntas (cape) ....
Trinidad (isl.) ....
Tronador (mt.) ....
Tunuyán (river) ....
Tupungato (mt.) ....
Uruguay (river) ....
Valdés (pen.) ....
Vallimanca (river) ....
Viedma (lake) ....
Zapaleri (mt.) ....

*City and suburbs.
†Population of department.

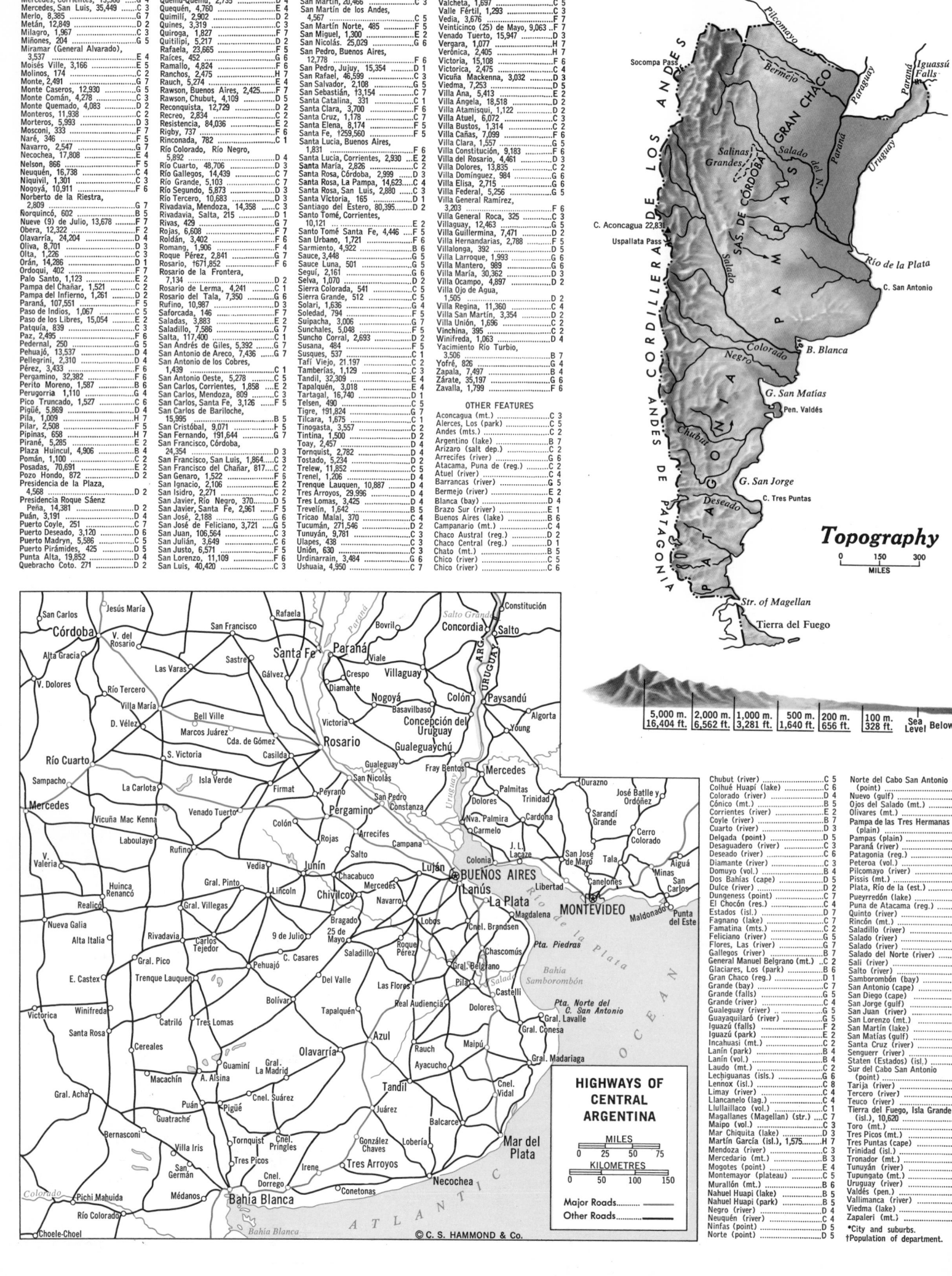

Topography

0   150   300
MILES

| 5,000 m. 16,404 ft. | 2,000 m. 6,562 ft. | 1,000 m. 3,281 ft. | 500 m. 1,640 ft. | 200 m. 656 ft. | 100 m. 328 ft. | Sea Level | Below |

HIGHWAYS OF CENTRAL ARGENTINA

MILES
0   25   50   75

KILOMETRES
0   50   100   150

Major Roads ....
Other Roads ....

© C. S. HAMMOND & Co.

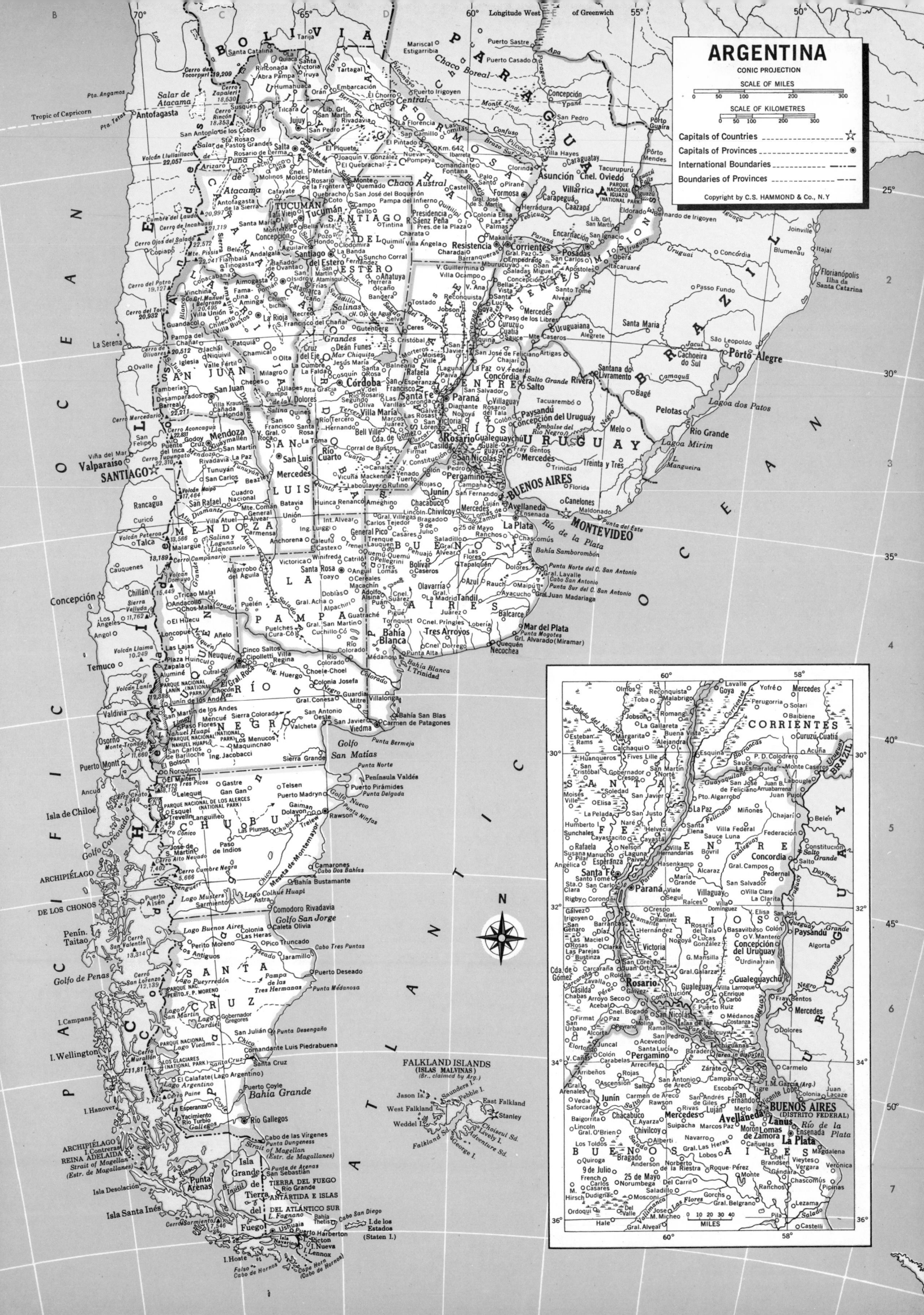

ARGENTINA
CONIC PROJECTION

SCALE OF MILES

SCALE OF KILOMETRES

Capitals of Countries .... ☆
Capitals of Provinces .... ◉
International Boundaries ....
Boundaries of Provinces ....

Copyright by C.S. Hammond & Co., N.Y

CORRIENTES

FALKLAND ISLANDS
(ISLAS MALVINAS)
(Br. claimed by Arg.)

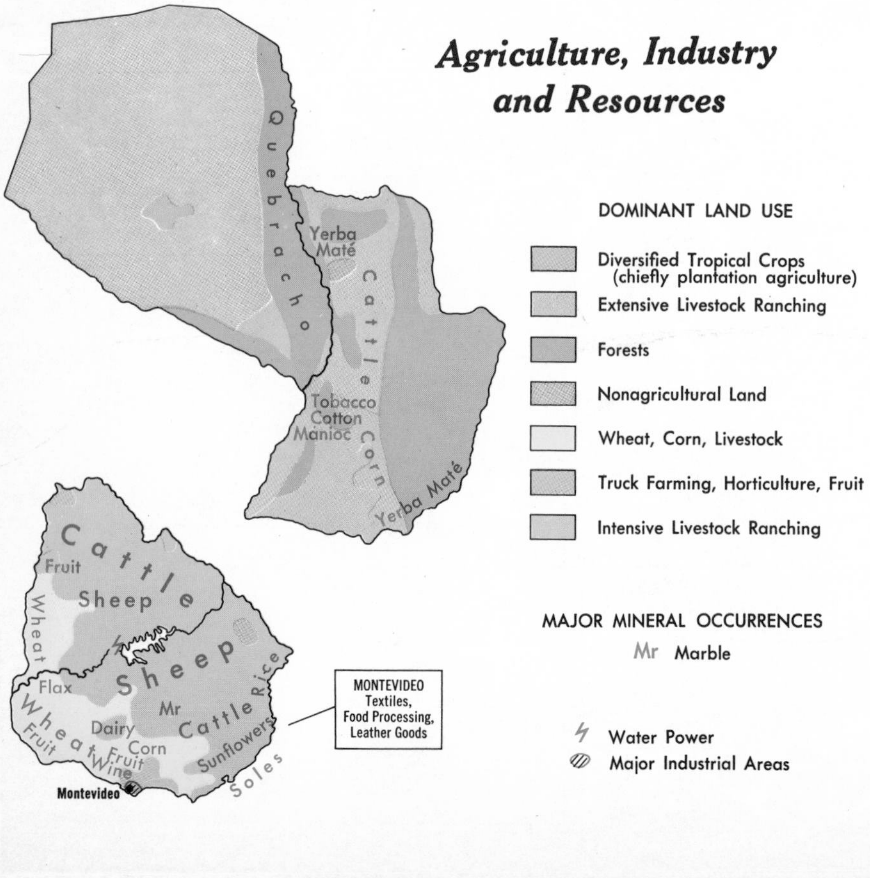

PARAGUAY

DEPARTMENTS

Agriculture, Industry and Resources

DOMINANT LAND USE

Diversified Tropical Crops (chiefly plantation agriculture)

Extensive Livestock Ranching

Forests

Nonagricultural Land

Wheat, Corn, Livestock

Truck Farming, Horticulture, Fruit

Intensive Livestock Ranching

MAJOR MINERAL OCCURRENCES

Mr Marble

MONTEVIDEO
Textiles,
Food Processing,
Leather Goods

Water Power

Major Industrial Areas

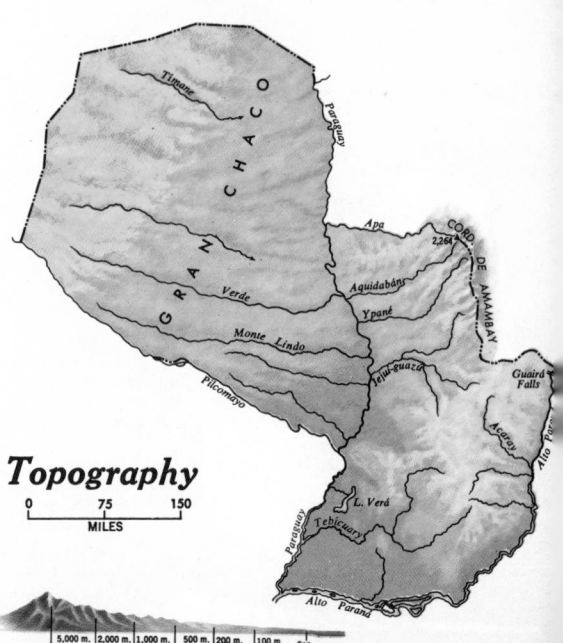

Topography

0 75 150
MILES

5,000 m. 2,000 m. 1,000 m. 500 m. 200 m. 100 m. Sea
16,404 ft. 6,562 ft. 3,281 ft. 1,640 ft. 656 ft. 328 ft. Level Below

URUGUAY

DEPARTMENTS

CITIES and TOWNS

OTHER FEATURES

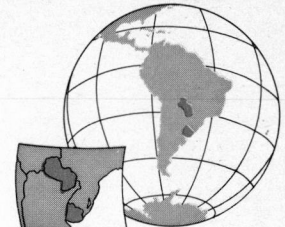

PARAGUAY

AREA 157,047 sq. mi.
POPULATION 2,314,000
CAPITAL Asunción
LARGEST CITY Asunción
HIGHEST POINT Amambay Range 2,264 ft.
MONETARY UNIT guaraní
MAJOR LANGUAGES Spanish, Guaraní
MAJOR RELIGION Roman Catholicism

URUGUAY

AREA 72,172 sq. mi.
POPULATION 2,900,000
CAPITAL Montevideo
LARGEST CITY Montevideo
HIGHEST POINT Mirador Nacional 1,644 ft.
MONETARY UNIT Uruguayan peso
MAJOR LANGUAGE Spanish
MAJOR RELIGION Roman Catholicism

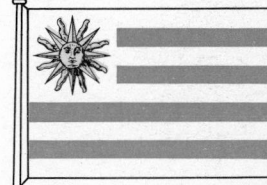

*City and suburbs.
†Population of district.

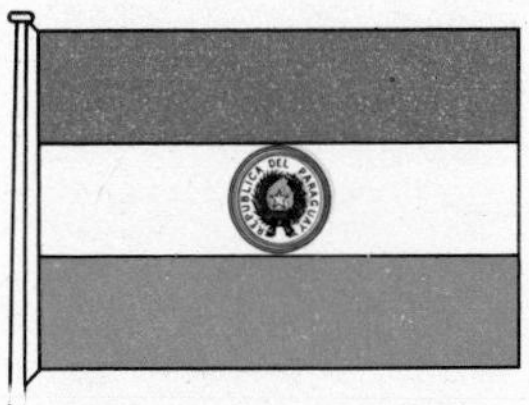

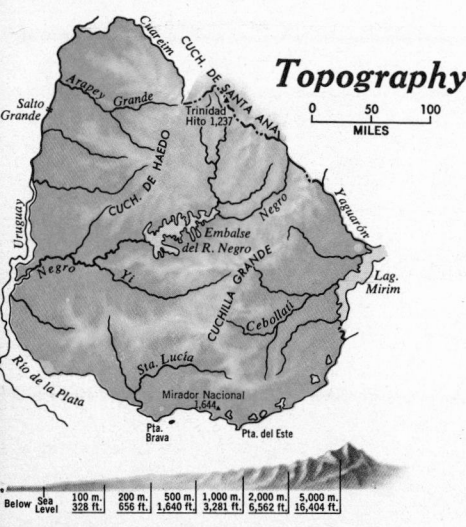

Topography
0 50 100
MILES
Cuareim
CUCH. DE SANTA ANA
Arapey Grande
Salto Grande
Trinidad Hito 1,237
CUCH. DE HAEDO
Uruguay
Yaguarón
Negro
Embalse del R. Negro
Negro
Yí
CUCHILLA GRANDE
Cebollatí
Lag. Mirim
Sta. Lucía
Río de la Plata
Mirador Nacional 1,644
Pta. Brava
Pta. del Este
Below Sea Level
100 m. 328 ft.
200 m. 656 ft.
500 m. 1,640 ft.
1,000 m. 3,281 ft.
2,000 m. 6,562 ft.
5,000 m. 16,404 ft.

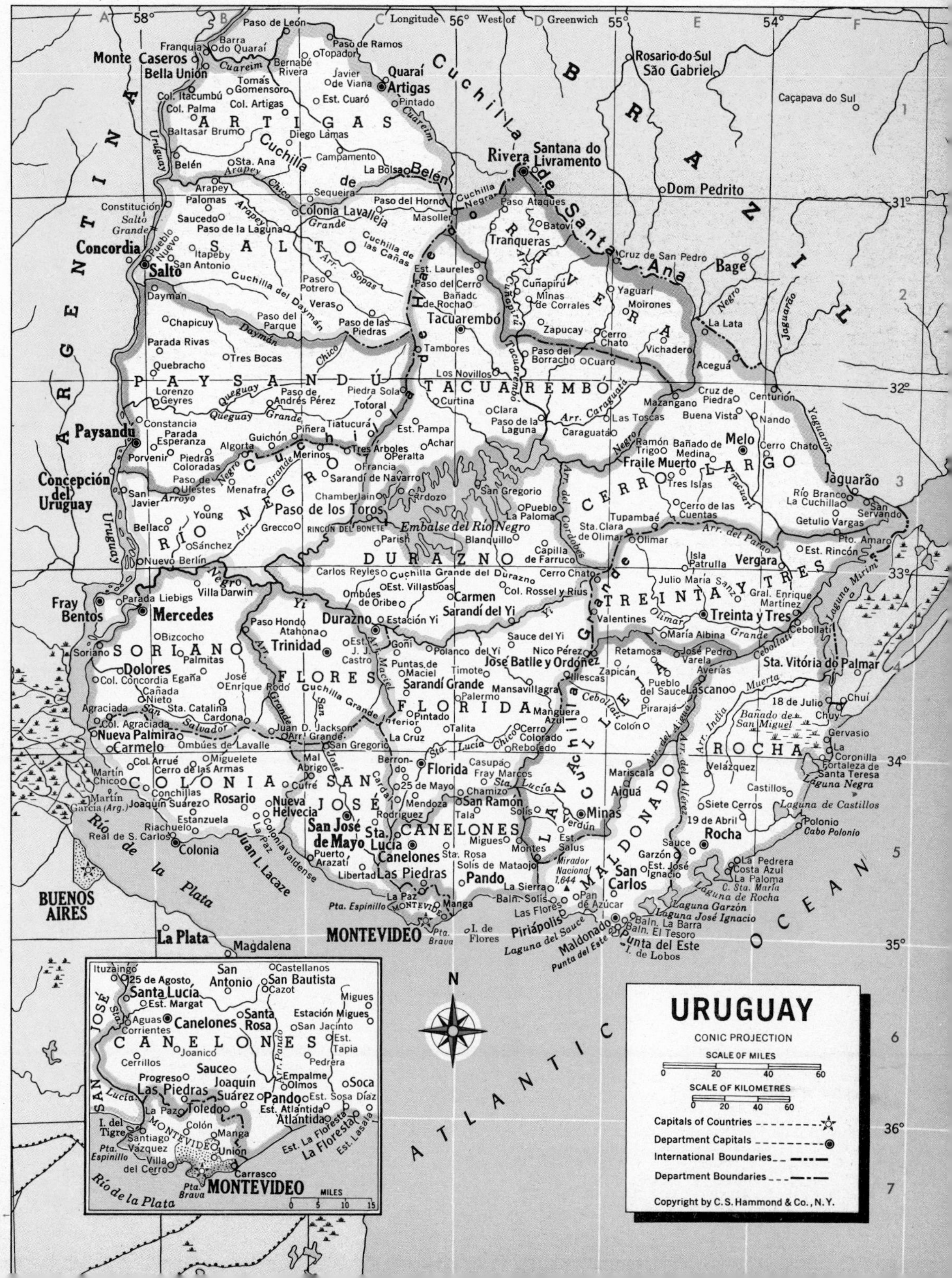

URUGUAY
CONIC PROJECTION
SCALE OF MILES
0 20 40 60
SCALE OF KILOMETRES
0 20 40 60
Capitals of Countries
Department Capitals
International Boundaries
Department Boundaries
Copyright by C.S. Hammond & Co., N.Y.
Longitude 56° West of Greenwich
ARGENTINA
BRAZIL
ATLANTIC OCEAN
ARTIGAS
SALTO
PAYSANDÚ
RÍO NEGRO
SORIANO
COLONIA
SAN JOSÉ
FLORES
FLORIDA
DURAZNO
TACUAREMBÓ
RIVERA
CERRO LARGO
TREINTA Y TRES
LAVALLEJA
CANELONES
MALDONADO
ROCHA
MONTEVIDEO
BUENOS AIRES
La Plata
Río de la Plata

NORTH AMERICA

LAMBERT AZIMUTHAL EQUAL-AREA PROJECTION

SCALE OF MILES
0 100 200   400   600   800

SCALE OF KILOMETRES
0   200   400   600   800

Capitals of Countries .... ☆
International Boundaries .... ▬ ▬ ▬
Other Boundaries .... ▬ ▬ ▬
Canals ....

© C.S. HAMMOND & CO., N.Y.

POPULATION DISTRIBUTION

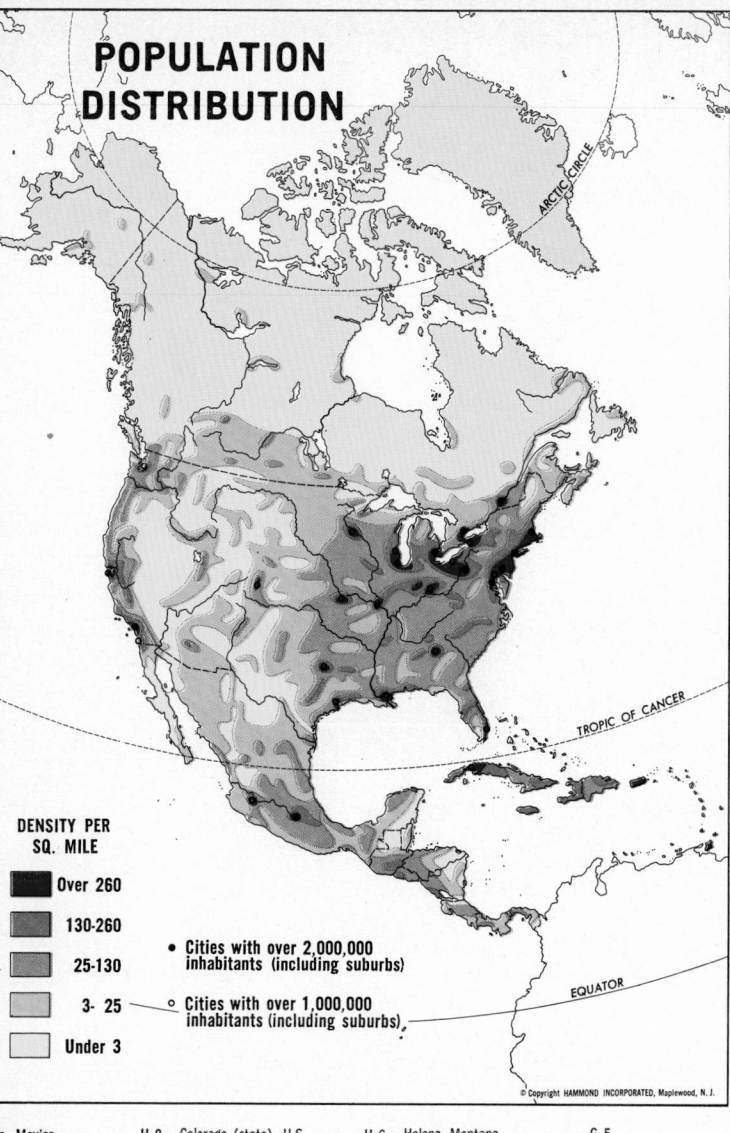

AREA 9,363,000 sq. mi.
POPULATION 314,000,000
LARGEST CITY New York
HIGHEST POINT Mt. McKinley 20,320 ft
LOWEST POINT Death Valley -282 ft.

DENSITY PER SQ. MILE

- Over 260
- 130-260
- 25-130
- 3- 25
- Under 3

• Cities with over 2,000,000 inhabitants (including suburbs)
○ Cities with over 1,000,000 inhabitants (including suburbs)

© Copyright HAMMOND INCORPORATED, Maplewood, N. J.

VEGETATION

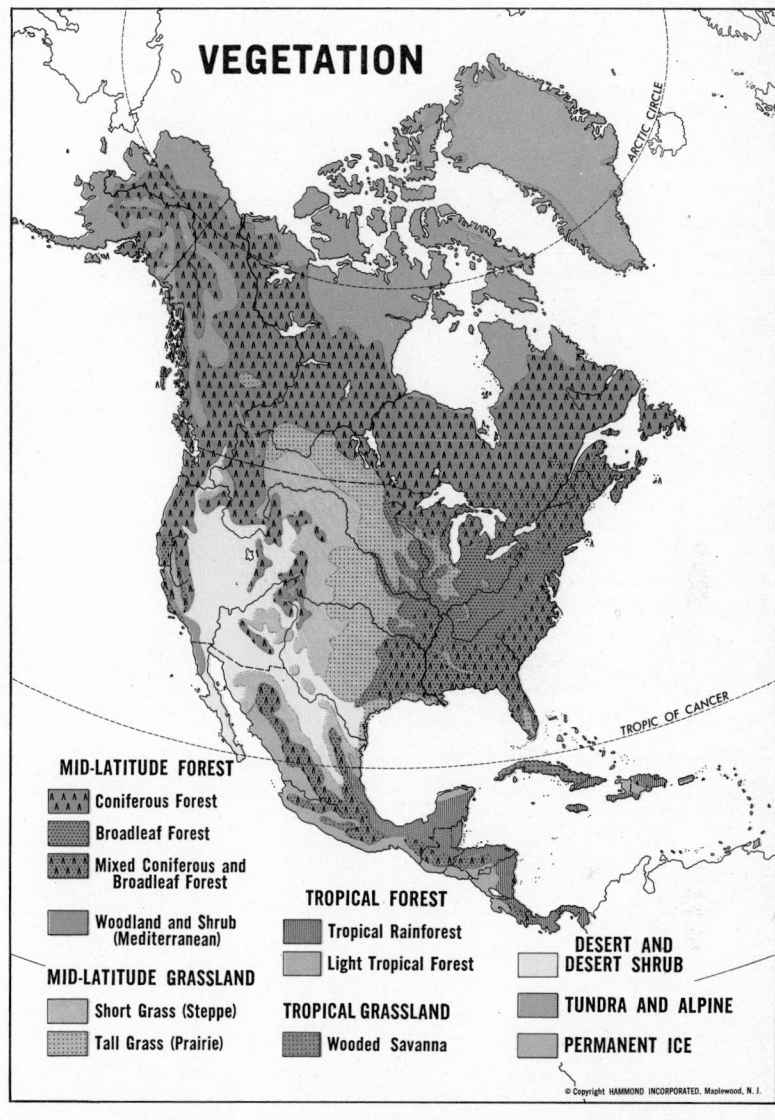

MID-LATITUDE FOREST
- Coniferous Forest
- Broadleaf Forest
- Mixed Coniferous and Broadleaf Forest
- Woodland and Shrub (Mediterranean)

MID-LATITUDE GRASSLAND
- Short Grass (Steppe)
- Tall Grass (Prairie)

TROPICAL FOREST
- Tropical Rainforest
- Light Tropical Forest

TROPICAL GRASSLAND
- Wooded Savanna

DESERT AND DESERT SHRUB

TUNDRA AND ALPINE

PERMANENT ICE

© Copyright HAMMOND INCORPORATED, Maplewood, N. J.

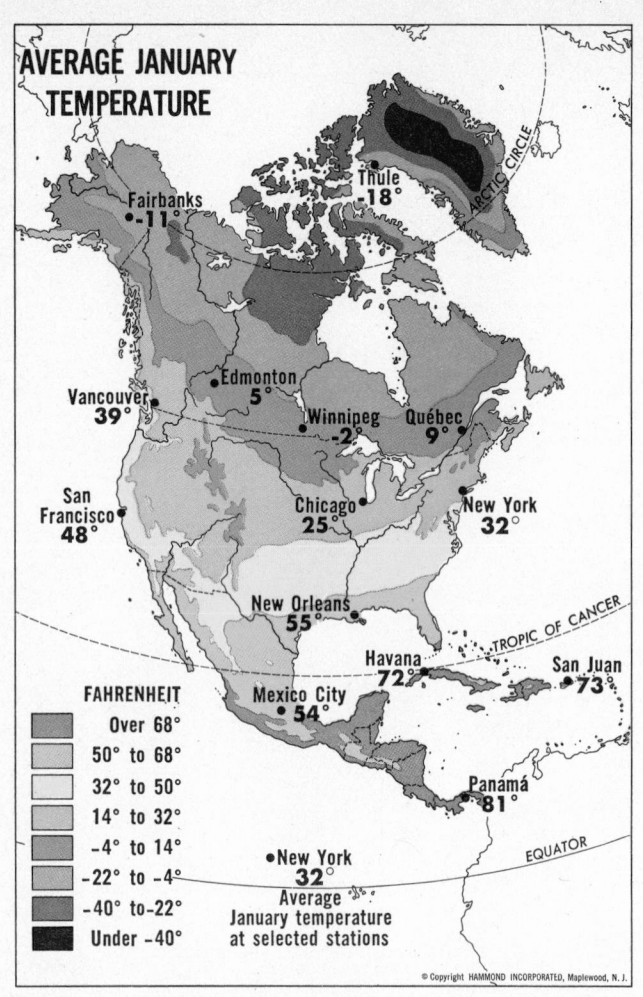

AVERAGE JANUARY TEMPERATURE

Fairbanks -11°
Thule -18°
Edmonton 5°
Vancouver 39°
Winnipeg -2°
Québec 9°
San Francisco 48°
Chicago 25°
New York 32°
New Orleans 55°
Havana 72°
San Juan 73°
Mexico City 54°
Panamá 81°

TROPIC OF CANCER
ARCTIC CIRCLE
EQUATOR

FAHRENHEIT

	Over 68°
	50° to 68°
	32° to 50°
	14° to 32°
	-4° to 14°
	-22° to -4°
	-40° to -22°
	Under -40°

• New York
32°
Average
January temperature
at selected stations

© Copyright HAMMOND INCORPORATED, Maplewood, N.J.

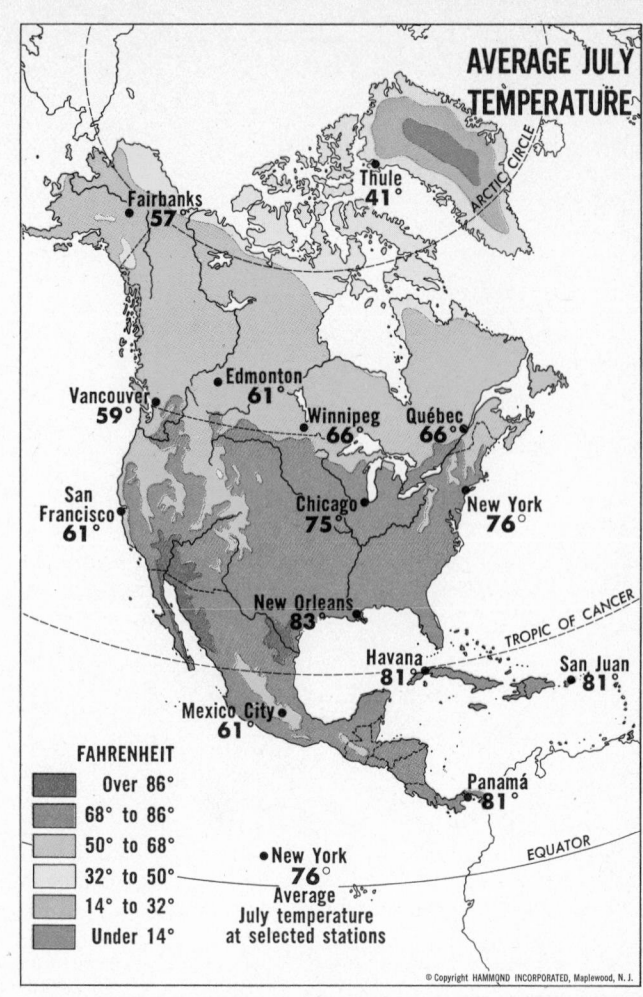

AVERAGE JULY TEMPERATURE

Fairbanks 57°
Thule 41°
Edmonton 61°
Vancouver 59°
Winnipeg 66°
Québec 66°
San Francisco 61°
Chicago 75°
New York 76°
New Orleans 83°
Havana 81°
San Juan 81°
Mexico City 61°
Panamá 81°

TROPIC OF CANCER
ARCTIC CIRCLE
EQUATOR

FAHRENHEIT

	Over 86°
	68° to 86°
	50° to 68°
	32° to 50°
	14° to 32°
	Under 14°

• New York
76°
Average
July temperature
at selected stations

© Copyright HAMMOND INCORPORATED, Maplewood, N.J.

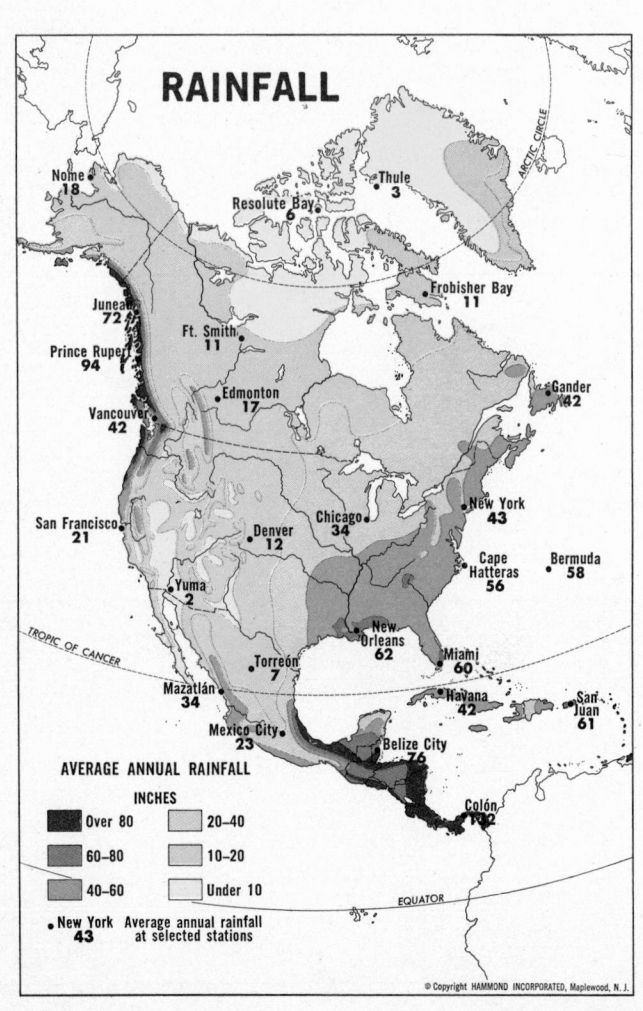

RAINFALL

Nome 18
Thule 3
Resolute Bay 6
Frobisher Bay 11
Juneau 72
Ft. Smith 11
Prince Rupert 94
Edmonton 17
Gander 42
Vancouver 42
San Francisco 21
Denver 12
Chicago 34
New York 43
Yuma 2
Cape Hatteras 56
Bermuda 58
New Orleans 62
Miami 60
Torreón 7
Mazatlán 34
Havana 42
San Juan 61
Mexico City 23
Belize City 76
Colón 122

ARCTIC CIRCLE
TROPIC OF CANCER
EQUATOR

AVERAGE ANNUAL RAINFALL
INCHES

	Over 80		20–40
	60–80		10–20
	40–60		Under 10

• New York   Average annual rainfall
43   at selected stations

© Copyright HAMMOND INCORPORATED, Maplewood, N.J.

VEGETATION/RELIEF

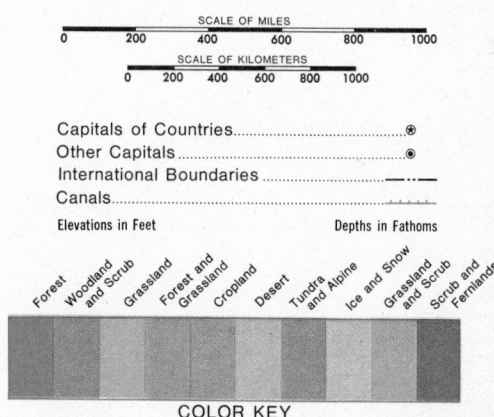

SCALE OF MILES
0   200   400   600   800   1000

SCALE OF KILOMETERS
0   200   400   600   800   1000

Capitals of Countries	⊛
Other Capitals	⊙
International Boundaries	—·—·—
Canals	

Elevations in Feet   Depths in Fathoms

Forest | Woodland and Scrub | Grassland | Forest and Grassland | Cropland | Desert | Tundra and Alpine | Ice and Snow | Grassland | Scrub and Farmlands

COLOR KEY

ASIA
U.S.S.R.

EAST SIBERIAN SEA

ARCTIC OCEAN

North Pole

GREENLAND SEA

GREENLAND (Den.)

ICELAND
Reykjavik

BERING SEA

Bering Strait

St. Lawrence I.

BEAUFORT SEA

Queen Elizabeth Islands

Banks I.

Melville I.

Devon I.

Baffin Bay

Arctic Circle

Denmark Strait

Alaska Pen.

Nome

Pt. Barrow

Kotzebue

Alaska Range

Anchorage

Juneau

Gulf of Alaska

Kodiak I.

Victoria I.

Great Bear L.

Mackenzie

Great Slave L.

Yellowknife

Laurentian

C. Farewell

Gothaab

Davis Strait

LABRADOR SEA

C. Chidley

Ungava Peninsula

Labrador Plateau

Smallwood Res.

Churchill

Newfoundland

Gander

St. John's

C. Race

Prince Rupert

Queen Charlotte Is.

Alexander Arch.

CANADA

Peace

L. Athabasca

Athabasca

North

Edmonton

Saskatchewan

Saskatoon

Calgary

South

Regina

Churchill

Nelson

L. Winnipeg

Albany

Hudson Bay

James Bay

Eastmain

Plateau

Appalachian

Gulf of St. Lawrence

Cape Breton I.

Quebec

St. Lawrence

St. John

Halifax

Vancouver I.

Victoria

Vancouver

Seattle

Winnipeg

Thunder Bay

Duluth

L. Superior

Sudbury

Montreal

Ottawa

Toronto

Boston

C. Cod

PACIFIC OCEAN

Portland

Missouri

Red

Minneapolis

Mississippi

Milwaukee

L. Michigan

L. Huron

Detroit

L. Erie

Cleveland

Buffalo

L. Ontario

Pittsburgh

New York

Philadelphia

Washington

San Francisco

C. Mendocino

Sierra Nevada

Rockies

Great Salt Lake

Salt Lake City

Mt. Whitney

Denver

Pikes Peak

South Platte

North Platte

Omaha

Chicago

Indianapolis

Cincinnati

Columbus

Ohio

Norfolk

C. Hatteras

Bermuda (U.K.)

Las Vegas

Great Basin

Colorado

UNITED STATES

Kansas City

St. Louis

Arkansas

Wichita

Nashville

Tennessee

Mt. Mitchell

Charlotte

Los Angeles

San Diego

Phoenix

Tucson

Albuquerque

Oklahoma City

Tulsa

Ozark Plateau

Memphis

Birmingham

Atlanta

El Paso

Ciudad Juarez

Rio Grande

Red

Fort Worth

Dallas

Jacksonville

C. Canaveral

Chihuahua

San Antonio

Houston

New Orleans

Tampa

Miami

BAHAMAS

Nassau

Tropic of Cancer

West Indies

Turks and Caicos Is. (U.K.)

Sierra Madre Occidental

Corpus Christi

Gulf of Mexico

C. San Lucas

Culiacan

Monterrey

Tampico

Bay of Campeche

Havana

CUBA

Santiago de Cuba

HAITI

Port-au-Prince

DOMINICAN REPUBLIC

Santo Domingo

San Juan

PUERTO RICO

Greater Antilles

Lower California

Gulf of California

Sierra Madre Oriental

MEXICO

Guadalajara

Mexico City

Popocatepetl 17,887

Veracruz

Acapulco

Merida

Yucatan Pen.

JAMAICA

Kingston

CARIBBEAN SEA

NETHERLANDS ANTILLES

Aruba

Curacao

Bonaire

Willemstad

GUATEMALA

Guatemala

BELIZE

HONDURAS

Tegucigalpa

San Salvador

EL SALVADOR

NICARAGUA

Managua

COSTA RICA

San Jose

CANAL ZONE

PANAMA

Barranquilla

Caracas

VENEZUELA

Bogota

COLOMBIA

SOUTH AMERICA

ATLANTIC OCEAN

© HAMMOND INCORPORATED, Maplewood, N.J.

Longitude 90° West of Greenwich

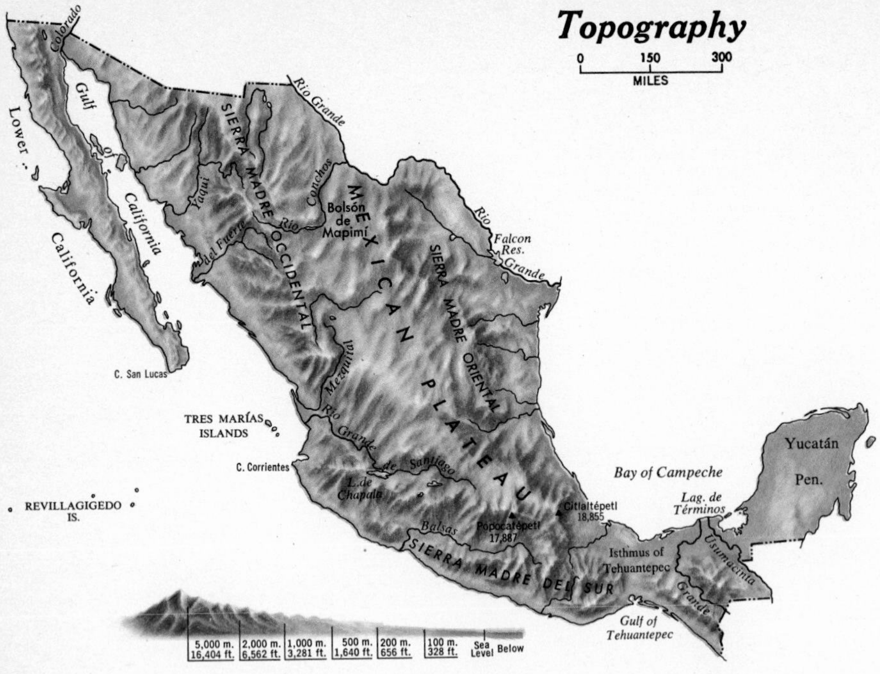

STATES and TERRITORIES

Aguascalientes, 334,936 ....H 6
Baja California Norte, 856,773 ....B 1
Baja California Sur, 123,786 ....C 3
Campeche, 250,391 ....O 7
Chiapas, 1,578,180 ....N 8
Chihuahua, 1,730,012 ....F 2
Coahuila, 1,140,989 ....H 3
Colima, 240,235 ....G 7
Distrito Federal, 7,005,855 ....L 1
Durango, 919,381 ....G 4
Guanajuato, 2,285,249 ....J 6
Guerrero, 1,573,098 ....J 8
Hidalgo, 1,156,177 ....K 6
Jalisco, 3,322,750 ....H 6
México, 3,797,861 ....K 7
Michoacán, 2,341,556 ....H 7
Morelos, 620,392 ....K 7
Nayarit, 547,992 ....G 6
Nuevo León, 1,653,808 ....K 4
Oaxaca, 2,011,946 ....L 8
Puebla, 2,483,770 ....L 7
Querétaro, 464,226 ....J 6
Quintana Roo, 91,044 ....P 7
San Luis Potosí, 1,257,028 ....J 5
Sinaloa, 1,273,228 ....F 4
Sonora, 1,092,458 ....D 2
Tabasco, 766,346 ....N 7
Tamaulipas, 1,438,350 ....K 4
Tlaxcala, 418,334 ....N 1
Veracruz, 3,813,613 ....L 7
Yucatán, 774,011 ....P 6
Zacatecas, 949,663 ....H 5

CITIES and TOWNS

Acámbaro, 80,259 ....J 7
Acaponeta, 29,829 ....G 5
Acapulco de Juárez, 234,866 ....J 8
Acatlán, 22,507 ....K 7
Acatzingo, 14,809 ....N 2
Acayucan, 36,352 ....M 8
Aconchi, 2,313 ....D 2
Actopan, 26,608 ....Q 1
Agualeguas, 5,536 ....J 3
Agua Prieta, 21,627 ....E 1
Aguascalientes, 222,105 ....H 6
Aguililla, 20,752 ....H 7
Ahuacatlán, 14,180 ....G 6
Ajalpan, 20,413 ....L 7
Alamos, 24,123 ....E 3
Aldama, Chihuahua, 14,117 ....G 2
Aldama, Tamaulipas, 15,336 ....L 5
Aljojuca, 5,520 ....O 1
Allende, Chihuahua, 11,039 ....G 3
Allende, Coahuila, 12,736 ....J 2
Allende, Nuevo León, 14,263 ....J 4
Almoloya del Río, 3,692 ....K 1
Altamira, 28,667 ....K 5
Altar, 3,811 ....D 1
Altotonga, 31,231 ....P 1
Alvarado, 33,152 ....M 7
Amatlán de los Reyes, 21,011 ....P 2
Amealco, 26,222 ....K 6
Ameca, 42,016 ....H 6
Amecameca de Juárez, 21,753 ....L 1
Amozoc de Mota, 13,381............N 2
Angostura, 29,709 ....E 4
Apan, 21,550 ....M 1
Apatzingán de la Constitución, 67,384 ....J 7
Apizaco, 20,998 ....N 1
Aquiles Serdán, 5,159 ....G 2
Aramberri, 16,051 ....J 5
Arandas, 41,958 ....H 6
Arcelia, 25,631 ....J 7
Arizpe, 4,415 ....D 1
Armeria, 16,334 ....G 7
Arriaga, 23,582 ....N 8
Arteaga, 17,455 ....H 7
Ascensión, 8,810 ....E 1
Atlixco, 72,256 ....M 2
Atotonilco, 35,297 ....H 6
Autlán de Navarro, 30,853 ....G 7
Ayutla de los Libres, 23,668 ....K 8
Azcapotzalco, 545,513 ....L 1
Azoyú, 23,554 ....K 8
Bacadéhuachi, 1,470 ....D 2
Bacerac, 2,306 ....E 1
Bácum, 17,598 ....D 3
Badiraguato, 28,995 ....F 4
Balancán, 27,241 ....O 8
Balleza, 15,122 ....F 3
Batopilas, 8,780 ....F 3
Baviácora, 4,202 ....E 2
Bavispe, 2,048 ....E 1
Benjamín Hill, 5,807 ....D 1
Boca del Río, 27,884 ....Q 1
Buenaventura, 14,629 ....F 2
Burgos, 5,529 ....K 4
Cadereyta, 28,093 ....K 6
Cadereyta, Jiménez, 30,429 ....K 4
Calera, 13,030 ....H 5
Calkiní, 24,503 ....O 6
Calpulalpan, 14,633 ....M 1
Calvillo, 24,039 ....H 6
Campeche, 81,147 ....O 7
Cananea, 21,824 ....D 1
Canatlán, 63,871 ....G 4
Cancún ....Q 6
Candela, 2,202 ....J 3
Carbo, 3,242 ....D 2
Cárdenas, S. Luis Potosí, 18,091 ....K 6
Cárdenas, Tabasco, 78,477 ....N 8
Carmen, 71,240 ....N 7
Casas Grandes, 11,207............F 1
Catemaco, 23,671 ....M 7
Cedral, 12,426 ....J 5
Celaya, 143,703 ....J 6
Celestún, 1,535 ....O 6
Cerralvo, 6,831 ....J 3
Cerritos, 18,868 ....K 5
Chalchihuites, 11,347 ....G 5
Chalco, 41,145 ....M 1
Champotón, 27,581 ....O 7
Chapulco, 2,807 ....O 2
Charcas, 22,388 ....J 5
Chetumal, 34,237 ....Q 7
Chiapa de Corzo, 22,640 ....N 8
Chiautempan, 33,820 ....N 1
Chicoloapan de Juárez, 8,995 ....M 1
Chietla, 26,921 ....M 2
Chignahuapan, 29,556 ....N 1
Chignautla, 8,348 ....N 1
Chihuahua, 363,850 ....G 2
Chilapa, 53,263 ....K 8
Chilpancingo, 56,904 ....K 8
China, 9,018 ....K 4
Chocamán, 7,270 ....P 2
Choix, 27,515 ....E 3
Cholula, 20,913 ....M 1
Cihuatlán, 16,314 ....G 7
Cintalapa, 31,252 ....M 8
Ciudad Acuña, 32,760 ....J 2
Ciudad Camargo, Chihuahua, 29,185 ....G 3
Ciudad Camargo, Tamaulipas, 16,097 ....K 3
Ciudad Delicias, 64,385 ....G 2
Ciudad del Maíz, 35,502 ....K 5
Ciudad de Valles, 71,098 ....K 5
Ciudad Guerrero, 35,631 ....F 2
Ciudad Guzmán, 48,142 ....H 7
Ciudad Juárez, 436,054 ....F 1
Ciudad Lerdo, 53,551 ....H 4
Ciudad Madero, 89,994 ....L 5
Ciudad Mante, 79,130 ....K 5
Ciudad Miguel Alemán, 18,134 ....K 3
Ciudad Obregón, 181,972 ....E 3
Ciudad Río Bravo, 70,814 ....K 4
Ciudad Serdán, 25,288 ....O 2
Ciudad Victoria, 94,304 ....K 5
Coalcomán de Matamoros, 13,480 ....H 7
Coatepec, 34,161 ....P 1
Coatzacoalcos, 108,818 ....M 7
Cocula, 20,273 ....G 6
Colima, 72,074 ....H 7
Colón, 20,392 ....K 6
Colotlán, 14,316 ....H 5
Comala, 13,715 ....G 7
Comalcalco, 71,651 ....N 7
Comitán, 38,137 ....O 8
Comondú, 30,872 ....D 3
Compostela, 59,422 ....G 6
Concepción del Oro, 15,711............J 4
Concordia, 21,023 ....G 5
Córdoba, 92,870 ....P 2
Cosalá, 16,202 ....F 4
Cosamaloapan de Carpio, 75,412 ....M 7
Cosautlán de Carvajal, 8,015 ....P 1
Coscomatepec de Bravo, 19,890 ....P 2
Cosío, 7,031 ....H 5
Cosoleacaque, 20,251 ....M 7
Cotija, 17,296 ....H 7
Coyame, 3,798 ....G 2
Coyoacán, 338,850 ....L 1
Coyotepec, 8,658 ....L 1
Coyuca, 25,128 ....J 7
Coyuca de Benítez, 36,032............J 8
Coyutla, 12,008 ....L 6
Cozumel, 12,634 ....Q 6
Cuatrociénegas de Carranza, 9,512 ....H 3
Cuauhtémoc, 65,160 ....F 2
Cuautitlán, 40,622 ....L 1
Cuautla Morelos, 67,869............L 2
Cuencamé, 31,170 ....H 4
Cuernavaca, 159,909 ....L 2
Cuicatlán, 45,013 ....L 8
Cuitlahuac, 13,078 ....P 2
Culiacán, 358,812 ....F 4
Cumpas, 6,186 ....D 2
Cuna de la Independencia Nacional, 71,212 ....J 6
Cunduacán, 42,872 ....N 7
Doctor Arroyo, 45,889 ....K 5
Durango, 192,934 ....G 4
Ejutla de Crespo, 34,890 ....L 8
El Ebano, 20,571 ....K 5
El Fuerte, 62,001 ....E 3
El Oro, Durango, 18,668 ....G 4
El Oro, México, 17,086 ....K 7
El Salto, 19,604 ....G 5
Empalme, 32,541 ....D 2
Encarnación de Díaz, 29,533 ....H 6
Ensenada, 113,320 ....A 1
Escuinapa de Hidalgo, 30,763 ....G 5
Escuintla, 13,754 ....N 9
Etchojoa, 53,767 ....E 3
Fortín de las Flores, 21,370............P 2
Fresnillo, 101,316 ....H 5
Frontera, 43,007 ....N 7
Galeana, Chihuahua, 3,176 ....F 1
Galeana, Nuevo León, 39,143............J 4
García de la Cadena, 4,755............H 6
General Bravo, 6,063 ....K 4
General Cepeda, 13,332 ....J 4
Gómez Palacio, 135,743 ....G 4
González, 23,748 ....K 5
Guadalajara, 1,196,218 ....H 6
Guadalupe, Nvo. León, 153,454 ....J 4
Guadalupe, Zacatecas, 31,976 ....H 5
Guadalupe-Bravos, 9,649 ....F 1
Guadalupe Victoria, 27,450 ....G 4
Guadalupe y Calvo, 31,131 ....F 2
Guanacevi, 12,035 ....G 4
Guanajuato, 65,258 ....J 6
Guasave, 148,475 ....E 4
Guaymas, 84,730 ....D 3
Gutiérrez Zamora, 20,534 ....L 6
Halachó, 8,547 ....O 6
Hecelchakán, 10,974 ....O 6
Hermosillo, 206,663 ....D 2
Heroica Caborca, 29,486 ....C 1
Heroica Huamantla, 26,191 ....N 1
Heroica Nogales, 52,865 ....D 1
Hidalgo, 21,434 ....K 4
Hopelchén, 23,509 ....P 7
Huajuapan de León, 83,939............L 8
Huaquechula, 16,702 ....M 2
Huatabampo, 43,963 ....D 3
Huatusco de Chicuellar, 20,621 ....P 2
Huauchinango, 37,211 ....L 6
Huehuetlán, 6,962 ....M 2
Huejotzingo, 21,728 ....M 1
Huejutla de Reyes, 45,771 ....K 6
Huetamo de Núñez, 35,414 ....J 7
Hueyotlipan, 6,786 ....M 1
Huimanguillo, 70,525 ....N 8
Huitzuco, 28,159 ....K 7
Huixtla, 25,884 ....N 9
Hunucmá, 10,600 ....O 6
Ignacio de la Llave, 16,345 ....Q 2
Iguala, 60,980 ....K 7
Imuris, 5,853 ....D 1
Indé, 11,969 ....G 4
Irapuato, 175,966 ....J 6
Isla de Aguada ....O 7
Isla Mujeres, 10,469 ....Q 6
Ixmiquilpan, 35,851 ....K 6
Ixtacalco, 474,700 ....L 1
Ixtapalapa, 533,569 ....L 1
Ixtlán del Río, 16,228 ....G 6
Izamal, 16,188 ....P 6
Izúcar de Matamoros, 44,074 ....M 2
Jala, 11,174 ....G 6
Jalacingo, 15,436 ....P 1
Jalapa Enríquez, 127,081 ....P 1
Jalpa, Tabasco, 29,904............N 7
Jalpa, Zacatecas, 26,050 ....H 6
Jalpan, 15,319 ....K 6
Jáltipan, 19,676 ....M 8
Jaumave, 13,504 ....K 5
Jerez de Garcia Salinas, 49,202 ....H 5
Jico, 14,153 ....P 1
Jilotepec, 34,866 ....K 7
Jiménez, Chihuahua, 27,044 ....G 3
Jiménez, Coahuila, 8,019 ....J 2
Jojutla de Juárez, 31,196............L 2
Jonacatepec, 7,478 ....M 2
Jonuta, 14,227 ....N 7
Juan Aldama, 13,661 ....H 4
Juárez, 1,664 ....J 3
Juchipila, 14,517 ....H 6
Juchique de Ferrer, 14,094 ....Q 1
Juchitán de Zaragoza, 178,388 ....M 8
La Barca, 40,331 ....H 6
La Concordia, 15,296 ....N 9
La Cruz, Chihuahua, 3,899 ....G 3
La Cruz, Sinaloa, 19,055 ....F 5
Lagos, 66,273 ....J 6
La Paz, 49,637 ....D 5
La Piedad, 51,484 ....H 6
La Trinitaria, 28,028 ....N 9
La Yesca, 9,010 ....G 6
León, 453,976 ....J 6
Libres, 12,973 ....O 1
Linares, 49,397 ....K 4
Llera de Canales, 21,117 ....K 5
Loreto, 21,544 ....J 5
Los Mochis, 165,612 ....E 4
Los Reyes, 33,879 ....H 7
Macuspana, 75,013 ....N 8
Madera, 32,367 ....F 2
Magdalena, 13,485 ....D 1
Manuel Benavides, 5,135 ....H 2
Manzanillo, 46,170 ....G 7
Mapastepec, 16,911 ....N 9
Mapimí, 19,053 ....G 4
Martínez de la Torre, 62,707 ....L 6
Mascota, 15,260 ....G 6
Matamoros, Coahuila, 44,103 ....H 4
Matamoros, Tamaulipas, 182,887 ....L 4
Matehuala, 48,368 ....J 5
Maxcanú, 10,620 ....O 6
Mazapil, 28,656 ....J 4
Mazatán, 1,561 ....E 2
Mazatlán, 171,835 ....F 5
Melchor Múzquiz, 45,945 ....J 3
Melchor Ocampo, 4,180 ....H 4
Melchor Ocampo del Balsas, 23,248 ....H 8
Meoquí, 27,000 ....G 2
Mérida, 253,856 ....P 6
Mexicali, 390,411 ....B 1
Mexico City (México) (capital), 7,005,855 ....L 1
Mexico City, *7,157,000 ....L 1
Mezquital, 4,663 ....G 5
Miacatlán, 12,579 ....L 2
Mier, 5,916 ....K 3
Miguel Azua, 15,330 ....H 4
Minatitlán, 89,412 ....M 8
Mineral del Monte, 10,943 ....K 6
Miquihuana, 3,099 ....K 5
Misantla, 44,268 ....P 1
Mocorito, 49,957 ....F 4
Moctezuma, S. L. Potosí, 13,628 ....J 5
Moctezuma, Sonora, 3,476 ....E 2
Monclova, 80,252 ....J 3
Montemorelos, 34,067 ....K 4
Monterrey, 830,336 ....J 4
Morelia, 209,507 ....J 7
Morelos, 4,721 ....J 2
Morelos Cañada, 11,463 ....O 2
Moroleón, 33,765 ....J 6
Motozintla de Mendoza, 31,518 ....N 9
Motul, 21,087 ....P 6
Mulegé, 19,282 ....C 3
Muna, 6,147 ....P 6
Naco, 3,639 ....D 1
Nacozari de García, 3,483 ....E 1
Nadadores, 3,869 ....J 3
Nanacamilpa, 8,658 ....M 1
Naolinco de Victoria, 11,077 ....P 1
Naranjos, 21,371 ....L 6
Naucalpan, 373,605 ....L 1
Nautla, 9,425 ....L 6
Nava, 5,669 ....J 2
Navojoa, 69,792 ....E 3
Nazas, 13,189 ....G 4
Nieves, 19,938 ....H 5
Nochistlán, Oaxaca, 58,609 ....L 8
Nochistlán, Zacatecas, 28,463 ....H 6
Nogales, 19,158 ....P 2
Nombre de Dios, 17,742 ....G 5
Nonoava, 4,054 ....F 3
Nopalucan, 8,401 ....O 1
Nueva Casas Grandes, 25,333 ....F 1
Nueva Ciudad Guerrero, 4,065 ....K 3
Nuevo Laredo, 150,922 ....J 3
Nuevo Morelos, 2,245 ....K 5
Oaxaca de Juárez, 156,587 ....L 8
Ocampo, Chihuahua, 4,947 ....E 2
Ocampo, Coahuila, 10,072 ....H 3
Ocampo, Tamaulipas, 15,998 ....K 5
Ocotlán, 43,394 ....H 6
Ocotlán de Morelos, 45,752 ....L 8
Ojinaga, 23,854 ....G 2
Ojocaliente, 20,280 ....H 5
Ometepec, 23,604 ....K 8
Opódepe, 3,312 ....D 2
Oriental, 7,375 ....O 1
Orizaba, 92,728 ....P 2
Otumba de Gómez Farías, 11,960 ....M 1
Oxkutzcab, 10,295 ....P 7
Ozuluama, 22,382 ....L 6
Ozumba, 11,013 ....M 1
Pachuca, 84,543 ....K 6
Padilla, 13,643 ....K 5
Palenque, 22,684 ....O 8
Palizada, 7,445 ....O 7
Palmar de Bravo, 15,898 ....O 2
Palmillas, 2,420 ....K 5
Pánuco, 49,077 ....K 6
Papantla de Olarte, 94,623 ....L 6
Paraíso, 30,439 ....N 7
Parral, 61,729 ....G 3
Parras, 32,664 ....H 4
Pátzcuaro, 44,591 ....J 7
Pedro Montoya, 10,760 ....K 6
Pénjamo, 89,548 ....J 6
Peñón Blanco, 10,541............H 4
Perote, 23,556 ....P 1
Petatlán, 31,088 ....J 8
Peto, 11,986 ....P 6
Piedras Negras, 65,883 ....J 2
Pijijiapan, 20,350 ....N 9
Pitiquito, 6,100 ....D 1
Pochutla, 84,033 ....L 9
Poza Rica de Hidalgo, 121,341 ....L 6
Progreso, 22,100 ....P 6

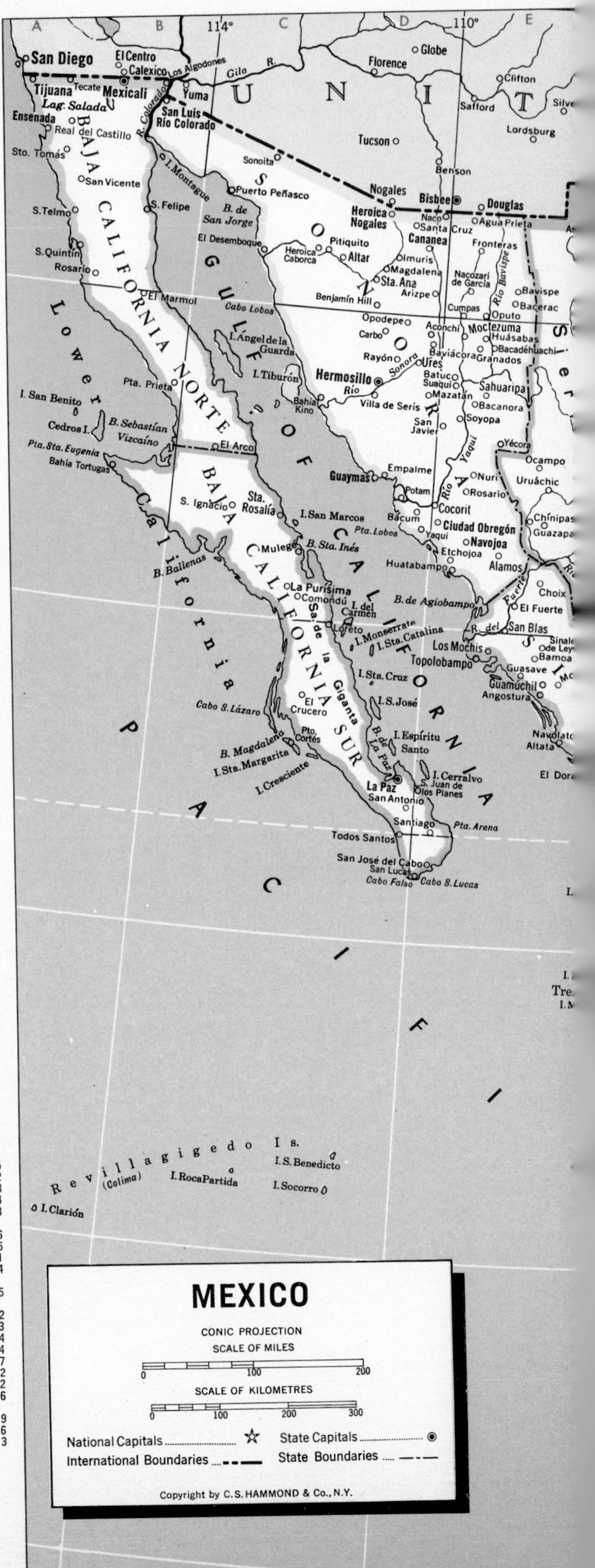

(continued on following page)

AREA 761,601 sq. mi.
POPULATION 48,313,438
CAPITAL Mexico City
LARGEST CITY Mexico City
HIGHEST POINT Citlaltépetl 18,855 ft.
MONETARY UNIT Mexican peso
MAJOR LANGUAGE Spanish
MAJOR RELIGION Roman Catholicism

States Indicated by Numbers

1	Tlaxcala	6	Querétaro
2	Morelos	7	Guanajuato
3	Distrito Federal	8	Aguascalientes
4	México	9	Nayarit
5	Hidalgo	10	Colima

San Gabriel Chilac, 7,303 ....K 7
San Ignacio, 22,116 ....F 5
San Javier, 390 ....D 2
San José del Cabo, 9,382 ....D 5
San Juan, Jalisco, 31,389 ....H 6
San Juan, Querétaro,
  53,332 ....K 6
San Juan de Guadalupe,
  8,877 ....H 4
San Juan del Río,
  14,639 ....G 4
San Juan Ixtenco, 4,894 ....N 1
San Juan Xiutetelco,
  11,771 ....O 1
San Luis de la Paz, 26,819....J 6
San Luis del Cordero,
  3,155 ....H 4
San Luis Potosí, 274,320 ....J 6
San Luis Río Colorado,
  63,644 ....B 1
San Marcos, 33,954 ....K 8
San Martín Texmelucan,
  50,071 ....M 1
San Martín Xaltocan,
  6,142 ....N 1
San Miguel, 63,937 ....J 6
San Nicolás, 1,023 ....K 4
San Nicolás Terrenate,
  7,160 ....K 4
San Pedro, 70,407 ....H 4
San Pedro del Gallo, 3,843....G 4
Santa Ana, 10,416 ....D 1
Santa Bárbara, 20,117 ....F 3
Santa Cruz, 1,659 ....D 1
Santa Inés Zacatelco,
  19,972 ....M 1
Santa María, 6,260 ....J 6
Santa María del Río, 30,072 ...J 6
Santa María del Tule ....K 8
Santander Jiménez, 5,323 ....K 4
Santa Rosalía ....C 3
Santiago, Baja California,
  4,978 ....E 5
Santiago, Nayarit, 84,167 ....G 6
Santiago Jamiltepec,
  104,275 ....K 8
Santiago Juxtlahuaca,
  37,095 ....K 8
Santiago Papasquiaro,
  35,828 ....F 4
Santiago Tuxtla, 33,471 ....M 7
Saucillo, 30,781 ....G 2
Sayula, 18,878 ....H 7
Sierra Mojada, 5,517 ....H 3
Silao, 69,866 ....J 6
Simojovel, 14,896 ....N 8
Sinaloa de Leyva, 53,639 ....E 4
Soledad de Doblado,
  19,467 ....Q 2
Soledad Díez Gutiérrez,
  28,337 ....J 5
Sombrerete, 48,411 ....H 5
Sotuta, 5,417 ....P 6
Soyopa, 2,314 ....E 2
Suaqui, 1,061 ....E 2
Tacámbaro de Codallos,
  33,690 ....J 7
Tacotalpa, 20,912 ....N 8
Tala, 33,369 ....G 6
Talpa de Allende, 13,027 ....G 6
Tamazunchale, 60,976 ....K 6
Tamiahua, 23,689 ....L 6
Tampico, 196,147 ....L 5
Tapachula, 108,464 ....N 9
Taxco de Alarcón, 64,368 ....K 7
Teapa, 19,787 ....N 8

Tecamachalco, 21,688 ....O 2
Tecate, 17,917 ....A 1
Tecomán, 45,933 ....H 7
Tecpan de Galeana,
  44,820 ....J 8
Tecuala, 41,129 ....G 5
Tehuacán, 67,520 ....L 7
Tehuantepec, 100,176 ....M 8
Tehuipango, 7,163 ....P 2
Tekax, 16,370 ....P 6
Teloloapan, 48,458 ....J 7
Temascalapa, 9,428 ....M 1
Temax, 5,821 ....P 6
Tenancingo, 31,808 ....K 7
Tenabo, 3,992 ....P 6
Tenango de Río Blanco ....O 2
Tenosique de Pino Suárez,
  26,954 ....O 6
Teocaltiche, 29,330 ....H 6
Teocelo, 7,441 ....P 1
Teotihuacán de Arista,
  15,704 ....L 1
Teotitlán, 103,209 ....L 8
Tepatitlán, 53,683 ....H 6
Tepatlaxco de Hidalgo,
  8,768 ....N 1
Tepeaca, 26,334 ....N 2
Tepeapulco, 26,254 ....M 1
Tepehuanes, 16,361 ....G 4
Tepeji, 24,107 ....K 6
Tepetlaoxtoc, 6,987 ....L 1
Tepexi de Rodríguez,
  12,655 ....O 2
Tepeyahualco, 9,504 ....N 1
Tepic, 111,344 ....G 6
Tepoztlán, 12,835 ....L 1
Texcoco de Mora,
  67,220 ....M 1
Teziutlán, 41,502 ....O 1
Ticul, 16,537 ....P 6
Tierra Blanca, 48,733 ....L 7
Tihuatlán, 53,447 ....L 6
Tijuana, 333,125 ....A 1
Tixtla, 19,735 ....K 8
Tizayuca, 8,717 ....L 1
Tizimín, 29,895 ....Q 6
Tlachichuca, 15,225 ....N 1
Tlacolula, 78,684 ....L 8
Tlacotalpan, 13,404 ....M 7
Tlacotepec de Mejía,
  1,948 ....P 1
Tlahuallilo de Zaragoza,
  21,646 ....H 3
Tlalixcoyan, 28,625 ....Q 2
Tlalmanalco de Velásquez,
  20,420 ....L 1
Tlalnepantla de Comonfort,
  373,657 ....K 1
Tlalpan, 115,528 ....L 1
Tlaltenango, 19,145 ....L 1
Tlaltizapán, 20,716 ....L 2
Tlapacoyan, 23,623 ....P 1
Tlapa de Comonfort,
  23,261 ....K 8
Tlaquiltenango, 16,335 ....L 2
Tlaxcala, 21,424 ....M 1
Tlaxco de Morelos,
  16,128 ....N 1
Tlaxiaco, 85,929 ....L 8
Tlayacapan, 5,240 ....L 1
Todos Santos, 4,506 ....D 5
Tolimán, 12,017 ....K 6
Toluca, 220,195 ....K 7
Tomatlán, 17,201 ....G 6

Tonalá, 41,562 ....N 8
Topolobampo, 45,449 ....E 4
Torreón, 257,045 ....H 4
Tula, 21,201 ....K 5
Tulancingo, 45,449 ....K 7
Tulcingo de Valle, 6,718 ....M 2
Tultepec, 13,693 ....L 1
Tuxpan, Jalisco, 23,569 ....H 7
Tuxpan, Nayarit, 28,345 ....G 6
Tuxpan de Rodríguez Cano,
  65,211 ....L 6
Tuxtepec, 184,757 ....L 7
Tuxtla Gutiérrez, 69,326 ....N 8
Umán, 14,258 ....P 6

Úrsulo Galván, 16,772 ....Q 1
Uruáchic, 7,585 ....E 3
Uruapan, 104,475 ....J 7
Valladolid, 25,367 ....P 6
Valle de Bravo, 23,591 ....J 7
Valle de Santiago, 80,504 ....J 6
Valle Hermoso, 41,546 ....L 4
Vanegas, 36,384 ....J 5
Venado, 12,147 ....J 5
Venustiano Carranza, 32,131 ...N 8
Veracruz Llave, 242,351 ....Q 1
Vicente Guerrero, Durango,
  13,529 ....G 5
Vicente Guerrero, Puebla,
  10,207 ....M 2

Viesca, 15,046 ....H 4
Villa de Cos, 18,012 ....H 5
Villa de Guadalupe, 12,436 ....J 5
Villa de Seris ....D 2
Villa Frontera, 31,055 ....J 3
Villa García, 9,116 ....J 5
Villagrán, 10,338 ....K 4
Villahermosa, 162,678 ....N 8
Villaldama, 4,639 ....J 3
Villa Matamoros, 5,928 ....G 3
Villanueva, 35,553 ....H 5
Villa Unión, 20,002 ....H 5
Xicoténcatl, 21,144 ....K 5

Xochihuehuetlán, 6,046 ....K 8
Xochimilco, 117,083 ....L 1
Xochitlán, 8,166 ....N 2
Yalalón, 29,497 ....N 8
Yautepec, 26,182 ....L 2
Yécora, 4,898 ....E 2
Yecuatla, 10,382 ....P 1
Zaachila, 22,739 ....L 8
Zacapoaxtla, 25,479 ....O 1
Zacapu, 52,649 ....J 7
Zacatecas, 56,829 ....J 5
Zacatlán, 37,261 ....N 1
Zacoalco, 21,929 ....H 6
Zamora, 82,712 ....H 7
Zaragoza, 8,955 ....H 2
Zimatlán de Álvarez,
  40,302 ....L 8
Zitácuaro, 67,173 ....J 7
Zongolica, 24,372 ....P 2
Zumpango, 35,035 ....L 1
Zumpango del Río, 21,894 ....J 8

OTHER FEATURES

Agiobampo (bay) ....E 3
Aguanaval (river) ....H 4
Amistad (res.) ....J 2
Ángel de la Guarda
  (island) ....C 2
Antigua (river) ....Q 1
Arena (point) ....Q 5
Arenas (cay) ....O 5
Atoyac (river) ....N 2
Atoyac (river) ....Q 2
Babia (river) ....J 2
Bacalar (lake) ....P 7
Ballenas (bay) ....C 3
Balsas (river) ....J 7
Banderas (bay) ....G 6
Bavispe (river) ....E 2
Blanco (river) ....P 2
Bravo (river) ....G 2
Burro, Sierra del (mts.) ....J 2
California (gulf) ....D 3
Campeche (bank) ....P 6
Campeche (bay) ....N 7
Candelaria (river) ....O 7
Carmen (island) ....D 4
Casas Grandes (river) ....F 1
Catoche (cape) ....Q 6
Cedros (island) ....B 4
Cerralvo (island) ....E 5
Chamela (bay) ....G 7
Chapala (lake) ....H 6
Chetumal (bay) ....P 7
Chichén-Itzá (ruins) ....P 6
Chixoy (river) ....N 8
Citlaltépetl (mt.) ....O 2
Clarión (island) ....B 7
Colorado (river) ....B 1
Conchos (river) ....G 3
Corrientes (cape) ....F 6
Coyuca (river) ....J 8
Crescente (island) ....D 3
Cuitzeo (lake) ....J 6
Delgada (point) ....J 7
Dzibilchaltún (ruins) ....P 6
El Azúcar (res.) ....K 3
Espíritu Santo (island) ....D 5
Falcón (res.) ....K 3
Falso (cape) ....D 5
Fuerte (river) ....E 3
Giganta, Sierra de la
  (mts.) ....D 4
Grande (river) ....D 4
Grande (river) ....G 2
Grande de Santiago
  (river) ....G 6
Grijalva (river) ....N 7
Guzmán (lake) ....F 1
Herrero (point) ....Q 7
Holbox (island) ....P 6
Hondo (river) ....P 7
Jesús María, Barra
  (inlet) ....L 6
La Boquilla (res.) ....G 3
La Paz (bay) ....D 5
Lobos (cape) ....D 2
Lobos (point) ....D 3

Lower California (pen.),
  980,559 ....B
Madre (lagoon) ....L 4
Madre del Sur, Sierra
  (mts.) ....J-L
Madre Occidental, Sierra
  (mts.) ....E 2
Madre Oriental, Sierra
  (mts.) ....H 4
Magdalena (bay) ....C 4
Maldonado (point) ....J 8
Mapimí, Bolsón de
  (depression) ....G 3
María Cleófas (island) ....F 6
María Madre (island) ....F 6
María Magdalena (island) ....F 6
Mexico (gulf) ....M 5
Mezquital (river) ....G 5
Mita (point) ....F 6
Mitla (ruins) ....L 8
Moctezuma (river) ....K 6
Monserrate (isl.) ....D 4
Montague (isl.) ....B 1
Muerto, Mar (lagoon) ....N 8
Nauhcampatépetl (mt.) ....O 1
Nayarit, Sierra (mts.) ....G 5
Nazas (river) ....G 4
Nuevo (cay) ....P 6
Orizaba (Citlaltépetl)
  (mt.) ....O 2
Palenque (ruins) ....N 8
Palmito de la Vírgen (isl.) ....F 5
Palmito del Verde (isl.) ....F 5
Pánuco (river) ....K 6
Paricutín (vol.) ....H 7
Pátzcuaro (lake) ....J 7
Pérez (isl.) ....P 6
Petacalco (bay) ....H 8
Popocatépetl (mt.) ....L 2
Ramos (river) ....G 4
Revillagigedo (isls.) ....B 7
Río Grande (river) ....G 2
Roca Partida (isl.) ....B 7
Sabinas (river) ....J 3
Salada (lagoon) ....B 1
San Antonio, Barra de
  (inlet) ....K 6
San Benedicto (isl.) ....B 7
San Benito (isl.) ....A 3
San Blas (river) ....J 2
San Jorge (bay) ....C 1
San José (isl.) ....D 4
San Lázaro (cape) ....C 4
San Lucas (cape) ....D 5
San Marcos (isl.) ....C 3
San Rafael, Barra de
  (inlet) ....L 5
Santa Ana, Barra de
  (inlet) ....L 5
Santa Catalina (isl.) ....D 4
Santa Cruz (isl.) ....D 4
Santa Eugenia (point) ....A 3
Santa Inés (isl.) ....C 3
Santa Margarita (isl.) ....C 5
Santa María (lake) ....F 1
Santa María (river) ....F 1
Santiaguillo (lake) ....G 4
Sebastián Vizcaíno (bay) ....B 3
Socorro (isl.) ....B 7
Sonora (river) ....D 2
Superior (lagoon) ....M 8
Teacapán, Boca (inlet) ....F 5
Tehuantepec (gulf) ....M 9
Tehuantepec (isthmus) ....M 8
Teotihuacán (ruins) ....L 1
Términos (lagoon) ....N 8
Tiburón (isl.) ....C 2
Tres Marías (isls.) ....F 6
Triángulo Este (isl.) ....O 7
Triángulo Oeste (isl.) ....O 7
Tula (ruins) ....K 5
Urique (river) ....E 3
Usumacinta (river) ....N 8
Uxmal (ruins) ....P 6
Valsequillo, Presa (res.) ....N 2
Verde (river) ....G 6
Verde (river) ....H 6
Yaqui (river) ....E 2

*City and suburbs.

HIGHWAYS OF MIDDLE AMERICA

0   200   400   600 MI.

0   200   400   600 KM.

Limited Access Highways
Major Highways
Other Important Roads
U.S. Interstate Numbers
U.S. Route Numbers
Other Route Numbers

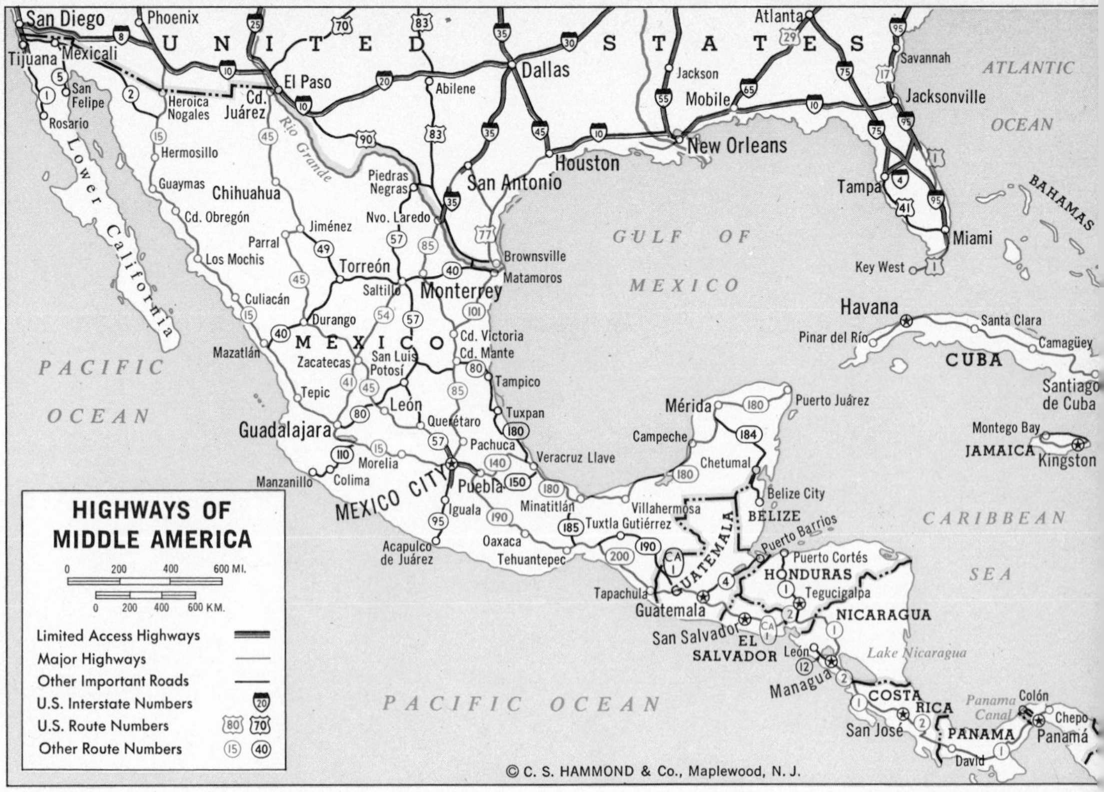

© C. S. HAMMOND & Co., Maplewood, N.J.

Agriculture, Industry and Resources

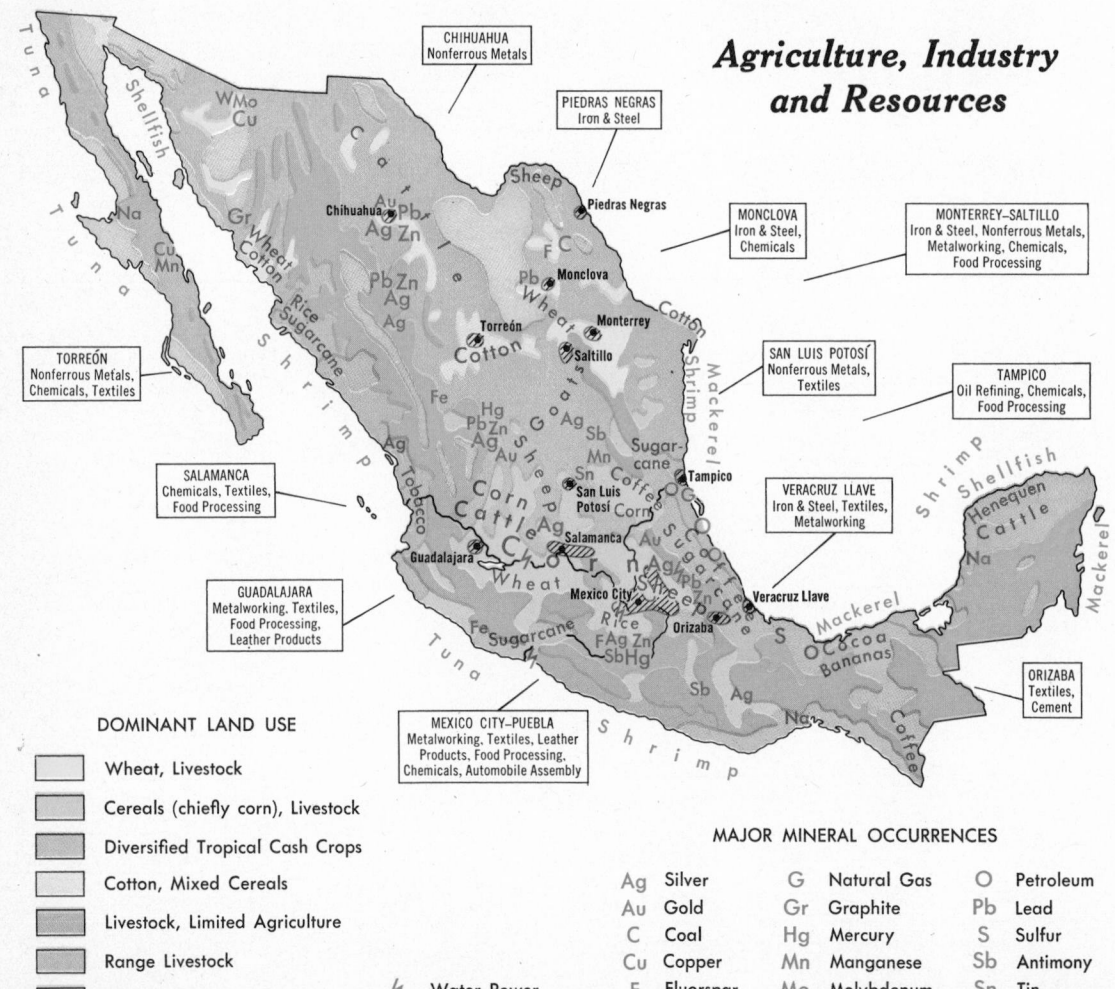

CHIHUAHUA
Nonferrous Metals

PIEDRAS NEGRAS
Iron & Steel

MONCLOVA
Iron & Steel,
Chemicals

MONTERREY–SALTILLO
Iron & Steel, Nonferrous Metals,
Metalworking, Chemicals,
Food Processing

TORREÓN
Nonferrous Metals,
Chemicals, Textiles

SAN LUIS POTOSÍ
Nonferrous Metals,
Textiles

TAMPICO
Oil Refining, Chemicals,
Food Processing

SALAMANCA
Chemicals, Textiles,
Food Processing

VERACRUZ LLAVE
Iron & Steel, Textiles,
Metalworking

GUADALAJARA
Metalworking, Textiles,
Food Processing,
Leather Products

ORIZABA
Textiles,
Cement

MEXICO CITY–PUEBLA
Metalworking, Textiles, Leather
Products, Food Processing,
Chemicals, Automobile Assembly

DOMINANT LAND USE

Wheat, Livestock
Cereals (chiefly corn), Livestock
Diversified Tropical Cash Crops
Cotton, Mixed Cereals
Livestock, Limited Agriculture
Range Livestock
Forests
Nonagricultural Land

Water Power
Major Industrial Areas

MAJOR MINERAL OCCURRENCES

Ag Silver
Au Gold
C   Coal
Cu Copper
F   Fluorspar
Fe Iron Ore

G   Natural Gas
Gr Graphite
Hg Mercury
Mn Manganese
Mo Molybdenum
Na Salt

O   Petroleum
Pb Lead
S   Sulfur
Sb Antimony
Sn Tin
W   Tungsten
Zn Zinc

GUATEMALA
AREA 42,042 sq. mi.
POPULATION 5,200,000
CAPITAL Guatemala
LARGEST CITY Guatemala
HIGHEST POINT Tajumulco 13,845 ft.
MONETARY UNIT quetzal
MAJOR LANGUAGES Spanish, Quiché
MAJOR RELIGION Roman Catholicism

BELIZE
AREA 8,867 sq. mi.
POPULATION 122,000
CAPITAL Belmopan
LARGEST CITY Belize City
HIGHEST POINT Victoria Peak, 3,681 ft.
MONETARY UNIT Belize dollar
MAJOR LANGUAGES English, Spanish, Mayan
MAJOR RELIGIONS Protestantism, Roman Catholicism

EL SALVADOR
AREA 8,260 sq. mi.
POPULATION 3,418,455
CAPITAL San Salvador
LARGEST CITY San Salvador
HIGHEST POINT Santa Ana 7,825 ft.
MONETARY UNIT colón
MAJOR LANGUAGE Spanish
MAJOR RELIGION Roman Catholicism

HONDURAS
AREA 43,277 sq. mi.
POPULATION 2,495,000
CAPITAL Tegucigalpa
LARGEST CITY Tegucigalpa
HIGHEST POINT Las Minas 9,347 ft.
MONETARY UNIT lempira
MAJOR LANGUAGE Spanish
MAJOR RELIGION Roman Catholicism

NICARAGUA
AREA 45,698 sq. mi.
POPULATION 1,984,000
CAPITAL Managua
LARGEST CITY Managua
HIGHEST POINT Cerro Mocotón 6,913 ft.
MONETARY UNIT córdoba
MAJOR LANGUAGE Spanish
MAJOR RELIGION Roman Catholicism

COSTA RICA
AREA 19,575 sq. mi.
POPULATION 1,800,000
CAPITAL San José
LARGEST CITY San José
HIGHEST POINT Chirripó Grande 12,530 ft.
MONETARY UNIT colón
MAJOR LANGUAGE Spanish
MAJOR RELIGION Roman Catholicism

PANAMA
AREA 29,209 sq. mi.
POPULATION 1,425,343
CAPITAL Panamá
LARGEST CITY Panamá
HIGHEST POINT Vol. Chiriquí 11,401 ft.
MONETARY UNIT balboa
MAJOR LANGUAGE Spanish
MAJOR RELIGION Roman Catholicism

CANAL ZONE
AREA 647 sq. mi.
POPULATION 44,650
CAPITAL Balboa Heights

Agriculture, Industry and Resources

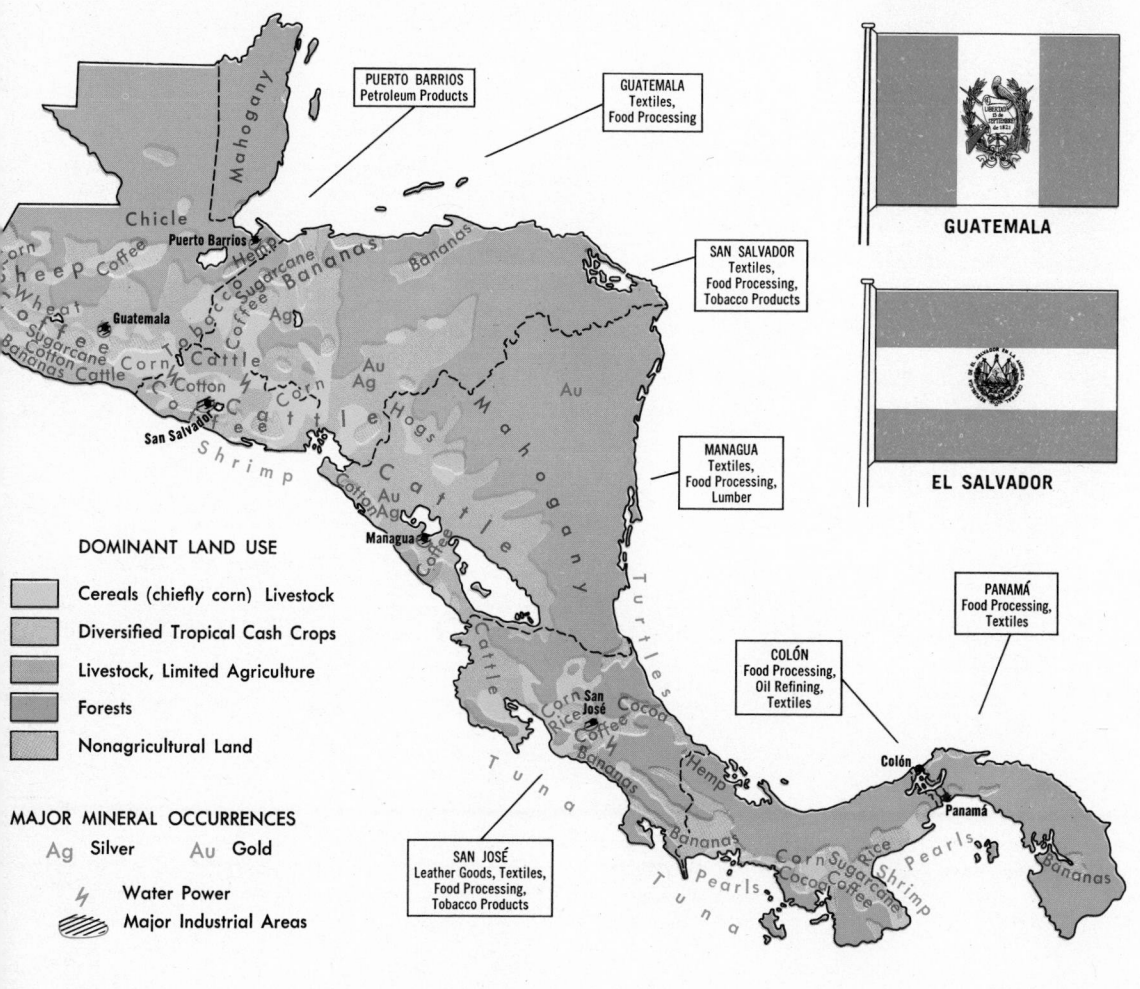

PUERTO BARRIOS
Petroleum Products

GUATEMALA
Textiles,
Food Processing

SAN SALVADOR
Textiles,
Food Processing,
Tobacco Products

MANAGUA
Textiles,
Food Processing,
Lumber

PANAMÁ
Food Processing,
Textiles

COLÓN
Food Processing,
Oil Refining,
Textiles

SAN JOSÉ
Leather Goods, Textiles,
Food Processing,
Tobacco Products

DOMINANT LAND USE
- Cereals (chiefly corn) Livestock
- Diversified Tropical Cash Crops
- Livestock, Limited Agriculture
- Forests
- Nonagricultural Land

MAJOR MINERAL OCCURRENCES
- Ag Silver
- Au Gold
- ⚡ Water Power
- Major Industrial Areas

BELIZE

GUATEMALA

HONDURAS

EL SALVADOR

NICARAGUA

COSTA RICA

PANAMA

COSTA RICA (continued)

Carreta (point) .... F 6
Chirripó Grande (mt.) .... F 6
Coronada (bay) .... F 6
Cuilapa Miravalles (volcano) .. E 5
Dulce (gulf) .... F 6
Góngora (mt.) .... E 6
Guionos (point) .... E 6
Irazú (mt.) .... F 6
Judas (point) .... F 6
Llerena (point) .... F 6
Matapalo (cape) .... E 6
Nicoya (gulf) .... E 6
Nicoya (pen.) .... E 6
Papagayo (gulf) .... E 5
Salinas (bay) .... D 5
San Juan (river) .... E, F 5
Santa Elena (cape) .... D 5
Talamanca (range) .... F 6
Velas (cape) .... D 5

EL SALVADOR

CITIES and TOWNS

Acajutla, 5,310 .... B 4
Ahuachapán, 16,180 .... B 4

Atiquizaya, 7,878 .... C 3
Chalatenango, 7,209 .... C 3
Chinameca, 7,020 .... C 4
Cojutepeque, 16,084 .... C 4
Estanzuelas, 2,785 .... C 4
Ilobasco, 6,432 .... C 4
Intipucá, 3,683 .... D 4
Jucuarán, 1,680 .... D 4
La Libertad, 7,015 .... C 4
La Palma, 1,992 .... C 3
La Unión, 16,459 .... D 4
Metapán, 4,896 .... C 3
Nueva San Salvador (Santa
  Tecla), 36,944 .... C 4
Puerto de la Concordia .... C 4
San Francisco Gotera, 4,638 .. C 4
San Miguel, 50,668 .... D 4
San Salvador (cap.), 349,725 .. C 4
Santa Ana, 102,301 .... C 3
Santa Rosa de Lima, 6,297 .. D 4
Santa Tecla, 36,944 .... C 4
San Vicente, 19,887 .... C 4
Sensuntepeque, 6,791 ...... C 4
Sonsonate, 32,675 .... C 4
Suchitoto, 5,758 .... C 4
Texistepeque, 1,723 .... C 3
Usulután, 17,796 .... C 4
Zacatecoluca, 16,189 ...... C 4

OTHER FEATURES

Fonseca (gulf) .... D 4
Güija (lake) .... C 4
Lempa (river) .... C 4
Remedios (point) .... B 4
Santa Ana (mt.) .... C 4

GUATEMALA

CITIES and TOWNS

Amatitlán, 12,225 .... B 3
Antigua, 13,576 .... B 3
Asunción Mita, 6,341 ...... C 3
Cahabón, 939 .... C 3
Chahal, 323 .... C 3
Chajul, 4,187 .... B 3
Champerico, 3,823 .... A 3
Chichicastenango, 2,099 ... B 3
Chimaltenango, 9,077 ...... B 3
Chinaja .... B 2
Chiquimula, 14,760 .... C 3
Chisec, 812 .... B 3
Coatepeque, 13,657 .... A 3
Cobán, 9,073 .... B 3
Comalapa, 9,202 .... B 3

Cubulco, 1,676 .... B 3
Cuilapa, 3,657 .... B 3
Cuilco, 728 .... B 3
Dolores, 630 .... C 2
El Cambio .... B 3
El Porvenir .... B 3
El Progreso, 3,458 .... B 3
Escuintla, 24,832 .... B 3
Flores, 1,503 .... C 2
Gualán, 4,425 .... C 3
Guatemala (cap.), 700,000 . B 3
Huehuetenango, 10,185 ..... B 3
Ipala, 3,190 .... C 3
Izabal .... C 3
Iztapa, 751 .... B 4
Jacaltenango, 3,873 .... A 3
Jalapa, 10,035 .... C 3
Jutiapa, 7,747 .... C 3
La Gomera, 1,397 .... B 3
La Libertad, 770 .... B 2
Livingston, 3,026 .... C 3
Los Amates, 1,131 .... C 3
Masagua, 1,100 .... B 3
Matías de Gálvez .... C 2
Mazatenango, 19,506 .... B 3
Momostenango, 3,148 .... B 3
Morales, 1,710 .... C 3
Nejapa .... C 3

Ocós, 576 .... A 3
Panzós, 1,803 .... C 3
Puerto Barrios, 22,242 .... C 2
Quezaltenango, 45,195 ..... B 3
Quezaltepeque, 2,578 ...... C 3
Rabinal, 4,155 .... B 3
Retalhuleu, 14,366 .... B 3
Río Hondo, 1,300 .... C 3
Sacapulas, 1,407 .... B 3
Salamá, 4,442 .... B 3
San Andrés, 939 .... B 2
San Felipe, 2,916 .... B 3
San José, 5,771 .... B 4
San Juan de Dios .... B 3
San Luis, 763 .... C 2
San Luis Jilotepeque, 5,795 .. C 3
San Marcos, 5,569 .... B 3
San Martín Jilotepeque, 2,806 .. B 3
San Mateo Ixtatán, 2,892 .. B 2
San Miguel .... C 2
San Pedro Carchá, 3,966 ... B 3
Santa Ana, 239 .... C 2
Santa Ana Mixtán .... B 3
Santa Cruz del Quiché, 6,472 .. B 3
Santa Rosa de Lima, 734 ... B 3
Sipacate .... B 3
Sololá, 3,957 .... B 3
Tacaná, 900 .... A 3

Tejutla, 973 .... B 3
Totonicapán, 7,292 .... B 3
Yaloch .... C 2
Zacapa, 11,173 .... C 3

OTHER FEATURES

Atitlán (lake) .... B 3
Atitlán (volcano) .... B 3
Azul (river) .... C 2
Chixoy (river) .... B 3
Dulce (Izabal) (lake) ..... C 3
Güija (lake) .... D 2
Honduras (gulf) .... C 2
Izabal (lake) .... C 3
Minas (mts.) .... B 3
Motagua (river) .... C 3
Pasión (river) .... B 2
Petén-Itzá (lake) .... C 2
San Pedro (river) .... B 2
Sarstun (river) .... C 3
Tacaná (volcano) .... A 3
Tajumulco (volcano) .... A 3
Tres Puntas (cape) .... C 3
Usumacinta (river) .... B 2

HONDURAS

CITIES and TOWNS

Ahuás .... E 3
Amapala, 3,491 .... D 4
Balana .... E 3
Balfate, 602 .... D 3
Belén, 201 .... E 3
Brus Laguna, 1,247 .... E 3
Caratasca .... F 3
Catacamas, 4,751 .... D 3
Cedros, 1,177 .... D 3
Chichicaste .... E 3
Choloma, 6,678 .... C 3
Choluteca, 17,350 .... D 4
Colorado .... E 3
Comayagua, 11,247 .... D 3
Comayagüela .... D 3
Concepción de María, 653 .. D 4
Concordia, 644 .... D 3
Copán, 2,190 .... C 3
Corquín, 2,817 .... C 3
Cruta .... F 3
Danlí, 8,242 .... D 3
Donel .... E 3
El Dulce Nombre, 145 ...... D 3

CENTRAL AMERICA

CONIC PROJECTION

SCALE OF MILES

0 25 50 100 150

SCALE OF KILOMETRES

0 25 50 100 150

Capitals of Countries .... ☆
International Boundaries ......
Canals ....

Copyright by C.S. Hammond & Co., N.Y.

El Paraíso, Copán, 1,787 .....C 3
El Paraíso, El Paraíso, 5,758 ..D 4
El Porvenir, 529 ....D 3
El Progreso, 8,718 ....D 3
El Triunfo, 2,136 ....D 4
Goascorán, 1,184 ....C 3
Gracias, 2,484 ....C 3
Guaimaca, 2,620 ....D 3
Gualpatanta ....
Guanaja, 1,253 ....E 2
Guarita, 599 ....C 3
Guayape, 610 ....D 3
Iriona, 119 ....E 2
Jacaleapa, 992 ....D 3
Jesús de Otoro, 2,775 ......D 3
Jutiapa, 1,711 ....D 3
Juticalpa, 7,912 ....D 3
La Ceiba, 33,934 ....D 3
La Concepción ....C 3
La Esperanza, 2,000 ....C 3
La Guata, 281 ....D 3
La Paz, 5,542 ....D 3
La Protección ....D 3
Lauterique, 272 ....D 4
Limón. 1.934 ....E 3
Manto, 943 ....D 3
Marcala, 1,968 ....C 3
Melcher ....D 3

Morazán, 3,924 ....D 3
Morocelí, 1,472 ....D 3
Nacaome, 4,376 ....D 4
Namasigüe, 1,024 ....D 4
Naranjito, 3,291 ....D 4
Nueva Armenia, 866 ....D 3
Nueva Ocotepeque, 4,608 ...C 3
Olanchito, 5,008 ....D 3
Omoa, 1,384 ....C 3
Paso Real ....
Patuca ....E 3
Pespire, 1,758 ....D 4
Puerto Castilla ....E 2
Puerto Cortés, 21,600 ......D 2
Roatán, 1,883 ....D 2
Sabanagrande, 1,657 ....D 4
Salado ....
San Esteban, 763 ....D 3
San Francisco, 1,122 ......D 3
San Francisco de la Paz,
  1,971 ....D 3
San Juan de Flores, 1,174 ..D 3
San Luis, 2,631 ....C 3
San Marcos, 1,576 ....C 3
San Pedro Sula, 90,538 ....D 3
San Pedro Zacapa, 765 .....D 3
Santa Bárbara, 6,129 ......C 3
Santa Cruz de Yojoa, 1,833 .D 3

Topography

5,000 m. / 16,404 ft. — 2,000 m. / 6,562 ft. — 1,000 m. / 3,281 ft. — 500 m. / 1,640 ft. — 200 m. / 656 ft. — 100 m. / 328 ft. — Sea Level — Below

0 — 75 — 150
MILES

JAMAICA inset

Montego Bay, Falmouth, St. Ann's Bay, Ewarton, Port María, Annotto Bay, Port Antonio, S. Negril Pt., Savanna la Mar, Black River, Spanish Town, Kingston, Blue Mountain Pk. 7,388, Morant Point, Portland Point

Walton Bank
Pedro Bank
Pedro Cays (Jamaica)
Morant Cays (Jamaica)
Serranilla Bank (Col.)
Bajo Nuevo (Col.)
Serrana Bank (Col.)
Roncador Bank (Col.)

CARIBBEAN SEA

Santa Rita, 3,976 ....D 3
Santa Rosa de Aguán, 1,701 .E 2
Santa Rosa de Copán, 9,109 .C 3
Siguatepeque, 9,462 ....C 3
Sinuapa, 882 ....C 3
Sonaguera, 1,344 ....D 3
Sulaco, 1,071 ....D 3
Tegucigalpa (cap.), 253,283 .D 3
Tela, 14,103 ....D 3
Teupasenti, 829 ....D 3
Tocoa, 1,605 ....E 3
Trinidad, 2,817 ....C 3
Trujillo, 4,656 ....E 3
Uji ....F 3
Utila, 957 ....D 2
Villa de San Antonio, 2,287 .D 3
Yocón, 269 ....D 3
Yorito, 869 ....D 3
Yoro, 4,129 ....D 3
Yuscarán, 1,854 ....D 4

OTHER FEATURES

Aguán (river) ....D 3
Bahía (isls.), 9,702 ......D 2
Bonacca (Guanaja) (isl.),
  2,039 ....E 2
Brus (lagoon) ....E 2
Camarón (cape) ....E 2
Caratasca (cays) ....F 2
Caratasca (lagoon) ....F 2
Choluteca (river) ....D 4
Cisne (isls.), 28 ....F 2
Coco (river) ....F 3
Colón (mts.) ....E 3
Esperanza (mts.) ....C 3
Falso (cape) ....F 3
Fonseca (gulf) ....D 4
Gorda (cay) ....F 3
Guanaja (isl.), 2,039 .....E 2
Half Moon (reefs) ....E 2
Honduras (cape) ....E 2
Honduras (gulf) ....D 2
Patuca (point) ....E 2
Patuca (river) ....E 3
Paulaya (river) ....E 3
Pigeon (cays) ....F 3
Pija (mts.) ....D 3
Roatán (isl.), 6,552 ......D 2
San Pablo, Sierra de (mts.) .E 3
Segovia (Coco) (river) ....E 3
Sico (river) ....E 3
Sulaco (river) ....D 3
Swan (Cisne) (isls.), 28 ...F 2
Ulúa (river) ....D 3
Utila (isl.), 1,111 ....D 2
Vivario (cays) ....F 3
Wanks (Coco) (river) .....D 3
Yojoa (lake) ....D 3

NICARAGUA

CITIES and TOWNS

Acoyapa, 1,755 ....E 5
Alamikamba ....E 4
Barra de Río Grande .....F 3
Bilwaskarma ....F 3
Bluefields, 9,292 ....F 4
Boaco, 4,656 ....E 4
Bocay ....E 3
Bonanza, 2,175 ....E 4
Bragman's Bluff (Puerto
  Cabezas), 5,983 ....F 3
Cabo Gracias a Dios, 511 ..F 3
Camoapa, 2,617 ....E 4

Chichigalpa, 6,657 ....D 4
Chinandega, 22,409 ......D 4
Ciudad Darío, 3,851 .....D 4
Comalapa, 441 ....E 4
Condega, 2,229 ....D 4
Corinto, 9,177 ....D 4
Cuicuina ....E 4
Cuyu Tigni ....F 3
Diriamba, 10,499 ....D 5
El Gallo ....F 4
El Jicaral, 239 ....D 4
El Jícaro, 1,114 ....D 4
El Sauce, 2,944 ....D 4
El Viejo, 7,190 ....D 4
Esquipulas, 1,636 ....E 4
Estelí, 12,742 ....D 4
Granada, 28,507 ....E 5
Greytown (San Juan del
  Norte), 199 ....F 5
Jalapa, 1,868 ....D 4
Jinotega, 7,693 ....E 4
Jinotepe, 9,113 ....D 5
Juigalpa, 6,146 ....E 4
La Conquista, 364 ....D 5
La Cruz, 155 ....E 4
Laguna de Perlas ....F 4
La Libertad, 1,355 ......E 4
La Paz Central, 4,431 ...D 4
La Paz de Oriente, 828 ..D 4
La Trinidad, 2,340 ......D 4
León, 44,053 ....D 4
Managua (capital),
  262,047 ....D 4
Masatepe, 4,831 ....D 5
Masaya, 23,402 ....D 5
Matagalpa, 15,030 ....E 4
Mateare, 1,254 ....D 4
Morrito, 324 ....E 5
Moyogalpa, 1,252 ....E 5
Muleculus ....E 4
Muy Muy, 691 ....E 4
Muy Muy Viejo ....E 4
Nagarote, 5,241 ....D 4
Nandaime, 5,051 ....D 5
Ocotal, 4,339 ....D 4
Ocotal ....D 4
Palsagua ....
Playa Grande ....D 4
Poneloya, 995 ....D 4
Poteca ....E 4
Prinzapolka, 230 ....F 4
Puerto Cabezas, 5,983 ..F 3
Quilalí, 710 ....D 4
Rama (El Rama),
  600 ....E 4
Rivas, 7,721 ....D 5
San Carlos, 1,547 ......E 5
Sandy Bay ....F 4
San Francisco ....E 5
San Jorge, 1,657 ......E 5
San Juan del Norte, 199 .F 5
San Juan del Sur, 2,103 .D 5
San Miguelito, 885 .....E 5
San Pedro ....
San Rafael del Norte, 1,298 .E 4
San Rafael del Sur, 2,411 .D 5
San Ramón, 436 ....E 4
Santa Cruz ....
Santo Domingo, 1,779 ...E 4
Santo Tomás, 1,530 .....E 5
Siuna, 3,743 ....E 4
Somotillo, 1,435 ....D 4
Somoto, 3,907 ....D 4
Telpaneca, 1,019 ......D 4
Terrabona, 690 ....D 4
Teustepe, 764 ....E 4
Tipitapa, 3,600 ....D 4
Tunki ....E 4
Waspán, 973 ....F 3
Yablis ....F 4

OTHER FEATURES

Alargate (reef) ....F 3
Coco (river) ....E 3
Coseguina (point) ......D 4
Dariense (range) ....E 4
Dipilto (range) ....D 4
Escondido (river) ......F 4
Fonseca (gulf) ....D 4
Gorda (point) ....F 5
Gracias a Dios (cape) ...F 3
Grande (river) ....E 4
Great Corn (isl.), 1,896 .F 4
Huapí (mts.) ....E 4
Isabelia (range) ....E 4
King (cays) ....F 4
Kukalaya (river) ....F 4
Little Corn (isl.) ......F 4
Managua (lake) ....D 4
Miskito (cays) ....F 3
Monkey (point) ....F 4
Mosquito Coast (reg.) ..E 4
Nicaragua (lake) ....E 5
Ometepe (isl.), 12,556 ..E 5
Pearl (cays) ....F 4
Perlas (lagoon) ....F 4
Prinzapolca (river) .....F 4
Salinas (bay) ....D 5
San Juan (river) ....E, F 5
San Juan del Norte (bay) .F 5
Solentiname (isls.) ....E 5
Tuma (river) ....E 4
Tyra (cays) ....F 4
Waspuk (river) ....E 3
Wawa (river) ....F 4
Zapatera (isl.) ....E 5

PANAMA

CITIES and TOWNS

Aguadulce, 8,192 ....G 6
Alanje, ‡1,544 ....F 6
Almirante, 4,134 ....F 6
Antón, 3,022 ....G 6
Bajo Boquete, 2,625 ....F 6
Belén ....G 6
Bocas del Toro, 2,462 ...F 6
Calobre, ‡1,933 ....G 6
Cañazas, 15,516 ....G 6
Capira, ‡2,168 ....G 6
Carreto ....J 6
Chepo, 1,598 ....H 6
Chimán, ‡1,972 ....H 6
Chiriquí Grande, †1,517 .F 6
Chitré, 12,575 ....G 7
Chorrera, 26,026 ......H 6
Coclé del Norte, ‡1,329 .G 6
Colón, 67,641 ....H 6
David, 35,538 ....F 6
Dolega, ‡3,710 ....F 6
El Real ....J 6
Garachiné, ‡1,471 .....J 6
Guabito, ‡3,531 ......F 6
Gualaca, ‡3,125 ......F 6
Horconcitos ....F 6
La Concepción, 9,179 ..F 6
La Palma, 1,845 ......H 6
Las Palmas, ‡3,115 ....G 6
Las Tablas, 3,571 .....G 7
Loma Escobar (La Pintada) .G 6
Los Santos, 3,940 .....G 7
Mandinga ....H 6
Miguel de la Borda .....G 6
Miramar, †132 ....H 6
Montijo, 13,600 ......G 6
Natá, 3,195 ....G 6
Nuevo Chagres ....G 6
Ocú, †5,267 ....G 7

Olá, †1987 ....G 6
Panamá (cap.), 418,013 .H 6
Parita, †2,320 ....G 6
Pedasí, ‡1,302 ....G 6
Penonomé, 5,067 ......G 6
Playón Chico ....H 6
Playón Grande ....H 6
Portobelo, †1,626 .....H 6
Potrerillos ....F 6
Puerto Armuelles, 12,022 .F 6
Puerto Obaldía ....J 6
San Carlos, ‡1,421 ....H 6
San Cristóbal ....G 6
San Félix, ‡1,314 .....G 6
San Francisco, ‡1,576 ..G 6
Santa Fé, ‡1,768 ......G 6
Santiago, 14,391 ......G 6
Soná, 4,066 ....G 6
Tocumen, ‡5,905 ......H 6
Tolé, 14,734 ....F 6
Tonosí, ‡1,301 ....G 7

OTHER FEATURES

Azuero (pen.) ....G 7
Bastimentos (isl.), 574 ..G 6
Brewster (mt.) ....H 6
Burica (point) ....F 7
Cébaco (isl.) ....G 7
Chepo (river) ....H 6
Chiriquí (gulf) ....F 7
Chiriquí (lagoon) ......F 6
Chiriquí (volcano) .....F 6
Chucunaque (river) ....J 6
Coiba (isl.) ....F 7
Colón (isl.) ....G 6
Contreras (isls.) ......F 7
Darién (mts.) ....J 6
Escudo de Veraguas (isl.) .G 6
Gatun (lake) ....G 6
Gorda (point) ....H 6
Jicarón (isl.) ....F 7
Ladrones (isls.) ......F 7
Manzanillo (point) ....H 6
Montijo (gulf) ....G 6
Mosquito (gulf) ......G 6
Mulatas (arch.) ......J 6
Panamá (gulf) ....H 7
Pando (mt.) ....F 6
Parida (isl.) ....F 6
Parita (gulf) ....G 6
Perlas (arch.) ....H 6
Puercos (prom.) ......H 7
Rey (isl.) ....H 6
Rincón (point) ....G 6
San Blas (gulf) ....H 6
San Blas (range) .....H 6
San José (isl.) ....H 6
San Miguel (bay) .....H 6
Santiago (mt.) ....G 6
Secas (isls.) ....F 6
Tabasará (mts.) ......G 6
Taboga (isl.), †1,747 ..H 6
Tiburón (cape) ....J 6
Urabá (gulf) ....G 6
Valiente (pen.) ....G 6

City and suburbs.
†Population of sub-district.
‡Population of district.

CUBA

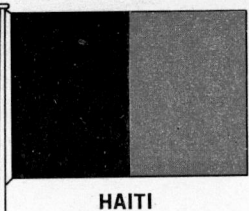
HAITI

DOMINICAN REPUBLIC

JAMAICA

TRINIDAD AND TOBAGO

BARBADOS

CUBA
AREA 44,206 sq. mi.
POPULATION 8,553,395
CAPITAL Havana
LARGEST CITY Havana
HIGHEST POINT Pico Turquino 6,561 ft.
MONETARY UNIT Cuban peso
MAJOR LANGUAGE Spanish
MAJOR RELIGION Roman Catholicism

HAITI
AREA 10,694 sq. mi.
POPULATION 4,867,190
CAPITAL Port-au-Prince
LARGEST CITY Port-au-Prince
HIGHEST POINT Pic La Selle 8,793 ft.
MONETARY UNIT gourde
MAJOR LANGUAGES Creole French, French
MAJOR RELIGION Roman Catholicism

DOMINICAN REPUBLIC
AREA 18,704 sq. mi.
POPULATION 4,011,589
CAPITAL Santo Domingo
LARGEST CITY Santo Domingo
HIGHEST POINT Pico Duarte 10,417 ft.
MONETARY UNIT Dominican peso
MAJOR LANGUAGE Spanish
MAJOR RELIGION Roman Catholicism

JAMAICA
AREA 4,411 sq. mi.
POPULATION 1,972,000
CAPITAL Kingston
LARGEST CITY Kingston
HIGHEST POINT Blue Mountain Peak, 7,402 ft.
MONETARY UNIT Jamaican pound
MAJOR LANGUAGE English
MAJOR RELIGIONS Protestantism, Roman Catholicism

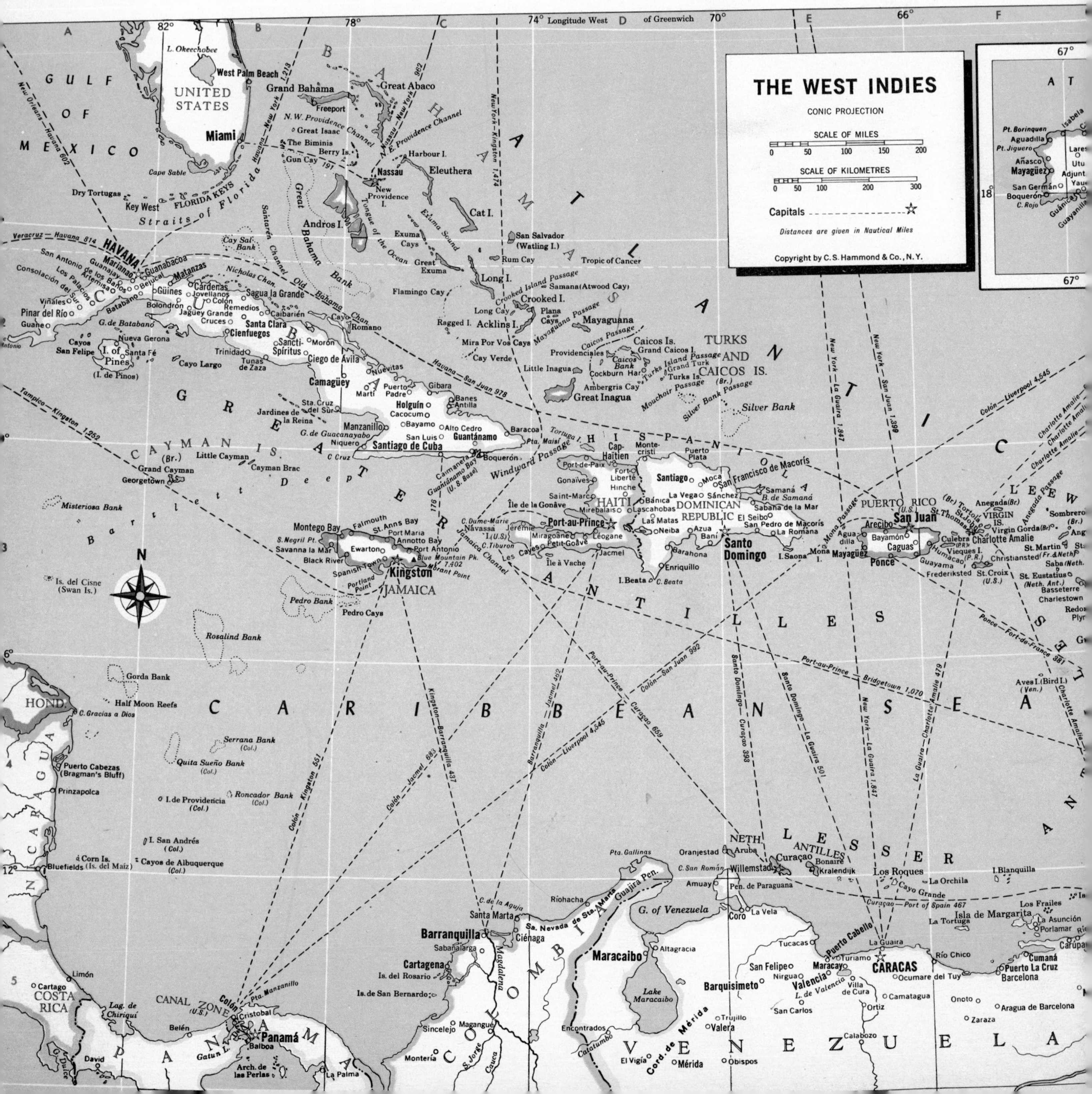

THE WEST INDIES
CONIC PROJECTION

SCALE OF MILES
0   50   100   150   200

SCALE OF KILOMETRES
0   50   100   200   300

Capitals - - - - - - - ☆

Distances are given in Nautical Miles

Copyright by C. S. Hammond & Co., N.Y.

GRENADA

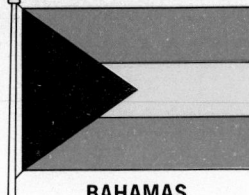

BAHAMAS

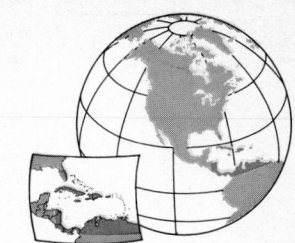

BARBADOS

AREA 166 sq. mi.
POPULATION 253,620
CAPITAL Bridgetown
LARGEST CITY Bridgetown
HIGHEST POINT Mt. Hillaby 1,104 ft.
MONETARY UNIT East Caribbean dollar
MAJOR LANGUAGE English
MAJOR RELIGION Protestantism

BAHAMAS

AREA 5,382 sq. mi.
POPULATION 197,000
CAPITAL Nassau
LARGEST CITY Nassau
HIGHEST POINT Mt. Alvernia 206 ft.
MONETARY UNIT Bahamian dollar
MAJOR LANGUAGE English
MAJOR RELIGIONS Roman Catholicism, Protestantism

GRENADA

AREA 133 sq. mi.
POPULATION 96,000
CAPITAL St. George's
LARGEST CITY St. George's
HIGHEST POINT Mt. St. Catherine 2,757 ft
MONETARY UNIT East Caribbean dollar
MAJOR LANGUAGES English, French patois
MAJOR RELIGIONS Roman Catholicism, Protestantism

TRINIDAD AND TOBAGO

AREA 1,980 sq. mi.
POPULATION 1,040,000
CAPITAL Port of Spain
LARGEST CITY Port of Spain
HIGHEST POINT Mt. Aripo 3,084 ft.
MONETARY UNIT Trinidad and Tobago dollar
MAJOR LANGUAGES English, Hindi
MAJOR RELIGIONS Roman Catholicism, Protestantism, Hinduism, Islam

VIRGIN ISLANDS (U.S.)

AREA 133 sq. mi.
POPULATION 62,468
CAPITAL Charlotte Amalie
MONETARY UNIT U.S. dollar
MAJOR LANGUAGES English, Creole
MAJOR RELIGIONS Roman Catholicism, Protestantism

VIRGIN ISLANDS (BR.)

AREA 59 sq. mi.
POPULATION 10,484
CAPITAL Road Town
MONETARY UNIT British West Indian dollar
MAJOR LANGUAGES English, Creole
MAJOR RELIGION Protestantism

PUERTO RICO

AREA 3,435 sq. mi.
POPULATION 2,712,033
CAPITAL San Juan
MONETARY UNIT U.S. dollar
MAJOR LANGUAGES Spanish, English
MAJOR RELIGION Roman Catholicism

BERMUDA

AREA 21 sq. mi.
POPULATION 52,000
CAPITAL Hamilton
MONETARY UNIT Bermuda dollar
MAJOR LANGUAGE English
MAJOR RELIGION Protestantism

NETHERLANDS ANTILLES

AREA 390 sq. mi.
POPULATION 220,000
CAPITAL Willemstad
MONETARY UNIT Antilles guilder
MAJOR LANGUAGES Dutch, Papiamento, English
MAJOR RELIGIONS Roman Catholicism, Protestantism

PUERTO RICO

BERMUDA ISLANDS

ANTIGUA
Barbuda (isl.), 1,145 ....G 3
Redonda (isl.) ....F 3
Saint John's (cap.), 24,367 ....G 3

BAHAMAS
Acklins (isl.), 1,160 ....C 2
Andros (isl.), 7,460 ....B 1
Atwood (Samana) (cay), 32......D 2
Berry (isls.), 266 ....B 1
Biminis, The (isls.), 1,576.........B 1
Cat (isl.), 3,131 ....C 1
Crooked (isl.), 764 ....C 1
Eleuthera (isl.), 7,247 ....C 1
Exuma (cays), 220 ....C 1
Exuma (Great Exuma) (isl.), 2,854 .....C 2
Grand Bahama (isl.), 7,847.......B 1
Great Abaco (isl.), 4,746 ....C 1
Great Exuma (isl.), 2,854 ....C 2
Great Inagua (isl.), 1,240 ....D 2
Great Issac (isl.), 5 ....B 1
Gun (cay), 3 ....B 1
Harbour (isl.), 997 ....C 1
Long (cay), 22 ....C 2
Long (isl.), 4,176 ....C 2
Mayaguana (isl.), 707 ....D 2
Nassau (cap.), *100,000............C 1
New Providence (isl.), 100,000...C 1
Plana (cays), 3 ....D 2
Ragged (isl.), 371 ....C 2
Rum (cay), 77 ....C 2
Samana (cays), 32 ....D 2
San Salvador (isl.), 968 ....C 1
Tongue of the Ocean (chan.).....C 1
Watling (San Salvador) (isl.), 968 .....C 1

BARBADOS
Bridgetown (cap.), 12,430........G 4

BERMUDA
Bermuda (isl.) ....H 3
Castle (harb.) ....H 2
Great (sound) ....G 2
Hamilton (cap.), 3,000 ....H 3
Hamilton, *14,156 ....H 3
Harrington (sound) ....G 3
Ireland (isl.) ....H 2
Saint David's (isl.) ....H 2
Saint George, 1,335 ....H 2
Saint George's (isl.) ....H 2
Somerset (isl.) ....G 3

CAYMAN ISLANDS
Total Population, 10,652

Cayman Brac (isl.), 1,240 ....B 3
Georgetown (cap.), 4,106 ....B 3
Grand Cayman (isl.), 9,309 ....B 3
Little Cayman (isl.), 23 ....B 3

CUBA
Bayamo, 45,400 ....C 2
Camagüey, 178,600 ....B 2
Cárdenas, 67,400 ....B 2
Ciego de Ávila, 54,700 ....B 2
Cienfuegos, 91,800 ....B 2
Florida (straits) ....B 1
Guanabacoa, 41,000 ....B 2
Guantánamo, 135,100 ....C 2
Güines, 45,000 ....B 2
Holguín, 100,500 ....C 2
Havana (cap.), *1,577,200 ....A 2
Manzanillo, 91,200 ....C 2
Mariano, 454,700 ....A 2
Matanzas, 84,100 ....B 2
Pinar del Río, 67,600 ....A 2
Pines (Pinos) (isl.), 20,630.........A 2
Sagua la Grande, 35,200 ....B 2
Sancti-Spíritus, 62,500 ....B 2
San Felipe (cay), 391 ....A 2
Santa Clara, 137,700 ....B 2
Santiago de Cuba, 259,000 ....B 2
Viñales, 1,602 ....A 2
Windward (passage) ....C 2

DOMINICA
Roseau (cap.), *16,677 ....G 4

DOMINICAN REPUBLIC
Barahona, 37,889 ....D 3
La Romana, 36,722 ....E 3
La Vega, 31,085 ....D 3
Puerto Plata, 32,181 ....D 3
San Francisco de Macorís, 43,941 .....E 3
San Pedro de Macorís, 42,473....E 3
Santiago, 155,151 ....D 3
Santo Domingo, 671,402...E 3

GRENADA
Carriacou (isl.), 6,958 ....G 4
Gouyave, 2,356 ....F 4
Grenadines (isls.), 5,612............G 4
Saint George's (cap.), *26,843....F 5

GUADELOUPE
Basse-Terre (cap.), 16,000 ....F 4
Saint-Barthélemy (isl.), 2,351.....F 3
Saint-Martin (isl.), 5,062 ....F 3

HAITI
Cap-Haïtien, 30,000 ....D 3
Gonâve (isl.), 45,411 ....D 3
Jacmel, 1199,598 ....D 3
Léogane, †140,607 ....D 3
Les Cayes, 195,446 ....C 3
Port-au-Prince (cap.), *352,681..D 3
Tortuga (Tortue) (isl.), 13,723..D 2

JAMAICA
Blue Mountain (peak) ....C 3
Jamaica (channel) ....C 3
Kingston (cap.), *376,520 ....C 3
Montego Bay, 23,610 ....B 3
Pedro (cays) ....C 3
Port Antonio, 7,830 ....C 3
Savanna la Mar, 9,789 ....B 3
Spanish Town, 14,706 ....C 3

MARTINIQUE
Forte-de-France (cap.), 100,000..G 4
Pelée (vol.) ....G 4

MONTSERRAT
Total Population, 12,300

Plymouth (cap.), 3,000 ....F 3

NETHERLANDS ANTILLES
Aruba (isl.), 58,868 ....E 4
Bonaire (isl.), 5,755 ....E 4
Curaçao (isl.), 196,170 ....E 4
Saba (isl.), 1,094 ....F 3
Sint Eustatius (isl.), 1,022..........F 3
Sint Maarten (Saint Martin) (isl.), 4,970 .....F 3
Willemstad (cap.), *94,133.........E 4

PUERTO RICO
Aguadilla, 21,031 ....F 1
Arecibo, 35,484 ....G 1
Bayamón, 147,552 ....G 1
Caguas, †95,661 ....G 1
Cataño, 26,459 ....G 1
Cayey, 21,562 ....G 1
Culebra (isl.), 732 ....H 1
Guayama, 20,318 ....G 1
Humacao, 12,411 ....G 1
Mayagüez, †85,857 ....F 1
Mona (isl.), 6 ....E 3
Ponce, †158,981 ....F 1
San 'Juan (cap.), †851,247 ....G 1
Vieques (isl.), 7,767 ....G 1

SAINT CHRISTOPHER-NEVIS-ANGUILLA
Anguilla (isl.), 5,605 ....F 3
Basseterre (cap.), 15,726 ....F 3
Sombrero (isl.), 5 ....F 3

SAINT LUCIA
Castries (cap.), *15,291 ....G 4

SAINT VINCENT
Bequia (isl.) ....G 4
Canouan (isl.) ....G 4
Grenadines (isls.), 6,428 ....G 4
Kingstown (cap.), *23,482 ....G 4
Union (isl.) ....G 4

TRINIDAD AND TOBAGO
Port of Spain (cap.), *250,000....G 5
Scarborough, 1,931 ....G 5
Tobago (isl.), 36,850 ....G 5
Trinidad (isl.), 973,250 ....G 5

TURKS AND CAICOS IS.
Total Population, 6,000

Caicos (isls.), 2,200 ....D 2
Cockburn Harbour, 866 ....D 2
Grand Turk (isl.), 2,339 ....D 2
Providenciales (isl.), 510 ....D 2
Turks (isls.), 3,800 ....D 2

VIRGIN ISLANDS (BRITISH)
Anegada (isl.), 290 ....H 1
Road Town (cap.), 2,183 ....H 1

VIRGIN ISLANDS (U.S.)
Charlotte Amalie (cap.), 12,220..H 1
Saint Croix (isl.), 31,779 ....H 2
Saint John (isl.), 1,729 ....H 1
Saint Thomas (isl.), 28,960 ....H 1

WEST INDIES
Antilles Gtr. (isls.), 22,094,100...D 3
Antilles, Lesser, 2,749,000 ....F 4
Hispaniola (isl.), 8,878,800 ....D 2
Leeward (isls.), 599,300 ....F 3
Navassa (isl.) ....C 3
Windward (isls.), 2,149,750........G 4

*City and suburbs.
†Population of commune.
‡Population of met. area.

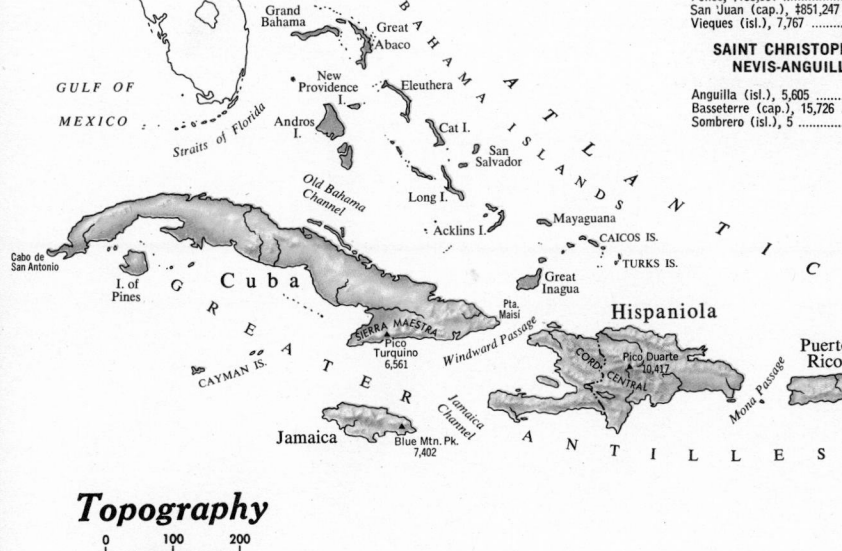

Topography

0   100   200
MILES

| Below Sea Level | 100 m. 328 ft. | 200 m. 656 ft. | 500 m. 1,640 ft. | 1,000 m. 3,281 ft. | 2,000 m. 6,562 ft. | 5,000 m. 16,404 ft. |

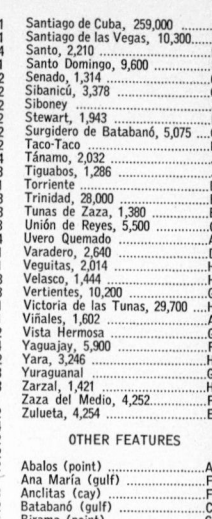

CUBA
SCALE OF MILES
SCALE OF KILOMETRES

HISPANIOLA
SCALE OF MILES
SCALE OF KILOMETRES

JAMAICA
SCALE OF MILES
SCALE OF KILOMETRES

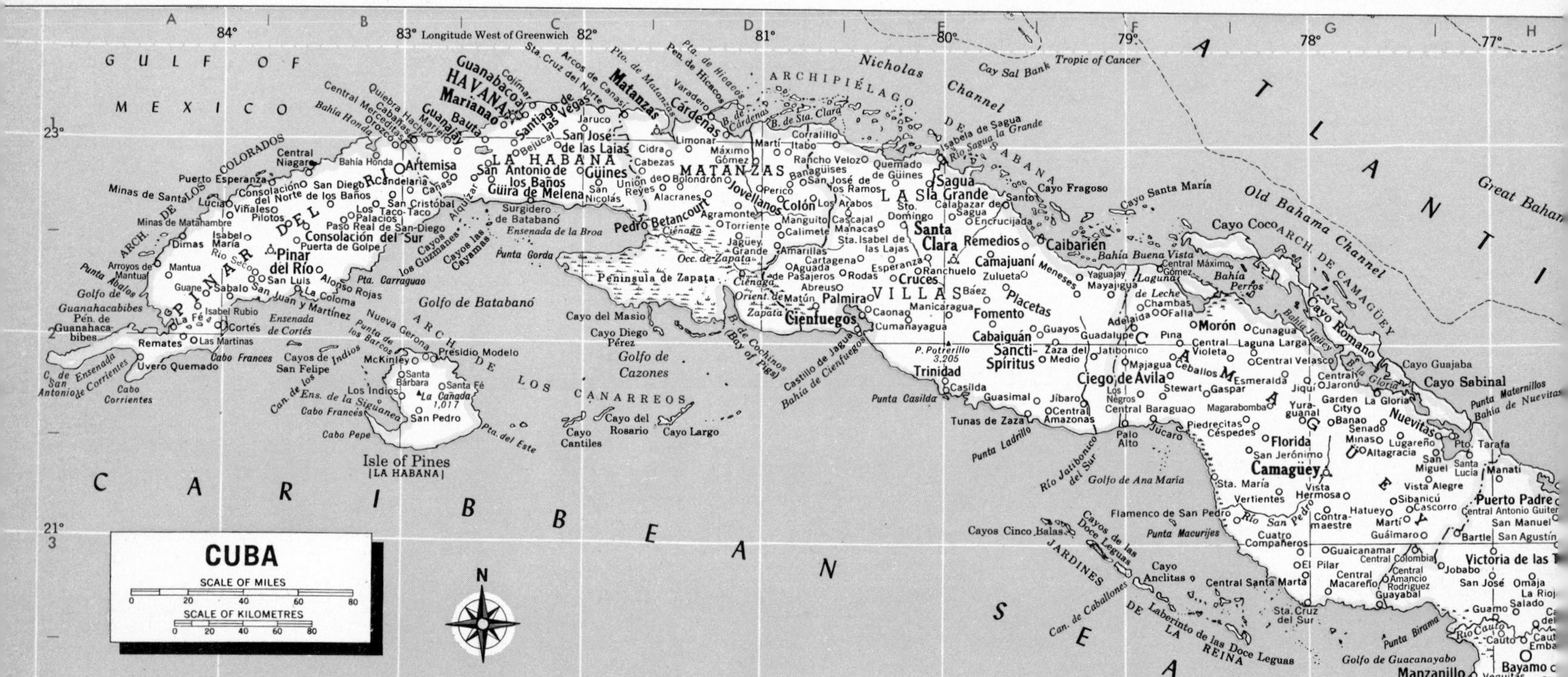

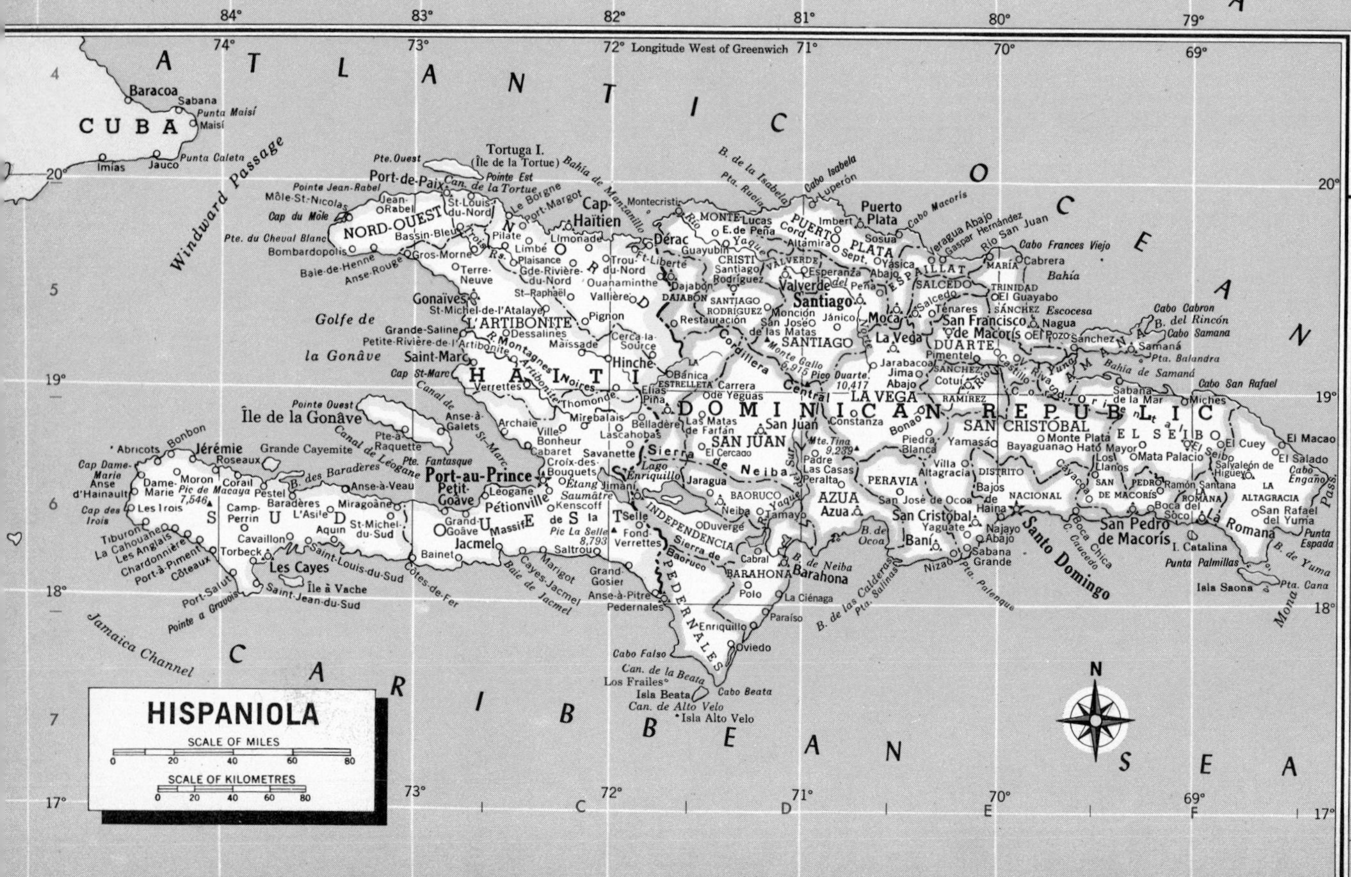

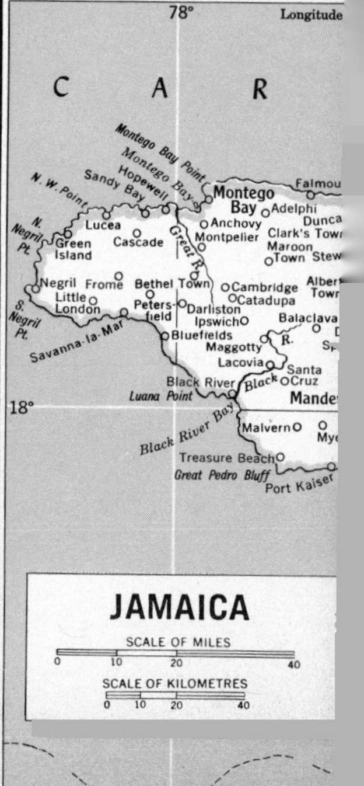

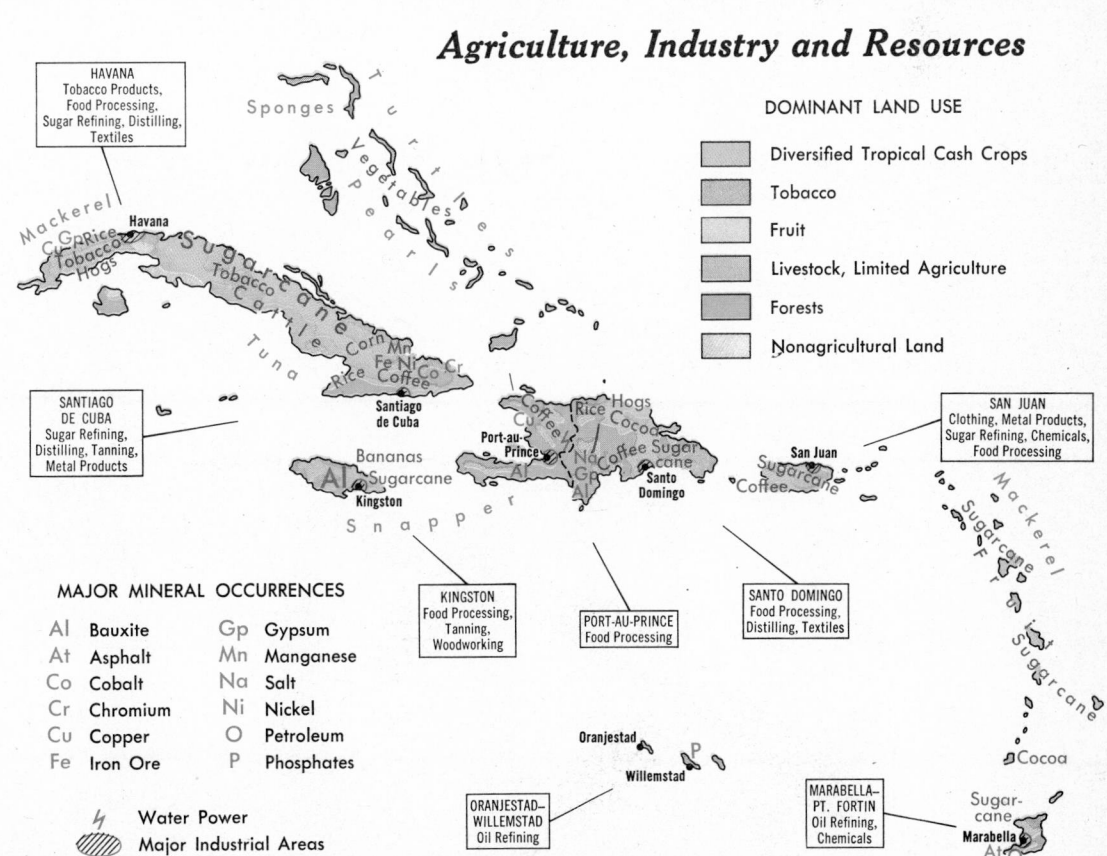

Agriculture, Industry and Resources

DOMINANT LAND USE

Diversified Tropical Cash Crops

Tobacco

Fruit

Livestock, Limited Agriculture

Forests

Nonagricultural Land

HAVANA
Tobacco Products,
Food Processing,
Sugar Refining, Distilling,
Textiles

SANTIAGO
DE CUBA
Sugar Refining,
Distilling, Tanning,
Metal Products

SAN JUAN
Clothing, Metal Products,
Sugar Refining, Chemicals,
Food Processing

KINGSTON
Food Processing,
Tanning,
Woodworking

PORT-AU-PRINCE
Food Processing

SANTO DOMINGO
Food Processing,
Distilling, Textiles

ORANJESTAD–
WILLEMSTAD
Oil Refining

MARABELLA–
PT. FORTIN
Oil Refining,
Chemicals

MAJOR MINERAL OCCURRENCES

Al Bauxite
At Asphalt
Co Cobalt
Cr Chromium
Cu Copper
Fe Iron Ore

Gp Gypsum
Mn Manganese
Na Salt
Ni Nickel
O Petroleum
P Phosphates

⚡ Water Power
🌧 Major Industrial Areas

(continued)

PUERTO RICO

DISTRICTS

Aguadilla, 284,983 A 1
Arecibo, 270,492 C 1
Bayamón, 359,499 D 1
Guayama, 335,305 D 2
Humacao, 283,481 F 2
Mayagüez, 267,731 B 2
Ponce, 308,988 C 2
San Juan, 601,554 E 1

CITIES and TOWNS

Adjuntas, 5,319 B 2
Aguada, 4,590 A 1
Aguadilla, 21,031 A 1
Aguas Buenas, 3,426 E 2
Aibonito, 7,582 E 2
Añasco, 4,416 A 1
Ángeles, †2,817 B 2
Arecibo, 35,484 B 1
Arroyo, 5,429 E 3
Arus C 3
Bahomamey, †146 A 1
Bajadero C 1
Barceloneta, 4,515 C 1
Barranquitas, 4,508 D 2
Bayamón, 147,552 D 1
Boquerón, 12,790 A 3
Cabo Rojo, 7,181 A 2
Caguas, 63,215 E 2
Caguas, ‡95,661 E 2
Camuy, 3,892 B 1
Carolina, 94,271 E 1
Cataño, 26,459 D 1
Cayey, 21,562 D 2
Ceiba, 2,147 F 2
Central Aguirre, 1,237 D 3
Ciales, 4,046 C 1
Cidra, 6,306 D 2
Coamo, 12,077 D 2
Comerío, 6,297 D 2
Coquí, 2,643 D 3
Corozal, 5,211 D 1
Corral Viejo C 2
Coto Laurel, 1,761 C 2
Culebra, 611 G 1
Dewey (Culebra), 611 G 1
Dorado, 4,388 D 1
Ensenada, 1,268 B 3
Esperanza, †1,312 G 2
Fajardo, 18,249 F 1
Florida, 1,716 C 1
Guánica, 8,979 B 3
Guayama, 20,318 E 3
Guayanilla, 5,189 B 3
Guaynabo, 55,310 D 1
Gurabo, 6,290 E 2
Hatillo, 2,760 B 1
Hato Rey, 160,539 E 1
Hormigüeros, 6,531 A 2
Humacao, 12,411 E 2
Isabela, 9,515 A 1
Isabel Segunda, 2,378 G 2
Jayuya, 3,826 C 2
Jobos, 2,720 D 3
Juana Díaz, 8,765 C 2
Juncos, 7,985 E 2
Lajas, 3,391 A 3
Lares, 4,545 B 2
Las Marías, 474 B 2
Las Piedras, 4,636 E 2
Levittown, 17,079 D 1
Loíza, 2,707 E 1
Loíza Aldea, 3,350 E 1
Luquillo, 2,459 F 1
Manatí, 13,483 C 1
Maricao, 1,492 B 2
Maunabo, 1,829 E 3
Mayagüez, 68,872 A 2
Mayagüez, ‡85,857 A 2
Moca, 2,378 A 1
Morovis, 2,892 D 1
Naguabo, 4,169 F 2
Naranjito, 3,283 D 1
Orocovis, 3,684 C 2
Palmer, 1,456 F 1
Palo Seco, †489 D 1
Parquera, 1,028 A 3
Patillas, 2,543 E 3
Peñuelas, 3,169 B 2
Playa de Fajardo F 1
Playa de Humacao, 1,912 F 2
Playa de Ponce, †15,574 C 3
Ponce, 128,233 C 3
Ponce, ‡158,981 C 3
Puerto Nuevo, †37,644 D 1
Puerto Real, 1,502 A 2
Puerto Real (Playa de Fajardo) F 1
Punta Santiago (Playa de Humacao), 1,912 F 2
Quebradillas, 2,840 B 1
Rincón, 1,538 A 1
Río Blanco, †2,659 F 2
Río Grande, 4,164 F 1
Río Piedras, †3,761 E 1
Rosario, 640 A 2
Sabana Grande, 5,561 B 2
Sabana Seca, 5,023 D 1
Salinas, 4,461 D 3
San Antonio, 2,484 A 1
San Germán, 11,613 A 2
San Juan (capital), 452,749 E 1
San Juan, ‡851,247 E 1
San Lorenzo, 7,702 E 2
San Sebastián, 7,169 B 1
Santa Isabel, 4,495 C 3
Santurce, †128,232 E 1
Tallaboa, 1,155 B 3
Toa Alta, 3,199 D 1
Toa Baja, 2,026 D 1
Trujillo Alto, 18,477 E 1
Utuado, 11,573 B 2
Vega Alta, 8,688 D 1
Vega Baja, 17,089 C 1
Vieques (Isabel Segunda), 2,378 G 2
Villalba, 4,134 C 2
Yabucoa, 5,119 E 2
Yauco, 12,922 B 2

OTHER FEATURES

Aguadillo (bay) A 1
Algarrobo (pt.) A 2
Añasco (bay) A 1
Arenas (pt.) F 2
Bauta (river) C 2
Bayamón (river) D 1
Boquerón (bay) A 3
Borinquen (pt.) A 1
Cabullón (pt.) C 3
Caja de Muertos (isl.) C 3
Camuy (river) B 1
Candelero (pt.) F 2
Canovanas (river) E 1
Caonillas (lake) C 2
Carite (lake) E 2
Carraízo (lake) E 1
Cayey, Sierra de (mts.) D 2
Central, Cordillera (range) C 2
Cerro Gordo (pt.) D 1
Coamo (res.) D 3
Coamo (river) D 3
Culebra (isl.), 732 G 1
Culebrinas (river) A 1
Culebrita (isl.) G 2
El Toro (mt.) F 2
El Yunque (mt.) F 1
Este (pt.) G 2
Fajardo (river) F 1
Figuras (pt.) E 3
Fosforescente (bay) A 3
Grande de Añasco (river) B 2
Grande de Arecibo (river) C 1
Grande de Loíza (river) E 1
Grande de Manatí (river) C 1
Guajataca (lake) B 1
Guanajibo (pt.) A 2
Guanajibo (river) A 2
Guánica (lake) B 3
Guaniquilla (pt.) A 2
Guayabal (lake) C 2
Guayanés (pt.) F 2
Guayanés (river) E 2
Guayanilla (bay) B 3
Guayo (lake) B 2
Guilarte (mt.) B 2
Honda (bay) F 2
Humacao (river) E 2
Jacaguas (river) C 2
Jaicoa (mts.) B 1
Jiguero (pt.) A 1
Jobos (bay) D 3
La Bandera (pt.) E 1
Lima (pt.) F 2
Lobo (cay) G 1
Luquillo, Sierra de (mts.) E 2
Manglillo (pt.) B 3
Mayagüez (bay) A 2
Miquillo (pt.) F 1
Molinos (pt.) G 1
Mona (passage) A 2
Negra (pt.) G 2
Nigua (river) D 2
Ola Grande (pt.) D 3
Palmas Altas (pt.) C 1
Patillas (lake) E 2
Peñón (pt.) B 1
Petrona (pt.) D 3
Pirata (mt.) F 2
Plata (river) D 2
Puerca (pt.) F 2
Puerto Medio Mundo (bay) F 2
Puerto Nuevo (pt.) C 1
Punta, Cerro de (mt.) C 2
Ramey A.F.B., 7,507 A 1
Rincón (bay) D 3
Rojo (cape) A 3
Salinas (pt.) D 1
San José (lake) E 1
San Juan, Cabezas de (prom.) F 1
San Juan National Hist. Site D 1
Sardina (pt.) A 1
Soldado (pt.) G 2
Sucia (bay) A 3
Tanamá (river) B 1
Torrecilla (lagoon) E 1
Tortuguero (lake) D 1
Tuna (pt.) E 3
Vacía Talega (pt.) E 1
Viento (pt.) E 3
Vieques (isl.), 7,767 G 2
Vieques (passage) F 2
Vieques (sound) G 2
Yagüez (river) A 2
Yauco (lake) B 2
Yeguas (pt.) F 3

ANTIGUA

Total Population, 63,000

CITIES and TOWNS

All Saints, 2,077 D11
Cedar Grove, 899 E11
Falmouth, 239 E11
Freetown, 1,026 E11
Jennings, 850 D11
Johnsons Point, 339 D11
Liberta, 1,988 E11
Old Road, 1,178 D11
Parham, 1,123 E11
Saint John's (capital) 24,367 E11
Willikies, 1,330 E11

OTHER FEATURES

Antigua (isl.), 54,304 E11
Boggy (peak) D11
Boon (pt.) E11
Green (isl.) E11
Guiana (isl.) E11
Long (isl.) E11
Saint John's (harb.) D11
Standfast (pt.) E11
Willoughby (bay) E11

BARBADOS

CITIES and TOWNS

Bathsheba B 8
Belleplaine B 8
Bridgetown (capital), 12,430 B 9
Carlton B 8
Cave Hill B 9
Checker Hall B 8
Codrington B 8
Crab Hill B 8
Crane C 9
Drax Hall B 8
Ellerton B 9
Greenland B 8
Holetown B 8
Kendal B 8
Lodge Hill B 8
Marchfield B 9
Maxwell B 9
Maxwell Hill B 9
Mount Standfast B 8
Portland B 8
Rose Hill B 8
Rouen B 9
Saint Lawrence B 9
Saint Martins B 9
Scarboro B 9
Seawell B 9
Six Mens B 8
Speightstown, 2,415 B 8
Spring Hall B 8
Welchman Hall B 8

OTHER FEATURES

Carlisle (bay) B 9
Hillaby (mt.) B 8
Long (bay) B 9
North (pt.) B 8
Oistins (bay) B 9
Pelican (isl.) B 9
Ragged (pt.) C 8
Sam Lord's Castle C 9
South (pt.) B 9

DOMINICA

Total Population, 70,302

CITIES and TOWNS

Barroui E 6
Castle Bruce, 1,474 F 6
Coulihaut, 972 E 6
Delice, 377 F 7
Grand Bay, 2,385 F 7
Hampstead, 559 E 5
La Plaine, 746 F 6
Laudat, 364 E 6
Mahaut, 1,688 E 6
Marigot, 3,200 E 6
Petit Soufrière, 799 F 6
Portsmouth, 4,146 E 5
Rosalie, 781 F 6
Roseau (capital), 10,157 E 7
Roseau, *16,677 E 7
Saint Joseph, 2,646 E 6
Salybia, 297 F 6
Soufrière, 934 E 7
Vieille Case, 1,372 E 5
Wesley, 2,063 F 5

OTHER FEATURES

Capuchin (cape) E 5
Carib Reserve, 1,974 F 6
Clyde (river) F 6
Crampton (pt.) F 5
Diablotin, Morne (mt.) E 6
Dominica (passage) E 5
Douglas (bay) E 5
Grand (bay) F 7
Jaquet (pt.) E 5
Layou (river) E 6
Martinique (passage) E 7
Micotrin (mt.) F 6
Pagoua (bay) F 6
Prince Rupert (bay) E 5
Roseau (river) E 7
Scotts (head) E 7
Soufrière (bay) E 7
Trois Pitons, Morne (mt.) E 6

GRENADA

Total Population, 105,000

CITIES and TOWNS

Crochu D 8
Gouyave, 2,356 C 8
Grand Anse C 9
Grand Roy C 8
Grenville, 1,747 D 8
Hermitage D 8
La Taste D 8
Marquis D 8
Mount Tivoli D 8
Providence D 9
Saint George's, (capital), 9,000 C 9
Saint George's, *26,843 C 9
Sauteurs, 925 D 8
Union D 8
Victoria, 1,692 D 8
Woburn C 9
Woodford C 8

OTHER FEATURES

Bedford (pt.) D 8
David (pt.) D 8
Great Bacolet (pt.) D 8
Green (isl.) D 8
Grenville (bay) D 8
Gros (pt.) C 8
Halifax (harb.) C 8
Irvins (bay) D 8
Les Tantes (isls.) D 7
Molinière (pt.) C 8
Prickly (pt.) C 9
Ronde (isl.) D 7
Saint Catherine (mt.) D 8
Saline (pt.) C 9
Sinai (mt.) D 8
Telescope (pt.) D 8

GUADELOUPE

Total Population, 324,000

CITIES and TOWNS

Anse-Bertrand, 2,597 B 5
Baie-Mahault, 2,518 A 6
Baillif, 3,056 A 7
Baninier A 6
Basse-Terre (capital), 16,000 A 7
Bouillante, 1,993 A 6
Bourg-des-Saintes, 1,174 A 7
Capesterre, 7,000 A 7
Capesterre, 861 B 7
Deshaies, 754 A 6
Ferry A 6
Gosier, 5,000 B 6
Gourbeyre, 3,024 A 7
Goyave, 1,191 A 6
Grand-Bourg, 3,299 B 7
Grippon B 6
Lamentin, 1,457 A 6
Le Moule, 8,000 B 6
Les Abymes, 6,600 B 6
Morne-à-l'Eau, 10,000 A 6
Petit-Bourg, 3,896 A 6
Petit-Canal, 1,725 A 6
Pigeon A 6
Pointe-à-Pitre, 50,000 B 6
Pointe-Noire, 2,473 A 6
Port-Louis, 5,000 B 5
Saint-Claude, 4,800 A 7
Saint-François, 3,200 B 6
Saint-Louis, 1,500 B 7
Sainte-Anne, 3,573 B 6
Sainte-Marguerite B 6
Sainte-Marie A 6
Sainte-Rose, 3,043 A 6
Trois-Rivières, 1,743 A 7
Vieux-Fort, 1,213 B 7
Vieux-Habitants, 1,621 A 7

OTHER FEATURES

Allègre (pt.) A 6
Antigues (pt.) A 5
Basse-Terre (isl.), 134,601 A 6
Châteaux (pt.) B 6
Constant, Morne (hill) B 7
Désirade (isl.), 1,559 B 6
Fajou (isl.) A 6
Grand Cul-de-Sac Marin (bay) A 6
Grand Îlet (isl.) A 7
Grande-Terre (isl.), 150,576 B 5
Grande Vigie (pt.) B 5
Guadeloupe (isl.), 285,177 B 6
Guadeloupe (passage) A 5
Kahouanne (isl.) A 6
Marie-Galante (isl.), 15,870 B 7
Nord (pt.) B 7
Nord-Est (bay) B 6
Petit Cul-de-Sac Marin (bay) A 6
Petite-Terre (isls.) B 6
Saintes (isls.), 3,272 A 7
Saintes, Canal des (chan.) A 7
Salée (river) A 6
Sans Toucher (mt.) A 6
Soufrière (mt.) A 7
Terre-de-Bas (isl.), 1,795 A 7
Terre-de-Haut (isl.), 1,477 A 7
Vieux-Fort (pt.) A 7

MARTINIQUE

Total Population, 332,000

CITIES and TOWNS

Ajoupa-Bouillon, 1,397 C 5
Anses-d'Arlet, 1,102 C 7
Basse-Pointe, 2,324 C 5
Belle-Fontaine, 1,082 C 6
Carbet, 2,593 C 6
Case-Pilote, 1,625 C 6
Diamant, 629 C 7
Ducos, 1,976 D 6
Fond-Lahaye C 6
Fonds-Saint-Denis, 780 C 6
Fort-de-France (capital), 100,000 C 6
Fort-Desaix D 6
François, 3,195 D 6
Grande-Rivière, 1,493 C 5
Gros-Morne, 979 D 6
Lamentin, 6,721 D 6
Lorrain, 1,848 D 5
Macouba, 1,329 C 5
Marigot, 1,449 D 5
Marin, 1,789 D 7
Morne-Rouge, 2,655 C 5
Morne-Vert, 493 C 6
Prêcheur, 2,312 C 5
Rivière-Pilote, 2,039 D 7
Rivière-Salée, 1,725 D 7
Robert, 2,077 D 6
Saint-Esprit, 3,214 D 6
Saint-Joseph, 1,995 D 6
Saint-Pierre, 5,556 C 6
Sainte-Anne, 960 D 7
Sainte-Luce, 1,243 D 7
Sainte-Marie, 2,933 D 5
Schoelcher, 10,817 C 6
Trinité, 3,566 D 6
Trois-Îlets, 1,400 C 6
Vauclin, 2,908 D 6
Vert-Pré D 6

OTHER FEATURES

Cabet, Pitons du (mt.) C 6
Cabri (isl.) D 7
Caravelle (pen.) D 6
Cul-de-Sac du Marin (bay) D 7
Diable (pt.) D 5
Ferré (cape) D 7
Fort-de-France (bay) C 6
Galion (bay) D 6
Lézarde (river) D 6
Long, Îlet (isl.) D 6
Lorrain (river) D 5
Martinique (passage) C 5
Pelée (vol.) C 5
Pilote (river) D 7
Ramiers, Îlet-à- (isl.) C 6
Ramville, Îlet (isl.) D 6
Robert (harb.) D 6
Rocher du Diamant (isl.) C 7
Rose (pt.) D 6
Saint-Martin (cape) C 5
Saint-Pierre (bay) C 5
Salines (pt.) D 7
Salomon (pt.) C 7
Vauclin (mt.) D 6

NETHERLANDS ANTILLES

CITIES and TOWNS

Aresji D 9
Ascension F 8
Bacuna E 8
Balashi E10
Boven Bolivia E 8
Bubali D10
Bushiribana D10
Dokterstuin D 8
Druif D10
Emmastad G 9
Entrejo E 8
Fontein E 8
Fuik G 9
Groot Sint Joris G 8
Hato G 8
Kralendijk (capital), Bonaire, 839 E 8
Lago E10
Lagoen F 8
Montanja di Reij G 9
New Port G 9
Noord di Salinja E 8
Onima E 8
Oranjestad (capital), Aruba, 15,398 D10
Otrabanda F 9
Patrick F 8
Rincon E 8
Rooi E 8
Sabana Westpunt F 8
Santa Barbara G 9
Santa Catharina E10
Savaneta E10
Savonet F 8
Sint Anna D10
Sint Jan D 8
Sint Kruis F 8
Sint Martha F 8
Sint Michiel F 9
Sint Nicolaas E10
Sint Willebrordus F 8
Terra Corra E 8
Westpunt D10
Willemstad (capital), 43,547 F 9
Willemstad, *94,133 F 9

OTHER FEATURES

Aruba (isl.), 58,868 E 9
Basora (pt.) E10
Bonaire (isl.), 5,755 E 9
Bullen (bay) F 9
Caracas (bay) G 9
Curaçao (isl.), 196,170 G 7
Goto (lake) D10
Jamanota (mt.) E10
Kanon (pt.) G 9
Klein Bonaire (isl.) E 8
Kudarebe (pt.) D 9
Lac (bay) D 9
Lacre (pt.) E 9
Malmok (mt.) E 9
Noord (pt.) D 8
Noord (pt.) F 8
Paarden (bay) D10
Palm (beach) D10
Pekelmeer (lake) E 9
Piscadera (bay) F 9
Schottegat (bay) G 9
Sint Anna (bay) F 9
Sint Christoffel Berg (mt.) F 8
Sint Joris (bay) G 9
Slag (bay) D 8
Vierkant (pt.) E 8

SAINT CHRISTOPHER-NEVIS-ANGUILLA

Total Population, 56,000

CITIES and TOWNS

Basseterre (capital), 15,726 C10
Cayon, 1,524 C10
Charlestown, 2,852 C11
Cotton Ground, 747 C11
Dieppe Bay, 949 C10
Gingerland D11
Golden Rock C10
Newcastle, 361 D11
Old Road, 1,206 C10
Sadlers Village, 1,091 C10
Sandy Point, 3,608 C10
Tabernacle, 1,250 C10
Zion Hill D11

OTHER FEATURES

Brimstone (hill) C10
Dogwood (pt.) D11
Fort (pt.) C11
Great Salt (pond) D10
Heldens (pt.) C10
Horse Shoe (pt.) C11
Misery (mt.) C10
Monkey (hill) C10
Muddy (pt.) C10
Narrows, The (str.) D11
Nevis (isl.), 12,762 D11
Nevis (peak) D11
North Friars (bay) D10
Palmetto (pt.) C10
Saint Christopher (isl.), 38,291 D10
Saint Kitts (Saint Christopher) (isl.), 38,291 D10
South Friars (bay) C10

SAINT LUCIA

Total Population, 110,000

CITIES and TOWNS

Anse la Raye, 2,053 F 6
Canaries, 1,676 G 6
Castries (capital), 4,353 G 6
Castries, *15,291 G 6
Choc G 5
Choiseul, 513 F 7
Dauphin G 5
Dennery, 2,252 G 6
Gros Islet, 1,016 G 5
Laborie, 1,591 G 7
Marigot G 6
Marquis G 6
Micoud, 2,040 G 6
Praslin G 6
Soufrière, 2,692 F 6
Vieux Fort, 3,228 G 7

OTHER FEATURES

Beaumont (pt.) F 6
Canaries, Piton (mt.) G 6
Cannelles (pt.) G 7
Cannelles (river) G 6
Cap (pt.) G 5
Choc (bay) G 5
Fond d'Or (bay) G 6
Gimie (mt.) G 6
Grand Caille (pt.) F 6
Grand Cul de Sac (river) G 6
Gros Islet (bay) G 5
Gros Piton (mt.) G 6
Maria (isl.) G 7
Ministre (pt.) G 7
Moule à Chique (cape) G 7
Petit Piton (mt.) G 6
Pigeon (isl.) G 5
Port Castries (harb.) G 6
Port Praslin (bay) G 6
Roseau (river) G 6
Saint Lucia (chan.) G 5
Saint Vincent (passage) G 7
Savannes (bay) G 7
Sorcière, La (mt.) G 6
Soufrière (bay) F 6
Vierge (pt.) G 6
Vieux Fort (river) G 6

SAINT VINCENT

Total Population, 89,129

CITIES and TOWNS

Barrouallie, †2,459 A 9
Calliaqua, †3,589 A 9
Camden Park A 9
Chateaubelair, †2,173 A 8
Colonarie, †1,550 A 9
Georgetown, †2,645 A 8
Kingstown (capital), 17,258 A 9
Kingstown, *23,482 A 9
Layou, †3,060 A 9
Turema A 8
Wallibu A 8

OTHER FEATURES

Colonarie (pt.) A 9
Cumberland (bay) A 8
Dark (head) A 8
De Volet (pt.) A 8
Espagnol (pt.) A 8
Greathead (bay) A 9
Kingstown (bay) A 9
Owia (bay) A 8
Porter (pt.) A 8
Richmond (peak) A 8
Saint Andrew (mt.) A 9
Saint Vincent (passage) A 8
Soufrière (mt.) A 8
Yambu (head) A 9

TRINIDAD and TOBAGO

CITIES and TOWNS

Arima, 10,982 B10
Arouca, 4,781 B10
Basse Terre B11
Biche, 1,986 B11
Blanchisseuse, 205 B10
California A11
Carapichaima B10
Caroni, 678 B10
Cedros, 1,388 A11
Chaguanas, 3,509 A10
Chaguaramas A10
Couva, 3,567 B10
Cunapo B10
Débé, 2,189 B11
Ecclesville B11
Flanagin Town B10
Fullarton A11
Fyzabad, 1,869 A11
Gran Couva B11
Grande Rivière, 301 B10
Guaico B10
Guayaguayare, 287 B11
La Brea, 4,828 A11
La Lune, 252 B11
Marabella, 8,937 A11
Matelot, 289 B10
Matura B10
Mayaro, 1,828 B11
Moruga, 656 B11
Mucurapo, 2,851 A10
Nestor B10
Palo Seco A11
Peñal, 3,594 B11
Piarco B10
Point Fortin, 8,753 A11
Port-of-Spain (capital), 86,150 A10
Port-of-Spain, *250,000 A10
Princes Town, 6,681 B11
Redhead, 302 B10
Rio Claro, 2,174 B11
Sadhoowa B11
Saint Joseph, 4,079 B10
Saint Joseph B11
San Fernando, 39,830 A11
San Francique A11
San Juan, 19,064 A10
Sangre Grande, 5,087 B10
Sans Souci, 295 B10
Siparia, 4,174 B11
Tabaquite B11
Tableland B11
Tacarigua, 6,704 B10
Talparo B10
Toco, 979 B10
Tunapuna, 11,287 B10
Upper Manzanilla B10
Valencia, 370 B10
Waterloo A10

OTHER FEATURES

Aripo, El Cerro del (mt.) B10
Boca Grande (passage) A10
Casa Cruz (cape) B11
Chacachacare (isl.) A10
Chupara (pt.) B10
Cocos (bay) B10
Dragons Mouth (passage) A10
Erin (bay) A11
Erin (pt.) A11
Galeota (pt.) B11
Galera (pt.) C10
Guapo (bay) A11
Guatuaro (pt.) B11
Icacos (pt.) A11
Matura (bay) B10
Mayaro (bay) B11
Monos (isl.) A10
Nariva (swamp) B10
Oropuche (river) B10
Ortoire (river) B11
Paria (gulf) A10
Pitch (lake) A11
Serpents Mouth (passage) A11
Tamana (mt.) B10
Trinidad (isl.), 973,250 A 9
Tucuche, El (mt.) B10
U.S. Naval Base A10

VIRGIN ISLANDS (BRITISH)

CITIES and TOWNS

Road Town (capital), 2,183 D 3
West End, 105 C 4

OTHER FEATURES

Flanagan (passage) D 4
Frenchman (cay) C 4
Great Thatch (isl.) C 4
Great Tobago (isl.) B 3
Jost Van Dyke (isl.), 124 C 3
Little Tobago (isl.) B 3
Narrow, The (str.) C 4
Norman (isl.) D 4
Peter (isl.) D 4
Road (bay) D 3
Sage (mt.) D 4
Sir Francis Drake (chan.) D 4
Tortola (isl.), 8,939 D 3

VIRGIN ISLANDS (U. S.)

CITIES and TOWNS

Bethlehem E 4
Canebay E 3
Charlotte Amalie (capital), 12,220 B 4
Christiansted, 3,020 F 4
Cruz Bay, †1,497 C 4
Diamond F 4
East End, †26 D 4
Emmaus C 4
Fredensdal F 4
Frederiksted, 1,531 E 4
Grove Place E 4
Kingshill F 4
Longford F 4
Negro Bay E 4

OTHER FEATURES

Altona (lagoon) F 4
Annaly (bay) E 3
Baron Bluff (prom.) E 3
Bordeaux (mt.) C 4
Brass (isls.) A 4
Buck (isl.) G 3
Buck Island (chan.) F 3
Buck Island Reef National Mon. G 3
Butler (bay) E 4
Caneel (bay) B 4
Capella (isls.) B 5
Christiansted National Hist. Site F 4
Coral (bay) D 4
Crown (mt.) A 4
Dutchcap (cay) A 4
Eagle (mt.) E 4
East (pt.) G 4
Flanagan (passage) D 4
Flat (cays) A 4
Grass (pt.) G 4
Great (pond) F 4
Great Pond (bay) F 4
Green (cay) F 4
Hams Bluff (prom.) E 3
Hans Lollik (isls.) B 3
Hassel (isl.) B 4
Jersey (bay) B 4
Krause (lagoon) F 4
Leeward (passage) B 4
Long (pt.) B 4
Long (pt.) E 4
Lovango (cay) C 4
Magens (bay) B 4
Maho (bay) C 4
Narrows, The (str.) C 4
Nulliberg (mt.) B 4
Perseverance (bay) A 4
Picara (pt.) B 4
Pillsbury (sound) B 4
Privateer (pt.) D 4
Pull (pt.) F 3
Ram (head) C 4
Red (pt.) C 4
Reef (bay) C 4
Saba (isl.) A 4
Saint Croix (isl.), 31,779 G 4
Saint James (isls.) B 4
Saint John (isl.), 1,729 C 4
Saint Thomas (harb.) B 4
Saint Thomas (isl.), 28,960 A 4
Salt (cay) A 4
Salt (river) F 4
Salt River (bay) F 4
Sandy (pt.) E 4
Savana (isl.) A 4
Southwest (cape) E 4
Tague (bay) G 4
Thatch (cay) B 4
Turner Hole (bay) G 4
U.S. Naval Air Sta. F 4
Vagthus (pt.) F 4
Virgin (passage) A 4
Virgin Islands National Park C 4
Water (isl.) A 4
Westend Saltpond (lagoon) E 4

*City and suburbs.
†Population of municipality or sub-division.

PUERTO RICO AND THE LESSER ANTILLES

Copyright by C.S. HAMMOND & CO., N.Y.

National, Territorial and Colonial Capitals .... ☆
Lesser Administrative Centers .... ◉
International Boundaries ....
Senatorial District Boundaries ....
Railroads ....

ISLANDS — POLITICAL UNITS

Puerto Rico .... Commonwealth of the United States
St. Thomas & St. John
St. Croix } .... Virgin Islands — U. S. Territory
Curaçao, Aruba
Bonaire } .... Neth. Antilles-Integral Part of Neth. Realm
Guadeloupe .... French Overseas Department
Martinique .... French Overseas Department
Dominica, St. Lucia, St. Vincent, Antigua
St. Christopher & Nevis } .... Associated Members of the British Commonwealth
Trinidad .... Trinidad & Tobago
Barbados, Grenada .... Independent Members of the British Commonwealth

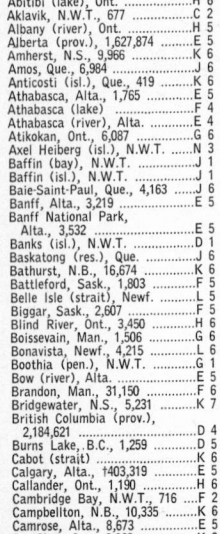

CANADA

SCALE

0 50 100 200 300 400 500 MI.

0 50 100 200 300 400 500 KM.

Capitals of Countries............☆
Provincial & Territorial Capitals....△
International Boundaries............ ‒ ‒ ‒
Provincial Boundaries.............. ‒ · ‒ ·
Canals.............................

Abitibi (lake), Ont.	H 6
Aklavik, N.W.T., 677	C 2
Albany (river), Ont.	H 5
Alberta (prov.), 1,627,874	E 4
Amherst, N.S., 9,966	K 6
Amos, Que., 6,984	J 6
Anticosti (isl.), Que., 419	K 6
Athabasca, Alta., 1,765	E 5
Athabasca (lake)	F 4
Athabasca (river), Alta.	E 4
Atikokan, Ont., 6,087	G 6
Axel Heiberg (isl.), N.W.T.	N 3
Baffin (bay), N.W.T.	J 1
Baffin (isl.), N.W.T.	K 2
Baie-Saint-Paul, Que., 4,163	J 6
Banff, Alta., 3,219	E 5
Banff National Park, Alta., 3,532	E 5
Banks (isl.), N.W.T.	D 1
Baskatong (res.), Que.	J 6
Bathurst, N.B., 16,674	K 6
Battleford, Sask., 1,803	F 5
Belle Isle (strait), Newf.	L 5
Biggar, Sask., 2,607	F 5
Blind River, Ont., 3,450	H 6
Boissevain, Man., 1,506	G 6
Bonavista, Newf., 4,215	L 6
Boothia (pen.), N.W.T.	G 1
Bow (river), Alta.	E 5
Brandon, Man., 31,150	F 6
Bridgewater, N.S., 5,231	K 7
British Columbia (prov.), 2,184,621	D 4
Burns Lake, B.C., 1,259	D 5
Cabot (strait)	L 6
Calgary, Alta., †403,319	E 5
Callander, Ont., 1,190	H 6
Cambridge Bay, N.W.T., 716	F 2
Campbellton, N.B., 10,335	K 6
Camrose, Alta., 8,673	E 5
Cap-Chat, Que., 3,868	K 6
Cape Breton (isl.), N.S., 162,989	K 6
Cardston, Alta., 2,685	E 5
Carman, Man., 2,030	G 6
Chandler, Que., 3,843	K 6
Channel-Port aux Basques, Newf., 5,942	L 6
Chapleau, Ont., 3,389	H 6
Charlottetown (cap.), P.E.I., 19,133	K 6
Chatham, N.B., 7,833	K 6
Chibougamau, Que., 9,701	J 6
Chicoutimi, Que., 33,893	J 6
Chicoutimi-Jonquière, †133,703	J 6
Chidley (cape)	K 3
Chilliwack, B.C., 9,135	D 6
Churchill, Man., 1,654	G 4
Churchill (falls), Newf.	L 5
Coast (mts.)	C 4
Cobalt, Ont., 2,197	H 6
Cochrane, Ont., 4,965	H 6
Coleman, Alta., 1,534	E 6
Columbia (river), B.C.	D 5
Coppermine, N.W.T., 637	E 2
Corner Brook, Newf., 26,309	L 6
Cornwall, Ont., 47,116	J 7
Courtenay, B.C., 7,152	D 6
Cranbrook, B.C., 12,000	E 6
Cree (lake), Sask.	F 4
Dartmouth, N.S., 64,770	K 6
Dauphin, Man., 8,891	F 5
Davis (strait)	K 1
Dawson, Yukon, 762	C 3
Devon (isl.), N.W.T.	M 3
Didsbury, Alta., 1,821	E 5
Drumheller, Alta., 5,446	E 5
Edmonton (cap.), Alta., †495,702	E 5
Edmundston, N.B., 12,365	K 6
Edson, Alta., 3,818	E 5
Ellesmere (isl.), N.W.T.	N 3
Englehart, Ont., 1,721	H 6
Eskimo Point, N.W.T., 598	G 3
Estevan, Sask., 9,150	F 6
Eston, Sask., 1,418	F 5
Fernie, B.C., 4,422	E 6
Finlay (river), B.C.	D 4
Flin Flon, Man.-Sask., 9,344	F 4
Fogo (isl.), Newf., 4,094	L 6
Fort-Chimo, Que., 693	K 4
Fort George, Que., 1,280	J 5
Fort Macleod, Alta., 2,715	E 6
Fort McMurray, Alta., 6,847	E 4
Fort McPherson, N.W.T., 679	C 2
Fort Nelson, B.C., 2,289	D 4
Fort Providence, N.W.T., 587	E 3
Fort Resolution, N.W.T., 623	E 3
Fort Saskatchewan, Alta., 5,726	E 5
Fort Simpson, N.W.T., 747	D 3
Fort Smith, N.W.T., 2,364	E 3
Foxe (basin), N.W.T.	J 2
Franklin (dist.), N.W.T., 7,747	H 1
Fraser (river), B.C.	D 5
Fredericton (cap.), N.B., 24,254	K 6
Frobisher Bay, N.W.T., 2,014	K 3
Fundy (bay)	K 6
Gagnon, Que., 3,787	K 5
Gander, Newf., 7,748	L 6
Gaspé, Que., 17,211	K 6
Georgian (bay), Ont.	H 6
Geraldton, Ont., 3,178	H 6
Glace Bay, N.S., 22,440	L 6
Goose Bay, Newf., 496	L 5
Gouin (res.), Que.	J 6
Grand Falls, Newf., 7,677	L 6
Grande Prairie, Alta., 13,079	E 4
Great Bear (lake), N.W.T.	D 2
Great Slave (lake), N.W.T.	E 3
Guelph, Ont., 60,087	H 7
Hamilton, Ont., †498,523	H 7
Hanna, Alta., 2,545	E 5
Harbour Grace, Newf., 2,771	L 6
Havre-Saint-Pierre, Que., 2,998	K 5
Hay River, N.W.T., 2,406	E 3
Hearst, Ont., 3,501	H 6
Hecate (strait), B.C.	C 5
High River, Alta., 2,676	E 5
Hope, B.C., 3,153	D 6
Hull, Que., 63,580	J 6
Humboldt, Sask., 3,881	F 5
Indian Head, Sask., 1,810	F 5
Inuvik, N.W.T., 2,669	C 2
Inverness, N.S., 1,846	K 6
Iroquois Falls, Ont., 7,271	H 6
Jasper, Alta., 2,932	D 5
Jasper Nat'l Park, Alta., 3,064	E 5
Jonquière, Que., 28,430	J 6
Juan de Fuca (strait), B.C.	D 6
Kamloops, B.C., 26,168	D 5
Kamsack, Sask., 2,783	F 5
Kane (basin), N.W.T.	N 3
Kapuskasing, Ont., 12,834	H 6
Keewatin (dist.), N.W.T., 3,403	G 3
Kelowna, B.C., 19,412	D 6
Kenora, Ont., 10,952	G 6
Killarney, Man., 2,074	F 6
Kindersley, Sask., 3,451	F 5
Kingston, Ont., 59,047	J 7
Kirkland Lake, Ont., 13,599	H 6
Kitimat, B.C., 11,824	C 5
Kluane (lake), Yukon	C 3
Kootenay (lake), B.C.	E 6
Labrador (reg.), Newf., 28,166	K 4
Labrador (sea)	L 4
Lac La Biche, Alta., 1,791	E 5
Lacombe, Alta., 3,436	E 5
Lake Louise, Alta., 165	E 5
Lancaster (sound), N.W.T.	H 1
La Sarre, Que., 5,185	J 6
La Tuque, Que., 13,099	J 6
Leduc, Alta., 4,000	E 5
Lesser Slave (lake), Alta.	E 4
Lethbridge, Alta., 41,217	E 6
Liard (river)	D 3
Lillooet, B.C., 1,514	D 5
Lloydminster, Alta.-Sask., 8,691	E 5
Logan (mt.), Yukon	B 3
London, Ont., †286,011	H 7
Lunenburg, N.S., 3,215	K 7
Mackenzie (dist.) N.W.T., 23,657	E 3
Mackenzie (river), N.W.T.	D 2
Magdalen (isls.), Que., 13,303	K 6
Manicouagan (riv.), Que.	K 5
Manitoba (prov.), 988,247	F 5
Manitoba (lake), Man.	F 5
Manitoulin (isl.), Ont.	H 6
Maple Creek, Sask., 2,268	F 6
Marathon, Ont., 2,456	H 6
Mattawa, Ont., 2,881	J 6
Mayo, Yukon, 381	C 3
M'Clintock (chan.), N.W.T.	F 1
Medicine Hat, Alta., 26,518	E 5
Melfort, Sask., 4,725	F 5
Melville, Sask., 5,375	F 5
Melville (isl.), N.W.T.	E 1
Melville (lake), Newf.	L 5
Merritt, B.C., 5,289	D 5
Minto (lake), Que.	J 4
Mistassibi (river), Que.	J 5
Mistassini (lake), Que.	J 5
Moncton, N.B., 47,891	K 6
Mont-Joli, Que., 6,698	K 6
Mont-Laurier, Que., 8,240	J 6
Montréal, Que., †2,743,208	J 6
Moose Jaw, Sask., 31,854	F 5
Moosomin, Sask., 2,407	F 5
Moosonee, Ont., 987	H 5
Morden, Man., 3,266	F 6
Nanaimo, B.C., 14,948	D 6
Nares (strait), N.W.T.	N 3
Nelson, B.C., 9,400	E 6
Nelson (river), Man.	G 4
Newcastle, N.B., 6,460	K 6
New Brunswick (prov.), 634,557	K 6
Newfoundland (prov.), 522,104	L 5
Newfoundland (isl.), 493,938	L 6
New Liskeard, Ont., 5,488	H 6
New Westminster, B.C., 42,835	D 6
Niagara Falls, Ont., 67,163	J 7
Nipigon, Ont., 2,141	H 6
Noranda, Que., 10,741	J 6
North Battleford, Sask., 12,698	F 5
North Bay, Ont., 49,187	J 6
North Magnetic Pole	F 1
North Saskatchewan (river)	E 5
North Vancouver, B.C., 31,847	D 6
Northwest Territories, 34,807	E 2
Nottaway (river), Que.	J 5
Nova Scotia (prov.), 788,960	K 7
Okanagan (lake), B.C.	D 6
Ontario (prov.), 7,703,106	H 5
Ottawa (cap.), Canada, 302,341	J 6
Ottawa-Hull, †602,510	J 6
Ottawa (river)	J 6
Owen Sound, Ont., 18,469	H 7
Parry (chan.), N.W.T.	E-H 1
Parry Sound, Ont., 5,842	J 6
Peace (river)	D 4
Peace River, Alta., 5,039	E 4
Peel (river)	C 2
Pelly (river), Yukon	C 3
Pembroke, Ont., 16,544	J 6
Péribonca (river), Que.	J 5
Peterborough, Ont., 58,111	J 7
Pincher Creek, Alta., 3,227	E 6
Portage la Prairie, Man., 12,950	G 5
Port-Cartier, Que., 3,730	K 6
Poste-de-la-Baleine, Que., 987	J 4
Povungnituk, Que., 676	J 3
Prince Albert, Sask., 28,464	F 5
Prince Albert Nat'l Park, Sask., 182	F 5
Prince Edward Island (prov.), 111,641	K 6
Prince George, B.C., 33,101	D 5
Prince Patrick (isl.), N.W.T.	M 3
Prince Rupert, B.C., 15,747	C 5
Québec (prov.), 6,027,764	J 5
Québec (cap.), Que., †480,502	J 6
Queen Charlotte (isls.), B.C., 2,390	B 5
Queen Elizabeth (isls.), N.W.T.	M 3
Quesnel, B.C., 6,252	D 5
Race (cape), Newf.	L 6
Radville, Sask., 1,024	F 6
Rae-Edzo, N.W.T., 1,081	E 3
Rainy (lake), Ont.	G 6
Rainy River, Ont., 1,196	G 6
Ray (cape), Newf.	L 6
Raymond, Alta., 2,156	E 6
Red Deer, Alta., 27,674	E 5
Regina (cap.), Sask., †140,734	F 5
Reindeer (lake)	F 4
Renfrew, Ont., 9,173	J 6
Revelstoke, B.C., 4,867	E 5
Riding Mtn. Nat'l Park, Man., 158	F 5
Rimouski, Que., 26,887	K 6
Rivière-du-Loup, Que., 12,760	K 6
Roberval, Que., 8,330	J 6
Robson (mt.), B.C.	E 5
Rocky (mts.)	D 4
Rocky Mtn. House, Alta., 2,968	E 5
Rosetown, Sask., 2,614	F 5
Rossland, B.C., 3,896	E 6
Rosthern, Sask., 1,431	F 5
Rouyn, Que., 17,821	J 6
Sable (cape), N.S.	K 7
Sable (isl.), N.S., 12	L 7
Saint Elias (mts.), Yukon	B 3
Saint John, N.B., †106,744	K 6
Saint John's (cap.), Newf., †131,814	L 6

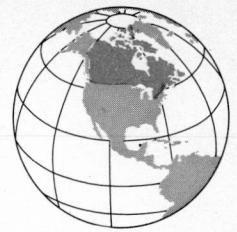

AREA 3,851,809 sq. mi.
POPULATION 21,489,000
CAPITAL Ottawa
LARGEST CITY Montréal
HIGHEST POINT Mt. Logan 19,850 ft.
MONETARY UNIT Canadian dollar
MAJOR LANGUAGES English, French
MAJOR RELIGIONS Protestantism, Roman Catholicism

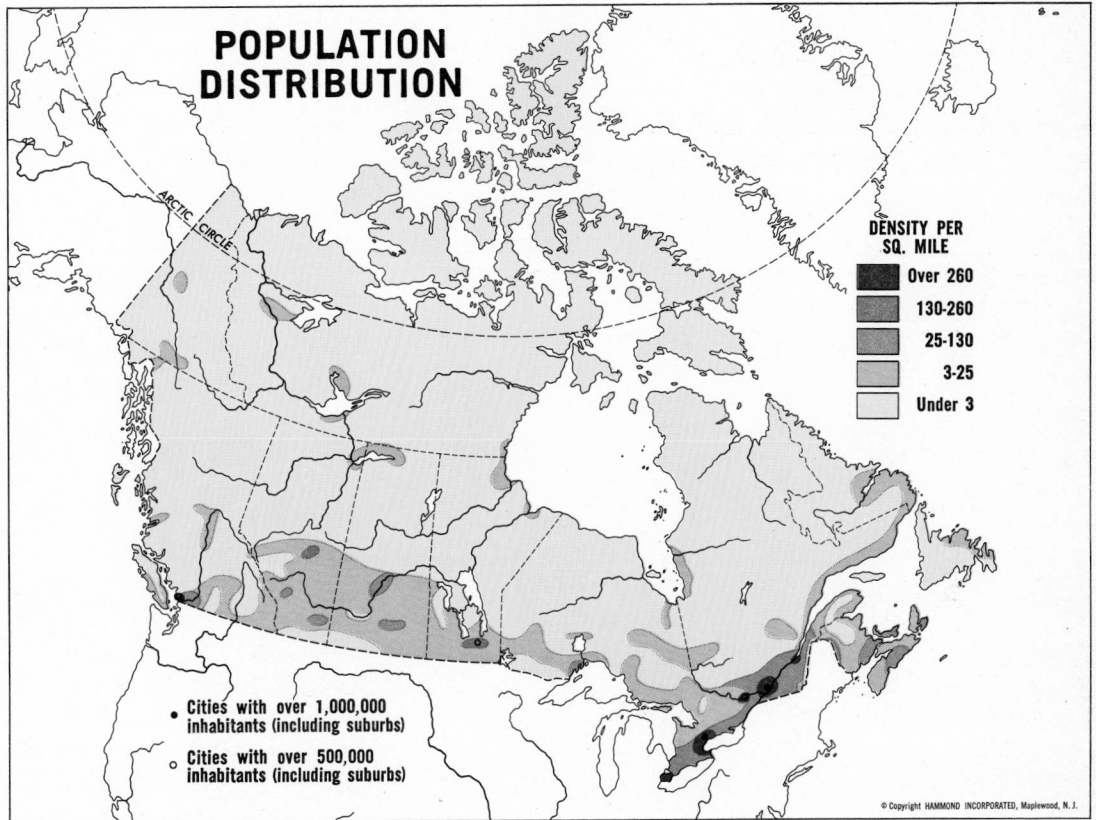

POPULATION DISTRIBUTION

DENSITY PER SQ. MILE

- Over 260
- 130-260
- 25-130
- 3-25
- Under 3

● Cities with over 1,000,000 inhabitants (including suburbs)
○ Cities with over 500,000 inhabitants (including suburbs)

© Copyright HAMMOND INCORPORATED, Maplewood, N.J.

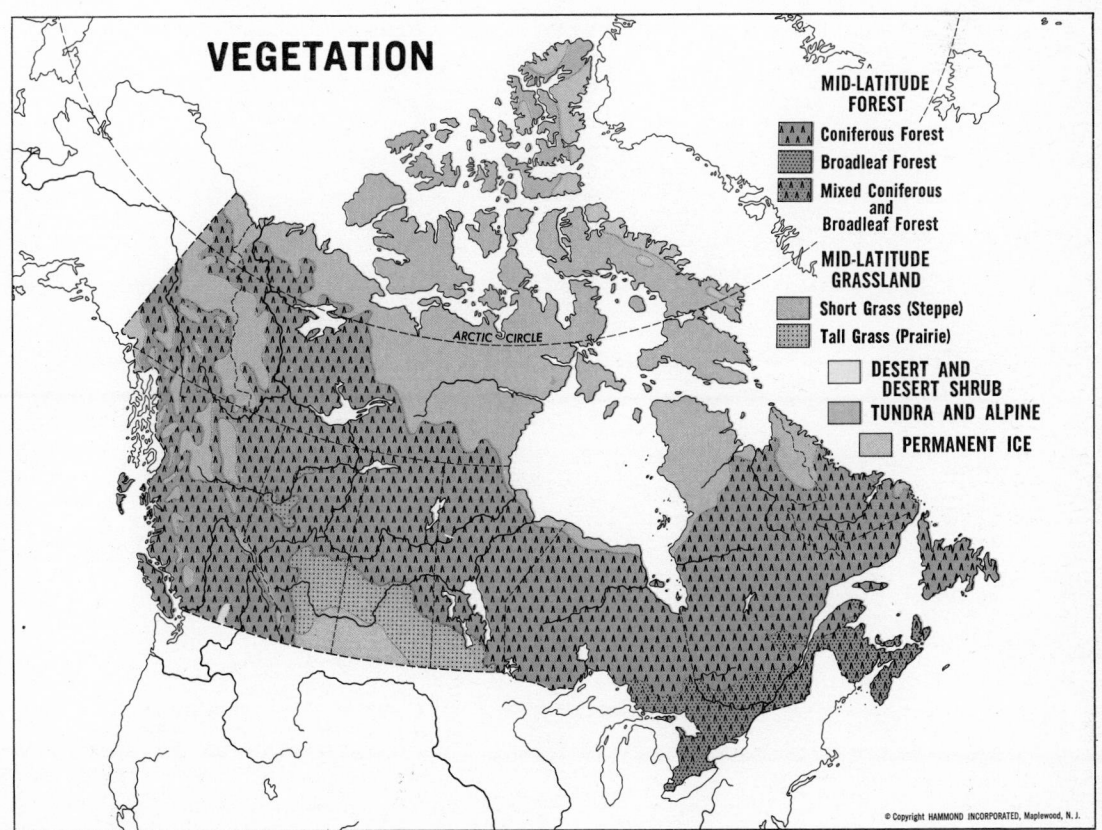

VEGETATION

MID-LATITUDE FOREST
- Coniferous Forest
- Broadleaf Forest
- Mixed Coniferous and Broadleaf Forest

MID-LATITUDE GRASSLAND
- Short Grass (Steppe)
- Tall Grass (Prairie)

- DESERT AND DESERT SHRUB
- TUNDRA AND ALPINE
- PERMANENT ICE

© Copyright HAMMOND INCORPORATED, Maplewood, N.J.

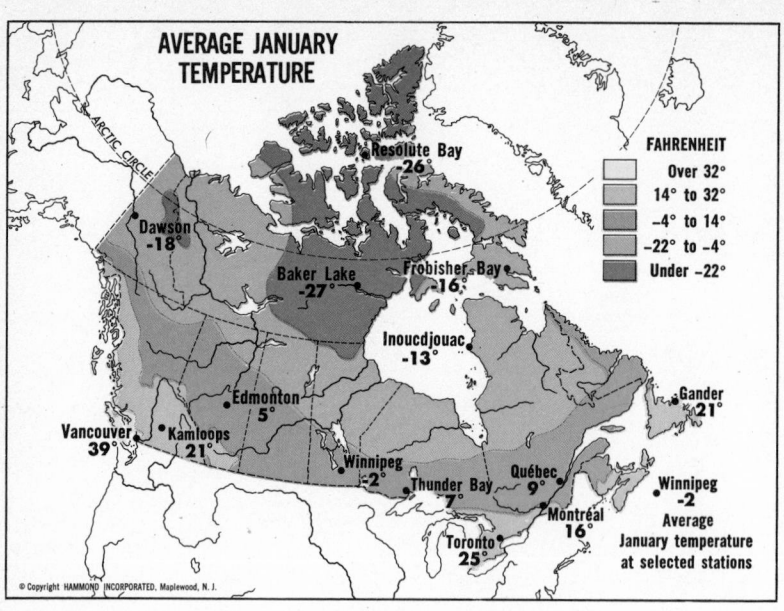

AVERAGE JANUARY TEMPERATURE
ARCTIC CIRCLE
FAHRENHEIT
Over 32°
14° to 32°
-4° to 14°
-22° to -4°
Under -22°
Resolute Bay -26°
Dawson -18°
Baker Lake -27°
Frobisher Bay -16°
Inoucdjouac -13°
Edmonton 5°
Gander 21°
Vancouver 39°
Kamloops 21°
Winnipeg -2°
Thunder Bay 7°
Québec 9°
Montréal 16°
Toronto 25°
Winnipeg -2
Average January temperature at selected stations
© Copyright HAMMOND INCORPORATED, Maplewood, N. J.

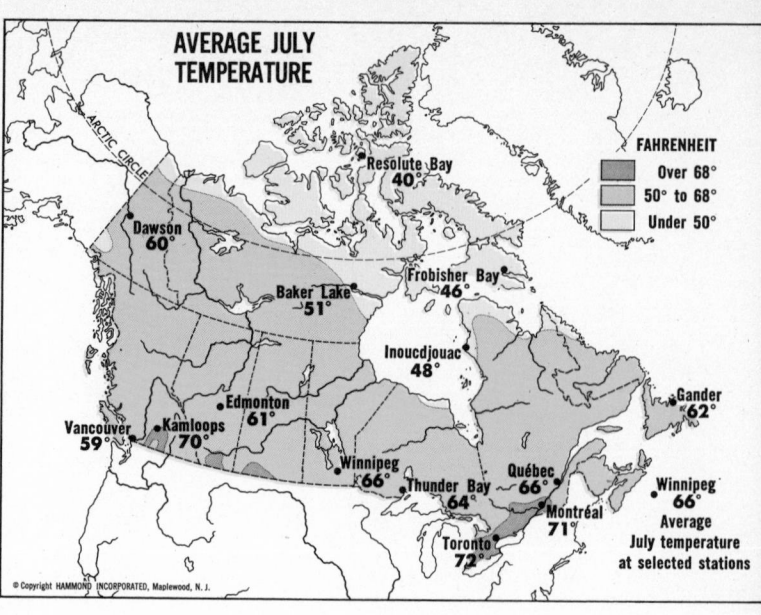

AVERAGE JULY TEMPERATURE
ARCTIC CIRCLE
FAHRENHEIT
Over 68°
50° to 68°
Under 50°
Resolute Bay 40°
Dawson 60°
Frobisher Bay 46°
Baker Lake 51°
Inoucdjouac 48°
Edmonton 61°
Gander 62°
Vancouver 59°
Kamloops 70°
Winnipeg 66°
Thunder Bay 64°
Québec 66°
Montréal 71°
Toronto 72°
Winnipeg 66°
Average July temperature at selected stations
© Copyright HAMMOND INCORPORATED, Maplewood, N. J.

Agriculture, Industry and Resources

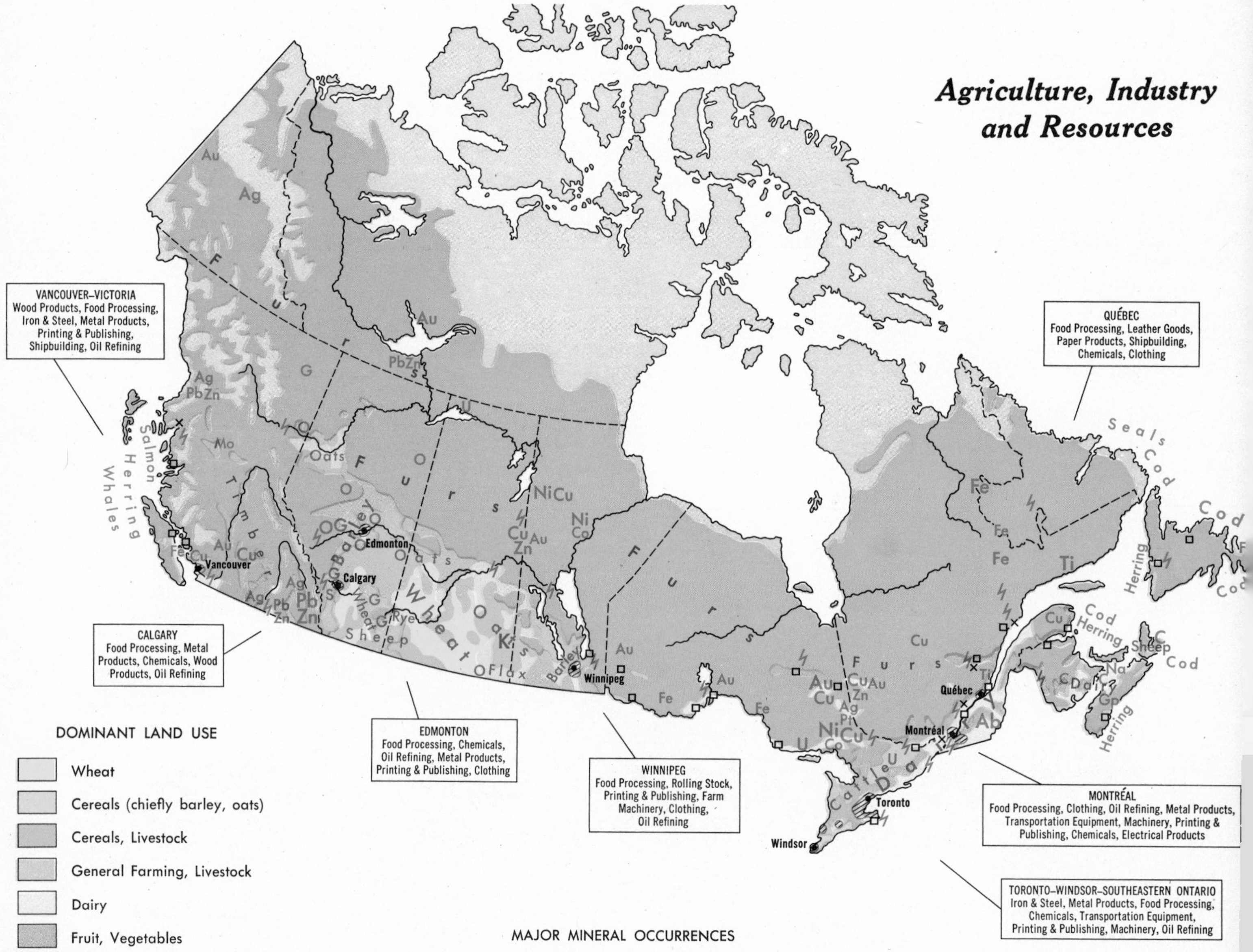

VANCOUVER–VICTORIA
Wood Products, Food Processing, Iron & Steel, Metal Products, Printing & Publishing, Shipbuilding, Oil Refining
QUÉBEC
Food Processing, Leather Goods, Paper Products, Shipbuilding, Chemicals, Clothing
CALGARY
Food Processing, Metal Products, Chemicals, Wood Products, Oil Refining
EDMONTON
Food Processing, Chemicals, Oil Refining, Metal Products, Printing & Publishing, Clothing
WINNIPEG
Food Processing, Rolling Stock, Printing & Publishing, Farm Machinery, Clothing, Oil Refining
MONTRÉAL
Food Processing, Clothing, Oil Refining, Metal Products, Transportation Equipment, Machinery, Printing & Publishing, Chemicals, Electrical Products
TORONTO–WINDSOR–SOUTHEASTERN ONTARIO
Iron & Steel, Metal Products, Food Processing, Chemicals, Transportation Equipment, Printing & Publishing, Machinery, Oil Refining
Furs
Timber
Oats
Wheat
Sheep
Flax
Rye
Barley
Cattle
Dairy
Salmon
Herring
Whales
Seals
Cod
Vancouver
Calgary
Edmonton
Winnipeg
Québec
Montréal
Toronto
Windsor

DOMINANT LAND USE

- Wheat
- Cereals (chiefly barley, oats)
- Cereals, Livestock
- General Farming, Livestock
- Dairy
- Fruit, Vegetables
- Pasture Livestock
- Range Livestock
- Forests
- Nonagricultural Land

MAJOR MINERAL OCCURRENCES

Ab	Asbestos	Cu	Copper	Mo	Molybdenum	Pt	Platinum
Ag	Silver	Fe	Iron Ore	Na	Salt	S	Sulfur
Au	Gold	G	Natural Gas	Ni	Nickel	Ti	Titanium
C	Coal	Gp	Gypsum	O	Petroleum	U	Uranium
Co	Cobalt	K	Potash	Pb	Lead	Zn	Zinc

- Water Power
- Major Industrial Areas
- Major Pulp & Paper Mills
- × Aluminum Smelters

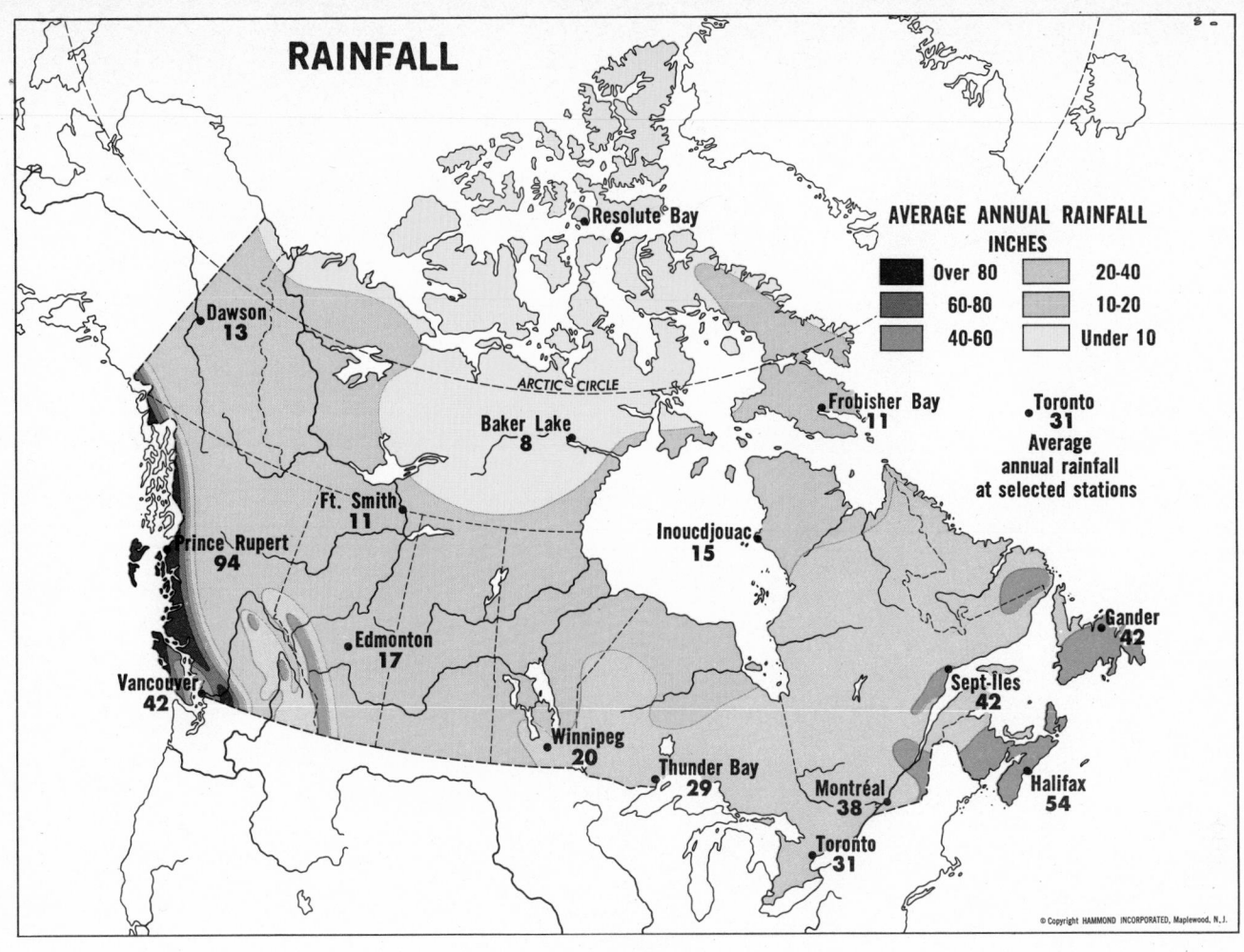

RAINFALL
AVERAGE ANNUAL RAINFALL
INCHES
Over 80
60-80
40-60
20-40
10-20
Under 10
Toronto
31
Average
annual rainfall
at selected stations
Resolute Bay
6
Dawson
13
ARCTIC CIRCLE
Frobisher Bay
11
Baker Lake
8
Ft. Smith
11
Inoucdjouac
15
Prince Rupert
94
Gander
42
Edmonton
17
Sept-Iles
42
Vancouver
42
Winnipeg
20
Thunder Bay
29
Montréal
38
Halifax
54
Toronto
31
© Copyright HAMMOND INCORPORATED, Maplewood, N.J.

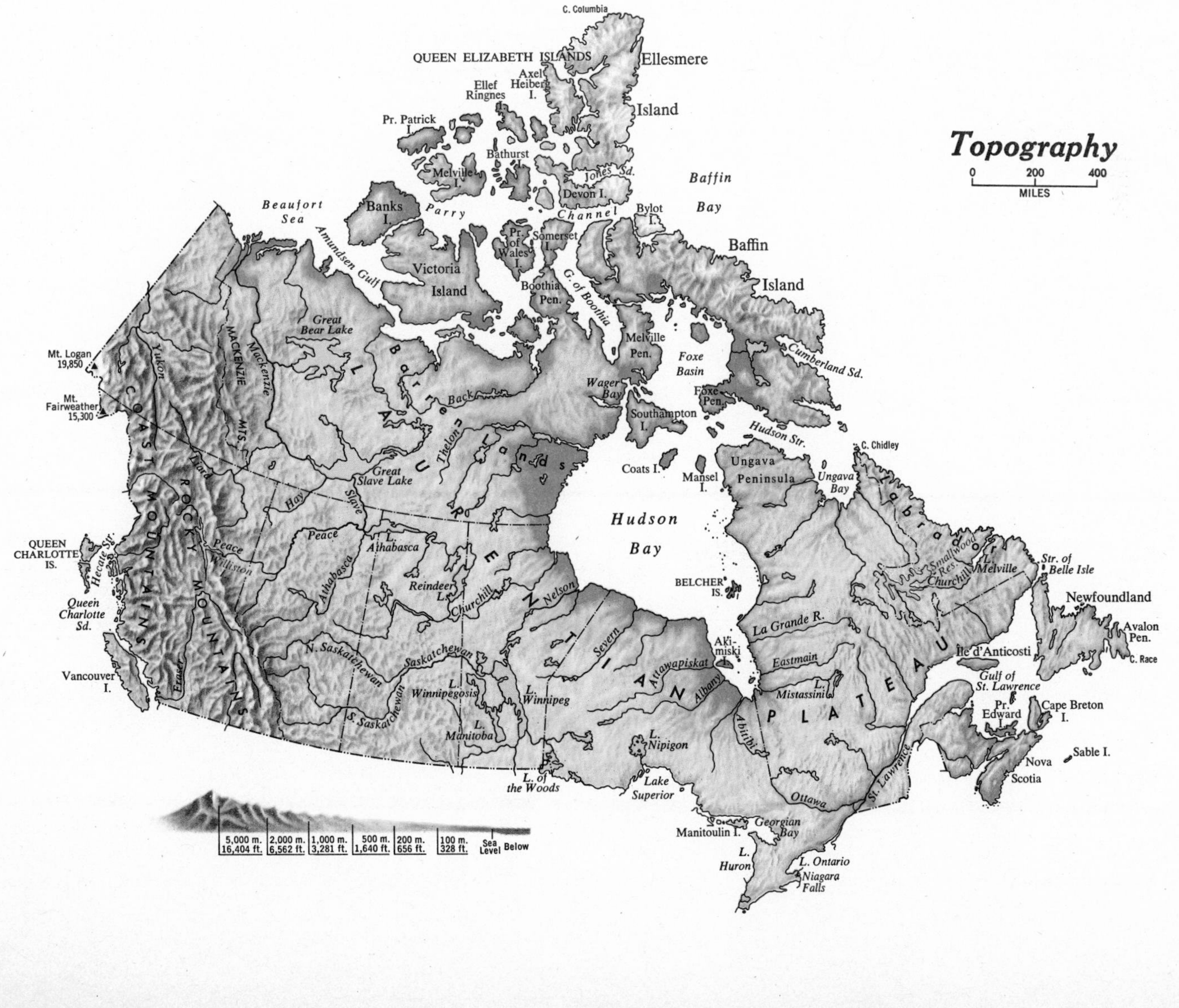

Topography
0
200
400
MILES
C. Columbia
QUEEN ELIZABETH ISLANDS
Ellesmere
Island
Axel Heiberg I.
Ellef Ringnes I.
Pr. Patrick I.
Bathurst I.
Melville I.
Jones Sd.
Devon I.
Baffin
Bay
Beaufort
Sea
Banks I.
Parry
Channel
Bylot I.
Amundsen Gulf
Victoria
Island
Pr. of Wales I.
Somerset I.
Baffin
Island
Boothia Pen.
G. of Boothia
Great Bear Lake
Melville Pen.
Foxe Basin
Cumberland Sd.
Mt. Logan 19,850
Mt. Fairweather 15,300
Yukon
MACKENZIE MTS.
Mackenzie
Barren Lands
LAURENTIAN
Back
Wager Bay
Southampton I.
Foxe Pen.
Hudson Str.
C. Chidley
COAST MOUNTAINS
ROCKY MOUNTAINS
Liard
Thelon
Great Slave Lake
Coats I.
Mansel I.
Ungava Peninsula
Ungava Bay
Labrador
Hay
Slave
Hudson
Bay
QUEEN CHARLOTTE IS.
Hecate Str.
Peace
Williston
Peace
Athabasca
L. Athabasca
Reindeer L.
Churchill
Nelson
BELCHER IS.
Smallwood Res.
Churchill
L. Melville
Str. of Belle Isle
Newfoundland
Queen Charlotte Sd.
N. Saskatchewan
Saskatchewan
Severn
Attawapiskat
Akimiski I.
La Grande R.
Avalon Pen.
C. Race
Île d'Anticosti
Vancouver I.
Fraser
S. Saskatchewan
L. Winnipegosis
L. Winnipeg
L. Manitoba
Albany
Eastmain
L. Mistassini
PLATEAU
Gulf of St. Lawrence
Pr. Edward I.
Cape Breton I.
L. Nipigon
Abitibi
St. Lawrence
Nova Scotia
Sable I.
L. of the Woods
Lake Superior
Ottawa
Manitoulin I.
Georgian Bay
L. Huron
L. Ontario
Niagara Falls
5,000 m. 16,404 ft.
2,000 m. 6,562 ft.
1,000 m. 3,281 ft.
500 m. 1,640 ft.
200 m. 656 ft.
100 m. 328 ft.
Sea Level
Below

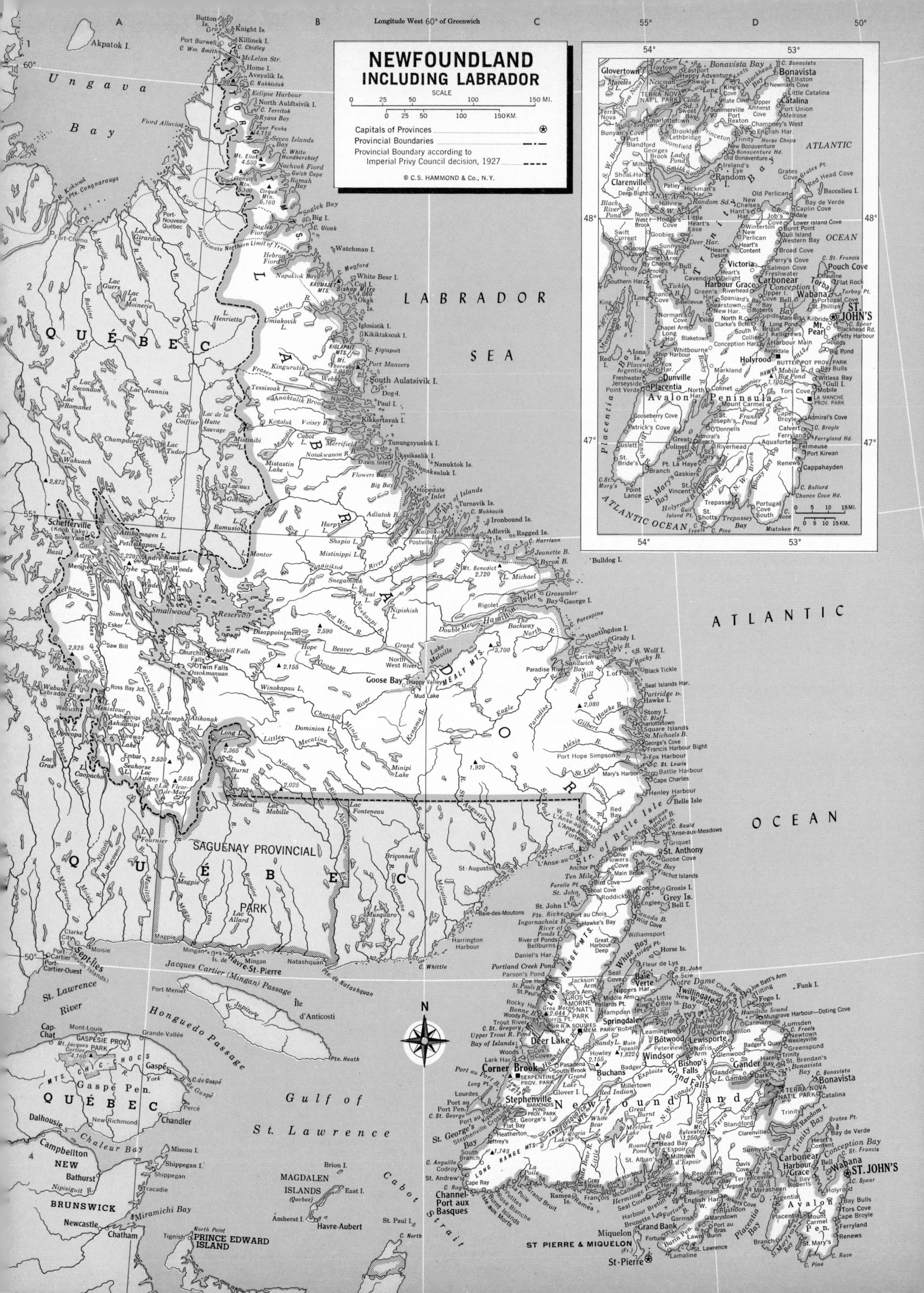

NEWFOUNDLAND INCLUDING LABRADOR

SCALE

0   25   50   100   150 MI.

0   25   50   100   150 KM.

Capitals of Provinces .... ⊛
Provincial Boundaries .... —·—·—
Provincial Boundary according to
Imperial Privy Council decision, 1927 .... — — — —

© C.S. HAMMOND & Co., N.Y.

Longitude West 60° of Greenwich

AREA 156,185 sq. mi.
POPULATION 620,000
CAPITAL St. John's
LARGEST CITY St. John's
HIGHEST POINT Cirque Mtn. 5,160 ft.
SETTLED IN 1610
ADMITTED TO CONFEDERATION 1949
PROVINCIAL FLOWER Pitcher Plant

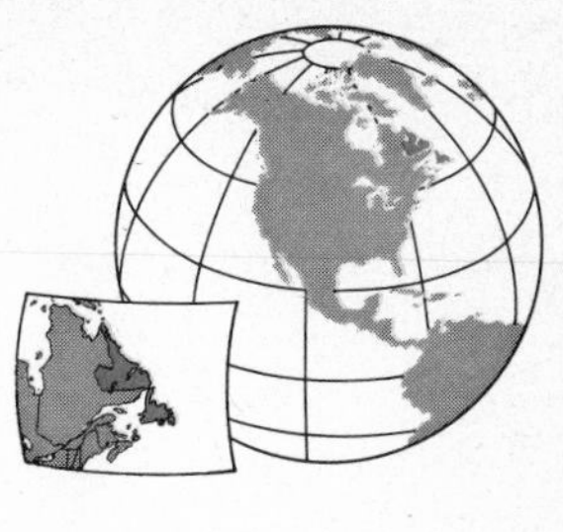

Agriculture, Industry and Resources

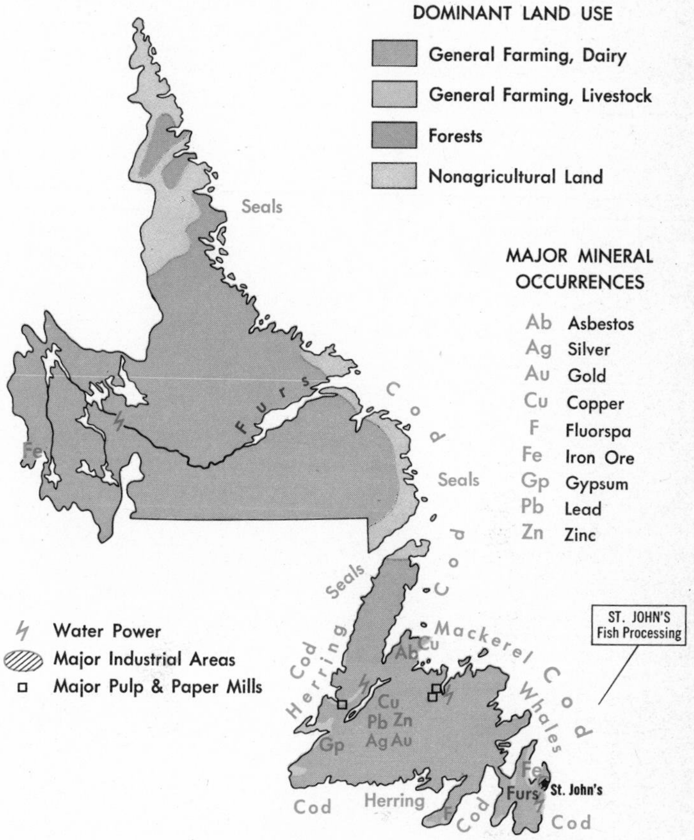

DOMINANT LAND USE
General Farming, Dairy
General Farming, Livestock
Forests
Nonagricultural Land
MAJOR MINERAL OCCURRENCES
Ab Asbestos
Ag Silver
Au Gold
Cu Copper
F Fluorspa
Fe Iron Ore
Gp Gypsum
Pb Lead
Zn Zinc
Water Power
Major Industrial Areas
Major Pulp & Paper Mills
ST. JOHN'S Fish Processing
Seals
Furs
Cod
Herring
Mackerel
Whales
Fe
Ab
Cu
Pb Zn
Ag Au
Gp
St. John's

CITIES and TOWNS

Admiral's Beach, 402 ....D 2
Admiral's Cove, 121 ....D 2
Anchor Point, 275 ....C 3
Aquaforte, 186 ....D 2
Argentia, 13 ....C 2
Arnold's Cove, 919 ....C 2
Avondale, 944 ....D 2
Badger, 1,187 ....C 4
Badger's Quay, 904 ....D 4
Baie Verte, 2,397 ....C 4
Battle Harbour, 75 ....C 3
Bauline, 297 ....D 2
Bay Bulls, 1,011 ....D 2
Bay de Verde, 826 ....D 2
Bay L'Argent, 453 ....D 4
Bay Roberts, 3,702 ....D 2
Bellburns, 165 ....C 3
Belleoram, 530 ....C 4
Bellevue, 293 ....D 2
Bird Cove, 339 ....C 3
Bishop's Falls, 4,133 ....C 4
Blackhead Road, 1,672 ....D 2
Black Tickle, 164 ....C 3
Blaketown, 399 ....D 2
Bloomfield, 597 ....D 2
Bonavista, 4,215 ....D 2
Botwood, 4,115 ....C 4
Branch, 516 ....D 2
Brigus, 746 ....D 2
Broad Cove, 198 ....D 2
Brooklyn, 167 ....D 2
Brownsdale, 189 ....D 2
Buchans, 1,907 ....C 4
Bunyan's Cove, 494 ....C 2
Burgeo, 2,226 ....C 4
Burin, 2,586 ....C 4
Burnt Islands, 799 ....C 4
Burnt Point, 257 ....D 2
Calvert, 470 ....D 2
Campbellton, 730 ....D 4
Cape Broyle, 677 ....D 2
Cape Ray, 302 ....C 4
Caplin Cove, 164 ....D 2
Carbonear, 4,732 ....D 2
Carmanville, 839 ....D 4
Cartwright, 752 ....C 3
Catalina, 1,131 ....D 2
Cavendish, 286 ....D 2
Champney's West, 195 ....D 2
Chance Cove, 446 ....D 2
Change Islands, 609 ....D 4
Channel-Port aux Basques, 5,942 ....C 4
Chapel Arm, 659 ....D 2
Charlottetown, 309 ....D 2
Churchill Falls, 2,357 ....B 3
Clarenville, 2,193 ....C 2
Clarke's Beach, 877 ....D 2
Codroy, 321 ....C 4
Colinet, 264 ....D 2
Colliers, 650 ....D 2
Come By Chance, 364 ....C 2
Conception Harbour, 783 ....D 2
Conche, 505 ....C 3
Cook's Harbour, 325 ....C 3
Corner Brook, 26,309 ....C 4
Cow Head, 501 ....C 4
Cox's Cove, 797 ....C 4
Cupids, 691 ....D 2
Cuslett, 124 ....C 2
Daniel's Harbour, 415 ....C 3
Dark Cove, 1,198 ....D 4
Davis Inlet, 193 ....B 2
Deep Bight, 169 ....C 2
Deer Lake, 4,421 ....C 4
Dildo, 878 ....D 2
Dunville, 1,742 ....D 2
Eastport, 438 ....D 1
Elliston, 551 ....D 2
Englee, 1,050 ....C 3
English Harbour West, 393 ....C 4
Fermeuse, 404 ....D 2
Ferryland, 716 ....D 2
Flat Bay, 357 ....C 4
Flat Rock, 680 ....D 2
Fleur de Lys, 672 ....C 3
Flowers Cove, 372 ....C 3
Fogo, 1,155 ....D 4
Forteau, 312 ....C 3
Fortune, 2,164 ....C 4
Fox Harbour, 214 ....C 3
Fox Harbour, 685 ....D 2
François, 220 ....C 4
Freshwater, 1,562 ....C 2
Freshwater, 222 ....D 2
Gambo, 491 ....D 4
Gander, 7,748 ....D 4
Garnish, 618 ....C 4
Gaskiers, 300 ....D 2
Gaultois, 509 ....C 4
Georges Brook, 209 ....D 2
Gillesport, 314 ....D 4
Glenwood, 979 ....D 4
Glovertown, 1,915 ....C 1
Goobies, 137 ....D 2
Goose Bay, 496 ....B 3
Gooseberry Cove, 145 ....C 2
Goose Cove, 239 ....C 2
Goose Cove, 349 ....C 3
Goulds, 4,695 ....D 2
Grand Bank, 3,476 ....C 4
Grand Falls, 7,677 ....C 4
Grates Cove, 328 ....D 2
Great Harbour Deep, 329 ....C 3
Green Island Cove, 224 ....C 3
Green's Harbour, 710 ....D 2
Greenspond, 449 ....D 4
Grey River, 204 ....C 4
Griquet, 825 ....C 3
Gull Island, 361 ....D 2
Hampden, 739 ....C 4
Hant's Harbour, 522 ....D 2
Happy Adventure, 364 ....D 2
Happy Valley, 4,937 ....B 3
Harbour Breton, 2,196 ....C 4
Harbour Grace, 2,771 ....D 2
Harbour Main, 652 ....D 2
Hare Bay, 1,485 ....D 4
Hawke's Bay, 462 ....C 3
Head of Bay d'Espoir, 514 ....C 4
Heart's Content, 599 ....D 2
Heart's Delight, 543 ....D 2
Heart's Desire, 347 ....D 2
Heatherton, 329 ....C 4
Hermitage, 520 ....C 4
Hickman's Harbour, 414 ....D 2
Hillview, 281 ....D 2
Hodge's Cove, 391 ....D 2
Holyrood, 1,282 ....D 2
Hopedale, 375 ....B 2
Howley, 409 ....C 4
Isle aux Morts, 1,158 ....C 4
Jackson's Arm, 491 ....C 4
Jeffrey's, 280 ....C 4
Jerseyside, 1,061 ....B 3
Job's Cove, 182 ....D 2
Joe Batt's Arm, 886 ....D 4
Keels, 146 ....D 1
Kelligrews, 2,046 ....D 2
Kilbride, 2,148 ....D 2
King's Cove, 271 ....D 1
King's Point, 651 ....C 4
Kippens, 1,383 ....C 4
Labrador City, 7,622 ....A 3
Lamaline, 553 ....C 4
L'Anse-au-Clair, 233 ....C 3
L'Anse-au-Loup, 448 ....C 3
La Poile, 173 ....C 4
Lark Harbour, 590 ....C 4
La Scie, 1,255 ....C 4
Lawn, 1,000 ....C 4
Lethbridge, 657 ....D 2
Lewisporte, 3,175 ....C 4
Little Bay Islands, 394 ....C 4
Little Catalina, 722 ....D 2
Little Heart's Ease, 395 ....D 2
Long Harbour, 376 ....D 2
Long Pond, 1,758 ....D 2
Lourdes, 903 ....C 4
Lower Island Cove, 406 ....D 2
Lumsden, 630 ....D 4
Main Brook, 590 ....C 3
Makkovik, 292 ....C 2
Manuels, 1,006 ....D 2
Markland, 311 ....D 2
Mary's Harbour, 134 ....C 3
Marystown, 4,960 ....D 4
McCallum, 216 ....C 4
Melrose, 378 ....D 2
Middle Arm, 474 ....C 4
Millertown, 316 ....C 4
Milltown, 712 ....C 4
Milton, 290 ....C 2
Mount Carmel, 435 ....D 2
Mount Pearl, 7,211 ....D 2
Musgrave Harbour-Doting Cove, 1,238 ....D 4
Musgravetown, 586 ....C 2
Nain, 708 ....B 2
New Chelsea, 215 ....D 2
New Harbour, 704 ....D 2
Newmans Cove, 235 ....D 2
New Perlican, 308 ....D 2
Newtown, 513 ....D 4
Nippers Harbour, 275 ....C 4
Norman's Cove, 997 ....C 2
Norris Arm, 1,191 ....C 4
Norris Point, 986 ....C 4
North Harbour, 146 ....D 2
North River, 256 ....D 2
North West Brook, 302 ....C 2
North West River, 931 ....B 3
O'Donnells, 268 ....D 2
Old Perlican, 597 ....D 2
Paradise River, 146 ....C 3
Parkers Cove, 405 ....D 4
Parson's Pond, 491 ....C 3
Pasadena, 964 ....C 4
Patrick's Cove, 170 ....C 2
Perry's Cove, 165 ....D 2
Peterview, 953 ....C 4
Petley, 177 ....D 2
Petty Harbour, 940 ....D 2
Pinware, 186 ....C 3
Placentia, 2,211 ....C 2
Plate Cove, 517 ....D 2
Point La Haye, 320 ....D 2
Point Lance, 133 ....C 2
Point Leamington, 940 ....C 4
Point Verde, 309 ....C 2
Pollards Point, 439 ....C 4
Port au Bras, 393 ....D 4
Port au Choix, 861 ....C 3
Port au Port, 605 ....C 4
Port Blandford, 779 ....C 2
Port Hope Simpson, 232 ....C 3
Port Kirwan, 159 ....D 2
Port Rexton, 384 ....D 2
Portugal Cove, 1,411 ....D 2
Portugal Cove South, 371 ....D 2
Port Union, 578 ....D 2
Pouch Cove, 1,483 ....D 2
Princeton, 180 ....D 2
Raleigh, 292 ....C 3
Ramea, 1,208 ....C 4
Red Bay, 296 ....C 3
Red Head Cove, 234 ....D 2
Rencontre East, 235 ....C 4
Renews, 497 ....D 2
Rigolet, 182 ....C 3
Riverhead, 329 ....D 2
River of Ponds, 258 ....C 3
Robert's Arm, 1,044 ....C 4
Rocky Harbour, 982 ....C 4
Roddickton, 1,239 ....C 3
Rose Blanche, 703 ....C 4
Rushoon, 506 ....D 4
Saint Alban's, 1,941 ....C 4
Saint Andrew's, 257 ....C 4
Saint Anthony, 2,593 ....C 3
Saint Brendan's, 276 ....D 4
Saint Bride's, 598 ....C 2
Saint George's, 2,082 ....C 4
Saint John's (cap.), 88,102 ....D 2
Saint John's, ‡131,814 ....D 2
Saint Joseph's, 305 ....D 2
Saint Lawrence, 2,173 ....C 4
Saint Mary's, 375 ....D 2
Saint Paul's, 347 ....C 4
Saint Phillips, 573 ....D 2
Saint Shotts, 226 ....D 2
Saint Vincent's, 593 ....D 2
Salmon Cove, 653 ....D 2
Seal Cove, 698 ....C 3
Seal Cove, 457 ....C 4
Seldom, 442 ....D 4
Ship Harbour, 255 ....D 2
Shoal Cove, 236 ....C 3
Shoal Harbour, 715 ....C 2
Sop's Arm, 382 ....C 4
South Branch, 339 ....C 4
South Brook, 802 ....C 4
Southern Harbour, 679 ....C 2
South River, 554 ....D 2
Spaniard's Bay, 1,764 ....D 2
Springdale, 3,224 ....C 4
Stephenville, 7,770 ....C 4
Stephenville Crossing, 2,129 ....C 4
Summerville, 374 ....D 2
Sunnyside, 716 ....D 2
Sweet Bay, 192 ....D 2
Swift Current, 426 ....C 2
Terrenceville, 700 ....D 4
Tilting, 406 ....D 4
Torbay, 2,090 ....D 2
Tors Cove, 325 ....D 2
Traytown, 344 ....D 1
Trepassey, 1,443 ....D 2
Trinity, 577 ....D 2
Trinity, 288 ....D 4
Trout River, 689 ....C 4
Twillingate, 1,437 ....C 4
Upper Island Cove, 1,819 ....D 2
Victoria, 1,601 ....D 2
Wabana, 5,421 ....D 2
Wabush, 3,387 ....A 3
Wesleyville, 1,142 ....D 4
Western Bay, 430 ....D 2
West Saint Modeste, 294 ....C 3
Whitbourne, 1,235 ....D 2
Wild Cove, 172 ....C 3
Windsor, 6,644 ....C 4
Winterton, 794 ....D 2
Witless Bay, 754 ....D 2
Woody Point, 300 ....C 4

OTHER FEATURES

Alexis (riv.) ....C 3
Anguille (cape) ....C 4
Annieopscotch (mts.) ....C 4
Ashuanipi (lake) ....A 3
Ashuanipi (riv.) ....A 3
Atikonak (lake) ....B 3
Attikamagen (lake) ....A 3
Avalon (pen.) ....D 2
Barachois Pond Prov. Park ....C 4
Bauld (cape) ....C 3
Bell (isl.) ....C 3
Bell (isl.), 6,079 ....D 2
Belle Isle (isl.), 25 ....C 3
Belle Isle (str.) ....C 3
Blackhead (bay) ....D 2
Bonavista (bay) ....D 1
Bonavista (cape) ....D 1
Bonne (bay) ....C 4
Broyle (cape) ....D 2
Bull Arm (inlet) ....D 2
Burin (pen.) ....C 4
Butter Pot Prov. Park ....D 2
Cabot (str.) ....B 4
Canada (bay) ....C 3
Chidley (cape) ....B 1
Churchill (falls) ....B 3
Churchill (riv.) ....B 3
Cirque (mt.) ....B 2
Clode (sound) ....D 2
Conception (bay) ....D 2
Deep (inlet) ....B 2
Double Mer (lake) ....C 3
Dyke (lake) ....A 3
Eagle (riv.) ....C 3
Espoir (bay) ....C 4
Exploits (bay) ....C 4
Exploits (riv.) ....C 4
Fogo (isl.), 4,094 ....D 4
Fortune (bay) ....C 4
Freels (cape) ....D 3
Gander (lake) ....D 4
Gander (riv.) ....D 4
Glover (isl.) ....C 4
Goose (riv.) ....B 3
Grand (lake) ....B 3
Grand (lake) ....C 4
Grates (pt.) ....D 2
Great Colinet (isl.) ....D 2
Grey (isls.) ....C 3
Groais (isl.) ....C 3
Gros Morne (mt.) ....C 4
Gros Morne Nat'l Park ....C 4
Groswater (bay) ....C 3
Hamilton (inlet) ....C 3
Hamilton (sound) ....D 4
Hare (bay) ....C 3
Hawke (hills) ....D 2
Hebron (fjord) ....B 2
Hermitage (bay) ....C 4
Holyrood (bay) ....D 2
Horse (isls.) ....D 3
Horse Chops (head) ....D 2
Humber (riv.) ....C 4
Ingornachoix (bay) ....C 3
Innuit (mt.) ....B 2
Ireland's Eye (isl.) ....D 2
Islands (bay) ....C 4
Kaipokok (bay) ....B 2
Kanairiktok (riv.) ....B 3
Kaumajet (mts.) ....B 2
Kingurutuk (lake) ....B 2
Labrador (reg.), 28,166 ....B 2
Labrador (sea) ....C 2
La Manche Prov. Park ....D 2
La Poile (bay) ....C 4
Little Mecatina (riv.) ....B 3
Long (isl.) ....C 4
Long (lake) ....A 3
Long (pt.) ....C 4
Long Range (mts.) ....C 4
Main Topsail (mt.) ....C 4
Makkovik (cape) ....C 2
McLelan (str.) ....B 1
Mealy (mts.) ....C 3
Meelpaeg (lake) ....C 4
Melville (lake) ....C 3
Menihek (lakes) ....A 3
Merasheen (isl.) ....C 2
Mistaken (pt.) ....D 2
Mistastin (lake) ....B 2
Nachvak (fjord) ....B 2
Naskaupi (riv.) ....B 3
Newfoundland (isl.), 493,938 ....C 4
Newman (sound) ....D 2
New World (isl.), 4,563 ....C 4
Norman (cape) ....C 3
North Aulatsivik (isl.) ....B 2
Notre Dame (bay) ....C 4
Okak (bay) ....B 2
Ossokmanuan (res.) ....B 3
Petitsikapau (lake) ....A 3
Pine (cape) ....D 2
Pinware (riv.) ....C 3
Pistolet (bay) ....C 3
Placentia (bay) ....C 2
Ponds (isl.), 164 ....C 3
Port au Port (bay) ....C 4
Port au Port (pen.) ....C 4
Port Manvers (harb.) ....B 2
Race (cape) ....D 2
Ramah (bay) ....B 2
Ramea (isls.), 1,208 ....C 4
Random (isl.), 1,353 ....D 2
Random (sound) ....D 2
Ray (cape) ....C 4
Red (isl.) ....C 2
Red Indian (lake) ....C 4
Red Wine (riv.) ....B 3
Rocky (riv.) ....D 2
Round (pond) ....C 4
Saglek (bay) ....B 2
Saint Francis (cape) ....D 2
Saint George (cape) ....C 4
Saint George's (bay) ....C 4
Saint John (bay) ....C 3
Saint John (cape) ....C 3
Saint Lawrence (gulf) ....B 4
Saint Lewis (cape) ....C 3
Saint Mary's (bay) ....C 2
Saint Mary's (cape) ....C 2
Saint Michaels (bay) ....C 3
Salmonier (riv.) ....D 2
Sandwich (bay) ....C 3
Serpentine Prov. Park ....C 4
Shabogamo (lake) ....A 3
Shoal (bay) ....D 2
Sir R.A. Squires Mem. Park ....C 4
Smallwood (res.) ....B 3
Smith (sound) ....D 2
South Aulatsivik (isl.) ....B 2
Spear (cape) ....D 2
Swale (isl.) ....D 1
Sylvester (mt.) ....C 4
Terra Nova (riv.) ....C 2
Terra Nova Nat'l Park ....D 2
Territok (cape) ....B 2
Thoresby (mt.) ....B 2
Tickle (bay) ....D 2
Torbay (pt.) ....D 2
Torngat (mts.) ....B 2
Trespassey (bay) ....D 2
Trinity (bay) ....D 2
Tunungayualok (isl.) ....B 2
Ukasiksalik (isl.), 193 ....B 2
Victoria (lake) ....C 4
Wabush (lake) ....A 3
White (bay) ....C 3
White Bear (lake) ....C 4
White Handkerchief (cape) ....B 2

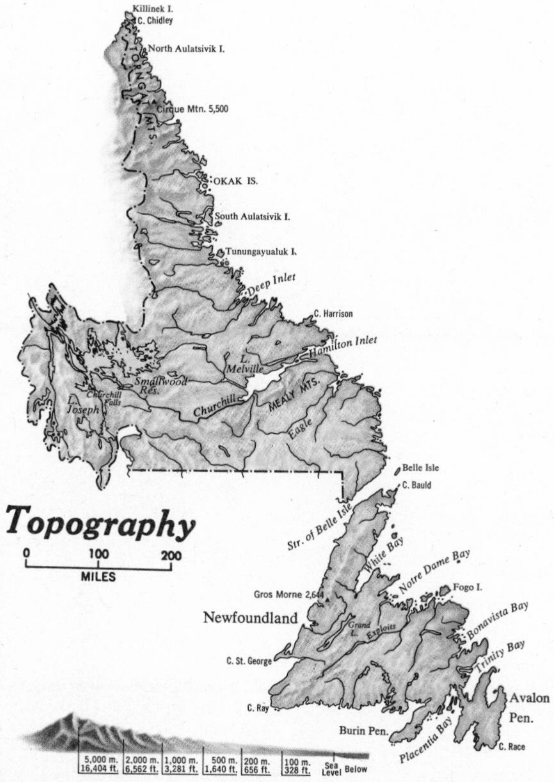

Topography
0 100 200
MILES
Killinek I.
C. Chidley
North Aulatsivik I.
Cirque Mtn. 5,500
OKAK IS.
South Aulatsivik I.
Tunungayualuk I.
Deep Inlet
C. Harrison
Hamilton Inlet
Melville
Smallwood Res.
Churchill
MEALY MTS.
Eagle
Belle Isle
C. Bauld
Str. of Belle Isle
White Bay
Notre Dame Bay
Fogo I.
Gros Morne 2,644
Newfoundland
Bonavista Bay
C. St. George
Trinity Bay
C. Ray
Avalon Pen.
Burin Pen.
Placentia Bay
C. Race
5,000 m. 16,404 ft.
2,000 m. 6,562 ft.
1,000 m. 3,281 ft.
500 m. 1,640 ft.
200 m. 656 ft.
100 m. 328 ft.
Sea Level
Below

SAINT PIERRE & MIQUELON

CITIES and TOWNS

Saint-Pierre (cap.), 4,565 C

OTHER FEATURES

Miquelon (isl.), 621 ....C 4
Saint Pierre (isl.), 4,565 ....C 4

‡ Population of metropolitan area.

NOVA SCOTIA

Yarmouth, 24,682..........C 5

COUNTIES

CITIES and TOWNS

Annapolis, 21,841..........C 4
Antigonish, 16,814..........F 3
Cape Breton, 129,075..........H 3
Colchester, 37,735..........D 3
Cumberland, 35,160..........D 3
Digby, 20,349..........C 4
Guysborough, 12,864..........F 3
Halifax, 261,461..........E 4
Hants, 28,935..........D 3
Inverness, 20,375..........G 2
Kings, 44,975..........D 3
Lunenburg, 38,422..........D 4
Pictou, 46,104..........F 3
Queens, 12,950..........D 4
Richmond, 12,734..........H 3
Shelburne, 16,661..........C 5
Victoria, 7,823..........H 2

Abercrombie, 532..........F 3
Alder Point, 844..........H 2
Aldershot, 1,729..........D 3
Amherst⊙, 9,966..........D 3
Annapolis Royal⊙, 758..........C 4
Antigonish⊙, 5,489..........F 3
Arcadia, 425..........B 5
Arichat⊙, 829..........H 3
Auburn, 519..........D 3
Aylesford, 680..........D 3
Baddeck⊙, 831..........H 2
Barrington Passage, 551..........C 5
Bear River, 733..........C 4
Beaverbank, 958..........E 4
Belliveau Cove, 486..........B 4
Belmont, 663..........E 3
Berwick, 1,412..........D 3

Bible Hill, 3,505..........E 3
Block House, 418..........D 4
Blue Rock, 394..........D 4
Bras d'Or, 655..........H 2
Bridgetown, 1,039..........C 4
Bridgewater, 5,231..........D 4
Brookfield, 658..........E 3
Brooklyn, 1,253..........D 4
Caledonia, 459..........C 4
Cambridge Station, 699..........D 3
Canning, 809..........D 3
Canso, 1,209..........H 3
Cape North, 118..........H 2
Centreville, 552..........D 3
Chester, 1,031..........D 4
Chester Basin, 588..........D 4
Chéticamp, 1,016..........G 2
Church Point, 258..........B 4
Clark's Harbour, 1,082..........C 5
Clementsport, 479..........C 4
Comeauville, 365..........B 4
Concession, 404..........B 4
Conquerall Bank, 480..........D 4

Conway, 363..........C 4
Dartmouth, 64,770..........E 4
Debert, 703..........E 3
Deep Brook, 494..........C 4
Digby⊙, 2,363..........C 4
Dominion, 2,879..........J 2
Donkin, 910..........J 2
East Chester, 485..........D 4
East Chezzetcook, 617..........E 4
Ellershouse, 427..........D 3
Elmsdale, 758..........E 4
Enfield, 1,056..........E 4
Fall River, 969..........E 4
Falmouth, 759..........D 3
Florence, 1,958..........H 2
Freeport, 475..........B 4
Glace Bay, 22,440..........J 2
Gold River, 448..........D 4
Granville Ferry, 445..........C 4
Great Village, 494..........E 3
Grosses Coques, 360..........B 4
Guysborough⊙, 494..........G 3
Halifax (cap.)⊙, 122,035..........E 4

Halifax, ‡222,637..........E 4
Hantsport, 1,447..........D 3
Havre Boucher, 385..........G 3
Head of Jeddore, 445..........E 4
Head of Saint Margarets
   Bay, 644..........E 4
Heatherton, 368..........G 3
Hebron, 463..........B 5
Herring Cove, 1,487..........E 4
Hilden, 803..........E 3
Hopewell, 439..........F 3
Hubbards, 427..........D 4
Ingonish, 338..........H 2
Ingonish Beach, 640..........H 2
Inverness, 1,846..........G 2
Joggins, 777..........D 3
Judique, 409..........G 3
Kentville⊙, 5,198..........D 3
Kingston, 1,429..........D 4
Lakeside, 1,687..........E 4
Lantz, 661..........E 4
L'Ardoise West, 432..........H 3
Lawrencetown, 512..........C 4

Lequille, 526..........C 4
Little Dover, 585..........G 3
Liverpool⊙, 3,654..........D 4
Lockeport, 1,208..........C 5
Louisbourg, 1,582..........J 3
Louisdale, 1,036..........H 3
Lower Wedgeport, 561..........C 5
Lower West Pubnico, 743..........C 5
Lower Woods Harbour,
   589..........C 5
Lunenburg⊙, 3,215..........D 4
Lyons Brook, 441..........F 3
Mabou, 421..........G 2
Maccan, 492..........D 3
Mahone Bay, 1,333..........D 4
Main-à-Dieu, 394..........J 2
Meaghers Grant, 388..........E 4
Melvern Square, 427..........C 3
Meteghan, 909..........B 4
Meteghan Centre, 368..........B 4
Meteghan River, 414..........B 4
Middle Musquodoboit
   638..........E 3

Middleton, 1,870..........C 4
Middlewood, 395..........D 4
Milford Station, 650..........E 3
Milton, 1,854..........D 4
Mira Road, 1,503..........H 2
Monastery, 418..........G 3
Mount Uniacke, 813..........E 4
Mulgrave, 1,196..........G 3
Musquodoboit Harbour,
   768..........E 4
New Germany, 584..........D 4
New Glasgow, 10,849..........F 3
New Minas, 1,503..........D 3
Newport, 471..........D 3
New Road, 1,333..........C 4
New Victoria, 1,377..........H 2
New Waterford, 9,579..........J 2
Nictaux, 578..........C 4
North Sydney, 8,604..........H 2
Oxford, 1,473..........D 3
Parkers Cove, 395..........C 4
Parrsboro, 1,807..........D 3
Petit-de-Grat, 1,032..........H 3

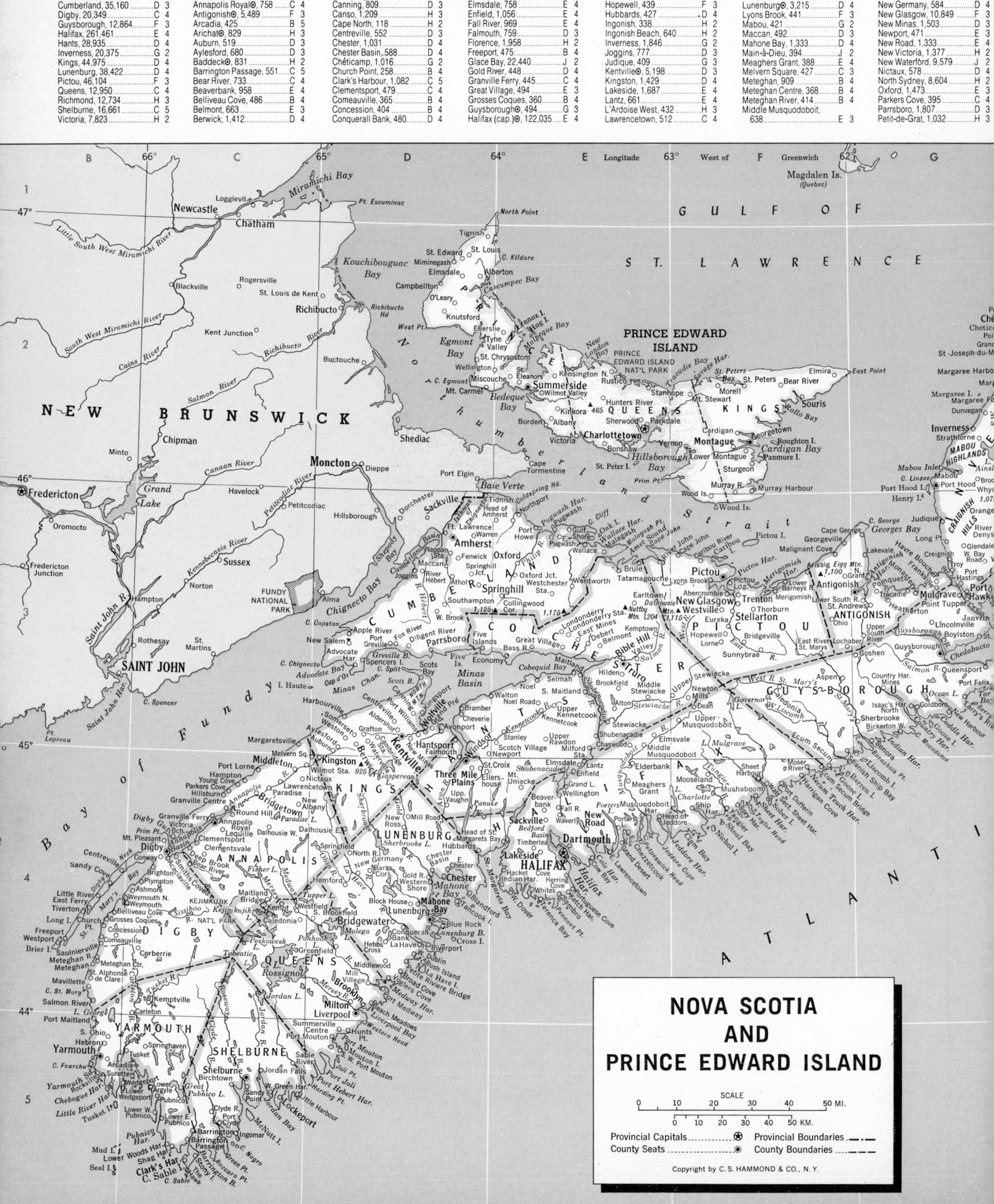

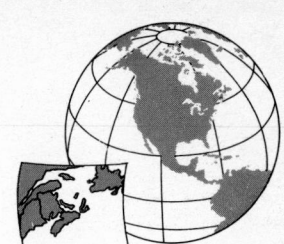

-Étang, 438	G 2	Shelburne⊙, 2,689	C 5	
ou, 4,250	F 3	Shubenacadie, 633	E 3	
u Landing, 435	F 3	Somerset, 371	D 3	
quet, 387	G 3	Springhill, 5,262	E 3	
rs Lake, 840	E 4	Stellarton, 5,357	F 3	
Hastings, 565	G 3	Stewiacke, 1,040	E 3	
Hawkesbury, 3,372	G 3	Sydney⊙, 33,230	H 2	
Hood⊙, 523	G 2	Sydney Mines, 8,991	H 2	
Maitland, 419	B 5	Sydney River, 2,009	H 2	
Morien, 470	H 3	Tatamagouche, 568	E 3	
Williams, 638	D 3	Terence Bay, 1,134	E 4	
wash, 644	E 3	Thorburn, 1,019	F 3	
rve Mines, 2,529	H 2	Three Mile Plains, 1,163	D 4	
Bourgeois, 445	H 3	Timberlea, 1,770	E 4	
Hébert, 862	G 2	Trenton, 3,331	F 3	
John, 468	E 3	Troy, 441	G 3	
port, 371	D 4	Truro⊙, 13,047	E 3	
ville, 5,701	F 4	Tusket, 423	C 5	
Croix, 375	E 4	Upper Musquodoboit, 362	F 3	
Peters, 663	H 3	Waterville, 552	D 3	
oro, 556	E 3	Waverley, 1,419	E 4	
nierville, 481	B 4	Wedgeport, 840	C 5	
t Harbour, 1,062	F 4	Wellington, 411	E 4	

PRINCE EDWARD ISLAND

AREA 2,184 sq. mi.
POPULATION 110,000
CAPITAL Charlottetown
LARGEST CITY Charlottetown
HIGHEST POINT 465 ft.
SETTLED IN 1720
ADMITTED TO CONFEDERATION 1873
PROVINCIAL FLOWER Lady's Slipper

NOVA SCOTIA

AREA 21,425 sq. mi.
POPULATION 767,000
CAPITAL Halifax
LARGEST CITY Halifax
HIGHEST POINT Cape Breton Highlands 1,747 ft.
SETTLED IN 1605
ADMITTED TO CONFEDERATION 1867
PROVINCIAL FLOWER Trailing Arbutus or Mayflower

West Arichat, 549	G 3
West Dover, 362	E 4
Western Shore, 774	D 4
Westmount, 1,790	H 2
Westport, 380	B 4
Westville, 3,898	F 3
Weymouth, 604	C 4
Whites Lake, 432	E 4
Wilmot Station, 597	D 4
Windsor⊙, 3,775	D 3
Wolfville, 2,861	D 3
Yarmouth⊙, 8,516	B 5

OTHER FEATURES

Ainslie (lake)	G 2
Annapolis (basin)	C 4
Annapolis (riv.)	C 4
Aspy (bay)	H 2
Avon (riv.)	D 4
Barachois (pt.)	G 4
Bedford (basin)	E 4
Boularderie (isl.), 1,902	H 2
Bras d'Or (lake)	H 3
Breton (cape)	J 3
Brier (isl.), 380	B 4
Canso (cape)	H 3
Canso (str.)	G 3
Cape Breton (isl.), 162,989	J 2
Cape Breton Highlands Nat'l Park	H 2
Cape Sable (isl.), 3,151	C 5
Caribou (isl.), 35	F 3
Carleton (riv.)	C 4
Chebogue (harb.)	B 5
Chedabucto (bay)	G 3
Chéticamp (isl.), 63	G 2
Chignecto (bay)	D 3
Chignecto (isth.)	D 3
Cobequid (bay)	E 3
Country (harb.)	G 3
Craignish (hills)	G 3
Cumberland (basin)	D 3
Digby Gut (chan.)	C 4
Digby Neck (pen.)	B 4
Egmont (cape)	H 2
Fourchu (cape)	B 5
Fundy (bay)	C 3
Gabarus (bay)	H 3
Gaspereau (lake)	D 4
George (bay)	G 3
Georges (bay)	G 3
Gold (riv.)	D 4
Great Bras d'Or (chan.)	H 2
Greville (bay)	D 3
Guysborough (riv.)	G 3
Halifax (harb.)	E 4
Hébert (riv.)	D 3
Ingonish North (bay)	H 2
Janvrin (isl.), 162	G 3
Jeddore (harb.)	F 4
John (cape)	E 3
Joli (pt.)	D 5
Jordan (riv.)	C 5
Kejimkujik Nat'l Park	C 4
Kennetcook (riv.)	E 3
La Have (isl.), 7	D 4
La Have (riv.)	D 4
Liscomb (isl.), 12	G 4
Lomond, Loch (lake)	H 3
Long (isl.), 846	B 4
Louisbourg Nat'l Hist. Park	J 3
Mabou Highlands (hills)	G 2
Madame (isl.), 3,767	H 3
Mahone (bay)	D 4
Malagash (pt.)	E 3
McNutt (isl.), 20	C 5
Medway (riv.)	C 4
Merigomish (harb.)	F 3
Mersey (riv.)	C 4
Minas (basin)	D 3
Minas (chan.)	D 3
Mira (bay)	J 2
Musquodoboit (riv.)	E
Necum Teuch (harb.)	F 4
Negro (cape)	C 5
North (cape)	H 1
North (isl.)	D 3
North Bay Ingonish (bay)	H 2
North East Margaree (riv.)	E 2
Northumberland (str.)	E 2
Nuttby (mt.)	E 3
Ohio (riv.)	D 4
Panuke (lake)	D 4
Pennant (pt.)	E 4
Percé (cape)	J 2
Petit-de-Grat (isl.), 1,032	H 3
Petpeswick (head)	E 4
Pictou (harb.)	F 3
Pictou (isl.), 69	F 3
Ponhook (lake)	D 4
Port Hood (isl.), 39	G 2
Port Joli (harb.)	D 5
Prim (pt.)	C 4

Roseway (riv.)	C 4
Rossignol (lake)	C 4
Sable (cape)	C 5
Sable (isl.), 12	
Saint Andrews (chan.)	H 2
Saint Ann's (bay)	H 2
Saint Lawrence (bay)	H 1
Saint Lawrence (cape)	H 1
Saint Margarets (bay)	E 4
Saint Mary's (bay)	B 4
Saint Mary's (riv.)	F 3
Saint Paul (isl.), 10	H 1
Saint Peters (bay)	H 3
Salmon (riv.)	E 3
Scatarie (isl.), 8	J 2
Scots (bay)	D 3
Seal (isl.), 10	B 5
Sheet (harb.)	F 4
Sherbrooke (lake)	D 4
Shubenacadie (lake)	E 3
Shubenacadie (riv.)	E 3
Sissiboo (riv.)	C 4
Sober (isl.), 113	F 4
Split (cape)	D 3
Stewiacke (riv.)	E 3

Sydney (harb.)	H 2
Tor (bay)	G 3
Tusket (riv.)	C 4
Verte (bay)	E 3
West (riv.)	F 3
West Liscomb (riv.)	F 3
Whitehaven (bay)	G 3
Yarmouth (sound)	B 5

PRINCE EDWARD ISLAND

COUNTIES

Kings, 18,424	F 2
Prince, 42,082	D 2
Queens, 51,135	E 2

CITIES and TOWNS

Alberton, 973	E 2

Borden, 624	E 2
Bunbury, 527	F 2
Charlottetown (cap.)⊙, 19,133	E 2
Cornwall, 557	E 2
Elmsdale, 403	D 2
Georgetown⊙, 767	F 2
Hunter River, 362	E 2
Kensington, 1,086	E 2
Miminegash, 417	D 2
Miscouche, 750	D 2
Montague, 1,608	F 2
Morell, 387	F 2
Mount Stewart, 413	F 2
Murray Harbour, 367	F 2
Murray River, 478	F 2
North Rustico, 767	E 2
O'Leary, 795	D 2
Parkdale, 2,313	E 2
Saint Edward, 537	D 2
Saint Eleanors, 1,621	E 2
Saint Peters, 370	F 2
Sherwood, 3,807	E 2
Souris, 1,393	F 2
Stanhope, 203	E 2

Summerside⊙, 9,439	E 2
Tignish, 1,060	D 2
Victoria, 171	E 2
Wilmot, 737	E 2

OTHER FEATURES

Bedeque (bay)	E 2
Cardigan (bay)	F 2
Cascumpeque (bay)	D 2
East (pt.)	G 2
Egmont (bay)	D 2
Hillsborough (bay)	E 2
Malpeque (bay)	E 2
North (pt.)	E 1
Panmure (isl.), 45	F 2
Prince Edward Island Nat'l Park	E 2
Saint Lawrence (gulf)	F 2
Tracadie (bay)	E 2
⊙ County seat.	

‡ Population of metropolitan area.

Topography

```
0    30    60
  MILES
```

Below Sea Level | 100 m. 328 ft. | 200 m. 656 ft. | 500 m. 1,640 ft. | 1,000 m. 3,281 ft. | 2,000 m. 6,562 ft. | 5,000 m. 16,404 ft.

Agriculture, Industry and Resources

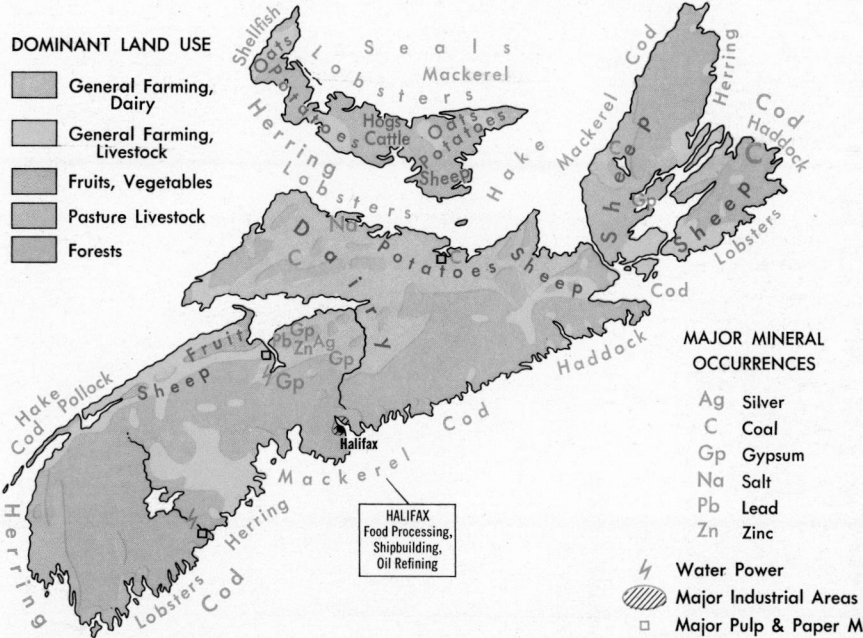

DOMINANT LAND USE

- General Farming, Dairy
- General Farming, Livestock
- Fruits, Vegetables
- Pasture Livestock
- Forests

HALIFAX
Food Processing,
Shipbuilding,
Oil Refining

MAJOR MINERAL OCCURRENCES

- Ag Silver
- C   Coal
- Gp Gypsum
- Na Salt
- Pb Lead
- Zn Zinc

⚡ Water Power
▨ Major Industrial Areas
▫ Major Pulp & Paper Mills

170 New Brunswick

COUNTIES

Albert, 16,307	F 3	
Carleton, 24,428	C 2	
Charlotte, 24,551	C 3	
Gloucester, 74,752	E 1	
Kent, 24,901	E 2	
King's, 33,285	E 3	
Madawaska, 34,976	B 1	
Northumberland, 51,561	D 2	
Queen's, 12,486	D 3	
Restigouche, 41,289	C 1	
Saint John, 92,162	E 3	
Sunbury, 21,268	C 1	
Victoria, 19,796	C 1	
Westmorland, 98,669	F 2	
York, 64,126	C 3	

CITIES and TOWNS

Acadie Siding, 112	E 2	Beechwood, 349	C 2	Bristol, 771	C 2	Chatham Head, 1,440	E 2	Doaktown, 938	D 2	Fosterville, 71	C 3
Acadieville, 144	E 2	Beersville, 85	E 2	Brockway, 68	C 3	Chipman, 1,977	E 2	Dorchester⊙, 1,199	F 3	Four Falls Corner, 97	C 2
Adamsville, 119	E 2	Belledune, 784	C 1	Browns Flats, 262	E 3	Clair, 704	B 1	Dorchester Crossing, 574	F 2	Fox Creek, 488	F 2
Albert Mines, 130	F 3	Bellefleur, 145	C 1	Buctouche, 1,964	F 2	Clarendon, 105	D 3	Douglas Harbour, 46	D 3	Fredericton (cap.)⊙,
Alcida, 222	E 1	Bellefond, 294	E 1	Burnsville, 179	E 1	Cliffordvale, 110	C 2	Douglastown, 637	E 2	24,254	D 3
Aldouane, 83	E 2	Belleisle Creek, 179	E 3	Burton⊙, 357	D 3	Clifton, 231	E 1	Drummond, 637	C 1	Fredericton Junction, 615	D 3
Allardville, 712	E 1	Benjamin, 65	D 1	Burtts Corner, 487	D 2	Cloverdale, 133	C 2	Duguayville, 372	E 1	Gagetown⊙, 609	D 3
Alma, 425	F 3	Benton, 149	C 3	Caissie-Village, 34	F 2	Coal Branch, 89	E 2	Dumbarton, 59	C 3	Gardner Creek, 47	E 3
Anagance, 109	E 3	Beresford, 2,325	E 1	Cambridge-Narrows, 416	E 3	Coal Creek, 71	E 2	Dumfries, 257	D 2	Geary, 1,023	D 3
Apohaqui, 352	E 3	Berry Mills, 349	E 2	Campbellton, 10,335	D 1	Cocagne, 234	F 2	Dupuis Corner, 378	F 2	Germantown, 71	F 3
Argyle, 63	C 2	Bertrand, 1,094	E 1	Canaan Road, 130	E 2	Cocagne Cape, 258	F 2	Durham Bridge, 182	D 2	Gillespie, 88	C 1
Armstrong Brook, 321	E 1	Berwick, 130	E 3	Canaan Station, 102	E 2	Codys, 571	E 3	East Shediac, 585	F 2	Glassville, 172	C 2
Arthurette, 299	C 2	Black Point, 150	D 1	Canterbury, 528	C 3	Coldstream, 160	C 2	Edmundston⊙, 12,365	B 1	Glencoe, 143	D 3
Astle, 194	D 2	Black River, 91	E 2	Cap-Bateau, 466	F 1	Coles Island, 121	E 3	Eel River Bridge, 487	C 1	Glenlivet, 231	C 1
Atholville, 2,108	D 1	Black River Bridge, 335	E 2	Cape Tormentine, 261	G 2	College Bridge, 545	F 3	Eel River Crossing, 1,075	D 1	Gloucester Junction, 167	C 1
Aulac, 128	F 3	Blackville, 915	E 2	Cap Lumière, 305	F 2	Collette, 178	E 2	Elgin, 283	E 3	Gondola Point, 850	D 3
Back Bay, 567	D 3	Blissfield, 130	D 2	Cap-Pelé, 2,081	F 2	Connell, 107	C 2	Elmwood, 78	C 2	Grafton, 359	C 2
Baie-Sainte-Anne, 735	E 2	Bloomfield Ridge, 218	D 2	Caraquet, 3,441	E 1	Connors, 231	B 1	Enniskillen, 77	D 3	Grand Bay, 1,066	E 3
Baie-Verte, 177	F 2	Blue Cove, 519	D 1	Caron Brook, 191	B 1	Cork Station, 241	C 2	Evandale, 33	E 3	Grande-Anse, 545	E 1
Bailey, 143	D 3	Bocabec, 59	C 3	Carrolls Crossing, 188	D 2	Cornhill, 83	E 3	Evangeline, 298	F 1	Grand Falls, 4,516	C 1
Bairdsville, 171	C 2	Boiestown, 332	D 2	Castalia, 199	D 3	Cross Creek, 241	D 2	Fairhaven, 118	C 4	Grand Falls Hill, 559	C 1
Baker Brook, 561	B 1	Bonny River, 134	D 3	Central Blissville (Bailey),		Cumberland Bay, 246	E 2	Fairisle, 444	E 1	Grand Harbour, 556	D 4
Balmoral, 896	D 1	Bossé, 134	C 1	143	D 3	Dalhousie⊙, 6,255	D 1	Fairvale, 2,050	E 3	Gray Rapids, 307	E 2
Barker's Point, 1,882	D 2	Bourgeois, 306	F 2	Centre-Acadie, 151	E 2	Dalhousie Junction, 275	D 1	Ferry Road, 520	E 1	Gunningsville, 1,669	F 2
Barnaby River, 87	E 2	Brantville, 1,072	E 1	Centre-Saint-Simon, 517	E 1	Darlington, 585	D 1	Fielding, 215	C 2	Hammondvale, 127	E 3
Barnettville, 182	E 2	Breau-Village, 249	F 2	Centreville, 566	C 2	Daulnay, 539	E 1	Five Fingers, 148	C 1	Hampstead, 118	D 3
Bartibog Bridge, 163	E 1	Brest, 117	C 1	Chance Harbour, 181	D 3	Dawsonville, 208	C 1	Flatlands, 280	D 1	Hampton⊙, 1,748	E 3
Bas-Caraquet, 1,685	F 1	Bridgedale, 416	F 2	Charlo, 1,621	D 1	Debec, 272	C 2	Florenceville, 584	C 2	Harcourt, 163	E 2
Bass River, 129	E 2	Briggs Corner, 138	E 2	Chartersville, 320	F 2	Dieppe, 4,277	F 2	Fontaine, 318	F 2	Hardwicke, 93	E 1
Bath, 920	C 2			Chatham, 7,833	E 1	Dipper Harbour, 109	D 3	Forest City, 55	C 3	Hardwood Ridge, 222	D 2
Bathurst⊙, 16,674	E 1										
Bathurst Mines, 45	E 1										
Bayfield, 178	G 2										
Bayside, 207	C 3										
Beaver Brook Station, 276	E 1										
Beaver Harbour, 355	D 3										

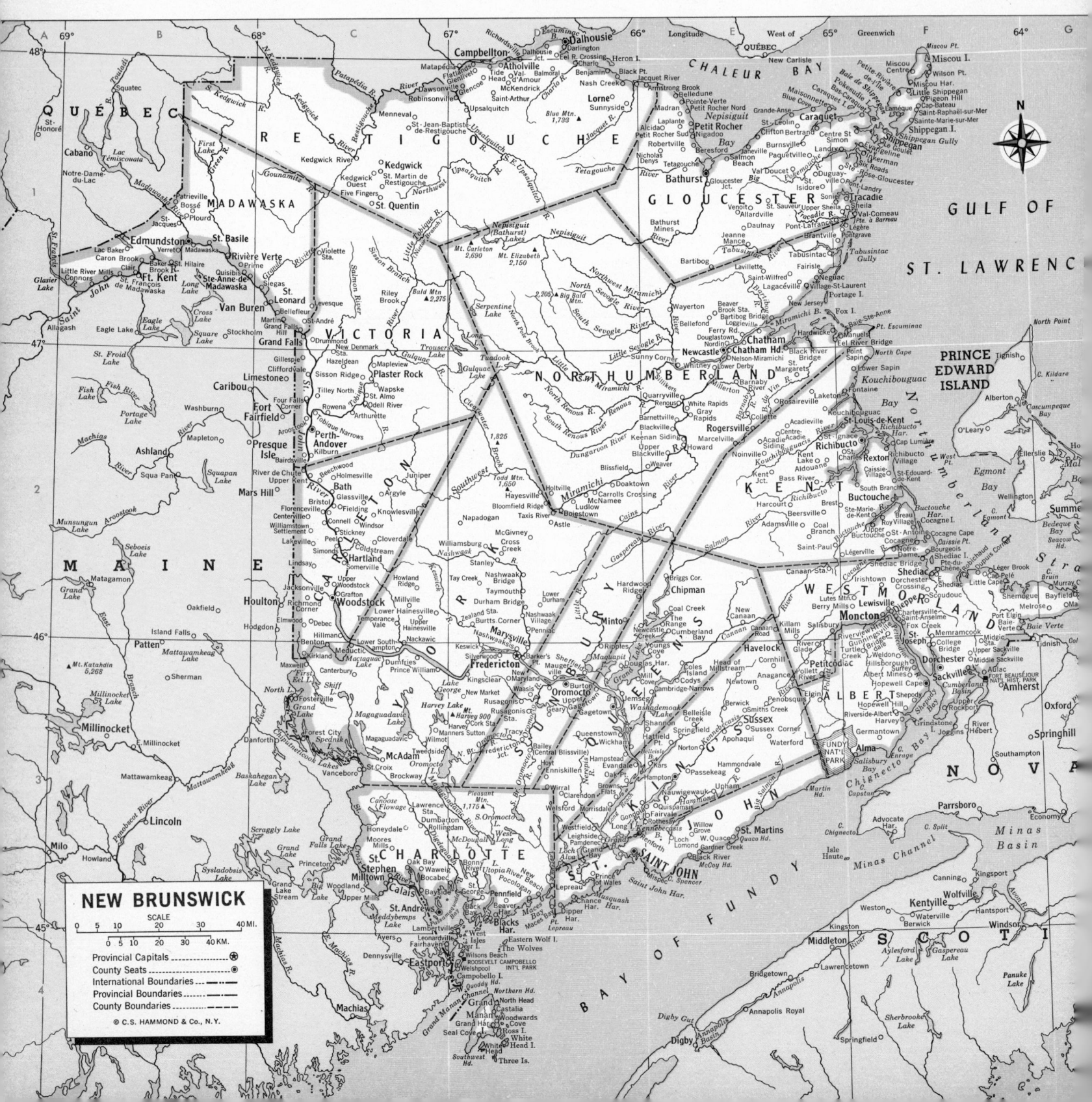

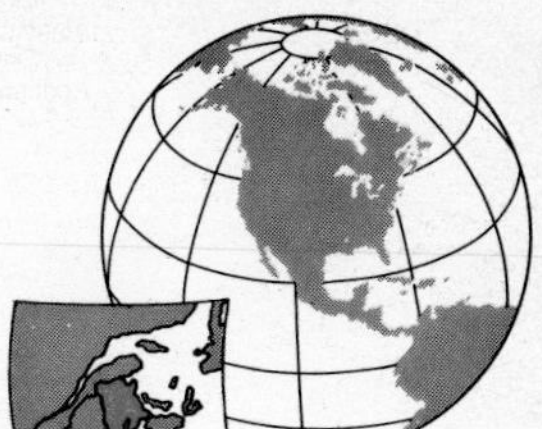

AREA 28,354 sq. mi.
POPULATION 624,000
CAPITAL Fredericton
LARGEST CITY Saint John
HIGHEST POINT Mt. Carleton 2,690 ft.
SETTLED IN 1611
ADMITTED TO CONFEDERATION 1867
PROVINCIAL FLOWER Purple Violet

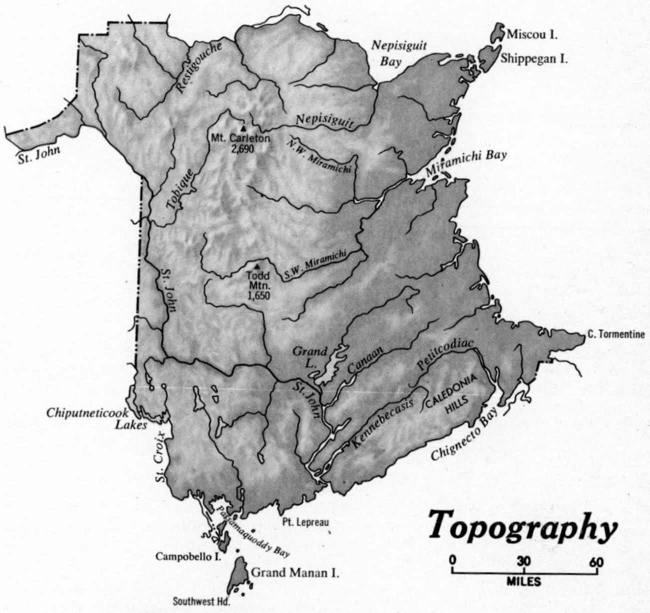
Miscou I.
Shippegan I.
Nepisiguit Bay
Restigouche
Nepisiguit
Mt. Carleton 2,690
N.W. Miramichi
St. John
Miramichi Bay
Tobique
Todd Mtn. 1,650
S.W. Miramichi
St. John
Grand L.
Canaan
Petitcodiac
C. Tormentine
Chiputneticook Lakes
St. Croix
St. John
Kennebecasis
CALEDONIA HILLS
Chignecto Bay
Pt. Lepreau
Passamaquoddy Bay
Campobello I.
Grand Manan I.
Southwest Hd.
MILES

Topography

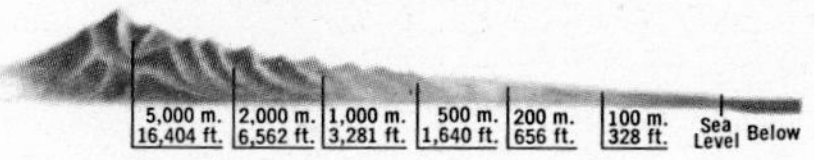
5,000 m. 16,404 ft.
2,000 m. 6,562 ft.
1,000 m. 3,281 ft.
500 m. 1,640 ft.
200 m. 656 ft.
100 m. 328 ft.
Sea Level
Below

:land, 1,009 C 2
vey, 54 F 3
vey, 383 D 3
ield Point, 181 E 3
elock, 513 E 3
esville, 120 D 2
eldean, 213 C 2
d of Millstream, 86 E 3
nan, 159 C 2
sborough, 781 F 3
nesville, 251 C 2
ville, 300 D 2
eydale, 90 C 3
ewell Cape⊙, 162 F 3
ewell Hill, 164 F 3
ard, 176 E 2
land Ridge, 56 C 2
, 97 D 3
rman, 500 F 1
town, 194 F 2
ksonville, 372 C 2
quet River, 866 E 1
eville, 164 E 1
nne Mance, 97 E 1
seg, 185 D 3
per, 585 C 2
, 76 E 3
gwick, 1,065 C 1
gwick Ouest, 101 C 1
gwick River, 25 C 1
han Siding, 74 E 2
Junction, 105 E 2
Lake, 50 E 2
wick, 308 D 3
urn, 167 C 2
m Mills, 60 E 2
sclear, 132 D 3
and, 91 C 3
wlesville, 58 C 2
chibouguac, 151 F 2
Baker, 360 B 1
acéville, 261 E 1
eton, 127 E 2
eville, 325 C 2
bertville, 181 C 3
èque, 933 F 1
ry, 268 E 1
ante, 240 E 1
llette, 500 E 1
rence Station, 221 C 3
er Brook, 339 F 2
ère, 514 F 1
erville, 199 F 2
oulet, 1,155 F 1
hside, 597 D 3
hardville, 179 C 4
reau, 162 D 3
esque, 225 C 1

Lewisville, 3,710 F 2
Lindsay, 108 C 2
Little Cape, 454 F 2
Little River Mills, 110 B 1
Little Shippegan, 100 F 1
Loch Lomond, 137 E 3
Loggieville, 877 E 1
Lorne, 999 D 1
Lower Derby, 260 E 2
Lower Durham, 115 D 2
Lower Hainesville, 119 C 2
Lower Millstream, 199 E 3
Lower Sapin, 186 F 2
Lower Southampton, 118 C 2
Ludlow, 193 D 2
Lutes Mountain, 234 E 2
Maces Bay, 133 D 3
Madran, 245 E 1
Magaguadavic, 121 C 3
Maisonnette, 620 E 1
Malden, 112 G 2
Manners Sutton, 199 D 3
Manuels, 546 F 1
Mapleview, 110 C 2
Marcelville, 78 E 2
Martin, 115 C 1
Marysville, 3,872 D 2
Maugerville, 346 D 3
Maxwell, 61 C 3
McAdam, 2,224 C 3
McGivney, 232 D 2
McKendrick, 594 D 1
McNamee, 189 D 2
Meductic, 172 C 3
Melrose, 144 F 2
Memramcook, 366 F 2
Menneval, 169 C 1
Middle Sackville, 311 F 3
Midgic Station, 211 F 3
Mill Cove, 227 D 3
Millerton, 199 E 2
Milltown, 1,893 C 3
Millville, 352 C 2
Minto, 3,880 D 2
Miscou Centre, 473 F 1
Miscou Harbour, 86 F 1
Mispec, 132 E 3
Moncton, 47,891 F 2
Moores Mills, 138 C 3
Morrisdale, 162 D 3
Murray Corner, 178 G 2
Nackawic, 1,324 C 2
Napadogan, 123 D 2
Nash Creek, 268 D 1
Nashwaak Bridge, 237 D 2
Nashwaaksis, 7,353 D 3
Nashwaak Village, 141 D 2
Nauwigewauk, 313 E 3

Neguac, 1,498 E 1
Nelson-Miramichi, 1,580 E 2
New Canaan, 44 E 2
Newcastle⊙, 6,460 E 2
Newcastle Creek, 205 D 2
New Denmark Station, 315 C 1
New Jersey, 117 E 1
New Market, 95 D 3
New Maryland, 643 D 3
New River Beach, 78 D 3
Newtown, 89 E 3
Nicholas Denys, 241 D 1
Nigadoo, 597 E 1
Noinville, 39 E 2
Nordin, 303 E 1
North Head, 649 D 4
Norton, 1,149 E 3
Notre-Dame, 362 F 2
Oak Bay, 232 C 3
Oak Point, 100 D 3
Odell River, 166 C 2
Oromocto, 11,427 D 3
Pamdenec, 422 D 3
Paquetville, 479 E 1
Passekeag, 169 E 3
Patrieville, 140 B 1
Peel, 82 C 2
Pennfield, 267 D 3
Penniac, 407 D 2
Penobsquis, 79 E 3
Perth-Andover⊙, 2,108 C 2
Petitcodiac, 1,569 E 3
Petite-Rivière-de-l'Île, 477 F 1
Petit Rocher, 1,624 E 1
Petit Rocher Nord, 414 E 1
Petit Rocher Sud, 538 E 1
Pigeon Hill, 445 F 1
Plaster Rock, 1,331 C 2
Plourd, 336 B 1
Pocologan, 108 D 3
Pointe-du-Chêne, 484 F 2
Pointe-Verte, 524 E 1
Point Sapin, 349 F 2
Pollett River, 64 E 3
Pontgrave, 202 F 1
Pont-Lafrance, 856 E 1
Pont-Landry, 562 F 1
Port Elgin, 553 F 2
Prime, 73 B 1
Prince of Wales, 131 D 3
Prince William, 236 C 3
Quarryville, 312 E 2
Queenstown, 105 D 3
Quisibis, 138 B 1
Quispamsis, 2,215 E 3
Renforth, 1,606 E 3
Renous, 211 E 2

Rexton, 755 F 2
Richardsville, 892 D 1
Richibucto⊙, 1,850 E 2
Richibucto Village, 357 F 2
Richmond Corner, 54 C 2
Riley Brook, 166 C 1
Ripples, 230 D 3
River de Chute, 57 C 2
River Glade, 242 E 3
Riverside-Albert, 509 F 3
Riverview Heights, 6,525 F 2
Rivière Verte, 1,657 B 1
Robertville, 954 E 1
Robichaud, 350 F 2
Robinsonville, 202 C 1
Rogersville, 1,077 E 2
Rollingdam, 124 C 3
Rosaireville, 87 E 2
Rothesay, 1,038 E 3
Rowena, 104 C 2
Roy, 115 F 2
Rusagonis, 182 D 3
Rusagonis Station, 76 D 3
Sackville, 3,180 F 3
Saint Almo, 53 C 2
Saint-André, 315 C 1
Saint Andrews⊙, 1,812 C 3
Saint-Anselme, 1,150 F 2
Saint-Antoine, 756 F 2
Saint-Arthur, 521 D 1
Saint Basile, 3,085 B 1
Saint-Charles, 381 F 2
Saint Croix, 50 C 3
Sainte-Anne-de-Madawaska, 1,253 B 1
Saint-Édouard-de-Kent, 207 F 2
Sainte-Marie-de-Kent, 269 F 2
Sainte-Marie-sur-Mer, 430 F 1
Sainte-Rose-Gloucester, 479 F 1
Saint François de Madawaska, 511 B 1
Saint George, 977 D 3
Saint Hilaire, 199 B 1
Saint-Ignace, 382 F 2
Saint-Isidore, 477 E 1
Saint-Jacques, 1,072 B 1
Saint-Jean-Baptiste-de-Restigouche, 293 C 1
Saint John⊙, 89,039 E 3
Saint John, ‡106,744 E 3
Saint-Joseph, 687 F 3
Saint-Léolin, 694 E 1
Saint Leonard, 1,478 C 1
Saint-Louis-de-Kent, 992 F 2
Saint Margarets, 213 E 2
Saint Martin de Restigouche, 145 C 1
Saint Martins, 484 E 3
Saint-Paul, 314 E 2
Saint Quentin, 2,093 C 1
Saint-Raphaël-sur-Mer, 588 F 1
Saint Sauveur, 626 E 1
Saint Stephen, 3,409 C 3
Saint-Wilfred, 307 E 1
Salisbury, 1,070 E 2
Salmon Beach, 382 E 1
Scoudouc, 250 F 2
Seal Cove, 613 D 4
Shannon, 72 E 3
Shediac, 2,203 F 2
Shediac Bridge, 347 F 2
Sheffield, 112 D 3
Sheila, 854 F 1
Shemogue, 189 F 2
Shepody, 88 F 3
Shippegan, 2,043 F 1
Siegas, 393 C 1
Sillikers, 275 E 2
Silverwood, 935 D 3
Simonds, 236 C 2
Sisson Ridge, 166 C 2
Six Roads, 441 F 1
Smiths Creek, 195 E 3
Somerville, 362 C 2
Sonier, 443 E 1
South Branch, 143 F 2
Springfield, 139 E 3
Stanley, 388 D 2
Stickney, 266 C 2
Sunny Corner, 572 E 2
Sunnyside, 79 D 1
Surrey, 286 F 3
Sussex, 3,942 E 3

Sussex Corner, 700 E 3
Tabusintac, 253 E 1
Taxis River, 172 D 2
Tay Creek, 177 D 2
Taymouth, 280 D 2
Temperance Vale, 323 C 2
Tetagouche, 359 E 1
The Range, 88 E 2
Thibault, 231 C 1
Tide Head, 797 D 1
Tilley North, 226 C 2
Tobique Narrows, 169 C 2
Tracadie, 2,222 F 1
Tracy, 610 D 3
Turtle Creek, 200 F 3
Tweedside, 125 C 3
Upham, 132 E 3
Upper Blackville, 224 E 2
Upper Buctouche, 155 F 2
Upper Gagetown, 299 D 3
Upper Hainesville, 217 C 2
Upper Kent, 301 C 2
Upper Mills, 143 C 3
Upper Rockport, 17 F 3
Upper Sackville, 234 F 3
Upper Sheila, 748 E 1
Upper Woodstock, 336 C 2
Upsalquitch, 135 D 1
Val-Comeau, 495 F 1
Val d'Amour, 580 D 1
Val Doucet, 486 E 1
Veniot, 560 E 1
Verret, 900 B 1
Village-Saint-Laurent, 164 E 1
Violette Station, 128 C 1
Waasis, 176 D 3
Wapske, 210 C 2
Waterford, 132 E 3
Waweig, 124 C 3
Wayerton, 161 E 1
Weaver, 112 E 2
Weldon, 199 F 3
Welsford, 293 D 3
Welshpool, 172 D 4
Westfield, 461 D 3
West Quaco, 102 E 3
White Head, 178 D 4
White Rapids, 304 E 2
Whitney, 282 E 2
Wickham, 86 D 3
Williamsburg, 333 D 2
Williamstown Settlement, 197 C 2
Willow Grove, 336 E 3
Wilmot, 127 C 3
Wilson Point, 70 F 1
Wilsons Beach, 911 D 4
Windsor, 56 C 2

Wirral, 115 D 3
Woodstock⊙, 4,846 C 2
Woodwards Cove, 180 D 4
Youngs Cove, 118 E 3
Zealand Station, 442 D 2

OTHER FEATURES

Bald (mt.) C 1
Bartibog (riv.) E 1
Bay du Vin (riv.) E 2
Big Tracadie (riv.) E 1
Buctouche (harb.) F 2
Buctouche (riv.) F 2
Campobello (isl.), 1,274 D 4
Canaan (riv.) E 2
Carleton (mt.) D 1
Chaleur (bay) E 1
Chignecto (bay) F 3
Chiputneticook (lakes) C 3
Cocagne (isl.) F 2
Cumberland (basin) F 3
Deer (isl.), 730 D 4
Digdeguash (riv.) C 3
Escuminac (bay) D 1
Escuminac (pt.) F 1
Fort Beauséjour Nat'l Hist. Park F 3
Fundy (bay) E 3
Fundy Nat'l Park E 3
Gaspereau (riv.) D 2
Grand (bay) D 3
Grand (lake) C 3
Grand (lake) D 3
Grande (riv.) C 1
Grand Manan (chan.) C 4
Grand Manan (isl.), 2,547 D 4
Green (riv.) B 1
Hammond (riv.) E 3
Harvey (lake) C 3
Heron (isl.) D 1
Kedgwick (riv.) C 1
Kennebecasis (riv.) E 3
Keswick (riv.) C 2
Kouchibouguac (bay) F 2
Kouchibouguacis (riv.) E 2
Lepreau (riv.) D 3
Little (riv.) D 2
Long (isl.) D 3
Long Reach (inlet) D 3
Maces (bay) D 3
Mactaquac (lake) C 3
Madawaska (riv.) B 1
Magaguadavic (lake) C 3
Magaguadavic (riv.) C 3
Miramichi (bay) E 1

Miscou (isl.), 728 F 1
Miscou (pt.) F 1
Musquash (harb.) D 3
Nashwaak (riv.) D 2
Nepisiguit (bay) E 1
Nepisiguit (riv.) D 1
Nerepis (riv.) D 3
Northern (head) D 4
North Sevogle (riv.) D 1
Northumberland (str.) F 2
Northwest Miramichi (riv.) D 1
Oromocto (lake) C 3
Oromocto (riv.) D 3
Passamaquoddy (bay) C 3
Patapédia (riv.) C 1
Petitcodiac (riv.) F 3
Pokemouche (riv.) E 1
Pokesudie (isl.), 368 F 1
Pollett (riv.) E 3
Quaco (head) E 3
Renous (riv.) D 2
Restigouche (riv.) C 1
Richibucto (harb.) F 2
Richibucto (riv.) E 2
Roosevelt Campobello Int'l Park D 4
Saint Croix (riv.) C 3
Saint Francis (riv.) A 1
Saint John (harb.) E 3
Saint John (riv.) C 2
Saint Lawrence (gulf) F 1
Salisbury (bay) F 3
Salmon (riv.) C 1
Salmon (riv.) E 2
Shediac (isl.) F 2
Shepody (bay) F 3
Shippegan (bay) E 1
Shippegan (gully) F 1
Shippegan (isl.), 7,745 F 1
South Sevogle (riv.) D 1
Southwest (head) D 4
Southwest Miramichi (riv.) D 2
Spear (cape) G 2
Spednik (lake) C 3
Spencer (cape) E 3
Tabusintac (gully) F 1
Tabusintac (riv.) E 1
Tetagouche (riv.) D 1
Tobique (riv.) C 2
Upsalquitch (riv.) D 1
Utopia (lake) D 3
Verte (bay) G 2
Washademoak (lake) E 3
West (isls.), 974 D 4
White Head (isl.), 178 D 4

⊙ County seat.
‡ Population of metropolitan area.

Agriculture, Industry and Resources

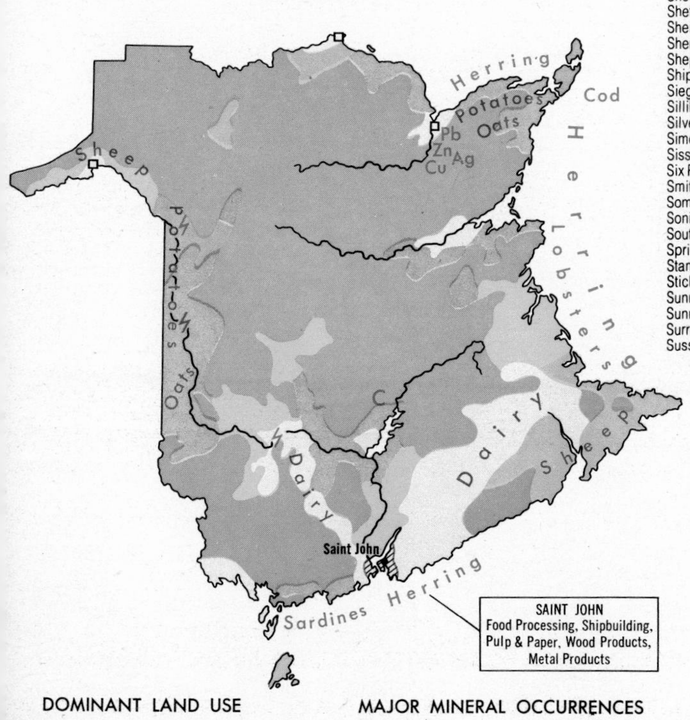
Herring
Potatoes
Cod
Oats
Pb
Zn
Ag
Cu
Sheep
Potatoes
Oats
Herring
Lobsters
Dairy
C
Dairy
Sheep
Saint John
Herring
Sardines
SAINT JOHN
Food Processing, Shipbuilding, Pulp & Paper, Wood Products, Metal Products

DOMINANT LAND USE

- Cereals, Livestock
- Dairy
- Potatoes
- General Farming, Livestock
- Pasture Livestock
- Forests

MAJOR MINERAL OCCURRENCES

- Ag Silver
- C Coal
- Cu Copper
- Pb Lead
- Zn Zinc

- Water Power
- Major Industrial Areas
- Major Pulp & Paper Mills

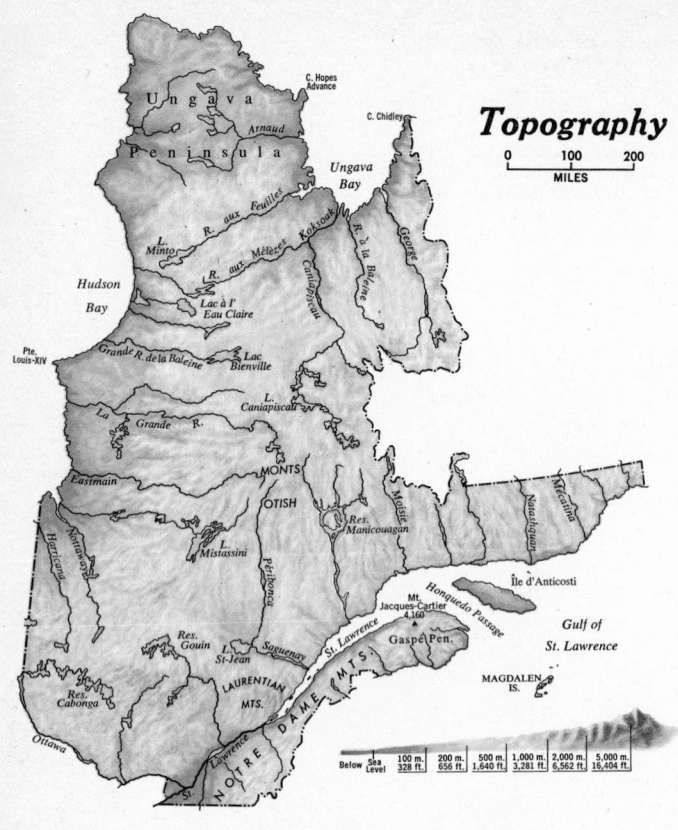

Topography

0   100   200
MILES

Below Sea Level | 100 m. 328 ft. | 200 m. 656 ft. | 500 m. 1,640 ft. | 1,000 m. 3,281 ft. | 2,000 m. 6,562 ft. | 5,000 m. 16,404 ft.

QUÉBEC
COUNTIES

Argenteuil, 31,319.....C 4
Arthabaska, 51,524.....E 4
Bagot, 23,591.....D 4
Beauce, 63,960.....G 3
Beauharnois, 52,137.....C 4
Bellechasse, 23,517.....G 3
Berthier, 27,288.....C 3
Bonaventure, 41,701.....C 2
Brome, 15,311.....E 4
Chambly, 231,590.....J 4
Champlain, 113,150.....E 2
Charlevoix-Est, 16,780.....G 2
Charlevoix-Ouest, 13,650.....G 2
Châteauguay, 53,737.....D 4
Chicoutimi, 163,348.....G 1
Compton, 21,367.....F 4
Deux-Montagnes, 52,369.....C 4
Dorchester, 32,473.....C 3

Drummond, 64,144.....E 4
Frontenac, 27,293.....G 4
Gaspé-Est, 41,727.....D 1
Gaspé-Ouest, 18,754.....C 1
Gatineau, 55,729.....B 3
Hull, 109,946.....B 4
Huntingdon, 15,358.....C 4
Iberville, 20,400.....D 4
Île-de-Montréal, 1,959,143.....H 4
Île-Jésus, 228,010.....H 4
Joliette, 52,088.....C 3
Kamouraska, 26,264.....H 2
Labelle, 30,582.....B 3
Lac-Saint-Jean-Est, 45,220.....F 1
Lac-Saint-Jean-Ouest, 57,074.....E 1
Laprairie, 61,691.....H 4
Lévis, 62,776.....J 3
L'Islet, 23,187.....G 2
Lotbinière, 27,373.....F 3

Maskinongé, 21,257.....D 3
Matane, 30,261.....B 1
Matapédia, 26,856.....B 2
Mégantic, 58,020.....F 3
Missisquoi, 33,953.....D 4
Montcalm, 21,546.....C 3
Montmagny, 26,307.....G 3
Montmorency No. 1, 20,401.....F 2
Montmorency No. 2, 5,435.....G 3
Napierville, 12,067.....D 4
Nicolet, 30,004.....E 3
Papineau, 31,793.....B 4
Pontiac, 19,570.....A 3
Portneuf, 51,540.....E 3
Québec, 423,162.....H 4
Richelieu, 47,093.....D 4
Richmond, 41,044.....E 4
Rimouski, 64,263.....J 1
Rivière-du-Loup, 39,488.....H 2
Rouville, 31,759.....D 4
Saguenay, 111,272.....H 1

Saint-Hyacinthe, 50,494.....D 4
Saint-Jean, 45,892.....D 4
Saint-Maurice, 108,366.....D 3
Shefford, 62,361.....E 4
Sherbrooke, 101,470.....E 4
Soulanges, 11,449.....C 4
Stanstead, 36,266.....F 4
Témiscouata, 23,189.....J 2
Terrebonne, 139,945.....H 4
Vaudreuil, 36,593.....C 4
Verchères, 35,273.....J 4
Wolfe, 16,197.....F 4
Yamaska, 15,206.....E 3

CITIES and TOWNS

Acton Vale, 4,564.....D 4
Albanel, 788.....E 1
Alma⊙, 22,622.....F 1
Amqui, 3,797.....B 2
Ancienne-Lorette, 8,304.....H 3
Angers, 881.....B 4
Anjou, 33,886.....H 4
Armagh, 987.....G 3
Arthabaska⊙, 4,479.....F 3
Arvida, 18,448.....F 1
Asbestos, 9,749.....E 4
Ayer's Cliff⊙, 873.....E 4
Aylmer, 7,198.....B 4
Bagotville, 6,041.....G 1
Baie-Comeau, 12,109.....A 1
Baie-de-Shawinigan, 847.....E 3
Baie-des-Sables, 638.....A 1
Baie-d'Urfé, 3,881.....G 4
Baie-Saint-Paul⊙, 4,163.....G 2
Baie-Trinité, 734.....A 1
Beaconsfield, 19,389.....H 4
Beauceville, 2,098.....G 3
Beauceville-Est⊙, 2,192.....G 3
Beauharnois⊙, 8,121.....D 4
Beaulieu, 659.....J 3
Beaumont, 630.....F 3
Beauport, 14,681.....J 3
Beaupré, 2,862.....G 3
Bécancour⊙, 8,182.....E 3
Bedford⊙, 2,786.....E 4
Beebe Plain, 1,236.....E 4
Bélair, 4,505.....H 3
Beloeil, 12,274.....D 4
Bernierville, 2,415.....F 3
Berthierville⊙, 4,080.....D 3
Bic, 1,157.....J 1
Black Lake, 4,123.....F 3
Blainville, 9,630.....H 4
Bois-des-Filion, 4,061.....H 4
Bolduc, 1,496.....G 4
Bonaventure, 1,079.....C 2
Boucherville, 19,997.....J 4
Breakeyville, 800.....J 3
Bromont, 1,089.....E 4
Bromptonville, 2,771.....F 4
Brossard, 23,452.....H 4
Brownsburg, 3,481.....C 4
Buckingham, 7,304.....B 4
Cabano, 3,063.....J 2
Calumet, 744.....C 4
Candiac, 5,185.....J 4
Cap-à-l'Aigle, 679.....G 2
Cap-Chat, 3,868.....B 1
Cap-de-la-Madeleine, 31,463.....E 3
Caplan, 693.....C 2
Cap-Rouge, 1,750.....H 3
Cap-Saint-Ignace, 1,338.....G 2
Cap-Santé⊙, 610.....F 3

Carignan, 3,340.....J 4
Carleton, 899.....C 2
Caughnawaga, 3,982.....H 4
Causapscal, 2,965.....B 2
Chambly, 11,469.....J 4
Chambord, 1,106.....E 1
Champlain, 632.....E 3
Chandler, 3,843.....D 2
Charlemagne, 4,111.....H 4
Charlesbourg, 33,443.....J 3
Charny, 5,175.....J 3
Châteauguay, 15,797.....H 4
Château-Richer⊙, 3,111.....J 3
Chénéville, 718.....B 4
Chicoutimi⊙, 33,893.....G 1
Chicoutimi-Jonquière, ‡133,703.....G 1
Chicoutimi-Nord, 14,086.....G 1
Chute-aux-Outardes, 1,930.....A 1
Clermont, 3,386.....G 2
Coaticook, 6,569.....F 4
Coleraine, 1,474.....F 4
Contrecoeur, 2,694.....D 4
Cookshire⊙, 1,484.....F 4
Coteau-du-Lac, 838.....C 4
Coteau-Landing⊙, 846.....C 4
Côte-Saint-Luc, 24,375.....H 4
Courcelles, 679.....G 4
Courville, 6,222.....J 3
Cowansville, 11,920.....E 4
Crabtree, 1,706.....D 4
Danville, 2,566.....E 4
Daveluyville, 998.....E 3
Deauville, 761.....E 4
Dégelis, 3,046.....J 2
Delson, 2,941.....H 4
Desbiens, 1,813.....E 1
Deschaillons-sur-Saint-Laurent, 1,176.....E 3
Deschambault, 995.....E 3
Deschênes, 1,806.....B 4
Deux-Montagnes, 8,631.....H 4
Didyme, 720.....E 1
Disraëli, 3,384.....F 4
Dolbeau, 7,633.....E 1
Dollard-des-Ormeaux, 25,217.....H 4
Donnacona, 5,940.....F 3
Dorion, 6,209.....C 4
Dorval, 20,469.....H 4
Douville, 3,267.....D 4
Drummondville⊙, 31,813.....E 4
Drummondville-Sud, 8,989.....E 4
East Angus, 4,715.....F 4
East Broughton, 1,380.....F 3
East Broughton Station, 1,127.....F 3
Escoumins, 1,968.....H 1
Farnham, 6,496.....E 4
Ferme-Neuve, 1,990.....B 3
Forestville, 1,606.....H 1
Frampton, 711.....G 3
Francoeur, 1,186.....F 3
Gaspé, 17,211.....D 1
Gatineau, 22,321.....B 4
Giffard, 13,135.....J 3
Girardville, 933.....E 1
Glenwood Domaine, 3,997.....B 4
Godbout, 653.....B 1
Gracefield, 1,049.....A 3
Granby, 34,385.....D 4
Grande-Rivière, 1,330.....D 2
Grandes-Bergeronnes, 802.....H 1
Grande-Vallée, 779.....D 1
Grand'Mère, 17,137.....E 3
Greenfield Park, 15,348.....J 4
Grenville, 1,495.....C 4
Hampstead, 7,033.....H 4
Ham-Sud⊙, 64.....F 4
Hauterive, 13,181.....A 1
Hébertville-Station, 1,163.....F 1
Hemmingford, 810.....D 4
Henryville, 666.....D 4
Hudson, 4,345.....C 4
Hull⊙, 63,580.....B 4
Huntingdon⊙, 3,087.....C 4
Iberville⊙, 9,331.....D 4
Île-Bizard, 2,950.....H 4
Île-Perrot, 4,021.....H 4
Inverness⊙, 362.....F 3
Joliette⊙, 20,127.....D 3
Jonquière, 28,430.....F 1
Kénogami, 10,970.....F 1
Kirkland, 2,917.....H 4
Labelle, 1,492.....B 3
Lac-au-Saumon, 1,314.....B 2
Lac-aux-Sables, 844.....E 3
Lac-Beauport, 42.....F 3
Lac-Bouchette, 954.....E 1
Lac-Brome⊙, 4,063.....C 3
Lac-Carré, 660.....C 3
Lac-Etchemin, 2,789.....G 3
Lachine, 44,423.....H 4
Lachute⊙, 11,813.....C 4
Lac-Mégantic⊙, 6,770.....G 4
Lacolle, 1,254.....D 4
Lac-Saint-Charles, 1,693.....H 3
Lafontaine, 2,980.....C 4
La Guadeloupe, 1,934.....G 3
La Malbaie⊙, 4,036.....G 2
Lambton, 767.....F 4
L'Ange-Gardien, 1,605.....F 3
L'Annonciation, 2,162.....C 3
Lanoraie, 1,151.....D 4
La Pérade, 1,123.....E 3
La Pocatière, 4,256.....H 2
La Prairie, 8,309.....H 4
La Providence, 4,709.....E 4
La Salle, 72,912.....H 4
L'Ascension, 1,034.....F 1
L'Assomption⊙, 4,915.....D 4
La Station-du-Coteau, 885.....C 4

La Tuque, 13,099.....E 2
Laurentides, 1,746.....D 4
Laurier-Station, 946.....F 3
Laurierville, 922.....F 3
Lauzon, 12,809.....J 3
Laval, 228,010.....H 4
Lavaltrie, 1,261.....D 4
Le Moyne, 8,194.....J 4
Lennoxville, 3,859.....F 4
L'Épiphanie, 2,752.....D 4
Léry, 2,247.....H 4
Les Méchins, 792.....B 1
Lévis, 16,597.....J 3
Linière, 1,220.....G 3
L'Islet, 1,195.....G 2
L'Islet-sur-Mer, 772.....G 2
L'Isle-Verte, 1,360.....G 1
Longueuil⊙, 97,590.....J 4
Loretteville⊙, 11,644.....H 3
Lorraine, 3,145.....H 4
Louiseville⊙, 4,042.....E 3
Luceville, 1,411.....J 1
Lyster, 879.....F 3
Magog, 13,281.....E 4
Maniwaki⊙, 6,689.....B 3
Manouane, 751.....C 2
Manseau, 756.....E 3
Maple Grove, 1,708.....H 4
Maria, 1,157.....C 2
Marieville, 4,563.....D 4
Mascouche, 8,812.....H 4
Maskinongé, 996.....E 3
Masson, 2,336.....R 4

Massueville, 632.....D 4
Matane⊙, 11,841.....B 1
Melocheville, 1,601.....C 4
Mercier, 4,011.....H 4
Mistassini, 3,601.....E 1
Mont-Carmel, 800.....H 2
Montebello, 1,285.....C 4
Mont-Joli, 6,698.....J 1
Mont-Laurier⊙, 8,240.....C 3
Mont-Louis, 815.....C 1
Montmagny⊙, 12,432.....G 3
Montmorency, 4,949.....J 3
Montréal⊙, 1,214,352.....H 4
Montréal, ‡2,743,208.....H 4
Montréal-Est, 5,076.....J 4
Montréal-Nord, 89,139.....H 4
Mont-Rolland, 1,503.....C 4
Mont-Royal, 21,561.....H 4
Mont-Saint-Hilaire, 5,758.....J 4
Morin Heights, 710.....C 4
Murdochville, 2,891.....C 1
Napierville, 1,987.....D 4
Neuville, 798.....F 3
New Carlisle⊙, 1,384.....C 2
New Richmond, 3,957.....C 2
Nicolet, 4,714.....E 3
Nitro, 1,827.....D 4
Nominingue, 699.....C 3
Normandin, 1,823.....E 1
North Hatley, 728.....F 4
Notre-Dame-de-la-Doré, 1,127.....E 1
Notre-Dame-des-Anges, 790.....F 3

Agriculture, Industry and Resources

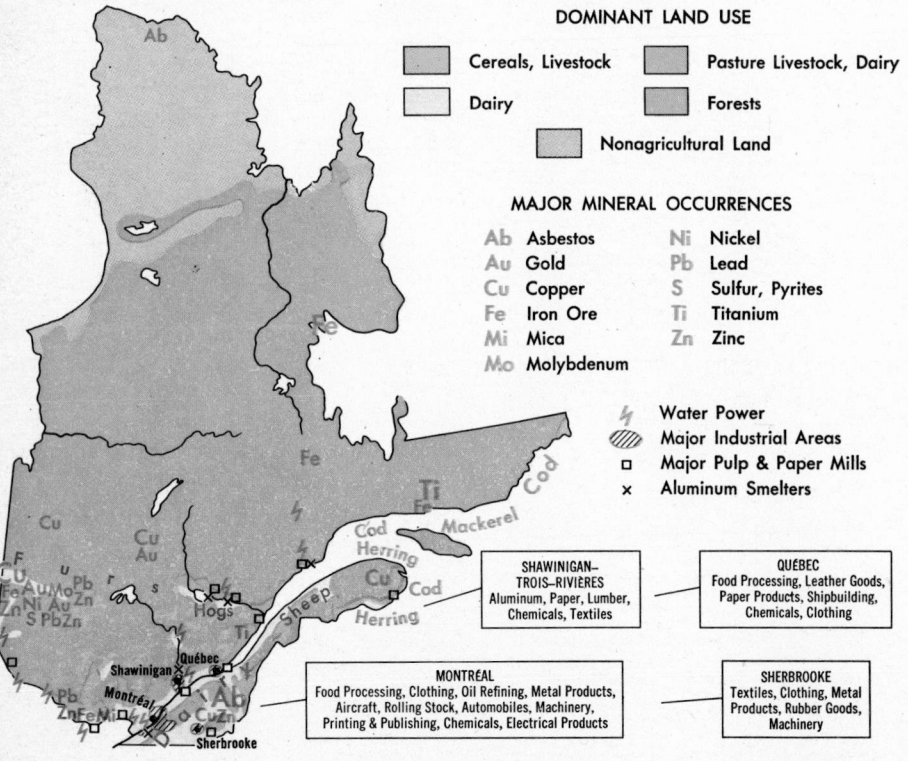

DOMINANT LAND USE

- Cereals, Livestock
- Pasture Livestock, Dairy
- Dairy
- Forests
- Nonagricultural Land

MAJOR MINERAL OCCURRENCES

Ab Asbestos
Au Gold
Cu Copper
Fe Iron Ore
Mi Mica
Mo Molybdenum
Ni Nickel
Pb Lead
S   Sulfur, Pyrites
Ti Titanium
Zn Zinc

⚡ Water Power
▨ Major Industrial Areas
□ Major Pulp & Paper Mills
× Aluminum Smelters

SHAWINIGAN–TROIS-RIVIÈRES
Aluminum, Paper, Lumber, Chemicals, Textiles

QUÉBEC
Food Processing, Leather Goods, Paper Products, Shipbuilding, Chemicals, Clothing

MONTRÉAL
Food Processing, Clothing, Oil Refining, Metal Products, Aircraft, Rolling Stock, Automobiles, Machinery, Printing & Publishing, Chemicals, Electrical Products

SHERBROOKE
Textiles, Clothing, Metal Products, Rubber Goods, Machinery

QUÉBEC SOUTHERN PART

SCALE
0 5 10   20   30   40 MI.
0 5 10 20   30   40 KM.

National Capital ⊛ Provincial & State
Provincial Capital ⊛ Boundaries
County Seats ⊙ County Boundaries
International Boundaries

Notre-Dame-des-
Laurentides, 5,080 ....H 3
Notre-Dame-des-Prairies,
3,541 ....D 3
Notre-Dame-
d'Hébertville, 1,506 ..F 1
Notre-Dame-du-Bon-
Conseil, 1,048 ....E 4
2,107 ....J 2
Nouvelle, 722 ....C 2
merville, 1,102 ....E 4
rmstown, 1,517 ....D 4
tterburn Park 3,512 ....H 4
utrabos-Mills, 668 ....D 2
apineauville⊙, 1,384 ....D 2
aspébiac, 1,317 ....B 2
etit-Matane, 668 ....B 1
etit-Saguenay (Saint-
Francois-d'Assise),
691 ....G 1
ierrefonds, 33,010 ....H 4
erreville, 1,455 ....E 3
incourt, 5,899 ....H 4
intendre, 796 ....J 3
aisance, 651 ....B 4
lessisville, 7,204 ....F 3
ointe-à-la-Croix, 753 ....C 2
ointe-au-Pic, 1,231 ....G 2
ointe-aux-Outardes, 836 ..A 1

Pointe-aux-Trembles,
35,567 ....J 4
Pointe-Calumet, 2,214 ..G 4
Pointe-Claire, 27,303 ..H 4
Pointe-du-Lac, 1,314 ..E 3
Pointe-Gatineau, 15,640 ..B 4
Pointe-Lebel, 756 ....A 1
Pont-Rouge, 3,272 ....F 3
Port-Alfred, 9,228 ....G 1
Portneuf, 1,347 ....F 3
Price, 2,740 ....A 1
Princeville, 3,829 ....F 3
Quebec (cap.), 186,088 ..H 3
Québec, ⊙480,502 ....H 3
Quyon, 879 ....A 4
Rawdon, 1,217 ....H 4
Repentigny, 19,520 ....J 4
Restigouche, 1,155 ....C 2
Richelieu, 1,777 ....J 4
Richmond⊙, 4,317 ....E 4
Rigaud, 2,138 ....H 4
Rimouski⊙, 26,887 ....J 1
Rimouski-Est, 2,069 ....J 1
Rivière-à-Pierre, 691 ....E 3
Rivière-du-Loup⊙, 12,760 ..H 2
Rivière-du-Moulin, 4,393 ..G 1
Rivière-Portneuf, 987 ....H 1
Robertsonville, 1,294 ..F 3
Roberval⊙, 8,330 ....E 1
Rock Forest, 793 ....E 4
Rock Island, 1,341 ....E 4
Rosemère, 6,710 ....H 4
Rougemont, 853 ....D 4
Roxboro, 7,633 ....H 4

Roxton Falls, 1,139 ....E 4
Sacré-Coeur-de-Jésus,
1,252 ....H 1
Saint-Adelphe, 708 ....E 3
Saint-Agapitville, 1,493 ..F 3
Saint-Alban, 770 ....E 3
Saint-Alexandre-de-
Kamouraska, 927 ....H 2
Saint-Alexis-des-Monts,
1,905 ....D 3
Saint-Amable, 1,051 ....J 4
Saint-Ambroise, 1,629 ..F 1
Saint-Anaclet, 955 ....J 1
Saint-André-Avellin, 1,088 ..B 4
Saint-André-Est, 1,201 ..C 4
Saint-Anselme, 1,400 ..F 3
Saint-Antonin, 748 ....H 2
Saint-Aubert, 952 ....G 2
Saint-Augustin-de-
Québec, 688 ....H 3
Saint-Basile-le-Grand,
4,402 ....J 4
Saint-Basile-Sud, 1,731 ..F 3
Saint-Bernard-sur-Mer,
667 ....G 2
Saint-Boniface-de-
Shawinigan, 2,581 ..D 3
Saint-Bruno-de-
Montarville, 15,780 ..J 4
Saint-Camille-de-
Bellechasse, 774 ....G 3
Saint-Casimir, 1,239 ..E 3

Saint-Césaire, 2,279 ..D 4
Saint-Charles, 969 ....G 3
Saint-Charles-de-
Drummond, 2,266 ..E 4
Saint-Charles-de-
Mandeville, 900 ....D 3
Saint-Chrysostome, 1,077 ..D 4
Saint-Coeur-de-Marie,
1,218 ....F 1
Saint-Côme, 914 ....D 3
Saint-Constant, 4,139 ..H 4
Saint-Cyprien
743 ....J 2
Saint-Cyrille, 1,125 ....E 4
Saint-Damien-de-
Buckland, 1,799 ....G 3
Saint-David-de-
Falardeau, 770 ....F 1
Saint-David-de-
l'Auberivière, 3,818 ..J 3
Saint-Denis, 899 ....D 4
Saint-Dominique, 1,722 ..J 4
Saint-Donat-de-
Montcalm, 1,536 ..C 3
Sainte-Adelaide-de-
Pabos, 853 ....D 2
Sainte-Adèle, 2,581 ..C 4
Sainte-Agathe, 646 ....C 4
Sainte-Agathe-des-
Monts, 5,532 ....C 4
Sainte-Angèle-de-Mérici,
688 ....J 1
Sainte-Anne-de-Beaupré,
1,797 ....F 2

Sainte-Anne-de-Bellevue,
4,976 ....H 4
Sainte-Anne-des-Monts⊙,
5,546 ....C 1
Sainte-Anne-des-Plaines,
2,093 ....H 4
Sainte-Blandine, 941 ....J 1
Sainte-Catherine, 913 ..F 3
Sainte-Claire-de-Joliette,
1,490 ....G 3
Sainte-Croix, 1,545 ....F 3
Sainte-Famille-
d'Orléans⊙, 295 ....G 3
Sainte-Félicité, 816 ....B 1
Sainte-Foy, 68,385 ....H 3
Sainte-Geneviève, 2,847 ..H 4
Sainte-Geneviève-de-
Batiscan⊙, 556 ....E 3

Sainte-Hedwidge-de-
Roberval⊙, 8,330 ....E 1
Sainte-Hélène-de-
Kamouraska, 656 ....H 2
Sainte-Hénédine⊙, 533 ..F 3
Sainte-Jeanne-d'Arc, 936 ..E 1
Sainte-Julie-de-
Verchères, 1,214 ..J 4
Sainte-Julienne⊙, 839 ..G 3
Sainte-Justine, 980 ....G 3
Sainte-Marie,
4,307 ....F 3
Sainte-Martine⊙, 1,931 ..D 4
Sainte-Émile, 2,645 ....H 3
Sainte-Monique, 697 ....F 3
Sainte-Perpétue-de-
L'Islet, 1,048 ....H 2

Saint-Éphrem-de-Tring, 954 G 3
Saint-Pudentienne, 799 ....E 4
Sainte-Scholastique⊙,
14,787 ....C 4
Saint-Esprit, 937 ....D 3
Sainte-Thècle, 1,725 ....E 3
Sainte-Thérèse, 17,175 ..H 4
Sainte-Thérèse-Ouest,
7,278 ....H 4
Saint-Étienne-des-Grès,
870 ....E 3
Saint-Eugène, 656 ....G 2
Saint-Eustache, 9,479 ..H 4
Saint-Eustache-Est, 4,993 ..H 4
Saint-Fabien, 1,537 ....J 1
Saint-Félicien, 4,952 ..E 1
Saint-Félix-de-Valois,
1,455 ....D 3

AREA 594,860 sq. mi.
POPULATION 6,023,000
CAPITAL Québec
LARGEST CITY Montréal
HIGHEST POINT Mt. Jacques Cartier 4,160 ft.
SETTLED IN 1608
ADMITTED TO CONFEDERATION 1867
PROVINCIAL FLOWER White Garden Lily

Saint-Féréol-les-Neiges, 692 ... G 2
Saint-Flavien, 645 ... F 3
Saint-François-d'Assise, 691 ... G 1
Saint-François-du-Lac⊙, 1,001 ... E 3
Saint-Fulgence, 999 ... G 1
Saint-Gabriel, 3,383 ... D 3
Saint-Gédéon, Frontenac, 1,174 ... G 4
Saint-Gédéon, Lac-St-Jean-E., 885 ... F 1
Saint-Georges, Beauce, 7,554 ... G 3
Saint-Georges, Champlain, 2,061 ... E 3
Saint-Georges-de-Cacouna, 1,001 ... H 2
Saint-Georges-Ouest, 6,000 ... G 3
Saint-Germain-de-Grantham, 1,104 ... E 4
Saint-Gilles, 694 ... F 3
Saint-Grégoire, 655 ... D 4
Saint-Grégoire-de-Greenlay, 694 ... E 4
Saint-Henri, 1,160 ... J 3
Saint-Honoré, Beauce, 1,045 ... G 4
Saint-Honoré, Chicoutimi, 1,055 ... F 1
Saint-Hubert, 36,854 ... J 4
Saint-Hubert-de-Témiscouata, 832 ... J 2
Saint-Hyacinthe⊙, 24,562 ... D 4
Saint-Isidore, 736 ... F 3
Saint-Isidore-de-Laprairie, 749 ... D 4
Saint-Jacques, 1,975 ... D 4
Saint-Jean⊙, 32,863 ... D 4
Saint-Jean-Chrysostome, 1,905 ... J 3
Saint-Jean-de-Boischatel, 1,685 ... J 3
Saint-Jean-de-Dieu, 1,148 ... J 1
Saint-Jean-de-Matha, 943 ... D 3
Saint-Jean-Port-Joli⊙, 1,795 ... G 2
Saint-Jérôme, Lac-St-Jean-E., 1,910 ... F 1
Saint-Jérôme, Terrebonne⊙, 26,524 ... H 4
Saint-Joachim, 920 ... G 2
Saint-Joachim-de-Tourelle, 1,021 ... D 4

Saint-Joseph, 4,945 ... E 4
Saint-Joseph-de-Beauce, 2,893 ... G 3
Saint-Joseph-de-la-Rivière-Bleue, 1,429 ... J 2
Saint-Joseph-de-Sorel, 3,290 ... D 3
Saint-Jovite, 3,132 ... C 3
Saint-Lambert, 18,616 ... J 4
Saint-Laurent, 62,955 ... H 4
Saint-Léonard, 52,040 ... H 4
Saint-Léonard-d'Aston, 995 ... E 3
Saint-Léon-de-Standon, 830 ... G 3
Saint-Léon-le-Grand, 695 ... B 2
Saint-Liboire⊙, 667 ... E 4
Saint-Louis-de-Terrebonne, 1,113 ... H 4
Saint-Louis-du-Ha! Ha!, 733 H 2
Saint-Luc, 4,850 ... D 4
Saint-Marc-des-Carrières, 2,650 ... E 3
Saint-Méthode-de-Frontenac, 793 ... F 3
Saint-Michel-de-Bellechasse, 967 ... G 3
Saint-Michel-des-Saints, 1,647 ... D 3
Saint-Nazaire-de-Chicoutimi, 884 ... F 1
Saint-Nicolas, 1,975 ... H 3
Saint-Noël, 910 ... B 1
Saint-Odilon, 704 ... G 3
Saint-Ours, 838 ... D 4
Saint-Pacôme, 1,180 ... G 2
Saint-Pamphile, 3,542 ... H 3
Saint-Pascal, 2,513 ... H 2
Saint-Paul-de-Montminy, 746 ... G 3
Saint-Paulin, 809 ... D 3
Saint-Paul-l'Ermite, 3,165 ... J 3
Saint-Philippe-de-Néri, 701 ... H 2
Saint-Pie, 1,709 ... E 4
Saint-Pierre, 6,801 ... H 4
Saint-Prime, 2,350 ... E 1
Saint-Prosper-de-Dorchester, 1,696 ... G 3
Saint-Raphaël⊙, 1,216 ... G 3
Saint-Raymond, 4,036 ... F 3
Saint-Rédempteur, 1,652 ... J 3
Saint-Régis, 727 ... C 4
Saint-Rémi, 2,282 ... D 4
Saint-Roch-de-l'Achigan, 962 ... D 4

Saint-Roch-de-Richelieu, 721 ... D 4
Saint-Romuald-d'Etchemin⊙, 8,394 ... J 3
Saint-Sauveur-des-Monts, 1,846 ... C 4
Saint-Siméon, 1,186 ... G 2
Saint-Thomas-de-Joliette, 728 ... D 3
Saint-Timothée, 1,613 ... D 4
Saint-Tite, 3,130 ... E 3
Saint-Ubald, 809 ... E 3
Saint-Ulric, 936 ... B 1
Saint-Urbain-de-Charlevoix, 1,172 ... G 2
Saint-Victor, 1,017 ... G 3
Saint-Zacharie, 1,390 ... G 3
Saint-Zotique, 1,243 ... C 4
Sault-au-Mouton, 951 ... H 1
Sawyerville, 864 ... F 4
Sayabec, 1,789 ... B 1
Scotstown, 917 ... F 4
Senneville, 1,412 ... H 4
Shawbridge, 969 ... C 4
Shawinigan, 27,792 ... E 3
Shawinigan-Sud, 11,470 ... E 3
Sherbrooke⊙, 80,711 ... E 4
Sillery, 13,932 ... J 3
Sorel⊙, 19,347 ... D 3
Squatec, 950 ... J 2
Stanstead Plain, 1,192 ... E 4
Sully, 776 ... H 2
Sutton, 1,684 ... E 4
Tadoussac⊙, 1,010 ... H 1
Templeton, 3,684 ... H 4
Terrebonne, 22,003 ... H 4
Thetford Mines, 22,003 ... F 3
Thurso, 3,219 ... B 4
Touraine, 6,978 ... H 2
Tourville, 678 ... H 2
Tracy, 11,842 ... D 3
Tring-Jonction, 1,283 ... F 3
Trois-Pistoles, 4,678 ... H 1
Trois-Rivières, 55,869 ... E 3
Trois-Rivières-Ouest, 8,057 ... E 3
Upton, 818 ... E 4
Val-Brillant, 690 ... B 1
Valcourt, 2,411 ... E 4
Val-David, 1,627 ... C 3
Vallée-Jonction, 1,295 ... G 3
Valleyfield, 30,173 ... C 4
Val-Saint-Michel, 2,050 ... H 3
Vanier, 9,717 ... J 3
Varennes, 2,382 ... J 4
Vaudreuil⊙, 3,843 ... C 4

Verchères⊙, 1,840 ... J 4
Verdun, 74,718 ... H 4
Victoriaville, 22,047 ... F 3
Villeneuve, 4,062 ... J 3
Warwick, 2,847 ... F 4
Waterloo⊙, 4,936 ... E 4
Waterville, 1,476 ... F 4
Weedon-Centre, 1,429 ... F 4
Westmount, 23,606 ... H 4
Windsor, 6,023 ... F 4
Wottonville, 683 ... F 4
Yamachiche⊙, 1,147 ... E 3

OTHER FEATURES

Alma (isl.) ... F 1
Aylmer (lake) ... E 1
Baskatong (res.) ... B 3
Batiscan (riv.) ... E 2
Bécancour (riv.) ... F 3
Bonaventure (isl.) ... D 1
Bonaventure (riv.) ... D 1
Brome (lake) ... E 4
Brompton (lake) ... E 4
Cascapédia (riv.) ... C 1
Chaleur (bay) ... C 2
Champlain (lake) ... D 4
Chaudière (riv.) ... F 3
Chic-Chocs (mts.) ... C 1
Chicoutimi (riv.) ... F 2
Coudres (isl.), 1,522 ... G 2
Deschênes (lake) ... A 4
Deux Montagnes (lake) ... C 4
Ditton (riv.) ... F 4
Forillon Nat'l Park ... D 1
Fort Chambly Nat'l Hist. Park ... J 4
Gaspé (bay) ... D 1
Gaspé (cape) ... D 1
Gaspé (pen.) ... C 1
Gaspésie Prov. Park ... C 1
Gatineau (riv.) ... B 3
Îles (lake) ... B 3
Jacques-Cartier (mt.) ... C 1
Jacques-Cartier (riv.) ... F 2
Kénogami (lake) ... F 1
Kiamika (res.) ... B 3
La Maurice Nat'l Park ... E 3
Laurentides Prov. Park ... F 2
La Vérendrye Prov. Park ... A 2
Lièvre (riv.) ... B 3
Lièvres (isl.) ... H 2
Maskinongé (riv.) ... D 3
Matane (riv.) ... B 1
Matane Prov. Park ... B 1
Matapédia (riv.) ... B 2
Matawin (res.) ... D 3

Mégantic (lake) ... G 4
Memphremagog (lake) ... E 4
Mercier (dam) ... A 3
Métabetchouane (riv.) ... F 1
Mille Îles (riv.) ... H 4
Montmorency (riv.) ... F 2
Mont-Tremblant Prov. Park ... C 3
Nicolet (riv.) ... E 3
Nominingue (lake) ... C 3
Nord (riv.) ... C 4
Orléans (isl.), 5,435 ... F 3
Ottawa (riv.) ... B 4
Ouareau (riv.) ... D 3
Patapédia (riv.) ... B 2
Péribonca (riv.) ... F 1
Petite Nation (riv.) ... B 4
Prairies (riv.) ... H 4
Rimouski (riv.) ... J 1
Ristigouche (riv.) ... B 2
Saguenay (riv.) ... G 1
Sainte-Anne (riv.) ... F 3
Sainte-Anne (riv.) ... B 1
Saint-François (lake) ... F 4
Saint-François (riv.) ... E 4
Saint-Jean (lake) ... E 1
Saint Lawrence (gulf) ... D 2
Saint Lawrence (riv.) ... H 1
Saint-Louis (lake) ... H 4
Saint-Maurice (riv.) ... E 3
Saint-Pierre (lake) ... E 3
Shawinigan (riv.) ... F 1
Shipshaw (riv.) ... F 1
Soeurs (isl.) ... H 4
Témiscouata (lake) ... H 2
Tremblant (lake) ... C 3
Trente et un Milles (lake) ... B 3
Verte (isl.), 175 ... H 1
Yamaska (riv.) ... E 4
York (riv.) ... D 1

⊙ County seat.
‡ Population of metropolitan area.

QUÉBEC, NORTHERN
INTERNAL DIVISIONS

Abitibi (co.), 112,244 ... B 2
Abitibi (terr.), 21,308 ... B 3
Chicoutimi (county), 163,348 ... C 2
Lac-Saint-Jean-Ouest (county), 57,074 ... C 2
Mistassini (terr.), 2,702 B 2
Nouveau-Québec (terr.), 10,002 ... E 1

Pontiac (co.), 19,570 ... B 3
Saguenay (co.), 111,272 D 2
Témiscamingue (county), 54,656 ... B 3

CITIES and TOWNS

Aguanish, 442 ... E 2
Amos⊙, 6,984 ... B 3
Angliers, 404 ... B 3
Baie-du-Poste, 1,598 ... C 2
Barraute, 1,288 ... B 3
Belleterre, 614 ... B 3
Betsiamites, 1,574 ... D 2
Cadillac, 1,102 ... B 3
Chapais, 2,914 ... C 2
Chibougamau, 9,701 ... C 2
Clarke City, 750 ... D 2
Dolbeau, 7,633 ... C 2
Duparquet, 786 ... B 3
Dupuy, 439 ... B 3
Évain, 605 ... B 3
Forestville, 1,606 ... D 2
Fort-Chimo, 693 ... F 1
Fort-George, 1,280 ... B 2
Gagnon, 3,787 ... D 2
Godbout, 653 ... D 2
Hauterive, 13,181 ... D 2
Havre-St-Pierre, 2,999 ... E 2
Inoucdjouac, 525 ... E 1
La Reine, 450 ... B 3
La Sarre, 5,185 ... B 3
La Tabatière, 475 ... F 2
Lebel-sur-Quevillon, 2,936 ... B 3
Lorrainville, 906 ... B 3
Macamic, 1,705 ... B 3
Malartic, 5,347 ... B 3
Manicouagan, 500 ... D 2
Matagami, 2,411 ... B 2
Micoua, 851 ... D 2
Moisie, 570 ... D 2
Noranda, 10,741 ... B 3
Normétal, 1,851 ... B 3
Nouveau-Comptoir, 514 ... B 2
Obedjiwan, 712 ... C 2
Parent, 452 ... C 3
Port-Cartier, 3,730 ... D 2
Port-Cartier-Ouest, 500 ... D 3
Port-Menier, 394 ... E 2
Poste-de-la-Baleine, 987 ... B 1
Povungnituk, 676 ... C 1
Rivière-au-Tonnerre, 520 ... D 2
Rouyn, 17,821 ... B 3
Rupert House, 757 ... B 2

Saglouc, 402 ... C 1
Saint-Augustin, 916 ... F 2
Schefferville, 3,271 ... D 2
Senneterre, 4,303 ... B 3
Sept-Îles, 24,320 ... D 2
Témiscaming, 2,428 ... B 3
Val-d'Or, 17,421 ... B 3
Ville-Marie⊙, 1,995 ... B 3

OTHER FEATURES

Anticosti (isl.), 419 ... E 2
Baleine, Grand Rivière de la (riv.) ... B 2
Betsiamites (riv.) ... D 2
Bienville (lake) ... C 2
Cabonga (res.) ... B 3
Caniapiscau (riv.) ... D 1
Daniel-Johnson (dam) ... D 2
Dozois (res.) ... B 3
Eastmain (riv.) ... B 2
George (riv.) ... E 1
Gouin (res.) ... C 2
Grande Rivière, La (riv.) ... B 2
Guillaume-Delisle (lake) ... B 1
Harricana (riv.) ... B 2
Honguedo (passg.) ... D 1
Hudson (bay) ... A 1
Hudson (str.) ... C 1
Jacques-Cartier (passg.) ... E 2
James (bay) ... A 2
Koksoak (riv.) ... D 1
La Vérendrye Prov. Park ... B 3
Louis-XIV (pt.) ... A 2
Manicouagan (res.) ... D 2
Mistassibi (riv.) ... C 2
Mistassini (lake) ... C 2
Moisie (riv.) ... D 2
Natashquan (riv.) ... E 2
Nottaway (riv.) ... B 2
Nouveau-Québec (crater) ... D 1
Otish (mts.) ... D 2
Ottawa (riv.) ... B 3
Reed (mt.) ... D 2
Romaine (riv.) ... E 2
Saguenay (riv.) ... D 2
Saguenay Prov. Park ... D 2
Saint Lawrence (gulf) ... E 2
Saint Lawrence (riv.) ... D 2
Ungava (bay) ... E 1
Ungava (pen.) ... D 1
Wolstenholme (cape) ... C 1
Wright (mt.) ... D 2

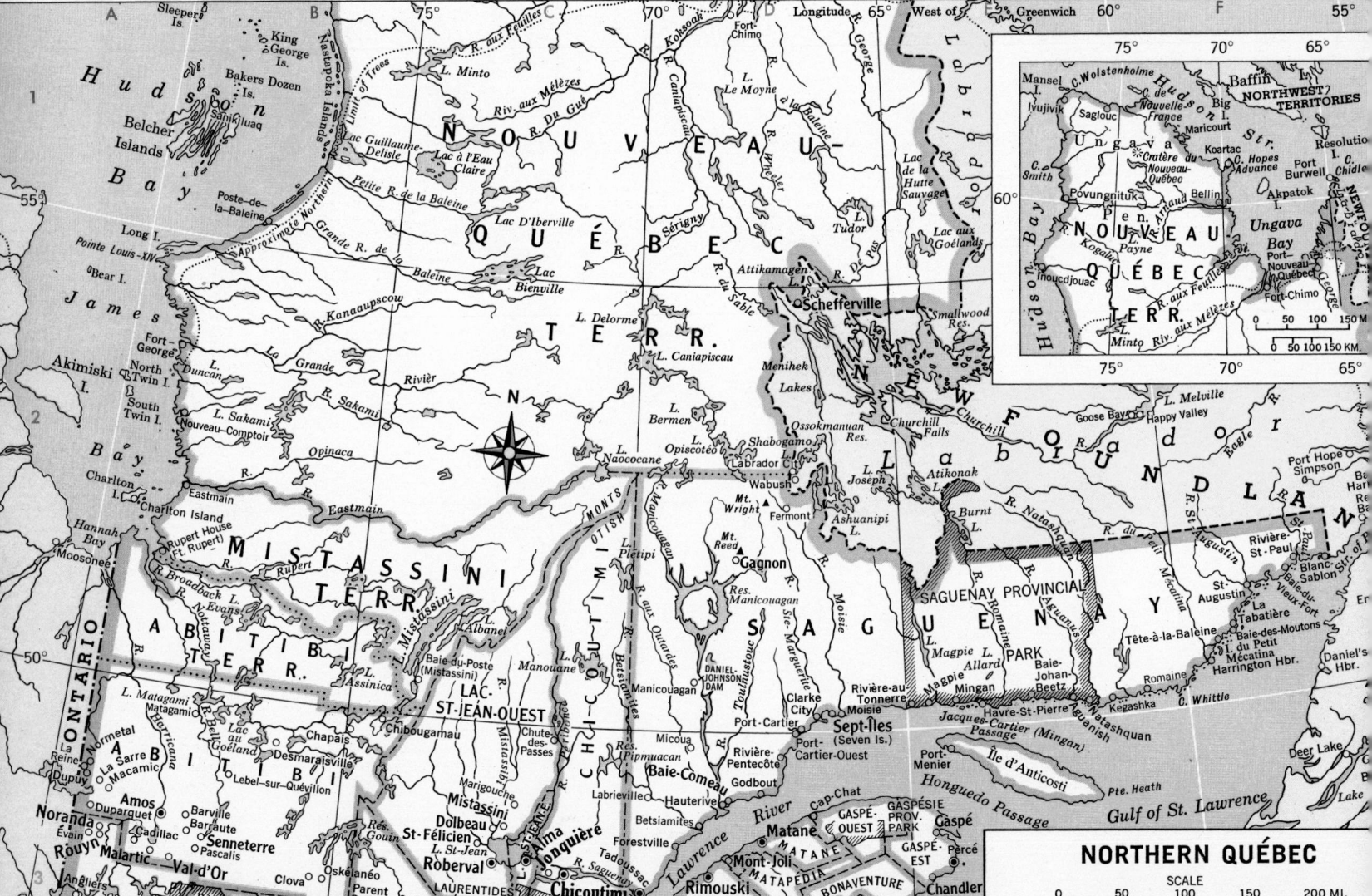

NORTHERN QUÉBEC

SCALE

0   50   100   150   200 MI.

0   50   100   150   200 KM.

Provincial Capital ... ⊛
County Seats ... ⊙
International Boundaries ... — · —
Provincial Boundaries
County Boundaries
Territorial Boundaries ... — · · —

© C.S. HAMMOND & Co., N.Y.

ONTARIO, NORTHERN

INTERNAL DIVISIONS

ma (terr. dist.),
21,937 . . . . .D 3
rane (terr. dist.),
5,836 . . . . .D 2
ra (terr. dist.), 53,230 C 2
toulin (terr. dist.),
0,931 . . . . .D 3
sing (terr. dist.),
'8,867 . . . . .E 3
Sound (terr. dist.),
0,244 . . . . .E 3
River (terr. dist.),
5,750 . . . . .B 3
rew (county), 90,875 .E 3
ury (reg. munic.),
68,224 . . . . .D 3
ury (terr. dist.),
98,079 . . . . .D 3
der Bay (terr. dist.),
45,390 . . . . .C 3
skaming (terr. dist.),
6,485 . . . . .D 3

CITIES and TOWNS

kan, 6,007 . . . . .B 3
River, 3,450 . . . . . . .D 3
eol, 3,994 . . . . .D 3
River, 1,094 . . . . . . .E 3
eau, 3,365 . . . . .D 3
rane ⊙, 4,965 . . . . . .D 3
River, 5,671 . . . . . . .E 3
en, 6,939 . . . . .B 3
Lake, 8,727 . . . . .D 3
nola, 6,045 . . . . .D 3
lbany, 25 . . . . .D 2
rances ⊙, 9,947 . . . .B 3
dton, 3,178 . . . . .C 3
ybury ⊙, 5,280 . . . . .D 3
st, 5,354 . . . . .D 3
sville, 9,784 . . . . .E 3
ois Falls, 7,055 . . . . .D 3
skasing, 12,834 . . . .D 3
ra ⊙, 10,952 . . . . . . .B 3
nd Lake, 13,599 . . . .D 3
ouwadge, 3,258 . . . .C 3
wa, 2,881 . . . . .E 3
se Factory, 849 . . . . . .D 2
sonee, 1,793 . . . . . . .D 2
New Liskeard, 5,488 . . . . .E 3
Nickel Centre, 13,037 . . . .D 3
North Bay ⊙, 49,187 . . . . .E 3
Onaping Falls, 7,511 . . . . .D 3
Parry Sound ⊙, 5,842 . . . .D 3
Pembroke ⊙, 16,544 . . . . .E 3
Renfrew, 9,173 . . . . .E 3
Sault Sainte Marie ⊙,
80,332 . . . . .D 3
Sturgeon Falls, 6,662 . . . .E 3
Sudbury, 99,512 . . . . .D 3
Sudbury, ‡155,424 . . . . . .D 3
Thunder Bay ⊙, 108,411 . .C 3
Thunder Bay, ‡112,093 . . .C 3
Timmins, 43,182 . . . . . . .D 3
Valley East, 17,937 . . . . . .D 3
Walden, 10,788 . . . . .D 3
Wawa, 4,375 . . . . .C 3

OTHER FEATURES

Abitibi (lake) . . . . .E 3
Abitibi (riv.) . . . . .D 2
Albany (riv.) . . . . .C 2
Algonquin Prov. Park, 337 E 3
Attawapiskat (riv.) . . . . . .C 2
Big Trout (lake) . . . . .B 2
Caribou (isl.), 3 . . . . .C 3
Eabamet (lake) . . . . .C 2
Ekwan (riv.) . . . . .C 2
English (riv.) . . . . .B 2
Groundhog (riv.) . . . . . . .D 3
Hannah (bay) . . . . .D 2
Henrietta Maria (cape) . . .D 1
Hudson (bay) . . . . .D 1
James (bay) . . . . .D 2
Kapuskasing (riv.) . . . . . .D 3
Kenogami (riv.) . . . . .C 2
Lake of the Woods (lake) .B 3
Lake Superior Prov. Park .D 3
Manitoulin (isl.), 10,064 .D 3
Mattagami (riv.) . . . . .D 3
Michipicoten (isl.), 4 . . . .C 3
Mille Lacs (lake) . . . . . . .B 3
Missinaibi (riv.) . . . . .D 2
Nipigon (lake) . . . . .C 3
North Caribou (lake) . . . . .B 2
Ogidaki (mt.) . . . . .D 3
Ogoki (riv.) . . . . .C 2
Ottawa (riv.) . . . . .E 3
Pipestone (riv.) . . . . .B 2
Polar Bear Prov. Park . . .D 2
Quetico Prov. Park . . . . . .B 3
Rainy (lake) . . . . .B 3
Red (lake) . . . . .B 2
Sachigo (riv.) . . . . .B 2
Saint Joseph (lake) . . . . . .B 2
Sandy (lake) . . . . .B 2
Seine (riv.) . . . . .B 3
Seul (lake) . . . . .B 2
Severn (riv.) . . . . .B 2
Sibley Prov. Park, 2 . . . . .C 3
Slate (isls.), 4 . . . . .C 3
Superior (lake) . . . . .C 3
Sutton (riv.) . . . . .D 2
Thunder (bay) . . . . .C 3
Timagami (lake) . . . . .D 3
Timiskaming (lake) . . . . . .E 3
Winisk (riv.) . . . . .C 2
Winnipeg (riv.) . . . . .A 2
Woods (lake) . . . . .B 3

ONTARIO

INTERNAL DIVISIONS

Algoma (terr. dist.),
121,937 . . . . .J 5
Brant (county), 96,767 . . .D 4
Bruce (county), 47,385 . . .C 3
Cochrane (terr. dist.),
95,836 . . . . .J 4
Dufferin (county), 21,200 .D 3
Dundas (county), 17,457 . .J 2
Durham (reg. munic.),
221,503 . . . . .F 4
Elgin (county), 66,608 . . . .C 5
Essex (county), 306,399 . .B 5
Frontenac (county),
101,692 . . . . .H 3
Glengarry (county), 18,480 K 2
Grenville (county), 24,316 .J 3
Grey (county), 66,403 . . . .D 3
Haldimand-Norfolk (reg.
munic.), 86,772 . . . . .D 5
Haliburton (county), 9,081 F 2
Hamilton-Wentworth (reg.
munic.), 401,883 . . . .D 4
Halton (reg. munic.),
190,469 . . . . .E 4
Hastings (county), 99,393 G 3
Huron (county), 52,951 . . .C 4
Kenora (terr. dist.), 53,230 G 5
Kent (county), 101,118 . . .B 5
Lambton (county),
114,314 . . . . .B 5
Lanark (county), 42,259 H 3
Leeds (county), 50,093 . . .H 3
Lennox and Addington
(county), 28,359 . . . . .G 3
Manitoulin (terr. dist.),
10,931 . . . . .B 2
Middlesex (county),
282,014 . . . . .C 4
Muskoka (dist. munic.)
31,938 . . . . .E 3
Niagara (reg. munic.),
347,328 . . . . .E 4
Nipissing (terr. dist.),
78,867 . . . . .F 2
Northumberland (county),
60,102 . . . . .G 3
Ottawa-Carleton (reg. munic.),
471,931 . . . . .J 2
Oxford (county), 80,349 .D 4
Parry Sound (terr. dist.),
30,244 . . . . .D 2
Peel (reg. munic.),
259,402 . . . . .E 4
Perth (county), 62,973 . . .C 4
Peterborough (county),
92,417 . . . . .F 3
Prescott (county),
27,832 . . . . .K 2
Prince Edward (county),
20,640 . . . . .G 3
Rainy River (terr. dist.),
25,750 . . . . .G 5
Renfrew (county),
90,875 . . . . .G 2
Russell (county), 16,287 . .J 2
Simcoe (county),
175,604 . . . . .E 3
Stormont (county),
61,302 . . . . .K 2
Sudbury (reg. munic.),
168,224 . . . . .K 6
Sudbury (terr. dist.),
198,079 . . . . .J 5
Thunder Bay (terr. dist.),
145,390 . . . . .H 5
Timiskaming (terr. dist.),
46,485 . . . . .K 5
Toronto (metro. munic.),
2,086,017 . . . . .K 4
Victoria (county),
36,641 . . . . .F 3
Waterloo (reg. munic.),
254,037 . . . . .D 4
Wellington (county),
108,581 . . . . .D 4
York (reg. munic.),
166,060 . . . . .E 4

AREA 412,582 sq. mi.
POPULATION 7,707,000
CAPITAL Toronto
LARGEST CITY Toronto
HIGHEST POINT Ogidaki Mtn. 2,183 ft.
SETTLED IN 1749
ADMITTED TO CONFEDERATION 1867
PROVINCIAL FLOWER White Trillium

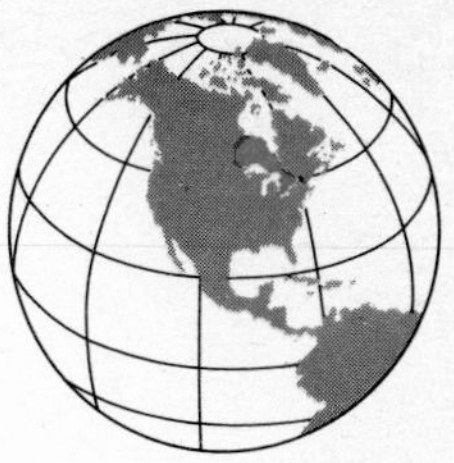

CITIES and TOWNS

Ailsa Craig, 608 . . . . .C 4
Ajax, 15,052 . . . . .E 4
Alban, 420 . . . . .D 1
Alcona Beach, 659 . . . . . . .E 3
Alexandria, 3,240 . . . . . . .K 2
Alfred, 1,230 . . . . .K 2
Alliston, 3,176 . . . . .E 3
Almonte, 3,696 . . . . .H 2
Alvinston, 702 . . . . .B 5
Amherstburg, 5,169 . . . . .A 5
Amherst View, 3,121 . . . . .H 3
Ancaster, 15,326 . . . . . . .D 4
Angus, 3,174 . . . . .E 3
Apple Hill, 318 . . . . .K 2
Arkona, 469 . . . . .C 4
Armstrong, 574 . . . . .H 4
Arnprior, 6,016 . . . . .H 2
Arthur, 1,414 . . . . .D 4
Athens, 1,071 . . . . .J 3
Atherley, 392 . . . . .E 3
Atikokan, 6,007 . . . . .G 5
Atwood, 690 . . . . .D 4
Aurora, 13,614 . . . . .J 3
Avonmore, 287 . . . . .K 2
Aylmer, 4,755 . . . . .C 5
Ayr, 1,272 . . . . .D 4
Ayton, 423 . . . . .D 3
Baden, 959 . . . . .D 4
Bala, 462 . . . . .E 2
Bancroft, 2,276 . . . . .G 2
Barrie ⊙, 27,676 . . . . .E 3
Barry's Bay, 1,432 . . . . . .G 2
Batawa, 667 . . . . .G 3
Batchawana Bay, 586 . . . .J 5
Bath, 810 . . . . .H 3
Bayfield, 503 . . . . .C 4
Bayside, 1,732 . . . . .G 3
Baysville, 283 . . . . .E 2
Beachburg, 549 . . . . .H 2
Beachville, 995 . . . . .D 4
Beardmore, 754 . . . . .H 5
Beaverton, 1,485 . . . . .E 3
Beeton, 1,061 . . . . .E 3
Belle River, 2,877 . . . . . . .B 5
Belleville ⊙, 35,128 . . . . .G 3
Belmont, 798 . . . . .C 5
Bethany, 325 . . . . .F 3
Bewdley, 446 . . . . .F 3
Bicroft, 576 . . . . .F 2
Blackburn, 3,841 . . . . .J 2
Blenheim, 3,490 . . . . .C 5
Blind River, 3,450 . . . . . . .J 5
Bloomfield, 730 . . . . .G 4
Blyth, 814 . . . . .C 4
Bobcaygeon, 1,518 . . . . . .F 3
Bonfield, 694 . . . . .E 1
Bothwell, 810 . . . . .C 5
Bourget, 855 . . . . .J 2
Bracebridge ⊙, 6,903 . . . .E 2
Bradford, 3,401 . . . . .E 3
Braeside, 522 . . . . .H 2
Brampton ⊙, 73,570 . . . . .J 4
Brantford ⊙, 64,421 . . . . .D 4
Bridgenorth, 1,380 . . . . . .F 3
Brigden, 582 . . . . .B 5
Brighton, 2,956 . . . . .G 3
Brights Grove, 730 . . . . . .B 4
Britt, 500 . . . . .D 2
Brockville ⊙, 19,765 . . . . .J 3
Bruce Mines, 505 . . . . .J 5
Brussels, 908 . . . . .C 4
Burford, 1,291 . . . . .D 4
Burgessville, 329 . . . . . . .D 4
Burk's Falls, 891 . . . . .E 2
Burlington, 87,023 . . . . . .E 4
Cache Bay, 727 . . . . .D 1
Caesarea, 352 . . . . .F 3
Calabogie, 299 . . . . .H 2
Caledon, 13,480 . . . . .E 4
Callander, 1,190 . . . . .E 1
Cambridge, 64,114 . . . . . .D 4
Campbellford, 3,522 . . . . .G 3
Cannington, 1,083 . . . . . . .E 3
Cape Croker, 681 . . . . .D 3
Capreol, 3,994 . . . . .K 5
Caramat, 520 . . . . .H 5
Cardinal, 1,865 . . . . .J 3
Carleton Place, 5,020 . . . .H 2
Carlisle, 488 . . . . .D 4
Carp, 516 . . . . .H 2
Cartier, 740 . . . . .J 5
Casselman, 1,337 . . . . . . .J 2
Castleton, 289 . . . . .F 3
Cedar Springs, 302 . . . . . .B 5
Chalk River, 1,094 . . . . . . .G 1
Chapleau, 3,365 . . . . .J 5
Charing Cross, 436 . . . . . .B 5
Chatham ⊙, 35,317 . . . . .B 5
Chatsworth, 399 . . . . .D 3
Chesley, 1,693 . . . . .C 3
Chesterville, 1,252 . . . . . . .J 2
Chute-à-Blondeau, 420 . . . K 2
City View, 4,500 . . . . .J 2
Clarence Creek, 411 . . . . . .J 2
Clarksburg, 389 . . . . .D 3
Clifford, 555 . . . . .D 4
Clinton, 3,154 . . . . .C 4
Cobalt, 2,197 . . . . .K 5
Cobden, 926 . . . . .H 2
Coboconk, 477 . . . . .F 3
Cobourg ⊙, 11,282 . . . . . .F 4
Cochrane ⊙, 4,965 . . . . . .K 5
Colborne, 1,588 . . . . .G 4
Colchester, 752 . . . . .B 6
Coldwater, 759 . . . . .E 3
Collingwood, 9,775 . . . . . .D 3
Collins Bay, 2,089 . . . . . . .H 3
Comber, 642 . . . . .B 5
Consecon, 332 . . . . .G 3
Cookstown, 847 . . . . .E 3
Cornwall ⊙, 47,116 . . . . . .K 2
Corunna, 3,052 . . . . .B 5
Cottam, 530 . . . . .B 5
Courtland, 574 . . . . .D 5
Courtright, 590 . . . . .B 5
Coverdale, 670 . . . . .F 4
Crediton, 409 . . . . .C 4
Creemore, 978 . . . . .D 3
Crysler, 481 . . . . .J 2
Cumberland, 581 . . . . .J 2
Cumberland Beach, 477 . . .E 3
Dashwood, 434 . . . . .C 4
Deep River, 5,671 . . . . . . .G 1
Delaware, 627 . . . . .C 5
Delhi, 3,894 . . . . .D 5
Delta, 465 . . . . .H 3
Deseronto, 1,863 . . . . . . .G 3
Dorchester, 1,796 . . . . . . .C 5
Douglas, 307 . . . . .H 2
Drayton, 752 . . . . .D 4
Dresden, 2,369 . . . . .B 5
Drumbo, 460 . . . . .D 4
Dryden, 6,939 . . . . .G 4
Dublin, 314 . . . . .C 4
Dubreuilville, 654 . . . . .J 5
Dundalk, 1,022 . . . . .D 3
Dundas, 17,208 . . . . .D 4
Dunnville, 11,422 . . . . . . .E 5
Durham, 2,448 . . . . .D 3
Dutton, 878 . . . . .C 5
East York, 104,784 . . . . . .J 4
Echo Bay, 493 . . . . .J 5
Eganville, 1,395 . . . . .G 2
Egmondville, 492 . . . . . . .C 4
Elgin, 322 . . . . .H 3
Elk Lake, 627 . . . . .K 5
Elliot Lake, 8,727 . . . . .B 1
Elmira, 4,730 . . . . .D 4
Elmvale, 1,103 . . . . .E 3
Elmwood, 345 . . . . .C 3
Elora, 1,904 . . . . .D 4
Embro, 703 . . . . .C 4
Embrun, 1,452 . . . . .J 2
Emeryville, 1,719 . . . . . . .B 5
Emo, 768 . . . . .F 5
Englehart, 1,721 . . . . .K 5
Erieau, 509 . . . . .C 5
Erin, 1,446 . . . . .D 4
Espanola, 6,045 . . . . .J 5
Essex, 4,002 . . . . .B 5
Etobicoke, 282,686 . . . . . .J 4
Everett, 405 . . . . .E 3
Exeter, 3,354 . . . . .C 4
Fauquier, 643 . . . . .J 5
Fenelon Falls, 1,616 . . . . . .F 3
Fergus, 5,433 . . . . .D 4
Field, 655 . . . . .E 1
Finch, 397 . . . . .J 2
Fingal, 322 . . . . .C 5
Fitzroy Harbour, 317 . . . . .H 2
Flesherton, 524 . . . . .D 3
Foleyet, 637 . . . . .J 5
Fordwich, 325 . . . . .C 4

(continued on following page)

NORTHERN ONTARIO
SCALE
0 25 50 100 150 200 MI.
0 25 50 100 150 200 KM.
Provincial and State Boundaries
County Boundaries
© C.S. HAMMOND & Co., N.Y.
Longitude West of Greenwich
Hudson Bay
James Bay
MANITOBA
KENORA
THUNDER BAY
COCHRANE
ALGOMA
SUDBURY
TIMISKAMING
NIPISSING
RAINY RIVER
MINNESOTA
MICHIGAN
QUEBEC
Lake Superior
L. Michigan
Georgian Bay
Thunder Bay
Sault Ste. Marie
Timmins
Kirkland Lake
Kenora
Dryden
Atikokan
Ft. Frances
Sudbury
North Bay
Pembroke
Renfrew
Parry Sound
Cochrane
Kapuskasing
Moosonee
Moose Factory
Fort Albany
Fort Severn
Wawa
Marquette
Escanaba
Noranda
Rouyn
Amos
Val-d'Or

ONTARIO CENTRAL PART

Copyright by C. S. HAMMOND & CO., N.Y.

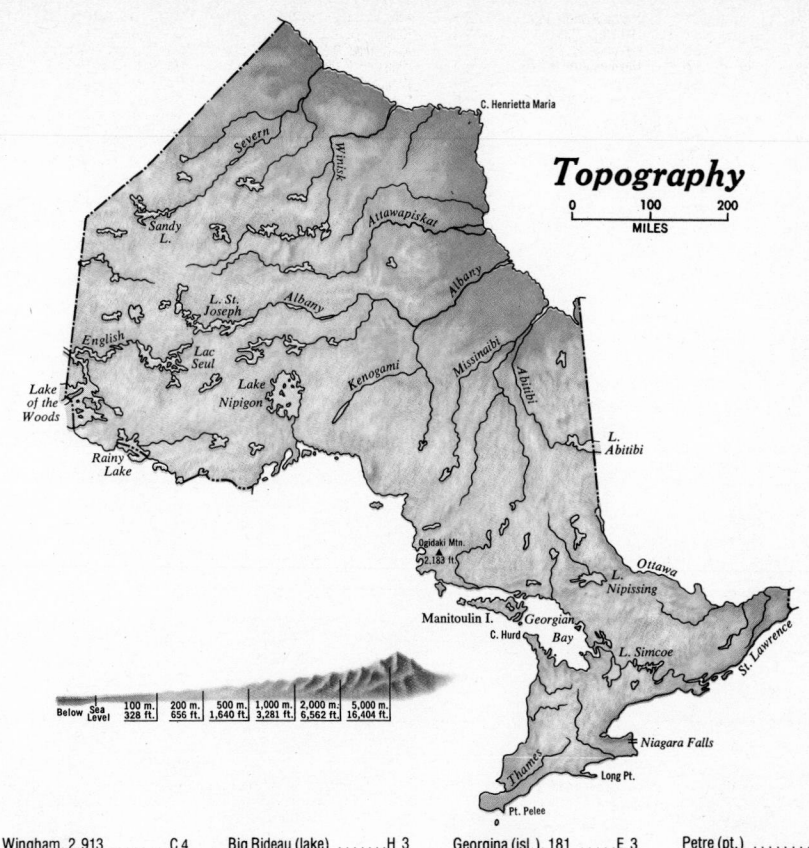

Topography

```
0    100    200
       MILES
```

Below Sea Level | 100 m. 328 ft. | 200 m. 656 ft. | 500 m. 1,640 ft. | 1,000 m. 3,281 ft. | 2,000 m. 6,562 ft. | 5,000 m. 16,404 ft.

ONTARIO
SOUTHERN PART

```
SCALE
0   10   20   30   40   50MI.
0  10  20  30  40  50KM.
```

ional Capital ....⊛
vincial Capital ....⊛
nty Seats ....◉
rnational
oundaries ....

Provincial & State
Boundaries ....
County Boundaries ---
Canals ....

*Agriculture, Industry
and Resources*

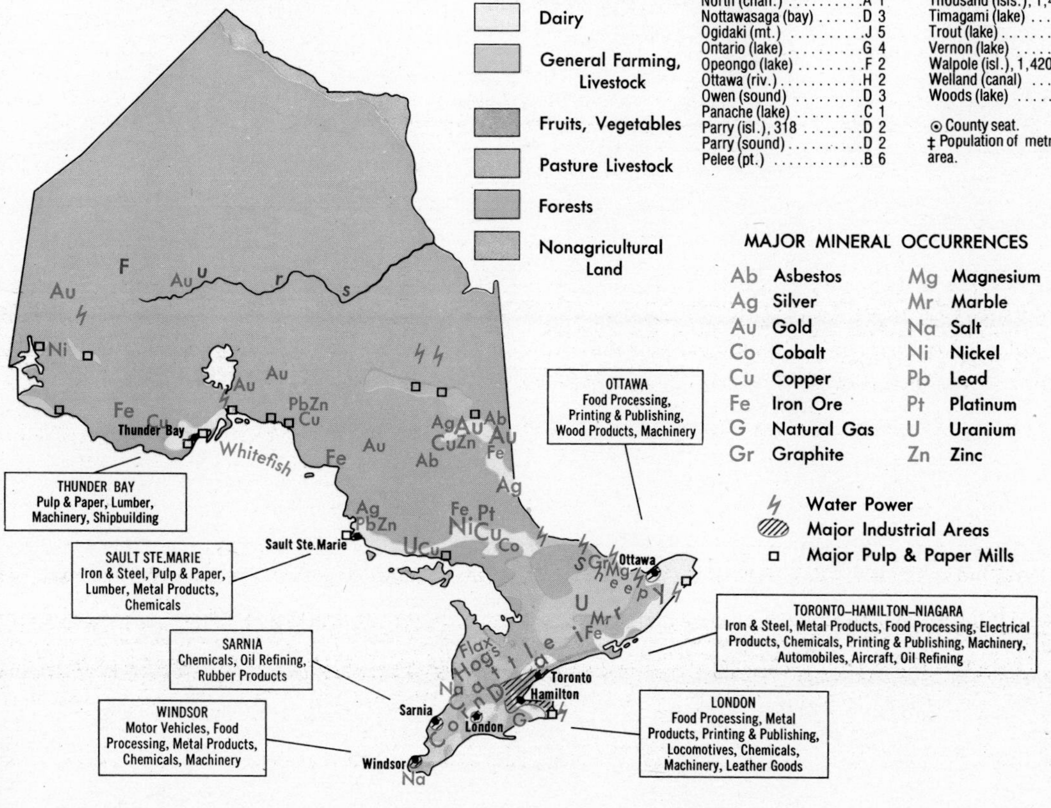

DOMINANT LAND USE

Cereals, Cash Crops, Livestock

Dairy

General Farming, Livestock

Fruits, Vegetables

Pasture Livestock

Forests

Nonagricultural Land

MAJOR MINERAL OCCURRENCES

Ab	Asbestos	Mg	Magnesium
Ag	Silver	Mr	Marble
Au	Gold	Na	Salt
Co	Cobalt	Ni	Nickel
Cu	Copper	Pb	Lead
Fe	Iron Ore	Pt	Platinum
G	Natural Gas	U	Uranium
Gr	Graphite	Zn	Zinc

⚡ Water Power
▨ Major Industrial Areas
□ Major Pulp & Paper Mills

OTTAWA
Food Processing, Printing & Publishing, Wood Products, Machinery

THUNDER BAY
Pulp & Paper, Lumber, Machinery, Shipbuilding

SAULT STE.MARIE
Iron & Steel, Pulp & Paper, Lumber, Metal Products, Chemicals

SARNIA
Chemicals, Oil Refining, Rubber Products

WINDSOR
Motor Vehicles, Food Processing, Metal Products, Chemicals, Machinery

TORONTO—HAMILTON—NIAGARA
Iron & Steel, Metal Products, Food Processing, Electrical Products, Chemicals, Printing & Publishing, Machinery, Automobiles, Aircraft, Oil Refining

LONDON
Food Processing, Metal Products, Printing & Publishing, Locomotives, Chemicals, Machinery, Leather Goods

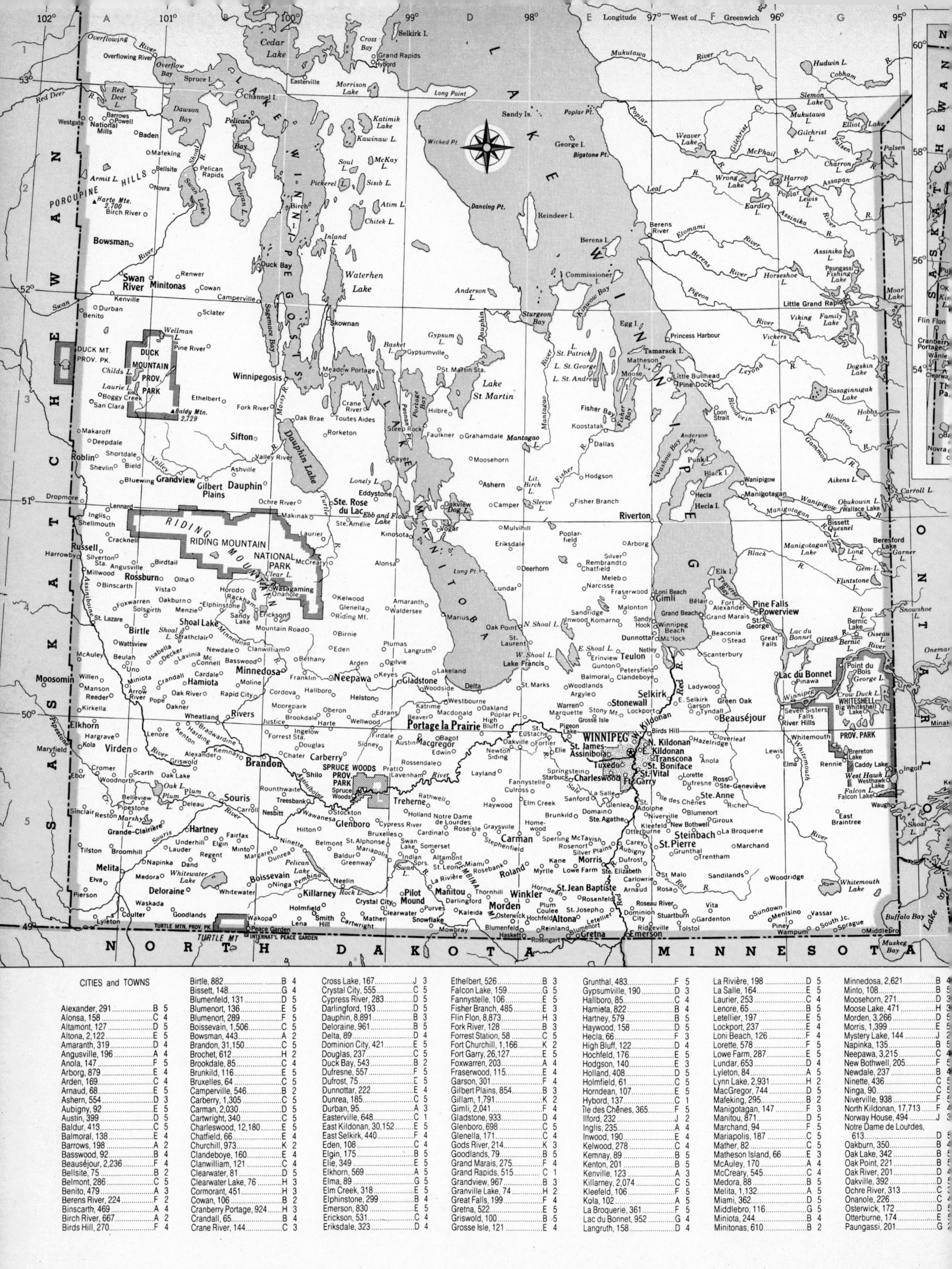

CITIES and TOWNS

Name	Pop.	Grid
Alexander	291	B 5
Alonsa	158	C 4
Altamont	127	D 5
Altona	2,122	E 5
Amaranth	319	C 4
Angusville	196	A 4
Anola	147	F 5
Arborg	879	E 4
Arden	169	C 4
Arnaud	68	E 5
Ashern	554	D 3
Aubigny	92	E 5
Austin	399	D 5
Baldur	413	C 5
Balmoral	138	E 4
Barrows	198	A 2
Basswood	92	B 4
Beauséjour	2,236	F 4
Bellsite	75	A 2
Belmont	286	C 5
Benito	479	A 2
Berens River	224	F 2
Binscarth	469	A 4
Birch River	667	A 2
Birds Hill	270	F 4
Birtle	882	B 4
Bissett	148	G 4
Blumenfeld	131	D 5
Blumenort	136	E 5
Blumenort	289	F 5
Boissevain	1,506	B 5
Bowsman	443	A 2
Brandon	31,150	B 5
Brochet	612	H 2
Brookdale	85	C 4
Brunkild	116	E 5
Bruxelles	64	C 5
Camperville	546	B 3
Carberry	1,305	C 5
Carman	2,030	D 5
Cartwright	340	C 5
Charleswood	12,180	E 4
Chatfield	66	E 4
Churchill	973	K 2
Clandeboye	160	E 4
Clanwilliam	121	C 4
Clearwater	81	D 5
Clearwater Lake	76	H 3
Cormorant	451	H 2
Cowan	106	B 3
Cranberry Portage	924	H 3
Crandall	65	B 4
Crane River	144	C 3
Cross Lake	167	J 3
Crystal City	555	C 5
Cypress River	283	D 5
Darlingford	193	D 5
Dauphin	8,891	B 3
Deloraine	961	B 5
Delta	89	D 4
Dominion City	421	E 5
Douglas	237	C 5
Duck Bay	543	B 2
Dufresne	557	F 5
Dufrost	75	E 5
Dunnottar	222	E 4
Dunrea	185	C 5
Durban	95	A 3
Easterville	648	C 1
East Kildonan	30,152	E 4
East Selkirk	440	E 4
Eden	108	C 4
Elgin	175	B 5
Elie	349	E 5
Elkhorn	569	A 5
Elma	89	G 5
Elm Creek	318	E 5
Elphinstone	299	C 4
Emerson	830	E 5
Erickson	531	C 4
Eriksdale	323	D 4
Ethelbert	526	B 3
Falcon Lake	159	G 5
Fannystelle	106	E 5
Fisher Branch	485	E 3
Flin Flon	8,873	H 3
Fork River	128	B 3
Forrest Station	58	C 5
Fort Churchill	1,166	K 2
Fort Garry	26,127	E 4
Foxwarren	203	A 4
Fraserwood	115	E 4
Garson	301	F 4
Gillam	1,791	K 2
Gilbert Plains	854	B 3
Gimli	2,041	F 4
Gladstone	933	D 4
Glenboro	698	C 5
Glenella	171	C 4
Gods River	214	K 3
Goodlands	79	B 5
Grand Marais	275	F 4
Grand Rapids	515	C 1
Grandview	967	B 3
Granville Lake	74	H 2
Great Falls	199	F 4
Gretna	522	E 5
Griswold	100	B 5
Grosse Isle	121	E 4
Grunthal	483	F 5
Gypsumville	190	D 3
Hallboro	85	C 4
Hamiota	822	B 4
Hartney	579	B 5
Haywood	158	D 5
Hecla	66	F 3
High Bluff	122	D 5
Hochfeld	176	E 5
Hodgson	140	E 3
Holland	408	D 5
Holmfield	61	C 5
Horndean	107	E 5
Hybord	137	C 1
Île des Chênes	365	F 5
Ilford	232	J 2
Inglis	235	A 4
Inwood	190	E 4
Kelwood	278	C 4
Kemnay	89	B 5
Kenton	201	B 5
Kenville	123	A 3
Killarney	2,074	C 5
Kleefeld	106	F 5
Kola	102	A 5
La Broquerie	361	F 5
Lac du Bonnet	952	G 4
Langruth	158	D 4
La Rivière	198	D 5
La Salle	164	E 5
Laurier	253	C 4
Lenore	65	B 5
Letellier	197	E 5
Lockport	237	E 4
Loni Beach	126	F 4
Lorette	653	F 5
Lowe Farm	287	E 5
Lundar	653	D 4
Lyleton	84	A 5
Lynn Lake	2,931	H 2
MacGregor	744	D 5
Mafeking	295	A 2
Manigotagan	147	F 3
Manitou	871	C 5
Marchand	94	F 5
Mariapolis	187	C 5
Mather	82	C 5
Matheson Island	66	E 3
McAuley	170	A 4
McCreary	545	C 4
Medora	88	B 5
Melita	1,132	A 5
Miami	362	D 5
Middlebro	116	G 5
Miniota	244	B 4
Minitonas	610	B 2
Minnedosa	2,621	B 4
Minto	108	
Moosehorn	271	D
Moose Lake	471	H
Morden	3,266	D
Morris	1,399	E
Mystery Lake	144	J
Napinka	135	
Neepawa	3,215	
New Bothwell	237	
Newdale	237	
Ninette	436	
Ninga	90	
Niverville	938	
North Kildonan	17,713	J
Norway House	494	
Notre Dame de Lourdes	613	
Oakburn	350	
Oak Lake	342	
Oak Point	221	
Oak River	201	
Oakville	392	
Ochre River	313	
Onanole	226	
Osterwick	172	D E
Otterburne	174	
Paungassi	201	

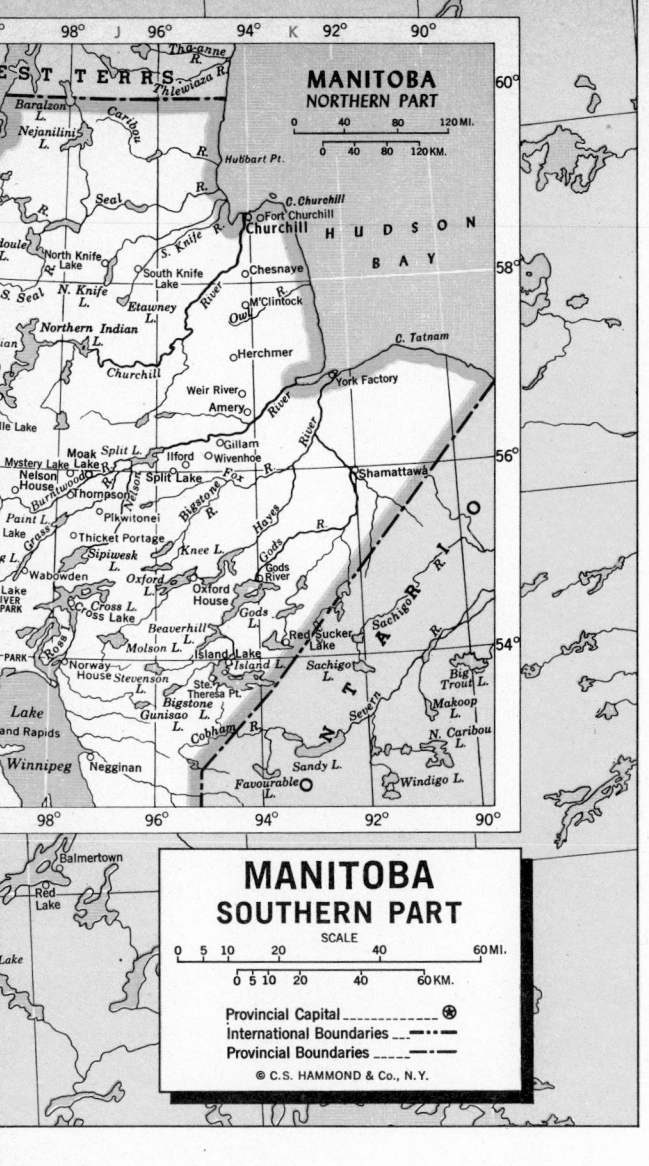

MANITOBA
NORTHERN PART

MANITOBA
SOUTHERN PART
SCALE

Provincial Capital ⊛
International Boundaries ━ ∙ ━ ∙
Provincial Boundaries ━ ∙∙ ━

© C.S. HAMMOND & Co., N.Y.

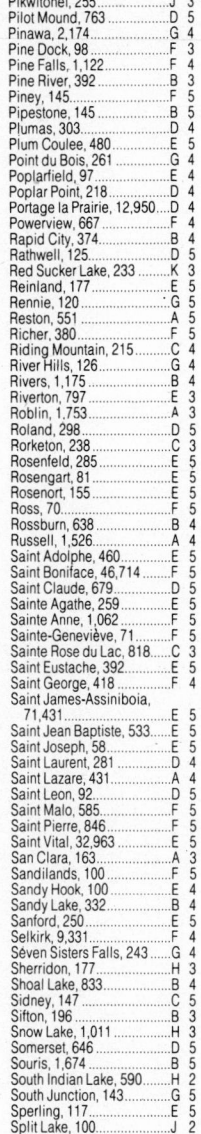

Pelican Rapids, 217 ....B 2
Petersfield, 146 ....E 4
Pierson, 228 ....A 5
Pikwitonei, 255 ....J 3
Pilot Mound, 763 ....D 5
Pinawa, 2,174 ....G 4
Pine Dock, 98 ....F 3
Pine Falls, 1,122 ....F 4
Pine River, 392 ....B 3
Piney, 145 ....F 5
Pipestone, 145 ....B 5
Plumas, 303 ....D 4
Plum Coulee, 480 ....E 5
Point du Bois, 261 ....G 4
Poplarfield, 97 ....E 4
Poplar Point, 218 ....D 4
Portage la Prairie, 12,950 ....D 4
Powerview, 667 ....F 4
Rapid City, 374 ....B 4
Rathwell, 125 ....D 5
Red Sucker Lake, 233 ....K 3
Reinland, 177 ....E 5
Rennie, 120 ....G 4
Reston, 551 ....A 5
Richer, 380 ....F 5
Riding Mountain, 215 ....C 4
River Hills, 126 ....G 4
Rivers, 1,175 ....B 4
Riverton, 797 ....E 3
Roblin, 1,753 ....A 3
Roland, 298 ....D 5
Rorketon, 238 ....C 3
Rosenfeld, 285 ....E 5
Rosengart, 81 ....E 5
Rosenort, 155 ....E 5
Ross, 70 ....F 5
Rossburn, 638 ....B 4
Russell, 1,526 ....A 4
Saint Adolphe, 460 ....E 5
Saint Boniface, 46,714 ....F 5
Saint Claude, 679 ....D 5
Sainte Agathe, 259 ....E 5
Sainte Anne, 1,062 ....F 5
Sainte-Geneviève, 71 ....F 5
Sainte Rose du Lac, 818 .....C 3
Saint Eustache, 392 ....E 5
Saint George, 418 ....F 4
Saint James-Assiniboia,
   71,431 ....F 5
Saint Jean Baptiste, 533 .....E 5
Saint Joseph, 58 ....E 5
Saint Laurent, 281 ....D 4
Saint Lazare, 431 ....A 4
Saint Leon, 92 ....D 5
Saint Malo, 585 ....F 5
Saint Pierre, 846 ....F 5
Saint Vital, 32,963 ....E 5
San Clara, 163 ....A 3
Sandilands, 100 ....F 5
Sandy Hook, 100 ....E 4
Sandy Lake, 332 ....B 4
Sanford, 250 ....E 5
Selkirk, 9,331 ....F 4
Séven Sisters Falls, 243 .....G 4
Sherridon, 177 ....H 3
Shoal Lake, 833 ....B 4
Sidney, 147 ....C 5
Sifton, 196 ....B 3
Snow Lake, 1,011 ....H 3
Somerset, 646 ....D 5
Souris, 1,674 ....B 5
South Indian Lake, 590 ......H 2
South Junction, 143 ....G 5
Sperling, 117 ....E 5
Split Lake, 100 ....J 2
Sprague, 195 ....G 5
Springstein, 117 ....E 5
Spruce Woods, 183 ....C 5

Starbuck, 263 ....E 5
Steep Rock, 146 ....D 3
Steinbach, 5,197 ....F 5
Stockton, 58 ....C 5
Stonewall, 1,583 ....E 4
Stony Mountain, 1,268 ......E 4
Strathclair, 404 ....B 4
Sundown, 296 ....F 5
Swan Lake, 300 ....D 5
Swan River, 3,522 ....A 2
Teulon, 828 ....E 4
The Pas, 19,001 ....H 3
Thicket Portage, 318 ....J 3
Thompson, 6,062 ....J 2
Tilston, 72 ....A 5
Tolstoi, 88 ....F 5
Transcona, 22,490 ....F 5
Treherne, 628 ....D 5
Tuxedo, 3,258 ....E 5
Tyndall, 400 ....F 4
Vassar, 240 ....G 5
Virden, 2,823 ....A 5
Vista, 71 ....B 4
Vita, 349 ....F 5
Vogar, 126 ....D 4
Wabowden, 809 ....J 3
Wanless, 123 ....H 3
Warren, 267 ....E 4
Wasagaming, 122 ....C 4
Waskada, 247 ....B 5
Wawanesa, 478 ....C 5
Wellwood, 79 ....C 4
Westbourne, 113 ....D 4
West Kildonan, 23,959 .....E 4
Wheatland, 67 ....B 4
Whitemouth, 366 ....G 5
Winkler, 2,983 ....E 5
Winnipeg (cap.), 246,246 ...E 5
Winnipeg, ‡540,262 ....E 5
Winnipeg Beach, 687 ....F 4
Winnipegosis, 887 ....B 3
Woodlands, 123 ....E 4
Woodridge, 228 ....G 5

OTHER FEATURES

Assiniboine (riv.) ....C 5
Assinika (riv.) ....G 2
Baldy (mt.) ....B 3
Berens (riv.) ....F 2
Bernic (lake) ....G 4
Birch (isl.) ....C 2
Black (isl.) ....F 3
Bloodvein (riv.) ....F 3
Bonnet (lake) ....G 4
Burntwood (riv.) ....J 2
Cedar (lake) ....B 1
Charron (lake) ....G 2

Childs (lake) ....A 3
Chitek (lake) ....C 2
Churchill (cape) ....K 2
Churchill (riv.) ....J 2
Clear (lake) ....C 4
Clearwater Prov. Park .....H 3
Cormorant (lake) ....H 3
Cross (lake) ....J 3
Crow Duck (lake) ....G 4
Dauphin (lake) ....C 3
Dauphin (riv.) ....D 3
Dawson (bay) ....B 2
Dog (lake) ....D 3
Duck Mountain Prov. Park .B 3
East Shoal (lake) ....E 4
Ebb and Flow (lake) ......C 3
Elk (isl.) ....F 4
Falcon (lake) ....G 5
Family (lake) ....G 3
Fisher (bay) ....E 3
Fishing (lake) ....G 2
Fox (riv.) ....K 2
Garner (lake) ....G 4
George (lake) ....G 4
Gods (lake) ....K 3
Gods (riv.) ....K 3
Granville (lake) ....H 2
Grass (riv.) ....J 3
Grass River Prov. Park ...H 3
Harte (mt.) ....A 2
Hayes (riv.) ....K 3
Hecla (isl.) ....F 3
Hudson (bay) ....K 2
International Peace
   Garden ....B 5
Island (lake) ....K 3
Kawinaw (lake) ....C 2
Kississing (lake) ....H 2
Lake of the Woods (lake) .H 5
Lonely (lake) ....C 3
Long (pt.) ....D 1
Manigotagan (riv.) .....G 3
Manitoba (lake) ....D 4
Mantagao (riv.) ....E 3
Minnedosa (riv.) ....B 4
Moose (isl.) ....E 3
Mossy (riv.) ....C 3
Mukutawa (riv.) ....E 1
Nejanilini (lake) ....J 1
Nelson (riv.) ....J 2
Northern Indian (lake) ..J 2
North Shoal (lake) .....E 4
Nueltin (lake) ....H 1
Oak (lake) ....B 5
Oiseau (riv.) ....G 4
Overflowing (riv.) .....A 1
Oxford (lake) ....J 3
Paint (lake) ....J 2
Pelican (bay) ....B 2
Pelican (lake) ....B 2

Pelican (lake) ....C 5
Pembina (mt.) ....D 5
Pembina (riv.) ....C 5
Peonan (pt.) ....D 3
Pigeon (riv.) ....F 2
Pipestone (creek) .....A 5
Plum (creek) ....B 5
Poplar (riv.) ....D 3
Porcupine (hills) ......A 2
Portage (bay) ....D 3
Rat (riv.) ....F 5
Red (riv.) ....F 4
Red Deer (lake) ......A 2
Reindeer (isl.) ....E 2
Reindeer (lake) ......H 2
Riding (mt.) ....B 4
Riding Mountain Nat'l
   Park, 158 ....B 4
Rock (lake) ....C 5
Ross (isl.) ....J 3
Sagemace (bay) ......B 3
Saint George (lake) ...E 3
Saint Martin (lake) ...D 3
Sale (riv.) ....E 5
Sasaginnigak (lake) ..G 3
Seal (riv.) ....J 2
Setting (lake) ....H 3
Shoal (riv.) ....B 2
Sipiweska (lake) .....J 3
Souris (riv.) ....B 5
Southern Indian (lake) .H 2
South Knife (riv.) ....J 2
Split (lake) ....J 2
Spruce Woods Prov. Park .C 5
Sturgeon (bay) ......E 3
Swan (lake) ....B 2
Swan (lake) ....D 5
Swan (riv.) ....A 3
Tadoule (lake) ......J 2
Tatnam (cape) ......K 2
Traverse (bay) ......F 4
Turtle (riv.) ....C 3
Turtle Mountain Prov. Park .B 5
Valley (riv.) ....B 3
Wanipigow (riv.) ....G 3
Washow (bay) ......F 3
Waterhen (lake) ....E 2
Weaver (lake) ......F 2
West Hawk (lake) ...G 5
West Shoal (lake) ...E 4
Whitemouth (lake) ..G 5
Whitemouth (riv.) ..G 5
Whiteshell Prov. Park .G 4
Whitewater (lake) ...B 5
Winnipeg (lake) .....E 2
Winnipeg (riv.) .....G 4
Winnipegosis (lake) ..C 2
Woods (lake) ....H 5
‡ Population of metropolitan
   area.

AREA   251,000 sq. mi.
POPULATION   979,000
CAPITAL   Winnipeg
LARGEST CITY   Winnipeg
HIGHEST POINT   Baldy Mtn. 2,729 ft.
SETTLED IN   1812
ADMITTED TO CONFEDERATION   1870
PROVINCIAL FLOWER   Prairie Crocus

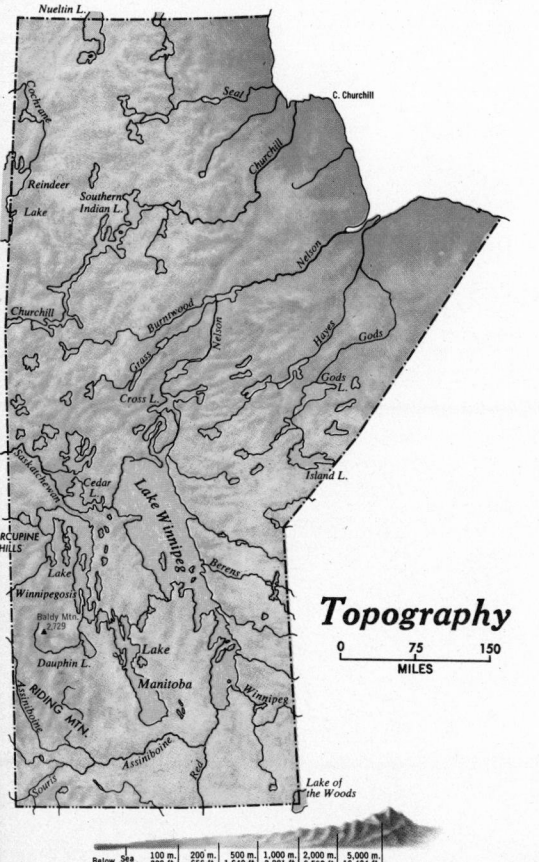

Topography

MILES

Below Sea | 100 m. | 200 m. | 500 m. | 1,000 m. | 2,000 m. | 5,000 m.
Level | 328 ft. | 656 ft. | 1,640 ft. | 3,281 ft. | 6,562 ft. | 16,404 ft.

Agriculture, Industry and Resources

DOMINANT LAND USE

Cereals (chiefly barley, oats)
Cereals, Livestock
Dairy
Livestock
Forests
Nonagricultural Land

MAJOR MINERAL OCCURRENCES

Au   Gold
Co   Cobalt
Cu   Copper
Na   Salt
Ni   Nickel
O   Petroleum
Pb   Lead
Pt   Platinum
Zn   Zinc

Water Power
Major Industrial Areas
Major Pulp & Paper Mills

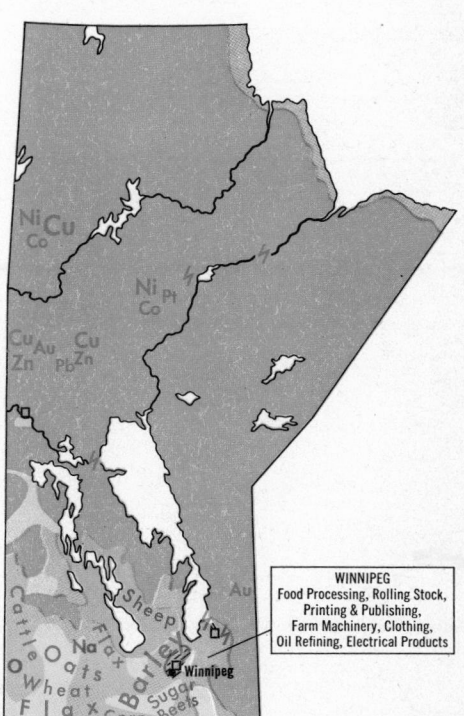

WINNIPEG
Food Processing, Rolling Stock,
Printing & Publishing,
Farm Machinery, Clothing,
Oil Refining, Electrical Products

Topography

0   60   120
MILES

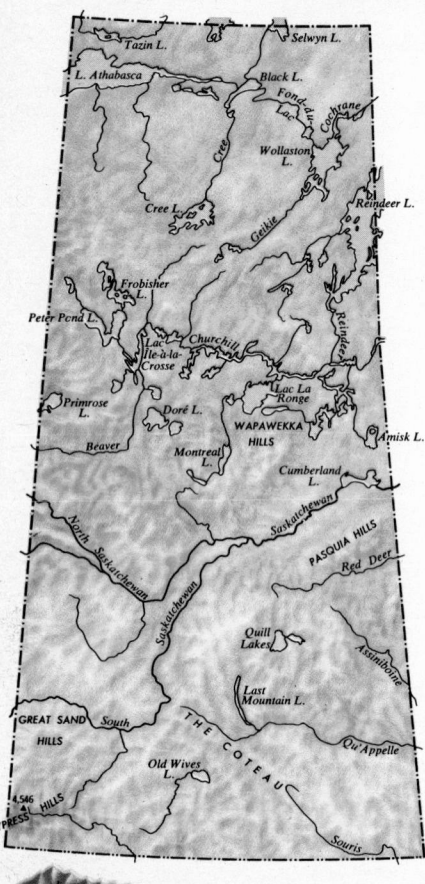

5,000 m.   2,000 m.   1,000 m.   500 m.   200 m.   100 m.   Sea   Below
16,404 ft. 6,562 ft. 3,281 ft. 1,640 ft. 656 ft. 328 ft. Level

Agriculture, Industry and Resources

DOMINANT LAND USE

Wheat

Cereals (chiefly barley, oats)

Cereals, Livestock

Livestock

Forests

MAJOR MINERAL OCCURRENCES

Au Gold
Cu Copper
G   Natural Gas
He Helium
K   Potash
Lg Lignite

Na Salt
O   Petroleum
S   Sulfur
U   Uranium
Zn Zinc

Water Power

Major Industrial Areas

REGINA
Food Processing, Machinery, Oil Refining

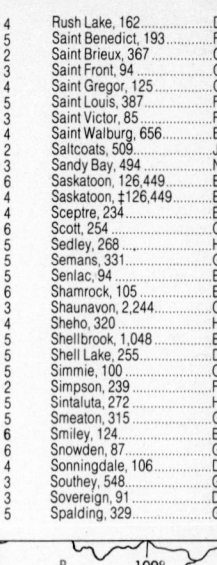

...ers, 117 ....D 3	Unity, 2,294 ....B 3	Wilkie, 1,642 ....C 3	Beaverlodge (lake) ....L 2
...ritwood, 719 ....D 2	Uranium City, 1,867 ....L 2	Willow Bunch, 482 ....F 6	Brightsand (lake) ....B 2
...ingside, 350 ....J 4	Val Marie, 307 ....D 6	Windthorst, 188 ....J 5	Candle (lake) ....E 2
...ingwater, 99 ....C 4	Vanguard, 315 ....D 6	Wiseton, 181 ....D 4	Carrot (lake) ....J 2
...uce Lake, 106 ....B 2	Vanscoy, 244 ....D 4	Wishart, 269 ....H 4	Churchill (riv.) ....M 3
...Hill, 384 ....K 5	Vawn, 119 ....C 2	Wolfe, 115 ....M 2	Coteau, The (hills) ....D 4
...City, 543 ....G 3	Veregin, 197 ....K 4	Wolseley, 975 ....H 5	Cowan (lake) ....D 4
...nen, 225 ....J 4	Vibank, 275 ....H 5	Wood Mountain, 86 ......E 6	Cree (riv.) ....J 1
...wart Valley, 138 ....D 5	Viceroy, 152 ....F 4	Wroxton, 92 ....K 4	Cumberland (lake) ....J 1
...kholm, 357 ....J 5	Viscount, 395 ....F 4	Wymark, 199 ....D 5	Cypress (hills) ....B 6
...ny Rapids, 147 ....M 2	Vonda, 258 ....E 2	Wynyard, 1,932 ....G 4	Cypress Hills Prov. Park ..B 6
...oughton, 751 ....E 4	Wadena, 1,382 ....H 4	Yarbo, 160 ....K 5	Delaronde (lake) ....E 1
...asbourg, 759 ....G 4	Wakaw, 1,009 ....F 3	Yellow Creek, 163 ....F 3	Diefenbaker (lake) ....D 4
...ongfield, 110 ....E 4	Waldeck, 242 ....D 5	Yellow Grass, 500 ....H 6	Doré (lake) ....E 1
...rgis, 617 ....J 4	Waldheim, 606 ....F 2	Yorkton, 13,430 ....J 5	Duck Mountain Prov. Park .K 4
...cess, 101 ....D 5	Wapella, 518 ....K 5	Young, 496 ....F 4	Eagle (lake) ....D 4
...ft Current, 15,415 ....D 5	Warman, 781 ....E 2	Zealandia, 155 ....D 4	Eaglehill (creek) ....D 4
...vania, 125 ....G 3	Waseca, 140 ....B 2	Zenon Park, 346 ....H 2	Fond du Lac (riv.) ....M 2
...ntallon, 174 ....K 5	Waskesiu Lake, 154 ....E 2		Fort Walsh Nat'l Hist. Park .A 6
...eodore, 434 ....J 4	Watrous, 1,541 ....F 4		Frenchman (riv.) ....C 6
...go, 227 ....K 4	Watson, 840 ....G 3		Frobisher (lake) ....C 2
...mpkins, 353 ....C 5	Wawota, 536 ....J 6	**OTHER FEATURES**	Gardiner (dam) ....D 4
...quay, 377 ....H 4	Webb, 105 ....C 5		Good Spirit (lake) ....J 4
...mping Lake, 241 ....B 3	Weekes, 183 ....J 3		Goodspirit Prov. Park ......J 4
...oune, 136 ....H 6	Weirdale, 108 ....F 2	Allan (hills) ....E 4	Great Sand (hills) ....B 5
...nor Lake, 276 ....L 3	Weldon, 254 ....F 2	Amisk (lake) ....M 4	Greenwater Lake Prov.
...tleford, 419 ....B 2	Welwyn, 231 ....K 5	Assiniboine (riv.) ....J 3	Park, 13 ....H 3
...ford, 153 ....F 2	Weyburn, 8,815 ....H 6	Athabasca (lake) ....L 2	
...ana, 86 ....H 5	White City, 129 ....G 5	Battle (creek) ....B 6	
	White Fox, 354 ....H 2	Battle (riv.) ....B 3	
	Whitewood, 1,098 ....J 5	Bear (hills) ....C 4	
	Wilcox, 189 ....G 5	Beaver (lake) ....H 4	
		Beaver (riv.) ....C 1	

Lenore (lake) ....G 3	Pheasant (hills) ....J 5	Thickwood (hills) ....D 2
Makwa (riv.) ....B 1	Prince Albert Nat'l Park,	Tobin (lake) ....H 2
Manito (lake) ....B 3	182 ....E 1	Torch (riv.) ....H 2
Meadow Lake Prov. Park ..G 1	Qu'Appelle (riv.) ....J 5	Touchwood (hills) ....G 4
Meeting (lake) ....D 2	Quill (lake) ....G 4	Turtle (lake) ....C 2
Missouri Coteau (hills) ....F 6	Redberry (lake) ....D 3	Wapakemka (hills) ....M 4
Montreal (lake) ....F 1	Red Deer (riv.) ....K 3	Waskesiu (lake) ....E 2
Moose Jaw (riv.) ....G 5	Reindeer (lake) ....N 3	Willow Bunch (lake) ....F 6
Moose Mountain Prov.	Rivers (lake) ....F 6	Witchekan (lake) ....D 2
Park ....J 6	Saskatchewan (riv.) ....H 2	Wollaston (lake) ....N 2
Nipawin Prov. Park ....J 6	Souris (riv.) ....H 6	Wood (mt.) ....E 6
North Saskatchewan (riv.) .D 3	South Saskatchewan (riv.) .C 5	Wood (riv.) ....E 6
Old Wives (lake) ....E 5	Sturgeon (riv.) ....E 2	
Pasquia (riv.) ....H 2	Swift Current (creek) ....D 5	‡ Population of metropolitan
Peter Pond (lake) ....L 2	Tazin (lake) ....L 2	area.

AREA 251,700 sq. mi.
POPULATION 933,000
CAPITAL Regina
LARGEST CITY Regina
HIGHEST POINT Cypress Hills 4,546 ft.
SETTLED IN 1774
ADMITTED TO CONFEDERATION 1905
PROVINCIAL FLOWER Prairie Lily

SASKATCHEWAN NORTHERN PART

SCALE
0 20 40 60 80 100 MI.
0 20 40 60 80 100 KM.

SASKATCHEWAN SOUTHERN PART

SCALE
0 5 10 20 40 60 MI.
0 5 10 20 40 60 KM.

Provincial Capital ....⊛
International Boundaries ......
Provincial Boundaries ....

© C.S. HAMMOND & Co., N.Y.

Alberta 183

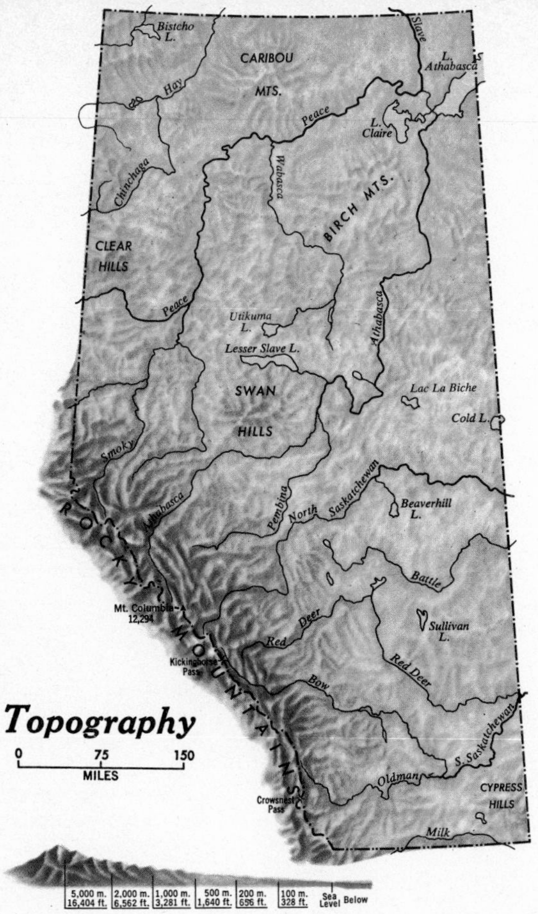
Bistcho L.
CARIBOU MTS.
Slave
L. Athabasca
Hay
Peace
L. Claire
Chinchaga
Wabasca
BIRCH MTS.
CLEAR HILLS
Peace
Utikuma L.
Athabasca
Lesser Slave L.
SWAN HILLS
Lac La Biche
Cold L.
Smoky
Athabasca
Pembina
North Saskatchewan
Beaverhill L.
ROCKY MOUNTAINS
Battle
Mt. Columbia 12,294
Red Deer
Sullivan L.
Kickinghorse Pass
Red Deer
Bow
S. Saskatchewan
Oldman
CYPRESS HILLS
Crowsnest Pass
Milk
Topography
0 75 150
MILES
5,000 m. 16,404 ft.
2,000 m. 6,562 ft.
1,000 m. 3,281 ft.
500 m. 1,640 ft.
200 m. 656 ft.
100 m. 328 ft.
Sea Level
Below

AREA 255,285 sq. mi.
POPULATION 1,614,000
CAPITAL Edmonton
LARGEST CITY Edmonton
HIGHEST POINT Mt. Columbia 12,294 ft.
SETTLED IN 1861
ADMITTED TO CONFEDERATION 1905
PROVINCIAL FLOWER Wild Rose

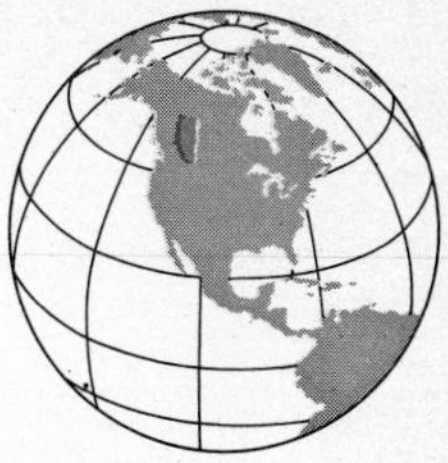

CITIES and TOWNS

adia Valley, 166 .... E 4
me, 300 .... D 4
rial, 151 .... D 4
rdrie, 1,089 .... C 4
berta Beach, 320 .... C 3
der Flats, 133 .... C 3
x, 565 .... D 3
iance, 230 .... E 3
nisk, 134 .... E 3
ndrew, 466 .... D 3
zac, 114 .... E 1
dmore, 230 .... E 2
drossan, 137 .... D 3
rowwood, 166 .... D 4
hmont, 150 .... E 2
habasca, 1,765 .... D 2
ikameg, 117 .... C 2
nff, 3,219 .... C 4
rnwell, 341 .... D 5
arons, 237 .... D 4
arrhead, 2,803 .... C 2
ashaw, 757 .... D 3
assano, 861 .... D 4
awlf, 182 .... D 3
eaumont, 337 .... D 3
eaverlodge, 1,157 .... A 2
eiseker, 414 .... D 4
ellevue, 1,242 .... C 5
entley, 621 .... C 3
erwyn, 474 .... B 1
g Valley, 306 .... D 3
ack Diamond, 945 .... C 4
ackfalds, 904 .... D 3
ackfoot, 175 .... E 3
ackie, 168 .... D 4
airmore, 2,037 .... C 5
ue Ridge, 239 .... C 2
uesky, 124 .... A 1
n Accord, 332 .... D 3
nnyville, 2,587 .... E 2
wden, 560 .... C 4
w Island, 1,159 .... E 5
yle, 460 .... D 2
agg Creek, 203 .... C 4
eton, 352 .... C 3
ooks, 3,986 .... E 4
ownvale, 161 .... B 1
uce, 110 .... E 3
uderheim, 350 .... D 3
ûlé, 104 .... B 3
ick Lake, 159 .... C 3
rdett, 206 .... E 5
adomin, 109 .... B 3
adotte Lake, 192 .... B 1
algary, 403,319 .... C 4
algary, ‡403,319 .... C 4
almar, 799 .... D 3
amrose, 8,673 .... D 3
anmore, 1,538 .... C 4
anyon Creek, 205 .... C 2
arbon, 343 .... D 4
arbondale, 115 .... D 3
ardston, 2,685 .... D 5
armangay, 230 .... D 4
Caroline, 339 .... C 3
Carseland, 105 .... D 4
Carstairs, 884 .... D 4
Caslan, 117 .... D 2
Castor, 1,166 .... D 3
Cayley, 122 .... D 4
Cereal, 220 .... E 4
Champion, 335 .... D 4
Chateh, 400 .... A 5
Chauvin, 349 .... E 3
Chipewyan Lake, 118 .... D 1
Chipman, 181 .... D 3
Clairmont, 309 .... A 2
Clandonald, 119 .... E 3
Claresholm, 2,935 .... D 4
Clive, 247 .... D 3
Clyde, 233 .... D 2
Coaldale, 2,798 .... D 5
Coalhurst, 426 .... D 5
Cochrane, 1,046 .... C 4
Cold Lake, 1,309 .... E 2
Coleman, 1,534 .... C 5
Colinton, 125 .... D 2
College Heights, 331 .... D 3
Conklin, 119 .... E 2
Consort, 659 .... E 3
Cooking Lake, 196 .... D 3
Coronation, 877 .... E 3
Coutts, 407 .... D 5
Cowley, 201 .... D 5
Cremona, 186 .... C 4
Crossfield, 638 .... C 4
Czar, 196 .... E 3
Daysland, 593 .... D 3
Delburne, 383 .... D 3
Delia, 241 .... D 4
Derwent, 203 .... E 3
Desmarais, 258 .... D 2
Devon, 1,468 .... D 3
Dewberry, 160 .... E 3
Didsbury, 1,821 .... C 4
Dixonville, 113 .... B 1
Donalda, 232 .... D 3
Donnelly, 274 .... B 2
Drayton Valley, 3,900 .... C 3
Drumheller, 5,446 .... D 4
Duchess, 228 .... E 4
Eaglesham, 218 .... B 2
East Coulée, 312 .... D 4
Eckville, 660 .... C 3
Edberg, 145 .... D 3
Edgerton, 296 .... E 3
Edmonton (cap.), 438,152 .... D 3
Edmonton, ‡495,702 .... D 3
Edmonton Beach, 148 .... C 3
Edson, 3,818 .... B 3
Elk Point, 729 .... E 3
Elnora, 213 .... D 3
Empress, 266 .... E 4
Enilda, 201 .... B 2
Entwistle, 353 .... C 3
Erskine, 233 .... D 3
Evansburg, 528 .... C 3
Exshaw, 548 .... C 4
Fairview, 2,109 .... A 1
Falher, 918 .... B 2
Faust, 353 .... C 2
Fawcett, 141 .... C 2
Ferintosh, 127 .... D 3
Foremost, 568 .... E 5
Forestburg, 669 .... E 3
Fort Assiniboine, 173 .... C 2
Fort Chipewyan, 1,122 .... C 5
Fort Kent, 113 .... E 2
Fort Macleod, 2,715 .... D 5
Fort McKay, 200 .... E 1
Fort McMurray, 6,847 .... E 1
Fort Saskatchewan, 5,726 .... D 3
Fort Vermilion, 740 .... B 5
Fox Creek, 1,281 .... B 2
Frank, 224 .... C 5
Galahad, 179 .... E 3
Garden River, 134 .... B 5
Gibbons, 551 .... D 3
Gift Lake, 379 .... C 2
Girouxville, 347 .... B 2
Gleichen, 367 .... D 4
Glendon, 354 .... E 2
Glenwood, 200 .... D 5
Grand Centre, 2,088 .... E 2
Grande Cache, 2,525 .... A 3
Grande Prairie, 13,079 .... A 2
Granum, 324 .... D 5
Grassy Lake, 196 .... E 5
Grimshaw, 1,714 .... B 1
Grouard Mission, 277 .... C 2
Halkirk, 136 .... D 3
Hanna, 2,545 .... E 4
Hardieville, 473 .... D 5
Hardisty, 594 .... E 3
Hay Lakes, 211 .... D 3
Heisler, 199 .... D 3
High Level, 1,614 .... A 5
High Prairie, 2,354 .... B 2
High River, 2,676 .... D 4
Hillcrest, 613 .... C 5
Hill Spring, 213 .... D 5
Hines Creek, 438 .... A 1
Hinton, 4,911 .... B 3
Holden, 448 .... D 3
Hughenden, 267 .... E 3
Hussar, 170 .... D 4
Hythe, 487 .... A 2
Imperial Mills, 118 .... E 2
Innisfail, 2,474 .... D 3
Innisfree, 252 .... E 3
Irma, 423 .... E 3
Irricana, 139 .... D 4
Irvine, 194 .... E 5
Jarvie, 104 .... D 2
Jasper, 2,932 .... B 3
Joussard, 269 .... B 2
Kikino, 202 .... D 2
Killam, 851 .... E 3
Kinuso, 267 .... C 2
Kitscoty, 320 .... E 3
Lac La Biche, 1,791 .... E 2
Lacombe, 3,436 .... D 3
Lake Louise, 165 .... B 4
Lamont, 899 .... D 3
Langdon, 109 .... D 4
Lavoy, 114 .... E 3
Leduc, 4,000 .... D 3
Legal, 563 .... D 3
Leslieville, 159 .... C 3
Lethbridge, 41,217 .... D 5
Linden, 226 .... D 4
Little Buffalo Lake, 165 .... B 1
Lloydminster, 4,738 .... E 3
Lodgepole, 144 .... C 3
Lomond, 165 .... D 4
Longview, 189 .... C 4
Loon Lake, 135 .... C 1
Lougheed, 217 .... E 3
Lundbreck, 113 .... C 5
Magrath, 1,215 .... D 5
Mallaig, 190 .... E 2
Manning, 1,071 .... B 1
Mannville, 646 .... E 3
Marlboro, 156 .... B 3
Marwayne, 351 .... E 3
Mayerthorpe, 1,036 .... C 3
McLennan, 1,090 .... B 2
Meander River, 233 .... A 5
Medicine Hat, 26,518 .... E 4
Midlandvale, 392 .... D 4
Milk River, 775 .... D 5
Millet, 456 .... D 3
Milo, 117 .... D 4
Minburn, 106 .... E 3
Mirror, 365 .... D 3
Monarch, 102 .... D 5
Morinville, 1,475 .... D 3
Morrin, 197 .... D 4
Mulhurst, 139 .... D 3
Mundare, 511 .... D 3
Myrnam, 403 .... E 3
Nacmine, 350 .... D 4
Nampa, 283 .... B 1
Nanton, 991 .... D 4
Newbrook, 154 .... D 2
New Norway, 200 .... D 3
New Sarepta, 202 .... D 3
Nobleford, 401 .... D 5
North Calling Lake, 103 .... D 2
Okotoks, 1,247 .... C 4
Olds, 3,376 .... D 4
Onoway, 496 .... C 3
Oyen, 929 .... E 4
Paradise Valley, 144 .... E 3
Peace River, 5,039 .... B 1
Peerless Lake, 134 .... C 1
Peers, 129 .... B 3
Penhold, 452 .... D 3
Pibroch, 112 .... D 2
Picardville, 130 .... D 2
Picture Butte, 1,008 .... D 5
Pincher Creek, 3,227 .... D 5
Plamondon, 189 .... D 2
Pollockville, 29 .... E 4
Ponoka, 4,414 .... D 3
Provost, 1,489 .... E 3
Radway, 170 .... D 2
Rainbow Lake, 355 .... A 5
Ralston, 475 .... E 4
Ranfurly, 110 .... E 3
Raymond, 2,156 .... D 5
Redcliff, 2,255 .... E 4
Red Deer, 27,674 .... D 3
Redwater, 1,287 .... D 3
Rimbey, 1,450 .... C 3
Robb, 256 .... B 3
Rochester, 111 .... D 2
Rockyford, 286 .... D 4
Rocky Mountain House,
2,968 .... C 3
Rolling Hills, 127 .... E 4
Rosalind, 203 .... D 3
Rosemary, 208 .... E 4
Rycroft, 461 .... A 2
Ryley, 428 .... D 3
Saint Albert, 11,800 .... D 3
Saint Paul, 4,161 .... E 3
Sangudo, 360 .... C 3
Seba Beach, 165 .... C 3
Sedgewick, 730 .... E 3
Seebe, 108 .... C 4
Sexsmith, 559 .... A 2
Shaughnessy, 323 .... D 5
Sherwood Park, 14,282 .... D 3
Slave Lake, 2,052 .... C 2
Smith, 445 .... D 2
Smoky Lake, 881 .... D 2
Spirit River, 1,091 .... A 2
Spruce Grove, 3,029 .... D 3
Spruce View, 104 .... C 3
Standard, 267 .... D 4
Stavely, 351 .... D 4
Stettler, 4,168 .... D 3
Stirling, 436 .... D 5
Stony Plain, 1,770 .... C 3
Strathmore, 1,148 .... D 4
Strome, 226 .... E 3
Sundre, 933 .... C 4
Swan Hills, 1,376 .... C 2
Sylvan Lake, 1,597 .... C 3
Taber, 4,765 .... E 5
Thorhild, 509 .... D 2
Thorsby, 595 .... C 3
Three Hills, 1,354 .... D 4
Tilley, 270 .... E 4
Tofield, 924 .... D 3
Torrington, 118 .... D 4
Trochu, 739 .... D 4
Trout Lake, 162 .... C 1
Turin, 102 .... D 5
Turner Valley, 766 .... C 4
Two Hills, 979 .... E 3
Valleyview, 1,708 .... B 2
Vauxhall, 1,016 .... D 4
Vegreville, 3,691 .... E 3
Vermilion, 2,915 .... E 3
Veteran, 267 .... E 3
Viking, 1,178 .... E 3
Vilna, 303 .... E 2
Vulcan, 1,384 .... D 4
Wabamun, 336 .... C 3
Wabasca, 172 .... D 2
Wainwright, 3,872 .... E 3
Wanham, 268 .... A 2
Warburg, 464 .... C 3
Warner, 408 .... D 5
Warspite, 110 .... D 2
Waskatenau, 233 .... D 2
Waterton Park, 236 .... D 5
Wembley, 348 .... A 2
Westlock, 3,246 .... C 2
Westward Ho, 104 .... C 4
Wetaskiwin, 6,267 .... D 3
Whitecourt, 3,202 .... C 2
Whitelaw, 192 .... A 1
Widewater, 126 .... C 2
Wildwood, 386 .... C 3
Willingdon, 325 .... E 3
Winfield, 209 .... C 3
Youngstown, 305 .... E 4

OTHER FEATURES

Alberta (mt.) .... B 3
Assiniboine (mt.) .... C 4
Athabasca (lake) .... C 5
Athabasca (riv.) .... D 1
Banff Nat'l Park, 3,532 .... B 4
Battle (riv.) .... D 3
Beaverhill (lake) .... D 3
Belly (riv.) .... D 5
Berry (creek) .... E 4
Biche (lake) .... E 2
Big Bend (res.) .... C 3
Bighorn (range) .... B 3
Birch (hills) .... A 2
Birch (lake) .... E 3
Birch (mts.) .... B 5
Bow (riv.) .... D 4
Boyer (riv.) .... A 5
Brazeau (mt.) .... B 3
Brazeau (riv.) .... B 3
Buffalo (lake) .... D 3
Buffalo Head (hills) .... B 5
Cadotte (riv.) .... B 1
Calling (lake) .... D 2
Caribou (mts.) .... B 5
Chinchaga (riv.) .... A 5
Chip (lake) .... C 3
Chipewyan (riv.) .... D 1
Christina (riv.) .... E 1
Claire (lake) .... B 5
Clear (hills) .... A 1
Clearwater (riv.) .... C 4
Clearwater (riv.) .... E 1
Cold (lake) .... E 2
Columbia (mt.) .... B 3
Crowsnest (pass) .... C 5
Cypress (hills) .... E 5
Cypress Hills Prov. Park .... E 5
Eisenhower (mt.) .... C 4
Elbow (riv.) .... C 4
Elk Island Nat'l Park, 46 .... D 3
Etzikom Coulee (riv.) .... E 5
Firebag (riv.) .... E 1
Forbes (mt.) .... B 4
Frog (lake) .... E 3
Gordon (lake) .... E 1
Gough (lake) .... D 3
Graham (lake) .... C 1
Gull (lake) .... C 3
Hawk (hills) .... B 1
Hay (riv.) .... A 5
Highwood (riv.) .... C 4
Iosegun (lake) .... B 2
Jasper Nat'l Park, 3,064 .... A 3
Kickinghorse (pass) .... B 4
Kimiwan (lake) .... B 2
Kitchener (mt.) .... B 3
Lesser Slave (lake) .... C 2
Little Bow (riv.) .... D 4
Little Smoky (riv.) .... B 2
Livingstone (range) .... C 4
Lyell (mt.) .... B 4
Maligne (lake) .... B 3
McGregor (lake) .... D 4
McLeod (riv.) .... B 3
Milk (riv.) .... D 5
Muriel (lake) .... E 2
Muskwa (riv.) .... C 1
North Saskatchewan (riv.) .... E 3
North Wabasca (lake) .... D 1
Notikewin (riv.) .... A 1
Oldman (riv.) .... D 5
Pakowki (lake) .... E 5
Peace (riv.) .... B 1
Peerless (lake) .... C 1
Pelican (mts.) .... D 2
Pembina (riv.) .... C 3
Pigeon (lake) .... D 3
Porcupine (hills) .... C 4
Red Deer (riv.) .... D 4
Rocky (mts.) .... C 4
Rosebud (riv.) .... D 4
Sainte Anne (lake) .... C 3
Saint Mary (riv.) .... D 5
Saulteaux (riv.) .... C 2
Slave (riv.) .... C 5
Smoky (riv.) .... A 2
Sounding (creek) .... E 4
South Saskatchewan (riv.) .... E 4
South Wabasca (lake) .... D 2
Spray (mts.) .... C 4
Sullivan (lake) .... D 3
Swan (hills) .... C 2
Temple (mt.) .... B 4
The Twins (mt.) .... B 3
Thickwood (hills) .... D 1
Utikuma (lake) .... C 2
Vermilion (riv.) .... E 3
Wabasca (riv.) .... C 1
Waterton-Glacier Int'l
Peace Park, 259 .... C 5
Waterton Lakes Nat'l Park,
259 .... C 5
Whitemud (riv.) .... A 1
Willmore Wilderness
Prov. Park .... A 3
Winagami (lake) .... B 2
Winefred (lake) .... E 2
Wood Buffalo Nat'l Park,
186 .... B 5
Yellowhead (pass) .... A 3

‡ Population of metropolitan area.

Agriculture, Industry and Resources

DOMINANT LAND USE

- Wheat
- Cereals (chiefly barley, oats)
- Cereals, Livestock
- Dairy
- Pasture Livestock
- Range Livestock
- Forests
- Nonagricultural Land

MAJOR MINERAL OCCURRENCES

- C Coal
- G Natural Gas
- Na Salt
- O Petroleum
- S Sulfur
- Water Power
- Major Industrial Areas

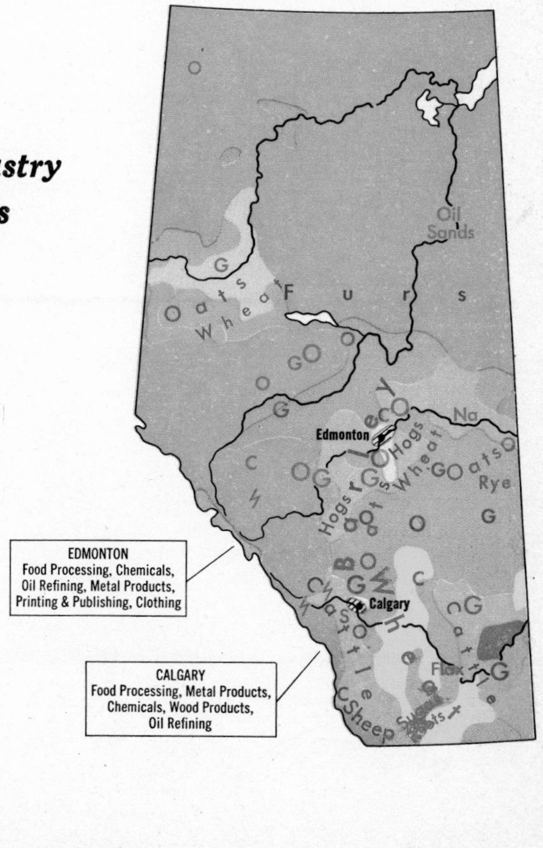
Oil Sands
Furs
Oats
Wheat
Edmonton
Hogs
Wheat
Oats
Rye
Na
Calgary
Cattle
Sheep
Flax
EDMONTON
Food Processing, Chemicals, Oil Refining, Metal Products, Printing & Publishing, Clothing
CALGARY
Food Processing, Metal Products, Chemicals, Wood Products, Oil Refining

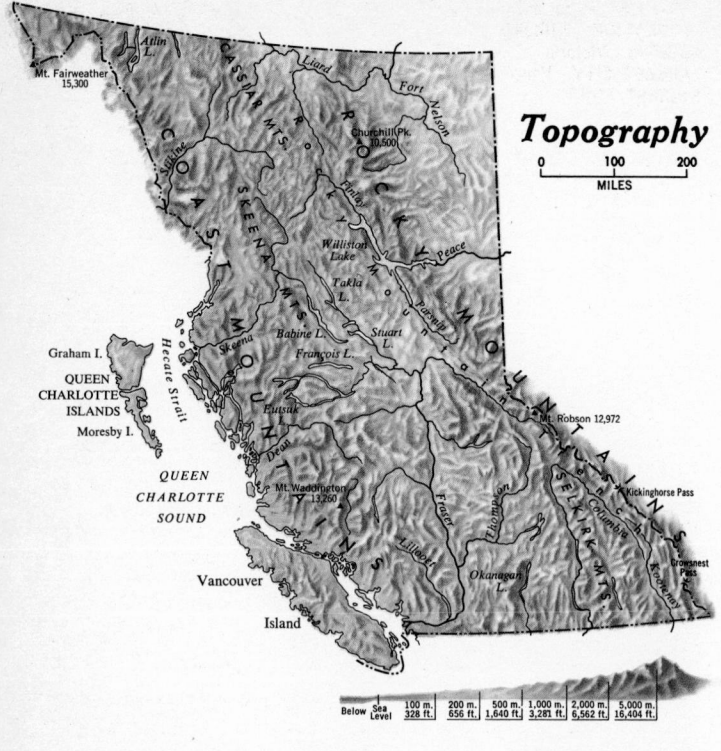

Topography

0 100 200
MILES

Below Sea Level | 100 m. 328 ft. | 200 m. 656 ft. | 500 m. 1,640 ft. | 1,000 m. 3,281 ft. | 2,000 m. 6,562 ft. | 5,000 m. 16,404 ft.

CITIES and TOWNS

Abbotsford, 706 .... L 3
Albert Head, 330 .... J 4
Alert Bay, 760 .... D 5
Alexandria, 168 .... F 4
Armstrong, 1,648 .... H 5
Ashcroft, 1,916 .... G 5
Ashton Creek, 318 .... H 5
Athalmer, 255 .... K 5
Atlin, 258 .... J 1
Avola, 265 .... H 4
Balfour, 195 .... J 5
Barrière, 829 .... H 4
Bear Lake, 302 .... F 3
Beaverdell, 241 .... H 5
Bella Coola, 273 .... D 4
Big Eddy, 654 .... H 4
Birch Island, 219 .... H 4
Blue River, 475 .... H 4
Boston Bar, 548 .... G 5
Bowen Island, 351 ...... K 3
Bowser, 169 .... H 2

Brackendale, 692 .... F 5
Bralorne, 379 .... J 5
Britannia Beach, 738 ... K 2
Brouse, 446 .... J 5
Burnaby, ●125,660 ...... K 3
Burns Lake, 1,259 .... D 3
Cache Creek, 1,013 ..... G 5
Campbell River, ●10,000 . E 5
Campbell River, 9,770 . E 5
Canal Flats, 902 .... K 5
Cassiar, 1,073 .... K 2
Castlegar, 3,072 .... J 5
Cawston, 642 .... H 5
Caycuse, 297 .... J 3
Cedarside, 218 .... H 4
Celista, 178 .... H 4
Central Saanich, ●5,136 . K 3
Charlie Lake, 214 .... G 2
Chase, 1,212 .... H 5
Chase River, 728 .... J 3
Chemainus, 2,129 .... J 3
Cherry Creek, 449 ...... G 5
Cherryville, 284 .... H 5
Chetwynd, 1,260 .... G 2

Chilliwack, 9,135 .... M 3
Chilliwhack, ●23,739 ... M 3
Clearbrook, 3,653 .... L 3
Clearwater, 513 .... G 4
Clinton, 905 .... G 4
Coal Harbour, 334 ...... D 5
Cobble Hill, 280 .... K 3
Coldstream, ●3,602 ..... H 5
Comox, 3,980 .... H 2
Coquitlam, ●53,073 ..... K 3
Courtenay, 7,152 .... E 5
Cranbrook, 12,000 ...... K 5
Crawford Bay, 244 ...... J 5
Creston, 3,204 .... J 5
Crofton, 972 .... J 3
Cultus Lake, 554 .... M 3
Cumberland, 1,718 ..... E 5
Dawson Creek, 11,885 . G 2
Delta, ●45,860 .... K 3
Departure Bay, 3,744 .. J 3
Donald, 235 .... J 4
Duncan, 4,388 .... J 3
East Kelowna, 826 ..... H 5
Eddontenajon, 180 ..... K 2

Edgewater, 346 .... J 5
Elko, 196 .... K 5
Endako, 242 .... E 3
Enderby, 1,158 .... H 5
Errington, 464 .... J 3
Esquimalt, ●12,922 .... K 4
Extension, 181 .... J 3
Falkland, 375 .... H 5
Fernie, 4,422 .... K 5
Field, 358 .... J 4
Flood, 295 .... M 3
Forest Grove, 238 ...... G 4
Fort Fraser, 385 .... E 3
Fort Langley, 1,342 .... L 3
Fort Nelson, 2,289 ..... M 2
Fort Saint James, 1,483 . E 3
Fort Saint John, 8,264 . G 2
Franklin River, 187 ..... H 3
Fraser Lake, 1,292 ..... E 3
Fraser Mills, ●157 ...... K 3
Fruitvale, 1,379 .... J 5
Gabriola Island, 655 ... J 3
Galiano Island, 412 .... K 3
Ganges, 333 .... K 3
Gibsons, 1,934 .... K 3
Gillies Bay, 543 .... H 2
Giscome, 416 .... F 3
Golden, 3,012 .... J 4
Gold River, 1,896 ...... D 5
Grand Forks, 3,173 .... H 6
Granisle, 451 .... D 3
Granthams Landing, 404 . J 3
Greenwood, 868 .... H 5
Grindrod, 283 .... H 5
Hagensborg, 315 .... D 4
Haney, 3,221 .... L 3
Harrison Hot Springs, 598 . M 3
Hatzic, 547 .... L 3
Hazelton, 351 .... D 2
Hedley, 385 .... G 5
Heffley Creek, 503 ..... G 5
Hendrix Lake, 341 ...... G 4
Heriot Bay, 187 .... H 2
Hixon, 385 .... F 3
Holberg, 333 .... C 5
Honeymoon Bay, 546 .. J 3
Hope, 3,153 .... M 3
Houston, ●2,232 .... D 3
Houston, 905 .... D 3
Hudson Hope, 1,116 ... F 2
Hudson's Hope, ●1,741 . F 2
Huntingdon, 202 .... L 3
Invermere, 1,065 ...... J 5
Ioco, 308 .... K 3
Jaffray, 193 .... K 5
Kaleden, 640 .... H 5
Kamloops, 26,168 ..... G 5
Kaslo, 755 .... J 5
Kelly Lake, 231 .... G 4
Kelowna, 19,412 ...... H 5
Kemano, 346 .... D 3
Kent, ●2,966 .... M 3
Keremeos, 605 .... G 5
Kimberley, 7,641 ...... K 5
Kinnaird, 2,846 .... J 5
Kitimat, 11,824 .... C 3
Kitsault, 343 .... C 2
Kitwanga, 217 .... D 2
Kokish, 222 .... D 5
Lac La Hache, 417 .... G 4
Ladysmith, 3,664 ..... J 3
Lake Cowichan, 2,364 . J 3

Lang Bay, 285 .... E 5
Langley, ●21,936 ..... L 3
Langley, 4,684 .... L 3
Lantzville, 565 .... J 3
Lillooet, 1,514 .... G 5
Lion's Bay, 396 .... K 3
Lone Butte, 206 ...... G 4
Louis Creek, 289 ..... H 4
Lower Nicola, 361 .... G 5
Lower Post, 206 ...... L 1
Lumby, 940 .... H 5
Lytton, 494 .... G 5
Mackenzie, ●2,332 ... F 2
Mackenzie, 1,976 .... F 2
Madeira Park, 351 ... J 2
Maple Bay, 509 ...... K 3
Maple Ridge, ●24,476 . L 3
Masset, 975 .... B 3
Matsqui, ●23,554 .... L 3
Mayne Island, 293 .. K 3
McBride, 658 .... G 3
McConnell Creek, 233 . D 2
McLure, 193 .... H 4
Merritt, 5,289 .... G 5
Merville, 227 .... E 5
Mesachie Lake, 266 . J 3
Metchosin, 540 ...... K 4
Mica Creek, 772 ..... H 4
Midway, 502 .... H 6
Mill Bay, 347 .... C 2
Milnes Landing, 254 . K 3
Mission, ●10,220 .... L 3
Mission City, 3,649 . L 3
Moberly, 175 .... J 4
Monte Lake, 176 .... G 5
Montrose, 1,137 ..... J 5
Nakusp, 1,163 .... J 5
Nanaimo, 14,948 .... J 3
Naramata, 461 .... H 5
Nelson, 9,400 .... J 5
New Denver, 644 .... J 5
New Hazelton, 475 .. D 2
New Westminster, 42,835 . K 3
Nicholson, 619 .... J 4
Nicomen Island, 527 . L 3
Nootka, 2 .... D 5
North Bend, 424 ..... G 5
North Cowichan, ●12,170 . J 3
North Pender Island, 407 . K 3
North Saanich, ●3,601 . K 3
North Vancouver, ●57,861 . K 3
North Vancouver, 31,847 . K 3
Nukko Lake, 182 ..... F 3
Oak Bay, ●18,426 ... K 4
Ocean Falls, 1,085 .. D 4
Okanagan Centre, 266 . H 5
Okanagan Falls, 621 . H 5
Okanagan Landing, 656 . H 5
Okanagan Mission, 857 . H 5
Old Barkerville, 3 ... G 3
Oliver, 1,615 .... H 5
One Hundred Mile House, 1,120 ...... G 4
Osoyoos, 1,285 ...... H 5
Oyama, 326 .... H 5
Parksville, 2,169 .... J 3
Parson, 306 .... J 4
Peachland, ●1,446 .. G 5
Penticton, 18,146 ... H 5
Pine Valley, 264 ..... F 2
Pitt Meadows, ●2,771 . L 3
Popkum, 286 .... M 3
Port Alberni, 20,063 . H 3
Port Alice, 1,507 .... D 5
Port Clements, 406 . B 3
Port Coquitlam, 19,560 . L 3
Port Edward, 1,019 . C 3
Port Hammond, 1,556 . L 3
Port Hardy, ●1,761 .. D 5
Port McNeill, 934 ... D 5
Port Moody, 10,778 . L 3
Port Renfrew, 362 .. J 3
Pouce-Coupé, 595 .. G 2
Powell River, ●13,726 . E 5
Prince George, 33,101 . F 3
Prince Rupert, 15,747 . B 3
Princeton, 2,601 .... G 5
Procter, 183 .... J 5
Qualicum Beach, 1,245 . J 3
Queen Charlotte, 665 . A 3
Quesnel, 6,252 ...... F 4
Radium Hot Springs, 393 . J 5
Rayleigh, 652 .... G 5
Revelstoke, 4,867 ... J 5
Richmond, ●62,121 .. K 3
Riondel, 572 .... J 5
Robson, 1,046 .... J 5
Rossland, 3,896 ..... H 6
Royston, 532 .... H 2
Rutland, 3,279 .... H 5
Saanich, ●65,040 ... K 3
Salmo, 872 .... J 5
Salmon Arm, ●7,793 . H 5
Salmon Arm, 1,981 . H 5
Saltair, 1,008 .... J 3
Sandspit, 459 .... B 3
Sardis, 1,194 .... M 3
Saseenos, 574 .... J 3
Saturna Island, 174 . K 3
Savona, 670 .... G 5
Sayward, 465 .... D 5
Sechelt, 590 .... J 2
Seventy Mile House, 225 . G 4
Shawnigan Lake, 213 . J 3
Shoreacres, 345 ..... J 5
Sicamous, 814 .... H 5
Sidney, 4,868 .... K 3
Silverton, 246 .... J 5
Slocan, 346 .... J 5
Slocan Park, 360 .... J 5
Smithers, 3,864 ..... D 3
Sointula, 575 .... D 5
Sooke, 836 .... J 3
Sorrento, 269 .... H 5
South Fort George, 1,282 . F 3
South Hazelton, 483 . D 2
South Slocan, 278 ... J 5

South Wellington, 460 . J 3
Sparwood, ●2,990 ... K 5
Sparwood, 2,154 .... K 5
Spences Bridge, 199 . G 5
Sproat Lake, 321 .... H 3
Squamish, ●6,121 ... F 5
Squamish, 1,597 .... F 5
Stewart, ●1,357 ..... C 2
Stoner, 182 .... F 3
Summerland, ●5,551 . H 5
Surrey, ●98,601 ..... K 3
Tahsis, 1,351 .... D 5
Tasu, 331 .... A 4
Taylor, 605 .... G 2
Telkwa, 712 .... D 3
Terrace, ●9,991 ..... C 3
Terrace, 7,820 ...... C 3
Thrums, 365 .... J 5
Tofino, 461 .... E 5
Trail, 11,149 .... J 5
Ucluelet, 1,018 ..... E 6
Union Bay, 407 ..... H 2
Upper Fraser, 339 .. G 3
Valemount, 693 .... G 3
Valleyview, 3,787 .. G 5
Vananda, 497 .... E 5
Vancouver, 426,256 . K 3
Vancouver, ‡1,082,352 . K 3
Vancouver (Greater), ●1,028,334 ... K 3
Vanderhoof, 1,653 . E 3
Vavenby, 331 .... H 4
Vernon, 13,283 ..... H 5

Victoria (cap.), 61,761 . K
Victoria, ‡195,800 .. K
Warfield, 2,132 ..... J
Wasa, 355 .... K 5
Wells, 409 .... G 3
Westbank, 747 ..... H 5
West Vancouver, ●36,440 . K 3
Westwold, 434 ...... H 5
White Rock, 10,349 . K 3
Williams Lake, 4,072 . F 4
Willow River, 422 .. F 3
Wilmer, 200 .... J 5
Wilson Creek, 408 .. J 2
Windermere, 421 ... K 5
Winfield, 875 .... H 5
Winlaw, 383 .... J 5
Woodfibre, 408 .... K 3
Woss Lake, 394 .... D 5
Wynndel, 579 .... J 5
Yahk, 192 .... J 5
Yale, 224 .... G 5
Yarrow, 1,039 ...... L 3
Ymir, 292 .... J 5
Youbou, 1,109 ..... J 3
Zeballos, 186 ...... D 5

OTHER FEATURES

Adams (riv.) ....
Alberni (inlet) ....
Alsek (riv.) ....

Agriculture, Industry and Resources

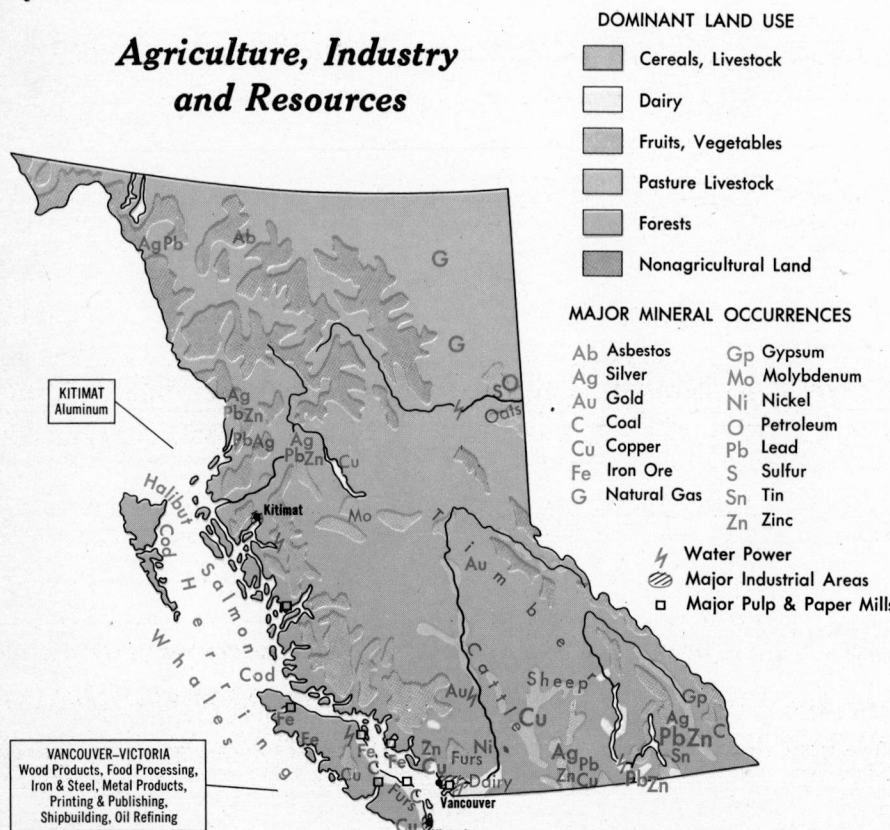

DOMINANT LAND USE

- Cereals, Livestock
- Dairy
- Fruits, Vegetables
- Pasture Livestock
- Forests
- Nonagricultural Land

MAJOR MINERAL OCCURRENCES

Ab	Asbestos	Gp	Gypsum
Ag	Silver	Mo	Molybdenum
Au	Gold	Ni	Nickel
C	Coal	O	Petroleum
Cu	Copper	Pb	Lead
Fe	Iron Ore	S	Sulfur
G	Natural Gas	Sn	Tin
		Zn	Zinc

⚡ Water Power
Major Industrial Areas
□ Major Pulp & Paper Mills

KITIMAT Aluminum

VANCOUVER–VICTORIA
Wood Products, Food Processing,
Iron & Steel, Metal Products,
Printing & Publishing,
Shipbuilding, Oil Refining

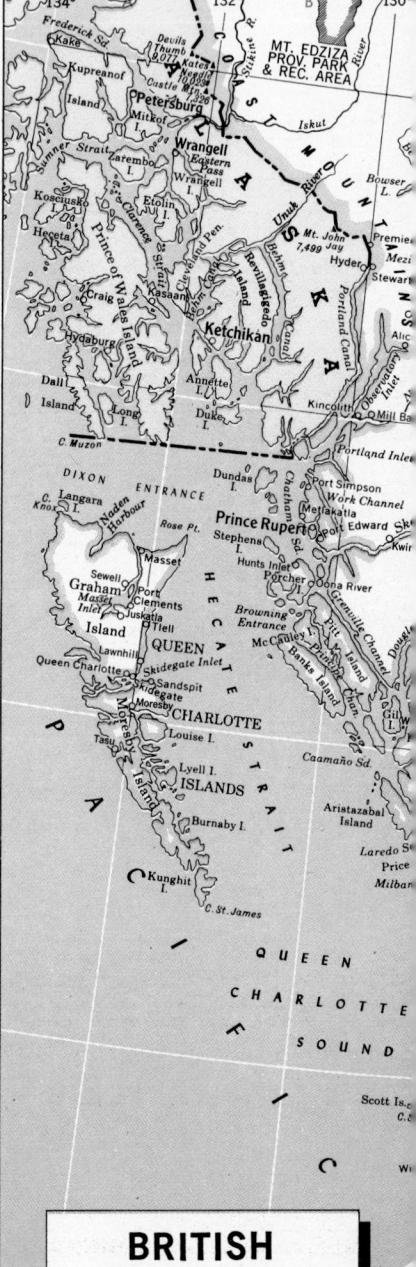

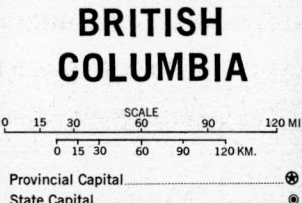

BRITISH COLUMBIA

SCALE
0 15 30   60   90   120 MI.
0 15 30   60   90   120 KM.

Provincial Capital .... ⊛
State Capital .... ◉
International Boundaries ....
Provincial Boundaries ....

© C.S. HAMMOND & Co., N.Y.

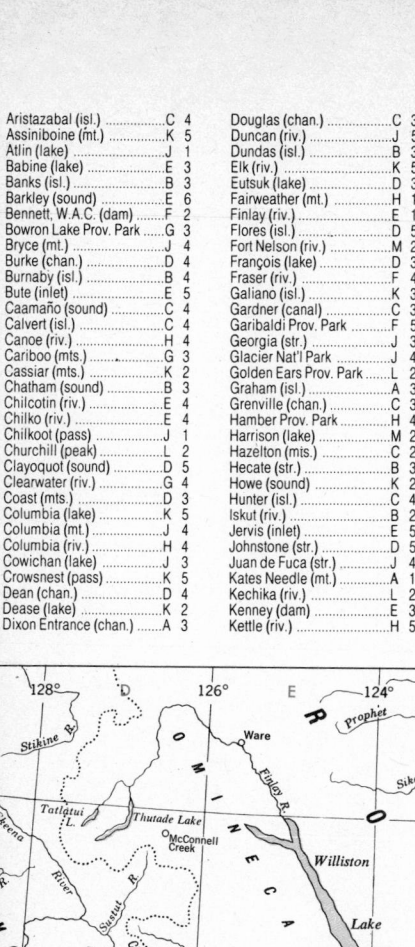

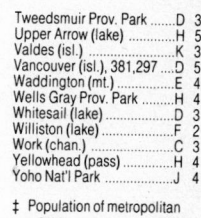

Aristazabal (isl.) ....C 4	Douglas (chan.) ....C 3	Kickinghorse (pass) ....J 4	Nanika (dam) ....D 3
Assiniboine (mt.) ....K 5	Duncan (riv.) ....J 5	King (isl.) ....D 4	Nass (riv.) ....B 2
Atlin (lake) ....J 1	Dundas (isl.) ....B 3	Klinaklini (riv.) ....E 4	Nechako (riv.) ....E 3
Babine (lake) ....E 3	Elk (riv.) ....K 5	Knight (inlet) ....D 4	Nootka (isl.) ....D 5
Banks (isl.) ....B 3	Eutsuk (lake) ....D 3	Knox (cape) ....A 3	Nootka (sound) ....D 5
Barkley (sound) ....D 5	Fairweather (mt.) ....H 1	Kokanee Glacier Prov.	North Thompson (riv.) ....G 4
Bennett, W.A.C. (dam) ....F 2	Finlay (riv.) ....E 1	Park ....J 5	Observatory (inlet) ......C 2
Bowron Lake Prov. Park ...G 3	Flores (isl.) ....D 5	Koocanusa (lake) ....K 6	Okanagan (lake) ....H 5
Bryce (mt.) ....J 4	Fort Nelson (riv.) ....M 2	Kootenay (lake) ....J 5	Okanogan (riv.) ....H 5
Burke (chan.) ....D 4	François (lake) ....D 3	Kootenay (riv.) ....J 5	Omineca (mts.) ....E 2
Burnaby (isl.) ....B 4	Fraser (riv.) ....F 3	Kootenay Nat'l Park .....J 4	Ootsa (lake) ....D 3
Bute (inlet) ....E 5	Galiano (isl.) ....K 3	Kunghit (isl.) ....B 4	Pacific Rim Nat'l Park ...E 5
Caamaño (sound) ....C 4	Gardner (canal) ....C 3	Kyuquot (sound) ....C 4	Parsnip (riv.) ....F 2
Calvert (isl.) ....C 4	Garibaldi Prov. Park .....F 5	Langara (isl.) ....A 3	Peace (riv.) ....G 2
Canoe (riv.) ....H 4	Georgia (str.) ....J 3	Liard (riv.) ....L 1	Pine (riv.) ....G 2
Cariboo (mts.) ....G 3	Glacier Nat'l Park ....J 4	Lillooet (riv.) ....F 5	Pitt (isl.) ....C 3
Cassiar (mts.) ....K 2	Golden Ears Prov. Park ...L 5	Lower Arrow (lake) ......H 5	Pitt (lake) ....L 5
Chatham (sound) ....B 3	Graham (isl.) ....A 3	Malaspina (str.) ....J 2	Porcher (isl.) ....B 3
Chilcotin (riv.) ....E 4	Grenville (chan.) ....C 3	Manning Prov. Park, 23 ..G 5	Portland (canal) ....B 2
Chilko (riv.) ....E 4	Hamber Prov. Park ....H 4	Masset (inlet) ....A 3	Portland (inlet) ....C 3
Chilkoot (pass) ....J 1	Harrison (lake) ....M 2	Milbanke (sound) ....C 4	Princess Royal (isl.) ....C 3
Churchill (peak) ....L 2	Hazelton (mts.) ....C 2	Monashee (mts.) ....H 4	Principe (chan.) ....C 3
Clayoquot (sound) ....D 5	Hecate (str.) ....B 3	Moresby (isl.) ....B 4	Prophet (riv.) ....M 2
Clearwater (riv.) ....G 4	Howe (sound) ....K 2	Morice (riv.) ....D 3	Purcell (mts.) ....J 5
Coast (mts.) ....D 3	Hunter (isl.) ....C 4	Mount Assiniboine Prov.	Quatsino (sound) ....C 4
Columbia (lake) ....K 5	Iskut (riv.) ....B 2	Park ....K 5	Queen Charlotte (isls.),
Columbia (mt.) ....J 4	Jervis (inlet) ....E 5	Mount Edziza Prov. Park	2,390. ....B 3
Columbia (riv.) ....H 4	Johnstone (str.) ....D 5	and Rec. Area ....B 1	Queen Charlotte (sound) ..C 4
Cowichan (lake) ....J 3	Juan de Fuca (str.) ......J 4	Mount Revelstoke Nat'l	Queen Charlotte (str.) ...D 5
Crowsnest (pass) ....K 5	Kates Needle (mt.) ....A 1	Park ....H 4	Quesnel (riv.) ....G 3
Dean (chan.) ....D 4	Kechika (riv.) ....L 2	Mount Robson Prov. Park .H 4	Rivers (inlet) ....C 4
Dease (lake) ....K 2	Kenney (dam) ....E 3	Muncho Lake Prov. Park ..L 2	Robson (mt.) ....H 3
Dixon Entrance (chan.) ....A 3	Kettle (riv.) ....H 5	Muskwa (riv.) ....M 2	Rocky (mts.) ....F 2

Rose (pt.) ....B 3	Smith (sound) ....C 4	Tweedsmuir Prov. Park ....D 3	
Saint James (cape) ....B 4	Stave (lake) ....L 5	Upper Arrow (lake) ....H 5	
Salmon (riv.) ....F 3	Stikine (riv.) ....B 1	Valdes (isl.) ....K 3	
Scott (cape) ....C 5	Stone Mountain Prov. Park .L 2	Vancouver (isl.), 381,297 ..D 5	
Seechelt (inlet) ....J 2	Strathcona Prov. Park .....E 5	Waddington (mt.) ....E 4	
Seechelt (pen.) ....J 2	Stuart (lake) ....E 3	Wells Gray Prov. Park ....H 4	
Selkirk (mts.) ....J 4	Tagish (lake) ....J 1	Whitesail (lake) ....D 3	
Seymour (inlet) ....D 4	Tahtsa (lake) ....D 3	Williston (lake) ....F 2	
Shuswap (lake) ....H 4	Takla (lake) ....D 2	Work (chan.) ....C 3	
Sikanni Chief (riv.) ....F 2	Taku (riv.) ....J 2	Yellowhead (pass) ....H 4	
Sir Sandford (mt.) ....J 4	Teslin (lake) ....K 1	Yoho Nat'l Park ....J 4	
Skeena (mts.) ....C 2	Tetachuck (lake) ....E 3		
Skeena (riv.) ....C 2	Texada (isl.) ....J 2	‡ Population of metropolitan	
Skidegate (inlet) ....B 3	Thompson (riv.) ....G 5	area.	
Slocan (lake) ....J 5	Tiedemann (mt.) ....E 4	• Population of municipality.	

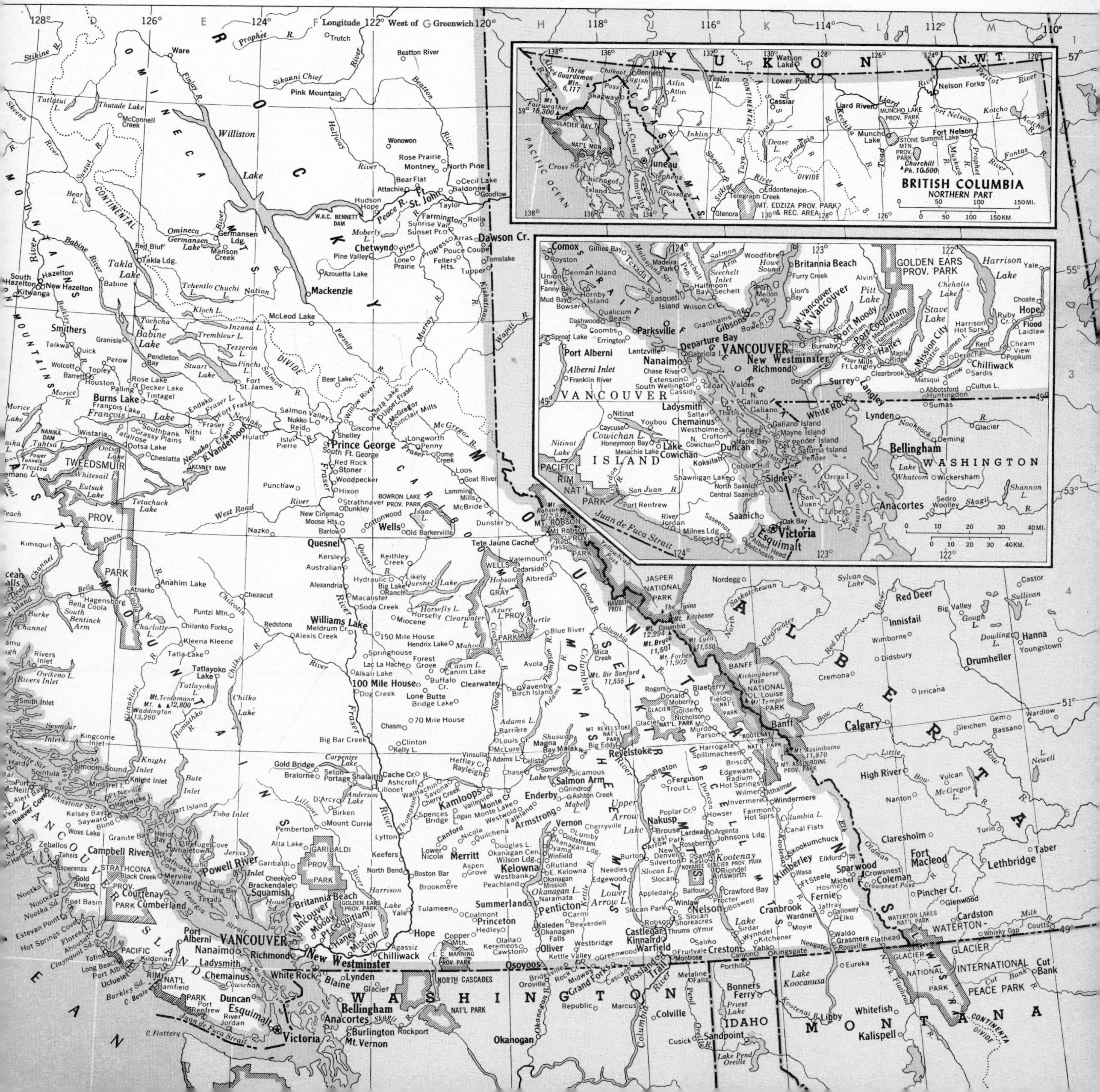

AREA 366,255 sq. mi.
POPULATION 2,161,000
CAPITAL Victoria
LARGEST CITY Vancouver
HIGHEST POINT Mt. Fairweather 15,300 ft.
SETTLED IN 1806
ADMITTED TO CONFEDERATION 1871
PROVINCIAL FLOWER Dogwood

NORTHWEST TERRITORIES

DISTRICTS

Franklin, 7,747.................K 2
Keewatin, 3,403................J 3
Mackenzie, 23,657.............G 3

CITIES and TOWNS

Aklavik, 677......................E 3
Alert, 15...........................M 1
Amadjuak, 5......................L 3
Arctic Bay, 269..................K 2
Arctic Red River, 108........E 3
Aston Bay, 8.....................J 2
Baker Lake, 756................J 3
Bell Rock, 1.......................G 3
Broughton Island, 334.......M 3
Buffalo River Junction, 3...G 3
Cambridge Bay, 716..........H 3
Cape Dorset, 597..............L 3
Cape Dyer, 10...................M 3
Cape Smith, 147................L 3
Chesterfield Inlet, 258.......K 3
Clyde, 274.........................M 2
Colville Lake, 65...............F 3
Coppermine, 637...............G 3
Coral Harbour, 355............K 3
Dory Point, 17...................G 3
Enterprise, 56...................G 3
Eskimo Point, 598.............K 3
Eureka, 10.........................K 2
Fort Franklin, 339..............F 3
Fort Good Hope, 327.........F 3
Fort Liard, 263...................F 3
Fort McPherson, 679.........E 3
Fort Norman, 248..............F 3
Fort Providence, 587..........G 3
Fort Resolution, 623..........G 3
Fort Simpson, 747.............F 3
Fort Smith, 2,364..............G 4
Frobisher Bay, 2,014.........M 3
Gjoa Haven, 276................J 3
Grise Fiord, 109.................K 2
Hall Beach, 263.................K 3
Hay River, 2,406...............G 3
Hislop Lake, 4...................G 3
Holman Island, 241...........G 2
Igloolik, 563.......................K 3
Inuvik, 2,669.....................E 3
Isachsen, 2........................H 2
Jean-Marie River, 47.........F 3
Kakisa, 42.........................G 3
Kipisa, 33..........................M 3
Lac la Martre, 161..............G 3
Lake Harbour, 189.............L 3
Marian Lake, 29................G 3
Mary River, 10...................L 2
Mould Bay, 6....................F 2
Nahanni Butte, 66.............F 3
Norman Wells, 301............F 3
Pangnirtung, 690...............M 3
Paulatuk, 95......................F 3
Pelly Bay, 215...................K 3
Pine Point, 1,225...............G 3
Pond Inlet, 416..................L 2
Port Burwell, 107...............M 3
Port Radium, 99................G 3
Rae-Edzo, 1,081...............G 3

Rae Lake, 73.....................G 3
Rankin Inlet, 566...............J 3
Repulse Bay, 242..............K 3
Resolute Bay, 184.............J 2
Resolution Island, 8...........M 3
Rocher River, 4.................G 3
Sachs Harbour, 143...........F 2
Salt River, 2......................G 3
Sawmill Bay, 10.................G 3
Snare Lake, 9....................G 3
Snowdrift, 221...................G 3
Spence Bay, 209...............J 3
Trout Lake, 48...................F 3
Tuktoyaktuk, 596...............E 3
Tungsten, 130....................F 3
Twin Gorges, 5.................G 3
Whale Cove, 213...............J 3
Wrigley, 152......................F 3
Yellowknife (cap.), 6,122...G 3

OTHER FEATURES

Adelaide (pen.)..................J 3
Admiralty (inlet).................K 2
Air Force (isl.)...................L 3
Akpatok (isl.).....................M 3
Amadjuak (lake).................L 3
Amund Ringnes (isl.).........H 1
Amundsen (gulf).................F 2
Arctic Red (riv.).................E 3
Artillery (lake)...................H 3
Auyuittuq Nat'l Park.........M 3
Axel Heiberg (isl.).............J 2
Aylmer (lake).....................H 3
Back (riv.).........................J 3
Baffin (bay).......................M 2
Baffin (isl.)........................L 3
Baker (lake).......................J 3
Banks (isl.)........................F 2
Barbeau (peak)...................L 1
Barrow (str.)......................J 2
Bathurst (cape)..................F 2
Bathurst (inlet)..................H 3
Bathurst (isl.)....................H 2
Beaufort (sea)...................D 2
Boothia (gulf).....................K 3
Boothia (pen.)....................J 3
Borden (isl.).......................G 2
Borden (pen.).....................K 2
Brodeur (pen.)....................K 2
Bruce (mts.)......................L 2
Buchan (gulf).....................L 2
Burnside (riv.)....................G 3
Byam Martin (chan.)..........H 2
Byam Martin (isl.).............H 2
Bylot (isl.).........................L 2
Camsell (riv.).....................G 3
Challenger (mts.)...............L 1
Chantrey (inlet)..................J 3
Chesterfield (inlet).............J 3
Chidley (cape)....................M 3
Clinton-Colden (lake).........H 3
Clyde (inlet).......................M 2
Coats (isl.)........................K 3
Coburg (isl.)......................L 2
Columbia (cape).................M 1
Colville (lake)....................F 3
Committee (bay).................K 3
Contwoyto (lake)................H 3
Coppermine (riv.)...............G 3
Cornwall (isl.)....................J 2
Cornwallis (isl.).................J 2
Coronation (gulf)................G 3

Croker (bay).......................K 2
Crown Prince Frederik
  (isl.).................................K 3
Cumberland (pen.).............M 3
Cumberland (sound)..........M 3
Davis (str.)........................M 3
Dease (str.).......................H 3
Denmark (bay)...................M 3
Devon (isl.).......................K 2
Dolphin and Union (str.)....G 3
Dubawnt (lake)...................H 3
Dubawnt (riv.)....................H 3
Dundas (cape)....................M 3
Dyer (cape).......................M 3
Eclipse (sound)..................L 2
Eglinton (isl.).....................F 2
Ellef Ringnes (isl.).............H 2
Ellesmere (isl.)..................K 2
Ennadai (lake)...................H 3
Eskimo (lakes)..................E 3
Eureka (sound)..................K 2
Evans (str.).......................K 3
Exeter (sound)...................M 3
Fisher (str.).......................K 3
Fosheim (pen.)...................K 1
Foxe (basin)......................L 3
Foxe (chan.)......................K 3
Foxe (pen.)........................L 3
Franklin (bay)....................F 2
Franklin (mts.)...................F 3
Franklin (str.).....................J 3
Frobisher (bay)..................M 3
Frozen (str.).......................K 3
Fury and Hecla (str.).........K 3
Gabriel (str.)......................M 3
Garry (lake).......................J 3
Gods Mercy (bay)..............K 3
Great Bear (lake)...............F 3
Great Bear (riv.)................F 3
Great Slave (lake).............G 3
Greely (fjord).....................K 1
Grinnell (pen.)....................J 2
Hadley (bay)......................H 2
Hall (basin).......................M 1
Hall (pen.).........................M 3
Hayes (riv.).......................J 3
Hazen (lake)......................L 1
Hazen (str.).......................G 2
Henik (lakes).....................J 3
Henry Kater (cape)............M 3
Home (bay)........................M 3
Hood (riv.).........................G 3
Horn (mts.)........................G 3
Hornaday (riv.)...................F 3
Horton (riv.).......................F 3
Hottah (lake)......................G 3
Hudson (bay).....................K 3
Hudson (str.).....................L 3
Isachsen (cape).................H 2
James Ross (str.)..............J 3
Jenny Lind (isl.)................H 3
Jens Munk (isl.)................K 3
Jones (sound)....................K 2
Kaminuriak (lake)..............J 3
Kane (basin)......................L 2
Kasba (lake)......................H 3
Kazan (riv.)........................J 3
Keele (riv.).........................F 3
Keith Arm (inlet)................F 3
Kellett (cape).....................F 2
Kellett (str.).......................G 2
Kennedy (chan.).................M 1
Kent (pen.).........................J 3
King Christian (isl.)............H 2
King William (isl.)..............J 3

Lady Ann (str.)..................K 2
La Martre (lake).................G 3
Lancaster (sound)..............K 2
Lands End (cape)...............F 2
Larsen (sound)...................J 3
Liard (riv.).........................F 4
Lincoln (sea).....................M 1
Liverpool (bay)...................E 3
Lockhart (riv.)....................H 3
Lougheed (isl.)..................H 2
Lyon (inlet)........................K 3
MacKay (lake)....................G 3
Mackenzie (bay).................E 3
Mackenzie (mts.)...............F 3
Mackenzie (riv.).................F 3
Mackenzie King (isl.).........G 2
Macmillan (pass)...............F 3
Maguse (lake)....................J 3
Makinson (inlet).................L 2
Mansel (isl.)......................K 3
Marian (lake).....................G 3
Markham (inlet).................L 1
McLeod (bay).....................H 3
M'Clintock (chan.)..............H 2
M'Clure (str.).....................F 2
McTavish Arm (inlet).........G 3
Meighen (isl.)....................H 1
Melville (isl.)......................G 2

Melville (pen.)....................K 3
Mercy (cape).....................M 3
Mills (lake).........................G 3
Minto (inlet).......................G 2
Mistake (bay)....................J 3
Nahanni Nat'l Park............F 3
Nansen (sound).................J 1
Nares (str.).........................L 2
Navy Board (inlet)..............K 2
Nettilling (lake)..................L 3
Nonacho (lake)..................H 3
North Arm (inlet)...............G 3
North Magnetic Pole..........H 2
Norwegian (bay).................J 2
Nottingham (isl.)................L 3
Nueltin (lake).....................H 3
Ommanney (bay)................H 2
Padloping (isl.)..................M 3
Parry (bay).........................K 3
Parry (chan.).....................G 2
Parry (isls.)........................G 2
Parry (pen.).......................F 2
Peary (chan.).....................H 2
Peel (sound)......................J 2
Pelly (bay).........................J 3
Penny (str.)........................J 2
Point (lake)........................G 3
Pond (inlet).......................L 2

DOMINANT LAND USE

 Forests

Nonagricultural Land

MAJOR MINERAL OCCURRENCES

Ab	Asbestos	Cu	Copper
Ag	Silver	Fe	Iron Ore
Au	Gold	O	Petroleum
C	Coal	Pb	Lead
		Zn	Zinc

Topography

0   200   400
MILES

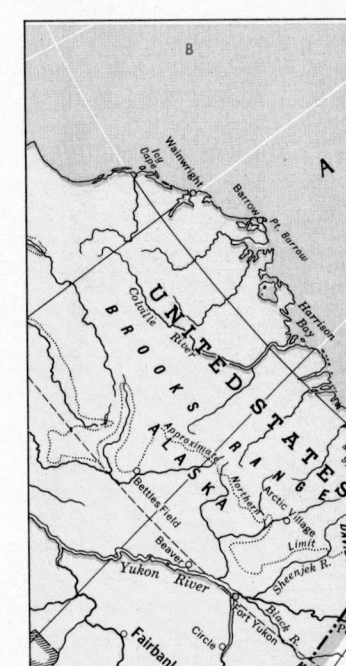

5,000 m.	2,000 m.	1,000 m.	500 m.	200 m.	100 m.	Sea
16,404 ft.	6,562 ft.	3,281 ft.	1,640 ft.	656 ft.	328 ft.	Level Below

Agriculture, Industry and Resources

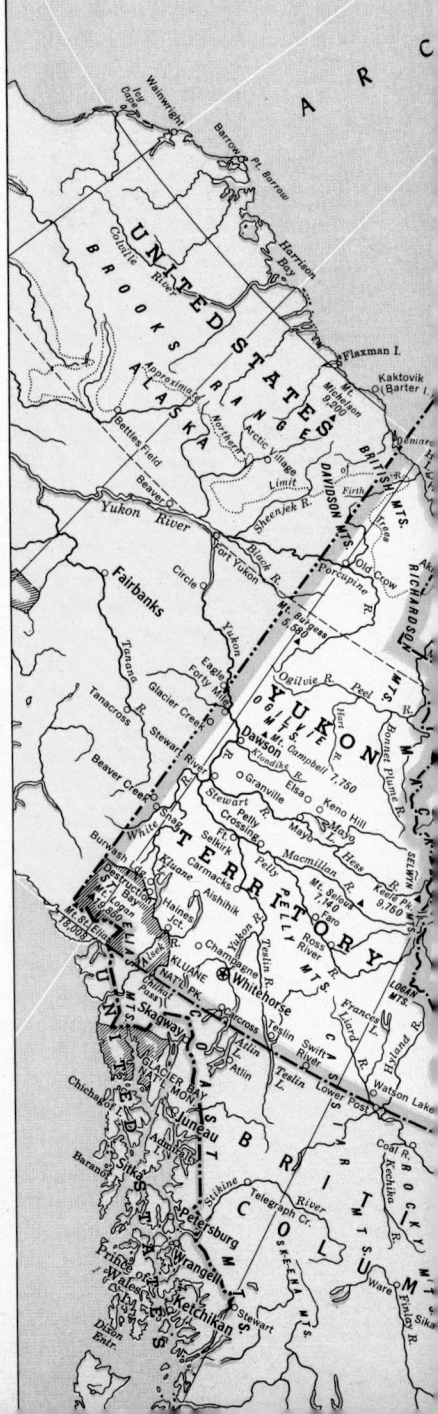

YUKON TERRITORY

AREA 207,076 sq. mi.
POPULATION 17,000
CAPITAL Whitehorse
LARGEST CITY Whitehorse
HIGHEST POINT Mt. Logan 19,850 ft.
SETTLED IN 1897
ADMITTED TO CONFEDERATION 1898
PROVINCIAL FLOWER Fireweed

NORTHWEST TERRITORIES

AREA 1,304,903 sq. mi.
POPULATION 34,000
CAPITAL Yellowknife
LARGEST CITY Yellowknife
HIGHEST POINT Barbeau Peak 8,540 ft.
SETTLED IN 1800
ADMITTED TO CONFEDERATION 1870
PROVINCIAL FLOWER Mountain Avens

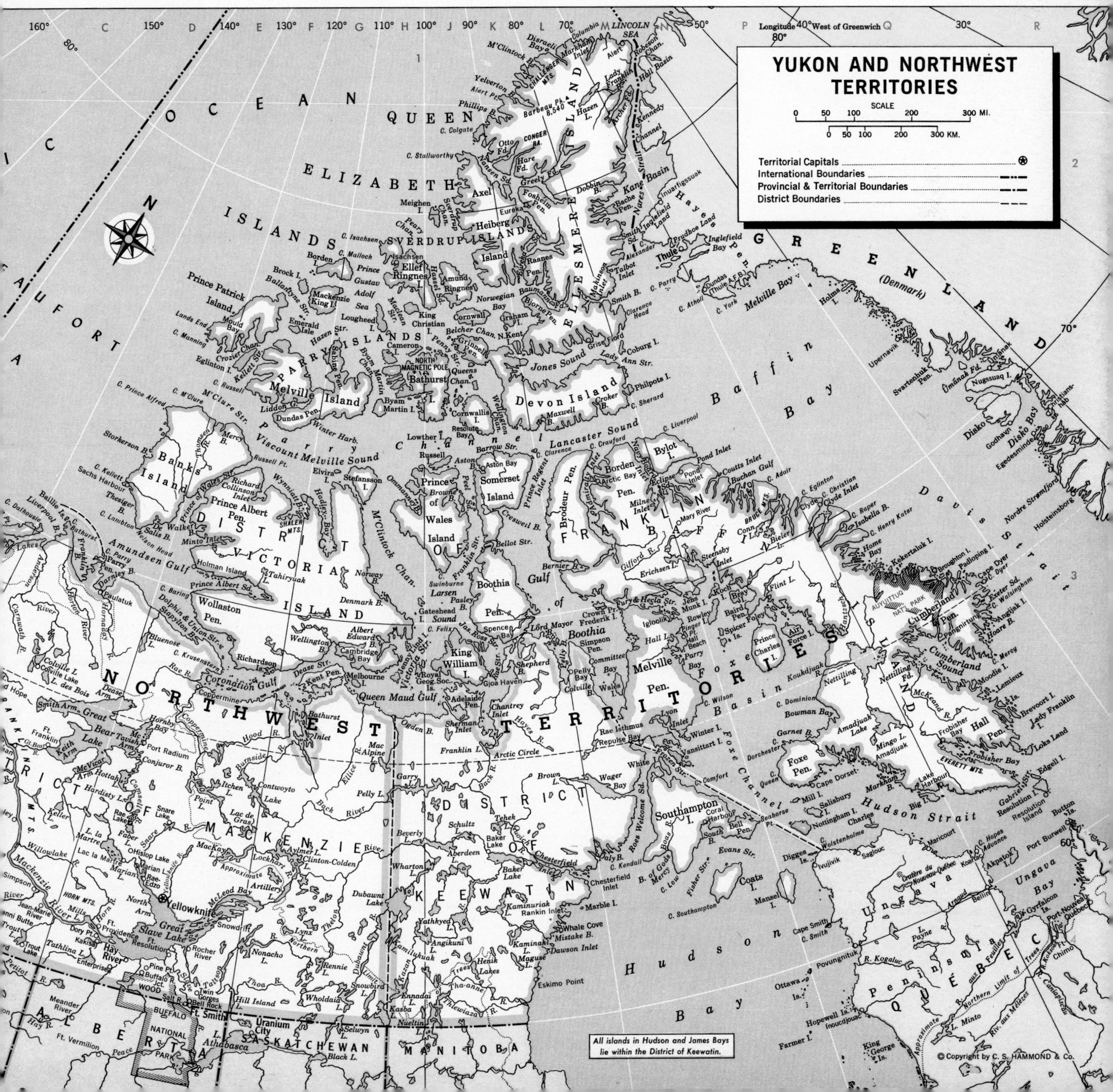

YUKON AND NORTHWEST TERRITORIES

SCALE

0   50   100   200   300 MI.

0 50 100   200   300 KM.

Territorial Capitals .... ⊛
International Boundaries ....
Provincial & Territorial Boundaries ......
District Boundaries ....

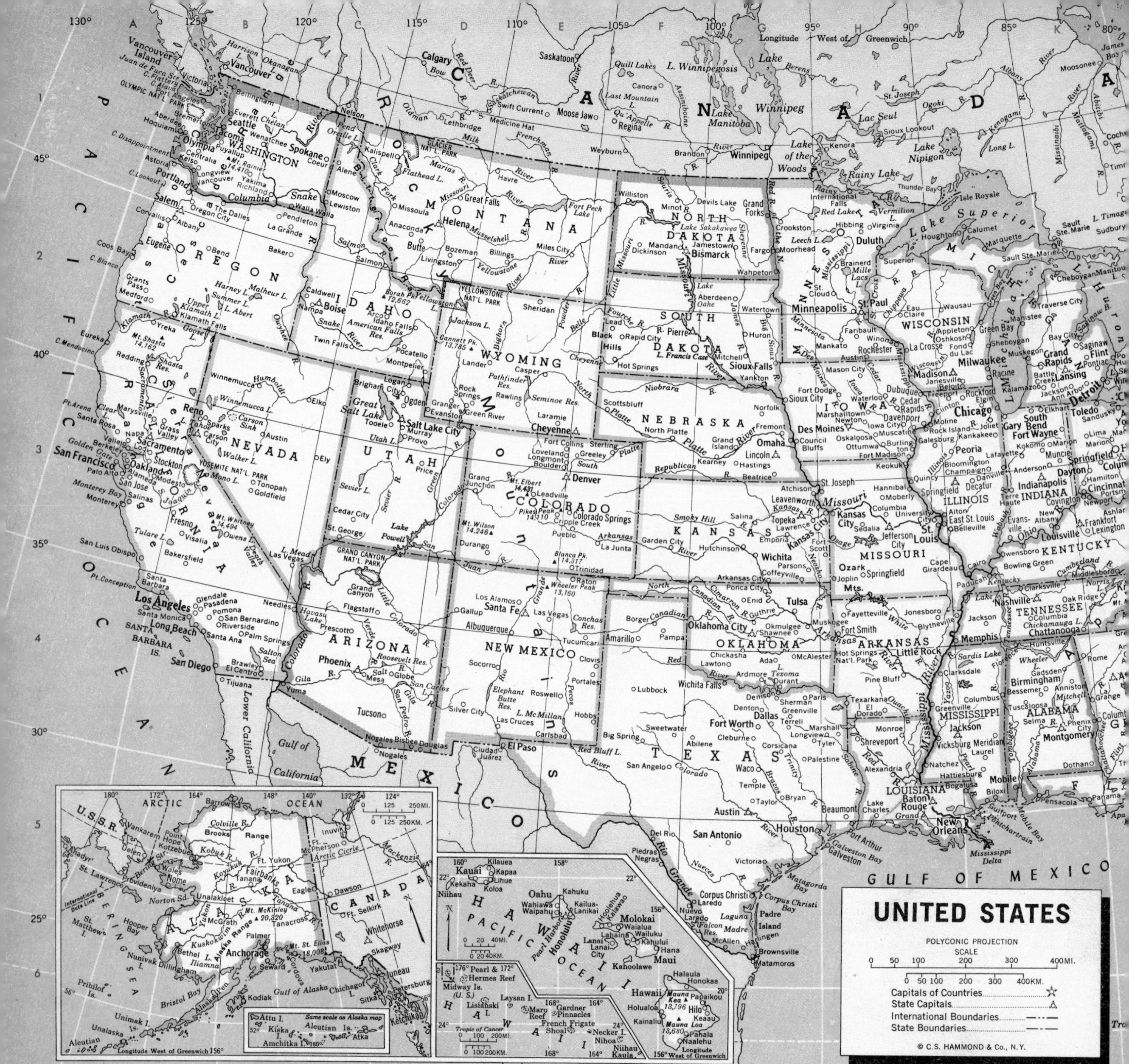

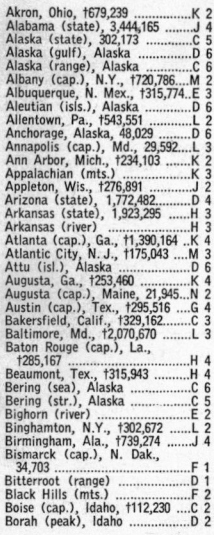

UNITED STATES
POLYCONIC PROJECTION
SCALE
0 50 100 200 300 400 MI.
0 50 100 200 300 400 KM.
Capitals of Countries
State Capitals
International Boundaries
State Boundaries
© C.S. HAMMOND & Co., N.Y.

Akron, Ohio, †679,239 ....K 2
Alabama (state), 3,444,165 ....J 4
Alaska (state), 302,173 ....C 5
Alaska (gulf), Alaska ....D 6
Alaska (range), Alaska ....C 6
Albany (cap.), N.Y., †720,786....M 2
Albuquerque, N. Mex., †315,774..E 3
Aleutian (isls.), Alaska ....D 6
Allentown, Pa., †543,551 ....L 2
Anchorage, Alaska, 48,029 ....D 6
Annapolis (cap.), Md., 29,592....L 3
Ann Arbor, Mich., †234,103 ....K 2
Appalachian (mts.) ....K 3
Appleton, Wis., †276,891 ....J 2
Arizona (state), 1,772,482..........D 4
Arkansas (state), 1,923,295 ......H 3
Arkansas (river) ....H 3
Atlanta (cap.), Ga., †1,390,164 ..K 4
Atlantic City, N. J., †175,043 ....M 3
Attu (isl.), Alaska ....D 6
Augusta, Ga., †253,460 ....K 4
Augusta (cap.), Maine, 21,945...N 2
Austin (cap.), Tex., †295,516 ....G 4
Bakersfield, Calif., †329,162........C 3
Baltimore, Md., †2,070,670 ....L 3
Baton Rouge (cap.), La.,
†285,167 ....H 4
Beaumont, Tex., †315,943 ....H 4
Bering (sea), Alaska ....C 6
Bering (str.), Alaska ....C 5
Bighorn (river) ....E 2
Binghamton, N.Y., †302,672 ......L 2
Birmingham, Ala., †739,274 ....J 4
Bismarck (cap.), N. Dak.,
34,703 ....F 1
Bitterroot (range) ....D 1
Black Hills (mts.) ....F 2
Boise (cap.), Idaho, †112,230 ....C 2
Borah (peak), Idaho ....D 2
Boston (cap.), Mass., †2,753,700 M 2
Brazos (river), Tex. ....G 4
Bridgeport, Conn., †388,953 ......M 2
Brooks (range), Alaska ....C 5
Buffalo, N.Y., †1,349,211 ....L 2
California (state), 19,953,134......B 3
Canadian (river) ....F 3
Canaveral (cape), Fla., ...L 5
Canton, Ohio, †372,210 ....K 2
Cape Fear (river), N.C. ....L 4
Carson City (cap.), Nev.,
15,468 ....C 3
Cascade (range) ....B 1
Cedar Rapids, Iowa, †163,213.....H 2
Champlain (lake) ....M 2
Charleston, S.C., †303,849 ....L 4
Charleston (cap.), W. Va.,
†229,515 ....K 3
Charlotte, N.C., †409,370 ....K 3
Chattahoochee (river) ....K 4
Chattanooga, Tenn., †304,927 ....J 3
Chesapeake (bay) ....L 3
Cheyenne (cap.), Wyo., 40,914....E 2
Cheyenne (river) ....F 2
Chicago, Ill., †6,978,947 ....J 2
Cimarron (river) ....G 3
Cincinnati, Ohio, †1,384,911 ......K 3
Cleveland, Ohio, †2,064,194 ....K 2
Coast (range) ....B 2
Cod (cape), Mass. ....N 2
Colorado (state), 2,207,259 ....E 3
Colorado (river) ....D 4
Colorado (river), Tex. ....G 4
Colorado Sprs., Colo., †235,972...F 3
Columbia (cap.), S.C., †322,880..K 4
Columbia (river) ....B 1
Columbus, Ga., †238,584 ....K 4
Columbus (cap.), Ohio, †916,228..K 3
Concord (cap.), N.H., 30,022 ....M 2
Connecticut (state), 3,032,217....M 2
Connecticut (river) ....M 2
Corpus Christi, Tex., †284,832 ....G 5
Cumberland (river) ....J 3
Dallas, Tex., †1,555,950 ....G 4
Davenport, Iowa, †362,638 ....H 2
Dayton, Ohio, †850,266 ....K 3
Death Valley (depr.), Calif. .....C 3
Delaware (state), 548,104..........L 3
Delaware (bay) ....M 3
Denver (cap.), Colo., †1,227,529..F 3
Des Moines (cap.), Iowa,
†286,101 ....H 2
Detroit, Mich., †4,199,931 ....K 2
District of Columbia, 756,510......L 3
Dover (cap.), Del., 17,488 ....L 3
Duluth, Minn., †265,350 ....H 1
Durham, N.C., †190,388 ....L 3
Elbert (mt.), Colo. ....E 3
El Paso, Tex., †359,291 ....E 4
Erie, Pa., †263,654 ....K 2
Erie (lake) ....K 2
Eugene, Oreg., †213,358 ....B 2
Evansville, Ind., †232,775 ....J 3
Everglades (swamp), Fla. ....K 5
Fayetteville, N.C., †212,042 ....L 3
Flint, Mich., †496,658 ....K 2
Florida (state), 6,789,443 ....K 5
Florida (keys), Fla. ....K 6
Ft. Smith, Ark., †160,421 ....H 3
Ft. Wayne, Ind., †280,455 ....J 2
Ft. Worth, Tex., †762,086 ....G 4
Frankfort (cap.), Ky., 21,356......K 3
Fresno, Calif., †413,053 ....C 3
Galveston, Tex., †169,812 ....H 5
Gary, Ind., †633,367 ....J 2
Georgia (state), 4,589,575 ....K 4
Gila (river) ....D 4
Glacier Nat'l Park, Mont. ....D 1
Golden Gate (chan.), Calif. ......B 3
Grand Canyon Nat'l Park, Ariz. ..D 3
Grand Rapids, Mich., †539,225 ....J 2
Great Salt (lake), Utah ....D 2
Greensboro, N.C., †603,895 ....K 3
Greenville, S.C., †299,502 ....K 4
Hamilton, Ohio, †226,207 ....K 3
Harrisburg (cap.), Pa., †410,626..L 2
Hartford (cap.), Conn.,
†663,891 ....M 2
Hatteras (cape), N.C. ....M 3
Havasu (lake) ....D 4
Hawaii (state), 769,913 ....F 6
Hawaii (isl.), Hawaii ....F 6
Helena (cap.), Mont., 22,730......D 1
Honolulu (cap.), Hawaii,
†629,176 ....F 5
Houston, Tex., †1,985,031 ....G 5
Huntington, W. Va., †253,743 ....K 3
Huntsville, Ala., †228,239 ....J 4
Huron (lake), Mich. ....K 2
Idaho (state), 713,008 ....D 2
Illinois (state), 11,113,976 ....J 3
Indiana (state), 5,193,669 ....J 3
Indianapolis (cap.), Ind.,
†1,109,882 ....J 3
Iowa (state), 2,825,041 ....H 2
Jackson (cap.), Miss., †258,906..H 4
Jacksonville, Fla., †528,865.........K 4
Jefferson City (cap.), Mo.
32,407 ....H 3
Jersey City, N. J., †609,266 ......M 2
Johnstown, Pa., †262,822 ....L 2
Juneau (cap.), Alaska, 13,556....E 6
Kalamazoo, Mich., †201,550........J 2
Kansas (state), 2,249,071 ....G 3
Kansas City, Kans.-Mo.,
†1,256,649 ....H 3
Kauai (isl.), Hawaii ....E 5
Kentucky (state), 3,219,311 ..... J 3
Kentucky (lake) .... J 3
Knoxville, Tenn., †400,337 .... K 3
Lancaster, Pa., †319,693 .... L 2
Lansing (cap.), Mich.,
†378,423 .... K 2
Las Vegas, Nev., †273,288 .... C 3
Lawrence, Mass., †232,395 .... M 2
Lexington, Ky., †174,323 .... K 3
Lima, Ohio, †171,472 .... K 2
Lincoln (cap.), Nebr., †167,972... G 2
Little Rock (cap.), Ark.,
†323.296 ....H 4
Long (isl.), N.Y. ....M 2
Long Beach, Calif., 358,633 ......C 4
Los Angeles, Calif., †7,032,075...C 4
Louisiana (state), 3,643,180 ......H 4
Louisville, Ky., †826,553 ....J 3
Lowell, Mass., †212,860 ....M 2
Lubbock, Tex., †179,295 ....F 4
Macon, Ga., †206,342 ....K 4
Madison (cap.), Wis., †290,272..H 2
Maine (state), 993,663 ....N 1
Maryland (state), 3,922,399 ......L 3
Massachusetts (state),
5,689,170 ....M 2
Maui (isl.), Hawaii ....F 5
Mauna Kea (mt.), Hawaii ....G 6
Mauna Loa (mt.), Hawaii ....G 6
May (cape), N. J. ....M 3
McKinley (mt.), Alaska ....D 5
Mead (lake) ....D 3
Memphis, Tenn., †770,120 ....J 3
Mendocino (cape), Calif. ....A 2
Mexico (gulf) ....J 5
Miami, Fla., †1,267,792 ....K 5
Michigan (state), 8,875,083 ....J 1
Michigan (lake) ....J 2
Milwaukee, Wis., †1,403,887........J 2
Minneapolis, Minn., †1,813,647....H 1
Minnesota (state), 3,805,069 .....H 1
Mississippi (state), 2,216,912 ....J 4
Mississippi (river) ....H 4
Missouri (state), 4,677,399 ....H 3
Missouri (river) ....H 3
Mitchell (mt.), N.C. ....K 3
Mobile, Ala., †376,690 ....J 4
Montana (state), 694,409 ....E 1
Montgomery (cap.), Ala.,
†201,325 ....J 4
Montpelier (cap.), Vt., 8,609 ....M 2
Nantucket (isl.), Mass. ....N 2
Nashville (cap.), Tenn., †540,982 J 3
Nebraska (state), 1,483,791 ......F 2
Nevada (state), 488,738 ....C 3
Newark, N. J., †1,856,556 ....M 2
New Hampshire(state), 737,681..M 2
New Haven, Conn., †355,538 .....M 2
New Jersey (state), 7,168,164....M 3
New Mexico (state), 1,016,000....E 4
New Orleans, La., †1,045,809 .....H 5
Newport News, Va., †292,159 ....L 3
New York (state), 18,190,740......L 2
New York, N.Y., †11,528,649 .....M 2
Norfolk, Va., †680,600 ....L 3
North Carolina(state), 5,082,059..L 3
North Dakota (state), 617,761 ....F 1
Oahu (isl.), Hawaii ....F 5
Oakland, Calif., 361,561 ....B 3
Ohio (state), 10,652,017 ....K 2
Ohio (river) ....J 3
Oklahoma (state), 2,559,253 ......G 3
Oklahoma City (cap.), Okla.,
†640,889 ....G 3
Olympia (cap.), Wash., 23,111....B 1
Olympic Nat'l Park, Wash. ....A 1
Omaha, Nebr., †541,453 ....G 2
Ontario (lake), N.Y. ....L 2
Oregon (state), 2,091,385 ....
Orlando, Fla., †428,003 ....
Ozark (mts.) ....
Paterson, N. J., †1,358,794.........M
Pennsylvania (state), 11,793,909..
Pensacola, Fla., †243,075 ....
Peoria, Ill., †341,979 ....
Philadelphia, Pa., †4,817,914 ....M
Phoenix (cap.), Ariz., †968,487..D
Pierre (cap.), S. Dak., 9,699 .....F
Pikes (peak), Colo. ....E
Pittsburgh, Pa., †2,401,245 L
Platte (river), Nebr. ....G
Pontchartrain (lake), La. ....J
Portland, Maine, †141,625 ....N
Portland, Oreg., †1,009,129 ....B
Potomac (river) L
Providence (cap.), R.I., †914,110 .M
Racine, Wis., †170,838 ....J
Rainier (mt.), Wash. ....B
Raleigh (cap.), N.C., †228,453 L
Reading, Pa., †296,382 L
Red (river) ....H
Red River of the North (river)..G
Rhode Island (state), 949,723....M
Richmond (cap.), Va., †518,319..L
Rio Grande (river) ....F
Roanoke, Va., †181,436 ....K
Rochester, N.Y., †882,667 L
Rockford, Ill., †272,063 ....J
Rocky (mts.) ....E
Sacramento (cap.), Calif.,
†800,592 ....B
Saginaw, Mich., †219,743 ....K
Saint Clair (lake), Mich. ....K
Saint Lawrence (river), N.Y. ....N
Saint Louis, Mo., †2,363,017 ......H
Saint Paul (cap.), Minn.,
309,980 ....H

AREA 3,615,123 sq. mi.
POPULATION 203,235,298
CAPITAL Washington
LARGEST CITY New York
HIGHEST POINT Mt. McKinley 20,320 ft.
MONETARY VALUE U.S. dollar
MAJOR LANGUAGE English
MAJOR RELIGIONS Protestantism, Roman Catholicism, Judaism

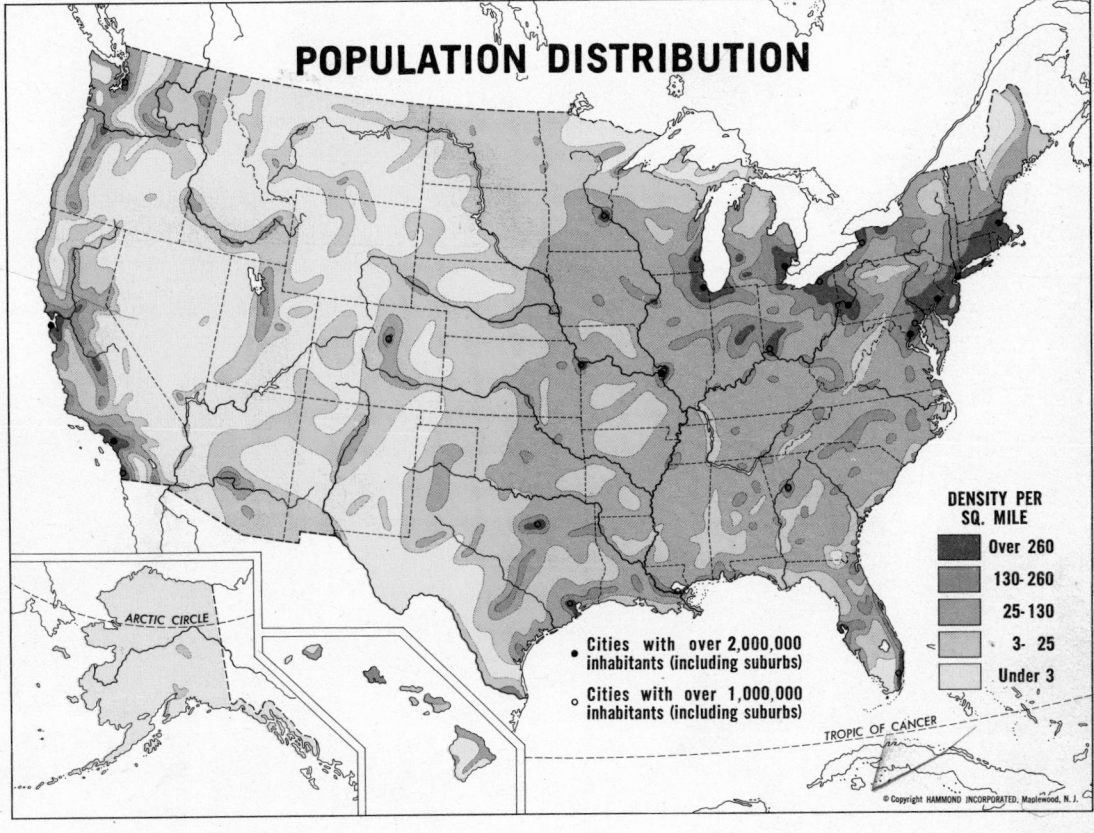

POPULATION DISTRIBUTION

DENSITY PER SQ. MILE
Over 260
130- 260
25- 130
3- 25
Under 3

• Cities with over 2,000,000 inhabitants (including suburbs)
○ Cities with over 1,000,000 inhabitants (including suburbs)

ARCTIC CIRCLE

TROPIC OF CANCER

© Copyright HAMMOND INCORPORATED, Maplewood, N.J.

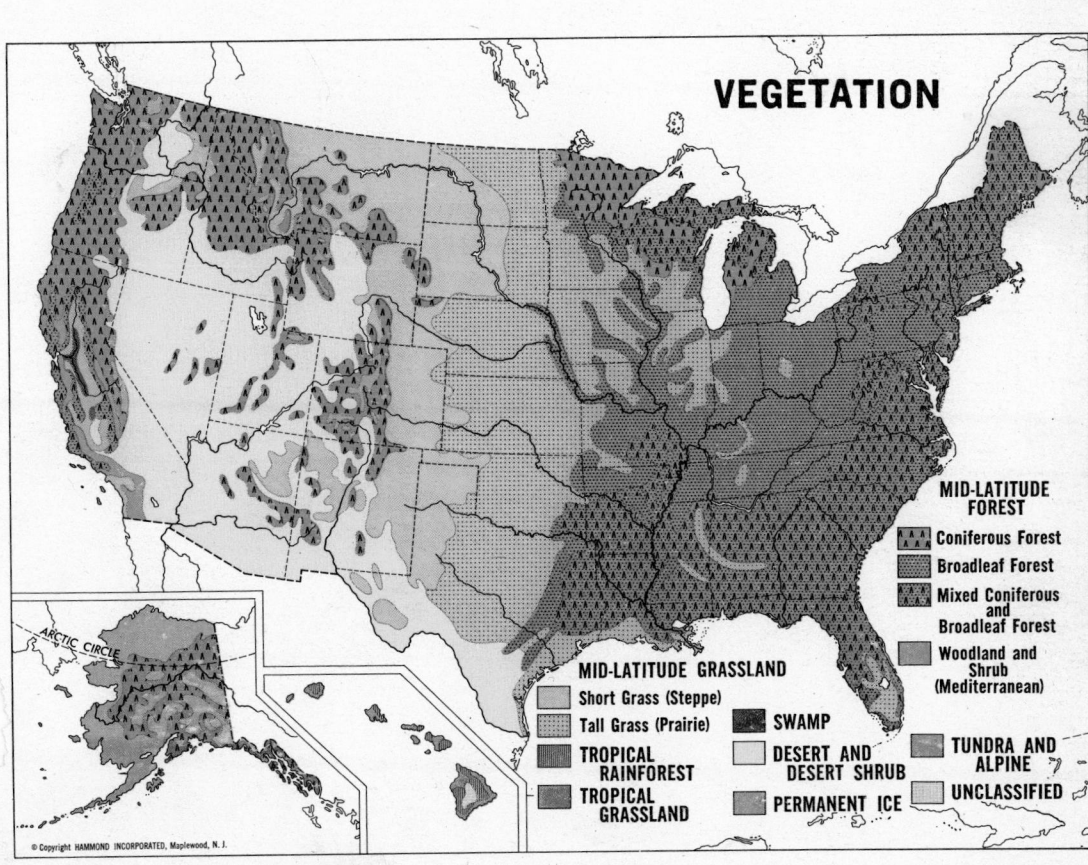

VEGETATION

MID-LATITUDE FOREST

Coniferous Forest
Broadleaf Forest
Mixed Coniferous and Broadleaf Forest
Woodland and Shrub (Mediterranean)

MID-LATITUDE GRASSLAND

Short Grass (Steppe)
Tall Grass (Prairie)
TROPICAL RAINFOREST
TROPICAL GRASSLAND

SWAMP
DESERT AND DESERT SHRUB
PERMANENT ICE

TUNDRA AND ALPINE
UNCLASSIFIED

ARCTIC CIRCLE

© Copyright HAMMOND INCORPORATED, Maplewood, N.J.

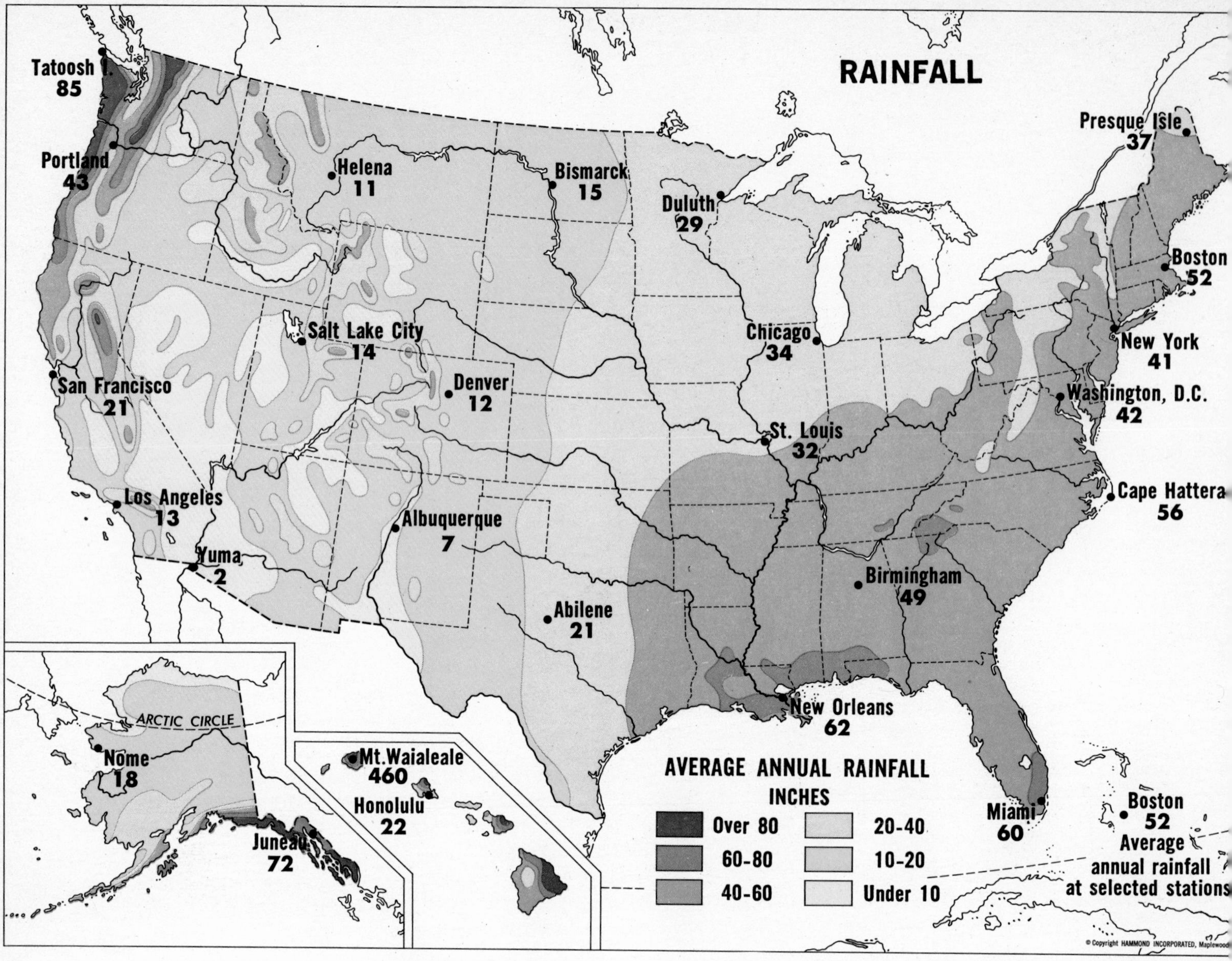

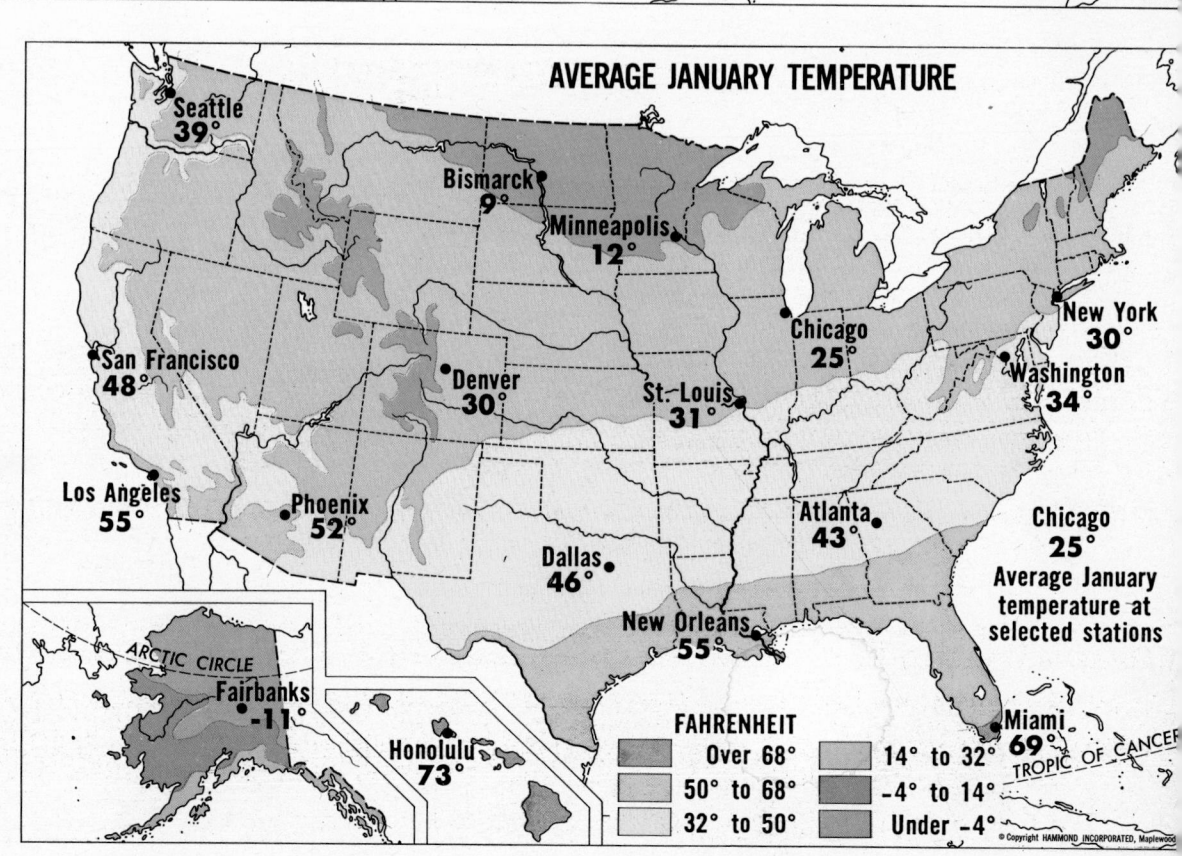

RAINFALL

Tatoosh I.
85

Portland
43

Helena
11

Bismarck
15

Duluth
29

Presque Isle
37

Boston
52

Chicago
34

New York
41

Salt Lake City
14

Washington, D.C.
42

San Francisco
21

Denver
12

St. Louis
32

Los Angeles
13

Albuquerque
7

Cape Hattera
56

Yuma
2

Abilene
21

Birmingham
49

New Orleans
62

ARCTIC CIRCLE

Nome
18

Mt. Waialeale
460

Honolulu
22

Juneau
72

Miami
60

AVERAGE ANNUAL RAINFALL
INCHES

Over 80		20-40
60-80		10-20
40-60		Under 10

Boston
52
Average
annual rainfall
at selected stations

© Copyright HAMMOND INCORPORATED, Maplewood

AVERAGE JANUARY TEMPERATURE

Seattle
39°

Bismarck
9°

Minneapolis
12°

Chicago
25°

New York
30°

San Francisco
48°

Denver
30°

St. Louis
31°

Washington
34°

Los Angeles
55°

Phoenix
52°

Atlanta
43°

Chicago
25°
Average January
temperature at
selected stations

Dallas
46°

New Orleans
55°

ARCTIC CIRCLE

Fairbanks
-11°

Honolulu
73°

Miami
69°

TROPIC OF CANCER

FAHRENHEIT

Over 68°		14° to 32°
50° to 68°		-4° to 14°
32° to 50°		Under -4°

© Copyright HAMMOND INCORPORATED, Maplewood

Topography

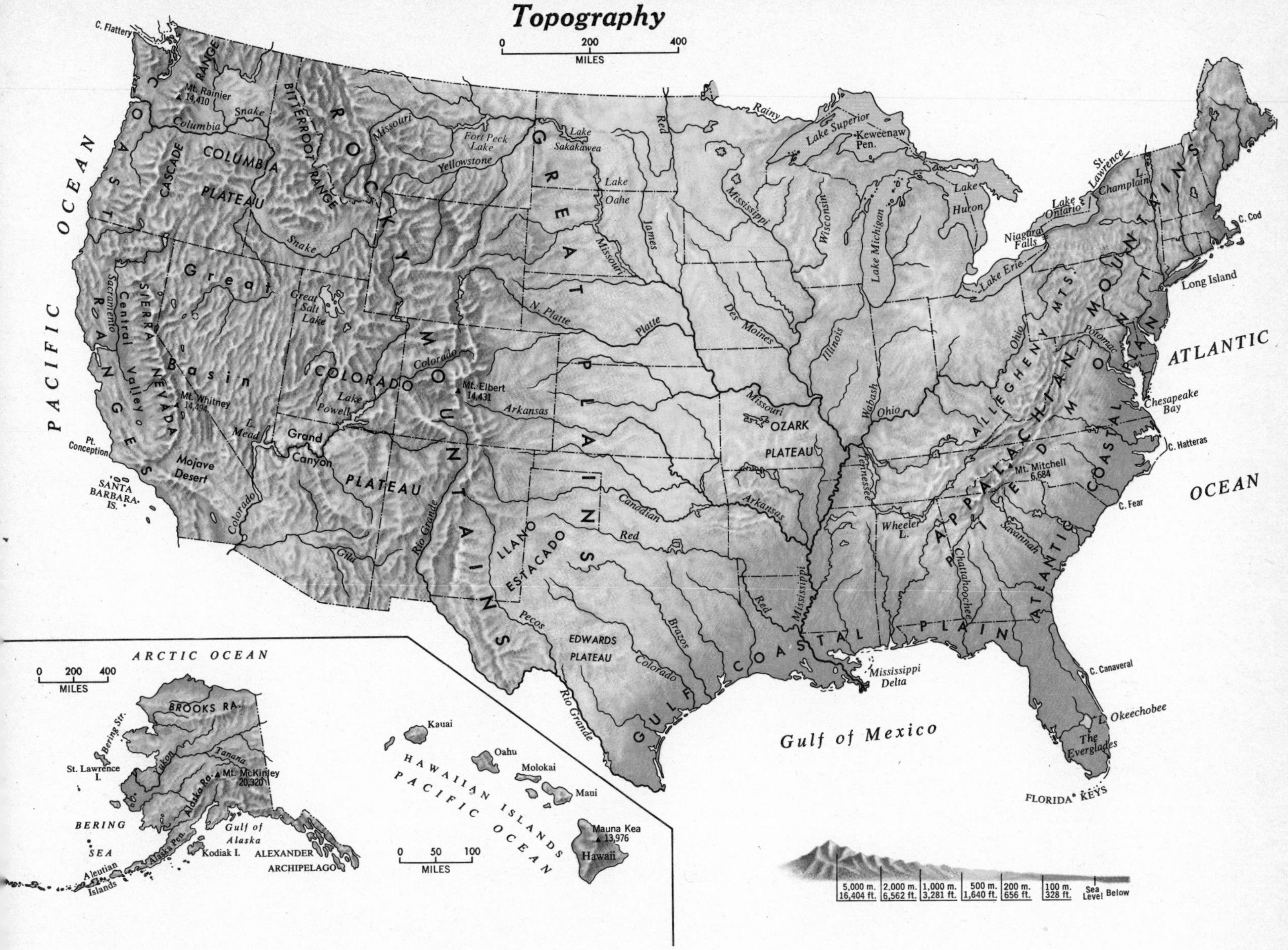

SCALE
0   200   400
MILES

PACIFIC OCEAN

C. Flattery
COAST RANGE
Mt. Rainier 14,410
CASCADE RANGE
COLUMBIA PLATEAU
Columbia
Snake
BITTERROOT RANGE
ROCKY MOUNTAINS
Missouri
Fort Peck Lake
Yellowstone
Snake
Great Salt Lake
Great Basin
SIERRA NEVADA
Sacramento
Central Valley
Mt. Whitney 14,494
Pt. Conception
Mojave Desert
SANTA BARBARA IS.
Colorado
COLORADO PLATEAU
Lake Powell
Grand Canyon
Lake Mead
Gila
Rio Grande
Colorado
Mt. Elbert 14,431
Pecos
LLANO ESTACADO
EDWARDS PLATEAU
Colorado
Brazos
Red
Canadian
Arkansas
N. Platte
Platte
GREAT PLAINS
Lake Oahe
James
Missouri
Lake Sakakawea
Red
Rainy
Lake Superior
Keweenaw Pen.
Des Moines
Wisconsin
Illinois
Lake Michigan
Lake Huron
Lake Erie
Lake Ontario
Niagara Falls
St. Lawrence
Lake Champlain
C. Cod
Long Island
ATLANTIC
Wabash
Ohio
Missouri
OZARK PLATEAU
Arkansas
Tennessee
Ohio
ALLEGHENY MTS.
APPALACHIAN MOUNTAINS
Wheeler
Chattahoochee
Chesapeake Bay
C. Hatteras
C. Fear
Mt. Mitchell 6,684
Potomac
Savannah
ATLANTIC COASTAL PLAIN
OCEAN
GULF COASTAL PLAIN
Mississippi
Mississippi Delta
C. Canaveral
L. Okeechobee
The Everglades
FLORIDA KEYS

Gulf of Mexico

ARCTIC OCEAN
SCALE
0   200   400
MILES
BROOKS RA.
Yukon
Tanana
St. Lawrence I.
Bering Str.
ALASKA RA.
Mt. McKinley 20,320
BERING SEA
Gulf of Alaska
Kodiak I.
Alaska Pen.
Aleutian Islands
ALEXANDER ARCHIPELAGO

Kauai
Oahu
Molokai
Maui
HAWAIIAN ISLANDS
PACIFIC OCEAN
Mauna Kea 13,976
Hawaii
SCALE
0   50   100
MILES

5,000 m. 16,404 ft. | 2,000 m. 6,562 ft. | 1,000 m. 3,281 ft. | 500 m. 1,640 ft. | 200 m. 656 ft. | 100 m. 328 ft. | Sea Level | Below

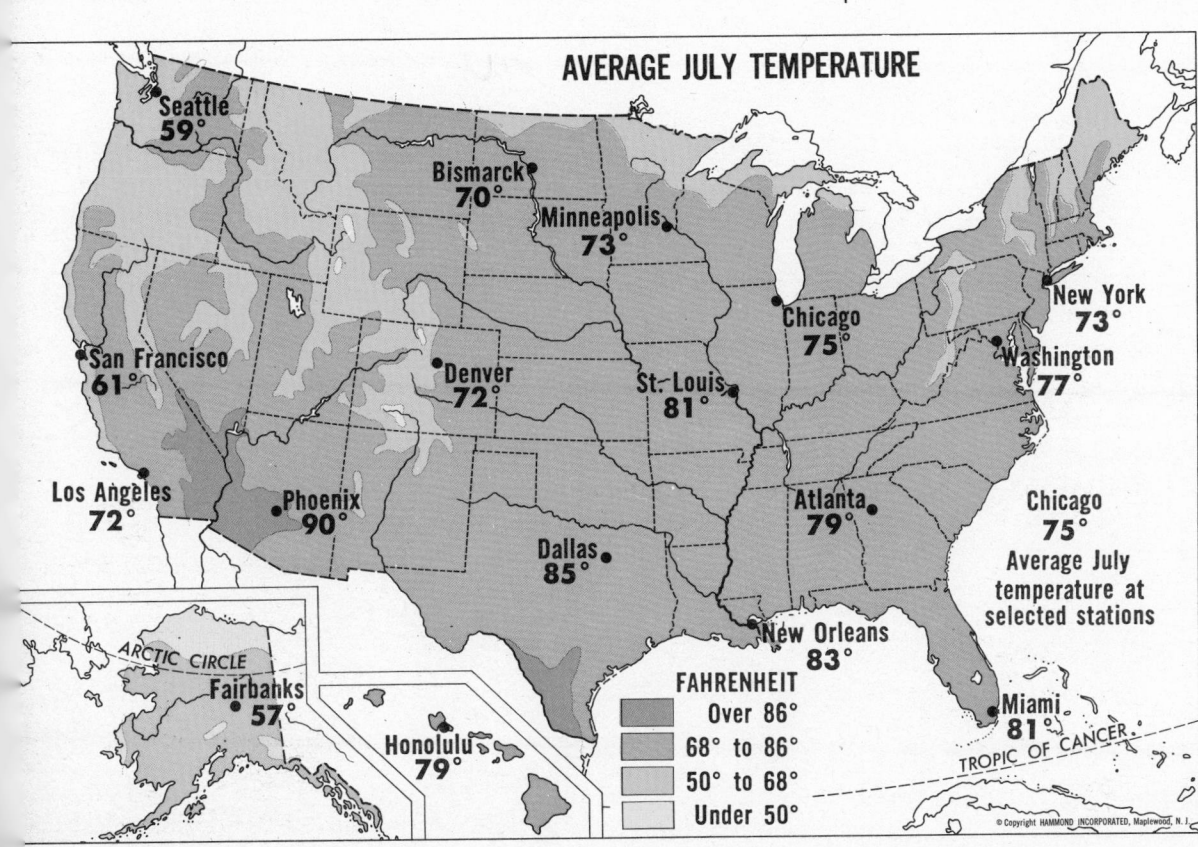

AVERAGE JULY TEMPERATURE

Seattle 59°
Bismarck 70°
Minneapolis 73°
New York 73°
Chicago 75°
San Francisco 61°
Denver 72°
St. Louis 81°
Washington 77°
Los Angeles 72°
Phoenix 90°
Atlanta 79°
Dallas 85°
Chicago 75°
Average July temperature at selected stations
New Orleans 83°
Miami 81°
ARCTIC CIRCLE
Fairbanks 57°
Honolulu 79°
TROPIC OF CANCER

FAHRENHEIT
Over 86°
68° to 86°
50° to 68°
Under 50°

LAND USE

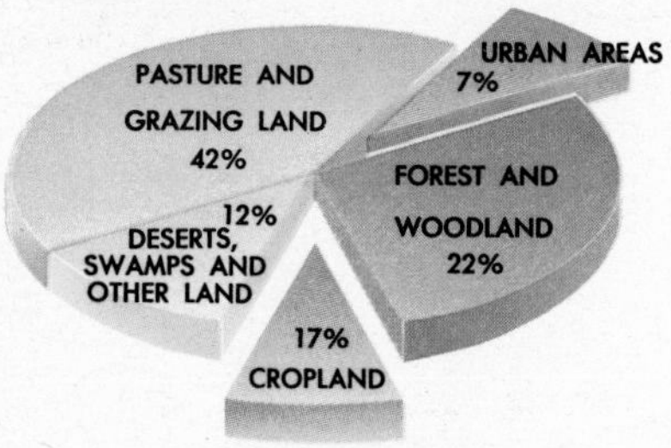

PASTURE AND GRAZING LAND 42%
URBAN AREAS 7%
FOREST AND WOODLAND 22%
12% DESERTS, SWAMPS AND OTHER LAND
17% CROPLAND

EMPLOYMENT

MANUFACTURING 27%
WHOLESALE AND RETAIL TRADE 19%
GOVERNMENT 17%
SERVICES 14%
AGRICULTURE 6%
TRANSPORTATION AND PUBLIC UTILITIES 6%
CONSTRUCTION 5%
FINANCE, INSURANCE, REAL ESTATE 5%
MINING 1%

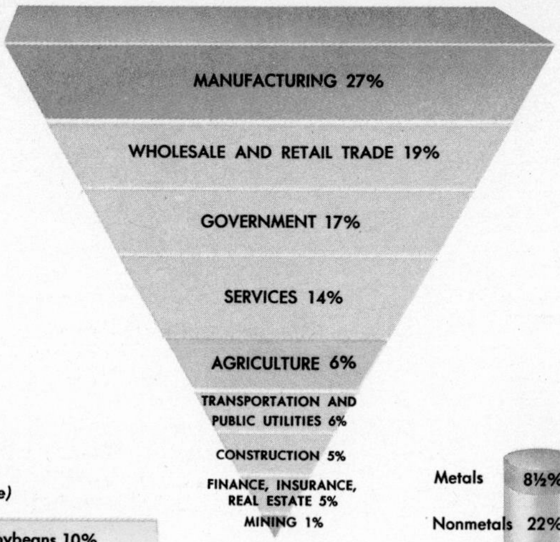

TOTAL VALUE ADDED BY MANUFACTURING

(percent by industry group)

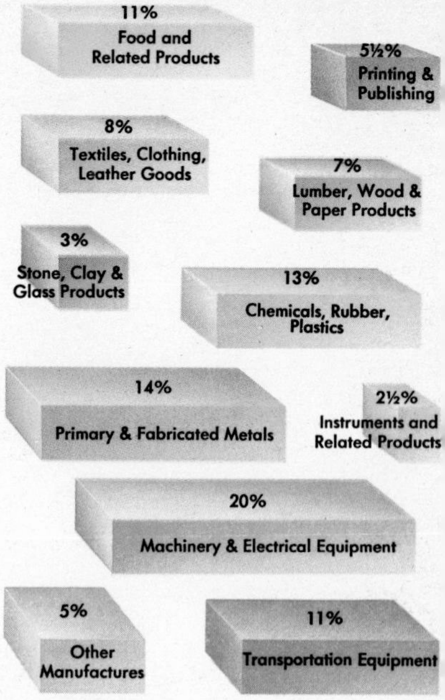

11% Food and Related Products
5½% Printing & Publishing
8% Textiles, Clothing, Leather Goods
7% Lumber, Wood & Paper Products
3% Stone, Clay & Glass Products
13% Chemicals, Rubber, Plastics
14% Primary & Fabricated Metals
2½% Instruments and Related Products
20% Machinery & Electrical Equipment
5% Other Manufactures
11% Transportation Equipment

CROPLAND *(percent of total acreage)*

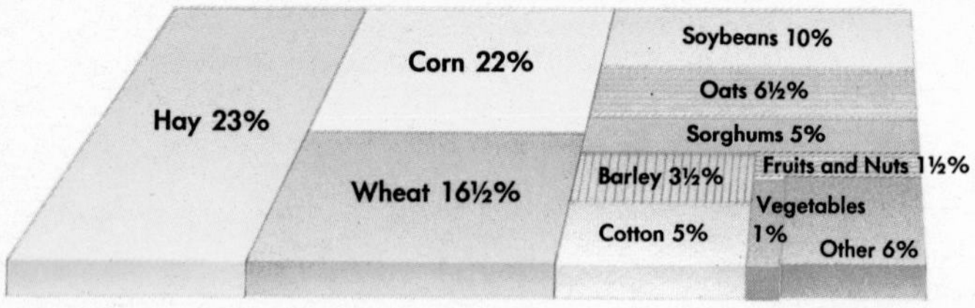

Hay 23%
Corn 22%
Soybeans 10%
Oats 6½%
Sorghums 5%
Wheat 16½%
Barley 3½%
Fruits and Nuts 1½%
Vegetables 1%
Cotton 5%
Other 6%

VALUE OF MINERAL PRODUCTION

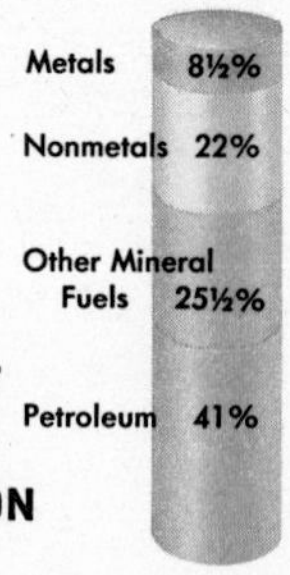

Metals 8½%
Nonmetals 22%
Other Mineral Fuels 25½%
Petroleum 41%

Agriculture, Industry and Resources

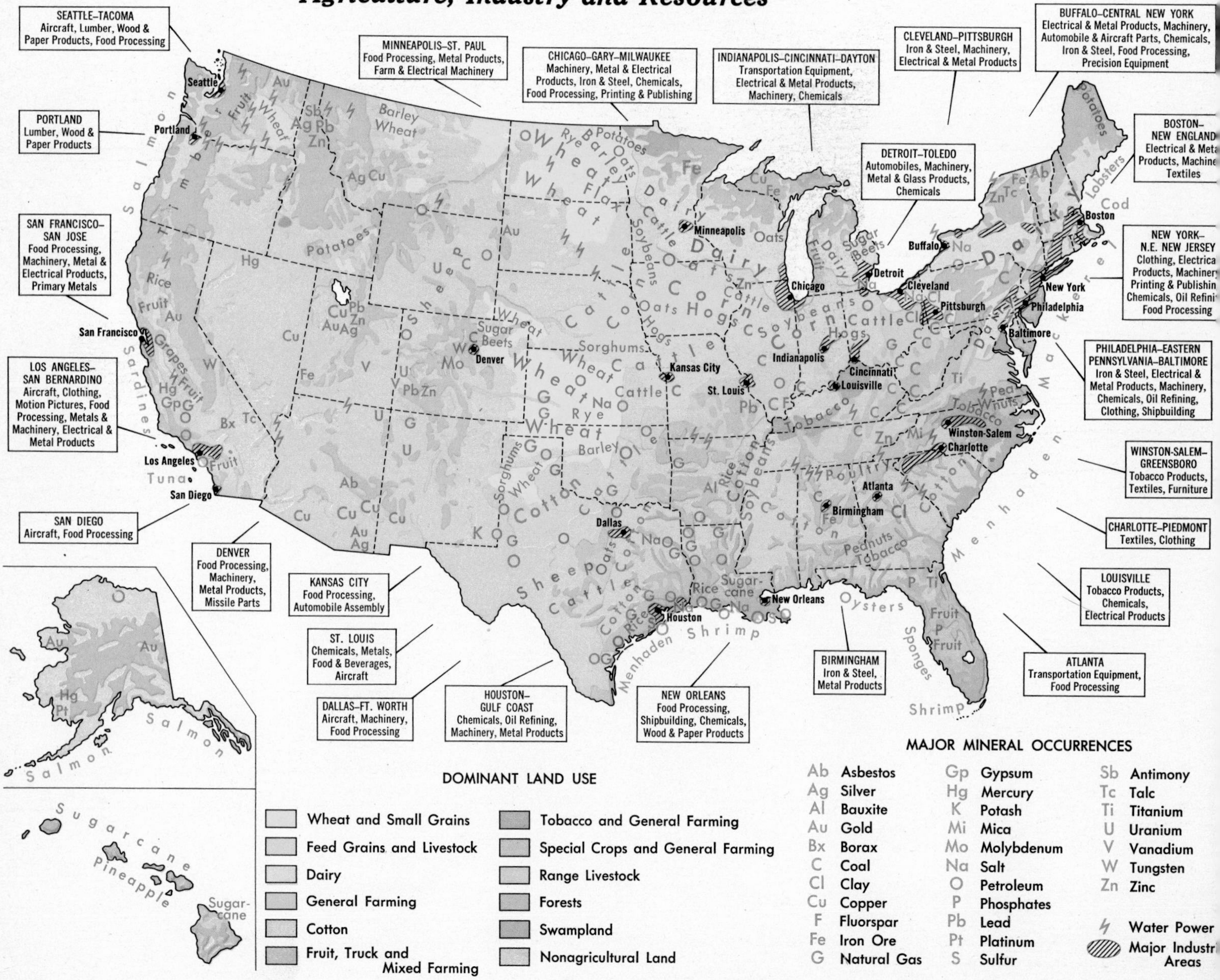

SEATTLE–TACOMA Aircraft, Lumber, Wood & Paper Products, Food Processing
MINNEAPOLIS–ST. PAUL Food Processing, Metal Products, Farm & Electrical Machinery
CHICAGO–GARY–MILWAUKEE Machinery, Metal & Electrical Products, Iron & Steel, Chemicals, Food Processing, Printing & Publishing
INDIANAPOLIS–CINCINNATI–DAYTON Transportation Equipment, Electrical & Metal Products, Machinery, Chemicals
CLEVELAND–PITTSBURGH Iron & Steel, Machinery, Electrical & Metal Products
BUFFALO–CENTRAL NEW YORK Electrical & Metal Products, Machinery, Automobile & Aircraft Parts, Chemicals, Iron & Steel, Food Processing, Precision Equipment
PORTLAND Lumber, Wood & Paper Products
DETROIT–TOLEDO Automobiles, Machinery, Metal & Glass Products, Chemicals
BOSTON–NEW ENGLAND Electrical & Metal Products, Machinery, Textiles
SAN FRANCISCO–SAN JOSE Food Processing, Machinery, Metal & Electrical Products, Primary Metals
NEW YORK–N.E. NEW JERSEY Clothing, Electrical Products, Machinery, Printing & Publishing, Chemicals, Oil Refining, Food Processing
LOS ANGELES–SAN BERNARDINO Aircraft, Clothing, Motion Pictures, Food Processing, Metals & Machinery, Electrical & Metal Products
PHILADELPHIA–EASTERN PENNSYLVANIA–BALTIMORE Iron & Steel, Electrical & Metal Products, Machinery, Chemicals, Oil Refining, Clothing, Shipbuilding
WINSTON-SALEM–GREENSBORO Tobacco Products, Textiles, Furniture
SAN DIEGO Aircraft, Food Processing
CHARLOTTE–PIEDMONT Textiles, Clothing
DENVER Food Processing, Machinery, Metal Products, Missile Parts
KANSAS CITY Food Processing, Automobile Assembly
LOUISVILLE Tobacco Products, Chemicals, Electrical Products
ST. LOUIS Chemicals, Metals, Food & Beverages, Aircraft
ATLANTA Transportation Equipment, Food Processing
DALLAS–FT. WORTH Aircraft, Machinery, Food Processing
HOUSTON–GULF COAST Chemicals, Oil Refining, Machinery, Metal Products
NEW ORLEANS Food Processing, Shipbuilding, Chemicals, Wood & Paper Products
BIRMINGHAM Iron & Steel, Metal Products
Seattle
Portland
San Francisco
Los Angeles
San Diego
Denver
Minneapolis
Chicago
Detroit
Buffalo
Cleveland
Pittsburgh
Boston
New York
Philadelphia
Baltimore
Indianapolis
Cincinnati
Louisville
Kansas City
St. Louis
Winston-Salem
Charlotte
Atlanta
Birmingham
Dallas
Houston
New Orleans
Salmon
Sardines
Tuna
Lobsters
Cod
Menhaden
Oysters
Shrimp
Sponges
Sugarcane
Pineapple
DOMINANT LAND USE
Wheat and Small Grains
Feed Grains and Livestock
Dairy
General Farming
Cotton
Fruit, Truck and Mixed Farming
Tobacco and General Farming
Special Crops and General Farming
Range Livestock
Forests
Swampland
Nonagricultural Land
MAJOR MINERAL OCCURRENCES
Ab Asbestos
Ag Silver
Al Bauxite
Au Gold
Bx Borax
C Coal
Cl Clay
Cu Copper
F Fluorspar
Fe Iron Ore
G Natural Gas
Gp Gypsum
Hg Mercury
K Potash
Mi Mica
Mo Molybdenum
Na Salt
O Petroleum
P Phosphates
Pb Lead
Pt Platinum
S Sulfur
Sb Antimony
Tc Talc
Ti Titanium
U Uranium
V Vanadium
W Tungsten
Zn Zinc
Water Power
Major Industrial Areas

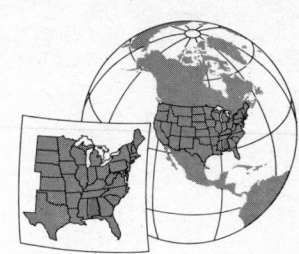

COUNTIES

Autauga, 24,460 .... E 5
Baldwin, 59,382 .... C 9
Barbour, 22,543 .... H 7
Bibb, 13,812 .... D 5
Blount, 26,853 .... E 2
Bullock, 11,824 .... G 6
Butler, 22,007 .... E 7
Calhoun, 103,092 .... G 3
Chambers, 36,356 .... H 5
Cherokee, 15,606 .... G 2
Chilton, 25,180 .... E 5
Choctaw, 16,589 .... C 7
Clarke, 26,724 .... C 7
Clay, 12,636 .... G 4
Cleburne, 10,996 .... G 3
Coffee, 34,872 .... G 8
Colbert, 49,632 .... C 1
Conecuh, 15,645 .... E 8
Coosa, 10,662 .... F 5
Covington, 34,079 .... F 8
Crenshaw, 13,188 .... F 7
Cullman, 52,445 .... E 2
Dale, 52,938 .... G 8
Dallas, 55,296 .... D 6
De Kalb, 41,981 .... F 2
Elmore, 33,535 .... F 5
Escambia, 34,906 .... D 8
Etowah, 94,144 .... F 2
Fayette, 16,252 .... C 3
Franklin, 23,933 .... C 2
Geneva, 21,924 .... G 8
Greene, 10,650 .... C 5
Hale, 15,888 .... C 5
Henry, 13,254 .... H 8
Houston, 56,574 .... H 8
Jackson, 39,202 .... F 1
Jefferson, 644,991 .... E 3
Lamar, 14,335 .... B 3
Lauderdale, 68,111 .... C 1
Lawrence, 27,281 .... D 1
Lee, 61,268 .... H 5
Limestone, 41,699 .... E 1
Lowndes, 12,897 .... E 6
Macon, 24,841 .... G 6
Madison, 186,540 .... E 1
Marengo, 23,819 .... C 6
Marion, 23,788 .... C 2
Marshall, 54,211 .... F 2
Mobile, 317,308 .... B 9
Monroe, 20,883 .... D 7
Montgomery, 167,790 .... F 6
Morgan, 77,306 .... E 2
Perry, 15,388 .... D 6
Pickens, 20,326 .... B 4
Pike, 25,038 .... G 7
Randolph, 18,331 .... H 4
Russell, 45,394 .... H 6
Saint Clair, 27,956 .... F 3
Shelby, 38,037 .... E 4
Sumter, 16,974 .... B 5
Talladega, 65,280 .... F 4
Tallapoosa, 33,840 .... G 5

Tuscaloosa, 116,029 .... C 4
Walker, 56,246 .... D 3
Washington, 16,241 .... B 8
Wilcox, 16,303 .... D 7
Winston, 16,654 .... D 2

CITIES and TOWNS

Zip	Name/Pop.	Key
36310	Abbeville⊙, 2,996	H 7
35440	Abernant, 602	D 4
35005	Adamsville, 2,412	D 3
35540	Addison, 692	D 2
35006	Adger, 1,550	D 4
35441	Akron, 535	C 5
35007	Alabaster, 2,642	E 4
35950	Albertville, 9,963	F 2
† 35115	Aldrich, 476	E 4
35010	Alexander City, 12,358	G 5
36250	Alexandria, 600	G 3
35442	Aliceville, 2,807	B 4
35013	Allgood, 272	E 3
† 35616	Allsboro, 300	B 1
35015	Alton, 500	E 3
35952	Altoona, 881	F 2
36420	Andalusia⊙, 10,092	F 8
35610	Anderson, 400	D 1
36201	Anniston⊙, 31,533	G 3
35016	Arab, 4,399	E 2
35805	Ardmore, 761	E 1
36311	Ariton, 643	G 7
35033	Arkadelphia, 325	E 3
† 35035	Ashby, 500	E 4
36312	Ashford, 1,980	H 8
36251	Ashland⊙, 1,921	G 4
35953	Ashville, 986	F 3
35611	Athens⊙, 14,360	E 1
36502	Atmore, 8,293	C 8
35954	Attalla, 7,510	F 2
36830	Auburn, 22,767	H 5
36003	Autaugaville, 870	E 6
† 36312	Avon, 374	H 8
36505	Axis, 600	B 9
35019	Baileyton, 500	E 2
36004	Baker Hill, 350	H 7
36506	Barlow Bend, 300	C 8
† 36532	Barnwell, 700	C 10
36533	Battles Wharf, 300	C 10
36507	Bay Minette⊙, 6,727	C 9
36509	Bayou La Batre, 2,664	B 10
35543	Bear Creek, 336	C 2
36425	Beatrice, 455	D 7
35544	Beaverton, 265	B 3
† 35653	Belgreen, 500	C 2
36901	Bellamy, 700	B 6
35546	Berry, 679	C 3
35020	Bessemer, 33,428	D 4
* 35201	Birmingham⊙, 300,910	D 4
	Birmingham, ‡739,274	D 3
36902	Bladon Springs, 300	B 7
† 36874	Bleecker, 250	H 5
35031	Blountsville, 1,254	E 2
36201	Blue Mountain, 446	G 3
35226	Bluff Park 12,372	E 4

35957	Boaz, 5,621	F 2
36903	Bolinger, 250	B 7
36007	Bolling, 250	E 7
36511	Bon Secour, 850	C 10
36110	Boylston, 2,943	F 6
36009	Brantley, 1,066	F 7
35034	Brent, 2,093	D 5
36426	Brewton⊙, 6,747	D 8
35740	Bridgeport, 2,908	G 1
35035	Brierfield, 950	E 4
35020	Brighton, 2,277	D 4
35548	Brilliant, 726	C 2
36429	Brooklyn, 350	E 8
35036	Brookside, 990	E 3
35444	Brookwood, 450	D 4
35445	Brownville, 300	C 4
35010	Brundidge, 2,709	G 7
35446	Buhl, 500	C 4
36725	Burkville, 250	E 6
36431	Burnt Corn, 250	D 7
36904	Butler⊙, 2,064	B 6
† 36767	Cahaba, 50	D 6
35040	Calera, 1,655	E 4
36012	Calhoun, 950	E 6
36513	Calvert, 500	B 8
36726	Camden⊙, 1,742	D 7
36850	Camp Hill, 1,554	G 5
36514	Canoe, 560	D 8
† 36726	Canton Bend, 250	D 6
35549	Carbon Hill, 1,929	C 3
36515	Carlton, 275	C 8
35447	Carrollton⊙, 923	B 4
† 36023	Carrville, 895	G 5
† 36548	Carson, 250	G 1
36432	Castleberry, 666	D 8
36013	Cecil, 250	F 6
35959	Cedar Bluff, 956	G 2
36014	Central, 300	D 6
35960	Centre⊙, 2,418	G 2
35042	Centreville⊙, 2,233	D 5
36729	Chance, 300	C 7
36015	Chapman, 400	E 7
36518	Chatom⊙, 1,059	B 8
35043	Chelsea, 615	E 4
35616	Cherokee, 1,484	C 1
36611	Chickasaw, 8,447	A 9
35044	Childersburg, 4,831	F 4
36254	Choccolocco, 300	G 3
36905	Choctaw, 600	B 6
36520	Chrysler, 300	C 8
36521	Chunchula, 400	B 9
36522	Citronelle, 1,935	B 8
35045	Clanton⊙, 5,868	E 5
36015	Clayton⊙, 1,626	G 7
35049	Cleveland, 413	E 3
36017	Clio, 1,065	G 7
35617	Cloverdale, 650	C 1
35449	Coaling, 300	D 4
36523	Coden, 500	B 10
36318	Coffee Springs, 329	G 8
36524	Coffeeville, 441	B 7
35452	Coker, 800	C 4
35961	Collinsville, 1,300	G 2
36319	Columbia, 891	H 8
35051	Columbiana⊙, 2,248	E 4

AREA 51,609 sq. mi.
POPULATION 3,444,165
CAPITAL Montgomery
LARGEST CITY Birmingham
HIGHEST POINT Cheaha Mtn. 2,407 ft.
SETTLED IN 1702
ADMITTED TO UNION December 14, 1819
POPULAR NAME Heart of Dixie; Cotton State
STATE FLOWER Camellia
STATE BIRD Yellowhammer

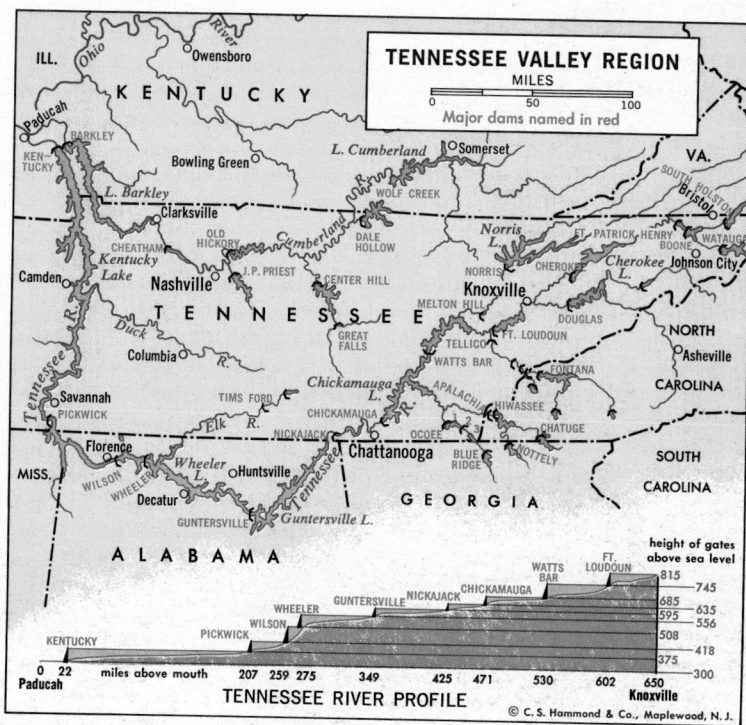

TENNESSEE VALLEY REGION
MILES
0 50 100
Major dams named in red

height of gates above sea level

TENNESSEE RIVER PROFILE

© C. S. Hammond & Co., Maplewood, N.J.

Agriculture, Industry and Resources

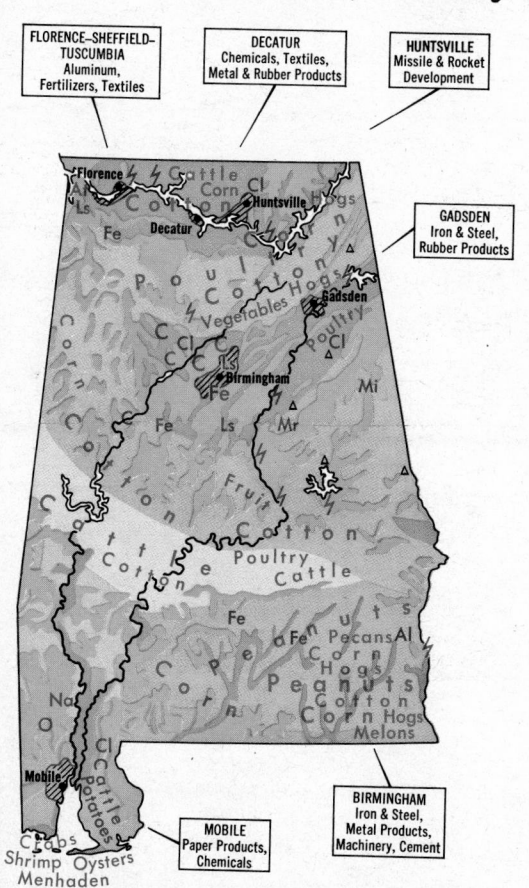

FLORENCE–SHEFFIELD–TUSCUMBIA
Aluminum, Fertilizers, Textiles

DECATUR
Chemicals, Textiles, Metal & Rubber Products

HUNTSVILLE
Missile & Rocket Development

GADSDEN
Iron & Steel, Rubber Products

MOBILE
Paper Products, Chemicals

BIRMINGHAM
Iron & Steel, Metal Products, Machinery, Cement

DOMINANT LAND USE

- Specialized Cotton
- Cotton, Livestock
- Cotton, General Farming
- Cotton, Hogs, Peanuts
- Cotton, Forest Products
- Peanuts, General Farming
- Truck and Mixed Farming
- Forests
- Swampland, Limited Agriculture

MAJOR MINERAL OCCURRENCES

Al   Bauxite   Ls   Limestone
At   Asphalt   Mi   Mica
C   Coal   Mr   Marble
Cl   Clay   Na   Salt
Fe   Iron Ore   O   Petroleum

⚡   Water Power
▨   Major Industrial Areas
△   Major Textile Manufacturing Centers

36019	Cooper, 250	E 5
36020	Coosada, 600	F 5
35550	Cordova, 2,750	D 3
† 35546	Corona, 300	C 3
35088	Cottage Grove, 300	F 5
35453	Cottondale, 600	D 4
36851	Cottonton, 415	H 6
36320	Cottonwood, 1,149	H 8
35618	Courtland, 547	D 1
36321	Cowarts, 350	H 8
36435	Coy 950	D 7
36525	Creola, 950	B 9
36906	Cromwell, 700	B 6
35962	Crossville, 1,035	G 2
36907	Cuba, 386	B 6
35055	Cullman⊙, 12,601	E 2
36920	Cullomburg, 325	B 7
36852	Cusseta, 250	H 5
36853	Dadeville⊙, 2,847	G 5
36322	Daleville, 5,182	G 8
35619	Danville, 400	D 2
36526	Daphne, 2,382	C 9
36528	Dauphin Island, 950	B 10
36256	Daviston, 247	G 4
36257	De Armanville, 500	G 3
36022	Deatsville, 350	F 5
35601	Decatur⊙, 38,044	D 1
36529	Deer Park, 300	B 8
36732	Demopolis, 7,651	C 6
36436	Dickinson, 350	C 7
36736	Dixons Mills, 285	C 7
35061	Dolomite, 1,237	D 4
35062	Dora, 1,862	D 3
36301	Dothan⊙, 36,733	H 8
35553	Double Springs⊙, 957	D 2
35964	Douglas, 527	F 2
36028	Dozier, 304	F 7
36259	Duke, 250	F 4
35744	Dutton, 423	G 1
† 36507	Dyas, 250	C 9
36260	Eastaboga, 500	F 3
36426	East Brewton, 2,336	E 8
35457	Echola, 300	C 4
36024	Eclectic, 1,184	F 5
† 36317	Edwin, 296	H 7
36323	Elba⊙, 4,634	F 8
36530	Elberta, 395	C 10
35554	Eldridge, 350	C 3
35620	Elkmont, 394	E 1
36025	Elmore, 656	F 5
35458	Elrod, 600	C 4
35459	Emelle, 300	B 5
35063	Empire, 300	D 3
36330	Enterprise, 15,591	G 8
35460	Epes, 293	B 5
36027	Eufaula, 9,102	H 7
35462	Eutaw⊙, 2,805	C 5
36401	Evergreen⊙, 3,924	E 8
36439	Excel, 422	D 8
35746	Fackler, 250	G 1

36854	Fairfax, 2,772	H 5
35064	Fairfield, 14,369	E 3
36532	Fairhope, 5,720	C 10
35208	Fairview, 313	E 2
35622	Falkville, 946	E 2
35555	Fayette⊙, 4,568	C 3
36440	Finchburg, 300	D 7
36855	Five Points, 247	H 4
† 35129	Flat Creek-Wegra, 1,066	D 3
35966	Flat Rock, 750	G 1
36739	Flatwood, 300	C 6
† 35601	Flint City, 404	D 1
36441	Flomaton, 1,584	D 8
36442	Florala, 2,701	F 8
35630	Florence⊙, 34,031	C 1
36535	Foley, 3,368	C 10
35214	Forestdale, 6,091	E 3
36030	Forest Home, 450	E 7
36740	Forkland, 400	C 5
36031	Fort Davis, 500	G 6
36032	Fort Deposit, 1,438	E 7
36856	Fort Mitchell, 500	H 6
35967	Fort Payne⊙, 8,435	G 2
35463	Fosters, 400	C 4
36444	Franklin, 500	D 7
36538	Frankville, 550	B 7
† 31833	Fredonia, 300	H 5
36445	Frisco City, 1,286	D 8
36539	Fruitdale, 275	B 8
36446	Fulton, 628	C 7
35068	Fultondale, 5,163	E 3
36741	Furman, 300	E 6
35971	Fyffe, 311	G 2
* 35901	Gadsden⊙, 53,928	G 2
	Gadsden, ‡94,144	G 2
36540	Gainestown, 300	C 8
35464	Gainesville, 255	B 5
35972	Gallant, 475	F 2
36038	Gantt, 380	F 8
35070	Garden City, 745	E 2
35071	Gardendale, 6,502	E 3
36340	Geneva⊙, 4,398	G 8
36033	Georgiana, 2,148	E 7
35974	Geraldine, 610	G 2
35559	Glen Allen, 276	C 3
35905	Glencoe, 2,901	G 3
36034	Glenwood, 378	F 7
† 36024	Good Hope, 840	E 2
35072	Goodwater, 2,172	F 4
35466	Gordo, 1,991	C 4
36343	Gordon, 312	H 8
35561	Gorgas, 500	D 3
36035	Goshen, 279	F 7
36450	Gosport, 400	C 7
36036	Grady, 298	F 7
36541	Grand Bay, 950	B 10
35747	Grant, 382	F 1
35073	Graysville, 3,182	D 3
35074	Green Pond, 500	D 4
36744	Greensboro⊙, 3,371	C 5

(continued on following page)

ALABAMA

SCALE
0 5 10   20   30   40 MI.

0 5 10   20   30   40 KM.

State Capitals............⊛
County Seats.............⊗

© C.S. HAMMOND & CO., N.Y.

Railroad tracks form tangled spider webs leading to voracious steel furnaces. Native coal, iron ore and limestone are delivered to Ensley (Birmingham), Alabama plant.

Topography

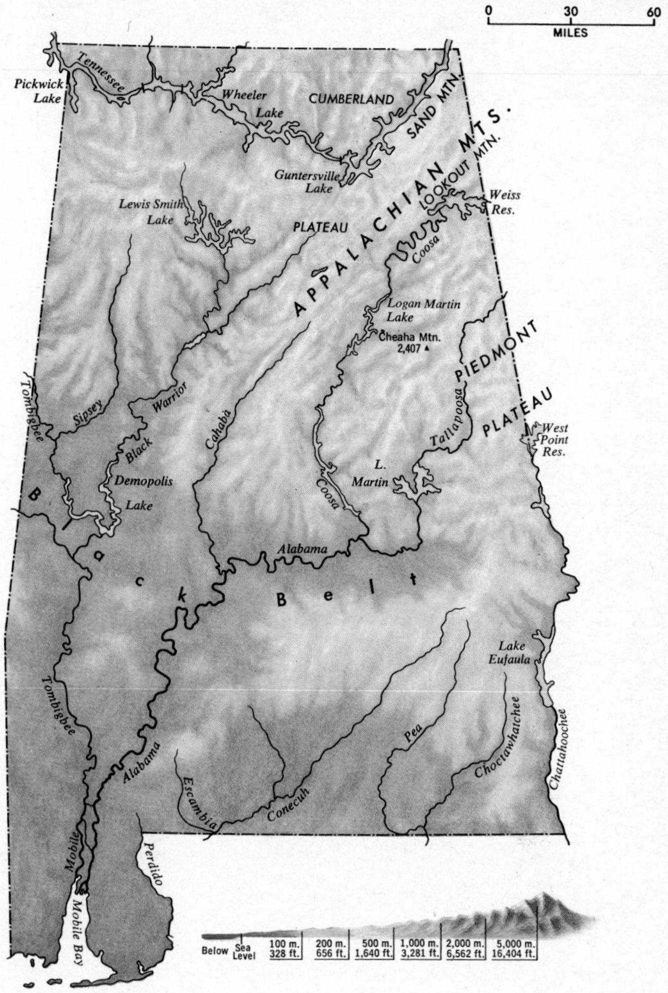

7 Greenville⊙, 8,033 E 7
1 Grove Hill⊙, 1,825 C 7
5 Groveoak, 275 F 2
3 Guin, 2,220 C 3
2 Gulf Shores, 909 C 10
6 Guntersville⊙, 6,491 F 2
8 Gurley, 647 F 1
4 Hackleburg, 726 C 2
5 Haleyville, 4,134 C 2
9 Halsell, 250 B 6
0 Hamilton⊙, 3,088 C 2
7 Hanceville, 2,027 E 2
9 Hardaway, 300 G 6
8 Harpersville, 639 F 4
4 Hartford, 2,648 G 8
0 Hartselle, 7,355 E 2
9 Harvest, 500 E 1
8 Hatchechubbee, 250 H 6
2 Hatton, 950 D 1
0 Hayneville⊙, 473 E 6
5 Headland, 2,545 H 8
4 Heflin⊙, 2,872 G 3
0 Helena, 1,110 E 4
8 Henagar, 812 G 1
9 Higdon, 450 G 1
1 Hissop, 250 F 5
1 Hobson City, 1,124 G 3
3 Hokes Bluff, 2,133 G 3
2 Hollins, 600 F 4
3 Holly Pond, 325 E 2
1 Hollytree, 245 F 1
2 Hollywood, 301 G 1
1 Holt, 2,000 D 4
9 Holy Trinity, 400 H 6
9 Homewood, 21,245 E 4
6 Hoover, 1,393 E 4
3 Hope Hull, 975 F 6
0 Horton, 271 F 2
0 Hueytown, 7,095 D 4
1 Huntsville⊙, 137,802 E 1
Huntsville, ‡228,339 E 1
7 Hurricane, 300 C 9
0 Hurtsboro, 937 H 6
2 Hybart, 250 D 7
1 Ider, 500 G 1
0 Irondale, 3,166 E 3
0 Jachin, 250 B 6
5 Jackson, 5,957 C 8
1 Jacksons Gap, 450 G 5
5 Jacksonville, 7,715 G 3
1 Jasper⊙, 10,798 D 3
5 Jefferson, 500 C 6
5 Jemison, 1,423 E 5
8 Jenifer, 300 G 3
6 Johns, 241 D 4
7 Joppa, 350 E 2
9 Kellyton, 500 F 5
4 Kennedy, 415 B 3
5 Kent, 500 G 5
5 Killen, 683 D 1

35091 Kimberly, 847 E 3
36746 Kimbrough, 250 C 6
36453 Kinston, 540 F 8
35469 Knoxville, 500 C 4
35754 Laceys Spring, 500 E 1
36862 Lafayette⊙, 3,530 H 5
36747 Lamison, 275 C 6
36863 Lanett, 6,908 H 5
36864 Langdale, 2,235 H 5
35755 Langston, 250 G 1
36046 Lapine, 300 F 7
† 35768 Larkinsville, 425 F 1
36911 Lavaca, 550 B 6
35094 Leeds, 6,991 E 3
35646 Leighton, 1,231 D 1
36548 Leroy, 350 B 8
36047 Letohatchee, 250 E 6
35648 Lexington, 278 D 1
36549 Lillian, 600 D 10
35096 Lincoln, 1,127 F 3
36748 Linden⊙, 2,697 C 6
36266 Lineville, 1,984 G 4
35020 Lipscomb, 3,225 E 4
36912 Lisman, 628 B 6
36550 Little River, 400 C 8
† 36876 Little Shawmut, 2,682 H 5
35654 Littleville, 858 C 1
35470 Livingston⊙, 2,358 B 5
36865 Loachapoka, 400 G 5
36455 Lockhart, 698 F 8
† 35045 Lomax, 300 E 5
36048 Louisville, 785 G 7
36751 Lower Peach Tree, 950 C 7
36551 Loxley, 859 C 9
36049 Luverne⊙, 2,440 F 7
35575 Lynn, 286 C 2
35758 Madison, 3,086 E 1
36754 Magnolia, 350 C 6
36555 Magnolia Springs, 726 C 10
36556 Malcolm, 300 B 8
† 35501 Manchester, 400 D 3
† 36586 Manila, 300 C 7
36750 Maplesville, 596 E 5
35112 Margaret, 685 F 3
† 35616 Margerum, 250 B 1
36756 Marion⊙, 4,289 D 5
36759 Marion Junction, 300 D 6
† 36801 Marvyn, 300 H 6
35111 McCalla, 450 E 4
36552 McCullough, 500 D 8
36553 McIntosh, 600 B 8
36456 McKenzie, 491 E 7
36753 McWilliams, 525 D 7
36913 Melvin, 300 B 7
35984 Mentone, 407 G 1
35759 Meridianville, 950 F 1
36458 Mexia, 250 D 8
35228 Midfield, 6,399 E 4
36350 Midland City, 1,172 H 8
36053 Midway, 558 H 6

† 35150 Mignon, 1,726 F 4
36054 Millbrook, 800 F 6
36760 Millers Ferry, 300 D 6
35576 Millport, 1,070 B 3
36558 Millry, 911 B 7
36761 Minter, 450 D 6
* 36601 Mobile⊙, 190,026 B 9
Mobile, ‡376,690 B 9
36460 Monroeville⊙, 4,846 D 7
† 35804 Monrovia, 500 E 1
35115 Montevallo, 3,719 E 4
* 36101 Montgomery (cap.)⊙, 133,386 F 6
Montgomery, ‡201,325 F 6
36559 Montrose, 900 C 9
† 35125 Moody, 504 F 3
35116 Morris, 519 E 3
36762 Morvin, 350 C 7
35650 Moulton⊙, 2,470 D 2
35474 Moundville, 996 C 5
† 35957 Mountainboro, 311 F 2
35223 Mountain Brook, 19,474 E 4
† 36047 Mount Carmel, 400 F 6
36057 Mount Meigs, 250 F 6
36560 Mount Vernon, 1,079 B 8
† 36012 Mount Willing, 364 E 6
36268 Munford, 950 F 3
35660 Muscle Shoals, 6,907 C 1
36763 Myrtlewood, 334 C 6
36764 Nanafalia, 250 B 6
35578 Nauvoo, 265 D 3
36765 Newbern, 286 C 5
36351 New Brockton, 1,374 G 8
35760 New Hope, 1,300 F 1
35761 New Market, 600 F 1
35010 New Site, 378 G 4
36352 Newton, 1,865 G 8
36353 Newville, 465 H 8
35476 Northport, 9,435 C 4
36866 Notasulga, 833 G 5
† 35014 Nottingham, 400 F 4
35579 Oakman, 853 D 3
35120 Odenville, 533 F 3
36271 Ohatchee, 445 G 3
35121 Oneonta⊙, 4,390 E 3
36801 Opelika⊙, 19,027 H 5
36467 Opp, 6,493 F 8
36561 Orange Beach, 300 C 10
36767 Orrville, 362 D 6
35763 Owens Cross Roads, 767 E 1
36201 Oxford, 4,361 G 3
36360 Ozark⊙, 13,555 G 8
35477 Panola, 300 B 5
36370 Pansey, 300 H 8
35580 Parrish, 1,742 D 3
35124 Pelham, 931 E 4
35125 Pell City⊙, 5,381 F 3
36916 Pennington, 276 B 6
36562 Perdido, 325 C 8
36530 Perdido Beach, 300 C 10

36471 Peterman, 750 D 7
35478 Peterson, 1,040 D 4
36867 Phenix City⊙, 25,281 H 6
35581 Phil Campbell, 1,230 C 2
36272 Piedmont, 5,063 G 3
36371 Pinckard, 609 G 8
36768 Pine Apple, 347 E 7
36769 Pine Hill, 697 C 7
36065 Pine Level, 300 F 6
35126 Pinson, 2,500 E 3
35765 Pisgah, 519 G 1
36871 Pittsview, 400 H 6
36758 Plantersville, 550 E 5
36564 Point Clear, 850 C 10
36067 Prattville⊙, 13,116 E 6
36610 Prichard, 41,578 B 9
35766 Princeton, 250 F 1
36772 Putnam, 305 B 6
† 36507 Rabun, 300 C 8
35131 Ragland, 1,239 F 3
35901 Rainbow City, 3,107 F 3
35986 Rainsville, 2,099 G 2
35480 Ralph, 500 C 4
36069 Ramer, 750 F 6
36273 Ranburne, 371 H 3
36473 Range, 275 D 8
35582 Red Bay, 2,464 B 2
36474 Red Level, 616 E 8
† 35954 Reece City, 496 G 2
35481 Reform, 1,893 C 4
† 36720 Rehoboth, 300 D 6
† 35160 Renfroe, 400 F 4
36475 Repton, 277 D 8
† 35203 Republic, 500 E 3
36918 Riderwood, 400 B 6
36476 River Falls, 580 E 8
35135 Riverside, 351 F 3
36872 River View, 1,109 H 5
36274 Roanoke, 5,251 H 4
36567 Robertsdale, 2,078 C 9
35136 Rockford⊙, 603 F 5
36274 Rock Mills, 800 H 4
35652 Rogersville, 950 D 1
† 35020 Roosevelt City, 3,663 E 4
35653 Russellville⊙, 7,814 C 2
36071 Rutledge, 353 F 7
35137 Saginaw, 300 E 4
35138 Saint Bernard, 896 E 2
† 35146 Saint Clair Springs, 300 F 3
36568 Saint Elmo, 650 B 10
36569 Saint Stephens, 400 B 7
36874 Salem, 475 H 5
36570 Salitpa, 500 C 7
36477 Samson, 2,257 F 8
36478 Sanford, 256 F 8
35583 Saragossa, 300 D 3
36571 Saraland, 7,840 B 9
36775 Sardis, 300 E 6
36775 Sardis, 368 F 2
36572 Satsuma, 2,035 B 9

35139 Sayre, 700 E 3
35768 Scottsboro⊙, 9,324 F 1
36875 Seale, 400 H 6
35771 Section, 702 G 1
36701 Selma⊙, 27,379 E 6
† 36701 Selmont, 2,270 E 6
36574 Seminole, 275 D 10
36575 Semmes, 800 B 9
36876 Shawmut, 2,181 H 5
35660 Sheffield, 13,115 C 1
35143 Shelby, 500 E 4
36075 Shorter, 500 G 6
36373 Shorterville, 330 H 7
36733 Shortleaf, 253 C 6
36919 Silas, 345 B 7
35144 Siluria, 678 E 4
36576 Silverhill, 552 C 9
† 36268 Silver Run, 250 G 3
35584 Sipsey, 608 D 3
36375 Slocomb, 1,883 G 8
36877 Smiths, 2,500 H 5
35952 Snead, 347 F 2
† 36104 Snowdoun, 250 F 6
36778 Snow Hill, 500 E 7
35901 Southside, 983 F 3
36527 Spanish Fort, 983 C 9
† 35674 Spring Valley, 600 C 1
35146 Springville, 1,153 E 3
35585 Spruce Pine, 600 C 2
36878 Standing Rock, 500 H 4
36578 Stapleton, 975 C 9
35987 Steele, 798 F 3
35147 Sterrett, 450 F 4
35772 Stevenson, 2,390 G 1
† 35150 Stewartville, 250 F 4
36579 Stockton, 1,400 C 9
35586 Sulligent, 1,762 B 3
35148 Sumiton, 2,374 D 3
36580 Summerdale, 550 C 10
36780 Sunny South, 250 C 7
36781 Suttle, 256 D 5
36782 Sweet Water, 265 C 6
35149 Sycamore, 800 F 4
35150 Sylacauga, 12,255 F 4
35988 Sylvania, 476 G 1
35160 Talladega⊙, 17,662 F 4
36078 Tallassee, 4,809 G 5
35671 Tanner, 600 E 1
35217 Tarrant, 6,835 E 3
36582 Theodore, 1,950 B 9
36783 Thomaston, 824 C 6
36784 Thomasville, 3,769 C 7
35171 Thorsby, 944 E 5
35672 Town Creek, 1,203 D 1
35587 Townley, 500 D 3
36921 Toxey, 304 B 7
35172 Trafford, 628 E 3
35673 Trinity, 881 D 1
36081 Troy⊙, 11,482 G 7
35173 Trussville, 2,985 E 3

36479 Tunnel Springs, 300 D 7
35401 Tuscaloosa⊙, 65,773 C 4
Tuscaloosa, ‡116,029 C 4
35674 Tuscumbia⊙, 8,828 C 1
36083 Tuskegee⊙, 11,028 G 6
36088 Tuskegee Institute, 5,800 G 6
36089 Union Springs⊙, 4,324 G 6
36786 Uniontown, 2,133 D 6
36480 Uriah, 1,200 D 8
35775 Valhermoso Springs, 500 E 2
35989 Valley Head, 470 G 1
35176 Vandiver, 700 F 4
36091 Verbena, 350 E 5
35592 Vernon⊙, 2,190 B 3
35216 Vestavia Hills, 8,311 E 4
35593 Vina, 366 B 2
35178 Vincent, 1,419 F 4
35179 Vinemont, 480 E 2
36481 Vredenburgh, 622 D 7
36276 Wadley, 626 G 4
36585 Wagarville, 350 B 8
36586 Walker Springs, 500 C 7
35180 Warrior, 2,621 E 3
35677 Waterloo, 262 B 1
35182 Wattsville, 500 F 3
36879 Waverly, 247 G 5
36277 Weaver, 2,091 G 3
36376 Webb, 354 H 8
36278 Wedowee⊙, 842 H 4
† 35129 Wegra-Flat Creek, 1,066 D 3
35183 Weogufka, 350 F 4
35184 West Blocton, 1,172 D 4
† 36201 West End-Cobb Town, 5,515 G 3
35185 Westover, 1,400 E 4
36092 Wetumpka⊙, 3,786 F 5
36482 Whatley, 500 C 7
† 35618 Wheeler, 300 D 1
† 36040 White Hall, 300 E 6
† 36862 White Plains, 350 G 3
† 35094 Whites Chapel, 334 F 3
36923 Whitfield, 500 B 6
† 36352 Wicksburg, 400 G 8
36587 Wilmer, 720 B 9
35186 Wilsonville, 659 E 4
35187 Wilton, 573 E 4
35594 Winfield, 3,292 C 3
35188 Woodstock, 320 D 4
35776 Woodville, 322 F 1
36924 Yantley, 500 B 6
36789 Yellow Bluff, 350 C 7
36925 York, 3,044 B 6

⊙ County seat.
‡ Population of metropolitan area.
† Zip of nearest p.o.
* Multiple zips

196 Alaska

Agriculture, Industry and Resources

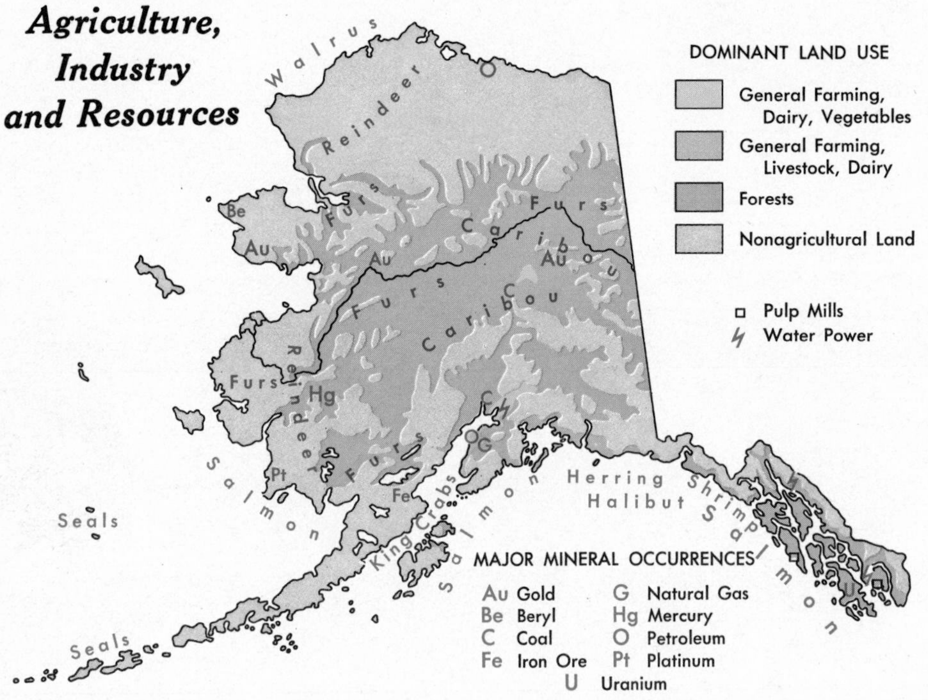

DOMINANT LAND USE

- General Farming, Dairy, Vegetables
- General Farming, Livestock, Dairy
- Forests
- Nonagricultural Land

▫ Pulp Mills

⚡ Water Power

MAJOR MINERAL OCCURRENCES

Au	Gold	G	Natural Gas
Be	Beryl	Hg	Mercury
C	Coal	O	Petroleum
Fe	Iron Ore	Pt	Platinum
U	Uranium		

Topography

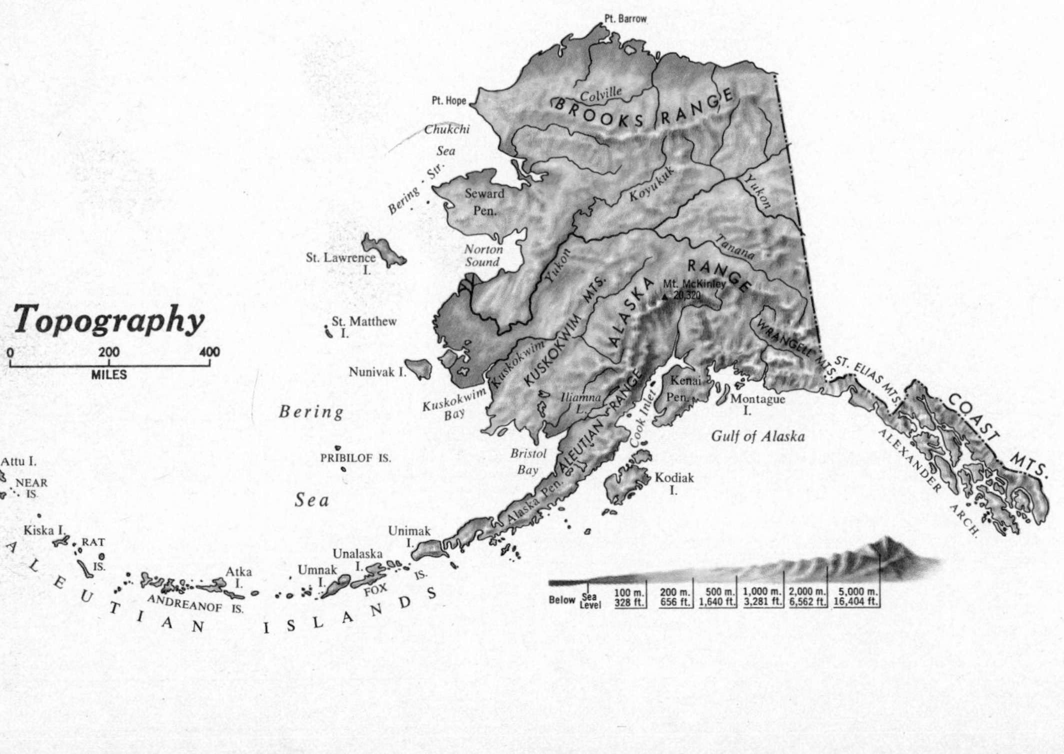

MILES
0 — 200 — 400

Below Sea Level | 100 m. 328 ft. | 200 m. 656 ft. | 500 m. 1,640 ft. | 1,000 m. 3,281 ft. | 2,000 m. 6,562 ft. | 5,000 m. 16,404 ft.

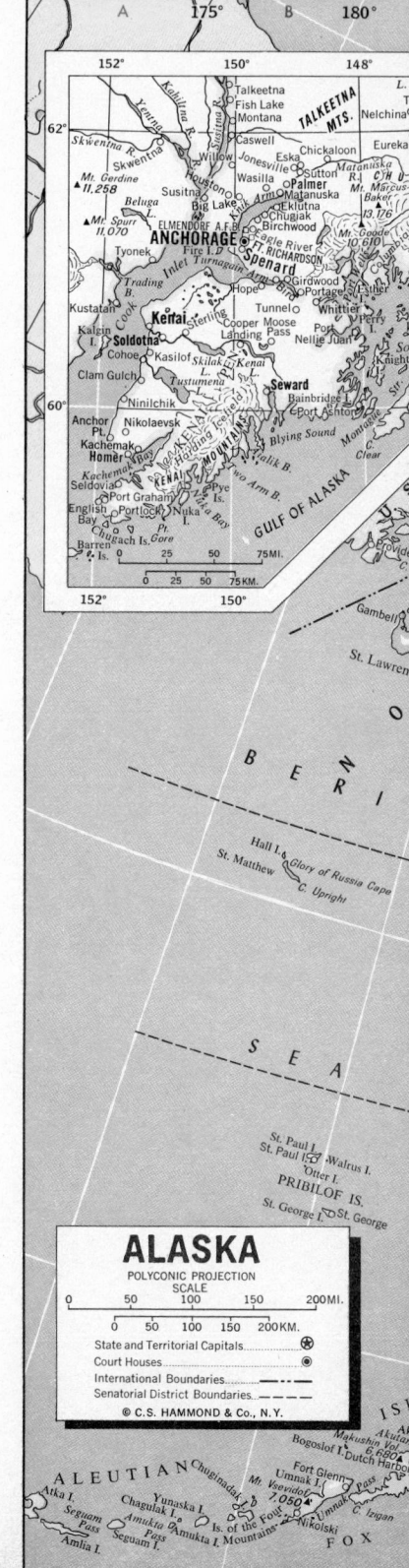

ALASKA

POLYCONIC PROJECTION

SCALE
0 — 50 — 100 — 150 — 200 MI.
0 — 50 — 100 — 150 — 200 KM.

State and Territorial Capitals ⊗
Court Houses ⊙
International Boundaries
Senatorial District Boundaries

© C.S. HAMMOND & Co., N.Y.

Arthur A. Twomey — Shostal Associates

Despite its deceptively calm exterior, the Vaughan Lewis Glacier is actually a river of ice, hundreds of feet deep, flowing steadily. Ridges (eskers) are formed by streams under the ice.

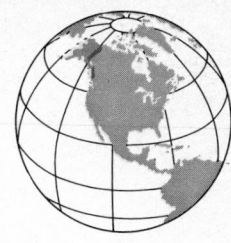

AREA 586,412 sq. mi.
POPULATION 302,173
CAPITAL Juneau
LARGEST CITY Anchorage
HIGHEST POINT Mt. McKinley 20,320 ft.
SETTLED IN 1801
ADMITTED TO UNION January 3, 1959
POPULAR NAME Great Land
STATE FLOWER Forget-me-not
STATE BIRD Willow Ptarmigan

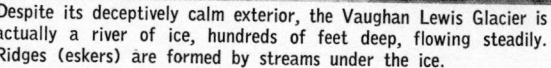

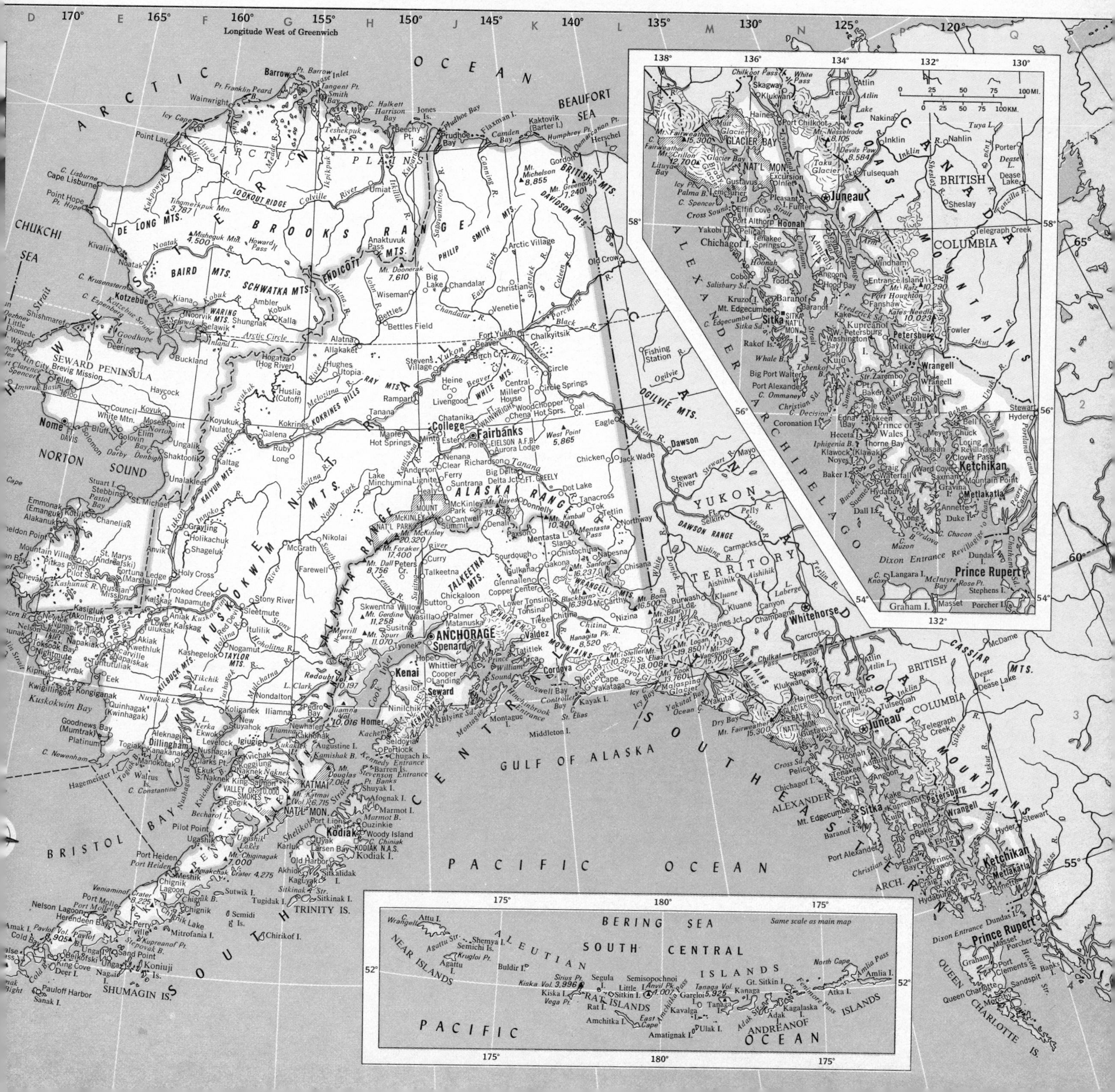

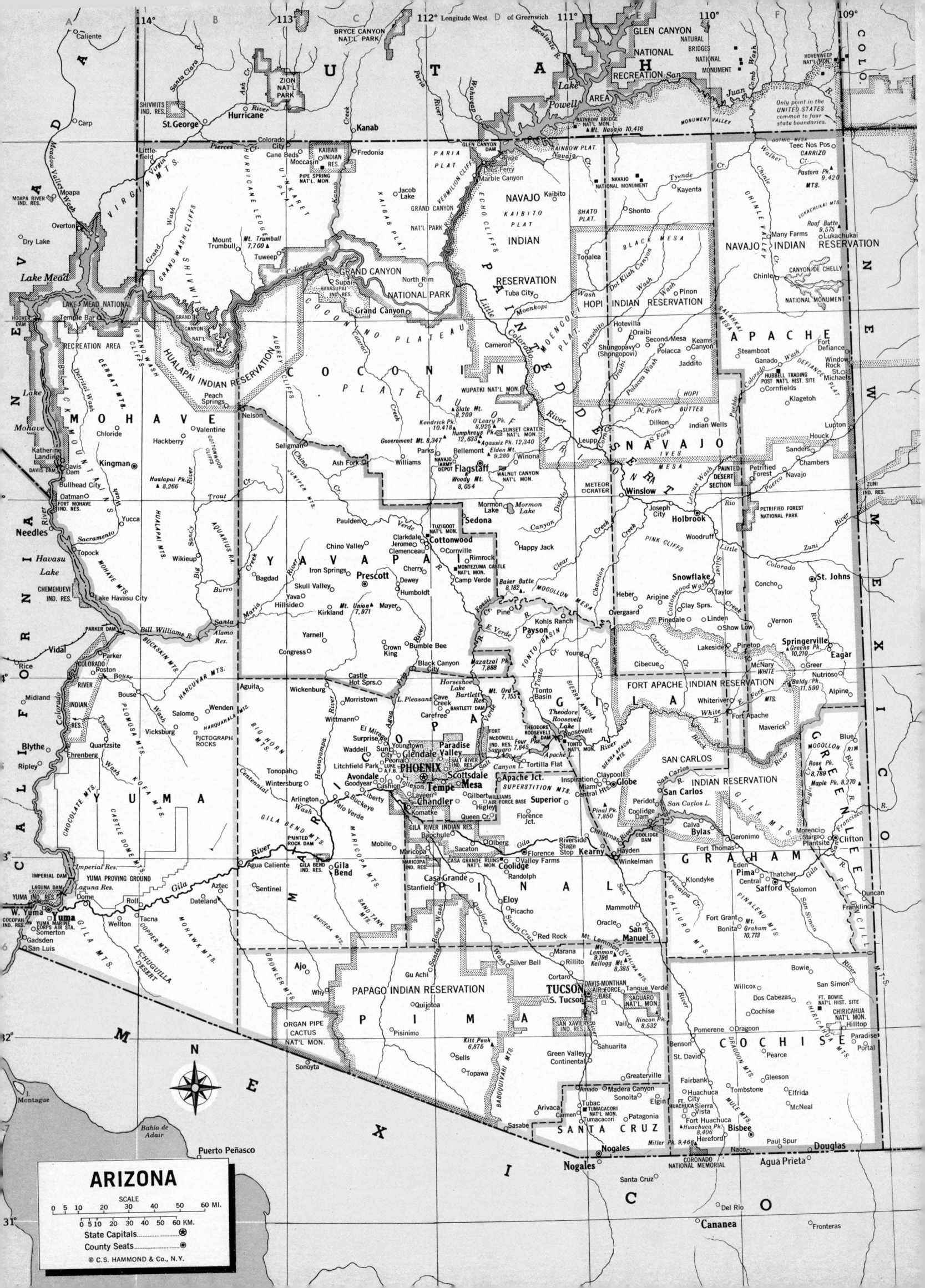

Topography

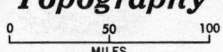

0   50   100
MILES

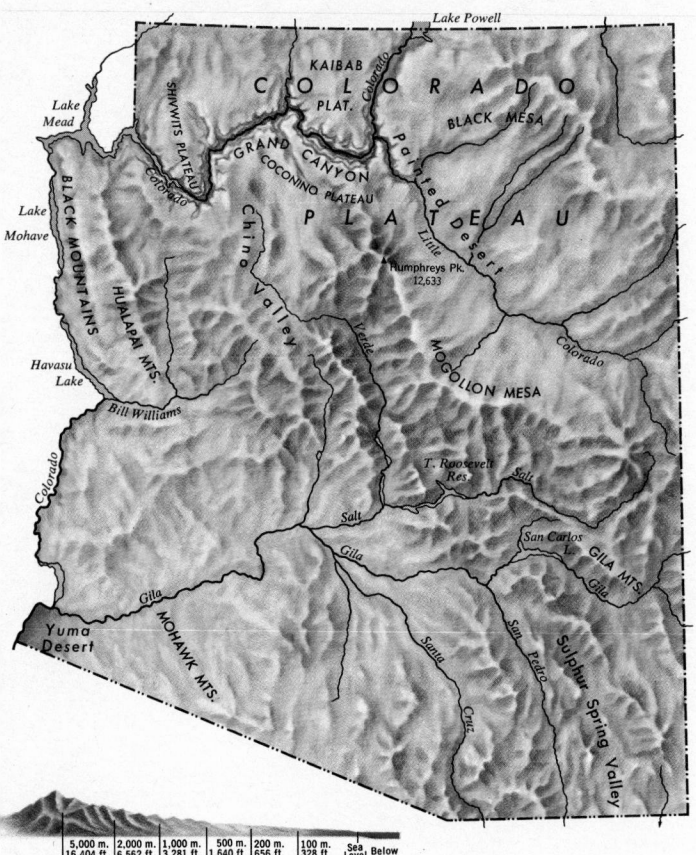

5,000 m. | 2,000 m. | 1,000 m. | 500 m. | 200 m. | 100 m. | Sea | Below
16,404 ft. | 6,562 ft. | 3,281 ft. | 1,640 ft. | 656 ft. | 328 ft. | Level |

AREA 113,909 sq. mi.
POPULATION 1,772,482
CAPITAL Phoenix
LARGEST CITY Phoenix
HIGHEST POINT Humphreys Pk. 12,633 ft.
SETTLED IN 1580
ADMITTED TO UNION February 14, 1912
POPULAR NAME Grand Canyon State
STATE FLOWER Saguaro Cactus Blossom
STATE BIRD Cactus Wren

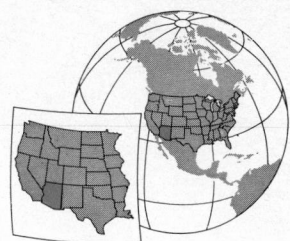

Agriculture, Industry and Resources

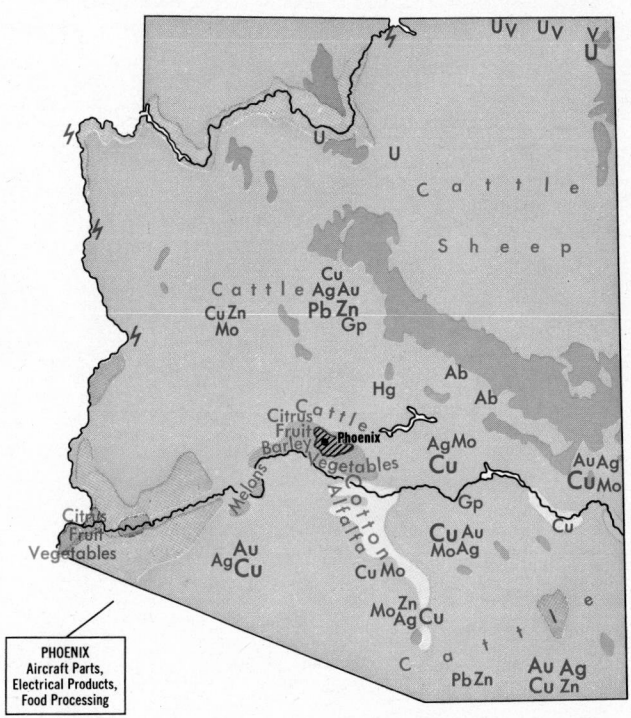

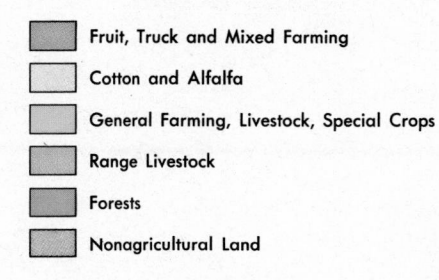

PHOENIX
Aircraft Parts,
Electrical Products,
Food Processing

MAJOR MINERAL OCCURRENCES

Ab	Asbestos	Gp	Gypsum	U	Uranium
Ag	Silver	Hg	Mercury	V	Vanadium
Au	Gold	Mo	Molybdenum	Zn	Zinc
Cu	Copper	Pb	Lead		

DOMINANT LAND USE

- Fruit, Truck and Mixed Farming
- Cotton and Alfalfa
- General Farming, Livestock, Special Crops
- Range Livestock
- Forests
- Nonagricultural Land

⚡ Water Power

▨ Major Industrial Areas

COUNTIES

e, 32,298	F 3
se, 61,910	F 7
ino, 48,326	C 3
9,255	E 5
m, 16,578	E 6
ee, 10,330	F 5
pa, 967,522	C 5
e, 25,857	A 3
E, 47,715	E 3
351,667	D 6
67,916	D 6
Cruz, 13,966	E 7
ai, 36,733	C 4
60,827	A 5

CITIES and TOWNS

Name/Pop.	Key
Agua Caliente, 30	B 6
Aguila, 450	B 5
Ajo, 5,881	C 6
Alpine, 450	F 5
Amado, 75	D 7
Apache Junction, 2,390	D 5
Aripine, 25	E 4
Arivaca, 165	D 7
Arlington, 950	C 5
Ash Fork, 800	C 3
Avondale, 6,304	C 5
Aztec, 20	B 6
Bagdad, 2,079	B 4
Bapchule, 300	D 5
Bellemont, 6	D 3
Benson, 2,839	E 7
Bisbee⊙, 8,328	F 7
Black Canyon City, 600	C 4
Blue, 50	F 5
Bonita, 20	E 6
Bouse, 200	A 5
Bowie, 600	F 6
Buckeye, 2,599	C 5
Bullhead City, 2,900	A 3
Bumble Bee, 15	C 4
Bylas, 1,125	E 6
Calva, 10	E 5
Cameron, 600	D 3
Camp Verde, 1,500	D 4
Cane Beds, 30	B 2
Carefree, 350	D 5
Carmen, 200	D 7
Casa Grande, 10,536	D 6
Cashion, 2,705	C 5
Castle Hot Springs, 50	C 5
Cave Creek, 300	D 5
Central, 300	F 6
Central Heights, 2,289	E 5
Chambers, 500	F 3

85224 Chandler, 13,763	D 5
† 86327 Cherry, 20	C 4
86503 Chinle, 500	F 2
86323 Chino Valley, 970	C 4
86431 Chloride, 225	A 3
† 85292 Christmas, 201	E 5
85901 Cibecue, 100	E 4
86024 Clarkdale, 892	C 4
85532 Claypool, 2,245	E 5
† 85934 Clay Springs, 225	E 4
† 86326 Clemenceau, 300	C 4
85533 Clifton⊙, 5,087	F 5
85606 Cochise, 150	F 6
86021 Colorado City, 350	B 2
85924 Concho, 100	F 4
85332 Congress, 350	C 4
† 85640 Continental, 250	D 7
85228 Coolidge, 4,651	D 6
† 85542 Coolidge Dam, 42	E 5
† 86505 Cornfields, 200	F 3
86325 Cornville, 425	D 4
85230 Cortaro, 75	D 6
86326 Cottonwood, 2,815	D 4
86333 Crown King, 100	C 4
85333 Dateland, 100	B 6
† 86430 Davis Dam, 125	A 3
86327 Dewey, 100	C 4
† 86047 Dilkon, 90	E 3
† 85364 Dome, 48	A 6
† 85643 Dos Cabezas, 30	F 6
85607 Douglas, 12,462	F 7
85609 Dragoon, 150	F 6
85534 Duncan, 773	F 6
85925 Eagar, 1,279	F 4
85535 Eden, 89	E 6
85334 Ehrenburg, 93	A 5
† 85617 Elfrida, 700	F 7
† 85637 Elgin, 247	E 7
85335 El Mirage, 3,258	C 5
85231 Eloy, 5,381	D 6
85612 Fairbank, 100	E 7
86001 Flagstaff⊙, 26,117	D 3
85232 Florence⊙, 2,173	D 5
85233 Florence Junction, 35	D 5
85926 Fort Apache, 500	F 4
86504 Fort Defiance, 900	F 3
85643 Fort Grant, 240	F 6
85613 Fort Huachuca, 159	E 7
85536 Fort Thomas, 450	E 6
85534 Franklin, 300	F 6
86022 Fredonia, 798	C 2
85336 Gadsden, 250	A 6
86505 Ganado, 300	F 3
† 85536 Geronimo, 25	E 6
85337 Gila Bend, 1,795	C 6
85234 Gilbert, 1,971	D 5
† 85617 Gleeson, 15	F 7
85301 Glendale⊙, 36,228	C 5
85501 Globe⊙, 7,333	E 5

85338 Goodyear, 2,140	C 5
86023 Grand Canyon, 1,011	C 2
† 85637 Greaterville, 15	E 7
85614 Green Valley, 5,971	D 7
85927 Greer, 60	F 4
85634 Gu-Achi, 339	C 6
86401 Hackberry, 250	B 3
86024 Happy Jack, 50	D 4
85235 Hayden, 1,283	E 5
85928 Heber, 750	E 4
85615 Hereford, 10	E 7
85236 Higley, 500	D 5
86301 Hillside, 100	B 4
† 85632 Hilltop, 9	F 6
86025 Holbrook⊙, 4,759	E 3
86030 Hotevilla, 600	E 3
86506 Houck, 325	F 3
85616 Huachuca City, 1,233	E 7
86329 Humboldt, 424	C 4
86031 Indian Wells, 150	E 3
85537 Inspiration, 500	D 5
86330 Iron Springs, 175	C 4
86022 Jacob Lake, 16	C 2
† 86025 Jeddito, 20	E 3
86331 Jerome, 290	C 4
86032 Joseph City, 650	E 4
86044 Kaibito, 275	D 2
† 86401 Katherine Landing, 102	A 3
86033 Kayenta, 500	E 2
86034 Keams Canyon, 400	E 3
85237 Kearny, 2,829	E 5
86401 Kingman⊙, 7,312	A 3
86332 Kirkland, 100	C 4
† 86505 Klagetoh, 200	F 3
85643 Klondyke, 86	E 6
85538 Kohls Ranch, 100	D 4
† 85339 Komatke, 300	C 5
86403 Lake Havasu City, 5,700	A 4
85929 Lakeside, 700	E 4
85339 Laveen, 800	C 5
† 86036 Lees Ferry, 10	D 2
86035 Leupp, 150	E 3
† 85326 Liberty, 150	C 5
† 85901 Linden, 50	E 4
85340 Litchfield Park, 1,664	C 5
86432 Littlefield, 40	B 2
86507 Lukachukai, 350	F 2
86508 Lupton, 250	F 3
85341 Lukeville, 50	C 7
† 85637 Madera Canyon, 75	E 7
85618 Mammoth, 1,953	E 6
86503 Many Farms, 250	F 2
85238 Marana, 2,900	D 6
86036 Marble Canyon, 6	D 2
85239 Maricopa, 750	C 5
† 85920 Maverick, 50	F 5
86333 Mayer, 810	C 4
85930 McNary, 950	F 4
85617 McNeal, 100	F 7

(continued on following page)

200 Arizona

(continued)

Indigo-blue Lake Mead is surrounded by color-streaked cliffs and ranges, set off by the bright concrete of Arizona's Hoover Dam. One of the world's largest man-made lakes, Lake Mead provides water storage, dependable water supply and water sports.

* 85201 Mesa, 62,853...........D 5	85624 Patagonia, 630............E 7	85242 Queen Creek, 600..........D 5
85539 Miami, 3,394..............E 5	86334 Paulden, 4................C 4	† 85634 Quijotoa, 107............C 6
† 85239 Mobile, 100.............C 5	† 85607 Paul Spur, 34...........F 7	85243 Randolph, 350.............D 6
86022 Moccasin, 60.............C 2	85541 Payson, 1,490............D 4	85333 Sentinel, 20.............B 6
85540 Morenci, 950.............F 5	86434 Peach Springs, 525.......B 3	85245 Red Rock, 100............D 6
86038 Mormon Lake, 20..........D 4	85625 Pearce, 300..............F 7	85246 Rillito, 400.............D 6
85342 Morristown, 250..........C 5	85345 Peoria, 4,792............C 5	86335 Rimrock, 217.............D 4
85619 Mount Lemmon, 75.........E 6	85542 Peridot, 950.............E 5	85237 Riverside Stage Stop, 418..D 5
† 84770 Mount Trumbull, 14......B 2	86025 Petrified Forest, 80......F 3	85347 Roll, 700...............A 6
85620 Naco, 750................E 7	* 85001 Phoenix (cap.)⊙, 581,562..C 5	85545 Roosevelt, 125...........D 5
86509 Navajo, 100..............F 3	Phoenix, ‡967,522.......C 5	85247 Sacaton, 300............D 5
† 86434 Nelson, 39.............B 3	85241 Picacho, 1,200...........D 6	85546 Safford⊙, 5,333..........F 6
85621 Nogales⊙, 8,946..........E 7	85543 Pima, 1,184..............F 6	85629 Sahuarita, 200...........E 7
86022 North Rim, 2.............C 2	85544 Pine, 800...............D 4	85630 Saint David, 1,250.......E 7
85932 Nutrioso, 67.............F 5	85934 Pinedale, 86.............E 4	85936 Saint Johns, 1,320........F 4
86433 Oatman, 175.............A 3	85935 Pinetop, 950.............F 4	86511 Saint Michaels, 250.......F 3
† 85247 Olberg, 65.............D 5	86510 Pinon, 100..............E 2	85348 Salome, 684.............B 5
85623 Oracle, 1,500............E 6	85634 Pisinimo, 187............C 6	85550 San Carlos, 2,542.........E 5
86039 Oraibi, 600..............E 3	† 85540 Plantsite, 1,077........F 5	86512 Sanders, 420.............F 3
85933 Overgaard, 300...........E 4	86042 Polacca, 500.............E 3	85349 San Luis, 280............A 6
86040 Page, 1,439..............D 2	86627 Pomerene, 365............E 6	85631 San Manuel, 4,332.........E 6
85343 Palo Verde, 500..........C 5	85632 Portal, 72...............F 7	85632 San Simon, 400...........F 6
85253 Paradise Valley, 7,155....D 5	85371 Poston, 500.............A 4	85633 Sasabe, 50..............D 7
85344 Parker, 1,948............A 4	86301 Prescott⊙, 13,030........C 4	85251 Scottsdale, 67,823.......D 5
86001 Parks, 175..............C 3	85346 Quartzsite, 255..........A 5	86043 Second Mesa, 30..........E 3
		86336 Sedona, 2,022...........D 4

86337 Seligman, 950............B 3	86514 Teec Nos Pos, 550.........F 2	85357 Wenden, 245.............F 5
85634 Sells, 1,245.............D 7	85281 Tempe, 62,907...........D 5	† 85364 West Yuma, 5,552........A 6
† 85333 Sentinel, 20...........B 6	86443 Temple Bar, 84...........A 2	85941 Whiteriver, 900..........F 4
86044 Shonto, 700..............E 2	85552 Thatcher, 2,320..........F 6	85321 Why, 65.
85901 Show Low, 2,285..........F 4	85353 Tolleson, 3,881..........C 5	85358 Wickenburg, 2,698........C 5
† 86043 Shungopavy (Shongopovi),	85638 Tombstone, 1,241.........F 7	85360 Wikieup, 150............B 3
570............E 3	86044 Tonalea, 125.............E 2	85643 Willcox, 2,568.
85635 Sierra Vista, 6,689.......E 7	85354 Tonopah, 54.............B 5	86046 Williams, 2,386..........C 3
85270 Silver Bell, 900.........D 6	85553 Tonto Basin, 69..........D 5	86515 Window Rock, 600.........F 2
85937 Snowflake, 1,833.........E 4	85639 Topawa, 500.............D 7	85292 Winkelman, 974...........E 6
85551 Solomon, 700............F 6	86436 Topock, 325.............A 4	86047 Winslow, 8,066.
85350 Somerton, 2,225..........A 6	85290 Tortilla Flat, 37.........D 5	† 86001 Winona, 25.
85637 Sonoita, 50.............E 7	85640 Tubac, 140.............E 7	85322 Wintersburg, 400.
85713 South Tucson, 6,220.......D 6	85741 Tuba City, 2,500.........D 2	85361 Wittmann, 600.
85938 Springerville, 1,038......F 4	86045 Tuba City, 2,500.........D 2	85942 Woodruff, 120.
85272 Stanfield, 150...........C 6	85272 Tumacacori, 100..........D 7	85362 Yarnell, 800.
† 85540 Stargo, 1,194..........F 5	85640 Tumacacori, 100..........D 7	† 86301 Yava, 40.
† 85505 Steamboat, 100.........F 3	† 84770 Tuweep, 14............B 2	85554 Young, 197.
85351 Sun City, 13,670.........D 5	85641 Vail, 175..............E 6	85363 Youngtown, 1,886.
86435 Supai, 190..............C 2	85291 Valentine, 120..........B 3	86438 Yucca, 250.
85273 Superior, 4,975..........D 5	85291 Valley Farms, 240........D 6	85364 Yuma⊙, 29,007.
85352 Tacna, 950..............B 6	85940 Vernon, 75.............F 4	
† 85701 Tanque Verde, 850.......E 6	* 85348 Vicksburg, 16..........B 5	⊙ County seat.
85939 Taylor, 888.............E 4	85355 Waddell, 100............C 5	‡ Population of metropolitan area
	85356 Wellton, 900............A 6	† Zip of nearest p.o.
		* Multiple zips

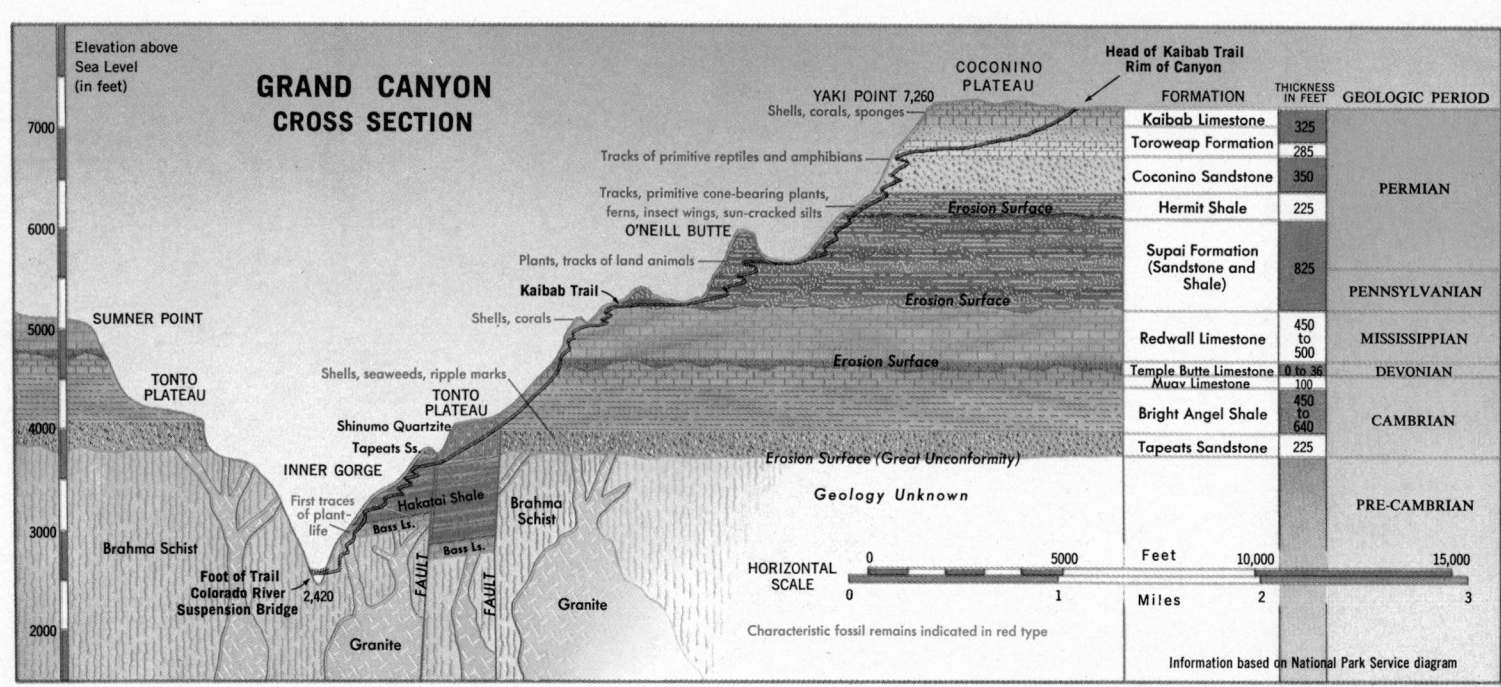

GRAND CANYON CROSS SECTION

Elevation above Sea Level (in feet)

FORMATION	THICKNESS IN FEET	GEOLOGIC PERIOD
Kaibab Limestone	325	PERMIAN
Toroweap Formation	285	PERMIAN
Coconino Sandstone	350	PERMIAN
Hermit Shale	225	PERMIAN
Supai Formation (Sandstone and Shale)	825	PENNSYLVANIAN
Redwall Limestone	450 to 500	MISSISSIPPIAN
Temple Butte Limestone	0 to 36	DEVONIAN
Muav Limestone	100	CAMBRIAN
Bright Angel Shale	450 to 640	CAMBRIAN
Tapeats Sandstone	225	CAMBRIAN
		PRE-CAMBRIAN

Head of Kaibab Trail Rim of Canyon

COCONINO PLATEAU

YAKI POINT 7,260 — Shells, corals, sponges

Tracks of primitive reptiles and amphibians

Tracks, primitive cone-bearing plants, ferns, insect wings, sun-cracked silts

O'NEILL BUTTE

Plants, tracks of land animals

Kaibab Trail

Shells, corals

SUMNER POINT

Erosion Surface

Erosion Surface

Erosion Surface

TONTO PLATEAU

Shells, seaweeds, ripple marks

TONTO PLATEAU

Shinumo Quartzite

Tapeats Ss.

INNER GORGE

Erosion Surface (Great Unconformity)

Geology Unknown

First traces of plant-life

Hakatai Shale

Bass Ls.

Bass Ls.

Brahma Schist

Brahma Schist

Foot of Trail
Colorado River
Suspension Bridge 2,420

FAULT

FAULT

Granite

Granite

Granite

HORIZONTAL SCALE

| 0 | 5000 | Feet | 10,000 | | 15,000 |

| 0 | | 1 | Miles | 2 | 3 |

Characteristic fossil remains indicated in red type

Information based on National Park Service diagram

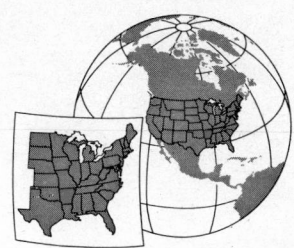

COUNTIES

...sas, 23,347	H 5	
...y, 24,976	G 7	
...r, 15,319	F 1	
...n, 50,476	B 1	
...e, 19,073	D 1	
...ey, 12,778	F 7	
...un, 5,573	E 6	
...ll, 12,301	C 1	
...ot, 18,164	H 7	
...n, 21,537	D 5	
...18,771	K 1	
...urne, 10,349	F 2	
...land, 6,605	F 6	
...mbia, 25,952	E 3	
...ay, 16,805	E 3	
...52,068	J 2	
...ord, 25,677	B 2	
...nden, 48,106	K 3	
...s, 19,783	J 3	
...s, 10,022	E 6	
...a, 18,761	H 6	
...15,157	G 6	
...ner, 31,572	F 3	

Franklin, 11,301	C 2	
Fulton, 7,699	G 1	
Garland, 54,131	D 4	
Grant, 9,711	F 5	
Greene, 24,765	J 1	
Hempstead, 19,308	C 6	
Hot Spring, 21,963	E 5	
Howard, 11,412	C 5	
Independence, 22,723	G 2	
Izard, 7,381	G 1	
Jackson, 20,452	H 2	
Jefferson, 85,329	G 5	
Johnson, 13,630	C 2	
Lafayette, 10,018	C 7	
Lawrence, 16,320	H 1	
Lee, 18,884	J 4	
Lincoln, 12,913	G 6	
Little River, 11,194	B 6	
Logan, 16,789	C 3	
Lonoke, 26,249	G 4	
Madison, 9,453	C 1	
Marion, 7,000	E 1	
Miller, 33,385	C 7	
Mississippi, 62,060	K 2	
Monroe, 15,657	H 4	
Montgomery, 5,821	C 4	

Nevada, 10,111	D 6	
Newton, 5,844	D 2	
Ouachita, 30,896	E 6	
Perry, 5,634	E 4	
Phillips, 40,046	J 5	
Pike, 8,711	C 5	
Poinsett, 26,822	J 2	
Polk, 13,297	B 5	
Pope, 28,607	D 3	
Prairie, 10,249	G 4	
Pulaski, 287,189	F 4	
Randolph, 12,645	H 1	
Saint Francis, 30,799	J 3	
Saline, 36,107	E 4	
Scott, 8,207	B 4	
Searcy, 7,731	E 2	
Sebastian, 79,237	B 3	
Sevier, 11,272	B 6	
Sharp, 8,233	G 1	
Stone, 6,838	F 2	
Union, 45,428	E 7	
Van Buren, 8,275	E 2	
Washington, 77,370	B 2	
White, 39,253	G 3	
Woodruff, 11,566	H 3	
Yell, 14,208	D 3	

AREA 53,104 sq. mi.
POPULATION 1,923,295
CAPITAL Little Rock
LARGEST CITY Little Rock
HIGHEST POINT Magazine Mtn. 2,753 ft.
SETTLED IN 1685
ADMITTED TO UNION June 15, 1836
POPULAR NAME Land of Opportunity; Wonder State
STATE FLOWER Apple Blossom
STATE BIRD Mockingbird

Agriculture, Industry and Resources

DOMINANT LAND USE

- Fruit and Mixed Farming
- Specialized Cotton
- Cotton, General Farming
- Rice, General Farming
- General Farming, Livestock, Truck Farming, Cotton
- Forests
- Swampland, Limited Agriculture

MAJOR MINERAL OCCURRENCES

Al	Bauxite		G	Natural Gas
Ba	Barite		Gp	Gypsum
C	Coal		Mr	Marble
Cl	Clay		O	Petroleum
D	Diamonds		Sp	Soapstone
		Zn	Zinc	

⚡ Water Power   ▨ Major Industrial Areas

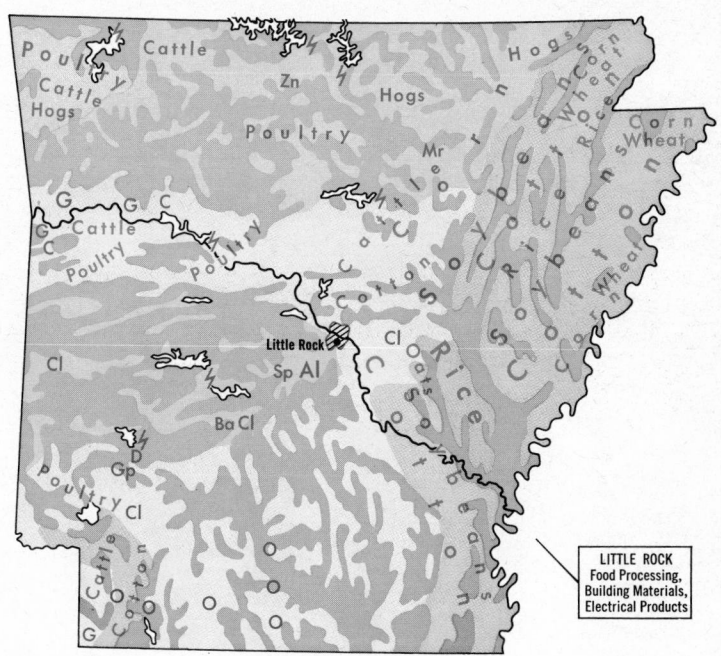

LITTLE ROCK
Food Processing,
Building Materials,
Electrical Products

Soybeans, Arkansas' leading cash crop, valued primarily as high protein food and feed, also has a wide range of uses, including plastics and agricultural sprays.

Eric Carle — Shostal Associates

CITIES and TOWNS

Zip	Name/Pop.	Key
72920	Abbott, 210	B 3
72001	Adona, 204	E 3
72510	Agnos, 130	G 1
72002	Alexander, 297	F 4
72410	Alicia, 246	H 2
72820	Alix, 250	C 3
† 72046	Allport, 307	G 4
72921	Alma, 1,613	B 3
72003	Almyra, 416	H 5
72611	Alpena, 309	D 1
72004	Altheimer, 1,037	G 5
72821	Altus, 418	C 3
72005	Amagon, 136	H 2
71921	Amity, 614	D 5
71922	Antoine, 182	D 5
72822	Appleton, 200	E 3
71923	Arkadelphia◉, 9,841	D 5
71630	Arkansas City◉, 615	H 6
† 72055	Arkansas Post, 15	H 5
72310	Armorel, 300	L 2
71822	Ashdown◉, 3,522	B 6
72513	Ash Flat◉, 211	G 1
72823	Atkins, 2,015	E 3
72311	Aubrey, 351	J 4
72006	Augusta◉, 2,777	H 3
72007	Austin, 236	G 4
72008	Auvergne, 150	H 2
72711	Avoca, 173	B 1
72010	Bald Knob, 2,094	G 3
72631	Banks, 189	F 6
72923	Barling, 1,739	B 3
72312	Barton, 400	J 4
72313	Bassett, 265	K 2
72501	Batesville◉, 7,209	G 2
72411	Bay, 751	J 2
71720	Bearden, 1,272	E 6
72012	Beebe, 2,805	G 3
72014	Beedeville, 144	H 3
71721	Beirne, 140	D 6
72712	Bella Vista, 500	B 1
† 72601	Bellefonte, 300	D 1
72824	Belleville, 379	D 3
71820	Ben Lomond, 155	B 6
72015	Benton◉, 16,499	F 4
72712	Bentonville◉, 5,508	B 1
72615	Bergman, 249	E 1
72616	Berryville◉, 2,271	C 1
† 72764	Bethel Heights, 284	B 1
† 72501	Bethesda, 285	G 2
72016	Bigelow, 258	E 3
72617	Bigflat, 189	F 1
72423	Biggers, 190	H 1
† 72386	Birdsong, 150	K 3
72017	Biscoe, 340	H 4
71929	Bismarck, 200	D 5

Zip	Name/Pop.	Key
72414	Black Oak, 272	K 2
72415	Black Rock, 498	H 1
† 72069	Blackton, 175	H 4
71825	Blevins, 265	C 6
† 72933	Bloomer, 150	B 3
71722	Bluff City, 244	D 6
72827	Bluffton, 198	C 4
72315	Blytheville◉, 24,752	L 2
72926	Boles, 163	B 4
† 71858	Bodcaw, 158	D 6
72921	Bono, 428	J 2
72927	Booneville◉, 3,239	C 3
72020	Bradford, 826	G 3
71826	Bradley, 706	C 7
72928	Branch, 325	C 3
† 72017	Brasfield, 200	H 4
72828	Briggsville, 200	C 4
72021	Brinkley, 5,275	H 4
72417	Brookland, 465	J 2
72618	Bruno, 130	E 1
72022	Bryant, 1,199	F 4
71827	Buckner, 392	D 7
72619	Bull Shoals, 430	E 1
72321	Burdette, 173	L 2
72023	Cabot, 2,903	F 4
72419	Caraway, 952	K 2
72024	Carlisle, 2,048	G 4
71725	Carthage, 566	E 5
72025	Casa, 208	D 3
72421	Cash, 265	J 2
72026	Casscoe, 200	H 4
† 72951	Caulksville, 208	C 3
72521	Cave City, 807	G 2
72718	Cave Springs, 469	B 1
72930	Cecil, 234	C 3
72450	Center Hill, 1,201	J 1
71830	Center Point, 144	C 5
72027	Center Ridge, 220	E 3
72719	Centerton, 312	B 1
71901	Central City, 150	B 3
† 71832	Chapel Hill, 154	B 5
72933	Charleston◉, 1,497	C 3
72522	Charlotte, 158	H 2
72323	Chatfield, 195	K 3
72542	Cherokee Village, 1,300	G 1
† 71953	Cherry Hill, 250	B 4
72324	Cherry Valley, 556	J 3
71726	Chidester, 232	D 6
72029	Clarendon◉, 2,563	H 4

Zip	Name/Pop.	Key
72325	Clarkedale, 250	K 3
72830	Clarksville◉, 4,616	D 3
72031	Clinton◉, 1,029	F 2
72832	Coal Hill, 733	C 3
72476	College City, 645	J 1
71655	College Heights, 2,050	G 6
72326	Colt, 301	J 3
71831	Columbus, 258	C 6
72523	Concord, 163	G 2
72032	Conway◉, 15,510	F 3
72422	Corning◉, 2,705	J 1
72626	Cotter, 858	E 1
72036	Cotton Plant, 1,657	H 3
71937	Cove, 334	B 5
72037	Coy, 240	G 4
72327	Crawfordsville, 831	K 3
71635	Crossett, 6,191	G 7
71728	Curtis, 500	D 6
72526	Cushman, 427	G 2
† 71923	Dalark, 132	E 5
72039	Damascus, 255	F 3
72833	Danville◉, 1,362	C 3
72834	Dardanelle◉, 3,297	D 3
72424	Datto, 142	J 1
72722	Decatur, 847	A 1
72723	Delaney, 150	C 2
72425	Delaplaine, 145	J 1
72835	Delaware, 200	D 3
71940	Delight, 439	C 5
72426	Dell, 358	K 2
72836	Denning, 203	C 3
71832	De Queen◉, 3,863	B 5
71638	Dermott, 4,250	H 7
72040	Des Arc◉, 1,714	G 4
72041	De Valls Bluff◉, 622	H 4
72042	De Witt◉, 3,728	H 5
72644	Diamond City, 282	E 1
72043	Diaz, 283	H 2
71833	Dierks, 1,101	B 5
71834	Doddridge, 125	C 7
71941	Donaldson, 500	E 5
72837	Dover, 662	D 3
72530	Drasco, 300	G 2
† 72943	Driggs, 125	C 3
71639	Dumas, 4,600	H 6
72935	Dyer, 486	B 3
71729	Eagle Mills, 149	E 6
72331	Earle, 3,146	K 3
71701	East Camden, 589	E 6
72044	Edgemont, 125	F 2
72332	Edmondson, 412	K 3
72333	Elaine, 1,210	J 5
71730	El Dorado◉, 25,283	E 7
72727	Elkins, 418	C 1
72728	Elm Springs, 260	B 1
72045	El Paso, 131	F 3
71740	Emerson, 393	D 7
71835	Emmet, 433	D 6

(continued on following page)

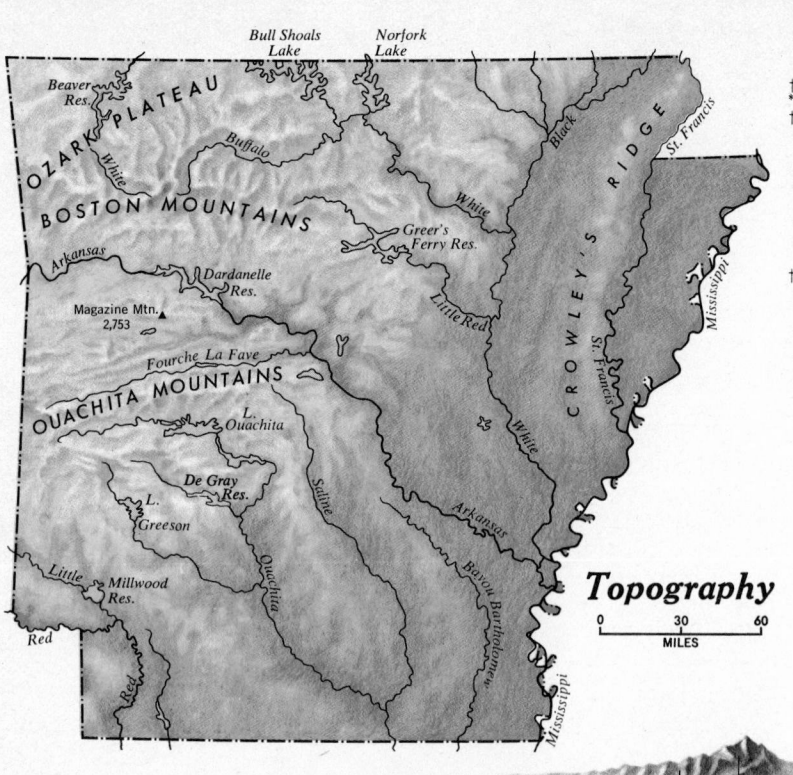

Topography

0   30   60
MILES

Below Sea Level | 100 m. 328 ft. | 200 m. 656 ft. | 500 m. 1,640 ft. | 1,000 m. 3,281 ft. | 2,000 m. 6,562 ft. | 5,000 m. 16,404 ft.

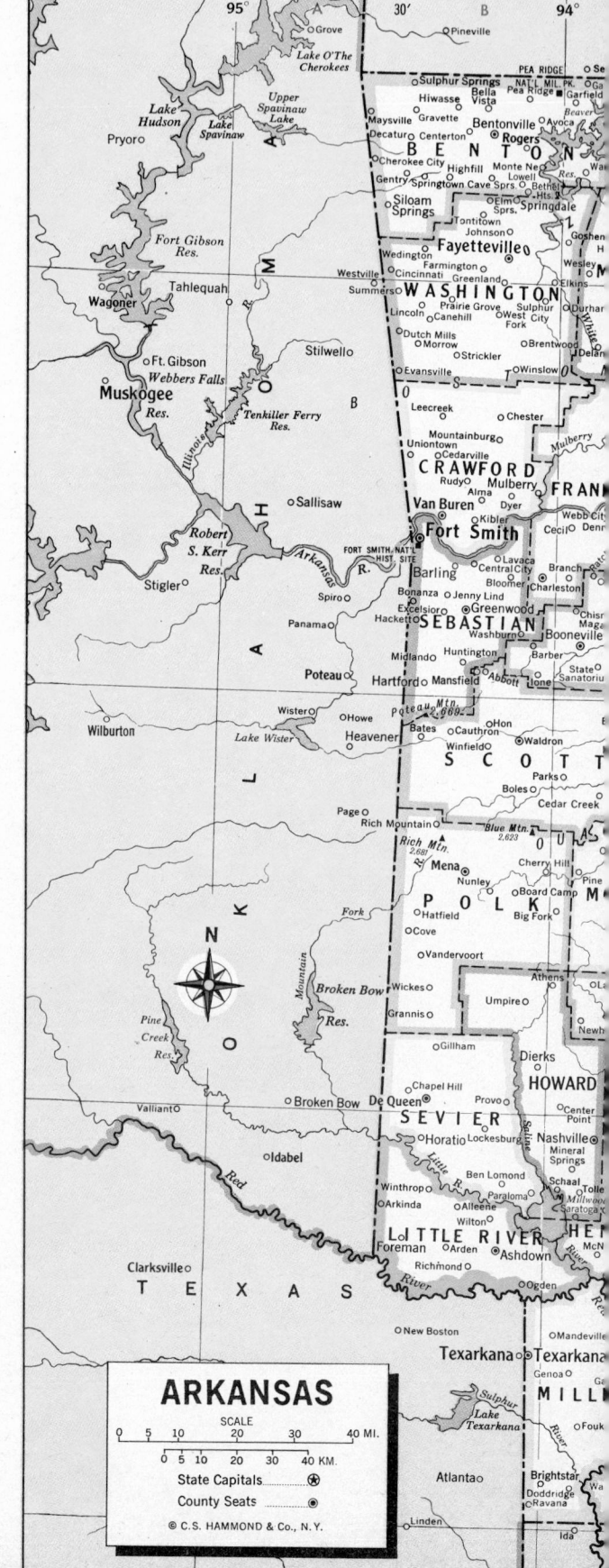

ARKANSAS

SCALE

0 5 10   20   30   40 MI.

0 5 10   20   30   40 KM.

State Capitals ....⊛
County Seats ....⊙

© C.S. HAMMOND & Co., N.Y.

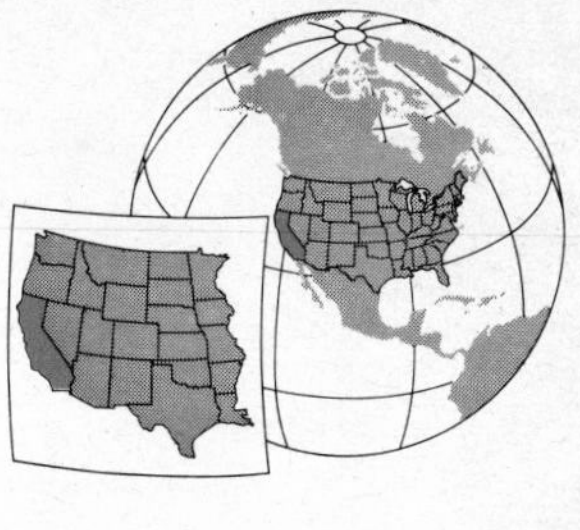

AREA 158,693 sq. mi.
POPULATION 19,953,134
CAPITAL Sacramento
LARGEST CITY Los Angeles
HIGHEST POINT Mt. Whitney 14,494 ft.
SETTLED IN 1769
ADMITTED TO UNION September 9, 1850
POPULAR NAME Golden State
STATE FLOWER Golden Poppy
STATE BIRD California Valley Quail

COUNTIES

Alameda, 1,073,184	D 6
Alpine, 484	F 5
Amador, 11,821	E 5
Butte, 101,969	D 4
Calaveras, 13,585	E 5
Colusa, 12,430	C 4
Contra Costa, 558,389	D 6
Del Norte, 14,580	B 2
El Dorado, 43,833	E 5
Fresno, 413,053	E 7
Glenn, 17,521	C 4
Humboldt, 99,692	B 3
Imperial, 74,492	K 10
Inyo, 15,571	H 7
Kern, 329,162	G 8
Kings, 64,610	F 8
Lake, 19,548	C 4
Lassen, 14,960	E 3
Los Angeles, 7,032,075	G 9
Madera, 41,519	F 6
Marin, 206,038	C 5
Mariposa, 6,015	E 6
Mendocino, 51,101	B 4
Merced, 104,629	E 6
Modoc, 7,469	E 2
Mono, 4,016	F 5
Monterey, 250,071	D 7
Napa, 79,140	C 5
Nevada, 26,346	E 4
Orange, 1,420,386	H 10
Placer, 77,306	E 4
Plumas, 11,707	E 4
Riverside, 459,074	J 10
Sacramento, 631,498	D 5
San Benito, 18,226	D 7
San Bernardino, 684,072	J 9
San Diego, 1,357,854	J 10
San Francisco (city county), 715,674	J 2
San Joaquin, 290,208	D 6
San Luis Obispo, 105,690	E 8
San Mateo, 556,234	C 6
Santa Barbara, 264,324	E 9
Santa Clara, 1,064,714	D 6
Santa Cruz, 123,790	C 6
Shasta, 77,640	C 3
Sierra, 2,365	E 4
Siskiyou, 33,225	C 2
Solano, 169,941	D 5
Sonoma, 204,885	C 5
Stanislaus, 194,506	D 6
Sutter, 41,935	D 4
Tehama, 29,517	C 3
Trinity, 7,615	B 3
Tulare, 188,322	G 7
Tuolumne, 22,169	F 5
Ventura, 376,430	F 9
Yolo, 91,788	D 5
Yuba, 44,736	D 4

CITIES and TOWNS

	Zip	Name/Pop.	Key
	92301	Adelanto, 2,115	H 9
	96006	Adin, 550	E 2
	93601	Ahwahnee, 503	F 6
	94501	Alameda, 70,968	J 2
	94507	Alamo-Danville, 14,059	K 2
	94706	Albany, 14,674	J 2
*	91801	Alhambra, 62,125	C 10
	93201	Alpaugh, 800	F 8
	92001	Alpine, 1,570	J 11
	91001	Altadena, 42,380	C 10
	91701	Alta Loma, 6,100	E 10
	96101	Alturas⊙, 2,799	E 2
†	95101	Alum Rock, 18,355	L 3
*	92801	Anaheim, 166,701	D 11
		Anaheim-Santa Ana-Garden Grove, ‡1,420,386	D 11
	96007	Anderson, 5,492	C 3
	95222	Angels Camp, 1,710	E 5
	94508	Angwin, 2,690	C 5
	94509	Antioch, 28,060	L 1
	92307	Apple Valley, 6,702	H 9
	95003	Aptos, 8,704	K 4
	95912	Arbuckle, 1,037	C 4
	95825	Arcade-Arden, 82,498	B 8
	91006	Arcadia, 42,868	C 10
	95521	Arcata, 8,985	A 3
	93202	Armona, 1,392	F 7
	93420	Arroyo Grande, 7,454	E 8
	90701	Artesia, 14,757	C 11
	93203	Arvin, 5,090	G 8
†	94578	Ashland, 14,810	K 2
	95413	Asti, 50	C 5
	93422	Atascadero, 10,290	E 8
	94025	Atherton, 8,085	K 3
	95301	Atwater, 11,640	E 6
	93602	Auberry, 515	F 6
	95603	Auburn⊙, 6,570	C 8
	90704	Avalon, 1,520	G 10
	93204	Avenal, 3,035	E 8
	91702	Azusa, 25,217	D 10
	92309	Baker, 600	J 8
*	93301	Bakersfield⊙ 69,515	G 8
		Bakersfield ‡, 329,271	G 8
	91706	Baldwin Park, 47,285	D 10
	92220	Banning, 12,034	J 10
	92311	Barstow, 17,442	H 9
†	95501	Bayview, 2,340	A 3
†	93401	Baywood Park-Los Osos, 3,487	E 8
	92223	Beaumont, 5,484	J 10
	90201	Bell, 21,836	C 11
	90706	Bellflower, 51,454	C 11
	94002	Belmont, 23,667	J 3
	94920	Belvedere, 2,599	H 2
	94510	Benicia, 8,783	K 1
	95005	Ben Lomond, 2,793	K 4
*	94701	Berkeley, 116,716	J 2
	94511	Bethel Island, 1,398	L 1
*	90210	Beverly Hills, 33,416	B 10
	92314	Big Bear City, 850	J 9
	92315	Big Bear Lake, 5,268	J 9
	95917	Biggs, 1,115	D 4
	93513	Big Pine, 839	G 6
	93920	Big Sur, 500	D 7
	93606	Biola, 950	E 7
	93514	Bishop, 3,498	G 6
†	94947	Black Point, 500	J 1
	92316	Bloomington, 11,957	E 10
	95525	Blue Lake, 1,112	A 3
	92225	Blythe, 7,047	L 10
	94923	Bodega Bay, 700	B 5
	94924	Bolinas, 700	H 1
	95415	Boonville, 715	B 5
	93516	Boron, 1,999	H 8
	92004	Borrego Springs, 860	J 10
	95006	Boulder Creek, 1,806	J 4
	95707	Bowman, 2,089	C 8
	91010	Bradbury, 1,098	D 10
	92227	Brawley, 13,746	K 11
	92621	Brea, 18,447	D 11
	94513	Brentwood, 2,649	L 2
	93517	Bridgeport⊙, 525	F 5
	94005	Brisbane, 3,003	J 2
	95605	Broderick-Bryte, 12,782	B 8
	95007	Brookdale, 630	J 4
	95605	Bryte-Broderick, 12,782	B 8
	93427	Buellton, 1,402	E 9
	90620	Buena Park, 63,646	D 11
*	91501	Burbank, 88,871	C 10
	94010	Burlingame, 27,320	J 2
	96013	Burney, 2,190	D 3
	93206	Buttonwillow, 1,193	F 8
	94514	Byron, 800	L 2
	92230	Cabazon, 598	J 10
	92231	Calexico, 10,625	K 11
	93501	California City, 1,309	H 8
	92233	Calipatria, 1,824	K 10
	94515	Calistoga, 1,882	C 5
	95418	Calpella, 900	B 4
	93745	Calwa, 5,191	F 7
	93010	Camarillo, 19,219	F 9
	93428	Cambria, 1,716	D 8
	95709	Camino, 800	E 5
	95008	Campbell, 24,770	K 3
	92006	Campo, 850	J 11
	95226	Campo Seco, 700	D 9
*	91303	Canoga Park, 109,127	B 10
	92672	Capistrano Beach, 4,149	H 10
	95010	Capitola, 5,080	K 4
	92007	Cardiff-by-the-Sea, 5,724	H 10
	92008	Carlsbad, 14,944	H 10
	93921	Carmel, 4,525	D 7
	93924	Carmel Valley, 3,026	D 7
	95608	Carmichael, 37,625	C 8
	93013	Carpinteria, 6,982	F 9
	90744	Carson, 71,150	C 11
	93609	Caruthers, 950	E 7
†	93001	Casitas Springs, 1,113	F 9
	95420	Caspar, 578	B 4
	91310	Castaic, 800	G 9
	94546	Castro Valley, 44,760	K 2
	95012	Castroville, 3,235	D 7
	92234	Cathedral City, 3,640	J 10
	93430	Cayucos, 1,772	E 8
	96104	Cedarville, 825	E 2
	96019	Central Valley, 2,361	C 3
	95307	Ceres, 6,029	D 6
	90701	Cerritos, 15,856	C 11
	91311	Chatsworth, 24,000	B 10
	95044	Chemeketa Park-Redwood Estates, 1,452	K 4
†	94521	Cherryland, 9,969	K 2
	96020	Chester, 1,531	D 3
	95926	Chico, 19,580	D 4
	93555	China Lake, 11,105	H 8
	95309	Chinese Camp, 150	E 6
	91710	Chino, 20,411	D 10
	93610	Chowchilla, 4,349	E 6
*	92010	Chula Vista, 67,901	J 11
	95610	Citrus Heights, 21,760	C 8
	91711	Claremont, 23,464	D 10
	95612	Clarksburg, 554	B 9
	94517	Clayton, 1,385	K 2
	95422	Clearlake Highlands, 2,836	C 5
	95423	Clearlake Oaks, 975	C 4
	95425	Cloverdale, 3,251	B 5
	93612	Clovis, 13,856	F 7
	92236	Coachella, 8,353	J 10
	93210	Coalinga, 6,161	E 7
	95713	Colfax, 798	E 4
	94014	Colma, 537	J 2
	92324	Colton, 19,974	E 10
	95932	Colusa⊙, 3,842	C 4
†	90001	Commerce, 10,536	C 10
*	90220	Compton, 78,611	C 11
*	94520	Concord, 85,164	K 1
	93212	Corcoran, 5,249	F 7
	96021	Corning, 3,573	C 4
	91720	Corona, 27,519	E 11
	92118	Coronado, 20,910	H 11
	95076	Corralitos, 600	L 4
	94925	Corte Madera, 8,464	J 2
*	92626	Costa Mesa, 72,660	D 11
	96022	Cottonwood, 1,288	C 3
	95428	Covelo, 900	B 4
	91722	Covina, 30,380	D 10
	95531	Crescent City⊙, 2,586	A 2
	92325	Crestline, 3,509	H 9
	94525	Crockett, 2,900	J 1
	91730	Cucamonga, 5,796	E 10
	90230	Culver City, 31,035	B 10
	95014	Cupertino, 18,216	K 3
	93615	Cutler, 2,503	F 7
	95534	Cutten, 2,228	A 3
	90630	Cypress, 31,026	D 11
	92327	Daggett, 950	H 9
*	94014	Daly City, 66,922	H 2
	92629	Dana Point, 4,745	H 10
	94526	Danville-Alamo, 14,059	K 2
	95616	Davis, 23,488	B 8
	94576	Deer Park, 975	C 5
	93215	Delano, 14,559	F 8
	95315	Delhi, 2,063	E 6
	92014	Del Mar, 3,956	H 11
	93940	Del Rey Oaks, 1,823	D 7
	92404	Del Rosa, 8,000	E 10
	92240	Desert Hot Springs, 2,738	J 9
†	93550	Desert View Highlands, 2,172	G 9
	94528	Diablo, 950	K 2
	95619	Diamond Springs, 900	D 8
	93618	Dinuba, 7,917	F 7
	95620	Dixon, 4,432	B 9
	96023	Dorris, 840	D 2
	93620	Dos Palos, 2,496	E 6
*	90240	Downey, 88,445	C 11
	95936	Downieville⊙, 375	E 4
	91010	Duarte, 14,981	D 10
	94566	Dublin, 13,641	K 2
	95937	Dunnigan, 550	C 5
	96025	Dunsmuir, 2,214	C 2
	95938	Durham, 700	D 4
	92241	Eagle Mountain, 2,453	K 10
	93219	Earlimart, 3,080	F 8
†	92225	East Blythe, 1,252	L 10
	90804	East Los Angeles, 105,033	C 10
	93706	Easton, 1,065	F 7
	93523	Edwards, 900	G 9
*	92020	El Cajon, 52,273	J 11
	92243	El Centro⊙, 19,272	K 11
	94530	El Cerrito, 25,190	J 2
	95623	El Dorado, 900	C 8
	95630	El Dorado Hills, 2,000	C 8
	94018	El Granada, 1,473	H 3
	95624	Elk Grove, 3,721	B 9
*	91731	El Monte, 69,837	D 10
	95318	El Portal, 675	F 6
	93030	El Rio, 6,173	F 9
	90245	El Segundo, 15,620	B 11
	92330	Elsinore, 3,530	F 11
	92630	El Toro, 8,654	E 11
	94608	Emeryville, 2,681	J 2
	95319	Empire, 2,016	D 6
	92024	Encinitas, 5,375	H 10
	91316	Encino, 40,000	B 10
	96001	Enterprise, 11,486	C 3
	95320	Escalon, 2,366	E 6
	92025	Escondido, 36,792	J 10
	95627	Esparto, 1,088	C 5
	91739	Etiwanda, 900	E 10
	96027	Etna, 667	C 2
	95501	Eureka⊙, 24,337	A 3
	93221	Exeter, 4,475	F 7
	94930	Fairfax, 7,661	H 1
	94533	Fairfield⊙, 44,146	K 1
	95628	Fair Oaks, 11,256	C 8
	92028	Fallbrook, 6,945	H 10
	96028	Fall River Mills, 600	D 3
	93223	Farmersville, 3,456	F 7
	93224	Fellows, 530	F 8
	95018	Felton, 2,062	K 4
	95536	Ferndale, 1,352	A 3
	93015	Fillmore, 6,285	G 9
	93622	Firebaugh, 2,517	E 7
	95828	Florin, 9,646	B 8
	95630	Folsom, 5,810	C 8
	92335	Fontana, 20,673	E 10
†	93268	Ford City, 3,503	F 8
†	95703	Foresthill, 900	E 4
	94933	Forest Knolls, 900	H 1
	95437	Fort Bragg, 4,455	B 4
	95538	Fort Dick, 850	A 2
	96032	Fort Jones, 515	C 2
	95540	Fortuna, 4,203	A 3
	94404	Foster City, 9,327	J 2
	92708	Fountain Valley, 31,826	D 11
	93625	Fowler, 2,239	F 7
	93225	Frazier Park, 1,167	F 9
	95019	Freedom, 5,563	L 4
*	94536	Fremont, 100,869	K 3
†	93701	Fresno⊙, 165,972	F 7
		Fresno, ‡413,053	F 7
*	92631	Fullerton, 85,987	D 11
	95632	Galt, 3,200	C 9
*	90247	Gardena, 41,021	C 11
*	92640	Garden Grove, 122,524	D 11
	95634	Georgetown, 700	E 5
	96035	Gerber, 800	C 3
	95441	Geyserville, 887	B 5
	95020	Gilroy, 12,665	D 6
†	92501	Glen Avon Heights, 5,759	E 10
*	91201	Glendale, 132,752	C 10
	91740	Glendora, 31,349	D 10
	93017	Goleta, 3,500	F 9
	93926	Gonzales, 2,575	D 7
	93227	Goshen, 1,324	F 7
	91344	Granada Hills, 50,000	B 10
	92324	Grand Terrace, 5,901	E 10
	95945	Grass Valley, 5,149	D 4
	95444	Graton, 975	C 5
	93308	Greenacres, 2,116	F 8
	93927	Greenfield, 2,608	D 7
	95947	Greenville, 1,073	E 3
	95948	Gridley, 3,534	D 4
	93433	Grover City, 5,939	E 8
	93434	Guadalupe, 3,145	E 9
	95445	Gualala, 585	B 5
	95446	Guerneville, 900	B 5
	95322	Gustine, 2,793	D 6
	94019	Half Moon Bay, 4,023	H 3
	95951	Hamilton City, 961	C 4
	93230	Hanford⊙, 15,179	F 7
	96039	Happy Camp, 925	B 2
	90710	Harbor City, 17,500	C 11
	90250	Hawthorne, 53,304	C 11
	96041	Hayfork, 900	B 3
*	94541	Hayward, 93,058	K 2
	95448	Healdsburg, 5,438	B 5
	92249	Heber, 875	K 11
	92343	Hemet, 12,252	H 10
	96113	Herlong, 900	E 3
	90254	Hermosa Beach, 17,412	B 11
	92345	Hesperia, 4,592	H 9
†	91302	Hidden Hills, 1,529	B 10
	92507	Highgrove, 2,158	E 10
	92346	Highland, 13,290	H 9
	95324	Hilmar, 813	E 6
	92347	Hinkley, 900	H 9
	95023	Hollister⊙, 7,663	D 7
	90028	Hollywood, 85,047	C 10
	92250	Holtville, 3,496	K 11
†	91720	Home Gardens, 5,116	E 11
	92348	Homeland, 1,187	H 10
	95546	Hoopa, 850	B 2
	95449	Hopland, 817	B 5
	95326	Hughson, 2,144	E 6
*	92646	Huntington Beach, 115,960	C 11
	90255	Huntington Park, 33,744	C 11
	93234	Huron, 1,525	E 7
	92349	Idyllwild, 950	J 10
	94947	Ignacio, 4,500	H 1
	92251	Imperial, 3,094	K 11
	92032	Imperial Beach, 20,244	H 11
	93526	Independence⊙, 748	H 7
	92201	Indio, 14,459	J 10
*	90301	Inglewood, 89,985	B 11
	94937	Inverness, 800	B 5
	95640	Ione, 2,369	C 9
	93017	Isla Vista, 13,441	E 9
	95641	Isleton, 909	L 1
	93235	Ivanhoe, 1,595	F 7
	95642	Jackson⊙, 1,924	C 9
	92034	Jacumba, 700	J 11
	95327	Jamestown, 950	E 6
	92252	Joshua Tree, 1,211	J 9
	95451	Kelseyville, 950	C 5
†	94701	Kensington, 5,823	J 2
	93600	Kerman, 2,667	E 7
	93238	Kernville, 900	G 8
	93239	Kettleman City, 600	E 7
	95328	Keyes, 1,875	E 6
	93930	King City, 3,717	D 7
	95719	Kings Beach, 600	F 4
	93631	Kingsburg, 3,843	F 7
	95645	Knights Landing, 846	B 8
	91011	La Canada, 20,652	C 10
	91214	La Crescenta-Montrose, 19,594	C 10
	94549	Lafayette, 20,484	K 2
*	92651	Laguna Beach, 14,550	G 10
	92653	Laguna Hills, 13,676	D 11
	92677	Laguna Niguel, 4,644	H 10
	90631	La Habra, 41,350	D 11
	94020	La Honda, 650	J 3
	92037	La Jolla, 30,000	H 11
	92352	Lake Arrowhead, 2,682	H 9
	93532	Lake Hughes, 750	G 9
	93240	Lake Isabella, 850	G 8
†	92330	Lakeland Village, 1,724	E 11
	95453	Lakeport⊙, 3,005	C 4
*	90712	Lakewood, 82,973	C 11
	92041	La Mesa, 39,178	H 11
	90638	La Mirada, 30,808	D 11
	93241	Lamont, 7,007	G 8
	93534	Lancaster, 30,948	G 9
*	91744	La Puente, 31,092	D 10
	94939	Larkspur, 10,487	H 1
	95076	La Selva Beach, 1,171	K 4
	95330	Lathrop, 2,137	D 6
	93242	Laton, 1,071	F 7
	91750	La Verne, 12,965	D 10

(continued on following page)

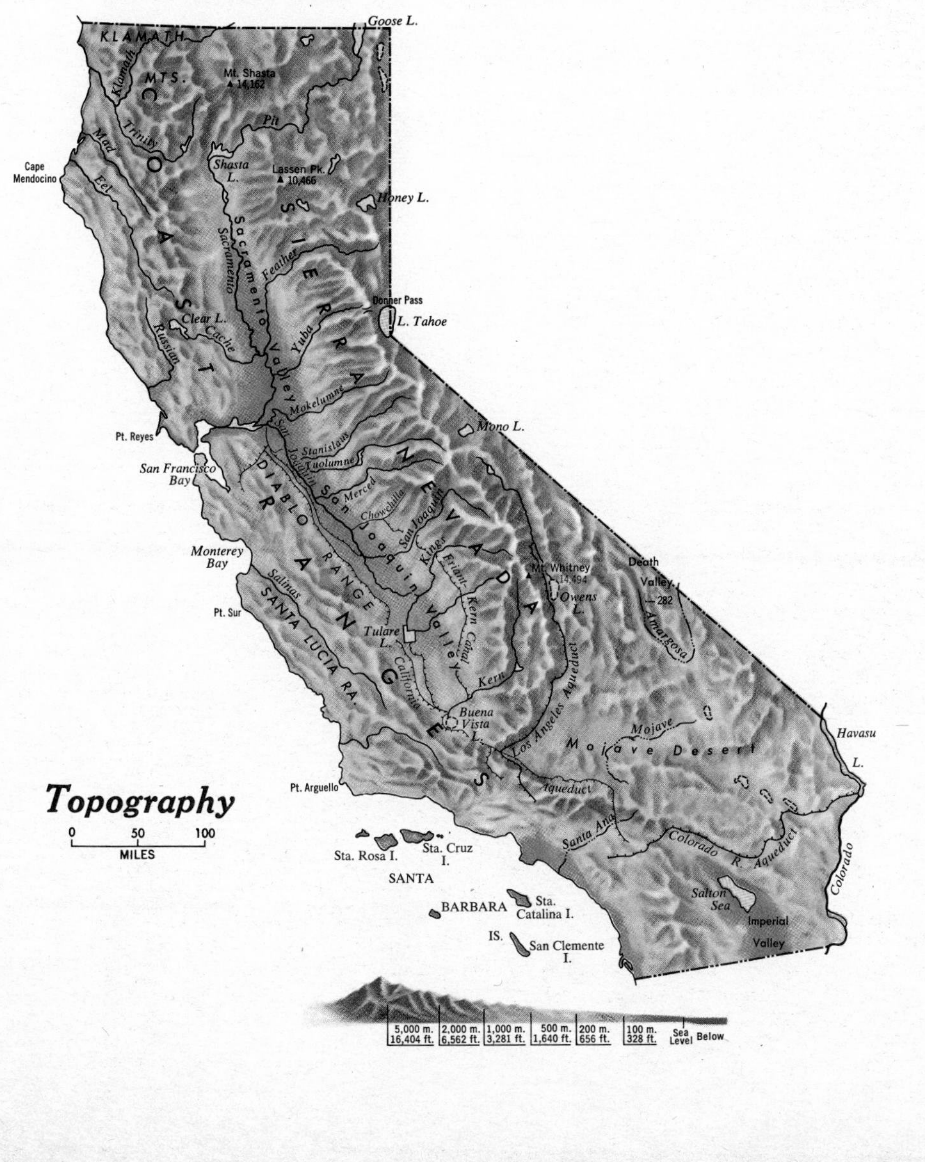
Goose L.
KLAMATH
MTS.
Klamath
Mt. Shasta 14,162
Pit
Trinity
Mad
Eel
Cape Mendocino
Shasta L.
Lassen Pk. 10,466
Honey L.
Sacramento
Feather
SIERRA
Yuba
Donner Pass
L. Tahoe
Clear L.
Cache
Russian
Valley
Mokelumne
Pt. Reyes
San Francisco Bay
Mono L.
Stanislaus
Tuolumne
Merced
Chowchilla
San Joaquin
DIABLO
RANGE
NEVADA
Kings
Mt. Whitney 14,494
Death Valley -282
Owens L.
Monterey Bay
Salinas
Pt. Sur
SANTA LUCIA RA.
Tulare L.
Kern
Amargosa
Buena Vista L.
Los Angeles Aqueduct
Mojave
Mojave Desert
Havasu L.
Pt. Arguello
Aqueduct
Santa Ana
Colorado R. Aqueduct
Colorado
Sta. Rosa I.
Sta. Cruz I.
SANTA
BARBARA
Sta. Catalina I.
IS.
San Clemente I.
Salton Sea
Imperial Valley
5,000 m. 16,404 ft.
2,000 m. 6,562 ft.
1,000 m. 3,281 ft.
500 m. 1,640 ft.
200 m. 656 ft.
100 m. 328 ft.
Sea Level
Below

Topography

0 50 100
MILES

(continued)

90260 Lawndale, 24,825 .... B 11
95454 Laytonville, 917 .... B 4
95333 Le Grand, 995 .... E 6
92045 Lemon Grove, 19,690 .... J 11
93245 Lemoore, 4,219 .... F 7
90304 Lennox, 16,121 .... B 11
92311 Lenwood, 3,834 .... H 9
92024 Leucadia, 5,900 .... H 10
95648 Lincoln, 3,176 .... B 8
† 95901 Linda, 7,731 .... D 4
93247 Lindsay, 5,206 .... F 7
95953 Live Oak, 2,645 .... D 4
95953 Live Oak, 6,443 .... K 4
94550 Livermore, 37,703 .... L 2
95334 Livingston, 2,588 .... E 6
95237 Lockeford, 890 .... C 9
95240 Lodi, 28,691 .... C 9
95551 Loleta, 800 .... A 3
92354 Loma Linda, 9,797 .... F 10
90717 Lomita, 19,784 .... C 11
93436 Lompoc, 25,284 .... E 9
93545 Lone Pine, 1,241 .... H 7
* 90801 Long Beach, 358,633 .... C 11
95650 Loomis, 1,108 .... C 8
90720 Los Alamitos, 11,346 .... D 11
93440 Los Alamos, 750 .... E 9
94022 Los Altos, 24,956 .... K 3
94022 Los Altos Hills, 6,865 .... J 3
* 90001 Los Angeles⊙, 2,816,061 .... C 10
Los Angeles-Long Beach, ‡7,032,075 .... C 10
93635 Los Banos, 9,188 .... E 6
95030 Los Gatos, 23,735 .... K 4
96055 Los Molinos, 900 .... D 3
† 93401 Los Osos-Baywood Park, 3,487 .... E 8
95457 Lower Lake, 850 .... C 5
96118 Loyalton, 945 .... E 4
95458 Lucerne, 1,300 .... C 4
92356 Lucerne Valley, 850 .... J 9
90262 Lynwood, 43,353 .... C 11
93637 Madera⊙, 16,044 .... E 7
90265 Malibu, 15,000 .... B 10
90266 Manhattan Beach, 35,352 .... B 11
95336 Manteca, 13,845 .... D 6
93252 Maricopa, 740 .... F 8
† 94901 Marinwood, 6,000 .... H 1
95338 Mariposa⊙, 900 .... F 6
96120 Markleeville⊙, 150 .... F 5
94553 Martinez⊙, 16,506 .... K 1
95901 Marysville⊙, 9,353 .... D 4
95955 Maxwell, 850 .... C 4
90270 Maywood, 16,996 .... C 10
96057 McCloud, 1,643 .... C 2
93250 McFarland, 4,177 .... F 8
92254 Mecca, 900 .... K 10
93023 Meiners Oaks, 7,025 .... F 9
95460 Mendocino, 975 .... B 4
93640 Mendota, 2,705 .... E 7
94025 Menlo Park, 26,734 .... J 3
92359 Mentone, 2,900 .... H 9
95340 Merced⊙, 22,670 .... E 6
95461 Middletown, 800 .... C 5
92655 Midway City, 5,900 .... D 11
94030 Millbrae, 20,781 .... J 2
94941 Mill Valley, 12,942 .... H 2
95035 Milpitas, 27,149 .... L 3
91752 Mira Loma, 8,482 .... E 10
92675 Mission Viejo, 11,933 .... D 11
* 95350 Modesto⊙, 61,712 .... D 6
93501 Mojave, 2,573 .... G 8
95245 Mokelumne Hill, 560 .... E 5
91016 Monrovia, 30,015 .... D 10
96064 Montague, 890 .... C 2
93003 Montalvo, 2,400 .... F 9
94037 Montara, 1,459 .... H 3
91763 Montclair, 22,546 .... D 10
90640 Montebello, 42,807 .... C 10
93103 Montecito, 4,900 .... F 9
93940 Monterey, 26,302 .... D 7
91754 Monterey Park, 49,166 .... C 10
95462 Monte Rio, 900 .... B 5
95030 Monte Sereno, 3,089 .... K 4
91020 Montrose-La Crescenta, 19,594 .... C 10
93021 Moorpark, 3,380 .... G 9
94556 Moraga, 14,205 .... K 2
95037 Morgan Hill, 6,485 .... L 4
93442 Morro Bay, 7,109 .... D 8
94038 Moss Beach, 700 .... H 3
95039 Moss Landing, 600 .... C 7
94040 Mountain View, 51,092 .... K 3
96067 Mount Shasta, 2,163 .... C 2
† 95926 Mulberry, 1,795 .... D 4
95247 Murphys, 780 .... E 5
92362 Murrieta, 850 .... H 10
92405 Muscoy, 7,091 .... E 10
94558 Napa⊙, 35,978 .... C 5
92050 National City, 43,184 .... J 11
92363 Needles, 4,051 .... L 9
95959 Nevada City⊙, 2,314 .... D 4
94560 Newark, 27,153 .... K 3
92365 Newberry Springs, 710 .... J 9
95658 Newcastle, 900 .... C 8
91321 Newhall, 9,651 .... G 9
95360 Newman, 2,505 .... D 6
* 92660 Newport Beach, 49,422 .... D 11
92257 Niland, 900 .... K 10
93444 Nipomo, 3,642 .... E 8
91760 Norco, 14,511 .... E 11
93643 North Fork, 575 .... F 6
95660 North Highlands, 31,854 .... B 8
* 91601 North Hollywood, 190,000 .... B 10
90650 Norwalk, 91,827 .... C 11
94947 Novato, 31,006 .... H 1
95361 Oakdale, 6,594 .... E 6
93644 Oakhurst, 800 .... F 6
* 94601 Oakland⊙, 361,561 .... J 2
94561 Oakley, 1,306 .... L 1
93022 Oak View, 4,872 .... F 9
93445 Oceano, 2,564 .... E 8
92054 Oceanside, 40,494 .... H 10
93308 Oildale, 20,879 .... F 8
93023 Ojai, 5,591 .... F 9
* 91761 Ontario, 64,118 .... D 10
95060 Opal Cliffs, 5,425 .... K 4
* 92666 Orange, 77,374 .... D 11

93646 Orange Cove, 3,392 .... F 7
93454 Orcutt, 8,500 .... E 9
95555 Orick, 950 .... A 2
94563 Orinda, 6,790 .... J 2
95963 Orland, 2,884 .... C 4
95556 Orleans, 850 .... B 2
92368 Oro Grande, 700 .... H 9
93647 Orosi, 2,757 .... F 7
95965 Oroville⊙, 7,536 .... D 4
93030 Oxnard, 71,225 .... F 9
Oxnard-Ventura, ‡376,430 .... F 9
94044 Pacifica, 36,020 .... H 2
92109 Pacific Beach, 59,000 .... H 11
93950 Pacific Grove, 13,505 .... C 7
† 95076 Pajaro, 1,407 .... D 7
95968 Palermo, 1,966 .... D 4
93550 Palmdale, 8,511 .... G 9
92260 Palm Desert, 6,171 .... J 10
92262 Palm Springs, 20,936 .... J 10
* 94301 Palo Alto, 55,966 .... K 3
90274 Palos Verdes Estates, 13,641 .... B 11
95969 Paradise, 14,539 .... D 4
90723 Paramount, 34,734 .... C 11
93648 Parlier, 1,993 .... F 7
* 91101 Pasadena, 113,327 .... C 10
† 95060 Pastiempo, 1,115 .... K 4
93446 Paso Robles, 7,168 .... E 8
95363 Patterson, 3,147 .... D 6
93553 Pearblossom, 900 .... H 9
93953 Pebble Beach, 5,000 .... C 7
92370 Perris, 4,228 .... F 11
94060 Pescadero, 625 .... J 4
94952 Petaluma, 24,870 .... H 1
95466 Philo, 700 .... B 4
90660 Pico Rivera, 54,170 .... C 10
94611 Piedmont, 10,917 .... J 2
93650 Pinedale, 1,900 .... F 7
94564 Pinole, 15,850 .... J 1
93040 Piru, 975 .... G 9
93449 Pismo Beach, 4,043 .... E 8
94565 Pittsburg, 20,651 .... L 1
93256 Pixley, 1,584 .... F 8
92670 Placentia, 21,948 .... D 11
95667 Placerville⊙, 5,416 .... C 8
95365 Planada, 2,056 .... E 6
94523 Pleasant Hill, 24,610 .... K 2
94566 Pleasanton, 18,328 .... L 2
95669 Plymouth, 501 .... C 8
95726 Pollock Pines, 850 .... E 5
* 91766 Pomona, 87,384 .... D 10
93257 Poplar, 1,239 .... F 7
93257 Porterville, 12,602 .... G 7
93041 Port Hueneme, 14,295 .... F 9
96122 Portola, 1,625 .... E 4
94025 Portola Valley, 4,999 .... J 3
95469 Potter Valley, 975 .... B 4
92064 Poway, 9,422 .... J 11
96079 Project City, 1,431 .... C 3
93534 Quartz Hill, 4,935 .... G 9
95971 Quincy⊙, 3,343 .... E 4
92065 Ramona, 3,554 .... J 10
95670 Rancho Cordova, 30,451 .... C 8
† 91321 Rancho Santa Clarita, 4,860 .... G 9
92067 Rancho Santa Fe, 975 .... H 10
96080 Red Bluff⊙, 7,676 .... C 3
96001 Redding⊙, 16,659 .... C 3
92373 Redlands, 36,355 .... H 9
* 90277 Redondo Beach, 56,075 .... B 11
* 94061 Redwood City⊙, 55,686 .... J 3
95044 Redwood Estates-Chemeketa Park, 1,452 .... K 4
93654 Reedley, 8,131 .... F 7
91335 Reseda, 60,862 .... B 10
92376 Rialto, 28,370 .... E 10
93261 Richgrove, 1,023 .... F 8
* 94801 Richmond, 79,043 .... J 1
93555 Ridgecrest, 7,629 .... H 8
95562 Rio Dell, 2,817 .... A 3
95673 Rio Linda, 7,524 .... B 8
94571 Rio Vista, 3,135 .... L 1
95366 Ripon, 2,679 .... D 6
95367 Riverbank, 3,949 .... E 6
93656 Riverdale, 1,722 .... E 7
* 92501 Riverside⊙, 140,089 .... E 11
95677 Rocklin, 3,039 .... B 8
94572 Rodeo, 5,356 .... J 1
94928 Rohnert Park, 6,133 .... C 5
95540 Rohnerville, 2,781 .... B 3
90274 Rolling Hills, 2,050 .... B 11
90274 Rolling Hills Estates, 6,027 .... B 11
93560 Rosamond, 2,281 .... G 9
91770 Rosemead, 40,972 .... C 10
95678 Roseville, 17,895 .... B 8
94957 Ross, 2,742 .... H 1
92509 Rubidoux, 13,969 .... E 10
* 95801 Sacramento (cap.)⊙, 254,413 .... B 8
Sacramento, ‡800,592 .... B 8
94574 Saint Helena, 3,173 .... C 5
93901 Salinas⊙, 58,896 .... D 7
Salinas-Monterey, ‡250,071 .... D 7
95563 Salyer, 700 .... B 3
95564 Samoa, 585 .... A 3
95249 San Andreas⊙, 1,564 .... E 5
94960 San Anselmo, 13,031 .... H 1
93450 San Ardo, 750 .... E 7
* 92401 San Bernardino⊙, 104,251 .... E 10
San Bernardino-Riverside-Ontario, ‡1,143,146 .... E 10
94066 San Bruno, 36,254 .... J 2
94070 San Carlos, 25,924 .... J 3
92672 San Clemente, 17,063 .... H 10
* 92101 San Diego⊙, 696,769 .... H 11
San Diego, ‡1,357,854 .... H 11
91773 San Dimas, 15,692 .... D 10
* 91340 San Fernando, 16,571 .... C 10
* 94101 San Francisco⊙, 715,674 .... H 2
San Francisco-Oakland, ‡3,109,519 .... H 2
* 91775 San Gabriel, 29,176 .... C 10
93657 Sanger, 10,088 .... F 7
92383 San Jacinto, 4,385 .... H 10
93660 San Joaquin, 1,506 .... E 7
* 95101 San Jose⊙, 445,779 .... L 3
San Jose, ‡1,064,714 .... L 3

Agriculture, Industry and Resources

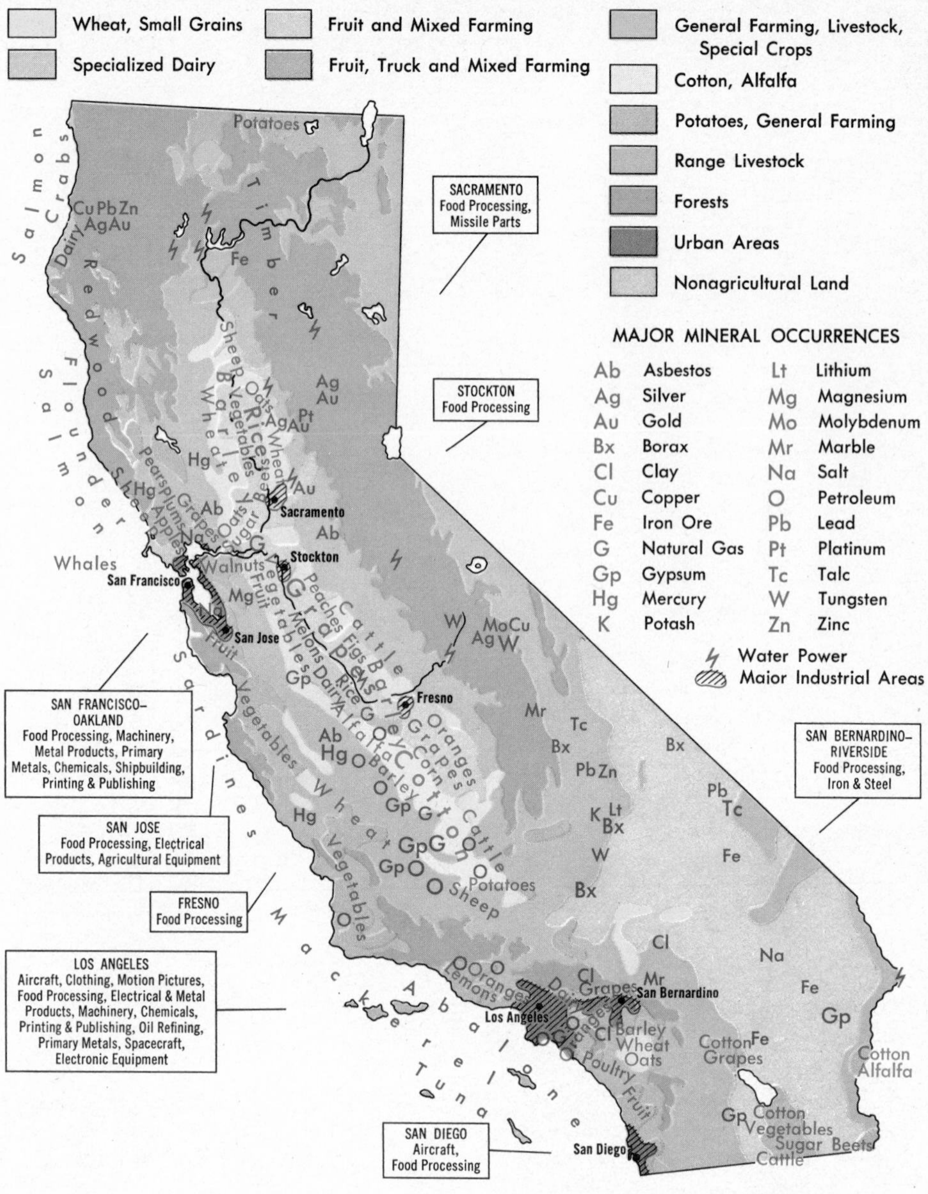
DOMINANT LAND USE
Wheat, Small Grains
Specialized Dairy
Fruit and Mixed Farming
Fruit, Truck and Mixed Farming
General Farming, Livestock, Special Crops
Cotton, Alfalfa
Potatoes, General Farming
Range Livestock
Forests
Urban Areas
Nonagricultural Land
MAJOR MINERAL OCCURRENCES
Ab Asbestos
Ag Silver
Au Gold
Bx Borax
Cl Clay
Cu Copper
Fe Iron Ore
G Natural Gas
Gp Gypsum
Hg Mercury
K Potash
Lt Lithium
Mg Magnesium
Mo Molybdenum
Mr Marble
Na Salt
O Petroleum
Pb Lead
Pt Platinum
Tc Talc
W Tungsten
Zn Zinc
Water Power
Major Industrial Areas
SACRAMENTO
Food Processing, Missile Parts
STOCKTON
Food Processing
SAN FRANCISCO–OAKLAND
Food Processing, Machinery, Metal Products, Primary Metals, Chemicals, Shipbuilding, Printing & Publishing
SAN JOSE
Food Processing, Electrical Products, Agricultural Equipment
FRESNO
Food Processing
LOS ANGELES
Aircraft, Clothing, Motion Pictures, Food Processing, Electrical & Metal Products, Machinery, Chemicals, Printing & Publishing, Oil Refining, Primary Metals, Spacecraft, Electronic Equipment
SAN DIEGO
Aircraft, Food Processing
SAN BERNARDINO–RIVERSIDE
Food Processing, Iron & Steel
Sacramento
Stockton
San Francisco
San Jose
Fresno
Los Angeles
San Bernardino
San Diego
Whales
Salmon
Crabs
Timber
Potatoes
Redwood
Flounder
Sardines
Mackerel
Tuna
Sheep
Cattle
Vegetables
Grapes
Apples
Walnuts
Peaches
Figs
Melons
Oranges
Cotton
Barley
Wheat
Oats
Lemons
Poultry
Fruit
Cotton Alfalfa
Sugar Beets

95045 San Juan Bautista, 1,164 .... D 7
92675 San Juan Capistrano, 3,781 .... H 10
* 94577 San Leandro, 68,698 .... J 2
94580 San Lorenzo, 24,633 .... K 2
93401 San Luis Obispo⊙, 28,036 .... E 8
92069 San Marcos, 3,896 .... H 10
91108 San Marino, 14,177 .... D 10
95046 San Martin, 1,392 .... L 4
* 94401 San Mateo, 78,911 .... J 3
93451 San Miguel, 600 .... E 8
94806 San Pablo, 21,461 .... J 1
* 90731 San Pedro, 91,000 .... C 11
* 94901 San Rafael⊙, 38,977 .... J 1
94583 San Ramon, 4,084 .... K 2
* 92701 Santa Ana⊙, 156,601 .... D 11
* 93101 Santa Barbara⊙, 70,215 .... F 9
Santa Barbara, ‡264,324 .... F 9
* 95050 Santa Clara, 87,717 .... K 3
95060 Santa Cruz⊙, 32,076 .... K 4
90670 Santa Fe Springs, 14,750 .... C 11
93453 Santa Margarita, 750 .... E 8
93454 Santa Maria, 32,749 .... E 9
* 90401 Santa Monica, 88,289 .... B 10
93060 Santa Paula, 18,001 .... F 9
* 95401 Santa Rosa⊙, 50,006 .... C 5
93063 Santa Susana, 2,900 .... B 10
† 94901 Santa Venetia, 2,500 .... J 1
92071 Santee, 21,107 .... J 11
95070 Saratoga, 27,110 .... K 4
93003 Saticoy, 2,400 .... F 9
94965 Sausalito, 6,158 .... H 2
95565 Scotia, 950 .... A 3
95060 Scotts Valley, 3,621 .... K 4
90740 Seal Beach, 24 441 .... C 11
93955 Seaside, 35,935 .... D 7
95472 Sebastopol, 3,993 .... C 5
92273 Seeley, 952 .... K 11
93662 Selma, 7,459 .... F 7
91343 Sepulveda, 40,000 .... B 10
93263 Shafter, 5,327 .... F 8
96087 Shasta, 750 .... C 3
93449 Shell Beach, 1,900 .... E 8
91024 Sierra Madre, 12,140 .... D 10
90806 Signal Hill, 5,582 .... C 11

92676 Silverado, 950 .... E 11
93065 Simi Valley, 56,464 .... G 9
92075 Solana Beach, 5,023 .... H 11
93960 Soledad, 6,843 .... D 7
93463 Solvang, 2,004 .... E 9
95476 Sonoma, 4,112 .... C 5
95370 Sonora⊙, 3,100 .... E 6
95073 Soquel, 5,795 .... K 4
93665 South Dos Palos, 850 .... E 7
91733 South El Monte, 13,443 .... C 10
90280 South Gate, 56,909 .... C 11
95705 South Lake Tahoe, 12,921 .... F 5
† 95965 South Oroville, 4,111 .... D 4
91030 South Pasadena, 22,979 .... C 10
† 95801 South Sacramento, 28,574 .... B 8
94080 South San Francisco, 46,646 .... J 2
† 93268 South Taft, 2,214 .... F 8
93265 Springville, 720 .... G 7
94305 Stanford, 8,691 .... J 3
90680 Stanton, 17,947 .... D 11
94970 Stinson Beach, 800 .... H 2
* 95201 Stockton⊙, 107,644 .... D 6
Stockton, ‡290,208 .... D 6
93266 Stratford, 750 .... F 7
93267 Strathmore, 1,221 .... F 7
94585 Suisun City, 2,917 .... K 1
93067 Summerland, 781 .... F 9
92381 Sun City, 5,519 .... F 11
96089 Summit City, 900 .... C 3
91040 Sunland, 22,200 .... C 10
92388 Sunnymead, 6,708 .... F 11
* 94086 Sunnyvale, 95,408 .... K 3
94586 Sunol, 750 .... L 2
90742 Sunset Beach, 1,900 .... C 11
96130 Susanville⊙, 6,608 .... E 3
95982 Sutter, 1,488 .... D 4
95685 Sutter Creek, 1,508 .... C 9
93268 Taft, 4,285 .... F 8
95730 Tahoe City, 1,394 .... E 4
91356 Tarzana, 24,165 .... B 10
93561 Tehachapi, 4,211 .... G 8
91780 Temple City, 29,673 .... D 10
93465 Templeton, 900 .... E 8

93270 Terra Bella, 1,037 .... G 8
92274 Thermal, 975 .... J 10
† 95965 Thermalito, 4,217 .... D 4
95686 Thornton, 850 .... B 9
91360 Thousand Oaks. 36,334 .... G 9
92276 Thousand Palms, 600 .... J 10
94920 Tiburon, 6,209 .... J 2
93272 Tipton, 969 .... F 7
90290 Topanga, 4,800 .... B 10
† 90290 Topanga Beach, 4,500 .... B 10
* 90501 Torrance, 134,584 .... C 11
95376 Tracy, 14,724 .... D 6
93668 Tranquillity, 800 .... E 7
93562 Trona, 975 .... H 8
95734 Truckee, 1,392 .... E 4
91042 Tujunga, 22,000 .... C 10
93274 Tulare, 16,235 .... F 7
96134 Tulelake, 857 .... D 2
95379 Tuolumne, 1,365 .... E 6
95380 Turlock, 13,992 .... E 6
92680 Tustin, 21,178 .... D 11
95383 Twain Harte, 1,484 .... E 6
92277 Twentynine Palms, 5,667 .... K 9
† 95060 Twin Lakes, 3,012 .... K 4
95482 Ukiah⊙, 10,095 .... B 4
94587 Union City, 14,724 .... K 2
90007 University Park, 3,100 .... D 11
91786 Upland, 32,551 .... E 10
95485 Upper Lake, 975 .... C 4
95688 Vacaville, 21,690 .... D 5
91355 Valencia, 4,243 .... G 9
94590 Vallejo, 66,733 .... J 1
Vallejo-Napa, ‡249,081 .... J 1
95252 Valley Springs, 800 .... C 9
* 91401 Van Nuys, 231,600 .... B 10
90291 Venice, 80,500 .... B 11
* 93001 Ventura⊙, 55,797 .... F 9
92392 Victorville, 10,845 .... H 9
92667 Villa Park, 2,723 .... D 11
93277 Visalia⊙, 27,268 .... F 7
92083 Vista, 24,688 .... H 10
91789 Walnut, 5,992 .... D 10
* 94595 Walnut Creek, 39,844 .... K 2
95690 Walnut Grove, 800 .... B 9

93280 Wasco, 8,269 .... F
95386 Waterford, 2,243 .... E
95076 Watsonville, 14,569 .... D
96093 Weaverville⊙, 1,489 .... B
96094 Weed, 2,983 C
* 91790 West Covina, 68,034 .... D 1
† 90025 West Hollywood, 29,448 .... B 1
90025 West Los Angeles, 38,805 .... B 1
92683 Westminster, 59,865 .... D 1
92281 Westmorland, 1,175 .... K 1
94565 West Pittsburg, 5,969 .... K
95255 West Point, 950 .... E
95691 West Sacramento, 12,002 .... B
96137 Westwood, Lassen, 1,862 .... D
90024 Westwood, L.A., 45,000 .... B 1
95692 Wheatland, 1,280 .... D
* 90601 Whittier, 72,863 .... D 1
95987 Williams, 1,571 C
95490 Willits, 3,091 .... B
95988 Willows⊙, 4,085 C
90744 Wilmington, 38,000 .... C 1
95492 Windsor, 2,359 C
92283 Winterhaven, 850 .... L 1
95694 Winters, 2,419 .... D
95388 Winton, 3,393 .... E
95258 Woodbridge, 1,397 .... B
93286 Woodlake, 3,371 .... G
95695 Woodland⊙, 20,677 .... B
91364 Woodland Hills, 56,420 .... B 1
94062 Woodside, 4,731 .... J
92398 Yermo, 1,304 .... J
92686 Yorba Linda, 11,856 .... D 1
95389 Yosemite National Park, 857 .... F
94599 Yountville, 2,332 C
96097 Yreka⊙, 5,394 C
95991 Yuba City⊙, 13,986 .... D
92399 Yucaipa, 19,284 .... J
92284 Yucca Valley, 3,893 .... J

⊙ County seat.
‡ Population of metropolitan area.
† Zip of nearest p.o.
* Multiple zips

AREA 104,247 sq. mi
POPULATION 2,207,259
CAPITAL Denver
LARGEST CITY Denver
HIGHEST POINT Mt. Elbert 14,433 ft.
SETTLED IN 1858
ADMITTED TO UNION August 1, 1876
POPULAR NAME Centennial State
STATE FLOWER Mountain Columbine
STATE BIRD Lark Bunting

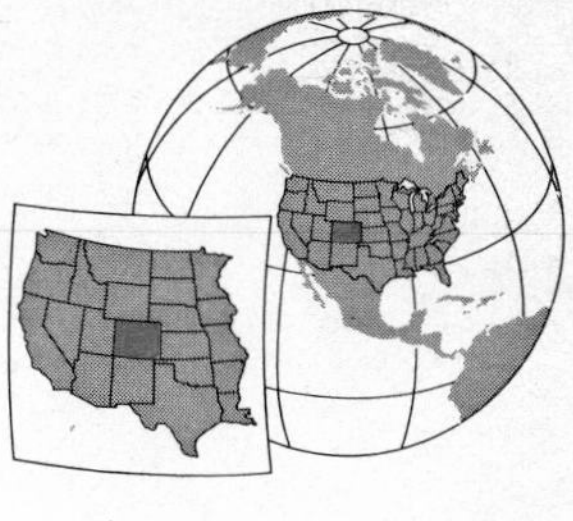

COUNTIES

Name/Pop.	Key
dams, 185,789	L 3
amosa, 11,422	H 7
apahoe, 162,142	L 3
chuleta, 2,733	E 8
aca, 5,674	O 8
ent, 6,493	N 7
oulder, 131,889	J 2
haffee, 10,162	G 5
heyenne, 2,396	O 5
ear Creek, 4,819	H 3
onejos, 7,846	G 8
ostilla, 3,091	J 8
rowley, 3,086	M 6
uster, 1,120	J 6
elta, 15,286	D 5
enver, 514,678	K 3
olores, 1,641	C 7
ouglas, 8,407	K 4
agle, 7,498	F 3
bert, 3,903	L 4
Paso, 235,972	K 5
emont, 21,942	J 5
arfield, 14,821	C 3
lpin, 1,272	H 3
rand, 4,107	G 2
unnison, 7,578	E 5
insdale, 202	E 7
uerfano, 6,590	K 7
ckson, 1,811	G 1
efferson, 233,031	J 3
owa, 2,029	O 6
t Carson, 7,530	O 4
ake, 8,282	G 4
a Plata, 19,199	D 8
arimer, 89,900	H 1
as Animas, 15,744	L 8
incoln, 4,836	M 5
ogan, 18,852	N 1
esa, 54,374	B 5
ineral, 786	F 7
offat, 6,525	C 1
ontezuma, 12,952	B 8
ontrose, 18,366	C 6
organ, 20,105	M 2
tero, 23,523	M 7
uray, 1,546	D 6
ark, 2,185	H 4
hillips, 4,131	P 1
itkin, 6,185	F 4
rowers, 13,258	P 7
ueblo, 118,238	K 6
o Blanco, 4,842	C 3
io Grande, 10,494	G 7
outt, 6,592	E 1
aguache, 3,827	G 6
an Juan, 831	D 7
an Miguel, 1,949	C 6
edgwick, 3,405	P 1
ummit, 2,665	G 3
eller, 3,316	J 5
ashington, 5,550	N 3
eld, 89,297	L 1
uma, 8,544	P 2

CITIES and TOWNS

Zip	Name/Pop.	Key
80101	Agate, 120	M 4
81020	Aguilar, 699	K 8
80720	Akron⊙, 1,775	N 2
81101	Alamosa⊙, 6,985	H 8
80510	Allenspark, 100	J 2
80420	Alma, 73	G 4
81210	Almont, 15	F 5
80721	Amherst, 105	P 1
80801	Anton, 65	N 3
81120	Antonito, 1,113	H 8
80802	Arapahoe, 100	P 5
81021	Arlington, 10	N 6
80804	Arriba, 254	N 4
† 81323	Arriola, 50	B 8
80002	Arvada, 46,814	J 3
81611	Aspen⊙, 2,404	F 4
80722	Atwood, 75	N 1
80610	Ault, 841	K 1
80010	Aurora, 74,974	K 3
81410	Austin, 1,163	D 5
81620	Avon, 50	F 3
81022	Avondale, 750	L 6
80421	Bailey, 200	H 4
† 80624	Barnesville, 20	L 2
81621	Basalt, 419	E 4
81122	Bayfield, 320	D 8
81411	Bedrock, 20	B 6
† 80758	Beecher Island, 5	P 3
80512	Bellvue, 335	J 1
80102	Bennett, 613	L 3
80513	Berthoud, 1,446	J 2
† 80438	Berthoud Pass, 200	H 3
80805	Bethune, 99	P 4
81023	Beulah, 425	K 6
80908	Black Forest, 700	K 4
80422	Black Hawk, 217	J 3
81123	Blanca, 212	H 8
† 81001	Blende, 950	K 6
† 80424	Blue River, 8	G 4
† 81155	Bonanza, 10	G 6
81024	Boncarbo, 50	K 8
80423	Bond, 63	F 3
81025	Boone, 448	L 6
* 80301	Boulder⊙, 66,870	J 2
† 81428	Bowie, 18	D 5
80806	Boyero, 25	N 5
81026	Brandon, 10	P 6
81027	Branson, 70	M 8
80424	Breckenridge⊙, 548	G 4
80611	Briggsdale, 440	L 1
80601	Brighton⊙, 8,309	K 3
81028	Bristol, 250	P 6
† 80901	Broadmoor, 3,871	K 5
† 81212	Brookside, 173	J 6
80020	Broomfield, 7,261	J 3
80723	Brush, 3,377	M 2
† 80742	Buckingham, 6	L 1
81211	Buena Vista, 1,962	G 5
80425	Buffalo Creek, 150	J 4
80807	Burlington⊙, 2,828	P 3
80426	Burns, 100	F 3
80103	Byers, 490	L 3
81320	Cahone, 125	B 7
80808	Calhan, 465	L 4
81029	Campo, 206	O 8
81212	Canon City⊙, 9,206	J 6
81124	Capulin, 600	G 8
81623	Carbondale, 726	E 4
80612	Carr, 47	K 1
80809	Cascade, 950	K 5
80104	Castle Rock⊙, 1,531	K 4
81413	Cedaredge, 581	D 5
81125	Center, 1,470	G 7
80427	Central City⊙, 228	J 3
81126	Chama, 400	J 8
81030	Cheraw, 129	N 6
80810	Cheyenne Wells⊙, 982	P 5
81127	Chimney Rock, 51	E 8
81031	Chivington, 15	O 6
81128	Chromo, 150	F 8
81220	Cimarron, 25	D 6
80428	Clark, 55	F 1
† 80731	Clarkville, 4	P 2
81520	Clifton, 950	C 4
80429	Climax, 975	G 4
81221	Coal Creek, 225	J 6
81222	Coaldale, 104	H 6
80430	Coalmont, 12	F 1
81032	Cokedale, 101	K 8
81624	Collbran, 225	C 4
† 81401	Colona, 54	D 6
81004	Colorado City, 411	K 6
* 80901	Colorado Springs⊙, 135,060	K 5
	Colorado Springs, ‡235,972	K 5
† 80428	Columbine, 12	E 1
80022	Commerce City, 17,407	K 3
80432	Como, 35	H 4
81129	Conejos⊙, 100	G 8
80812	Cope, 125	O 3
80611	Cornish, 2	L 2
81321	Cortez⊙, 6,032	B 8
81223	Cotopaxi, 150	H 6
80434	Cowdrey, 10	G 1
81625	Craig⊙, 4,205	D 2
81415	Crawford, 171	D 5
81130	Creede⊙, 653	E 7
81224	Crested Butte, 372	E 5
81131	Crestone, 34	H 7
80813	Cripple Creek⊙, 425	J 5
80726	Crook, 199	O 1
81033	Crowley, 216	M 6
81055	Cuchara, 43	J 8
80514	Dacono, 360	K 2
† 80728	Dailey, 20	O 1
81630	De Beque, 155	C 4
† 80135	Deckers, 4	J 4
80105	Deer Trail, 374	M 3
81034	Delhi, 10	M 7
81132	Del Norte⊙, 1,569	G 7
81416	Delta⊙, 3,694	D 5
* 80201	Denver (cap.)⊙, 514,678	K 3
	Denver, ‡1,227,529	K 3
81035	Deora, 2	O 7
80435	Dillon, 182	H 3
81610	Dinosaur, 247	B 2
80814	Divide, 50	J 5
81323	Dolores, 820	C 8
81324	Dove Creek⊙, 619	A 7
† 81239	Doyleville, 75	F 6
80515	Drake, 75	J 2
81301	Durango⊙, 10,333	D 8
81036	Eads⊙, 795	O 6
81631	Eagle⊙, 790	F 3
† 81212	East Canon, 1,805	J 6
80615	Eaton, 1,389	K 1
81418	Eckert, 850	C 5
80727	Eckley, 193	P 2
80214	Edgewater, 4,866	J 3
81632	Edwards, 100	F 3
81325	Egnar, 84	B 7
80106	Elbert, 150	L 4
80437	Eldora, 100	H 3
80107	Elizabeth, 493	K 4
81633	Elk Springs, 56	C 2
80438	Empire, 249	H 3
80110	Englewood, 33,695	K 3
80516	Erie, 1,090	K 2
80517	Estes Park, 1,616	J 2
† 81433	Eureka, 25	D 7
80620	Evans, 2,570	K 2
80439	Evergreen, 2,321	J 3
80440	Fairplay⊙, 419	H 4
81037	Farisita, 45	J 7
† 80030	Federal Heights, 1,502	J 3
80520	Firestone, 570	K 2
† 80810	Firstview, 6	O 5
80815	Flagler, 615	N 4
80728	Fleming, 349	O 1
81226	Florence, 2,846	J 6
80816	Florissant, 75	J 5
80521	Fort Collins⊙, 43,337	J 1
81133	Fort Garland, 400	J 8
80621	Fort Lupton, 2,489	K 2
81038	Fort Lyon, 135	N 6
80701	Fort Morgan⊙, 7,594	M 2
80817	Fountain, 3,515	K 5
81039	Fowler, 1,241	L 6
80441	Foxton, 75	J 4
80116	Franktown, 157	K 4
80442	Fraser, 221	H 3
80530	Frederick, 696	K 2
80820	Freshwater (Guffey), 24	H 5
80443	Frisco, 471	G 3
81521	Fruita, 1,822	B 4
† 81501	Fruitvale, 950	C 4
80622	Galeton, 200	K 1
81134	Garcia, 90	J 8
81040	Gardner, 75	J 7
81227	Garfield, 11	G 5
81522	Gateway, 250	B 5
80818	Genoa, 161	N 4
80444	Georgetown⊙, 542	H 3
80623	Gilcrest, 382	K 2
80624	Gill, 250	L 2
81634	Gilman, 400	G 3
81523	Glade Park, 69	B 5
80485	Glendevey, 50	H 1
80532	Glen Haven, 50	H 2
81601	Glenwood Springs⊙, 4,106	E 4
80401	Golden⊙, 9,817	J 3
80625	Goodrich, 85	M 2
80445	Gould, 12	G 2
81041	Granada, 551	P 6
80446	Granby, 554	H 2
81501	Grand Junction⊙, 20,170	B 4
80447	Grand Lake, 189	H 2
81635	Grand Valley, 270	D 4
81228	Granite, 23	G 4
80448	Grant, 50	H 4
80631	Greeley⊙, 38,902	K 2
† 80118	Greenland, 47	K 4
80819	Green Mountain Falls, 359	K 5
81636	Greystone, 2	B 1
80729	Grover, 121	L 1
80820	Guffey, 24	H 5
81042	Gulnare, 100	K 8
81230	Gunnison⊙, 4,613	E 5
81637	Gypsum, 420	F 3
80730	Hale, 12	P 3
81638	Hamilton, 30	D 2
81043	Hartman, 129	P 6
80449	Hartsel, 75	H 4
81044	Hasty, 150	O 6
81045	Haswell, 135	N 6
80731	Haxtun, 899	O 1
81639	Hayden, 763	E 2
80732	Hereford, 50	L 1
81326	Hesperus, 78	C 8
80733	Hillrose, 121	N 2
81232	Hillside, 79	H 6
81046	Hoehne, 400	L 8
81047	Holly, 993	P 6
80734	Holyoke⊙, 1,640	P 1
81136	Hooper, 80	H 7
81419	Hotchkiss, 507	D 5
80451	Hot Sulphur Springs⊙, 220	H 2
81233	Howard, 175	H 6
80641	Hoyt, 175	L 2
80642	Hudson, 518	K 2
80821	Hugo⊙, 759	N 4
80533	Hygiene, 400	J 2
80452	Idaho Springs, 2,003	H 3
80735	Idalia, 100	P 3
81137	Ignacio, 613	D 8
80736	Iliff, 193	N 1
81427	Ironton,	D 7
† 80901	Ivywild, 12,000	K 5
80455	Jamestown, 185	J 2
81048	Jansen, 267	K 8
81138	Jaroso, 56	H 8
80456	Jefferson, 45	H 4
80822	Joes, 100	O 3
80534	Johnstown, 1,191	K 2
80737	Julesburg⊙, 1,578	P 1
80823	Karval, 70	N 5
80643	Keenesburg, 427	L 2
80738	Keota, 6	L 1
80644	Kersey, 474	L 2
81049	Kim, 200	N 8
80117	Kiowa⊙, 235	L 4
80824	Kirk, 100	P 3
80825	Kit Carson, 220	O 5
† 80435	Kokomo, 75	G 4
80459	Kremmling, 764	G 2
80826	Kutch, 2	M 5
80026	Lafayette, 3,498	K 3
81139	La Garita, 50	G 7
80739	Laird, 105	P 2
81140	La Jara, 768	H 8
81050	La Junta⊙, 7,938	M 7
81235	Lake City⊙, 91	E 6
80827	Lake George, 29	J 5
80215	Lakewood, 92,787	J 3
81052	Lamar⊙, 7,797	O 6
80535	Laporte, 950	J 1
80118	Larkspur, 350	K 4
80645	La Salle, 1,227	K 2
81054	Las Animas⊙, 3,148	N 6
† 81151	Lasauces, 120	H 8
† 81153	Lavalley, 237	J 8
81055	La Veta, 589	J 8
† 80452	Lawson, 108	H 3
81625	Lay, 8	D 2
81420	Lazear, 60	D 5
80461	Leadville⊙, 4,314	G 4
† 81323	Lebanon, 50	B 8
81327	Lewis, 350	B 8
80828	Limon, 1,814	M 4
† 81212	Lincoln Park, 2,984	J 6
80740	Lindon, 50	N 3
80120	Littleton⊙, 26,466	K 3
80536	Livermore, 20	J 1
† 80701	Log Lane Village, 329	M 2
81524	Loma, 100	B 4
80501	Longmont, 23,209	J 2
† 80135	Longview, 10	J 4
80027	Louisville, 2,409	J 3
80131	Louviers, 306	K 4
80537	Loveland, 16,220	J 2
80646	Lucerne, 150	K 2
81056	Lycan, 4	P 7
80540	Lyons, 958	J 2
81525	Mack, 175	B 4
81421	Maher, 80	D 5
† 80461	Malta, 200	G 4
81141	Manassa, 814	H 8
81328	Mancos, 709	C 8
80829	Manitou Springs, 4,278	J 5
81058	Manzanola, 451	M 6
† 81623	Marble, 1	E 4
81329	Marvel, 100	C 8
80541	Masonville, 200	J 2
† 80649	Masters, 50	L 2
80830	Matheson, 100	M 4
81640	Maybell, 82	C 2
81057	McClave, 165	O 6
80463	McCoy, 14	F 3
80542	Mead, 195	K 2
81641	Meeker⊙, 1,597	D 2
81642	Meredith, 48	F 4
80741	Merino, 260	N 2
81005	Mesa, 295	C 4
81330	Mesa Verde National Park, 70	C 8
81142	Mesita, 50	H 8
80543	Milliken, 702	K 2
80477	Milner, 75	F 2
81645	Minturn, 706	G 3
81059	Model, 19	L 8
81143	Moffat, 98	H 6
81646	Molina, 120	D 4
81144	Monte Vista, 3,909	G 7
80464	Montezuma, 6	H 3

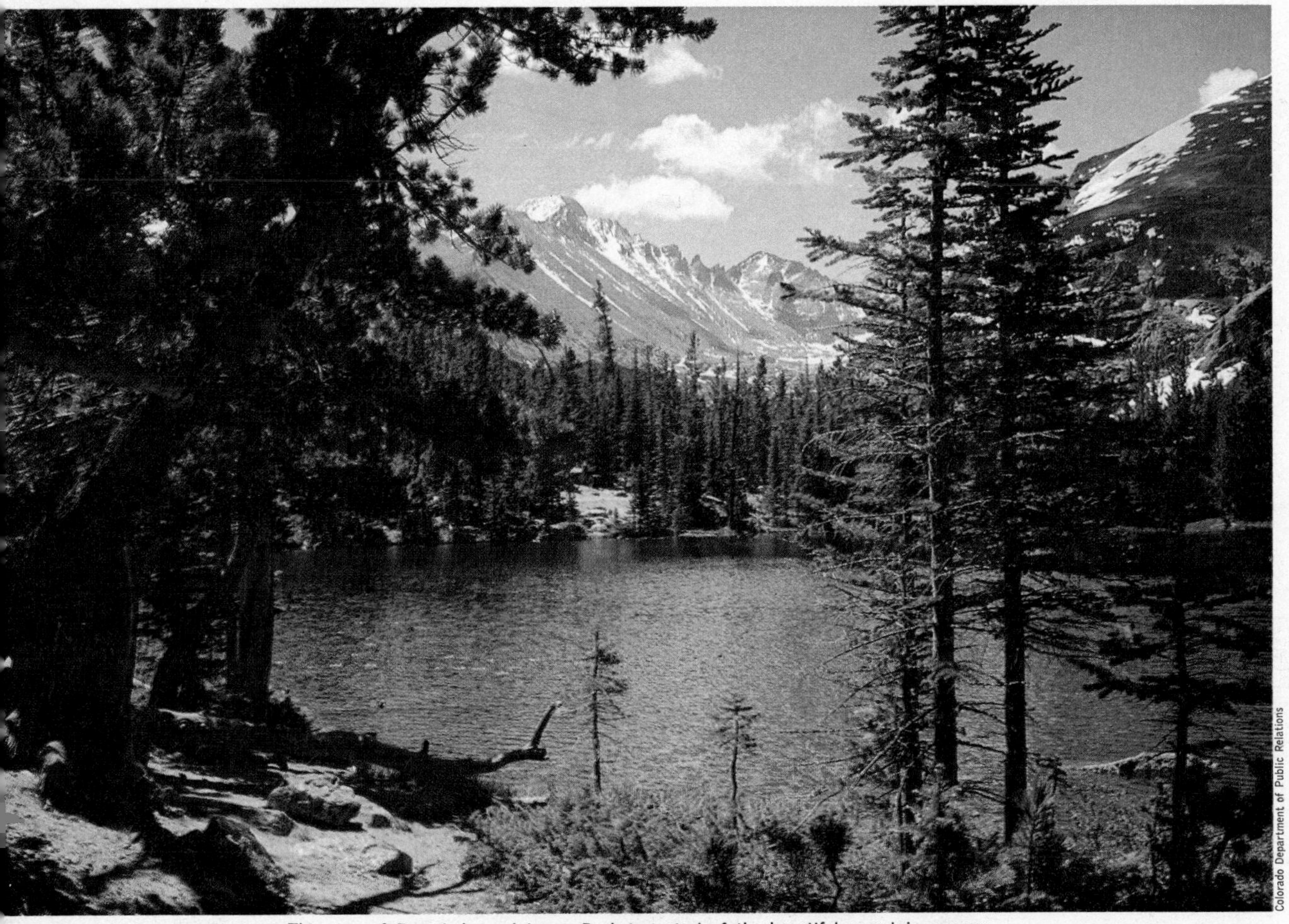

Colorado Department of Public Relations

This view of Bear Lake and Longs Peak is typical of the beautiful mountain scenery found in Rocky Mountain National Park, an area which many call "the roof of America."

(continued on following page)

Topography

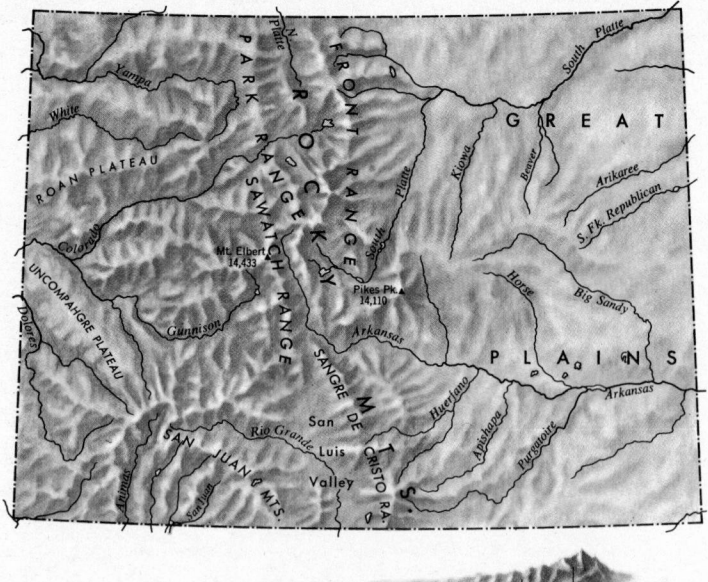

Agriculture, Industry and Resources

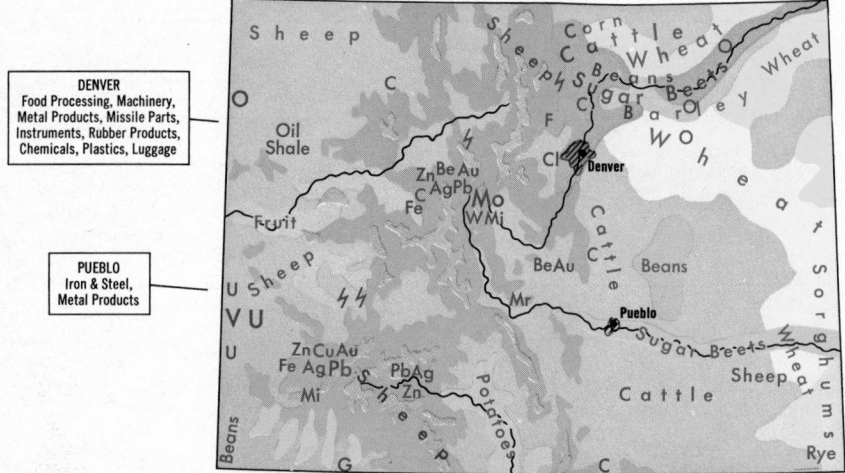

DENVER
Food Processing, Machinery, Metal Products, Missile Parts, Instruments, Rubber Products, Chemicals, Plastics, Luggage

PUEBLO
Iron & Steel, Metal Products

DOMINANT LAND USE

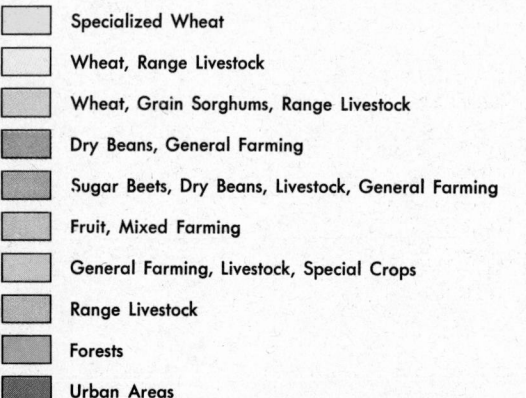

- Specialized Wheat
- Wheat, Range Livestock
- Wheat, Grain Sorghums, Range Livestock
- Dry Beans, General Farming
- Sugar Beets, Dry Beans, Livestock, General Farming
- Fruit, Mixed Farming
- General Farming, Livestock, Special Crops
- Range Livestock
- Forests
- Urban Areas
- Nonagricultural Land

MAJOR MINERAL OCCURRENCES

Ag	Silver	Mi	Mica
Au	Gold	Mo	Molybdenum
Be	Beryl	Mr	Marble
C	Coal	O	Petroleum
Cl	Clay	Pb	Lead
Cu	Copper	U	Uranium
F	Fluorspar	V	Vanadium
Fe	Iron Ore	W	Tungsten
G	Natural Gas	Zn	Zinc

⚡ Water Power

▨ Major Industrial Areas

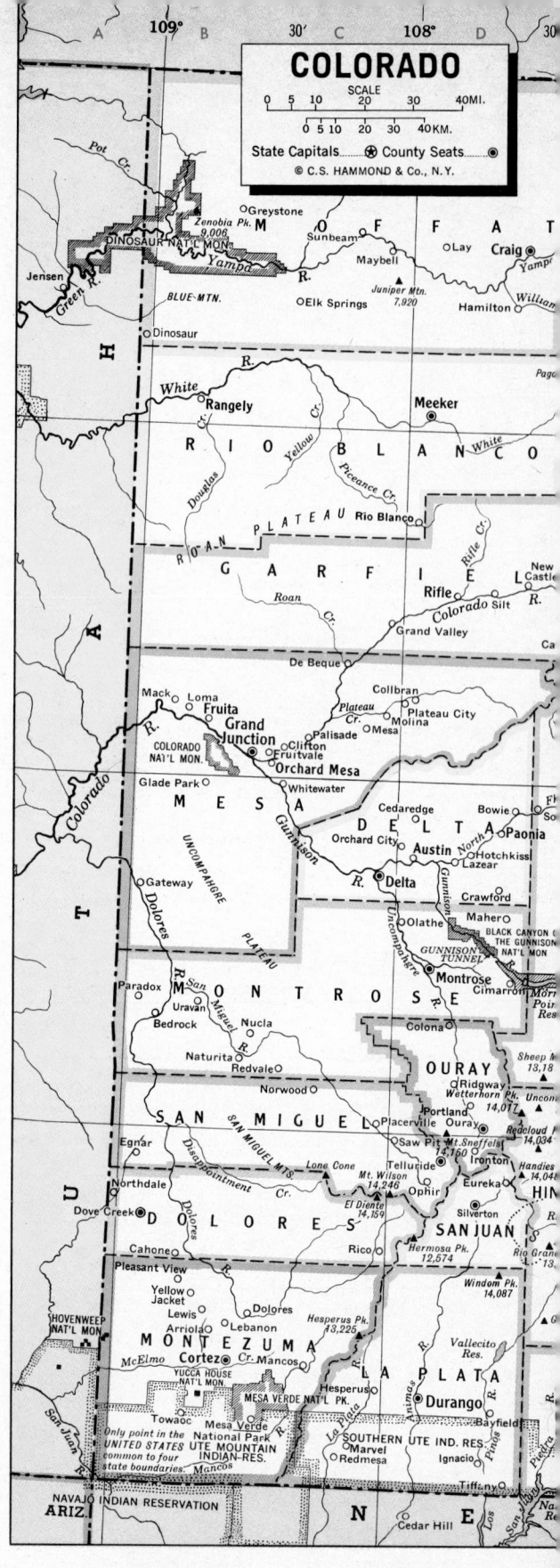

COLORADO
SCALE
0 5 10 20 30 40 MI.
0 5 10 20 30 40 KM.
State Capitals ⊛ County Seats ◉
© C.S. HAMMOND & Co., N.Y.

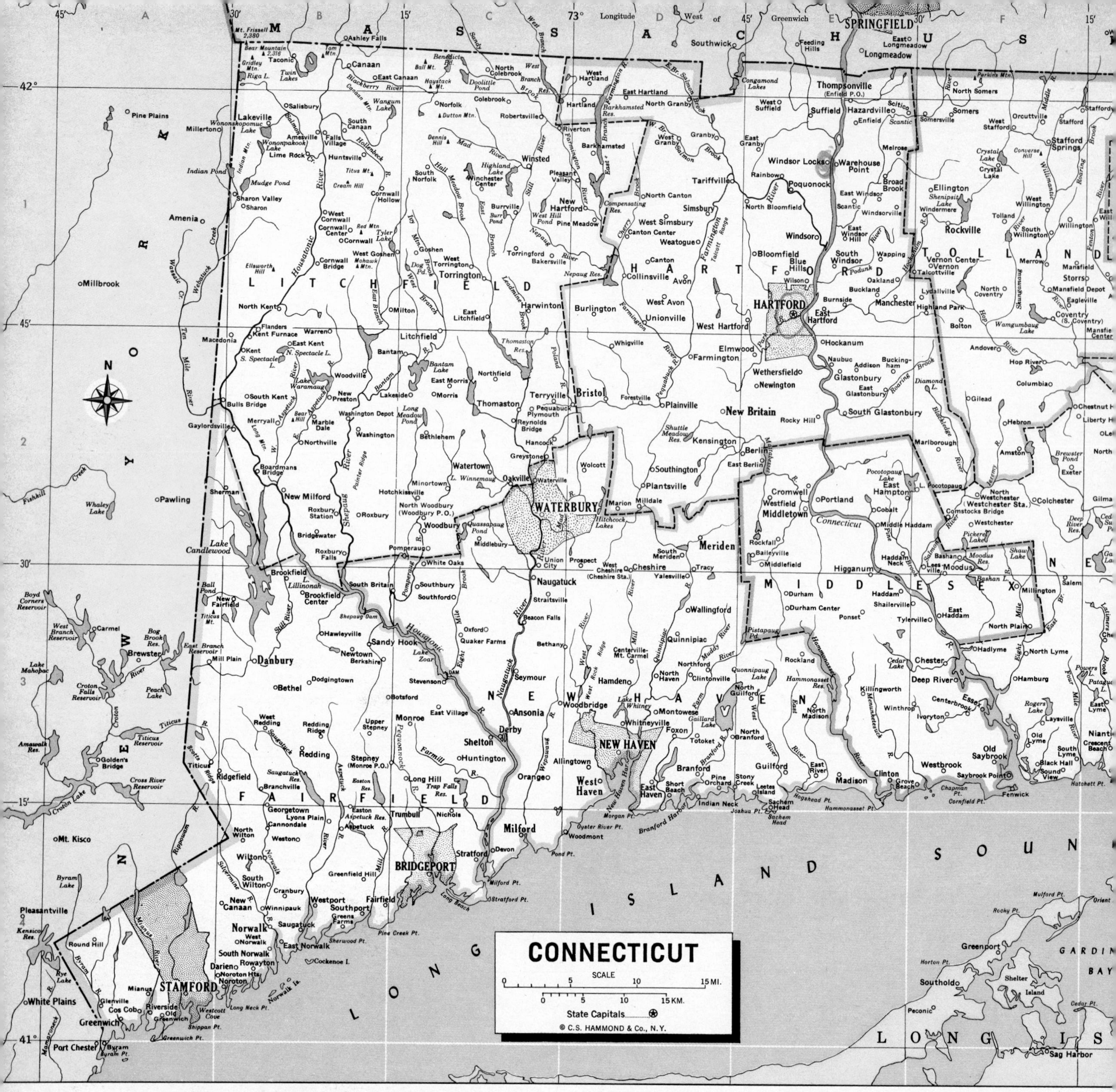

CONNECTICUT

SCALE

0 ... 5 ... 10 ... 15 MI.

0 ... 5 ... 10 ... 15 KM.

State Capitals .... ⊛

© C.S. Hammond & Co., N.Y.

Topography

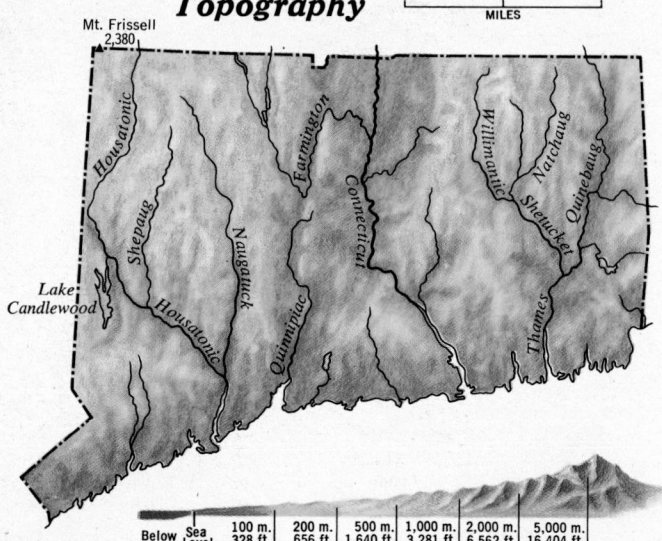

Mt. Frissell
2,380

Lake Candlewood

Housatonic · Shepaug · Naugatuck · Farmington · Connecticut · Quinnipiac · Willimantic · Shetucket · Natchaug · Quinebaug · Thames

	Below Sea Level	100 m. 328 ft.	200 m. 656 ft.	500 m. 1,640 ft.	1,000 m. 3,281 ft.	2,000 m. 6,562 ft.	5,000 m. 16,404 ft.

0 ... 15 ... 30
MILES

COUNTIES

	Name/Pop.	Key
	Fairfield, 792,814	B 3
	Hartford, 816,737	D 1
	Litchfield, 144,091	B 1
	Middlesex, 114,816	E 3
	New Haven, 744,948	D 3
	New London, 230,348	G 2
	Tolland, 103,448	F 1
	Windham, 84,515	H 1

CITIES and TOWNS

Zip	Name/Pop.	Key
† 06516	Allingtown, 7,000	D 3
06231	Amston, 1,963	F 2
06232	Andover, ▲2,099	F 2
06401	Ansonia, 21,160	C 3
† 06250	Ashford, ▲2,156	G 1
06001	Avon, ▲8,352	D 1
06330	Baltic, 1,500	G 2
† 06063	Barkhamsted, ▲2,066	D 1
06403	Beacon Falls, ▲3,546	C 3
06037	Berlin, ▲14,149	E 2
† 06501	Bethany, ▲3,857	C 3
06751	Bethlehem, ▲1,923	C 2
06002	Bloomfield, ▲18,301	E 1
06002	Bloomfield, 8,000	E 1
06112	Blue Hills, 5,000	E 1
06040	Bolton, ▲3,691	F 1
06405	Branford, ▲20,444	D 3
06405	Branford, 2,080	D 3
* 06601	Bridgeport, 156,542	C 4
	Bridgeport, ‡388,953	C 4
06752	Bridgewater, ▲1,277	B 2
06010	Bristol, 55,487	D 2
06016	Broad Brook, 1,548	E 1
06804	Brookfield, ▲9,688	B 3
06804	Brookfield, 6,000	B 3
06805	Brookfield Center, 3,000	B 3
06234	Brooklyn, ▲4,965	H 1
06085	Burlington, ▲4,070	D 1
06085	Burlington, 950	D 1
10573	Byram, 5,631	A 4
06018	Canaan, ▲931	B 1
06018	Canaan, 1,083	B 1
06331	Canterbury, ▲2,673	H 2
06019	Canton, ▲6,868	D 1
06332	Central Village, 1,200	H 2
06235	Chaplin, ▲1,621	G 1
06410	Cheshire, ▲19,051	D 2
06412	Chester, ▲2,982	F 3
06412	Chester, 1,569	F 3
06413	Clinton, ▲10,267	E 3
06413	Clinton, 5,957	E 3
† 06473	Clintonville, 1,300	D 3
06415	Colchester, ▲6,603	F 2
06415	Colchester, 3,529	F 2
06021	Colebrook, ▲1,020	C 1
06022	Collinsville, 2,897	D 1
06238	Coventry, ▲8,140	F 1
06238	Coventry, 3,735	F 1
06416	Cromwell, ▲7,400	E 2
06405	Branford, 2,080	D 3
06010	Bristol, 55,487	D 2
06016	Broad Brook, 1,548	E 1
06804	Brookfield, ▲9,688	B 3
06804	Brookfield, 6,000	B 3
06805	Brookfield Center, 3,000	B 3
06234	Brooklyn, ▲4,965	H 1
06085	Burlington, ▲4,070	D 1
06085	Burlington, 950	D 1
10573	Byram, 5,631	A 4
06810	Danbury, 50,781	B 3
06239	Danielson, 4,580	H 1
06820	Darien, ▲20,411	B 4
06241	Dayville, ▲950	H 1
06417	Deep River, ▲3,690	F 3
06417	Deep River, 2,333	F 3
06418	Derby, 12,599	C 3
† 06460	Devon, 2,750	C 4
06422	Durham, ▲4,489	E 3
06023	East Berlin, 1,100	E 2
† 06239	East Brooklyn, 1,377	H 1
06242	Eastford, ▲922	G 1
06026	East Granby, ▲3,352	E 1
06423	East Haddam, ▲4,474	F 2
06424	East Hampton, ▲7,078	E 2
06424	East Hampton, 1,982	E 2
06108	East Hartford, ▲57,583	E 1
06512	East Haven, 25,120	D 3
06333	East Lyme, ▲11,399	G 3
† 06856	East Norwalk, 9,500	B 4
06425	Eastondale, ▲4,885	B 3
† 06088	East Windsor, ▲8,513	E 1
06029	Ellington, ▲7,707	F 1
06110	Elmwood, 18,500	E 1
06082	Enfield, ▲46,189	E 1
06082	Enfield P.O. (Thompsonville), 27,000	E 1
06426	Essex, ▲4,911	F 3
06426	Essex, 2,473	F 3
06430	Fairfield, ▲56,487	B 4
06032	Farmington, ▲14,390	D 2
† 06010	Forestville, 20,000	D 2

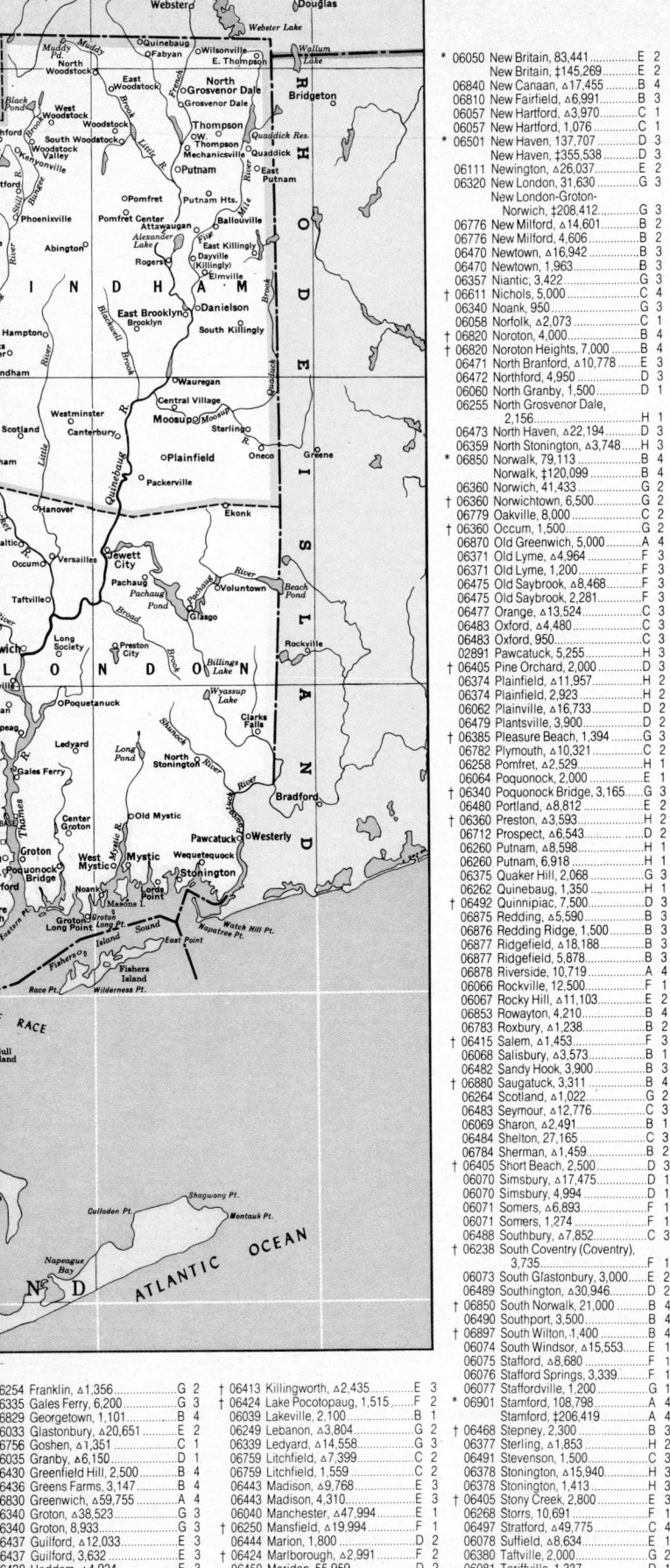

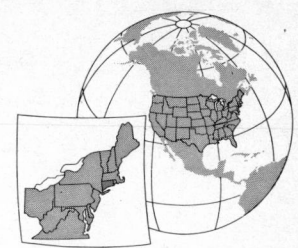

AREA 5,009 sq. mi.
POPULATION 3,032,217
CAPITAL Hartford
LARGEST CITY Hartford
HIGHEST POINT Mt. Frissell (S. Slope) 2,380 ft.
SETTLED IN 1635
ADMITTED TO UNION January 9, 1788
POPULAR NAME Constitution State; Nutmeg State
STATE FLOWER Mountain Laurel
STATE BIRD Robin

Agriculture, Industry and Resources

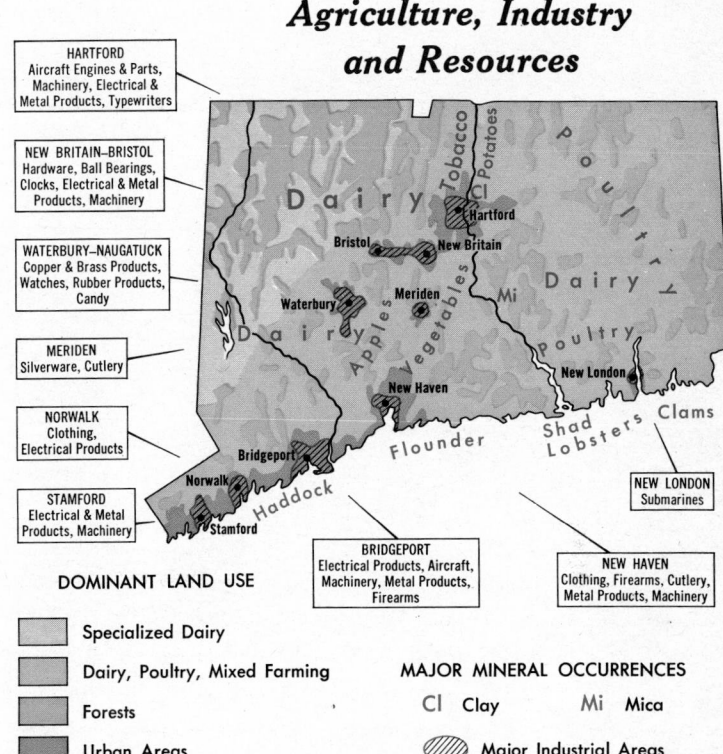

HARTFORD
Aircraft Engines & Parts, Machinery, Electrical & Metal Products, Typewriters

NEW BRITAIN–BRISTOL
Hardware, Ball Bearings, Clocks, Electrical & Metal Products, Machinery

WATERBURY–NAUGATUCK
Copper & Brass Products, Watches, Rubber Products, Candy

MERIDEN
Silverware, Cutlery

NORWALK
Clothing, Electrical Products

STAMFORD
Electrical & Metal Products, Machinery

BRIDGEPORT
Electrical Products, Aircraft, Machinery, Metal Products, Firearms

NEW LONDON
Submarines

NEW HAVEN
Clothing, Firearms, Cutlery, Metal Products, Machinery

DOMINANT LAND USE

- Specialized Dairy
- Dairy, Poultry, Mixed Farming
- Forests
- Urban Areas

MAJOR MINERAL OCCURRENCES
Cl Clay   Mi Mica

Major Industrial Areas

06050	New Britain, 83,441	E	2
	New Britain, ‡145,269	E	2
06840	New Canaan, ▲17,455	B	4
06810	New Fairfield, ▲6,991	B	3
06057	New Hartford, ▲3,970	C	1
06057	New Hartford, 1,076	C	1
06501	New Haven, 137,707	D	3
	New Haven, ‡355,538	D	3
06111	Newington, ▲26,037	E	2
06320	New London, 31,630	G	3
	New London-Groton- Norwich, ‡208,412	G	3
06776	New Milford, ▲14,601	B	2
06776	New Milford, 4,606	B	2
06470	Newtown, ▲16,942	B	3
06470	Newtown, 1,963	B	3
06357	Niantic, 3,422	G	3
06611	Nichols, 5,000	C	4
06340	Noank, 950	G	3
06058	Norfolk, ▲2,073	C	1
06820	Noroton, 4,000	B	4
06820	Noroton Heights, 7,000	B	4
06471	North Branford, ▲10,778	E	3
06472	Northford, 4,950	D	3
06060	North Granby, 1,500	D	1
06255	North Grosvenor Dale, 2,156	H	1
06473	North Haven, ▲22,194	D	3
06359	North Stonington, ▲3,748	H	3
06850	Norwalk, 79,113	B	4
	Norwalk, ‡120,099	B	4
06360	Norwich, 41,433	G	2
06360	Norwichtown, 6,500	G	2
06779	Oakville, 8,000	C	2
06360	Occum, 1,500	G	2
06870	Old Greenwich, 5,000	A	4
06371	Old Lyme, ▲4,964	F	3
06371	Old Lyme, 1,200	F	3
06475	Old Saybrook, ▲8,468	F	3
06475	Old Saybrook, 2,281	F	3
06477	Orange, ▲13,524	C	3
06483	Oxford, ▲4,480	C	3
06483	Oxford, 950	C	3
02891	Pawcatuck, 5,255	H	3
06405	Pine Orchard, 2,000	D	3
06374	Plainfield, ▲11,957	H	2
06374	Plainfield, 2,923	H	2
06062	Plainville, ▲16,733	D	2
06479	Plantsville, 3,900	D	2
06385	Pleasure Beach, 1,394	G	3
06782	Plymouth, ▲10,321	C	2
06258	Pomfret, ▲2,529	H	1
06064	Poquonock, 2,000	E	1
06340	Poquonock Bridge, 3,165	G	3
06480	Portland, ▲8,812	E	2
06360	Preston, ▲3,593	H	2
06712	Prospect, ▲6,543	D	2
06260	Putnam, ▲8,598	H	1
06260	Putnam, 6,918	H	1
06375	Quaker Hill, 2,068	G	3
06262	Quinebaug, 1,350	H	1
06492	Quinnipiac, 7,500	D	3
06875	Redding, 5,590	B	3
06876	Redding Ridge, 1,500	B	3
06877	Ridgefield, ▲18,188	B	3
06877	Ridgefield, 5,878	B	3
06878	Riverside, 10,719	A	4
06066	Rockville, 12,500	F	1
06067	Rocky Hill, ▲11,103	E	2
06853	Rowayton, 4,210	B	4
06783	Roxbury, ▲1,238	B	2
06415	Salem, ▲1,453	F	3
06068	Salisbury, ▲3,573	B	1
06482	Sandy Hook, 3,900	B	3
06880	Saugatuck, 3,311	B	4
06264	Scotland, ▲1,022	G	2
06483	Seymour, ▲12,776	C	3
06069	Sharon, ▲2,491	B	1
06484	Shelton, 27,165	C	3
06784	Sherman, ▲1,459	B	2
06405	Short Beach, 2,500	D	3
06070	Simsbury, ▲17,475	D	1
06070	Simsbury, 4,994	D	1
06071	Somers, ▲6,893	F	1
06071	Somers, 1,274	F	1
06488	Southbury, ▲7,852	C	3
06238	South Coventry (Coventry), 3,735	F	1
06073	South Glastonbury, 3,000	E	2
06489	Southington, ▲30,946	D	2
06850	South Norwalk, 21,000	B	4
06490	Southport, 3,500	B	4
06897	South Wilton, 1,400	B	4
06074	South Windsor, ▲15,553	E	1
06075	Stafford, ▲8,680	F	1
06076	Stafford Springs, 3,339	F	1
06077	Staffordville, 1,200	G	1
06901	Stamford, 108,798	A	4
	Stamford, ‡206,419	A	4
06468	Stepney, 2,300	B	3
06377	Sterling, ▲1,853	H	2
06491	Stevenson, 1,500	C	3
06378	Stonington, ▲15,940	H	3
06378	Stonington, 1,413	H	3
06405	Stony Creek, 2,800	E	3
06268	Storrs, 10,691	F	1
06497	Stratford, ▲49,775	C	4
06078	Suffield, ▲8,634	E	1
06380	Taftville, 2,000	G	2
06081	Tariffville, 1,337	D	1
06786	Terryville, 6,900	C	2
06360	Thamesville, 1,500	G	2
06087	Thomaston, ▲6,233	C	2
06277	Thompson, ▲7,580	H	1
06277	Thompson, 1,200	H	1
06082	Thompsonville, 27,000	E	1
06084	Tolland, ▲7,857	F	1
06790	Torrington, ▲3,500	C	1
06790	Torrington, 31,952	C	1
06405	Totoket, 950	D	3
06611	Trumbull, ▲31,394	C	4
06611	Trumbull, 10,000	C	4
06382	Uncasville, 1,750	G	3
06076	Union, ▲443	G	1
06770	Union City, 5,000	C	2
06085	Unionville, 2,900	D	2
06086	Vernon, ▲27,237	F	1
06384	Voluntown, ▲1,452	H	2

06492	Wallingford, ▲35,714	D	3
06074	Wapping, 1,600	E	1
06088	Warehouse Point, 2,400	E	1
06754	Warren, ▲827	B	2
06793	Washington, ▲3,121	B	2
06701	Waterbury, 108,033	C	2
	Waterbury, ‡208,956	C	2
06385	Waterford, ▲17,227	G	3
06795	Watertown, ▲18,610	C	2
06795	Watertown, 9,000	C	2
06714	Waterville, 4,295	C	2
06387	Wauregan, 1,100	H	2
06089	Weatogue, 2,396	D	1
06001	West Avon, 4,500	D	1
06498	Westbrook, ▲3,820	F	3
06498	Westbrook, 1,507	F	3
06410	West Cheshire, 2,000	D	3
06457	Westfield, 9,000	E	2
06107	West Hartford, ▲68,031	D	1
06516	West Haven, 52,851	D	3
06388	West Mystic, 3,694	H	3
06856	West Norwalk, 950	B	4
06880	Weston, ▲7,417	B	4
06880	Weston, 3,000	B	4
06880	Westport, ▲27,414	B	4
06896	West Redding, 1,200	B	3
06092	West Simsbury, 1,419	D	1
06093	West Suffield, 2,400	E	1
06109	Wethersfield, 26,662	E	2
06517	Whitneyville, 18,438	D	3
06226	Willimantic, 14,402	G	2
06279	Willington, ▲3,755	F	1
06897	Wilton, ▲13,572	B	4
06897	Wilton, 4,200	B	4
06094	Winchester, ▲11,106	C	1
06094	Winchester Center, 350	C	1
06280	Windham, ▲19,626	G	2
06095	Windsor, ▲22,502	E	1
06096	Windsor Locks, ▲15,080	E	1
06098	Winsted, 8,954	C	1
06716	Wolcott, ▲12,495	D	2
06501	Woodbridge, ▲7,673	D	3
06798	Woodbury, ▲5,869	C	2
06798	Woodbury, 1,800	C	2
06798	Woodbury P.O. (North Woodbury), 1,342	C	2
06460	Woodmont, 2,400	C	3
06281	Woodstock, ▲4,311	H	1
06492	Yalesville, 3,500	D	3
06389	Yantic, 1,200	G	2

06254	Franklin, ▲1,356	G	2
06335	Gales Ferry, 6,200	G	3
06829	Georgetown, 1,101	B	4
06033	Glastonbury, ▲20,651	E	2
06756	Goshen, ▲1,351	C	1
06035	Granby, ▲6,150	D	1
06430	Greenfield Hill, 2,500	B	4
06436	Greens Farms, 3,147	A	4
06830	Greenwich, ▲59,755	A	4
06340	Groton, ▲38,523	G	3
06340	Groton, 8,933	G	3
06437	Guilford, ▲12,033	E	3
06437	Guilford, 3,632	E	3
06438	Haddam, ▲4,934	E	3
06438	Haddam, 950	E	3
06514	Hamden, ▲49,357	D	3
06247	Hampton, ▲1,129	G	1
06101	Hartford (cap.), 158,017	E	1
	Hartford, ‡663,891	E	1
06091	Hartland, ▲1,303	D	1
06790	Harwinton, ▲4,318	C	1
06082	Hazardville, 10,000	E	1
06248	Hebron, ▲3,815	F	2
06441	Higganum, 2,600	E	2
06108	Hockanum, 6,500	E	2
06484	Huntington, 2,000	C	3
06405	Indian Neck, 1,500	D	3
06442	Ivoryton, 1,500	F	3
06351	Jewett City, 3,372	H	2
06037	Kensington, 6,000	D	2
06757	Kent, ▲1,990	B	2
06241	Killingly, ▲13,573	H	2
06413	Killingworth, ▲2,435	E	3
06424	Lake Pocotopaug, 1,515	F	2
06039	Lakeville, 2,100	B	1
06249	Lebanon, ▲3,804	G	2
06339	Ledyard, ▲14,558	G	3
06759	Litchfield, ▲7,399	C	2
06759	Litchfield, 1,559	C	2
06443	Madison, ▲9,768	E	3
06443	Madison, 4,310	E	3
06040	Manchester, ▲47,994	E	1
06250	Mansfield, ▲19,994	F	1
06444	Marion, 1,800	D	2
06424	Marlborough, ▲2,991	F	2
06450	Meriden, 55,959	D	2
	Meriden, ‡55,959	D	2
06762	Middlebury, ▲5,542	C	2
06455	Middlefield, ▲4,132	E	2
06457	Middletown, 36,924	E	2
06460	Milford, 50,858	C	4
06467	Milldale, 1,175	D	2
06468	Monroe, ▲12,047	C	3
06468	Monroe P.O. (Stepney), 3,000	B	3
06473	Montowese, 2,500	D	3
06353	Montville, 1,688	G	3
06353	Montville, ▲15,662	G	3
06469	Moodus, 1,352	F	2
06354	Moosup, 3,376	H	2
06385	Morningside Park, 3,458	G	3
06763	Morris, ▲1,609	C	2
06355	Mystic, 2,568	H	3
06770	Naugatuck, 23,034	C	3

‡ Population of metropolitan area.
▲ Population of town or township.
† Zip of nearest p.o.
* Multiple zips

Bark whaler "Charles W. Morgan," on view at Mystic, Connecticut, covered more miles and caught more whales than any other ship of her kind.

Edmund V. Ballman

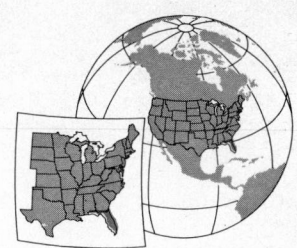

COUNTIES

...hua, 104,764	D 2
...er, 9,242	D 1
...75,283	D 2
...lford, 14,625	D 2
...ard, 230,006	F 5
...vard, 620,100	F 5
...oun, 7,624	D 6
...arlotte, 27,559	E 5
...us, 19,196	D 3
..., 32,059	E 2
...umbia, 25,250	C 1
...e, 1,287,792	F 6
...Soto, 13,060	E 4
...e, 5,480	C 2
...al, 528,865	B 6
...ambia, 205,334	B 6
...ler, 4,454	E 2
...ranklin, 7,065	B 2
...dsen, 39,184	B 1
...christ, 3,551	D 2
...des, 3,669	E 5
...f, 10,096	D 7
...milton, 7,787	D 1
...dee, 14,889	E 4
...ndry, 11,859	E 5
...rnando, 17,004	D 3
...hlands, 29,507	E 4
...lsborough, 490,265	D 4
...mes, 10,720	D 2
...an River, 35,992	F 4
...kson, 34,434	D 5
...erson, 8,778	C 1
...ayette, 2,892	E 3
...e, 69,305	E 5
..., 105,216	E 5
...n, 103,047	B 1
...y, 12,756	D 2
...erty, 3,379	C 1
...dison, 13,481	C 1
...natee, 97,115	D 4
...rion, 69,030	D 2
...tin, 28,035	F 4
...nroe, 52,586	E 7
...ssau, 20,626	E 1
...aloosa, 88,187	C 6
...eechobee, 11,233	F 4
...nge, 344,311	E 3
...ceola, 25,267	E 3
...m Beach, 348,753	F 5
...co, 75,955	D 3
...ellas, 522,329	D 4
...k, 227,222	E 4
...nam, 36,290	E 2
...t Johns, 30,727	E 2
...t Lucie, 50,836	F 4
...ta Rosa, 37,741	B 6
...asota, 120,413	D 4
...minole, 83,692	E 3
...nter, 14,839	D 3
Suwannee, 15,559	C 1
Taylor, 13,641	C 1
Union, 8,112	D 1
Volusia, 169,487	E 2
Wakulla, 6,308	B 1
Walton, 16,087	C 6
Washington, 11,453	C 6

CITIES and TOWNS

Zip	Name/Pop.	Key
32615	Alachua, 2,252	D 2
32420	Alford, 402	D 6
32421	Altha, 423	A 1
32702	Altoona, 800	E 3
33820	Alturas, 468	E 4
33920	Alva, 900	E 5
33501	Anna Maria, 1,137	D 4
32617	Anthony, 500	D 2
32320	Apalachicola⊙, 3,102	A 2
33570	Apollo Beach, 1,042	C 3
32703	Apopka, 4,045	E 3
33821	Arcadia⊙, 5,658	E 4
32618	Archer, 898	D 2
32422	Argyle, 155	C 6
† 32327	Arran, 160	B 1
32705	Astatula, 388	E 3
32002	Astor, 300	E 2
32823	Auburndale, 5,386	E 3
† 32344	Aucilla, 150	C 1
33825	Avon Park, 6,712	E 4
33827	Babson Park, 950	E 4
32530	Bagdad, 850	B 6
32531	Baker, 500	C 5
32234	Baldwin, 1,272	E 1
† 33101	Bal Harbour, 2,038	B 4
32005	Barberville, 300	E 2
32533	Barrineau Park, 150	B 6
32532	Barth, 200	B 6
33830	Bartow⊙, 12,891	E 4
32423	Bascom, 200	A 1
33428	Basinger, 300	F 4
† 33101	Bay Harbour Islands, 4,619	B 4
33504	Bay Pines, 1,100	B 3
33902	Bayshore, 150	E 5
† 36502	Bay Springs, 125	B 6
33429	Bean City, 155	F 5
33578	Bee Ridge, 2,100	D 4
32619	Bell, 227	D 2
33540	Belleair, 2,962	B 2
† 33540	Belleair Beach, 952	B 2
33540	Belleair Bluffs, 1,910	B 3
33430	Belle Glade, 15,949	F 5
† 33430	Belle Glade Camp, 1,892	F 5
† 32801	Belle Isle, 2,705	E 3
32620	Belleview, 916	D 2
33152	Biscayne Park, 2,717	B 4
† 32801	Bithlo, 684	E 3
32424	Blountstown⊙, 2,384	A 1
† 32535	Bluffsprings, 160	B 5
33921	Boca Grande, 600	D 5
33432	Boca Raton, 28,506	F 5
33922	Bokeelia, 750	D 5
32425	Bonifay⊙, 2,068	C 5
33923	Bonita Springs, 1,932	E 5
32007	Bostwick, 500	E 2
33834	Bowling Green, 1,357	E 4
33435	Boynton Beach, 18,115	F 5
33505	Bradenton⊙, 21,040	D 4
33510	Bradenton Beach, 1,370	D 4
33835	Bradley, 1,276	D 4
33511	Brandon, 12,749	D 4
32008	Branford, 820	D 2
† 33435	Briny Breezes, 481	G 5
32321	Bristol⊙, 626	B 1
32621	Bronson⊙, 698	D 2
32622	Brooker, 340	D 2
33512	Brooksville⊙, 4,060	D 3

AREA 58,560 sq. mi.
POPULATION 6,789,443
CAPITAL Tallahassee
LARGEST CITY Jacksonville
HIGHEST POINT 345 ft. (Walton County)
SETTLED IN 1565
ADMITTED TO UNION March 3, 1845
POPULAR NAME Sunshine State; Peninsula State
STATE FLOWER Orange Blossom
STATE BIRD Mockingbird

Topography

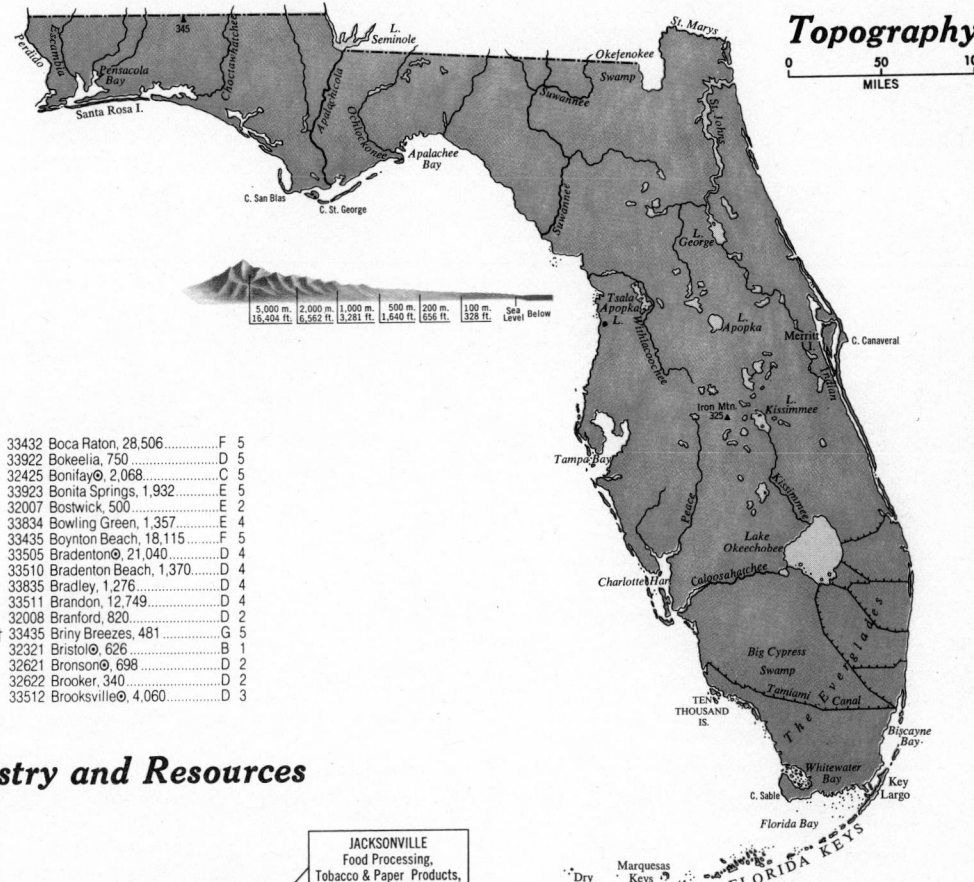

Agriculture, Industry and Resources

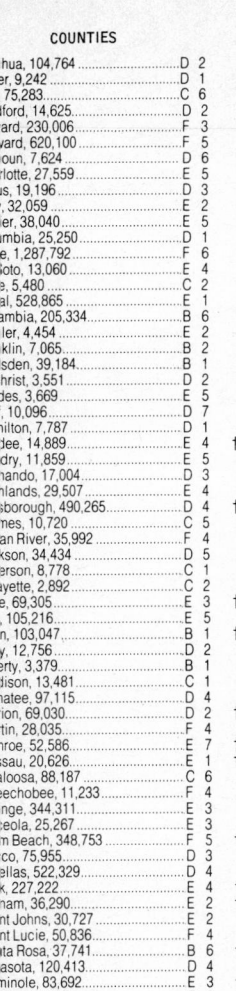

DOMINANT LAND USE

- Fruit, Truck & Mixed Farming
- Truck & Mixed Farming
- Truck Farming
- Cotton, Tobacco, Hogs, Peanuts
- Peanuts, General Farming
- General Farming, Forest Products, Truck Farming, Cotton
- Livestock Grazing
- Forests
- Swampland, Limited Agriculture
- Urban Areas
- Nonagricultural Land

MAJOR MINERAL OCCURRENCES

Cl	Clay	Pe	Peat
Ls	Limestone	Ti	Titanium
P	Phosphates	Zr	Zirconium
⚡	Water Power		Major Industrial Areas

JACKSONVILLE
Food Processing,
Tobacco & Paper Products,
Chemicals

PENSACOLA
Lumber, Wood & Paper
Products, Chemicals

TAMPA– ST. PETERSBURG
Food Processing,
Chemicals, Cigars

MIAMI– WEST PALM BEACH
Aircraft, Metal & Electrical
Products, Food Processing,
Clothing, Furniture

† 33101	Browns Village, 23,442	B 4
32455	Bruce, 221	C 6
33439	Bryant, 400	F 5
† 33054	Bunche Park, 5,773	B 4
32010	Bunnell⊙, 1,687	E 2
33513	Bushnell⊙, 700	D 3
32011	Callahan, 772	E 1
32401	Callaway, 3,240	D 6
33426	Campbellton, 304	D 5
33438	Canal Point, 900	F 5
32624	Candler, 500	E 2
32920	Cape Canaveral, 4,258	F 3
33904	Cape Coral, 10,193	E 5
33924	Captiva, 150	D 5
33054	Carol City, 27,361	B 4
32322	Carrabelle, 1,044	B 2
32427	Caryville, 724	C 6
32706	Cassadaga, 250	E 3
32707	Casselberry, 9,438	E 3
† 32401	Cedar Grove, 689	D 6
32625	Cedar Key, 714	C 2
33514	Center Hill, 371	D 3
32535	Century, 2,679	B 5
† 32302	Chaires, 150	B 1
33950	Charlotte Harbor, 990	E 5
32324	Chattahoochee, 7,944	B 1
† 32350	Cherry Lake Farms, 400	C 1
32626	Chiefland, 1,965	D 2
32428	Chipley⊙, 3,347	D 6
33925	Chokoloskee, 300	E 6
32709	Christmas, 800	E 3
† 32548	Cinco Bayou, 362	B 6
32627	Citra, 500	D 2
† 32922	City Point, 350	F 3
32430	Clarksville, 250	D 6
* 33515	Clearwater⊙, 52,074	B 2
32711	Clermont, 3,661	E 3
† 33950	Cleveland, 150	E 5
33440	Clewiston, 3,896	E 5
32922	Cocoa, 16,110	F 3
32931	Cocoa Beach, 9,952	F 3
† 33060	Coconut Creek, 1,359	F 5
33521	Coleman, 614	D 3
32448	Compass Lake, 200	D 6
† 32333	Concord, 300	B 1
33314	Cooper City, 2,535	F 5
33926	Copeland, 500	E 6
† 83559	Coral Cove, 1,520	D 4
33134	Coral Gables, 42,494	B 5
33836	Cornwell, 700	E 4
33522	Cortez, 600	D 4
32533	Cottagehill, 500	B 6
32431	Cottondale, 765	D 6
32327	Crawfordville⊙, 750	B 1
32012	Crescent City, 1,734	E 2
32536	Crestview⊙, 7,952	C 6
32628	Cross City⊙, 2,268	C 1
32463	Crystal Lake, 125	D 6
32629	Crystal River, 1,696	D 3
33524	Crystal Springs, 300	D 3
33157	Cutler Ridge, 17,441	F 6
32432	Cypress, 266	A 1
33880	Cypress Gardens, 3,757	E 4
† 33472	Cypress Quarters, 1,310	F 4
33525	Dade City⊙, 4,241	D 3
33004	Dania, 9,013	B 4
† 32464	Darlington, 175	C 5
33837	Davenport, 828	E 3
33314	Davie, 2,856	B 4
32013	Day, 200	C 1
* 32014	Daytona Beach, 45,327	F 2
32016	Daytona Beach Shores, 768	F 2
32713	De Bary, 3,154	E 3
33441	Deerfield Beach, 17,130	F 5
32433	De Funiak Springs⊙, 4,966	C 6
32720	De Land⊙, 11,641	E 2
32028	De Leon Springs, 1,134	E 2
33444	Delray Beach, 19,366	F 5
32763	Deltona, 4,868	E 3
† 33870	De Soto City, 250	E 4
32541	Destin, 1,536	C 6
32030	Doctors Inlet, 800	E 1
33527	Dover, 2,094	D 4
† 32060	Dowling Park, 200	C 1
33838	Dundee, 1,660	E 3
33528	Dunedin, 17,639	B 2
32630	Dunnellon, 1,146	D 2
33839	Eagle Lake, 1,373	E 4
32631	Earleton, 350	D 2
† 33601	East Lake-Orient Park, 5,697	C 2
† 33940	East Naples, 6,152	E 5
32031	East Palatka, 1,446	E 2
32328	Eastpoint, 1,188	B 2
32437	Ebro, 125	C 6
32032	Edgewater, 3,348	F 3
32801	Edgewood, 392	E 3
† 33601	Egypt Lake, 7,556	C 2
33531	Elfers, 500	D 3
32033	Elkton, 240	E 2
† 33101	El Portal, 2,068	B 4
33533	Englewood, 5,182	D 5
32504	Ensley, 2,400	B 6

(continued on following page)

(continued)

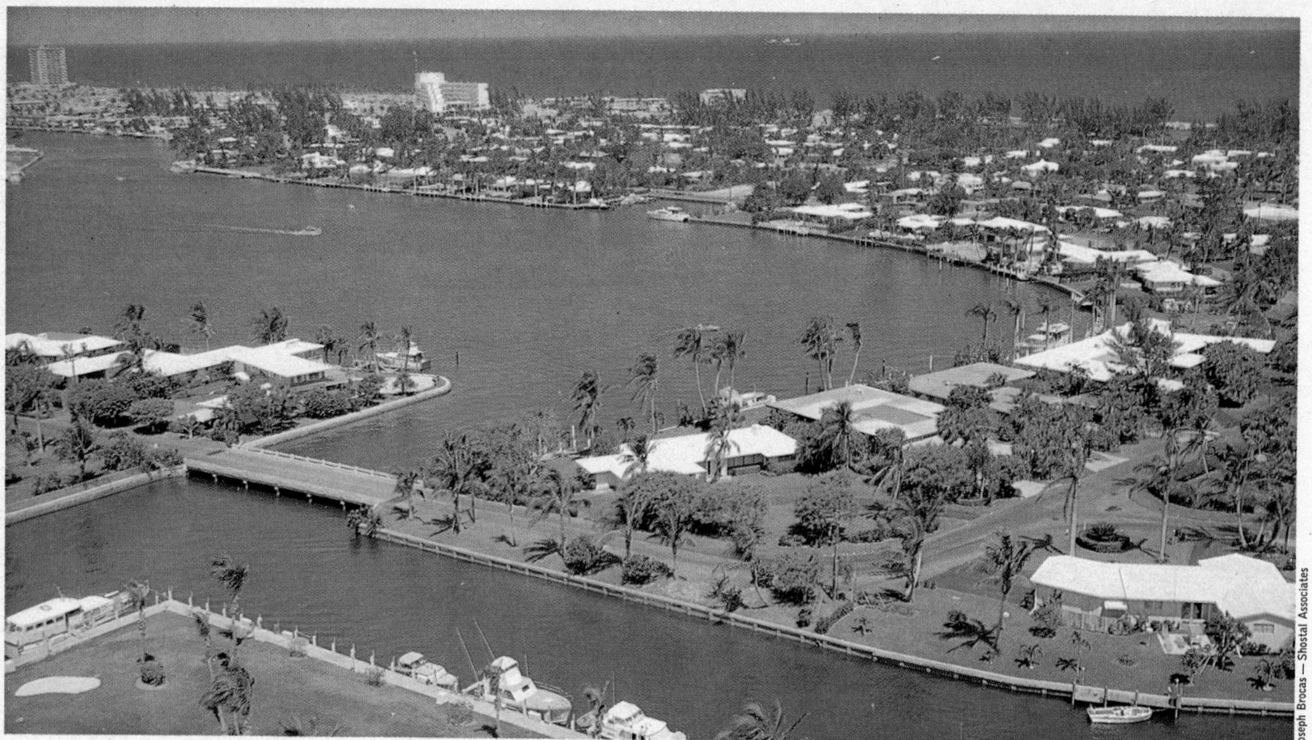

Joseph Brocas — Shostal Associates

Over 150 miles of inland waterways provide a Venetian atmosphere in the modern city of Fort Lauderdale, Florida.

† 32010 Espanola, 300 ....E 2
33928 Estero, 950 ....E 5
32425 Esto, 210 ....C 5
32726 Eustis, 6,722 ....E 3
33929 Everglades City, 462 ....E 6
† 32601 Fairbanks, 380 ....D 2
† 32804 Fairvilla, 950 ....E 3
33930 Felda, 125 ....E 5
32948 Fellsmere, 813 ....F 4
32034 Fernandina Beach⊙, 6,955 ...E 1
† 33301 Fern Crest Village, 1,009 ....B 4
32036 Flagler Beach, 1,042 ....E 2
32635 Florahome, 400 ....E 2
32636 Floral City, 975 ....D 3
33030 Florida City, 5,133 ....F 6
† 32570 Floridatown, 297 ....B 6
† 32569 Florosa, 200 ....B 6
† 32347 Foley, 500 ....C 1
† 33935 Fort Denaud, 300 ....E 5
† 33472 Fort Drum, 100 ....F 4
33834 Fort Green, 300 ....E 4
* 33301 Fort Lauderdale⊙, 139,590 ...C 4
Fort Lauderdale-Hollywood, ‡620,100 ....C 4
32637 Fort McCoy, 900 ....E 2
33841 Fort Meade, 4,374 ....E 4
* 33901 Fort Myers⊙, 27,351 ....E 5
33931 Fort Myers Beach, 4,305 ....E 5
33842 Fort Ogden, 700 ....E 4
33450 Fort Pierce⊙, 29,721 ....F 4
32548 Fort Walton Beach, 19,994 ....C 6
32038 Fort White, 365 ....D 2
32438 Fountain, 650 ....D 6
32439 Freeport, 950 ....C 6
† 32430 Frink, 275 ....D 6
33843 Frostproof, 2,814 ....E 4
32731 Fruitland Park, 1,359 ....D 3
33578 Fruitville, 1,531 ....D 4
32601 Gainesville⊙, 64,510 ....D 2
32732 Geneva, 950 ....E 3
32039 Georgetown, 687 ....E 2
33534 Gibsonton, 1,900 ....C 3
32960 Gifford, 5,772 ....F 4
32040 Glen Saint Mary, 357 ....D 1
32722 Glenwood, 400 ....E 2
33160 Golden Beach, 849 ....C 4
33940 Golden Gate, 1,410 ....E 5
† 33455 Gomez, 400 ....F 4
32560 Gonzalez, 750 ....B 6
33933 Goodland, 500 ....E 6
† 32502 Goulding, 500 ....B 6
33170 Goulds, 6,690 ....F 6
32440 Graceville, 2,560 ....D 5
32042 Graham, 150 ....D 2
32638 Grandin, 150 ....E 2
32442 Grand Ridge, 512 ....A 1
32949 Grant, 500 ....F 4
33460 Greenacres City, 1,731 ....F 5
32043 Green Cove Springs⊙, 3,857 ....E 2
32330 Greensboro, 716 ....B 1
32331 Greenville, 1,141 ....C 1
32443 Greenwood, 515 ....A 1
32332 Gretna, 883 ....B 1
33533 Grove City, 1,178 ....F 5
32736 Groveland, 1,928 ....E 3
32561 Gulf Breeze, 4,190 ....B 6
32639 Gulf Hammock, 300 ....D 2
† 33552 Gulf Harbors, 1,177 ....D 3
33737 Gulfport, 9,730 ....B 3
† 33444 Gulf Stream, 408 ....F 5
† 32601 Hague, 200 ....D 2
33844 Haines City, 8,956 ....E 3
33009 Hallandale, 23,849 ....B 4
32044 Hampton, 386 ....D 2
33440 Harlem, 2,006 ....F 5
32563 Harold, 150 ....B 6
32045 Hastings, 320 ....E 2

32333 Havana, 2,022 ....B 1
32640 Hawthorne, 1,126 ....D 2
32642 Hernando, 524 ....D 3
* 33010 Hialeah, 102,297 ....B 4
† 33010 Hialeah Gardens, 492 ....B 4
33846 Highland City, 900 ....E 4
† 33515 High Point, 800 ....B 3
32643 High Springs, 2,787 ....D 2
32401 Hiland Park, 3,691 ....C 6
† 33827 Hillcrest Heights, 154 ....E 4
32046 Hilliard, 1,205 ....E 1
† 32327 Hilliardville, 150 ....B 1
† 33060 Hillsboro Beach, 713 ....F 5
† 32333 Hinson, 250 ....B 1
33455 Hobe Sound, 2,029 ....F 4
32645 Holder, 134 ....D 3
32047 Hollister, 500 ....E 2
32017 Holly Hill, 8,191 ....E 2
* 33020 Hollywood, 106,873 ....B 4
† 33020 Hollywood Ridge Farms, 302 ....B 4
33509 Holmes Beach, 2,699 ....D 4
32564 Holt, 850 ....C 6
33030 Homestead, 13,674 ....F 6
32646 Homosassa, 850 ....D 3
32647 Homosassa Springs, 550 ......D 3
32334 Hosford, 975 ....B 1
32737 Howey In The Hills, 466 ....E 3
33568 Hudson, 2,278 ....D 3
† 33460 Hypoluxo, 336 ....F 5
33934 Immokalee, 3,764 ....E 5
32901 Indialantic, 2,685 ....F 3
32935 Indian Harbour Beach, 5,371 ....F 3
33535 Indian Rocks Beach, 2,666 ...B 3
† 33535 Indian Rocks Beach South Shore, 791 ....B 3
33456 Indiantown, 2,283 ....F 4
32649 Inglis, 449 ....D 2
33848 Intercession City, 600 ....E 3
32048 Interlachen, 478 ....E 2
32650 Inverness⊙, 2,299 ....D 3
33036 Islamorada, 1,251 ....F 7
32654 Island Grove, 200 ....D 2
* 32201 Jacksonville⊙, 528,865 ....E 1
Jacksonville, ‡528,865 ....E 1
32250 Jacksonville Beach, 12,049 ..E 1
32052 Jasper⊙, 2,221 ....D 1
32565 Jay, 646 ....B 5
32053 Jennings, 582 ....C 1
33457 Jensen Beach, 3,000 ....F 4
† 32901 June Park, 3,090 ....F 3
† 33404 Juno Beach, 747 ....F 5
33458 Jupiter, 3,136 ....F 5
† 33455 Jupiter Island, 295 ....F 4
33849 Kathleen, 900 ....D 3
32739 Kenansville, 450 ....F 4
33156 Kendall, 35,497 ....B 5
† 32670 Kendrick, 200 ....D 2
33709 Kenneth City, 3,862 ....B 3
33149 Key Biscayne, 4,563 ....B 5
33051 Key Colony Beach, 371 ....F 7
33037 Key Largo, 2,866 ....F 6
32656 Keystone Heights, 800 ....E 2
33040 Key West⊙, 27,563 ....E 7
32449 Kinard, 450 ....D 6
32741 Kissimmee⊙, 7,119 ....E 3
† 32010 Korona, 200 ....E 2
33935 La Belle⊙, 1,823 ....E 5
33537 Lacoochee, 1,380 ....D 3
32658 La Crosse, 365 ....D 2
32659 Lady Lake, 382 ....E 3
33850 Lake Alfred, 2,847 ....E 3
32054 Lake Butler⊙, 1,598 ....D 1
† 33601 Lake Carroll, 5,577 ....C 2
32055 Lake City⊙, 10,575 ....D 1
32057 Lake Como, 340 ....E 2
33459 Lake Harbor, 300 ....F 5

32744 Lake Helen, 1,303 ....E 3
32745 Lake Jem, 314 ....E 3
* 33801 Lakeland, 41,550 ....D 3
† 33601 Lake Magdalene, 9,266 ....D 3
32746 Lake Mary, 900 ....E 3
32747 Lake Monroe, 500 ....E 3
33403 Lake Park, 6,993 ....F 5
33852 Lake Placid, 656 ....E 4
† 33471 Lakeport, 375 ....E 5
33853 Lake Wales, 8,240 ....E 4
32566 Lakewood, 525 ....C 5
33460 Lake Worth, 23,714 ....G 5
32336 Lamont, 500 ....C 1
33539 Land O'Lakes, 900 ....D 3
33460 Lantana, 7,126 ....F 5
33540 Largo, 22,031 ....B 3
33308 Lauderdale-by-the-Sea, 2,879 ....C 3
† 33301 Lauderdale Lakes, 10,577 .....B 4
33313 Lauderhill, 8,465 ....B 4
32567 Laurel Hill, 418 ....C 5
33545 Laurel-Nokomis, 3,238 ....D 4
32058 Lawtey, 636 ....D 1
32661 Lecanto, 125 ....D 3
32059 Lee, 240 ....C 1
32748 Leesburg, 11,869 ....E 3
33936 Lehigh Acres, 4,394 ....E 5
33030 Leisure City, 2,900 ....F 6
† 33601 Leto, 8,458 ....C 2
33064 Lighthouse Point, 9,071 ....F 5
† 33865 Limestone, 200 ....E 4
32060 Live Oak⊙, 6,830 ....D 1
32337 Lloyd, 225 ....C 1
32662 Lochloosa, 175 ....E 2
33548 Longboat Key, 2,850 ....D 4
33001 Long Key, 150 ....F 7
32750 Longwood, 3,203 ....E 3
33857 Lorida, 950 ....E 4
33858 Loughman, 950 ....E 3
32663 Lowell, 350 ....D 2
33470 Loxahatchee, 950 ....F 5
33549 Lutz, 950 ....D 3
32444 Lynn Haven, 4,044 ....C 6
32063 Macclenny⊙, 2,733 ....D 1
33738 Madeira Beach, 4,158 ....B 3
32340 Madison⊙, 3,737 ....C 1
32751 Maitland, 7,157 ....E 3
32950 Malabar, 634 ....F 3
32445 Malone, 667 ....A 1
33550 Mango, 950 ....D 4
33050 Marathon, 4,397 ....E 7
33937 Marco, 900 ....E 6
33063 Margate, 8,867 ....F 5
32446 Marianna⊙, 6,741 ....A 1
† 32084 Marineland, 13 ....E 2
32569 Mary Esther, 3,192 ....B 6
33512 Masaryktown, 389 ....D 3
32753 Mascotte, 966 ....E 3
32066 Mayo⊙, 793 ....C 1
32568 McDavid, 500 ....B 5
32664 McIntosh, 287 ....D 2
† 33101 Medley, 351 ....B 4
32901 Melbourne, 40,236 ....F 3
32951 Melbourne Beach, 2,262 ....F 3
32666 Melrose, 950 ....D 2
† 33301 Melrose Park, 6,111 ....B 4
† 33561 Memphis, 3,207 ....D 4
32952 Merritt Island, 29,233 ....F 3
32410 Mexico Beach, 588 ....D 6
* 33101 Miami⊙, 334,859 ....B 5
Miami, ‡1,267,792 ....B 5
33139 Miami Beach, 87,072 ....C 5
† 33101 Miami Lakes, 3,500 ....B 4
33153 Miami Shores, 9,425 ....B 4
33166 Miami Springs, 13,279 ....B 5
32667 Micanopy, 759 ....D 2
† 32960 Micco, 400 ....F 4
32309 Miccosukee, 275 ....B 1

32068 Middleburg, 950 ....E 1
32343 Midway, 900 ....B 1
32537 Milligan, 950 ....C 6
32570 Milton⊙, 5,360 ....B 6
32754 Mims, 8,309 ....F 3
32755 Minneola, 878 ....E 3
33023 Miramar, 23,973 ....B 4
32577 Molino, 850 ....B 6
† 32696 Montbrook, 250 ....D 2
32344 Monticello⊙, 2,473 ....C 1
32756 Montverde, 308 ....E 3
33471 Moore Haven⊙, 974 ....E 5
32434 Mossy Head, 160 ....C 6
32757 Mount Dora, 4,543 ....E 3
32352 Mount Pleasant, 150 ....B 1
33860 Mulberry, 2,701 ....E 4
33551 Myakka City, 672 ....D 4
32506 Myrtle Grove, 16,186 ....B 6
33940 Naples⊙, 12,042 ....E 5
† 33940 Naples Park, 1,522 ....E 5
33030 Naranja, 2,900 ....F 6
32233 Neptune Beach, 2,868 ....E 1
32669 Newberry, 1,247 ....D 2
33552 New Port Richey, 6,098 ....D 3
32069 New Smyrna Beach, 10,580 ..F 2
32578 Niceville, 4,024 ....C 6
33863 Nichols, 300 ....E 4
33864 Nocatee, 950 ....E 4
33555 Nokomis-Laurel, 3,238 ....D 4
32452 Noma, 234 ....C 5
33141 North Bay Village, 4,831 ....B 4
33903 North Fort Myers, 8,798 ....E 5
33161 North Miami, 34,767 ....B 4
33161 North Miami Beach, 30,723...C 4
† 33940 North Naples, 3,201 ....E 5
33403 North Palm Beach, 9,035 ....F 5
33595 North Port Charlotte, 2,244 ....D 4
† 33708 North Redington Beach, 768 ....B 3
† 33054 Norwood, 14,973 ....B 4
32759 Oak Hill, 747 ....F 3
32760 Oakland, 672 ....E 3
33307 Oakland Park, 16,261 ....B 3
32071 O'Brien, 200 ....D 1
32670 Ocala⊙, 22,583 ....D 2
† 33457 Ocean Breeze, 714 ....F 4
33444 Ocean Ridge, 1,074 ....F 5
33943 Ochopee, 200 ....E 6
32761 Ocoee, 3,937 ....E 3
33556 Odessa, 500 ....D 3
33163 Ojus, 12,000 ....B 4
32762 Okahumpka, 470 ....D 3
33472 Okeechobee⊙, 3,715 ....F 4
32679 Oklawaha, 700 ....E 2
33557 Oldsmar, 1,538 ....B 2
32680 Old Town, 500 ....C 2
32072 Olustee, 400 ....D 1
33865 Ona, 236 ....E 4
33558 Oneco, 3,246 ....D 4
33054 Opa-locka, 11,902 ....B 4
32763 Orange City, 1,777 ....E 3
32681 Orange Lake, 900 ....D 2
32073 Orange Park, 7,619 ....E 1
32682 Orange Springs, 500 ....E 2
* 32801 Orlando⊙, 99,006 ....E 3
Orlando, ‡428,003 ....E 3
32074 Ormond Beach, 14,063 ....E 2
33559 Osprey, 1,115 ....D 4
32764 Osteen, 875 ....E 3
32683 Otter Creek, 400 ....D 2
32765 Oviedo, 1,870 ....E 3
32684 Oxford, 490 ....D 3
33560 Ozona, 900 ....D 3
32570 Pace, 1,776 ....B 6
33476 Pahokee, 5,663 ....F 5
32077 Palatka⊙, 9,310 ....E 2
32901 Palm Bay, 6,927 ....F 3
33480 Palm Beach, 9,086 ....G 4

† 33404 Palm Beach Shores, 1,214 ....G 5
33490 Palm City, 900 ....F 4
33561 Palmetto, 7,422 ....D 4
33563 Palm Harbor, 1,763 ....D 3
33619 Palm River-Clair Mel, 8,536 ..C 3
32935 Palm Shores, 202 ....F 3
33460 Palm Springs, 4,340 ....F 5
32346 Panacea, 950 ....B 1
32401 Panama City⊙, 32,096 ....C 6
32401 Parker, 4,212 ....C 6
33564 Parrish, 950 ....D 4
32538 Paxton, 243 ....C 5
† 33023 Pembroke Park, 2,949 ....B 4
33023 Pembroke Pines, 15,520 ....B 4
32079 Penney Farms, 561 ....E 2
* 32501 Pensacola⊙, 59,507 ....B 6
Pensacola, ‡243,075 ....B 6
33157 Perrine, 10,257 ....F 6
32347 Perry⊙, 7,701 ....C 1
33867 Pierce, 500 ....E 4
32080 Pierson, 654 ....E 2
33565 Pinellas Park, 22,287 ....B 3
32350 Pinetta, 300 ....C 1
† 33042 Pirates Cove, 150 ....E 7
33946 Placida, 250 ....D 5
33314 Plantation, 23,523 ....B 4
33566 Plant City, 15,451 ....D 3
32768 Plymouth, 950 ....E 3
33868 Polk City, 151 ....E 3
32081 Pomona Park, 578 ....E 2
* 33060 Pompano Beach, 37,724 ....F 5
32455 Ponce de Leon, 288 ....C 6
† 32019 Ponce Inlet, 328 ....F 2
32082 Ponte Vedra Beach, 2,100 .....E 1
33950 Port Charlotte, 10,769 ....D 5
† 32439 Portland, 228 ....C 6
† 33438 Port Mayaca, 400 ....F 5
32019 Port Orange, 3,781 ....F 2
33568 Port Richey, 1,259 ....D 3
32456 Port Saint Joe, 4,401 ....D 6
33450 Port Saint Lucie, 330 ....F 4
33492 Port Salerno, 1,161 ....F 4
33171 Princeton, 1,900 ....F 6
† 33619 Progress, 1,328 ....C 3
† 32061 Providence, 150 ....D 2
33950 Punta Gorda⊙, 3,879 ....E 5
32351 Quincy⊙, 8,334 ....B 1
32083 Raiford, 500 ....D 1
† 32696 Raleigh, 275 ....D 2
32455 Redbay, 500 ....C 6
32686 Reddick, 305 ....D 2
33708 Redington Beach, 1,583 ....B 3
† 33708 Redington Shores, 1,733 ....B 3
† 33599 Richland, 928 ....D 3
† 33158 Richmond Heights, 6,663 ......F 6
33569 Riverview, 2,225 ....D 4
33404 Riviera Beach, 21,401 ....G 5
32955 Rockledge, 10,523 ....F 3
32957 Roseland, 550 ....F 4
32447 Round Lake, 275 ....D 6
33570 Ruskin, 2,414 ....C 3
33572 Safety Harbor, 3,103 ....B 2
32084 Saint Augustine⊙, 12,352 .....E 2
32084 Saint Augustine Beach, 632 ..E 2
33573 Saint Catherine, 350 ....D 3
32769 Saint Cloud, 5,041 ....E 3
33956 Saint James City, 500 ....D 5
33574 Saint Leo, 1,145 ....D 3
† 33450 Saint Lucie, 428 ....F 4
32355 Saint Marks, 366 ....B 1
* 33701 Saint Petersburg, 216,232 .....B 3
33736 Saint Petersburg Beach, 8,024 ....B 3
32356 Salem, 150 ....C 2
33505 Samoset, 4,070 ....D 4
† 32069 Samsula, 270 ....E 2
33576 San Antonio, 473 ....D 3
32087 Sanderson, 150 ....D 1

32771 Sanford⊙, 17,393 ....
33957 Sanibel, 750 ....
32088 San Mateo, 975 ....
† 32670 Santos, 150 ....
* 33577 Sarasota⊙, 40,237 ....
32935 Satellite Beach, 6,558 ....
32089 Satsuma, 610 ....
32775 Scottsmoor, 850 ....
† 33301 Sea Ranch Lakes, 660 ....
32958 Sebastian, 825 ....
33870 Sebring⊙, 7,223 ....
33584 Seffner, 2,000 ....
33540 Seminole, 2,410 ....
32090 Seville, 500 ....
† 33457 Sewalls Point, 298 ....
32579 Shalimar, 578 ....
† 32628 Shamrock, 200 ....
32959 Sharpes, 427 ....
32688 Silver Springs, 500 ....
32460 Sneads, 1,550 ....
32358 Sopchoppy, 460 ....
32776 Sorrento, 500 ....
33493 South Bay, 2,958 ....
32021 South Daytona, 4,979 ....
† 36441 South Flomaton, 329 ....
33143 South Miami, 19,571 ....
33707 South Pasadena, 2,063 ....
† 32401 Southport, 1,560 ....
32690 Sparr, 450 ....
32401 Springfield, 5,949 ....
32091 Starke⊙, 4,848 ....
32359 Steinhatchee, 800 ....
33494 Stuart⊙, 4,820 ....
32335 Sumatra, 150 ....
32691 Summerfield, 450 ....
33042 Summerland Key, 350 ....
33586 Sun City, 2,143 ....
† 33450 Sunland Gardens, 1,900 ....F
33160 Sunny Isles, 950 C
† 33577 Sunnyland, 4,900 ....D
32461 Sunnyside, 370 C
33313 Sunrise Golf Village, 7,403....E
33154 Surfside, 3,614 ....E
32692 Suwannee, 203 C
† 33144 Sweetwater, 3,307 ....E
† 33601 Sweetwater Creek, 19,453.....E
† 32043 Switzerland, 500 ....E
32809 Taft, 1,183 ....E
* 32301 Tallahassee (cap.)⊙, 71,897 ....E
Tallahassee, ‡103,047 ....E
† 33301 Tamarac, 5,078 ....E
* 33601 Tampa⊙, 277,767 C
Tampa-Saint Petersburg, ‡1,012,594 C
33589 Tarpon Springs, 7,118 ....D
32778 Tavares⊙, 3,261 ....E
33070 Tavernier, 900 ....F
32360 Telogia, 300 ....E
33617 Temple Terrace, 7,347 C
33458 Tequesta, 2,642 ....F
33591 Terra Ceia, 450 ....D
33592 Thonotosassa, 900 ....D
33905 Tice, 7,254 ....E
32780 Titusville⊙, 30,515 ....F
33740 Treasure Island, 6,120 ....B
32693 Trenton⊙, 1,074 ....D
33593 Trilby, 930 ....D
32784 Umatilla, 1,600 ....E
32580 Valparaiso, 6,504 C
33595 Venice, 6,648 ....D
33960 Venus, 300 ....E
32462 Vernon, 691 C
32960 Vero Beach⊙, 11,908 ....F
† 32548 Villa Tasso, 200 C
† 33166 Virginia Gardens, 2,524 ....B
32970 Wabasso, 950 ....F
32361 Wacissa, 275 ....B
† 32327 Wakulla, 225 ....B
32694 Waldo, 800 ....D
32568 Walnut Hill, 500 ....B
32507 Warrington, 15,848 ....B
† 32055 Watertown, 3,624 ....D
33873 Wauchula⊙, 3,007 ....E
32463 Wausau, 288 ....D
33877 Waverly, 1,172 ....E
33597 Webster, 739 ....D
32695 Weirsdale, 995 ....D
32093 Welaka, 496 ....E
32094 Wellborn, 600 ....D
32401 Westbay, 350 C
† 32901 West Melbourne, 3,050 ....F
† 33101 West Miami, 5,494 ....B
* 33401 West Palm Beach⊙, 57,375...F
West Palm Beach, ‡348,753 ....F
32401 West Panama City Beach, 1,052 C
32505 West Pensacola, 20,924 ....B
32464 Westville, 475 C
† 33101 Westwood Lakes, 12,811 ....B
32465 Wewahitchka⊙, 1,733 ....D
† 32465 White City, 600 ....F
32096 White Springs, 767 ....D
32785 Wildwood, 2,082 ....D
32696 Williston, 1,939 ....D
33305 Wilton Manors, 10,948 ....B
33598 Wimauma, 650 ....D
32786 Windermere, 894 ....E
32971 Winter Beach, 350 ....F
32787 Winter Garden, 5,153 ....E
33880 Winter Haven, 16,136 ....E
32789 Winter Park, 21,895 ....E
32362 Woodville, 900 ....B
32697 Worthington Springs, 214 ......D
32797 Yalaha, 675 ....E
32698 Yankeetown, 490 ....D
32466 Youngstown, 400 ....D
32097 Yulee, 950 ....E
32798 Zellwood, 550 ....E
33599 Zephyrhills, 3,369 ....D
33890 Zolfo Springs, 1,117 ....E

⊙ County seat.
‡ Population of metropolitan area.
† Zip of nearest p.o.
* Multiple zips

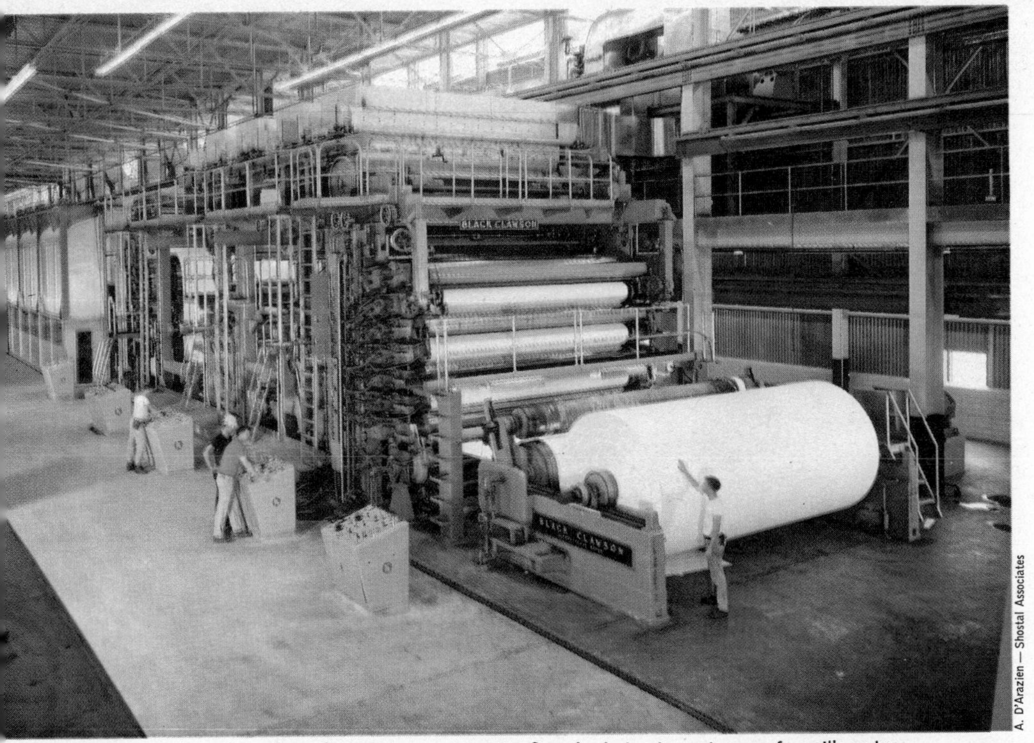

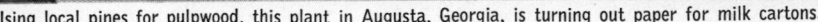

Using local pines for pulpwood, this plant in Augusta, Georgia, is turning out paper for milk cartons.

A. D'Arazien — Shostal Associates

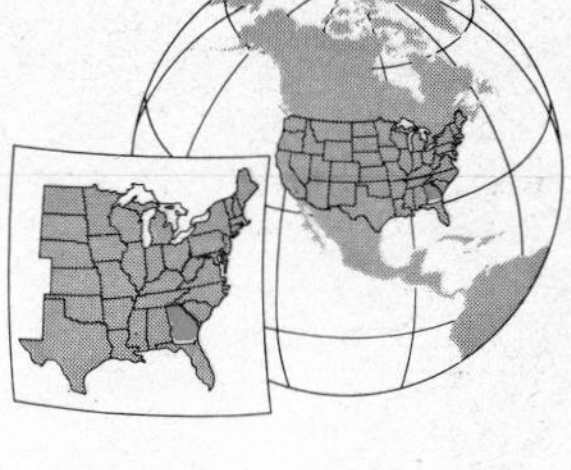

AREA 58,876 sq. mi.
POPULATION 4,589,575
CAPITAL Atlanta
LARGEST CITY Atlanta
HIGHEST POINT Brasstown Bald 4,784 ft.
SETTLED IN 1733
ADMITTED TO UNION January 2, 1788
POPULAR NAME Empire State of the South; Peach State
STATE FLOWER Cherokee Rose
STATE BIRD Brown Thrasher

COUNTIES

pling, 12,726	H 7
inson, 5,879	G 8
con, 8,233	G 7
ker, 3,875	D 8
ldwin, 34,240	F 4
nks, 6,833	E 2
rrow, 16,859	E 2
rtow, 32,663	C 2
n Hill, 13,171	F 7
rrien, 11,556	F 8
bb, 143,418	E 5
eckley, 10,291	F 6
antley, 5,940	J 8
ooks, 13,739	E 9
yan, 6,539	K 6
lloch, 31,585	J 6
rke, 18,255	J 4
tts, 10,560	E 4
lhoun, 6,606	C 7
mden, 11,334	J 9
ndler, 6,412	H 6
rroll, 45,404	B 3
atoosa, 28,271	B 1
arlton, 5,680	H 9
atham, 187,767	K 6
attahoochee, 25,813	C 6
attooga, 20,541	B 1
erokee, 31,059	D 2
arke, 65,177	F 3
ay, 3,636	B 7
ayton, 98,043	D 3
inch, 6,405	G 9
bb, 196,793	C 3
ffee, 22,828	G 8
lquitt, 32,200	E 8
lumbia, 22,327	H 3
ok, 12,129	F 8
weta, 32,310	C 4
awford, 5,748	E 5
isp, 18,087	E 7
ade, 9,910	A 1
awson, 3,639	D 2
ecatur, 22,310	C 9
e Kalb, 415,387	D 3
odge, 15,658	F 6
ooly, 10,404	E 6
ougherty, 89,639	D 7
ouglas, 28,659	C 3
arly, 12,682	C 8
chols, 1,924	G 9
ffingham, 13,632	K 6
lbert, 17,262	G 2
manuel, 18,189	H 5
vans, 7,290	J 6
annin, 13,357	D 1
ayette, 11,364	C 4
loyd, 73,742	B 2
orsyth, 16,928	D 2
ranklin, 12,784	F 2
ulton, 607,592	D 3
ilmer, 8,956	D 1
lascock, 2,280	G 4
lynn, 50,528	J 8
ordon, 23,570	C 2
rady, 17,826	D 9
reene, 10,212	F 3
winnett, 72,349	D 2
abersham, 20,691	E 1
all, 59,405	E 2
ancock, 9,019	G 4
aralson, 15,927	B 3
arris, 11,520	C 5
art, 15,814	G 2
eard, 5,354	B 4
enry, 23,724	D 4
ouston, 62,924	E 6
Irwin, 8,036	F 7
Jackson, 21,093	E 2
Jasper, 5,760	E 4
Jeff Davis, 9,425	G 7
Jefferson, 17,174	H 4
Jenkins, 8,332	J 5
Johnson, 7,727	G 5
Jones, 12,218	E 5
Lamar, 10,688	D 4
Lanier, 5,031	F 8
Laurens, 32,738	G 6
Lee, 7,044	D 7
Liberty, 17,569	J 7
Lincoln, 5,895	H 3
Long, 3,746	J 7
Lowndes, 55,112	F 9
Lumpkin, 8,728	D 1
Macon, 12,933	D 6
Madison, 13,517	F 2
Marion, 5,099	C 6
McDuffie, 15,276	H 4
McIntosh, 7,371	K 7
Meriwether, 19,461	C 4
Miller, 6,397	C 8
Mitchell, 18,956	D 8
Monroe, 10,991	E 4
Montgomery, 6,099	G 6
Morgan, 9,904	F 3
Murray, 12,986	C 1
Muscogee, 167,377	C 6
Newton, 26,282	E 3
Oconee, 7,915	F 3
Oglethorpe, 7,598	F 3
Paulding, 17,520	C 3
Peach, 15,990	E 5
Pickens, 9,620	D 2
Pierce, 9,281	H 8
Pike, 7,316	D 4
Polk, 29,656	B 3
Pulaski, 8,066	E 6
Putnam, 8,394	F 4
Quitman, 2,180	B 7
Rabun, 8,327	F 1
Randolph, 8,734	C 7
Richmond, 162,347	H 4
Rockdale, 18,152	D 3
Schley, 3,097	D 6
Screven, 12,591	J 5
Seminole, 7,059	C 9
Spalding, 39,514	D 4
Stephens, 20,331	F 1
Stewart, 6,511	C 6
Sumter, 26,931	D 6
Talbot, 6,625	C 5
Taliaferro, 2,423	G 3
Tattnall, 16,557	J 6
Taylor, 7,865	D 5
Telfair, 11,381	G 7
Terrell, 11,416	D 7
Thomas, 34,515	E 9
Tift, 27,288	E 7
Toombs, 19,151	H 6
Towns, 4,565	E 1
Treutlen, 5,647	G 6
Troup, 44,466	B 4
Turner, 8,790	E 7
Twiggs, 8,222	F 5
Union, 6,811	E 1
Upson, 23,505	D 5
Walker, 50,691	B 1
Walton, 23,404	E 3
Ware, 33,525	H 8
Warren, 6,669	G 4
Washington, 17,480	G 4
Wayne, 17,858	J 7
Webster, 2,362	C 6
Wheeler, 4,596	G 6
White, 7,742	E 1
Whitfield, 55,108	B 1
Wilcox, 6,998	F 7
Wilkes, 10,184	G 3
Wilkinson, 9,393	F 5
Worth, 14,770	E 8

CITIES and TOWNS

Zip	*Name/Pop.*	*Key*
31001	Abbeville⊙, 781	F 7
30101	Acworth, 3,929	C 2
30103	Adairsville, 1,676	C 2
31620	Adel⊙, 4,972	F 8
31002	Adrian, 705	G 5
30410	Ailey, 487	G 6
30411	Alamo⊙, 833	G 6
31622	Alapaha, 633	F 8
* 31701	Albany⊙, 72,623	D 7
	Albany, ‡89,639	D 7
† 30204	Aldora, 322	D 4
30801	Alexander, 200	J 4
31301	Allenhurst, 230	J 7
31003	Allentown, 295	F 5
31510	Alma⊙, 3,756	G 7
† 30209	Almon, 400	E 3
30201	Alpharetta, 2,455	D 2
30510	Alto, 372	E 2
† 30161	Alto Park, 2,963	B 2
31512	Ambrose, 253	G 7
31709	Americus⊙, 16,091	D 6
31711	Andersonville, 274	D 6
30802	Appling⊙, 212	H 3
31712	Arabi, 305	E 7
30104	Aragon, 850	B 2
† 30549	Arcade, 229	E 2
31520	Arco, 6,009	J 8
31623	Argyle, 206	G 8
31713	Arlington, 1,698	C 8
30105	Armuchee, 600	B 2
31714	Ashburn⊙, 4,209	E 7
† 30521	Ashland, 350	F 2
30601	Athens⊙, 44,342	F 3
* 30301	Atlanta (cap.)⊙, 496,973	D 3
	Atlanta, ‡1,390,164	D 3
31715	Attapulgus, 513	D 9
30203	Auburn, 361	E 2
* 30901	Augusta⊙, 59,864	J 4
	Augusta, ‡253,460	J 4
30001	Austell, 2,632	C 3
† 30557	Avalon, 204	F 1
30803	Avera, 217	G 4
30002	Avondale Estates, 1,735	D 3
31624	Axson, 250	G 8
31716	Baconton, 710	D 8
31717	Bainbridge⊙, 10,887	C 9
30511	Baldwin, 772	E 2
30107	Ball Ground, 617	D 2
30204	Barnesville⊙, 4,935	D 4
† 31601	Barretts, 275	F 8
30413	Bartow, 333	G 5
31720	Barwick, 381	E 9
31513	Baxley⊙, 3,503	H 7
† 31792	Beachton, 200	D 9
30414	Bellville, 234	H 6
† 31601	Bemiss, 325	F 9
31722	Berlin, 422	E 8
30748	Berryton, 200	B 2
30620	Bethlehem, 304	E 3
31904	Bibb City, 812	B 5
30621	Bishop, 235	F 3
31516	Blackshear⊙, 2,624	H 8
30512	Blairsville⊙, 491	E 1
31723	Blakely⊙, 5,267	C 8
† 31308	Blitchton, 256	J 6
31302	Bloomingdale, 1,588	K 6
30513	Blue Ridge⊙, 1,602	D 1
30805	Blythe, 333	H 4
30622	Bogart, 667	E 3
31626	Boston, 1,443	E 9
30623	Bostwick, 289	E 3
30108	Bowdon, 1,753	B 3
30109	Bowdon Junction, 200	B 3
30516	Bowersville, 301	G 2
30624	Bowman, 724	G 2
31801	Box Springs, 600	C 5
30517	Braselton, 386	E 2
30110	Bremen, 3,484	B 3
31701	Bridgeboro, 250	E 8
31725	Brinson, 231	C 9
31726	Bronwood, 500	D 7
31727	Brookfield, 860	F 8
30415	Brooklet, 683	J 6
31519	Broxton, 957	G 7
31520	Brunswick⊙, 19,585	K 8
30113	Buchanan⊙, 800	B 3
31803	Buena Vista⊙, 1,486	C 6
30518	Buford, 4,640	D 2
† 31020	Bullard, 230	F 5
31006	Butler⊙, 1,589	D 5
31007	Byromville, 419	E 6
31008	Byron, 1,368	E 5
31009	Cadwell, 354	G 6
31728	Cairo⊙, 8,061	D 9
30701	Calhoun⊙, 4,748	C 1
31729	Calvary, 500	D 9
30807	Camak, 224	G 4
31730	Camilla⊙, 4,987	D 8
30520	Canon, 709	F 2
30114	Canton⊙, 3,654	C 2
† 30720	Carbondale, 300	B 1
30203	Carl, 234	E 3
30627	Carlton, 294	F 2
30521	Carnesville⊙, 510	F 2
30117	Carrollton⊙, 13,520	C 3
† 30540	Cartecay, 250	D 1
30120	Cartersville⊙, 9,929	C 2
30123	Cassville, 350	C 2
31804	Cataula, 500	C 5
30124	Cave Spring, 1,305	B 2
31627	Cecil, 265	F 8
30125	Cedartown⊙, 9,253	B 2
† 30601	Center, 213	F 2
31093	Centerville, 1,725	E 5
† 31816	Chalybeate Springs, 266	C 5
30341	Chamblee, 9,127	D 3
30705	Chatsworth⊙, 2,706	C 1
31011	Chauncey, 308	F 6
31012	Chester, 409	F 6
30707	Chickamauga, 1,842	B 1
† 30512	Choestoe, 215	E 1
31733	Chula, 300	E 7
30523	Clarkesville⊙, 1,294	F 1
30021	Clarkston, 3,127	D 3
30417	Claxton⊙, 2,669	J 6
30525	Clayton⊙, 1,569	F 1
30128	Clem, 350	B 3
30527	Clermont, 290	E 2
30528	Cleveland⊙, 1,353	E 1
31734	Climax, 275	D 9
31604	Clyattville, 500	F 9
31303	Clyo, 300	K 6
30420	Cobbtown, 321	H 6
31014	Cochran⊙, 5,161	F 6
30710	Cohutta, 300	C 1
30628	Colbert, 532	F 2
30337	College Park, 18,203	C 3
30421	Collins, 574	H 6
31737	Colquitt⊙, 2,026	C 8
* 31901	Columbus⊙, 154,168	C 6
	Columbus, ‡238,584	C 6
30629	Comer, 828	F 2
30529	Commerce, 3,702	E 2
30206	Concord, 312	D 4
30207	Conyers⊙, 4,890	D 3
31738	Coolidge, 717	E 8
30129	Coosa, 600	B 2
31015	Cordele⊙, 10,733	E 7
30531	Cornelia, 3,014	E 1
30209	Covington⊙, 10,267	E 3
30630	Crawford, 624	F 3
30631	Crawfordville⊙, 735	G 3
† 30105	Crystal Springs, 500	B 2
31016	Culloden, 272	D 5
30130	Cumming⊙, 2,031	D 2
31805	Cusseta⊙, 1,251	C 6
31740	Cuthbert⊙, 3,972	C 7
30211	Dacula, 782	E 3
30533	Dahlonega⊙, 2,658	D 1
30132	Dallas⊙, 2,133	C 3
30720	Dalton⊙, 18,872	C 1
31741	Damascus, 272	C 8
30633	Danielsville⊙, 378	F 2
31017	Danville, 515	F 5
31305	Darien⊙, 1,826	K 8
31601	Dasher, 452	F 9
31018	Davisboro, 476	G 5
31742	Dawson⊙, 5,383	D 7
30534	Dawsonville⊙, 288	D 2
30808	Dearing, 555	H 4
* 30030	Decatur⊙, 21,943	D 3
† 31501	Deenwood, 3,015	H 8
30535	Demorest, 1,070	F 1
31532	Denton, 244	G 7
31743	De Soto, 321	D 7
31019	Dexter, 438	G 6
† 31520	Dock Junction (Arco), 6,009	J 8
31744	Doerun, 1,157	E 8
31745	Donalsonville⊙, 2,907	C 8
30340	Doraville, 9,039	D 3
31533	Douglas⊙, 10,195	G 7
30134	Douglasville⊙, 5,472	C 3
31020	Dry Branch, 700	F 5
31021	Dublin⊙, 15,143	G 5
31022	Dudley, 423	F 5
30136	Duluth, 1,810	D 2
31630	Du Pont, 252	G 9
30538	Eastanollee, 365	F 1
31021	East Dublin, 1,986	G 5
30539	East Ellijay, 488	C 1
31023	Eastman⊙, 5,416	F 6
† 30263	East Newnan, 1,634	C 4
30344	East Point, 39,315	C 3
31024	Eatonton⊙, 4,125	F 4
31307	Eden, 300	K 6
31746	Edison, 1,210	C 7
† 31093	Elberta, 500	E 5
30635	Elberton⊙, 6,438	G 2
30060	Elizabeth, 950	C 2
31025	Elko, 450	E 6
31308	Ellabell, 400	K 6
31806	Ellaville⊙, 1,391	D 6
31747	Ellenton, 337	E 8
31807	Ellerslie, 615	C 5
30540	Ellijay⊙, 1,326	C 1
30137	Emerson, 813	C 2
31026	Empire, 325	F 6
31749	Enigma, 505	F 8
† 30217	Ephesus, 212	B 4
30541	Epworth, 300	D 1
30724	Eton, 286	C 1
† 31331	Eulonia, 500	K 7
30809	Evans, 1,500	H 3
31536	Everett, 300	J 8
30212	Experiment, 2,256	D 4
30213	Fairburn, 3,143	C 3
30139	Fairmount, 623	C 2
31631	Fargo, 800	G 9
30214	Fayetteville⊙, 2,160	C 4
30140	Felton, 300	B 3
31750	Fitzgerald⊙, 8,015	F 7
† 31313	Flemington, 265	K 7
30215	Flippen, 600	D 3
30216	Flovilla, 289	E 4
30542	Flowery Branch, 779	E 2
31537	Folkston⊙, 2,112	H 9
30050	Forest Park, 19,994	D 3
31029	Forsyth⊙, 3,736	E 4
31751	Fort Gaines⊙, 1,255	C 7
30741	Fort Oglethorpe, 3,869	B 1
31030	Fort Valley⊙, 9,251	E 5
31752	Fowlstown, 400	D 9
30217	Franklin⊙, 749	B 4
30639	Franklin Springs, 501	F 2
37317	Fry, 300	D 1
31753	Funston, 293	E 8
30501	Gainesville⊙, 15,459	E 2
31408	Garden City, 5,741	K 6
30425	Garfield, 214	H 5
31810	Geneva, 250	C 5
31754	Georgetown⊙, 578	B 7
30810	Gibson⊙, 701	G 4
30426	Girard, 241	J 4
30427	Glennville, 2,965	J 7
30428	Glenwood, 670	G 6
30641	Good Hope, 202	E 3
31031	Gordon, 2,553	F 5
30811	Gough, 300	H 4
30812	Gracewood, 1,200	H 4
30220	Grantville, 1,128	C 4
31032	Gray⊙, 2,014	F 4
30221	Grayson, 366	E 3
30642	Greensboro⊙, 2,583	F 3
30222	Greenville⊙, 1,085	C 4
† 31620	Greggs, 250	F 8
30223	Griffin⊙, 22,734	D 4
† 31036	Grovania, 300	E 6
30813	Grovetown, 3,169	H 4
31312	Guyton, 742	K 6
30544	Habersham, 225	F 1
31033	Haddock, 600	F 4
30429	Hagan, 572	J 6
31632	Hahira, 1,326	F 9
31811	Hamilton⊙, 357	C 5
30228	Hampton, 1,551	D 4
30354	Hapeville, 9,567	D 3
31034	Hardwick, 14,047	F 4
30814	Harlem, 1,540	H 4
31035	Harrison, 329	G 5
30643	Hartwell⊙, 4,865	G 2
31036	Hawkinsville⊙, 4,077	E 6
31539	Hazlehurst⊙, 4,065	G 7
30545	Helen, 252	E 1
31037	Helena, 1,230	G 6
30815	Hephzibah, 987	H 4
30546	Hiawassee⊙, 415	E 1
31038	Hillsboro, 250	E 4
30467	Hilltonia, 294	J 5
31313	Hinesville⊙, 4,115	J 7
30141	Hiram, 441	C 3
31542	Hoboken, 424	H 8
30230	Hogansville, 3,075	C 4
30142	Holly Springs, 575	D 2
30523	Hollywood, 300	E 1
† 31537	Homeland, 595	H 9
30547	Homer⊙, 365	F 2
31634	Homerville⊙, 3,025	G 8
31543	Hortense, 400	J 8
30548	Hoschton, 509	E 2
30646	Hull, 222	F 2
30561	Hurst, 216	D 1
31041	Ideal, 543	D 6
30647	Ila, 202	F 2
30231	Indian Springs, 300	E 4
30232	Inman, 475	D 4
31759	Iron City, 351	C 8
31042	Irwinton⊙, 757	F 5
31760	Irwinville, 550	F 7
31406	Isle of Hope, 975	K 7
† 31031	Ivey, 245	F 5
30233	Jackson⊙, 3,778	E 4
31544	Jacksonville, 214	G 7
30143	Jasper⊙, 1,202	D 2

(continued on following page)

30549 Jefferson⊙, 1,647 .... F 2
31044 Jeffersonville⊙, 1,302 .... F 5
30234 Jenkinsburg, 382 .... E 4
31545 Jesup⊙, 9,091 .... J 7
30236 Jonesboro⊙, 4,105 .... D 4
31046 Juliette, 600 .... E 4
31812 Junction City, 269 .... C 5
31813 Juniper, 525 .... C 6
30551 Juno, 522 .... D 2
30144 Kennesaw, 3,548 .... C 2
30214 Kenwood, 500 .... D 3
30816 Keysville, 300 .... H 4
31548 Kingsland, 1,831 .... J 9
30145 Kingston, 714 .... C 2
1049 Kite, 336 .... G 5
1050 Knoxville⊙, 25 .... E 5
30728 La Fayette⊙, 6,044 .... B 1
0240 La Grange⊙, 23,301 .... B 4
0260 Lake, 2,306 .... D 3
1635 Lakeland⊙, 2,569 .... F 8
0552 Lakemont, 295 .... F 1
1636 Lake Park, 361 .... F 9
0553 Lavonia, 2,044 .... F 2
0245 Lawrenceville⊙, 5,115 .... D 3
1650 Lax, 350 .... F 8
0528 Leaf, 250 .... E 1
0802 Leah, 210 .... H 3
1762 Leary, 907 .... C 8
0146 Lebanon, 500 .... D 2
1763 Leesburg⊙, 996 .... D 7
1637 Lenox, 860 .... F 8
1764 Leslie, 562 .... D 7
0648 Lexington⊙, 322 .... F 3
0247 Lilburn, 1,668 .... D 3
0286 Lincoln Park, 1,852 .... D 5
0817 Lincolnton⊙, 1,442 .... G 3
0147 Lindale, 2,768 .... B 2
0728 Linwood, 588 .... B 1
0057 Lithia Springs, 950 .... C 3
0058 Lithonia, 2,270 .... D 3
1052 Lizella, 975 .... E 5
0248 Locust Grove, 642 .... D 4
0249 Loganville, 1,318 .... E 3
0741 Lookout Mountain, 1,538 .... B 1
0434 Louisville⊙, 2,691 .... H 4
814 Louvale, 263 .... C 6
316 Ludowici⊙, 1,419 .... J 7
0175 Ludville, 205 .... C 2
554 Lula, 736 .... E 2
549 Lumber City, 1,377 .... G 7
815 Lumpkin⊙, 1,431 .... C 6
251 Luthersville, 400 .... C 4
730 Lyerly, 426 .... B 2
436 Lyons⊙, 3,739 .... H 6
059 Mableton, 9,500 .... C 3
201 Macon⊙, 122,423 .... E 5
Macon, ‡206,342 .... E 5
650 Madison⊙, 2,890 .... F 3
816 Manchester, 4,779 .... C 5
550 Manor, 500 .... G 8
255 Mansfield, 340 .... E 4
148 Marblehill, 300 .... D 2
060 Marietta⊙, 27,216 .... D 3
312 Marlow, 500 .... K 6
057 Marshallville, 1,376 .... D 6

30557 Martin, 201 .... F 2
30907 Martinez, 950 .... H 3
30671 Maxeys, 229 .... F 3
30558 Maysville, 553 .... E 2
† 30908 McBean, 300 .... J 4
30555 McCaysville, 1,619 .... D 1
30253 McDonough⊙, 2,675 .... D 4
31054 McIntyre, 471 .... F 5
31055 McRae⊙, 3,151 .... G 6
30256 Meansville, 313 .... D 4
31765 Meigs, 1,226 .... D 8
31318 Meldrim, 500 .... K 6
30731 Menlo, 593 .... B 2
30819 Mesena, 400 .... G 4
† 31792 Metcalf, 213 .... E 9
30439 Metter⊙, 2,912 .... H 6
31820 Midland, 250 .... C 5
30441 Midville, 665 .... H 5
31060 Milan, 1,084 .... G 6
31061 Milledgeville⊙, 11,601 .... F 4
30442 Millen⊙, 3,713 .... J 5
30257 Milner, 270 .... D 4
30207 Milstead, 1,157 .... D 3
30258 Molena, 389 .... D 4
30655 Monroe⊙, 8,071 .... E 3
31063 Montezuma, 4,125 .... E 6
31064 Monticello⊙, 2,132 .... E 4
30259 Moreland, 363 .... C 4
31766 Morgan⊙, 280 .... C 7
30560 Morganton, 205 .... D 1
31638 Morven, 449 .... E 9
31768 Moultrie⊙, 14,302 .... E 8
30562 Mountain City, 594 .... F 1
† 30075 Mountain Park, 268 .... D 2
30563 Mount Airy, 463 .... F 1
30149 Mount Berry, 1,500 .... B 2
30445 Mount Vernon⊙, 1,579 .... G 6
30261 Mountville, 218 .... C 4
30150 Mount Zion, 264 .... B 3
30564 Murrayville, 550 .... E 2
31769 Mystic, 250 .... F 7
31553 Nahunta⊙, 974 .... H 8
† 31808 Nankipooh, 500 .... C 5
31639 Nashville⊙, 4,323 .... F 8
31641 Naylor, 244 .... F 9
30151 Nelson, 613 .... D 2
30262 Newborn, 294 .... E 3
† 30501 New Holland, 950 .... E 2
30446 Newington, 402 .... J 5
30263 Newnan⊙, 11,205 .... C 4
31770 Newton⊙, 624 .... D 8
31554 Nicholls, 1,150 .... G 7
30565 Nicholson, 397 .... F 2
† 30728 Noble, 250 .... B 1
30071 Norcross, 2,755 .... D 3
31771 Norman Park, 912 .... E 8
30114 North Canton, 950 .... C 2
† 30645 North High Shoals, 165 .... F 3
30821 Norwood, 272 .... G 4
31903 Oak Park, 226 .... H 6
30566 Oakwood, 250 .... E 2
31773 Ochlocknee, 611 .... E 9
31774 Ocilla⊙, 3,185 .... F 7
31067 Oconee, 262 .... G 5
31555 Odum, 379 .... H 7

31556 Offerman, 500 .... H 8
31406 Oglethorpe⊙, 1,286 .... D 6
30449 Oliver, 217 .... J 5
31775 Omega, 831 .... E 8
† 30701 Oostanaula, 300 .... B 1
30267 Oxford, 1,373 .... E 3
30268 Palmetto, 2,045 .... C 3
31777 Parrott, 222 .... D 7
31557 Patterson, 788 .... H 8
31778 Pavo, 775 .... E 9
† 31201 Payne, 236 .... E 5
† 30214 Peachtree City, 793 .... C 4
31642 Pearson⊙, 1,700 .... G 8
31779 Pelham, 4,539 .... D 8
31321 Pembroke⊙, 1,361 .... J 6
30567 Pendergrass, 267 .... E 2
30822 Perkins, 250 .... J 5
31069 Perry⊙, 7,771 .... E 6
† 31794 Phillipsburg, 2,335 .... E 8
† 31629 Pidcock, 210 .... E 9
31071 Pinehurst, 405 .... E 6
30152 Pine Log, 205 .... C 2
31822 Pine Mountain, 862 .... C 5
† 31312 Pineora, 266 .... K 6
† 31728 Pine Park, 330 .... D 9
31071 Pineview, 528 .... F 6
31072 Pitts, 345 .... E 7
31780 Plains, 683 .... D 6
31322 Pooler, 1,517 .... K 6
30450 Portal, 643 .... J 5
30270 Porterdale, 1,773 .... E 3
31407 Port Wentworth, 3,905 .... K 6
31781 Poulan, 766 .... E 8
30073 Powder Springs, 2,559 .... C 3
31824 Preston⊙, 226 .... C 6
30451 Pulaski, 230 .... J 6
31782 Putney, 750 .... D 8
31643 Quitman⊙, 4,818 .... E 9
30568 Rabun Gap, 250 .... F 1
31645 Ray City, 617 .... F 8
30660 Rayle, 300 .... G 3
31783 Rebecca, 266 .... E 7
30272 Red Oak, 3,500 .... C 3
30452 Register, 300 .... J 6
30453 Reidsville⊙, 1,806 .... H 6
31601 Remerton, 523 .... F 9
31075 Rentz, 392 .... G 6
30735 Resaca, 500 .... C 1
31076 Reynolds, 1,253 .... D 5
31077 Rhine, 471 .... F 7
31323 Riceboro, 252 .... K 7
31825 Richland, 1,823 .... C 6
31324 Richmond Hill, 826 .... K 7
31326 Rincon, 1,854 .... K 6
30736 Ringgold⊙, 1,381 .... B 1
30738 Rising Fawn, 400 .... A 1
30274 Riverdale, 2,521 .... D 3
31204 Riverside, 1,159 .... B 2
31078 Roberta, 746 .... D 5
† 30545 Robertstown, 290 .... E 1
31079 Rochelle, 1,380 .... F 7
30153 Rockmart, 3,857 .... B 2
30740 Rocky Face, 500 .... C 1
30455 Rocky Ford, 252 .... J 5
30161 Rome⊙, 30,759 .... B 2

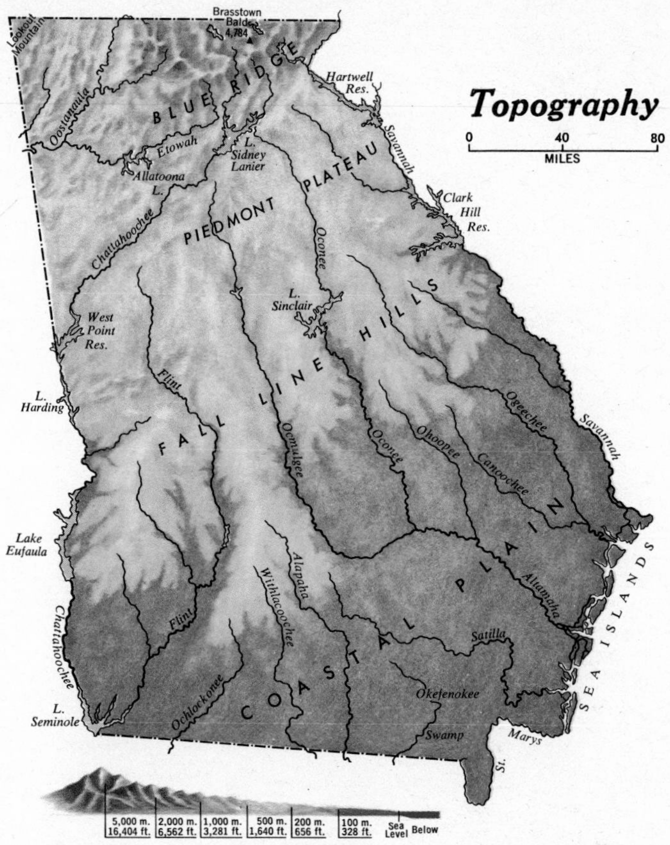
Topography
0
40
80
MILES
Brasstown Bald
4,784
Lookout Mountain
BLUE RIDGE
Hartwell Res.
Oostanaula
Etowah
Sidney Lanier
Savannah
Allatoona L.
PIEDMONT PLATEAU
Clark Hill Res.
Chattahoochee
Oconee
L. Sinclair
West Point Res.
FALL LINE HILLS
Flint
L. Harding
Ocmulgee
Oconee
Ohoopee
Ogeechee
Canoochee
Savannah
Lake Eufaula
COASTAL PLAIN
Altamaha
SEA ISLANDS
Chattahoochee
Alapaha
Withlacoochee
Flint
Satilla
Ochlockonee
Okefenokee Swamp
L. Seminole
Marys
St.
5,000 m. 16,404 ft.
2,000 m. 6,562 ft.
1,000 m. 3,281 ft.
500 m. 1,640 ft.
200 m. 656 ft.
100 m. 328 ft.
Sea Level
Below

30170 Roopville, 221 .... B 4
30741 Rossville, 3,869 .... B 1
30075 Roswell, 5,430 .... D 2
30662 Royston, 2,428 .... F 2
† 30680 Russell, 378 .... E 3
30663 Rutledge, 628 .... E 3
31646 Saint George, 600 .... H 9
31558 Saint Marys, 3,408 .... J 9
31522 Saint Simons Island, 5,346 .... K 8
31784 Sale City, 323 .... D 8
31082 Sandersville⊙, 5,546 .... G 5
31327 Sapelo Island, 250 .... K 8
30456 Sardis, 643 .... J 5
30275 Sargent, 800 .... C 4
31785 Sasser, 339 .... D 7
30571 Sautee-Nacoochee, 350 .... E 1
* 31401 Savannah⊙, 118,349 .... L 6
Savannah, ‡187,767 .... L 6
31328 Savannah Beach, 1,786 .... L 6
31083 Scotland, 261 .... G 6
31095 Scott, 215 .... G 5
31560 Screven, 936 .... H 7
31561 Sea Island, 600 .... K 8
30276 Senoia, 910 .... C 4
30172 Shannon, 1,563 .... B 2
31786 Shellman, 1,166 .... C 7
31826 Shiloh, 298 .... C 5
† 31781 Shingler, 300 .... E 7
30665 Siloam, 319 .... F 3
30173 Silver Creek, 450 .... B 2
31086 Smarr, 350 .... E 5
31787 Smithville, 713 .... D 7
30080 Smyrna, 19,157 .... D 3
30278 Snellville, 1,990 .... D 3
30279 Social Circle, 1,961 .... E 3
30457 Soperton⊙, 2,596 .... G 6
31647 Sparks, 1,337 .... F 8
31087 Sparta⊙, 2,172 .... F 4
31329 Springfield⊙, 1,001 .... K 6
30705 Spring Place, 241 .... C 1
30823 Stapleton, 390 .... H 4
31648 Statenville⊙, 700 .... G 9
30458 Statesboro⊙, 14,616 .... J 6
30666 Statham, 817 .... E 3
31088 Stevens Pottery, 350 .... F 5
30464 Stillmore, 354 .... H 6
30281 Stockbridge, 1,561 .... D 3
31649 Stockton, 500 .... G 9
30083 Stone Mountain, 1,899 .... D 3
30282 Stonewall, 950 .... C 3
† 30747 Subligna, 300 .... B 1
30572 Suches, 400 .... E 1
30518 Sugar Hill, 1,745 .... E 2
30747 Summerville⊙, 5,043 .... B 2
31789 Sumner, 207 .... E 7
30284 Sunny Side, 209 .... D 4
31563 Surrency, 352 .... H 7
30174 Suwanee, 615 .... D 2
30401 Swainsboro⊙, 7,325 .... H 5
31790 Sycamore, 547 .... E 7
30467 Sylvania⊙, 3,199 .... J 5
31791 Sylvester⊙, 4,226 .... E 7
31827 Talbotton⊙, 1,045 .... C 5
30176 Tallapoosa, 2,896 .... B 3
30573 Tallulah Falls, 255 .... F 1
30177 Tate, 950 .... D 2
30178 Taylorsville, 253 .... C 2
30179 Temple, 864 .... B 3
30751 Tennga, 300 .... C 1
31089 Tennille, 1,753 .... G 5
30286 Thomaston⊙, 10,024 .... D 5
31792 Thomasville⊙, 18,155 .... E 9

30824 Thomson⊙, 6,503 .... H 4
31404 Thunderbolt, 2,750 .... K 6
31794 Tifton⊙, 12,179 .... F 8
30576 Tiger, 312 .... F 1
30668 Tignall, 756 .... G 3
30577 Toccoa⊙, 6,971 .... F 1
31090 Toorhsboro, 682 .... F 5
31331 Townsend, 300 .... J 7
30752 Trenton⊙, 1,523 .... A 1
30753 Trion, 1,965 .... B 1
30755 Tunnel Hill, 900 .... C 1
30289 Turin, 242 .... C 4
30471 Twin City, 1,119 .... H 5
31795 Ty Ty, 447 .... E 8
31091 Unadilla, 1,457 .... E 6
30291 Union City, 3,031 .... D 3
30669 Union Point, 1,624 .... F 3
31794 Unionville, 1,646 .... F 8
30473 Uvalda, 663 .... H 6
31601 Valdosta⊙, 32,303 .... F 9
30756 Varnell, 400 .... C 1
30474 Vidalia, 9,507 .... H 6
31092 Vienna⊙, 2,341 .... E 6
30180 Villa Rica, 3,922 .... C 3
30182 Waco, 431 .... B 3
30477 Wadley, 1,989 .... H 5
30183 Waleska, 487 .... D 2
31333 Walthourville, 300 .... J 7
31564 Waresboro, 350 .... H 8
31830 Warm Springs, 523 .... C 5
31093 Warner Robins, 33,491 .... E 5
30828 Warrenton⊙, 2,073 .... G 4
31796 Warwick, 466 .... E 7
30673 Washington⊙, 4,094 .... G 3
30677 Watkinsville⊙, 986 .... E 3
31565 Waverly, 250 .... J 8
31831 Waverly Hall, 671 .... C 5
31501 Waycross⊙, 18,996 .... H 8
30830 Waynesboro⊙, 5,530 .... J 4
31566 Waynesville, 500 .... J 8
31833 West Point, 4,232 .... B 5
31797 Whigham, 381 .... D 9
30184 White, 462 .... C 2
30603 White Hall, 400 .... F 3
30678 White Plains, 236 .... F 4
30185 Whitesburg, 720 .... B 4
30186 Whitestone, 450 .... C 1
† 31833 Whitesville, 250 .... C 5
30581 Wiley, 300 .... F 1
31650 Willacoochee, 1,120 .... G 8
30292 Williamson, 284 .... D 4
31404 Wilmington Island, 3,284 .... L 7
30680 Winder⊙, 6,605 .... E 3
† 30824 Winfield, 444 .... H 3
30187 Winston, 625 .... C 3
30683 Winterville, 551 .... F 3
31569 Woodbine⊙, 1,002 .... J 9
30293 Woodbury, 1,422 .... C 5
31836 Woodland, 689 .... D 5
30188 Woodstock, 870 .... D 2
30670 Woodville, 379 .... F 3
30833 Wrens, 2,204 .... H 4
31096 Wrightsville⊙, 2,106 .... G 5
31097 Yatesville, 423 .... D 5
30582 Young Harris, 544 .... E 1
30295 Zebulon⊙, 776 .... D 4

⊙ County seat.
‡ Population of metropolitan area.
† Zip of nearest p.o.
* Multiple zips

Agriculture, Industry and Resources

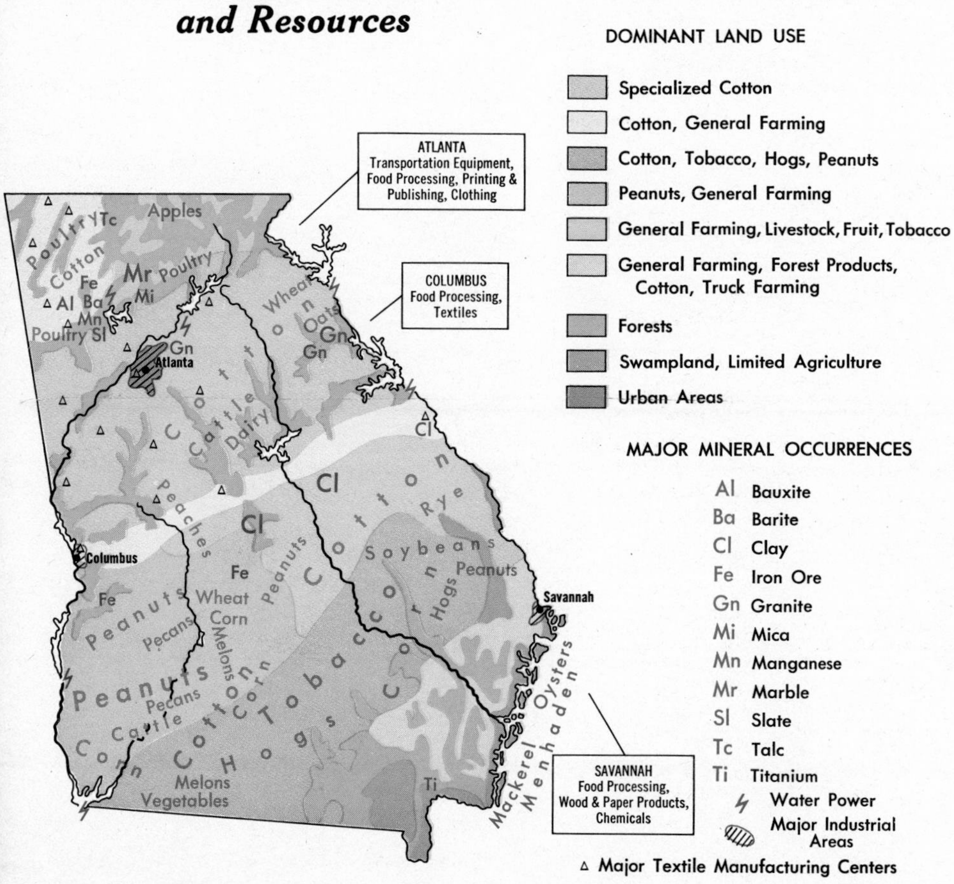
DOMINANT LAND USE
Specialized Cotton
Cotton, General Farming
Cotton, Tobacco, Hogs, Peanuts
Peanuts, General Farming
General Farming, Livestock, Fruit, Tobacco
General Farming, Forest Products, Cotton, Truck Farming
Forests
Swampland, Limited Agriculture
Urban Areas
MAJOR MINERAL OCCURRENCES
Al Bauxite
Ba Barite
Cl Clay
Fe Iron Ore
Gn Granite
Mi Mica
Mn Manganese
Mr Marble
Sl Slate
Tc Talc
Ti Titanium
Water Power
Major Industrial Areas
Major Textile Manufacturing Centers
ATLANTA
Transportation Equipment, Food Processing, Printing & Publishing, Clothing
COLUMBUS
Food Processing, Textiles
SAVANNAH
Food Processing, Wood & Paper Products, Chemicals
Apples
Poultry
Cotton
Atlanta
Columbus
Savannah
Cattle
Dairy
Peaches
Wheat
Oats
Peanuts
Soybeans
Rye
Corn
Pecans
Melons
Tobacco
Hogs
Vegetables
Oysters
Menhaden
Mackerel

Topography

0   40   80
MILES

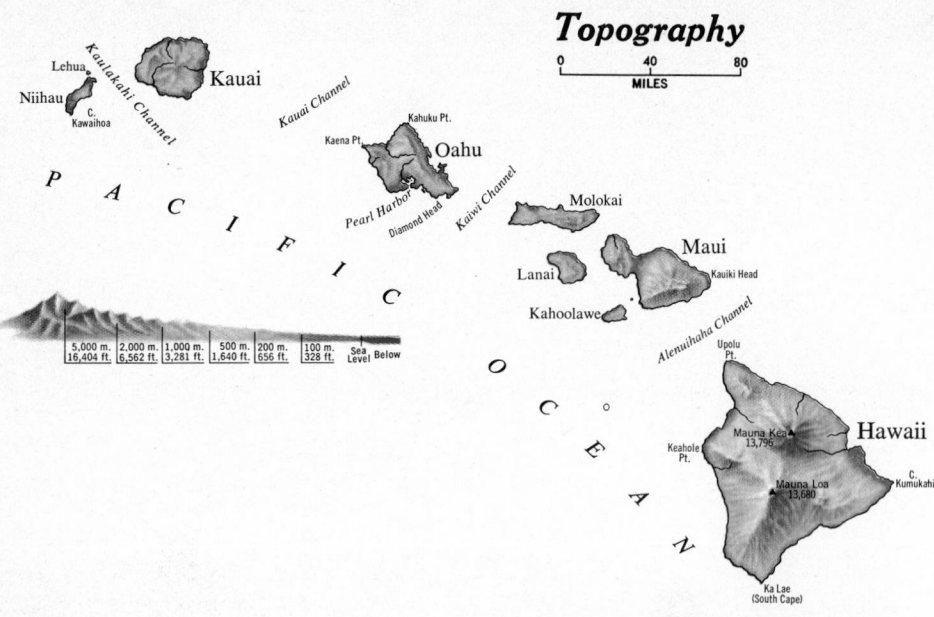

PACIFIC OCEAN

Kauai
Lehua
Niihau
C. Kawaihoa
Kaulakahi Channel
Kauai Channel
Kahuku Pt.
Kaena Pt.
Oahu
Pearl Harbor
Diamond Head
Kaiwi Channel
Molokai
Lanai
Maui
Kauiki Head
Kahoolawe
Alenuihaha Channel
Upolu Pt.
Keahole Pt.
Mauna Kea 13,796
Hawaii
Mauna Loa 13,680
C. Kumukahi
Ka Lae (South Cape)

5,000 m. 16,404 ft. | 2,000 m. 6,562 ft. | 1,000 m. 3,281 ft. | 500 m. 1,640 ft. | 200 m. 656 ft. | 100 m. 328 ft. | Sea Level | Below

COUNTIES

Hawaii, 63,468	K	7
Honolulu, 629,176	D	3
Kalawao, 172	G	1
Kauai, 29,761	A	1
Maui, 45,984	J	1

CITIES and TOWNS

Zip	Name/Pop.	Key
96701	Aiea, 12,560	B 3
96821	Aina Haina, 15,000	F 2
96703	Anahola, 638	C 1
† 96706	Barbers Point Housing, 1,947	E 2
96704	Captain Cook, 1,263	G 5
96705	Eleele, 758	C 2
96706	Ewa, 2,906	A 4
96706	Ewa Beach, 7,765	A 4
† 96701	Foster Village, 3,755	B 3
† 96714	Haena, 75	C 1
96708	Haiku, 464	J 2
96709	Haina, 333	H 3
96710	Hakalau, 742	J 4
† 96701	Halawa Heights, 5,809	B 3
96712	Haleiwa, 2,626	E 1
96787	Haliimaile, 638	J 2
96713	Hana, 459	K 2
96714	Hanalei, 153	C 1
96715	Hanamaulu, 2,461	C
96716	Hanapepe, 1,388	C
96717	Hauula, 2,048	E
96718	Hawaii National Park, 100	J
96719	Hawi, 797	G
96824	Hickam Housing, 7,352	C
96720	Hilo⊙, 26,353	J
96725	Holualoa, 850	J
96726	Honaunau, 950	J
† 96710	Honohina, 125	H
96727	Honokaa, 1,555	H
† 96761	Honokahua, 431	H
96740	Honokohau, 200	G
* 96801	Honolulu (cap.)⊛, 324,871	C
	Honolulu, ‡630,528	
96728	Honomu, 737	J
† 96706	Honouliuli, 600	A
96729	Hoolehua, 1,090	G
† 96740	Huehue, 100	G
† 96706	Iroquois Point, 4,572	A
† 96801	Iwilei, 1,835	C
96730	Kaaawa, 848	F
† 96761	Kaanapali, 250	H
† 96801	Kahala, 14,288	F
† 96744	Kahaluu, 1,657	F
96731	Kahuku, 917	E
96732	Kahului, 8,280	J
96734	Kailua, 33,783	F
† 96740	Kailua, 365	J
† 96740	Kailua Kona (Kailua), 365	F
96816	Kaimuki, 25,315	D

A   B

Sharp spikes bristle protectively around their precious fruit crop on Pineapple Hill, west Maui. Second only to sugarcane, pineapples rank high in Hawaii's economy.

David Muench — Shostal Associates

Agriculture, Industry and Resources

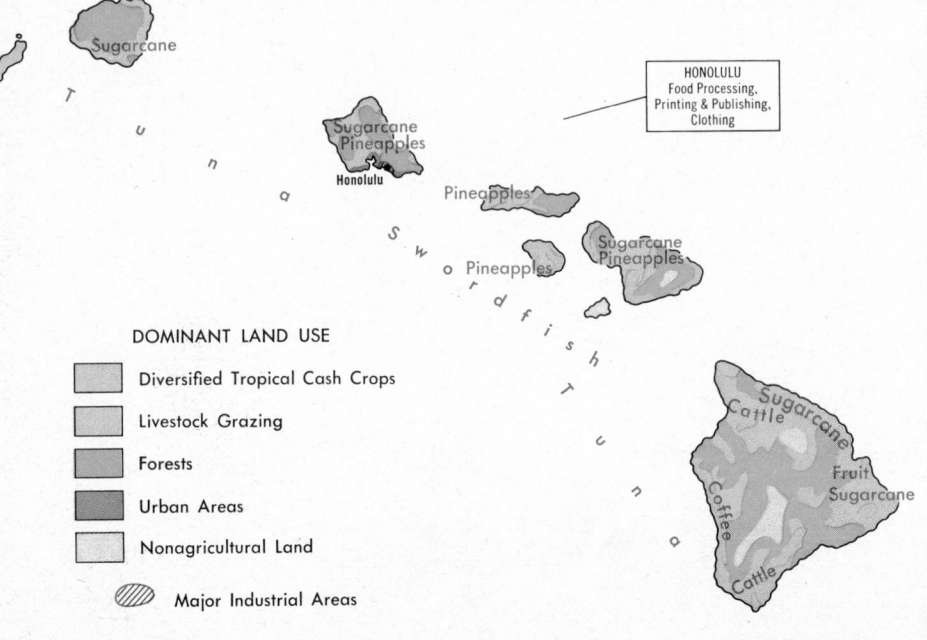

Sugarcane

Tuna

Sugarcane Pineapples
Honolulu

Pineapples

Swordfish

Pineapples

Sugarcane Pineapples

HONOLULU
Food Processing, Printing & Publishing, Clothing

Tuna

Sugarcane
Cattle
Sugarcane
Coffee
Fruit Sugarcane
Cattle

DOMINANT LAND USE

- Diversified Tropical Cash Crops
- Livestock Grazing
- Forests
- Urban Areas
- Nonagricultural Land
- Major Industrial Areas

KAUAI COUNTY

160°   Longitude West of Greenwich

SCALE
0   5   10   15 MI.
0   5   10   15KM

Hanalei
Haena Pt.
Haena
Wainiha
Makaha Pt.
Nohili Pt.
K A U
Lehua
Mana
Kawaili R.
Kaunuopou Pt.
Kokole Pt.
Kekaha
Kaulakahi Channel
Paniau Pk. 1,281
Puuwai
Pueo Pt.
Waimea
Waimea Bay
Makaweli
Makakilo
Hanap—
Elee
NIIHAU
Kamalino
Halalii Lake
Kaumakani
Puolo Pt.
Hanapepe Bay
Cape Kawaihoa

158°
Waipahu
Pearl City
Waimalu Halawa Hts.
Aiea
East Loch
Ford I.
Halawa Stream
Moanalua
Honouliuli
West Loch
Middle Loch
FORD I. N.A.S.
Foster Village
Kahi
Salt Lake
FT. SHAFTER
Ewa
O
PEARL
HARBOR
Southeast Loch
Hickam Housing
HICKAM A.F.B.
A
H
Kalihi
Puur
Waipio Pen.
Waipio
Iroquois Point
Keahi Pt.
HONOLULU INTERNAT'L AIRPORT
Keehi Lagoon
Kalihi
Iwilei
Ewa Beach
M A M A L A
Ahua Pt.
Kalihi Entrance
Anuenue
Honolulu Harbor
B

HONOLULU & PEARL HARBOR

SCALE
0   1   2 MI.
0   1   2KM.

180°   Kure   176°   Eastern I.   Midway Is. (U.S.)   172°   16
Sand I.
International Date Line
H
A
Pearl and Hermes Reef
W
A
I
I
A
Lisianski I.
Laysan I.
Maro Reef
P
A
C
I
F
Frenc S.
O
C
E
A
Johnston Ato " (U.S.)

HAWAII

State Capital .... ⊛

County Seats .... ⊙

© C.S. HAMMOND & Co., N.Y.

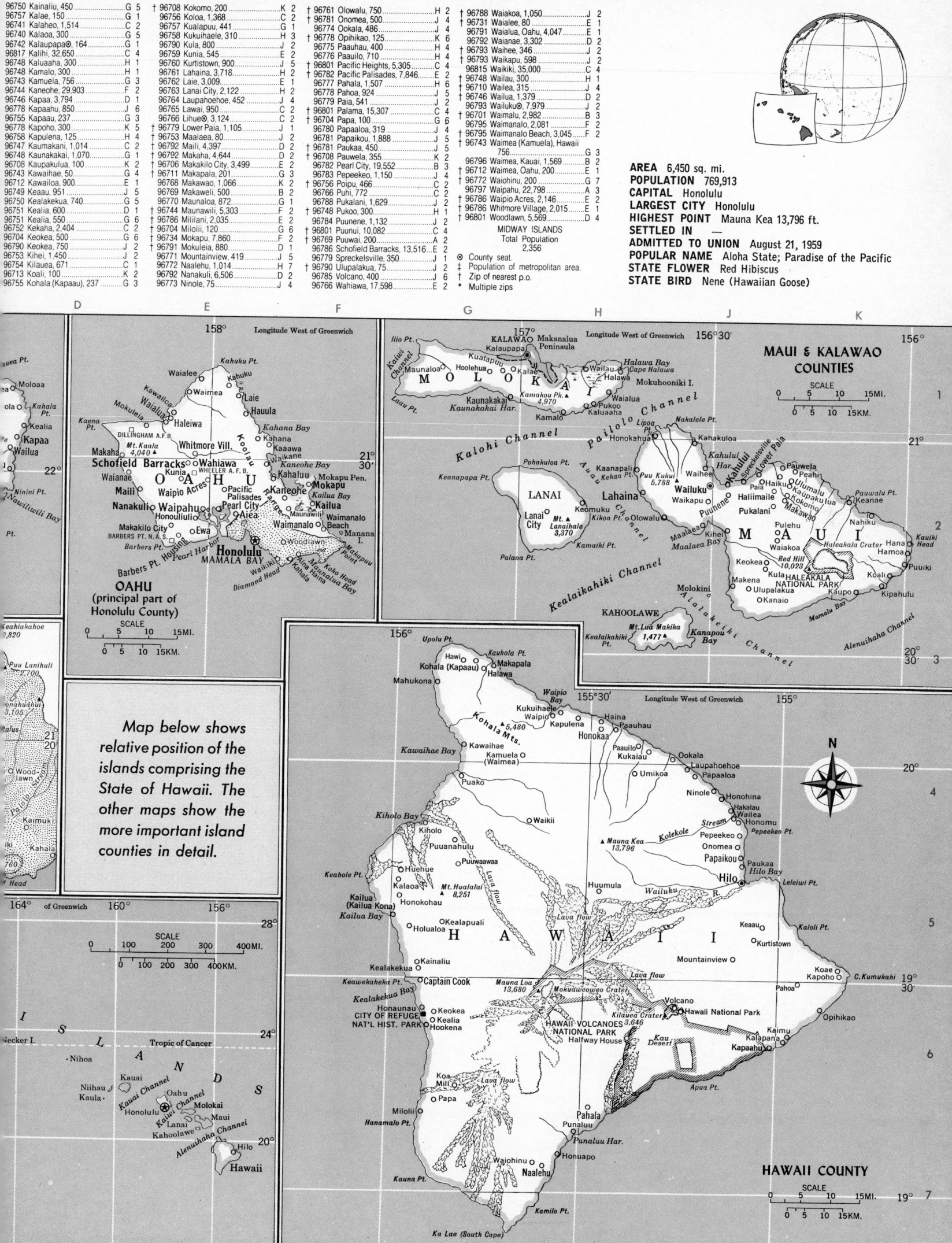

96750 Kainaliu, 450 .... G 5
96757 Kalae, 150 .... G 1
96741 Kalaheo, 1,514 .... C 2
96740 Kalaoa, 300 .... G 5
96742 Kalaupapa⊙, 164 .... G 1
96817 Kalihi, 32,650 .... C 4
96748 Kaluaaha, 300 .... H 1
96748 Kamalo, 300 .... H 1
96743 Kamuela, 756 .... G 3
96744 Kaneohe, 29,903 .... F 2
96746 Kapaa, 3,794 .... D 1
96778 Kapaahu, 850 .... J 6
96755 Kapaau, 237 .... G 3
96778 Kapoho, 300 .... K 5
96758 Kapulena, 125 .... H 4
96747 Kaumakani, 1,014 .... C 2
96748 Kaunakakai, 1,070 .... G 1
96708 Kawailoa, 100 .... K 2
96743 Kawaihae, 50 .... G 4
96712 Kawailoa, 900 .... C 1
96749 Keaau, 951 .... J 5
96750 Kealakekua, 740 .... G 5
96751 Kealia, 600 .... D 1
96751 Keanae, 550 .... G 6
96752 Kekaha, 2,404 .... C 2
96704 Keokea, 500 .... G 6
96790 Keokea, 750 .... J 2
96753 Kihei, 1,450 .... J 2
96754 Kilauea, 671 .... C 1
96713 Koali, 100 .... K 2
96755 Kohala (Kapaau), 237 .... G 3

†96708 Kokomo, 200 .... K 2
96756 Koloa, 1,368 .... C 2
96757 Kualapuu, 441 .... G 1
96758 Kukuihaele, 310 .... H 3
96790 Kula, 800 .... J 2
96759 Kunia, 545 .... E 2
96760 Kurtistown, 900 .... J 5
96761 Lahaina, 3,718 .... H 2
96762 Laie, 3,009 .... E 1
96763 Lanai City, 2,122 .... H 2
96764 Laupahoehoe, 452 .... J 4
96765 Lawai, 950 .... C 2
†96766 Lihue⊙, 3,124 .... C 2
†96779 Lower Paia, 1,105 .... J 1
96753 Maalaea, 80 .... J 2
96792 Maili, 4,397 .... D 2
†96792 Makaha, 4,644 .... D 2
96706 Makakilo City, 3,499 .... E 2
96769 Makaweli, 500 .... B 2
96768 Makawao, 1,066 .... K 2
96769 Makaweli, 500 .... B 2
96770 Makaalaloa, 872 .... G 1
†96744 Maunawili, 5,303 .... F 2
†96786 Mililani, 2,035 .... E 2
96704 Miloli'i, 120 .... G 6
96734 Mokapu, 7,860 .... F 2
96791 Mokuleia, 880 .... D 1
96771 Mountainview, 419 .... J 5
96772 Naalehu, 1,014 .... H 7
96792 Nanakuli, 6,506 .... D 2
96773 Ninole, 75 .... J 4

†96761 Olowalu, 750 .... H 2
†96774 Onomea, 500 .... J 4
†96778 Ookala, 486 .... J 4
†96778 Opihikao, 125 .... K 6
96775 Paauhau, 400 .... H 4
96776 Paauilo, 710 .... H 4
†96801 Pacific Heights, 5,305 .... C 4
†96782 Pacific Palisades, 7,846 .... E 2
96777 Pahala, 1,507 .... H 6
96778 Pahoa, 924 .... J 5
96779 Paia, 541 .... J 2
†96801 Palama, 15,307 .... C 4
96704 Papa, 100 .... G 6
96780 Papaaloa, 319 .... J 4
96781 Papaikou, 1,888 .... J 5
96781 Paukaa, 450 .... J 5
96782 Pearl City, 19,552 .... B 3
96783 Pepeekeo, 1,150 .... J 4
96756 Poipu, 466 .... C 2
96766 Puhi, 772 .... C 2
96788 Pukalani, 1,629 .... J 2
96748 Pukoo, 300 .... H 1
96784 Puunene, 1,132 .... J 2
†96801 Puunui, 10,082 .... C 4
96769 Puuwai, 200 .... A 2
96786 Schofield Barracks, 13,516 .... E 2
96779 Spreckelsville, 350 .... J 1
†96790 Ulupalakua, 75 .... J 2
96785 Volcano, 400 .... J 6
96766 Wahiawa, 17,598 .... E 2

†96788 Waiakoa, 1,050 .... J 2
†96731 Waialee, 80 .... E 1
96791 Waialua, Oahu, 4,047 .... D 1
96792 Waianae, 3,302 .... D 2
†96793 Waihee, 346 .... J 2
†96793 Waikapu, 598 .... J 2
96815 Waikiki, 35,000 .... C 4
96748 Wailau, 300 .... H 1
96710 Wailea, 315 .... J 4
96746 Wailua, 1,379 .... D 2
†96793 Wailuku⊙, 7,979 .... J 2
†96701 Waimalu, 2,982 .... B 3
†96795 Waimanalo, 2,081 .... F 2
†96795 Waimanalo Beach, 3,045 .... F 2
†96743 Waimea (Kamuela), Hawaii
756 .... G 3
†96796 Waimea, Kauai, 1,569 .... C 2
†96712 Waimea, Oahu, 200 .... E 1
96772 Waiohinu, 200 .... G 7
96797 Waipahu, 22,798 .... A 3
†96786 Waipio Acres, 2,146 .... E 2
†96786 Whitmore Village, 2,015 .... E 1
†96801 Woodlawn, 5,569 .... D 4

MIDWAY ISLANDS
Total Population
2,356

⊙ County seat.
‡ Population of metropolitan area.
† Zip of nearest p.o.
* Multiple zips

AREA 6,450 sq. mi.
POPULATION 769,913
CAPITAL Honolulu
LARGEST CITY Honolulu
HIGHEST POINT Mauna Kea 13,796 ft.
SETTLED IN —
ADMITTED TO UNION August 21, 1959
POPULAR NAME Aloha State; Paradise of the Pacific
STATE FLOWER Red Hibiscus
STATE BIRD Nene (Hawaiian Goose)

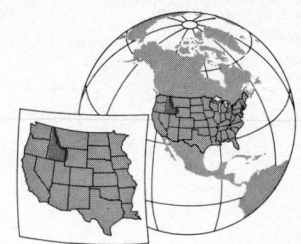

COUNTIES

Ada, 112,230.....................B 6
Adams, 2,877....................B 5
Bannock, 52,200................F 7
Bear Lake, 5,801...............G 7
Benewah, 6,230.................B 2
Bingham, 29,167...............F 6
Blaine, 5,749....................D 6
Boise, 1,763.....................C 6
Bonner, 15,560.................B 1
Bonneville, 51,250.............G 6
Boundary, 6,371...............B 1
Butte, 2,925.....................E 6
Camas, 728......................D 6
Canyon, 61,288................B 6
Caribou, 6,534..................G 7
Cassia, 17,017..................E 7
Clark, 741........................F 5
Clearwater, 10,871............C 3
Custer, 2,967...................D 5
Elmore, 17,479.................C 6
Franklin, 7,373.................G 7
Fremont, 8,710.................G 5
Gem, 9,387......................B 6
Gooding, 8,645.................D 6
Idaho, 12,891...................C 4
Jefferson, 11,619..............F 6
Jerome, 10,253.................D 7
Kootenai, 35,332..............B 2
Latah, 24,891...................B 3
Lemhi, 5,566....................D 4
Lewis, 3,867.....................B 3
Lincoln, 3,057...................D 6
Madison, 13,452...............G 6
Minidoka, 15,731..............E 7
Nez Perce, 30,376.............B 3
Oneida, 2,864...................F 7
Owyhee, 6,422.................B 7
Payette, 12,401.................B 5
Power, 4,864.....................F 7
Shoshone, 19,718.............B 2
Teton, 2,351.....................G 6
Twin Falls, 41,807.............D 7
Valley, 3,609.....................C 5
Washington, 7,633............B 5

CITIES and TOWNS

Zip	Name/Pop.	Key
83210	Aberdeen, 1,542	F 7
83310	Acequia, 107	E 7
83520	Ahsahka, 500	B 3
83311	Albion, 229	E 7
83312	Almo, 170	E 7
83211	American Falls⊙, 2,769	E 7
83401	Ammon, 1,338	G 6
83212	Arbon, 75	F 7
83213	Arco⊙, 1,244	E 6
83214	Arimo, 252	F 7
83420	Ashton, 1,187	G 5
83801	Athol, 190	B 2
83601	Atlanta, 50	C 6
83215	Atomic City, 24	F 6
83802	Avery, 250	C 2
83461	Baker, 98	E 4
83217	Bancroft, 366	G 7
83264	Banida, 76	G 7
83602	Banks, 49	B 5
83218	Basalt, 349	F 6
83803	Bayview, 300	B 2
83313	Bellevue, 537	D 6
83219	Bennington, 60	G 7
83220	Bern, 135	G 7
83221	Blackfoot⊙, 8,716	F 6
83804	Blanchard, 120	A 1
83314	Bliss, 114	D 7
83223	Bloomington, 186	G 7
83701	Boise (cap.)⊙, 74,990	B 6
	Boise, ‡112,230	B 6
83805	Bonners Ferry⊙, 2,796	B 1
83806	Bovill, 343	B 3
83651	Bowmont, 100	B 6
83315	Bridge, 140	E 7
83604	Bruneau, 150	C 7
83316	Buhl, 2,975	D 7
83307	Burke, 150	C 2
83318	Burley⊙, 8,279	E 7
83213	Butte City, 42	E 6
83308	Calder, 200	B 2
83605	Caldwell⊙, 14,219	B 6
83610	Cambridge, 383	B 5
83320	Carey, 750	E 6
83609	Careywood, 60	B 1
83462	Carmen, 40	E 4
83611	Cascade⊙, 833	C 5
83421	Castleford, 174	C 7
83810	Cataldo, 275	B 2
83241	Central, 60	G 7
83226	Challis⊙, 784	D 5
83451	Chatcolet, 95	B 2
83421	Chester, 206	G 5
83217	Chesterfield, 50	G 7
83201	Chubbuck, 2,924	F 7
83811	Clark Fork, 367	B 1
83812	Clarkia, 147	B 2
83227	Clayton, 36	D 5
83221	Clearwater, 110	C 3
83463	Cleveland, 60	G 7
83228	Clifton, 137	F 7
83229	Cobalt, 35	D 4
83814	Coeur d'Alene⊙, 16,228	B 2
83235	Colburn, 200	B 1
83230	Conda, 250	G 7
83821	Coolin, 110	B 1
83322	Corral, 21	D 6
83522	Cottonwood, 867	B 3
83612	Council⊙, 899	B 5
83523	Craigmont, 554	B 3
83522	Crouch, 71	B 5
83524	Culdesac, 211	B 3
83815	Dalton Gardens, 1,559	B 2
83232	Dayton, 198	F 7
83323	Deary, 411	B 3
83323	Declo, 251	E 7
83524	Desmet, 154	B 2
83324	Dietrich, 84	D 7

83233	Dingle, 300	G 7
83615	Donnelly, 114	B 5
83825	Dover, 300	B 1
83234	Downey, 586	F 7
83422	Driggs⊙, 727	G 6
83423	Dubois⊙, 400	F 5
83616	Eagle, 525	B 6
83836	East Hope, 175	B 1
83826	Eastport, 83	B 1
83325	Eden, 343	D 7
83326	Elba, 87	E 7
83525	Elk City, 500	C 4
83827	Elk River, 383	B 3
83235	Ellis, 75	D 5
83828	Emida, 135	B 2
83617	Emmett⊙, 3,945	B 6
83829	Enaville, 90	B 2
83327	Fairfield⊙, 157	D 6
83424	Felt, 90	G 6
83531	Fenn, 45	B 4
83526	Ferdinand, 157	B 3
83830	Fernwood, 360	B 2
83328	Filer, 1,173	D 7
83236	Firth, 362	F 6
83261	Fish Haven, 120	G 7
83203	Fort Hall, 750	F 6
83237	Franklin, 402	G 7
83619	Fruitland, 1,576	B 6
83620	Fruitvale, 90	B 5
83704	Garden City, 2,368	B 6
83622	Garden Valley, 100	C 5
83873	Gem, 50	C 2
83832	Genesee, 619	B 3
83238	Geneva, 200	G 7
83239	Georgetown, 421	G 7
83463	Gibbonsville, 85	E 4
83623	Glenns Ferry, 1,386	D 7
83330	Gooding⊙, 2,599	D 7
83241	Grace, 826	G 7
83624	Grand View, 450	B 7
83530	Grangeville⊙, 3,636	B 4
83533	Greencreek, 72	B 3
83626	Greenleaf, 425	B 6
83854	Greer, 70	B 3
83332	Hagerman, 436	D 7
83333	Hailey⊙, 1,425	D 6
83627	Hammett, 653	C 7
83334	Hansen, 415	D 7
83521	Harpster, 250	C 4
83833	Harrison, 249	B 2
83834	Harvard, 50	B 3
83854	Hauser, 349	A 2
83835	Hayden, 1,285	B 2
83835	Hayden Lake, 260	B 2
83335	Hazelton, 396	E 7
83534	Headquarters, 350	C 3
83443	Heise, 84	G 6
83336	Heyburn, 1,637	E 7
83337	Hill City, 30	D 6
83243	Holbrook, 100	F 7
83301	Hollister, 57	D 7
83628	Homedale, 1,411	A 6
83836	Hope, 63	B 1
83629	Horseshoe Bend, 511	B 6
83244	Howe, 428	F 6
83854	Huetter, 49	B 2
83631	Idaho City⊙, 164	C 6
83401	Idaho Falls⊙, 35,776	F 6
83632	Indian Valley, 72	B 5
83245	Inkom, 522	F 7
83427	Iona, 890	G 6
83428	Irwin, 228	G 6
83429	Island Park, 136	G 5
83338	Jerome⊙, 4,183	D 7
83355	Juliaetta, 423	B 3
83536	Kamiah, 1,307	B 3
83837	Kellogg, 3,811	B 2
83537	Kendrick, 426	B 3
83340	Ketchum, 1,454	D 6
83538	Keuterville, 26	B 3
83423	Kilgore, 50	G 5
83341	Kimberly, 1,557	D 7
83633	King Hill, 150	C 6
83539	Kooskia, 809	C 3
83840	Kootenai, 168	B 1
83634	Kuna, 593	B 6
83841	Laclede, 200	B 1
83635	Lake Fork, 141	B 5
83430	Lamont, 30	G 6
83540	Lapwai, 400	B 3
83246	Lava Hot Springs, 516	F 7
83464	Leadore, 111	E 5
83465	Lemhi, 100	E 5
83249	Leslie, 100	E 6
83636	Letha, 115	B 6
83501	Lewiston⊙, 26,068	A 3
83341	Lewisville, 468	F 6
83432	Lorenzo, 125	G 6
83242	Lost River, 58	E 6
83637	Lowman, 45	C 5
83542	Lucile, 105	B 4
83241	Lund, 100	G 7
83251	Mackay, 539	E 6
83433	Macks Inn, 150	G 5
83252	Malad City⊙, 1,848	F 7
83342	Malta, 199	E 7
83639	Marsing, 610	B 6
83253	May, 120	E 5
83638	McCall, 1,758	C 5
83250	McCammon, 623	F 7
83640	Meadows, 250	B 5
83641	Melba, 197	B 6
83434	Menan, 545	F 6
83642	Meridian, 2,616	B 6
83463	Mesa, 25	B 5
83644	Middleton, 739	B 6
83645	Midvale, 176	B 5
83343	Minidoka, 131	E 7
83435	Monteview, 110	F 6
83466	Montour, 138	B 6
83254	Montpelier, 2,604	G 7
83255	Moore, 156	E 6
83256	Moreland, 500	F 6
83843	Moscow⊙, 14,146	B 3
83647	Mountain Home⊙, 6,451	C 6

83845	Moyie Springs, 203	B 1
83450	Mud Lake, 194	F 6
83846	Mullan, 1,279	C 2
83650	Murphy⊙, 75	B 6
83874	Murray, 100	C 2
83344	Murtaugh, 124	D 7
83345	Naf, 42	E 7
83651	Nampa, 20,768	B 6
83847	Naples, 463	B 1
83436	Newdale, 267	G 6
83654	New Meadows, 605	B 4
83655	New Plymouth, 986	B 6
83543	Nezperce⊙, 555	B 3
83848	Nordman, 168	B 1
83466	North Fork, 150	D 4
83656	Notus, 304	B 6
83254	Nounan, 92	G 7
83346	Oakley, 656	D 7
83259	Obsidian, 22	D 6
83657	Ola, 78	B 5
99156	Oldtown, 161	A 1
83855	Onaway, 166	B 3
83659	Oreana, 100	B 6
83544	Orofino⊙, 3,883	B 3
83525	Orogrande, 34	C 4
83849	Osburn, 2,248	B 2
83260	Ovid, 150	G 7
83263	Oxford, 75	F 7
83437	Palisades, 95	G 6
83261	Paris⊙, 615	G 7
83438	Parker, 266	G 6
83660	Parma, 1,228	B 6
83347	Paul, 911	E 7
83661	Payette⊙, 4,521	B 5
83545	Peck, 238	B 3
83348	Picabo, 50	D 6
83546	Pierce, 1,218	C 3
83850	Pinehurst, 1,934	B 2
83262	Pingree, 115	F 6
83851	Plummer, 443	B 2
83201	Pocatello⊙, 40,036	F 7
83547	Pollock, 50	B 4
83852	Ponderay, 275	B 1
83853	Porthill, 39	B 1
83854	Post Falls, 2,371	A 2
83855	Potlatch, 871	A 3
83263	Preston⊙, 3,310	G 7
83856	Priest River, 1,493	A 1
83857	Princeton, 124	B 3
83858	Rathdrum, 741	A 2
83114	Raymond, 65	G 7
83548	Reubens, 81	B 3
83440	Rexburg⊙, 8,272	G 6
83349	Richfield, 290	D 6
83832	Riddle, 44	B 7
83442	Rigby⊙, 2,293	F 6
83549	Riggins, 533	B 4
83443	Ririe, 575	G 6
83867	Roberts, 393	F 6
83221	Rockford, 150	F 6
83271	Rockland, 209	F 7
83302	Rogerson, 45	D 7
83660	Roswell, 65	A 6
83350	Rupert⊙, 4,563	E 7
83860	Sagle, 100	B 1
83445	Saint Anthony⊙, 2,877	G 6
83272	Saint Charles, 200	G 7
83861	Saint Joe, 50	B 2
83861	Saint Maries⊙, 2,571	B 2
83467	Salmon⊙, 2,910	D 4
83252	Samaria, 137	F 7
83862	Samuels, 467	B 1
83863	Sanders, 27	B 2
83864	Sandpoint⊙, 4,144	B 1
83866	Santa, 100	B 2
83274	Shelley, 2,614	F 6
83352	Shoshone⊙, 1,233	D 7
83650	Silver City, 1	B 6
83423	Small, 35	F 5
83868	Smelterville, 967	B 2
83276	Soda Springs⊙, 2,977	G 7
83550	Southwick, 38	B 3
83446	Spencer, 45	F 5
83869	Spirit Lake, 622	A 2
83277	Springfield, 180	F 6
83447	Squirrel, 43	G 5
83278	Stanley, 47	D 5
83669	Star, 500	B 6
83279	Sterling, 73	F 6
83552	Stites, 263	C 3
83280	Stone, 114	F 7
83448	Sugar City, 617	G 6
83353	Sun Valley, 180	D 6
83281	Swanlake, 145	F 7
83449	Swan Valley, 235	G 6
83670	Sweet, 120	B 6
83468	Tendoy, 150	E 5
83870	Tensed, 151	B 2
83450	Terreton, 42	F 6
83451	Teton, 390	G 6
83452	Tetonia, 176	G 6
83283	Thatcher, 300	G 7
83453	Thornton, 177	G 6
83871	Troy, 541	B 3
83354	Tuttle, 53	D 7
83301	Twin Falls⊙, 21,914	D 7
83454	Ucon, 664	F 6
83455	Victor, 241	G 6
83872	Viola, 300	B 3
83234	Virginia, 100	F 7
83873	Wallace⊙, 2,206	C 2
83875	Wardner, 492	B 2
83611	Warm Lake, 200	C 5
83285	Wayan, 50	G 7
83553	Weippe, 713	C 3
83672	Weiser⊙, 4,108	B 5
83355	Wendell, 1,122	D 7
83286	Weston, 230	F 7
83354	White Bird, 185	B 4
83676	Wilder, 564	A 6
83555	Winchester, 274	B 3
83876	Worley, 230	B 2
83677	Yellow Pine, 45	C 4

⊙ County seat.
‡ Population of metropolitan area.
† Zip of nearest p.o.
* Multiple zips

AREA 83,557 sq. mi.
POPULATION 713,008
CAPITAL Boise
LARGEST CITY Boise
HIGHEST POINT Borah Pk. 12,662 ft.
SETTLED IN 1842
ADMITTED TO UNION July 3, 1890
POPULAR NAME Gem State
STATE FLOWER Syringa
STATE BIRD Mountain Bluebird

Agriculture, Industry and Resources

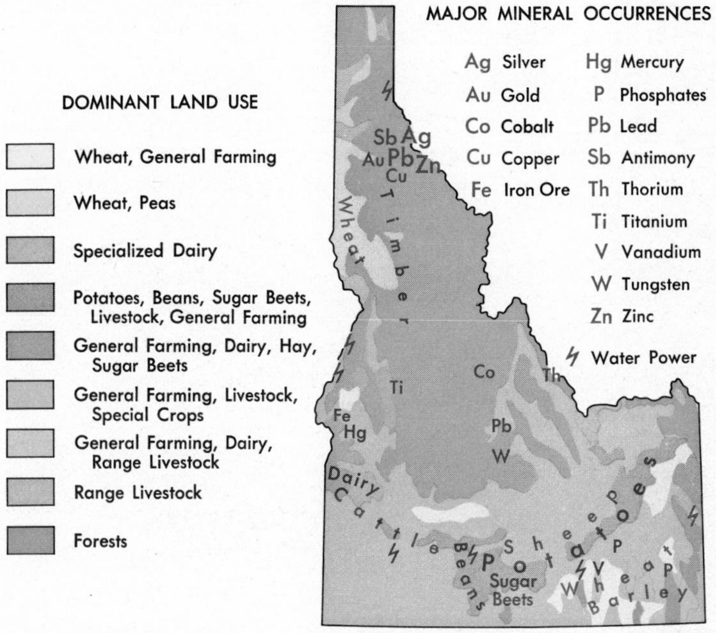

MAJOR MINERAL OCCURRENCES

Ag Silver   Hg Mercury
Au Gold   P Phosphates
Co Cobalt   Pb Lead
Cu Copper   Sb Antimony
Fe Iron Ore   Th Thorium
  Ti Titanium
  V Vanadium
  W Tungsten
  Zn Zinc
  ⚡ Water Power

DOMINANT LAND USE

Wheat, General Farming

Wheat, Peas

Specialized Dairy

Potatoes, Beans, Sugar Beets, Livestock, General Farming

General Farming, Dairy, Hay, Sugar Beets

General Farming, Livestock, Special Crops

General Farming, Dairy, Range Livestock

Range Livestock

Forests

The Sun Valley Ski Patrol adds a touch of color to the slopes of Baldy Mountain. Here, in one of the country's most popular resorts, visitors acquire tropical tans while swimming in heated pools, skiing, skijoring, dogsledding or just sunbathing in the glacial air.

Bob Lee—Shostal Associates

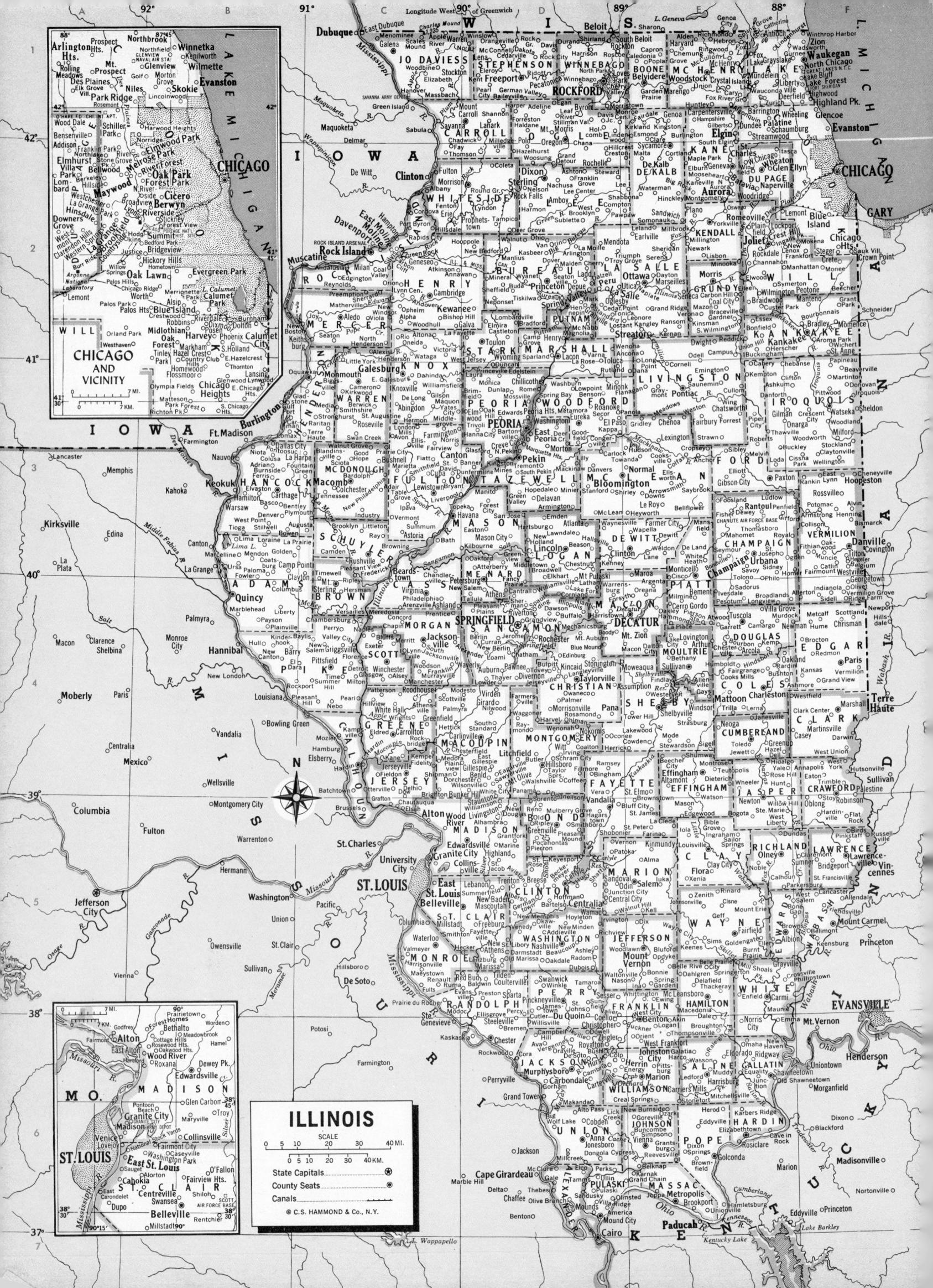

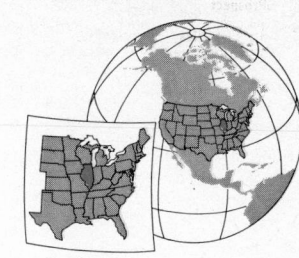

COUNTIES

Adams, 70,861	B 4
Alexander, 12,015	D 6
ond, 14,012	D 5
oone, 25,440	E 1
rown, 5,586	C 4
ureau, 38,541	D 2
alhoun, 5,675	C 4
arroll, 19,276	D 1
ass, 14,219	C 4
hampaign, 163,281	E 4
hristian, 35,948	D 4
lark, 16,216	F 4
lay, 14,735	E 5
linton, 28,315	D 5
oles, 47,815	E 4
ook, 5,492,369	F 2
rawford, 19,824	F 4
umberland, 9,772	E 4
e Kalb, 71,654	E 2
ouglas, 18,997	E 4
u Page, 491,882	F 2
gar, 21,591	F 4
dwards, 7,090	E 5
ingham, 24,608	E 4
ayette, 20,752	D 4
rd, 16,382	E 3
anklin, 38,329	E 5
lton, 41,890	C 3
allatin, 7,418	E 6
reene, 17,014	C 4
undy, 26,535	E 2
amilton, 8,665	E 5
ncock, 23,645	B 3
rdin, 4,914	E 6
enderson, 8,451	C 3
nry, 53,217	C 2
quois, 33,532	F 3
ckson, 55,008	D 6
sper, 10,741	E 4
fferson, 31,446	E 5
Daviess, 21,766	C 1
nson, 7,550	E 6
ne, 251,005	F 2
nkakee, 97,250	F 2
dall, 26,374	E 2
x, 61,280	C 3
Salle, 111,409	E 2
rence, 17,522	F 5
, 37,947	D 2
ngston, 40,690	E 3
an, 33,538	D 3
Macon, 125,010	E 4
Macoupin, 44,557	D 4
Madison, 250,934	D 5
Marion, 38,986	D 5
Marshall, 13,302	D 2
Mason, 16,161	D 3
Massac, 13,889	E 6
McDonough, 36,653	C 3
McHenry, 111,555	E 1
McLean, 104,389	D 3
Menard, 9,685	D 3
Mercer, 17,294	C 2
Monroe, 18,831	D 5
Montgomery, 30,260	D 4
Morgan, 36,174	C 4
Moultrie, 13,263	E 4
Ogle, 42,867	D 1
Peoria, 195,318	D 3
Perry, 19,757	D 5
Piatt, 15,509	E 4
Pike, 19,185	C 4
Pope, 3,857	E 6
Pulaski, 8,741	D 6
Putnam, 5,007	D 2
Randolph, 31,379	D 5
Richland, 16,829	E 5
Rock Island, 166,734	C 2
Saint Clair, 285,176	D 5
Saline, 25,721	E 6
Sangamon, 161,335	D 4
Schuyler, 8,135	C 3
Scott, 6,096	C 4
Shelby, 22,589	E 4
Stark, 7,510	D 2
Stephenson, 48,861	D 1
Tazewell, 118,649	D 3
Union, 16,071	D 6
Vermilion, 97,047	F 3
Wabash, 12,841	F 5
Warren, 21,595	C 3
Washington, 13,780	D 5
Wayne, 17,004	E 5
White, 17,312	E 5
Whiteside, 62,877	D 2
Will, 249,498	F 2
Williamson, 49,021	E 6
Winnebago, 246,623	D 1
Woodford, 28,012	D 3

CITIES and TOWNS

Zip	Name/Pop.	Key
61410	Abingdon, 3,936	C 3
60101	Addison, 24,482	A 2
61230	Albany, 942	C 2
62215	Albers, 656	D 5
62806	Albion⊙, 1,791	E 5
61231	Aledo⊙, 3,325	C 2
61412	Alexis, 946	C 2
60102	Algonquin, 3,515	E 1
62001	Alhambra, 594	D 5
† 62207	Alorton, 3,573	B 6
61413	Alpha, 771	C 2
† 60601	Alsip, 11,141	B 2
62411	Altamont, 1,929	E 4
62002	Alton, 39,700	A 6
61310	Amboy, 2,184	D 2
61232	Andalusia, 950	C 2
62906	Anna, 4,766	D 6
61234	Annawan, 787	C 2
60002	Antioch, 3,189	E 1
61910	Arcola, 2,276	E 4
62501	Argenta, 1,034	E 4
* 60004	Arlington Heights, 64,884	A 1
60910	Aroma Park, 896	F 2
61911	Arthur, 2,214	E 4
60911	Ashkum, 590	E 3
62612	Ashland, 1,128	C 4
62808	Ashley, 655	D 5
61006	Ashton, 1,112	D 2
62510	Assumption, 1,487	E 4
61501	Astoria, 1,281	C 3
62613	Athens, 1,158	C 4
61235	Atkinson, 1,053	C 2
61723	Atlanta, 1,640	D 3
61913	Atwood, 1,264	E 4
62615	Auburn, 2,594	D 4
62311	Augusta, 824	C 3
* 60504	Aurora, 74,182	E 2
62907	Ava, 728	D 6
62216	Aviston, 828	D 5
61415	Avon, 1,013	C 3
61007	Baileyville, 600	D 1
60010	Barrington, 7,701	E 1
62312	Barry, 1,444	B 4
61607	Bartonville, 7,221	D 3
62219	Beckemeyer, 1,069	D 5
† 60601	Bedford Park, 583	B 2
60401	Beecher, 1,770	F 2
† 61883	Belgium, 578	F 3
* 62220	Belleville⊙, 41,699	B 6
60104	Bellwood, 22,096	A 2
61008	Belvidere⊙, 14,061	E 1
61813	Bement, 1,638	E 4
62009	Benld, 1,736	D 4
60106	Bensenville, 12,833	A 1
62812	Benton⊙, 6,833	E 6
60162	Berkeley, 6,152	A 2
60402	Berwyn, 52,502	B 2
62010	Bethalto, 7,074	B 6
61914	Bethany, 1,235	E 4
61420	Blandinsville, 922	C 3
61701	Bloomington⊙, 39,992	D 3
	Bloomington-Normal, ‡104,389	D 3
60406	Blue Island, 22,958	B 2
62513	Blue Mound, 1,181	D 4
62621	Bluffs, 866	C 4
60914	Bourbonnais, 5,909	F 2
60407	Braceville, 668	E 2
61421	Bradford, 885	D 2
60915	Bradley, 9,881	F 2
60408	Braidwood, 2,323	E 2
62230	Breese, 2,885	D 5
62417	Bridgeport, 2,262	F 5
60455	Bridgeview, 12,522	B 2
62012	Brighton, 1,889	C 4
61517	Brimfield, 729	D 3
60153	Broadview, 9,307	A 2
60513	Brookfield, 20,284	A 2
† 62059	Brooklyn (Lovejoy), 1,702	A 6
62910	Brookport, 1,046	E 6
62418	Brownstown, 689	E 5
60918	Buckley, 680	E 3
61314	Buda, 675	D 2
62014	Bunker Hill, 1,465	D 4
† 60601	Burnham, 3,634	B 2
† 60558	Burr Ridge, 1,637	A 2
61422	Bushnell, 3,703	C 3
61010	Byron, 1,749	D 1
62606	Cahokia, 20,649	B 6
62914	Cairo⊙, 6,277	D 6
60409	Calumet City, 32,956	B 2
† 60601	Calumet Park, 10,069	B 2
62915	Cambria, 798	D 6
61238	Cambridge⊙, 2,095	C 2
62320	Camp Point, 1,143	B 3
61520	Canton, 14,217	C 3
61012	Capron, 654	E 1
61239	Carbon Cliff, 1,369	C 2
62901	Carbondale, 22,816	D 6
62626	Carlinville⊙, 5,675	C 4
62231	Carlyle⊙, 3,139	D 5
62821	Carmi⊙, 6,033	E 5
60110	Carpentersville, 24,059	E 1
62917	Carriers Mills, 2,013	E 6
62016	Carrollton⊙, 2,866	C 4
62918	Carterville, 3,061	D 6
62321	Carthage⊙, 3,350	B 3
60013	Cary, 4,358	E 1
62420	Casey, 2,994	F 4
62232	Caseyville, 3,411	B 6
61817	Catlin, 2,093	F 3
61013	Cedarville, 578	D 1
† 62801	Central City, 1,377	D 5
62801	Centralia, 15,217	D 5
62206	Centreville, 11,378	B 6
61818	Cerro Gordo, 1,368	E 4
61014	Chadwick, 605	D 1
61820	Champaign, 56,532	E 3
	Champaign-Urbana, ‡163,281	E 3
62627	Chandlerville, 762	C 3
60410	Channahon, 1,505	E 2
62628	Chapin, 552	C 4
61920	Charleston⊙, 16,421	E 4
62629	Chatham, 2,788	D 4
60921	Chatsworth, 1,255	E 3
60922	Chebanse, 1,185	F 3
61726	Chenoa, 1,860	E 3
61016	Cherry Valley, 952	D 1
62233	Chester⊙, 5,310	D 6
* 60601	Chicago⊙, 3,366,957	B 2
60411	Chicago Heights, 40,900	B 3
60415	Chicago Ridge, 9,187	A 2
61523	Chillicothe, 6,052	D 3
61924	Chrisman, 1,285	F 4
62822	Christopher, 2,910	D 6
60650	Cicero, 67,058	B 2
62823	Cisne, 615	E 5
60924	Cissna Park, 773	F 3
60514	Clarendon Hills, 6,750	A 2
62824	Clay City, 1,049	E 5
62334	Clayton, 727	B 3
60927	Clifton, 1,339	F 3
61727	Clinton⊙, 7,570	D 3
60416	Coal City, 3,040	E 2
61240	Coal Valley, 3,088	C 2
62920	Cobden, 1,114	D 6
62017	Coffeen, 641	D 4
62326	Colchester, 1,747	C 3
61728	Colfax, 935	E 3
62234	Collinsville, 17,773	B 6
62236	Columbia, 4,188	C 5
61242	Cordova, 589	C 2
62018	Cottage Hills, 1,261	B 6
62237	Coulterville, 1,186	D 5
60477	Country Club Hills, 6,920	B 3
† 60525	Countryside, 2,888	A 2
62922	Creal Springs, 830	E 6
60928	Crescent City, 597	F 3
60435	Crest Hill, 7,460	E 2
60113	Creston, 595	D 2
60445	Crestwood, 5,543	B 2
60417	Crete, 4,656	F 2
61611	Creve Coeur, 6,440	D 3
62827	Crossville, 860	F 5
60014	Crystal Lake, 14,541	E 1
61427	Cuba, 1,581	C 3
60929	Cullom, 572	E 3
62330	Dallas City, 1,284	B 3
61320	Dalzell, 579	D 2
61732	Danvers, 854	D 3
61832	Danville⊙, 42,570	F 3
* 62521	Decatur⊙, 90,397	E 4
	Decatur, ‡125,010	E 4

(continued on following page)

AREA 56,400 sq. mi.
POPULATION 11,113,976
CAPITAL Springfield
LARGEST CITY Chicago
HIGHEST POINT Charles Mound 1,235 ft.
SETTLED IN 1720
ADMITTED TO UNION December 3, 1818
POPULAR NAME Prairie State
STATE FLOWER Violet
STATE BIRD Cardinal

Agriculture, Industry and Resources

DOMINANT LAND USE

- Cash Corn, Oats, Soybeans
- Hogs, Soft Winter Wheat
- Cattle Feed, Hogs
- Hogs, Dairy
- Specialized Dairy
- General Farming, Dairy, Livestock, Poultry
- Pasture Livestock
- Urban Areas

MAJOR MINERAL OCCURRENCES

- C — Coal
- Cl — Clay
- F — Fluorspar
- Ls — Limestone
- O — Petroleum
- Pb — Lead
- Zn — Zinc

Major Industrial Areas

ROCKFORD Machine Tools, Machinery, Metal Products, Screws & Bolts, Farm Equipment

CHICAGO—NORTHEASTERN ILLINOIS Machinery, Metal & Electrical Products, Food Processing, Printing & Publishing, Chemicals, Iron & Steel, Clothing, Transportation Equipment

ROCK ISLAND—MOLINE Machinery, Metal Products, Ordnance, Farm Equipment

PEORIA Machinery, Metal Products, Chemicals, Food Processing, Distilling, Earth Movers

DECATUR Machinery, Metal Products, Soybean & Corn Processing, Food Processing

SPRINGFIELD Electrical & Metal Products, Machinery, Tractors

EAST ST. LOUIS Primary Metals, Aluminum Products, Chemicals, Food Processing, Oil Refining, Building Materials

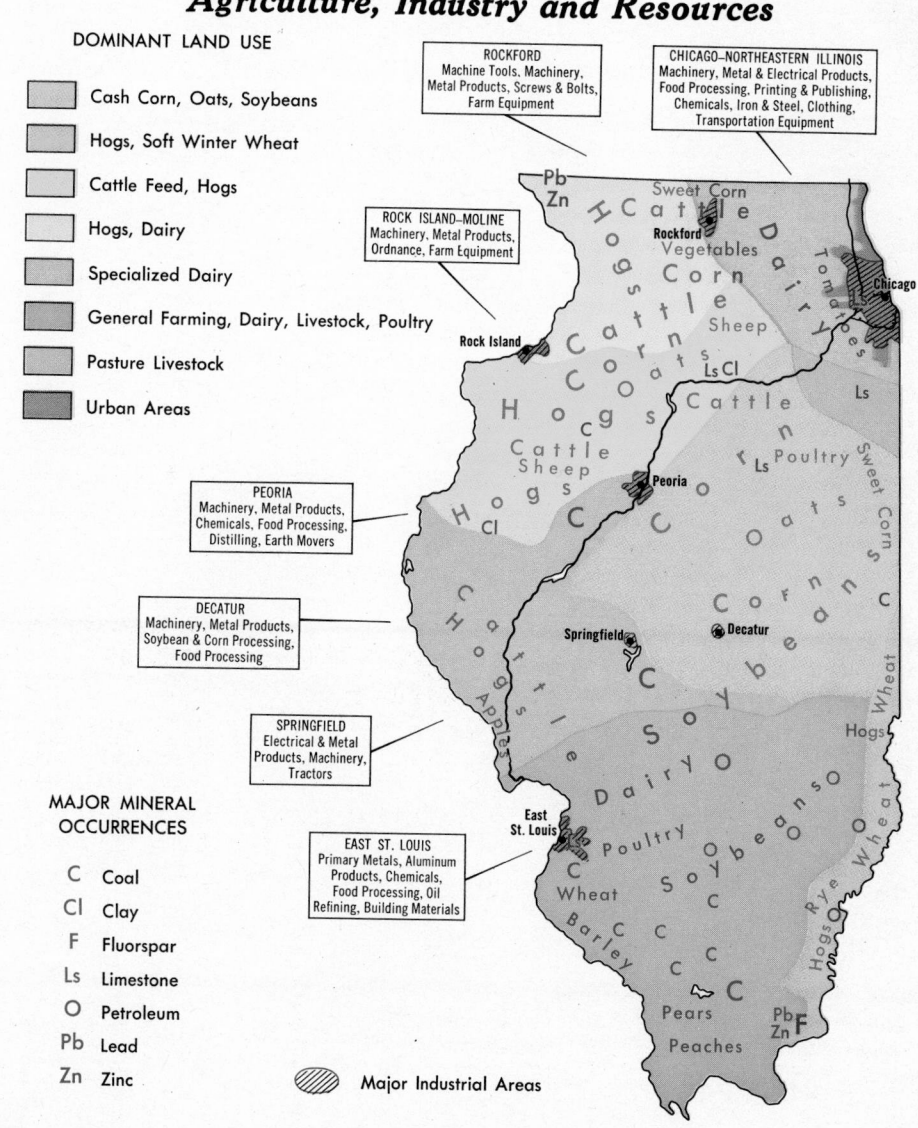

Topography

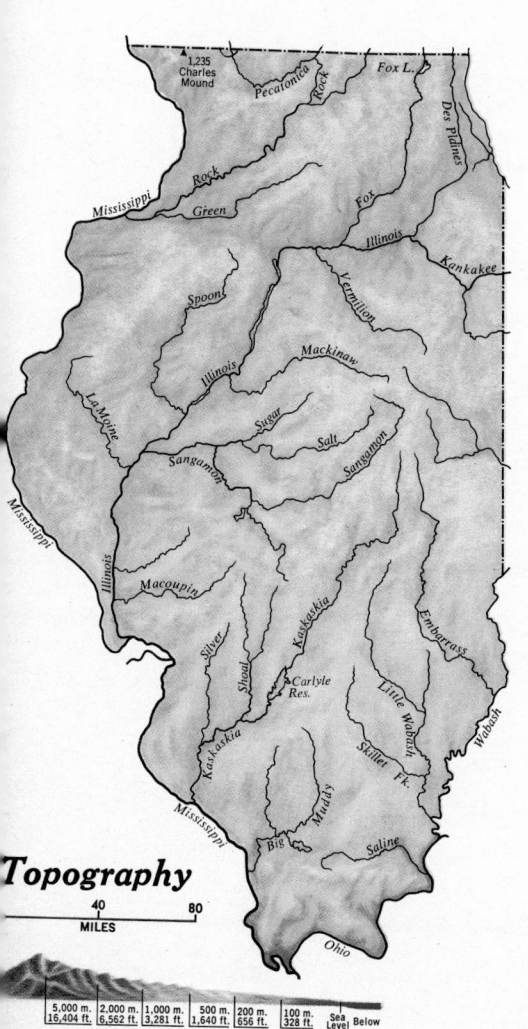

MILES

| 5,000 m. 16,404 ft. | 2,000 m. 6,562 ft. | 1,000 m. 3,281 ft. | 500 m. 1,640 ft. | 200 m. 656 ft. | 100 m. 328 ft. | Sea Level | Below |

(continued)

61733 Deer Creek, 647 D 3
60015 Deerfield, 18,949 F 1
60115 De Kalb, 32,949 E 2
61734 Delavan, 1,844 D 3
61322 Depue, 1,919 D 2
62924 De Soto, 966 D 6
* 60016 Des Plaines, 57,239 A 1
† 62025 Dewey Park, 2,029 B 6
62530 Divernon, 1,010 D 4
† 60469 Dixmoor, 4,735 B 2
61021 Dixon⊙, 18,147 D 2
60419 Dolton, 25,937 B 2
62926 Dongola, 825 D 6
60515 Downers Grove, 32,751 A 2
61736 Downs, 651 E 3
60118 Dundee (East and West Dundee), 6,215 E 1
61525 Dunlap, 656 D 3
62239 Dupo, 2,842 A 6
62832 Du Quoin, 6,691 D 5
61024 Durand, 972 D 1
60420 Dwight, 3,841 E 2
60518 Earlville, 1,410 E 2
62024 East Alton, 7,309 B 6
† 60411 East Chicago Heights, 5,000 B 3
61025 East Dubuque, 2,408 C 1
† 60118 East Dundee (Dundee), 2,920 E 1
61430 East Galesburg, 706 C 3
† 60429 East Hazelcrest, 1,885 B 2
61244 East Moline, 20,832 C 2
61611 East Peoria, 18,455 D 3
* 62201 East Saint Louis, 69,996 B 6
62531 Edinburg, 1,153 D 4
62025 Edwardsville⊙, 11,070 B 6
62401 Effingham⊙, 9,458 E 4
60119 Elburn, 1,122 E 2
62930 Eldorado, 3,876 E 6
60120 Elgin, 55,691 E 1
61028 Elizabeth, 707 C 1
62931 Elizabethtown⊙, 436 E 6
60007 Elk Grove Village, 24,516 A 1
62932 Elkville, 850 D 6
60126 Elmhurst, 50,547 A 2
61529 Elmwood, 2,014 D 3
60635 Elmwood Park, 26,160 B 2
61738 El Paso, 2,291 D 3
60421 Elwood, 794 E 2
62635 Emden, 552 D 3
62933 Energy, 812 E 6
62835 Enfield, 764 E 5
62934 Equality, 732 E 6
62250 Erie, 1,566 C 2
61530 Eureka⊙, 3,028 D 3
* 60201 Evanston, 79,808 B 1
62242 Evansville, 838 D 5
60642 Evergreen Park, 25,487 B 2
61739 Fairbury, 3,359 E 3
62837 Fairfield⊙, 5,897 E 5
† 62002 Fairmont, 1,521 A 6
† 62201 Fairmont City, 2,769 B 6
61841 Fairmount, 785 F 3
61432 Fairview, 601 C 3
62232 Fairview Heights, 8,625 B 6
62838 Farina, 634 E 5
61842 Farmer City, 2,217 E 3
61531 Farmington, 2,959 C 3
62534 Findlay, 809 E 4
61843 Fisher, 1,525 E 3
61844 Fithian, 562 F 3
61740 Flanagan, 878 E 3
62839 Flora, 5,283 E 5
60422 Flossmoor, 7,846 B 3
† 62018 Forest Homes, 1,998 B 6
60130 Forest Park, 15,472 B 2
† 60402 Forest View, 927 B 2
61741 Forrest, 1,219 E 3
61030 Forreston, 1,227 D 1
60020 Fox Lake, 4,511 E 1
60021 Fox River Grove, 2,245 E 1
60423 Frankfort, 2,325 F 2
62638 Franklin, 565 C 4
61031 Franklin Grove, 968 D 2
60131 Franklin Park, 20,497 A 2

62243 Freeburg, 2,495 D 5
61032 Freeport⊙, 27,736 D 1
61252 Fulton, 3,630 C 2
62935 Galatia, 792 E 6
61036 Galena⊙, 3,930 C 1
61401 Galesburg⊙, 36,290 C 3
61434 Galva, 3,061 D 2
60424 Gardner, 1,212 E 2
61254 Geneseo, 5,840 C 2
60134 Geneva⊙, 9,115 E 2
60135 Genoa, 3,003 E 1
61846 Georgetown, 3,984 F 4
62245 Germantown, 1,108 D 5
60936 Gibson City, 3,454 E 3
61847 Gifford, 814 E 3
62033 Gillespie, 3,457 D 4
60938 Gilman, 1,786 E 3
62640 Girard, 1,881 D 4
61533 Glasford, 1,066 D 3
62034 Glen Carbon, 1,897 B 6
60022 Glencoe, 10,542 F 1
60137 Glen Ellyn, 21,909 F 2
60025 Glenview, 24,880 B 1
60425 Glenwood, 7,416 B 3
62035 Godfrey, 1,225 A 6
62938 Golconda⊙, 922 E 6
62339 Golden, 571 B 3
62939 Goreville, 1,109 E 6
62037 Grafton, 1,018 C 5
61325 Grand Ridge, 698 E 2
62942 Grand Tower, 664 D 6
† 62701 Grandview, 2,242 D 4
62040 Granite City, 40,440 B 6
60940 Grant Park, 801 F 2
61326 Granville, 1,232 D 2
60030 Grayslake, 4,907 E 1
62844 Grayville, 2,035 E 5
62044 Greenfield, 1,179 C 4
† 61241 Green Rock, 2,744 C 2
62248 Greenup, 1,618 E 4
61534 Green Valley, 617 D 3
62642 Greenview, 740 D 3
62246 Greenville⊙, 4,631 D 5
61744 Gridley, 1,007 E 3
62340 Griggsville, 1,245 C 4
60031 Gurnee, 2,738 F 1
62341 Hamilton, 2,764 B 3
60140 Hampshire, 1,611 E 1
62256 Hampton, 1,612 C 2
61536 Hanna City, 1,282 D 3
61041 Hanover, 1,243 C 1
62047 Hardin⊙, 1,035 C 4
62946 Harrisburg⊙, 9,535 E 6
62048 Hartford, 2,243 B 6
60033 Harvard, 5,177 E 1
60426 Harvey, 34,636 B 2
60656 Harwood Heights, 9,060 B 1
62644 Havana⊙, 4,376 D 3
60429 Hazel Crest, 10,329 B 2
60034 Hebron, 781 E 1
† 61832 Hegeler, 1,595 F 3
61327 Hennepin⊙, 535 D 2
61537 Henry, 2,610 D 2
62948 Herrin, 9,623 E 6
60941 Herscher, 988 E 2
61745 Heyworth, 1,441 E 3
60457 Hickory Hills, 13,176 B 2
62249 Highland, 5,981 D 5
60035 Highland Park, 32,263 F 1
60040 Highwood, 4,973 F 1
61244 Hillcrest, 630 D 2
62049 Hillsboro⊙, 4,267 D 4
60162 Hillside, 8,888 A 2
60520 Hinckley, 1,053 E 2
60521 Hinsdale, 15,918 A 2
60525 Hodgkins, 2,270 A 2
61849 Homer, 1,354 F 3
60456 Hometown, 6,729 B 2
60430 Homewood, 18,871 B 3
60942 Hoopeston, 6,461 F 3
61747 Hopedale, 923 D 3
61748 Hudson, 802 E 3
62343 Hull, 585 B 4
60142 Huntley, 1,432 E 1
62949 Hurst, 934 D 6

62539 Illiopolis, 1,122 D 4
61440 Industry, 558 C 3
† 60431 Ingalls Park, 5,615 F 2
61441 Ipava, 608 C 3
62051 Irving, 599 D 4
60042 Island Lake, 1,973 E 1
60143 Itasca, 4,638 F 2
62650 Jacksonville⊙, 20,553 C 4
† 62701 Jerome, 1,673 D 4
62052 Jerseyville⊙, 7,446 C 4
62951 Johnston City, 3,928 E 6
* 60431 Joliet⊙, 80,378 E 2
62952 Jonesboro⊙, 1,676 D 6
† 60453 Justice, 9,473 A 2
60901 Kankakee⊙, 30,944 F 2
61933 Kansas, 779 F 4
62956 Karnak, 641 E 6
† 63673 Kaskaskia, 79 C 6
61442 Keithsburg, 836 B 2
60043 Kenilworth, 2,980 B 1
61443 Kewanee, 15,762 C 2
62540 Kincaid, 1,424 D 4
62854 Kinmundy, 759 E 5
60146 Kirkland, 1,138 E 1
61447 Kirkwood, 817 C 3
61448 Knoxville, 2,930 C 3
61540 Lacon⊙, 2,147 D 2
61329 Ladd, 1,328 D 2
60525 La Grange, 16,773 A 2
60525 La Grange Park, 15,626 A 2
61450 La Harpe, 1,240 C 3
60044 Lake Bluff, 4,979 F 1
† 60002 Lake Catherine, 1,219 E 1
60045 Lake Forest, 15,642 F 1
60047 Lake Zurich, 4,082 E 1
61330 La Moille, 669 D 2
61046 Lanark, 1,495 D 1
60438 Lansing, 25,805 B 3
61301 La Salle, 10,736 E 2
62439 Lawrenceville⊙, 5,863 F 5
61047 Leaf River, 633 D 1
62254 Lebanon, 3,564 D 5
60531 Leland, 743 E 2
60439 Lemont, 5,080 A 2
61048 Lena, 1,691 D 1
61752 Le Roy, 2,435 E 3
61542 Lewistown⊙, 2,706 C 3
61753 Lexington, 1,615 E 3
60048 Libertyville, 11,684 F 1
62656 Lincoln⊙, 17,582 D 3
† 60601 Lincolnwood, 12,929 B 1
60046 Lindenhurst, 3,141 F 1
62056 Litchfield, 7,190 D 4
62058 Livingston, 916 D 5
60441 Lockport, 9,985 F 2
61454 Lomax, 565 B 3
60148 Lombard, 35,977 A 2
61544 London Mills, 600 C 3
62858 Louisville⊙, 1,020 E 5
62059 Lovejoy, 1,702 A 6
61111 Loves Park, 12,390 E 1
61937 Lovington, 1,303 E 4
61261 Lyndon, 673 D 2
† 60411 Lynwood, 1,042 B 3
60534 Lyons, 11,124 B 2
61755 Mackinaw, 1,293 D 3
61455 Macomb⊙, 19,643 C 3
62544 Macon, 1,249 E 4
62060 Madison, 7,042 B 6
61853 Mahomet, 1,296 E 3
60150 Malta, 961 E 2
60442 Manhattan, 1,530 F 2
61546 Manito, 1,334 D 3
61854 Mansfield, 870 E 3
60950 Manteno, 2,864 F 2
60151 Maple Park, 660 E 2
60152 Marengo, 4,235 E 1
62061 Marine, 882 D 5
62959 Marion⊙, 11,724 E 6
62257 Marissa, 2,004 D 5
60426 Markham, 15,987 B 2
61756 Maroa, 1,467 E 3
† 61554 Marquette Heights, 2,758 D 3
61341 Marseilles, 4,320 E 2
62441 Marshall⊙, 3,468 F 4

62442 Martinsville, 1,374 F 4
62062 Maryville, 809 B 6
62258 Mascoutah, 5,045 D 5
62664 Mason City, 2,611 D 3
61263 Matherville, 699 C 2
60443 Matteson, 4,741 B 3
61938 Mattoon, 19,681 E 4
60153 Maywood, 30,036 A 2
60444 Mazon, 727 E 2
62957 McClure, 800 D 6
† 60050 McCullom Lake, 873 E 1
60050 McHenry, 6,772 E 1
61754 McLean, 820 D 3
62859 McLeansboro⊙, 2,630 E 5
† 62010 Meadowbrook, 1,295 B 6
* 60160 Melrose Park, 22,706 A 2
62351 Mendon, 883 B 3
61342 Mendota, 6,902 D 2
62665 Meredosia, 1,178 C 4
† 60601 Merrionette Park, 2,303 B 2
61548 Metamora, 2,176 D 3
62960 Metropolis⊙, 6,940 E 6
62666 Middletown, 626 D 3
60445 Midlothian, 15,939 B 2
61264 Milan, 4,873 C 2
60953 Milford, 1,656 F 3
61051 Milledgeville, 1,130 D 1
62260 Millstadt, 2,168 B 6
61759 Minier, 986 D 3
61760 Minonk, 2,267 D 3
60447 Minooka, 768 E 2
60448 Mokena, 1,643 F 2
61265 Moline, 46,237 C 2
60954 Momence, 2,836 F 2
60449 Monee, 940 F 2
61462 Monmouth⊙, 11,022 C 3
60538 Montgomery, 3,278 E 2
61856 Monticello⊙, 4,130 E 3
60539 Mooseheart, 850 E 2
60450 Morris⊙, 8,194 E 2
61270 Morrison⊙, 4,387 C 2
62546 Morrisonville, 1,178 D 4
† 61101 Morristown, 669 D 1
61550 Morton, 10,419 D 3
60053 Morton Grove, 26,369 B 1
62963 Mound City⊙, 1,177 D 6
62964 Mounds, 1,718 D 6
62863 Mount Carmel⊙, 8,096 F 5
61053 Mount Carroll⊙, 2,143 D 1
61054 Mount Morris, 3,173 D 1
62069 Mount Olive, 2,288 D 4
60056 Mount Prospect, 34,995 A 1
62548 Mount Pulaski, 1,677 D 3
62353 Mount Sterling⊙, 2,182 C 4
62864 Mount Vernon⊙, 15,980 E 5
62549 Mount Zion, 2,343 E 4
62550 Moweaqua, 1,687 E 4
62262 Mulberry Grove, 697 D 5
60060 Mundelein, 16,128 E 1
62966 Murphysboro⊙, 10,013 D 6
62668 Murrayville, 595 C 4
60540 Naperville, 23,885 E 2
† 61350 Naplate, 686 E 2
62263 Nashville⊙, 3,027 D 5
62354 Nauvoo, 1,047 B 3
62447 Neoga, 1,270 E 4
60541 Newark, 590 E 2
62264 New Athens, 2,000 D 5
62265 New Baden, 1,953 D 5
62670 New Berlin, 754 D 4
61272 New Boston, 706 B 2
62867 New Haven, 606 E 6
60451 New Lenox, 2,855 F 2
61942 Newman, 1,018 F 4
62448 Newton⊙, 3,024 E 5
61465 New Windsor, 723 C 2
62551 Niantic, 705 D 4
60648 Niles, 31,432 A 1
62868 Noble, 719 E 5
62075 Nokomis, 2,532 D 4
61761 Normal, 26,396 E 3
† 60601 Norridge, 16,880 B 1
62869 Norris City, 1,319 E 6
60542 North Aurora, 4,833 E 2
60062 Northbrook, 27,297 A 1
60064 North Chicago, 47,275 F 1
60093 Northfield, 5,010 B 1
60164 Northlake, 14,212 A 2
† 61101 North Park, 15,679 D 1
† 61554 North Pekin, 1,886 D 3
60546 North Riverside, 8,097 B 2
† 61373 North Utica (Utica), 974 E 2
60452 Oak Forest, 17,870 B 2
61943 Oakland, 1,012 F 4
* 60453 Oak Lawn, 60,305 B 2
60303 Oak Park, 62,511 B 2
61858 Oakwood, 1,367 F 3
† 62095 Oakwood Heights, 3,229 B 6
62449 Oblong, 1,860 F 5
60460 Odell, 1,076 E 2
62870 Odin, 1,263 D 5
62269 O'Fallon, 7,268 B 6
61348 Oglesby, 4,175 D 2
62271 Okawville, 992 D 5
62969 Olive Branch, 600 D 6
62450 Olney⊙, 8,974 E 5
60461 Olympia Fields, 3,478 B 3
60955 Onarga, 1,436 F 3
61467 Oneida, 728 C 3
61469 Oquawka⊙, 1,352 C 3
62554 Oreana, 1,092 E 4
61061 Oregon⊙, 3,539 D 1
61273 Orion, 1,801 C 2
60462 Orland Park, 6,391 E 2
60543 Oswego, 1,862 E 2
61350 Ottawa⊙, 18,716 E 2
60067 Palatine, 25,904 E 1
62451 Palestine, 1,640 F 4
62674 Palmyra, 776 C 4
60463 Palos Heights, 9,915 A 2
60465 Palos Hills, 6,629 A 2
60464 Palos Park, 3,297 A 2
62557 Pana, 6,326 D 4
61944 Paris⊙, 9,971 F 4
60466 Park Forest, 30,638 B 3
60068 Park Ridge, 42,466 A 1
62875 Patoka, 562 D 5

62558 Pawnee, 1,936 D 4
61353 Pawpaw, 846 E 2
60957 Paxton⊙, 4,373 E 3
62360 Payson, 589 B 4
61063 Pecatonica, 1,781 D 1
61554 Pekin⊙, 31,375 D 3
* 61601 Peoria⊙, 126,963 D 3
Peoria, ‡341,979 D 3
61614 Peoria Heights, 7,943 D 3
60468 Peotone, 2,345 F 2
62272 Percy, 967 D 5
61354 Peru, 11,772 D 2
62675 Petersburg⊙, 2,632 D 4
61864 Philo, 1,022 E 3
† 60426 Phoenix, 3,596 B 2
62274 Pinckneyville⊙, 3,377 D 5
60959 Piper City, 817 E 3
62363 Pittsfield⊙, 4,244 C 4
60544 Plainfield, 2,928 E 2
60545 Plano, 4,664 E 2
62366 Pleasant Hill, 1,064 C 4
62677 Pleasant Plains, 644 D 4
62367 Plymouth, 740 C 3
62275 Pocahontas, 764 D 5
61074 Polo, 2,542 D 2
61764 Pontiac⊙, 9,031 E 3
61065 Poplar Grove, 607 E 1
61275 Port Byron, 1,222 C 2
60469 Posen, 5,498 B 2
61865 Potomac, 909 F 3
61470 Prairie City, 630 C 3
62277 Prairie du Rocher, 658 C 5
61356 Princeton⊙, 6,959 D 2
61559 Princeville, 1,455 D 3
61277 Prophetstown, 1,915 D 2
60070 Prospect Heights, 13,333 A 1
62301 Quincy⊙, 45,288 B 4
62080 Ramsey, 830 D 4
60960 Rankin, 727 F 3
61866 Rantoul, 25,562 E 3
61278 Rapids City, 656 C 2
62560 Raymond, 890 D 4
62278 Red Bud, 2,559 D 5
61279 Reynolds, 610 C 2
60071 Richmond, 1,153 E 1
60471 Richton Park, 2,558 B 3
61870 Ridge Farm, 1,015 F 4
62979 Ridgway, 1,160 E 6
60627 Riverdale, 15,806 B 2
60305 River Forest, 13,402 B 2
60171 River Grove, 11,465 A 2
60546 Riverside, 10,432 B 2
62561 Riverton, 2,090 D 4
61561 Roanoke, 2,040 D 3
60472 Robbins, 9,641 B 2
62454 Robinson⊙, 7,178 F 5
61068 Rochelle, 8,594 D 2
62563 Rochester, 1,667 D 4
60436 Rockdale, 2,085 E 2
61071 Rock Falls, 10,287 D 2
* 61101 Rockford⊙, 147,370 D 1
Rockford, ‡272,063 D 1
61201 Rock Island⊙, 50,166 C 2
Rock Island-Moline-Davenport, ‡362,638 C 2
61072 Rockton, 2,099 E 1
60008 Rolling Meadows, 19,178 A 1
61562 Rome, 1,919 D 3
† 60441 Romeoville, 12,674 E 2
62082 Roodhouse, 2,357 C 4
61073 Roscoe, 949 D 1
60018 Rosemont, 4,360 A 1
61473 Roseville, 1,111 C 3
† 62024 Rosewood Heights, 3,391 B 6
62982 Rosiclare, 1,421 E 6
60963 Rossville, 1,420 F 3
62084 Roxana, 1,882 B 6
62983 Royalton, 1,166 D 6
62681 Rushville⊙, 3,300 C 3
60964 Saint Anne, 1,271 F 2
60174 Saint Charles, 12,928 E 2
61563 Saint David, 773 C 3
62458 Saint Elmo, 1,676 E 4
62460 Saint Francisville, 997 F 5
62281 Saint Jacob, 659 D 5
61873 Saint Joseph, 1,554 E 3
62881 Salem⊙, 6,187 E 5
62882 Sandoval, 1,332 D 5
60548 Sandwich, 5,056 E 2
62682 San Jose, 681 D 3
60411 Sauk Village, 7,479 F 2
61074 Savanna, 4,942 C 1
61874 Savoy, 592 E 3
61770 Saybrook, 814 E 3
60172 Schaumburg, 18,730 E 1
60176 Schiller Park, 12,712 A 1
† 62049 Schram City, 657 D 4
61360 Seneca, 1,781 E 2
62884 Sesser, 2,125 D 5
61875 Seymour, 850 E 3
60550 Shabbona, 730 E 2
61078 Shannon, 848 D 1
62984 Shawneetown⊙, 1,742 E 6
61361 Sheffield, 1,038 D 2
62565 Shelbyville⊙, 4,597 E 4
60966 Sheldon, 1,455 F 3
60551 Sheridan, 724 E 2
61281 Sherrard, 808 C 2
† 62220 Shiloh, 945 B 6
61876 Sidell, 645 F 4
61877 Sidney, 915 E 3
61282 Silvis, 5,907 C 2
60076 Skokie, 68,627 B 1
62285 Smithton, 847 C 5
60552 Somonauk, 1,112 E 2
62086 Sorento, 625 D 5
61080 South Beloit, 3,804 E 1
60411 South Chicago Heights, 4,923 B 3
60177 South Elgin, 4,289 E 2
60473 South Holland, 23,931 B 2
62650 South Jacksonville, 2,950 C 4
61564 South Pekin, 955 D 3
60474 South Wilmington, 725 E 2
61565 Sparland, 585 D 2
62286 Sparta, 4,307 D 5
* 62701 Springfield (cap.)⊙, 91,753 D 4
Springfield, ‡161,335 D 4

61362 Spring Valley, 5,605 D
61774 Stanford, 657 D
62088 Staunton, 4,396 D
62288 Steeleville, 1,957 D
60475 Steger, 8,104 F
61081 Sterling, 16,113 D
62463 Stewardson, 729 E
60402 Stickney, 6,601 B
61084 Stillman Valley, 871 D
61085 Stockton, 1,930 C
60165 Stone Park, 4,451 A
62567 Stonington, 1,096 D
60103 Streamwood, 18,176 E
61364 Streator, 15,600 E
61480 Stronghurst, 836 C
61951 Sullivan⊙, 4,112 E
60501 Summit, 11,569 B
62466 Sumner, 1,201 F
62221 Swansea, 5,432 B
60178 Sycamore⊙, 7,843 E
62688 Tallula, 643 D
62888 Tamaroa, 799 D
62988 Tamms, 645 D
61283 Tampico, 838 D
62089 Taylor Springs, 620 D
62568 Taylorville⊙, 10,644 D
62467 Teutopolis, 1,249 E
62689 Thayer, 616 D
61878 Thomasboro, 806 E
61285 Thomson, 617 C
60476 Thornton, 3,714 B
62292 Tilden, 909 D
† 61832 Tilton, 2,544 F
60477 Tinley Park, 12,382 B
61368 Tiskilwa, 973 D
62468 Toledo⊙, 1,068 E
61880 Tolono, 2,027 E
61369 Toluca, 1,319 D
61370 Tonica, 821 E
61483 Toulon⊙, 1,207 D
61776 Towanda, 578 E
62571 Tower Hill, 683 E
61568 Tremont, 1,942 D
62293 Trenton, 2,328 D
62294 Troy, 2,144 B
61953 Tuscola⊙, 3,917 E
60180 Union, 579 E
61801 Urbana⊙, 32,800 E
61373 Utica, 974 E
62891 Valier, 628 D
62295 Valmeyer, 733 C
62471 Vandalia⊙, 5,160 D
62090 Venice, 4,680 A
61484 Vermont, 947 C
61485 Victoria, 782 C
62995 Vienna⊙, 1,325 E
61956 Villa Grove, 2,605 E
60181 Villa Park, 25,891 A
61486 Viola, 946 C
62690 Virden, 3,504 D
62691 Virginia⊙, 1,814 C
60083 Wadsworth, 756 F
61376 Walnut, 1,295 D
† 62801 Wamac, 1,347 D
61777 Wapella, 572 E
61087 Warren, 1,523 C
62573 Warrensburg, 738 D
62379 Warsaw, 1,758 B
61570 Washburn, 1,173 D
61571 Washington, 6,790 D
62204 Washington Park, 9,524 B
61488 Wataga, 570 C
62298 Waterloo⊙, 4,546 C
60556 Waterman, 990 E
60970 Watseka⊙, 5,294 F
60084 Wauconda, 5,460 E
60085 Waukegan⊙, 65,269 F
62692 Waverly, 1,442 D
62895 Wayne City, 985 E
61882 Weldon, 553 E
61377 Wenona, 1,080 E
60153 Westchester, 20,033 A
60185 West Chicago, 10,111 E
† 62812 West City, 637 E
† 60118 West Dundee (Dundee), 3,295 E
60558 Western Springs, 12,147
62474 Westfield, 678
62896 West Frankfort, 8,836
60559 Westmont, 8,482
62476 West Salem, 979
61883 Westville, 3,655
60187 Wheaton⊙, 31,138
60090 Wheeling, 14,746
62092 White Hall, 2,979
61489 Williamsfield, 552
62693 Williamsville, 923
62997 Willisville, 659
60480 Willow Springs, 3,318
60091 Wilmette, 32,134
60481 Wilmington, 4,335
62093 Wilsonville, 691
62694 Winchester⊙, 1,788
61957 Windsor, 1,126
† 61465 Windsor (New Windsor), 723
60190 Winfield, 4,285
61088 Winnebago, 1,285
60093 Winnetka, 14,131
60096 Winthrop Harbor, 4,794
62094 Witt, 1,040
60191 Wood Dale, 8,831
61490 Woodhull, 898
60515 Woodridge, 11,028
62095 Wood River, 13,186
60098 Woodstock⊙, 10,226
62097 Worden, 1,091
60482 Worth, 11,999
61379 Wyanet, 1,005
61491 Wyoming, 1,563
61572 Yates City, 840
60560 Yorkville⊙, 2,049
62999 Zeigler, 1,940
60099 Zion, 17,268

⊙ County seat.
‡ Population of metropolitan area
† Zip of nearest p.o.
* Multiple zips

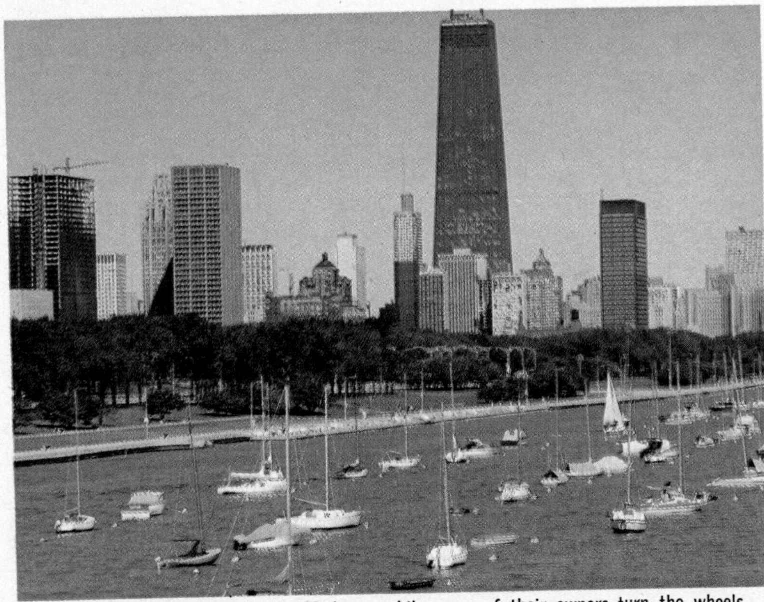
Fred Boler—Shostal Associates

Sailboats lie anchored in Lake Michigan while many of their owners turn the wheels of industry behind Chicago's steel and glass facade.

COUNTIES

County	Key
Adams, 26,871	H 3
Allen, 280,455	G 2
Bartholomew, 57,022	F 6
Benton, 11,262	C 3
Blackford, 15,888	G 4
Boone, 30,870	E 4
Brown, 9,057	E 6
Carroll, 17,734	D 3
Cass, 40,456	E 3
Clark, 75,876	F 8
Clay, 23,933	C 6
Clinton, 30,547	E 4
Crawford, 8,033	E 8
Daviess, 26,602	C 7
Dearborn, 29,430	H 6
Decatur, 22,738	G 6
De Kalb, 30,837	H 2
Delaware, 129,219	G 4
Dubois, 30,934	D 8
Elkhart, 126,529	F 1
ayette, 26,216	G 5
loyd, 55,622	F 8
ountain, 18,257	C 4
ranklin, 16,943	G 6
ulton, 16,984	E 2
ibson, 30,444	B 8
rant, 83,955	F 3
reene, 26,894	D 6
lamilton, 54,532	E 4
lancock, 35,096	F 5
larrison, 20,423	E 8
endricks, 53,974	D 5
enry, 52,603	G 5
loward, 83,198	E 4
luntington, 34,970	G 3
ackson, 33,187	E 7
asper, 20,429	C 2
ay, 23,575	G 4
efferson, 27,006	G 7
ennings, 19,454	F 7
ohnson, 61,138	E 6
nox, 41,546	C 7
osciusko, 48,127	F 2
agrange, 20,890	G 1
ake, 546,253	C 2
aPorte, 105,342	D 1
awrence, 38,038	E 7
adison, 138,451	F 4
arion, 792,299	E 5
arshall, 34,986	E 2
artin, 10,969	D 7
ami, 39,246	E 3
onroe, 84,849	D 6
ontgomery, 33,930	D 4
organ, 44,176	E 6
ewton, 11,606	C 3
oble, 31,382	G 2
io, 4,289	H 7
ange, 16,968	E 7
wen, 12,163	D 6
rke, 14,600	C 5
rry, 19,075	D 8
ke, 12,281	C 8
rter, 87,114	C 2
sey, 21,740	B 8
aski, 12,534	D 2
tnam, 26,932	D 5
ndolph, 28,915	G 4
oley, 21,138	G 6
sh, 20,352	G 5
nt Joseph, 245,045	E 1
ott, 17,144	F 7
elby, 37,797	F 5
encer, 17,134	C 9
rke, 19,280	D 2
uben, 20,159	G 1
livan, 19,889	C 6
tzerland, 6,306	G 7
pecanoe, 109,378	D 4
ton, 16,650	E 4
on, 6,582	H 5
derburgh, 168,772	B 8
million, 16,793	C 5
o, 114,528	C 6
bash, 35,553	F 3
rren, 8,705	C 4
rrick, 27,972	C 8
shington, 19,278	E 7
yne, 79,109	G 5
ls, 23,821	G 3
te, 20,995	D 3
tley, 23,395	F 2

CITIES and TOWNS

	Name/Pop.	*Key*
40	Adams, 300	F 6
47	Adamsboro, 325	E 3
2	Advance, 561	D 5
0	Akron, 1,019	E 2
20	Albany, 2,293	G 4
1	Albion⊙, 1,498	G 2
33	Alert, 210	F 6
1	Alexandria, 5,097	F 4
8	Altona, 209	G 2
7	Ambia, 300	C 4
1	Amboy, 473	F 3
1	Amity, 400	E 6
3	Amo, 422	D 5
1	Anderson⊙, 70,787	F 4
	Anderson, ‡138,451	F 4
4	Andersonville, 250	G 5
2	Andrews, 1,207	F 3
3	Angola⊙, 5,117	G 1
0	Arcadia, 1,338	E 4
4	Arcola, 325	G 2
4	Ardmore, 800	E 1
1	Argos, 1,393	E 2
4	Arlington, 550	F 5
5	Ashley, 721	G 1
1	Atlanta, 620	E 4
8	Attica, 4,262	C 4
2	Atwood, 300	F 2
6	Auburn⊙, 7,337	G 2
1	Aurora, 4,293	H 6
47102	Austin, 4,902	F 7
46710	Avilla, 881	G 2
47420	Avoca, 400	D 7
46105	Bainbridge, 703	D 5
46106	Bargersville, 873	E 5
47006	Batesville, 3,799	G 6
47920	Battle Ground, 818	D 3
47421	Bedford⊙, 13,087	E 7
46107	Beech Grove, 13,468	E 5
† 46526	Benton, 221	F 2
46711	Berne, 2,988	H 3
46301	Beverly Shores, 946	C 1
47512	Bicknell, 3,717	C 7
46713	Bippus, 220	F 3
47513	Birdseye, 404	D 8
† 46401	Blackoak, 9,624	C 1
47831	Blanford, 700	B 5
47170	Blocher, 350	F 7
47424	Bloomfield⊙, 2,565	D 6
47832	Bloomingdale, 391	C 5
47401	Bloomington⊙, 42,890	D 6
† 47360	Blountsville, 220	G 4
† 46176	Blue Ridge, 236	F 5
46714	Bluffton⊙, 8,297	G 3
46110	Boggstown, 200	F 5
46302	Boone Grove, 225	C 2
47601	Boonville⊙, 5,736	C 8
47106	Borden, 337	F 8
47324	Boston, 210	H 5
47921	Boswell, 998	C 3
46504	Bourbon, 1,606	E 2
47833	Bowling Green, 200	D 6
47107	Bradford, 400	E 8
47834	Brazil⊙, 8,163	C 5
46506	Bremen, 3,487	E 2
47836	Bridgeton, 350	C 5
† 45030	Bright, 450	H 6
46720	Brimfield, 258	G 2
46913	Bringhurst, 250	E 3
46507	Bristol, 1,100	F 1
† 47354	Bronson (Losantville), 212	G 4
47922	Brook, 919	C 3
46111	Brooklyn, 911	E 5
47923	Brookston, 1,232	D 3
47012	Brookville⊙, 2,864	G 6
46112	Brownsburg, 5,186	E 5
47220	Brownstown⊙, 2,376	F 7
47325	Brownsville, 285	H 5
47516	Bruceville, 627	C 7
47326	Bryant, 320	G 3
47924	Buck Creek, 260	D 4
47517	Buckskin, 275	C 8
47925	Buffalo, 350	D 3
46914	Bunker Hill, 956	E 3
46508	Burket, 210	F 2
46915	Burlington, 685	E 4
47926	Burnettsville, 510	D 3
47222	Burney, 344	F 6
† 46401	Burns Harbor, 1,284	C 1
46916	Burrows, 259	E 3
46721	Butler, 2,394	H 2
47223	Butlerville, 275	F 6
† 46371	Byron, 200	C 5
† 47362	Cadiz, 207	G 5
47327	Cambridge City, 2,481	G 5
46917	Camden, 577	D 3
47108	Campbellsburg, 678	E 7
47520	Cannelton⊙, 2,280	D 9
47837	Carbon, 344	C 5
47838	Carlisle, 714	C 7
46032	Carmel, 6,568	E 5
46114	Cartersburg, 400	E 5
46115	Carthage, 946	F 5
† 47460	Cataract, 200	D 6
47928	Cayuga, 1,090	C 5
47016	Cedar Grove, 248	H 6
46303	Cedar Lake, 7,589	C 2
47521	Celestine, 300	D 8
† 47842	Centenary, 225	B 5
46918	Center, 310	E 4
47840	Centerpoint, 275	C 6
46116	Centerton, 250	E 5
47330	Centerville, 2,380	H 5
47929	Chalmers, 544	D 3
47610	Chandler, 2,032	C 8
47111	Charlestown, 5,890	F 8
46117	Charlottesville, 500	F 5
† 47138	Chelsea, 200	F 7
46017	Chesterfield, 3,001	F 4
46304	Chesterton, 6,177	D 1
47611	Chrisney, 550	C 8
46723	Churubusco, 1,528	G 2
46034	Cicero, 1,378	E 4
47225	Clarksburg, 347	G 6
47930	Clarks Hill, 741	D 4
47130	Clarksville, 13,806	F 8
47841	Clay City, 900	C 6
46510	Claypool, 468	F 2
46118	Clayton, 736	D 5
47426	Clear Creek, 250	E 6
† 46737	Clear Lake, 271	H 1
47226	Clifford, 275	F 6
47842	Clinton, 5,340	C 5
46120	Cloverdale, 870	D 5
47427	Coal City, 300	D 6
47845	Coalmont, 400	C 6
46121	Coatesville, 453	D 5
47931	Colburn, 300	D 3
46035	Colfax, 633	D 4
47978	Collegeville, 1,700	C 3
46725	Columbia City⊙, 4,911	G 2
47201	Columbus⊙, 27,141	E 6
47331	Connersville⊙, 17,604	G 5
46919	Converse, 1,163	F 3
47228	Cortland, 200	F 7
46730	Corunna, 359	G 2
47112	Corydon⊙, 2,719	E 8
47932	Covington⊙, 2,641	C 4
† 47302	Cowan, 428	G 4
47522	Crane, 339	D 7
47933	Crawfordsville⊙, 13,842	D 4
46732	Cromwell, 475	F 2
47229	Crothersville, 1,663	F 7
46307	Crown Point⊙, 10,931	C 2
46511	Culver, 1,783	E 2
46229	Cumberland, 479	E 5
47612	Cynthiana, 793	B 8
47523	Dale, 1,113	D 8
47334	Daleville, 1,730	F 4
47847	Dana, 720	C 5
46122	Danville⊙, 3,771	D 5
47940	Darlington, 802	D 4
47941	Dayton, 840	D 4
46733	Decatur⊙, 8,445	H 3
47524	Decker, 268	B 7
† 46917	Deer Creek, 250	E 3
46923	Delphi⊙, 2,582	D 3
46310	Demotte, 1,697	C 2
46926	Denver, 566	E 3
47230	Deputy, 255	F 7
47302	Desoto, 385	G 4
47018	Dillsboro, 840	G 6
46513	Donaldson, 250	E 2
† 47118	Doolittle Mills, 200	D 8
47335	Dublin, 1,021	G 5
47525	Dubois, 500	D 8
47848	Dugger, 1,150	C 6
† 46304	Dune Acres, 301	C 1
47336	Dunkirk, 3,465	G 4
† 46514	Dunlap, 1,900	F 1
47337	Dunreith, 200	F 5
47231	Dupont, 357	G 7
46311	Dyer, 4,906	C 1
† 46074	Eagletown, 365	E 4
47942	Earl Park, 478	C 3
46312	East Chicago, 46,982	C 1
47019	East Enterprise, 250	H 7
46405	East Gary, 9,858	C 1
† 47370	East Germantown (Pershing), 447	G 5
47338	Eaton, 1,594	G 4
47116	Eckerty, 200	D 8
47339	Economy, 285	G 5
† 46011	Edgewood, 2,326	F 4
46124	Edinburg, 4,906	E 6
47528	Edwardsport, 482	C 7
† 47150	Edwardsville, 700	F 8
47613	Elberfeld, 834	C 8
47232	Elizabethtown, 519	F 6
46514	Elkhart, 43,152	F 1
47429	Ellettsville, 1,627	D 6
47529	Elnora, 873	C 7
† 47018	Elrod, 200	G 6
† 47901	Elston, 500	D 4
46036	Elwood, 11,196	F 4
46125	Eminence, 200	D 5
47118	English⊙, 664	E 8
46524	Etna Green, 516	E 2
† 47928	Eugene, 300	B 5
* 47701	Evansville⊙, 138,764	C 9
	Evansville, ‡232,775	C 9
46126	Fairland, 950	F 5
46928	Fairmount, 3,427	F 4
† 47842	Fairview Park, 1,067	C 5
47850	Farmersburg, 962	C 6
47340	Farmland, 1,262	G 4
47532	Ferdinand, 1,432	D 8
46128	Fillmore, 600	D 5
46129	Finly, 350	F 5
46038	Fishers, 628	E 5
47234	Flat Rock, 289	F 6
46929	Flora, 1,877	E 3
47119	Floyds Knobs, 350	F 8
47851	Fontanet, 200	C 5
46039	Forest, 400	E 4
47533	Fort Branch, 2,535	B 8
46040	Fortville, 2,460	F 5
* 46801	Fort Wayne⊙, 177,671	G 2
	Fort Wayne, ‡280,455	G 2
47341	Fountain City, 852	H 5
46130	Fountaintown, 225	F 5
47944	Fowler⊙, 2,643	C 3
46930	Fowlerton, 337	F 4
47946	Francesville, 1,015	D 3
47534	Francisco, 621	B 8
46041	Frankfort⊙, 14,956	E 4
46131	Franklin⊙, 11,477	E 6
46044	Frankton, 1,796	F 4
47120	Fredericksburg, 207	E 8
47431	Freedom, 262	D 6
47535	Freelandville, 710	C 7
47235	Freetown, 550	E 7
46737	Fremont, 1,043	H 1
47432	French Lick, 2,059	D 7
46931	Fulton, 372	E 3
† 47119	Galena, 250	F 8
46932	Galveston, 1,284	E 3
46738	Garrett, 4,715	G 2
* 46401	Gary, 175,415	C 1
	Gary-Hammond-East Chicago, ‡633,367	C 1
46933	Gas City, 5,742	F 4
47342	Gaston, 928	G 4
46740	Geneva, 1,100	H 3
47537	Gentryville, 281	C 8
47122	Georgetown, 1,273	F 8
47343	Glenwood, 452	G 5
† 47567	Glezen, 300	C 8
46045	Goldsmith, 235	E 4
47948	Goodland, 1,176	C 3
46526	Goshen⊙, 17,171	F 1
47433	Gosport, 692	D 6
46741	Grabill, 570	H 2
47615	Grandview, 696	C 9
46530	Granger, 200	E 1
46135	Greencastle⊙, 8,852	D 5
† 47025	Greendale, 3,783	H 6
46140	Greenfield⊙, 9,986	F 5
47344	Greensboro, 225	G 5
47240	Greensburg⊙, 8,620	G 6
47345	Greens Fork, 444	H 5
46936	Greentown, 1,870	E 4
47124	Greenville, 611	F 8
46142	Greenwood, 11,408	E 5
46319	Griffith, 18,168	C 1
46144	Gwynneville, 240	F 5
47346	Hagerstown, 2,059	G 5
46742	Hamilton, 537	H 1
46532	Hamlet, 761	D 2
* 46320	Hammond, 107,790	B 1
46340	Hanna, 500	D 2
47243	Hanover, 3,018	F 7
47125	Hardinsburg, 263	E 8

AREA 36,291 sq. mi.
POPULATION 5,193,669
CAPITAL Indianapolis
LARGEST CITY Indianapolis
HIGHEST POINT 1,257 ft. (Wayne County)
SETTLED IN 1730
ADMITTED TO UNION December 11, 1816
POPULAR NAME Hoosier State
STATE FLOWER Peony
STATE BIRD Cardinal

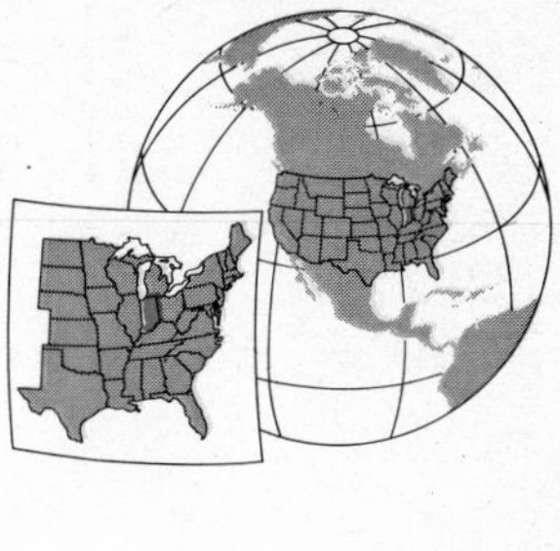

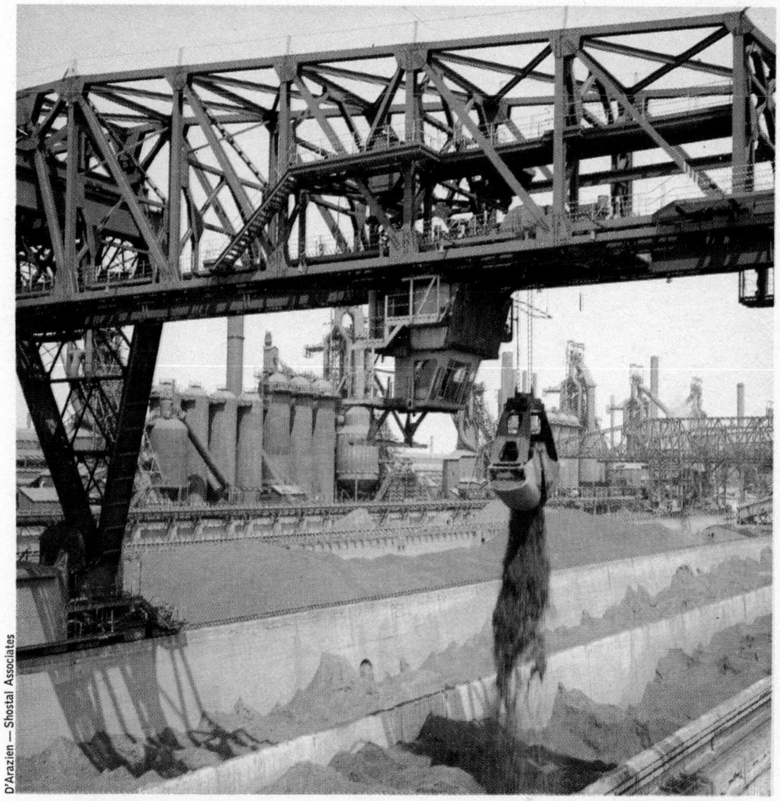

D'Arazien — Shostal Associates

Ore being unloaded in the storage yard at steel plant docks in Gary, Indiana. Aided by the state's outstanding natural supply of limestone, mills in the Lake Michigan area produce more than 15 million tons of steel yearly.

46743	Harlan, 840	H 2
47853	Harmony, 750	C 5
47434	Harrodsburg, 400	D 6
47348	Hartford City⊙, 8,207	G 4
47244	Hartsville, 434	F 6
47617	Hatfield, 800	C 9
47539	Haubstadt, 1,171	B 8
† 47546	Haysville, 585	D 8
47540	Hazleton, 416	B 8
46341	Hebron, 1,624	C 2
47436	Heltonville, 400	E 7
46937	Hemlock, 200	F 4
47126	Henryville, 1,500	F 7
46322	Highland, 24,947	B 1
46046	Hillisburg, 225	E 4
47949	Hillsboro, 505	C 4
47854	Hillsdale, 500	C 5
46745	Hoagland, 530	H 3
46342	Hobart, 21,485	C 1
46047	Hobbs, 400	F 4
47541	Holland, 662	C 8
47023	Holton, 610	G 6
46146	Homer, 245	F 5
47246	Hope, 1,603	F 6
† 46069	Hortonville, 240	E 4
46746	Howe, 800	G 1
46747	Hudson, 464	G 1
46552	Hudson Lake, 1,134	D 1
46748	Huntertown, 775	G 2
47542	Huntingburg, 4,794	D 8
46750	Huntington⊙, 16,217	G 3
† 46064	Huntsville, 450	G 4
47437	Huron, 580	D 7
47855	Hymera, 907	C 6
47950	Idaville, 600	D 3
* 46201	Indianapolis (cap.)⊙ 744,624	E 5
	Indianapolis, ‡1,109,882	E 5
46048	Ingalls, 888	F 5
47545	Ireland, 527	C 8
46147	Jamestown, 938	D 5
47438	Jasonville, 2,335	C 6
47546	Jasper⊙, 8,641	D 8
47130	Jeffersonville⊙, 20,008	F 8
† 47565	Johnson, 250	B 8
† 46074	Jolietville, 265	E 4
46938	Jonesboro, 2,466	F 4
47247	Jonesville, 202	F 6
46049	Kempton, 469	E 4
46755	Kendallville, 6,838	G 2
47351	Kennard, 518	G 5
47951	Kentland⊙, 1,864	C 3
46939	Kewanna, 614	E 2
46759	Keystone, 200	G 3
46760	Kimmell, 350	F 2
47952	Kingman, 530	C 5
46345	Kingsbury, 314	D 1
46346	Kingsford Heights, 1,200	D 2
46050	Kirklin, 736	E 4
46148	Knightstown, 2,456	F 5
47857	Knightsville, 788	C 5
46534	Knox⊙, 3,519	D 2
46901	Kokomo⊙, 44,042	E 4
† 46574	Koontz Lake, 900	D 2
46347	Kouts, 1,388	C 2
46348	La Crosse, 696	D 2
47954	Ladoga, 1,099	D 5
* 47901	Lafayette⊙, 44,955	D 4
	Lafayette-West Lafayette, ‡109,378	D 4
46940	La Fontaine, 793	F 3
46761	Lagrange⊙, 2,053	F 1
46941	Lagro, 552	F 3
† 46703	Lake James, 400	H 1
46943	Laketon, 500	F 3
46349	Lake Village, 600	C 2
46536	Lakeville, 712	E 1
† 46567	Lake Wawasee, 600	F 2
47136	Lanesville, 586	E 8
46763	Laotto, 312	G 2
46537	Lapaz, 604	E 2
46051	Lapel, 1,725	F 4
46350	LaPorte⊙, 22,140	D 1
46764	Larwill, 324	F 2
47024	Laurel, 753	G 6
46226	Lawrence, 16,646	E 5
47025	Lawrenceburg⊙, 4,636	H 6
47137	Leavenworth, 330	E 8
46052	Lebanon⊙, 9,766	D 4
46538	Leesburg, 561	F 2
46945	Leiters Ford, 250	E 2
46765	Leo, 500	G 2
46355	Leroy, 350	C 2
† 47240	Letts, 247	F 6
47352	Lewisville, 530	G 5
47138	Lexington, 400	F 7
47353	Liberty⊙, 1,831	H 5
46766	Liberty Center, 300	G 3
46946	Liberty Mills, 200	F 2
46767	Ligonier, 3,034	F 2
47955	Linden, 713	D 4
46769	Linn Grove, 300	H 3
47441	Linton, 5,450	C 6
† 46755	Lisbon, 200	G 2
46149	Lizton, 397	D 5
46947	Logansport⊙, 19,255	E 3
† 46360	Long Beach, 2,740	D 1
47553	Loogootee, 2,953	D 7
47354	Losantville, 212	G 4
46356	Lowell, 3,839	C 2
† 46601	Lydick, 1,341	E 1
† 47874	Lyford, 400	C 5
47355	Lynn, 1,360	H 4
47619	Lynnville, 556	C 8
47443	Lyons, 702	C 7
46951	Macy, 273	E 3
47250	Madison⊙, 13,081	G 7
† 47001	Manchester, 250	H 6
46150	Manilla, 300	F 5
† 47872	Mansfield, 200	C 5
47140	Marengo, 767	E 8
47556	Mariah Hill, 275	D 8
† 46176	Marietta, 280	F 6
46952	Marion⊙, 39,607	F 3
46770	Markle, 963	G 3
46056	Markleville, 457	F 5
47859	Marshall, 365	C 5
46151	Martinsville⊙, 9,723	D 6
46957	Matthews, 728	F 4
46154	Maxwell, 245	F 5
46055	McCordsville, 500	F 5
47860	Mecca, 800	C 5
47957	Medaryville, 732	D 2
47260	Medora, 788	E 7
47958	Mellott, 325	C 4
47143	Memphis, 324	F 8
46539	Mentone, 830	E 2
47861	Merom, 305	B 6
46410	Merrillville, 15,918	C 2
47030	Metamora, 400	G 6
† 46703	Metz, 200	H 1
46958	Mexico, 850	E 3
46959	Miami, 420	E 3
46360	Michigan City, 39,369	C 1

(continued on following page)

(continued)

46057 Michigantown, 457 .... E 4
46540 Middlebury, 1,055 .... F 1
47356 Middletown, 2,046 .... F 4
47445 Midland, 220 .... C 6
47031 Milan, 1,260 .... G 6
46542 Milford, 1,264 .... F 2
46543 Millersburg, 618 .... F 1
47261 Millhousen, 252 .... G 6
47145 Milltown, 829 .... E 8
† 47362 Millville, 275 .... G 5
46156 Milroy, 750 .... G 6
47357 Milton, 694 .... G 5
46544 Mishawaka, 35,517 .... E 1
47446 Mitchell, 4,092 .... E 7
47358 Modoc, 275 .... G 4
46771 Mongo, 225 .... G 1
47959 Monon, 1,548 .... D 3
46772 Monroe, 622 .... H 3
47557 Monroe City, 603 .... C 7
46773 Monroeville, 1,353 .... H 3
46157 Monrovia, 750 .... E 5
46960 Monterey, 268 .... D 2
47862 Montezuma, 1,192 .... C 5
47558 Montgomery, 411 .... C 7
47960 Monticello⊙, 4,869 .... D 3
47962 Montmorenci, 350 .... D 4
47359 Montpelier, 2,093 .... G 3
47360 Mooreland, 495 .... G 5
47032 Moores Hill, 616 .... G 6
46158 Mooresville, 5,800 .... E 5
46160 Morgantown, 1,134 .... E 6
47963 Morocco, 1,285 .... C 3
47033 Morris, 435 .... G 6
46161 Morristown, 838 .... F 5
47361 Mount Summit, 395 .... G 4
47620 Mount Vernon⊙, 6,770 .... B 9
46058 Mulberry, 1,075 .... D 4
* 47302 Muncie⊙, 69,080 .... G 4
Muncie, ‡129,219 .... G 4
46321 Munster, 16,514 .... B 1
47147 Nabb, 204 .... F 7
47034 Napoleon, 282 .... G 6
46550 Nappanee, 4,159 .... F 2
47448 Nashville⊙, 527 .... E 6
† 47421 Needmore, 200 .... E 7
47150 New Albany⊙, 38,402 .... F 8
47449 Newberry, 295 .... C 7
47630 Newburgh, 2,302 .... C 9
46552 New Carlisle, 1,434 .... E 1
47362 New Castle⊙, 21,215 .... G 5
† 46342 New Chicago, 2,231 .... C 1
47863 New Goshen, 500 .... B 5
47631 New Harmony, 971 .... B 8
46774 New Haven, 5,728 .... H 2
47366 New Lisbon, 350 .... G 5
† 46979 New London, 200 .... E 4
47965 New Market, 640 .... D 5
46163 New Palestine, 863 .... F 5
46553 New Paris, 1,080 .... F 2
† 47165 New Pekin, 912 .... F 7
47263 New Point, 381 .... G 6
47966 Newport⊙, 708 .... C 5
† 47106 New Providence (Borden), 337 .... F 8
47967 New Richmond, 381 .... D 4
47968 New Ross, 318 .... D 5
† 46173 New Salem, 270 .... G 5
47161 New Salisbury, 350 .... E 8
47969 Newtown, 286 .... C 4
47035 New Trenton, 200 .... H 6
47162 New Washington, 1,100 .... F 7
46184 New Whiteland, 4,200 .... E 5
46060 Noblesville⊙, 7,548 .... F 4
46366 North Judson, 1,738 .... D 2
46554 North Liberty, 1,259 .... E 1
46962 North Manchester, 5,791 .... F 3
46165 North Salem, 601 .... D 5
47805 North Terre Haute, 1,400 .... C 5
47265 North Vernon, 4,582 .... F 6
46555 North Webster, 456 .... F 2
† 47960 Norway, 250 .... D 3
46556 Notre Dame, 8,400 .... E 1
† 47331 Nulltown, 250 .... G 5
46965 Oakford, 300 .... E 4
47560 Oakland City, 3,289 .... C 8
47561 Oaktown, 726 .... C 7
47367 Oakville, 250 .... G 4
47562 Odon, 1,433 .... C 7
† 46401 Ogden Dunes, 1,361 .... C 1
47036 Oldenburg, 758 .... G 6
47451 Oolitic, 1,155 .... E 7
† 47343 Orange, 200 .... G 5
46063 Orestes, 519 .... F 4
46776 Orland, 457 .... G 1
47452 Orleans, 1,834 .... D 7
46561 Osceola, 1,572 .... E 1
47037 Osgood, 1,346 .... G 6
46777 Ossian, 1,538 .... G 3
46367 Otis, 300 .... D 1
47163 Otisco, 375 .... F 7
47970 Otterbein, 899 .... C 4
47564 Otwell, 850 .... C 8
47453 Owensburg, 700 .... D 7
47565 Owensville, 1,056 .... B 8
47971 Oxford, 1,098 .... C 3
† 46508 Palestine, 200 .... F 2
47164 Palmyra, 483 .... E 8
47454 Paoli⊙, 3,281 .... E 7
46166 Paragon, 538 .... D 6
47368 Parker, 1,179 .... G 4
47566 Patoka, 529 .... B 8
47455 Patricksburg, 265 .... D 6
47038 Patriot, 216 .... H 7
47865 Paxton, 250 .... C 6
47165 Pekin, 950 .... E 7
46064 Pendleton, 2,243 .... F 5
47369 Pennville, 798 .... G 4
† 46011 Perkinsville, 300 .... F 4
47974 Perrysville, 510 .... C 4
47370 Pershing, 447 .... G 5
† 46975 Pershing, 425 .... E 2
46970 Peru⊙, 14,139 .... E 3
47567 Petersburg⊙, 2,697 .... C 7
46778 Petroleum, 200 .... G 3
46562 Pierceton, 1,175 .... F 2
47866 Pimento, 200 .... C 6
† 46350 Pine Lake, 1,954 .... D 1
47975 Pine Village, 291 .... C 4
46167 Pittsboro, 867 .... D 5
46168 Plainfield, 8,211 .... E 5
47568 Plainville, 538 .... C 7
46779 Pleasant Lake, 650 .... H 1
46563 Plymouth⊙, 7,661 .... E 2
47868 Poland, 300 .... C 6
46781 Poneto, 286 .... G 3
46368 Portage, 19,127 .... C 1
46304 Porter, 3,058 .... C 1
47371 Portland⊙, 7,115 .... H 4
47633 Poseyville, 1,035 .... B 8
† 46360 Pottawattamie Park, 374 .... C 1
47869 Prairie Creek, 225 .... C 6
47870 Prairieton, 400 .... B 6
† 46164 Princes Lakes, 597 .... E 6
47570 Princeton⊙, 7,431 .... B 8
46170 Putnamville, 200 .... D 5
47456 Quincy, 250 .... D 6
47573 Ragsdale, 200 .... C 7
46737 Ray, 200 .... H 1
† 47274 Reddington, 245 .... F 6
47373 Redkey, 1,667 .... G 4
46171 Reelsville, 210 .... D 5
47977 Remington, 1,127 .... C 3
47978 Rensselaer⊙, 4,688 .... C 3
47980 Reynolds, 641 .... D 3
47634 Richland, 650 .... C 9
47374 Richmond⊙, 43,999 .... H 5
47380 Ridgeville, 924 .... G 4
47871 Riley, 257 .... C 6
47040 Rising Sun⊙, 2,305 .... H 7
46172 Roachdale, 1,004 .... D 5
46974 Roann, 509 .... F 3
46783 Roanoke, 858 .... G 3
46975 Rochester⊙, 4,631 .... E 2
46977 Rockfield, 300 .... D 3
47635 Rockport⊙, 2,565 .... C 9
47872 Rockville⊙, 2,820 .... C 5
46371 Rolling Prairie, 2,500 .... D 1
47574 Rome, 1,354 .... D 9
46784 Rome City, 1,385 .... G 1
47981 Romney, 420 .... D 4
47874 Rosedale, 817 .... C 5
† 46601 Roseland, 895 .... E 1
46372 Roselawn, 200 .... C 2
46065 Rossville, 830 .... D 4
46978 Royal Center, 987 .... E 3
† 47302 Royerton, 411 .... G 4
46173 Rushville⊙, 6,686 .... G 5
46175 Russellville, 390 .... D 5
46975 Russiaville, 844 .... E 4
47575 Saint Anthony, 460 .... D 8
47875 Saint Bernice, 900 .... C 5
46785 Saint Joe, 564 .... H 2
46373 Saint John, 1,757 .... C 2
† 45030 Saint Leon, 435 .... H 6
47876 Saint Mary-of-the-Woods, 1,200 .... B 6
† 46556 Saint Marys, 1,600 .... E 1
47577 Saint Meinrad, 1,100 .... D 8
47272 Saint Paul, 785 .... F 6
† 47012 Saint Peter, 200 .... H 6
† 47620 Saint Philip, 400 .... B 9
† 47638 Saint Wendel, 250 .... B 8
47167 Salem⊙, 5,041 .... E 7
47578 Sandborn, 528 .... C 7
† 47401 Sanders, 200 .... E 6
46374 San Pierre, 300 .... D 2
47579 Santa Claus, 125 .... D 8
47382 Saratoga, 406 .... H 4
† 47283 Sardinia, 225 .... F 6
46375 Schererville, 3,663 .... C 2
46376 Schneider, 426 .... C 2
47273 Scipio, 250 .... F 6
47170 Scottsburg⊙, 4,791 .... F 7
47878 Seelyville, 1,195 .... C 6
47172 Sellersburg, 3,177 .... F 8
47383 Selma, 890 .... G 4
47274 Seymour, 13,352 .... F 7
46068 Sharpsville, 672 .... E 4
47879 Shelburn, 1,281 .... C 6
46377 Shelby, 400 .... C 2
46176 Shelbyville⊙, 15,094 .... F 6
47880 Shepardsville, 325 .... B 5
46069 Sheridan, 2,137 .... E 4
† 47338 Shideler, 275 .... G 4
46565 Shipshewana, 448 .... F 1
47384 Shirley, 958 .... F 5

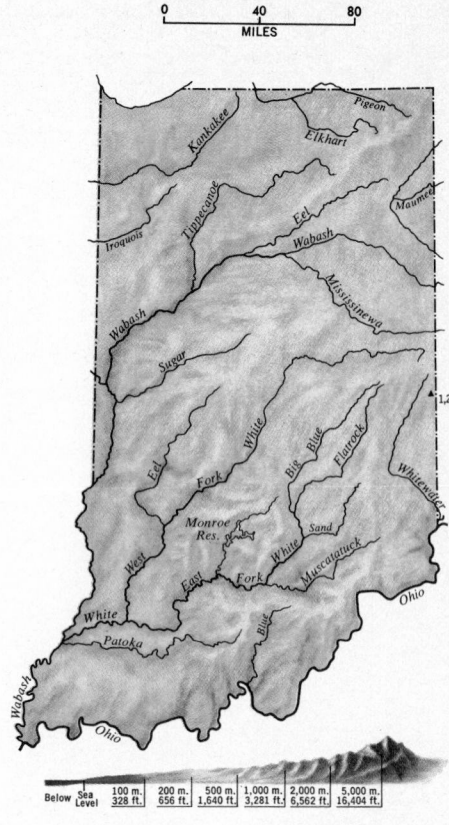

Topography

0 40 80
MILES
Pigeon
Kankakee
Elkhart
Maumee
Iroquois
Tippecanoe
Eel
Wabash
Mississinewa
Wabash
Sugar
White
Eel
Big Blue
Flatrock
Whitewater
Fork
Monroe Res.
Sand
West
East
White
Fork
Muscatatuck
Ohio
White
Patoka
Blue
Wabash
Ohio
Below Sea Level
100 m. 328 ft.
200 m. 656 ft.
500 m. 1,640 ft.
1,000 m. 3,281 ft.
2,000 m. 6,562 ft.
5,000 m. 16,404 ft.

Agriculture, Industry and Resources

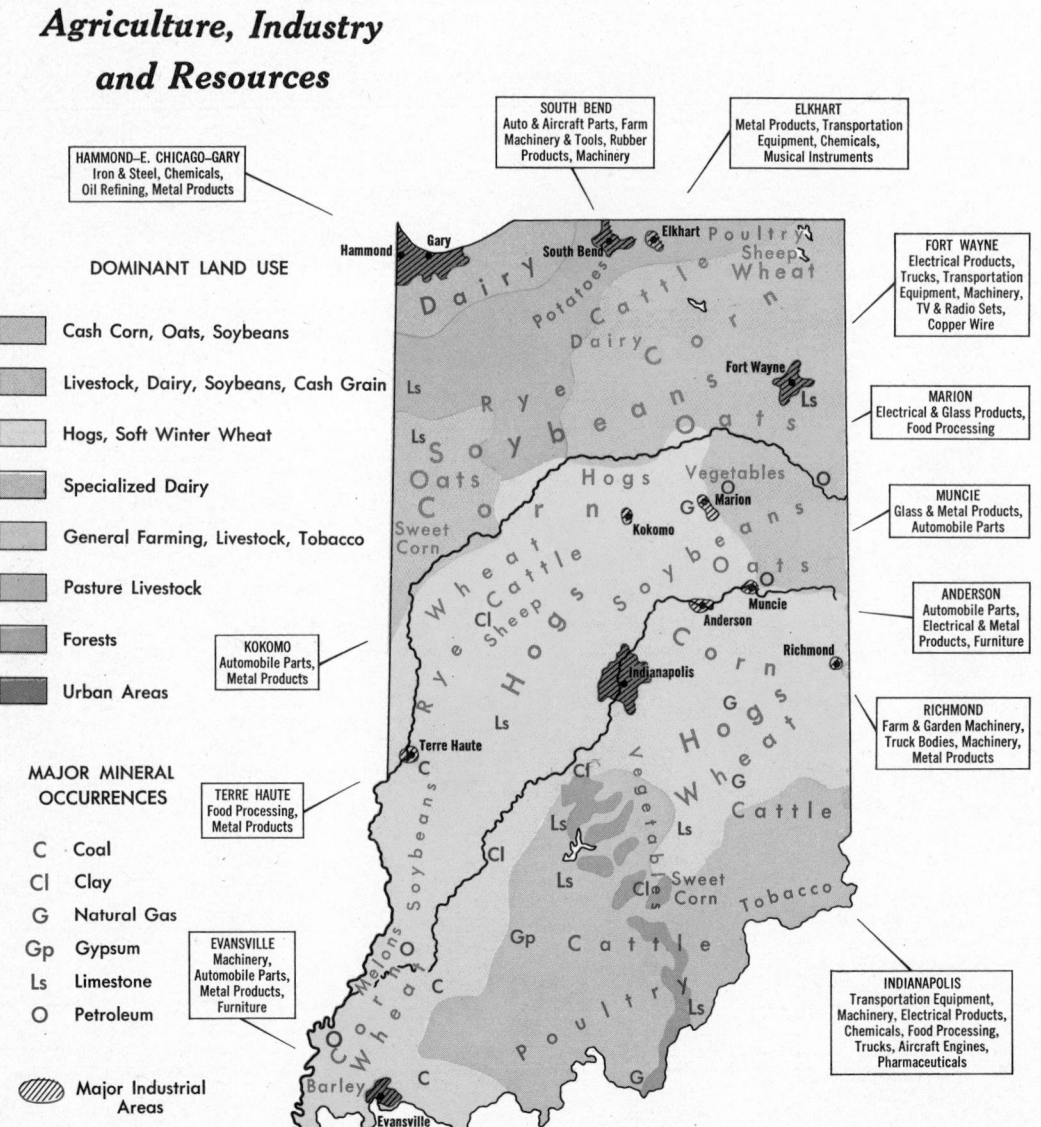

HAMMOND–E. CHICAGO–GARY
Iron & Steel, Chemicals, Oil Refining, Metal Products
SOUTH BEND
Auto & Aircraft Parts, Farm Machinery & Tools, Rubber Products, Machinery
ELKHART
Metal Products, Transportation Equipment, Chemicals, Musical Instruments
FORT WAYNE
Electrical Products, Trucks, Transportation Equipment, Machinery, TV & Radio Sets, Copper Wire
MARION
Electrical & Glass Products, Food Processing
MUNCIE
Glass & Metal Products, Automobile Parts
ANDERSON
Automobile Parts, Electrical & Metal Products, Furniture
KOKOMO
Automobile Parts, Metal Products
RICHMOND
Farm & Garden Machinery, Truck Bodies, Machinery, Metal Products
TERRE HAUTE
Food Processing, Metal Products
EVANSVILLE
Machinery, Automobile Parts, Metal Products, Furniture
INDIANAPOLIS
Transportation Equipment, Machinery, Electrical Products, Chemicals, Food Processing, Trucks, Aircraft Engines, Pharmaceuticals
DOMINANT LAND USE
Cash Corn, Oats, Soybeans
Livestock, Dairy, Soybeans, Cash Grain
Hogs, Soft Winter Wheat
Specialized Dairy
General Farming, Livestock, Tobacco
Pasture Livestock
Forests
Urban Areas
MAJOR MINERAL OCCURRENCES
C Coal
Cl Clay
G Natural Gas
Gp Gypsum
Ls Limestone
O Petroleum
Major Industrial Areas
Hammond
Gary
South Bend
Elkhart
Fort Wayne
Marion
Kokomo
Muncie
Anderson
Indianapolis
Richmond
Terre Haute
Evansville
Poultry
Sheep
Wheat
Dairy
Potatoes
Cattle
Corn
Rye
Soybeans
Oats
Hogs
Vegetables
Sweet Corn
Tobacco
Melons
Barley

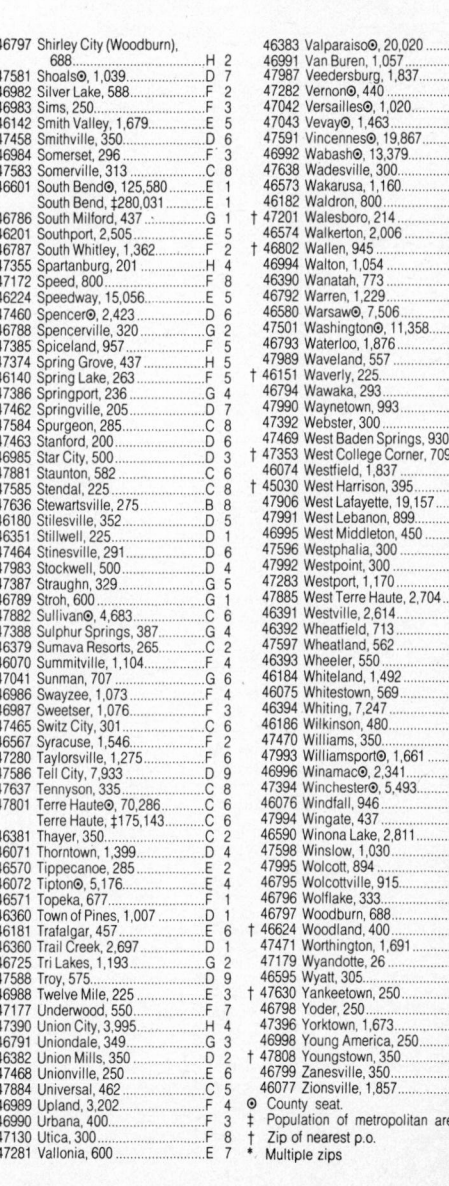

† 46797 Shirley City (Woodburn), 688 .... H 2
47581 Shoals⊙, 1,039 .... D 7
46982 Silver Lake, 588 .... F 2
46983 Sims, 250 .... F 3
† 46142 Smith Valley, 1,679 .... E 5
47458 Smithville, 350 .... D 6
46984 Somerset, 296 .... F 3
47583 Somerville, 313 .... C 8
* 46601 South Bend⊙, 125,580 .... E 1
South Bend, ‡280,031 .... E 1
46786 South Milford, 437 .... G 1
† 46201 Southport, 2,505 .... E 5
46787 South Whitley, 1,362 .... F 2
† 47355 Spartanburg, 201 .... H 4
47172 Speed, 800 .... F 8
46224 Speedway, 15,056 .... E 5
47460 Spencer⊙, 2,423 .... D 6
46788 Spencerville, 320 .... G 2
47385 Spiceland, 957 .... F 5
† 47374 Spring Grove, 437 .... H 5
† 46140 Spring Lake, 263 .... F 5
47386 Springport, 236 .... G 4
47462 Springville, 205 .... D 7
47584 Spurgeon, 285 .... C 8
47463 Stanford, 200 .... D 6
46985 Star City, 500 .... D 3
47881 Staunton, 582 .... C 6
47585 Stendal, 225 .... C 8
47636 Stewartsville, 275 .... B 8
46180 Stilesville, 352 .... D 5
46351 Stillwell, 225 .... D 1
47464 Stinesville, 291 .... D 6
47983 Stockwell, 500 .... D 4
47387 Straughn, 329 .... G 5
46789 Stroh, 600 .... G 1
47882 Sullivan⊙, 4,683 .... C 6
47388 Sulphur Springs, 387 .... G 4
46379 Sumava Resorts, 265 .... C 2
46070 Summitville, 1,104 .... F 4
47041 Sunman, 707 .... G 6
46986 Swayzee, 1,073 .... F 4
46987 Sweetser, 1,076 .... F 3
47465 Switz City, 301 .... C 6
46567 Syracuse, 1,546 .... F 2
47280 Taylorsville, 1,275 .... F 6
47586 Tell City, 7,933 .... D 9
47637 Tennyson, 335 .... C 8
* 47801 Terre Haute⊙, 70,286 .... C 6
Terre Haute, ‡175,143 .... C 6
46381 Thayer, 350 .... C 2
46071 Thorntown, 1,399 .... D 4
46570 Tippecanoe, 285 .... E 2
46072 Tipton⊙, 5,176 .... E 4
46571 Topeka, 677 .... F 1
† 46360 Town of Pines, 1,007 .... D 1
46181 Trafalgar, 457 .... E 6
† 46360 Trail Creek, 2,697 .... D 1
† 46725 Tri Lakes, 1,193 .... G 2
47588 Troy, 575 .... D 9
46988 Twelve Mile, 225 .... E 3
47177 Underwood, 550 .... F 7
47390 Union City, 3,995 .... H 4
46791 Uniondale, 349 .... G 3
46382 Union Mills, 350 .... D 2
47468 Unionville, 250 .... E 6
47884 Universal, 462 .... C 5
46989 Upland, 3,202 .... F 4
46990 Urbana, 400 .... F 3
† 47130 Utica, 300 .... F 8
47281 Vallonia, 600 .... E 7
46383 Valparaiso⊙, 20,020 ....
46991 Van Buren, 1,057 ....
47987 Veedersburg, 1,837 ....
47282 Vernon⊙, 440 ....
47042 Versailles⊙, 1,020 ....
47043 Vevay⊙, 1,463 ....
47591 Vincennes⊙, 19,867 ....
46992 Wabash⊙, 13,379 ....
47638 Wadesville, 300 ....
46573 Wakarusa, 1,160 ....
46182 Waldron, 800 ....
† 47201 Walesboro, 214 ....
46574 Walkerton, 2,006 ....
† 46802 Wallen, 945 ....
46994 Walton, 1,054 ....
46390 Wanatah, 773 ....
46792 Warren, 1,229 ....
46580 Warsaw⊙, 7,506 ....
47501 Washington⊙, 11,358 ....
46793 Waterloo, 1,876 ....
47989 Waveland, 557 ....
† 46151 Waverly, 225 ....
46794 Wawaka, 293 ....
47990 Waynetown, 993 ....
47392 Webster, 300 ....
47469 West Baden Springs, 930 ...
† 47353 West College Corner, 709 ..
46074 Westfield, 1,837 ....
† 45030 West Harrison, 395 ....
47906 West Lafayette, 19,157 ....
47991 West Lebanon, 899 ....
46995 West Middleton, 450 ....
47596 Westphalia, 300 ....
47992 Westpoint, 300 ....
47283 Westport, 1,170 ....
47885 West Terre Haute, 2,704 ....
46391 Westville, 2,614 ....
46392 Wheatfield, 713 ....
47597 Wheatland, 562 ....
46393 Wheeler, 550 ....
46184 Whiteland, 1,492 ....
46075 Whitestown, 569 ....
46394 Whiting, 7,247 ....
46186 Wilkinson, 480 ....
47470 Williams, 350 ....
47993 Williamsport⊙, 1,661 ....
46996 Winamac⊙, 2,341 ....
47394 Winchester⊙, 5,493 ....
46076 Windfall, 946 ....
47994 Wingate, 437 ....
46590 Winona Lake, 2,811 ....
47598 Winslow, 1,030 ....
47995 Wolcott, 894 ....
46795 Wolcottville, 915 ....
46796 Wolflake, 333 ....
46797 Woodburn, 688 ....
† 46624 Woodland, 400 ....
47471 Worthington, 1,691 ....
47179 Wyandotte, 26 ....
46595 Wyatt, 305 ....
† 47630 Yankeetown, 250 ....
46798 Yoder, 250 ....
47396 Yorktown, 1,673 ....
46998 Young America, 250 ....
† 47808 Youngstown, 350 ....
46799 Zanesville, 350 ....
46077 Zionsville, 1,857 ....

⊙ County seat.
‡ Population of metropolitan area
† Zip of nearest p.o.
* Multiple zips

INDIANA

SCALE

0 5 10   20   30   40 MI.

0 5 10   20   30   40 KM.

State Capitals .... ⊛

County Seats .... ○

© C.S. Hammond & Co., N.Y.

COUNTIES

Adair, 9,487	E 6	
Adams, 6,322	D 6	
Allamakee, 14,968	L 2	
Appanoose, 15,007	H 7	
Audubon, 9,595	D 5	
Benton, 22,885	J 4	
Black Hawk, 132,916	J 4	
Boone, 26,470	F 4	
Bremer, 22,737	J 3	
Buchanan, 21,746	K 4	
Buena Vista, 20,693	C 3	
Butler, 16,953	H 3	
Calhoun, 14,287	D 4	
Carroll, 22,912	D 4	
Cass, 17,007	D 6	
Cedar, 17,655	L 5	
Cerro Gordo, 49,335	G 2	
Cherokee, 17,269	B 3	
Chickasaw, 14,969	J 2	
Clarke, 7,581	F 6	
Clay, 18,464	C 2	
Clayton, 20,606	L 3	
Clinton, 56,749	M 5	
Crawford, 18,780	C 4	
Dallas, 26,085	E 5	

Davis, 8,207	J 7	
Decatur, 9,737	F 7	
Delaware, 18,770	L 4	
Des Moines, 46,982	L 7	
Dickinson, 12,565	C 2	
Dubuque, 90,609	M 4	
Emmet, 14,009	D 2	
Fayette, 26,898	K 3	
Floyd, 19,860	H 2	
Franklin, 13,255	G 3	
Fremont, 9,282	B 7	
Greene, 12,716	E 5	
Grundy, 14,119	H 4	
Guthrie, 12,243	D 5	
Hamilton, 18,383	F 4	
Hancock, 13,227	F 2	
Hardin, 22,248	G 4	
Harrison, 16,240	B 5	
Henry, 18,114	K 6	
Howard, 11,442	J 2	
Humboldt, 12,519	E 3	
Ida, 9,190	C 4	
Iowa, 15,419	J 5	
Jackson, 20,839	M 4	
Jasper, 35,425	G 5	
Jefferson, 15,774	K 6	
Johnson, 72,127	K 5	

Jones, 19,868	L 4	
Keokuk, 13,943	J 6	
Kossuth, 22,937	E 2	
Lee, 42,996	L 7	
Linn, 163,213	K 4	
Louisa, 10,682	L 6	
Lucas, 10,163	G 6	
Lyon, 13,340	A 2	
Madison, 11,558	E 6	
Mahaska, 22,177	H 6	
Marion, 26,352	G 6	
Marshall, 41,076	G 4	
Mills, 11,606	B 6	
Mitchell, 13,108	H 2	
Monona, 12,069	B 4	
Monroe, 9,357	H 7	
Montgomery, 12,781	C 6	
Muscatine, 37,181	L 5	
O'Brien, 17,522	B 2	
Osceola, 8,555	B 2	
Page, 18,507	C 7	
Palo Alto, 13,289	D 2	
Plymouth, 24,312	A 3	
Pocahontas, 12,729	D 3	
Polk, 286,101	F 5	
Pottawattamie, 86,991	B 6	
Poweshiek, 18,803	H 5	

Ringgold, 6,373	E 7	
Sac, 15,573	C 4	
Scott, 142,687	M 5	
Shelby, 15,528	C 5	
Sioux, 27,996	A 2	
Story, 62,783	G 4	
Tama, 20,147	H 4	
Taylor, 8,790	D 7	
Union, 13,557	E 6	
Van Buren, 8,643	K 7	
Wapello, 42,149	J 6	
Warren, 27,432	F 6	
Washington, 18,967	K 6	
Wayne, 8,405	G 7	
Webster, 48,391	E 4	
Winnebago, 12,990	F 2	
Winneshiek, 21,758	K 2	
Woodbury, 103,052	A 4	
Worth, 8,968	G 2	
Wright, 17,294	F 3	

CITIES and TOWNS

Zip	Name/Pop.	Key
50601	Ackley, 1,794	G 3
50002	Adair, 750	D 6
50003	Adel ⊙, 2,419	E 5

Zip	Name/Pop.	Key
50830	Afton, 823	E 6
52530	Agency, 610	J 6
52201	Ainsworth, 455	K 6
51001	Akron, 1,324	A 3
50510	Albert City, 683	C 3
52531	Albia ⊙, 4,151	H 6
50005	Albion, 772	H 4
52202	Alburnett, 418	K 4
50006	Alden, 876	G 3
50420	Alexander, 249	G 3
50511	Algona ⊙, 6,032	E 2
50008	Allerton, 643	G 7
50602	Allison ⊙, 1,071	H 3
51002	Alta, 1,717	C 3
50603	Alta Vista, 283	J 2
51003	Alton, 1,018	A 2
50009	Altoona, 2,854	G 5
52203	Amana, 610	K 4
50010	Ames, 39,505	F 4
52205	Anamosa ⊙, 4,389	L 4
52030	Andrew, 335	M 4
50020	Anita, 1,101	D 6
50021	Ankeny, 9,151	F 5
51004	Anthon, 711	B 4
50604	Aplington, 936	H 3
51430	Arcadia, 414	C 4
50606	Arlington, 481	K 3

Zip	Name/Pop.	Key
50514	Armstrong, 1,061	D 2
51331	Arnolds Park, 970	C 2
51431	Arthur, 273	C 4
† 52001	Asbury, 410	M 4
51232	Ashton, 483	B 2
52720	Atalissa, 244	L 5
52206	Atkins, 581	K 4
50022	Atlantic ⊙, 7,306	D 6
51433	Auburn, 329	C 4
50025	Audubon ⊙, 2,907	D 5
51005	Aurelia, 1,065	C 3
50607	Aurora, 229	K 3
51521	Avoca, 1,535	C 6
50515	Ayrshire, 243	D 3
50516	Badger, 465	E 3
50026	Bagley, 365	E 5
50517	Bancroft, 1,103	E 2
50027	Barnes City, 238	H 5
52533	Batavia, 525	J 6
51006	Battle Creek, 837	B 4
50028	Baxter, 788	G 5
50029	Bayard, 628	D 5
52534	Beacon, 338	H 6
50609	Beaman, 222	H 4
50833	Bedford ⊙, 1,733	D 7
52208	Belle Plaine, 2,810	J 4
52031	Bellevue, 2,336	M 4

421 Belmond, 2,358...F 3	50044 Bussey, 498...H 6	51012 Cherokee⊙, 7,272...B 3
721 Bennett, 385...L 5	52729 Calamus, 396...M 5	50050 Churdan, 598...D 4
722 Bettendorf, 22,126...N 5	50523 Callender, 421...E 4	52549 Cincinnati, 570...G 7
535 Birmingham, 452...K 7	52132 Calmar, 1,941...K 2	50524 Clare, 249...E 3
034 Blairsburg, 287...F 4	51009 Calumet, 219...B 3	52216 Clarence, 981...M 5
209 Blairstown, 612...J 5	52730 Camanche, 3,470...N 5	51632 Clarinda⊙, 5,420...C 7
536 Blakesburg, 403...H 7	50046 Cambridge, 661...G 5	50525 Clarion⊙, 2,972...F 3
523 Blencoe, 255...A 5	52542 Cantril, 258...J 7	50619 Clarksville, 1,360...H 3
836 Blockton, 273...D 7	50047 Carlisle, 2,246...G 5	50840 Clearfield, 430...D 7
631 Bloomfield, 2,718...J 7	51401 Carroll⊙, 8,716...D 4	50428 Clear Lake, 6,430...G 2
726 Blue Grass, 1,032...M 5	51525 Carson, 756...C 6	51014 Cleghorn, 274...B 3
519 Bode, 372...E 3	† 68101 Carter Lake, 3,268...B 6	52135 Clermont, 582...K 3
620 Bonaparte, 517...K 7	52033 Cascade, 1,744...L 4	52732 Clinton⊙, 34,719...N 5
035 Bondurant, 462...G 5	50048 Casey, 561...D 5	50053 Clive, 3,005...F 5
036 Boone⊙, 12,468...F 4	52133 Castalia, 210...K 2	52217 Clutier, 275...J 4
040 Boxholm, 242...E 4	51010 Castana, 211...B 4	† 50501 Coalville, 275...E 4
234 Boyden, 670...B 2	50613 Cedar Falls, 29,597...H 3	52218 Coggon, 656...L 4
210 Brandon, 432...K 4	* 52401 Cedar Rapids⊙, 110,642...K 5	51636 Coin, 294...C 7
436 Breda, 518...C 4	Cedar Rapids, ‡163,213...K 5	52035 Colesburg, 379...L 3
540 Brighton, 632...K 6	52213 Center Point, 1,456...K 4	50054 Colfax, 2,293...G 5
611 Bristow, 230...F 2	52544 Centerville⊙, 6,531...H 7	51637 College Springs, 295...C 7
423 Britt, 2,069...F 2	52214 Central City, 1,116...K 4	50055 Collins, 404...G 5
211 Brooklyn, 1,410...J 5	50049 Chariton⊙, 5,009...G 6	50056 Colo, 606...G 5
728 Buffalo, 1,513...M 6	50616 Charles City⊙, 9,268...H 2	52737 Columbus City, 312...L 6
24 Buffalo Center, 1,118...F 2	52737 Charlotte, 444...M 5	52738 Columbus Junction, 1,205...L 6
601 Burlington⊙, 32,366...L 7	51439 Charter Oak, 715...C 4	52739 Conesville, 295...L 6
522 Burt, 608...E 2	52215 Chelsea, 381...J 5	50631 Conrad, 932...H 4

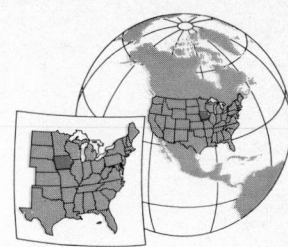

AREA 56,290 sq. mi.
POPULATION 2,825,041
CAPITAL Des Moines
LARGEST CITY Des Moines
HIGHEST POINT Ocheyedan Mound 1,675 ft.
SETTLED IN 1788
ADMITTED TO UNION December 28, 1846
POPULAR NAME Hawkeye State
STATE FLOWER Wild Rose
STATE BIRD Eastern Goldfinch

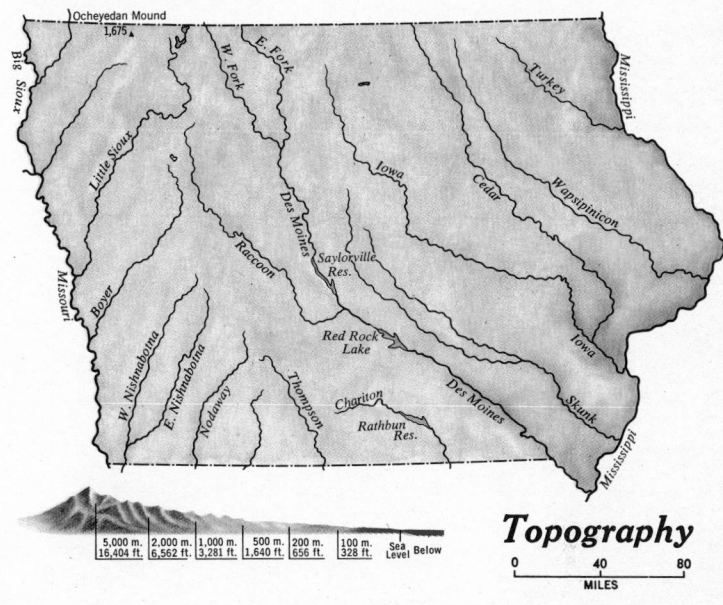

Topography

50058 Coon Rapids, 1,381...D 5	52553 Eddyville, 945...H 6	50108 Grand River, 211...F 7
52240 Coralville, 6,130...K 5	52042 Edgewood, 786...K 3	52752 Grandview, 357...L 6
50841 Corning⊙, 2,095...D 7	52554 Eldon, 1,319...J 7	50109 Granger, 661...F 5
51016 Correctionville, 870...B 4	50627 Eldora⊙, 3,223...G 4	51022 Granville, 383...B 3
50430 Corwith, 407...F 3	52748 Eldridge, 1,535...M 5	50848 Gravity, 286...D 7
50060 Corydon⊙, 1,745...G 7	52141 Elgin, 613...K 3	52050 Greeley, 323...L 3
50431 Coulter, 262...G 3	52043 Elkader⊙, 1,592...L 3	50636 Greene, 1,363...H 3
51501 Council Bluffs⊙, 60,348...B 6	50073 Elkhart, 269...F 5	50849 Greenfield⊙, 2,212...D 6
52621 Crawfordsville, 288...K 6	51531 Elk Horn, 667...C 5	50111 Grimes, 834...F 5
51526 Crescent, 284...B 6	† 50700 Elk Run Heights, 1,175...J 4	50112 Grinnell, 8,402...H 5
52136 Cresco⊙, 3,927...J 2	51532 Elliott, 423...C 6	51535 Griswold, 1,181...C 6
50801 Creston⊙, 8,234...E 6	50075 Ellsworth, 443...F 4	50638 Grundy Center⊙, 2,712...H 4
50432 Crystal Lake, 276...F 2	50628 Elma, 601...J 2	50115 Guthrie Center⊙, 1,834...D 5
50843 Cumberland, 385...D 6	52227 Ely, 275...K 5	52052 Guttenberg, 2,177...L 3
50529 Dakota City, 746...E 3	51533 Emerson, 484...C 6	51444 Halbur, 235...D 4
50062 Dallas, 438...G 6	50536 Emmetsburg⊙, 4,150...D 2	51640 Hamburg, 1,649...B 7
50063 Dallas Center, 1,128...E 5	52045 Epworth, 1,132...M 4	50441 Hampton⊙, 4,376...G 3
51019 Danbury, 527...B 4	52626 Essex, 770...C 7	51536 Hancock, 228...C 6
52623 Danville, 948...L 7	50707 Evansdale, 5,038...J 4	50544 Harcourt, 305...E 4
* 52801 Davenport⊙, 98,469...M 5	51338 Everly, 699...C 2	51537 Harlan⊙, 5,049...C 5
Davenport-Rock Island-	50076 Exira, 966...D 5	52146 Harpers Ferry, 227...L 2
Moline, ‡362,638...M 5	52555 Exline, 224...H 7	50118 Hartford, 582...G 6
50065 Davis City, 301...F 7	50629 Fairbank, 810...K 3	51346 Hartley, 1,694...C 2
50066 Dawson, 232...E 5	52228 Fairfax, 635...K 5	50119 Harvey, 217...H 6
50530 Dayton, 909...E 4	52556 Fairfield⊙, 8,715...J 6	51540 Hastings, 229...C 6
52101 Decorah⊙, 7,458...K 2	52046 Farley, 1,096...L 3	50546 Havelock, 220...D 3
51440 Dedham, 325...D 5	52047 Farmersburg, 232...L 3	51023 Hawarden, 2,789...A 2
52222 Deep River, 323...J 5	52626 Farmington, 634...J 7	52147 Hawkeye, 529...J 3
51527 Defiance, 392...C 5	50538 Farnhamville, 393...D 4	50641 Hazleton, 826...K 3
52223 Delhi, 527...L 4	51639 Farragut, 521...C 7	52563 Hedrick, 790...J 6
52037 Delmar, 599...M 4	52142 Fayette, 1,947...K 3	51541 Henderson, 211...C 6
51441 Deloit, 279...C 4	50539 Fenton, 403...E 2	52233 Hiawatha, 2,416...K 4
52550 Delta, 475...J 6	50434 Fertile, 394...G 2	52235 Hills, 507...K 6
51442 Denison⊙, 5,882...C 5	50435 Floyd, 380...H 2	52630 Hillsboro, 252...K 7
52624 Denmark, 375...L 7	50540 Fonda, 980...D 3	51024 Hinton, 488...A 4
50622 Denver, 1,169...J 3	50846 Fontanelle, 752...E 6	50642 Holland, 258...H 4
* 50301 Des Moines (cap.)⊙,	50436 Forest City⊙, 3,841...F 2	51025 Holstein, 1,445...B 4
200,587...G 5	52144 Fort Atkinson, 339...J 2	52053 Holy Cross, 290...L 3
Des Moines, ‡286,101...G 5	50501 Fort Dodge⊙, 31,263...E 3	52237 Hopkinton, 800...L 4
50069 De Soto, 369...E 5	52627 Fort Madison⊙, 13,996...L 7	51026 Hornick, 250...A 4
52742 De Witt, 3,647...N 5	51340 Fostoria, 219...C 2	51238 Hospers, 646...B 2
50070 Dexter, 652...E 5	50630 Fredericksburg, 912...J 3	50122 Hubbard, 846...G 4
50845 Diagonal, 327...E 7	52561 Fremont, 480...H 6	50643 Hudson, 1,535...H 4
51333 Dickens, 240...C 2	51020 Galva, 319...C 3	51239 Hull, 1,523...A 2
50624 Dike, 794...H 4	50103 Garden Grove, 285...F 7	50548 Humboldt, 4,665...E 3
52745 Dixon, 276...M 5	52049 Garnavillo, 634...L 3	50133 Humeston, 673...G 7
52746 Donahue, 216...M 5	50438 Garner⊙, 2,217...F 2	50124 Huxley, 937...F 5
52625 Donnellson, 798...K 7	52229 Garrison, 383...J 4	51445 Ida Grove⊙, 2,261...B 4
51235 Doon, 423...A 2	50632 Garwin, 563...H 4	50644 Independence⊙, 5,910...K 4
52551 Douds, 247...J 7	51237 Geneva, 194...G 3	50125 Indianola⊙, 8,852...F 6
51528 Dow City, 571...B 5	50105 Gilbert, 521...F 5	51240 Inwood, 644...A 2
50071 Dows, 777...F 3	50634 Gilbertville, 655...J 4	50645 Ionia, 270...J 2
52001 Dubuque⊙, 62,309...M 3	50106 Gilman, 513...H 5	52240 Iowa City⊙, 46,850...K 5
Dubuque, ‡90,609...M 3	50541 Gilmore City, 766...D 3	50126 Iowa Falls, 6,454...G 3
50625 Dumont, 724...H 3	50635 Gladbrook, 961...H 4	51027 Ireton, 582...A 3
52532 Duncombe, 418...E 4	51534 Glenwood⊙, 4,195...B 6	51446 Irwin, 446...C 5
50626 Dunkerton, 563...J 3	51443 Glidden, 964...D 4	50128 Jamaica, 271...E 5
51529 Dunlap, 1,292...B 5	50542 Goldfield, 722...F 3	52647 Janesville, 741...J 3
52747 Durant, 1,472...M 5	50439 Goodell, 218...F 3	50129 Jefferson⊙, 4,735...E 4
52040 Dyersville, 3,437...L 3	52750 Gooselake, 218...N 5	50648 Jesup, 1,662...J 4
52224 Dysart, 1,251...J 4	50543 Gowrie, 1,225...D 4	50130 Jewell, 1,152...F 4
50533 Eagle Grove, 4,489...F 3	51342 Graettinger, 907...D 2	50131 Johnston, 222...F 5
50072 Earlham, 974...E 5	50440 Grafton, 254...G 2	52247 Kalona, 1,488...K 6
51530 Earling, 573...C 5	50107 Grand Junction, 967...E 4	50132 Kamrar, 243...F 4
52041 Earlville, 751...L 4	52751 Grand Mound, 627...M 5	50447 Kanawha, 705...F 3
50535 Early, 727...C 4		50133 Kellerton, 299...E 7

(continued on following page)

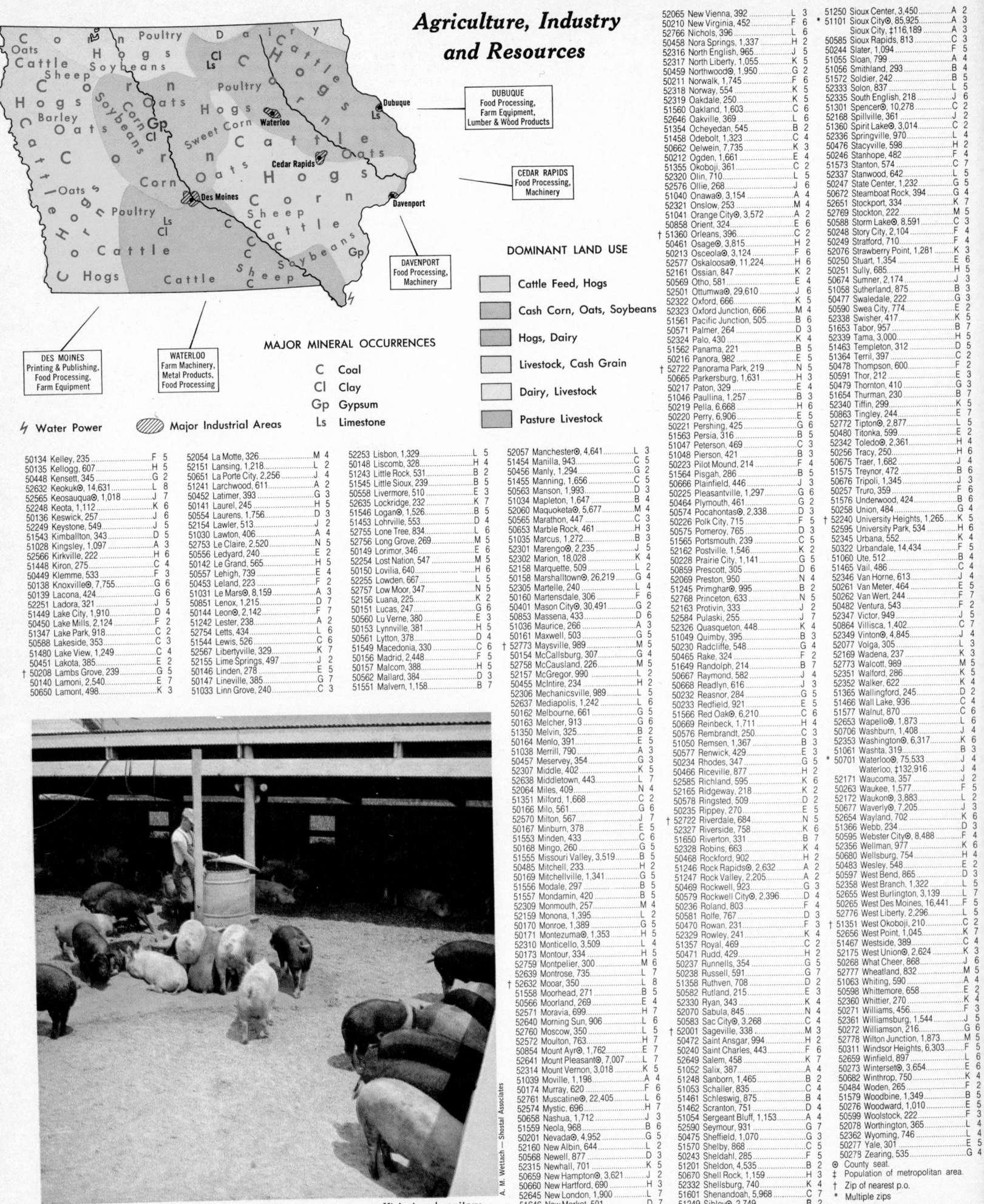

Agriculture, Industry and Resources

DUBUQUE Food Processing, Farm Equipment, Lumber & Wood Products

CEDAR RAPIDS Food Processing, Machinery

DAVENPORT Food Processing, Machinery

DES MOINES Printing & Publishing, Food Processing, Farm Equipment

WATERLOO Farm Machinery, Metal Products, Food Processing

⚡ Water Power   Major Industrial Areas

MAJOR MINERAL OCCURRENCES

C   Coal
Cl   Clay
Gp   Gypsum
Ls   Limestone

DOMINANT LAND USE

- Cattle Feed, Hogs
- Cash Corn, Oats, Soybeans
- Hogs, Dairy
- Livestock, Cash Grain
- Dairy, Livestock
- Pasture Livestock

This Iowa farmer confines his hogs to concrete pens as a more efficient and sanitary method of raising healthy animals for market. Iowa's record-breaking hog production is due largely to the availability of corn for fodder.

A. M. Wetach — Shostal Associates

Agriculture, Industry and Resources

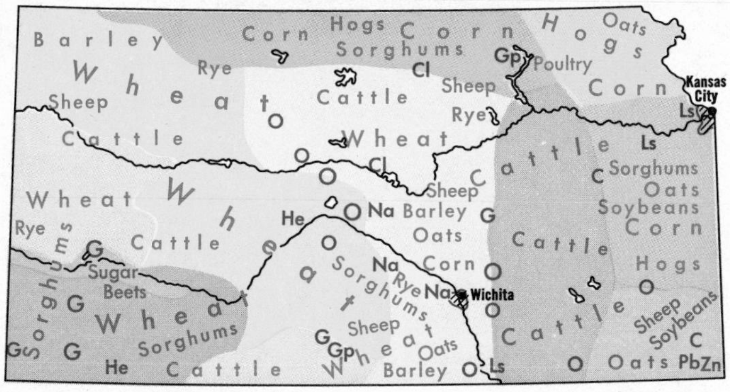

WICHITA
Aircraft, Food Processing

KANSAS CITY
Food Processing, Chemicals, Automobiles, Machinery, Metal Products

AREA 82,264 sq. mi.
POPULATION 2,249,071
CAPITAL Topeka
LARGEST CITY Wichita
HIGHEST POINT Mt. Sunflower 4,039 ft.
SETTLED IN 1831
ADMITTED TO UNION January 29, 1861
POPULAR NAME Sunflower State
STATE FLOWER Sunflower
STATE BIRD Western Meadowlark

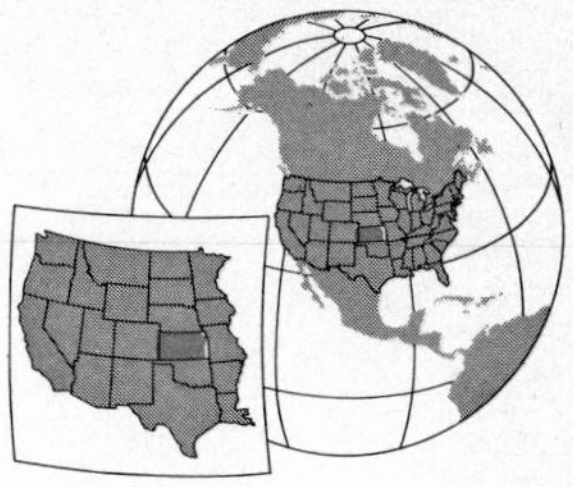

DOMINANT LAND USE

- Specialized Wheat
- Wheat, General Farming
- Wheat, Range Livestock
- Wheat, Grain Sorghums, Range Livestock
- Cattle Feed, Hogs
- Livestock, Cash Grain
- Livestock, Cash Grain, Dairy
- General Farming, Livestock, Cash Grain
- General Farming, Livestock, Special Crops
- Range Livestock

MAJOR MINERAL OCCURRENCES

C	Coal	Ls	Limestone
Cl	Clay	Na	Salt
G	Natural Gas	O	Petroleum
Gp	Gypsum	Pb	Lead
He	Helium	Zn	Zinc

Major Industrial Areas

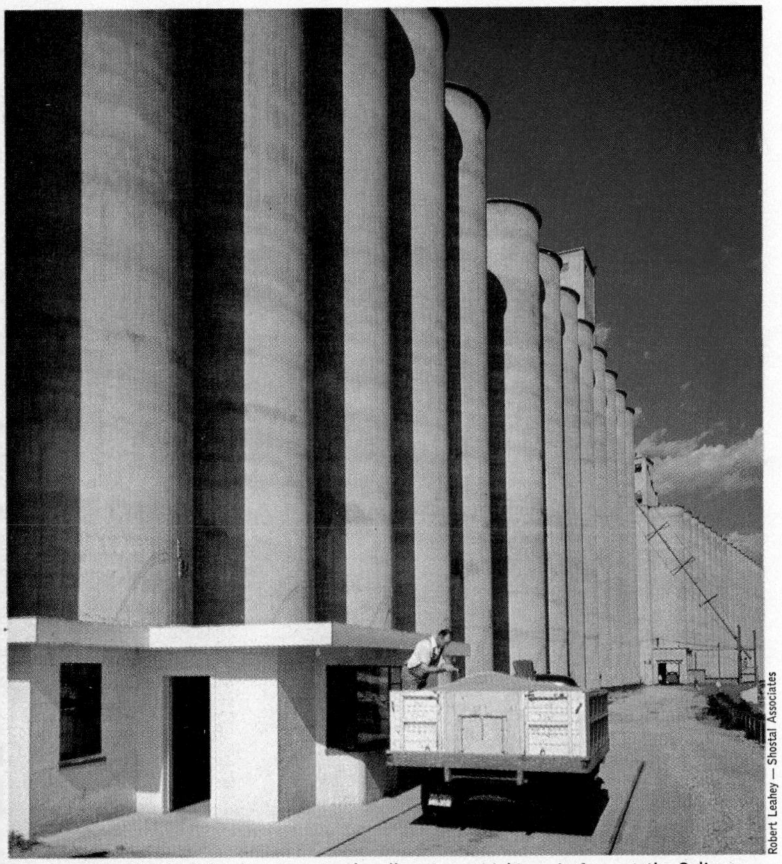

Robert Leahey — Shostal Associates

Loaded with wheat for storage, a truck pulls onto a weighing platform at the Salina grain elevators. Wheat is grown here on such a scale that Kansas is known as the Breadbasket of the World.

COUNTIES

Name/Pop.	Key
Allen, 15,043	G 4
Anderson, 8,501	G 3
Atchison, 19,165	G 2
Barber, 7,016	D 4
Barton, 30,663	D 3
Bourbon, 15,215	H 4
Brown, 11,685	G 2
Butler, 38,658	F 4
Chase, 3,408	F 3
Chautauqua, 4,642	F 4
Cherokee, 21,549	H 4
Cheyenne, 4,256	A 2
Clark, 2,896	C 4
Clay, 9,890	E 2
Cloud, 13,466	E 2
Coffey, 7,397	G 3
Comanche, 2,702	C 4
Cowley, 35,012	F 4
Crawford, 37,850	H 4
Decatur, 4,988	B 2
Dickinson, 19,993	E 3
Doniphan, 9,107	G 2
Douglas, 57,932	G 3
Edwards, 4,581	C 4
Elk, 3,858	F 4
Ellis, 24,730	C 3
Ellsworth, 6,146	D 3
Finney, 18,947	B 3
Ford, 22,587	C 4
Franklin, 19,548	G 3
Geary, 28,111	F 3
Gove, 3,940	B 3
Graham, 4,751	C 2
Grant, 5,961	A 4
Gray, 4,516	B 4
Greeley, 1,819	A 3
Greenwood, 9,141	F 4
Hamilton, 2,747	A 3
Harper, 7,871	D 4
Harvey, 27,236	E 3
Haskell, 3,672	B 4
Hodgeman, 2,662	C 3
Jackson, 10,342	G 2
Jefferson, 11,945	G 2
Jewell, 6,099	D 2
Johnson, 217,662	H 3
Kearny, 3,047	A 3
Kingman, 8,886	D 4
Kiowa, 4,088	C 4
Labette, 25,775	G 4
Lane, 2,707	B 3
Leavenworth, 53,340	G 2
Lincoln, 4,582	D 2
Linn, 7,770	H 3
Logan, 3,814	A 3
Lyon, 32,071	F 3
Marion, 13,935	E 3
Marshall, 13,139	F 2
McPherson, 24,778	E 3
Meade, 4,912	B 4
Miami, 19,254	H 3
Mitchell, 8,010	D 2
Montgomery, 39,949	G 4
Morris, 6,432	F 3
Morton, 3,576	A 4
Nemaha, 11,825	F 2
Neosho, 18,812	G 4
Ness, 4,791	C 3
Norton, 7,279	C 2
Osage, 13,352	G 3
Osborne, 6,416	D 2
Ottawa, 6,183	E 2
Pawnee, 8,484	C 3
Phillips, 7,888	C 2
Pottawatomie, 11,755	F 2
Pratt, 10,056	D 4
Rawlins, 4,393	A 2
Reno, 60,765	D 4
Republic, 8,498	E 2
Rice, 12,320	D 3
Riley, 56,788	F 2
Rooks, 7,628	C 2
Rush, 5,117	C 3
Russell, 9,428	D 3
Saline, 46,592	E 3
Scott, 5,606	B 3
Sedgwick, 350,694	E 4
Seward, 15,744	B 4
Shawnee, 155,322	G 2
Sheridan, 3,859	B 2
Sherman, 7,792	A 2
Smith, 6,757	D 2
Stafford, 5,943	D 3
Stanton, 2,287	A 4
Stevens, 4,198	A 4
Sumner, 23,553	E 4
Thomas, 7,501	A 2
Trego, 4,436	C 3
Wabaunsee, 6,397	F 3
Wallace, 2,215	A 3
Washington, 9,249	E 2
Wichita, 3,274	A 3
Wilson, 11,317	G 4
Woodson, 4,789	G 4
Wyandotte, 186,845	H 2

CITIES and TOWNS

	Zip	Name/Pop.	Key
	67510	Abbyville, 143	D 4
	67410	Abilene⊙, 6,661	E 3
	67414	Ada, 120	E 2
	66830	Admire, 144	F 3
	66930	Agenda, 107	E 2
	67621	Agra, 294	C 2
	67511	Albert, 235	C 3
	67512	Alden, 238	D 3
	67513	Alexander, 129	C 3
	66833	Allen, 175	F 3
	66401	Alma⊙, 905	F 2
	67622	Almena, 489	C 2
	67330	Altamont, 845	G 4
	66834	Alta Vista, 402	F 3
	67623	Alton, 214	D 2
	66710	Altoona, 475	G 4
	66835	Americus, 441	F 3
	67001	Andale, 500	E 4
	67002	Andover, 1,880	E 4
	67003	Anthony⊙, 2,653	D 4
	66711	Arcadia, 388	H 4
	67004	Argonia, 591	E 4
	67005	Arkansas City, 13,216	E 4
	67514	Arlington, 503	D 4
	66712	Arma, 1,348	H 4
	67831	Ashland⊙, 1,244	C 4
	67416	Assaria, 303	E 3
	66002	Atchison⊙, 12,565	G 2
	66932	Athol, 108	D 2
	67008	Atlanta, 216	F 4
	67009	Attica, 639	D 4
	67730	Atwood⊙, 1,658	B 2
	66402	Auburn, 261	G 3
	67010	Augusta, 5,977	F 4
	67417	Aurora, 120	E 2
	66403	Axtell, 456	F 2
	66404	Baileyville, 110	F 2
	66006	Baldwin City, 2,520	G 3
	67418	Barnard, 190	D 2
	66933	Barnes, 209	F 2
	67332	Bartlett, 138	G 4
	66007	Basehor, 724	G 2
	66713	Baxter Springs, 4,489	H 4
	67516	Bazine, 386	C 3
	66406	Beattie, 288	F 2
	67012	Beaumont, 135	F 4
	67013	Belle Plaine, 1,553	E 4
	66935	Belleville⊙, 3,063	E 2
	67420	Beloit⊙, 4,121	D 2
	67519	Belpre, 191	C 4
	66407	Belvue, 161	F 2
	67422	Bennington, 561	E 2
	67016	Bentley, 260	E 4
	67017	Benton, 517	E 4
	66408	Bern, 191	F 2
	67423	Beverly, 193	E 2
	67731	Bird City, 671	A 2
	67520	Bison, 285	C 3
	66010	Blue Mound, 308	H 3
	66411	Blue Rapids, 1,148	F 2
	67018	Bluff City, 109	E 4
	67625	Bogue, 257	C 2
	66012	Bonner Springs, 3,662	H 2
	67732	Brewster, 320	A 2
	66716	Bronson, 397	H 4
	67425	Brookville, 238	E 3
	67834	Bucklin, 771	C 4
	66013	Bucyrus, 196	H 3
	66717	Buffalo, 321	G 4
	67522	Buhler, 1,019	E 3
	67626	Bunker Hill, 181	D 3
	67019	Burden, 503	F 4
	67523	Burdett, 285	C 3
	66838	Burdick, 120	F 3
	66413	Burlingame, 999	G 3
	66839	Burlington⊙, 2,099	G 3
	66840	Burns, 268	F 3
	66936	Burr Oak, 426	D 2
	67020	Burrton, 808	E 3
	67427	Bushton, 397	D 3
	67022	Caldwell, 1,540	E 4
	67023	Cambridge, 110	F 4
	67333	Caney, 2,192	G 4
	67428	Canton, 893	E 3
	66414	Carbondale, 1,041	G 3
	66842	Cassoday, 123	F 3
	67627	Catharine, 126	C 3
	67430	Cawker City, 726	D 2
	67024	Cedar Vale, 665	F 4
	66415	Centralia, 511	F 2
	66720	Chanute, 10,341	G 4
	67431	Chapman, 1,132	E 3
	67524	Chase, 800	D 3
	67334	Chautauqua, 137	F 4
	67025	Cheney, 1,160	E 4
	66724	Cherokee, 790	H 4
	67335	Cherryvale, 2,609	G 4
	67336	Chetopa, 1,596	G 4
†	66762	Chicopee, 300	H 4
	87835	Cimarron⊙, 1,373	B 4
	66416	Circleville, 178	G 2
	67525	Claflin, 887	D 3
	67432	Clay Center⊙, 4,963	E 2
	67629	Clayton, 127	B 2
	67026	Clearwater, 1,435	E 4
	66937	Clifton, 718	E 2
	66938	Clyde, 946	E 2
	67028	Coats, 152	D 4
	67337	Coffeyville, 15,116	G 4
	67701	Colby⊙, 4,658	A 2
	67029	Coldwater⊙, 1,016	C 4
	67631	Collyer, 182	B 2
	66015	Colony, 382	G 3
	66725	Columbus⊙, 3,356	H 4
	67030	Colwich, 879	E 4
	66901	Concordia⊙, 7,221	E 2
	67031	Conway Springs, 1,153	E 4
	67836	Coolidge, 102	A 3
	67837	Copeland, 267	B 4
	66417	Corning, 162	F 2
	66845	Cottonwood Falls⊙, 987	F 3
	66846	Council Grove⊙, 2,403	F 3
	66939	Courtland, 403	E 2
	66728	Crestline, 102	H 4
	66940	Cuba, 290	E 2
†	67124	Cullison, 117	D 4
	67435	Culver, 148	E 3
	66016	Cummings, 826	G 2
	67035	Cunningham, 483	D 4
	67632	Damar, 245	C 2
	67340	Dearing, 338	G 4
	67838	Deerfield, 474	A 4
	66418	Delia, 168	G 2
	67436	Delphos, 599	E 2
	66419	Denison, 248	G 2
	67341	Dennis, 120	G 4
	66017	Denton, 162	G 2
	67037	Derby, 7,947	E 4
	66018	De Soto, 1,839	H 3
	67038	Dexter, 286	F 4
	67839	Dighton⊙, 1,540	B 3
	67801	Dodge City⊙, 14,127	B 4
	67634	Dorrance, 234	D 3
	67039	Douglass, 1,126	F 4
	66420	Dover, 122	G 3
	67437	Downs, 1,268	D 2
	67635	Dresden, 103	B 2
	66848	Dunlap, 102	F 3
	67438	Durham, 143	E 3
	66849	Dwight, 322	F 3
	66731	Earlton, 102	G 4
†	67201	Eastborough, 1,141	E 4
	66020	Easton, 435	G 2
	66021	Edgerton, 513	H 3
	67342	Edna, 418	G 4
	66022	Edwardsville, 619	H 2
	66023	Effingham, 605	G 2
	67041	Elbing, 128	E 3
	67042	El Dorado⊙, 12,308	F 4
	67361	Elgin, 115	F 4
	67344	Elk City, 432	G 4
	67345	Elk Falls, 124	F 4
	67950	Elkhart⊙, 2,089	A 4
	67526	Ellinwood, 2,416	D 3
	67637	Ellis, 2,137	C 3

(continued on following page)

67439 Ellsworth⊙, 2,080......D 3
66850 Elmdale, 102......F 3
† 66603 Elmont, 112......G 2
66732 Elsmore, 116......G 4
66024 Elwood, 1,283......H 2
66422 Emmett, 156......F 2
66801 Emporia⊙, 23,327......F 3
67840 Englewood, 158......C 3
67841 Ensign, 237......B 4
67441 Enterprise, 868......E 3
66733 Erie⊙, 1,414......G 4
66941 Esbon, 206......D 2
66423 Eskridge, 589......F 3
66025 Eudora, 2,071......H 3
67045 Eureka⊙, 3,576......F 4
66424 Everest, 304......G 2
66425 Fairview, 283......G 2
67047 Fall River, 191......F 4
67442 Falun, 105......E 3
66851 Florence, 716......E 3
66026 Fontana, 160......H 3
67842 Ford, 246......C 4
66942 Formoso, 180......D 2
67843 Fort Dodge, 450......C 4
66027 Fort Leavenworth, 8,060......H 2
66701 Fort Scott⊙, 8,967......H 4

67844 Fowler, 588......B 4
66427 Frankfort, 960......F 2
66735 Franklin, 620......H 4
66736 Fredonia⊙, 3,080......G 4
66762 Frontenac, 2,223......H 4
66738 Fulton, 213......H 4
66739 Galena, 3,712......H 4
66740 Galesburg, 146......G 4
67443 Galva, 522......E 3
67846 Garden City⊙, 14,708......B 4
67050 Garden Plain, 678......E 4
66030 Gardner, 1,839......H 3
67529 Garfield, 261......C 3
66741 Garland, 125......H 4
66032 Garnett⊙, 3,169......G 3
66742 Gas, 438......G 4
67638 Gaylord, 211......D 2
67444 Geneseo, 453......D 3
67051 Geuda Springs, 223......E 4
67743 Girard⊙, 2,591......H 4
67639 Glade, 180......C 2
67445 Glasco, 767......E 2
67446 Glen Elder, 422......D 2
67052 Goddard, 955......E 4
67053 Goessel, 386......E 3
66428 Goff, 207......F 2

67735 Goodland⊙, 5,510......A 2
67640 Gorham, 379......D 3
67736 Gove⊙, 172......B 3
67737 Grainfield, 374......B 3
† 66441 Grandview Plaza, 734......F 2
66429 Grantville, 190......G 2
67530 Great Bend⊙, 16,133......D 3
66033 Greeley, 368......G 3
66943 Greenleaf, 448......E 2
67054 Greensburg⊙, 1,907......C 4
67346 Grenola, 290......F 4
66852 Gridley, 328......G 3
67738 Grinnell, 449......B 2
67448 Gypsum, 391......E 3
66744 Hallowell, 135......H 4
67056 Halstead, 1,716......E 4
66853 Hamilton, 349......F 4
66945 Hanover, 793......E 2
67849 Hanston, 282......C 4
67057 Hardtner, 300......D 4
67058 Harper, 1,665......D 4
66854 Hartford, 478......F 3
66431 Harveyville, 279......F 3
67347 Havana, 144......G 4

67543 Haven, 1,146......E 4
66432 Havensville, 163......F 2
67059 Haviland, 705......C 4
67601 Hays⊙, 15,396......C 3
67060 Haysville, 6,483......E 4
67061 Hazelton, 176......D 4
67850 Healy, 251......B 3
66746 Hepler, 152......H 4
67449 Herington, 3,165......E 3
67739 Herndon, 268......B 2
67062 Hesston, 1,926......E 3
66434 Hiawatha⊙, 3,365......G 2
66035 Highland, 899......G 2
67642 Hill City⊙, 2,071......C 2
67063 Hillsboro, 2,730......E 3
66036 Hillsdale, 250......H 3
67544 Hoisington, 3,710......D 3
67851 Holcomb, 272......B 3
66436 Holton⊙, 3,063......G 2
67450 Holyrood, 593......D 3
66438 Home, 120......F 2
67451 Hope, 438......E 3
† 67879 Horace, 137......A 3
66439 Horton, 2,177......G 2
67349 Howard⊙, 918......F 4
67740 Hoxie⊙, 1,419......B 2

66440 Hoyt, 420......G 2
67545 Hudson, 181......D 3
67951 Hugoton⊙, 2,739......A 4
66748 Humboldt, 2,249......G 4
67452 Hunter, 150......D 2
66038 Huron, 106......G 2
67501 Hutchinson⊙, 36,885......D 3
67301 Independence⊙, 10,347......G 4
67853 Ingalls, 235......B 4
67546 Inman, 836......E 3
66749 Iola⊙, 6,493......G 4
67065 Isabel, 147......D 4
67066 Iuka, 210......D 4
66948 Jamestown, 470......E 2
67643 Jennings, 224......B 2
67854 Jetmore⊙, 936......C 3
66949 Jewell, 569......D 2
67855 Johnson⊙, 1,283......A 4
66441 Junction City⊙, 19,018......E 2
67454 Kanopolis, 626......D 3
67741 Kanorado, 278......A 2
* 66101 Kansas City⊙, 168,213......H 2
    Kansas City, ‡1,253,916......H 2
67067 Kechi, 229......E 4
67857 Kendall, 160......A 4
66951 Kensington, 653......C 2

66039 Kincaid, 189......G 3
67068 Kingman⊙, 3,622......D 4
67547 Kinsley⊙, 2,212......C 3
67070 Kiowa, 1,414......D 4
67644 Kirwin, 293......D 2
67859 Kismet, 294......B 4
67350 Labette, 105......G 4
67548 La Crosse⊙, 1,583......C 3
66040 La Cygne, 989......H 3
66750 Lafontaine, 140......G 4
66751 La Harpe, 509......G 4
67860 Lakin⊙, 1,570......A 4
66041 Lancaster, 279......G 2
66042 Lane, 254......G 3
66043 Lansing, 3,797......H 2
67550 Larned⊙, 4,567......C 3
67072 Latham, 156......F 4
66044 Lawrence⊙, 45,698......H 3
66048 Leavenworth⊙, 25,147......H 2
66206 Leawood, 10,349......H 2
66952 Lebanon, 517......D 2
66856 Lebo, 589......F 3
66050 Lecompton, 434......G 3
67073 Lehigh, 168......E 3
67645 Lenora, 439......C 2
67074 Leon, 510......F 4

Map

Longitude West of Greenwich

Bordering states: NEBRASKA, COLORADO, OKLAHOMA, TEXAS, MISSOURI

Counties: CHEYENNE, RAWLINS, DECATUR, NORTON, PHILLIPS, SMITH, JEWELL, REPUBLIC, WASHINGTON, MARSHALL, NEMAHA, BROWN, DONIPHAN, SHERMAN, THOMAS, SHERIDAN, GRAHAM, ROOKS, OSBORNE, MITCHELL, CLOUD, CLAY, RILEY, POTTAWATOMIE, JACKSON, ATCHISON, JEFFERSON, LEAVENWORTH, WALLACE, LOGAN, GOVE, TREGO, ELLIS, RUSSELL, LINCOLN, OTTAWA, DICKINSON, GEARY, SALINE, WABAUNSEE, SHAWNEE, DOUGLAS, WYANDOTTE, JOHNSON, GREELEY, WICHITA, SCOTT, LANE, NESS, RUSH, BARTON, ELLSWORTH, RICE, MCPHERSON, MARION, MORRIS, LYON, OSAGE, FRANKLIN, MIAMI, HAMILTON, KEARNY, FINNEY, HODGEMAN, PAWNEE, STAFFORD, RENO, HARVEY, SEDGWICK, BUTLER, CHASE, COFFEY, ANDERSON, LINN, STANTON, GRANT, HASKELL, GRAY, FORD, EDWARDS, PRATT, KINGMAN, KIOWA, MORTON, STEVENS, SEWARD, MEADE, CLARK, COMANCHE, BARBER, HARPER, SUMNER, COWLEY, CHAUTAUQUA, MONTGOMERY, LABETTE, CHEROKEE, CRAWFORD, NEOSHO, WILSON, ELK, GREENWOOD, WOODSON, ALLEN, BOURBON

Legend

KANSAS

SCALE
0 5 10 20 30 40 50 MI.
0 5 10 20 30 40 50 KM.

State Capitals ⊛
County Seats ⊙

© C.S. HAMMOND & CO., N.Y.

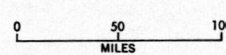

6449 Leonardville, 412 .... F 2
7861 Leoti◉, 1,916 .... A 3
6857 Le Roy, 551 .... G 3
7743 Levant, 425 .... A 2
7552 Lewis, 525 .... C 4
7901 Liberal, 13,471 .... B 4
7351 Liberty, 185 .... G 4
7553 Liebenthal, 169 .... C 3
6858 Lincoln◉, 1,582 .... D 2
7455 Lincolnville, 218 .... F 3
7453 Lindsborg, 2,764 .... E 3
6953 Linn, 388 .... F 2
6052 Linwood, 323 .... G 2
7457 Little River, 493 .... E 3
7646 Logan, 760 .... C 2
7647 Long Island, 195 .... C 2
7352 Longton, 304 .... F 4
7459 Lorraine, 202 .... D 3
6859 Lost Springs, 103 .... H 3
6053 Louisburg, 1,033 .... H 3
6450 Louisville, 204 .... F 2
7648 Lucas, 524 .... D 2
7649 Luray, 303 .... D 2
6451 Lyndon◉, 958 .... G 3
7554 Lyons◉, 4,355 .... D 3
7557 Macksville, 484 .... D 4

66860 Madison, 1,061 .... F 3
66955 Mahaska, 122 .... E 2
67101 Maize, 785 .... E 4
66502 Manhattan◉, 27,575 .... F 2
66956 Mankato◉, 1,287 .... D 2
67862 Manter, 219 .... A 4
67507 Maple Hill, 327 .... F 2
66754 Mapleton, 112 .... H 3
67863 Marienthal, 120 .... A 4
66861 Marion◉, 2,052 .... E 3
67464 Marquette, 578 .... E 3
66508 Marysville◉, 3,588 .... F 2
66509 Mayetta, 246 .... G 2
67103 Mayfield, 110 .... E 4
67556 McCracken, 333 .... C 3
66753 McCune, 487 .... H 4
67745 McDonald, 269 .... A 2
66501 McFarland, 209 .... F 2
66054 McLouth, 623 .... G 2
67460 McPherson◉, 10,851 .... E 3
67864 Meade◉, 1,899 .... B 4
67104 Medicine Lodge◉, 2,545 .... D 4
67558 Medora, 110 .... E 3
66510 Melvern, 455 .... G 3
66512 Meriden, 472 .... G 2
66203 Merriam, 10,851 .... H 3

Topography

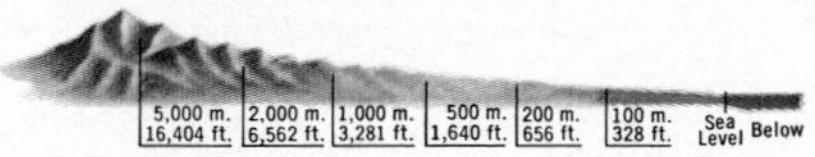

0   50   100
MILES

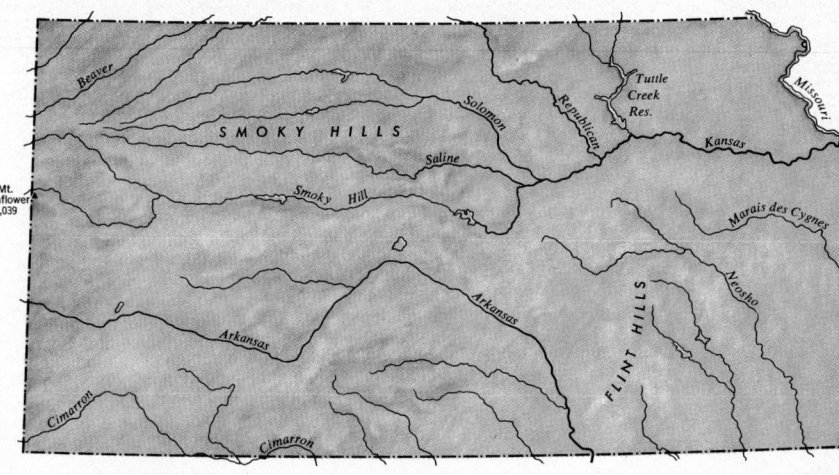

5,000 m. 2,000 m. 1,000 m. 500 m. 200 m. 100 m. Sea Level Below
16,404 ft. 6,562 ft. 3,281 ft. 1,640 ft. 656 ft. 328 ft.

67105 Milan, 162 .... E 4
66514 Milford, 296 .... F 2
67466 Miltonvale, 718 .... E 2
67467 Minneapolis◉, 1,971 .... E 2
67865 Minneola, 630 .... C 4
66222 Mission, 8,376 .... H 2
67353 Moline, 555 .... F 4
67867 Montezuma, 606 .... B 4
66755 Moran, 550 .... G 4
67468 Morganville, 257 .... E 2
67650 Morland, 300 .... B 2
66515 Morrill, 308 .... G 2
66958 Morrowville, 201 .... E 2
67952 Moscow, 228 .... A 4
66056 Mound City◉, 714 .... H 3
67107 Moundridge, 1,271 .... E 3
67354 Mound Valley, 467 .... G 4
67108 Mount Hope, 665 .... E 4
66758 Mulberry, 622 .... H 4
67109 Mullinville, 376 .... C 4
67110 Mulvane, 3,185 .... E 4
66959 Munden, 123 .... E 2
† 67601 Munjor, 200 .... C 3
66960 Narka, 130 .... E 2
67112 Nashville, 107 .... D 4
67651 Natoma, 603 .... D 2
66757 Neodesha, 3,295 .... G 4
66758 Neosho Falls, 184 .... G 3
66864 Neosho Rapids, 234 .... F 3
67560 Ness City◉, 1,756 .... C 3
66516 Netawaka, 192 .... G 2
67470 New Cambria, 160 .... E 3
67114 Newton◉, 15,439 .... E 3
67561 Nickerson, 1,187 .... D 3
67653 Norcatur, 284 .... B 2
67117 North Newton, 963 .... E 3
67654 Norton◉, 3,627 .... C 2
66060 Nortonville, 727 .... G 2
67118 Norwich, 414 .... E 4
67748 Oakley◉, 2,173 .... B 2
67749 Oberlin◉, 2,291 .... B 2
67562 Odin, 117 .... D 3
67656 Offerle, 212 .... C 4
67656 Ogallah, 110 .... C 3
66517 Ogden, 1,491 .... F 2
66518 Oketo, 133 .... F 2
66061 Olathe◉, 17,917 .... H 3
67564 Olmitz, 161 .... D 3
66865 Olpe, 453 .... F 3
66520 Olsburg, 151 .... F 2
66521 Onaga, 761 .... F 2
66522 Oneida, 112 .... G 2
66760 Opolis, 160 .... H 4
66523 Osage City, 2,600 .... G 3
66064 Osawatomie, 4,294 .... H 3
67473 Osborne◉, 1,980 .... D 2
66066 Oskaloosa◉, 955 .... G 2
67356 Oswego◉, 2,200 .... G 4
67565 Otis, 387 .... C 3
66067 Ottawa◉, 11,036 .... G 3
66524 Overbrook, 748 .... G 3
66204 Overland Park, 76,623 .... H 3
67119 Oxford, 1,113 .... E 4
66070 Ozawkie, 137 .... G 2
67657 Palco, 398 .... C 2
66962 Palmer, 166 .... E 2
66071 Paola◉, 4,622 .... H 3
67658 Paradise, 145 .... D 2
67751 Park, 178 .... B 2
67219 Park City, 2,529 .... E 4
66072 Parker, 255 .... H 3
67357 Parsons, 13,015 .... G 4
67566 Partridge, 302 .... D 4
66619 Pauline, 800 .... G 3
67567 Pawnee Rock, 442 .... D 3
66526 Paxico, 216 .... F 2
66866 Peabody, 1,368 .... E 3
67120 Peck, 150 .... E 4
66073 Perry, 664 .... G 2
67360 Peru, 289 .... F 4
67660 Pfeifer, 175 .... C 3
67661 Phillipsburg◉, 3,241 .... C 2
67122 Piedmont, 116 .... F 4
67868 Pierceville, 175 .... B 4

66761 Piqua, 107 .... G 4
66762 Pittsburg, 20,171 .... H 4
67869 Plains, 857 .... B 4
67663 Plainville, 2,627 .... C 2
66075 Pleasanton, 1,216 .... H 3
67568 Plevna, 124 .... D 4
66076 Pomona, 541 .... G 3
67474 Portis, 178 .... D 2
67123 Potwin, 497 .... F 4
66527 Powhattan, 111 .... G 2
67664 Prairie View, 201 .... C 2
66208 Prairie Village, 28,138 .... H 2
67124 Pratt◉, 6,736 .... D 4
67767 Prescott, 222 .... H 3
67569 Preston, 239 .... D 4
67570 Pretty Prairie, 561 .... D 4
67078 Princeton, 159 .... G 3
67127 Protection, 673 .... C 4
66528 Quenemo, 429 .... G 3
67752 Quinter, 930 .... B 2
67475 Ramona, 121 .... E 3
66963 Randall, 195 .... D 2
66554 Randolph, 106 .... F 2
67572 Ransom, 416 .... C 3
66079 Rantoul, 163 .... G 3
67573 Raymond, 133 .... D 3
66868 Reading, 247 .... F 3
67769 Redfield, 138 .... H 4
66964 Republic, 243 .... E 2
66529 Reserve, 117 .... G 2
67753 Rexford, 231 .... B 2
66080 Richmond, 464 .... G 3
66531 Riley, 668 .... F 2
66770 Riverton, 500 .... H 4
66532 Robinson, 278 .... G 2
† 66205 Roeland Park, 9,974 .... H 2
67954 Rolla, 400 .... A 4
67132 Rosalia, 130 .... F 4
67133 Rose Hill, 387 .... E 4
66533 Rossville, 934 .... G 2
67476 Roxbury, 110 .... E 3
67574 Rozel, 236 .... C 3
67575 Rush Center, 237 .... C 3
67665 Russell◉, 5,371 .... D 3
66534 Sabetha, 2,376 .... G 2
67756 Saint Francis◉, 1,725 .... A 2
67135 Saint George, 241 .... F 2
67576 Saint John◉, 1,477 .... D 3
66536 Saint Marys, 1,434 .... F 2
66771 Saint Paul, 804 .... G 4
67401 Salina◉, 37,714 .... E 3
67870 Satanta, 1,161 .... B 4
66772 Savonburg, 109 .... G 4
67134 Sawyer, 164 .... D 4
66773 Scammon, 457 .... H 4
66966 Scandia, 567 .... E 2
67667 Schoenchen, 207 .... C 3
67871 Scott City◉, 4,001 .... B 3
66537 Scranton, 575 .... G 3
67361 Sedan◉, 1,555 .... F 4
67135 Sedgwick, 1,083 .... E 4
67757 Selden, 271 .... B 2
66538 Seneca◉, 2,182 .... F 2
66081 Severance, 128 .... G 2
67137 Severy, 384 .... F 4
67872 Shallow Water, 106 .... B 3
67138 Sharon, 265 .... D 4
67758 Sharon Springs◉, 1,012 .... A 3
66203 Shawnee, 20,482 .... H 2
67874 Shields, 101 .... B 3
66539 Silver Lake, 811 .... G 2
67478 Simpson, 131 .... E 2
66967 Smith Center◉, 2,389 .... D 2
67479 Smolan, 175 .... E 3
66540 Soldier, 173 .... G 2
67480 Solomon, 973 .... E 3
67140 South Haven, 413 .... E 4
† 67501 South Hutchinson, 1,879 .... D 3
67578 Spearville, 738 .... C 3
66083 Spring Hill, 1,186 .... H 3
67578 Stafford, 1,414 .... D 4
66084 Stanley, 450 .... H 3
66775 Stark, 124 .... G 4
67579 Sterling, 2,312 .... D 3
66085 Stilwell, 350 .... H 3

66669 Stockton◉, 1,818 .... C 2
66869 Strong City, 545 .... F 3
67877 Sublette◉, 1,208 .... B 4
66541 Summerfield, 254 .... F 2
67143 Sun City, 119 .... D 4
66019 Sunflower, 1,744 .... H 3
67363 Sycamore, 125 .... G 4
67581 Sylvia, 390 .... D 4
67878 Syracuse◉, 1,720 .... A 3
67482 Talmage, 125 .... E 2
67483 Tampa, 154 .... E 3
66542 Tecumseh, 270 .... G 2
67484 Tescott, 393 .... E 2
66776 Thayer, 430 .... G 4
67582 Timken, 123 .... C 3
67485 Tipton, 315 .... D 2
66086 Tonganoxie, 1,717 .... G 2
* 66601 Topeka (cap.)◉, 125,011 .... G 2
    Topeka, ‡155,322 .... G 2
66777 Toronto, 431 .... G 4
67144 Towanda, 1,190 .... E 4
66778 Treece, 225 .... H 4
67879 Tribune◉, 1,013 .... A 3
67087 Troy◉, 1,047 .... G 2
67583 Turon, 430 .... D 4
67364 Tyro, 206 .... G 4
67146 Udall, 668 .... E 4
67880 Ulysses◉, 3,779 .... A 4
66543 Uniontown, 286 .... G 4
67584 Utica, 297 .... B 3
67147 Valley Center, 2,551 .... E 4
66088 Valley Falls, 1,169 .... G 2
66544 Vermillion, 191 .... F 2
67671 Victoria, 1,246 .... C 3
67149 Viola, 193 .... E 4
66870 Virgil, 179 .... F 4
67672 WaKeeney◉, 2,334 .... C 2
67487 Wakefield, 583 .... E 2
67673 Waldo, 123 .... D 2
67761 Wallace, 112 .... A 3
66780 Walnut, 330 .... G 4
67151 Walton, 211 .... E 3
66547 Wamego, 2,507 .... F 2
66968 Washington◉, 1,584 .... F 2
66548 Waterville, 632 .... F 2
66090 Wathena, 1,150 .... H 2
66871 Waverly, 510 .... G 3
66781 Weir, 740 .... H 4
66091 Welda, 149 .... G 3
67152 Wellington◉, 8,072 .... E 4
66092 Wellsville, 1,183 .... G 3
67762 Weskan, 350 .... A 3
66782 West Mineral, 232 .... H 4
66549 Westmoreland◉, 485 .... F 2
66093 Westphalia, 185 .... G 3
67869 West Plains (Plains), 857 .... B 4
66550 Wetmore, 392 .... G 2
66551 Wheaton, 106 .... F 2
66872 White City, 458 .... F 3
66094 White Cloud, 210 .... G 2
67154 Whitewater, 520 .... E 4
66552 Whiting, 256 .... G 2
* 67201 Wichita◉, 276,554 .... E 4
    Wichita, ‡389,352 .... E 4
† 66601 Willard, 124 .... G 2
66095 Williamsburg, 286 .... G 3
66873 Wilsey, 169 .... F 3
67490 Wilson, 870 .... D 3
66097 Winchester, 287 .... G 2
67491 Windom, 183 .... E 3
67156 Winfield◉, 11,405 .... F 4
67764 Winona, 293 .... A 2
67492 Woodbine, 170 .... E 3
67675 Woodston, 211 .... C 2
67882 Wright, 173 .... C 4
66783 Yates Center◉, 1,967 .... G 4
67585 Yoder, 155 .... D 4
67159 Zenda, 142 .... D 4
67676 Zurich, 189 .... C 2

◉ County seat.
‡ Population of metropolitan area.
† Zip of nearest p.o.
* Multiple zips

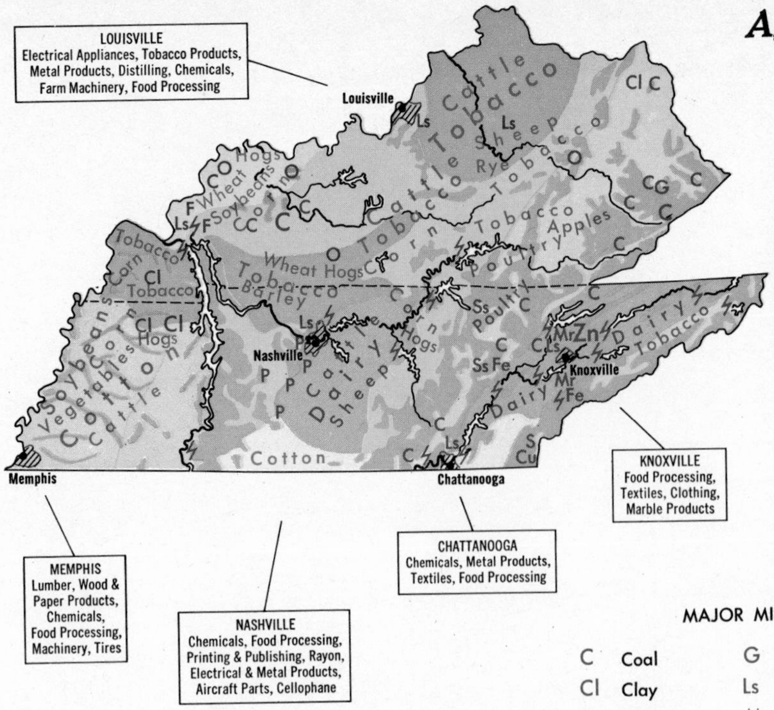
LOUISVILLE
Electrical Appliances, Tobacco Products, Metal Products, Distilling, Chemicals, Farm Machinery, Food Processing
Louisville
Nashville
Knoxville
Memphis
Chattanooga
KNOXVILLE
Food Processing, Textiles, Clothing, Marble Products
CHATTANOOGA
Chemicals, Metal Products, Textiles, Food Processing
MEMPHIS
Lumber, Wood & Paper Products, Chemicals, Food Processing, Machinery, Tires
NASHVILLE
Chemicals, Food Processing, Printing & Publishing, Rayon, Electrical & Metal Products, Aircraft Parts, Cellophane

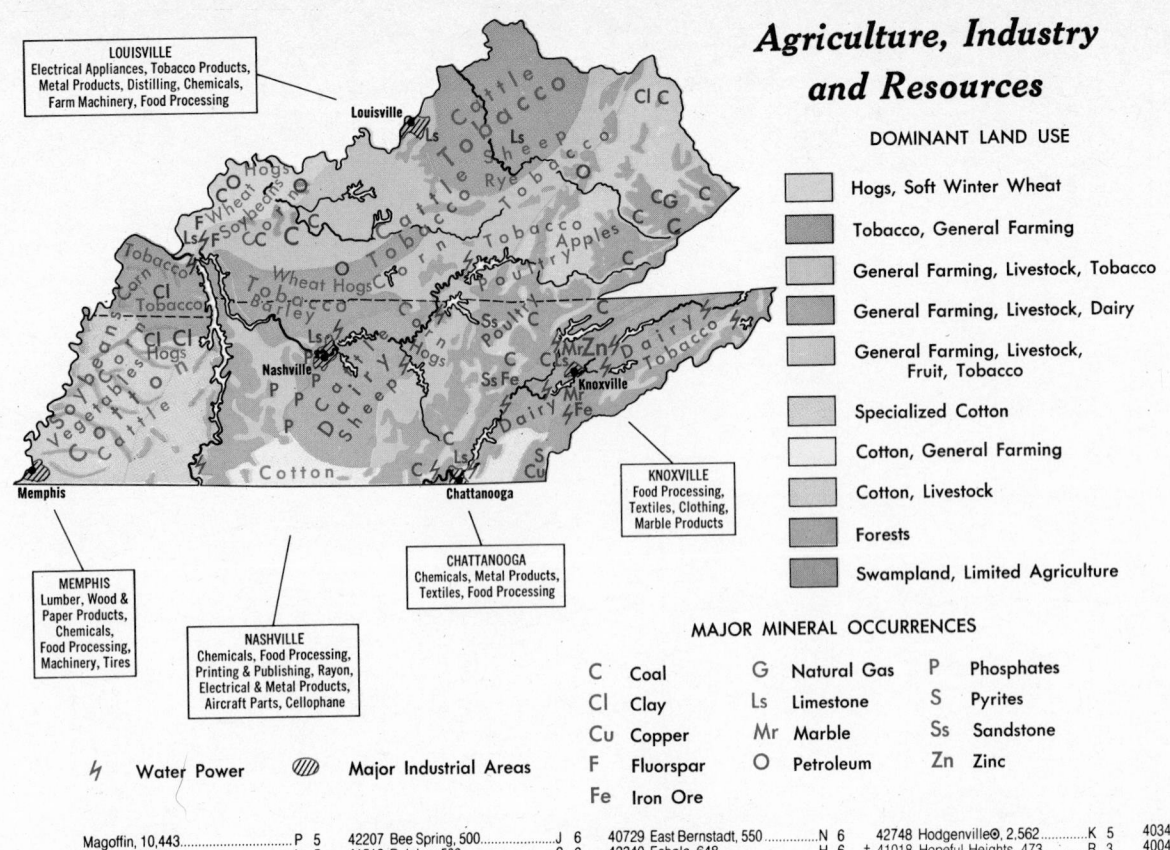

Agriculture, Industry and Resources

DOMINANT LAND USE

- Hogs, Soft Winter Wheat
- Tobacco, General Farming
- General Farming, Livestock, Tobacco
- General Farming, Livestock, Dairy
- General Farming, Livestock, Fruit, Tobacco
- Specialized Cotton
- Cotton, General Farming
- Cotton, Livestock
- Forests
- Swampland, Limited Agriculture

MAJOR MINERAL OCCURRENCES

C	Coal	G	Natural Gas	P	Phosphates
Cl	Clay	Ls	Limestone	S	Pyrites
Cu	Copper	Mr	Marble	Ss	Sandstone
F	Fluorspar	O	Petroleum	Zn	Zinc
Fe	Iron Ore				

ϟ Water Power

▨ Major Industrial Areas

KENTUCKY

COUNTIES

Adair, 13,037	L 6
Allen, 12,598	J 7
Anderson, 9,358	M 5
Ballard, 8,276	C 6
Barren, 28,677	K 7
Bath, 9,235	O 4
Bell, 31,087	O 7
Boone, 32,812	M 3
Bourbon, 18,476	N 4
Boyd, 52,376	R 4
Boyle, 21,090	M 5
Bracken, 7,227	N 3
Breathitt, 14,221	P 5
Breckinridge, 14,789	H 5
Bullitt, 26,090	K 5
Butler, 9,723	H 6
Caldwell, 13,179	F 6
Calloway, 27,692	E 7
Campbell, 88,501	N 3
Carlisle, 5,354	C 7
Carroll, 8,523	L 3
Carter, 19,850	P 4
Casey, 12,930	M 6
Christian, 56,224	F 7
Clark, 24,090	N 4
Clay, 18,481	O 6
Clinton, 8,174	L 7
Crittenden, 8,493	E 6
Cumberland, 6,850	L 7
Daviess, 79,486	G 5
Edmonson, 8,751	J 6
Elliott, 5,933	P 4
Estill, 12,752	O 5
Fayette, 174,323	N 4
Fleming, 11,366	O 4
Floyd, 35,889	R 5
Franklin, 34,481	M 4
Fulton, 10,183	C 7
Gallatin, 4,134	M 3
Garrard, 9,457	M 5
Grant, 9,999	M 3
Graves, 30,939	D 7
Grayson, 16,445	J 5
Green, 10,350	K 6
Greenup, 33,192	R 3
Hancock, 7,080	H 5
Hardin, 78,421	K 5
Harlan, 37,370	P 7
Harrison, 14,158	N 4
Hart, 13,980	K 6
Henderson, 36,031	F 5
Henry, 10,910	L 4
Hickman, 6,264	C 7
Hopkins, 38,167	F 6
Jackson, 10,005	N 6
Jefferson, 695,055	K 4
Jessamine, 17,430	M 5
Johnson, 17,539	R 5
Kenton, 129,440	M 3
Knott, 14,698	R 6
Knox, 23,689	O 7
Larue, 10,672	K 5
Laurel, 27,386	N 6
Lawrence, 10,726	R 4
Lee, 6,587	O 5
Leslie, 11,623	P 6
Letcher, 23,165	R 6
Lewis, 12,355	P 3
Lincoln, 16,663	M 6
Livingston, 7,596	E 6
Logan, 21,793	H 7
Lyon, 5,562	E 6
Madison, 42,730	N 5
Magoffin, 10,443	P 5
Marion, 16,714	L 5
Marshall, 20,381	E 7
Martin, 9,377	R 5
Mason, 17,273	O 3
McCracken, 58,281	D 6
McCreary, 12,548	N 7
McLean, 9,062	G 5
Meade, 18,796	J 5
Menifee, 4,050	O 5
Mercer, 15,960	M 5
Metcalfe, 8,177	K 7
Monroe, 11,642	K 7
Montgomery, 15,364	O 4
Morgan, 10,019	P 5
Muhlenberg, 27,537	G 6
Nelson, 23,477	K 5
Nicholas, 6,508	N 4
Ohio, 18,790	H 6
Oldham, 14,687	L 4
Owen, 7,470	M 3
Owsley, 5,023	O 6
Pendleton, 9,949	N 3
Perry, 25,714	P 6
Pike, 61,059	S 6
Powell, 7,704	O 5
Pulaski, 35,234	M 6
Robertson, 2,163	N 3
Rockcastle, 12,305	N 6
Rowan, 17,010	P 4
Russell, 10,542	L 7
Scott, 17,948	M 4
Shelby, 18,999	L 4
Simpson, 13,054	H 7
Spencer, 5,488	L 4
Taylor, 17,138	L 6
Todd, 10,823	G 7
Trigg, 8,620	F 7
Trimble, 5,349	L 3
Union, 15,882	F 5
Warren, 57,432	H 6
Washington, 10,728	L 5
Wayne, 14,268	M 7
Webster, 13,282	F 5
Whitley, 24,145	N 7
Wolfe, 5,669	O 5
Woodford, 14,434	M 4

CITIES and TOWNS

Zip	Name/Pop.	Key
42202	Adairville, 973	H 7
41510	Aflex, 475	S 5
42602	Albany⊙, 1,891	L 7
41001	Alexandria⊙, 3,844	N 3
41601	Allen, 724	R 5
40223	Anchorage, 1,477	K 4
40402	Annville, 500	O 6
40902	Arjay, 975	O 7
42021	Arlington, 549	D 7
41101	Ashland, 29,245	R 4
	Ashland-Huntington, ‡253,743	R 4
42206	Auburn, 1,160	H 7
† 40201	Audubon Park, 1,862	K 4
41002	Augusta, 1,434	N 3
41602	Auxier, 900	R 5
41603	Banner, 550	R 5
40906	Barbourville⊙, 3,549	O 7
40004	Bardstown⊙, 5,816	L 5
42023	Bardwell⊙, 1,049	D 7
42024	Barlow, 746	D 6
41311	Beattyville⊙, 923	O 5
41203	Beauty, 800	S 5
42320	Beaver Dam, 2,622	H 6
40006	Bedford⊙, 780	L 3
40359	Beechwood, 1,788	K 4
42207	Bee Spring, 500	J 6
41513	Belcher, 500	S 6
41514	Belfry, 800	S 5
41073	Bellevue, 8,847	S 2
40807	Benham, 1,000	R 7
42025	Benton⊙, 3,652	E 7
40403	Berea, 6,956	N 5
41605	Betsy Layne, 975	R 5
40914	Big Creek, 473	O 6
41804	Blackey, 500	R 6
40008	Bloomfield, 1,072	L 5
† 41501	Boldman, 500	R 5
41719	Bonnyman, 800	P 6
41314	Booneville⊙, 126	O 6
42101	Bowling Green⊙, 36,253	H 7
40108	Brandenburg⊙, 1,637	J 4
40409	Brodhead, 769	N 6
† 41016	Bromley, 1,069	S 2
40109	Brooks, 850	K 4
41004	Brooksville⊙, 609	N 3
42326	Browder, 450	H 6
42210	Brownsville⊙, 542	J 6
41125	Bruin, 500	P 4
40218	Buechel, 5,359	K 4
41722	Bulan, 800	P 6
40310	Burgin, 1,002	M 5
42717	Burkesville⊙, 1,717	L 7
41005	Burlington⊙, 500	R 3
42519	Burnside, 586	M 6
41006	Butler, 558	N 3
42211	Cadiz⊙, 1,987	F 7
42327	Calhoun⊙, 901	G 5
42029	Calvert City, 2,104	E 6
40011	Campbellsburg, 479	L 3
42718	Campbellsville⊙, 7,598	L 6
41301	Campton⊙, 419	O 5
42721	Caneyville, 530	J 6
40311	Carlisle⊙, 1,579	N 4
41008	Carrollton⊙, 3,884	L 3
41129	Catlettsburg⊙, 3,420	R 4
42127	Cave City, 1,818	K 6
40815	Cawood, 800	P 7
42724	Cecilia, 500	K 5
42330	Central City, 3,455	G 6
41727	Chavies, 500	P 6
42726	Clarkson, 660	J 6
42404	Clay, 1,426	F 6
40312	Clay City, 983	O 5
40313	Clearfield, 550	P 4
42031	Clinton⊙, 1,618	D 7
40414	Clover Bottom, 600	N 5
40111	Cloverport, 1,388	H 5
41076	Cold Spring, 5,348	T 3
42728	Columbia⊙, 3,234	L 6
41729	Combs, 900	P 6
42609	Cooper, 500	M 7
40701	Corbin, 7,317	N 7
42406	Corydon, 880	F 5
* 41011	Covington, 52,535	S 2
40419	Crab Orchard, 861	M 6
† 41016	Crescent Springs, 1,662	R 2
† 41076	Crestview, 657	S 2
† 41017	Crestview Hills, 1,114	R 3
42217	Crofton, 631	G 6
42034	Crutchfield, 500	D 7
40823	Cumberland, 3,317	R 6
42035	Cunningham, 700	D 7
41031	Cynthiana⊙, 6,356	N 4
41733	Daisy, 500	P 6
40422	Danville⊙, 11,542	M 5
42408	Dawson Springs, 2,830	F 6
41074	Dayton, 8,691	T 2
42409	Dixon⊙, 572	F 5
41520	Dorton, 750	R 6
42337	Drakesboro, 907	H 6
41035	Dry Ridge, 1,100	M 3
42410	Earlington, 2,321	F 6
40729	East Bernstadt, 550	N 6
42340	Echols, 648	H 6
42038	Eddyville⊙, 1,981	F 6
† 41017	Edgewood, 4,139	S 3
42129	Edmonton⊙, 958	K 7
42701	Elizabethtown⊙, 11,748	K 5
41522	Elkhorn City, 1,081	S 6
42220	Elkton⊙, 1,612	G 7
† 41018	Elsmere, 5,161	R 3
40019	Eminence, 2,225	L 4
40826	Eolia, 768	R 6
41018	Erlanger, 12,676	R 3
40828	Evarts, 1,182	P 7
41039	Ewing, 525	O 4
40118	Fairdale, 12,079	K 4
41426	Falcon, 450	P 5
40119	Falls of Rough, 700	J 5
41040	Falmouth⊙, 2,593	N 3
42039	Fancy Farm, 850	D 7
42532	Faubush, 496	M 6
41524	Fedscreek, 950	S 6
42533	Ferguson, 507	M 6
41427	Flat Fork, 500	P 5
41219	Flatgap, 450	R 5
40935	Flat Lick, 500	O 7
41139	Flatwoods, 7,380	R 4
41816	Fleming, 473	R 6
41041	Flemingsburg⊙, 2,483	O 4
41042	Florence, 11,457	R 3
42343	Fordsville, 489	H 5
40121	Fort Knox, 37,608	K 5
41017	Fort Mitchell, 6,982	S 3
41075	Fort Thomas, 16,338	S 2
† 41011	Fort Wright-Lookout Heights, 4,819	S 3
40601	Frankfort (cap.)⊙, 21,356	M 4
42134	Franklin⊙, 6,553	J 7
42411	Fredonia, 450	E 6
40322	Frenchburg⊙, 467	O 5
† 41175	Fullerton, 950	P 3
42041	Fulton, 3,250	D 7
41630	Garrett, 985	R 6
41141	Garrison, 800	P 3
40324	Georgetown⊙, 8,629	M 4
40943	Girdler, 500	O 7
42141	Glasgow⊙, 11,301	J 7
41046	Glencoe, 500	M 3
42232	Gracey, 450	F 7
42344	Graham, 500	G 6
41142	Grahn, 450	P 4
40734	Gray, 800	O 7
40434	Gray Hawk, 500	N 6
41143	Grayson⊙, 2,184	R 4
42743	Greensburg⊙, 1,990	K 6
41144	Greenup⊙, 1,284	R 3
42345	Greenville⊙, 3,875	G 6
41329	Guage, 450	P 5
42234	Guthrie, 1,200	G 7
41820	Hall, 500	R 6
40947	Hammond, 500	O 7
42048	Hardin, 522	E 7
40143	Hardinsburg⊙, 1,547	H 5
41531	Hardy, 950	S 5
40831	Harlan⊙, 3,318	P 7
40330	Harrodsburg⊙, 6,741	M 5
42347	Hartford⊙, 1,868	H 6
41514	Hatfield, 700	S 5
42348	Hawesville⊙, 1,262	H 5
41701	Hazard⊙, 5,459	P 6
41048	Hebron, 550	R 2
42420	Henderson⊙, 22,976	F 5
42050	Hickman⊙, 3,048	C 7
41076	Highland Heights, 4,400	T 3
40951	Hima, 600	O 6
† 41203	Himlerville (Beauty), 800	S 5
41822	Hindman⊙, 808	R 6
41146	Hitchins, 500	R 4
42748	Hodgenville⊙, 2,562	K 5
† 41018	Hopeful Heights, 473	R 3
42240	Hopkinsville⊙, 21,250	F 7
42749	Horse Cave, 2,068	K 6
41749	Hyden⊙, 482	P 6
† 42408	Ilsley, 500	F 6
41051	Independence⊙, 1,784	M 3
41224	Inez⊙, 469	S 5
40336	Irvine⊙, 2,918	O 5
40146	Irvington, 1,300	J 5
41339	Jackson⊙, 1,887	P 5
42629	Jamestown⊙, 1,027	L 7
41751	Jeff, 615	P 6
40299	Jeffersontown, 9,701	L 4
40337	Jeffersonville, 800	O 5
41537	Jenkins, 2,552	R 6
40440	Junction City, 1,046	M 5
40737	Keavy, 500	N 6
40847	Kenvir, 800	P 7
42053	Kevil, 504	D 6
40848	Kitts, 950	P 7
42055	Kuttawa, 453	E 6
42056	La Center, 1,044	C 6
40031	La Grange⊙, 1,713	L 4
† 41017	Lakeside Park, 2,511	R 3
40444	Lancaster⊙, 3,230	M 5
40342	Lawrenceburg⊙, 3,579	M 4
41756	Leatherwood, 750	P 6
40033	Lebanon⊙, 5,528	L 5
40150	Lebanon Junction, 1,571	K 5
41343	Leeco, 475	O 5
42754	Leitchfield⊙, 2,983	J 6
40849	Lejunior, 597	P 7
42256	Lewisburg, 651	G 6
42351	Lewisport, 1,595	H 5
* 40501	Lexington⊙, 108,137	N 4
	Lexington, ‡174,323	N 4
42539	Liberty⊙, 1,765	M 6
41646	Ligon, 500	R 6
40740	Lily, 800	N 6
41834	Littcarr, 550	R 6
42352	Livermore, 1,594	G 5
42059	Lola, 600	E 6
40741	London⊙, 4,337	N 6
42001	Lone Oak, 3,759	D 6
41542	Lookout, 600	S 6
40037	Loretto, 985	L 5
41348	Lost Creek, 500	P 6
41701	Lothair, 800	P 6
41230	Louisa⊙, 1,781	R 4
* 40201	Louisville⊙, 361,472	K 4
	Louisville, ‡826,553	K 4
41231	Lovely, 500	S 5
41232	Lowmansville, 500	R 5
40854	Loyall, 1,212	P 7
41016	Ludlow, 5,815	S 2
40855	Lynch, 800	R 7
† 40201	Lynnview, 1,165	K 4
42431	Madisonville⊙, 15,332	F 6
41547	Majestic, 600	S 5
40962	Manchester⊙, 1,664	O 6
42064	Marion⊙, 3,008	E 6
42631	Marshes Siding, 950	M 7
41649	Martin, 786	R 5
42066	Mayfield⊙, 10,724	D 7
41056	Maysville⊙, 7,411	O 3
41543	McAndrews, 975	S 5
40447	McKee⊙, 255	O 6
40448	McKinney, 475	M 6
41835	McRoberts, 1,037	R 6
41546	McVeigh, 700	S 5
41059	Melbourne, 500	T 3
41501	Meta, 600	S 5
40965	Middlesboro, 11,844	O 7
40243	Middletown, 2,500	L 4
40347	Midway, 1,278	M 4
41501	Millard, 600	S 6
40348	Millersburg, 788	N 4
40045	Milton, 756	L 3
42633	Monticello⊙, 3,618	M 7
40351	Morehead⊙, 7,191	P 4
42437	Morganfield⊙, 3,563	E 5
42261	Morgantown⊙, 1,394	H 6
42440	Mortons Gap, 1,169	F 6
41064	Mount Olivet⊙, 442	N 3
40353	Mount Sterling⊙, 5,083	N 4
40456	Mount Vernon⊙, 1,639	N 6
40047	Mount Washington, 2,020	K 4
40155	Muldraugh, 1,773	J 5
42765	Munfordville⊙, 1,233	J 6
42071	Murray⊙, 13,537	E 7
42544	Nancy, 600	M 6
41840	Neon, 705	R 6
40050	New Castle⊙, 755	L 4
40051	New Haven, 977	K 5
* 41071	Newport, 25,988	S 2
40356	Nicholasville⊙, 5,829	N 5
41357	Noctor, 500	P 5
42442	Nortonville, 699	G 6
41238	Oil Springs, 900	P 5
40219	Okolona, 17,643	K 4
41164	Olive Hill, 1,197	P 4
40972	Oneida, 700	O 6
42301	Owensboro⊙, 50,329	G 5
40359	Owenton⊙, 1,280	M 3
40360	Owingsville⊙, 1,381	O 4
42001	Paducah⊙, 31,627	D 6
41240	Paintsville⊙, 3,868	R 5
40361	Paris⊙, 7,823	N 4
42160	Park City, 567	J 6
† 41011	Park Hills, 3,999	S 2
40464	Parksville, 560	M 5
42266	Pembroke, 634	G 7
40468	Perryville, 730	M 5
40056	Pewee Valley, 950	L 4
41553	Phelps, 770	S 6
42366	Philpot, 531	H 5
41501	Pikeville⊙, 4,576	S 6
42635	Pine Knot, 950	M 7
40977	Pineville⊙, 2,817	O 7
40755	Pittsburg, 938	N 6
40258	Pleasure Ridge Park, 28,566	J 4
40057	Pleasureville, 747	L 4
42367	Powderly, 631	G 6
41845	Premium, 489	R 6
41653	Prestonsburg⊙, 3,422	R 5
42445	Princeton⊙, 6,292	F 6
40059	Prospect, 500	K 4
42450	Providence, 4,270	F 6
41169	Raceland, 1,857	R 3
40160	Radcliff, 7,881	K 5
40472	Ravenna, 784	O 5
42638	Revelo, 500	N 7
40475	Richmond⊙, 16,861	N 5
42452	Robards, 701	F 5
41169	Russell, 1,982	R 3
42642	Russell Springs, 1,641	L 6
42276	Russellville⊙, 6,456	H 7
40207	Saint Matthews, 13,152	K 4
42078	Salem, 650	E 6
40371	Salt Lick, 441	O 4
40372	Salvisa, 500	M 5
41465	Salyersville⊙, 1,196	P 5
41171	Sandy Hook⊙, 192	P 4
40982	Scalf, 500	O 7
42553	Science Hill, 470	M 6
42164	Scottsville⊙, 3,584	J 7
42455	Sebree, 1,092	F 5
† 41385	Sewell, 500	P 5
40983	Sextons Creek, 975	O 6
41562	Shelbiana, 800	R 6
40065	Shelbyville⊙, 4,182	L 4
40165	Shepherdsville⊙, 2,769	K 4

Zip	Name/Pop.	Key
40216	Shively, 19,223	K 4
40984	Sibert, 500	O 6
41085	Silver Grove, 1,365	T 3
40067	Simpsonville, 628	L 4
41763	Slemp, 500	P 6
41764	Smilax, 856	P 6
42081	Smithland⊙, 514	E 6
42171	Smiths Grove, 756	J 6
42646	Smith Town, 500	M 7
41173	Soldier, 600	P 4
42501	Somerset⊙, 10,436	M 6
41071	Southgate, 3,212	S 2
41174	South Portsmouth, 950	P 3
41175	South Shore, 676	R 3
25661	South Williamson, 850	S 5
42458	Spottsville, 914	G 5
40069	Springfield⊙, 2,961	L 5
41256	Staffordsville, 700	R 5
40484	Stanford⊙, 2,474	M 5
40380	Stanton⊙, 2,037	O 5
42647	Stearns, 900	N 7
40170	Stephensport, 500	H 5
41567	Stone, 850	S 5
42459	Sturgis, 2,210	F 5
42558	Tateville, 680	M 7
41011	Taylor Mill, 3,253	S 3
40071	Taylorsville⊙, 897	L 4
41259	Thealka, 550	R 5
41189	Tollesboro, 500	O 3
42167	Tompkinsville⊙, 2,207	K 7
42286	Trenton, 496	G 7
40486	Tyner, 590	O 6
41091	Union, 500	M 3
42461	Uniontown, 1,255	F 5
42784	Upton, 552	K 6
40272	Valley Station, 24,471	K 4
41179	Vanceburg⊙, 1,773	P 3
41265	Van Lear, 1,033	R 5
40872	Verda, 950	P 7
41092	Verona, 500	M 3
40383	Versailles⊙, 5,679	M 4
41017	Villa Hills, 1,647	R 2
40175	Vine Grove, 2,987	K 5
41572	Virgie, 600	R 6
41094	Walton, 1,801	M 3
41095	Warsaw⊙, 1,232	M 3
41667	Weeksbury, 950	R 6
41472	West Liberty⊙, 1,387	P 5
40177	West Point, 1,741	J 4
42564	West Somerset, 850	M 6
41268	West Van Lear, 975	R 5
41101	Westwood, 2,900	R 4
41669	Wheelwright, 793	R 6
42464	White Plains, 729	G 6
41858	Whitesburg⊙, 1,137	R 6
42378	Whitesville, 752	H 5
42653	Whitley City⊙, 1,060	N 7
42087	Wickliffe⊙, 1,211	C 7
41071	Wilders, 823	S 3
40769	Williamsburg⊙, 3,687	N 7
41097	Williamstown⊙, 2,063	M 3
40390	Wilmore, 3,466	M 5
40391	Winchester⊙, 13,402	N 4
42088	Wingo, 593	D 7
41011	Winston Park, 578	S 3
41394	Wolverine, 500	P 5
40771	Woodbine, 700	N 7
42001	Woodlawn, 1,639	D 6
41071	Woodlawn, 525	S 2
41776	Wooton, 750	P 6
41183	Worthington, 1,364	R 3
41501	Zebulon, 800	R 5

TENNESSEE

COUNTIES

Name/Pop.	Key
Anderson, 60,300	N 8
Bedford, 25,039	J 9
Benton, 12,126	E 8
Bledsoe, 7,643	L 9
Blount, 63,744	O 9
Bradley, 50,686	M10
Campbell, 26,045	N 8
Cannon, 8,467	J 9
Carroll, 25,741	E 9
Carter, 42,575	S 8
Cheatham, 13,199	G 8
Chester, 9,927	D 10
Claiborne, 19,420	O 8
Clay, 6,624	K 7
Cocke, 25,283	P 9
Coffee, 32,572	J 9
Crockett, 14,402	C 9
Cumberland, 20,733	L 9
Davidson, 447,877	H 8
Decatur, 9,457	E 9
De Kalb, 11,151	K 9
Dickson, 21,977	G 8
Dyer, 30,427	C 8
Fayette, 22,692	C 10
Fentress, 12,593	M 8
Franklin, 27,244	J 10
Gibson, 47,871	D 9
Giles, 22,138	G 10
Grainger, 13,948	O 8
Greene, 47,630	R 8
Grundy, 10,631	K 10
Hamblen, 38,696	P 8
Hamilton, 254,236	L 10
Hancock, 6,719	P 7
Hardeman, 22,435	C 10
Hardin, 18,212	E 10
Hawkins, 33,726	P 8
Haywood, 19,596	C 9
Henderson, 17,291	E 9
Henry, 23,749	E 8
Hickman, 12,096	G 9
Houston, 5,845	F 8
Humphreys, 13,560	F 8
Jackson, 8,141	K 8
Jefferson, 24,940	P 8
Johnson, 11,569	T 7
Knox, 276,293	O 9
Lake, 7,896	B 8
Lauderdale, 20,271	B 9
Lawrence, 29,097	G 10
Lewis, 6,761	F 9
Lincoln, 24,318	H 10
Loudon, 24,266	N 9
Macon, 12,315	J 7
Madison, 65,727	D 9
Marion, 20,577	K 10
Marshall, 17,319	H 10
Maury, 43,376	G 9
McMinn, 35,462	M10
McNairy, 18,369	D 10
Meigs, 5,219	M 9
Monroe, 23,475	N 10
Montgomery, 62,721	G 8
Moore, 3,568	J 10
Morgan, 13,619	M 8
Obion, 29,936	C 8
Overton, 14,866	L 8
Perry, 5,238	F 9
Pickett, 3,774	M 7
Polk, 11,669	N 10
Putnam, 35,487	K 8
Rhea, 17,202	M 9
Roane, 38,881	M 9
Robertson, 29,102	H 7
Rutherford, 59,428	J 9
Scott, 14,762	M 8
Sequatchie, 6,331	L 10
Sevier, 28,241	O 9
Shelby, 722,014	B 10
Smith, 12,509	J 8
Stewart, 7,319	F 7
Sullivan, 127,329	S 7
Sumner, 56,106	J 8
Tipton, 28,001	B 9
Trousdale, 5,155	J 8
Unicoi, 15,254	S 8
Union, 9,072	O 8
Van Buren, 3,758	L 9
Warren, 26,972	K 9
Washington, 73,924	R 8
Wayne, 12,365	F 10
Weakley, 28,827	D 8
White, 17,088	L 9
Williamson, 34,330	H 9
Wilson, 36,999	J 8

KENTUCKY

AREA 40,395 sq. mi.
POPULATION 3,219,311
CAPITAL Frankfort
LARGEST CITY Louisville
HIGHEST POINT Black Mtn. 4,145 ft.
SETTLED IN 1774
ADMITTED TO UNION June 1, 1792
POPULAR NAME Blue Grass State
STATE FLOWER Goldenrod
STATE BIRD Cardinal

TENNESSEE

AREA 42,244 sq. mi.
POPULATION 3,924,164
CAPITAL Nashville
LARGEST CITY Memphis
HIGHEST POINT Clingmans Dome 6,643 ft.
SETTLED IN 1757
ADMITTED TO UNION June 1, 1796
POPULAR NAME Volunteer State
STATE FLOWER Iris
STATE BIRD Mockingbird

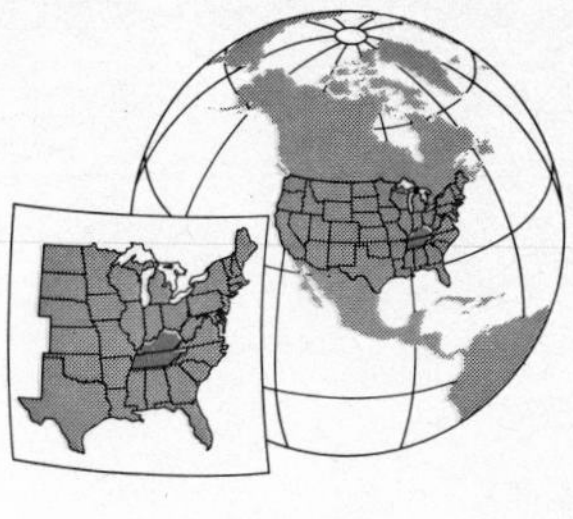

CITIES and TOWNS

Zip	Name/Pop.	Key
37010	Adams, 458	G 7
38310	Adamsville, 1,344	E 10
37616	Afton, 550	R 8
38001	Alamo⊙, 2,499	C 9
37701	Alcoa, 7,739	N 9
37012	Alexandria, 680	J 8
38501	Algood, 1,808	K 8
38504	Allardt, 610	M 8
38541	Allons, 600	L 8
37301	Altamont⊙, 546	K 10
38449	Ardmore, 601	H 10
38002	Arlington, 1,349	B 10
38506	Armathwaite, 625	M 8
37707	Arthur, 500	O 7
37015	Ashland City⊙, 2,027	G 8
37303	Athens⊙, 11,790	M10
38004	Atoka, 446	B 10
38220	Atwood, 937	D 9
37304	Bakewell, 600	L 10
† 37650	Banner Hill, 2,517	R 8
38005	Bartlett, 1,150	B 10
38311	Bath Springs, 725	E 10
38544	Baxter, 1,229	K 8
37708	Bean Station, 500	P 8
37018	Beechgrove, 600	J 9
37305	Beersheba Springs, 560	K 10
37205	Belle Meade	H 8
38006	Bells, 1,474	C 9
38314	Bemis, 1,883	D 9
37307	Benton⊙, 749	M10
† 37201	Berry Hill	H 8
† 37027	Berry's Chapel, 1,345	H 9
38315	Bethel Springs, 781	D 10
38221	Big Sandy, 539	E 8
37308	Birchwood, 900	M10
37709	Blaine, 650	O 8
37660	Bloomingdale, 3,120	R 7
38545	Bloomington Springs, 800	K 8
37617	Blountville⊙, 900	S 7
37618	Bluff City, 947	S 8
38008	Bolivar⊙, 6,674	C 10
38316	Bradford, 968	D 8
37658	Braemar-Hampton, 1,100	S 8
37027	Brentwood, 1,091	H 8
37710	Briceville, 850	N 8
38011	Brighton, 952	B 10
37620	Bristol, 20,064	S 7
38012	Brownsville⊙, 7,011	C 9
38317	Bruceton, 1,450	E 8
38014	Brunswick, 500	B 10
38318	Buena Vista, 500	E 9
37711	Bulls Gap, 774	P 8
37640	Butler, 500	T 8
38549	Byrdstown⊙, 582	L 7
37309	Calhoun, 624	M10
38320	Camden⊙, 3,052	E 8
38129	Capleville, 450	B 10
37030	Carthage⊙, 2,491	K 8
37714	Caryville, 648	N 8
38551	Celina⊙, 1,370	K 7
37033	Centerville⊙, 2,592	G 9
37034	Chapel Hill, 752	H 9
37310	Charleston, 792	M10
37036	Charlotte⊙, 610	G 8
* 37401	Chattanooga⊙, 119,082	K 10
	Chattanooga, ‡304,927	K 10
37642	Church Hill, 2,822	R 7
37715	Clairfield, 650	O 7
38553	Clarkrange, 675	L 8
37040	Clarksville⊙, 31,719	G 7
37311	Cleveland⊙, 20,651	M10
38425	Clifton, 737	F 10
37716	Clinton⊙, 4,794	N 8
37719	Coalfield, 712	N 8
37313	Coalmont, 518	K 10
37314	Cokercreek, 500	N 10
37315	Collegedale, 3,031	M10
38017	Collierville, 3,625	B 10
38450	Collinwood, 922	F 10
37663	Colonial Heights, 3,027	R 8
38401	Columbia⊙, 21,471	G 9
37720	Concord, 500	N 9
38501	Cookeville⊙, 14,270	L 8
37317	Copperhill, 563	N 10
38018	Cordova, 600	B 10
37047	Cornersville, 655	H 10
37721	Corryton, 500	O 8
38326	Counce, 975	E 10
38019	Covington⊙, 5,801	B 9
37318	Cowan, 1,772	K 10
37723	Crab Orchard, 900	M 9
38555	Crossville⊙, 5,381	L 9
37051	Cumberland Furnace, 800	G 8
38452	Cypress Inn, 500	F 10
37725	Dandridge⊙, 1,270	O 8
37321	Dayton⊙, 4,361	L 9
37322	Decatur⊙, 698	M 9
38329	Decaturville⊙, 958	E 9
37324	Decherd, 2,148	J 10
37055	Dickson, 5,665	G 8
37214	Donelson	H 8
37058	Dover⊙, 1,179	F 8
38559	Doyle, 1,205	K 9
38225	Dresden⊙, 1,939	D 8
38023	Drummonds, 700	A 10
37326	Ducktown, 562	N 10
37327	Dunlap⊙, 1,672	L 10
38330	Dyer, 2,501	D 8
38024	Dyersburg⊙, 14,523	C 8
† 37801	Eagleton, 5,345	O 9
† 37311	East Cleveland, 1,870	M10
37412	East Ridge, 21,799	L 11
37732	Elgin, 500	M 8
37643	Elizabethton⊙, 12,269	S 8
37734	Elk Valley, 750	N 7
38029	Ellendale, 1,500	B 10
† 37601	Embreeville Junction, 1,293	R 8
37735	Emory Gap, 500	M 9
37329	Englewood, 1,878	M10
37061	Erin⊙, 1,157	F 8
37650	Erwin⊙, 4,715	S 8
37330	Estill Springs, 919	J 10
38456	Ethridge, 600	G 10
37331	Etowah, 3,736	M10
37332	Evensville, 475	M 9
37062	Fairview, 1,630	G 9
37656	Fall Branch, 825	R 8
37334	Fayetteville⊙, 7,030	H 10
38030	Finley, 950	B 8
37335	Flintville, 500	H 10
38031	Forest Hill, 850	B 10
† 37201	Forest Hills	H 8
38032	Fort Pillow, 700	B 9
37064	Franklin⊙, 9,404	H 9
38034	Friendship, 441	C 9
37737	Friendsville, 575	N 9
38337	Gadsden, 523	D 9
38562	Gainesboro⊙, 1,101	K 8
37066	Gallatin⊙, 13,093	H 8
38037	Gates, 523	C 9
37738	Gatlinburg, 2,329	O 9
38038	Germantown, 3,474	B 10
37071	Gladeville, 500	J 8
38229	Gleason, 1,314	D 8
37072	Goodlettsville	H 8
38563	Gordonsville, 601	K 8
37337	Grandview, 1,250	M 9
37338	Graysville, 951	L 10
37073	Green Brier, 2,279	H 8
37743	Greeneville⊙, 13,722	R 8
38230	Greenfield, 2,050	D 8
38565	Grimsley, 500	L 2
37339	Gruetli, 910	K 10
† 37766	Habersham, 800	N 8
38040	Halls, 2,323	C 9
38461	Hampshire, 500	G 9
37658	Hampton-Braemar, 1,100	S 8
37748	Harriman, 8,734	M 9
37341	Harrison, 500	L 10
37752	Harrogate, 950	O 8
37074	Hartsville⊙, 2,243	J 8
37755	Helenwood, 675	M 8
38340	Henderson⊙, 3,581	D 10
38041	Henning, 605	B 9
37343	Hixson, 6,188	L 10
38462	Hohenwald⊙, 3,385	F 9
38342	Hollow Rock, 722	E 8
38343	Humboldt, 10,066	D 9
38344	Huntingdon⊙, 3,661	E 8
37345	Huntland, 849	J 10
37756	Huntsville⊙, 337	N 8
37079	Indian Mound, 600	F 7
† 37201	Inglewood	H 8
38463	Iron City, 504	F 10
37757	Jacksboro⊙, 689	N 8
38301	Jackson⊙, 39,996	D 9
38556	Jamestown⊙, 1,899	M 8
37347	Jasper⊙, 1,811	K 10
37760	Jefferson City, 5,124	P 8
37762	Jellico, 2,235	N 7
37601	Johnson City, 33,770	S 8
37659	Jonesboro⊙, 1,510	R 8
37921	Karns, 1,105	N 9
38233	Kenton, 1,439	C 8
† 34347	Kimball, 807	K 10
* 37660	Kingsport, 31,938	R 7
37763	Kingston⊙, 4,142	N 9
* 37901	Knoxville⊙, 174,587	O 9
	Knoxville, ‡400,337	O 9
37349	Laager, 675	K 10
37083	Lafayette⊙, 2,583	J 7
37766	La Follette, 6,902	N 8
37769	Lake City, 1,923	N 8
37416	Lake Hills-Murray Hills, 7,806	L 10
† 37138	Lakewood, 2,500	H 8
37086	La Vergne, 2,825	H 9
38464	Lawrenceburg⊙, 8,889	G 10
37087	Lebanon⊙, 12,492	J 8
37771	Lenoir City, 5,324	N 9
37091	Lewisburg⊙, 7,207	H 10
38351	Lexington⊙, 4,955	E 9
37681	Limestone, 500	R 8
37096	Linden⊙, 1,062	F 9
38570	Livingston⊙, 3,050	L 8
37097	Lobelville, 773	F 9
† 37662	Long Island, 1,352	S 7
37350	Lookout Mountain, 1,741	L 11
38469	Loretto, 1,375	G 10
37774	Loudon⊙, 3,728	N 9
37777	Louisville, 500	N 9
37351	Lupton City, 750	L 10
37779	Luttrell, 819	O 8
38471	Lutts, 850	F 10

(continued on following page)

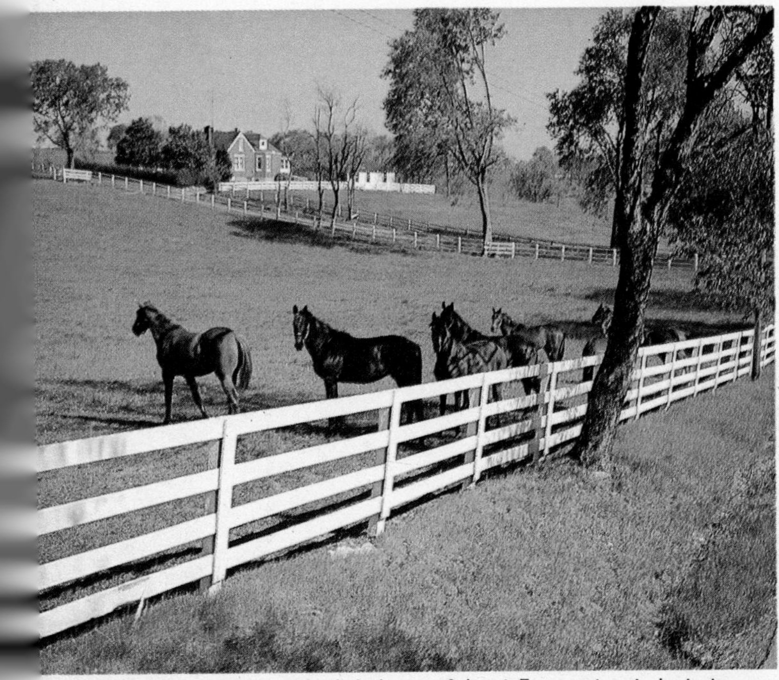

Jack Zehrt — Shostal Associates

Sleek racehorses enjoy a patch of shade on a Calumet Farm pasture in Lexington, Kentucky. More than half the country's winning racehorses are from Inner Bluegrass area farms.

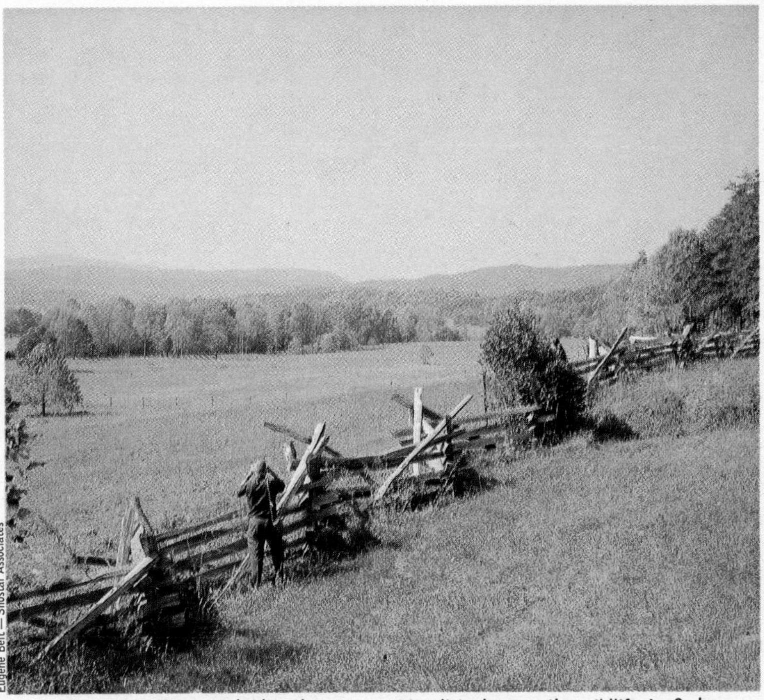

Eugene Belt — Shostal Associates

Using field glasses to bridge the gap, a naturalist observes the wildlife in Cades Cove, Tennessee. Mist-shrouded Great Smoky Mountains are in the distance.

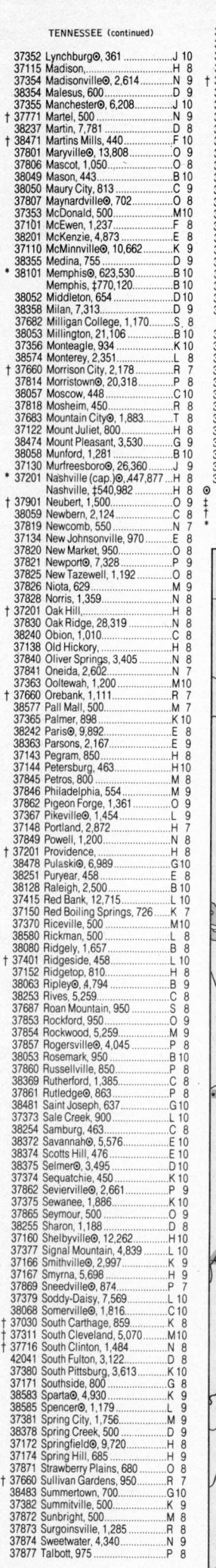

TENNESSEE (continued)

37352 Lynchburg⊙, 361 .....J 10
37115 Madison, ...H 8
37354 Madisonville⊙, 2,614 .....N 9
38354 Malesus, 600 .....D 9
37355 Manchester⊙, 6,208 .....J 10
† 37771 Martel, 500 .....N 9
38237 Martin, 7,781 .....D 8
† 38471 Martins Mills, 440 .....F 10
37801 Maryville⊙, 13,808 .....O 9
37806 Mascot, 1,050 .....O 8
38049 Mason, 443 .....B 10
38050 Maury City, 813 .....D 9
37807 Maynardville⊙, 702 .....O 8
37353 McDonald, 500 .....M 10
37101 McEwen, 1,237 .....F 8
38201 McKenzie, 4,873 .....D 8
37110 McMinnville⊙, 10,662 .....K 9
38355 Medina, 755 .....D 9
* 38101 Memphis⊙, 623,530 .....B 10
        Memphis, ‡770,120 .....B 10
38052 Middleton, 654 .....D 10
38358 Milan, 7,313 .....D 9
37682 Milligan College, 1,170 .....S, 8
38053 Millington, 21,106 .....B 10
37356 Monteagle, 934 .....K 10
38574 Monterey, 2,351 .....L 8
† 37660 Morrison City, 2,178 .....R 7
37814 Morristown⊙, 20,318 .....P 8
38057 Moscow, 448 .....C 10
37818 Mosheim, 450 .....P 8
37683 Mountain City⊙, 1,883 .....T 7
37122 Mount Juliet, 800 .....H 8
38474 Mount Pleasant, 3,530 .....G 9
38058 Munford, 1,281 .....B 10
37130 Murfreesboro⊙, 26,360 .....J 9
* 37201 Nashville (cap.)⊙, 447,877 .....H 8
        Nashville, ‡540,982 .....H 8
† 37901 Neubert, 1,500 .....O 9
38059 Newbern, 2,124 .....C 8
37819 Newcomb, 550 .....N 7
37134 New Johnsonville, 970 .....E 8
37820 New Market, 950 .....O 8
37821 Newport⊙, 7,328 .....P 9
37825 New Tazewell, 1,192 .....N 8
37826 Niota, 629 .....M 9
37828 Norris, 1,359 .....N 8
† 37201 Oak Hill, ...H 8
37830 Oak Ridge, 28,319 .....N 8
38240 Obion, 1,010 .....C 8
37138 Old Hickory, ...H 8
37840 Oliver Springs, 3,405 .....N 8
37841 Oneida, 2,602 .....N 7
37363 Ooltewah, 1,200 .....M 10
† 37660 Orebank, 1,111 .....R 7
38577 Pall Mall, 500 .....M 7
37365 Palmer, 898 .....K 10
38242 Paris⊙, 9,892 .....E 8
38363 Parsons, 2,167 .....E 9
37143 Pegram, 850 .....H 8
37144 Petersburg, 463 .....H 10
37845 Petros, 800 .....N 8
37846 Philadelphia, 554 .....M 9
37862 Pigeon Forge, 1,361 .....P 9
37367 Pikeville⊙, 1,454 .....L 9
37148 Portland, 2,872 .....H 7
37849 Powell, 1,200 .....N 8
† 37201 Providence, ...H 8
38478 Pulaski⊙, 6,989 .....G 10
38251 Puryear, 458 .....E 8
38128 Raleigh, 2,500 .....B 10
37415 Red Bank, 12,715 .....L 10
37150 Red Boiling Springs, 726 .....K 7
37370 Riceville, 500 .....M 10
38580 Rickman, 500 .....L 8
38080 Ridgely, 1,657 .....B 8
† 37401 Ridgeside, 458 .....L 10
37152 Ridgetop, 810 .....H 8
38063 Ripley⊙, 4,794 .....B 9
38253 Rives, 5,259 .....C 8
37687 Roan Mountain, 950 .....S 8
37853 Rockford, 950 .....O 9
37854 Rockwood, 5,259 .....M 9
37857 Rogersville⊙, 4,045 .....P 8
38053 Rosemark, 950 .....B 10
37860 Russellville, 850 .....P 8
38369 Rutherford, 1,385 .....C 8
37861 Rutledge⊙, 863 .....P 8
38481 Saint Joseph, 637 .....G 10
37773 Sale Creek, 900 .....L 10
38254 Samburg, 463 .....C 8
38372 Savannah⊙, 5,576 .....E 10
38374 Scotts Hill, 476 .....E 10
38375 Selmer⊙, 3,495 .....D 10
37374 Sequatchie, 450 .....K 10
37862 Sevierville⊙, 2,661 .....P 9
37375 Sewanee, 1,886 .....K 10
37865 Seymour, 500 .....O 9
38255 Sharon, 1,188 .....D 8
37160 Shelbyville⊙, 12,262 .....H 10
37377 Signal Mountain, 4,839 .....L 10
37166 Smithville⊙, 2,997 .....K 9
37167 Smyrna, 5,698 .....H 9
37869 Sneedville⊙, 874 .....P 7
37379 Soddy-Daisy, 7,569 .....L 10
† 37311 South Cleveland, 5,070 .....M 10
† 37716 South Clinton, 1,484 .....N 8
42041 South Fulton, 3,122 .....D 8
37380 South Pittsburg, 3,613 .....K 10
37171 Southside, 800 .....G 8
38583 Sparta⊙, 4,930 .....K 9
38585 Spencer⊙, 1,179 .....L 9
37381 Spring City, 1,756 .....M 9
38878 Spring Creek, 500 .....D 9
37172 Springfield⊙, 9,720 .....H 8
37174 Spring Hill, 685 .....H 9
37871 Strawberry Plains, 680 .....O 9
† 37660 Sullivan Gardens, 950 .....R 7
38483 Summertown, 700 .....G 10
37382 Summitville, 500 .....K 9
37872 Sunbright, 500 .....M 8
37873 Surgoinsville, 1,285 .....R 8
37874 Sweetwater, 4,340 .....N 9
37877 Talbott, 975 .....P 8

37879 Tazewell⊙, 1,860 .....O 8
37385 Tellico Plains, 773 .....N 10
37880 Ten Mile, 700 .....M 9
37178 Tennessee Ridge, 664 .....F 8
† 37401 Tiftona, 1,750 .....L 11
38079 Tiptonville⊙, 2,229 .....B 8
37387 Tracy City, 1,388 .....K 10
37883 Treadway, 712 .....P 8
38382 Trenton⊙, 4,226 .....D 9
38258 Trezevant, 877 .....D 8
37259 Trimble, 675 .....C 8
38260 Troy, 826 .....C 8
37388 Tullahoma, 15,311 .....J 10
37743 Tusculum, 1,157 .....P 8
37692 Unicoi, 500 .....S 8
38261 Union City⊙, 11,925 .....C 8
37393 Victoria, 800 .....K 10
37885 Vonore, 524 .....N 9
37887 Wartburg⊙, 541 .....M 8
37183 Wartrace, 616 .....J 9
37184 Watertown, 1,061 .....J 8
37185 Waverly⊙, 3,794 .....F 8
38485 Waynesboro⊙, 1,983 .....F 10
38074 Western State Hospital,
        2,900 .....C 10
37186 Westmoreland, 1,423 .....J 7
37187 White Bluff, 516 .....G 8
38116 Whitehaven, 19,000 .....A 10
37188 White House, 650 .....H 8
37890 White Pine, 1,532 .....P 8
37891 Whitesburg, 500 .....P 8
37396 Whiteside, 523 .....K 10
38075 Whiteville, 992 .....C 10
37397 Whitwell, 1,669 .....L 10
37398 Winchester⊙, 5,211 .....J 10
37892 Winfield, 950 .....M 7
37190 Woodbury⊙, 1,725 .....J 9
37191 Woodlawn, 500 .....G 7

⊙ County seat.
‡ Population of metropolitan area.
† Zip of nearest p.o.
* Multiple zips

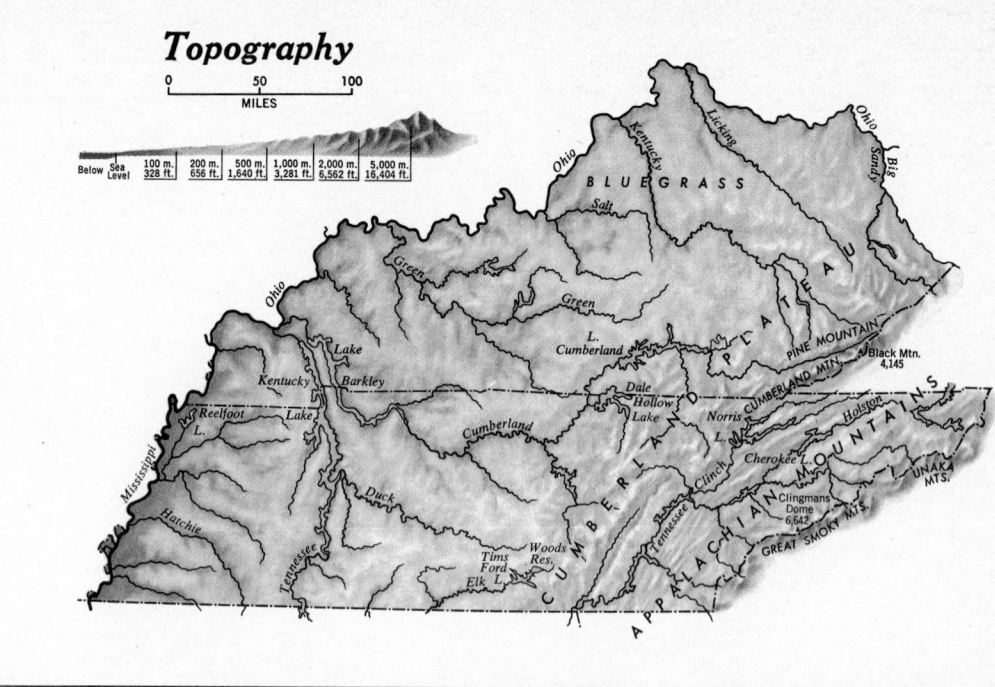

Topography

0   50   100
MILES

| Below Sea Level | 100 m. 328 ft. | 200 m. 656 ft. | 500 m. 1,640 ft. | 1,000 m. 3,281 ft. | 2,000 m. 6,562 ft. | 5,000 m. 16,404 ft. |

KENTUCKY
and
TENNESSEE

SCALE
0 5 10   20   30   40MI.
0 5 10 20   30   40KM.
State Capitals.........................⊛
County Seats..........................◉
C.S. HAMMOND & Co., N.Y.

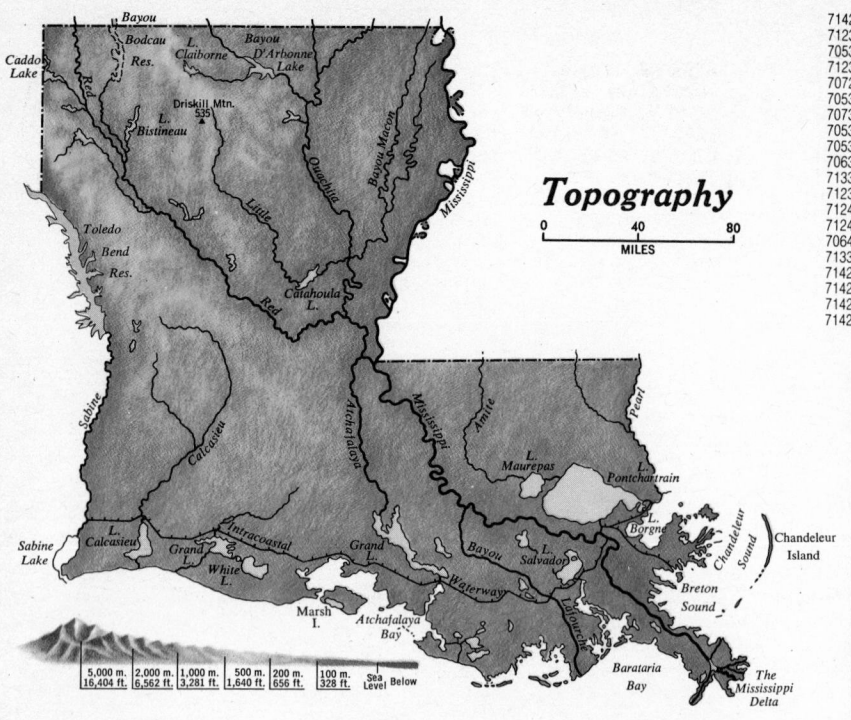

Topography

0   40   80
MILES

5,000 m. 2,000 m. 1,000 m. 500 m. 200 m. 100 m. Sea
16,404 ft. 6,562 ft. 3,281 ft. 1,640 ft. 656 ft. 328 ft. Level Below

PARISHES

Acadia, 52,109		F 6
Allen, 20,794		E 5
Ascension, 37,086		J 6
Assumption, 19,654		H 7
Avoyelles, 37,751		G 4
Beauregard, 22,888		D 5
Bienville, 16,024		D 2
Bossier, 64,519		C 1
Caddo, 230,184		C 1
Calcasieu, 145,415		D 6
Caldwell, 9,354		F 2
Cameron, 8,194		D 7
Catahoula, 11,769		G 3
Claiborne, 17,024		D 1
Concordia, 22,578		G 4
De Soto, 22,764		C 2
East Baton Rouge, 285,167		K 1
East Carroll, 12,884		H 1
East Feliciana, 17,657		H 5
Evangeline, 31,932		F 5
Franklin, 23,946		G 2
Grant, 13,671		E 3
Iberia, 57,397		G 7
Iberville, 30,746		H 6
Jackson, 15,963		E 2
Jefferson, 337,568		K 7
Jefferson Davis, 29,554		E 6
Lafayette, 109,716		F 6
Lafourche, 68,941		J 7
La Salle, 13,295		F 3
Lincoln, 33,800		E 1
Livingston, 36,511		L 2
Madison, 15,065		H 2
Morehouse, 32,463		G 1
Natchitoches, 35,219		D 3
Orleans, 593,471		L 6
Ouachita, 115,387		F 1
Plaquemines, 25,225		L 8
Pointe Coupee, 22,022		G 5
Rapides, 118,078		E 4
Red River, 9,226		D 2
Richland, 21,774		G 2
Sabine, 18,638		C 3
Saint Bernard, 51,185		L 7
Saint Charles, 29,550		K 7
Saint Helena, 9,937		J 5
Saint James, 19,733		J 3
Saint John the Baptist, 23,813		M 3
Saint Landry, 80,364		F 5
Saint Martin, 32,453		G 6
Saint Mary, 60,752		H 7
Saint Tammany, 63,585		L 6
Tangipahoa, 65,875		K 5
Tensas, 9,732		H 2
Terrebonne, 76,049		J 8
Union, 18,447		F 1
Vermilion, 43,071		F 7
Vernon, 53,794		D 4
Washington, 41,987		K 5
Webster, 39,939		D 1
West Baton Rouge, 16,864		H 6
West Carroll, 13,028		H 1
West Feliciana, 11,376		H 5
Winn, 16,369		E 3

CITIES and TOWNS

Zip	Name/Pop.	Key
70510	Abbeville⊙, 10,996	F 7
70420	Abita Springs, 839	L 6
71316	Acme, 212	G 4
† 70774	Acy, 570	L 3
70710	Addis, 724	J 2
70544	Adeline, 200	H 7
† 70711	Albany, 700	M 1
71016	Alberta, 300	L 2
† 71301	Alexandria⊙, 41,557	E 4
70340	Amelia, 2,292	H 7
70422	Amite⊙, 3,593	K 5
71403	Anacoco, 575	D 4
† 71301	Anandale, 1,779	F 4
70426	Angie, 317	L 5
70712	Angola, 550	G 5
70032	Arabi, 12,000	K 7
† 70736	Arbroth, 250	H 5
71001	Arcadia⊙, 2,970	E 1
71218	Archibald, 300	G 2
† 71343	Archie, 200	G 3
† 70456	Arcola, 200	K 5
70512	Arnaudville, 1,673	G 6
71002	Ashland, 211	D 2
71003	Athens, 387	E 1
71404	Atlanta, 342	E 3
70513	Avery Island, 591	G 7
70713	Bains, 400	H 5
70714	Baker, 8,281	K 1
70514	Baldwin, 2,117	H 7
71405	Ball, 500	F 4
† 70401	Baptist, 150	M 1
70036	Barataria, 950	K 7
71320	Bordelonville, 450	G 4
70515	Basile, 1,779	E 5
71219	Baskin, 177	G 2
71220	Bastrop⊙, 14,713	G 1
* 70801	Baton Rouge (cap.)⊙, 165,963	K 2
	Baton Rouge, ‡285,167	K 2
† 70754	Bayou Barbary, 200	M 2
† 70360	Bayou Cane, 9,077	J 7
70716	Bayou Goula, 850	J 3
70380	Bayou Vista, 5,121	H 7
71220	Beekman, 300	G 1
70675	Bel, 150	C 6
71004	Belcher, 400	C 1
70630	Bell City, 350	D 6
† 70341	Belle Alliance, 350	K 3
70037	Belle Chasse, 950	O 4
† 71330	Belledeau, 450	F 4
† 70341	Belle Rose, 900	K 3
† 71468	Bellwood, 150	D 3
71406	Belmont, 150	C 3
71005	Benson, 200	C 3
71407	Bentley, 300	E 3
71006	Benton⊙, 1,493	C 1
71222	Bernice, 1,794	E 1
† 70040	Bertrandville, 175	L 7
70342	Berwick, 4,168	H 7
71007	Bethany, 250	B 2
71008	Bienville, 287	D 2
71009	Blanchard, 806	C 1
70427	Bogalusa, 18,412	L 5
† 71064	Bolinger, 250	C 1
71223	Bonita, 533	G 1
70038	Boothville, 300	M 8
71320	Bordelonville, 450	G 4
71224	Bosco, 480	F 2
71010	Bossier City, 41,595	C 1
† 70353	Boudreaux, 275	J 8
70343	Bourg, 900	J 7
70039	Boutte, 950	N 4
71409	Boyce, 1,240	E 4
† 70040	Braithwaite, 550	P 4
70517	Breaux Bridge, 4,942	G 6
70718	Brittany, 290	L 3
70518	Broussard, 1,707	F 6
70719	Brusly, 1,282	J 2
71322	Bunkie, 4,395	F 4
70041	Buras-Triumph, 4,113	L 8
70738	Burnside, 500	L 3
70431	Bush, 275	L 5
71225	Cade, 800	G 6
71433	Calcasieu, 400	E 4
71225	Calhoun, 653	F 2
71410	Calvin, 286	E 3
70631	Cameron⊙, 975	D 7
71411	Campti, 1,078	D 3
70584	Cankton, 260	F 6
70520	Carencro, 2,302	F 6
70042	Carlisle, 975	L 7
70721	Carville, 950	K 3
71016	Castor, 178	D 2
70521	Cecelia, 550	G 6
71323	Center Point, 850	F 4
70522	Centerville, 500	H 7
70723	Central, 546	L 3
† 70395	Chacahoula, 150	J 7
70043	Chalmette⊙, 15,000	P 4
70523	Charenton, 950	H 7
71324	Chase, 150	G 2
70524	Chataignier, 725	F 5
71226	Chatham, 827	F 2
70344	Chauvin, 900	J 8
71325	Cheneyville, 1,082	F 4
71227	Choudrant, 555	F 1
70525	Church Point, 3,865	F 6
71414	Clarence, 448	E 3
71415	Clarks, 889	F 2
71228	Clay, 400	E 2
71326	Clayton, 1,103	H 3
70722	Clinton⊙, 1,884	J 5
71416	Cloutierville, 250	E 3
71417	Colfax⊙, 1,892	E 3
71229	Collinston, 397	G 1
71418	Columbia⊙, 1,000	F 2
70723	Convent⊙, 650	L 3
71419	Converse, 375	C 3
† 70785	Corbin, 189	L 1
71327	Cottonport, 1,846	F 5
71018	Cotton Valley, 1,261	D 1
† 71018	Couchwood, 150	D 1
71019	Coushatta⊙, 1,492	D 2
70433	Covington⊙, 7,170	K 5
† 70656	Cravens, 475	E 5
70632	Creole, 175	D 7
† 70764	Crescent, 300	J 2
71020	Creston, 150	E 3
70526	Crowley⊙, 16,104	F 6
71230	Crowville, 400	G 2
71021	Cullen, 1,956	D 1
70345	Cut Off, 750	K 7
† 70040	Dalcour, 275	P 4
70725	Darrow, 500	K 3
70046	Davant, 650	L 7
70528	Delcambre, 1,975	F 7
71232	Delhi, 2,887	H 2
71233	Delta, 153	J 2
70726	Denham Springs, 6,752	L 1
70633	De Quincy, 3,448	D 6
70634	De Ridder⊙, 8,030	D 5
70030	Des Allemands, 2,318	N 4
70047	Destrehan, 800	N 4
71328	Deville, 500	F 4
70048	Diamond, 370	L 7
71022	Dixie, 330	C 1
† 71055	Dixie Inn, 456	D 1
71422	Dodson, 457	E 2
70346	Donaldsonville⊙, 7,367	J 3
70352	Donner, 500	J 7
71234	Downsville, 250	F 1
71023	Doyline, 716	D 1
70637	Dry Creek, 480	D 5
71423	Dry Prong, 352	E 3
71235	Dubach, 1,096	E 1
71024	Dubberly, 212	D 1
70353	Dulac, 225	J 8
71236	Dunn, 225	G 2
70728	Duplessis, 700	K 2
70529	Duson, 1,199	F 6
71247	East Hodge, 200	E 2
70530	Easton, 365	F 6
71025	East Point, 200	D 2
71330	Echo, 450	F 4
70049	Edgard⊙, 300	M 3
71019	Edgefield, 201	D 2
† 70668	Edgerly, 250	C 6
71331	Effie, 950	F 4
70638	Elizabeth, 504	E 4
71424	Elmer, 445	E 4
† 71051	Elm Grove, 350	C 2
† 70775	Elm Park, 200	H 5
70532	Elton, 1,598	E 6
71425	Enterprise, 300	G 3
71237	Epps, 448	G 1
70533	Erath, 2,024	F 7
71238	Eros, 164	F 2
70729	Erwinville, 790	H 5
70534	Estherwood, 661	F 6
70730	Ethel, 350	H 5
70535	Eunice, 11,390	F 6
70537	Evangeline, 400	F 6
70639	Evans, 400	D 5
71333	Evergreen, 307	F 5
71239	Extension, 950	G 3
71240	Fairbanks, 150	F 1
71241	Farmerville⊙, 3,416	F 1
70640	Fenton, 404	E 6
71334	Ferriday, 5,239	H 3
71426	Fisher, 300	D 4
71427	Flatwoods, 450	E 4
71428	Flora, 200	D 3
71429	Florien, 639	D 4
70436	Fluker, 400	K 5
70437	Folsom, 249	K 5
70732	Fordoche, 488	G 5
71242	Forest, 221	H 1
71430	Forest Hill, 370	E 4
† 71449	Fort Jesup, 950	C 3
71243	Fort Necessity, 150	G 2
70538	Franklin⊙, 9,325	H 7
70438	Franklinton⊙, 3,562	K 5
71027	Frierson, 700	C 2
71039	Fryeburg, 150	D 2
† 70769	Galvez, 200	L 2
70540	Garden City, 515	H 7
70051	Garyville, 2,474	M 3
70734	Geismar, 300	K 3
71432	Georgetown, 306	F 3
71028	Gibsland, 1,380	E 1
70356	Gibson, 950	H 7
71336	Gilbert, 746	G 2
71029	Gilliam, 211	C 1
71244	Girard, 250	G 2
† 70538	Glencoe, 200	H 7
71433	Glenmora, 1,651	E 4
71030	Gloster, 975	C 2
70736	Glynn, 400	H 5
70357	Golden Meadow, 2,681	K 7
71031	Goldonna, 337	E 2
70737	Gonzales, 4,512	K 2
70079	Good Hope, 950	N 4
71337	Good Pine, 535	F 3
71245	Grambling, 4,407	E 1
70052	Gramercy, 2,567	M 3
71032	Grand Cane, 284	C 2
70643	Grand Chenier, 710	E 7
70541	Grand Coteau, 1,301	F 6
70358	Grand Isle, 2,236	L 8
70601	Grand Lake, 400	D 7

LOUISIANA

SCALE
0 5 10   20   30   40 MI.
0 5 10   20   30   40 KM.

State Capitals .... ⊛
Parish Seats .... ⊙
Canals .... ––––

© C.S. HAMMOND & Co., N.Y.

(continued on following page)

AREA 48,523 sq. mi.
POPULATION 3,643,180
CAPITAL Baton Rouge
LARGEST CITY New Orleans
HIGHEST POINT Driskill Mtn. 535 ft.
SETTLED IN 1699
ADMITTED TO UNION April 30, 1812
POPULAR NAME Pelican State
STATE FLOWER Magnolia
STATE BIRD Eastern Brown Pelican

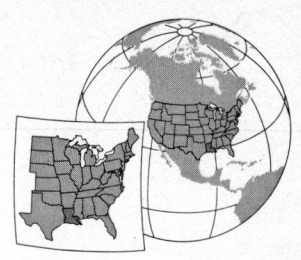

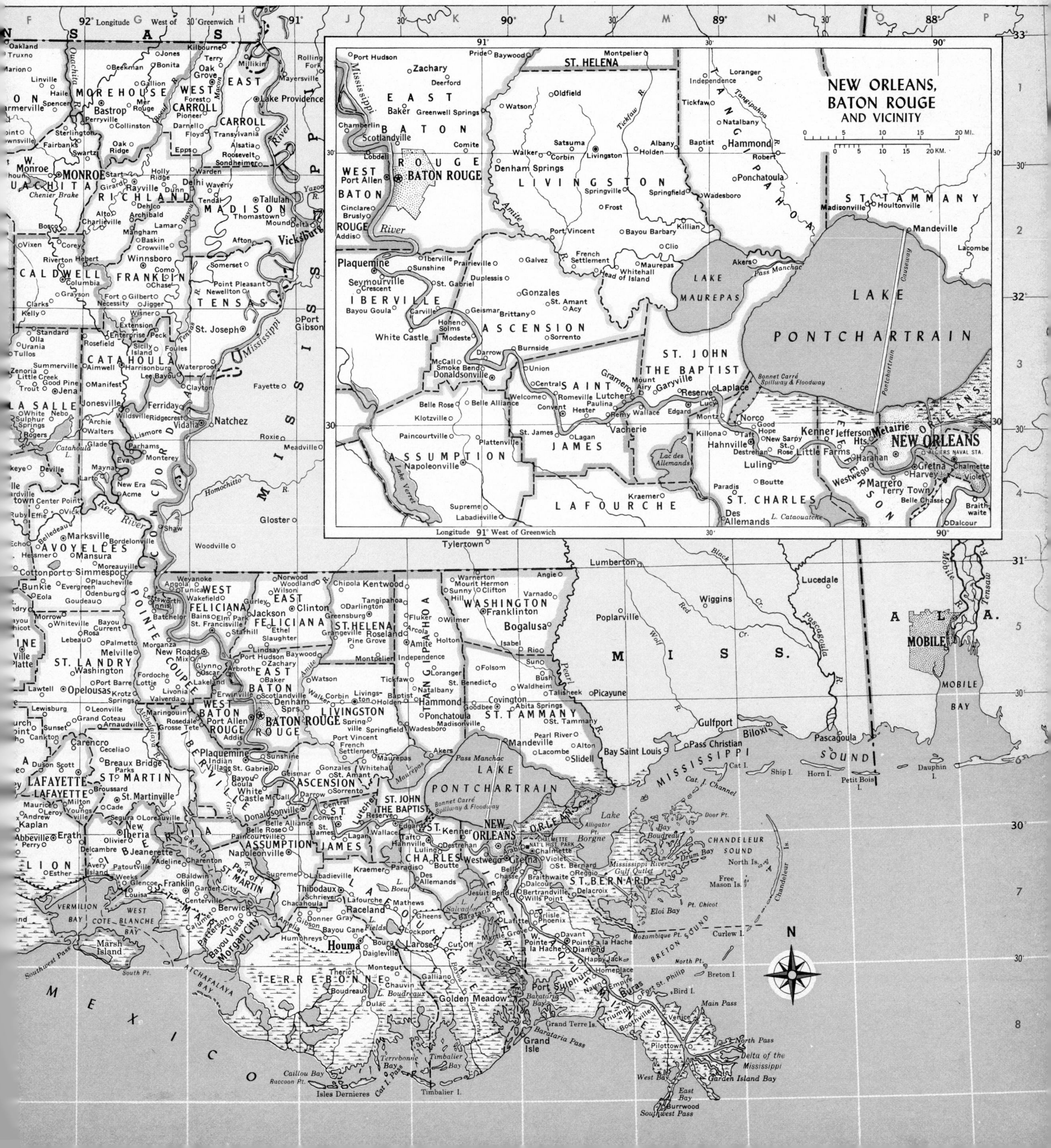

(continued)

Agriculture, Industry and Resources

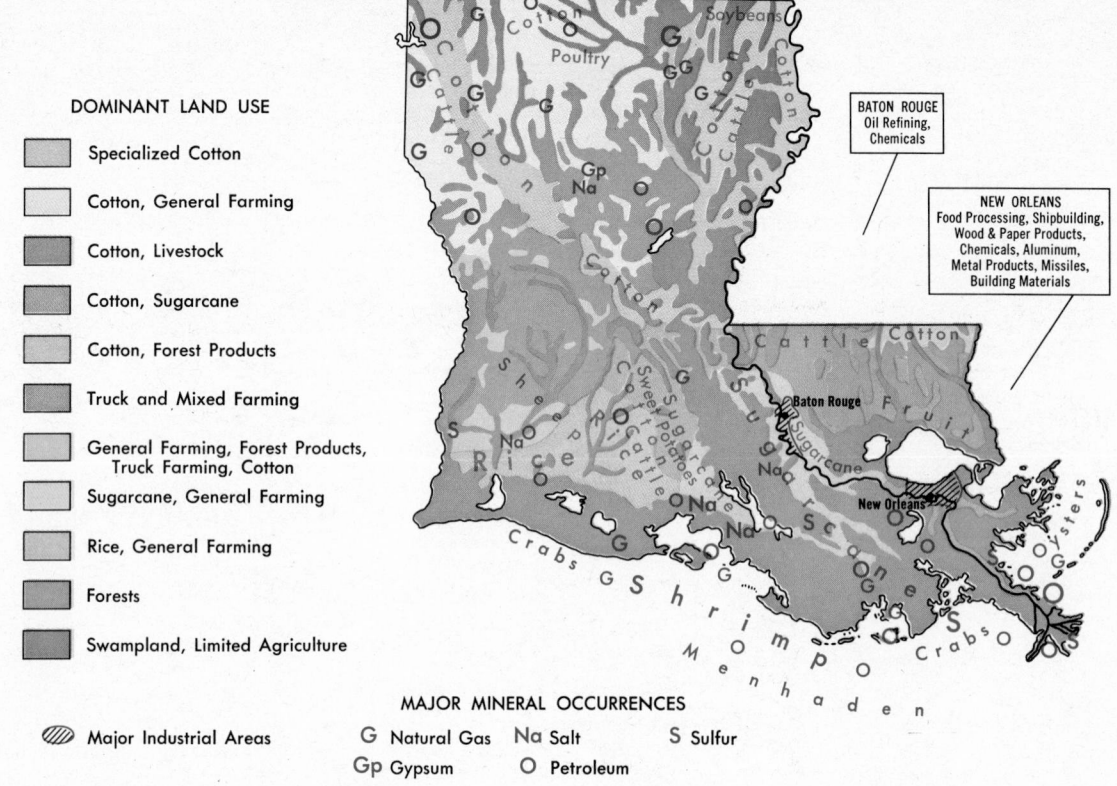

DOMINANT LAND USE

- Specialized Cotton
- Cotton, General Farming
- Cotton, Livestock
- Cotton, Sugarcane
- Cotton, Forest Products
- Truck and Mixed Farming
- General Farming, Forest Products, Truck Farming, Cotton
- Sugarcane, General Farming
- Rice, General Farming
- Forests
- Swampland, Limited Agriculture

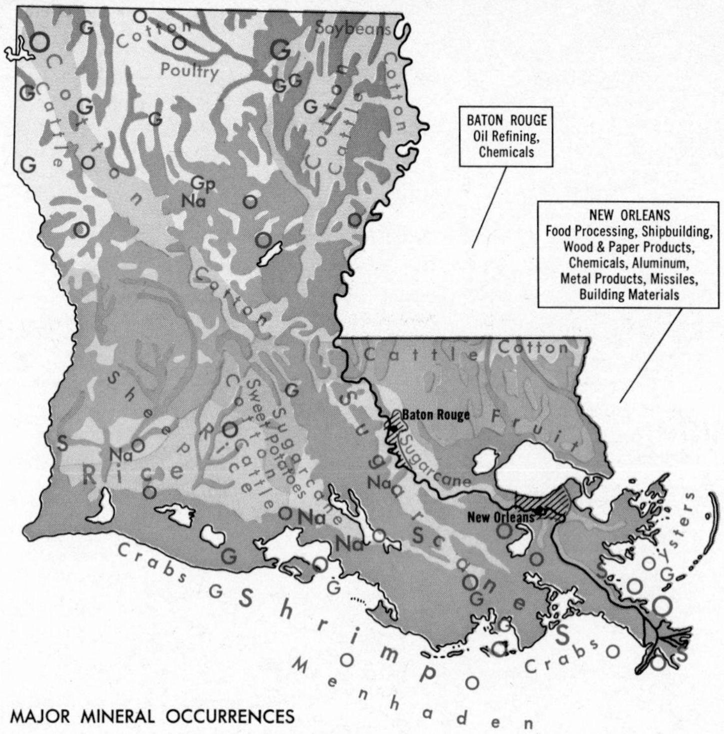

BATON ROUGE
Oil Refining, Chemicals
NEW ORLEANS
Food Processing, Shipbuilding, Wood & Paper Products, Chemicals, Aluminum, Metal Products, Missiles, Building Materials
Soybeans
Cotton
Poultry
Cattle
Sheep
Rice
Sugarcane
Sweet Potatoes
Fruit
Baton Rouge
New Orleans
Oysters
Crabs
Shrimp
Menhaden

MAJOR MINERAL OCCURRENCES

Major Industrial Areas — G Natural Gas — Na Salt — S Sulfur — Gp Gypsum — O Petroleum

71047 Keithville, 500 C 2
71441 Kelly, 250 F 3
70062 Kenner, 29,858 N 4
70444 Kentwood, 2,736 J 5
71253 Kilbourne, 370 H 1
† 70462 Killian, 275 M 2
70066 Killona, 600 M 3
70648 Kinder, 2,307 E 6
70370 Klotzville, 248 K 3
70371 Kraemer, 510 M 4
70750 Krotz Springs, 1,435 G 5
70372 Labadieville, 700 K 4
70650 Lacassine, 494 E 6
70445 Lacombe, 750 L 6
70501 Lafayette⊙, 68,908 F 6
Lafayette, ‡109,716 F 6
70067 Lafitte, 1,223 K 7
† 70301 Lafourche, 200 J 7
70549 Lake Arthur, 3,551 E 6
70601 Lake Charles⊙, 77,998 D 6
Lake Charles, ‡145,415 D 6
70752 Lakeland, 400 H 5
71254 Lake Providence⊙, 6,183 H 1
70068 Laplace, 5,953 N 3
70373 Larose, 4,267 K 7
71344 Larto, 500 G 4
70550 Lawtell, 600 F 5
71345 Lebeau, 270 F 5
71346 Lecompte, 1,518 F 4
71446 Leesville⊙, 8,928 D 4
71447 Lena, 250 E 4
70551 Leonville, 512 G 6
70753 Lettsworth, 200 G 5
† 70525 Lewisburg, 265 F 6
71348 Libuse, 500 F 4
71256 Lillie, 160 E 1
71048 Lisbon, 151 E 1
† 71343 Lismore, 380 G 3
† 70062 Little Farms, 15,713 N 4
70754 Livingston⊙, 1,398 L 1
70755 Livonia, 611 G 5
70374 Lockport, 1,995 K 7
71049 Logansport, 1,330 C 3
† 71367 Lonepine, 850 F 5
71448 Longleaf, 250 E 4
71050 Longstreet, 182 B 2
70652 Longville, 250 D 5
70446 Loranger, 200 N 1
70552 Loreauville, 728 G 6
70756 Lottie, 350 G 5
70069 Lucy, 825 M 3
70070 Luling, 3,255 N 4
70071 Lutcher, 3,911 L 3
70447 Madisonville, 801 K 6
70554 Mamou, 3,275 F 5
70448 Mandeville, 2,282 L 6
71259 Mangham, 544 G 2
71052 Mansfield⊙, 6,432 C 2
71350 Mansura, 1,699 G 4
71449 Many⊙, 3,112 C 3
70663 Maplewood, 1,900 D 6
70757 Maringouin, 1,365 G 6
71260 Marion, 796 F 1
71351 Marksville⊙, 4,519 G 4
70072 Marrero, 29,015 O 4
70375 Mathews, 600 J 7
70449 Maurepas, 200 M 2
70555 Maurice, 476 F 6
† 71433 McNary, 220 E 5
71451 Melder, 200 E 4
71353 Melville, 2,076 G 5
70556 Mermentau, 756 E 6
71261 Mer Rouge, 819 G 1
70653 Merryville, 1,286 D 5
* 70001 Metairie, 135,816 O 4
70557 Midland, 500 F 6
70558 Milton, 500 F 6
71055 Minden⊙, 13,996 D 1
70376 Modeste, 230 K 3
71201 Monroe⊙, 56,374 F 1
Monroe, ‡115,387 F 1
70377 Montegut, 950 J 8
71354 Monterey, 800 G 4
71454 Montgomery, 923 E 3
70422 Montpelier, 211 M 1
† 70068 Montz, 200 M 3
71060 Mooringsport, 830 B 1
71455 Mora, 378 E 4
71355 Moreauville, 807 G 4
70380 Morgan City, 16,586 H 7
70759 Morganza, 836 G 5
71356 Morrow, 350 F 5
70559 Morse, 759 F 6
70076 Mount Airy, 700 M 3
70077 Nairn, 500 L 8
70390 Napoleonville⊙, 1,008 K 4
70451 Natalbany, 900 N 1
71456 Natchez, 600 D 3
71457 Natchitoches⊙, 15,974 D 3
† 71342 Nebo, 200 F 3
71460 Negreet, 200 C 4
71357 Newellton, 1,403 H 2
† 71354 New Era, 200 G 4
70560 New Iberia⊙, 30,147 G 6
71461 Newllano, 1,800 D 4
* 70101 New Orleans⊙, 593,471 O 4
New Orleans, ‡1,045,809 O 4
70760 New Roads⊙, 3,945 G 5
70078 New Sarpy, 1,643 N 4
71462 Noble, 209 C 3
70079 Norco, 4,773 N 3
† 71247 North Hodge, 640 E 2
70761 Norwood, 348 H 5
71463 Oakdale, 7,301 E 5
71263 Oak Grove⊙, 1,980 H 1
71264 Oak Ridge, 276 G 1
70655 Oberlin⊙, 1,857 E 5
† 71369 Odenburg, 175 G 5
71061 Oil City, 907 C 1
† 70560 Olivier, 300 G 7
71465 Olla, 1,387 F 3
70570 Opelousas⊙, 20,121 G 5
70762 Oscar, 700 H 5
71358 Palmetto, 312 G 5
70391 Paincourtville, 600 K 3
70080 Paradis, 750 M 4
70582 Parks, 491 G 6
† 70544 Patoutville, 230 G 7
70392 Patterson, 4,409 H 7
70763 Paulina, 500 L 3
70452 Pearl River, 1,361 L 6
† 70548 Pecan Island, 480 F 7
70575 Perry, 225 F 7
† 70042 Phoenix, 525 L 7
70453 Pine Grove, 500 J 5
70576 Pine Prairie, 515 E 5
71360 Pineville, 8,951 F 4
71266 Pioneer, 188 H 1
70656 Pitkin, 700 E 5
71064 Plain Dealing, 2,116 C 1
70764 Plaquemine⊙, 7,739 J 2
70393 Plattenville, 400 K 4
71362 Plaucheville, 224 G 5
71065 Pleasant Hill, 826 C 3
70082 Pointe a la Hache⊙, 750 L 7
71467 Pollock, 341 F 3
70454 Ponchatoula, 4,545 N 2
70767 Port Allen⊙, 5,728 J 2
70577 Port Barre, 2,133 G 5
† 70791 Port Hudson, 200 J 1
70083 Port Sulphur, 3,022 L 8
† 70726 Port Vincent, 387 L 2
71066 Powhatan, 277 D 3
70769 Prairieville, 500 K 2
71067 Princeton, 350 C 1
71468 Provencal, 530 D 3
71268 Quitman, 169 E 2
70394 Raceland, 4,880 J 7
70578 Rayne, 9,510 F 6
71269 Rayville⊙, 3,962 G 2
70580 Reddell, 800 F 5
70658 Reeves, 214 D 5
† 70085 Reggio, 400 L 7
† 70763 Remy, 850 L 3
70084 Reserve, 6,381 M 3
71334 Ridgecrest, 1,076 G 3
71068 Ringgold, 1,731 D 2
† 70427 Rio, 250 L 5
70581 Roanoke, 640 E 6
71469 Robeline, 274 D 3
70455 Robert, 600 N 1
71069 Rodessa, 273 B 1
70772 Rosedale, 621 G 6
70456 Roseland, 1,273 J 5
70659 Rosepine, 587 D 5
71365 Ruby, 350 F 4
71270 Ruston⊙, 17,365 E 1
70774 Saint Amant, 900 L 2
70457 Saint Benedict, 200 K 5
70085 Saint Bernard, 750 L 7
70775 Saint Francisville⊙ 1,603 H 5
70776 Saint Gabriel, 975 K 2
70086 Saint James, 600 L 3
71366 Saint Joseph⊙, 1,864 H 3
71367 Saint Landry, 950 F 5
70582 Saint Martinville⊙, 7,153 G 6
71471 Saint Maurice, 650 E 3
70087 Saint Rose, 2,106 N 4
71070 Saline, 307 E 2
71301 Samtown, 4,210 F 4
71071 Sarepta, 882 D 1
70395 Schriever, 700 J 7
70807 Scotlandville, 22,557 J 1
70583 Scott, 1,334 F 6
† 70560 Segura, 200 G 6
† 70764 Seymourville, 2,506 J 2
71072 Shongaloo, 173 D 1
* 71101 Shreveport⊙, 182,064 C 1
Shreveport, ‡294,703 C 1
71073 Sibley, 869 D 1
71368 Sicily Island. 630 G 3
71472 Sieper, 200 E 4
71473 Sikes, 237 F 2
71369 Simmesport, 2,027 G 5
71474 Simpson, 491 D 4
71275 Simsboro, 412 E 1
70660 Singer, 400 D 5
71475 Slagle, 200 D 4
70777 Slaughter, 580 H 5
70458 Slidell, 16,101 L 6
† 70346 Smoke Bend, 300 K 3
71276 Sondheimer, 325 H 1
70778 Sorrento, 1,182 L 3
† 71052 South Mansfield, 439 C 3
71277 Spearsville, 197 E 1
70462 Springfield, 423 M 2
71075 Springhill, 6,496 D 1
† 71465 Standard, 190 F 3
70661 Starks, 750 C 6
71279 Start, 200 G 2
71280 Sterlington, 1,118 F 1
71078 Stonewall, 500 C 2
70663 Sulphur, 13,551 D 6
71079 Summerfield, 170 E 1
70463 Sun, 288 L 5
70584 Sunset, 1,675 F 6
70780 Sunshine, 900 K 2
70396 Supreme, 617 K 4
71281 Swartz, 650 G 1
† 70601 Sweet Lake, 300 D 7
70464 Talisheek, 292 L 5
71282 Tallulah⊙, 9,643 H 2
70465 Tangipahoa, 469 J 5
71080 Taylor, 500 D 1
† 71290 Tendal, 200 H 2
† 70053 Terry Town, 13,832 O 4
70397 Theriot, 950 J 8
70301 Thibodaux⊙, 14,925 J 7
70466 Tickfaw, 370 M 1
71477 Tioga, 457 F 4
71286 Transylvania, 400 H 1
71081 Trees, 247 B 1
† 70041 Triumph-Buras, 4,113 L 8
71371 Trout, 500 F
71479 Tullos, 600 F
70782 Tunica, 475 G 5
70585 Turkey Creek, 280 F
70723 Union, 665 L
71480 Urania, 950 F
70090 Vacherie, 2,145 L
† 70757 Valverda, 200 G
70467 Varnado, 320 L
70091 Venice, 900 M
71372 Vick, 500 F
71373 Vidalia⊙, 5,538 G
71270 Vienna, 250 E
70586 Ville Platte⊙, 9,692 F
70668 Vinton, 3,454 C
70092 Violet, 975 P
71082 Vivian, 4,046 B
70784 Wakefield, 200 H
70785 Walker, 1,363 L
† 70049 Wallace, 200 M
71374 Walters, 500 G
71289 Warden, 350 H
† 71301 Wardville, 1,087 F
70589 Washington, 1,473 G
71375 Waterproof, 1,438 H
70786 Watson, 700 L
71290 Waverly, 350 H
† 70569 Weeks, 400 G
70093 Welcome, 450 L
70591 Welsh, 3,203 E
70669 Westlake, 4,082 D
71291 West Monroe, 14,868 F
† 70082 West Pointe a la Hache, 250 L
70094 Westwego, 11,402 O
70787 Weyanoke, 500 H
70788 White Castle, 2,206 J
† 70462 Whitehall, 380 M
71376 Whiteville, 450 F
71377 Wildsville. 650 G
70789 Wilson, 606 H
71483 Winnfield⊙, 7,142 E
71295 Winnsboro⊙, 5,349 G
71378 Wisner, 1,339 G
71485 Woodworth, 409 E
70592 Youngsville, 1,002 G
70791 Zachary, 4,964 K
71486 Zwolle, 2,169 C

⊙ Parish seat.
‡ Population of metropolitan area.
† Zip of nearest p.o.
* Multiple zips

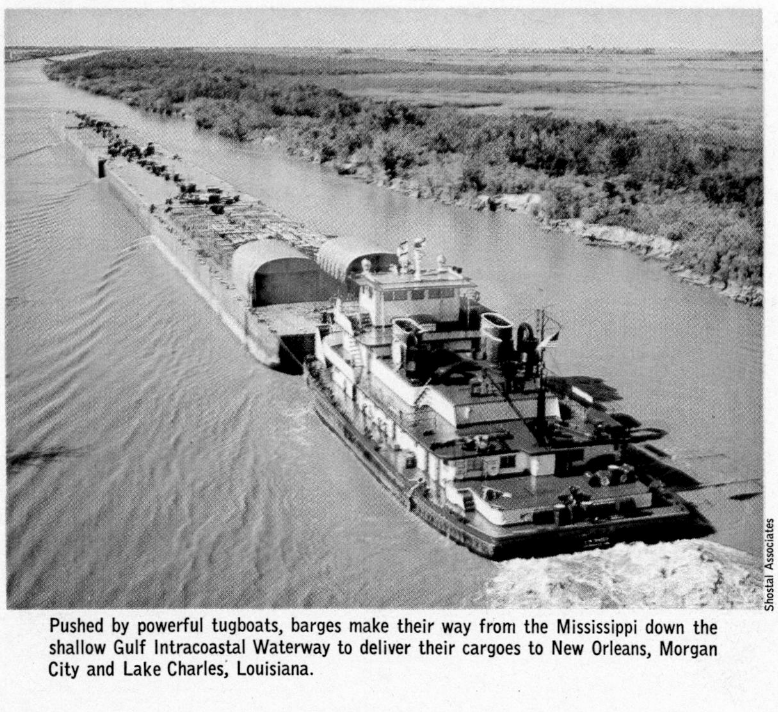

Shostal Associates

Pushed by powerful tugboats, barges make their way from the Mississippi down the shallow Gulf Intracoastal Waterway to deliver their cargoes to New Orleans, Morgan City and Lake Charles, Louisiana.

AREA 33,215 sq. mi.
POPULATION 993,663
CAPITAL Augusta
LARGEST CITY Portland
HIGHEST POINT Katahdin 5,268 ft.
SETTLED IN 1624
ADMITTED TO UNION March 15, 1820
POPULAR NAME Pine Tree State
STATE FLOWER Pine Cone & Tassel
STATE BIRD Chickadee

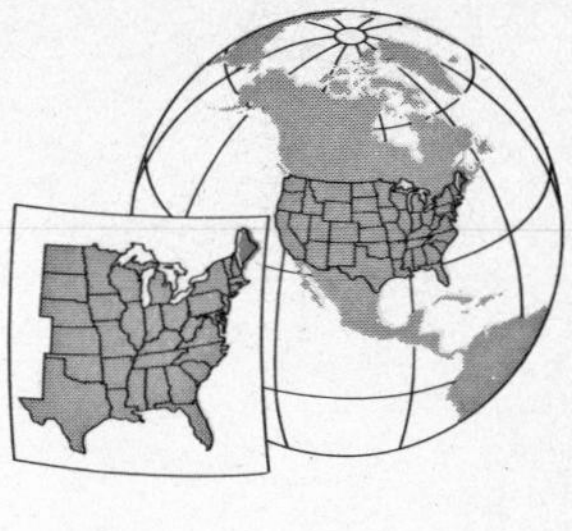

COUNTIES

Androscoggin, 91,279	C 7
Aroostook, 92,463	F 2
Cumberland, 192,528	C 8
Franklin, 22,444	B 5
Hancock, 34,590	G 6
Kennebec, 95,247	D 7
Knox, 29,013	E 7
Lincoln, 20,537	D 7
Oxford, 43,457	B 7
Penobscot, 125,393	F 5
Piscataquis, 16,285	E 4
Sagadahoc, 23,452	D 7
Somerset, 40,597	C 4
Waldo, 23,328	E 6
Washington, 29,859	H 6
York, 111,576	B 9

CITIES and TOWNS

Zip	Name/Pop.	Key
04406	Abbot Village, ∆453	D 5
04001	Acton, ∆697	B 8
04606	Addison, ∆773	H 6
04910	Albion, ∆1,056	E 6
04610	Alexander, ∆169	H 5
04002	Alfred⊙, ∆1,211	B 9
04774	Allagash, ∆456	F 1
04938	Allens Mills, 150	C 6
4535	Alna, ∆315	D 7
4468	Alton, ∆340	F 5
4408	Amherst, ∆148	G 6
4216	Andover, ∆791	B 6
4216	Andover, 350	B 6
4911	Anson, ∆2,168	D 6
4911	Anson, 950	D 6
4862	Appleton, ∆628	E 7
4732	Ashland, ∆1,761	G 2
4732	Ashland, 750	G 2
4912	Athens, ∆592	D 6
4912	Athens, 200	D 6
4426	Atkinson, ∆213	E 5
4210	Auburn⊙, 24,151	C 7
4330	Augusta (cap.)⊙, 21,945	D 7
4408	Aurora, ∆72	G 6
4003	Bailey Island, 400	D 8
4409	Bancroft, ∆53	H 4
4401	Bangor⊙, 33,168	F 6
4609	Bar Harbor, ∆3,716	G 7
4609	Bar Harbor, 2,392	G 7
4610	Baring, 150	J 5
4004	Bar Mills, 800	C 8
4653	Bass Harbor, 413	G 7
4530	Bath⊙, 9,679	D 8
4915	Bayside, 238	F 7
4611	Beals, ∆663	H 7
4622	Beddington, ∆32	H 6
4915	Belfast⊙, 5,957	F 7
4917	Belgrade, ∆1,302	D 7
917	Belgrade, 300	D 7
918	Belgrade Lakes, 700	D 6
915	Belmont, ∆349	E 7
733	Benedicta, ∆177	G 4
919	Benton, ∆1,729	D 6
901	Berwick, ∆3,136	B 9
901	Berwick, 1,765	B 9
285	Berry Mills, 245	C 6
217	Bethel, ∆2,220	B 7
217	Bethel, 750	B 7
005	Biddeford, 19,983	B 9
006	Biddeford Pool, 500	C 9
920	Bingham, ∆1,254	D 5
920	Bingham, 1,184	D 5
613	Birch Harbor, 210	H 7
734	Blaine, ∆903	H 2
734	Blaine-Mars Hill, 1,854	H 2
406	Blanchard, ∆56	D 5
614	Blue Hill, ∆1,367	F 7
615	Blue Hill Falls, 850	F 7
040	Bolsters Mills, 150	B 7
537	Boothbay, ∆1,814	D 8
04537	Boothbay, 700	D 8
04538	Boothbay Harbor, 2,320	D 8
04008	Bowdoinham, ∆1,294	D 7
04481	Bowerbank, ∆29	E 5
04410	Bradford, ∆569	F 5
04410	Bradford, 150	F 5
04411	Bradley, ∆1,010	F 6
04412	Brewer, 9,300	F 6
04735	Bridgewater, ∆895	H 3
04009	Bridgton, ∆2,967	B 7
04009	Bridgton, 1,779	B 7
† 04990	Brighton, ∆58	D 5
04539	Bristol, ∆1,721	D 8
04539	Bristol, 160	D 8
04616	Brooklin, ∆598	F 7
04921	Brooks, ∆751	E 6
04617	Brooksville, ∆673	F 7
04413	Brookton, 225	H 4
04010	Brownfield, ∆478	B 8
04010	Brownfield, 200	B 8
04414	Brownville, ∆1,490	E 5
04414	Brownville, 1,641	E 5
04415	Brownville Junction, 950	E 5
04011	Brunswick, ∆16,195	C 8
04011	Brunswick, 10,867	C 8
04219	Bryant Pond, 350	B 7
04220	Buckfield, ∆929	C 7
04618	Bucks Harbor, 161	J 6
04416	Bucksport, ∆3,756	F 6
04416	Bucksport, 2,456	F 6
04417	Burlington, ∆266	G 5
04922	Burnham, ∆802	E 6
† 04093	Buxton, ∆3,135	C 8
† 04275	Byron, ∆132	B 6
04619	Calais, 4,044	J 5
04923	Cambridge, ∆281	E 5
04843	Camden, ∆4,115	F 7
04843	Camden, 3,492	F 7
04924	Canaan, ∆904	D 6
04221	Canton, ∆742	C 7
03902	Cape Neddick, 850	B 9
04014	Cape Porpoise, 500	C 9
04925	Caratunk, ∆96	C 5
04418	Cardville, 223	F 5
04736	Caribou, 10,419	G 2
04419	Carmel, ∆1,301	E 6
04420	Carroll, ∆132	G 5
† 04224	Carthage, ∆354	C 6
† 04465	Cary, ∆184	H 4
04015	Casco, ∆1,256	B 7
04015	Casco, 250	B 7
04421	Castine, ∆1,080	F 7
† 04623	Centerville, ∆19	H 6
† 04757	Chapman, ∆328	G 2
04422	Charleston, ∆909	F 5
† 04666	Charlotte, ∆199	J 5
04017	Chebeague Island, 400	C 8
† 04345	Chelsea, ∆2,095	D 7
04622	Cherryfield, ∆771	H 6
† 04458	Chester, ∆255	F 5
† 04938	Chesterville, ∆643	C 6
04926	China, ∆1,850	E 7
04926	China, 336	E 7
04222	Chisholm, 1,530	C 7
† 04428	Clifton, ∆233	G 6
04927	Clinton, ∆1,971	D 6
04927	Clinton, 1,124	D 6
† 04623	Columbia, ∆162	H 6
04623	Columbia Falls, ∆367	H 6
† 04638	Cooper, ∆88	H 6
04341	Coopers Mills, 200	E 7
04624	Corea, 300	H 7
04928	Corinna, ∆1,700	E 6
04020	Cornish, ∆839	B 8
† 04976	Cornville, ∆623	D 6
04423	Costigan, 200	F 5
04625	Cranberry Isles, ∆186	G 7
† 04610	Crawford, ∆74	H 5
† 04015	Crescent Lake, 175	C 7
04738	Crouseville, 300	G 2
† 04747	Crystal, ∆281	G 4
04021	Cumberland Center, ∆4,096	C 8
04021	Cumberland Center, 950	C 8
04011	Cundys Harbor, 150	D 8
† 04563	Cushing, ∆522	E 7
04626	Cutler, ∆588	J 6
04626	Cutler, 153	J 6
04543	Damariscotta, ∆1,264	E 7
04543	Damariscotta-Newcastle, 1,188	E 7
04424	Danforth, ∆794	H 4
04424	Danforth, 650	H 4
† 04622	Deblois, ∆20	H 6
† 04429	Dedham, ∆522	F 6
04627	Deer Isle, ∆1,211	F 7
04627	Deer Isle, 600	F 7
04022	Denmark, ∆397	B 8
04628	Dennysville, ∆278	J 6
04425	Derby, 300	E 5
04929	Detroit, ∆663	E 6
04930	Dexter, ∆3,725	E 5
04936	Dexter, 2,732	E 5
04224	Dixfield, ∆2,188	C 6
04224	Dixfield, 1,535	C 6
04932	Dixmont, ∆559	E 6
04426	Dover-Foxcroft, ∆4,178	E 5
04426	Dover-Foxcroft⊙, 3,102	E 5
04342	Dresden, ∆787	D 7
04225	Dryden, 675	C 6
† 04039	Dry Mills, 700	C 8
† 04747	Dyer Brook, ∆165	G 3
04739	Eagle Lake, ∆908	F 1
04739	Eagle Lake, 675	F 1
04226	East Andover, 194	B 6
04024	East Baldwin, 175	B 8
04629	East Blue Hill, 150	G 7
04544	East Boothbay, 400	D 8
04427	East Corinth, 525	F 5
04227	East Dixfield, 288	C 6
04428	East Eddington, 200	F 6
04026	East Hiram, 198	B 8
04429	East Holden, 450	F 6
04027	East Lebanon, 950	B 9
† 04049	East Limington, 200	B 8
04228	East Livermore, 290	C 7
04630	East Machias, ∆1,057	J 6
04630	East Machias, 750	J 6
† 04950	East Madison, 400	D 6
04430	East Millinocket, ∆2,567	F 4
04430	East Millinocket, 2,564	F 4
04740	Easton, ∆1,305	H 2
† 04270	East Otisfield, 200	B 7
04229	East Peru, 350	C 7
04230	East Poland, 700	C 7
04631	Eastport, 1,989	K 6
04231	East Stoneham, 150	B 7
04632	East Sullivan, 300	G 6
† 04862	East Union, 220	E 7
04935	East Vassalboro, 300	D 7
04030	East Waterboro, 365	B 8
04234	East Wilton, 650	C 6
† 04428	Eddington, ∆1,358	F 6
† 04428	Eddington, 250	F 6
04545	Edgecomb, ∆549	D 8
† 04628	Edmunds, 229	J 6
03903	Eliot, ∆3,497	B 9
04605	Ellsworth⊙, 4,603	G 6
04433	Enfield, ∆1,148	F 5
04433	Enfield, 150	F 5
04434	Etna, ∆526	E 6
04936	Eustis, ∆595	B 5
04435	Exeter, ∆663	E 6
† 04938	Fairbanks, 300	C 6
04937	Fairfield, ∆5,684	D 6
04937	Fairfield, 3,694	D 6
† 04937	Fairfield Center, 975	D 6
04105	Falmouth, ∆6,291	C 8
04105	Falmouth, 1,621	C 8
† 04105	Falmouth Foreside (Falmouth), 1,621	C 8
† 04345	Farmingdale, ∆2,423	D 7
† 04345	Farmingdale, 1,832	D 7
04938	Farmington, ∆5,657	C 6
04938	Farmington⊙, 3,096	C 6
04940	Farmington Falls, 500	C 6
04344	Fayette, ∆447	C 7
04546	Five Islands, 161	D 8
04742	Fort Fairfield, ∆4,859	H 2
04742	Fort Fairfield, 2,322	H 2
04743	Fort Kent, ∆4,575	F 1
04743	Fort Kent, 2,876	F 1
04744	Fort Kent Mills, 300	F 1
04438	Frankfort, ∆620	F 6
04634	Franklin, ∆708	G 6
04634	Franklin, 350	G 6
04941	Freedom, ∆373	E 7
04032	Freeport, ∆4,781	C 8
04032	Freeport, 1,822	C 8
04745	Frenchville, ∆1,375	G 1
04745	Frenchville, 800	G 1
04547	Friendship, ∆834	E 7
04547	Friendship, 700	E 7
04037	Fryeburg, ∆2,208	A 7
04037	Fryeburg, 1,075	A 7
04345	Gardiner, 6,685	D 7
04939	Garland, ∆596	E 5
04939	Garland, 300	E 5
04548	Georgetown, ∆464	D 8
04548	Georgetown, 190	D 8
† 04217	Gilead, ∆153	B 7
† 04401	Glenburn, ∆1,196	F 6
04846	Glen Cove, 300	E 7
† 04005	Goodwins Mills, 340	B 8
† 04046	Goose Rocks Beach, 200	C 9
04038	Gorham, ∆7,839	C 8
04038	Gorham, 3,337	C 8
04636	Gouldsboro, ∆1,310	H 7
04636	Gouldsboro, 296	H 7
04746	Grand Isle, ∆797	G 1
04746	Grand Isle, 400	G 1
04637	Grand Lake Stream, ∆186	H 5
04039	Gray, ∆2,939	C 8
04039	Gray, 525	C 8
04236	Greene, ∆1,772	C 7
04441	Greenville, ∆1,894	D 5
04441	Greenville, 1,714	D 5
04442	Greenville Junction, 150	D 5
04443	Guilford, ∆1,694	E 5
04443	Guilford, 1,216	E 5
04347	Hallowell, 2,814	D 7
† 04785	Hamlin, ∆357	H 1
04444	Hampden, ∆4,693	F 6
04444	Hampden, 2,207	F 6
04445	Hampden Highlands, 950	F 6
04640	Hancock, ∆1,070	G 6
04237	Hanover, ∆275	B 7
04942	Harmony, ∆650	D 6
04942	Harmony, 350	D 6
† 04011	Harpswell, ∆2,552	D 8
04643	Harrington, ∆553	H 6
04040	Harrison, ∆1,045	B 7
† 04221	Hartford, ∆312	C 7
04943	Hartland, ∆1,414	D 6
04943	Hartland, 975	D 6
04446	Haynesville, ∆157	G 4
04238	Hebron, ∆532	C 7
† 04401	Hermon, ∆2,376	F 6
† 04082	Highland Lake, 600	C 8
04944	Hinckley, 317	D 6
04041	Hiram, ∆686	B 8
04041	Hiram, 175	B 8
04730	Hodgdon, ∆933	H 3
† 04429	Holden, ∆1,789	H 3
† 04429	Holden, 900	H 3
04042	Hollis Center, ∆1,560	B 8
04847	Hope, ∆500	E 7
04847	Hope, 175	E 7
04730	Houlton, ∆8,111	H 3
04730	Houlton⊙, 6,760	H 3
04448	Howland, ∆1,468	F 5
04448	Howland, 1,418	F 5
04449	Hudson, ∆482	F 5
04644	Hulls Cove, 200	G 7
04747	Island Falls, ∆913	G 3
04645	Isle au Haut, ∆45	F 7
04848	Islesboro, ∆421	F 7
04848	Islesboro, 200	F 7
04945	Jackman, ∆848	C 4
04945	Jackman, 700	C 4
04647	Jacksonville, 200	J 6
04239	Jay, ∆3,954	C 7
04239	Jay, 850	C 7
04348	Jefferson, ∆1,242	D 7
04648	Jonesboro, ∆448	J 6
04649	Jonesport, ∆1,326	H 6
04649	Jonesport, 1,073	H 6
04748	Keegan, 450	G 1
04450	Kenduskeag, ∆733	E 6
04043	Kennebunk, ∆5,646	B 9
04043	Kennebunk, 2,764	B 9
04046	Kennebunkport, ∆2,160	C 9
04046	Kennebunkport, 1,097	C 9
04349	Kents Hill, 250	D 7
04047	Kezar Falls, 680	B 8
04947	Kingfield, ∆877	C 6
04451	Kingman, 250	G 4
† 04990	Kingsbury, ∆7	D 5
03904	Kittery, ∆11,028	B 9
03904	Kittery, 7,363	B 9
03905	Kittery Point, 1,172	B 9
† 04986	Knox, ∆443	E 6
04453	La Grange, ∆393	F 5
04453	La Grange, 250	F 5
† 04463	Lake View, ∆16	F 5
† 04605	Lamoine, ∆615	G 7
04455	Lee, ∆599	G 5
† 04263	Leeds, ∆1,031	C 7
04456	Levant, ∆862	F 6
04240	Lewiston, 41,779	C 7
	Lewiston-Auburn, ‡72,474	C 7
04949	Liberty, ∆515	E 7
04949	Liberty, 200	E 7
04749	Lille, 300	G 1
04048	Limerick, ∆963	B 8
04750	Limestone, ∆8,745	H 2
04750	Limestone, 1,572	H 2
04049	Limington, ∆1,066	B 8
04049	Limington, 250	B 8
04457	Lincoln, ∆4,759	G 5
04457	Lincoln, 3,482	G 5
04458	Lincoln Center, 325	G 5
04849	Lincolnville, ∆955	E 7
04849	Lincolnville, 800	E 7
04755	Linneus, ∆608	H 3
04250	Lisbon, ∆6,544	C 7
* 04250	Lisbon-Lisbon Center, 1,475	C 7
04252	Lisbon Falls, 3,257	D 7
04350	Litchfield, ∆1,222	D 7
04650	Little Deer Isle, 275	F 7
† 04760	Littleton, ∆958	H 3
04253	Livermore, ∆1,610	C 7
04253	Livermore, 280	C 7
04254	Livermore Falls, ∆3,450	C 7
04254	Livermore Falls, 2,378	C 7
04255	Locke Mills, 300	B 7
04051	Lovell, ∆607	B 7
04051	Lovell, 180	B 7
† 04433	Lowell, ∆154	F 5
04652	Lubec, ∆1,949	K 6
04652	Lubec, 900	K 6
† 04730	Ludlow, ∆259	G 3
04654	Machias, ∆2,441	J 6
04654	Machias⊙, 1,368	J 6
04655	Machiasport, ∆887	H 6
04655	Machiasport, 374	H 6
† 04451	Macwahoc, ∆126	G 4
04756	Madawaska, ∆5,585	G 1
04756	Madawaska, 4,452	G 1
04950	Madison, ∆4,278	D 6
04950	Madison, 2,920	D 6
† 04966	Madrid, ∆107	B 6
04351	Manchester, ∆1,331	D 7
04757	Mapleton, ∆1,598	G 2
04758	Mars Hill, ∆1,875	H 2
04758	Mars Hill-Blaine, 1,854	H 2
04759	Masardis, ∆317	G 3
04459	Mattawamkeag, ∆988	G 5
04256	Mechanic Falls, ∆2,193	C 7
04256	Mechanic Falls, 1,872	C 7
04657	Meddybemps, ∆76	J 5
† 04453	Medford, ∆146	F 5
04460	Medway, ∆1,491	G 4
04957	Mercer, ∆313	D 6
04257	Mexico, ∆4,309	B 6
04257	Mexico, 3,325	B 6
04658	Milbridge, ∆1,154	H 6
04461	Milford, ∆1,828	F 6
04461	Milford, 1,519	F 6
04462	Millinocket, ∆7,742	F 4
04462	Millinocket, 7,558	F 4
04463	Milo, ∆2,572	F 5
04463	Milo, 1,514	F 5
04258	Minot, ∆919	C 7
04258	Minot, 250	C 7
04852	Monhegan, ∆44	E 7
04259	Monmouth, ∆2,062	D 7

(continued on following page)

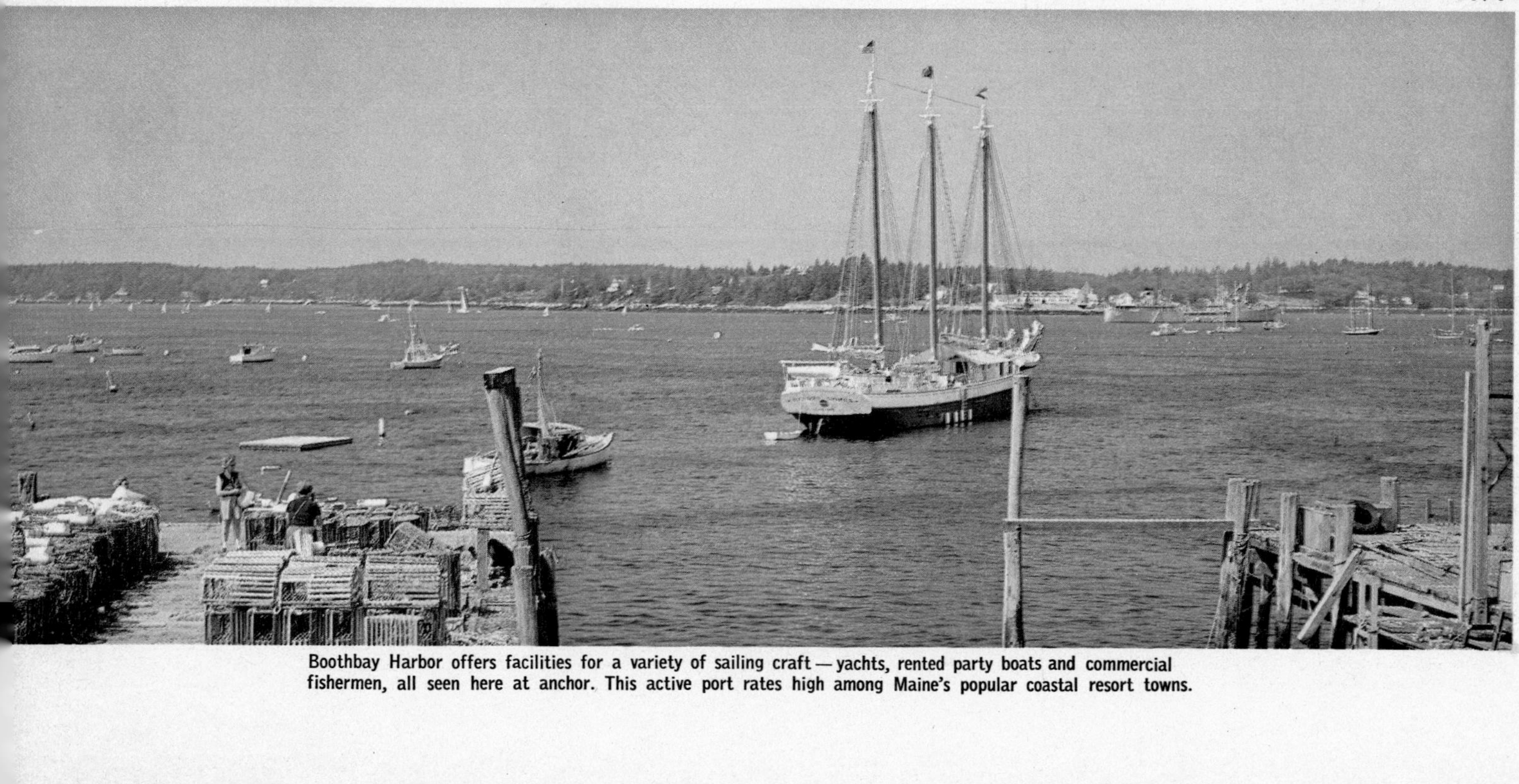

Boothbay Harbor offers facilities for a variety of sailing craft — yachts, rented party boats and commercial fishermen, all seen here at anchor. This active port rates high among Maine's popular coastal resort towns.

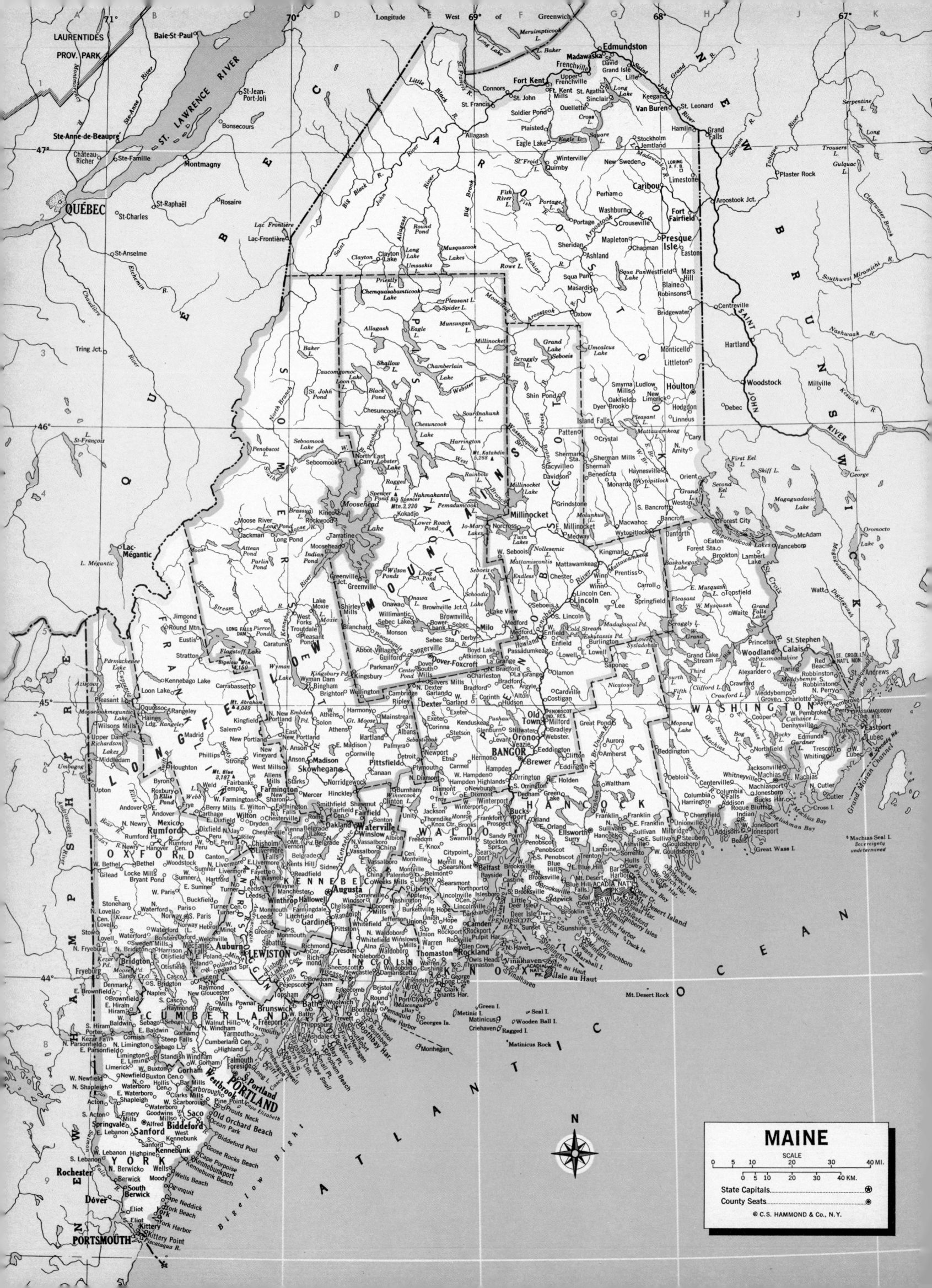

MAINE

SCALE

0   5   10   20   30   40 MI.

0 5 10   20   40 KM.

State Capitals .... ⊛

County Seats .... ⊙

© C.S. HAMMOND & Co., N.Y.

Agriculture, Industry and Resources

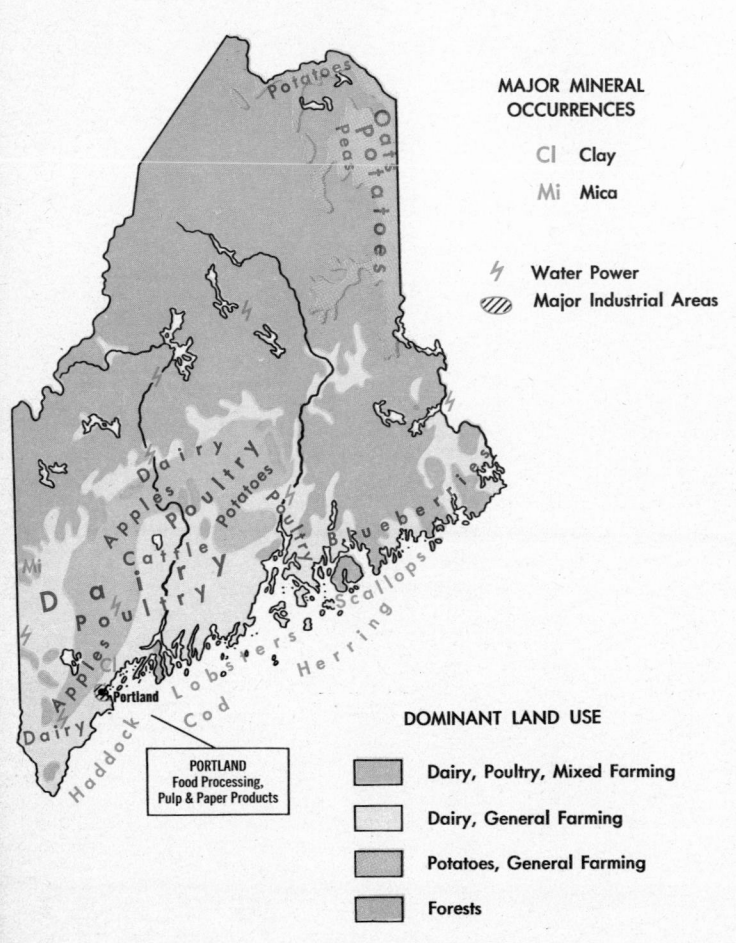

MAJOR MINERAL OCCURRENCES

Cl Clay

Mi Mica

⚡ Water Power

▨ Major Industrial Areas

PORTLAND
Food Processing,
Pulp & Paper Products

DOMINANT LAND USE

▨ Dairy, Poultry, Mixed Farming

▨ Dairy, General Farming

▨ Potatoes, General Farming

▨ Forests

Topography

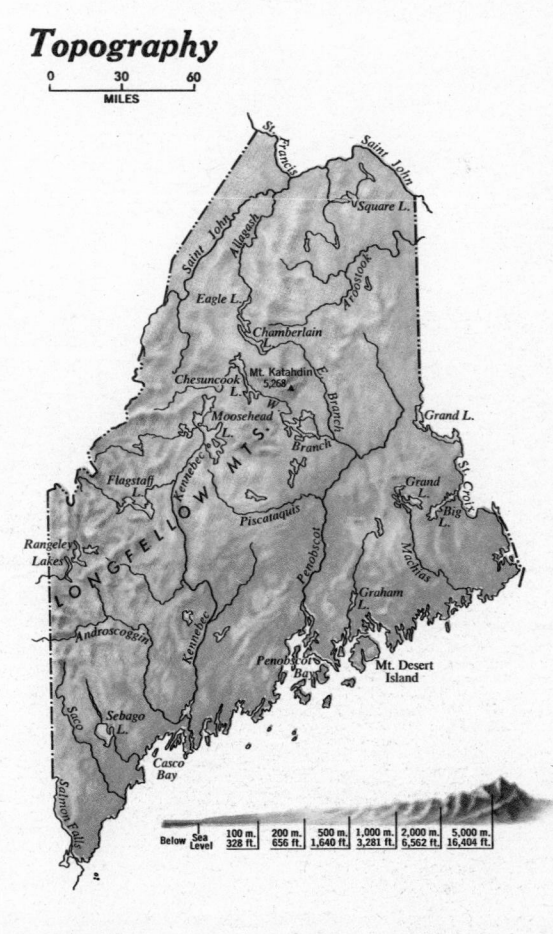

0   30   60
MILES

Below Sea Level | 100 m. 328 ft. | 200 m. 656 ft. | 500 m. 1,640 ft. | 1,000 m. 3,281 ft. | 2,000 m. 6,562 ft. | 5,000 m. 16,404 ft.

MARYLAND
COUNTIES

Allegany, 84,044 .... C 2
Anne Arundel, 297,539 ...... M 4
Baltimore, 621,077 .... M 3
Baltimore (city county), 905,759 .. M 3
Calvert, 20,682 .... M 6
Caroline, 19,781 .... P 5
Carroll, 69,006 .... K 2
Cecil, 53,291 .... P 2
Charles, 47,678 .... K 6
Dorchester, 29,405 .... O 7
Frederick, 84,927 .... J 3
Garrett, 21,476 .... A 2
Harford, 115,378 .... N 2
Howard, 61,911 .... L 4
Kent, 16,146 .... O 3
Montgomery, 522,809 .... J 4
Prince Georges, 660,567 .... L 5
Queen Annes, 18,422 .... P 4
Saint Marys, 47,388 .... M 7
Somerset, 18,924 .... R 8
Talbot, 23,692 .... O 5
Washington, 103,829 .... G 2
Wicomico, 54,236 .... R 7
Worcester, 24,442 .... S 8

CITIES and TOWNS

Zip   Name/Pop. .... Key
21001 Aberdeen, 12,375 .... O 2
21009 Abingdon, 3,000 .... N 3
21520 Accident, 237 .... A 2
20607 Accokeek, 450 .... L 6
21710 Adamstown, 265 .... H 3
21810 Allen, 200 .... R 7
† 21043 Allview, 2,314 .... L 4
† 21401 Annapolis (cap.)⊙, 29,592 .. M 5
20701 Annapolis Junction, 775 .. M 4
† 21782 Antietam, 150 .... H 3
20608 Aquasco, 950 .... L 6
† 20785 Ardmore, 500 .... G 4
* 20015 Aspen Hill, 16,799 .... K 4
* 21201 Baltimore, 905,759 .... M 3
     Baltimore, ‡2,070,670 .. M 3
21607 Barclay, 187 .... P 4
20703 Barnesville, 162 .... J 4
20610 Barston, 500 .... M 6
21521 Barton, 723 .... B 3
† 21901 Bayview, 250 .... P 2
21014 Bel Air⊙, 6,307 .... N 2
20611 Bel Alton, 675 .... L 7
† 21662 Bellevue, 500 .... O 6
20705 Beltsville, 8,912 ...... G 3
20612 Benedict, 700 .... M 6
21811 Berlin, 1,942 .... T 7
† 20740 Berwyn Heights, 3,934 .. G 4
20014 Bethesda, 71,621 ..... E 4
21609 Bethlehem, 200 .... P 6
21610 Betterton, 327 .... O 3
21611 Bishops Head, 250 .... O 7
21813 Bishopville, 300 .... T 7
21814 Bivalve, 450 .... P 7
20710 Bladensburg, 7,488 ... G 4
21523 Bloomington, 235 ..... B 3
21713 Boonsboro, 1,410 ..... H 2
† 21532 Borden Shaft, 208 .... B 2
21020 Boring, 283 .... L 2
† 20027 Boulevard Heights, 500 .. F 5
20678 Bowens, 250 .... M 6
20715 Bowie, 35,028 .... H 4
20720 Boyds, 300 .... J 4
21612 Bozman, 500 .... N 5
20613 Brandywine, 525 ..... L 6
20722 Brentwood, 3,426 .... F 4
21715 Brownsville, 185 ..... H 3
21716 Brunswick, 3,566 .... H 3
21717 Buckeystown, 400 .... J 3
21718 Burkittsville, 221 .... H 3
20730 Burtonsville, 3,000 ... L 4
20618 Bushwood, 675 .... L 7
21023 Butler, 150 .... L 2
20731 Cabin John, 2,500 ... E 4
20619 California, 350 .... M 7
* 20705 Calverton, 6,453 ..... L 4
21613 Cambridge⊙, 11,595 . O 6
20031 Camp Springs, 22,776 . G 5
20027 Capitol Heights, 2,852 . G 5
21024 Cardiff, 510 .... N 2
* 20780 Carrollton, 13,395 ... G 4
21025 Carrollton, 174 ...... L 2
† 21034 Castleton, 675 ...... N 2
† 21788 Catoctin Furnace, 516 . J 2
21228 Catonsville, 54,812 .. M 3
21720 Cavetown, 325 ...... H 2
21913 Cecilton, 581 .... P 3
† 20767 Cedar Grove, 300 .... K 4
* 20027 Cedar Heights, 6,049 . G 5
21617 Centreville⊙, 1,853 .. O 4
21816 Chance, 500 .... P 8
20621 Chaptico, 300 .... M 7
21914 Charlestown, 721 .... P 2
20622 Charlotte Hall, 200 .. M 7
21027 Chase, 900 .... N 3
20623 Cheltenham, 950 .... L 6
† 21921 Cherry Hill, 214 ..... P 2
20732 Chesapeake Beach, 934 . N 6
21915 Chesapeake City, 1,031 . P 2
21619 Chester, 950 .... N 5
21620 Chestertown⊙, 3,476 . O 4
20785 Cheverly, 6,696 ..... G 4
* 20015 Chevy Chase, 16,424 . E 4
21721 Chewsville, 350 ..... H 2
20783 Chillum, 35,656 ..... F 4
21623 Church Hill, 247 ..... O 4
21028 Churchville, 500 .... N 2
21624 Claiborne, 150 ...... N 5
20734 Clarksburg, 400 .... J 4
21029 Clarksville, 500 ..... L 4
21722 Clear Spring, 499 ... G 2
20624 Clements, 800 ...... L 7
20735 Clinton, 1,900 ...... G 6
21030 Cockeysville, 2,900 . L 2
20740 College Park, 26,156 . G 4
† 20722 Colmar Manor, 1,715 . F 4
21917 Colora, 500 .... O 2

20626 Coltons Point, 310 ... M 8
21043 Columbia, 8,815 .... L 5
20627 Compton, 500 ...... M 7
21918 Conowingo, 150 .... O 2
21723 Cooksville, 497 .... K 3
† 20027 Coral Hills, 7,105 ... G 5
21625 Cordova, 365 ...... O 5
21524 Corriganville, 850 .. C 2
20722 Cottage City, 993 ... F 4
20611 Cox Station (Bel Alton), 675 . L 7
21788 Creagerstown, 240 .. J 2
21525 Crellin, 500 .... A 3
21502 Cresaptown, 1,731 . C 2
21817 Crisfield, 3,078 .... P 9
21627 Crocheron, 150 .... O 8
21113 Crofton, 4,478 ..... M 4
21032 Crownsville, 1,900 . M 4
21628 Crumpton, 375 ..... P 4
21502 Cumberland⊙, 29,724 . D 2
20750 Damascus, 2,638 ... K 3
20628 Dameron, 500 ...... N 8
21820 Dames Quarter, 300 . P 8
21035 Davidsonville, 250 . M 5

20751 Deale, 1,059 .... M 5
21821 Deal Island, 800 .... P 8
21550 Deer Park, 310 ..... A 3
† 19940 Delmar, 1,191 .... R 7
21629 Denton⊙, 1,561 ..... P 5
20855 Derwood, 450 .... K 4
20753 Dickerson, 500 ..... J 4
20028 District Heights, 8,424 . G 5
† 21710 Doubs, 273 .... J 3
21795 Downsville, 255 .... G 2
20630 Drayden, 450 .... N 8
† 21154 Dublin, 366 .... N 2
21222 Dundalk, 85,377 .... N 3
20608 Eagle Harbor, 200 .. M 6
† 21146 Earleigh Heights, 1,500 . M 4
21631 East New Market, 251 . P 6
21601 Easton⊙, 6,809 ..... O 5
21528 Eckhart Mines, 900 . C 2
21040 Edgewood, 8,551 ... N 3
20781 Edmonston, 1,441 .. F 4
21784 Eldersburg, 1,739 .. L 3
21920 Elk Mills, 500 ...... P 2
† 21901 Elk Neck, 700 ...... P 2
21227 Elkridge, 4,900 ..... M 4
21921 Elkton⊙, 5,362 ..... P 2
21529 Ellerslie, 950 ...... C 2

21043 Ellicott City⊙, 9,506 . L 3
21727 Emmitsburg, 1,532 .. J 2
21221 Essex, 38,193 ...... N 3
21824 Ewell, 350 .... O 9
† 21620 Fairlee, 300 .... O 4
† 20027 Fairmont Heights, 1,972 . G 5
21047 Fallston, 617 ...... N 2
21632 Federalsburg, 1,917 . P 6
21061 Ferndale, 9,929 .... M 4
21048 Finksburg, 950 ..... L 3
21634 Fishing Creek, 595 . N 7
21530 Flintstone, 395 .... D 2
† 20907 Forest Glen, 1,900 .. F 4
† 20001 Forest Heights, 3,600 . F 5
21050 Forest Hill, 450 .... N 2
† 20028 Forestville, 16,152 .. G 5
20013 Fort Foote, 700 .... F 6
20735 Fort Washington, 1,650 . L 6
21740 Fountain Head, 2,029 . H 2
21760 Foxville, 400 .... J 2
21701 Frederick⊙, 23,641 . J 3
21053 Freeland, 500 ...... M 2
21531 Friendsville, 566 ... A 2
† 21157 Frizzellburg, 300 ... K 2
21532 Frostburg, 7,327 ... C 2
21826 Fruitland, 2,315 .... R 8

21734 Funkstown, 1,051 ... H 2
20760 Gaithersburg, 8,344 . K 4
21635 Galena, 361 .... P 3
21054 Gambrills, 460 ..... M 4
20766 Garrett Park, 1,258 . E 3
21055 Garrison, 950 ...... L 3
20767 Germantown, 260 .. J 4
21829 Girdletree, 850 .... S 8
20801 Glenarden, 4,502 .. G 4
21057 Glen Arm, 350 ..... N 3
21061 Glen Burnie, 38,608 . M 4
20768 Glen Echo, 297 .... E 4
† 20013 Glen Echo Heights, 2,025 . E 4
21737 Glenelg, 400 .... L 3
21071 Glyndon-Reisterstown,
     14,037 .... L 3
21636 Goldsboro, 231 .... P 4
* 20715 Good Luck, 10,584 . G 4
† 21788 Graceham, 300 ..... J 2
21163 Granite, 950 .... L 3
21536 Grantsville, 517 ... B 2
21638 Grasonville, 1,182 . O 5
20770 Greenbelt, 18,199 .. G 4
21122 Green Haven, 1,841 . M 4
21072 Greenmount, 325 .. L 2
21639 Greensboro, 1,173 . P 5

21740 Hagerstown⊙, 35,862 . H 2
† 21740 Halfway, 6,106 ..... H 2
† 20850 Halpine, 5,912 ..... K 4
21074 Hampstead, 961 .... L 2
21750 Hancock, 1,832 .... F 2
21201 Hanover, 500 ...... L 3
† 21787 Harney, 250 .... J 2
21078 Havre de Grace, 9,791 . N 2
21830 Hebron, 705 .... R 8
21080 Henryton, 400 ..... L 3
† 21111 Hereford, 680 ..... L 2
21753 Highfield, 500 ..... H 2
20901 Hillandale, 19,520 .. F 4
† 20013 Hillcrest Heights, 24,037 . F 5
21641 Hillsboro, 177 ..... P 5
20636 Hollywood, 500 .... M 7
21642 Hoopersville, 500 .. N 8
20637 Hughesville, 500 .. M 6
20639 Huntingtown, 450 .. M 6
21643 Hurlock, 1,056 .... P 6
† 21864 Hursley Station (Stockton),
     500 .... S 8
20734 Hyattstown, 150 ... J 4
* 20780 Hyattsville, 14,998 . F 4
20640 Indian Head, 1,350 . K 6
21644 Ingleside, 180 ..... P 5

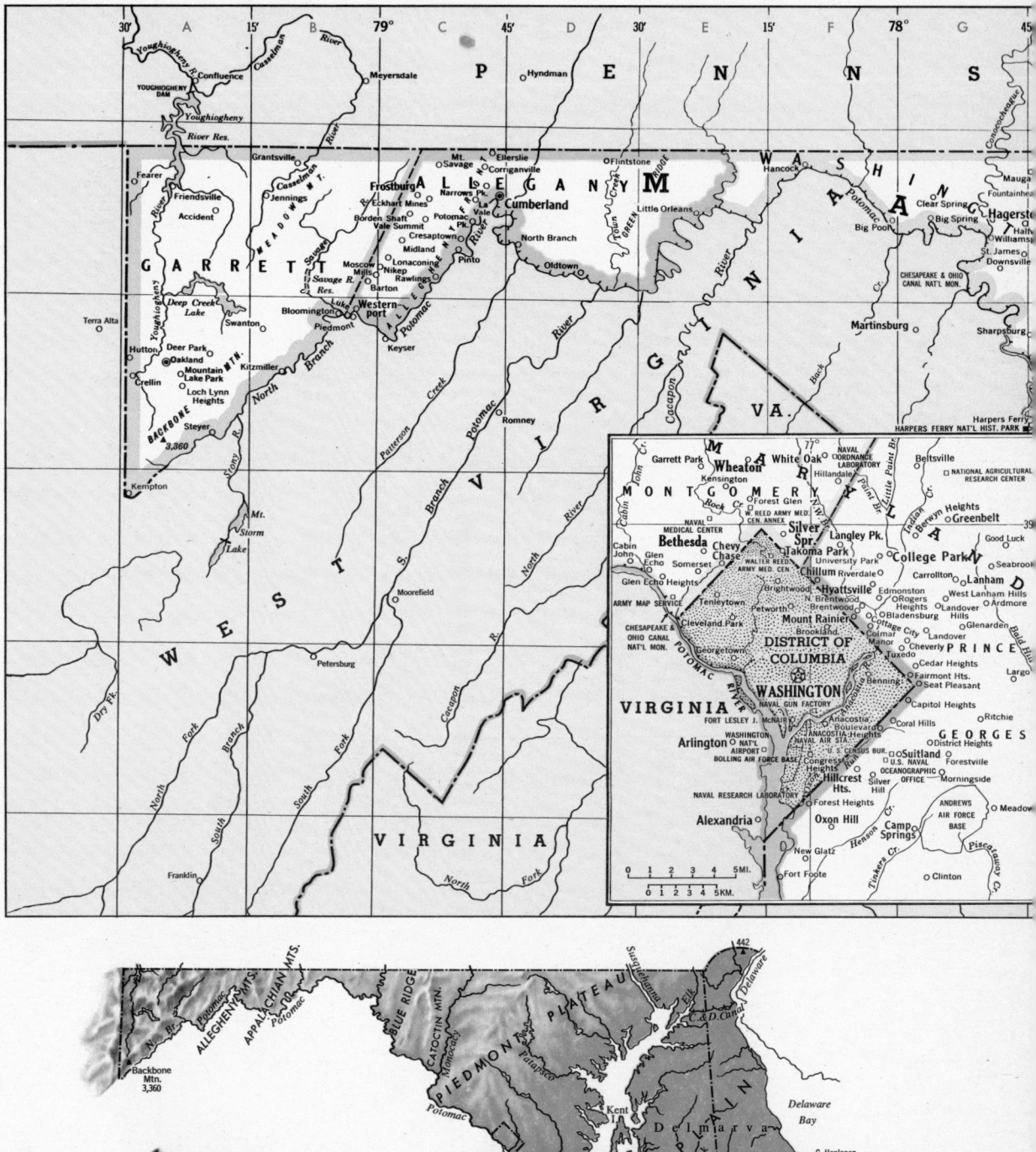

Topography

5,000 m.   2,000 m.   1,000 m.   500 m.   200 m.   100 m.   Sea   Below
16,404 ft.   6,562 ft.   3,281 ft.   1,640 ft.   656 ft.   328 ft.   Level

0   30   60
MILES

(continued on following page)

MARYLAND
AREA 10,577 sq. mi.
POPULATION 3,922,399
CAPITAL Annapolis
LARGEST CITY Baltimore
HIGHEST POINT Backbone Mtn. 3,360 ft.
SETTLED IN 1634
ADMITTED TO UNION April 28, 1788
POPULAR NAME Old Line State; Free State
STATE FLOWER Black-eyed Susan
STATE BIRD Baltimore Oriole

DELAWARE
AREA 2,057 sq. mi.
POPULATION 548,104
CAPITAL Dover
LARGEST CITY Wilmington
HIGHEST POINT Ebright Road 442 ft.
SETTLED IN 1631
ADMITTED TO UNION December 7, 1787
POPULAR NAME First State; Diamond State
STATE FLOWER Peach Blossom
STATE BIRD Blue Hen Chicken

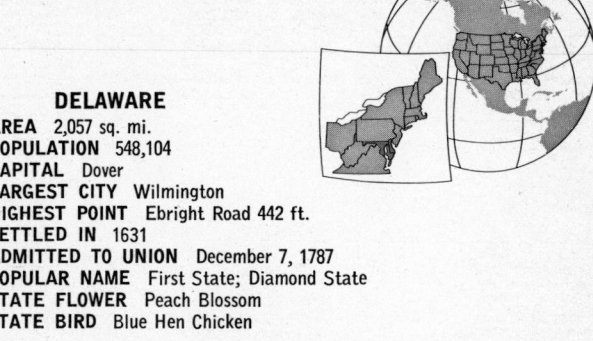

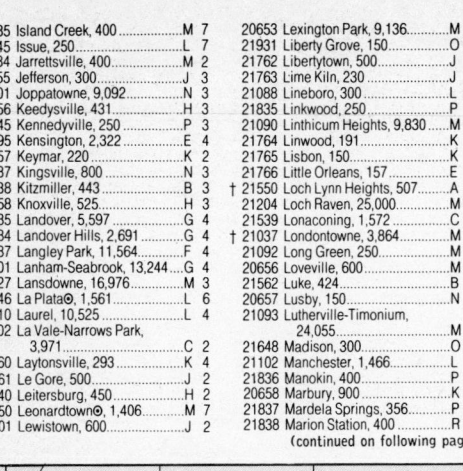

MARYLAND and DELAWARE

SCALE

0 5 10 20 30 MI.

0 5 10 20 30 KM.

National Capital ... ⊛
State Capitals ... ☆
County Seats ... ⊙
Canals

© C.S. HAMMOND & Co., N.Y.

Antietam Battlefield, near Sharpsburg, Maryland, the scene of the country's bloodiest one-day battle on September 17, 1862. A national battlefield site today, it is surrounded by farms, some of whose cattle graze among the cannons and monuments.

In Lewes, Delaware, settled by the Dutch in 1631, the Thompson Country Store sign establishes its origin as c.1800. The home of generations of Delaware River ship pilots, this seafaring town survives a history of shipwreck, bombardment and plundering.

Agriculture, Industry and Resources

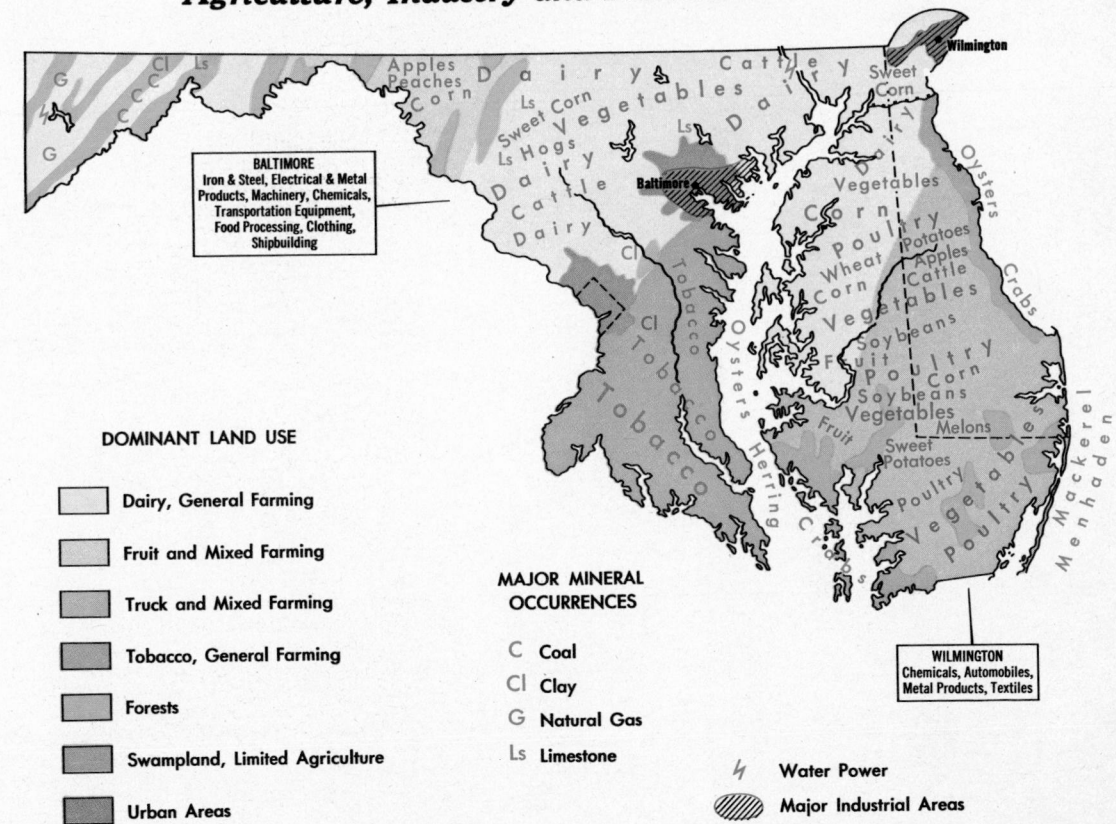

BALTIMORE
Iron & Steel, Electrical & Metal Products, Machinery, Chemicals, Transportation Equipment, Food Processing, Clothing, Shipbuilding

WILMINGTON
Chemicals, Automobiles, Metal Products, Textiles

DOMINANT LAND USE

- Dairy, General Farming
- Fruit and Mixed Farming
- Truck and Mixed Farming
- Tobacco, General Farming
- Forests
- Swampland, Limited Agriculture
- Urban Areas

MAJOR MINERAL OCCURRENCES

- C Coal
- Cl Clay
- G Natural Gas
- Ls Limestone

- ⚡ Water Power
- ▨ Major Industrial Areas

MASSACHUSETTS
AREA 8,257 sq. mi.
POPULATION 5,689,170
CAPITAL Boston
LARGEST CITY Boston
HIGHEST POINT Mt. Greylock 3,491 ft.
SETTLED IN 1620
ADMITTED TO UNION February 6, 1788
POPULAR NAME Bay State; Old Colony
STATE FLOWER Mayflower
STATE BIRD Chickadee

RHODE ISLAND
AREA 1,214 sq. mi.
POPULATION 949,723
CAPITAL Providence
LARGEST CITY Providence
HIGHEST POINT Jerimoth Hill 812 ft.
SETTLED IN 1636
ADMITTED TO UNION May 29, 1790
POPULAR NAME Little Rhody
STATE FLOWER Violet
STATE BIRD Rhode Island Red

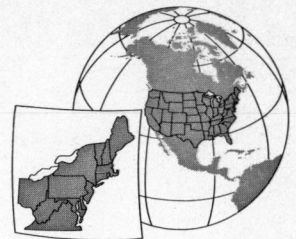

Agriculture, Industry and Resources

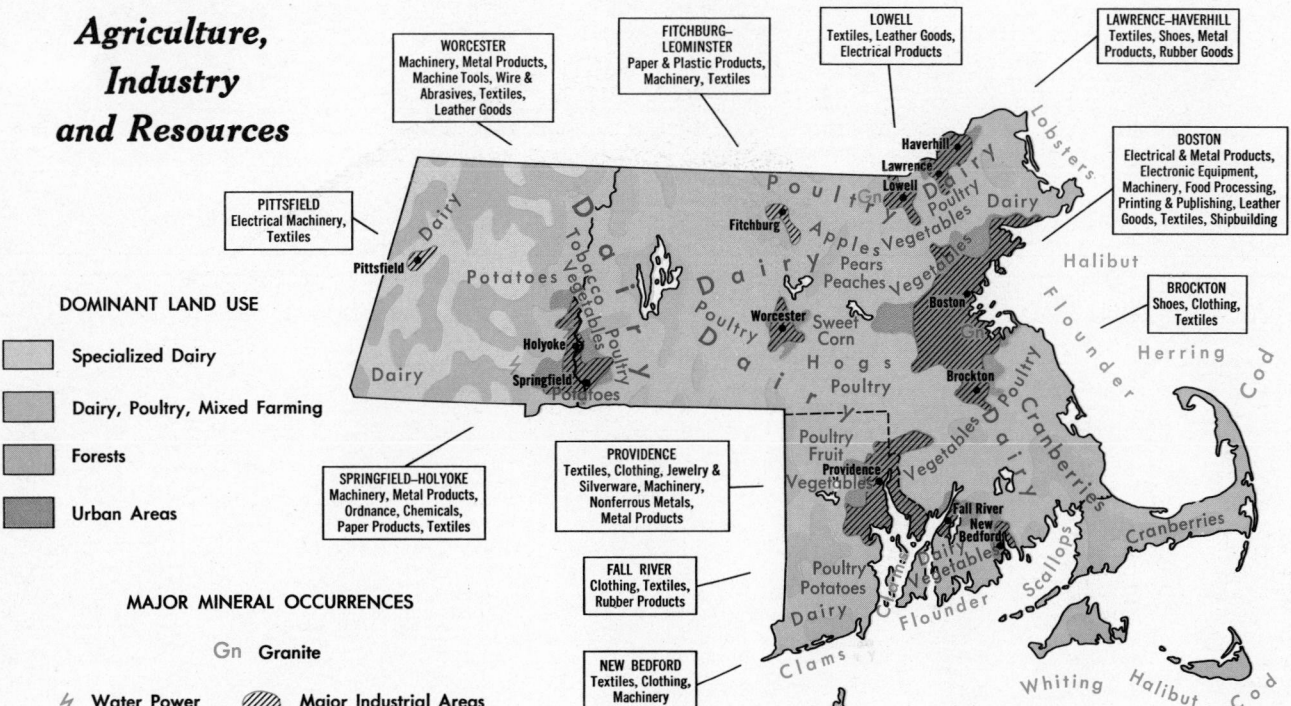

PITTSFIELD
Electrical Machinery, Textiles

WORCESTER
Machinery, Metal Products, Machine Tools, Wire & Abrasives, Textiles, Leather Goods

FITCHBURG–LEOMINSTER
Paper & Plastic Products, Machinery, Textiles

LOWELL
Textiles, Leather Goods, Electrical Products

LAWRENCE–HAVERHILL
Textiles, Shoes, Metal Products, Rubber Goods

BOSTON
Electrical & Metal Products, Electronic Equipment, Machinery, Food Processing, Printing & Publishing, Leather Goods, Textiles, Shipbuilding

BROCKTON
Shoes, Clothing, Textiles

SPRINGFIELD–HOLYOKE
Machinery, Metal Products, Ordnance, Chemicals, Paper Products, Textiles

PROVIDENCE
Textiles, Clothing, Jewelry & Silverware, Machinery, Nonferrous Metals, Metal Products

FALL RIVER
Clothing, Textiles, Rubber Products

NEW BEDFORD
Textiles, Clothing, Machinery

DOMINANT LAND USE
- Specialized Dairy
- Dairy, Poultry, Mixed Farming
- Forests
- Urban Areas

MAJOR MINERAL OCCURRENCES
Gn Granite

⚡ Water Power   ▨ Major Industrial Areas

(continued on following page)

MASSACHUSETTS (continued)

01550 Southbridge, ○17,057....G 4
01550 Southbridge, 14,261....G 4
02748 South Dartmouth, 9,209....L 6
02375 South Easton, 4,400....K 4
01075 South Hadley, 17,033....D 4
01075 South Hadley Falls, 6,500....D 4
† 02190 South Weymouth, 17,500....E 8
01077 Southwick, 6,330....D 4
02664 South Yarmouth, 5,380....O 6
01562 Spencer, 8,779....F 3
01562 Spencer, 5,895....F 3
* 01101 Springfield○, 163,905....D 4
  Springfield-Chicopee-
  Holyoke, †529,921....D 4
01564 Sterling, △4,247....G 3
01262 Stockbridge, △2,312....A 3
01262 Stockbridge, 1,147....A 3
02180 Stoneham, △20,725....C 6
02072 Stoughton, △23,459....K 4
01775 Stow, △3,984....H 3
01566 Sturbridge, △4,878....F 4

01776 Sudbury, △13,506....A 6
01375 Sunderland, △2,236....D 3
† 01527 Sutton, △4,590....G 4
01907 Swampscott, △13,578....E 6
02777 Swansea, △12,640....K 5
02780 Taunton○, 43,756....K 5
01468 Templeton, △5,863....F 2
01876 Tewksbury, △22,755....K 2
01034 Tolland, △172....D 4
01983 Topsfield, △5,225....L 1
01469 Townsend, △4,281....H 2
02666 Truro, △1,234....O 5
01376 Turners Falls, 5,168....D 2
01879 Tyngsboro, △4,204....J 2
01264 Tyringham, △234....A 4
01568 Upton, △3,484....H 4
01569 Uxbridge, △8,253....H 5
02568 Vineyard Haven, 1,599....M 7
† 02168 Waban, 6,871....B 7
01880 Wakefield, △25,402....C 5
01081 Wales, △852....F 4
02081 Walpole, △18,149....B 8
02154 Waltham, 61,582....B 6

01082 Ware, △8,187....E 3
01082 Ware, 6,509....E 3
02571 Wareham, △11,492....L 5
01083 Warren, △3,633....F 4
01378 Warwick, △492....E 2
† 01223 Washington, △406....B 3
02172 Watertown, △39,307....C 6
02172 Waverley, 15,000....B 6
01778 Wayland, △13,461....A 7
01570 Webster, △14,917....G 4
01570 Webster, 12,432....G 4
02181 Wellesley, △28,051....B 7
02181 Wellesley Hills, 15,000....B 7
02667 Wellfleet, △1,743....O 5
01379 Wendell, △405....E 2
01984 Wenham, △3,849....L 1
01581 Westboro, △12,594....H 3
01581 Westborough, 4,474....H 3
02379 West Bridgewater, △7,152....K 4
01585 West Brookfield, △2,653....F 3
01085 Westfield, 31,433....D 4
01886 Westford, △10,368....J 2

01027 Westhampton, △793....C 3
01473 Westminster, △4,273....G 2
01985 West Newbury, △2,254....L 1
† 02165 West Newton, 13,500....B 7
02193 Windsor, △10,870....B 6
02790 Westport, △9,791....K 6
02790 Westport P.O. (North
  Westport), 4,000....K 6
01089 West Springfield, △28,461....D 4
01266 West Stockbridge, △1,354....A 3
02575 West Tisbury, △453....M 7
02090 Westwood, △12,750....B 8
02673 West Yarmouth, 3,699....N 6
† 02188 Weymouth, 54,610....D 8
01093 Whately, △1,145....D 3
01588 Whitinsville, 5,210....H 4
02382 Whitman, △13,059....L 4
01095 Wilbraham, △11,984....E 4
01095 Wilbraham, 3,540....E 4
01096 Williamsburg, △2,342....C 3
01267 Williamstown, △8,454....B 2
01267 Williamstown, 4,285....B 2
01887 Wilmington, △17,102....C 5

01887 Wilmington, 3,900....C 5
01475 Winchendon, △6,635....F 2
01475 Winchendon, 3,997....F 2
01890 Winchester, △22,269....C 6
01270 Windsor, △468....B 2
02152 Winthrop, △20,335....D 6
01801 Woburn, 37,406....C 6
02543 Woods Hole, 750....M 6
* 01601 Worcester○, 176,572....H 3
  Worcester, †339,730....H 3
01098 Worthington, △712....C 3
02093 Wrentham, △7,315....J 4
† 02675 Yarmouth, △12,033....O 6

CITIES and TOWNS

Zip	Name/Pop.
02816	Anthony, 7,000
02887	Apponaug, 6,533
02806	Barrington, △17,554
02806	Barrington, 13,000
02809	Bristol○, △17,860
02809	Bristol○, 14,000
02911	Centerdale, 8,000
02863	Central Falls, 18,716
02813	Charlestown, △2,863
02816	Coventry, △22,947
02816	Coventry, 7,000
02910	Cranston, 73,037
02818	East Greenwich○, △9,577
02914	East Providence, 48,151
02822	Exeter, △3,245
02825	Foster, △2,626
02828	Greenville, 3,500
02833	Hopkinton, △5,392
02835	Jamestown, △2,911

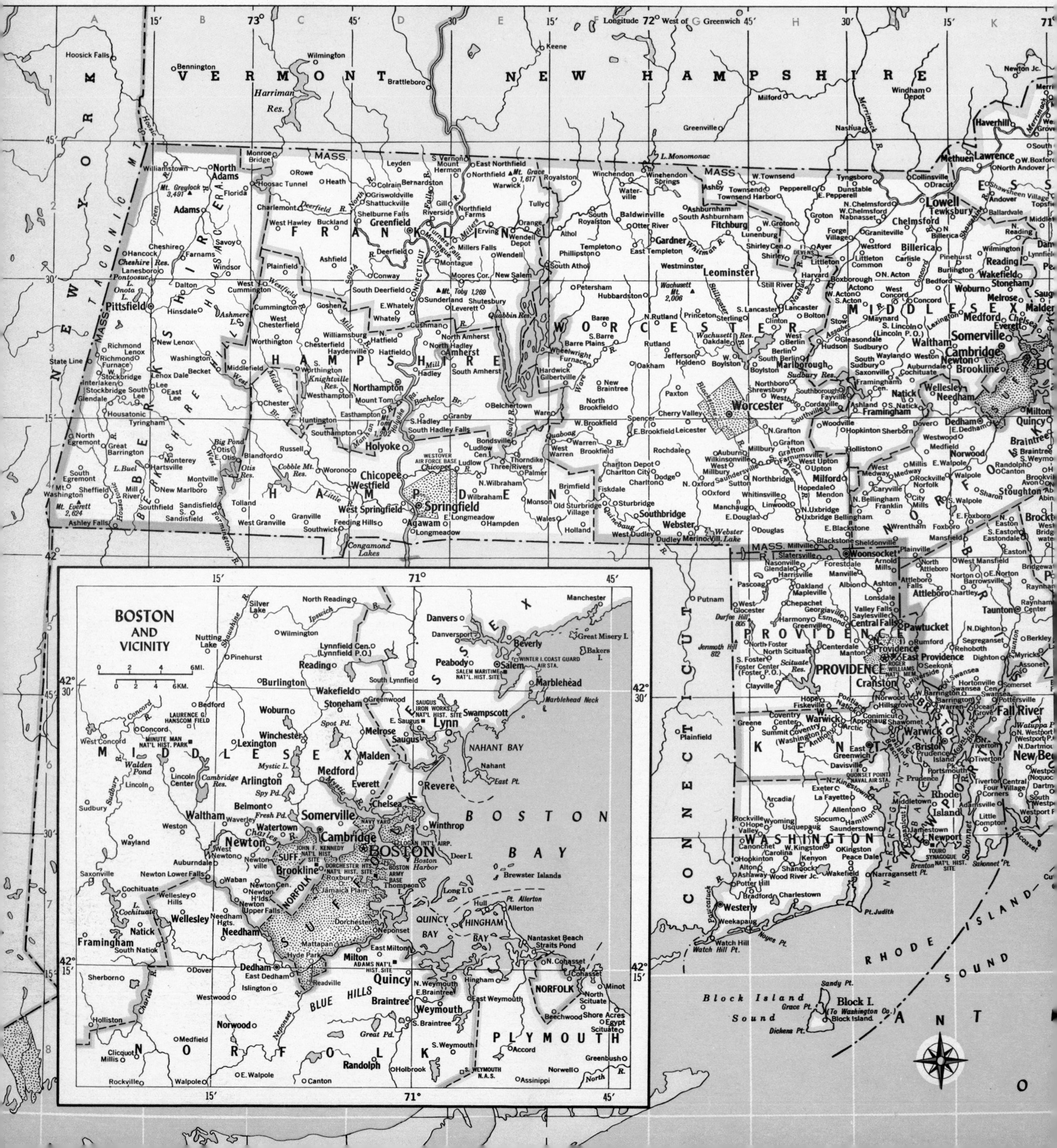

RHODE ISLAND

COUNTIES

Bristol, 45,937....J 6
Kent, 142,382....H 6
Newport, 94,559....K 6
Providence, 580,261....H 5
Washington, 83,586....H 7

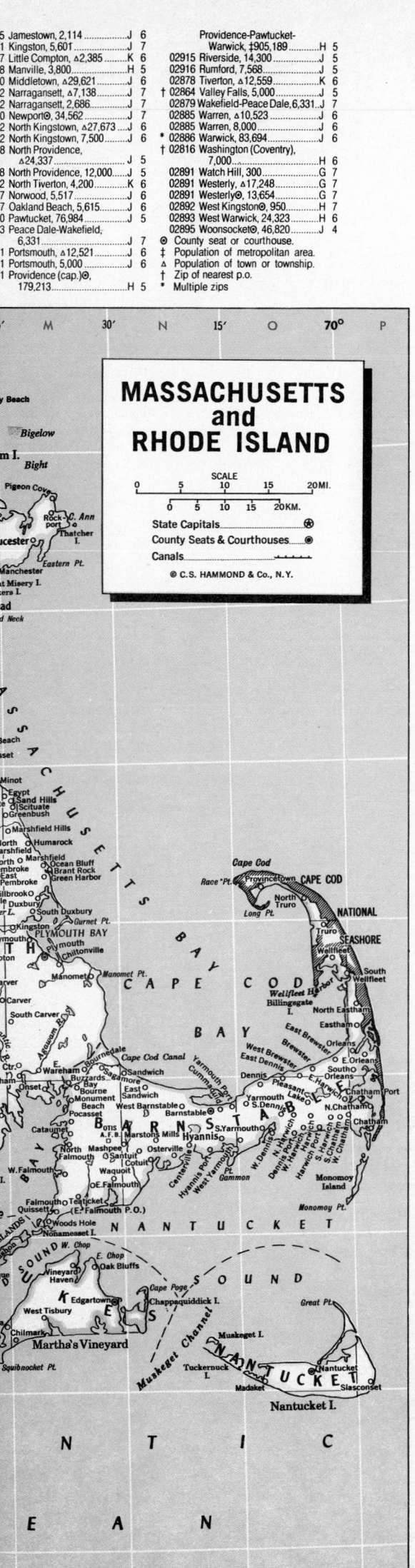

MASSACHUSETTS and RHODE ISLAND

SCALE
0 5 10 15 20 MI.
0 5 10 15 20 KM.

State Capitals ⊛
County Seats & Courthouses ⊙
Canals

© C.S. HAMMOND & Co., N.Y.

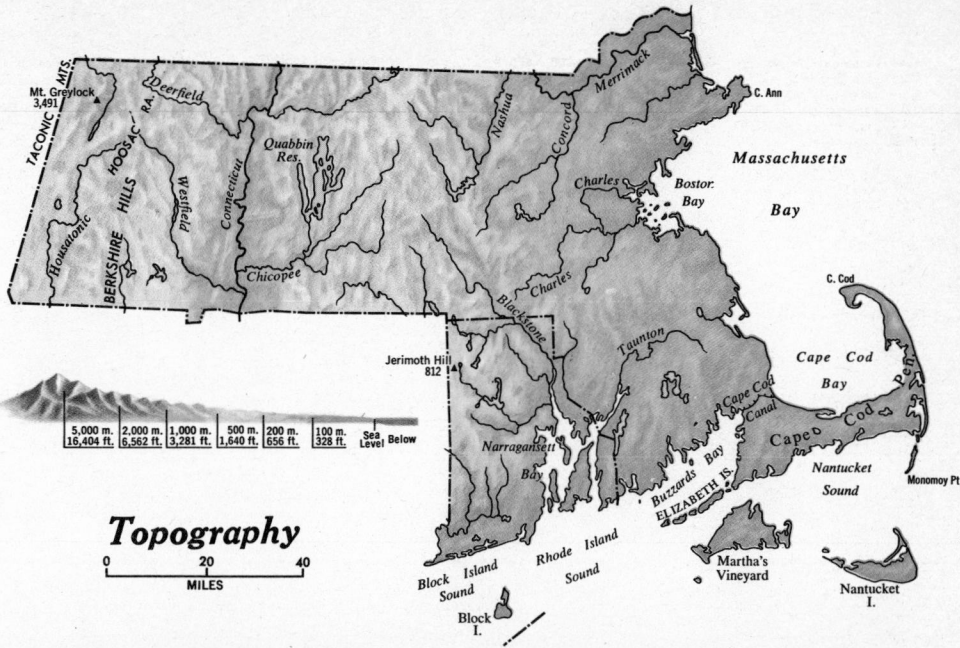

Topography

Marking the site of the first battle of the Revolutionary War on April 19, 1775, the Minuteman Statue faces the line of advancing Redcoats at Lexington, Massachusetts.

Typical Newport turn-of-the-century grandeur in a French chalet-style mansion, with mansard roof and wrought iron gates.

AREA 58,216 sq. mi.
POPULATION 8,875,083
CAPITAL Lansing
LARGEST CITY Detroit
HIGHEST POINT Mt. Curwood 1,980 ft.
SETTLED IN 1650
ADMITTED TO UNION January 26, 1837
POPULAR NAME Wolverine State
STATE FLOWER Apple Blossom
STATE BIRD Robin

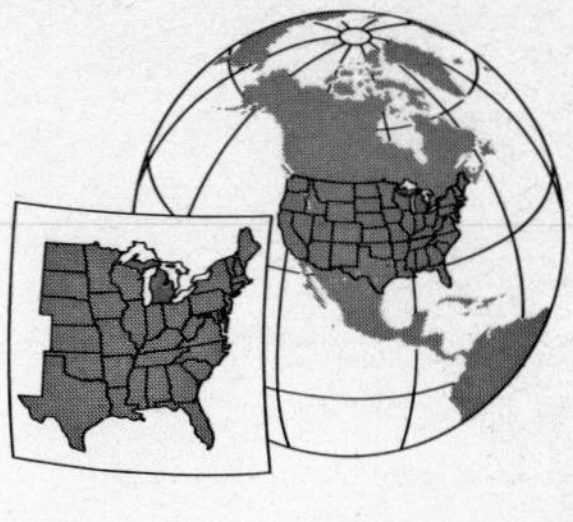

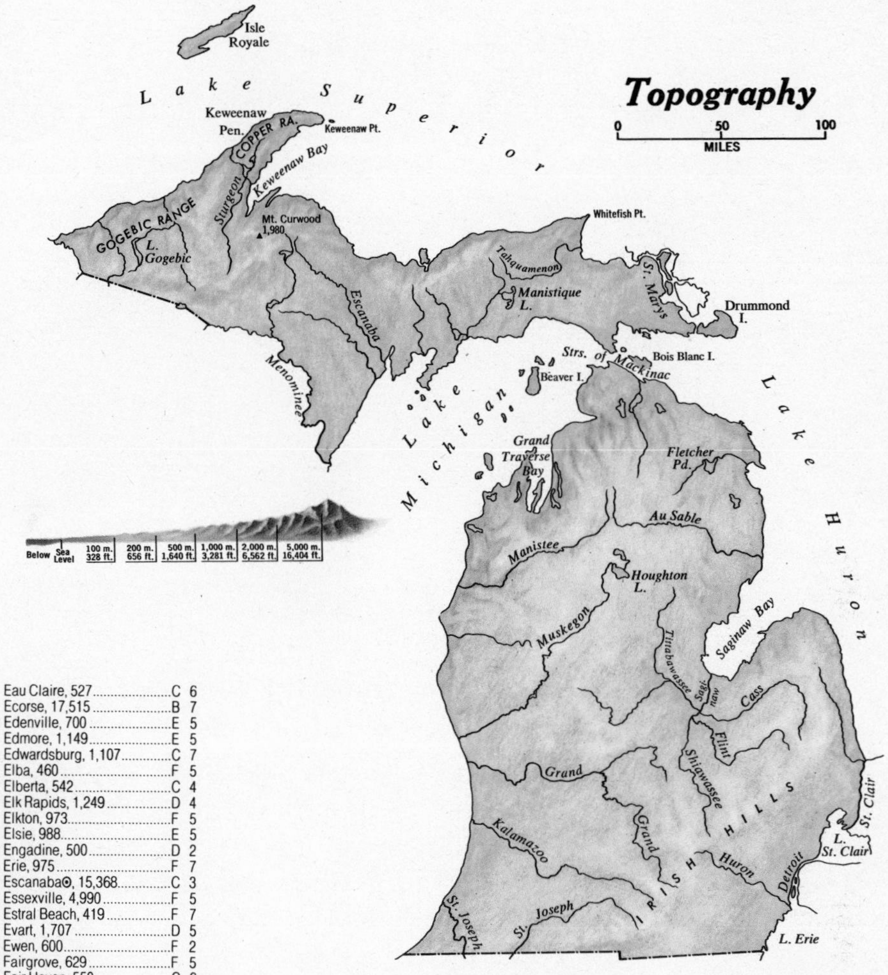

COUNTIES

ona, 7,113	F 4
er, 8,568	C 2
gan, 66,575	D 6
ena, 30,708	F 4
im, 12,612	D 3
nac, 11,149	F 4
aga, 7,789	A 2
ry, 38,166	D 6
, 117,339	E 5
zie, 8,593	C 4
ien, 163,875	C 7
nch, 37,906	D 7
houn, 141,963	D 6
s, 43,312	C 7
arlevoix, 16,541	D 3
boygan, 16,573	E 3
opewa, 32,412	E 2
re, 16,695	E 5
ton, 48,492	E 6
wford, 6,482	E 4
ta, 35,924	C 2
kinson, 23,753	B 2
on, 68,892	E 6
net, 18,331	E 3
esee, 444,341	F 5
dwin, 13,471	E 4
gebic, 20,676	F 2
nd Traverse, 39,175	D 4
tiot, 39,246	E 5
sdale, 37,171	E 7
ghton, 34,652	G 1
on, 34,083	F 5
ham, 261,039	E 6
a, 45,848	D 6
co, 24,905	F 4
, 13,813	G 2
bella, 44,594	E 5
kson, 143,274	E 6
amazoo, 201,550	D 6
kaska, 5,272	D 4
t, 411,044	D 5
weenaw, 2,264	A 1
e, 5,661	D 5
eer, 52,317	F 5
lanau, 10,872	D 4
awee, 81,609	E 7
ngston, 58,967	F 6
e, 6,789	D 2
ckinac, 9,660	D 2
comb, 625,309	G 6
nistee, 20,094	C 4
rquette, 64,686	B 2
son, 22,612	C 4
costa, 27,992	D 5
nominee, 24,587	B 3
land, 63,769	E 5
saukee, 7,126	D 4
nroe, 118,479	F 7
ntcalm, 39,660	D 5
ntmorency, 5,247	E 3
skegon, 157,246	C 5
waygo, 27,992	D 5
kland, 907,871	F 6
eana, 17,984	C 5
emaw, 11,903	E 4
onagon, 10,548	F 1
ceola, 14,838	D 5
coda, 4,726	E 4
ego, 10,422	E 3
awa, 128,181	C 6
sque Isle, 12,836	F 3
scommon, 9,892	E 4
ginaw, 219,743	E 5
nt Clair, 120,175	G 6
nt Joseph, 47,392	D 7
nilac, 34,889	G 5
hoolcraft, 8,226	C 2
awassee, 63,075	E 6
scola, 48,603	F 5
n Buren, 56,173	C 6
shtenaw, 234,103	F 6
yne, 2,666,751	F 6
xford, 19,717	D 4

CITIES and TOWNS

p	*Name/Pop.*	*Key*
220	Addison, 595	E 7
221	Adrian⊙, 20,382	F 7
701	Akron, 525	F 5
764	Alabaster, 46	F 4
224	Albion, 12,112	E 6
001	Algonac, 3,684	G 6
10	Allegan⊙, 4,516	D 6
101	Allen Park, 40,747	B 7
801	Alma, 9,790	E 5
003	Almont, 1,634	F 6
707	Alpena⊙, 13,805	F 3
903	Amasa, 450	G 2
004	Anchorville, 440	G 6
103	Ann Arbor⊙, 99,797	F 6
	Ann Arbor, ‡234,103	F 6
659	Antrim, 475	D 4
10	Argyle, 800	G 5
005	Armada, 1,352	G 6
806	Ashley, 521	E 5
011	Athens, 996	D 6
709	Atlanta⊙, 475	E 3
905	Atlantic Mine, 785	G 1
11	Auburn, 1,919	F 5
57	Auburn Heights, 7,500	F 6
703	Au Gres, 564	F 4
12	Augusta, 1,025	D 6
750	Au Sable-Oscoda, 3,475	F 4
640	Averill, 800	E 5
413	Bad Axe⊙, 2,999	G 5
304	Baldwin⊙, 612	D 5
414	Bancroft, 724	E 6
013	Bangor, 2,050	C 6
908	Baraga, 1,116	G 1
307	Bark River, 550	B 3
101	Baroda, 439	C 7
308	Bath, 600	E 6
014	Battle Creek, 38,931	D 6
48706	Bay City⊙, 49,449	F 5
	Bay City, ‡117,339	F 5
48720	Bay Port, 600	F 5
49770	Bay View, 500	E 3
48612	Beaverton, 954	E 5
49020	Bedford, 450	D 6
† 49423	Beechwood, 2,714	C 6
48809	Belding, 5,121	D 5
49615	Bellaire⊙, 897	D 4
48111	Belleville, 2,406	F 6
49021	Bellevue, 1,297	E 6
49022	Benton Harbor, 16,481	C 6
† 49022	Benton Heights, 8,067	C 6
49910	Bergland, 635	F 1
48072	Berkley, 22,618	B 6
49103	Berrien Springs, 1,951	C 7
49911	Bessemer⊙, 2,805	F 2
49617	Beulah⊙, 461	C 4
49307	Big Rapids⊙, 11,995	D 5
48415	Birch Run, 932	F 5
* 48008	Birmingham, 26,170	B 6
49228	Blissfield, 2,753	F 7
48013	Bloomfield Hills, 3,672	B 6
49026	Bloomingdale, 496	C 6
49712	Boyne City, 2,969	E 3
48615	Breckenridge, 1,257	E 5
48722	Bridgeport, 1,900	F 5
49106	Bridgman, 1,621	C 7
48116	Brighton, 2,457	F 6
49715	Brimley, 490	E 2
49229	Britton, 697	F 6
49028	Bronson, 2,390	D 7
49230	Brooklyn, 1,112	E 6
48416	Brown City, 1,142	G 5
49716	Brutus, 431	E 3
49107	Buchanan, 4,645	C 7
49314	Burnips, 725	D 6
49030	Burr Oak, 873	D 7
48418	Byron, 655	E 6
49315	Byron Center, 900	D 6
49601	Cadillac⊙, 9,990	D 4
49316	Caledonia, 716	D 6
49913	Calumet, 1,007	A 1
48014	Capac, 1,279	G 5
48117	Carleton, 1,503	F 6
48723	Caro⊙, 3,701	F 5
48724	Carrollton, 7,300	E 5
48811	Carson City, 1,217	E 5
48419	Carsonville, 621	G 5
48725	Caseville, 607	F 5
49915	Caspian, 1,165	G 2
48726	Cass City, 1,974	F 5
49031	Cassopolis⊙, 2,108	C 7
49422	Castle Park, 500	C 6
49319	Cedar Springs, 1,807	D 5
49719	Cedarville, 800	E 2
49233	Cement City, 531	E 6
48015	Center Line, 10,379	B 6
49622	Central Lake, 741	D 3
49032	Centreville⊙, 1,044	D 7
49814	Champion, 550	B 2
49815	Channing, 550	B 2
49720	Charlevoix⊙, 3,519	D 3
48813	Charlotte⊙, 8,244	E 6
49623	Chase, 534	D 5
49721	Cheboygan⊙, 5,553	E 3
48118	Chelsea, 3,858	E 6
48616	Chesaning, 2,876	E 5
48617	Clare, 2,639	E 5
49234	Clarklake, 500	E 6
48016	Clarkston, 1,034	F 6
48017	Clawson, 17,617	B 6
49235	Clayton, 505	E 7
48727	Clifford, 472	F 5
49034	Climax, 594	D 6
49236	Clinton, 1,677	F 6
48420	Clio, 2,357	F 5
49036	Coldwater⊙, 9,099	D 7
48618	Coleman, 1,295	E 5
49038	Coloma, 1,814	C 6
49040	Colon, 1,172	D 7
48421	Columbiaville, 935	F 5
49041	Comstock, 5,003	D 6
49237	Concord, 983	E 6
49042	Constantine, 1,733	D 7
49722	Conway, 560	E 3
49404	Coopersville, 2,129	C 5
49818	Cornell, 640	B 3
48817	Corunna⊙, 2,829	E 6
49043	Covert, 650	C 6
48422	Croswell, 1,954	G 5
48818	Crystal, 649	E 5
49920	Crystal Falls⊙, 2,000	A 2
† 49501	Cutlerville, 6,267	D 6
48819	Dansville, 486	E 6
48423	Davison, 5,259	F 5
* 48120	Dearborn, 104,199	B 7
48127	Dearborn Heights, 80,069	B 7
49045	Decatur, 1,764	C 6
48427	Deckerville, 817	G 5
49238	Deerfield, 834	F 7
49725	De Tour Village, 494	E 3
* 48201	Detroit⊙, 1,511,482	B 7
	Detroit, ‡4,199,931	B 7
† 48161	Detroit Beach, 2,053	F 7
48820	De Witt, 1,829	E 6
48130	Dexter, 1,729	F 6
48821	Dimondale, 970	E 6
49922	Dollar Bay, 950	G 1
49323	Dorr, 550	D 6
49406	Douglas, 813	C 6
49047	Dowagiac, 6,583	D 6
48020	Drayton Plains, 16,462	F 6
49726	Drummond Island, 700	F 3
48428	Dryden, 654	F 6
48131	Dundee, 2,472	F 7
48429	Durand, 3,678	E 6
49924	Eagle River⊙, 36	A 1
48021	East Detroit, 45,920	B 6
† 49506	East Grand Rapids, 12,565	D 6
49727	East Jordan, 2,041	D 3
† 49801	East Kingsford, 1,155	A 3
49626	Eastlake, 512	C 4
48823	East Lansing, 47,540	E 6
48730	East Tawas, 2,372	F 4
† 49001	Eastwood, 9,682	D 6
48827	Eaton Rapids, 4,494	E 6
49111	Eau Claire, 527	C 6
48229	Ecorse, 17,515	B 7
48620	Edenville, 700	E 5
48829	Edmore, 1,149	E 5
49112	Edwardsburg, 1,107	C 7
† 48446	Elba, 460	F 5
49628	Elberta, 542	C 4
49629	Elk Rapids, 1,249	D 4
48731	Elkton, 973	F 5
48831	Elsie, 988	E 5
49827	Engadine, 500	D 2
48133	Erie, 975	F 7
49829	Escanaba⊙, 15,368	C 3
48732	Essexville, 4,990	F 5
† 48166	Estral Beach, 419	F 7
49631	Evart, 1,707	D 5
49925	Ewen, 600	F 2
48733	Fairgrove, 629	F 5
48023	Fair Haven, 550	G 6
49022	Fair Plain, 3,680	C 6
48621	Fairview, 600	F 4
48024	Farmington, 13,337	F 6
48622	Farwell, 777	E 5
49408	Fennville, 811	C 6
48430	Fenton, 8,284	F 6
48220	Ferndale, 30,850	B 6
49409	Ferrysburg, 2,196	C 5
48134	Flat Rock, 5,643	F 6
* 48501	Flint⊙, 193,317	F 6
	Flint, ‡496,658	F 6
48433	Flushing, 7,190	F 5
48835	Fowler, 1,020	E 5
48836	Fowlerville, 1,978	F 6
48734	Frankenmuth, 2,834	F 5
49635	Frankfort, 1,660	C 4
48025	Franklin, 3,344	B 6
48026	Fraser, 11,868	B 6
48623	Freeland, 1,303	E 5
49325	Freeport, 501	D 6
49412	Fremont, 3,465	D 5
49415	Fruitport, 1,409	C 5
49052	Fulton, 500	D 6
49927	Gaastra, 479	G 2
49053	Galesburg, 1,355	D 6
49113	Galien, 691	C 7
49735	Gaylord⊙, 3,012	E 3
48437	Genesee, 950	F 5
49836	Germfask, 750	C 2
48173	Gibraltar, 3,325	F 6
49837	Gladstone, 5,237	C 3
48624	Gladwin⊙, 2,071	E 5
49055	Gobles, 801	D 6
49737	Good Hart, 500	D 3
48438	Goodrich, 774	F 6
48439	Grand Blanc, 5,132	F 6
49417	Grand Haven⊙, 11,884	C 5
48837	Grand Ledge, 6,032	E 6
49839	Grand Marais, 650	D 2
* 49501	Grand Rapids⊙, 197,649	D 5
	Grand Rapids, ‡539,225	D 5
49418	Grandville, 10,764	D 6
49327	Grant, 772	D 5
49240	Grass Lake, 1,061	E 6
49738	Grayling⊙, 2,143	E 4
48738	Greenbush, 650	F 4
48838	Greenville, 7,493	D 5
48138	Grosse Ile, 7,799	B 7
48236	Grosse Pointe, 6,637	B 7
† 48236	Grosse Pointe Farms, 11,701	B 6
† 48236	Grosse Pointe Park, 15,585	B 7
† 48236	Grosse Pointe Shores, 3,042	B 6
† 48236	Grosse Pointe Woods, 21,878	B 6
49840	Gulliver, 962	D 2
49841	Gwinn, 1,054	B 2
48739	Hale, 500	F 4
48139	Hamburg, 500	F 6
49419	Hamilton, 950	C 6
48212	Hamtramck, 27,245	B 6
49930	Hancock, 4,820	G 1
49241	Hanover, 513	E 6
48441	Harbor Beach, 2,134	G 5
49740	Harbor Springs, 1,662	D 3
48236	Harper Woods, 20,186	B 6
48625	Harrison⊙, 1,460	E 4
48740	Harrisville⊙, 541	F 4
48028	Harsens Island, 750	G 6
49420	Hart⊙, 2,139	C 5
49057	Hartford, 2,508	C 6
48840	Haslett, 3,492	E 6
49058	Hastings⊙, 6,501	D 6
48030	Hazel Park, 23,784	B 6
48626	Hemlock, 900	E 5
48841	Henderson, 600	E 5
49847	Hermansville, 950	B 3
49744	Herron, 950	F 3
49421	Hesperia, 877	D 5
49745	Hessel, 500	E 2
48203	Highland Park, 35,444	B 6
49242	Hillsdale⊙, 7,728	E 7
49423	Holland, 26,337	C 6
48442	Holly, 4,355	F 6
48842	Holt, 6,980	E 6
49425	Holton, 500	C 5
49245	Homer, 1,617	E 6
49328	Hopkins, 566	D 6
49931	Houghton⊙, 6,067	G 1
48629	Houghton Lake, 500	E 4
48630	Houghton Lake Heights, 1,252	E 4
49329	Howard City, 1,060	D 5
48843	Howell⊙, 5,224	E 6
49934	Hubbell, 1,251	A 1
49247	Hudson, 2,618	E 7
49426	Hudsonville, 3,523	D 6
48140	Ida, 970	F 7
49642	Idlewild, 800	D 5
48444	Imlay City, 1,980	F 5
49749	Indian River, 950	E 3
48141	Inkster, 38,595	B 7
49643	Interlochen, 800	D 4
48846	Ionia⊙, 6,361	D 6
49801	Iron Mountain⊙, 8,702	B 3
49935	Iron River, 2,684	G 2
49938	Ironwood, 8,711	F 2
49849	Ishpeming, 8,245	B 2
48847	Ithaca⊙, 2,749	E 5
* 49201	Jackson⊙, 45,484	E 6
	Jackson, ‡143,274	E 6
49428	Jenison, 11,266	D 6
49061	Jones, 420	D 7
49250	Jonesville, 2,081	E 6
* 49001	Kalamazoo⊙, 85,555	D 6
	Kalamazoo, ‡201,550	D 6
49646	Kalkaska⊙, 1,475	D 4
48631	Kawkawlin, 450	F 5
48030	Keego Harbor, 3,092	F 6
49330	Kent City, 686	D 5
49508	Kentwood, 20,310	D 6
48445	Kinde, 618	G 5
49801	Kingsford, 5,276	A 3
49649	Kingsley, 632	D 4
48741	Kingston, 464	F 5
48848	Laingsburg, 1,159	E 6
48632	Lake, 600	E 5
49651	Lake City⊙, 704	D 4
48143	Lakeland, 720	F 6
49945	Lake Linden, 1,214	A 1
† 49039	Lake Michigan Beach, 1,201	C 6
48849	Lake Odessa, 1,924	D 6
48850	Lakeview, 1,198	D 5
† 49440	Lakewood Club, 590	C 5
48144	Lambertville, 5,721	F 7
49946	L'Anse⊙, 2,538	G 1
* 48901	Lansing (cap.), 131,546	E 6
	Lansing, ‡378,423	E 6
48446	Lapeer⊙, 6,270	F 5
49913	Laurium, 2,868	A 1
49064	Lawrence, 790	C 6
49065	Lawton, 1,358	D 6
49654	Leland⊙, 776	D 3
49251	Leslie, 1,894	E 6
49755	Levering, 967	E 3
49756	Lewiston, 750	E 4
48450	Lexington, 834	G 5
48146	Lincoln Park, 52,984	B 7
48451	Linden, 1,546	F 6
48634	Linwood, 950	F 5
49252	Litchfield, 1,167	E 6
49833	Little Lake, 950	B 2
* 48150	Livonia, 110,109	F 6
48743	Long Lake, 900	F 4
49331	Lowell, 3,068	D 6
49431	Ludington⊙, 9,021	C 5
48157	Luna Pier, 1,418	F 7
48851	Lyons, 758	E 6
49757	Mackinac Island, 517	E 3
49701	Mackinaw City, 810	E 3
48071	Madison Heights, 38,599	F 6
49659	Mancelona, 1,255	E 4
48158	Manchester, 1,650	E 6
49660	Manistee⊙, 7,723	C 4
49854	Manistique⊙, 4,324	C 3
49663	Manton, 1,107	D 4
48853	Maple Rapids, 683	E 5
49067	Marcellus, 1,139	D 6
49947	Marenisco, 865	F 2
48039	Marine City, 4,567	G 6
49665	Marion, 891	D 4
48453	Marlette, 1,706	G 5
49435	Marne, 950	D 5
49855	Marquette⊙, 21,967	B 2
49068	Marshall⊙, 7,253	E 6
49070	Martin, 502	D 6
48040	Marysville, 5,610	G 6
48854	Mason⊙, 5,468	E 6
49948	Mass, 850	G 1
49071	Mattawan, 1,569	D 6
48159	Maybee, 485	F 6
48744	Mayville, 872	F 5
49657	McBain, 520	D 4
48122	Melvindale, 13,862	B 7
48041	Memphis, 1,121	G 6
49072	Mendon, 949	D 7
49858	Menominee⊙, 10,748	B 3

(continued on following page)

Turning out more than one car a minute keeps these inspectors on their toes during the final step on an assembly line in Detroit, Michigan.

A. D'Arazien — Shostal Associates

Agriculture, Industry and Resources

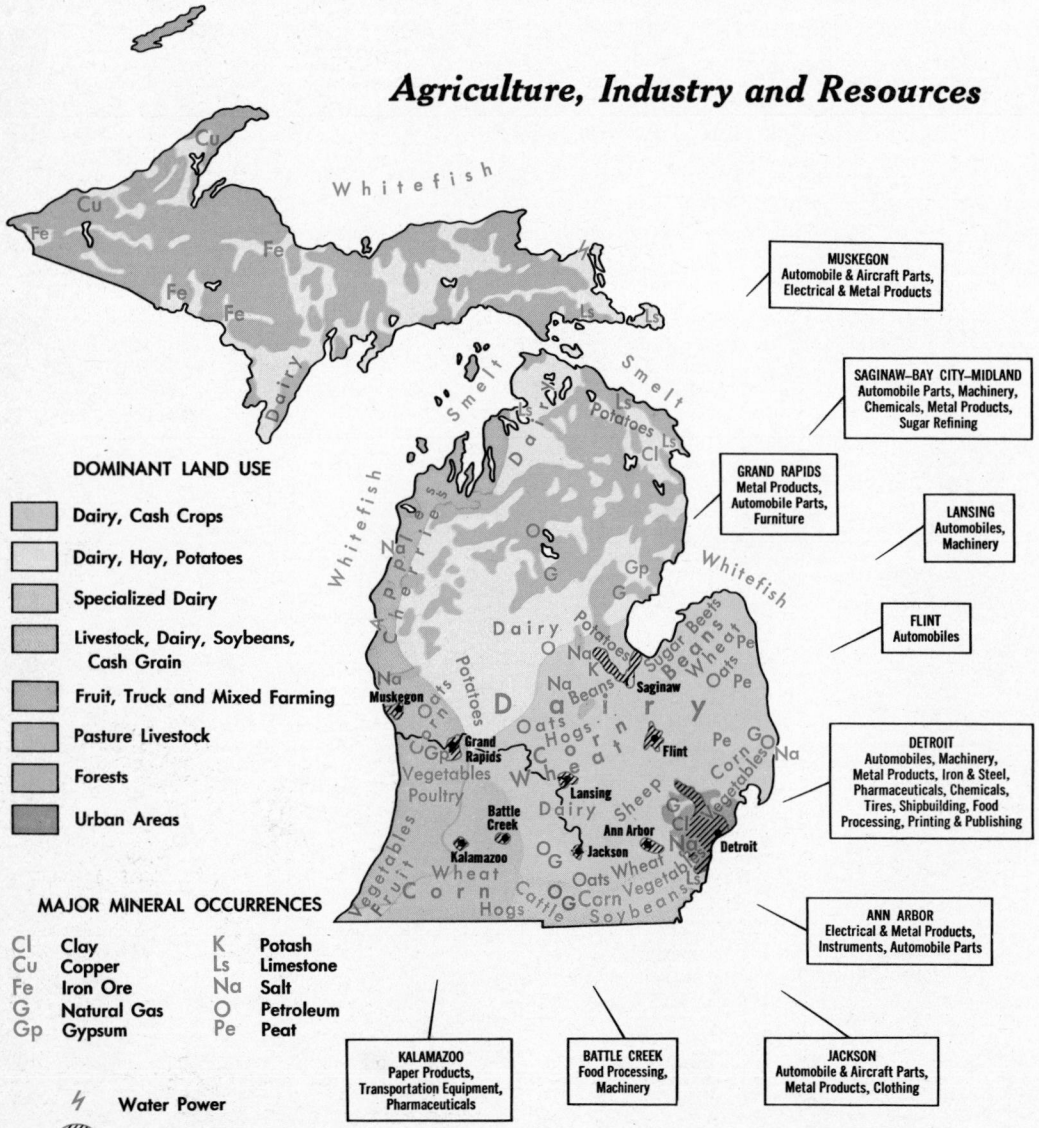

MUSKEGON
Automobile & Aircraft Parts,
Electrical & Metal Products

SAGINAW–BAY CITY–MIDLAND
Automobile Parts, Machinery,
Chemicals, Metal Products,
Sugar Refining

GRAND RAPIDS
Metal Products,
Automobile Parts,
Furniture

LANSING
Automobiles,
Machinery

FLINT
Automobiles

DETROIT
Automobiles, Machinery,
Metal Products, Iron & Steel,
Pharmaceuticals, Chemicals,
Tires, Shipbuilding, Food
Processing, Printing & Publishing

ANN ARBOR
Electrical & Metal Products,
Instruments, Automobile Parts

KALAMAZOO
Paper Products,
Transportation Equipment,
Pharmaceuticals

BATTLE CREEK
Food Processing,
Machinery

JACKSON
Automobile & Aircraft Parts,
Metal Products, Clothing

DOMINANT LAND USE

- Dairy, Cash Crops
- Dairy, Hay, Potatoes
- Specialized Dairy
- Livestock, Dairy, Soybeans, Cash Grain
- Fruit, Truck and Mixed Farming
- Pasture Livestock
- Forests
- Urban Areas

MAJOR MINERAL OCCURRENCES

Cl	Clay	K	Potash
Cu	Copper	Ls	Limestone
Fe	Iron Ore	Na	Salt
G	Natural Gas	O	Petroleum
Gp	Gypsum	Pe	Peat

Water Power

Major Industrial Areas

48637	Merrill, 961	E 5
48455	Metamora, 468	F 6
49758	Metz, 495	F 3
49254	Michigan Center, 4,900	E 6
48856	Middleton, 500	E 5
49333	Middleville, 1,865	D 6
48640	Midland⊙, 35,176	E 5
48160	Milan, 4,533	F 6
48042	Milford, 4,699	F 6
48746	Millington, 1,099	F 5
48647	Mio⊙, 975	E 4
49950	Mohawk, 800	A 1
49335	Moline, 750	D 6
48161	Monroe⊙, 23,894	F 7
49437	Montague, 2,396	C 5
48457	Montrose, 1,789	F 5
49256	Morenci, 2,132	E 7
49336	Morley, 481	D 5
48857	Morrice, 734	E 6
48043	Mount Clemens⊙, 20,476	G 6
48458	Mount Morris, 3,778	F 5
48858	Mount Pleasant⊙, 20,504	E 5
48860	Muir, 617	D 5
48861	Mulliken, 454	E 6
48747	Munger, 432	F 5
49862	Munising⊙, 3,677	C 2
* 49440	Muskegon⊙, 44,631	C 5
	Muskegon-Muskegon Heights, ‡157,426	C 5
49444	Muskegon Heights, 17,304	C 5
49261	Napoleon, 950	E 6
49073	Nashville, 1,558	D 6
49865	National Mine, 565	B 2
49866	Negaunee, 5,248	B 2
49337	Newaygo, 1,381	D 5
48047	New Baltimore, 4,132	G 6
49868	Newberry⊙, 2,334	D 2
48164	New Boston, 800	F 6
49117	New Buffalo, 2,784	C 7
49446	New Era, 466	C 5
48048	New Haven, 1,855	G 6
48460	New Lothrop, 596	F 5
49119	New Troy, 430	C 7
49120	Niles, 12,988	C 7
49262	North Adams, 574	E 7
48461	North Branch, 932	F 5
49445	North Muskegon, 4,243	C 5
49670	Northport, 594	D 3
48167	Northville, 5,400	F 6
* 49444	Norton Shores, 22,271	C 5
49870	Norway, 3,033	B 3
48050	Novi, 9,668	F 6
48237	Oak Park, 36,762	B 6
49763	Ocqueoc, 500	F 3
48864	Okemos, 7,770	E 6
49076	Olivet, 1,629	E 6
49765	Onaway, 1,262	E 3
49675	Onekama, 638	C 4
49265	Onsted, 555	E 6
49953	Ontonagon⊙, 2,432	F 1
48033	Orchard Lake, 1,487	F 6
48462	Ortonville, 983	F 6
48750	Oscoda-Au Sable, 3,475	F 4
48463	Otisville, 724	F 5
49078	Otsego, 3,957	D 6
† 49735	Otsego Lake, 500	E 4
48464	Otter Lake, 551	F 5
48866	Ovid, 1,650	E 5
48867	Owosso, 17,179	E 5
48051	Oxford, 2,536	F 6
49955	Painesdale, 600	G 1
49871	Palmer, 950	B 2
49268	Palmyra, 600	E 7
49269	Parma, 880	E 6
49079	Paw Paw, 3,160	D 6
† 49038	Paw Paw Lake, 3,726	C 6
48052	Pearl Beach, 1,744	G 6
48466	Peck, 580	G 5
49769	Pellston, 469	E 3
49449	Pentwater, 993	C 5
48871	Perrinton, 489	E 5
48872	Perry, 1,531	E 6
49270	Petersburg, 1,227	F 7
49770	Petoskey⊙, 6,342	E 3
48873	Pewamo, 498	E 5
49774	Pickford, 800	E 2
48755	Pigeon, 1,174	F 5
48169	Pinckney, 921	F 6
48650	Pinconning, 1,320	F 5
49271	Pittsford, 610	E 7
49080	Plainwell, 3,195	D 6
48069	Pleasant Ridge, 3,989	B 6
48170	Plymouth, 11,758	F 6
* 48053	Pontiac⊙, 85,279	F 6
49081	Portage, 33,590	D 6
48467	Port Austin, 883	F 4
48060	Port Huron⊙, 35,794	G 6
48875	Portland, 3,817	E 6
48469	Port Sanilac, 493	G 5
48876	Potterville, 1,280	E 6
49874	Powers, 560	B 3
48651	Prudenville, 500	E 4
49082	Quincy, 1,540	E 7
49876	Quinnesec, 770	A 3
49959	Ramsay, 1,068	F 2
49676	Rapid City, 450	D 4
49878	Rapid River, 950	C 3
49451	Ravenna, 1,048	D 5
49274	Reading, 1,125	E 7
49677	Reed City⊙, 2,286	D 5
48757	Reese, 1,050	F 5
49340	Remus, 425	D 5
49879	Republic, 900	B 2
49083	Richland, 728	D 6
48062	Richmond, 3,234	G 6
48758	Richville, 650	F 5
48218	River Rouge, 15,947	B 7
49084	Riverside, 650	C 6
48192	Riverview, 11,342	F 6
48063	Rochester, 7,054	F 6
49341	Rockford, 2,428	D 5
49960	Rockland, 450	G 1
48173	Rockwood, 3,119	F 6
49779	Rogers City⊙, 4,275	F 3
48065	Romeo, 4,012	F 6
48174	Romulus, 3,900	F 6
49444	Roosevelt Park, 4,176	C 5

48653	Roscommon⊙, 810	E 4
48878	Rosebush, 439	E 5
48654	Rose City, 530	E 4
48066	Roseville, 60,529	B 6
48067	Royal Oak, 85,499	B 6
49780	Rudyard, 950	E 2
* 48601	Saginaw⊙, 91,849	F 5
	Saginaw, ‡219,743	F 5
48655	Saint Charles, 2,046	E 5
48079	Saint Clair, 4,770	G 6
* 48080	Saint Clair Shores, 88,093	B 6
48656	Saint Helen, 700	E 4
49781	Saint Ignace⊙, 2,892	E 2
48879	Saint Johns⊙, 6,672	E 5
49085	Saint Joseph⊙, 11,042	C 6
48880	Saint Louis, 4,101	E 5
48176	Saline, 4,811	F 6
48471	Sandusky⊙, 2,071	G 5
48657	Sanford, 818	E 5
48881	Saranac, 1,223	D 6
49453	Saugatuck, 1,022	C 6
49783	Sault Sainte Marie⊙, 15,136	E 2
49125	Sawyer, 650	C 6
49087	Schoolcraft, 1,277	D 6
49454	Scottville, 1,202	C 5
49455	Shelby, 1,703	C 5
48759	Sebewaing, 2,053	F 5
48883	Shepherd, 1,416	E 5
48884	Sheridan, 653	D 5
† 49085	Shoreham, 666	C 6
† 49125	Shorewood Hills, 1,629	C 6
49047	Sister Lakes, 700	C 6
48075	Southfield, 69,285	B 6
48192	Southgate, 33,909	F 6
49090	South Haven, 6,471	C 6
48178	South Lyon, 2,675	F 6
† 48161	South Monroe, 3,012	F 7
49963	South Range, 898	G 1
48179	South Rockwood, 1,477	F 6
49486	Spalding, 600	B 3
† 48060	Sparlingville, 1,845	G 6
49345	Sparta, 3,094	D 5
49283	Spring Arbor, 1,832	E 6
49015	Springfield, 3,994	D 6
49456	Spring Lake, 3,034	C 5
49284	Springport, 723	E 6
49688	Stambaugh, 1,458	A 2
48658	Standish⊙, 1,184	F 5
48888	Stanton⊙, 1,089	E 5
49887	Stephenson, 800	B 3
49659	Sterling, 507	E 4
* 48077	Sterling Heights, 61,365	F 6
49127	Stevensville, 1,107	C 6
49285	Stockbridge, 1,190	E 6
49681	Stronach, 500	C 4
49790	Strongs, 450	E 2
49091	Sturgis, 9,295	D 7
48890	Sunfield, 497	E 6
49682	Suttons Bay, 522	D 3
48473	Swartz Creek, 4,928	F 6
† 48053	Sylvan Lake, 2,219	F 6
48763	Tawas City⊙, 1,666	F 4
48180	Taylor, 70,020	F 6
49286	Tecumseh, 7,120	E 6
49092	Tekonsha, 739	E 6
48182	Temperance, 2,900	F 7
49128	Three Oaks, 1,750	C 7
49093	Three Rivers, 7,355	D 6
49792	Tower, 425	E 3
49684	Traverse City⊙, 18,048	D 4
48183	Trenton, 24,127	B 7
48084	Troy, 39,419	B 6
49347	Trufant, 600	D 5
48475	Ubly, 899	G 5
49094	Union City, 1,740	D 6
49129	Union Pier, 900	C 7
48767	Unionville, 647	F 5
48087	Utica, 3,504	F 6
49095	Vandalia, 427	D 7
49795	Vanderbilt, 522	E 3
48768	Vassar, 2,802	F 5
49096	Vermontville, 857	E 6
48476	Vernon, 818	E 5
48891	Vestaburg, 680	E 5
49097	Vicksburg, 2,139	D 6
49892	Vulcan, 975	B 3
49968	Wakefield, 2,757	F 2
49288	Waldron, 564	E 7
49504	Walker, 11,492	D 5
48088	Walled Lake, 3,759	F 6
49796	Walloon Lake, 550	E 3
48089	Warren, 179,260	F 6
49969	Watersmeet, 700	A 2
49098	Watervliet, 2,059	C 6
49348	Wayland, 2,054	D 6
48184	Wayne, 21,054	F 6
48892	Webberville, 1,251	E 6
48893	Weidman, 450	E 5
49894	Wells, 1,085	B 3
48661	West Branch⊙, 1,912	E 4
48185	Westland, 86,749	F 6
48894	Westphalia, 806	E 6
49349	White Cloud⊙, 1,044	D 5
49461	Whitehall, 3,017	C 5
49099	White Pigeon, 1,455	D 7
49971	White Pine, 1,218	F 1
48189	Whitmore Lake, 2,763	F 6
48190	Whittaker, 500	F 6
48770	Whittemore, 460	F 4
48895	Williamston, 2,600	E 6
48191	Willis, 500	F 6
49896	Wilson, 500	B 3
48896	Winn, 600	E 5
48096	Wixom, 2,010	F 6
49442	Wolf Lake, 2,258	C 5
48183	Woodhaven, 3,330	B 7
48897	Woodland, 473	D 6
48192	Wyandotte, 41,061	B 7
49509	Wyoming, 56,560	D 6
48097	Yale, 1,505	G 5
48197	Ypsilanti, 29,538	F 6
49464	Zeeland, 4,734	C 6
† 48601	Zilwaukee, 2,072	F 5

⊙ County seat.
‡ Population of metropolitan area.
† Zip of nearest p.o.
* Multiple zips

AREA 84,068 sq. mi.
POPULATION 3,805,069
CAPITAL St. Paul
LARGEST CITY Minneapolis
HIGHEST POINT Eagle Mtn. 2,301 ft.
SETTLED IN 1805
ADMITTED TO UNION May 11, 1858
POPULAR NAME North Star State; Gopher State
STATE FLOWER Lady-slipper
STATE BIRD Loon

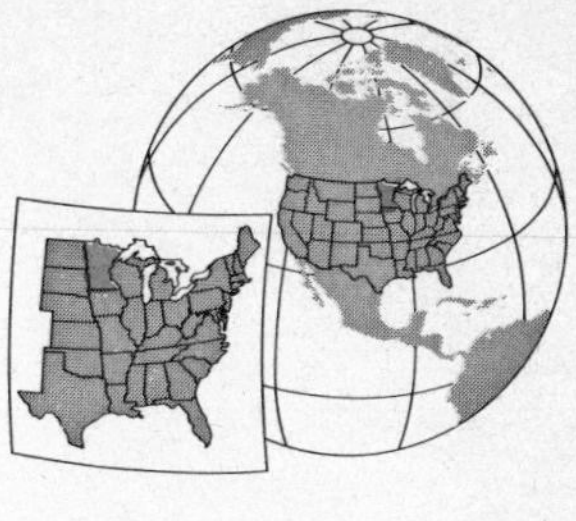

COUNTIES

Aitkin, 11,403 E 4
Anoka, 154,556 E 5
Becker, 24,372 C 4
Beltrami, 26,373 C 2
Benton, 20,841 D 5
Big Stone, 7,941 B 5
Blue Earth, 52,322 D 6
Brown, 28,887 D 6
Carlton, 28,072 F 4
Carver, 28,310 E 6
Cass, 17,323 D 4
Chippewa, 15,109 C 5
Chisago, 17,492 F 5
Clay, 46,585 B 4
Clearwater, 8,013 C 3
Cook, 3,423 H 3
Cottonwood, 14,887 C 6
Crow Wing, 34,826 D 4
Dakota, 139,808 E 6
Dodge, 13,037 F 7
Douglas, 22,892 C 5
Faribault, 20,896 D 7
Fillmore, 21,916 F 7
Freeborn, 38,064 E 7
Goodhue, 34,763 F 6
Grant, 7,462 B 5
Hennepin, 960,080 E 5
Houston, 17,556 G 7
Hubbard, 10,583 D 3
Isanti, 16,560 E 5
Itasca, 35,530 E 3
Jackson, 14,352 C 7
Kanabec, 9,775 E 5
Kandiyohi, 30,548 C 5
Kittson, 6,853 B 2
Koochiching, 17,731 E 2
Lac qui Parle, 11,164 B 6
Lake, 13,351 G 3
Lake of the Woods, 3,987 D 2
Le Sueur, 21,332 E 6
Lincoln, 8,143 B 6
Lyon, 24,273 C 6
Mahnomen, 5,638 C 3
Marshall, 13,060 B 2
Martin, 24,316 D 7
McLeod, 27,662 D 6
Meeker, 18,810 D 5
Mille Lacs, 15,703 E 5
Morrison, 26,949 D 4
Mower, 43,783 F 7
Murray, 12,508 C 6
Nicollet, 24,518 D 6
Nobles, 23,208 C 7
Norman, 10,008 B 3
Olmsted, 84,104 F 7
Otter Tail, 46,097 C 4
Pennington, 13,266 B 2
Pine, 16,821 F 4
Pipestone, 12,791 B 6
Polk, 34,435 B 3
Pope, 11,107 C 5
Ramsey, 476,255 E 5
Red Lake, 5,388 B 3
Redwood, 20,024 C 6
Renville, 21,139 C 6
Rice, 41,582 E 6
Rock, 11,346 B 7
Roseau, 11,569 C 2
Saint Louis, 220,693 F 3
Scott, 32,423 E 6
Sherburne, 18,344 E 5
Sibley, 15,845 D 6
Stearns, 95,400 D 5
Steele, 26,931 E 7
Stevens, 11,218 B 5
Swift, 13,177 C 5
Todd, 22,114 D 4
Traverse, 6,254 B 5
Wabasha, 17,224 F 6
Wadena, 12,412 D 4
Waseca, 16,663 E 6
Washington, 82,948 F 5
Watonwan, 13,298 D 7
Wilkin, 9,389 B 4
Winona, 44,409 G 6
Wright, 38,933 D 5
Yellow Medicine, 14,418 B 6

CITIES and TOWNS

Zip Name/Pop. Key

56510 Ada⊙, 2,076 B 3
55909 Adams, 771 F 7
56110 Adrian, 1,350 C 7
55001 Afton, 248 F 6
56430 Ah-Gwah-Ching, 500 D 3
56431 Aitkin⊙, 1,553 E 4
56433 Akeley, 468 D 3
56307 Albany, 1,599 D 5
56207 Alberta, 140 B 5
56007 Albert Lea⊙, 19,418 E 7
55301 Albertville, 451 E 5
56009 Alden, 713 E 7
56308 Alexandria⊙, 6,973 C 5
55002 Almelund, 150 F 5
56111 Alpha, 179 D 7
55910 Altura, 334 G 6
56710 Alvarado, 302 B 2
56010 Amboy, 571 D 7
55703 Angora, 287 F 3
55302 Annandale, 1,234 D 5
55303 Anoka⊙, 13,489 E 5
56208 Appleton, 1,789 C 5
55378 Apple Valley, 8,502 G 6
56113 Arco, 121 B 6
56713 Argyle, 739 B 2
55307 Arlington, 1,823 D 6
55801 Arnold, 750 F 4
56309 Ashby, 415 C 4
55704 Askov, 287 F 4
56209 Atwater, 956 D 5
56511 Audubon, 297 C 4
55705 Aurora, 2,531 F 3
55912 Austin⊙, 25,074 E 7
56114 Avoca, 203 C 7
56310 Avon, 725 D 5
55706 Babbitt, 3,076 G 3
56435 Backus, 257 D 4
56714 Badger, 327 B 2
56621 Bagley⊙, 1,314 C 3
56115 Balaton, 649 C 6
56622 Ball Club, 150 E 3
56514 Barnesville, 1,782 B 4
55707 Barnum, 382 F 4
56311 Barrett, 342 B 5
56515 Battle Lake, 772 C 4
56623 Baudette⊙, 1,547 D 2
† 56401 Baxter, 1,556 D 4
† 56444 Bay Lake, 250 E 4
55003 Bayport, 2,987 F 5
56211 Beardsley, 366 B 5
† 55723 Bear River, 250 E 3
55601 Beaver Bay, 362 G 3
56116 Beaver Creek, 235 B 7
55308 Becker, 365 E 5
56516 Bejou, 157 B 3
56312 Belgrade, 713 C 5
† 55027 Bellechester, 199 F 6
56011 Belle Plaine, 2,328 E 6
56212 Bellingham, 263 B 5
56517 Beltrami, 171 B 3
56214 Belview, 429 C 6
56601 Bemidji⊙, 11,490 D 3
56626 Bena, 169 D 3
56215 Benson⊙, 3,484 C 5
56437 Bertha, 512 C 4
56117 Bigelow, 262 C 7
56627 Big Falls, 534 E 2
56628 Bigfork, 399 E 3
55309 Big Lake, 1,015 E 5
56118 Bingham Lake, 214 C 7
55310 Bird Island, 1,309 D 6
55708 Biwabik, 1,483 F 3
56630 Blackduck, 595 D 3
† 55303 Blaine, 20,640 G 5
† 56011 Blakeley, 125 E 6
56216 Blomkest, 172 D 6
55917 Blooming Prairie, 1,804 E 7
55420 Bloomington, 81,970 G 6
56013 Blue Earth⊙, 3,965 D 7
56518 Bluffton, 195 C 4
56519 Borup, 128 B 3
55709 Bovey, 858 E 3
56314 Bowlus, 268 D 5
56218 Boyd, 311 C 6
55006 Braham, 744 E 5
56401 Brainerd⊙, 11,667 D 4
† 55056 Branch, 880 F 5
56315 Brandon, 414 C 5
56520 Breckenridge⊙, 4,200 B 4
† 56472 Breezy Point Village, 233 D 4
56119 Brewster, 563 C 7
56014 Bricelyn, 470 E 7
55710 Britt, 175 F 3
55429 Brooklyn Center, 35,173 G 5
† 55401 Brooklyn Park, 26,230 G 5
56715 Brooks, 163 B 3
55711 Brookston, 137 F 4
56316 Brooten, 615 C 5
56438 Browerville, 665 D 4
55918 Brownsdale, 625 F 7
56219 Browns Valley, 906 B 5
55919 Brownsville, 417 G 7
55312 Brownton, 688 D 6
55712 Bruno, 130 F 4
† 55051 Brunswick, 144 E 5
56317 Buckman, 158 D 5
55313 Buffalo⊙, 3,275 E 5
55314 Buffalo Lake, 758 D 6
55713 Buhl, 1,303 F 3
55378 Burnsville, 19,940 E 6
56318 Burtrum, 135 D 5
56120 Butterfield, 619 D 7
† 56723 Bygland, 475 B 3
55920 Byron, 1,419 F 6
55921 Caledonia⊙, 2,619 G 7
56521 Callaway, 233 C 3
55716 Calumet, 460 E 3
55008 Cambridge⊙, 3,467 E 5
56522 Campbell, 339 B 4
56220 Canby, 2,081 B 6
55009 Cannon Falls, 2,072 F 6
55922 Canton, 391 F 7
55717 Canyon, 125 F 3
56319 Carlos, 260 C 5
55718 Carlton⊙, 884 F 4
55315 Carver, 669 E 6
56633 Cass Lake, 1,317 D 3
55010 Castle Rock, 150 E 6
55012 Center City⊙, 324 F 5
† 55038 Centerville, 534 E 5
56121 Ceylon, 487 D 7
55316 Champlin, 2,275 G 5
56122 Chandler, 319 C 7
55317 Chanhassen, 4,879 F 6
55318 Chaska⊙, 4,352 F 6
55923 Chatfield, 1,885 F 7
55013 Chisago City, 1,068 F 5
55719 Chisholm, 5,913 E 3
56221 Chokio, 455 B 5
55014 Circle Pines, 3,918 G 5
56222 Clara City, 1,491 C 6
55924 Claremont, 520 E 6
56440 Clarissa, 599 C 4
56223 Clarkfield, 1,084 C 6
56016 Clarks Grove, 480 E 7
56634 Clearbrook, 599 C 3
55319 Clear Lake, 280 E 5
55320 Clearwater, 282 D 5
56224 Clements, 252 D 6
56017 Cleveland, 492 E 6
56523 Climax, 255 B 3
56225 Clinton, 608 B 5
56524 Clitherall, 131 C 4
56226 Clontarf, 147 C 5
55720 Cloquet, 8,699 F 4
55015 Cloverton, 150 F 4
55721 Cohasset, 536 E 3
55321 Cokato, 1,735 D 5
56320 Cold Spring, 2,006 D 5
55722 Coleraine, 1,086 E 3
56321 Collegeville, 1,600 D 5
55322 Cologne, 518 E 6
55421 Columbia Heights, 23,997 G 5
56019 Comfrey, 525 D 6
56525 Comstock, 135 B 4
56020 Conger, 167 E 7
55723 Cook, 687 F 3
55433 Coon Rapids, 30,505 G 5
† 55340 Corcoran, 1,656 F 5
56228 Cosmos, 570 D 6
55016 Cottage Grove, 13,419 F 6
55724 Cotton, 350 F 3
56229 Cottonwood, 794 C 6
56021 Courtland, 360 D 6
55725 Crane Lake, 350 F 2
55726 Cromwell, 181 F 4
56716 Crookston⊙, 8,312 B 3
56441 Crosby, 2,241 D 4
56442 Crosslake, 358 E 4
† 55005 Crown, 200 E 5
† 55401 Crystal, 30,925 G 5
55323 Crystal Bay, 6,787 F 5
56123 Currie, 368 C 6
56323 Cyrus, 289 C 5
55925 Dakota, 369 G 7
56324 Dalton, 221 C 4
56230 Danube, 497 C 6
56231 Danvers, 136 C 5
56022 Darfur, 179 D 6
55324 Darwin, 224 D 5
55325 Dassel, 1,058 D 5
56232 Dawson, 1,699 B 6
55327 Dayton, 517 E 5
55391 Deephaven, 3,853 G 5
56527 Deer Creek, 287 C 4
56636 Deer River, 815 E 3
56444 Deerwood, 448 E 4
56233 De Graff, 195 C 5
55328 Delano, 1,851 E 5
56023 Delavan, 281 D 7
56234 Delhi, 154 C 6
† 55110 Dellwood, 514 F 5
55018 Dennison, 162 E 6
56528 Dent, 156 C 4
56501 Detroit Lakes⊙, 5,797 C 4
55926 Dexter, 252 F 7
56529 Dilworth, 2,321 B 4
55927 Dodge Center, 1,603 F 6
56235 Donnelly, 252 B 5
55929 Dover, 321 F 7
55930 Dresbach, 250 G 7
* 55801 Duluth⊙, 100,578 F 4
Duluth-Superior, ‡265,350 F 4
56236 Dumont, 204 B 5
55019 Dundas, 460 E 6
56126 Dundee, 138 C 7
56127 Dunnell, 237 D 7
56446 Eagle Bend, 557 D 4
† 55005 East Bethel, 2,586 E 5
56024 Eagle Lake, 839 E 6
† 56031 East Chain, 171 D 7
56721 East Grand Forks, 7,607 B 3
† 56401 East Gull Lake, 440 D 4
56025 Easton, 352 E 7
56237 Echo, 356 C 6
55343 Eden Prairie, 6,938 G 6
55329 Eden Valley, 776 D 5
56128 Edgerton, 1,119 B 7
55424 Edina, 44,046 G 5
56639 Effie, 165 E 3
55931 Eitzen, 208 G 7
† 55910 Elba, 158 F 6
56531 Elbow Lake⊙, 1,484 B 5
55932 Elgin, 580 F 6
56533 Elizabeth, 188 B 4
55330 Elk River⊙, 2,252 E 5
55933 Elkton, 134 F 7
56026 Ellendale, 569 E 7
56129 Ellsworth, 588 C 7
56027 Elmore, 910 D 7
56325 Elrosa, 203 C 5
55731 Ely, 4,904 G 3
56028 Elysian, 445 E 6
55732 Embarrass, 195 F 3
56447 Emily, 386 E 4
56029 Emmons, 412 E 7
56534 Erhard, 748 B 4
56640 Ericsburg, 300 E 2
56535 Erskine, 571 B 3
55733 Esko, 500 F 4
56722 Euclid, 130 B 3
56238 Evan, 126 D 6
56326 Evansville, 553 C 4
55734 Eveleth, 4,721 F 3
55331 Excelsior, 2,563 F 6
55934 Eyota, 639 F 6
55332 Fairfax, 1,432 D 6
55383 Fairhaven, 129 D 5
56031 Fairmont⊙, 10,751 D 7
55113 Falcon Heights, 5,507 G 5
55021 Faribault⊙, 16,595 E 6
55024 Farmington, 3,104 E 6
56641 Federal Dam, 147 D 3
56536 Felton, 232 B 3
56537 Fergus Falls⊙, 12,443 B 4
56540 Fertile, 955 B 3
56448 Fifty Lakes, 143 D 4
55603 Finland, 300 G 3
55735 Finlayson, 192 F 4
56723 Fisher, 383 B 3
56328 Flensburg, 259 D 5
55736 Floodwood, 650 E 4
† 55792 Florenton, 635 F 3
56329 Foley⊙, 1,271 D 5
† 56308 Forada, 158 C 5
55738 Forbes, 225 F 3
55025 Forest Lake, 3,207 F 5
56330 Foreston, 273 E 5
56542 Fosston, 1,684 C 3
55935 Fountain, 347 F 7
56543 Foxhome, 185 B 4
55333 Franklin, 557 D 6
56544 Frazee, 1,015 C 4
56032 Freeborn, 296 E 7
56331 Freeport, 593 D 5
† 55801 French River, 200 G 4
55421 Fridley, 29,233 G 5
55026 Frontenac, 223 F 6
56033 Frost, 290 D 7
56131 Fulda, 1,226 C 7
56034 Garden City, 270 D 6
56332 Garfield, 198 C 5
56450 Garrison, 125 E 4
56132 Garvin, 201 C 6
56545 Gary, 265 B 3
55334 Gaylord⊙, 1,720 D 6
56035 Geneva, 358 E 7
56717 Gentilly, 163 B 3
56546 Georgetown, 141 B 3
55740 Gheen, 145 F 3
56239 Ghent, 301 C 6
55335 Gibbon, 877 D 6
55741 Gilbert, 2,287 F 3
† 56431 Glen, 125 E 4
55336 Glencoe⊙, 4,217 D 6
56036 Glenville, 740 E 7
56334 Glenwood⊙, 2,584 C 5
56547 Glyndon, 674 B 4
55427 Golden Valley, 24,246 G 5
56644 Gonvick, 344 C 3
55027 Goodhue, 539 F 6
55742 Goodland, 175 E 3
56725 Goodridge, 144 C 2
56037 Good Thunder, 489 D 6
55027 Goodview, 1,829 G 6
56240 Graceville, 735 B 5
56039 Granada, 381 D 7
55604 Grand Marais⊙, 1,301 G 2
55936 Grand Meadow, 869 F 7
55744 Grand Rapids⊙, 7,247 E 3
55029 Grandy, 155 E 5
56241 Granite Falls⊙, 3,225 C 6
55030 Grasston, 132 E 5
56726 Greenbush, 787 B 2
† 55373 Greenfield, 977 F 5
55338 Green Isle, 363 E 6
56242 Green Valley, 129 C 6
56335 Greenwald, 244 D 5
56336 Grey Eagle, 325 D 5
56243 Grove City, 502 D 5
56727 Grygla, 211 C 2
56452 Hackensack, 220 D 4
56133 Hadley, 119 C 7
56728 Hallock⊙, 1,477 A 2
56548 Halstad, 598 B 3
55339 Hamburg, 377 D 6
55340 Hamel, 2,396 F 5
55938 Hammond, 179 F 6
55031 Hampton, 369 E 6
56244 Hancock, 806 C 5
56245 Hanley Falls, 265 C 6
55341 Hanover, 365 E 5
56041 Hanska, 442 D 6
56364 Harding, 119 E 4
56134 Hardwick, 274 B 7
55939 Harmony, 1,130 F 7
55032 Harris, 559 F 5
56042 Hartland, 331 E 7
† 55374 Hassan, 778 E 5
55033 Hastings⊙, 12,195 F 6
56549 Hawley, 1,371 B 4
55940 Hayfield, 939 F 7
56043 Hayward, 261 E 7
55342 Hector, 1,178 D 6
56044 Henderson, 730 E 6
56136 Hendricks, 712 B 6
56550 Hendrum, 311 B 3
56551 Henning, 850 C 4
56248 Herman, 619 B 5
56137 Heron Lake, 777 C 7
56453 Hewitt, 198 C 4
55746 Hibbing, 16,104 F 3
55748 Hill City, 357 E 4
56138 Hills, 571 B 7
55037 Hinckley, 885 E 4
56552 Hitterdal, 178 B 4
56339 Hoffman, 627 C 5
55941 Hokah, 697 G 7
56340 Holdingford, 551 D 5
56139 Holland, 263 B 6
56045 Hollandale, 287 E 7
56249 Holloway, 146 C 5
55749 Holyoke, 190 F 4
55942 Homer, 150 G 6
56045 Hope, 125 E 6
55343 Hopkins, 13,428 G 5
55943 Houston, 1,090 G 7
55606 Hovland, 150 G 2
55349 Howard Lake, 1,162 D 5
55750 Hoyt Lakes, 3,634 F 3
55038 Hugo, 751 E 5
56047 Huntley, 139 D 7
55350 Hutchinson, 8,031 D 6
56140 Ihlen, 132 B 7
† 55359 Independence, 1,993 F 5
56649 International Falls⊙, 6,439 E 2
55075 Inver Grove Heights, 12,148 E 6
56141 Iona, 260 C 7
55751 Iron, 150 F 3
56455 Ironton, 562 D 4
55040 Isanti, 679 E 5
56342 Isle, 551 E 4
56142 Ivanhoe⊙, 738 B 6
56143 Jackson⊙, 3,550 C 7
55752 Jacobson, 225 E 4
56048 Janesville, 1,557 E 6
56144 Jasper, 754 B 7
56145 Jeffers, 436 C 6
56456 Jenkins, 148 D 4
55352 Jordan, 1,836 E 6
† 56669 Kabetogama, 150 F 2
56251 Kandiyohi, 295 D 5
56732 Karlstad, 727 B 2
56050 Kasota, 732 D 6
55944 Kasson, 1,883 F 6
55753 Keewatin, 1,382 E 3
56650 Kelliher, 289 D 3
55945 Kellogg, 403 G 6
55754 Kelly Lake, 950 F 3
55755 Kelsey, 151 F 3
56733 Kennedy, 424 B 2
56343 Kensington, 308 C 5
56553 Kent, 139 B 4
55946 Kenyon, 1,575 E 6
56252 Kerkhoven, 641 C 5
55757 Kettle River, 173 E 4
56051 Kiester, 681 E 7
56052 Kilkenny, 182 E 6
55353 Kimball, 567 D 5
55758 Kinney, 325 F 3
55609 Knife River, 350 G 4
55947 La Crescent, 3,142 G 7
56054 Lafayette, 498 D 6
56149 Lake Benton, 759 B 6
56734 Lake Bronson, 325 B 2
55041 Lake City, 3,594 F 6
56055 Lake Crystal, 1,807 D 6
55042 Lake Elmo, 4,032 F 6
56150 Lakefield, 1,820 C 7
† 55398 Lake Fremont (Zimmerman), 495 E 5
56458 Lake George, 200 D 3
55043 Lakeland, 962 F 6
56253 Lake Lillian, 316 C 6
56554 Lake Park, 658 B 4
† 55043 Lake Saint Croix Beach, 1,111 F 6
† 56401 Lake Shore, 410 D 4
55044 Lakeville, 7,556 E 6
56151 Lake Wilson, 378 B 7
56152 Lamberton, 962 C 6
56735 Lancaster, 382 B 2
55949 Lanesboro, 850 G 7
55950 Lansing, 300 F 7
56461 Laporte, 154 D 3
† 55744 La Prairie, 413 E 3
56056 La Salle, 132 D 6

(continued on following page)

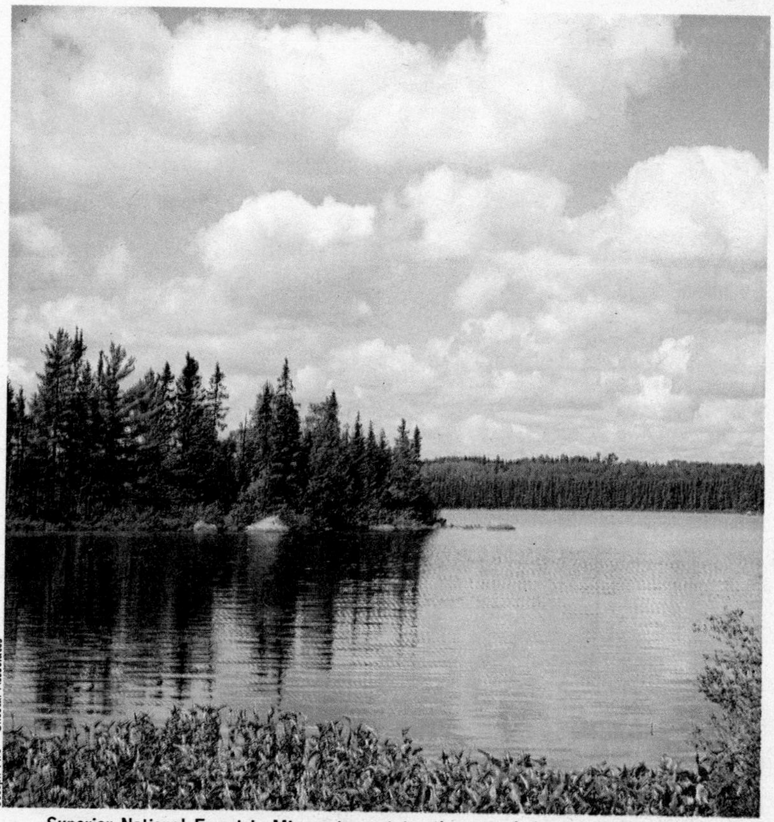

Joseph Fire—Shostal Associates

Superior National Forest in Minnesota contains the nation's largest wilderness park with primitive virgin timberlands, protected wildlife and 5,000 restocked lakes.

56344 Lastrup, 161 .... D 4
† 55101 Lauderdale, 2,419 .... G 5
56057 Le Center⊙, 1,890 .... E 6
56651 Lengby, 140 .... C 3
† 55734 Leonidas, 157 .... F 3
56153 Leota, 285 .... C 7
55951 Le Roy, 870 .... F 7
55354 Lester Prairie, 1,162 .... D 6
56058 Le Sueur, 3,745 .... E 6
55952 Lewiston, 1,000 .... G 7
56060 Lewisville, 291 .... D 7
† 55014 Lexington, 1,926 .... G 5
† 55050 Lilydale, 664 .... G 5
55045 Lindstrom, 1,260 .... F 5
† 55038 Lino Lakes, 3,692 .... G 5
56155 Lismore, 323 .... B 7
55355 Litchfield⊙, 5,262 .... D 5
56345 Little Falls⊙, 7,467 .... D 5
56653 Littlefork, 824 .... E 2
55611 Little Marais, 175 .... G 3
† 56334 Long Beach, 219 .... C 5
55356 Long Lake, 1,506 .... F 5
56347 Long Prairie⊙, 2,416 .... D 5
56655 Longville, 171 .... D 4
55046 Lonsdale, 622 .... E 6
55357 Loretto, 340 .... F 5
56349 Lowry, 257 .... C 5
56255 Lucan, 254 .... C 6
55612 Lutsen, 620 .... F 2
56156 Luverne⊙, 4,703 .... B 7
55953 Lyle, 522 .... F 7
56157 Lynd, 267 .... C 6
55954 Mabel, 888 .... G 7
56062 Madelia, 2,316 .... D 6
56256 Madison⊙, 2,242 .... B 5
56063 Madison Lake, 587 .... E 6
56158 Magnolia, 233 .... B 7
56557 Mahnomen⊙, 1,313 .... C 3
55115 Mahtomedi, 2,640 .... F 5
55762 Mahtowa, 167 .... F 4
56001 Mankato⊙, 30,895 .... E 6
55955 Mantorville⊙, 479 .... F 6
† 55369 Maple Grove, 6,275 .... F 5
55358 Maple Lake, 1,124 .... D 5
55359 Maple Plain, 1,169 .... F 5
56065 Mapleton, 1,307 .... E 7
† 55912 Mapleview, 328 .... E 7
55109 Maplewood, 25,222 .... G 5
55764 Marble, 682 .... E 3
56657 Marcell, 350 .... E 3
56257 Marietta, 264 .... B 5
55047 Marine on Saint Croix, 513 .... F 5
56258 Marshall⊙, 9,886 .... C 6
55360 Mayer, 325 .... E 6
56260 Maynard, 455 .... C 6
55956 Mazeppa, 498 .... F 6
55760 McGregor, 331 .... E 4
56556 McIntosh, 753 .... C 3
55761 McKinley, 317 .... F 3
55765 Meadowlands, 128 .... F 3
55049 Medford, 690 .... E 6
55427 Medicine Lake, 930 .... G 5
† 55340 Medina (Hamel), 2,396 .... F 5
† 56352 Meire Grove, 171 .... C 5
56352 Melrose, 2,273 .... D 5
56464 Menahga, 835 .... C 4
55050 Mendota, 327 .... G 5
† 55050 Mendota Heights, 6,165 .... G 6
56736 Mentor, 236 .... B 3
56465 Merrifield, 300 .... D 4
56737 Middle River, 369 .... B 2
† 55033 Miesville, 192 .... F 6
56353 Milaca⊙, 1,940 .... E 5
56262 Milan, 427 .... C 5
55957 Millville, 139 .... F 6
56263 Milroy, 247 .... C 6
56354 Miltona, 172 .... C 4
* 55401 Minneapolis⊙, 434,400 .... G 5
Minneapolis-Saint Paul, ‡1,813,647 .... G 5
56264 Minneota, 1,320 .... C 6
55959 Minnesota City, 301 .... G 6
56068 Minnesota Lake, 738 .... E 7
55343 Minnetonka, 35,776 .... G 5
† 55364 Minnetrista, 2,878 .... F 5
56265 Montevideo⊙, 5,661 .... C 6
56069 Montgomery, 2,281 .... E 6
55362 Monticello, 1,636 .... E 5
55363 Montrose, 379 .... E 5
56560 Moorhead⊙, 29,687 .... B 4
Moorhead-Fargo, ‡120,238 .... B 4
55767 Moose Lake, 1,400 .... F 4
56266 Mora⊙, 2,582 .... E 5
56266 Morgan, 972 .... D 6
56267 Morris⊙, 5,366 .... C 5
55052 Morristown, 659 .... E 6
56270 Morton, 591 .... C 6
56466 Motley, 351 .... D 4
55364 Mound, 7,572 .... E 6
† 55112 Mounds View, 9,988 .... G 5
55768 Mountain Iron, 1,698 .... F 3
56159 Mountain Lake, 1,986 .... D 7
56271 Murdock, 358 .... C 5
55769 Nashwauk, 1,341 .... E 3
56272 Nassau, 126 .... B 5
56566 Naytahwaush, 350 .... C 3
56355 Nelson, 175 .... C 5
55053 Nerstrand, 231 .... E 6
55772 Nett Lake, 470 .... E 2
56467 Nevis, 308 .... D 4
55366 New Auburn, 274 .... D 6
55112 New Brighton, 19,507 .... G 5
56738 Newfolden, 390 .... B 2
55367 New Germany, 303 .... E 6
56273 New London, 736 .... C 5
55054 New Market, 215 .... E 6
56356 New Munich, 307 .... D 5
55055 Newport, 2,922 .... F 6
56071 New Prague, 2,680 .... E 6
56072 New Richland, 1,113 .... E 7
† 55031 New Trier, 153 .... F 6
56073 New Ulm⊙, 13,051 .... D 6
56567 New York Mills, 791 .... C 4
† 56431 Nichols, 125 .... E 4
56074 Nicollet, 618 .... D 6
56568 Nielsville, 156 .... B 3
56468 Nisswa, 1,011 .... D 4
55770 Nopeming, 268 .... F 4
56274 Norcross, 137 .... B 5
55056 North Branch, 1,106 .... F 5
† 56442 North Crosslake, 362 .... D 4
55057 Northfield, 10,235 .... E 6
56001 North Mankato, 7,347 .... D 6
56661 Northome, 351 .... D 3
56275 North Redwood, 155 .... D 6
56075 Northrop, 188 .... D 7
55109 North Saint Paul, 11,950 .... E 5
55368 Norwood, 1,058 .... E 6
56276 Odessa, 194 .... B 5
56160 Odin, 166 .... D 7
56569 Ogema, 236 .... C 3
56358 Ogilvie, 384 .... E 5
56161 Okabena, 237 .... C 7
56742 Oklee, 536 .... C 3
56277 Olivia⊙, 2,553 .... C 6
56359 Onamia, 670 .... E 4
† 55044 Orchard Lake, 200 .... E 6
56162 Ormsby, 199 .... D 7
† 55323 Orono (Crystal Bay), 6,787 .... F 5
55960 Oronoco, 564 .... F 6
55771 Orr, 315 .... F 2
56278 Ortonville⊙, 2,665 .... B 5
56570 Osage, 175 .... C 4
56360 Osakis, 1,306 .... C 5
56744 Oslo, 417 .... A 2
55369 Osseo, 2,908 .... G 5
55961 Ostrander, 216 .... F 7
† 56058 Ottawa, 125 .... E 6
56571 Ottertail, 180 .... C 4
56662 Outing, 425 .... E 4
55060 Owatonna⊙, 15,341 .... E 6
56469 Palisade, 149 .... E 4
† 55801 Palmers, 150 .... G 4
† 55705 Palo, 158 .... F 3
56361 Parkers Prairie, 882 .... C 4
56470 Park Rapids⊙, 2,772 .... D 4
56362 Paynesville, 1,920 .... D 5
56363 Pease, 187 .... E 5
† 56472 Pelican Lakes (Breezy Point Village), 233 .... D 4
56572 Pelican Rapids, 1,835 .... B 4
56078 Pemberton, 128 .... E 7
55775 Pengilly, 625 .... E 3
56279 Pennock, 255 .... C 5
56472 Pequot Lakes, 499 .... D 4
56573 Perham, 1,933 .... C 4
56574 Perley, 149 .... B 3
55962 Peterson, 269 .... G 7
† 55948 Pickwick, 150 .... G 7
56364 Pierz, 893 .... D 5
56473 Pillager, 374 .... D 4
55063 Pine City⊙, 2,143 .... F 5
55963 Pine Island, 1,640 .... F 6
56474 Pine River, 803 .... D 4
56164 Pipestone⊙, 5,328 .... B 7
55964 Plainview, 2,093 .... F 6
55370 Plato, 303 .... D 6
56748 Plummer, 285 .... B 3
† 55401 Plymouth, 17,593 .... G 5
56666 Ponemah, 531 .... D 2
56280 Porter, 207 .... B 6
55965 Preston⊙, 1,413 .... F 7
55371 Princeton, 2,531 .... E 5
56281 Prinsburg, 448 .... C 6
55372 Prior Lake, 1,114 .... E 6
55810 Proctor, 3,123 .... F 4
† 55752 Rabey, 125 .... E 4
55967 Racine, 197 .... F 7
56475 Randall, 536 .... D 4
55065 Randolph, 350 .... E 6
56668 Ranier, 255 .... E 2
56669 Ray, 200 .... E 2
56282 Raymond, 589 .... C 5
56165 Reading, 150 .... C 7
55968 Reads Landing, 150 .... F 6
56670 Redby, 475 .... D 3
56671 Redlake, 300 .... C 3
56750 Red Lake Falls⊙, 1,740 .... B 3
55066 Red Wing⊙, 10,441 .... F 6
56283 Redwood Falls⊙, 4,774 .... C 6
56672 Remer, 403 .... E 3
56284 Renville, 1,252 .... C 6
56166 Revere, 166 .... C 6
56367 Rice, 366 .... D 5
55423 Richfield, 47,231 .... G 6
56368 Richmond, 866 .... D 5
55422 Robbinsdale, 16,845 .... G 5
55901 Rochester⊙, 53,766 .... F 6
55067 Rock Creek, 805 .... F 5
55373 Rockford, 730 .... F 5
56369 Rockville, 302 .... D 5
55374 Rogers, 544 .... E 5
55969 Rollingstone, 450 .... G 6
56371 Roscoe, 195 .... D 5
56751 Roseau⊙, 2,552 .... C 2
55970 Rose Creek, 390 .... F 7
† 56216 Roseland, 123 .... C 6
55068 Rosemount, 1,337 .... E 6
55113 Roseville, 34,518 .... G 5
56579 Rothsay, 448 .... B 4
56167 Round Lake, 506 .... C 7
56373 Royalton, 534 .... D 5
55069 Rush City, 1,130 .... F 5
55971 Rushford, 1,318 .... G 7
56168 Rushmore, 394 .... C 7
56169 Russell, 398 .... C 6
56170 Ruthton, 405 .... B 6
55778 Rutledge, 123 .... F 4
56580 Sabin, 333 .... B 4
56285 Sacred Heart, 707 .... C 6
55779 Saginaw, 407 .... F 4
55414 Saint Anthony Falls, 9,239 .... G 5
55375 Saint Bonifacius, 685 .... F 5
55972 Saint Charles, 1,942 .... F 7
56080 Saint Clair, 488 .... E 6
56301 Saint Cloud⊙, 39,691 .... D 5
55070 Saint Francis, 897 .... E 5
56554 Saint Hilaire, 337 .... B 2
56081 Saint James⊙, 4,027 .... D 7
56374 Saint Joseph, 1,786 .... D 5
55426 Saint Louis Park, 48,883 .... G 5
56376 Saint Martin, 188 .... D 5
55376 Saint Michael, 1,021 .... E 5
* 55101 Saint Paul (cap.)⊙, 309,980 .... G 6
55071 Saint Paul Park, 5,587 .... G 6
56082 Saint Peter⊙, 8,339 .... E 6
56375 Saint Stephen, 331 .... D 5
56755 Saint Vincent, 177 .... A 2
56083 Sanborn, 505 .... C 6
55072 Sandstone, 1,641 .... F 4
56377 Sartell, 1,323 .... D 5
56378 Sauk Centre, 3,750 .... C 5
56379 Sauk Rapids, 5,051 .... D 5
55378 Savage, 3,611 .... G 6
55780 Sawyer, 200 .... F 4
55073 Scandia, 200 .... F 5
† 55720 Scanlon, 1,132 .... F 4
55613 Schroeder, 550 .... G 3
56287 Seaforth, 132 .... C 6
56084 Searles, 160 .... D 6
56477 Sebeka, 668 .... C 4
55074 Shafer, 149 .... F 5
55379 Shakopee⊙, 6,876 .... F 6
56581 Shelly, 260 .... B 3
56171 Sherburn, 1,190 .... D 7
56676 Shevlin, 185 .... C 3
† 55021 Shieldsville, 150 .... E 6
† 55331 Shorewood, 4,223 .... F 5
55614 Silver Bay, 3,504 .... G 3
55380 Silver Creek, 125 .... D 5
55381 Silver Lake, 694 .... D 6
† 56001 Skyline, 400 .... D 6
56172 Slayton⊙, 2,351 .... C 7
56085 Sleepy Eye, 3,461 .... D 6
† 56345 Sobieski, 189 .... D 5
55782 Soudan, 900 .... F 3
55382 South Haven, 238 .... D 5
56679 South International Falls, 2,116 .... E 2
55075 South Saint Paul, 25,016 .... G 6
56288 Spicer, 586 .... C 5
56087 Springfield, 2,530 .... C 6
55974 Spring Grove, 1,290 .... G 7
55432 Spring Lake Park, 6,417 .... E 5
55384 Spring Park, 1,087 .... F 5
55975 Spring Valley, 2,572 .... F 7
55079 Stacy, 278 .... E 5
55080 Stanchfield, 155 .... E 5
56479 Staples, 2,657 .... D 4
56381 Starbuck, 1,138 .... C 5
56173 Steen, 191 .... B 7
56757 Stephen, 904 .... A 2
55385 Stewart, 666 .... D 6
55976 Stewartville, 2,802 .... F 7
55082 Stillwater⊙, 10,191 .... F 5
55988 Stockton, 346 .... G 6
56174 Storden, 364 .... C 6
56758 Strandquist, 138 .... B 2
55783 Sturgeon Lake, 167 .... F 4
56289 Sunburg, 144 .... C 5
† 55075 Sunfish Lake, 269 .... E 6
56290 Svea, 125 .... C 6
56382 Swanville, 300 .... D 5
55785 Swatara, 250 .... E 4
55786 Taconite, 352 .... E 3
56291 Taunton, 195 .... B 6
55084 Taylors Falls, 587 .... F 5
56683 Tenstrike, 138 .... D 3
56701 Thief River Falls⊙, 8,618 .... B 2
† 56319 Thomson, 159 .... F 4
56583 Tintah, 167 .... B 5
55615 Tofte, 400 .... H 3
55789 Toivola, 185 .... F 3
† 55331 Tonka Bay, 1,397 .... F 5
55790 Tower, 699 .... F 3
56175 Tracy, 2,516 .... C 6
56176 Trimont, 835 .... D 7
56088 Truman, 1,137 .... D 7
55791 Twig, 165 .... F 4
56089 Twin Lakes, 230 .... E 7
56584 Twin Valley, 868 .... B 3
55616 Two Harbors⊙, 4,437 .... G 3
56178 Tyler, 1,069 .... B 6
56585 Ulen, 486 .... B 3
56586 Underwood, 278 .... C 4
56384 Upsala, 312 .... D 5
† 56361 Urbank, 125 .... C 4
55979 Utica, 240 .... G 7
† 55101 Vadnais Heights, 3,391 .... G 5
56587 Vergas, 281 .... C 4
55085 Vermillion, 359 .... F 6
56481 Verndale, 570 .... C 4
† 55752 Verndon, 135 .... E 4
56090 Vernon Center, 347 .... D 7
55086 Veseli, 150 .... E 6
56292 Vesta, 330 .... C 6
55386 Victoria, 850 .... F 6
56385 Villard, 221 .... C 5
56588 Vining, 121 .... C 4
55792 Virginia, 12,450 .... F 3
55981 Wabasha⊙, 2,371 .... G 6
56293 Wabasso, 738 .... C 6
55387 Waconia, 2,445 .... E 6
56482 Wadena⊙, 4,640 .... C 4
56386 Wahkon, 208 .... E 4
56387 Waite Park, 2,824 .... D 5
56091 Waldorf, 285 .... E 7
56484 Walker⊙, 2,073 .... D 3
56180 Walnut Grove, 756 .... C 6
56092 Walters, 152 .... E 7
55982 Waltham, 189 .... F 7
55983 Wanamingo, 574 .... F 6
56294 Wanda, 124 .... C 6
55743 Warba, 148 .... E 3
56762 Warren⊙, 1,999 .... B 2
56763 Warroad, 1,086 .... C 2
55087 Warsaw, 200 .... E 6
56093 Waseca⊙, 6,789 .... E 6
55388 Watertown, 1,390 .... E 6
56096 Waterville, 1,539 .... E 6
55389 Watkins, 785 .... D 5
56295 Watson, 228 .... C 5
56589 Waubun, 345 .... C 3
55390 Waverly, 546 .... E 5
55391 Wayzata, 3,700 .... G 5
55088 Webster, 175 .... E 6
56181 Welcome, 694 .... D 7
56097 Wells, 2,791 .... E 7
56590 Wendell, 247 .... B 4
56183 Westbrook, 990 .... C 6
55985 West Concord, 718 .... F 6
55118 West Saint Paul, 18,799 .... G 5
56296 Wheaton⊙, 2,029 .... B 5
56485 Whipholt, 142 .... D 3
55110 White Bear Lake, 23,313 .... G 5
56591 White Earth, 150 .... C 3
56184 Wilder, 132 .... C 7
55090 Willernie, 697 .... G 5
56686 Williams, 220 .... D 2
56201 Willmar⊙, 12,869 .... C 5
55795 Willow River, 331 .... F 4
56185 Wilmont, 390 .... C 7
56687 Wilton, 119 .... C 3
56101 Windom⊙, 3,952 .... C 7
56592 Winger, 228 .... B 3
56098 Winnebago, 1,791 .... D 7
55987 Winona⊙, 26,438 .... G 6
55395 Winsted, 1,266 .... D 6
55396 Winthrop, 1,391 .... D 6
55796 Winton, 193 .... G 3
56594 Wolverton, 171 .... B 4
† 55798 Woodbury, 6,184 .... F 6
56297 Wood Lake, 418 .... C 6
56186 Woodstock, 217 .... B 7
56187 Worthington⊙, 9,825 .... C 7
55797 Wrenshall, 147 .... F 4
55798 Wright, 132 .... E 4
55990 Wykoff, 450 .... F 7
55092 Wyoming, 695 .... F 5
55397 Young America, 611 .... E 6
55799 Zim, 608 .... F 3
55398 Zimmerman, 495 .... E 5
55991 Zumbro Falls, 203 .... F 6
55992 Zumbrota, 1,929 .... F 6

⊙ County seat.
‡ Population of metropolitan area.
† Zip of nearest p.o.
* Multiple zips

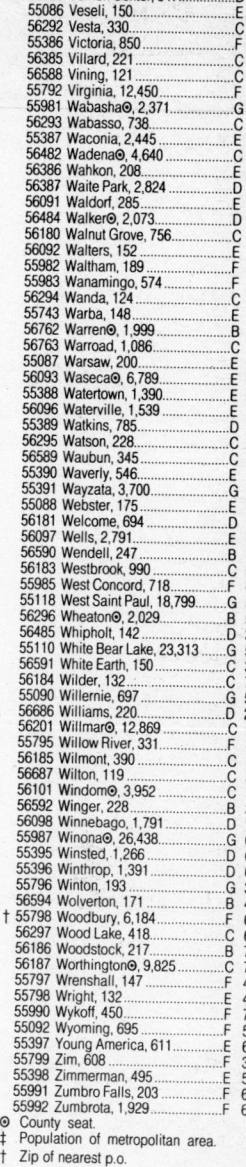

Agriculture, Industry and Resources

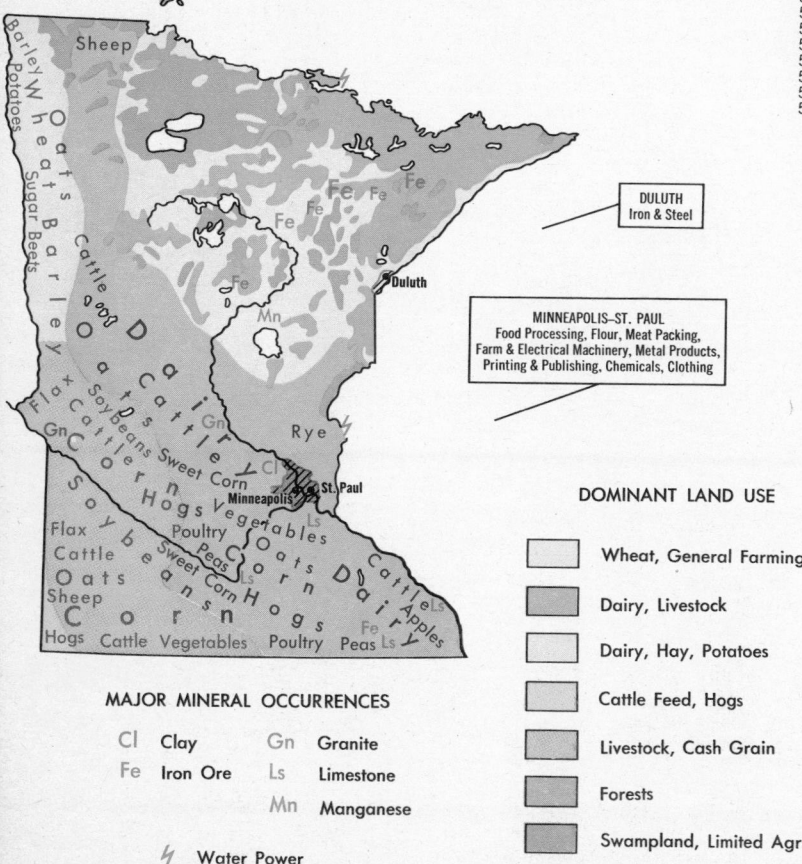

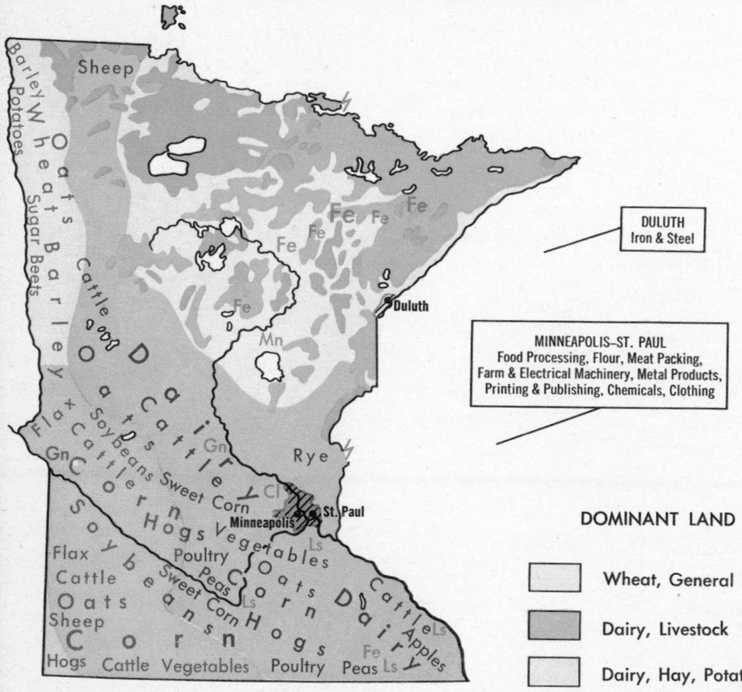
Sheep
Barley
Wheat
Potatoes
Oats
Sugar Beets
Cattle
Barley
Dairy
Oats
Flax
Soybeans
Cattle
Corn
Sweet Corn
Hogs
Vegetables
Poultry
Peas
Flax
Cattle
Oats
Sheep
Corn
Hogs
Cattle
Vegetables
Poultry
Peas
Apples
Dairy
Rye
Fe
Mn
Gn
Cl
Ls
Duluth
Minneapolis
St. Paul
DULUTH
Iron & Steel
MINNEAPOLIS-ST. PAUL
Food Processing, Flour, Meat Packing, Farm & Electrical Machinery, Metal Products, Printing & Publishing, Chemicals, Clothing

DOMINANT LAND USE

- Wheat, General Farming
- Dairy, Livestock
- Dairy, Hay, Potatoes
- Cattle Feed, Hogs
- Livestock, Cash Grain
- Forests
- Swampland, Limited Agriculture
- Urban Areas

MAJOR MINERAL OCCURRENCES

Cl	Clay	Gn	Granite
Fe	Iron Ore	Ls	Limestone
		Mn	Manganese

ϟ Water Power

Major Industrial Areas

Topography

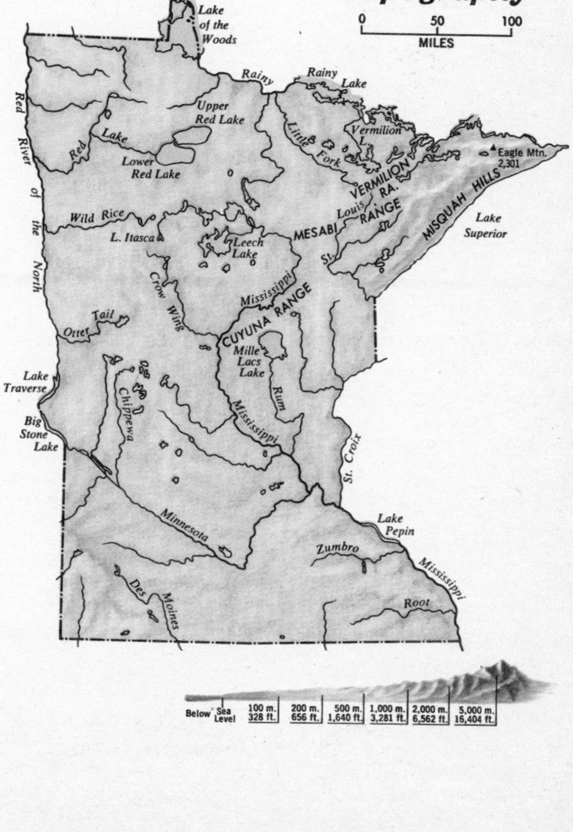
0
50
100
MILES
Lake of the Woods
Rainy
Rainy Lake
Upper Red Lake
Lower Red Lake
Red Lake
Red River of the North
Little Fork
Vermilion
Eagle Mtn. 2,301
VERMILION RA.
MISQUAH HILLS
Lake Superior
MESABI RANGE
St. Louis
Wild Rice
L. Itasca
Leech Lake
Crow Wing
Mississippi
CUYUNA RANGE
Otter Tail
Mille Lacs Lake
Rum
Lake Traverse
Big Stone Lake
Chippewa
St. Croix
Minnesota
Lake Pepin
Zumbro
Root
Des Moines
Below Sea Level
100 m. 328 ft.
200 m. 656 ft.
500 m. 1,640 ft.
1,000 m. 3,281 ft.
2,000 m. 6,562 ft.
5,000 m. 16,404 ft.

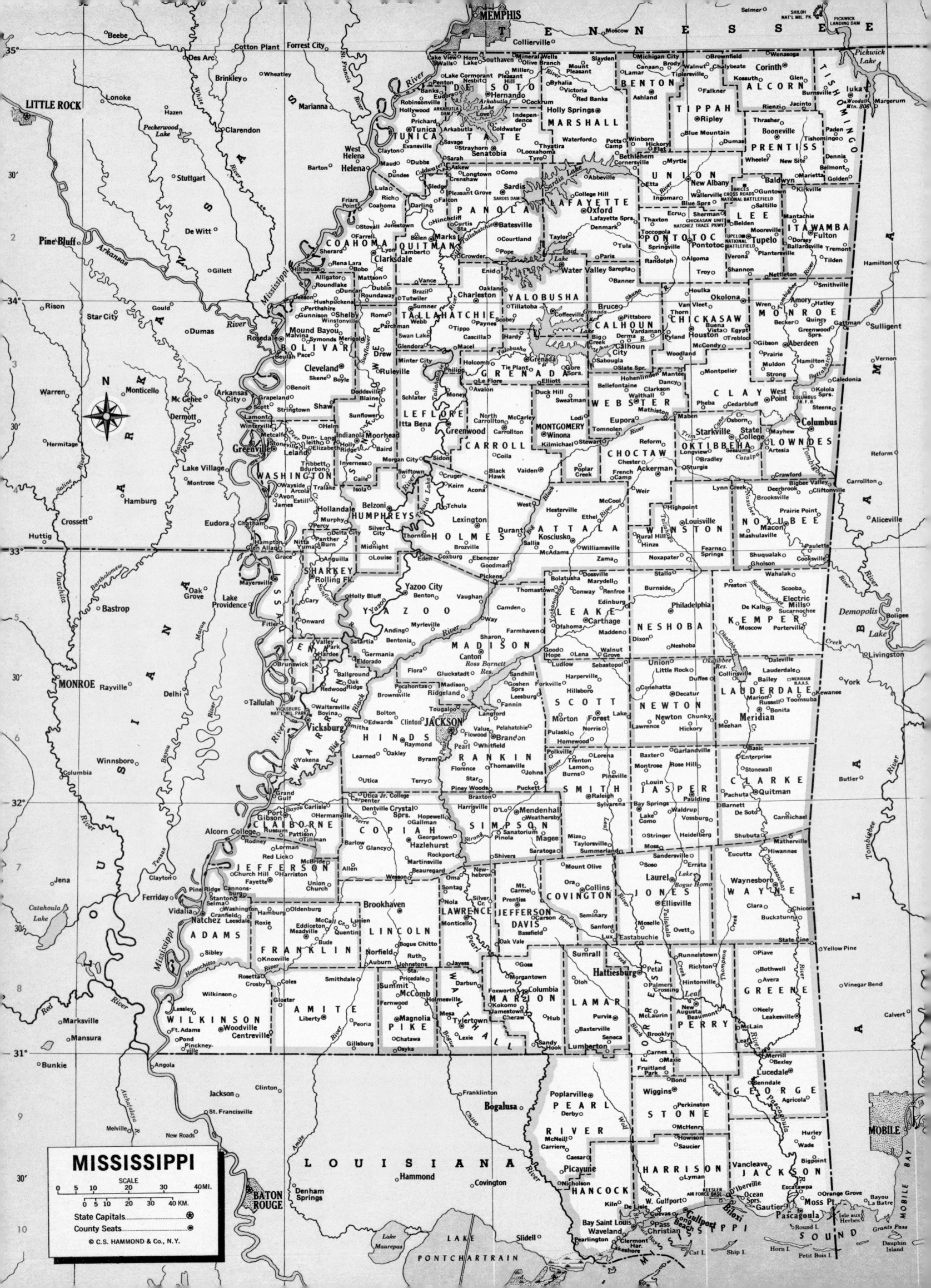

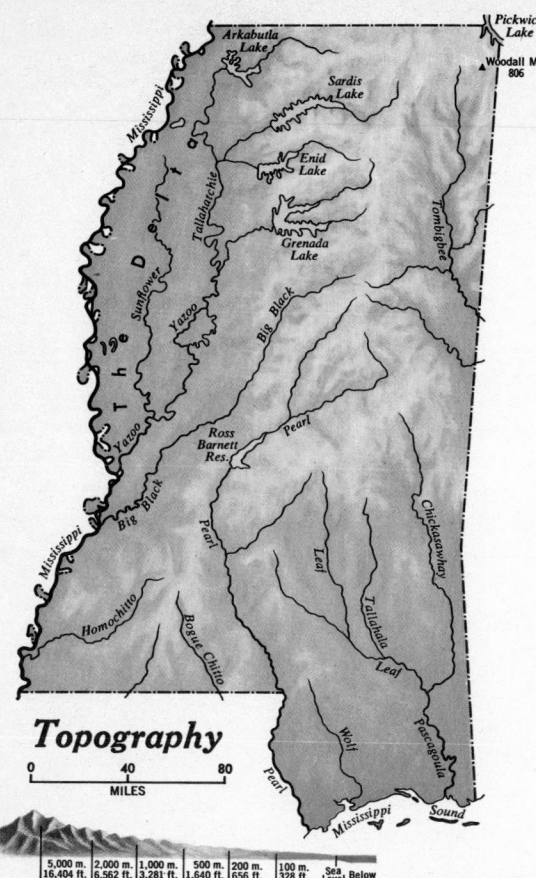

Topography

0 · 40 · 80
MILES

5,000 m. / 2,000 m. / 1,000 m. / 500 m. / 200 m. / 100 m. / Sea / Below
16,404 ft. / 6,562 ft. / 3,281 ft. / 1,640 ft. / 656 ft. / 328 ft. / Level

AREA 47,716 sq. mi.
POPULATION 2,216,912
CAPITAL Jackson
LARGEST CITY Jackson
HIGHEST POINT Woodall Mtn. 806 ft.
SETTLED IN 1716
ADMITTED TO UNION December 10, 1817
POPULAR NAME Magnolia State
STATE FLOWER Magnolia
STATE BIRD Mockingbird

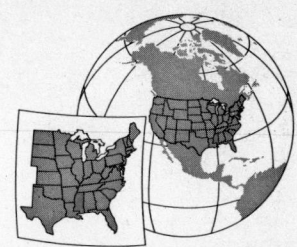

Jack Zehrt — Shostal Associates

Gracious antebellum houses of brick and stucco, shaded by moss-draped oaks, add a sense of permanence to the older section of Biloxi, Mississippi.

† 38769 Malvina, 100......C 3
38855 Mantachie, 200......H 2
39751 Mantee, 142......F 3
38856 Marietta, 250......H 2
39342 Marion, 550......G 6
38646 Marks⊙, 2,609......D 2
† 39083 Martinsville, 250......D 7
† 39051 Marydell, 125......F 5
† 39341 Mashulaville, 227......G 4
† 39360 Matherville, 150......G 7
39752 Mathiston, 570......F 3
38758 Mattson, 200......C 2
† 39425 Maxie, 100......F 9
39113 Mayersville⊙, 500......B 5
39753 Mayhew, 200......G 4
39107 McAdams, 240......E 4
39647 McCall Creek, 250......C 7
38943 McCarley, 250......E 3
39648 McComb, 11,969......D 8
38854 McCondy, 150......G 3
39108 McCool, 225......F 4
39561 McHenry, 550......F 9
39456 McLain, 632......G 8
† 39401 McLaurin, 100......F 8
39457 McNeill, 800......F 9
39653 Meadville⊙, 594......C 8
† 39301 Meehan, 100......G 6
39114 Mendenhall⊙, 2,402......E 7
39301 Meridian⊙, 45,083......G 6
38759 Merigold, 772......C 3
† 39452 Merrill, 100......G 9
38760 Metcalfe, 600......B 4
38647 Michigan City, 350......F 1
39115 Midnight, 450......C 4
38648 Mineral Wells, 250......E 3
38944 Minter City, 300......D 3
39116 Mize, 372......E 7
38945 Money, 350......D 3
39654 Monticello⊙, 1,790......D 7
39754 Montpelier, 200......G 3
39343 Montrose, 160......F 6
38857 Mooreville, 200......G 2
38761 Moorhead, 2,284......C 4
38946 Morgan City, 300......D 4
39484 Morgantown, 305......E 6
39117 Morton, 2,672......E 6
39459 Moselle, 525......F 7
39460 Moss, 150......F 7
39563 Moss Point, 19,321......G 10
38762 Mound Bayou, 2,134......C 3
39119 Mount Olive, 923......E 7
38649 Mount Pleasant, 250......C 4
† 38748 Murphy, 100......C 4
38650 Myrtle, 308......F 1
39120 Natchez⊙, 19,704......B 7
39461 Neely, 200......G 8
38651 Nesbit, 300......D 1
39344 Neshoba, 250......F 5
38858 Nettleton, 1,591......G 2
38652 New Albany⊙, 6,426......G 2
39462 New Augusta⊙, 511......F 8
39140 Newhebron, 456......D 7
39345 Newton, 3,556......F 6
39463 Nicholson, 400......E 10
38763 Nitta Yuma, 150......C 4
† 39665 Nola, 120......D 7
† 39629 Norfield, 225......C 8
38947 North Carrollton, 611......E 3

39346 Noxapater, 554......F 5
38948 Oakland, 493......E 2
† 39154 Oakley, 420......D 6
39180 Oak Ridge, 350......C 5
39656 Oak Vale, 166......E 8
39564 Ocean Springs, 9,580......G 10
39141 Ofahoma, 850......E 5
38860 Okolona⊙, 3,002......G 2
38654 Olive Branch, 1,513......E 1
† 39482 Oloh, 100......E 8
39142 Oma, 100......D 7
39428 Ora, 140......E 7
† 39501 Orange Grove, 200......H 10
39657 Osyka, 628......D 8
39464 Ovett, 250......F 8
38655 Oxford⊙, 13,846......F 2
38764 Pace, 629......C 3
39347 Pachuta, 271......G 6
38861 Paden, 97......H 1
† 39401 Palmers Crossing, 250......F 8
38765 Panther Burn, 400......C 4
38738 Parchman, 200......D 3
38949 Paris, 253......F 2
39567 Pascagoula⊙, 27,264......G 10
39571 Pass Christian, 2,979......F 10
39144 Pattison, 540......C 7
39348 Paulding⊙, 769......F 6
39349 Paulette, 230......H 4
† 38920 Paynes, 100......D 6
39208 Pearl, 9,623......D 6
39572 Pearlington, 500......E 10
39145 Pelahatchie, 1,306......E 6
38664 Penton, 175......D 1
† 39645 Peoria, 100......C 8
39573 Perkinston, 950......F 9
39465 Petal, 6,986......F 8
39755 Pheba, 280......G 3
39350 Philadelphia⊙, 6,274......F 5
38950 Philipp, 975......D 3
39476 Piave, 500......E 8
39466 Picayune, 10,467......E 9
39146 Pickens, 1,012......E 5
39120 Pine Ridge, 175......B 7
39148 Piney Woods, 300......D 6
39149 Pinola, 102......E 7
38951 Pittsboro⊙, 188......F 3
38862 Plantersville, 910......G 2
38657 Pleasant Grove, 150......D 2
† 38651 Pleasant Hill, 400......E 1
39118 Polkville, 500......E 6
38863 Pontotoc⊙, 3,453......G 2
38568 Pope, 210......E 2
39747 Poplar Creek, 100......E 4
39470 Poplarville⊙, 2,312......E 9
39352 Porterville, 150......G 5
39150 Port Gibson⊙, 2,589......B 7
38659 Potts Camp, 459......F 1
39353 Prairie Point, 150......H 4
39474 Prentiss⊙, 1,789......E 7
39354 Preston, 120......G 5
† 39666 Pricedale, 400......D 8
38660 Prichard, 250......D 1
39151 Puckett, 333......E 6
39152 Pulaski, 108......E 6
39475 Purvis⊙, 1,860......F 8
† 38851 Pyland, 120......F 3
39660 Quentin, 150......C 8
39355 Quitman⊙, 2,702......G 6

39153 Raleigh⊙, 1,018......F 6
38864 Randolph, 205......F 2
39154 Raymond⊙, 1,620......D 6
38661 Red Banks, 350......F 1
† 39096 Red Lick, 250......B 7
39156 Redwood, 400......C 6
39757 Reform, 150......F 4
39462 Rena Lara, 400......C 2
39140 Renfroe, 100......F 5
39476 Richton, 1,110......G 8
39157 Ridgeland, 1,650......D 6
38865 Rienzi, 363......G 1
38663 Ripley⊙, 3,482......G 1
38664 Robinsonville, 285......D 1

† 39083 Rockport, 100......D 7
39096 Rodney, 200......B 7
39159 Rolling Fork⊙, 2,034......C 5
38768 Rome, 171......D 3
† 38769 Rosedale⊙, 2,599......B 3
39356 Rose Hill, 300......F 6
38614 Roundaway, 175......C 2
† 38740 Roundlake, 105......C 2
39681 Roxie, 662......B 8
38771 Ruleville, 2,351......D 3
† 39401 Runnelstown, 200......F 8
39108 Rural Hill, 125......F 4
39357 Russell, 300......G 6
39662 Ruth, 150......D 8

39955 Sabougla, 100......F 3
39160 Sallis, 213......E 4
38866 Saltillo, 836......G 2
39112 Sanatorium, 400......E 7
39477 Sandersville, 694......F 7
39161 Sandhill, 392......E 6
39478 Sandy Hook, 108......E 8
39479 Sanford, 150......E 7
38665 Sarah, 300......D 1
38666 Sardis⊙, 2,391......E 2
38867 Sarepta, 650......F 2
39574 Saucier, 100......F 9
38667 Savage, 100......D 1
38952 Schlater, 398......D 3
38953 Scobey, 100......E 3
39358 Scooba, 626......G 5
38772 Scott, 500......B 3
39359 Sebastopol, 268......F 5
39479 Seminary, 269......E 7
38668 Senatobia⊙, 4,247......E 1
39758 Sessums, 100......G 4
38868 Shannon, 575......G 2
38773 Shaw, 2,513......C 3
38774 Shelby, 2,645......C 3
38669 Sherard, 160......C 2
38869 Sherman, 468......G 2
39164 Shivers, 100......E 7
39360 Shubuta, 602......G 7
39361 Shuqualak, 591......G 5
39165 Sibley, 250......B 8
38954 Sidon, 348......D 4
39166 Silver City, 370......C 4
39663 Silver Creek, 257......D 7
38775 Skene, 300......C 3
38955 Slate Spring, 105......F 3
† 38642 Slayden, 310......F 1
38670 Sledge, 516......D 2
39664 Smithdale, 200......C 8
38870 Smithville, 552......H 2
39665 Sontag, 200......D 7
39480 Soso, 230......F 7
38671 Southaven, 8,931......E 1
† 38863 Springville, 100......F 2
† 39350 Stallo, 100......F 5
39167 Star, 575......D 6
39759 Starkville⊙, 11,369......G 4
39762 State College, 4,595......G 4
39362 State Line, 598......G 8
39766 Steens, 125......H 3
39767 Stewart, 150......F 4
38776 Stoneville, 700......C 4
39363 Stonewall, 1,161......G 6
38672 Stovall, 260......C 2
† 38665 Strayhorn, 800......D 1
39481 Stringer, 340......F 7
38777 Stringtown, 300......C 3
39769 Sturgis, 321......F 4
39168 Summerland, 150......F 7
39666 Summit, 1,640......D 8
38957 Sumner⊙, 533......D 3
39482 Sumrall, 955......E 8
38778 Sunflower, 983......C 3
38958 Swan Lake, 250......D 3
38959 Swiftown, 400......D 4
39153 Sylvarena, 115......F 6
† 39776 Symonds, 200......C 3
38673 Taylor, 92......E 2
39168 Taylorsville, 1,299......F 7
39169 Tchula, 1,729......D 4
39170 Terry, 546......D 6
38871 Thaxton, 250......F 2
39171 Thomastown, 350......E 5
39172 Thorn, 125......F 3
39172 Thornton, 120......D 4

† 38829 Thrasher, 800......G 1
† 38668 Thyatira, 100......E 1
38960 Tie Plant, 950......E 3
† 38843 Tilden, 250......H 2
38961 Tillatoba, 102......E 3
38674 Tiplersville, 120......G 1
38962 Tippo, 200......D 3
38873 Tishomingo, 410......H 1
38874 Toccopola, 175......F 2
39770 Tomnolen, 225......F 4
39364 Toomsuba, 500......G 6
39174 Tougaloo, 1,720......D 6
38757 Tralake, 200......C 4
38875 Trebloc, 750......G 3
38876 Tremont, 250......H 2
38779 Tribbett, 200......C 4
† 38863 Troy, 150......G 2
38675 Tula, 100......F 2
38676 Tunica⊙, 1,685......D 1
38801 Tupelo⊙, 20,471......G 2
38963 Tutwiler, 1,103......D 2
39667 Tylertown⊙, 1,736......D 8
39365 Union, 1,856......F 5
39668 Union Church, 194......C 7
39175 Utica, 1,019......C 6
39175 Utica Junior College, 700......C 6
39176 Vaiden⊙, 716......E 4
39177 Valley Park, 350......C 5
39178 Value, 327......D 6
38964 Vance, 500......D 2
† 39564 Vancleave, 505......G 9
† 38851 Van Vleet, 300......G 3
38878 Vardaman, 777......F 3
38879 Verona, 1,877......G 2
39180 Vicksburg⊙, 25,478......C 6
38679 Victoria, 400......E 1
39366 Vossburg, 250......F 7
39575 Wade, 800......G 9
† 39422 Waldrup, 125......F 7
38680 Walls, 850......D 1
38683 Walnut, 458......G 1
39189 Walnut Grove, 398......F 5
† 39180 Waltersville, 150......C 6
39771 Walthall⊙, 161......F 3
39190 Washington, 250......B 7
38685 Waterford, 375......F 1
38965 Water Valley⊙, 3,285......E 2
39576 Waveland, 3,108......F 10
39367 Waynesboro⊙, 4,368......G 7
38780 Wayside, 250......C 4
38966 Webb, 751......D 3
39772 Weir, 573......F 4
38886 Wenasoga, 125......G 1
39191 Wesson, 1,253......D 7
39192 West, 305......E 4
† 39501 West-Gulfport, 6,996......F 10
39773 West Point⊙, 8,714......G 3
38880 Wheeler, 600......G 1
39193 Whitfield, 6,200......E 6
39577 Wiggins⊙, 2,995......F 9
† 39090 Williamsville, 250......F 4
38659 Winborn, 122......F 1
38967 Winona⊙, 5,521......E 4
38781 Winstonville, 536......C 3
38782 Winterville, 500......B 4
39776 Woodland, 130......F 4
39669 Woodville⊙, 1,734......A 8
39730 Wren, 150......G 2
39194 Yazoo City⊙, 10,796......D 5
39090 Zama, 125......F 5

⊙ County seat.
* Population of metropolitan area.
○ Zip of nearest p.o.
† Multiple zips

Agriculture, Industry and Resources

DOMINANT LAND USE

- Specialized Cotton
- Cotton, Livestock
- Cotton, General Farming
- Cotton, Forest Products
- Truck and Mixed Farming
- Forests
- Swampland, Limited Agriculture

MAJOR MINERAL OCCURRENCES

Cl Clay
Fe Iron Ore
G Natural Gas
O Petroleum
▨ Major Industrial Areas

PASCAGOULA
Shipbuilding,
Oil Refining

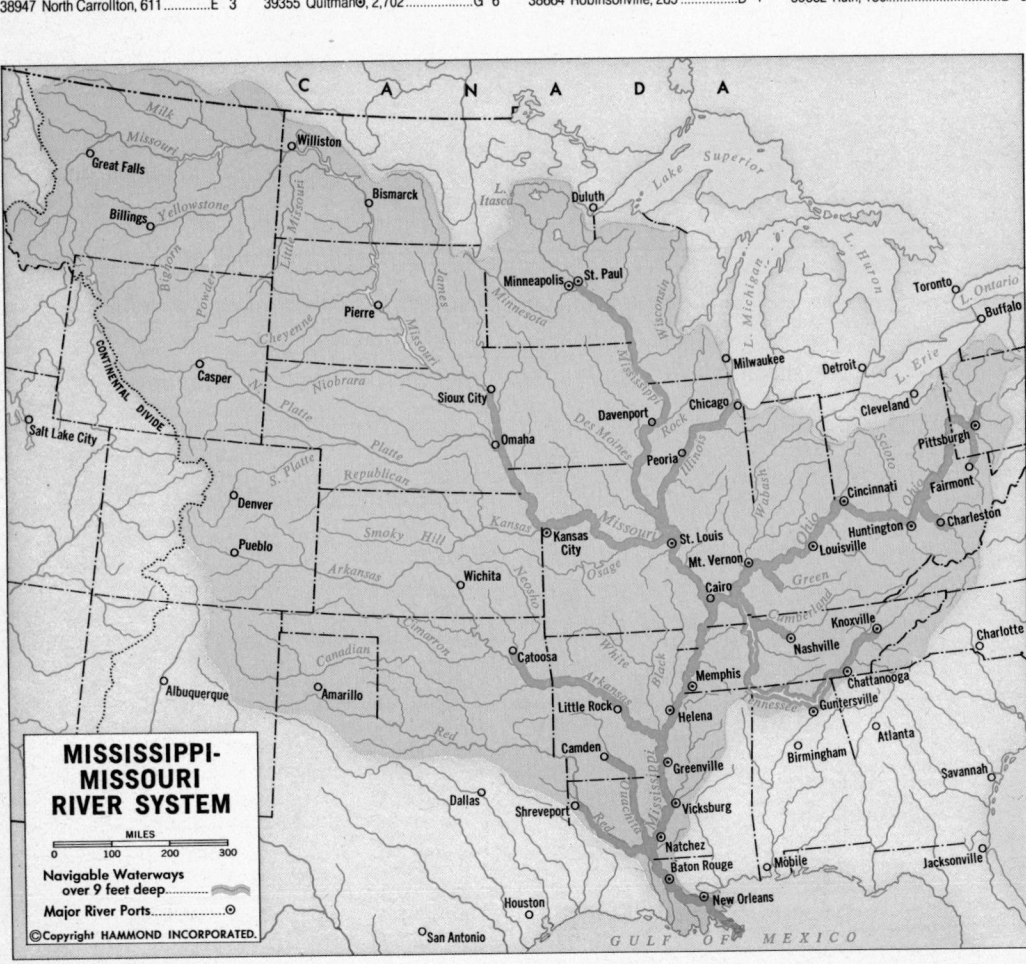

MISSISSIPPI-MISSOURI RIVER SYSTEM

MILES
0   100   200   300

Navigable Waterways over 9 feet deep
Major River Ports......⊙

©Copyright HAMMOND INCORPORATED.

AREA 69,686 sq. mi.
POPULATION 4,677,399
CAPITAL Jefferson City
LARGEST CITY St. Louis
HIGHEST POINT Taum Sauk Mtn. 1,772 ft.
SETTLED IN 1764
ADMITTED TO UNION August 10, 1821
POPULAR NAME Show Me State
STATE FLOWER Hawthorn
STATE BIRD Bluebird

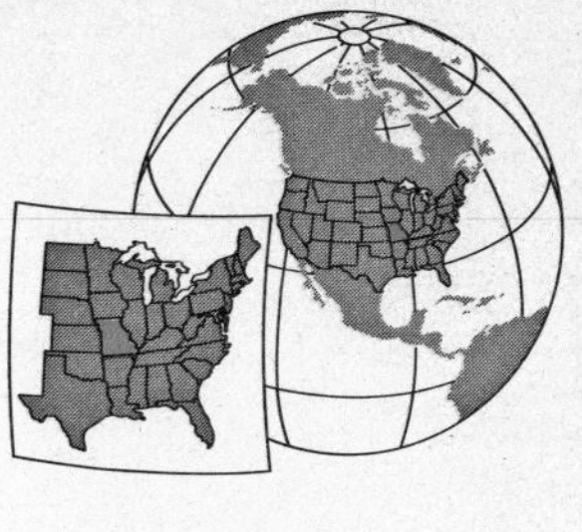

COUNTIES

Name/Pop.	Key
r, 22,472	G 2
ew, 11,913	C 3
ison, 9,240	B 2
ain, 25,362	J 4
y, 19,597	E 9
on, 10,431	D 7
s, 15,468	D 6
on, 9,695	F 6
nger, 8,820	M 8
ne, 80,911	H 4
hanan, 86,915	C 3
er, 33,529	M 9
well, 8,351	E 3
away, 25,850	J 5
den, 13,315	G 6
e Girardeau, 49,350	N 8
oll, 12,565	F 4
er, 3,878	L 9
s, 39,448	D 5
ar, 9,424	E 7
riton, 11,084	F 3
stian, 15,124	F 9
k, 8,260	J 2
, 123,322	D 4
ton, 12,462	D 3
e, 46,228	H 6
per, 14,732	G 5
wford, 14,828	K 7
e, 6,850	E 8
as, 10,054	F 7
iess, 8,420	E 3
Kalb, 7,305	D 3
t, 11,457	J 7
glas, 9,268	G 9
klin, 33,742	M10
nklin, 55,116	K 6
conade, 11,878	J 6
ntry, 8,060	D 2
ene, 152,929	F 8
ndy, 11,819	E 2
rison, 10,257	E 2
ry, 18,451	E 6
kory, 4,481	F 7
t, 6,654	B 2
ward, 10,561	G 4
well, 23,521	J 9
, 9,529	L 7
kson, 654,558	D 5
per, 79,852	D 8
erson, 105,248	L 6
nson, 34,172	E 5
x, 5,692	H 2
lede, 19,944	G 7
ayette, 26,626	E 4
vrence, 24,585	E 8
vis, 10,993	J 2
coln, 18,041	L 4
n, 15,125	F 3
ngston, 15,368	E 3
con, 15,432	G 3
dison, 8,641	M 8
ries, 6,851	J 6
rion, 28,121	J 3
Donald, 12,357	D 9
rcer, 4,910	E 2
er, 15,026	H 6
sissippi, 16,647	O 9
niteau, 10,742	G 5
nroe, 9,542	H 3
ntgomery, 11,000	K 5
rgan, 10,068	G 6
v Madrid, 23,420	N 9
wton, 32,901	D 9
daway, 22,467	C 2
egon, 9,180	K 9
age, 10,994	J 6
ark, 6,226	H 9
miscot, 26,373	N10
ry, 14,393	N 7
tis, 34,137	F 5
elps, 29,481	J 7
e, 16,928	K 4
tte, 32,081	C 4
k, 15,415	F 7
laski, 53,781	H 7
nam, 5,916	F 2
lls, 7,764	J 3
ndolph, 22,434	G 3
y, 17,599	E 4
ynolds, 6,106	L 8
pley, 9,803	L 9
int Charles, 92,954	L 5
int Clair, 7,667	E 6
inte Genevieve, 12,867	M 7
nt Francois, 36,818	M 7
int Louis, 951,353	M 5
int Louis (city county), 622,236	M 5
line, 24,633	F 4
huyler, 4,665	G 2
otland, 5,499	H 2
ott, 33,250	N 8
annon, 7,196	K 8
elby, 7,906	H 3
oddard, 25,771	N 9
one, 9,921	F 9
llivan, 7,572	F 2
ney, 13,023	F 9
xas, 18,320	J 8
rnon, 19,065	D 7
arren, 9,699	K 5
ashington, 15,086	L 7
ayne, 8,546	L 8
ebster, 15,562	G 8
orth, 3,359	D 2
right, 13,667	H 8

CITIES and TOWNS

ip	Name/Pop.	Key
720	Adrian, 1,259	D 6
730	Advance, 903	N 8
123	Affton, 24,067	P 3
836	Airport Drive, 300	C 8
830	Alba, 365	D 8
402	Albany⊙, 1,804	D 2
63430	Alexandria, 453	K 2
63001	Allenton, 800	N 3
64001	Alma, 380	E 4
64620	Altamont, 225	D 3
63732	Altenburg, 277	O 7
65606	Alton⊙, 715	K 9
64421	Amazonia, 326	C 3
64722	Amoret, 219	C 6
64831	Anderson, 1,065	D 9
63620	Annapolis, 330	L 8
63820	Anniston, 515	O 9
64724	Appleton City, 1,058	D 6
63821	Arbyrd, 575	M10
63621	Arcadia, 627	L 7
64725	Archie, 525	D 5
65001	Argyle, 262	J 6
65230	Armstrong, 354	G 4
63010	Arnold, 11,994	P 4
65604	Ash Grove, 934	E 8
65010	Ashland, 769	H 5
63530	Atlanta, 377	H 3
63332	Augusta, 259	M 3
65605	Aurora, 5,359	E 9
65231	Auxvasse, 808	J 4
65608	Ava⊙, 2,504	G 9
64010	Avondale, 748	P 5
63011	Ballwin, 10,656	O 3
63531	Baring, 206	H 2
64423	Barnard, 206	C 2
64011	Bates City, 229	E 5
† 65619	Battlefield, 291	F 8
63622	Belgrade, 349	L 7
63735	Bell City, 424	N 8
65013	Belle, 1,133	J 6
† 63101	Bellefontaine Neighbors, 13,987	R 2
63623	Belleview, 225	L 7
63333	Bellflower, 360	K 4
64012	Belton, 9,783	C 5
63736	Benton⊙, 640	O 8
63014	Berger, 226	K 5
63134	Berkeley, 19,743	P 2
63822	Bernie, 1,641	M 9
63823	Bertrand, 604	O 9
64424	Bethany⊙, 2,914	E 2
63532	Bevier, 806	G 3
65610	Billings, 760	F 8
65438	Birch Tree, 573	K 9
† 64068	Birmingham, 266	P 5
63624	Bismarck, 1,387	L 7
65321	Blackburn, 294	F 4
† 63031	Black Jack, 3,500	P 2
65322	Blackwater, 249	G 5
65014	Bland, 621	J 6
63824	Blodgett, 220	O 8
63825	Bloomfield⊙, 1,584	M 9
63627	Bloomsdale, 411	M 6
64015	Blue Springs, 6,779	R 6
† 64101	Blue Summit, 1,283	R 5
64426	Blythedale, 213	E 2
64622	Bogard, 294	E 4
65612	Bois D'Arc, 250	F 8
64427	Bolckow, 225	C 2
65613	Bolivar⊙, 4,769	F 7
63628	Bonne Terre, 3,622	L 7
65016	Bonnots Mill, 210	J 5
65233	Boonville⊙, 7,514	G 5
64723	Bosworth, 386	F 4
65441	Bourbon, 955	K 6
63334	Bowling Green⊙, 2,936	K 4
63826	Braggadocio, 285	N10
63827	Bragg City, 210	N10
65616	Branson, 2,175	F 9
63533	Brashear, 316	H 2
64624	Braymer, 919	E 3
64625	Breckenridge, 598	E 3
† 63101	Breckenridge Hills, 7,011	O 2
63144	Brentwood, 11,248	P 3
63044	Bridgeton, 19,992	O 2
64728	Bronaugh, 203	C 7
64628	Brookfield, 5,491	F 3
64630	Browning, 412	F 2
65236	Brunswick, 1,870	F 4
64631	Bucklin, 654	G 3
64016	Buckner, 1,695	R 5
65622	Buffalo⊙, 1,915	F 7
65237	Bunceton, 437	G 5
63629	Bunker, 447	K 8
64428	Burlington Junction, 634	B 2
64730	Butler⊙, 3,984	D 6
65689	Cabool, 1,848	H 8
63630	Cadet, 300	L 6
64632	Cainsville, 454	E 2
65239	Cairo, 248	H 4
65323	Calhoun, 360	E 6
65018	California⊙, 3,105	H 5
63534	Callao, 373	G 3
64017	Camden, 286	D 4
65020	Camdenton⊙, 1,636	G 6
64429	Cameron, 3,960	D 3
63933	Campbell, 1,979	M 9
63828	Canalou, 358	N 9
63435	Canton, 2,680	J 2
63701	Cape Girardeau, 31,282	O 8
63829	Cardwell, 859	M10
64834	Carl Junction, 1,661	C 8
64633	Carrollton⊙, 4,847	E 4
64835	Carterville, 1,716	D 8
64836	Carthage⊙, 11,035	D 8
63830	Caruthersville⊙, 7,350	N10
65625	Cassville⊙, 1,910	E 9
63015	Catawissa, 250	N 4
65022	Cedar City, 454	H 5
63016	Cedar Hill, 500	L 6
63436	Center, 588	J 3
65023	Centertown, 277	H 5
64019	Centerview, 234	E 5
63633	Centerville⊙, 209	L 8
65240	Centralia, 3,618	H 4
63740	Chaffee, 2,793	N 8
65024	Chamois, 615	J 5
63834	Charleston⊙, 5,131	O 9
63017	Chesterfield, 13,000	O 3
64733	Chilhowee, 297	E 5
64601	Chillicothe⊙, 9,519	E 3
64635	Chula, 244	F 3
63437	Clarence, 1,050	H 3
65243	Clark, 271	H 4
65025	Clarksburg, 343	G 5
64430	Clarksdale, 248	D 3
63336	Clarksville, 668	K 4
63837	Clarkton, 1,177	M10
64119	Claycomo, 1,841	P 5
63105	Clayton⊙, 16,222	P 3
64431	Clearmont, 226	C 1
64734	Cleveland, 256	C 5
65631	Clever, 430	F 8
64735	Clinton⊙, 7,504	E 6
65325	Cole Camp, 1,038	F 6
65201	Columbia⊙, 58,804	H 5
63742	Commerce, 234	O 8
64434	Conception Junction, 237	C 2
64020	Concordia, 1,854	E 5
65632	Conway, 547	G 7
63839	Cooter, 414	N10
64021	Corder, 476	E 4
63338	Cottleville, 275	N 2
† 64501	Country Club Village, 221	C 3
64637	Cowgill, 232	E 3
64437	Craig, 369	B 2
65633	Crane, 1,003	E 9
64739	Creighton, 294	D 6
63018	Crescent, 425	N 3
† 63101	Crestwood, 15,398	O 3
63141	Creve Coeur, 8,967	O 3
65452	Crocker, 814	H 7
65634	Cross Timbers, 204	F 6
63019	Crystal City, 3,898	M 6
65453	Cuba, 2,070	K 6
63339	Curryville, 337	K 4
64439	Dearborn, 543	C 3
64740	Deepwater, 565	E 6
64440	De Kalb, 287	C 3
63744	Delta, 462	N 8
63636	Des Arc, 222	L 8
63601	Desloge, 2,818	M 7
63020	De Soto, 5,984	M 6
63131	Des Peres, 5,333	O 3
63841	Dexter, 6,024	N 9
64840	Diamond, 554	D 9
65459	Dixon, 1,387	H 6
63637	Doe Run, 900	M 7
63935	Doniphan⊙, 1,850	L 9
† 65550	Doolittle, 509	J 7
63844	Dorena, 500	O 9
63536	Downing, 406	H 2
64742	Drexel, 723	C 6
63936	Dudley, 248	M 9
64841	Duenweg, 656	D 8
† 64801	Duquesne, 738	D 8
64442	Eagleville, 388	D 2
64743	East Lynne, 255	D 5
63845	East Prairie, 3,275	O 9
65462	Edgar Springs, 450	J 7
64444	Edgerton, 477	C 4
63537	Edina⊙, 1,574	H 2
65026	Eldon, 3,520	G 6
64744	El Dorado Springs, 3,300	E 7
63638	Ellington, 1,094	L 8
63011	Ellisville, 4,681	N 3
63937	Ellsinore, 342	L 9
63343	Elsberry, 1,398	L 4
63639	Elvins, 1,603	L 7
65466	Eminence⊙, 520	K 8
65327	Emma, 224	F 5
63344	Eolia, 321	L 4
63846	Essex, 493	N 9
† 63601	Esther, 1,040	M 7
63025	Eureka, 2,384	N 3
65646	Everton, 264	E 8
63440	Ewing, 330	J 2
64024	Excelsior Springs, 9,411	R 4
65647	Exeter, 434	D 9
64446	Fairfax, 835	B 2
65648	Fair Grove, 431	F 8
65649	Fair Play, 328	E 7
64842	Fairview, 263	D 9
63345	Farber, 470	J 4
63640	Farmington⊙, 6,590	M 7
65248	Fayette⊙, 3,520	G 4
63026	Fenton, 2,275	P 3
63135	Ferguson, 28,915	P 2
63028	Festus, 7,530	M 6
64449	Fillmore, 251	C 2
63940	Fisk, 503	M 9
63601	Flat River, 4,550	M 7
* 63031	Florissant, 65,908	P 2
63347	Foley, 224	L 4
65652	Fordland, 399	G 8
64451	Forest City, 365	B 3
63348	Foristell, 273	M 2
65653	Forsyth⊙, 803	F 9
63441	Frankford, 472	K 4
65250	Franklin, 252	G 4
63645	Fredericktown⊙, 3,799	M 7
65035	Freeburg, 577	J 6
64746	Freeman, 417	C 5
63748	Frohna, 225	N 7
† 63101	Frontenac, 3,920	O 3
65251	Fulton⊙, 12,148	J 5
65655	Gainesville⊙, 627	G 9
65656	Galena⊙, 391	F 9
64640	Gallatin⊙, 1,833	E 3
64641	Galt, 261	F 2
64747	Garden City, 633	D 5
65036	Gasconade, 235	J 5
63037	Gerald, 762	K 6
63848	Gideon, 1,112	N10
65330	Gilliam, 248	F 4
64642	Gilman City, 376	D 2
64118	Gladstone, 23,128	P 5
65254	Glasgow, 1,336	G 4
† 64068	Glenaire, 505	R 5
63038	Glencoe, 2,500	N 3
63122	Glendale, 6,891	P 3
64748	Golden City, 810	D 8
63843	Goodman, 565	C 9
63543	Gorin, 220	H 2
64454	Gower, 758	C 3
64455	Graham, 213	C 2
64029	Grain Valley, 709	S 6
64844	Granby, 1,678	D 9
63943	Grandin, 243	L 9
64030	Grandview, 17,456	P 6
63650	Graniteville, 375	L 7
64456	Grant City⊙, 1,095	D 2
65037	Gravois Mills, 994	G 6
63850	Grayridge, 300	N 9
63039	Gray Summit, 950	M 3
63544	Green Castle, 235	G 2
63545	Green City, 629	F 2
65661	Greenfield⊙, 1,172	E 8
65332	Green Ridge, 403	F 5
63546	Greentop, 351	H 2
63944	Greenville⊙, 328	M 8
64034	Greenwood, 925	R 6
63040	Grover, 550	O 3
64643	Hale, 461	F 3
65255	Hallsville, 790	H 4
64644	Hamilton, 1,645	E 3
63401	Hannibal, 18,609	K 3
64035	Hardin, 683	E 4
64701	Harrisonville⊙, 4,928	D 5
65667	Hartville⊙, 524	G 8
63349	Hawk Point, 354	K 5
63851	Hayti, 3,841	N10
* 63042	Hazelwood, 14,082	P 2
63047	Hematite, 300	L 6
64460	Hemple, 350	D 3
64036	Henrietta, 466	E 4
63048	Herculaneum, 1,885	M 6
65041	Hermann⊙, 2,658	K 5
65668	Hermitage⊙, 284	F 7
65257	Higbee, 641	H 4
64037	Higginsville, 4,318	E 4
63049	High Ridge, 350	O 4
63050	Hillsboro⊙, 432	L 6
63852	Holcomb, 593	N10
64040	Holden, 2,089	E 5
63853	Holland, 329	N10
65672	Hollister, 906	F 9
64048	Holt, 319	D 4
64461	Hopkins, 656	C 1
† 63070	Horine, 850	M 6
63855	Hornersville, 693	M10
63051	House Springs, 500	O 4
65483	Houston⊙, 2,178	J 8
65333	Houstonia, 312	F 5
65674	Humansville, 825	E 7
64752	Hume, 350	C 6
63443	Hunnewell, 304	J 3
65259	Huntsville⊙, 1,442	H 4
63547	Hurdland, 225	H 2
65486	Iberia, 741	H 6
63754	Illmo, 1,232	O 8
63052	Imperial, 900	P 4
* 64050	Independence⊙, 111,662	R 5
63648	Irondale, 319	L 7
63650	Ironton⊙, 1,452	L 7
63755	Jackson⊙, 5,896	N 8
64648	Jamesport, 614	E 3
65046	Jamestown, 243	G 5
64755	Jasper, 796	D 8
65101	Jefferson City (cap.)⊙, 32,407	H 5
63136	Jennings, 19,379	P 2
63351	Jonesburg, 479	K 5
64801	Joplin, 39,256	C 8
† 63385	Josephville, 250	N 2
63445	Kahoka⊙, 2,207	J 2
* 64101	Kansas City, 507,087	P 5
	Kansas City, ‡1,253,916	P 5
64060	Kearney, 984	D 4
63758	Kelso, 401	O 8
63857	Kennett⊙, 9,852	M10
65261	Keytesville⊙, 730	G 4
64649	Kidder, 231	D 3
63053	Kimmswick, 268	M 6
64463	King City, 1,023	D 2
64650	Kingston⊙, 291	E 3
64061	Kingsville, 284	D 5
63140	Kinloch, 5,629	P 2
63501	Kirksville⊙, 15,560	H 2
63122	Kirkwood, 31,890	O 3
65336	Knob Noster, 2,264	E 5
63446	Knox City, 284	H 2
63054	Koch, 600	P 4
65692	Koshkonong, 216	J 9
† 63090	Krakow, 300	K 6
63055	Labadie, 350	N 3
63447	La Belle, 848	J 2
64651	Laclede, 430	F 3
63352	Laddonia, 745	J 4
† 64758	Ladue, 10,491	P 3
63448	La Grange, 1,237	K 2
64063	Lake Lotawana, 1,786	R 6
65049	Lake Ozark, 507	G 6
† 64015	Lake Tapawingo, 867	R 6
† 64034	Lake Winnebago, 432	R 6
64759	Lamar⊙, 3,760	D 8
65337	La Monte, 814	F 5
64847	Lanagan, 374	C 9
63548	Lancaster⊙, 821	H 1
63549	La Plata, 1,377	H 2
64652	Laredo, 383	E 2
64465	Lathrop, 1,268	D 3
64062	Lawson, 1,034	D 4
† 63640	Leadington, 299	M 7
63653	Leadwood, 1,397	L 7
65535	Leasburg, 218	K 6
65536	Lebanon⊙, 8,616	G 7
64063	Lee's Summit, 16,230	R 6
64761	Leeton, 425	E 5
63125	Lemay, 40,115	P 3
63654	Lesterville, 275	L 8
64066	Levasy, 283	S 5
63452	Lewistown, 615	J 2
64067	Lexington⊙, 5,388	E 4
64762	Liberal, 644	D 7
64068	Liberty⊙, 13,679	R 5
65542	Licking, 1,002	J 8
63862	Lilbourn, 1,152	N 9
65338	Lincoln, 574	F 6
65051	Linn⊙, 1,289	J 5
65052	Linn Creek, 268	G 6
64653	Linneus⊙, 400	F 3
65682	Lockwood, 887	E 8
65054	Loose Creek, 370	J 5
63353	Louisiana, 4,533	K 4
64763	Lowry City, 520	E 6
63762	Lutesville, 626	M 8
63552	Macon⊙, 5,301	H 3
65263	Madison, 540	H 4
64466	Maitland, 319	B 2
63863	Malden, 5,374	M 9
65339	Malta Bend, 342	F 4
65704	Mansfield, 1,056	G 8
63143	Maplewood, 12,785	P 3
63764	Marble Hill⊙, 589	N 8
64658	Marceline, 2,622	F 3
65705	Marionville, 1,496	E 8
63655	Marquand, 400	M 8
65340	Marshall⊙, 11,847	F 4
65706	Marshfield⊙, 2,961	G 8
63866	Marston, 666	N 9
63357	Marthasville, 415	L 5
65264	Martinsburg, 318	J 4
64468	Maryville⊙, 9,970	C 2
63857	Matthews, 538	N 9
64469	Maysville⊙, 1,045	D 3
64071	Mayview, 330	E 4
64657	McFall, 203	D 2
64659	Meadville, 409	F 3
63555	Memphis⊙, 2,081	H 2
64660	Mendon, 289	F 3
64661	Mercer, 364	F 2
65058	Meta, 387	H 6
65265	Mexico⊙, 11,807	J 4
65344	Miami, 205	F 4
63359	Middletown, 235	J 4
63556	Milan⊙, 1,794	F 2
65707	Miller, 676	E 8
63952	Mill Spring, 207	L 8
64769	Mindenmines, 279	D 8
63659	Mine La Motte, 200	M 7
† 63801	Miner, 640	N 9
63660	Mineral Point, 369	L 7
64072	Missouri City, 375	R 5
65270	Moberly, 12,988	G 4

(continued on following page)

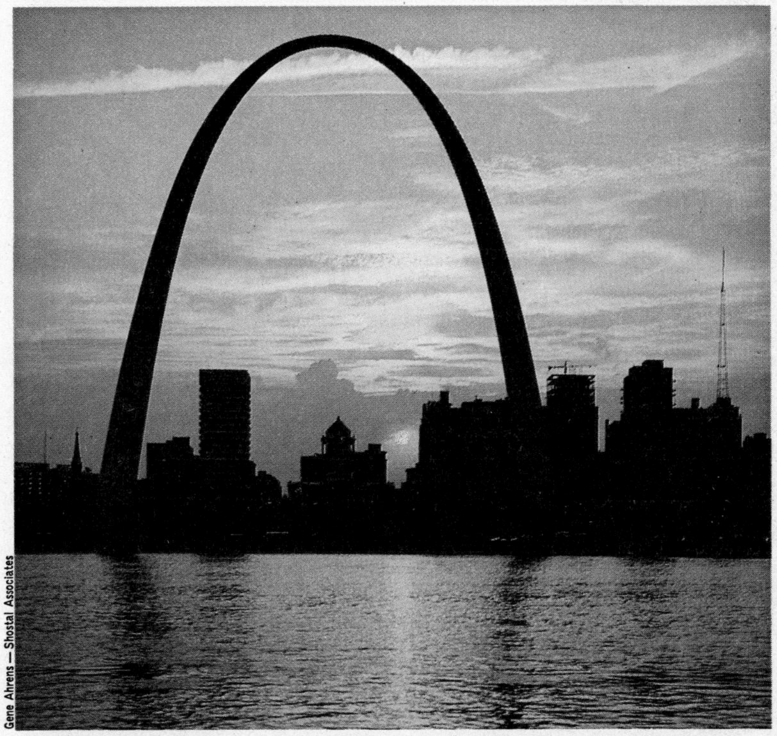

Gene Ahrens — Shostal Associates

The Gateway Arch soars in silhouette against the St. Louis skyline. A Saarinen design, the monument is the centerpiece of the Jefferson National Expansion Memorial. Internal passenger trains carry sightseers up either leg to the long observation room.

Agriculture, Industry and Resources

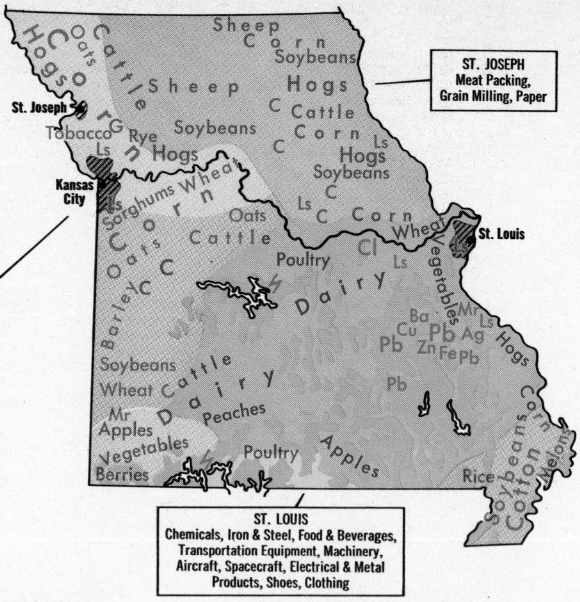

St. Joseph

ST. JOSEPH
Meat Packing,
Grain Milling, Paper

Kansas City

KANSAS CITY
Food Processing, Flour, Automobile
Assembly, Chemicals, Aircraft Parts,
Metal Products, Printing & Publishing

St. Louis

ST. LOUIS
Chemicals, Iron & Steel, Food & Beverages,
Transportation Equipment, Machinery,
Aircraft, Spacecraft, Electrical & Metal
Products, Shoes, Clothing

DOMINANT LAND USE

- Cattle Feed, Hogs
- Livestock, Cash Grain, Dairy
- Pasture Livestock
- Specialized Cotton
- General Farming, Dairy, Livestock, Poultry
- General Farming, Livestock, Truck Farming, Cotton
- Fruit and Mixed Farming
- Forests
- Urban Areas

MAJOR MINERAL OCCURRENCES

Ag	Silver	G	Natural Gas
Ba	Barite	Ls	Limestone
C	Coal	Mr	Marble
Cl	Clay	Pb	Lead
Cu	Copper	Zn	Zinc
Fe	Iron Ore		

Water Power   Major Industrial Areas

65059 Mokane, 398	J 5	
65708 Monett, 5,937	E 9	
63456 Monroe City, 2,456	J 3	
63361 Montgomery City⊙, 2,187	K 5	
63457 Monticello⊙, 157	J 2	
64770 Montrose, 531	E 6	
63868 Morehouse, 1,332	N 9	
63767 Morley, 528	N 8	
65061 Morrison, 234	J 5	
65710 Morrisville, 256	F 8	
64073 Mosby, 337	R 4	
63362 Moscow Mills, 399	M 1	
64470 Mound City, 1,202	B 2	
65711 Mountain Grove, 3,377	H 8	
65548 Mountain View, 1,320	J 8	
65712 Mount Vernon⊙, 2,600	E 8	
† 63088 Murphy, 900	O 4	
64074 Napoleon, 263	E 4	
63953 Naylor, 586	L 9	
63954 Neelyville, 231	M 9	
65347 Nelson, 230	F 4	
64850 Neosho⊙, 7,517	D 9	
64772 Nevada⊙, 9,736	D 7	
65063 New Bloomfield, 427	J 5	
65550 Newburg, 806	J 7	
63558 New Cambria, 260	G 3	

63363 New Florence, 635	K 5	
65274 New Franklin, 1,122	G 4	
64471 New Hampton, 327	D 2	
63068 New Haven, 1,474	K 5	
63459 New London⊙, 967	K 3	
63869 New Madrid⊙, 2,719	O 9	
63365 New Melle, 225	M 2	
64667 Newtown, 211	F 2	
63559 Niangua, 309	G 8	
65714 Nixa, 1,636	F 8	
64854 Noel, 924	D 9	
64668 Norborne, 950	E 4	
63121 Normandy, 6,306	P 3	
64116 North Kansas City, 5,183	P 5	
† 64152 Northmoor, 562	P 5	
63101 Northwoods, 4,611	P 3	
65717 Norwood, 294	H 8	
65536 Novinger, 547	G 2	
64075 Oak Grove, 2,025	S 6	
† 63080 Oak Grove, 340	K 6	
63101 Oakland, 1,609	P 3	
64116 Oakview, 541	P 5	
† 63125 Oakville, 11,612	P 4	
65070 Odessa, 2,839	E 5	
63366 O'Fallon, 7,018	N 2	
63369 Old Monroe, 330	N 1	

63132 Olivette, 9,341	P 3	
63771 Oran, 1,226	N 8	
64473 Oregon⊙, 789	B 2	
64855 Oronogo, 492	D 8	
64077 Orrick, 883	D 4	
65065 Osage Beach, 1,091	G 6	
64474 Osborn, 338	D 3	
64776 Osceola⊙, 874	E 6	
65348 Otterville, 440	G 5	
63114 Overland, 24,949	P 3	
65066 Owensville, 2,416	K 6	
65721 Ozark⊙, 2,384	F 8	
63069 Pacific, 3,247	N 4	
† 63101 Pagedale, 5,571	P 3	
63461 Palmyra⊙, 3,188	J 3	
65725 Paris⊙, 1,442	J 4	
64152 Parkville, 1,253	O 5	
63870 Parma, 1,051	N 9	
64475 Parnell, 232	C 2	
64670 Pattonsburg, 540	D 2	
64078 Peculiar, 705	D 5	
63462 Perry, 839	J 4	
63775 Perryville⊙, 5,149	M 7	
63070 Pevely, 517	N 6	
64476 Pickering, 245	C 2	
63957 Piedmont, 1,906	L 8	

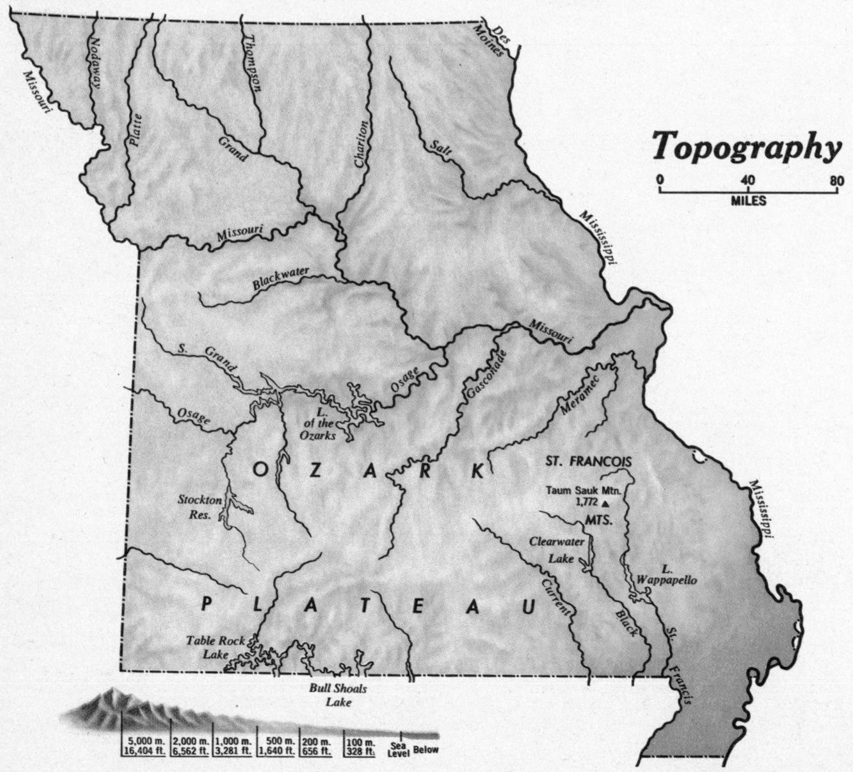

65723 Pierce City, 1,097	E 8	
65276 Pilot Grove, 701	G 5	
63663 Pilot Knob, 588	L 7	
63120 Pine Lawn, 5,773	P 3	
64856 Pineville⊙, 444	D 9	
64079 Platte City⊙, 2,022	C 4	
† 64152 Platte Woods, 484	O 5	
64477 Plattsburg⊙, 1,832	D 3	
64080 Pleasant Hill, 3,396	D 5	
65725 Pleasant Hope, 265	F 7	
† 64836 Pleasant Valley, 1,535	R 5	
63779 Pocahontas, 604	M 7	
64671 Polo, 438	D 3	
65789 Pomona, 250	J 9	
63901 Poplar Bluff⊙, 16,653	L 9	
63373 Portage Des Sioux, 509	P 2	
63873 Portageville, 3,117	N 10	
65067 Portland, 250	J 5	
63664 Potosi⊙, 2,761	L 7	
65068 Prairie Home, 231	G 5	
64673 Princeton⊙, 1,328	E 2	
64857 Purcell, 325	D 8	
64674 Purdin, 236	F 3	

65734 Purdy, 588	E	
63960 Puxico, 759	M	
63561 Queen City, 588	H	
63961 Qulin, 496	H	
64858 Racine, 274	D	
64479 Ravenwood, 336	C	
65555 Raymondville, 284	J	
64083 Raymore, 587	D	
64133 Raytown, 33,632	R	
65737 Reeds Spring, 286	F	
65738 Republic, 2,411	E	
64779 Rich Hill, 1,661	D	
65556 Richland, 1,783	H	
64085 Richmond⊙, 4,948	D	
63117 Richmond Heights, 13,802	P	
64481 Ridgeway, 469	D	
63874 Risco, 412	N	
† 63601 Rivermines, 402	L	
64168 Riverside, 2,123	P	
† 63101 Riverview, 3,741	R	
65279 Rocheport, 307	G	
63101 Rock Hill, 7,275	P	
64482 Rock Port⊙, 1,575	B	

Topography

0   40   80
MILES

OZARK PLATEAU

ST. FRANCOIS
Taum Sauk Mtn.
1,772 ▲
MTS.

Clearwater Lake

L. Wappello

Stockton Res.

L. of the Ozarks

Table Rock Lake

Bull Shoals Lake

5,000 m. | 2,000 m. | 1,000 m. | 500 m. | 200 m. | 100 m. | Sea Level
16,404 ft. | 6,562 ft. | 3,281 ft. | 1,640 ft. | 656 ft. | 328 ft. | Below

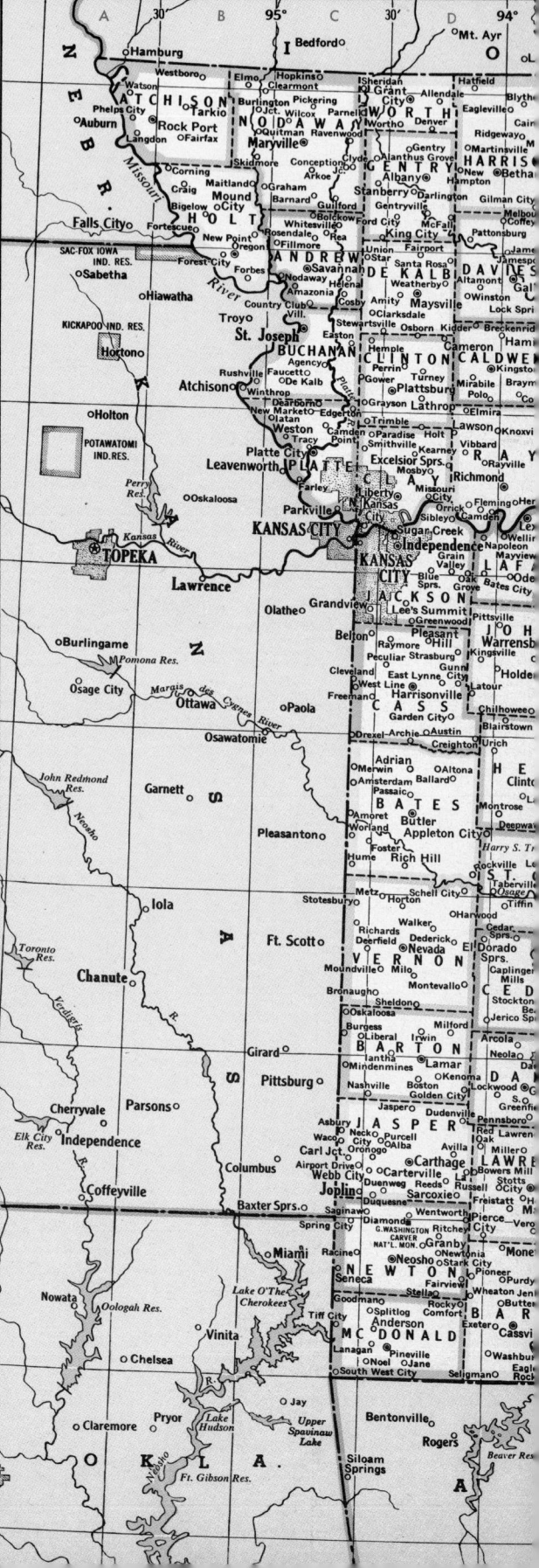

COUNTIES

Beaverhead, 8,187 ....C 5
Big Horn, 10,057 ....J 5
Blaine, 6,727 ....G 2
Broadwater, 2,526 ....E 4
Carbon, 7,080 ....G 5
Carter, 1,956 ....M 5
Cascade, 81,804 ....E 3
Chouteau, 6,473 ....F 3
Custer, 12,174 ....L 4
Daniels, 3,083 ....L 2
Dawson, 11,269 ....M 3
Deer Lodge, 15,652 ....C 5
Fallon, 4,050 ....M 4
Fergus, 12,611 ....G 3
Flathead, 39,460 ....B 2
Gallatin, 32,505 ....E 5
Garfield, 1,796 ....J 3
Glacier, 10,783 ....C 2
Golden Valley, 931 ....G 4
Granite, 2,737 ....C 4
Hill, 17,358 ....F 2
Jefferson, 5,238 ....D 4
Judith Basin, 2,667 ....F 3
Lake, 14,445 ....B 3
Lewis and Clark, 33,281 ....D 3
Liberty, 2,359 ....E 2
Lincoln, 18,063 ....A 2
Madison, 5,014 ....D 5
McCone, 2,875 ....L 3
Meagher, 2,122 ....F 4
Mineral, 2,958 ....B 3
Missoula, 58,263 ....C 3
Musselshell, 3,734 ....H 4
Park, 11,197 ....F 5
Petroleum, 675 ....H 3
Phillips, 5,386 ....J 2
Pondera, 6,611 ....D 2
Powder River, 2,862 ....L 5
Powell, 6,660 ....D 4
Prairie, 1,752 ....L 4
Ravalli, 14,409 ....B 4
Richland, 9,837 ....M 3
Roosevelt, 10,365 ....L 2
Rosebud, 6,032 ....K 4
Sanders, 7,093 ....A 3
Sheridan, 5,779 ....M 2
Silver Bow, 41,981 ....D 5
Stillwater, 4,632 ....G 5
Sweet Grass, 2,980 ....G 5

Teton, 6,116 ....D 3
Toole, 5,839 ....E 2
Treasure, 1,069 ....J 4
Valley, 11,471 ....K 2
Wheatland, 2,529 ....G 4
Wibaux, 1,465 ....M 4
Yellowstone, 87,367 ....H 4
Yellowstone Nat'l Park, 64 ..F 6

CITIES and TOWNS

Zip	Name/Pop.	Key
59001	Absarokee, 700	G 5
59820	Alberton, 363	B 3
59710	Alder, 100	D 5
† 59634	Alhambra, 50	E 4
† 59741	Amsterdam, 200	E 5
59711	Anaconda⊙, 9,771	C 4
59211	Antelope, 95	M 2
59821	Arlee, 220	B 3
† 59412	Armington, 62	F 3
59003	Ashland, 200	K 5
59410	Augusta, 400	D 3
59713	Avon, 250	D 4
59411	Babb, 50	C 2
59212	Bainville, 217	M 2
59313	Baker⊙, 2,584	M 4
59006	Ballantine, 350	J 5
† 59725	Bannack, 20	C 5
59613	Basin, 230	D 4
59007	Bearcreek, 31	G 5
† 59441	Becket, 35	F 4
59008	Belfry, 250	H 5
59714	Belgrade, 1,307	E 5
† 59046	Belmont, 75	H 4
59412	Belt, 656	E 3
† 59462	Benchland, 100	F 3
59314	Biddle, 83	L 5
59910	Big Arm, 100	B 3
59911	Bigfork, 500	C 2
59010	Big Sandy, 827	F 2
59520	Big Sandy, 827	D 4
59011	Big Timber⊙, 1,592	G 5
* 59101	Billings⊙, 61,581	H 5
	Billings, ‡87,367	H 5
59414	Black Eagle, 1,500	E 3
59415	Blackfoot, 100	D 2
59823	Bonner, 250	C 4
59632	Boulder⊙, 1,342	E 4
59521	Box Elder, 200	F 2
† 59715	Bozeman⊙, 18,670	E 5

Zip	Name/Pop.	Key
59416	Brady, 230	E 2
59014	Bridger, 717	H 5
59317	Broadus⊙, 799	L 5
59015	Broadview, 123	H 4
59213	Brockton, 401	M 2
59214	Brockway, 80	L 3
59417	Browning, 1,700	C 2
59016	Busby, 600	J 5
59701	Butte⊙, 23,368	D 5
† 59857	Camas Prairie, 160	B 3
59601	Canyon Ferry, 100	E 4
59721	Cardwell, 36	E 5
59420	Carter, 100	E 3
59347	Cartersville, 140	K 4
59421	Cascade, 714	E 3
59701	Centerville, 2,284	D 4
59834	Charlo, 150	B 3
59522	Chester⊙, 936	E 2
59523	Chinook⊙, 1,813	G 2
59422	Choteau⊙, 1,586	D 3
59423	Christina, 44	D 3
59215	Circle⊙, 964	L 3
59634	Clancy, 550	E 4
59825	Clinton, 250	C 4
59018	Clyde Park, 244	F 5
59924	Coffee Creek, 79	F 3
59323	Colstrip, 160	K 5
59912	Columbia Falls, 2,652	B 2
59019	Columbus⊙, 1,173	G 5
59826	Condon, 250	C 3
59827	Conner, 150	B 5
59425	Conrad⊙, 2,770	D 2
59020	Cooke City, 45	G 6
59913	Coram, 450	C 2
59828	Corvallis, 467	B 4
† 59648	Craig, 100	D 3
59217	Crane, 152	M 3
59022	Crow Agency, 975	J 5
59218	Culbertson, 821	M 2
59024	Custer, 193	J 4
59427	Cut Bank⊙, 4,004	D 2
59219	Dagmar, 55	M 2
59829	Darby, 538	B 4
59027	Dayton, 60	B 3
† 59028	Dean, 32	G 5
59830	De Borgia, 80	A 3
59722	Deer Lodge⊙, 4,306	D 4
59013	Dell, 50	D 5
† 59053	Delpine, 33	F 4
59430	Denton, 398	G 3
59431	Devon, 33	E 2

Zip	Name/Pop.	Key
59725	Dillon⊙, 4,548	D 5
59727	Divide, 105	D 5
59831	Dixon, 300	B 3
59524	Dodson, 196	H 2
59832	Drummond, 494	D 4
59832	Dupuyer, 105	D 2
59433	Dutton, 415	E 3
59829	East Glacier Park, 340	C 2
59635	East Helena, 1,651	E 4
59026	Edgar, 150	H 5
59434	Ekalaka⊙, 663	M 5
† 59701	Elk Park, 53	D 4
59728	Elliston, 300	D 4
59915	Elmo, 150	B 3
59729	Ennis, 501	E 5
59325	Epsie, 60	L 5

Zip	Name/Pop.	Key
59916	Essex, 35	C 2
† 59075	Eureka, 1,195	B 1
59436	Fairfield, 638	D 3
59221	Fairview, 956	M 3
59326	Fallon, 200	L 4
59028	Fishtail, 52	G 5
59222	Flaxville, 185	L 2
† 59701	Floral Park, 5,113	D 5
59833	Florence, 500	B 4
59026	Floweree, 306	E 3
59441	Forestgrove, 90	G 3
59327	Forsyth⊙, 1,873	K 4
† 59701	Fort Belknap, 185	H 2
59442	Fort Benton⊙, 1,863	F 3
59223	Fort Peck, 975	K 2

Zip	Name/Pop.	Key
59443	Fort Shaw, 450	E 3
† 59075	Fort Smith, 300	J 5
59224	Four Buttes, 50	L 2
59225	Frazer, 300	K 2
59834	Frenchtown, 300	B 3
59226	Froid, 330	M 2
59029	Fromberg, 364	H 5
59444	Galata, 48	E 2
† 59722	Galen, 210	D 5
59730	Gallatin Gateway, 200	E 5
59030	Gardiner, 479	F 5
59445	Garneill, 55	G 3
59731	Garrison, 350	D 4
59446	Geraldine, 370	F 3
59447	Geyser, 567	F 3
59525	Gildford, 285	F 2

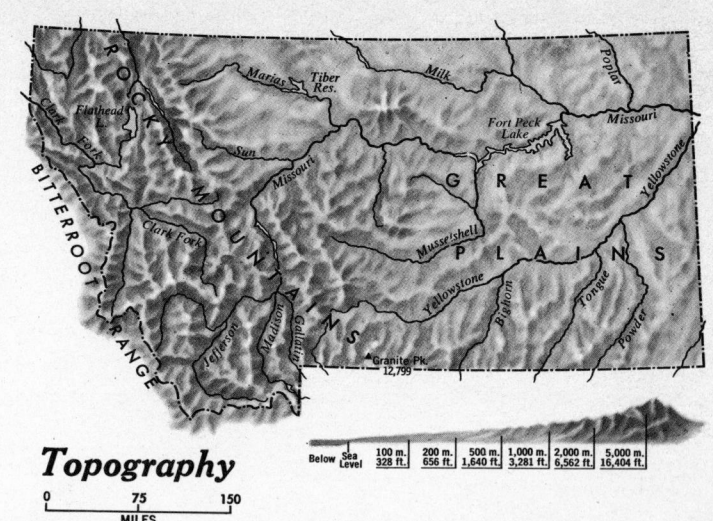

Topography

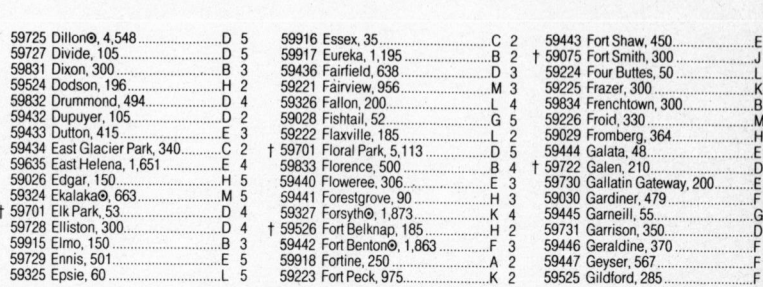

Below Sea Level	100 m. 328 ft.	200 m. 656 ft.	500 m. 1,640 ft.	1,000 m. 3,281 ft.	2,000 m. 6,562 ft.	5,000 m. 16,404 ft.

0   75   150
MILES

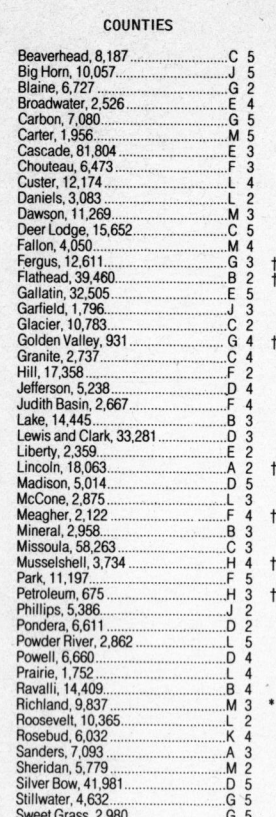

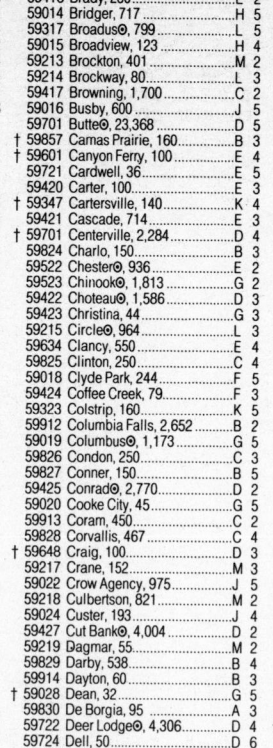

Surrounded by the wide open spaces, a Montana ranch basks in the reflected glory of the Rocky Mountains while it awaits cattle returning from the range. Ranches accommodate so many head of cattle that the state's residents are outnumbered six to one.

Ray Manley — Shostal Associates

AREA 147,138 sq. mi.
POPULATION 694,409
CAPITAL Helena
LARGEST CITY Billings
HIGHEST POINT Granite Pk. 12,799 ft.
SETTLED IN 1809
ADMITTED TO UNION November 8, 1889
POPULAR NAME Treasure State
STATE FLOWER Bitterroot
STATE BIRD Western Meadowlark

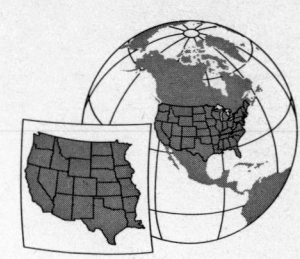

Agriculture, Industry and Resources

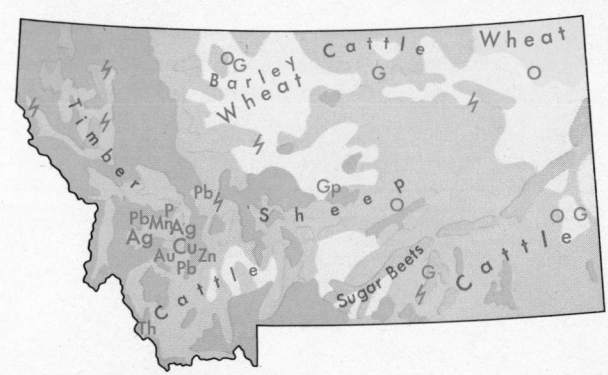

DOMINANT LAND USE

- Specialized Wheat
- Wheat, Range Livestock
- General Farming, Dairy, Range Livestock
- General Farming, Livestock, Special Crops
- Range Livestock
- Sugar Beets, Beans, Livestock, General Farming
- Forests

MAJOR MINERAL OCCURRENCES

Ag	Silver	O	Petroleum
Au	Gold	P	Phosphates
Cu	Copper	Pb	Lead
G	Natural Gas	Th	Thorium
Gp	Gypsum	Zn	Zinc
Mn	Manganese		
		⚡	Water Power

59230 Glasgow⊙, 4,700	K	2
† 59725 Glen, 100	D	5
59330 Glendive⊙, 6,305	M	3
59240 Glentana, 40	K	2
59733 Goldcreek, 76	D	4
59835 Grantsdale, 250	B	4
59032 Grassrange, 181	H	3
59401 Great Falls⊙, 60,091	E	3
Great Falls, ‡81,804	E	3
59836 Greenough, 100	C	4
59837 Hall, 95	C	4
59840 Hamilton⊙, 2,499	B	4
59034 Hardin⊙, 2,733	J	5
59526 Harlem, 1,094	H	2
59036 Harlowton⊙, 1,375	F	4
59735 Harrison, 275	E	5
59333 Hathaway, 45	K	4
59842 Haugan, 40	A	3
59501 Havre⊙, 10,558	G	2
59527 Hays, 950	H	2
59448 Heart Butte, 450	C	2
59601 Helena (cap.)⊙, 22,730	E	4
59843 Helmville, 76	C	4
59844 Heron, 185	A	2
59450 Highwood, 360	F	3
59451 Hilger, 40	G	3
59528 Hingham, 262	F	2
59241 Hinsdale, 500	K	2
59452 Hobson, 192	G	4
† 59353 Hodges, 50	M	4
59529 Hogeland, 68	H	2
59242 Homestead, 75	M	2
59845 Hot Springs, 664	B	3
59919 Hungry Horse, 700	C	2
59037 Huntley, 225	H	5
59846 Huson, 40	B	3
59038 Hysham⊙, 373	J	4
59039 Ingomar, 55	J	4
59335 Intake, 60	M	3
59530 Inverness, 150	F	2
59336 Ismay, 40	M	4
59736 Jackson, 196	C	5
59737 Jeffers, 70	E	5
59638 Jefferson City, 99	E	4
† 59721 Jefferson Island, 31	E	5
59041 Joliet, 412	G	5
59531 Joplin, 350	F	2
59337 Jordan⊙, 529	J	3
59453 Judith Gap, 160	G	4
59901 Kalispell⊙, 10,526	B	2
59454 Kevin, 250	D	2
59920 Kila, 44	B	2
† 59072 Klein, 200	H	4
59532 Kremlin, 347	F	2
59922 Lakeside, 663	B	2
59243 Lambert, 141	M	3
59043 Lame Deer, 460	K	5
59533 Landusky, 50	H	3
59244 Larslan, 140	K	2
59044 Laurel, 4,454	H	5

59738 Laurin, 60	D	5
59046 Lavina, 169	H	4
59457 Lewistown⊙, 6,437	G	3
59923 Libby⊙, 3,286	A	2
59739 Lima, 351	D	6
59639 Lincoln, 473	D	4
59339 Lindsay, 40	L	3
59047 Livingston⊙, 6,883	F	5
59535 Lloyd, 70	G	2
59340 Locate, 49	L	4
† 59101 Lockwood, 950	H	5
59050 Lodge Grass, 806	J	5
† 59524 Lodgepole, 39	H	2
59763 Logan, 53	E	5
59847 Lolo, 300	B	4
59460 Loma, 172	F	3
59461 Lothair, 35	E	2
59538 Malta⊙, 2,195	J	2
59741 Manhattan, 816	E	5
59925 Marion, 120	B	2
59053 Martinsdale, 203	F	4
59640 Marysville, 42	D	4
59742 Maudlow, 75	E	4
53850 Maxville, 44	C	4
59740 McAllister, 62	E	5
59247 Medicine Lake, 393	M	2
59743 Melrose, 350	D	5
59054 Melstone, 227	H	4
59055 Melville, 150	F	4
59301 Miles City⊙, 9,023	L	4
59851 Milltown, 500	C	4
59801 Missoula⊙, 29,497	C	4
59462 Moccasin, 100	F	3
59643 Monarch, 80	F	3
59464 Moore, 219	G	4
59059 Musselshell, 32	H	4
59248 Nashua, 513	K	2
59465 Neihart, 109	F	4
59745 Norris, 37	E	5
† 59501 North Havre, 1,073	G	2
59050 Noxon, 250	A	3
† 59936 Nyack, 31	C	2
59061 Nye, 65	G	5
59466 Oilmont, 75	E	2
59927 Olney, 250	B	2
59250 Opheim, 306	K	2
59251 Oswego, 75	L	2
59252 Outlook, 153	M	2
59854 Ovando, 102	C	3
59855 Pablo, 350	B	3
59856 Paradise, 500	B	3
59063 Park City, 400	H	5
59253 Peerless, 100	L	2
59467 Pendroy, 35	D	2
59858 Philipsburg⊙, 1,128	C	4
59859 Plains, 1,046	B	3
59254 Plentywood⊙, 2,381	M	2
59344 Plevna, 189	M	4
59860 Polson⊙, 2,464	B	3
59064 Pompeys Pillar, 69	J	5

59747 Pony, 111	E	5
59255 Poplar, 1,389	L	2
59862 Potomac, 58	C	4
59468 Power, 91	E	3
59929 Proctor, 108	B	3
59066 Pryor, 150	H	5
59641 Radersburg, 65	E	4
59748 Ramsay, 140	D	4
59067 Rapelje, 295	G	5
59863 Ravalli, 150	B	3
59256 Raymond, 34	M	2
59469 Raynesford, 100	F	3
59068 Red Lodge⊙, 1,844	G	5
59257 Redstone, 77	M	2
59069 Reedpoint, 125	G	5
59258 Reserve, 90	M	2
59930 Rexford, 243	A	2
59259 Richey, 389	L	3
59260 Richland, 37	K	2
59642 Ringling, 51	F	4
59070 Roberts, 291	G	5
† 59521 Rocky Boy, 150	G	2
59931 Rollins, 200	B	3
59864 Ronan, 1,347	C	3
59337 Rosebud, 120	K	4
59072 Roundup⊙, 2,116	H	4
59471 Roy, 175	H	3
59540 Rudyard, 550	F	2
59074 Ryegate⊙, 261	G	4
59261 Saco, 356	J	2
59865 Saint Ignatius, 925	C	3
59866 Saint Regis, 500	A	3
59075 Saint Xavier, 110	J	5
59867 Saltese, 95	A	3
59472 Sand Coulee, 500	E	3
59076 Sanders, 50	J	4
59473 Santa Rita, 125	D	2
59262 Savage, 300	M	3
59263 Scobey⊙, 1,486	L	2
59868 Seeley Lake, 400	C	3
59078 Shawmut, 60	G	4
† 59347 Sheffield, 40	K	4
59474 Shelby⊙, 3,111	E	2
59079 Shepherd, 100	H	5
59799 Sheridan, 636	D	5
59270 Sidney⊙, 4,543	M	3
59080 Silesia, 90	H	5
† 59701 Silver Bow Park, 5,524	D	4
59751 Silver Star, 100	D	5
59477 Simms, 299	E	3
59541 Simpson, 70	F	2
59932 Somers, 950	B	2
59348 Sonnette, 42	L	5
† 59442 Square Butte, 48	F	3
59479 Stanford⊙, 505	F	3
† 59846 Stark, 51	B	3
59870 Stevensville, 829	C	4
59480 Stockett, 500	E	3
59933 Stryker, 60	B	2
59481 Suffolk, 45	G	3

59482 Sunburst, 604	E	2
59483 Sun River, 190	E	3
59872 Superior⊙, 993	B	3
59911 Swan Lake, 200	C	3
59484 Sweetgrass, 120	E	2
59349 Terry⊙, 870	L	4
59873 Thompson Falls⊙, 1,356	A	3
59752 Three Forks, 1,188	E	5
† 59347 Thurlow, 40	K	4
59643 Toston, 75	E	4
59644 Townsend⊙, 1,371	E	4
59934 Trego, 50	B	2
59753 Trident, 50	E	5
59874 Trout Creek, 200	A	3
59935 Troy, 1,046	A	2
59542 Turner, 175	H	2
59754 Twin Bridges, 613	D	5
59085 Twodot, 118	F	4
59485 Ulm, 450	E	3
59452 Utica, 40	F	4
59486 Valier, 651	D	2
† 59237 Vananda, 50	K	4
59487 Vaughn, 345	E	3
59875 Victor, 500	B	4
59274 Vida, 52	L	3
59755 Virginia City⊙, 149	E	5
59701 Walkerville, 1,097	D	4
59756 Warmsprings, 1,600	D	4
59757 Waterloo, 50	D	5
† 59214 Watkins, 40	K	3
59275 Westby, 287	M	2
59936 West Glacier, 348	C	2
59758 West Yellowstone, 756	E	6
59937 Whitefish, 3,349	B	2
59759 Whitehall, 1,035	D	5
† 59784 Whitepine, 50	A	3
59645 White Sulphur Springs⊙, 1,200	E	4
59276 Whitetail, 125	L	2
59544 Whitewater, 100	J	2
59353 Wibaux⊙, 643	M	3
59760 Willow Creek, 325	E	5
59086 Wilsall, 200	F	5
59488 Windham, 60	F	3
59489 Winifred, 190	G	3
59087 Winnett⊙, 271	H	4
59647 Winston, 150	E	4
59761 Wisdom, 155	C	5
59762 Wise River, 125	C	5
59648 Wolf Creek, 90	E	4
59201 Wolf Point⊙, 3,095	L	2
† 59875 Woodside, 80	B	4
59088 Worden, 350	H	5
59089 Wyola, 110	J	5
† 59935 Yaak, 75	A	2
59547 Zurich, 89	G	2

⊙ County seat.
‡ Population of metropolitan area.
† Zip of nearest p.o.
* Multiple zips

COUNTIES

Adams, 30,553 ....F 4
Antelope, 9,047 ....F 2
Arthur, 606 ....C 3
Banner, 1,034 ....A 3
Blaine, 847 ....E 3
Boone, 8,190 ....F 3
Box Butte, 10,094 ....A 2
Boyd, 3,752 ....F 2
Brown, 4,021 ....E 2
Buffalo, 31,222 ....E 4
Burt, 9,247 ....H 3
Butler, 9,461 ....G 3
Cass, 18,076 ....H 4
Cedar, 12,192 ....G 2
Chase, 4,129 ....C 4
Cherry, 6,846 ....C 2
Cheyenne, 10,778 ....A 3
Clay, 8,266 ....F 4
Colfax, 9,498 ....G 3
Cuming, 12,034 ....H 3
Custer, 14,092 ....E 3
Dakota, 13,137 ....H 2
Dawes, 9,693 ....A 2
Dawson, 19,467 ....E 4
Deuel, 2,717 ....B 3
Dixon, 7,453 ....H 2
Dodge, 34,782 ....H 3
Douglas, 389,455 ....H 3
Dundy, 2,926 ....C 4
Fillmore, 8,137 ....G 4
Franklin, 4,566 ....E 4
Frontier, 3,982 ....D 4
Furnas, 6,897 ....D 4
Gage, 25,719 ....H 4
Garden, 2,929 ....B 3
Garfield, 2,411 ....E 3
Gosper, 2,178 ....E 4
Grant, 1,019 ....C 3
Greeley, 4,000 ....F 3
Hall, 42,851 ....F 4
Hamilton, 8,867 ....F 4
Harlan, 4,357 ....E 4
Hayes, 1,530 ....C 4
Hitchcock, 4,051 ....C 4
Holt, 12,933 ....F 2
Hooker, 939 ....C 3
Howard, 6,807 ....F 3
Jefferson, 10,436 ....G 4
Johnson, 5,743 ....H 4
Kearney, 6,707 ....F 4
Keith, 8,487 ....C 3
Keya Paha, 1,340 ....E 2
Kimball, 6,009 ....A 3
Knox, 11,723 ....G 2
Lancaster, 167,972 ....H 4
Lincoln, 29,538 ....D 3
Logan, 991 ....D 3
Loup, 854 ....E 3
Madison, 27,402 ....G 3
McPherson, 623 ....C 3
Merrick, 8,751 ....F 3
Morrill, 5,813 ....A 3
Nance, 5,142 ....F 3
Nemaha, 8,976 ....J 4
Nuckolls, 7,404 ....F 4
Otoe, 15,576 ....H 4
Pawnee, 4,473 ....H 4
Perkins, 3,423 ....C 4
Phelps, 9,553 ....E 4
Pierce, 8,493 ....G 2
Platte, 26,508 ....G 3
Polk, 6,468 ....G 3
Red Willow, 12,191 ....D 4
Richardson, 12,277 ....J 4
Rock, 2,231 ....E 2
Saline, 12,809 ....G 4
Sarpy, 63,696 ....H 3
Saunders, 17,018 ....H 3
Scotts Bluff, 36,432 ......A 3
Seward, 14,460 ....G 4
Sheridan, 7,285 ....B 2
Sherman, 4,725 ....F 3

Sioux, 2,034 ....A 2
Stanton, 5,758 ....G 3
Thayer, 7,779 ....G 4
Thomas, 954 ....D 3
Thurston, 6,942 ....H 2
Valley, 5,783 ....E 3
Washington, 13,310 ....H 3
Wayne, 10,400 ....G 2
Webster, 6,477 ....F 4
Wheeler, 1,054 ....F 3
York, 13,685 ....G 4

CITIES and TOWNS

Zip	Name/Pop.	Key
68301	Adams, 463	H 4
69210	Ainsworth⊙, 2,073	D 2
68620	Albion⊙, 2,074	F 3
68810	Alda, 456	F 4
68710	Allen, 309	H 2
69301	Alliance⊙, 6,862	A 2
68920	Alma⊙, 1,299	E 4
68814	Ansley, 631	E 3
68922	Arapahoe, 1,147	E 4
68815	Arcadia, 418	F 3
68002	Arlington, 910	H 3
69120	Arnold, 752	D 3
69121	Arthur⊙, 175	C 3
68003	Ashland, 2,176	H 3
68713	Atkinson, 1,406	E 2
68305	Auburn⊙, 3,650	J 4
68818	Aurora⊙, 3,180	F 4
68924	Axtell, 500	E 4
68004	Bancroft, 545	H 2
68622	Bartlett⊙, 193	F 3
69020	Bartley, 283	D 4
68714	Bassett⊙, 983	E 2
68715	Battle Creek, 1,158	G 3
69334	Bayard, 1,338	A 3
68310	Beatrice⊙, 12,389	H 4
68926	Beaver City⊙, 802	D 4
68313	Beaver Crossing, 400	G 4
68716	Beemer, 699	H 3
68005	Bellevue, 19,449	J 3
68624	Bellwood, 361	G 3
69021	Benkelman⊙, 1,349	C 4
68317	Bennet, 489	H 4
68007	Bennington, 683	H 3
68927	Bertrand, 662	E 4
69122	Big Springs, 472	B 3
68928	Bladen, 293	F 4
68008	Blair⊙, 6,106	H 3
68718	Bloomfield, 1,287	G 2
68930	Blue Hill, 1,201	F 4
68318	Blue Springs, 494	H 4
68010	Boys Town, 989	H 3
68819	Bradshaw, 347	G 4
69123	Brady, 311	D 3
68626	Brainard, 309	G 3
68821	Brewster⊙, 54	D 3
69336	Bridgeport⊙, 1,490	A 3
68822	Broken Bow⊙, 3,734	E 3
68321	Brownville, 174	J 4
69127	Brule, 423	C 3
68322	Bruning, 315	G 4
68823	Burwell⊙, 1,341	E 3
68722	Butte⊙, 575	F 2
68824	Cairo, 686	F 4
68825	Callaway, 523	D 3
69022	Cambridge, 1,145	D 4
68932	Campbell, 447	F 4
68015	Cedar Bluffs, 616	H 3
68627	Cedar Rapids, 449	F 3
68724	Center⊙, 111	G 2
68826	Central City⊙, 2,803	F 3
68017	Ceresco, 474	H 3
69337	Chadron⊙, 5,853	B 2
68725	Chambers, 321	F 2
68827	Chapman, 371	F 3
69129	Chappell⊙, 1,204	B 3
68327	Chester, 459	G 4
68628	Clarks, 480	G 3
68629	Clarkson, 805	G 3

Zip	Name/Pop.	Key
68933	Clay Center⊙, 952	F 4
68726	Clearwater, 398	F 2
68727	Coleridge, 608	G 2
68601	Columbus⊙, 15,471	G 3
68329	Cook, 328	H 4
68331	Cortland, 326	H 4
69130	Cozad, 4,219	E 4
68019	Craig, 295	H 3
69339	Crawford, 1,291	A 2
68729	Creighton, 1,461	G 2
68730	Crofton, 677	G 2
69024	Culbertson, 801	C 4
69025	Curtis, 1,166	D 4
68731	Dakota City⊙, 1,057	H 2
69131	Dalton, 354	B 3
68831	Dannebrog, 384	F 3
68635	Davenport, 427	G 4
68632	David City⊙, 2,380	G 3
68020	Decatur, 679	H 2
68340	Deshler, 937	G 4
68341	De Witt, 651	H 4
68342	Diller, 287	H 4
69133	Dix, 342	A 3
68633	Dodge, 704	H 3
68832	Doniphan, 542	F 4
68343	Dorchester, 492	G 4
68634	Duncan, 298	G 3
68347	Eagle, 441	H 4
68935	Edgar, 707	F 4
68636	Elgin, 917	F 3
68022	Elkhorn, 1,184	H 3
68836	Elm Creek, 798	E 4
68349	Elmwood, 548	H 4
68937	Elwood⊙, 601	E 4
68733	Emerson, 850	H 2
69028	Eustis, 400	D 4
68735	Ewing, 552	F 2
68351	Exeter, 759	G 4
68352	Fairbury⊙, 5,265	G 4
68938	Fairfield, 487	G 4
68354	Fairmont, 761	G 4
68355	Falls City⊙, 5,444	J 4
68358	Firth, 328	H 4
68023	Fort Calhoun, 642	J 3
68939	Franklin⊙, 1,193	E 4
68025	Fremont⊙, 22,962	H 3
68359	Friend, 1,126	G 4
68638	Fullerton⊙, 1,444	F 3
68361	Geneva⊙, 2,275	G 4
68640	Genoa, 1,174	G 3
69341	Gering⊙, 5,639	A 3
68840	Gibbon, 1,388	F 4
68841	Giltner, 408	F 4
68941	Glenvil, 332	F 4
69343	Gordon, 2,106	B 2
69138	Gothenburg, 3,154	D 4
68801	Grand Island⊙, 31,269	F 4
69140	Grant⊙, 1,099	C 4
68842	Greeley⊙, 580	F 3
68366	Greenwood, 506	H 3
68028	Gretna, 1,557	H 3
68942	Guide Rock, 318	F 4
68843	Hampton, 387	G 4
69345	Harrisburg⊙, 80	A 3
69346	Harrison⊙, 377	A 2
68739	Hartington⊙, 1,581	G 2
68944	Harvard, 1,230	F 4
68901	Hastings⊙, 23,580	F 4
69032	Hayes Center⊙, 237	C 4
69347	Hay Springs, 682	B 2
68370	Hebron⊙, 1,667	G 4
69348	Hemingford, 734	A 2
68371	Henderson, 901	G 4
68029	Herman, 323	H 3
69143	Hershey, 526	D 3
68372	Hickman, 415	H 4
68947	Hildreth, 352	E 4
68948	Holbrook, 307	D 4
68949	Holdrege⊙, 5,635	E 4
68030	Homer, 457	H 2
68031	Hooper, 895	H 3
68641	Howells, 682	H 3
68376	Humboldt, 1,194	J 4

Miles of pens hold thousands of head of cattle in the Union Stockyards, Omaha. Next stop — the meat packers' plant.

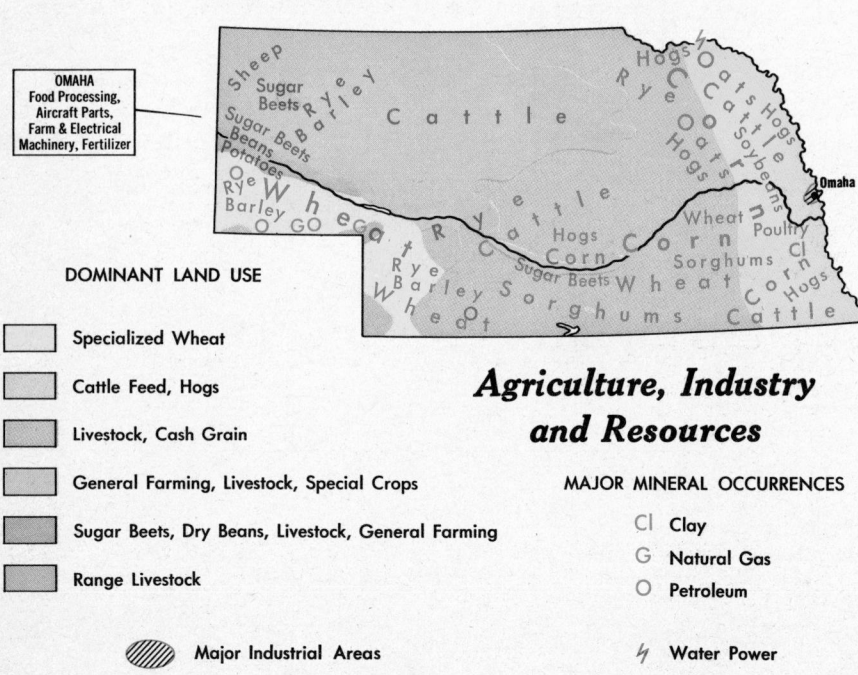

OMAHA
Food Processing, Aircraft Parts, Farm & Electrical Machinery, Fertilizer

DOMINANT LAND USE

- Specialized Wheat
- Cattle Feed, Hogs
- Livestock, Cash Grain
- General Farming, Livestock, Special Crops
- Sugar Beets, Dry Beans, Livestock, General Farming
- Range Livestock

▨ Major Industrial Areas

Agriculture, Industry and Resources

MAJOR MINERAL OCCURRENCES

- Cl Clay
- G Natural Gas
- O Petroleum
- ⚡ Water Power

NEBRASKA

SCALE

0 5 10 20 30 40 50 60 MI.

0 5 10 20 30 40 50 60 KM.

State Capitals ....⊛

County Seats ....⊙

© C.S. HAMMOND & Co., N.Y.

68642 Humphrey, 862......................G 3
69350 Hyannis◉, 345......................D 2
69033 Imperial◉, 1,589..................C 4
69034 Indianola, 672.....................D 4
68378 Johnson, 350.......................J 4
68955 Juniata, 480........................F 4
68847 Kearney◉, 19,181................E 4
68956 Kenesaw, 728......................F 4
68034 Kennard, 336......................H 3
69145 Kimball◉, 3,680..................A 3
68745 Laurel, 1,009......................G 2
68046 La Vista, 4,807...................J 3
68957 Lawrence, 343....................H 4
68643 Leigh, 501...........................G 3
69147 Lewellen, 376.....................B 3
68850 Lexington◉, 5,618..............E 4
68501 Lincoln (cap.) 149,518.......H 4
      Lincoln, ‡167,972...............H 4
68644 Lindsay, 291.......................G 3
69149 Lodgepole, 407..................B 3
69217 Long Pine, 363...................E 2
68958 Loomis, 323........................E 4
68037 Louisville, 1,036.................J 3
68853 Loup City◉, 1,456..............F 3
69352 Lyman, 561.........................A 3
68746 Lynch, 375..........................F 2
68038 Lyons, 1,177.......................H 3
68039 Macy, 550...........................G 2
68748 Madison◉, 1,595................G 3
69038 Maywood, 309....................D 4
69001 McCook◉, 8,285................D 4
68401 McCool Junction, 289........G 4
68041 Mead, 488...........................H 3
68752 Meadow Grove, 372...........G 2
68856 Merna, 322..........................E 3
68405 Milford, 1,846.....................H 4
68137 Millard, 7,460.....................H 3
68406 Milligan, 319.......................G 4
69356 Minatare, 939.....................A 3
68959 Minden◉, 2,669..................F 4
69357 Mitchell, 1,842....................A 3
69358 Morrill, 937.........................A 3
69152 Muilen◉, 667......................C 2
68409 Murray, 286........................J 3
68410 Nebraska City◉, 7,441.......J 4
68413 Nehawka, 298.....................H 4
68756 Neligh◉, 1,764...................F 4
68961 Nelson◉, 746......................F 4
68757 Newcastle, 347...................G 2
68758 Newman Grove, 863..........G 3
68760 Niobrara, 602......................G 2
68701 Norfolk, 16,607..................H 2
68649 North Bend, 1,350.............H 3
68859 North Loup, 441.................F 3
69101 North Platte◉, 19,447.......D 3
68761 Oakdale, 322.......................F 2

68045 Oakland, 1,355....................H 3
68415 Odell, 349............................H 4
69153 Ogallala◉, 4,976................C 3
* 68101 Omaha◉, 347,328.............J 3
      Omaha, ‡540,142................J 3
68763 O'Neill◉, 3,753..................F 2
68764 Orchard, 467.......................F 2
68862 Ord◉, 2,439.......................E 3
68966 Orleans, 592.......................E 4
68651 Osceola◉, 923....................G 3
69154 Oshkosh◉, 1,067..............B 3
68765 Osmond, 883......................G 2
68863 Overton, 506......................E 4
68967 Oxford, 1,116.....................E 4
69040 Palisade, 372......................C 4
68864 Palmer, 391........................F 3
68418 Palmyra, 386......................H 4
68046 Papillion◉, 5,606...............J 3
† 68801 Parkview, 1,089.................G 3
68420 Pawnee City◉, 1,267.........H 4
69155 Paxton, 503.........................C 3
68047 Pender◉, 1,229..................H 2
68421 Peru, 1,380.........................J 4
68652 Petersburg, 370..................G 3
68865 Phillips, 341........................F 4
68767 Pierce◉, 1,360...................G 2
68768 Pilger, 470...........................G 2
68769 Plainview, 1,494................G 2
68653 Platte Center, 384.............G 3
68048 Plattsmouth◉, 6,371.........J 3
68424 Plymouth, 424.....................G 4
68654 Polk, 413.............................G 3
68770 Ponca◉, 984......................H 2
68050 Prague, 291.........................H 3
68127 Ralston, 4,265.....................J 3
68771 Randolph, 1,130.................G 2
68869 Ravenna, 1,356..................F 4
68970 Red Cloud◉, 2,195...........F 4
68658 Rising City, 344..................G 3
68431 Rulo, 299............................J 4
69360 Rushville◉, 1,137..............B 2
68660 Saint Edward, 853.............G 3
68873 Saint Paul◉, 2,026............F 3
68874 Sargent, 789........................E 3
68661 Schuyler◉, 3,597..............G 3
68875 Scotia, 354..........................F 3
69361 Scottsbluff, 14,507............A 3
68057 Scribner, 1,031...................H 3
68434 Seward◉, 5,294.................H 4
68662 Shelby, 647.........................G 3
68876 Shelton, 1,028.....................F 4
68436 Shickley, 385......................G 4
69162 Sidney◉, 6,403..................B 3
68663 Silver Creek, 483...............G 3
68664 Snyder, 383........................H 3

68776 South Sioux City, 7,920.....H 2
68665 Spalding, 676......................F 3
68777 Spencer, 606......................F 2
68059 Springfield, 795..................H 3
68778 Springview◉, 260..............E 2
68779 Stanton◉, 1,369................G 3
69163 Stapleton◉, 311................D 3
68443 Sterling, 476.......................H 4
69042 Stockville◉, 61..................D 4
69043 Stratton, 481......................C 4
68666 Stromsburg, 1,215............G 3
68780 Stuart, 561..........................E 2
68978 Superior, 2,779..................F 4
69165 Sutherland, 840..................C 3
68979 Sutton, 1,361.....................G 4
68446 Syracuse, 1,562.................H 4
68447 Table Rock, 429................H 4
68448 Talmage, 285.....................H 4
68879 Taylor◉, 240......................E 3
68450 Tecumseh◉, 2,058............H 4
68061 Tekamah◉, 1,848.............H 3
† 69341 Terrytown, 747.................A 3
69166 Thedford◉, 303.................D 3
68781 Tilden, 947..........................G 2
69044 Trenton◉, 770...................D 4
69167 Tryon◉, 138.......................C 3
68669 Ulysses, 312........................G 3
68456 Utica, 602............................G 4
69201 Valentine◉, 2,662.............D 2
68064 Valley, 1,595.......................H 3
68065 Valparaiso, 415...................H 3
68783 Verdigre, 570......................F 2
68066 Wahoo◉, 3,835..................H 3
68784 Wakefield, 1,160................H 2
68067 Walthill, 897........................H 2
69045 Wauneta, 738.....................C 4
68786 Wausa, 720.........................G 2
68462 Waverly, 1,152...................H 4
68787 Wayne◉, 5,379..................G 2
68463 Weeping Water, 1,143.......J 3
68464 Western, 344......................G 4
68070 Weston, 285........................H 3
68788 West Point◉, 3,385...........H 3
68465 Wilber◉, 1,483...................H 4
68071 Winnebago, 675.................H 2
68790 Winside, 453.......................H 2
68791 Wisner, 1,315.....................H 2
68882 Wolbach, 968......................F 3
68883 Wood River, 1,061............F 4
68466 Wymore, 1,790..................G 4
68467 York◉, 6,778......................G 4
68073 Yutan, 507..........................H 3

◉ County seat
‡ Population of metropolitan area.
† Zip of nearest p.o.
* Multiple zips

AREA 77,227 sq. mi.
POPULATION 1,483,791
CAPITAL Lincoln
LARGEST CITY Omaha
HIGHEST POINT 5,426 ft. (Kimball Co.)
SETTLED IN 1847
ADMITTED TO UNION March 1, 1867
POPULAR NAME Cornhusker State
STATE FLOWER Goldenrod
STATE BIRD Western Meadowlark

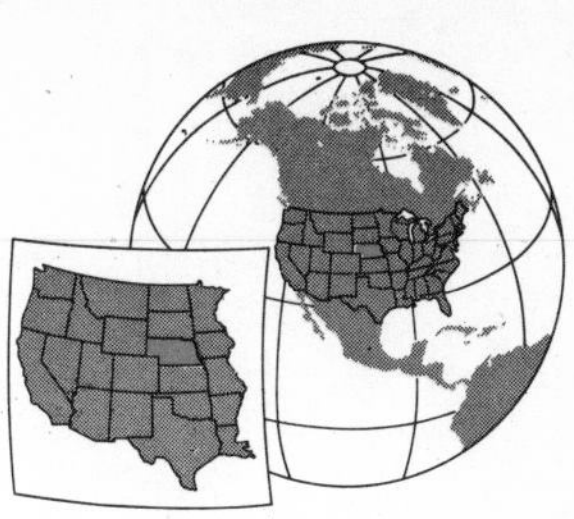

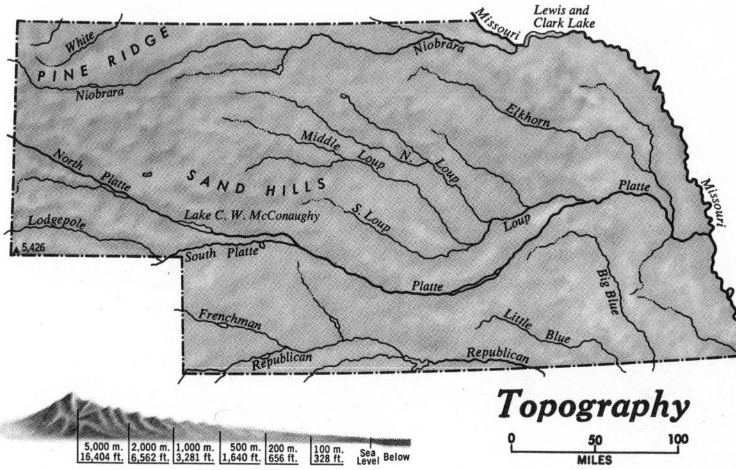

Topography

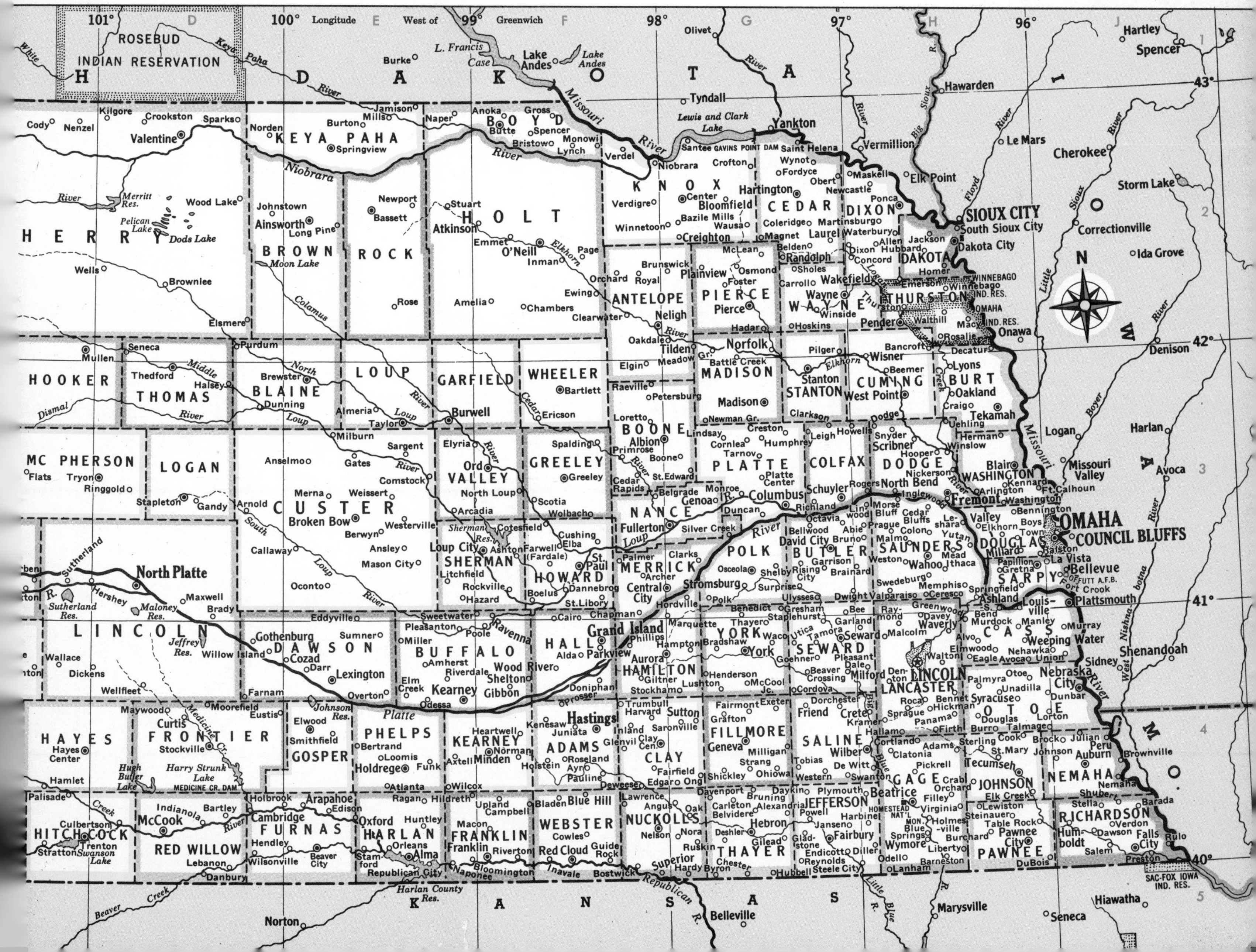

MILES 0 50 100

5,000 m. / 16,404 ft.   2,000 m. / 6,562 ft.   1,000 m. / 3,281 ft.   500 m. / 1,640 ft.   200 m. / 656 ft.   100 m. / 328 ft.   Sea Level   Below

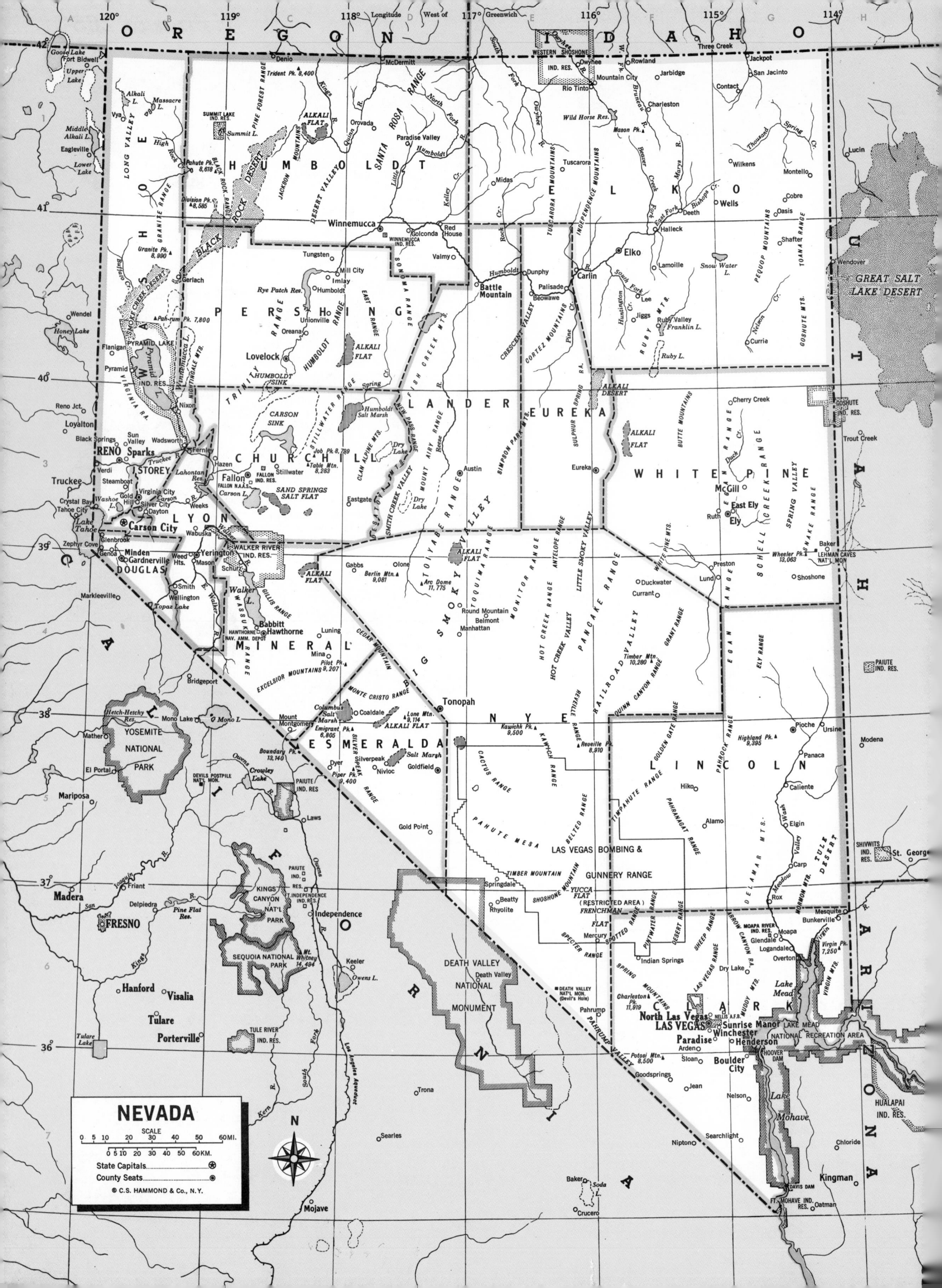

NEVADA

SCALE
0 5 10 20 30 40 50 60 MI.
0 10 20 30 40 50 60 KM.

State Capitals .... ⊛
County Seats .... ⊙

© C.S. HAMMOND & CO., N.Y.

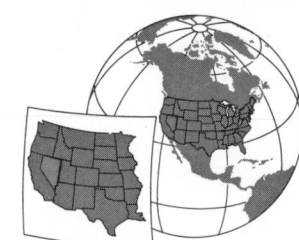

COUNTIES

Carson City (city), 15,468........B 3
Churchill, 10,513...................C 3
Clark, 273,288......................F 6
Douglas, 6,882......................B 4
Elko, 13,958.........................F 1
Esmeralda, 629......................D 5
Eureka, 948..........................E 3
Humboldt, 6,375....................C 1
Lander, 2,666........................D 3
Lincoln, 2,557.......................F 5
Lyon, 8,221..........................B 3
Mineral, 7,051.......................C 4
Nye, 5,599...........................E 4
Pershing, 2,670......................C 2
Storey, 695..........................B 3
Washoe, 121,068....................B 2
White Pine, 10,150..................F 3

CITIES and TOWNS

Zip   Name/Pop.   Key
89001 Alamo, 300....................F 5
89310 Austin⊙, 300.................E 3
89416 Babbitt, 1,579...............C 4
89311 Baker, 75....................G 3
89820 Battle Mountain, 1,856.....E 2
89003 Beatty, 570.................E 6
89045 Belmont, 25.................E 4
89821 Beowawe, 104...............E 2
89508 Black Springs, 2,500.......B 3
89005 Boulder City, 5,223........G 7
89007 Bunkerville, 150...........G 6
89008 Caliente, 916..............G 5
89822 Carlin, 1,313..............E 2
89009 Carp, 32...................G 5
89701 Carson City (cap.),15,468..B 3
89801 Charleston, 14.............F 1
89312 Cherry Creek, 75...........G 3
89049 Coaldale, 31...............D 4
89830 Cobre, 14..................G 1
89825 Contact, 9.................G 1
89402 Crystal Bay, 950...........A 3
89314 Currant, 30................F 4
89313 Currie, 15.................G 2
89403 Dayton, 350................B 3
89823 Deeth, 27..................F 1
89404 Denio, 28..................C 1
89040 Dry Lake, 5................G 6
89314 Duckwater, 85..............F 4
89821 Dunphy, 25.................E 2
89010 Dyer, 60...................C 5
89315 East Ely, 1,992............G 3
89406 Eastgate, 17...............D 3
89112 East Las Vegas, 6,501......F 6
89009 Elgin, 8...................G 5
89801 Elko⊙, 7,621...............F 2
89301 Ely⊙, 4,176................G 3
89316 Eureka⊙, 300...............E 3
89406 Fallon⊙, 2,959.............C 3
89408 Fernley, 750...............B 3
89409 Gabbs, 874.................D 4
89410 Gardnerville, 800..........B 4
89411 Genoa, 170.................B 4
89412 Gerlach, 150...............B 2
89413 Glenbrook, 800.............B 3
89025 Glendale, 20...............G 6
89414 Golconda, 350..............D 2
89013 Goldfield⊙, 213............D 5
89013 Gold Hill, 50..............B 3
89013 Gold Point, 10.............D 5
89019 Goodsprings, 120...........F 7
89824 Halleck, 50................F 1
89415 Hawthorne⊙, 3,539..........C 4
89417 Hazen, 60..................C 3

89015 Henderson, 16,395..........G 6
89017 Hiko, 150..................F 5
† 89418 Humboldt, 12.............C 2
89418 Imlay, 150.................C 2
89018 Indian Springs, 500........F 6
† 89310 Ione, 15.................D 4
89825 Jackpot, 400...............G 1
89826 Jarbidge, 25...............F 1
89019 Jean, 100..................F 7
89827 Jiggs, 6...................F 2
89828 Lamoille, 51...............F 2
* 89101 Las Vegas⊙, 125,787.....F 6
        Las Vegas, ‡273,288.....F 6
89829 Lee, 180...................F 2
89021 Logandale, 410.............G 6
89419 Lovelock⊙, 1,571...........C 2
89317 Lund, 300..................F 4
89420 Luning, 55.................C 4
89022 Manhattan, 28..............E 4
† 89447 Mason, 200...............B 4
89421 McDermitt, 300.............D 1
89318 McGill, 2,164..............G 3
89023 Mercury, 2,200.............E 5
89024 Mesquite, 500..............G 6
† 89414 Midas, 6.................E 1
† 89418 Mill City, 4.............D 2
89422 Mina, 375..................C 4
89423 Minden⊙, 520...............B 4
89025 Moapa, 250.................G 6
89830 Montello, 150..............G 1
89831 Mountain City, 80..........F 1
† 89422 Mount Montgomery, 10.....C 5
† 89046 Nelson, 67...............G 7
89024 Nixon, 300.................B 3
89030 North Las Vegas, 36,216....F 6
† 89830 Oasis, 5.................G 1
89419 Oreana, 18.................C 2
89425 Orovada, 250...............D 1
89040 Overton, 900...............G 6
89832 Owyhee, 100................F 1
89041 Pahrump, 400...............E 6
† 89822 Palisade, 5..............E 2
89042 Panaca, 500................G 5
89101 Paradise, 24,477...........F 6
89426 Paradise Valley, 110.......D 1
89043 Pioche⊙, 525...............G 5
89301 Preston, 44................G 4
† 89414 Red House, 4.............D 2
* 89501 Reno⊙, 72,863............B 3
        Reno, ‡121,068..........B 3
89003 Rhyolite, 8................E 6
89831 Rio Tinto, 5...............F 1
89045 Round Mountain, 100........E 4
89831 Rowland, 10................F 1
† 89009 Rox, 12..................G 6
89833 Ruby Valley, 225...........F 2
89319 Ruth, 750..................F 3
† 89825 San Jacinto, 8...........G 1
89427 Schurz, 350................C 4
89046 Searchlight, 279...........F 7
89835 Shafter, 7.................G 1
† 89301 Shoshone, 15.............G 4
89428 Silver City, 100...........B 3
89047 Silverpeak, 80.............D 5
† 89114 Sloan, 25................F 7
89430 Smith, 300.................B 4
89431 Sparks, 24,187.............B 3
89436 Steamboat, 560.............B 3
† 89406 Stillwater, 30...........C 3
† 89101 Sunrise Manor, 10,886....F 6
† 89431 Sun Valley, 2,414........B 3
89049 Tonopah⊙, 1,716............D 5
89834 Tuscarora, 15..............E 1
† 89418 Unionville, 18...........C 2
† 89043 Ursine, 40...............G 5
89438 Valmy, 50..................D 2

89439 Verdi, 100.................B 3
89440 Virginia City⊙, 300........B 3
† 96104 Vya, 12..................B 1
† 89447 Wabuska, 50..............B 3
89442 Wadsworth, 375.............B 3
89443 Weed Heights, 750..........B 4
† 89447 Weeks, 15................B 3
89835 Wells, 1,081...............G 1
† 89835 Wilkins, 6...............G 1
† 89101 Winchester, 13,981.......F 6
89445 Winnemucca⊙, 3,587.........D 2
89447 Yerington⊙, 2,010..........B 4
89449 Zephyr Cove, 400...........A 3

⊙ County seat.
‡ Population of metropolitan area.
† Zip of nearest p.o.
* Multiple zips

AREA 110,540 sq. mi.
POPULATION 488,738
CAPITAL Carson City
LARGEST CITY Las Vegas
HIGHEST POINT Boundary Pk. 13,140 ft.
SETTLED IN 1850
ADMITTED TO UNION October 31, 1864
POPULAR NAME Silver State
STATE FLOWER Sagebrush
STATE BIRD Mountain Bluebird

An incandescent oasis in the Nevada desert, Reno beckons travelers to its varied diversions — from games of chance and nightclub entertainment to annual rodeos and skiing in the Sierra Nevada.

Bill McKinney — Shostal Associates

Agriculture, Industry and Resources

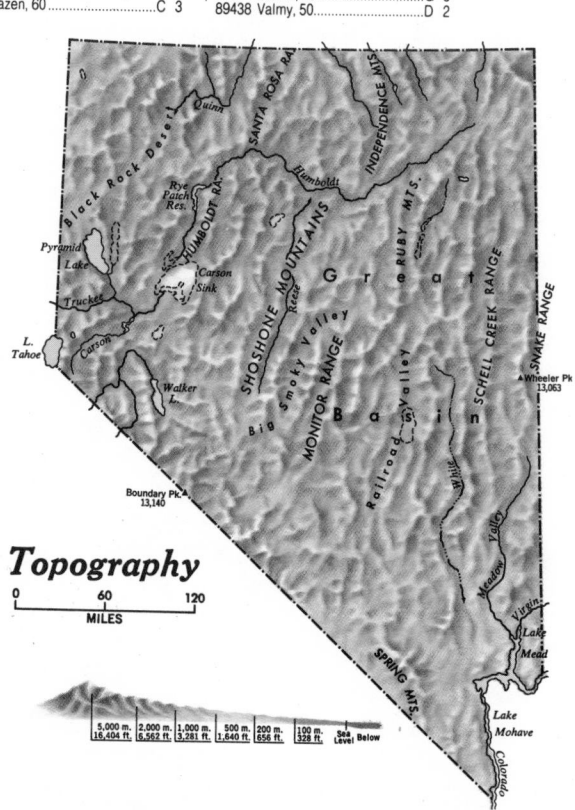

Topography

MILES
0   60   120

5,000 m. 2,000 m. 1,000 m. 500 m. 200 m. 100 m. Sea Below
16,404 ft. 6,562 ft. 3,281 ft. 1,640 ft. 656 ft. 328 ft. Level

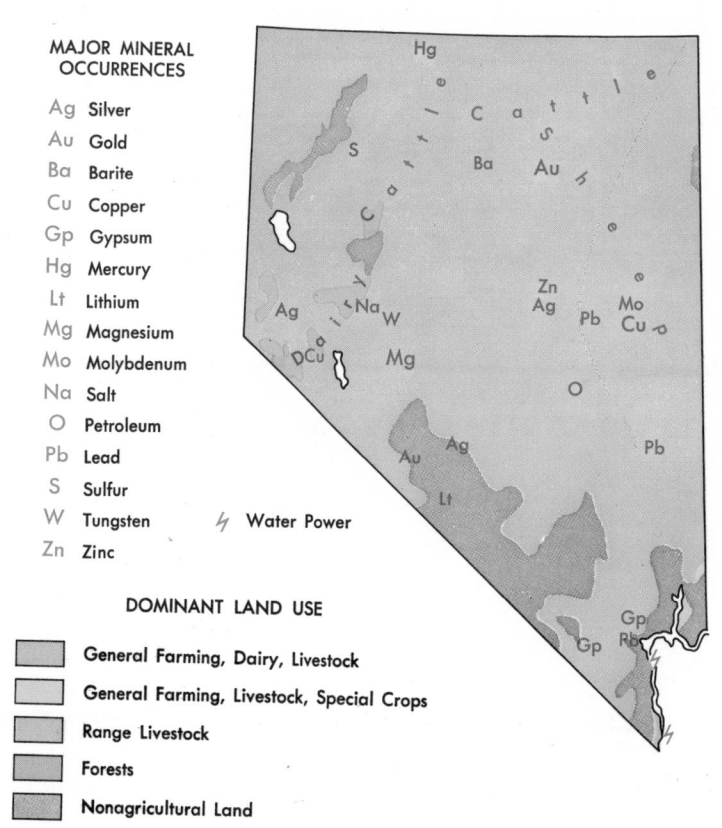

MAJOR MINERAL OCCURRENCES

Ag Silver
Au Gold
Ba Barite
Cu Copper
Gp Gypsum
Hg Mercury
Lt Lithium
Mg Magnesium
Mo Molybdenum
Na Salt
O   Petroleum
Pb Lead
S   Sulfur
W   Tungsten   ⚡ Water Power
Zn Zinc

DOMINANT LAND USE

General Farming, Dairy, Livestock
General Farming, Livestock, Special Crops
Range Livestock
Forests
Nonagricultural Land

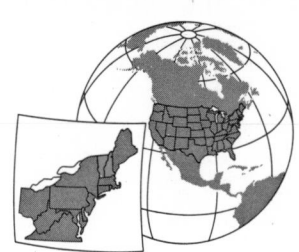

NEW HAMPSHIRE

COUNTIES

Belknap, 32,367	D 4
Carroll, 18,548	E 4
Cheshire, 52,364	C 6
Coos, 34,291	E 2
Grafton, 54,914	D 4
Hillsboro, 223,941	D 6
Merrimack, 80,925	D 5
Rockingham, 138,951	E 5
Strafford, 70,431	E 5
Sullivan, 30,949	C 5

CITIES and TOWNS

Zip	Name/Pop.	Key
03601	Acworth, ▵459	C 5
† 03864	Albany, ▵259	E 3
† 03222	Alexandria, ▵466	D 4
† 03275	Allenstown, ▵2,732	E 5
03602	Alstead, ▵1,185	C 5
03602	Alstead, 450	C 5
03809	Alton, ▵1,647	E 5
03809	Alton, 450	E 5
03031	Amherst, ▵4,605	D 6
03810	Amherst, 600	D 6
03216	Andover, ▵1,138	D 5
03216	Andover, 500	D 5
03440	Antrim, ▵2,122	D 5
03440	Antrim, 750	D 5
03217	Ashland, ▵1,599	D 4
03217	Ashland, 1,391	D 4
03441	Ashuelot, 750	C 6
03811	Atkinson, ▵2,291	E 6
03032	Auburn, ▵2,035	E 5
03218	Barnstead, ▵1,119	E 5
03218	Barnstead, 400	E 5
† 03825	Barrington, ▵1,865	F 5
03812	Bartlett, ▵1,098	E 3
03812	Bartlett, 600	E 3
03740	Bath, ▵607	D 3
03102	Bedford, ▵5,859	D 6
03220	Belmont, ▵2,493	E 5
03220	Belmont, 900	E 5
03442	Bennington, ▵639	D 5
† 03785	Benton, ▵194	D 3
03570	Berlin, 15,256	E 3
03574	Bethlehem, ▵1,142	D 3
03574	Bethlehem, 500	D 3
03301	Boscawen, ▵3,162	D 5
† 03301	Bow Mills, 600	D 5
03221	Bradford, ▵679	D 5
† 03833	Brentwood, ▵1,468	E 6
03575	Bretton Woods, 6	E 3
† 03222	Bridgewater, ▵398	D 4
03222	Bristol, ▵1,670	D 4
03222	Bristol, 1,080	D 4
† 03872	Brookfield, ▵198	E 4
03033	Brookline, ▵1,167	D 6
03223	Campton, ▵1,171	D 4
03741	Canaan, ▵1,923	C 4
03741	Canaan, 500	C 4
03034	Candia, ▵1,997	E 5
03079	Canobie Lake, 500	E 6
03224	Canterbury, ▵895	D 5
† 03595	Carroll, ▵310	D 3
03813	Center Conway, 450	E 4
03226	Center Harbor, ▵540	E 4
03814	Center Ossipee, 550	E 4
03603	Charlestown, ▵3,274	C 5
03603	Charlestown, 1,285	C 5
† 04037	Chatham, ▵134	E 3
03036	Chester, ▵1,382	E 6
03443	Chesterfield, ▵1,817	C 6
03443	Chesterfield, 450	C 5
† 03258	Chichester, ▵1,083	E 5
03743	Claremont, 14,221	C 5
05902	Clarksville, ▵166	E 1
03576	Colebrook, ▵2,094	E 2
03576	Colebrook, 1,070	E 2
03301	Concord (cap.)⊙, 30,022	D 5
03229	Contoocook, 975	D 5
03818	Conway, ▵4,865	E 4
03818	Conway, 1,489	E 4
† 03753	Croydon, ▵396	C 5
† 03598	Dalton, ▵425	D 3
03230	Danbury, ▵489	D 4
03819	Danville, ▵924	E 6
03037	Deerfield, ▵1,178	E 6
† 03244	Deering, ▵578	D 5
03038	Derry,, ▵11,712	E 6
03038	Derry, 6,090	E 6

† 03266	Dorchester, ▵141	D 4
03820	Dover⊙, 20,850	F 5
03444	Dublin, ▵837	C 6
† 03588	Dummer, ▵225	E 2
† 03301	Dunbarton, ▵825	D 5
03824	Durham, ▵8,869	F 5
03824	Durham, 7,221	F 5
03231	East Andover, 450	D 5
03041	East Derry, 600	E 6
03827	East Kingston, ▵838	F 6
03580	Easton, ▵92	D 3
03446	East Swanzey, 500	C 6
03894	East Wolfeboro, 400	E 4
03832	Eaton, ▵221	E 4
† 03264	Ellsworth, ▵13	D 4
03748	Enfield, ▵2,345	C 4
03748	Enfield, 1,408	C 4
03042	Epping, ▵2,356	E 5
03042	Epping, 1,097	E 5
03234	Epsom, ▵1,469	E 5
03579	Errol, ▵199	E 2
03750	Etna, 550	C 4
03833	Exeter, ▵8,892	F 6
03833	Exeter⊙, 6,439	F 6
03835	Farmington, ▵3,588	E 5
03835	Farmington, 2,884	E 5
03447	Fitzwilliam, ▵1,362	C 6
03447	Fitzwilliam, 750	C 6
03043	Francestown, ▵525	D 6
03580	Franconia, ▵655	D 3
03235	Franklin, 7,292	D 5
03836	Freedom, ▵387	E 4

NEW HAMPSHIRE

AREA 9,304 sq. mi.
POPULATION 737,681
CAPITAL Concord
LARGEST CITY Manchester
HIGHEST POINT Mt. Washington 6,288 ft.
SETTLED IN 1623
ADMITTED TO UNION June 21, 1788
POPULAR NAME Granite State
STATE FLOWER Purple Lilac
STATE BIRD Purple Finch

VERMONT

AREA 9,609 sq. mi.
POPULATION 444,732
CAPITAL Montpelier
LARGEST CITY Burlington
HIGHEST POINT Mt. Mansfield 4,393 ft.
SETTLED IN 1764
ADMITTED TO UNION March 4, 1791
POPULAR NAME Green Mountain State
STATE FLOWER Red Clover
STATE BIRD Hermit Thrush

Topography

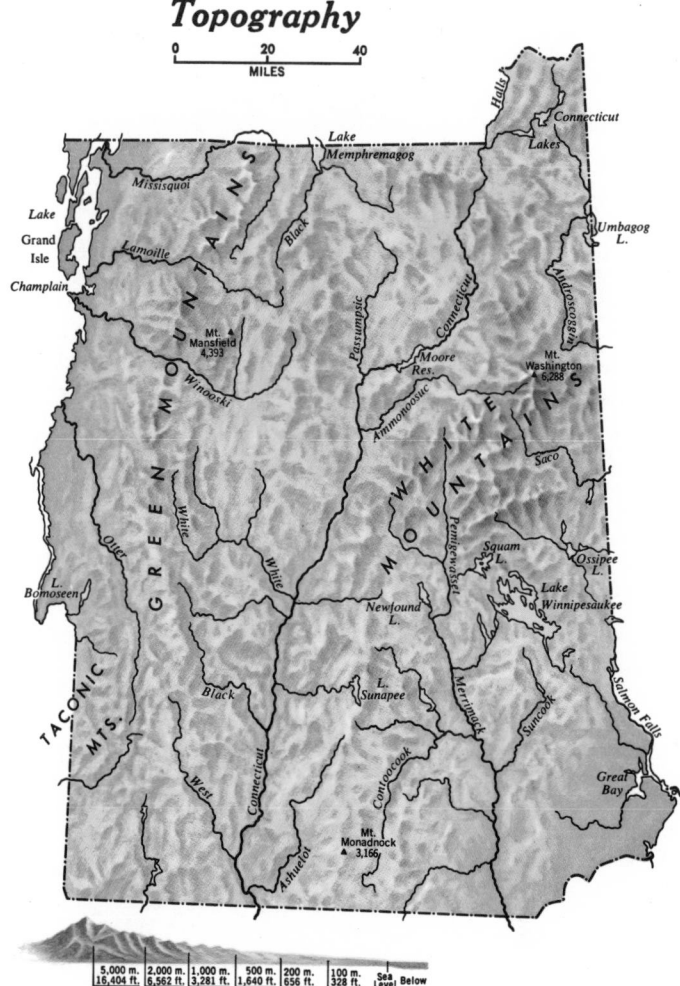

0   20   40
MILES

5,000 m. 16,404 ft.	2,000 m. 6,562 ft.	1,000 m. 3,281 ft.	500 m. 1,640 ft.	200 m. 656 ft.	100 m. 328 ft.	Sea Level Below

Agriculture, Industry and Resources

DOMINANT LAND USE

- Specialized Dairy
- Dairy, General Farming
- Dairy, Poultry, Mixed Farming
- Forests
- ⚡ Water Power
- Major Industrial Areas

MANCHESTER
Leather Goods, Textiles,
Electrical Products

MAJOR MINERAL OCCURRENCES

Ab	Asbestos		Mr	Marble
Be	Beryl		Sl	Slate
Gn	Granite		Tc	Talc
Mi	Mica		Th	Thorium

03044	Fremont, ▵993	E 6
† 03246	Gilford, ▵3,219	E 4
03237	Gilmanton, ▵1,010	E 5
03448	Gilsum, ▵570	C 5
03045	Goffstown, ▵9,284	D 5
03045	Goffstown, 2,272	D 5
03581	Gorham, ▵2,998	E 3
03581	Gorham, 2,020	E 3
03752	Goshen, ▵395	C 5
03239	Gossville, 800	E 5
03240	Grafton, ▵370	D 4
03753	Grantham, ▵366	C 5
03045	Grasmere, 513	D 5
03047	Greenfield, ▵1,058	D 6
03840	Greenland, ▵1,784	F 5
03048	Greenville, ▵1,587	D 6
03048	Greenville, 1,332	D 6
† 03241	Groton, ▵120	D 4
03582	Groveton, 1,597	D 2
03841	Hampstead, ▵2,401	E 6
03841	Hampstead, 500	E 6
03842	Hampton, ▵8,011	F 6
03842	Hampton, 5,407	F 6
03842	Hampton Beach, 975	F 6
03844	Hampton Falls, ▵1,254	F 6
03449	Hancock, ▵909	C 6
03755	Hanover, ▵8,494	C 4
03755	Hanover, 6,147	C 4
03450	Harrisville, ▵584	C 6
03765	Haverhill, ▵3,090	D 3
03765	Haverhill, 400	D 3
03241	Hebron, ▵234	D 4
03242	Henniker, ▵2,348	D 5
03242	Henniker, 950	D 5
03243	Hill, ▵909	D 5
03244	Hillsboro, ▵2,775	D 5
03244	Hillsboro, 1,784	D 5
03451	Hinsdale, ▵3,276	C 6
03451	Hinsdale, 1,059	C 6
03245	Holderness, ▵1,048	D 4
03049	Hollis, ▵2,616	D 6
03049	Hollis, 500	D 6
03106	Hooksett, ▵5,564	E 5
03106	Hooksett, 1,303	E 5

03301	Hopkinton, ▵3,007	D 5
03301	Hopkinton, 500	D 5
03051	Hudson, ▵10,638	E 6
03051	Hudson, 4,900	E 6
03845	Intervale, 500	E 3
03846	Jackson, ▵404	E 3
03452	Jaffrey, ▵3,353	C 6
03452	Jaffrey, 1,922	C 6
03583	Jefferson, ▵714	D 3
03431	Keene⊙, 20,467	C 6
03848	Kingston, ▵2,882	E 6
03246	Laconia⊙, 14,888	E 4
03584	Lancaster, ▵3,166	D 3
03584	Lancaster⊙, 2,120	D 3
† 03585	Landaff, ▵292	D 3
† 03602	Landaff, ▵337	C 5
03766	Lebanon, 9,725	C 4
† 03857	Lee, ▵1,481	F 5
03606	Lempster, ▵360	C 5
03251	Lincoln, ▵1,341	D 3
03251	Lincoln, 900	D 3
03585	Lisbon, ▵1,480	D 3
03585	Lisbon, 1,247	D 3
† 03051	Litchfield, ▵1,420	E 6
03561	Littleton, ▵5,290	D 3
03561	Littleton, 4,180	D 3
03252	Lochmere, 500	D 5
03053	Londonderry, ▵5,346	E 6
03301	Loudon, ▵1,707	E 5
† 03585	Lyman, ▵213	D 3
03768	Lyme, ▵1,112	C 4
03768	Lyme, 400	C 4
† 03082	Lyndeboro, ▵789	D 6
† 03820	Madbury, ▵704	F 5
03849	Madison, ▵572	E 4
* 03101	Manchester, 87,754	E 6
	Manchester, ‡108,461	E 6
03455	Marlborough, ▵1,671	C 6
03455	Marlborough, 1,231	C 6
03456	Marlow, ▵390	C 5
03253	Meredith, ▵2,904	D 4
03253	Meredith, 1,017	D 4
03770	Meriden, 495	C 4
03054	Merrimack, ▵8,595	D 6

03054	Merrimack, 850	D 6
† 03887	Middleton, ▵430	E 5
03588	Milan, ▵713	E 2
03055	Milford, ▵6,622	D 6
03055	Milford, 4,997	D 6
03851	Milton, ▵1,859	F 5
03851	Milton, 750	F 5
03771	Monroe, ▵385	C 3
03057	Mont Vernon, ▵906	D 6
03254	Moultonboro, ▵1,310	E 4
03060	Nashua⊙, 55,820	D 6
03457	Nelson, ▵304	C 5
03070	New Boston, ▵1,390	D 6
03070	New Boston, 450	D 6
03255	Newbury, ▵509	C 5
03854	New Castle, ▵975	F 5
03855	New Durham, ▵583	E 5
03856	Newfields, ▵843	F 5
03256	New Hampton, ▵946	D 4
† 03801	Newington, ▵798	F 5
03071	New Ipswich, ▵1,803	D 6
03257	New London, ▵2,236	D 5
03257	New London, 1,347	D 5
03857	Newmarket, ▵3,361	F 5
03857	Newmarket, 2,645	F 5
03773	Newport, ▵5,899	C 5
03773	Newport⊙, 3,296	C 5
03858	Newton, ▵1,920	E 6
03858	Newton, 483	E 6
03859	Newton Junction, 500	E 6
03258	North Chichester, 450	E 5
03860	North Conway, 1,723	E 3
† 03276	Northfield, ▵2,193	D 5
03276	Northfield-Tilton, 2,420	D 5
03862	North Hampton, ▵3,259	F 6
03862	North Hampton, 750	F 6
03774	North Haverhill, 750	D 3
† 03773	North Newport, 500	C 5
03073	North Salem, 950	E 6
03590	North Stratford, 650	D 2
† 03582	Northumberland, ▵2,493	D 2
† 03608	North Walpole, 950	C 5
03281	North Weare, 600	D 5
03261	Northwood, ▵1,526	E 5

(continued on following page)

(continued)

NEW HAMPSHIRE
(continued)

03262 North Woodstock, 650 D 3
03290 Nottingham, ▵952 E 5
† 03741 Orange, ▵103 D 4
03777 Orford, ▵793 C 4
03864 Ossipee⊙, ▵1,647 E 4
03076 Pelham, ▵5,408 E 6
† 03275 Pembroke, ▵4,261 E 5
03458 Peterborough, ▵3,807 D 6
03458 Peterborough, 2,078 D 6
03779 Piermont, ▵462 C 4
03592 Pittsburg, ▵726 E 1
03263 Pittsfield, ▵2,517 E 5
03263 Pittsfield, 1,662 E 5
03781 Plainfield, ▵1,323 C 4
03865 Plaistow, ▵4,712 E 6
03865 Plaistow, 950 E 6
03264 Plymouth, ▵4,225 D 4
03264 Plymouth, 3,109 D 4
03801 Portsmouth, 25,717 F 5
03593 Randolph, ▵169 E 3
03077 Raymond, ▵3,003 E 5
† 03470 Richmond, ▵287 C 6
03461 Rindge, ▵2,175 C 6
03867 Rochester, 17,938 E 5
† 03431 Roxbury, ▵161 C 6
03266 Rumney, ▵870 D 4
03870 Rye, ▵4,083 F 5
03870 Rye, 750 F 5
03871 Rye Beach, 750 F 6
† 03870 Rye North Beach, 700 F 5
03079 Salem, ▵20,142 E 6
03079 Salem, 950 E 6
† 03079 Salem Depot, 975 E 6
03268 Salisbury, ▵589 D 5
† 03820 Salmon Falls, 950 F 5
03269 Sanbornton, ▵1,022 D 5
03872 Sanbornville, 550 F 4
03873 Sandown, ▵741 E 6
03270 Sandwich, ▵666 E 4
03874 Seabrook, ▵3,053 F 6
03874 Seabrook, 950 F 6
† 03458 Sharon, ▵136 D 6
† 03581 Shelburne, ▵199 E 3
03878 Somersworth, 9,026 F 5
† 03037 South Deerfield, 500 E 5
† 01913 South Hampton, ▵558 F 6
03083 South Merrimack, 650 D 6
† 03874 South Seabrook, 500 F 6
03462 Spofford, 631 C 6
† 03284 Springfield, ▵310 C 4
† 03582 Stark, ▵343 E 2
† 03576 Stewartstown, ▵1,008 E 2
03464 Stoddard, ▵242 C 5
03884 Strafford, ▵965 E 5
† 03590 Stratford, ▵980 D 2
03885 Stratham, ▵1,512 F 5
03585 Sugar Hill, ▵336 D 3
† 03445 Sullivan, ▵376 C 5
03782 Sunapee, ▵1,384 C 5
03782 Sunapee, 750 C 5
03275 Suncook, 4,280 D 5
03431 Surry, ▵507 C 5
† 03260 Sutton, ▵642 D 5
† 03431 Swanzey, ▵4,254 C 6
† 03431 Swanzey, 950 C 6
03886 Tamworth, ▵1,054 E 4
03084 Temple, ▵441 D 6
† 03285 Thornton, ▵594 D 4
03276 Tilton, ▵2,579 D 5
03276 Tilton-Northfield, 2,420 D 5
03465 Troy, ▵1,713 C 6
† 03816 Tuftonboro, ▵910 E 4
† 03743 Unity, ▵709 C 5
03888 Wakefield, ▵1,420 F 4
03608 Walpole, ▵2,966 C 5
03608 Walpole, 900 C 5
03278 Warner, ▵1,441 D 5
03278 Warner, 600 D 5
03279 Warren, ▵539 D 4
03280 Washington, ▵248 C 5
03223 Waterville Valley, ▵109 D 4
03281 Weare, ▵1,851 D 5
03281 Weare P.O. (North Weare), 600 D 5
† 03301 Webster, ▵680 D 5
03282 Wentworth, ▵376 D 4
† 03579 Wentworths Location, ▵37 E 2
† 03038 West Derry (Derry), 6,090 E 6
03784 West Lebanon, 4,200 C 4
03467 Westmoreland, ▵998 C 6
03597 West Stewartstown, 600 E 2
03469 West Swanzey, 950 C 6
03892 Westville, 500 E 6
03598 Whitefield, ▵1,538 D 3
03598 Whitefield, 1,093 D 3
† 03287 Wilmot, ▵516 D 5
03086 Wilton, ▵2,276 D 6
03086 Wilton, 1,161 D 6
03470 Winchester, ▵2,869 C 6
03470 Winchester, 938 C 6
03087 Windham, ▵3,008 E 6
03289 Winnisquam, 500 E 5
03894 Wolfeboro, ▵3,036 E 4
03894 Wolfeboro, 1,718 E 4
03896 Wolfeboro Falls, 650 E 4
03293 Woodstock, ▵897 D 4
03785 Woodsville⊙, 1,336 C 3

VERMONT

COUNTIES

Addison, 24,266 A 3
Bennington, 29,282 A 6
Caledonia, 22,789 C 2
Chittenden, 99,131 A 3
Essex, 5,416 D 2
Franklin, 31,282 B 2
Grand Isle, 3,574 A 2
Lamoille, 13,309 B 2
Orange, 17,676 C 3
Orleans, 20,153 C 2
Rutland, 52,637 A 4
Washington, 47,659 B 3
Windham, 33,074 B 5
Windsor, 44,082 B 4

CITIES and TOWNS

Zip *Name/Pop.* *Key*

† 05491 Addison, ▵717 A 3
05820 Albany, ▵528 C 2
05440 Alburg, ▵1,271 A 2
05440 Alburg, 520 A 2
† 05143 Andover, ▵239 B 5
05250 Arlington, ▵1,934 A 5
05250 Arlington, 1,212 A 5
05030 Ascutney, 500 C 5
05901 Averill, ▵8 D 2
05441 Bakersfield, ▵635 B 2
05031 Barnard, ▵569 B 4
05821 Barnet, ▵1,342 C 3
05641 Barre, 10,209 C 3
05641 Barre, ▵6,509 C 3
05822 Barton, ▵2,874 C 2
05822 Barton, 1,051 C 2
05902 Beecher Falls, 640 D 2
05101 Bellows Falls, 3,505 C 5
05442 Belvidere, ▵189 B 2
05201 Bennington, ▵14,586 A 6
05201 Bennington⊙, 7,950 A 6
05731 Benson, ▵583 A 4
† 05476 Berkshire, ▵931 B 2
05032 Bethel, ▵1,347 B 4
† 03590 Bloomfield, ▵196 D 2
† 05466 Bolton, ▵427 B 3
05732 Bomoseen, 500 A 4
05033 Bradford, ▵1,627 C 3
05033 Bradford, 709 C 3
05646 Braintree, ▵751 B 4
05733 Brandon, ▵3,697 A 4
05733 Brandon, 1,720 A 4
05301 Brattleboro, ▵12,239 B 6
05301 Brattleboro, 9,055 B 6
05034 Bridgewater, ▵783 B 4
05734 Bridport, ▵809 A 4
05443 Bristol, ▵2,744 A 3
05443 Bristol, 1,737 A 3
05036 Brookfield, ▵606 B 3
† 05345 Brookline, ▵180 B 5
† 05860 Brownington, ▵522 C 2
† 05871 Burke, ▵1,053 D 2
05401 Burlington⊙, 38,633 A 3
05647 Cabot, ▵663 C 3
05648 Calais, ▵749 B 3
05444 Cambridge, ▵1,528 B 2
05903 Canaan, ▵949 D 2
05735 Castleton, ▵2,837 A 4
05735 Castleton, 450 A 4
05142 Cavendish, ▵1,264 B 5
05736 Center Rutland, 500 A 4
05445 Charlotte, ▵1,802 A 3
05038 Chelsea⊙, ▵983 C 4
05038 Chelsea, 525 C 4
05143 Chester, ▵2,371 B 5
05143 Chester, 950 B 5
05144 Chester Depot, 500 B 5
05737 Chittenden, ▵646 B 4
05737 Chittenden, 525 B 4
† 05759 Clarendon, ▵1,537 A 4
05446 Colchester, ▵8,776 A 2
05824 Concord, ▵896 D 3
05039 Corinth, ▵683 C 3
† 05753 Cornwall, ▵900 A 4
05825 Coventry, ▵492 C 2
05826 Craftsbury, ▵632 C 2
05739 Danby, ▵910 A 5
05828 Danville, ▵1,405 C 3
05828 Danville, 450 C 3
05829 Derby, ▵3,252 C 2
05829 Derby (Derby Center), 547 C 2
05830 Derby Line, 834 C 2
05251 Dorset, ▵1,293 A 5
05251 Dorset, 450 A 5
† 05676 Duxbury, ▵621 B 3
05252 East Arlington, 500 A 5
05649 East Barre, 950 C 3
05448 East Fairfield, 700 B 2
05837 East Haven, ▵197 D 2
05740 East Middlebury, 500 A 4
05651 East Montpelier, ▵1,597 B 3
05651 East Montpelier, 550 B 3
05652 Eden, ▵513 B 2
05450 Enosburg Falls, 1,266 B 2
05451 Essex, ▵10,951 A 2
05451 Essex, 850 A 2
05452 Essex Junction, 6,511 A 3
05454 Fairfax, ▵1,366 B 2
05455 Fairfield, ▵1,285 B 2
05743 Fair Haven, ▵2,777 A 4
05743 Fair Haven, 2,287 A 4
05045 Fairlee, ▵604 C 4
05045 Fairlee, 425 C 4
05456 Ferrisburg, ▵1,875 A 3
† 05444 Fletcher, ▵456 B 2
05745 Forest Dale, 500 A 4
05457 Franklin, ▵821 B 2
† 05478 Georgia, ▵1.711 A 2
05904 Gilman, 700 D 3
05839 Glover, ▵649 C 2
05146 Grafton, ▵465 B 5
05840 Granby, ▵52 D 2
05458 Grand Isle, ▵809 A 2
05654 Graniteville, 1,120 C 3
05747 Granville, ▵255 B 4
05841 Greensboro, ▵593 C 2
05046 Groton, ▵666 C 3
05046 Groton, 438 C 3
05905 Guildhall⊙, ▵169 D 2
† 05301 Guilford, ▵1,108 B 6
† 05358 Halifax, ▵295 B 6
05748 Hancock, ▵283 B 4
05843 Hardwick, ▵2,466 C 2
05843 Hardwick, 1,503 C 2
05047 Hartford, ▵6,477 C 4
05047 Hartford, 650 C 4
05047 Hartland, ▵1,806 C 4
† 05459 Highgate, ▵1,936 B 2
05459 Highgate Center, 927 B 2
05461 Hinesburg, ▵1,775 A 3
† 05830 Holland, ▵383 D 2
05749 Hubbardton, ▵228 A 4
05462 Huntington, ▵748 B 3
05655 Hyde Park, ▵1,347 B 2
05655 Hyde Park⊙, 418 B 2
05750 Hydeville, 450 A 4
† 05777 Ira, ▵284 A 4
05845 Irasburg, ▵775 C 2
05846 Island Pond, 1,123 D 2
05463 Isle La Motte, ▵262 A 2
05343 Jamaica, ▵590 B 5
† 05859 Jay, ▵182 C 2
05465 Jericho, ▵2,343 B 3
05465 Jericho, 450 A 2
05656 Johnson, ▵1,927 B 2
05656 Johnson, 1,296 B 2
† 05752 Leicester, ▵583 A 4
† 03576 Lemington, ▵120 D 2
† 05443 Lincoln, ▵599 B 3
05148 Londonderry, ▵1,037 B 5
05847 Lowell, ▵515 C 2
05149 Ludlow, ▵2,463 B 5
05149 Ludlow, 1,508 B 5
05906 Lunenburg, ▵1,061 D 3
05849 Lyndon, ▵3,705 C 2
05851 Lyndonville, 1,415 D 2
† 05905 Maidstone, ▵94 D 2
05254 Manchester, ▵2,919 A 5
05254 Manchester⊙, 435 A 5
05255 Manchester Center, 900 A 5
05256 Manchester Depot, 1,560 B 5
05344 Marlboro, ▵592 B 6
05658 Marshfield, ▵1,033 C 3
† 05701 Mendon, ▵743 B 4
05753 Middlebury, ▵6,532 A 3
05753 Middlebury⊙, 4,500 A 3
† 05602 Middlesex, ▵857 B 3
05757 Middletown Springs, ▵426 A 5
05468 Milton, ▵4,495 A 2
05468 Milton, 1,164 A 2
05469 Monkton, ▵765 A 3
05470 Montgomery, ▵651 B 2
05602 Montpelier (cap.)⊙, 8,609 B 3
05660 Moretown, ▵904 B 3
05853 Morgan, ▵286 D 2
† 05661 Morristown, ▵4,052 B 2
05661 Morrisville, 2,116 B 2
05758 Mount Holly, ▵687 B 5
† 05739 Mount Tabor, ▵184 B 5
† 05871 Newark, ▵144 D 2
05051 Newbury, ▵1,440 C 3
05051 Newbury, 450 C 3
05345 Newfane, ▵900 B 6
05345 Newfane⊙, 183 B 6
05472 New Haven, ▵1,039 A 3
05855 Newport, ▵1,125 C 2
05855 Newport⊙, 4,664 C 2
05257 North Bennington, 984 A 6
05759 North Clarendon, 750 B 4
05663 Northfield, ▵4,870 B 3
05663 Northfield, 2,139 B 3
05664 Northfield Falls, 700 B 3
05474 North Hero⊙, ▵364 A 2
05260 North Pownal, 600 A 6
05150 North Springfield, 1,100 B 5
05859 North Troy, 774 C 2
05907 Norton, ▵207 D 2
05055 Norwich, ▵1,966 C 4
05055 Norwich, 500 C 4
† 05649 Orange, ▵540 C 3
05860 Orleans, 1,138 C 2
05760 Orwell, ▵851 A 4
† 05491 Panton, ▵416 A 3
05761 Pawlet, ▵1,184 A 5
05862 Peacham, ▵446 C 3
05152 Peru, ▵243 B 5
05762 Pittsfield, ▵249 B 4
05763 Pittsford, ▵2,306 A 4
05763 Pittsford, 682 A 4
05667 Plainfield, ▵1,399 C 3
05667 Plainfield, 949 C 3
05056 Plymouth, ▵283 B 4
† 05067 Pomfret, ▵620 B 4
05764 Poultney, ▵3,217 A 4
05764 Poultney, 1,914 A 4
05261 Pownal, ▵2,441 A 6
05261 Pownal, 700 A 6
05765 Proctor, ▵2,095 A 4
05765 Proctor, 1,950 A 4
05153 Proctorsville, 512 B 5
05346 Putney, ▵1,727 B 6
05346 Putney, 1,115 B 6
05059 Quechee, 420 C 4
05060 Randolph, ▵3,882 B 4
05060 Randolph, 2,115 B 4
05062 Reading, ▵564 B 5
05350 Readsboro, ▵638 B 6
05350 Readsboro, 469 B 6
05476 Richford, ▵2,116 B 2
05476 Richford, 1,527 B 2
05477 Richmond, ▵2,249 A 3
05477 Richmond, 935 A 3
05766 Ripton, ▵187 A 4
05767 Rochester, ▵884 B 4
† 05101 Rockingham, ▵5,501 C 5
05669 Roxbury, ▵354 B 3
05063 Royalton, ▵1,399 B 4
05768 Rupert, ▵582 A 5
05701 Rutland, ▵2,248 B 4
05701 Rutland⊙, 19,293 B 4
05042 Ryegate, ▵830 C 3
05478 Saint Albans, ▵3,270 A 2
05478 Saint Albans⊙, 8,082 A 2
† 05401 Saint George, ▵477 A 2
05819 Saint Johnsbury, ▵8,409 D 3
05819 Saint Johnsbury⊙, 7,000 D 3
05769 Salisbury, ▵649 A 4
† 05250 Sandgate, ▵127 A 5
05154 Saxtons River, 581 B 5
† 05363 Searsburg, ▵84 A 6
05262 Shaftsbury, ▵2,411 A 6
05065 Sharon, ▵541 C 4
05866 Sheffield, ▵307 C 2
05482 Shelburne, ▵3,728 A 3
05482 Shelburne, 2,591 A 3
05483 Sheldon, ▵1,481 B 2
05770 Shoreham, ▵790 A 4
† 05738 Shrewsbury, ▵570 B 4
05670 South Barre, 865 B 3
05401 South Burlington, ▵10,032 A 3
05486 South Hero, ▵868 A 2
05155 South Londonderry, 600 B 5
05068 South Royalton, 625 C 4
05156 Springfield, ▵10,063 B 5
05156 Springfield, 5,632 B 5
† 01247 Stamford, ▵752 A 6
05487 Starksboro, ▵668 A 3
05772 Stockbridge, ▵389 B 4
05672 Stowe, ▵2,388 B 3
05672 Stowe, 435 B 3
05072 Strafford, ▵536 C 4
† 05360 Stratton, ▵104 B 5
† 05733 Sudbury, ▵253 A 4
† 05250 Sunderland, ▵601 A 5
05867 Sutton, ▵438 C 2
05488 Swanton, ▵4,622 A 2
05488 Swanton, 2,630 A 2
05074 Thetford, ▵1,422 C 4
† 05773 Tinmouth, ▵268 A 5
05076 Topsham, ▵686 C 3
05353 Townshend, ▵668 B 5
05868 Troy, ▵1,457 C 2
05077 Tunbridge, ▵791 C 4
05489 Underhill, ▵1,198 B 2
05491 Vergennes, 2,242 A 3
05354 Vernon, ▵1,024 B 6
05079 Vershire, ▵299 C 4
05673 Waitsfield, ▵837 B 3
† 05873 Walden, ▵442 C 3
05773 Wallingford, ▵1,676 B 5
05773 Wallingford, 815 B 5
† 05491 Waltham, ▵265 A 3
05355 Wardsboro, ▵391 B 5
05674 Warren, ▵588 B 3
05675 Washington, ▵667 C 3
05676 Waterbury, ▵4,614 B 3
05676 Waterbury, 2,840 B 3
05677 Waterbury Center, 900 B 3
05492 Waterville, ▵397 B 2
05678 Websterville, 700 B 3
05774 Wells, ▵560 A 5
05081 Wells River, 419 C 3
05301 West Brattleboro, 2,200 B 6
05083 West Fairlee, ▵337 C 4
05874 Westfield, ▵375 C 2
05494 Westford, ▵991 A 2
† 05743 West Haven, ▵240 A 4
05158 Westminster, ▵1,875 C 5
† 05860 Westmore, ▵195 C 2
05161 Weston, ▵507 B 5
05161 Weston, 450 B 5
05777 West Rutland, ▵2,381 A 4
05777 West Rutland, 1,875 A 4
† 05753 Weybridge, ▵618 A 3
† 05851 Wheelock, ▵238 C 2
05001 White River Junction, 2,379 C 4
05778 Whiting, ▵359 A 4
05361 Whitingham, ▵1,011 B 6
05088 Wilder, 1,328 C 4
05679 Williamstown, ▵1,822 B 3
05679 Williamstown, 650 B 3
05495 Williston, ▵3,187 A 3
05363 Wilmington, ▵1,184 B 6
05363 Wilmington, 544 B 6
† 05359 Windham, ▵174 B 5
05089 Windsor, ▵4,158 C 5
05089 Windsor, 3,400 C 5
05404 Winooski, 7,309 A 3
05680 Wolcott, ▵676 C 2
† 05681 Woodbury, ▵399 C 3
† 05201 Woodford, ▵286 A 6
05091 Woodstock, ▵2,608 B 4
05091 Woodstock⊙, 1,154 B 4
05682 Worcester, ▵505 B 3

⊙ County seat.
▵ Population of town or township.
‡ Population of metropolitan area.
† Zip of nearest p.o.
* Multiple zips

Edmund V. Ballman

Designed to protect wooden structures from the ravages of weather, a few early covered bridges are still standing in New Hampshire. This barn-red relic is in Jackson.

Located in the heart of Vermont, Barre rightfully boasts of its granite quarries which provide a sculptured panorama set off by surrounding green hills.

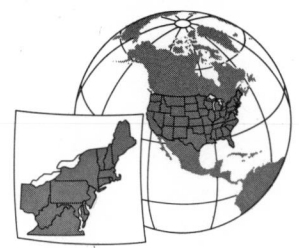

COUNTIES

Atlantic, 175,043 ....D 5
Bergen, 898,012 ....E 2
Burlington, 323,132 ....D 4
Camden, 456,291 ....D 4
Cape May, 59,554 ....D 6
Cumberland, 121,374 ....C 5
Essex, 929,986 ....E 2
Gloucester, 172,681 ....C 4
Hudson, 609,266 ....E 2
Hunterdon, 69,718 ....D 2
Mercer, 303,968 ....D 3
Middlesex, 583,813 ....E 3
Monmouth, 459,379 ....E 3
Morris, 383,454 ....D 2
Ocean, 208,470 ....E 4
Passaic, 460,782 ....E 1
Salem, 60,346 ....C 4
Somerset, 198,372 ....D 2
Sussex, 77,528 ....D 1
Union, 543,116 ....E 2
Warren, 73,879 ....C 2

CITIES and TOWNS

Zip	Name/Pop.	Key
08201	Absecon, 6,094	D 5
07820	Allamuchy, 600	D 2
07401	Allendale, 6,240	B 1
07711	Allenhurst, 1,012	F 3
08501	Allentown, 1,603	D 3
08720	Allenwood, 2,200	E 3
08001	Alloway, 850	C 4
08865	Alpha, 2,829	C 2
07620	Alpine, 1,344	C 1
07821	Andover, 813	D 2
08801	Annandale, 675	D 2
07712	Asbury Park, 16,533	F 3
† 08033	Ashland, 2,500	B 3
08004	Atco, 2,980	D 4
08401	Atlantic City, 47,859	E 5
	Atlantic City, ‡175,043	E 5
07716	Atlantic Highlands, 5,102	F 3
08106	Audubon, 10,802	B 3
08106	Audubon Park, 1,492	B 3
08202	Avalon, 1,283	D 5
07001	Avenel, 10,250	E 2
07717	Avon by the Sea, 2,163	F 3
08005	Barnegat, 900	E 4
08006	Barnegat Light, 554	E 4
08007	Barrington, 8,409	B 3
07920	Basking Ridge, 2,500	D 2
08742	Bay Head, 1,083	E 3
07002	Bayonne, 72,743	E 2
08721	Bayville, 6,000	E 4
08008	Beach Haven, 1,488	E 4
08722	Beachwood, 4,390	E 4
07921	Bedminster, 1,250	D 2
07718	Belford, 7,000	E 3
08502	Belle Mead, 1,950	D 3
07109	Belleville, 34,643	B 2
08030	Bellmawr, 15,618	B 3
07719	Belmar, 5,782	E 3
07823	Belvidere◉, 2,641	C 2
07621	Bergenfield, 33,131	C 2
07922	Berkeley Heights, ▲13,078	E 2
08009	Berlin, 4,997	D 4
07924	Bernardsville, 6,652	D 2
08010	Beverly, 3,105	D 3
08012	Blackwood, 9,500	C 4
07825	Blairstown, 1,900	C 2
07003	Bloomfield, 52,029	B 2
07403	Bloomingdale, 7,797	E 1
08804	Bloomsbury, 879	C 2
07603	Bogota, 8,125	B 2
07005	Boonton, 9,261	E 2
08505	Bordentown, 4,490	D 3
08805	Bound Brook, 10,450	D 2
07720	Bradley Beach, 4,163	F 3
08826	Branchville, 911	D 1
08723	Breton Woods, 1,900	E 3
08723	Brick Town, ▲35,057	E 3
08014	Bridgeport, 950	C 4
08302	Bridgeton◉, 20,435	C 5
08730	Brielle, 3,594	E 3
08203	Brigantine, 6,741	E 5
08030	Brooklawn, 2,870	B 3
07926	Brookside, 1,300	D 2
08015	Browns Mills, 7,144	D 4
07828	Budd Lake, 3,168	D 2
08310	Buena, 3,283	D 4
08016	Burlington, 11,991	D 3
07405	Butler, 7,051	E 2
07006	Caldwell, 8,719	B 2
07830	Califon, 970	D 2
* 08101	Camden◉, 102,551	B 3
† 08701	Candlewood, 5,629	E 3
08204	Cape May, 4,392	D 6
08210	Cape May Court House◉, 2,062	D 5
07072	Carlstadt, 7,947	B 2
08069	Carneys Point, 3,900	C 4
07008	Carteret, 23,137	E 2
08018	Cedar Brook, 600	D 4
07009	Cedar Grove, ▲15,582	B 2
07927	Cedar Knolls, 3,900	E 2
08311	Cedarville, 900	C 5
† 08723	Cedarwood Park, 1,400	E 3
07928	Chatham, 9,566	E 2
08019	Chatsworth, 700	D 4
08879	Cheesequake, 2,900	E 3
08034	Cherry Hill, ▲64,395	B 3
† 08089	Chesilhurst, 801	D 4
07930	Chester, 1,299	D 2
* 08505	Chesterfield, ▲3,190	D 3
07066	Clark, ▲18,829	A
08020	Clarksboro, 1,500	C 4
08510	Clarksburg, 800	E 3
08312	Clayton, 5,193	C 4
08021	Clementon, 4,492	D 4
07010	Cliffside Park, 14,387	C 2
08721	Cliffwood, 7,056	E 3
* 07011	Clifton, 82,437	B 2
08809	Clinton, 1,742	D 2
07624	Closter, 8,604	C 1
08108	Collingswood, 17,422	B 3
08213	Cologne, 800	D 4
07067	Colonia, 12,000	E 2
07722	Colts Neck, 950	E 3
08022	Columbus, 800	D 3
07961	Convent Station, 6,587	E 2
08512	Cranbury, 1,253	D 3
07016	Cranford, ▲27,391	E 2
07626	Cresskill, 7,164	C 1
08515	Crosswicks, 700	D 3
07723	Deal, 2,401	F 3
08023	Deepwater, 800	C 4
08110	Delair, 2,800	B 3
08075	Delanco, ▲4,157	D 3
08075	Delran, 675	B 3
07627	Demarest, 6,262	C 1
08214	Dennisville, 990	D 5
07834	Denville, ▲14,045	E 2
08096	Deptford, ▲24,232	B 4
08317	Dorothy, 850	D 5
07801	Dover, 15,039	D 2

07628	Dumont, 17,534	C 1
08812	Dunellen, 7,072	D 2
08816	East Brunswick, ▲34,166	E 3
07936	East Hanover, ▲7,734	E 2
07734	East Keansburg, 5,000	E 3
08873	East Millstone, 950	D 3
† 07100	East Newark, 1,922	B 2
* 07017	East Orange, 75,471	B 2
07407	East Paterson, 22,749	B 2
07073	East Rutherford, 8,536	B 2
07724	Eatontown, 14,619	E 3
07020	Edgewater, 4,849	C 2
† 08010	Edgewater Park, ▲7,412	D 3
08817	Edison, ▲67,120	E 2
08215	Egg Harbor City, 4,304	D 4
07740	Elberon, 2,900	F 3
* 07201	Elizabeth◉, 112,654	B 2
08318	Elmer, 1,592	C 4
07630	Emerson, 8,428	B 1
* 07631	Englewood, 24,985	C 2
07632	Englewood Cliffs, 5,938	C 2
† 08330	English Creek, 950	D 5
† 07726	Englishtown, 1,048	E 3
07849	Espanong (Lake Hopatcong), 1,941	D 2
07021	Essex Fells, 2,541	B 2
07006	Fairfield, 6,731	A 2
07701	Fair Haven, 6,142	E 3
07410	Fair Lawn, 37,975	B 1
08320	Fairton, 600	C 5
07022	Fairview, 10,698	C 2
07023	Fanwood, 8,920	E 2
07931	Far Hills, 780	D 2
07727	Farmingdale, 1,148	E 3
† 08505	Fieldsboro, 615	D 3
08821	Flagtown, 800	D 2
07836	Flanders, 3,875	D 2
08822	Flemington◉, 3,917	D 2
08518	Florence-Roebling, 7,551	D 3
07932	Florham Park, 8,094	E 2
† 08037	Folsom, 1,767	D 4
08863	Fords, 14,000	E 2
08731	Forked River, 1,422	E 4
07024	Fort Lee, 30,631	C 2
07416	Franklin, ▲30,389	D 3
07416	Franklin, 4,236	D 1
07417	Franklin Lakes, 7,550	B 1
08322	Franklinville, 2,500	C 4
07728	Freehold◉, 10,545	E 3
08825	Frenchtown, 1,459	C 2
07026	Garfield, 30,722	B 2
07027	Garwood, 5,260	E 2
08026	Gibbsboro, 2,634	B 4
08027	Gibbstown, 3,400	C 4
† 08753	Gilford Park, 4,007	E 4

07933	Gillette, 2,950	E 2
08028	Glassboro, 12,938	C 4
08029	Glendora, 10,280	B 4
08826	Glen Gardner, 874	D 2
07028	Glen Ridge, 8,518	B 2
07452	Glen Rock, 13,011	B 1
08030	Gloucester City, 14,707	B 3
08219	Green Creek, 975	D 5
07435	Green Pond, 800	E 1
07935	Green Village, 800	D 2
08323	Greenwich, ▲963	C 5
08032	Grenloch, 950	C 4
07950	Greystone Park, 5,500	D 2
08620	Groveville, 2,800	D 3
07093	Guttenberg, 5,754	C 2
* 07601	Hackensack◉, 35,911	B 2
07840	Hackettstown, 9,472	D 2
08033	Haddonfield, 13,118	B 3
08035	Haddon Heights, 9,365	B 3
08036	Hainesport, ▲2,990	D 4
07508	Haledon, 6,767	B 1
07419	Hamburg, 1,820	D 1
08690	Hamilton Square, 11,300	D 3
08037	Hammonton, 11,464	D 4
08827	Hampton, 1,386	D 2
07640	Harrington Park, 4,841	C 1
07029	Harrison, 11,811	B 2
08039	Harrisonville, 950	C 4
† 08057	Hartford, 650	D 4
07604	Hasbrouck Heights, 13,651	B 2
07641	Haworth, 3,760	C 1
07507	Hawthorne, 19,173	B 2
07730	Hazlet, 15,000	E 3
08828	Helmetta, 955	E 3
07421	Hewitt, 950	E 1
08829	High Bridge, 2,606	D 2
08904	Highland Park, 14,385	E 2
07732	Highlands, 3,916	F 3
08520	Hightstown, 5,431	D 3
07502	Hillcrest, 1,975	C 2
07642	Hillsdale, 11,768	B 1
07205	Hillside, ▲21,636	B 2
† 08083	Hi-Nella, 1,195	B 4
07030	Hoboken, 45,380	C 2
07423	Ho-ho-kus, 4,348	B 1
07733	Holmdel, 5,500	E 3
07843	Hopatcong, 9,052	D 2
07844	Hope, 950	C 2
08525	Hopewell, 2,271	D 3
07727	Howell, ▲21,756	E 3
† 08865	Huntington, 1,900	C 2
† 07712	Interlaken, 1,182	F 3
07845	Ironia, 1,500	D 2
07111	Irvington, 59,743	B 2
08830	Iselin, 19,000	E 2

(continued on following page)

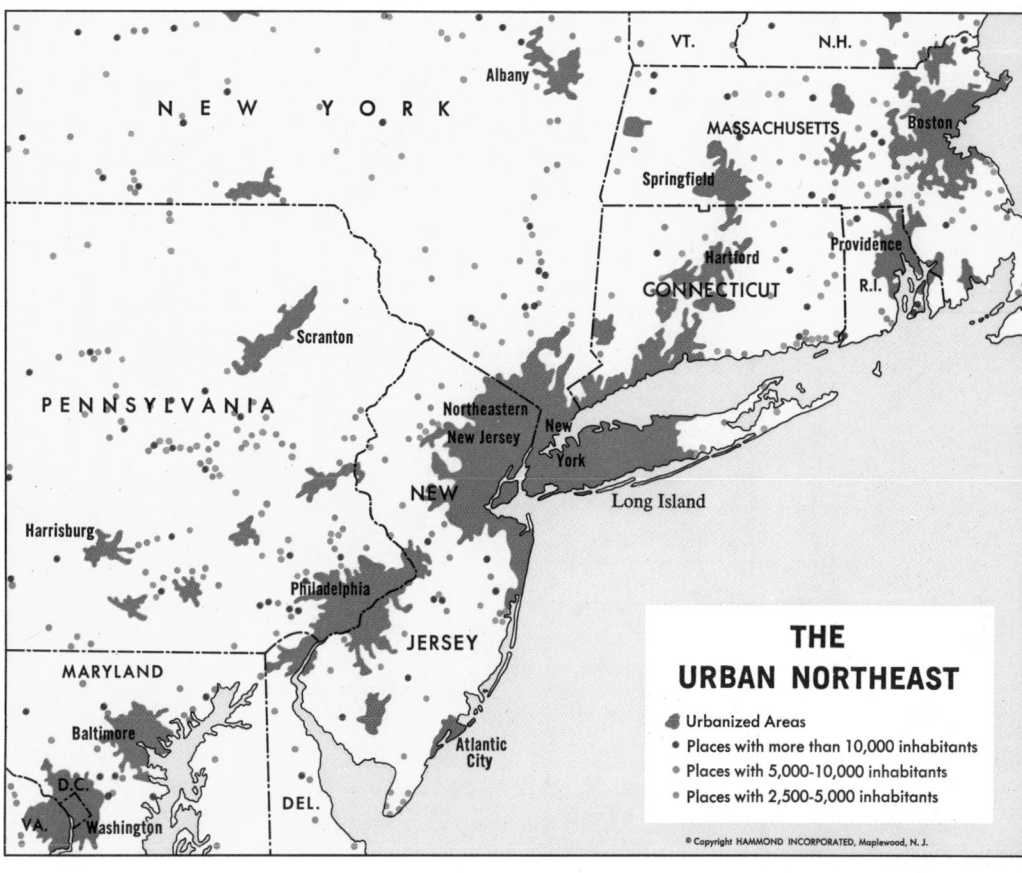

THE URBAN NORTHEAST

AREA 7,836 sq. mi.
POPULATION 7,168,164
CAPITAL Trenton
LARGEST CITY Newark
HIGHEST POINT High Point 1,803 ft.
SETTLED IN 1617
ADMITTED TO UNION December 18, 1787
POPULAR NAME Garden State
STATE FLOWER Violet
STATE BIRD Eastern Goldfinch

● Urbanized Areas
● Places with more than 10,000 inhabitants
● Places with 5,000-10,000 inhabitants
● Places with 2,500-5,000 inhabitants

® Copyright HAMMOND INCORPORATED, Maplewood, N.J.

Agriculture, Industry and Resources

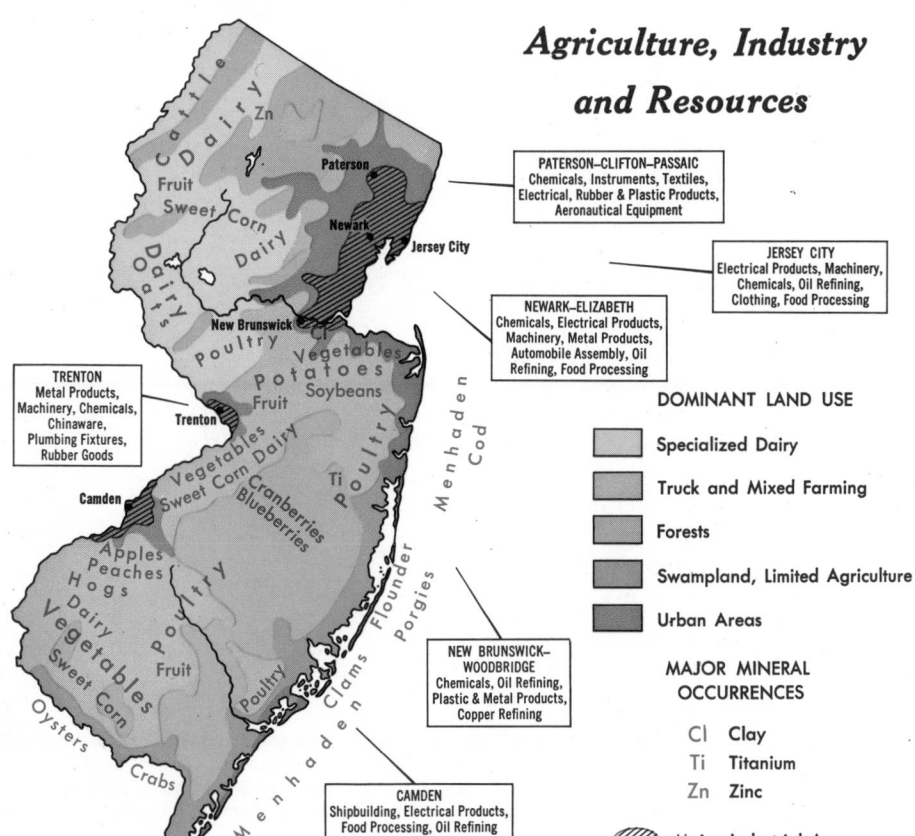

PATERSON–CLIFTON–PASSAIC
Chemicals, Instruments, Textiles, Electrical, Rubber & Plastic Products, Aeronautical Equipment

JERSEY CITY
Electrical Products, Machinery, Chemicals, Oil Refining, Clothing, Food Processing

NEWARK–ELIZABETH
Chemicals, Electrical Products, Machinery, Metal Products, Automobile Assembly, Oil Refining, Food Processing

TRENTON
Metal Products, Machinery, Chemicals, Chinaware, Plumbing Fixtures, Rubber Goods

NEW BRUNSWICK–WOODBRIDGE
Chemicals, Oil Refining, Plastic & Metal Products, Copper Refining

CAMDEN
Shipbuilding, Electrical Products, Food Processing, Oil Refining

DOMINANT LAND USE

Specialized Dairy

Truck and Mixed Farming

Forests

Swampland, Limited Agriculture

Urban Areas

MAJOR MINERAL OCCURRENCES

Cl Clay
Ti Titanium
Zn Zinc

Major Industrial Areas

Topography

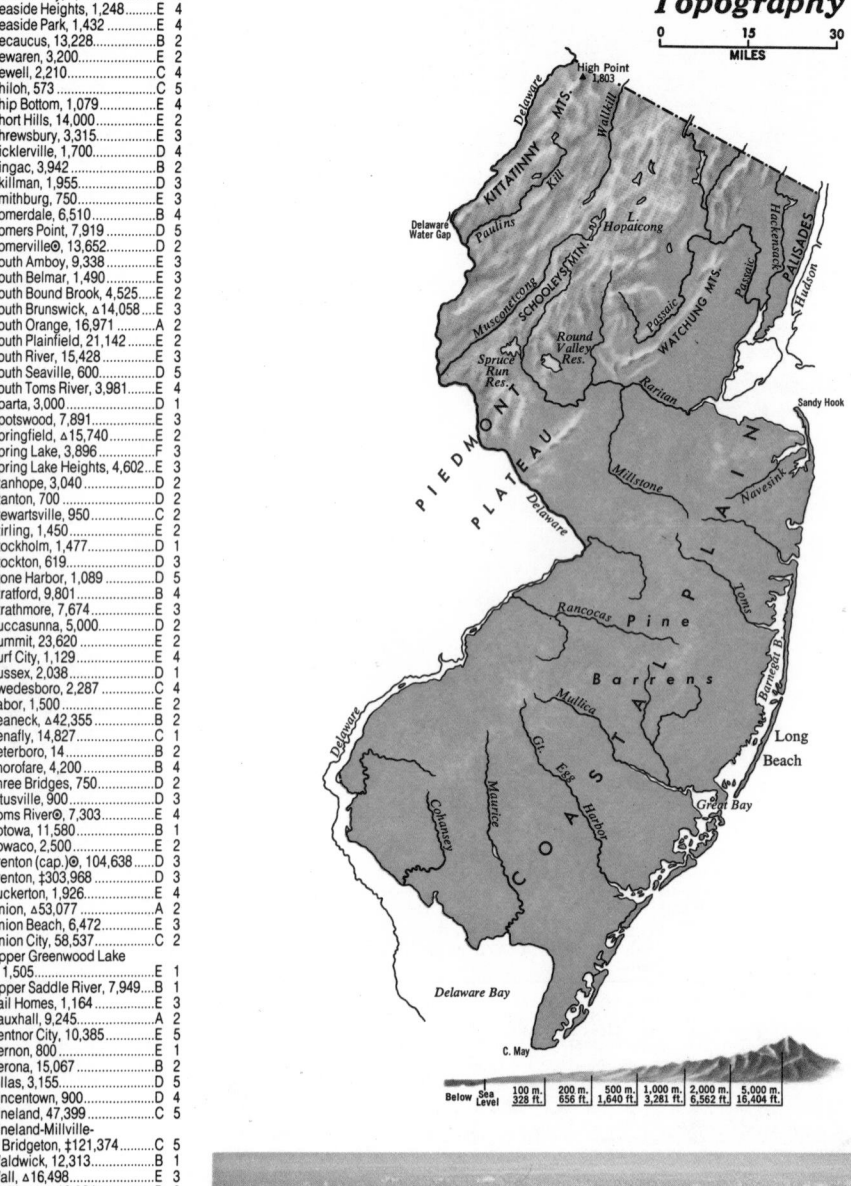

Below Sea Level | 100 m. 328 ft. | 200 m. 656 ft. | 500 m. 1,640 ft. | 1,000 m. 3,281 ft. | 2,000 m. 6,562 ft. | 5,000 m. 16,404 ft.

New Jersey towns become suburbs of Manhattan, thanks to connecting links like the Holland and Lincoln Tunnels and the George Washington Bridge. Scene above is the Fort Lee approach to the Bridge.

Michael Lewy — Shostal Associates

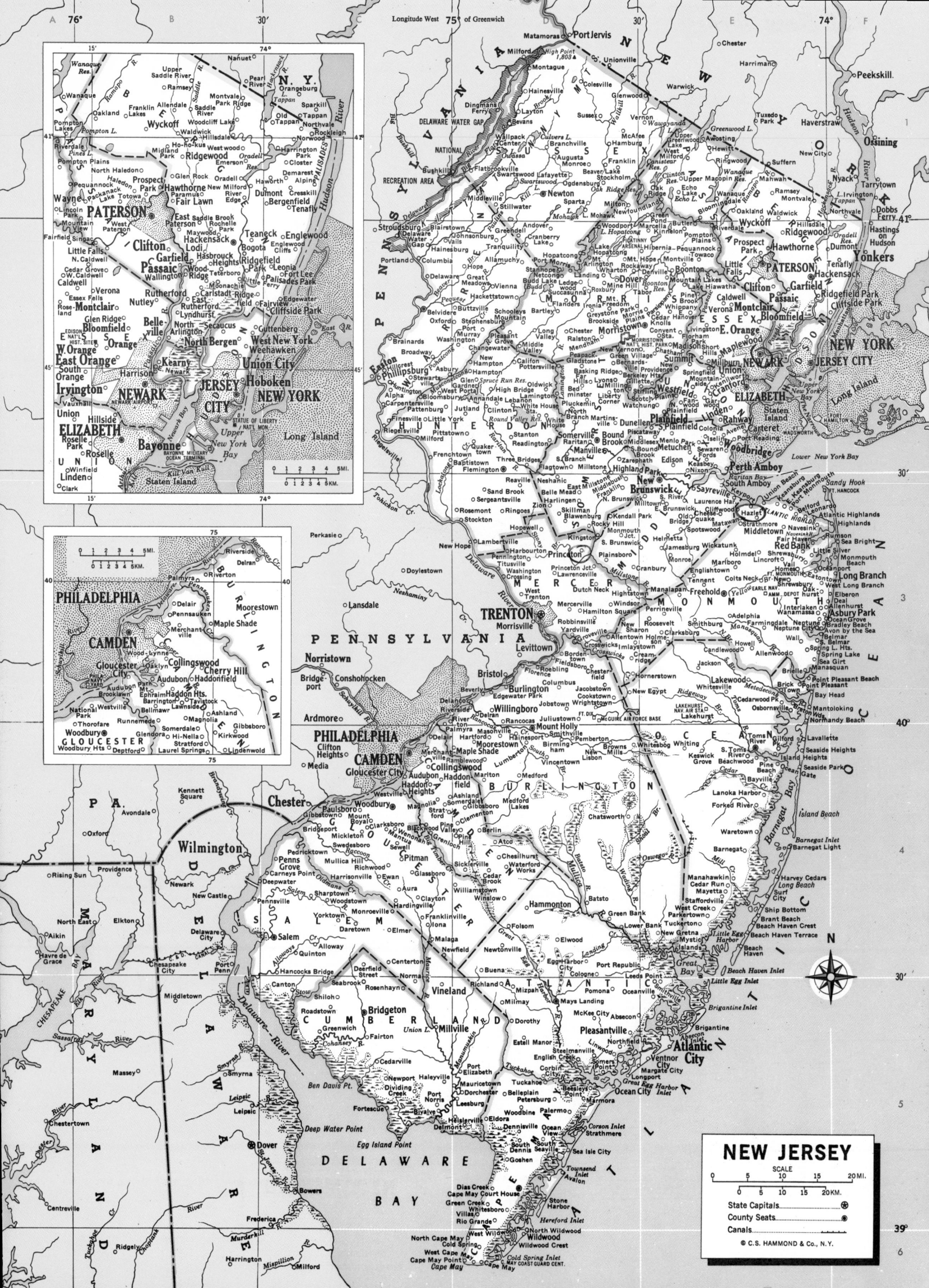

NEW JERSEY

SCALE

0 5 10 15 20 MI.

0 5 10 15 20 KM.

State Capitals........⊛

County Seats.........◉

Canals...................

© C.S. HAMMOND & Co., N.Y.

COUNTIES

Bernalillo, 315,774	C 4	
Catron, 2,198	A 4	
Chaves, 43,335	E 5	
Colfax, 12,170	E 2	
Curry, 39,517	F 4	
De Baca, 2,547	E 4	
Dona Ana, 69,773	C 6	
Eddy, 41,119	E 6	
Grant, 22,030	A 6	
Guadalupe, 4,969	E 4	
Harding, 1,348	F 3	
Hidalgo, 4,734	A 7	
Lea, 49,554	F 6	
Lincoln, 7,560	D 5	
Los Alamos, 15,198	C 3	
Luna, 11,706	B 6	
McKinley, 43,208	A 3	
Mora, 4,673	E 3	
Otero, 41,097	D 6	
Quay, 10,903	F 3	
Rio Arriba, 25,170	B 2	

Roosevelt, 16,479	F 4
Sandoval, 17,492	C 3
San Juan, 52,517	A 2
San Miguel, 21,951	D 3
Santa Fe, 53,756	C 3
Sierra, 7,189	B 5
Socorro, 9,763	C 5
Taos, 17,516	D 2
Torrance, 5,290	D 4
Union, 4,925	F 2
Valencia, 40,539	A 4

CITIES and TOWNS

Zip	Name/Pop.	Key
87510	Abiquiu, 310	C 2
† 87049	Acoma, 150	B 4
† 87049	Acomita, 975	B 4
87114	Alameda, 5,000	C 3
88310	Alamogordo⊙, 23,035	C 6
* 87101	Albuquerque⊙, 243,751	C 3
	Alburquerque⊙, ★315,774	C 3
87511	Alcalde, 975	C 2

Zip	Name/Pop.	Key
87001	Algodones, 195	C 3
88312	Alto, 104	D 5
87512	Amalia, 200	D 2
88020	Animas, 75	A 7
88021	Anthony, 1,728	C 6
† 87711	Anton Chico, 600	D 3
† 88351	Arabela, 65	D 5
87820	Aragon, 85	A 5
87930	Arrey, 367	B 6
87513	Arroyo Hondo, 400	D 2
87514	Arroyo Seco, 500	D 2
87210	Artesia, 10,315	E 6
88023	Bayard, 2,908	A 6
87002	Belen, 4,823	C 4
88334	Bent, 157	D 5
88024	Berino, 300	C 6
87004	Bernalillo, 2,016	C 3
87815	Bingham, 60	C 5
87412	Blanco, 150	B 2
87413	Bloomfield, 1,574	A 2
87005	Bluewater, 300	A 3
87006	Bosque, 300	C 4

Zip	Name/Pop.	Key
87712	Buena Vista, 178	D 3
87515	Canjilon, 300	C 2
87516	Canones, 200	C 2
88316	Capitan, 439	D 5
88414	Capulin, 100	F 2
88220	Carlsbad⊙, 21,297	E 6
88301	Carrizozo⊙, 1,123	D 5
87007	Casa Blanca, 560	B 4
88113	Causey, 150	F 4
87518	Cebolla, 150	C 2
87008	Cedar Crest, 600	C 3
† 87410	Cedar Hill, 145	B 2
88026	Central, 1,864	A 6
87010	Cerrillos, 118	D 3
87519	Cerro, 400	D 2
87713	Chacon, 200	D 3
87520	Chama, 899	C 2
88027	Chamberino, 400	C 6
88021	Chamisal, 637	D 2
† 87059	Chilili, 80	C 4
87522	Chimayo, 900	D 3
87714	Cimarron, 927	E 3
88415	Clayton⊙, 2,931	F 2

Zip	Name/Pop.	Key
87715	Cleveland, 500	D 2
88028	Cliff, 350	A 6
88317	Cloudcroft, 525	D 6
88101	Clovis⊙, 28,495	F 4
† 87041	Cochiti, 300	C 3
88029	Columbus, 241	B 7
88416	Conchas Dam, 192	D 3
87523	Cordova, 600	D 2
88318	Corona, 262	D 4
87048	Corrales, 975	C 3
87524	Costilla, 400	D 2
87012	Coyote, 125	C 2
87313	Crownpoint, 876	A 3
† 86504	Crystal, 200	A 2
87013	Cuba, 750	B 2
87014	Cubero, 300	B 3
88417	Cuervo, 150	E 3
87522	Cundiyo, 98	D 3
87821	Datil, 150	A 4
88030	Deming, 8,343	B 6
87933	Derry, 75	B 6
88418	Des Moines, 204	F 2
88230	Dexter, 746	E 5

Zip	Name/Pop.	Key
† 87711	Dilia, 125	D 3
87527	Dixon, 640	D 2
88032	Dona Ana, 800	C 6
88115	Dora, 196	F 5
87528	Dulce, 450	B 2
88319	Duran, 100	D 4
87718	Eagle Nest, 300	D 2
87015	Edgewood, 75	C 3
87935	Elephant Butte, 75	B 5
88116	Elida, 233	F 5
† 87731	El Porvenir, 90	D 3
87529	El Prado, 200	D 2
87530	El Rito, 475	C 2
87531	Embudo, 400	D 2
88321	Encino, 250	D 4
87532	Espanola, 4,528	C 2
87016	Estancia, 721	C 4
88231	Eunice, 2,641	F 6
88033	Fairacres, 500	C 6
87720	Farley, 81	E 2
87401	Farmington, 21,979	A 2
88034	Faywood, 75	A 6
† 88041	Fierro, 200	A 6

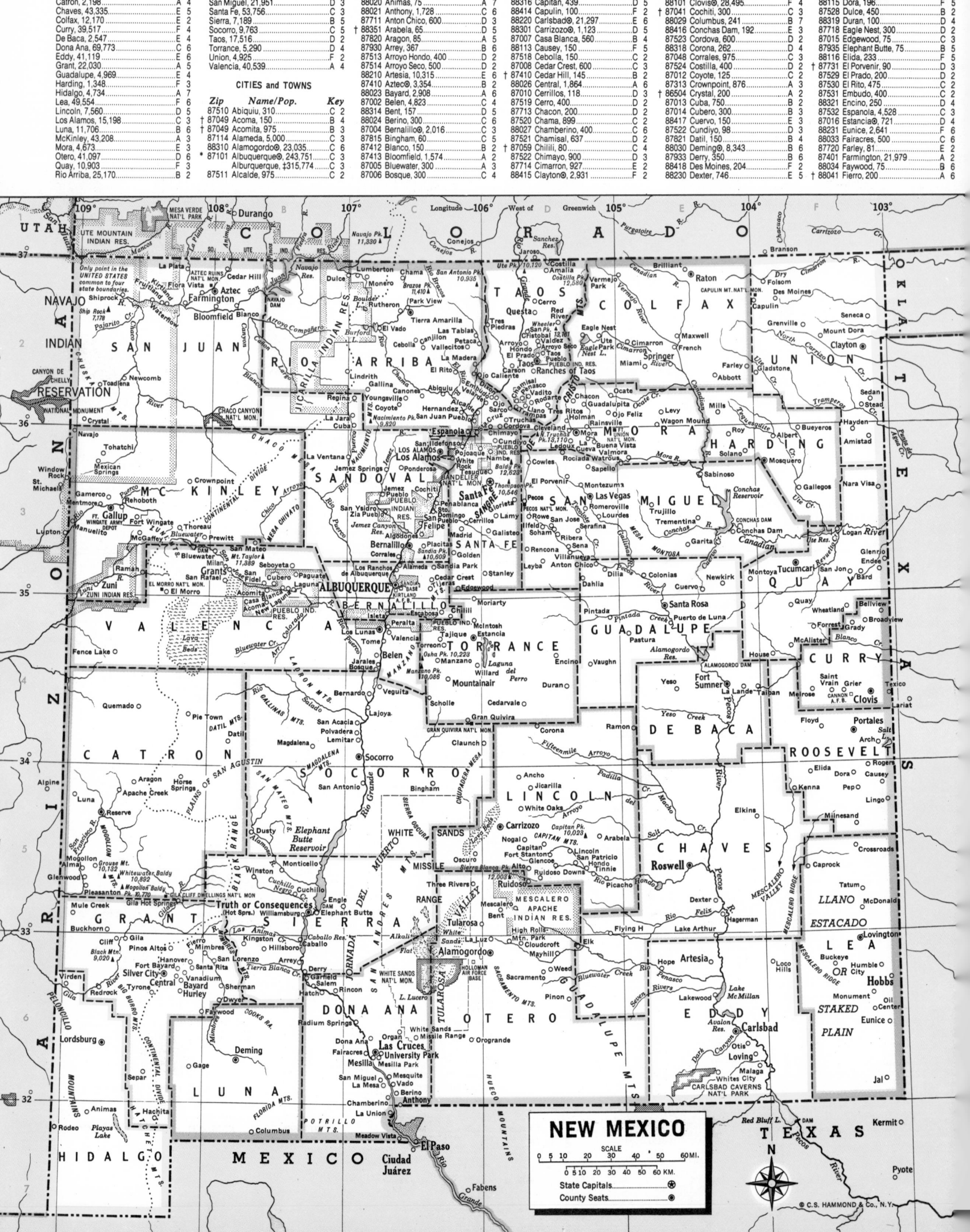

NEW MEXICO

SCALE
0 5 10 20 30 40 50 60 MI.
0 5 10 20 30 40 50 60 KM.

State Capitals ⊛
County Seats ⊙

© C.S. HAMMOND & Co., N.Y.

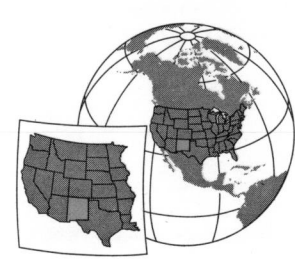

Golden adobe against the blue Sangre de Cristo Mountains. Clear, pure colors, magnificent surroundings and congenial atmosphere combine to draw artists and writers to Taos, New Mexico.

AREA 121,666 sq. mi.
POPULATION 1,016,000
CAPITAL Santa Fe
LARGEST CITY Albuquerque
HIGHEST POINT Wheeler Pk. 13,161 ft.
SETTLED IN 1605
ADMITTED TO UNION January 6, 1912
POPULAR NAME Land of Enchantment
STATE FLOWER Yucca
STATE BIRD Road Runner

Topography

0 50 100 MILES

Below Sea Level | 100 m. 328 ft. | 200 m. 656 ft. | 500 m. 1,640 ft. | 1,000 m. 3,281 ft. | 2,000 m. 6,562 ft. | 5,000 m. 16,404 ft.

Agriculture, Industry and Resources

DOMINANT LAND USE

Wheat, Grain Sorghums, Range Livestock

General Farming, Livestock, Special Crops

General Farming, Livestock, Cash Grain

Dry Beans, General Farming

Cotton, Forest Products

Range Livestock

Forests

Nonagricultural Land

MAJOR MINERAL OCCURRENCES

Ag Silver
Au Gold
C Coal
Cu Copper
G Natural Gas
Gp Gypsum
K Potash
Mo Molybdenum
Mr Marble
Na Salt
O Petroleum
Pb Lead
U Uranium
V Vanadium
Zn Zinc
⚡ Water Power

NEW YORK

SCALE
0 5 10 20 30 40 MI.
0 5 10 20 30 40 KM.

State Capitals........⊛
County Seats..........◉
Canals................

© C.S. HAMMOND & Co., N.Y.

COUNTIES

County	Pop.	Key
Albany, 285,618		M 5
Allegany, 46,458		D 6
Bronx, 1,472,216		N 9
Broome, 221,815		J 6
Cattaraugus, 81,666		C 6
Cayuga, 77,439		G 4
Chautauqua, 147,305		B 6
Chemung, 101,537		G 6
Chenango, 46,368		J 6
Clinton, 72,934		N 1
Columbia, 51,519		N 6
Cortland, 45,894		H 5
Delaware, 44,718		K 6
Dutchess, 222,295		N 7
Erie, 1,113,491		C 5
Essex, 34,631		N 2
Franklin, 43,931		M 1
Fulton, 52,637		M 4
Genesee, 58,722		D 4
Greene, 33,136		M 6
Hamilton, 4,714		L 3
Herkimer, 67,440		L 4
Jefferson, 88,508		J 2
Kings, 2,601,852		N 9
Lewis, 23,644		K 3
Livingston, 54,041		E 5
Madison, 62,864		J 5
Monroe, 711,917		E 4
Montgomery, 55,883		M 5
Nassau, 1,422,905		N 9
New York, 1,524,541		N 9
Niagara, 235,720		C 4
Oneida, 273,037		J 4
Onondaga, 472,185		H 5
Ontario, 78,849		F 5
Orange, 220,558		M 8
Orleans, 37,305		D 4

County	Pop.	Key
Oswego, 100,897		H 4
Otsego, 56,181		K 5
Putnam, 56,696		N 8
Queens, 1,973,708		N 9
Rensselaer, 152,510		O 5
Richmond, 295,443		M 9
Rockland, 229,903		N 8
Saint Lawrence, 111,991		K 2
Saratoga, 121,679		N 4
Schenectady, 160,979		M 5
Schoharie, 24,750		M 5
Schuyler, 16,737		G 6
Seneca, 35,083		G 5
Steuben, 99,546		F 6
Suffolk, 1,116 672		O 9
Sullivan, 52,580		L 7
Tioga, 46,513		H 6
Tompkins, 76,879		H 6
Ulster, 141,241		M 7
Warren, 49,402		N 3
Washington, 52,725		O 4
Wayne, 79,404		F 4
Westchester, 891,409		N 8
Wyoming, 37,688		D 5
Yates, 19,831		F 5

CITIES and TOWNS

Zip	Name/Pop.	Key
13605	Adams, 1,951	J 3
13606	Adams Center, 900	H 3
14801	Addison, 2,104	F 6
13730	Afton, 1,064	J 6
14001	Akron, 2,863	C 4
*12201	Albany (cap.)◉, 114,873	N 5
	Albany-Schenectady-Troy, ‡720,786	N 5
14411	Albion◉, 5,122	D 4
14004	Alden, 2,651	C 5
10507	Bedford Hills, 3,900	N 8

Zip	Name/Pop.	Key
13607	Alexandria Bay, 1,440	J 2
14802	Alfred, 3,804	E 6
14706	Allegany, 2,050	C 6
12009	Altamont, 1,561	M 5
11930	Amagansett, 900	R 9
12501	Amenia, 1,157	N 7
11701	Amityville, 9,857	O 9
*12010	Amsterdam◉, 25,524	M 5
14806	Andover, 1,214	E 6
14709	Angelica, 948	D 6
14006	Angola, 2,676	C 5
13732	Apalachin, 1,233	H 6
14009	Arcade, 1,972	D 5
10502	Ardsley, 4,470	O 7
14807	Arkport, 984	E 6
12603	Arlington, 11,203	N 7
12015	Athens, 1,718	N 6
14808	Atlanta, 900	F 5
11509	Atlantic Beach, 1,640	N 9
14011	Attica, 2,911	D 5
13021	Auburn◉, 34,599	G 5
13026	Aurora, 1,072	G 5
12912	Au Sable Forks, 1,900	N 2
12018	Averill Park, 1,471	O 5
14809	Avoca, 1,153	F 6
14414	Avon, 3,260	E 5
*11702	Babylon, 12,588	O 9
13733	Bainbridge, 1,674	J 6
11510	Baldwin, 34,525	R 7
13027	Baldwinsville, 6,298	H 4
12020	Ballston Spa◉, 4,968	N 5
†12550	Balmville, 3,214	M 7
14020	Batavia◉, 17,338	D 5
14810	Bath◉, 6,053	F 6
11705	Bayport, 7,995	O 9
11706	Bay Shore, 11,119	O 9
11709	Bayville, 6,147	R 6
12508	Beacon, 13,255	N 7

Zip	Name/Pop.	Key
11426	Bellerose, 1,654	R 7
11710	Bellmore, 18,431	R 7
11713	Bellport, 3,046	P 9
14813	Belmont◉, 1,102	E 6
14416	Bergen, 1,018	E 4
12022	Berlin, 975	O 5
14814	Big Flats, 2,509	G 6
*13901	Binghamton◉, 64,123	J 6
	Binghamton, ‡302,672	J 6
13612	Black River, 1,307	J 3
14219	Blasdell, 3,910	C 5
14024	Bliss, 950	D 5
14715	Bolivar, 1,379	D 6
12814	Bolton Landing, 950	N 3
13309	Boonville, 2,488	K 4
14025	Boston, 950	C 5
12815	Brant Lake, 1,200	N 3
13613	Brasher Falls, 950	L 1
14816	Breesport, 950	G 6
11717	Brentwood, 27,868	O 9
13029	Brewerton, 1,985	H 4
10509	Brewster, 1,638	N 8
11932	Bridgehampton, 900	R 9
12025	Broadalbin, 1,452	M 4
14420	Brockport, 7,878	D 4
14716	Brocton, 1,450	B 6
10401	Bronx (borough)◉, 1,472,216	N 9
10708	Bronxville, 6,674	O 7
*11201	Brooklyn◉, 2,601,852	N 9
13615	Brownville, 1,187	H 3
10511	Buchanan, 2,110	N 8
*14201	Buffalo◉, 462,768	B 5
	Buffalo, ‡1,349,211	B 5
12413	Cairo, 950	M 6
14423	Caledonia, 2,327	E 5
12723	Callicoon, 950	K 7
13624	Clayton, 1,970	J 3

Zip	Name/Pop.	Key
13031	Camillus, 1,534	H 4
13317	Canajoharie, 2,686	L 5
14424	Canandaigua◉, 10,488	F 5
13032	Canastota, 5,033	J 4
13743	Candor, 939	H 6
14823	Canisteo, 2,772	E 6
13617	Canton◉, 6,398	K 1
10512	Carmel◉, 3,395	N 8
13619	Carthage, 3,889	J 3
14718	Cassadaga, 905	B 6
14427	Castile, 1,330	D 5
12033	Castleton-on-Hudson, 1,730	N 5
12414	Catskill◉, 5,317	N 6
14719	Cattaraugus, 1,200	C 6
13035	Cazenovia, 3,031	J 5
11516	Cedarhurst, 6,941	R 7
14720	Celoron, 1,456	B 6
11720	Centereach, 9,427	O 9
11934	Center Moriches, 3,802	P 9
11722	Central Islip, 36,369	O 9
13036	Central Square, 1,298	H 4
10917	Central Valley, 975	M 8
13319	Chadwicks, 975	K 4
12919	Champlain, 1,426	N 1
12920	Chateaugay, 976	M 1
12037	Chatham, 2,239	N 6
14225	Chautauqua, 500	A 6
14225	Cheektowaga, △113,844	C 5
13745	Chenango Bridge, 5,059	J 6
10918	Chester, 1,627	M 8
12817	Chestertown, 950	N 3
13037	Chittenango, 3,605	J 4
14428	Churchville, 1,065	E 4
13040	Cincinnatus, 900	J 5
14031	Clarence, 2,014	C 5
14430	Clarkson, 1,300	D 4
†12118	Clifton Park, △14,867	N 5

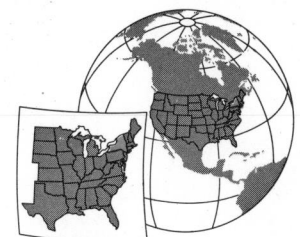

AREA 49,576 sq. mi.
POPULATION 18,241,266
CAPITAL Albany
LARGEST CITY New York
HIGHEST POINT Mt. Marcy 5,344 ft.
SETTLED IN 1614
ADMITTED TO UNION July 26, 1788
POPULAR NAME Empire State
STATE FLOWER Rose
STATE BIRD Bluebird

Topography

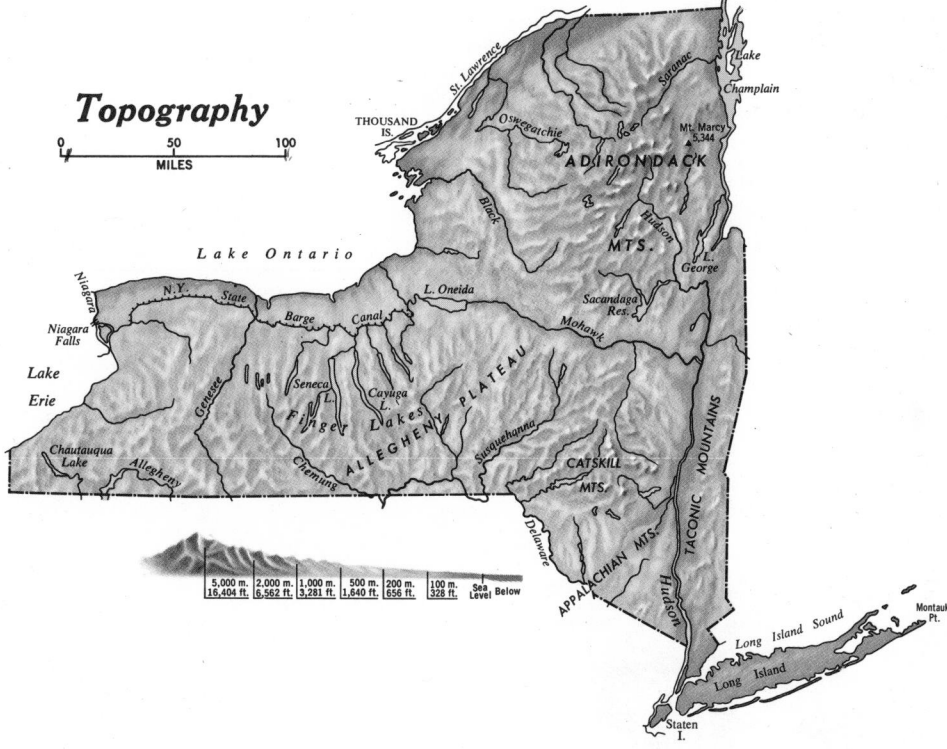

14432 Clifton Springs, 2,058	F 4	
13323 Clinton, 2,271	K 4	
14433 Clyde, 2,828	G 4	
12043 Cobleskill, 4,368	L 5	
12045 Coeymans, 975	N 6	
12047 Cohoes, 18,613	N 5	
14033 Colden, 950	C 5	
10516 Cold Spring, 2,083	N 8	
† 12201 Colonie, 8,701	N 5	
13326 Cooperstown⊙, 2,403	L 5	
12822 Corinth, 3,267	N 4	
14830 Corning, 15,792	F 6	
12518 Cornwall, 2,032	M 8	
13045 Cortland, 19,621	H 5	
12051 Coxsackie, 2,399	N 6	
10519 Croton Falls, 950	N 8	
10520 Croton-on-Hudson, 7,523	N 8	
14727 Cuba, 1,735	D 6	
12929 Dannemora, 3,735	N 1	
14437 Dansville, 5,436	E 5	
11729 Deer Park, 31,120	O 9	
14042 Delevan, 994	D 6	
12753 Delhi⊙, 3,017	L 6	
12054 Delmar, 7,500	N 5	
14043 Depew, 22,158	C 5	
13754 Deposit, 2,061	K 6	
14047 Derby, 4,900	B 5	
13214 DeWitt, 10,032	H 4	
13634 Dexter, 1,061	J 2	
10522 Dobbs Ferry, 10,353	O 6	
13329 Dolgeville, 2,872	L 4	
12522 Dover Plains, 975	O 7	
13053 Dryden, 1,490	H 6	
14837 Dundee, 1,539	F 5	
14048 Dunkirk, 16,855	B 5	
13054 Durhamville, 975	J 4	
13332 Earlville, 1,050	J 5	
14052 East Aurora, 7,033	C 5	
12061 East Greenbush, 985	N 5	
11937 East Hampton, 1,753	R 8	
11554 East Meadow, 46,252	R 7	
11940 East Moriches, 1,702	P 9	
11731 East Northport, 12,392	O 9	
11941 Eastport, 1,308	P 9	
14445 East Rochester, 8,347	F 4	
11518 East Rockaway, 10,323	R 7	
13057 East Syracuse, 4,333	H 4	
14057 Eden, 2,962	C 5	
† 14226 Eggertsville, 55,000	C 5	
13060 Elbridge, 1,040	G 5	
12932 Elizabethtown⊙, 607	N 2	
12428 Ellenville, 4,482	M 7	
14731 Ellicottville, 955	C 6	
14059 Elma, 2,784	C 5	
* 14901 Elmira⊙, 39,945	G 6	
14903 Elmira Heights, 4,906	G 6	
11003 Elmont, 29,363	R 7	
10523 Elmsford, 3,911	O 6	
13760 Endicott, 16,556	H 6	
13760 Endwell, 15,999	H 6	
14450 Fairport, 6,474	F 4	
† 12601 Fairview, 8,517	N 7	
14733 Falconer, 2,983	B 6	
11735 Farmingdale, 9,297	N 9	
13066 Fayetteville, 4,996	J 4	
12524 Fishkill, 913	N 7	
* 11001 Floral Park, 18,422	R 7	
10921 Florida, 1,674	M 8	
13337 Fly Creek, 910	K 5	
12068 Fonda⊙, 1,120	M 5	
14062 Forestville, 908	B 6	
12937 Fort Covington, 983	M 1	
12828 Fort Edward, 3,733	O 4	
13339 Fort Plain, 2,809	L 5	
13340 Frankfort, 3,305	K 4	
14737 Franklinville, 1,948	D 6	
14063 Fredonia, 10,326	B 6	
11520 Freeport, 40,374	R 7	
14738 Frewsburg, 1,772	B 6	
14739 Friendship, 1,285	D 6	
13069 Fulton, 14,003	H 4	
11530 Garden City, 25,373	R 7	
10524 Garrison, 975	N 8	
14067 Gasport, 950	C 4	
14454 Geneseo⊙, 5,714	E 5	
14456 Geneva, 16,793	G 5	
14740 Gerry, 950	B 6	
12432 Glasco, 1,169	M 6	
11542 Glen Cove, 25,770	R 7	
11545 Glen Head, 4,000	R 7	
12801 Glens Falls, 17,222	N 4	
12078 Gloversville, 19,677	M 4	
10526 Golden's Bridge, 1,101	N 8	
10924 Goshen⊙, 4,342	M 8	
13642 Gouverneur, 4,574	K 2	
14070 Gowanda, 3,110	B 6	
12434 Grand Gorge, 950	L 6	
14072 Grand Island, 900	B 5	
12832 Granville, 2,784	O 4	
* 11020 Great Neck, 10,724	R 7	
14616 Greene, ∆75,136	E 4	
13778 Greene, 1,874	J 6	
12183 Green Island, 3,297	N 5	
11944 Greenport, 2,481	R 8	
12834 Greenwich, 2,092	O 4	
10925 Greenwood Lake, 2,262	M 8	
13073 Groton, 2,112	H 5	
13780 Guilford, 995	J 6	
12086 Hagaman, 1,410	M 5	
14075 Hamburg, 10,215	C 5	
13346 Hamilton, 3,636	J 5	
14840 Hammondsport, 1,066	F 6	
11946 Hampton Bays, 1,862	P 9	
13783 Hancock, 1,688	K 7	
10926 Harriman, 955	M 8	
14926 Harrison, 9,250	P 7	
10706 Hastings on Hudson, 9,479	O 6	
10927 Haverstraw, 8,198	M 8	
14532 Hawthorne, 5,000	O 6	
* 11550 Hempstead, 39,411	R 7	
13650 Henderson, 900	H 3	
13350 Herkimer⊙, 8,960	L 4	

(continued on following page)

(continued)

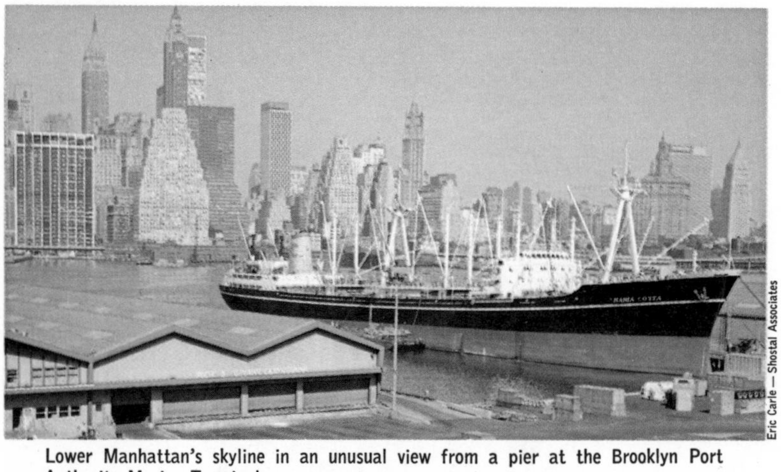
Eric Carle—Shostal Associates

Lower Manhattan's skyline in an unusual view from a pier at the Brooklyn Port Authority Marine Terminal.

11557 Hewlett, 6,796 ....R 7
* 11801 Hicksville, 48,075 ....R 7
12440 High Falls, 950 ....M 7
12528 Highland, 2,184 ....M 7
10928 Highland Falls, 4,638 ....M 8
10931 Hillburn, 1,058 ....M 8
14468 Hilton, 2,440 ....E 4
14080 Holland, 950 ....C 5
14470 Holley, 1,868 ....D 4
13077 Homer, 4,143 ....H 5
14472 Honeoye Falls, 2,248 ....F 5
12090 Hoosick Falls, 3,897 ....O 5
12533 Hopewell Junction, 2,055 ....N 7
14843 Hornell, 12,144 ....E 6
14845 Horseheads, 7,989 ....G 6
14744 Houghton, 1,620 ....D 6
12534 Hudson⊙, 8,940 ....N 6
12839 Hudson Falls⊙, 7,917 ....O 4
11743 Huntington, 12,130 ....O 9
11746 Huntington Station, 28,817 ....O 9
12443 Hurley, 4,081 ....M 7
12538 Hyde Park, 2,805 ....N 6
13357 Ilion, 9,808 ....K 5
12842 Indian Lake, 950 ....M 3
11696 Inwood, 8,433 ....R 7
14617 Irondequoit, ∆63,675 ....E 4
10533 Irvington, 5,878 ....O 6
11558 Island Park, 5,396 ....R 8
11751 Islip, 7,962 ....O 9
14850 Ithaca⊙, 26,226 ....G 6
* 11401 Jamaica⊙, 765,078 ....N 9
14701 Jamestown, 39,795 ....B 6
13078 Jamesville, 900 ....H 5
11753 Jericho, 14,010 ....S 7
13790 Johnson City, 18,025 ....J 6
12095 Johnstown⊙, 10,045 ....M 4
13080 Jordan, 1,493 ....H 4
10536 Katonah, 4,189 ....N 8
12944 Keeseville, 2,122 ....O 2
14271 Kenmore, 20,980 ....C 5
14747 Kennedy, 950 ....B 6
12446 Kerhonkson, 1,243 ....M 7
14478 Keuka Park, 990 ....F 5
12106 Kinderhook, 1,233 ....N 6
* 11201 Kings (Brooklyn) (borough), 2,601,852 ....N 9
11754 Kings Park, 5,555 ....O 9
11024 Kings Point, 5,525 ....R 7
12401 Kingston⊙, 25,544 ....M 7
14218 Lackawanna, 28,657 ....B 5
10512 Lake Carmel, 4,796 ....N 8
12845 Lake George⊙, 1,046 ....N 4
12449 Lake Katrine, 1,092 ....M 7
12846 Lake Luzerne, 900 ....N 4
12946 Lake Placid, 2,731 ....N 2
12108 Lake Pleasant⊙, 364 ....M 4
11040 Lake Success, 3,254 ....R 7
14085 Lake View, 6,000 ....B 5
14750 Lakewood, 3,864 ....B 6
14086 Lancaster, 13,365 ....C 5
10538 Larchmont, 7,203 ....P 7
11559 Lawrence, 6,566 ....R 7
14482 Le Roy, 5,118 ....E 5
11756 Levittown, 65,440 ....S 7
14092 Lewiston, 3,292 ....B 4
12754 Liberty, 4,293 ....L 7
14485 Lima, 1,686 ....E 5
11757 Lindenhurst, 28,338 ....O 9
13365 Little Falls, 7,629 ....L 4
14755 Little Valley⊙, 1,340 ....C 6
13088 Liverpool, 3,307 ....H 4
12758 Livingston Manor, 1,522 ....L 7
14487 Livonia, 1,278 ....E 5
14094 Lockport⊙, 25,399 ....C 4
11561 Long Beach, 33,127 ....R 8
13367 Lowville, 3,671 ....J 3
11563 Lynbrook, 23,776 ....R 7
12952 Lyon Mountain, 1,200 ....N 1
14489 Lyons⊙, 4,496 ....F 4
14502 Macedon, 1,168 ....F 4
13660 Madrid, 950 ....K 1
10541 Mahopac, 5,265 ....N 8
13103 Mallory, 900 ....H 4
12953 Malone⊙, 8,048 ....M 1
11565 Malverne, 10,036 ....R 7
10543 Mamaroneck, 18,909 ....P 7
14504 Manchester, 1,305 ....F 5
11030 Manhasset, 8,541 ....R 7
* 10001 Manhattan (borough), 1,524,541 ....M 9
13104 Manlius, 4,295 ....J 5
13803 Marathon, 1,053 ....J 6
13108 Marcellus, 1,456 ....H 5
13403 Marcy, 2,417 ....K 4
14505 Marion, 925 ....F 4
12542 Marlboro, 1,580 ....M 7
11758 Massapequa, 26,951 ....O 9
11762 Massapequa Park, 22,112 ....O 9
13662 Massena, 14,042 ....L 1
11950 Mastic Beach, 4,870 ....P 9
11952 Mattituck, 1,995 ....P 9
12543 Maybrook, 1,536 ....M 8
12117 Mayfield, 981 ....M 4
14757 Mayville⊙, 1,567 ....A 6
13101 McGraw, 1,319 ....H 5
12118 Mechanicville, 6,247 ....N 5
14103 Medina, 6,415 ....D 4
† 13021 Melrose Park, 2,189 ....G 5
† 12201 Menands, 3,449 ....N 5
11566 Merrick, 25,904 ....S 7
13114 Mexico, 1,555 ....H 4
12122 Middleburg, 1,410 ....M 5
12550 Middle Hope, 2,327 ....M 7
14105 Middleport, 2,132 ....C 4
10940 Middletown, 22,607 ....L 8
12545 Millbrook, 1,735 ....N 7
12546 Millerton, 1,042 ....O 7
11765 Mill Neck, 982 ....R 6
12547 Milton, 1,900 ....M 7
12547 Milton, 1,861 ....N 4
11501 Mineola⊙, 21,845 ....R 7
13115 Minetto, 950 ....H 4
12956 Mineville-Witherbee, 1,967 ....O 2
13407 Mohawk, 3,301 ....L 4
10950 Monroe, 4,439 ....M 8
12549 Montgomery, 1,533 ....M 7
12701 Monticello⊙, 5,991 ....L 7
14865 Montour Falls, 1,534 ....G 6
13118 Moravia, 1,642 ....H 5
12960 Moriah, 953 ....N 2
12962 Morrisonville, 1,276 ....N 1
13408 Morrisville, 2,296 ....J 5
12763 Mountain Dale, 950 ....L 7
10549 Mount Kisco, 8,172 ....N 8
14510 Mount Morris, 3,417 ....E 5
* 10550 Mount Vernon, 72,778 ....O 7
12458 Napanoch, 975 ....M 7
14512 Naples, 1,324 ....F 5
12123 Nassau, 1,466 ....N 5
14513 Newark, 11,644 ....G 4
13811 Newark Valley, 1,286 ....H 6
13411 New Berlin, 1,369 ....K 5
12550 Newburgh, 26,219 ....M 7
10956 New City⊙, 27,344 ....N 8
14108 Newfane, 2,588 ....C 4
13413 New Hartford, 2,433 ....K 4
11040 New Hyde Park, 10,116 ....R 7
12561 New Paltz, 6,058 ....M 7
13416 Newport, 908 ....K 4
* 10801 New Rochelle, 75,385 ....P 7
12550 New Windsor, 8,803 ....N 8
* 10001 New York (5 boroughs)⊙, 7,867,760 ....M 9
New York, ‡11,517,483 ....M 9
13417 New York Mills, 3,805 ....K 4
* 14301 Niagara Falls, 85,615 ....C 4
12309 Niskayuna, 6,186 ....N 5
13667 Norfolk, 1,379 ....K 1
14110 North Boston, 1,635 ....C 5
14514 North Chili, 3,163 ....E 4
14111 North Collins, 1,675 ....C 5
15853 North Creek, 950 ....M 3
14113 North Java, 950 ....D 5
11768 Northport, 7,440 ....O 9
13212 North Syracuse, 8,687 ....H 4
10591 North Tarrytown, 8,334 ....O 6
14120 North Tonawanda, 36,012 ....C 4
12134 Northville, 1,192 ....M 4
13815 Norwich⊙, 8,843 ....J 5
13668 Norwood, 2,098 ....L 1
14517 Nunda, 1,254 ....E 5
10960 Nyack, 6,659 ....N 8
14125 Oakfield, 1,964 ....D 4
11572 Oceanside, 35,028 ....R 7
13669 Ogdensburg, 14,554 ....K 1
14126 Olcott, 1,592 ....C 4
13420 Old Forge, 950 ....L 3
14760 Olean, 19,169 ....D 6
13421 Oneida, 11,658 ....J 4
13820 Oneonta, 16,030 ....K 6
14127 Orchard Park, 3,732 ....C 5
13424 Oriskany, 1,627 ....K 4
13425 Oriskany Falls, 927 ....J 5
10562 Ossining, 21,659 ....N 8
13126 Oswego⊙, 23,844 ....G 4
13825 Otego, 956 ....K 6
10963 Otisville, 933 ....L 8
14521 Ovid⊙, 779 ....G 5
13827 Owego⊙, 5,152 ....H 6
13830 Oxford, 1,944 ....J 6
11771 Oyster Bay, 14,330 ....S 6
14870 Painted Post, 2,496 ....F 6
14522 Palmyra, 3,776 ....F 4
12768 Parksville, 950 ....L 7
11772 Patchogue, 11,582 ....P 9
12563 Patterson, 975 ....N 7
12137 Pattersonville, 950 ....M 5
12564 Pawling, 1,914 ....N 7
10965 Pearl River, 17,146 ....M 8
10566 Peekskill, 18,881 ....N 8
† 10803 Pelham Manor, 6,673 ....O 7
14526 Penfield, 8,904 ....F 4
14527 Penn Yan⊙, 5,168 ....F 5
14530 Perry, 4,538 ....D 5
12972 Peru, 1,261 ....N 1
14532 Phelps, 1,989 ....F 5
12565 Philmont, 1,674 ....N 6
13135 Phoenix, 2,617 ....H 4
10968 Piermont, 2,386 ....M 8
12566 Pine Bush, 1,183 ....M 7
10969 Pine Island, 925 ....L 8
12567 Pine Plains, 950 ....N 7
14534 Pittsford, 1,755 ....E 4
11803 Plainview, 32,195 ....O 9
12901 Plattsburgh⊙, 18,715 ....O 1
10570 Pleasantville, 7,110 ....N 8
13140 Port Byron, 1,330 ....G 4
10573 Port Chester, 25,803 ....P 7
12466 Port Ewen, 2,882 ....N 7
12974 Port Henry, 1,532 ....O 2
11777 Port Jefferson, 5,515 ....P 9
12771 Port Jervis, 8,852 ....L 8
14770 Portville, 1,304 ....D 6
11050 Port Washington, 15,923 ....R 6
13676 Potsdam, 9,985 ....K 1
* 12601 Poughkeepsie⊙, 32,029 ....N 7
13142 Pulaski, 2,480 ....H 3
10577 Purchase, 2,900 ....P 7
10579 Putnam Valley, ∆975 ....N 8
* 11101 Queens (borough), 1,973,708 ....N 9
11429 Queens Village, 72,000 ....R 7
14772 Randolph, 1,498 ....C 6
14131 Ransomville, 1,034 ....C 4
12143 Ravena, 2,797 ....N 6
12571 Red Hook, 1,680 ....N 7
12144 Rensselaer, 10,136 ....N 5
12572 Rhinebeck, 2,336 ....N 7
13439 Richfield Springs, 1,540 ....K 5
14775 Ripley, 1,173 ....A 6
11901 Riverhead⊙, 7,585 ....P 9
† 14830 Riverside, 911 ....F 6
* 14601 Rochester⊙, 296,233 ....E 4
Rochester, ‡882,667 ....E 4
* 11570 Rockville Centre, 27,444 ....R 7
13440 Rome, 50,148 ....J 4
11779 Ronkonkoma, 7,284 ....O 9
11575 Roosevelt, 15,008 ....R 7
12776 Roscoe, 1,300 ....L 7
12472 Rosendale, 1,220 ....M 7
11576 Roslyn, 2,546 ....R 7
12979 Rouses Point, 2,250 ....O 1
10580 Rye, 15,869 ....P 7
13685 Sackets Harbor, 1,202 ....H 3
11963 Sag Harbor, 2,363 ....R 8
10301 Saint George⊙, 13,000 ....M 9
13452 Saint Johnsville, 2,089 ....L 5
14779 Salamanca, 7,877 ....C 6
12865 Salem, 1,025 ....O 4
† 11050 Sands Point, 2,916 ....N 9
12983 Saranac Lake, 6,086 ....M 2
12866 Saratoga Springs, 18,845 ....N 4
12477 Saugerties, 4,190 ....M 6
13456 Sauquoit, 1,900 ....K 5
14879 Savona, 933 ....F 6
11782 Sayville, 11,680 ....O 9
10583 Scarsdale, 19,229 ....P 7
* 12301 Schenectady⊙, 77,859 ....M 5
12157 Schoharie⊙, 1,125 ....M 5
12870 Schroon Lake, 950 ....N 3
12871 Schuylerville, 1,402 ....N 4
12302 Scotia, 8,224 ....N 5
14546 Scottsville, 1,967 ....E 4
† 14075 Scranton, 925 ....C 5
† 14617 Sea Breeze, 1,200 ....F 4
11579 Sea Cliff, 5,890 ....R 6
13148 Seneca Falls, 7,794 ....G 5
13460 Sherburne, 1,613 ....K 5
13461 Sherrill, 2,986 ....J 4
14548 Shortsville, 1,516 ....F 5
13838 Sidney, 4,789 ....K 6
14136 Silver Creek, 3,182 ....B 5
13152 Skaneateles, 3,055 ....H 5
† 14201 Sloan, 5,216 ....C 5
10974 Sloatsburg, 3,134 ....M 8
11787 Smithtown, 15,000 ....O 9
14551 Sodus, 1,813 ....G 4
14555 Sodus Point, 1,172 ....G 4
13209 Solvay, 8,280 ....H 4
11968 Southampton, 4,904 ....R 9
14830 South Corning, 1,414 ....F 6
12779 South Fallsburg, 1,590 ....L 7
† 12801 South Glens Falls, 4,013 ....N 4
11971 Southold, 2,030 ....P 8
† 14901 Southport, 8,685 ....G 6
14559 Spencerport, 2,929 ....E 4
10977 Spring Valley, 18,112 ....M 8
14141 Springville, 4,350 ....C 5
12167 Stamford, 1,286 ....L 6
* 10301 Staten Island (borough), 295,443 ....M 9
12170 Stillwater, 1,428 ....N 5
11790 Stony Brook, 6,391 ....O 9
10980 Stony Point, 8,270 ....M 8
12172 Stottville, 1,106 ....N 6
10901 Suffern, 8,273 ....M 8
11791 Syosset, 9,970 ....S 7
* 13201 Syracuse⊙, 197,208 ....H 4
Syracuse, ‡635,946 ....H 4
10591 Tarrytown, 11,115 ....O 6
13691 Theresa, 985 ....J 2
† 11020 Thomaston, 2,486 ....R 7
12883 Ticonderoga, 3,268 ....N 3
12486 Tillson, 1,256 ....M 7
14150 Tonawanda, 21,898 ....B 4
* 12180 Troy⊙, 62,918 ....N 5
14886 Trumansburg, 1,618 ....G 5
10707 Tuckahoe, 6,236 ....O 7
12986 Tupper Lake, 4,854 ....M 2
13849 Unadilla, 1,489 ....K 6
13160 Union Springs, 1,183 ....G 5
* 13501 Utica⊙, 91,611 ....K 4
Utica-Rome, ‡337,477 ....K 4
12184 Valatie, 1,288 ....N 6
10595 Valhalla, 6,000 ....P 6
* 11580 Valley Stream, 40,413 ....N 9
13850 Vestal, 8,303 ....H 6
14564 Victor, 2,187 ....F 5
12186 Voorheesville, 2,826 ....N 5
13694 Waddington, 955 ....K 1
11792 Wading River, 975 ....P 9
12586 Walden, 5,277 ....M 7
12589 Wallkill, 1,849 ....M 7
13856 Walton, 3,744 ....K 6
13163 Wampsville⊙, 586 ....J 4
† 14075 Wanakah, 1,600 ....C 5
11793 Wantagh, 21,873 ....N 9
12590 Wappingers Falls, 5,607 ....N 7
12885 Warrensburg, 2,743 ....N 3
14569 Warsaw⊙, 3,619 ....D 5
10990 Warwick, 3,604 ....M 8
12188 Waterford, 2,879 ....N 5
13165 Waterloo⊙, 5,418 ....G 5
13601 Watertown⊙, 30,787 ....J 3
13480 Waterville, 1,808 ....K 5
12189 Watervliet, 12,404 ....N 5
14891 Watkins Glen⊙, 2,716 ....G 6
14892 Waverley, 5,261 ....G 7
14572 Wayland, 2,022 ....E 5
14580 Webster, 5,037 ....F 4
13166 Weedsport, 1,900 ....G 4
14895 Wellsville, 5,815 ....E 6
11590 Westbury, 15,362 ....R 7
† 13619 West Carthage, 2,047 ....J 3
† 14901 West Elmira, 5,901 ....G 6
14787 Westfield, 3,651 ....A 6
† 12801 West Glens Falls, 3,363 ....N 4
11977 Westhampton, 1,156 ....P 9
11978 Westhampton Beach, 1,926 ....P 9
10996 West Point, 8,100 ....M 8
11796 West Sayville, 7,386 ....O 9
14224 West Seneca, ∆48,404 ....C 5
13491 West Winfield, 1,018 ....K 5
12887 Whitehall, 3,764 ....O 3
* 10601 White Plains⊙, 50,220 ....P 6
13492 Whitesboro, 4,805 ....K 4
13862 Whitney Point, 1,058 ....J 6
14589 Williamson, 1,991 ....F 4
14221 Williamsville, 6,835 ....C 5
11596 Williston Park, 9,154 ....R 7
12996 Willsboro, 950 ....N 2
14172 Wilson, 1,284 ....C 4
13865 Windsor, 1,098 ....J 6
12998 Witherbee-Mineville, 1,967 ....N 2
14590 Wolcott, 1,617 ....G 4
12788 Woodbourne, 1,155 ....M 7
11598 Woodmere, 19,831 ....R 7
12789 Woodridge, 1,071 ....L 7
12498 Woodstock, 1,073 ....M 6
* 10701 Yonkers, 204,370 ....O 7
† 10598 Yorktown, 9,008 ....N 8
13495 Yorkville, 3,425 ....K 4
14174 Youngstown, 2,169 ....C 4

⊙ County seat.
‡ Population of metropolitan area.
∆ Population of town or township.
† Zip of nearest p.o.
* Multiple zips

Agriculture, Industry and Resources

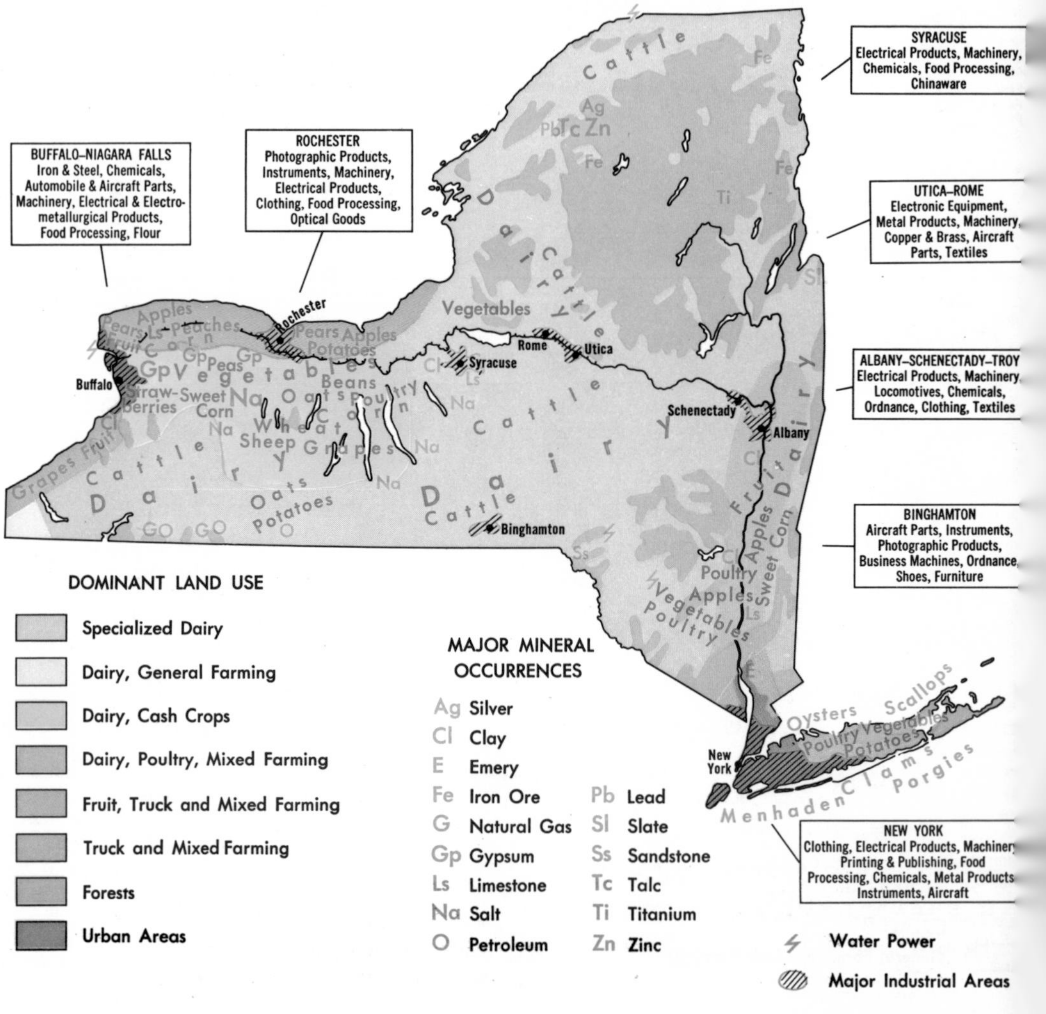
BUFFALO–NIAGARA FALLS
Iron & Steel, Chemicals, Automobile & Aircraft Parts, Machinery, Electrical & Electro-metallurgical Products, Food Processing, Flour
ROCHESTER
Photographic Products, Instruments, Machinery, Electrical Products, Clothing, Food Processing, Optical Goods
SYRACUSE
Electrical Products, Machinery, Chemicals, Food Processing, Chinaware
UTICA–ROME
Electronic Equipment, Metal Products, Machinery, Copper & Brass, Aircraft Parts, Textiles
ALBANY–SCHENECTADY–TROY
Electrical Products, Machinery, Locomotives, Chemicals, Ordnance, Clothing, Textiles
BINGHAMTON
Aircraft Parts, Instruments, Photographic Products, Business Machines, Ordnance, Shoes, Furniture
NEW YORK
Clothing, Electrical Products, Machinery, Printing & Publishing, Food Processing, Chemicals, Metal Products, Instruments, Aircraft
Buffalo
Rochester
Syracuse
Rome
Utica
Schenectady
Albany
Binghamton
New York
Cattle
Dairy
Vegetables
Apples
Pears
Peaches
Fruit
Corn
Peas
Potatoes
Beans
Oats
Wheat
Sheep
Grapes
Sweet Corn
Poultry
Oysters
Scallops
Clams
Porgies
Menhaden
DOMINANT LAND USE
Specialized Dairy
Dairy, General Farming
Dairy, Cash Crops
Dairy, Poultry, Mixed Farming
Fruit, Truck and Mixed Farming
Truck and Mixed Farming
Forests
Urban Areas
MAJOR MINERAL OCCURRENCES
Ag Silver
Cl Clay
E Emery
Fe Iron Ore
G Natural Gas
Gp Gypsum
Ls Limestone
Na Salt
O Petroleum
Pb Lead
Sl Slate
Ss Sandstone
Tc Talc
Ti Titanium
Zn Zinc
Water Power
Major Industrial Areas

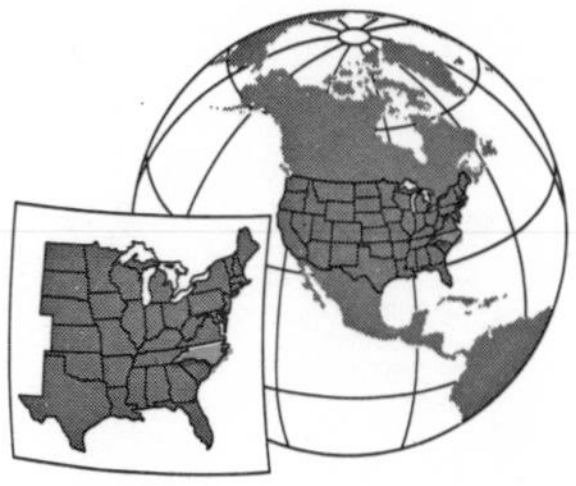

AREA 52,586 sq. mi.
POPULATION 5,082,059
CAPITAL Raleigh
LARGEST CITY Charlotte
HIGHEST POINT Mt. Mitchell 6,684 ft.
SETTLED IN 1650
ADMITTED TO UNION November 21, 1789
POPULAR NAME Tarheel State
STATE FLOWER Flowering Dogwood
STATE BIRD Cardinal

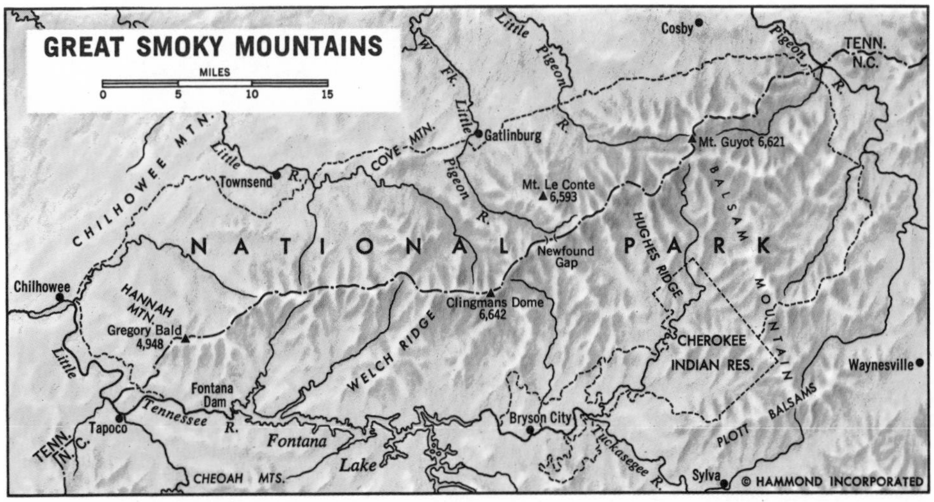
GREAT SMOKY MOUNTAINS
MILES
0 5 10 15
NATIONAL PARK
Cosby
TENN.
N.C.
Little Pigeon R.
W. Fk. Little Pigeon R.
Pigeon R.
Gatlinburg
Mt. Guyot 6,621
CHILHOWEE MTN.
Little R.
Townsend
COVE MTN.
Mt. Le Conte 6,593
BALSAM MOUNTAIN
HUGHES RIDGE
Newfound Gap
Chilhowee
HANNAH MTN.
Gregory Bald 4,948
Clingmans Dome 6,642
CHEROKEE INDIAN RES.
Waynesville
WELCH RIDGE
Fontana Dam
Tennessee R.
Fontana Lake
Bryson City
TENN. N.C.
Tapoco
PLOTT BALSAMS
Tuckasegee R.
CHEOAH MTS.
Sylva
© HAMMOND INCORPORATED

COUNTIES

amance, 96,362	L	3
exander, 19,466	G	3
eghany, 8,134	G	1
son, 23,488	J	4
he, 19,571	F	2
ery, 12,655	F	2
aufort, 35,980	R	4
rtie, 20,528	P	2
aden, 26,477	M	5
unswick, 24,223	N	6
ncombe, 145,056	D	3
rke, 60,364	F	3
barrus, 74,629	H	4
ldwell, 56,699	F	3
amden, 5,453	S	2
rteret, 31,603	R	5
swell, 19,055	L	2
tawba, 90,873	G	3
atham, 29,554	L	3
erokee, 16,330	A	4
owan, 10,764	R	2
ay, 5,180	B	4
eveland, 72,556	F	4
olumbus, 46,937	M	6
aven, 62,554	P	4
mberland, 212,042	M	4
rrituck, 6,976	S	2
re, 6,995	T	3
vidson, 95,627	J	3
vie, 18,855	H	3
plin, 38,015	O	5
rham, 132,681	M	3
lgecombe, 52,341	O	3
rsyth, 214,348	J	2
anklin, 26,820	N	2
aston, 148,415	G	4
ates, 8,524	R	2
aham, 6,562	B	4
anville, 32,762	M	2
eene, 14,967	O	3
uilford, 288,590	K	3
alifax, 53,884	O	2
arnett, 49,667	M	4
aywood, 41,710	C	3
enderson, 42,804	D	4
ertford, 23,529	P	2
oke, 16,436	L	4
yde, 5,571	S	3
dell, 72,197	H	3
ckson, 21,593	C	4
hnston, 61,737	N	4
nes, 9,779	P	4
e 30,467	L	4
noir, 55,204	O	4
ncoln, 32,682	G	3
acon, 15,788	B	4
adison, 16,003	D	3
artin, 24,730	P	3
cDowell, 30,648	E	3
ecklenburg, 354,656	H	4
tchell, 13,447	E	2
ontgomery, 19,267	K	4
oore, 39,048	L	4
ash, 59,122	O	2
ew Hanover, 82,996	O	6
orthampton, 24,009	P	2
nslow, 103,126	P	5
ange, 57,707	L	2
amlico, 9,467	R	4
asquotank, 26,824	S	2
ender, 18,149	O	5
erquimans, 8,351	S	2
erson, 25,914	M	2
Pitt, 73,900	P	3
Polk, 11,735	E	4
Randolph, 76,358	K	3
Richmond, 39,889	K	4
Robeson, 84,842	L	5
Rockingham, 72,402	K	2
Rowan, 90,035	H	3
Rutherford, 47,337	E	4
Sampson, 44,954	N	4
Scotland, 26,929	L	5
Stanly, 42,822	J	4
Stokes, 23,782	J	2
Surry, 51,415	H	2
Swain, 7,861	B	3
Transylvania, 19,713	D	4
Tyrrell, 3,806	S	3
Union, 54,714	H	4
Vance, 32,691	N	2
Wake, 228,453	M	3
Warren, 15,810	N	2
Washington, 14,038	R	3
Watauga, 23,404	F	2
Wayne, 85,408	N	4
Wilkes, 49,524	G	2
Wilson, 57,486	O	3
Yadkin, 24,599	H	2
Yancey, 12,629	E	3

CITIES and TOWNS

Zip	Name/Pop.	Key
28321	Abbottsburg, 425	M 5
28315	Aberdeen, 1,592	L 4
27006	Advance, 206	J 3
27910	Ahoskie, 5,105	P 2
27201	Alamance, 450	K 2
† 28713	Alarka, 900	C 4
28001	Albemarle⊙, 11,126	J 4
† 27589	Alert, 200	N 2
28701	Alexander, 200	D 3
28509	Alliance, 577	R 4
† 28364	Alma, 200	L 5
28702	Almond, 200	B 4
27202	Altamahaw, 900	L 2
28901	Andrews, 1,384	B 4
27501	Angier, 1,431	M 4
28007	Ansonville, 694	J 4
27502	Apex, 2,192	M 3
28510	Arapahoe, 212	R 4
27263	Archdale, 6,103	K 3
27589	Arcola, 300	N 2
28704	Arden, 850	D 4
† 28642	Arlington, 711	H 2
28420	Ash, 250	N 6
27203	Asheboro⊙, 10,797	K 3
* 28801	Asheville⊙, 57,681	D 3
	Asheville, ‡145,056	D 3
28603	Ashford, 225	F 3
† 27983	Askewville, 247	R 2
28421	Atkinson, 325	N 5
28511	Atlantic, 950	S 5
28512	Atlantic Beach, 300	R 5
27805	Aulander, 947	P 2
27806	Aurora, 620	R 4
28318	Autryville, 213	M 4
27915	Avon, 400	U 4
† 28076	Avondale-Henrietta, 1,307	F 4
28513	Ayden, 3,450	P 4
28009	Badin, 1,626	J 4
27503	Bahama, 280	M 2
27807	Bailey, 724	N 3
28705	Bakersville⊙, 409	E 2
28706	Balfour, 2,014	E 4
† 27203	Balfours, 4,836	K 3
28707	Balsam, 300	C 4
† 27030	Bannertown, 1,138	H 1
27917	Barco, 325	T 2
† 28739	Barker Heights, 2,933	D 4
28710	Bat Cave, 400	E 4
27808	Bath, 231	R 4
27809	Battleboro, 688	O 2
28515	Bayboro⊙, 665	R 4
27207	Bear Creek, 500	L 3
28516	Beaufort⊙, 3,368	R 5
27810	Belhaven, 2,259	R 3
28012	Belmont, 4,814	H 4
27919	Belvidere, 275	S 2
† 28621	Benham, 400	G 2
27208	Bennett, 200	K 3
27504	Benson, 2,267	N 4
† 27565	Berea, 200	M 2
28016	Bessemer City, 5,217	G 4
† 28779	Beta, 500	C 4
27812	Bethel, 1,514	P 3
28518	Beulaville, 1,156	O 5
† 28803	Biltmore Forest, 1,298	E 3
27209	Biscoe, 1,244	K 4
27813	Black Creek, 449	O 3
28711	Black Mountain, 3,204	E 3
28320	Bladenboro, 783	M 5
27212	Blanch, 210	L 2
28605	Blowing Rock, 801	F 2
† 28438	Boardman, 233	M 6
28092	Boger City, 2,203	G 4
† 28570	Bogue, 600	R 5
28461	Boiling Spring Lakes, 245	N 7
28017	Boiling Springs, 2,284	F 4
28423	Bolton, 534	N 6
27213	Bonlee, 275	L 3
28606	Boomer, 212	G 2
28607	Boone⊙, 8,754	F 2
27011	Boonville, 687	H 2
28322	Bowdens, 250	N 4
28712	Brevard⊙, 5,243	D 4
28519	Bridgeton, 520	R 4
27505	Broadway, 694	L 4
28601	Brookford, 590	G 3
27214	Browns Summit, 500	K 2
28424	Brunswick, 206	M 6
28713	Bryson City⊙, 1,290	C 4
† 28377	Buies, 275	L 5
27506	Buies Creek, 2,024	M 4
27507	Bullock, 550	M 2
27508	Bunn, 284	N 3
28323	Bunnlevel, 200	M 4
28425	Burgaw⊙, 1,744	N 5
27215	Burlington, 35,930	K 2
28714	Burnsville⊙, 1,348	E 3
27509	Butner, 3,538	M 2
28324	Butters, 225	M 5
27920	Buxton, 700	U 4
27228	Bynum, 400	L 3
28325	Calypso, 462	N 4
27921	Camden⊙, 300	S 2
28326	Cameron, 204	L 4
28715	Candler, 950	D 3
27229	Candor, 561	K 4
28716	Canton, 5,158	D 3
28019	Caroleen, 975	F 4
28428	Carolina Beach, 1,663	O 6
27510	Carrboro, 3,472	L 3
28327	Carthage⊙, 1,034	K 4
27511	Cary, 7,430	M 3
28020	Casar, 350	F 3
28717	Cashiers, 230	C 4
27816	Castalia, 265	O 2
28429	Castle Hayne, 900	O 6
28609	Catawba, 565	G 3
† 28754	Catharine Lake, 500	O 5
27230	Cedar Falls, 500	K 3
28520	Cedar Island, 250	S 5
28718	Cedar Mountain, 250	D 4
28431	Chadbourn, 2,213	M 6
27514	Chapel Hill, 25,537	M 3
* 28201	Charlotte⊙, 241,178	H 4
	Charlotte, ‡409,370	H 4
28719	Cherokee, 975	C 4
28021	Cherryville, 5,258	G 4
28023	China Grove, 1,788	H 3
28521	Chinquapin, 350	O 5
27817	Chocowinity, 566	P 4
28610	Claremont, 788	G 3
28432	Clarendon, 300	M 6
28433	Clarkton, 662	M 6
27520	Clayton, 3,103	N 3
27012	Clemmons, 4,900	J 2
27013	Cleveland, 614	H 3
28024	Cliffside, 950	F 4
27233	Climax, 475	K 3
28328	Clinton⊙, 7,157	N 5
28721	Clyde, 900	D 3
27521	Coats, 1,051	M 4
27922	Cofield, 422	R 2
27923	Coinjock, 650	S 2
27924	Colerain, 373	R 2
27234	Coleridge, 600	K 3
28611	Collettsville, 275	F 3
27925	Columbia⊙, 902	S 3
28722	Columbus⊙, 731	E 4
28522	Comfort, 340	O 5
27818	Como, 211	P 1
28025	Concord⊙, 18,464	H 4
28612	Connellys Springs, 500	F 3
28613	Conover, 3,355	G 3
27820	Conway, 694	P 2
27014	Cooleemee, 1,115	H 3
28031	Cornelius, 1,296	H 4
28523	Cove City, 485	P 4
28032	Cramerton, 2,142	G 4
27522	Creedmoor, 1,405	M 2
27928	Creswell, 633	S 3
28033	Crouse, 850	G 4
† 28716	Cruso, 800	D 4
28723	Cullowhee, 6,300	C 4
28331	Cumberland, 800	M 5
28435	Currie, 294	N 6
27929	Currituck⊙, 500	T 2
27015	Cycle, 210	H 2
28034	Dallas, 4,059	G 4
† 27043	Dalton, 400	J 2
27016	Danbury⊙, 152	J 2
28036	Davidson, 2,931	H 4
28524	Davis, 600	R 5
28436	Delco, 450	N 6
27239	Denton, 1,017	J 3
28725	Dillsboro, 215	C 4
27017	Dobson⊙, 933	H 2
† 28685	Dockery, 300	G 2
28526	Dover, 585	P 4
28619	Drexel, 1,431	F 3
28332	Dublin, 283	M 5
28334	Dunn, 8,302	M 4
* 27701	Durham⊙, 95,438	M 2
	Durham, ‡190,388	M 2
† 28761	Dysartsville, 950	F 3
27242	Eagle Springs, 500	K 4
28038	Earl, 300	F 4
27018	East Bend, 485	H 2
28726	East Flat Rock, 2,627	E 4
28352	East Laurinburg, 487	L 5
† 28752	East Marion, 3,015	F 3
28039	East Spencer, 2,217	J 3
27288	Eden, 15,871	K 1
27932	Edenton⊙, 4,766	R 2
27243	Efland, 600	L 2
27909	Elizabeth City⊙, 14,069	S 2
28337	Elizabethtown⊙, 1,418	M 5
28621	Elkin, 2,899	H 2
28622	Elk Park, 503	F 2
28040	Ellenboro, 465	F 4
28338	Ellerbe, 913	K 4
27822	Elm City, 1,201	O 3
27244	Elon College, 2,150	L 2
27823	Enfield, 3,272	O 2
27824	Engelhard, 500	T 3
28728	Enka, 500	D 3
27527	Ernul, 350	P 4
28339	Erwin, 2,852	M 4
27247	Ether, 375	K 4
28729	Etowah, 700	D 4
27830	Eureka, 263	O 3
28438	Evergreen, 250	M 6
28439	Fair Bluff, 1,039	M 6
27826	Fairfield, 954	S 3
28340	Fairmont, 2,827	L 6
28730	Fairview, 800	D 3
28341	Faison, 598	N 4
28041	Faith, 506	J 3
28342	Falcon, 357	M 4
† 27028	Farmington, 300	H 3
27828	Farmville, 4,424	O 3
* 28301	Fayetteville⊙, 53,510	M 4
	Fayetteville, ‡212,042	M 4
28731	Flat Rock, 650	E 4
28732	Fletcher, 950	E 4
28043	Forest City, 7,179	E 4
† 27028	Fork, 250	J 3
27829	Fountain, 434	O 3
27524	Four Oaks, 1,057	M 4
28734	Franklin⊙, 2,336	C 4
27525	Franklinton, 1,459	N 2
27248	Franklinville, 794	K 3
28440	Freeland, 500	N 6
27830	Fremont, 1,596	N 3
27936	Frisco, 325	T 4
27526	Fuquay-Varina, 3,576	M 3
28441	Garland, 656	N 5
27529	Garner, 4,923	M 3
27831	Garysburg, 231	O 2

(continued on following page)

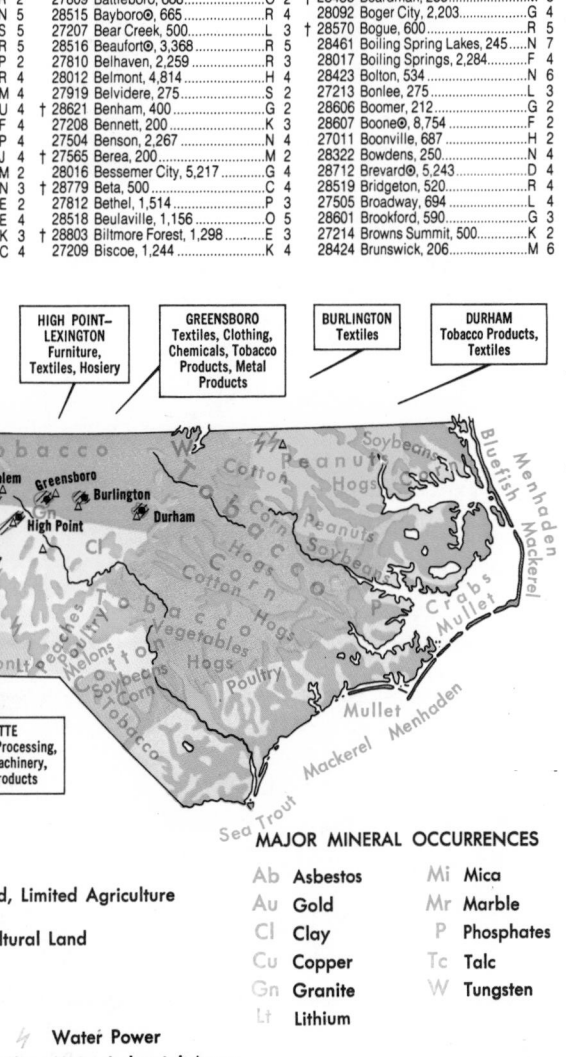

Agriculture, Industry and Resources

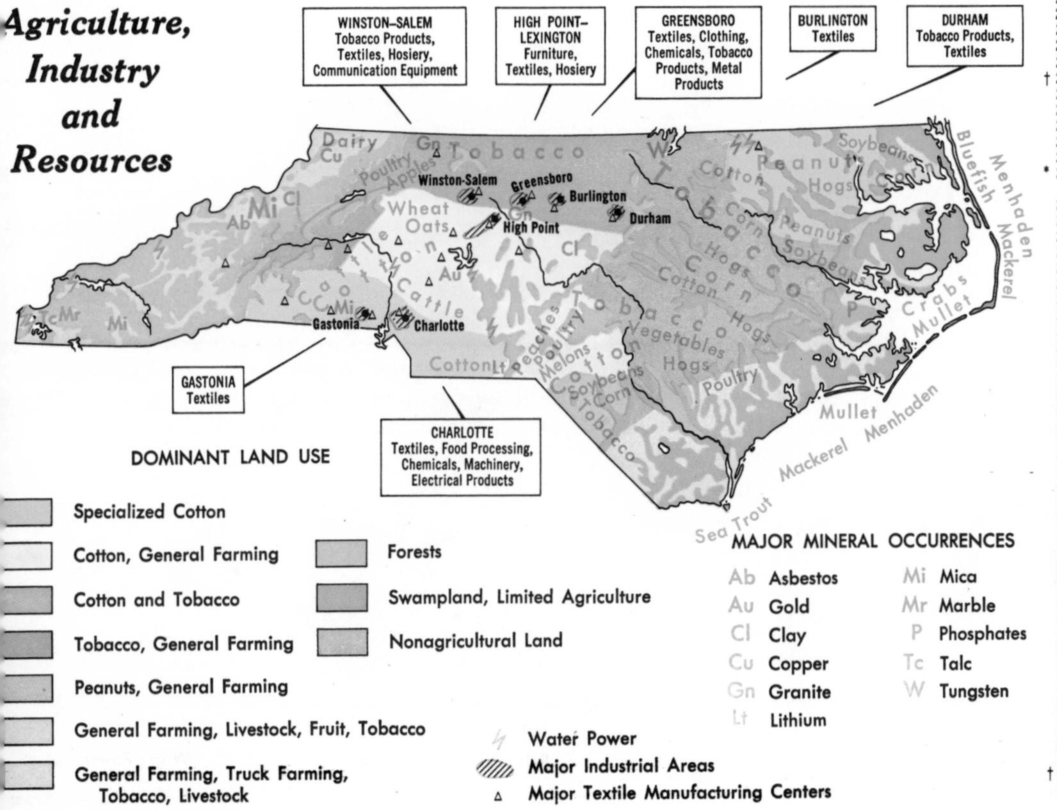
WINSTON-SALEM
Tobacco Products, Textiles, Hosiery, Communication Equipment
HIGH POINT-LEXINGTON
Furniture, Textiles, Hosiery
GREENSBORO
Textiles, Clothing, Chemicals, Tobacco Products, Metal Products
BURLINGTON
Textiles
DURHAM
Tobacco Products, Textiles
GASTONIA
Textiles
CHARLOTTE
Textiles, Food Processing, Chemicals, Machinery, Electrical Products
Winston-Salem
Greensboro
Burlington
Durham
High Point
Gastonia
Charlotte
Dairy
Tobacco
Poultry
Apples
Wheat
Oats
Cattle
Cotton
Peanuts
Soybeans
Hogs
Corn
Peaches
Melons
Vegetables
Bluefish
Menhaden
Mackerel
Crabs
Mullet
Sea Trout
DOMINANT LAND USE
Specialized Cotton
Cotton, General Farming
Cotton and Tobacco
Tobacco, General Farming
Peanuts, General Farming
General Farming, Livestock, Fruit, Tobacco
General Farming, Truck Farming, Tobacco, Livestock
Forests
Swampland, Limited Agriculture
Nonagricultural Land
MAJOR MINERAL OCCURRENCES
Ab Asbestos
Au Gold
Cl Clay
Cu Copper
Gn Granite
Lt Lithium
Mi Mica
Mr Marble
P Phosphates
Tc Talc
W Tungsten
Water Power
Major Industrial Areas
Major Textile Manufacturing Centers

28052 Gastonia◉, 47,142....G 4
27937 Gates, 225....R 2
27938 Gatesville◉, 338....R 2
28343 Gibson, 502....K 5
27249 Gibsonville, 2,019....J 2
28628 Glen Alpine, 797....F 3
27251 Glendon, 250....L 2
27215 Glen Raven, 2,848....L 2
28736 Glenville, 400....C 4
28737 Glenwood, 400....F 3
28071 Gold Hill, 350....J 3
27530 Goldsboro◉, 26,810....O 4
27252 Goldston, 364....L 3
27253 Graham◉, 8,172....L 2
27939 Grandy, 425....T 2
28630 Granite Falls, 2,388....G 3
28072 Granite Quarry, 1,344....H 3
28529 Grantsboro, 900....Q 4
28740 Greenmountain, 500....E 3
* 27401 Greensboro◉, 144,076....K 2
  Greensboro-Winston-Salem-High Point, ‡603,895....K 2
27834 Greenville◉, 29,063....P 3
28530 Grifton, 1,860....P 4
27837 Grimesland, 394....P 3
28073 Grover, 555....G 4
27256 Gulf, 300....L 3
27839 Halifax◉, 335....O 2
28442 Hallsboro, 300....M 6
27840 Hamilton, 579....P 3
28345 Hamlet, 4,627....K 5
28443 Hampstead, 400....O 6
27020 Hamptonville, 250....H 2
27941 Harbinger, 460....T 2
28531 Harkers Island, 1,633....R 5
28634 Harmony, 377....H 3
28444 Harrells, 249....N 5
28075 Harrisburg, 800....H 4
27943 Hatteras, 500....T 4
28532 Havelock, 5,283....P 5
27258 Haw River, 1,542....L 2
28739 Hayesville◉, 428....B 4
† 28318 Hayne, 300....M 5
28635 Hays, 750....G 2
† 27559 Haywood, 500....L 3
28738 Hazelwood, 2,057....C 4
27536 Henderson◉, 13,896....N 2
28739 Hendersonville◉, 6,443....E 4
28076 Henrietta-Avondale, 1,307....G 4
27944 Hertford◉, 2,023....S 2
28601 Hickory, 20,569....G 3
28636 Hiddenite, 800....G 3
28741 Highlands, 583....C 4
* 27260 High Point, 63,204....J 2
28077 High Shoals, 900....G 4
28637 Hildebran, 481....F 3
27278 Hillsborough◉, 1,444....L 2
27843 Hobgood, 530....P 2
28537 Hobucken, 500....S 4
28347 Hoffman, 434....K 4
27844 Hollister, 750....O 2
28445 Holly Ridge, 415....P 6
27540 Holly Springs, 697....M 3
28538 Hookerton, 441....O 4
28348 Hope Mills, 1,721....N 5
28743 Hot Springs, 653....D 3
28539 Hubert, 980....P 5
28638 Hudson, 2,820....G 3
28078 Huntersville, 1,538....H 4
28666 Icard, 1,100....G 3
28079 Indian Trail, 405....H 4
27589 Inez, 250....N 2
28080 Iron Station, 250....G 4
27845 Jackson◉, 762....P 2
28540 Jacksonville◉, 16,021....O 5
28550 James City, 2,577....R 4
27282 Jamestown, 1,297....K 3
27846 Jamesville, 533....R 3
27947 Jarvisburg, 350....T 2
28640 Jefferson◉, 943....G 2
† 28352 Johns, 250....K 5
28642 Jonesville, 1,659....H 2
27283 Julian, 300....K 3
28787 Jupiter, 208....D 3
28081 Kannapolis, 36,293....H 4
27847 Kelford, 295....P 2
28349 Kenansville◉, 762....O 5
27542 Kenly, 1,370....N 3
27284 Kernersville, 4,815....J 2
27948 Kill Devil Hills, 357....T 3
27021 King, 1,033....J 2
28086 Kings Mountain, 8,465....G 4
28501 Kinston◉, 22,309....O 4
27544 Kittrell, 427....M 2
27949 Kitty Hawk, 600....T 2

27545 Knightdale, 815....N 3
27950 Knotts Island, 450....T 2
28449 Kure Beach, 394....O 7
28551 La Grange, 2,558....O 4
28746 Lake Lure, 500....E 4
28747 Lake Toxaway, 750....D 4
28350 Lakeview, 449....L 4
28450 Lake Waccamaw, 924....M 6
28088 Landis, 2,297....H 3
28643 Lansing, 388....F 1
28089 Lattimore, 257....F 4
28351 Laurel Hill, 1,215....K 5
† 28739 Laurel Park, 581....D 4
28352 Laurinburg◉, 8,859....K 5
28090 Lawndale, 544....F 4
27291 Leasburg, 400....L 2
28748 Leicester, 265....D 3
28451 Leland, 500....N 6
28645 Lenoir◉, 14,705....G 3
27849 Lewiston, 327....P 2
27292 Lexington◉, 17,205....J 3
27298 Liberty, 2,167....K 3
28091 Lilesville, 641....K 5
27546 Lillington◉, 1,155....M 4
28092 Lincolnton◉, 5,293....G 4
28356 Linden, 205....M 4
28646 Linville, 400....F 2
27299 Linwood, 300....J 3
27850 Littleton, 903....O 2
28461 Long Beach, 493....N 7
28548 Longhurst, 1,485....L 2
28648 Longisland, 350....H 3
28601 Long View, 3,360....F 3
28452 Longwood, 650....N 6
† 28345 Longwood Park, 1,284....K 5
27549 Louisburg◉, 2,941....N 2
28098 Lowell, 3,307....G 4
27024 Lowgap, 660....H 1
28552 Lowland, 538....S 4
27851 Lucama, 610....N 3

28358 Lumberton◉, 16,961....L 5
28750 Lynn, 550....E 4
27852 Macclesfield, 536....O 3
27951 Mackeys, 250....R 3
27025 Madison, 2,018....J 2
28751 Maggie, 400....C 3
28453 Magnolia, 614....O 5
28650 Maiden, 2,416....G 3
27552 Mamers, 500....L 4
† 28387 Manly, 225....L 4
27953 Manns Harbor, 365....T 3
27954 Manteo◉, 547....T 3
27855 Mapleton, 250....P 2
28905 Marble, 300....B 4
28752 Marion◉, 3,335....E 3
28753 Marshall◉, 982....D 3
28553 Marshallberg, 700....S 5
28754 Mars Hill, 1,623....D 3
28103 Marshville, 1,405....J 4
28105 Matthews, 783....H 4
28554 Maury, 421....O 4
28364 Maxton, 1,885....L 5
27027 Mayodan, 2,875....K 2
28555 Maysville, 912....P 5
28361 McCain, 950....L 4
27302 Mebane, 2,433....L 2
† 28646 Merrimon, 500....R 5
27555 Micro, 300....N 3
27557 Middlesex, 729....N 3
28107 Midland, 950....J 4
† 28377 Midstate Mill, 925....L 5
28544 Midway Park, 4,900....O 5
27305 Milton, 235....L 1
27854 Milwaukee, 376....P 2
28212 Mint Hill, 1,200....H 4
28109 Misenheimer, 1,923....J 3
28115 Mocksville◉, 2,529....H 3
27559 Moncure, 800....L 3
28110 Monroe◉, 11,282....J 5
28757 Montreat, 450....E 3

28114 Mooresboro, 275....F 4
28115 Mooresville, 8,808....H 3
28654 Moravian Falls, 375....G 2
28557 Morehead City, 5,233....R 5
28655 Morganton◉, 13,625....F 3
28119 Morven, 562....J 5
27030 Mount Airy, 7,325....H 1
27306 Mount Gilead, 1,286....K 4
28120 Mount Holly, 5,107....H 4
28123 Mount Mourne, 950....H 4
28365 Mount Olive, 4,914....O 4
28124 Mount Pleasant, 1,174....J 4
27345 Mount Vernon Springs, 225....L 3
27958 Moyock, 350....S 1
27855 Murfreesboro, 3,508....R 2
28906 Murphy◉, 2,082....A 4
27959 Nags Head, 414....T 3
27856 Nashville◉, 1,670....O 3
27561 Neuse, 500....M 3
28560 New Bern◉, 14,660....P 4
28657 Newland◉, 524....F 2
28127 New London, 285....J 4
28570 Newport, 1,735....R 5
28658 Newton◉, 7,857....G 3
28366 Newton Grove, 546....N 4
27563 Norlina, 969....N 2
28752 North Cove, 257....F 2
28532 North Harlowe, 975....R 5
28659 North Wilkesboro, 3,357....G 2
28564 Northside, 400....M 2
28128 Norwood, 1,896....J 4
28129 Oakboro, 568....J 4
27857 Oak City, 559....P 3
27310 Oak Ridge, 950....K 2
27960 Ocracoke, 500....T 4
28762 Old Fort, 676....E 3
27961 Old Trap, 400....T 2
28368 Olivia, 400....L 4
28571 Oriental, 445....R 4
28805 Oteen, 2,863....E 3

27565 Oxford◉, 7,178....M 2
27860 Pantego, 218....R 3
28371 Parkton, 550....M 5
27861 Parmele, 373....P 3
28661 Patterson, 344....G 2
28133 Peachland, 556....J 5
† 28091 Pee Dee, 210....K 5
27311 Pelham, 350....L 1
28372 Pembroke, 1,982....L 5
28766 Penrose, 600....D 4
28716 Phillipsville, 1,239....C 3
27863 Pikeville, 580....N 4
27041 Pilot Mountain, 1,309....H 2
28373 Pinebluff, 570....K 4
27042 Pine Hall, 550....J 2
28374 Pinehurst, 1,056....K 4
27568 Pine Level, 983....N 4
28662 Pineola, 875....F 2
27864 Pinetops, 1,379....O 3
27865 Pinetown, 278....R 3
28134 Pineville, 1,948....H 4
28572 Pink Hill, 522....O 4
27043 Pinnacle, 725....J 2
28768 Pisgah Forest, 850....D 4
27312 Pittsboro◉, 1,447....L 3
27866 Pleasant Hill, 250....P 2
27962 Plymouth◉, 4,774....R 3
28135 Polkton, 845....J 4
28136 Polkville, 450....F 4
28573 Pollocksville, 456....P 4
27965 Poplar Branch, 400....T 2
27966 Powells Point, 375....T 2
27967 Powellsville, 247....R 2
27858 Princeton, 1,044....N 4
† 27886 Princeville, 654....P 3
28363 Raeford◉, 3,180....L 5
* 27601 Raleigh (cap.)◉, 121,577....M 3
  Raleigh, ‡228,453....M 3
27316 Ramseur, 1,328....K 3
27317 Randleman, 2,312....K 3

† 28906 Ranger, 500....A 4
28052 Ranlo, 2,092....G 4
27868 Red Oak, 359....O 3
28377 Red Springs, 3,383....L 5
27320 Reidsville, 13,636....K 2
28378 Rex, 975....F 4
28667 Rhodhiss, 784....F 3
28092 Rhyne, 2,273....G 4
28137 Richfield, 306....J 3
28574 Richlands, 935....O 5
27869 Rich Square, 1,254....P 2
27570 Ridgeway, 500....N 2
28456 Riegelwood, 459....N 6
27870 Roanoke Rapids, 13,508....O 2
28668 Roaring Gap, 450....G 2
28669 Roaring River, 500....G 2
27325 Robbins, 1,059....K 3
28771 Robbinsville◉, 777....B 4
† 28379 Roberdel, 350....K 5
27871 Robersonville, 1,910....P 3
28379 Rockingham◉, 5,852....K 5
28138 Rockwell, 999....J 3
27801 Rocky Mount, 34,284....O 3
28457 Rocky Point, 500....N 6
27571 Rolesville, 529....N 3
28670 Ronda, 465....G 2
27970 Roper, 649....R 3
28382 Roseboro, 1,235....N 5
28458 Rose Hill, 1,448....O 5
28772 Rosman, 407....D 4
27572 Rougemont, 400....L 2
28383 Rowland, 1,358....L 5
27573 Roxboro◉, 5,370....L 2
28384 Rockobel, 347....L 5
† 27587 Royal Cotton Mills, 600....M 3
27326 Ruffin, 600....K 1
27045 Rural Hall, 2,338....J 2
† 28139 Ruth, 360....F 4
28671 Rutherford College, 950....F 3
28139 Rutherfordton◉, 3,245....F 4

Topography

0   40   80
MILES

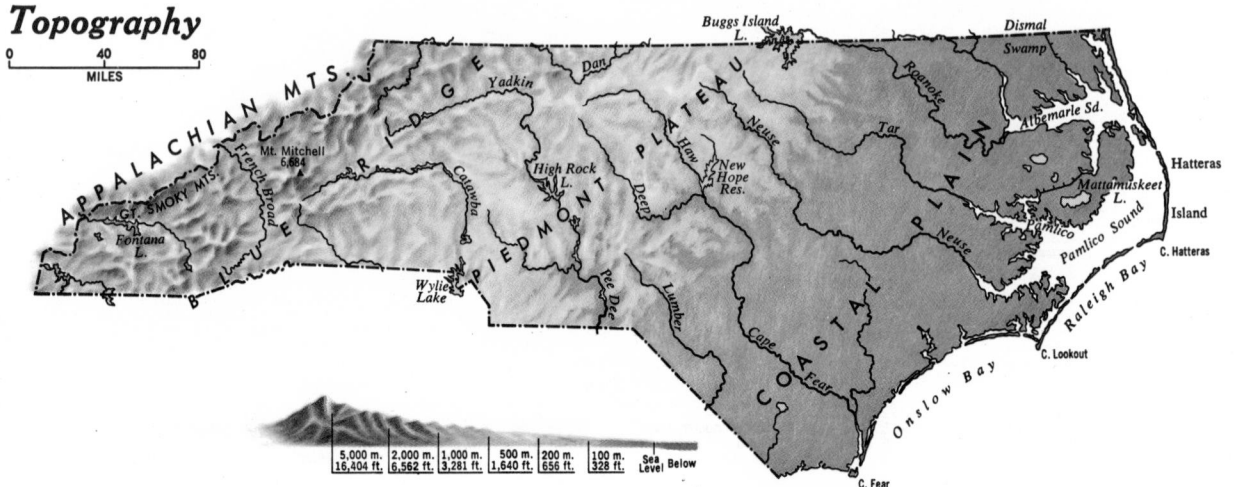

5,000 m. / 16,404 ft.   2,000 m. / 6,562 ft.   1,000 m. / 3,281 ft.   500 m. / 1,640 ft.   200 m. / 656 ft.   100 m. / 328 ft.   Sea Level   Below

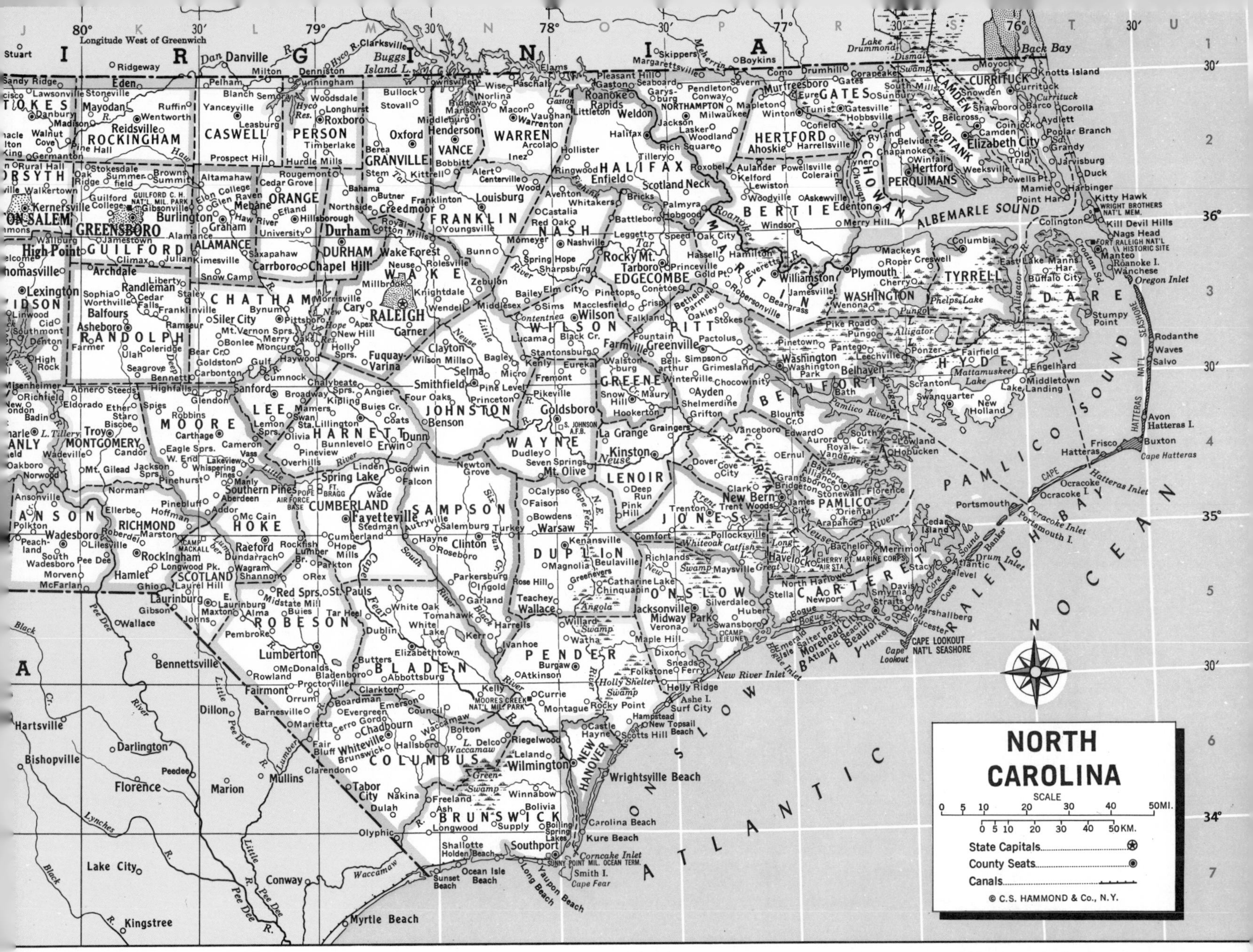

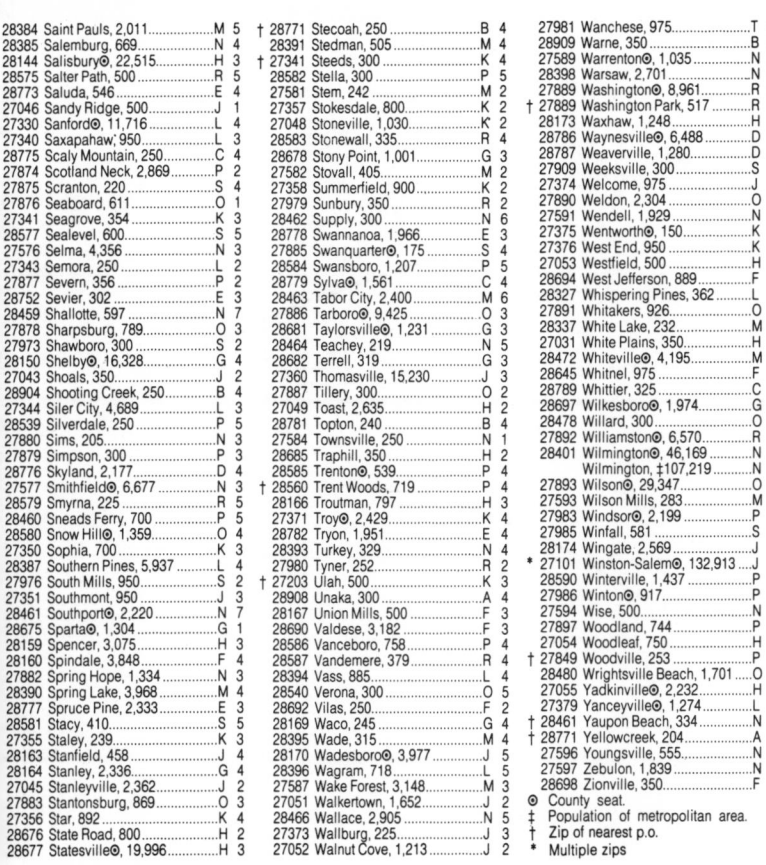

28384 Saint Pauls, 2,011........M 5
28385 Salemburg, 669........N 4
28144 Salisbury⊙, 22,515........H 3
28575 Salter Path, 500........R 5
28773 Saluda, 546........E 4
27046 Sandy Ridge, 500........J 1
27330 Sanford⊙, 11,716........L 3
27340 Saxapahaw; 950........L 3
28775 Scaly Mountain, 250........C 4
27874 Scotland Neck, 2,869........P 2
27875 Scranton, 220........S 3
27876 Seaboard, 611........O 1
27341 Seagrove, 354........K 3
28577 Sealevel, 600........S 5
27576 Selma, 4,356........N 3
27343 Semora, 250........L 1
27877 Severn, 356........P 2
28752 Sevier, 302........E 3
28459 Shallotte, 597........N 7
27878 Sharpsburg, 789........O 3
27973 Shawboro, 300........S 2
28150 Shelby⊙, 16,328........G 4
27043 Shoals, 350........J 2
28904 Shooting Creek, 250........B 4
27344 Siler City, 4,689........L 3
28539 Silverdale, 250........P 5
27880 Sims, 205........N 3
27879 Simpson, 300........P 3
28776 Skyland, 2,177........D 4
27577 Smithfield⊙, 6,677........N 3
28579 Smyrna, 225........R 5
28460 Sneads Ferry, 700........P 5
28580 Snow Hill⊙, 1,359........O 4
27350 Sophia, 700........K 3
28387 Southern Pines, 5,937........L 4
27976 South Mills, 950........S 2
27351 Southmont, 950........J 3
28461 Southport⊙, 2,220........N 7
28675 Sparta⊙, 1,304........G 1
28159 Spencer, 3,075........H 3
28160 Spindale, 3,848........F 4
27882 Spring Hope, 1,334........N 3
28390 Spring Lake, 3,968........L 4
28777 Spruce Pine, 2,333........E 3
28581 Stacy, 410........S 5
27355 Staley, 239........K 3
28163 Stanfield, 458........H 4
28164 Stanley, 2,336........G 4
27045 Stanleyville, 2,362........J 2
27883 Stantonsburg, 869........O 3
28356 Star, 892........K 4
28676 State Road, 800........H 2
28677 Statesville⊙, 19,996........H 3

† 28771 Stecoah, 250........B 4
28391 Stedman, 505........M 4
† 27341 Steeds, 300........K 4
28582 Stella, 300........P 5
27581 Stem, 242........M 2
27357 Stokesdale, 800........K 2
27048 Stoneville, 1,030........K 2
28583 Stonewall, 335........R 4
28678 Stony Point, 1,001........G 3
27582 Stovall, 405........M 2
27358 Summerfield, 900........K 2
27979 Sunbury, 539........R 2
28462 Supply, 300........N 6
28778 Swannanoa, 1,966........E 3
27885 Swanquarter⊙, 175........S 4
28584 Swansboro, 1,207........P 5
28779 Sylva⊙, 1,561........C 4
28463 Tabor City, 2,400........M 6
27886 Tarboro⊙, 9,425........O 3
28681 Taylorsville⊙, 1,231........G 3
28464 Teachey, 219........N 5
28682 Terrell, 319........G 3
27360 Thomasville, 15,230........J 3
27887 Tillery, 300........O 2
27049 Toast, 2,635........H 2
28781 Topton, 240........B 4
27584 Townsville, 250........N 1
28685 Traphill, 350........H 2
28585 Trenton⊙, 539........P 4
† 28560 Trent Woods, 719........P 4
28166 Troutman, 797........H 3
27371 Troy⊙, 2,429........K 4
28782 Tryon, 1,951........E 4
28393 Turkey, 329........N 4
27980 Tyner, 252........R 2
† 27203 Ulah, 500........K 3
28908 Unaka, 300........A 4
28167 Union Mills, 500........F 3
28690 Valdese, 3,182........F 3
28586 Vanceboro, 758........P 4
28587 Vandemere, 379........R 4
28394 Vass, 885........L 4
28540 Verona, 300........O 5
28692 Vilas, 250........F 2
28169 Waco, 245........G 4
28395 Wade, 315........M 4
28170 Wadesboro⊙, 3,977........J 5
28396 Wagram, 718........L 5
27587 Wake Forest, 3,148........M 3
27051 Walkertown, 1,652........J 2
28466 Wallace, 2,905........N 5
27373 Wallburg, 225........J 2
27052 Walnut Cove, 1,213........J 2

27981 Wanchese, 975........T 3
28909 Warne, 350........B 5
27589 Warrenton⊙, 1,035........N 2
28398 Warsaw, 2,701........N 4
27889 Washington⊙, 8,961........R 3
† 27889 Washington Park, 517........R 3
28173 Waxhaw, 1,248........H 5
28786 Waynesville⊙, 6,488........D 4
28787 Weaverville, 1,280........D 4
27909 Weeksville, 300........S 2
27374 Welcome, 975........J 3
27890 Weldon, 2,304........O 2
27591 Wendell, 1,929........N 3
27375 Wentworth⊙, 150........K 2
27376 West End, 950........K 4
27053 Westfield, 500........H 2
28694 West Jefferson, 889........F 2
28327 Whispering Pines, 362........L 4
27891 Whitakers, 926........O 2
28337 White Lake, 232........M 5
27031 White Plains, 350........H 2
28472 Whiteville⊙, 4,195........M 6
28645 Whitnel, 975........F 3
28789 Whittier, 325........C 4
28697 Wilkesboro⊙, 1,974........G 2
28478 Willard, 300........O 5
27892 Williamston⊙, 6,570........R 3
28401 Wilmington⊙, 46,169........N 6
      Wilmington, ‡107,219........N 6
27893 Wilson⊙, 29,347........O 3
27593 Wilson Mills, 283........M 3
27983 Windsor⊙, 2,199........P 2
27985 Winfall, 581........S 2
28174 Wingate, 2,569........J 5
* 27101 Winston-Salem⊙, 132,913........J 2
28590 Winterville, 1,437........P 3
27986 Winton⊙, 917........P 2
27594 Wise, 500........N 1
27897 Woodland, 744........P 2
27054 Woodleaf, 750........H 3
† 27849 Woodville, 253........P 2
28480 Wrightsville Beach, 1,701........O 6
27055 Yadkinville⊙, 2,232........H 2
27379 Yanceyville⊙, 1,274........L 2
28461 Yaupon Beach, 334........N 7
† 28771 Yellowcreek, 204........B 4
27596 Youngsville, 555........M 3
27597 Zebulon, 1,839........N 3
28698 Zionville, 350........F 2

⊙ County seat.
‡ Population of metropolitan area.
§ Zip of nearest p.o.
* Multiple zips

Weeding "green gold" — tobacco is North Carolina's money crop.

NORTH DAKOTA

SCALE
0 5 10 20 30 MI.
0 5 10 20 30 KM.

State Capitals............⊛
County Seats..............⊛

© C.S. HAMMOND & Co., N.Y.

COUNTIES

Adams, 3,832 ....F 7
Barnes, 14,669 ....O 5
Benson, 8,245 ....M 3
Billings, 1,198 ....D 5
Bottineau, 9,496 ....J 2
Bowman, 3,901 ....C 7
Burke, 4,739 ....E 2
Burleigh, 40,714 ....J 6
Cass, 73,653 ....R 5
Cavalier, 8,213 ....N 2
Dickey, 6,976 ....N 7
Divide, 4,564 ....C 2
Dunn, 4,895 ....E 5
Eddy, 4,103 ....M 4
Emmons, 7,200 ....K 7
Foster, 4,832 ....N 5
Golden Valley, 2,611 ....C 5
Grand Forks, 61,102 ....P 3
Grant, 5,009 ....G 6
Griggs, 4,184 ....O 5
Hettinger, 5,075 ....E 7
Kidder, 4,362 ....K 6
La Moure, 7,117 ....N 7
Logan, 4,245 ....L 7
McHenry, 8,977 ....J 3
McIntosh, 5,545 ....L 7
McKenzie, 6,127 ....D 4
McLean, 11,251 ....G 4
Mercer, 6,175 ....G 5
Morton, 20,310 ....H 6
Mountrail, 8,437 ....E 3
Nelson, 5,776 ....O 4
Oliver, 2,322 ....H 5

Pembina, 10,728 ....P 2
Pierce, 6,323 ....K 3
Ramsey, 12,915 ....N 3
Ransom, 7,102 ....P 7
Renville, 3,828 ....G 2
Richland, 18,089 ....R 7
Rolette, 11,549 ....L 2
Sargent, 5,937 ....P 7
Sheridan, 3,232 ....K 4
Sioux, 3,632 ....H 7
Slope, 1,484 ....C 7
Stark, 19,613 ....E 6
Steele, 3,749 ....P 5
Stutsman, 23,550 ....M 5
Towner, 4,645 ....M 2
Traill, 9,571 ....R 5
Walsh, 16,251 ....P 3
Ward, 58,560 ....G 3
Wells, 7,847 ....L 4
Williams, 19,301 ....C 3

CITIES and TOWNS

Zip	Name/Pop.	Key
58001	Abercrombie, 262	S 7
58210	Adams, 284	O 3
58830	Alamo, 124	D 2
58831	Alexander, 208	D 4
58003	Alice, 83	P 6
58520	Almont, 109	H 6
58311	Alsen, 201	N 2
58833	Ambrose, 82	D 1
58620	Amidon⊙, 54	D 7
58710	Anamoose, 401	K 4

58212	Aneta, 376	P 4
58711	Antler, 135	H 2
58005	Argusville, 118	R 5
58835	Arnegard, 141	D 4
58006	Arthur, 412	R 5
58214	Arvilla, 115	P 4
58413	Ashley⊙, 1,236	M 7
58712	Balfour, 93	J 4
58313	Balta, 133	K 3
58008	Barney, 81	S 7
58216	Bathgate, 133	P 2
58621	Beach⊙, 1,408	C 6
58316	Belcourt, 950	L 2
58622	Belfield, 1,130	D 6
58718	Berthold, 398	G 3
58523	Beulah, 1,344	G 5
58416	Binford, 242	O 4
58317	Bisbee, 305	M 2
58501	Bismarck (cap.)⊛, 34,703	J 6
58318	Bottineau⊙, 2,760	J 2
58721	Bowbells⊙, 584	F 2
58418	Bowdon, 229	L 5
58623	Bowman⊙, 1,762	D 7
58524	Braddock, 106	K 6
58321	Brocket, 95	O 3
58420	Buchanan, 100	N 5
58011	Buffalo, 241	R 6
58722	Burlington, 247	H 3
58723	Butte, 193	J 4
58218	Buxton, 235	R 4
58324	Cando⊙, 1,512	M 2
58528	Cannon Ball, 550	J 7
58627	Carson⊙ (Hensel), 81	P 2 †
58725	Carpio, 215	G 3
58421	Carrington⊙, 2,491	M 5

58529	Carson⊙, 466	H 7
58012	Casselton, 1,485	R 6
58422	Cathay, 110	M 4
58220	Cavalier⊙, 1,381	P 2
58013	Cayuga, 116	P 7
58530	Center⊙, 619	H 5
58014	Chaffee, 99	R 6
58015	Christine, 108	S 6
58325	Church's Ferry, 139	M 3
58424	Cleveland, 128	M 6
58016	Clifford, 84	P 5
58017	Cogswell, 203	P 7
58727	Columbus, 465	E 2
58425	Cooperstown⊙, 1,485	O 5
58426	Courtenay, 125	N 5
58327	Crary, 150	N 3
58730	Crosby⊙, 1,545	D 2
58222	Crystal, 272	P 2
58021	Davenport, 147	R 6
58428	Dawson, 131	L 6
58429	Dazey, 128	O 5
58430	Denhoff, 85	K 5
58733	Des Lacs, 197	G 3
58601	Dickinson⊙, 12,405	E 6
58625	Dodge, 121	F 5
58734	Donnybrook, 163	G 2
58735	Douglas, 144	G 4
58736	Drake, 636	K 4
58730	Drayton, 1,095	P 2
58532	Driscoll, 128	K 6
58626	Dunn Center, 107	E 5
58329	Dunseith, 811	L 2
58024	Dwight, 93	S 7

58432	Eckelson, 100	O 6
58433	Edgeley, 888	N 7
58227	Edinburg, 315	P 3
58830	Edmore, 398	O 3
58331	Egeland, 96	M 2
58533	Elgin, 839	G 7
58436	Ellendale⊙, 1,517	N 7
58027	Enderlin, 1,343	P 6
58843	Epping, 140	D 3
58029	Erie, 100	P 5
58332	Esmond, 416	L 3
58229	Fairdale, 102	O 3
58030	Fairmount, 412	S 7
58102	Fargo⊙, 53,365	S 6
	Fargo-Moorhead, ‡120,238	S 6
58438	Fessenden⊙, 815	L 4
58031	Fingal, 166	P 6
58230	Finley⊙, 809	P 4
58535	Flasher, 467	H 7
58737	Flaxton, 286	F 2
58439	Forbes, 88	N 8
58231	Fordville, 361	P 3
58233	Forest River, 169	P 3
58032	Forman⊙, 596	P 7
58033	Fort Ransom, 121	P 6
58335	Fort Totten, 550	M 4
58844	Fortuna, 216	C 2
58538	Fort Yates⊙, 1,153	J 7
58440	Fredonia, 100	M 7
58441	Fullerton, 120	O 7
58442	Gackle, 470	M 6
58035	Galesburg, 134	R 5
58739	Gardena, 84	J 2
58036	Gardner, 96	R 5

58540	Garrison, 1,614	H 4
58235	Gilby, 268	R 3
58630	Gladstone, 222	F 6
58740	Glenburn, 381	H 2
58443	Glenfield, 127	N 5
58631	Glen Ullin, 1,070	G 6
58541	Goldenvalley, 235	F 5
58632	Golva, 104	C 6
58444	Goodrich, 300	K 5
58445	Grace City, 87	N 4
58237	Grafton⊙, 5,946	P 3
58201	Grand Forks⊙, 39,008	R 4
58038	Grandin, 187	R 5
58741	Granville, 282	J 3
58039	Great Bend, 86	S 7
58845	Grenora, 401	C 2
58040	Gwinner, 623	P 7
58542	Hague, 146	L 7
58636	Halliday, 413	F 5
58238	Hamilton, 110	P 2
58338	Hampden, 114	N 2
58041	Hankinson, 1,125	S 7
58448	Hannaford, 244	O 5
58239	Hannah, 145	M 2
58340	Harlow, 85	M 3
58341	Harvey, 2,361	L 4
58042	Harwood, 200	R 5
58240	Hatton, 808	R 4
58043	Havana, 156	P 7
58544	Hazelton, 374	K 7
58545	Hazen, 1,240	G 5
58638	Hebron, 1,103	G 6
58342	Heimdal, 101	L 4
58547	Hensler, 100	H 5
58639	Hettinger⊙, 1,655	F 7

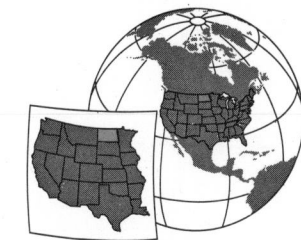

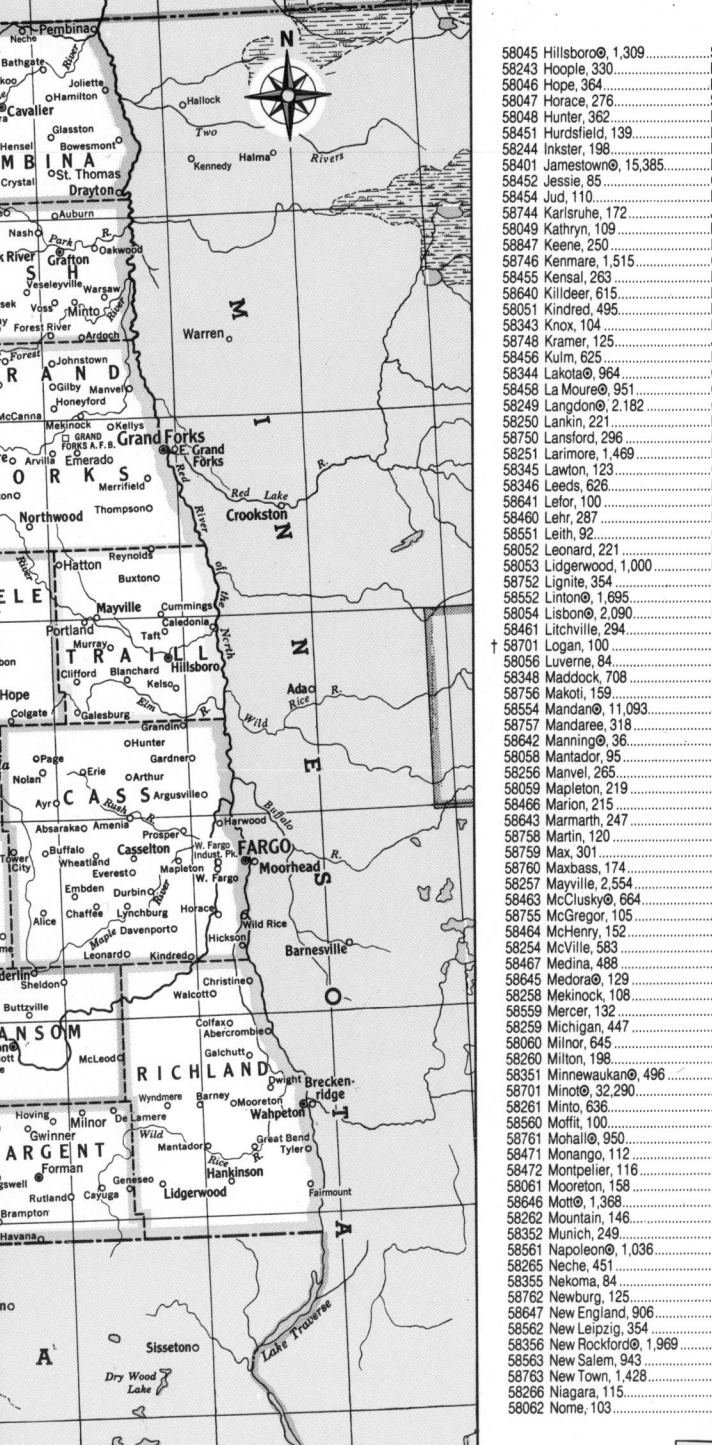

AREA 70,665 sq. mi.
POPULATION 617,761
CAPITAL Bismarck
LARGEST CITY Fargo
HIGHEST POINT White Butte 3,506 ft.
SETTLED IN 1780
ADMITTED TO UNION November 2, 1889
POPULAR NAME Flickertail State; Sioux State
STATE FLOWER Prairie Rose
STATE BIRD Meadowlark

Topography

5,000 m. 16,404 ft. | 2,000 m. 6,562 ft. | 1,000 m. 3,281 ft. | 500 m. 1,640 ft. | 200 m. 656 ft. | 100 m. 328 ft. | Sea Level | Below

0   50   100
MILES

Zip	Place	Col/Row
58045	Hillsboro⊙, 1,309	S 5
58243	Hoople, 330	P 2
58046	Hope, 364	P 5
58047	Horace, 276	S 6
58048	Hunter, 362	R 5
58451	Hurdsfield, 139	L 4
58244	Inkster, 198	P 3
58401	Jamestown⊙, 15,385	N 6
58452	Jessie, 85	O 4
58454	Jud, 110	N 6
58744	Karlsruhe, 172	J 3
58049	Kathryn, 109	P 6
58847	Keene, 250	E 4
58746	Kenmare, 1,515	G 2
58455	Kensal, 263	N 5
58640	Killdeer, 615	E 5
58051	Kindred, 495	R 6
58343	Knox, 104	L 3
58748	Kramer, 125	J 2
58456	Kulm, 625	N 7
58344	Lakota⊙, 964	O 3
58458	La Moure⊙, 951	O 7
58249	Langdon⊙, 2,182	O 2
58250	Lankin, 221	P 3
58750	Lansford, 296	H 2
58251	Larimore, 1,469	P 4
58345	Lawton, 123	O 3
58346	Leeds, 626	M 3
58641	Lefor, 100	F 6
58460	Lehr, 287	M 7
58551	Leith, 92	G 7
58052	Leonard, 221	R 6
58053	Lidgerwood, 1,000	R 7
58752	Lignite, 354	F 2
58552	Linton⊙, 1,695	K 7
58054	Lisbon⊙, 2,090	P 7
58461	Litchville, 294	O 6
† 58701	Logan, 100	H 3
58056	Luverne, 84	P 5
58348	Maddock, 708	L 4
58756	Makoti, 159	G 4
58554	Mandan⊙, 11,093	J 6
58757	Mandaree, 318	E 4
58642	Manning, 36	E 5
58058	Mantador, 95	R 7
58256	Manvel, 265	R 3
58059	Mapleton, 219	R 6
58466	Marion, 215	O 6
58643	Marmarth, 247	B 7
58758	Martin, 120	K 4
58759	Max, 301	H 4
58760	Maxbass, 174	H 2
58257	Mayville, 2,554	R 4
58463	McClusky⊙, 664	K 4
58755	McGregor, 105	D 2
58464	McHenry, 152	N 4
58254	McVille, 583	O 4
58467	Medina, 488	M 6
58645	Medora⊙, 129	C 6
58258	Mekinock, 108	R 4
58559	Mercer, 132	J 5
58259	Michigan, 447	O 3
58060	Milnor, 645	R 7
58260	Milton, 198	O 2
58351	Minnewaukan⊙, 496	M 3
58701	Minot⊙, 32,290	H 3
58261	Minto, 636	R 3
58759	Moffit, 100	K 6
58761	Mohall⊙, 950	G 2
58471	Monango, 112	N 7
58472	Montpelier, 116	N 6
58061	Mooreton, 158	S 7
58646	Mott⊙, 1,368	F 7
58262	Mountain, 146	P 2
58352	Munich, 249	N 2
58561	Napoleon⊙, 1,036	L 7
58265	Neche, 451	P 2
58355	Nekoma, 84	O 2
58762	Newburg, 125	J 2
58647	New England, 906	E 6
58562	New Leipzig, 354	G 7
58356	New Rockford⊙, 1,969	N 4
58563	New Salem, 943	G 6
58763	New Town, 1,428	F 4
58266	Niagara, 115	P 4
58062	Nome, 103	P 6
58765	Noonan, 403	D 2
58267	Northwood, 1,189	P 4
58473	Nortonville, 90	N 6
58474	Oakes, 1,742	O 7
† 58237	Oakwood, 91	R 3
58357	Oberon, 151	M 4
58063	Oriska, 128	P 6
58269	Osnabrock, 255	O 2
58064	Page, 367	P 5
58769	Palermo, 146	F 3
58270	Park River, 1,680	P 3
58770	Parshall, 1,246	F 4
58361	Pekin, 120	O 4
58271	Pembina, 741	R 2
58272	Petersburg, 266	P 3
58475	Pettibone, 173	L 5
† 58545	Pick City, 119	G 5
58273	Pisek, 154	P 3
58771	Plaza, 291	G 3
58772	Portal, 251	E 2
58274	Portland, 534	R 5
58773	Powers Lake, 523	E 2
58849	Ray, 776	D 3
58649	Reeder, 306	E 7
58650	Regent, 344	E 7
58275	Reynolds, 236	R 4
58651	Rhame, 206	C 7
58652	Richardton, 799	F 6
58565	Riverdale, 600	H 4
58478	Robinson, 125	L 5
58365	Rocklake, 270	M 2
58479	Rogers, 96	O 5
58366	Rolette, 579	L 2
58367	Rolla⊙, 1,458	L 2
58776	Ross, 135	F 3
58368	Rugby⊙, 2,889	L 3
58067	Rutland, 225	P 7
58779	Ryder, 211	G 4
58369	Saint John, 367	L 2
58276	Saint Thomas, 508	R 2
58480	Sanborn, 255	O 6
58780	Sanish, 25	E 4
58372	Sarles, 148	N 2
58781	Sawyer, 373	H 3
58653	Scranton, 360	D 7
58568	Selfridge, 346	J 7
58373	Selz, 110	L 4
58654	Sentinel Butte, 125	C 6
58277	Sharon, 201	P 4
58068	Sheldon, 192	P 6
58782	Sherwood, 369	G 2
58374	Sheyenne, 362	M 4
58569	Shields, 125	H 7
58570	Solen, 180	J 7
58783	Souris, 151	J 2
58655	South Heart, 132	D 6
58481	Spiritwood, 100	N 6
58784	Stanley⊙, 1,581	F 3
58571	Stanton⊙, 517	H 5
58377	Starkweather, 193	N 3
58482	Steele⊙, 692	L 6
58573	Strasburg, 642	K 7
58483	Streeter, 324	M 6
58785	Surrey, 361	H 3
58484	Sutton, 87	M 5
58486	Sykeston, 232	M 5
58487	Tappen, 294	L 6
58656	Taylor, 162	E 6
58278	Thompson, 291	R 4
58852	Tioga, 1,667	E 3
58379	Tokio, 130	N 4
58787	Tolley, 163	G 2
58380	Tolna, 247	O 4
58071	Tower City, 289	P 6
58788	Towner⊙, 870	K 3
58853	Trenton, 150	C 3
58575	Turtle Lake, 712	J 4
58488	Tuttle, 216	L 5
58576	Underwood, 781	H 5
58789	Upham, 272	J 2
58072	Valley City⊙, 7,843	P 6
58790	Velva, 1,241	J 3
58490	Verona, 140	O 7
58075	Wahpeton⊙, 7,076	S 7
58077	Walcott, 175	R 6
58281	Wales, 116	N 2
58282	Walhalla, 1,471	P 2
58577	Washburn⊙, 804	J 5
58854	Watford City⊙, 1,768	D 4
58078	West Fargo, 5,161	S 6
† 58078	West Fargo Industrial Park, 104	S 6
58793	Westhope, 705	H 2
58794	White Earth, 128	E 3
58795	Wildrose, 235	D 2
58801	Williston⊙, 11,280	C 3
58384	Willow City, 403	K 2
58579	Wilton, 695	J 5
58492	Wimbledon, 337	O 5
58494	Wing, 223	K 5
58495	Wishek, 1,275	L 7
58496	Woodworth, 139	M 5
58081	Wyndmere, 516	R 7
58386	York, 102	L 3
58497	Ypsilanti, 139	N 6
58580	Zap, 271	G 5
58581	Zeeland, 313	L 8

⊙ County seat.
‡ Population of metropolitan area.
† Zip of nearest p.o.
* Multiple zips

North Dakota's wealth springs from her soil. The state has the largest farms and leads in production of barley, wheat and flaxseed.

COMPIX

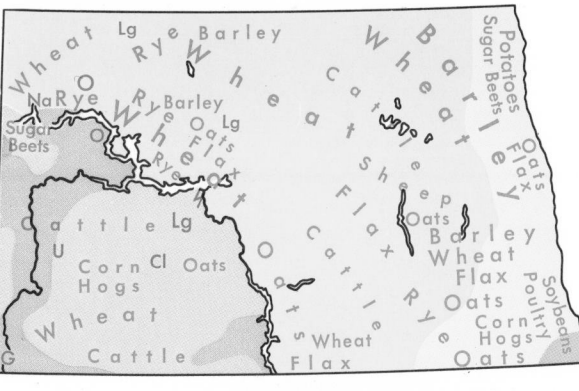

DOMINANT LAND USE

☐ Specialized Wheat

☐ Wheat, General Farming

☐ Wheat, Range Livestock

☐ Livestock, Cash Grain

☐ Sugar Beets, Dry Beans, Livestock, General Farming

☐ Range Livestock

⚡ Water Power

Agriculture, Industry and Resources

MAJOR MINERAL OCCURRENCES

Cl Clay
G   Natural Gas
Lg Lignite
Na Salt
O   Petroleum
U   Uranium

OHIO

SCALE
0 5 10   20   30   40 MI.
0 5 10 20   30   40 KM.

State Capitals .... ⊛
County Seats .... ⊛

© C.S. HAMMOND & Co., N.Y.

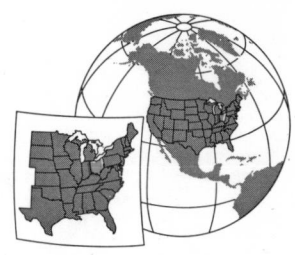

COUNTIES

Adams, 18,957..................D 8
Allen, 111,144...................B 4
Ashland, 43,303.................F 4
Ashtabula, 98,237..............J 2
Athens, 54,889..................F 7
Auglaize, 38,602................B 4
Belmont, 80,917................J 5
Brown, 26,635...................C 8
Butler, 226,207.................A 7
Carroll, 21,579..................H 4
Champaign, 30,491.............C 5
Clark, 157,115...................C 6
Clermont, 95,725...............B 7
Clinton, 31,464..................C 7
Columbiana, 108,310...........J 4
Coshocton, 33,486.............G 5
Crawford, 50,364...............E 4
Cuyahoga, 1,721,300..........G 3
Darke, 49,141...................A 5
Defiance, 36,949...............A 3
Delaware, 42,908..............D 5
Erie, 75,909.....................E 3
Fairfield, 73,301................E 6
Fayette, 25,461................D 6
Franklin, 833,249..............D 6
Fulton, 33,071..................B 2
Gallia, 25,239...................F 8
Geauga, 62,977...............H 3
Greene, 125,057...............C 6
Guernsey, 37,665.............H 5
Hamilton, 924,018.............A 7
Hancock, 61,217...............C 3
Hardin, 30,813.................C 4
Harrison, 17,013...............H 5
Henry, 27,058..................B 3
Highland, 28,996..............C 7
Hocking, 20,322...............F 6
Holmes, 23,024................G 4
Huron, 49,587.................E 3
Jackson, 27,174..............E 7
Jefferson, 96,193.............J 5
Knox, 41,795..................F 5
Lake, 197,200.................H 2
Lawrence, 56,868............E 8
Licking, 107,799..............F 5
Logan, 35,072.................C 5
Lorain, 256,843...............F 3
Lucas, 484,370................C 2
Madison, 28,318..............D 6
Mahoning, 303,424...........J 4
Marion, 64,724................D 4
Medina, 82,717...............G 3
Meigs, 19,799.................F 7
Mercer, 35,265................A 4
Miami, 84,342.................B 5
Monroe, 15,739..............H 6
Montgomery, 606,148........B 6
Morgan, 12,375...............G 6
Morrow, 21,348...............E 4
Muskingum, 77,826...........G 5
Noble, 10,428.................G 6
Ottawa, 37,099...............D 2
Paulding, 19,329..............A 3
Perry, 27,434..................F 6
Pickaway, 40,071.............D 7
Pike, 19,114....................D 7
Portage, 125,868.............H 3
Preble, 34,719................A 6
Putnam, 31,134...............B 3
Richland, 129,997............E 4
Ross, 61,211...................D 7
Sandusky, 60,983.............D 3
Scioto, 76,951.................D 8
Seneca, 60,696...............D 3
Shelby, 37,748................B 5
Stark, 372,210................H 4
Summit, 553,371..............G 3
Trumbull, 232,579............J 3
Tuscarawas, 77,211..........H 5
Union, 23,786.................D 5
Van Wert, 29,194............A 4
Vinton, 9,420..................E 7
Warren, 84,925...............B 7
Washington, 57,160..........H 7
Wayne, 87,123................G 4
Williams, 33,669..............A 2
Wood, 89,722..................C 3
Wyandot, 21,826.............D 4

CITIES and TOWNS

Zip	Name/Pop.	Key
45101	Aberdeen, 1,165	C 8
45810	Ada, 5,309	C 4
45001	Addyston, 1,336	B 9
43901	Adena, 1,134	J 5
44301	Akron⊙, 275,425	G 3
	Akron, ‡679,239	G 3
45710	Albany, 899	F 7
43001	Alexandria, 588	E 5
45812	Alger, 1,071	C 4
44601	Alliance, 26,547	H 4
43102	Amanda, 788	E 6
45201	Amberley, 5,574	C 9
45102	Amelia, 820	D10
44001	Amherst, 9,902	F 3
43903	Amsterdam, 882	J 5
44003	Andover, 1,179	J 2
45302	Anna, 792	B 5
45303	Ansonia, 1,044	A 5
45813	Antwerp, 1,735	A 3
44606	Apple Creek, 784	G 4
44804	Arcadia, 689	D 3
45304	Arcanum, 1,993	A 6
43502	Archbold, 3,047	B 2
45814	Arlington, 1,066	C 4
45201	Arlington Heights, 1,476	C 9
44805	Ashland⊙, 19,872	F 4
43003	Ashley, 1,034	E 5
44004	Ashtabula, 24,313	J 2
43103	Ashville, 1,772	E 6
45701	Athens⊙, 23,310	F 7
44807	Attica, 1,005	E 3
44201	Atwater, 975	H 3

Zip	Name/Pop.	Key
44202	Aurora, 6,549	H 3
44010	Austinburg, 900	J 2
44515	Austintown, 29,393	J 3
44011	Avon, 7,214	F 3
44012	Avon Lake, 12,261	F 2
† 43512	Ayersville, 950	B 3
45612	Bainbridge, 1,057	D 7
† 43420	Ballville, 1,652	D 3
43804	Baltic, 571	G 5
43105	Baltimore, 2,418	E 6
44203	Barberton, 33,052	G 4
43713	Barnesville, 4,292	H 6
43905	Barton, 975	J 5
45103	Batavia⊙, 1,894	B 7
† 44870	Bay View, 798	E 3
44140	Bay Village, 18,163	G 4
44608	Beach City, 1,133	G 4
† 44101	Beachwood, 9,631	J 2
45808	Beaverdam, 525	C 4
44146	Bedford, 17,552	H 9
† 44146	Bedford Heights, 13,063	J 9
43906	Bellaire, 9,655	J 5
45305	Bellbrook, 1,268	C 6
43310	Belle Center, 985	C 4
43311	Bellefontaine⊙, 11,255	C 5
44811	Bellevue, 8,604	E 3
44813	Bellville, 1,685	E 4
43718	Belmont, 666	H 5
44609	Beloit, 921	J 4
45714	Belpre, 7,189	G 7
44017	Berea, 22,396	G10
43908	Bergholz, 914	J 5
44814	Berlin Heights, 828	F 3
45106	Bethel, 2,214	B 8
43719	Bethesda, 1,157	H 5
44815	Bettsville, 833	D 3
45715	Beverly, 1,396	G 6
43209	Bexley, 14,888	E 6
45107	Blanchester, 3,080	C 7
44817	Bloomdale, 727	D 3
43106	Bloomingburg, 895	D 6
44818	Bloomville, 884	D 3
† 45201	Blue Ash, 8,324	C 9
45817	Bluffton, 2,935	C 4
44512	Boardman, 30,852	J 3
44612	Bolivar, 1,084	G 4
† 44264	Boston Heights, 846	J 10
45306	Botkins, 1,057	B 5
43402	Bowling Green⊙, 21,760	C 3
45308	Bradford, 2,163	B 5
43406	Bradner, 1,140	C 3
† 44101	Bratenahl, 1,613	H 9
44141	Brecksville, 9,137	H10
43107	Bremen, 1,413	F 6
44613	Brewster, 2,020	G 4
† 44215	Briarwood Beach, 508	G 3
43912	Bridgeport, 3,001	J 5
† 45201	Bridgetown, 13,352	B 9
43913	Brilliant, 2,178	J 5
44240	Brimfield, 950	H 3
44402	Bristolville, 900	J 3
† 44141	Broadview Heights, 11,463	H10
44403	Brookfield, 1,200	J 3
44144	Brooklyn, 13,142	H 9
† 44131	Brooklyn Heights, 1,527	H 9

Zip	Name/Pop.	Key
44142	Brook Park, 30,774	G 9
† 43912	Brookside, 939	J 5
45309	Brookville, 4,403	B 6
44212	Brunswick, 15,852	G 3
43506	Bryan⊙, 7,008	A 3
45716	Buchtel, 592	F 7
43008	Buckeye Lake, 2,961	F 6
44820	Bucyrus⊙, 13,111	E 4
43722	Buffalo, 710	G 6
† 45680	Burlington, 900	F 9
44021	Burton, 1,214	H 3
44822	Butler, 1,052	E 4
43723	Byesville, 2,097	G 6
43907	Cadiz⊙, 3,060	J 5
45820	Cairo, 587	B 4
43920	Calcutta, 2,900	J 4
44614	Canal Fulton, 2,367	G 4
43110	Canal Winchester, 2,412	E 6
44406	Canfield, 4,997	J 3
* 44701	Canton⊙, 110,053	H 4
	Canton, ‡372,210	H 4
43315	Cardington, 1,730	E 5
43316	Carey, 3,523	D 4
45005	Carlisle, 3,821	B 6
43112	Carroll, 614	E 6
44615	Carrollton⊙, 2,817	J 4
44824	Castalia, 1,045	E 3
45314	Cedarville, 2,342	C 6
45822	Celina⊙, 7,779	A 4
43011	Centerburg, 1,038	E 5
45459	Centerville, 10,333	B 6
44022	Chagrin Falls, 4,848	J 2
45719	Chauncey, 1,117	F 7
† 45202	Cherry Grove, 850	C10
45619	Chesapeake, 1,364	E 9
44026	Chesterland, 11,500	H 2
45211	Cheviot, 11,135	B 9
45601	Chillicothe⊙, 24,842	E 7
45389	Christiansburg, 724	C 5
* 45201	Cincinnati⊙, 452,524	B 9
	Cincinnati, ‡1,384,851	B 9
43113	Circleville, 11,687	D 6
45113	Clarksville, 574	C 7
45315	Clayton, 773	B 6
* 44101	Cleveland⊙, 750,903	H 9
	Cleveland, ‡2,074,194	H 9
44118	Cleveland Heights, 60,767	H 9
45002	Cleves, 2,044	B 9
44216	Clinton, 1,335	G 4
43410	Clyde, 5,503	E 3
† 45638	Coal Grove, 2,759	E 9
45621	Coalton, 550	E 7
45828	Coldwater, 3,533	A 5
† 44034	Colebrook, 700	J 2
44028	Columbia Station, 518	G10
44408	Columbiana, 4,959	J 4
* 43201	Columbus (cap.)⊙, 539,677	E 6
	Columbus, ‡916,228	E 6
45830	Columbus Grove, 2,290	B 4

(continued on following page)

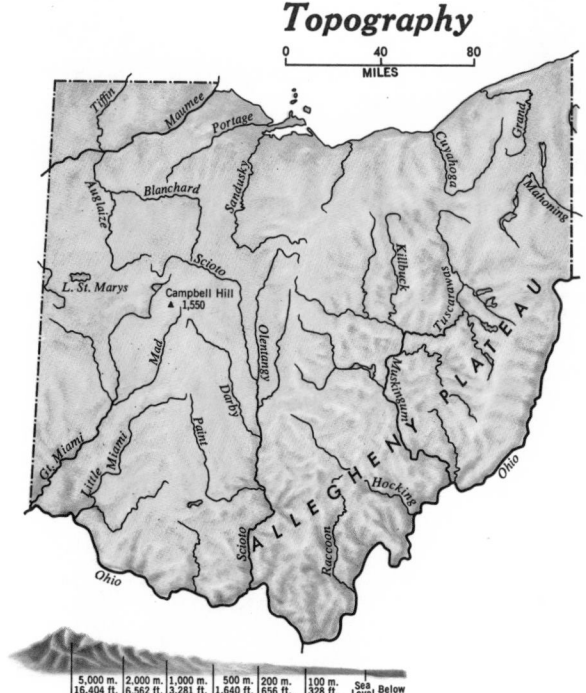

AREA 41,222 sq. mi.
POPULATION 10,652,017
CAPITAL Columbus
LARGEST CITY Cleveland
HIGHEST POINT Campbell Hill 1,550 ft.
SETTLED IN 1788
ADMITTED TO UNION March 1, 1803
POPULAR NAME Buckeye State
STATE FLOWER Scarlet Carnation
STATE BIRD Cardinal

Topography

0   40   80
MILES

5,000 m. | 2,000 m. | 1,000 m. | 500 m. | 200 m. | 100 m. | Sea Level Below
16,404 ft. | 6,562 ft. | 3,281 ft. | 1,640 ft. | 656 ft. | 328 ft.

Agriculture, Industry and Resources

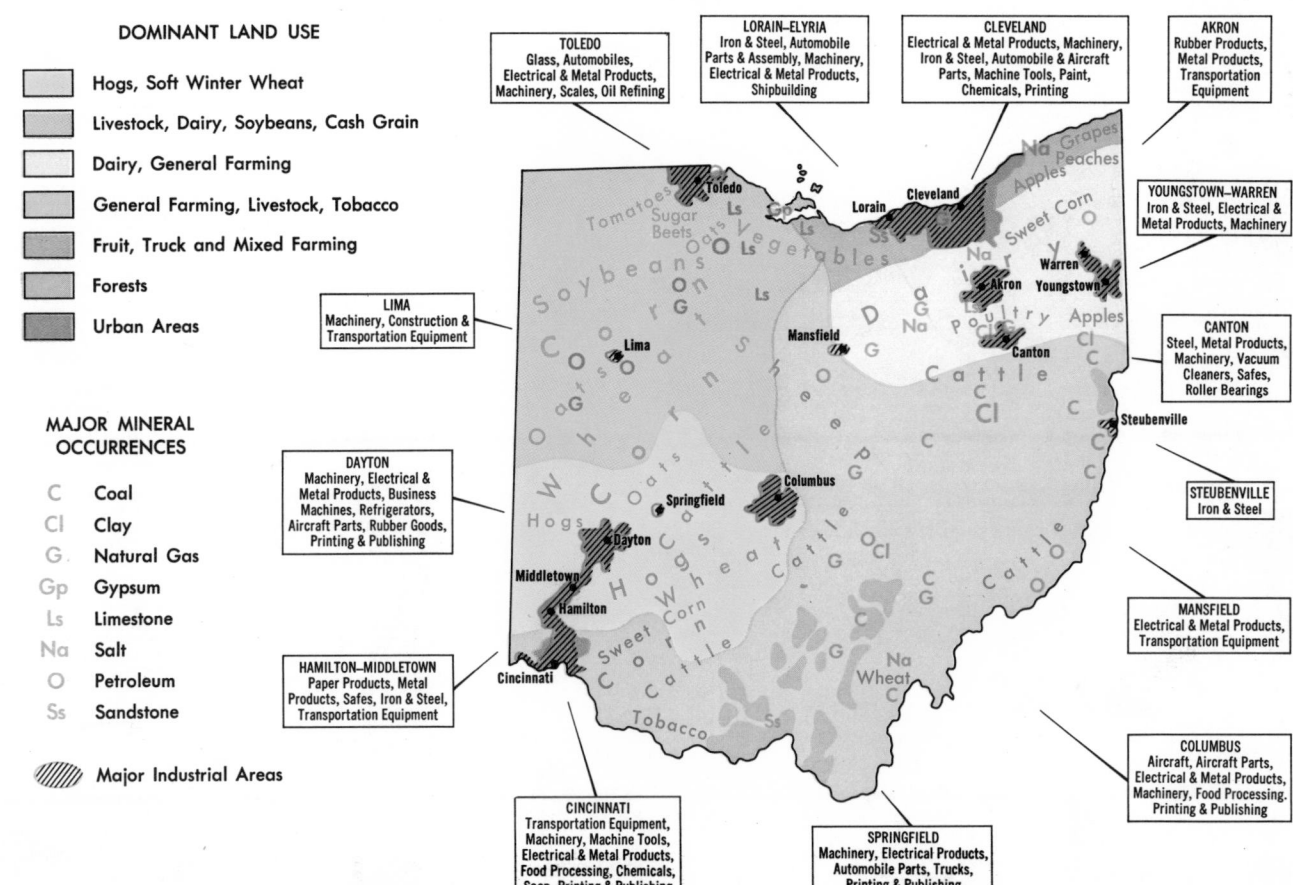

DOMINANT LAND USE

- Hogs, Soft Winter Wheat
- Livestock, Dairy, Soybeans, Cash Grain
- Dairy, General Farming
- General Farming, Livestock, Tobacco
- Fruit, Truck and Mixed Farming
- Forests
- Urban Areas

MAJOR MINERAL OCCURRENCES

- C — Coal
- Cl — Clay
- G — Natural Gas
- Gp — Gypsum
- Ls — Limestone
- Na — Salt
- O — Petroleum
- Ss — Sandstone

- ///// Major Industrial Areas

TOLEDO
Glass, Automobiles, Electrical & Metal Products, Machinery, Scales, Oil Refining

LORAIN–ELYRIA
Iron & Steel, Automobile Parts & Assembly, Machinery, Electrical & Metal Products, Shipbuilding

CLEVELAND
Electrical & Metal Products, Machinery, Iron & Steel, Automobile & Aircraft Parts, Machine Tools, Paint, Chemicals, Printing

AKRON
Rubber Products, Metal Products, Transportation Equipment

YOUNGSTOWN–WARREN
Iron & Steel, Electrical & Metal Products, Machinery

LIMA
Machinery, Construction & Transportation Equipment

CANTON
Steel, Metal Products, Machinery, Vacuum Cleaners, Safes, Roller Bearings

DAYTON
Machinery, Electrical & Metal Products, Business Machines, Refrigerators, Aircraft Parts, Rubber Goods, Printing & Publishing

STEUBENVILLE
Iron & Steel

MANSFIELD
Electrical & Metal Products, Transportation Equipment

HAMILTON–MIDDLETOWN
Paper Products, Metal Products, Safes, Iron & Steel, Transportation Equipment

COLUMBUS
Aircraft, Aircraft Parts, Electrical & Metal Products, Machinery, Food Processing, Printing & Publishing

CINCINNATI
Transportation Equipment, Machinery, Machine Tools, Electrical & Metal Products, Food Processing, Chemicals, Soap, Printing & Publishing

SPRINGFIELD
Machinery, Electrical Products, Automobile Parts, Trucks, Printing & Publishing

(continued)

Lou Moore—Shostal Associates

Reminiscent of children's book illustrations, the tugboat "Washington" guides ore-carrier "Peter Robertson" through Cleveland's Industrial Flats, past a Milwaukee fuel tanker.

44030 Conneaut, 14,552 J 2
45831 Continental, 1,185 B 3
45832 Convoy, 991 A 4
45723 Coolville, 672 G 7
43730 Corning, 838 F 6
44410 Cortland, 2,525 J 3
43812 Coshocton⊙, 13,747 G 5
† 45201 Covedale, 6,639 B 10
45318 Covington, 2,575 B 5
† 44429 Craig Beach, 1,451 H 3
44827 Crestline, 5,947 E 4
44217 Creston, 1,632 G 3
45806 Cridersville, 1,103 B 4
43731 Crooksville, 2,828 F 6
† 45341 Crystal Lakes, 5,851 C 6
* 44221 Cuyahoga Falls, 49,678 G 3
† 44101 Cuyahoga Heights, 866 H 9
43413 Cygnet, 629 C 3
44618 Dalton, 1,177 G 4
43014 Danville, 1,025 F 5
43123 Darbydale, 743 D 6
* 45401 Dayton⊙, 243,601 B 6
Dayton, ‡850,266 B 6
44411 Deerfield, 800 H 3
45236 Deer Park, 7,415 C 9
43512 Defiance⊙, 16,281 B 3
43318 Degraff, 1,117 C 5
43015 Delaware⊙, 15,008 E 5
45833 Delphos, 7,608 B 4
43515 Delta, 2,544 B 2
44621 Dennison, 3,506 H 5
† 45202 Dent, 800 B 9
43516 Deshler, 1,938 C 3
45750 Devola, 1,989 H 7
43917 Dillonvale, 1,095 J 5
44622 Dover, 11,516 G 4
44230 Doylestown, 2,373 G 4
43821 Dresden, 1,516 G 5
43017 Dublin, 681 D 5
43734 Duncan Falls, 900 G 6
45836 Dunkirk, 1,036 C 4
44730 East Canton, 1,631 H 4
44112 East Cleveland, 39,600 H 9
44094 Eastlake, 19,690 J 8
43920 East Liverpool, 20,020 J 4
44413 East Palestine, 5,604 J 4
44626 East Sparta, 959 H 4
45320 Eaton⊙, 6,020 A 6
† 44035 Eaton Estates, 2,076 G 3
43517 Edgerton, 2,126 A 3
44004 Edgewood, 3,437 J 2
43320 Edison, 569 E 4
43518 Edon, 803 A 2
45807 Elida, 1,211 B 4
43416 Elmore, 1,316 D 3
45216 Elmwood Place, 3,525 B 9
* 44035 Elyria⊙, 53,427 F 3
45322 Englewood, 7,885 B 6
45323 Enon, 1,929 C 6
44117 Euclid, 71,552 J 9
† 45201 Evendale, 1,967 C 9
45042 Excello, 900 B 7
45324 Fairborn, 32,267 B 6
† 45201 Fairfax, 2,705 C 9
45014 Fairfield, 14,680 A 7
44313 Fairlawn, 6,102 G 3
44077 Fairport Harbor, 3,665 H 2
44126 Fairview Park, 21,681 G 9
45325 Farmersville, 865 A 6
43521 Fayette, 1,175 B 2
45120 Felicity, 786 B 8
45840 Findlay⊙, 35,800 C 3
45326 Fletcher, 539 B 5
43977 Flushing, 1,207 J 5
45843 Forest, 1,535 C 4
45405 Forest Park, 15,139 B 9
† 45202 Forestville, 950 C 10
45844 Fort Jennings, 533 B 4
45845 Fort Loramie, 744 B 5
† 45401 Fort McKinley, 11,536 B 6
45846 Fort Recovery, 1,348 A 5
† 45801 Fort Shawnee, 3,436 B 4
44830 Fostoria, 16,037 D 3
45628 Frankfort, 949 D 7
45005 Franklin, 10,075 B 6
45629 Franklin Furnace, 975 E 8
43822 Frazeysburg, 941 F 5
44627 Fredericksburg, 601 G 4
43019 Fredericktown, 1,935 F 5
43420 Fremont⊙, 18,490 D 3
45630 Friendship, 600 D 8
43230 Gahanna, 12,400 E 5
44833 Galion, 13,123 E 4
45631 Gallipolis⊙, 7,490 F 8
43022 Gambier, 1,571 F 5
44125 Garfield Heights, 41,417 J 9
44231 Garrettsville, 1,718 H 3
44040 Gates Mills, 2,378 J 9
44041 Geneva, 6,449 J 2
44043 Geneva-on-the-Lake, 877 H 2
43430 Genoa, 2,139 D 2
45121 Georgetown⊙, 2,949 C 8
45327 Germantown, 4,088 B 6
45328 Gettysburg, 526 A 5
43431 Gibsonburg, 2,585 D 3
44420 Girard, 14,119 J 3
45848 Glandorf, 732 B 3
45246 Glendale, 2,690 C 9
† 44139 Glenwillow, 526 J 10
45732 Glouster, 2,121 F 6
44629 Gnadenhutten, 1,466 G 5
† 45201 Golf Manor, 5,170 C 9
45122 Goshen, 1,174 B 7
44044 Grafton, 1,771 F 3
43522 Grand Rapids, 976 C 3
44045 Grand River, 613 H 2
† 43201 Grandview Heights, 8,460 D 6
43023 Granville, 3,963 F 5
45330 Gratis, 621 A 6
43322 Green Camp, 537 D 4
45123 Greenfield, 4,780 D 7
45218 Greenhills, 6,092 B 9
44232 Greensburg, 950 G 4
44836 Green Springs, 1,279 E 3
44630 Greentown, 1,150 H 4
45331 Greenville⊙, 12,380 A 5
44837 Greenwich, 1,473 E 3
45239 Groesbeck, 5,000 B 9
43123 Grove City, 13,911 D 6
43125 Groveport, 2,490 E 6
45849 Grover Hill, 536 B 3
45634 Hamden, 953 F 7
45130 Hamersville, 567 C 8
* 45011 Hamilton⊙, 67,865 A 7
Hamilton-Middletown, ‡226,207 A 7
43524 Hamler, 681 B 3
43931 Hannibal, 550 J 6
† 43055 Hanover, 626 F 5
43126 Harrisburg, 556 D 6
45030 Harrison, 4,408 A 9
45850 Harrod, 533 C 4
† 44085 Hartsgrove, 775 J 2
44632 Hartville, 1,752 H 4
43525 Haskins, 549 C 3
43127 Haydenville, 650 F 7
43055 Heath, 6,768 F 5
43025 Hebron, 1,699 E 6
43526 Hicksville, 3,461 A 3
† 44143 Highland Heights, 5,926 J 9
43026 Hilliard, 8,369 D 5
45133 Hillsboro⊙, 5,584 C 7
44234 Hiram, 1,484 H 3
43527 Holgate, 1,541 B 3
43528 Holland, 1,108 C 2
45033 Hooven, 550 A 9
43976 Hopedale, 916 J 5
44425 Hubbard, 8,583 J 3
45424 Huber Heights, 18,943 B 6
44236 Hudson, 3,933 H 3
† 44022 Hunting Valley, 797 J 9
44839 Huron, 6,896 E 3
44131 Independence, 7,034 H 9
† 45201 Indian Hill, 5,651 C 9
† 43932 Irondale, 602 J 4
45638 Ironton⊙, 15,030 E 8
45640 Jackson⊙, 6,843 E 7
45334 Jackson Center, 1,119 B 5
45740 Jacksonville, 545 F 7
45335 Jamestown, 1,790 C 6
44047 Jefferson⊙, 2,472 J 2
† 43162 Jefferson (West Jefferson), 3,664 D 6
43128 Jeffersonville, 1,031 C 6
44840 Jeromesville, 659 F 4
43986 Jewett, 901 H 5
43031 Johnstown, 3,208 E 5
43748 Junction City, 732 F 6
45853 Kalida, 900 B 4
44240 Kent, 28,183 H 3
43326 Kenton⊙, 8,315 C 4
45429 Kettering, 69,599 B 6
44637 Killbuck, 893 G 5
45034 Kings Mills, 800 B 7
45644 Kingston, 1,157 E 7
44048 Kingsville, 1,129 J 2
44428 Kinsman, 900 J 3
43033 Kirkersville, 578 E 6
44094 Kirtland, 5,530 H 2
43951 Lafferty, 900 H 5
44050 Lagrange, 1,074 F 3
44250 Lakemore, 2,708 H 3
43440 Lakeside, 850 E 2
43331 Lakeview, 1,026 C 4
44107 Lakewood, 70,173 G 9
43130 Lancaster⊙, 32,911 E 6
43934 Lansing, 950 J 5
43332 La Rue, 867 D 4
43135 Laurelville, 624 E 7
† 45501 Lawrenceville, 687 C 6
44430 Leavittsburg, 4,979 J 3
45036 Lebanon⊙, 7,934 B 7
45135 Leesburg, 984 D 7
44431 Leetonia, 2,342 J 4
45856 Leipsic, 2,072 C 3
44251 Leroy, 715 G 3
45338 Lewisburg, 1,553 A 6
44904 Lexington, 2,972 E 4
43532 Liberty Center, 1,007 B 3
* 45801 Lima⊙, 53,734 B 4
Lima, ‡171,472 B 4
† 45201 Lincoln Heights, 6,099 C 9
43442 Lindsey, 652 D 3
44432 Lisbon⊙, 3,521 J 4
44253 Litchfield, 650 F 3
43136 Lithopolis, 705 E 6
45742 Little Hocking, 520 G 7
45215 Lockland, 5,288 C 9
44254 Lodi, 2,399 F 3
43138 Logan⊙, 6,269 F 6
43140 London⊙, 6,481 C 6
* 44052 Lorain, 78,185 F 3
Lorain-Elyria, ‡256,843 F 3
44842 Loudonville, 2,865 F 4
44641 Louisville, 6,298 H 4
45140 Loveland, 7,144 D 9
45744 Lowell, 852 H 6
44436 Lowellville, 1,836 J 3
44843 Lucas, 771 F 4
45648 Lucasville, 900 E 8
43443 Luckey, 996 D 3
45142 Lynchburg, 1,186 C 7
44124 Lyndhurst, 19,749 J 9
43533 Lyons, 630 B 2
44056 Macedonia, 6,375 J 10
† 45202 Mack, 5,000 B 9
45243 Madeira, 6,713 C 9
44057 Madison, 1,678 H 2
44643 Magnolia, 1,064 H 4
43758 Malta, 1,017 G 6
44644 Malvern, 1,256 H 4
45144 Manchester, 2,195 C 8
* 44901 Mansfield⊙, 55,047 F 4
Mansfield, ‡129,997 F 4
44255 Mantua, 1,199 H 3
44137 Maple Heights, 34,093 H 9
† 43440 Marblehead, 726 E 2
45860 Maria Stein, 950 A 5
45227 Mariemont, 4,540 C 9
45750 Marietta⊙, 16,861 G 7
43302 Marion⊙, 38,646 D 4
44645 Marshallville, 693 G 4
43935 Martins Ferry, 10,757 J 5
43040 Marysville⊙, 5,744 D 5
45040 Mason, 5,677 B 7
44646 Massillon, 32,539 H 4
44438 Masury, 2,060 J 3
45069 Maud, 550 B 7
43537 Maumee, 15,937 C 2
† 44121 Mayfield, 3,548 J 9
† 44101 Mayfield Heights, 22,139 J 9
45651 McArthur⊙, 1,543 F 7
43534 McClure, 699 C 3
45858 McComb, 1,329 C 3
43756 McConnelsville⊙, 2,107 G 6
44437 McDonald, 3,177 J 3
45859 McGuffey, 704 C 4
43044 Mechanicsburg, 1,686 D 5
44256 Medina⊙, 10,913 G 3
45862 Mendon, 672 A 4
44060 Mentor, 36,912 H 2
44060 Mentor-on-the-Lake, 6,517 G 2
43540 Metamora, 594 C 2
45342 Miamisburg, 14,797 B 6
45041 Miamitown, 800 A 9
44652 Middlebranch, 600 H 4
† 44017 Middleburg Heights, 12,367 G 10
44062 Middlefield, 1,726 H 3
45863 Middle Point, 543 B 4
45760 Middleport, 2,784 F 7
45042 Middletown, 48,767 A 6
44653 Midvale, 636 H 5
44846 Milan, 1,405 E 3
45150 Milford, 4,828 D 9
43045 Milford Center, 753 D 5
43447 Millbury, 771 D 2
44654 Millersburg⊙, 2,979 F 4
43046 Millersport, 777 E 6
45013 Millville, 697 A 7
44656 Mineral City, 860 H 4
44440 Mineral Ridge, 1,500 J 3
44657 Minerva, 4,359 H 4
† 43201 Minerva Park, 1,402 E 5
43938 Mingo Junction, 5,278 J 5
45865 Minster, 2,405 B 5
44260 Mogadore, 3,858 H 3
45050 Monroe, 3,492 B 7
44847 Monroeville, 1,455 E 3
45242 Montgomery, 5,683 C 9
43543 Montpelier, 4,184 A 2
45439 Moraine, 4,898 B 6
† 44022 Moreland Hills, 3,000 J 9
45152 Morrow, 1,486 B 7
43338 Mount Gilead⊙, 2,971 E 4
45231 Mount Healthy, 7,446 B 9
45154 Mount Orab, 1,306 C 7
43939 Mount Pleasant, 635 J 5
43143 Mount Sterling, 1,536 D 6
43050 Mount Vernon⊙, 13,373 E 5
43340 Mount Victory, 633 D 4
44262 Munroe Falls, 3,794 H 3
43144 Murray City, 562 F 6
43545 Napoleon⊙, 7,791 B 3
44662 Navarre, 1,607 H 4
43940 Neffs, 900 J 5
44441 Negley, 600 J 4
45764 Nelsonville, 4,812 F 7
44849 Nevada, 917 D 4
43054 New Albany, 513 E 5
43055 Newark⊙, 41,836 F 5
45662 New Boston, 3,325 E 8
45869 New Bremen, 2,185 B 5
† 44101 Newburgh Heights, 3,396 H 9
† 45201 New Burlington, 900 B 9
45344 New Carlisle, 6,112 C 6
43832 Newcomerstown, 4,155 G 5
43762 New Concord, 2,318 G 6
43145 New Holland, 796 D 6
45871 New Knoxville, 852 B 5
45345 New Lebanon, 4,248 B 6
43764 New Lexington⊙, 4,921 F 6
44851 New London, 2,336 F 3
45346 New Madison, 959 A 6
45767 New Matamoras, 940 J 6
45011 New Miami, 3,273 A 7
44442 New Middletown, 1,664 J 4
45347 New Paris, 1,692 A 6
44663 New Philadelphia⊙, 15,184 G 5
45768 Newport, 975 H 7
45157 New Richmond, 2,650 B 8
43766 New Straitsville, 947 F 6
44444 Newton Falls, 5,378 J 3
45244 Newtown, 2,047 C 10
45159 New Vienna, 849 C 7
44854 New Washington, 1,251 E 4
44445 New Waterford, 735 J 4
44446 Niles, 21,581 J 3
45872 North Baltimore, 3,143 C 3
45052 North Bend, 638 B 9
44450 North Bloomfield, 650 J 3
44720 North Canton, 15,228 H 4
45239 North College Hill, 12,363 B 9
44855 North Fairfield, 540 E 3
44067 Northfield, 1,089 J 10
44707 North Industry, 2,000 H 4
44068 North Kingsville, 2,458 J 2
43060 North Lewisburg, 840 C 5
44452 North Lima, 800 J 4
44070 North Olmsted, 34,861 G 9
† 44081 North Perry, 851 H 2
† 44101 North Randall, 1,212 H 9
44035 North Ridgeville, 13,152 F 3
44133 North Royalton, 12,807 H 10
† 43601 Northwood, 4,222 D 2
† 43701 North Zanesville, 3,399 G 6
44203 Norton, 12,308 G 3
44857 Norwalk⊙, 13,386 E 3
45212 Norwood, 30,420 C 9
43449 Oak Harbor, 2,807 D 2
45656 Oak Hill, 1,642 E 8
45873 Oakwood, 10,095 B 6
45873 Oakwood, 3,127 B 3
45873 Oakwood, 804 B 3
44074 Oberlin, 8,761 F 3
43207 Obetz, 2,248 E 6
45874 Ohio City, 816 A 4
44138 Olmsted Falls, 2,504 G 9
44862 Ontario, 4,345 E 4
† 44101 Orange, 2,112 H 9
43616 Oregon, 16,563 D 2
44667 Orrville, 7,408 G 4
44076 Orwell, 965 J 2
45875 Ottawa⊙, 3,622 B 3
† 43601 Ottawa Hills, 4,270 C 2
45876 Ottoville, 914 B 4
45160 Owensville, 707 B 8
45056 Oxford, 15,868 A 6
44077 Painesville⊙, 16,536 H 2
45877 Pandora, 857 C 4
44080 Parkman, 750 H 3
44129 Parma, 100,216 H 9
† 44129 Parma Heights, 27,192 G 9
43062 Pataskala, 1,831 E 5
45879 Paulding⊙, 2,983 A 3
45880 Payne, 1,351 A 3
45660 Peebles, 1,629 D 8
43450 Pemberville, 1,301 C 3
44264 Peninsula, 692 G 3
44124 Pepper Pike, 5,933 J 9
44081 Perry, 917 H 2
43551 Perrysburg, 7,693 C 2
44864 Perrysville, 752 F 4
45354 Phillipsburg, 831 B 6
43771 Philo, 846 G 6
43147 Pickerington, 696 E 6
45661 Piketon, 1,347 E 7
43554 Pioneer, 968 A 2
45356 Piqua, 20,741 B 5
43064 Plain City, 2,254 D 5
45359 Pleasant Hill, 1,025 B 5
43148 Pleasantville, 754 F 6
44865 Plymouth, 1,993 E 4
† 45042 Poasttown, 650 B 6
44514 Poland, 3,097 J 3
45769 Pomeroy⊙, 2,672 G 7
43452 Port Clinton⊙, 7,202 E 2
45770 Portland, 550 G 7
45662 Portsmouth⊙, 27,633 D 8
43837 Port Washington, 550 G 5
43942 Powhatan Point, 2,167 J 6
45669 Proctorville, 881 F 9
43342 Prospect, 1,031 D 5
43456 Put-in-Bay, 135 E 2
43773 Quaker City, 510 H 6
43343 Quincy, 686 C 5
45771 Racine, 583 G 8
43066 Radnor, 950 D 5
44265 Randolph, 900 H 3
44266 Ravenna⊙, 11,780 H 3
43943 Rayland, 617 J 5
45215 Reading, 14,303 C 9
† 45202 Remington, 600 C 9
45773 Reno, 576 H 7
† 43412 Reno Beach, 1,049 D 2
44867 Republic, 705 D 3
43068 Reynoldsburg, 13,921 E 6
44286 Richfield, 3,228 G 3
43944 Richmond, 777 J 5
† 44045 Richmond (Grand River), 613 H 2
45673 Richmond Dale, 950 E 7
44143 Richmond Heights, 9,220 H 9
43344 Richwood, 2,072 D 5
45674 Rio Grande, 814 F 8
45167 Ripley, 2,745 C 8
43457 Risingsun, 730 C 3
44270 Rittman, 6,308 G 4
† 43085 Riverlea, 558 D 5
44670 Robertsville, 600 H 4
45766 Rock Creek, 731 J 2
45882 Rockford, 1,207 A 4
44116 Rocky River, 22,958 G 9
44085 Rome, 648 J 2
44272 Rootstown, 900 H 3
† 45662 Rosemount, 1,786 D 8
43777 Roseville, 1,767 F 6
45061 Ross (Venice), 1,661 B 9
43460 Rossford, 5,302 C 2
45236 Rossmoyne, 2,900 C 9
† 43943 Rush Run, 560 J 5
43347 Rushsylvania, 526 C 5
43348 Russells Point, 1,104 C 5
45775 Rutland, 663 F 7
45169 Sabina, 2,160 C 7
† 44067 Sagamore Hills, 4,100 J 10
45217 Saint Bernard, 6,080 B 9
43950 Saint Clairsville⊙, 4,754 J 5
45883 Saint Henry, 1,276 A 5
45885 Saint Marys, 7,699 B 4
43072 Saint Paris, 1,646 C 5
44460 Salem, 14,186 J 4
43945 Salineville, 1,686 J 4
44870 Sandusky⊙, 32,674 E 3
44671 Sandyville, 543 H 4
45171 Sardinia, 824 C 7
43946 Sardis, 700 J 6
43988 Scio, 1,002 H 5
† 45662 Sciotodale, 950 E 8
45679 Seaman, 866 C 8
44672 Sebring, 4,954 H 4
† 44101 Seven Hills, 12,700 H 9
45062 Seven Mile, 699 A 7
44273 Seville, 1,402 G 3
43947 Shadyside, 5,070 J 6
44120 Shaker Heights, 36,306 H 9
45241 Sharonville, 10,985 C 9
43782 Shawnee, 914 F 6
† 44052 Sheffield, 1,730 F 3
44054 Sheffield Lake, 8,734 F 3
44875 Shelby, 9,847 E 4
43556 Sherwood, 784 A 3
44878 Shiloh, 817 E 4
44676 Shreve, 1,635 F 4
45365 Sidney⊙, 16,332 B 5
† 44221 Silver Lake, 3,637 G 3
† 45201 Silverton, 6,588 C 9
43948 Smithfield, 1,245 J 5
44677 Smithville, 1,278 G 4
44139 Solon, 11,519 J 9
43783 Somerset, 1,417 F 6
† 44001 South Amherst, 2,913 F 3
† 43103 South Bloomfield, 610 D 6
45368 South Charleston, 1,500 C 6
44121 South Euclid, 29,579 H 9
45065 South Lebanon, 3,014 B 7
45680 South Point, 2,243 E 9
† 44022 South Russell, 2,673 H 3
45369 South Vienna, 545 C 6
45682 South Webster, 825 E 8
43701 South Zanesville, 1,436 F 6
44275 Spencer, 758 F 3
45887 Spencerville, 2,241 B 4
45066 Springboro, 2,799 B 6
45246 Springdale, 8,127 B 9
* 45501 Springfield⊙, 81,926 C 6
Springfield, ‡157,115 C 6
45370 Spring Valley, 667 C 6
44276 Sterling, 550 G 4
43952 Steubenville⊙, 30,771 J 5
Steubenville-Weirton, ‡165,627 J 5
43154 Stoutsville, 573 E 6
44224 Stow, 19,847 H 3
44680 Strasburg, 1,874
44240 Streetsboro, 7,966
44136 Strongsville, 15,182
44471 Struthers, 15,343 J
43557 Stryker, 1,296
† 44260 Suffield, 650
44681 Sugarcreek, 1,771
43074 Sunbury, 2,512 E
43558 Swanton, 2,927 C
44882 Sycamore, 1,096 D
43560 Sylvania, 12,031 C
45779 Syracuse, 684 C
44278 Tallmadge, 15,274 H
† 43771 Taylorsville (Philo), 846 C
45174 Terrace Park, 2,266 D
45780 The Plains, 1,568 F
43076 Thornville, 679 F
44883 Tiffin⊙, 21,596 D
43963 Tiltonsville, 2,123 J
† 44094 Timberlake, 964 J
45371 Tipp City, 5,090 B
† 45245 Tobasco, 950 C
* 43601 Toledo⊙, 383,818 D
Toledo, ‡692,571 D
43964 Toronto, 7,705 J
45067 Trenton, 5,278 B
45782 Trimble, 542 F
45373 Troy⊙, 17,186 B
44682 Tuscarawas, 830 H
44087 Twinsburg, 6,432 J
44683 Uhrichsville, 5,731 H
45322 Union, 3,654 B
† 47390 Union City, 1,808 A
44685 Uniontown, 875 H
44118 University Heights, 17,055 H
43221 Upper Arlington, 38,630 D
43351 Upper Sandusky⊙, 5,645 D
43078 Urbana⊙, 11,237 C
† 43123 Urbancrest, 754 D
43080 Utica, 1,977 F
† 43201 Valley View, 909 D
† 44101 Valley View, 1,422 H
45377 Vandalia, 10,796 B
45890 Vanlue, 539 C
45891 Van Wert⊙, 11,320 A
44870 Venice, 1,661 B
44089 Vermilion, 9,872 F
45378 Verona, 593 A
45380 Versailles, 2,441 A
44473 Vienna, 1,200 J
† 44473 Vienna (South Vienna), 545 C
44281 Wadsworth, 13,142 G
† 44094 Waite Hill, 514 H
44889 Wakeman, 514 F
43465 Walbridge, 3,208 C
44687 Walnut Creek, 550 G
† 44146 Walton Hills, 2,508 J
45895 Wapakoneta⊙, 7,324 B
* 44481 Warren⊙, 63,494 J
† 44100 Warrensville Heights, 18,925 H
43844 Warsaw, 725 G
43160 Washington Court House⊙, 12,495 D
44490 Washingtonville, 747 J
45786 Waterford, 600 G
43566 Waterville, 2,940 C
43567 Wauseon⊙, 4,932 B
45690 Waverly⊙, 4,858 D
43466 Wayne, 921 C
44688 Waynesburg, 1,337 H
45896 Waynesfield, 704 C
45068 Waynesville, 1,638 B
44090 Wellington, 4,137 F
45692 Wellston, 5,410 F
43968 Wellsville, 5,891 J
45381 West Alexandria, 1,553 A
45449 West Carrollton, 10,748 B
43081 Westerville, 12,530 D
44491 West Farmington, 650 J
43162 West Jefferson, 3,664 D
43845 West Lafayette, 1,719 G
44145 Westlake, 15,689 G
43357 West Liberty, 1,580 C
43358 West Mansfield, 753 C
45383 West Milton, 3,696 B
43569 Weston, 1,269 C
† 45662 West Portsmouth, 3,396 D
44287 West Salem, 1,058 F
45693 West Union⊙, 1,951 C
43570 West Unity, 1,589 B
† 44138 Westview, 2,523 G
45694 Wheelersburg, 3,709 E
43213 Whitehall, 25,263 E
43571 Whitehouse, 1,542 C
44092 Wickliffe, 21,354 J
44890 Willard, 5,510 E
45176 Williamsburg, 2,054 B
44093 Williamsfield, 950 J
43164 Williamsport, 857 D
44094 Willoughby, 18,634 J
† 44094 Willoughby Hills, 5,247 J
44094 Willowick, 21,237 J
45898 Willshire, 623 A
45177 Wilmington⊙, 10,051 C
45697 Winchester, 760 C
44288 Windham, 3,360 H
43952 Wintersville, 4,921 J
45245 Withamsville, 975 C
† 45201 Woodlawn, 3,251 C
† 44101 Woodmere, 976 J
43793 Woodsfield⊙, 3,239 H
43469 Woodville, 1,834 D
44691 Wooster⊙, 18,703 G
43085 Worthington, 15,326 E
45215 Wyoming, 9,089 C
45385 Xenia⊙, 25,373 C
45387 Yellow Springs, 4,624 C
43971 Yorkville, 1,656 J
* 44501 Youngstown⊙, 139,788 J
Youngstown-Warren, ‡536,003 J
43701 Zanesville⊙, 33,045 G

⊙ County seat.
‡ Population of metropolitan area.
† Zip of nearest p.o.
* Multiple zips

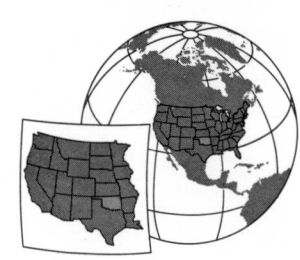

AREA 69,919 sq. mi.
POPULATION 2,559,253
CAPITAL Oklahoma City
LARGEST CITY Oklahoma City
HIGHEST POINT Black Mesa 4,973 ft.
SETTLED IN 1889
ADMITTED TO UNION November 16, 1907
POPULAR NAME Sooner State
STATE FLOWER Mistletoe
STATE BIRD Scissor-tailed Flycatcher

(continued on following page)

Agriculture, Industry and Resources

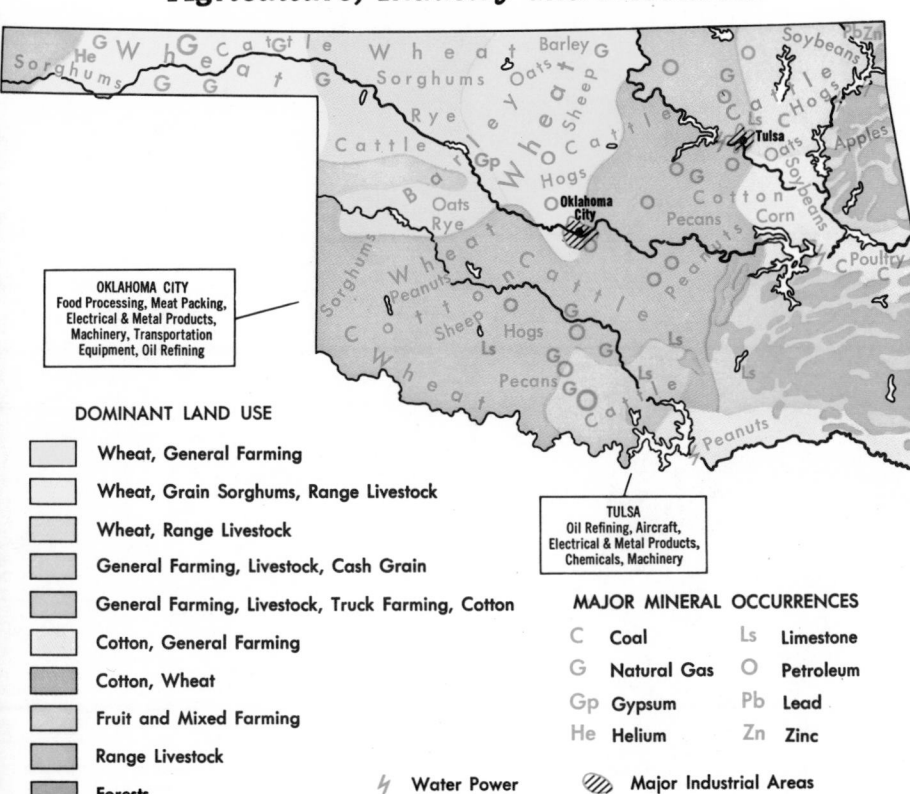

OKLAHOMA CITY
Food Processing, Meat Packing, Electrical & Metal Products, Machinery, Transportation Equipment, Oil Refining

TULSA
Oil Refining, Aircraft, Electrical & Metal Products, Chemicals, Machinery

DOMINANT LAND USE

- Wheat, General Farming
- Wheat, Grain Sorghums, Range Livestock
- Wheat, Range Livestock
- General Farming, Livestock, Cash Grain
- General Farming, Livestock, Truck Farming, Cotton
- Cotton, General Farming
- Cotton, Wheat
- Fruit and Mixed Farming
- Range Livestock
- Forests

⚡ Water Power   ▨ Major Industrial Areas

MAJOR MINERAL OCCURRENCES

C	Coal	Ls	Limestone
G	Natural Gas	O	Petroleum
Gp	Gypsum	Pb	Lead
He	Helium	Zn	Zinc

D. Elliott Stribling — Shostal Associates

Aesthetic drawbacks are outweighed by substantial revenues from oil wells obstructing the view of Oklahoma's capitol building.

OKLAHOMA

SCALE
0 5 10 20 30 40 MI.
0 5 10 20 30 40 KM.

State Capitals........⊛
County Seats........⊙
© C.S. HAMMOND & Co., N.Y.

Topography

0 50 100
MILES

5,000 m. 2,000 m. 1,000 m. 500 m. 200 m. 100 m. Sea Below
16,404 ft. 6,562 ft. 3,281 ft. 1,640 ft. 656 ft. 328 ft. Level

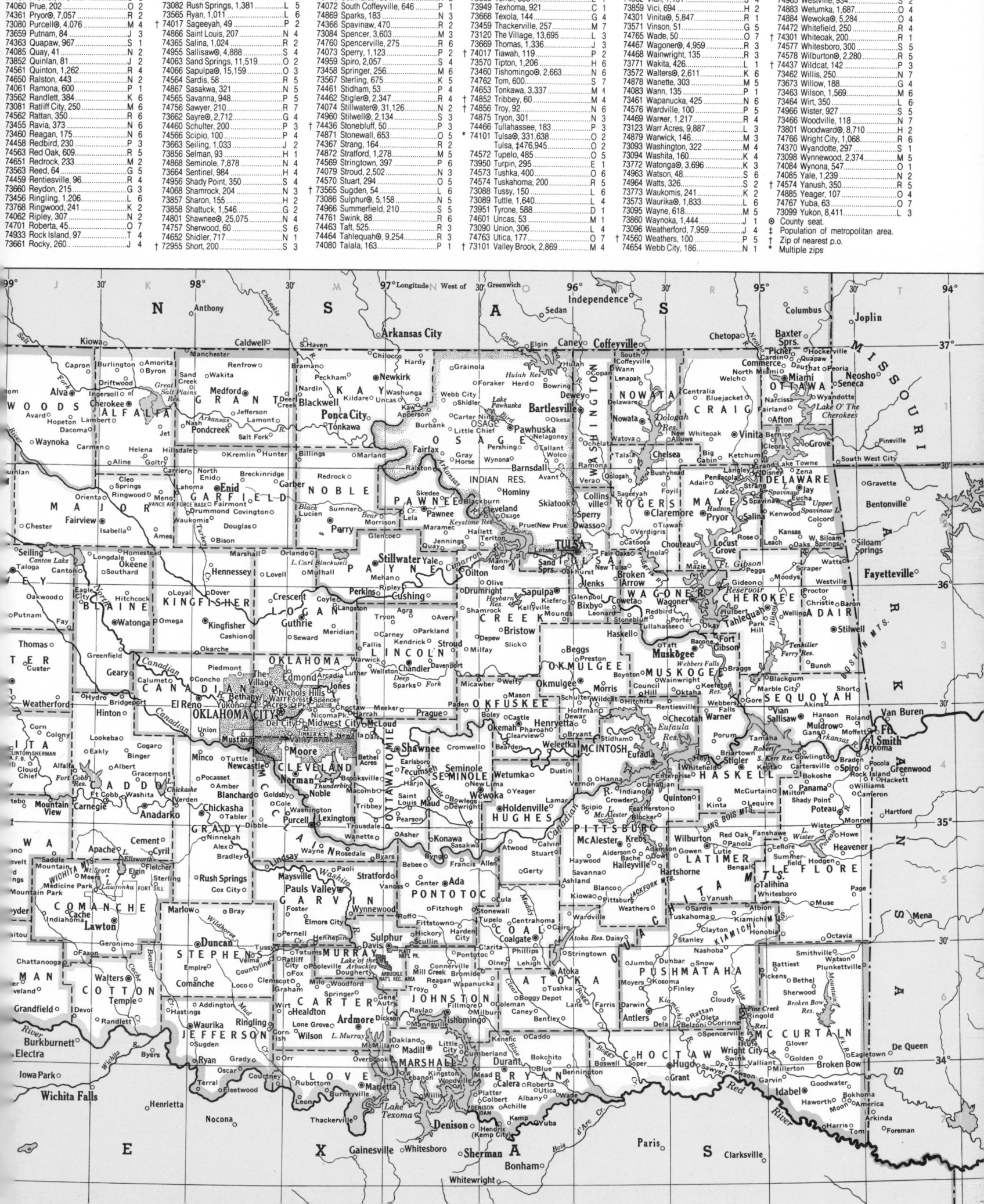

COUNTIES

Baker, 14,919 ....K 3
Benton, 53,776 ....D 3
Clackamas, 166,088 ....E 2
Clatsop, 28,473 ....D 1
Columbia, 28,790 ....D 2
Coos, 56,515 ....C 4
Crook, 9,985 ....G 3
Curry, 13,006 ....C 5
Deschutes, 30,442 ....F 4
Douglas, 71,743 ....D 4
Gilliam, 2,342 ....G 2
Grant, 6,996 ....J 3
Harney, 7,215 ....H 4
Hood River, 13,187 ....F 2
Jackson, 94,533 ....E 5
Jefferson, 8,548 ....F 3
Josephine, 35,746 ....D 5
Klamath, 50,021 ....F 5
Lake, 6,343 ....G 5
Lane, 213,358 ....E 4
Lincoln, 25,755 ....C 3
Linn, 71,914 ....E 3
Malheur, 23,169 ....K 4

Marion, 151,309 ....E 3
Morrow, 4,465 ....H 2
Multnomah, 556,667 ....E 2
Polk, 35,349 ....D 3
Sherman, 2,139 ....G 2
Tillamook, 17,930 ....D 2
Umatilla, 44,923 ....J 2
Union, 19,377 ....J 2
Wallowa, 6,247 ....K 2
Wasco, 20,133 ....F 2
Washington, 157,920 ....D 2
Wheeler, 1,849 ....G 3
Yamhill, 40,213 ....D 2

CITIES and TOWNS

Zip	Name/Pop.	Key
97810	Adams, 219	J 2
97620	Adel, 200	H 5
97901	Adrian, 200	K 4
97320	Agate Beach, 975	C 3
97406	Agness, 120	C 5
† 97361	Airlie, 45	D 3
97321	Albany◉, 18,181	D 3
† 97601	Algoma, 77	F 5
97811	Alicel, 30	J 2
97407	Allegany, 200	D 4
97006	Aloha, 6,000	A 2
97408	Alpine, 80	D 3
97324	Alsea, 600	D 3
† 97601	Altamont, 15,746	F 5
97409	Alvadore, 350	D 3
97101	Amity, 708	D 2
97001	Antelope, 51	F 3
97530	Applegate, 125	D 5
97458	Arago, 200	C 4
97812	Arlington, 375	G 2
97473	Ash, 80	D 4
97520	Ashland, 12,342	E 5
97103	Astoria◉, 10,244	D 1
97813	Athena, 872	J 2
97325	Aumsville, 590	E 3
97002	Aurora, 306	B 2
97817	Austin, 170	J 3
97410	Azalea, 40	D 5
97814	Baker◉, 9,354	K 3
97378	Ballston, 120	D 2
97458	Bancroft, 45	D 5
97411	Bandon, 1,832	C 4
97106	Banks, 430	A 1

97003	Barlow, 105	B 2
† 97009	Barton, 100	B 2
† 97136	Bar View, 75	C 2
97817	Bates, 430	J 3
97107	Bay City, 898	D 2
97621	Beatty, 50	F 5
97108	Beaver, 450	D 2
97004	Beavercreek, 708	B 2
97005	Beaverton, 18,577	A 2
97456	Bellfountain, 50	D 3
† 97701	Bend◉, 13,710	F 3
97058	Biggs, 50	G 2
97016	Birkenfeld, 45	D 1
97412	Blachly, 425	D 3
97108	Blaine, 150	D 2
97326	Blodgett, 150	D 3
97413	Blue River, 350	E 3
97622	Bly, 50	F 5
97818	Boardman, 192	H 2
97623	Bonanza, 230	F 5
97002	Bonneville, 130	E 2
97009	Boring, 150	B 2
† 97021	Boyd, 26	F 2
97342	Breitenbush, 50	F 3
97010	Bridal Veil, 155	E 2

† 97458	Bridge, 250	D 4
97819	Bridgeport, 45	K 3
97001	Brightwood, 420	E 2
97032	Broadacres, 80	A 3
97414	Broadbent, 265	C 4
97903	Brogan, 140	K 3
97415	Brookings, 2,720	C 5
97305	Brooks, 490	A 3
† 97840	Brownlee, 50	L 3
† 97524	Brownsboro, 150	E 5
97327	Brownsville, 1,034	E 3
97351	Buena Vista, 90	D 3
97420	Bunker Hill, 1,549	C 4
97720	Burns◉, 3,293	H 4
97522	Butte Falls, 358	E 5
† 97002	Butteville, 385	A 2
97109	Buxton, 163	D 2
97416	Camas Valley, 665	C 4
97730	Camp Sherman, 87	F 3
† 97493	Canary, 50	D 3
97013	Canby, 3,813	B 2
97110	Cannon Beach, 500	D 1
97820	Canyon City◉, 600	J 3
97417	Canyonville, 940	D 5

97111	Carlton, 1,126	D
† 97415	Carpenterville, 30	C
97015	Carver, 50	B
97014	Cascade Locks, 574	E
97329	Cascadia, 150	E
97523	Cave Junction, 415	D
97821	Cayuse, 300	J
97822	Cecil, 75	H
† 97225	Cedar Hills, 2,900	A
† 97005	Cedar Mill, 1,500	A
† 97058	Celilo, 50	G
97501	Central Point, 4,004	D
97420	Charleston, 500	C
97306	Chemawa, 900	A
97731	Chemult, 580	E
† 97058	Chenoweth, 2,329	F
97119	Cherry Grove, 200	D
† 97055	Cherryville, 280	C
97419	Cheshire, 750	C
97624	Chiloquin, 826	F
97015	Clackamas, 6,000	D
97016	Clatskanie, 1,286	D
97112	Cloverdale, 151	D
97401	Coburg, 665	E
97017	Colton, 305	B

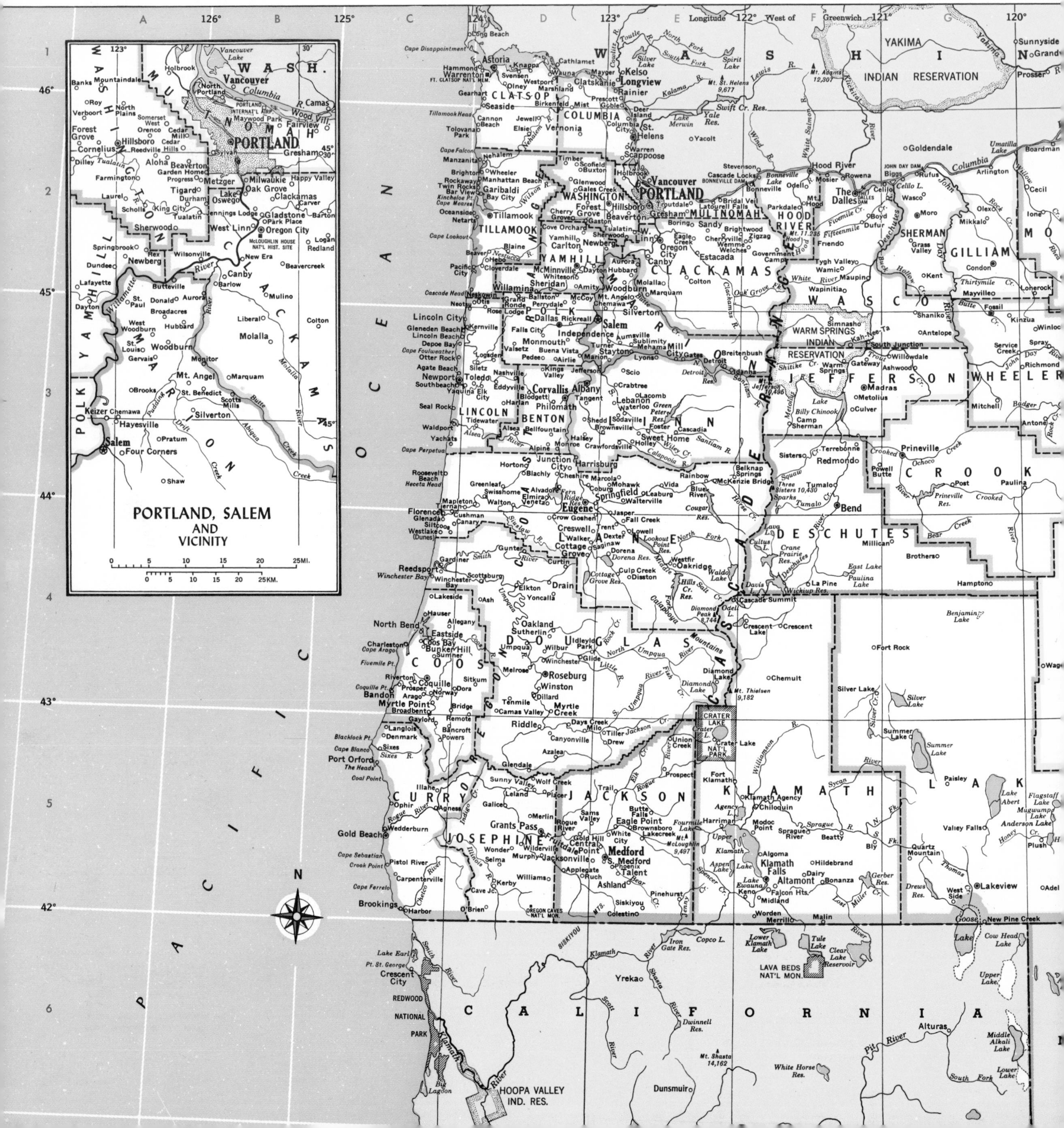

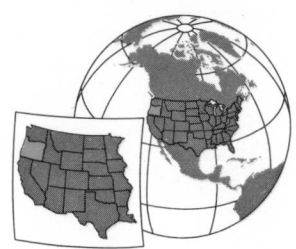

AREA 96,981 sq. mi.
POPULATION 2,091,385
CAPITAL Salem
LARGEST CITY Portland
HIGHEST POINT Mt. Hood 11,235 ft.
SETTLED IN 1810
ADMITTED TO UNION February 14, 1859
POPULAR NAME Beaver State
STATE FLOWER Oregon Grape
STATE BIRD Western Meadowlark

Topography

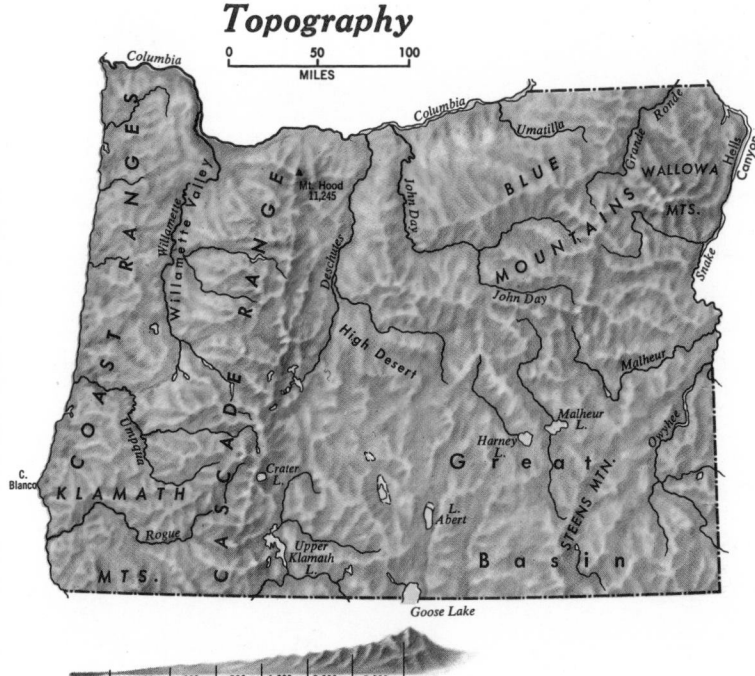

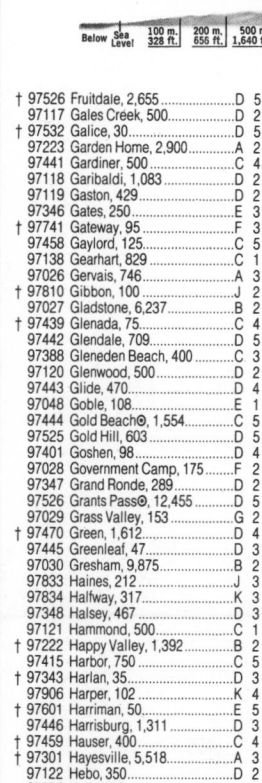

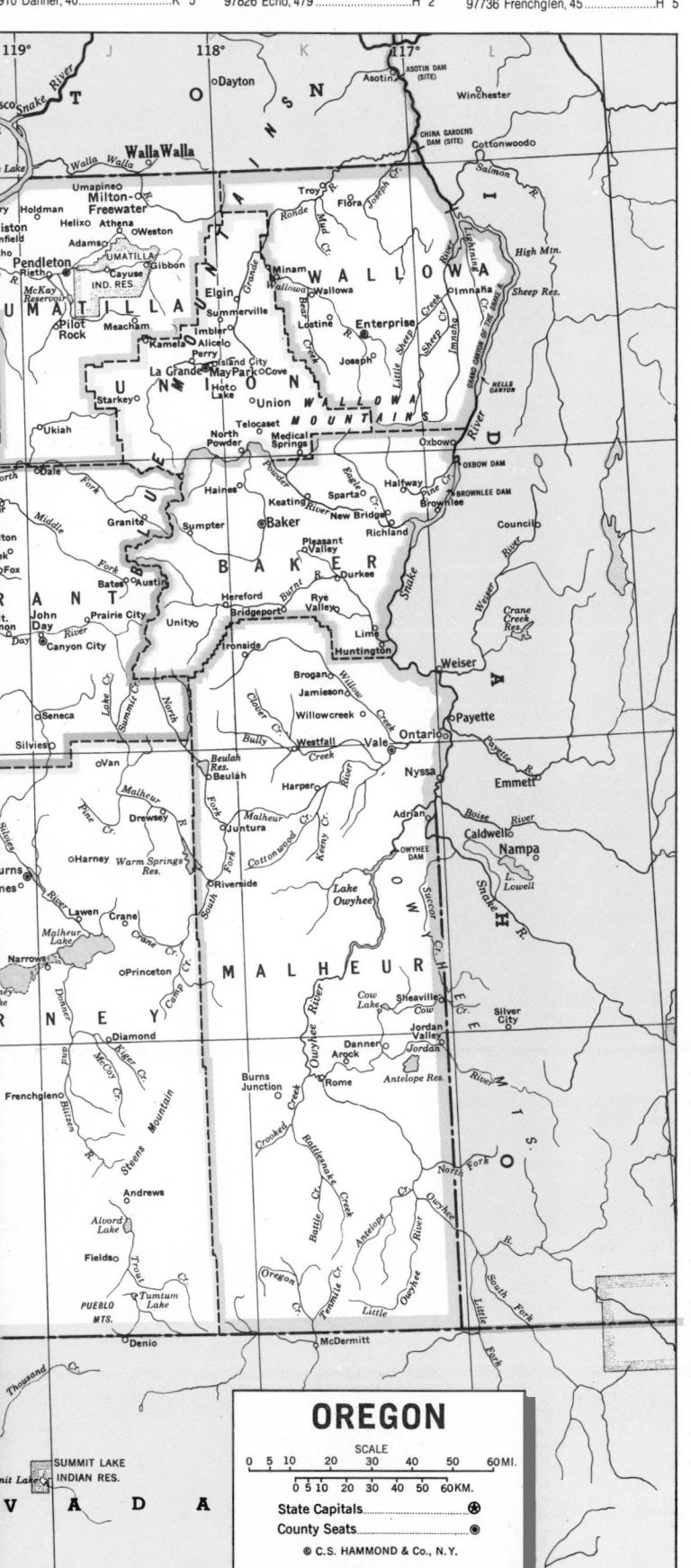

OREGON

SCALE

0 5 10 20 30 40 50 60 MI.

0 5 10 20 30 40 50 60 KM.

State Capitals ⊛
County Seats ⊗

© C.S. HAMMOND & Co., N.Y.

(continued on following page)

Agriculture, Industry and Resources

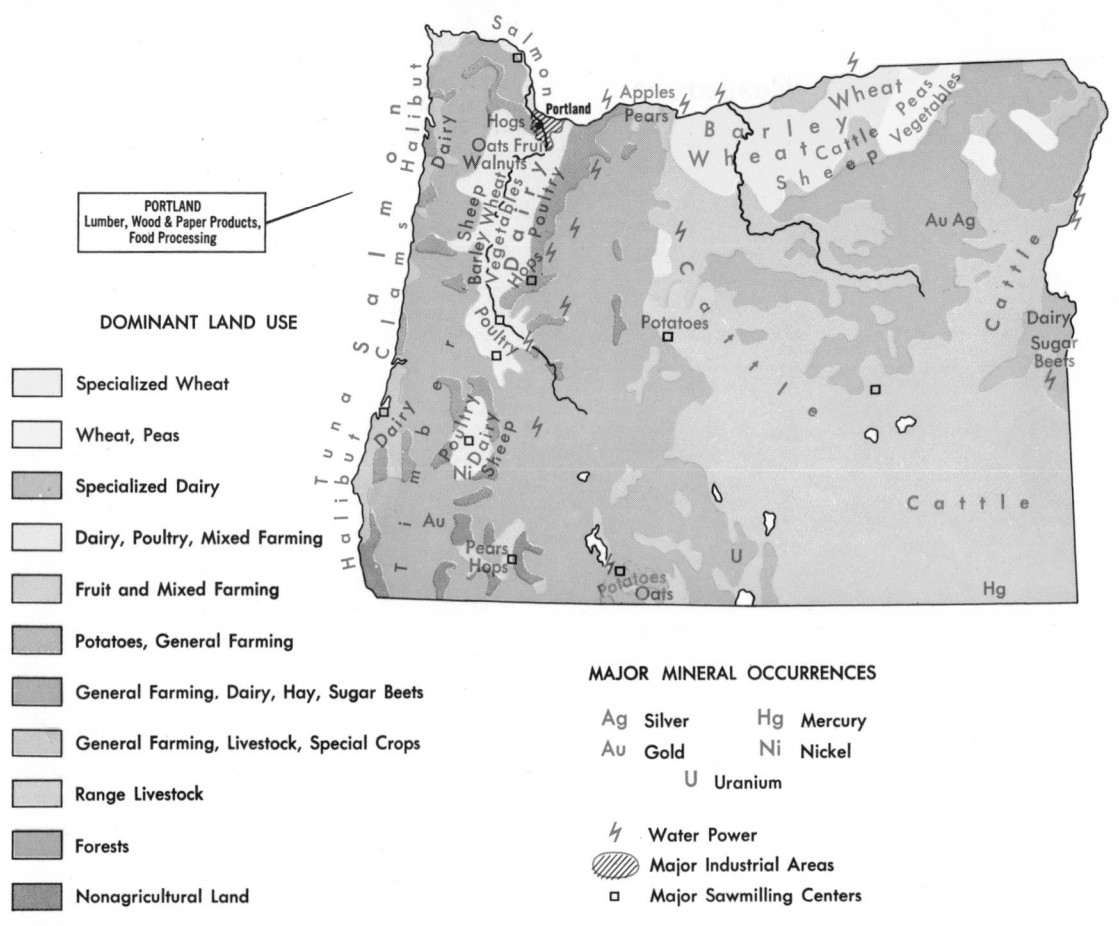

PORTLAND
Lumber, Wood & Paper Products,
Food Processing

DOMINANT LAND USE

- Specialized Wheat
- Wheat, Peas
- Specialized Dairy
- Dairy, Poultry, Mixed Farming
- Fruit and Mixed Farming
- Potatoes, General Farming
- General Farming, Dairy, Hay, Sugar Beets
- General Farming, Livestock, Special Crops
- Range Livestock
- Forests
- Nonagricultural Land

MAJOR MINERAL OCCURRENCES

Ag	Silver	Hg	Mercury
Au	Gold	Ni	Nickel
	U	Uranium	

- ⚡ Water Power
- Major Industrial Areas
- ▫ Major Sawmilling Centers

Oregon's magnificently rugged coastline — sandy beaches interspersed with rock fragments ("stacks") torn from the cliffs.

Oregon State Highway Department

◉ County seat.
‡ Population of metropolitan area.
† Zip of nearest p.o.
* Multiple zips

Agriculture, Industry and Resources

DOMINANT LAND USE

- Specialized Dairy
- Dairy, General Farming
- Fruit and Mixed Farming
- Fruit, Truck and Mixed Farming
- General Farming, Livestock, Tobacco
- General Farming, Livestock, Fruit, Tobacco
- Forests
- Urban Areas

AREA 45,333 sq. mi.
POPULATION 11,793,909
CAPITAL Harrisburg
LARGEST CITY Philadelphia
HIGHEST POINT Mt. Davis 3,213 ft.
SETTLED IN 1682
ADMITTED TO UNION December 12, 1787
POPULAR NAME Keystone State
STATE FLOWER Mountain Laurel
STATE BIRD Ruffed Grouse

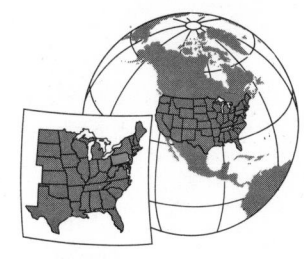

MAJOR MINERAL OCCURRENCES

C Coal G Natural Gas Sl Slate
Cl Clay Ls Limestone Ss Sandstone
Co Cobalt O Petroleum Zn Zinc
Fe Iron Ore

⚡ Water Power
▨ Major Industrial Areas

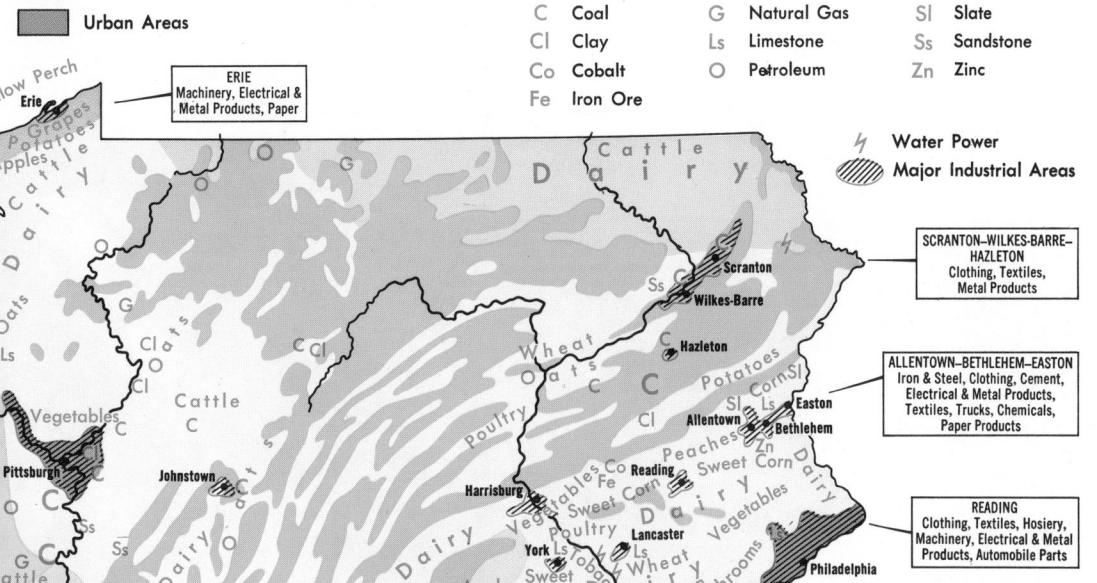

ERIE Machinery, Electrical & Metal Products, Paper

SCRANTON–WILKES-BARRE–HAZLETON Clothing, Textiles, Metal Products

ALLENTOWN–BETHLEHEM–EASTON Iron & Steel, Clothing, Cement, Electrical & Metal Products, Textiles, Trucks, Chemicals, Paper Products

READING Clothing, Textiles, Hosiery, Machinery, Electrical & Metal Products, Automobile Parts

PITTSBURGH Iron & Steel, Machinery, Electrical & Metal Products, Chemicals, Paint, Glass, Barges, Food Processing

JOHNSTOWN Iron & Steel

HARRISBURG Food Processing, Iron & Steel, Clothing, Metal Products

YORK Machinery, Metal Products, Paper Products, Air Conditioning Equipment, Clothing & Textiles

LANCASTER Machinery, Textiles, Food Processing, Clothing, Electrical & Metal Products, Watches, Farm Equipment, Floor Coverings

PHILADELPHIA Machinery, Textiles, Clothing, Electrical & Metal Products, Chemicals, Oil Refining, Food Processing, Printing & Publishing, Iron & Steel, Rugs & Carpets, Leather Goods, Cigars, Instruments

(continued on following page)

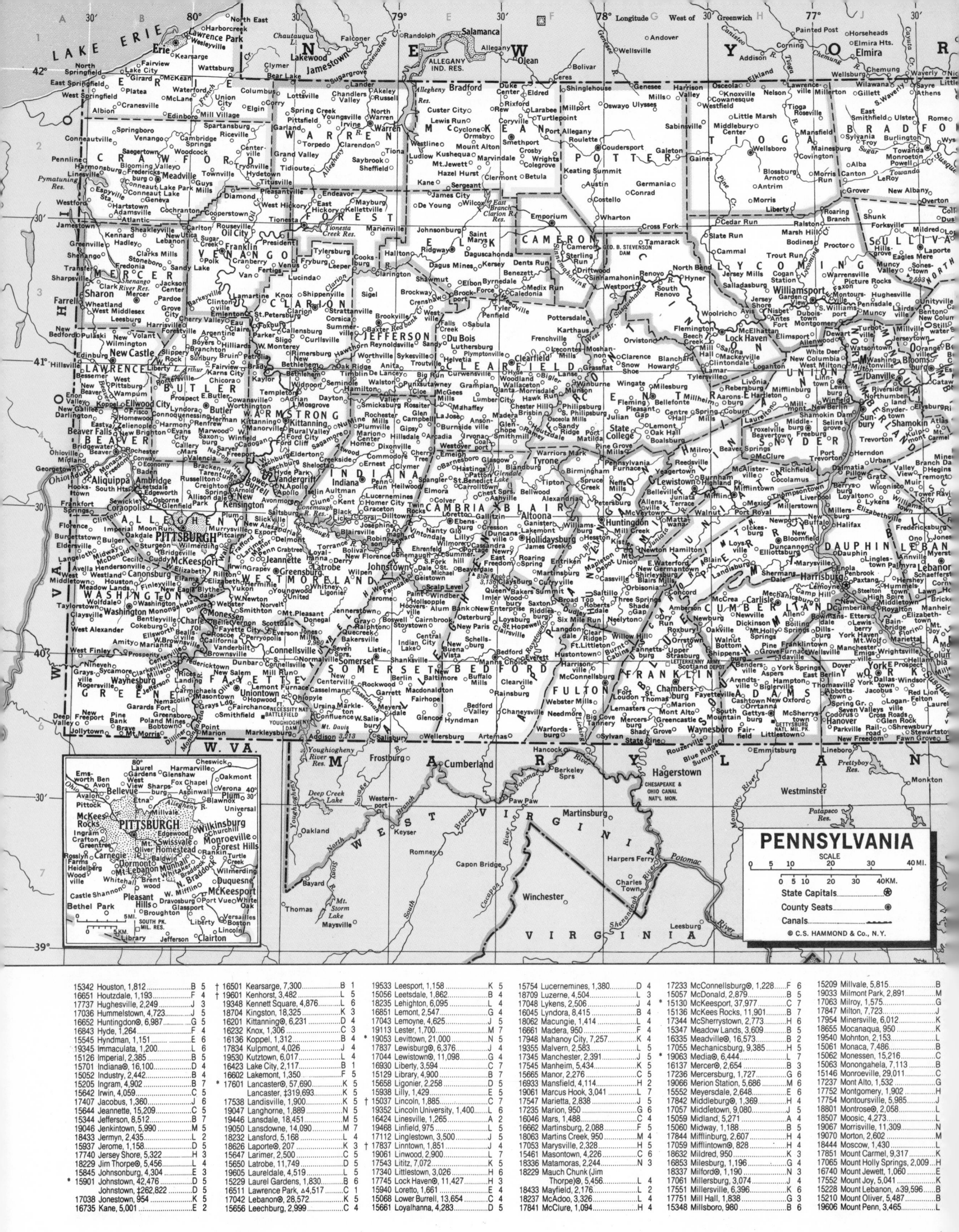

PENNSYLVANIA

SCALE
0 5 10 20 30 40 MI.
0 5 10 20 30 40KM.

State Capitals .... ⊛
County Seats .... ⊙
Canals .... ‒ ‒ ‒

Ⓒ C.S. HAMMOND & Co., N.Y.

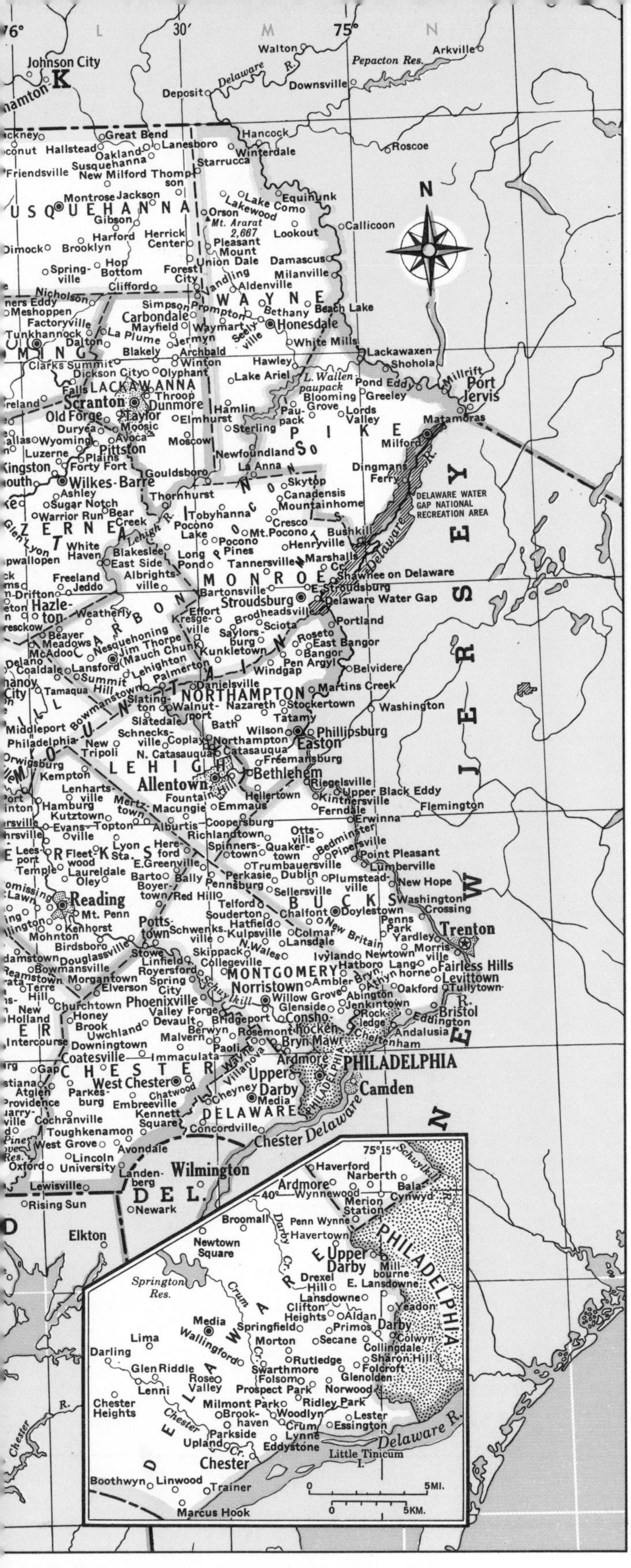

19074	Norwood, 7,229	M 7	16345	Russell, 950	D 2	16947	Troy, 1,315	J 2
18636	Noxen, 950	K 3	15076	Russellton, 1,597	C 4	19007	Tullytown, 2,194	N 5
18241	Nuremberg, 950	K 4	19070	Rutledge, 1,167	M 7	18657	Tunkhannock⊙, 2,251	L 2
15071	Oakdale, 1,614	B 5	16433	Saegertown, 1,348	B 2	15145	Turtle Creek, 8,308	C 7
† 19047	Oakford, 3,800	N 5	17970	Saint Clair, 4,576	K 4	15960	Twin Rocks, 975	F 4
16139	Oakmont, 7,550	C 4	15857	Saint Marys, 7,470	E 3	16686	Tyrone, 7,072	F 4
† 15059	Ohioville, 3,918	B 4	15951	Saint Michael, 1,248	E 5	16438	Union City, 3,631	C 2
16301	Oil City, 15,033	D 3	15681	Saltsburg, 1,037	C 4	15401	Uniontown⊙, 16,282	C 6
18518	Old Forge, 9,522	L 3	† 15801	Sandy, 2,000	E 3	15689	United, 975	D 5
15472	Oliver, 3,091	C 5	16056	Saxonburg, 1,191	C 4	15235	Universal, 1,900	C 7
18447	Olyphant, 5,422	L 3	18840	Sayre, 7,473	K 2	† 19013	Upland, 3,930	L 7
17961	Orwigsburg, 2,661	K 4	15963	Scalp Level, 1,353	E 5	* 19082	Upper Darby, △95,910	M 6
16666	Osceola Mills, 1,671	F 4	17088	Schaefferstown, 1,027	K 5	19481	Valley Forge, 400	L 5
19363	Oxford, 3,658	L 6	18078	Schnecksville, 1,550	L 4	17983	Valley View, 1,585	J 4
15963	Paint, 1,233	E 5	17972	Schuylkill Haven, 6,125	K 4	15690	Vandergrift, 7,873	D 4
18071	Palmerton, 5,620	L 4	18354	Sciota, 950	M 4	15147	Verona, 3,737	C 6
17078	Palmyra, 7,615	J 5	15683	Scottdale, 5,818	C 5	15132	Versailles, 2,754	C 7
19301	Paoli, 5,835	M 5	* 18501	Scranton⊙, 103,564	L 3	19085	Villanova, 5,250	M 6
17562	Paradise, 975	K 5		Scranton, ‡234,107	L 3	15148	Wall, 1,265	C 7
19365	Parkesburg, 2,701	L 6	19018	Secane, 5,700	M 7	19086	Wallingford, 3,500	L 7
† 19013	Parkside, 2,343	M 7	17870	Selinsgrove, 5,116	J 4	18088	Walnutport, 1,942	L 4
† 17331	Parkville, 5,120	J 6	18960	Sellersville, 2,829	M 5	16157	Wampum, 1,189	B 4
16668	Patton, 2,762	E 4	15143	Sewickley, 5,660	B 4	16365	Warren⊙, 12,998	D 2
17111	Paxtang, 2,160	J 5	17872	Shamokin, 11,719	J 4	15301	Washington⊙, 19,827	B 5
18072	Pen Argyl, 3,668	M 4	17876	Shamokin Dam, 1,562	J 4	16441	Waterford, 1,468	B 2
17103	Penbrook, 3,379	J 5	16146	Sharon, 22,653	B 3	17777	Watsontown, 2,514	J 3
18073	Pennsburg, 2,260	M 5	19079	Sharon Hill, 7,464	N 7	18472	Waymart, 1,122	M 2
† 19003	Penn Wynne, 6,038	M 6	15215	Sharpsburg, 5,499	C 4	19087	Wayne, 12,500	M 6
18944	Perkasie, 5,451	M 5	16150	Sharpsville, 6,126	A 3	17268	Waynesboro, 10,011	G 6
15473	Perryopolis, 2,043	C 5	16347	Sheffield, 1,564	D 2	15370	Waynesburg⊙, 5,152	B 6
* 19101	Philadelphia⊙, 1,948,609	N 6	17976	Shenandoah, 8,287	K 4	18255	Weatherly, 2,554	L 4
	Philadelphia, ‡4,817,914	N 6	18655	Shickshinny, 1,685	K 3	16901	Wellsboro⊙, 4,003	H 2
16866	Philipsburg, 3,700	F 4	19607	Shillington, 6,249	K 5	19565	Wernersville, 1,761	K 5
19460	Phoenixville, 14,823	L 5	16748	Shinglehouse, 1,320	F 2	16510	Wesleyville, 3,920	C 1
17963	Pine Grove, 2,197	K 4	17257	Shippensburg, 6,536	H 5	15417	West Brownsville, 1,426	C 5
16868	Pine Grove Mills, 950	G 4	19555	Shoemakersville, 1,427	K 4	19380	West Chester⊙, 19,301	L 6
15140	Pitcairn, 4,741	C 5	17361	Shrewsbury, 1,716	J 6	16950	Westfield, 1,273	H 2
* 15201	Pittsburgh⊙, 520,117	B 7	18407	Simpson, 1,900	L 2	19390	West Grove, 1,870	L 6
	Pittsburgh, ‡2,401,245	B 7	19608	Sinking Spring, 2,862	K 5	18201	West Hazleton, 6,059	K 4
* 18640	Pittston, 11,113	L 3	19474	Skippack, 975	M 5	† 16201	West Kittanning, 956	C 4
18705	Plains, 6,606	L 3	18080	Slatington, 4,687	L 4	19609	West Lawn, 1,973	K 5
16823	Pleasant Gap, 1,773	G 4	15684	Slickville, 1,066	C 5	† 15656	West Leechburg, 1,422	C 4
15236	Pleasant Hills, 10,409	B 7	16057	Slippery Rock, 4,949	B 3	16159	West Middlesex, 1,293	B 3
16341	Pleasantville, 1,005	C 2	16749	Smethport⊙, 1,883	F 2	15122	West Mifflin, 28,070	C 7
15239	Plum, 21,932	C 5	15478	Smithfield, 969	C 6	† 15901	Westmont, 6,673	D 5
18651	Plymouth, 9,536	K 3	15501	Somerset⊙, 6,269	D 6	15089	West Newton, 3,648	C 5
† 18651	Plymptonville, 1,040	E 3	18964	Souderton, 6,366	M 5	15229	West View, 8,312	B 6
15474	Point Marion, 1,750	C 5	15425	South Connellsville, 2,385	C 5	† 17401	West York, 5,314	J 6
16342	Polk, 3,673	C 2	15956	South Fork, 1,661	E 5	16161	Wheatland, 1,421	B 3
15946	Portage, 4,151	E 5	14892	South Waverly, 1,307	J 2	15120	Whitaker, 1,697	C 7
16743	Port Allegany, 2,703	F 2	17701	South Williamsport, 7,153	J 3	18052	Whitehall, 16,551	L 4
17965	Port Carbon, 2,717	K 4	15775	Spangler, 3,109	E 4	18661	White Haven, 2,134	L 3
15133	Port Vue, 5,862	C 7	19475	Spring City, 3,578	L 5	15131	White Oak, 9,304	C 7
19464	Pottstown, 25,355	L 5	15144	Springdale, 5,202	C 5	17097	Wiconisco, 1,236	J 4
17901	Pottsville⊙, 19,715	K 4	19064	Springfield, △2,446	M 7	15870	Wilcox, 950	E 2
19018	Primos, 3,900	M 7	17362	Spring Grove, 1,669	J 6	* 18701	Wilkes-Barre⊙, 58,856	L 3
16052	Prospect, 973	B 4	16801	State College, 33,778	G 4		Wilkes-Barre-Hazleton, ‡342,301	L 3
19076	Prospect Park, 7,250	M 7	17113	Steelton, 8,556	J 5	15221	Wilkinsburg, 26,780	C 7
15767	Punxsutawney, 7,792	E 4	17363	Stewartstown, 1,157	K 6	16693	Williamsburg, 1,704	F 5
18951	Quakertown, 7,276	M 5	16153	Stoneboro, 1,129	B 3	17701	Williamsport⊙, 37,918	H 3
17566	Quarryville, 1,571	K 5	19464	Stowe, 3,596	L 5	17098	Williamstown, 1,919	J 4
† 15104	Rankin, 3,817	C 7	17579	Strasburg, 1,897	K 6	19090	Willow Grove, 16,494	M 5
* 19601	Reading⊙, 87,643	L 5	18360	Stroudsburg⊙, 5,451	M 4	15148	Wilmerding, 3,218	C 7
	Reading, ‡415,056	L 5	† 16323	Sugarcreek, 5,944	C 3	15025	Wilson, 8,482	M 4
17567	Reamstown, 1,050	K 5	18706	Sugar Notch, 1,333	L 3	15963	Windber, 6,332	E 5
18076	Red Hill, 1,201	L 5	18250	Summit Hill, 3,811	L 4	18091	Windgap, 2,270	M 4
17356	Red Lion, 5,645	J 6	17801	Sunbury⊙, 13,025	J 4	17366	Windsor, 1,298	J 6
17084	Reedsville, 950	G 4	18847	Susquehanna, 2,319	L 2	† 18434	Winton, 4,948	M 3
17764	Renovo, 2,620	G 3	19081	Swarthmore, 6,156	M 7	† 15301	Wolfdale, 1,202	B 5
15851	Reynoldsville, 2,771	D 3	15218	Swissvale, 13,821	C 7	19567	Womelsdorf, 1,551	K 5
17087	Richland, 1,444	K 5	15865	Sykesville, 1,311	E 3	19094	Woodlyn, 6,500	M 7
15853	Ridgway⊙, 6,022	E 2	18252	Tamaqua, 9,246	L 4	17368	Wrightsville, 2,668	J 5
19078	Ridley Park, 9,025	M 7	15084	Tarentum, 7,379	C 4	19096	Wynnewood, 9,200	M 6
18077	Riegelsville, 1,050	M 4	18517	Taylor, 6,977	L 3	18644	Wyoming, 4,195	L 3
15678	Rillton, 975	C 5	18969	Telford, 3,409	M 5	19610	Wyomissing, 7,136	K 5
16248	Rimersburg, 1,146	D 3	19560	Temple, 1,667	L 5	19067	Yardley, 2,616	N 5
17868	Riverside, 1,905	J 4	16259	Templeton, 950	C 4	19050	Yeadon, 12,136	N 7
16673	Roaring Spring, 2,811	F 5	17581	Terre Hill, 1,129	K 5	17099	Yeagertown, 1,363	G 4
19551	Robesonia, 1,685	K 5	18512	Throop, 4,307	L 3	* 17401	York⊙, 50,335	J 6
15949	Robinson, 975	D 5	19562	Topton, 1,744	L 5		York, ‡329,540	J 6
15074	Rochester, 4,819	B 4	19374	Toughkenamon, 1,233	L 6	16371	Youngsville, 2,158	D 2
19111	Rockledge, 2,564	M 5	18848	Towanda⊙, 4,224	J 2	15697	Youngwood, 3,057	D 5
15557	Rockwood, 1,051	D 6	17980	Tower City, 1,774	J 4	16063	Zelienople, 3,602	B 4
15477	Roscoe, 1,176	C 5	15085	Trafford, 4,383	C 5			
19010	Rosemont, 4,900	M 6	16353	Tionesta⊙, 711	C 2	⊙	County seat.	
18013	Roseto, 1,538	M 4	16354	Titusville, 7,331	C 2	‡	Population of metropolitan area.	
17250	Rouzerville, 1,419	G 6	19560	Temple...		△	Population of town or township.	
† 17067	Royalton, 1,040	J 5	18848	Towanda...		†	Zip of nearest p.o.	
19468	Royersford, 4,235	L 5	18254	Trescow, 1,146	K 4	*	Multiple zips	
16249	Rural Valley, 962	D 4	17881	Trevorton, 2,196	J 4			

666	Mount Pleasant, 5,895	D 5	17349	New Freedom, 1,495	J 6
444	Mount Pocono, 1,019	M 3	17557	New Holland, 3,971	K 5
666	Mount Union, 3,662	G 5	18938	New Hope, 978	N 5
654	Mountville, 1,454	K 5	15068	New Kensington, 20,312	C 4
447	Mount Wolf, 1,811	J 5	18834	New Milford, 1,143	L 2
756	Muncy, 2,872	J 3	17350	New Oxford, 1,495	H 5
20	Munhall, 16,674	C 7	17959	New Philadelphia, 1,528	K 4
968	Murrysville, 3,900	C 5	17074	Newport, 1,747	H 5
067	Myerstown, 3,645	K 5	15468	New Salem, 1,337	C 6
634	Nanticoke, 14,632	K 3	15626	New Salem (Delmont), 1,934	D 5
043	Nanty Glo, 4,298	E 5	18940	Newtown, 2,216	N 5
072	Narberth, 5,151	M 6	19073	Newtown Square, 16,000	L 5
065	Natrona Heights, 15,000	C 4	17241	Newville, 1,631	H 5
064	Nazareth, 5,815	M 4	16142	New Wilmington, 2,721	B 3
351	Nemacolin, 1,273	B 6	17759	Nisbet, 950	H 3
066	Nescopeck, 1,897	K 3	* 19401	Norristown⊙, 38,169	M 5
240	Nesquehoning, 3,338	L 4	18067	Northampton, 8,389	M 4
141	New Beaver, 1,426	A 4	15673	North Apollo, 1,618	D 4
140	New Bedford, 950	A 3	15104	North Braddock, 10,838	C 7
242	New Bethlehem, 1,406	D 3	18032	North Catasauqua, 2,941	L 4
068	New Bloomfield⊙, 1,032	H 5	16428	North East, 3,846	C 1
066	New Brighton, 7,637	B 4	17857	Northumberland, 4,102	J 4
901	New Britain, 2,428	M 5	19454	North Wales, 3,911	M 5
070	New Cumberland, 9,803	J 5	16365	North Warren, 1,360	D 2
070	New Eagle, 2,497	B 5	15674	Norvelt, 2,588	C 5

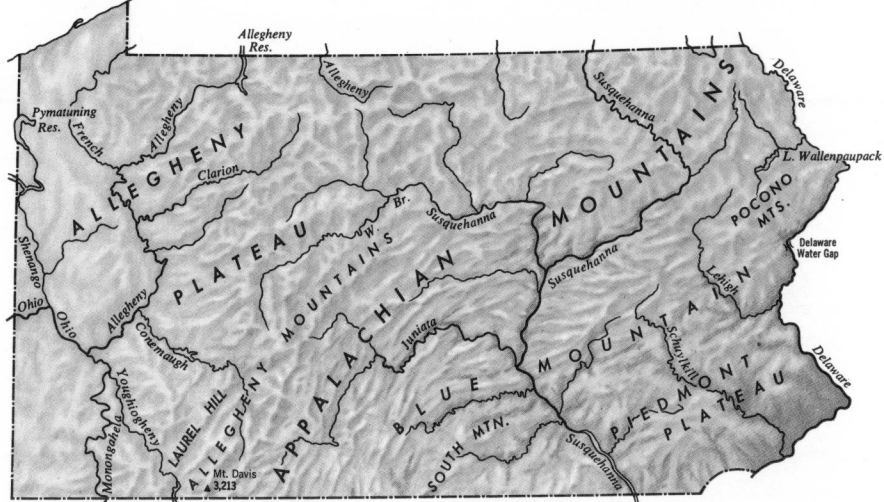

Topography

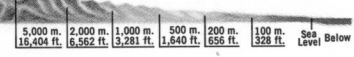

0   30   60
MILES

| 5,000 m. 16,404 ft. | 2,000 m. 6,562 ft. | 1,000 m. 3,281 ft. | 500 m. 1,640 ft. | 200 m. 656 ft. | 100 m. 328 ft. | Sea Level Below |

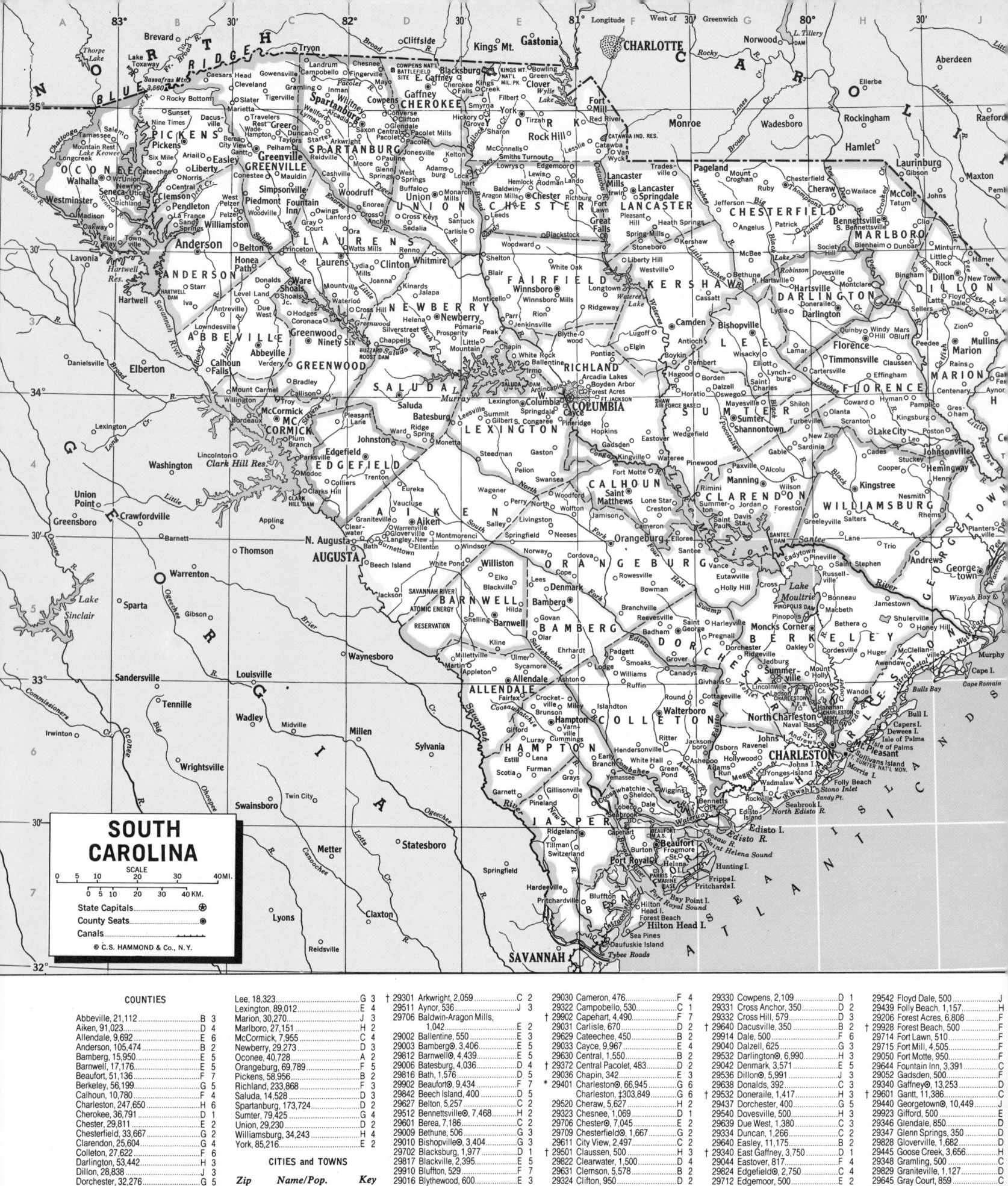

SOUTH CAROLINA

SCALE

0 5 10 20 30 40 MI.

0 5 10 20 30 40 KM.

State Capitals ⊛

County Seats ◉

Canals ----

© C.S. HAMMOND & Co., N.Y.

COUNTIES

Abbeville, 21,112........B 3
Aiken, 91,023........D 4
Allendale, 9,692........E 6
Anderson, 105,474........B 2
Bamberg, 15,950........E 5
Barnwell, 17,176........E 5
Beaufort, 51,136........F 7
Berkeley, 56,199........G 5
Calhoun, 10,780........F 4
Charleston, 247,650........H 6
Cherokee, 36,791........D 1
Chester, 29,811........E 2
Chesterfield, 33,667........G 2
Clarendon, 25,604........G 4
Colleton, 27,622........G 6
Darlington, 53,442........H 3
Dillon, 28,838........J 3
Dorchester, 32,276........G 6
Edgefield, 15,692........D 4
Fairfield, 19,999........E 3
Florence, 89,636........H 3
Georgetown, 33,500........J 5
Greenville, 240,546........C 2
Greenwood, 49,686........C 3
Hampton, 15,878........E 6
Horry, 69,992........J 4
Jasper, 11,885........E 6
Kershaw, 34,727........F 3
Lancaster, 43,328........F 2
Laurens, 49,713........D 2

CITIES and TOWNS

Zip	Name/Pop.	Key
29620	Abbeville⊙, 5,515	C 3
29426	Adams Run, 500	G 6
29801	Aiken⊙, 13,436	D 4
29001	Alcolu, 600	G 4
29810	Allendale⊙, 3,620	E 5
29621	Anderson⊙, 27,556	B 2
29510	Andrews, 2,879	H 5
† 29020	Antioch, 500	F 3
29320	Arcadia, 1,887	C 2
† 29201	Arcadia Lakes, 741	F 3
† 29201	Ardincaple, 726	E 3
29640	Ariail, 1,150	B 2

Lee, 18,323........G 3
Lexington, 89,012........E 4
Marion, 30,270........J 3
Marlboro, 27,151........H 2
McCormick, 7,955........C 4
Newberry, 29,273........D 3
Oconee, 40,728........A 2
Orangeburg, 69,789........F 5
Pickens, 58,956........B 2
Richland, 233,868........F 3
Saluda, 14,528........D 3
Spartanburg, 173,724........D 2
Sumter, 79,425........G 4
Union, 29,230........D 2
Williamsburg, 34,243........H 4
York, 85,216........E 2

† 29301 Arkwright, 2,059........C 2
29511 Aynor, 536........J 3
29706 Baldwin-Aragon Mills, 1,042........E 2
29002 Ballentine, 550........E 3
29003 Bamberg⊙, 3,406........E 5
29812 Barnwell⊙, 4,439........E 5
29006 Batesburg, 4,036........D 4
29816 Bath, 1,576........D 5
29627 Belton, 5,257........C 2
29512 Bennettsville⊙, 7,468........H 2
29601 Berea, 7,186........C 2
29009 Bethune, 506........F 3
29010 Bishopville⊙, 3,404........G 3
29702 Blacksburg, 1,977........D 1
29817 Blackville, 2,395........E 5
29910 Bluffton, 529........F 7
29016 Blythewood, 600........F 3
29431 Bonneau, 365........H 5
29703 Bowling Green, 542........E 1
29018 Bowman, 1,095........F 5
† 29201 Boyden Arbor, 416........F 3
29019 Boykin, 350........F 3
29432 Branchville, 1,011........F 5
29911 Brunson, 559........E 6
29321 Buffalo, 1,461........D 2
† 29834 Burnettown, 434........D 5
29902 Burton, 900........F 7
29628 Calhoun Falls, 2,234........B 3
29020 Camden⊙, 8,532........F 3

29030 Cameron, 476........F 4
29322 Campobello, 530........C 1
† 29902 Capehart, 4,490........F 7
29031 Carlisle, 670........D 2
29629 Cateechee, 450........B 2
29033 Cayce, 9,967........E 4
29630 Central, 1,550........B 2
† 29372 Central Pacolet, 483........D 2
29036 Chapin, 342........E 3
* 29401 Charleston⊙, 66,945........G 6
        Charleston, ‡303,849........G 6
29520 Cheraw, 5,627........H 2
29323 Chesnee, 1,069........D 1
29706 Chester⊙, 7,045........E 2
29709 Chesterfield⊙, 1,667........G 2
29611 City View, 2,497........C 2
† 29501 Claussen, 600........H 3
29631 Clemson, 5,578........B 2
29325 Clinton, 8,138........D 3
29525 Clio, 936........H 2
29710 Clover, 3,506........E 1
29016 Conestee, 600........C 2
29636 Converse, 900........D 2
29329 Coosawhatchie, 500........F 6
29526 Conway⊙, 8,151........J 4
29912 Cordesville, 900........H 5
29434 Cottageville, 497........G 6
29435 Coward, 466........H 4
29530 Coward, 466........H 4

29330 Cowpens, 2,109........D 1
29331 Cross Anchor, 350........D 2
29332 Cross Hill, 579........D 3
† 29640 Dacusville, 350........B 2
29914 Dale, 500........F 6
29040 Dalzell, 625........G 3
29532 Darlington⊙, 6,990........H 3
29042 Denmark, 3,571........E 5
29536 Dillon⊙, 5,991........J 3
29638 Donalds, 392........C 3
† 29532 Doneraile, 1,417........H 3
29437 Dorchester, 400........G 5
29540 Dovesville, 500........H 3
29639 Due West, 1,380........C 3
29334 Duncan, 1,266........C 2
29640 Easley, 11,175........B 2
† 29340 East Gaffney, 3,750........D 1
29044 Eastover, 817........F 4
29824 Edgefield⊙, 2,750........C 4
29712 Edgemoor, 500........E 2
29438 Edisto Island, 900........G 6
29081 Ehrhardt, 478........E 5
29045 Elgin, 374........F 3
29046 Elliott, 500........G 3
29047 Elloree, 940........F 4
29335 Enoree, 850........D 2
29918 Estill, 1,954........E 6
29048 Eutawville, 386........G 5
29827 Fairfax, 1,937........E 6
29643 Fair Play, 500........A 2
29501 Florence⊙, 25,997........H 3

29542 Floyd Dale, 500........J
29439 Folly Beach, 1,157........H
29206 Forest Acres, 6,808........F
† 29928 Forest Beach, 500........F
29714 Fort Lawn, 510........F
29715 Fort Mill, 4,505........E
29050 Fort Motte, 950........F
29644 Fountain Inn, 3,391........C
29052 Gadsden, 500........F
29340 Gaffney⊙, 13,253........D
† 29601 Gantt, 11,386........C
29440 Georgetown⊙, 10,449........J
29923 Gifford, 500........E
29346 Glendale, 850........D
29347 Glenn Springs, 350........D
29828 Gloverville, 1,682........D
29445 Goose Creek, 3,656........H
29829 Gramling, 500........C
29348 Gray Court, 859........C
29645 Greelyville, 542........H
29446 Green Pond, 500........G
29055 Great Falls, 2,727........F
29056 Greeleyville, 542........H
29446 Green Pond, 500........G
29468 Green Sea, 500........J
* 29601 Greenville⊙, 61,208........C
        Greenville, ‡299,502........C
29646 Greenwood⊙, 21,069........C
29651 Greer, 10,642........C
29546 Gresham, 500........J
29569 Gurley, 425........J
29924 Hampton⊙, 2,845........E
29410 Hanahan, 8,376........H

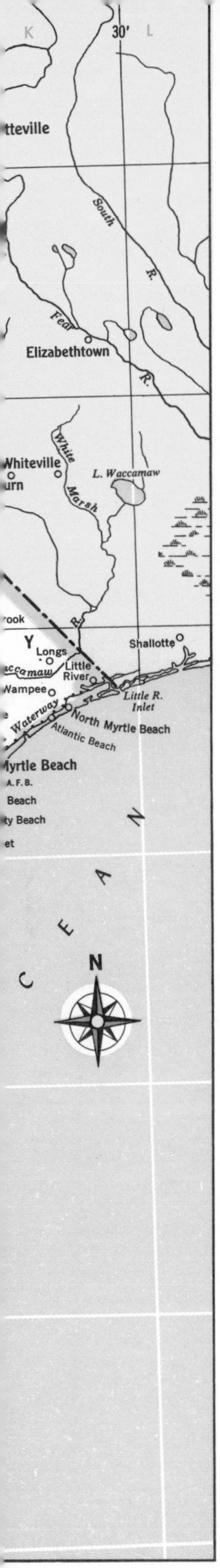

K
30'
L
tteville
South
R.
Fear
Elizabethtown
R.
White
Whiteville
urn
L. Waccamaw
Marsh
rook
Y
Longs
Shallotte
Little River
Waccamaw
Wampee
Little R. Inlet
Waterway
North Myrtle Beach
Atlantic Beach
Myrtle Beach
A.F.B.
Beach
ty Beach
et
C
E
A
N
N

927 Hardeeville, 853 .... E 7
448 Harleyville, 704 .... G 5
550 Hartsville, 8,017 .... G 3
058 Heath Springs, 955 .... F 2
554 Hemingway, 1,026 .... J 4
706 Hemlock, 1,524 .... E 2
717 Hickory Grove, 377 .... E 2
813 Hilda, 331 .... E 5
928 Hilton Head Island, 450 .... F 7
059 Holly Hill, 1,178 .... G 5
449 Hollywood, 339 .... G 6
654 Honea Path, 3,707 .... C 3
062 Horatio, 500 .... F 3
450 Huger, 500 .... H 5
349 Inman, 1,661 .... C 1
063 Irmo, 517 .... E 3
720 Irwin, 1,424 .... F 2
451 Isle of Palms, 2,657 .... H 6
655 Iva, 1,114 .... B 3
831 Jackson, 1,928 .... D 5
452 Jacksonboro, 550 .... G 6
483 Jedburg, 900 .... G 5
718 Jefferson, 709 .... G 2
351 Joanna, 1,631 .... D 3
455 Johns Island, 675 .... G 6
555 Johnsonville, 1,267 .... J 4
832 Johnston, 2,552 .... D 4
353 Jonesville, 1,447 .... D 2
067 Kershaw, 1,818 .... G 2
556 Kingstree⊙, 3,381 .... H 4
814 Kline, 305 .... E 5
456 Ladson, 600 .... G 6

Agriculture, Industry and Resources

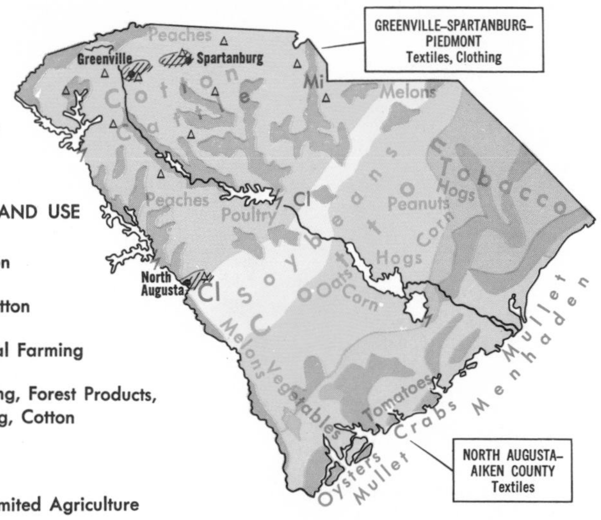

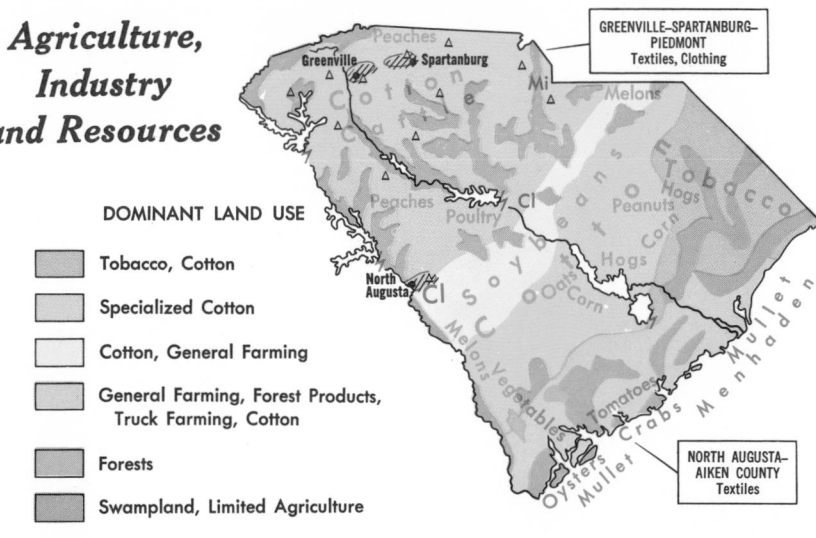

GREENVILLE–SPARTANBURG–PIEDMONT
Textiles, Clothing
Peaches
Greenville
Spartanburg
Mi
Melons
Cotton
Tobacco
Peaches
Poultry
Cl
Peanuts
Hogs
Corn
Soybeans
Hogs
North Augusta
Cl
Oats
Corn
Mullet
Menhaden
Melons
Vegetables
Tomatoes
Crabs
Oysters
Mullet
NORTH AUGUSTA–AIKEN COUNTY
Textiles
DOMINANT LAND USE
Tobacco, Cotton
Specialized Cotton
Cotton, General Farming
General Farming, Forest Products, Truck Farming, Cotton
Forests
Swampland, Limited Agriculture
MAJOR MINERAL OCCURRENCES
Cl Clay
Mi Mica
Major Industrial Areas
Water Power
Major Textile Centers

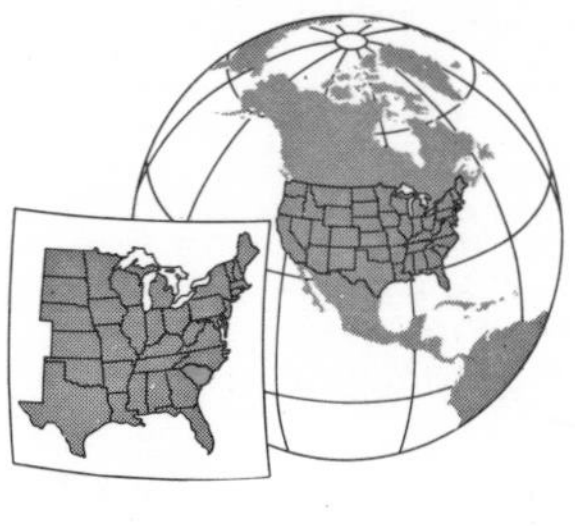

AREA 31,055 sq. mi.
POPULATION 2,590,516
CAPITAL Columbia
LARGEST CITY Columbia
HIGHEST POINT Sassafras Mtn. 3,560 ft.
SETTLED IN 1670
ADMITTED TO UNION May 23, 1788
POPULAR NAME Palmetto State
STATE FLOWER Yellow Jessamine
STATE BIRD Carolina Wren

29656 La France, 875 .... B 2
29560 Lake City, 6,247 .... H 4
29563 Lake View, 949 .... J 3
29069 Lamar, 1,250 .... G 3
29720 Lancaster⊙, 9,186 .... F 2
† 29720 Lancaster Mills, 2,558 .... F 2
29724 Lando, 775 .... E 2
29356 Landrum, 1,859 .... C 1
29564 Lane, 517 .... H 5
29834 Langley, 975 .... D 4
29565 Latta, 1,764 .... J 3
29360 Laurens⊙, 10,298 .... C 3
29070 Leesville, 1,907 .... E 4
29734 Lesslie, 500 .... E 2
29072 Lexington⊙, 969 .... E 4
29657 Liberty, 2,860 .... B 2
† 29483 Lincolnville, 504 .... G 6
29566 Little River, 500 .... K 4
29931 Lobeco, 350 .... F 6
29569 Loris, 1,741 .... K 3
29078 Lugoff, 500 .... F 3
29079 Lydia, 400 .... G 3
29325 Lydia Mills, 925 .... D 3
29365 Lyman, 1,159 .... C 2
29080 Lynchburg, 546 .... G 3
29660 Madison, 350 .... A 2
29102 Manning⊙, 4,025 .... G 4
29661 Marietta-Slater, 1,764 .... C 1
29571 Marion⊙, 7,435 .... J 3
29662 Mauldin, 3,797 .... C 2
29104 Mayesville, 757 .... G 4
29368 Mayo, 800 .... D 1
29101 McBee, 592 .... G 3
29570 McColl, 2,524 .... H 2
29835 McCormick⊙, 1,864 .... C 4
† 29379 Monarch Mills, 1,726 .... D 2
29461 Moncks Corner⊙, 2,314 .... G 5
29105 Monetta, 850 .... D 4
29839 Montmorenci, 700 .... D 4
29664 Mountain Rest, 500 .... A 2
29464 Mount Pleasant, 6,155 .... H 6
29574 Mullins, 6,006 .... J 3
29576 Murrells Inlet, 850 .... K 4
29577 Myrtle Beach, 8,536 .... K 4
29408 Naval Base, 13,565 .... G 6
29107 Neeses, 388 .... E 4
29580 Nesmith, 350 .... H 4
29108 Newberry⊙, 9,218 .... D 3
29809 New Ellenton, 2,546 .... D 5
29665 Newry, 874 .... B 2
† 29536 New Town, 950 .... J 3
29581 Nichols, 549 .... J 3
29666 Ninety Six, 2,166 .... C 3
29667 Norris, 757 .... B 2
29112 North, 1,076 .... E 4
29841 North Augusta, 12,883 .... C 5
29406 North Charleston, 19,854 .... G 6
† 29550 North Hartsville, 1,485 .... G 3
29582 North Myrtle Beach, 1,957 .... K 4
29113 Norway, 579 .... E 5
29114 Olanta, 640 .... H 4
29843 Olar, 423 .... E 5
29115 Orangeburg⊙, 13,252 .... F 4
29372 Pacolet, 1,418 .... D 2
29373 Pacolet Mills, 1,504 .... D 2
29728 Pageland, 2,122 .... G 2
29583 Pamplico, 1,068 .... H 4
29584 Patrick, 421 .... G 2
29374 Pauline, 750 .... D 2
29585 Pawleys Island, 650 .... J 5
29670 Pendleton, 2,615 .... B 2
29671 Pickens⊙, 2,954 .... B 2
29673 Piedmont, 2,242 .... C 2
† 29169 Pineridge, 633 .... E 4
29468 Pineville, 900 .... H 5
29125 Pinewood, 687 .... G 4
29469 Pinopolis, 788 .... G 5
29935 Port Royal, 2,865 .... F 7
29127 Prosperity, 762 .... D 3
† 29501 Quinby, 788 .... H 3
29589 Rains, 600 .... J 3
29470 Ravenel, 931 .... G 6
29375 Reidville, 460 .... C 2
29128 Rembert, 350 .... G 3
29936 Ridgeland⊙, 1,165 .... E 7

29129 Ridge Spring, 644 .... D 4
29472 Ridgeville, 563 .... G 5
29130 Ridgeway, 437 .... F 3
29131 Rimini, 400 .... G 4
29473 Ritter, 350 .... F 6
29730 Rock Hill, 33,846 .... E 2
29740 Rodman, 500 .... E 2
29133 Rowesville, 392 .... F 5
29741 Ruby, 306 .... G 2
29475 Ruffin, 400 .... F 6
29407 Saint Andrews, 9,202 .... G 6
29134 Saint Charles, 350 .... G 3
29477 Saint George⊙, 1,806 .... F 5
29135 Saint Matthews⊙, 2,403 .... F 4
† 29148 Saint Paul, 725 .... G 4
29479 Saint Stephen, 1,506 .... H 5
29137 Salley, 450 .... E 4
29138 Saluda⊙, 2,442 .... D 4
† 29301 Saxon, 4,807 .... D 2
29591 Scranton, 732 .... H 4
29940 Seabrook, 500 .... F 6
29592 Sellers, 561 .... H 3
29678 Seneca, 6,027 .... A 2
† 29150 Shannontown, 7,491 .... G 4
29941 Sheldon, 950 .... F 6
29480 Shulerville, 375 .... H 5
29681 Simpsonville, 3,308 .... C 2
29682 Six Mile, 361 .... B 2
29683 Slater-Marietta, 1,764 .... C 1
29593 Society Hill, 806 .... H 2
† 29512 South Bennettsville, 1,726 .... H 2
† 29169 South Congaree, 1,434 .... E 4
* 29301 Spartanburg⊙, 44,546 .... C 1
29169 Springdale, 2,638 .... E 4
† 29720 Springdale, 3,193 .... F 2
29146 Springfield, 724 .... E 4
† 29067 Spring Mills, 975 .... F 2
29377 Startex, 1,203 .... C 2
29482 Sullivans Island, 1,426 .... H 6
29148 Summerton, 1,305 .... G 4
29483 Summerville, 3,839 .... G 5
29150 Sumter⊙, 24,435 .... G 4
29685 Sunset, 450 .... B 2
29577 Surfside Beach, 1,329 .... K 4
29160 Swansea, 691 .... E 4
29686 Tamassee, 420 .... A 2
29687 Taylors, 6,831 .... C 2
29688 Tigerville, 975 .... C 1
29161 Timmonsville, 2,246 .... H 3
29690 Travelers Rest, 2,241 .... C 2
29847 Trenton, 362 .... D 4
29162 Turbeville, 442 .... G 4
29379 Union⊙, 10,775 .... D 2
† 29678 Utica, 1,299 .... B 2
29944 Varnville, 1,555 .... E 6
29850 Vaucluse, 575 .... D 7
29607 Wade-Hampton, 17,152 .... C 2
29164 Wagener, 723 .... E 4
29691 Walhalla⊙, 3,662 .... A 2
29488 Walterboro⊙, 6,257 .... F 6
29692 Ware Shoals, 2,480 .... C 3
29851 Warrenville, 1,059 .... D 4
† 29360 Watts Mills, 1,181 .... D 2
29385 Wellford, 1,298 .... C 2
29169 West Columbia, 7,838 .... E 4
29693 Westminster, 2,521 .... A 2
29669 West Pelzer, 861 .... B 2
29696 West Union, 388 .... B 2
29178 Whitmire, 2,226 .... D 3
29303 Whitney, 2,891 .... D 1
29697 Williamston, 3,991 .... B 2
29853 Williston, 2,594 .... E 5
29856 Windsor, 590 .... E 5
† 29501 Windy Hill, 1,671 .... H 3
29180 Winnsboro⊙, 3,411 .... E 3
† 29180 Winnsboro Mills, 2,312 .... E 3
29388 Woodruff, 4,576 .... D 2
29945 Yemassee, 745 .... F 6
29494 Yonges Island, 350 .... G 6
29745 York⊙, 5,081 .... E 1
† 29574 Zion, 400 .... J 3

⊙ County seat.
‡ Population of metropolitan area.
† Zip of nearest p.o.
* Multiple zips

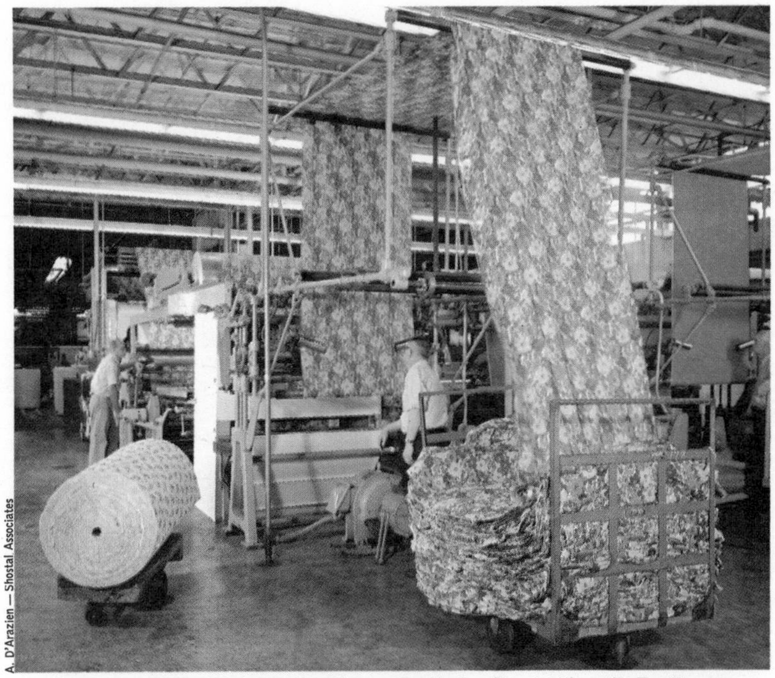

A. D'Arazien — Shostal Associates

Colorful materials being Sanforized in a South Carolina textile mill. Textiles are by far the most important of the state's industries.

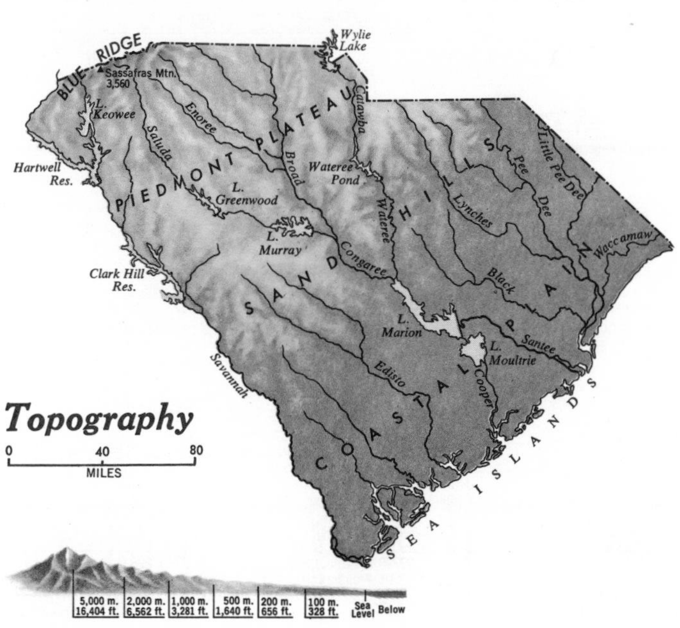

BLUE RIDGE
Sassafras Mtn. 3,560
Wylie Lake
L. Keowee
PIEDMONT PLATEAU
Catawba
Enoree
Saluda
Broad
Wateree Pond
Hartwell Res.
L. Greenwood
Wateree
SAND HILLS
Lynches
Pee Dee
Little Pee Dee
L. Murray
Congaree
Waccamaw
Clark Hill Res.
Black
L. Marion
Santee
L. Moultrie
Savannah
Edisto
Cooper
COASTAL PLAIN
SEA ISLANDS
Topography
0 40 80
MILES
5,000 m. 16,404 ft.
2,000 m. 6,562 ft.
1,000 m. 3,281 ft.
500 m. 1,640 ft.
200 m. 656 ft.
100 m. 328 ft.
Sea Level
Below

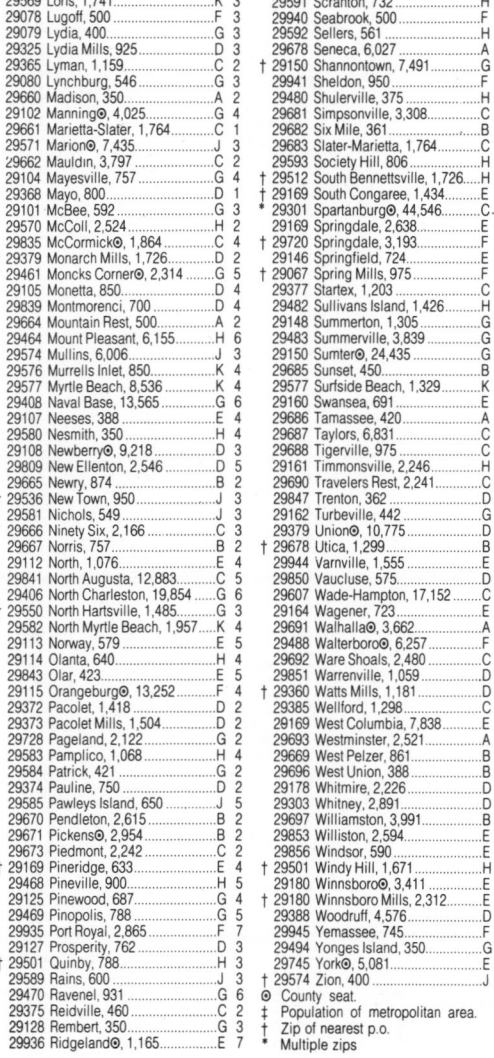

COUNTIES

Aurora, 4,183....................M 6
Beadle, 20,877..................N 5
Bennett, 3,088..................F 7
Bon Homme, 8,577.............O 7
Brookings, 22,158..............R 5
Brown, 36,920...................N 2
Brule, 5,870......................L 6
Buffalo, 1,739....................L 5
Butte, 7,825......................B 4
Campbell, 2,866................J 2
Charles Mix, 9,994.............M 7
Clark, 5,515......................O 4
Clay, 12,923......................P 8
Codington, 19,140.............P 4
Corson, 4,994....................G 2
Custer, 4,698.....................B 6
Davison, 17,319.................N 6
Day, 8,713........................O 3
Deuel, 5,686......................R 4
Dewey, 5,170....................G 3
Douglas, 4,569..................N 7
Edmunds, 5,548................L 3
Fall River, 7,505................B 7
Faulk, 3,893......................L 3

Grant, 9,005......................R 3
Gregory, 6,710..................L 7
Haakon, 2,802..................F 5
Hamlin, 5,172...................P 4
Hand, 5,883......................L 4
Hanson, 3,781..................O 6
Harding, 1,855..................B 2
Hughes, 11,632.................J 5
Hutchinson, 10,379...........O 7
Hyde, 2,515......................K 4
Jackson, 1,531..................F 6
Jerauld, 3,310..................M 5
Jones, 1,882.....................H 6
Kingsbury, 7,657...............O 5
Lake, 11,456.....................P 5
Lawrence, 17,453..............B 5
Lincoln, 11,761.................R 7
Lyman, 4,060....................J 6
Marshall, 5,965.................O 2
McCook, 7,246..................P 6
McPherson, 5,022.............L 2
Meade, 16,618..................D 5
Mellette, 2,420..................H 6
Miner, 4,454.....................O 5
Minnehaha, 95,209...........R 6
Moody, 7,622....................R 5

Pennington, 59,349...........C 6
Perkins, 4,769...................D 3
Potter, 4,449.....................J 3
Roberts, 11,678.................P 2
Sanborn, 3,697.................N 5
Shannon, 8,198................D 7
Spink, 10,595...................N 4
Stanley, 2,457..................H 5
Sully, 2,362......................J 4
Todd, 6,606......................H 7
Tripp, 8,171......................K 7
Turner, 9,872....................P 7
Union, 9,643.....................R 8
Walworth, 7,842...............J 3
Washabaugh, 1,389...........F 6
Yankton, 19,039................P 7
Ziebach, 2,221..................F 4

CITIES and TOWNS

Zip	Name/Pop.	Key
57401	Aberdeen⊚, 26,476	M 3
57310	Academy, 17	M 7
57520	Agar, 156	J 4
57420	Akaska, 46	J 3
57210	Albee, 26	S 3
57001	Alcester, 627	R 7
57311	Alexandria⊚, 598	O 6
57714	Allen, 150	F 7
57312	Alpena, 307	N 5
57211	Altamont, 54	R 4
57421	Amherst, 75	O 2
57422	Andover, 138	O 3
57715	Ardmore, 14	B 7
57212	Arlington, 954	P 5
57313	Armour⊚, 925	N 7
57423	Artas, 73	K 2
57314	Artesian, 277	O 6
57424	Ashton, 137	N 4
57213	Astoria, 153	J 3
57425	Athol, 50	M 3
57002	Aurora, 237	R 6
57315	Avon, 610	N 8
57214	Badger, 122	P 4
57003	Baltic, 364	R 6
57316	Bancroft, 48	O 4
57716	Barnard, 72	N 2
57716	Batesland, 135	E 7
57717	Bath, 150	N 3
57521	Belvidere, 96	G 6
57215	Bemis, 28	R 4
57004	Beresford, 1,655	R 7
57216	Big Stone City, 631	S 3
† 57310	Bijou Hills, 12	L 6
57620	Bison⊚, 406	E 2
57718	Black Hawk, 550	C 5
57522	Blunt, 445	J 4
57317	Bonesteel, 354	M 7
57318	Bonilla, 33	N 4
57719	Box Elder, 607	C 5
57217	Bradley, 157	O 3
57218	Brandt, 132	S 4
57429	Brentford, 94	N 3
57319	Bridgewater, 633	P 6
57219	Bristol, 470	O 3
57430	Britton⊚, 1,465	O 2
† 57350	Broadland, 45	N 4
57006	Brookings⊚, 13,717	R 5
57220	Bruce, 217	R 5
57221	Bryant, 502	P 4
57720	Buffalo⊚, 393	D 2
57722	Buffalo Gap, 155	C 6
57621	Bullhead, 449	G 2
57010	Burbank, 96	R 8
57523	Burke⊚, 892	L 7
57011	Bushnell, 65	R 5
57222	Butler, 38	R 4
57724	Camp Crook, 150	C 2
57012	Canistota, 636	P 6
57524	Canning, 40	J 5
57321	Canova, 204	O 6
57013	Canton⊚, 2,665	R 7
57725	Caputa, 43	C 6
† 57533	Carlock, 13	L 7
57428	Bowdle, 667	K 3
57322	Carpenter, 50	O 4
57526	Carter, 17	J 7
57323	Carthage, 362	O 5
57223	Castlewood, 523	R 4
57324	Cavour, 134	N 5
† 57058	Center, 18	P 6
57014	Centerville, 910	R 7
57727	Central City, 188	B 5
57325	Chamberlain⊚, 2,626	L 6
57015	Chancellor, 220	R 7
57431	Chelsea, 45	M 3
57622	Cherry Creek, 275	F 4
57016	Chester, 260	R 6
57224	Claire City, 100	R 2
57432	Claremont, 214	N 2
57225	Clark⊚, 1,356	O 4

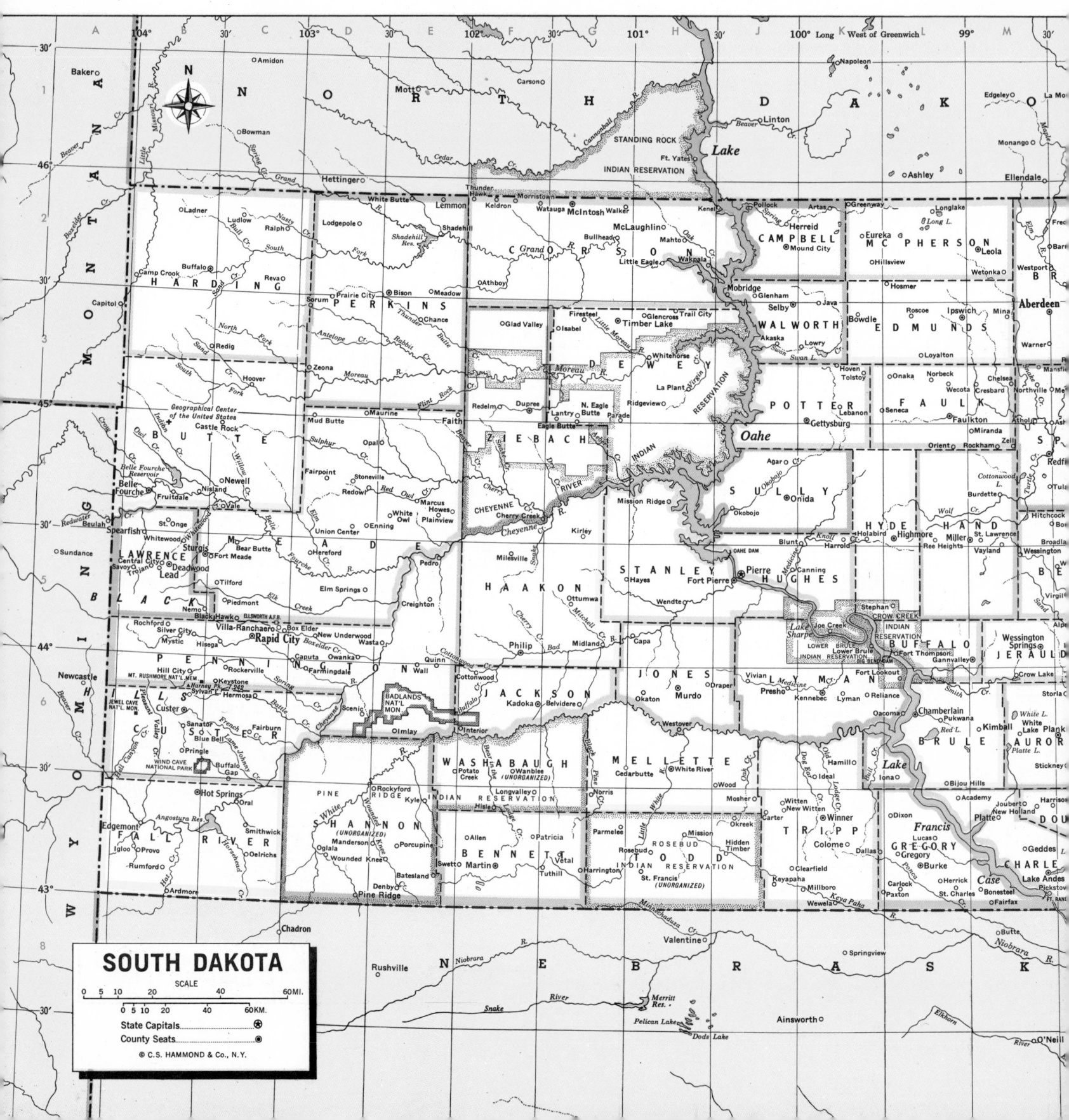

SOUTH DAKOTA

SCALE

0 5 10 20   40   60 MI.

0 5 10 20   40   60 KM.

State Capitals.................⊛

County Seats..................⊚

© C.S. HAMMOND & Co., N.Y.

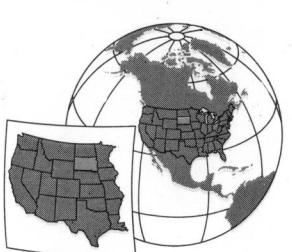

(continued on following page)

AREA 77,047 sq. mi.
POPULATION 666,257
CAPITAL Pierre
LARGEST CITY Sioux Falls
HIGHEST POINT Harney Pk. 7,242 ft.
SETTLED IN 1856
ADMITTED TO UNION November 2, 1889
POPULAR NAME Coyote State; Sunshine State
STATE FLOWER Pasqueflower
STATE BIRD Ring-necked Pheasant

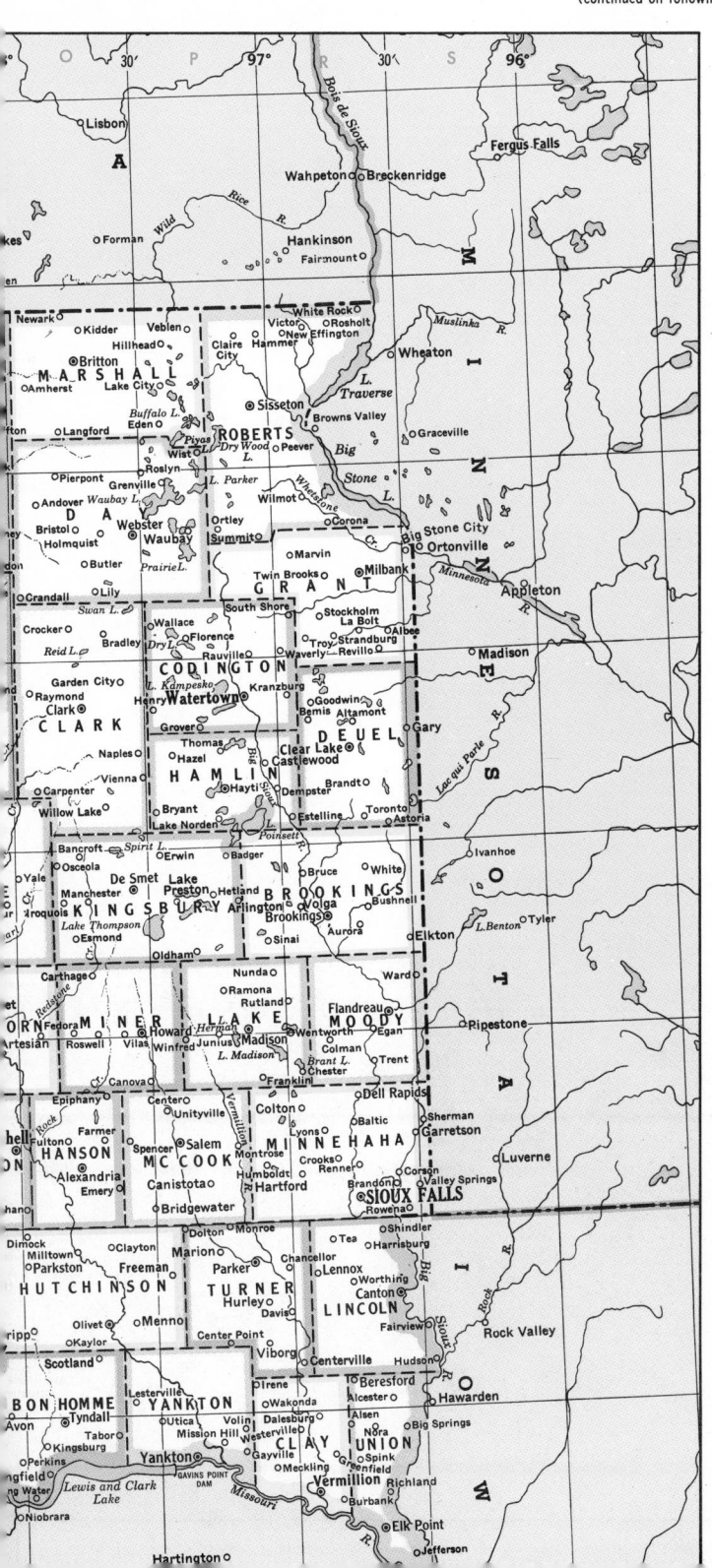

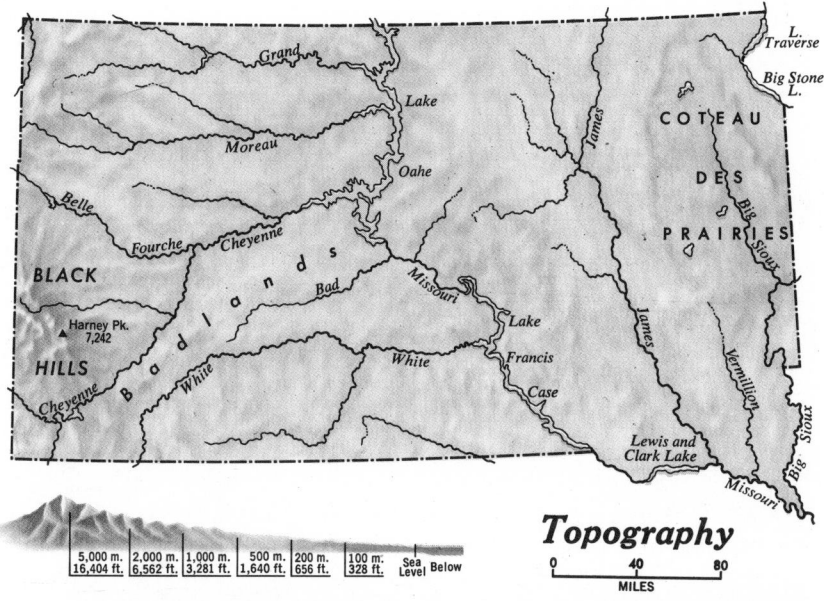

Topography

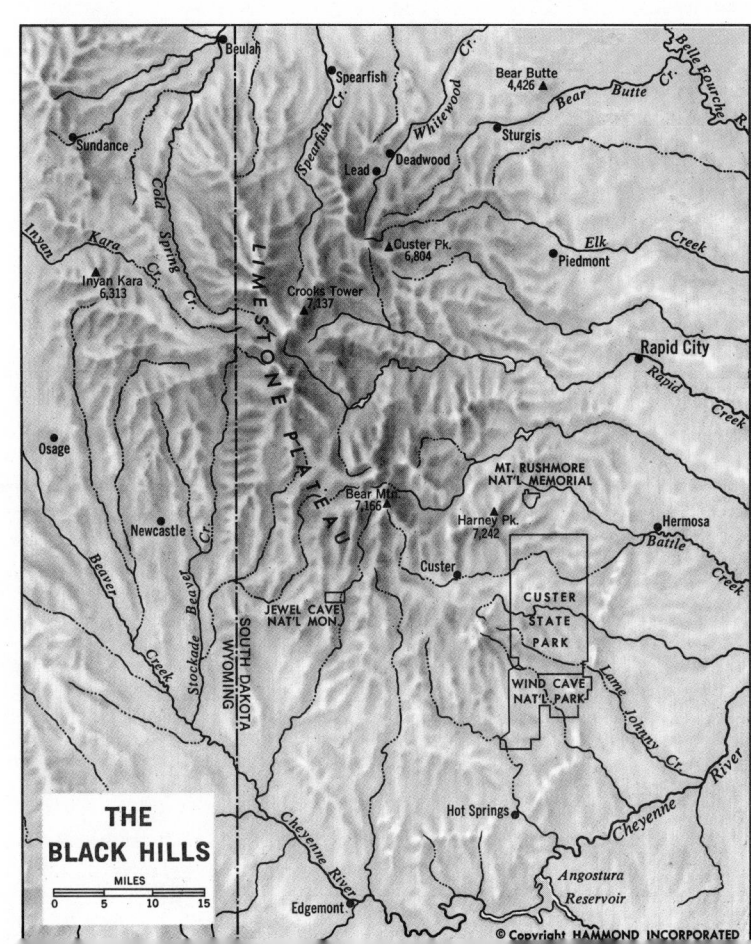

THE BLACK HILLS

† 57010 Greenfield, 12 ....R 8
† 57380 Greenwood, 90 ....N 8
57533 Gregory, 1,756 ....L 7
57239 Grenville, 154 ....O 3
57445 Groton, 1,021 ....N 3
† 57201 Grover, 12 ....P 4
57534 Hamill, 57 ....K 6
57240 Hammer, 30 ....R 2
57535 Harrington, 54 ....G 7
57032 Harrisburg, 338 ....R 7
57344 Harrison, 68 ....M 7
57536 Harrold, 184 ....K 4
57033 Hartford, 800 ....P 6
57537 Hayes, 28 ....H 5
57241 Hayti◉, 393 ....P 4
57242 Hazel, 101 ....P 4
57446 Hecla, 407 ....N 2
57243 Henry, 182 ....P 4
57744 Hermosa, 150 ....C 6
57632 Herreid, 672 ....K 2
57538 Herrick, 126 ....L 7
57244 Hetland, 81 ....P 5
† 69501 Hidden Timber, 30 ....J 7
57345 Highmore◉, 1,173 ....L 4
57745 Hill City, 389 ....B 6
† 57270 Hillhead, 26 ....O 2
† 57437 Hillsview, 19 ....L 2
† 57701 Hisega, 36 ....C 5
57348 Hitchcock, 150 ....M 4
57540 Holabird, 32 ....K 4
† 57274 Holmquist, 13 ....O 3
57448 Hosmer, 437 ....L 2
57747 Hot Springs◉, 4,434 ....C 7
57449 Houghton, 90 ....N 2
57450 Hoven, 671 ....K 3
57349 Howard◉, 1,175 ....P 5
57034 Hudson, 366 ....R 7
57035 Humboldt, 411 ....P 6
57036 Hurley, 399 ....P 7
57350 Huron◉, 14,299 ....N 5
57541 Ideal, 135 ....K 6
† 57774 Igloo, 20 ....B 7
57750 Interior, 81 ....F 6
57451 Ipswich◉, 1,187 ....L 3
57037 Irene, 461 ....P 7
57353 Iroquois, 375 ....O 5
57633 Isabel, 394 ....G 3
57452 Java, 305 ....K 3
57038 Jefferson, 474 ....S 8
† 57042 Junius, 50 ....P 6
57543 Kadoka◉, 815 ....F 6
57354 Kaylor, 110 ....O 7
57634 Keldron, 35 ....F 2
57642 Kenel, 245 ....H 2
57544 Kennebec◉, 372 ....K 6
57751 Keystone, 475 ....C 6
57453 Kidder, 140 ....O 2
57355 Kimball, 825 ....M 6
57245 Kranzburg, 143 ....R 4
57752 Kyle, 500 ....E 7
57246 La Bolt, 90 ....R 4
57356 Lake Andes◉, 948 ....M 7
57247 Lake City, 44 ....O 2
57248 Lake Norden, 393 ....P 4
57249 Lake Preston, 812 ....P 5
57358 Lane, 94 ....N 5
57454 Langford, 328 ....O 2
57636 Lantry, 52 ....G 3
57637 La Plant, 165 ....H 3
57754 Lead, 5,420 ....B 5
57455 Lebanon, 182 ....K 3
57638 Lemmon, 1,997 ....E 2
57039 Lennox, 1,487 ....R 7
57456 Leola◉, 787 ....M 2
57040 Lesterville, 181 ....O 7
57359 Letcher, 201 ....N 6
57250 Lily, 62 ....O 3
57639 Little Eagle, 975 ....H 2
57640 Lodgepole, 25 ....D 2
57457 Longlake, 128 ....L 2
57547 Longvalley, 16 ....F 7
57360 Loomis, 150 ....N 6
57548 Lower Brule, 500 ....K 5
57458 Lowry, 35 ....K 3
57549 Lucas, 13 ....L 7
† 57569 Lyman, 15 ....K 6
57041 Lyons, 89 ....R 6
57042 Madison◉, 6,315 ....P 6
57643 Mahto, 23 ....H 2
† 57353 Manchester, 25 ....O 5
57756 Manderson, 350 ....D 7
57460 Mansfield, 150 ....N 3
57043 Marion, 844 ....P 7
57551 Martin◉, 1,248 ....F 7
57361 Marty, 225 ....N 8
57251 Marvin, 65 ....R 3
57627 Maurine, 12 ....E 3
57641 McIntosh◉, 563 ....G 2
57642 McLaughlin, 863 ....H 2
57044 Meckling, 100 ....R 8
57461 Mellette, 199 ....N 3
57045 Menno, 796 ....P 7
57552 Midland, 270 ....G 5
57252 Milbank◉, 3,727 ....R 3
57362 Miller◉, 2,148 ....L 4
† 57366 Milltown, 28 ....O 7
57462 Mina, 18 ....M 3
57463 Miranda, 60 ....M 4
57555 Mission, 739 ....H 7
57046 Mission Hill, 161 ....P 8
57301 Mitchell◉, 13,425 ....N 6
57601 Mobridge, 4,545 ....J 2
57047 Monroe, 134 ....P 7
57048 Montrose, 377 ....P 6
57645 Morristown, 144 ....F 2
57558 Mosher, 19 ....J 7
57646 Mound City◉, 164 ....K 2
57363 Mount Vernon, 398 ....N 6
57559 Murdo◉, 865 ....H 6
† 57778 Mystic, 16 ....B 6
57254 Naples, 38 ....O 4
57759 Nemo, 100 ....B 5
57364 New Holland, 131 ....M 7
† 57453 Newark, 25 ....J 7
57255 New Effington, 258 ....R 2
57760 Newell, 664 ....C 4
57364 New Holland, 131 ....M 7
57761 New Underwood, 416 ....D 5

57762 Nisland, 157 ....C 4
57560 Norris, 42 ....G 7
† 57543 North Eagle Butte, 1,351 ....G 3
57049 North Sioux City, 860 ....R 8
57465 Northville, 119 ....M 3
57050 Nunda, 85 ....P 5
57365 Oacoma, 215 ....L 6
57763 Oelrichs, 94 ....C 7
57764 Oglala, 250 ....D 7
57562 Okaton, 65 ....H 6
† 57501 Okobojo, 15 ....J 4
57563 Okreek, 300 ....J 7
57051 Oldham, 244 ....O 5
57052 Olivet◉, 103 ....O 7
57466 Onaka, 69 ....L 3
57564 Onida◉, 785 ....K 4
57766 Oral, 45 ....C 7
57467 Orient, 131 ....L 4
57256 Ortley, 111 ....P 3
† 57353 Osceola, 32 ....O 5
57053 Parker◉, 1,005 ....P 7
57366 Parkston, 1,611 ....O 7
57566 Parmelee, 475 ....G 7
† 57529 Paxton, 18 ....L 7
† 57729 Pedro, 15 ....E 5
57257 Peever, 202 ....R 2
57567 Philip◉, 983 ....F 5
57367 Pickstown, 300 ....M 7
57769 Piedmont, 650 ....C 5
57468 Pierpont, 241 ....O 3
† 57501 Pierre (cap.)◉, 9,699 ....J 5
57770 Pine Ridge, 2,768 ....E 7
57368 Plankinton◉, 613 ....N 6
57369 Platte, 1,351 ....M 7
57648 Pollock, 341 ....J 2
57772 Porcupine, 200 ....E 7
† 57750 Potato Creek, 40 ....F 6
57649 Prairie City, 55 ....D 2
57568 Presho, 922 ....J 6
57773 Pringle, 86 ....B 7
57774 Provo, 45 ....B 7
57370 Pukwana, 208 ....L 6
57402 Putney, 24 ....N 2
57775 Quinn, 105 ....E 5
57054 Ramona, 227 ....P 5
57701 Rapid City◉, 43,836 ....C 5
57357 Ravinia, 109 ....N 7
57258 Raymond, 114 ....O 4
57469 Redfield◉, 2,943 ....N 4
57776 Redig, 13 ....C 3
57777 Redowl, 14 ....D 4
57371 Ree Heights, 183 ....L 4
57569 Reliance, 204 ....K 6
57055 Renner, 260 ....R 6
57259 Revillo, 142 ....R 3
† 57025 Richland, 70 ....R 8
57652 Ridgeview, 65 ....H 3
57778 Rochford, 20 ....B 5
57701 Rockerville, 48 ....C 6
57470 Rockham, 60 ....M 4
† 57772 Rockyford, 50 ....E 7
57471 Roscoe, 398 ....L 3
57570 Rosebud, 650 ....H 7
57260 Rosholt, 456 ....R 2
57261 Roslyn, 250 ....P 2
57372 Roswell, 32 ....O 6
57056 Rowena, 76 ....R 6
57057 Rutland, 100 ....P 5
57571 Saint Charles, 33 ....L 7
57572 Saint Francis, 300 ....H 7
57373 Saint Lawrence, 249 ....M 4
57779 Saint Onge, 200 ....B 4
57058 Salem◉, 1,391 ....P 6
† 57730 Sanator, 150 ....B 6
† 57754 Savoy, 15 ....B 5
57780 Scenic, 56 ....D 6
57059 Scotland, 984 ....O 7
57472 Selby◉, 957 ....J 3

57653 Shadehill, 186 ....E 2
57060 Sherman, 82 ....S 6
† 57101 Shindler, 20 ....R 7
57781 Silver City, 40 ....B 5
57061 Sinai, 147 ....P 5
* 57101 Sioux Falls◉, 72,488 ....R 6
Sioux Falls, †95,209 ....R 6
57262 Sisseton◉, 3,094 ....R 2
57782 Smithwick, 25 ....C 7
57263 South Shore, 199 ....P 3
57783 Spearfish, 4,661 ....B 5
57374 Spencer, 385 ....O 6
† 57010 Spink, 21 ....R 8
57062 Springfield, 1,566 ....N 8
57346 Stephan, 60 ....K 5
57375 Stickney, 421 ....M 6
57264 Stockholm, 116 ....R 3
† 57359 Storla, 75 ....M 6
57265 Strandburg, 98 ....R 3
57474 Stratford, 106 ....N 3
57785 Sturgis◉, 4,536 ....B 5
57266 Summit, 332 ....P 3
† 57551 Swett, 20 ....E 7
57063 Tabor, 388 ....O 8
57433 Tacoma Park, 18 ....N 2
57064 Tea, 302 ....R 7
† 57242 Thomas, 15 ....P 4

57655 Thunder Hawk, 45 ....F 2
† 57769 Tilford, 162 ....C 5
57656 Timber Lake◉, 625 ....H 3
57475 Tolstoy, 99 ....K 3
57268 Toronto, 216 ....R 4
57657 Trail City, 75 ....H 3
57065 Trent, 177 ....R 6
57376 Tripp, 851 ....N 7
† 57754 Trojan, 25 ....B 5
† 57265 Troy, 13 ....R 3
57476 Tulare, 211 ....N 4
57477 Turton, 121 ....N 3
57574 Tuthill, 73 ....G 7
57269 Twin Brooks, 122 ....R 3
57066 Tyndall◉, 1,245 ....O 8
57787 Union Center, 50 ....D 4
† 57058 Unityville, 30 ....P 6
57067 Utica, 89 ....P 8
57788 Vale, 89 ....C 4
57068 Valley Springs, 566 ....S 6
57270 Veblen, 377 ....P 2
57478 Verdon, 18 ....N 3
57069 Vermillion◉, 9,128 ....R 8
57575 Vetal, 17 ....G 7
57575 Viborg, 662 ....P 7
† 57260 Victor, 22 ....R 2
57271 Vienna, 119 ....O 4

† 57349 Vilas, 33 ....O 6
† 57701 Villa Ranchaero 3,171 ....C 5
57379 Virgil, 43 ....N 5
57576 Vivian, 200 ....J 6
57071 Volga, 982 ....R 5
57072 Volin, 157 ....P 8
57380 Wagner, 1,655 ....N 7
57073 Wakonda, 290 ....P 7
57658 Wakpala, 500 ....H 2
57790 Wall, 786 ....E 6
57272 Wallace, 95 ....P 3
57577 Wanblee, 500 ....F 6
57074 Ward, 57 ....R 5
57479 Warner, 175 ....M 3
57791 Wasta, 127 ....D 5
57660 Watauga, 76 ....F 2
57201 Watertown◉, 13,388 ....P 4
57273 Waubay, 696 ....P 3
57202 Waverly, 40 ....R 3
57274 Webster◉, 2,252 ....P 3
57480 Wecota, 50 ....L 3
† 57532 Wendte, 20 ....H 5
57075 Wentworth, 196 ....R 6
57781 Wessington, 380 ....M 5
57382 Wessington Springs◉, 1,300 ....M 5

57481 Westport, 136 ....M
57482 Wetonka, 31 ....M
57578 Wewela, 16 ....K
57276 White, 418 ....R
† 57638 White Butte, 15 ....E
57661 Whitehorse, 100 ....H
57383 White Lake, 395 ....M
57579 White River◉, 617 ....H
57277 White Rock, 35 ....R
57793 Whitewood, 689 ....B
57278 Willow Lake, 353 ....O
57279 Wilmot, 518 ....R
57076 Winfred, 110 ....P
57580 Winner◉, 3,789 ....K
57584 Witten, 140 ....J
57384 Wolsey, 436 ....N
57585 Wood, 132 ....J
57385 Woonsocket◉, 852 ....N
57077 Worthing, 294 ....R
57794 Wounded Knee, 500 ....O
57386 Yale, 148 ....O
57078 Yankton◉, 11,919 ....P
57483 Zell, 87 ....M

◉ County seat.
‡ Population of metropolitan area.
† Zip of nearest p.o.
* Multiple zips

Agriculture, Industry and Resources

DOMINANT LAND USE

- Specialized Wheat
- Wheat, General Farming
- Wheat, Range Livestock
- Cattle Feed, Hogs
- Livestock, Cash Grain
- General Farming, Livestock, Special Crops
- Range Livestock
- Forests

⚡ Water Power

MAJOR MINERAL OCCURRENCES

Ag Silver
Au Gold
Be Beryl
Gn Granite

Mi Mica
O Petroleum
U Uranium
V Vanadium

Beds of fossils await paleontologists in the vast, semi-arid buttes of the Badlands, east of the Black Hills

E. C. Werner—Shostal Associates

Texas 301

COUNTIES

County	Key
Anderson, 27,789	J 6
Andrews, 10,372	B 5
Angelina, 49,349	K 6
Aransas, 8,902	H 10
Archer, 5,759	F 4
Armstrong, 1,895	C 3
Atascosa, 18,696	F 9
Austin, 13,831	H 8
Bailey, 8,487	B 3
Bandera, 4,747	E 8
Bastrop, 17,297	G 7
Baylor, 5,221	E 4
Bee, 22,737	G 9
Bell, 124,483	G 6
Bexar, 830,460	F 8
Blanco, 3,567	F 7
Borden, 888	C 5
Bosque, 10,966	G 6
Bowie, 67,813	K 4
Brazoria, 108,312	J 8
Brazos, 57,978	H 7
Brewster, 7,780	A 8
Briscoe, 2,794	C 3
Brooks, 8,005	F 11
Brown, 25,877	F 6
Burleson, 9,999	H 7
Burnet, 11,420	F 7
Caldwell, 21,178	G 8
Calhoun, 17,831	H 9
Callahan, 8,205	E 5
Cameron, 140,368	G 11
Camp, 8,005	K 5
Carson, 6,358	C 2
Cass, 24,133	K 4
Castro, 10,394	B 3
Chambers, 12,187	K 8
Cherokee, 32,008	J 6
Childress, 6,605	D 3
Clay, 8,079	F 4
Cochran, 5,326	B 4
Coke, 3,087	D 6
Coleman, 10,288	E 6
Collin, 66,920	H 4
Collingsworth, 4,755	D 3
Colorado, 17,638	H 8
Comal, 24,165	F 8
Comanche, 11,898	F 6
Concho, 2,937	E 6
Cooke, 23,471	G 4
Coryell, 35,311	G 6
Cottle, 3,204	D 3
Crane, 4,172	B 6
Crockett, 3,885	C 7
Crosby, 9,085	C 4
Culberson, 3,429	C 11
Dallam, 6,012	B 1
Dallas, 1,327,321	H 5
Dawson, 16,604	C 5
Deaf Smith, 18,999	B 3
Delta, 4,927	J 4
Denton, 75,633	G 4
De Witt, 18,660	G 9
Dickens, 3,737	D 4
Dimmit, 9,039	E 9
Donley, 3,641	D 2
Duval, 11,722	F 10
Eastland, 18,092	F 5
Ector, 91,805	B 6
Edwards, 2,107	D 7
Ellis, 46,638	H 5
El Paso, 359,291	A 10
Erath, 18,141	F 5
Falls, 17,300	H 6
Fannin, 22,705	H 4
Fayette, 17,650	H 8
Fisher, 6,344	D 5
Floyd, 11,044	C 3
Foard, 2,211	E 3
Fort Bend, 52,314	J 8
Franklin, 5,291	J 4
Freestone, 11,116	H 6
Frio, 11,159	E 9
Gaines, 11,593	B 5
Galveston, 169,812	K 8
Garza, 5,289	C 4
Gillespie, 10,553	F 7
Glasscock, 1,155	C 6
Goliad, 4,869	G 9
Gonzales, 16,375	G 8
Gray, 26,949	D 2
Grayson, 83,225	H 4
Gregg, 75,929	K 5
Grimes, 11,855	J 7
Guadalupe, 33,554	G 8
Hale, 34,137	C 3
Hall, 6,015	D 3
Hamilton, 7,198	F 6
Hansford, 6,351	C 1
Hardeman, 6,795	E 3
Hardin, 29,996	K 7
Harris, 1,741,912	J 8
Harrison, 44,841	K 5
Hartley, 2,782	B 2
Haskell, 8,512	E 4
Hays, 27,642	F 7
Hemphill, 3,084	D 2
Henderson, 26,466	J 5
Hidalgo, 181,535	F 11
Hill, 22,596	G 5
Hockley, 20,396	B 4
Hood, 6,368	G 5
Hopkins, 20,710	J 4
Houston, 17,855	J 6
Howard, 37,796	C 5
Hudspeth, 2,392	B 10
Hunt, 47,948	H 4
Hutchinson, 24,443	C 2
Irion, 1,070	C 6
Jack, 6,711	F 4
Jackson, 12,975	H 9
Jasper, 24,692	K 7
Jeff Davis, 1,527	C 11
Jefferson, 244,773	K 8
Jim Hogg, 4,654	F 11
Jim Wells, 33,032	F 10
Johnson, 45,769	G 5
Jones, 16,106	E 5
Karnes, 13,462	G 9
Kaufman, 32,392	H 5
Kendall, 6,964	F 8
Kenedy, 678	G 11
Kent, 1,434	D 4
Kerr, 19,454	E 7
Kimble, 3,904	E 7
King, 464	D 4
Kinney, 2,006	D 8
Kleberg, 33,166	G 10
Knox, 5,972	E 4
Lamar, 36,062	J 4
Lamb, 17,770	B 3
Lampasas, 9,323	F 6
La Salle, 5,014	E 9
Lavaca, 17,903	H 8
Lee, 8,048	H 7
Leon, 8,738	J 6
Liberty, 33,014	K 7
Limestone, 18,100	H 6
Lipscomb, 3,486	D 1
Live Oak, 6,697	F 9
Llano, 6,979	F 7
Loving, 164	D 10
Lubbock, 179,295	C 4
Lynn, 9,107	C 4
Madison, 7,693	J 6
Marion, 8,517	K 5
Martin, 4,774	C 5
Mason, 3,356	E 7
Matagorda, 27,913	H 9
Maverick, 18,093	D 9
McCulloch, 8,571	E 6
McLennan, 147,553	G 6
McMullen, 1,095	F 9
Medina, 20,249	E 8
Menard, 2,646	E 7
Midland, 65,433	B 6
Milam, 20,028	H 7
Mills, 4,212	F 6
Mitchell, 9,073	D 5
Montague, 15,326	G 4
Montgomery, 49,479	J 7
Moore, 14,060	C 2
Morris, 12,310	K 4
Motley, 2,178	D 3
Nacogdoches, 36,362	K 6
Navarro, 31,150	H 5
Newton, 11,657	L 7
Nolan, 16,220	D 5
Nueces, 237,544	G 10
Ochiltree, 9,704	D 1
Oldham, 2,258	B 2
Orange, 71,170	L 7
Palo Pinto, 28,962	F 5
Panola, 15,894	K 5
Parker, 33,888	G 5
Parmer, 10,509	B 3
Pecos, 13,748	B 7
Polk, 14,457	K 7
Potter, 90,511	C 2
Presidio, 4,842	C 12
Rains, 3,752	J 5
Randall, 53,885	C 2
Reagan, 3,239	C 6
Real, 2,013	E 8
Red River, 14,298	J 4
Reeves, 16,526	D 11
Refugio, 9,494	G 9
Roberts, 967	D 2
Robertson, 14,389	H 6
Rockwall, 7,046	H 5
Runnels, 12,108	E 6
Rusk, 34,102	K 5
Sabine, 7,187	L 6
San Augustine, 7,858	K 6
San Jacinto, 6,702	J 7
San Patricio, 47,288	G 10
San Saba, 5,540	F 6
Schleicher, 2,277	D 7
Scurry, 15,760	D 5
Shackelford, 3,323	E 5
Shelby, 19,672	K 6
Sherman, 3,657	C 1
Smith, 97,096	J 5
Somervell, 2,793	G 5
Starr, 17,707	F 11
Stephens, 8,414	F 5
Sterling, 1,056	C 6
Stonewall, 2,397	D 4
Sutton, 3,175	D 7
Swisher, 10,373	C 3
Tarrant, 716,317	G 5
Taylor, 97,853	E 5
Terrell, 1,940	B 7
Terry, 14,118	B 4
Throckmorton, 2,205	E 4
Titus, 16,702	K 4
Tom Green, 71,047	D 6
Travis, 295,516	G 7
Trinity, 7,628	J 6
Tyler, 12,417	K 7
Upshur, 20,976	K 5
Upton, 4,697	B 6
Uvalde, 17,348	E 8
Val Verde, 27,471	C 8
Van Zandt, 22,155	J 5
Victoria, 53,766	H 9
Walker, 27,680	J 7
Waller, 14,285	J 8
Ward, 13,019	A 6
Washington, 18,842	H 7
Webb, 72,859	E 10
Wharton, 36,729	H 8
Wheeler, 6,434	D 2
Wichita, 121,862	F 3
Wilbarger, 15,355	E 3
Willacy, 15,570	G 11
Williamson, 37,305	G 7
Wilson, 13,041	F 8
Winkler, 9,640	A 6
Wise, 19,687	G 4
Wood, 18,589	J 5
Yoakum, 7,344	B 4
Young, 15,400	F 4
Zapata, 4,352	E 11
Zavala, 11,370	E 9

AREA 267,339 sq. mi.
POPULATION 11,196,730
CAPITAL Austin
LARGEST CITY Houston
HIGHEST POINT Guadalupe Pk. 8,751 ft.
SETTLED IN 1686
ADMITTED TO UNION December 29, 1845
POPULAR NAME Lone Star State
STATE FLOWER Bluebonnet
STATE BIRD Mockingbird

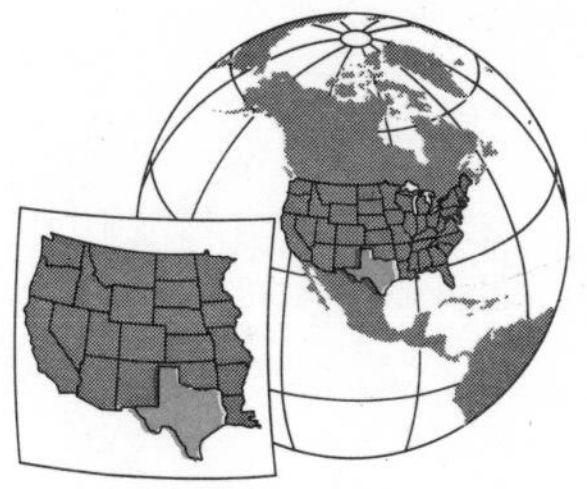

CITIES and TOWNS

	Zip	Name/Pop.	Key
	79311	Abernathy, 2,625	B 4
*	79601	Abilene⊙, 89,653	E 5
		Abilene, ‡113,959	E 5
	78516	Alamo, 4,291	F 11
	78209	Alamo Heights, 6,933	F 8
	76430	Albany⊙, 1,978	E 5
	78332	Alice⊙, 20,121	F 10
	79830	Alpine⊙, 5,971	D 11
	77510	Alta Loma, 1,536	K 3
	75925	Alto, 1,045	J 6
	76009	Alvarado, 2,129	G 5
	77511	Alvin, 10,671	J 3
*	79101	Amarillo⊙, 127,010	C 2
		Amarillo, ‡144,396	C 2
	77514	Anahuac⊙, 1,881	K 8
	77830	Anderson⊙, 500	J 7
	79714	Andrews⊙, 8,625	B 5
	77515	Angleton⊙, 9,770	J 8
	79501	Anson⊙, 2,615	E 5
	88021	Anthony, 2,154	A 10
	79313	Anton, 1,034	B 4
	78336	Aransas Pass, 5,813	G 10
	77517	Arcadia, 1,200	K 3
	76351	Archer City⊙, 1,722	F 4
*	76010	Arlington, 90,643	F 2
	78827	Asherton, 1,645	E 9
	79502	Aspermont⊙, 1,198	D 4
	75751	Athens⊙, 9,582	J 5
	75551	Atlanta, 5,007	K 4
*	78701	Austin (cap.)⊙, 251,808	G 7
		Austin, ‡295,516	G 7
	76020	Azle, 4,493	E 1
	77518	Bacliff, 1,900	K 2
	79504	Baird⊙, 1,538	E 5
	75149	Balch Springs, 10,464	H 2
	76821	Ballinger⊙, 4,203	E 6
	78003	Bandera⊙, 891	F 8
	76823	Bangs, 1,214	E 6
	77532	Barrett, 2,750	K 1
	76511	Bartlett, 1,622	G 7
	78602	Bastrop⊙, 3,112	G 7
	77414	Bay City⊙, 11,733	H 9
	77520	Baytown, 43,980	L 2
	77701	Beaumont⊙, 115,919	K 7
		Beaumont-Port Arthur-Orange, ‡315,943	K 7
	76021	Bedford, 10,049	F 2
	78102	Beeville⊙, 13,506	G 9
	77401	Bellaire, 19,009	J 2
	76705	Bellmead, 7,698	H 6
	77418	Bellville⊙, 2,371	H 8
	76513	Belton⊙, 8,696	G 7
	78341	Benavides, 2,112	F 10
	76126	Benbrook, 8,169	E 2
	79505	Benjamin⊙, 308	E 4
	76932	Big Lake⊙, 2,489	C 6
	79720	Big Spring⊙, 28,735	C 5
	78343	Bishop, 3,466	G 10
	77951	Bloomington, 1,676	H 9
	76131	Blue Mound, 1,283	F 1
	78006	Boerne⊙, 2,432	F 8
	75417	Bogata, 1,287	J 4
	75418	Bonham⊙, 7,698	H 4
	79007	Borger, 14,195	C 2
	75557	Boston⊙, 500	K 4
	79009	Bovina, 1,428	A 3
	76230	Bowie, 5,185	G 4
	78832	Brackettville⊙, 1,539	D 8
	76825	Brady⊙, 5,557	E 6
	77422	Brazoria, 1,681	J 9
	76024	Breckenridge⊙, 5,944	F 5
	77833	Brenham⊙, 8,922	H 7
	77611	Bridge City, 8,164	L 7
	76026	Bridgeport, 3,614	G 4
	77423	Brookshire, 1,683	J 8
	77581	Brookside Village, 1,507	J 2
	79316	Brownfield⊙, 9,647	B 4
	78520	Brownsville⊙, 52,522	G 12
		Brownsville-Harlingen-San Benito, ‡140,368	G 12
	76801	Brownwood⊙, 17,368	F 6
	77801	Bryan⊙, 33,719	H 7
		Bryan-College Station, ‡57,978	H 7
	75831	Buffalo, 1,242	J 6
	77612	Buna, 1,649	L 7
†	79007	Bunavista, 1,402	C 2
†	77001	Bunker Hill Village, 3,977	J 1
	76354	Burkburnett, 9,230	F 3
	76028	Burleson, 7,713	F 2
	78611	Burnet⊙, 2,864	F 7
	77836	Caldwell⊙, 2,308	H 7
	77837	Calvert, 2,072	H 7
	76520	Cameron⊙, 5,546	H 7
	79014	Canadian⊙, 2,292	D 2
	75103	Canton⊙, 2,283	J 5
	79835	Canutillo, 1,588	A 10
	79015	Canyon⊙, 8,333	C 3

(continued on following page)

Agriculture, Industry and Resources

DOMINANT LAND USE

- Wheat, Grain Sorghums, Range Livestock
- Cotton, Wheat
- Specialized Cotton
- Cotton, General Farming
- Cotton, Forest Products
- Cotton, Range Livestock
- Rice, General Farming
- Peanuts, General Farming
- General Farming, Livestock, Cash Grain
- General Farming, Forest Products, Truck Farming, Cotton
- Fruit, Truck and Mixed Farming
- Range Livestock
- Forests
- Swampland, Limited Agriculture
- Nonagricultural Land
- Urban Areas

MAJOR MINERAL OCCURRENCES

- At Asphalt
- Cl Clay
- Fe Iron Ore
- G Natural Gas
- Gn Granite
- Gp Gypsum
- Gr Graphite
- He Helium
- Ls Limestone
- Na Salt
- O Petroleum
- S Sulfur
- Tc Talc
- U Uranium

- Water Power
- Major Industrial Areas

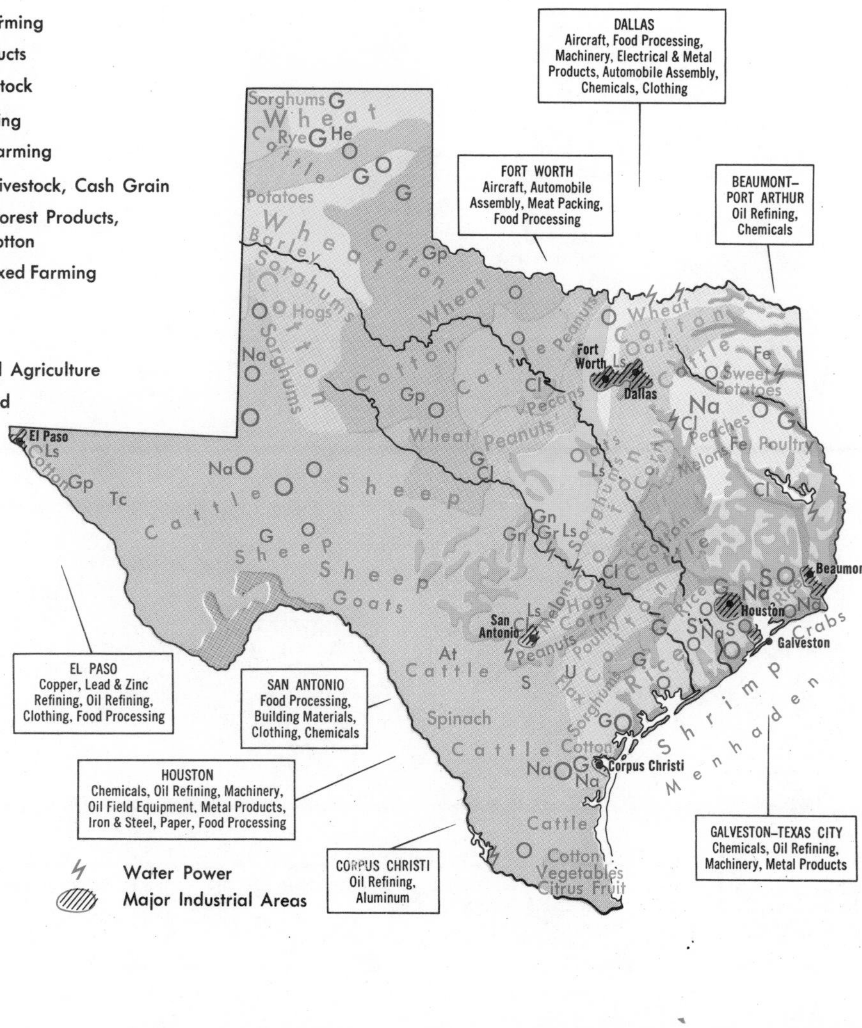
DALLAS
Aircraft, Food Processing, Machinery, Electrical & Metal Products, Automobile Assembly, Chemicals, Clothing
FORT WORTH
Aircraft, Automobile Assembly, Meat Packing, Food Processing
BEAUMONT–PORT ARTHUR
Oil Refining, Chemicals
EL PASO
Copper, Lead & Zinc Refining, Oil Refining, Clothing, Food Processing
SAN ANTONIO
Food Processing, Building Materials, Clothing, Chemicals
HOUSTON
Chemicals, Oil Refining, Machinery, Oil Field Equipment, Metal Products, Iron & Steel, Paper, Food Processing
CORPUS CHRISTI
Oil Refining, Aluminum
GALVESTON–TEXAS CITY
Chemicals, Oil Refining, Machinery, Metal Products
El Paso
Fort Worth
Dallas
San Antonio
Houston
Beaumont
Galveston
Corpus Christi
Sorghums
Wheat
Rye
Cattle
Potatoes
Barley
Cotton
Hogs
Peanuts
Pecans
Oats
Sweet Potatoes
Peaches
Melons
Poultry
Sheep
Goats
Corn
Rice
Flax
Spinach
Shrimp
Menhaden
Crabs
Vegetables
Citrus Fruit

TEXAS

State Capitals ⊛
County Seats ◉

⊛ C.S. HAMMOND & CO., N.Y.

WESTERN PART OF TEXAS
Same scale as main map

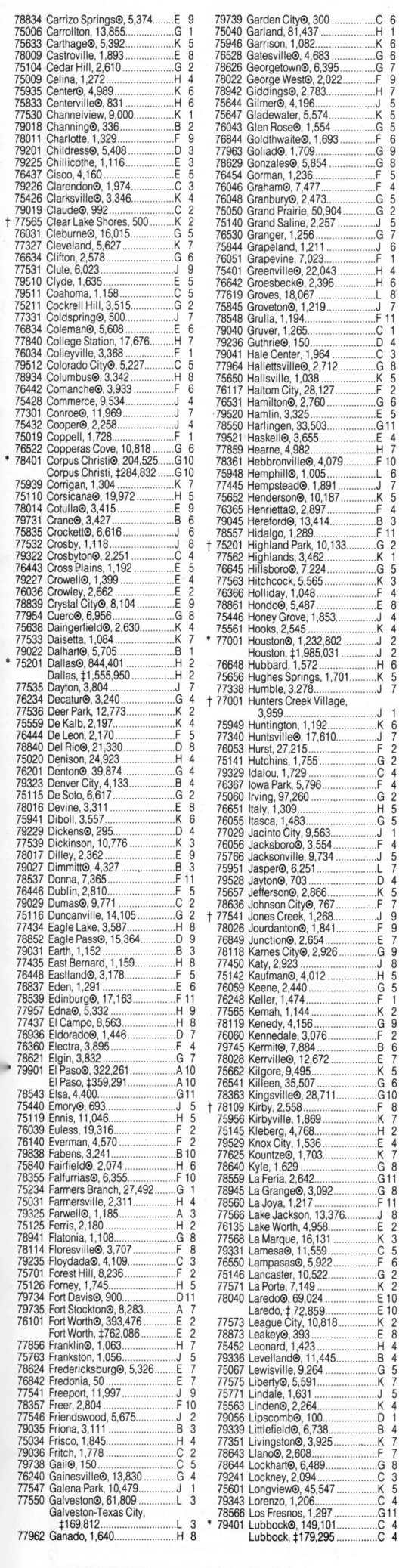

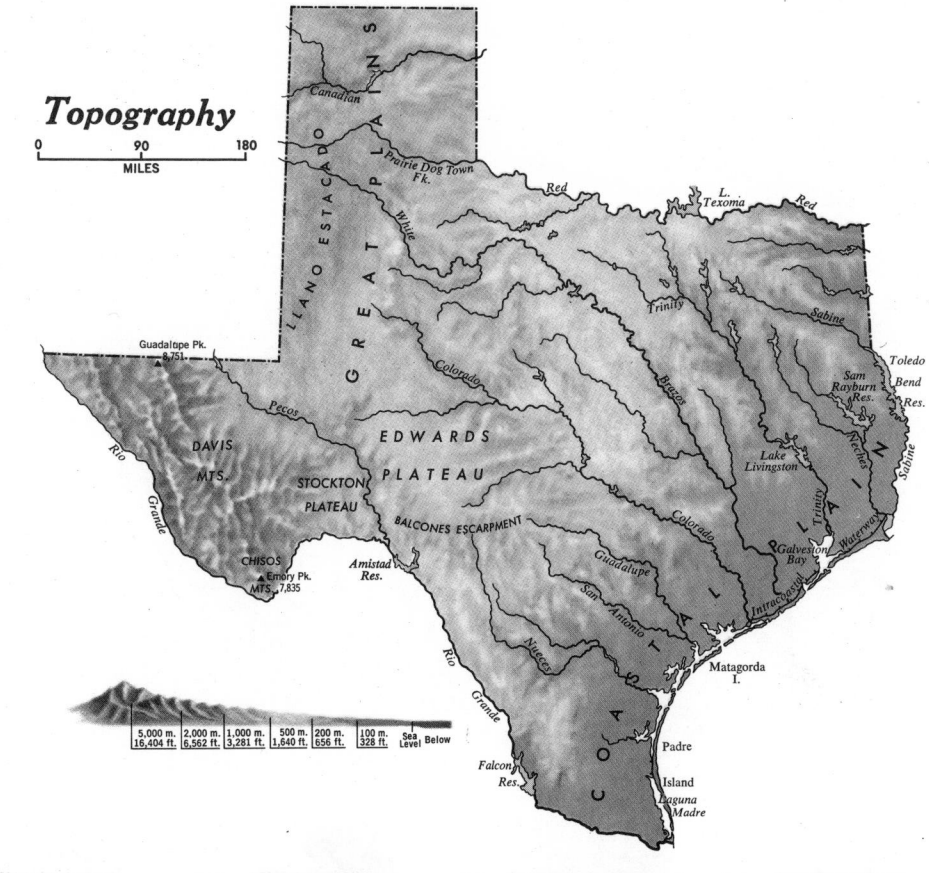

Topography

0   90   180
MILES

5,000 m. / 16,404 ft. · 2,000 m. / 6,562 ft. · 1,000 m. / 3,281 ft. · 500 m. / 1,640 ft. · 200 m. / 656 ft. · 100 m. / 328 ft. · Sea Level · Below

78834 Carrizo Springs⊙, 5,374......E 9
75006 Carrollton, 13,855......G 1
75633 Carthage⊙, 5,392......K 5
78009 Castroville, 1,893......E 8
75104 Cedar Hill, 2,610......G 2
75009 Celina, 1,272......H 4
75935 Center⊙, 4,989......K 6
75833 Centerville⊙, 831......H 6
77530 Channelview, 9,000......K 1
79018 Channing⊙, 336......B 2
78011 Charlotte, 1,329......F 9
79201 Childress⊙, 5,408......D 3
79225 Chillicothe, 1,116......E 3
76437 Cisco, 4,160......E 5
79226 Clarendon⊙, 1,974......C 3
75426 Clarksville⊙, 3,346......K 4
79019 Claude⊙, 992......C 2
† 77565 Clear Lake Shores, 500......K 2
76031 Cleburne⊙, 16,015......G 5
77327 Cleveland, 5,627......K 7
76634 Clifton, 2,578......G 6
77531 Clute, 6,023......J 9
79510 Clyde, 1,635......E 5
75211 Cockrell Hill, 3,515......G 2
77331 Coldspring⊙, 500......J 7
76834 Coleman⊙, 5,608......E 6
77840 College Station, 17,676......H 7
76034 Colleyville, 3,368......F 1
79512 Colorado City⊙, 5,227......C 5
78934 Columbus⊙, 3,342......H 8
76442 Comanche⊙, 3,933......F 6
75428 Commerce, 9,534......J 4
77301 Conroe⊙, 11,969......J 7
75432 Cooper⊙, 2,258......J 4
75019 Coppell, 1,728......F 1
76522 Copperas Cove, 10,818......G 6
* 78401 Corpus Christi⊙, 204,525......G10
   Corpus Christi, ‡284,832......G10
75939 Corrigan, 1,304......K 7
75110 Corsicana⊙, 19,972......H 5
78014 Cotulla⊙, 3,415......E 9
79731 Crane⊙, 3,427......B 6
75835 Crockett⊙, 6,616......J 6
77532 Crosby, 1,118......J 8
79322 Crosbyton⊙, 2,251......C 4
76443 Cross Plains, 1,192......E 5
79227 Crowell⊙, 1,399......E 4
76036 Crowley, 2,662......F 2
78839 Crystal City⊙, 8,104......E 9
77954 Cuero⊙, 6,956......G 9
75638 Daingerfield⊙, 2,630......K 4
77533 Daisetta, 1,084......K 7
79022 Dalhart⊙, 5,705......B 1
* 75201 Dallas⊙, 844,401......H 2
   Dallas, ‡1,555,950......H 2
77535 Dayton, 3,804......J 7
76234 Decatur⊙, 3,240......G 4
77536 Deer Park, 12,773......K 2
75559 De Kalb, 2,197......K 4
76444 De Leon, 2,170......F 5
78840 Del Rio⊙, 21,330......D 8
75020 Denison, 24,923......H 4
76201 Denton⊙, 39,874......G 4
79323 Denver City, 4,133......B 4
75115 De Soto, 6,617......G 2
78016 Devine, 3,311......E 8
75941 Diboll, 3,557......K 6
79229 Dickens⊙, 295......D 4
77539 Dickinson, 10,776......K 3
78017 Dilley, 2,362......E 9
79027 Dimmitt⊙, 4,327......B 3
78537 Donna, 7,365......F 5
76446 Dublin, 2,810......F 5
79029 Dumas⊙, 9,771......C 2
75116 Duncanville, 14,105......G 2
77434 Eagle Lake, 3,587......H 8
78852 Eagle Pass⊙, 15,364......D 9
79031 Earth, 1,152......B 3
77435 East Bernard, 1,159......H 8
76448 Eastland⊙, 3,178......F 5
76837 Eden, 1,291......E 6
78539 Edinburg⊙, 17,163......F11
77957 Edna⊙, 5,332......H 9
77437 El Campo, 8,563......H 8
76936 Eldorado⊙, 1,446......D 7
76360 Electra, 3,895......F 4
78621 Elgin, 3,832......G 7
79901 El Paso⊙, 322,261......A 10
   El Paso, ‡359,291......A 10
78543 Elsa, 4,400......G 11
75440 Emory⊙, 693......J 5
75119 Ennis, 11,046......H 5
76039 Euless, 19,316......F 2
76140 Everman, 4,570......F 2
79838 Fabens, 3,241......B 10
78355 Falfurrias⊙, 6,355......F 10
75234 Farmers Branch, 27,492......G 1
75031 Farmersville, 2,311......H 4
79325 Farwell⊙, 1,185......A 3
75125 Ferris, 2,180......H 5
78941 Flatonia, 1,108......G 8
78114 Floresville⊙, 3,707......F 8
79235 Floydada⊙, 4,109......C 3
75701 Forest Hill, 8,236......F 2
75126 Forney, 1,745......H 5
79734 Fort Davis⊙, 900......D 11
79735 Fort Stockton⊙, 8,283......A 7
76101 Fort Worth⊙, 393,476......E 2
   Fort Worth, ‡762,086......E 2
77856 Franklin, 1,063......H 7
75763 Frankston, 1,056......J 5
78624 Fredericksburg⊙, 5,326......E 7
76842 Fredonia, 50......E 7
77541 Freeport, 11,997......J 9
78357 Freer, 2,804......F 10
77546 Friendswood, 5,675......J 2
79035 Friona, 3,111......A 3
75034 Frisco, 1,845......H 4
75417 Fritch, 1,778......C 2
79738 Gail⊙, 150......C 5
76240 Gainesville⊙, 13,830......G 4
77547 Galena Park, 10,479......L 1
75550 Galveston⊙, 61,809......L 3
   Galveston-Texas City,
   ‡169,812......L 3
77962 Ganado, 1,640......H 8

79739 Garden City⊙, 300......C 6
75040 Garland, 81,437......H 1
75946 Garrison, 1,082......K 6
76528 Gatesville⊙, 4,683......G 6
78626 Georgetown⊙, 6,395......G 7
76022 George West⊙, 2,022......F 9
78942 Giddings⊙, 2,783......H 7
75644 Gilmer⊙, 4,196......J 5
75647 Gladewater, 5,574......K 5
76043 Glen Rose⊙, 1,554......G 5
76844 Goldthwaite⊙, 1,693......F 6
77963 Goliad⊙, 1,709......G 9
78629 Gonzales⊙, 5,854......G 8
76454 Gorman, 1,236......F 5
76046 Graham⊙, 7,477......F 4
76048 Granbury⊙, 2,473......G 5
75050 Grand Prairie, 50,904......G 2
75140 Grand Saline, 2,257......J 5
76530 Granger, 1,256......G 7
75844 Grapeland, 1,211......J 6
75051 Grapevine, 7,023......F 1
75401 Greenville⊙, 22,043......H 4
76642 Groesbeck⊙, 2,396......H 6
77619 Groves, 18,067......L 8
75845 Groveton⊙, 1,219......J 7
78548 Grulla, 1,194......F 11
79040 Gruver, 1,265......C 1
79236 Guthrie⊙, 150......D 4
79041 Hale Center, 1,964......C 3
77964 Hallettsville⊙, 2,712......G 8
75650 Hallsville, 1,038......K 5
76117 Haltom City, 28,127......F 2
76531 Hamilton⊙, 2,760......G 6
79520 Hamlin, 3,325......D 4
78550 Harlingen, 33,503......G11
75521 Haskell⊙, 3,655......E 4
77859 Hearne, 4,982......H 7
78361 Hebbronville⊙, 4,079......F 10
77445 Hempstead⊙, 1,891......H 7
75652 Henderson⊙, 10,187......K 5
76365 Henrietta⊙, 2,897......F 4
79045 Hereford⊙, 13,414......B 3
78557 Hidalgo, 1,289......F 11
† 75201 Highland Park⊙, 10,133......G 2
77562 Highlands, 3,462......K 1
76645 Hillsboro⊙, 7,224......G 5
77563 Hitchcock, 5,565......K 3
76366 Holliday, 1,048......F 4
75446 Honey Grove, 1,853......J 4
75561 Hooks, 2,545......K 4
* 77001 Houston⊙, 1,232,802......J 2
   Houston, ‡1,985,031......J 2
76648 Hubbard, 1,572......H 6
75656 Hughes Springs, 1,701......K 5
77338 Humble, 3,278......J 7
† 77001 Hunters Creek Village,
   3,959......J 1
75949 Huntington, 1,192......K 6
77340 Huntsville⊙, 17,610......J 7
76053 Hurst, 27,215......F 2
75141 Hutchins, 1,755......G 2
79329 Idalou, 1,729......C 4
75060 Irving, 97,260......G 2
76651 Italy, 1,309......H 5
76055 Itasca, 1,483......G 5
77029 Jacinto City, 9,563......J 1
76056 Jacksboro⊙, 3,554......F 4
75766 Jacksonville, 9,734......J 5
75951 Jasper⊙, 6,251......L 7
79528 Jayton⊙, 703......D 4
75657 Jefferson⊙, 2,866......K 5
78380 Johnson City⊙, 767......F 7
† 77541 Jones Creek, 1,268......J 9
78026 Jourdanton⊙, 1,841......F 9
76849 Junction⊙, 2,654......E 7
78118 Karnes City⊙, 2,926......F 9
77450 Katy, 2,923......J 8
75142 Kaufman⊙, 4,012......H 5
76248 Keller, 1,474......F 1
77565 Kemah, 1,144......K 2
78119 Kenedy, 4,156......G 9
76060 Kennedale, 3,076......F 2
79745 Kermit⊙, 7,884......B 6
78028 Kerrville⊙, 12,672......E 7
76541 Killeen, 35,507......G 6
78363 Kingsville⊙, 28,711......G10
75956 Kirbyville, 1,869......K 7
75145 Kleberg, 4,768......G 2
79529 Knox City, 1,536......E 4
77625 Kountze⊙, 1,703......K 7
78640 Kyle, 1,629......G 8
78559 La Feria, 2,642......G11
78945 La Grange⊙, 3,092......G 8
78560 La Joya, 1,217......F 11
77566 Lake Jackson, 13,376......J 8
76135 Lake Worth, 4,958......E 2
77568 La Marque, 16,131......K 3
79331 Lamesa⊙, 11,559......C 5
76550 Lampasas⊙, 5,922......F 6
75146 Lancaster, 10,522......G 2
77571 La Porte, 7,149......K 2
78040 Laredo⊙, 69,024......E 10
   Laredo, ‡72,859......E 10
77573 League City, 10,818......K 2
78873 Leakey⊙, 393......E 8
75452 Leonard, 1,423......H 4
79336 Levelland⊙, 11,445......B 4
75067 Lewisville, 9,264......G 5
77575 Liberty⊙, 5,591......K 7
75771 Lindale, 1,631......J 5
75563 Linden⊙, 2,264......K 4
79056 Lipscomb⊙, 100......D 1
75339 Littlefield⊙, 6,738......B 4
77351 Livingston⊙, 3,925......K 7
78643 Llano⊙, 2,608......F 7
76854 Lockhart⊙, 6,489......G 8
79241 Lockney, 2,094......C 3
75601 Longview⊙, 45,547......K 5
79343 Lorenzo, 1,206......C 4
76655 Los Fresnos, 1,297......G11
* 79401 Lubbock⊙, 149,101......C 4
   Lubbock, ‡179,295......C 4

75901 Lufkin⊙, 23,049......K 6
78648 Luling, 4,719......G 8
78569 Lyford, 1,425......G11
78052 Lytle, 1,271......F 8
75147 Mabank, 1,239......H 5
77864 Madisonville⊙, 2,881......J 7
75148 Malakoff, 2,045......H 5
76063 Mansfield, 3,658......F 2
78654 Marble Falls, 2,209......F 7
79843 Marfa⊙, 2,647......C12
76661 Marlin⊙, 6,351......H 6
75670 Marshall⊙, 22,937......K 5
76664 Mart, 2,183......H 6
76856 Mason⊙, 1,806......E 7
79244 Matador⊙, 1,091......D 3
78368 Mathis, 5,351......G 9
75567 Maud, 1,107......K 4
78501 McAllen, 37,636......F 11
   McAllen-Pharr-Edinburg,
   ‡181,535......F 11
79752 McCamey, 2,647......B 6
76657 McGregor, 4,365......G 6
75069 McKinney⊙, 15,193......H 4
79057 McLean, 1,183......D 2
77520 McNair, 2,039......K 1
79245 Memphis⊙, 3,227......D 3
76859 Menard⊙, 1,740......E 7
79754 Mentone⊙, 50......D10
75570 Mercedes, 9,355......F 12
76665 Meridian⊙, 1,162......G 6
75936 Merkel, 2,163......E 5
76941 Mertzon⊙, 513......C 6
75149 Mesquite, 55,131......H 2
76667 Mexia, 5,943......H 6
79059 Miami⊙, 611......D 2
79701 Midland⊙, 59,463......C 6
   Midland, ‡65,433......C 6
76065 Midlothian, 2,322......G 5
75773 Mineola, 3,926......J 5
76067 Mineral Wells, 18,411......F 5
78572 Mission, 13,043......F 11
77449 Missouri City, 4,136......J 2
79756 Monahans⊙, 8,333......B 6
76251 Montague⊙, 490......G 4
78059 Mont Belvieu, 1,144......L 1
76557 Moody, 1,286......G 6
79346 Morton⊙, 2,738......B 4
75455 Mount Pleasant⊙, 8,877......K 4
75457 Mount Vernon⊙, 1,806......J 4
76252 Muenster, 1,411......G 4
79347 Muleshoe⊙, 4,525......B 3
76371 Munday, 1,726......E 4
75961 Nacogdoches⊙, 22,544......K 6
75568 Naples, 1,726......K 4
75569 Nash, 1,961......K 4
78059 Natalia, 1,296......F 8
77868 Navasota, 5,111......J 7
77461 Needville, 1,024......J 8
75570 New Boston, 4,199......K 4
78130 New Braunfels⊙, 17,859......F 8
75966 Newton⊙, 1,529......L 7
78140 Nixon, 1,925......G 8
76255 Nocona, 2,871......G 4
† 76118 North Richland Hills, 16,514..F 1
79760 Odessa⊙, 78,380......B 6
   Odessa, ‡91,805......B 6
79351 O'Donnell, 1,148......C 5
76374 Olney, 3,624......F 4
79064 Olton, 1,782......B 3
78372 Orange Grove, 1,075......F 10
75684 Overton, 2,084......K 5

76943 Ozona⊙, 2,864......C 7
79248 Paducah⊙, 2,052......D 4
78866 Paint Rock⊙, 193......E 6
77465 Palacios, 3,642......H 9
75801 Palestine⊙, 14,525......J 6
76072 Palo Pinto⊙, 250......F 5
79065 Pampa⊙, 21,726......D 2
79068 Panhandle⊙, 2,141......C 2
75460 Paris⊙, 23,441......J 4
* 77501 Pasadena, 89,277......J 2
77581 Pearland, 6,444......J 2
78061 Pearsall⊙, 5,545......E 9
79772 Pecos⊙, 12,682......D 10
79070 Perryton⊙, 7,810......D 1
79250 Petersburg, 1,300......C 4
78577 Pharr, 15,829......F 11
79071 Phillips, 2,515......C 2
76258 Pilot Point, 1,663......H 4
75968 Pineland, 1,127......L 6
† 77001 Piney Point Village, 2,548......J 1
75686 Pittsburg⊙, 3,844......J 4
79355 Plains⊙, 1,087......B 4
79072 Plainview⊙, 19,096......C 3
75074 Plano, 17,872......H 4
78064 Pleasanton, 5,407......F 9
77978 Point Comfort, 1,446......H 9
78373 Port Aransas, 1,218......H10
77640 Port Arthur, 57,371......K 8
77365 Porter, 1,900......J 7
78578 Port Isabel, 3,067......G11
78374 Portland, 7,302......G10
77979 Port Lavaca⊙, 10,491......H 9
77651 Port Neches, 10,894......K 7
79356 Post⊙, 3,854......C 4
78065 Poteet, 3,013......F 8
78147 Poth, 1,598......F 8
77445 Prairie View, 3,589......J 7
78375 Premont, 3,282......F 10
79845 Presidio, 850......C12
79252 Quanah⊙, 2,959......E 3
75572 Queen City, 1,227......L 4
75783 Quitman⊙, 1,494......J 5
79357 Ralls, 1,962......C 4
76470 Ranger, 3,094......F 5
79778 Rankin⊙, 1,105......B 6
78580 Raymondville⊙, 7,987......G11
78377 Refugio⊙, 4,340......G 9
75080 Richardson, 48,582......G 1
76118 Richland Hills, 8,865......F 2
77469 Richmond⊙, 5,777......J 8
78582 Rio Grande City⊙, 5,676......F 11
78583 Rio Hondo, 1,167......G11
77019 River Oaks, 8,193......E 2
78380 Robstown, 11,217......G10
76945 Robert Lee⊙, 1,119......D 6
78664 Round Rock, 2,811......G 7
76567 Rockdale, 4,655......G 7
78382 Rockport⊙, 3,879......H 9
78880 Rocksprings⊙, 1,221......D 8
75087 Rockwall⊙, 3,121......H 5
76569 Rogers, 1,030......G 7
78584 Roma-Los Saenz, 2,154......E 11
79545 Roscoe, 1,580......D 5
76570 Rosebud, 1,597......G 7
77471 Rosenberg, 12,098......J 8
79546 Rotan, 2,804......D 5
78664 Round Rock, 2,811......G 7
75088 Rowlett, 1,696......H 1
75189 Royse City, 1,535......H 4
78151 Runge, 1,147......G 8
75785 Rusk⊙, 4,681......J 6
78881 Sabinal, 1,554......E 8
76079 Saginaw, 2,382......E 1

76265 Saint Jo, 1,054......G 4
76901 San Angelo⊙, 63,884......D 6
   San Angelo, ‡71,047......D 6
* 78201 San Antonio⊙, 654,153......F 8
   San Antonio, ‡864,014......F 8
75972 San Augustine⊙, 2,539......K 6
78586 San Benito, 15,176......G12
79848 Sanderson⊙, 1,229......B 7
78384 San Diego⊙, 4,490......F 10
78289 San Juan, 5,070......F 11
77539 San Leon, 1,500......L 2
78666 San Marcos⊙, 18,860......F 8
78070 San Saba⊙, 2,555......F 6
† 76101 Sansom Park Village, 4,771..E 2
76878 Santa Anna, 1,310......E 6
78385 Sarita⊙, 250......G10
78154 Schertz, 4,061......F 8
78956 Schulenburg, 2,294......H 8
77586 Seabrook, 3,811......K 2
77983 Seadrift, 1,092......H 9
75159 Seagoville, 4,390......H 2
79359 Seagraves, 2,440......B 5
77474 Sealy, 2,685......H 8
78155 Seguin⊙, 15,934......G 8
79360 Seminole⊙, 5,007......B 5
76380 Seymour⊙, 3,349......E 4
79363 Shallowater, 1,339......B 4
77565 Shamrock, 2,644......D 2
77001 Sheldon, 1,665......K 1
75090 Sherman⊙, 29,061......H 4
   Sherman-Denison, ‡83,225..H 4
77984 Shiner, 2,102......G 8
77571 Shore Acres, 1,872......K 2
79851 Sierra Blanca⊙, 900......B11
77556 Silsbee, 7,271......K 7
79257 Silverton⊙, 1,026......C 3
78387 Sinton⊙, 5,563......G 9
79364 Slaton, 6,583......C 4
78957 Smithville, 2,959......G 8
79549 Snyder⊙, 11,171......D 5
77879 Somerville, 1,250......H 7
78884 Sonora⊙, 2,149......D 7
77659 Sourlake, 1,694......K 7
77587 South Houston, 11,527......J 2
76051 Southlake, 2,031......F 1
† 77001 Southside Place, 1,466......J 2
79081 Spearman⊙, 3,435......C 1
77373 Spring, 1,900......J 2
76082 Springtown, 1,194......G 5
† 77001 Spring Valley, 3,170......J 1
79370 Spur, 1,747......D 4
77477 Stafford, 2,906......J 2
79553 Stamford, 4,558......E 5
79782 Stanton⊙, 2,117......C 5
76401 Stephenville⊙, 9,277......F 5
79083 Sterling City⊙, 780......D 6
79083 Stinnett⊙, 2,014......C 2
78160 Stockdale, 1,132......G 8
79084 Stratford⊙, 2,139......C 1
77478 Sugar Land, 3,318......J 2
75482 Sulphur Springs⊙, 10,642......J 4
79372 Sundown, 1,329......B 4
79086 Sunray, 1,854......C 1
77480 Sweeny, 3,191......J 8
79556 Sweetwater⊙, 12,020......D 5
78390 Taft, 3,274......G 10
79373 Tahoka⊙, 2,956......C 4
76574 Taylor, 9,616......G 7
75860 Teague, 2,867......H 6
76501 Temple, 33,431......G 6
75974 Tenaha, 1,094......K 6
79852 Terlingua, 100......D12

75160 Terrell, 14,182......H 5
† 78201 Terrell Hills, 5,225......F 8
75501 Texarkana, 30,497......L 4
   Texarkana, ‡101,198......L 4
77590 Texas City, 38,908......L 3
73949 Texhoma, 356......C 1
78071 Three Rivers, 1,761......F 9
76083 Throckmorton⊙, 1,105......F 4
78072 Tilden⊙, 600......F 9
75975 Timpson, 1,254......K 6
77375 Tomball, 2,734......J 7
75163 Trinidad, 1,079......H 5
75862 Trinity, 2,512......J 7
75789 Troup, 1,668......J 5
79088 Tulia⊙, 5,294......C 3
75701 Tyler⊙, 57,770......J 5
   Tyler, ‡97,096......J 5
78228 University Park, 23,498......H 2
78801 Uvalde⊙, 10,764......E 8
75790 Van, 1,593......J 5
75095 Van Alstyne, 1,981......H 4
79855 Van Horn⊙, 2,240......C11
79092 Vega⊙, 839......B 2
76384 Vernon⊙, 11,454......E 3
77901 Victoria⊙, 41,349......H 9
76662 Vidor, 9,738......L 7
* 76701 Waco⊙, 95,326......G 6
   Waco, ‡147,553......G 6
78959 Waelder, 1,138......G 8
75501 Wake Village, 2,408......L 4
77485 Wallis, 1,028......H 8
75692 Waskom, 1,460......L 5
75165 Waxahachie⊙, 13,452......H 5
76086 Weatherford⊙, 11,750......G 5
77598 Webster, 2,231......K 2
78962 Weimar, 2,104......H 8
79095 Wellington⊙, 2,884......D 3
78596 Weslaco, 15,313......G11
76691 West, 2,406......G 6
77486 West Columbia, 3,335......J 8
77630 West Orange, 4,787......L 7
† 77001 West University Place,
   13,317......J 2
† 76101 Westworth, 4,578......E 2
77488 Wharton⊙, 7,881......J 8
79096 Wheeler⊙, 1,116......D 2
79097 White Deer, 1,092......C 2
76273 Whitesboro, 2,927......H 4
76108 White Settlement, 13,449......E 2
75491 Whitewright, 1,742......H 4
76692 Whitney, 1,371......G 6
* 76301 Wichita Falls⊙, 97,564......F 4
   Wichita Falls, ‡127,621......F 4
77378 Willis, 1,571......J 7
75169 Wills Point, 2,636......J 5
75172 Wilmer, 1,922......H 2
77665 Winnie, 1,116......K 7
75494 Winnsboro, 3,064......J 5
79567 Winters, 2,907......D 5
75496 Wolfe City, 1,433......J 4
79382 Wolfforth, 1,002......B 4
78393 Woodsboro, 1,839......G 9
79579 Woodville⊙, 2,636......L 7
76693 Wortham, 1,036......H 6
75098 Wylie, 2,675......H 5
77995 Yoakum, 5,755......G 8
78164 Yorktown, 2,411......G 9
78076 Zapata⊙, 2,102......E 11

⊙ County seat.
‡ Population of metropolitan area.
‡ Zip of nearest p.o.
* Multiple zips

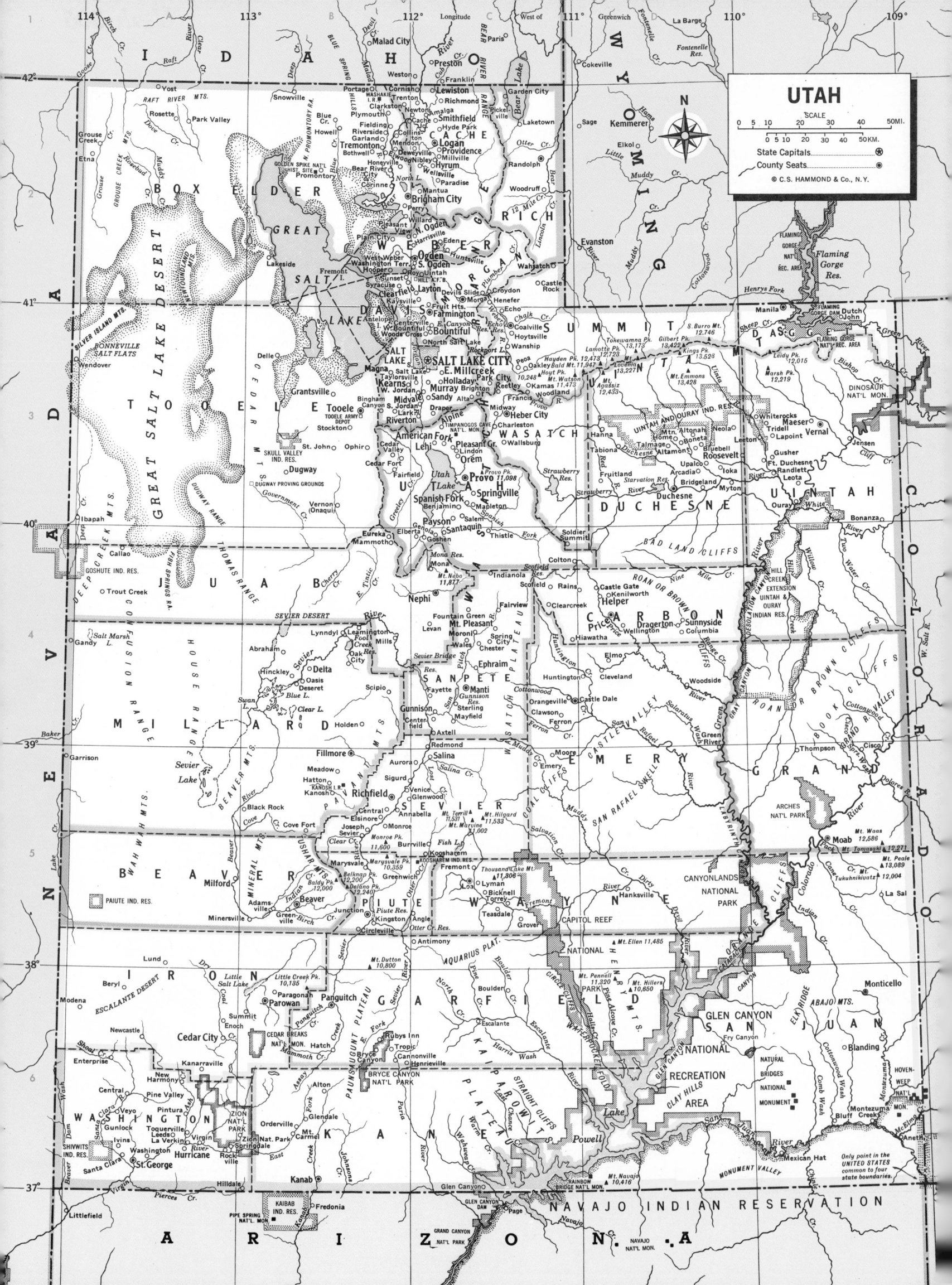

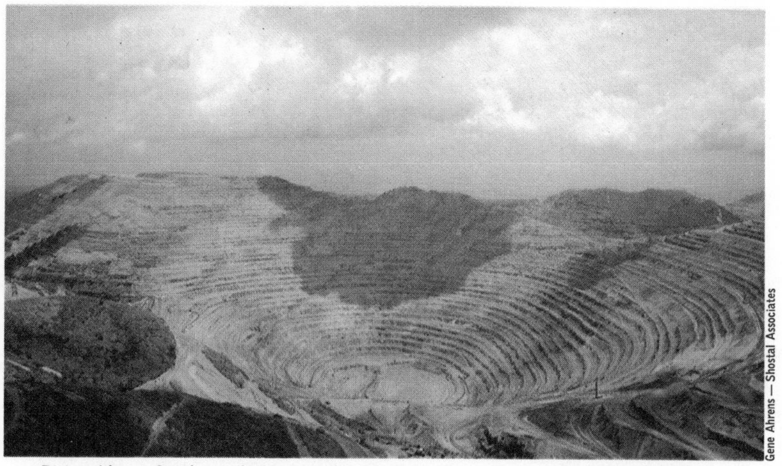
Gene Ahrens — Shostal Associates

Rising like a Greek amphitheater, the Bingham Open Pit Copper Mine in Utah is constantly changing as giant electric shovels remove seven tons of earth at a time.

AREA 84,916 sq. mi.
POPULATION 1,059,273
CAPITAL Salt Lake City
LARGEST CITY Salt Lake City
HIGHEST POINT Kings Pk. 13,528 ft.
SETTLED IN 1847
ADMITTED TO UNION January 4, 1896
POPULAR NAME Beehive State
STATE FLOWER Sego Lily
STATE BIRD Sea Gull

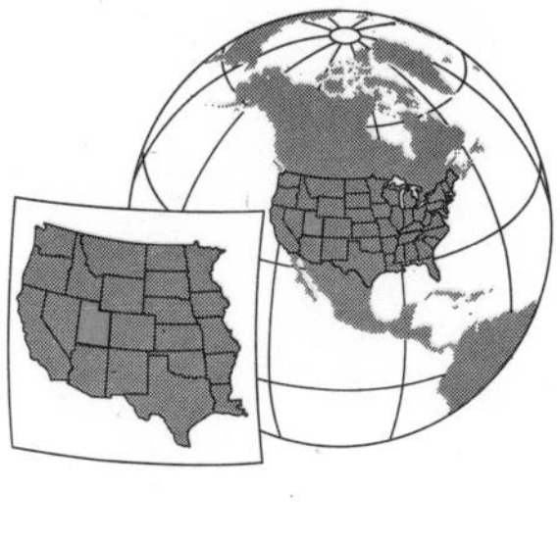

COUNTIES

Beaver, 3,800	A 5
Box Elder, 28,129	A 2
Cache, 42,331	C 2
Carbon, 15,647	D 4
Daggett, 666	E 3
Davis, 99,028	B 3
Duchesne, 7,299	D 3
Emery, 5,137	D 4
Garfield, 3,157	C 6
Grand, 6,688	E 5
Iron, 12,177	A 6
Juab, 4,574	A 4
Kane, 2,421	B 6
Millard, 6,988	A 4
Morgan, 3,983	C 2
Piute, 1,164	B 5
Rich, 1,615	C 2
Salt Lake, 458,607	B 3
San Juan, 9,606	E 6
Sanpete, 10,976	C 4
Sevier, 10,103	C 5
Summit, 5,879	D 3
Tooele, 21,545	A 3
Uintah, 12,684	E 3
Utah, 137,776	C 3
Wasatch, 5,863	C 3
Washington, 13,669	A 6
Wayne, 1,483	C 5
Weber, 126,278	B 2

CITIES and TOWNS

Zip	*Name/Pop.*	*Key*
84003	Alpine, 1,047	C 3
84001	Altamont, 129	D 3
84002	Altonah, 225	D 3
84335	Amalga, 207	C 2
84003	American Fork, 7,713	C 3
84510	Aneth, 250	E 6
84711	Annabella, 221	B 5
84712	Antimony, 113	C 5
84005	Arcadia, 150	D 3
84620	Aurora, 493	B 5
84621	Axtell, 150	C 4
84301	Bear River City, 445	B 2
84713	Beaver⊙, 1,453	B 5
† 84660	Benjamin, 503	C 3
84715	Bicknell, 264	C 5
84511	Blanding, 2,250	E 6
84007	Bluebell, 210	D 3
84512	Bluff, 300	E 6
84008	Bonanza, 150	E 3
† 84337	Bothwell, 300	B 2
84716	Boulder, 93	C 6
84010	Bountiful, 27,853	C 3
84012	Bridgeland, 150	D 3
84302	Brigham City⊙, 14,007	C 2
84117	Brighton, 150	C 3
84717	Bryce Canyon, 229	B 6
84718	Cannonville, 113	B 6
84513	Castle Dale⊙, 541	D 4
84514	Castle Gate, 205	D 4
84720	Cedar City, 8,946	A 6
† 84013	Cedar Fort, 188	B 3
84013	Cedar Valley, 290	B 3
84622	Centerfield, 419	C 4
84014	Centerville, 3,268	C 3
84722	Central, 154	B 5
† 84032	Charleston, 196	C 3
84623	Chester, 130	C 4
84723	Circleville, 443	B 5
84305	Clarkston, 420	B 2
84516	Clawson, 95	C 4
84015	Clearfield, 13,316	B 2
84518	Cleveland, 244	D 4
84017	Coalville⊙, 864	C 3
84519	Columbia, 380	D 4
84307	Corinne, 471	B 2
84308	Cornish, 173	B 2
84018	Croydon, 90	C 2
84624	Delta, 1,610	B 4
84625	Deseret, 215	B 4
84309	Deweyville, 248	B 2
84520	Dragerton, 1,614	D 4
84020	Draper, 4,000	C 3
84021	Duchesne⊙, 1,094	D 3
84022	Dugway, 2,357	B 3
84023	Dutch John, 263	E 3
† 84101	East Millcreek, 26,579	C 3
84310	Eden, 421	C 2
84626	Elberta, 325	B 4
84521	Elmo, 141	D 4
84724	Elsinore, 357	B 5
† 84337	Elwood, 294	B 2
84522	Emery, 216	C 5
† 84720	Enoch, 120	A 6
84725	Enterprise, 844	A 6
84627	Ephraim, 2,127	C 4
84726	Escalante, 638	C 6
84628	Eureka, 753	B 4
84629	Fairview, 696	C 4
84025	Farmington⊙, 2,526	C 3
84630	Fayette, 93	C 4
84523	Ferron, 663	C 4
84311	Fielding, 254	B 2
84631	Fillmore⊙, 1,411	B 5
84026	Fort Duchesne, 300	E 3
84632	Fountain Green, 467	C 4
† 84036	Francis, 268	C 3
84727	Fremont, 160	C 5
† 84037	Fruit Heights, 800	C 2
84028	Garden City, 134	C 2
84312	Garland, 1,187	B 2
† 84655	Genola, 424	C 4
84729	Glendale, 200	B 6
84730	Glenwood, 212	C 5
84633	Goshen, 459	C 4
84029	Grantsville, 2,931	B 3
84525	Green River, 1,033	D 4
84731	Greenville, 97	B 5
84313	Grouse Creek, 100	A 2
84733	Gunlock, 93	A 6
84634	Gunnison, 1,073	C 4
84030	Gusher, 125	E 3
84734	Hanksville, 224	D 5
84031	Hanna, 135	D 3
† 84401	Harrisville, 603	C 2
84735	Hatch, 139	B 6
84032	Heber City⊙, 3,245	C 3
84526	Helper, 1,964	D 4
84033	Henefer, 446	C 2
84736	Henrieville, 145	C 6
84527	Hiawatha, 166	D 4
† 84767	Hilldale, 480	B 6
84635	Hinckley, 400	B 4
84636	Holden, 351	B 4
84117	Holladay, 23,014	C 3
84314	Honeyville, 640	B 2
84315	Hooper, 1,705	B 2
84316	Howell, 146	B 2
† 84017	Hoytsville, 500	C 3
84528	Huntington, 857	C 4
84317	Huntsville, 553	C 2
84737	Hurricane, 1,408	A 6
84318	Hyde Park, 1,025	C 2
84319	Hyrum, 2,340	C 2
84034	Ibapah, 135	A 3
† 84052	Ioka, 115	D 3
84738	Ivins, 137	A 6
84035	Jensen, 360	E 3
84739	Joseph, 125	B 5
84740	Junction⊙, 135	B 5
84036	Kamas, 806	C 3
84741	Kanab⊙, 1,381	B 6
84742	Kanarraville, 204	A 6
84637	Kanosh, 319	B 5
84037	Kaysville, 6,192	B 2
84118	Kearns, 17,071	B 3
84529	Kenilworth, 500	D 4
84743	Kingston, 114	B 5
84744	Koosharem, 141	C 5
84038	Laketown, 208	C 2
84039	Lapoint, 335	E 3
84040	Lark, 728	B 3
84530	La Sal, 200	E 5
84745	La Verkin, 463	A 6
84041	Layton, 13,603	C 2
84638	Leamington, 112	B 4
84746	Leeds, 151	A 6
84043	Lehi, 4,659	C 3
84639	Levan, 376	C 4
84320	Lewiston, 1,244	C 2
† 84062	Lindon, 1,644	C 3
84747	Loa⊙, 324	C 5
84321	Logan⊙, 22,333	C 2
84749	Lyman, 180	C 5
84640	Lynndyl, 111	B 4
† 84078	Maeser, 1,248	E 3
84044	Magna, 5,509	B 3
84046	Manila⊙, 226	E 3
84642	Manti⊙, 1,803	C 4
† 84302	Mantua, 413	C 2
† 84663	Mapleton, 1,980	C 3
84750	Marysvale, 289	B 5
84643	Mayfield, 267	C 4
84644	Meadow, 238	B 5
84325	Mendon, 345	B 2
84531	Mexican Hat, 100	E 6
84047	Midvale, 7,840	B 3
84049	Midway, 804	C 3
84751	Milford, 1,304	A 5
84326	Millville, 441	C 2
84752	Minersville, 448	A 5
84532	Moab⊙, 4,793	E 5
84645	Mona, 309	C 4
84754	Monroe, 918	B 5
84534	Montezuma Creek, 500	E 6
84535	Monticello⊙, 1,431	E 6
84050	Morgan⊙, 1,586	C 2
84646	Moroni, 894	C 4
84051	Mountain Home, 140	D 3
84647	Mount Pleasant, 1,516	C 4
84107	Murray, 21,206	C 3
84052	Myton, 322	D 3
84053	Neola, 600	D 3
84648	Nephi⊙, 2,699	C 4
84756	Newcastle, 150	A 6
84327	Newton, 444	C 2
† 84321	Nibley, 367	C 2
† 84401	North Ogden, 5,257	C 2
84054	North Salt Lake, 2,143	C 3
84649	Oak City, 278	B 4
84055	Oakley, 265	C 3
84650	Oasis, 150	B 4
* 84401	Ogden⊙, 69,478	C 2
	Ogden, ‡126,278	C 4
† 84080	Onaqui (Vernon), 541	B 3
84537	Orangeville, 511	C 4
84758	Orderville, 399	B 6
84057	Orem, 25,729	C 3
84059	Ouray, 100	E 3
84759	Panguitch⊙, 1,318	B 6
84328	Paradise, 399	C 2
84760	Paragonah, 275	B 6
84060	Park City, 1,193	C 3
84329	Park Valley, 100	A 2
84761	Parowan⊙, 1,423	B 6
84651	Payson, 4,501	C 3
84061	Peoa, 230	C 3
† 84302	Perry, 909	C 2
† 84028	Pickleville, 106	C 2
† 84401	Plain City, 1,543	B 2
84062	Pleasant Grove, 5,327	C 3
† 84401	Pleasant View, 2,028	B 2
84330	Plymouth, 203	B 2
84331	Portage, 144	B 2
84501	Price⊙, 6,218	D 4
84332	Providence, 1,608	C 2
84601	Provo⊙, 53,131	C 3
	Provo-Orem, ‡137,776	C 3
84063	Randlett, 350	E 3
84064	Randolph⊙, 500	C 2
84652	Redmond, 409	C 4
84701	Richfield⊙, 4,471	B 5
84333	Richmond, 1,000	C 2
84334	Riverside, 290	B 2
84065	Riverton, 2,820	B 3
84763	Rockville, 110	A 6
84066	Roosevelt, 2,005	D 3
84067	Roy, 14,356	C 2
84770	Saint George⊙, 7,097	A 6
84069	Saint John, 200	B 3
84653	Salem, 1,081	C 3
84654	Salina, 1,494	C 5
* 84101	Salt Lake City (cap.)⊙, 175,885	B 3
	Salt Lake City, ‡557,635	B 3
84070	Sandy, 6,438	C 3
84765	Santa Clara, 271	A 6
84655	Santaquin, 1,236	C 4
84656	Scipio, 264	B 4
84657	Sigurd, 291	B 5
84335	Smithfield, 3,342	C 2
84336	Snowville, 174	B 2
† 84065	South Jordan, 2,942	B 3
† 84401	South Ogden, 9,991	C 2
84115	South Salt Lake, 7,810	C 3
84660	Spanish Fork, 7,284	C 3
84662	Spring City, 456	C 4
84767	Springdale, 172	B 6
84663	Springville, 8,790	C 3
84665	Sterling, 144	C 4
84071	Stockton, 469	B 3
84772	Summit, 150	B 6
84539	Sunnyside, 485	D 4
† 84015	Sunset, 6,268	B 2
† 84041	Syracuse, 1,843	B 2
84072	Tabiona, 125	D 3
84073	Talmage, 140	D 3
† 84101	Taylorsville, 12,522	B 3
84773	Teasdale, 160	C 5
84074	Tooele⊙, 12,539	B 3
84774	Toquerville, 185	A 6
84337	Tremonton, 2,794	B 2
84338	Trenton, 390	B 2
84076	Tridell, 212	E 3
84776	Tropic, 329	B 6
† 84401	Uintah, 400	C 2
† 84007	Upalco, 150	D 3
84777	Venice, 220	C 5
84078	Vernal⊙, 3,908	E 3
84080	Vernon, 541	B 3
† 84722	Veyo, 144	A 6
84779	Virgin, 119	A 6
84082	Wallsburg, 211	C 3
† 84017	Wanship, 175	C 3
84780	Washington, 750	A 6
† 84401	Washington Terrace, 7,241	B 2
84542	Wellington, 922	D 4
84339	Wellsville, 1,267	C 2
84083	Wendover, 781	A 3
† 84087	West Bountiful, 1,246	B 3
84084	West Jordan, 4,221	B 3
† 84401	West Weber, 750	B 2
84085	Whiterocks, 600	E 3
84340	Willard, 1,045	C 2
† 84036	Woodland, 190	C 3
84086	Woodruff, 173	C 2
84087	Woods Cross, 3,124	B 3

⊙ County seat.
‡ Population of metropolitan area.
† Zip of nearest p.o.
* Multiple zips

Agriculture, Industry and Resources

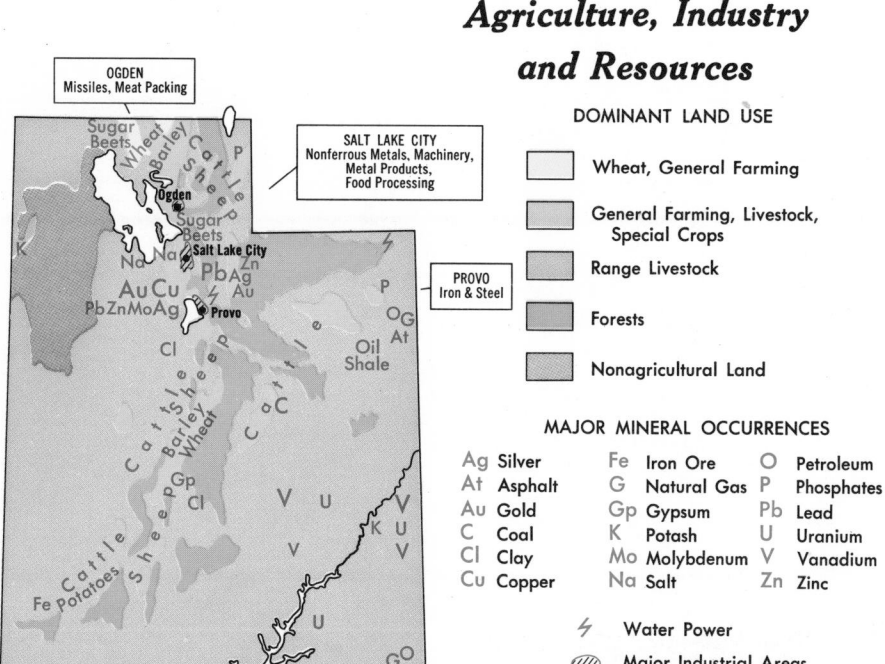

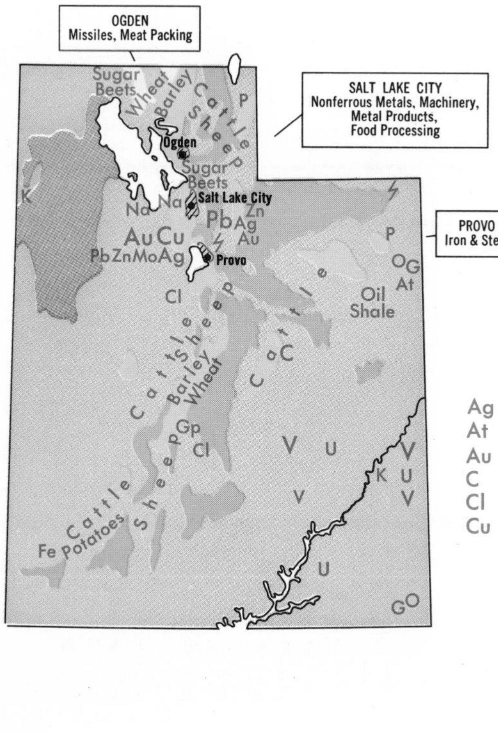
OGDEN
Missiles, Meat Packing
SALT LAKE CITY
Nonferrous Metals, Machinery, Metal Products, Food Processing
PROVO
Iron & Steel
Ogden
Salt Lake City
Provo
Sugar Beets
Wheat
Barley
Cattle
Sheep
Oil Shale
Potatoes

DOMINANT LAND USE

- Wheat, General Farming
- General Farming, Livestock, Special Crops
- Range Livestock
- Forests
- Nonagricultural Land

MAJOR MINERAL OCCURRENCES

Ag	Silver	Fe	Iron Ore	O	Petroleum
At	Asphalt	G	Natural Gas	P	Phosphates
Au	Gold	Gp	Gypsum	Pb	Lead
C	Coal	K	Potash	U	Uranium
Cl	Clay	Mo	Molybdenum	V	Vanadium
Cu	Copper	Na	Salt	Zn	Zinc

Water Power

Major Industrial Areas

Topography

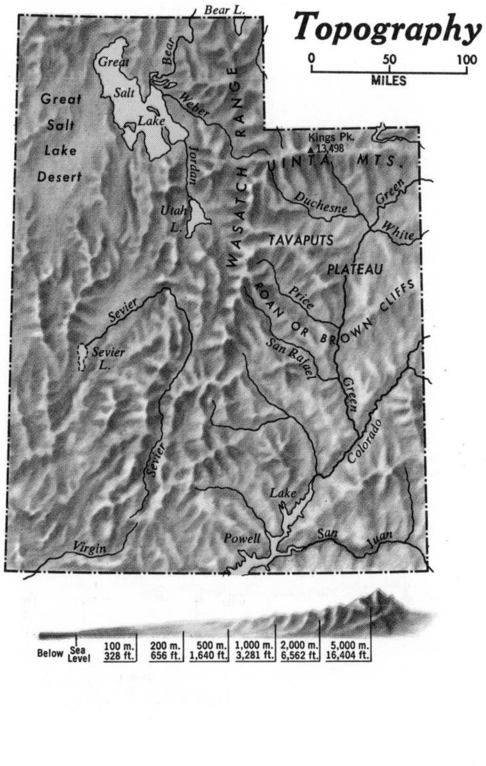
0 50 100
MILES
Bear L.
Great Salt Lake
Bear
Weber
Great Salt Lake Desert
Jordan
Utah L.
WASATCH RANGE
Kings Pk. 13,498
UINTA MTS.
Duchesne
Green
White
TAVAPUTS PLATEAU
Price
ROAN OR BROWN CLIFFS
San Rafael
Sevier
Sevier L.
Colorado
Green
Lake Powell
San Juan
Virgin
Below Sea Level
100 m. 328 ft.
200 m. 656 ft.
500 m. 1,640 ft.
1,000 m. 3,281 ft.
2,000 m. 6,562 ft.
5,000 m. 16,404 ft.

Topography

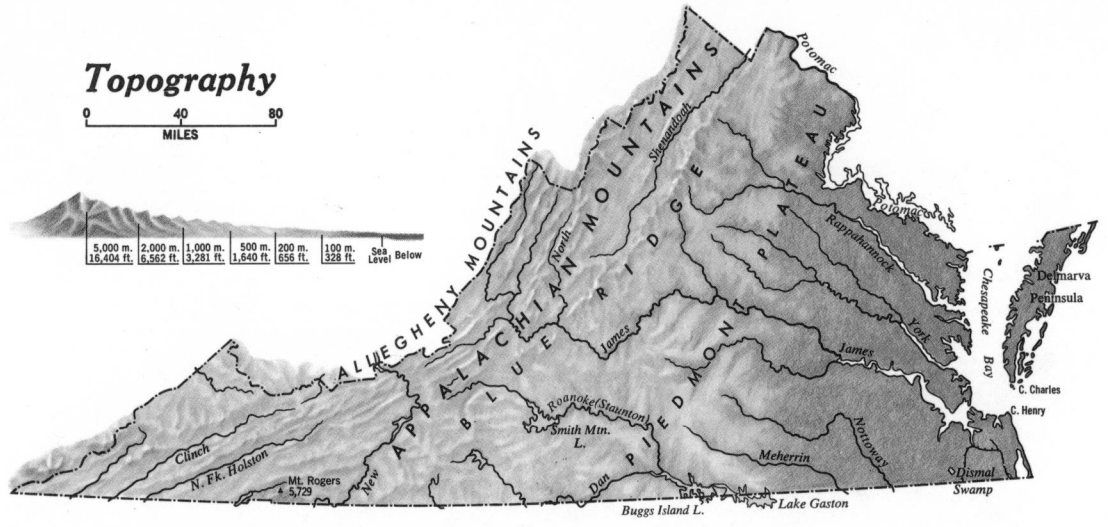

MILES
0   40   80

5,000 m. / 2,000 m. / 1,000 m. / 500 m. / 200 m. / 100 m. / Sea Level
16,404 ft. / 6,562 ft. / 3,281 ft. / 1,640 ft. / 656 ft. / 328 ft. / Below

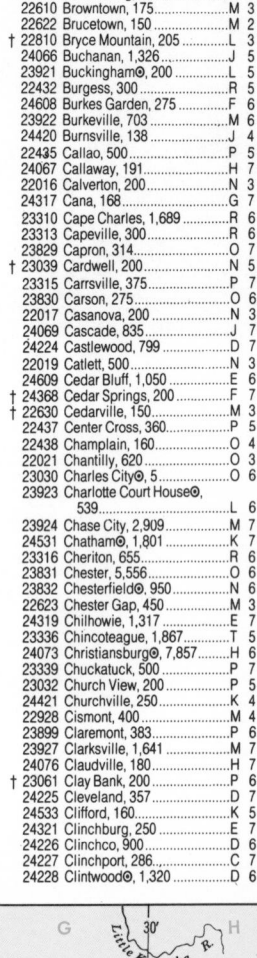

22715 Brightwood, 250	......	M 4
24316 Broadford, 850	......	E 7
22815 Broadway, 887	......	L 3
23920 Brodnax, 569	......	N 7
22430 Brooke, 275	......	O 4
24528 Brookneal, 1,037	......	L 6
24415 Brownsburg, 200	......	K 5
22610 Browntown, 175	......	M 3
22622 Brucetown, 150	......	M 2
† 22810 Bryce Mountain, 205	......	L 3
24066 Buchanan, 1,326	......	J 5
23921 Buckingham⊙, 200	......	L 5
22432 Burgess, 300	......	R 5
24608 Burkes Garden, 275	......	F 6
23922 Burkeville, 703	......	M 6
24420 Burnsville, 138	......	J 4
22435 Callao, 500	......	R 5
24067 Callaway, 191	......	H 7
22016 Calverton, 200	......	N 3
24317 Cana, 168	......	G 7
23310 Cape Charles, 1,689	......	R 6
23313 Capeville, 300	......	R 6
23829 Capron, 314	......	O 7
† 23039 Cardwell, 200	......	N 5
23315 Carrsville, 375	......	P 7
23830 Carson, 275	......	O 6
22017 Casanova, 200	......	N 3
24069 Cascade, 835	......	J 7
22019 Catlett, 500	......	N 3
24609 Cedar Bluff, 1,050	......	E 6
24368 Cedar Springs, 200	......	F 7
† 22630 Cedarville, 150	......	M 3
22437 Center Cross, 360	......	P 5
22438 Champlain, 160	......	O 4
22021 Chantilly, 620	......	O 3
23030 Charles City⊙, 5	......	O 6
23923 Charlotte Court House⊙, 539	......	L 6
23924 Chase City, 2,909	......	M 7
24531 Chatham⊙, 1,801	......	K 7
23316 Cheriton, 655	......	R 6
23831 Chester, 5,556	......	O 6
23832 Chesterfield⊙, 950	......	N 6
22623 Chester Gap, 450	......	M 3
24319 Chilhowie, 2,511	......	E 7
23336 Chincoteague, 1,867	......	T 5
24073 Christiansburg, 7,857	......	H 6
23339 Chuckatuck, 500	......	P 7
23032 Church View, 200	......	P 5
24421 Churchville, 250	......	K 4
22928 Cismont, 400	......	M 4
23899 Claremont, 383	......	P 6
23927 Clarksville, 1,641	......	M 7
24076 Claudville, 180	......	H 7
† 23061 Clay Bank, 200	......	P 6
24225 Cleveland, 357	......	D 7
24533 Clifford, 160	......	K 5
24321 Clinchburg, 250	......	C 6
24226 Clinchco, 900	......	D 6
24227 Clinchport, 286	......	C 7
24228 Clintwood⊙, 1,320	......	D 6

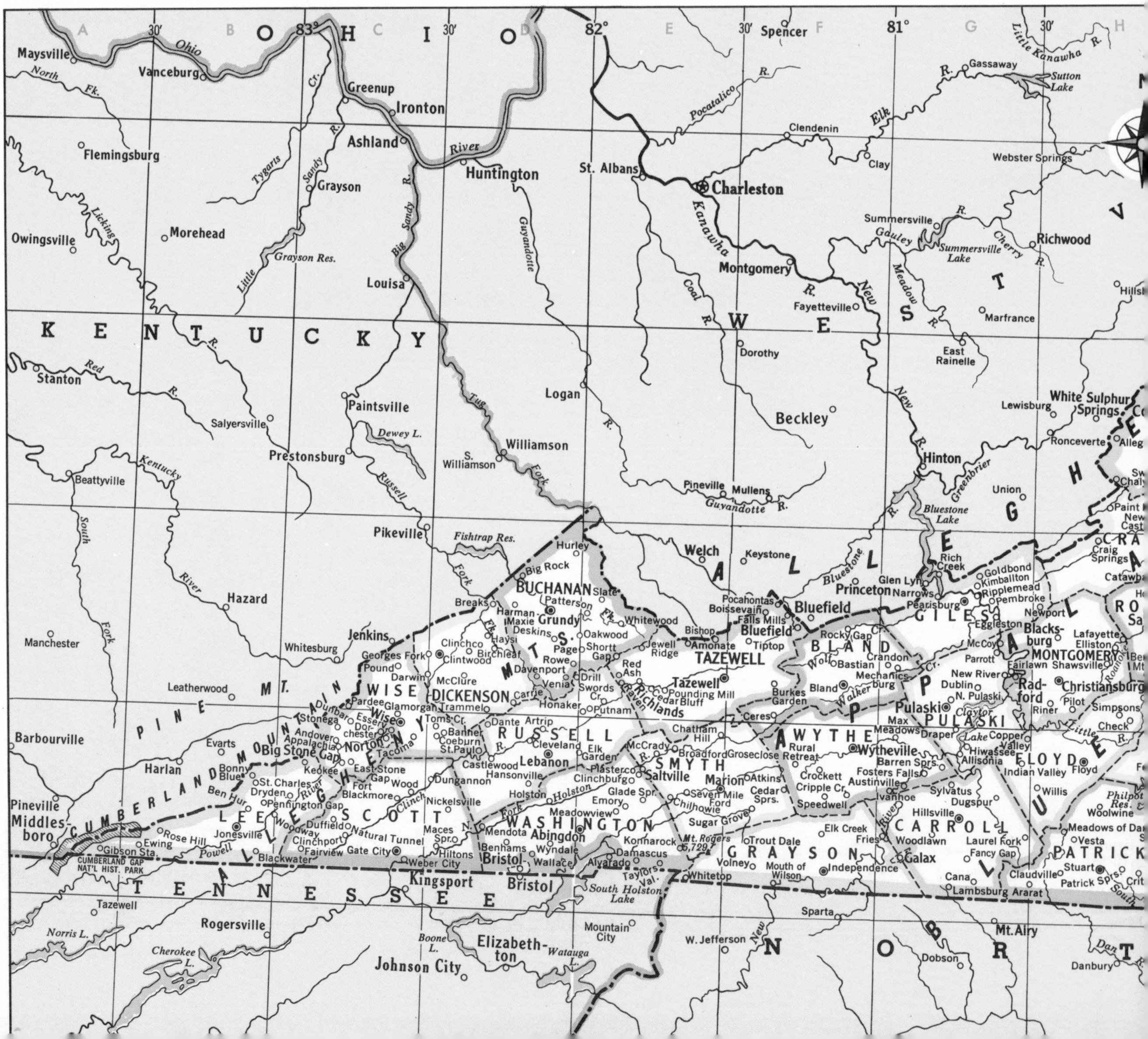

COUNTIES

Accomack, 29,004 ...... S 5
Albemarle, 37,780 ...... L 5
Alleghany, 12,461 ...... H 5
Amelia, 7,592 ...... M 6
Amherst, 26,072 ...... K 5
Appomattox, 9,784 ...... L 6
Arlington, 174,284 ...... O 3
Augusta, 44,220 ...... K 4
Bath, 5,192 ...... J 4
Bedford, 26,728 ...... J 6
Bland, 5,423 ...... F 6
Botetourt, 18,193 ...... J 5
Brunswick, 16,172 ...... N 7
Buchanan, 32,071 ...... D 6
Buckingham, 10,597 ...... L 5
Campbell, 43,319 ...... K 6
Caroline, 13,925 ...... O 4
Carroll, 23,092 ...... G 7
Charles City, 6,158 ...... O 6
Charlotte, 11,551 ...... L 6
Chesterfield, 76,855 ...... N 6
Clarke, 8,102 ...... M 2
Craig, 3,524 ...... H 6
Culpeper, 18,218 ...... M 3
Cumberland, 6,179 ...... L 5
Danville, 46,391 ...... J 7
Dickenson, 16,077 ...... D 6
Dinwiddie, 25,046 ...... N 6
Essex, 7,099 ...... P 5
Fairfax, 455,021 ...... O 3
Fauquier, 26,375 ...... N 3
Floyd, 9,775 ...... H 7
Fluvanna, 7,621 ...... M 5
Franklin, 26,858 ...... J 6
Frederick, 28,893 ...... M 2
Giles, 16,741 ...... G 6
Gloucester, 14,059 ...... P 6
Goochland, 10,069 ...... N 5
Grayson, 15,439 ...... F 7
Greene, 5,248 ...... M 4
Greensville, 9,604 ...... N 7
Halifax, 30,076 ...... L 7
Hanover, 37,479 ...... N 5
Henrico, 154,364 ...... N 6
Henry, 50,901 ...... J 7
Highland, 2,529 ...... J 4
Isle of Wight, 18,285 ...... P 7
James City, 17,853 ...... P 6
King and Queen, 5,491 ...... P 5
King George, 8,039 ...... O 4
King William, 7,497 ...... O 5
Lancaster, 9,126 ...... R 5
Lee, 20,321 ...... B 7
Loudoun, 37,150 ...... N 3
Louisa, 14,004 ...... N 5
Lunenburg, 11,687 ...... M 7
Madison, 8,638 ...... M 4
Mathews, 7,168 ...... R 6
Mecklenburg, 29,426 ...... M 7
Middlesex, 6,295 ...... P 5
Montgomery, 47,157 ...... H 6
Nansemond, 35,166 ...... P 7
Nelson, 11,702 ...... L 5
New Kent, 5,300 ...... P 5
Northampton, 14,442 ...... S 5
Northumberland, 9,239 ...... R 5
Nottoway, 14,260 ...... M 6
Orange, 13,792 ...... M 4
Page, 16,581 ...... M 3
Patrick, 15,282 ...... H 7
Pittsylvania, 58,789 ...... K 7
Powhatan, 7,696 ...... N 5
Prince Edward, 14,379 ...... L 6
Prince George, 29,092 ...... O 6
Prince William, 111,102 ...... O 3
Pulaski, 29,564 ...... G 6
Rappahannock, 5,199 ...... M 3
Richmond, 5,841 ...... P 5
Roanoke, 67,339 ...... H 6
Rockbridge, 16,637 ...... K 5
Rockingham, 47,890 ...... L 4
Russell, 24,533 ...... D 7
Scott, 24,376 ...... C 7
Shenandoah, 22,852 ...... L 3
Smyth, 31,349 ...... E 7
Southampton, 18,582 ...... O 7
Spotsylvania, 16,424 ...... N 4
Stafford, 24,587 ...... O 4
Surry, 5,882 ...... P 6
Sussex, 11,464 ...... N 7
Tazewell, 39,816 ...... E 6
Warren, 15,301 ...... M 3
Washington, 40,835 ...... D 7
Westmoreland, 12,142 ...... P 4

Wise, 35,947 ...... C 6
Wythe, 22,139 ...... F 7
York, 33,203 ...... P 6

INDEPENDENT CITIES

Zip	Name/Pop.	Key
* 22301	Alexandria, 110,938	P 3
24523	Bedford⊙, 6,011	J 6
24201	Bristol, 14,857	D 7
24416	Buena Vista, 6,425	K 5
* 22901	Charlottesville⊙, 38,880	M 4
23320	Chesapeake, 89,580	R 7
24422	Clifton Forge, 5,501	J 5
23834	Colonial Heights, 15,097	O 6
24426	Covington, 10,060	H 5
24541	Danville, 46,391	J 7
23847	Emporia⊙, 5,300	N 7
22030	Fairfax⊙, 21,970	O 3
22040	Falls Church, 10,772	O 3
23851	Franklin, 6,880	P 7
22401	Fredericksburg, 14,450	N 4
24333	Galax⊙, 6,278	G 7
* 23360	Hampton, 120,779	R 6
22801	Harrisonburg⊙, 14,605	K 4
23860	Hopewell, 23,471	O 6
24450	Lexington⊙, 7,597	J 5
24501	Lynchburg⊙, 54,083	K 6
24112	Martinsville⊙, 19,653	J 7
* 23601	Newport News, 138,177	P 6
23501	Norfolk, 307,951	R 7
24273	Norton, 4,001	C 7
23803	Petersburg, 36,103	N 6
* 23701	Portsmouth⊙, 110,963	R 7
24141	Radford, 11,596	G 6
23201	Richmond (cap.)⊙, 249,621	O 5
* 24001	Roanoke, 92,115	H 6
24153	Salem⊙, 21,982	H 6
24592	South Boston, 6,889	L 7
24401	Staunton, 24,504	K 4
23434	Suffolk⊙, 9,858	P 7
* 23450	Virginia Beach, 172,106	S 7
22980	Waynesboro, 16,707	L 4
23185	Williamsburg, 9,069	P 6
22601	Winchester⊙, 14,643	M 2

CITIES and TOWNS

24210 Abingdon⊙, 4,376		D 7
23301 Accomac⊙, 373		S 5
23001 Achilles, 525		R 6
22920 Afton, 525		L 4
† 22959 Alberene, 200		L 5
23821 Alberta, 466		N 7
24310 Allisonia, 350		G 7
24517 Altavista, 2,708		K 6
24520 Alton, 250		K 7
23002 Amelia Court House⊙, 537		N 6
24521 Amherst⊙, 1,108		K 5
22002 Amissville, 150		M 3
24601 Amonate, 500		E 6
24215 Andover, 300		C 7
22003 Annandale, 27,428		O 3
24216 Appalachia, 2,161		C 7
24522 Appomattox⊙, 1,400		L 6
24053 Ararat, 500		G 7
* 22201 Arlington⊙, 174,284		P 3
22922 Arrington, 350		L 5
23004 Arvonia, 300		M 5
22011 Ashburn, 345		O 2
23005 Ashland, 2,934		N 5
24311 Atkins, 500		F 7
24411 Augusta Springs, 400		K 4
24312 Austinville, 750		F 7
24054 Axton, 540		J 7
23009 Aylett, 300		O 5
24602 Bandy, 500		E 6
24231 Banner, 350		D 7
22923 Barboursville, 207		M 4
24313 Barren Springs, 150		G 7
24055 Bassett, 3,058		J 7
24314 Bastian, 450		F 6
22924 Batesville, 450		L 5
23016 Beaverlett, 178		R 6
† 23201 Bellbluff, 3,900		M 7
23306 Belle Haven, 504		S 5
22307 Belleview, 8,299		O 3
24218 Ben Hur, 300		B 7
24059 Bent Mountain, 140		H 6
22610 Bentonville, 700		M 3
22811 Bergton, 150		L 3
22611 Berryville⊙, 1,569		M 2
24526 Big Island, 500		K 5
24603 Big Rock, 350		D 6
24219 Big Stone Gap, 4,153		C 7
24220 Birchleaf, 650		D 6
23307 Birdsnest, 250		S 6
24604 Bishop, 400		E 6
23916 Blackridge, 140		M 7
24060 Blacksburg, 9,384		H 6
23824 Blackstone, 3,412		N 6
24221 Blackwater, 205		B 7
24527 Blairs, 500		K 7
24415 Bland⊙, 950		F 6
23308 Bloxom, 391		S 5
24605 Bluefield, 5,286		E 6
22012 Bluemont, 310		N 2
24064 Blue Ridge, 926		J 6
24606 Boissevain, 975		F 6
24065 Boones Mill, 363		J 6
23235 Bon Air, 10,562		N 5
24427 Bowling Green⊙, 528		O 4
22620 Boyce, 378		M 2
23917 Boydton⊙, 541		M 7
23827 Boykins, 742		O 7
23828 Branchville, 189		O 7
22714 Brandy Station, 530		N 4
24607 Breaks, 500		D 6
23022 Bremo Bluff, 200		M 5
22812 Bridgewater, 2,828		K 4

24534 Clover, 227	L	7
24077 Cloverdale, 850	J	6
24535 Cluster Springs, 500	L	7
23035 Cobbs Creek, 600	R	6
24230 Coeburn, 2,362	D	7
24536 Coleman Falls, 250	K	6
22442 Coles Point, 200	P	4
24450 Collierstown, 125	J	5
24078 Collinsville, 6,015	J	7
22443 Colonial Beach, 2,058	P	4
23038 Columbia, 125	M	5
24538 Concord, 400	K	6
24080 Copper Valley, 425	G	7
23837 Courtland⊙, 899	O	7
22931 Covesville, 500	L	5
24430 Craigsville, 988	J	4
24315 Crandon, 250	G	6
23930 Crewe, 1,433	M	6
24431 Crimora, 450	L	4
24322 Cripple Creek, 200	F	7
24082 Critz, 150	H	7
24323 Crockett, 300	F	7
22625 Cross Junction, 200	M	2
22932 Crozet, 1,433	L	4
23039 Crozier, 300	N	5
24539 Crystal Hill, 475	L	7
23934 Cullen, 140	L	6
22701 Culpeper⊙, 6,056	M	4
23040 Cumberland⊙, 500	M	6
22448 Dahlgren, 950	O	4
† 22172 Dale City, 13,857	O	3
24083 Daleville, 450	J	6
24236 Damascus, 1,230	E	7
24237 Dante, 1,153	D	7
24239 Davenport, 300	D	6
22821 Dayton, 978	L	4
24432 Deerfield, 200	K	4
22025 Delaplane, 164	N	3
23043 Deltaville, 950	R	5
23839 Dendron, 336	P	6
23840 De Witt, 140	N	6
23936 Dillwyn, 497	M	5
23841 Dinwiddie⊙, 500	N	6
23842 Disputanta, 500	O	6
23047 Doswell, 200	N	5
23937 Drakes Branch, 702	L	7
24324 Draper, 276	G	7
23844 Drewryville, 250	O	7
24242 Drill, 192	E	6
23346 Driver, 250	P	7
24243 Dryden, 400	B	7
24084 Dublin, 1,653	G	6
22026 Dumfries, 1,890	O	3
23938 Dundas, 200	M	7
24245 Dungannon, 282	D	7
22454 Dunnsville, 312	P	5
24085 Eagle Rock, 750	J	5
22936 Earlysville, 210	M	4
24246 East Stone Gap, 500	C	7
23347 Eastville⊙, 203	R	6
23845 Ebony, 150	N	7
23349 Eclipse, 295	R	7
† 22485 Edgehill, 225	O	4
22824 Edinburg, 766	M	3
24086 Eggleston, 500	G	6
23846 Elberon, 200	P	6
22827 Elkton, 1,511	L	4
24087 Elliston, 700	H	6
24327 Emory, 458	E	7
22937 Esmont, 950	L	5
24274 Esserville, 975	G	2
23803 Ettrick, 3,950	O	6
23939 Evergreen, 300	L	6
24550 Evington, 175	K	6
24248 Ewing, 700	B	7
23350 Exmore, 1,421	S	5
24435 Fairfield, 465	K	5
24141 Fairlawn, 1,767	G	6
† 22539 Fairport, 175	R	5
24613 Falls Mills, 500	F	6
22401 Falmouth, 2,139	O	4
23901 Farmville⊙, 4,331	M	6
22460 Farnham, 150	P	5
24088 Ferrum, 200	H	7
24089 Fieldale, 1,337	H	7
24090 Fincastle⊙, 397	J	6
22939 Fishersville, 975	K	4
22627 Flint Hill, 200	M	3
24091 Floyd⊙, 474	H	7
24551 Forest, 497	K	6
23055 Fork Union, 350	M	5
24250 Fort Blackmore, 600	C	7
22578 Foxwells, 400	R	5
24330 Fries, 885	F	7
22630 Front Royal⊙, 8,211	M	3
22830 Fulks Run, 130	L	3
22065 Gainesville, 600	N	3
22463 Garrisonville, 200	N	4
23857 Gasburg, 150	N	7
24251 Gate City⊙, 1,914	C	7
† 24228 Georges Fork, 500	C	6
† 24248 Gibson Station, 200	A	7
24340 Glade Spring, 1,615	E	7
24554 Gladys, 312	K	6
24555 Glasgow, 1,304	K	5
23060 Glen Allen, 985	N	5
24093 Glen Lyn, 191	G	6
24438 Glen Wilton, 280	J	5
† 24541 Glenwood, 1,295	K	7
23061 Gloucester⊙, 700	P	6
23062 Gloucester Point, 850	R	6
24094 Goldbond, 250	G	6
22720 Goldvein, 350	N	4
23063 Goochland⊙, 800	N	5
24556 Goode, 200	K	6
22942 Gordonsville, 1,253	M	4
22637 Gore, 150	M	2
23490 Grafton, 500	P	6
23356 Greenbackville, 300	T	5
23942 Green Bay, 150	M	6

(continued on following page)

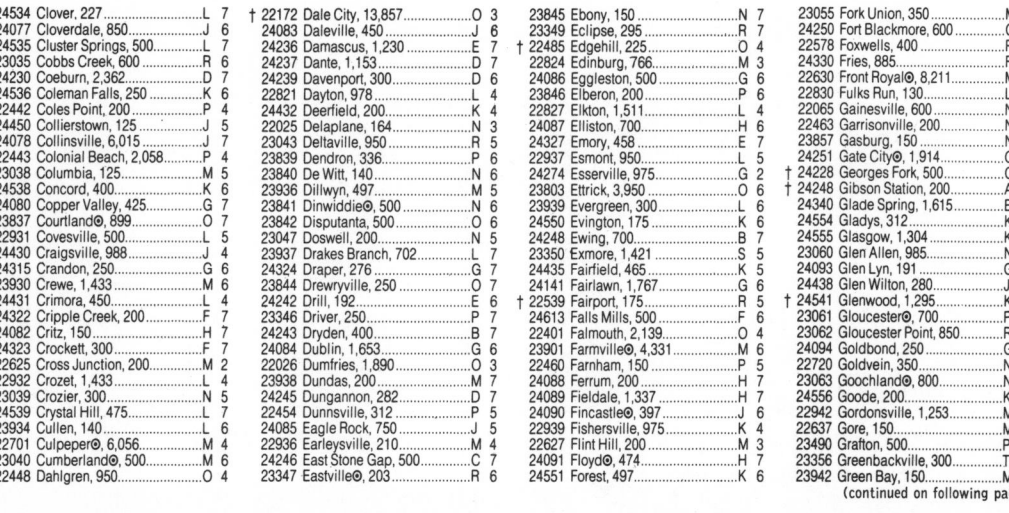

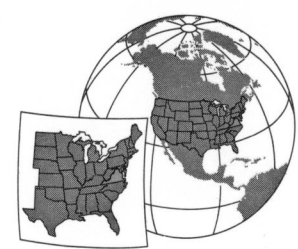

AREA 40,817 sq. mi.
POPULATION 4,648,494
CAPITAL Richmond
LARGEST CITY Norfolk
HIGHEST POINT Mt. Rogers 5,729 ft.
SETTLED IN 1607
ADMITTED TO UNION June 26, 1788
POPULAR NAME Old Dominion
STATE FLOWER Dogwood
STATE BIRD Cardinal

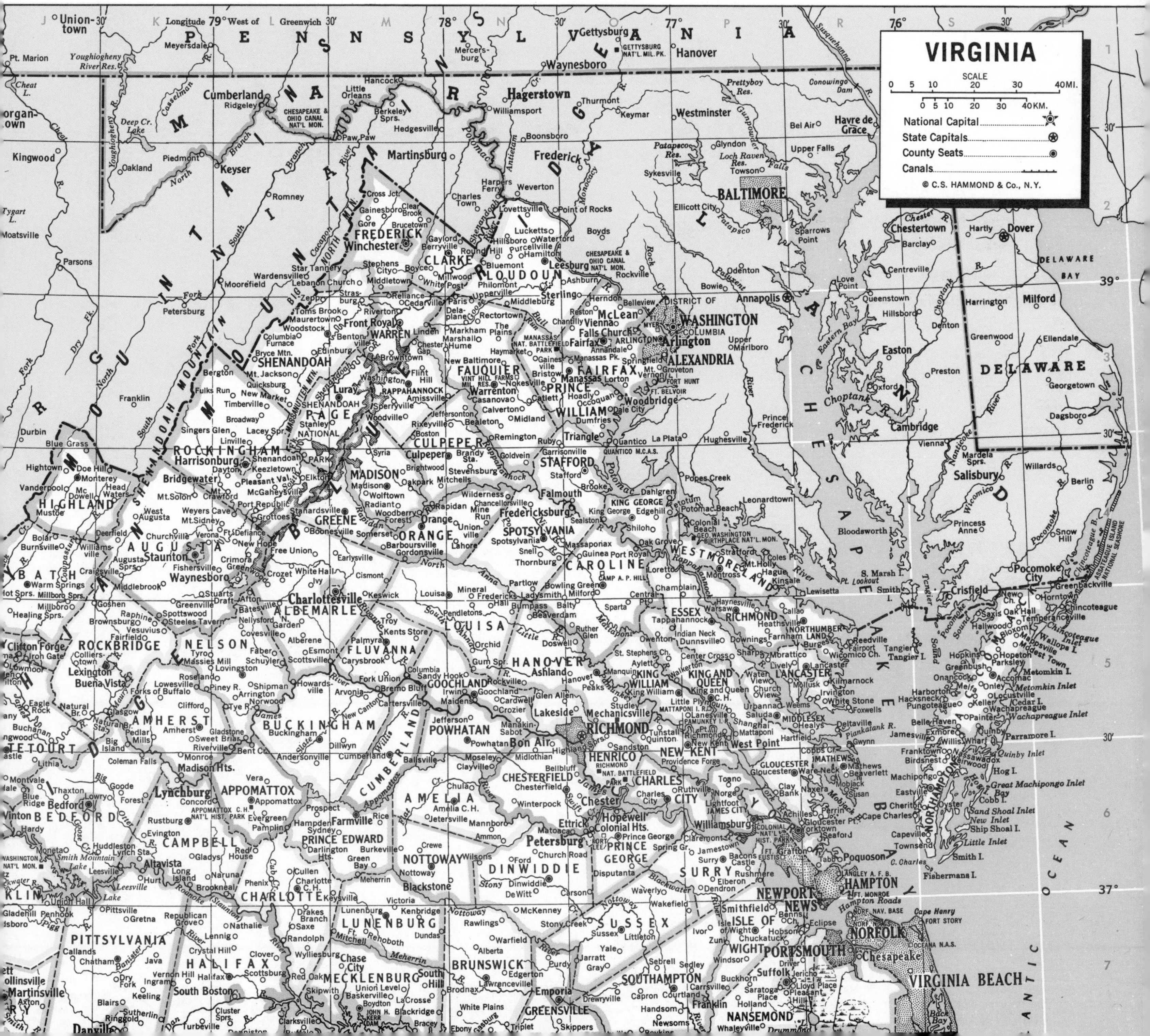

VIRGINIA
SCALE
0 5 10 20 30 40 MI.
0 5 10 20 30 40 KM.
National Capital
State Capitals
County Seats
Canals
© C.S. HAMMOND & Co., N.Y.

Agriculture, Industry and Resources

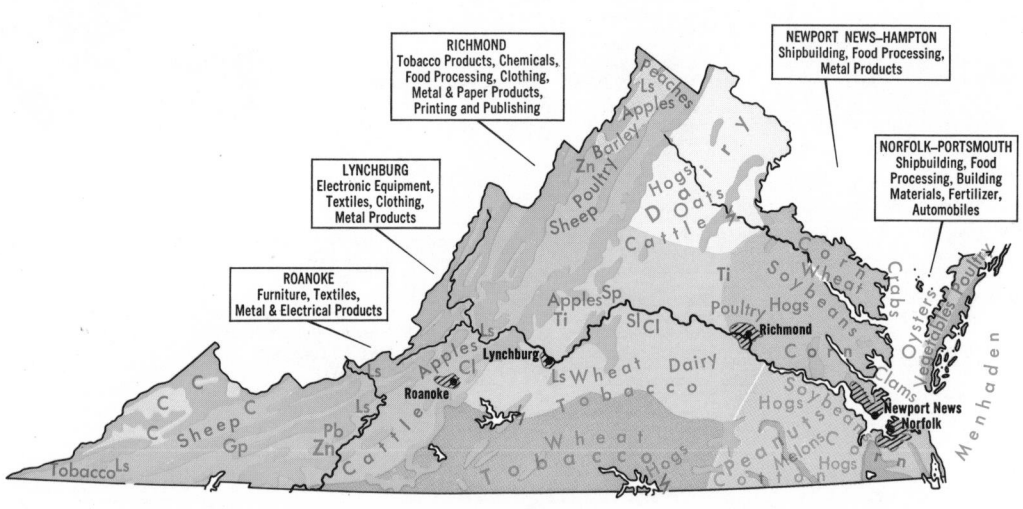

RICHMOND
Tobacco Products, Chemicals, Food Processing, Clothing, Metal & Paper Products, Printing and Publishing

LYNCHBURG
Electronic Equipment, Textiles, Clothing, Metal Products

ROANOKE
Furniture, Textiles, Metal & Electrical Products

NEWPORT NEWS–HAMPTON
Shipbuilding, Food Processing, Metal Products

NORFOLK–PORTSMOUTH
Shipbuilding, Food Processing, Building Materials, Fertilizer, Automobiles

MAJOR MINERAL OCCURRENCES

C	Coal	Sl	Slate
Cl	Clay	Sp	Soapstone
Gp	Gypsum	Ti	Titanium
Ls	Limestone	Zn	Zinc
Pb	Lead		

⚡ Water Power
▨ Major Industrial Areas

DOMINANT LAND USE

- Dairy, General Farming
- General Farming, Livestock, Dairy
- General Farming, Livestock, Tobacco
- General Farming, Livestock, Fruit, Tobacco
- General Farming, Truck Farming, Tobacco, Livestock
- Tobacco, General Farming
- Peanuts, General Farming
- Fruit and Mixed Farming
- Truck and Mixed Farming
- Forests
- Swampland, Limited Agriculture

The Governor's Palace in Williamsburg, Virginia, typifies the splendor enjoyed by the royal governors in residence from 1720 to 1780.

Eric Carle – Shostal Associates

◉ County seat.
‡ Population of metropolitan area.
† Zip of nearest p.o.
* Multiple zips

Agriculture, Industry and Resources

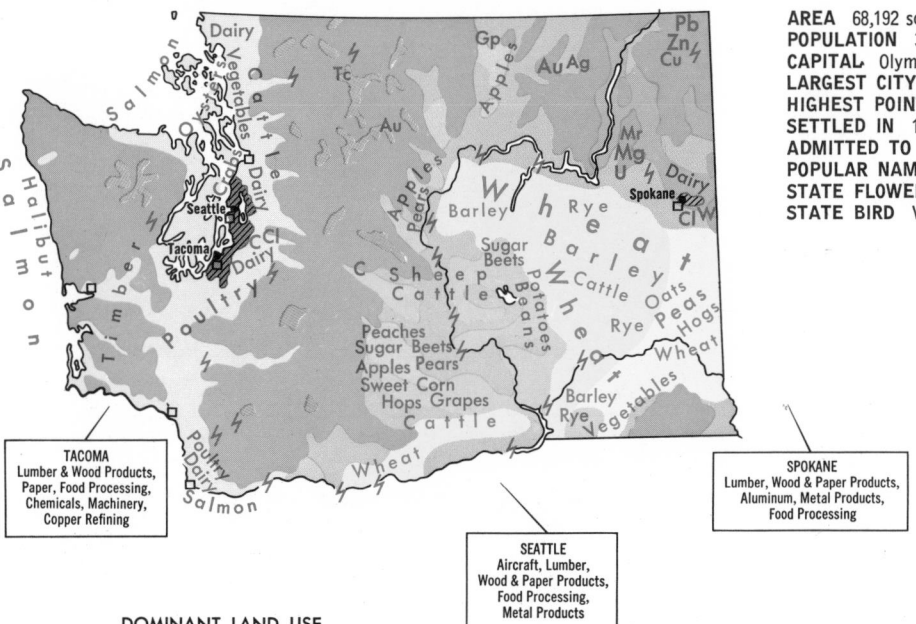

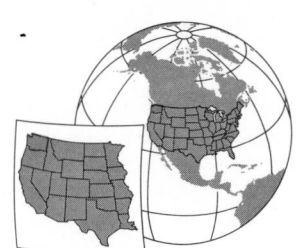

AREA 68,192 sq. mi.
POPULATION 3,409,169
CAPITAL Olympia
LARGEST CITY Seattle
HIGHEST POINT Mt. Rainier 14,410 ft.
SETTLED IN 1811
ADMITTED TO UNION November 11, 1889
POPULAR NAME Evergreen State
STATE FLOWER Coast Rhododendron
STATE BIRD Willow Goldfinch

TACOMA
Lumber & Wood Products,
Paper, Food Processing,
Chemicals, Machinery,
Copper Refining

SEATTLE
Aircraft, Lumber,
Wood & Paper Products,
Food Processing,
Metal Products

SPOKANE
Lumber, Wood & Paper Products,
Aluminum, Metal Products,
Food Processing

DOMINANT LAND USE

- Specialized Wheat
- Wheat, Peas
- Dairy, Poultry, Mixed Farming
- Fruit and Mixed Farming
- General Farming, Dairy, Range Livestock
- General Farming, Livestock, Special Crops
- Range Livestock
- Forests
- Urban Areas
- Nonagricultural Land

MAJOR MINERAL OCCURRENCES

Ag	Silver	Mr	Marble
Au	Gold	Pb	Lead
C	Coal	Tc	Talc
Cl	Clay	U	Uranium
Cu	Copper	W	Tungsten
Gp	Gypsum	Zn	Zinc
Mg	Magnesium		

⚡ Water Power
▨ Major Industrial Areas
□ Major Sawmilling Centers

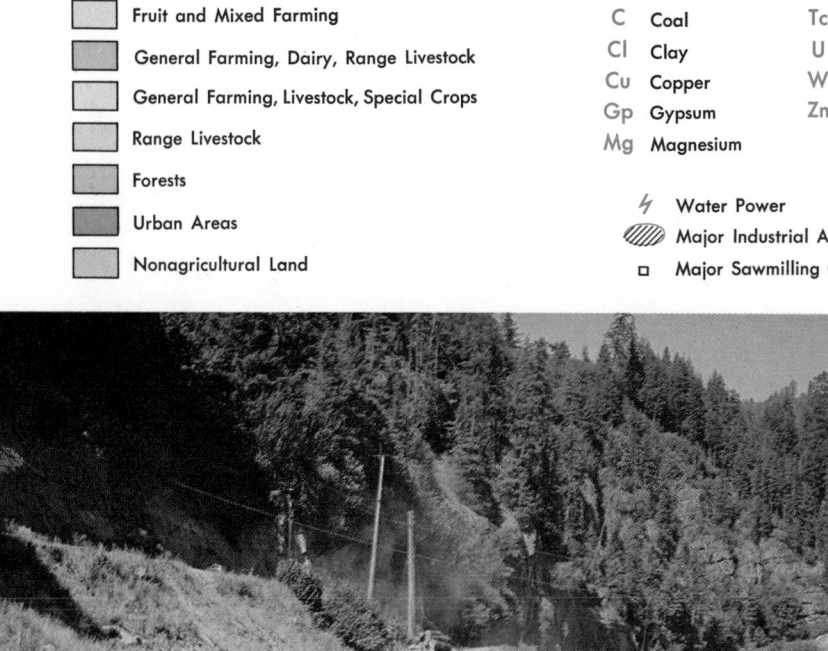

Pulpwood being rafted to the mills is a familiar sight in the Northwest, the region which leads the country in lumber production.

Warren Dick—Shostal Associates

COUNTIES

Adams, 12,014	G	3
Asotin, 13,799	H	4
Benton, 67,540	F	4
Chelan, 41,355	E	3
Clallam, 34,770	B	2
Clark, 128,454	C	5
Columbia, 4,439	H	4
Cowlitz, 68,616	C	4
Douglas, 16,787	F	3
Ferry, 3,655	G	2
Franklin, 25,816	G	4
Garfield, 2,911	H	4
Grant, 41,881	F	3
Grays Harbor, 59,533	B	3
Island, 27,011	C	2
Jefferson, 10,661	B	3
King, 1,156,633	D	3
Kitsap, 101,732	C	3
Kittitas, 25,039	E	3
Klickitat, 12,138	E	5
Lewis, 45,467	C	4
Lincoln, 9,572	G	3
Mason, 20,918	B	3
Okanogan, 25,867	F	2
Pacific, 15,796	B	4
Pend Oreille, 6,025	H	2
Pierce, 411,027	C	3
San Juan, 3,856	C	2
Skagit, 52,381	D	2
Skamania, 5,845	D	5
Snohomish, 265,236	D	2
Spokane, 287,487	H	3
Stevens, 17,405	H	2
Thurston, 76,894	C	4
Wahkiakum, 3,592	B	4
Walla Walla, 42,176	G	4
Whatcom, 81,950	D	2
Whitman, 37,900	H	4
Yakima, 144,971	E	4

CITIES and TOWNS

Zip	Name/Pop.	Key	
98520	Aberdeen, 18,489	B	3
98220	Acme, 170	C	2
99101	Addy, 141	H	2
98522	Adna, 150	B	4
98810	Aeneas, 85	F	2
99001	Airway Heights, 744	H	3
99102	Albion, 687	H	4
98301	Alder, 300	C	4
98002	Algona, 1,276	C	3
98524	Allyn, 850	C	3
99103	Almira, 376	G	3
98525	Aloha, 140	A	3
† 98643	Altoona, 66	B	4
98526	Amanda Park, 495	A	3
99002	Amber, 32	H	3
98601	Amboy, 480	C	5
98221	Anacortes, 7,701	C	2
99401	Anatone, 70	H	4
98602	Appleton, 40	D	5
† 99114	Arden, 30	H	2
98811	Ardenvoir, 350	E	3
98603	Ariel, 386	C	5
98223	Arlington, 2,261	C	2
98304	Ashford, 415	C	4
99402	Asotin⊙, 637	H	4
98002	Auburn, 21,817	C	3
† 99348	Ayer, 70	G	4
98816	Azwell, 152	F	3
98110	Bainbridge Island-Winslow, 1,461	A	2
98224	Baring, 75	D	3
98604	Battle Ground, 1,438	C	5
98527	Bay Center, 350	A	4
† 98520	Bay City, 58	B	4
† 98004	Beaux Arts, 475	B	2
98305	Beaver, 450	A	2
98528	Belfair, 500	C	3
* 98004	Bellevue, 61,102	B	2
98225	Bellingham⊙, 39,375	C	2
99104	Belmont, 59	H	3
99105	Benge, 45	G	4
99320	Benton City, 1,070	F	4
99321	Beverly, 86	F	4
98322	Bickleton, 200	E	5
† 98273	Biglake, 105	C	2
98605	Bingen, 671	D	5
98010	Black Diamond, 1,160	D	3
98230	Blaine, 1,955	C	2
98231	Blanchard, 200	C	2
99106	Bluecreek, 40	H	2
98382	Blyn, 350	B	3
† 98532	Boistfort, 55	B	4
98390	Bonney Lake, 2,313	C	3
† 99126	Bossburg, 66	H	2
98011	Bothell, 4,883	B	1
98232	Bow, 975	C	3
99107	Boyds, 68	G	2
98310	Bremerton, 35,307	A	2
98812	Brewster, 1,059	F	2
98813	Bridgeport, 952	F	3
98036	Brier, 3,093	C	3
98320	Brinnon, 500	B	3
† 98537	Brooklyn, 50	B	4
98920	Brownstown, 80	E	4
† 98310	Brownsville, 50	A	2
98606	Brush Prairie, 200	C	5
† 98101	Bryn Mawr, 4,589	B	2
98321	Buckley, 3,446	C	3
98530	Bucoda, 421	C	4
98921	Buena, 590	E	4
99323	Burbank, 800	G	4
98166	Burien, 2,000	A	2
98322	Burley, 200	C	3
98233	Burlington, 3,138	C	2
98013	Burton, 650	C	3
98607	Camas, 5,790	C	5
98323	Carbonado, 394	D	3
98324	Carlsborg, 500	B	2
98814	Carlton, 120	F	2
98014	Carnation, 530	D	3
98609	Carrolls, 400	C	4
98610	Carson, 500	D	5
98815	Cashmere, 1,976	E	3
98611	Castle Rock, 1,647	B	4
98612	Cathlamet⊙, 647	B	4
† 98045	Cedar Falls, 200	D	3
98613	Centerville, 100	D	5
98531	Centralia, 10,054	C	4
98520	Central Park, 2,720	B	3
99003	Chattaroy, 250	H	3
98532	Chehalis⊙, 5,727	C	4
98816	Chelan, 2,430	E	3
98817	Chelan Falls, 200	E	3
99004	Cheney, 6,358	H	3
98818	Chesaw, 32	G	2
99109	Chewelah, 1,365	H	2
98325	Chimacum, 275	C	3
98614	Chinook, 445	B	4
98533	Cinebar, 35	C	4
98326	Clallam Bay, 750	A	2
99403	Clarkston, 6,312	H	4
99110	Clayton, 204	H	3
98235	Clearlake, 750	C	2
98399	Clearwater, 155	A	3
98922	Cle Elum, 1,725	E	3
† 98937	Cliffdell, 50	E	4
98236	Clinton, 500	C	3
98244	Clipper, 25	C	2
† 99402	Cloverland, 80	H	4
98004	Clyde Hill, 2,987	B	2
† 98055	Coalfield, 500	B	2
99005	Colbert, 225	H	3
† 98366	Colby, 150	A	2
99111	Colfax⊙, 2,664	H	4
99324	College Place, 4,510	G	4
99113	Colton, 279	H	4
† 98632	Columbia Heights, 1,572	C	4
99114	Colville⊙, 3,742	H	2
98819	Conconully, 122	F	2
98827	Concrete, 573	D	2
99326	Connell, 1,161	G	4
98238	Conway, 120	C	2
98605	Cook, 240	D	5
98535	Copalis Beach, 481	A	3
98536	Copalis Crossing, 200	B	3
98537	Cosmopolis, 1,599	B	4
98616	Cougar, 76	C	4
99115	Coulee City, 558	F	3
99116	Coulee Dam, 1,425	G	3
98239	Coupeville⊙, 678	C	2
98923	Cowiche, 150	E	4
99117	Creston, 325	G	3
98015	Cumberland, 250	D	3
99118	Curlew, 200	G	2
98538	Curtis, 200	B	4
99119	Cusick, 257	H	2
98240	Custer, 315	C	2
98617	Dallesport, 400	D	5
99121	Danville, 108	G	2
98241	Darrington, 1,094	D	2
99122	Davenport⊙, 1,363	G	3
99328	Dayton⊙, 2,596	H	4
99010	Deepcreek, 73	H	3
98618	Deep River, 500	B	4
98243	Deer Harbor, 200	B	2
99006	Deer Park, 1,295	H	3
† 99006	Denison, 100	H	3
98188	Des Moines, 3,871	B	2
98283	Diablo, 200	D	2
† 99111	Diamond, 49	H	4
99213	Dishman, 9,079	H	3
99329	Dixie, 200	G	4
† 98279	Doebay, 100	B	2
† 98951	Donald, 100	E	4
98539	Doty, 210	B	4
† 98858	Douglas, 27	F	3
† 98532	Dryad, 184	B	4
98821	Dryden, 550	E	3
† 98382	Dungeness, 675	B	2
98327	Du Pont, 384	C	3
98019	Duvall, 607	D	3
98540	East Olympia, 300	B	4
98925	Easton, 300	D	3
98245	Eastsound, 800	B	2
98801	East Wenatchee, 913	E	3
98328	Eatonville, 2,446	C	4
98246	Edison, 250	C	2
98020	Edmonds, 23,998	C	3

(continued on following page)

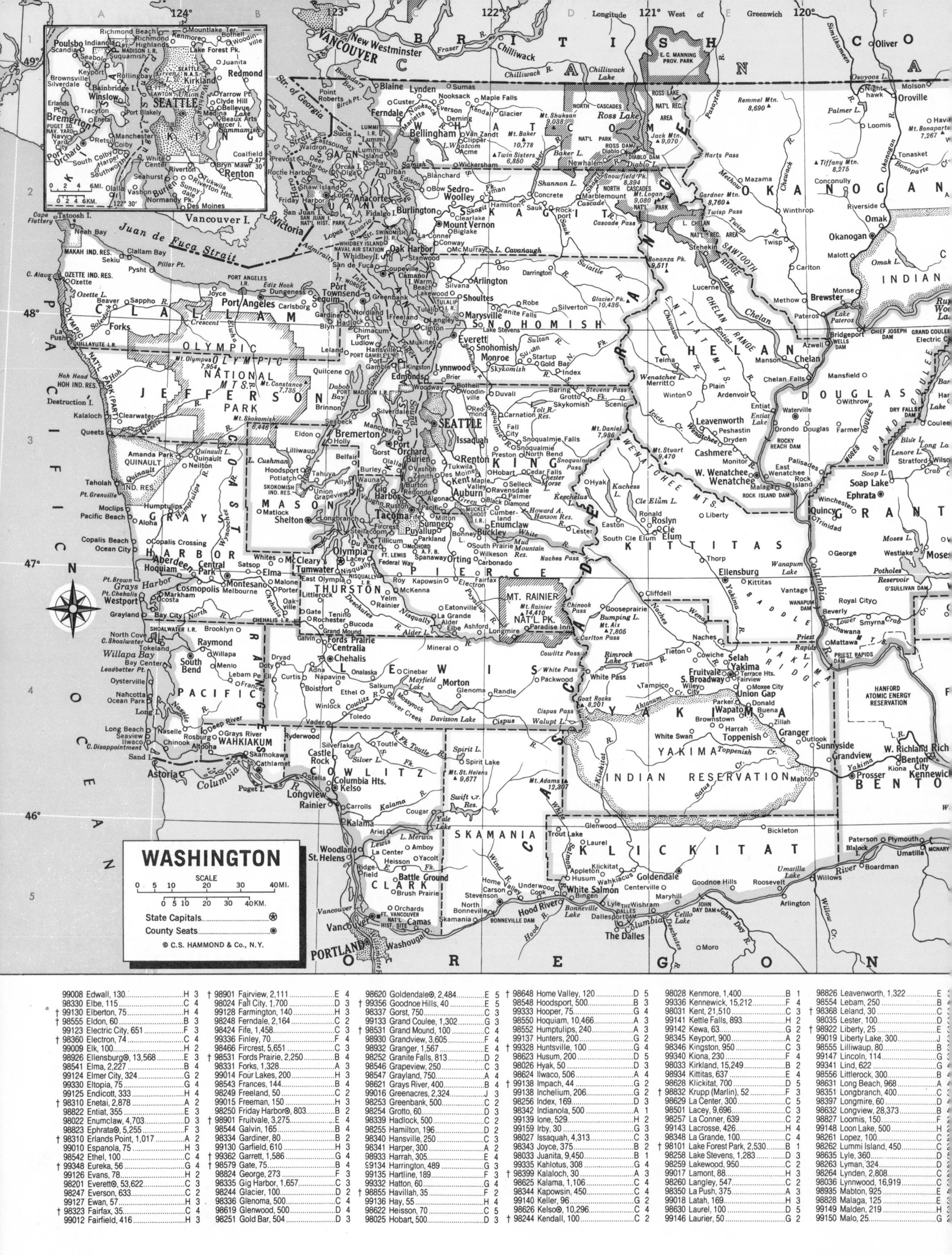

WASHINGTON

SCALE
0 5 10 20 30 40 MI.
0 5 10 20 30 40 KM.

State Capitals.....⊛
County Seats.....⊙

© C.S. HAMMOND & Co., N.Y.

ZIP	Place, Population	Ref
99008	Edwall, 130	H 3
98330	Elbe, 115	C 4
† 98901	Elberton, 75	H 3
98555	Eldon, 60	B 3
† 99123	Electric City, 651	F 3
† 98360	Electron, 74	D 3
99009	Elk, 100	H 2
98926	Ellensburg⊙, 13,568	E 3
98541	Elma, 2,227	B 4
99124	Elmer City, 324	G 2
99330	Eltopia, 75	G 4
99125	Endicott, 333	H 3
† 98310	Enetai, 2,878	A 2
98822	Entiat, 355	E 3
98022	Enumclaw, 4,703	D 3
98823	Ephrata⊙, 5,255	F 3
† 98310	Erlands Point, 1,017	A 2
99010	Espanola, 75	H 2
98542	Ethel, 100	C 4
† 99348	Eureka, 56	G 4
99126	Evans, 78	H 2
98201	Everett⊙, 53,622	C 2
98247	Everson, 633	C 2
99127	Ewan, 57	H 3
† 98323	Fairfax, 35	C 4
99012	Fairfield, 416	H 3
† 98901	Fairview, 2,111	E 4
99356	Fall City, 1,700	D 3
99128	Farmington, 140	H 3
98248	Ferndale, 2,164	C 2
98424	Fife, 1,458	C 3
99336	Finley, 70	F 4
98466	Fircrest, 5,651	C 3
† 98531	Fords Prairie, 2,250	B 4
98331	Forks, 1,328	A 3
99014	Four Lakes, 200	H 3
98543	Frances, 144	B 4
99016	Freeman, 150	H 3
† 98250	Friday Harbor⊙, 803	B 2
† 98901	Fruitvale, 3,275	E 4
98544	Galvin, 165	B 4
98334	Gardiner, 80	B 2
99130	Garfield, 610	H 3
† 99362	Garrett, 1,586	G 4
98579	Gate, 75	B 4
98824	George, 273	F 3
98335	Gig Harbor, 1,657	C 3
98244	Glacier, 100	D 2
98336	Glenoma, 500	C 4
98619	Glenwood, 500	D 4
98251	Gold Bar, 504	D 3
98620	Goldendale⊙, 2,484	E 5
† 99356	Goodnoe Hills, 40	E 5
98337	Gorst, 750	B 3
99133	Grand Coulee, 1,302	G 3
† 98531	Grand Mound, 100	C 4
98930	Grandview, 3,605	F 4
98932	Granger, 1,567	E 4
98252	Granite Falls, 813	D 2
98546	Grapeview, 250	C 3
98547	Grayland, 750	A 4
98621	Grays River, 400	B 4
99016	Greenacres, 2,324	J 3
98253	Greenbank, 500	C 2
98254	Grotto, 60	D 3
98339	Hadlock, 500	B 2
98255	Hamilton, 196	D 2
98340	Hansville, 250	A 2
98341	Harper, 300	B 3
98933	Harrah, 305	E 4
99134	Harrington, 489	G 3
99135	Hartline, 189	G 3
99332	Hatton, 60	G 4
† 98544	Havillah, 35	F 2
98936	Hay, 55	H 4
99622	Heisson, 70	C 5
98025	Hobart, 500	D 3
† 98648	Home Valley, 120	D 5
98548	Hoodsport, 500	B 3
99333	Hooper, 75	G 4
98550	Hoquiam, 10,466	A 3
98552	Humptulips, 240	A 3
99137	Hunters, 200	G 2
† 99328	Huntsville, 100	G 4
98623	Husum, 200	D 5
98026	Hyak, 50	D 3
† 98624	Ilwaco, 506	A 4
99138	Impach, 44	G 2
99138	Inchelium, 206	G 2
98256	Index, 169	D 3
98342	Indianola, 500	A 1
99139	Ione, 529	H 2
99159	Irby, 30	G 3
98027	Issaquah, 4,313	D 3
98343	Joyce, 375	B 2
98033	Juanita, 9,450	B 1
† 98399	Kalaloch, 308	G 4
98625	Kalama, 1,106	C 4
98344	Kapowsin, 450	D 3
98140	Keller, 96	G 2
98626	Kelso⊙, 10,296	C 4
† 98244	Kendall, 100	C 2
98028	Kenmore, 1,400	B 1
99336	Kennewick, 15,212	F 4
98031	Kent, 21,510	C 3
98550	Kettle Falls, 893	G 2
99142	Kewa, 63	G 2
98345	Keyport, 900	A 2
98346	Kingston, 950	A 2
98340	Kiona, 230	F 4
98033	Kirkland, 15,249	B 1
98934	Kittitas, 637	E 4
98628	Klickitat, 700	D 5
† 98832	Krupp (Marlin), 52	F 3
98629	La Center, 300	C 5
98501	Lacey, 9,696	C 3
98257	La Conner, 639	C 2
99143	Lacrosse, 426	H 4
98348	La Grande, 100	C 3
† 98101	Lake Forest Park, 2,530	B 1
98258	Lake Stevens, 1,283	D 3
98259	Lakewood, 950	C 3
99017	Lamont, 88	H 3
98260	Langley, 547	C 2
98350	La Push, 375	A 3
99018	Latah, 169	H 3
98630	Laurel, 100	D 5
99146	Laurier, 50	G 2
98826	Leavenworth, 1,322	E 3
98554	Lebam, 250	B 4
† 98368	Leland, 30	C 2
98035	Lester, 100	D 3
† 98922	Liberty, 25	E 3
99019	Liberty Lake, 300	J 3
99147	Lincoln, 114	G 3
99341	Lind, 622	G 3
98556	Littlerock, 300	B 4
98631	Long Beach, 968	A 4
98351	Longbranch, 400	C 3
98397	Longmire, 60	C 4
99632	Longview, 28,373	B 4
98827	Loomis, 150	F 2
99148	Loon Lake, 500	H 2
98261	Lopez, 100	C 2
98262	Lummi Island, 450	C 2
98635	Lyle, 360	D 5
98263	Lyman, 324	D 2
99264	Lynden, 2,808	C 2
98036	Lynnwood, 16,919	C 2
98935	Mabton, 925	E 4
98828	Malaga, 125	E 3
99149	Malden, 219	H 3
99150	Malo, 25	G 2

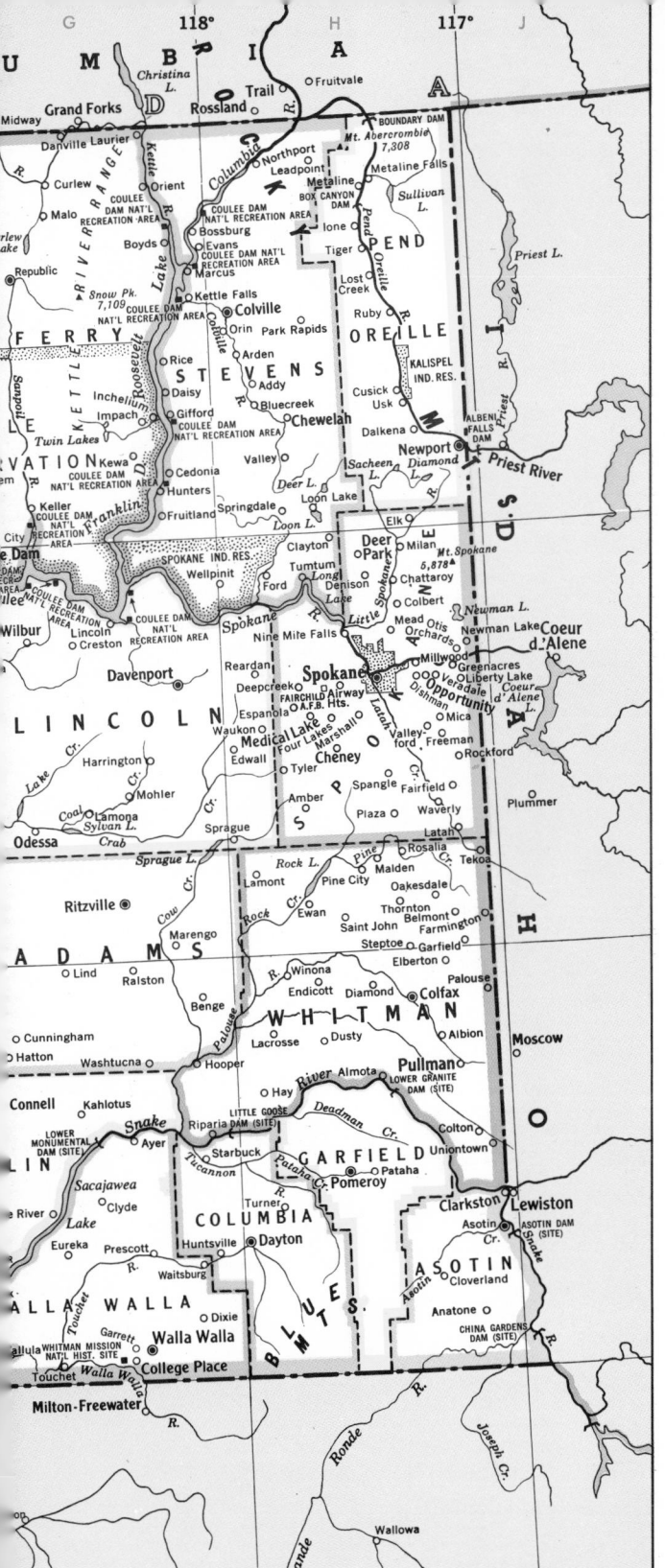

Topography

0   40   80
MILES

Below Sea Level | 100 m. 328 ft. | 200 m. 656 ft. | 500 m. 1,640 ft. | 1,000 m. 3,281 ft. | 2,000 m. 6,562 ft. | 5,000 m. 16,404 ft.

98501 Olympia (cap.)◉, 23,111....C 3	98940 Ronald, 200....................E 3	98492 Tillicum, 1,900................C 3
98841 Omak, 4,164.....................F 2	99356 Roosevelt, 60..................E 5	98590 Tokeland, 300................A 4
98570 Onalaska, 288..................C 4	99170 Rosalia, 569....................H 3	98591 Toledo, 654....................C 4
98566 Neilton, 250.....................A 3	99643 Rosburg, 250..................B 4	98855 Tonasket, 951................F 2
99214 Opportunity, 16,604.........H 3	98941 Roslyn, 1,031.................E 3	98948 Toppenish, 5,744............E 4
98662 Orchards, 800.................C 5	98843 Orondo, 130...................E 3	99360 Touchet, 250..................G 4
99160 Orient, 200.....................G 2	† 98832 Ruff, 40.........................F 3	98649 Toutle, 813....................C 4
98843 Orondo, 130...................E 3	99357 Royal City, 477...............F 4	98393 Tracyton, 1,413..............C 2
98844 Oroville, 1,555................F 2	† 98401 Ruston, 668..................C 3	† 98848 Trinidad, 30.................F 3
98360 Orting, 1,643..................C 3	98581 Ryderwood, 345..............B 4	98650 Trout Lake, 500...............D 5
98223 Oso, 150........................D 2	99171 Saint John, 575...............H 3	98188 Tukwila, 3,496...............B 2
99344 Othello, 4,122.................F 4	99027 Otis Orchards, 900..........H 3	† 98270 Tulalip, 325.................C 2
99027 Otis Orchards, 900..........H 3	98239 San de Fuca, 80.............C 2	99034 Tumtum, 100.................H 3
98938 Outlook, 300...................E 4	98379 Sappho, 200..................A 2	98579 Tumwater, 5,373............B 3
98641 Oysterville, 86.................A 4	98583 Satsop, 300..................B 3	† 99328 Turner, 25...................H 4
† 98326 Ozette, 50...................A 2	† 98283 Sauk, 50....................D 2	98856 Twisp, 756....................E 2
† 98047 Pacific, 1,831...............C 3	98370 Scandia, 75...................A 1	99035 Tyler, 69......................H 3
98571 Pacific Beach, 975...........A 3	† 99321 Schawana, 100.............F 4	98651 Underwood, 500.............D 5
98361 Packwood, 800...............D 4	98380 Seabeck, 200...............C 3	98592 Union, 380...................B 3
98845 Palisades, 200................E 3	† 98110 Seabold, 250...............A 1	98903 Union Gap, 2,040...........E 4
98048 Palmer, 250....................D 3	98062 Seahurst, 3,000.............A 2	99179 Uniontown, 310.............H 4
99161 Palouse, 948..................H 4	* 98101 Seattle◉, 530,831.........A 2	98180 Usk, 250......................H 2
98398 Paradise Inn, 200.............D 4	Seattle-Everett, ‡1,421,869.....A 2	98593 Vader, 387...................B 4
98939 Parker, 700....................E 4	98644 Seaview, 950.................A 4	98181 Valley, 156....................H 2
98444 Parkland, 21,012.............C 3	98284 Sedro-Woolley, 4,598......C 2	99036 Valleyford, 250..............H 3
99301 Pasco◉, 13,920..............F 4	98381 Sekiu, 500....................A 2	* 98660 Vancouver◉, 42,493......C 5
† 99347 Pataha, 97..................H 4	98942 Selah, 3,070.................E 4	98950 Vantage, 125................E 4
98846 Pateros, 472..................E 2	98064 Selleck, 300..................D 3	99244 Van Zandt, 25..............C 2
99345 Paterson, 50..................F 5	98382 Sequim, 1,549...............B 2	98070 Vashon, 350................A 2
98572 Pe Ell, 582.....................B 4	98286 Shaw Island, 95.............B 2	98394 Vaughn, 600................C 3
98847 Peshastin, 200...............E 3	98584 Shelton◉, 6,515.............B 3	99037 Veradale, 5,320............H 3
99162 Pine City, 48..................H 3	98270 Shoultes, 4,754............C 2	98670 Wahkiacus, 65.............D 5
† 98826 Plain, 75.....................E 3	98287 Silvana, 300................C 2	99361 Waitsburg, 953............G 4
99028 Plaza, 50.......................H 3	98585 Silver Creek, 382...........C 4	98297 Waldron, 75...............B 2
99346 Plymouth, 89.................F 5	98383 Silverdale, 950.............C 2	99362 Walla Walla◉, 23,619.....G 4
98281 Point Roberts, 400...........B 2	† 98645 Silverlake, 42..............C 4	99363 Wallula, 89.................G 4
† 99347 Pomeroy◉, 1,823.........H 4	98252 Silverton, 65................D 2	98951 Wapato, 2,841............E 4
98362 Port Angeles◉, 16,367......B 2	98646 Skamania, 250.............C 5	98857 Warden, 1,254............F 4
98110 Port Blakely, 600.............A 2	98647 Skamokawa, 500..........B 4	† 98292 Warm Beach, 225........C 2
98573 Porter, 200....................B 4	98288 Skykomish, 283............D 3	98671 Washougal, 3,388.........C 5
98364 Port Gamble, 425............C 3	98290 Snohomish, 5,174..........C 2	99371 Washtucna, 316............H 4
98365 Port Ludlow, 200.............C 3	98065 Snoqualmie, 1,260.........D 3	98858 Waterville◉, 919...........E 3
98366 Port Orchard◉, 3,904.......C 3	98066 Snoqualmie Falls, 250......D 3	99038 Waukon, 41................H 3
98368 Port Townsend◉, 5,241.....C 2	98851 Soap Lake, 1,064...........F 3	98395 Wauna, 300...............C 3
98574 Potlatch, 350..................B 3	98586 South Bend◉, 1,795........B 4	99039 Waverly, 48................H 3
98370 Poulsbo, 1,856...............A 1	† 98901 South Broadway, 3,298...E 4	98801 Wenatchee◉, 16,912......E 3
99348 Prescott, 242..................G 4	98943 South Cle Elum, 374........D 3	† 98837 Westlake, 258.............F 3
98050 Preston, 500...................D 3	98384 South Colby, 450...........A 2	98595 Westport, 1,364...........A 4
† 98250 Prevost, 25.................B 2	98385 South Prairie, 206..........C 3	99352 West Richland, 1,107......F 4
† 99350 Prosser◉, 2,954...........F 4	98386 Southworth, 425............A 2	† 98801 West Wenatchee, 2,134...E 3
99163 Pullman, 20,509..............H 4	98387 Spanaway, 5,768...........C 3	† 98837 Wheeler, 75...............F 3
98371 Puyallup, 14,742.............C 3	99031 Spangle, 179.................H 3	98146 White Center, 17,300......A 2
† 98399 Queets, 180................A 3	* 99201 Spokane◉, 170,516......H 3	† 98541 Whites, 70................B 3
98376 Quilcene, 900.................C 3	Spokane, ‡287,487.............H 3	98675 White Salmon, 1,585......D 5
98575 Quinault, 340.................A 3	99032 Sprague, 550...............G 3	98952 White Swan, 270..........E 4
98848 Quincy, 3,237.................F 3	99165 Ralston, 35..................G 4	98285 Wickersham, 200.........C 2
98576 Rainier, 382...................C 4	99377 Randle, 950.................D 4	99185 Wilbur, 1,074.............G 3
99173 Springdale, 215...............H 3	98292 Stanwood, 1,347...........C 2	98906 Wiley City, 250...........E 4
98377 Randle, 950...................D 4	99359 Starbuck, 216..............G 4	98396 Wilkeson, 317.............D 3
98051 Ravensdale, 400..............D 3	98293 Startup, 450................D 3	98577 Willapa, 300..............B 4
98577 Raymond, 3,126..............B 4	98852 Stehekin, 40................D 2	98860 Wilson Creek, 184.........F 3
99029 Reardan, 389.................H 3	98388 Steilacoom, 2,850..........C 3	98848 Winchester, 70............F 3
98052 Redmond, 11,031.............B 1	99174 Steptoe, 200...............H 3	98596 Winlock, 890..............C 4
98054 Redondo, 950.................C 3	98648 Stevenson◉, 916...........C 5	99186 Winona, 51................H 4
98055 Renton, 25,258...............B 2	98853 Stratford, 160..............F 3	† 98110 Winslow (Bainbridge Island–
99166 Republic◉, 862...............G 2	98294 Sultan, 1,119...............C 3	Winslow), 1,461..........A 2
98378 Retsil, 419.....................A 2	98295 Sumas, 689.................C 2	98862 Winthrop, 371.............E 2
99352 Richland, 26,290.............F 4	98390 Sumner, 4,325.............C 3	98673 Wishram, 575.............D 5
98160 Richmond Beach, 2,550......A 1	98100 Sunnydale, 1,850..........B 2	98863 Withrow, 90...............E 3
† 98133 Richmond Highlands, 6,854.....A 1	98944 Sunnyside, 6,751..........F 4	98072 Woodinville, 2,900........B 1
98642 Ridgefield, 1,004.............C 5	99352 Suquamish, 950...........A 2	98604 Woodland, 1,622..........C 5
99169 Ritzville◉, 1,876.............G 3	* 98401 Tacoma◉, 154,581.......C 3	98020 Woodway, 879............C 3
98849 Riverside, 228................F 2	Tacoma, ‡411,027.............C 3	98675 Yacolt, 488...............C 5
† 98188 Riverton, 23,160...........B 2	98587 Taholah, 550...............A 3	* 98901 Yakima◉, 45,588........E 4
98188 Riverton Heights, 34,800....B 2	98588 Tahuya, 260................B 3	† 98498 Yarrow Point, 1,103......B 2
98252 Roche Harbor, 175............B 2	99033 Tekoa, 808.................H 4	98004 Yarrow Point, 1,103......B 2
98579 Rochester, 325...............C 4	† 98826 Telma, 150................E 3	98597 Yelm, 628................C 4
99030 Rockford, 327................H 3	98589 Tenino, 962................C 4	98188 Zenith, 1,900............C 3
† 98801 Rock Island, 191...........E 3	98901 Terrace Heights, 1,033......E 4	98953 Zillah, 1,138.............E 4
98283 Rockport, 350................D 2	99176 Thornton, 97...............H 4	◉ County seat.
† 98626 Rocky Point, 1,733.........A 2	98946 Thorp, 350.................D 3	‡ Population of metropolitan area.
98061 Rollingbay, 950...............A 2	98947 Tieton, 415................E 4	† Zip of nearest p.o.
	99177 Tiger, 69...................H 2	* Multiple zips

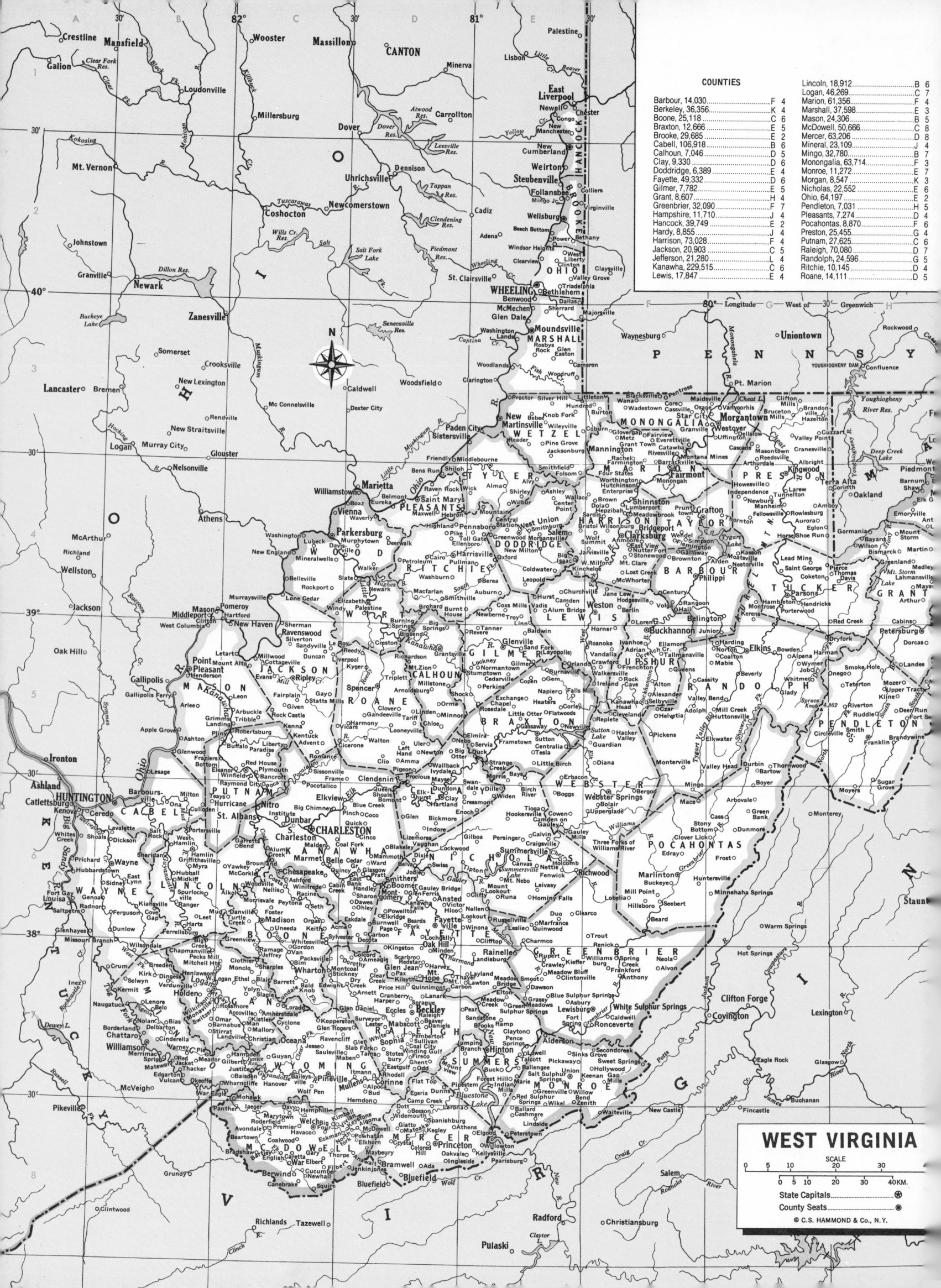

COUNTIES

County	Population	Grid
Barbour	14,030	F 4
Berkeley	36,356	K 4
Boone	25,118	C 6
Braxton	12,666	E 5
Brooke	29,685	E 2
Cabell	106,918	B 6
Calhoun	7,046	D 5
Clay	9,330	D 6
Doddridge	6,389	E 4
Fayette	49,332	D 6
Gilmer	7,782	E 5
Grant	8,607	H 4
Greenbrier	32,090	F 7
Hampshire	11,710	J 4
Hancock	39,749	E 2
Hardy	8,855	J 4
Harrison	73,028	F 4
Jackson	20,903	C 5
Jefferson	21,280	L 4
Kanawha	229,515	C 6
Lewis	17,847	E 4
Lincoln	18,912	B 6
Logan	46,269	C 7
Marion	61,356	F 4
Marshall	37,598	E 3
Mason	24,306	B 5
McDowell	50,666	C 8
Mercer	63,206	D 8
Mineral	23,109	J 4
Mingo	32,780	B 7
Monongalia	63,714	F 3
Monroe	11,272	E 7
Morgan	8,547	K 3
Nicholas	22,552	E 6
Ohio	64,197	E 2
Pendleton	7,031	H 5
Pleasants	7,274	D 4
Pocahontas	8,870	G 6
Preston	25,455	G 4
Putnam	27,625	C 6
Raleigh	70,080	D 7
Randolph	24,596	G 5
Ritchie	10,145	D 4
Roane	14,111	D 5

WEST VIRGINIA

SCALE

0 5 10   20   30

0 5 10   20   30   40KM.

State Capitals .... ⊛

County Seats .... ◉

© C.S. HAMMOND & Co., N.Y.

Summers, 13,213 ... E 7
Taylor, 13,878 ... F 4
Tucker, 7,447 ... G 4
Tyler, 9,929 ... E 4
Upshur, 19,092 ... F 5
Wayne, 37,581 ... B 6
Webster, 9,809 ... F 6
Wetzel, 20,314 ... E 3
Wirt, 4,154 ... D 4
Wood, 86,818 ... D 4
Wyoming, 30,095 ... C 7

CITIES and TOWNS

Zip *Name/Pop.* *Key*
25606 Accoville, 975 ... C 7
† 24701 Ada, 250 ... D 8
† 26288 Addison (Webster Springs)⊙, 1,038 ... F 6
26210 Adrian, 500 ... F 5
26519 Albright, 319 ... G 3
24910 Alderson, 1,278 ... E 7
24807 Algoma, 400 ... D 8
25501 Alkol, 500 ... C 6
26320 Alma, 296 ... E 4
24710 Alpoca, 200 ... D 7
25003 Alum Creek, 900 ... C 6
25004 Ameagle, 210 ... D 7
25607 Amherstdale, 1,602 ... C 4
24808 Anawalt, 801 ... D 8
26323 Anmoore, 944 ... F 4
25812 Ansted, 1,511 ... D 6
24915 Arbovale, 300 ... G 6
25006 Arbuckle, 300 ... C 5
26324 Arden, 200 ... G 4
25007 Arnett, 300 ... D 7
25234 Arnoldsburg, 175 ... D 5
26816 Arthur, 200 ... H 4
26520 Arthurdale, 950 ... G 3
24916 Asbury, 280 ... E 7
24809 Asco, 200 ... C 8
25009 Ashford, 400 ... C 6
24712 Athens, 967 ... E 8
26704 Augusta, 550 ... J 4
26705 Aurora, 275 ... G 4
24811 Avondale, 250 ... C 8
24812 Baileysville, 800 ... C 7
25608 Baisden, 500 ... C 7
26801 Baker, 200 ... J 4
25410 Bakerton, 250 ... L 4
25010 Bald Knob, 356 ... C 7
24918 Ballard, 220 ... E 8
25011 Bancroft, 446 ... C 5
25504 Barboursville, 2,279 ... B 6
25609 Barnabus, 750 ... C 7
26559 Barrackville, 1,596 ... F 3
25013 Barrett, 950 ... C 7
24813 Bartley, 600 ... C 8
† 25411 Bath, 944 ... K 3
26707 Bayard, 475 ... H 4
† 26629 Bays, 186 ... E 5
25014 Beards Fork, 350 ... D 6
24814 Beartown, 500 ... C 8
25813 Beaver (Glen Hedrick), 1,711 ... D 7
25801 Beckley⊙, 19,884 ... D 7
26030 Beech Bottom, 544 ... E 2
24714 Beeson, 250 ... D 8
26250 Belington, 1,567 ... F 4

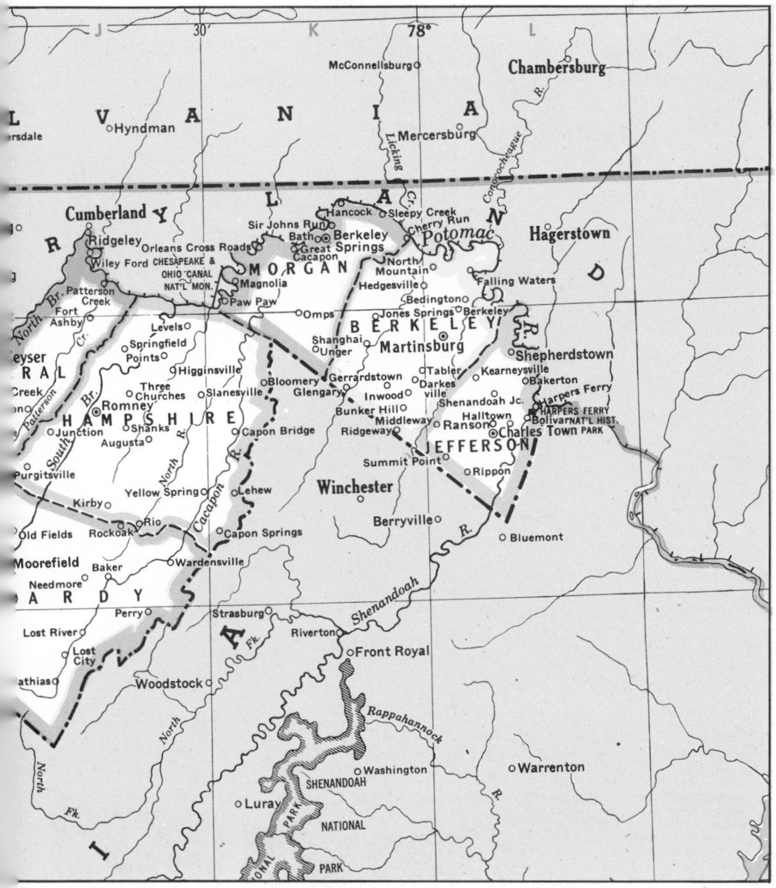
J
K
L
30'
78°
McConnellsburg
Chambersburg
Hyndman
Mercersburg
Cumberland
Hagerstown
Hancock
Sleepy Creek
Cherry Run
Potomac
Sir Johns Run
Bath
Berkeley
Great Springs
Cacapon
MORGAN
North Mountain
Falling Waters
Ridgeley
Orleans Cross Roads
Wiley Ford
CHESAPEAKE & OHIO CANAL NAT'L MON.
Magnolia
Paw Paw
Hedgesville
Bedington
Jones Springs
Berkeley
Omps
BERKELEY
Shanghai
Unger
Martinsburg
Shepherdstown
Fort Ashby
Patterson Creek
Levels
Springfield
Points
Higginsville
Three Churches
Slanesville
Romney
HAMPSHIRE
Augusta
Shanks
Junction
Purgitsville
Bloomery
Gerrardstown
Glengary
Tabler
Darkesville
Kearneysville
Bakerton
Inwood
Bunker Hill
Middleway
Shenandoah Jc.
Halltown
Ranson
Charles Town
Harpers Ferry
HARPERS FERRY
BOLIVAR NAT'L HIST. PARK
Capon Bridge
Ridgeway
JEFFERSON
Summit Point
Rippon
Winchester
Yellow Spring
Lehew
Kirby
Rio
Old Fields
Rockoak
Capon Springs
Berryville
Bluemont
Moorefield
Baker
Wardensville
Needmore
HARDY
Perry
Strasburg
Riverton
Shenandoah
Lost River
Lost City
Front Royal
Mathias
Woodstock
Rappahannock
Washington
Warrenton
SHENANDOAH
Luray
NATIONAL
PARK

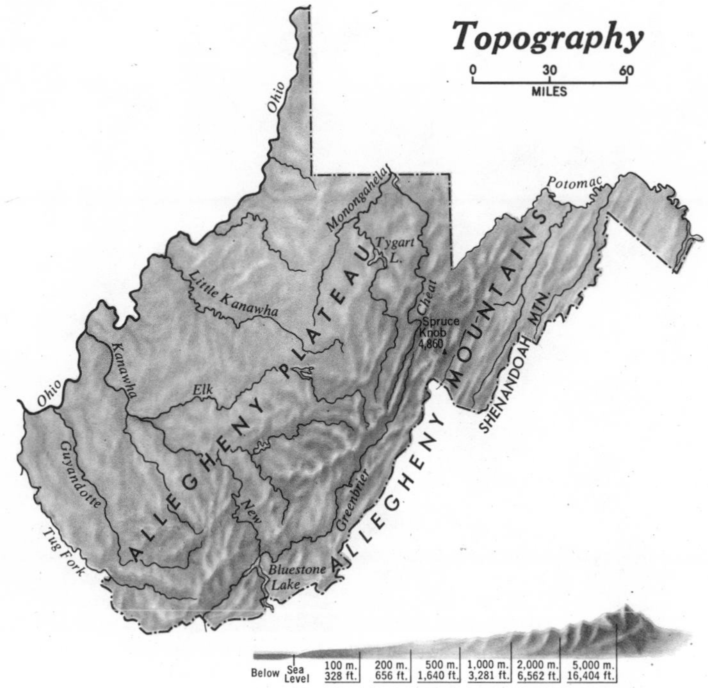
Topography
0
30
60
MILES
Ohio
Monongahela
Potomac
Tygart L.
Little Kanawha
ALLEGHENY PLATEAU
Spruce Knob 4,860
Cheat
ALLEGHENY MOUNTAINS
SHENANDOAH MTN.
Kanawha
Elk
Ohio
Guyandotte
New
Greenbrier
Tug Fork
Bluestone Lake
ALLEGHENY
Below
Sea Level
100 m. 328 ft.
200 m. 656 ft.
500 m. 1,640 ft.
1,000 m. 3,281 ft.
2,000 m. 6,562 ft.
5,000 m. 16,404 ft.

AREA 24,181 sq. mi.
POPULATION 1,744,237
CAPITAL Charleston
LARGEST CITY Huntington
HIGHEST POINT Spruce Knob 4,862 ft.
SETTLED IN 1774
ADMITTED TO UNION June 20, 1863
POPULAR NAME Mountain State
STATE FLOWER Rhododendron
STATE BIRD Cardinal

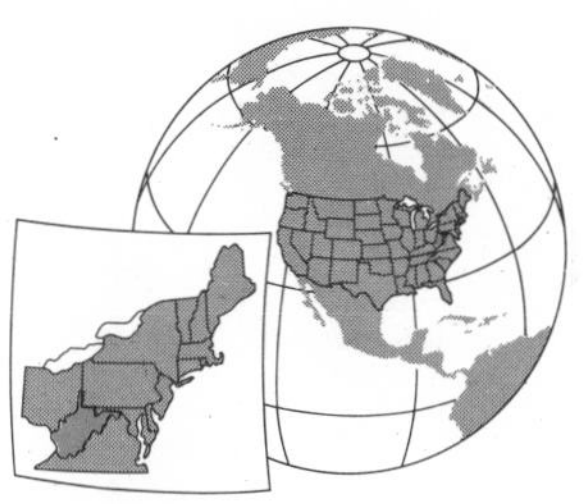

25015 Belle, 1,786 ... C 6
26134 Belmont, 802 ... D 4
26656 Belva, 550 ... D 6
26031 Benwood, 2,737 ... E 2
26298 Bergoo, 260 ... F 6
† 25401 Berkeley, 600 ... L 4
25411 Berkeley Springs⊙, 2,200 ... K 3
24815 Berwind, 675 ... C 8
26032 Bethany, 602 ... E 2
† 26003 Bethlehem, 2,461 ... E 2
26253 Beverly, 470 ... G 5
25019 Bickmore, 375 ... D 6
25302 Big Chimney, 450 ... C 6
25505 Big Creek, 500 ... B 7
† 24853 Big Four, 200 ... C 8
25021 Bim, 395 ... C 7
26610 Birch River, 650 ... E 6
26521 Blacksville, 264 ... F 3
25022 Blair, 700 ... C 7
25023 Blakeley, 260 ... D 6
25026 Blue Creek, 300 ... D 6
24701 Bluefield, 15,921 ... D 8
26288 Bolair, 450 ... F 6
25426 Bolivar, 943 ... L 4
25030 Bomont, 412 ... D 6
25031 Boomer, 1,261 ... D 6
25665 Borderland, 250 ... B 7
24817 Bradshaw, 1,048 ... C 8
24715 Bramwell, 1,125 ... D 8
26802 Brandywine, 188 ... H 5
25666 Breeden, 300 ... B 7
26330 Bridgeport, 4,777 ... F 4
† 25314 Brounland, 900 ... C 6
26334 Brownton, 700 ... F 4
26525 Bruceton Mills, 209 ... G 3
26201 Buckhannon⊙, 7,261 ... F 5
24716 Bud, 400 ... D 7
25033 Buffalo, 831 ... C 5
25413 Bunker Hill, 500 ... K 4
26710 Burlington, 338 ... J 4
26335 Burnsville, 591 ... E 5
26562 Burton, 250 ... F 3
25035 Cabin Creek, 900 ... C 6
26855 Cabins, 300 ... H 4
26337 Cairo, 412 ... D 4
24925 Caldwell, 425 ... F 7
26660 Calvin, 200 ... E 6
26208 Camden on Gauley, 243 ... E 6
26033 Cameron, 1,537 ... E 3
25820 Camp Creek, 200 ... D 7
24819 Canebrake, 250 ... C 8
26662 Canvas, 300 ... E 6
26711 Capon Bridge, 211 ... K 4
26823 Capon Springs, 250 ... K 4
25037 Carbon, 200 ... D 6
24821 Caretta, 650 ... C 8
26527 Cassville, 800 ... F 3
26564 Catawba, 186 ... F 3
25039 Cedar Grove, 1,275 ... D 6
26340 Central Station, 275 ... E 4
26214 Century, 239 ... F 4
25507 Ceredo, 1,583 ... B 6
25508 Chapmanville, 1,175 ... B 7
* 25301 Charleston (cap.)⊙, 71,505 ... C 6
Charleston, ‡229,515 ... C 6
25414 Charles Town⊙, 3,023 ... L 4
25958 Charmco, 900 ... E 6
25667 Chattaroy, 1,145 ... B 7
25315 Chesapeake, 2,428 ... C 6
26034 Chester, 3,614 ... E 1
25306 Cinco, 500 ... D 6
26804 Circleville, 180 ... H 5
26301 Clarksburg⊙, 24,864 ... F 4
25043 Clay⊙, 479 ... D 6
25044 Clear Creek, 300 ... D 7
† 26003 Clearview, 512 ... E 2
25045 Clendenin, 1,438 ... D 5
25237 Clifton, 358 ... B 5
† 25854 Clifty, 250 ... E 6
† 26058 Clinton, 350 ... E 2
25046 Clio, 300 ... D 5
25047 Clothier, 950 ... C 7
25238 Clover, 350 ... D 5
24929 Clover Lick, 250 ... F 6
25823 Coal City, 1,089 ... D 7
25306 Coal Fork, 950 ... D 6
26257 Coalton, 234 ... G 5
24824 Coalwood, 650 ... C 8
26565 Coburn, 230 ... F 3
25048 Colcord, 600 ... D 7
26035 Colliers, 500 ... E 2
† 24740 Colored Hill, 1,031 ... D 8
26615 Copen, 312 ... E 5
25826 Corinne, 1,090 ... D 7
26713 Corinth, 195 ... H 4
25051 Costa, 500 ... C 6
25239 Cottageville, 500 ... C 5
25509 Cove Gap, 650 ... B 6
26206 Cowen, 467 ... E 6
26205 Craigsville, 300 ... E 6
25828 Cranberry, 297 ... D 7
25669 Crum, 300 ... B 7
24826 Cucumber, 275 ... C 8
25510 Culloden, 1,033 ... B 6
24827 Cyclone, 500 ... C 7
25832 Daniels, 950 ... D 7
25053 Danville, 580 ... C 6
† 25428 Darkesville, 375 ... L 4
26260 Davis, 868 ... H 4
26142 Davisville, 200 ... C 4
24828 Davy, 993 ... C 8
25054 Dawes, 800 ... D 6
24932 Dawson, 200 ... E 7
25055 Decota, 800 ... D 6
25670 Delbarton, 903 ... B 7
26531 Dellslow, 500 ... G 3
26217 Diana, 600 ... F 5
† 25535 Dickson, 200 ... B 6
26617 Dille, 300 ... E 6
25671 Dingess, 600 ... B 7
25059 Dixie, 800 ... D 6
† 26386 Dola, 200 ... F 4
26835 Dorcas, 250 ... H 5
25060 Dorothy, 400 ... D 7
25062 Dry Creek, 290 ... D 7
26263 Dryfork, 208 ... H 5
25063 Duck, 500 ... E 5
25064 Dunbar, 9,151 ... C 6
24934 Dunmore, 200 ... G 6
26264 Durbin, 347 ... G 5
25067 East Bank, 1,025 ... D 6
25835 Eastgulf, 300 ... D 7
25512 East Lynn, 500 ... B 6
† 26301 East View, 1,618 ... F 4
25836 Eccles, 1,105 ... D 7
24829 Eckman, 850 ... C 8
25672 Edgarton, 415 ... B 7
† 24954 Edray, 175 ... F 6
24830 Elbert, 400 ... C 8
25070 Eleanor, 1,035 ... C 5
26143 Elizabeth⊙, 821 ... D 4
26717 Elk Garden, 291 ... H 4
26241 Elkins⊙, 8,287 ... G 5
† 24868 Elkridge, 500 ... D 6
25071 Elkview, 1,486 ... C 6
26267 Ellamore, 400 ... F 5
26346 Ellenboro, 267 ... D 4
25965 Elton, 320 ... E 7
24832 English, 500 ... C 8
26568 Enterprise, 975 ... F 4
26203 Erbacon, 350 ... E 5
25075 Eskdale, 500 ... D 6
25076 Ethel, 450 ... C 7
25241 Evans, 400 ... C 5
26533 Everettville, 200 ... F 3
26554 Fairmont, 26,093 ... F 4
† 25271 Fairplain, 200 ... C 5
26570 Fairview, 640 ... F 3
† 24966 Falling Springs (Renick), 255 ... F 6
26571 Farmington, 595 ... F 3
25840 Fayetteville⊙, 1,712 ... D 6
26202 Fenwick, 500 ... E 6
25513 Ferrellsburg, 300 ... B 6
25823 Fireco, 300 ... D 7
26818 Fisher, 250 ... H 4
25841 Flat Top, 550 ... D 7
26621 Flatwoods, 220 ... E 5
26347 Flemington, 458 ... F 4
26037 Follansbee, 3,883 ... E 2
26348 Folsom, 325 ... E 4
24935 Forest Hill, 314 ... E 7
26719 Fort Ashby, 1,225 ... J 4
25514 Fort Gay, 792 ... A 6
26806 Fort Seybert, 208 ... H 5
24936 Fort Spring, 250 ... E 7
26572 Four States, 300 ... F 4
25071 Frame, 200 ... C 5
26623 Frametown, 600 ... E 5
24938 Frankford, 200 ... F 7
26807 Franklin⊙, 695 ... H 5
26218 French Creek, 200 ... F 5
26219 Frenchton, 212 ... F 5
26146 Friendly, 190 ... D 3
25515 Gallipolis Ferry, 325 ... B 5
26349 Galloway, 289 ... F 4
25243 Gandeeville, 271 ... D 5
24836 Gary, 850 ... C 8
26624 Gassaway, 1,253 ... E 5
25085 Gauley Bridge, 1,800 ... D 6
25420 Gerrardstown, 258 ... K 4
25843 Ghent, 450 ... D 7
† 24736 Giatto, 400 ... D 8
25621 Gilbert, 778 ... C 7
26671 Gilboa, 375 ... E 6
25086 Glasgow, 904 ... D 6
26038 Glen Dale, 2,150 ... E 3
25844 Glen Daniel, 300 ... D 7
25090 Glen Ferris, 275 ... D 6
† 25813 Glen Hedrick (Beaver), 1,711 ... D 7
25846 Glen Jean, 1,510 ... D 7
25848 Glen Rogers, 500 ... D 7
26351 Glenville⊙, 2,183 ... E 5
25849 Glen White, 600 ... D 7
25520 Glenwood, 400 ... B 5
25093 Gordon, 500 ... C 7
26720 Gormania, 250 ... H 4
26354 Grafton⊙, 6,433 ... G 4
26147 Grantsville⊙, 795 ... D 5
26574 Grant Town, 946 ... F 3
26534 Granville, 1,027 ... F 3
25422 Great Cacapon, 750 ... K 3
25966 Green Sulphur Springs, 300 ... E 7
† 25166 Greenview, 250 ... C 6
26360 Greenwood, 460 ... E 4
25521 Griffithsville, 300 ... B 6
25095 Grimms Landing, 350 ... B 5
26221 Guardian, 200 ... F 5
24838 Guyan, 250 ... C 7
25423 Halltown, 325 ... L 4
26269 Hambleton, 328 ... G 4
25523 Hamlin⊙, 1,024 ... B 6
25623 Hampden, 251 ... C 7
25102 Handley, 500 ... D 6
24839 Hanover, 300 ... C 7
† 26250 Harding, 200 ... G 5
25851 Harper, 300 ... D 7
25425 Harpers Ferry, 423 ... L 4
26362 Harrisville⊙, 1,464 ... E 4
25247 Hartford, 527 ... C 4
25852 Harvey, 500 ... D 7
24841 Havaco, 329 ... C 8
26627 Heaters, 343 ... E 5
25427 Hedgesville, 274 ... K 3
26224 Helvetia, 269 ... F 5
24842 Hemphill, 785 ... C 8
25106 Henderson, 496 ... B 5
26271 Hendricks, 317 ... G 4
25624 Henlawson, 900 ... B 7
26369 Hepzibah, 600 ... F 4
24726 Herndon, 500 ... D 7
25854 Hico, 750 ... D 6
24946 Hillsboro, 267 ... F 6
25951 Hinton⊙, 4,503 ... E 7
26262 Holcomb, 200 ... E 6
25625 Holden, 2,325 ... B 7
† 26651 Hookersville, 250 ... E 6
26575 Hundred, 475 ... E 3
* 25701 Huntington⊙, 74,315 ... A 6
Huntington-Ashland, ‡253,743 ... A 6
25526 Hurricane, 3,491 ... C 6
24844 Iaeger, 822 ... C 8
25111 Indore, 200 ... D 6
25112 Institute, 3,100 ... C 6
25428 Inwood, 600 ... K 4
24847 Itmann, 500 ... D 7
25113 Ivydale, 700 ... D 5
26377 Jacksonburg, 735 ... E 3
26378 Jane Lew, 397 ... F 4
† 26462 Jarvisville, 250 ... F 4
25114 Jeffrey, 900 ... C 7
24848 Jenkinjones, 800 ... D 8
26674 Jodie, 300 ... D 6
25969 Jumping Branch, 297 ... E 7
26275 Junior, 513 ... G 5
24851 Justice, 600 ... C 7
25430 Kearneysville, 250 ... L 4
24731 Kegley, 450 ... D 8
24732 Kellysville, 200 ... E 8
25248 Kenna, 380 ... C 5
25530 Kenova, 4,860 ... A 6
25674 Kermit, 716 ... B 7
26726 Keyser⊙, 6,586 ... J 4
24852 Keystone, 1,008 ... D 8
25859 Kilsyth, 450 ... D 7
24853 Kimball, 962 ... C 8
26537 Kingwood⊙, 2,550 ... G 4
† 25671 Kirk, 400 ... B 7
25628 Kistler, 750 ... C 7
24854 Kopperston, 900 ... C 7
25860 Lanark, 375 ... D 7
† 25831 Landisburg, 250 ... E 7
25629 Landville, 250 ... C 7
25535 Lavalette, 600 ... B 6
25864 Layland, 455 ... E 7
† 26430 Layopolis (Sand Fork), 252 ... E 5
25251 Left Hand, 200 ... D 5
26676 Leivasy, 450 ... E 6
25676 Lenore, 800 ... B 7
25123 Leon, 192 ... C 5
25971 Lerona, 350 ... D 8
25537 Lesage, 600 ... B 5
25972 Leslie, 500 ... E 6
25865 Lester, 507 ... D 7
25253 Letart, 250 ... C 5
24901 Lewisburg⊙, 2,407 ... E 7
24951 Lindside, 225 ... E 8
26384 Linn, 212 ... E 4
26629 Little Birch, 180 ... E 5
† 26624 Little Otter, 250 ... E 5
26581 Littleton, 333 ... F 3
25125 Lizemores, 400 ... D 6
26677 Lockwood, 300 ... D 6
25601 Logan⊙, 3,311 ... B 7
25868 Lookout, 200 ... E 6
25630 Lorado, 400 ... C 7
26385 Lost Creek, 571 ... F 4
† 26101 Lubeck, 500 ... C 4
26386 Lumberport, 957 ... F 4
25631 Lundale, 700 ... C 7
25870 Maben, 200 ... D 7
26278 Mabie, 366 ... G 5
25871 Mabscott, 1,254 ... D 7
25873 MacArthur, 1,614 ... D 7
25130 Madison⊙, 2,342 ... C 6
26541 Maidsville, 485 ... F 3
25306 Malden, 900 ... C 6
25634 Mallory, 1,240 ... C 7
25132 Mammoth, 576 ... D 6
25635 Man, 1,201 ... C 7
26582 Mannington, 2,747 ... F 3
25975 Marfrance, 240 ... E 6
24954 Marlinton⊙, 1,286 ... F 6
25315 Marmet, 2,339 ... C 6
25401 Martinsburg⊙, 14,626 ... K 4
25260 Mason, 1,319 ... B 4
26542 Masontown, 868 ... G 3
25678 Matewan, 651 ... B 7
24736 Matoaka, 608 ... D 8
24861 Maybeury, 850 ... D 8

(continued on following page)

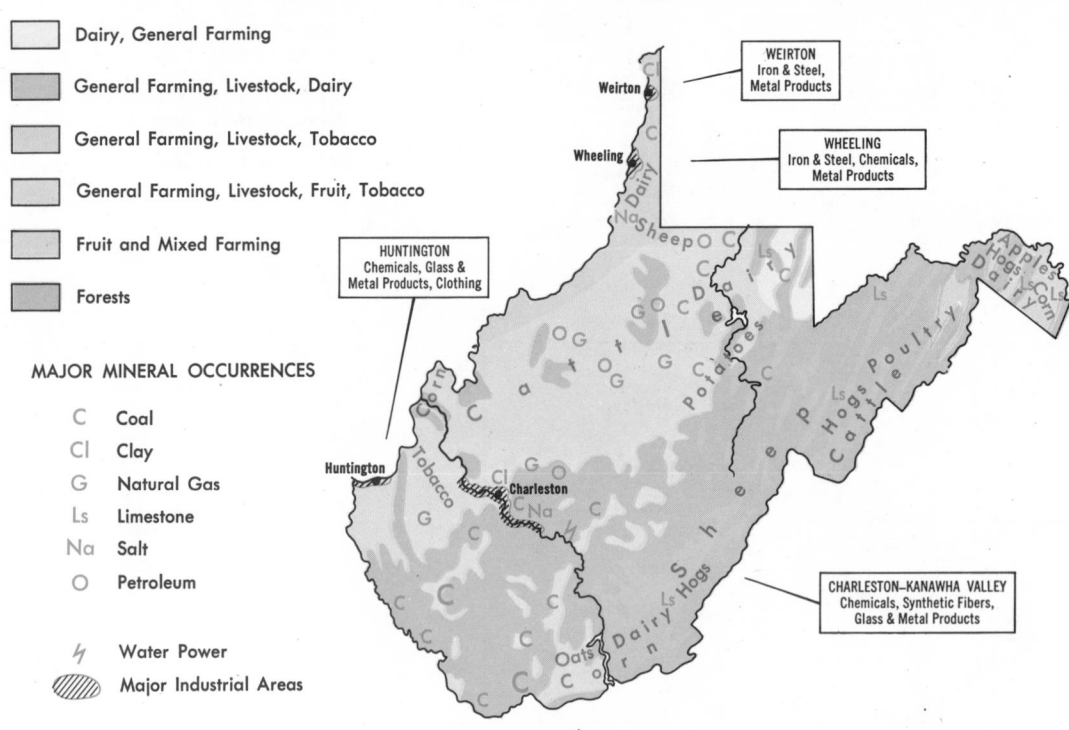

Agriculture, Industry and Resources

DOMINANT LAND USE

- Dairy, General Farming
- General Farming, Livestock, Dairy
- General Farming, Livestock, Tobacco
- General Farming, Livestock, Fruit, Tobacco
- Fruit and Mixed Farming
- Forests

MAJOR MINERAL OCCURRENCES

- C — Coal
- Cl — Clay
- G — Natural Gas
- Ls — Limestone
- Na — Salt
- O — Petroleum
- ⚡ Water Power
- Major Industrial Areas

WEIRTON
Iron & Steel, Metal Products

WHEELING
Iron & Steel, Chemicals, Metal Products

HUNTINGTON
Chemicals, Glass & Metal Products, Clothing

CHARLESTON–KANAWHA VALLEY
Chemicals, Synthetic Fibers, Glass & Metal Products

At one of Clarksburg, West Virginia's glass plants, liquid glass is poured into a machine and becomes beautifully textured stained-glass panels.

A. D'Arazien — Shostal Associates

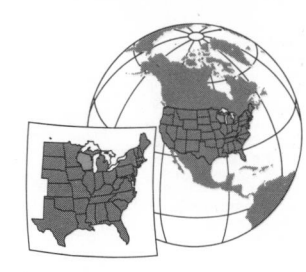

AREA 56,154 sq. mi.
POPULATION 4,417,933
CAPITAL Madison
LARGEST CITY Milwaukee
HIGHEST POINT Timms Hill 1,952 ft.
SETTLED IN 1670
ADMITTED TO UNION May 29, 1848
POPULAR NAME Badger State
STATE FLOWER Wood Violet
STATE BIRD Robin

Shostal Associates

Topography

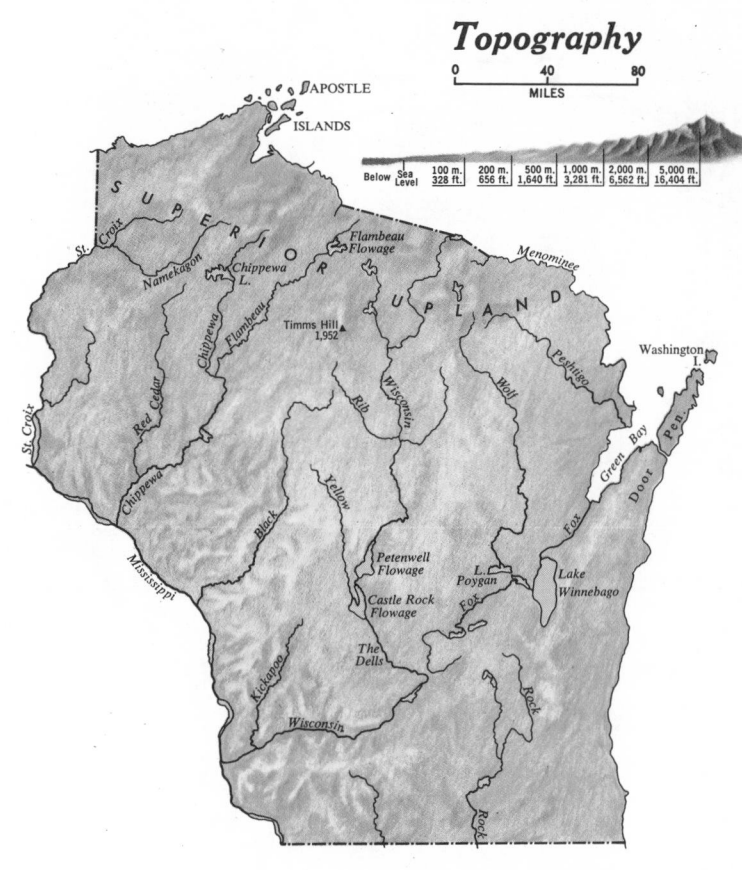

Agriculture, Industry and Resources

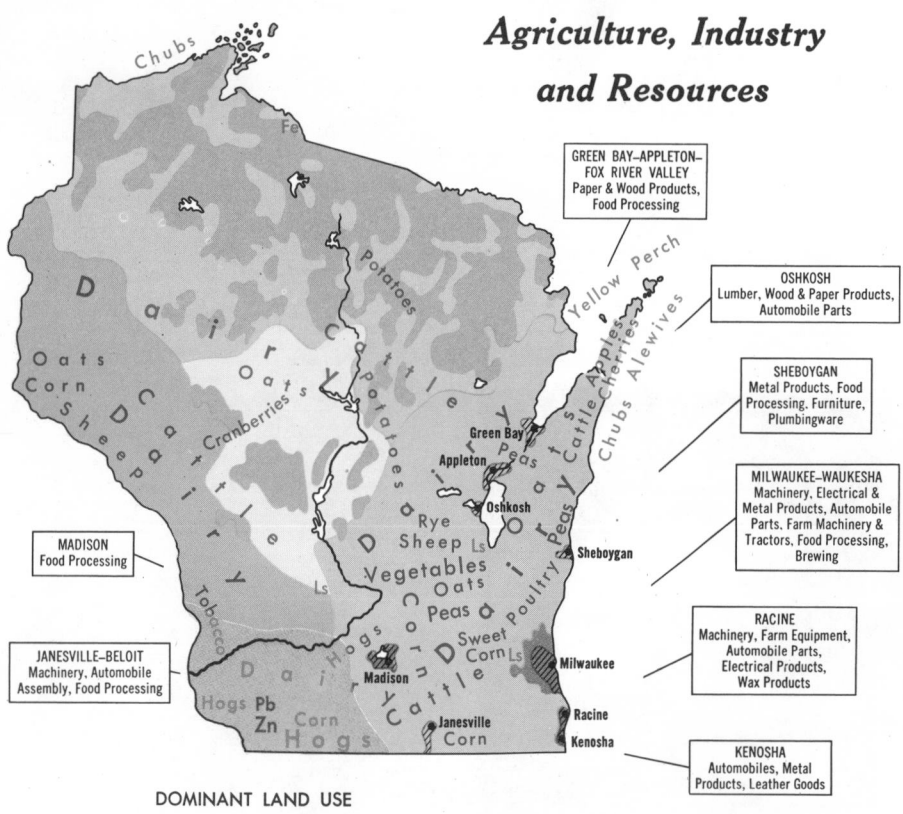

DOMINANT LAND USE

Specialized Dairy

Dairy, Hay, Potatoes

Dairy, General Farming

Hogs, Dairy

MAJOR MINERAL OCCURRENCES

Fe Iron Ore   Pb Lead

WISCONSIN

SCALE
0 5 10   20   30   40 MI.
0 5 10 20 30 40 KM.

State Capitals .... ⊛
County Seats .... ◉
Canals .... ━━━

© C.S. HAMMOND & Co., N.Y.

Agriculture, Industry and Resources

DOMINANT LAND USE

- Specialized Wheat
- Specialized Dairy
- General Farming, Livestock, Special Crops
- Sugar Beets, Dry Beans, Livestock, General Farming
- Range Livestock
- Forests
- Nonagricultural Land

MAJOR MINERAL OCCURRENCES

C	Coal	G	Natural Gas	P	Phosphates
Cl	Clay	O	Petroleum	U	Uranium
Fe	Iron Ore			V	Vanadium

⚡ Water Power

COUNTIES

Albany, 26,431		G 4
Big Horn, 10,202		E 1
Campbell, 12,957		G 1
Carbon, 13,354		F 4
Converse, 5,938		G 3
Crook, 4,535		H 1
Fremont, 28,352		D 2
Goshen, 10,885		H 4
Hot Springs, 4,952		D 2
Johnson, 5,587		F 1
Laramie, 56,360		H 4
Lincoln, 8,640		B 3
Natrona, 51,264		F 3
Niobrara, 2,924		H 2
Park, 17,752		C 1
Platte, 6,486		H 4
Sheridan, 17,852		F 1
Sublette, 3,755		C 3
Sweetwater, 18,391		D 4
Teton, 4,823		B 2
Uinta, 7,100		B 4
Washakie, 7,569		E 2
Weston, 6,307		H 2

CITIES and TOWNS

Zip	Name/Pop.	Key
82830	Acme, 98	E 1
83110	Afton, 1,290	B 3

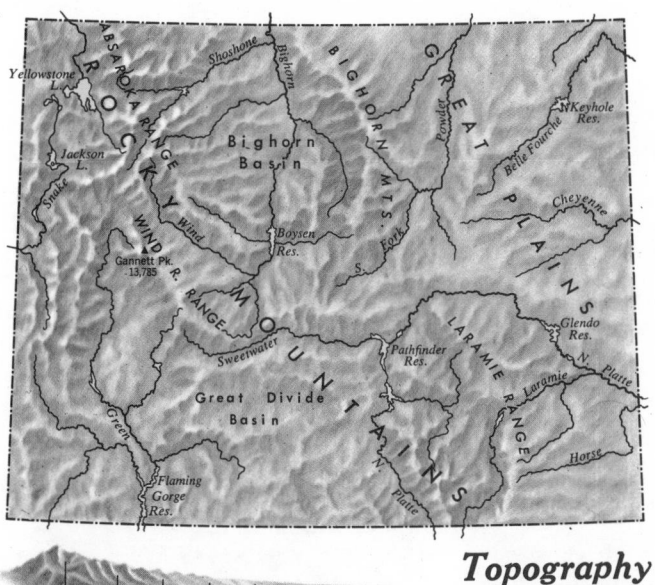

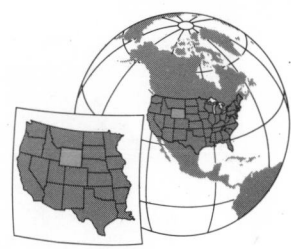

WYOMING

SCALE
0 5 10 20 30 40 MI.
0 5 10 20 30 40 KM.

State Capitals .... ⊛
County Seats .... ⊙

© C.S. HAMMOND & Co., N.Y.

Topography

| 5,000 m. 16,404 ft. | 2,000 m. 6,562 ft. | 1,000 m. 3,281 ft. | 500 m. 1,640 ft. | 200 m. 656 ft. | 100 m. 328 ft. | Sea Level | Below |

0   50   100
MILES

AREA 97,914 sq. mi.
POPULATION 332,416
CAPITAL Cheyenne
LARGEST CITY Cheyenne
HIGHEST POINT Gannett Pk. 13,785 ft.
SETTLED IN 1834
ADMITTED TO UNION July 10, 1890
POPULAR NAME Equality State
STATE FLOWER Indian Paintbrush
STATE BIRD Meadowlark

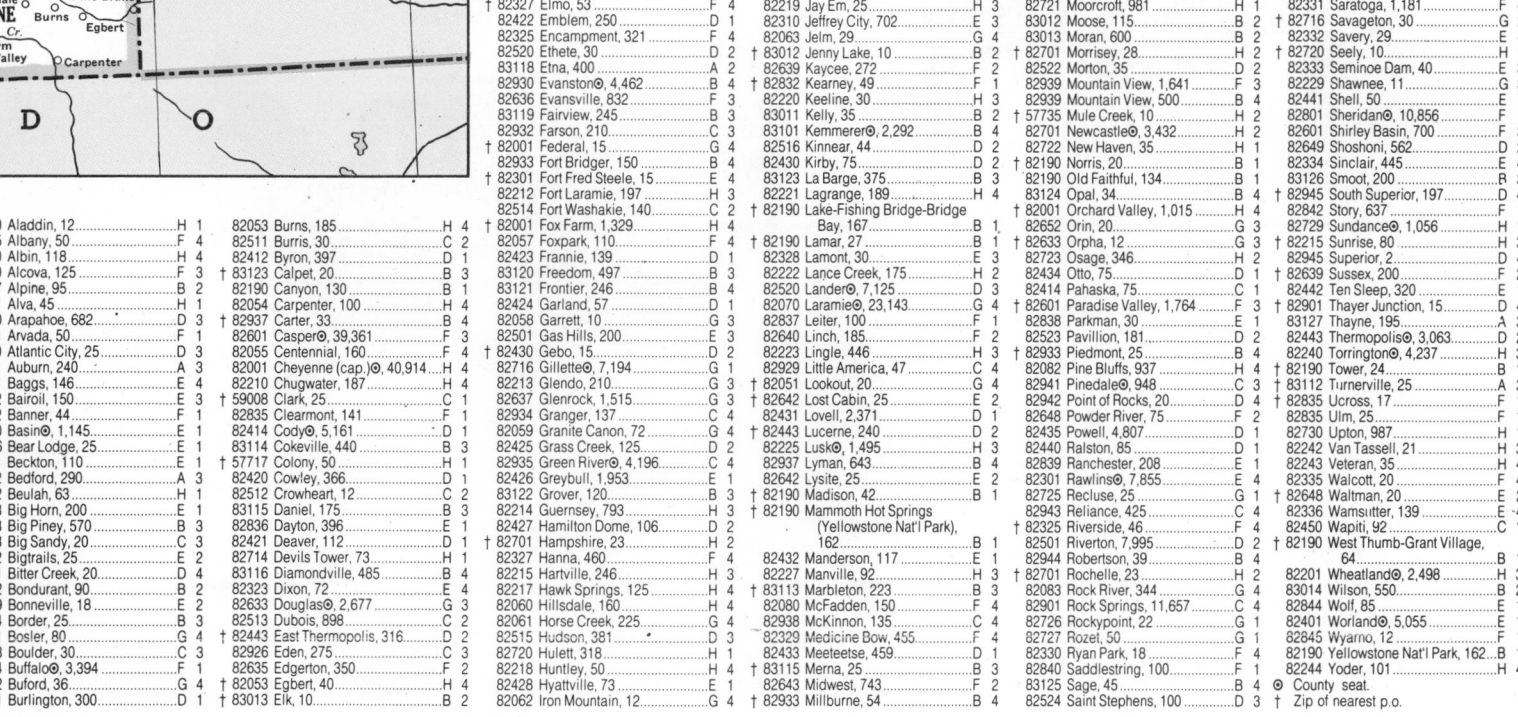

Jack Zehrt — Shostal Associates

Intrepid mountain climbers are challenged by the sheer granite cliffs of Wyoming's Teton Range. Lowland meadows and trails attract less ambitious sportsmen.

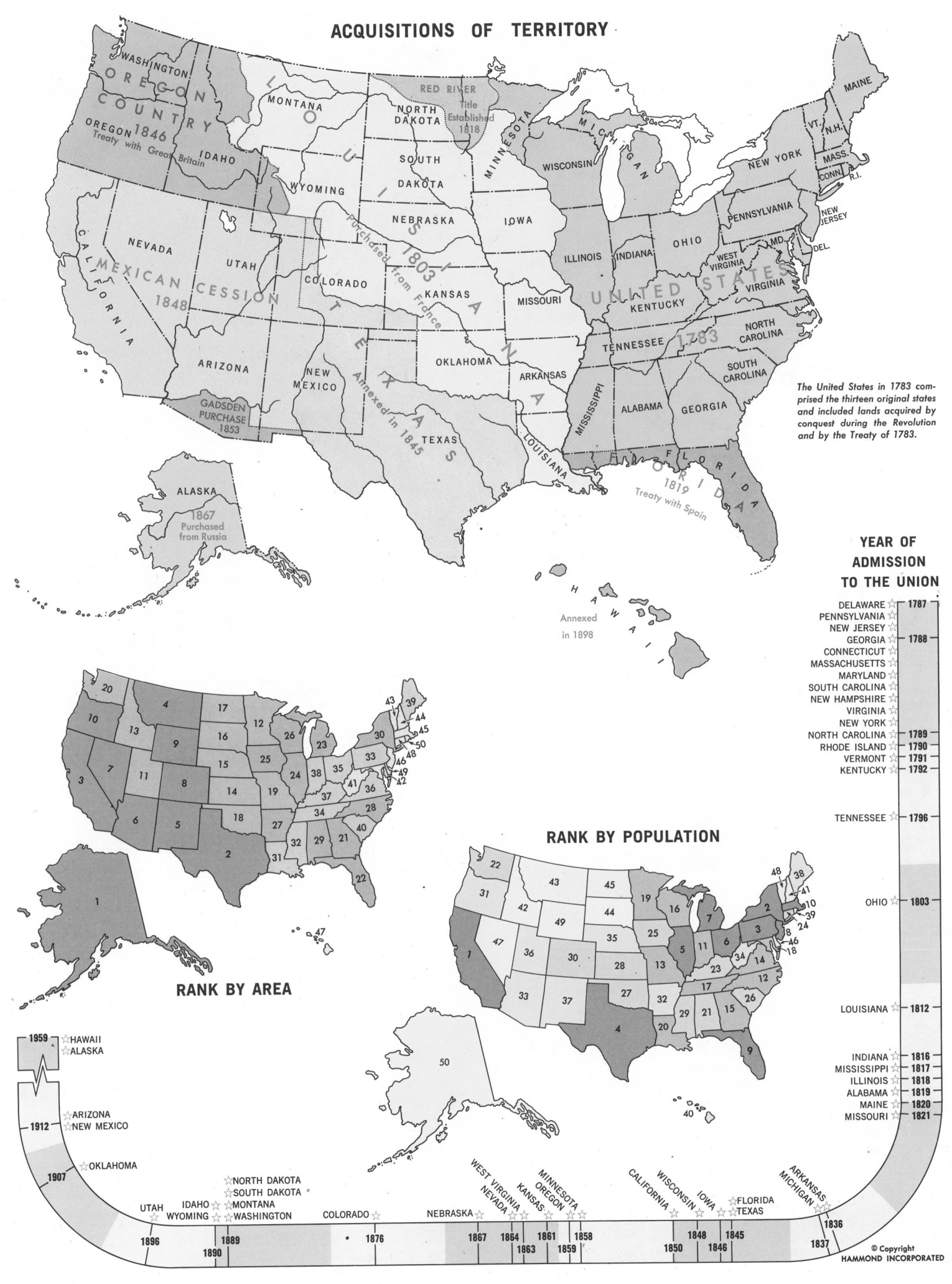

ACQUISITIONS OF TERRITORY

The United States in 1783 comprised the thirteen original states and included lands acquired by conquest during the Revolution and by the Treaty of 1783.

YEAR OF ADMISSION TO THE UNION

DELAWARE ☆	1787
PENNSYLVANIA ☆	
NEW JERSEY ☆	
GEORGIA ☆	1788
CONNECTICUT ☆	
MASSACHUSETTS ☆	
MARYLAND ☆	
SOUTH CAROLINA ☆	
NEW HAMPSHIRE ☆	
VIRGINIA ☆	
NEW YORK ☆	
NORTH CAROLINA ☆	1789
RHODE ISLAND ☆	1790
VERMONT ☆	1791
KENTUCKY ☆	1792
TENNESSEE ☆	1796
OHIO ☆	1803
LOUISIANA ☆	1812
INDIANA ☆	1816
MISSISSIPPI ☆	1817
ILLINOIS ☆	1818
ALABAMA ☆	1819
MAINE ☆	1820
MISSOURI ☆	1821

RANK BY AREA

RANK BY POPULATION

1959 ☆HAWAII ☆ALASKA
1912 ☆ARIZONA ☆NEW MEXICO
1907 ☆OKLAHOMA
☆NORTH DAKOTA
☆SOUTH DAKOTA
UTAH ☆IDAHO ☆MONTANA
☆WYOMING ☆WASHINGTON
COLORADO ☆
NEBRASKA
WEST VIRGINIA
NEVADA KANSAS
MINNESOTA OREGON
CALIFORNIA WISCONSIN IOWA
MICHIGAN ARKANSAS
FLORIDA TEXAS

1896 1889 1890 1876 1867 1864 1863 1861 1859 1858 1850 1848 1846 1845 1836 1837

© Copyright
HAMMOND INCORPORATED

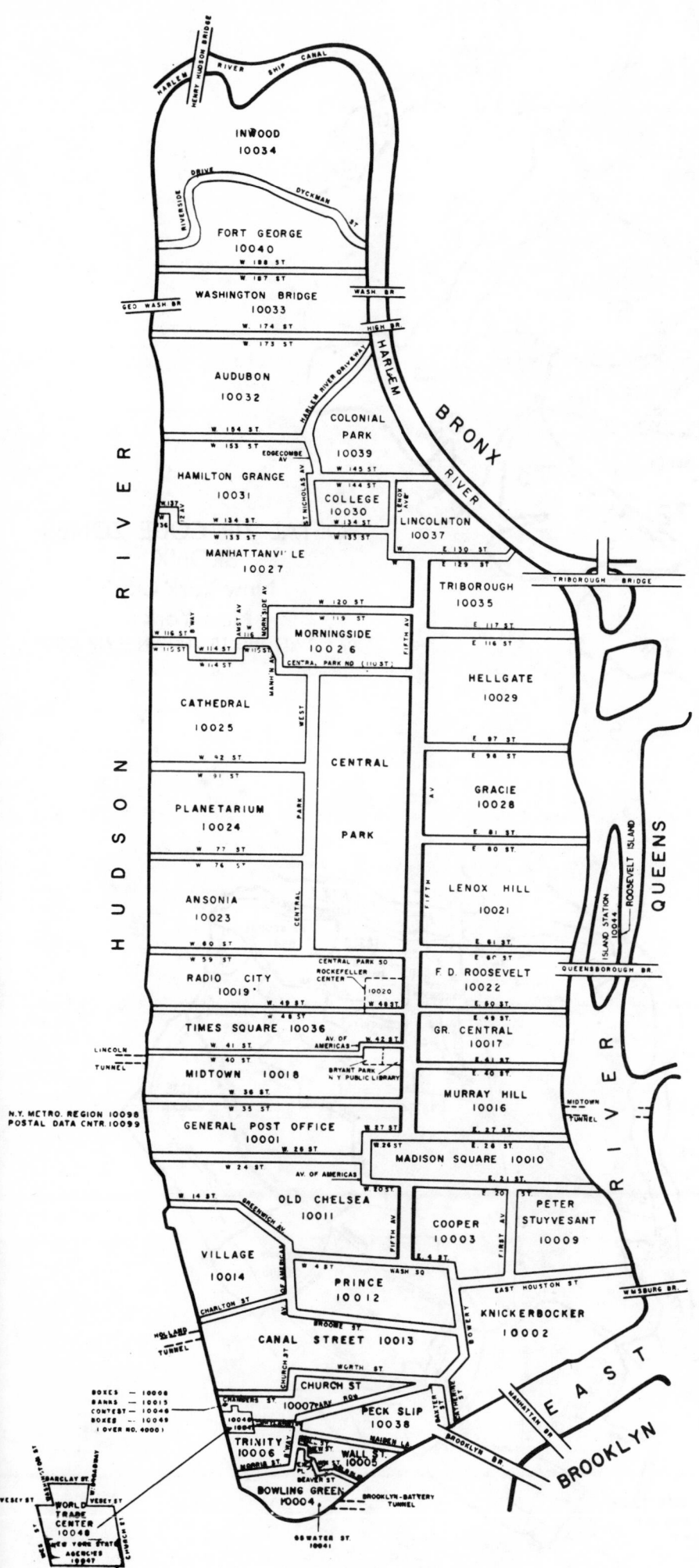

POSTAL ZIP CODE ZONES
MANHATTAN
New York City
New York
100+ TWO DIGITS SHOWN = ZIP CODE

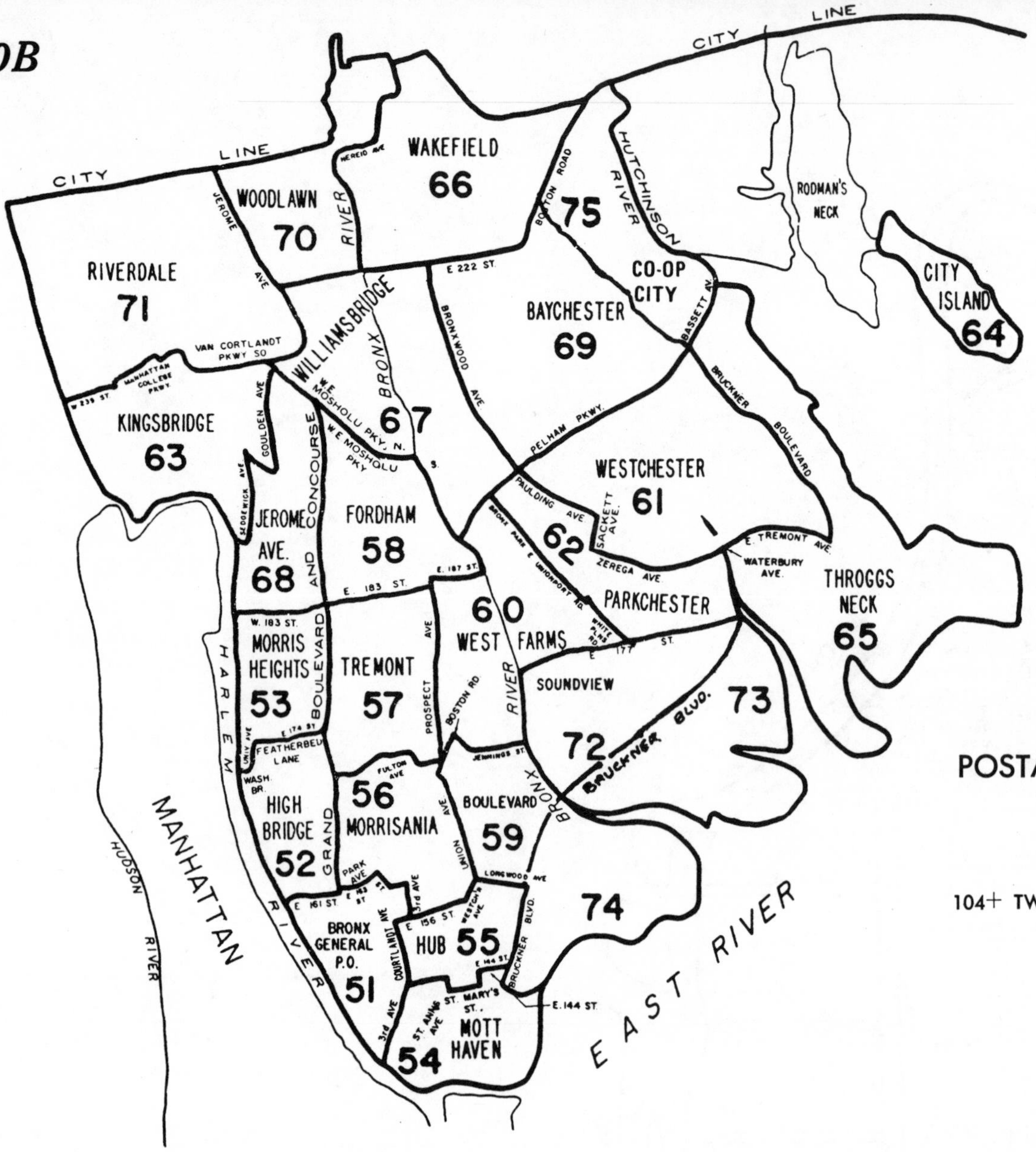
CITY LINE
CITY LINE
WAKEFIELD
66
WOODLAWN
70
RIVER
JEROME AVE.
NEREID AVE
75
BOSTON ROAD
HUTCHINSON RIVER
RODMAN'S NECK
CITY ISLAND
64
RIVERDALE
71
E 222 ST.
CO-OP CITY
BAYCHESTER
69
BAYCHESTER AVE.
BRONXWOOD AVE
VAN CORTLANDT PKWY SO.
WILLIAMSBRIDGE
BRONX
67
W 238 ST.
MANHATTAN COLLEGE PKWY
KINGSBRIDGE
63
GOULDEN AVE.
W.E. MOSHOLU PKY. N.
W.E. MOSHOLU PKY. S.
CONCOURSE
PELHAM PKWY.
BRUCKNER BOULEVARD
WESTCHESTER
61
SEDGWICK AVE
JEROME AVE.
68
FORDHAM
58
PAULDING AVE
SACKETT AVE.
62
BRONX PARK E.
UNIONPORT RD.
E. TREMONT AVE.
WATERBURY AVE.
ZEREGA AVE.
THROGGS NECK
65
AND
E. 187 ST.
E. 183 ST.
60
PARKCHESTER
W. 183 ST.
MORRIS HEIGHTS
53
BOULEVARD
TREMONT
57
PROSPECT AVE
WEST FARMS
WHITE PLAINS RD.
E. 177 ST.
SOUNDVIEW
73
BOSTON RD
RIVER
72
BRUCKNER BLVD.
UNIV AVE
E. 174 ST.
FEATHERBED LANE
WASH. BR.
JENNINGS ST.
FULTON AVE
56
MORRISANIA
BOULEVARD
59
BRONX
HIGH BRIDGE
52
GRAND
PARK AVE.
UNION AVE.
LONGWOOD AVE
74
E 161 ST.
E 163 ST.
3rd AVE
E 156 ST.
WESTCHESTER AVE.
BRONX GENERAL P.O.
51
COURTLANDT AVE
HUB
55
E 144 ST.
BRUCKNER BLVD.
E. 144 ST.
ST. ANNS AVE
ST. MARY'S ST.
MOTT HAVEN
54
MANHATTAN
HARLEM RIVER
HUDSON RIVER
EAST RIVER

POSTAL ZIP CODE ZONES
BRONX
New York City
New York
104+ TWO DIGITS SHOWN = ZIP CODE

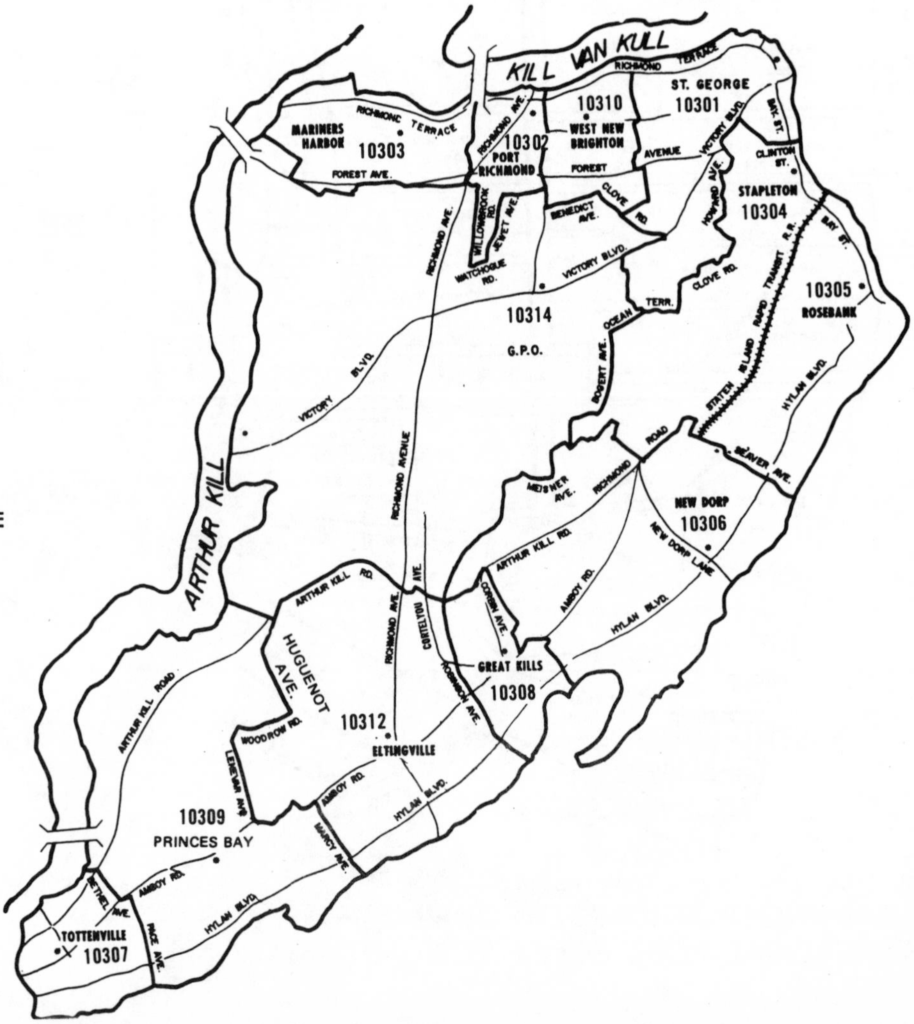
KILL VAN KULL
RICHMOND TERRACE
ST. GEORGE
10301
10310
WEST NEW BRIGHTON
MARINERS HARBOR
10303
RICHMOND TERRACE
RICHMOND AVE.
10302
PORT RICHMOND
FOREST AVE.
FOREST
AVENUE
VICTORY BLVD.
BAY ST.
CLINTON ST.
STAPLETON
10304
RICHMOND AVE.
WILLOWBROOK RD.
JEWETT AVE.
BENEDICT AVE.
CLOVE RD.
HOWARD AVE.
WATCHOGUE RD.
VICTORY BLVD.
CLOVE RD.
TERR.
OCEAN
10305
ROSEBANK
10314
G.P.O.
VICTORY BLVD.
BOGERT AVE.
STATEN ISLAND RAPID TRANSIT R.R.
HYLAN BLVD.
RICHMOND AVENUE
ROAD
BEAVER AVE.
MEISNER AVE.
RICHMOND
ARTHUR KILL
NEW DORP
10306
ARTHUR KILL RD.
NEW DORP LANE
AMBOY RD.
ARTHUR KILL RD.
RICHMOND AVE.
CLARKE AVE.
CORTELYOU AVE.
HYLAN BLVD.
HUGUENOT AVE.
GREAT KILLS
10308
ROBINSON AVE.
ARTHUR KILL ROAD
10312
WOODROW RD.
ELTINGVILLE
LENEVAR AVE.
AMBOY RD.
HYLAN BLVD.
10309
PRINCES BAY
MARCY AVE.
BETHEL AVE.
AMBOY RD.
PAGE AVE.
HYLAN BLVD.
TOTTENVILLE
10307

POSTAL ZIP CODE ZONES
STATEN ISLAND
New York City
New York
103+ TWO DIGITS SHOWN = ZIP CODE

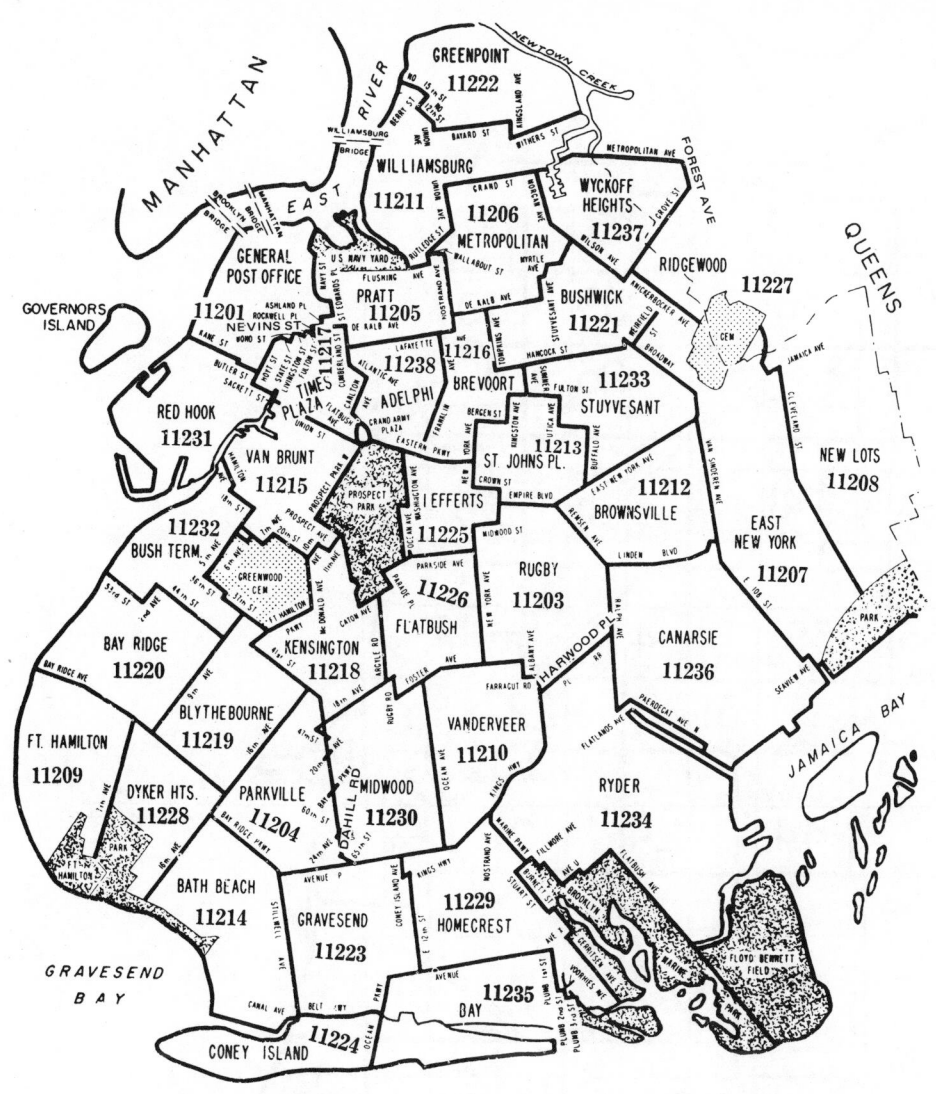

POSTAL ZIP CODE ZONES
BROOKLYN
New York City
New York
112+ TWO DIGITS SHOWN = ZIP CODE

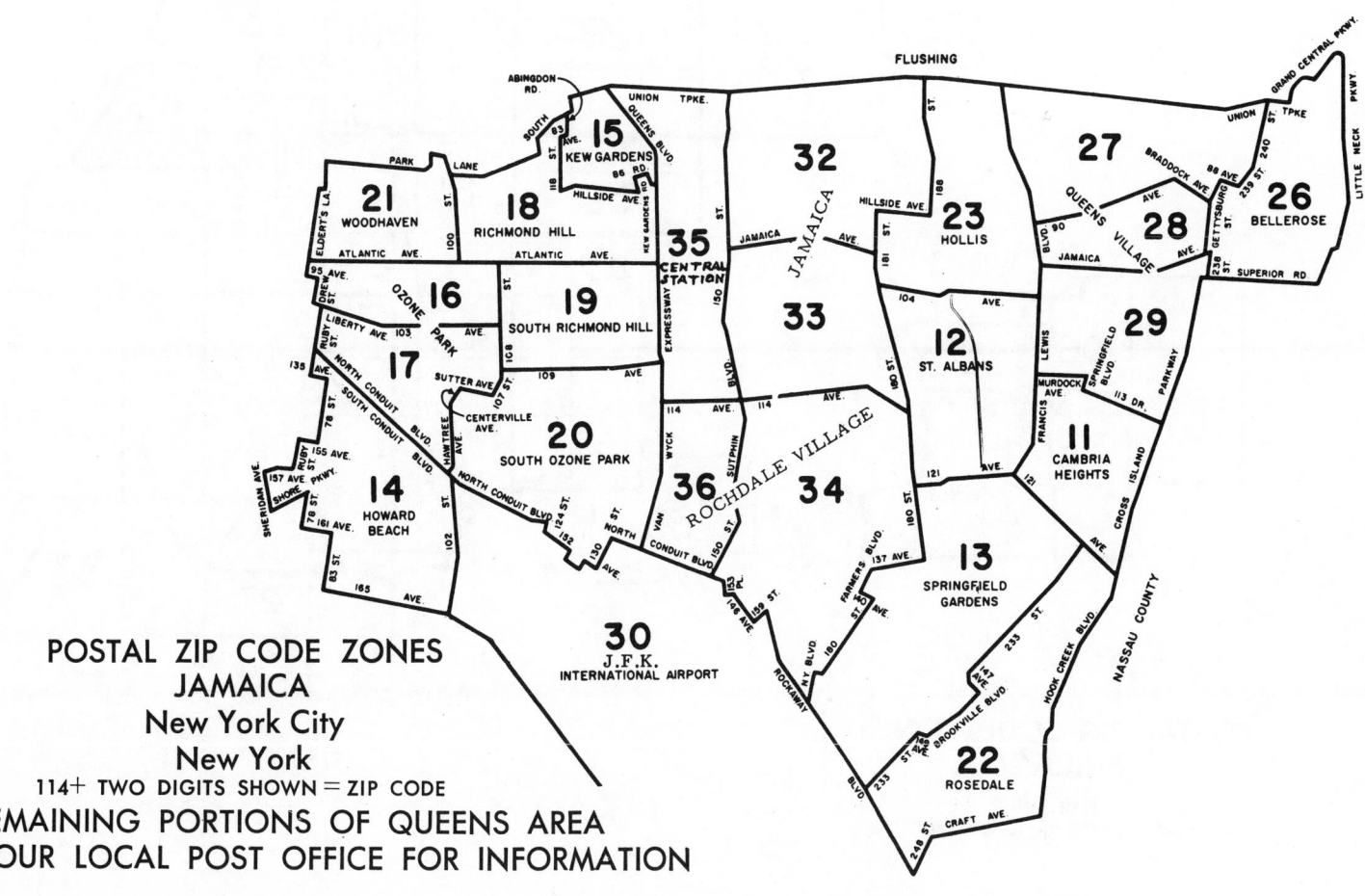

POSTAL ZIP CODE ZONES
JAMAICA
New York City
New York
114+ TWO DIGITS SHOWN = ZIP CODE
FOR REMAINING PORTIONS OF QUEENS AREA
CONTACT YOUR LOCAL POST OFFICE FOR INFORMATION

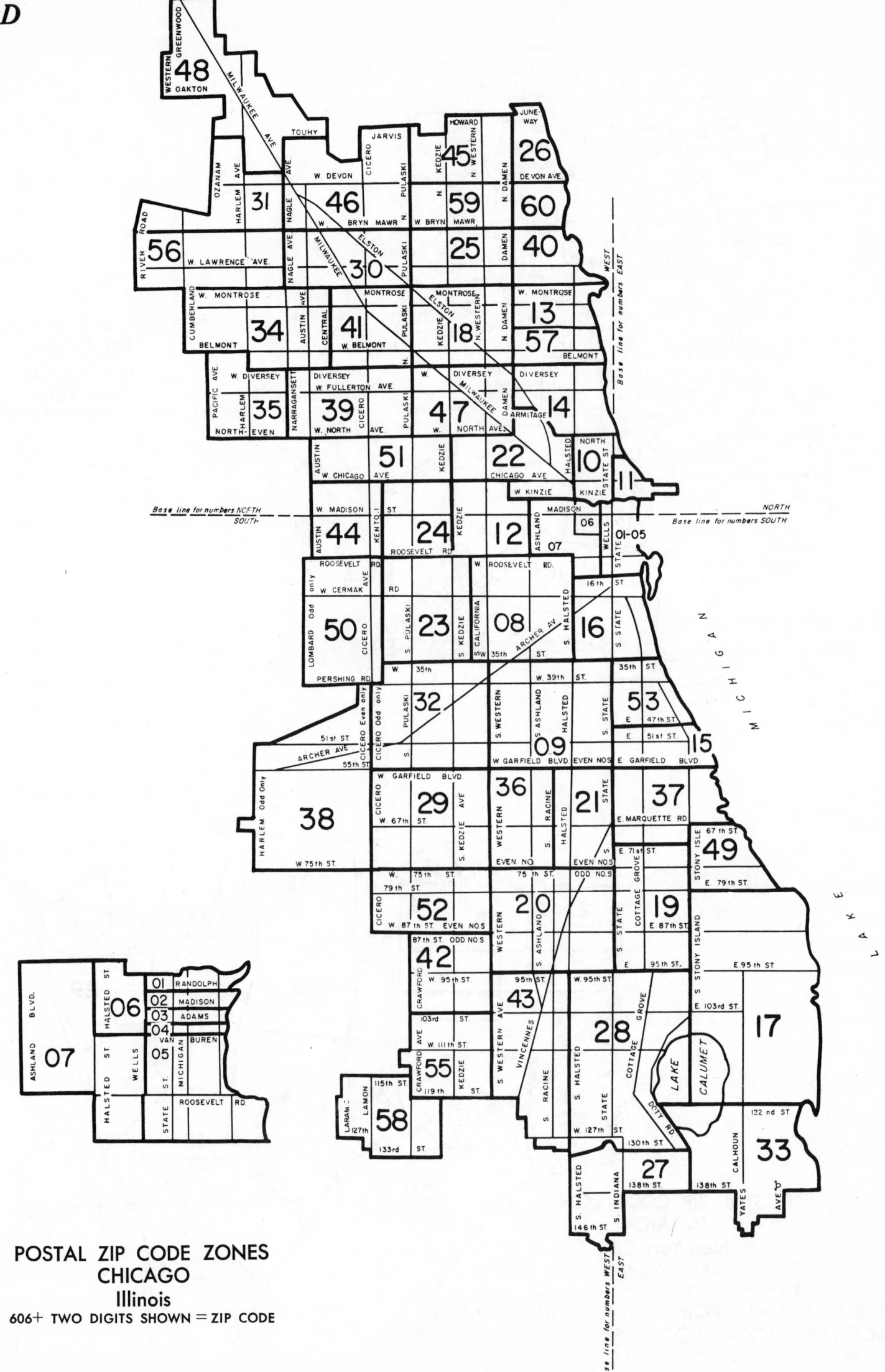

320D

POSTAL ZIP CODE ZONES
CHICAGO
Illinois
606+ TWO DIGITS SHOWN = ZIP CODE

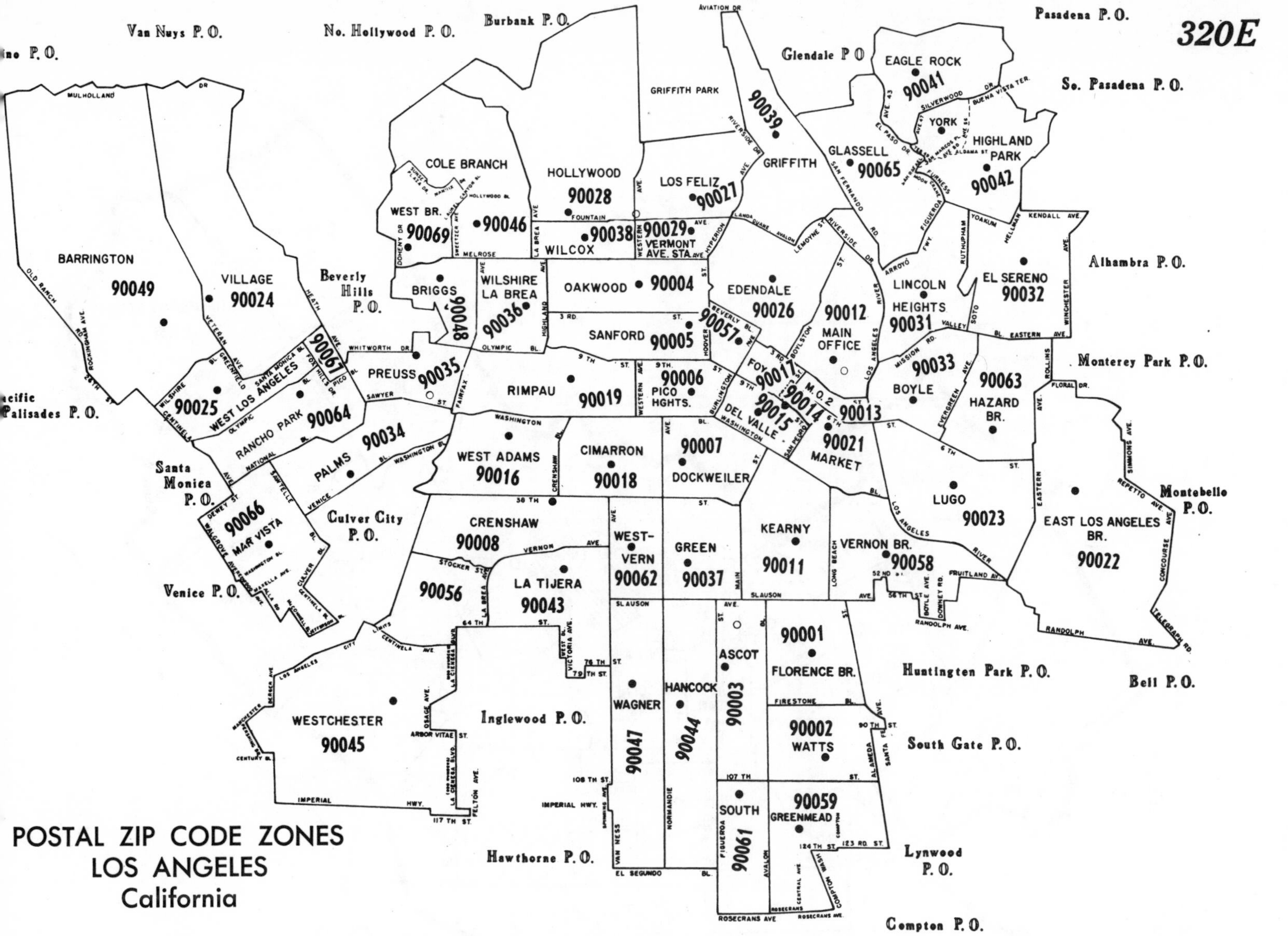

POSTAL ZIP CODE ZONES
LOS ANGELES
California

Van Nuys P.O.   No. Hollywood P.O.   Burbank P.O.   Pasadena P.O.

...no P.O.   Glendale P O   EAGLE ROCK 90041   So. Pasadena P.O.

GRIFFITH PARK   90039   YORK   HIGHLAND PARK

COLE BRANCH   HOLLYWOOD 90028   LOS FELIZ   GRIFFITH   GLASSELL 90065   90042

WEST BR. 90069   90046   90038 WILCOX   90027   90029 VERMONT AVE. STA.   Alhambra P.O.

BARRINGTON 90049   VILLAGE 90024   Beverly Hills P.O.   BRIGGS   WILSHIRE LA BREA   OAKWOOD 90004   EDENDALE 90026   LINCOLN HEIGHTS 90031   EL SERENO 90032

90068   90036   SANFORD 90005   90057   90012 MAIN OFFICE   90033 BOYLE   Monterey Park P.O.

90061   PREUSS 90035   RIMPAU   90019   90006 PICO HGHTS.   90017   M.O.2 90014   90013   90063 HAZARD BR.

Pacific Palisades P.O.   90025   WEST LOS ANGELES   90064   RANCHO PARK   90034   DEL VALLE 90015   90021 MARKET

Santa Monica P.O.   90066 MAR VISTA   PALMS   Culver City P.O.   WEST ADAMS 90016   CIMARRON 90018   90007 DOCKWEILER   LUGO 90023   EAST LOS ANGELES BR. 90022   Montebello P.O.

Venice P.O.   CRENSHAW 90008   90056   LA TIJERA 90043   WEST-VERN 90062   GREEN 90037   KEARNY 90011   VERNON BR. 90058

WESTCHESTER 90045   Inglewood P.O.   WAGNER 90047   HANCOCK 90044   ASCOT 90003   90001 FLORENCE BR.   Huntington Park P.O.   Bell P.O.

90002 WATTS   South Gate P.O.

SOUTH 90061   90059 GREENMEAD   Lynwood P.O.

Hawthorne P.O.   Compton P.O.

POSTAL ZIP CODE ZONES
NO. HOLLYWOOD
California

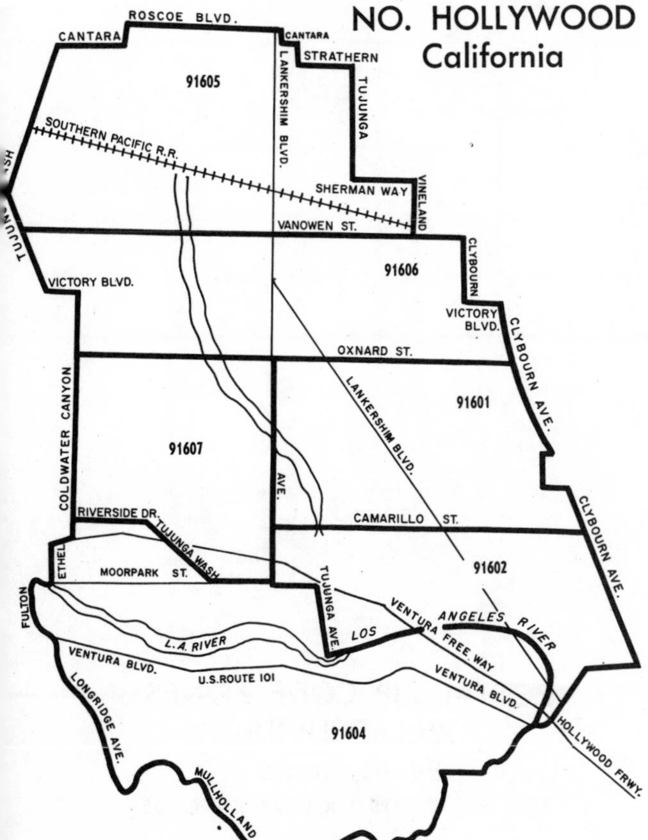

91605   91606   91601   91607   91602   91604

ROSCOE BLVD.   CANTARA   STRATHERN   SOUTHERN PACIFIC R.R.   SHERMAN WAY   VANOWEN ST.   VICTORY BLVD.   OXNARD ST.   CAMARILLO ST.   MOORPARK ST.   VENTURA BLVD.   U.S. ROUTE 101   MULHOLLAND DR.

POSTAL ZIP CODE ZONES
SANTA MONICA
California

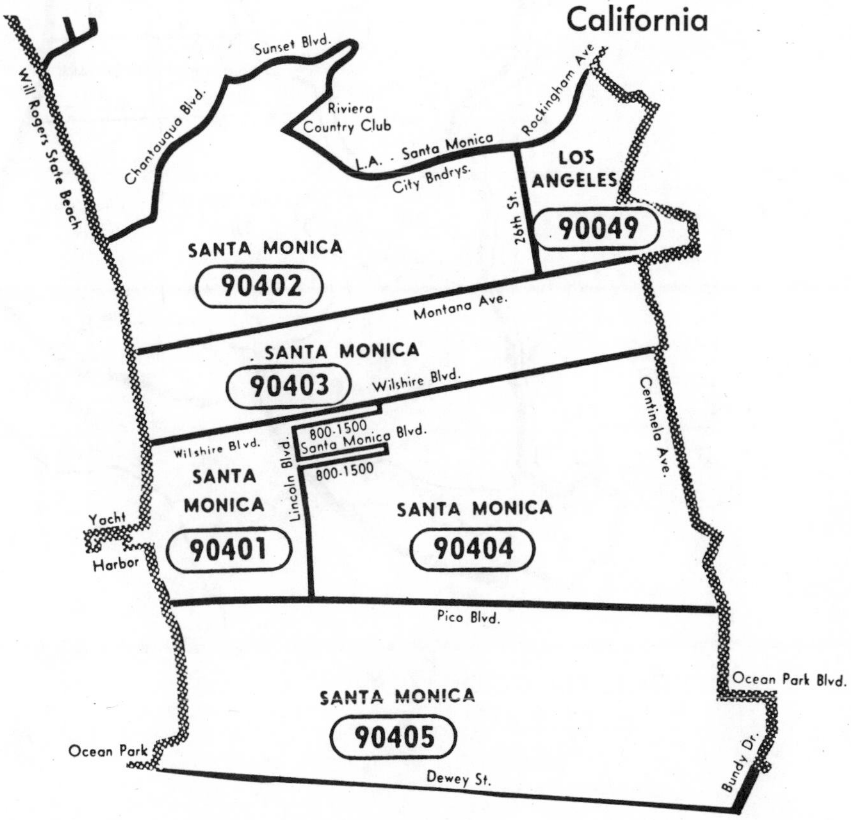

Sunset Blvd.   Riviera Country Club   L.A. - Santa Monica City Bndrys.   LOS ANGELES 90049

SANTA MONICA 90402   Montana Ave.

SANTA MONICA 90403   Wilshire Blvd.

SANTA MONICA 90401   SANTA MONICA 90404   Pico Blvd.

SANTA MONICA 90405   Ocean Park Blvd.   Dewey St.

FOR REMAINING PORTIONS OF LOS ANGELES AREA CONTACT YOUR LOCAL POST OFFICE FOR INFORMATION

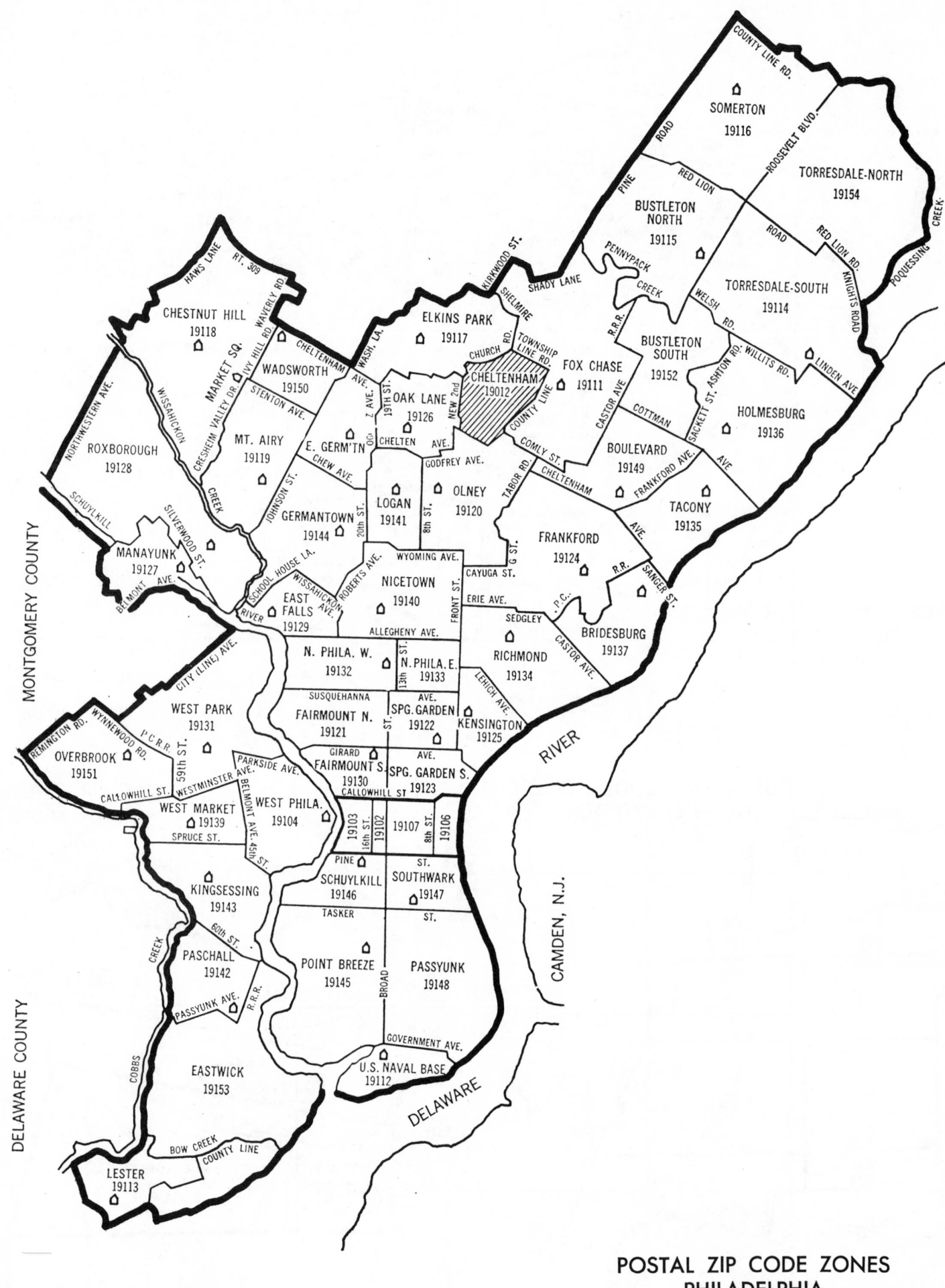

POSTAL ZIP CODE ZONES
PHILADELPHIA
Pennsylvania
191+ TWO DIGITS SHOWN = ZIP CODE

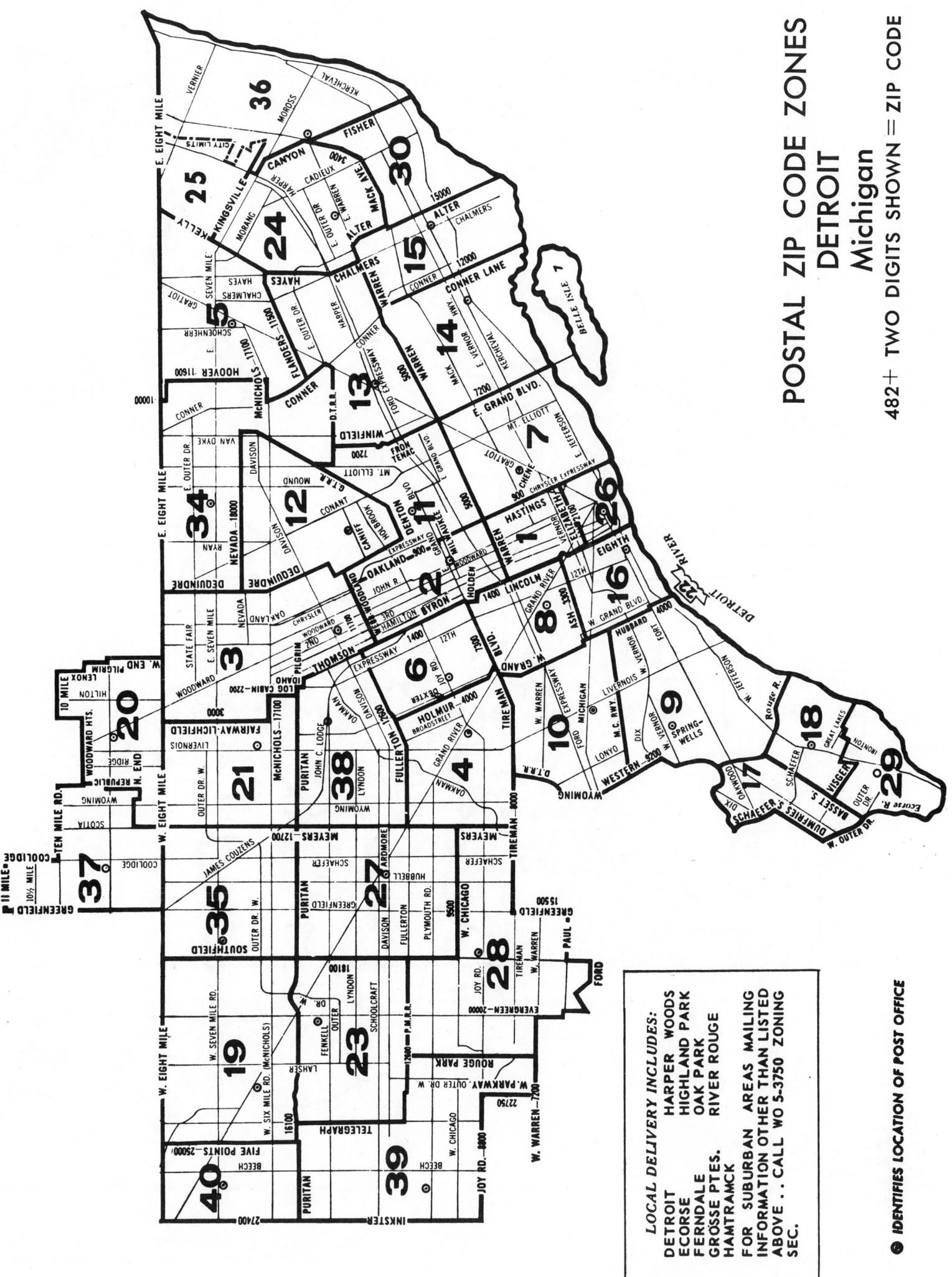

320G

POSTAL ZIP CODE ZONES
DETROIT
Michigan

482+ TWO DIGITS SHOWN = ZIP CODE

LOCAL DELIVERY INCLUDES:

DETROIT	HARPER WOODS
ECORSE	HIGHLAND PARK
FERNDALE	OAK PARK
GRÖSSE PTES.	RIVER ROUGE
HAMTRAMCK	

FOR SUBURBAN AREAS MAILING
INFORMATION OTHER THAN LISTED
ABOVE .. CALL WO 5-3750 ZONING
SEC.

● IDENTIFIES LOCATION OF POST OFFICE

POSTAL ZIP CODE ZONES
HOUSTON
Texas
770 + TWO DIGITS SHOWN = ZIP CODE

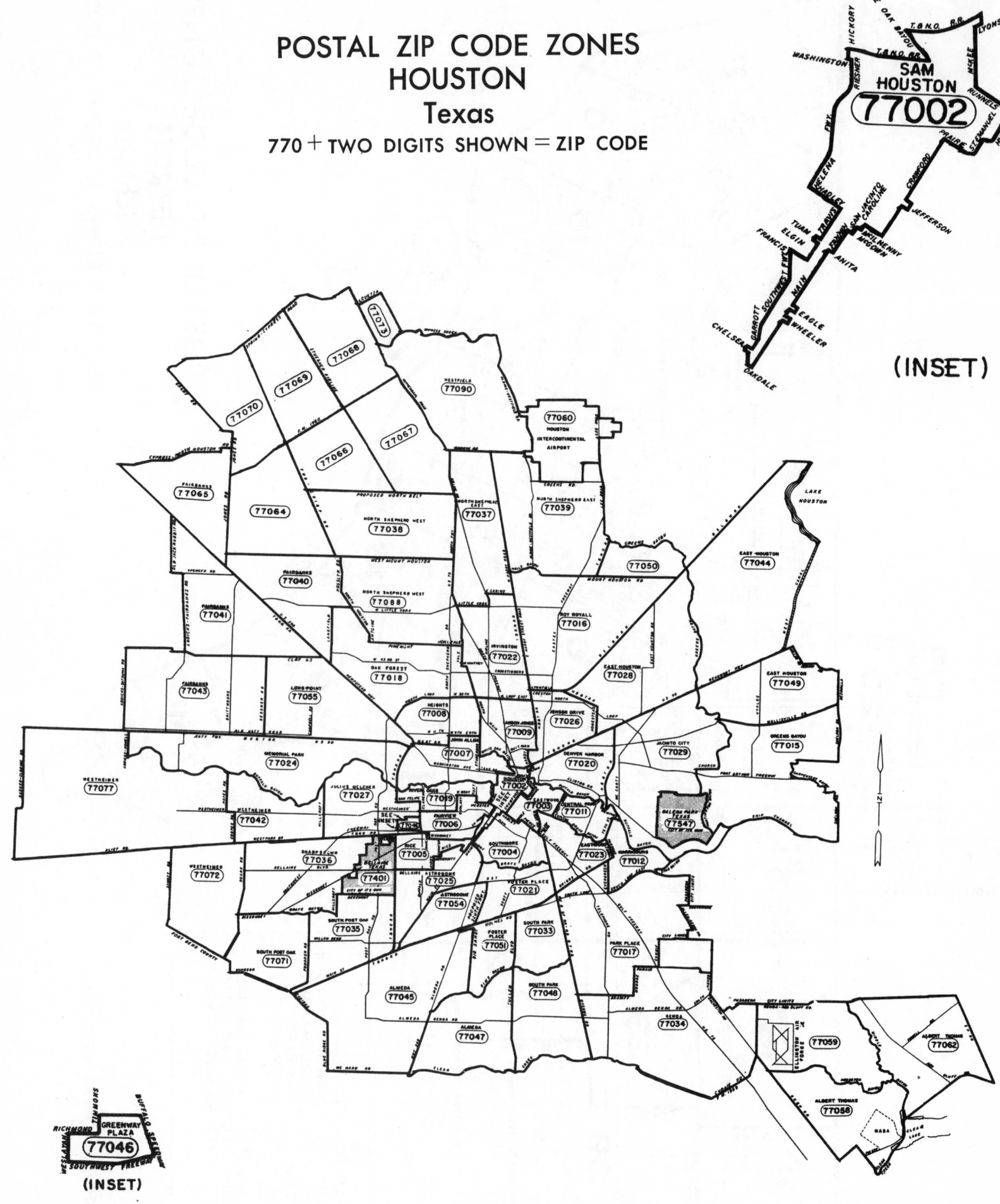

(INSET)

(INSET)

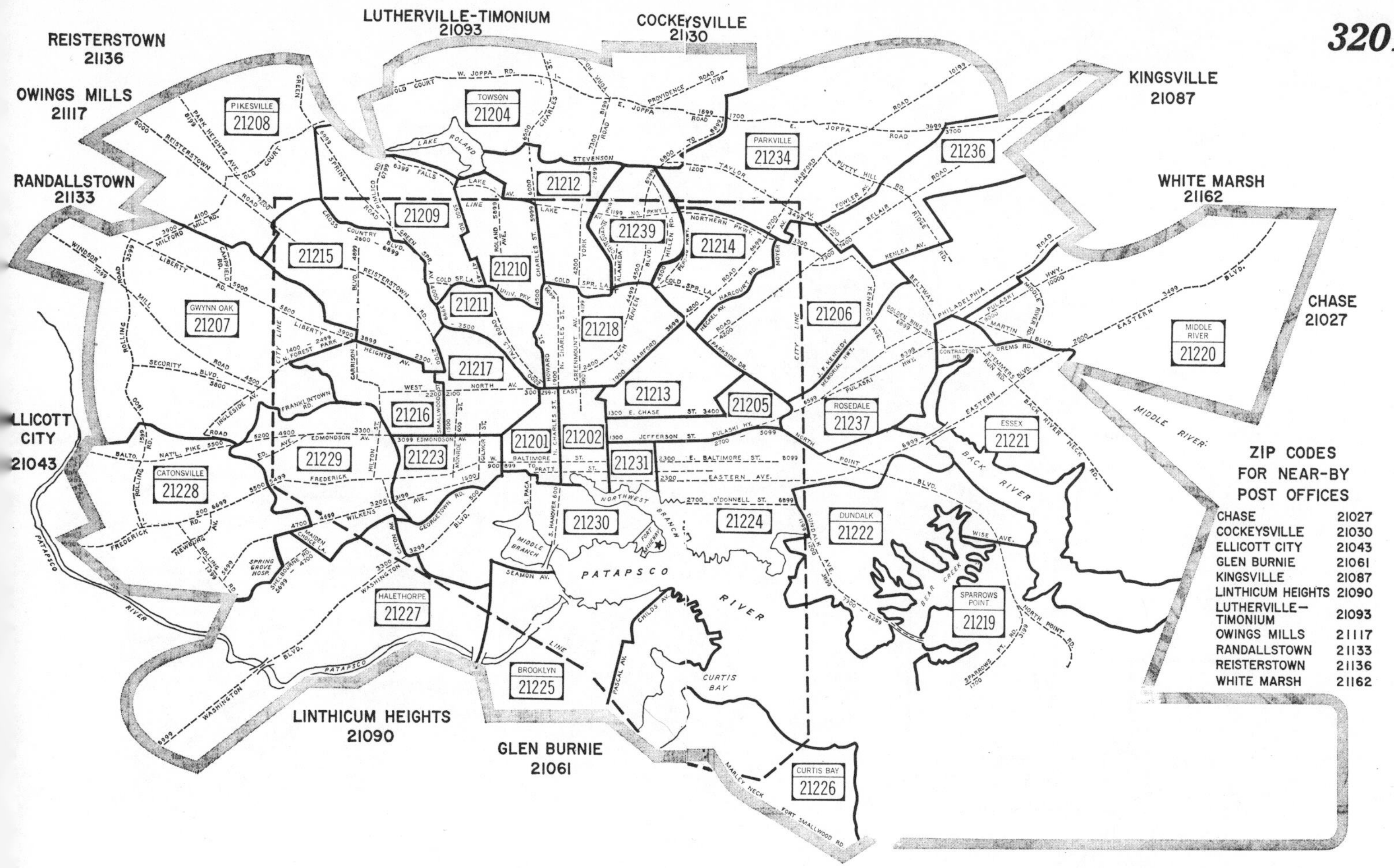

POSTAL ZIP CODE ZONES
BALTIMORE
Maryland

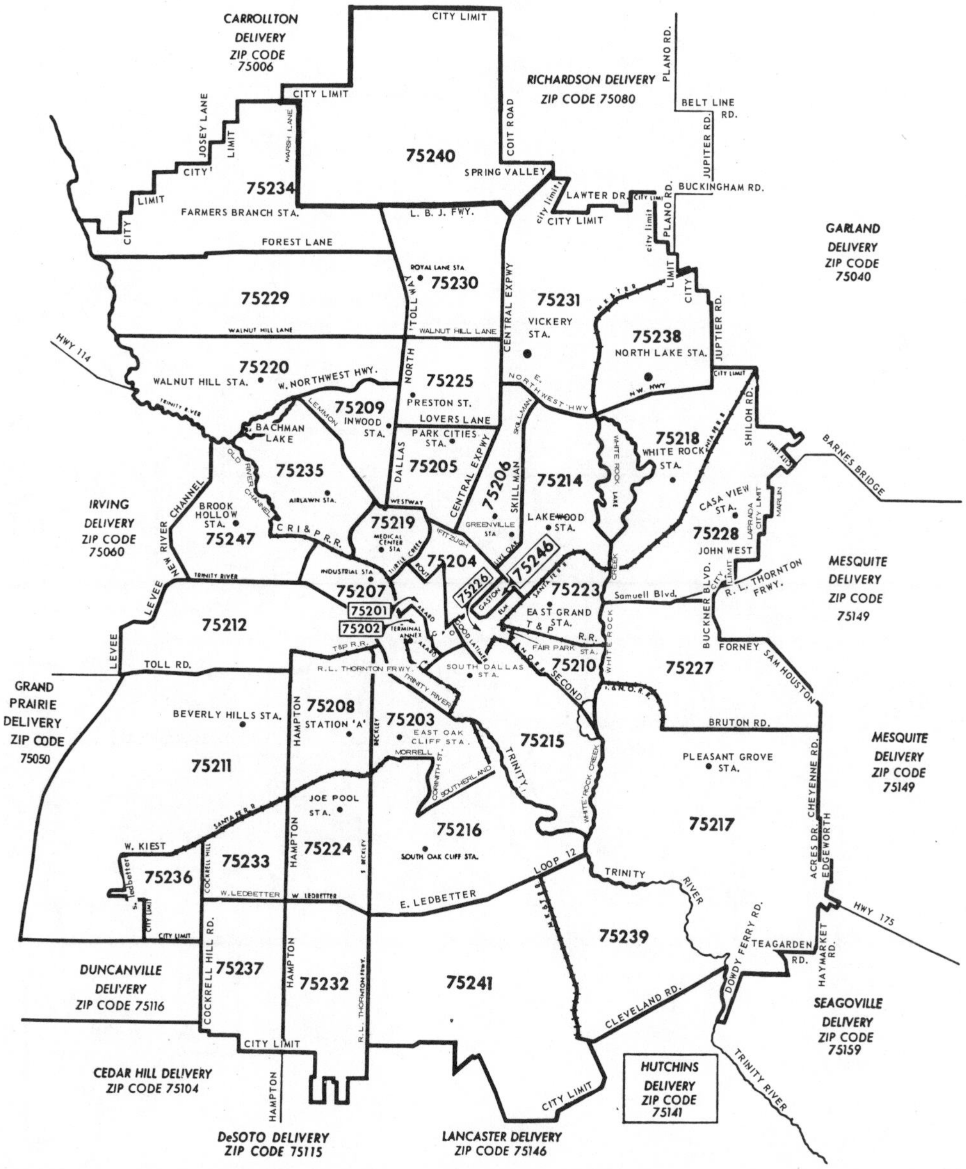

REISTERSTOWN 21136

OWINGS MILLS 21117

RANDALLSTOWN 21133

ELLICOTT CITY 21043

LUTHERVILLE-TIMONIUM 21093

COCKEYSVILLE 21130

KINGSVILLE 21087

WHITE MARSH 21162

CHASE 21027

PIKESVILLE 21208
TOWSON 21204
PARKVILLE 21234
21236
MIDDLE RIVER 21220
21212
21209
21215
21210
21239
21214
GWYNN OAK 21207
21211
21218
21206
CATONSVILLE 21228
21217
21213
21205
ROSEDALE 21237
ESSEX 21221
21216
21201
21202
21231
21229
21223
21230
21224
DUNDALK 21222
HALETHORPE 21227
SPARROWS POINT 21219
BROOKLYN 21225
CURTIS BAY 21226

LINTHICUM HEIGHTS 21090

GLEN BURNIE 21061

ZIP CODES FOR NEAR-BY POST OFFICES

CHASE	21027
COCKEYSVILLE	21030
ELLICOTT CITY	21043
GLEN BURNIE	21061
KINGSVILLE	21087
LINTHICUM HEIGHTS	21090
LUTHERVILLE–TIMONIUM	21093
OWINGS MILLS	21117
RANDALLSTOWN	21133
REISTERSTOWN	21136
WHITE MARSH	21162

POSTAL ZIP CODE ZONES
DALLAS
Texas

CARROLLTON DELIVERY ZIP CODE 75006

RICHARDSON DELIVERY ZIP CODE 75080

GARLAND DELIVERY ZIP CODE 75040

75240
75234
75229
75230
75231
75238
75220
75225
75209
75235
75205
75206
75214
75218
75247
75219
75228
75204
75248
75207
75226
75223
75201
75202
75210
75227
75212
75208
75203
75215
75211
75224
75216
75217
75233
75236
75237
75232
75241
75239

IRVING DELIVERY ZIP CODE 75060

GRAND PRAIRIE DELIVERY ZIP CODE 75050

MESQUITE DELIVERY ZIP CODE 75149

DUNCANVILLE DELIVERY ZIP CODE 75116

CEDAR HILL DELIVERY ZIP CODE 75104

DeSOTO DELIVERY ZIP CODE 75115

LANCASTER DELIVERY ZIP CODE 75146

HUTCHINS DELIVERY ZIP CODE 75141

SEAGOVILLE DELIVERY ZIP CODE 75159

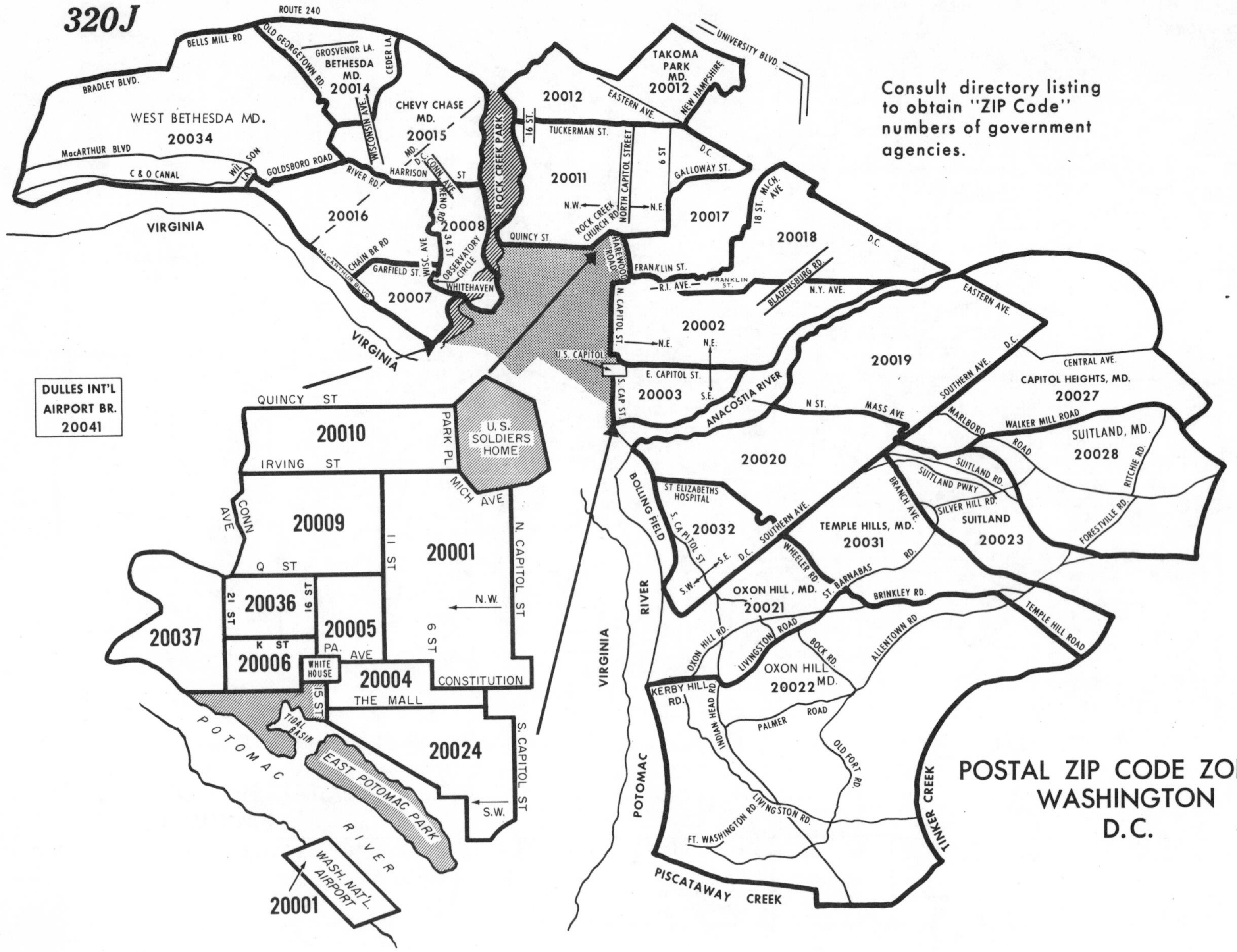

320J

POSTAL ZIP CODE ZONES WASHINGTON D.C.

Consult directory listing to obtain "ZIP Code" numbers of government agencies.

ROUTE 240
BELLS MILL RD
OLD GEORGETOWN RD.
GROSVENOR LA.
CEDER LA.
BRADLEY BLVD.
BETHESDA MD. 20014
UNIVERSITY BLVD.
TAKOMA PARK MD. 20012
WEST BETHESDA MD. 20034
CHEVY CHASE MD. 20015
NEW HAMPSHIRE
20012
EASTERN AVE.
MacARTHUR BLVD
WISCONSIN AVE.
TUCKERMAN ST.
16 ST
WILSON
GOLDSBORO ROAD
HARRISON
CONN ST
D.C.
20011
6 ST
GALLOWAY ST.
D.C.
C & O CANAL
RIVER RD.
ROCK CREEK PARK
N.W.
N.E.
20017
18 ST
MICH. AVE
VIRGINIA
20016
RENO RD.
34 ST.
20008
QUINCY ST.
ROCK CREEK CHURCH
NORTH CAPITOL STREET
20018
D.C.
CHAIN BR RD
OBSERVATORY CIRCLE
FRANKLIN ST.
FRANKLIN ST.
N.Y. AVE.
GARFIELD ST.
WISC. AVE.
R.I. AVE.
BLADENSBURG RD.
EASTERN AVE.
20007
WHITEHAVEN
20002
N.E.
N.E.
CENTRAL AVE.
VIRGINIA
U.S. CAPITOL
20003
E. CAPITOL ST.
S.E.
20019
D.C.
CAPITOL HEIGHTS, MD. 20027
DULLES INT'L AIRPORT BR. 20041
QUINCY ST.
PARK PL
MICH. AVE
ANACOSTIA RIVER
N ST.
SOUTHERN AVE.
WALKER MILL ROAD
SUITLAND, MD. 20028
RITCHIE RD.
20010
U.S. SOLDIERS HOME
MASS AVE
MARLBORO
SUITLAND RD.
IRVING ST
S. CAPITOL ST.
20020
SUITLAND PWKY
SILVER HILL RD.
FORESTVILLE RD.
CONN AVE
20009
Q ST
II ST
20001
ST ELIZABETHS HOSPITAL
S. CAPITOL ST.
S.E. D.C.
20032
SOUTHERN AVE.
BRANCH AVE.
SUITLAND 20023
21 ST
16 ST
20036
N.W.
BOLLING FIELD
TEMPLE HILLS, MD. 20031
TEMPLE HILL ROAD
20037
20005
6 ST
WHEELER RD.
ST. BARNABAS RD.
20006
K ST
PA. AVE.
RIVER
OXON HILL, MD. 20021
BRINKLEY RD.
WHITE HOUSE
15 ST
20004
CONSTITUTION
OXON HILL RD.
LIVINGSTON ROAD
ALLENTOWN RD.
TIDAL BASIN
THE MALL
KERBY HILLS RD.
INDIAN HEAD RD.
ROCK RD
OLD FORT RD.
POTOMAC RIVER
EAST POTOMAC PARK
20024
S. CAPITOL ST.
S.W.
OXON HILL MD. 20022
PALMER ROAD
VIRGINIA
WASH. NAT'L. AIRPORT
LIVINGSTON RD.
TINKER CREEK
20001
FT. WASHINGTON RD
LIVINGSTON RD.
POTOMAC
PISCATAWAY CREEK

POSTAL ZIP CODE ZONES INDIANAPOLIS Indiana
462+ TWO DIGITS SHOWN = ZIP CODE

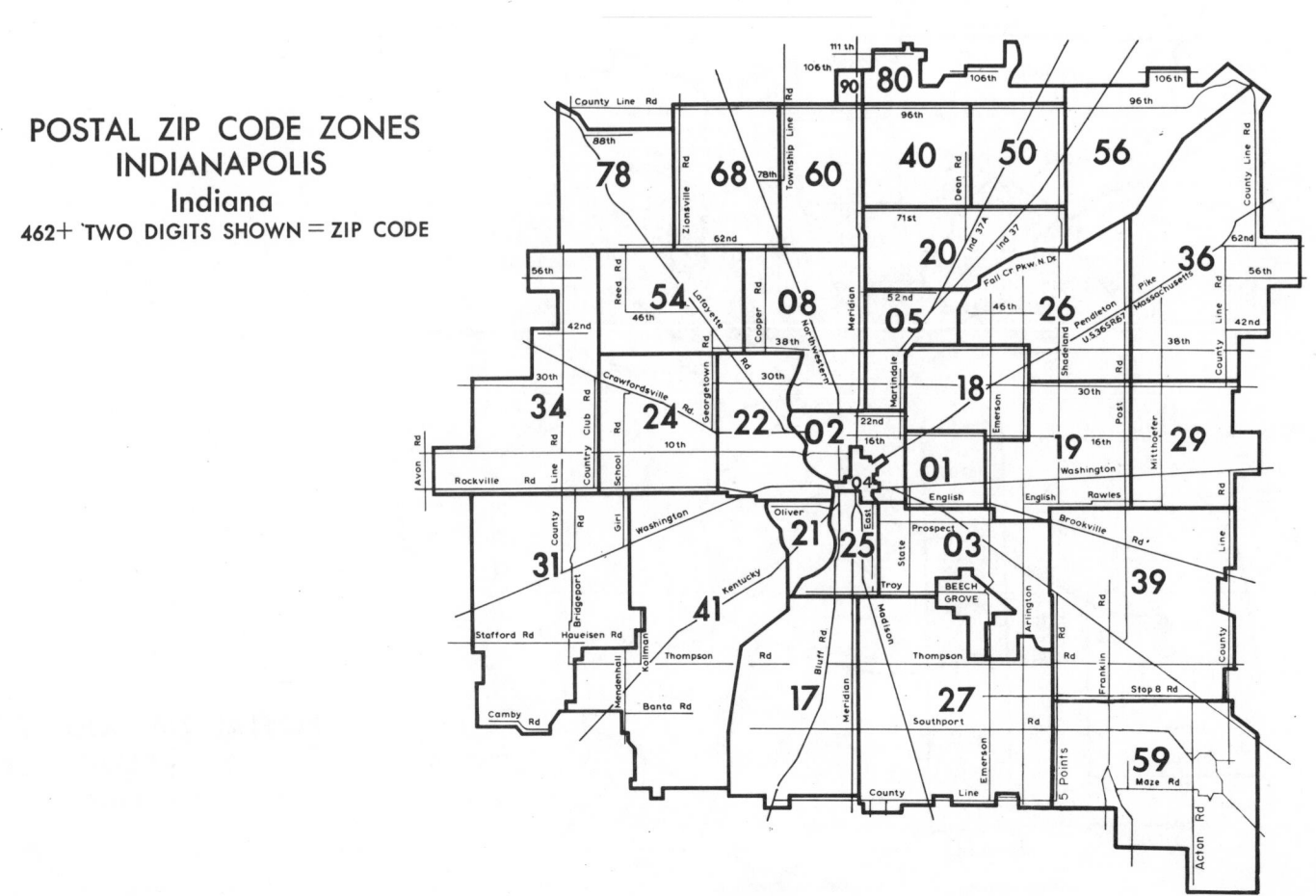

POSTAL ZIP CODE ZONES
CLEVELAND
Ohio
441+ TWO DIGITS SHOWN = ZIP CODE

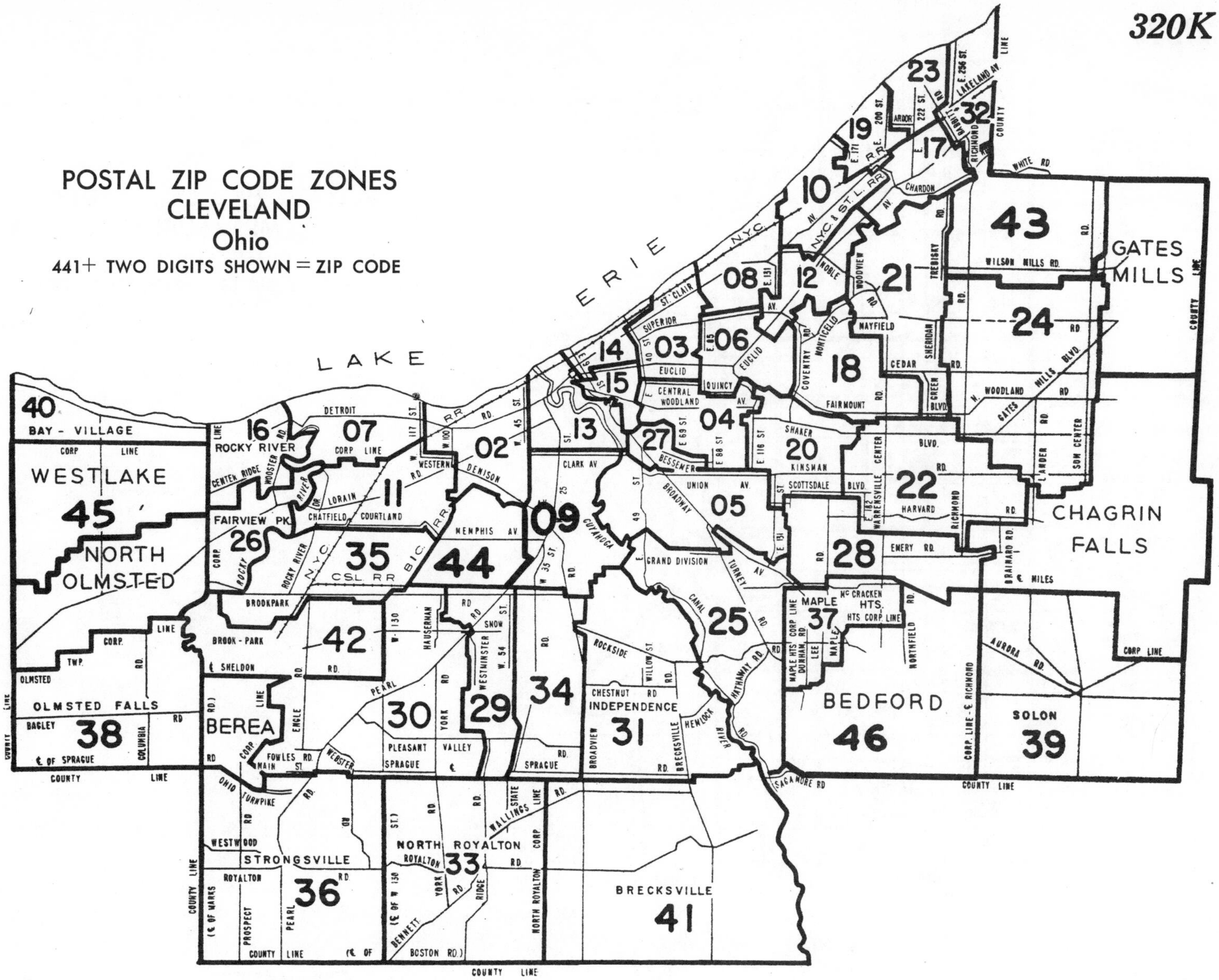

LAKE ERIE

LAKE

40 BAY - VILLAGE

WESTLAKE 45

NORTH OLMSTED

16 ROCKY RIVER

07

FAIRVIEW PK. 26

OLMSTED FALLS

BAGLEY 38

BEREA

BROOKPARK

BROOK - PARK

SHELDON

42

35 CSL RR

44

11

02

13

27

09

14

15

03 06

08 12

04

05

20 KINSMAN SHAKER

18

21

43

GATES MILLS

24

22 HARVARD

28

25

37 MAPLE HTS.

BEDFORD 46

CHAGRIN FALLS

SOLON 39

30

29 34

31 INDEPENDENCE

CHESTNUT

STRONGSVILLE

36

NORTH ROYALTON 33

BRECKSVILLE 41

POSTAL ZIP CODE ZONES
SAN FRANCISCO
California

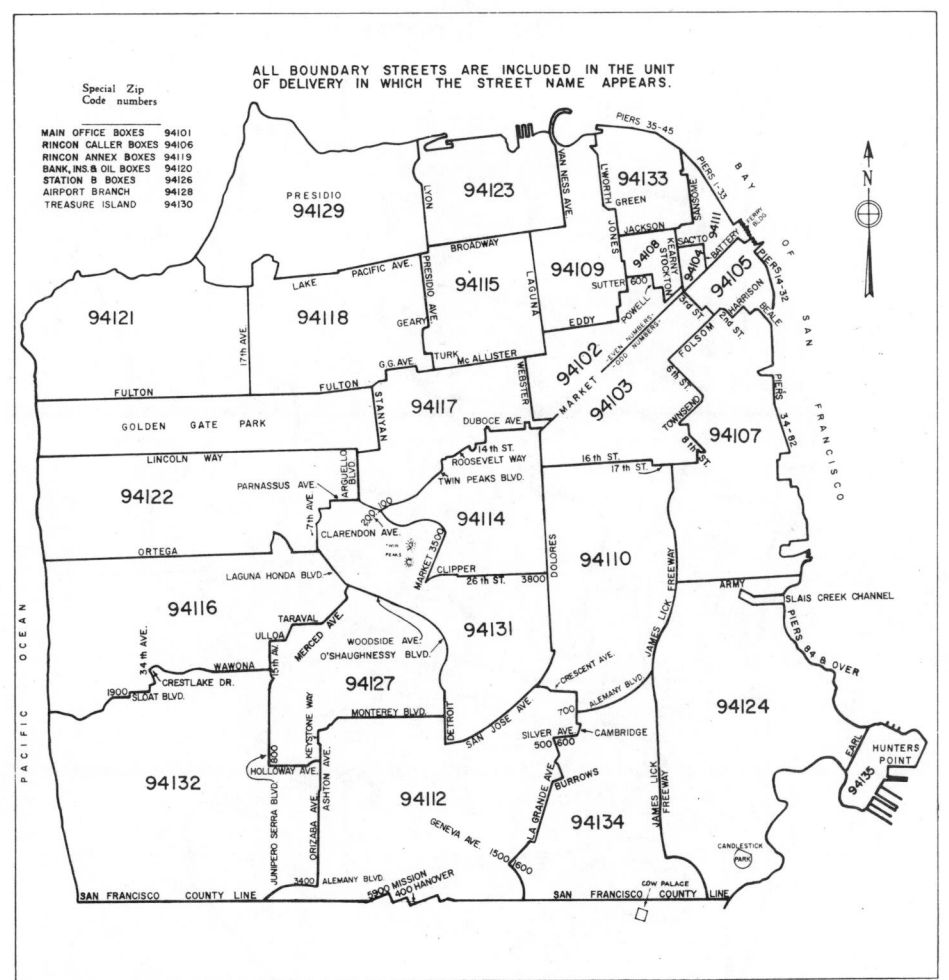

Special Zip Code numbers

MAIN OFFICE BOXES	94101
RINCON CALLER BOXES	94106
RINCON ANNEX BOXES	94119
BANK, INS.& OIL BOXES	94120
STATION B BOXES	94126
AIRPORT BRANCH	94128
TREASURE ISLAND	94130

ALL BOUNDARY STREETS ARE INCLUDED IN THE UNIT OF DELIVERY IN WHICH THE STREET NAME APPEARS.

PRESIDIO

94129

94123

94133

94121

94118

94115

94109

94108 94111 94104 94105

94102

94103

94107

94117

94122

94116

94114

94110

94131

94127

94132

94112

94134

94124

94135 HUNTERS POINT

CANDLESTICK PARK

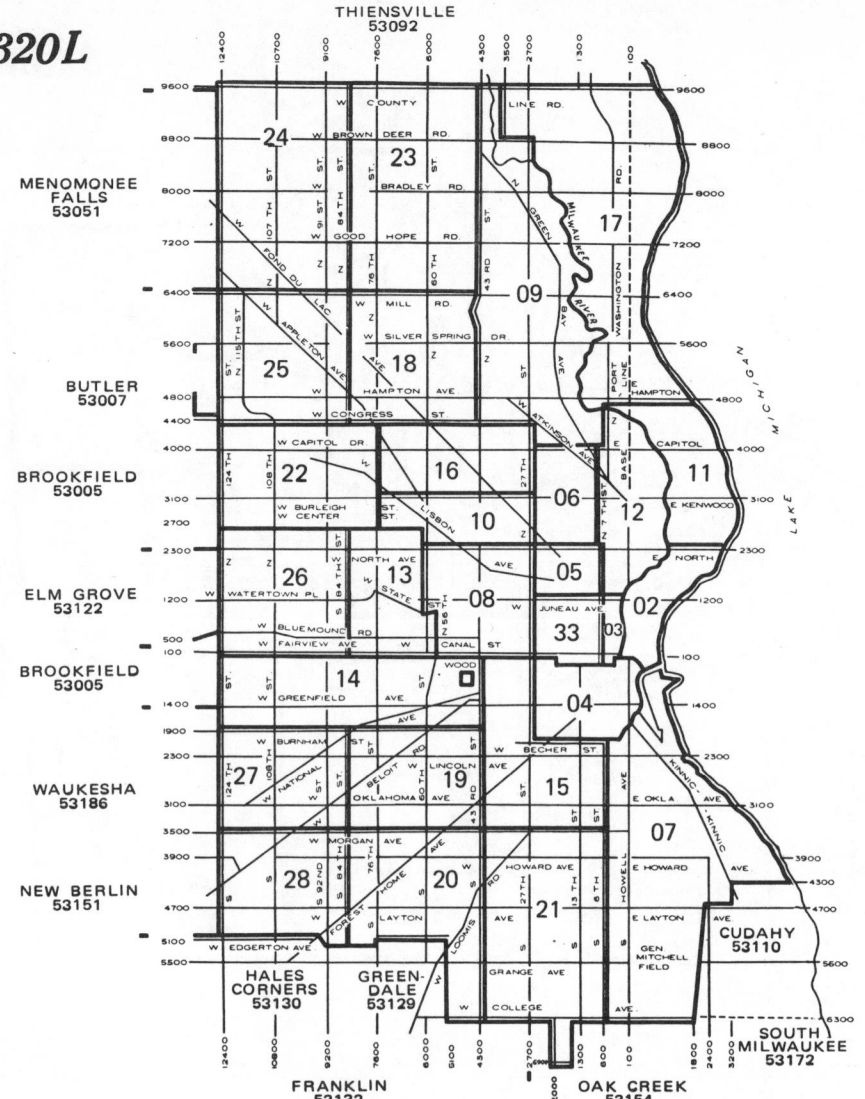

POSTAL ZIP CODE ZONES
MILWAUKEE
Wisconsin
532+ TWO DIGITS SHOWN = ZIP CODE

POSTAL ZIP CODE ZONES
SAN DIEGO
California

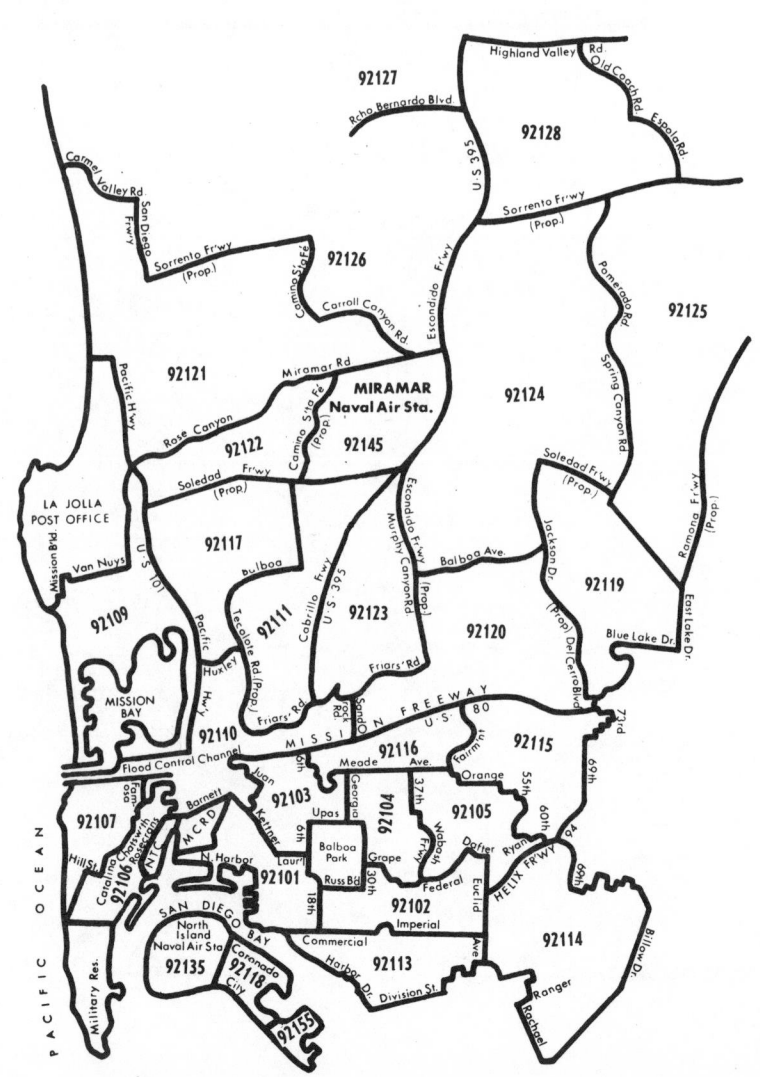

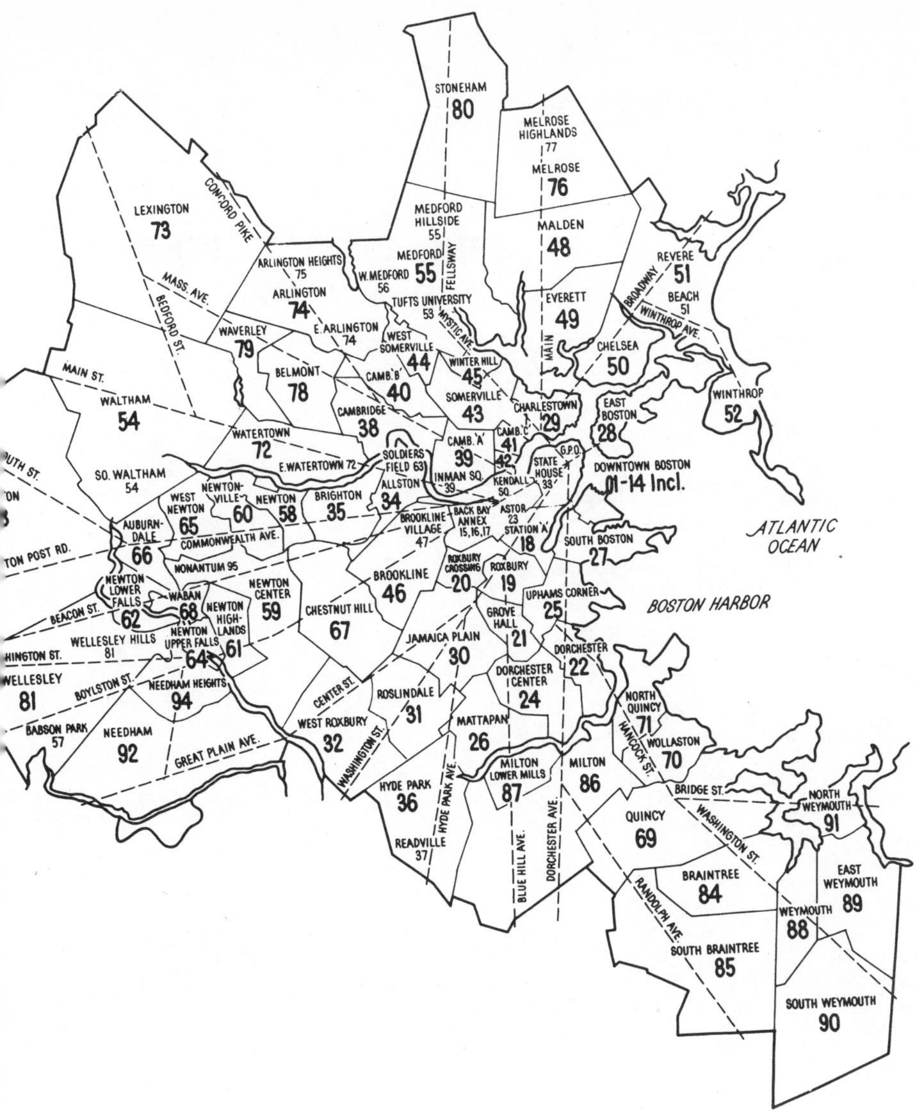

POSTAL ZIP CODE ZONES
BOSTON
Massachusetts
021+ TWO DIGITS SHOWN = ZIP CODE

ATLANTIC OCEAN

BOSTON HARBOR

STONEHAM 80

MELROSE HIGHLANDS 77

MELROSE 76

MEDFORD HILLSIDE 55

MALDEN 48

LEXINGTON 73

ARLINGTON HEIGHTS 75

ARLINGTON 74

W. MEDFORD 55

MEDFORD 55

EVERETT 49

REVERE 51

BEACH 51

CHELSEA 50

WINTHROP 52

EAST BOSTON 28

WAVERLEY 79

E. ARLINGTON 74

WEST SOMERVILLE 44

WINTER HILL 45

SOMERVILLE 43

CHARLESTOWN 29

BELMONT 78

CAMB. "B" 40

CAMBRIDGE 38

WALTHAM 54

SO. WALTHAM 54

WATERTOWN 72

E. WATERTOWN 72

CAMB. "A" 39

SOLDIERS FIELD 63

INMAN SQ. 39

ALLSTON 34

KENDALL 42

STATE HOUSE 33

DOWNTOWN BOSTON 01-14 Incl.

WEST NEWTON 65

NEWTONVILLE 60

NEWTON 58

BRIGHTON 35

BACK BAY ANNEX 15,16,17

ASTOR STATION "A" 23

SOUTH BOSTON 27

AUBURNDALE 66

NONANTUM 95

BROOKLINE VILLAGE 47

ROXBURY CROSSING 20

ROXBURY 19

UPHAMS CORNER 25

NEWTON LOWER FALLS 62

WABAN 68

NEWTON HIGHLANDS

NEWTON CENTER 59

CHESTNUT HILL 67

BROOKLINE 46

GROVE HALL 21

DORCHESTER 22

WELLESLEY HILLS 81

NEWTON UPPER FALLS 61

64

JAMAICA PLAIN 30

DORCHESTER CENTER 24

NORTH QUINCY 71

WOLLASTON 70

WELLESLEY 81

NEEDHAM HEIGHTS 94

CENTER ST.

ROSLINDALE 31

MATTAPAN 26

MILTON LOWER MILLS 87

MILTON 86

NORTH WEYMOUTH 91

BABSON PARK 57

NEEDHAM 92

WEST ROXBURY 32

HYDE PARK 36

QUINCY 69

EAST WEYMOUTH 89

READVILLE 37

BRAINTREE 84

WEYMOUTH 88

SOUTH BRAINTREE 85

SOUTH WEYMOUTH 90

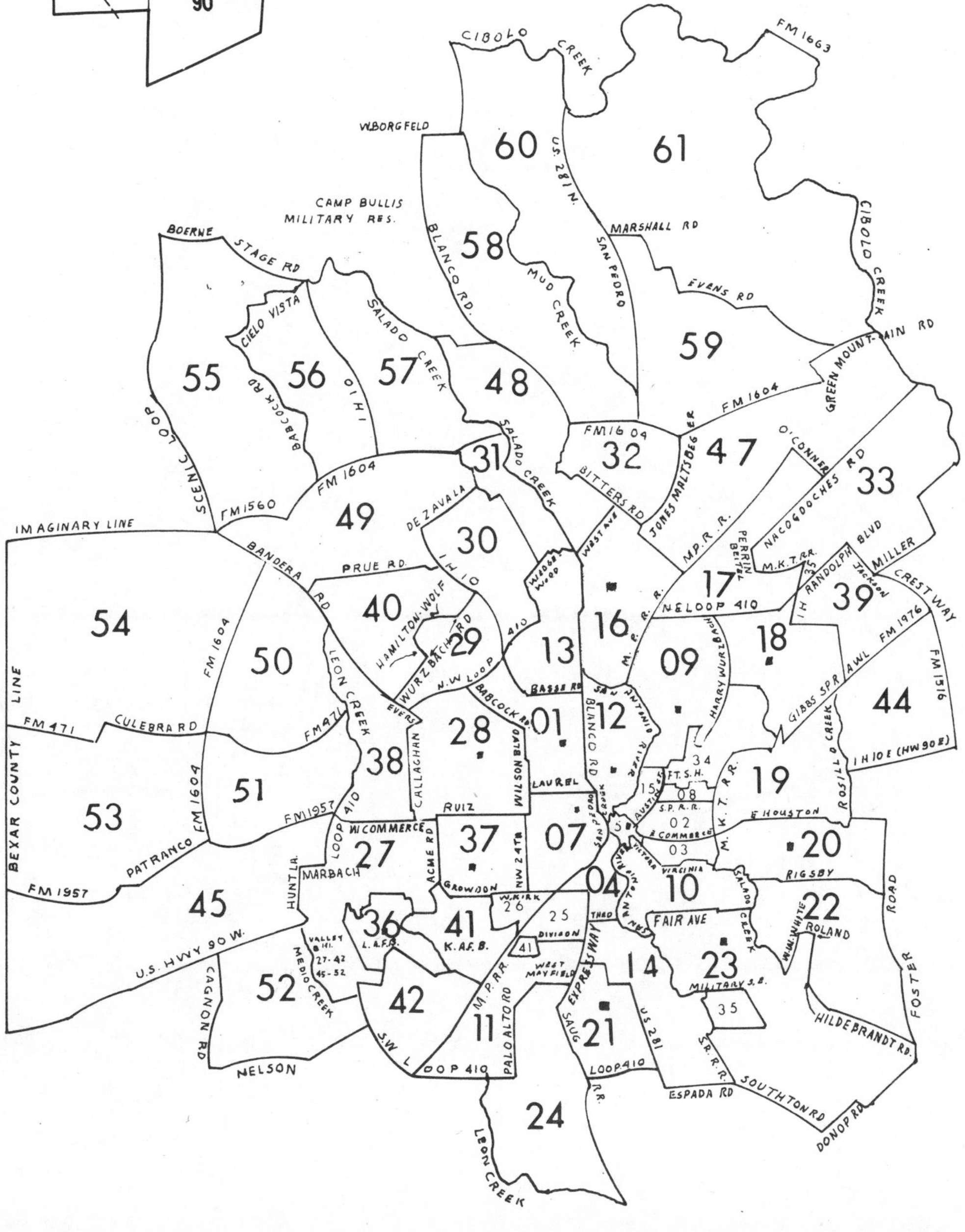

POSTAL ZIP CODE ZONES
SAN ANTONIO
Texas
782+ TWO DIGITS SHOWN = ZIP CODE

CIBOLO CREEK   FM 1663

VBORGFELD

60   61

CAMP BULLIS MILITARY RES.

58   59

BOERNE   STAGE RD

CIELO VISTA

55 56 57 48 32 47 33

31

49 30

54 50 40 29 16 17 39 18

13 09 44

28 01 12

38 27 37 07 19

51 53 45 36 41 04 10 20 22

52 42 11 14 21 23 24

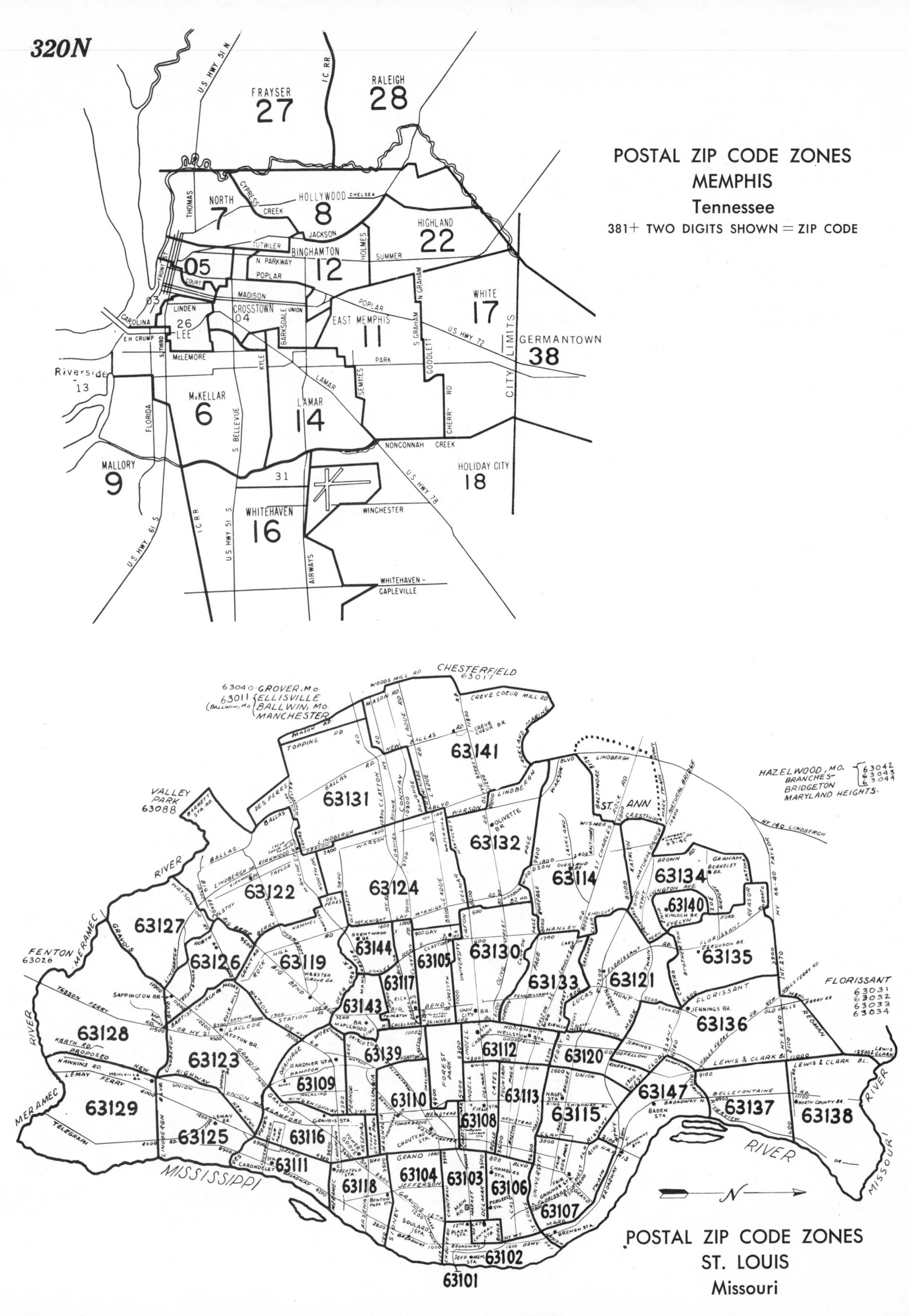

POSTAL ZIP CODE ZONES
MEMPHIS
Tennessee
381+ TWO DIGITS SHOWN = ZIP CODE

FRAYSER 27
RALEIGH 28
NORTH 7
HOLLYWOOD 8
HIGHLAND 22
05
BINGHAMTON 12
WHITE 17
03
CROSSTOWN 04
GERMANTOWN 38
LEE 26
EAST MEMPHIS 11
Riverside 13
McKELLAR 6
LAMAR 14
MALLORY 9
31
HOLIDAY CITY 18
WHITEHAVEN 16
WHITEHAVEN – CAPLEVILLE

POSTAL ZIP CODE ZONES
ST. LOUIS
Missouri

CHESTERFIELD 63017
63040 GROVER, MO.
63011 ELLISVILLE
BALLWIN, MO.
(BALLWIN, MO.)
MANCHESTER
63141
63131
HAZELWOOD, MO. 63042 63043 63044
BRANCHES–
BRIDGETON
MARYLAND HEIGHTS
VALLEY PARK 63088
63132
63114
63134
63140
63122
63124
63127
63126 63119 63144 63105 63130 63133 63121 63135
FENTON 63026
63117
63143
63136
FLORISSANT 63031 63032 63033 63034
63128 63123 63139 63112 63120
63129 63109 63110 63113 63115 63147 63137 63138
63125 63116 63108
63111 63104 63103 63106
63118 63107
63102
63101

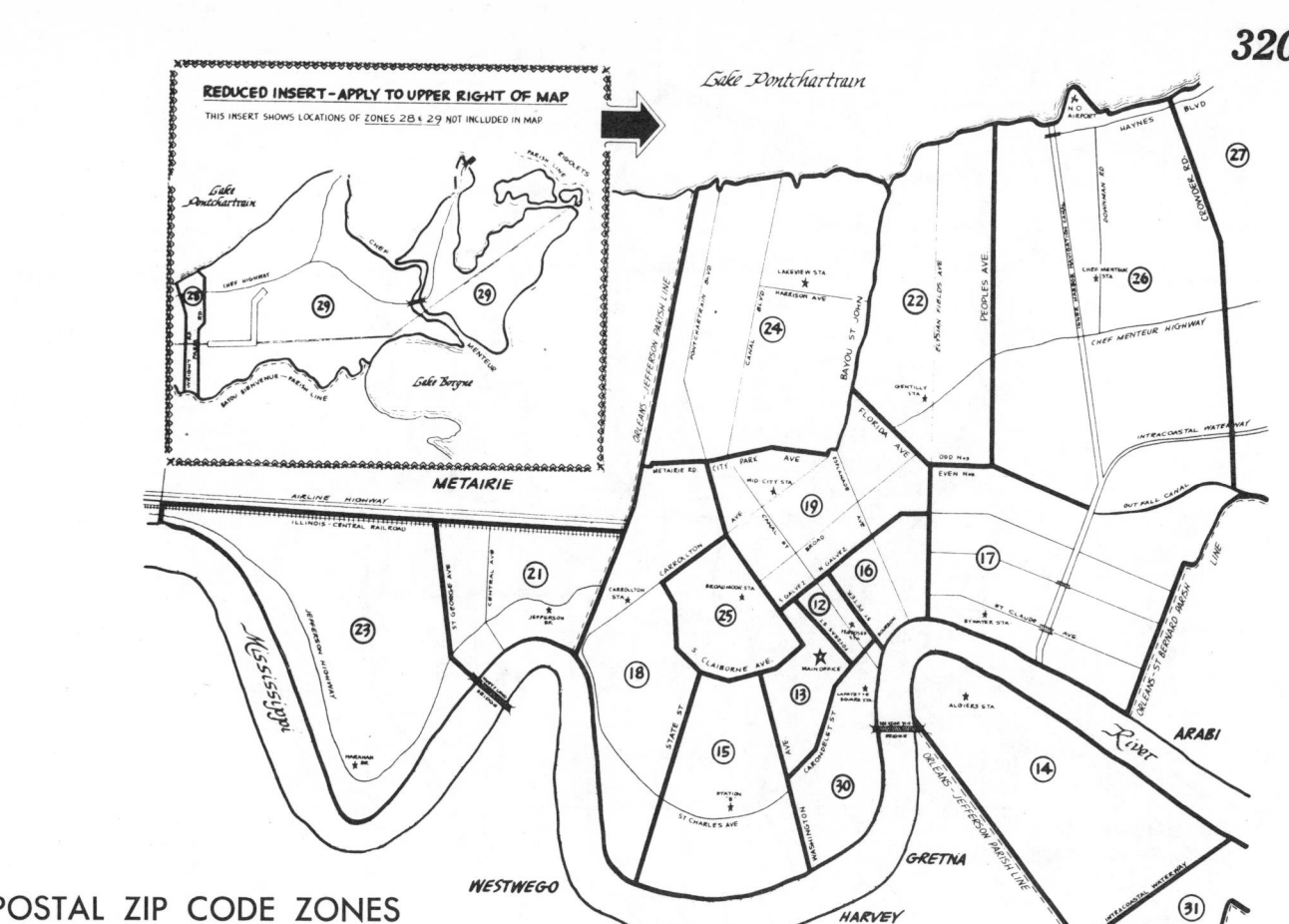

POSTAL ZIP CODE ZONES
NEW ORLEANS
Louisiana
701+ TWO DIGITS SHOWN = ZIP CODE

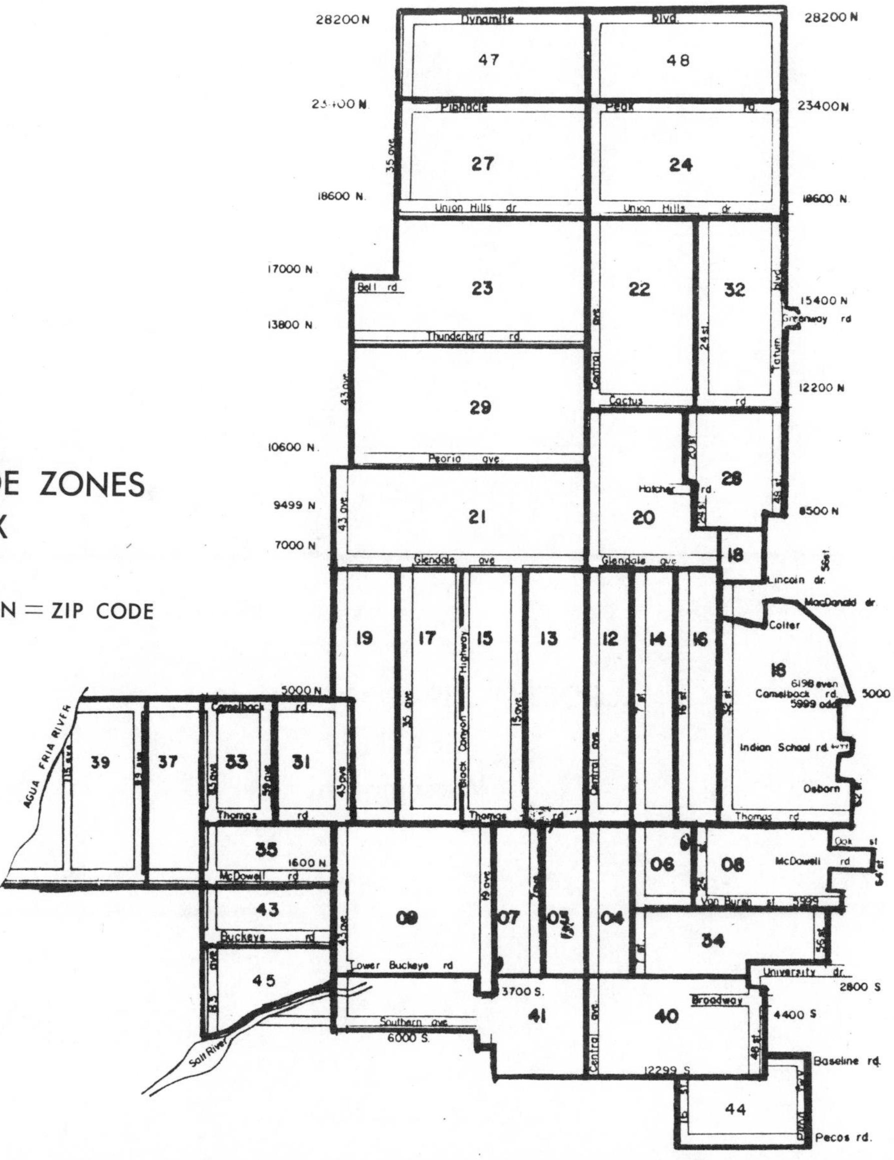

POSTAL ZIP CODE ZONES
PHOENIX
Arizona
850+ TWO DIGITS SHOWN = ZIP CODE

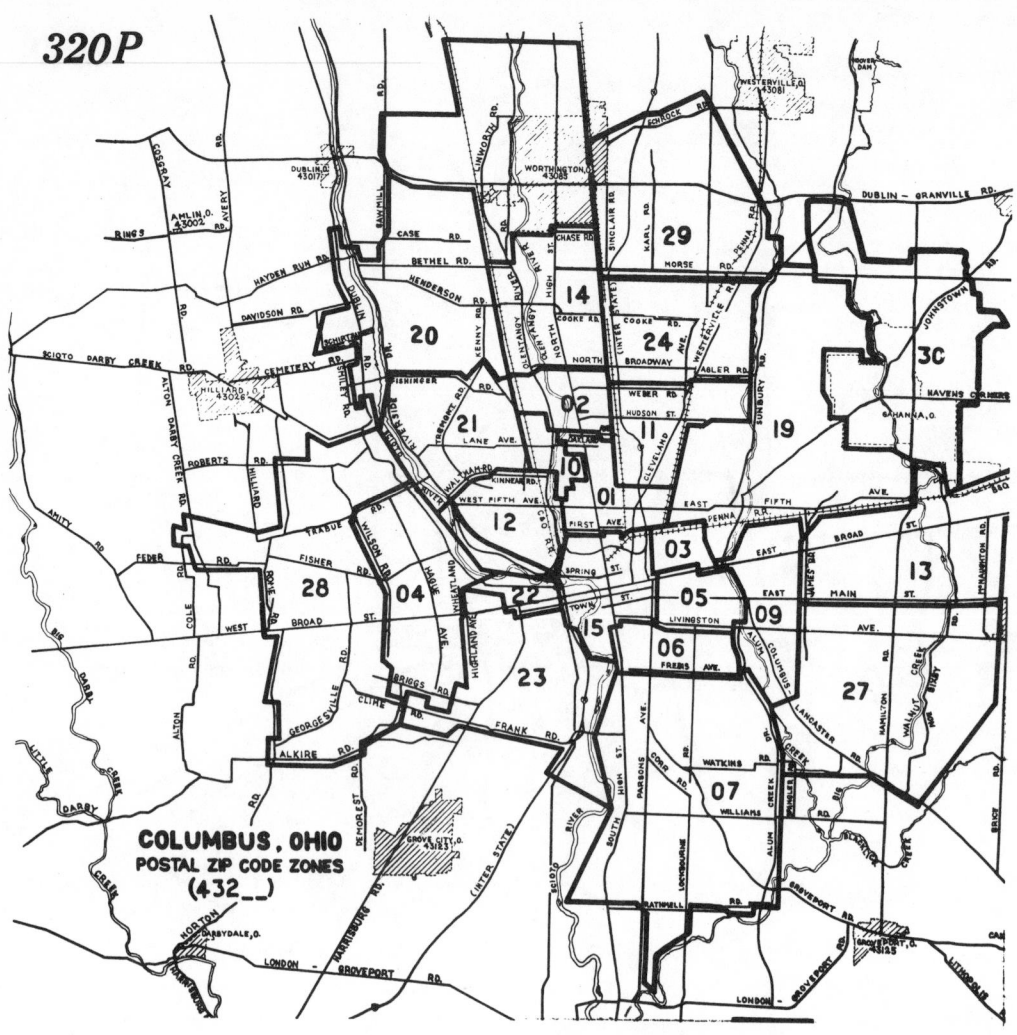

POSTAL ZIP CODE ZONES
COLUMBUS
Ohio
432+ TWO DIGITS SHOWN = ZIP CODE

COLUMBUS, OHIO
POSTAL ZIP CODE ZONES
(432__)

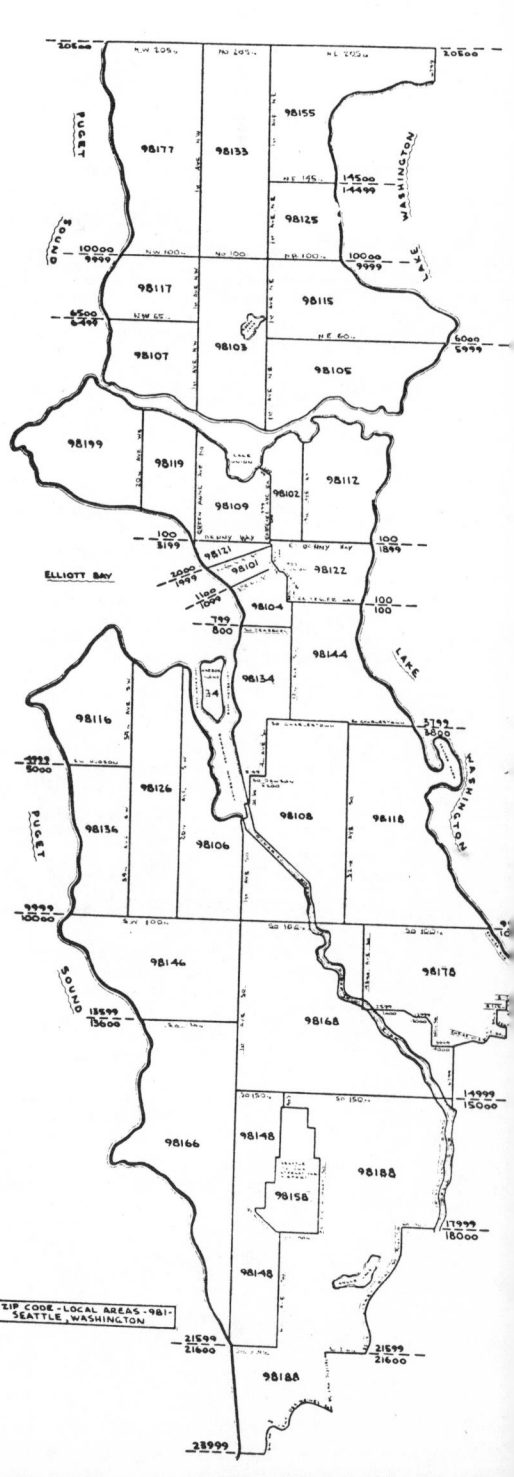

POSTAL ZIP CODE ZONES
SEATTLE
Washington

ZIP CODE - LOCAL AREAS - 981 -
SEATTLE, WASHINGTON

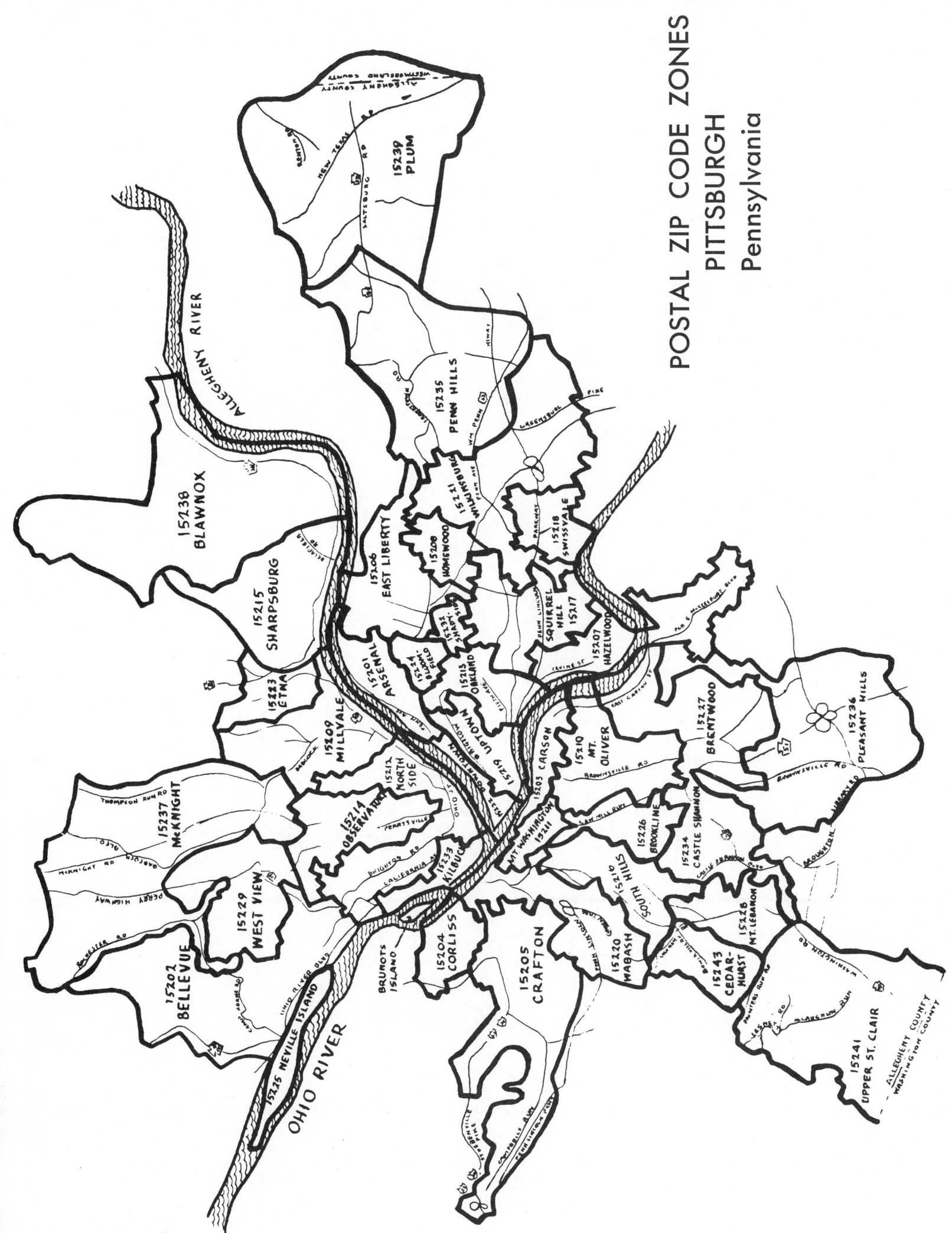

POSTAL ZIP CODE ZONES
PITTSBURGH
Pennsylvania

POSTAL ZIP CODE ZONES
DENVER
Colorado

802+ TWO DIGITS SHOWN = ZIP CODE

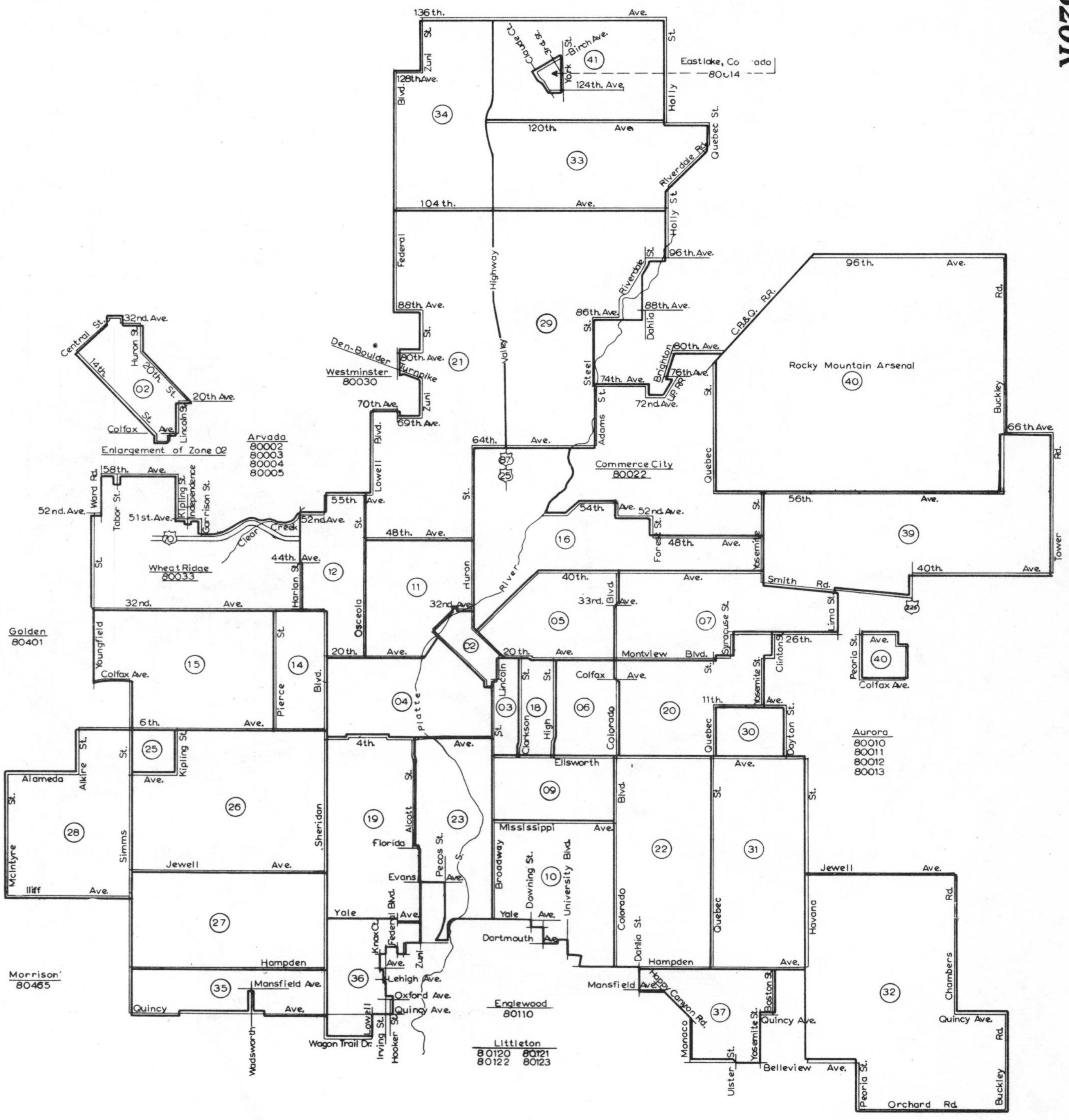

Rocky Mountain Arsenal

Aurora
80010
80011
80012
80013

Commerce City
80022

Eastlake, Colorado
80614

Westminster
80030

Den-Boulder

Arvada
80002
80003
80004
80005

Wheat Ridge
80033

Enlargement of Zone 02

Golden
80401

Morrison
80465

Englewood
80110

Littleton
80120
80121
80122
80123

Street labels (partial): Tower Rd., Buckley Rd., 96th Ave., 66th Ave., 40th, Lima St., Peoria St., Colfax Ave., Buckley Rd., Chambers, Quincy Ave., Orchard Rd., Peoria St., Belleview Ave., Quincy Ave., Boston St., Ulster St., Monaco, Havana, Jewell, Dayton St., Quebec, Hampden, Yosemite St., 11th Ave., Colorado, Dahlia St., Monsfield Ave., Happy Canyon Rd., University Blvd., Broadway, Mississippi, Downing St., Yale Ave., Dartmouth, Clarkson St., High St., Lincoln, Huron, Platte River, Pecos St., Alcott, Federal Blvd., Florida, Evans, Zuni, Lehigh Ave., Oxford Ave., Irving St., Knox Ct., Hooker St., Lowell, Wagon Trail Dr., Sheridan, Kipling St., Hampden, Mansfield Ave., Wadsworth, Jewell, Simms, Quincy, Alkire St., McIntyre St., Iliff, Alameda, 6th Ave., Youngfield, Colfax Ave., Garrison St., Independence, Kipling St., Tabor St., Ward Rd., 32nd., 44th Ave., 52nd Ave., Clear Creek, Harlan St., Osceola, 55th, Lowell Blvd., 70th Ave., Zuni, Empire, Tennyson, 80th Ave., Federal, 128th Ave., Zuni St., 136th St., 104th Ave., 120th, Claude Ct., York, 124th Ave., 3rd & 4th St., Holly St., Quebec St., Riverdale Rd., Dahlia, 96th Ave., 88th Ave., 86th St., Steel St., Adams St., 74th Ave., 72nd Ave., Brighton, 76th Ave., Forest St., 52nd Ave., 54th, 48th, Yosemite St., Smith Rd., C&SRR, 56th, Valley Highway, 64th, 32nd St., 20th, 4th, Evans

Zone numbers shown: 02, 03, 04, 05, 06, 07, 08, 09, 10, 11, 12, 14, 15, 16, 18, 19, 20, 21, 22, 23, 25, 26, 27, 28, 29, 30, 31, 32, 33, 34, 35, 36, 37, 39, 40, 41

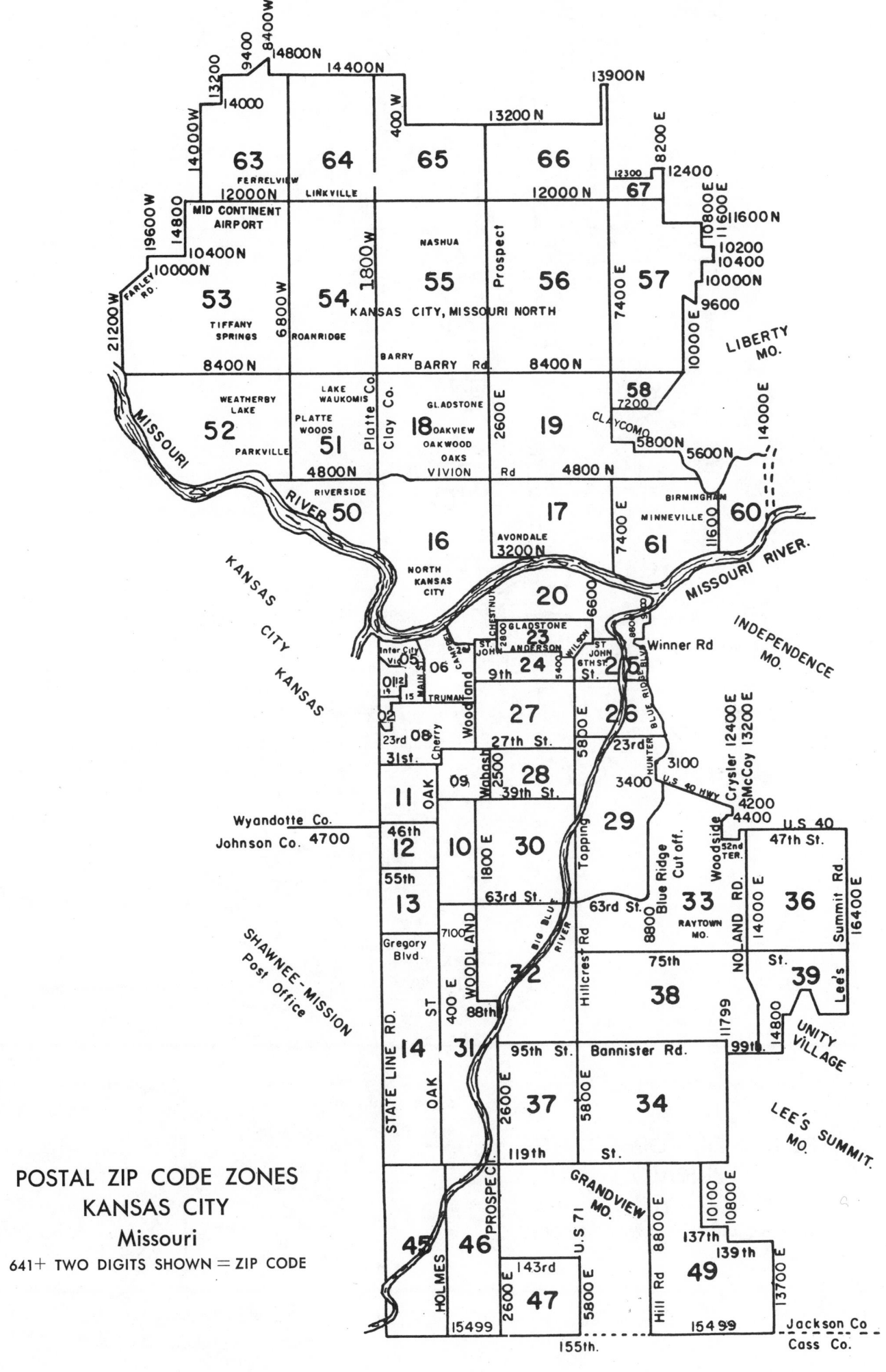

POSTAL ZIP CODE ZONES
KANSAS CITY
Missouri
641+ TWO DIGITS SHOWN = ZIP CODE

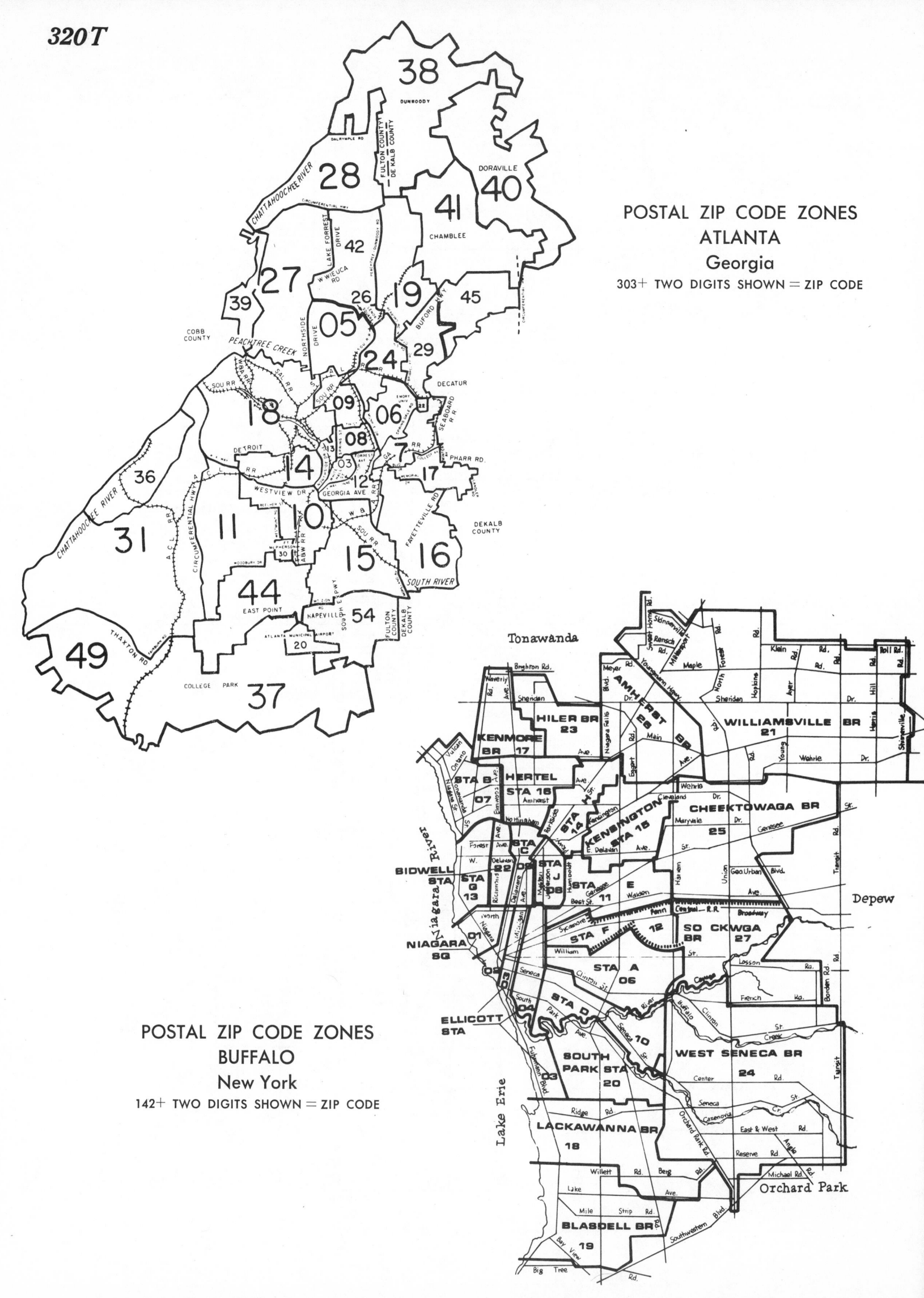

320T

POSTAL ZIP CODE ZONES
ATLANTA
Georgia
303+ TWO DIGITS SHOWN = ZIP CODE

POSTAL ZIP CODE ZONES
BUFFALO
New York
142+ TWO DIGITS SHOWN = ZIP CODE

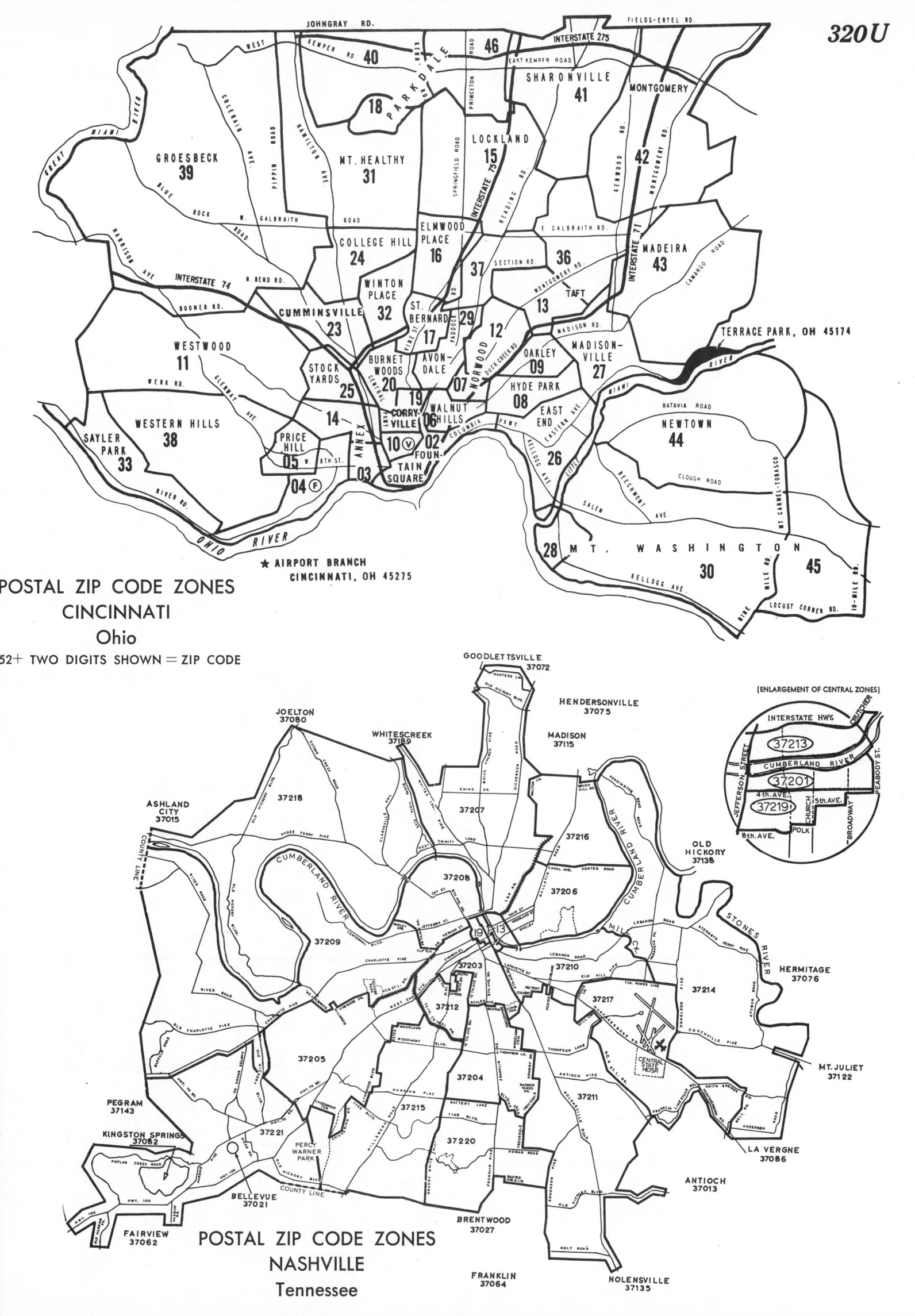

320U

POSTAL ZIP CODE ZONES
CINCINNATI
Ohio
52+ TWO DIGITS SHOWN = ZIP CODE

★ AIRPORT BRANCH
CINCINNATI, OH 45275

TERRACE PARK, OH 45174

GROESBECK 39
MT. HEALTHY 31
COLLEGE HILL 24
WINTON PLACE 32
CUMMINSVILLE 23
WESTWOOD 11
STOCK YARDS 25
WESTERN HILLS 38
SAYLER PARK 33
PRICE HILL 05
ANNEX 03
04 (F)
14
10 (V)
02 FOUNTAIN SQUARE
CORRYVILLE 06
WALNUT HILLS 06
BURNET WOODS 20
19
AVONDALE 07
ST. BERNARD 17
29
12
NORWOOD
OAKLEY 09
HYDE PARK 08
EAST END 26
MADISONVILLE 27
MADEIRA 43
TAFT
13
36
37
ELMWOOD PLACE 16
LOCKLAND 15
MONTGOMERY
SHARONVILLE 41
42
40
46
18
NEWTOWN 44
MT. WASHINGTON 28 30 45

POSTAL ZIP CODE ZONES
NASHVILLE
Tennessee

(ENLARGEMENT OF CENTRAL ZONES)
37213
37201
37219

GOODLETTSVILLE 37072
HENDERSONVILLE 37075
MADISON 37115
JOELTON 37080
WHITESCREEK 37189
ASHLAND CITY 37015
37218
37207
37216
37208
37206
37209
37203
37210
37212
37217
37214
OLD HICKORY 37138
HERMITAGE 37076
MT. JULIET 37122
37205
37204
37211
37215
37220
PEGRAM 37143
KINGSTON SPRINGS 37082
FAIRVIEW 37062
BELLEVUE 37021
LA VERGNE 37086
ANTIOCH 37013
BRENTWOOD 37027
FRANKLIN 37064
NOLENSVILLE 37135
1973

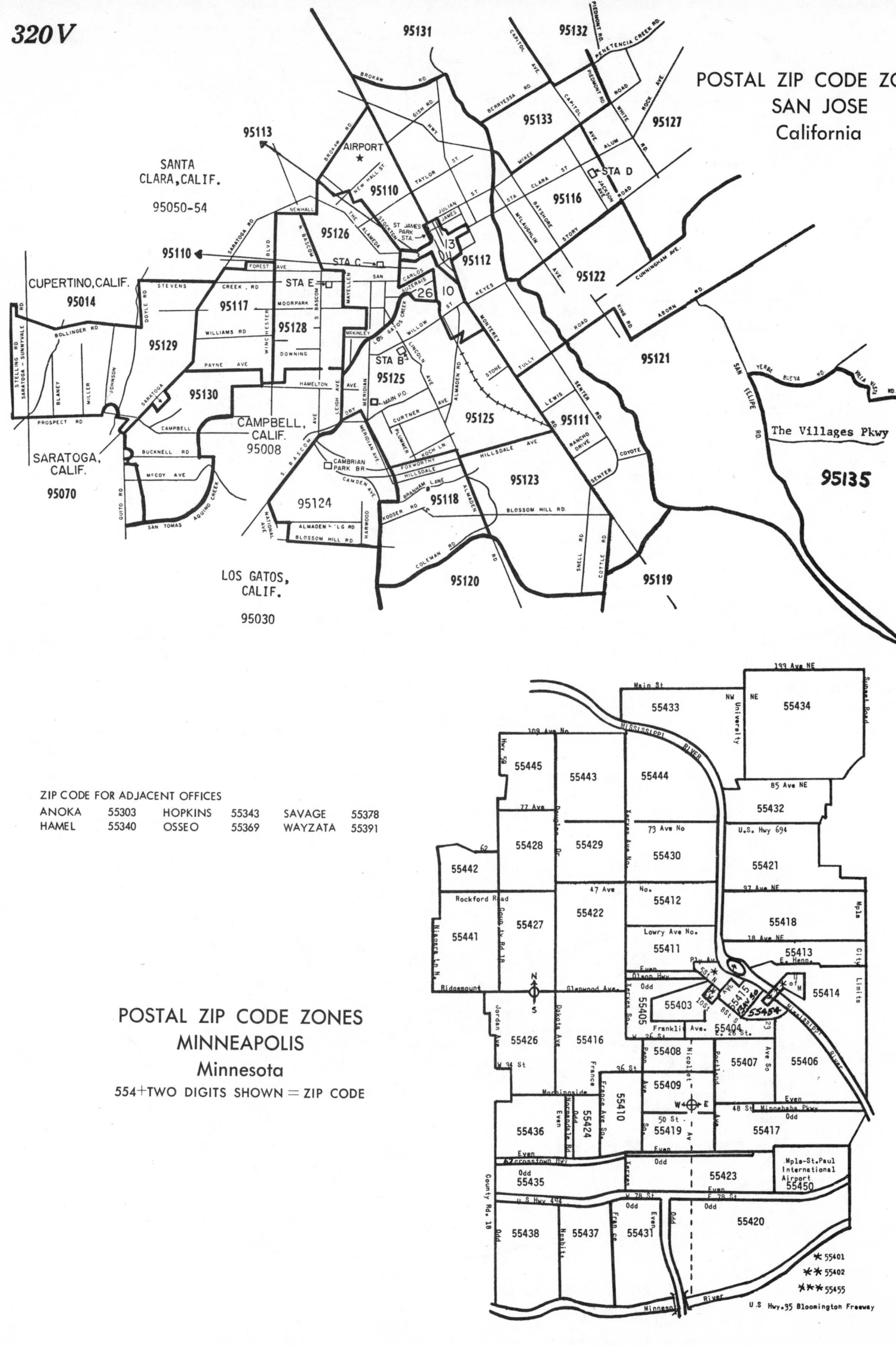

POSTAL ZIP CODE ZONES
SAN JOSE
California

SANTA CLARA, CALIF.
95050-54

CUPERTINO, CALIF.
95014

SARATOGA, CALIF.
95070

CAMPBELL, CALIF.
95008

LOS GATOS, CALIF.
95030

The Villages Pkwy
95135

95131   95132
95113
95133   95127
95110   STA D
95126   95116
95117   95112
95128   95122
95129   95130
95125   95121
95124   95125   95111
95118   95123
95120   95119

ZIP CODE FOR ADJACENT OFFICES
ANOKA   55303   HOPKINS   55343   SAVAGE   55378
HAMEL   55340   OSSEO   55369   WAYZATA   55391

POSTAL ZIP CODE ZONES
MINNEAPOLIS
Minnesota
554+TWO DIGITS SHOWN = ZIP CODE

55433   55434
55445   55443   55444
55432
55428   55429   55430   55421
55442
55441   55427   55422   55412   55418
55411   55413
55426   55416   55403   55415   55414
55405   55454
55408   55404   55407   55406
55409
55436   55424   55410   55419   55417
55435   55423   55420
55438   55437   55431   55450

★ 55401
★★ 55402
★★★ 55455

U.S Hwy.95 Bloomington Freeway

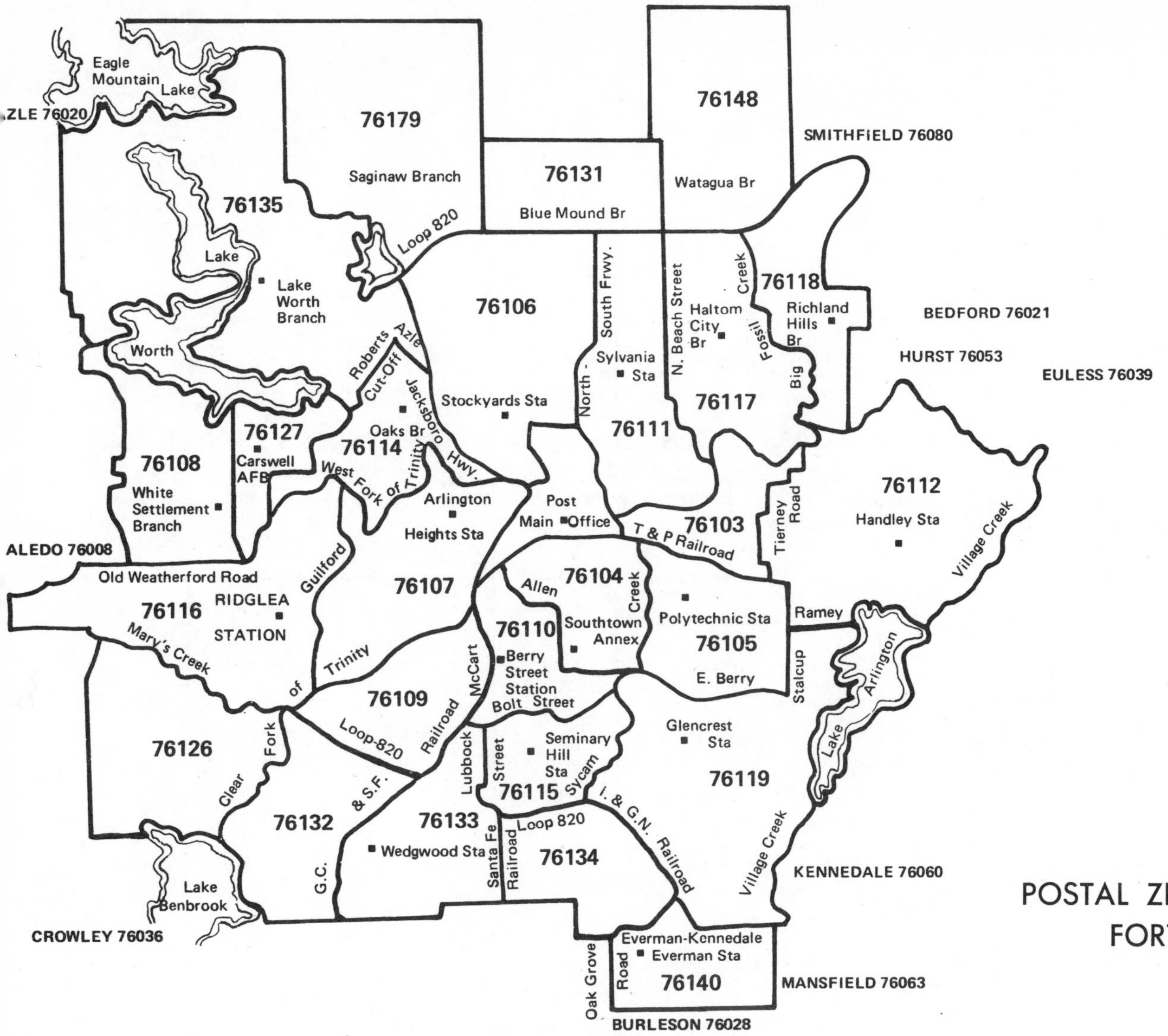

Eagle Mountain Lake

ZLE 76020

76179

Saginaw Branch

76148

SMITHFIELD 76080

76131

Blue Mound Br

Watagua Br

76135

Loop 820

Lake Worth Branch

Lake

Worth

76106

South Frwy.

N. Beach Street

Creek

76118

Haltom City Br

Richland Hills Br

Fossil

BEDFORD 76021

Sylvania Sta

76117

HURST 76053

EULESS 76039

Roberts Cut-Off

Azle

Jacksboro Hwy.

Stockyards Sta

76111

Big

76127

Carswell AFB

Oaks Br

76114

Arlington Heights Sta

Post Office

Main

76103

Tierney Road

76112

Handley Sta

Village Creek

76108

White Settlement Branch

West Fork of Trinity

ALEDO 76008

Old Weatherford Road

Guilford

76107

Allen

76104

Creek

T & P Railroad

Ramey

Stalcup

Lake Arlington

76116

RIDGLEA STATION

Mary's Creek

Trinity

76110

Southtown Annex

Polytechnic Sta

76105

E. Berry

Village Creek

Berry Street Station

Bolt Street

McCart

Railroad

76109

Lubbock Street

Loop-820

& S.F.

Seminary Hill Sta

Glencrest Sta

76119

76126

Clear Fork of Trinity

G.C.

76132

Wedgwood Sta

76133

Santa Fe Railroad

76115

Sycam

Loop 820

I. & G.N. Railroad

76134

Village Creek

KENNEDALE 76060

Lake Benbrook

CROWLEY 76036

Oak Grove Road

Everman-Kennedale Everman Sta

76140

MANSFIELD 76063

BURLESON 76028

POSTAL ZIP CODE ZONES
FORT WORTH
Texas

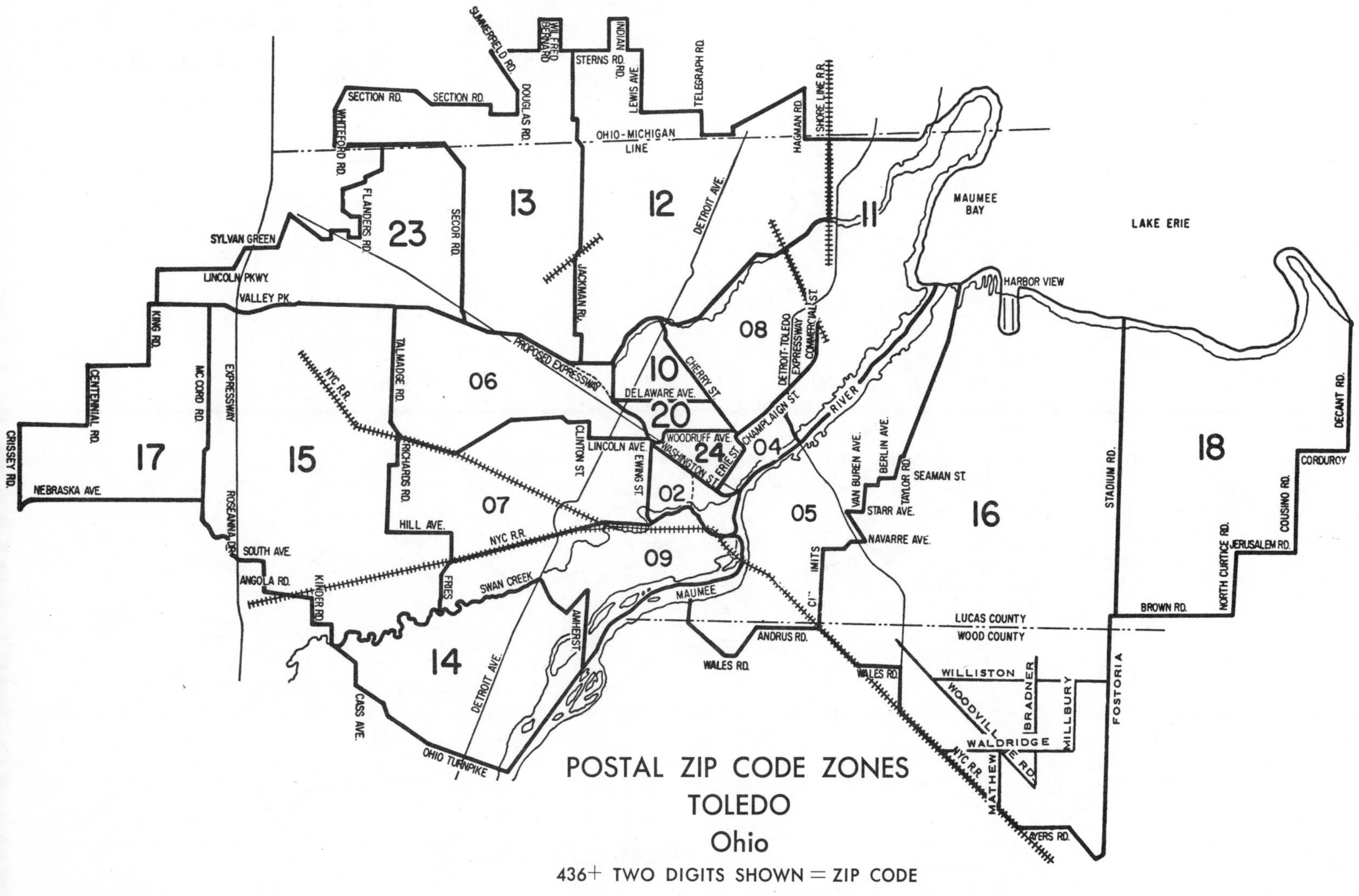

S.MMERFIELD RD.

WM. FRED BERNARD

Sterns Rd.

INDIAN

Lewis Ave.

Telegraph Rd.

SHORE LINE R.R.

SECTION RD.

SECTION RD.

Douglas Rd.

OHIO-MICHIGAN LINE

Hagman Rd.

MAUMEE BAY

LAKE ERIE

WHITEFORD RD.

13

12

Detroit Ave.

Flanders Rd.

23

Secor Rd.

Jackman Rd.

HARBOR VIEW

Sylvan Green

Lincoln Pkwy.

Valley Pk.

08

Detroit-Toledo Expressway

Commercial St.

RIVER

King Rd.

Talmadge Rd.

06

Proposed Expressway

10

Cherry St.

Centennial Rd.

McCord Rd.

Expressway

NYC R.R.

Richards Rd.

Delaware Ave.

20

Crissey Rd.

17

15

07

Hill Ave.

Roseanna Rd.

Clinton St.

Lincoln Ave.

Ewing St.

Woodruff Ave.

Washington St.

Champlaign St.

ERIE ST.

04

Van Buren Ave.

Berlin Ave.

Taylor Rd.

Seaman St.

Starr Ave.

05

Stadium Rd.

18

Decant Rd.

Corduroy

Cousino Rd.

Nebraska Ave.

02

Navarre Ave.

16

North Curtice Rd.

Jerusalem Rd.

South Ave.

NYC R.R.

Angola Rd.

Kinder Rd.

Freds

Swan Creek

09

Maumee

CITY LIMITS

14

Amherst

Wales Rd.

Andrus Rd.

Wales Rd.

LUCAS COUNTY

WOOD COUNTY

Brown Rd.

FOSTORIA

Cass Ave.

Detroit Ave.

Ohio Turnpike

Williston

Woodville Rd.

Bradner Rd.

Millbury

Waldridge

Mathew Rd.

NYC R.R.

Ayers Rd.

POSTAL ZIP CODE ZONES
TOLEDO
Ohio

436+ TWO DIGITS SHOWN = ZIP CODE

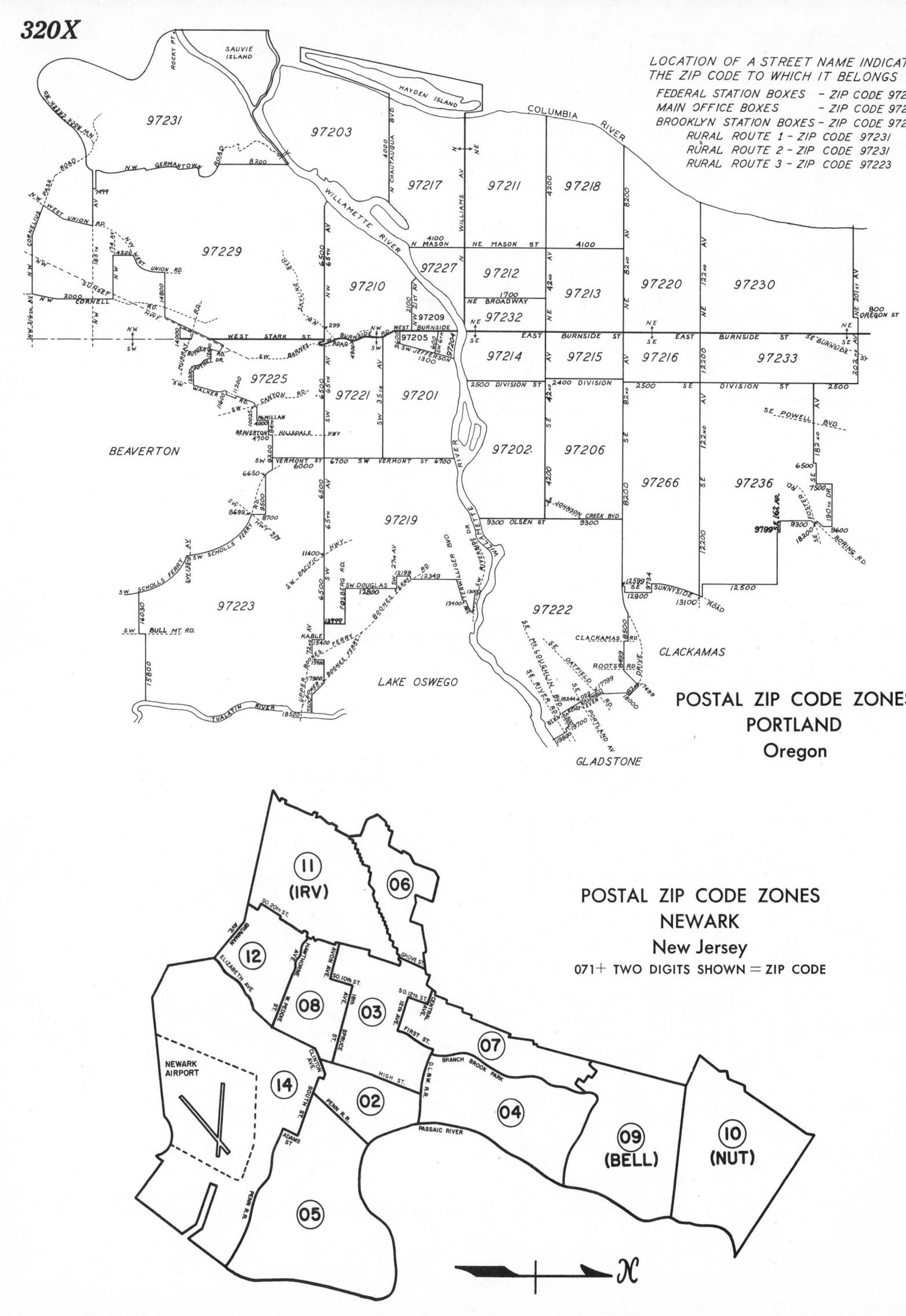

LOCATION OF A STREET NAME INDICATES
THE ZIP CODE TO WHICH IT BELONGS
FEDERAL STATION BOXES – ZIP CODE 97207
MAIN OFFICE BOXES – ZIP CODE 97208
BROOKLYN STATION BOXES – ZIP CODE 97242
RURAL ROUTE 1 – ZIP CODE 97231
RURAL ROUTE 2 – ZIP CODE 97231
RURAL ROUTE 3 – ZIP CODE 97223

POSTAL ZIP CODE ZONES
PORTLAND
Oregon

POSTAL ZIP CODE ZONES
NEWARK
New Jersey
071+ TWO DIGITS SHOWN = ZIP CODE

INDEX OF THE WORLD

Introduction

This index is a directory to the atlas as a whole. It contains an alphabetical listing of the major political divisions (countries and administrative subdivisions, i.e., states, provinces, departments), principal cities and towns, and geographical features, such as mountains, rivers, bays, islands, shown on the maps contained in this atlas.

Entries are generally indexed to the map or inset having the largest scale, but in some cases, where the entry has equal coverage or is important to its surroundings on more than one map, more than one reference is given.

Each entry gives the political division in which it is located, or in the case of certain geographical features the appropriate continent or regional name, and the page number of the map on which the name will be found. The user who is unfamiliar with a place name will thus be able to identify the political division to which it belongs and to locate quickly the appropriate map or maps.

Once having found the map listed in this index, the user will easily find the place name on the map by first locating it in the accompanying map index. Here the user will find the necessary index key reference. When there is more than one place of the same name on the same map, only one reference is given. The individual map index will give the multiple listings of names and key references. A glance at adjacent pages will show whether there are additional maps on which the place name may be found, by referring to the accompanying index or by looking in the same relative location on the map.

The abbreviations for the political division names and geographical terms are explained in the glossary in the front of the atlas. In some cases place names have been shortened here. The full name will be found in the individual index accompanying the map itself.

A

Aa (river), Switz., 39
Aachen, W. Ger., 22
Aalen, W. Ger., 22
Aalst, Belg., 27
Äänekoski, Fin., 18
Aarau, Switz., 39
Aare (river), Switz., 39
Aargau (canton), Switz., 39
Aba, Nigeria, 106
Abacaxis (riv.), Braz., 132
Abadan, Iran, 66
Abadeh, Iran, 66
Abadla, Alg., 106
Abaetetuba, Braz., 132
Abaiang (atoll), Gilb. & Ell. Is., 87
Abajo (mts.), Utah, 304
Abakan, U.S.S.R., 48
Abancay, Peru, 128
Abarquh, Iran, 66
Abashiri, Japan, 81
Abau, P.N.G., 85
Abaya (lake), Eth., 111
Abbai (riv.), Eth., 111
Abbe (lake), Africa, 111
Abbeville, Ala., 194
Abbeville, France, 28
Abbeville, La., 238
Abbeville, S.C., 296
Abbeyfeale, Ire., 17
Abbottabad, Pak., 68
Abdanan, Iran, 66
Abdulino, U.S.S.R., 52
Abécher, Chad, 111
Abemama (atoll), Gilb. & Ell. Is., 87
Abengourou, Ivory Coast, 106
Åbenrå, Den., 21
Abeokuta, Nigeria, 106
Aberaeron, Wales, 13
Abercorn (Mbala), Zambia, 115
Aberdare, Wales, 13
Aberdeen, Md., 245
Aberdeen, Miss., 256
Aberdeen (lake), N.W.T., 187
Aberdeen (county), Scot., 15
Aberdeen, Scot., 15
Aberdeen, S. Dak., 298
Aberdeen, Wash., 310
Aberfeldy, Scot., 15
Abergavenny, Wales, 13
Abergele, Wales, 13
Abertillery, Wales, 13
Aberystwyth, Wales, 13
Abha, Saudi Ar., 59
Ab-i-Diz (river), Iran, 66
Abidjan (cap.), Ivory Coast, 106
Abilene, Kans., 232
Abilene, Tex., 302
Abingdon, Eng., 13
Abingdon, Ill., 222
Abingdon, Va., 307
Abington, Pa., 294
Abitibi (lake), Ont., 177
Abitibi (riv.), Ont., 177
Abkhaz A.S.S.R., U.S.S.R., 52
Abnûb, Egypt, 111
Åbo (Turku), Fin., 18
Abomey, Benin,106
Abony, Hung., 41
Abor (hills), India, 68
Abqaiq, Saudi Ar., 59
Abra (prov.), Phil., 82
Abraham Lincoln Birthplace Nat'l Hist. Site, Ky., 237
Abruzzi (reg.), Italy, 34
Absecon, N. J., 273
Abu 'Arish, Saudi Ar., 59
Abu Dara, Ras (cape), Sudan, 111
Abu Dhabi (cap.), U.A.E., 59
Abu Hadriya, Saudi Ar., 59
Abu Hamed, Sudan, 111
Abu Kemal, Syria, 63
Abu-mad, Ras (cape), Saudi Ar., 59
Abu Road, India, 68
Abu Shagara, Ras (cape), Sudan, 111
Abu Zabad, Sudan, 111
Abydos (ruins), Egypt, 111
Abydos (ruins), Turkey, 63
Acadia Nat'l Park, Maine, 242
Acadia Valley, Alta., 182
Acajutla, El Sal., 154
Acámbaro, Mex., 150
Acaponeta, Mex., 150
Acapulco, Mex., 150
Acarigua, Venez., 124
Acatlán, Mex., 150
Acatzingo, Mex., 150
Accra (cap.), Ghana, 106
Accrington, Eng., 10
Achacachi, Bol., 136
Achalpur, India, 68
Achill (isl.), Ire., 17
Achnasheen, Scot., 15
Acireale, Italy, 34
Acklins (isl.), Bah., 156
Aconcagua (prov.), Chile, 138
Aconcagua (mt.), Arg., 143
Aconchi, Mex., 150
Acoyapa, Nic., 154
Acqui Terme, Italy, 34
Acre (state), Braz., 132
Acre (riv.), Braz., 132
Acre, Israel, 65
Acri, Italy, 34
Actopan, Mex., 150
Ada, Minn., 254
Ada, Ohio, 284
Ada, Okla., 288
Adam, Oman, 59
Adamawa (reg.), Africa, 115
Adam's (peak), Sri Lanka, 68
Adams, Mass., 249
Adams (mt.), Wash., 310
Adam's Bridge (shoals), Asia, 68
Adams Nat'l Hist. Site, Mass., 249
Adamstown (cap.), Pitcairn Is., 87
Adana (prov.), Turkey, 63
Adana, Turkey, 63
Adapazarı, Turkey, 63
Adare (cape), Ant., 5
Adda (riv.), Italy, 34
Addis Ababa (cap.), Eth., 111
Addis Alam, Eth., 111
Addison, Ill., 222
Ad Diwaniya, Iraq, 66
Adel, Ga., 216
Adelaide (isl.), Ant., 5
Adelaide (cap.), S. Austral., 94
Adelaide (pen.), N.W.T., 187
Adelaide River, N. Terr., 93
Adelanto, Calif., 204
Adélie Coast (reg.), Ant., 5
Aden (gulf), 54
Aden (cap.), P.D.R. Yemen, 59
Adige (riv.), Italy, 34
Adilabad, India, 68
Adimi, U.S.S.R., 48
Adirondack (mts.), N.Y., 276
Adıyaman (prov.), Turkey, 63
Adjuntas, P. Rico, 161
Admiralty (gulf), W. Austral., 92
Admiralty (isls.), P.N.G., 87
Ado, Nigeria, 106
Adoni, India, 68
Adour (riv.), France, 28
Adra, Spain, 33
Adrano, Italy, 34
Adrar, Alg., 106
Adrar (reg.), Mauritania, 106
Adrar des Iforas (plat.), Africa, 106
Adria, Italy, 34
Adrian, Mich., 250
Adriatic (sea), Europe, 7
Adwa, Eth., 111
Adygey Aut. Obl., U.S.S.R., 52
Adzhar A.S.S.R., U.S.S.R., 52
Aegean (sea), 45
Aegean Islands (reg.), Greece, 45
Afars & Issas, Terr. of the, 111
Afghanistan, 68
Åfjord, Norway, 18
Afmadu, Somalia, 115
Africa, 102
Afton, Wyo., 319
Afyon, Turkey, 63
Afyon-Karahisar (prov.), Turkey, 63
Agadès, Niger, 106
Agadir, Mor., 106
Agaña (cap.), Guam, 87
Agartala, India, 68
Agate Fossil Beds Nat'l Mon., Nebr., 264
Agats, Indonesia, 85
Agatti (isl.), India, 68
Agboville, Ivory Coast, 106
Agdam, U.S.S.R., 52
Agde, France, 28
Agen, France, 28
Aginsk Buryat Nat'l Okrug, U.S.S.R., 48
Aginskoye, U.S.S.R., 48
Agiobampo (bay), Mex., 150
Agira, Italy, 34
Agordat, Eth., 111
Agra, India, 68
Ağrı (prov.), Turkey, 63
Agrigento (prov.), Italy, 34
Agrigento, Italy, 34
Agrihan (isl.), Pac. Is., 87
Agrínion, Greece, 45
Agryz, U.S.S.R., 52
Aguada, P. Rico, 161
Aguadilla (dist.), P. Rico, 161
Aguadilla, P. Rico, 161
Aguadulce, Pan., 154
Aguán (riv.), Hond., 154
Aguanaval (riv.), Mex., 150
Aguanus (riv.), Canada,174
Agua Prieta, Mex., 150
Aguarico (riv.), S. Amer., 128
Aguas Buenas, P. Rico, 161
Aguascalientes (state), Mex., 150
Aguascalientes, Mex., 150
Águeda, Port., 33
Aguilar, Colo., 208
Aguilar, Spain, 33
Aguilas, Spain, 33
Aguililla, Mex., 150
Aguja (pt.), Peru, 128
Agulhas (cape), S. Afr., 118
Agusan del Norte (prov.), Phil., 82
Agusan del Sur (prov.), Phil., 82
Ahaggar (range), Alg., 106
Ahau, Fiji, 87
Ahlen, W. Ger., 22
Ahmadabad, India, 68
Ahmadnagar, India, 68
Ahmadpur East, Pak., 68
Ahoskie, N.C., 281
Ahrensburg, W. Ger., 22
Ahuacatlán, Mex., 150
Ahuachapán, El Sal., 154
Ahuás, Hond., 154
Ahurei, Fr. Poly., 87
Åhus, Sweden, 18
Ahvenanmaa (prov.), Fin., 18
Ahwar, P.D.R. Yemen, 59
Ahwaz, Iran, 66
Aibonito, P. Rico, 161
Aichi (prefecture), Japan, 81
Aiea, Hawaii, 218
Aiguá, Urug., 145
Aigun (Aihui), China, 77
Aiken, S.C., 296
Ailinglapalap (atoll), Pac. Is., 87
Ailuk (atoll), Pac. Is., 87
Ain (dept.), France, 28
Ain (riv.), France, 28
Aina Haina, Hawaii, 218
'Ain al Mubarrak, Saudi Ar., 59
Aïn-Béïda, Alg., 106
Aïn-Sefra, Alg., 106
Ainsworth, Nebr., 264
Aïn-Témouchent, Alg., 106
Aïoun el Atrous, Mauritania, 106
Air (mts.), Niger, 106
Airdrie, Scot., 15
Aire (riv.), Eng., 13
Air Force (isl.), N.W.T., 187
Air Force Acad., Colo., 208
Aisén (prov.), Chile, 138
Aishihik, Yukon, 187
Aisne (dept.), France, 28
Aisne (riv.), France, 28
Aitape, P.N.G., 85
Aitkin, Minn., 254
Aitutaki (atoll), Cook Is., 87
Aiud, Rum., 45
Aix-en-Provence, France, 28
Aix-les-Bains, France, 28
Aíyina, Greece, 45
Aíyion, Greece, 45
Aizuwakamatsu, Japan, 81
Aizwal, India, 68
Ajaccio, France, 28
Ajaccio (gulf), France, 28
Ajanta, India, 68
Ajax, Ont., 177
Ajedabia, Libya, 111
Ajka, Hung., 41
'Ajlun (dist.), Jordan, 65
'Ajman, U.A.E., 59
Ajmer, India, 68
Ajo, Ariz., 198
Ak Dağ (mts.), Turkey, 63
Akarai (mts.), Guyana, 131
Akashi, Japan, 81
Aken, E. Ger., 22
Akershus (county), Norway, 18
Aketi, Zaire, 115
Akhaltsikhe, U.S.S.R., 52
Akhdar, Jebel (mts.), Libya, 111
Akhdar, Jebel (range), Oman, 59
Akhisar, Turkey, 63
Akhtopol, Bulg., 45
Akhtubinsk, U.S.S.R., 52
Akhtyrka, U.S.S.R., 52
Akimiski (isl.), N.W.T., 187
Akim Oda, Ghana, 106
Akita (prefecture), Japan, 81
Akita, Japan, 81
Akjoujt, Mauritania, 106
Akkerman (Belgorod-Dnestrovskiy), U.S.S.R., 52
Aklan (prov.), Phil., 82
Aklavik, N.W.T., 187
Akmolinsk (Tselinograd), U.S.S.R., 48
Akobo (riv.), Africa, 111
Akola, India, 68
Akpatok (isl.), N.W.T., 187
Akrítas (cape), Greece, 45
Akron, N.Y., 276
Akron, Ohio, 284
Akşehir, Turkey, 63
Aksum, Eth., 111
Aktí (pen.), Greece, 45
Aktyubinsk, U.S.S.R., 48
Akureyri, Ice., 21
Akyab (Sittwe), Burma, 72
Al, Norway, 18
Alabama (riv.), Ala., 194
Alabama (state), U.S., 194
Alabat (isl.), Phil., 82
Alagir, U.S.S.R., 52
Alagoas (state), Braz., 132
Alagoinhas, Braz., 132
Alagón, Spain, 33
Al Ahqaf (Bahr es Safi) (des.), Arabia, 59
Alajuela, C. Rica, 154
Alakol' (lake), U.S.S.R., 48
Alameda, Calif., 204
Alamikamba, Nic., 154
Alamo, Tex., 302
Alamogordo, N. Mex., 274
Alamo Hts., Tex., 302
Alamos, Mex., 150
Alamosa, Colo., 208
Åland (isls.), Fin., 18
Alanje, Pan., 154
Alanya, Turkey, 63
Alaotra (lake), Malag. Rep., 118
Alaşehir, Turkey, 63
Alashan (des.), China, 77
Alaska (gulf), Alaska, 196
Alaska (pen.), Alaska, 196
Alaska (range), Alaska, 196
Alaska (state), U.S., 196
Alassio, Italy, 34
Alatri, Italy, 34
Alatyr', U.S.S.R., 52
Alausí, Ecua., 128
Álava (prov.), Spain, 33
Alavus, Fin., 18
Alayor, Spain, 33
Al 'Aziziya, Iraq, 66
Alba, Italy, 34
Alba Iulia, Rum., 45
Albacete (prov.), Spain, 33
Albacete, Spain, 33
Albania, 45
Albano (lake), Italy, 34
Albano Laziale, Italy, 34
Albany, Calif., 204
Albany, Ga., 216
Albany, Ind., 227
Albany, Jam., 158
Albany (cap.), N.Y., 276
Albany (riv.), Ont., 177
Albany, Oreg., 291
Albany, P.E.I., 169
Albany, W. Austral., 92
Albany N.A.S., Ga., 216
Albay (prov.), Phil., 82
Albemarle (pt.), Ecuador, 128
Albemarle, N.C., 281
Alberni, Br. Col., 184
Albert (lake), Africa, 115
Albert, France, 28
Alberta (mt.), Alta., 182
Alberta (prov.), Canada, 182
Albert Lea, Minn., 254
Alberton, P.E.I., 169
Alberton, S. Afr., 118
Albertville, Ala., 194
Albertville, France, 28
Albi, France, 28
Albia, Iowa, 229
Albina, Surinam, 131
Albino, Italy, 34
Albion, Mich., 250
Albion, Nebr., 264
Albion, N.Y., 276
Alborán (isl.), Spain, 33
Ålborg, Den., 21
Albox, Spain, 33
Albuquerque, N. Mex., 274
Alburquerque, Spain, 33
Albury, N.S.W., 97
Alcácer do Sal, Port., 33
Alcalá de Guadaira, Spain, 33
Alcalá de Henares, Spain, 33
Alcalá de los Gazules, Spain, 33
Alcalá la Real, Spain, 33
Alcamo, Italy, 34
Alcanar, Spain, 33
Alcañiz, Spain, 33
Alcántara, Port., 33
Alcántara, Spain, 33
Alcantarilla, Spain, 33
Alcaraz (mts.), Spain, 33
Alcaudete, Spain, 33
Alcázar de San Juan, Spain, 33
Alcira, Spain, 33
Alcoa, Tenn., 237
Alcobaça, Port., 33
Alcoy, Spain, 33
Alcudia (bay), Spain, 33
Aldabra (isls.), Br. Indian Ocean Terr., 118
Aldama, Mex., 150
Aldan, Pa., 294
Aldan, U.S.S.R., 48
Aldan (plat.), U.S.S.R., 48
Aldeia Nova, Port., 33
Alderney (isl.), Chan. Is., 13
Aldershot, Eng.,13
Aldershot, N.S., 168
Aldridge-Brownhills, Eng., 10
Aledo, Ill., 222
Aleg, Mauritania, 106
Alegrete, Braz., 132
'Aleih, Leb., 63
Aleksandriya, U.S.S.R., 52
Aleksandrovsk-Sakhalinskiy, U.S.S.R., 48
Alekseyevka, U.S.S.R., 52
Aleksin, U.S.S.R., 52
Aleksinac, Yugo., 45
Além Paraíba, Braz., 135
Alençon, France, 28
Aleppo (gov.), Syria, 63
Aleppo, Syria, 63
Alert, N.W.T., 187
Alert Bay, Br. Col., 184
Alès, France, 28
Alessandria (prov.), Italy, 34
Alessandria, Italy, 34
Ålesund, Norway, 18
Aleutian (isls.), Alaska, 196
Alexander (arch.), Alaska, 196
Alexander (isl.), Ant., 5
Alexander, Minn., 254
Alexander City, Ala., 194
Alexandra, N.Z., 101
Alexandra (falls), N.W.T., 187
Alexandra Land (isl.), U.S.S.R., 48
Alexandretta (Iskenderun), Turkey, 63
Alexandria, Egypt, 111
Alexandria, Ind., 227
Alexandria, La., 238
Alexandria, Minn., 254
Alexandria, Rum., 45
Alexandria, Scot., 15
Alexandria, Va., 307
Alexandroúpolis, Greece, 45
Aleysk, U.S.S.R., 48
Al Falluja, Iraq, 66
Alfaro, Spain, 33
Alfatar, Bulg., 45
Alfeld, W. Ger., 22
Alfenas, Braz., 135
Alford, Scot., 15
Alfred, N.Y., 276
Alga, U.S.S.R., 48
Algarve (prov.), Port., 33
Algeciras, Spain, 33
Algemesí, Spain, 33
Algeria, 106
Algés, Port., 33
Alghero, Italy, 34
Algiers (cap.), Alg., 106
Algoa (bay), S. Afr., 118
Algoma, Wis., 317
Algona, Iowa, 229
Algonac, Mich., 250
Algonquin Prov. Park, Ont., 177
Alhama de Granada, Spain, 33
Alhama de Murcia, Spain, 33
Alhambra, Calif., 204
Al Hoceima, Mor., 106
Alhos Vedros, Port., 33
Ali-Bayramly, U.S.S.R., 52
Alicante (prov.), Spain, 33
Alicante, Spain, 33
Alice, Tex., 302
Alice Arm, Br. Col., 184
Alice Springs, N. Terr., 93
Aliceville, Ala., 194
Aligarh, India, 68
Alingsås, Sweden, 18
Aliquippa, Pa., 294
Alivérion, Greece, 45
Aliwal North, S. Afr., 118
Aljezur, Port., 33
Aljojuca, Mex., 150
Aljustrel, Port., 33
Alkmaar, Neth., 27
Al Kufa, Iraq, 66
Al Kuwait (cap.), Kuwait, 59
Allahabad, India, 68
Allakh-Yun', U.S.S.R., 48
Allanmyo, Burma, 72
Allegan, Mich., 250
Allen (lake), Ire., 17
Allendale, N. J., 273
Allendale, S.C., 296
Allende, Mex., 150
Allen Park, Mich., 250
Allentown, Pa., 294
Alleppey, India, 68
Aller (riv.), W. Ger., 22
Allgäu (reg.), W. Ger., 22
Alliance, Nebr., 264
Alliance, Ohio, 284
Allier (dept.), France, 28
Allinge-Sandvig, Den., 21
Allingtown, Conn., 210
Allison Pk., Pa., 294
Al Lith, Saudi Ar., 59
Alloa, Scot., 15
All Saints, Antigua, 161
Alma, Ga., 216
Alma, Mich., 250
Alma, Nebr., 264
Alma, Que., 172
Alma-Ata, U.S.S.R., 48
Almada, Port., 33
Almadén, Spain, 33
Almagro, Spain, 33
Almansa, Spain, 33
Almanzor (mt.), Spain, 33
Almanzora (riv.), Spain, 33
Almeirim, Port., 33
Almelo, Neth., 27
Almendralejo, Spain, 33
Almería (prov.), Spain, 33
Almería, Spain, 33
Almería (gulf), Spain, 33
Al'met'yevsk, U.S.S.R., 52
Älmhult, Sweden, 18
Almirante, Pan., 154
Almirós, Greece, 45
Almodóvar del Campo, Spain, 33
Almoloya, Mex., 150
Almonte, Spain, 33
Almora, India, 68
Almuñécar, Spain, 33
Alofi (cap.), Niue, 87
Álora, Spain, 33
Alor Setar, Malaysia, 72
Alorton, Ill., 222
Alpena, Mich., 250
Alpes-de-Haute-Provence (dept.), France, 28
Alpes-Maritimes (dept.), France, 28
Alpiarça, Port., 33
Alpine, Tex., 302
Alps (mts.), Europe, 7
Al Qaiyara, Iraq, 66
Al Qatn, P.D.R. Yemen, 59
Alsask, Sask., 181
Alsdorf, W. Ger., 22
Alsek (riv.), Yukon, 187
Alsip, Ill., 222
Alsten (isl.), Norway, 18
Alta (riv.), Norway, 18
Altadena, Calif., 204
Alta Gracia, Arg., 143
Altagracia, Venez., 124
Altamira, Mex., 150
Altamont, Oreg., 291
Altar, Mex., 150
Altavista, Va., 307
Altay (mts.), Asia, 54
Altay (Yusun Bulak), Mong., 77
Alte (lake), Norway, 18
Altena, W. Ger., 22
Altenburg, E. Ger., 22
Altındağ, Turkey, 63
Altmark (reg.), E. Ger., 22
Alto Alentejo (prov.), Port., 33
Alto Araguaia, Braz., 132
Alton, Ill., 222
Altona, Man., 179
Altona, W. Ger., 22
Altoona, Pa., 294
Alto Paraguay (dept.), Par., 144
Alto Paraná (dept.), Par., 144
Alto Park, Ga., 216
Alto Ritacuva (mt.), Col.,126
Altotonga, Mex., 150
Altrincham, Eng., 10
Alturas, Calif., 204
Altus, Okla., 288
Altyn Tagh (mts.), China, 77
Alula, Somalia, 115
Alum Rock, Calif., 204
Alushta, U.S.S.R., 52
Alva, Okla., 288
Alva, Scot., 15
Alvarado, Mex., 150
Alvesta, Sweden, 18
Alvin, Tex., 302
Älvsborg (county), Sweden, 18
Älvsbyn, Sweden, 18
Alwar, India, 68
Alyth, Scot., 15
Alz (riv.), W. Ger., 22
Alzey, W. Ger., 22
Amadeus (lake), N. Terr., 93
'Amadiya, Iraq, 66
Amadora, Port., 33
Amagasaki, Japan, 81
Amakusa (isls.), Japan, 81
Åmål, Sweden, 18
Amaliás, Greece, 45
Amalner, India, 68
Amambaí, Braz., 132
Amambay (dept.), Par., 144
Amami (isls.), Japan, 81
Amami-O-Shima (isl.), Japan, 81
Amanos (mts.), Turkey, 63
Amapá (terr.), Braz., 132
Amapala, Hond., 154
Amaparí (riv.), Braz., 132
'Amara, Iraq, 66
Amarante, Braz., 132
Amarapura, Burma, 72
Amarillo, Tex., 302
Amasya (prov.), Turkey, 63
Amasya, Turkey, 63
Amatitlán, Guat., 154
Amatlán, Mex., 150
Amazon (riv.), S. Amer., 120
Amazonas (state), Braz., 132
Amazonas (intendency), Col., 126
Amazonas (dept.), Peru, 128
Amazonas (terr.), Venez., 124
Ambala, India, 68
Ambarchik, U.S.S.R., 48
Ambato, Ecuador, 128
Ambatondrazaka, Malag. Rep., 118
Amber (cape), Malag. Rep., 118
Amberg, W. Ger., 22
Ambergris (cay), Belize, 154
Ambérieu, France, 28
Amberley, Ohio, 284
Ambler, Pa., 294
Amboina, Indon., 85
Amboise, France, 28
Ambon (Amboina), Indon., 85
Ambositra, Malag. Rep., 118
Ambridge, Pa., 294
Ambriz, Angola, 115
Ambrizete, Angola, 115
Ambrym (isl.), New Hebr., 87
Ambunti, P.N.G., 85
Amchitka (isl.), Alaska, 196
Amealco, Mex., 150
Ameca, Mex., 150
Amecameca, Mex., 150
Americana, Braz., 135
American Highland, Ant., 5
American Falls, Idaho, 220
American Fork, Utah, 304
American Samoa, 87
Americus, Ga., 216
Amersfoort, Neth., 27
Amery Ice Shelf, Ant., 5
Ames, Iowa, 229
Amesbury, Mass., 249
Amfilokhía, Greece, 45
Ámfissa, Greece, 45
Amhara (reg.), Eth., 111
Amherst, Burma, 72
Amherst, Mass., 249
Amherst, N.S., 169
Amherst, Ohio, 284
Amherstburg, Ont., 177
Amiens, France, 28
Amindivi (isls.), India, 68
Amindiri (Amini) (isl.), India, 68
Amisk (lake), Sask., 181
Amistad (res.), 150
Amistad Nat'l Rec. Area, Tex., 302
Amite, La., 238
Amityville, N.Y., 276
Amlwch, Wales, 13
Amman (dist.), Jordan, 65
Amman (cap.), Jordan, 65
Ammanford, Wales, 13
Ammersee (lake), W. Ger., 22
Amnat, Thai., 72
Amne Machin (mts.), China, 77
Amorgós (isl.), Greece, 45
Amory, Miss., 256
Amos, Que., 174
Amoy, China, 77
Amozoc de Mota, Mex., 150
Amposta, Spain, 33
Amqui, Que., 172
Amravati, India, 68
Amreli, India, 68
Amritsar, India, 68
Amsterdam (isl.), 3
Amsterdam (cap.), Neth., 27
Amsterdam, N.Y., 276
Amstetten, Austria, 41
Am-Timan, Chad, 111
Amuay, Venez., 124
Amu-Dar'ya (riv.), Asia, 48
Amuku (mts.), Guyana, 131
Amul, Iran, 66
Amund Ringnes (isl.), N.W.T., 187
Amundsen (bay), Ant., 5
Amundsen (sea), Ant., 5
Amundsen (gulf), N.W.T., 187
Amur (riv.), Asia, 48
Amya (pass), Asia, 72
'Ana, Iraq, 66
Anaa (atoll), Fr. Poly., 87
Anaco, Venez., 124
Anaconda, Mont., 262
Anacortes, Wash., 310
Anadarko, Okla., 288
Anadyr', U.S.S.R., 48
Anadyr' (gulf), U.S.S.R., 48
Anadyr' (range), U.S.S.R., 48
Anadyr' (riv.), U.S.S.R., 48
Anáfi (isl.), Greece, 45
Anaheim, Calif., 204
Anai Mudi (mt.), India, 68
'Anaiza, Saudi Ar., 59
Anakapalle, India, 68
Anambas (isls.), Indon., 85
Anamosa, Iowa, 229
Anamur (cape),Turkey, 63
Anan, Japan, 81
Anandale, La., 238
Anantapur, India, 68
Anantnag, India, 68
Anapa, U.S.S.R., 52
Anápolis, Braz., 132
Anasco, P. Rico, 161
Añatuya, Arg., 143
Anauá (riv.), Braz., 132
Anbar (prov.), Iraq, 66
Ancash (dept.), Peru, 128
Ancaster, Ont., 177
Anchorage, Alaska, 196
Ancohuma (mt.), Bol., 136
Ancona (prov.), Italy, 34
Ancona, Italy, 34
Ancón de Sardinas (bay), Ecuador, 128
Ancud, Chile, 138
Andalgalá, Arg., 143
Åndalsnes, Norway, 18
Andalusia, Ala., 194
Andalusia (reg.), Spain, 33
Andaman (sea), Asia, 54
Andaman (isls.), India, 68
Andaman and Nicobar Islands (terr.), India, 68
Anderlecht, Belg., 27
Andernach, W. Ger., 22
Anderson, Calif., 204
Anderson, Ind., 227
Anderson (riv.), N.W.T., 187
Anderson, S.C., 296
Andes (mts.), S. Amer., 120
Andheri, India, 68
Andhra Pradesh (state), India, 68
Andikíthira (isl.), Greece, 45
Andizhan, U.S.S.R., 48
Andkhui, Afghan., 68
Ándissa, Greece, 45
Andong, S. Korea, 81
Andorra, 33
Andorra la Vella (cap.), Andorra, 33
Andover, Eng., 13
Andravídha, Greece, 45
Andreas (cape), Cyprus, 63
Andrew Johnson Nat'l Hist. Site, Tenn., 237
Andrews, S.C., 296
Andrews, Tex., 302
Andros (isl.), Bah., 156
Ándros, Greece, 45
Ándros (isl.), Greece, 45
Androth (isl.), India, 68
Ands (fjord), Norway, 18
Andújar, Spain, 33
Andulo, Ang., 115
Anécho, Togo, 106
Anegada (isl.), Virgin Is. (Br.), 156
Aneityum (isl.), New Hebr., 87
'Aneiza, Jebel (mt.), Asia, 59
Aneto (mt.), Spain, 33
Angara (riv.), U.S.S.R., 48
Angarsk, U.S.S.R., 48
Angaur (isl.), Pac. Is., 87
Ånge, Sweden, 18
Angel (fall), Venez., 124
Ángel de la Guarda (isl.), Mex., 150
Angeles, Phil., 82
Ängelholm, Sweden, 18
Angerman (riv.), Sweden, 18
Angermünde, E. Ger., 22
Angers, France, 28
Angikuni (lake), N.W.T., 187
Angkor Wat (ruins), Cambodia, 72
Anglesey (county), Wales, 13
Angleton, Tex., 302
Angliers, Que., 174
Angmagssalik, Greenl., 4
Ango, Dem. Rep. of the Congo, 115
Angoche (isl.), Mozamb., 118
Angol, Chile, 138
Angola, 115
Angola, Ind., 227
Angoram, P.N.G., 85
Angostura, Mex., 150
Angoulême, France, 28
Angra do Heroísmo, Port., 32
Anguilla (isl.), St. Chr.-N.-A., 156
Angus (county), Scot., 15
Anholt (isl.), Den., 21
Anhwei (prov.), China, 77
Aniene (riv.), Italy, 34
Anina, Rum., 45
Anjou, Que., 172
Anjouan (isl.), Comoro Is., 118
Ankara (prov.), Turkey, 63
Ankara (cap.), Turkey, 63
Ankeny, Iowa, 229
Anker (riv.), Eng., 10
Anking, China, 77
Anklam, E. Ger., 22
Ankober, Eth., 111
An Loc, S. Vietnam, 72
Ann (cape), Mass., 249
Anna, Ill., 222
Annaba, Alg., 106
Annaberg-Buchholz, E. Ger., 22
An Najaf, Iraq, 66
Annan, Scot., 15
Annandale, Va., 307
Annapolis (cap.), Md., 245
Annapolis (basin), N.S., 169
Annapolis Royal, N.S., 169
Annapurna (mt.), Nepal, 68
Ann Arbor, Mich., 250
An Nasiriya, Iraq, 66
Annecy, France, 28
Anniston, Ala., 194
Annobón (Pagalu) (isl.), Eq. Guin., 102
Annonay, France, 28
Annotto Bay, Jam., 158
Annville, Pa., 294
Anoka, Minn., 254
Anóyia, Greece, 45
Áno Viánnos, Greece, 45
Ansbach, W. Ger., 22
Anse la Raye, St. Lucia, 161
Anshan, China, 77
Anshun, China, 77
Ansŏng, S. Korea, 81
Ansonia, Conn., 210
Antâkya, Turkey, 63
Antalaha, Malag. Rep., 118
Antalya (prov.), Turkey, 63
Antalya, Turkey, 63
Antalya (gulf), Turkey, 63
Antarctic (pen.), Ant., 5
Antarctica, 5
Antequera, Spain, 33
Anthony, Kans., 232
Anthony, N. Mex., 274
Anti-Atlas (ranges), Mor., 106
Antibes, France, 28
Anticosti (isl.), Que., 174
Antietam Nat'l Battlef. Site, Md., 245
Antigo, Wis., 317
Antigonish, N.S., 169
Antigua, 161
Antigua, Guat., 154
Antigua (riv.), Mex., 150
Antilla, Cuba, 158
Antilles, Greater (isls.), W. Indies, 156, 158, 161
Antilles, Lesser (isls.), W. Indies, 156,161
Antioch, Calif., 204
Antioch, Ill., 222
Antioquia (dept.), Col., 126
Antipodes (isls.), N.Z., 5
Antique (prov.), Phil., 82
Anti-Taurus (mts.), Turkey, 63
Antlers, Okla., 288
Antofagasta (prov.), Chile, 138
Antofagasta, Chile, 138
Antofagasta de la Sierra, Arg., 143
Antón, Pan., 154
Antongil (bay), Malag. Rep., 118
António Enes, Mozamb., 118
Antony, France, 28
Antrim (county), N. Ire., 17
Antrim, N. Ire., 17
Antsirabe, Malag. Rep., 118
Antung (Tantung), China, 77
Antwerp (prov.), Belg., 27
Antwerp, Belg., 27
An Uaimh, Ire., 17
Anuradhapura, Sri Lanka, 68
Anyang, China, 72
Anzhero-Sudzhensk, U.S.S.R., 48
Anzoátegui (state), Venez., 124
Aomori (prefecture), Japan, 81
Aomori, Japan, 81
Aosta (reg.), Italy, 34
Aosta (prov.), Italy, 34
Aosta, Italy, 34
Aoulef, Alg., 106
Apa (riv.), S. Amer., 144
Apache Jct., Ariz., 198
Apalachee (bay), Fla., 212
Apalachicola, Fla., 212
Apan, Mex., 150
Apaporis (riv.), Col., 126
Aparri, Phil., 82
Apatity, U.S.S.R., 52
Apatzingán de la Constitución, Mex., 150
Apeldoorn, Neth., 27
Apennines (mts.), Italy, 34
Apennines, Central (range), Italy, 34
Apennines, Northern (range), Italy, 34
Apennines, Southern (range), Italy, 34
Apia (cap.), W. Samoa, 87
Apizaco, Mex., 150
Apo (vol.), Phil., 82
Apolda, E. Ger., 22
Apollo, Pa., 294
Apopka, Fla., 212
Aporé (riv.), Braz., 132
Appalachian (mts.), U.S., 188
Appenzell Ausser-Rhoden (canton), Switz., 39
Appenzell Inner-Rhoden (canton), Switz., 39
Appleton, Wis., 317
Appleton City, Mo., 261
Apple Valley, Calif., 204
Apple Valley, Minn., 254
Appomattox C.H. Nat'l Hist. Pk., Va., 307
Apponaug, R.I., 249
Approuague (riv.), Fr. Guiana, 131
Apsheron (pen.), U.S.S.R., 52
Apsheronsk, U.S.S.R., 52
Apt, France, 28
Apulia (reg.), Italy, 34
Apure (state), Venez., 124
Apure (riv.), Venez., 124
Apurímac (dept.), Peru, 128
Apurímac (riv.), Peru, 128
'Aqaba (gulf), Asia, 59
'Aqaba, Jordan, 65
Aqsu, China, 77
Aquidauana, Braz., 132
Aquiles Serdán, Mex., 150
Aquin, Haiti, 158
Arab, Ala., 194
'Arab, Shatt-al- (riv.), Asia, 66
'Araba, Wadi (dry river), Asia, 65
Arabia (pen.), Asia, 54
Arabian (sea), Asia, 54
Arabian (des.), Egypt, 111
Aracaju, Braz., 132
Aracati, Braz., 132
Araçatuba, Braz., 135
Aracena, Spain, 33
Arad, Rum., 45
'Arafat, Jebel (mt.), Saudi Ar., 59
Arafura (sea), 85
Aragón (reg.), Spain, 33
Aragón (riv.), Spain, 33
Aragua (state), Venez., 124
Aragua de Barcelona, Venez., 124
Araguaia (riv.), Braz., 132
Araguari, Braz., 132
Araguari (riv.), Braz., 132
Arak, Iran, 66
Arakan (state), Burma, 72
Arakan Yoma (mts.), Burma, 72
Araks (riv.), Asia, 59
Aral (sea), U.S.S.R., 48
Aral'sk, U.S.S.R., 48
Aramberri, Mex., 150
Aran (isl.), Ire., 17
Aran (isls.), Ire., 17
Aranda de Duero, Spain, 33
Arandas, Mex., 150
Aranjuez, Spain, 33
Aransas Pass, Tex., 302
Arapey Grande (riv.), Urug., 145
Arapkir, Turkey, 63
Araranguá, Braz., 132
Araraquara, Braz., 135
Araras, Braz., 135
Ararat (mt.), Turkey, 63
Ararat, Vic., 97
Arauca (commissary), Col., 126
Arauca, Col., 126
Arauca (riv.), S. Amer., 120
Arauco (prov.), Chile, 138
Arauco, Chile, 138
Araxá, Braz., 132
Arbai Khere, Mong., 77
Arbela (Erbil), Iraq, 66
Arboga, Sweden, 18
Arborfield, Sask., 181
Arborg, Man., 179
Arbroath, Scot., 15
Arbuckle Nat'l Rec. Area, Okla., 288
Arcachon, France, 28
Arcadia, Calif., 204
Arcadia, Fla., 212
Arcadia, La., 238
Arcata, Calif., 204
Arcelia, Mex., 150
Archangel, U.S.S.R., 52
Archbald, Pa., 294
Archena, Spain, 33
Arches Nat'l Park, Utah, 304
Archidona, Spain, 33
Arco, Ga., 216
Arco, Idaho, 220
Arcola, Sask., 181
Arcos de la Frontera, Spain, 33
Arcot, India, 68
Arcoverde, Braz., 132
Arctic Circle, 4
Arctic Ocean, 4
Arctic Red River, N.W.T., 187
Arda (riv.), Europe, 45
Ardahan, Turkey, 63
Ardebil, Iran, 66
Ardèche (dept.), France, 28
Ardee, Ire., 17
Ardennes (plat.), Belg., 27
Ardennes (dept.), France, 28
Ardhéa, Greece, 45
Ardino, Bulg., 45
Ardistan, Iran, 66
Ardmore, Ind., 227
Ardmore, Okla., 288
Ardmore, Pa., 294
Ardrossan, Scot., 15
Ardsley, N.Y., 276
Arecibo (dist.), P. Rico, 161
Arecibo, P. Rico, 161
Areia Branca, Braz., 132
Arena (pt.), Mex., 150
Arenas (cay), Mex., 150
Arenas de San Pedro, Spain, 33
Arendal, Norway, 18
Arenys de Mar, Spain, 33

Arequipa (dept.), Peru, 128
Arequipa, Peru, 128
Arezzo (prov.), Italy, 34
Arezzo, Italy, 34
Argalastí, Greece, 45
Argamasilla de Alba, Spain, 33
Arganda, Spain, 33
Argentan, France, 28
Argenteuil, France, 28
Argentia, Newf., 166
Argentina, 143
Argentino (lake), Arg., 143
Argeş (riv.), Rum., 45
Argo, Sudan, 111
Argolís (gulf), Greece, 45
Argonne Nat'l Lab., Ill., 222
Árgos, Greece, 45
Argostólion, Greece, 45
Arguin (bay), Mauritania, 106
Argun (riv.), Asia, 77
Argyll (county), Scot., 15
Århus, Den., 21
Arica, Chile, 138
Arichat, N.S., 169
Ariège (dept.), France, 28
Arima, Trinidad and Tobago, 161
Arinos (riv.), Braz., 132
Aripuanã (riv.), Braz., 132
Arivonimamo, Malag. Rep., 118
Arizaro (salt dep.), Arg.,143
Arizona (state), U.S., 198
Arizpe, Mex., 150
Årjang, Sweden, 18
Arkadelphia, Ark., 203
Arkaig (lake), Scot., 15
Arkansas (state), U.S., 203
Arkansas (riv.), U.S., 188
Arkansas City, Kans., 232
Arkansas Post Nat'l Mem., Ark., 203
Arkhángelos, Greece, 45
Arkhangel'sk (Archangel), U.S.S.R., 52
Arklow, Ire., 17
Arkona (cape), E. Ger., 22
Arles, France, 28
Arlington, Mass., 249
Arlington, N.Y., 276
Arlington, Oreg., 291
Arlington, Tex., 302
Arlington, Va., 307
Arlington Heights, Ill., 222
Arlon, Belg., 27
Arma (plat.), Saudi Ar., 59
Armadale, Scot., 15
Armagh (county), N. Ire., 17
Armagh, N. Ire., 17
Armavir, U.S.S.R., 52
Armdale, N.S., 169
Armenia, Col., 126
Armenian S.S.R., U.S.S.R., 52
Armentières, France, 28
Armeria, Mex., 150
Armidale, N.S.W., 97
Armstrong, Br. Col., 184
Armstrong, Ont., 175
Arnaía, Greece, 45
Arnaud (riv.), Que., 174
Arnauti (cape), Cyprus, 63
Arnhem, Neth., 27
Arnhem (cape), N. Terr., 93
Arnhem Land (reg.), N. Terr., 93
Arno (riv.), Italy, 34
Arno (atoll), Pac. Is., 87
Arnold, Mo., 261
Arnold, Pa., 294
Arnprior, Ont., 177
Arnsberg, W. Ger., 22
Arnstadt, E. Ger., 22
Aroche, Spain, 33
Arorae (atoll), Gilb. & Ell. Is., 87
Arouca, Trinidad and Tobago, 161
Arrah, India, 68
Arran (isl.), Scot., 15
Arras, France, 28
Arrecife, Spain, 33
Arrecifes, Arg., 143
Arrecifes (riv.), Arg., 143
Arrowhead, Br. Col., 184
Arroyo, P. Rico, 161
Arroyo Grande, Calif., 204
Árta, Greece, 45
Arta, Spain, 33
Artem, U.S.S.R., 48
Artemisa, Cuba, 158
Artemovskiy, U.S.S.R., 48
Artesia, Calif., 204
Artesia, N. Mex., 274
Arthabaska, Que., 172
Arthur's (pass), N.Z., 101
Artibonite (dept.), Haiti, 158
Artibonite (river), Haiti, 158
Artigas (dept.), Urug., 145
Artigas, Urug., 145
Artillery (lake), N.W.T., 187
Artvin (prov.), Turkey, 63
Artvin, Turkey, 63
Aru (isls.), Indon., 85
Arua, Uganda, 115
Aruba (isl.), Neth. Ant., 161
Arucas, Spain, 33
Arunachal Pradesh (terr.), India, 68
Aruppukkottai, India, 68
Arusha (reg.), Tanz., 115
Arusha, Tanz., 115
Arusi (gov.), Eth., 111
Aruwimi (riv.), Zaire, 115
Arvada, Colo., 208
Arvi, India, 68
Arvida, Que., 172
Arvidsjaur, Sweden, 18
Arvika, Sweden, 18
Arvin, Calif., 204
Arzamas, U.S.S.R., 52
Aš, Czech., 41
Asahan (riv.), Indon., 85
Asahi (mt.), Japan, 81
Asahikawa, Japan, 81
Asansol, India, 68
Asbestos, Que., 172
Asbury Park, N. J., 273
Ascensión, Bol., 136
Ascensión, Mex., 150
Ascension (isl.), St. Helena, 102
Aschaffenburg, W. Ger., 22
Ascoli Piceno (prov.), Italy, 34
Ascoli Piceno, Italy, 34
Ascope, Peru, 128
Ascot, Queensland, 95
Åseda, Sweden, 18
Åsele, Sweden, 18
Asenovgrad, Bulg., 45
Ashanti (reg.), Ghana, 106
Ashburn, Ga., 216
Ashburton, N.Z., 101
Ashburton (riv.), W. Austral., 92
Ashcroft, Br. Col., 184
Ashdod, Israel, 65
Ashdown, Ark., 203
Asheboro, N.C., 281
Ashern, Man., 179
Asheville, N.C., 281
Ashfield, N.S.W., 97
Ashford, Eng., 13
Ash Fork, Ariz., 198
Ashibetsu, Japan, 81
Ashikaga, Japan, 81
Ashington, Eng., 13
Ashiya, Japan, 81
Ashkhabad, U.S.S.R., 48
Ashland, Kans., 232
Ashland, Ky., 237
Ashland, Ohio, 284
Ashland, Oreg., 291
Ashland, Pa., 294
Ashland, Va., 307
Ashland, Wis., 317
Ashley, N. Dak., 283
Ashley, Pa., 294
Ashmore and Cartier Islands (terr.), Austral., 88
Ashqelon, Israel, 65
Ash Shabicha, Iraq, 66
Ashtabula, Ohio, 284
Ashton-under-Lyne, Eng., 10
Ashwaubenon, Wis., 317
'Asi (riv.), Syria, 63
Asia, 54
Asilah, Mor., 106
Asinara (isl.), Italy, 34
Asino, U.S.S.R., 48
'Asir (reg.), Saudi Ar., 59
Askim, Norway, 18
Asmara, Eth., 111
Åsnen (lake), Sweden, 18
Asnières, France, 28
Aso (mt.), Japan, 81
Aspe, Spain, 33
Aspen, Colo., 208
Aspinwall, Pa., 294
Aspiring (mt.), N.Z., 101
Assab, Eth., 111
Assaba (reg.), Mauritania, 106
Assam (state), India, 68
Assateague Isl. Nat'l Seashore, Va., 307
Asselle, Eth., 111
Assiniboia, Sask., 181
Assiniboine (mt.), Canada, 182
Assis, Braz., 135
Assumption (isl.), Seych., 118
Astara, U.S.S.R., 52
Asterabad (Gurgan), Iran, 66
Asti (prov.), Italy, 34
Asti, Italy, 34
Astipálaia, Greece, 45
Astipálaia (isl.), Greece, 45
Astorga, Spain, 33
Astoria, Oreg., 291
Astove (isl.), Seych., 118
Astrakhan', U.S.S.R., 52
Asturias (reg.), Spain, 33
Asunción (cap.), Par., 144
Asunción Mita, Guat., 154
Aswân, Egypt, 111
Aswân High (dam), Egypt, 111
Asyût, Egypt, 111
Atacama (prov.), Chile, 138
Atacama (des.), Chile, 138
Atafu (atoll), Tokelau Is., 87
Atakpamé, Togo, 106
Atalándi, Greece, 45
Atalaya, Peru, 128
Atami, Japan, 81
Atar, Mauritania, 106
Atascadero, Calif., 204
Atbara, Sudan, 111
Atbara (riv.), Africa, 111
Atbasar, U.S.S.R., 48
Atchison, Kans., 232
Atco, N. J., 273
Atenas, C. Rica, 154
Athabasca, Alta., 182
Athabasca (riv.), Alta., 182
Athabasca (lake), Canada, 163
Athens, Ala., 194
Athens, Ga., 216
Athens (cap.), Greece, 45
Athens, N.Y., 276
Athens, Ohio, 284
Athens, Pa., 294
Athens, Tenn., 237
Athens, Tex., 302
Atherton, Calif., 204
Athlone, Ire., 17
Athol, Mass., 249
Athol (dist.), Scotland, 15
Atholville, N.B., 170
Áthos (mt.), Greece, 45
Athy, Ire., 17
Ati, Chad, 111
Atikameg, Alta., 182
Atikokan, Ont., 175
Atikonak (lake), Newf., 166
Atiquizaya, El Sal., 154
Atitlán (lake), Guat., 154
Atitlán (vol.), Guat., 154
Atiu (isl.), Cook Is., 87
Atka (isl.), Alaska, 196
Atkarsk, U.S.S.R., 52
Atkinson, Nebr., 264
Atlanta, C. Rica, 154
Atlanta (cap.), Ga., 216
Atlanta, Tex., 302
Atlantic, Iowa, 229
Atlantic Beach, Fla., 212
Atlantic City, N. J., 273
Atlantic Highlands, N. J., 273
Atlántico (dept.), Col., 126
Atlantic Ocean, North, 3
Atlantic Ocean, South, 3
Atlas (mts.), Africa, 106
Atlin, Br. Col., 184
Atlixco, Mex., 150
Atmore, Ala., 194
Atoka, Okla., 288
Atotonilco, Mex., 150
Atoyac (riv.), Mex., 150
Atrek (riv.), Asia, 66
Attalla, Ala., 194
Attawapiskat (riv.), Ont., 175
Attica, Ind., 227
Attica, N.Y., 276
Attikamagen (lake), Newf., 166
Attleboro, Mass., 249
Attopeu, Laos, 72
Attu (isl.), Alaska, 196
Atuel (riv.), Arg., 143
Atuntaqui, Ecuador, 128
Atuona, Fr. Poly., 87
Atwater, Calif., 204
Atwood (Samana) (cay), Bah., 156
Aubagne, France, 28
Aube (dept.), France, 28
Aube (riv.), France, 28
Aubenas, France, 28
Aubervilliers, France, 28
Auburn, Ala., 194
Auburn, Calif., 204
Auburn, Ind., 227
Auburn, Maine, 242
Auburn, Mass., 249
Auburn, Nebr., 264
Auburn, N.S.W., 97
Auburn, N.Y., 276
Auburn, Wash., 310
Auburndale, Fla., 212
Auburndale, Mass., 249
Auburn Hts., Mich.,250
Aubusson, France, 28
Auch, France, 28
Auchterarder, Scot., 15
Auckland (prov. dist.), N.Z., 101
Auckland, N.Z., 101
Aude (dept.), France, 28
Audincourt, France, 28
Audubon, Iowa, 229
Audubon, N. J., 273
Aue, E. Ger., 22
Auerbach, E. Ger., 22
Augsburg, W. Ger., 22
Augusta, Ga., 216
Augusta, Kans., 232
Augusta (cap.), Maine, 242
Aujila, Libya, 111
Aulnay-sous-Bois, France, 28
Aur, Pulau (isl.), Malaysia, 72
Aurangabad, India, 68
Auray, France, 28
Aurès (mts.), Alg., 106
Aurich, W. Ger., 22
Aurignac, France, 28
Aurillac, France, 28
Aurora, Colo., 208
Aurora, Ill., 222
Aurora, Ind., 227
Aurora, Minn., 254
Aurora, Mo., 261
Aurora, Nebr., 264
Aurora, Ohio, 284
Aurora, Ont., 177
Aus, S.W. Afr., 118
Aust-Agder (county), Norway, 18
Austin, Ind., 227
Austin, Minn., 254
Austin, Nev., 266
Austin (cap.), Tex., 302
Austral (isls.), Fr. Poly., 87
Australia, 88
Australian Alps (mts.), Austral., 97
Australian Capital (terr.), Austral., 97
Austria, 41
Autlan, Mex., 150
Autun, France, 28
Auvergne (mts.), France, 28
Auxerre, France, 28
Auyuittuq Nat'l Park, N.W.T., 187
Avallon, France, 28
Avalon, Calif., 204
Avalon (pen.), Newf., 166
Avalon, Pa., 294
Avaré, Braz., 135
Avarua (cap.), Cook Is., 87
Aveiro, Port., 33
Avellaneda, Arg., 143
Avellino (prov.), Italy, 34
Avellino, Italy, 34
Avenal, Calif., 204
Avenel, N. J., 273
Avesnes, France, 28
Avesta, Sweden, 18
Aveyron (dept.), France, 28
Avignon, France, 28
Ávila (prov.), Spain, 33
Ávila, Spain, 33
Avion, France, 28
Avoca, Pa., 294
Avon (riv.), Eng., 13
Avon, N.Y., 276
Avon, Ohio, 284
Avondale, Ariz., 198
Avon Lake, Ohio, 284
Avon Park, Fla., 212
Avranches, France, 28
Awaji (isl.), Japan, 81
Awash (riv.), Eth., 111
Awe (lake), Scot., 15
Axel Heiberg (isl.), N.W.T., 187
Axim, Ghana, 106
Ayabe, Japan, 81
Ayacucho, Arg., 143
Ayacucho (dept.), Peru, 128
Ayacucho, Peru, 128
Ayaguz, U.S.S.R., 48
Ayamonte, Spain, 33
Ayapel, Col., 126
Ayden, N.C., 281
Aydın (prov.), Turkey, 63
Aydın, Turkey, 63
Ayer, Mass., 249
Ayer's Cliff, Que., 172
Ayers Rock (mt.), N. Terr., 93
Áyion Óros (aut. dist.), Greece, 45
Áyios Evstrátios (isl.), Greece, 45
Áyios Matthaíos, Greece, 45
Áyios Nikólaos, Greece, 45
Áyios Yeóryios (cape), Greece, 45
Aykhal, U.S.S.R., 48
Aylesbury, Eng., 13
Aylmer (lake), N.W.T., 187
Aylmer, Ont., 177
Ayora, Spain, 33
Ayr, Queensland, 95
Ayr (county), Scot., 15
Ayr, Scot., 15
Ayre (pt.), I. of Man, 13
Aytos, Bulg., 45
Ayutla, Mex., 150
Ayutthaya, Thai., 72
Ayvalik, Turkey, 63
Azamgarh, India, 68
Azcapotzalco, Mex., 150
Azemmour, Mor., 106
Azerbaidzhan S.S.R., U.S.S.R., 52
Azle, Tex., 302
Azogues, Ecuador, 128
Azores (isls.), Port., 32
Azov, U.S.S.R., 52
Azov (sea), U.S.S.R., 52
Azoyú, Mex., 150
Azpeitia, Spain, 33
Azrou, Mor., 106
Aztec, N. Mex., 274
Aztec Ruins Nat'l Mon., N. Mex., 274
Azua (prov.), Dom. Rep., 158
Azua, Dom. Rep., 158
Azuaga, Spain, 33
Azuay (prov.), Ecuador, 128
Azuero (pen.), Pan., 154
Azul, Arg., 143
Azul (riv.), Guat., 154
Azul (mts.), Peru, 128
Azusa, Calif., 204
Az Zubair, Iraq, 66

B

Ba'albek, Leb., 63
Baba (cape), Turkey, 63
Babahoyo, Ecua., 128
Babar (isls.), Indon., 85
Babbitt, Minn., 254
Babbitt, Nev., 266
Bab el Mandeb (strait), 111
Babelthuap (isl.), Pac. Is., 87
Babia (riv.), Mex., 150
Babil (prov.), Iraq, 66
Babine (riv.), Br. Col., 184
Babol, Iran, 66
Babuyan (isls.), Phil., 82
Babylon (ruins), Iraq, 66
Babylon, N.Y., 276
Bacalar (lake), Mex., 150
Bacău, Rum., 45
Bacchus Marsh, Vic., 97
Bach Long Vi (Nightingale) (isl.), N. Vietnam, 72
Bačka Topola, Yugo., 45
Backnang, W. Ger., 22
Bac Lieu (Vinh Loi), S. Vietnam, 72
Bac Ninh, N. Vietnam, 72
Bacolod, Phil., 82
Bács-Kiskun (county), Hung., 41
Bacup, Eng., 10
Badagara, India, 68
Badajoz (prov.), Spain, 33
Badajoz, Spain, 33
Badalona, Spain, 33
Bad Axe, Mich., 250
Bad Doberan, E. Ger., 22
Bad Dürkheim, W. Ger., 22
Bad Dürrenberg, E. Ger., 22
Baden, Austria, 41
Baden, Pa., 294
Baden, Switz., 39
Baden-Baden, W. Ger., 22
Baden-Württemberg (state), W. Ger., 22
Badgastein, Austria, 41
Bad Hersfeld, W. Ger., 22
Bad Homburg, W. Ger., 22
Bad Ischl, Austria, 41
Bad Kissingen, W. Ger., 22
Bad Kreuznach, W. Ger., 22
Badlands Nat'l Mon., S. Dak., 298
Bad Langensalza, E. Ger., 22
Badr, Saudi Ar., 59
Bad Salzuflen, W. Ger., 22
Bad Tölz, W. Ger., 22
Badulla, Sri Lanka, 68
Baffin (bay), N. Amer., 187
Baffin (isl.), N.W.T., 187
Bafq, Iran, 66
Bafra, Turkey, 63
Bagalkot, India, 68
Bagamoyo, Tanz., 115
Bagé, Braz., 132
Bagenalstown (Muinebeag) Ire., 17
Baghdad (prov.), Iraq, 66
Baghdad (cap.), Iraq, 66
Baghlan, Afghan., 68
Bagnères-de-Bigorre, France, 28
Bagnolet, France, 28
Bago, Phil., 82
Bagotville, Que., 172
Baguio, Phil., 82
Baguirmi (reg.), Chad, 111
Bahamas, 156
Bahariya (oasis), Egypt, 111
Bahawalnagar, Pak., 68
Bahawalpur, Pak., 68
Bahia (state), Braz., 132
Bahia (Salvador), Braz., 132
Bahía (isls.), Hond., 154
Bahía Blanca, Arg., 143
Bahía de Caráquez, Ecua., 128
Bahraich, India, 68
Bahrain, 59
Bahramabad, Iran, 66
Bahr el Ghazal (prov.), Sudan, 111
Bahr es Safi (des.), Arabia, 59
Baia Mare, Rum., 45
Baida, Libya, 111
Baidoa, Somalia, 115
Baie-Comeau, Que., 172
Baie-Saint-Paul, Que., 172
Baie-Trinité, Que., 172
Baie Verte, Newf., 166
Baile Atha Cliath (Dublin) (cap.), Ire., 17
Băileşti, Rum., 45
Bainbridge, Ga., 216
Bainbridge Naval Train. Ctr., Md., 245
Bairiki (cap.), Gilb. & Ell. Is., 87
Bairnsdale, Vic., 97
Bais, Phil., 82
Baixo Alentejo (prov.), Port., 33
Baja, Hung., 41
Baja California Norte (state), Mex., 150
Baja California Sur (state), Mex., 150
Bajo Boquete, Pan., 154
Baker, La., 238
Baker, Mont., 262
Baker, Oreg., 291
Baker (isl.), Pacific, 87
Baker (mt.), Wash., 310
Baker Lake, N.W.T., 187
Bakersfield, Calif., 204
Bakewell, Eng., 10
Bakhchisaray, U.S.S.R., 52
Bakhmach, U.S.S.R., 52
Bakhtiari (governorate), Iran, 66
Bakırköy, Turkey, 63
Bakony (mts.), Hung., 41
Baku, U.S.S.R., 52
Bala, Wales, 13
Balabac (isl.), Phil., 82
Bala Cynwyd, Pa., 294
Balakhna, U.S.S.R., 52
Balaklava, U.S.S.R., 52
Balakovo, U.S.S.R., 52
Bala Murghab, Afghan., 68
Balashov, U.S.S.R., 52
Balasore, India, 68
Balaton (lake), Hung., 41
Balboa, C.Z., 154
Balbriggan, Ire., 17
Balcarce, Arg., 143
Balchik, Bulg., 45
Balch Sprs., Tex., 302
Balclutha, N.Z., 101
Baldwin, N.Y., 276
Baldwin, Pa., 294
Baldwin Pk., Calif., 204
Baldwinsville, N.Y., 276
Baleares (prov.), Spain, 33
Balearic (isls.), Spain, 33
Baleine (riv.), Que., 174
Balhaf, P.D.R., Yemen, 59
Bali (isl.), Indon., 85
Bali (sea), Indon., 85
Balıkesir (prov.), Turkey, 63
Balıkesir, Turkey, 63
Balikpapan, Indon., 85
Balkan (mts.), Bulg., 45
Balkh, Afghan., 68
Balkhash, U.S.S.R., 48
Balkhash (lake), U.S.S.R., 48
Ballarat, Vic., 97
Ballater, Scot., 15
Ballenas (bay), Mex., 150
Ballerup, Den., 21
Ballia, India, 68
Ballina, Ire., 17
Ballina, N.S.W., 97
Ballinasloe, Ire., 17
Ballinger, Tex., 302
Ballinrobe, Ire., 17
Ballston Spa, N.Y., 276
Bally, India, 68
Ballybunion, Ire., 17
Ballycastle, N. Ire., 17
Ballymoney, N. Ire., 17
Ballymote, Ire., 17
Ballyshannon, Ire., 17
Balmoral, Queensland, 95
Balmoral Castle, Scot., 15
Balonne (riv.), Queensland, 95
Balrampur, India, 68
Balsas (riv.), Mex., 150
Baltic (sea), Europe, 18
Baltimore, Ire., 17
Baltimore, Md., 245
Baltistan (reg.), India, 68
Baltit, India, 68
Baltiysk, U.S.S.R., 52
Baluchistan (reg.), Iran, 66
Baluchistan (prov.), Pak., 68
Bam, Iran, 66
Bamako (cap.), Mali, 106
Bambari, Centr. Afr. Rep., 115
Bamberg, S.C., 296
Bamberg, W. Ger., 22
Bamenda, Cameroon, 115
Bamian, Afghan., 68
Bam Tso (lake), China, 77
Banana, Zaire, 115
Bananal (isl.), Braz., 132
Bânâs, Ras (cape), Egypt, 111
Banbury, Eng., 13
Banchory, Scot., 15
Bancroft, Ont., 175
Banda, India, 68
Banda (sea), Indon., 85
Banda Atjeh, Indon., 85
Bandar 'Abbas, Iran, 66
Bandar Maharani, Malaysia, 72
Bandar Penggaram, Malaysia, 72
Bandar Seri Begawan (cap.), Brunei, 85
Bandar Shah, Iran, 66
Bandar Shahpur, Iran, 66
Bandeira (mt.), Braz., 132
Bandelier Nat'l Mon., N. Mex., 274
Banderas (bay), Mex., 150
Bandiagara, Mali, 106
Bandırma, Turkey, 63
Bandjarmasin, Indon., 85
Bandon, Ire., 17
Bandra, India, 68
Bandundu (reg.), Zaire, 115
Bandundu, Zaire, 115
Bandung, Indon., 85
Banes, Cuba, 158
Banff, Alta., 182
Banff (county), Scot., 15
Banff, Scot., 15
Banff Nat'l Park, Alta., 182
Bangalore, India, 68
Bangassou, Centr. Afr. Rep., 115
Banggai (arch.), Indon., 85
Bangka (isl.), Indon., 85
Bangkok (cap.), Thai., 72
Bangladesh, 68
Bangor, Maine, 242
Bangor, N. Ire., 17
Bangor, Pa., 294
Bangor, Wales, 13
Bangued, Phil., 82
Bangui (cap.), Centr. Afr. Rep., 115
Bangweulu (lake), Zambia, 115
Baní, Dom. Rep., 158
Baniara, P.N.G., 85
Baniyas, Syria, 63
Banja Luka, Yugo., 45
Banjul (cap.), Gambia, 106
Banjuwangi, Indon., 85
Banks (isl.), Br. Col., 184
Banks (isls.), New Hebr., 87
Banks (isl.), N.W.T., 187
Banks (strait), Tas., 99
Bankstown, N.S.W., 97
Bankura, India, 68
Ban Me Thuot, S. Vietnam, 72
Banning, Calif., 204
Bannockburn, Scot., 15
Bannu, Pak., 68
Ban Pua, Thai., 72
Bansberia, India, 68
Banská Bystrica, Czech., 41
Banstead, Eng., 10
Bantry, Ire., 17
Bantry (bay), Ire., 17
Bantul, Indon., 85
Banzare Coast (reg.), Ant., 5
Banzyville, Zaire, 115
Baoruco (prov.), Dom. Rep., 158
Ba'quba, Iraq, 66
Baqura, Jordan, 65
Bar, Yugo., 45
Barabinsk, U.S.S.R., 48
Baraboo, Wis., 317
Baracoa, Cuba, 158
Baradero, Arg., 143
Barahona (prov.), Dom. Rep., 158
Barahona, Dom. Rep., 158
Baranovichi, U.S.S.R., 52
Baranya (county), Hung., 41
Barawa (Brava), Somalia, 115
Barbacena, Braz., 135
Barbados, 161
Barbate (riv.), Spain, 33
Barbeau (peak), N.W.T., 187
Barberton, Ohio, 284
Barbourville, Ky., 237
Barbuda (isl.), Antigua, 156
Barce (El Marj), Libya, 111
Barcellona Pozzo di Gotto, Italy, 34
Bareclona (prov.), Spain, 33
Barcelona, Spain, 33
Barcelona, Venez., 124
Bardera, Somalia, 115
Bardstown, Ky., 237
Bareilly, India, 68
Barents (sea), 48
Barentsburg, Norway, 18
Bar Harbor, Maine, 242
Bari (prov.), Italy, 34
Bari, Italy, 34
Barinas (state), Venez., 124
Barinas, Venez., 124
Barisal, Bang., 68
Barisan (mts.), Indon., 85
Barito (riv.), Indon., 85
Barking, Eng., 10
Barkly (tableland), N. Terr., 93
Bar-le-Duc, France, 28
Barlee (lake), W. Austral., 92
Barletta, Italy, 34
Barmer, India, 68
Barmouth, Wales, 13
Barnagore, India, 68
Barnaul, U.S.S.R., 48
Barnesboro, Pa., 294
Barnesville, Ga., 216
Barnet, Eng., 10
Barnsley, Eng., 13
Barnstaple, Eng., 13
Barnwell, S.C., 296
Baroda, India, 68
Barogbil (pass), Asia, 68
Barotseland (reg.), Zambia, 115
Barpeta, India, 68
Barquisimeto, Venez., 124
Barra (isl.), Scot., 15
Barra (isls.), Scot., 15
Barrackpore, India, 68
Barrackville, W. Va., 313
Barra do Piraí, Braz., 135
Barra Mansa, Braz., 135
Barranca, Peru, 128
Barrancabermeja, Col., 126
Barranquilla, Col., 126
Barraute, Que., 174
Barre, Vt., 268
Barrhead, Alta., 182
Barrhead, Scot., 15
Barrie, Ont., 177
Barrington, Ill., 222
Barrington, N. J., 273
Barrington, R.I., 249
Barrow, Alaska, 196
Barrow (pt.), Alaska, 196
Barrow (riv.), Ire., 17
Barrow (isl.), W. Austral.,92
Barrow-in-Furness, Eng., 13
Barr Smith (mt.), Ant., 5
Barry, Wales, 13
Barry's Bay, Ont., 175
Barsi, India, 68
Barstow, Calif., 204
Bartica, Guyana, 131
Bartin, Turkey, 63
Bartlesville, Okla., 288
Bartolomeu Dias, Mozamb., 118
Bartonville, Ill., 222
Bartow, Fla., 212
Baruun Urta, Mong., 77
Barvas, Scot., 15
Barwon (riv.), N.S.W., 97
Basankusu, Zaire, 115
Basco, Phil., 82
Basel, Switz., 39
Baselland (canton), Switz., 39
Basestadt (canton), Switz., 39
Bashi (chan.), Asia, 82
Bashkir A.S.S.R., U.S.S.R., 52
Basilan (prov.), Phil., 82
Basilan (isl.), Phil., 82
Basildon, Eng., 13
Basilicata (reg.), Italy, 34
Basin, Wyo., 319
Basingstoke, Eng., 13
Basirhat, India, 68
Basra (prov.), Iraq, 66
Basra, Iraq, 66
Bas-Rhin (dept.), France, 28
Bass (strait), Austral., 88
Bassano, Alta., 182
Bassano del Grappa, Italy, 34
Bassein, Burma, 72
Bassein, India, 68
Basse-Terre (cap.), Guad., 161
Basseterre (cap.), St. Chr.-N.-A., 161
Bassett, Va., 307
Bastia, France, 28
Bastogne, Belg., 27
Bastrop, La., 238
Bastrop, Tex., 302
Bas-Zaïre(reg.), Zaire, 115
Bata, Eq. Guin., 115
Bataan (prov.), Phil., 82
Batabanó (gulf), Cuba, 158
Batala, India, 68
Batalha, Port., 33
Batan (isls.), Phil., 82
Batanes (prov.), Phil., 82
Batang, China, 77
Batang, Indon., 85
Batangan (cape), S. Vietnam, 72
Batangas (prov.), Phil., 82
Batangas, Phil., 82
Batavia, Ill., 222
Batavia (Djakarta)(cap.), Indon., 85
Batavia, N.Y., 276
Bataysk, U.S.S.R., 52
Batesburg, S.C., 296
Batesville, Ark., 203
Batesville, Ind., 227
Batesville, Miss., 256
Bath, Eng., 13
Bath, Maine, 242
Bath, N.Y., 276
Bathgate, Scot., 15
Bathurst, N.B., 170
Bathurst, N.S.W., 97
Bathurst (isl.), N. Terr., 93
Bathurst (isl.), N.W.T., 187
Batina (reg.), Oman, 59
Batjan (isls.), Indon., 85
Batley, Eng., 13
Batman, Turkey, 63
Batna, Alg., 106
Bato-Bato, Phil., 82
Baton Rouge (cap.), La., 238
Batouri, Cameroon, 115
Battambang, Cambodia, 72
Batterbee (cape), Ant., 5
Batticaloa, Sri Lanka, 68
Battle Creek, Mich., 250
Battleford, Sask., 181
Battle Harbour, Newf., 166
Batu (isls.), Indon., 85
Batu Gajah, Malaysia, 72
Batumi, U.S.S.R., 52
Bat Yam, Israel, 65
Bauchi, Nigeria, 106
Baudouinville, Zaire, 115
Bauld (cape), Newf., 166
Baulkham Hills, N.S.W., 97
Bauru, Braz., 135
Bautzen, E. Ger., 22
Bavaria (state), W. Ger., 22
Bavarian (for.), W. Ger., 22
Bavarian Alps (mts.), Europe, 22
Bavispe (riv.), Mex., 150
Bawean (isl.), Indon., 85
Baxley, Ga., 216
Baxter Sprs., Kans., 232
Bayamo, Cuba, 158
Bayamón (dist.), P. Rico, 161
Bayamón, P. Rico, 161
Bayan Kara Shan (range), China, 77
Bayan Khongor (prov.), Mong., 77
Bayan Khongor, Mong., 77
Bayan Tumen (Choibalsan), Mong., 77
Bayan Ulegei (prov.), Mong., 77
Bayan Ulegei, Mong., 77
Bayard, N. Mex., 274
Bayburt, Turkey, 63
Bay City, Mich., 250
Bay City, Tex., 302
Bayeux, France, 28
Baykal (lake), U.S.S.R., 48
Baykonur, U.S.S.R., 48
Bay Minette, Ala., 194
Bayombong, Phil., 82
Bayonne, France, 28
Bayonne, N. J., 273
Bayport, Minn., 254
Bayport, N.Y., 276
Bayram-Ali, U.S.S.R., 48
Bayreuth, W. Ger., 22
Bay Roberts, Newf., 166
Bay Saint Louis, Miss., 256
Bay Shore, N.Y., 276
Bayside, Wis., 317
Bay Village, Ohio, 284
Bayville, N.Y., 276
Baza, Spain, 33
Bazaruto (isl.), Mozamb., 118
Beaconsfield, Que., 172
Beachwood, N. J., 273
Beachwood, Ohio, 284
Beachy (head), Eng., 13
Beacon, N.Y., 276
Beagle (chan.), Chile, 138
Bear (lake), U.S., 304
Beardmore (glac.), Ant., 5
Beardstown, Ill., 222
Bearpaw (mts.), Mont., 262
Beata (isl.), Dom. Rep., 158
Beatrice, Nebr., 264
Beatton (riv.), Br. Col., 184
Beaufort, Malaysia, 85
Beaufort (sea), N. Amer., 187
Beaufort, N.C., 281
Beaufort, S.C., 296
Beaufort West, S. Afr., 118
Beauharnois, Que., 172
Beauly, Scot., 15
Beaumaris, Wales, 13
Beaumont, Calif., 204
Beaumont, Tex., 302
Beauport, Que., 172
Beauséjour, Man., 179
Beauvais, France, 28
Beaver, Okla., 288
Beaver, Pa., 294
Beaver Dam, Wis., 317
Beaver Falls, Pa., 294
Beaverhead (mts.), Idaho, 220
Beaverlodge, Alta., 182
Beaverton, Oreg., 291
Bebington, Eng., 10
Bečej, Yugo., 45
Béchar, Alg., 106
Beckley, W. Va., 313
Bedeque (bay), P.E.I., 169
Bedford, Eng., 13
Bedford, Ind., 227
Bedford, Ohio, 284
Bedford, Pa., 294
Bedford, Tex., 302
Bedford, Va., 307
Bedfordshire (county), Eng., 13
Bedlington Sta., Eng., 13
Bedworth, Eng., 13
Będzin, Poland, 47
Beersheba, Israel, 65
Beeston and Stapleford, Eng., 13
Beeville, Tex., 302
Bega, N.S.W., 97
Begemdir and Simen (gov.), Eth., 111
Behbehan, Iran, 66
Beira (dist.), Mozamb., 118
Beira, Mozamb., 118
Beira Alta (prov.), Port., 33
Beira Baixa (prov.), Port., 33
Beira Litoral (prov.), Port., 33
Beirut (cap.), Leb., 63
Beith, Scot., 15
Beit Jala, Jordan, 65
Beit Sahur, Jordan, 65
Beja, Port., 33
Beja, Tunisia, 106
Béjaïa, Alg., 106
Béjar, Spain, 33
Bekasi, Indon., 85
Békés (county), Hung., 41
Békéscsaba, Hung., 41
Bela, Pak., 68
Bela Crkva, Yugo., 45
Bel Air, Md., 245
Belaya (riv.), U.S.S.R., 52
Belaya Tserkov', U.S.S.R., 52
Belding, Mich., 250
Belebey, U.S.S.R., 52
Belém, Braz., 132
Belém, Port., 33
Belen, N. Mex., 274
Belep (isls.), New Cal., 87
Belet Uen, Somalia, 115
Belfast, Maine, 242
Belfast (cap.), N. Ire., 17
Belfast (inlet), N. Ire., 17
Belford, N. J., 273
Belfort (terr.), France, 28
Belfort, France, 28
Belgaum, India, 68
Belgium, 27
Belgorod, U.S.S.R., 52
Belgorod-Dnestrovskiy, U.S.S.R., 52
Belgrade (cap.), Yugo., 45
Belitung (Billiton) (isl.), Indon., 85
Belize, 154
Belize City, Belize, 154
Bell, Calif., 204
Bell (isl.), Newf., 166
Bella Coola, Br. Col., 184
Bellaire, Ohio, 284
Bellaire, Tex., 302
Bellary, India, 68
Bella Unión, Urug., 145
Bell Bay, Tas., 99
Bellefontaine, Ohio, 284
Bellefonte, Pa., 294
Belle Fourche, S. Dak., 298
Belle Glade, Fla., 212
Belle-Île (isl.), France, 28
Belle Isle (str.), Newf., 166
Belle Mead, N.J., 273
Belle Meade, Tenn., 237
Belleoram, Newf., 166
Belle Plaine, Iowa, 229
Belleville, Ill., 222
Belleville, Kans., 232
Belleville, N. J., 273
Belleville, Ont., 177
Bellevue, Alta., 182
Bellevue, Ky., 237
Bellevue, Nebr., 264
Bellevue, Ohio, 284
Bellevue, Pa., 294
Bellevue, Wash., 310
Bellflower, Calif., 204
Bellingham, Wash., 310
Bellingshausen (sea), Ant., 5
Bellinzona, Switz., 39
Bellmawr, N. J., 273
Bellmead, Tex., 302
Bellmore, N.Y., 276
Bellows Falls, Vt., 268
Belluno (prov.), Italy, 34
Belluno, Italy, 34
Bell Ville, Arg., 143
Bellville, S. Afr., 118
Bellwood, Ill., 222
Belmar, N. J., 273
Belmont, Calif., 204
Belmont, Mass., 249
Belmont, N.C., 281
Belmopan (cap.), Belize, 154
Belogorsk, U.S.S.R., 48
Belo Horizonte, Braz., 135
Beloit, Kans., 232
Beloit, Wis., 317
Beloretsk, U.S.S.R., 52
Belo-sur-Tsiribihina, Malag. Rep., 118
Beloye (lake), U.S.S.R., 52
Belper, Eng., 13
Belpre, Ohio, 284
Belton, Mo., 261
Belton, S.C., 296
Belton, Tex., 302
Beltsville, Md., 245
Bel'tsy, U.S.S.R., 52
Belur, India, 68
Belvidere, Ill., 222
Belzoni, Miss., 256
Bemidji, Minn., 254
Bemis, Tenn., 237
Benadir (prov.), Somalia, 115
Benalla, Vic., 97
Benares (Varanasi), India, 68
Ben Avon Pa., 294
Benbecula (isl.), Scot., 15
Benbrook, Tex., 302
Bend, Oreg., 291
Bendery, U.S.S.R., 52
Bendigo, Vic., 97
Bene Beraq, Israel, 65
Benevento (prov.), Italy, 34
Benevento, Italy, 34
Benfleet, Eng., 13
Bengal (bay), Asia, 68
Benghazi (prov.), Libya, 111
Benghazi, Libya, 111
Bengkalis, Indon., 85
Bengkulu, Indon., 85

Bên Gôi (bay), S. Vietnam, 72
Benguela (dist.), Angola, 115
Benguela, Angola, 115
Benguet (prov.), Phil., 82
Benha, Egypt, 111
Beni, El (dept.), Bolivia, 136
Benicia, Calif., 204
Beni Mazar, Egypt, 111
Beni-Mellal, Mor., 106
Benin, 106
Benin (bight), Africa, 106
Benin City, Nigeria, 106
Beni Suef, Egypt, 111
Benjamín Hill, Mex., 150
Bennettsville, S.C., 296
Ben Nevis (mt.), Scot., 15
Bennington, Vt., 268
Benoni, S. Africa, 118
Benque Viejo, Belize, 154
Bensenville, Ill., 222
Bensheim, W. Ger., 22
Benson, Ariz., 198
Benson, Minn., 254
Bentleyville, Pa., 294
Benton, Ark., 204
Benton, Ill., 222
Benton, Ky., 237
Bentong, Malaysia, 72
Benton Harbor, Mich., 250
Bentonville, Ark., 203
Bent's Old Fort Nat'l Hist. Site, Colo., 209
Benue (riv.), Africa, 106
Benue-Plateau (state), Nigeria, 106
Benwood, W. Va., 313
Beograd (Belgrade) (cap.), Yugo., 45
Beppu, Japan, 81
Bequia (isl.), St. Vincent, 156
Berar (reg.), India, 68
Berat, Albania, 45
Berau (bay), Indon., 85
Berber, Sudan, 111
Berbera, Somalia, 115
Berbérati, Centr. Afr. Rep., 115
Berchem, Belg., 27
Berchtesgaden, W. Ger., 22
Berdichev, U.S.S.R., 52
Berdyansk, U.S.S.R., 52
Berea, Ky., 237
Berea, Ohio, 284
Beregovo, U.S.S.R., 52
Berens (riv.), Canada, 179
Berezina (riv.), U.S.S.R., 52
Berezniki, U.S.S.R., 52
Bergama, Turkey, 63
Bergamo (prov.), Italy, 34
Bergamo, Italy, 34
Bergen, Neth., 27
Bergen, Norway, 18
Bergenfield, N. J., 273
Bergen op Zoom, Neth., 27
Bergerac, France, 28
Bergisch Gladbach, W. Ger., 22
Berhampore, India, 68
Berhampur, India, 68
Bering (sea), 3
Bering (strait), 196
Bering (isl.), U.S.S.R., 48
Berkeley, Calif., 204
Berkeley, Ill., 222
Berkeley, Mo., 261
Berkeley Hts., N. J., 273
Berkeley Sprs., W. Va., 313
Berkley, Mich., 250
Berkshire (county), Eng., 13
Berkshire (hills), Mass., 249
Berlin, Conn., 210
Berlin, N.H., 268
Berlin, N. J., 373
Berlin, Wis., 317
Berlin, East (cap.), E. Ger., 22
Berlin, West, W. Ger., 22
Bermeo, Spain, 33
Bermuda, 156
Bermuda (isl.), Berm., 156
Bern (canton), Switz., 39
Bern (cap.), Switz., 39
Bernalillo, N. Mex., 274
Bernardsville, N. J., 273
Bernburg, E. Ger., 22
Bernese Oberland (reg.), Switz., 39
Bernierville, Que., 172
Bernina (pass), Switz., 39
Beroun, Czech., 41
Berry (isls.), Bah., 156
Berthierville, Que., 172
Beru (atoll), Gilb. & Ellice Is., 87
Berwick, La., 238
Berwick, Pa., 294
Berwick (county), Scot., 15
Berwick, Vic., 97
Berwick-upon-Tweed, Eng., 13
Berwyn, Ill., 222
Berwyn, Pa., 294
Berwyn (mts.), Wales, 13
Besançon, France, 28
Beşiktaş, Turkey, 63
Beskids (mts.), Europe, 41
Beslan, U.S.S.R., 52
Besni, Turkey, 63
Bessemer, Ala., 194
Bessemer, Mich., 250
Bessemer City, N.C., 281
Bethalto, Ill., 222
Bethanie, S.W. Afr., 118
Bethany, Mo., 261
Bethany, Okla., 288
Bethel, Alaska, 196
Bethel, Conn., 210
Bethel Park, Pa., 294
Bethesda, Md., 245
Bethesda, Wales, 13
Bethlehem, Jordan, 65
Bethlehem, Pa., 294
Bethlehem, S. Africa, 118
Béthune, France, 28
Bet She'an, Israel, 65
Betsiamites (riv.), Que., 174
Bettendorf, Iowa, 229
Bettiah, India, 68
Betws-y-coed, Wales, 13
Beverley, Eng., 13
Beverly, Mass., 249
Beverly, N. J., 273
Beverly Hills, Calif., 204
Beverwijk, Neth., 27
Bewdley, Eng., 10
Bexhill, Eng., 13
Bexley, Eng., 10
Bexley, Ohio, 284
Beykoz, Turkey, 63
Beyla, Guinea, 106
Beyoğlu, Turkey, 63
Beyşehir (lake), Turkey, 63
Bezhetsk, U.S.S.R., 52
Béziers, France, 28
Bhadrak, India, 68
Bhadravati, India, 68
Bhadreswar, India, 68
Bhagalpur, India, 68
Bhaktapur, Nepal, 68
Bhamo, Burma, 72
Bhandara, India, 68
Bhandup, India, 68
Bharatpur, India, 68
Bhatinda, India, 68
Bhatpara, India, 68
Bhavnagar, India, 68
Bheri (riv.), Nepal, 68
Bhilwara, India, 68
Bhimavaram, India, 68
Bhir (Bir), India, 68
Bhiwandi, India, 68
Bhiwani, India, 68
Bhopal, India, 68
Bhubaneswar, India, 68
Bhuj, India, 68
Bhusawal, India, 68
Bhutan, 68
Biafra (bight), Africa, 106
Biak (isl.), Indon., 85
Biała Podlaska, Poland, 47
Białogard, Poland, 47
Białystok (prov.), Poland, 47
Białystok, Poland, 47
Biarritz, France, 28
Bibai, Japan, 81
Biberach, W. Ger., 22
Bicknell, Ind., 227
Bicroft, Ont., 177
Bidar, India, 68
Biddeford, Maine, 242
Bideford, Eng., 13
Bié (dist.), Angola, 115
Biel, Switz., 39
Bielawa, Poland, 47
Bielefeld, W. Ger., 22
Biella, Italy, 34
Bielsko-Biała, Poland, 47
Bienfait, Sask., 181
Bien Hoa, S. Vietnam, 72
Bienville (lake), Que., 174
Biga, Turkey, 63
Big Bend (res.), Alta., 182
Big Bend Nat'l Park, Tex., 302
Biggar, Sask., 181
Biggar, Scot., 15
Big Hole Nat'l Battlefield, Mont., 262
Bighorn (riv.), U.S., 188
Bighorn Canyon Nat'l Rec. Area, U.S., 318
Big Lake, Tex., 302
Big Rapids, Mich., 250
Big River, Sask., 181
Big Spring, Tex., 302
Big Stone Gap, Va., 307
Big Timber, Mont., 262
Bihać, Yugo., 45
Bihar (state), India, 68
Bihar, India, 68
Bijagós (isls.), Guinea-Bissau, 106
Bijapur, India, 68
Bijeljina, Yugo., 45
Bijnor, India, 68
Bikaner, India, 68
Bikini (atoll), Pac. Is., 87
Bilaspur, India, 68
Bilauktaung (range), Asia, 72
Bilbao, Spain, 33
Bilecik (prov.), Turkey, 63
Bilibino, U.S.S.R., 48
Billings, Mont., 262
Billiton (isl.), Indon., 85
Biloxi, Miss., 256
Biminis, The (isls.), Bah., 156
Bina, India, 68
Bindjai, Indon., 85
Bingen, W. Ger., 22
Bingerville, Ivory Coast, 106
Binghamton, N.Y., 276
Bingöl (prov.), Turkey, 63
Binh Dinh, S. Vietnam, 72
Binningen, Switz., 39
Bintan (isl.), Indon., 85
Bintulu, Malaysia, 85
Bío-Bío (prov.), Chile, 138
Biograd, Yugo., 45
Bir, India, 68
Bir 'Ali, P.D.R. Yemen, 59
Biratnagar, Nepal, 68
Birchwood, Alaska, 196
Birdsboro, Pa., 294
Birecik, Turkey, 63
Birganj, Nepal, 68
Birjand, Iran, 66
Birkenhead, Eng., 10
Birkerød, Den., 21
Bîrlad, Rum., 45
Birmingham, Ala., 194
Birmingham, Eng., 10
Birmingham, Mich., 250
Bir-Mogrein, Mauritania, 106
Birni-N'Konni, Niger, 106
Birobidzhan, U.S.S.R., 48
Birr, Ire., 17
Birsk, U.S.S.R., 52
Bir Zeit, Jordan, 65
Bisbee, Ariz., 198
Biscay (bay), Europe, 7
Biscayne Nat'l Mon., Fla., 212
Bisceglie, Italy, 34
Biscoe (isls.), Ant., 5
Bishop, Calif., 204
Bishop, Tex., 302
Bishop Auckland, Eng., 13
Bishop's Falls, Newf., 166
Bishop's Stortford, Eng., 13
Bishopville, S.C., 296
Biskra, Alg., 106
Bismarck (cap.), N. Dak., 283
Bismarck (arch), P.N.G., 87
Bissau (cap.), Guinea-Bissau, 106
Bissett, Man., 179
Bistriţa, Rum., 45
Bitam, Gabon, 115
Bitlis (prov.), Turkey, 63
Bitlis, Turkey, 63
Bitola, Yugo., 45
Bitterfeld, E. Ger., 22
Bitterroot (range), U.S., 188
Biwa (lake), Japan, 81
Biysk, U.S.S.R., 48
Bizerte, Tun., 106
Bjelovar, Yugo., 45
Bjørnoya (isl.), Norway, 18
Black (sea), 52
Black (riv.), Asia, 72
Black (for.), W. Ger., 22
Blackburn, Eng., 10
Black Canyon of the Gunnison Nat'l Mon., Colo., 208
Black Diamond, Alta., 182
Black Elster (riv.), E. Ger., 22
Blackfoot, Idaho, 220
Black Forest, Colo., 208
Black Hills (mts.), U.S., 188
Blackoak, Ind., 227
Blackpool, Eng., 10
Black River, Jam., 158
Black River Falls, Wis., 317
Black Rock (des.), Nev., 266
Blacksburg, Va., 307
Blackstone, Va., 307
Blacktown, N.S.W., 97
Blackwater (riv.), Eng., 13
Blackwater (riv.), Ire., 17
Blackwater (riv.), N. Ire., 17
Blackwater (res.), Scot., 15
Blackwell, Okla., 288
Blackwood (Ngundju) (cape), Indon., 85
Bladensburg, Md., 245
Blagoveshchensk, U.S.S.R., 48
Blagoyevgrad, Bulg., 45
Blaine, Minn., 254
Blair, Nebr., 264
Blair-Atholl, Scot., 15
Blairgowrie and Rattray, Scot., 15
Blairmore, Alta., 182
Blairsville, Pa., 294
Blaj, Rum., 45
Blakely, Ga., 216
Blakely, Pa., 294
Blanc (cape), Africa, 102
Blanc (mt.), Europe, 28
Blanc (cape), Tun., 106
Blanca (peak), Colo., 208
Blanche (lake), S. Austral., 94
Blanchester, Ohio, 284
Blanco (riv.), Mex., 150
Blanco (cape), Oreg., 291
Blankenburg, E. Ger., 22
Blantyre, Malawi, 115
Blantyre, Scot., 15
Blarney, Ire., 17
Blasdell, N.Y., 276
Blasket (isls.), Ire., 17
Blaydon, Eng., 13
Bled, Yugo., 45
Blekinge (county), Sweden, 18
Blenheim, N.Z., 101
Bletchley, Eng., 13
Blida, Alg., 106
Blind River, Ont., 177
Blissfield, Mich., 250
Blitar, Indon., 85
Block (isl.), R.I., 249
Bloemfontein, S. Africa, 118
Blois, France, 28
Bloodvein (riv.), Man., 179
Bloody Foreland (prom.), Ire., 17
Bloomer, Wis., 317
Bloomfield, N. J., 273
Bloomfield Hills, Mich., 250
Bloomington, Calif., 204
Bloomington, Ill., 222
Bloomington, Ind., 227
Bloomington, Minn., 254
Bloomsburg, Pa., 294
Blora, Indon., 85
Bludenz, Austria, 41
Blue (mts.), Oreg., 291
Blue Ash, Ohio, 284
Blue Earth, Minn., 254
Bluefield, Va., 307
Bluefield, W. Va., 313
Bluefields, Nic., 154
Blue Hills, Conn., 210
Blue Island, Ill., 222
Blue Mountain (peak), Jam., 158
Blue Mountains, N.S.W., 97
Blue Nile (riv.), Africa, 111
Blue Nile (prov.), Sudan, 111
Blue Springs, Mo., 261
Blue Stack (mts.), Ire., 17
Bluff, N.Z., 101
Bluff Park, Ala., 194
Bluffton, Ind., 227
Bluffton, Ohio, 284
Blumenau, Braz., 132
Blyth, Eng., 13
Blythe, Calif., 204
Blytheville, Ark., 203
Bo, S. Leone, 106
Boardman, Ohio, 284
Boa Vista, Braz., 132
Boaz, Ala., 194
Bobigny, France, 28
Böblingen, W. Ger., 22
Bobo-Dioulasso, Upp. Volta,106
Bobotov Kuk (mt.), Yugo., 45
Bobrinets, U.S.S.R., 52
Bobruysk, U.S.S.R., 52
Boca Raton, Fla., 212
Bocas del Toro, Pan., 154
Bochnia, Poland, 47
Bocholt, W. Ger., 22
Bochum, W. Ger., 22
Bodaybo, U.S.S.R., 48
Bodélé (depr.), Chad, 111
Boden, Sweden, 18
Bodensee (Constance) (lake), Europe, 39
Bodinayakkanur, India, 68
Bodjonegoro, Indon., 85
Bodø, Norway, 18
Bogalusa, La., 238
Bogatynia, Poland, 47
Bogdo Ula (mts.), China, 77
Boggeragh (mts.), Ire., 17
Boghé, Mauritania, 106
Bogia, P.N.G., 85
Bognor Regis, Eng., 13
Bogor, Indon., 85
Bogotá (cap.), Col., 126
Bogota, N. J., 273
Bogra, Bang., 68
Bohemian (for.), Europe, 22
Bohol (prov.), Phil., 82
Bohol (isl.), Phil., 82
Boisdale (inlet), Scot., 15
Boise (cap.), Idaho, 220
Boise City, Okla., 288
Boissevain, Man., 179
Bojador (cape), Sp. Sahara, 106
Boké, Guinea, 106
Boksburg, S. Africa, 118
Bokungu, Zaire, 115
Bolama, Guinea-Bissau, 106
Bolan (pass), Pak., 68
Bolesławiec, Poland, 47
Bolívar, Arg., 143
Bolívar (dept.), Col., 126
Bolívar (prov.), Ecua., 128
Bolivar, Mo., 261
Bolivar, Tenn., 237
Bolívar (state), Venez., 124
Bolívar (mt.), Venez., 124
Bolivia, 136
Bollington, Eng., 10
Bolligen, Switz., 39
Bollnäs, Sweden, 18
Bologna (prov.), Italy, 34
Bologna, Italy, 34
Bologoye, U.S.S.R., 52
Bolomba, Zaire, 115
Bolovens (plat.), Laos, 72
Bolsena (lake), Italy, 34
Bolsover, Eng., 13
Bolton, Eng., 10
Bolu (prov.), Turkey, 63
Bolu, Turkey, 63
Bolvadin, Turkey, 63
Bolvanskiy Nos (cape), U.S.S.R., 48
Bolzano (prov.), Italy, 34
Bolzano, Italy, 34
Boma, Zaire, 115
Bombay, India, 68
Bomi Hills, Liberia, 106
Bomu (riv.), Africa, 115
Bon (cape), Tun., 106
Bonacca (Guanaja) (isl.), Hond., 154
Bonaire (isl.), Neth. Ant., 161
Bonanza, Nic., 154
Bonavista, Newf., 166
Bondi (beach), N.S.W., 97
Bondo, Zaire, 115
Bone (gulf), Indon., 85
Bo'ness, Scot., 15
Bongor, Chad, 111
Bonham, Tex., 302
Bonifacio (strait), Europe, 34
Bonin (isls.), Japan, 81
Bonn (cap.), W. Ger., 22
Bonners Ferry, Idaho, 220
Bonner Sprs., Kans., 232
Bonne Terre, Mo., 261
Bonneville (dam), U.S., 310
Bonny, Nigeria, 106
Bonnyrigg and Lasswade, Scot., 15
Bonnyville, Alta., 182
Bonthain, Indon., 85
Bonthe, S. Leone, 106
Bontoc, Phil., 82
Booker T. Washington Nat'l Mon., Va., 307
Boone, Iowa, 229
Boone, N.C., 281
Booneville, Ark., 203
Booneville, Miss., 256
Boonton, N. J., 273
Boonville, Mo., 261
Boothbay Hbr., Maine, 242
Boothia (gulf), N.W.T., 187
Boothia (pen.), N.W.T., 187
Boothwyn, Pa., 294
Bootle, Eng., 10
Boquerón (dept.), Par., 144
Boquerón (bay), P. Rico, 161
Bor, Yugo., 45
Bora-Bora (isl.), Fr. Poly., 87
Borah (peak), Idaho, 220
Borama, Somalia, 115
Borås, Sweden, 18
Borazjun, Iran, 66
Bordeaux, France, 28
Bordentown, N. J., 273
Bordj-Bou-Arréridj, Alg., 106
Borgå, Fin., 18
Borger, Tex., 302
Borgerhout, Belg., 27
Borgomanero, Italy, 34
Borikhane, Laos, 72
Borinquen (pt.), P. Rico, 161
Borislav, U.S.S.R., 52
Borisoglebsk, U.S.S.R., 52
Borisov, U.S.S.R., 52
Borku (reg.), Chad, 111
Borlänge, Sweden, 18
Borneo (isl.), Asia, 85
Borneo (Kalimantan)(reg.), Indon., 85
Bornholm (isl.), Den., 21
Bor Nor (lake), Asia, 77
Bornova, Turkey, 63
Bornu (reg.), Nigeria, 106
Borovichi, U.S.S.R., 52
Borsod-Abaúj-Zemplen (county), Hung., 41
Boruca, C. Rica, 154
Borzhomi, U.S.S.R., 52
Borzya, U.S.S.R., 48
Bosanski Brod, Yugo., 45
Bosanski Novi, Yugo., 45
Bosaso, Somalia, 115
Boscobel, Wis., 317
Bosna (riv.), Yugo., 45
Bosnia and Hercegovina (rep.), Yugo., 45
Boso (pen.), Japan, 81
Bosobolo, Zaire, 115
Bosporus (str.), Turkey, 63
Bossangoa, Centr. Afr. Rep., 115
Bossier City, La., 238
Boston, Eng., 13
Boston (cap.), Mass., 249
Botany, N.S.W., 97
Botany (bay), N.S.W., 97
Botevgrad, Bulg., 45
Bothnia (gulf), Europe, 18
Botoşani, Rum., 45
Botswana, 118
Bottineau, N. Dak., 283
Bottrop, W. Ger., 22
Botucatu, Braz., 135
Botwood, Newf., 166
Bouaké, Ivory Coast, 106
Bouar, Centr. Afr. Rep., 115
Bouches-du-Rhône (dept.), France, 28
Bougainville (isl.), P.N.G., 87
Bougainville (cape), W. Austral., 92
Bougouni, Mali, 106
Boulder, Colo., 208
Boulder, W. Austral., 92
Boulder City, Nev., 266
Boulogne-Billancourt, France, 28
Boulogne-sur-Mer, France, 28
Boundary (peak), Nev., 266
Bound Brook, N. J., 273
Bountiful, Utah, 304
Bourail, New Cal., 87
Bourbonnais, Ill., 222
Bourg, France, 28
Bourges, France, 28
Bourke, N.S.W., 97
Bourlamaque, Que., 174
Bournemouth, Eng., 13
Boutilimit, Mauritania, 106
Bouvet (isl.), Ant., 5
Bow (riv.), Alta., 182
Bowen, Queensland, 95
Bowie, Tex., 302
Bow Island, Alta., 182
Bowling Green, Ky., 237
Bowling Green, Mo., 261
Bowling Green, Ohio, 284
Bowling Green (cape), Queensland, 95
Bowmore, Scot., 15
Bowral, N.S.W., 97
Box Hill, Vic., 97
Boyacá (dept.), Col., 126
Boyer Ahmedi & Kohkiluye (governorate), Iran, 66
Boyertown, Pa., 294
Boyle, Ire., 17
Boyne (river), Ire., 17
Boyne City, Mich., 250
Boynton Beach, Fla., 212
Bozeman, Mont., 262
Bozoum, Centr. Afr. Rep., 115
Bra, Italy, 34
Brabant (prov.), Belg., 27
Brač (isl.), Yugo., 45
Bracciano (lake), Italy, 34
Bracebridge, Ont., 177
Brackenridge, Pa., 294
Bracknell, Eng., 13
Brackwede, W. Ger., 22
Brad, Rum., 45
Braddock, Pa., 294
Bradenton, Fla., 212
Bradford, Eng., 10
Bradford, Pa., 294
Bradley, Ill., 222
Bradley Beach, N. J., 273
Brady, Tex., 302
Braemar, Scot., 15
Braga, Port., 33
Bragado, Arg., 143
Bragança, Port., 33
Bragança Paulista, Braz., 135
Bragman's Bluff (Puerto Cabezas), Nic., 154
Brahmaputra (riv.), Asia, 68
Braich-y-pwll (prom.), Wales, 13
Brăila, Rum., 45
Brainerd, Minn., 254
Braintree, Mass., 249
Braintree and Bocking, Eng., 13
Brakpan, S. Africa, 118
Bralorne, Br. Col., 184
Bramble (bay), Queensland, 95
Brampton, Ont., 177
Brandenburg, E. Ger., 22
Brandenburg (reg.), E. Ger., 22
Brandon, Man., 179
Brandon and Byshottles, Eng., 13
Bransfield (str.), Ant., 5
Brantford, Ont., 177
Brasília (cap.), Braz., 132
Braşov, Rum., 45
Bratislava, Czech., 41
Bratsk, U.S.S.R., 48
Bratsk (res.), U.S.S.R., 48
Brattleboro, Vt., 268
Braunau, Austria, 41
Braunschweig (Brunswick), W. Ger., 22
Brava, Somalia, 115
Bravo (Grande)(riv.), Mex., 150
Brawley, Calif., 204
Bray, Ire., 17
Brazeau (riv.), Alta., 182
Brazil, 132
Brazil, Ind., 227
Brazos (riv.), Tex., 302
Brazzaville (cap.), Congo, 115
Brčko, Yugo., 45
Brea, Calif., 204
Breaux Bridge, La., 238
Brechin, Scot., 15
Breckenridge, Minn., 254
Breckenridge, Tex., 302
Breckenridge Hills, Mo., 261
Brecknock, Wales, 13
Brecksville, Ohio, 284
Břeclav, Czech., 41
Breconshire (county), Wales, 13
Breda, Neth., 27
Bregenz, Austria, 41
Breidhafjördhur (fjord), Ice., 21
Breisgau (reg.), W. Ger., 22
Bremanger (isl.), Norway, 18
Bremen, Ga., 216
Bremen, Ind., 227
Bremen (state), W. Ger., 22
Bremen, W. Ger., 22
Bremerhaven, W. Ger., 22
Bremerton, Wash., 310
Brenham, Tex., 302
Brenner (pass), Europe, 41
Brent, Eng., 10
Brentwood, Eng., 10
Brentwood, Md., 245
Brentwood, N.Y., 276
Brentwood, Pa., 294
Brescia (prov.), Italy, 34
Brescia, Italy, 34
Bressanone, Italy, 34
Bressay (isl.), Scot., 15
Brest, France, 28
Brest, U.S.S.R., 52
Breton (sound), La., 238
Breton (cape), N.S., 169
Brevard, N.C., 281
Brewer, Maine, 242
Brewood, Eng., 10
Brewton, Ala., 194
Briançon, France, 28
Brices Cross Roads Nat'l Battlef. Site, Miss., 256
Bridgend, Wales, 13
Bridge of Allan, Scot., 15
Bridgeport, Ala., 194
Bridgeport, Conn., 210
Bridgeport, Ohio, 284
Bridgeport, Pa., 294
Bridgeport, Tex., 302
Bridgeport, W. Va., 313
Bridgeton, N. J., 273
Bridgetown (cap.), Barb., 161
Bridgeville, Pa., 294
Bridgewater, Mass., 249
Bridgewater, N.S., 169
Bridgwater, Eng., 13
Bridlington, Eng., 13
Brielle, N. J., 273
Brienz (lake), Switz., 39
Brierfield, Eng., 10
Brigantine, N. J., 273
Brigham City, Utah, 304
Brighouse, Eng., 13
Brighton, Ala., 194
Brighton, Colo., 208
Brighton, Eng., 13
Brighton, S. Austral., 94
Brighton, Vic., 97
Brikama, Gambia, 106
Brinkley, Ark., 203
Brindisi (prov.), Italy, 34
Brindisi, Italy, 34
Brisbane, Calif., 204
Brisbane (cap.), Queensland, 95
Bristol (bay), Alaska, 196
Bristol, Conn., 210
Bristol, Eng., 13
Bristol, Pa., 294
Bristol, R.I., 249
Bristol, Tenn., 237
Bristol (chan.), U.K., 13
Bristol, Va., 307
Bristow, Okla., 288
British Columbia (prov.), Canada, 184
British Indian Ocean Terr., 54, 119
Brive, France, 28
Brno, Czech., 41
Broach, India, 68
Broad (sound), Queensland, 95
Broadmeadows, Vic., 97
Broadmoor, Colo., 209
Broadstairs and St. Peter's, Eng., 13
Broadview, Sask., 181
Brockport, N.Y., 276
Brockton, Mass., 249
Brockville, Ont., 177
Brockway, Pa., 294
Brod, Yugo., 45
Brodick, Scot., 15
Brodnica, Poland, 47
Broken Arrow, Okla., 288
Broken Bow, Nebr., 264
Broken Bow, Okla., 288
Broken Hill, N.S.W., 97
Brokopondo (dist.), Sur., 131
Bromley, Eng., 10
Bromsgrove, Eng., 10
Brønderslev, Den., 21
Bronte, Italy, 34
Bronx, N.Y., 276
Bronxville, N.Y., 276
Brookfield, Ill., 222
Brookfield, Mo., 261
Brookfield, Wis., 317
Brookhaven, Miss., 256
Brookhaven, Pa., 294
Brookhaven Nat'l Lab., N.Y., 276
Brookings, S. Dak., 298
Brookline, Mass., 249
Brooklyn, N.Y., 276
Brook Park, Ohio, 284
Brooks (range), Alaska, 196
Brooks, Alta., 182
Brooksville, Fla., 212
Brookville, Pa., 294
Broomall, Pa., 294
Broome, W. Austral., 92
Broomfield, Colo., 208
Brossard, Que., 172
Brown Deer, Wis., 317
Brownfield, Tex., 302
Browning, Mont., 262
Brownsburg, Ind., 227
Browns Village, Fla., 212
Brownsville, Pa., 294
Brownsville, Tenn., 237
Brownsville, Tex., 302
Brownwood, Tex., 302
Bruay-en-Artois, France, 28
Bruce (mt.), W. Austral., 92
Bruchsal, W. Ger., 22
Bruck, Austria, 41
Bruges, Belg., 27
Brühl, W. Ger., 22
Brundidge, Ala., 194
Brunei, 85
Brunswick, Ga., 216
Brunswick, Maine, 242
Brunswick, Md., 245
Brunswick, Vic., 97
Brunswick, W. Ger., 22
Brus (lag.), Hond., 154
Brush, Colo., 208
Brussels (cap.), Belg., 27
Bryan, Ohio, 284
Bryan, Tex., 302
Bryansk, U.S.S.R., 52
Bryce Canyon Nat'l Park, Utah, 304
Bryn Mawr, Pa., 294
Brynmawr, Wales, 13
Bryn Mawr, Wash., 310
Brzeg, Poland, 47
Bubiyan (isl.), Kuwait, 59
Bucaramanga, Col., 126
Buchanan, Liberia, 106
Buchanan, Mich., 250
Buchans, Newf., 166
Bucharest (cap.), Rum., 45
Buckeye, Ariz., 198
Buckhannon, W. Va., 313
Buckhaven and Methil, Scot., 15
Buckie, Scot., 15
Buckingham, Que., 172
Buckinghamshire (county), Eng., 13
Buck Isl. Reef Nat'l Mon., Virgin Is. (U.S.), 161
Buckley, Wash., 310
Buctouche (riv.), N.B., 170
Bucureşti (Bucharest) (cap.), Rum., 45
Bucyrus, Ohio, 284
Budafok, Hung., 41
Budapest (cap.), Hung., 41
Budaun, India, 68
Budd Coast (reg.), Ant., 5
Budge-Budge, India, 68
Buea, Cameroon, 115
Buechel, Ky., 237
Buena, N. J., 273
Buena Park, Calif., 204
Buenaventura, Col., 126
Buenaventura, Mex., 150
Buena Vista, Va., 307
Buenos Aires (prov.), Arg., 143
Buenos Aires (cap.), Arg., 143
Buenos Aires, C. Rica, 154
Buenos Aires (lake), S. Amer., 120
Buffalo, N.Y., 276
Buffalo, Wyo., 319
Buffalo Head (hills), Alta., 182
Buford, Ga., 216
Bug (riv.), Europe, 47
Bug (riv.), U.S.S.R., 52
Buga, Col., 126
Bugojno, Yugo., 45
Bugul'ma, U.S.S.R., 52
Buguruslan, U.S.S.R., 52
Buhl, Idaho, 220
Builth Wells, Wales, 13
Bujalance, Spain, 33
Bujnurd, Iran, 66
Bujumbura (cap.), Burundi, 115
Bukama, Zaire, 115
Bukavu, Zaire, 115
Bukhara, U.S.S.R., 48
Bukidnon (prov.), Phil., 82
Bukittinggi, Indon., 85
Bulacan (prov.), Phil., 82
Bulagan (prov.), Mong., 77
Bulagan, Mong., 77
Bulawayo, Rhod., 118
Buldan, Turkey, 63
Bulgaria, 45
Buller (riv.), N.Z., 101
Buller (mt.), Vic., 97
Bulloo (lake), Queensland, 95
Bulo Burti, Somalia, 115
Bulolo, P.N.G., 85
Bulsar, India, 68
Bulun, U.S.S.R., 48
Buna, P.N.G., 85
Bunbury, W. Austral., 92
Buncrana, Ire., 17
Bundaberg, Queensland, 95
Bundi, India, 68
Bungo (strait), Japan, 81
Bunguran (Natuna) (isls.), Indon., 85
Bunia, Zaire, 115
Bunkie, La., 238
Bur Acaba, Somalia, 115
Buraida, Saudi Ar., 59
Buraimi, Asia, 59
Burao, Somalia, 115
Buras, La., 238
Burbank, Calif., 204
Burdekin (riv.), Queensland, 95
Burdur (prov.), Turkey, 63
Burdur, Turkey, 63
Burdwan, India, 68
Burg, E. Ger., 22
Burgas, Bulg., 45
Burgdorf, Switz., 39
Burgenland (prov.), Austria, 41
Burgeo, Newf., 166
Burgess Hill, Eng., 13
Burghead, Scot., 15
Burgos (prov.), Spain, 33
Burgos, Spain, 33
Burhanpur, India, 68
Burica (pt.), Cent. Amer., 154
Burien, Wash., 310
Burin, Newf., 166
Buriram, Thai., 72
Burkburnett, Tex., 302
Burley, Idaho, 220
Burlingame, Calif., 204
Burlington, Iowa, 229
Burlington, N. J., 273
Burlington, N.C., 281
Burlington, Ont., 177
Burlington, Vt., 268
Burlington, Wash., 310
Burlington, Wis., 317
Burma, 72
Burnaby, B.C., 184
Burnham, Pa., 294
Burnham-on-Sea, Eng., 13
Burnley, Eng., 10
Burns, Oreg., 291
Burns Harbor, Ind., 227
Burnside (riv.), N.W.T., 187
Burnside, S. Austral., 94
Burns Lake, Br. Col., 184
Burnsville, Minn., 254
Burntisland, Scot., 15
Burntwood, Eng., 10
Burntwood (riv.), Man., 179
Burriana, Spain, 33
Burry Port, Wales, 13
Bursa (prov.), Turkey, 63
Bursa, Turkey, 63
Bur Sa'id (Port Said), Egypt, 111
Burtonport, Ire., 17
Burton upon Trent, Eng., 10
Burtonwood, Eng., 10
Burträsk, Sweden, 18
Buru (isl.), Indon., 85
Burujird, Iran, 66
Burundi, 115
Burwood, N.S.W., 97
Bury, Eng., 10
Buryat A.S.S.R., U.S.S.R., 48
Burye, Eth., 111
Bury Saint Edmunds, Eng., 13
Bushey, Eng., 10
Bushire, Iran, 66
Buskerud (county), Norway, 18
Busselton, W. Austral., 92
Bussum, Neth., 27
Busto Arsizio, Italy, 34
Busuanga (isl.), Phil., 82
Buta, Zaire, 115
Butare, Rwanda, 115
Butaritari (atoll), Gilb. & Ell. Is., 87
Bute (county), Scot., 15
Bute (isl.), Scot., 15
Butler, Mo., 261
Butler, N. J., 273
Butler, Pa., 294
Butte, Mont., 262
Butterworth, Malaysia, 72
Butuan, Phil., 82
Butung (isl.), Indon., 85
Buxtehude, W. Ger., 22
Buxton, Eng., 10
Buy, U.S.S.R., 52
Buynaksk, U.S.S.R., 52
Büyük Ağrı (Ararat) (mt.), Turkey, 63
Buzău, Rum., 45
Buziaş, Rum., 45
Buzuluk, U.S.S.R., 52
Buzzards (bay), Mass., 249
Byala, Bulg., 45
Byala Slatina, Bulg., 45
Bydgoszcz (prov.), Poland, 47
Bydgoszcz, Poland, 47
Bylot (isl.), N.W.T., 187
Byram, Conn., 210
Byrd Sta., Ant., 5
Byron (cape), N.S.W., 97
Bytom, Poland, 47
Bytów, Poland, 47

C

Caacupé, Par., 144
Caaguazú (dept.), Par., 144
Caatingas (reg.), Braz., 120
Caazapá (dept.), Par., 144
Caazapá, Par., 144
Cabaiguán, Cuba, 158
Cabanatuan, Phil., 82
Cabarroquis, Phil., 82
Cabimas, Venez., 124
Cabinda (dist.), Angola, 115
Cabo Delgado (dist.), Mozamb., 118
Cabonga (res.), Que., 174
Cabot (str.), Canada, 163
Cabrillo Nat'l Mon., Calif., 204
Čačak, Yugo., 45
Cáceres (prov.), Spain, 33
Cáceres, Spain, 33
Cacheu, Guinea-Bissau, 106
Cachoeira do Sul, Braz., 132
Cachoeiro de Itapemirim, Braz., 132
Caconda, Angola, 115
Cader Idris (mts.), Wales, 13
Cadillac, Mich., 250
Cadiz, Ohio, 284
Cádiz (prov.), Spain, 33
Cádiz, Spain, 33
Cádiz (gulf), Spain, 33
Caen, France, 28
Caerleon, Wales, 13
Caernarvon, Wales, 13
Caernarvonshire (county), Wales, 13
Caerphilly, Wales, 13
Cagayan (prov.), Phil., 82
Cagayan de Oro, Phil., 82
Cagayan Sulu (isl.), Phil., 82
Cagliari (prov.), Italy, 34
Cagliari, Italy, 34
Cagliari (gulf), Italy, 34
Cagua, Venez., 124
Caguán (riv.), Col., 126
Caguas, P. Rico, 161
Cahir, Ire., 17
Cahirciveen, Ire., 17
Cahokia, Ill., 222
Cahors, France, 28
Caibarién, Cuba, 158
Caicos (isls.), Turks & Caicos Is., 156
Caimanera, Cuba, 158
Caird Coast (reg.), Ant., 5
Cairngorm (mts.), Scot., 15
Cairns, Queensland, 95
Cairo (cap.), Egypt, 111
Cairo, Ga., 216
Cairo, Ill., 222
Caithness (county), Scot., 15
Cajamarca (dept.), Peru, 128
Cajamarca, Peru, 128
Calabar, Nigeria, 106
Calabozo, Venez., 124
Calabria (reg.), Italy, 34
Calahorra, Spain, 33
Calais, France, 28
Calais, Maine, 242
Calama, Chile, 138
Calamian Group (isls.), Phil., 82
Călăraşi, Rum., 45
Calatayud, Spain, 33
Calcasieu (lake), La., 238
Calcutta, India, 68
Caldas (dept.), Col., 126
Caldas da Rainha, Port., 33
Caldwell, Idaho, 220
Caldwell, N. J., 273
Caldy (isl.), Wales, 13
Caledon, Ont., 177
Caledonia, Minn., 254
Caledonian (canal), Scot., 15
Calexico, Calif., 204
Calf of Man (isl.), Isle of Man, 13
Calgary, Alta., 182
Calheta, Port., 33
Calhoun, Ga., 216
Calhoun Falls, S.C., 296
Cali, Col., 126
Calicut (Kozhikode), India, 68
Caliente, Nev., 266
California (gulf), Mex., 150
California, Mo., 261
California, Pa., 294
California (state), U.S., 204
Calipatria, Calif., 204
Callao, Peru, 128
Callao (prov.), Peru, 128
Caltagirone, Italy, 34
Caltanissetta (prov.), Italy, 34
Caltanissetta, Italy, 34
Caluire, France, 28
Calumet City, Ill., 222
Calumet Park, Ill., 222
Calvados (dept.), France, 28
Calvinia, S. Afr., 118

Camagüey (prov.), Cuba, 158
Camagüey, Cuba, 158
Camajuani, Cuba, 158
Camarillo, Calif., 204
Camarines Norte (prov.), Phil., 82
Camarines Sur (prov.), Phil., 82
Camarón (cape), Hond., 154
Camas, Wash., 310
Ca Mau (Mui Bai Bung) (pt.), S. Vietnam, 72
Cambay, India, 68
Cambay (gulf), India, 68
Camberwell, Vic., 97
Cambodia, 72
Camborne-Redruth, Eng., 13
Cambrai, France, 28
Cambrian (mts.), Wales, 13
Cambridge, Eng., 13
Cambridge, Md., 245
Cambridge, Mass., 249
Cambridge, Minn., 254
Cambridge, Ohio, 284
Cambridge, Ont., 177
Cambridge Bay, N.W.T., 187
Cambridge City, Ind., 227
Cambridgeshire and the Isle of Ely (county), Eng., 13
Camden, Ark., 203
Camden, Eng., 10
Camden, Maine, 242
Camden, N. J., 273
Camden, N.S.W., 97
Camden, N.Y., 276
Camden, S.C., 296
Camden, Tenn., 237
Cameron, Mo., 261
Cameron (mts.), N.Z., 101
Cameron, Tex., 302
Cameron Highlands, Malaysia, 72
Cameroon, 115
Cameroon (mt.), Cameroon, 115
Camiguin (prov.), Phil., 82
Camilla, Ga., 216
Camiri, Bol., 136
Camoapa, Nic., 154
Camopi, Fr. Gui., 131
Camotes (isls.), Phil., 82
Campana, Arg., 143
Campana (isl.), Chile, 138
Campania (reg.), Italy, 34
Campbell, Calif., 204
Campbell, Ohio, 284
Campbellford, Ont., 177
Campbellpore, Pak., 68
Campbell River, Br. Col., 184
Campbellsville, Ky., 237
Campbellton, N.B., 170
Campbelltown, N.S.W., 97
Campbelltown, S. Austral., 94
Campbeltown, Scot., 15
Campeche (state), Mex., 150
Campeche, Mex., 150
Campeche (bay), Mex., 150
Campechuela, Cuba, 158
Camp Hill, Pa., 294
Camp Hill, Queensland, 95
Campina Grande, Braz., 132
Campinas, Braz., 135
Campobasso (prov.), Italy, 34
Campobasso, Italy, 34
Campobello (isl.), N.B., 170
Campo Grande, Braz., 132
Campo Maior, Port., 33
Campos, Braz., 135
Campos (reg.), Braz., 120
Cam Ranh (bay), S. Vietnam, 72
Camrose, Alta., 182
Camuy, P. Rico, 161
Canada, 163
Cañada de Gómez, Arg., 143
Canadian (riv.), U.S., 188
Canajoharie, N.Y., 276
Çanakkale (prov.), Turkey, 63
Çanakkale, Turkey, 63
Canal Zone, 154
Canandaigua, N.Y., 276
Cananea, Mex., 150
Cañar (prov.), Ecua., 128
Canary (isls.), Spain, 33
Cañas, C. Rica, 154
Canastota, N.Y., 276
Canaveral (cape), Fla., 212
Canavieiras, Braz., 132
Canberra (cap.), Austral., 97
Cancer, Tropic of, 3
Candala, Somalia, 115
Candelaria (riv.), Mex., 150
Candia (Iráklion), Greece, 45
Candlewood (lake), Conn., 210
Canea (Khaniá), Greece, 45
Caneel (bay), Virgin Is. (U.S.), 161
Canelones (dept.), Urug., 145
Canelones, Urug., 145
Canendiyu (dept.), Par., 144
Cañete, Chile, 138
Caney, Kans., 232
Canfield, Ohio, 284
Caniapiscau (riv.), Que., 174
Caniçado, Mozamb., 118
Canisteo, N.Y., 276
Çankaya, Turkey, 63
Çankırı (prov.), Turkey, 63
Çankırı, Turkey, 63
Canlaon, Phil., 82
Canmore, Alta., 182
Cannanore, India, 68
Cannes, France, 28
Cannock, Eng., 10
Caño (isl.), C. Rica, 154
Canoas, Brazil, 132
Canoga Park, Calif., 204
Canon City, Colo., 208
Canonsburg, Pa., 294
Canora, Sask., 181
Canosa di Puglia, Italy, 34
Canouan (isl.), St. Vincent, 156
Can Phumo (dist.), Mozamb., 118
Can Phumo (cap.), Mozamb., 118
Canso (str.), N.S., 169
Cantabrian (mts.), Spain, 33
Cantal (dept.), France, 28
Cantaura, Venez., 124
Canterbury, Eng., 13
Canterbury, N.S.W., 97
Canterbury (prov. dist.), N.Z., 101
Canterbury (bight), N.Z., 101
Canton, China, 77
Canton (isl.), Gilb. and Ell. Is., 87
Canton, Ill., 222
Canton, Miss., 256
Canton, Mo., 261
Canton, N.Y., 276
Canton, N.C., 281
Canton, Ohio, 284
Canton, S. Dak., 298
Canumã (riv.), Braz., 132
Canyon, Tex., 302
Canyon de Chelly Nat'l Mon., Ariz., 198
Canyon Ferry (lake), Mont., 262
Canyonlands Nat'l Park, Utah, 304
Cao Bang, N. Vietnam, 72
Caparica, Port., 33
Cap-Chat, Que., 172
Cap-de-la-Madeleine, Que., 172
Cape (pen.), S. Africa, 118
Cape Barren (isl.), Tas., 99
Cape Breton (isl.), N.S., 169
Cape Breton Highlands Nat'l Park, N.S., 169
Cape Canaveral, Fla., 212
Cape Charles, Va., 307
Cape Coast, Ghana, 106
Cape Cod Nat'l Seashore, Mass., 249
Cape Coral, Fla., 212
Cape Girardeau, Mo., 261
Cape Hatteras Nat'l Seashore, N.C., 281
Cape Lookout Nat'l Seashore, N.C., 281
Cape May, N. J., 273
Cape of Good Hope (prov.), S. Africa, 118
Capesterre, Guad., 161
Cape Town (cap.), S. Africa, 118
Cape Verde, 106
Cape York (pen.), Queensland, 95
Cap-Haïtien, Haiti, 158
Capim (riv.), Braz., 132
Capitol Reef Nat'l Park, Utah, 304
Capiz (prov.), Phil., 82
Capraia (isl.), Italy, 34
Capreol, Ont., 175
Capri (isl.), Italy, 34
Capricorn, Tropic of, 3
Capricorn Group (isls.), Queensland, 95
Caprivi Strip (reg.), S.W. Afr., 118
Cap Saint-Jacques (Vung Tau), S. Vietnam, 72
Captain Cook, Hawaii, 218
Capua, Italy, 34
Capulin Mtn. Nat'l Mon., N. Mex., 274
Caquetá (intendency), Col., 126
Caquetá (riv.), Col., 126
Carabobo (state), Venez., 124
Caracal, Rum., 45
Caracas (cap.), Venez., 124
Carahue, Chile, 138
Carajás (range), Braz., 132
Carapeguá, Par., 144
Caratasca (lag.), Hond., 154
Caratinga, Braz., 135
Caravelas, Braz., 132
Carbet, Mart., 161
Carbonara (cape), Italy, 34
Carbondale, Ill., 222
Carbondale, Pa., 294
Carbonear, Newf., 166
Carcassonne, France, 28
Carchi (prov.), Ecua., 128
Cárdenas, Cuba, 158
Cárdenas, Mex., 150
Cardiff, Wales, 13
Cardiff-by-the-Sea, Calif., 204
Cardigan, Wales, 13
Cardigan (bay), Wales, 13
Cardiganshire (county), Wales, 13
Cardona, Urug., 145
Cardston, Alta., 182
Carey, Ohio, 284
Cariamanga, Ecua., 128
Caribbean (sea), 156
Cariboo (mts.), Br. Col., 184
Caribou, Maine, 242
Carib Reserve, Dominica, 161
Carinthia (prov.), Austria, 41
Caripito, Venez., 124
Carleton Place, Ont., 177
Carlin, Nev., 266
Carlingford (inlet), Ire., 17
Carlinville, Ill., 222
Carlisle, Eng., 13
Carlisle, Pa., 294
Carlow (county), Ire., 17
Carlow, Ire., 17
Carl Sandburg Home Nat'l Hist. Site, N.C., 281
Carlsbad, Calif., 204
Carlsbad, N. Mex., 274
Carlsbad Caverns Nat'l Park, N. Mex., 274
Carlstadt, N. J., 273
Carlton, Eng., 13
Carluke, Scot., 15
Carlyle, Ill., 222
Carlyle, Sask., 181
Carmacks, Yukon, 187
Carman, Man., 179
Carmarthen, Wales, 13
Carmarthenshire (county), Wales, 13
Carmel, Calif., 204
Carmel (mt.), Israel, 65
Carmelo, Urug., 145
Carmen, Mex., 150
Carmen de Patagones, Arg., 143
Carmi, Ill., 222
Carmichael, Calif., 204
Carmiel, Israel, 65
Carmona, Angola, 115
Carmona, Spain, 33
Carnarvon, W. Austral., 92
Carnaxide, Port., 33
Carnduff, Sask., 181
Carnegie, Okla., 288
Carnegie, Pa., 294
Carnic Alps (range), Europe, 41
Carnot, Centr. Afr. Rep., 115
Carnoustie, Scot., 15
Carnsore (pt.), Ire., 17
Caro, Mich., 250
Carol City, Fla., 212
Carolina, P. Rico, 161
Caroline (isls.), Pac. Is., 87
Caroní (riv.), Venez., 124
Carora, Venez., 124
Carouge, Switz., 39
Carpathians (mts.), Europe, 7
Carpentaria (gulf), Austral., 88
Carpentersville, Ill., 222
Carpi, Italy, 34
Carpinteria, Calif., 204
Carrantuohill (mt.), Ire., 17
Carrara, Italy, 34
Carriacou (isl.), Grenada, 156
Carrick (dist.), Scot., 15
Carrickfergus, N. Ire., 17
Carrickmacross, Ire., 17
Carrick-on-Shannon, Ire., 17
Carrick-on-Suir, Ire., 17
Carrington, N. Dak., 283
Carrizo Springs, Tex., 302
Carrizozo, N. Mex., 274
Carroll, Iowa, 229
Carrollton, Ga., 216
Carrollton, Ill., 222
Carrollton, Ky., 237
Carrollton, Mich., 250
Carrollton, Mo., 261
Carrollton, Ohio, 284
Carrollton, Tex., 302
Carrot River, Sask., 181
Carson, Calif., 204
Carson City (cap.), Nev., 266
Carson Sink (depr.), Nev., 266
Cartagena, Chile, 138
Cartagena, Col., 126
Cartagena, Spain, 33
Cartago, Col., 126
Cartago, C. Rica, 154
Carteret, N. J., 273
Cartersville, Ga., 216
Carterville, Ill., 222
Carthage, Ill., 222
Carthage, Mo., 261
Carthage, N.Y., 276
Carthage, Tex., 302
Cartwright, Newf., 166
Caruaru, Braz., 132
Carúpano, Venez., 124
Caruthersville, Mo., 261
Cary, Ill., 222
Cary, N.C., 281
Casablanca, Mor., 106
Casa Grande, Ariz., 198
Casa Grande Ruins Nat'l Mon., Ariz., 198
Casale Monferrato, Italy, 34
Casamance (riv.), Sen., 106
Casanare (intendency), Col., 126
Casas Grandes (riv.), Mex., 150
Cascade (range), U.S., 188
Cascais, Port., 33
Cascina, Italy, 34
Caserta (prov.), Italy, 34
Caserta, Italy, 34
Casey, Ill., 222
Cashel, Ire., 17
Casilda, Arg., 143
Casino, N.S.W., 97
Casiquiare, Brazo (riv.), Venez., 124
Casper, Wyo., 319
Caspian (sea), 54
Cassiar (mts.), Canada, 184
Cassino, Italy, 34
Castel Gandolfo, Italy, 34
Castellammare di Stabia, Italy, 34
Castellón (prov.), Spain, 33
Castellón de la Plana, Spain, 33
Castelo Branco, Port., 33
Castelvetrano, Italy, 34
Castile, New (reg.), Spain, 33
Castile, Old (reg.), Spain, 33
Castilla, Peru, 128
Castillo de San Marcos Nat'l Mon., Fla., 212
Castillos, Urug., 145
Castle (harb.), Berm., 156
Castlebar, Ire., 17
Castleblayney, Ire., 17
Castle Bromwich, Eng., 10
Castlecomer-Donaguile, Ire., 17
Castle Douglas, Scot., 15
Castleford, Eng., 13
Castlegar, Br. Col., 184
Castlemaine, Vic., 97
Castlerea, Ire., 17
Castle Shannon, Pa., 294
Castor, Alta., 182
Castres, France, 28
Castries (cap.), St. Lucia, 161
Castro, Chile, 138
Castro del Río, Spain, 33
Castro Valley, Calif., 204
Castroville, Calif., 204
Cat (isl.), Bah., 156
Catacamas, Hond., 154
Catacaos, Peru, 128
Cataguases, Braz., 135
Catalão, Braz., 132
Catalonia (reg.), Spain, 33
Catamarca (prov.), Arg., 143
Catamarca, Arg., 143
Catanduanes (prov.), Phil., 82
Catanduanes (isl.), Phil., 82
Catanduva, Braz., 135
Catania (prov.), Italy, 34
Catania, Italy, 34
Cataño, P. Rico, 161
Catanzaro (prov.), Italy, 34
Catanzaro, Italy, 34
Catarman, Phil., 82
Catasauqua, Pa., 294
Catbalogan, Phil., 82
Catemaco, Mex., 150
Caterham and Warlingham, Eng., 10
Catlettsburg, Ky., 237
Catonsville, Md., 245
Catskill, N.Y., 276
Catskill (mts.), N.Y., 276
Catumbela, Angola, 115
Cauca (dept.), Col., 126
Cauca (riv.), Col., 126
Caucasus (mts.), U.S.S.R., 52
Caulfield, Vic., 97
Cauquenes, Chile, 138
Caura (riv.), Venez., 124
Causapscal, Que., 172
Causses (reg.), France, 28
Cautín (prov.), Chile, 138
Cauto (riv.), Cuba, 158
Cava, Italy, 34
Cavalier, N. Dak., 283
Cavally (riv.), Africa, 106
Cavan (county), Ire., 17
Cavan, Ire., 17
Caviana (isl.), Braz., 132
Cavite (prov.), Phil., 82
Cavite, Phil., 82
Cawnpore (Kanpur), India, 68
Cawood, Ky., 237
Caxias, Braz., 132
Caxias do Sul, Braz., 132
Cayambe, Ecua., 128
Cayce, S.C., 296
Cayenne (cap.), Fr. Gui., 131
Cayey, P. Rico, 161
Cayman Brac (isl.), Cayman Is., 156
Cayman Islands, 156
Cayo, Belize, 154
Cayuga (lake), N.Y., 276
Cazenovia, N.Y., 276
Ceanannus Mór, Ire., 17
Ceará (state), Braz., 132
Ceará (Fortaleza), Braz., 132
Cébaco (isl.), Pan., 154
Cebeci, Turkey, 63
Cebu (prov.), Phil., 82
Cebu, Phil., 82
Cebu (isl.), Phil., 82
Cedar Breaks Nat'l Mon., Utah, 304
Cedarburg, Wis., 317
Cedar City, Utah, 304
Cedar Falls, Iowa, 229
Cedar Grove, N. J., 273
Cedarhurst, N.Y., 276
Cedar Lake, Ind., 227
Cedar Rapids, Iowa, 229
Cedartown, Ga., 216
Cedros (isl.), Mex., 150
Cegléd, Hung., 41
Cehegín, Spain, 33
Celaya, Mex., 150
Celebes (sea), Asia, 85
Celebes (isl.), Indon., 85
Celina, Ohio, 284
Celje, Yugo., 45
Celle, W. Ger., 22
Center, Tex., 302
Centereach, N.Y., 276
Center Line, Mich., 250
Centerville, Iowa, 229
Centerville, Ohio, 284
Central (prov.), Iran, 66
Central (dist.), Israel, 65
Central (prov.), Kenya, 115
Central (prov.), Mong., 77
Central (dept.), Par., 144
Central African Rep., 115
Central America, 154
Central City, Nebr., 264
Central Falls, R.I., 249
Central Greece and Euboea (reg.), Greece, 45
Centralia, Ill., 222
Centralia, Mo., 261
Centralia, Wash., 310
Central Islip, N.Y., 276
Central Valley, Calif., 204
Centreville, Ill., 222
Cephalonia (Kefallinía) (isl.), Greece, 45
Ceram (isl.), Indon., 85
Ceres, Calif., 204
Ceres, S. Africa, 118
Cerf (isl.), Seych., 118
Cerignola, Italy, 34
Cerritos, Calif., 204
Cerritos, Mex., 150
Cerro de Pasco, Peru, 128
Cerro Largo (dept.), Urug., 145
Cervera, Spain, 33
César (dept.), Col., 126
Cesena, Italy, 34
Cēsis, U.S.S.R., 53
České Budějovice, Czech., 41
Český Těšín, Czech., 41
Cessnock, N.S.W., 97
Cetinje, Yugo., 45
Ceuta, Spain, 33
Cévennes (mts.), France, 28
Ceyhan, Turkey, 63
Ceylon (Sri Lanka), 68
Chacabuco, Arg., 143
Chachapoyas, Peru, 128
Chachoengsao, Thai., 72
Chaco (prov.), Arg., 143
Chaco (riv.), N. Mex., 274
Chaco (dept.), Par., 144
Chaco, Gran (reg.), S. Amer., 120
Chaco Canyon Nat'l Mon., N. Mex., 274
Chad, 111
Chad (lake), Africa, 111
Chadron, Nebr., 264
Chaffee, Mo., 261
Chagai (hills), Asia, 68
Chagos (arch.), Br. Indian Ocean Terr., 54
Chagrin Falls, Ohio, 284
Chaguanas, Trin. & Tob., 161
Chaibasa, India, 68
Chai Buri, Thai., 72
Chaiyaphum, Thai., 68
Chajul, Guat., 154
Chalatenango, El Sal., 154
Chalco, Mex., 150
Chaleur (bay), Canada, 170
Chalk River, Ont., 177
Challapata, Bol., 136
Chalmette Nat'l Hist. Pk., La., 238
Châlons-sur-Marne, France, 28
Chalon-sur-Saône, France, 28
Chalus, Iran, 66
Chambal (riv.), India, 68
Chamberlain, S. Dak., 298
Chambersburg, Pa., 294
Chambéry, France, 28
Chamblee, Ga., 216
Chambly, Que., 172
Chamdo, China, 77
Chamizal Nat'l Mem., Tex., 302
Chamonix, France, 28
Champaign, Ill., 222
Champassak, Laos, 72
Champdani, India, 68
Champerico, Guat., 154
Champigny-sur-Marne, France, 28
Champlain (lake), N. Amer., 268
Chañaral, Chile, 138
Chanda, India, 68
Chandeleur (isls.), La., 238
Chandernagore, India, 68
Chandigarh, India, 68
Chandler, Ariz., 198
Chandler, Okla., 288
Chandler, Que., 172
Changchih, China, 77
Changchow, China, 77
Changchun, China, 77
Chang Pai Shan (range), N. Korea, 81
Changsha, China, 77
Chang Tang (plat.), China, 77
Changteh, China, 77
Changyeh, China, 77
Chankiang, China, 77
Channel (isl.), 13
Channel Isls. Nat'l Mon., Calif., 204
Channel-Port aux Basques, Newf., 166
Channelview, Tex., 302
Chanthaburi, Thai., 72
Chantilly, France, 28
Chanute, Kans., 232
Chaoan (Chaochow), China, 77
Chaoking, China, 77
Chao Phraya (riv.), Thai., 72
Chaotung, China, 77
Chaoyang, China, 77
Chapala (lake), Mex., 150
Chapayevsk, U.S.S.R., 52
Chapel Hill, N.C., 281
Chapelton, Jam., 158
Chapleau, Ont., 175
Chapra, India, 68
Charcas, Mex., 150
Charcot (isl.), Ant., 5
Chardon, Ohio, 284
Chardzhou, U.S.S.R., 48
Charente (dept.), France, 28
Charente (riv.), France, 28
Charente-Maritime (dept.), France, 28
Charenton-le-Pont, France, 28
Charikar, Afghan., 68
Chariton, Iowa, 229
Charity, Guyana, 131
Charleroi, Belg., 27
Charleroi, Pa., 294
Charlesbourg, Que., 172
Charles City, Iowa, 229
Charleston, Ill., 222
Charleston, Miss., 256
Charleston, Mo., 261
Charleston (peak), Nev., 266
Charleston, S.C., 296
Charleston (cap.), W. Va., 313
Charlestown, Ind., 227
Charlestown (cap.), Nevis, 161
Charles Town, W. Va., 313
Charleville, Queensland, 95
Charleville-Mézières, France, 28
Charlevoix, Mich., 250
Charlotte (harb.), Fla., 212
Charlotte, Mich., 250
Charlotte, N.C., 281
Charlotte Amalie (cap.), Virgin Is. (U.S.), 161
Charlottenburg, W. Ger., 22
Charlottesville, Va., 307
Charlottetown (cap.), P.E.I., 169
Charny, Que., 172
Charters Towers, Queensland, 95
Chartres, France, 28
Chascomús, Arg., 143
Chase City, Va., 307
Chaska, Minn., 254
Châteaudun, France, 28
Château-Gontier, France, 28
Châteauguay, Que., 172
Châteauroux, France, 28
Château-Thierry, France, 28
Châtellerault, France, 28
Chatham, Eng., 13
Chatham, N.B., 170
Chatham, N. J., 273
Chatham (isls.), N.Z., 101
Chatham, Ont., 177
Châtillon, France, 28
Chatou, France, 28
Chatsworth, Calif., 204
Chattahoochee, Fla., 212
Chattahoochee (riv.), U.S., 188
Chattanooga, Tenn., 237
Chauk, Burma, 72
Chaumont, France, 28
Chau Phu, S. Vietnam, 72
Chauvin, La., 238
Chaves, Port., 33
Chaykovskiy, U.S.S.R., 52
Cheadle and Gatley, Eng., 10
Cheb, Czech., 41
Cheboksary, U.S.S.R., 52
Cheboygan, Mich., 250
Chechaouen, Mor., 106
Chechen-Ingush A.S.S.R., U.S.S.R., 52
Chech Erg (des.), Africa, 106
Checotah, Okla., 288
Cheduba (isl.), Burma, 72
Cheektowaga, N.Y., 276
Chefoo, China, 77
Chehalis, Wash., 310
Cheju (isl.), S. Korea, 81
Chekiang (prov.), China, 77
Chelan (lake), Wash., 310
Chéliff (riv.), Alg., 106
Chelkar, U.S.S.R., 48
Chelles, France, 28
Chełm, Poland, 47
Chełmno, Poland, 47
Chelmsford, Eng., 13
Chelsea, Mass., 249
Chelsea, Mich., 250
Chelsea, Vic., 97
Cheltenham, Eng., 13
Cheltenham, Pa., 294
Chelyabinsk, U.S.S.R., 48
Chelyuskin (cape), U.S.S.R., 48
Chemainus, Br. Col., 184
Chemba, Mozamb., 118
Chembur, India, 68
Chemnitz (Karl-Marx-Stadt), E. Ger., 22
Chenab (riv.), Asia, 68
Cheney, Wash., 310
Chengchow, China, 77
Chengteh, China, 77
Chengtu, China, 77
Chepo (riv.), Pan., 154
Chepstow, Wales, 13
Cher (dept.), France, 28
Cher (riv.), France, 28
Cheraw, S.C., 296
Cherbourg, France, 28
Cherchen (riv.), China, 77
Cheremkhovo, U.S.S.R., 48
Cherepovets, U.S.S.R., 52
Cherial (riv.), India, 68
Cherkassy, U.S.S.R., 52
Cherkessk, U.S.S.R., 52
Chermside, Queensland, 95
Chernigov, U.S.S.R., 52
Chernovtsy, U.S.S.R., 52
Cherokee, Iowa, 229
Cherokee, Okla., 288
Cherrapunji, India, 68
Cherry Hill, N. J., 273
Cherryvale, Kans., 232
Cherryville, N.C., 281
Cherskiy (range), U.S.S.R., 48
Chertsey, Eng., 10
Chesaning, Mich., 250
Chesapeake (bay), U.S., 188
Chesapeake, Va., 307
Chesapeake, W. Va., 313
Chesapeake & Ohio Canal Nat'l Hist. Pk., Md., 245
Chesham, Eng., 13
Cheshire, Conn., 210
Cheshire (county), Eng., 13
Cheshskaya (bay), U.S.S.R., 52
Cheshunt, Eng., 10
Chester, Eng., 13
Chester, Ill., 222
Chester, Pa., 294
Chester, S.C., 296
Chester, W. Va., 313
Chesterfield, Eng., 13
Chesterfield, Ind., 227
Chesterfield (inlet), N.W.T., 187
Chester-le-Street, Eng., 13
Chesterton, Ind., 227
Chestertown, Md., 245
Cheswick, Pa., 294
Chetlat (isl.), India, 68
Chetumal, Mex., 150
Chetwynd, Br. Col., 184
Cheverly, Md., 245
Cheviot, Ohio, 284
Cheviot (hills), U.K., 13
Chevy Chase, Md., 245
Cheyenne (riv.), U.S., 188
Cheyenne (cap.), Wyo., 319
Chhatarpur, India, 68
Chhindwara, India, 68
Chhlong, Cambodia, 72
Chi (riv.), Thai., 72
Chiai, China, 77
Chiang Rai, Thai., 72
Chiapas (state), Mex., 150
Chiatura, U.S.S.R., 52
Chiautempan, Mex., 150
Chiba (pref.), Japan, 81
Chiba, Japan, 81
Chibougamau, Que., 174
Chibuto, Mozamb., 118
Chicago, Ill., 222
Chicago Heights, Ill., 222
Chicago Portage Nat'l Hist. Site, Ill., 222
Chicago Ridge, Ill., 222
Chicapa (riv.), Africa, 115
Chichagof (isl.), Alaska, 196
Chichén-Itzá (ruins), Mex., 150
Chichester, Eng., 13
Chichi (isl.), Japan, 81
Chichicastenango, Guat., 154
Chichigalpa, Nic., 154
Chickamauga and Chattanooga Nat'l Mil. Pk., U.S., 237
Chickasaw, Ala., 194
Chickasha, Okla., 288
Chiclana de la Frontera, Spain, 33
Chiclayo, Peru, 128
Chico (riv.), Arg., 143
Chico, Calif., 204
Chicopee, Mass., 249
Chicoutimi, Que., 172
Chidambaram, India, 68
Chidley (cape), Canada, 166
Chiemsee (lake), W. Ger., 22
Chiengmai, Thai., 72
Chieti (prov.), Italy, 34
Chieti, Italy, 34
Chignecto (isthmus), N.S.-N.Br., 168
Chigwell, Eng., 10
Chihfeng, China, 77
Chihli (gulf), China, 77
Chihuahua (state), Mex., 150
Chihuahua, Mex., 150
Chik Ballapur, India, 68
Chikmagalur, India, 68
Chilapa, Mex., 150
Childersburg, Ala., 194
Childress, Tex., 302
Chile, 138
Chililabombwe, Zambia, 115
Chilka (lake), India, 68
Chillán, Chile, 138
Chillicothe, Ill., 222
Chillicothe, Mo., 261
Chillicothe, Ohio, 284
Chilliwack, Br. Col., 184
Chillum, Md., 245
Chiloé (prov.), Chile, 138
Chiloé (isl.), Chile, 138
Chilpancingo, Mex., 150
Chilton, Wis., 317
Chilwa (lake), Africa, 115
Chimaltenango, Guat., 154
Chimborazo (prov.), Ecua., 128
Chimborazo (mt.), Ecua., 128
Chimbote, Peru, 128
Chimkent, U.S.S.R., 48
Chimney Rock Nat'l Hist. Site, Nebr., 264
Chin (hills), Burma, 72
China, 77
China, Maine, 242
China Lake, Calif., 204
Chinameca, El Sal., 154
Chinandega, Nic., 154
Chincha Alta, Peru, 128
Chinchow, China, 77
Chindwin (riv.), Burma, 72
Chingleput, India, 68
Chingola, Zambia, 115
Chinguetti, Mauritania, 106
Chin (state), Burma, 72
Chinju, S. Korea, 81
Chinkiang, China, 77
Chino, Calif., 204
Chinook, Mont., 262
Chinwangtao, China, 77
Chioggia, Italy, 34
Chipata, Zambia, 115
Chipley, Fla., 212
Chippewa Falls, Wis., 317
Chiquimula, Guat., 154
Chiquinquirá, Col., 126
Chir (riv.), U.S.S.R., 52
Chirala, India, 68
Chiricahua Nat'l Mon., Ariz., 198
Chiriquí (gulf), Pan., 154
Chiriquí (vol.), Pan., 154
Chirpan, Bulg., 45
Chisholm, Minn., 254
Chistopol', U.S.S.R., 52
Chita, U.S.S.R., 48
Chitradurga, India, 68
Chitral, Pak., 68
Chitré, Pan., 154
Chittagong, Bang., 68
Chittenango, N.Y., 276
Chittoor, India, 68
Chivacoa, Venez., 124
Chivilcoy, Arg., 143
Chkalov (Orenburg), U.S.S.R., 52
Chocó (dept.), Col., 126
Choibalsan, Mong., 77
Choiseul (isl.), Sol. Is., 87
Choisy-le-Roi, France, 28
Chojnice, Poland, 47
Cholet, France, 28
Choloma, Hond., 154
Cholula, Mex., 150
Choluteca, Hond., 154
Chomo Lhari (mt.), Asia, 68
Chomutov, Czech., 41
Chon Buri, Thai., 72
Chone, Ecua., 128
Ch'ŏngjin, N. Korea, 81
Ch'ongju, S. Korea, 81
Chŏnju, S. Korea, 81
Chonos (arch.), Chile, 138
Chorley, Eng., 10
Chorrera, Pan., 154
Chorrillos, Peru, 128
Chorzów, Poland, 47
Choshi, Japan, 81
Chowchilla, Calif., 204
Christchurch, Eng., 13
Christchurch, N.Z., 101
Christiana, Jam., 158
Christiansburg, Va., 307
Christiansted, Virgin Is. (U.S.), 161
Christiansted Nat'l Hist. Site, Virgin Is. (U.S.), 161
Christmas (isl.), Austral., 54
Christmas (isl.), Gilb. and Ell. Is., 87
Christopher, Ill., 222
Chrudim, Czech., 41
Chrzanów, Poland, 47
Chu (riv.), U.S.S.R., 48
Chüanchow, China, 77
Chubut (prov.), Arg., 143
Chubut (riv.), Arg., 143
Chuchow, China, 77
Chukai, Malaysia, 72
Chukchi (sea), 48
Chukchi (pen.), U.S.S.R., 48
Chukchi Nat'l Okrug, U.S.S.R., 48
Chu Lai, S. Vietnam, 72
Chula Vista, Calif., 204
Chulucanas, Peru, 128
Chulumani, Bol., 136
Chulym (riv.), U.S.S.R., 48
Chumatien, China, 77
Ch'unch'ŏn, S. Korea, 81
Ch'ungju, S. Korea, 81
Chungking, China, 77
Chungshan, China, 77
Chuquicamata, Chile, 138
Chuquisaca (dept.), Bol., 136
Chur, Switz., 39
Churchill (peak), Br. Col., 184
Churchill (riv.), Canada, 163
Churchill, Man., 179
Churchill (falls), Newf., 166
Churchill (riv.), Newf., 166
Churchill, Pa., 294
Churchill (lake), Sask., 181
Church Point, La., 238
Churu, India, 68
Chushan (arch.), China, 77
Chusovoy, U.S.S.R., 52
Chuvash A.S.S.R., U.S.S.R., 52
Ciampino, Italy, 34
Cicero, Ill., 222
Ciego de Avila, Cuba, 158
Ciénaga, Col., 126
Cienfuegos, Cuba, 158
Cieszyn, Poland, 47
Cieza, Spain, 33
Cimarron (riv.), U.S., 188
Cîmpina, Rum., 45
Cîmpulung, Rum., 45
Cinca (riv.), Spain, 33
Cincinnati, Ohio, 284
Cintalapa, Mex., 150
Circeo (cape), Italy, 34
Circle Pines, Minn., 254
Circleville, Ohio, 284
Cirencester, Eng., 13
Cisco, Tex., 302
Cisne (isls.), Hond., 154
Citlaltépetl (mt.), Mex., 150
Citrus Hts., Calif., 204
City of Refuge Nat'l Hist. Pk., Hawaii, 218
City View, Ont., 177
Ciudad Acuña, Mex., 150
Ciudad Bolívar, Venez., 124
Ciudad Camargo, Mex., 150
Ciudad Darío, Nic., 154
Ciudad Delicias, Mex., 150
Ciudad de Valles, Mex., 150
Ciudad Guayana, Venez., 124
Ciudad Guzmán, Mex., 150
Ciudad Juárez, Mex., 150
Ciudad Lerdo, Mex., 150
Ciudad Madero, Mex., 150
Ciudad Mante, Mex., 150
Ciudad Obregón, Mex., 150
Ciudad Ojeda, Venez., 124
Ciudad Piar, Venez., 124
Ciudad Real (prov.), Spain, 33
Ciudad Real, Spain, 33
Ciudad Río Bravo, Mex., 150
Ciudad Serdán, Mex., 150
Ciudad Victoria, Mex., 150
Civitavecchia, Italy, 34
Clackamas, Oreg., 291
Clackmannan (county), Scot., 15
Clackmannan, Scot., 15
Clacton, Eng., 13
Clairton, Pa., 294
Clamart, France, 28
Clanton, Ala., 194
Clara, Ire., 17
Clare (county), Ire., 17
Claremont, Calif., 204
Claremont, N.H., 268
Claremore, Okla., 288
Claremorris, Ire., 17
Clarence (isl.), Chile, 138
Clarendon Hills, Ill., 222
Claresholm, Alta., 182
Clarinda, Iowa, 229
Clarion, Iowa, 229
Clarion, Pa., 294
Clark, N. J., 273
Clarksburg, W. Va., 313
Clarksdale, Miss., 256
Clarkston, Wash., 310
Clarksville, Ark., 203
Clarksville, Ind., 227
Clarksville, Tenn., 237
Clarksville, Tex., 302
Claro (riv.), Braz., 132
Clausthal-Zellerfeld, W. Ger., 22
Clawson, Mich., 250
Claxton, Ga., 216
Clay Center, Kans., 232
Claymont, Del., 245
Clayton, Mo., 261
Clayton, N. J., 273
Clayton, N. Mex., 274
Clayton, N.C., 281
Clear, Alaska, 196
Clear (lake), Calif., 204
Clear (cape), Ire., 17
Clearfield, Pa., 294
Clearfield, Utah, 304
Clear Lake, Iowa, 229
Clearwater, Fla., 212
Clearwater (mts.), Idaho, 220
Cleburne, Tex., 302
Cleethorpes, Eng., 13
Clementon, N. J., 273
Clerf (river), Lux., 27
Clermont, Fla., 212
Clermont-Ferrand, France, 28
Cleveland, Miss., 256
Cleveland, Ohio, 284
Cleveland, Okla., 288
Cleveland, Tenn., 237
Cleveland, Tex., 302
Cleveland Heights, Ohio, 284
Clew (bay), Ire., 17
Clewiston, Fla., 212
Clichy, France, 28
Clifden, Ire., 17
Cliffside Park, N. J., 273
Cliffwood, N. J., 273
Clifton, Ariz., 198
Clifton, N. J., 273
Clifton Forge, Va., 307
Clifton Hts., Pa., 294
Clifton Park, N.Y., 276
Clinton, Br. Col., 184
Clinton, Conn., 210
Clinton, Ill., 222
Clinton, Ind., 227
Clinton, Iowa, 229
Clinton, Mass., 249
Clinton, Miss., 256
Clinton, Mo., 261
Clinton, N.C., 281
Clinton, Okla., 288
Clinton, Ont., 177
Clinton, S.C., 296
Clinton, Tenn., 237
Clintonville, Wis., 317
Clipperton (isl.), Fr. Poly., 3
Clitheroe, Eng., 10
Cliza, Bol., 136
Clonakilty, Ire., 17
Clondalkin, Ire., 17
Clones, Ire., 17
Clonmel, Ire., 17
Cloquet, Minn., 254
Closter, N. J., 273
Cloudy (bay), N.Z., 101
Clover, S.C., 296
Cloverdale, Calif., 204
Clovis, Calif., 204
Clovis, N. Mex., 274
Cluj, Rum., 45
Cluny, France, 28
Clute, Tex., 302
Clutha (riv.), N.Z., 101
Clwyd (riv.), Wales, 13
Clyde, N.Y., 276
Clyde (inlet), N.W.T., 187
Clyde, Ohio, 284
Clyde (firth), Scot., 15
Clyde (riv.), Scot., 15
Clydebank, Scot., 15
Coachella, Calif., 204
Coahuila (state), Mex., 150
Coal City, Ill., 222
Coalcomán, Mex., 150
Coaldale, Alta., 182
Coal Grove, Ohio, 284
Coalinga, Calif., 204
Coalville, Eng., 13
Coamo, P. Rico, 161
Coast (mts.), Br. Col., 184
Coast (ranges), Calif., 204
Coast (prov.), Kenya, 115
Coast (reg.), Tanz., 115
Coatbridge, Scot., 15
Coatepec, Mex., 150
Coatepeque, Guat., 154
Coatesville, Pa., 294
Coaticook, Que., 172
Coats Land (reg.), Ant., 5
Coatzacoalcos, Mex., 150
Cobalt, Ont., 175
Cobán, Guat., 154
Cóbh, Ire., 17
Cobija, Bol., 136
Cobleskill, N.Y., 276
Cobourg, Ont., 177
Coburg, Vic., 97
Coburg, W. Ger., 22
Cocanada (Kakinada), India, 68
Cochabamba (dept.), Bol., 136

E

F

G

H

Kaya, Upp. Volta, 106
Kayah (state), Burma, 72
Kayes, Mali, 106
Kayseri (prov.), Turkey, 63
Kayseri, Turkey, 63
Kaysville, Utah, 304
Kazach'ye, U.S.S.R., 48
Kazakh S.S.R., U.S.S.R., 48
Kazalinsk, U.S.S.R., 48
Kazan (riv.), N.W.T., 187
Kazan', U.S.S.R., 52
Kazandzhik, U.S.S.R., 48
Kazanlůk, Bulg., 45
Kazatin, U.S.S.R., 52
Kazerun, Iran, 66
Kazvin, Iran, 66
Kéa (isl.), Greece, 45
Keansburg, N. J., 273
Kearney, Nebr., 264
Kearns, Utah, 304
Kearny, N. J., 273
Kearsarge, Pa., 294
Kebnekaise (mt.), Sweden, 18
Kebumen, Indon., 85
Kecskemét, Hung., 41
Kedah (state), Malaysia, 72
Kedainiai, U.S.S.R., 53
Kediri, Indon., 85
Kédougou, Sen., 106
Kedzierzyn, Poland, 47
Keego Hbr., Mich., 250
Keele (peak), Yukon, 187
Keelung, China, 77
Keene, N.H., 268
Keetmanshoop, S.W. Afr., 118
Keewatin (dist.), N.W.T., 187
Keewatin, Ont., 175
Kefallinia (isl.), Greece, 45
Kefar Atta, Israel, 65
Kefar Sava, Israel, 65
Keflavík, Iceland, 21
Ke Ga (pt.), S. Vietnam, 72
Kehl, W. Ger., 22
Keighley, Eng., 10
Keilor, Vic., 97
Keitele (lake), Fin., 18
Keith, Scot., 15
Keizer, Oreg., 291
Kejimkujik Nat'l Park, N.S., 168
Kékes (mt.), Hung., 41
Kelang, Malaysia, 72
Kelantan (state), Malaysia, 72
Kelheim, W. Ger., 22
Kelkit (riv.), Turkey, 63
Kellogg, Idaho, 220
Kells (Ceanannus Mór), Ire., 17
Kélo, Chad, 111
Kelowna, Br. Col., 184
Kelso, Scot., 15
Kelso, Wash., 310
Kelston West, N.Z., 101
Keltie (lake), Ant., 5
Keluang, Malaysia, 72
Kem', U.S.S.R., 52
Kemerovo, U.S.S.R., 48
Kemi, Fin., 18
Kemi (lake), Fin., 18
Kemi (riv.), Fin., 18
Kemijärvi, Fin., 18
Kemmerer, Wyo., 319
Kemp Coast (reg.), Ant., 5
Kempsey, N.S.W., 97
Kempten, W. Ger., 22
Kempton Park, S. Afr., 118
Kenadsa, Alg., 106
Kenai, Alaska, 196
Kendal, Eng., 13
Kendal, Indon., 85
Kendall Park, N.J., 273
Kendallville, Ind., 227
Kendari, Indon., 85
Kenedy, Tex., 302
Kenema, S. Leone, 106
Keng Kok, Laos, 72
Kenhorst, Pa., 294
Kenilworth, Eng., 10
Kenilworth, Ill., 222
Kenilworth, N. J., 273
Keningau, Malaysia, 85
Kénitra, Mor., 106
Kenmare, Ire., 17
Kenmore, N.Y., 276
Kenmore, Wash., 310
Kennebunk, Maine, 242
Kenner, La., 238
Kennesaw Mtn. Nat'l Battlef. Park, Ga., 216
Kennett, Mo., 261
Kennett Square, Pa., 294
Kennewick, Wash., 310
Kenogami (riv.), Ont., 175
Kénogami, Que., 172
Keno Hill, Yukon, 187
Kenora, Ont., 175
Kenosha, Wis., 317
Kenova, W. Va., 313
Kensington, Conn., 210
Kensington, P.E.I., 169
Kensington and Chelsea, Eng., 10
Kensington and Norwood, S. Austral., 94
Kent (county), Eng., 13
Kent (pen.), N.W.T., 187
Kent, Ohio, 284
Kent, Wash., 310
Kenton, Ohio, 284
Kentucky (state), U.S., 237
Kentucky (lake), U.S., 237
Kentville, N.S., 169
Kentwood, La., 238
Kentwood, Mich., 250
Kenya, 115
Kenya (mt.), Kenya, 115
Keokuk, Iowa, 229
Kerala (state), India, 68
Kerava, Fin., 18
Kerch', U.S.S.R., 52
Kerema, P.N.G., 85
Kerguélen (isls.), 3
Kericho, Kenya, 115
Kerintji (mt.), Indon., 85
Keriya, China, 77
Kerkennah (isls.), Tun., 106
Kerki, U.S.S.R., 48
Kérkira, Greece, 45
Kérkira (isl.), Greece, 45
Kermadec (isls.), N.Z., 87
Kerman (prov.), Iran, 66
Kerman, Iran, 66
Kermanshah (prov.), Iran, 66
Kermanshah, Iran, 66
Kerme (gulf), Turkey, 63

Kermit, Tex., 302
Kernersville, N.C., 281
Kerrobert, Sask., 181
Kerrville, Tex., 302
Kerry (county), Ire., 17
Kerulen (riv.), Asia, 77
Kesagami (lake), Ont., 177
Kesennuma, Japan, 81
Keski-Suomi (prov.), Fin., 18
Keta, Ghana, 106
Ketchikan, Alaska, 196
Kete Krakye, Ghana, 106
Kętrzyn, Poland, 47
Kettering, Eng., 13
Kettering, Ohio, 284
Kevelaer, W. Ger., 22
Kew, Vic., 97
Kewanee, Ill., 222
Kewaunee, Wis., 317
Keweenaw (pt.), Mich., 250
Keynsham, Eng., 13
Keyport, N. J., 273
Keyser, W. Va., 313
Key West, Fla., 212
Kezhma, U.S.S.R., 48
Khabarovsk, U.S.S.R., 48
Khabur (riv.), Syria, 63
Khachmas, U.S.S.R., 52
Khaibar, Saudi Ar., 59
Khairpur, Pak., 68
Khakass Aut. Oblast, U.S.S.R., 48
Khalkís, Greece, 45
Khamgaon, India, 68
Khan Abasa, China, 77
Khanabad, Afghan., 68
Khanaqin, Iraq, 66
Khandwa, India, 68
Khandyga, U.S.S.R., 48
Khangai (mts.), Mong., 77
Khanh Hoa, S. Vietnam, 72
Khanh Hung, S. Vietnam, 72
Khaniá, Greece, 45
Khanka (lake), Asia, 77
Khan Yunis, Gaza Strip, 65
Kharagpur, India, 68
Kharan, Pak., 68
Khara Usu (lake), Mong., 77
Khârga (oasis), Egypt, 111
Khar'kov, U.S.S.R., 52
Kharmanlii, Bulg., 45
Kharovsk, U.S.S.R., 52
Khartoum (prov.), Sudan, 111
Khartoum (cap.), Sudan, 111
Khartoum North, Sudan, 111
Khasavyurt, U.S.S.R., 52
Khashm el Girba, Sudan, 111
Khaskovo, Bulg., 45
Khatanga, U.S.S.R., 48
Khemis Miliana, Alg., 106
Khenifra, Mor., 106
Khentei (prov.), Mong., 77
Kherson, U.S.S.R., 52
Kheta (riv.), U.S.S.R., 48
Khilok, U.S.S.R., 48
Khíos, Greece, 45
Khíos (isl.), Greece, 45
Khirbet Qumran (site), Jordan, 65
Khiva, U.S.S.R., 48
Khmel'nitskiy, U.S.S.R., 52
Khodzheyli, U.S.S.R., 48
Khoi, Iran, 66
Kholmsk, U.S.S.R., 48
Khone, Laos, 72
Khong, Laos, 72
Khong Sédone, Laos, 72
Khon Kaen, Thai., 72
Khoper (riv.), U.S.S.R., 52
Khorat (Nakhon Ratchasima), Thai., 72
Khorog, U.S.S.R., 48
Khorol, U.S.S.R., 52
Khorramshahr, Iran, 66
Khotan, China, 77
Khotin, U.S.S.R., 52
Khouribga, Mor., 106
Khubsugul (prov.), Mong., 77
Khubsugul (lake), Mong., 77
Khu Khan, Thai., 72
Khulna, Bang., 68
Khurasan (prov.), Iran, 66
Khurramabad, Iran, 66
Khuzistan (prov.), Iran, 66
Khvalynsk, U.S.S.R., 52
Khyber (pass), Pak., 68
Kialing Kiang (riv.), China, 77
Kiama, N.S.W., 97
Kiamusze, China, 77
Kian, China, 77
Kiangsi (prov.), China, 77
Kiangsu (prov.), China, 77
Kianta (lake), Fin., 18
Kiaohsien, China, 77
Kiayükwan, China, 77
Kibombo, Zaire, 115
Kičevo, Yugo., 45
Kidapawan, Phil., 82
Kidderminster, Eng., 10
Kidwelly, Wales, 13
Kiel, W. Ger., 22
Kiel (canal), W. Ger., 22
Kiel, Wis., 317
Kielce (prov.), Poland, 47
Kielce, Poland, 47
Kienow, China, 77
Kienshui, China, 77
Kienyang, China, 77
Kieta, P.N.G., 87
Kiev, U.S.S.R., 52
Kiffa, Mauritania, 106
Kigali (cap.), Rwanda, 115
Kigoma (reg.), Tanz., 115
Kigoma-Ujiji, Tanz., 115
Kikinda, Yugo., 45
Kikwit, Zaire, 115
Kilauea (crater), Hawaii, 218
Kildare (county), Ire., 17
Kildare, Ire., 17
Kil'din (isl.), U.S.S.R., 52
Kilgore, Tex., 302
Kili (atoll), Pac. Is., 87
Kilimanjaro (reg.), Tanz., 115
Kilimanjaro (mt.), Tanz., 115
Kilis, Turkey, 63
Kiliya, U.S.S.R., 52
Kilkee, Ire., 17
Kilkenny (county), Ire., 17

Kilkenny, Ire., 17
Kilkís, Greece, 45
Killaloe, Ire., 17
Killarney, Ire., 17
Killarney, Man., 179
Killeen, Tex., 302
Killinek (isl.), Canada, 166
Killingley, Conn., 210
Kilmarnock, Scot., 15
Kilmory, Scot., 15
Kilosa, Tanz., 115
Kilpis (lake), Europe, 18
Kilrenny and Anstruther, Scot., 15
Kilrush, Ire., 17
Kilsyth, Scot., 15
Kilwa Kivinje, Tanz., 115
Kilwa Masoko, Tanz., 115
Kimball, Nebr., 264
Kimberley, Br. Col., 184
Kimberley, S. Afr., 118
Kimberley (plat.), W. Austral., 92
Kimberly, Wis., 317
Kimchaek, N. Korea, 81
Kimch'ŏn, S. Korea, 81
Kimovsk, U.S.S.R., 52
Kimry, U.S.S.R., 52
Kinabalu (mt.), Malaysia, 85
Kincardine, Ont., 177
Kincardine (county), Scot., 15
Kindersley, Sask., 181
Kindia, Guinea, 106
Kindu, Zaire, 115
Kinel', U.S.S.R., 52
Kinel' (riv.), U.S.S.R., 52
Kineshma, U.S.S.R., 52
King (isl.), Br. Col., 184
King (isl.), Tas., 99
King (sound), W. Austral., 92
Kingaroy, Queensland, 95
King Christian IX Land (reg.), Greenl., 4
King Christian X Land (reg.), Greenl., 4
King City, Calif., 204
Kingfisher, Okla., 288
King Frederik VIII Land (reg.), Greenl., 4
King Frederik VI Land (reg.), Greenl., 4
King George's (falls), S. Afr. 118
King Leopold (range), W. Austral., 92
Kingman, Ariz., 198
Kingman, Kans., 232
Kingman Reef (isl.), Pacific, 87
Kings (peak), Utah, 304
Kingsburg, Calif., 204
Kings Canyon Nat'l Park, Calif., 204
Kingscourt, Ire., 17
Kingsford, Mich., 250
King's Lynn, Eng., 13
Kings Mtn., N.C., 281
Kings Mtn. Nat'l Mil. Park, S.C., 296
Kings Park, N.Y., 276
Kings Point, N.Y., 276
Kingsport, Tenn., 237
Kingston (bay), Jam., 158
Kingston, N.Y., 276
Kingston (cap.), Norfolk I., 88
Kingston, Ont., 177
Kingston, Pa., 294
Kingston upon Thames, Eng., 10
Kingston (Dún Laoghaire), Ire., 17
Kingstown (cap.), St. Vincent, 161
Kingstree, S.C., 296
Kingsville, Md., 245
Kingsville, Ont., 177
Kingsville, Tex., 302
Kingswood, Eng., 13
Kingtehchen, China, 77
Kingussie, Scot., 15
King William's Town, S. Afr., 118
Kingwood, W. Va., 313
Kinhwa, China, 77
Kinloch, Mo., 261
Kinlochleven, Scot., 15
Kinnairds (head), Scot., 15
Kinnelon, N.J., 273
Kinross (county), Scot., 15
Kinross, Scot., 15
Kinsale, Ire., 17
Kinshasa (cap.), Zaire, 115
Kinston, N.C., 281
Kinta, China, 77
Kintampo, Ghana, 106
Kintyre (dist.), Scot., 15
Kioga (lake), Uganda, 115
Kipárissía (gulf), Greece, 45
Kipushi, Zaire, 115
Kirchberg, Switz., 39
Kirchheim, W. Ger., 22
Kirensk, U.S.S.R., 48
Kirgiz (no lake), Mong., 77
Kirgiz S.S.R., U.S.S.R., 48
Kirigalpotta (mt.), Sri Lanka, 68
Kirin (prov.), China, 77
Kirin, China, 77
Kirkby, Eng., 10
Kirkby-in-Ashfield, Eng., 13
Kirkcaldy, Scot., 15
Kirkcudbright (county), Scot., 15
Kirkcudbright, Scot., 15
Kirkee, India, 68
Kirkenes, Norway, 18
Kirkham, Eng., 10
Kirkintilloch, Scot., 15
Kirkland, Wash., 310
Kirkland Lake, Ont., 175
Kírklareli (prov.), Turkey, 63
Kírklareli, Turkey, 63
Kirkpatrick (mt.), Ant., 5
Kirksville, Mo., 261
Kirkuk (prov.), Iraq, 66
Kirkuk, Iraq, 66
Kirkwall, Scot., 15
Kirkwood, Mo., 261
Kirov, U.S.S.R., 52
Kirovabad, U.S.S.R., 52
Kirovakan, U.S.S.R., 52
Kirovo-Chepetsk, U.S.S.R., 52
Kirovograd, U.S.S.R., 52
Kirovsk, U.S.S.R., 52
Kirriemuir, Scot., 15

Kirsanov, U.S.S.R., 52
Kirşehir (prov.), Turkey, 63
Kirşehir, Turkey, 63
Kiruna, Sweden, 18
Kiryu, Japan, 81
Kisa, Sweden, 18
Kisangani, Zaire, 115
Kisar (isl.), Indon., 85
Kisarazu, Japan, 81
Kiselevsk, U.S.S.R., 48
Kishinev, U.S.S.R., 52
Kishiwada, Japan, 81
Kisi, China, 77
Kiska (isl.), Alaska, 196
Kiskunfélegyháza, Hung., 41
Kiskunhalas, Hung., 41
Kislovodsk, U.S.S.R., 52
Kismayu, Somalia, 111
Kispest, Hung., 41
Kissidougou, Guinea, 106
Kissimmee, Fla., 212
Kississing (lake), Man.,179
Kistna (riv.), India, 68
Kisumu, Kenya, 115
Kita, Mali, 106
Kitai, China, 77
Kitaibaraki, Japan, 81
Kita Iwo (isl.), Japan, 81
Kitakyushu, Japan, 81
Kitale, Kenya, 115
Kitami, Japan, 81
Kitchener, Ont., 177
Kíthira (isl.), Greece, 45
Kitimat, Br. Col., 184
Kitinen (riv.), Fin., 18
Kittanning, Pa., 294
Kittery, Maine, 242
Kittilä, Fin., 18
Kitwe, Zambia, 115
Kitzbühel, Austria, 41
Kitzingen, W. Ger., 22
Kiuchüan, China, 77
Kiukiang, China, 77
Kiungchow (strait), China, 77
Kiungshan, China, 77
Kivi (lake), Fin., 18
Kivu (lake), Africa, 115
Kivu (reg.), Zaire, 115
Kizel', U.S.S.R., 52
Kızılırmak (riv.), Turkey, 63
Kızıltoprak, Turkey, 63
Kizlyar, U.S.S.R., 52
Kizyl-Arvat, U.S.S.R., 48
Kjölen (range), Europe, 18
Kladno, Czech., 41
Klagenfurt, Austria, 41
Klaipéda, U.S.S.R., 53
Klamath Falls, Oreg., 291
Klaten, Indon., 85
Klatovy, Czech., 41
Kleberg, Tex., 302
Kleinmachnow, E. Ger., 22
Klerksdorp, S. Afr., 118
Kleve, W. Ger., 22
Klimovichi, U.S.S.R., 52
Klingenthal, E. Ger., 22
Klintsy, U.S.S.R., 52
Kłodzko, Poland, 47
Klondike (riv.), Yukon, 187
Kloten, Switz., 39
Klosterneuburg, Austria, 41
Kluane (lake), Yukon, 187
Kluane Nat'l Park, Yukon, 187
Klyuchevskaya Sopka (vol.), U.S.S.R., 48
Knighton, Wales, 13
Knittelfeld, Austria, 41
Knob Lake (Schefferville), Que., 174
Knox, Ind., 227
Knox Coast (reg.), Ant., 5
Knoxville, Ill., 222
Knoxville, Iowa, 229
Knoxville, Tenn., 237
Knutsford, Eng., 10
Knysna, S. Afr., 118
Kobdo (prov.), Mong., 77
Kobdo, Mong., 77
Kobe, Japan, 81
København (Copenhagen) (cap.), Den., 21
Koblenz, Switz., 39
Koblenz, W. Ger., 22
Kobrin, U.S.S.R., 52
Kobuk (riv.), Alaska, 196
Kobuleti, U.S.S.R., 52
Kocaeli (prov.), Turkey, 63
Koch'ang, S. Korea, 81
Kochi (pref.), Japan, 81
Kochi, Japan, 81
Kodaira, Japan, 81
Kodiak, Alaska, 196
Kodiak (isl.), Alaska, 196
Kodok, Sudan, 111
Koforidua, Ghana, 106
Kofu, Japan, 81
Kogarah, N.S.W., 97
Kohat, Pak., 68
Kohima, India, 68
Kohtla-Järve, U.S.S.R., 53
Koitere (lake), Fin., 18
Kŏje (isl.), S. Korea, 81
Kokanee Glacier Prov. Park, Br. Col., 184
Kokchetav, U.S.S.R., 48
Kokemäki, Fin., 18
Kokiu, China, 77
Kokkola, Fin., 18
Kokomo, P.N.G., 85
Kokomo, Ind., 227
Koko Nor (lake), China, 77
Koksoak (riv.), Que., 174
Kola (riv.), U.S.S.R., 52
Kolahun, Liberia, 106
Kolar Gold Fields, India, 68
Kolarovgrad, Bulg., 45
Kolding, Den., 21
Kolguyev (isl.), U.S.S.R., 52
Kolhapur, India, 68
Kolín, Czech., 41
Kołobrzeg, Poland, 47
Kolomna, U.S.S.R., 52
Kolpashevo, U.S.S.R., 48
Kolva (riv.), U.S.S.R., 52
Kolwezi, Zaire, 115
Kolyma (range), U.S.S.R., 48
Kolyma (riv.), U.S.S.R., 48
Komandorskiye (isls.), U.S.S.R., 48
Komárno, Czech., 41
Komárom (county), Hung., 41
Komatsu, Japan, 81
Komi A.S.S.R., U.S.S.R., 52
Komi-Permyak Nat'l Okrug, U.S.S.R., 48

Komló, Hung., 41
Kommunarsk, U.S.S.R., 52
Komodo (isl.), Indon., 85
Kôm Ombo, Egypt, 111
Komotiní, Greece, 45
Kompong Cham, Cambodia, 72
Kompong Chhnang, Cambodia, 72
Kompong Som, Cambodia, 72
Kompong Speu, Cambodia, 72
Kompong Thom, Cambodia, 72
Kompong Trabek, Cambodia, 72
Komrat, U.S.S.R., 52
Komsomolets (isl.), U.S.S.R., 48
Komsomol'sk, U.S.S.R., 48
Kondoa, Tanz., 115
Kondopoga, U.S.S.R., 52
Kong, Ivory Coast, 106
Kongju, S. Korea, 81
Kong Karls Land (isl.), Norway, 18
Kongmoon, China, 77
Kongolo, Zaire, 115
Kongsberg, Norway, 18
Kongsvinger, Norway, 18
Kongwa, Tanz., 115
Königsberg (Kaliningrad), U.S.S.R., 52
Königssee (lake), W. Ger., 22
Konin, Poland, 47
Koniz, Switz., 39
Konstantinovka, U.S.S.R., 52
Konstanz, W. Ger., 22
Kontum, S. Vietnam, 72
Kontum (plat.), S. Vietnam, 72
Konya (prov.), Turkey, 63
Konya, Turkey, 63
Kootenay (lake), Br. Col., 184
Kootenay (riv.), Br. Col., 184
Kootenay Nat'l Park, Br. Col., 184
Köpenick, E. Ger., 22
Koper, Yugo., 45
Kopeysk, U.S.S.R., 48
Köping, Sweden, 18
Kopparberg (county), Sweden, 18
Kopparberg, Sweden, 18
Koprivnica, Yugo., 45
Korab (mt.), Europe, 45
Korçë, Alb., 45
Korčula (isl.), Yugo., 45
Kordofan (prov.), Sudan, 111
Korea, 81
Korea (strait), Asia, 81
Korf, U.S.S.R., 48
Korhogo, Ivory Coast, 106
Koriyama, Japan, 81
Korkino, U.S.S.R., 48
Kornwestheim, W. Ger., 22
Köröglu (mts.), Turkey, 63
Koronadal, Phil., 82
Koror, Pac. Is., 87
Kororoit (creek), Vic., 97
Körös (riv.), Hung., 41
Korosten', U.S.S.R., 52
Korsakov, U.S.S.R., 48
Korsør, Den., 21
Koryak (range), U.S.S.R., 48
Koryak Nat'l Okrug, U.S.S.R., 48
Kos (isl.), Greece, 45
Kosciusko, Miss., 256
Kosciusko (mt.), N.S.W., 97
Koshigaya, Japan, 81
Košice, Czech., 41
Koslan, U.S.S.R., 52
Kosovo (aut. prov.), Yugo., 45
Kosovska Mitrovica, Yugo., 45
Kosti, Sudan, 111
Kostroma, U.S.S.R., 52
Koszalin (prov.), Poland, 47
Koszalin, Poland, 47
Kota, India, 68
Kotaagung, Indon., 85
Kota Baharu, Malaysia, 72
Kota Kinabalu, Malaysia, 72
Kotel'nich, U.S.S.R., 52
Kotel'nikovo, U.S.S.R., 52
Kotel'nyy (isl.), U.S.S.R., 48
Köthen, E. Ger., 22
Kotka, Fin., 18
Kotlas, U.S.S.R., 52
Kotor, Yugo., 45
Kotovsk, U.S.S.R., 52
Kottayam, India, 68
Kotuy (riv.), U.S.S.R., 48
Kötzebue, Alaska, 196
Koudougou, Upp. Volta, 106
Koula-Moutou, Gabon, 115
Koulikoro, Mali, 106
Koumra, Chad, 111
Kouroussa, Guinea, 106
Koutiala, Mali, 106
Kouvola, Fin., 18
Kovel', U.S.S.R., 52
Kovrov, U.S.S.R., 52
Kowloon, Hong Kong, 77
Koyukuk (riv.), Alaska, 196
Koza, Japan, 81
Kozáni, Greece, 45
Kozhevnikovo, U.S.S.R., 48
Kozhikode, India, 68
Kpandu, Ghana, 106
Kra (isth.), Thai., 72
Kragan, Indon., 85
Kragerø, Norway, 18
Kragujevac, Yugo., 45
Krakatau (Rakata) (isl.), Indon., 85
Kralendijk, Neth. Ant., 161
Kraljevo (Rankovićevo), Yugo., 45
Kramatorsk, U.S.S.R., 52
Kramfors, Sweden, 18
Kranj, Yugo., 45
Krasino, U.S.S.R., 48
Krasnik, Poland, 47
Krasnoarmeysk, U.S.S.R., 52
Krasnodar, U.S.S.R., 52
Krasnograd, U.S.S.R., 52
Krasnokamsk, U.S.S.R., 52
Krasnoslobodsk, U.S.S.R., 52
Krasnotur'insk, U.S.S.R., 48

Krasnoural'sk, U.S.S.R., 48
Krasnovishersk, U.S.S.R., 48
Krasnovodsk, U.S.S.R., 48
Krasnoyarsk, U.S.S.R., 48
Krasnyy Luch, U.S.S.R., 52
Kratie, Cambodia, 72
Krauchmar, Cambodia, 72
Kraulshavn, Greenl., 4
Krawang, Indon., 85
Krefeld, W. Ger., 22
Kremenchug, U.S.S.R., 52
Krems, Austria, 41
Kreuzlingen, Switz., 39
Kribi, Cameroon, 115
Krichev, U.S.S.R., 52
Kriens, Switz., 39
Krishna (riv.), India, 68
Krishna (Kistna) (riv.), India, 68
Krishnanagar, India, 68
Kristiansand, Norway, 18
Kristianstad (county), Sweden, 18
Kristiansund, Norway, 18
Kristiinankaupunki (Kristinestad), Fin., 18
Kristinehamn, Sweden, 18
Krivoy Rog, U.S.S.R., 52
Krk (isl.), Yugo., 45
Krnov, Czech., 41
Krolevets, U.S.S.R., 52
Kronoberg (county), Sweden, 18
Kronshtadt, U.S.S.R., 52
Kroonstad, S. Afr., 118
Kropotkin, U.S.S.R., 52
Krosno Ordz., Poland, 47
Kru Coast (reg.), Liberia, 106
Kruě, Alb., 45
Kruger Nat'l Park, S. Afr., 118
Krugersdorp, S. Afr., 118
Krung Thep (Bangkok) (cap.), Thai., 72
Kruševac, Yugo., 45
Krymsk, U.S.S.R., 52
Ksar-el-Kebir, Mor., 106
Ksar-es-Souk, Mor., 106
Kuala Lipis, Malaysia, 72
Kuala Lumpur (cap.), Malaysia, 72
Kuala Pilah, Malaysia, 72
Kuala Selangor, Malaysia, 72
Kuala Terengganu, Malaysia, 72
Kuantan, Malaysia, 72
Kuba, U.S.S.R., 52
Kubeno (lake), U.S.S.R., 52
Kucha, China, 77
Kuching, Malaysia, 85
Kuçove (Stalin), Alb., 45
Kudat, Malaysia, 85
Kudus, Indon., 85
Kudymkar, U.S.S.R., 52
Kufra (oasis), Libya, 111
Kuhmo, Fin., 18
Kukawa, Nigeria, 106
Kulai, Malaysia, 72
Kula Kangri (mt.), Asia, 68
Kuldiga, U.S.S.R., 52
Kuldja, China, 77
Kulebaki, U.S.S.R., 52
Kulmbach, W. Ger., 22
Kulpmont, Pa., 294
Kul'sary, U.S.S.R., 48
Kuma (riv.), U.S.S.R., 52
Kumagaya, Japan, 81
Kumamoto (pref.), Japan, 81
Kumamoto, Japan, 81
Kumanovo, Yugo., 45
Kumasi, Ghana, 106
Kumba, Cameroon, 115
Kumbakonam, India, 68
Kumbi Saleh (ruins), Mauritania, 106
Kumla, Sweden, 18
Kunar (riv.), Asia, 68
Kungälv, Sweden, 18
Kungsbacka, Sweden, 18
Kungu, Zaire, 115
Kungur, U.S.S.R., 52
Kuningan, Indon., 85
Kunlun (mts.), Asia, 77
Kunming, China, 77
Kunsan, S. Korea, 81
Kuopio (prov.), Fin., 18
Kuopio, Fin., 18
Kupang, Indon., 85
Kupino, U.S.S.R., 48
Kupyansk, U.S.S.R., 52
Kura (riv.), U.S.S.R., 52
Kurashiki, Japan, 81
Kurdistan (prov.), Iran, 66
Kürdzhali, Bulg., 45
Kure (bay), Hawaii, 218
Kure, Japan, 81
Kure (mts.), Turkey, 63
Kuressaare, U.S.S.R., 53
Kurgan, U.S.S.R., 48
Kurgan-Tyube, U.S.S.R., 48
Kuria Muria (isls.), Oman, 59
Kurikka, Fin., 18
Kuril (isls.), U.S.S.R., 48
Kurla, China, 77
Kurla, India, 68
Kurmuk, Sudan, 111
Kurnool, India, 68
Kurri Kurri-Weston, N.S.W., 97
Kursk, U.S.S.R., 52
Kuruma, Japan, 81
Kurunegala, Sri Lanka, 68
Kusadası, Turkey, 63
Kusaie (isl.), Pac. Is., 87
Kushiro, Japan, 81
Kushk, Afghan., 68
Kushka, U.S.S.R., 48
Kuskokwim (riv.), Alaska, 196
Küsnacht, Switz., 39
Küssnacht, Switz., 39
Kustanay, U.S.S.R., 48
Kütahya (prov.), Turkey, 63
Kütahya, Turkey, 63
Kutaisi, U.S.S.R., 52
Kutaradja (Banda Atjeh), Indon., 85
Kutch (gulf), India, 68
Kutch, Rann of (salt marsh), Asia, India, 68
Kutno, Poland, 47
Kutu, Zaire, 115
Kutztown, Pa., 294
Kuusamo, Fin., 18
Kuvándyk, U.S.S.R., 48

Kuwait, 59
Kuybyshev, U.S.S.R., 52
Kuybyshev (res.), U.S.S.R., 52
Kuyto (lake), U.S.S.R., 52
Kuznetsk, U.S.S.R., 52
Kvalöy (isl.), Norway, 18
Kvarner (gulf), Yugo., 45
Kvichak (riv.), Alaska, 196
Kvikkjokk, Sweden, 18
Kviteseid, Norway, 18
Kwajalein (atoll), Pac. Is., 87
Kwando (riv.), Africa, 115
Kwanghwa, China, 77
Kwangju, S. Korea, 81
Kwangnan, China, 77
Kwango (riv.), Africa, 115
Kwangsi Chuang Aut. Reg., China, 77
Kwangtung (prov.), China, 77
Kwara (state), Nigeria, 106
Kwatta, Sur., 131
Kweichow (prov.), China, 77
Kweilin, China, 77
Kweiping, China, 77
Kweisui (Huhehot), China, 77
Kweiyang, China, 77
Kwidzyn, Poland, 47
Kwilu (riv.), Africa, 115
Kwinana, W. Austral., 92
Kyabé, Chad, 111
Kyabram, Vic., 97
Kyaikto, Burma, 72
Kyakhta, U.S.S.R., 48
Kyangin, Burma, 72
Kyaring Tso (lake), China, 77
Kyaukpadaung, Burma, 72
Kyaukpyu, Burma, 72
Kyaukse, Burma, 72
Kymi (prov.), Fin., 18
Kyneton, Vic., 97
Kyogle, N.S.W., 97
Kyŏngju, S. Korea, 81
Kyoto (pref.), Japan, 81
Kyoto, Japan, 81
Kyrenia, Cyprus, 63
Kyushu (isl.), Japan, 81
Kyusyur, U.S.S.R., 48
Kyustendil, Bulg., 45
Kyusyur, U.S.S.R., 48
Kywebwe, Burma, 72
Kyzyl, U.S.S.R., 48
Kyzyl-Kum (des.), U.S.S.R., 48
Kzyl-Orda, U.S.S.R., 48

L

La Asunción, Venez., 124
La Barca, Mex., 150
La Baule, France, 28
Labe (riv.), Czech., 41
Labé, Guinea, 106
Labinsk, U.S.S.R., 52
Laborie, St. Lucia, 161
Labrador (sea), 166
Labrador (dist.), Newf., 166
La Brea, Trin. & Tobago, 161
Labuan, Phil., 85
Labuan (isl.), Malaysia, 85
Labuk (bay), Malaysia, 85
Labutta, Burma, 72
La Calera, Chile, 138
La Canada, Calif., 204
La Carlota, Phil. Is., 82
Laccadive (isls.), India, 68
La Ceiba, Hond., 154
Lacepede (isls.), W. Austral., 92
Lacey, Wash., 310
La Chaux-de-Fonds, Switz., 39
Lachine, Que., 172
Lachlan (riv.), N.S.W., 97
Lachute, Que., 172
Lackawanna, N.Y., 276
Lac La Biche, Alta., 182
La Colle, Que., 172
Lacombe, Alta., 182
La Concepción, Pan., 154
La Concepción, Venez., 124
Laconia, N.H., 268
La Coruña (prov.), Spain, 33
La Coruña, Spain, 33
La Courneuve, France, 28
La Crescent, Minn., 254
La Crescenta, Calif., 204
La Crosse, Wis., 317
Ladakh (reg.), India, 68
La Digue (isl.), Seych., 118
Lado, Sudan, 111
Ladoga (lake), U.S.S.R., 52
La Dorada, Col., 126
Ladue, Mo., 261
Ladysmith, Br. Col., 184
Ladysmith, S. Afr., 118
Ladysmith, Wis., 317
Lae, P.N.G., 85
Laesø (isl.), Den., 21
La Esperanza, Hond., 154
Lafayette, Ala., 194
Lafayette, Calif., 204
Lafayette, Colo., 208
La Fayette, Ga., 216
Lafayette, Ind., 227
Lafayette, La., 238
La Feria, Tex., 302
Lafitte, La., 238
La Follette, Tenn., 237
Lagan (riv.), N. Ire., 17
Lagawe, Phil., 82
Laghouat, Alg., 106
La Gomera, Guat., 154
Lagos (state), Nigeria, 106
Lagos (cap.), Nigeria, 106
Lagos, Port., 33
Lagosta (Lastovo) (isl.), Yugo., 45
La Grande, Oreg., 291
La Grange, Ga., 216
La Grange, Ill., 222
La Grange, Tex., 302
La Grange Park, Ill., 222
La Guajira (department), Col., 126
Laguna, Braz., 132

Laguna (prov.), Phil., 82
Laguna Beach, Calif., 204
Laguna Hills, Calif., 204
La Habana (cap.), Cuba, 158
La Habra, Calif., 204
Lahad Datu, Malaysia, 85
Lahaina, Hawaii, 218
Lahej, P.D.R. Yemen, 59
Lahijan, Iran, 66
Lahn (riv.), W. Ger., 22
Lahore, Pak., 68
Lahr, W. Ger., 22
Lahti, Fin., 18
Lai, Chad, 111
Lai Chau, N. Vietnam, 72
Laila, Saudi Ar., 59
La Jara, N. Mex., 274
Lajes, Braz., 132
La Jolla, Calif., 204
La Junta, Colo., 208
Lake Arthur, La., 238
Lake Bluff, Ill., 222
Lake Carmel, N.Y., 276
Lake Charles, La., 238
Lake Chelan Nat'l Rec. Area, Wash., 310
Lake City, Fla., 212
Lake City, Minn., 254
Lake City, S.C., 296
Lake Forest, Ill., 222
Lake Geneva, Wis., 317
Lake Havasu City, Ariz., 198
Lake Hiawatha, N. J., 273
Lake Hopatcong, N. J., 273
Lakehurst, N. J., 273
Lake Jackson, Tex., 302
Lakeland, Fla., 212
Lakeland Vill., Calif., 204
Lake Louise, Alta., 182
Lake Mead Nat'l Recr. Area, U.S., 198
Lake Mills, Wis., 317
Lake Mohawk, N. J., 273
Lakemore, Ohio, 284
Lake of the Woods (lake), N. Amer., 175
Lake Oswego, Oreg., 291
Lake Park, Fla., 212
Lake Placid, N.Y., 276
Lake Providence, La., 238
Lake Success, N.Y., 276
Lake Superior Prov. Park, Ont., 175
Lakeview, Oreg., 291
Lake Village, Ark., 203
Lake Wales, Fla., 212
Lakewood, Calif., 204
Lakewood, Colo., 208
Lakewood, N. J., 273
Lakewood, Ohio, 284
Lake Worth, Fla., 212
Lake Worth, Tex., 302
Lake Zurich, Ill., 222
Lakónia (gulf), Greece, 45
Lakse (fjord), Norway, 18
Lakshadweep (terr.), India, 68
La Libertad, Ecua., 128
La Libertad, El Sal., 154
La Libertad, Nic., 154
La Libertad (dept.), Peru, 128
La Ligua, Chile, 138
La Línea, Spain, 33
Lalitpur, Nepal, 68
La Louvière, Belg., 27
Lama-Kara, Togo, 106
La Malbaie, Que., 172
La Manche (English) (chan.), Europe, 28
Lamar, Colo., 208
Lamar, Mo., 261
La Marque, Tex., 302
La Maya, Cuba, 158
Lambaré, Par., 144
Lambaréné, Gabon, 115
Lambayeque (dept.), Peru, 128
Lambayeque, Peru, 128
Lambertville, N. J., 273
Lambeth, Eng., 10
Lambeth, Ont., 177
Lamego, Port., 33
Lamentin, Guad., 161
Lamentin, Mart., 161
La Mesa, Calif., 204
Lamesa, Tex., 302
Lamía, Greece, 45
La Mirada, Calif., 204
Lamongan, Indon., 85
Lamont, Calif., 204
Lamotrek (atoll), Pac. Is., 87
Lampang, Thai., 72
Lampasas, Tex., 302
Lampedusa (isl.), Italy, 34
Lampeter, Wales, 13
Lamphun, Thai., 72
Lamu, Kenya, 115
Lanai (isl.), Hawaii, 218
Lanao del Norte (prov.), Phil., 82
Lanao del Sur (prov.), Phil., 82
Lanark (county), Scot., 15
Lancashire (county), Eng., 13
Lancaster, Calif., 204
Lancaster, Eng., 13
Lancaster, Ky., 237
Lancaster, N.Y., 276
Lancaster (sound), N.W.T., 187
Lancaster, Ohio, 284
Lancaster, Pa., 294
Lancaster, S.C., 296
Lancaster, Tex., 302
Lancaster, Wis., 317
Lanchow, China, 77
Lanciano, Italy, 34
Landau, W. Ger., 22
Land Between The Lakes Rec. Area, Ky.-Tenn., 236
Lander, Wyo., 319
Landes (dept.), France, 28
Land's End (prom.), Eng., 13
Lands End (cape), N.W.T., 187
Landshut, W. Ger., 22
Landskrona, Sweden, 18
Lane Cove, N.S.W., 97
Lanett, Ala., 194
Langdale, Ala., 194
Langdon, N. Dak., 283

Langeland (isl.), Den., 21
Langenhagen, W. Ger., 22
Langenthal, Switz., 39
Langley Park, Md., 245
Langøy (isl.), Norway, 18
Langsa, Indon., 85
Lang Son, N. Vietnam, 72
Lanham, Md., 245
Lanin (vol.), S. Amer., 138
Lansdale, Pa., 294
Lansdowne, Md., 245
Lansdowne, Pa., 294
L'Anse, Mich., 250
Lansford, Pa., 294
Lansing, Ill., 222
Lansing (cap.), Mich., 250
Lantana, Fla., 212
Lantsang, China, 77
Lanús, Arg., 143
Lanzarote (isl.), Spain, 33
Laoag, Phil., 82
Laoighis (county), Ire., 17
Laon, France, 28
La Oroya, Peru, 128
Laos, 72
La Palma, El Sal., 154
La Palma, Pan., 154
La Palma (isl.), Spain, 33
La Pampa (prov.), Arg., 143
La Paz, Arg., 143
La Paz (dept.), Bol., 136
La Paz (cap.), Bol., 136
La Paz, Hond., 154
La Paz, Mex., 150
La Paz Central, Nic., 154
Lapeer, Mich., 250
La Pérouse (str.), Asia, 48
La Piedad, Mex., 150
Laplace, La., 238
La Plaine, Dominica, 161
La Plata, Arg., 143
La Pocatière, Que., 172
LaPorte, Ind., 227
La Porte, Tex., 302
Lappeenranta, Fin., 18
Lappi (prov.), Fin., 18
La Prairie, Que., 172
Laptev (sea), U.S.S.R., 48
La Puente, Calif., 204
Lapu-Lapu, Phil., 82
La Quiaca, Arg., 143
L'Aquila (prov.), Italy, 34
L'Aquila, Italy, 34
Lar, Iran, 66
Lara (state), Venez., 124
Larache, Mor., 106
Laramie (range), U.S., 208, 319
Laramie, Wyo., 319
Larchmont, N.Y., 276
Larder Lake, Ont., 177
Laredo, Tex., 302
Lares, P. Rico, 161
Largeau, Chad, 111
Largo, Fla., 212
Largs, Scot., 15
La Rioja (prov.), Arg., 143
La Rioja, Arg., 143
La Rioja, Cuba, 158
Lárisa, Greece, 45
Laristan (reg.), Iran, 66
Larkana, Pak., 68
Larkhall, Scot., 15
Larkspur, Calif., 204
Larnaca, Cyprus, 63
Larne, N. Ire., 17
Larned, Kans., 232
La Rochelle, France, 28
La Roche-sur-Yon, France, 28
La Romana (prov.), Dom. Rep., 158
La Romana, Dom. Rep., 158
Larose, La., 238
Larsen Ice Shelf, Ant., 5
Larvik, Norway, 18
La Salle, Ill., 222
La Salle, Que., 172
Las Animas, Colo., 208
Las Anod, Somalia, 115
La Sarre, Que., 174
Lascahobas, Haiti, 158
Las Cruces, N. Mex., 274
La Selle (peak), Haiti, 158
La Serena, Chile, 138
La Seyne-sur-Mer, France, 28
Las Flores, Arg., 143
Lashio, Burma, 72
La Skhirra, Tun., 106
Las Matas, Dom. Rep., 158
Las Palmas (prov.), Spain, 33
Las Palmas de Gran Canaria, Spain, 33
La Spezia (prov.), Italy, 34
La Spezia, Italy, 34
Las Piedras, P. Rico, 161
Las Piedras, Urug., 145
Las Plumas, Arg., 143
Lassen (peak), Calif., 204
Lassen Vol. Nat'l Park, Calif., 204
L'Assomption, Que., 172
Las Tablas, Pan., 154
Last Mountain (lake), Sask., 181
Lastoursville, Gabon, 115
Lastovo (isl.), Yugo., 45
Las Vegas, Nev., 266
Las Vegas, N. Mex., 274
Las Villas (prov.), Cuba, 158
Latacunga, Ecua., 128
Latakia (gov.), Syria, 63
Latakia, Syria, 63
Latina (prov.), Italy, 34
Latina, Italy, 34
Latium (reg.), Italy, 34
La Tortuga (isl.), Venez., 124
La Trinidad, Nic., 154
La Trinidad, Phil., 82
Latrobe, Pa., 294
Latrobe, Tas., 99
La Tuque, Que., 172
Latur, India, 68
Latvian S.S.R., U.S.S.R., 52
Lauchhammer, E. Ger., 22
Lauderdale Lakes, Fla., 212
Lau Group (isls.), Fiji, 87
Launceston, Tas., 99
La Unión, Chile, 138
La Unión, El Sal., 154
La Union (prov.), Phil., 82
Laurel, Del., 245
Laurel, Md., 245
Laurel, Miss., 256

Laurel, Mont., 262
Laureldale, Pa., 294
Laurence Harbor, N.J., 273
Laurens, S.C., 296
Laurentides Prov. Park, Que., 172
Lauringburg, N.C., 281
Laurium, Mich., 250
Lausanne, Switz., 39
Laut (isl.), Indon., 85
Lauwers Zee (bay), Neth., 27
Lauzon, Que., 172
Lava Beds Nat'l Mon., Calif., 204
Laval, Que., 172
La Vale, Md., 245
La Vega (prov.), Dom. Rep., 158
La Vega, Dom. Rep., 158
La Vérendrye Prov. Park, Que., 172
La Verne, Calif., 204
Laverton, Vic., 97
La Victoria, Venez., 124
Lavras, Braz., 135
Lawang, Indon., 85
Lawndale, Calif., 204
Lawrence, Ind., 227
Lawrence, Kans., 232
Lawrence, Mass., 249
Lawrence, N.Y., 276
Lawrenceburg, Ind., 227
Lawrenceburg, Ky., 237
Lawrenceburg, Tenn., 237
Lawrence Park, Pa., 294
Lawrenceville, Ga., 216
Lawrenceville, Ill., 222
Lawton, Okla., 288
Lay (cape), N. Vietnam, 72
Layou (riv.), Dominica, 161
Layou, St. Vincent, 161
Laysan (isl.), Hawaii, 218
Layton, Utah, 304
Lazarev Sta., Ant., 5
Lead, S. Dak., 298
Leader, Sask., 181
Leadville, Colo., 208
League City, Tex., 302
Lealui, Zambia, 115
Leamington, Ont., 177
Leamington, Eng., 13
Leatherhead, Eng., 13
Leavenworth, Kans., 232
Leawood, Kans., 232
Lebanon, 63
Lebanon, Ill., 222
Lebanon, Ind., 227
Lebanon, Ky., 237
Lebanon (mts.), Leb., 63
Lebanon, Mo., 261
Lebanon, Ohio, 284
Lebanon, Oreg., 291
Lebanon, Pa., 294
Lebanon, Tenn., 237
Lebedin, U.S.S.R., 52
Le Blanc-Mesnil, France, 28
Lębork, Poland, 47
Le Bourget, France, 28
Lebu, Chile, 138
Lecce (prov.), Italy, 34
Lecce, Italy, 34
Lecco, Italy, 34
Lech (riv.), W. Ger., 22
Le Creusot, France, 28
Ledo, India, 68
Leduc, Alta., 182
Ledyard, Conn., 210
Lee, Mass., 249
Lee (riv.), Ire., 17
Leech (lake), Minn., 254
Leechburg, Pa., 294
Leeds, Ala., 194
Leeds, Eng., 13
Leek, Eng., 13
Leesburg, Fla., 212
Leesburg, Va., 307
Lee's Summit, Mo., 261
Leesville, La., 238
Leeton, N.S.W., 97
Leetonia, Ohio, 284
Leeuwarden, Neth., 27
Leeuwin (cape), W. Austral., 92
Leeward (passage), Virgin Is. (U.S.), 161
Leeward (isls.), W. Indies, 156
Legazpi, Phil., 82
Legges Tor (peak), Tas., 99
Leghorn (prov.), Italy, 34
Leghorn, Italy, 34
Legionowo, Poland, 47
Legnica, Poland, 47
Leguan (isl.), Guyana, 131
Leh, India, 68
Le Havre, France, 28
Lehi, Utah, 304
Lehigh Acres, Fla., 212
Lehighton, Pa., 294
Lehman Caves Nat'l Mon., Nev., 266
Leicester, Eng., 13
Leicestershire (county), Eng., 13
Leichhardt, N.S.W., 97
Leichhardt (riv.), Queensland, 95
Leiden, Neth., 27
Leigh, Eng., 10
Leine (riv.), W. Ger., 22
Leinster (prov.), Ire., 17
Leipzig (dist.), E. Ger., 22
Leipzig, E. Ger., 22
Leiria, Port., 33
Leisure City, Fla., 212
Leitchfield, Conn., 210
Leith, Scot., 15
Leitrim (county), Ire., 17
Leix (Laoighis) (county), Ire., 17
Lek (river), Neth., 27
Lekoni, Gabon, 115
Leland, Miss., 256
Le Locle, Switz., 39
Lelydorp, Sur., 131
Le Mans, France, 28
Le Mars, Iowa, 229
Lemmon, S. Dak., 298
Lemon Grove, Calif., 204
Lemont, Ill., 222
Lemoore, Calif., 204
Le Moule, Guad., 161
Lemoyne, Pa., 294
Lempa (riv.), El Sal., 154
Lena (riv.), U.S.S.R., 48
Leninabad, U.S.S.R., 48
Leninakan, U.S.S.R., 52

Leningrad, U.S.S.R., 52
Leninogorsk, U.S.S.R., 48
Leninsk-Kuznetskiy, U.S.S.R., 48
Lenkoran', U.S.S.R., 52
Lennox, Calif., 204
Lennoxville, Que., 172
Lenoir, N.C., 281
Lenoir City, Tenn., 237
Lens, France, 28
Lentini, Italy, 34
Lenvik, Norway, 18
Leoben, Austria, 41
Léogane, Haiti, 158
Leominster, Mass., 249
León, Mex., 150
León, Nic., 154
León (riv.), Spain, 33
León (prov.), Spain, 33
León, Spain, 33
Leonardo, N. J., 273
Leonforte, Italy, 34
Leongatha, Vic., 97
Leonia, N. J., 273
Leopold II (lake), Zaire, 115
Lephepe, Botswana, 118
L'Épiphanie, Que., 172
Lepontine Alps (range), Europe, 39
Le Port, Réunion, 118
Leptis Magna (ruins), Libya, 111
Le Puy, France, 28
Léré, Chad, 111
Leribe, Lesotho, 118
Lérida (prov.), Spain, 33
Lérida, Spain, 33
Léros (isl.), Greece, 45
Le Roy, N.Y., 276
Lerwick, Scot., 15
Les Cayes, Haiti, 158
Leskovac, Yugo., 45
Lesotho, 118
Lesozavodsk, U.S.S.R., 48
Lesser Antilles (isls.), N. Amer., 156
Lesser Slave (lake), Alta., 182
Le Sueur, Minn., 254
Lésvos (isl.), Greece, 45
Leszno, Poland, 47
Letchworth, Eng., 13
Lethbridge, Alta., 182
Leticia, Col., 126
Letpadan, Burma, 72
Letterkenny, Ire., 17
Leucadia, Calif., 204
Leuser (mt.), Indon., 85
Levádhia, Greece, 45
Levallois-Perret, France, 28
Levelland, Tex., 302
Leven, Scot., 15
Leverkusen, W. Ger., 22
Levice, Czech., 41
Levin, N.Z., 101
Lévis, Que., 172
Levittown, N.Y., 276
Levittown, Pa., 294
Levkás (isl.), Greece, 45
Lévrier (bay), Mauritania, 106
Levskigrad, Bulg., 45
Levuka, Fiji, 87
Lewes, Del., 245
Lewes, Eng., 13
Lewis (dist.), Scot., 15
Lewisburg, Pa., 294
Lewisburg, Tenn., 237
Lewisham, Eng., 10
Lewisporte, Newf., 166
Lewiston, Idaho, 220
Lewiston, Maine, 242
Lewiston, N.Y., 276
Lewistown, Ill., 222
Lewistown, Mont., 262
Lewistown, Pa., 294
Lewisville, N. Br., 170
Lewisville, Tex., 302
Lexington, Ky., 237
Lexington, Mass., 249
Lexington, Miss., 256
Lexington, Mo., 261
Lexington, Nebr., 264
Lexington, N.C., 281
Lexington, Tenn., 237
Lexington, Va., 307
Lexington Park, Md., 245
Leyland, Eng., 10
Leyte (prov.), Phil., 82
Leyte (isl.), Phil., 82
Lezh, Alb., 45
L'gov, U.S.S.R., 52
Lhasa, China, 77
Lhatse Dzong, China, 77
Liao Ho (riv.), China, 77
Liaoning (prov.), China, 77
Liaotung (pen.), China, 77
Liaoyang, China, 77
Liaoyüan, China, 77
Liard (riv.), Canada, 187
Líbano, Col., 126
Libby, Mont., 262
Libenge, Zaire, 115
Liberal, Kans., 232
Liberec, Czech., 41
Liberia, 106
Liberia, C. Rica, 154
Liberta, Antigua, 161
Liberty, Mo., 261
Liberty, N.Y., 276
Liberty, Pa., 294
Liberty, S.C., 296
Liberty, Tex., 302
Libertyville, Ill., 222
Libya, 111
Libyan (des.), Africa, 111
Licata, Italy, 34
Lichfield, Eng., 10
Lichtenberg, E. Ger., 22
Lichtenfels, Minn., 254
Lichtenburg, S. Afr., 118
Lida, U.S.S.R., 52
Lidice, Czech., 41
Lidingö, Sweden, 18
Lidköping, Sweden, 18
Lido di Ostia, Italy, 34
Lido di Venezia, Italy, 34
Liechtenstein, 39
Liège (prov.), Belg., 27
Liège, Belg., 27
Lienyünkang, China, 77
Lienz, Austria, 41
Liepāja, U.S.S.R., 53
Lier, Belg., 27
Liestal, Switz., 39
Liévin, France, 28
Liffey (riv.), Ire., 17
Lifford, Ire., 17
Lifu (isl.), New Cal., 87

Ligonha (riv.), Mozamb., 118
Ligonier, Ind., 227
Lillehampton, Eng., 13
Liguria (reg.), Italy, 34
Ligurian (sea), Italy, 34
Lihue, Hawaii, 218
Likasi, Zaire, 115
Likiang, China, 77
Lille, France, 28
Lille Bælt (chan.), Den., 21
Lillehammer, Norway, 18
Lillestrøm, Norway, 18
Lillooet, Br. Col., 184
Lillydale, Vic., 97
Lilongwe (cap.), Malawi, 115
Lim (fjord), Den., 21
Lim (riv.), Yugo., 45
Lima (riv.), Europe, 33
Lima, Ohio, 284
Lima (dept.), Peru, 128
Lima (cap.), Peru, 128
Limache, Chile, 138
Limassol, Cyprus, 63
Limavady, N. Ire., 17
Limbach-Oberfrohna, E. Ger., 22
Limbé, Haiti, 158
Limburg (prov.), Belg., 27
Limburg (prov.), Neth., 27
Limeira, Braz., 135
Limerick (county), Ire., 17
Limerick, Ire., 17
Limmat (riv.), Switz., 39
Limmen (bight), N. Terr., 93
Límnos (isl.), Greece, 45
Limoeiro, Braz., 132
Limoges, France, 28
Limón, C. Rica, 154
Limón, Hond., 154
Limousin (reg.), France, 28
Limpopo (riv.), Africa, 118
Linares (prov.), Chile, 138
Linares, Chile, 138
Linares, Mex., 150
Linares, Spain, 33
Linchwan, China, 77
Lincoln, Arg., 143
Lincoln, Calif., 204
Lincoln, Eng., 13
Lincoln, Ill., 222
Lincoln, Maine, 242
Lincoln, Mass., 249
Lincoln (cap.), Nebr., 264
Lincoln (sea), N. Amer., 146
Lincoln, Ont., 117
Lincoln Boyhood Nat'l Mem., Ind., 227
Lincoln City, Oreg., 291
Lincoln Park, Mich., 250
Lincoln Park, N. J., 273
Lincolnshire-Holland (county), Eng., 13
Lincolnshire-Kesteven (county), Eng., 13
Lincolnshire-Lindsey (county), Eng., 13
Lincolnton, N.C., 281
Lincolnwood, Ill., 222
Lincroft, N. J., 273
Linda, Calif., 204
Lindau, W. Ger., 22
Linden, Ala., 194
Linden, Guyana, 131
Linden, N. J., 273
Lindenhurst, N.Y., 276
Lindenwold, N. J., 273
Lindesnes (cape), Norway, 18
Lindi (riv.), Tanz., 115
Lindi, Tanz., 115
Lindsay, Calif., 204
Lindsay, Okla., 288
Lindsay, Ont., 177
Lindsborg, Kans., 232
Line (isls.), Pacific, 87
Linfen, China, 77
Lingen, W. Ger., 22
Lingga (arch.), Indon., 85
Linhai, China, 77
Linhsien, China, 77
Linköping, Sweden, 18
Linlithgow, Scot., 15
Linnhe (inlet), Scot., 15
Linosa (isl.), Italy, 34
Lins, Braz., 135
Linstead, Jam., 158
Linton, Ind., 227
Lintsing, China, 77
Linwood, N. J., 273
Linwood, Pa., 294
Linz, Austria, 41
Lionel Town, Jam., 158
Lions (gulf), France, 28
Lipa, Phil., 82
Lipari (isls.), Italy, 34
Lipetsk, U.S.S.R., 52
Lippe (riv.), W. Ger., 22
Lippstadt, W. Ger., 22
Lipscomb, Ala., 194
Liri (riv.), Italy, 34
Lisala, Zaire, 115
Lisbon, N. Dak., 283
Lisbon, Ohio, 284
Lisbon (Lisboa)(cap.), Port., 33
Lisburn, N. Ire., 17
Lisianski (isl.), Hawaii, 218
Lisichansk, U.S.S.R., 52
Lisieux, France, 28
Lismore, Ire., 17
Lismore, N.S.W., 97
Lista (pen.), Norway, 18
Lister (mt.), Ant., 5
Listowel, Ire., 17
Listowel, Ont., 177
Litani (riv.), Leb., 63
Litani (riv.), Sur., 131
Litchfield, Conn., 210
Litchfield, Ill., 222
Litchfield, Minn., 254
Litchfield Park, Ariz., 198
Litherland, Eng., 10
Lithgow, N.S.W., 97
Lithuanian S.S.R., U.S.S.R., 52
Lititz, Pa., 294
Litoměřice, Czech., 41
Little America, Ant., 5
Little Cayman (isl.), Cayman Is., 156
Little Chute, Wis., 317
Little Colorado (riv.), U.S., 198
Little Corn (isl.), Nic., 154
Little Current, Ont., 177
Little Falls, Minn., 254
Little Falls, N. J., 273
Little Falls, N.Y., 276

Little Ferry, N. J., 273
Littlefield, Tex., 302
Littlehampton, Eng., 13
Little Inagua (isl.), Bah., 156
Little Makin (isl.), Gilb. & Ell. Is., 87
Little Minch (sound), Scot., 15
Little Namaland (reg.), S. Afr., 118
Little Rock (cap.), Ark., 203
Little Saint Bernard (pass), Europe, 28
Little Shawmut, Ala., 194
Little Silver, N. J., 273
Littlestown, Pa., 294
Little Tobago (isl.), Virgin Is. (Br.), 161
Littleton, Colo., 208
Littleton, N.H., 268
Litvínov, Czech., 41
Liuchow, China, 77
Live Oak, Fla., 212
Livermore, Calif., 204
Livermore Falls, Maine, 242
Liverpool, Eng., 10
Liverpool, N.S.W., 97
Liverpool, N.S., 169
Livingston (cap.), Guat., 154
Livingston, Mont., 262
Livingston, N. J., 273
Livingston, Tex., 302
Livingstone, Zambia, 115
Livingstonia, Malawi, 115
Livonia, Mich., 250
Livorno (Leghorn), Italy, 34
Liwale, Tanz., 115
Lizard (head), Eng., 13
Ljubljana, Yugo., 45
Llandeilo, Wales, 13
Llandovery, Wales, 13
Llandrindod Wells, Wales, 13
Llandudno, Wales, 13
Llanelli, Wales, 13
Llanfairfechan, Wales, 13
Llanfyllin, Wales, 13
Llangefni, Wales, 13
Llangollen, Wales, 13
Llanidloes, Wales, 13
Llano, Tex., 302
Llano Estacado (plain), U.S., 274, 302
Llanos del Orinoco (plains), S. Amer., 120
Llanquihue (prov.), Chile, 138
Llanrwst, Wales, 13
Llerena (pt.), C. Rica, 154
Lleyn (pen.), Wales, 13
Llobregat (riv.), Spain, 33
Llolleo, Chile, 138
Lloydminster, Sask.-Alta., 181, 182
Llullaillaco (vol.), S. Amer., 138
Loa (riv.), Chile, 138
Lobatse, Botswana, 118
Lobaye (riv.), Centr. Afr. Rep., 115
Lobito, Angola, 115
Lobos (cape), Mex., 150
Lobos de Afuera (isl.), Peru, 128
Lobos de Tierra (isl.), Peru, 128
Locarno, Switz., 39
Lochaber (dist.), Scot., 15
Lochgelly, Scot., 15
Lochy (lake), Scot., 15
Lockeport, N.S., 169
Lockhart, Tex., 302
Lock Haven, Pa., 294
Lockland, Ohio, 284
Lockport, Ill., 222
Lockport, N.Y., 276
Loc Ninh, S. Vietnam, 72
Lod (Lydda), Israel, 65
Lodar, P.D.R. Yemen, 59
Lodi, Calif., 204
Lodi, Italy, 34
Lodi, N. J., 273
Lodja, Zaire, 115
Łódź (prov.), Poland, 47
Łódź, Poland, 47
Loei, Thai., 72
Lofoten (isls.), Norway, 18
Lofty (mt.), S. Austral., 94
Lofty (range), Tas., 99
Logan, Ohio, 284
Logan, Utah, 304
Logan, W. Va., 313
Logan (mt.), Yukon, 187
Logansport, Ind., 227
Logone (riv.), Africa, 111
Logroño (prov.), Spain, 33
Logroño, Spain, 33
Loho, China, 77
Loir (riv.), France, 28
Loire (dept.), France, 28
Loire (riv.), France, 28
Loire-Atlantique (dept.), France, 28
Loiret (dept.), France, 28
Loir-et-Cher (dept.), France, 28
Loíza, P. Rico, 161
Loíza Aldea, P. Rico, 161
Loja (prov.), Ecua., 128
Loja, Ecua., 128
Lokeren, Belg., 27
Lokoja, Nigeria, 106
Lolland (isl.), Den., 21
Lolo (pass), Idaho, 220
Lom (riv.), Cameroon, 115
Lom (riv.), Togo, 106
Lomas de Zamora, Arg., 143
Lombard, Ill., 222
Lombardy (reg.), Italy, 34
Lombok (isl.), Indon., 85
Lomela, Zaire, 115
Lomita, Calif., 204
Lomond (lake), Scot., 15
Lompoc, Calif., 204
Lom Sak, Thai., 72
Łomża, Poland, 47
London, Eng. (cap.), U.K., 10, 13
London, Ky., 237
London, Ohio, 284
London, Ont., 177
Londonderry (county), N. Ire., 17
Londonderry, N. Ire., 17

Londonderry (cape), W. Austral., 92
Londrina, Braz., 132
Long (cay), Bah., 156
Long (isl.), Bah., 156
Long (isl.), N.Y., 276
Long (pt.), Ont., 177
Long (inlet), Scot., 15
Long Beach, Calif., 204
Long Beach, Miss., 256
Long Beach, N.Y., 276
Long Branch, N. J., 273
Long Eaton, Eng., 13
Longford (county), Ire., 17
Longford, Ire., 17
Long Island (sound), U.S., 276
Longlac, Ont., 177
Longmeadow, Mass., 249
Longmont, Colo., 208
Long Range (mts.), Newf., 166
Longreach, Queensland, 95
Longridge, Eng., 10
Longueuil, Que., 172
Long View, N.C., 281
Longview, Tex., 302
Longview, Wash., 310
Longwy, France, 28
Long Xuyen, S. Vietnam, 72
Longyearbyen, Norway, 18
Lookout Mtn., Ga., 216
Loop (head), Ire., 17
Lopatka (cape), U.S.S.R., 48
Lop Buri, Thai., 72
Lopez (cape), Gabon, 115
Lop Nor (dry lake), China, 77
Lorain, Ohio, 284
Loralai, Pak., 68
Lorca, Spain, 33
Lord Howe (isl.), N.S.W., 97
Lord Howe (Ontong Java) (isl.), Sol. Is., 87
Lordsburg, N. Mex., 274
Lorena, Braz., 135
Loreto (dept.), Peru, 128
Lorettville, Que., 172
Lorica, Col., 126
Lorient, France, 28
Lorne (dist.), Scot., 15
Lörrach, W. Ger., 22
Lorraine, Mart., 161
Lorrain (reg.), Sask.-Alta., 181, 182
Los Alamitos, Calif., 204
Los Alamos, N. Mex., 274
Los Altos, Calif., 204
Los Amates, Guat., 154
Los Andes, Chile, 138
Los Angeles, Calif., 204
Los Angeles, Chile, 138
Loshan, China, 77
Lošinj (isl.), Yugo., 45
Los Mochis, Mex., 150
Los Palacios, Cuba, 158
Los Ranchos de Albuquerque, N.M., 274
Los Reyes, Mex., 150
Los Roques (isls.), Venez., 124
Los Ríos (prov.), Ecua., 128
Los Santos, Pan., 154
Los Teques, Venez., 124
Lot (dept.), France, 28
Lot (riv.), France, 28
Lot-et-Garonne (dept.), France, 28
Lothians (dist.), Scot., 15
Lötschberg (tunnel), Switz., 39
Loudon, Tenn., 237
Loudonville, Ohio, 284
Louga, Sen., 106
Loughborough, Eng., 13
Loughrea, Ire., 17
Louisburg, N.C., 281
Louisburg, N.S., 168
Louisiade (arch.), P.N.G., 85
Louisiana, Mo., 261
Louisiana (state), U.S., 238
Louis Trichardt, S. Afr., 118
Louisville, Ky., 237
Louisville, Miss., 256
Louisville, Ohio, 284
Loulé, Port., 33
Louny, Czech., 41
Lourdes, France, 28
Lourenço Marques (Can Phumo) (cap.), Mozamb., 118
Lourinhã, Port., 33
Lousã, Port., 33
Louth (county), Ire., 17
Louth, Eng., 13
Louvain, Belg., 27
Lovech, Bulg., 45
Loveland, Colo., 208
Loveland, Ohio, 284
Lovell, Wyo., 319
Lovelock, Nev., 266
Loves Park, Ill., 222
Lovington, N. Mex., 274
Lovisa, Fin., 18
Low, Zaire, 115
Lowell, Mass., 249
Lowell, Mich., 250
Lowell, N.C., 281
Lower Arrow (lake), Br. Col., 184
Lower Austria (prov.), Austria, 41
Lower California (pen.), Mex., 150
Lower Caraquet, N. Br., 170
Lower Engadine (dist.), Switz., 39
Lower Hutt, N.Z., 101
Lower Juba (prov.), Somalia, 115
Lower Rhine (riv.), Neth., 27
Lower Saxony (state), W. Ger., 22
Lower Tunguska (riv.), U.S.S.R., 48
Lowestoft, Eng., 13
Lowville, N.Y., 276
Loyalty (isls.), New Cal., 87
Loyang, China, 77
Lozère (dept.), France, 28
Loznica, Yugo., 45
Lozovaya, U.S.S.R., 52
Luanda (dist.), Angola, 115
Luanda (cap.), Angola, 115
Luang (mt.), Thai., 72

Luang Prabang, Laos, 72
Luanshya, Zambia, 115
Luba, Eq. Guin., 115
Lübbecke, W. Ger., 22
Lübbenau, E. Ger., 22
Lubbock, Tex., 302
Lübeck, W. Ger., 22
Lublin (prov.), Poland, 47
Lublin, Poland, 47
Lubudi, Zaire, 115
Lubumbashi, Zaire, 115
Luc An Chau, N. Vietnam, 72
Lucan-Doddsborough, Ire., 17
Lucas E. de Peña, Dom. Rep., 158
Lucca (prov.), Italy, 34
Lucca, Italy, 34
Luce (bay), Scot., 15
Lucea, Jam., 158
Lucena, Phil., 82
Lucena, Spain, 33
Lucenec, Czech., 41
Lucera, Italy, 34
Lucerne (lake), Switz., 39
Lucerne, Switz., 39
Luchow, China, 77
Lucknow, India, 68
Lüdenscheid, W. Ger., 22
Lüderitz, S.W. Afr., 118
Ludhiana, India, 68
Ludington, Mich., 250
Ludlow, Ky., 237
Ludlow, Mass., 249
Ludvika, Sweden, 18
Ludwigsburg, W. Ger., 22
Ludwigshafen, W. Ger., 22
Luebo, Zaire, 115
Lufira, Zaire, 115
Lufkin, Tex., 302
Lugano, Switz., 39
Lugansk (Voroshilovgrad), U.S.S.R., 52
Lugenda (riv.), Mozamb., 118
Lugh, Somalia, 115
Lugo, Italy, 34
Lugo (prov.), Spain, 33
Lugo, Spain, 33
Lugoj, Rum., 45
Luhaiya, Yemen Arab Rep., 59
Luichow (pen.), China, 77
Luilaka (riv.), Zaire, 115
Luimneach (Limerick), Ire., 17
Luitpold Coast (reg.), Ant., 5
Luján, Arg., 143
Lukenie (riv.), Zaire, 115
Lule (riv.), Sweden, 18
Luleå, Sweden, 18
Lüleburgaz, Turkey, 63
Luling, Tex., 302
Lulua (riv.), Zaire, 115
Lumadjang, Indon., 85
Lumberton, N.C., 281
Lumut, Malaysia, 72
Lund, Sweden, 18
Lunda (dist.), Angola, 115
Lundy (isl.), Eng., 13
Lune (riv.), Eng., 13
Lüneburg, W. Ger., 22
Lüneburger Heide (dist.), W. Ger., 22
Lünen, W. Ger., 22
Lunenburg, Mass., 249
Lunenburg, N.S., 169
Lunéville, France, 28
Lungchen, China, 77
Lungi, S. Leone, 106
Lungwebungu (riv.), Africa, 115
Luozi, Zaire, 115
Lupeni, Rum., 45
Luque, Par., 144
Luray, Va., 307
Luristan (governorate), Iran, 66
Lusaka (cap.), Zambia, 115
Lusambo, Zaire, 115
Lusatia (reg.), E. Ger., 22
Lushnje, Alb., 45
Lushoto, Tanz., 115
Lusk, Wyo., 319
Luso, Angola, 115
Lustenau, Austria, 41
Lüta, China, 77
Lutcher, La., 238
Lutherville, Md., 245
Luton, Eng., 13
Lutsk, U.S.S.R., 52
Lützow-Holm (bay), Ant., 5
Luverne, Minn., 254
Luvua (riv.), Zaire, 115
Luxembourg, 27
Luxembourg (prov.), Belg., 27
Luxembourg (cap.), Lux., 27
Luxor, Egypt, 111
Luzern (canton), Switz., 39
Luzern (Lucerne), Switz., 39
Luzerne, Pa., 294
Luzon (isl.), Phil., 82
L'vov (Łwów), U.S.S.R., 52
Lyallpur, Pak., 68
Lydda, Israel, 65
Lydenburg, S. Afr., 118
Lyell (mt.), Tas., 99
Lykens, Pa., 294
Lyman, Miss., 256
Lyme (bay), Eng., 13
Lymington, Eng., 13
Lymm, Eng., 10
Lynbrook, N.Y., 276
Lynch, Ky., 237
Lynchburg, Va., 307
Lynden, Wash., 310
Lyndhurst, N. J., 273
Lyndhurst, Ohio, 284
Lyndon B. Johnson Nat'l Hist. Site, Tex., 302
Lyndora, Pa., 294
Lyngby, Den., 21
Lynn, Mass., 249
Lynnfield Ctr., Mass., 249
Lynn Haven, Fla., 212
Lynn Lake, Man., 179
Lynwood, Calif., 204
Lynnwood, Wash., 310
Lyon, France, 28
Lyons, Ga., 216
Lyons, Ill., 222
Lyons, Kans., 232
Lyons, N. J., 273
Lyons, N.Y., 276
Lysaker, Norway, 18
Lys'va, U.S.S.R., 52

Lytham Saint Anne's, Eng., 10
Lyttelton, N.Z., 101
Lyubertsy, U.S.S.R., 52
Lyubotin, U.S.S.R., 52

M

Ma'an (dist.), Jordan, 65
Ma'an, Jordan, 65
Maarianhamina (Mariehamn), Fin., 18
Maas (riv.), Neth., 27
Maasin, Phil., 82
Maastricht, Neth., 27
Mableton, Ga., 216
Macaé, Braz., 135
Macamic, Que., 174
Macao, 77
Macao (cap.), Macao, 77
Macapá, Braz., 132
Macará, Ecua., 128
Macau, Braz., 132
Macclenny, Fla., 212
Macclesfield, Eng., 10
Macdonald (lake), Austral., 92
Macdonnell (ranges), N. Terr., 93
Macduff, Scot., 15
Macedonia (reg.), Greece, 45
Macedonia, Ohio, 284
Macedonia (rep.), Yugo., 45
Maceió, Braz., 132
Macenta, Guinea, 106
Macerata (prov.), Italy, 34
Macerata, Italy, 34
Macgillicuddy's Reeks (mts.), Ire., 17
Machacamarca, Bol., 136
Machala, Ecua., 128
Machali, Chile, 138
Machico, Port., 33
Machida, Japan, 81
Machilipatnam, India, 68
Machiques, Venez., 124
Machupicchu, Peru, 128
Macías Nguema Biyogo (prov.), Eq. Guin., 115
Macina (dep.), Mali, 106
Mackay, Queensland, 95
Mackenzie (bay), Ant., 5
Mackenzie (mts.), Canada, 187
Mackenzie (dist.), N.W.T., 187
Mackenzie (riv.), N.W.T., 187
Mackinac (isl.), Mich., 250
Mackinaw City, Mich., 250
Macksville, N.S.W., 97
Maclear (cape), S. Afr., 118
Macmillan (riv.), Yukon, 187
Macomb, Ill., 222
Mâcon, France, 28
Macon, Ga., 216
Macon, Mo., 261
Macoris (cape), Dom. Rep., 158
Macquarie (isl.), Austral., 3
Macquarie (harb.), Tas., 99
Mac-Robertson Land (reg.), Ant., 5
Macroom, Ire., 17
Mactan (isl.), Phil., 82
Macuspana, Mex., 150
Ma'daba, Jordan, 65
Madagascar (isl.), Malag. Rep., 118
Madame (isl.), N.S., 169
Madang, P.N.G., 85
Madawaska, Maine, 242
Madeira (riv.), Braz., 132
Madeira (isls.), Port., 33
Madeira (prov.), Port., 33
Madeira Beach, Fla., 212
Madera, Calif., 204
Madera, Mex., 150
Madhubani, India, 68
Madhya Pradesh (state), India, 68
Madill, Okla., 288
Madinat ash Sha'b, P.D.R., Yemen, 58
Madison, Fla., 212
Madison, Ga., 216
Madison, Ill., 222
Madison, Ind., 227
Madison, Maine, 242
Madison, N. J., 273
Madison, S. Dak., 298
Madison (cap.), Wis., 317
Madison Hts., Mich., 250
Madison Hts., Va., 307
Madisonville, Ky., 237
Madiun, Indon., 85
Madjalengka, Indon., 85
Madjene, Indon., 85
Madras, India, 68
Madras, Oreg., 291
Madre (lag.), Mex., 150
Madre de Dios (prov.), Peru, 128
Madre del Sur, Sierra (mts.), Mex., 150
Madre Occidental, Sierra (mts.), Mex., 150
Madre Oriental, Sierra (mts.), Mex., 150
Madrid (prov.), Spain, 33
Madrid (cap.), Spain, 33
Madura, India, 68
Madura (isl.), Indon., 85
Maebashi, Japan, 81
Maestra, Sierra (mts.), Cuba, 158
Maevatanana, Malag. Rep., 118
Mafeking, S. Afr., 118
Mafeteng, Lesotho, 118
Maffra, Vic., 97
Mafia (isl.), Tanz., 115
Mafra, Braz., 132
Magadan, U.S.S.R., 48
Magadi, Kenya, 115
Magallanes (prov.), Chile, 138
Magangué, Col., 126
Maganoy, Phil., 82
Magaria, Niger, 106
Magdala, Eth., 111
Magdalen (isls.), Que., 163

Oriente (prov.), Cuba, 158
Orillia, Ont., 177
Orinda, Calif., 204
Orinoco (riv.), S. Amer., 124
Orissa (state), India, 68
Oristano (gulf), Italy, 34
Orituco (riv.), Venez., 124
Orizaba, Mex., 150
Orkhon (riv.), Mong., 77
Orkney (county), Scot., 15
Orkney (isls.), Scot., 15
Orland, Calif., 204
Orlândia, Braz., 135
Orlando, Fla., 212
Orland Park, Ill., 222
Orléans, France, 28
Orléans (isl.), Que., 172
Orléansville (El Asnam), Alg., 106
Orlice (riv.), Czech., 41
Orlová, Czech., 41
Orly, France, 28
Ormoc, Phil., 82
Ormond Beach, Fla., 212
Ormskirk, Eng., 10
Orne (dept.), France, 28
Orne (riv.), France, 28
Ornsköldsvik, Sweden, 18
Orocovis, P. Rico, 161
Orofino, Idaho, 220
Oroluk (atoll), Pac. Is., 87
Oromocto, N.B., 170
Orona (Hull)(isl.), Gilb. and Ell. Is., 87
Orono, Maine, 242
Orono, Minn., 254
Orontes ('Asi)(riv.), Syria, 63
Oropuche (riv.), Trin. & Tob., 161
Oroquieta, Phil., 82
Orosei (gulf), Italy, 34
Orosháza, Hung., 41
Orotina, C. Rica, 154
Oroville, Calif., 204
Orrville, Ohio, 284
Orsha, U.S.S.R., 52
Orsk, U.S.S.R., 52
Ortega, Col., 126
Ortegal (cape), Spain, 33
Orteguaza (riv.), Col., 126
Ortles (range), Europe, 34
Ortoire (riv.), Trin. & Tob., 161
Ortón (riv.), Bol., 136
Ortona, Italy, 34
Ortonville, Minn., 254
Oruro (dept.), Bol., 136
Oruro, Bol., 136
Osage, Iowa, 229
Osaka (pref.), Japan, 81
Osaka, Japan, 81
Osawatomie, Kans., 232
Osceola, Ark., 203
Osceola, Iowa, 229
Oscoda, Mich., 250
Osh, U.S.S.R., 48
Oshawa, Ont., 177
Oshima (isl.), Japan, 81
Oshkosh, Wis., 317
Oshogbo, Nigeria, 106
Oshwe, Zaire, 115
Osijek, Yugo., 45
Osipenko (Berdyansk), U.S.S.R., 52
Oskaloosa, Iowa, 229
Oskarshamn, Sweden, 18
Oslo (cap.), Norway, 18
Osmaniye, Turkey, 63
Osnabrück, W. Ger., 22
Osorno (prov.), Chile, 138
Osorno, Chile, 138
Osoyoos, Br. Col., 184
Oss, Neth., 27
Ossa (mt.), Greece, 45
Ossining, N.Y., 276
Ossokmanuan (res.), Newf., 166
Ostend, Belg., 27
Östergotland (county), Sweden, 18
Östersund, Sweden, 18
Østfold (county), Norway, 18
Ostrava, Czech., 41
Ostrogozhsk, U.S.S.R., 52
Ostrov, Czech., 41
Ostrowiec Swkrz., Poland, 47
Ostrów Wlkp., Poland, 47
Ostuni, Italy, 34
Osům (riv.), Bulg., 45
Osumi (isls.), Japan, 81
Oswego, N.Y., 276
Oświęcim, Poland, 47
Ota, Japan, 81
Otago (land dist.), N.Z., 101
Otaru, Japan, 81
Otava (riv.), Czech., 41
Otavalo, Ecua., 128
Otavi, S.W. Afr., 118
Otematata, N.Z., 101
Othello, Wash., 310
Otjiwarongo, S.W. Afr., 118
Otley, Eng., 13
Otradnyy, U.S.S.R., 52
Otranto (strait), Europe, 34, 45
Otsego, Mich., 250
Otsu, Japan, 81
Ottawa (cap.), Canada, 177
Ottawa (riv.), Canada, 163, 177
Ottawa, Ill., 222
Ottawa, Kans., 232
Ottawa (isls.), N.W.T., 187
Ottawa, Ohio, 284
Ottawa Hills, Ohio, 284
Ottumwa, Iowa, 229
Otuzco, Peru, 128
Otway (sound), Chile, 138
Otwock, Poland, 47
Ötztal Alps (mts.), Europe, 41
Ouachita (mts.), U.S., 203, 288
Ouadda, Centr. Afr. Rep., 115
Ouagadougou (cap.), Upp. Volta, 106
Ouahigouya, Upp. Volta, 106
Oualata, Mauritania, 106
Ouanaminthe, Haiti, 158
Ouanary, Fr. Gui., 131
Ouanda-Djalé, Centr. Afr. Rep., 115
Ouargla, Alg., 106
Oudtshoorn, S. Afr., 118
Oued-Zem, Mor., 106
Ouessant (isl.), France, 28
Ouesso, Congo, 115
Ouest (dept.), Haiti, 158
Ouest (pt.), Haiti, 158
Ouezzane, Mor., 106
Ougrée, Belg., 27
Ouidah, Benin, 106
Oujda, Mor., 106
Ouled-Djellal, Alg., 106
Oullins, France, 28
Oulu (prov.), Fin., 18
Oulu, Fin., 18
Oulu (riv.), Fin., 18
Oum Hadjer, Chad, 111
Ou Neua, Laos, 72
Our (riv.), Europe, 27
Ourinhos, Braz., 135
Ouro Fino, Braz., 135
Ouro Prêto, Braz., 135
Ourthe (riv.), Belg., 27
Ouse (riv.), Eng., 13
Outardes (riv.), Que., 174
Outer Hebrides (isls.), Scot., 15
Outjo, S.W. Afr., 118
Outlook, Sask., 181
Outokumpu, Fin., 18
Outremont, Que., 172
Ovalle, Chile, 138
Ovamboland (reg.), S.W. Afr., 118
Overflakkee (isl.), Neth., 27
Overijssel (prov.), Neth., 27
Overland, Mo., 261
Overland Park, Kans., 232
Overlea, Md., 245
Overton, Nev., 266
Oviedo (prov.), Spain, 33
Oviedo, Spain, 33
Owatonna, Minn., 254
Owego, N.Y., 276
Owen Falls (dam), Uganda, 115
Owensboro, Ky., 237
Owen Sound, Ont., 177
Owia (bay), St. Vincent, 161
Owings Mills, Md., 245
Owo, Nigeria, 106
Owosso, Mich., 250
Owyhee (lake), Oreg., 291
Oxapampa, Peru, 128
Oxbow, Sask., 181
Oxelösund, Sweden, 18
Oxford, Ala., 194
Oxford, Eng., 13
Oxford (lake), Man., 179
Oxford, Mass., 249
Oxford, Mich., 250
Oxford, Miss., 256
Oxford, N.C., 281
Oxford, N.S., 169
Oxford, Ohio, 284
Oxford, Pa., 294
Oxfordshire (county), Eng., 13
Oxkutzcab, Mex., 150
Oxnard, Calif., 204
Oyama, Japan, 81
Oyapock (riv.), S. Amer., 131
Oyem, Gabon, 115
Oyo, Nigeria, 106
Oyón, Peru, 128
Oyster Bay, N.Y., 276
Ozamiz, Phil., 82
Ozark, Ala., 194
Ozark (mts.), U.S., 203, 261
Ozarks, Lake of the (lake), Mo., 261
Ózd, Hung., 41
Ozona, Tex., 302
Ozumba, Mex., 150

P

Paarl, S. Afr., 118
Pabianice, Poland, 47
Pabna, Bang., 68
Pacajá Grande (riv.), Braz., 132
Pacaraima (range), S. Amer., 132
Pacasmayo, Peru, 128
Pachen, China, 77
Pacho, Col., 126
Pachuca, Mex., 150
Pachung, China, 77
Pacific, Mo., 261
Pacifica, Calif., 204
Pacific Beach, Calif., 204
Pacific Grove, Calif., 204
Pacific Islands, Territory of the, 87
Pacific Ocean, 87
Pacific Palisades, Hawaii, 218
Packanack Lake, N. J., 273
Padang, Indon., 85
Padangpandjang, Indon., 85
Padangsidimpuan, Indon., 85
Paden City, W. Va., 313
Paderborn, W. Ger., 22
Padilla, Bol., 136
Padre Isl. Nat'l Seashore, Tex., 302
Padre Las Casas, Dom. Rep., 158
Padua (prov.), Italy, 34
Padua, Italy, 34
Paducah, Ky., 237
Pafúri, Mozamb., 118
Pag (isl.), Yugo., 45
Pagadian, Phil., 82
Pagalu (isl.), Eq. Guin., 102
Pagan, Burma, 72
Pagan (isl.), Pac. Is., 87
Page, Ariz., 198
Pagedale, Mo., 261
Pago Pago (cap.), Amer. Samoa, 87
Pagoua (bay), Dominica, 161
Pahala, Hawaii, 218
Pahang (state), Malaysia, 72
Pahang (riv.), Malaysia, 72
Pahlevi, Iran, 66
Pahokee, Fla., 212
Paia, Hawaii, 218
Paicheng, China, 77
Paiján, Peru, 128
Päijänne (lake), Fin., 18
Pailin, Cambodia, 72
Pailingmiao, China, 77
Paillaco, Chile, 138
Paine, Chile, 138
Painesville, Ohio, 284
Painted (des.), Ariz., 198
Painted Post, N.Y., 276
Paintsville, Ky., 237
Paipote, Chile, 138
Paisley, Scot., 15
Paita, Peru, 128
Paiyin, China, 77
Pajakumbuh, Indon., 85
Pakanbaru, Indon., 85
Pak Beng, Laos, 72
Pakch'ŏn, N. Korea, 81
Pak Hin Boun, Laos, 72
Pakhoi, China, 77
Pakistan, 68
Paklay, Laos, 72
Pakokku, Burma, 72
Pak Sane, Laos, 72
Pakse, Laos, 72
Pakwach, Uganda, 115
Pala, Chad, 111
Palacios, Tex., 302
Palana, U.S.S.R., 48
Palanpur, India, 68
Palapye, Botswana, 118
Palatine, Ill., 222
Palatka, Fla., 212
Palau (isls.), Pac. Is., 87
Palawan (prov.), Phil., 82
Palawan (isl.), Phil., 82
Palayan, Phil., 82
Palayankottai, India, 68
Palembang, Indon., 85
Palena (river), S. Amer., 138
Palencia (prov.), Spain, 33
Palencia, Spain, 33
Palenque (pt.), Dom. Rep., 158
Palenque (ruins), Mex., 150
Palermo (prov.), Italy, 34
Palermo, Italy, 34
Palestine, Tex., 302
Palghat, India, 68
Pali, India, 68
Palimé, Togo, 106
Palisades Park, N. J., 273
Palk (strait), Asia, 68
Palliser (cape), N.Z., 101
Palma, Mozamb., 118
Palma, Spain, 33
Palmares, Braz., 132
Palmares, C. Rica, 154
Palmarola (isl.), Italy, 34
Palmas (cape), Liberia, 106
Palmas Altas (pt.), P. Rico, 161
Palm Bay, Fla., 212
Palm Beach, Fla., 212
Palmdale, Calif., 204
Palmeira, Braz., 135
Palmeirinhas (pt.), Angola, 115
Palmer, Alaska, 196
Palmer, Mass., 249
Palmer Land (reg.), Ant., 5
Palmer Sta., Ant., 5
Palmerston (atoll), Cook Is., 87
Palmerston North, N.Z., 101
Palmerton, Pa., 294
Palmetto, Fla., 212
Palmetto (pt.), St. Chr.-N.-A., 161
Palmiet (river), S. Afr., 118
Palmillas (pt.), Dom. Rep., 158
Palmira, Col., 126
Palmira, Cuba, 158
Palmitas, Urug., 145
Palm Springs, Calif., 204
Palm Springs, Fla., 212
Palmyra, Mo., 261
Palmyra, N. J., 273
Palmyra, N.Y., 276
Palmyra (isl.), Pacific, 87
Palmyra, Pa., 294
Palmyra (Tadmor), Syria, 63
Palmyras (pt.), India, 68
Palni, India, 68
Palo, Phil., 82
Palo Alto, Calif., 204
Palomar (mt.), Calif., 204
Palos (cape), Spain, 33
Palos Hts., Ill., 222
Palos Hills, Ill., 222
Palos Verdes Estates, Calif., 204
Palpa, Peru, 128
Pamekasan, Indon., 85
Pameungpeuk, Indon., 85
Pamir (plat.), Asia, 54
Pamlico (sound), N.C., 281
Pampa, Tex., 302
Pampanga (prov.), Phil., 82
Pampas (plain), Arg., 143
Pampas, Peru, 128
Pamplona, Col., 126
Pamplona, Spain, 33
Pana, Ill., 222
Panagyurishte, Bulg., 45
Panama, 154
Panama (canal), C.Z., 154
Panamá (cap.), Pan., 154
Panamá (gulf), Pan., 154
Panama City, Fla., 212
Panaon (isl.), Phil., 82
Panarea (isl.), Italy, 34
Panaro (riv.), Italy, 34
Panay (isl.), Phil., 82
Pančevo, Yugo., 45
Panchur, India, 68
Panda, Mozamb., 118
Pan de Azúcar, Urug., 145
Pandeglang, Indon., 85
Pandharpur, India, 68
Pando (dept.), Bol., 136
Pando (mt.), Bol., 136
Pando, Urug., 145
Panevėžys, U.S.S.R., 53
Panfilov, U.S.S.R., 48
Pangai, Tonga, 87
Pangala, Congo, 115
Pangani, Tanz., 115
Pangasinan (prov.), Phil., 82
Pangi, Zaire, 115
Pangkalanberandan, Indon., 85
Pangkalpinang, Indon., 85
Pangkiang, China, 77
Panglao (isl.), Phil., 82
Pangong Tso (lake), Asia, 68
Panguipulli, Chile, 138
Panguitch, Utah, 304
Pangutaran Group (isls.), Phil., 82
Panihati, India, 68
Panipat, India, 68
Panjao, Afghan., 68
Panjim, India, 68
Pankow, E. Ger., 22
P'anmunjŏm, Korea, 81
Pantelleria (isl.), Italy, 34
Pantin, France, 28
Pánuco, Mex., 150
Panuke (lake), N.S., 169
Panzós, Guat., 154
Pao (river), Venez., 124
Paochang, China, 77
Paoki, China, 77
Paola, Kans., 232
Paoli, Ind., 227
Paoli, Pa., 294
Paoshan, China, 77
Paoting, China, 77
Paotow, China, 77
Paoua, Centr. Afr. Rep., 115
Pápa, Hung., 41
Papagaio (riv.), Braz., 132
Papagayo (gulf), C. Rica, 154
Papaikou, Hawaii, 218
Papantla de Olarte, Mex., 150
Papar, Malaysia, 85
Papa Stour (isl.), Scot., 15
Papeete (cap.), Fr. Poly., 87
Paphos, Cyprus, 63
Papineauville, Que., 172
Papua (gulf), P.N.G., 85
Papua New Guinea, 85, 87
Papun, Burma, 72
Papunáua (riv.), Col., 126
Pará (state), Braz., 132
Pará (Belém), Braz., 132
Paracas (pen.), Peru, 128
Paracatu, Braz., 132
Parachinar, Pak., 68
Paraćin, Yugo., 45
Pará de Minas, Braz., 135
Paradise, Calif., 204
Paradise, Nev., 266
Paradise Valley, Ariz., 198
Paragould, Ark., 203
Paraguá (riv.), Bol., 136
Paragua (riv.), Venez., 124
Paraguaçu Paulista, Braz., 132
Paraguaná (pen.), Venez., 124
Paraguarí (dept.), Par., 144
Paraguarí, Par., 144
Paraguay, 144
Paraguay (riv.), S. Amer., 120
Paraíba (state), Braz., 132
Paraíba do Sul, Braz., 135
Paraíso, C. Rica, 154
Paraíso, Mex., 150
Parakou, Benin, 106
Paramaribo (dist.), Sur., 131
Paramaribo (cap.), Sur., 131
Paramount, Calif., 204
Paramus, N. J., 273
Paramushir (isl.), U.S.S.R., 48
Paraná, Arg., 143
Paraná (state), Braz., 132
Paraná (riv.), Braz., 132
Paraná (riv.), S. Amer., 120
Paranaguá, Braz., 135
Paranaíba, Braz., 132
Paranam, Sur., 131
Paranapanema (riv.), Braz., 132
Paranapiacaba (range), Braz., 135
Paranatinga (riv.), Braz., 132
Parao (riv.), Urug., 145
Parapetí (riv.), Bol., 136
Parati, Braz., 135
Paratinga, Braz., 132
Parbhani, India, 68
Pardo (riv.), Braz., 132, 135
Pardubice, Czech., 41
Pare, Indon., 85
Parent, Que., 174
Parepare, Indon., 85
Parham, Antigua, 161
Paria (gulf), 124
Paria (pen.), Venez., 124
Pariaguán, Venez., 124
Pariaman, Indon., 85
Parícutin (vol.), Mex., 150
Parida (isl.), Pan., 154
Parika, Guyana, 131
Parima (mts.), S. Amer., 124
Parinacochas (lake), Peru, 128
Pariñas (pt.), Peru, 128
Parintins, Braz., 132
Paris, Ark., 203
Paris (dept.), France, 28
Paris (cap.), France, 28
Paris, Ill., 222
Paris, Ky., 237
Paris, Maine, 242
Paris, Ont., 177
Paris, Tenn., 237
Paris, Tex., 302
Parita, Pan., 154
Park (range), Colo., 208
Park City, Kans., 232
Parkdale, P.E.I., 169
Parker, Fla., 212
Parker (dam), U.S., 198
Parkersburg, W. Va., 313
Parkes, N.S.W., 97
Parkesburg, Pa., 294
Park Falls, Wis., 317
Park Forest, Ill., 222
Park Hills, Ky., 237
Parkland, Wash., 310
Park Rapids, Minn., 254
Park Ridge, Ill., 222
Park Ridge, N. J., 273
Park River, N. Dak., 283
Parksville, Br. Col., 184
Parkville, Md., 245
Parkville, Pa., 294
Parlakhemundi, India, 68
Parma (prov.), Italy, 34
Parma, Italy, 34
Parma, Ohio, 284
Parma Hts., Ohio, 284
Parnaíba, Braz., 132
Parnaíba (riv.), Braz., 132
Parnassus (mt.), Greece, 45
Pärnu, U.S.S.R., 53
Paro Dzong, Bhutan, 68
Paropamisus (range), Afghan., 68
Páros (isl.), Greece, 45
Parow, S. Afr., 118
Parowan, Utah, 304
Parral, Chile, 138
Parral, Mex., 150
Parramatta, N.S.W., 97
Parras, Mex., 150
Parrsboro, N.S., 169
Parry (chan.), N.W.T., 187
Parry Sound, Ont., 177
Parsippany, N. J., 273
Parsnip (riv.), Br. Col., 184
Parsons, Kans., 232
Partinico, Italy, 34
Partry (mts.), Ire., 17
Parvatipuram, India, 68
Parys, S. Afr., 118
Pasadena, Calif., 204
Pasadena, Tex., 302
Pasado (cape), Ecua., 128
Pasaje, Ecua., 128
Pasargadae (ruins), Iran, 66
Pascagoula, Miss., 256
Paşcani, Rum., 45
Pasco (dept.), Peru, 128
Pasco, Wash., 310
Pascua (riv.), Chile, 138
Pas-de-Calais (dept.), France, 28
Pasión (riv.), Guat., 154
Paso de los Libres, Arg., 143
Paso de los Toros, Urug., 145
Pasorapa, Bol., 136
Paso Robles, Calif., 204
Passage West, Ire., 17
Passaic, N. J., 273
Passamaquoddy (bay), N. Amer., 170
Passau, W. Ger., 22
Pass Christian, Miss., 256
Passo Fundo, Braz., 132
Passos, Braz., 135
Pastaza (prov.), Ecua., 128
Pastaza (riv.), S. Amer., 128
Pasto, Col., 126
Pasuruan, Indon., 85
Pasvik (riv.), Europe, 18
Patacamaya, Bol., 136
Patagonia (reg.), Arg., 143
Patan, India, 68
Patapédia (riv.), Canada, 170, 172
Patchogue, N.Y., 276
Paternion, Austria, 41
Paterno, Italy, 34
Paterson, N. J., 273
Pathfinder (res.), Wyo., 319
Pati, Indon., 85
Patía (riv.), Col., 126
Patiala, India, 68
Patillas, P. Rico, 161
Pativilca (riv.), Peru, 128
Patjitan, Indon., 85
Pátmos (isl.), Greece, 45
Patna, India, 68
Patos, Braz., 132
Pátrai, Greece, 45
Patrocínio, Braz., 132
Patta (isl.), Kenya, 115
Pattani, Thai., 72
Patterson, La., 238
Patton, Pa., 294
Patuca (riv.), Hond., 154
Pátzcuaro (lake), Mex., 150
Pau, France, 28
Paucartambo, Peru, 128
Paul (isl.), Newf., 166
Paulaya (riv.), Hond., 154
Paulding, Ohio, 284
Paulo de Faria, Braz., 135
Paulsboro, N. J., 273
Pauls Valley, Okla., 288
Pauto (riv.), Col., 126
Pavia (prov.), Italy, 34
Pavia, Italy, 34
Pāvilosta, U.S.S.R., 53
Pavlodar, U.S.S.R., 48
Pavlovo, U.S.S.R., 52
Pawcatuck, Conn., 210
Pawhuska, Okla., 288
Paw Paw, Mich., 250
Pawtucket, R.I., 249
Paxoí (isl.), Greece, 45
Paxton, Ill., 222
Paya Lebar, Sing., 72
Payette, Idaho, 220
Payneham, S. Austral., 94
Paysandú (dept.), Urug., 145
Paysandú, Urug., 145
Payson, Utah, 304
Paz, Arg., 143
Pazardzhik, Bulg., 45
Peabody, Mass., 249
Peace (riv.), Canada, 163
Peace River, Alta., 182
Peak, The (mt.), Eng., 13
Pea Ridge Nat'l Mil. Park, Ark., 203
Pearl (harb.), Hawaii, 218
Pearl, Miss., 256
Pearl and Hermes (reef), Hawaii, 218
Pearl City, Hawaii, 218
Pearl River, N.Y., 276
Pearsall, Tex., 302
Peary Land (reg.), Greenl., 4
Pebane, Mozamb., 118
Peć, Yugo., 45
Pechora, U.S.S.R., 52
Pechora (riv.), U.S.S.R., 52
Pecos, Tex., 302
Pecos (riv.), U.S., 274, 302
Pecos Nat'l Mon., N. Mex., 274
Pécs, Hung., 41
Pedasí, Pan., 154
Pedernales (prov.), Dom. Rep., 158
Pedernales, Dom. Rep., 158
Pedernales (riv.), Tex., 302
Pedra Azul, Braz., 132
Pedraza, Col., 126
Pedreiras, Braz., 132
Pedro de Valdivia, Chile, 138
Pedro Juan Caballero, Par., 144
Pedro Montoya, Mex., 150
Peebles (county), Scot., 15
Peebles, Scot., 15
Peekskill, N.Y., 276
Peel (riv.), Canada, 162, 187
Peel, I. of Man, 13
Pegasus (bay), N.Z., 101
Pegu (div.), Burma, 72
Pegu, Burma, 72
Pegu Yoma (mts.), Burma, 72
Pehuajó, Arg., 143
Peihai (Pakhoi), China, 77
Peine, W. Ger., 22
Peiping (Peking) (cap.), China, 77
Peipus (lake), U.S.S.R., 53
Peixoto (dam), Braz., 135
Pekalongan, Indon., 85
Pekan, Malaysia, 72
Pekan Nanas, Malaysia, 72
Pekin, Ill., 222
Peking (cap.), China, 77
Pelagie (isls.), Italy, 34
Pelagruž (Pelagosa) (isl.), Yugo., 45
Pelée (vol.), Mart., 161
Pelée (pt.), Ont., 177
Peleliu (isl.), Pac. Is., 87
Pelham, Ga., 216
Pelham, Ont., 177
Pelham Manor, N.Y., 276
Pelileo, Ecua., 128
Pella, Iowa, 229
Pell City, Ala., 194
Pellegrini, Arg., 143
Pelly (riv.), Yukon, 187
Pelopónnisos (reg.), Greece, 45
Pelotas, Braz., 132
Pemalang, Indon., 85
Pematangsiantar, Indon., 85
Pemba, Mozamb., 118
Pemba (reg.), Tanz., 115
Pemba (isl.), Tanz., 115
Pemberton, W. Austral., 92
Pembroke, N.H., 268
Pembroke, Ont., 177
Pembroke, Wales, 13
Pembrokeshire (county), Wales, 13
Peña, Dom. Rep., 158
Peñablanca, Chile, 138
Peñaflor, Chile, 138
Peñal, Trin. & Tob., 161
Peñalara (mt.), Spain, 33
Penápolis, Braz., 135
Pen Argyl, Pa., 294
Peñarroya-Pueblonuevo, Spain, 33
Penarth, Wales, 13
Penas (gulf), Chile, 138
Penbrook, Pa., 294
Penco, Chile, 138
Pendé (river), Centr. Afr. Rep., 115
Pendembu, S. Leone, 106
Pendleton, Oreg., 291
Pend Oreille (lake), Idaho, 220
Penedo, Braz., 132
Penetanguishene, Ont., 177
Penganga (riv.), India, 68
Penghu (isls.), China, 77
Pengpu, China, 77
Penibética (mts.), Spain, 33
Penicuik, Scot., 15
Pénjamo, Mex., 150
Penki, China, 77
Penmarch (pt.), France, 28
Penner (riv.), India, 68
Pennine (range), Eng., 13
Pennine Alps (range), Europe, 39
Pennsauken, N. J., 273
Penns Grove, N. J., 273
Pennsville, N. J., 273
Pennsylvania (state), U.S., 294
Penn Yan, N.Y., 276
Penola, S. Austral., 94
Peñón Blanco, Mex., 150
Penonomé, Pan., 154
Penrhyn (Tongareva) (atoll), Cook Is., 87
Penrith, Eng., 13
Penrith, N.S.W., 97
Pensacola, Fla., 212
Penticton, Br. Col., 184
Pentland (firth), Scot., 15
Peñuelas, P. Rico, 161
Penza, U.S.S.R., 52
Penzance, Eng., 13
Penzhina (bay), U.S.S.R., 48
Peoria, Ariz., 198
Peoria, Ill., 222
Peoria Hts., Ill., 222
Pepe (cape), Cuba, 158
Pepper Pike, Ohio, 284
Peqin, Alb., 45
Pequannock, N. J., 273
Pera (head), Queensland, 95
Pera (Beyoğlu), Turkey, 63
Perabumulih, Indon., 85
Perak (state), Malaysia, 72
Perales (riv.), Spain, 33
Peralta, Dom. Rep., 158
Peravia (prov.), Dom. Rep., 158
Percé, Que., 172
Perche (reg.), France, 28
Perdido (mt.), Spain, 33
Pereira, Col., 126
Pereira d'Eça, Angola, 115
Pérez, Arg., 143
Pergamino, Arg., 143
Péribonca (riv.), Que., 174
Perico, Cuba, 158
Périgueux, France, 28
Perijá (mts.), S. Amer., 126
Perim (isl.), P.D.R. Yemen, 59
Periyar (lake), India, 68
Perkam (cape), Indon., 85
Perkasie, Pa., 294
Perlas (lag.), Nic., 154
Perlas (arch.), Pan., 154
Perlis (state), Malaysia, 72
Perm', U.S.S.R., 52
Përmet, Alb., 45
Pernambuco (state), Braz., 132
Pernambuco (Recife), Braz., 132
Pernik, Bulg., 45
Perote, Mex., 150
Perpignan, France, 28
Perrine, Fla., 212
Perris, Calif., 204
Perros (bay), Cuba, 158
Perry, Fla., 212
Perry, Ga., 216
Perry, Iowa, 229
Perry, N.Y., 276
Perry, Okla., 288
Perrygo Place, Wis., 317
Perrysburg, Ohio, 284
Perrys Victory & Int'l Peace Mem., Ohio, 284
Perryton, Tex., 302
Perryville, Mo., 261
Persepolis (ruins), Iran, 66
Persia (Iran), 66
Persian (gulf), Asia, 59
Perth, Ont., 177
Perth (county), Scot., 15
Perth, Scot., 15
Perth (cap.), W. Austral., 92
Perth Amboy, N. J., 273
Perth-Andover, N.B., 170
Peru, 128
Peru, Ill., 222
Peru, Ind., 227
Perugia (prov.), Italy, 34
Perugia, Italy, 34
Pervomaysk, U.S.S.R., 52
Pesaro, Italy, 34
Pesaro e Urbino (prov.), Italy, 34
Pescadores (Penghu)(isls.), China, 77
Pescara (prov.), Italy, 34
Pescara, Italy, 34
Peshawar, Pak., 68
Peshkopi, Alb., 45
Peshtera, Bulg., 45
Peshtigo, Wis., 317
Pespire, Hond., 154
Pessac, France, 28
Pest (county), Hung., 41
Petachalco (bay), Mex., 150
Petah Tiqwa, Israel, 65
Petal, Miss., 256
Petaluma, Calif., 204
Pétange, Lux., 27
Petatlán, Mex., 150
Petauke, Zambia, 115
Petawawa, Ont., 177
Petén-Itzá (lake), Guat., 154
Peter (isl.), Virgin Is. (Br.), 161
Peter I (isl.), Ant., 5
Peterborough, Eng., 13
Peterborough, Ont., 177
Peterborough, S.Austral., 94
Peterhead, Scot., 15
Petermann (ranges), Austral., 93
Petersburg, Alaska, 196
Petersburg, Ind., 227
Petersburg, Va., 307
Pétionville, Haiti, 158
Petit-Bourg, Guad., 161
Petitcodiac, N.B., 170
Petite Rivière de la Baleine (riv.), Que., 174
Petite-Rivière-de-l'Artibonite, Haiti, 158
Petite-Terre (isls.), Guad., 161
Petit-Goâve, Haiti, 158
Petit-Mécatina (riv.), Que., 174
Petitot (riv.), Canada, 187
Peto, Mex., 150
Petone, N.Z., 101
Petoskey, Mich., 250
Petra (ruins), Jordan, 65
Petrich, Bulg., 45
Petrified Forest Nat'l Park, Ariz., 198
Petrila, Rum., 45
Petrolia, Ont., 177
Petrolina, Braz., 132
Petrona (pt.), P. Rico, 161
Petropavlovsk, U.S.S.R., 48
Petropavlovsk-Kamchatskiy, U.S.S.R., 48
Petrópolis, Braz., 135
Petroşeni, Rum., 45
Petrovsk, U.S.S.R., 52
Petrovsk-Zabaykal'skiy, U.S.S.R., 48
Petrozavodsk, U.S.S.R., 52
Peu, Sol. Is., 87
Peumo, Chile, 138
Pezinok, Czech., 41
Pforzheim, W. Ger., 22
Phan Rang, S. Vietnam, 72
Phan Ri, S. Vietnam, 72
Phan Thiet, S. Vietnam, 72
Pharr, Tex., 302
Phatthalung, Thai., 72
Phayao, Thai., 72
Phelps (peak), Venez., 124
Phenix City, Ala., 194
Phet Buri, Thai., 72
Phichit, Thai., 72
Philadelphia, Miss., 256
Philadelphia, Pa., 294
Philippeville (Skikda), Alg., 106
Philippine (sea), 87
Philippines, 82
Philipsburg, Pa., 294
Phillips, Tex., 302
Phillipsburg, Kans., 232
Phillipsburg, N. J., 273
Phitsanulok, Thai., 72
Phnom Penh (cap.), Cambodia, 72
Phoenix (cap.), Ariz., 198
Phoenix (isls.), Gilb. & Ell. Is., 87
Phoenix, Ill., 222
Phoenixville, Pa., 294
Phong Saly, Laos, 72
Phrae, Thai., 72
Phsar Oudong, Cambodia, 72
Phu Bia (mt.), Laos, 72
Phuc Loi, N. Vietnam, 72
Phu Co Pi (mt.), Laos, 72
Phu Cuong, S. Vietnam, 72
Phu Dien, N. Vietnam, 72
Phuket, Thai., 72
Phu Loc, S. Vietnam, 72
Phum Rovieng, Cambodia, 72
Phu My, S. Vietnam, 72
Phu Qui, N. Vietnam, 72
Phu Quoc, Dao (isl.), S. Vietnam, 72
Phu Rieng, S. Vietnam, 72
Phu Tho, N. Vietnam, 72
Phutthaisong, Thai., 72
Phu Vinh (Tra Vinh), S. Vietnam, 72
P. I. (Paul Isnard), Fr. Gui., 131
Piacenza (prov.), Italy, 34
Piacenza, Italy, 34
Pianosa (isl.), Italy, 34
Piatra Neamţ, Rum., 45
Piauí (state), Braz., 132
Piauí (riv.), Braz., 132
Piave (riv.), Italy, 34
Piazza Armerina, Italy, 34
Pibor Post, Sudan, 111
Picayune, Miss., 256
Picher, Okla., 288
Pichilemu, Chile, 138
Pichincha (prov.), Ecua., 128
Pickering, Ont., 177
Pickersgill, Guyana, 131
Pico (isl.), Port., 32
Pico Rivera, Calif., 204
Picos, Braz., 132
Picota, Peru, 128
Picton, N.Z., 101
Picton, Ont., 177
Pictou, N.S., 169
Picture Butte, Alta., 182
Pictured Rocks Nat'l Lakeshore, Mich., 250
Pidurutalagala (mt.), Sri Lanka, 68
Piedecuesta, Col., 126
Piedmont, Ala., 194
Piedmont, Calif., 204
Piedmont (reg.), Italy, 34
Piedras Negras, Mex., 150
Piekary Śląskie, Poland, 47
Pieksämäki, Fin., 18
Pielinen (lake), Fin., 18
Pierre (cap.), S. Dak., 298
Pierrefonds, Que., 172
Piešt'any, Czech., 41
Pietarsaari (Jakobstad), Fin., 18
Pietermaritzburg, S. Africa, 118
Pietersburg, S. Afr., 118
Piet Retief, S. Afr., 118
Pietrosul (mt.), Rum., 45
Pigeon (riv.), N. Amer., 179
Piggott, Ark., 203
Pigs (Cochinos)(bay), Cuba, 158
Pigüé, Arg., 143
Pija (mts.), Hond., 154
Pijijiapan, Mex., 150
Pikes (peak), Colo., 208
Pikesville, Md., 245
Piketberg, S. Afr., 118
Pikeville, Ky., 237
Piła, Poland, 47
Pilar, Arg., 143
Pilar, Braz., 132
Pilar, Par., 144
Pilatus (mt.), Switz., 39
Pilaya (riv.), Bol., 136
Pilcomayo (riv.), S. Amer., 143
Pili, Phil., 82
Pilibhit, India, 68
Píllaro, Ecua., 128
Pillsbury (sound), Virgin Is. (U.S.), 161
Pilote (riv.), Mart., 161
Pimentel, Dom. Rep., 158
Pimentel, Peru, 128
Pina, Cuba, 158
Pinang (state), Malaysia, 72
Pinang, Malaysia, 72
Pinang (isl.), Malaysia, 72
Pinar del Río (prov.), Cuba, 158
Pinar del Río, Cuba, 158
Piñas, Ecua., 128
Pincher Creek, Alta., 182
Pinckneyville, Ill., 222
Pindo (riv.), Ecua., 128
Pindus (mts.), Greece, 45
Pine Bluff, Ark., 203
Pine Creek, N. Terr., 93
Pine Falls, Man., 179
Pinega (riv.), U.S.S.R., 52
Pine Hill, N. J., 273
Pinelands, S. Afr., 118
Pine Lawn, Mo., 261
Pinellas Park, Fla., 212
Pine Ridge, S. Dak., 298
Pinerolo, Italy, 34
Pines, Isle of (isl.), Cuba, 158
Pines, Isle of (isl.), New Cal., 87
Pinetown, S. Afr., 118
Pineville, Ky., 237
Pineville, La., 238
Pingchüan, China, 77
Pingelap (atoll), Pac. Is., 87
Pingelly, W. Austral., 92
Pingliang, China, 77
Pinglo, China, 77
Pingsiang, China, 77
Pingtung, China, 77
Pingwu, China, 77
Pinhal, Braz., 135
Piniós (riv.), Greece, 45
Pinnacles Nat'l Mon., Calif., 204
Pinneberg, W. Ger., 22
Pinole, Calif., 204
Pinsk, U.S.S.R., 52
Pinta (isl.), Ecua., 128
Piombino, Italy, 34
Piotrków Tryb., Poland, 47
Pipe Spring Nat'l Mon., Ariz., 198
Pipestone, Minn., 254
Pipestone Nat'l Mon., Minn., 254
Piqua, Ohio, 284
Piquete, Braz., 135
Piracicaba, Braz., 135
Piraiévs, Greece, 45
Piraju, Braz., 135
Pirámide (mt.), Chile, 138
Piraně, Arg., 143
Pirapora, Braz., 132
Pirassununga, Braz., 135
Pirata (mt.), P. Rico, 161
Piray (riv.), Bol., 136
Pirayú, Par., 144
Pires do Rio, Braz., 132
Pírgos, Greece, 45
Piriápolis, Urug., 145
Piribebuy, Par., 144
Piripiri, Braz., 132
Píritu, Venez., 124
Pirmasens, W. Ger., 22
Pirna, E. Ger., 22
Pirot, Yugo., 45
Pisa (prov.), Italy, 34
Pisa, Italy, 34
Piscataway, N. J., 273
Pisco, Peru, 128
Písek, Czech., 41
Pistoia (prov.), Italy, 34
Pistoia, Italy, 34
Pistolet (bay), Newf., 166
Pitalito, Col., 126

Q

R

Widnes, Eng., 10
Wieliczka, Poland, 47
Wieluń, Poland, 47
Wien (Vienna) (cap.), Austria, 41
Wiener Neustadt, Austria, 41
Wieringermeer Polder, Neth., 27
Wiesbaden, W. Ger., 22
Wigan, Eng., 10
Wight (isl.), Eng., 13
Wight, Isle of (county), Eng., 13
Wigston, Eng., 13
Wigtown (county), Scot., 15
Wigtown (bay), Scot., 15
Wil, Switz., 39
Wildhorn (mt.), Switz., 39
Wildspitze (mt.), Austria, 41
Wildwood, N. J., 273
Wildwood Crest, N. J., 273
Wilhelm II Coast (reg.), Ant., 5
Wilhelmina (canal), Neth., 27
Wilhelmina (mts.), Sur., 131
Wilhelm-Pieck-Stadt, E. Ger., 22
Wilhelmshaven, W. Ger., 22
Wilkes-Barre, Pa., 294
Wilkes Land (reg.), Ant., 5
Wilkie, Sask., 181
Wilkinsburg, Pa., 294
Willamette (riv.), Oreg., 291
Willard, Ohio, 284
Willcox, Ariz., 198
Willebroek, Belg., 27
Willems (canal), Neth., 27
Willemstad (cap.), Neth. Ant., 161
William (riv.), Sask., 181
William H. Taft Nat'l Hist. Site, Ohio, 284
Williams, Ariz., 198
Williamsburg, Ky., 237
Williamsburg, Va., 307
Williams Lake, Br. Col., 184
Williamson, W. Va., 313
Williamsport, Pa., 294
Williamston, N.C., 281
Williamston, S.C., 296
Williamstown, Mass., 249
Williamstown, N. J., 273
Williamstown, Vic., 97
Williamstown, W. Va., 313
Williamsville, N.Y., 276
Willikies, Antigua, 161
Willimantic, Conn., 210
Willingboro, N. J., 273
Williston (lake), Br. Col., 184
Williston, N. Dak., 283
Williston, S.C., 296
Williston Park, N.Y., 276
Willits, Calif., 204
Willmar, Minn., 254
Willmore Wilderness Prov. Park, Alta., 182
Willoughby, N.S.W., 97
Willoughby, Ohio, 284
Willoughby (lake), Vt., 268
Willoughby Hills, Ohio, 284
Willow Bunch, Sask., 181
Willow Grove, Pa., 294
Willowick, Ohio, 284
Willows, Calif., 204
Wilmerding, Pa., 294
Wilmette, Ill., 222
Wilmington, Calif., 204
Wilmington, Del., 245
Wilmington, Ill., 222
Wilmington, N.C., 281
Wilmington, Ohio, 284
Wilmore, Ky., 237
Wilmslow, Eng., 10
Wilson (mt.), Calif., 204
Wilson, N.C., 281
Wilson, Pa., 294
Wilsons (prom.), Vic., 97
Wilson's Creek Nat'l Battlefield, Mo., 261
Wilton, Conn., 210
Wilton Manors, Fla., 212
Wiltshire (county), Eng., 13
Wiltz, Lux., 27
Wimbledon, Eng., 10
Wimmera (riv.), Vic., 97
Winchelsea, Vic., 97
Winchendon, Mass., 249
Winchester, Eng., 13
Winchester, Ind., 227
Winchester, Ky., 237
Winchester, Mass., 249
Winchester, Nev., 266
Winchester, Tenn., 237
Winchester, Va., 307
Windber, Pa., 294
Wind Cave Nat'l Park, S. Dak., 298
Winder, Ga., 216
Windham, Conn., 210
Windham, Ohio, 284
Windhoek (cap.), S.W. Afr., 118
Windisch, Switz., 39
Windom, Minn., 254
Window Rock, Ariz., 198
Wind River (range), Wyo., 319
Windsor, Conn., 210
Windsor, Mo., 261
Windsor, Newf., 166
Windsor, N.S.W., 97
Windsor, N.S., 169
Windsor, Ont., 177
Windsor, Que., 172
Windsor, Queensland, 95
Windsor, Vt., 268
Windsor Hts., Iowa, 229
Windward (isls.), W. Indies, 156
Windward (passage), W. Indies, 156
Winefred (lake), Alta., 182
Winfield, Ala., 194
Winfield, Kans., 232
Winfield, N. J., 273
Wingham, N.S.W., 97
Wingham, Ont., 177
Winisk (riv.), Ont., 177
Winkelman, Ariz., 198
Winkler, Man., 179
Winneba, Ghana, 106
Winnebago (lake), Wis., 317
Winnemucca, Nev., 266
Winnemucca (lake), Nev., 266
Winner, S. Dak., 298
Winnetka, Ill., 222
Winnfield, La., 238
Winnibigoshish (lake), Minn., 254
Winnipeg (cap.), Man., 179
Winnipeg (lake), Man., 179
Winnipegosis, Man., 179
Winnipegosis (lake), Man., 179
Winnipesaukee (lake), N.H., 268
Winnsboro, La., 238
Winnsboro, S.C., 296
Winnsboro, Tex., 302
Winona, Minn., 254
Winona, Miss., 256
Winooski, Vt., 268
Winooski (riv.), Vt., 268
Winschoten, Neth., 27
Winsford, Eng., 10
Winslow, Ariz., 198
Winslow, Maine, 242
Winsted, Conn., 210
Winston-Salem, N.C., 281
Winter Garden, Fla., 212
Winter Haven, Fla., 212
Winter Park, Fla., 212
Winters, Tex., 302
Winterset, Iowa, 229
Wintersville, Ohio, 284
Winterswijk, Neth., 27
Winterthur, Switz., 39
Winthrop, Mass., 249
Winthrop Harbor, Ill., 222
Winton, N.Z., 101
Winton, Pa., 294
Winyah (bay), S.C., 296
Wirral, Eng., 10
Wisbech, Eng., 13
Wisconsin (state), U.S., 317
Wisconsin (riv.), Wis., 317
Wisconsin Dells, Wis., 317
Wisconsin Rapids, Wis., 317
Wise, Va., 307
Wisła (Vistula) (riv.), Poland, 47
Wismar, E. Ger., 22
Witbank, S. Afr., 118
Witham (riv.), Eng., 13
Withamsville, Ohio, 284
Withlacoochee (riv.), Fla., 212
Witten, W. Ger., 22
Wittenberg, E. Ger., 22
Wittenberge, E. Ger., 22
Wittenoom Gorge, W. Austral., 92
Witu, Kenya, 115
Witvlei, S.W. Afr., 118
Witwatersrand (reg.), S. Afr., 118
Włocławek, Poland, 47
Woburn, Mass., 249
Wodonga, Vic., 97
Woerden, Neth., 27
Wohlen, Switz., 39
Woking, Eng., 10
Wokingham, Eng., 13
Woleai (atoll), Pac. Is., 87
Wolf (riv.), Tenn., 237
Wolfenbüttel, W. Ger., 22
Wolf Lake, Mich., 250
Wolf Point, Mont., 262
Wolfsberg, Austria, 41
Wolfsburg, W. Ger., 22
Wolfville, N.S., 169
Wolgast, E. Ger., 22
Wolin (isl.), Poland, 47
Wollaston (isls.), Chile, 138
Wollaston (lake), Sask., 181
Wollongong, N.S.W., 97
Wolmaransstad, S. Afr., 118
Wołomin, Poland, 47
Wolseley, Sask., 181
Wolstenholme (cape), Que., 174
Woluwe-Saint-Lambert, Belg., 27
Woluwe-Saint-Pierre, Belg., 27
Wolverhampton, Eng., 10
Wolverton, Eng., 13
Wombwell, Eng., 13
Wŏnju, S. Korea, 81
Wonogiri, Indon., 85
Wonosobo, Indon., 85
Wŏnsan, N. Korea, 81
Wonthaggi, Vic., 97
Woodall (mt.), Miss., 256
Woodbine, N. J., 273
Woodbridge, N. J., 273
Wood Buffalo Nat'l Park, Canada, 182, 187
Woodburn, Oreg., 291
Woodbury, Conn., 210
Woodbury, N. J., 273
Woodcliff Lake, N.J., 273
Wood Dale, Ill., 222
Woodend, Vic., 97
Woodlake, Calif., 204
Woodland, Calif., 204
Woodland Hills, Calif., 204
Woodlands, Sing., 72
Woodlark (isl.), P.N.G., 85
Woodlawn, Md., 245
Woodlawn, Ohio, 284
Woodlyn, Pa., 294
Wood-Lynne, N. J., 273
Woodmere, N.Y., 276
Woodmont, Conn., 210
Woodridge, Ill., 222
Wood-Ridge, N. J., 273
Wood River, Ill., 222
Woodroffe (mt.), S. Austral., 94
Woodruff, S.C., 296
Woods, Lake of the (lake), N. Amer., 179, 254
Woods (lake), N. Terr., 93
Woodsfield, Ohio, 284
Woods Hole, Mass., 249
Woodside, Calif., 204
Woodson Terr., Mo., 261
Woodstock, Ill., 222
Woodstock, N.B., 170
Woodstock, Ont., 177
Woodstock, Vt., 268
Woodstown, N. J., 273
Woodville, N.Z., 101
Woodville, S. Austral., 94
Woodward, Okla., 288
Woody Point, Newf., 166
Woolgoolga, N.S.W., 97
Woollahra, N.S.W., 97
Woomera, S. Austral., 94
Woonsocket, R.I., 249
Woonsocket, S. Dak., 298
Wooramel (riv.), W. Austral., 92
Wooster, Ohio, 284
Worb, Switz., 39
Worcester, Eng., 13
Worcester, Mass., 249
Worcester, S. Afr., 118
Worcestershire (county), Eng., 13
Wörgl, Austria, 41
Workington, Eng., 13
Worksop, Eng., 13
Worland, Wyo., 319
Wormerveer, Neth., 27
Worms, W. Ger., 22
Worth, Ill., 222
Worth (lake), Tex., 302
Worthing, Eng., 13
Worthington, Minn., 254
Worthington, Ohio, 284
Wotje (atoll), Pac. Is., 87
Wounded Knee (creek), S. Dak., 298
Woy Woy-Ettalong, N.S.W., 97
Wrangel (isl.), U.S.S.R., 48
Wrangell, Alaska, 196
Wrangell (mts.), Alaska, 196
Wrath (cape), Scot., 15
Wray, Colo., 208
Wrexham, Wales, 13
Wright Bros. Nat'l Mon., N.C., 281
Wrightstown, N. J., 273
Wrigley, N.W.T., 187
Wrocław (prov.), Poland, 47
Wrocław, Poland, 47
Września, Poland, 47
Wuchow, China, 77
Wuchung, China, 77
Wuhan, China, 77
Wuhing, China, 77
Wuhu, China, 77
Wukari, Nigeria, 106
Wu Kiang (riv.), China, 77
Wum, Cameroon, 115
Wundowie, W. Austral., 92
Wunstorf, W. Ger., 22
Wupatki Nat'l Mon., Ariz., 198
Wuppertal, W. Ger., 22
Würmsee (Starnbergersee) (lake), W. Ger., 22
Würzburg, W. Ger., 22
Wurzen, E. Ger., 22
Wusih, China, 77
Wusu, China, 77
Wuwei, China, 77
Wuyi Shan (range), China, 77
Wuyüan, China, 77
Wyandotte, Mich., 250
Wyangala (res.), N.S.W., 97
Wyckoff, N. J., 273
Wye (riv.), U.K., 13
Wyndham, W. Austral., 92
Wynne, Ark., 203
Wynnewood, Okla., 288
Wynnewood, Pa., 294
Wynnum, Queensland, 95
Wynyard, Sask., 181
Wynyard, Tas., 99
Wyoming, Mich., 250
Wyoming, Ohio, 284
Wyoming, Pa., 294
Wyoming (state), U.S., 319
Wyoming (range), Wyo., 319
Wyomissing, Pa., 294
Wyong, N.S.W., 97
Wytheville, Va., 307

X

Xánthi, Greece, 45
Xarrama (riv.), Port., 33
Xenia, Ohio, 284
Xicoténcatl, Mex., 150
Xicotepec, Mex., 150
Xieng Khouang, Laos, 72
Xingu (riv.), Braz., 132
Xique-Xique, Braz., 132
Xochihuehuetlán, Mex., 150
Xochimilco, Mex., 150
Xochitlán, Mex., 150

Y

Yaan, China, 77
Ya'bad, Jordan, 65
Yablonovyy (range), U.S.S.R., 48
Yabucoa, P. Rico, 161
Yacuiba, Bol., 136
Yacuma (riv.), Bol., 136
Yaeyama (isls.), Japan, 81
Yaguajay, Cuba, 158
Yaguarón, Par., 144
Yaguarón (riv.), Urug., 145
Yaguas (riv.), Peru, 128
Yaizu, Japan, 81
Yajalón, Mex., 150
Yakima, Wash., 310
Yakima (riv.), Wash., 310
Yako, Upp. Volta, 106
Yaku (isl.), Japan, 81
Yakut A.S.S.R., U.S.S.R., 48
Yakutat, Alaska, 196
Yakutsk, U.S.S.R., 48
Yala, Thai., 72
Yalesville, Conn., 210
Yalinga, Cent. Afr. Rep., 115
Yallourn, Vic., 97
Yalova, Turkey, 63
Yalta, U.S.S.R., 52
Yalu (riv.), Asia, 81
Yalung Kiang (riv.), China, 77
Yamagata (prefecture), Japan, 81
Yamagata, Japan, 81
Yamaguchi (prefecture), Japan, 81
Yamaguchi, Japan, 81
Yamal (pen.), U.S.S.R., 48
Yamal-Nenets Nat'l Okrug, U.S.S.R., 48
Yamama, Saudi Ar., 59
Yamanashi (prefecture), Japan, 81
Yamantau (mt.), U.S.S.R., 52
Yamaska (riv.), Que., 172
Yambio, Sudan, 111
Yambol, Bulg., 45
Yamdrok Tso (lake), China, 77
Yamethin, Burma, 72
Yampa (riv.), Colo., 208
Yampi Sound, W. Austral., 92
Yamun, Jordan, 65
Yana (riv.), U.S.S.R., 48
Yanam, India, 68
Yandoon, Burma, 72
Yangambi, Zaire, 115
Yangchow, China, 77
Yangchüan, China, 77
Yangdŏk, N. Korea, 81
Yangi Hissar, China, 77
Yangtze Kiang (riv.), China, 77
Yangyang, S. Korea, 81
Yankton, S. Dak., 298
Yao, Japan, 81
Yaoundé (cap.), Cameroon, 115
Yap (isl.), Pac. Is., 87
Yara, Cuba, 158
Yaracuy, Venez., 124
Yare (riv.), Eng., 13
Yarí (riv.), Col., 126
Yarim, Yemen Arab Rep., 59
Yaritagua, Venez., 124
Yarkand, China, 77
Yarkand (riv.), China, 77
Yarmouth, Maine, 242
Yarmouth, Mass., 249
Yarmouth, N.S., 169
Yarmuk (riv.), Asia, 65
Yaroslavl', U.S.S.R., 52
Yarra (riv.), Vic., 97
Yarram, Vic., 97
Yarrawonga, Vic., 97
Yartsevo, U.S.S.R., 52
Yarumal, Col., 126
Yas (isl.), U.A.E., 59
Yasothon, Thai., 72
Yass, N.S.W., 97
Yataity, Par., 144
Yathkyed (lake), N.W.T., 187
Yatsushiro, Japan, 81
Yatta, Jordan, 65
Yatung, China, 77
Yauco, P. Rico, 161
Yautepec, Mex., 150
Yavarí (riv.), Peru, 128
Yavero (riv.), Peru, 128
Yavne, Israel, 65
Yawatahama, Japan, 81
Yazoo (riv.), Miss., 256
Yazoo City, Miss., 256
Ybycuí, Par., 144
Ybytimí, Par., 144
Yding Skovhøj (mt.), Den., 21
Ye, Burma, 72
Yea, Vic., 97
Yeadon, Pa., 294
Yecla, Spain, 33
Yefremov, U.S.S.R., 52
Yegros, Par., 144
Yeguas (pt.), P. Rico, 161
Yehsien, China, 77
Yehud, Israel, 65
Yei, Sudan, 111
Yelets, U.S.S.R., 52
Yelimané, Mali, 106
Yelizaveta (cape), U.S.S.R., 48
Yell (isl.), Scot., 15
Yellow (sea), Asia, 77
Yellow (Hwang Ho)(riv.), China, 77
Yellowknife (cap.), N.W.T., 187
Yellowknife (riv.), N.W.T., 187
Yellow Sprs., Ohio, 284
Yellowstone (riv.), U.S., 262, 283, 319
Yellowstone (lake), Wyo., 319
Yellowstone Nat'l Park, U.S., 319
Yelwa, Nigeria, 106
Yemen Arab Republic, 59
Yemen, Peoples Democratic Republic of, 59
Yenakiyevo, U.S.S.R., 52
Yenan, China, 77
Yenangyaung, Burma, 72
Yen Bai, N. Vietnam, 72
Yenbo, Saudi Ar., 59
Yendi, Ghana, 106
Yeniköy, Turkey, 63
Yenimahalle, Turkey, 63
Yenişehir, Turkey, 63
Yenisey (riv.), U.S.S.R., 48
Yeniseysk, U.S.S.R., 48
Yenki, China, 77
Yenyüan, China, 77
Yeo (lake), W. Austral., 92
Yeola, India, 68
Yeotmal, India, 68
Yeovil, Eng., 13
Yeppoon, Queensland, 95
Yerington, Nev., 266
Yeronga, Queensland, 95
Yesagyo, Burma, 72
Yeshbum, P.D.R. Yemen, 59
Yeşilırmak (riv.), Turkey, 63
Yeşilköy, Turkey, 63
Yessentuki, U.S.S.R., 52
Yeu (isl.), France, 28
Yevpatoria, U.S.S.R., 52
Yeysk, U.S.S.R., 52
Yezd (gov.), Iran, 66
Yezd, Iran, 66
Yhú, Par., 144
Yi (riv.), Urug., 145
Yialousa, Cyprus, 63
Yiannitsá, Greece, 45
Yinchwan, China, 77
Yingkow, China, 77
Yirga Alam, Eth., 111
Yirol, Sudan, 111
Yiyang, China, 77
Ylikitka (lake), Fin., 18
Yoakum, Tex., 302
Yodo (riv.), Japan, 81
Yog (pt.), Phil., 82
Yoho Nat'l Park, Br. Col., 184
Yojoa (lake), Hond., 154
Yokkaichi, Japan, 81
Yokohama, Japan, 81
Yokosuka, Japan, 81
Yokote, Japan, 81
Yola, Nigeria, 106
Yonago, Japan, 81
Yonaguni (isl.), Japan, 81
Yonezawa, Japan, 81
Yongamp'o, N. Korea, 81
Yŏngch'ŏn, S. Korea, 81
Yŏngdŏk, S. Korea, 81
Yŏngju, S. Korea, 81
Yonkers, N.Y., 276
Yonne (dept.), France, 28
Yonne (riv.), France, 28
Yopal, Col., 126
York, Ala., 194
York, Eng., 13
York (cape), Greenl., 4
York, Nebr., 264
York, Ont., 177
York, Pa., 294
York (cape), Queensland, 95
York, S.C., 296
York (riv.), Va., 307
York, W. Austral., 92
Yorke (pen.), S. Austral., 94
York Landing, Man., 179
Yorkshire-East Riding (county), Eng., 13
Yorkshire-North Riding (county), Eng., 13
Yorkshire-West Riding (county), Eng., 13
Yorkton, Sask., 181
Yorktown, N.Y., 276
Yorktown, Tex., 302
Yorktown, Va., 307
Yorkville, N.Y., 276
Yoro, Hond., 154
Yoron (isl.), Japan, 81
Yosemite Nat'l Park, Calif., 204
Yoshino (riv.), Japan, 81
Yoshkar-Ola, U.S.S.R., 52
Yŏsu, S. Korea, 81
Yotala, Bol., 136
Youghal, Ire., 17
Youghal (bay), Ire., 17
Youghiogheny (riv.), U.S., 245, 294
Young, N.S.W., 97
Young, Urug., 145
Youngstown, Ohio, 284
Youngtown, Ariz., 198
Youngwood, Pa., 294
Yousouffia, Mor., 106
Yozgat (prov.), Turkey, 63
Yozgat, Turkey, 63
Ypacaraí, Par., 144
Ypané, Par., 144
Ypoá (lake), Par., 144
Ypres (Ieper), Belg., 27
Ypsilanti, Mich., 250
Yreka, Calif., 204
Yser (riv.), Belg., 27
Ystad, Sweden, 18
Yüan Kiang (riv.), China, 77
Yüanling, China, 77
Yuba City, Calif., 204
Yubari, Japan, 81
Yucaipa, Calif., 204
Yucatán (state), Mex., 150
Yucatán (pen.), Mex., 150
Yucatán (chan.), N. Amer., 156
Yucca Flat (basin), Nev., 266
Yucca House Nat'l Mon., Colo., 208
Yugodzyr, Mong., 77
Yugorskiy (pen.), U.S.S.R., 48
Yugoslavia, 45
Yühsien, China, 77
Yühwan (isl.), China, 77
Yü Kiang (riv.), China, 77
Yukon (terr.), Canada, 187
Yukon (riv.), N. Amer., 187, 196
Yukon, Okla., 288
Yule (riv.), W. Austral., 92
Yülin, China, 77
Yuma, Ariz., 198
Yuma (bay), Dom. Rep., 158
Yuma Proving Ground, Ariz., 198
Yümen, China, 77
Yungan, China, 77
Yungas, Las (dist.), Bol., 136
Yungkia (Wenchow), China, 77
Yungteng, China, 77
Yünhsien, China, 77
Yünnan (prov.), China, 77
Yurimaguas, Peru, 128
Yur'yevets, U.S.S.R., 52
Yuscarán, Hond., 154
Yüshashan, China, 77
Yütze, China, 77
Yuty, Par., 144
Yuzhno-Sakhalinsk, U.S.S.R., 48
Yverdon, Switz., 39
Yvelines (dept.), France, 28

Z

Zaachila, Mex., 150
Zaandam, Neth., 27
Zabid, Yemen Arab Rep., 59
Ząbkowice Śląskie, Poland, 47
Zabrze, Poland, 47
Zabul, Iran, 66
Zacapa, Guat., 154
Zacapoaxtla, Mex., 150
Zacapu, Mex., 150
Zacatecas (state), Mex., 150
Zacatecas, Mex., 150
Zacatecoluca, El Sal., 154
Zacatepec, Mex., 150
Zacatlán, Mex., 150
Zachary, La., 238
Zacoalco, Mex., 150
Zadar, Yugo., 45
Zafra, Spain, 33
Żagań, Poland, 47
Zagazig, Egypt, 111
Zagora, Mor., 106
Zagorsk, U.S.S.R., 52
Zagreb, Yugo., 45
Zagros (mts.), Iran, 66
Zahidan, Iran, 66
Zahle, Leb., 63
Zaire, 115
Zaire (Congo) (riv.), Africa, 115
Zaire (dist.), Angola, 115
Zaječar, Yugo., 45
Zákinthos, Greece, 45
Zákinthos (isl.), Greece, 45
Zakopane, Poland, 47
Zala (county), Hung., 41
Zalaegerszeg, Hung., 41
Zalamea, Spain, 33
Zalău, Rum., 45
Zalingei, Sudan, 111
Zambales (prov.), Phil., 82
Zambezi (riv.), Africa, 118
Zambézia (dist.), Mozamb., 118
Zambia, 115
Zamboanga, Phil., 82
Zamboanga del Norte (prov.), Phil., 82
Zamboanga del Sur (prov.), Phil., 82
Zambrów, Poland, 47
Zamora, Ecua., 128
Zamora, Mex., 150
Zamora (prov.), Spain, 33
Zamora, Spain, 33
Zamora-Chinchipe (prov.), Ecua., 128
Zamość, Poland, 47
Zanaga, Congo, 115
Zandvoort, Neth., 27
Zanesville, Ohio, 284
Zante (Zákinthos) (isl.), Greece, 45
Zanzibar (reg's), Tanz., 115
Zanzibar, Tanz., 115
Zanzibar (isl.), Tanz., 115
Zao (mt.), Japan, 81
Zaouiet-el-Kahla, Alg., 106
Západočeský (reg.), Czech., 41
Západoslovenský (reg.), Czech., 41
Zapala, Arg., 143
Zapaleri, Cerro (mt.), S. Amer., 136
Zapata (pen.), Cuba, 158
Zapatera (isl.), Nic., 154
Zapatoca, Col., 126
Zaporozh'ye, U.S.S.R., 52
Zara, Turkey, 63
Zara (Zadar), Yugo., 45
Zaragoza, Mex., 150
Zaragoza (Saragossa), Spain, 33
Zarand, Iran, 66
Zárate, Arg., 143
Zaraza, Venez., 124
Zaria, Nigeria, 106
Zarqa' (riv.), Jordan, 65
Zaruma, Ecua., 128
Żary, Poland, 47
Zarzal, Col., 126
Zarzis, Tun., 106
Zaskar (mts.), India, 68
Žatec, Czech., 41
Zavitinsk, U.S.S.R., 48
Zawia (prov.), Libya, 111
Zawia, Libya, 111
Zawiercie, Poland, 47
Zaysan (lake), U.S.S.R., 48
Zaza del Medio, Cuba, 158
Zduńska Wola, Poland, 47
Zebak, Afghan., 68
Zebdani, Syria, 63
Zeehan, Tas., 99
Zeeland, Mich., 250
Zeeland (prov.), Neth., 27
Zeerust, S. Africa, 118
Zefat, Israel, 65
Zegharta, Leb., 63
Zehdenick, E. Ger., 22
Zeila, Somalia, 115
Zeist, Neth., 27
Zeitz, E. Ger., 22
Zele, Belg., 27
Zelenodol'sk, U.S.S.R., 52
Zelienople, Pa., 294
Zell, Austria, 41
Zella, Libya, 111
Zella-Mehlis, E. Ger., 22
Zellersee (lake), Switz., 39
Zelten, Jebel (mts.), Libya, 111
Zelzate, Belg., 27
Zémio, Centr. Afr. Rep., 115
Zenica, Yugo., 45
Zenjan (gov.), Iran, 66
Zenjan, Iran, 66
Zephyrhills, Fla., 212
Zerbst, E. Ger., 22
Zermatt, Switz., 39
Zetland (county), Scot., 15
Zeulenroda, E. Ger., 22
Zeytinburnu, Turkey, 63
Zgierz, Poland, 47
Zgorzelec, Poland, 47
Zhdanov, U.S.S.R., 52
Zhelaniye (cape), U.S.S.R., 48
Zhigulevsk, U.S.S.R., 52
Zhitomir, U.S.S.R., 52
Zhmerinka, U.S.S.R., 52
Zhob (riv.), Pak., 68
Zhodino, U.S.S.R., 52
Ziębice, Poland, 47
Zielona Góra (prov.), Poland, 47
Zielona Góra, Poland, 47
Zifta, Egypt, 111
Ziguei, Chad, 111
Ziguinchor, Sen., 106
Zile, Turkey, 63
Žilina, Czech., 41
Zilling Tso (lake), China, 77
Zima, U.S.S.R., 48
Zimatlán de Álvarez, Mex., 150
Zimbabwe Nat'l Park, Rhod., 118
Zimnicea, Rum., 45
Zinder, Niger, 106
Zinjibar, P.D.R. Yemen, 59
Zion, Ill., 222
Zion Nat'l Park, Utah, 304
Zipaquirá, Col., 126
Zirko (isl.), U.A.E., 59
Zirndorf, W. Ger., 22
Zitácuaro, Mex., 150
Zittau, E. Ger., 22
Zivarık, Turkey, 63
Ziz, Wadi (dry riv.), Mor., 106
Zlatoust, U.S.S.R., 48
Zlín (Gottwaldov), Czech., 41
Zliten, Libya, 111
Znamenka, U.S.S.R., 52
Znojmo, Czech., 41
Zollikofen, Switz., 39
Zolotonosha, U.S.S.R., 52
Zomba, Malawi, 115
Zonderend (riv.), S. Africa, 118
Zonguldak (prov.), Turkey, 63
Zonguldak, Turkey, 63
Zonhoven, Belg., 27
Zouar, Chad, 111
Zrenjanin, Yugo., 45
Zuarungu, Ghana, 106
Zudáñez, Bol., 136
Zug (canton), Switz., 39
Zug, Switz., 39
Zug (lake), Switz., 39
Zugdidi, U.S.S.R., 52
Zugspitze (mt.), Europe, 22
Zula, Eth., 111
Zulia (state), Venez., 124
Zulueta, Cuba, 158
Zululand (reg.), S. Africa, 118
Zumbo, Mozamb., 118
Zumpango, Mex., 150
Zuni, N. Mex., 274
Zuni (riv.), U.S., 198, 274
Zürich (canton), Switz., 39
Zürich, Switz., 39
Zürich (lake), Switz., 39
Zutphen, Neth., 27
Zvolen, Czech., 41
Zwara, Libya, 111
Zweibrücken, W. Ger., 22
Zweisimmen, Switz., 39
Zwickau, E. Ger., 22
Zwijndrecht, Neth., 27
Zwischenahn, W. Ger., 22
Zwolle, Neth., 27
Żyrardów, Poland, 47
Żywiec, Poland, 47

GEOGRAPHICAL TERMS

A. = Arabic Camb. = Cambodian Ch. = Chinese Czech. = Czechoslovakian Dan. = Danish Du. = Dutch Finn. = Finnish Fr. = French Ger. = German Ice. = Icelandic It. = Italian Jap. = Japanese Mong. = Mongol Nor. = Norwegian Per. = Persian Port. = Portuguese Russ. = Russian Sp. = Spanish Sw. = Swedish Turk. = Turkish

Å	Nor., Sw.	Stream
Aas	Dan., Nor.	Hills
Abajo	Sp.	Lower
Ada, Adasi	Turk.	Island
Altipiano	It.	Plateau
Altiplano	Sp.	Plateau
Alv, Alf, Elf	Sw.	River
Arrecife	Sp.	Reef
Asa	Nor., Sw.	Hill
Asaga	Turk.	Lower
Austral	Sp.	Southern
Baai	Du.	Bay
Bab	Arabic	Gate or Strait
Bahia	Sp.	Bay
Bahr	Arabic	Marsh, Lake, Sea, River
Baia	Port.	Bay
Baie	Fr.	Bay, Gulf
Baizo	Port.	Low
Bakke	Dan.	Hill
Bana	Jap.	Cape
Bañados	Sp.	Marshes
Band	Per.	Mt. Range
Barra	Sp.	Reef
Bel	Turk.	Pass
Belt	Ger.	Strait
Ben	Gaelic	Mountain
Bera	Du.	Mountain
Berg	Ger., Du.	Mountain
Bir	Arabic	Well
Birket	Arabic	Pond
Boca	Sp.	Gulf, Inlet
Boğhaz	Turk.	Strait
Bolshoi, Bolshaya	Russ.	Big
Bolson	Sp.	Depression
Bong	Korean	Mountain
Boreal	Sp.	Northern
Breen	Nor.	Glacier
Bro	Dan., Nor., Sw.	Bridge
Bucht	Ger.	Bay
Bugt	Dan.	Bay
Bukhta	Russ.	Bay
Bukit	Malay	Hill, Mountain
Bukt	Nor., Sw.	Bay, Gulf
Burnu, Burun	Turk.	Cape, Point
By	Dan., Nor., Sw.	Town
Cabo	Port., Sp.	Cape
Campos	Port.	Plains
Canal	Port., Sp.	Channel
Cap, Capo	Fr., It.	Cape
Cataratas	Sp.	Falls
Catena	It.	Mt. Range
Catingas	Port.	Open Woodlands
Central, Centrale	Fr., It.	Middle
Cerrito, Cerro	Sp.	Hill
Cerros	Sp.	Hills, Mountains
Chai	Turk.	River
Chow	Ch.	Town of the second rank
Ciénaga	Sp.	Swamp
Ciudad	Sp.	City
Col	Fr.	Pass
Cordillera	Sp.	Mt. Range, Mts.
Côte	Fr.	Coast
Csatoria	Magyar	Canal
Cuchilla	Sp.	Mt. Range
Curiche	Sp.	Swamp
Dag, Dagh	Turk.	Mountain
Dağlari	Turk.	Mt. Range
Dal	Nor., Sw.	Valley
Dar	Arabic	Land
Darya	Per.	Salt Lake
Dasht	Per.	Desert, Plain
Deniz, Denizi	Turk.	Sea, Lake
Desierto	Sp.	Desert
Détroit	Fr.	Strait
Djeziret	Arabic, Turk.	Island
Do	Korean	Island
Doi	Thai	Mountain
Eiland	Du.	Island
Elv	Dan., Nor.	River
Embalse	Sp.	Reservoir
Emi	Berber	Mountain
Erg	Arabic	Dune, Desert
Eski	Turk.	Old
Est, Este	Fr., Port., Sp.	East
Estero	Sp.	Estuary, Creek
Estrecho, Estreito	Sp., Port.	Strait
Etang	Fr.	Pond, Lagoon, Lake
Fedja, Feij	Arabic	Pass
Fiume	It.	River
Fjäll	Sw.	Mountain
Fjeld, Fjell	Nor.	Hills, Mountain
Fjord	Dan., Nor., Sw.	Fiord
Fleuve	Fr.	River
Fljót	Icelandic	Stream
Fluss	Ger.	River
Fokani, Fukani	Arabic	Upper
Fors	Sw.	Waterfall
Fos, Foss	Dan., Nor.	Waterfall
Fu	Ch.	Town of importance
Gamla	Nor.	Old
Gamle	Dan.	Old
Gata	Jap.	Lake
Gawa	Jap.	River
Gebel	Arabic	Mountain
Gebergte	Du.	Mt. Range
Gebirge	Ger.	Mt. Range
Ghubbet	Arabic	Bay
Gobi	Mongol	Desert
Goe	Jap.	Pass
Gol	Mongol, Turk.	Lake, Stream
Golf	Ger., Du.	Gulf
Golfe	Fr.	Gulf
Golfo	Sp., It., Port.	Gulf
Gölü	Turk.	Lake
Gora	Russ.	Mountain
Grand, Grande	Fr., Sp.	Big
Groot	Du.	Big
Gross	Ger.	Big
Grosso	It., Port.	Big
Guba	Russ.	Bay, Gulf
Gunto	Jap.	Archipelago
Gunung	Malay	Mountain
Hai	Ch.	Sea
Halbinsel	Ger.	Peninsula
Hamáda, Hammada	Arabic	Rocky Plateau
Hamn	Sw.	Harbor
Hamún	Per.	Marsh
Hanto	Jap.	Peninsula
Has, Hassi	Arabic	Well
Hav	Dan., Nor., Sw.	Sea, Ocean
Havet	Nor.	Bay
Havn	Dan., Nor.	Harbor
Havre	Fr.	Harbor
Higashi, Higasi	Jap.	East
Ho	Ch.	River
Hochebene	Ger.	Plateau
Hoek	Du.	Cape
Hoku	Jap.	North
Holm	Dan., Nor., Sw.	Island
Hory	Czech.	Mountains
Hoved	Dan., Nor.	Cape, Promontory
Hsien	Ch.	Town of the third class
Hu	Ch.	Lake
Huk	Dan., Nor., Sw.	Point
Hus, Huus	Dan., Nor., Sw.	House
Hwang	Ch.	Yellow
Ile	Fr.	Island
Ilet	Fr.	Islet
Ilot	Fr.	Islet
Indre	Dan., Nor.	Inner
Inferieur, Inferiore	Fr., It.	Lower
Inner, Inre	Sw.	Inner
Insel	Ger.	Island
Irmak	Turk.	River
Isla	Sp.	Island
Isola	It.	Island
Jabal, Jebel	Arabic	Mountains
Järvi	Finn.	Lake
Jaure	Sw.	Lake
Jezira	Arabic	Island
Jima	Jap.	Island
Joki	Finn.	River
Kaap	Du.	Cape
Kabir, Kebir	Arabic	Big
Kai	Jap.	Sea
Kaikyo	Jap.	Strait
Kami	Turk.	Upper
Kanaal	Du.	Canal
Kanal	Russ., Ger.	Canal, Channel
Kao	Thai	Mountain
Kap, Kapp	Nor., Sw., Ice.	Cape
Kaupunki	Finn.	Town
Kawa	Jap.	River
Khao	Thai	Mountain
Khrebet	Russ.	Mt. Range
Kiang	Ch.	River
Kiao	Ch.	Point
Kita	Jap.	North
Klein	Du., Ger.	Small
Klint	Dan.	Promontory
Kô	Jap.	Lake
Ko	Thai	Island
Koh	Camb., Khmer	Island
Kong	Ch.	River
Kop	Du.	Peak, Head
Köping	Sw.	Market, Borough
Körfez, Körfezi	Turk.	Gulf
Kosa	Russ.	Spit
Kosui	Jap.	Lake
Kraal	Du.	Native Village
Kuchuk	Turk.	Small
Kuh	Per.	Mountain
Kul	Sinkiang Turki	Lake
Kum	Turk.	Desert
Kuro	Jap.	Black
Laag	Du.	Low
Lac	Fr.	Lake
Lago	Port., Sp., It.	Lake
Lagoa	Port.	Lagoon
Laguna	Sp.	Lagoon
Lagune	Fr.	Lagoon
Lahti	Finn.	Bay, Bight
Län	Sw.	County
Lilla	Sw.	Small
Lille	Dan., Nor.	Small
Ling	Ch.	Mountain
Llanos	Sp.	Plains
Mae Nam	Thai	River
Mali, Malaya	Russ.	Small
Man	Korean	Bay
Mar	Sp., Port.	Sea
Mare	It.	Sea
Medio	Sp.	Middle
Meer	Du.	Lake
Meer	Ger.	Sea
Mer	Fr.	Sea
Meridionale	It.	Southern
Meseta	Sp.	Plateau
Middelst, Midden	Du.	Middle
Minami	Jap.	Southern
Mir	Per.	Mountain
Mis	Russ.	Cape
Misaki	Jap.	Cape
Mittel	Ger.	Middle
Mont	Fr.	Mountain
Montagne	Fr.	Mountain
Montaña	Sp.	Mountains
Monte	Sp., It., Port.	Mountain
More	Russ.	Sea
Morro	Port., Sp.	Mountain, Promontory
Morue	Fr.	Hill
Moyen	Fr.	Middle
Muong	Siamese	Town
Mys	Russ.	Cape
Nada	Jap.	Sea
Naka	Jap.	Middle
Nam	Burm., Lao	River
Nan	Ch., Jap.	South
Nes	Nor.	Cape, Point
Nevado	Sp.	Snow covered peak
Nieder	Ger.	Lower
Nishi, Nisi	Jap.	West
Nizhni, Nizhnyaya	Russ.	Lower
Njarga	Finn.	Peninsula, Promontory
Nong	Thai	Lake
Noord	Du.	North
Nor	Mong.	Lake
Nord	Fr., Ger.	North
Norte	Sp., It., Port.	North
Nos	Russ.	Cape
Novi, Novaya	Russ.	New
Nusa	Malay	Island
Ny, Nya	Nor., Sw.	New
O	Jap.	Big
Ö	Nor., Sw.	Island
Ober	Ger.	Upper
Occidental, Occidentale	Sp., It.	Western
Odde	Dan.	Point
Oeste	Port.	West
Ola	Mong.	Mountains
Ooster	Du.	Eastern
Opper, Over	Du.	Upper
Oriental	Sp., Fr.	Eastern
Orientale	It.	Eastern
Orta	Turk.	Middle
Ost	Ger.	East
Ostrov	Russ.	Island
Ouest	Fr.	West
öy	Nor.	Island
Ozero	Russ.	Lake
Pampa	Sp.	Plain
Pas	Fr.	Channel, Strait
Paso	Sp.	Pass
Passo	It., Port.	Pass
Peh, Pei	Ch.	North
Peña	Sp.	Rock, Mountain
Penisola	It.	Peninsula
Pequeño	Sp.	Small
Pereval	Russ.	Pass
Peski	Russ.	Desert
Petit	Fr.	Small
Phu	Lao, Annamese	Mtn.
Pic	Fr.	Mountain
Piccolo	It.	Small
Pico	Port., Sp.	Mountain, Peak
Pik	Russ.	Mountain, Peak
Piton	Fr.	Mountain, Peak
Planalto	Port.	Plateau
Plato	Russ.	Plateau
Pointe	Fr.	Point
Poluostrov	Russ.	Peninsula
Ponta	Port.	Point
Presa	Sp.	Reservoir
Presqu'île	Fr.	Peninsula
Proliv	Russ.	Strait
Pulou, Pulo	Malay	Island
Punt	Du.	Point
Punta	Sp., It., Port.	Point
Qum	Turk.	Desert
Rada	Sp.	Inlet
Rade	Fr.	Bay, Inlet
Ras	Arabic	Cape
Reka	Russ.	River
Retto	Jap.	Archipelago
Ria	Sp.	Estuary
Río	Sp.	River
Rivier, Rivière	Du., Fr.	River
Rud	Per.	River
Saghir	Arabic	Small
Sai	Jap.	West
Saki	Jap.	Cape
Salar, Salina	Sp.	Salt Deposit
Salto	Sp., Port.	Falls
San	Ch., Jap., Korean	Hill
Sanmaek	Korean	Mt. Range
Schiereiland	Du.	Peninsula
Se	Camb., Khmer	River
See	Ger.	Sea, Lake
Selvas	Sp., Port.	Woods, Forest
Seno	Sp.	Bay, Gulf
Serra	Port.	Mts.
Serranía	Sp.	Mts.
Seto	Jap.	Strait
Settentrionale	It.	Northern
Severni, Severnaya	Russ.	North
Shan	Ch., Jap.	Hill, Mts.
Shang	Ch.	Upper
Shatt	Arabic	River
Shima	Jap.	Island
Shimo	Jap.	Lower
Shin	Jap.	Land
Shiro	Jap.	White
Shoto	Jap.	Islands
Si	Ch.	West
Siao	Ch.	Small
Sierra	Sp.	Mt. Range, Mts.
Sjö	Nor., Sw.	Lake, Sea
Sok, Suk, Souk	Arabic, Ar. Fr.	Market
Song	Annamese	River
Sopka	Russ.	Volcano
Spitze	Ger.	Mt. Peak
Sredni, Srednyaya	Russ.	Middle
Stad	Dan., Nor., Sw.	City
Stari, Staraya	Russ.	Old
Step	Russ.	Treeless Plain
Straat	Du.	Strait
Strasse	Ger.	Strait
Stretto	It.	Strait
Ström	Dan., Nor., Sw.	Sound
Stung	Camb., Khmer	River
Su	Turk.	River
Sud, Süd	Sp., Fr., Ger.	South
Suido	Jap.	Strait, Channel
Sul	Port.	South
Sund	Dan., Nor., Sw.	Sound
Sungei	Malay	River
Supérieur	Fr.	Upper
Superior, Superiore	Sp., It.	Upper
Sur	Sp.	South
Suyu	Turk.	River
Ta	Ch.	Big
Tafelland	Du.	Plateau
Tagh	Turk.	Mt. Range
Take	Jap.	Peak, Ridge
Takht	Arabic	Lower
Tal	Ger.	Valley
Tandjong, Tanjung	Malay	Cape, Point
Tao	Ch.	Island
Tell	Arabic	Hill
Thale	Thai	Sea, Lake
Tind	Nor.	Peak
Tö	Jap.	East
To	Jap.	Island
Toge	Jap.	Pass
Trask	Finn.	Lake
Tso	Tibetan	Lake
Tugh	Somali	Dry River
Tung	Ch.	Eastern
Udjung	Malay	Point
Umi	Jap.	Bay
Unter	Ger.	Lower
Ura	Jap.	Inlet
Val	Fr.	Valley
Vatn	Nor.	Lake
Vecchio	It.	Old
Veld	Du.	Plain, Field
Velho	Port.	Old
Verkhni	Russ.	Upper
Vesi	Finn.	Lake
Vieho	Sp.	Old
Vik	Nor., Sw.	Bay
Vishni, Vishnyaya	Russ.	High
Vodokhranilishche	Russ.	Reservoir
Volcán	Sp.	Volcano
Vostochni, Vostochnaya	Russ.	East, Eastern
Wadi	Arabic	Dry River
Wald	Ger.	Forest
Wan	Jap.	Bay
Westersch	Du.	Western
Wüste	Ger.	Desert
Yama	Jap.	Mountain
Yarim Ada	Turk.	Peninsula
Yokara	Turk.	Upper
Yug, Yuzhni, Yuzhnaya	Russ.	South, Southern
Zaki	Jap.	Cape
Zaliv	Russ.	Bay, Gulf
Zapadni, Zapadnaya	Russ.	Western
Zee	Du.	Sea
Zemlya	Russ.	Land
Zuid	Du.	South

Between Principal Cities in the United States

FROM/TO	Albuquerque, N. Mex.	Atlanta, Ga.	Baltimore, Md.	Boise, Idaho	Boston, Mass.	Brownsville, Tex.	Buffalo, N. Y.	Chicago, Ill.	Cincinnati, Ohio	Cleveland, Ohio	Denver, Colo.	Des Moines, Iowa	Detroit, Mich.	El Paso, Tex.	Fargo, N. Dak.	Fort Worth, Tex.	Galveston, Tex.	Hastings, Nebr.	Hot Springs, Ark.	Houghton, Mich.	Jacksonville, Fla.	Kansas City, Mo.	Los Angeles, Calif.	Louisville, Ky.	Memphis, Tenn.	Miami, Fla.	Minneapolis, Minn.	Missoula, Mont.	Nashville, Tenn.	New Orleans, La.	New York, N. Y.	Norfolk, Va.	Oklahoma, Okla.	Omaha, Nebr.	Philadelphia, Pa.	Phoenix, Ariz.	Pittsburgh, Pa.
Albuquerque, N. Mex.	....	1273	1670	774	1967	838	1577	1126	1248	1417	332	833	1360	228	968	561	803	588	773	1252	1492	717	663	1174	938	1710	980	895	1117	1030	1810	1696	518	718	1748	330	1498
Atlanta, Ga	1273	....	575	1830	933	960	695	583	368	550	1208	738	595	1293	1112	750	688	901	498	947	286	675	1935	317	335	610	905	1790	218	427	747	507	753	815	663	1592	520
Baltimore, Md	1670	575	....	2055	358	1525	273	603	423	305	1505	913	398	1750	1143	1239	1245	1154	964	808	682	962	2313	498	792	958	948	1947	597	1001	170	167	1173	1026	90	2002	194
Boise, Idaho	774	1830	2055	....	2266	1610	1872	1453	1663	1754	637	1155	1671	969	975	1263	1538	934	1384	1367	2098	1158	663	1623	1506	2368	1140	252	1631	1713	2153	2137	1138	1044	2113	733	1863
Boston, Mass	1967	933	358	2266	....	1881	398	849	737	550	1766	1159	613	2067	1304	1574	1598	1415	1302	922	1015	1250	2590	823	1133	1258	1125	2124	941	1359	188	467	1490	1280	268	2295	478
Brownsville, Tex	838	960	1525	1610	1881	....	1575	1234	1184	1402	1047	1102	1398	682	1445	471	287	1013	650	1543	1025	923	1370	1093	777	1100	1335	1706	952	536	1695	1465	659	1061	1614	1023	1424
Buffalo, N. Y	1577	695	273	1872	398	1575	....	454	392	175	1368	762	218	1690	923	1221	1289	1019	956	560	880	862	2195	483	802	1184	733	1740	626	1087	291	435	1117	883	278	1904	178
Chicago, Ill	1126	583	603	1453	849	1234	454	....	249	307	918	310	236	1249	571	820	954	566	585	367	861	413	1741	268	481	1190	356	1348	394	831	711	696	689	432	664	1451	411
Cincinnati, Ohio	1248	368	423	1663	737	1184	392	249	....	218	1090	509	234	1333	818	839	897	742	569	589	628	541	1892	92	410	957	603	1578	239	708	568	474	755	620	501	1578	258
Cleveland, Ohio	1417	550	305	1754	550	1402	175	307	218	....	1223	617	94	1521	838	1046	1116	871	787	518	768	700	2044	309	627	1088	632	1640	456	922	404	429	946	738	343	1745	115
Denver, Colo	332	1208	1505	637	1766	1047	1368	918	1090	1223	....	607	1153	554	642	643	925	353	749	970	1468	555	828	1035	878	1732	699	670	1018	1079	1628	1562	503	485	1575	585	1320
Des Moines, Iowa	833	738	913	1155	1159	1102	762	310	509	617	607	....	545	980	397	640	851	256	488	458	1024	180	1433	477	485	1338	235	1074	523	825	1023	983	469	122	972	1154	718
Detroit, Mich	1360	595	398	1671	613	1398	218	236	234	94	1153	545	....	1475	745	1018	1111	800	761	427	832	643	1976	315	621	1156	542	1552	468	938	483	522	905	666	444	1685	208
El Paso, Tex	228	1293	1750	969	2067	682	1690	1249	1333	1521	554	980	1475	....	1161	543	723	757	802	1422	1481	836	702	1253	978	1662	1156	1115	1169	986	1902	1755	578	875	1834	347	1592
Fargo, N. Dak	968	1112	1143	975	1304	1445	923	571	818	838	642	397	745	1161	....	973	1218	440	875	393	1400	548	1426	818	882	1721	219	819	900	1221	1213	1258	786	390	1186	1225	952
Fort Worth, Tex	561	750	1239	1263	1574	471	1221	820	839	1046	643	640	1018	543	973	....	283	544	273	1093	943	460	1212	751	448	1150	870	1312	643	470	1398	1226	188	590	1324	858	1097
Galveston, Tex	803	688	1245	1538	1598	287	1289	954	897	1116	925	851	1111	723	1218	283	....	808	375	1277	799	677	1423	807	492	941	1087	1595	666	288	1415	1195	456	828	1336	1065	1140
Hastings, Nebr	588	901	1154	934	1415	1013	1019	566	742	871	353	256	800	757	440	544	808	....	513	666	1178	226	1177	693	591	1468	399	891	697	870	1275	1216	357	135	1222	901	967
Hot Springs, Ark	773	498	964	1384	1302	650	956	585	569	787	749	488	761	802	875	273	375	513	....	901	728	326	1437	480	176	983	722	1385	370	358	1125	955	260	490	1051	1094	825
Houghton, Mich	1252	947	808	1367	922	1543	560	367	589	518	970	458	427	1422	393	1093	1277	666	901	....	1216	633	1787	636	830	1545	272	1208	760	1187	849	946	926	547	827	1550	630
Jacksonville, Fla	1492	286	682	2098	1015	1025	880	861	628	768	1468	1024	832	1481	1400	943	799	1178	728	1216	....	952	2153	595	591	328	1192	2070	502	511	838	548	988	1098	758	1800	703
Kansas City, Mo	717	675	962	1158	1250	923	862	413	541	700	555	180	643	836	548	460	677	226	326	633	952	....	1352	480	370	1247	413	1117	472	678	1097	1009	293	165	1037	1045	784
Los Angeles, Calif	663	1935	2313	663	2590	1370	2195	1741	1892	2044	828	1433	1976	702	1426	1212	1423	1177	1437	1787	2153	1352	....	1825	1602	2355	1522	910	1777	1675	2446	2352	1182	1312	2388	357	2135
Louisville, Ky	1174	317	498	1623	823	1093	483	268	92	309	1035	477	315	1253	818	751	807	693	480	636	595	480	1825	....	319	923	605	1550	153	623	650	528	675	579	580	1512	345
Memphis, Tenn	938	335	792	1506	1133	777	802	481	410	627	878	485	621	978	882	448	492	591	176	830	591	370	1602	319	....	878	700	1483	195	358	953	778	422	529	878	1264	660
Miami, Fla	1710	610	958	2368	1258	1100	1184	1190	957	1088	1732	1338	1156	1662	1721	1150	941	1468	983	1545	328	1247	2355	923	878	....	1516	2359	821	681	1095	802	1233	1402	1023	1998	1014
Minneapolis, Minn	980	905	948	1140	1125	1335	733	356	603	632	699	235	542	1156	219	870	1087	399	722	272	1192	413	1522	605	700	1516	....	1010	695	1050	1019	1047	692	291	985	1279	745
Missoula, Mont	895	1790	1947	252	2124	1706	1740	1348	1578	1640	670	1074	1552	1115	819	1312	1595	891	1385	1208	2070	1117	910	1550	1483	2359	1010	....	1582	1733	2030	2045	1162	978	1997	932	1754
Nashville, Tenn	1117	218	597	1631	941	952	626	394	239	456	1018	523	468	1169	900	643	666	697	370	760	502	472	1777	153	195	821	695	1582	....	470	758	586	602	604	683	1445	472
New Orleans, La	1030	427	1001	1713	1359	536	1087	831	708	922	1079	825	938	986	1221	470	288	870	358	1187	511	678	1675	623	358	681	1050	1733	470	....	1173	932	575	845	1090	1318	923
New York, N. Y	1810	747	170	2153	188	1695	291	711	568	404	1628	1023	483	1902	1213	1398	1415	1275	1125	849	838	1097	2446	650	953	1095	1019	2030	758	1173	....	293	1324	1144	83	2142	313
Norfolk, Va	1696	507	167	2137	467	1465	435	696	474	429	1562	983	522	1755	1258	1226	1195	1216	955	946	548	1009	2352	528	778	802	1047	2045	586	932	293	....	1186	1095	220	2027	316
Oklahoma, Okla	518	753	1173	1138	1490	659	1117	689	755	946	503	469	905	578	786	188	456	357	260	926	988	293	1182	675	422	1233	692	1162	602	575	1324	1186	....	405	1256	843	1013
Omaha, Nebr	718	815	1026	1044	1280	1061	883	432	620	738	485	122	666	875	390	590	828	135	490	547	1098	165	1312	579	529	1402	291	978	604	845	1144	1095	405	....	1094	1032	837
Philadelphia, Pa	1748	663	90	2113	268	1614	278	664	501	343	575	972	444	1834	1186	1324	1335	1222	1051	827	758	1037	2388	580	878	1023	985	1997	683	1090	83	220	1256	1094	....	2079	254
Phoenix, Ariz	330	1592	2002	733	2295	1023	1904	1451	1578	1745	585	1154	1685	347	1225	858	1065	901	1094	1550	1800	1045	357	1512	1264	1998	1279	932	1445	1318	2142	2027	843	1032	2079	....	1829
Pittsburgh, Pa	1498	520	194	1863	478	1424	178	411	258	115	1320	718	208	1592	952	1097	1140	967	825	530	703	784	2135	345	660	1014	745	1754	472	923	313	316	1013	837	254	1829	....
Portland, Me	2015	1022	446	2282	100	1961	438	892	802	603	1803	1197	657	2126	1313	1642	1678	1454	1371	924	1113	1300	2631	892	1205	1357	1145	2133	1015	1445	277	565	1550	1318	360	2345	545
Portland, Oreg	1107	2172	2367	349	2553	1944	2167	1765	1987	2063	985	1479	1975	1286	1248	1612	1885	1271	1733	1638	2442	1397	825	1953	1852	2716	1435	430	1970	2063	2455	2458	1488	1373	2419	1007	2174
Richmond, Va	1628	470	128	2060	471	1428	375	618	399	353	1488	905	445	1695	1180	1170	1154	1142	897	870	953	937	2283	457	722	831	968	1967	526	899	287	79	1122	1020	205	1960	242
St. Louis, Mo	938	467	731	1389	1036	975	662	259	308	490	793	270	452	1033	658	568	697	455	325	591	755	238	1585	242	242	1067	464	1331	253	599	873	771	456	352	808	1270	561
Salt Lake City, Utah	483	1580	1858	292	2099	1317	1701	1260	1450	1567	372	952	1490	689	865	977	1249	708	1116	1242	1840	922	577	1400	1250	2098	988	435	1390	1433	1972	1925	862	833	1923	504	1670
San Francisco, Calif	893	2133	2451	516	2696	1675	2298	1855	2037	2163	946	1547	2087	993	1447	1454	1693	1297	1648	1833	2375	1500	345	1983	1800	2603	1585	762	1958	1923	2568	2510	1386	1425	2518	652	2264
Schenectady, N. Y	1823	840	278	2120	150	1770	249	702	605	408	1618	1012	467	1930	1157	1445	1487	1267	1175	776	960	1107	2445	695	1010	1229	975	1978	820	1259	142	426	1354	1133	205	2152	350
Seattle, Wash	1178	2180	2341	405	2508	2015	2130	1743	1974	2035	1020	1470	1945	1373	1206	1658	1938	1288	1759	1588	2450	1505	956	1945	1867	2740	1403	395	1973	2098	2419	2440	1523	1372	2388	1112	2145
Shreveport, La	764	548	1064	1433	1410	510	1080	725	688	904	799	624	891	752	1002	209	233	615	142	1043	733	326	1420	598	279	950	859	1457	470	280	1230	1037	297	617	1153	1067	939
Spokane, Wash	1028	1960	2110	290	2279	1852	1900	1514	1746	1804	827	1243	1715	1238	976	1470	1753	1061	1552	1360	2239	1286	939	1720	1652	2528	1173	170	1752	1898	2190	2211	1324	1149	2159	1020	1918
Springfield, Mass	1889	863	282	2196	79	1805	325	774	659	473	1692	1085	540	1990	1240	1495	1524	1340	1224	860	957	1173	2515	745	1055	1210	1056	2060	863	1287	120	411	1412	1205	201	2220	400
Vermillion, S. Dak	742	917	1083	973	1314	1161	916	479	694	785	468	187	705	920	284	689	938	167	605	510	1203	280	1291	663	642	1510	238	887	704	960	1189	1166	502	115	1143	1043	891
Washington, D. C	1648	542	33	2045	392	1493	290	594	403	303	1490	895	397	1726	1141	1210	1214	1139	936	813	647	943	2295	473	763	927	936	1940	567	968	204	145	1150	1012	122	1980	188

Between Principal Cities of Europe

	Amsterdam	Athens	Baku	Barcelona	Belgrade	Berlin	Brussels	Bucharest	Budapest	Cologne	Copenhagen	Istanbul	Dresden	Dublin	Frankfort	Hamburg	Leningrad	Lisbon	London	Lyon	Madrid	Marseilles	Milan	Moscow	Munich	Oslo	Paris	Riga	Rome	Sofia	Stockholm	Toulouse	Warsaw	Vienna	Zurich
Amsterdam	....	1340	2218	770	875	365	105	1100	710	128	381	1360	385	468	228	232	1090	1140	220	458	912	627	517	1325	415	568	257	820	808	1073	695	625	673	580	375
Athens	1340	....	1395	1160	500	1112	1292	460	698	1200	1320	350	1022	1765	1113	1250	1535	1770	1476	1100	1463	1025	900	1388	925	1610	1300	1310	650	335	1495	1215	990	795	1000
Baku	2218	1395	....	2427	1487	1867	2240	1220	1562	2127	1980	1070	1837	2490	2055	2020	1570	3050	2435	2238	2742	2238	2028	1175	1912	2118	2335	1590	1900	1360	1862	2425	1555	1700	2050
Barcelona	770	1160	2427	....	998	925	658	1210	924	692	1085	1380	860	919	665	910	1740	610	707	327	316	211	450	1852	648	1330	518	1440	530	1072	1410	156	1150	830	513
Belgrade	875	500	1487	998	....	618	850	295	205	750	840	502	530	1327	652	760	1165	1555	1040	752	1235	750	540	1160	475	1112	890	855	440	231	1005	930	510	300	590
Berlin	365	1112	1867	925	618	....	401	798	425	300	225	1068	95	815	268	165	815	1410	575	601	1149	730	570	995	310	520	540	520	730	810	503	815	320	322	410
Brussels	105	1292	2240	658	850	401	....	1110	700	110	475	1345	407	480	198	301	1175	998	202	352	807	521	435	1392	372	672	170	900	730	945	793	515	720	568	312
Bucharest	1100	460	1220	1210	295	798	1110	....	295	982	970	272	725	1560	890	950	1080	1842	1285	1025	1518	1020	819	920	725	1245	1152	870	700	194	1080	1210	580	520	855
Budapest	710	698	1562	924	205	425	700	295	....	590	629	650	345	1176	504	572	965	1515	900	680	1214	718	476	965	350	920	770	685	500	395	820	883	342	128	498
Cologne	128	1200	2127	692	750	300	110	982	590	....	400	1240	292	585	93	228	1090	1126	308	370	875	528	390	1285	282	635	250	805	675	945	722	875	602	460	259
Copenhagen	381	1320	1960	1085	840	225	475	970	629	400	....	1240	315	768	412	180	708	1520	590	760	1272	906	720	970	520	303	634	453	948	1010	330	962	415	538	595
Istanbul	1360	350	1070	1380	502	1068	1345	272	650	1240	1240	....	995	1830	1150	1222	1292	2005	1540	1238	1690	1205	1030	1180	975	1505	1390	1115	840	315	1340	1400	852	790	1090
Dresden	385	1022	1837	860	530	95	407	725	345	292	315	995	....	852	236	238	885	1380	592	540	1100	655	435	1200	227	620	523	585	630	730	598	762	325	235	342
Dublin	468	1765	2490	919	1327	815	480	1560	1176	585	768	1830	852	....	671	668	1440	1015	300	720	902	875	880	1728	855	786	480	1210	1175	1525	1010	761	1130	1040	768
Frankfort	228	1113	2055	665	652	268	198	890	504	93	412	1150	236	671	....	250	1075	1160	392	350	888	492	323	1240	193	675	295	780	698	860	730	560	550	370	193
Hamburg	232	1250	2020	910	760	165	301	950	572	228	180	1222	238	668	250	....	880	1301	448	580	1098	730	570	1100	378	445	459	600	810	954	502	780	462	460	432
Leningrad	1090	1535	1570	1740	1165	815	1175	1080	965	1090	708	1292	885	1440	1075	880	....	2235	1300	1420	1980	1540	1315	391	1100	670	1335	300	1440	1218	435	1635	640	975	1225
Lisbon	1140	1770	3050	610	1555	1410	998	1842	1515	1126	1520	2005	1380	1015	1160	1301	2235	....	975	850	313	810	1350	430	1208	1690	890	1940	1150	1685	1848	640	1700	1415	1058
London	220	1476	2435	707	1040	575	202	1285	900	308	590	1540	592	300	392	448	1300	975	....	455	777	620	595	1540	526	720	210	1035	890	1235	885	550	890	762	480
Lyon	458	1100	2238	327	752	601	352	1025	680	370	760	1238	540	720	350	580	1420	850	455	....	577	170	210	1560	352	1005	248	1122	462	928	1080	228	850	562	206
Madrid	912	1463	2742	316	1235	1149	807	1518	1214	875	1272	1690	1100	902	888	1098	1980	313	777	557	....	394	728	2120	910	1474	645	1670	840	1385	1598	344	1410	1110	765
Marseilles	627	1025	2238	211	750	730	521	1020	718	528	906	1205	655	875	492	730	1540	810	620	170	394	....	238	1642	445	1165	410	1238	372	895	1225	196	950	620	318
Milan	517	900	2028	450	540	570	435	819	476	390	720	1030	435	880	323	570	1315	1350	595	210	728	238	....	1408	215	1000	400	1010	295	715	1020	400	705	385	137
Moscow	1325	1388	1175	1852	1160	995	1392	920	965	1285	970	1180	1200	1728	1240	1100	391	430	1540	1560	2120	1642	1408	....	1220	1030	1538	520	1462	1100	770	1770	710	1028	1350
Munich	415	925	1912	648	475	310	372	725	350	282	520	975	227	855	193	378	1100	1208	526	352	910	445	215	1220	....	810	425	800	430	672	811	570	500	222	158
Oslo	568	1610	2118	1330	1112	520	672	1245	920	635	303	1505	620	786	675	445	670	1690	720	1005	1474	1165	1000	1030	810	....	830	531	1242	1295	267	1140	653	835	869
Paris	257	1300	2335	518	890	540	170	1152	770	250	634	1390	523	480	295	459	1335	890	210	248	645	410	400	1538	425	830	....	1050	690	1080	950	431	845	770	295
Riga	820	1310	1590	1440	855	520	900	870	685	805	453	1115	585	1210	780	600	300	1940	1035	1122	1670	1238	1010	520	800	531	1050	....	1155	985	276	1335	350	685	930
Rome	808	650	1900	530	440	730	730	700	500	675	948	840	630	1175	698	810	1440	1150	890	462	840	372	295	1462	430	1242	690	1155	....	545	1220	569	810	470	421
Sofia	1073	335	1360	1072	231	810	945	194	395	945	1010	315	730	1525	860	954	1218	1685	1235	928	1385	895	715	1100	672	1295	1080	985	545	....	1170	1080	662	500	780
Stockholm	695	1495	1862	1410	1005	503	793	1080	820	722	330	1340	598	1010	730	502	435	1848	885	1080	1598	1225	1020	770	811	267	950	276	1220	1170	....	1281	500	770	908
Toulouse	625	1215	2425	156	930	815	515	1210	883	875	962	1400	762	761	560	780	1635	640	550	228	344	196	400	1770	570	1140	431	1335	569	1080	1281	....	1062	725	425
Warsaw	673	990	1555	1150	510	320	720	580	342	602	415	852	325	1130	550	462	640	1700	890	850	1410	950	705	710	500	653	845	350	810	662	500	1062	....	345	640
Vienna	580	795	1700	830	300	322	568	520	128	460	538	790	235	1040	370	460	975	1415	762	562	1110	620	385	1028	222	835	770	685	470	500	770	725	345	....	365
Zurich	375	1000	2050	513	590	410	312	855	498	259	595	1090	342	768	193	432	1225	1058	480	206	765	318	137	1350	158	869	295	930	421	780	908	425	640	365	....

Richmond, Va.	St. Louis, Mo.	Salt Lake City, Utah	San Francisco, Calif.	Schenectady, N. Y.	Seattle, Wash.	Shreveport, La.	Spokane, Wash.	Springfield, Mass.	Vermillion, S. Dak.	Washington, D.
1628	938	483	893	1823	1178	764	1028	1889	742	1648
470	467	1580	2133	840	2180	548	1960	863	917	542
128	731	1858	2451	278	2341	1064	2110	282	1083	33
2060	1389	292	516	2120	405	1433	290	2196	973	2045
471	1036	2099	2696	150	2508	1410	2279	79	1314	392
1428	975	1317	1675	1770	2015	510	1852	1805	1161	1493
375	662	1701	2298	249	2130	1080	1900	325	916	290
618	259	1260	1855	702	1743	725	1514	774	479	594
399	308	1450	2037	605	1974	688	1746	659	694	403
353	490	1567	2163	408	2035	904	1804	478	785	303
1488	793	372	946	1618	1020	799	827	1692	468	1490
905	270	952	1547	1012	1470	624	1243	1085	187	895
445	452	1490	2087	467	1945	891	1715	540	705	397
1695	1033	689	993	1930	1373	752	1238	1990	920	1726
1180	658	865	1447	1157	1206	1002	976	1240	284	1141
1170	568	977	1454	1445	1658	209	1470	1495	689	1210
1154	697	1249	1693	1487	1938	233	1753	1524	938	1214
1142	455	708	1297	1267	1288	615	1061	1340	167	1139
897	325	1116	1648	1175	1759	142	1552	1224	605	936
870	591	1242	1833	776	1588	1043	1360	860	510	813
953	755	1840	2375	960	2450	733	2239	957	1203	647
937	238	922	1500	1107	1505	326	1286	1173	280	943
2283	1585	577	345	2445	956	1420	939	2515	1291	2295
457	242	1400	1983	695	1945	598	1720	745	663	473
722	242	1250	1800	1010	1867	279	1652	1055	642	763
831	1067	2098	2603	1229	2740	950	2528	1210	1510	927
968	464	988	1585	975	1403	859	1173	1056	238	936
1967	1331	435	762	1978	395	1457	170	2060	887	1940
526	253	1390	1958	820	1973	470	1752	863	704	567
899	599	1433	1923	1259	2098	280	1898	1287	960	968
287	873	1972	2568	142	2419	1230	2190	120	1189	204
79	771	1925	2510	426	2440	1037	2211	411	1166	145
1122	456	862	1386	1354	1523	297	1324	1412	502	1150
1020	352	833	1425	1133	1372	617	1149	1205	115	1012
205	808	1923	2518	205	2388	1153	2159	201	1143	122
1960	1270	504	652	2152	1112	1067	1020	2220	1043	1980
242	561	1670	2264	350	2145	939	1918	400	891	188
565	1094	2127	2725	197	2513	1484	2285	159	1345	480
2381	1723	636	536	2405	143	1783	295	2488	1293	2360
....	699	1850	2436	406	2362	985	2133	407	1089	96
699	....	1158	1738	898	1722	466	1500	958	450	710
1850	1158	....	592	1950	697	1155	548	2027	785	1845
2436	1738	592	....	2548	680	1655	730	2625	1383	2437
406	898	1950	2548	....	2363	1290	2139	86	1165	313
2362	1722	697	680	2363	....	1820	229	2445	1282	2335
985	466	1155	1655	1290	1820	....	1621	1333	726	1035
2133	1500	548	730	2139	229	1621	....	2216	1055	2105
407	958	2027	2625	86	2445	1333	2216	....	1242	321
1089	450	785	1383	1165	1282	726	1055	1242	....	1073
96	710	1845	2437	313	2335	1035	2105	321	1073	....

New York to	Miles	San Francisco to	Miles	Seattle to	Miles	Washington to	Miles
Buenos Aires	5,295	Buenos Aires	6,487	Buenos Aires	6,956	Buenos Aires	5,205
Bogota	2,474	Bogota	3,863	Bogota	4,166	Bogota	2,344
Caracas	2,100	Caracas	3,900	Caracas	4,100	Caracas	2,040
Guatemala City	2,060	Guatemala City	2,525	Guatemala City	2,930	Guatemala City	1,835
Havana	1,302	Havana	2,600	Havana	2,805	Havana	1,110
La Paz	3,905	La Paz	5,080	La Paz	5,110	La Paz	3,780
Panama	2,211	Panama	3,349	Panama	3,680	Panama	2,020
Para	3,281	Para	5,430	Para	5,550	Para	3,270
Managua	2,100	Managua	2,860	Managua	3,240	Managua	1,920
Rio de Janeiro	4,810	Rio de Janeiro	6,655	Rio de Janeiro	6,945	Rio de Janeiro	4,710
San Jose	2,200	San Jose	3,070	San Jose	3,430	San Jose	2,030
Santiago	5,134	Santiago	5,960	Santiago	6,466	Santiago	4,965
Tampico	1,880	Tampico	1,790	Tampico	2,200	Tampico	1,665

Between Representative Cities of the United States and Latin America

Chicago to	Miles	Denver to	Miles	Los Angeles to	Miles	New Orleans to	Miles
Buenos Aires	5,598	Buenos Aires	5,935	Buenos Aires	6,148	Buenos Aires	4,902
Bogota	2,691	Bogota	3,100	Bogota	3,515	Bogota	1,996
Caracas	2,480	Caracas	3,105	Caracas	3,610	Caracas	1,990
Guatemala City	1,870	Guatemala City	1,935	Guatemala City	2,190	Guatemala City	1,050
Havana	1,315	Havana	1,760	Havana	2,320	Havana	672
La Paz	4,130	La Paz	4,445	La Paz	4,805	La Paz	3,480
Panama	2,320	Panama	2,620	Panama	3,025	Panama	1,600
Para	3,820	Para	4,580	Para	5,110	Para	3,470
Managua	2,060	Managua	2,230	Managua	2,540	Managua	1,250
Rio de Janeiro	5,320	Rio de Janeiro	5,900	Rio de Janeiro	6,330	Rio de Janeiro	4,798
San Jose	2,100	San Jose	2,420	San Jose	2,725	San Jose	1,425
Santiago	5,320	Santiago	5,495	Santiago	5,595	Santiago	4,553
Tampico	1,460	Tampico	1,240	Tampico	1,470	Tampico	720

TABLES OF AIRLINE DISTANCES

All Distances in Statute Miles

Between Principal Cities of the World

FROM/TO	Azores	Bagdad	Berlin	Bombay	Buenos Aires	Callao	Cairo	Cape Town	Chicago	Istanbul	Guam	Honolulu	Juneau	London	Los Angeles	Melbourne	Mexico City	Montreal	New Orleans	New York	Panama	Paris	Rio de Janeiro	San Francisco	Santiago	Seattle	Shanghai	Singapore	Tokyo	Wellington
Azores	....	3906	2148	5930	5385	4825	3325	5670	3305	2880	8985	7421	4715	1562	5034	12190	4584	2548	3718	2604	3918	1617	4312	5114	5718	4720	7324	8338	7370	11475
Bagdad	3906	....	2040	2022	8215	8618	785	4923	6490	1085	6380	8445	6180	2568	7695	8150	8155	5814	7212	6066	7807	2385	7012	7521	8876	6848	4468	4443	5242	9782
Berlin	2148	2040	....	3947	7411	6937	1823	5949	4458	1068	7158	7384	4638	575	5849	9992	6119	3776	5182	4026	5902	540	6246	5744	7842	5121	5323	6226	5623	11384
Bombay	5930	2022	3947	....	9380	10530	2698	5133	8144	3043	4831	8172	6992	4526	8810	6140	9818	7582	8952	7875	9832	4391	8438	8523	10127	7830	3219	2425	4247	7752
Buenos Aires	5385	8215	7411	9380	....	1982	7428	4332	5598	7638	10516	7653	7964	6919	6148	7336	4609	5619	4902	5295	3319	6891	1230	6487	731	6956	12295	9940	11601	6341
Callao	4825	8618	6937	10530	1982	....	7870	6195	3765	7666	9760	5993	5806	6376	4155	8196	2619	3954	2990	3633	1450	6455	2400	4500	1548	4964	10760	11700	9740	6696
Cairo	3325	785	1823	2698	7428	7870	....	4476	6231	780	7175	8925	6352	2218	7675	8720	7807	5502	6862	5701	7230	2020	6242	7554	8100	6915	5290	5152	6005	10360
Cape Town	5670	4923	5949	5133	4332	6195	4476	....	8551	5210	8918	11655	10382	5975	10165	6510	8620	7975	8390	7845	7090	5732	3850	10340	5080	10305	8179	6025	9234	7149
Chicago	3305	6490	4458	8144	5598	3765	6231	8551	....	5530	7510	4315	2310	4015	1741	9837	1690	750	827	727	2320	4219	5320	1875	5325	1753	7155	9475	6410	8465
Istanbul	2880	1085	1068	3043	7638	7666	780	5210	5530	....	7015	8200	5665	1540	6895	9189	7160	4825	6220	5060	6797	1390	6420	6770	8230	6124	5084	5440	5649	10790
Guam	8985	6380	7158	4831	10516	9760	7175	8918	7510	7015	....	3896	5225	7605	6255	3497	7690	7840	7895	8115	9220	7675	11710	5952	9946	5785	1945	2990	1596	4206
Honolulu	7421	8445	7384	8172	7653	5993	8925	11655	4315	8200	3896	....	2825	7320	2620	5581	3846	4992	4305	5051	5347	7525	8400	2407	6935	2707	5009	6874	3940	4676
Juneau	4715	6180	4638	6992	7964	5806	6352	10382	2310	5665	5225	2825	....	4496	1835	8162	3210	2647	2860	2874	4456	4700	7611	1530	7320	870	4968	7375	4117	7501
London	1562	2568	575	4526	6919	6376	2218	5975	4015	1540	7605	7320	4496	....	5496	10590	5605	3370	4656	3500	5310	210	5747	5440	7275	4850	5841	6818	6050	11790
Los Angeles	5034	7695	5849	8810	6148	4155	7675	10165	1741	6895	6255	2620	1835	5496	....	8098	1445	2468	1695	2466	3025	5711	6330	345	5595	961	6598	8955	5600	6806
Melbourne	12190	8150	9992	6140	7336	8196	8720	6510	9837	9189	3497	5581	8162	10590	8098	....	8599	10553	9455	10541	9211	10500	8340	7970	7130	8330	4967	3768	5172	1655
Mexico City	4584	8155	6119	9818	4609	2619	7807	8620	1690	7160	7690	3846	3210	5605	1445	8599	....	2247	940	2110	1532	5800	4810	1870	4122	2339	8120	10495	7190	7003
Montreal	2548	5814	3776	7582	5619	3954	5502	7975	750	4825	7840	4992	2647	3370	2468	10553	2247	....	1390	340	2545	3490	5110	2557	5461	2309	7141	9280	6546	9206
New Orleans	3718	7212	5182	8952	4902	2990	6862	8390	827	6220	7895	4305	2860	4656	1695	9455	940	1390	....	1161	1600	4846	4798	1960	4553	2137	7830	10255	6993	7950
New York	2604	6066	4026	7875	5295	3633	5701	7845	727	5060	8115	5051	2874	3500	2466	10541	2110	340	1161	....	2211	3600	4810	2606	5134	2440	7460	9617	6846	9067
Panama	3918	7807	5902	9832	3319	1450	7230	7090	2320	6797	9220	5347	4456	5310	3025	9211	1532	2545	1600	2211	....	5440	3311	3349	3000	3680	9430	11800	8560	7580
Paris	1617	2385	540	4391	6891	6455	2020	5762	4219	1390	7675	7525	4700	210	5711	10500	5800	3490	4846	3600	5440	....	5710	5680	7300	5080	5855	6730	6132	11865
Rio de Janeiro	4312	7012	6246	8438	1230	2400	6242	3850	5320	6420	11710	8400	7611	5747	6330	8340	4810	5110	4798	4810	3311	5710	....	6655	1852	6945	11510	9875	11600	7510
San Francisco	5114	7521	5744	8523	6487	4500	7554	10340	1875	6770	5952	2407	1530	5440	345	7970	1870	2557	1960	2606	3349	5680	6655	....	5960	692	6245	8440	5250	6800
Santiago	5718	8876	7842	10127	731	1548	8100	5080	5325	8230	9946	6935	7320	7275	5595	7130	4122	5461	4553	5134	3000	7300	1852	5960	....	6466	11850	10270	10850	5925
Seattle	4720	6848	5121	7830	6956	4964	6915	10305	1753	6124	5785	2707	870	4850	961	8330	2339	2309	2137	2440	3680	5080	6945	692	6466	....	5780	8200	4863	7310
Shanghai	7324	4468	5323	3219	12295	10760	5290	8179	7155	5084	1945	5009	4968	5841	6598	4967	8120	7141	7830	7460	9430	5855	11510	6245	11850	5780	....	2395	1095	6080
Singapore	8338	4443	6226	2425	9940	11700	5152	6025	9475	5440	2990	6874	7375	6818	8955	3768	10495	9280	10255	9617	11800	6730	9875	8440	10270	8200	2395	....	3350	5360
Tokyo	7370	5242	5623	4247	11601	9740	6005	9234	6410	5649	1596	3940	4117	6050	5600	5172	7190	6546	6993	6846	8560	6132	11600	5250	10850	4863	1095	3350	....	5730
Wellington	11475	9782	11384	7752	6341	6696	10360	7149	8465	10790	4206	4676	7501	11790	6806	1655	7003	9206	7950	9067	7580	11865	7510	6800	5925	7310	6080	5360	5730	......

WORLD STATISTICAL TABLES

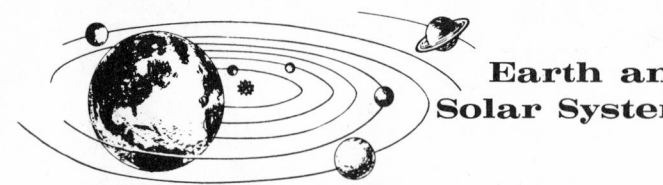

Earth and Solar System

Elements of the Solar System

	Mean Distance From Sun in Miles	Period of Revolution Around Sun	Period of Rotation on Axis	Equatorial Diameter in Miles	Surface Gravity (Earth=1)	Mean Density (Water=1)	Number of Satellites
SUN	....	....	25.4 days	864,000	27.95	1.4	....
MERCURY	36,001,000	87.97 days	59 days (?)	3,100	0.38	5.3	0
VENUS	67,272,000	224.70 days	247 days (?)	7,700	0.88	4.9	0
EARTH	93,003,000	365.26 days	23h 56m	7,927	1.00	5.5	1
MARS	141,708,000	687 days	24h 37m	4,200	0.39	4.0	2
JUPITER	483,880,000	11.86 years	9h 50m	88,698	2.65	1.3	12
SATURN	887,141,000	29.46 years	10h 14m	75,060	1.17	0.7	10
URANUS	1,782,000,000	84.02 years	10h 45m	29,200	1.05	1.3	5
NEPTUNE	2,792,000,000	164.79 years	15h 48m	27,700	1.23	1.6	2
PLUTO	3,664,000,000	247.7 years	6.4 days (?)	8,700 (?)	0.7 (?)	?	0

Dimensions of the Earth

Superficial area	197,272,000	sq. miles
Land surface	57,491,000	" "
North America	9,363,000	" "
South America	6,875,000	" "
Europe	4,063,000	" "
Asia	17,032,000	" "
Africa	11,682,000	" "
Australia	2,967,741	" "
Water surface	139,781,000	" "
Atlantic Ocean	31,862,000	" "
Pacific Ocean	64,186,000	" "
Indian Ocean	28,350,000	" "
Arctic Ocean	3,662,000	" "
Equatorial circumference	24,902	miles
Meridional circumference	24,860	"
Equatorial diameter	7,926.677	"
Polar diameter	7,899.988	"
Equatorial radius	3,963.34	"
Polar radius	3,949.99	"
Volume of the Earth	260,000,000,000	cubic miles
Mass, or weight	6,592,000,000,000,000,000,000	tons
Mean distance from the Sun	93,003,000	miles

The Moon is the Earth's natural satellite. The mean distance which separates the Earth from the Moon is 238,857 miles. The Moon's true period of revolution (sidereal month) is 27⅓ days. The Moon rotates on its own axis once during this time. The phase period or time between new moons (synodic month) is 29½ days. The Moon's diameter is 2,160 miles, its density is 3.3 and its surface gravity is 0.2.

Oceans and Seas of the World

	AREA IN SQ. MILES	GREATEST DEPTH IN FEET	VOLUME IN CUBIC MILES
Pacific Ocean	64,186,000	36,198	167,025,000
Atlantic Ocean	31,862,000	28,374	77,580,000
Indian Ocean	28,350,000	25,344	68,213,000
Arctic Ocean	3,662,000	17,880	3,026,000
Mediterranean Sea	960,000	16,896	1,019,400
Bering Sea	875,000	13,422	788,500
Caribbean Sea	970,000	24,720	2,298,400
Sea of Okhotsk	590,000	11,070	454,700
East China Sea	482,000	10,500	52,700
Hudson Bay	476,000	1,500	37,590
Japan Sea	389,000	13,242	383,200
North Sea	222,000	2,654	12,890
Red Sea	169,000	7,254	53,700
Black Sea	185,000	7,200	....
Baltic Sea	163,000	1,506	5,360

Principal Lakes and Inland Seas

	AREA IN SQ. MILES
Caspian Sea	143,200
Lake Superior	32,483
Lake Victoria	26,828
Aral Sea	24,630
Lake Huron	23,860
Lake Michigan	22,178
Lake Tanganyika	12,700
Great Bear Lake	12,275
Lake Baykal	12,162
Lake Nyasa	11,500
Great Slave Lake	10,980
Lake Erie	9,889
Lake Winnipeg	9,465
Lake Ontario	7,313
Lake Ladoga	7,100
Lake Balkhash	6,700
Lake Chad	6,500
Lake Onega	3,765
Lake Titicaca	3,200
Lake Athabasca	3,120
Lake Nicaragua	3,100
Lake Rudolf	2,473
Reindeer Lake	2,467
Issyk-Kul'	2,276
Vänern	2,149
Lake Winnipegosis	2,103
Kariba Lake	2,050
Lake Urmia	1,795
Lake Albert	1,640
Lake Peipus	1,400
Lake Tana	1,219
Great Salt Lake	1,100
Lake Bangweulu	Approx. 1,000
Vättern	733
Dead Sea	405
Lake Balaton	266
Lake Geneva	225
Lake of Constance	208
Lake Garda	143
Lake of Neuchâtel	83
Lake Maggiore	82
Lake Como	56
Lake of Lucerne	44.5
Lake of Zurich	34

Great Ship Canals

	LENGTH IN MILES	DEPTH IN FEET
Baltic-White Sea, U.S.S.R.	141	....
Suez, U.A.R.	100.76	34
Albert, Belgium	81	16.5
Moscow-Volga, U.S.S.R.	80	18
Kiel, West Germany	61	37
Göta, Sweden	54	10
Panama, Canal Zone	50.72	41
Houston Ship, U.S.A.	50	36
Amsterdam-Rhine, Netherlands	45	41
Beaumont-Port Arthur, U.S.A.	40	32
Manchester Ship, England	35.5	28
Chicago Sanitary and Ship, U.S.A.	30	22
Welland, Canada	27.6	30
Juliana, Netherlands	21	11.8
Chesapeake and Delaware, U.S.A.	19	27
Cape Cod, U.S.A.	13	25
Lake Washington, U.S.A.	8	30
Corinth, Greece	4	26.25
Sault Ste. Marie, U.S.A.	1.6	24.5
Sault Ste. Marie, Canada	1.4	18.25

Principal Islands of the World

	AREA IN SQ. MILES		AREA IN SQ. MILES		AREA IN SQ. MILES		AREA IN SQ. MILES
Greenland	840,000	Tierra del Fuego	18,500	Wrangel	2,819	Orkney Islands	376
New Guinea	320,000	Melville	16,369	Canary Islands	2,808	Madeira Islands	308
Borneo	287,000	Kyushu	16,200	Kerguélen	2,700	Dominica	290
Madagascar	226,467	Southampton	15,700	Prince Edward	2,184	Tonga	270
Baffin	183,810	Solomon Islands	15,580	Trinidad and Tobago	1,980	Caroline Islands	267
Sumatra	164,148	New Britain	14,098	Balearic Islands	1,936	Molokai	261
Philippines	115,707	Taiwan (Formosa)	13,948	Madura	1,752	St. Lucia	238
New Zealand	103,736	Hainan	13,000	South Georgia	1,600	Corfu	229
Honshu	88,923	Prince of Wales	12,830	Cape Verde Islands	1,557	Bornholm	227
England-Scotland-Wales	88,755	Vancouver	12,408	Long I., New York	1,401	Isle of Man	227
Ellesmere	82,119	Timor	11,527	Socotra	1,400	Singapore	226
Victoria	81,930	Sicily	9,926	Gotland	1,225	Guam	212
Celebes	72,986	Somerset	9,370	Isle of Pines	1,180	Isle Royale	210
Java	48,842	Sardinia	9,301	Samoa	1,173	Virgin Islands	192
Cuba	44,206	Shikoku	7,244	Réunion	969	Curaçao	182
Newfoundland	43,359	New Caledonia	7,335	Azores	893	Barbados	166
Luzon	40,420	Fiji Islands	7,015	Ryukyu Islands	848	St. Vincent	150
Iceland	39,768	New Hebrides	5,700	Fernando Po	786	Isle of Wight	147
Mindanao	36,537	Kuril Islands	5,700	Tenerife	785	Lanai	141
Ireland	32,059	Falkland Islands	4,618	Maui	728	Grenada	133
Novaya Zemlya	31,900	Jamaica	4,411	Mauritius	709	Maltese Islands	122
Hokkaido	30,305	Bahama Islands	4,404	Zanzibar	640	Tobago	116
Molucca Islands	30,168	Hawaii	4,036	Oahu	604	Seychelles	109
Hispaniola	29,398	Cape Breton	3,970	Guadeloupe	583	Martha's Vinyard	109
Sakhalin	28,215	New Ireland	3,800	Ahvenanmaa (Aland Is.)	564	Channel Islands	75
Tasmania	26,215	Cyprus	3,473	Kauai	551	Nantucket	57
Ceylon	25,332	Puedto Rico	3,435	Shetland Islands	551	St. Helena	47
Svalbard	23,958	Corsica	3,368	Rhodes	542	Ascension	34
Banks	23,230	Crete	3,218	Martinique	425	Hong Kong	29
Devon	20,861	Galápagos Islands	3,042	Tahiti	402	Manhattan, New York	22
Bismarck Arch.	18,770	Hebrides	3,000	Pemba	380	Bermudas	21

Principal Mountains of the World

	FEET		FEET
Everest, Nepal-China	29,028	Dykh-Tau, U.S.S.R.	17,054
Godwin Austen (K2), India	28,250	Ararat, Turkey	16,946
Kanchenjunga, Nepal-India	28,208	Vinson Massif, Antarctica	16,864
Dhaulagiri, Nepal	26,810	Margherita (Ruwenzori), Africa	16,795
Nanga Parbat, India	26,660	Kazbek, U.S.S.R.	16,558
Annapurna, Nepal	26,504	Djaja, Indonesia	16,503
Nanda Devi, India	25,645	Blanc, France	15,771
Kamet, India	25,447	Klyuchevskaya Sopka, U.S.S.R.	15,584
Gurla Mandhata, China	25,355	Rosa (Dufourspitze), Italy-Switzerland	15,203
Tirich Mir, Pakistan	25,230	Ras Dashan, Ethiopia	15,157
Minya Konka, China	24,902	Matterhorn, Switzerland	14,688
Muztagh Ata, China	24,757	Whitney, California	14,494
Communism, U.S.S.R.	24,590	Elbert, Colorado	14,433
Pobeda Peak, U.S.S.R.	24,406	Rainer, Washington	14,410
Chomo Lhari, India-China	23,997	Markham, Antarctica	14,272
Muztagh, China	23,891	Shasta, California	14,162
Aconcagua, Argentina	22,831	Pikes Peak, Colorado	14,110
Ojos del Salado, Chile-Arg.	22,572	Finsteraarhorn, Switzerland	14,022
Tupungato, Chile-Argentina	22,310	Tajumulco, Guatemala	13,845
Mercedario, Argentina	22,211	Mauna Kea, Hawaii	13,796
Huascarán, Peru	22,205	Mauna Loa, Hawaii	13,680
Llullaillaco Volcano, Chile-Arg.	22,057	Toubkal, Morocco	13,665
Ancohuma, Bolivia	21,489	Jungfrau, Switzerland	13,642
Illampu, Bolivia	21,276	Cameroon, Cameroon	13,350
Chimborazo, Ecuador	20,561	Gran Paradiso, Italy	13,323
McKinley, Alaska	20,320	Robson, British Columbia	12,972
Logan, Yukon	19,850	Grossglockner, Austria	12,461
Cotopaxi, Ecuador	19,347	Fuji, Japan	12,389
Kilimanjaro, Tanzania	19,340	Cook, New Zealand	12,349
El Misti, Peru	19,199	Pico de Teide, Canary Is.	12,172
Citlaltépetl (Orizaba), Mexico	18,855	Semeru, Java, Indonesia	12,060
El'brus, U.S.S.R.	18,481	Mulhacén, Spain	11,411
Demavend, Iran	18,376	Etna, Italy	11,053
St. Elias, Alaska-Yukon	18,008	Lassen Peak, California	10,457
Vilcanota, Peru	17,999	Kosciusko, Australia	7,316
Popocatépetl, Mexico	17,887	Mitchell, North Carolina	6,684
Kenya, Kenya	17,058		

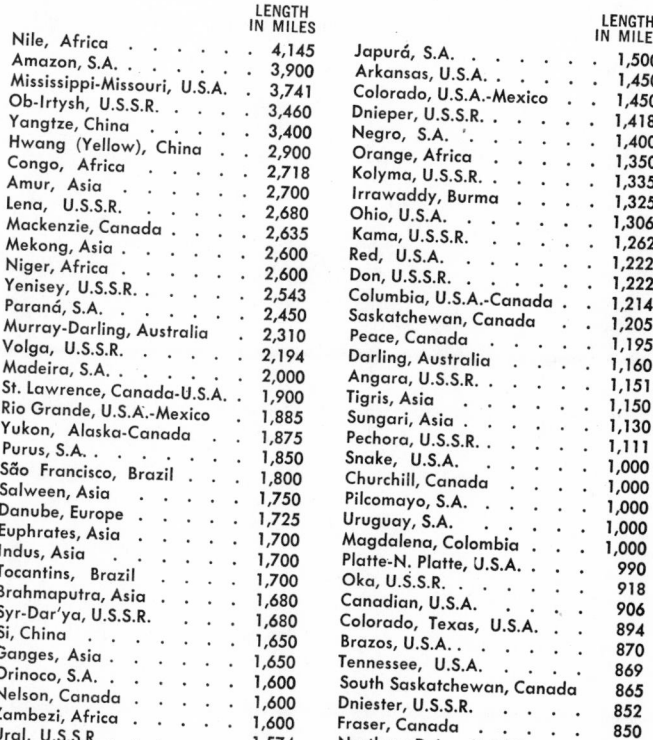

Longest Rivers of the World

	LENGTH IN MILES		LENGTH IN MILES
Nile, Africa	4,145	Japurá, S.A.	1,500
Amazon, S.A.	3,900	Arkansas, U.S.A.	1,450
Mississippi-Missouri, U.S.A.	3,741	Colorado, U.S.A.-Mexico	1,450
Ob-Irtysh, U.S.S.R.	3,460	Dnieper, U.S.S.R.	1,418
Yangtze, China	3,400	Negro, S.A.	1,400
Hwang (Yellow), China	2,900	Orange, Africa	1,350
Congo, Africa	2,718	Kolyma, U.S.S.R.	1,335
Amur, Asia	2,700	Irrawaddy, Burma	1,325
Lena, U.S.S.R.	2,680	Ohio, U.S.A.	1,306
Mackenzie, Canada	2,635	Kama, U.S.S.R.	1,262
Mekong, Asia	2,600	Red, U.S.A.	1,222
Niger, Africa	2,600	Don, U.S.S.R.	1,222
Yenisey, U.S.S.R.	2,543	Columbia, U.S.A.-Canada	1,214
Paraná, S.A.	2,450	Saskatchewan, Canada	1,205
Murray-Darling, Australia	2,310	Peace, Canada	1,195
Volga, U.S.S.R.	2,194	Darling, Australia	1,160
Madeira, S.A.	2,000	Angara, U.S.S.R.	1,151
St. Lawrence, Canada-U.S.A.	1,900	Tigris, Asia	1,150
Rio Grande, U.S.A.-Mexico	1,885	Sungari, Asia	1,130
Yukon, Alaska-Canada	1,875	Pechora, U.S.S.R.	1,111
Purus, S.A.	1,850	Snake, U.S.A.	1,000
São Francisco, Brazil	1,800	Churchill, Canada	1,000
Salween, Asia	1,750	Pilcomayo, S.A.	1,000
Danube, Europe	1,725	Uruguay, S.A.	1,000
Euphrates, Asia	1,700	Magdalena, Colombia	1,000
Indus, Asia	1,700	Platte-N. Platte, U.S.A.	990
Tocantins, Brazil	1,700	Oka, U.S.S.R.	918
Brahmaputra, Asia	1,680	Canadian, U.S.A.	906
Syr-Dar'ya, U.S.S.R.	1,680	Colorado, Texas, U.S.A.	894
Si, China	1,650	Brazos, U.S.A.	870
Ganges, Asia	1,650	Tennessee, U.S.A.	869
Orinoco, S.A.	1,600	South Saskatchewan, Canada	865
Nelson, Canada	1,600	Dniester, U.S.S.R.	852
Zambezi, Africa	1,600	Fraser, Canada	850
Ural, U.S.S.R.	1,574	Northern Dvina, U.S.S.R.	803
Amu-Dar'ya, Asia	1,550	Tisza, Europe	800
Olenek, U.S.S.R.	1,500	North Canadian, U.S.A.	784
Paraguay, S.A.	1,500	Athabasca, Canada	765

MAP PROJECTIONS

by Erwin Raisz

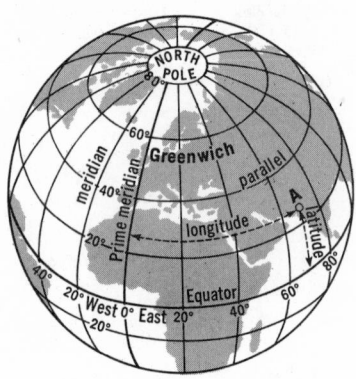

Our earth is rotating around its *axis* once a day. The two end points of its axis are the *poles;* the line circling the earth midway between the poles is the *equator*. The arc from either of the poles to the equator is divided into 90 *degrees*. The distance, expressed in degrees, from the equator to any point is its *latitude* and circles of equal latitude are the *parallels*. On maps it is customary to show parallels of evenly-spaced degrees such as every fifth or every tenth.

The equator is divided into 360 degrees. Lines circling from pole to pole through the degree points on the equator are called *meridians*. They are all equal in length but by international agreement the meridian passing through the Greenwich Observatory in London has been chosen as *prime meridian*. The distance, expressed in degrees, from the prime meridian to any point is its *longitude*. While meridians are all equal in length, parallels become shorter and shorter as they approach the poles. Whereas one degree of latitude represents everywhere approximately 69 miles, one degree of longitude varies from 69 miles at the equator to nothing at the poles.

Each degree is divided into 60 minutes and each minute into 60 seconds. One minute of latitude equals a nautical mile.

The map is flat but the earth is nearly spherical. Neither a rubber ball nor any part of a rubber ball may be flattened without stretching or tearing unless the part is very small. To present the curved surface of the earth on a flat map is not difficult as long as the areas under consideration are small, but the mapping of countries, continents, or the whole earth requires some kind of *projection*. Any regular set of parallels and meridians upon which a map can be drawn makes a map projection. Many systems are used.

In any projection only the parallels or the meridians or some other set of lines can be *true* (the same length as on the globe of corresponding scale); all other lines are too long or too short. Only on a globe is it possible to have both the parallels and the meridians true. The scale given on a flat map cannot be true everywhere. The construction of the various projections begins usually with laying out the parallels or meridians which have true lengths.

RECTANGULAR PROJECTION — This is a set of evenly-placed meridians and horizontal parallels. The central or *standard parallel* and all meridians are true. All other parallels are either too long or too short. The projection is used for simple maps of small areas, as city plans, etc.

MERCATOR PROJECTION — In this projection the meridians are evenly-spaced vertical lines. The parallels are horizontal, spaced so that their length has the same relation to the meridians as on a globe. As the meridians converge at higher latitudes on the globe, while on the map they do not, the parallels have to be drawn also farther and farther apart to maintain the correct relationship. When every very small area has the same shape as on a globe we call the projection *conformal*. The most interesting quality of this projection is that all *compass directions* appear as straight lines. For this reason it is generally used for marine charts. It is also frequently used for world maps in spite of the fact that the high latitudes are very much exaggerated in size. Only the equator is true to scale; all other parallels and meridians are too long. The Mercator projection did *not* derive from projecting a globe upon a cylinder.

SINUSOIDAL PROJECTION — The parallels are truly-spaced horizontal lines. They are divided truly and the connecting curves make the meridians. It does not make a good world map because the outer regions are distorted, but the

Rectangular Projection

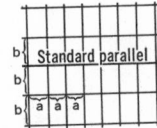

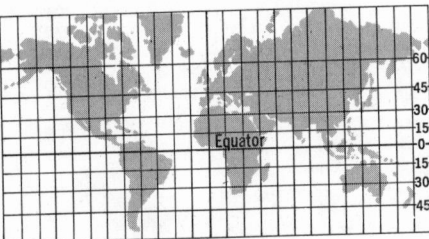

Mercator Projection

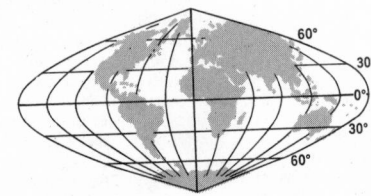

Sinusoidal Projection

central portion is good and this part is often used for maps of Africa and South America. Every part of the map has the same area as the corresponding area on the globe. It is an *equal-area* projection.

MOLLWEIDE PROJECTION — The meridians are equally-spaced ellipses; the parallels are horizontal lines spaced so that every belt of latitude should have the same area as on a globe. This projection is popular for world maps, especially in European atlases.

GOODE'S INTERRUPTED PROJECTIONS—Only the good central part of the Mollweide or sinusoidal (or both) projection is used and the oceans are cut. This makes an equal-area map with little distortion of shape. It is commonly used for world maps.

ECKERT PROJECTIONS — These are similar to the sinusoidal or the Mollweide projections, but the poles are shown as lines half the length of the equator. There are several variants; the meridians are either sine curves or ellipses; the parallels are horizontal and spaced either evenly or so as to make the projection equal area. Their use for world maps is increasing. The figure shows the elliptical equal-area variant.

CONIC PROJECTION — The original idea of the conic projection is that of capping the globe by a cone upon which both the parallels and meridians are projected from the center of the globe. The cone is then cut open and laid flat. A cone can be made tangent to any chosen *standard parallel*.

The actually-used conic projection is a modification of this idea. The radius of the standard parallel is obtained as above. The meridians are straight radiating lines spaced truly on the standard parallel. The parallels are concentric circles spaced at true distances. All parallels except the standard are too long. The projection is used for maps of countries in middle latitudes, as it presents good shapes with small scale error.

There are several variants: The use of *two standard parallels*, one near the top, the other near the bottom of the map, reduces the scale error. In the *Albers projection* the parallels are spaced unevenly, to make the projection equal-area. This is a good projection for the United States. In the *Lambert conformal conic projection* the parallels are spaced so that any small quadrangle of the grid should have the same shape as on the globe. This is the best projection for air-navigation charts as it has relatively straight azimuths.

An *azimuth* is a great-circle direction reckoned clockwise from north. A *great-circle direction* points to a place along the shortest line on the earth's surface. This is not the same as compass direction. The center of a great circle is the center of the globe.

BONNE PROJECTION — The parallels are laid out exactly as in the conic projection. All parallels are divided truly and the connecting curves make the meridians. It is an equal-area projection. It is used for maps of the northern continents, as Asia, Europe, and North America.

POLYCONIC PROJECTION — The central meridian is divided truly. The parallels are non-concentric circles, the radii of which are obtained by drawing tangents to the globe as though the globe were covered by several cones rather than by only one. Each parallel is divided truly and the connecting curves make the meridians. All meridians except the central one are too long. This projection is used for large-scale topographic sheets — less often for countries or continents.

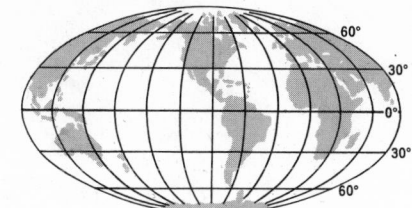

Mollweide Projection

Goode's Interrupted Projection

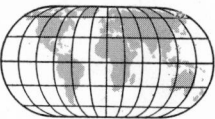

Eckert Projection

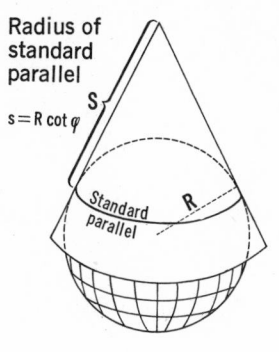

Radius of standard parallel

$s = R \cot \varphi$

Conic Projection

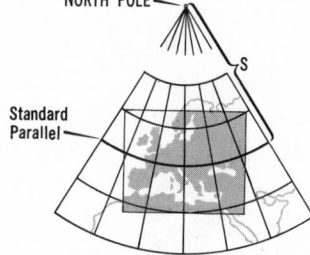

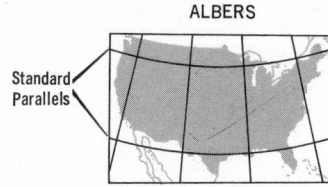

ALBERS

Albers Projection

LAMBERT

Lambert Conformal Conic Projection

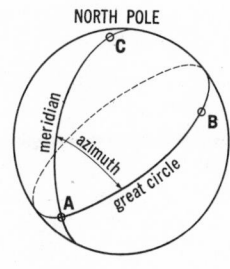

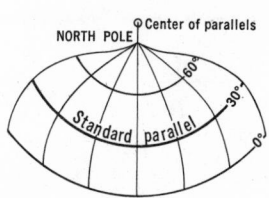

Bonne Projection

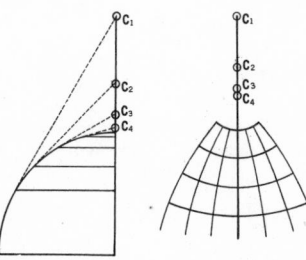

Polyconic Projection

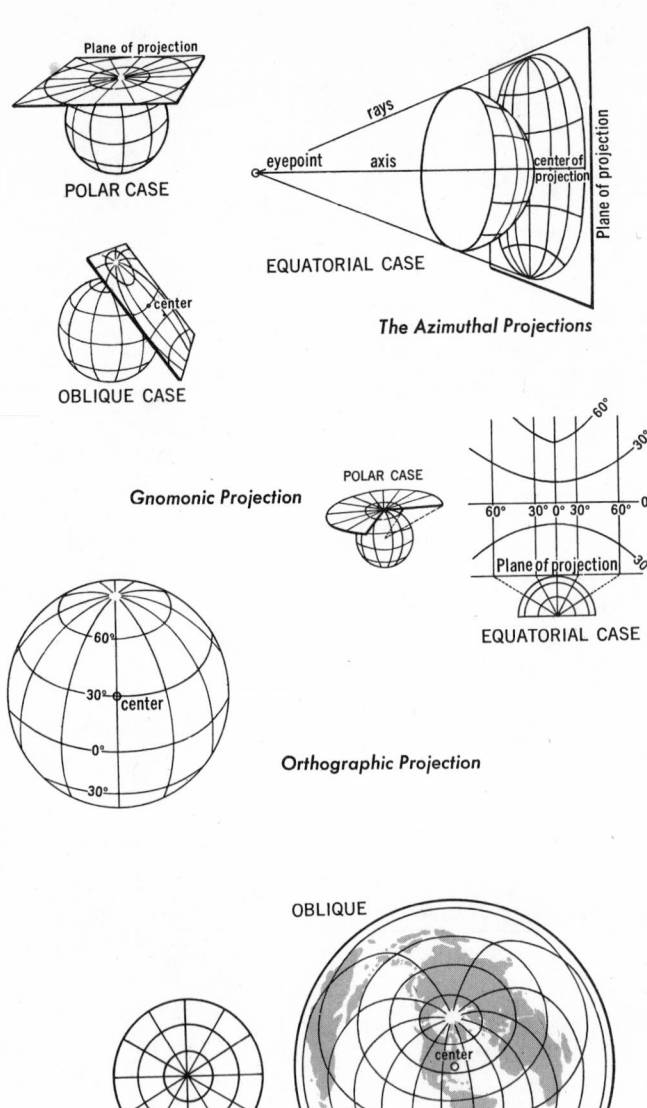

The Azimuthal Projections

Gnomonic Projection

Orthographic Projection

Azimuthal Equidistant Projection

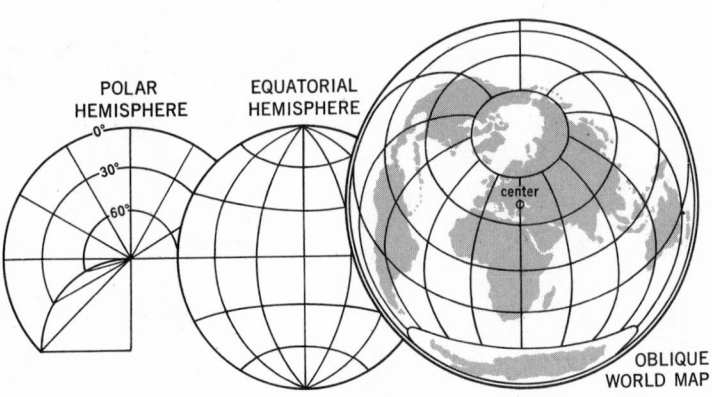

Lambert Azimuthal Equal-Area Projection

THE AZIMUTHAL PROJECTIONS — In this group a part of the globe is projected from an eyepoint onto a plane. The eyepoint can be at different distances, making different projections. The plane of projection can be tangent at the equator, at a pole, or at any other point on which we want to focus attention. The most important quality of all azimuthal projections is that they show every point at its true direction (azimuth) from the center point, and all points equally distant from the center point will be equally distant on the map also.

GNOMONIC PROJECTION — This projection has the eyepoint at the center of the globe Only the central part is good; the outer regions are badly distorted. Yet the projection has one important quality, all great circles being shown as straight lines. For this reason it is used for laying out the routes for long range flying or trans-oceanic navigation.

ORTHOGRAPHIC PROJECTION — This projection has the eyepoint at infinite distance and the projecting rays are parallel. The polar or equatorial varieties are rare but the oblique case became very popular on account of its visual quality. It looks like a picture of a globe. Although the distortion on the peripheries is extreme, we see it correctly because the eye perceives it not as a map but as a picture of a three-dimensional globe. Obviously only a hemisphere (half globe) can be shown.

Some azimuthal projections do not derive from the actual process of projecting from an eyepoint, but are arrived at by other means:

AZIMUTHAL EQUIDISTANT PROJECTION — This is the only projection in which every point is shown both at true great-circle direction and at true distance from the center point, but all other directions and distances are distorted. The principle of the projection can best be understood from the polar case. Most polar maps are in this projection. The oblique case is used for radio direction finding, for earthquake research, and in long-distance flying. A separate map has to be constructed for each central point selected.

LAMBERT AZIMUTHAL EQUAL-AREA PROJECTION — The construction of this projection can best be understood from the polar case. All three cases are widely used. It makes a good polar map and it is often extended to include the southern continents. It is the most common projection used for maps of the Eastern and Western Hemispheres, and it is a good projection for continents as it shows correct areas with relatively little distortion of shape. Most of the continent maps in this atlas are in this projection.

IN THIS ATLAS, on almost all maps, parallels and meridians have been marked because they are useful for the following:

(a) They show the north-south and east-west directions which appear on many maps at oblique angles especially near the margins.

(b) With the help of parallels and meridians every place can be exactly located; for instance, New York City is at 41° N and 74° W on any map.

(c) They help to measure distances even in the distorted parts of the map. The scale given on each map is true only along certain lines which are specified in the foregoing discussion for each projection. One degree of latitude equals nearly 69 statute miles or 60 nautical miles. The length of one degree of longitude varies (1° long. = 1° lat. × cos lat.).